D1606075

THE PASSAGES OF LIFE™ BIBLE

This Bible belongs to

Date

Nourishment
for the Body, Mind,
and Spirit in Every
Season of Life

THE PASSAGES OF LIFE™

Significant Passages for My Family and Friends

Name	*Event*	*Date*
Name	*Event*	*Date*
Name	*Event*	*Date*
Name	*Event*	*Date*
Name	*Event*	*Date*
Name	*Event*	*Date*

THE PASSAGES OF LIFE™

Significant Passages for My Family and Friends

Name	*Event*	*Date*

Name	*Event*	*Date*

Name	*Event*	*Date*

Name	*Event*	*Date*

Name	*Event*	*Date*

Name	*Event*	*Date*

THE PASSAGES OF LIFE™

Significant Passages for My Family and Friends

Name	*Event*	*Date*

Name	*Event*	*Date*

Name	*Event*	*Date*

Name	*Event*	*Date*

Name	*Event*	*Date*

Name	*Event*	*Date*

THE PASSAGES OF LIFE™ BIBLE

Dale Hanson Bourke
General Editor

Laura Barker
Associate Editor

The New King James Version

THOMAS NELSON PUBLISHERS

Nashville • Atlanta • London • Vancouver

Developed in association with the literary agency of
Alive Communications.

Title page logo: The triquetra (from a Latin word meaning "three-cornered") is an ancient symbol for the Trinity. It comprises three interwoven arcs, distinct yet equal and inseparable, symbolizing that the Father, Son, and Holy Spirit are three distinct yet equal Persons and indivisibly One God.

Printed in the United States of America
1 2 3 4 5 6 7 8 9 10 — 99 98 97 96 95

Welcome

*T*here comes a time in our lives when things begin to change. We notice crinkles becoming wrinkles and those extra holiday pounds come to visit and decide to stay. A game of tennis becomes a time to get a little exercise and have some fun instead of an occasion to wipe the other person off the map and prove our superiority once and for all.

Our children don't really need us anymore and we compete for their attention, wondering when it was that they stopped whining and began negotiating. Marriage settles in and we discover the joy of companionship and shared memories and what it means to bear one another's burdens. We begin to understand that things don't change overnight—but they do change. We learn to wait and watch and rejoice in the small signs of miracles in process.

We still work long and hard for raises and promotions, but our career is no longer the most important thing in life. We begin to realize that life isn't always fair, but we also realize that we've had our share of breaks along the way. Friendships become precious and we value those people who have loved us through the good times and the bad. We make new friends carefully and know that they are to be treasured. Our parents age and pass away and we are left with the daunting responsibility of being the matriarchs and patriarchs of our families.

The Bible, which we once searched for answers and read out of obligation, becomes a daily nourisher. Old passages take on new meaning. Verses we once memorized in order to earn a prize come back to us in times of joy and pain and we are glad we have hidden them in our hearts.

We pray often because we know it makes a difference. We talk to God about everything and we understand that nothing in our lives is hidden from Him. We learn to listen for His

voice and we trust Him to teach us gently. We discover the joy of surrender and the foolishness of pride. We learn to listen and really hear what people have to say. We choose our words carefully because we have learned that they can build up or tear down someone else.

The Passages of Life™ Bible is for those of us who aren't necessarily old, but aren't young anymore. It's for those of us who know that life has its seasons and that being younger isn't necessarily being better.

It is for me, because I have a different faith than I had ten years ago, and for my grandmother who is still growing and learning and discovering God in new ways.

This Bible is for you, too. I pray that it will guide you and comfort you, bring you peace and joy, whatever your passage of life.

Dale Hanson Bourke

✦Contents✦

of the Passages of Life™ Bible

I. Text

II. Study Helps

✦Books of the Bible✦

In Sequence

The Old Testament

New Testament

✦Books of the Bible✦

Alphabetically

The Old Testament

New Testament

✦Index of Features✦

Passing It On

Legacy

Aspirations

Study Articles

Questions and Answers

Portraits

✦Preface✦

Purpose

In the preface to the 1611 edition, the translators of the Authorized Version, known popularly as the King James Bible, state that it was not their purpose "to make a new translation . . . . but to make a good one better." Indebted to the earlier work of William Tyndale and others, they saw their best contribution to consist in revising and enhancing the excellence of the English versions which had sprung from the Reformation of the sixteenth century. In harmony with the purpose of the King James scholars, the translators and editors of the present work have not pursued a goal of innovation. They have perceived the Holy Bible, New King James Version, as a continuation of the labors of the earlier translators, thus unlocking for today's readers the spiritual treasures found especially in the Authorized Version of the Holy Scriptures.

A Living Legacy

For nearly four hundred years, and throughout several revisions of its English form, the King James Bible has been deeply revered among the English-speaking peoples of the world. The precision of translation for which it is historically renowned, and its majesty of style, have enabled that monumental version of the Word of God to become the mainspring of the religion, language, and legal foundations of our civilization.

Although the Elizabethan period and our own cra share in zeal for technical advance, the former period was more aggressively devoted to classical learning. Along with this awakened concern for the classics came a flourishing companion interest in the Scriptures, an interest that was enlivened by the conviction that the manuscripts were providentially handed down and were a trustworthy record of the inspired Word of God. The King James translators were committed to producing an English Bible that would be a precise translation, and by no means a paraphrase or a broadly approximate rendering. On the one hand, the scholars were almost as familiar with the original languages of the Bible as with their native English. On the other hand, their reverence for the divine Author and His Word assured a translation of the Scriptures in which only a principle of utmost accuracy could be accepted. Therefore, while seeking to unveil the excellent *form* of the traditional English Bible, special care has also been taken in the present edition to preserve the work of *precision* which is the legacy of the 1611 translators.

Complete Equivalence in Translation

Where new translation has been necessary in the New King James Version, the most complete representation of the original has been ren-

dered by considering the history of usage and etymology of words in their contexts. This principle of complete equivalence seeks to preserve *all* of the information in the text, while presenting it in good literary form. Dynamic equivalence, a recent procedure in Bible translation, commonly results in paraphrasing where a more literal rendering is needed to reflect a specific and vital sense. For example, complete equivalence truly renders the original text in expressions such as "lifted her voice and wept" (Gen. 21:16); "I gave you cleanness of teeth" (Amos 4:6); "Jesus met them, saying, 'Rejoice!' " (Matt. 28:9); and " 'Woman, what does your concern have to do with Me?' " (John 2:4). Complete equivalence translates fully, in order to provide an English text that is both accurate and readable.

In keeping with the principle of complete equivalence, it is the policy to translate interjections which are commonly omitted in modern language renderings of the Bible. As an example, the interjection *behold,* in the older King James editions, continues to have a place in English usage, especially in dramatically calling attention to a spectacular scene, or an event of profound importance such as the Immanuel prophecy of Isaiah 7:14. Consequently, *behold* is retained for these occasions in the present edition. However, the Hebrew and Greek originals for this word can be translated variously, depending on the circumstances in the passage. Therefore, in addition to *behold,* words such as *indeed, look, see,* and *surely* are also rendered to convey the appropriate sense suggested by the context in each case.

In faithfulness to God and to our readers, it was deemed appropriate that all participating scholars sign a statement affirming their belief in the verbal and plenary inspiration of Scripture, and in the inerrancy of the original autographs.

The Style

Students of the Bible applaud the timeless devotional character of our historic Bible. Yet it is also universally understood that our language, like all living languages, has undergone profound change since 1611. Subsequent revisions of the King James Bible have sought to keep abreast of changes in English speech. The present work is a further step toward this objective. Where obsolescence and other reading difficulties exist, present-day vocabulary, punctuation, and grammar have been carefully integrated. Words representing ancient objects, such as *chariot* and *phylactery,* have no modern substitutes and are therefore retained.

In the discipline of translating biblical and other ancient languages, a standard method of transliteration, that is, the English spelling of untranslated words, such as names of persons and places, has never been

commonly adopted. In keeping with the design of the present work, the King James spelling of untranslated words is retained, although made uniform throughout. For example, instead of the spellings *Isaiah* and *Elijah* in the Old Testament, and *Esaias* and *Elias* in the New Testament, *Isaiah* and *Elijah* now appear in both Testaments.

King James doctrinal and theological terms, for example, *propitiation, justification,* and *sanctification,* are generally familiar to English-speaking peoples. Such terms have been retained except where the original language indicates need for a more precise translation.

Readers of the Authorized Version will immediately be struck by the absence of several pronouns: *thee, thou,* and *ye* are replaced by the simple *you,* while *your* and *yours* are substituted for *thy* and *thine* as applicable. *Thee, thou, thy,* and *thine* were once forms of address to express a special relationship to human as well as divine persons. These pronouns are no longer part of our language. However, reverence for God in the present work is preserved by capitalizing pronouns, including *You, Your,* and *Yours,* which refer to Him. Additionally, capitalization of these pronouns benefits the reader by clearly distinguishing divine and human persons referred to in a passage. Without such capitalization the distinction is often obscure, because the antecedent of a pronoun is not always clear in the English translation.

In addition to the pronoun usages of the seventeenth century, the *-eth* and *-est* verb endings are now obsolete. Contemporary English usage has been substituted for the previous verb endings.

The real character of the Authorized Version does not reside in its archaic pronouns or verbs or other grammatical forms of the seventeenth century, but rather in the care taken by its scholars to impart the letter and spirit of the original text in a majestic and reverent style.

The Format

The format of the New King James Version is designed to enhance the vividness and devotional quality of the Holy Scriptures:

- Subject headings assist the reader to identify topics and transitions in the biblical content.
- Words or phrases in *italics* indicate expressions in the original language which require clarification by additional English words, as also done throughout the history of the King James Bible.
- Verse numbers within a paragraph are easily distinguishable.
- Oblique type in the New Testament indicates a quotation from the Old Testament.
- Prose is divided into paragraphs to indicate the structure of thought.

- Poetry is structured as contemporary verse to reflect the poetic form and beauty of the passage in the original language.
- The covenant name of God was usually translated from the Hebrew as "LORD" or "GOD" (using capital letters as shown) in the King James Old Testament. This tradition is maintained. In the present edition the name is so capitalized whenever the covenant name is quoted in the New Testament from a passage in the Old Testament.

The Old Testament Text

The Hebrew Bible has come down to us through the scrupulous care of ancient scribes who copied the original text in successive generations. By the sixth century A.D. the scribes were succeeded by a group known as the Masoretes, who continued to preserve the sacred Scriptures for another five hundred years in a form known as the Masoretic Text. Babylonia, Palestine, and Tiberias were the main centers of Masoretic activity; but by the tenth century A.D. the Masoretes of Tiberias, led by the family of ben Asher, gained the ascendancy. Through subsequent editions, the ben Asher text became in the twelfth century the only recognized form of the Hebrew Scriptures.

Daniel Bomberg printed the first Rabbinic Bible in 1516–17; that work was followed in 1524–25 by a second edition prepared by Jacob ben Chayyim and also published by Bomberg. The text of ben Chayyim was adopted in most subsequent Hebrew Bibles, including those used by the King James translators. The ben Chayyim text was also used for the first two editions of Rudolph Kittel's *Biblia Hebraica* of 1906 and 1912. In 1937 Paul Kahle published a third edition of *Biblia Hebraica.* This edition was based on the oldest dated manuscript of the ben Asher text, the Leningrad Manuscript B19a (A.D. 1008), which Kahle regarded as superior to that used by ben Chayyim.

For the New King James Version the text used was the 1967/1977 Stuttgart edition of the *Biblia Hebraica,* with frequent comparisons being made with the Bomberg edition of 1524–25. The Septuagint (Greek) Version of the Old Testament and the Latin Vulgate also were consulted. In addition to referring to a variety of ancient versions of the Hebrew Scriptures, the New King James Version draws on the resources of relevant manuscripts from the Dea Sea caves. In the few places where the Hebrew was so obscure that the 1611 King James was compelled to follow one of the versions, but where information is now available to resolve the problems, the New King James Version follows the Hebrew text. Significant variations are recorded in the side reference column.

The New Testament Text

There is more manuscript support for the New Testament than for any other body of ancient literature. Over five thousand Greek, eight thousand Latin, and many more manuscripts in other languages attest the integrity of the New Testament. There is only one basic New Testament used by Protestants, Roman Catholics, and Orthodox, by conservatives and liberals. Minor variations in hand copying have appeared through the centuries, before mechanical printing began about A.D. 1450.

Some variations exist in the spelling of Greek words, in word order, and in similar details. These ordinarily do not show up in translation and do not affect the sense of the text in any way.

Other manuscript differences such as omission or inclusion of a word or a clause, and two paragraphs in the Gospels, should not overshadow the overwhelming degree of *agreement* which exists among the ancient records. Bible readers may be assured that the most important differences in English New Testaments of today are due, not to manuscript divergence, but to the way in which translators view the task of translation: How literally should the text be rendered? How does the translator view the matter of biblical inspiration? Does the translator adopt a paraphrase when a literal rendering would be quite clear and more to the point? The New King James Version follows the historic precedent of the Authorized Version in maintaining a literal approach to translation, except where the idiom of the original language cannot be translated directly into our tongue.

The King James New Testament was based on the traditional text of the Greek-speaking churches, first published in 1516, and later called the Textus Receptus or Received Text. Although based on the relatively few available manuscripts, these were representative of many more which existed at the time but only became known later. In the late nineteenth century, B. Westcott and F. Hort taught that this text had been officially edited by the fourth-century church, but a total lack of historical evidence for this event has forced a revision of the theory. It is now widely held that the Byzantine Text that largely supports the Textus Receptus has as much right as the Alexandrian or any other tradition to be weighed in determining the text of the New Testament. Those readings in the Textus Receptus which have weak support are indicated in the side reference column as being opposed by both Critical and Majority Texts (see "Side-Column Notes").

Since the 1880s most contemporary translations of the New Testament have relied upon a relatively few manuscripts discovered chiefly in the late nineteenth and early twentieth centuries. Such translations depend primarily on two manuscripts, Codex Vaticanus and Codex Sinaiti-

cus, because of their greater age. The Greek text obtained by using these sources and the related papyri (our most ancient manuscripts) is known as the Alexandrian Text. However, some scholars have grounds for doubting the faithfulness of Vaticanus and Sinaiticus, since they often disagree with one another, and Sinaiticus exhibits excessive omission.

A third viewpoint of New Testament scholarship holds that the best text is based on the consensus of the majority of existing Greek manuscripts. This text is called the Majority Text. Most of these manuscripts are in substantial agreement. Even though many are late, and none is earlier than the fifth century, usually their readings are verified by papyri, ancient versions, quotations from the early church fathers, or a combination of these. The Majority Text is similar to the Textus Receptus, but it corrects those readings which have little or no support in the Greek manuscript tradition.

Today, scholars agree that the science of New Testament textual criticism is in a state of flux. Very few scholars still favor the Textus Receptus as such, and then often for its historical prestige as the text of Luther, Calvin, Tyndale, and the King James Version. For about a century most have followed a Critical Text (so called because it is edited according to specific principles of textual criticism) which depends heavily upon the Alexandrian type of text. More recently many have abandoned this Critical Text (which is quite similar to the one edited by Westcott and Hort) for one that is more eclectic. Finally, a small but growing number of scholars prefer the Majority Text, which is close to the traditional text except in the Revelation.

In light of these facts, and also because the New King James Version is the fifth revision of a historic document translated from specific Greek texts, the editors decided to retain the traditional text in the body of the New Testament and to indicate major Critical and Majority Text variant readings in the side reference column. Although these variations are duly indicated in the side-column notes of the present edition, it is most important to emphasize that fully eighty-five percent of the New Testament text is the same in the Textus Receptus, the Alexandrian Text, and the Majority Text.

Side-Column Notes

Significant explanatory notes, alternate translations, and cross-references, as well as New Testament citations of Old Testament passages, are supplied in the side reference column.

Important textual variants in the Old Testament are identified in a standard form.

The textual notes in the present edition of the New Testament make

no evaluation of readings, but do clearly indicate the manuscript sources of readings. They objectively present the facts without such tendentious remarks as "the best manuscripts omit" or "the most reliable manuscripts read." Such notes are value judgments that differ according to varying viewpoints on the text. By giving a clearly defined set of variants the New King James Version benefits readers of all textual persuasions.

Where significant variations occur in the New Testament Greek manuscripts, textual notes are classified as follows:

1. NU-Text
   These variations from the traditional text generally represent the Alexandrian or Egyptian type of text described previously in "The New Testament Text." They are found in the Critical Text published in the twenty-seventh edition of the Nestle-Aland Greek New Testament (N) and in the United Bible Societies' fourth edition (U), hence the acronym, "NU-Text."

2. M-Text
   This symbol indicates points of variation in the Majority Text from the traditional text, as also previously discussed in "The New Testament Text." It should be noted that M stands for whatever reading is printed in the published *Greek New Testament According to the Majority Text*, whether supported by overwhelming, strong, or only a divided majority textual tradition.

The textual notes reflect the scholarship of the past 150 years and will assist the reader to observe the variations between the different manuscript traditions of the New Testament. Such information is generally not available in English translations of the New Testament.

THE
OLD TESTAMENT

✦Genesis✦

Genesis describes the beginning of many things—the world, life, death, humanity, sin, family, marriage, and sacrifice. Although Genesis does not name its author, the early church believed that Moses wrote the Pentateuch (the first five books of the Bible), and several places in Scripture support this (Lev. 1:1, 2; Neh. 13:1; Matt. 8:4; Acts 26:22). Moses may have written Genesis following the Israelites' departure from Egypt in around 1446 B.C.

Genesis contains many essential doctrines of the Bible. It affirms God as the Creator of the universe and the initiator of the covenant with man. Chapters 12 and 15 detail the Abrahamic Covenant, explaining God's plan of salvation for the world through Israel, the chosen nation.

The first eleven chapters lay the foundation of the entire Bible and focus on four key events: creation, the Fall, the Flood, and the Tower of Babel. Chapters 12—50 show how God set Abraham apart and blessed the world through his descendants—Isaac, Jacob, and Joseph. The continued faithfulness and service of people such as Noah and Abraham show that God can use people of any age in fulfillment of His plan for His children. ✦

CHAPTER 1

The History of Creation

In the beginning God created the heavens and the earth. 2The earth was without
form, and void; and darkness *was*[a] on the
face of the deep. And the Spirit of God was
hovering over the face of the waters.
3Then God said, "Let there be light";
and there was light. 4And God saw the
light, that *it was* good; and God divided
the light from the darkness. 5God called the
light Day, and the darkness He called
Night. So the evening and the morning
were the first day.
6Then God said, "Let there be a firmament in the midst of the waters, and let it
divide the waters from the waters." 7Thus
God made the firmament, and divided the
waters which *were* under the firmament
from the waters which *were* above the firmament; and it was so. 8And God called

1:2 [a]Words in italic type have been added for clarity. They are not found in the original Hebrew or Aramaic.

1:1–5 Time and matter had no existence before **the beginning**; only the one living **God**, who had no beginning, was in existence. **created**: Here a bringing into existence from nothing. **the heavens and the earth**: The entire universe. "New heavens and a new earth," as part of a new creation, are anticipated by Isaiah and John. **without form**, and void: The unordered conditions on earth before God made it habitable for man. The **Spirit of God**, the third member of the Trinity, was overseeing this unordered creation. **God said**: By the power of His spoken word, God willed creation into existence. Christ the Word, the Second Person of the Trinity, was the agent of this creative process. **called**: Or named. To have the right of naming something expresses ownership and lordship.

God's Kaleidoscope Creation

Claire Cloninger

I see the "color" of God's creation not only in the visual beauty of the world around me; I am also learning to see it in the incredibly diverse beauty of His children as well. Each of us has been made so uniquely, designed so specifically, that not one other person on earth is exactly like us (Ps. 139:14). We truly are what my friend, Mickey Smith, calls "human snowflakes." Every finger on every hand on every person in every land who has ever lived contains a unique fingerprint!

"Each of us has been made so uniquely that not one other person on earth is exactly like us."

What a colorful creation this is! Think of it. God has delighted to give each one of us a special identity, and yet many of us spend our lives trying to conform to some self-imposed "norm." We deny our own individuality and that of others. We insist on playing out God's drama in black and white, ignoring the many colorful brush strokes of His hand.

If creativity and individuality should flourish in any place on earth, it should be in the church of Jesus Christ. As the Holy Spirit is given full rein, each member of Christ's body should be moving toward the total fulfillment of his or her unique destiny. The separate gifts and abilities of each Christian should be lovingly sought out, coaxed, challenged, and encouraged by other members of the body. ✦

the firmament Heaven. So the evening and
the morning were the second day.
9Then God said, "Let the waters under
the heavens be gathered together into one
place, and let the dry *land* appear"; and it
was so. 10And God called the dry *land*
Earth, and the gathering together of the
waters He called Seas. And God saw that *it*
was good.
11Then God said, "Let the earth bring
forth grass, the herb *that* yields seed, *and*
the fruit tree *that* yields fruit according to
its kind, whose seed *is* in itself, on the
earth"; and it was so. 12And the earth
brought forth grass, the herb *that* yields
seed according to its kind, and the tree *that*
yields fruit, whose seed *is* in itself accord-
ing to its kind. And God saw that *it was*
good. 13So the evening and the morning
were the third day.
14Then God said, "Let there be lights in
the firmament of the heavens to divide the
day from the night; and let them be for
signs and seasons, and for days and years;
15and let them be for lights in the firma-
ment of the heavens to give light on the
earth"; and it was so. 16Then God made
two great lights: the greater light to rule
the day, and the lesser light to rule the
night. *He made* the stars also. 17God set
them in the firmament of the heavens to
give light on the earth, 18and to rule over
the day and over the night, and to divide
the light from the darkness. And God saw

that *it was* good. 19So the evening and the
morning were the fourth day.
20Then God said, "Let the waters
abound with an abundance of living crea-
tures, and let birds fly above the earth
across the face of the firmament of the
heavens." 21So God created great sea crea-
tures and every living thing that moves,
with which the waters abounded, accord-
ing to their kind, and every winged bird
according to its kind. And God saw that *it
was* good. 22And God blessed them, saying,
"Be fruitful and multiply, and fill the wa-
ters in the seas, and let birds multiply on
the earth." 23So the evening and the morn-
ing were the fifth day.
24Then God said, "Let the earth bring
forth the living creature according to its
kind: cattle and creeping thing and beast of
the earth, *each* according to its kind"; and it
was so. 25And God made the beast of the
earth according to its kind, cattle according
to its kind, and everything that creeps on
the earth according to its kind. And God
saw that *it was* good.
26Then God said, "Let Us make man in
Our image, according to Our likeness; let
them have dominion over the fish of the
sea, over the birds of the air, and over the
cattle, over all[a] the earth and over every
creeping thing that creeps on the earth."
27So God created man in His *own* image; in
the image of God He created him; male
and female He created them. 28Then God
blessed them, and God said to them, "Be
fruitful and multiply; fill the earth and
subdue it; have dominion over the fish of
the sea, over the birds of the air, and over
every living thing that moves on the
earth."
29And God said, "See, I have given you
every herb *that* yields seed which *is* on the
face of all the earth, and every tree whose
fruit yields seed; to you it shall be for food.
30Also, to every beast of the earth, to every
bird of the air, and to everything that
creeps on the earth, in which *there is* life, *I
have given* every green herb for food"; and
it was so. 31Then God saw everything that
He had made, and indeed *it was* very good.
So the evening and the morning were the
sixth day.

> All things bright and beautiful,
> All creatures great and small,
> All things wise and wonderful,
> The Lord God made them all.
> Cecil Frances Alexander

CHAPTER 2

Thus the heavens and the earth, and all
the host of them, were finished. 2And on
the seventh day God ended His work
which He had done, and He rested on the
seventh day from all His work which He
had done. 3Then God blessed the seventh
day and sanctified it, because in it He
rested from all His work which God had
created and made.

1:26 [a]Syriac reads *all the wild animals of.*

1:24, 25 According to its kind: indicates God's establishment of order within creation. Although biological variations may occur within different "kinds of plant and animal life, there is no provision for evolution from one "kind" to another.

1:26–28 Let Us: Perhaps a reference to the Trinity. The Hebrew word here for "man" is *'adam*, to be understood as "humankind" (and so in v. 27 and chapter 2). It is the same word used for the proper name "Adam" in 2:19 and subsequent verses. *'Adam* is related to the Hebrew word for ground, *'adamah*, from which humankind was "formed" (2:7). **in Our image**: The essence of the image of God is not stated here, but dominion over all of creation (v. 28) is the functional result of bearing God's image. Humans are to be God's visible representatives, ruling creation as God would rule it. In addition, the image of God points to their distinctive dignity—endowed with reason, moral self-consciousness, freedom of choice, imagination, immortality, and at least limited creativity.

> Every minute life begins all over again.
> Thomas Merton

4This *is* the history[a] of the heavens and
the earth when they were created, in the
day that the LORD God made the earth and
the heavens, 5before any plant of the field
was in the earth and before any herb of the
field had grown. For the LORD God had not
caused it to rain on the earth, and *there was*
no man to till the ground; 6but a mist went
up from the earth and watered the whole
face of the ground.
7And the LORD God formed man *of* the
dust of the ground, and breathed into his
nostrils the breath of life; and man became
a living being.

Life in God's Garden

8The LORD God planted a garden east-
ward in Eden, and there He put the man
whom He had formed. 9And out of the
ground the LORD God made every tree
grow that is pleasant to the sight and good
for food. The tree of life *was* also in the
midst of the garden, and the tree of the
knowledge of good and evil.
10Now a river went out of Eden to water
the garden, and from there it parted and
became four riverheads. 11The name of the
first *is* Pī'shon; it *is* the one which skirts the
whole land of Hav'i·lah, where *there is*
gold. 12And the gold of that land *is* good.
Bdellium and the onyx stone *are* there.
13The name of the second river *is* Gī'hon; it
is the one which goes around the whole
land of Cush. 14The name of the third river
is Hid'de·kel;[a] it *is* the one which goes to-
ward the east of Assyria. The fourth river *is*
the Eū·phrā'tēs.

15Then the LORD God took the man and
put him in the garden of Eden to tend and
keep it. 16And the LORD God commanded
the man, saying, "Of every tree of the gar-
den you may freely eat; 17but of the tree of
the knowledge of good and evil you shall
not eat, for in the day that you eat of it you
shall surely die."
18And the LORD God said, "*It is* not good
that man should be alone; I will make him
a helper comparable to him." 19Out of the
ground the LORD God formed every beast
of the field and every bird of the air, and
brought *them* to Adam to see what he
would call them. And whatever Adam
called each living creature, that *was* its
name. 20So Adam gave names to all cattle,
to the birds of the air, and to every beast of
the field. But for Adam there was not
found a helper comparable to him.
21And the LORD God caused a deep sleep
to fall on Adam, and he slept; and He took
one of his ribs, and closed up the flesh in
its place. 22Then the rib which the LORD
God had taken from man He made into
a woman, and He brought her to the
man.
23And Adam said:

"This *is* now bone of my bones
And flesh of my flesh;
She shall be called Woman,
Because she was taken out of Man."

24Therefore a man shall leave his father and
mother and be joined to his wife, and they
shall become one flesh.
25And they were both naked, the man
and his wife, and were not ashamed.

2:4 [a]Hebrew *toledoth*, literally *generations* 2:14 [a]Or *Tigris*

2:15 tend . . . keep: Man's first assignment in ruling creation as God's representative. Man was to enhance earth's vegetation through cultivation so that it will further glorify the Creator.

2:17 The prohibition regarding **the tree of the knowledge of good and evil** provided an opportunity for man to express his love for God through obedience to Him.

CHAPTER 3

The Temptation and Fall of Man

Now the serpent was more cunning
than any beast of the field which the LORD
God had made. And he said to the woman,
"Has God indeed said, 'You shall not eat of
every tree of the garden'?"
2And the woman said to the serpent,
"We may eat the fruit of the trees of the
garden; 3but of the fruit of the tree which *is*
in the midst of the garden, God has said,
'You shall not eat it, nor shall you touch it,
lest you die.' "
4Then the serpent said to the woman,
"You will not surely die. 5For God knows
that in the day you eat of it your eyes will
be opened, and you will be like God,
knowing good and evil."
6So when the woman saw that the tree
was good for food, that it *was* pleasant to
the eyes, and a tree desirable to make *one*
wise, she took of its fruit and ate. She also
gave to her husband with her, and he ate.
7Then the eyes of both of them were
opened, and they knew that they *were*
naked; and they sewed fig leaves together
and made themselves coverings.
8And they heard the sound of the LORD
God walking in the garden in the cool of
the day, and Adam and his wife hid them-
selves from the presence of the LORD God
among the trees of the garden.
9Then the LORD God called to Adam and
said to him, "Where *are* you?"
10So he said, "I heard Your voice in the
garden, and I was afraid because I was
naked; and I hid myself."
11And He said, "Who told you that you
were naked? Have you eaten from the tree
of which I commanded you that you
should not eat?"
12Then the man said, "The woman
whom You gave *to be* with me, she gave me
of the tree, and I ate."
13And the LORD God said to the woman,
"What *is* this you have done?"
The woman said, "The serpent deceived
me, and I ate."
14So the LORD God said to the serpent:

"Because you have done this,
You *are* cursed more than all cattle,
And more than every beast of the
field;
On your belly you shall go,
And you shall eat dust
All the days of your life.
15 And I will put enmity
Between you and the woman,
And between your seed and her Seed;
He shall bruise your head,
And you shall bruise His heel."

16To the woman He said:

"I will greatly multiply your sorrow
and your conception;
In pain you shall bring forth children;
Your desire *shall be* for your husband,
And he shall rule over you."

3:6 Satan's invasions represent three God-given areas of human life: **good for food** (physical), **pleasant to the eyes** (emotional), and **desirable to make one wise** (spiritual). **gave to her husband**: God has endowed us with the power of influence—for good and for evil.

3:7, 8 made . . . coverings: Shame always seeks to conceal. Prior to their disobedience the man and woman had experienced no guilt in their relationship with each other or with God (see 2:25). **hid themselves**: When we have sinned, our inclination is to hide from God's presence (see Luke 23:30).

3:14–19 Because of Adam and Eve's disobedience the serpent (v. 15) and the ground (v. 17) were **cursed**. The serpent's curse was to **eat dust**, a parallel of "lick dust," figurative for being humbled or defeated (see Ps. 72:9; Mic. 7:16, 17). The **serpent**, the **woman**, and **Adam** all sinned, and all were punished.

Adam and Eve: In the Beginning

During the seven days of creation, God paused several times to examine His work, and He "saw that it was good" (Gen. 1:25). Everything He created was in perfect balance: day and night, water and land, man and woman.

Then God planted a garden full of beautiful trees that produced delicious fruit, and He made Adam and Eve the caretakers.

Within the garden of Eden existed an answer for every possible need. The trees provided food for Adam and Eve's physical requirements. The presence of Eve supplied Adam's social needs and vice versa, and the Lord Himself was available for their spiritual and mental nourishment.

But, just as God did not force Adam and Eve to feed themselves or talk with each other, He did not compel them to fellowship with Him. He provided for their every need, but He allowed them to choose whether or not they would take advantage of His blessings.

In their free will, Adam and Eve chose not to stay close to Him or to seek His guidance. When they decided to eat the fruit of the tree of the knowledge of good and evil, they also chose to break fellowship with God.

The consequences of the first sin—the curses upon the serpent, the woman, and the man—created imbalance throughout the world. All of nature suffered because of the Fall (Jer. 12:4; Rom. 8:20). Man and the serpent became enemies (Gen. 3:15). Pain became a part of life, and conflict arose between husband and wife (v. 16). The earth became a battleground between man and nature (vv. 17–19).

But in the midst of all these tragic changes came a blessed assurance that one day all would be restored. Verse 15, long recognized as the first messianic prophecy of the Bible, tells of a Deliverer who would conquer Satan but, in so doing, be "bruised" Himself. This promise refers to Christ's bruising on the Cross, which led to the destruction of Satan and his kingdom.

Christ's death gives us the opportunity to embrace the gift of eternal life, which once could be found only in the Garden of Eden. However, just as God answered Adam and Eve's needs without forcing them to accept His provision, so He has given us the freedom to accept or reject His gift of life.

Only when we submit to His will and pursue fellowship with God will we be able to achieve the balanced life that He intended in the beginning. He has provided the answer for our every need, but we must choose to accept it. ✦

17 Then to Adam He said, "Because you
have heeded the voice of your wife, and
have eaten from the tree of which I com-
manded you, saying, 'You shall not eat of
it':

"Cursed *is* the ground for your sake;
In toil you shall eat *of* it
All the days of your life.
18 Both thorns and thistles it shall bring
forth for you,
And you shall eat the herb of the
field.
19 In the sweat of your face you shall eat
bread
Till you return to the ground,
For out of it you were taken;
For dust you *are*,
And to dust you shall return."

20 And Adam called his wife's name
Eve, because she was the mother of all liv-
ing.
21 Also for Adam and his wife the LORD
God made tunics of skin, and clothed
them.
22 Then the LORD God said, "Behold, the
man has become like one of Us, to know
good and evil. And now, lest he put out his
hand and take also of the tree of life, and
eat, and live forever"— 23 therefore the
LORD God sent him out of the garden of
Eden to till the ground from which he was
taken. 24 So He drove out the man; and He
placed cherubim at the east of the garden
of Eden, and a flaming sword which
turned every way, to guard the way to the
tree of life.

CHAPTER 4

Cain Murders Abel

Now Adam knew Eve his wife, and she
conceived and bore Cain, and said, "I have
acquired a man from the LORD." 2 Then she
bore again, this time his brother Abel. Now
Abel was a keeper of sheep, but Cain was a
tiller of the ground. 3 And in the process of
time it came to pass that Cain brought an
offering of the fruit of the ground to the
LORD. 4 Abel also brought of the firstborn of
his flock and of their fat. And the LORD re-
spected Abel and his offering, 5 but He did
not respect Cain and his offering. And
Cain was very angry, and his countenance
fell.
6 So the LORD said to Cain, "Why are you
angry? And why has your countenance
fallen? 7 If you do well, will you not be ac-
cepted? And if you do not do well, sin lies
at the door. And its desire *is* for you, but
you should rule over it."
8 Now Cain talked with Abel his
brother;[a] and it came to pass, when they
were in the field, that Cain rose up against
Abel his brother and killed him.
9 Then the LORD said to Cain, "Where *is*
Abel your brother?"
He said, "I do not know. *Am* I my
brother's keeper?"
10 And He said, "What have you done?
The voice of your brother's blood cries out
to Me from the ground. 11 So now you *are*
cursed from the earth, which has opened
its mouth to receive your brother's blood

4:8 [a]Samaritan Pentateuch, Septuagint, Syriac, and Vulgate add *"Let us go out to the field."*

4:4, 5 The two offerings (vv. 3, 4) indicate humanity's early knowledge of divine worship and its significance. The NT explains that the Lord **respected Abel** and his offering because by faith he offered a better sacrifice. Probably the sacrifice was better because it involved the shedding of blood, as God had done for the first time while making coverings for Adam and Eve (3:21), suggesting that shedding blood was required to cover the guilt of human sin. The Lord **did not respect Cain** and his offering because "his works were evil" (see 1 John 3:12). This may mean that Cain knew plants could not atone for sin, but offered them anyway. Cain's response to the rejection was resentment, leading to deep anger and eventually to the first murder.

from your hand. 12When you till the
ground, it shall no longer yield its strength
to you. A fugitive and a vagabond you
shall be on the earth."

13And Cain said to the LORD, "My pun-
ishment *is* greater than I can bear! 14Surely
You have driven me out this day from the
face of the ground; I shall be hidden from
Your face; I shall be a fugitive and a
vagabond on the earth, and it will hap-
pen *that* anyone who finds me will kill
me."

15And the LORD said to him, "Therefore,[a]
whoever kills Cain, vengeance shall be
taken on him sevenfold." And the LORD set
a mark on Cain, lest anyone finding him
should kill him.

The Family of Cain

16Then Cain went out from the presence
of the LORD and dwelt in the land of Nod
on the east of Eden. 17And Cain knew his
wife, and she conceived and bore Ē'noch.
And he built a city, and called the name of
the city after the name of his son—Ē'noch.
18To Ē'noch was born Ī'rad; and Ī'rad begot
Me·hū'ja·el, and Me·hū'ja·el begot Me-
thū'sha·el, and Me·thū'sha·el begot Lā'-
mech.

19Then Lā'mech took for himself two
wives: the name of one *was* Ā'dah, and the
name of the second *was* Zil'lah. 20And
Ā'dah bore Jā'bal. He was the father of
those who dwell in tents and have live-
stock. 21His brother's name *was* Jū'bal. He
was the father of all those who play the
harp and flute. 22And as for Zil'lah, she
also bore Tū'bal-Cāin, an instructor of
every craftsman in bronze and iron. And
the sister of Tū'bal-Cāin *was* Nā'a·mah.

23Then Lā'mech said to his wives:

"Ā'dah and Zil'lah, hear my voice;
Wives of Lā'mech, listen to my
speech!
For I have killed a man for wounding
me,
Even a young man for hurting me.
24 If Cain shall be avenged sevenfold,
Then Lā'mech seventy-sevenfold."

A New Son

25And Adam knew his wife again, and
she bore a son and named him Seth, "For
God has appointed another seed for me in-
stead of Abel, whom Cain killed." 26And as
for Seth, to him also a son was born; and he
named him Ē'nosh.[a] Then *men* began to
call on the name of the LORD.

CHAPTER 5

The Family of Adam

This is the book of the genealogy of
Adam. In the day that God created man,
He made him in the likeness of God. 2He
created them male and female, and blessed
them and called them Mankind in the day
they were created. 3And Adam lived one
hundred and thirty years, and begot *a son*
in his own likeness, after his image, and
named him Seth. 4After he begot Seth, the
days of Adam were eight hundred years;
and he had sons and daughters. 5So all the
days that Adam lived were nine hundred
and thirty years; and he died.

6Seth lived one hundred and five years,
and begot Ē'nosh. 7After he begot Ē'nosh,
Seth lived eight hundred and seven years,
and had sons and daughters. 8So all the

4:15 [a]Following Masoretic Text and Targum; Septuagint, Syriac, and Vulgate read *Not so.* 4:26 [a]Greek *Enos*

4:26 Enosh, "Frail Man," was to begin a new line who, in contrast to the self-reliance of Cain, would live in reliance upon the **name** (character) **of the LORD**. The Messiah would eventually come through this line of descent.

5:4–32 The genealogies recorded here indicate that ten generations linked the event of Creation with the Flood. The frequent occurrence of the phrase "and he died" demonstrates the fulfillment of the curse that resulted from Adam's sin.

days of Seth were nine hundred and
twelve years; and he died.
9Ē'nosh lived ninety years, and begot
Cā·ī'nan.[a] 10After he begot Cā·ī'nan,
Ē'nosh lived eight hundred and fifteen
years, and had sons and daughters. 11So all
the days of Ē'nosh were nine hundred and
five years; and he died.
12Cā·ī'nan lived seventy years, and be-
got Ma·hal'a·lel. 13After he begot Ma-
hal'a·lel, Cā·ī'nan lived eight hundred and
forty years, and had sons and daughters.
14So all the days of Cā·ī'nan were nine
hundred and ten years; and he died.
15Ma·hal'a·lel lived sixty-five years, and
begot Jar'ed. 16After he begot Jar'ed,
Ma·hal'a·lel lived eight hundred and
thirty years, and had sons and daughters.
17So all the days of Ma·hal'a·lel were eight
hundred and ninety-five years; and he
died.
18Jar'ed lived one hundred and sixty-
two years, and begot Ē'noch. 19After he be-
got Ē'noch, Jar'ed lived eight hundred
years, and had sons and daughters. 20So all
the days of Jar'ed were nine hundred and
sixty-two years; and he died.
21Ē'noch lived sixty-five years, and be-
got Me·thū'se·lah. 22After he begot
Me·thū'se·lah, Ē'noch walked with God
three hundred years, and had sons and
daughters. 23So all the days of Ē'noch were
three hundred and sixty-five years. 24And
Ē'noch walked with God; and he *was* not,
for God took him.
25Me·thū'se·lah lived one hundred and
eighty-seven years, and begot Lā'mech.
26After he begot Lā'mech, Me·thū'se·lah
lived seven hundred and eighty-two years,
and had sons and daughters. 27So all the
days of Me·thū'se·lah were nine hundred
and sixty-nine years; and he died.
28Lā'mech lived one hundred and
eighty-two years, and had a son. 29And he
called his name Noah, saying, "This *one*
will comfort us concerning our work and
the toil of our hands, because of the
ground which the LORD has cursed." 30Af-
ter he begot Noah, Lā'mech lived five hun-
dred and ninety-five years, and had sons
and daughters. 31So all the days of Lā'mech
were seven hundred and seventy-seven
years; and he died.
32And Noah was five hundred years old,
and Noah begot Shem, Ham, and Jā'pheth.

CHAPTER 6

The Wickedness and Judgment of Man

Now it came to pass, when men began
to multiply on the face of the earth, and
daughters were born to them, 2that the
sons of God saw the daughters of men, that
they *were* beautiful; and they took wives
for themselves of all whom they chose.
3And the LORD said, "My Spirit shall not
strive[a] with man forever, for he *is* indeed
flesh; yet his days shall be one hundred
and twenty years." 4There were giants on
the earth in those days, and also afterward,
when the sons of God came in to the
daughters of men and they bore *children* to
them. Those *were* the mighty men who *were*
of old, men of renown.
5Then the LORD[a] saw that the wicked-
ness of man *was* great in the earth, and *that*
every intent of the thoughts of his heart
was only evil continually. 6And the LORD
was sorry that He had made man on the
earth, and He was grieved in His heart. 7So
the LORD said, "I will destroy man whom I
have created from the face of the earth,
both man and beast, creeping thing and

5:9 [a]Hebrew *Qenan* 6:3 [a]Septuagint, Syriac, Targum, and Vulgate read *abide*. 6:5 [a]Following Masoretic Text and Targum; Vulgate reads *God;* Septuagint reads *LORD God.*

5:24 Enoch's relationship with God provides an inspiring example for all believers. The statement that he "walked with God" indicates a continuing, intimate relationship with the Lord.

birds of the air, for I am sorry that I have
made them." 8But Noah found grace in the
eyes of the LORD.

Noah Pleases God

9This is the genealogy of Noah. Noah
was a just man, perfect in his generations.
Noah walked with God. 10And Noah begot
three sons: Shem, Ham, and Jā′pheth.
11The earth also was corrupt before God,
and the earth was filled with violence. 12So
God looked upon the earth, and indeed it
was corrupt; for all flesh had corrupted
their way on the earth.

The Ark Prepared

13And God said to Noah, "The end of all
flesh has come before Me, for the earth is
filled with violence through them; and be-
hold, I will destroy them with the earth.
14Make yourself an ark of gopherwood;
make rooms in the ark, and cover it inside
and outside with pitch. 15And this is how
you shall make it: The length of the ark
shall be three hundred cubits, its width fifty
cubits, and its height thirty cubits. 16You
shall make a window for the ark, and you
shall finish it to a cubit from above; and set
the door of the ark in its side. You shall
make it *with* lower, second, and third *decks*.
17And behold, I Myself am bringing
floodwaters on the earth, to destroy from
under heaven all flesh in which *is* the
breath of life; everything that *is* on the
earth shall die. 18But I will establish My
covenant with you; and you shall go into
the ark—you, your sons, your wife, and
your sons' wives with you. 19And of every
living thing of all flesh you shall bring two
of every *sort* into the ark, to keep *them* alive
with you; they shall be male and female.
20Of the birds after their kind, of animals
after their kind, and of every creeping
thing of the earth after its kind, two of
every *kind* will come to you to keep *them*
alive. 21And you shall take for yourself of
all food that is eaten, and you shall gather
it to yourself; and it shall be food for you
and for them."
22Thus Noah did; according to all that
God commanded him, so he did.

CHAPTER 7

The Great Flood

Then the LORD said to Noah, "Come into
the ark, you and all your household, be-
cause I have seen *that* you *are* righteous be-
fore Me in this generation. 2You shall take
with you seven each of every clean animal,
a male and his female; two each of animals
that *are* unclean, a male and his female;
3also seven each of birds of the air, male
and female, to keep the species alive on the
face of all the earth. 4For after seven more
days I will cause it to rain on the earth forty
days and forty nights, and I will destroy
from the face of the earth all living things
that I have made." 5And Noah did accord-
ing to all that the LORD commanded him.
6Noah *was* six hundred years old when the
floodwaters were on the earth.
7So Noah, with his sons, his wife, and
his sons' wives, went into the ark because

6:14–16 cubits: Length—450 feet (135 m); width—75 feet (22.5 m); height—45 feet (13.5 m). These dimensions would produce an interior volume of about 150,000 cubic feet (41,000 cu m). No keel, oars, or rudder are mentioned. The **ark** was probably like a very large barge of three stories divided into **rooms** (compartments). It had one **door** in its **side** and a **window** (opening) for light and air just below the roof.

7:2, 3 The distinction between **clean** and **unclean** animals was religious. Clean animals could be used for sacrificial purposes. This distinction did not yet apply to which animals could be eaten. Permission to eat animal flesh was granted only after the Flood. Verses 2, 3 elaborate on the basic command already given in 6:19. One pair was a minimum. **seven each**: The Hebrew expression can be translated as three pairs plus one extra. The extra clean animal may have been used for the sacrifice.

NOAH: MAN OF FAITH

Although nothing is known about Noah's early life, the Bible tells us that at five hundred years of age, "Noah found grace in the eyes of the LORD. . . . [He] was a just man, perfect in his generations. Noah walked with God" (Gen. 6:8, 9).

These simple statements reveal a wealth of information about this Old Testament hero. First, the root word for *just* implies conformity to a moral or ethical standard, while *perfect* means "blameless." Noah had the strength of character to withstand the corruption all around him ("in his generations"). Noah resisted temptation and served God even as the rest of the world was filled with such wickedness that God had decided to destroy man from the face of the earth. In a world of physical giants (6:4), Noah was a spiritual giant—just the man for the task God had in mind.

Second, the spiritual foundation laid by his great-grandfather Enoch must have greatly impacted Noah's own relationship with God. Enoch, who "walked with God," escaped death because of his faithfulness; God simply "took him" (5:24). Noah's relationship with the Lord is described in exactly the same words.

Upon receiving instructions from God, Noah did not make excuses about his age or physical condition. He did not ask God for a sign or for a simpler assignment. He simply acted in total faith and trust, "according to all that God commanded him" (v. 22).

He continued to fulfill his appointed task for one hundred years. We are not told whether God spoke to him at all during this time, but we do know that he persisted despite the unbelievers who must have mocked him. In fact, he apparently preached to his tormentors (2 Pet. 2:5), warning them of the wrath to come.

Although faithful in many things, Noah was not flawless. How sad that the only event described between the Flood and Noah's death was his drunkenness and nakedness.

But God recognizes that His children are not always perfect and, despite his sin, Noah is listed as one of the three most righteous men in the history of God's people. Job and Daniel are the other two (Ezek. 14:14, 20). Noah also appears in the "Hall of Faith" in Hebrews 11.

No matter how old we grow, we must never assume that we are above temptation and sin. Constant vigilance of our spiritual lives is essential. When we do fall into sin, God waits only for us to confess and repent before restoring us into fellowship with Him. Remember that, like Enoch and Noah, we're leaving behind a spiritual legacy—whether of faith or disobedience—that will influence future generations. ✦

of the waters of the flood. [8]Of clean ani-
mals, of animals that *are* unclean, of birds,
and of everything that creeps on the earth,
[9]two by two they went into the ark to
Noah, male and female, as God had com-
manded Noah. [10]And it came to pass after
seven days that the waters of the flood
were on the earth. [11]In the six hundredth
year of Noah's life, in the second month,
the seventeenth day of the month, on that
day all the fountains of the great deep were
broken up, and the windows of heaven
were opened. [12]And the rain was on the
earth forty days and forty nights.

[13]On the very same day Noah and
Noah's sons, Shem, Ham, and Jā'pheth,
and Noah's wife and the three wives of his
sons with them, entered the ark— [14]they
and every beast after its kind, all cattle af-
ter their kind, every creeping thing that
creeps on the earth after its kind, and every
bird after its kind, every bird of every sort.
[15]And they went into the ark to Noah, two
by two, of all flesh in which *is* the breath of
life. [16]So those that entered, male and fe-
male of all flesh, went in as God had com-
manded him; and the LORD shut him in.

[17]Now the flood was on the earth forty
days. The waters increased and lifted up
the ark, and it rose high above the earth.
[18]The waters prevailed and greatly in-
creased on the earth, and the ark moved
about on the surface of the waters. [19]And
the waters prevailed exceedingly on the
earth, and all the high hills under the
whole heaven were covered. [20]The waters
prevailed fifteen cubits upward, and the
mountains were covered. [21]And all flesh
died that moved on the earth: birds and
cattle and beasts and every creeping thing
that creeps on the earth, and every man.
[22]All in whose nostrils *was* the breath of the
spirit[a] of life, all that *was* on the dry *land*,
died. [23]So He destroyed all living things
which were on the face of the ground: both
man and cattle, creeping thing and bird of
the air. They were destroyed from the
earth. Only Noah and those who *were* with
him in the ark remained *alive*. [24]And the
waters prevailed on the earth one hundred
and fifty days.

CHAPTER 8

Noah's Deliverance

Then God remembered Noah, and
every living thing, and all the animals that
were with him in the ark. And God made a
wind to pass over the earth, and the waters
subsided. [2]The fountains of the deep and
the windows of heaven were also stopped,
and the rain from heaven was restrained.
[3]And the waters receded continually from
the earth. At the end of the hundred and
fifty days the waters decreased. [4]Then the
ark rested in the seventh month, the seven-
teenth day of the month, on the mountains
of Ar'a·rat. [5]And the waters decreased con-
tinually until the tenth month. In the tenth
month, on the first *day* of the month, the
tops of the mountains were seen.

[6]So it came to pass, at the end of forty
days, that Noah opened the window of the
ark which he had made. [7]Then he sent out
a raven, which kept going to and fro until
the waters had dried up from the earth.
[8]He also sent out from himself a dove, to
see if the waters had receded from the face
of the ground. [9]But the dove found no rest-
ing place for the sole of her foot, and she
returned into the ark to him, for the waters
were on the face of the whole earth. So he
put out his hand and took her, and drew
her into the ark to himself. [10]And he waited
yet another seven days, and again he sent
the dove out from the ark. [11]Then the dove
came to him in the evening, and behold, a
freshly plucked olive leaf *was* in her

7:22 [a]Septuagint and Vulgate omit *of the spirit*.

8:4 Ararat: A mountain range southeast of the Black Sea and west of the Caspian Sea. Thus, the Flood carried the ark northwestward toward the Black Sea.

mouth; and Noah knew that the waters
had receded from the earth. 12So he waited
yet another seven days and sent out the
dove, which did not return again to him
anymore.
13And it came to pass in the six hundred
and first year, in the first *month,* the first
day of the month, that the waters were
dried up from the earth; and Noah re-
moved the covering of the ark and looked,
and indeed the surface of the ground was
dry. 14And in the second month, on the
twenty-seventh day of the month, the
earth was dried.
15Then God spoke to Noah, saying,
16"Go out of the ark, you and your wife,
and your sons and your sons' wives with
you. 17Bring out with you every living
thing of all flesh that *is* with you: birds and
cattle and every creeping thing that creeps
on the earth, so that they may abound on
the earth, and be fruitful and multiply on
the earth." 18So Noah went out, and his
sons and his wife and his sons' wives with
him. 19Every animal, every creeping thing,
every bird, *and* whatever creeps on the
earth, according to their families, went out
of the ark.

God's Covenant with Creation

20Then Noah built an altar to the LORD,
and took of every clean animal and of
every clean bird, and offered burnt offer-
ings on the altar. 21And the LORD smelled a
soothing aroma. Then the LORD said in His
heart, "I will never again curse the ground
for man's sake, although the imagination
of man's heart *is* evil from his youth; nor
will I again destroy every living thing as I
have done.

22 "While the earth remains,
Seedtime and harvest,
Cold and heat,
Winter and summer,
And day and night
Shall not cease."

CHAPTER 9

So God blessed Noah and his sons, and
said to them: "Be fruitful and multiply, and
fill the earth.[a] 2And the fear of you and the
dread of you shall be on every beast of the
earth, on every bird of the air, on all that
move *on* the earth, and on all the fish of the
sea. They are given into your hand. 3Every
moving thing that lives shall be food for
you. I have given you all things, even as
the green herbs. 4But you shall not eat flesh
with its life, *that is,* its blood. 5Surely for
your lifeblood I will demand *a reckoning;*
from the hand of every beast I will require
it, and from the hand of man. From the
hand of every man's brother I will require
the life of man.

6 "Whoever sheds man's blood,
By man his blood shall be shed;
For in the image of God
He made man.
7 And as for you, be fruitful and
multiply;
Bring forth abundantly in the earth
And multiply in it."

8Then God spoke to Noah and to his
sons with him, saying: 9"And as for Me,

9:1 [a]Compare Genesis 1:28

8:22 The omission of spring and autumn is not an oversight; a rainy **winter** and a dry **summer** were the two chief seasons that assured crops in OT agricultural societies.

9:3 This is the first mention of animals as appropriate **food** for humans. Previously, God had only mentioned herbs and fruit trees as suitable for eating (1:29).

9:8–17 A **covenant** (v. 9) binds two parties together. In the God-human covenants of the Bible, God is the initiator. He is willing to commit Himself before He asks a commitment from us. God's covenant with Noah was promised before the Flood, and He promised never again to destroy the earth by a flood. That covenant was universal applying to **every living creature** (vv. 10, 12). It was unconditional and **perpetual** (v. 12).

behold, I establish My covenant with you
and with your descendants[a] after you,
10and with every living creature that *is* with
you: the birds, the cattle, and every beast of
the earth with you, of all that go out of the
ark, every beast of the earth. 11Thus I estab-
lish My covenant with you: Never again
shall all flesh be cut off by the waters of the
flood; never again shall there be a flood to
destroy the earth."

12And God said: "This *is* the sign of the
covenant which I make between Me and
you, and every living creature that *is* with
you, for perpetual generations: 13I set My
rainbow in the cloud, and it shall be for the
sign of the covenant between Me and the
earth. 14It shall be, when I bring a cloud
over the earth, that the rainbow shall be
seen in the cloud; 15and I will remember
My covenant which *is* between Me and
you and every living creature of all flesh;
the waters shall never again become a
flood to destroy all flesh. 16The rainbow
shall be in the cloud, and I will look on it to
remember the everlasting covenant be-
tween God and every living creature of all
flesh that *is* on the earth." 17And God said
to Noah, "This *is* the sign of the covenant
which I have established between Me and
all flesh that *is* on the earth."

Noah and His Sons

18Now the sons of Noah who went out
of the ark were Shem, Ham, and Jā'pheth.
And Ham *was* the father of Cā'naan.
19These three *were* the sons of Noah, and
from these the whole earth was populated.

20And Noah began *to be* a farmer, and he
planted a vineyard. 21Then he drank of the
wine and was drunk, and became uncov-
ered in his tent. 22And Ham, the father of
Cā'naan, saw the nakedness of his father,
and told his two brothers outside. 23But
Shem and Jā'pheth took a garment, laid *it*
on both their shoulders, and went back-
ward and covered the nakedness of their
father. Their faces *were* turned away, and
they did not see their father's nakedness.
24So Noah awoke from his wine, and
knew what his younger son had done to
him. 25Then he said:

"Cursed *be* Cā'naan;
A servant of servants
He shall be to his brethren."

26And he said:

"Blessed *be* the LORD,
The God of Shem,
And may Cā'naan be his servant.
27 May God enlarge Jā'pheth,
And may he dwell in the tents of
Shem;
And may Cā'naan be his servant."

28And Noah lived after the flood three
hundred and fifty years. 29So all the days of
Noah were nine hundred and fifty years;
and he died.

CHAPTER 10

Nations Descended from Noah

Now this *is* the genealogy of the sons of
Noah: Shem, Ham, and Jā'pheth. And sons
were born to them after the flood.

9:9 [a]Literally *seed*

9:25–27 Cursed be Canaan: It is not clear why Canaan should be cursed for his father's sin. At any rate it was the later Canaanites' sexual promiscuity which made them an abomination in God's sight. The greatest blessing is given to Shem, from whose line Abraham and the Israelites would descend.

10:1–32 The **nations** of **earth**, as Moses knew them, are classified under the three **sons of Noah** (v. 32). The peoples are categorized according to various criteria: clan, language, location, and nationality. However, the primary grouping here is genealogical because the Canaanites and others listed as Hamitic also spoke Semitic languages. The locations of these groups are: (1) those descending from **Japheth** (vv. 2–5), 14 nations, primarily north and west of Canaan, who spoke the Indo-European languages; (2) those descending from

2The sons of Jā′pheth *were* Gō′mer, Mā′gog, Mā′daī, Jā′van, Tū′bal, Mē′shech, and Tī′ras. 3The sons of Gō′mer *were* Ash′ke·naz, Rī′phath,[a] and Tō·gar′mah. 4The sons of Jā′van *were* E·li′shah, Tar′shish, Kit′tim, and Dō′da·nim.[a] 5From these the coastland *peoples* of the Gentiles were separated into their lands, everyone according to his language, according to their families, into their nations.

6The sons of Ham *were* Cush, Miz′ra·im, Put,[a] and Cā′naan. 7The sons of Cush *were* Sē′ba, Hav′i·lah, Sab′tah, Rā′a·mah, and Sab′te·chah; and the sons of Rā′a·mah *were* Shē′ba and Dē′dan.

8Cush begot Nim′rod; he began to be a mighty one on the earth. 9He was a mighty hunter before the LORD; therefore it is said, "Like Nim′rod the mighty hunter before the LORD." 10And the beginning of his kingdom was Bā′bel, Ē′rech, Ac′cad, and Cal′neh, in the land of Shī′nar. 11From that land he went to Assyria and built Nin′e·veh, Re·hō′both Ir, Cā′lah, 12and Rē′sen between Nin′e·veh and Cā′lah (that *is* the principal city).

13Miz′ra·im begot Lū′dim, An′a·mim, Le·hā′bim, Naph′tū·him, 14Path·rū′sim, and Cas·lū′him (from whom came the Phi·lis′tines and Caph′to·rim).

15Cā′naan begot Sī′don his firstborn, and Heth; 16the Jeb′ū·sīte, the Am′o·rīte, and the Gir′ga·shīte; 17the Hī′vīte, the Ar′kīte, and the Sī′nīte; 18the Ar′vad·īte, the Zem′a·rīte, and the Hā′math·īte. Afterward the families of the Cā′naan·ītes were dispersed. 19And the border of the Cā′naan·ītes was from Sī′don as you go toward Gē′rar, as far as Gā′za; then as you go toward Sod′om, Go·mor′rah, Ad′mah, and Ze·boi′im, as far as Lā′sha. 20These *were* the sons of Ham, according to their families, according to their languages, in their lands *and* in their nations.

21And *children* were born also to Shem, the father of all the children of Ē′ber, the brother of Jā′pheth the elder. 22The sons of Shem *were* Ē′lam, As′shur, Ar·phā′xad, Lud, and Ar′am. 23The sons of Ar′am *were* Uz, Hul, Gē′ther, and Mash.[a] 24Ar·phā′xad begot Sā′lah,[a] and Sā′lah begot Ē′ber. 25To Ē′ber were born two sons: the name of one *was* Pē′leg, for in his days the earth was divided; and his brother's name *was* Jok′tan. 26Jok′tan begot Al·mō′dad, Shē′leph, Hā·zar·mā′veth, Jē′rah, 27Ha·dor′am, Ū′zal, Dik′lah, 28Ō′bal,[a] A·bim′a·el, Shē′ba, 29Ō′phir, Hav′i·lah, and Jō′bab. All these *were* the sons of Jok′tan. 30And their dwelling place was from Mē′sha as you go toward Sē′phar, the mountain of the east. 31These *were* the sons of Shem, according to their families, according to their languages, in their lands, according to their nations.

32These *were* the families of the sons of Noah, according to their generations, in their nations; and from these the nations were divided on the earth after the flood.

CHAPTER 11

The Tower of Babel

Now the whole earth had one language and one speech. 2And it came to pass, as they journeyed from the east, that they found a plain in the land of Shī′nar, and they dwelt there. 3Then they said to one another, "Come, let us make bricks and bake *them* thoroughly." They had brick for

10:3 [a]Spelled *Diphath* in 1 Chronicles 1:6
10:4 [a]Spelled *Rodanim* in Samaritan Pentateuch and 1 Chronicles 1:7
10:6 [a]Or *Phut*
10:23 [a]Called *Meshech* in Septuagint and 1 Chronicles 1:17
10:24 [a]Following Masoretic Text, Vulgate, and Targum; Septuagint reads *Arphaxad begot Cainan, and Cainan begot Salah* (compare Luke 3:35, 36).
10:28 [a]Spelled *Ebal* in 1 Chronicles 1:22

Ham (vv. 6–20), 30 nations, primarily in southwest Asia and northeast Africa, who spoke the Hamitic languages; (3) those descending from **Shem** (vv. 21–31), 26 nations, primarily in Canaan and west of Canaan, who spoke the Semitic languages.

stone, and they had asphalt for mortar.
4And they said, "Come, let us build our-
selves a city, and a tower whose top *is* in
the heavens; let us make a name for our-
selves, lest we be scattered abroad over the
face of the whole earth."
5But the LORD came down to see the city
and the tower which the sons of men had
built. 6And the LORD said, "Indeed the peo-
ple *are* one and they all have one language,
and this is what they begin to do; now
nothing that they propose to do will be
withheld from them. 7Come, let Us go
down and there confuse their language,
that they may not understand one an-
other's speech." 8So the LORD scattered
them abroad from there over the face of all
the earth, and they ceased building the
city. 9Therefore its name is called Bā′bel,
because there the LORD confused the lan-
guage of all the earth; and from there the
LORD scattered them abroad over the face
of all the earth.

Shem's Descendants

10This *is* the genealogy of Shem: Shem
was one hundred years old, and begot
Ar·phā′xad two years after the flood. 11Af-
ter he begot Ar·phā′xad, Shem lived five
hundred years, and begot sons and daugh-
ters.
12Ar·phā′xad lived thirty-five years, and
begot Sā′lah. 13After he begot Sā′lah,
Ar·phā′xad lived four hundred and three
years, and begot sons and daughters.
14Sā′lah lived thirty years, and begot
Ē′ber. 15After he begot Ē′ber, Sā′lah lived
four hundred and three years, and begot
sons and daughters.
16Ē′ber lived thirty-four years, and begot
Pē′leg. 17After he begot Pē′leg, Ē′ber lived
four hundred and thirty years, and begot
sons and daughters.
18Pē′leg lived thirty years, and begot
Rē′ū. 19After he begot Rē′ū, Pē′leg lived
two hundred and nine years, and begot
sons and daughters.
20Rē′ū lived thirty-two years, and begot
Sē′rug. 21After he begot Sē′rug, Rē′ū lived
two hundred and seven years, and begot
sons and daughters.
22Sē′rug lived thirty years, and begot
Nā′hor. 23After he begot Nā′hor, Sē′rug
lived two hundred years, and begot sons
and daughters.
24Nā′hor lived twenty-nine years, and
begot Tē′rah. 25After he begot Tē′rah,
Nā′hor lived one hundred and nineteen
years, and begot sons and daughters.
26Now Tē′rah lived seventy years, and
begot Abram, Nā′hor, and Har′an.

Terah's Descendants

27This *is* the genealogy of Tē′rah: Tē′rah
begot Abram, Nā′hor, and Har′an. Har′an
begot Lot. 28And Har′an died before his fa-
ther Tē′rah in his native land, in Ūr of the
Chal·dē′ans. 29Then Abram and Nā′hor
took wives: the name of Abram's wife *was*
Sar′aī, and the name of Nā′hor's wife,
Mil′cah, the daughter of Har′an the father
of Mil′cah and the father of Is′cah. 30But
Sar′aī was barren; she had no child.
31And Tē′rah took his son Abram and
his grandson Lot, the son of Har′an, and
his daughter-in-law Sar′aī, his son
Abram's wife, and they went out with
them from Ūr of the Chal·dē′ans to go to
the land of Cā′naan; and they came to
Har′an and dwelt there. 32So the days of
Tē′rah were two hundred and five years,
and Tē′rah died in Har′an.

11:7, 9 Us: Perhaps a second reference to the Trinity (see 1:26; 3:22 and note on 1:26–28). The Hebrew word for **confuse** *(balal)* is similar in sound to **Babel**, which means "Gate of God." The proposed Gate of God became only confusion. This is always the case when we try to elevate ourselves to His level.

CHAPTER 12

Promises to Abram

Now the LORD had said to Abram:

"Get out of your country,
From your family
And from your father's house,
To a land that I will show you.
2 I will make you a great nation;
I will bless you
And make your name great;
And you shall be a blessing.
3 I will bless those who bless you,
And I will curse him who curses you;
And in you all the families of the
earth shall be blessed."

4So Abram departed as the LORD had
spoken to him, and Lot went with him.
And Abram *was* seventy-five years old
when he departed from Har'an. 5Then
Abram took Sar'aī his wife and Lot his
brother's son, and all their possessions that
they had gathered, and the people whom
they had acquired in Har'an, and they de-
parted to go to the land of Cā'naan. So they
came to the land of Cā'naan. 6Abram
passed through the land to the place of
Shē'chem, as far as the terebinth tree of
Mō'reh.[a] And the Cā'naan·ītes *were* then in
the land.
7Then the LORD appeared to Abram and
said, "To your descendants I will give this
land." And there he built an altar to the
LORD, who had appeared to him. 8And he
moved from there to the mountain east of
Beth'el, and he pitched his tent *with* Beth'el
on the west and Aī on the east; there he
built an altar to the LORD and called on the
name of the LORD. 9So Abram journeyed,
going on still toward the South.[a]

Abram in Egypt

10Now there was a famine in the land,
and Abram went down to Egypt to dwell
there, for the famine *was* severe in the land.
11And it came to pass, when he was close to
entering Egypt, that he said to Sar'aī his
wife, "Indeed I know that you *are* a woman
of beautiful countenance. 12Therefore it
will happen, when the Egyptians see you,
that they will say, 'This *is* his wife'; and
they will kill me, but they will let you live.
13Please say you *are* my sister, that it may
be well with me for your sake, and that I[a]
may live because of you."
14So it was, when Abram came into
Egypt, that the Egyptians saw the woman,
that she *was* very beautiful. 15The princes of
Pharaoh also saw her and commended her
to Pharaoh. And the woman was taken to
Pharaoh's house. 16He treated Abram well
for her sake. He had sheep, oxen, male
donkeys, male and female servants, female
donkeys, and camels.
17But the LORD plagued Pharaoh and his
house with great plagues because of Sar'aī,
Abram's wife. 18And Pharaoh called
Abram and said, "What *is* this you have
done to me? Why did you not tell me that
she *was* your wife? 19Why did you say, 'She

12:6 [a]Hebrew *Alon Moreh* 12:9 [a]Hebrew *Negev*
12:13 [a]Literally *my soul*

12:1 God called Abram to give up all that was dear to him so that he could experience God's blessing. Today, God calls us to give up the things that are important in the eyes of the world so that we too can experience His fullest blessing.

12:6 Shechem: An ancient city in central Palestine. It is present-day Nablus, about 41 miles (66 km) north of Jerusalem between Mt. Ebal and Mt. Gerizim. **tree of Moreh**: Probably a place already sacred to the Canaanites.

12:9 Laws known from this period specified that an alien could not remain in one place for more than six months at a time.

12:11–13 my sister (v. 13): Sarai was his half-sister, the daughter of Abram's father, Terah. She was perhaps a legal sister as well through a marriage practice peculiar to Haran's Hurrian culture. But half-truths bring negative consequences.

Abraham: Father of the Faithful

If the Lord told you to pack up your household, say good-bye to your family and friends, and relocate to an unknown, unspecified destination, how would you respond?

Very few people would react with the extraordinary faith exhibited by Abraham in a similar situation. The Bible tells us that when God told him to go, "Abram departed as the LORD had spoken to him" (Gen. 12:4).

Yet despite his close relationship with God, Abraham's courage often failed when it came to risking his own life. Everywhere he traveled, he lied about his relationship to Sarah, leading people to believe she was his sister rather than his wife (20:13). Although Abraham failed to foresee the consequences of his lie, the Lord protected both Sarah and Abraham and brought the truth to light.

This Old Testament hero also failed in one other area. At the same time God sent Abraham on his travels, He promised to make him the father of a great nation. When ten years passed and Abraham was still without an heir, his faith began to falter. He and Sarah decided to help things along, and he fathered a child by her handmaid, Hagar.

Looking back with the wisdom of hindsight, we may wonder how a man of such faith could be so foolish. Yet how often do we tire of waiting on the Lord and decide to give events a little nudge in the direction we believe they should go? How many times have we said, "Lord, I can't take this waiting anymore; I've got to *do* something"?

Abraham's impatience did not stop God from honoring His commitment. However, the consequences of Abraham's impatience can be seen today in the centuries-old conflict between Jews and Arabs. All-powerful God is not detoured by our interference, but He doesn't always save us from the repercussions of our foolish choices.

Before we dismiss Abraham because of his shortcomings, however, we should take another look at some of his spiritual successes. In addition to obeying God's call, Abraham showed himself to be unselfish and courageous in his dealings with his self-centered nephew, Lot. At Lot's request, he generously gave up the best land in Jordan. Then, instead of holding a grudge, he twice saved Lot's life (14:14–16; 19:29).

The high mark of Abraham's faithfulness came when God asked him to sacrifice Isaac, the son of promise (ch. 22). The Lord wanted to see if Abraham still trusted God to honor His promise to make Isaac a father. Abraham's instant response to God's request reflects his obedient attitude, and his statement to those accompanying him demonstrates his immense faith: "The lad and I will go yonder and worship, and *we will come back to you*" (v. 5). Hebrews 11:17–19 reveals that Abraham believed God would raise Isaac from the

dead, if need be, in order to fulfill His promise concerning Abraham's descendants.

Like most Christians, Abraham's spiritual life experienced some ups and downs, and parents and grandparents should take caution: Our actions can affect future generations. Yet we can still draw comfort from God's patience with the failings of the patriarch of Israel, even as we are inspired by Abraham's acts of faith. ✦

is my sister'? I might have taken her as my
wife. Now therefore, here is your wife;
take *her* and go your way." [20]So Pharaoh
commanded *his* men concerning him; and
they sent him away, with his wife and all
that he had.

CHAPTER 13

Abram Inherits Canaan

Then Abram went up from Egypt, he
and his wife and all that he had, and Lot
with him, to the South.[a] [2]Abram *was* very
rich in livestock, in silver, and in gold.
[3]And he went on his journey from the
South as far as Beth'el, to the place where
his tent had been at the beginning, between Beth'el and Aī, [4]to the place of the
altar which he had made there at first. And
there Abram called on the name of the
LORD.

[5]Lot also, who went with Abram, had
flocks and herds and tents. [6]Now the land
was not able to support them, that they
might dwell together, for their possessions
were so great that they could not dwell together. [7]And there was strife between the
herdsmen of Abram's livestock and the
herdsmen of Lot's livestock. The Cā'naan·ītes and the Per'iz·zītes then dwelt in
the land.

[8]So Abram said to Lot, "Please let there
be no strife between you and me, and between my herdsmen and your herdsmen;
for we *are* brethren. [9]*Is* not the whole land
before you? Please separate from me. If *you*
take the left, then I will go to the right; or, if
you go to the right, then I will go to the
left."

[10]And Lot lifted his eyes and saw all the
plain of Jordan, that it *was* well watered
everywhere (before the LORD destroyed
Sod'om and Go·mor'rah) like the garden
of the LORD, like the land of Egypt as you
go toward Zō'ar. [11]Then Lot chose for himself all the plain of Jordan, and Lot journeyed east. And they separated from each
other. [12]Abram dwelt in the land of Cā'naan, and Lot dwelt in the cities of the
plain and pitched *his* tent even as far as
Sod'om. [13]But the men of Sod'om *were* exceedingly wicked and sinful against the
LORD.

[14]And the LORD said to Abram, after Lot
had separated from him: "Lift your eyes
now and look from the place where
you are—northward, southward, eastward, and westward; [15]for all the land
which you see I give to you and your descendants[a] forever. [16]And I will make your

13:1 [a]Hebrew *Negev* throughout the book

13:15 [a]Literally *seed,* and so

13:8, 9 Abram's response to the conflict demonstrates the unselfish love all Christians are to have for one another. He valued his relationship with Lot above any material gain.

13:10–12 From a high spot in the Bethel/Ai area one can see to the **east** the well-watered irrigated greenness of Jericho in the lower Jordan valley. South of this is the Dead Sea which may now cover the sites of **Sodom** and **Gomorrah**. Lot lifted his eyes in greed, inwardly envisioning the **plain of Jordan** as including also all the eastern slope of the Dead Sea to **Zoar** at its southern tip. The wealth of **Egypt** had left its mark on Lot.

descendants as the dust of the earth; so that if a man could number the dust of the earth, *then* your descendants also could be numbered. 17Arise, walk in the land through its length and its width, for I give it to you."

18Then Abram moved *his* tent, and went and dwelt by the terebinth trees of Mam′re,[a] which *are* in Hē′bron, and built an altar there to the LORD.

CHAPTER 14

Lot's Captivity and Rescue

And it came to pass in the days of Am′ra·phel king of Shī′nar, Ar′i·och king of El·lā′sar, Ched·or·la·ō′mer king of Ē′lam, and Tidal king of nations,[a] 2*that* they made war with Bē′ra king of Sod′om, Bir′sha king of Go·mor′rah, Shī′nab king of Ad′mah, Shem·ē′ber king of Ze·boi′im, and the king of Bē′la (that is, Zō′ar). 3All these joined together in the Valley of Sid′dim (that is, the Salt Sea). 4Twelve years they served Ched·or·la·ō′mer, and in the thirteenth year they rebelled.

5In the fourteenth year Ched·or-la·ō′mer and the kings that *were* with him came and attacked the Reph′a·im in Ash′te·roth Kar·nā′im, the Zū′zim in Ham, the Ē′mim in Shā′veh Kir·i·a·thā′im, 6and the Hor′ītes in their mountain of Sē′ir, as far as El Par′an, which *is* by the wilderness. 7Then they turned back and came to En Mish′pat (that *is,* Kā′desh), and attacked all the country of the A·mal′e·kītes, and also the Am′o·rītes who dwelt in Ha·zē′-zon Tā′mar.

8And the king of Sod′om, the king of Go·mor′rah, the king of Ad′mah, the king of Ze·boi′im, and the king of Bē′la (that *is,* Zō′ar) went out and joined together in battle in the Valley of Sid′dim 9against Ched·or·la·ō′mer king of Ē′lam, Tidal king of nations,[a] Am′ra·phel king of Shī′nar, and Ar′i·och king of El·lā′sar—four kings against five. 10Now the Valley of Sid′dim *was full of* asphalt pits; and the kings of Sod′om and Go·mor′rah fled; *some* fell there, and the remainder fled to the mountains. 11Then they took all the goods of Sod′om and Go·mor′rah, and all their provisions, and went their way. 12They also took Lot, Abram's brother's son who dwelt in Sod′om, and his goods, and departed.

13Then one who had escaped came and told Abram the Hebrew, for he dwelt by the terebinth trees of Mam′re[a] the Am′-o·rīte, brother of Esh′col and brother of Ā′ner; and they *were* allies with Abram. 14Now when Abram heard that his brother was taken captive, he armed his three hundred and eighteen trained *servants* who were born in his own house, and went in pursuit as far as Dan. 15He divided his forces against them by night, and he and his servants attacked them and pursued them as far as Hō′bah, which *is* north of Damascus. 16So he brought back all the goods, and also brought back his brother Lot and his goods, as well as the women and the people.

17And the king of Sod′om went out to meet him at the Valley of Shā′veh (that *is,* the King's Valley), after his return from the defeat of Ched·or·la·ō′mer and the kings who *were* with him.

13:18 [a]Hebrew *Alon Mamre* 14:1 [a]Hebrew *goyim* 14:9 [a]Hebrew *goyim* 14:13 [a]Hebrew *Alon Mamre*

14:17–20 Melchizedek (meaning "My King Is Righteousness" or "King of Righteousness") represents the order through which the messianic King would be ordained. **God Most High** (also vv. 19, 20): A title for the Lord (see v. 22). That Melchizedek knew of the living God, the **Possessor** (Creator) **of heaven and earth** suggests that the true knowledge of God had not yet been supplanted by polytheism everywhere. Melchizedek is a mysterious figure who in his role of priest and king supplies a type of Christ (see Heb. 7:1–10 and notes). He is construed by many to be a theophany or an actual preincarnate appearance of Christ.

Abram and Melchizedek

18 Then Mel·chiz'e·dek king of Sā'lem
brought out bread and wine; he *was* the
priest of God Most High. 19 And he blessed
him and said:

"Blessed be Abram of God Most High,
Possessor of heaven and earth;
20 And blessed be God Most High,
Who has delivered your enemies into
your hand."

And he gave him a tithe of all.
21 Now the king of Sod'om said to
Abram, "Give me the persons, and take the
goods for yourself."
22 But Abram said to the king of Sod'om,
"I have raised my hand to the LORD, God
Most High, the Possessor of heaven and
earth, 23 that I *will take* nothing, from a
thread to a sandal strap, and that I will not
take anything that *is* yours, lest you should
say, 'I have made Abram rich'— 24 except
only what the young men have eaten, and
the portion of the men who went with me:
Ā'ner, Esh'col, and Mam're; let them take
their portion."

CHAPTER 15

God's Covenant with Abram

After these things the word of the LORD
came to Abram in a vision, saying, "Do not
be afraid, Abram. I *am* your shield, your
exceedingly great reward."
2 But Abram said, "Lord GOD, what will
You give me, seeing I go childless, and the
heir of my house *is* El·i·ē'zer of Damas-
cus?" 3 Then Abram said, "Look, You have
given me no offspring; indeed one born in
my house is my heir!"
4 And behold, the word of the LORD *came*
to him, saying, "This one shall not be your
heir, but one who will come from your
own body shall be your heir." 5 Then He
brought him outside and said, "Look now
toward heaven, and count the stars if you
are able to number them." And He said to
him, "So shall your descendants be."
6 And he believed in the LORD, and He
accounted it to him for righteousness.
7 Then He said to him, "I *am* the LORD,
who brought you out of Ūr of the Chal-
dē'ans, to give you this land to inherit it."
8 And he said, "Lord GOD, how shall I
know that I will inherit it?"
9 So He said to him, "Bring Me a three-
year-old heifer, a three-year-old female
goat, a three-year-old ram, a turtledove,
and a young pigeon." 10 Then he brought
all these to Him and cut them in two,
down the middle, and placed each piece
opposite the other; but he did not cut the
birds in two. 11 And when the vultures
came down on the carcasses, Abram drove
them away.
12 Now when the sun was going down, a
deep sleep fell upon Abram; and behold,
horror *and* great darkness fell upon him.
13 Then He said to Abram: "Know certainly
that your descendants will be strangers in
a land *that is* not theirs, and will serve
them, and they will afflict them four hun-
dred years. 14 And also the nation whom
they serve I will judge; afterward they
shall come out with great possessions.
15 Now as for you, you shall go to your fa-
thers in peace; you shall be buried at a
good old age. 16 But in the fourth genera-
tion they shall return here, for the iniquity
of the Am'o·rītes *is* not yet complete."
17 And it came to pass, when the sun

15:2, 3 Hurrian law of Abram's time provided that a man with no son could adopt a servant as his **heir** to carry on his name, receive his estate, and give him a proper burial. Perhaps Abram had adopted **Eliezer**.

15:10 down the middle: Partners in a covenant ceremony stood between the bleeding halves of a sacrificial animal and called a similar fate upon themselves if they failed to keep the covenant promises (see Jer. 34:18 and note). Here, only God—in symbolic form—passed between the pieces (v. 17); thus, He was the only obligated party.

went down and it was dark, that behold, there appeared a smoking oven and a burning torch that passed between those pieces. 18On the same day the LORD made a covenant with Abram, saying:

"To your descendants I have given this land, from the river of Egypt to the great river, the River Eū·phrā'tēs— 19the Ken'-ītes, the Kē'nez·zītes, the Kad'mon·ītes, 20the Hit'tītes, the Per'iz·zītes, the Reph'-a·im, 21the Am'o·rītes, the Cā'naan·ītes, the Gir'ga·shītes, and the Jeb'ū·sītes."

CHAPTER 16

Hagar and Ishmael

Now Sar'aī, Abram's wife, had borne him no *children*. And she had an Egyptian maidservant whose name was Hā'gar. 2So Sar'aī said to Abram, "See now, the LORD has restrained me from bearing *children*. Please, go in to my maid; perhaps I shall obtain children by her." And Abram heeded the voice of Sar'aī. 3Then Sar'aī, Abram's wife, took Hā'gar her maid, the Egyptian, and gave her to her husband Abram to be his wife, after Abram had dwelt ten years in the land of Cā'naan. 4So he went in to Hā'gar, and she conceived. And when she saw that she had conceived, her mistress became despised in her eyes.

5Then Sar'aī said to Abram, "My wrong *be* upon you! I gave my maid into your embrace; and when she saw that she had conceived, I became despised in her eyes. The LORD judge between you and me."

6So Abram said to Sar'aī, "Indeed your maid *is* in your hand; do to her as you please." And when Sar'aī dealt harshly with her, she fled from her presence.

7Now the Angel of the LORD found her by a spring of water in the wilderness, by the spring on the way to Shūr. 8And He said, "Hā'gar, Sar'aī's maid, where have you come from, and where are you going?"

She said, "I am fleeing from the presence of my mistress Sar'aī."

9The Angel of the LORD said to her, "Return to your mistress, and submit yourself under her hand." 10Then the Angel of the LORD said to her, "I will multiply your descendants exceedingly, so that they shall not be counted for multitude." 11And the Angel of the LORD said to her:

"Behold, you *are* with child,
And you shall bear a son.
You shall call his name Ish'ma·el,
Because the LORD has heard your affliction.
12 He shall be a wild man;
His hand *shall be* against every man,
And every man's hand against him.
And he shall dwell in the presence of all his brethren."

13Then she called the name of the LORD who spoke to her, You-Are-the-God-Who-Sees; for she said, "Have I also here seen Him who sees me?" 14Therefore the well was called Bē'er La·haī' Roi;[a] observe, *it is* between Kā'desh and Bē'red.

15So Hā'gar bore Abram a son; and Abram named his son, whom Hā'gar bore, Ish'ma·el. 16Abram *was* eighty-six years old when Hā'gar bore Ish'ma·el to Abram.

CHAPTER 17

The Sign of the Covenant

When Abram was ninety-nine years old, the LORD appeared to Abram and said to him, "I *am* Almighty God; walk before Me and be blameless. 2And I will make My

16:14 [a]Literally *Well of the One Who Lives and Sees Me*

16:2 go in to my maid: This was Sarai's attempt in human strength to help the Lord fulfill His promise to Abram (see 13:16; 15:5). But attempts on our part to do God's work will always fail. God must supply in His way.

covenant between Me and you, and will
multiply you exceedingly." 3Then Abram
fell on his face, and God talked with him,
saying: 4"As for Me, behold, My covenant
is with you, and you shall be a father of
many nations. 5No longer shall your name
be called Abram, but your name shall be
Abraham; for I have made you a father of
many nations. 6I will make you exceed-
ingly fruitful; and I will make nations of
you, and kings shall come from you. 7And
I will establish My covenant between Me
and you and your descendants after you in
their generations, for an everlasting
covenant, to be God to you and your de-
scendants after you. 8Also I give to you and
your descendants after you the land in
which you are a stranger, all the land of
Cā'naan, as an everlasting possession; and
I will be their God."

9And God said to Abraham: "As for
you, you shall keep My covenant, you and
your descendants after you throughout
their generations. 10This *is* My covenant
which you shall keep, between Me and
you and your descendants after you: Every
male child among you shall be circum-
cised; 11and you shall be circumcised in the
flesh of your foreskins, and it shall be a
sign of the covenant between Me and you.
12He who is eight days old among you
shall be circumcised, every male child in
your generations, he who is born in your
house or bought with money from any for-
eigner who is not your descendant. 13He
who is born in your house and he who is
bought with your money must be circum-
cised, and My covenant shall be in your
flesh for an everlasting covenant. 14And the
uncircumcised male child, who is not cir-
cumcised in the flesh of his foreskin, that
person shall be cut off from his people; he
has broken My covenant."

15Then God said to Abraham, "As for
Sar'aī your wife, you shall not call her
name Sar'aī, but Sarah *shall be* her name.
16And I will bless her and also give you a
son by her; then I will bless her, and she
shall be *a mother* of nations; kings of peo-
ples shall be from her."

17Then Abraham fell on his face and
laughed, and said in his heart, "Shall *a child*
be born to a man who is one hundred years
old? And shall Sarah, who is ninety years
old, bear *a child?*" 18And Abraham said to
God, "Oh, that Ish'ma•el might live before
You!"

19Then God said: "No, Sarah your wife
shall bear you a son, and you shall call his
name Isaac; I will establish My covenant
with him for an everlasting covenant, *and*
with his descendants after him. 20And as
for Ish'ma•el, I have heard you. Behold, I
have blessed him, and will make him fruit-
ful, and will multiply him exceedingly. He
shall beget twelve princes, and I will make
him a great nation. 21But My covenant I
will establish with Isaac, whom Sarah shall
bear to you at this set time next year."
22Then He finished talking with him, and
God went up from Abraham.

23So Abraham took Ish'ma•el his son, all
who were born in his house and all who
were bought with his money, every male
among the men of Abraham's house, and
circumcised the flesh of their foreskins that
very same day, as God had said to him.
24Abraham *was* ninety-nine years old when
he was circumcised in the flesh of his fore-
skin. 25And Ish'ma•el his son *was* thirteen
years old when he was circumcised in the
flesh of his foreskin. 26That very same day
Abraham was circumcised, and his son
Ish'ma•el; 27and all the men of his house,
born in the house or bought with money
from a foreigner, were circumcised with him.

17:9–14 Circumcision was established as a sign of the Abrahamic covenant. It was an act of obedience and faith but of itself could not obtain righteousness; only faith in the Lord can achieve that (15:6). Likewise, baptism is an act of obedience for believers today, but it is meaningless without sincere faith.

CHAPTER 18

The Son of Promise

Then the LORD appeared to him by the
terebinth trees of Mam're,[a] as he was sit-
ting in the tent door in the heat of the day.
2So he lifted his eyes and looked, and be-
hold, three men were standing by him; and
when he saw *them,* he ran from the tent
door to meet them, and bowed himself to
the ground, 3and said, "My Lord, if I have
now found favor in Your sight, do not pass
on by Your servant. 4Please let a little water
be brought, and wash your feet, and rest
yourselves under the tree. 5And I will
bring a morsel of bread, that you may re-
fresh your hearts. After that you may pass
by, inasmuch as you have come to your
servant."

They said, "Do as you have said."

6So Abraham hurried into the tent to Sa-
rah and said, "Quickly, make ready three
measures of fine meal; knead *it* and make
cakes." 7And Abraham ran to the herd,
took a tender and good calf, gave *it* to a
young man, and he hastened to prepare it.
8So he took butter and milk and the calf
which he had prepared, and set *it* before
them; and he stood by them under the tree
as they ate.

9Then they said to him, "Where *is* Sarah
your wife?"

So he said, "Here, in the tent."

10And He said, "I will certainly return to
you according to the time of life, and be-
hold, Sarah your wife shall have a son."

(Sarah was listening in the tent door
which *was* behind him.) 11Now Abraham
and Sarah were old, well advanced in age;
and Sarah had passed the age of childbear-
ing.[a] 12Therefore Sarah laughed within her-
self, saying, "After I have grown old, shall
I have pleasure, my lord being old also?"

13And the LORD said to Abraham, "Why
did Sarah laugh, saying, 'Shall I surely
bear *a child,* since I am old?' 14Is anything
too hard for the LORD? At the appointed
time I will return to you, according to the
time of life, and Sarah shall have a son."

15But Sarah denied *it,* saying, "I did not
laugh," for she was afraid.

And He said, "No, but you did laugh!"

Abraham Intercedes for Sodom

16Then the men rose from there and
looked toward Sod'om, and Abraham
went with them to send them on the way.
17And the LORD said, "Shall I hide from
Abraham what I am doing, 18since Abra-
ham shall surely become a great and
mighty nation, and all the nations of the
earth shall be blessed in him? 19For I have
known him, in order that he may com-
mand his children and his household after
him, that they keep the way of the LORD, to
do righteousness and justice, that the LORD
may bring to Abraham what He has spo-
ken to him." 20And the LORD said, "Because
the outcry against Sod'om and Go·mor'rah
is great, and because their sin is very grave,
21I will go down now and see whether they
have done altogether according to the out-
cry against it that has come to Me; and if
not, I will know."

18:1 [a]Hebrew *Alon Mamre* 18:11 [a]Literally *the manner of women had ceased to be with Sarah*

18:1-33 In the most human of His visits to Abraham, God appeared as one of **three men** (v. 2). Throughout this story the narrator and God Himself use the name *Yahweh*, the LORD. Abraham, however, uses the title of humble address, *'adonay*, "Lord."

18:5-8 In keeping with Near Eastern hospitality, Abraham's offer of a **morsel** is in stark contrast to the actual feast he produced: **cakes** (v. 6), tender veal, **butter**, and **milk** (vv. 7, 8).

18:16-33 God's ultimate purpose with Abraham was to reveal Himself. If he was to bring up his children to know God (v. 19), Abraham himself must know Him. In this incident God all but asks Abraham to intercede for Sodom and Gomorrah. Out of this experience Abraham learned something about God's patience and compassion. Almost any excuse is enough for God to refrain from exercising His wholly justified wrath (see Ps. 103:8).

Sarah's Faltering Faith

When Sarah first left Haran with her husband, Abraham, she must have wondered into what he was getting them. At the call of God, they had left family and home to travel to an unknown land. In fact, the Bible tells us that Abraham "went out, not knowing where he was going" (Heb. 11:8).

At that time, women did not have much autonomy, and Sarah had little choice but to accompany her husband. However, she could certainly have made his life extremely difficult had she chosen to do so. Many other women throughout Scripture—Michal, Job's wife, and Rebekah—did not hesitate to criticize, belittle, and even deceive their husbands as they attempted to direct things their own way. But at age sixty-five, when Sarah found herself traveling in a foreign country, she willingly submitted to her husband's authority, and the New Testament presents her as a model of wifely obedience (1 Pet. 3:6).

However, as the years went by, Sarah became disenchanted with the waiting game. The Lord's promise of a son had not been fulfilled after several years, and she was not getting any younger. In accordance with a legal—but ungodly—custom of the day, she urged Abraham to obtain a child through her handmaid Hagar (Gen. 16).

God once again appeared to Abraham and made it clear that Hagar's child was not the son of promise. He assured Abraham that Sarah would bear a son the following year (17:21). She overheard and laughed in unbelief: "After I have grown old, shall I have pleasure, my lord being old also?" (18:12).

We can easily criticize Sarah for her skepticism of the Lord's power, until we picture ourselves in her place. She and Abraham had passed their prime. The literal translation of Genesis 18:11 is "the manner of women had ceased to be with Sarah." Medically speaking, she had no reason to believe she could ever bear a child.

In spite of Sarah's doubts, she allowed the Lord to use her. The writer of Hebrews tells us that "by faith Sarah . . . received strength to conceive seed, and she bore a child when she was past the age, because she judged Him faithful who had promised" (11:11). At the age of ninety, Sarah "conceived and bore Abraham a son in his old age, at the set time of which God had spoken to him" (Gen. 21:2).

Suddenly, her laughter changed from sarcasm into genuine joy. "God has made me laugh, and all who hear will laugh with me" (v. 6). According to God's instructions, Sarah and Abraham named their son Isaac, which means laughter.

The Lord not only overcame Sarah's physical inadequacies but He also strengthened her sagging faith. Her life shows that God can conquer our physical, emotional, and spiritual deficiencies when we allow Him to do so. ✦

22Then the men turned away from there
and went toward Sod'om, but Abraham
still stood before the LORD. 23And Abraham
came near and said, "Would You also de-
stroy the righteous with the wicked? 24Sup-
pose there were fifty righteous within the
city; would You also destroy the place and
not spare *it* for the fifty righteous that were
in it? 25Far be it from You to do such a thing
as this, to slay the righteous with the
wicked, so that the righteous should be as
the wicked; far be it from You! Shall not the
Judge of all the earth do right?"

26So the LORD said, "If I find in Sod'om
fifty righteous within the city, then I will
spare all the place for their sakes."

27Then Abraham answered and said,
"Indeed now, I who *am* but dust and ashes
have taken it upon myself to speak to the
Lord: 28Suppose there were five less than
the fifty righteous; would You destroy all
of the city for *lack of* five?"

So He said, "If I find there forty-five, I
will not destroy *it.*"

29And he spoke to Him yet again and
said, "Suppose there should be forty found
there?"

So He said, "I will not do *it* for the sake
of forty."

30Then he said, "Let not the Lord be an-
gry, and I will speak: Suppose thirty
should be found there?"

So He said, "I will not do *it* if I find
thirty there."

31And he said, "Indeed now, I have
taken it upon myself to speak to the Lord:
Suppose twenty should be found there?"

So He said, "I will not destroy *it* for the
sake of twenty."

32Then he said, "Let not the Lord be an-
gry, and I will speak but once more: Sup-
pose ten should be found there?"

And He said, "I will not destroy *it* for
the sake of ten." 33So the LORD went His
way as soon as He had finished speaking
with Abraham; and Abraham returned to
his place.

CHAPTER 19

Sodom's Depravity

Now the two angels came to Sod'om in
the evening, and Lot was sitting in the gate
of Sod'om. When Lot saw *them,* he rose to
meet them, and he bowed himself with his
face toward the ground. 2And he said,
"Here now, my lords, please turn in to
your servant's house and spend the night,
and wash your feet; then you may rise
early and go on your way."

And they said, "No, but we will spend
the night in the open square."

3But he insisted strongly; so they turned
in to him and entered his house. Then he
made them a feast, and baked unleavened
bread, and they ate.

4Now before they lay down, the men of
the city, the men of Sod'om, both old and
young, all the people from every quarter,
surrounded the house. 5And they called to
Lot and said to him, "Where are the men
who came to you tonight? Bring them out
to us that we may know them *carnally.*"

6So Lot went out to them through the
doorway, shut the door behind him, 7and
said, "Please, my brethren, do not do so
wickedly! 8See now, I have two daughters
who have not known a man; please, let me
bring them out to you, and you may do to
them as you wish; only do nothing to these
men, since this is the reason they have
come under the shadow of my roof."

9And they said, "Stand back!" Then they
said, "This one came in to stay *here,* and he
keeps acting as a judge; now we will deal
worse with you than with them." So they
pressed hard against the man Lot, and
came near to break down the door. 10But

19:16 Lot's hesitancy contrasts sharply with Abraham's willingness to obey God (17:26). Like many today, he had lost sight of his priorities and become attached to the things of the world.

the men reached out their hands and pulled Lot into the house with them, and shut the door. 11And they struck the men who *were* at the doorway of the house with blindness, both small and great, so that they became weary *trying* to find the door.

Sodom and Gomorrah Destroyed

12Then the men said to Lot, "Have you anyone else here? Son-in-law, your sons, your daughters, and whomever you have in the city—take *them* out of this place! 13For we will destroy this place, because the outcry against them has grown great before the face of the LORD, and the LORD has sent us to destroy it."

14So Lot went out and spoke to his sons-in-law, who had married his daughters, and said, "Get up, get out of this place; for the LORD will destroy this city!" But to his sons-in-law he seemed to be joking.

15When the morning dawned, the angels urged Lot to hurry, saying, "Arise, take your wife and your two daughters who are here, lest you be consumed in the punishment of the city." 16And while he lingered, the men took hold of his hand, his wife's hand, and the hands of his two daughters, the LORD being merciful to him, and they brought him out and set him outside the city. 17So it came to pass, when they had brought them outside, that he[a] said, "Escape for your life! Do not look behind you nor stay anywhere in the plain. Escape to the mountains, lest you be destroyed."

18Then Lot said to them, "Please, no, my lords! 19Indeed now, your servant has found favor in your sight, and you have increased your mercy which you have shown me by saving my life; but I cannot escape to the mountains, lest some evil overtake me and I die. 20See now, this city *is* near *enough* to flee to, and it *is* a little one; please let me escape there (*is* it not a little one?) and my soul shall live."

21And he said to him, "See, I have favored you concerning this thing also, in that I will not overthrow this city for which you have spoken. 22Hurry, escape there. For I cannot do anything until you arrive there."

Therefore the name of the city was called Zō'ar.

23The sun had risen upon the earth when Lot entered Zō'ar. 24Then the LORD rained brimstone and fire on Sod'om and Go·mor'rah, from the LORD out of the heavens. 25So He overthrew those cities, all the plain, all the inhabitants of the cities, and what grew on the ground.

26But his wife looked back behind him, and she became a pillar of salt.

27And Abraham went early in the morning to the place where he had stood before the LORD. 28Then he looked toward Sod'om and Go·mor'rah, and toward all the land of the plain; and he saw, and behold, the smoke of the land which went up like the smoke of a furnace. 29And it came to pass, when God destroyed the cities of the plain, that God remembered Abraham, and sent Lot out of the midst of the overthrow, when He overthrew the cities in which Lot had dwelt.

The Descendants of Lot

30Then Lot went up out of Zō'ar and dwelt in the mountains, and his two daughters were with him; for he was afraid to dwell in Zō'ar. And he and his two daughters dwelt in a cave. 31Now the firstborn said to the younger, "Our father *is* old, and *there is* no man on the earth to come in to us as is the custom of all the earth. 32Come, let us make our father drink wine, and we will lie with him, that we may preserve the lineage of our father." 33So they made their father drink wine that night. And the firstborn went in and lay with her father, and he did not know when she lay down or when she arose.

34It happened on the next day that the firstborn said to the younger, "Indeed I lay with my father last night; let us make him drink wine tonight also, and you go in *and* lie with him, that we may preserve the lineage of our father." 35Then they made

their father drink wine that night also. And
the younger arose and lay with him, and
he did not know when she lay down or
when she arose.
36Thus both the daughters of Lot were
with child by their father. 37The firstborn
bore a son and called his name Mō′ab; he *is*
the father of the Mō′ab·ītes to this day.
38And the younger, she also bore a son and
called his name Ben-Am′mī; he *is* the
father of the people of Am′mon to this
day.

CHAPTER 20

Abraham and Abimelech

And Abraham journeyed from there to
the South, and dwelt between Kā′desh and
Shūr, and stayed in Gē′rar. 2Now Abraham
said of Sarah his wife, "She *is* my sister."
And A·bim′e·lech king of Gē′rar sent and
took Sarah.
3But God came to A·bim′e·lech in a
dream by night, and said to him, "Indeed
you *are* a dead man because of the woman
whom you have taken, for she *is* a man's
wife."
4But A·bim′e·lech had not come near
her; and he said, "Lord, will You slay a
righteous nation also? 5Did he not say to
me, 'She *is* my sister'? And she, even she
herself said, 'He *is* my brother.' In the in-
tegrity of my heart and innocence of my
hands I have done this."
6And God said to him in a dream, "Yes,
I know that you did this in the integrity of
your heart. For I also withheld you from
sinning against Me; therefore I did not let
you touch her. 7Now therefore, restore the
man's wife; for he *is* a prophet, and he will
pray for you and you shall live. But if you
do not restore *her,* know that you shall
surely die, you and all who *are* yours."
8So A·bim′e·lech rose early in the morn-
ing, called all his servants, and told all
these things in their hearing; and the men
were very much afraid. 9And A·bim′e·lech
called Abraham and said to him, "What
have you done to us? How have I offended
you, that you have brought on me and on
my kingdom a great sin? You have done
deeds to me that ought not to be done."
10Then A·bim′e·lech said to Abraham,
"What did you have in view, that you have
done this thing?"
11And Abraham said, "Because I
thought, surely the fear of God *is* not in
this place; and they will kill me on account
of my wife. 12But indeed *she is* truly my sis-
ter. She *is* the daughter of my father, but
not the daughter of my mother; and she
became my wife. 13And it came to pass,
when God caused me to wander from my
father's house, that I said to her, 'This *is*
your kindness that you should do for me:
in every place, wherever we go, say of me,
"He *is* my brother." ' "
14Then A·bim′e·lech took sheep, oxen,
and male and female servants, and gave
them to Abraham; and he restored Sarah
his wife to him. 15And A·bim′e·lech said,
"See, my land *is* before you; dwell where it
pleases you." 16Then to Sarah he said, "Be-
hold, I have given your brother a thousand
pieces of silver; indeed this vindicates you[a]
before all who *are* with you and before
everybody." Thus she was rebuked.
17So Abraham prayed to God; and God
healed A·bim′e·lech, his wife, and his fe-
male servants. Then they bore *children;*
18for the LORD had closed up all the wombs
of the house of A·bim′e·lech because of
Sarah, Abraham's wife.

19:17 [a]Septuagint, Syriac, and Vulgate read *they.*
20:16 [a]Literally *it is a covering of the eyes for you*

20:3 This pagan king, **Abimelech**, apparently had some knowledge of God, though Abraham assumed there was no "fear of God" in Gerar (v. 11). In OT times God sometimes communicated His will in a **dream** (see 37:5; 1 Kin. 3:5). **a dead man** (also v. 7): Not an immediate execution, but a dying out of Abimelech's line (see vv. 17, 18).

CHAPTER 21

Isaac Is Born

And the LORD visited Sarah as He had
said, and the LORD did for Sarah as He had
spoken. 2For Sarah conceived and bore
Abraham a son in his old age, at the set
time of which God had spoken to him.
3And Abraham called the name of his son
who was born to him—whom Sarah bore
to him—Isaac. 4Then Abraham circum-
cised his son Isaac when he was eight days
old, as God had commanded him. 5Now
Abraham was one hundred years old
when his son Isaac was born to him. 6And
Sarah said, "God has made me laugh, *and*
all who hear will laugh with me." 7She also
said, "Who would have said to Abraham
that Sarah would nurse children? For I
have borne *him* a son in his old age."

Hagar and Ishmael Depart

8So the child grew and was weaned.
And Abraham made a great feast on the
same day that Isaac was weaned.

9And Sarah saw the son of Hā'gar the
Egyptian, whom she had borne to Abra-
ham, scoffing. 10Therefore she said to Abra-
ham, "Cast out this bondwoman and her
son; for the son of this bondwoman shall
not be heir with my son, *namely* with
Isaac." 11And the matter was very displeas-
ing in Abraham's sight because of his son.

12But God said to Abraham, "Do not let
it be displeasing in your sight because of
the lad or because of your bondwoman.
Whatever Sarah has said to you, listen to
her voice; for in Isaac your seed shall be
called. 13Yet I will also make a nation of the son
of the bondwoman, because he *is* your seed."

14So Abraham rose early in the morning,
and took bread and a skin of water; and
putting *it* on her shoulder, he gave *it* and
the boy to Hā'gar, and sent her away. Then
she departed and wandered in the Wilder-
ness of Bē·er·shē'ba. 15And the water in the
skin was used up, and she placed the boy
under one of the shrubs. 16Then she went
and sat down across from *him* at a distance
of about a bowshot; for she said to herself,
"Let me not see the death of the boy." So
she sat opposite *him*, and lifted her voice
and wept.

17And God heard the voice of the lad.
Then the angel of God called to Hā'gar out
of heaven, and said to her, "What ails you,
Hā'gar? Fear not, for God has heard the
voice of the lad where he *is*. 18Arise, lift up
the lad and hold him with your hand, for I
will make him a great nation."

19Then God opened her eyes, and she
saw a well of water. And she went and
filled the skin with water, and gave the lad
a drink. 20So God was with the lad; and he
grew and dwelt in the wilderness, and be-
came an archer. 21He dwelt in the Wilder-
ness of Par'an; and his mother took a wife
for him from the land of Egypt.

A Covenant with Abimelech

22And it came to pass at that time that
A·bim'e·lech and Phī'chol, the comman-
der of his army, spoke to Abraham, saying,
"God *is* with you in all that you do. 23Now

21:9 Hagar's **son**, Ishmael, was now at least 15 years old, being 13 at his circumcision (17:25) before Sarah's conception of Isaac.

21:10–14 Hurrian law prohibited the disinheriting of a firstborn son of a slave wife (Ishmael) in the event that the barren upper-class wife should later bear a son (Isaac). However, the upper-class wife's son would supersede the slave wife's son as the legal "firstborn." Sarah was wrong in her demand to cast out Hagar and her child (v. 10). Only upon God's command did Abraham send her away (v. 14). **I will also** (v. 13): God can sometimes do things differently from the way we do but still be loving and fair to all persons involved.

21:25–32 The Bible's first example of a **covenant** between equals, **Abraham** and **Abimelech** (v. 27), heads of two tribal groups. **well of water**: The dispute over its ownership occasioned the covenant. In accepting a gift of **seven ewe lambs** (v. 29), Abimelech publicly affirmed that the disputed well belonged to Abraham.

therefore, swear to me by God that you will not deal falsely with me, with my offspring, or with my posterity; but that according to the kindness that I have done to you, you will do to me and to the land in which you have dwelt."

24And Abraham said, "I will swear."

25Then Abraham rebuked A·bim'e·lech because of a well of water which A·bim'e·lech's servants had seized. 26And A·bim'e·lech said, "I do not know who has done this thing; you did not tell me, nor had I heard *of it* until today." 27So Abraham took sheep and oxen and gave them to A·bim'e·lech, and the two of them made a covenant. 28And Abraham set seven ewe lambs of the flock by themselves.

29Then A·bim'e·lech asked Abraham, "What *is the meaning of* these seven ewe lambs which you have set by themselves?"

30And he said, "You will take *these* seven ewe lambs from my hand, that they may be my witness that I have dug this well." 31Therefore he called that place Bē·er-shē'ba,[a] because the two of them swore an oath there.

32Thus they made a covenant at Bē·er·shē'ba. So A·bim'e·lech rose with Phī'chol, the commander of his army, and they returned to the land of the Phi·lis'tines. 33Then *Abraham* planted a tamarisk tree in Bē·er·shē'ba, and there called on the name of the LORD, the Everlasting God. 34And Abraham stayed in the land of the Phi·lis'tines many days.

CHAPTER 22

Abraham's Faith Confirmed

Now it came to pass after these things that God tested Abraham, and said to him, "Abraham!"

And he said, "Here I am."

2Then He said, "Take now your son, your only *son* Isaac, whom you love, and go to the land of Mō·rī'ah, and offer him there as a burnt offering on one of the mountains of which I shall tell you."

3So Abraham rose early in the morning and saddled his donkey, and took two of his young men with him, and Isaac his son; and he split the wood for the burnt offering, and arose and went to the place of which God had told him. 4Then on the third day Abraham lifted his eyes and saw the place afar off. 5And Abraham said to his young men, "Stay here with the donkey; the lad[a] and I will go yonder and worship, and we will come back to you."

6So Abraham took the wood of the burnt offering and laid *it* on Isaac his son; and he took the fire in his hand, and a knife, and the two of them went together. 7But Isaac spoke to Abraham his father and said, "My father!"

And he said, "Here I am, my son."

Then he said, "Look, the fire and the wood, but where *is* the lamb for a burnt offering?"

8And Abraham said, "My son, God will provide for Himself the lamb for a burnt offering." So the two of them went together.

9Then they came to the place of which God had told him. And Abraham built an altar there and placed the wood in order; and he bound Isaac his son and laid him on the altar, upon the wood. 10And Abraham stretched out his hand and took the knife to slay his son.

21:31 [a]Literally *Well of the Oath* or *Well of the Seven*
22:5 [a]Or *young man*

22:2 only son (also vv. 12, 16): Ishmael was also Abraham's son (16:16), but Isaac was the only son of the promise (see Heb. 11:17–19).

22:5 we will come back: How could this be if he were to sacrifice Isaac? Abraham's obedience included faith that "God was able to raise him up, even from the dead" (Heb. 11:19).

22:7–9 where is the lamb? . . . God will provide: Abraham's answer was not an evasion of the question but a statement of faith, even if the lamb was his son.

11But the Angel of the LORD called to him
from heaven and said, "Abraham, Abra-
ham!"
So he said, "Here I am."
12And He said, "Do not lay your hand
on the lad, or do anything to him; for now
I know that you fear God, since you have
not withheld your son, your only *son*, from
Me."
13Then Abraham lifted his eyes and
looked, and there behind *him was* a ram
caught in a thicket by its horns. So Abra-
ham went and took the ram, and offered it
up for a burnt offering instead of his son.
14And Abraham called the name of the
place, The-LORD-Will-Provide;[a] as it is said
to this day, "In the Mount of the LORD it
shall be provided."
15Then the Angel of the LORD called to
Abraham a second time out of heaven,
16and said: "By Myself I have sworn,
says the LORD, because you have done
this thing, and have not withheld your
son, your only *son*— 17blessing I will
bless you, and multiplying I will multiply
your descendants as the stars of the heaven
and as the sand which *is* on the seashore;
and your descendants shall possess the
gate of their enemies. 18In your seed all
the nations of the earth shall be blessed,
because you have obeyed My voice."
19So Abraham returned to his young men,
and they rose and went together to
Bē·er shē′ba; and Abraham dwelt at
Bē·er·shē′ba.

The Family of Nahor

20Now it came to pass after these things
that it was told Abraham, saying, "Indeed
Mil′cah also has borne children to your
brother Nā′hor: 21Huz his firstborn, Buz
his brother, Ke·mū′el the father of Ar′am,
22Chē′sed, Hā′zō, Pil′dash, Jid′laph, and
Be·thū′el." 23And Be·thū′el begot Re-
bekah.[a] These eight Mil′cah bore to Nā′hor,
Abraham's brother. 24His concubine,
whose name was Re·ū′mah, also bore
Tē′bah, Gā′ham, Thā′hash, and Mā′a-
chah.

CHAPTER 23

Sarah's Death and Burial

Sarah lived one hundred and twenty-
seven years; *these were* the years of the life
of Sarah. 2So Sarah died in Kir′jath Ar′ba
(that *is,* Hē′bron) in the land of Cā′naan,
and Abraham came to mourn for Sarah
and to weep for her.
3Then Abraham stood up from before
his dead, and spoke to the sons of Heth,
saying, 4"I *am* a foreigner and a visitor
among you. Give me property for a burial
place among you, that I may bury my dead
out of my sight."
5And the sons of Heth answered Abra-
ham, saying to him, 6"Hear us, my lord:
You *are* a mighty prince among us; bury
your dead in the choicest of our burial
places. None of us will withhold from you
his burial place, that you may bury your
dead."
7Then Abraham stood up and bowed
himself to the people of the land, the sons
of Heth. 8And he spoke with them, saying,
"If it is your wish that I bury my dead out
of my sight, hear me, and meet with
Ē′phron the son of Zō′har for me, 9that he
may give me the cave of Mach·pē′lah
which he has, which *is* at the end of his
field. Let him give it to me at the full price,
as property for a burial place among you."
10Now Ē′phron dwelt among the sons of
Heth; and Ē′phron the Hit′tīte answered
Abraham in the presence of the sons of
Heth, all who entered at the gate of his city,
saying, 11"No, my lord, hear me: I give you
the field and the cave that *is* in it; I give it to
you in the presence of the sons of my peo-
ple. I give it to you. Bury your dead!"
12Then Abraham bowed himself down
before the people of the land; 13and he
spoke to Ē′phron in the hearing of the peo-
ple of the land, saying, "If you *will give it,*
please hear me. I will give you money for

22:14 [a]Hebrew *YHWH Yireh* 22:23 [a]Spelled *Rebecca* in Romans 9:10

the field; take *it* from me and I will bury my dead there."

14And Ē′phron answered Abraham, saying to him, 15"My lord, listen to me; the land *is worth* four hundred shekels of silver. What *is* that between you and me? So bury your dead." 16And Abraham listened to Ē′phron; and Abraham weighed out the silver for Ē′phron which he had named in the hearing of the sons of Heth, four hundred shekels of silver, currency of the merchants.

17So the field of Ē′phron which *was* in Mach·pē′lah, which *was* before Mam′re, the field and the cave which *was* in it, and all the trees that *were* in the field, which *were* within all the surrounding borders, were deeded 18to Abraham as a possession in the presence of the sons of Heth, before all who went in at the gate of his city.

19And after this, Abraham buried Sarah his wife in the cave of the field of Mach·pē′lah, before Mam′re (that *is,* Hē′bron) in the land of Cā′naan. 20So the field and the cave that *is* in it were deeded to Abraham by the sons of Heth as property for a burial place.

CHAPTER 24

A Bride for Isaac

Now Abraham was old, well advanced in age; and the LORD had blessed Abraham in all things. 2So Abraham said to the oldest servant of his house, who ruled over all that he had, "Please, put your hand under my thigh, 3and I will make you swear by the LORD, the God of heaven and the God of the earth, that you will not take a wife for my son from the daughters of the Cā′naan·ītes, among whom I dwell; 4but you shall go to my country and to my family, and take a wife for my son Isaac."

5And the servant said to him, "Perhaps the woman will not be willing to follow me to this land. Must I take your son back to the land from which you came?"

6But Abraham said to him, "Beware that you do not take my son back there. 7The LORD God of heaven, who took me from my father's house and from the land of my family, and who spoke to me and swore to me, saying, 'To your descendants[a] I give this land,' He will send His angel before you, and you shall take a wife for my son from there. 8And if the woman is not willing to follow you, then you will be released from this oath; only do not take my son back there." 9So the servant put his hand under the thigh of Abraham his master, and swore to him concerning this matter.

10Then the servant took ten of his master's camels and departed, for all his master's goods *were in* his hand. And he arose and went to Mes·o·po·tā′mi·a, to the city of Nā′hor. 11And he made his camels kneel down outside the city by a well of water at evening time, the time when women go out to draw *water.* 12Then he said, "O LORD God of my master Abraham, please give me success this day, and show kindness to my master Abraham. 13Behold, *here* I stand by the well of water, and the daughters of the men of the city are coming out to draw water. 14Now let it be that the young woman to whom I say, 'Please let down your pitcher that I may drink,' and she says, 'Drink, and I will also give your camels a drink'—*let* her *be the one* You have appointed for Your servant Isaac. And by this I will know that You have shown kindness to my master."

15And it happened, before he had finished speaking, that behold, Rebekah, who was born to Be·thū′el, son of Mil′cah, the wife of Nā′hor, Abraham's brother, came

24:7 [a]Literally *seed*

24:14 An intelligent sign to request. Such a woman would be possessed of both exceptional kindness and energy. Ten camels could easily drink 200 gallons (909 l) of water before they finished (v. 19).

out with her pitcher on her shoulder. 16Now
the young woman *was* very beautiful to
behold, a virgin; no man had known her.
And she went down to the well, filled her
pitcher, and came up. 17And the servant
ran to meet her and said, "Please let me
drink a little water from your pitcher."

18So she said, "Drink, my lord." Then
she quickly let her pitcher down to her
hand, and gave him a drink. 19And when
she had finished giving him a drink, she
said, "I will draw *water* for your camels
also, until they have finished drinking."
20Then she quickly emptied her pitcher
into the trough, ran back to the well to
draw *water,* and drew for all his camels.
21And the man, wondering at her, re-
mained silent so as to know whether the
LORD had made his journey prosperous or
not.

22So it was, when the camels had fin-
ished drinking, that the man took a golden
nose ring weighing half a shekel, and two
bracelets for her wrists weighing ten
shekels of gold, 23and said, "Whose daugh-
ter *are* you? Tell me, please, is there room *in*
your father's house for us to lodge?"

24So she said to him, "I *am* the daughter
of Be·thū'el, Mil'cah's son, whom she bore
to Nā'hor." 25Moreover she said to him,
"We have both straw and feed enough, and
room to lodge."

26Then the man bowed down his head
and worshiped the LORD. 27And he said,
"Blessed *be* the LORD God of my master
Abraham, who has not forsaken His mercy
and His truth toward my master. As for
me, being on the way, the LORD led me to
the house of my master's brethren." 28So
the young woman ran and told her
mother's household these things.

29Now Rebekah had a brother whose
name *was* Lā'ban, and Lā'ban ran out to
the man by the well. 30So it came to pass,
when he saw the nose ring, and the
bracelets on his sister's wrists, and when
he heard the words of his sister Rebekah,
saying, "Thus the man spoke to me," that
he went to the man. And there he stood by
the camels at the well. 31And he said,
"Come in, O blessed of the LORD! Why do
you stand outside? For I have prepared the
house, and a place for the camels."

32Then the man came to the house. And
he unloaded the camels, and provided
straw and feed for the camels, and water to
wash his feet and the feet of the men who
were with him. 33*Food* was set before him to
eat, but he said, "I will not eat until I have
told about my errand."

And he said, "Speak on."

34So he said, "I *am* Abraham's servant.
35The LORD has blessed my master greatly,
and he has become great; and He has given
him flocks and herds, silver and gold, male
and female servants, and camels and don-
keys. 36And Sarah my master's wife bore a
son to my master when she was old; and to
him he has given all that he has. 37Now my
master made me swear, saying, 'You shall
not take a wife for my son from the daugh-
ters of the Cā'naan·ītes, in whose land I
dwell; 38but you shall go to my father's
house and to my family, and take a wife for
my son.' 39And I said to my master, 'Per-
haps the woman will not follow me.' 40But
he said to me, 'The LORD, before whom I
walk, will send His angel with you and
prosper your way; and you shall take a
wife for my son from my family and from
my father's house. 41You will be clear from
this oath when you arrive among my fam-
ily; for if they will not give *her* to you, then
you will be released from my oath.'

42"And this day I came to the well and
said, 'O LORD God of my master Abraham,
if You will now prosper the way in which I
go, 43behold, I stand by the well of water;
and it shall come to pass that when the vir-
gin comes out to draw *water,* and I say to

24:33 The servant's sense of urgency to convey his master's message before eating was caught by the host, and a concession to proper Near Eastern hospitality was made.

her, "Please give me a little water from your pitcher to drink," 44and she says to me, "Drink, and I will draw for your camels also,"—*let* her *be* the woman whom the LORD has appointed for my master's son.'

45"But before I had finished speaking in my heart, there was Rebekah, coming out with her pitcher on her shoulder; and she went down to the well and drew *water.* And I said to her, 'Please let me drink.' 46And she made haste and let her pitcher down from her *shoulder,* and said, 'Drink, and I will give your camels a drink also.' So I drank, and she gave the camels a drink also. 47Then I asked her, and said, 'Whose daughter *are* you?' And she said, 'The daughter of Be·thū'el, Nā'hor's son, whom Mil'cah bore to him.' So I put the nose ring on her nose and the bracelets on her wrists. 48And I bowed my head and worshiped the LORD, and blessed the LORD God of my master Abraham, who had led me in the way of truth to take the daughter of my master's brother for his son. 49Now if you will deal kindly and truly with my master, tell me. And if not, tell me, that I may turn to the right hand or to the left."

50Then Lā'ban and Be·thū'el answered and said, "The thing comes from the LORD; we cannot speak to you either bad or good. 51Here *is* Rebekah before you; take *her* and go, and let her be your master's son's wife, as the LORD has spoken."

52And it came to pass, when Abraham's servant heard their words, that he worshiped the LORD, *bowing himself* to the earth. 53Then the servant brought out jewelry of silver, jewelry of gold, and clothing, and gave *them* to Rebekah. He also gave precious things to her brother and to her mother.

54And he and the men who *were* with him ate and drank and stayed all night. Then they arose in the morning, and he said, "Send me away to my master."

55But her brother and her mother said, "Let the young woman stay with us *a few* days, at least ten; after that she may go."

56And he said to them, "Do not hinder me, since the LORD has prospered my way; send me away so that I may go to my master."

57So they said, "We will call the young woman and ask her personally." 58Then they called Rebekah and said to her, "Will you go with this man?"

And she said, "I will go."

59So they sent away Rebekah their sister and her nurse, and Abraham's servant and his men. 60And they blessed Rebekah and said to her:

"Our sister, *may* you *become*
The mother of thousands of ten
thousands;
And may your descendants possess
The gates of those who hate them."

61Then Rebekah and her maids arose, and they rode on the camels and followed the man. So the servant took Rebekah and departed.

62Now Isaac came from the way of Bē'er La·haī' Roi, for he dwelt in the South. 63And Isaac went out to meditate in the field in the evening; and he lifted his eyes and looked, and there, the camels *were* coming. 64Then Rebekah lifted her eyes, and when she saw Isaac she dismounted from her camel; 65for she had said to the servant, "Who *is* this man walking in the field to meet us?"

The servant said, "It *is* my master." So she took a veil and covered herself.

66And the servant told Isaac all the

24:50 Family authority in Hurrian society allowed one son to have jurisdiction over his brothers and sisters. Thus, Laban the brother is named before Bethuel the father, and received gifts (v. 53) while the father received none.

24:57, 58 Hurrian marriage law provided that the consent of the bride must also be obtained.

things that he had done. 67Then Isaac
brought her into his mother Sarah’s tent;
and he took Rebekah and she became his
wife, and he loved her. So Isaac was com-
forted after his mother’s *death.*

CHAPTER 25

Abraham and Keturah

Abraham again took a wife, and her
name *was* Ke·tū′rah. 2And she bore him
Zim′ran, Jok′shan, Mē′dan, Mid′i·an,
Ish′bak, and Shū′ah. 3Jok′shan begot
Shē′ba and Dē′dan. And the sons of Dē′-
dan were As·shū′rim, Le·tū′shim, and Le-
um′mim. 4And the sons of Mid′i·an *were*
Ē′phah, Ē′pher, Hā′noch, A·bī′dah, and
El·dā′ah. All these *were* the children of
Ke·tū′rah.

5And Abraham gave all that he had to
Isaac. 6But Abraham gave gifts to the sons
of the concubines which Abraham had;
and while he was still living he sent them
eastward, away from Isaac his son, to the
country of the east.

Abraham’s Death and Burial

7This *is* the sum of the years of Abra-
ham’s life which he lived: one hundred
and seventy-five years. 8Then Abraham
breathed his last and died in a good old
age, an old man and full *of years,* and was
gathered to his people. 9And his sons Isaac
and Ish′ma·el buried him in the cave of
Mach·pē′lah, which *is* before Mam′re, in
the field of Ē′phron the son of Zō′har the
Hit′tīte, 10the field which Abraham pur-
chased from the sons of Heth. There Abra-
ham was buried, and Sarah his wife. 11And
it came to pass, after the death of Abraham,
that God blessed his son Isaac. And Isaac
dwelt at Bē′er La·haī′ Roi.

The Families of Ishmael and Isaac

12Now this *is* the genealogy of Ish′ma·el,
Abraham’s son, whom Hā′gar the Egyp-
tian, Sarah’s maidservant, bore to Abra-
ham. 13And these *were* the names of the
sons of Ish′ma·el, by their names, accord-
ing to their generations: The firstborn of
Ish′ma·el, Ne·bā′joth; then Kē′dar,
Ad′bē·el, Mib′sam, 14Mish′ma, Dū′mah,
Mas′sa, 15Hā′dar,[a] Tē′ma, Jē′tur, Nā′phish,
and Ked′e·mah. 16These *were* the sons of
Ish′ma·el and these *were* their names, by
their towns and their settlements, twelve
princes according to their nations. 17These
were the years of the life of Ish′ma·el: one
hundred and thirty-seven years; and he
breathed his last and died, and was gath-
ered to his people. 18(They dwelt from
Hav′i·lah as far as Shūr, which *is* east of
Egypt as you go toward Assyria.) He died
in the presence of all his brethren.

19This *is* the genealogy of Isaac, Abra-
ham’s son. Abraham begot Isaac. 20Isaac
was forty years old when he took Rebekah
as wife, the daughter of Be·thū′el the Syr-
ian of Pad′an Ar′am, the sister of Lā′ban
the Syrian. 21Now Isaac pleaded with the
LORD for his wife, because she *was* barren;
and the LORD granted his plea, and Re-
bekah his wife conceived. 22But the chil-
dren struggled together within her; and
she said, “If *all is* well, why *am I like* this?”
So she went to inquire of the LORD.

23And the LORD said to her:

“Two nations *are* in your womb,
Two peoples shall be separated from
your body;

25:15 [a]Masoretic Text reads *Hadad.*

25:1–6 a wife . . . Keturah: Not of Sarah’s status, but a concubine (see 1 Chr. 1:32), a slave woman raised to secondary-wife status. Abraham had several such concubines (see v. 6).

25:23 older . . . serve . . . younger: This was contrary to what would be culturally expected. But God’s people are always subject to His intervention into purely human customs. God’s use of what society considers weaker or lesser is a common theme in the Bible.

One people shall be stronger than the
other,
And the older shall serve the
younger."

[24]So when her days were fulfilled *for her* to give birth, indeed *there were* twins in her womb. [25]And the first came out red. *He was* like a hairy garment all over; so they called his name Esau.[a] [26]Afterward his brother came out, and his hand took hold of Esau's heel; so his name was called Jacob.[a] Isaac *was* sixty years old when she bore them.

[27]So the boys grew. And Esau was a skillful hunter, a man of the field; but Jacob was a mild man, dwelling in tents. [28]And Isaac loved Esau because he ate *of his* game, but Rebekah loved Jacob.

Esau Sells His Birthright

[29]Now Jacob cooked a stew; and Esau came in from the field, and he *was* weary. [30]And Esau said to Jacob, "Please feed me with that same red *stew,* for I *am* weary." Therefore his name was called Ē'dom.[a]

[31]But Jacob said, "Sell me your birthright as of this day."

[32]And Esau said, "Look, I *am* about to die; so what *is* this birthright to me?"

[33]Then Jacob said, "Swear to me as of this day."

So he swore to him, and sold his birthright to Jacob. [34]And Jacob gave Esau bread and stew of lentils; then he ate and drank, arose, and went his way. Thus Esau despised *his* birthright.

CHAPTER 26

Isaac and Abimelech

There was a famine in the land, besides the first famine that was in the days of Abraham. And Isaac went to A·bim'e·lech king of the Phi·lis'tines, in Gē'rar.

[2]Then the LORD appeared to him and said: "Do not go down to Egypt; live in the land of which I shall tell you. [3]Dwell in this land, and I will be with you and bless you; for to you and your descendants I give all these lands, and I will perform the oath which I swore to Abraham your father. [4]And I will make your descendants multiply as the stars of heaven; I will give to your descendants all these lands; and in your seed all the nations of the earth shall be blessed; [5]because Abraham obeyed My voice and kept My charge, My commandments, My statutes, and My laws."

[6]So Isaac dwelt in Gē'rar. [7]And the men of the place asked about his wife. And he said, "She *is* my sister"; for he was afraid to say, "*She is* my wife," *because he thought,* "lest the men of the place kill me for Rebekah, because she *is* beautiful to behold." [8]Now it came to pass, when he had been there a long time, that A·bim'e·lech king of the Phi·lis'tines looked through a window, and saw, and there was Isaac, showing endearment to Rebekah his wife. [9]Then A·bim'e·lech called Isaac and said, "Quite obviously she *is* your wife; so how could you say, 'She *is* my sister'?"

25:25 [a]Literally *Hairy* 25:26 [a]Literally *Supplanter*
25:30 [a]Literally *Red*

25:29–34 Sell me your birthright: The firstborn son would normally inherit a double portion of his father's estate, exercise authority over the household, and bear the honor of his father's name. The father, however, legally could name a younger son to "firstborn" status. Hurrian law also provided that such a birthright could be sold. Esau's action was legally right but morally wrong: he **despised** his birthright as having no value in light of his immediate hunger—and bartered it for a bit of **bread** and **stew**. Jacob acted in the spirit of Cain: he failed to guard his brother from committing foolishness in his weakened condition, and thus failed to be his "brother's keeper" (4:9). As Christians, we are to keep things in their proper perspective, realizing that the things of this world are as nothing compared to the blessings that are ours in Christ.

Isaac said to him, "Because I said, 'Lest I
die on account of her.' "
10And A·bim'e·lech said, "What *is* this
you have done to us? One of the people
might soon have lain with your wife, and
you would have brought guilt on us." 11So
A·bim'e·lech charged all *his* people, say-
ing, "He who touches this man or his wife
shall surely be put to death."
12Then Isaac sowed in that land, and
reaped in the same year a hundredfold;
and the LORD blessed him. 13The man be-
gan to prosper, and continued prospering
until he became very prosperous; 14for he
had possessions of flocks and possessions
of herds and a great number of servants. So
the Phi·lis'tines envied him. 15Now the
Phi·lis'tines had stopped up all the wells
which his father's servants had dug in the
days of Abraham his father, and they had
filled them with earth. 16And A·bim'e·lech
said to Isaac, "Go away from us, for you
are much mightier than we."
17Then Isaac departed from there and
pitched his tent in the Valley of Gē'rar, and
dwelt there. 18And Isaac dug again the
wells of water which they had dug in
the days of Abraham his father, for the
Phi·lis'tines had stopped them up after
the death of Abraham. He called them by
the names which his father had called them.
19Also Isaac's servants dug in the valley,
and found a well of running water there.
20But the herdsmen of Gē'rar quarreled
with Isaac's herdsmen, saying, "The water
is ours." So he called the name of the well
Ē'sek,[a] because they quarreled with him.
21Then they dug another well, and they
quarreled over that *one* also. So he called its
name Sit'nah.[a] 22And he moved from there
and dug another well, and they did not
quarrel over it. So he called its name
Re·hō'both,[a] because he said, "For now the
LORD has made room for us, and we shall
be fruitful in the land."
23Then he went up from there to Bē-
er·shē'ba. 24And the LORD appeared to him
the same night and said, "I *am* the God of
your father Abraham; do not fear, for I *am*
with you. I will bless you and multiply
your descendants for My servant Abra-
ham's sake." 25So he built an altar there and
called on the name of the LORD, and he
pitched his tent there; and there Isaac's ser-
vants dug a well.
26Then A·bim'e·lech came to him from
Gē'rar with A·huz'zath, one of his friends,
and Phī'chol the commander of his army.
27And Isaac said to them, "Why have you
come to me, since you hate me and have
sent me away from you?"
28But they said, "We have certainly seen
that the LORD is with you. So we said, 'Let
there now be an oath between us, between
you and us; and let us make a covenant
with you, 29that you will do us no harm,
since we have not touched you, and since
we have done nothing to you but good and
have sent you away in peace. You *are* now
the blessed of the LORD.' "
30So he made them a feast, and they ate
and drank. 31Then they arose early in the
morning and swore an oath with one an-
other; and Isaac sent them away, and they
departed from him in peace.
32It came to pass the same day that
Isaac's servants came and told him about
the well which they had dug, and said to
him, "We have found water." 33So he called
it Shē'bah.[a] Therefore the name of the city
is Bē·er·shē'ba[b] to this day.
34When Esau was forty years old, he
took as wives Judith the daughter of
Be·ē'rī the Hit'tīte, and Bas'e·math the
daughter of Ē'lon the Hit'tīte. 35And they
were a grief of mind to Isaac and Rebekah.

26:20 [a]Literally *Quarrel* 26:21 [a]Literally *Enmity*
26:22 [a]Literally *Spaciousness* 26:33 [a]Literally *Oath* or *Seven* [b]Literally *Well of the Oath* or *Well of the Seven*

26:11 This is not the outcome one would have expected from the deception. God's providence continually gives us more than we deserve.

CHAPTER 27

Isaac Blesses Jacob

Now it came to pass, when Isaac was
old and his eyes were so dim that he could
not see, that he called Esau his older son
and said to him, "My son."

And he answered him, "Here I am."

2Then he said, "Behold now, I am old. I
do not know the day of my death. 3Now
therefore, please take your weapons, your
quiver and your bow, and go out to the
field and hunt game for me. 4And make me
savory food, such as I love, and bring *it* to
me that I may eat, that my soul may bless
you before I die."

5Now Rebekah was listening when Isaac
spoke to Esau his son. And Esau went to
the field to hunt game and to bring *it*. 6So
Rebekah spoke to Jacob her son, saying,
"Indeed I heard your father speak to Esau
your brother, saying, 7'Bring me game and
make savory food for me, that I may eat it
and bless you in the presence of the LORD
before my death.' 8Now therefore, my son,
obey my voice according to what I com-
mand you. 9Go now to the flock and bring
me from there two choice kids of the goats,
and I will make savory food from them for
your father, such as he loves. 10Then you
shall take *it* to your father, that he may eat
it, and that he may bless you before his
death."

11And Jacob said to Rebekah his mother,
"Look, Esau my brother *is* a hairy man,
and I *am* a smooth-*skinned* man. 12Perhaps
my father will feel me, and I shall seem to
be a deceiver to him; and I shall bring a
curse on myself and not a blessing."

13But his mother said to him, "*Let* your
curse *be* on me, my son; only obey my
voice, and go, get *them* for me." 14And he
went and got *them* and brought *them* to his
mother, and his mother made savory food,
such as his father loved. 15Then Rebekah
took the choice clothes of her elder son
Esau, which *were* with her in the house,
and put them on Jacob her younger son.
16And she put the skins of the kids of the
goats on his hands and on the smooth
part of his neck. 17Then she gave the
savory food and the bread, which she had
prepared, into the hand of her son Jacob.

18So he went to his father and said, "My
father."

And he said, "Here I am. Who *are* you,
my son?"

19Jacob said to his father, "I *am* Esau
your firstborn; I have done just as you told
me; please arise, sit and eat of my game,
that your soul may bless me."

20But Isaac said to his son, "How *is it*
that you have found *it* so quickly, my son?"

And he said, "Because the LORD your
God brought *it* to me."

21Isaac said to Jacob, "Please come near,
that I may feel you, my son, whether you
are really my son Esau or not." 22So Jacob
went near to Isaac his father, and he felt
him and said, "The voice *is* Jacob's voice,
but the hands *are* the hands of Esau." 23And
he did not recognize him, because his
hands were hairy like his brother Esau's
hands; so he blessed him.

24Then he said, "*Are* you really my son
Esau?"

He said, "I *am*."

25He said, "Bring *it* near to me, and I will
eat of my son's game, so that my soul may
bless you." So he brought *it* near to him,
and he ate; and he brought him wine, and
he drank. 26Then his father Isaac said to
him, "Come near now and kiss me, my
son." 27And he came near and kissed him;

27:5–10 in the presence of the LORD: The highest witness possible, binding the blessing. **that he may bless you** (v. 10): Rebekah sought to ensure that Isaac would not ignore Esau's sale of his birthright to Jacob (25:33), which could not be separated from the blessing.

27:20 your God: Jacob had not yet recognized the Lord as his God (see 28:21). Involving God in this lie made it the more despicable.

and he smelled the smell of his clothing, and blessed him and said:

"Surely, the smell of my son
Is like the smell of a field
Which the LORD has blessed.
28 Therefore may God give you
Of the dew of heaven,
Of the fatness of the earth,
And plenty of grain and wine.
29 Let peoples serve you,
And nations bow down to you.
Be master over your brethren,
And let your mother's sons bow
down to you.
Cursed *be* everyone who curses you,
And blessed *be* those who bless you!"

Esau's Lost Hope

30Now it happened, as soon as Isaac had
finished blessing Jacob, and Jacob had
scarcely gone out from the presence of Isaac
his father, that Esau his brother came in from
his hunting. 31He also had made savory
food, and brought it to his father, and
said to his father, "Let my father arise and
eat of his son's game, that your soul may
bless me."
32And his father Isaac said to him, "Who
are you?"
So he said, "I *am* your son, your first-
born, Esau."
33Then Isaac trembled exceedingly, and
said, "Who? Where *is* the one who hunted
game and brought *it* to me? I ate all *of it* be-
fore you came, and I have blessed him—
and indeed he shall be blessed."
34When Esau heard the words of his fa-
ther, he cried with an exceedingly great
and bitter cry, and said to his father, "Bless
me—me also, O my father!"
35But he said, "Your brother came with
deceit and has taken away your blessing."
36And *Esau* said, "Is he not rightly
named Jacob? For he has supplanted me
these two times. He took away my
birthright, and now look, he has taken
away my blessing!" And he said, "Have
you not reserved a blessing for me?"
37Then Isaac answered and said to Esau,
"Indeed I have made him your master, and
all his brethren I have given to him as ser-
vants; with grain and wine I have sus-

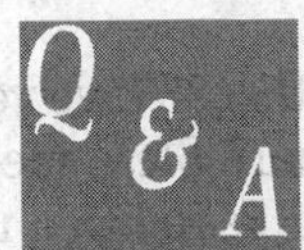

Does everyone need a will?

Elmer L. Gray

You have the right and even the responsibility to tell what you want done with what you have or might come to have after your death. You do that through a will.

What should happen to your money and possessions when you die? The simplest answer to that question is—whatever you want to be done. Of course, you have a number of possibilities, such as giving your possessions to your family, godly causes, or personal interests, and even your pets. Your will can show your appreciation, show what you care about, and be a message and a guide to others.

This Old Testament prayer can give you guidance: "Now also when I am old and grayheaded, O God, do not forsake me, until I declare Your strength to this generation, Your power to everyone who is to come" (Ps. 71:18).

Ask God for guidance in using what you have for the good of others and to His glory, now and for all time to come. ✦

27:27–29 blessed him: Jacob's blessing included physical prosperity (v. 28) and authority over **peoples** outside the family, and over **brethren** within the clan (v. 29).

tained him. What shall I do now for you, my son?"

38And Esau said to his father, "Have you only one blessing, my father? Bless me—me also, O my father!" And Esau lifted up his voice and wept.

39Then Isaac his father answered and said to him:

"Behold, your dwelling shall be of the
 fatness of the earth,
And of the dew of heaven from above.
40 By your sword you shall live,
And you shall serve your brother;
And it shall come to pass, when you
 become restless,
That you shall break his yoke from
 your neck."

Jacob Escapes from Esau

41So Esau hated Jacob because of the blessing with which his father blessed him, and Esau said in his heart, "The days of mourning for my father are at hand; then I will kill my brother Jacob."

42And the words of Esau her older son were told to Rebekah. So she sent and called Jacob her younger son, and said to him, "Surely your brother Esau comforts himself concerning you *by intending* to kill you. 43Now therefore, my son, obey my voice: arise, flee to my brother Lā'ban in Har'an. 44And stay with him a few days, until your brother's fury turns away, 45until your brother's anger turns away from you, and he forgets what you have done to him; then I will send and bring you from there. Why should I be bereaved also of you both in one day?"

46And Rebekah said to Isaac, "I am weary of my life because of the daughters of Heth; if Jacob takes a wife of the daughters of Heth, like these *who are* the daughters of the land, what good will my life be to me?"

CHAPTER 28

Then Isaac called Jacob and blessed him, and charged him, and said to him: "You shall not take a wife from the daughters of Cā'naan. 2Arise, go to Pad'an Ar'am, to the house of Be·thū'el your mother's father; and take yourself a wife from there of the daughters of Lā'ban your mother's brother.

3 "May God Almighty bless you,
And make you fruitful and multiply
 you,
That you may be an assembly of
 peoples;
4 And give you the blessing of Abra-
 ham,
To you and your descendants with
 you,
That you may inherit the land
In which you are a stranger,
Which God gave to Abraham."

5So Isaac sent Jacob away, and he went to Pad'an Ar'am, to Lā'ban the son of Be·thū'el the Syrian, the brother of Rebekah, the mother of Jacob and Esau.

Esau Marries Mahalath

6Esau saw that Isaac had blessed Jacob and sent him away to Pad'an Ar'am to take himself a wife from there, *and that* as he blessed him he gave him a charge, saying, "You shall not take a wife from the daughters of Cā'naan," 7and that Jacob had obeyed his father and his mother and had gone to Pad'an Ar'am. 8Also Esau saw that the daughters of Cā'naan did not please his father Isaac. 9So Esau went to Ish'ma·el and took Mā'ha·lath the daughter of Ish'ma·el, Abraham's son, the sister of Ne·bā'joth, to be his wife in addition to the wives he had.

Jacob's Vow at Bethel

10Now Jacob went out from Bē·er·shē'ba and went toward Har'an. 11So he came to a certain place and stayed there all night, because the sun had set. And he took one of the stones of that place and put it at his head, and he lay down in that place to

sleep. 12Then he dreamed, and behold, a
ladder *was* set up on the earth, and its top
reached to heaven; and there the angels of
God were ascending and descending on it.
13And behold, the LORD stood above it
and said: "I *am* the LORD God of Abraham
your father and the God of Isaac; the land
on which you lie I will give to you and
your descendants. 14Also your descen-
dants shall be as the dust of the earth; you
shall spread abroad to the west and the
east, to the north and the south; and in you
and in your seed all the families of the
earth shall be blessed. 15Behold, I *am* with
you and will keep you wherever you go,
and will bring you back to this land; for I
will not leave you until I have done what I
have spoken to you."
16Then Jacob awoke from his sleep and
said, "Surely the LORD is in this place, and
I did not know *it*." 17And he was afraid and
said, "How awesome *is* this place! This *is*
none other than the house of God, and this
is the gate of heaven!"
18Then Jacob rose early in the morning,
and took the stone that he had put at his
head, set it up as a pillar, and poured oil on
top of it. 19And he called the name of that
place Beth'el;[a] but the name of that city had
been Luz previously. 20Then Jacob made a
vow, saying, "If God will be with me, and
keep me in this way that I am going, and
give me bread to eat and clothing to put
on, 21so that I come back to my father's
house in peace, then the LORD shall be my
God. 22And this stone which I have set as a
pillar shall be God's house, and of all that
You give me I will surely give a tenth to
You."

28:19 [a]Literally *House of God*

CHAPTER 29

Jacob Meets Rachel

So Jacob went on his journey and came
to the land of the people of the East. 2And
he looked, and saw a well in the field; and
behold, there *were* three flocks of sheep ly-
ing by it; for out of that well they watered
the flocks. A large stone *was* on the well's
mouth. 3Now all the flocks would be gath-
ered there; and they would roll the stone
from the well's mouth, water the sheep,
and put the stone back in its place on the
well's mouth.
4And Jacob said to them, "My brethren,
where *are* you from?"
And they said, "We *are* from Har'an."
5Then he said to them, "Do you know
Lā'ban the son of Nā'hor?"
And they said, "We know him."

28:12 a ladder: Not one with rungs but a stairlike pavement. **Ascending** and **descending** describes the ministry of the **angels**, supernaturally created messengers between God in **heaven** and humankind on **earth**.

28:13–15 In wonderful condescension toward one who had shown no previous concern for God's ways, God extends the promises of Abraham to Jacob (vv. 13, 14), and adds personal promises of protection and care (v. 15).

28:17–19 gate of heaven: A figure expressing the belief that there was a narrow opening through which communication took place between heaven and earth. John depicts this gate as a "door . . . open in heaven" (Rev. 4:1).

28:20, 21 Jacob's **vow** sounds like a bargain with God. If God will keep His end of the deal—providing bread and clothing—then would his father's God, **the LORD** (see 27:20), become his God.

29:1–30 A description of what may have been an adoption-marriage contract: Jacob, received into his uncle Laban's **house** (v. 13) in **Haran** (v. 4), a Hurrian city, served Laban 14 years for his two daughters, Leah and Rachel (vv. 18, 30). At the time of Jacob's appearance, Laban had no sons. In this situation he would desire an heir to receive his estate. In such case, Hurrian law provided for adoption. The daughter and any resulting grandchildren remained the "property" of the father's house. The adopted son-in-law could leave the adoptive father's house to establish his "own house" (see 30:30) only with the father's permission.

6So he said to them, "Is he well?"
And they said, "*He is* well. And look, his
daughter Rachel is coming with the
sheep."
7Then he said, "Look, *it is* still high day;
it is not time for the cattle to be gathered to-
gether. Water the sheep, and go and feed
them."
8But they said, "We cannot until all the
flocks are gathered together, and they have
rolled the stone from the well's mouth;
then we water the sheep."
9Now while he was still speaking with
them, Rachel came with her father's sheep,
for she was a shepherdess. 10And it came to
pass, when Jacob saw Rachel the daughter
of Lā'ban his mother's brother, and the
sheep of Lā'ban his mother's brother, that
Jacob went near and rolled the stone from
the well's mouth, and watered the flock of
Lā'ban his mother's brother. 11Then Jacob
kissed Rachel, and lifted up his voice and
wept. 12And Jacob told Rachel that he *was*
her father's relative and that he *was* Re-
bekah's son. So she ran and told her father.
13Then it came to pass, when Lā'ban
heard the report about Jacob his sister's
son, that he ran to meet him, and embraced
him and kissed him, and brought him to
his house. So he told Lā'ban all these
things. 14And Lā'ban said to him, "Surely
you *are* my bone and my flesh." And he
stayed with him for a month.

Jacob Marries Leah and Rachel

15Then Lā'ban said to Jacob, "Because
you *are* my relative, should you therefore
serve me for nothing? Tell me, what *should*
your wages *be?* " 16Now Lā'ban had two
daughters: the name of the elder *was* Leah,
and the name of the younger *was* Rachel.
17Leah's eyes *were* delicate, but Rachel was
beautiful of form and appearance.
18Now Jacob loved Rachel; so he said, "I
will serve you seven years for Rachel your
younger daughter."
19And Lā'ban said, "*It is* better that I
give her to you than that I should give her
to another man. Stay with me." 20So Jacob
served seven years for Rachel, and they
seemed *only* a few days to him because of
the love he had for her.
21Then Jacob said to Lā'ban, "Give *me*
my wife, for my days are fulfilled, that I
may go in to her." 22And Lā'ban gathered
together all the men of the place and made
a feast. 23Now it came to pass in the
evening, that he took Leah his daughter
and brought her to Jacob; and he went in to
her. 24And Lā'ban gave his maid Zil'pah to
his daughter Leah *as* a maid. 25So it came
to pass in the morning, that behold, it *was*
Leah. And he said to Lā'ban, "What is this
you have done to me? Was it not for Rachel
that I served you? Why then have you de-
ceived me?"
26And Lā'ban said, "It must not be done
so in our country, to give the younger be-
fore the firstborn. 27Fulfill her week, and
we will give you this one also for the ser-
vice which you will serve with me still an-
other seven years."
28Then Jacob did so and fulfilled her
week. So he gave him his daughter Rachel
as wife also. 29And Lā'ban gave his maid
Bil'hah to his daughter Rachel as a maid.
30Then *Jacob* also went in to Rachel, and he
also loved Rachel more than Leah. And he
served with Lā'ban still another seven
years.

The Children of Jacob

31When the LORD saw that Leah *was* un-
loved, He opened her womb; but Rachel
was barren. 32So Leah conceived and bore a
son, and she called his name Reuben;[a] for
she said, "The LORD has surely looked on

29:32 [a]Literally *See, a Son*

29:28–30 At the end of **her week**—the seven-day celebration of his marriage to **Leah**—Jacob received **Rachel** also. He paid another seven years of service after marrying Rachel.

my affliction. Now therefore, my husband
will love me." 33Then she conceived again
and bore a son, and said, "Because the
LORD has heard that I *am* unloved, He has
therefore given me this *son* also." And she
called his name Sim'ē·on.[a] 34She conceived
again and bore a son, and said, "Now this
time my husband will become attached to
me, because I have borne him three sons."
Therefore his name was called Levi.[a] 35And
she conceived again and bore a son, and
said, "Now I will praise the LORD." There-
fore she called his name Judah.[a] Then she
stopped bearing.

CHAPTER 30

Now when Rachel saw that she bore Ja-
cob no children, Rachel envied her sister,
and said to Jacob, "Give me children, or
else I die!"

2And Jacob's anger was aroused against
Rachel, and he said, "*Am* I in the place of
God, who has withheld from you the fruit
of the womb?"

3So she said, "Here is my maid Bil'hah;
go in to her, and she will bear *a child* on my
knees, that I also may have children by
her." 4Then she gave him Bil'hah her maid
as wife, and Jacob went in to her. 5And
Bil'hah conceived and bore Jacob a son.
6Then Rachel said, "God has judged my
case; and He has also heard my voice and
given me a son." Therefore she called his
name Dan.[a] 7And Rachel's maid Bil'hah
conceived again and bore Jacob a second
son. 8Then Rachel said, "With great
wrestlings I have wrestled with my sister,
and indeed I have prevailed." So she called
his name Naph'ta·lī.[a]

9When Leah saw that she had stopped
bearing, she took Zil'pah her maid and
gave her to Jacob as wife. 10And Leah's
maid Zil'pah bore Jacob a son. 11Then Leah
said, "A troop comes!"[a] So she called his
name Gad.[b] 12And Leah's maid Zil'pah
bore Jacob a second son. 13Then Leah
said, "I am happy, for the daughters will
call me blessed." So she called his name
Ash'er.[a]

14Now Reuben went in the days of
wheat harvest and found mandrakes in the
field, and brought them to his mother
Leah. Then Rachel said to Leah, "Please
give me *some* of your son's mandrakes."

15But she said to her, "*Is it* a small matter
that you have taken away my husband?
Would you take away my son's mandrakes
also?"

And Rachel said, "Therefore he will lie
with you tonight for your son's man-
drakes."

16When Jacob came out of the field in the
evening, Leah went out to meet him and
said, "You must come in to me, for I have
surely hired you with my son's man-
drakes." And he lay with her that night.

17And God listened to Leah, and she
conceived and bore Jacob a fifth son. 18Leah
said, "God has given me my wages, be-
cause I have given my maid to my hus-
band." So she called his name Is'sa·char.[a]
19Then Leah conceived again and bore Ja-
cob a sixth son. 20And Leah said, "God has
endowed me *with* a good endowment;
now my husband will dwell with me, be-
cause I have borne him six sons." So she
called his name Zeb'ū·lun.[a] 21Afterward

29:33 [a]Literally *Heard* 29:34 [a]Literally *Attached*
29:35 [a]Literally *Praise* 30:6 [a]Literally *Judge*
30:8 [a]Literally *My Wrestling* 30:11 [a]Following Qere, Syriac, and Targum; Kethib, Septuagint, and Vulgate read *in fortune.* [b]Literally *Troop* or *Fortune*
30:13 [a]Literally *Happy* 30:18 [a]Literally *Wages*
30:20 [a]Literally *Dwelling*

29:34, 35 she called his name (also vv. 32, 33; 30:1–24): Names given to children were often descriptive of circumstances or the mother's desires at the time of birth.

30:14–16 mandrakes: An uncultivated plant of the potato family, ripening during wheat harvest. Its root, if eaten, was believed to induce fertility, and the fragrance of its flower to increase sexual desire (see Song 7:13).

she bore a daughter, and called her name Dī′nah.

22 Then God remembered Rachel, and God listened to her and opened her womb. 23 And she conceived and bore a son, and said, "God has taken away my reproach." 24 So she called his name Joseph,[a] and said, "The LORD shall add to me another son."

Jacob's Agreement with Laban

25 And it came to pass, when Rachel had borne Joseph, that Jacob said to Lā′ban, "Send me away, that I may go to my own place and to my country. 26 Give *me* my wives and my children for whom I have served you, and let me go; for you know my service which I have done for you."

27 And Lā′ban said to him, "Please *stay,* if I have found favor in your eyes, *for* I have learned by experience that the LORD has blessed me for your sake." 28 Then he said, "Name me your wages, and I will give *it.*"

29 So *Jacob* said to him, "You know how I have served you and how your livestock has been with me. 30 For what you had before I *came was* little, and it has increased to a great amount; the LORD has blessed you since my coming. And now, when shall I also provide for my own house?"

31 So he said, "What shall I give you?"

And Jacob said, "You shall not give me anything. If you will do this thing for me, I will again feed and keep your flocks: 32 Let me pass through all your flock today, removing from there all the speckled and spotted sheep, and all the brown ones among the lambs, and the spotted and speckled among the goats; and *these* shall be my wages. 33 So my righteousness will answer for me in time to come, when the subject of my wages comes before you: every one that *is* not speckled and spotted among the goats, and brown among the lambs, will be considered stolen, if *it is* with me."

34 And Lā′ban said, "Oh, that it were according to your word!" 35 So he removed that day the male goats that were speckled and spotted, all the female goats that were speckled and spotted, every one that had *some* white in it, and all the brown ones among the lambs, and gave *them* into the hand of his sons. 36 Then he put three days' journey between himself and Jacob, and Jacob fed the rest of Lā′ban's flocks.

37 Now Jacob took for himself rods of green poplar and of the almond and chestnut trees, peeled white strips in them, and exposed the white which *was* in the rods. 38 And the rods which he had peeled, he set before the flocks in the gutters, in the watering troughs where the flocks came to drink, so that they should conceive when they came to drink. 39 So the flocks conceived before the rods, and the flocks brought forth streaked, speckled, and spotted. 40 Then Jacob separated the lambs, and made the flocks face toward the streaked and all the brown in the flock of Lā′ban; but he put his own flocks by themselves and did not put them with Lā′ban's flock.

41 And it came to pass, whenever the stronger livestock conceived, that Jacob placed the rods before the eyes of the livestock in the gutters, that they might conceive among the rods. 42 But when the flocks were feeble, he did not put *them* in;

30:24 [a]Literally *He Will Add*

30:30 my own house: Jacob was yet subject to Laban's authority and must have Laban's permission to leave (see v. 25; 31:26–28).

30:35 Laban removed the livestock that should have been Jacob's and **gave** it to **his sons**. His deceitful character showed again (see 29:23) in this premeditated double cross.

30:37–43 rods of . . . poplar . . . almond . . . chestnut: The methods Jacob used to increase his proposed wages (v. 28) were a combination of superstition and selective breeding. They appeared to increase production of the various colored sheep and goats; the increase, however, was the work of God (see 31:7–9, 42).

so the feebler were Lā′ban's and the
stronger Jacob's. 43Thus the man became
exceedingly prosperous, and had large
flocks, female and male servants, and
camels and donkeys.

CHAPTER 31

Jacob Flees from Laban

Now *Jacob* heard the words of Lā′ban's
sons, saying, "Jacob has taken away all
that was our father's, and from what was
our father's he has acquired all this
wealth." 2And Jacob saw the countenance
of Lā′ban, and indeed it *was* not *favorable*
toward him as before. 3Then the LORD said
to Jacob, "Return to the land of your fa-
thers and to your family, and I will be with
you."

4So Jacob sent and called Rachel and
Leah to the field, to his flock, 5and said to
them, "I see your father's countenance,
that it *is* not *favorable* toward me as before;
but the God of my father has been with me.
6And you know that with all my might I
have served your father. 7Yet your father
has deceived me and changed my wages
ten times, but God did not allow him to
hurt me. 8If he said thus: 'The speckled
shall be your wages,' then all the flocks
bore speckled. And if he said thus: 'The
streaked shall be your wages,' then all the
flocks bore streaked. 9So God has taken
away the livestock of your father and
given *them* to me.

10"And it happened, at the time when
the flocks conceived, that I lifted my eyes
and saw in a dream, and behold, the rams
which leaped upon the flocks *were*
streaked, speckled, and gray-spotted.
11Then the Angel of God spoke to me in a
dream, saying, 'Jacob.' And I said, 'Here I
am.' 12And He said, 'Lift your eyes now
and see, all the rams which leap on the
flocks *are* streaked, speckled, and gray-
spotted; for I have seen all that Lā′ban is
doing to you. 13I *am* the God of Beth′el,
where you anointed the pillar *and* where
you made a vow to Me. Now arise, get out
of this land, and return to the land of your
family.'"

14Then Rachel and Leah answered and
said to him, "Is there still any portion or in-
heritance for us in our father's house?
15Are we not considered strangers by him?
For he has sold us, and also completely
consumed our money. 16For all these riches
which God has taken from our father are
really ours and our children's; now then,
whatever God has said to you, do it."

17Then Jacob rose and set his sons and
his wives on camels. 18And he carried
away all his livestock and all his posses-
sions which he had gained, his acquired
livestock which he had gained in Pad′an
Ar′am, to go to his father Isaac in the land
of Cā′naan. 19Now Lā′ban had gone to
shear his sheep, and Rachel had stolen the
household idols that were her father's.
20And Jacob stole away, unknown to
Lā′ban the Syrian, in that he did not tell
him that he intended to flee. 21So he fled
with all that he had. He arose and crossed
the river, and headed toward the moun-
tains of Gil′ē·ad.

Laban Pursues Jacob

22And Lā′ban was told on the third day
that Jacob had fled. 23Then he took his
brethren with him and pursued him for
seven days' journey, and he overtook him
in the mountains of Gil′ē·ad. 24But God
had come to Lā′ban the Syrian in a dream
by night, and said to him, "Be careful that
you speak to Jacob neither good nor bad."
25So Lā′ban overtook Jacob. Now Jacob

31:19 Early spring was the time to **shear** sheep. The **household idols** (also vv. 34, 35) were figurines representing gods (see vv. 30, 32), often in human form used in divination. Rachel yet practiced pagan worship (see 35:2). These figurines may also have been linked to family leadership and land ownership. They are sometimes called teraphim (see Hos. 3:4).

had pitched his tent in the mountains, and
Lā'ban with his brethren pitched in the
mountains of Gil'ē·ad.
26And Lā'ban said to Jacob: "What have
you done, that you have stolen away un-
known to me, and carried away my
daughters like captives *taken* with the
sword? 27Why did you flee away secretly,
and steal away from me, and not tell me;
for I might have sent you away with joy
and songs, with timbrel and harp? 28And
you did not allow me to kiss my sons and
my daughters. Now you have done fool-
ishly in *so* doing. 29It is in my power to do
you harm, but the God of your father
spoke to me last night, saying, 'Be careful
that you speak to Jacob neither good nor
bad.' 30And now you have surely gone be-
cause you greatly long for your father's
house, *but* why did you steal my gods?"
31Then Jacob answered and said to
Lā'ban, "Because I was afraid, for I said,
'Perhaps you would take your daughters
from me by force.' 32With whomever you
find your gods, do not let him live. In the
presence of our brethren, identify what I
have of yours and take *it* with you." For Ja-
cob did not know that Rachel had stolen
them.
33And Lā'ban went into Jacob's tent, into
Leah's tent, and into the two maids' tents,
but he did not find *them.* Then he went out
of Leah's tent and entered Rachel's tent.
34Now Rachel had taken the household
idols, put them in the camel's saddle, and
sat on them. And Lā'ban searched all
about the tent but did not find *them.* 35And
she said to her father, "Let it not displease
my lord that I cannot rise before you, for
the manner of women *is* with me." And he
searched but did not find the household
idols.
36Then Jacob was angry and rebuked
Lā'ban, and Jacob answered and said to
Lā'ban: "What *is* my trespass? What *is* my
sin, that you have so hotly pursued me?
37Although you have searched all my
things, what part of your household things
have you found? Set *it* here before my
brethren and your brethren, that they may
judge between us both! 38These twenty
years I *have been* with you; your ewes and
your female goats have not miscarried
their young, and I have not eaten the rams
of your flock. 39That which was torn *by*
beasts I did not bring to you; I bore the loss
of it. You required it from my hand, *whether*
stolen by day or stolen by night. 40*There* I
was! In the day the drought consumed me,
and the frost by night, and my sleep de-
parted from my eyes. 41Thus I have been in
your house twenty years; I served you
fourteen years for your two daughters, and
six years for your flock, and you have
changed my wages ten times. 42Unless the
God of my father, the God of Abraham and
the Fear of Isaac, had been with me, surely
now you would have sent me away
empty-handed. God has seen my affliction
and the labor of my hands, and rebuked
you last night."

Laban's Covenant with Jacob

43And Lā'ban answered and said to Ja-
cob, "*These* daughters *are* my daughters,
and *these* children *are* my children, and *this*
flock *is* my flock; all that you see *is* mine.
But what can I do this day to these my
daughters or to their children whom they
have borne? 44Now therefore, come, let us
make a covenant, you and I, and let it be a
witness between you and me."
45So Jacob took a stone and set it up *as* a
pillar. 46Then Jacob said to his brethren,

31:35 manner of women: Monthly menstruation. Whether fact or not, Rachel's explanation deflected Laban's search. The entire family—Laban, Rebekah, Jacob, and Rachel—seem to have been cursed with a need to deceive.

31:44–54 they ate bread (v. 54): A common meal, indicating that both Jacob and his brethren (vv. 46, 54) accepted the terms of the covenant (v. 44).

"Gather stones." And they took stones and made a heap, and they ate there on the heap. 47Lā'ban called it Jē'gar Sā·ha·dū'tha,[a] but Jacob called it Gal'e·ed.[b] 48And Lā'ban said, "This heap *is* a witness between you and me this day." Therefore its name was called Gal'e·ed, 49also Miz'pah,[a] because he said, "May the LORD watch between you and me when we are absent one from another. 50If you afflict my daughters, or if you take *other* wives besides my daughters, *although* no man *is* with us—see, God *is* witness between you and me!"

51Then Lā'ban said to Jacob, "Here is this heap and here is *this* pillar, which I have placed between you and me. 52This heap *is* a witness, and *this* pillar *is* a witness, that I will not pass beyond this heap to you, and you will not pass beyond this heap and this pillar to me, for harm. 53The God of Abraham, the God of Nā'hor, and the God of their father judge between us." And Jacob swore by the Fear of his father Isaac. 54Then Jacob offered a sacrifice on the mountain, and called his brethren to eat bread. And they ate bread and stayed all night on the mountain. 55And early in the morning Lā'ban arose, and kissed his sons and daughters and blessed them. Then Lā'ban departed and returned to his place.

CHAPTER 32

Esau Comes to Meet Jacob

So Jacob went on his way, and the angels of God met him. 2When Jacob saw them, he said, "This *is* God's camp." And he called the name of that place Mā·ha·na'im.[a]

3Then Jacob sent messengers before him to Esau his brother in the land of Sē'ir, the country of Ē'dom. 4And he commanded them, saying, "Speak thus to my lord Esau, 'Thus your servant Jacob says: "I have dwelt with Lā'ban and stayed there until now. 5I have oxen, donkeys, flocks, and male and female servants; and I have sent to tell my lord, that I may find favor in your sight." ' "

6Then the messengers returned to Jacob, saying, "We came to your brother Esau, and he also is coming to meet you, and four hundred men *are* with him." 7So Jacob was greatly afraid and distressed; and he divided the people that *were* with him, and the flocks and herds and camels, into two companies. 8And he said, "If Esau comes to the one company and attacks it, then the other company which is left will escape."

9Then Jacob said, "O God of my father Abraham and God of my father Isaac, the LORD who said to me, 'Return to your country and to your family, and I will deal well with you': 10I am not worthy of the least of all the mercies and of all the truth which You have shown Your servant; for I crossed over this Jordan with my staff, and now I have become two companies. 11Deliver me, I pray, from the hand of my brother, from the hand of Esau; for I fear him, lest he come and attack me *and* the mother with the children. 12For You said, 'I will surely treat you well, and make your descendants as the sand of the sea, which cannot be numbered for multitude.' "

31:47 [a]Literally, in Aramaic, *Heap of Witness* [b]Literally, in Hebrew, *Heap of Witness* 31:49 [a]Literally *Watch*
32:2 [a]Literally *Double Camp*

31:49, 50 May the LORD watch: Not a benediction but a curse. They called on God to kill them if they should violate the terms of the agreement.

31:52 Among pagans, the various idols were called upon to witness a covenant. Jacob was enough of a follower of the true God to simply use a heap of stones (v. 46) as historical evidence that a covenant had been entered into (see also Ex. 24:4; Josh. 4:7; 24:26, 27).

32:6–8 It was bad enough that Esau was coming to meet him instead of waiting for Jacob's arrival, but to come with **four hundred men** was a very bad sign indeed. What else could be their purpose but to make war?

Jacob: Time for a Change

Jacob, the son of Isaac and Rebekah, illustrates God's amazing power to change the direction of someone's life. Although Jacob's early years demonstrated his tendency toward craftiness and deceit, an encounter with God turned him into the man of faith mentioned in Hebrews 11:21.

The first indication of Jacob's character came in Genesis 25 when he saw an opportunity to take advantage of his brother and acted upon it. While we notice his callous craftiness, we must also acknowledge Jacob's keen grasp of the importance of the birthright. Esau, on the other hand, is said to have despised it, demonstrating an amazing lack of interest in the honors and responsibilities it represented.

Just a few chapters later, Jacob's craftiness has evolved into full-blown deceit. While his sin cannot be excused, it should be noted that his parents' actions led to this turn of events. Despite God's promise to Rebekah that the younger would rule the older (25:23) and the fact that Esau had already sold his birthright, Isaac still planned to bless Esau over Jacob. Because Rebekah favored her youngest son, she told him to deceive his father and steal the blessing from Esau.

When Esau sought to kill Jacob in revenge, he fled to the house of his uncle, Laban. En route, the Lord appeared to him in a dream and gave him the same promise He had given to Abraham and Isaac: "Your descendants shall be as the dust of the earth . . . and in your seed all the families of the earth shall be blessed" (28:14).

After building a memorial to the Lord, Jacob continued on to Haran, where he met his crafty match in Laban. Through Laban's treachery in giving him Leah for his wife instead of Rachel, Jacob tasted his own medicine. For the rest of his life, Jacob reaped the agony of the conflict this situation produced.

After twenty years of serving Laban, Jacob packed up his household and headed home. As he traveled, word came that Esau was coming with four hundred men to meet him. Jacob's prayerful response reveals the change that God had begun to work in his heart (32:9–12).

Soon after, a face-to-face encounter with God brought his lifelong spiritual struggle to a physical level. Both his name and his attitude changed through this experience. No longer "Supplanter" or "Deceiver," Jacob would now be called Israel, meaning "Prince with God" (v. 28). The change in his attitude can be seen in Jacob's generosity and honesty toward Esau and in his willingness to give God the glory for his prosperity (33:11).

Although Jacob's actions were not always guided by wisdom—as in his demonstration of favoritism toward Joseph—we never again see the cunning deception or pride that marked his early years. Instead we

see a man obedient to God and full of faith (see 35:1–4; 46:2–7).

No matter how sinful and contemptible a person has been, God's transforming power can work a miracle. He can change the bitter for the better, the sinner into a soul-winner, and the self-centered to the selfless. It's never too late to pray for a change. ✦

[13]So he lodged there that same night, and took what came to his hand as a present for Esau his brother: [14]two hundred female goats and twenty male goats, two hundred ewes and twenty rams, [15]thirty milk camels with their colts, forty cows and ten bulls, twenty female donkeys and ten foals. [16]Then he delivered *them* to the hand of his servants, every drove by itself, and said to his servants, "Pass over before me, and put some distance between successive droves." [17]And he commanded the first one, saying, "When Esau my brother meets you and asks you, saying, 'To whom do you belong, and where are you going? Whose *are* these in front of you?' [18]then you shall say, 'They *are* your servant Jacob's. It *is* a present sent to my lord Esau; and behold, he also *is* behind us.' " [19]So he commanded the second, the third, and all who followed the droves, saying, "In this manner you shall speak to Esau when you find him; [20]and also say, 'Behold, your servant Jacob *is* behind us.' " For he said, "I will appease him with the present that goes before me, and afterward I will see his face; perhaps he will accept me." [21]So the present went on over before him, but he himself lodged that night in the camp.

Wrestling with God

[22]And he arose that night and took his two wives, his two female servants, and his eleven sons, and crossed over the ford of Jab′bok. [23]He took them, sent them over the brook, and sent over what he had. [24]Then Jacob was left alone; and a Man wrestled with him until the breaking of day. [25]Now when He saw that He did not prevail against him, He touched the socket of his hip; and the socket of Jacob's hip was out of joint as He wrestled with him. [26]And He said, "Let Me go, for the day breaks."

But he said, "I will not let You go unless You bless me!"

[27]So He said to him, "What *is* your name?"

He said, "Jacob."

[28]And He said, "Your name shall no longer be called Jacob, but Israel;[a] for you have struggled with God and with men, and have prevailed."

[29]Then Jacob asked, saying, "Tell *me* Your name, I pray."

And He said, "Why *is* it *that* you ask about My name?" And He blessed him there.

[30]So Jacob called the name of the place Pe·nī′el:[a] "For I have seen God face to face, and my life is preserved." [31]Just as he crossed over Pe·nū′el[a] the sun rose on him, and he limped on his hip. [32]Therefore to

32:28 [a]Literally *Prince with God* 32:30 [a]Literally *Face of God* 32:31 [a]Same as *Peniel*, verse 30

32:22–30 Jacob's struggle with the **Man**, while physical, was a spiritual confrontation with God (see Hos. 12:2–4). His name change from **Jacob** ("Deceitful") to **Israel** ("Prince with God") depicts an inner spiritual change as well as a change in character. He was now ready, come what may, to meet Esau. Jacob's experience of God had a two-stage development: first at Bethel (28:10–22) and now 20 years later at Peniel.

this day the children of Israel do not eat the muscle that shrank, which *is* on the hip socket, because He touched the socket of Jacob's hip in the muscle that shrank.

CHAPTER 33

Jacob and Esau Meet

Now Jacob lifted his eyes and looked, and there, Esau was coming, and with him were four hundred men. So he divided the children among Leah, Rachel, and the two maidservants. 2And he put the maidservants and their children in front, Leah and her children behind, and Rachel and Joseph last. 3Then he crossed over before them and bowed himself to the ground seven times, until he came near to his brother.

4But Esau ran to meet him, and embraced him, and fell on his neck and kissed him, and they wept. 5And he lifted his eyes and saw the women and children, and said, "Who *are* these with you?"

So he said, "The children whom God has graciously given your servant." 6Then the maidservants came near, they and their children, and bowed down. 7And Leah also came near with her children, and they bowed down. Afterward Joseph and Rachel came near, and they bowed down.

8Then Esau said, "What *do* you *mean by* all this company which I met?"

And he said, "*These are* to find favor in the sight of my lord."

9But Esau said, "I have enough, my brother; keep what you have for yourself."

10And Jacob said, "No, please, if I have now found favor in your sight, then receive my present from my hand, inasmuch as I have seen your face as though I had seen the face of God, and you were pleased with me. 11Please, take my blessing that is brought to you, because God has dealt graciously with me, and because I have enough." So he urged him, and he took *it*.

12Then Esau said, "Let us take our journey; let us go, and I will go before you."

13But Jacob said to him, "My lord knows that the children *are* weak, and the flocks and herds which are nursing *are* with me. And if the men should drive them hard one day, all the flock will die. 14Please let my lord go on ahead before his servant. I will lead on slowly at a pace which the livestock that go before me, and the children, are able to endure, until I come to my lord in Sē'ir."

15And Esau said, "Now let me leave with you *some* of the people who *are* with me."

But he said, "What need is there? Let me find favor in the sight of my lord." 16So Esau returned that day on his way to Sē'ir. 17And Jacob journeyed to Suc'coth, built himself a house, and made booths for his livestock. Therefore the name of the place is called Suc'coth.[a]

Jacob Comes to Canaan

18Then Jacob came safely to the city of Shē'chem, which *is* in the land of Cā'naan, when he came from Pad'an Ar'am; and he pitched his tent before the city. 19And he bought the parcel of land, where he had pitched his tent, from the children of Hā'mor, Shē'chem's father, for one hundred pieces of money. 20Then he erected an altar there and called it El Ē·lō'he Israel.[a]

33:17 [a]Literally *Booths* 33:20 [a]Literally *God, the God of Israel*

33:3 crossed over before: Jacob was now willing to sacrifice himself. Signaling his complete submission to his elder brother, Jacob **bowed** himself, either in full prostration or upon his knees with hands and face on the **ground**. Such sevenfold bowing of minor city princes before Pharaoh is documented from Egypt.

33:9, 10 my brother: Esau verbally restored Jacob to a brother status (see 1 Kin. 20:32, 33). To receive the present was to physically signal forgiveness and restoration of status. **the face of God**: Jacob now knew that God is a God of grace and forgiveness.

CHAPTER 34

The Dinah Incident

Now Dī'nah the daughter of Leah,
whom she had borne to Jacob, went out to
see the daughters of the land. 2And when
Shē'chem the son of Hā'mor the Hī'vīte,
prince of the country, saw her, he took her
and lay with her, and violated her. 3His
soul was strongly attracted to Dī'nah the
daughter of Jacob, and he loved the young
woman and spoke kindly to the young
woman. 4So Shē'chem spoke to his father
Hā'mor, saying, "Get me this young
woman as a wife."

5And Jacob heard that he had defiled
Dī'nah his daughter. Now his sons were
with his livestock in the field; so Jacob held
his peace until they came. 6Then Hā'mor
the father of Shē'chem went out to Jacob to
speak with him. 7And the sons of Jacob
came in from the field when they heard *it;*
and the men were grieved and very angry,
because he had done a disgraceful thing in
Israel by lying with Jacob's daughter, a
thing which ought not to be done. 8But
Hā'mor spoke with them, saying, "The
soul of my son Shē'chem longs for your
daughter. Please give her to him as a wife.
9And make marriages with us; give your
daughters to us, and take our daughters to
yourselves. 10So you shall dwell with us,
and the land shall be before you. Dwell
and trade in it, and acquire possessions for
yourselves in it."

11Then Shē'chem said to her father and
her brothers, "Let me find favor in your
eyes, and whatever you say to me I will
give. 12Ask me ever so much dowry and
gift, and I will give according to what you
say to me; but give me the young woman
as a wife."

13But the sons of Jacob answered Shē'-
chem and Hā'mor his father, and spoke de-
ceitfully, because he had defiled Dī'nah
their sister. 14And they said to them, "We
cannot do this thing, to give our sister to
one who is uncircumcised, for that *would be*
a reproach to us. 15But on this *condition* we
will consent to you: If you will become as
we *are,* if every male of you is circumcised,
16then we will give our daughters to you,
and we will take your daughters to us; and
we will dwell with you, and we will be-
come one people. 17But if you will not heed
us and be circumcised, then we will take
our daughter and be gone."

18And their words pleased Hā'mor and
Shē'chem, Hā'mor's son. 19So the young
man did not delay to do the thing, because
he delighted in Jacob's daughter. He *was*
more honorable than all the household of
his father.

20And Hā'mor and Shē'chem his son
came to the gate of their city, and spoke
with the men of their city, saying: 21"These
men *are* at peace with us. Therefore let
them dwell in the land and trade in it. For
indeed the land *is* large enough for them.
Let us take their daughters to us as wives,
and let us give them our daughters. 22Only
on this *condition* will the men consent to
dwell with us, to be one people: if every
male among us is circumcised as they *are*
circumcised. 23*Will* not their livestock, their
property, and every animal of theirs *be*
ours? Only let us consent to them, and they
will dwell with us." 24And all who went
out of the gate of his city heeded Hā'mor
and Shē'chem his son; every male was

34:7 a disgraceful thing in Israel: a sin that has affected an entire family or community (see Josh 7:15).

34:24, 25 all who went out: A special class trained in defense of the city. It was they who were **circumcised. In pain** from circumcision, the defenders were incapacitated, making possible such a slaughter by only two attackers. It is possible, however, that Jacob's sons had their personal retainers with them. Simeon and Levi received great punishment for their abuse of the sign of the covenant; they lost their father's blessing and their tribes were dispersed throughout the land (49:5–7).

circumcised, all who went out of the gate
of his city.
25Now it came to pass on the third day,
when they were in pain, that two of the
sons of Jacob, Sim'ē·on and Levi, Dī'nah's
brothers, each took his sword and came
boldly upon the city and killed all the
males. 26And they killed Hā'mor and
Shē'chem his son with the edge of the
sword, and took Dī'nah from Shē'chem's
house, and went out. 27The sons of Jacob
came upon the slain, and plundered the
city, because their sister had been defiled.
28They took their sheep, their oxen, and
their donkeys, what *was* in the city and
what *was* in the field, 29and all their wealth.
All their little ones and their wives they
took captive; and they plundered even all
that *was* in the houses.
30Then Jacob said to Sim'ē·on and Levi,
"You have troubled me by making me ob-
noxious among the inhabitants of the land,
among the Cā'naan·ītes and the Per'iz-
zītes; and since I *am* few in number, they
will gather themselves together against me
and kill me. I shall be destroyed, my
household and I."
31But they said, "Should he treat our sis-
ter like a harlot?"

CHAPTER 35

Jacob's Return to Bethel

Then God said to Jacob, "Arise, go up to
Beth'el and dwell there; and make an altar
there to God, who appeared to you when
you fled from the face of Esau your
brother."
2And Jacob said to his household and to
all who *were* with him, "Put away the for-
eign gods that *are* among you, purify your-
selves, and change your garments. 3Then
let us arise and go up to Beth'el; and I will
make an altar there to God, who answered
me in the day of my distress and has been
with me in the way which I have gone."
4So they gave Jacob all the foreign gods
which *were* in their hands, and the earrings
which *were* in their ears; and Jacob hid
them under the terebinth tree which *was* by
Shē'chem.
5And they journeyed, and the terror of
God was upon the cities that *were* all
around them, and they did not pursue the
sons of Jacob. 6So Jacob came to Luz (that
is, Beth'el), which *is* in the land of Cā'naan,
he and all the people who *were* with him.
7And he built an altar there and called the
place El Beth'el,[a] because there God ap-
peared to him when he fled from the face
of his brother.
8Now Deb'or·ah, Rebekah's nurse, died,
and she was buried below Beth'el under
the terebinth tree. So the name of it was
called Al'lon Bach'uth.[a]
9Then God appeared to Jacob again,
when he came from Pad'an Ar'am, and
blessed him. 10And God said to him, "Your
name *is* Jacob; your name shall not be
called Jacob anymore, but Israel shall be
your name." So He called his name Israel.
11Also God said to him: "I *am* God
Almighty. Be fruitful and multiply; a na-
tion and a company of nations shall pro-
ceed from you, and kings shall come from
your body. 12The land which I gave Abra-
ham and Isaac I give to you; and to your
descendants after you I give this land."
13Then God went up from him in the place
where He talked with him. 14So Jacob set
up a pillar in the place where He talked
with him, a pillar of stone; and he poured a
drink offering on it, and he poured oil on
it. 15And Jacob called the name of the place
where God spoke with him, Beth'el.

Death of Rachel

16Then they journeyed from Beth'el.
And when there was but a little distance to
go to Eph'rath, Rachel labored *in childbirth,*
and she had hard labor. 17Now it came to
pass, when she was in hard labor, that the
midwife said to her, "Do not fear; you will
have this son also." 18And so it was, as her
soul was departing (for she died), that she

35:7 [a]Literally *God of the House of God*
35:8 [a]Literally *Terebinth of Weeping*

called his name Ben-Ō'ni;[a] but his father called him Benjamin.[b] 19So Rachel died and was buried on the way to Eph'rath (that *is,* Bethlehem). 20And Jacob set a pillar on her grave, which *is* the pillar of Rachel's grave to this day.

21Then Israel journeyed and pitched his tent beyond the tower of Ē'der. 22And it happened, when Israel dwelt in that land, that Reuben went and lay with Bil'hah his father's concubine; and Israel heard *about it.*

Jacob's Twelve Sons

Now the sons of Jacob were twelve: 23the sons of Leah *were* Reuben, Jacob's firstborn, and Sim'ē·on, Levi, Judah, Is'sa·char, and Zeb'ū·lun; 24the sons of Rachel *were* Joseph and Benjamin; 25the sons of Bil'hah, Rachel's maidservant, *were* Dan and Naph'ta·lī; 26and the sons of Zil'pah, Leah's maidservant, *were* Gad and Ash'er. These *were* the sons of Jacob who were born to him in Pad'an Ar'am.

Death of Isaac

27Then Jacob came to his father Isaac at Mam're, or Kir'jath Ar'ba[a] (that *is,* Hē'bron), where Abraham and Isaac had dwelt. 28Now the days of Isaac were one hundred and eighty years. 29So Isaac breathed his last and died, and was gathered to his people, *being* old and full of days. And his sons Esau and Jacob buried him.

CHAPTER 36

The Family of Esau

Now this *is* the genealogy of Esau, who is Ē'dom. 2Esau took his wives from the daughters of Cā'naan: Ā'dah the daughter of Ē'lon the Hit'tīte; A·hol·i·bā'mah the daughter of An'ah, the daughter of Zib'ē·on the Hī'vīte; 3and Bas'e·math, Ish'ma·el's daughter, sister of Ne·bā'joth. 4Now Ā'dah bore E·lī'phaz to Esau, and Bas'e·math bore Reū'el. 5And A·hol·i·bā'mah bore Jē'ush, Jā'a·lam, and Kō'rah. These *were* the sons of Esau who were born to him in the land of Cā'naan.

6Then Esau took his wives, his sons, his daughters, and all the persons of his household, his cattle and all his animals, and all his goods which he had gained in the land of Cā'naan, and went to a country away from the presence of his brother Jacob. 7For their possessions were too great for them to dwell together, and the land where they were strangers could not support them because of their livestock. 8So Esau dwelt in Mount Sē'ir. Esau *is* Ē'dom.

9And this *is* the genealogy of Esau the father of the Ē'dom·ītes in Mount Sē'ir. 10These *were* the names of Esau's sons: E·lī'phaz the son of Ā'dah the wife of Esau, and Reū'el the son of Bas'e·math the wife of Esau. 11And the sons of E·lī'phaz were Tē'man, Ō'mar, Zē'phō,[a] Gā'tam, and Kē'naz.

12Now Tim'na was the concubine of E·lī'phaz, Esau's son, and she bore Am'a·lek to E·lī'phaz. These *were* the sons of Ā'dah, Esau's wife.

13These *were* the sons of Reū'el: Nā'hath, Zē'rah, Sham'mah, and Miz'zah. These were the sons of Bas'e·math, Esau's wife.

14These were the sons of A·hol·i·bā'mah, Esau's wife, the daughter of An'ah, the daughter of Zib'ē·on. And she bore to Esau: Jē'ush, Jā'a·lam, and Kō'rah.

The Chiefs of Edom

15These *were* the chiefs of the sons of Esau. The sons of E·lī'phaz, the firstborn *son* of Esau, were Chief Tē'man, Chief

35:18 [a]Literally *Son of My Sorrow* [b]Literally *Son of the Right Hand* 35:27 [a]Literally *Town of Arba*
36:11 [a]Spelled *Zephi* in 1 Chronicles 1:36

35:22 An attempt by **Reuben**, Jacob's oldest son, to usurp some of his father's authority. His sin caused him to lose his birthright (49:3, 4). See 2 Sam. 16:21.

AGE IS A BLESSING

Leslie E. Moser, Ph.D.

Since the beginning, God has made old age a blessing. Consider the blessing of one of the Ten Commandments: "Honor your father and your mother, that your days may be long upon the land which the Lord your God is giving you" (Ex. 20:12). God applauds longevity as a virtue and a gift. Although He wrote in His master plan that every person will die, again and again He glorified long life as a blessing.

"God applauds longevity as a virtue and a gift."

God covenanted with Abraham, who was age ninety-nine, that he and ninety-year-old Sarah would have a son and that Abraham would become the father of many nations. Let me remind you that God is here for you and me right now—regardless of our ages—just as He was there for proud parents Abraham and Sarah. ✦

Ō'mar, Chief Zē'phō, Chief Kē'naz, 16Chief
Kō'rah,[a] Chief Gā'tam, *and* Chief Am'a·lek.
These *were* the chiefs of E·lī'phaz in the
land of Ē'dom. They *were* the sons of
Ā'dah.

17These *were* the sons of Reū'el, Esau's
son: Chief Nā'hath, Chief Zē'rah, Chief
Sham'mah, and Chief Miz'zah. These *were*
the chiefs of Reū'el in the land of Ē'dom.
These *were* the sons of Bas'e·math, Esau's
wife.

18And these *were* the sons of A·hol·i·bā'-
mah, Esau's wife: Chief Jē'ush, Chief
Jā'a·lam, and Chief Kō'rah. These *were* the
chiefs *who descended* from A·hol·i·bā'mah,
Esau's wife, the daughter of An'ah. 19These
were the sons of Esau, who is Ē'dom, and
these *were* their chiefs.

The Sons of Seir

20These *were* the sons of Sē'ir the Hor'īte
who inhabited the land: Lō'tan, Shō'bal,
Zib'ē·on, An'ah, 21Dī'shon, Ē'zer, and Dī'-
shan. These *were* the chiefs of the Hor'ītes,
the sons of Sē'ir, in the land of Ē'dom.

22And the sons of Lō'tan were Hō'rī and
Hē'mam.[a] Lō'tan's sister *was* Tim'na.

23These *were* the sons of Shō'bal: Al'van,[a]
Man'a·hath, Ē'bal, Shē'phō,[b] and Ō'nam.

24These *were* the sons of Zib'ē·on: both
Ā'jah and An'ah. This *was the* An'ah who
found the water[a] in the wilderness as he
pastured the donkeys of his father Zib'-
ē·on. 25These *were* the children of An'ah:
Dī'shon and A·hol·i·bā'mah the daughter
of An'ah.

26These *were* the sons of Dī'shon:[a]
Hem'dan,[b] Esh'ban, Ith'ran, and Chē'ran.
27These *were* the sons of Ē'zer: Bil'han,
Zā'a·van, and Ā'kan.[a] 28These *were* the sons
of Dī'shan: Uz and Ar'an.

29These *were* the chiefs of the Hor'ītes:
Chief Lō'tan, Chief Shō'bal, Chief Zib'ē·on,

36:16 [a]Samaritan Pentateuch omits *Chief Korah.*
36:22 [a]Spelled *Homam* in 1 Chronicles 1:39
36:23 [a]Spelled *Alian* in 1 Chronicles 1:40 [b]Spelled *Shephi* in 1 Chronicles 1:40 36:24 [a]Following Masoretic Text and Vulgate (*hot springs*); Septuagint reads *Jamin;* Targum reads *mighty men;* Talmud interprets as *mules.* 36:26 [a]Hebrew *Dishan* [b]Spelled *Hamran* in 1 Chronicles 1:41 36:27 [a]Spelled *Jaakan* in 1 Chronicles 1:42

Chief An'ah, 30Chief Dī'shon, Chief Ē'zer,
and Chief Dī'shan. These *were* the chiefs of
the Hor'ītes, according to their chiefs in
the land of Sē'ir.

The Kings of Edom

31Now these *were* the kings who reigned
in the land of Ē'dom before any king
reigned over the children of Israel: 32Bē'la
the son of Bē'or reigned in Ē'dom, and the
name of his city *was* Din'ha·bah. 33And
when Bē'la died, Jō'bab the son of Zē'rah
of Boz'rah reigned in his place. 34When
Jō'bab died, Hū'sham of the land of the
Tē'man·ītes reigned in his place. 35And
when Hū'sham died, Hā'dad the son of
Bē'dad, who attacked Mid'i·an in the
field of Mō'ab, reigned in his place. And
the name of his city *was* Ā'vith. 36When
Hā'dad died, Sam'lah of Mas·rē'kah
reigned in his place. 37And when Sam'lah
died, Saul of Re·hō'both-*by*-the-River
reigned in his place. 38When Saul died,
Bā'al-Hā'nan the son of Ach'bor reigned in
his place. 39And when Bā'al-Hā'nan the
son of Ach'bor died, Hā'dar[a] reigned in his
place; and the name of his city *was* Pā'ū.[b]
His wife's name *was* Me·het'a·bel, the
daughter of Mā'tred, the daughter of
Mez'a·hab.

The Chiefs of Esau

40And these *were* the names of the chiefs
of Esau, according to their families and
their places, by their names: Chief Tim'-
nah, Chief Al'vah,[a] Chief Jē'theth, 41Chief
A·hol·i·bā'mah, Chief Ē'lah, Chief Pī'non,
42Chief Kē'naz, Chief Tē'man, Chief Mib'-
zar, 43Chief Mag'di·el, and Chief Ī'ram.
These *were* the chiefs of Ē'dom, according
to their dwelling places in the land of their
possession. Esau *was* the father of the
Ē'dom·ītes.

CHAPTER 37

Joseph Dreams of Greatness

Now Jacob dwelt in the land where his
father was a stranger, in the land of
Cā'naan. 2This *is* the history of Jacob.

Joseph, *being* seventeen years old, was
feeding the flock with his brothers. And
the lad *was* with the sons of Bil'hah and the
sons of Zil'pah, his father's wives; and Jo-
seph brought a bad report of them to his
father.

3Now Israel loved Joseph more than all
his children, because he *was* the son of his
old age. Also he made him a tunic of *many*
colors. 4But when his brothers saw that
their father loved him more than all his
brothers, they hated him and could not
speak peaceably to him.

5Now Joseph had a dream, and he told *it*
to his brothers; and they hated him even
more. 6So he said to them, "Please hear this
dream which I have dreamed: 7There we
were, binding sheaves in the field. Then
behold, my sheaf arose and also stood up-
right; and indeed your sheaves stood all
around and bowed down to my sheaf."

8And his brothers said to him, "Shall
you indeed reign over us? Or shall you in-
deed have dominion over us?" So they

36:39 [a]Spelled *Hadad* in Samaritan Pentateuch, Syriac, and 1 Chronicles 1:50 [b]Spelled *Pai* in 1 Chronicles 1:50 36:40 [a]Spelled *Aliah* in 1 Chronicles 1:51

37:2–4 Because of the **bad report** Joseph's brothers **hated** him. A deeper reason was Jacob's favoritism. His special love for Joseph prompted the gift of a royal tunic. The description **many colors** comes from the Septuagint (the Greek translation of the OT). The precise meaning of the Hebrew word is unknown. In 2 Sam. 13:18 it refers to robes worn by the king's daughters. With this gift, Jacob had raised Joseph, the second youngest of 12, to a preferred status.

37:5–11 Joseph the dreamer (see v. 19) later became an interpreter of dreams (see 40:9–19; 41:25–32). At this point Joseph seems to have been quite naive or unwisely boastful. The Bible depicts its heroes honestly.

hated him even more for his dreams and
for his words.

9Then he dreamed still another dream
and told it to his brothers, and said, "Look,
I have dreamed another dream. And this
time, the sun, the moon, and the eleven
stars bowed down to me."

10So he told *it* to his father and his broth-
ers; and his father rebuked him and said to
him, "What *is* this dream that you have
dreamed? Shall your mother and I and
your brothers indeed come to bow down
to the earth before you?" 11And his broth-
ers envied him, but his father kept the mat-
ter *in mind*.

Joseph Sold by His Brothers

12Then his brothers went to feed their fa-
ther's flock in Shē'chem. 13And Israel said
to Joseph, "Are not your brothers feeding
the flock in Shē'chem? Come, I will send
you to them."

So he said to him, "Here I am."

14Then he said to him, "Please go and
see if it is well with your brothers and well
with the flocks, and bring back word to
me." So he sent him out of the Valley of
Hē'bron, and he went to Shē'chem.

15Now a certain man found him, and
there he was, wandering in the field. And
the man asked him, saying, "What are you
seeking?"

16So he said, "I am seeking my brothers.
Please tell me where they are feeding *their
flocks*."

17And the man said, "They have de-
parted from here, for I heard them say, 'Let
us go to Dō'than.' " So Joseph went after
his brothers and found them in Dō'than.

18Now when they saw him afar off, even
before he came near them, they conspired
against him to kill him. 19Then they said to
one another, "Look, this dreamer is com-
ing! 20Come therefore, let us now kill him
and cast him into some pit; and we shall
say, 'Some wild beast has devoured him.'
We shall see what will become of his
dreams!"

21But Reuben heard *it*, and he delivered
him out of their hands, and said, "Let us
not kill him." 22And Reuben said to them,
"Shed no blood, *but* cast him into this pit
which *is* in the wilderness, and do not lay a
hand on him"—that he might deliver him
out of their hands, and bring him back to
his father.

23So it came to pass, when Joseph had
come to his brothers, that they stripped Jo-
seph *of* his tunic, the tunic of *many* colors
that *was* on him. 24Then they took him and
cast him into a pit. And the pit *was* empty;
there was no water in it.

25And they sat down to eat a meal. Then
they lifted their eyes and looked, and there
was a company of Ish'ma·el·ītes, coming
from Gil'ē·ad with their camels, bearing
spices, balm, and myrrh, on their way to
carry *them* down to Egypt. 26So Judah said
to his brothers, "What profit *is there* if we
kill our brother and conceal his blood?
27Come and let us sell him to the Ish'ma-
el·ītes, and let not our hand be upon him,
for he *is* our brother *and* our flesh." And his
brothers listened. 28Then Mid'i·an·īte
traders passed by; so *the brothers* pulled Jo-
seph up and lifted him out of the pit, and
sold him to the Ish'ma·el·ītes for twenty
shekels of silver. And they took Joseph to
Egypt.

29Then Reuben returned to the pit, and
indeed Joseph *was* not in the pit; and he
tore his clothes. 30And he returned to his
brothers and said, "The lad *is* no *more;* and
I, where shall I go?"

37:25–28 Ishmaelites: The various tribal descendants of Ishmael, occupants of most of Arabia. **Midianites**: A subgroup of the Ishmaelites (v. 27) from Midian in Arabia. **sold him**: In so doing the brothers reduced Joseph from a brother to a slave. However, God used their treachery to help fulfill His plan (see 50:20), just as He can use trials in our lives to suit His purpose.

31So they took Joseph's tunic, killed a
kid of the goats, and dipped the tunic in
the blood. 32Then they sent the tunic of
many colors, and they brought *it* to their fa-
ther and said, "We have found this. Do you
know whether it *is* your son's tunic or
not?"

33And he recognized it and said, "*It is*
my son's tunic. A wild beast has devoured
him. Without doubt Joseph is torn to
pieces." 34Then Jacob tore his clothes, put
sackcloth on his waist, and mourned for
his son many days. 35And all his sons and
all his daughters arose to comfort him; but
he refused to be comforted, and he said,
"For I shall go down into the grave to my
son in mourning." Thus his father wept for
him.

36Now the Mid'i·an·ītes[a] had sold him
in Egypt to Pot'i·phar, an officer of
Pharaoh *and* captain of the guard.

CHAPTER 38

Judah and Tamar

It came to pass at that time that Judah
departed from his brothers, and visited a
certain A·dul'lam·īte whose name *was*
Hī'rah. 2And Judah saw there a daughter
of a certain Cā'naan·īte whose name *was*
Shū'a, and he married her and went in to
her. 3So she conceived and bore a son, and
he called his name Er. 4She conceived again
and bore a son, and she called his name
Ō'nan. 5And she conceived yet again and
bore a son, and called his name Shē'lah. He
was at Chē'zib when she bore him.

6Then Judah took a wife for Er his first-
born, and her name *was* Tā'mar. 7But Er, Ju-
dah's firstborn, was wicked in the sight of
the LORD, and the LORD killed him. 8And
Judah said to Ō'nan, "Go in to your
brother's wife and marry her, and raise up
an heir to your brother." 9But Ō'nan knew
that the heir would not be his; and it came
to pass, when he went in to his brother's
wife, that he emitted on the ground, lest he
should give an heir to his brother. 10And
the thing which he did displeased the
LORD; therefore He killed him also.

11Then Judah said to Tā'mar his daugh-
ter-in-law, "Remain a widow in your fa-
ther's house till my son Shē'lah is grown."
For he said, "Lest he also die like his broth-
ers." And Tā'mar went and dwelt in her fa-
ther's house.

12Now in the process of time the daugh-
ter of Shū'a, Judah's wife, died; and Judah
was comforted, and went up to his
sheepshearers at Tim'nah, he and his
friend Hī'rah the A·dul'lam·īte. 13And it
was told Tā'mar, saying, "Look, your
father-in-law is going up to Tim'nah to
shear his sheep." 14So she took off her
widow's garments, covered *herself* with a
veil and wrapped herself, and sat in an
open place which *was* on the way to
Tim'nah; for she saw that Shē'lah was
grown, and she was not given to him as a
wife. 15When Judah saw her, he thought
she *was* a harlot, because she had covered
her face. 16Then he turned to her by the
way, and said, "Please let me come in to
you"; for he did not know that she *was* his
daughter-in-law.

So she said, "What will you give me,
that you may come in to me?"

17And he said, "I will send a young goat
from the flock."

So she said, "Will you give *me* a pledge
till you send *it?*"

18Then he said, "What pledge shall I
give you?"

So she said, "Your signet and cord, and

37:36 [a]Masoretic Text reads *Medanites.*

38:8–11 raise up an heir to your brother: This custom, called levirate marriage, was widely practiced. It was later regulated by law for Israel (see Deut. 25:5–10). The practice, alluded to by Naomi (Ruth 1:11–13), is illustrated by Boaz's marriage to Ruth (Ruth 4:5–11). See Matt. 22:23–28.

your staff that *is* in your hand." Then he gave *them* to her, and went in to her, and she conceived by him. [19]So she arose and went away, and laid aside her veil and put on the garments of her widowhood.

[20]And Judah sent the young goat by the hand of his friend the A·dul'lam·īte, to receive *his* pledge from the woman's hand, but he did not find her. [21]Then he asked the men of that place, saying, "Where is the harlot who *was* openly by the roadside?"

And they said, "There was no harlot in this *place*."

[22]So he returned to Judah and said, "I cannot find her. Also, the men of the place said there was no harlot in this *place*."

[23]Then Judah said, "Let her take *them* for herself, lest we be shamed; for I sent this young goat and you have not found her."

[24]And it came to pass, about three months after, that Judah was told, saying, "Tā'mar your daughter-in-law has played the harlot; furthermore she *is* with child by harlotry."

So Judah said, "Bring her out and let her be burned!"

[25]When she *was* brought out, she sent to her father-in-law, saying, "By the man to whom these belong, I *am* with child." And she said, "Please determine whose these *are*—the signet and cord, and staff."

[26]So Judah acknowledged *them* and said, "She has been more righteous than I, because I did not give her to Shē'lah my son." And he never knew her again.

[27]Now it came to pass, at the time for giving birth, that behold, twins *were* in her womb. [28]And so it was, when she was giving birth, that *the one* put out *his* hand; and the midwife took a scarlet *thread* and bound it on his hand, saying, "This one came out first." [29]Then it happened, as he drew back his hand, that his brother came out unexpectedly; and she said, "How did you break through? *This* breach *be* upon you!" Therefore his name was called Per'ez.[a] [30]Afterward his brother came out who had the scarlet *thread* on his hand. And his name was called Zē'rah.

CHAPTER 39

Joseph a Slave in Egypt

Now Joseph had been taken down to Egypt. And Pot'i·phar, an officer of Pharaoh, captain of the guard, an Egyptian, bought him from the Ish'ma·el·ītes who had taken him down there. [2]The LORD was with Joseph, and he was a successful man; and he was in the house of his master the Egyptian. [3]And his master saw that the LORD *was* with him and that the LORD made all he did to prosper in his hand. [4]So Joseph found favor in his sight, and served him. Then he made him overseer of his house, and all *that* he had he put under his authority. [5]So it was, from the time *that* he had made him overseer of his house and all that he had, that the LORD blessed the Egyptian's house for Joseph's sake; and the blessing of the LORD was on all that he had in the house and in the field. [6]Thus he left all that he had in Joseph's hand, and he did not know what he had except for the bread which he ate.

Now Joseph was handsome in form and appearance.

[7]And it came to pass after these things that his master's wife cast longing eyes on Joseph, and she said, "Lie with me."

[8]But he refused and said to his master's

38:29 [a]Literally *Breach* or *Breakthrough*

39:4 overseer: The highest position to which a household slave could rise. He had responsibility for the food, clothing, finances, and property of the master. Though Joseph was sold as a slave, the Lord had overturned the intent of his brothers.

39:8, 9 How . . . can I . . . sin against God? Joseph's commitment to God was the basis for his loyalty to his master. The sin of adultery might remain hidden from Potiphar, but never from God. Like Joseph, we should be infinitely more concerned about offending God than about angering those around us.

wife, "Look, my master does not know
what *is* with me in the house, and he has
committed all that he has to my hand.
9*There is* no one greater in this house than I,
nor has he kept back anything from me but
you, because you *are* his wife. How then
can I do this great wickedness, and sin
against God?"

10So it was, as she spoke to Joseph day
by day, that he did not heed her, to lie with
her *or* to be with her.

11But it happened about this time, when
Joseph went into the house to do his work,
and none of the men of the house *was* in-
side, 12that she caught him by his garment,
saying, "Lie with me." But he left his gar-
ment in her hand, and fled and ran out-
side. 13And so it was, when she saw that he
had left his garment in her hand and fled
outside, 14that she called to the men of her
house and spoke to them, saying, "See, he
has brought in to us a Hebrew to mock us.
He came in to me to lie with me, and I cried
out with a loud voice. 15And it happened,
when he heard that I lifted my voice and
cried out, that he left his garment with me,
and fled and went outside."

16So she kept his garment with her until
his master came home. 17Then she spoke to
him with words like these, saying, "The
Hebrew servant whom you brought to us
came in to me to mock me; 18so it hap-
pened, as I lifted my voice and cried out,
that he left his garment with me and fled
outside."

19So it was, when his master heard the
words which his wife spoke to him, saying,
"Your servant did to me after this manner,"
that his anger was aroused. 20Then Jo-
seph's master took him and put him into
the prison, a place where the king's prison-
ers *were* confined. And he was there in the
prison. 21But the LORD was with Joseph and
showed him mercy, and He gave him favor
in the sight of the keeper of the prison.
22And the keeper of the prison committed
to Joseph's hand all the prisoners who *were*
in the prison; whatever they did there, it
was his doing. 23The keeper of the prison
did not look into anything *that was* under
Joseph's authority,[a] because the LORD was
with him; and whatever he did, the LORD
made *it* prosper.

CHAPTER 40

The Prisoners' Dreams

It came to pass after these things *that* the
butler and the baker of the king of Egypt
offended their lord, the king of Egypt.
2And Pharaoh was angry with his two offi-
cers, the chief butler and the chief baker.
3So he put them in custody in the house of
the captain of the guard, in the prison, the
place where Joseph *was* confined. 4And the
captain of the guard charged Joseph with
them, and he served them; so they were in
custody for a while.

5Then the butler and the baker of the
king of Egypt, who *were* confined in the
prison, had a dream, both of them, each
man's dream in one night *and* each man's
dream with its *own* interpretation. 6And Jo-
seph came in to them in the morning and
looked at them, and saw that they *were* sad.
7So he asked Pharaoh's officers who *were*

39:23 [a]Literally *his hand*

39:12 his garment: A man's clothing consisted of two pieces: an undergarment, tied about the hips, and an outergarment, a coat-like cape. Only the undergarment was worn when working indoors. Joseph fled naked.

39:20–23 Because Potiphar, **Joseph's master**, was a royal officer (see v. 1), his slave would be a legal member of his household. Joseph was therefore put in a special prison with the **king's prisoners**.

40:1, 2 The chief butler had charge of wines and other drinks (see vv. 11, 21). He must protect his master's life from plots of poison. In a royal household there would be several butlers with a chief over them.

with him in the custody of his lord's house, saying, "Why do you look *so* sad today?"

8And they said to him, "We each have had a dream, and *there is* no interpreter of it."

So Joseph said to them, "Do not interpretations belong to God? Tell *them* to me, please."

9Then the chief butler told his dream to Joseph, and said to him, "Behold, in my dream a vine *was* before me, 10and in the vine *were* three branches; it *was* as though it budded, its blossoms shot forth, and its clusters brought forth ripe grapes. 11Then Pharaoh's cup *was* in my hand; and I took the grapes and pressed them into Pharaoh's cup, and placed the cup in Pharaoh's hand."

12And Joseph said to him, "This *is* the interpretation of it: The three branches *are* three days. 13Now within three days Pharaoh will lift up your head and restore you to your place, and you will put Pharaoh's cup in his hand according to the former manner, when you were his butler. 14But remember me when it is well with you, and please show kindness to me; make mention of me to Pharaoh, and get me out of this house. 15For indeed I was stolen away from the land of the Hebrews; and also I have done nothing here that they should put me into the dungeon."

16When the chief baker saw that the interpretation was good, he said to Joseph, "I also *was* in my dream, and there *were* three white baskets on my head. 17In the uppermost basket *were* all kinds of baked goods for Pharaoh, and the birds ate them out of the basket on my head."

18So Joseph answered and said, "This *is* the interpretation of it: The three baskets *are* three days. 19Within three days Pharaoh will lift off your head from you and hang you on a tree; and the birds will eat your flesh from you."

20Now it came to pass on the third day, *which was* Pharaoh's birthday, that he made a feast for all his servants; and he lifted up the head of the chief butler and of the chief baker among his servants. 21Then he restored the chief butler to his butlership again, and he placed the cup in Pharaoh's hand. 22But he hanged the chief baker, as Joseph had interpreted to them. 23Yet the chief butler did not remember Joseph, but forgot him.

CHAPTER 41

Pharaoh's Dreams

Then it came to pass, at the end of two full years, that Pharaoh had a dream; and behold, he stood by the river. 2Suddenly there came up out of the river seven cows, fine looking and fat; and they fed in the meadow. 3Then behold, seven other cows came up after them out of the river, ugly and gaunt, and stood by the *other* cows on the bank of the river. 4And the ugly and gaunt cows ate up the seven fine looking and fat cows. So Pharaoh awoke. 5He slept and dreamed a second time; and suddenly seven heads of grain came up on one stalk, plump and good. 6Then behold, seven thin heads, blighted by the east wind, sprang up after them. 7And the seven thin heads devoured the seven plump and full heads. So Pharaoh awoke, and indeed, *it was* a dream. 8Now it came to pass in the morning that his spirit was troubled, and he sent and called for all the magicians of Egypt and all its wise men. And Pharaoh told them his dreams, but *there was* no one who could interpret them for Pharaoh.

9Then the chief butler spoke to Pharaoh, saying: "I remember my faults this day. 10When Pharaoh was angry with his servants, and put me in custody in the house of the captain of the guard, *both* me and the chief baker, 11we each had a dream in one night, he and I. Each of us dreamed according to the interpretation of his *own* dream. 12Now there *was* a young Hebrew man with us there, a servant of the captain of the guard. And we told him, and he interpreted our dreams for us; to each man he interpreted according to his *own* dream.

13And it came to pass, just as he interpreted
for us, so it happened. He restored me to
my office, and he hanged him."
14Then Pharaoh sent and called Joseph,
and they brought him quickly out of the
dungeon; and he shaved, changed his
clothing, and came to Pharaoh. 15And
Pharaoh said to Joseph, "I have had a
dream, and *there is* no one who can inter-
pret it. But I have heard it said of you *that*
you can understand a dream, to interpret
it."
16So Joseph answered Pharaoh, saying,
"*It is* not in me; God will give Pharaoh an
answer of peace."
17Then Pharaoh said to Joseph: "Behold,
in my dream I stood on the bank of the
river. 18Suddenly seven cows came up out
of the river, fine looking and fat; and they
fed in the meadow. 19Then behold, seven
other cows came up after them, poor and
very ugly and gaunt, such ugliness as I
have never seen in all the land of Egypt.
20And the gaunt and ugly cows ate up the
first seven, the fat cows. 21When they had
eaten them up, no one would have known
that they had eaten them, for they *were* just
as ugly as at the beginning. So I awoke.
22Also I saw in my dream, and suddenly
seven heads came up on one stalk, full and
good. 23Then behold, seven heads, with-
ered, thin, *and* blighted by the east wind,
sprang up after them. 24And the thin heads
devoured the seven good heads. So I told
this to the magicians, but *there was* no one
who could explain *it* to me."
25Then Joseph said to Pharaoh, "The
dreams of Pharaoh *are* one; God has shown
Pharaoh what He *is* about to do: 26The
seven good cows *are* seven years; and
the seven good heads *are* seven years; the
dreams *are* one. 27And the seven thin and
ugly cows which came up after them *are*
seven years, and the seven empty heads
blighted by the east wind are seven years
of famine. 28This *is* the thing which I have
spoken to Pharaoh. God has shown
Pharaoh what He *is* about to do. 29Indeed
seven years of great plenty will come
throughout all the land of Egypt; 30but after
them seven years of famine will arise, and
all the plenty will be forgotten in the land
of Egypt; and the famine will deplete the
land. 31So the plenty will not be known in
the land because of the famine following,
for it *will be* very severe. 32And the dream
was repeated to Pharaoh twice because the
thing *is* established by God, and God will
shortly bring it to pass.
33"Now therefore, let Pharaoh select a
discerning and wise man, and set him over
the land of Egypt. 34Let Pharaoh do *this*,
and let him appoint officers over the land,
to collect one-fifth *of the produce* of the land
of Egypt in the seven plentiful years. 35And
let them gather all the food of those good
years that are coming, and store up grain
under the authority of Pharaoh, and let
them keep food in the cities. 36Then that
food shall be as a reserve for the land for
the seven years of famine which shall be in
the land of Egypt, that the land may not
perish during the famine."

Joseph's Rise to Power

37So the advice was good in the eyes of
Pharaoh and in the eyes of all his servants.
38And Pharaoh said to his servants, "Can

41:16 Joseph's humility and readiness to give God the glory is another indication of his virtue. The spiritual gifts given to us by the Lord should be used for His purposes and glory; we should resist the temptation to take credit for the work He has enabled us to do.

41:34 One-fifth was a larger than usual grain tax. It was normal, however, for Egyptian authorities to tax grain and store it in royal granaries for distribution during low production years.

41:38 Spirit of God: A pagan king recognized that Joseph possessed supernatural ability—something beyond what the human spirit could do. This is the basic understanding of the work of the Spirit in the OT: divine empowerment and enabling (see Ex. 35:31; Dan.

we find *such a one* as this, a man in whom *is*
the Spirit of God?"
39Then Pharaoh said to Joseph, "Inas-
much as God has shown you all this, *there*
is no one as discerning and wise as you.
40You shall be over my house, and all my
people shall be ruled according to your
word; only in regard to the throne will I be
greater than you." 41And Pharaoh said to
Joseph, "See, I have set you over all the
land of Egypt."

42Then Pharaoh took his signet ring off
his hand and put it on Joseph's hand; and
he clothed him in garments of fine linen
and put a gold chain around his neck.
43And he had him ride in the second char-
iot which he had; and they cried out before
him, "Bow the knee!" So he set him over all
the land of Egypt. 44Pharaoh also said to Jo-
seph, "I *am* Pharaoh, and without your
consent no man may lift his hand or foot in
all the land of Egypt." 45And Pharaoh
called Joseph's name Zaph'nath-Pā·a-
nē'ah. And he gave him as a wife As'e-
nath, the daughter of Pō·ti'-Phe·rah' priest
of On. So Joseph went out over *all* the land
of Egypt.

46Joseph was thirty years old when he
stood before Pharaoh king of Egypt. And
Joseph went out from the presence of
Pharaoh, and went throughout all the land
of Egypt. 47Now in the seven plentiful
years the ground brought forth abun-
dantly. 48So he gathered up all the food of
the seven years which were in the land of
Egypt, and laid up the food in the cities; he
laid up in every city the food of the fields
which surrounded them. 49Joseph gathered
very much grain, as the sand of the sea, un-
til he stopped counting, for *it was* immea-
surable.

50And to Joseph were born two sons be-
fore the years of famine came, whom
As'e·nath, the daughter of Pō·ti'-Phe·rah'
priest of On, bore to him. 51Joseph called
the name of the firstborn Ma·nas'seh:[a] "For
God has made me forget all my toil and all
my father's house." 52And the name of the
second he called Ē'phra·im:[a] "For God has
caused me to be fruitful in the land of my
affliction."

53Then the seven years of plenty which
were in the land of Egypt ended, 54and the
seven years of famine began to come, as Jo-
seph had said. The famine was in all lands,
but in all the land of Egypt there was
bread. 55So when all the land of Egypt was
famished, the people cried to Pharaoh for
bread. Then Pharaoh said to all the Egyp-
tians, "Go to Joseph; whatever he says to
you, do." 56The famine was over all the face
of the earth, and Joseph opened all the
storehouses[a] and sold to the Egyptians.
And the famine became severe in the land
of Egypt. 57So all countries came to Joseph
in Egypt to buy *grain*, because the famine
was severe in all lands.

CHAPTER 42

Joseph's Brothers Go to Egypt

When Jacob saw that there was grain in
Egypt, Jacob said to his sons, "Why do you

41:51 [a]Literally *Making Forgetful* 41:52 [a]Literally *Fruitfulness* 41:56 [a]Literally *all that was in them*

4:9). Ultimately God revealed the most serious human inability to be in the moral realm. This is where the work of the Holy Spirit is most needed.

41:42–44 signet ring: A carved stone of the common Egyptian scarab beetle, mounted with a swivel on a gold finger ring. Its underside bore a person's name or other personal identification. When removed from the finger it functioned as a seal for authenticating documents. As Pharaoh's personal signet ring, it empowered Joseph to do business in the king's name. **gold chain**: The usual reward to an officer who had pleased the Pharaoh. **second chariot**: In Egypt the use of chariots was limited to the Pharaoh, his second-in-command, army generals, and ranking officials. **without your consent**: Joseph was given absolute authority.

look at one another?" 2And he said, "In-
deed I have heard that there is grain in
Egypt; go down to that place and buy for
us there, that we may live and not die."
3So Joseph's ten brothers went down to
buy grain in Egypt. 4But Jacob did not send
Joseph's brother Benjamin with his broth-
ers, for he said, "Lest some calamity befall
him." 5And the sons of Israel went to buy
grain among those who journeyed, for the
famine was in the land of Cā'naan.
6Now Joseph *was* governor over the
land; and it was he who sold to all the peo-
ple of the land. And Joseph's brothers
came and bowed down before him with
their faces to the earth. 7Joseph saw his
brothers and recognized them, but he
acted as a stranger to them and spoke
roughly to them. Then he said to them,
"Where do you come from?"
And they said, "From the land of
Cā'naan to buy food."
8So Joseph recognized his brothers, but
they did not recognize him. 9Then Joseph
remembered the dreams which he had
dreamed about them, and said to them,
"You *are* spies! You have come to see the
nakedness of the land!"
10And they said to him, "No, my lord,
but your servants have come to buy food.
11We *are* all one man's sons; we *are* honest
men; your servants are not spies."
12But he said to them, "No, but you have
come to see the nakedness of the land."
13And they said, "Your servants *are*
twelve brothers, the sons of one man in the
land of Cā'naan; and in fact, the youngest
is with our father today, and one *is* no
more."
14But Joseph said to them, "It *is* as I
spoke to you, saying, 'You *are* spies!' 15In
this *manner* you shall be tested: By the life
of Pharaoh, you shall not leave this place
unless your youngest brother comes here.
16Send one of you, and let him bring your
brother; and you shall be kept in prison,
that your words may be tested to see
whether *there is* any truth in you; or else, by
the life of Pharaoh, surely you *are* spies!"
17So he put them all together in prison
three days.
18Then Joseph said to them the third day,
"Do this and live, *for* I fear God: 19If you *are*
honest *men,* let one of your brothers be
confined to your prison house; but you, go
and carry grain for the famine of your
houses. 20And bring your youngest brother
to me; so your words will be verified, and
you shall not die."
And they did so. 21Then they said to one
another, "We *are* truly guilty concerning
our brother, for we saw the anguish of his
soul when he pleaded with us, and we
would not hear; therefore this distress has
come upon us."
22And Reuben answered them, saying,
"Did I not speak to you, saying, 'Do not sin
against the boy'; and you would not listen?
Therefore behold, his blood is now re-
quired of us." 23But they did not know that
Joseph understood *them,* for he spoke to
them through an interpreter. 24And he
turned himself away from them and wept.
Then he returned to them again, and
talked with them. And he took Sim'ē·on
from them and bound him before their
eyes.

The Brothers Return to Canaan

25Then Joseph gave a command to fill
their sacks with grain, to restore every
man's money to his sack, and to give them
provisions for the journey. Thus he did for
them. 26So they loaded their donkeys with

42:18 I fear God: Concerned lest unnecessary cruelty should be counted against him in the heavenly record. The statement would not necessarily reveal to Joseph's brothers his identity and knowledge of the biblical God. Egyptian faith believed in a future life after death.

42:24 wept: An indication of Joseph's heart. His motivation in putting pressure on them was not the bitter revenge one might expect. As Christians, we should allow the love of God to fill our hearts.

the grain and departed from there. 27But as
one *of them* opened his sack to give his don-
key feed at the encampment, he saw his
money; and there it was, in the mouth of
his sack. 28So he said to his brothers, "My
money has been restored, and there it is, in
my sack!" Then their hearts failed *them* and
they were afraid, saying to one another,
"What *is* this *that* God has done to us?"

29Then they went to Jacob their father in
the land of Cā'naan and told him all that
had happened to them, saying: 30"The man
who is lord of the land spoke roughly to us,
and took us for spies of the country. 31But
we said to him, 'We *are* honest *men;* we are
not spies. 32We *are* twelve brothers, sons of
our father; one *is* no *more,* and the youngest
is with our father this day in the land of
Cā'naan.' 33Then the man, the lord of the
country, said to us, 'By this I will know that
you *are* honest *men:* Leave one of your
brothers *here* with me, take *food for* the
famine of your households, and be gone.
34And bring your youngest brother to me;
so I shall know that you *are* not spies, but
that you *are* honest *men.* I will grant your
brother to you, and you may trade in the
land.' "

35Then it happened as they emptied
their sacks, that surprisingly each man's
bundle of money *was* in his sack; and when
they and their father saw the bundles of
money, they were afraid. 36And Jacob their
father said to them, "You have bereaved
me: Joseph is no *more,* Sim'ē·on is no *more,*
and you want to take Benjamin. All these
things are against me."

37Then Reuben spoke to his father, say-
ing, "Kill my two sons if I do not bring him
back to you; put him in my hands, and I
will bring him back to you."

38But he said, "My son shall not go
down with you, for his brother is dead,
and he is left alone. If any calamity should
befall him along the way in which you go,
then you would bring down my gray hair
with sorrow to the grave."

CHAPTER 43

Joseph's Brothers Return with Benjamin

Now the famine *was* severe in the land.
2And it came to pass, when they had eaten
up the grain which they had brought from
Egypt, that their father said to them, "Go
back, buy us a little food."

3But Judah spoke to him, saying, "The
man solemnly warned us, saying, 'You
shall not see my face unless your brother *is*
with you.' 4If you send our brother with us,
we will go down and buy you food. 5But if
you will not send *him,* we will not go
down; for the man said to us, 'You shall not
see my face unless your brother *is* with
you.' "

6And Israel said, "Why did you deal *so*
wrongfully with me *as* to tell the man
whether you had still *another* brother?"

7But they said, "The man asked us
pointedly about ourselves and our family,
saying, '*Is* your father still alive? Have you
another brother?' And we told him accord-
ing to these words. Could we possibly
have known that he would say, 'Bring your
brother down'?"

8Then Judah said to Israel his father,
"Send the lad with me, and we will arise
and go, that we may live and not die, both
we and you *and* also our little ones. 9I my-
self will be surety for him; from my hand
you shall require him. If I do not bring him
back to you and set him before you, then let
me bear the blame forever. 10For if we had
not lingered, surely by now we would
have returned this second time."

11And their father Israel said to them, "If
it must be so, then do this: Take some of the

43:8, 9 In the 22 years since they had sold Joseph, his brothers had become better men. **Judah**, who had suggested selling Joseph, now offered his own life as surety for Benjamin's life.

best fruits of the land in your vessels and carry down a present for the man—a little balm and a little honey, spices and myrrh, pistachio nuts and almonds. [12]Take double money in your hand, and take back in your hand the money that was returned in the mouth of your sacks; perhaps it was an oversight. [13]Take your brother also, and arise, go back to the man. [14]And may God Almighty give you mercy before the man, that he may release your other brother and Benjamin. If I am bereaved, I am bereaved!"

[15]So the men took that present and Benjamin, and they took double money in their hand, and arose and went down to Egypt; and they stood before Joseph. [16]When Joseph saw Benjamin with them, he said to the steward of his house, "Take *these* men to my home, and slaughter an animal and make ready; for *these* men will dine with me at noon." [17]Then the man did as Joseph ordered, and the man brought the men into Joseph's house.

[18]Now the men were afraid because they were brought into Joseph's house; and they said, "*It is* because of the money, which was returned in our sacks the first time, that we are brought in, so that he may make a case against us and seize us, to take us as slaves with our donkeys."

[19]When they drew near to the steward of Joseph's house, they talked with him at the door of the house, [20]and said, "O sir, we indeed came down the first time to buy food; [21]but it happened, when we came to the encampment, that we opened our sacks, and there, *each* man's money *was* in the mouth of his sack, our money in full weight; so we have brought it back in our hand. [22]And we have brought down other money in our hands to buy food. We do not know who put our money in our sacks."

[23]But he said, "Peace *be* with you, do not be afraid. Your God and the God of your father has given you treasure in your sacks; I had your money." Then he brought Sim'ē·on out to them.

[24]So the man brought the men into Joseph's house and gave *them* water, and they washed their feet; and he gave their donkeys feed. [25]Then they made the present ready for Joseph's coming at noon, for they heard that they would eat bread there.

[26]And when Joseph came home, they brought him the present which *was* in their hand into the house, and bowed down before him to the earth. [27]Then he asked them about *their* well-being, and said, "*Is* your father well, the old man of whom you spoke? *Is* he still alive?"

[28]And they answered, "Your servant our father *is* in good health; he *is* still alive." And they bowed their heads down and prostrated themselves.

[29]Then he lifted his eyes and saw his brother Benjamin, his mother's son, and said, "*Is* this your younger brother of whom you spoke to me?" And he said, "God be gracious to you, my son." [30]Now his heart yearned for his brother; so Joseph made haste and sought *somewhere* to weep. And he went into *his* chamber and wept there. [31]Then he washed his face and came out; and he restrained himself, and said, "Serve the bread."

[32]So they set him a place by himself, and them by themselves, and the Egyptians who ate with him by themselves; because the Egyptians could not eat food with the Hebrews, for that *is* an abomination to the Egyptians. [33]And they sat before him, the firstborn according to his birthright and the youngest according to his youth; and the men looked in astonishment at one another. [34]Then he took

43:32 could not eat food with the Hebrews: A religious separation; these Hebrews from Canaan ate animals, some of which were sacred to the Egyptians.

43:34 five times: To give extra portions signified a special relationship (see 1 Sam. 1:5); Benjamin was Joseph's full brother, his mother's son (v. 29).

servings to them from before him, but Ben-
jamin's serving was five times as much as
any of theirs. So they drank and were
merry with him.

CHAPTER 44

Joseph's Cup

And he commanded the steward of his
house, saying, "Fill the men's sacks with
food, as much as they can carry, and put
each man's money in the mouth of his
sack. 2Also put my cup, the silver cup, in
the mouth of the sack of the youngest, and
his grain money." So he did according to
the word that Joseph had spoken. 3As soon
as the morning dawned, the men were sent
away, they and their donkeys. 4When they
had gone out of the city, *and* were not *yet*
far off, Joseph said to his steward, "Get up,
follow the men; and when you overtake
them, say to them, 'Why have you repaid
evil for good? 5*Is* not this *the one* from
which my lord drinks, and with which he
indeed practices divination? You have
done evil in so doing.' "

6So he overtook them, and he spoke to
them these same words. 7And they said
to him, "Why does my lord say these
words? Far be it from us that your servants
should do such a thing. 8Look, we brought
back to you from the land of Cā'naan the
money which we found in the mouth of
our sacks. How then could we steal silver
or gold from your lord's house? 9With
whomever of your servants it is found, let
him die, and we also will be my lord's
slaves."

10And he said, "Now also *let* it *be* accord-
ing to your words; he with whom it is
found shall be my slave, and you shall be
blameless." 11Then each man speedily let
down his sack to the ground, and each
opened his sack. 12So he searched. He be-
gan with the oldest and left off with the
youngest; and the cup was found in Benja-
min's sack. 13Then they tore their clothes,
and each man loaded his donkey and re-
turned to the city.

14So Judah and his brothers came to Jo-
seph's house, and he *was* still there; and
they fell before him on the ground. 15And
Joseph said to them, "What deed *is* this
you have done? Did you not know that
such a man as I can certainly practice
divination?"

16Then Judah said, "What shall we say
to my lord? What shall we speak? Or how
shall we clear ourselves? God has found
out the iniquity of your servants; here we
are, my lord's slaves, both we and *he* also
with whom the cup was found."

17But he said, "Far be it from me that I
should do so; the man in whose hand the
cup was found, he shall be my slave. And
as for you, go up in peace to your father."

Judah Intercedes for Benjamin

18Then Judah came near to him and said:
"O my lord, please let your servant speak a
word in my lord's hearing, and do not let
your anger burn against your servant; for
you *are* even like Pharaoh. 19My lord asked
his servants, saying, 'Have you a father or
a brother?' 20And we said to my lord, 'We
have a father, an old man, and a child of *his*
old age, *who is* young; his brother is dead,
and he alone is left of his mother's chil-
dren, and his father loves him.' 21Then you
said to your servants, 'Bring him down to
me, that I may set my eyes on him.' 22And
we said to my lord, 'The lad cannot leave
his father, for *if* he should leave his father,
his father would die.' 23But you said to your
servants, 'Unless your youngest brother
comes down with you, you shall see my
face no more.'

44:9, 10 let him die: They were that confident of their innocence. The steward, however, knowing the eventual outcome (vv. 1, 2), reduced the proposed punishment from death to slavery.

Joseph: Victory over Bitterness

Prejudice, abuse, and injustice often plant roots of bitterness in the souls of their victims. As the years pass, this bitterness may develop into a deep, abiding anger that encompasses everyone and everything—including God and self—and erodes spiritual and physical health. Yet one Old Testament hero, who experienced many forms of persecution, resisted the temptation to become bitter and learned to reward good for evil.

Even as a young man, Joseph was hated by his own brothers (Gen. 37:2, 3). They resented the favoritism Jacob unwisely showed toward him and the fact that he had disclosed their evil deeds to their father. When he told them of his dreams, which predicted his family would one day be subservient to him, they envied him and hated him all the more (vv. 10, 11). The brothers plotted to kill him but were sidetracked by the lure of profit. They sold Joseph for twenty pieces of silver, and he became a slave in Egypt.

There, the injustice continued. When Joseph refused the advances of Potiphar's wife, she accused him of attempting to rape her. Her husband threw his erstwhile slave into prison without a hearing, but God showed mercy to Joseph and brought him into the jailer's good favor (39:10–21).

While in prison, Joseph interpreted two dreams for the king's butler and baker. Although the baker's dream signified his imminent death, the butler's dream meant he would soon return to Pharaoh's service. At Joseph's request, the butler promised to use his position to help gain Joseph's release from prison. Yet in another example of the unfairness of life, the butler failed to keep his word and promptly forgot about his friend.

Finally, the Lord provided an opportunity for Joseph to gain his release from prison by interpreting Pharaoh's disturbing dreams, which foretold of a coming famine. He gave God credit for his insight and at last was rewarded for his years of faith. At the age of thirty, Joseph held a position of great authority in Egypt, preparing the nation for the coming famine.

The land of Canaan, however, was not prepared for the disaster, and when his brothers came to buy food, Joseph had the perfect opportunity for revenge. Although he tested his brothers—perhaps to determine whether they would treat Benjamin as cruelly as they had treated him—he did not take advantage of them.

When his brothers recognized Joseph and realized their vulnerability, he reassured them, giving glory to God for His hand in the situation. He even refused to allow them to blame themselves (45:5–8). What an inspiring example of forgiveness!

No matter how badly others treat

us, Christians have no excuse for allowing themselves to become bitter. True forgiveness frees us from emotional bondage and allows us to regain our spiritual, physical, and mental health. When we are tempted to allow our resentment to take hold, we can say with Joseph: "You meant evil against me; but God meant it for good" (50:20). ✦

24"So it was, when we went up to your servant my father, that we told him the words of my lord. 25And our father said, 'Go back *and* buy us a little food.' 26But we said, 'We cannot go down; if our youngest brother is with us, then we will go down; for we may not see the man's face unless our youngest brother *is* with us.' 27Then your servant my father said to us, 'You know that my wife bore me two sons; 28and the one went out from me, and I said, "Surely he is torn to pieces"; and I have not seen him since. 29But if you take this one also from me, and calamity befalls him, you shall bring down my gray hair with sorrow to the grave.'

30"Now therefore, when I come to your servant my father, and the lad *is* not with us, since his life is bound up in the lad's life, 31it will happen, when he sees that the lad *is* not *with us,* that he will die. So your servants will bring down the gray hair of your servant our father with sorrow to the grave. 32For your servant became surety for the lad to my father, saying, 'If I do not bring him *back* to you, then I shall bear the blame before my father forever.' 33Now therefore, please let your servant remain instead of the lad as a slave to my lord, and let the lad go up with his brothers. 34For how shall I go up to my father if the lad *is* not with me, lest perhaps I see the evil that would come upon my father?"

CHAPTER 45

Joseph Revealed to His Brothers

Then Joseph could not restrain himself before all those who stood by him, and he cried out, "Make everyone go out from me!" So no one stood with him while Joseph made himself known to his brothers. 2And he wept aloud, and the Egyptians and the house of Pharaoh heard *it.*

3Then Joseph said to his brothers, "I *am* Joseph; does my father still live?" But his brothers could not answer him, for they were dismayed in his presence. 4And Joseph said to his brothers, "Please come near to me." So they came near. Then he said: "I *am* Joseph your brother, whom you sold into Egypt. 5But now, do not therefore be grieved or angry with yourselves because you sold me here; for God sent me before you to preserve life. 6For these two years the famine *has been* in the land, and *there are* still five years in which *there will be* neither plowing nor harvesting. 7And God sent me before you to preserve a posterity for you in the earth, and to save your lives

44:33, 34 let your servant remain . . . a slave: A great change had occurred; 22 years earlier Judah had sold a younger brother into slavery and lied to his father (see 37:26, 27). Now he offered to become a slave in order to free a younger brother, and spare his father from sorrow.

45:5–8 you sold me . . . God sent me: The doctrinal highlight of the Joseph story: What his brothers meant for evil, God meant for good (50:20). **to save your lives** (v. 7): And preserve their descendants. Joseph was an OT type of "Christ . . . who . . . when He suffered . . . committed Himself to Him who judges righteously . . . that we . . . might live" (1 Pet. 2:21–24).

by a great deliverance. 8So now *it was* not
you *who* sent me here, but God; and He has
made me a father to Pharaoh, and lord of
all his house, and a ruler throughout all the
land of Egypt.
9"Hurry and go up to my father, and say
to him, 'Thus says your son Joseph: "God
has made me lord of all Egypt; come down
to me, do not tarry. 10You shall dwell in the
land of Gō'shen, and you shall be near to
me, you and your children, your children's
children, your flocks and your herds, and
all that you have. 11There I will provide for
you, lest you and your household, and all
that you have, come to poverty; for *there
are* still five years of famine." '
12"And behold, your eyes and the eyes
of my brother Benjamin see that *it is* my
mouth that speaks to you. 13So you shall
tell my father of all my glory in Egypt, and
of all that you have seen; and you shall
hurry and bring my father down here."
14Then he fell on his brother Benjamin's
neck and wept, and Benjamin wept on his
neck. 15Moreover he kissed all his brothers
and wept over them, and after that his
brothers talked with him.
16Now the report of it was heard in
Pharaoh's house, saying, "Joseph's broth-
ers have come." So it pleased Pharaoh and
his servants well. 17And Pharaoh said to Jo-
seph, "Say to your brothers, 'Do this: Load
your animals and depart; go to the land of
Cā'naan. 18Bring your father and your
households and come to me; I will give
you the best of the land of Egypt, and you
will eat the fat of the land. 19Now you are
commanded—do this: Take carts out of the
land of Egypt for your little ones and your
wives; bring your father and come. 20Also
do not be concerned about your goods, for
the best of all the land of Egypt *is* yours.' "
21Then the sons of Israel did so; and Jo-
seph gave them carts, according to the
command of Pharaoh, and he gave them
provisions for the journey. 22He gave to all
of them, to each man, changes of garments;
but to Benjamin he gave three hundred
pieces of silver and five changes of gar-
ments. 23And he sent to his father these
things: ten donkeys loaded with the good
things of Egypt, and ten female donkeys
loaded with grain, bread, and food for his
father for the journey. 24So he sent his
brothers away, and they departed; and he
said to them, "See that you do not become
troubled along the way."
25Then they went up out of Egypt, and
came to the land of Cā'naan to Jacob their
father. 26And they told him, saying, "Jo-
seph *is* still alive, and he *is* governor over
all the land of Egypt." And Jacob's heart
stood still, because he did not believe
them. 27But when they told him all the
words which Joseph had said to them, and
when he saw the carts which Joseph had
sent to carry him, the spirit of Jacob their
father revived. 28Then Israel said, "*It is*
enough. Joseph my son *is* still alive. I will
go and see him before I die."

CHAPTER 46

Jacob's Journey to Egypt

So Israel took his journey with all that
he had, and came to Bē·er·shē'ba, and of-
fered sacrifices to the God of his father
Isaac. 2Then God spoke to Israel in the vi-
sions of the night, and said, "Jacob, Jacob!"
And he said, "Here I am."

45:16–24 It was unprecedented for an Egyptian pharaoh to show such generosity toward Semites from Canaan. The Egyptians tended to hold the Canaanites in contempt (see 43:32). However, between about 1800 and 1550 B.C. (the time of Joseph) Semitic-speaking peoples had established themselves in northern Egypt, and eventually ruled that area. Although becoming thoroughly assimilated to Egyptian culture, they still did not have the ingrained hostility of native Egyptians to the Canaanites.

45:24 Do not become troubled about your former evil. Joseph had already forgiven them (see 50:19–21).

3So He said, "I *am* God, the God of your father; do not fear to go down to Egypt, for I will make of you a great nation there. 4I will go down with you to Egypt, and I will also surely bring you up *again;* and Joseph will put his hand on your eyes."

5Then Jacob arose from Bē·er·shē'ba; and the sons of Israel carried their father Jacob, their little ones, and their wives, in the carts which Pharaoh had sent to carry him. 6So they took their livestock and their goods, which they had acquired in the land of Cā'naan, and went to Egypt, Jacob and all his descendants with him. 7His sons and his sons' sons, his daughters and his sons' daughters, and all his descendants he brought with him to Egypt.

8Now these *were* the names of the children of Israel, Jacob and his sons, who went to Egypt: Reuben *was* Jacob's firstborn. 9The sons of Reuben *were* Hā'noch, Pal'lū, Hez'ron, and Car'mī. 10The sons of Sim'ē·on *were* Je·mū'el,[a] Jā'min, Ō'had, Jā'chin,[b] Zō'har,[c] and Shā'ūl, the son of a Cā'naan·īte woman. 11The sons of Levi *were* Ger'shon, Kō'hath, and Me·rar'ī. 12The sons of Judah *were* Er, Ō'nan, Shē'lah, Per'ez, and Zē'rah (but Er and Ō'nan died in the land of Cā'naan). The sons of Per'ez were Hez'ron and Hā'mul. 13The sons of Is'sa·char *were* Tō'la, Pū'vah,[a] Job,[b] and Shim'ron. 14The sons of Zeb'ū·lun *were* Sē'red, Ē'lon, and Jah'lē·el. 15These *were* the sons of Leah, whom she bore to Jacob in Pad'an Ar'am, with his daughter Dī'nah. All the persons, his sons and his daughters, *were* thirty-three.

16The sons of Gad *were* Ziph'i·on,[a] Hag'gī, Shū'nī, Ez'bon,[b] Ē'rī, A·rō'dī,[c] and A·rē'lī. 17The sons of Ash'er *were* Jim'nah, Ish'ū·ah, Is'ū·ī, Bē·rī'ah, and Sē'rah, their sister. And the sons of Bē·rī'ah *were* Hē'ber and Mal'chi·el. 18These *were* the sons of Zil'pah, whom Lā'ban gave to Leah his daughter; and these she bore to Jacob: sixteen persons.

19The sons of Rachel, Jacob's wife, *were* Joseph and Benjamin. 20And to Joseph in the land of Egypt were born Ma·nas'seh and Ē'phra·im, whom As'e·nath, the daughter of Pō·ti'-Phe·rah' priest of On, bore to him. 21The sons of Benjamin *were* Bē'lah, Bē'cher, Ash'bel, Gē'ra, Nā'a·man, Ē'hī, Rosh, Mup'pim, Hup'pim,[a] and Ard. 22These *were* the sons of Rachel, who were born to Jacob: fourteen persons in all.

23The son of Dan *was* Hū'shim.[a] 24The sons of Naph'ta·lī *were* Jah'zē·el,[a] Gū'nī, Jē'zer, and Shil'lem.[b] 25These *were* the sons of Bil'hah, whom Lā'ban gave to Rachel his daughter, and she bore these to Jacob: seven persons in all.

26All the persons who went with Jacob to Egypt, who came from his body, besides Jacob's sons' wives, *were* sixty-six persons in all. 27And the sons of Joseph who were born to him in Egypt *were* two persons. All the persons of the house of Jacob who went to Egypt were seventy.

Jacob Settles in Goshen

28Then he sent Judah before him to Joseph, to point out before him *the way* to

46:10 [a]Spelled *Nemuel* in 1 Chronicles 4:24 [b]Called *Jarib* in 1 Chronicles 4:24 [c]Called *Zerah* in 1 Chronicles 4:24 46:13 [a]Spelled *Puah* in 1 Chronicles 7:1 [b]Same as *Jashub* in Numbers 26:24 and 1 Chronicles 7:1 46:16 [a]Spelled *Zephon* in Samaritan Pentateuch, Septuagint, and Numbers 26:15 [b]Called *Ozni* in Numbers 26:16 [c]Spelled *Arod* in Numbers 26:17 46:21 [a]Called *Hupham* in Numbers 26:39 46:23 [a]Called *Shuham* in Numbers 26:42 46:24 [a]Spelled *Jahziel* in 1 Chronicles 7:13 [b]Spelled *Shallum* in 1 Chronicles 7:13

46:4 his hand on your eyes: Joseph would be present when his father died and would close Israel's eyes at the time of his death.

46:8–27 This genealogy marks a sharp change in the story: the next 400 years would be in Egypt. For a genealogy of an earlier time in Israel's history see 36:1–43.

46:10 Two of Jacob's sons, Simeon and Judah, married Canaanite women (see 38:2) against the tradition of Abraham and Isaac (see 24:3; 28:1).

Gō′shen. And they came to the land of
Gō′shen. 29So Joseph made ready his char-
iot and went up to Gō′shen to meet his fa-
ther Israel; and he presented himself to
him, and fell on his neck and wept on his
neck a good while.

30And Israel said to Joseph, "Now let me
die, since I have seen your face, because
you *are* still alive."

31Then Joseph said to his brothers and to
his father's household, "I will go up and
tell Pharaoh, and say to him, 'My brothers
and those of my father's house, who *were*
in the land of Cā′naan, have come to me.
32And the men *are* shepherds, for their oc-
cupation has been to feed livestock; and
they have brought their flocks, their herds,
and all that they have.' 33So it shall be,
when Pharaoh calls you and says, 'What is
your occupation?' 34that you shall say,
'Your servants' occupation has been with
livestock from our youth even till now,
both we *and* also our fathers,' that you may
dwell in the land of Gō′shen; for every
shepherd *is* an abomination to the Egyp-
tians."

CHAPTER 47

Then Joseph went and told Pharaoh,
and said, "My father and my brothers,
their flocks and their herds and all that
they possess, have come from the land of
Cā′naan; and indeed they *are* in the land of
Gō′shen." 2And he took five men from
among his brothers and presented them to
Pharaoh. 3Then Pharaoh said to his broth-
ers, "What *is* your occupation?"

And they said to Pharaoh, "Your
servants *are* shepherds, both we *and* also
our fathers." 4And they said to Pharaoh,
"We have come to dwell in the land, be-
cause your servants have no pasture for
their flocks, for the famine *is* severe in the
land of Cā′naan. Now therefore, please let
your servants dwell in the land of
Gō′shen."

5Then Pharaoh spoke to Joseph, saying,
"Your father and your brothers have come
to you. 6The land of Egypt *is* before you.
Have your father and brothers dwell in the
best of the land; let them dwell in the land
of Gō′shen. And if you know *any* compe-
tent men among them, then make them
chief herdsmen over my livestock."

7Then Joseph brought in his father Ja-
cob and set him before Pharaoh; and
Jacob blessed Pharaoh. 8Pharaoh said to
Jacob, "How old *are* you?"

9And Jacob said to Pharaoh, "The days
of the years of my pilgrimage *are* one hun-
dred and thirty years; few and evil have
been the days of the years of my life, and
they have not attained to the days of the
years of the life of my fathers in the days
of their pilgrimage." 10So Jacob blessed
Pharaoh, and went out from before Pha-
raoh.

11And Joseph situated his father and his
brothers, and gave them a possession in
the land of Egypt, in the best of the land, in
the land of Ram′e·sēs, as Pharaoh had
commanded. 12Then Joseph provided his
father, his brothers, and all his father's
household with bread, according to the
number in *their* families.

46:31–34 An example of Near Eastern diplomacy. Joseph wanted his family settled in the **land of Goshen** (v. 34) on Egypt's northeastern border. But strangers from Canaan, being suspect in Egypt, were not allowed to settle in such a sensitive border area. On the other hand, a settlement of shepherds anywhere in the center of the country would not work out because every shepherd was an abomination to the Egyptians (v. 34). They considered shepherding a loathsome occupation practiced only by the barbarian Semites of northern lands. However, some sheep-keeping was practiced in the Nile delta region of Goshen. Thus, careful instructions for his brothers not to hide their occupation from Pharaoh would, Joseph hoped, result in their settlement in Goshen.

Joseph Deals with the Famine

[13]Now *there was* no bread in all the land; for the famine *was* very severe, so that the land of Egypt and the land of Cā′naan languished because of the famine. [14]And Joseph gathered up all the money that was found in the land of Egypt and in the land of Cā′naan, for the grain which they bought; and Joseph brought the money into Pharaoh's house.

[15]So when the money failed in the land of Egypt and in the land of Cā′naan, all the Egyptians came to Joseph and said, "Give us bread, for why should we die in your presence? For the money has failed."

[16]Then Joseph said, "Give your livestock, and I will give you *bread* for your livestock, if the money is gone." [17]So they brought their livestock to Joseph, and Joseph gave them bread *in exchange* for the horses, the flocks, the cattle of the herds, and for the donkeys. Thus he fed them with bread *in exchange* for all their livestock that year.

[18]When that year had ended, they came to him the next year and said to him, "We will not hide from my lord that our money is gone; my lord also has our herds of livestock. There is nothing left in the sight of my lord but our bodies and our lands. [19]Why should we die before your eyes, both we and our land? Buy us and our land for bread, and we and our land will be servants of Pharaoh; give *us* seed, that we may live and not die, that the land may not be desolate."

[20]Then Joseph bought all the land of Egypt for Pharaoh; for every man of the Egyptians sold his field, because the famine was severe upon them. So the land became Pharaoh's. [21]And as for the people, he moved them into the cities,[a] from *one* end of the borders of Egypt to the *other* end. [22]Only the land of the priests he did not buy; for the priests had rations *allotted to them* by Pharaoh, and they ate their rations which Pharaoh gave them; therefore they did not sell their lands.

[23]Then Joseph said to the people, "Indeed I have bought you and your land this day for Pharaoh. Look, *here is* seed for you, and you shall sow the land. [24]And it shall come to pass in the harvest that you shall give one-fifth to Pharaoh. Four-fifths shall be your own, as seed for the field and for your food, for those of your households and as food for your little ones."

[25]So they said, "You have saved our lives; let us find favor in the sight of my lord, and we will be Pharaoh's servants." [26]And Joseph made it a law over the land of Egypt to this day, *that* Pharaoh should have one-fifth, except for the land of the priests only, *which* did not become Pharaoh's.

Joseph's Vow to Jacob

[27]So Israel dwelt in the land of Egypt, in the country of Gō′shen; and they had possessions there and grew and multiplied exceedingly. [28]And Jacob lived in the land of Egypt seventeen years. So the length of Jacob's life was one hundred and forty-seven years. [29]When the time drew near that Israel must die, he called his son Joseph and said to him, "Now if I have found favor in your sight, please put your hand under my thigh, and deal kindly and truly with me. Please do not bury me in Egypt, [30]but let me lie with my fathers; you shall carry me out of Egypt and bury me in their burial place."

47:21 [a]Following Masoretic Text and Targum; Samaritan Pentateuch, Septuagint, and Vulgate read *made the people virtual slaves.*

47:17 he fed them with bread: Lit. "he guided them with bread." Like a shepherd, Joseph carefully brought the hungering people through **that year**.

47:29 put your hand under my thigh: A Near Eastern practice to confirm an oath (see 24:2).

And he said, "I will do as you have
said."
[31]Then he said, "Swear to me." And he
swore to him. So Israel bowed himself on
the head of the bed.

CHAPTER 48

Jacob Blesses Joseph's Sons

Now it came to pass after these things
that Joseph was told, "Indeed your father
is sick"; and he took with him his two sons,
Ma·nas'seh and Ē'phra·im. [2]And Jacob
was told, "Look, your son Joseph is com-
ing to you"; and Israel strengthened him-
self and sat up on the bed. [3]Then Jacob said
to Joseph: "God Almighty appeared to me
at Luz in the land of Cā'naan and blessed
me, [4]and said to me, 'Behold, I will make
you fruitful and multiply you, and I will
make of you a multitude of people, and
give this land to your descendants after
you *as* an everlasting possession.' [5]And
now your two sons, Ē'phra·im and Ma-
nas'seh, who were born to you in the land
of Egypt before I came to you in Egypt, *are*
mine; as Reuben and Sim'ē·on, they shall
be mine. [6]Your offspring whom you beget
after them shall be yours; they will be
called by the name of their brothers in their
inheritance. [7]But as for me, when I came
from Pad'an, Rachel died beside me in the
land of Cā'naan on the way, when *there was*
but a little distance to go to Eph'rath; and I
buried her there on the way to Eph'rath
(that is, Bethlehem)."
[8]Then Israel saw Joseph's sons, and said,
"Who *are* these?"
[9]Joseph said to his father, "They *are* my
sons, whom God has given me in this
place."
And he said, "Please bring them to me,
and I will bless them." [10]Now the eyes
of Israel were dim with age, *so that* he
could not see. Then Joseph brought them
near him, and he kissed them and em-
braced them. [11]And Israel said to Joseph, "I
had not thought to see your face; but in
fact, God has also shown me your off-
spring!"
[12]So Joseph brought them from beside
his knees, and he bowed down with his
face to the earth. [13]And Joseph took them
both, Ē'phra·im with his right hand to-
ward Israel's left hand, and Ma·nas'seh
with his left hand toward Israel's right
hand, and brought *them* near him. [14]Then
Israel stretched out his right hand and laid
it on Ē'phra·im's head, who *was* the
younger, and his left hand on Ma·nas'seh's
head, guiding his hands knowingly, for

Creative Grandparents

Jerry and Jack Schreur

There are biological grandparents and there are creative grandparents. Biological grandparents carry pictures in their wallets and hang photos on the wall. They have sporadic contact with their grandchildren and limited input into their lives. Biological grandparents are gift-givers and perfunctory hug-receivers.

Creative grandparents carry memories in their hearts and love in their souls. Creative grandparents go beyond showing off their grandchildren as trophies. Creative grandparents want to be an integral part of their grandchildren's lives. They want to impart to them their Christian values. They want to shower them with love and acceptance. They want to build a relationship that will last a lifetime. Creative grandparents put their hearts and souls into grandparenting, and they make a difference in the lives of their grandchildren. ✦

Ma·nas'seh *was* the firstborn. [15]And he blessed Joseph, and said:

"God, before whom my fathers Abraham and Isaac walked,
The God who has fed me all my life long to this day,
16 The Angel who has redeemed me from all evil,
Bless the lads;
Let my name be named upon them,
And the name of my fathers Abraham and Isaac;
And let them grow into a multitude in the midst of the earth."

[17]Now when Joseph saw that his father laid his right hand on the head of Ē'phra·im, it displeased him; so he took hold of his father's hand to remove it from Ē'phra·im's head to Ma·nas'seh's head. [18]And Joseph said to his father, "Not so, my father, for this *one is* the firstborn; put your right hand on his head."

[19]But his father refused and said, "I know, my son, I know. He also shall become a people, and he also shall be great; but truly his younger brother shall be greater than he, and his descendants shall become a multitude of nations."

[20]So he blessed them that day, saying, "By you Israel will bless, saying, 'May God make you as Ē'phra·im and as Ma·nas'seh!' " And thus he set Ē'phra·im before Ma·nas'seh.

[21]Then Israel said to Joseph, "Behold, I am dying, but God will be with you and bring you back to the land of your fathers. [22]Moreover I have given to you one portion above your brothers, which I took from the hand of the Am'o·rīte with my sword and my bow."

CHAPTER 49

Jacob's Last Words to His Sons

And Jacob called his sons and said, "Gather together, that I may tell you what shall befall you in the last days:

2 "Gather together and hear, you sons of Jacob,
And listen to Israel your father.

3 "Reuben, you are my firstborn,
My might and the beginning of my strength,
The excellency of dignity and the excellency of power.
4 Unstable as water, you shall not excel,
Because you went up to your father's bed;
Then you defiled *it*—
He went up to my couch.

5 "Sim'ē·on and Levi *are* brothers;
Instruments of cruelty *are in* their dwelling place.
6 Let not my soul enter their council;
Let not my honor be united to their assembly;
For in their anger they slew a man,
And in their self-will they hamstrung an ox.
7 Cursed *be* their anger, for *it is* fierce;
And their wrath, for it is cruel!
I will divide them in Jacob
And scatter them in Israel.

8 "Judah, you *are he* whom your brothers shall praise;
Your hand *shall be* on the neck of your enemies;
Your father's children shall bow down before you.

49:3–12 Later rulers of Israel and the Messiah (v. 10) would be descendants of Judah (v. 8), the fourth son. Thus, the royal line did not come from **Reuben**, the first son, who had shown himself of immoral character (v. 4; see 35:22), nor from **Simeon** and **Levi**, the second and third sons, who had shown characters of cruelty (v. 6; see 34:25, 26).

9 Judah *is* a lion's whelp;
From the prey, my son, you have
gone up.
He bows down, he lies down as a
lion;
And as a lion, who shall rouse him?
10 The scepter shall not depart from Judah,
Nor a lawgiver from between his feet,
Until Shī'lōh comes;
And to Him *shall be* the obedience of
the people.
11 Binding his donkey to the vine,
And his donkey's colt to the choice
vine,
He washed his garments in wine,
And his clothes in the blood of
grapes.
12 His eyes *are* darker than wine,
And his teeth whiter than milk.

13 "Zeb'ū·lun shall dwell by the haven of
the sea;
He *shall become* a haven for ships,
And his border shall adjoin Sī'don.

14 "Is'sa·char is a strong donkey,
Lying down between two burdens;
15 He saw that rest *was* good,
And that the land *was* pleasant;
He bowed his shoulder to bear *a
burden*,
And became a band of slaves.

16 "Dan shall judge his people
As one of the tribes of Israel.
17 Dan shall be a serpent by the way,
A viper by the path,
That bites the horse's heels
So that its rider shall fall backward.
18 I have waited for your salvation, O
LORD!

19 "Gad, a troop shall tramp upon him,
But he shall triumph at last.

20 "Bread from Ash'er *shall be* rich,
And he shall yield royal dainties.

21 "Naph'ta·lī *is* a deer let loose;
He uses beautiful words.

22 "Joseph *is* a fruitful bough,
A fruitful bough by a well;
His branches run over the wall.
23 The archers have bitterly grieved him,
Shot *at him* and hated him.
24 But his bow remained in strength,
And the arms of his hands were made
strong
By the hands of the Mighty *God* of Jacob
(From there *is* the Shepherd, the Stone
of Israel),
25 By the God of your father who will
help you,
And by the Almighty who will bless
you
With blessings of heaven above,
Blessings of the deep that lies
beneath,
Blessings of the breasts and of the
womb.
26 The blessings of your father
Have excelled the blessings of my
ancestors,
Up to the utmost bound of the
everlasting hills.
They shall be on the head of Joseph,
And on the crown of the head of him
who was separate from his
brothers.

49:14, 15 The descendants of **Issachar** did not drive out the Canaanites from the allotted territory and thus became a band of slaves to the Canaanites (see Judg. 1:30). Their territory was the Valley of Jezreel between two **burdens** (piles or hills), the mountains of Galilee and Gilboa.

49:22–26 **Joseph** includes both the tribes of Ephraim and Manasseh (48:14).

27 "Benjamin is a ravenous wolf;
In the morning he shall devour the
prey,
And at night he shall divide the
spoil."

28All these *are* the twelve tribes of Israel,
and this *is* what their father spoke to them.
And he blessed them; he blessed each one
according to his own blessing.

Jacob's Death and Burial

29Then he charged them and said to
them: "I am to be gathered to my people;
bury me with my fathers in the cave that *is*
in the field of Ē'phron the Hit'tīte, 30in the
cave that *is* in the field of Mach·pē'lah,
which *is* before Mam're in the land of
Cā'naan, which Abraham bought with the
field of Ē'phron the Hit'tīte as a possession
for a burial place. 31There they buried
Abraham and Sarah his wife, there they
buried Isaac and Rebekah his wife, and
there I buried Leah. 32The field and the
cave that *is* there *were* purchased from the
sons of Heth." 33And when Jacob had fin-
ished commanding his sons, he drew his
feet up into the bed and breathed his last,
and was gathered to his people.

CHAPTER 50

Then Joseph fell on his father's face and
wept over him, and kissed him. 2And Jo-
seph commanded his servants the physi-
cians to embalm his father. So the physi-
cians embalmed Israel. 3Forty days were
required for him, for such are the days re-
quired for those who are embalmed; and
the Egyptians mourned for him seventy
days.

4Now when the days of his mourning
were past, Joseph spoke to the household
of Pharaoh, saying, "If now I have found
favor in your eyes, please speak in the
hearing of Pharaoh, saying, 5'My father
made me swear, saying, "Behold, I am dy-
ing; in my grave which I dug for myself in
the land of Cā'naan, there you shall bury
me." Now therefore, please let me go up
and bury my father, and I will come
back.' "

6And Pharaoh said, "Go up and bury
your father, as he made you swear."

7So Joseph went up to bury his father;
and with him went up all the servants of
Pharaoh, the elders of his house, and all
the elders of the land of Egypt, 8as well as
all the house of Joseph, his brothers, and
his father's house. Only their little ones,
their flocks, and their herds they left in the
land of Gō'shen. 9And there went up with
him both chariots and horsemen, and it
was a very great gathering.

10Then they came to the threshing floor
of Ā'tad, which *is* beyond the Jordan, and
they mourned there with a great and very
solemn lamentation. He observed seven
days of mourning for his father. 11And
when the inhabitants of the land, the Cā'-
naan·ītes, saw the mourning at the thresh-
ing floor of Ā'tad, they said, "This *is* a deep
mourning of the Egyptians." Therefore its
name was called Abel Miz'ra·im,[a] which *is*
beyond the Jordan.

50:11 [a]Literally *Mourning of Egypt*

49:27 The characterization of the descendants of **Benjamin** as a **ravenous wolf** was apt (see Judg. 19). They were famous for their swordsmen and left-handed stone slingers (see Judg. 20:15, 16). Saul and Jonathan from the tribe of Benjamin fearlessly pursued the Philistines to defeat (1 Sam. 14:46).

49:29–33 gathered to my people (also v. 33): An expression of death. **bury me**: God's promise was not of Egypt but of **Canaan**, and Jacob did not want them to forget that while they were in Egypt.

50:2, 3 Seventy days was a customary time period for mourning in Egypt, especially for people of importance.

12So his sons did for him just as he had
commanded them. 13For his sons carried
him to the land of Cā'naan, and buried
him in the cave of the field of Mach·pē'lah,
before Mam're, which Abraham bought
with the field from Ē'phron the Hit'tīte as
property for a burial place. 14And after he
had buried his father, Joseph returned to
Egypt, he and his brothers and all who
went up with him to bury his father.

Joseph Reassures His Brothers

15When Joseph's brothers saw that their
father was dead, they said, "Perhaps Jo-
seph will hate us, and may actually repay
us for all the evil which we did to him."
16So they sent *messengers* to Joseph, saying,
"Before your father died he commanded,
saying, 17'Thus you shall say to Joseph: "I
beg you, please forgive the trespass of
your brothers and their sin; for they did
evil to you." ' Now, please, forgive the tres-
pass of the servants of the God of your fa-
ther." And Joseph wept when they spoke
to him.

18Then his brothers also went and fell
down before his face, and they said, "Be-
hold, we *are* your servants."

19Joseph said to them, "Do not be afraid,
for *am* I in the place of God? 20But as for
you, you meant evil against me; *but* God
meant it for good, in order to bring it about
as *it is* this day, to save many people alive.

> For both parties, forgiveness means the freedom again to be at peace inside their own skins and to be glad in each other's presence.
>
> Frederick Buechner

21Now therefore, do not be afraid; I will
provide for you and your little ones." And
he comforted them and spoke kindly to
them.

Death of Joseph

22So Joseph dwelt in Egypt, he and his
father's household. And Joseph lived one
hundred and ten years. 23Joseph saw
Ē'phra·im's children to the third *generation.*
The children of Mā'chir, the son of Ma-
nas'seh, were also brought up on Joseph's
knees.

24And Joseph said to his brethren, "I am
dying; but God will surely visit you, and
bring you out of this land to the land of
which He swore to Abraham, to Isaac, and
to Jacob." 25Then Joseph took an oath from
the children of Israel, saying, "God will
surely visit you, and you shall carry up my
bones from here." 26So Joseph died, *being*
one hundred and ten years old; and they
embalmed him, and he was put in a coffin
in Egypt.

50:15–21 Jacob's presence as Joseph's father protected his 10 sons from any revenge Joseph might take for the **evil** they had done. However, Jacob's death revived their feelings of guilt. Had they truly been forgiven? The reconciliation is effected in two stages. In true Near Eastern protocol, **messengers** (v. 16) were sent first; in the event of refusal, a different approach could be made. But the request was met with weeping (v. 17), giving the brothers courage to appear in person (v. 18). Joseph's indication of forgiveness was his offer: **I will provide for you** (v. 21).

50:26 embalmed: Embalming was a practice that originated in Egypt (see vv. 2, 3); the end product was a mummy. In Egyptian fashion the coffin for one of Joseph's rank would include several inner wooden coffins in the shape of the mummy, enclosed by two or three more rectangular wooden coffins, the outer one painted to resemble a house.

✦Exodus✦

Like Genesis, Exodus was most likely written by Moses (see John 1:45; Mark 7:10; 12:26; Luke 20:37) sometime after the Israelites left Egypt and before his death around 1400 B.C. The book covers the Israelites' escape from Egypt and their two-year trip through the wilderness toward Mount Sinai to receive instruction from God through Moses.

Exodus illustrates the central concept of redemption; Israel was saved from slavery in Egypt and given a covenant relationship with God. The climax occurs in chapters 12—14, when Israel was saved through the blood of the Passover Lamb and God's power over the Red Sea. Several parallels exist between events in Exodus and events during the ministry of Jesus. For example, the Passover Lamb was a symbol of Christ, and it demonstrated the necessity of a blood sacrifice.

Called to lead the Israelites at age eighty, Moses demonstrates that a call to minister to other believers can come at any age. Moses not only led the Israelites out of Egypt, he also received the Ten Commandments from God and oversaw the building of the tabernacle, which symbolized Christ and the way of redemption. ✦

CHAPTER 1

Israel's Suffering in Egypt

Now these *are* the names of the children
of Israel who came to Egypt; each man and
his household came with Jacob: 2Reuben,
Sim'ē·on, Levi, and Judah; 3Is'sa·char,
Zeb'ū·lun, and Benjamin; 4Dan, Naph'-
ta·lī, Gad, and Ash'er. 5All those who were
descendants[a] of Jacob were seventy[b] per-
sons (for Joseph was in Egypt *already*).
6And Joseph died, all his brothers, and all
that generation. 7But the children of Israel
were fruitful and increased abundantly,
multiplied and grew exceedingly mighty;
and the land was filled with them.
8Now there arose a new king over
Egypt, who did not know Joseph. 9And he
said to his people, "Look, the people of the
children of Israel *are* more and mightier
than we; 10come, let us deal shrewdly with
them, lest they multiply, and it happen, in
the event of war, that they also join our en-
emies and fight against us, and *so* go up
out of the land." 11Therefore they set

1:5 [a]Literally *who came from the loins of* [b]Dead Sea Scrolls and Septuagint read *seventy-five* (compare Acts 7:14).

1:1 Here, the reference to "the children of Israel" identifies Jacob's immediate family; all succeeding references signify the nation that descended from him, God's chosen people.

1:8 An early date for the Exodus would suggest that the **new king** was Thutmosis III (1490 to 1436 B.C.). That he **did not know Joseph** means he did not acknowledge Joseph's descendants as legitimate residents of Egypt.

taskmasters over them to afflict them with their burdens. And they built for Pharaoh supply cities, Pī'thom and Rā·am'sēs. 12But the more they afflicted them, the more they multiplied and grew. And they were in dread of the children of Israel. 13So the Egyptians made the children of Israel serve with rigor. 14And they made their lives bitter with hard bondage—in mortar, in brick, and in all manner of service in the field. All their service in which they made them serve *was* with rigor.

15Then the king of Egypt spoke to the Hebrew midwives, of whom the name of one *was* Shiph'rah and the name of the other Pū'ah; 16and he said, "When you do the duties of a midwife for the Hebrew women, and see *them* on the birthstools, if it *is* a son, then you shall kill him; but if it *is* a daughter, then she shall live." 17But the midwives feared God, and did not do as the king of Egypt commanded them, but saved the male children alive. 18So the king of Egypt called for the midwives and said to them, "Why have you done this thing, and saved the male children alive?"

19And the midwives said to Pharaoh, "Because the Hebrew women *are* not like the Egyptian women; for they *are* lively and give birth before the midwives come to them."

20Therefore God dealt well with the midwives, and the people multiplied and grew very mighty. 21And so it was, because the midwives feared God, that He provided households for them.

22So Pharaoh commanded all his people, saying, "Every son who is born[a] you shall cast into the river, and every daughter you shall save alive."

CHAPTER 2

Moses Is Born

And a man of the house of Levi went and took *as wife* a daughter of Levi. 2So the woman conceived and bore a son. And when she saw that he *was* a beautiful *child*, she hid him three months. 3But when she could no longer hide him, she took an ark of bulrushes for him, daubed it with asphalt and pitch, put the child in it, and laid *it* in the reeds by the river's bank. 4And his sister stood afar off, to know what would be done to him.

5Then the daughter of Pharaoh came down to bathe at the river. And her maidens walked along the riverside; and when she saw the ark among the reeds, she sent her maid to get it. 6And when she opened *it,* she saw the child, and behold, the baby wept. So she had compassion on him, and said, "This is one of the Hebrews' children."

7Then his sister said to Pharaoh's daughter, "Shall I go and call a nurse for you from the Hebrew women, that she may nurse the child for you?"

8And Pharaoh's daughter said to her, "Go." So the maiden went and called the child's mother. 9Then Pharaoh's daughter said to her, "Take this child away and nurse him for me, and I will give *you* your wages." So the woman took the child and nursed him. 10And the child grew, and she brought him to Pharaoh's daughter, and he became her son. So she called his name Moses,[a] saying, "Because I drew him out of the water."

1:22 [a]Samaritan Pentateuch, Septuagint, and Targum add *to the Hebrews.* 2:10 [a]Literally *Drawn Out*

1:15 Shiphrah and **Puah**, the midwives, are named, yet the mighty Pharaoh is not identified. Who is really great in this story?

2:1 The **man** was Amram and the **wife**, Jochebed (see 6:20).

2:7–9 Moses' **sister** was Miriam (Num. 26:59). **wages**: Jochebed is to be paid for being nurse to her own child. This provided an opportunity for her to train him in the Hebrew faith.

Moses Flees to Midian

[11]Now it came to pass in those days,
when Moses was grown, that he went out
to his brethren and looked at their bur-
dens. And he saw an Egyptian beating a
Hebrew, one of his brethren. [12]So he looked
this way and that way, and when he saw
no one, he killed the Egyptian and hid him
in the sand. [13]And when he went out the
second day, behold, two Hebrew men were
fighting, and he said to the one who did
the wrong, "Why are you striking your
companion?"

[14]Then he said, "Who made you a prince
and a judge over us? Do you intend to kill
me as you killed the Egyptian?"

So Moses feared and said, "Surely this
thing is known!" [15]When Pharaoh heard of
this matter, he sought to kill Moses. But
Moses fled from the face of Pharaoh and
dwelt in the land of Mid'i·an; and he sat
down by a well.

[16]Now the priest of Mid'i·an had seven
daughters. And they came and drew wa-
ter, and they filled the troughs to water
their father's flock. [17]Then the shepherds
came and drove them away; but Moses
stood up and helped them, and watered
their flock.

[18]When they came to Reū'el their father,
he said, "How *is it that* you have come so
soon today?"

[19]And they said, "An Egyptian deliv-
ered us from the hand of the shepherds,
and he also drew enough water for us and
watered the flock."

[20]So he said to his daughters, "And
where *is* he? Why *is* it *that* you have left the
man? Call him, that he may eat bread."

[21]Then Moses was content to live with
the man, and he gave Zip·pō'rah his
daughter to Moses. [22]And she bore *him* a
son. He called his name Ger'shom,[a] for he
said, "I have been a stranger in a foreign
land."

[23]Now it happened in the process of
time that the king of Egypt died. Then the
children of Israel groaned because of the
bondage, and they cried out; and their cry
came up to God because of the bondage.
[24]So God heard their groaning, and God re-
membered His covenant with Abraham,
with Isaac, and with Jacob. [25]And God
looked upon the children of Israel, and
God acknowledged *them*.

CHAPTER 3

Moses at the Burning Bush

Now Moses was tending the flock of
Jeth'rō his father-in-law, the priest of
Mid'i·an. And he led the flock to the back
of the desert, and came to Hō'reb, the
mountain of God. [2]And the Angel of the
LORD appeared to him in a flame of fire
from the midst of a bush. So he looked, and
behold, the bush was burning with fire,
but the bush *was* not consumed. [3]Then Mo-
ses said, "I will now turn aside and see this
great sight, why the bush does not burn."

[4]So when the LORD saw that he turned
aside to look, God called to him from the
midst of the bush and said, "Moses, Mo-
ses!"

And he said, "Here I am."

[5]Then He said, "Do not draw near this
place. Take your sandals off your feet, for
the place where you stand *is* holy ground."
[6]Moreover He said, "I *am* the God of your
father—the God of Abraham, the God of
Isaac, and the God of Jacob." And Moses
hid his face, for he was afraid to look upon
God.

[7]And the LORD said: "I have surely seen

2:22 [a]Literally *Stranger There*

2:11 Was grown is defined as "forty years old" in Acts 7:23.

2:16 The **priest of Midian** is called Jethro (3:1), Reuel (2:18), and Hobab (Num. 10:29). It was not uncommon in Bible times for a person to bear more than one name.

3:2 The Angel of the LORD in this verse appears to be the Lord Himself. **a flame of fire**: Often a symbol of God's presence—either for judgment or for cleansing.

the oppression of My people who *are* in Egypt, and have heard their cry because of their taskmasters, for I know their sorrows. 8So I have come down to deliver them out of the hand of the Egyptians, and to bring them up from that land to a good and large land, to a land flowing with milk and honey, to the place of the Cā′naan·ītes and the Hit′tītes and the Am′o·rītes and the Per′iz·zītes and the Hī′vītes and the Jeb′ū·sītes. 9Now therefore, behold, the cry of the children of Israel has come to Me, and I have also seen the oppression with which the Egyptians oppress them. 10Come now, therefore, and I will send you to Pharaoh that you may bring My people, the children of Israel, out of Egypt."

11But Moses said to God, "Who *am* I that I should go to Pharaoh, and that I should bring the children of Israel out of Egypt?"

12So He said, "I will certainly be with you. And this *shall be* a sign to you that I have sent you: When you have brought the people out of Egypt, you shall serve God on this mountain."

13Then Moses said to God, "Indeed, *when* I come to the children of Israel and say to them, 'The God of your fathers has sent me to you,' and they say to me, 'What *is* His name?' what shall I say to them?"

14And God said to Moses, "I AM WHO I AM." And He said, "Thus you shall say to the children of Israel, 'I AM has sent me to you.' " 15Moreover God said to Moses, "Thus you shall say to the children of Israel: 'The LORD God of your fathers, the God of Abraham, the God of Isaac, and the God of Jacob, has sent me to you. This *is* My name forever, and this *is* My memorial to all generations.' 16Go and gather the elders of Israel together, and say to them, 'The LORD God of your fathers, the God of Abraham, of Isaac, and of Jacob, appeared to me, saying, "I have surely visited you and *seen* what is done to you in Egypt; 17and I have said I will bring you up out of the affliction of Egypt to the land of the Cā′naan·ītes and the Hit′tītes and the Am′o·rītes and the Per′iz·zītes and the Hī′vītes and the Jeb′ū·sītes, to a land flowing with milk and honey." ' 18Then they will heed your voice; and you shall come, you and the elders of Israel, to the king of Egypt; and you shall say to him, 'The LORD God of the Hebrews has met with us; and now, please, let us go three days' journey into the wilderness, that we may sacrifice to the LORD our God.' 19But I am sure that the king of Egypt will not let you go, no, not even by a mighty hand. 20So I will stretch out My hand and strike Egypt with all My wonders which I will do in its midst; and after that he will let you go. 21And I will give this people favor in the sight of the Egyptians; and it shall be, when you go, that you shall not go empty-handed. 22But every woman shall ask of her neighbor, namely, of her who dwells near her house, articles of silver, articles of gold, and clothing; and you shall put *them* on your sons and on your daughters. So you shall plunder the Egyptians."

3:11—4:17 Moses' objections to serving are all ultimately questions about God: (1) Will He be with me? (3:11, 12); (2) What is He like? (3:13–25); (3) Is His power enough? (4:1–9); (4) Can He accommodate Himself to me? (4:10–17). God answers these underlying questions. Moses thought only in terms of his own resources when challenged by the will of God for his life. Instead of asking **Who am I**? he should have thought "Whose am I?"

3:14–17 This is the only place in the Bible where there is any explanation of the Hebrew name *YHWH*. The name *Yahweh* (Jehovah) is a form of the verb "to be" here translated **I AM**. The significance of this name is "the present One, He who is." To prisoners in a foreign land, feeling perhaps that even God had turned His back on them, this would be exhilarating news. Your God is present, even in Egypt.

3:22 The items that the Israelite women were to request from the Egyptians were considered to be compensation for the years of slave labor the Israelites had provided.

CHAPTER 4

Miraculous Signs for Pharaoh

Then Moses answered and said, "But
suppose they will not believe me or listen
to my voice; suppose they say, 'The LORD
has not appeared to you.' "
[2]So the LORD said to him, "What *is* that
in your hand?"
He said, "A rod."
[3]And He said, "Cast it on the ground."
So he cast it on the ground, and it became a
serpent; and Moses fled from it. [4]Then the
LORD said to Moses, "Reach out your hand
and take *it* by the tail" (and he reached out
his hand and caught it, and it became a rod
in his hand), [5]"that they may believe that
the LORD God of their fathers, the God of
Abraham, the God of Isaac, and the God of
Jacob, has appeared to you."
[6]Furthermore the LORD said to him,
"Now put your hand in your bosom." And
he put his hand in his bosom, and when he
took it out, behold, his hand *was* leprous,
like snow. [7]And He said, "Put your hand in
your bosom again." So he put his hand in
his bosom again, and drew it out of his bo-
som, and behold, it was restored like his
other flesh. [8]"Then it will be, if they do not
believe you, nor heed the message of the
first sign, that they may believe the mes-
sage of the latter sign. [9]And it shall be, if
they do not believe even these two signs,
or listen to your voice, that you shall take
water from the river[a] and pour *it* on the
dry *land*. The water which you take from
the river will become blood on the dry
land."

4:9 [a]That is, the Nile

GOD IS CALLING YOU

Sherwood Eliot Wirt

Find your calling! It may come to you in prayer or Bible study; it may emerge from daily circumstances; it may come as a result of great and sudden need; it may even come through your own vocational skills and interests. Find it! Listen for it!

A word to remind you: Other voices are in the world, and they, too, have their calls. Some are pleasant; many are tempting. Make sure that the Word of God validates the call to which you are listening. Talk to Christian friends about your call. Get all the help you can, but remember that in the ultimate sense, your call is not coming from king or priest or family or friends or anyone else but God Himself. Further, the call of God is irrevocable.

When Moses first heard God's call to go to Egypt and demand the release of his countrymen, he resisted it. "What if they don't believe me?" he asked. "What if they won't listen?" God's reply was in the form of another question: "What is that in your hand?" (Ex. 4:2). It was a state-of-the-art question. Today God may be asking you the same question: What is that in your hand? What are you doing right now? Why aren't you doing it for God? Paul says that God's call is irrevocable (Rom. 11:29). Once He calls, He never takes it back. ✦

Moses: The Reluctant Leader

The prophet Moses was a man of God, mighty in words and deeds (Acts 7:22). Through the power of the Lord, he performed many miracles, led the children of Israel out of Egypt, and served as their spiritual guide for more than forty years.

This eulogy accompanies the mention of his death in Scripture:

> "Since then there has not arisen in Israel a prophet like Moses, whom the LORD knew face to face, in all the signs and wonders which the LORD sent him to do in the land of Egypt . . . and by all that mighty power and all the great terror which Moses performed in the sight of all Israel" (Deut. 34:10–12).

What an incredible man he must have been to deserve such praise!

Yet Moses was not a natural-born leader. After one disastrous attempt at leadership when he was forty, he fled in fear to Midian where he worked as a shepherd in almost total obscurity for forty years (Ex. 2:11–15; Acts 7:23, 30).

One day, as he was tending the flock on the backside of the desert, Moses encountered God in a burning bush. When the Lord explained that He had chosen Moses to lead the children of Israel out of Egypt, the fearful shepherd quickly presented three "reasons" he could not answer the call:

(1) "Who am I that I should go to Pharaoh, and . . . bring the people of Israel out of Egypt?" (Ex. 3:11).

(2) "Suppose they will not believe me" (4:1).

(3) "I am not eloquent . . . but I am slow of speech and slow of tongue" (4:10).

The Lord responded to each of these excuses with essentially the same answer: "I will certainly be with you" (3:12). He promised to give Moses His divine presence, authority, and power, as well as guidance for his speech (3:12–14; 4:2–8, 12). Yet Moses still resisted, begging the Lord to send someone else (4:13). Despite all of God's assurances, he still refused to believe he was the right man for the job.

Finally, the Lord agreed to send Aaron to accompany the reluctant Moses and act as his spokesman, but He did not release Moses from his post. The mild-mannered shepherd reluctantly became the champion of Israel.

During Moses' forty-year tenure as Israel's leader, God kept each of His promises to supply the prophet's needs and compensate for his shortcomings. His presence took the form of a pillar of fire and a pillar of cloud as He led Moses and the Israelites. He gave Moses the power to perform a multitude of miracles both before and after the Exodus from Egypt.

As passage after passage reveals, God gave Moses the eloquence and persuasiveness he once lacked. We never again read that Moses exhib-

ited any fear of public speaking! Long after Aaron's death, Moses continued to speak to the children of Israel under the guidance of the Lord.

Although Moses' leadership was not problem-free, any troubles that came resulted from disobedience or lack of faith. We can clearly see that whenever he looked to the Lord to provide for his own insufficiency, Moses was not disappointed.

God will not assign His children a task without providing everything they need to bring it to completion. Just as He supplied Moses' spiritual, physical, and emotional needs, God will fully equip each of us to serve Him as He sees fit. ✦

10 Then Moses said to the LORD, "O my
Lord, I *am* not eloquent, neither before nor
since You have spoken to Your servant; but
I *am* slow of speech and slow of tongue."
11 So the LORD said to him, "Who has
made man's mouth? Or who makes the
mute, the deaf, the seeing, or the blind?
Have not I, the LORD? 12 Now therefore, go,
and I will be with your mouth and teach
you what you shall say."
13 But he said, "O my Lord, please send
by the hand of whomever *else* You may
send."
14 So the anger of the LORD was kindled
against Moses, and He said: "Is not Aaron
the Lē'vīte your brother? I know that he
can speak well. And look, he is also coming
out to meet you. When he sees you, he will
be glad in his heart. 15 Now you shall speak
to him and put the words in his mouth.
And I will be with your mouth and with
his mouth, and I will teach you what you
shall do. 16 So he shall be your spokesman
to the people. And he himself shall be as a
mouth for you, and you shall be to him as
God. 17 And you shall take this rod in your
hand, with which you shall do the signs."

Moses Goes to Egypt

18 So Moses went and returned to Jeth'rō
his father-in-law, and said to him, "Please
let me go and return to my brethren who
are in Egypt, and see whether they are still
alive."
And Jeth'rō said to Moses, "Go in
peace."
19 Now the LORD said to Moses in Mid'-
i·an, "Go, return to Egypt; for all the men
who sought your life are dead." 20 Then
Moses took his wife and his sons and set
them on a donkey, and he returned to the
land of Egypt. And Moses took the rod of
God in his hand.
21 And the LORD said to Moses, "When
you go back to Egypt, see that you do all
those wonders before Pharaoh which I
have put in your hand. But I will harden
his heart, so that he will not let the people

✦ ✦

4:10 Moses' fourth excuse is that he is not **eloquent**. Not according to Stephen (Acts 7:22)! It is no mark of humility to deny the presence of a gift one has received from God. Indeed, it is an implied criticism of one's Creator (vv. 11, 12). We are to use our talents to the utmost in the area of ministry to which God has called us.

4:13 Moses' last statement is not an excuse, but an open attempt to dodge obedience—**send** someone **else**. In sharp contrast is Isaiah's "Here am I! Send me" (Is. 6:8).

4:21 harden his heart: Not against Pharaoh's will, but in accordance with it. God confirms for us decisions we have made. Pharaoh would never voluntarily allow the people of Israel to go free, thus acknowledging some other god than himself (Egyptian pharaohs considered themselves divine). And by confirming his denial, God shows that Pharaoh is not God and does not have absolute freedom. Only God is truly sovereign; His freedom is without limit.

go. 22Then you shall say to Pharaoh, 'Thus
says the LORD: "Israel *is* My son, My first-
born. 23So I say to you, let My son go that
he may serve Me. But if you refuse to let
him go, indeed I will kill your son, your
firstborn." ' "

24And it came to pass on the way, at the
encampment, that the LORD met him and
sought to kill him. 25Then Zip·pō'rah took
a sharp stone and cut off the foreskin of her
son and cast *it* at *Moses'*[a] feet, and said,
"Surely you *are* a husband of blood to me!"
26So He let him go. Then she said, "*You are*
a husband of blood!"—because of the cir-
cumcision.

27And the LORD said to Aaron, "Go into
the wilderness to meet Moses." So he went
and met him on the mountain of God, and
kissed him. 28So Moses told Aaron all the
words of the LORD who had sent him, and
all the signs which He had commanded
him. 29Then Moses and Aaron went and
gathered together all the elders of the chil-
dren of Israel. 30And Aaron spoke all the
words which the LORD had spoken to Mo-
ses. Then he did the signs in the sight of the
people. 31So the people believed; and when
they heard that the LORD had visited the
children of Israel and that He had looked
on their affliction, then they bowed their
heads and worshiped.

CHAPTER 5

First Encounter with Pharaoh

Afterward Moses and Aaron went in
and told Pharaoh, "Thus says the LORD
God of Israel: 'Let My people go, that they
may hold a feast to Me in the wilderness.' "
2And Pharaoh said, "Who *is* the LORD,
that I should obey His voice to let Israel
go? I do not know the LORD, nor will I let
Israel go."
3So they said, "The God of the Hebrews
has met with us. Please, let us go three
days' journey into the desert and sacrifice
to the LORD our God, lest He fall upon us
with pestilence or with the sword."
4Then the king of Egypt said to them,
"Moses and Aaron, why do you take the
people from their work? Get *back* to your
labor." 5And Pharaoh said, "Look, the peo-
ple of the land *are* many now, and you
make them rest from their labor!"
6So the same day Pharaoh commanded
the taskmasters of the people and their of-
ficers, saying, 7"You shall no longer give
the people straw to make brick as before.
Let them go and gather straw for them-
selves. 8And you shall lay on them the
quota of bricks which they made before.
You shall not reduce it. For they are idle;
therefore they cry out, saying, 'Let us go
and sacrifice to our God.' 9Let more work
be laid on the men, that they may labor in
it, and let them not regard false words."
10And the taskmasters of the people and
their officers went out and spoke to the
people, saying, "Thus says Pharaoh: 'I will
not give you straw. 11Go, get yourselves
straw where you can find it; yet none of
your work will be reduced.' " 12So the peo-
ple were scattered abroad throughout all
the land of Egypt to gather stubble instead
of straw. 13And the taskmasters forced *them*
to hurry, saying, "Fulfill your work, *your*
daily quota, as when there was straw."
14Also the officers of the children of Israel,
whom Pharaoh's taskmasters had set over
them, were beaten *and* were asked, "Why
have you not fulfilled your task in making
brick both yesterday and today, as before?"
15Then the officers of the children of Is-
rael came and cried out to Pharaoh, saying,
"Why are you dealing thus with your ser-
vants? 16There is no straw given to your
servants, and they say to us, 'Make brick!'
And indeed your servants *are* beaten, but
the fault *is* in your *own* people."
17But he said, "You *are* idle! Idle! There-
fore you say, 'Let us go *and* sacrifice to the
LORD.' 18Therefore go now *and* work; for no
straw shall be given you, yet you shall de-
liver the quota of bricks." 19And the offi-
cers of the children of Israel saw *that* they

4:25 [a]Literally *his*

were in trouble after it was said, "You shall not reduce *any* bricks from your daily quota."

[20]Then, as they came out from Pharaoh, they met Moses and Aaron who stood there to meet them. [21]And they said to them, "Let the LORD look on you and judge, because you have made us abhorrent in the sight of Pharaoh and in the sight of his servants, to put a sword in their hand to kill us."

Israel's Deliverance Assured

[22]So Moses returned to the LORD and said, "Lord, why have You brought trouble on this people? Why *is* it You have sent me? [23]For since I came to Pharaoh to speak in Your name, he has done evil to this people; neither have You delivered Your people at all."

CHAPTER 6

Then the LORD said to Moses, "Now you shall see what I will do to Pharaoh. For with a strong hand he will let them go, and with a strong hand he will drive them out of his land."

[2]And God spoke to Moses and said to him: "I *am* the LORD. [3]I appeared to Abraham, to Isaac, and to Jacob, as God Almighty, but *by* My name LORD[a] I was not known to them. [4]I have also established My covenant with them, to give them the land of Cā'naan, the land of their pilgrimage, in which they were strangers. [5]And I have also heard the groaning of the children of Israel whom the Egyptians keep in bondage, and I have remembered My covenant. [6]Therefore say to the children of Israel: 'I *am* the LORD; I will bring you out from under the burdens of the Egyptians, I will rescue you from their bondage, and I will redeem you with an outstretched arm and with great judgments. [7]I will take you as My people, and I will be your God. Then you shall know that I *am* the LORD your God who brings you out from under the burdens of the Egyptians. [8]And I will bring you into the land which I swore to give to Abraham, Isaac, and Jacob; and I will give it to you *as* a heritage: I *am* the LORD.' " [9]So Moses spoke thus to the children of Israel; but they did not heed Moses, because of anguish of spirit and cruel bondage.

[10]And the LORD spoke to Moses, saying, [11]"Go in, tell Pharaoh king of Egypt to let the children of Israel go out of his land."

[12]And Moses spoke before the LORD, saying, "The children of Israel have not heeded me. How then shall Pharaoh heed me, for I *am* of uncircumcised lips?"

[13]Then the LORD spoke to Moses and Aaron, and gave them a command for the children of Israel and for Pharaoh king of Egypt, to bring the children of Israel out of the land of Egypt.

The Family of Moses and Aaron

[14]These *are* the heads of their fathers' houses: The sons of Reuben, the firstborn of Israel, *were* Hā'noch, Pal'lū, Hez'ron, and Car'mī. These are the families of Reuben. [15]And the sons of Sim'ē·on *were* Jemū'el,[a] Jā'min, Ō'had, Jā'chin, Zō'har, and

6:3 [a]Hebrew *YHWH*, traditionally *Jehovah*
6:15 [a]Spelled *Nemuel* in Numbers 26:12

5:22, 23 Lord, why? Moses had not yet learned that God's delays are not necessarily God's denials. In fact, the delay had served to put all the issues in clearer relief. Nothing short of God's power could deliver Israel now.

6:3 God Almighty represents the Hebrew *El Shaddai*. **I was not known to them** surely does not mean that the patriarchs were unfamiliar with the name **LORD** since Gen. 12:8; 15:2; 24:3 indicate they knew of that name for God. What must be intended is that God did not reveal the full meaning of His covenant name to Abraham and his kin. With the advent of Moses a new and fuller perception of God was achieved.

6:9 Instead of the promised deliverance, the Israelites were experiencing a more **cruel** form of **bondage** than before. They had lost confidence in Moses.

Shā’ūl the son of a Cā’naan·īte woman.
These *are* the families of Sim’ē·on. 16These
are the names of the sons of Levi according
to their generations: Ger’shon, Kō’hath,
and Me·rar’ī. And the years of the life of
Levi *were* one hundred and thirty-seven.
17The sons of Ger’shon *were* Lib’nī and
Shim’ī according to their families. 18And
the sons of Kō’hath *were* Am’ram, Iz’har,
Hē’bron, and Uz’zi·el. And the years of the
life of Kō’hath *were* one hundred and
thirty-three. 19The sons of Me·rar’ī *were*
Mah’lī and Mū’shī. These *are* the families
of Levi according to their generations.

20Now Am’ram took for himself Joch’-
e·bed, his father’s sister, as wife; and she
bore him Aaron and Moses. And the years
of the life of Am’ram *were* one hundred
and thirty-seven. 21The sons of Iz’har *were*
Kō’rah, Nē’pheg, and Zich’rī. 22And the
sons of Uz’zi·el *were* Mish’a·el, El’za·phan,
and Zith’rī. 23Aaron took to himself
E·lish’e·ba, daughter of Am·min’a·dab,
sister of Nah’shon, as wife; and she bore
him Nā’dab, A·bī’hū, El·ē·ā’zar, and
Ith’a·mar. 24And the sons of Kō’rah *were*
As’sir, El·kā’nah, and A·bī’a·saph. These
are the families of the Kō’ra·hītes. 25El·ē·ā’-
zar, Aaron’s son, took for himself one of
the daughters of Pū’ti·el as wife; and she
bore him Phin’e·has. These *are* the heads of
the fathers’ houses of the Lē’vītes accord-
ing to their families.

26These *are the same* Aaron and Moses to
whom the LORD said, "Bring out the chil-
dren of Israel from the land of Egypt ac-
cording to their armies." 27These *are* the
ones who spoke to Pharaoh king of Egypt,
to bring out the children of Israel from
Egypt. These *are the same* Moses and
Aaron.

Aaron Is Moses’ Spokesman

28And it came to pass, on the day the
LORD spoke to Moses in the land of Egypt,
29that the LORD spoke to Moses, saying, "I
am the LORD. Speak to Pharaoh king of
Egypt all that I say to you."

30But Moses said before the LORD, "Be-
hold, I *am* of uncircumcised lips, and how
shall Pharaoh heed me?"

CHAPTER 7

So the LORD said to Moses: "See, I have
made you *as* God to Pharaoh, and Aaron
your brother shall be your prophet. 2You
shall speak all that I command you. And
Aaron your brother shall tell Pharaoh to
send the children of Israel out of his land.
3And I will harden Pharaoh’s heart, and
multiply My signs and My wonders in the
land of Egypt. 4But Pharaoh will not heed
you, so that I may lay My hand on Egypt
and bring My armies *and* My people, the
children of Israel, out of the land of Egypt
by great judgments. 5And the Egyptians
shall know that I *am* the LORD, when I
stretch out My hand on Egypt and bring
out the children of Israel from among
them."

6Then Moses and Aaron did *so;* just as
the LORD commanded them, so they did.
7And Moses *was* eighty years old and
Aaron eighty-three years old when they
spoke to Pharaoh.

Aaron’s Miraculous Rod

8Then the LORD spoke to Moses and
Aaron, saying, 9"When Pharaoh speaks to
you, saying, ‘Show a miracle for your-
selves,’ then you shall say to Aaron, ‘Take
your rod and cast *it* before Pharaoh, *and* let
it become a serpent.’ " 10So Moses and
Aaron went in to Pharaoh, and they did so,
just as the LORD commanded. And Aaron
cast down his rod before Pharaoh and be-
fore his servants, and it became a serpent.

11But Pharaoh also called the wise men
and the sorcerers; so the magicians of

7:7 At a time when many people are slowing down, God called both Moses and Aaron to active duty.

Egypt, they also did in like manner with
their enchantments. [12]For every man threw
down his rod, and they became serpents.
But Aaron's rod swallowed up their rods.
[13]And Pharaoh's heart grew hard, and he
did not heed them, as the LORD had said.

The First Plague: Waters Become Blood

[14]So the LORD said to Moses: "Pharaoh's
heart *is* hard; he refuses to let the people
go. [15]Go to Pharaoh in the morning, when
he goes out to the water, and you shall
stand by the river's bank to meet him; and
the rod which was turned to a serpent you
shall take in your hand. [16]And you shall
say to him, 'The LORD God of the Hebrews
has sent me to you, saying, "Let My people
go, that they may serve Me in the wilder-
ness"; but indeed, until now you would
not hear! [17]Thus says the LORD: "By this
you shall know that I *am* the LORD. Behold,
I will strike the waters which *are* in the
river with the rod that *is* in my hand, and
they shall be turned to blood. [18]And the
fish that *are* in the river shall die, the river
shall stink, and the Egyptians will loathe to
drink the water of the river." ' "

[19]Then the LORD spoke to Moses, "Say to
Aaron, 'Take your rod and stretch out your
hand over the waters of Egypt, over their
streams, over their rivers, over their ponds,
and over all their pools of water, that they
may become blood. And there shall be
blood throughout all the land of Egypt,
both in *buckets of* wood and *pitchers of*
stone.' " [20]And Moses and Aaron did so,
just as the LORD commanded. So he lifted
up the rod and struck the waters that *were*
in the river, in the sight of Pharaoh and in
the sight of his servants. And all the waters
that *were* in the river were turned to blood.
[21]The fish that *were* in the river died, the
river stank, and the Egyptians could not
drink the water of the river. So there was
blood throughout all the land of Egypt.

[22]Then the magicians of Egypt did so
with their enchantments; and Pharaoh's
heart grew hard, and he did not heed
them, as the LORD had said. [23]And Pharaoh
turned and went into his house. Neither
was his heart moved by this. [24]So all the
Egyptians dug all around the river for wa-
ter to drink, because they could not drink
the water of the river. [25]And seven days
passed after the LORD had struck the river.

CHAPTER 8

The Second Plague: Frogs

And the LORD spoke to Moses, "Go to
Pharaoh and say to him, 'Thus says the
LORD: "Let My people go, that they may
serve Me. [2]But if you refuse to let *them* go,
behold, I will smite all your territory with
frogs. [3]So the river shall bring forth frogs
abundantly, which shall go up and come
into your house, into your bedroom, on
your bed, into the houses of your servants,
on your people, into your ovens, and into
your kneading bowls. [4]And the frogs shall
come up on you, on your people, and on
all your servants." ' "

[5]Then the LORD spoke to Moses, "Say to
Aaron, 'Stretch out your hand with your
rod over the streams, over the rivers, and
over the ponds, and cause frogs to come
up on the land of Egypt.' " [6]So Aaron
stretched out his hand over the waters of
Egypt, and the frogs came up and covered
the land of Egypt. [7]And the magicians did
so with their enchantments, and brought
up frogs on the land of Egypt.

[8]Then Pharaoh called for Moses and
Aaron, and said, "Entreat the LORD that He
may take away the frogs from me and from

7:14—8:2 At the same time He judged the Egyptians with the plagues, God demonstrated the powerlessness of their various gods. The Nile-goddess was a major deity as was the goddess Heqt, who represented the amphibian and reptilian worlds—thus the frogs.

7:20 There was no inherent power in the rod, which was but a symbol. God's power, not the rod, evoked the plague.

my people; and I will let the people go, that they may sacrifice to the LORD."

9And Moses said to Pharaoh, "Accept the honor of saying when I shall intercede for you, for your servants, and for your people, to destroy the frogs from you and your houses, *that* they may remain in the river only."

10So he said, "Tomorrow." And he said, "*Let it be* according to your word, that you may know that *there is* no one like the LORD our God. 11And the frogs shall depart from you, from your houses, from your servants, and from your people. They shall remain in the river only."

12Then Moses and Aaron went out from Pharaoh. And Moses cried out to the LORD concerning the frogs which He had brought against Pharaoh. 13So the LORD did according to the word of Moses. And the frogs died out of the houses, out of the courtyards, and out of the fields. 14They gathered them together in heaps, and the land stank. 15But when Pharaoh saw that there was relief, he hardened his heart and did not heed them, as the LORD had said.

The Third Plague: Lice

16So the LORD said to Moses, "Say to Aaron, 'Stretch out your rod, and strike the dust of the land, so that it may become lice throughout all the land of Egypt.' " 17And they did so. For Aaron stretched out his hand with his rod and struck the dust of the earth, and it became lice on man and beast. All the dust of the land became lice throughout all the land of Egypt.

18Now the magicians so worked with their enchantments to bring forth lice, but they could not. So there were lice on man and beast. 19Then the magicians said to Pharaoh, "This *is* the finger of God." But Pharaoh's heart grew hard, and he did not heed them, just as the LORD had said.

The Fourth Plague: Flies

20And the LORD said to Moses, "Rise early in the morning and stand before Pharaoh as he comes out to the water. Then say to him, 'Thus says the LORD: "Let My people go, that they may serve Me. 21Or else, if you will not let My people go, behold, I will send swarms *of flies* on you and your servants, on your people and into your houses. The houses of the Egyptians shall be full of swarms *of flies,* and also the ground on which they *stand.* 22And in that day I will set apart the land of Gō'shen, in which My people dwell, that no swarms *of flies* shall be there, in order that you may know that I *am* the LORD in the midst of the land. 23I will make a difference[a] between My people and your people. Tomorrow this sign shall be." ' " 24And the LORD did so. Thick swarms *of flies* came into the house of Pharaoh, *into* his servants' houses, and into all the land of Egypt. The land was corrupted because of the swarms *of flies.*

25Then Pharaoh called for Moses and Aaron, and said, "Go, sacrifice to your God in the land."

26And Moses said, "It is not right to do so, for we would be sacrificing the abomination of the Egyptians to the LORD our God. If we sacrifice the abomination of

8:23 [a]Literally *set a ransom* (compare Exodus 9:4 and 11:7)

8:15 Pharaoh's change of **heart** was short-lived. The removal of the annoying frogs meant back to business as usual. So it often is with our vows.

8:22, 23 Goshen, the portion of the Nile delta where the Israelites lived, was to be exempt from the flies. Here is the first of six places where God put a distinction between His own and the Egyptians (9:4, 6, 26; 10:23; 11:7), making the source of the plagues obvious and demonstrating His protection of His chosen people. See also 9:11; 10:6.

8:26 The Egyptians would be offended by the Israelite form of worship because it involved the sacrifice of certain animals that were worshiped by the Egyptians.

the Egyptians before their eyes, then will they not stone us? 27We will go three days' journey into the wilderness and sacrifice to the LORD our God as He will command us."

28So Pharaoh said, "I will let you go, that you may sacrifice to the LORD your God in the wilderness; only you shall not go very far away. Intercede for me."

29Then Moses said, "Indeed I am going out from you, and I will entreat the LORD, that the swarms *of flies* may depart tomorrow from Pharaoh, from his servants, and from his people. But let Pharaoh not deal deceitfully anymore in not letting the people go to sacrifice to the LORD."

30So Moses went out from Pharaoh and entreated the LORD. 31And the LORD did according to the word of Moses; He removed the swarms *of flies* from Pharaoh, from his servants, and from his people. Not one remained. 32But Pharaoh hardened his heart at this time also; neither would he let the people go.

CHAPTER 9

The Fifth Plague: Livestock Diseased

Then the LORD said to Moses, "Go in to Pharaoh and tell him, 'Thus says the LORD God of the Hebrews: "Let My people go, that they may serve Me. 2For if you refuse to let *them* go, and still hold them, 3behold, the hand of the LORD will be on your cattle in the field, on the horses, on the donkeys, on the camels, on the oxen, and on the sheep—a very severe pestilence. 4And the LORD will make a difference between the livestock of Israel and the livestock of Egypt. So nothing shall die of all *that* belongs to the children of Israel." ' " 5Then the LORD appointed a set time, saying, "Tomorrow the LORD will do this thing in the land."

6So the LORD did this thing on the next day, and all the livestock of Egypt died; but of the livestock of the children of Israel, not one died. 7Then Pharaoh sent, and indeed, not even one of the livestock of the Israelites was dead. But the heart of Pharaoh became hard, and he did not let the people go.

The Sixth Plague: Boils

8So the LORD said to Moses and Aaron, "Take for yourselves handfuls of ashes from a furnace, and let Moses scatter it toward the heavens in the sight of Pharaoh. 9And it will become fine dust in all the land of Egypt, and it will cause boils that break out in sores on man and beast throughout all the land of Egypt." 10Then they took ashes from the furnace and stood before Pharaoh, and Moses scattered *them* toward heaven. And *they* caused boils that break out in sores on man and beast. 11And the magicians could not stand before Moses because of the boils, for the boils were on the magicians and on all the Egyptians. 12But the LORD hardened the heart of Pharaoh; and he did not heed them, just as the LORD had spoken to Moses.

The Seventh Plague: Hail

13Then the LORD said to Moses, "Rise early in the morning and stand before Pharaoh, and say to him, 'Thus says the LORD God of the Hebrews: "Let My people go, that they may serve Me, 14for at this time I will send all My plagues to your very heart, and on your servants and on your people, that you may know that *there is* none like Me in all the earth. 15Now if I had stretched out My hand and struck you and your people with pestilence, then you would have been cut off from the earth. 16But indeed for this *purpose* I have raised you up, that I may show My power *in* you, and that My name may be declared in all the earth. 17As yet you exalt yourself against My people in that you will not let them go. 18Behold, tomorrow about this time I will cause very heavy hail to rain down, such as has not been in Egypt since

its founding until now. [19]Therefore send
now *and* gather your livestock and all that
you have in the field, for the hail shall
come down on every man and every ani-
mal which is found in the field and is not
brought home; and they shall die." ' "

[20]He who feared the word of the LORD
among the servants of Pharaoh made his
servants and his livestock flee to the
houses. [21]But he who did not regard the
word of the LORD left his servants and his
livestock in the field.

[22]Then the LORD said to Moses, "Stretch
out your hand toward heaven, that there
may be hail in all the land of Egypt—on
man, on beast, and on every herb of the
field, throughout the land of Egypt." [23]And
Moses stretched out his rod toward
heaven; and the LORD sent thunder and
hail, and fire darted to the ground. And the
LORD rained hail on the land of Egypt. [24]So
there was hail, and fire mingled with the
hail, so very heavy that there was none like
it in all the land of Egypt since it became a
nation. [25]And the hail struck throughout
the whole land of Egypt, all that *was* in the
field, both man and beast; and the hail
struck every herb of the field and broke
every tree of the field. [26]Only in the land of
Gō'shen, where the children of Israel *were,*
there was no hail.

[27]And Pharaoh sent and called for Mo-
ses and Aaron, and said to them, "I have
sinned this time. The LORD *is* righteous,
and my people and I *are* wicked. [28]Entreat
the LORD, that there may be no *more* mighty
thundering and hail, for *it is* enough. I will
let you go, and you shall stay no longer."

[29]So Moses said to him, "As soon as I
have gone out of the city, I will spread out
my hands to the LORD; the thunder will
cease, and there will be no more hail, that
you may know that the earth *is* the LORD's.
[30]But as for you and your servants, I know
that you will not yet fear the LORD God."

[31]Now the flax and the barley were
struck, for the barley *was* in the head and
the flax *was* in bud. [32]But the wheat and the
spelt were not struck, for they *are* late
crops.

[33]So Moses went out of the city from
Pharaoh and spread out his hands to the
LORD; then the thunder and the hail ceased,
and the rain was not poured on the earth.
[34]And when Pharaoh saw that the rain, the
hail, and the thunder had ceased, he
sinned yet more; and he hardened his
heart, he and his servants. [35]So the heart of
Pharaoh was hard; neither would he let the
children of Israel go, as the LORD had spo-
ken by Moses.

CHAPTER 10

The Eighth Plague: Locusts

Now the LORD said to Moses, "Go in to
Pharaoh; for I have hardened his heart and
the hearts of his servants, that I may show
these signs of Mine before him, [2]and that
you may tell in the hearing of your son and
your son's son the mighty things I have
done in Egypt, and My signs which I have
done among them, that you may know
that I *am* the LORD."

[3]So Moses and Aaron came in to
Pharaoh and said to him, "Thus says the
LORD God of the Hebrews: 'How long will
you refuse to humble yourself before Me?
Let My people go, that they may serve Me.
[4]Or else, if you refuse to let My people go,
behold, tomorrow I will bring locusts into
your territory. [5]And they shall cover the
face of the earth, so that no one will be able
to see the earth; and they shall eat the

9:19 The Lord always tempers His justice with mercy. Here He provides protection for those who heed His word.

9:31, 32 Flax and **barley** were harvested in February-March. **Wheat** and **spelt** were harvested later in March-April. This dates the plagues to mid-February.

10:3 humble yourself: Pharaoh's real problem was that he would not surrender his self-assertiveness and the maintenance of his sovereignty. Here is the essence of sin.

residue of what is left, which remains to you from the hail, and they shall eat every tree which grows up for you out of the field. 6They shall fill your houses, the houses of all your servants, and the houses of all the Egyptians—which neither your fathers nor your fathers' fathers have seen, since the day that they were on the earth to this day.' " And he turned and went out from Pharaoh.

7Then Pharaoh's servants said to him, "How long shall this man be a snare to us? Let the men go, that they may serve the LORD their God. Do you not yet know that Egypt is destroyed?"

8So Moses and Aaron were brought again to Pharaoh, and he said to them, "Go, serve the LORD your God. Who *are* the ones that are going?"

9And Moses said, "We will go with our young and our old; with our sons and our daughters, with our flocks and our herds we will go, for we must hold a feast to the LORD."

10Then he said to them, "The LORD had better be with you when I let you and your little ones go! Beware, for evil is ahead of you. 11Not so! Go now, you *who are* men, and serve the LORD, for that is what you desired." And they were driven out from Pharaoh's presence.

12Then the LORD said to Moses, "Stretch out your hand over the land of Egypt for the locusts, that they may come upon the land of Egypt, and eat every herb of the land—all that the hail has left." 13So Moses stretched out his rod over the land of Egypt, and the LORD brought an east wind on the land all that day and all *that* night. When it was morning, the east wind brought the locusts. 14And the locusts went up over all the land of Egypt and rested on all the territory of Egypt. *They were* very severe; previously there had been no such locusts as they, nor shall there be such after them. 15For they covered the face of the whole earth, so that the land was darkened; and they ate every herb of the land and all the fruit of the trees which the hail had left. So there remained nothing green on the trees or on the plants of the field throughout all the land of Egypt.

16Then Pharaoh called for Moses and Aaron in haste, and said, "I have sinned against the LORD your God and against you. 17Now therefore, please forgive my sin only this once, and entreat the LORD your God, that He may take away from me this death only." 18So he went out from Pharaoh and entreated the LORD. 19And the LORD turned a very strong west wind, which took the locusts away and blew them into the Red Sea. There remained not one locust in all the territory of Egypt. 20But the LORD hardened Pharaoh's heart, and he did not let the children of Israel go.

The Ninth Plague: Darkness

21Then the LORD said to Moses, "Stretch out your hand toward heaven, that there may be darkness over the land of Egypt, darkness *which* may even be felt." 22So Moses stretched out his hand toward heaven, and there was thick darkness in all the land of Egypt three days. 23They did not see one another; nor did anyone rise from his place for three days. But all the children of Israel had light in their dwellings.

24Then Pharaoh called to Moses and said, "Go, serve the LORD; only let your flocks and your herds be kept back. Let your little ones also go with you."

25But Moses said, "You must also give us sacrifices and burnt offerings, that we may sacrifice to the LORD our God. 26Our livestock also shall go with us; not a hoof shall be left behind. For we must take some of them to serve the LORD our God, and even we do not know with what we must serve the LORD until we arrive there."

10:21–29 Darkness, the ninth plague, would be a special test of power in a country accustomed to worshiping the sun-god, Re.

27But the LORD hardened Pharaoh's
heart, and he would not let them go. 28Then
Pharaoh said to him, "Get away from me!
Take heed to yourself and see my face no
more! For in the day you see my face you
shall die!"
29So Moses said, "You have spoken well.
I will never see your face again."

CHAPTER 11

Death of the Firstborn Announced

And the LORD said to Moses, "I will
bring one more plague on Pharaoh and on
Egypt. Afterward he will let you go from
here. When he lets *you* go, he will surely
drive you out of here altogether. 2Speak
now in the hearing of the people, and let
every man ask from his neighbor and
every woman from her neighbor, articles of
silver and articles of gold." 3And the LORD
gave the people favor in the sight of the
Egyptians. Moreover the man Moses *was*
very great in the land of Egypt, in the sight
of Pharaoh's servants and in the sight of
the people.
4Then Moses said, "Thus says the LORD:
'About midnight I will go out into the
midst of Egypt; 5and all the firstborn in the
land of Egypt shall die, from the firstborn
of Pharaoh who sits on his throne, even to
the firstborn of the female servant who *is*
behind the handmill, and all the firstborn
of the animals. 6Then there shall be a great
cry throughout all the land of Egypt, such
as was not like it *before,* nor shall be like it
again. 7But against none of the children of
Israel shall a dog move its tongue, against
man or beast, that you may know that the
LORD does make a difference between the
Egyptians and Israel.' 8And all these your
servants shall come down to me and bow
down to me, saying, 'Get out, and all the
people who follow you!' After that I will
go out." Then he went out from Pharaoh in
great anger.
9But the LORD said to Moses, "Pharaoh
will not heed you, so that My wonders
may be multiplied in the land of Egypt."
10So Moses and Aaron did all these won-
ders before Pharaoh; and the LORD hard-
ened Pharaoh's heart, and he did not let
the children of Israel go out of his land.

CHAPTER 12

The Passover Instituted

Now the LORD spoke to Moses and
Aaron in the land of Egypt, saying, 2"This
month *shall be* your beginning of months; it
shall be the first month of the year to you.
3Speak to all the congregation of Israel,
saying: 'On the tenth of this month every
man shall take for himself a lamb, accord-
ing to the house of *his* father, a lamb for a
household. 4And if the household is too
small for the lamb, let him and his neigh-
bor next to his house take *it* according to
the number of the persons; according to
each man's need you shall make your
count for the lamb. 5Your lamb shall be
without blemish, a male of the first year.
You may take *it* from the sheep or from the
goats. 6Now you shall keep it until the
fourteenth day of the same month. Then
the whole assembly of the congregation of
Israel shall kill it at twilight. 7And they
shall take *some* of the blood and put *it* on
the two doorposts and on the lintel of the
houses where they eat it. 8Then they shall
eat the flesh on that night; roasted in fire,
with unleavened bread *and* with bitter
herbs they shall eat it. 9Do not eat it raw, nor
boiled at all with water, but roasted in

12:2, 3 This month falls in March-April. It was called "Abib" at that time (13:4), but later called "Nisan." The beginning of life is recalled by observing the beginning of a new year. The Lamb of God, Jesus, made His triumphal entry into Jerusalem on the tenth of Nisan.

12:7, 21–28 The key ingredient in the Passover rituals was the brushing of the **blood** on the doors. The absence of the blood would destroy the Passover observance.

12:8 The **bitter herbs** represented the bitterness of the Israelites' bondage in Egypt.

fire—its head with its legs and its entrails. [10]You shall let none of it remain until morning, and what remains of it until morning you shall burn with fire. [11]And thus you shall eat it: *with* a belt on your waist, your sandals on your feet, and your staff in your hand. So you shall eat it in haste. It *is* the LORD's Passover.

[12]'For I will pass through the land of Egypt on that night, and will strike all the firstborn in the land of Egypt, both man and beast; and against all the gods of Egypt I will execute judgment: I *am* the LORD. [13]Now the blood shall be a sign for you on the houses where you *are.* And when I see the blood, I will pass over you; and the plague shall not be on you to destroy *you* when I strike the land of Egypt.

[14]'So this day shall be to you a memorial; and you shall keep it as a feast to the LORD throughout your generations. You shall keep it as a feast by an everlasting ordinance. [15]Seven days you shall eat unleavened bread. On the first day you shall remove leaven from your houses. For whoever eats leavened bread from the first day until the seventh day, that person shall be cut off from Israel. [16]On the first day *there shall be* a holy convocation, and on the seventh day there shall be a holy convocation for you. No manner of work shall be done on them; but *that* which everyone must eat—that only may be prepared by you. [17]So you shall observe *the Feast of* Unleavened Bread, for on this same day I will have brought your armies out of the land of Egypt. Therefore you shall observe this day throughout your generations as an everlasting ordinance. [18]In the first *month,* on the fourteenth day of the month at evening, you shall eat unleavened bread, until the twenty-first day of the month at evening. [19]For seven days no leaven shall be found in your houses, since whoever eats what is leavened, that same person shall be cut off from the congregation of Israel, whether *he is* a stranger or a native of the land. [20]You shall eat nothing leavened; in all your dwellings you shall eat unleavened bread.' "

[21]Then Moses called for all the elders of Israel and said to them, "Pick out and take lambs for yourselves according to your families, and kill the Passover *lamb.* [22]And you shall take a bunch of hyssop, dip *it* in the blood that *is* in the basin, and strike the lintel and the two doorposts with the blood that *is* in the basin. And none of you shall go out of the door of his house until morning. [23]For the LORD will pass through to strike the Egyptians; and when He sees the blood on the lintel and on the two doorposts, the LORD will pass over the door and not allow the destroyer to come into your houses to strike *you.* [24]And you shall observe this thing as an ordinance for you and your sons forever. [25]It will come to pass when you come to the land which the LORD will give you, just as He promised, that you shall keep this service. [26]And it shall be, when your children say to you, 'What do you mean by this service?' [27]that you shall say, 'It *is* the Passover sacrifice of the LORD, who passed over the houses of the children of Israel in Egypt when He struck the Egyptians and delivered our households.' " So the people bowed their heads and worshiped. [28]Then the children of Israel went away and did *so;* just as the

---

12:13 blood shall be a sign: The purpose of the blood was not simply to mark the Israelite homes. The Hebrews were already by themselves in Goshen. Rather, the lamb's blood was clearly in substitution for the blood of those within the house. Later, Christ became the sacrificial Lamb without blemish, shedding His blood to save us from spiritual death.

12:17 Following the Passover is the **Feast of Unleavened Bread**. Passover celebrated the deliverance from the death angel, while the Feast of Unleavened Bread celebrated the Exodus itself.

LORD had commanded Moses and Aaron, so they did.

The Tenth Plague: Death of the Firstborn

29And it came to pass at midnight that the LORD struck all the firstborn in the land of Egypt, from the firstborn of Pharaoh who sat on his throne to the firstborn of the captive who *was* in the dungeon, and all the firstborn of livestock. 30So Pharaoh rose in the night, he, all his servants, and all the Egyptians; and there was a great cry in Egypt, for *there was* not a house where *there was* not one dead.

The Exodus

31Then he called for Moses and Aaron by night, and said, "Rise, go out from among my people, both you and the children of Israel. And go, serve the LORD as you have said. 32Also take your flocks and your herds, as you have said, and be gone; and bless me also."

33And the Egyptians urged the people, that they might send them out of the land in haste. For they said, "We *shall* all *be* dead." 34So the people took their dough before it was leavened, having their kneading bowls bound up in their clothes on their shoulders. 35Now the children of Israel had done according to the word of Moses, and they had asked from the Egyptians articles of silver, articles of gold, and clothing. 36And the LORD had given the people favor in the sight of the Egyptians, so that they granted them *what they requested*. Thus they plundered the Egyptians.

37Then the children of Israel journeyed from Ram'e·sēs to Suc'coth, about six hundred thousand men on foot, besides children. 38A mixed multitude went up with them also, and flocks and herds—a great deal of livestock. 39And they baked unleavened cakes of the dough which they had brought out of Egypt; for it was not leavened, because they were driven out of Egypt and could not wait, nor had they prepared provisions for themselves.

40Now the sojourn of the children of Israel who lived in Egypt[a] *was* four hundred and thirty years. 41And it came to pass at the end of the four hundred and thirty years—on that very same day—it came to pass that all the armies of the LORD went out from the land of Egypt. 42It *is* a night of solemn observance to the LORD for bringing them out of the land of Egypt. This *is* that night of the LORD, a solemn observance for all the children of Israel throughout their generations.

Passover Regulations

43And the LORD said to Moses and Aaron, "This *is* the ordinance of the Passover: No foreigner shall eat it. 44But every man's servant who is bought for money, when you have circumcised him, then he may eat it. 45A sojourner and a

12:40 [a]Samaritan Pentateuch and Septuagint read *Egypt and Canaan.*

12:38 mixed multitude: The Hebrews did not leave Egypt by themselves, but were accompanied by others. This group was probably composed of those who had but one Hebrew parent, other oppressed or enslaved peoples, and maybe even some Egyptians who were impressed by the plagues.

12:40, 41 four hundred and thirty years: A precise reckoning. Gen. 15:13 uses the round number of 400.

12:43–50 Three classes of individuals are designated as ineligible to participate in the Passover: the **foreigner** (v. 43); the **sojourner** (v. 45, a transient alien); and the **hired servant** (v. 45, a foreigner hired as a day laborer). On the other hand, a **servant . . . bought for money** (v. 44) and the **stranger** (v. 48, a permanent alien) could observe Passover if they joined the family of God and submitted to its religious practices (v. 48). Because Israel was now joined by a "mixed multitude" (v. 38), the question of the participation of non-Israelites became significant.

hired servant shall not eat it. 46In one house it shall be eaten; you shall not carry any of the flesh outside the house, nor shall you break one of its bones. 47All the congregation of Israel shall keep it. 48And when a stranger dwells with you *and wants* to keep the Passover to the LORD, let all his males be circumcised, and then let him come near and keep it; and he shall be as a native of the land. For no uncircumcised person shall eat it. 49One law shall be for the native-born and for the stranger who dwells among you."

50Thus all the children of Israel did; as the LORD commanded Moses and Aaron, so they did. 51And it came to pass, on that very same day, that the LORD brought the children of Israel out of the land of Egypt according to their armies.

CHAPTER 13

The Firstborn Consecrated

Then the LORD spoke to Moses, saying, 2"Consecrate to Me all the firstborn, whatever opens the womb among the children of Israel, *both* of man and beast; it is Mine."

The Feast of Unleavened Bread

3And Moses said to the people: "Remember this day in which you went out of Egypt, out of the house of bondage; for by strength of hand the LORD brought you out of this *place.* No leavened bread shall be eaten. 4On this day you are going out, in the month Ā'bib. 5And it shall be, when the LORD brings you into the land of the Cā'naan·ītes and the Hit'tītes and the Am'o·rītes and the Hī'vītes and the Jeb'ū·sītes, which He swore to your fathers to give you, a land flowing with milk and honey, that you shall keep this service in this month. 6Seven days you shall eat unleavened bread, and on the seventh day *there shall be* a feast to the LORD. 7Unleavened bread shall be eaten seven days. And no leavened bread shall be seen among you, nor shall leaven be seen among you in all your quarters. 8And you shall tell your son in that day, saying, '*This is done* because of what the LORD did for me when I came up from Egypt.' 9It shall be as a sign to you on your hand and as a memorial between your eyes, that the LORD's law may be in your mouth; for with a strong hand the LORD has brought you out of Egypt. 10You shall therefore keep this ordinance in its season from year to year.

The Law of the Firstborn

11"And it shall be, when the LORD brings you into the land of the Cā'naan·ītes, as He swore to you and your fathers, and gives it to you, 12that you shall set apart to the LORD all that open the womb, that is, every firstborn that comes from an animal which you have; the males *shall be* the LORD's. 13But every firstborn of a donkey you shall redeem with a lamb; and if you will not redeem *it,* then you shall break its neck. And all the firstborn of man among your sons you shall redeem. 14So it shall be, when your son asks you in time to come, saying, 'What *is* this?' that you shall say to him, 'By strength of hand the LORD brought us out of Egypt, out of the house of bondage. 15And it came to pass, when Pharaoh was stubborn about letting us go, that the LORD killed all the firstborn in the land of Egypt, both the firstborn of man and the firstborn of beast. Therefore I sacrifice to the LORD all males that open the womb, but all the firstborn of my sons I redeem.' 16It shall be as a sign on your hand

---

13:1, 2, 11–16 Consecrate, in connection with the **firstborn**, means "to set apart." They belonged to God. He has exclusive claim on our choicest possessions, even the firstborn. The donkey was a valuable work animal. Probably because it was unclean, it could be redeemed with a lamb. That the firstborn of man must be redeemed (v. 15) indicates that children were not themselves to be sacrificed. All redemption required the provision of a substitute.

and as frontlets between your eyes, for by strength of hand the LORD brought us out of Egypt."

The Wilderness Way

17 Then it came to pass, when Pharaoh had let the people go, that God did not lead them *by* way of the land of the Phi·lis'tines, although that *was* near; for God said, "Lest perhaps the people change their minds when they see war, and return to Egypt." 18 So God led the people around *by* way of the wilderness of the Red Sea. And the children of Israel went up in orderly ranks out of the land of Egypt.

19 And Moses took the bones of Joseph with him, for he had placed the children of Israel under solemn oath, saying, "God will surely visit you, and you shall carry up my bones from here with you."[a]

20 So they took their journey from Suc'coth and camped in Ē'tham at the edge of the wilderness. 21 And the LORD went before them by day in a pillar of cloud to lead the way, and by night in a pillar of fire to give them light, so as to go by day and night. 22 He did not take away the pillar of cloud by day or the pillar of fire by night *from* before the people.

CHAPTER 14

The Red Sea Crossing

Now the LORD spoke to Moses, saying: 2 "Speak to the children of Israel, that they turn and camp before Pī Ha·hī'roth, between Mig'dōl and the sea, opposite Bā'al Zē'phon; you shall camp before it by the sea. 3 For Pharaoh will say of the children of Israel, 'They *are* bewildered by the land; the wilderness has closed them in.' 4 Then I will harden Pharaoh's heart, so that he will pursue them; and I will gain honor over Pharaoh and over all his army, that the Egyptians may know that I *am* the LORD." And they did so.

5 Now it was told the king of Egypt that the people had fled, and the heart of Pharaoh and his servants was turned against the people; and they said, "Why have we done this, that we have let Israel go from serving us?" 6 So he made ready his chariot and took his people with him. 7 Also, he took six hundred choice chariots, and all the chariots of Egypt with captains over every one of them. 8 And the LORD hardened the heart of Pharaoh king of Egypt, and he pursued the children of Israel; and the children of Israel went out with boldness. 9 So the Egyptians pursued them, all the horses *and* chariots of Pharaoh, his horsemen and his army, and overtook them camping by the sea beside Pī Ha·hī'roth, before Bā'al Zē'phon.

10 And when Pharaoh drew near, the children of Israel lifted their eyes, and behold, the Egyptians marched after them. So they were very afraid, and the children of Israel cried out to the LORD. 11 Then they said to Moses, "Because *there were* no graves in Egypt, have you taken us away to die in the wilderness? Why have you so dealt with us, to bring us up out of Egypt? 12 *Is* this not the word that we told you in Egypt, saying, 'Let us alone that we may serve the Egyptians'? For *it would have been* better for us to serve the Egyptians than that we should die in the wilderness."

13 And Moses said to the people, "Do not

13:19 [a]Genesis 50:25

13:17 The road to Philistia was heavily guarded by Egypt, and thus could lead the Israelites straight into battle. The Lord recognized that the people were not yet ready for such a test of their faith.

13:19 By carrying the bones of Joseph out of Egypt, Moses fulfilled Gen. 50:25, 26.

14:4 so that he will pursue: Pharaoh's plan to pursue the Hebrews was really a part of the Lord's plan. It was the Lord's plan versus Pharaoh's plan.

14:13, 14 A great statement of faith from Moses. Sometimes the most difficult thing to do is to **stand still** and trust God. They needed to **see the salvation of the LORD** more clearly

be afraid. Stand still, and see the salvation
of the LORD, which He will accomplish for
you today. For the Egyptians whom you
see today, you shall see again no more for-
ever. 14The LORD will fight for you, and you
shall hold your peace."

15And the LORD said to Moses, "Why do
you cry to Me? Tell the children of Israel to
go forward. 16But lift up your rod, and
stretch out your hand over the sea and di-
vide it. And the children of Israel shall go
on dry *ground* through the midst of the sea.
17And I indeed will harden the hearts of the
Egyptians, and they shall follow them. So I
will gain honor over Pharaoh and over all
his army, his chariots, and his horsemen.
18Then the Egyptians shall know that I *am*
the LORD, when I have gained honor for
Myself over Pharaoh, his chariots, and his
horsemen."

19And the Angel of God, who went be-
fore the camp of Israel, moved and went
behind them; and the pillar of cloud went
from before them and stood behind them.
20So it came between the camp of the Egyp-
tians and the camp of Israel. Thus it was a
cloud and darkness *to the one,* and it gave
light by night *to the other,* so that the one
did not come near the other all that night.

21Then Moses stretched out his hand
over the sea; and the LORD caused the sea
to go *back* by a strong east wind all that
night, and made the sea into dry *land,* and
the waters were divided. 22So the children
of Israel went into the midst of the sea on
the dry *ground,* and the waters *were* a wall
to them on their right hand and on their
left. 23And the Egyptians pursued and
went after them into the midst of the sea,
all Pharaoh's horses, his chariots, and his
horsemen.

24Now it came to pass, in the morning
watch, that the LORD looked down upon
the army of the Egyptians through the pil-
lar of fire and cloud, and He troubled the
army of the Egyptians. 25And He took off[a]
their chariot wheels, so that they drove
them with difficulty; and the Egyptians
said, "Let us flee from the face of Israel, for
the LORD fights for them against the Egyp-
tians."

26Then the LORD said to Moses, "Stretch
out your hand over the sea, that the waters
may come back upon the Egyptians, on
their chariots, and on their horsemen."
27And Moses stretched out his hand over
the sea; and when the morning appeared,
the sea returned to its full depth, while the
Egyptians were fleeing into it. So the LORD
overthrew the Egyptians in the midst of
the sea. 28Then the waters returned and
covered the chariots, the horsemen, *and* all
the army of Pharaoh that came into the sea
after them. Not so much as one of them re-
mained. 29But the children of Israel had
walked on dry *land* in the midst of the sea,
and the waters *were* a wall to them on their
right hand and on their left.

30So the LORD saved Israel that day out
of the hand of the Egyptians, and Israel
saw the Egyptians dead on the seashore.
31Thus Israel saw the great work which the
LORD had done in Egypt; so the people
feared the LORD, and believed the LORD
and His servant Moses.

CHAPTER 15

The Song of Moses

Then Moses and the children of Israel
sang this song to the LORD, and spoke, say-
ing:

"I will sing to the LORD,
For He has triumphed gloriously!
The horse and its rider
He has thrown into the sea!
2 The LORD *is* my strength and song,

14:25 [a]Samaritan Pentateuch, Septuagint, and Syriac read *bound.*

than the approaching Egyptians. We need to realize that God is not bound by human methods of deliverance as He works in our lives today.

And He has become my salvation;
He *is* my God, and I will praise Him;
My father's God, and I will exalt
Him.
3 The LORD *is* a man of war;
The LORD *is* His name.
4 Pharaoh's chariots and his army He
has cast into the sea;
His chosen captains also are drowned
in the Red Sea.
5 The depths have covered them;
They sank to the bottom like a stone.

6 "Your right hand, O LORD, has become
glorious in power;
Your right hand, O LORD, has dashed
the enemy in pieces.
7 And in the greatness of Your
excellence
You have overthrown those who rose
against You;
You sent forth Your wrath;
It consumed them like stubble.
8 And with the blast of Your nostrils
The waters were gathered together;
The floods stood upright like a heap;
The depths congealed in the heart of
the sea.
9 The enemy said, 'I will pursue,
I will overtake,
I will divide the spoil;
My desire shall be satisfied on them.
I will draw my sword,
My hand shall destroy them.'
10 You blew with Your wind,
The sea covered them;
They sank like lead in the mighty
waters.

11 "Who *is* like You, O LORD, among the
gods?
Who *is* like You, glorious in holiness,
Fearful in praises, doing wonders?
12 You stretched out Your right hand;
The earth swallowed them.
13 You in Your mercy have led forth
The people whom You have
redeemed;
You have guided *them* in Your
strength
To Your holy habitation.

14 "The people will hear *and* be afraid;
Sorrow will take hold of the
inhabitants of Phi·lis'ti·a.
15 Then the chiefs of Ē'dom will be
dismayed;
The mighty men of Mō'ab,
Trembling will take hold of them;
All the inhabitants of Cā'naan will
melt away.
16 Fear and dread will fall on them;
By the greatness of Your arm
They will be *as* still as a stone,
Till Your people pass over, O LORD,
Till the people pass over
Whom You have purchased.
17 You will bring them in and plant
them
In the mountain of Your inheritance,
In the place, O LORD, *which* You have
made
For Your own dwelling,
The sanctuary, O LORD, *which* Your
hands have established.

18 "The LORD shall reign forever and
ever."

19For the horses of Pharaoh went with
his chariots and his horsemen into the sea,
and the LORD brought back the waters of
the sea upon them. But the children of Is-
rael went on dry *land* in the midst of the
sea.

The Song of Miriam

20Then Miriam the prophetess, the sister
of Aaron, took the timbrel in her hand; and
all the women went out after her with tim-
brels and with dances. 21And Miriam an-
swered them:

"Sing to the LORD,
For He has triumphed gloriously!
The horse and its rider
He has thrown into the sea!"

Bitter Waters Made Sweet

[22]So Moses brought Israel from the Red Sea; then they went out into the Wilderness of Shūr. And they went three days in the wilderness and found no water. [23]Now when they came to Mar'ah, they could not drink the waters of Mar'ah, for they *were* bitter. Therefore the name of it was called Mar'ah.[a] [24]And the people complained against Moses, saying, "What shall we drink?" [25]So he cried out to the LORD, and the LORD showed him a tree. When he cast *it* into the waters, the waters were made sweet.

There He made a statute and an ordinance for them, and there He tested them, [26]and said, "If you diligently heed the voice of the LORD your God and do what is right in His sight, give ear to His commandments and keep all His statutes, I will put none of the diseases on you which I have brought on the Egyptians. For I *am* the LORD who heals you."

[27]Then they came to Ē'lim, where there *were* twelve wells of water and seventy palm trees; so they camped there by the waters.

CHAPTER 16

Bread from Heaven

And they journeyed from Ē'lim, and all the congregation of the children of Israel came to the Wilderness of Sin, which is between Ē'lim and Sinai, on the fifteenth day of the second month after they departed from the land of Egypt. [2]Then the whole congregation of the children of Israel complained against Moses and Aaron in the wilderness. [3]And the children of Israel said to them, "Oh, that we had died by the hand of the LORD in the land of Egypt, when we sat by the pots of meat *and* when we ate bread to the full! For you have brought us out into this wilderness to kill this whole assembly with hunger."

[4]Then the LORD said to Moses, "Behold, I will rain bread from heaven for you. And the people shall go out and gather a certain quota every day, that I may test them, whether they will walk in My law or not. [5]And it shall be on the sixth day that they shall prepare what they bring in, and it shall be twice as much as they gather daily."

[6]Then Moses and Aaron said to all the children of Israel, "At evening you shall know that the LORD has brought you out of the land of Egypt. [7]And in the morning you shall see the glory of the LORD; for He hears your complaints against the LORD. But what *are* we, that you complain against us?" [8]Also Moses said, "*This shall be seen* when the LORD gives you meat to eat in the evening, and in the morning bread to the full; for the LORD hears your complaints which you make against Him. And what *are* we? Your complaints *are* not against us but against the LORD."

[9]Then Moses spoke to Aaron, "Say to all the congregation of the children of Israel, 'Come near before the LORD, for He has heard your complaints.' " [10]Now it came to pass, as Aaron spoke to the whole congregation of the children of Israel, that they looked toward the wilderness, and behold, the glory of the LORD appeared in the cloud.

[11]And the LORD spoke to Moses, saying, [12]"I have heard the complaints of the

15:23 [a]Literally *Bitter*

16:3 Meat was a rare delicacy for the average citizen in the ancient Near East. The people also asserted that in Egypt they **ate bread to the full**. Probably both were exaggerations from complaining people.

16:4 I will rain bread: A loving God answers human need even for grumbling people. **a certain quota every day**: They were to collect only as much as they could eat in one day. They could not insulate themselves from having to trust God for daily bread. In this way God would **test** them.

children of Israel. Speak to them, saying,
'At twilight you shall eat meat, and in the
morning you shall be filled with bread.
And you shall know that I *am* the LORD
your God.' "
[13]So it was that quails came up at
evening and covered the camp, and in the
morning the dew lay all around the camp.
[14]And when the layer of dew lifted, there,
on the surface of the wilderness, was a
small round substance, *as* fine as frost on
the ground. [15]So when the children of Israel
saw *it,* they said to one another, "What is
it?" For they did not know what it *was.*
And Moses said to them, "This *is* the
bread which the LORD has given you to eat.
[16]This is the thing which the LORD has com-
manded: 'Let every man gather it accord-
ing to each one's need, one omer for each
person, *according to the* number of persons;
let every man take for *those* who *are* in his
tent.' "
[17]Then the children of Israel did so and
gathered, some more, some less. [18]So when
they measured *it* by omers, he who gath-
ered much had nothing left over, and he
who gathered little had no lack. Every man
had gathered according to each one's need.
[19]And Moses said, "Let no one leave any of
it till morning." [20]Notwithstanding they
did not heed Moses. But some of them left
part of it until morning, and it bred worms
and stank. And Moses was angry with
them. [21]So they gathered it every morning,
every man according to his need. And
when the sun became hot, it melted.
[22]And so it was, on the sixth day, *that*
they gathered twice as much bread, two
omers for each one. And all the rulers of
the congregation came and told Moses.
[23]Then he said to them, "This *is what* the
LORD has said: 'Tomorrow *is* a Sabbath rest,
a holy Sabbath to the LORD. Bake what you
will bake *today,* and boil what you will boil;
and lay up for yourselves all that remains,
to be kept until morning.' " [24]So they laid it
up till morning, as Moses commanded;
and it did not stink, nor were there
any worms in it. [25]Then Moses said, "Eat
that today, for today *is* a Sabbath to the
LORD; today you will not find it in the field.
[26]Six days you shall gather it, but on the
seventh day, the Sabbath, there will be
none."
[27]Now it happened *that some* of the peo-
ple went out on the seventh day to gather,
but they found none. [28]And the LORD said
to Moses, "How long do you refuse to keep
My commandments and My laws? [29]See!
For the LORD has given you the Sabbath;
therefore He gives you on the sixth day
bread for two days. Let every man remain
in his place; let no man go out of his place
on the seventh day." [30]So the people rested
on the seventh day.
[31]And the house of Israel called its name
Manna.[a] And it *was* like white coriander
seed, and the taste of it *was* like wafers
made with honey.
[32]Then Moses said, "This *is* the thing
which the LORD has commanded: 'Fill an
omer with it, to be kept for your genera-
tions, that they may see the bread with
which I fed you in the wilderness, when I
brought you out of the land of Egypt.' "
[33]And Moses said to Aaron, "Take a pot
and put an omer of manna in it, and lay it
up before the LORD, to be kept for your
generations." [34]As the LORD commanded
Moses, so Aaron laid it up before the Testi-
mony, to be kept. [35]And the children of Is-
rael ate manna forty years, until they came
to an inhabited land; they ate manna until
they came to the border of the land of
Cā'naan. [36]Now an omer *is* one-tenth of an
ephah.

16:31 [a]Literally *What?* (compare Exodus 16:15)

16:32 your generations: By preserving some manna, Israel would perpetually recall how dependent she was on God for her life.

16:35 The Hebrews ate manna only until they entered Canaan. Miraculous provision is not supplied when not needed.

CHAPTER 17

Water from the Rock

Then all the congregation of the children of Israel set out on their journey from the Wilderness of Sin, according to the commandment of the LORD, and camped in Reph'i·dim; but *there was* no water for the people to drink. 2Therefore the people contended with Moses, and said, "Give us water, that we may drink."

So Moses said to them, "Why do you contend with me? Why do you tempt the LORD?"

3And the people thirsted there for water, and the people complained against Moses, and said, "Why *is* it you have brought us up out of Egypt, to kill us and our children and our livestock with thirst?"

4So Moses cried out to the LORD, saying, "What shall I do with this people? They are almost ready to stone me!"

5And the LORD said to Moses, "Go on before the people, and take with you some of the elders of Israel. Also take in your hand your rod with which you struck the river, and go. 6Behold, I will stand before you there on the rock in Hō'reb; and you shall strike the rock, and water will come out of it, that the people may drink."

And Moses did so in the sight of the elders of Israel. 7So he called the name of the place Mas'sah[a] and Mer'i·bah,[b] because of the contention of the children of Israel, and because they tempted the LORD, saying, "Is the LORD among us or not?"

Victory over the Amalekites

8Now Am'a·lek came and fought with Israel in Reph'i·dim. 9And Moses said to Joshua, "Choose us some men and go out, fight with Am'a·lek. Tomorrow I will stand on the top of the hill with the rod of God in my hand." 10So Joshua did as Moses said to him, and fought with Am'a·lek. And Moses, Aaron, and Hur went up to the top of the hill. 11And so it was, when Moses held up his hand, that Israel prevailed; and when he let down his hand, Am'a·lek prevailed. 12But Moses' hands *became* heavy; so they took a stone and put *it* under him, and he sat on it. And Aaron and Hur supported his hands, one on one side, and the other on the other side; and his hands were steady until the going down of the sun. 13So Joshua defeated Am'a·lek and his people with the edge of the sword.

14Then the LORD said to Moses, "Write this *for* a memorial in the book and recount *it* in the hearing of Joshua, that I will utterly blot out the remembrance of Am'a·lek from under heaven." 15And Moses built an altar and called its name, The-LORD-Is-My-Banner;[a] 16for he said, "Because the LORD has sworn: the LORD *will have* war with Am'a·lek from generation to generation."

CHAPTER 18

Jethro's Advice

And Jeth'rō, the priest of Mid'i·an, Moses' father-in-law, heard of all that God had done for Moses and for Israel His people—that the LORD had brought Israel out of Egypt. 2Then Jeth'rō, Moses' father-in-law, took Zip·pō'rah, Moses' wife, after he had sent her back, 3with her two sons, of whom

17:7 [a]Literally *Tempted* [b]Literally *Contention*
17:15 [a]Hebrew *YHWH Nissi*

17:2 The Hebrew word *rib,* meaning "contend," is part of Me*rib*ah, the place name of v. 7. **tempt**: The same word used of God's test of Abraham in Gen. 22:1. To test God in this way is to dare Him to prove His power to the unbelieving mob.

18:1–6 Frequently in this chapter Jethro is described as Moses' father-in-law. In ancient Near Eastern society the "counsel" (v. 19) of the father-in-law was well respected. When Jethro heard what God had done for his son-in-law, he joined Moses and the Israelites in the wilderness (v. 5).

the name of one *was* Ger'shom (for he said,
"I have been a stranger in a foreign land")[a]
4and the name of the other *was* El·i·ē'zer[a]
(for *he said,* "The God of my father *was* my
help, and delivered me from the sword of
Pharaoh"); 5and Jeth'rō, Moses' father-in-
law, came with his sons and his wife to
Moses in the wilderness, where he was en-
camped at the mountain of God. 6Now he
had said to Moses, "I, your father-in-law
Jeth'rō, am coming to you with your wife
and her two sons with her."

7So Moses went out to meet his father-
in-law, bowed down, and kissed him. And
they asked each other about *their* well-
being, and they went into the tent. 8And
Moses told his father-in-law all that the
LORD had done to Pharaoh and to the
Egyptians for Israel's sake, all the hardship
that had come upon them on the way, and
how the LORD had delivered them. 9Then
Jeth'rō rejoiced for all the good which the
LORD had done for Israel, whom He had
delivered out of the hand of the Egyptians.
10And Jeth'rō said, "Blessed *be* the LORD,
who has delivered you out of the hand of
the Egyptians and out of the hand of
Pharaoh, *and* who has delivered the people
from under the hand of the Egyptians.
11Now I know that the LORD *is* greater than
all the gods; for in the very thing in which
they behaved proudly, *He was* above
them." 12Then Jeth'rō, Moses' father-in-law,
took[a] a burnt offering and *other* sacrifices *to
offer* to God. And Aaron came with all the
elders of Israel to eat bread with Moses'
father-in-law before God.

13And so it was, on the next day, that
Moses sat to judge the people; and the peo-
ple stood before Moses from morning until
evening. 14So when Moses' father-in-law
saw all that he did for the people, he said,
"What *is* this thing that you are doing for
the people? Why do you alone sit, and all
the people stand before you from morning
until evening?"

15And Moses said to his father-in-law,
"Because the people come to me to inquire
of God. 16When they have a difficulty, they
come to me, and I judge between one and
another; and I make known the statutes of
God and His laws."

17So Moses' father-in-law said to him,
"The thing that you do *is* not good. 18Both
you and these people who *are* with you
will surely wear yourselves out. For this
thing *is* too much for you; you are not able
to perform it by yourself. 19Listen now to
my voice; I will give you counsel, and God
will be with you: Stand before God for the
people, so that you may bring the difficul-
ties to God. 20And you shall teach them the
statutes and the laws, and show them the
way in which they must walk and
the work they must do. 21Moreover you
shall select from all the people able men,
such as fear God, men of truth, hating cov-
etousness; and place *such* over them *to be*
rulers of thousands, rulers of hundreds,
rulers of fifties, and rulers of tens. 22And let
them judge the people at all times. Then it
will be *that* every great matter they shall
bring to you, but every small matter they
themselves shall judge. So it will be easier
for you, for they will bear *the burden* with
you. 23If you do this thing, and God *so* com-
mands you, then you will be able to en-
dure, and all this people will also go to
their place in peace."

24So Moses heeded the voice of his
father-in-law and did all that he had said.
25And Moses chose able men out of all
Israel, and made them heads over the

18:3 [a]Compare Exodus 2:22 18:4 [a]Literally *My God Is Help* 18:12 [a]Following Masoretic Text and Septuagint; Syriac, Targum, and Vulgate read *offered.*

18:11 Now I know: Jethro is typical of many who would believe on the basis of the testimony of others (see John 20:29).

18:19–23 Jethro's advice to Moses provides important principles of leadership, which can be successfully incorporated today.

people: rulers of thousands, rulers of hun-
dreds, rulers of fifties, and rulers of tens.
26So they judged the people at all times; the
hard cases they brought to Moses, but they
judged every small case themselves.
27Then Moses let his father-in-law de-
part, and he went his way to his own land.

CHAPTER 19

Israel at Mount Sinai

In the third month after the children of
Israel had gone out of the land of Egypt, on
the same day, they came *to* the Wilderness
of Sinai. 2For they had departed from
Reph'i·dim, had come *to* the Wilderness of
Sinai, and camped in the wilderness. So Is-
rael camped there before the mountain.
3And Moses went up to God, and the
LORD called to him from the mountain,
saying, "Thus you shall say to the house of
Jacob, and tell the children of Israel: 4'You
have seen what I did to the Egyptians, and
how I bore you on eagles' wings and
brought you to Myself. 5Now therefore, if
you will indeed obey My voice and keep
My covenant, then you shall be a special
treasure to Me above all people; for all the
earth *is* Mine. 6And you shall be to Me a
kingdom of priests and a holy nation.'
These *are* the words which you shall speak
to the children of Israel."
7So Moses came and called for the elders
of the people, and laid before them all
these words which the LORD commanded
him. 8Then all the people answered to-
gether and said, "All that the LORD has
spoken we will do." So Moses brought
back the words of the people to the LORD.
9And the LORD said to Moses, "Behold, I
come to you in the thick cloud, that the
people may hear when I speak with you,
and believe you forever."
So Moses told the words of the people to
the LORD.
10Then the LORD said to Moses, "Go to
the people and consecrate them today and
tomorrow, and let them wash their clothes.
11And let them be ready for the third day.
For on the third day the LORD will come
down upon Mount Sinai in the sight of all
the people. 12You shall set bounds for the
people all around, saying, 'Take heed to
yourselves *that* you do *not* go up to the
mountain or touch its base. Whoever
touches the mountain shall surely be put to
death. 13Not a hand shall touch him, but he
shall surely be stoned or shot *with an arrow;*
whether man or beast, he shall not live.'
When the trumpet sounds long, they shall
come near the mountain."
14So Moses went down from the moun-
tain to the people and sanctified the peo-
ple, and they washed their clothes. 15And
he said to the people, "Be ready for the
third day; do not come near *your* wives."
16Then it came to pass on the third day,
in the morning, that there were thunder-
ings and lightnings, and a thick cloud on
the mountain; and the sound of the trum-
pet was very loud, so that all the people
who *were* in the camp trembled. 17And Mo-
ses brought the people out of the camp to
meet with God, and they stood at the foot
of the mountain. 18Now Mount Sinai *was*
completely in smoke, because the LORD

19:4 I bore you on eagles' wings: A delightful metaphor, describing God bringing His own from Egypt to Sinai.

19:6 kingdom of priests: This is a word of responsibility. A priest is a ministering servant, a bridge builder; Israel was to be the bridge between God and the nations of the earth. How could she do this? By being a **holy nation**. It is doubtful if Israel had yet much understanding of the word *holy*. Perhaps one function of the Ten Commandments was to make that meaning clear.

19:10 consecrate: The same Hebrew root as "holy" in v. 6. This was an awesome moment, and not one to be entered into casually. We are not to rush into God's presence unclean or unprepared (but see 1 John 1:9).

descended upon it in fire. Its smoke as-
cended like the smoke of a furnace, and the
whole mountain[a] quaked greatly. [19]And
when the blast of the trumpet sounded
long and became louder and louder, Moses
spoke, and God answered him by voice.
[20]Then the LORD came down upon Mount
Sinai, on the top of the mountain. And the
LORD called Moses to the top of the moun-
tain, and Moses went up.

[21]And the LORD said to Moses, "Go
down and warn the people, lest they break
through to gaze at the LORD, and many of
them perish. [22]Also let the priests who
come near the LORD consecrate themselves,
lest the LORD break out against them."

[23]But Moses said to the LORD, "The peo-
ple cannot come up to Mount Sinai; for You
warned us, saying, 'Set bounds around the
mountain and consecrate it.' "

[24]Then the LORD said to him, "Away! Get
down and then come up, you and Aaron
with you. But do not let the priests and the
people break through to come up to the
LORD, lest He break out against them." [25]So
Moses went down to the people and spoke
to them.

CHAPTER 20

The Ten Commandments

And God spoke all these words, saying:

2 "I *am* the LORD your God, who brought
you out of the land of Egypt, out of
the house of bondage.

3 "You shall have no other gods before
Me.

4 "You shall not make for yourself a
carved image—any likeness *of any-
thing* that *is* in heaven above, or
that *is* in the earth beneath, or that
is in the water under the earth; [5]you
shall not bow down to them nor
serve them. For I, the LORD your
God, *am* a jealous God, visiting the
iniquity of the fathers upon the
children to the third and fourth
generations of those who hate Me,
[6]but showing mercy to thousands,
to those who love Me and keep My
commandments.

7 "You shall not take the name of the
LORD your God in vain, for the
LORD will not hold *him* guiltless
who takes His name in vain.

8 "Remember the Sabbath day, to keep it
holy. [9]Six days you shall labor and
do all your work, [10]but the seventh
day *is* the Sabbath of the LORD your
God. *In it* you shall do no work:
you, nor your son, nor your daugh-
ter, nor your male servant, nor your
female servant, nor your cattle, nor
your stranger who *is* within your
gates. [11]For *in* six days the LORD
made the heavens and the earth,
the sea, and all that *is* in them, and
rested the seventh day. Therefore
the LORD blessed the Sabbath day
and hallowed it.

12 "Honor your father and your mother,
that your days may be long upon
the land which the LORD your God
is giving you.

13 "You shall not murder.

14 "You shall not commit adultery.

15 "You shall not steal.

16 "You shall not bear false witness against
your neighbor.

17 "You shall not covet your neighbor's
house; you shall not covet your

19:18 [a]Septuagint reads *all the people.*

19:21 break through: How can a holy God not destroy a sinful people by His very presence? Either by absolute separation (as here), or by employing a Mediator (as the rest of the Bible teaches).

20:1—23:33 The terms of the covenant. If Israel is to live with the Holy God, she must share His holy nature. These commandments are first presented in a short form stated as absolute principles (20:3–17), then in a longer form expressed in examples (20:22—23:33).

neighbor's wife, nor his male servant, nor his female servant, nor his ox, nor his donkey, nor anything that *is* your neighbor's."

The People Afraid of God's Presence

18Now all the people witnessed the thunderings, the lightning flashes, the sound of the trumpet, and the mountain smoking; and when the people saw *it,* they trembled and stood afar off. 19Then they said to Moses, "You speak with us, and we will hear; but let not God speak with us, lest we die."

20And Moses said to the people, "Do not fear; for God has come to test you, and that His fear may be before you, so that you may not sin." 21So the people stood afar off, but Moses drew near the thick darkness where God *was.*

The Law of the Altar

22Then the LORD said to Moses, "Thus you shall say to the children of Israel: 'You have seen that I have talked with you from heaven. 23You shall not make *anything to be* with Me—gods of silver or gods of gold you shall not make for yourselves. 24An altar of earth you shall make for Me, and you shall sacrifice on it your burnt offerings and your peace offerings, your sheep and your oxen. In every place where I record My name I will come to you, and I will bless you. 25And if you make Me an altar of stone, you shall not build it of hewn stone; for if you use your tool on it, you have profaned it. 26Nor shall you go up by steps to My altar, that your nakedness may not be exposed on it.'

CHAPTER 21

The Law Concerning Servants

"Now these *are* the judgments which you shall set before them: 2If you buy a Hebrew servant, he shall serve six years; and in the seventh he shall go out free and pay nothing. 3If he comes in by himself, he shall go out by himself; if he *comes in* married, then his wife shall go out with him. 4If his master has given him a wife, and she has borne him sons or daughters, the wife and her children shall be her master's, and he shall go out by himself. 5But if the servant plainly says, 'I love my master, my wife, and my children; I will not go out free,' 6then his master shall bring him to the judges. He shall also bring him to the door, or to the doorpost, and his master shall pierce his ear with an awl; and he shall serve him forever.

7"And if a man sells his daughter to be a female slave, she shall not go out as the male slaves do. 8If she does not please her master, who has betrothed her to himself, then he shall let her be redeemed. He shall have no right to sell her to a foreign people, since he has dealt deceitfully with her. 9And if he has betrothed her to his son, he shall deal with her according to the custom of daughters. 10If he takes another *wife,* he shall not diminish her food, her clothing, and her marriage rights. 11And if he does not do these three for her, then she shall go out free, without *paying* money.

The Law Concerning Violence

12"He who strikes a man so that he dies shall surely be put to death. 13However, if

---

20:22—23:33 The long form of the terms of the covenant, referred to in 24:7 as "the Book of the Covenant." These laws bear resemblance to other ancient Near Eastern legal codes, such as the Code of Hammurabi and the Hittite Code. God used the writing forms of this time and culture to convey His message to His people.

21:7–11 sells his daughter . . . takes another wife: These concessions to the culture of that time are not commands to do so, nor even approval of the practice. They simply recognize a situation and attempt to curb its worst abuses. **Redeemed** (v. 8) means to be married, probably by some relative. The Bible does not permit a woman to be treated merely as a possession. She is a person with dignity and rights.

he did not lie in wait, but God delivered *him* into his hand, then I will appoint for you a place where he may flee.

14"But if a man acts with premeditation against his neighbor, to kill him by treachery, you shall take him from My altar, that he may die.

15"And he who strikes his father or his mother shall surely be put to death.

16"He who kidnaps a man and sells him, or if he is found in his hand, shall surely be put to death.

17"And he who curses his father or his mother shall surely be put to death.

18"If men contend with each other, and one strikes the other with a stone or with *his* fist, and he does not die but is confined to *his* bed, 19if he rises again and walks about outside with his staff, then he who struck *him* shall be acquitted. He shall only pay *for* the loss of his time, and shall provide *for him* to be thoroughly healed.

20"And if a man beats his male or female servant with a rod, so that he dies under his hand, he shall surely be punished. 21Notwithstanding, if he remains alive a day or two, he shall not be punished; for he *is* his property.

22"If men fight, and hurt a woman with child, so that she gives birth prematurely, yet no harm follows, he shall surely be punished accordingly as the woman's husband imposes on him; and he shall pay as the judges *determine*. 23But if *any* harm follows, then you shall give life for life, 24eye for eye, tooth for tooth, hand for hand, foot for foot, 25burn for burn, wound for wound, stripe for stripe.

26"If a man strikes the eye of his male or female servant, and destroys it, he shall let him go free for the sake of his eye. 27And if he knocks out the tooth of his male or female servant, he shall let him go free for the sake of his tooth.

Animal Control Laws

28"If an ox gores a man or a woman to death, then the ox shall surely be stoned, and its flesh shall not be eaten; but the owner of the ox *shall be* acquitted. 29But if the ox tended to thrust with its horn in times past, and it has been made known to his owner, and he has not kept it confined, so that it has killed a man or a woman, the ox shall be stoned and its owner also shall be put to death. 30If there is imposed on him a sum of money, then he shall pay to redeem his life, whatever is imposed on him. 31Whether it has gored a son or gored a daughter, according to this judgment it shall be done to him. 32If the ox gores a male or female servant, he shall give to their master thirty shekels of silver, and the ox shall be stoned.

33"And if a man opens a pit, or if a man digs a pit and does not cover it, and an ox or a donkey falls in it, 34the owner of the pit shall make *it* good; he shall give money to their owner, but the dead *animal* shall be his.

35"If one man's ox hurts another's, so that it dies, then they shall sell the live ox and divide the money from it; and the dead *ox* they shall also divide. 36Or if it was known that the ox tended to thrust in time past, and its owner has not kept it confined, he shall surely pay ox for ox, and the dead animal shall be his own.

CHAPTER 22

Responsibility for Property

"If a man steals an ox or a sheep, and slaughters it or sells it, he shall restore five

---

21:24, 25 eye for eye: This famous dictum, quoted by Jesus (Matt. 5:38), does not endorse primitive retaliation. Rather, it teaches the principle that the penalty must match the crime—not exceed it, as some might wish (see Gen. 4:23, 24). There must be equal justice for all.

22:1 Four sheep for a sheep reminds us of Zacchaeus's offer to restore fourfold to

oxen for an ox and four sheep for a sheep.
2If the thief is found breaking in, and he is
struck so that he dies, *there shall be* no guilt
for his bloodshed. 3If the sun has risen on
him, *there shall be* guilt for his bloodshed.
He should make full restitution; if he has
nothing, then he shall be sold for his theft.
4If the theft is certainly found alive in his
hand, whether it is an ox or donkey or
sheep, he shall restore double.
5"If a man causes a field or vineyard to
be grazed, and lets loose his animal, and it
feeds in another man's field, he shall make
restitution from the best of his own field
and the best of his own vineyard.
6"If fire breaks out and catches in thorns,
so that stacked grain, standing grain, or the
field is consumed, he who kindled the fire
shall surely make restitution.
7"If a man delivers to his neighbor
money or articles to keep, and it is stolen
out of the man's house, if the thief is found,
he shall pay double. 8If the thief is not
found, then the master of the house shall
be brought to the judges *to see* whether he
has put his hand into his neighbor's goods.
9"For any kind of trespass, *whether it
concerns* an ox, a donkey, a sheep, or cloth-
ing, *or* for any kind of lost thing which *an-
other* claims to be his, the cause of both par-
ties shall come before the judges; *and*
whomever the judges condemn shall pay
double to his neighbor. 10If a man delivers
to his neighbor a donkey, an ox, a sheep, or
any animal to keep, and it dies, is hurt, or
driven away, no one seeing *it*, 11*then* an
oath of the LORD shall be between them
both, that he has not put his hand into his
neighbor's goods; and the owner of it shall
accept *that*, and he shall not make *it* good.
12But if, in fact, it is stolen from him, he
shall make restitution to the owner of it. 13If
it is torn to pieces *by a beast, then* he shall
bring it as evidence, *and* he shall not make
good what was torn.
14"And if a man borrows *anything* from
his neighbor, and it becomes injured or
dies, the owner of it not *being* with it, he
shall surely make *it* good. 15If its owner *was*
with it, he shall not make *it* good; if it *was*
hired, it came for its hire.

Moral and Ceremonial Principles

16"If a man entices a virgin who is not
betrothed, and lies with her, he shall surely
pay the bride-price for her *to be* his wife.
17If her father utterly refuses to give her to
him, he shall pay money according to the
bride-price of virgins.
18"You shall not permit a sorceress to
live.
19"Whoever lies with an animal shall
surely be put to death.
20"He who sacrifices to *any* god, except
to the LORD only, he shall be utterly de-
stroyed.
21"You shall neither mistreat a stranger
nor oppress him, for you were strangers in
the land of Egypt.
22"You shall not afflict any widow or fa-
therless child. 23If you afflict them in any
way, *and* they cry at all to Me, I will surely
hear their cry; 24and My wrath will become
hot, and I will kill you with the sword;
your wives shall be widows, and your chil-
dren fatherless.
25"If you lend money to *any of* My peo-
ple *who are* poor among you, you shall not
be like a moneylender to him; you shall not
charge him interest. 26If you ever take your
neighbor's garment as a pledge, you shall
return it to him before the sun goes down.
27For that *is* his only covering, it *is* his gar-
ment for his skin. What will he sleep in?

anyone whom he had cheated (Luke 19:8). True repentance issues in restitution, where necessary.

22:21–27 God has a special concern for the **stranger** (v. 21), **widow** (v. 22), the **fatherless child** (v. 22), and the **poor** (vv. 25–27). They represent the powerless, and hence vulnerable people of society. God is their protector.

And it will be that when he cries to Me, I
will hear, for I *am* gracious.
28"You shall not revile God, nor curse a
ruler of your people.
29"You shall not delay *to offer* the first of
your ripe produce and your juices. The
firstborn of your sons you shall give to Me.
30Likewise you shall do with your oxen *and*
your sheep. It shall be with its mother
seven days; on the eighth day you shall
give it to Me.
31"And you shall be holy men to Me:
you shall not eat meat torn *by beasts* in the
field; you shall throw it to the dogs.

CHAPTER 23

Justice for All

"You shall not circulate a false report.
Do not put your hand with the wicked to
be an unrighteous witness. 2You shall not
follow a crowd to do evil; nor shall you tes-
tify in a dispute so as to turn aside after
many to pervert *justice.* 3You shall not
show partiality to a poor man in his dis-
pute.
4"If you meet your enemy's ox or his
donkey going astray, you shall surely bring
it back to him again. 5If you see the donkey
of one who hates you lying under its bur-
den, and you would refrain from helping
it, you shall surely help him with it.
6"You shall not pervert the judgment of
your poor in his dispute. 7Keep yourself far
from a false matter; do not kill the innocent
and righteous. For I will not justify the
wicked. 8And you shall take no bribe, for a
bribe blinds the discerning and perverts
the words of the righteous.
9"Also you shall not oppress a stranger,
for you know the heart of a stranger, be-
cause you were strangers in the land of
Egypt.

The Law of Sabbaths

10"Six years you shall sow your land and
gather in its produce, 11but the seventh *year*
you shall let it rest and lie fallow, that the
poor of your people may eat; and what
they leave, the beasts of the field may eat.
In like manner you shall do with your
vineyard *and* your olive grove. 12Six days
you shall do your work, and on the sev-
enth day you shall rest, that your ox and
your donkey may rest, and the son of your
female servant and the stranger may be re-
freshed.
13"And in all that I have said to you, be
circumspect and make no mention of the
name of other gods, nor let it be heard from
your mouth.

Three Annual Feasts

14"Three times you shall keep a feast to
Me in the year: 15You shall keep the Feast of
Unleavened Bread (you shall eat unleav-
ened bread seven days, as I commanded
you, at the time appointed in the month of
Ā'bib, for in it you came out of Egypt; none
shall appear before Me empty); 16and the
Feast of Harvest, the firstfruits of your
labors which you have sown in the field;
and the Feast of Ingathering at the end of
the year, when you have gathered in *the
fruit of* your labors from the field.
17"Three times in the year all your males
shall appear before the Lord GOD.[a]
18"You shall not offer the blood of My
sacrifice with leavened bread; nor shall the
fat of My sacrifice remain until morning.
19The first of the firstfruits of your land you
shall bring into the house of the LORD your
God. You shall not boil a young goat in its
mother's milk.

23:17 [a]Hebrew *YHWH*, usually translated *LORD*

23:15, 16 The Feast of Unleavened Bread occurred in March-April. **The Feast of Harvest**, also known as Pentecost, commemorated the end of the grain harvest in late May. **The Feast of Ingathering**, also known as Tabernacles, celebrated the harvest of olives and grapes in the fall.

The Angel and the Promises

20"Behold, I send an Angel before you to keep you in the way and to bring you into the place which I have prepared. 21Beware of Him and obey His voice; do not provoke Him, for He will not pardon your transgressions; for My name *is* in Him. 22But if you indeed obey His voice and do all that I speak, then I will be an enemy to your enemies and an adversary to your adversaries. 23For My Angel will go before you and bring you in to the Am'o·rītes and the Hit'tītes and the Per'iz·zītes and the Cā'naan·ītes and the Hī'vītes and the Jeb'ū·sītes; and I will cut them off. 24You shall not bow down to their gods, nor serve them, nor do according to their works; but you shall utterly overthrow them and completely break down their *sacred* pillars.

25"So you shall serve the LORD your God, and He will bless your bread and your water. And I will take sickness away from the midst of you. 26No one shall suffer miscarriage or be barren in your land; I will fulfill the number of your days.

> ***I pray, O God, that my child shall serve You, the Lord his God.***
>
> *adapted from* Exodus 23:25

27"I will send My fear before you, I will cause confusion among all the people to whom you come, and will make all your enemies turn *their* backs to you. 28And I will send hornets before you, which shall drive out the Hī'vīte, the Cā'naan·īte, and the Hit'tīte from before you. 29I will not drive them out from before you in one year, lest the land become desolate and the beasts of the field become too numerous for you. 30Little by little I will drive them out from before you, until you have increased, and you inherit the land. 31And I will set your bounds from the Red Sea to the sea, Phi·lis'ti·a, and from the desert to the River.[a] For I will deliver the inhabitants of the land into your hand, and you shall drive them out before you. 32You shall make no covenant with them, nor with their gods. 33They shall not dwell in your land, lest they make you sin against Me. For *if* you serve their gods, it will surely be a snare to you."

CHAPTER 24

Israel Affirms the Covenant

Now He said to Moses, "Come up to the LORD, you and Aaron, Nā'dab and A·bī'hū, and seventy of the elders of Israel, and worship from afar. 2And Moses alone shall come near the LORD, but they shall not come near; nor shall the people go up with him."

3So Moses came and told the people all the words of the LORD and all the judgments. And all the people answered with one voice and said, "All the words which the LORD has said we will do." 4And Moses wrote all the words of the LORD. And he rose early in the morning, and built an altar at the foot of the mountain, and twelve pillars according to the twelve tribes of Israel. 5Then he sent young men of the

23:31 [a]Hebrew *Nahar,* the Euphrates

23:20, 21 My name is in Him: The full presence of God dwells with the Angel. See also Col. 2:9. The "Angel of the LORD" in the OT is a visible manifestation of God Himself. In many passages He is also called "the LORD" (see Gen. 16:7, 13; Judg. 6:12, 14; 13:21, 22) and speaks as God Himself (Gen. 22:11, 12; 31:11–13). Evidently He is the second Person of the Trinity, who later became incarnate as Jesus Christ (see John 1:18; also Is. 6:1 and John 12:41).

23:32, 33 God's people are not to compromise their standards but are to be separated from the world.

children of Israel, who offered burnt offer-
ings and sacrificed peace offerings of oxen
to the LORD. 6And Moses took half the
blood and put *it* in basins, and half the
blood he sprinkled on the altar. 7Then he
took the Book of the Covenant and read in
the hearing of the people. And they said,
"All that the LORD has said we will do, and
be obedient." 8And Moses took the blood,
sprinkled *it* on the people, and said, "This
is the blood of the covenant which the
LORD has made with you according to all
these words."

On the Mountain with God

9Then Moses went up, also Aaron,
Nā'dab, and A·bī'hū, and seventy of the
elders of Israel, 10and they saw the God of
Israel. And *there was* under His feet as it
were a paved work of sapphire stone, and
it was like the very heavens in *its* clarity.
11But on the nobles of the children of Israel
He did not lay His hand. So they saw God,
and they ate and drank.

12Then the LORD said to Moses, "Come
up to Me on the mountain and be there;
and I will give you tablets of stone, and the
law and commandments which I have
written, that you may teach them."

13So Moses arose with his assistant
Joshua, and Moses went up to the moun-
tain of God. 14And he said to the elders,
"Wait here for us until we come back to
you. Indeed, Aaron and Hur *are* with you.
If any man has a difficulty, let him go to
them." 15Then Moses went up into the
mountain, and a cloud covered the moun-
tain.

16Now the glory of the LORD rested on
Mount Sinai, and the cloud covered it six
days. And on the seventh day He called to
Moses out of the midst of the cloud. 17The
sight of the glory of the LORD *was* like a
consuming fire on the top of the mountain
in the eyes of the children of Israel. 18So
Moses went into the midst of the cloud and
went up into the mountain. And Moses
was on the mountain forty days and forty
nights.

CHAPTER 25

Offerings for the Sanctuary

Then the LORD spoke to Moses, saying:
2"Speak to the children of Israel, that they
bring Me an offering. From everyone who
gives it willingly with his heart you shall
take My offering. 3And this *is* the offering
which you shall take from them: gold, sil-
ver, and bronze; 4blue, purple, and scarlet
thread, fine linen, and goats' *hair;* 5ram
skins dyed red, badger skins, and acacia
wood; 6oil for the light, and spices for the
anointing oil and for the sweet incense;
7onyx stones, and stones to be set in the
ephod and in the breastplate. 8And let
them make Me a sanctuary, that I may
dwell among them. 9According to all that I
show you, *that is,* the pattern of the taber-
nacle and the pattern of all its furnishings,
just so you shall make *it.*

The Ark of the Testimony

10"And they shall make an ark of acacia
wood; two and a half cubits *shall be* its
length, a cubit and a half its width, and a
cubit and a half its height. 11And you shall
overlay it with pure gold, inside and out
you shall overlay it, and shall make on it a
molding of gold all around. 12You shall cast
four rings of gold for it, and put *them* in its
four corners; two rings *shall be* on one side,

24:6 A covenant was sealed by solemn oaths in which each party called down retribution upon his own head if he broke the agreement. These oaths were sealed in blood. **The blood** thrown on the altar symbolized God's oath, while that thrown on the people (v. 8) symbolized theirs. In such covenants both parties called upon God to strike them dead if they broke their oath (for God swearing by Himself, see Heb. 6:13, 14).

25:8 The tabernacle was to provide a place where God might dwell among His people. His glory previously covered the mountain. Now it would fill the place of worship.

and two rings on the other side. 13And you
shall make poles *of* acacia wood, and over-
lay them with gold. 14You shall put the
poles into the rings on the sides of the ark,
that the ark may be carried by them. 15The
poles shall be in the rings of the ark; they
shall not be taken from it. 16And you shall
put into the ark the Testimony which I will
give you.
17"You shall make a mercy seat of pure
gold; two and a half cubits *shall be* its
length and a cubit and a half its width.
18And you shall make two cherubim of
gold; of hammered work you shall make
them at the two ends of the mercy seat.
19Make one cherub at one end, and the
other cherub at the other end; you shall
make the cherubim at the two ends of it *of*
one piece with the mercy seat. 20And the
cherubim shall stretch out *their* wings
above, covering the mercy seat with their
wings, and they shall face one another; the
faces of the cherubim *shall be* toward the
mercy seat. 21You shall put the mercy seat
on top of the ark, and in the ark you shall
put the Testimony that I will give you.
22And there I will meet with you, and I will
speak with you from above the mercy seat,
from between the two cherubim which *are*
on the ark of the Testimony, about every-
thing which I will give you in command-
ment to the children of Israel.

The Table for the Showbread

23"You shall also make a table of acacia
wood; two cubits *shall be* its length, a cubit
its width, and a cubit and a half its height.
24And you shall overlay it with pure gold,
and make a molding of gold all around.
25You shall make for it a frame of a hand-
breadth all around, and you shall make a
gold molding for the frame all around.
26And you shall make for it four rings of
gold, and put the rings on the four corners
that *are* at its four legs. 27The rings shall be
close to the frame, as holders for the poles
to bear the table. 28And you shall make the
poles of acacia wood, and overlay them
with gold, that the table may be carried
with them. 29You shall make its dishes, its
pans, its pitchers, and its bowls for pour-
ing. You shall make them of pure gold.
30And you shall set the showbread on the
table before Me always.

The Gold Lampstand

31"You shall also make a lampstand of
pure gold; the lampstand shall be of ham-
mered work. Its shaft, its branches, its
bowls, its *ornamental* knobs, and flowers
shall be *of one piece*. 32And six branches
shall come out of its sides: three branches
of the lampstand out of one side, and three
branches of the lampstand out of the other
side. 33Three bowls *shall be* made like al-
mond *blossoms* on one branch, *with* an *orna-*
mental knob and a flower, and three bowls
made like almond *blossoms* on the other
branch, *with* an *ornamental* knob and a
flower—and so for the six branches that
come out of the lampstand. 34On the lamp-
stand itself four bowls *shall be* made like al-
mond *blossoms, each with* its *ornamental*
knob and flower. 35And *there shall be* a knob
under the *first* two branches of the same, a
knob under the *second* two branches of the
same, and a knob under the *third* two
branches of the same, according to the six
branches that extend from the lampstand.
36Their knobs and their branches *shall be of*
one piece; all of it *shall be* one hammered
piece of pure gold. 37You shall make seven
lamps for it, and they shall arrange its
lamps so that they give light in front of it.
38And its wick-trimmers and their trays
shall be of pure gold. 39It shall be made of a
talent of pure gold, with all these utensils.

25:21 The **mercy seat** was a covering for the ark, and as such covered the law inside the ark. The blood sprinkled on that cover (Lev. 16:14) would silence the broken law's cries for Israel's destruction because of their broken oath.

40And see to it that you make *them* accord-
ing to the pattern which was shown you on
the mountain.

CHAPTER 26

The Tabernacle

"Moreover you shall make the taberna-
cle *with* ten curtains *of* fine woven linen
and blue, purple, and scarlet *thread;* with
artistic designs of cherubim you shall
weave them. 2The length of each curtain
shall be twenty-eight cubits, and the width
of each curtain four cubits. And every one
of the curtains shall have the same mea-
surements. 3Five curtains shall be coupled
to one another, and *the other* five curtains
shall be coupled to one another. 4And you
shall make loops of blue *yarn* on the edge
of the curtain on the selvedge of *one* set,
and likewise you shall do on the outer
edge of *the other* curtain of the second set.
5Fifty loops you shall make in the one cur-
tain, and fifty loops you shall make on the
edge of the curtain that *is* on the end of the
second set, that the loops may be clasped
to one another. 6And you shall make fifty
clasps of gold, and couple the curtains to-
gether with the clasps, so that it may be
one tabernacle.

7"You shall also make curtains of goats'
hair, to be a tent over the tabernacle. You
shall make eleven curtains. 8The length of
each curtain *shall be* thirty cubits, and the
width of each curtain four cubits; and the
eleven curtains shall all have the same
measurements. 9And you shall couple five
curtains by themselves and six curtains by
themselves, and you shall double over the
sixth curtain at the forefront of the tent.
10You shall make fifty loops on the edge of
the curtain that is outermost in *one* set, and
fifty loops on the edge of the curtain of the
second set. 11And you shall make fifty
bronze clasps, put the clasps into the loops,
and couple the tent together, that it may be
one. 12The remnant that remains of the cur-
tains of the tent, the half curtain that re-
mains, shall hang over the back of the
tabernacle. 13And a cubit on one side and a
cubit on the other side, of what remains of
the length of the curtains of the tent, shall
hang over the sides of the tabernacle, on
this side and on that side, to cover it.

14"You shall also make a covering of ram
skins dyed red for the tent, and a covering
of badger skins above that.

15"And for the tabernacle you shall
make the boards of acacia wood, standing
upright. 16Ten cubits *shall be* the length of a
board, and a cubit and a half *shall be* the
width of each board. 17Two tenons *shall be*
in each board for binding one to another.
Thus you shall make for all the boards of
the tabernacle. 18And you shall make the
boards for the tabernacle, twenty boards
for the south side. 19You shall make forty
sockets of silver under the twenty boards:
two sockets under each of the boards for its
two tenons. 20And for the second side of
the tabernacle, the north side, *there shall be*
twenty boards 21and their forty sockets of
silver: two sockets under each of the
boards. 22For the far side of the tabernacle,
westward, you shall make six boards.
23And you shall also make two boards for
the two back corners of the tabernacle.
24They shall be coupled together at the bot-
tom and they shall be coupled together at
the top by one ring. Thus it shall be for
both of them. They shall be for the two cor-
ners. 25So there shall be eight boards with
their sockets of silver—sixteen sockets—
two sockets under each of the boards.

26"And you shall make bars of acacia
wood: five for the boards on one side of the
tabernacle, 27five bars for the boards on the
other side of the tabernacle, and five bars

25:40 Moses was to follow strictly the **pattern** God showed him. Nothing was left to his own ingenuity. In all spiritual matters we are to follow the Lord's leading precisely; any deviation from His will can be disastrous.

for the boards of the side of the tabernacle, for the far side westward. 28The middle bar shall pass through the midst of the boards from end to end. 29You shall overlay the boards with gold, make their rings of gold *as* holders for the bars, and overlay the bars with gold. 30And you shall raise up the tabernacle according to its pattern which you were shown on the mountain.

31"You shall make a veil woven of blue, purple, and scarlet *thread,* and fine woven linen. It shall be woven with an artistic design of cherubim. 32You shall hang it upon the four pillars of acacia *wood* overlaid with gold. Their hooks *shall be* gold, upon four sockets of silver. 33And you shall hang the veil from the clasps. Then you shall bring the ark of the Testimony in there, behind the veil. The veil shall be a divider for you between the holy *place* and the Most Holy. 34You shall put the mercy seat upon the ark of the Testimony in the Most Holy. 35You shall set the table outside the veil, and the lampstand across from the table on the side of the tabernacle toward the south; and you shall put the table on the north side.

36"You shall make a screen for the door of the tabernacle, *woven of* blue, purple, and scarlet *thread,* and fine woven linen, made by a weaver. 37And you shall make for the screen five pillars of acacia *wood,* and overlay them with gold; their hooks *shall be* gold, and you shall cast five sockets of bronze for them.

CHAPTER 27

The Altar of Burnt Offering

"You shall make an altar of acacia wood, five cubits long and five cubits wide—the altar shall be square—and its height *shall be* three cubits. 2You shall make its horns on its four corners; its horns shall be of one piece with it. And you shall overlay it with bronze. 3Also you shall make its pans to receive its ashes, and its shovels and its basins and its forks and its firepans; you shall make all its utensils of bronze. 4You shall make a grate for it, a network of bronze; and on the network you shall make four bronze rings at its four corners. 5You shall put it under the rim of the altar beneath, that the network may be midway up the altar. 6And you shall make poles for the altar, poles of acacia wood, and overlay them with bronze. 7The poles shall be put in the rings, and the poles shall be on the two sides of the altar to bear it. 8You shall make it hollow with boards; as it was shown you on the mountain, so shall they make *it.*

The Court of the Tabernacle

9"You shall also make the court of the tabernacle. For the south side *there shall be* hangings for the court *made of* fine woven linen, one hundred cubits long for one side. 10And its twenty pillars and their twenty sockets *shall be* bronze. The hooks of the pillars and their bands *shall be* silver. 11Likewise along the length of the north side *there shall be* hangings one hundred *cubits* long, with its twenty pillars and their twenty sockets of bronze, and the hooks of the pillars and their bands of silver.

12"And along the width of the court on the west side *shall be* hangings of fifty cubits, with their ten pillars and their ten sockets. 13The width of the court on the east side *shall be* fifty cubits. 14The hangings on *one* side *of the gate shall be* fifteen cubits,

---

26:31–35 Entering the tabernacle complex from the east and moving westward, one would encounter, in order, the altar of burnt offering, the bronze laver, and the tabernacle proper. *Tabernacle* here refers to the tent, including the **holy place** and the **Most Holy**; in other places it refers to the entire complex, including the curtained court in which the tent stood. Continuing westward into the holy place, one would find the table of showbread on the north side facing the gold **lampstand** to the south, then the altar of incense, and finally the **veil**, beyond which lay the Most Holy, containing the ark.

with their three pillars and their three sock-
ets. 15And on the other side *shall be* hang-
ings of fifteen *cubits, with* their three pillars
and their three sockets.
16"For the gate of the court *there shall be* a
screen twenty cubits long, *woven of* blue,
purple, and scarlet *thread,* and fine woven
linen, made by a weaver. It *shall have* four
pillars and four sockets. 17All the pillars
around the court shall have bands of silver;
their hooks *shall be* of silver and their sock-
ets of bronze. 18The length of the court *shall*
be one hundred cubits, the width fifty
throughout, and the height five cubits,
made of fine woven linen, and its sockets of
bronze. 19All the utensils of the tabernacle
for all its service, all its pegs, and all the
pegs of the court, *shall be* of bronze.

The Care of the Lampstand

20"And you shall command the children
of Israel that they bring you pure oil of
pressed olives for the light, to cause the
lamp to burn continually. 21In the taberna-
cle of meeting, outside the veil which *is* be-
fore the Testimony, Aaron and his sons
shall tend it from evening until morning
before the LORD. *It shall be* a statute forever
to their generations on behalf of the chil-
dren of Israel.

CHAPTER 28

Garments for the Priesthood

"Now take Aaron your brother, and his
sons with him, from among the children of
Israel, that he may minister to Me as priest,
Aaron *and* Aaron's sons: Nā'dab, A·bī'hū,
El·ē·ā'zar, and Ith'a·mar. 2And you shall
make holy garments for Aaron your
brother, for glory and for beauty. 3So you
shall speak to all *who are* gifted artisans,
whom I have filled with the spirit of wis-
dom, that they may make Aaron's gar-
ments, to consecrate him, that he may min-
ister to Me as priest. 4And these *are* the
garments which they shall make: a breast-
plate, an ephod,[a] a robe, a skillfully woven
tunic, a turban, and a sash. So they shall
make holy garments for Aaron your
brother and his sons, that he may minister
to Me as priest.

The Ephod

5"They shall take the gold, blue, purple,
and scarlet *thread,* and the fine linen, 6and
they shall make the ephod of gold, blue,
purple, *and* scarlet *thread,* and fine woven
linen, artistically worked. 7It shall have
two shoulder straps joined at its two
edges, and *so* it shall be joined together.
8And the intricately woven band of the
ephod, which *is* on it, shall be of the same
workmanship, *made of* gold, blue, purple,
and scarlet *thread,* and fine woven linen.
9"Then you shall take two onyx stones
and engrave on them the names of the sons
of Israel: 10six of their names on one stone
and six names on the other stone, in order
of their birth. 11With the work of an en-
graver in stone, *like* the engravings of a
signet, you shall engrave the two stones
with the names of the sons of Israel. You
shall set them in settings of gold. 12And
you shall put the two stones on the shoul-
ders of the ephod *as* memorial stones for
the sons of Israel. So Aaron shall bear
their names before the LORD on his two
shoulders as a memorial. 13You shall also

28:4 [a]That is, an ornamented vest

27:20, 21 The **oil** used in the lampstand was obtained by beating or pressing olives. A symbol for the Holy Spirit, the oil was to be **pure**, the best. We are never to offer God anything that is mediocre.

28:2–14 Even the choice of clothing was not left to the personal tastes of those who wore them. For sacred duties they were to be dressed in carefully specified holy garments. The **ephod** (v. 6) was a multicolored apron for the lower part of the body, and held up by **two shoulder straps** (v. 7). On each shoulder was set an onyx stone engraved with the names of six tribes of Israel.

make settings of gold, [14]and you shall make two chains of pure gold like braided cords, and fasten the braided chains to the settings.

The Breastplate

[15]"You shall make the breastplate of judgment. Artistically woven according to the workmanship of the ephod you shall make it: of gold, blue, purple, and scarlet *thread,* and fine woven linen, you shall make it. [16]It shall be doubled into a square: a span *shall be* its length, and a span *shall be* its width. [17]And you shall put settings of stones in it, four rows of stones: *The first* row *shall be* a sardius, a topaz, and an emerald; *this shall be* the first row; [18]the second row *shall be* a turquoise, a sapphire, and a diamond; [19]the third row, a jacinth, an agate, and an amethyst; [20]and the fourth row, a beryl, an onyx, and a jasper. They shall be set in gold settings. [21]And the stones shall have the names of the sons of Israel, twelve according to their names, *like* the engravings of a signet, each one with its own name; they shall be according to the twelve tribes.

[22]"You shall make chains for the breastplate at the end, like braided cords of pure gold. [23]And you shall make two rings of gold for the breastplate, and put the two rings on the two ends of the breastplate. [24]Then you shall put the two braided *chains* of gold in the two rings which are on the ends of the breastplate; [25]and the *other* two ends of the two braided *chains* you shall fasten to the two settings, and put them on the shoulder straps of the ephod in the front.

[26]"You shall make two rings of gold, and put them on the two ends of the breastplate, on the edge of it, which is on the inner side of the ephod. [27]And two *other* rings of gold you shall make, and put them on the two shoulder straps, underneath the ephod toward its front, right at the seam above the intricately woven band of the ephod. [28]They shall bind the breastplate by means of its rings to the rings of the ephod, using a blue cord, so that it is above the intricately woven band of the ephod, and so that the breastplate does not come loose from the ephod.

[29]"So Aaron shall bear the names of the sons of Israel on the breastplate of judgment over his heart, when he goes into the holy *place,* as a memorial before the LORD continually. [30]And you shall put in the breastplate of judgment the Ū'rim and the Thum'mim,[a] and they shall be over Aaron's heart when he goes in before the LORD. So Aaron shall bear the judgment of the children of Israel over his heart before the LORD continually.

Other Priestly Garments

[31]"You shall make the robe of the ephod all of blue. [32]There shall be an opening for his head in the middle of it; it shall have a woven binding all around its opening, like the opening in a coat of mail, so that it does not tear. [33]And upon its hem you shall make pomegranates of blue, purple, and scarlet, all around its hem, and bells of gold between them all around: [34]a golden bell and a pomegranate, a golden bell and a pomegranate, upon the hem of the robe all around. [35]And it shall be upon Aaron when he ministers, and its sound will be heard when he goes into the holy *place*

28:30 [a]Literally *the Lights and the Perfections* (compare Leviticus 8:8)

28:16, 17 The breastplate, attached to the ephod and made of similar materials. On the breastplate were 12 precious stones arranged in **four rows**. Each stone was engraved with the name of one of the tribes of Israel. Thus the names of God's people were always over the heart (v. 29) of the priest when he entered God's presence.

28:35 Only the high priest could represent the people before God, and only he could wear this robe. If he appeared before God except in his office as high priest, God's holiness would destroy him.

before the LORD and when he comes out, that he may not die.

[36]"You shall also make a plate of pure gold and engrave on it, *like* the engraving of a signet:

HOLINESS TO THE LORD.

[37]And you shall put it on a blue cord, that it may be on the turban; it shall be on the front of the turban. [38]So it shall be on Aaron's forehead, that Aaron may bear the iniquity of the holy things which the children of Israel hallow in all their holy gifts; and it shall always be on his forehead, that they may be accepted before the LORD.

[39]"You shall skillfully weave the tunic of fine linen *thread,* you shall make the turban of fine linen, and you shall make the sash of woven work.

[40]"For Aaron's sons you shall make tunics, and you shall make sashes for them. And you shall make hats for them, for glory and beauty. [41]So you shall put them on Aaron your brother and on his sons with him. You shall anoint them, consecrate them, and sanctify them, that they may minister to Me as priests. [42]And you shall make for them linen trousers to cover their nakedness; they shall reach from the waist to the thighs. [43]They shall be on Aaron and on his sons when they come into the tabernacle of meeting, or when they come near the altar to minister in the holy *place,* that they do not incur iniquity and die. *It shall be* a statute forever to him and his descendants after him.

CHAPTER 29

Aaron and His Sons Consecrated

"And this is what you shall do to them to hallow them for ministering to Me as priests: Take one young bull and two rams without blemish, [2]and unleavened bread, unleavened cakes mixed with oil, and unleavened wafers anointed with oil (you shall make them of wheat flour). [3]You shall put them in one basket and bring them in the basket, with the bull and the two rams.

[4]"And Aaron and his sons you shall bring to the door of the tabernacle of meeting, and you shall wash them with water. [5]Then you shall take the garments, put the tunic on Aaron, and the robe of the ephod, the ephod, and the breastplate, and gird him with the intricately woven band of the ephod. [6]You shall put the turban on his head, and put the holy crown on the turban. [7]And you shall take the anointing oil, pour *it* on his head, and anoint him. [8]Then you shall bring his sons and put tunics on them. [9]And you shall gird them with sashes, Aaron and his sons, and put the hats on them. The priesthood shall be theirs for a perpetual statute. So you shall consecrate Aaron and his sons.

[10]"You shall also have the bull brought before the tabernacle of meeting, and Aaron and his sons shall put their hands on the head of the bull. [11]Then you shall kill the bull before the LORD, *by* the door of the tabernacle of meeting. [12]You shall take *some* of the blood of the bull and put *it* on the horns of the altar with your finger, and

---

28:36–38 The **plate** was part of the crown of gold worn by the priest. The words inscribed on it, **HOLINESS TO THE LORD**, reminded everyone that the priest was set apart for God's work. It also reminds us of God's nonnegotiable summons to a holy life.

29:1–46 The entire chapter is devoted to instructions for the consecration of Aaron and his sons to the priesthood. It is not enough that the priests be correctly dressed. Moses must **hallow them for ministering** (v. 1). The Hebrew verb means to "be holy, be sanctified, be set apart." Holiness on the turban (28:36, 37) must be matched by holiness of heart. This emphasis permeates the chapter from beginning to end.

29:9 Consecrate in this verse is not "sanctify," but "ordain." The Hebrew is lit. "fill the hand of." The ordained are those whose hands are full of the things involved in doing God's work.

pour all the blood beside the base of the al-
tar. 13And you shall take all the fat that cov-
ers the entrails, the fatty lobe *attached* to the
liver, and the two kidneys and the fat that
is on them, and burn *them* on the altar. 14But
the flesh of the bull, with its skin and its of-
fal, you shall burn with fire outside the
camp. It *is* a sin offering.

15"You shall also take one ram, and
Aaron and his sons shall put their hands
on the head of the ram; 16and you shall kill
the ram, and you shall take its blood and
sprinkle *it* all around on the altar. 17Then
you shall cut the ram in pieces, wash its en-
trails and its legs, and put *them* with its
pieces and with its head. 18And you shall
burn the whole ram on the altar. It *is* a
burnt offering to the LORD; it *is* a sweet
aroma, an offering made by fire to the
LORD.

19"You shall also take the other ram, and
Aaron and his sons shall put their hands
on the head of the ram. 20Then you shall
kill the ram, and take some of its blood and
put *it* on the tip of the right ear of Aaron
and on the tip of the right ear of his sons,
on the thumb of their right hand and on
the big toe of their right foot, and sprinkle
the blood all around on the altar. 21And
you shall take some of the blood that is on
the altar, and some of the anointing oil, and
sprinkle *it* on Aaron and on his garments,
on his sons and on the garments of his sons
with him; and he and his garments shall be
hallowed, and his sons and his sons' gar-
ments with him.

22"Also you shall take the fat of the ram,
the fat tail, the fat that covers the entrails,
the fatty lobe *attached to* the liver, the two
kidneys and the fat on them, the right
thigh (for it *is* a ram of consecration), 23one
loaf of bread, one cake *made with* oil, and
one wafer from the basket of the unleav-
ened bread that *is* before the LORD; 24and
you shall put all these in the hands of
Aaron and in the hands of his sons, and
you shall wave them *as* a wave offering be-
fore the LORD. 25You shall receive them
back from their hands and burn *them* on
the altar as a burnt offering, as a sweet
aroma before the LORD. It *is* an offering
made by fire to the LORD.

26"Then you shall take the breast of the
ram of Aaron's consecration and wave it *as*
a wave offering before the LORD; and it
shall be your portion. 27And from the ram
of the consecration you shall consecrate
the breast of the wave offering which is
waved, and the thigh of the heave offering
which is raised, of *that* which *is* for Aaron
and of *that* which is for his sons. 28It shall be
from the children of Israel *for* Aaron and
his sons by a statute forever. For it is a
heave offering; it shall be a heave offering
from the children of Israel from the sacri-
fices of their peace offerings, *that is,* their
heave offering to the LORD.

29"And the holy garments of Aaron shall
be his sons' after him, to be anointed in
them and to be consecrated in them. 30That
son who becomes priest in his place shall
put them on for seven days, when he en-
ters the tabernacle of meeting to minister
in the holy *place.*

31"And you shall take the ram of the
consecration and boil its flesh in the holy
place. 32Then Aaron and his sons shall eat
the flesh of the ram, and the bread that *is* in
the basket, *by* the door of the tabernacle of
meeting. 33They shall eat those things with
which the atonement was made, to conse-
crate *and* to sanctify them; but an outsider
shall not eat *them,* because they *are* holy.
34And if any of the flesh of the consecra-
tion offerings, or of the bread, remains un-
til the morning, then you shall burn the
remainder with fire. It shall not be eaten,
because it *is* holy.

29:20 Many scholars believe that the blood of the ram was applied to the **right ear** to signify that the priest would hear only the word of the Lord, to his **thumb** to symbolize his dedication to properly fulfill his duties as priest, and to his **toe** to demonstrate that he would walk in the path of righteousness.

35"Thus you shall do to Aaron and his
sons, according to all that I have com-
manded you. Seven days you shall conse-
crate them. 36And you shall offer a bull
every day *as* a sin offering for atonement.
You shall cleanse the altar when you make
atonement for it, and you shall anoint it to
sanctify it. 37Seven days you shall make
atonement for the altar and sanctify it. And
the altar shall be most holy. Whatever
touches the altar must be holy.[a]

The Daily Offerings

38"Now this *is* what you shall offer on
the altar: two lambs of the first year, day by
day continually. 39One lamb you shall offer
in the morning, and the other lamb you
shall offer at twilight. 40With the one lamb
shall be one-tenth *of an ephah* of flour
mixed with one-fourth of a hin of pressed
oil, and one-fourth of a hin of wine *as* a
drink offering. 41And the other lamb you
shall offer at twilight; and you shall offer
with it the grain offering and the drink of-
fering, as in the morning, for a sweet
aroma, an offering made by fire to the
LORD. 42*This shall be* a continual burnt offer-
ing throughout your generations *at* the
door of the tabernacle of meeting before
the LORD, where I will meet you to speak
with you. 43And there I will meet with the
children of Israel, and *the tabernacle* shall be
sanctified by My glory. 44So I will conse-
crate the tabernacle of meeting and the al-
tar. I will also consecrate both Aaron and
his sons to minister to Me as priests. 45I will
dwell among the children of Israel and will
be their God. 46And they shall know that I
am the LORD their God, who brought them
up out of the land of Egypt, that I may dwell
among them. I *am* the LORD their God.

CHAPTER 30

The Altar of Incense

"You shall make an altar to burn incense
on; you shall make it of acacia wood. 2A cu-

An Altar of Remembrance

Jay Kesler

In Sunday school, many children are taught to sing "Count your blessings, name them one by one . . . ." It might be of great value to us as grandparents to take time to start at the beginning of our experience—perhaps the beginning of our marriage—and list the examples of God's faithfulness in our lives during this period. Then, during times of family conversation, we can share with our grandchildren these signs of God's faithfulness and His provision. Our experiences will give them "stones" in their lives which, combined with their own experience of God's goodness, will enable them to build an altar of remembrance unto the Lord. ✦

bit *shall be* its length and a cubit its width—
it shall be square—and two cubits *shall be*
its height. Its horns *shall be* of one piece
with it. 3And you shall overlay its top, its
sides all around, and its horns with pure
gold; and you shall make for it a molding
of gold all around. 4Two gold rings you
shall make for it, under the molding on
both its sides. You shall place *them* on its
two sides, and they will be holders for the
poles with which to bear it. 5You shall
make the poles of acacia wood, and over-
lay them with gold. 6And you shall put it
before the veil that *is* before the ark of the
Testimony, before the mercy seat that *is*
over the Testimony, where I will meet with
you.

7"Aaron shall burn on it sweet incense
every morning; when he tends the lamps,
he shall burn incense on it. 8And when
Aaron lights the lamps at twilight, he shall

29:37 [a]Compare Numbers 4:15 and Haggai 2:11–13

burn incense on it, a perpetual incense be-
fore the LORD throughout your genera-
tions. [9]You shall not offer strange incense
on it, or a burnt offering, or a grain offer-
ing; nor shall you pour a drink offering on
it. [10]And Aaron shall make atonement
upon its horns once a year with the blood
of the sin offering of atonement; once a
year he shall make atonement upon it
throughout your generations. It *is* most
holy to the LORD."

The Ransom Money

[11]Then the LORD spoke to Moses, saying:
[12]"When you take the census of the chil-
dren of Israel for their number, then every
man shall give a ransom for himself to the
LORD, when you number them, that there
may be no plague among them when *you*
number them. [13]This is what everyone
among those who are numbered shall give:
half a shekel according to the shekel of the
sanctuary (a shekel *is* twenty gerahs). The
half-shekel *shall be* an offering to the LORD.
[14]Everyone included among those who are
numbered, from twenty years old and
above, shall give an offering to the LORD.
[15]The rich shall not give more and the poor
shall not give less than half a shekel, when
you give an offering to the LORD, to make
atonement for yourselves. [16]And you shall
take the atonement money of the children
of Israel, and shall appoint it for the service
of the tabernacle of meeting, that it may be
a memorial for the children of Israel before
the LORD, to make atonement for your-
selves."

The Bronze Laver

[17]Then the LORD spoke to Moses, saying:
[18]"You shall also make a laver of bronze,
with its base also of bronze, for washing.
You shall put it between the tabernacle of
meeting and the altar. And you shall put
water in it, [19]for Aaron and his sons shall
wash their hands and their feet in water
from it. [20]When they go into the tabernacle
of meeting, or when they come near the al-
tar to minister, to burn an offering made by
fire to the LORD, they shall wash with wa-
ter, lest they die. [21]So they shall wash their
hands and their feet, lest they die. And it
shall be a statute forever to them—to him
and his descendants throughout their gen-
erations."

The Holy Anointing Oil

[22]Moreover the LORD spoke to Moses,
saying: [23]"Also take for yourself quality
spices—five hundred *shekels* of liquid
myrrh, half as much sweet-smelling cinna-
mon (two hundred and fifty *shekels*), two
hundred and fifty *shekels* of sweet-smelling
cane, [24]five hundred *shekels* of cassia, ac-
cording to the shekel of the sanctuary, and
a hin of olive oil. [25]And you shall make
from these a holy anointing oil, an oint-
ment compounded according to the art of
the perfumer. It shall be a holy anointing
oil. [26]With it you shall anoint the tabernacle
of meeting and the ark of the Testimony;
[27]the table and all its utensils, the lamp-
stand and its utensils, and the altar of in-
cense; [28]the altar of burnt offering with all
its utensils, and the laver and its base.
[29]You shall consecrate them, that they may
be most holy; whatever touches them must
be holy.[a] [30]And you shall anoint Aaron and
his sons, and consecrate them, that *they*
may minister to Me as priests.

[31]"And you shall speak to the children
of Israel, saying: 'This shall be a holy
anointing oil to Me throughout your gen-
erations. [32]It shall not be poured on man's
flesh; nor shall you make *any other* like it,
according to its composition. It *is* holy, *and*
it shall be holy to you. [33]Whoever com-
pounds *any* like it, or whoever puts *any* of

30:29 [a]Compare Numbers 4:15 and Haggai 2:11–13

30:10 Once a year, on the Day of Atonement (Lev. 16). Not only were priests holy (ch. 29), but so were altars. Because of their relation to the Holy One, sanctity extended to Israel's days, seasons, individuals, places, and objects.

it on an outsider, shall be cut off from his
people.' "

The Incense

[34]And the LORD said to Moses: "Take
sweet spices, stacte and onycha and gal-
banum, and pure frankincense with *these*
sweet spices; there shall be equal amounts
of each. [35]You shall make of these an in-
cense, a compound according to the art of
the perfumer, salted, pure, *and* holy. [36]And
you shall beat *some* of it very fine, and put
some of it before the Testimony in the
tabernacle of meeting where I will meet
with you. It shall be most holy to you. [37]But
as for the incense which you shall make,
you shall not make any for yourselves, ac-
cording to its composition. It shall be to
you holy for the LORD. [38]Whoever makes
any like it, to smell it, he shall be cut off
from his people."

CHAPTER 31

Artisans for Building the Tabernacle

Then the LORD spoke to Moses, saying:
[2]"See, I have called by name Bez'a·lel the
son of Ū'rī, the son of Hur, of the tribe of
Judah. [3]And I have filled him with the
Spirit of God, in wisdom, in understand-
ing, in knowledge, and in all *manner of*
workmanship, [4]to design artistic works,
to work in gold, in silver, in bronze, [5]in
cutting jewels for setting, in carving
wood, and to work in all *manner of* work-
manship.

[6]"And I, indeed I, have appointed with
him A·hō'li·ab the son of A·his'a·mach, of
the tribe of Dan; and I have put wisdom in
the hearts of all the gifted artisans, that
they may make all that I have commanded
you: [7]the tabernacle of meeting, the ark of
the Testimony and the mercy seat that *is* on
it, and all the furniture of the tabernacle—
[8]the table and its utensils, the pure *gold*
lampstand with all its utensils, the altar of
incense, [9]the altar of burnt offering with all
its utensils, and the laver and its base—
[10]the garments of ministry,[a] the holy gar-
ments for Aaron the priest and the gar-
ments of his sons, to minister as priests,
[11]and the anointing oil and sweet incense
for the holy *place*. According to all that I
have commanded you they shall do."

The Sabbath Law

[12]And the LORD spoke to Moses, saying,
[13]"Speak also to the children of Israel, say-
ing: 'Surely My Sabbaths you shall keep,
for it *is* a sign between Me and you
throughout your generations, that *you* may
know that I *am* the LORD who sanctifies
you. [14]You shall keep the Sabbath, there-
fore, for *it is* holy to you. Everyone who
profanes it shall surely be put to death; for
whoever does *any* work on it, that person
shall be cut off from among his people.
[15]Work shall be done for six days, but the
seventh *is* the Sabbath of rest, holy to the
LORD. Whoever does *any* work on the Sab-
bath day, he shall surely be put to death.
[16]Therefore the children of Israel shall keep
the Sabbath, to observe the Sabbath
throughout their generations *as* a perpet-
ual covenant. [17]It *is* a sign between Me and

31:10 [a]Or *woven garments*

30:33 any like it: The prohibition against duplicating the oil (or incense, v. 38) was a way of emphasizing God's transcendence. He is absolutely *other,* not a part of this world and not to be confused with it.

30:34–38 The **incense** was also to be **holy** (vv. 35–37). God's primary concern is that His people should be holy, as evidenced by the recurrence of that word in this section. By contrast "happy" does not appear at all. God wants His people to be happy, but holiness should be our priority. When our priorities are in proper order, we experience a deep peace and a satisfying joy that transcend temporal happiness.

31:3 The first person described in Scripture as **filled . . . with the Spirit of God** is not a patriarch or a prophet, but a craftsman. The work which Bezalel did could not have been done by the ordinary human spirit.

the children of Israel forever; for *in* six days
the LORD made the heavens and the earth,
and on the seventh day He rested and was
refreshed.' "

18 And when He had made an end of
speaking with him on Mount Sinai, He
gave Moses two tablets of the Testimony,
tablets of stone, written with the finger of
God.

CHAPTER 32

The Gold Calf

Now when the people saw that Moses
delayed coming down from the mountain,
the people gathered together to Aaron, and
said to him, "Come, make us gods that
shall go before us; for *as for* this Moses, the
man who brought us up out of the land of
Egypt, we do not know what has become
of him."

2 And Aaron said to them, "Break off the
golden earrings which *are* in the ears of
your wives, your sons, and your daugh-
ters, and bring *them* to me." 3 So all the peo-
ple broke off the golden earrings which
were in their ears, and brought *them* to
Aaron. 4 And he received *the gold* from their
hand, and he fashioned it with an engrav-
ing tool, and made a molded calf.

Then they said, "This *is* your god, O Is-
rael, that brought you out of the land of
Egypt!"

5 So when Aaron saw *it,* he built an altar
before it. And Aaron made a proclamation
and said, "Tomorrow *is* a feast to the
LORD." 6 Then they rose early on the next
day, offered burnt offerings, and brought
peace offerings; and the people sat down
to eat and drink, and rose up to play.

7 And the LORD said to Moses, "Go, get
down! For your people whom you brought
out of the land of Egypt have corrupted
themselves. 8 They have turned aside
quickly out of the way which I com-
manded them. They have made them-
selves a molded calf, and worshiped it and
sacrificed to it, and said, 'This *is* your god,
O Israel, that brought you out of the land
of Egypt!' " 9 And the LORD said to Moses,
"I have seen this people, and indeed it *is* a
stiff-necked people! 10 Now therefore, let
Me alone, that My wrath may burn hot
against them and I may consume them.
And I will make of you a great nation."

11 Then Moses pleaded with the LORD his
God, and said: "LORD, why does Your
wrath burn hot against Your people whom
You have brought out of the land of Egypt
with great power and with a mighty hand?
12 Why should the Egyptians speak, and
say, 'He brought them out to harm them, to
kill them in the mountains, and to con-
sume them from the face of the earth'?
Turn from Your fierce wrath, and relent
from this harm to Your people. 13 Remem-
ber Abraham, Isaac, and Israel, Your ser-
vants, to whom You swore by Your own
self, and said to them, 'I will multiply your
descendants as the stars of heaven; and all
this land that I have spoken of I give to
your descendants, and they shall inherit *it*
forever.' "[a] 14 So the LORD relented from the
harm which He said He would do to His
people.

15 And Moses turned and went down
from the mountain, and the two tablets of
the Testimony *were* in his hand. The tablets
were written on both sides; on the one *side*
and on the other they were written. 16 Now
the tablets *were* the work of God, and the
writing *was* the writing of God engraved
on the tablets.

17 And when Joshua heard the noise of

32:13 [a]Genesis 13:15 and 22:17

32:10–14 let Me alone: The people had broken the covenant and now deserved the death which their own blood oath (24:7, 8) called upon them. Yet God's compassion is so great that when one person interceded for them, His just anger was stayed. He did relent and change His mind about the harm He was going to do.

the people as they shouted, he said to Mo-
ses, "*There is* a noise of war in the camp."
[18]But he said:

"*It is* not the noise of the shout of
victory,
Nor the noise of the cry of defeat,
But the sound of singing I hear."

[19]So it was, as soon as he came near the
camp, that he saw the calf *and* the dancing.
So Moses' anger became hot, and he cast
the tablets out of his hands and broke them
at the foot of the mountain. [20]Then he took
the calf which they had made, burned *it* in
the fire, and ground *it* to powder; and he
scattered *it* on the water and made the chil-
dren of Israel drink *it*. [21]And Moses said to
Aaron, "What did this people do to you
that you have brought *so* great a sin upon
them?"
[22]So Aaron said, "Do not let the anger of
my lord become hot. You know the people,
that they *are set* on evil. [23]For they said to
me, 'Make us gods that shall go before us;
as for this Moses, the man who brought us
out of the land of Egypt, we do not know
what has become of him.' [24]And I said to
them, 'Whoever has any gold, let them
break *it* off.' So they gave *it* to me, and I
cast it into the fire, and this calf came
out."
[25]Now when Moses saw that the people
were unrestrained (for Aaron had not re-
strained them, to *their* shame among their
enemies), [26]then Moses stood in the en-
trance of the camp, and said, "Whoever *is*
on the LORD's side—*come* to me!" And all
the sons of Levi gathered themselves to-
gether to him. [27]And he said to them,
"Thus says the LORD God of Israel: 'Let
every man put his sword on his side, and
go in and out from entrance to entrance
throughout the camp, and let every man
kill his brother, every man his companion,
and every man his neighbor.' " [28]So the
sons of Levi did according to the word of
Moses. And about three thousand men of
the people fell that day. [29]Then Moses said,
"Consecrate yourselves today to the LORD,
that He may bestow on you a blessing this
day, for every man has opposed his son
and his brother."
[30]Now it came to pass on the next day
that Moses said to the people, "You have
committed a great sin. So now I will go up
to the LORD; perhaps I can make atonement
for your sin." [31]Then Moses returned to the
LORD and said, "Oh, these people have
committed a great sin, and have made for
themselves a god of gold! [32]Yet now, if You
will forgive their sin—but if not, I pray,
blot me out of Your book which You have
written."
[33]And the LORD said to Moses, "Who-
ever has sinned against Me, I will blot him
out of My book. [34]Now therefore, go, lead
the people to *the place* of which I have spo-
ken to you. Behold, My Angel shall go be-
fore you. Nevertheless, in the day when I
visit for punishment, I will visit punish-
ment upon them for their sin."
[35]So the LORD plagued the people be-
cause of what they did with the calf which
Aaron made.

CHAPTER 33

The Command to Leave Sinai

Then the LORD said to Moses, "Depart
and go up from here, you and the people
whom you have brought out of the land of
Egypt, to the land of which I swore to
Abraham, Isaac, and Jacob, saying, 'To
your descendants I will give it.' [2]And I will
send *My* Angel before you, and I will drive
out the Cā'naan·īte and the Am'o·rīte and
the Hit'tīte and the Per'iz·zīte and the

32:19 Moses could intercede for mercy on behalf of his people but that did not eliminate his feeling of great **anger** at their backsliding. The broken tablets represented the breaking of the covenant between the Israelites and God.

Hī′vīte and the Jeb′ū·sīte. 3*Go up* to a land flowing with milk and honey; for I will not go up in your midst, lest I consume you on the way, for you *are* a stiff-necked people."

4And when the people heard this bad news, they mourned, and no one put on his ornaments. 5For the LORD had said to Moses, "Say to the children of Israel, 'You *are* a stiff-necked people. I could come up into your midst in one moment and consume you. Now therefore, take off your ornaments, that I may know what to do to you.' " 6So the children of Israel stripped themselves of their ornaments by Mount Hō′reb.

Moses Meets with the LORD

7Moses took his tent and pitched it outside the camp, far from the camp, and called it the tabernacle of meeting. And it came to pass *that* everyone who sought the LORD went out to the tabernacle of meeting which *was* outside the camp. 8So it was, whenever Moses went out to the tabernacle, *that* all the people rose, and each man stood *at* his tent door and watched Moses until he had gone into the tabernacle. 9And it came to pass, when Moses entered the tabernacle, that the pillar of cloud descended and stood *at* the door of the tabernacle, and *the LORD* talked with Moses. 10All the people saw the pillar of cloud standing *at* the tabernacle door, and all the people rose and worshiped, each man *in* his tent door. 11So the LORD spoke to Moses face to face, as a man speaks to his friend. And he would return to the camp, but his servant Joshua the son of Nun, a young man, did not depart from the tabernacle.

The Promise of God's Presence

12Then Moses said to the LORD, "See, You say to me, 'Bring up this people.' But You have not let me know whom You will send with me. Yet You have said, 'I know you by name, and you have also found grace in My sight.' 13Now therefore, I pray, if I have found grace in Your sight, show me now Your way, that I may know You and that I may find grace in Your sight. And consider that this nation *is* Your people."

14And He said, "My Presence will go *with you,* and I will give you rest."

15Then he said to Him, "If Your Presence does not go *with us,* do not bring us up from here. 16For how then will it be known that Your people and I have found grace in Your sight, except You go with us? So we shall be separate, Your people and I, from all the people who *are* upon the face of the earth."

17So the LORD said to Moses, "I will also do this thing that you have spoken; for you have found grace in My sight, and I know you by name."

18And he said, "Please, show me Your glory."

19Then He said, "I will make all My goodness pass before you, and I will proclaim the name of the LORD before you. I will be gracious to whom I will be gracious, and I will have compassion on whom I will have compassion." 20But He said, "You cannot see My face; for no man shall see Me, and live." 21And the LORD said, "Here is a place by Me, and you shall stand on the rock. 22So it shall be, while My glory passes by, that I will put you in the cleft of the rock, and will cover you with My hand while I pass by. 23Then I will take

---

33:18–23 Moses requests to see God's **glory**, a physical manifestation of His transcendent reality; God responds that Moses cannot see His **face** (v. 20). There are limits placed on even a saint like Moses. All that he was granted was a fleeting sight of God's back (v. 23). God's **goodness** probably refers to all of His previous redemptive activities toward Israel. God is known not by appearance but by actions. The same should be true of His children.

away My hand, and you shall see My back;
but My face shall not be seen."

CHAPTER 34

Moses Makes New Tablets

And the LORD said to Moses, "Cut two
tablets of stone like the first *ones,* and I will
write on *these* tablets the words that were
on the first tablets which you broke. 2So be
ready in the morning, and come up in the
morning to Mount Sinai, and present your-
self to Me there on the top of the mountain.
3And no man shall come up with you, and
let no man be seen throughout all the
mountain; let neither flocks nor herds feed
before that mountain."

4So he cut two tablets of stone like the
first *ones.* Then Moses rose early in the
morning and went up Mount Sinai, as
the LORD had commanded him; and he
took in his hand the two tablets of
stone.

5Now the LORD descended in the cloud
and stood with him there, and proclaimed
the name of the LORD. 6And the LORD
passed before him and proclaimed, "The
LORD, the LORD God, merciful and gra-
cious, longsuffering, and abounding in
goodness and truth, 7keeping mercy for
thousands, forgiving iniquity and trans-
gression and sin, by no means clearing *the
guilty,* visiting the iniquity of the fathers
upon the children and the children's chil-
dren to the third and the fourth genera-
tion."

8So Moses made haste and bowed his
head toward the earth, and worshiped.
9Then he said, "If now I have found grace
in Your sight, O Lord, let my Lord, I pray,
go among us, even though we *are* a stiff-
necked people; and pardon our iniquity
and our sin, and take us as Your inheri-
tance."

The Covenant Renewed

10And He said: "Behold, I make a
covenant. Before all your people I will do
marvels such as have not been done in all
the earth, nor in any nation; and all the
people among whom you *are* shall see the
work of the LORD. For it *is* an awesome
thing that I will do with you. 11Observe
what I command you this day. Behold, I
am driving out from before you the
Am'o·rīte and the Cā'naan·īte and the
Hit'tīte and the Per'iz·zīte and the Hī'vīte
and the Jeb'ū·sīte. 12Take heed to yourself,
lest you make a covenant with the inhab-
itants of the land where you are going, lest
it be a snare in your midst. 13But you shall
destroy their altars, break their *sacred* pil-
lars, and cut down their wooden images
14(for you shall worship no other god, for
the LORD, whose name *is* Jealous, *is* a jeal-
ous God), 15lest you make a covenant with
the inhabitants of the land, and they play
the harlot with their gods and make sacri-
fice to their gods, and *one of them* invites
you and you eat of his sacrifice, 16and you
take of his daughters for your sons, and his
daughters play the harlot with their gods
and make your sons play the harlot with
their gods.

17"You shall make no molded gods for
yourselves.

18"The Feast of Unleavened Bread you
shall keep. Seven days you shall eat un-
leavened bread, as I commanded you, in
the appointed time of the month of Ā'bib;
for in the month of Ā'bib you came out
from Egypt.

19"All that open the womb *are* Mine, and
every male firstborn among your live-
stock, *whether* ox or sheep. 20But the

34:6, 7 Of all that God reveals about Himself, the most beautiful characteristic is that He is **forgiving**. To recent idolators who ought to have done better, He is the God of the second chance. The effects of our sin may reach out to the **third and the fourth generation**, but no farther (see Deut. 7:9). **by no means clearing the guilty**: Though God is great in mercy, the unrepentant wicked will be destroyed.

firstborn of a donkey you shall redeem with a lamb. And if you will not redeem *him,* then you shall break his neck. All the firstborn of your sons you shall redeem.

"And none shall appear before Me empty-handed.

21 "Six days you shall work, but on the seventh day you shall rest; in plowing time and in harvest you shall rest.

22 "And you shall observe the Feast of Weeks, of the firstfruits of wheat harvest, and the Feast of Ingathering at the year's end.

23 "Three times in the year all your men shall appear before the Lord, the LORD God of Israel. 24 For I will cast out the nations before you and enlarge your borders; neither will any man covet your land when you go up to appear before the LORD your God three times in the year.

25 "You shall not offer the blood of My sacrifice with leaven, nor shall the sacrifice of the Feast of the Passover be left until morning.

26 "The first of the firstfruits of your land you shall bring to the house of the LORD your God. You shall not boil a young goat in its mother's milk."

27 Then the LORD said to Moses, "Write these words, for according to the tenor of these words I have made a covenant with you and with Israel." 28 So he was there with the LORD forty days and forty nights; he neither ate bread nor drank water. And He wrote on the tablets the words of the covenant, the Ten Commandments.[a]

The Shining Face of Moses

29 Now it was so, when Moses came down from Mount Sinai (and the two tablets of the Testimony *were* in Moses' hand when he came down from the mountain), that Moses did not know that the skin of his face shone while he talked with Him. 30 So when Aaron and all the children of Israel saw Moses, behold, the skin of his face shone, and they were afraid to come near him. 31 Then Moses called to them, and Aaron and all the rulers of the congregation returned to him; and Moses talked with them. 32 Afterward all the children of Israel came near, and he gave them as commandments all that the LORD had spoken with him on Mount Sinai. 33 And when Moses had finished speaking with them, he put a veil on his face. 34 But whenever Moses went in before the LORD to speak with Him, he would take the veil off until he came out; and he would come out and speak to the children of Israel whatever he had been commanded. 35 And whenever the children of Israel saw the face of Moses, that the skin of Moses' face shone, then Moses would put the veil on his face again, until he went in to speak with Him.

CHAPTER 35

Sabbath Regulations

Then Moses gathered all the congregation of the children of Israel together, and said to them, "These *are* the words which the LORD has commanded *you* to do: 2 Work shall be done for six days, but the seventh day shall be a holy day for you, a Sabbath of rest to the LORD. Whoever does any work on it shall be put to death. 3 You shall kindle no fire throughout your dwellings on the Sabbath day."

Offerings for the Tabernacle

4 And Moses spoke to all the congregation of the children of Israel, saying, "This *is* the thing which the LORD commanded, saying: 5 'Take from among you an offering to the LORD. Whoever *is* of a willing heart,

34:28 [a]Literally *Ten Words*

34:35 The glow on Moses' **face** was not something of his own, but a reflection of the face of God (see 33:11). Paul refers to Moses' **veil** in 2 Cor. 3:12–16.

let him bring it as an offering to the LORD:
gold, silver, and bronze; [6]blue, purple, and
scarlet *thread,* fine linen, and goats' *hair;*
[7]ram skins dyed red, badger skins, and
acacia wood; [8]oil for the light, and spices
for the anointing oil and for the sweet in-
cense; [9]onyx stones, and stones to be set in
the ephod and in the breastplate.

Articles of the Tabernacle

[10]'All *who are* gifted artisans among you
shall come and make all that the LORD has
commanded: [11]the tabernacle, its tent, its
covering, its clasps, its boards, its bars, its
pillars, and its sockets; [12]the ark and
its poles, *with* the mercy seat, and the veil
of the covering; [13]the table and its poles, all
its utensils, and the showbread; [14]also the
lampstand for the light, its utensils, its
lamps, and the oil for the light; [15]the in-
cense altar, its poles, the anointing oil, the
sweet incense, and the screen for the door
at the entrance of the tabernacle; [16]the altar
of burnt offering with its bronze grating,
its poles, all its utensils, *and* the laver and
its base; [17]the hangings of the court, its pil-
lars, their sockets, and the screen for the
gate of the court; [18]the pegs of the taberna-
cle, the pegs of the court, and their cords;
[19]the garments of ministry,[a] for ministering
in the holy *place*—the holy garments for
Aaron the priest and the garments of his
sons, to minister as priests.' "

The Tabernacle Offerings Presented

[20]And all the congregation of the chil-
dren of Israel departed from the presence
of Moses. [21]Then everyone came whose
heart was stirred, and everyone whose
spirit was willing, *and* they brought the
LORD's offering for the work of the taber-
nacle of meeting, for all its service, and for
the holy garments. [22]They came, both men
and women, as many as had a willing
heart, *and* brought earrings and nose rings,
rings and necklaces, all jewelry of gold,
that is, every man who *made* an offering of
gold to the LORD. [23]And every man, with
whom was found blue, purple, and scarlet
thread, fine linen, goats' *hair,* red skins of
rams, and badger skins, brought *them.*
[24]Everyone who offered an offering of sil-
ver or bronze brought the LORD's offering.
And everyone with whom was found aca-
cia wood for any work of the service,
brought *it.* [25]All the women *who were*
gifted artisans spun yarn with their
hands, and brought what they had spun, of
blue, purple, *and* scarlet, and fine
linen. [26]And all the women whose
hearts stirred with wisdom spun yarn of
goats' *hair.* [27]The rulers brought onyx
stones, and the stones to be set in the
ephod and in the breastplate, [28]and spices
and oil for the light, for the anointing oil,
and for the sweet incense. [29]The children of
Israel brought a freewill offering to the
LORD, all the men and women whose
hearts were willing to bring *material* for all
kinds of work which the LORD, by the
hand of Moses, had commanded to be
done.

The Artisans Called by God

[30]And Moses said to the children of Is-
rael, "See, the LORD has called by name
Bez'a·lel the son of Ū'rī, the son of Hur, of
the tribe of Judah; [31]and He has filled him
with the Spirit of God, in wisdom and un-
derstanding, in knowledge and all manner
of workmanship, [32]to design artistic works,
to work in gold and silver and bronze, [33]in
cutting jewels for setting, in carving wood,
and to work in all manner of artistic work-
manship.

[34]"And He has put in his heart the abil-
ity to teach, *in* him and A·hō'li·ab the son
of A·his'a·mach, of the tribe of Dan. [35]He

35:19 [a]Or *woven garments*

35:30–35 The tabernacle workers were as much **called** by God to manual work as was Moses to his work. A calling from God is a serious, sacred matter.

has filled them with skill to do all manner of work of the engraver and the designer and the tapestry maker, in blue, purple, and scarlet *thread,* and fine linen, and of the weaver—those who do every work and those who design artistic works.

CHAPTER 36

"And Bez'a·lel and A·hō'li·ab, and every gifted artisan in whom the LORD has put wisdom and understanding, to know how to do all manner of work for the service of the sanctuary, shall do according to all that the LORD has commanded."

The People Give More than Enough

[2]Then Moses called Bez'a·lel and A·hō'li·ab, and every gifted artisan in whose heart the LORD had put wisdom, everyone whose heart was stirred, to come and do the work. [3]And they received from Moses all the offering which the children of Israel had brought for the work of the service of making the sanctuary. So they continued bringing to him freewill offerings every morning. [4]Then all the craftsmen who were doing all the work of the sanctuary came, each from the work he was doing, [5]and they spoke to Moses, saying, "The people bring much more than enough for the service of the work which the LORD commanded *us* to do."

[6]So Moses gave a commandment, and they caused it to be proclaimed throughout the camp, saying, "Let neither man nor woman do any more work for the offering of the sanctuary." And the people were restrained from bringing, [7]for the material they had was sufficient for all the work to be done—indeed too much.

Building the Tabernacle

[8]Then all the gifted artisans among them who worked on the tabernacle made ten curtains woven of fine linen, and of blue, purple, and scarlet thread; *with* artistic designs of cherubim they made them. [9]The length of each curtain *was* twenty-eight cubits, and the width of each curtain four cubits; the curtains *were* all the same size. [10]And he coupled five curtains to one another, and *the other* five curtains he coupled to one another. [11]He made loops of blue *yarn* on the edge of the curtain on the selvedge of one set; likewise he did on the outer edge of *the other* curtain of the second set. [12]Fifty loops he made on one curtain, and fifty loops he made on the edge of the curtain on the end of the second set; the loops held one *curtain* to another. [13]And he made fifty clasps of gold, and coupled the curtains to one another with the clasps, that it might be one tabernacle.

[14]He made curtains of goats' *hair* for the tent over the tabernacle; he made eleven curtains. [15]The length of each curtain *was* thirty cubits, and the width of each curtain four cubits; the eleven curtains *were* the same size. [16]He coupled five curtains by themselves and six curtains by themselves. [17]And he made fifty loops on the edge of the curtain that is outermost in one set, and fifty loops he made on the edge of the curtain of the second set. [18]He also made fifty bronze clasps to couple the tent together, that it might be one. [19]Then he made a covering for the tent of ram skins dyed red, and a covering of badger skins above *that.*

[20]For the tabernacle he made boards of acacia wood, standing upright. [21]The length of each board *was* ten cubits, and the width of each board a cubit and a half.

36:2 In God's plan **everyone** is involved. In the human plan the people watch the priest do the work (32:4).

36:8—39:31 A report of the work done in building the tabernacle. See 25:10—28:43, where the plans were given. This double description indicates something of the importance attached to these events of the Exodus. The Exodus finds its meaning in God being able to take a residence appropriate to His character in the midst of His people.

22Each board had two tenons for binding one to another. Thus he made for all the boards of the tabernacle. 23And he made boards for the tabernacle, twenty boards for the south side. 24Forty sockets of silver he made to go under the twenty boards: two sockets under each of the boards for its two tenons. 25And for the other side of the tabernacle, the north side, he made twenty boards 26and their forty sockets of silver: two sockets under each of the boards. 27For the west side of the tabernacle he made six boards. 28He also made two boards for the two back corners of the tabernacle. 29And they were coupled at the bottom and coupled together at the top by one ring. Thus he made both of them for the two corners. 30So there were eight boards and their sockets—sixteen sockets of silver—two sockets under each of the boards.

31And he made bars of acacia wood: five for the boards on one side of the tabernacle, 32five bars for the boards on the other side of the tabernacle, and five bars for the boards of the tabernacle on the far side westward. 33And he made the middle bar to pass through the boards from one end to the other. 34He overlaid the boards with gold, made their rings of gold *to be* holders for the bars, and overlaid the bars with gold.

35And he made a veil of blue, purple, and scarlet *thread,* and fine woven linen; it was worked *with* an artistic design of cherubim. 36He made for it four pillars of acacia *wood,* and overlaid them with gold, with their hooks of gold; and he cast four sockets of silver for them.

37He also made a screen for the tabernacle door, of blue, purple, and scarlet *thread,* and fine woven linen, made by a weaver, 38and its five pillars with their hooks. And he overlaid their capitals and their rings with gold, but their five sockets *were* bronze.

CHAPTER 37

Making the Ark of the Testimony

Then Bez'a·lel made the ark of acacia wood; two and a half cubits *was* its length, a cubit and a half its width, and a cubit and a half its height. 2He overlaid it with pure gold inside and outside, and made a molding of gold all around it. 3And he cast for it four rings of gold *to be set* in its four corners: two rings on one side, and two rings on the other side of it. 4He made poles of acacia wood, and overlaid them with gold. 5And he put the poles into the rings at the sides of the ark, to bear the ark. 6He also made the mercy seat of pure gold; two and a half cubits *was* its length and a cubit and a half its width. 7He made two cherubim of beaten gold; he made them of one piece at the two ends of the mercy seat: 8one cherub at one end on this side, and the other cherub at the *other* end on that side. He made the cherubim at the two ends *of one piece* with the mercy seat. 9The cherubim spread out *their* wings above, *and* covered the mercy seat with their wings. They faced one another; the faces of the cherubim were toward the mercy seat.

Making the Table for the Showbread

10He made the table of acacia wood; two cubits *was* its length, a cubit its width, and a cubit and a half its height. 11And he overlaid it with pure gold, and made a molding of gold all around it. 12Also he made a frame of a handbreadth all around it, and made a molding of gold for the frame all around it. 13And he cast for it four rings of

---

37:1–28 A description of six pieces of furniture used for worship in the tabernacle: **the ark** (vv. 1–5), the **mercy seat** covering the ark (vv. 6–9), the **table** of showbread (vv. 10–16), the **lampstand** (vv. 17–24), and the **incense altar** (vv. 25–28). **acacia wood** (v. 1): Probably the *Acacia Seyal,* which grows to a height of 20 feet (6 m). Its wood is close-grained and not readily attacked by insects, thus well suited for use in the ark and boards of the tabernacle.

gold, and put the rings on the four corners that *were* at its four legs. 14The rings were close to the frame, as holders for the poles to bear the table. 15And he made the poles of acacia wood to bear the table, and overlaid them with gold. 16He made of pure gold the utensils which were on the table: its dishes, its cups, its bowls, and its pitchers for pouring.

Making the Gold Lampstand

17He also made the lampstand of pure gold; of hammered work he made the lampstand. Its shaft, its branches, its bowls, its *ornamental* knobs, and its flowers were of the same piece. 18And six branches came out of its sides: three branches of the lampstand out of one side, and three branches of the lampstand out of the other side. 19There were three bowls made like almond *blossoms* on one branch, with an *ornamental* knob and a flower, and three bowls made like almond *blossoms* on the other branch, with an *ornamental* knob and a flower—and so for the six branches coming out of the lampstand. 20And on the lampstand itself *were* four bowls made like almond *blossoms, each with* its *ornamental* knob and flower. 21*There was* a knob under the *first* two branches of the same, a knob under the *second* two branches of the same, and a knob under the *third* two branches of the same, according to the six branches extending from it. 22Their knobs and their branches were of one piece; all of it *was* one hammered piece of pure gold. 23And he made its seven lamps, its wick-trimmers, and its trays of pure gold. 24Of a talent of pure gold he made it, with all its utensils.

Making the Altar of Incense

25He made the incense altar of acacia wood. Its length *was* a cubit and its width a cubit—*it was* square—and two cubits *was* its height. Its horns were *of one piece* with it. 26And he overlaid it with pure gold: its top, its sides all around, and its horns. He also made for it a molding of gold all around it. 27He made two rings of gold for it under its molding, by its two corners on both sides, as holders for the poles with which to bear it. 28And he made the poles of acacia wood, and overlaid them with gold.

Making the Anointing Oil and the Incense

29He also made the holy anointing oil and the pure incense of sweet spices, according to the work of the perfumer.

CHAPTER 38

Making the Altar of Burnt Offering

He made the altar of burnt offering of acacia wood; five cubits *was* its length and five cubits its width—*it was* square—and its height *was* three cubits. 2He made its horns on its four corners; the horns were *of one piece* with it. And he overlaid it with bronze. 3He made all the utensils for the altar: the pans, the shovels, the basins, the forks, and the firepans; all its utensils he made of bronze. 4And he made a grate of bronze network for the altar, under its rim, midway from the bottom. 5He cast four rings for the four corners of the bronze grating, *as* holders for the poles. 6And he made the poles of acacia wood, and overlaid them with bronze. 7Then he put the poles into the rings on the sides of the altar, with which to bear it. He made the altar hollow with boards.

Making the Bronze Laver

8He made the laver of bronze and its base of bronze, from the bronze mirrors of

---

38:8 Just as the priests were to use the laver to wash their hands and feet in preparation for service, so Christians are to keep themselves clean for their duties through confession and the Word of God (John 13:10 and 15:3; Eph. 5:26; 1 John 1:9). The basis for such cleansing, of course, is the blood of Christ (1 John 1:7).

the serving women who assembled at the door of the tabernacle of meeting.

Making the Court of the Tabernacle

[9]Then he made the court on the south side; the hangings of the court *were of* fine woven linen, one hundred cubits long. [10]There *were* twenty pillars for them, with twenty bronze sockets. The hooks of the pillars and their bands *were* silver. [11]On the north side *the hangings were* one hundred cubits *long,* with twenty pillars and their twenty bronze sockets. The hooks of the pillars and their bands *were* silver. [12]And on the west side *there were* hangings of fifty cubits, with ten pillars and their ten sockets. The hooks of the pillars and their bands *were* silver. [13]For the east side *the hangings were* fifty cubits. [14]The hangings of one side *of the gate were* fifteen cubits *long, with* their three pillars and their three sockets, [15]and the same for the other side of the court gate; on this side and that *were* hangings of fifteen cubits, *with* their three pillars and their three sockets. [16]All the hangings of the court all around *were of* fine woven linen. [17]The sockets for the pillars *were* bronze, the hooks of the pillars and their bands *were* silver, and the overlay of their capitals *was* silver; and all the pillars of the court had bands of silver. [18]The screen for the gate of the court *was* woven of blue, purple, and scarlet *thread,* and of fine woven linen. The length *was* twenty cubits, and the height along its width *was* five cubits, corresponding to the hangings of the court. [19]And *there were* four pillars *with* their four sockets of bronze; their hooks *were* silver, and the overlay of their capitals and their bands *was* silver. [20]All the pegs of the tabernacle, and of the court all around, *were* bronze.

Materials of the Tabernacle

[21]This is the inventory of the tabernacle, the tabernacle of the Testimony, which was counted according to the commandment of Moses, for the service of the Lē′vītes, by the hand of Ith′a·mar, son of Aaron the priest.

[22]Bez′a·lel the son of Ū′rī, the son of Hur, of the tribe of Judah, made all that the LORD had commanded Moses. [23]And with him *was* A·hō′li·ab the son of A·his′-a·mach, of the tribe of Dan, an engraver and designer, a weaver of blue, purple, and scarlet *thread,* and of fine linen.

[24]All the gold that was used in all the work of the holy *place,* that is, the gold of the offering, was twenty-nine talents and seven hundred and thirty shekels, according to the shekel of the sanctuary. [25]And the silver from those who were numbered of the congregation *was* one hundred talents and one thousand seven hundred and seventy-five shekels, according to the shekel of the sanctuary: [26]a bekah for each man (*that is,* half a shekel, according to the shekel of the sanctuary), for everyone included in the numbering from twenty years old and above, for six hundred and three thousand, five hundred and fifty *men.* [27]And from the hundred talents of silver were cast the sockets of the sanctuary and the bases of the veil: one hundred sockets from the hundred talents, one talent for each socket. [28]Then from the one thousand seven hundred and seventy-five *shekels* he made hooks for the pillars, overlaid their capitals, and made bands for them.

[29]The offering of bronze *was* seventy talents and two thousand four hundred shekels. [30]And with it he made the sockets for the door of the tabernacle of meeting, the bronze altar, the bronze grating for it,

38:21–31 If the **talent** (v. 24) is approximately 75 pounds (34 kg) and the **shekel** four-tenths of an ounce (12 g), then in the tabernacle complex there were approximately 2,193 pounds (996 kg) of **gold** (v. 24), 7,544 pounds (3,425 kg) of silver (v. 25), and 5,310 pounds (2,411 kg) of bronze (v. 29).

and all the utensils for the altar, 31the sockets for the court all around, the bases for the court gate, all the pegs for the tabernacle, and all the pegs for the court all around.

CHAPTER 39

Making the Garments of the Priesthood

Of the blue, purple, and scarlet *thread* they made garments of ministry,[a] for ministering in the holy *place,* and made the holy garments for Aaron, as the LORD had commanded Moses.

Making the Ephod

2He made the ephod of gold, blue, purple, and scarlet *thread,* and of fine woven linen. 3And they beat the gold into thin sheets and cut *it into* threads, to work *it* in *with* the blue, purple, and scarlet *thread,* and the fine linen, *into* artistic designs. 4They made shoulder straps for it to couple *it* together; it was coupled together at its two edges. 5And the intricately woven band of his ephod that *was* on it *was* of the same workmanship, *woven of* gold, blue, purple, and scarlet *thread,* and of fine woven linen, as the LORD had commanded Moses.

6And they set onyx stones, enclosed in settings of gold; they were engraved, as signets are engraved, with the names of the sons of Israel. 7He put them on the shoulders of the ephod *as* memorial stones for the sons of Israel, as the LORD had commanded Moses.

Making the Breastplate

8And he made the breastplate, artistically woven like the workmanship of the ephod, of gold, blue, purple, and scarlet *thread,* and of fine woven linen. 9They made the breastplate square by doubling it; a span *was* its length and a span its width when doubled. 10And they set in it four rows of stones: a row with a sardius, a topaz, and an emerald was the first row; 11the second row, a turquoise, a sapphire, and a diamond; 12the third row, a jacinth, an agate, and an amethyst; 13the fourth row, a beryl, an onyx, and a jasper. *They were* enclosed in settings of gold in their mountings. 14*There were* twelve stones according to the names of the sons of Israel: according to their names, *engraved like* a signet, each one with its own name according to the twelve tribes. 15And they made chains for the breastplate at the ends, like braided cords of pure gold. 16They also made two settings of gold and two gold rings, and put the two rings on the two ends of the breastplate. 17And they put the two braided *chains* of gold in the two rings on the ends of the breastplate. 18The two ends of the two braided *chains* they fastened in the two settings, and put them on the shoulder straps of the ephod in the front. 19And they made two rings of gold and put *them* on the two ends of the breastplate, on the edge of it, which *was* on the inward side of the ephod. 20They made two *other* gold rings and put them on the two shoulder straps, underneath the ephod toward its front, right at the seam above the intricately woven band of the ephod. 21And they bound the breastplate by means of its rings to the rings of the ephod with a blue cord, so that it would be above the intricately woven band of the ephod, and that the breastplate would not come loose from the ephod, as the LORD had commanded Moses.

Making the Other Priestly Garments

22He made the robe of the ephod of woven work, all of blue. 23And *there was* an opening in the middle of the robe, like the opening in a coat of mail, *with* a woven binding all around the opening, so that it would not tear. 24They made on the hem of the robe pomegranates of blue, purple, and scarlet, and of fine woven *linen.* 25And they made bells of pure gold, and put the bells between the pomegranates on the hem of

39:1 [a]Or *woven garments*

the robe all around between the pome-
granates: [26]a bell and a pomegranate, a bell
and a pomegranate, all around the hem of
the robe to minister in, as the LORD had
commanded Moses.
[27]They made tunics, artistically woven
of fine linen, for Aaron and his sons, [28]a
turban of fine linen, exquisite hats of fine
linen, short trousers of fine woven linen,
[29]and a sash of fine woven linen with blue,
purple, and scarlet *thread,* made by a
weaver, as the LORD had commanded Mo-
ses.
[30]Then they made the plate of the holy
crown of pure gold, and wrote on it an in-
scription *like* the engraving of a signet:

HOLINESS TO THE LORD.

[31]And they tied to it a blue cord, to fasten *it*
above on the turban, as the LORD had com-
manded Moses.

The Work Completed

[32]Thus all the work of the tabernacle of
the tent of meeting was finished. And the
children of Israel did according to all that
the LORD had commanded Moses; so they
did. [33]And they brought the tabernacle to
Moses, the tent and all its furnishings: its
clasps, its boards, its bars, its pillars, and
its sockets; [34]the covering of ram skins
dyed red, the covering of badger skins,
and the veil of the covering; [35]the ark of the
Testimony with its poles, and the mercy
seat; [36]the table, all its utensils, and the
showbread; [37]the pure *gold* lampstand with
its lamps (the lamps set in order), all its
utensils, and the oil for light; [38]the gold al-
tar, the anointing oil, and the sweet in-
cense; the screen for the tabernacle door;
[39]the bronze altar, its grate of bronze, its
poles, and all its utensils; the laver with its
base; [40]the hangings of the court, its pillars
and its sockets, the screen for the court
gate, its cords, and its pegs; all the utensils
for the service of the tabernacle, for the tent
of meeting; [41]and the garments of min-
istry,[a] to minister in the holy *place:* the holy
garments for Aaron the priest, and his
sons' garments, to minister as priests.
[42]According to all that the LORD had
commanded Moses, so the children of Is-
rael did all the work. [43]Then Moses looked
over all the work, and indeed they had
done it; as the LORD had commanded, just
so they had done it. And Moses blessed
them.

CHAPTER 40

The Tabernacle Erected and Arranged

Then the LORD spoke to Moses, saying:
[2]"On the first day of the first month you
shall set up the tabernacle of the tent of
meeting. [3]You shall put in it the ark of the
Testimony, and partition off the ark with
the veil. [4]You shall bring in the table and
arrange the things that are to be set in or-
der on it; and you shall bring in the lamp-
stand and light its lamps. [5]You shall also

39:41 [a]Or *woven garments*

40:1–8 The entire tabernacle was symbolic of God's character or activity. Each element reflected a spiritual significance, illustrating and teaching concepts common to both OT and NT. The closed *court* (27:9–19) barred entry to all but the consecrated priests—no unholy person may approach Him. The *altar of burnt offering* (27:1–8) shows that only the shedding of blood provides remission for sin. The *laver* (30:17–21) symbolizes that one must appropriate the cleansing that God provides in order to come into His presence. The *table of showbread* (25:23–30) reflects God's provision for temporal needs. The lamps (25:31–40) indicate guidance from God. The *altar of incense* (30:1–10) suggests that God provides access to Himself through prayer. The *veil* suggests the barrier that sin placed between God and humanity (the tearing of the veil at Christ's death showed that He had created the way through that barrier; see Matt 27:51; Heb. 10:19, 20). Finally, the *ark* (25:10–22), with its contents and its blood-sprinkled mercy seat, represents (among many other things) God's initiative in reestablishing fellowship between Himself and humanity.

set the altar of gold for the incense before the ark of the Testimony, and put up the screen for the door of the tabernacle. 6Then you shall set the altar of the burnt offering before the door of the tabernacle of the tent of meeting. 7And you shall set the laver between the tabernacle of meeting and the altar, and put water in it. 8You shall set up the court all around, and hang up the screen at the court gate.

9"And you shall take the anointing oil, and anoint the tabernacle and all that *is* in it; and you shall hallow it and all its utensils, and it shall be holy. 10You shall anoint the altar of the burnt offering and all its utensils, and consecrate the altar. The altar shall be most holy. 11And you shall anoint the laver and its base, and consecrate it.

12"Then you shall bring Aaron and his sons to the door of the tabernacle of meeting and wash them with water. 13You shall put the holy garments on Aaron, and anoint him and consecrate him, that he may minister to Me as priest. 14And you shall bring his sons and clothe them with tunics. 15You shall anoint them, as you anointed their father, that they may minister to Me as priests; for their anointing shall surely be an everlasting priesthood throughout their generations."

16Thus Moses did; according to all that the LORD had commanded him, so he did.

17And it came to pass in the first month of the second year, on the first *day* of the month, *that* the tabernacle was raised up. 18So Moses raised up the tabernacle, fastened its sockets, set up its boards, put in its bars, and raised up its pillars. 19And he spread out the tent over the tabernacle and put the covering of the tent on top of it, as the LORD had commanded Moses. 20He took the Testimony and put *it* into the ark, inserted the poles through the rings of the ark, and put the mercy seat on top of the ark. 21And he brought the ark into the tabernacle, hung up the veil of the covering, and partitioned off the ark of the Testimony, as the LORD had commanded Moses.

22He put the table in the tabernacle of meeting, on the north side of the tabernacle, outside the veil; 23and he set the bread in order upon it before the LORD, as the LORD had commanded Moses. 24He put the lampstand in the tabernacle of meeting, across from the table, on the south side of the tabernacle; 25and he lit the lamps before the LORD, as the LORD had commanded Moses. 26He put the gold altar in the tabernacle of meeting in front of the veil; 27and he burned sweet incense on it, as the LORD had commanded Moses. 28He hung up the screen *at* the door of the tabernacle. 29And he put the altar of burnt offering *before* the door of the tabernacle of the tent of meeting, and offered upon it the burnt offering and the grain offering, as the LORD had commanded Moses. 30He set the laver between the tabernacle of meeting and the altar, and put water there for washing; 31and Moses, Aaron, and his sons would wash their hands and their feet *with water* from it. 32Whenever they went into the tabernacle of meeting, and when they came near the altar, they washed, as the LORD had commanded Moses. 33And he raised up the court all around the tabernacle and the altar, and hung up the screen of the court gate. So Moses finished the work.

The Cloud and the Glory

34Then the cloud covered the tabernacle of meeting, and the glory of the LORD filled the tabernacle. 35And Moses was not able to enter the tabernacle of meeting, because the cloud rested above it, and the glory of

---

40:34–38 The same divine **glory** that once flooded the summit of Sinai now filled the tabernacle. God's glory moved from an unmovable mountain to a movable building. Sinai must be left behind. God's presence, however, would remain a reality, not a mere memory.

the LORD filled the tabernacle. [36]Whenever
the cloud was taken up from above the
tabernacle, the children of Israel would go
onward in all their journeys. [37]But if the
cloud was not taken up, then they did not
journey till the day that it was taken up.
[38]For the cloud of the LORD *was* above the
tabernacle by day, and fire was over it by
night, in the sight of all the house of Israel,
throughout all their journeys.

✦Leviticus✦

Some scholars believe that Leviticus was assembled anonymously after Moses' death, but this is doubtful because, in many instances, God spoke directly to Moses, who wrote down instructions for the Israelites (4:1; 6:1; 8:1; 11:1). The book describes the period when Israel camped at the foot of Mount Sinai after fleeing from Egypt, and it was probably written after the building of the tabernacle and before the Israelites' departure from the Sinai, or shortly thereafter.

Leviticus serves as a manual for the priests, providing instructions and regulations for worship. Chapters 1—17 detail the requirements of sacrifice and the need for forgiveness. The blood of an innocent animal became the substitute for the life of the sinner to satisfy a holy God. Chapters 18—27 outline the guidelines for Israel to be set apart from the world through ceremonial holiness (rituals) and moral holiness (pure living). Holiness is a key theme in the book, along with atonement and sacrifice, demonstrated by the Day of Atonement in chapter 16. Leviticus sets the foundation for Christ's death on the Cross as the once-for-all sacrifice for man's sin.

While some modern-day Christians may find the details of ancient Jewish ritual irrelevant, Leviticus demonstrates the importance God places on holy living. When we realize how quickly Israel strayed from the conduct clearly outlined in this book, we are reminded of the need to remain vigilant in our own spiritual walks. ✦

CHAPTER 1

The Burnt Offering

Now the LORD called to Moses, and spoke to him from the tabernacle of meet-
ing, saying, [2]"Speak to the children of Is-
rael, and say to them: 'When any one of you brings an offering to the LORD, you shall bring your offering of the livestock—of the herd and of the flock.

[3]'If his offering *is* a burnt sacrifice of the herd, let him offer a male without blemish; he shall offer it of his own free will at the door of the tabernacle of meeting before
the LORD. [4]Then he shall put his hand on the head of the burnt offering, and it will be accepted on his behalf to make atone-
ment for him. [5]He shall kill the bull before the LORD; and the priests, Aaron's sons, shall bring the blood and sprinkle the

---

1:2–17 The **burnt offering** is the only sacrifice that was totally consumed on the altar, hence it is often called the "whole burnt offering."

1:3 The animal presented could be from the **herd**, from the **flocks** (v. 10), or from **birds** (v. 14), and was to be without blemish. God wants our best. He merits that which is perfect (see Mal. 1:6–8). This perfect sacrifice also points us to Christ's offering of Himself as the spotless Lamb (1 Pet. 1:19).

blood all around on the altar that *is by* the
door of the tabernacle of meeting. 6And he
shall skin the burnt offering and cut it into
its pieces. 7The sons of Aaron the priest
shall put fire on the altar, and lay the
wood in order on the fire. 8Then the
priests, Aaron's sons, shall lay the parts,
the head, and the fat in order on the
wood that *is* on the fire upon the altar;
9but he shall wash its entrails and its legs
with water. And the priest shall burn all
on the altar as a burnt sacrifice, an offer-
ing made by fire, a sweet aroma to the
LORD.

10'If his offering *is* of the flocks—of the
sheep or of the goats—as a burnt sacrifice,
he shall bring a male without blemish. 11He
shall kill it on the north side of the altar be-
fore the LORD; and the priests, Aaron's
sons, shall sprinkle its blood all around on
the altar. 12And he shall cut it into its
pieces, with its head and its fat; and the
priest shall lay them in order on the wood
that *is* on the fire upon the altar; 13but he
shall wash the entrails and the legs with
water. Then the priest shall bring *it* all and
burn *it* on the altar; it *is* a burnt sacrifice, an
offering made by fire, a sweet aroma to the
LORD.

14'And if the burnt sacrifice of his offer-
ing to the LORD *is* of birds, then he shall
bring his offering of turtledoves or young
pigeons. 15The priest shall bring it to the al-
tar, wring off its head, and burn *it* on the al-
tar; its blood shall be drained out at the
side of the altar. 16And he shall remove its
crop with its feathers and cast it beside the
altar on the east side, into the place for
ashes. 17Then he shall split it at its wings,
but shall not divide *it* completely; and the
priest shall burn it on the altar, on the
wood that *is* on the fire. It *is* a burnt sacri-
fice, an offering made by fire, a sweet
aroma to the LORD.

CHAPTER 2

The Grain Offering

'When anyone offers a grain offering to
the LORD, his offering shall be *of* fine flour.
And he shall pour oil on it, and put frank-
incense on it. 2He shall bring it to Aaron's
sons, the priests, one of whom shall take
from it his handful of fine flour and oil
with all the frankincense. And the priest
shall burn *it as* a memorial on the altar, an
offering made by fire, a sweet aroma to the
LORD. 3The rest of the grain offering *shall be*
Aaron's and his sons'. *It is* most holy of the
offerings to the LORD made by fire.

4'And if you bring as an offering a grain
offering baked in the oven, *it shall be* un-
leavened cakes of fine flour mixed with oil,
or unleavened wafers anointed with oil.
5But if your offering *is* a grain offering
baked in a pan, *it shall be of* fine flour, un-
leavened, mixed with oil. 6You shall break
it in pieces and pour oil on it; it *is* a grain
offering.

7'If your offering *is* a grain offering *baked*
in a covered pan, it shall be made *of* fine
flour with oil. 8You shall bring the grain of-
fering that is made of these things to the
LORD. And when it is presented to the
priest, he shall bring it to the altar. 9Then
the priest shall take from the grain offering
a memorial portion, and burn *it* on the al-
tar. *It is* an offering made by fire, a sweet
aroma to the LORD. 10And what is left of the
grain offering *shall be* Aaron's and his
sons'. *It is* most holy of the offerings to the
LORD made by fire.

11'No grain offering which you bring to
the LORD shall be made with leaven, for
you shall burn no leaven nor any honey in
any offering to the LORD made by fire. 12As
for the offering of the firstfruits, you shall
offer them to the LORD, but they shall not
be burned on the altar for a sweet aroma.

2:1–16 It is possible that the **grain offering** was the poor person's burnt offering, or eventually became so. Not everybody had birds, but every Hebrew had at least some grain.

13And every offering of your grain offering
you shall season with salt; you shall not al-
low the salt of the covenant of your God to
be lacking from your grain offering. With
all your offerings you shall offer salt.
14'If you offer a grain offering of your
firstfruits to the LORD, you shall offer for
the grain offering of your firstfruits green
heads of grain roasted on the fire, grain
beaten from full heads. 15And you shall put
oil on it, and lay frankincense on it. It *is* a
grain offering. 16Then the priest shall burn
the memorial portion: *part* of its beaten
grain and *part* of its oil, with all the frank-
incense, as an offering made by fire to the
LORD.

CHAPTER 3

The Peace Offering

'When his offering *is* a sacrifice of a
peace offering, if he offers *it* of the herd,
whether male or female, he shall offer it
without blemish before the LORD. 2And he
shall lay his hand on the head of his offer-
ing, and kill it *at* the door of the tabernacle
of meeting; and Aaron's sons, the priests,
shall sprinkle the blood all around on the
altar. 3Then he shall offer from the sacrifice
of the peace offering an offering made by
fire to the LORD. The fat that covers the en-
trails and all the fat that *is* on the entrails,
4the two kidneys and the fat that *is* on them
by the flanks, and the fatty lobe *attached* to
the liver above the kidneys, he shall re-
move; 5and Aaron's sons shall burn it on
the altar upon the burnt sacrifice, which *is*
on the wood that *is* on the fire, *as* an offer-
ing made by fire, a sweet aroma to the
LORD.
6'If his offering as a sacrifice of a peace
offering to the LORD *is* of the flock, *whether*
male or female, he shall offer it without
blemish. 7If he offers a lamb as his offering,
then he shall offer it before the LORD. 8And
he shall lay his hand on the head of his of-
fering, and kill it before the tabernacle of
meeting; and Aaron's sons shall sprinkle
its blood all around on the altar.
9'Then he shall offer from the sacrifice of
the peace offering, as an offering made by
fire to the LORD, its fat *and* the whole fat tail
which he shall remove close to the back-
bone. And the fat that covers the entrails
and all the fat that *is* on the entrails, 10the
two kidneys and the fat that *is* on them by
the flanks, and the fatty lobe *attached* to the
liver above the kidneys, he shall remove;
11and the priest shall burn *them* on the altar
as food, an offering made by fire to the
LORD.
12'And if his offering *is* a goat, then he
shall offer it before the LORD. 13He shall lay
his hand on its head and kill it before the
tabernacle of meeting; and the sons of
Aaron shall sprinkle its blood all around
on the altar. 14Then he shall offer from it his
offering, as an offering made by fire to the
LORD. The fat that covers the entrails and
all the fat that *is* on the entrails, 15the two
kidneys and the fat that *is* on them by the
flanks, and the fatty lobe *attached* to the
liver above the kidneys, he shall remove;
16and the priest shall burn them on the al-
tar *as* food, an offering made by fire for a
sweet aroma; all the fat *is* the LORD's.

2:13 Salt was prescribed because it preserves. Num. 18:19 and 2 Chr. 13:5 speak of "a covenant of salt," possibly describing the covenant God had established with Israel as one He would preserve forever.

3:1–17 The third sacrifice is a **peace offering**, or fellowship sacrifice. This offering seems to be an expression of thanks for God's present fellowship, as well as a request that it may continue. Although the first part of the ritual is much like the burnt offering, not all of the flesh was consumed on the altar. Part was given to the priests (7:31–35) and part went back to the offerer to be eaten in the Lord's presence (7:15–17). The peace offering points us to Him who "is our peace" (Eph. 2:14), and who "made peace through the blood of His cross" (Col. 1:20).

LOW-FAT LIFESTYLE

Pam Smith

These days it is hard to pick up a magazine or newspaper without reading something about cutting the fat from our diets. The excess fat calories we consume are converted and stored as fat more readily than those from other sources. Fat is a more concentrated source of calories (all fats contain about nine calories per gram, or 120 calories per tablespoon). In addition, the body is more efficient in storing fat as fat. This is why the weight-control experts of today consider "trimming the fat" from our diets to be much more important in losing weight than just watching our calories.

In God's plan for the Israelites, He prohibited them from eating fat (Lev. 3:17); it was reserved for the Lord. Like many other restrictions at the time, this regulation served to help keep God's chosen people healthy.

Scientists today have determined that too much fat intake can have a severe effect on physical health. Consider these vital facts about fat:

✦ Excess fat increases our cholesterol levels and our risk of heart disease and stroke. While research shows that saturated fat is the main culprit, it also shows that any type of fat can cause problems.

✦ Excess fat increases our risk of cancer, particularly of the colon and breast. Fat alone is presently implicated in one-third of all cancer deaths.

✦ Excess fat increases our risk of gallbladder disease.

✦ Excess fat elevates blood pressure, regardless of weight.

✦ Excess fat fed to animals with a genetic susceptibility to diabetes has made them more likely to develop the disease. People with a family history of diabetes can cut the percentage of fat in their diet as one step toward prevention.

✦ Fat makes us fat!

If your cholesterol is normal, your blood pressure is low, and your family tree free from cancer, heart disease, and diabetes, these facts may seem irrelevant to you. But being free from all risk factors is a blessing that can be enhanced with healthy eating. Foods low in fat, such as whole grains, fruits, and vegetables, give us higher levels of energy, better stress management, and improved memory and sleep. ✦

17 '*This shall be* a perpetual statute throughout your generations in all your dwellings: you shall eat neither fat nor blood.' "

3:17 Both fat and **blood** belonged to the Lord and were thus forbidden to the children of Israel. In addition, the prohibition on eating fat may have been a form of preventive medicine, and another example of God's protection of His people in ways no one could understand at the time.

CHAPTER 4

The Sin Offering

Now the LORD spoke to Moses, saying,
2"Speak to the children of Israel, saying: 'If
a person sins unintentionally against any
of the commandments of the LORD *in any-*
thing which ought not to be done, and does
any of them, 3if the anointed priest sins,
bringing guilt on the people, then let him
offer to the LORD for his sin which he has
sinned a young bull without blemish as a
sin offering. 4He shall bring the bull to the
door of the tabernacle of meeting before
the LORD, lay his hand on the bull's head,
and kill the bull before the LORD. 5Then the
anointed priest shall take some of the
bull's blood and bring it to the tabernacle
of meeting. 6The priest shall dip his finger
in the blood and sprinkle some of the
blood seven times before the LORD, in front
of the veil of the sanctuary. 7And the priest
shall put some of the blood on the horns of
the altar of sweet incense before the LORD,
which is in the tabernacle of meeting; and
he shall pour the remaining blood of the
bull at the base of the altar of the burnt of-
fering, which is at the door of the taberna-
cle of meeting. 8He shall take from it all the
fat of the bull as the sin offering. The fat
that covers the entrails and all the fat
which *is* on the entrails, 9the two kidneys
and the fat that *is* on them by the flanks,
and the fatty lobe *attached* to the liver
above the kidneys, he shall remove, 10as it
was taken from the bull of the sacrifice of
the peace offering; and the priest shall
burn them on the altar of the burnt offer-
ing. 11But the bull's hide and all its flesh,
with its head and legs, its entrails and of-
fal— 12the whole bull he shall carry outside
the camp to a clean place, where the ashes
are poured out, and burn it on wood with
fire; where the ashes are poured out it shall
be burned.

13'Now if the whole congregation of Is-
rael sins unintentionally, and the thing is
hidden from the eyes of the assembly, and
they have done *something against* any of the
commandments of the LORD *in anything*
which should not be done, and are guilty;
14when the sin which they have committed
becomes known, then the assembly shall
offer a young bull for the sin, and bring it
before the tabernacle of meeting. 15And the
elders of the congregation shall lay their
hands on the head of the bull before the
LORD. Then the bull shall be killed before
the LORD. 16The anointed priest shall bring
some of the bull's blood to the tabernacle
of meeting. 17Then the priest shall dip his
finger in the blood and sprinkle *it* seven
times before the LORD, in front of the veil.
18And he shall put *some* of the blood on the
horns of the altar which *is* before the LORD,
which *is* in the tabernacle of meeting; and
he shall pour the remaining blood at the
base of the altar of burnt offering, which is
at the door of the tabernacle of meeting.
19He shall take all the fat from it and burn *it*
on the altar. 20And he shall do with the bull
as he did with the bull as a sin offering;

4:2 If a person sins: The sin offering was mandatory, unlike the previous three offerings, which were voluntary. It was offered because of particular acts of sin. These sacrifices made forgiveness available only to the one who sinned **unintentionally**, either through ignorance or negligence. By our very nature, we are inclined to sin; every human being has broken God's law, whether intentionally or not.

4:6, 7 In the sin offering for the **priest**, and for the whole congregation (v. 13), the blood was brought into the sanctuary before the **veil** to the **altar of sweet incense**. This was not required for the sin offering of the ruler (v. 22) or of the common people (v. 27). In those offerings the blood was applied to the horn of the altar of burnt offering (vv. 30, 34). The sin of the first two was greater; it affected a wider circle of people. Also, the sin of priest and community required the offering of a bull or young bull (vv. 3, 4, 14, 15), an expensive animal. The offering for a ruler or commoner required only a male or female goat (vv. 23, 28) or a female lamb (v. 32). On the veil see Ex. 26:31–35.

thus he shall do with it. So the priest shall
make atonement for them, and it shall be
forgiven them. [21]Then he shall carry the
bull outside the camp, and burn it as he
burned the first bull. It *is* a sin offering for
the assembly.

[22]'When a ruler has sinned, and done
something unintentionally *against* any of
the commandments of the LORD his God *in*
anything which should not be done, and is
guilty, [23]or if his sin which he has commit-
ted comes to his knowledge, he shall bring
as his offering a kid of the goats, a male
without blemish. [24]And he shall lay his
hand on the head of the goat, and kill it at
the place where they kill the burnt offering
before the LORD. It *is* a sin offering. [25]The
priest shall take some of the blood of the
sin offering with his finger, put *it* on
the horns of the altar of burnt offering, and
pour its blood at the base of the altar of
burnt offering. [26]And he shall burn all its
fat on the altar, like the fat of the sacrifice of
the peace offering. So the priest shall make
atonement for him concerning his sin, and
it shall be forgiven him.

[27]'If anyone of the common people sins
unintentionally by doing *something against*
any of the commandments of the LORD *in*
anything which ought not to be done, and
is guilty, [28]or if his sin which he has com-
mitted comes to his knowledge, then he
shall bring as his offering a kid of the
goats, a female without blemish, for his sin
which he has committed. [29]And he shall lay
his hand on the head of the sin offering,
and kill the sin offering at the place of the
burnt offering. [30]Then the priest shall take
some of its blood with his finger, put *it* on
the horns of the altar of burnt offering, and
pour all *the remaining* blood at the base of
the altar. [31]He shall remove all its fat, as fat
is removed from the sacrifice of the peace
offering; and the priest shall burn it on the
altar for a sweet aroma to the LORD. So the
priest shall make atonement for him, and it
shall be forgiven him.

[32]'If he brings a lamb as his sin offering,
he shall bring a female without blemish.
[33]Then he shall lay his hand on the head of
the sin offering, and kill it as a sin offering
at the place where they kill the burnt offer-
ing. [34]The priest shall take *some* of the
blood of the sin offering with his finger,
put *it* on the horns of the altar of burnt of-
fering, and pour all *the remaining* blood at
the base of the altar. [35]He shall remove all
its fat, as the fat of the lamb is removed
from the sacrifice of the peace offering.
Then the priest shall burn it on the altar, ac-
cording to the offerings made by fire to the
LORD. So the priest shall make atonement
for his sin that he has committed, and it
shall be forgiven him.

CHAPTER 5

The Trespass Offering

'If a person sins in hearing the utterance
of an oath, and *is* a witness, whether he has
seen or known *of the matter*—if he does not
tell *it*, he bears guilt.

[2]'Or if a person touches any unclean
thing, whether *it is* the carcass of an un-
clean beast, or the carcass of unclean live-
stock, or the carcass of unclean creeping
things, and he is unaware of it, he also
shall be unclean and guilty. [3]Or if he
touches human uncleanness—whatever
uncleanness with which a man may be de-
filed, and he is unaware of it—when he re-
alizes *it*, then he shall be guilty.

[4]'Or if a person swears, speaking
thoughtlessly with *his* lips to do evil or to
do good, whatever *it is* that a man may
pronounce by an oath, and he is unaware
of it—when he realizes *it*, then he shall be
guilty in any of these *matters*.

[5]'And it shall be, when he is guilty in

5:5 When an individual realizes the wrongness of his action, whether from the jogging of his memory, or because another person points out the sin, he is to **confess** (see 1 John 1:9). There must be acknowledgment and full acceptance of responsibility.

any of these *matters*, that he shall confess
that he has sinned in that *thing;* 6and he
shall bring his trespass offering to the LORD
for his sin which he has committed, a fe-
male from the flock, a lamb or a kid of the
goats as a sin offering. So the priest shall
make atonement for him concerning his
sin.

7'If he is not able to bring a lamb, then he
shall bring to the LORD, for his trespass
which he has committed, two turtledoves
or two young pigeons: one as a sin offering
and the other as a burnt offering. 8And he
shall bring them to the priest, who shall of-
fer *that* which *is* for the sin offering first,
and wring off its head from its neck, but
shall not divide *it* completely. 9Then he
shall sprinkle *some* of the blood of the sin
offering on the side of the altar, and the rest
of the blood shall be drained out at the
base of the altar. It *is* a sin offering. 10And
he shall offer the second *as* a burnt offering
according to the prescribed manner. So the
priest shall make atonement on his behalf
for his sin which he has committed, and it
shall be forgiven him.

11'But if he is not able to bring two
turtledoves or two young pigeons, then he
who sinned shall bring for his offering one-
tenth of an ephah of fine flour as a sin of-
fering. He shall put no oil on it, nor shall he
put frankincense on it, for it *is* a sin offer-
ing. 12Then he shall bring it to the priest,
and the priest shall take his handful of it as
a memorial portion, and burn *it* on the al-
tar according to the offerings made by fire
to the LORD. It *is* a sin offering. 13The priest
shall make atonement for him, for his sin
that he has committed in any of these mat-
ters; and it shall be forgiven him. *The rest*
shall be the priest's as a grain offering.' "

Offerings with Restitution

14Then the LORD spoke to Moses, saying:
15"If a person commits a trespass, and sins
unintentionally in regard to the holy things
of the LORD, then he shall bring to the LORD
as his trespass offering a ram without
blemish from the flocks, with your valua-
tion in shekels of silver according to the
shekel of the sanctuary, as a trespass offer-
ing. 16And he shall make restitution for the
harm that he has done in regard to the holy
thing, and shall add one-fifth to it and give
it to the priest. So the priest shall make
atonement for him with the ram of the tres-
pass offering, and it shall be forgiven him.

17"If a person sins, and commits any of
these things which are forbidden to be
done by the commandments of the LORD,
though he does not know *it*, yet he is guilty
and shall bear his iniquity. 18And he shall
bring to the priest a ram without blemish
from the flock, with your valuation, as a
trespass offering. So the priest shall make
atonement for him regarding his ignorance
in which he erred and did not know *it*, and
it shall be forgiven him. 19It is a trespass of-
fering; he has certainly trespassed against
the LORD."

CHAPTER 6

And the LORD spoke to Moses, saying:
2"If a person sins and commits a trespass
against the LORD by lying to his neighbor
about what was delivered to him for
safekeeping, or about a pledge, or about a
robbery, or if he has extorted from his
neighbor, 3or if he has found what was lost
and lies concerning it, and swears falsely—
in any one of these things that a man may
do in which he sins: 4then it shall be, be-

5:14—6:7 The **trespass offering** was a particular type of sin offering required when the sin committed resulted in another party suffering some kind of loss of what was rightfully his. This sin could be committed against God (5:14–19) or against other people (6:1–7). At the heart of this offering was **restitution**, full repayment to the injured party (v. 16). The law required payment of 20% more than had been taken. In the NT, Zacchaeus illustrates this disposition to make wrongs right (Luke 19:8).

cause he has sinned and is guilty, that he
shall restore what he has stolen, or the
thing which he has extorted, or what was
delivered to him for safekeeping, or the
lost thing which he found, 5or all that
about which he has sworn falsely. He shall
restore its full value, add one-fifth more to
it, *and* give it to whomever it belongs, on
the day of his trespass offering. 6And he
shall bring his trespass offering to the
LORD, a ram without blemish from the
flock, with your valuation, as a trespass of-
fering, to the priest. 7So the priest shall
make atonement for him before the LORD,
and he shall be forgiven for any one of
these things that he may have done in
which he trespasses."

The Law of the Burnt Offering

8Then the LORD spoke to Moses, saying,
9"Command Aaron and his sons, saying,
'This *is* the law of the burnt offering: The
burnt offering *shall be* on the hearth upon
the altar all night until morning, and the
fire of the altar shall be kept burning on it.
10And the priest shall put on his linen gar-
ment, and his linen trousers he shall put on
his body, and take up the ashes of the burnt
offering which the fire has consumed on
the altar, and he shall put them beside the
altar. 11Then he shall take off his garments,
put on other garments, and carry the ashes
outside the camp to a clean place. 12And
the fire on the altar shall be kept burning
on it; it shall not be put out. And the priest
shall burn wood on it every morning, and
lay the burnt offering in order on it; and he
shall burn on it the fat of the peace offer-
ings. 13A fire shall always be burning on the
altar; it shall never go out.

The Law of the Grain Offering

14'This *is* the law of the grain offering:
The sons of Aaron shall offer it on the altar
before the LORD. 15He shall take from it his
handful of the fine flour of the grain offer-
ing, with its oil, and all the frankincense
which *is* on the grain offering, and shall
burn *it* on the altar *for* a sweet aroma, as a
memorial to the LORD. 16And the remain-
der of it Aaron and his sons shall eat; with
unleavened bread it shall be eaten in a holy
place; in the court of the tabernacle of
meeting they shall eat it. 17It shall not be
baked with leaven. I have given it *as* their
portion of My offerings made by fire; it *is*
most holy, like the sin offering and the tres-
pass offering. 18All the males among the
children of Aaron may eat it. *It shall be* a
statute forever in your generations con-
cerning the offerings made by fire to the
LORD. Everyone who touches them must
be holy.' "[a]

19And the LORD spoke to Moses, saying,
20"This *is* the offering of Aaron and his
sons, which they shall offer to the LORD, *be-
ginning* on the day when he is anointed:
one-tenth of an ephah of fine flour as a
daily grain offering, half of it in the morn-
ing and half of it at night. 21It shall be
made in a pan with oil. *When it is* mixed,
you shall bring it in. The baked pieces of
the grain offering you shall offer *for* a
sweet aroma to the LORD. 22The priest
from among his sons, who is anointed in
his place, shall offer it. *It is* a statute forever
to the LORD. It shall be wholly burned.
23For every grain offering for the priest
shall be wholly burned. It shall not be
eaten."

The Law of the Sin Offering

24Also the LORD spoke to Moses, saying,
25"Speak to Aaron and to his sons, saying,
'This *is* the law of the sin offering: In the
place where the burnt offering is killed, the
sin offering shall be killed before the LORD.
It *is* most holy. 26The priest who offers it for
sin shall eat it. In a holy place it shall be

6:18 [a]Compare Numbers 4:15 and Haggai 2:11–13

6:12, 13 This never-ending **fire** should be reflected today in our constant zeal and devotion to the Lord.

Dreams for the Grandchildren

Charles R. Swindoll

I want my grandchildren to see that life is a kaleidoscope of color and studies and realms. I want them to be whole and not have a fixation on just one interest. I want them to enjoy their parents and to realize what their parents have done. I think one of the jobs of grandparents is to convince grandkids what great parents they have.

I want them to have an authentic relationship with God. I want it to be real. I would like them to be secure. If I could give them a gift, it would be security within themselves. I would like them to make great mates. I think one of the great challenges for parents is to remember they are training somebody else's husband or wife. ✦

eaten, in the court of the tabernacle of
meeting. 27Everyone who touches its flesh
must be holy.[a] And when its blood is sprin-
kled on any garment, you shall wash that
on which it was sprinkled, in a holy place.
28But the earthen vessel in which it is
boiled shall be broken. And if it is boiled in
a bronze pot, it shall be both scoured and
rinsed in water. 29All the males among the
priests may eat it. It *is* most holy. 30But no
sin offering from which *any* of the blood is
brought into the tabernacle of meeting, to
make atonement in the holy *place*,[a] shall be
eaten. It shall be burned in the fire.

CHAPTER 7

The Law of the Trespass Offering

7'Likewise this *is* the law of the trespass
offering (it *is* most holy): 2In the place
where they kill the burnt offering they
shall kill the trespass offering. And its
blood he shall sprinkle all around on the
altar. 3And he shall offer from it all its fat.
The fat tail and the fat that covers the en-
trails, 4the two kidneys and the fat that *is*
on them by the flanks, and the fatty lobe *at-*
tached to the liver above the kidneys, he
shall remove; 5and the priest shall burn
them on the altar *as* an offering made by
fire to the LORD. It *is* a trespass offering.
6Every male among the priests may eat it.
It shall be eaten in a holy place. It *is* most
holy. 7The trespass offering *is* like the sin
offering; *there is* one law for them both: the
priest who makes atonement with it shall
have *it*. 8And the priest who offers any-
one's burnt offering, that priest shall have
for himself the skin of the burnt offering
which he has offered. 9Also every grain of-
fering that is baked in the oven and all that
is prepared in the covered pan, or in a pan,
shall be the priest's who offers it. 10Every
grain offering, *whether* mixed with oil or
dry, shall belong to all the sons of Aaron, to
one *as much* as the other.

The Law of Peace Offerings

11'This *is* the law of the sacrifice of peace
offerings which he shall offer to the LORD:
12If he offers it for a thanksgiving, then he
shall offer, with the sacrifice of thanksgiv-
ing, unleavened cakes mixed with oil, un-
leavened wafers anointed with oil, or
cakes of blended flour mixed with oil. 13Be-
sides the cakes, *as* his offering he shall offer
leavened bread with the sacrifice of

6:27 [a]Compare Numbers 4:15 and Haggai 2:11–13
6:30 [a]The Most Holy Place when capitalized

7:11–21 Practices concerning the **peace offerings** which applied especially to the priests. The peace sacrifice was offered for either a **thanksgiving** (v. 12), a **vow**, or a **voluntary offering** (v. 16).

thanksgiving of his peace offering. [14]And
from it he shall offer one cake from each of-
fering *as* a heave offering to the LORD. It
shall belong to the priest who sprinkles the
blood of the peace offering.

[15]'The flesh of the sacrifice of his peace
offering for thanksgiving shall be eaten the
same day it is offered. He shall not leave
any of it until morning. [16]But if the sacrifice
of his offering *is* a vow or a voluntary of-
fering, it shall be eaten the same day that
he offers his sacrifice; but on the next day
the remainder of it also may be eaten; [17]the
remainder of the flesh of the sacrifice on
the third day must be burned with fire.
[18]And if *any* of the flesh of the sacrifice of
his peace offering is eaten at all on the third
day, it shall not be accepted, nor shall it be
imputed to him; it shall be an abomination
to him who offers it, and the person who
eats of it shall bear guilt.

[19]'The flesh that touches any unclean
thing shall not be eaten. It shall be burned
with fire. And as for the *clean* flesh, all who
are clean may eat of it. [20]But the person
who eats the flesh of the sacrifice of the
peace offering that *belongs* to the LORD,
while he is unclean, that person shall be
cut off from his people. [21]Moreover the per-
son who touches any unclean thing, *such as*
human uncleanness, *an* unclean animal, or
any abominable unclean thing,[a] and who
eats the flesh of the sacrifice of the peace
offering that *belongs* to the LORD, that per-
son shall be cut off from his people.' "

Fat and Blood May Not Be Eaten

[22]And the LORD spoke to Moses, saying,
[23]"Speak to the children of Israel, saying:
'You shall not eat any fat, of ox or sheep or
goat. [24]And the fat of an animal that dies
naturally, and the fat of what is torn by
wild beasts, may be used in any other way;
but you shall by no means eat it. [25]For who-
ever eats the fat of the animal of which
men offer an offering made by fire to the
LORD, the person who eats *it* shall be cut off
from his people. [26]Moreover you shall not
eat any blood in any of your dwellings,
whether of bird or beast. [27]Whoever eats
any blood, that person shall be cut off from
his people.' "

The Portion of Aaron and His Sons

[28]Then the LORD spoke to Moses, saying,
[29]"Speak to the children of Israel, saying:
'He who offers the sacrifice of his peace of-
fering to the LORD shall bring his offering
to the LORD from the sacrifice of his peace
offering. [30]His own hands shall bring the
offerings made by fire to the LORD. The fat
with the breast he shall bring, that the
breast may be waved *as* a wave offering be-
fore the LORD. [31]And the priest shall burn
the fat on the altar, but the breast shall be
Aaron's and his sons'. [32]Also the right
thigh you shall give to the priest *as* a heave
offering from the sacrifices of your peace
offerings. [33]He among the sons of Aaron,
who offers the blood of the peace offering
and the fat, shall have the right thigh for
his part. [34]For the breast of the wave offer-
ing and the thigh of the heave offering I
have taken from the children of Israel,
from the sacrifices of their peace offerings,
and I have given them to Aaron the priest
and to his sons from the children of Israel
by a statute forever.' "

[35]This *is* the consecrated portion for
Aaron and his sons, from the offerings
made by fire to the LORD, on the day when

7:21 [a]Following Masoretic Text, Septuagint, and Vulgate; Samaritan Pentateuch, Syriac, and Targum read *swarming thing* (compare 5:2).

7:22–27 Neither **fat** (v. 23) nor **blood** (v. 26) were to be eaten. To eat the fat was to rob God of what was rightfully His. To eat blood, which is synonymous with life, would be to misuse it. Some pagan religions practiced drinking blood as a way to increase vitality magically. Such magical attempts to supply human needs were forbidden to the Hebrews. The penalty for breaking either of these laws was to be **cut off**—separated from the covenant community, either through excommunication or by death (vv. 25, 27; 20:2, 3).

Moses presented them to minister to the LORD as priests. 36The LORD commanded this to be given to them by the children of Israel, on the day that He anointed them, *by* a statute forever throughout their generations.

37This *is* the law of the burnt offering, the grain offering, the sin offering, the trespass offering, the consecrations, and the sacrifice of the peace offering, 38which the LORD commanded Moses on Mount Sinai, on the day when He commanded the children of Israel to offer their offerings to the LORD in the Wilderness of Sinai.

CHAPTER 8

Aaron and His Sons Consecrated

And the LORD spoke to Moses, saying: 2"Take Aaron and his sons with him, and the garments, the anointing oil, a bull as the sin offering, two rams, and a basket of unleavened bread; 3and gather all the congregation together at the door of the tabernacle of meeting."

4So Moses did as the LORD commanded him. And the congregation was gathered together at the door of the tabernacle of meeting. 5And Moses said to the congregation, "This *is* what the LORD commanded to be done."

6Then Moses brought Aaron and his sons and washed them with water. 7And he put the tunic on him, girded him with the sash, clothed him with the robe, and put the ephod on him; and he girded him with the intricately woven band of the ephod, and with it tied *the ephod* on him. 8Then he put the breastplate on him, and he put the Ū'rim and the Thum'mim[a] in the breastplate. 9And he put the turban on his head. Also on the turban, on its front, he put the golden plate, the holy crown, as the LORD had commanded Moses.

10Also Moses took the anointing oil, and anointed the tabernacle and all that *was* in it, and consecrated them. 11He sprinkled some of it on the altar seven times, anointed the altar and all its utensils, and the laver and its base, to consecrate them. 12And he poured some of the anointing oil on Aaron's head and anointed him, to consecrate him.

13Then Moses brought Aaron's sons and put tunics on them, girded them with sashes, and put hats on them, as the LORD had commanded Moses.

14And he brought the bull for the sin offering. Then Aaron and his sons laid their hands on the head of the bull for the sin offering, 15and Moses killed *it*. Then he took the blood, and put *some* on the horns of the altar all around with his finger, and purified the altar. And he poured the blood at the base of the altar, and consecrated it, to make atonement for it. 16Then he took all the fat that *was* on the entrails, the fatty lobe *attached to* the liver, and the two kidneys with their fat, and Moses burned *them* on the altar. 17But the bull, its hide, its flesh, and its offal, he burned with fire outside the camp, as the LORD had commanded Moses.

18Then he brought the ram as the burnt offering. And Aaron and his sons laid their hands on the head of the ram, 19and Moses killed *it*. Then he sprinkled the blood all around on the altar. 20And he cut the ram into pieces; and Moses burned the head, the pieces, and the fat. 21Then he washed the entrails and the legs in water. And Moses burned the whole ram on the altar. It *was* a burnt sacrifice for a sweet aroma, an offering made by fire to the LORD, as the LORD had commanded Moses.

8:8 [a]Literally *the Lights and the Perfections* (compare Exodus 28:30)

8:14–17 This sin offering demonstrates that a calling from God does not make anyone automatically righteous; Christians in positions of leadership need God's forgiveness as much as any other person.

[22]And he brought the second ram, the ram of consecration. Then Aaron and his sons laid their hands on the head of the ram, [23]and Moses killed *it.* Also he took *some* of its blood and put it on the tip of Aaron's right ear, on the thumb of his right hand, and on the big toe of his right foot. [24]Then he brought Aaron's sons. And Moses put *some* of the blood on the tips of their right ears, on the thumbs of their right hands, and on the big toes of their right feet. And Moses sprinkled the blood all around on the altar. [25]Then he took the fat and the fat tail, all the fat that *was* on the entrails, the fatty lobe *attached to* the liver, the two kidneys and their fat, and the right thigh; [26]and from the basket of unleavened bread that was before the LORD he took one unleavened cake, a cake of bread *anointed with* oil, and one wafer, and put *them* on the fat and on the right thigh; [27]and he put all *these* in Aaron's hands and in his sons' hands, and waved them *as* a wave offering before the LORD. [28]Then Moses took them from their hands and burned *them* on the altar, on the burnt offering. They *were* consecration offerings for a sweet aroma. That *was* an offering made by fire to the LORD. [29]And Moses took the breast and waved it *as* a wave offering before the LORD. It was Moses' part of the ram of consecration, as the LORD had commanded Moses.

[30]Then Moses took some of the anointing oil and some of the blood which *was* on the altar, and sprinkled *it* on Aaron, on his garments, on his sons, and on the garments of his sons with him; and he consecrated Aaron, his garments, his sons, and the garments of his sons with him.

[31]And Moses said to Aaron and his sons, "Boil the flesh *at* the door of the tabernacle of meeting, and eat it there with the bread that *is* in the basket of consecration offerings, as I commanded, saying, 'Aaron and his sons shall eat it.' [32]What remains of the flesh and of the bread you shall burn with fire. [33]And you shall not go outside the door of the tabernacle of meeting *for* seven days, until the days of your consecration are ended. For seven days he shall consecrate you. [34]As he has done this day, *so* the LORD has commanded to do, to make atonement for you. [35]Therefore you shall stay *at* the door of the tabernacle of meeting day and night for seven days, and keep the charge of the LORD, so that you may not die; for so I have been commanded." [36]So Aaron and his sons did all the things that the LORD had commanded by the hand of Moses.

CHAPTER 9

The Priestly Ministry Begins

It came to pass on the eighth day that Moses called Aaron and his sons and the elders of Israel. [2]And he said to Aaron, "Take for yourself a young bull as a sin offering and a ram as a burnt offering, without blemish, and offer *them* before the LORD. [3]And to the children of Israel you shall speak, saying, 'Take a kid of the goats as a sin offering, and a calf and a lamb, *both* of the first year, without blemish, as a burnt offering, [4]also a bull and a ram as peace offerings, to sacrifice before the LORD, and a grain offering mixed with oil; for today the LORD will appear to you.' "

[5]So they brought what Moses commanded before the tabernacle of meeting. And all the congregation drew near and stood before the LORD. [6]Then Moses said, "This *is* the thing which the LORD commanded you to do, and the glory of the LORD will appear to you." [7]And Moses said to Aaron, "Go to the altar, offer your sin offering and your burnt offering, and make atonement for yourself and for the people. Offer the offering of the people, and make atonement for them, as the LORD commanded."

[8]Aaron therefore went to the altar and killed the calf of the sin offering, which *was* for himself. [9]Then the sons of Aaron brought the blood to him. And he dipped his finger in the blood, put *it* on the horns of the altar, and poured the blood at the base of the altar. [10]But the fat, the kidneys,

and the fatty lobe from the liver of the sin
offering he burned on the altar, as the LORD
had commanded Moses. 11The flesh and
the hide he burned with fire outside the
camp.

12And he killed the burnt offering; and
Aaron's sons presented to him the blood,
which he sprinkled all around on the altar.
13Then they presented the burnt offering to
him, with its pieces and head, and he
burned *them* on the altar. 14And he washed
the entrails and the legs, and burned *them*
with the burnt offering on the altar.

15Then he brought the people's offering,
and took the goat, which *was* the sin offer-
ing for the people, and killed it and offered
it for sin, like the first one. 16And he
brought the burnt offering and offered it
according to the prescribed manner. 17Then
he brought the grain offering, took a hand-
ful of it, and burned *it* on the altar, besides
the burnt sacrifice of the morning.

18He also killed the bull and the ram *as*
sacrifices of peace offerings, which *were* for
the people. And Aaron's sons presented to
him the blood, which he sprinkled all
around on the altar, 19and the fat from the
bull and the ram—the fatty tail, what cov-
ers *the entrails* and the kidneys, and the
fatty lobe *attached to* the liver; 20and they
put the fat on the breasts. Then he burned
the fat on the altar; 21but the breasts and the
right thigh Aaron waved *as* a wave offer-
ing before the LORD, as Moses had com-
manded.

22Then Aaron lifted his hand toward the
people, blessed them, and came down
from offering the sin offering, the burnt of-
fering, and peace offerings. 23And Moses
and Aaron went into the tabernacle of
meeting, and came out and blessed the
people. Then the glory of the LORD ap-
peared to all the people, 24and fire came out
from before the LORD and consumed the
burnt offering and the fat on the altar.
When all the people saw *it,* they shouted
and fell on their faces.

CHAPTER 10

The Profane Fire of Nadab and Abihu

Then Nā′dab and A·bī′hū, the sons of
Aaron, each took his censer and put fire in
it, put incense on it, and offered profane
fire before the LORD, which He had not
commanded them. 2So fire went out from
the LORD and devoured them, and they
died before the LORD. 3And Moses said to
Aaron, "This is what the LORD spoke, say-
ing:

'By those who come near Me
I must be regarded as holy;
And before all the people
I must be glorified.' "

So Aaron held his peace.

4Then Moses called Mish′a·el and
El′za·phan, the sons of Uz′zi·el the uncle
of Aaron, and said to them, "Come near,
carry your brethren from before the sanc-
tuary out of the camp." 5So they went near
and carried them by their tunics out of the
camp, as Moses had said.

6And Moses said to Aaron, and to
El·ē·ā′zar and Ith′a·mar, his sons, "Do not
uncover your heads nor tear your clothes,
lest you die, and wrath come upon all the
people. But let your brethren, the whole
house of Israel, bewail the burning which
the LORD has kindled. 7You shall not go out
from the door of the tabernacle of meeting,
lest you die, for the anointing oil of the
LORD *is* upon you." And they did accord-
ing to the word of Moses.

Conduct Prescribed for Priests

8Then the LORD spoke to Aaron, saying:
9"Do not drink wine or intoxicating drink,
you, nor your sons with you, when you go

10:6, 7 Aaron and his two remaining sons were not to mourn the deaths of Nadab and Abihu; instead, they were to remain within the tabernacle and fulfill their priestly duties.

> I see children as where tomorrow begins. Those children will be mothers and fathers of family units and leaders in the church. If we don't raise up strong leaders, we fail.
>
> Wallace Erickson

into the tabernacle of meeting, lest you die.
It shall be a statute forever throughout your
generations, [10]that you may distinguish be-
tween holy and unholy, and between un-
clean and clean, [11]and that you may teach
the children of Israel all the statutes which
the LORD has spoken to them by the hand
of Moses."

[12]And Moses spoke to Aaron, and to
El·ē·ā'zar and Ith'a·mar, his sons who
were left: "Take the grain offering that re-
mains of the offerings made by fire to the
LORD, and eat it without leaven beside the
altar; for it *is* most holy. [13]You shall eat it in
a holy place, because it *is* your due and
your sons' due, of the sacrifices made by
fire to the LORD; for so I have been com-
manded. [14]The breast of the wave offering
and the thigh of the heave offering you
shall eat in a clean place, you, your sons,
and your daughters with you; for *they are*
your due and your sons' due, *which* are
given from the sacrifices of peace offerings
of the children of Israel. [15]The thigh of the
heave offering and the breast of the wave
offering they shall bring with the offerings
of fat made by fire, to offer *as* a wave offer-
ing before the LORD. And it shall be yours
and your sons' with you, by a statute for-
ever, as the LORD has commanded."

[16]Then Moses made careful inquiry
about the goat of the sin offering, and there
it was—burned up. And he was angry
with El·ē·ā'zar and Ith'a·mar, the sons of
Aaron *who were* left, saying, [17]"Why have
you not eaten the sin offering in a holy
place, since it *is* most holy, and *God* has
given it to you to bear the guilt of the con-
gregation, to make atonement for them be-
fore the LORD? [18]See! Its blood was not
brought inside the holy *place;*[a] indeed you
should have eaten it in a holy *place,* as I
commanded."

[19]And Aaron said to Moses, "Look, this
day they have offered their sin offering
and their burnt offering before the LORD,
and such things have befallen me! *If* I had
eaten the sin offering today, would it have
been accepted in the sight of the LORD?"
[20]So when Moses heard *that,* he was con-
tent.

10:18 [a]The Most Holy Place when capitalized

CHAPTER 11

Foods Permitted and Forbidden

Now the LORD spoke to Moses and
Aaron, saying to them, [2]"Speak to the chil-
dren of Israel, saying, 'These *are* the ani-
mals which you may eat among all the an-
imals that *are* on the earth: [3]Among the
animals, whatever divides the hoof, hav-
ing cloven hooves *and* chewing the cud—
that you may eat. [4]Nevertheless these you
shall not eat among those that chew the
cud or those that have cloven hooves: the
camel, because it chews the cud but does
not have cloven hooves, is unclean to you;
[5]the rock hyrax, because it chews the cud
but does not have cloven hooves, *is* un-
clean to you; [6]the hare, because it chews
the cud but does not have cloven hooves, *is*
unclean to you; [7]and the swine, though it
divides the hoof, having cloven hooves,
yet does not chew the cud, *is* unclean to
you. [8]Their flesh you shall not eat, and
their carcasses you shall not touch. They
are unclean to you.

[9]'These you may eat of all that *are* in the
water: whatever in the water has fins and

11:1—15:33 Ultimately, only moral impurity prevents a person from experiencing God's holiness.

scales, whether in the seas or in the rivers—that you may eat. 10But all in the seas or in the rivers that do not have fins and scales, all that move in the water or any living thing which *is* in the water, they *are* an abomination to you. 11They shall be an abomination to you; you shall not eat their flesh, but you shall regard their carcasses as an abomination. 12Whatever in the water does not have fins or scales—that *shall be* an abomination to you.

13'And these you shall regard as an abomination among the birds; they shall not be eaten, they *are* an abomination: the eagle, the vulture, the buzzard, 14the kite, and the falcon after its kind; 15every raven after its kind, 16the ostrich, the short-eared owl, the sea gull, and the hawk after its kind; 17the little owl, the fisher owl, and the screech owl; 18the white owl, the jackdaw, and the carrion vulture; 19the stork, the heron after its kind, the hoopoe, and the bat.

20'All flying insects that creep on *all* fours *shall be* an abomination to you. 21Yet these you may eat of every flying insect that creeps on *all* fours: those which have jointed legs above their feet with which to leap on the earth. 22These you may eat: the locust after its kind, the destroying locust after its kind, the cricket after its kind, and the grasshopper after its kind. 23But all *other* flying insects which have four feet *shall be* an abomination to you.

Unclean Animals

24'By these you shall become unclean; whoever touches the carcass of any of them shall be unclean until evening; 25whoever carries part of the carcass of any of them shall wash his clothes and be unclean until evening: 26*The carcass* of any animal which divides the foot, but is not cloven-hoofed or does not chew the cud, *is* unclean to you. Everyone who touches it shall be unclean. 27And whatever goes on its paws, among all kinds of animals that go on *all* fours, those *are* unclean to you. Whoever touches any such carcass shall be unclean until evening. 28Whoever carries *any such* carcass shall wash his clothes and be unclean until evening. It *is* unclean to you.

29'These also *shall be* unclean to you among the creeping things that creep on the earth: the mole, the mouse, and the large lizard after its kind; 30the gecko, the monitor lizard, the sand reptile, the sand lizard, and the chameleon. 31These *are* unclean to you among all that creep. Whoever touches them when they are dead shall be unclean until evening. 32Anything on which *any* of them falls, when they are dead shall be unclean, whether *it is* any item of wood or clothing or skin or sack, whatever item *it is,* in which *any* work is done, it must be put in water. And it shall be unclean until evening; then it shall be clean. 33Any earthen vessel into which *any* of them falls you shall break; and whatever *is* in it shall be unclean: 34in such a vessel, any edible food upon which water falls becomes unclean, and any drink that may be drunk from it becomes unclean. 35And everything on which *a part* of *any such* carcass falls shall be unclean; *whether it is* an oven or cooking stove, it shall be broken down; *for* they *are* unclean, and shall be unclean to you. 36Nevertheless a spring or a cistern, *in which there is* plenty of water, shall be clean, but whatever touches any such carcass becomes unclean. 37And if a part of *any such* carcass falls on any planting seed which is to be sown, it *remains* clean. 38But if water is put on the seed, and if *a part* of *any such* carcass falls on it, it *becomes* unclean to you.

39'And if any animal which you may eat dies, he who touches its carcass shall be unclean until evening. 40He who eats of its carcass shall wash his clothes and be unclean until evening. He also who carries its carcass shall wash his clothes and be unclean until evening.

41'And every creeping thing that creeps on the earth *shall be* an abomination. It shall not be eaten. 42Whatever crawls on its belly, whatever goes on *all* fours, or what-

ever has many feet among all creeping
things that creep on the earth—these you
shall not eat, for they *are* an abomination.
[43]You shall not make yourselves abomina-
ble with any creeping thing that creeps;
nor shall you make yourselves unclean
with them, lest you be defiled by them.
[44]For I *am* the LORD your God. You shall
therefore consecrate yourselves, and you
shall be holy; for I *am* holy. Neither shall
you defile yourselves with any creeping
thing that creeps on the earth. [45]For I *am* the
LORD who brings you up out of the land of
Egypt, to be your God. You shall therefore
be holy, for I *am* holy.

[46]'This *is* the law of the animals and the
birds and every living creature that moves
in the waters, and of every creature that
creeps on the earth, [47]to distinguish be-
tween the unclean and the clean, and be-
tween the animal that may be eaten and
the animal that may not be eaten.' "

CHAPTER 12

The Ritual After Childbirth

Then the LORD spoke to Moses, saying,
[2]"Speak to the children of Israel, saying: 'If
a woman has conceived, and borne a male
child, then she shall be unclean seven days;
as in the days of her customary impurity
she shall be unclean. [3]And on the eighth
day the flesh of his foreskin shall be cir-
cumcised. [4]She shall then continue in the
blood of *her* purification thirty-three days.
She shall not touch any hallowed thing,
nor come into the sanctuary until the days
of her purification are fulfilled.

[5]'But if she bears a female child, then
she shall be unclean two weeks, as in her
customary impurity, and she shall con-
tinue in the blood of *her* purification sixty-
six days.

[6]'When the days of her purification are
fulfilled, whether for a son or a daughter,
she shall bring to the priest a lamb of the
first year as a burnt offering, and a young
pigeon or a turtledove as a sin offering, to
the door of the tabernacle of meeting.
[7]Then he shall offer it before the LORD, and
make atonement for her. And she shall be
clean from the flow of her blood. This *is* the
law for her who has borne a male or a fe-
male.

[8]'And if she is not able to bring a lamb,
then she may bring two turtledoves or two
young pigeons—one as a burnt offering
and the other as a sin offering. So the priest
shall make atonement for her, and she will
be clean.' "

CHAPTER 13

The Law Concerning Leprosy

And the LORD spoke to Moses and
Aaron, saying: [2]"When a man has on the
skin of his body a swelling, a scab, or a
bright spot, and it becomes on the skin of

12:4, 5 The period of uncleanness from the birth of a daughter is 80 days, but only 40 days for a son. This does not suggest that God values males more than females. Male and female believers are of equal worth (Gal. 3:28). He does distinguish between them, however. For example, Eve was created separately from Adam and responded to temptation differently, and for this reason women in the church differ from men in function and authority (1 Tim. 2:12–14). The present verse may have been intended simply to show that such a distinction exists.

12:6, 7 Bringing a sin **offering** after giving birth to a child did not mean that procreation was a sin. This offering was for purposes of purification, necessitated by the postnatal **flow of her blood**. These procedures, though strange to us, may underscore the sacredness that birth held for the ancient Hebrew.

12:8 Jesus' family offered two small birds for Mary's purification sacrifice, indicating they were unable to afford a lamb.

13:2 The priest's role was to care for the sick while protecting the health of the community.

his body *like* a leprous[a] sore, then he shall be brought to Aaron the priest or to one of his sons the priests. [3]The priest shall examine the sore on the skin of the body; and if the hair on the sore has turned white, and the sore appears *to be* deeper than the skin of his body, it *is* a leprous sore. Then the priest shall examine him, and pronounce him unclean. [4]But if the bright spot *is* white on the skin of his body, and does not appear *to be* deeper than the skin, and its hair has not turned white, then the priest shall isolate *the one who has* the sore seven days. [5]And the priest shall examine him on the seventh day; and indeed *if* the sore appears to be as it was, *and* the sore has not spread on the skin, then the priest shall isolate him another seven days. [6]Then the priest shall examine him again on the seventh day; and indeed *if* the sore has faded, *and* the sore has not spread on the skin, then the priest shall pronounce him clean; it *is only* a scab, and he shall wash his clothes and be clean. [7]But if the scab should at all spread over the skin, after he has been seen by the priest for his cleansing, he shall be seen by the priest again. [8]And *if* the priest sees that the scab has indeed spread on the skin, then the priest shall pronounce him unclean. It *is* leprosy.

[9]"When the leprous sore is on a person, then he shall be brought to the priest. [10]And the priest shall examine *him;* and indeed *if* the swelling on the skin *is* white, and it has turned the hair white, and *there is* a spot of raw flesh in the swelling, [11]it *is* an old leprosy on the skin of his body. The priest shall pronounce him unclean, and shall not isolate him, for he *is* unclean.

[12]"And if leprosy breaks out all over the skin, and the leprosy covers all the skin of *the one who has* the sore, from his head to his foot, wherever the priest looks, [13]then the priest shall consider; and indeed *if* the leprosy has covered all his body, he shall pronounce *him* clean *who has* the sore. It has all turned white. He *is* clean. [14]But when raw flesh appears on him, he shall be unclean. [15]And the priest shall examine the raw flesh and pronounce him to be unclean; *for* the raw flesh *is* unclean. It *is* leprosy. [16]Or if the raw flesh changes and turns white again, he shall come to the priest. [17]And the priest shall examine him; and indeed *if* the sore has turned white, then the priest shall pronounce *him* clean *who has* the sore. He *is* clean.

[18]"If the body develops a boil in the skin, and it is healed, [19]and in the place of the boil there comes a white swelling or a bright spot, reddish-white, then it shall be shown to the priest; [20]and *if,* when the priest sees it, it indeed *appears* deeper than the skin, and its hair has turned white, the priest shall pronounce him unclean. It *is* a leprous sore which has broken out of the boil. [21]But if the priest examines it, and indeed *there are* no white hairs in it, and it *is* not deeper than the skin, but has faded, then the priest shall isolate him seven days; [22]and if it should at all spread over the skin, then the priest shall pronounce him unclean. It *is* a leprous sore. [23]But if the bright spot stays in one place, *and* has not spread, it *is* the scar of the boil; and the priest shall pronounce him clean.

[24]"Or if the body receives a burn on its skin by fire, and the raw *flesh* of the burn becomes a bright spot, reddish-white or white, [25]then the priest shall examine it; and indeed *if* the hair of the bright spot has turned white, and it appears deeper than the skin, it *is* leprosy broken out in the burn. Therefore the priest shall pronounce him unclean. It *is* a leprous sore. [26]But if the priest examines it, and indeed *there are* no white hairs in the bright spot, and it *is* not deeper than the skin, but has faded, then the priest shall isolate him seven days. [27]And the priest shall examine him on the seventh day. If it has at all spread over the skin, then the priest shall pronounce him unclean. It *is* a leprous sore. [28]But if the bright spot stays in one place, *and* has not spread on the skin, but has faded, it *is* a

13:2 [a]Hebrew *saraath,* disfiguring skin diseases, including leprosy, and so in verses 2–46 and 14:1–32

swelling from the burn. The priest shall
pronounce him clean, for it *is* the scar from
the burn.

29"If a man or woman has a sore on the
head or the beard, 30then the priest shall ex-
amine the sore; and indeed if it appears
deeper than the skin, *and there is* in it thin
yellow hair, then the priest shall pro-
nounce him unclean. It *is* a scaly leprosy of
the head or beard. 31But if the priest exam-
ines the scaly sore, and indeed it does not
appear deeper than the skin, and *there is* no
black hair in it, then the priest shall isolate
the one who has the scale seven days. 32And
on the seventh day the priest shall examine
the sore; and indeed *if* the scale has not
spread, and there is no yellow hair in it,
and the scale does not appear deeper than
the skin, 33he shall shave himself, but the
scale he shall not shave. And the priest
shall isolate *the one who has* the scale an-
other seven days. 34On the seventh day the
priest shall examine the scale; and indeed
if the scale has not spread over the skin,
and does not appear deeper than the skin,
then the priest shall pronounce him clean.
He shall wash his clothes and be clean.
35But if the scale should at all spread over
the skin after his cleansing, 36then the
priest shall examine him; and indeed *if* the
scale has spread over the skin, the priest
need not seek for yellow hair. He *is* un-
clean. 37But if the scale appears to be at a
standstill, and there is black hair grown up
in it, the scale has healed. He *is* clean, and
the priest shall pronounce him clean.

38"If a man or a woman has bright spots
on the skin of the body, *specifically* white
bright spots, 39then the priest shall look;
and indeed *if* the bright spots on the skin of
the body *are* dull white, it *is* a white spot
that grows on the skin. He *is* clean.

40"As for the man whose hair has fallen
from his head, he *is* bald, *but* he *is* clean.
41He whose hair has fallen from his fore-
head, he *is* bald on the forehead, *but* he *is*
clean. 42And if there is on the bald head or
bald forehead a reddish-white sore, it *is*
leprosy breaking out on his bald head or
his bald forehead. 43Then the priest shall
examine it; and indeed *if* the swelling of
the sore *is* reddish-white on his bald head
or on his bald forehead, as the appearance
of leprosy on the skin of the body, 44he is a
leprous man. He *is* unclean. The priest
shall surely pronounce him unclean; his
sore *is* on his head.

45"Now the leper on whom the sore *is,*
his clothes shall be torn and his head bare;
and he shall cover his mustache, and cry,
'Unclean! Unclean!' 46He shall be unclean.
All the days he has the sore he shall be un-
clean. He *is* unclean, and he shall dwell
alone; his dwelling *shall be* outside the
camp.

The Law Concerning Leprous Garments

47"Also, if a garment has a leprous
plague[a] in it, *whether it is* a woolen garment
or a linen garment, 48whether *it is* in the
warp or woof of linen or wool, whether in
leather or in anything made of leather,
49and if the plague is greenish or reddish in
the garment or in the leather, whether in
the warp or in the woof, or in anything
made of leather, it *is* a leprous plague and
shall be shown to the priest. 50The priest
shall examine the plague and isolate *that
which has* the plague seven days. 51And he
shall examine the plague on the seventh
day. If the plague has spread in the gar-
ment, either in the warp or in the woof, in
the leather *or* in anything made of leather,
the plague *is* an active leprosy. It *is* un-
clean. 52He shall therefore burn that gar-
ment in which is the plague, whether warp
or woof, in wool or in linen, or anything of
leather, for it *is* an active leprosy; *the gar-
ment* shall be burned in the fire.

53"But if the priest examines *it,* and in-
deed the plague has not spread in the gar-
ment, either in the warp or in the woof, or
in anything made of leather, 54then the
priest shall command that they wash *the*

13:47 [a]A mold, fungus, or similar infestation, and so in verses 47–59

thing in which *is* the plague; and he shall isolate it another seven days. 55Then the priest shall examine the plague after it has been washed; and indeed *if* the plague has not changed its color, though the plague has not spread, it *is* unclean, and you shall burn it in the fire; it continues eating away, *whether* the damage *is* outside or inside. 56If the priest examines *it*, and indeed the plague has faded after washing it, then he shall tear it out of the garment, whether out of the warp or out of the woof, or out of the leather. 57But if it appears again in the garment, either in the warp or in the woof, or in anything made of leather, it *is* a spreading *plague;* you shall burn with fire that in which is the plague. 58And if you wash the garment, either warp or woof, or whatever is made of leather, if the plague has disappeared from it, then it shall be washed a second time, and shall be clean.

59"This *is* the law of the leprous plague in a garment of wool or linen, either in the warp or woof, or in anything made of leather, to pronounce it clean or to pronounce it unclean."

CHAPTER 14

The Ritual for Cleansing Healed Lepers

Then the LORD spoke to Moses, saying, 2"This shall be the law of the leper for the day of his cleansing: He shall be brought to the priest. 3And the priest shall go out of the camp, and the priest shall examine *him;* and indeed, *if* the leprosy is healed in the leper, 4then the priest shall command to take for him who is to be cleansed two living *and* clean birds, cedar wood, scarlet, and hyssop. 5And the priest shall command that one of the birds be killed in an earthen vessel over running water. 6As for the living bird, he shall take it, the cedar wood and the scarlet and the hyssop, and dip them and the living bird in the blood of the bird *that was* killed over the running water. 7And he shall sprinkle it seven times on him who is to be cleansed from the leprosy, and shall pronounce him clean, and shall let the living bird loose in the open field. 8He who is to be cleansed shall wash his clothes, shave off all his hair, and wash himself in water, that he may be clean. After that he shall come into the camp, and shall stay outside his tent seven days. 9But on the seventh day he shall shave all the hair off his head and his beard and his eyebrows—all his hair he shall shave off. He shall wash his clothes and wash his body in water, and he shall be clean.

10"And on the eighth day he shall take two male lambs without blemish, one ewe lamb of the first year without blemish, three-tenths *of an ephah* of fine flour mixed with oil as a grain offering, and one log of oil. 11Then the priest who makes *him* clean shall present the man who is to be made clean, and those things, before the LORD, *at* the door of the tabernacle of meeting. 12And the priest shall take one male lamb and offer it as a trespass offering, and the log of oil, and wave them *as* a wave offering before the LORD. 13Then he shall kill the lamb in the place where he kills the sin offering and the burnt offering, in a holy place; for as the sin offering *is* the priest's, so *is* the trespass offering. It *is* most holy. 14The priest shall take *some* of the blood of the trespass offering, and the priest shall put *it* on the tip of the right ear of him who is to be cleansed, on the thumb of his right hand, and on the big toe of his right foot. 15And the priest shall take *some* of the log of oil, and pour *it* into the palm of his own left hand. 16Then the priest shall dip his right finger in the oil that *is* in his left hand, and shall sprinkle some of the oil with his finger seven times before the LORD. 17And of

---

14:3 The phrase **if the leprosy is healed** shows clearly that the purpose of these rituals was not to remove the disease, but to witness to the fact that it had already been cured. The ritual is symbolic and religious, but not therapeutic.

the rest of the oil in his hand, the priest
shall put *some* on the tip of the right ear of
him who is to be cleansed, on the thumb of
his right hand, and on the big toe of his
right foot, on the blood of the trespass of-
fering. 18The rest of the oil that *is* in the
priest's hand he shall put on the head of
him who is to be cleansed. So the priest
shall make atonement for him before the
LORD.

19"Then the priest shall offer the sin of-
fering, and make atonement for him who
is to be cleansed from his uncleanness. Af-
terward he shall kill the burnt offering.
20And the priest shall offer the burnt offer-
ing and the grain offering on the altar. So
the priest shall make atonement for him,
and he shall be clean.

21"But if he *is* poor and cannot afford it,
then he shall take one male lamb *as* a tres-
pass offering to be waved, to make atone-
ment for him, one-tenth *of an ephah* of fine
flour mixed with oil as a grain offering, a
log of oil, 22and two turtledoves or two
young pigeons, such as he is able to afford:
one shall be a sin offering and the other a
burnt offering. 23He shall bring them to the
priest on the eighth day for his cleansing,
to the door of the tabernacle of meeting,
before the LORD. 24And the priest shall take
the lamb of the trespass offering and the
log of oil, and the priest shall wave them *as*
a wave offering before the LORD. 25Then he
shall kill the lamb of the trespass offering,
and the priest shall take *some* of the blood
of the trespass offering and put *it* on the tip
of the right ear of him who is to be
cleansed, on the thumb of his right hand,
and on the big toe of his right foot. 26And
the priest shall pour some of the oil into the
palm of his own left hand. 27Then the priest
shall sprinkle with his right finger *some* of
the oil that *is* in his left hand seven times
before the LORD. 28And the priest shall put
some of the oil that *is* in his hand on the
tip of the right ear of him who is to be
cleansed, on the thumb of the right hand,
and on the big toe of his right foot, on the
place of the blood of the trespass offering.
29The rest of the oil that *is* in the priest's
hand he shall put on the head of him who
is to be cleansed, to make atonement for
him before the LORD. 30And he shall offer
one of the turtledoves or young pigeons,
such as he can afford— 31such as he is able
to afford, the one *as* a sin offering and the
other *as* a burnt offering, with the grain of-
fering. So the priest shall make atonement
for him who is to be cleansed before the
LORD. 32This *is* the law *for one* who had a
leprous sore, who cannot afford the usual
cleansing."

The Law Concerning Leprous Houses

33And the LORD spoke to Moses and
Aaron, saying: 34"When you have come
into the land of Cā'naan, which I give you
as a possession, and I put the leprous
plague[a] in a house in the land of your pos-
session, 35and he who owns the house
comes and tells the priest, saying, 'It seems
to me that *there is* some plague in the
house,' 36then the priest shall command
that they empty the house, before the
priest goes *into it* to examine the plague,
that all that *is* in the house may not be
made unclean; and afterward the priest
shall go in to examine the house. 37And he
shall examine the plague; and indeed *if* the
plague *is* on the walls of the house with in-
grained streaks, greenish or reddish,
which appear to be deep in the wall, 38then
the priest shall go out of the house, to the
door of the house, and shut up the house
seven days. 39And the priest shall come
again on the seventh day and look; and in-
deed *if* the plague has spread on the walls
of the house, 40then the priest shall com-
mand that they take away the stones in
which *is* the plague, and they shall cast
them into an unclean place outside the city.
41And he shall cause the house to be
scraped inside, all around, and the dust
that they scrape off they shall pour out
in an unclean place outside the city.

14:34 [a]Decomposition by mildew, mold, dry rot, etc., and so in verses 34–53

42Then they shall take other stones and put
them in the place of *those* stones, and he
shall take other mortar and plaster the
house.
43"Now if the plague comes back and
breaks out in the house, after he has taken
away the stones, after he has scraped the
house, and after it is plastered, 44then the
priest shall come and look; and indeed *if*
the plague has spread in the house, it *is* an
active leprosy in the house. It *is* unclean.
45And he shall break down the house, its
stones, its timber, and all the plaster of the
house, and he shall carry *them* outside the
city to an unclean place. 46Moreover he
who goes into the house at all while it is
shut up shall be unclean until evening.
47And he who lies down in the house shall
wash his clothes, and he who eats in the
house shall wash his clothes.
48"But if the priest comes in and exam-
ines *it,* and indeed the plague has not
spread in the house after the house was
plastered, then the priest shall pronounce
the house clean, because the plague is
healed. 49And he shall take, to cleanse the
house, two birds, cedar wood, scarlet, and
hyssop. 50Then he shall kill one of the birds
in an earthen vessel over running water;
51and he shall take the cedar wood, the hys-
sop, the scarlet, and the living bird, and
dip them in the blood of the slain bird and
in the running water, and sprinkle the
house seven times. 52And he shall cleanse
the house with the blood of the bird and
the running water and the living bird, with
the cedar wood, the hyssop, and the scar-
let. 53Then he shall let the living bird loose
outside the city in the open field, and make
atonement for the house, and it shall be
clean.
54"This *is* the law for any leprous sore
and scale, 55for the leprosy of a garment
and of a house, 56for a swelling and a scab
and a bright spot, 57to teach when *it is* un-
clean and when *it is* clean. This *is* the law of
leprosy."

CHAPTER 15

The Law Concerning Bodily Discharges

And the LORD spoke to Moses and
Aaron, saying, 2"Speak to the children of
Israel, and say to them: 'When any man
has a discharge from his body, his dis-
charge *is* unclean. 3And this shall be his
uncleanness in regard to his discharge—
whether his body runs with his discharge,
or his body is stopped up by his discharge,
it *is* his uncleanness. 4Every bed is unclean
on which he who has the discharge lies,
and everything on which he sits shall be
unclean. 5And whoever touches his bed
shall wash his clothes and bathe in water,
and be unclean until evening. 6He who sits
on anything on which he who has the dis-
charge sat shall wash his clothes and bathe
in water, and be unclean until evening.
7And he who touches the body of him who
has the discharge shall wash his clothes
and bathe in water, and be unclean until
evening. 8If he who has the discharge spits
on him who is clean, then he shall wash his
clothes and bathe in water, and be unclean
until evening. 9Any saddle on which he
who has the discharge rides shall be un-
clean. 10Whoever touches anything that
was under him shall be unclean until
evening. He who carries *any of* those things
shall wash his clothes and bathe in water,
and be unclean until evening. 11And
whomever the one who has the discharge
touches, and has not rinsed his hands in
water, he shall wash his clothes and bathe
in water, and be unclean until evening.
12The vessel of earth that he who has the
discharge touches shall be broken, and
every vessel of wood shall be rinsed in
water.

15:1–18 Discharge (v. 2) refers to abnormal emissions of men, possibly due to infection or disease. **Semen** (vv. 16–18) is the normal emission of men.

13‘And when he who has a discharge is
cleansed of his discharge, then he shall
count for himself seven days for his cleans-
ing, wash his clothes, and bathe his body
in running water; then he shall be clean.
14On the eighth day he shall take for him-
self two turtledoves or two young pigeons,
and come before the LORD, to the door of
the tabernacle of meeting, and give them to
the priest. 15Then the priest shall offer
them, the one *as* a sin offering and the
other *as* a burnt offering. So the priest shall
make atonement for him before the LORD
because of his discharge.

16‘If any man has an emission of semen,
then he shall wash all his body in water,
and be unclean until evening. 17And any
garment and any leather on which there is
semen, it shall be washed with water, and
be unclean until evening. 18Also, when a
woman lies with a man, and *there is* an
emission of semen, they shall bathe in wa-
ter, and be unclean until evening.

19‘If a woman has a discharge, *and* the
discharge from her body is blood, she
shall be set apart seven days; and who-
ever touches her shall be unclean until
evening. 20Everything that she lies on dur-
ing her impurity shall be unclean; also
everything that she sits on shall be un-
clean. 21Whoever touches her bed shall
wash his clothes and bathe in water, and
be unclean until evening. 22And who-
ever touches anything that she sat on shall
wash his clothes and bathe in water, and be
unclean until evening. 23If *anything* is on
her bed or on anything on which she sits,
when he touches it, he shall be unclean
until evening. 24And if any man lies with
her at all, so that her impurity is on him,
he shall be unclean seven days; and
every bed on which he lies shall be un-
clean.

25‘If a woman has a discharge of blood
for many days, other than at the time of her
customary impurity, or if it runs beyond her
usual time of impurity, all the days of
her unclean discharge shall be as the days
of her *customary* impurity. She *shall be* un-
clean. 26Every bed on which she lies all the
days of her discharge shall be to her as the
bed of her impurity; and whatever she sits
on shall be unclean, as the uncleanness of
her impurity. 27Whoever touches those
things shall be unclean; he shall wash his
clothes and bathe in water, and be unclean
until evening.

28‘But if she is cleansed of her discharge,
then she shall count for herself seven days,
and after that she shall be clean. 29And on
the eighth day she shall take for herself
two turtledoves or two young pigeons,
and bring them to the priest, to the door of
the tabernacle of meeting. 30Then the priest
shall offer the one *as* a sin offering and
the other *as* a burnt offering, and the priest
shall make atonement for her before
the LORD for the discharge of her unclean-
ness.

31‘Thus you shall separate the children
of Israel from their uncleanness, lest they
die in their uncleanness when they defile
My tabernacle that *is* among them. 32This *is*
the law for one who has a discharge, and
for him who emits semen and is unclean
thereby, 33and for her who is indisposed
because of her *customary* impurity, and for
one who has a discharge, either man or
woman, and for him who lies with her
who is unclean.’ ”

15:19–24 discharge . . . is blood: The normal menstruation of women.

15:25–33 For many days indicates abnormal emissions for women. In the two normal cases (vv. 16–24), impurity is removed by bathing. In the prolonged and critical emissions the **sin** and **burnt offerings** are required (vv. 15, 30). The rationale behind these laws is not clear. At the least they promoted sexual hygiene and care in sexual relations. This passage details the isolation of the NT woman with the issue of blood and explains why she was so desperate to receive healing (see Matt. 9:20–22; Mark 5:25–34; Luke 8:43–48).

CHAPTER 16

The Day of Atonement

Now the LORD spoke to Moses after the death of the two sons of Aaron, when they offered *profane fire* before the LORD, and died; 2and the LORD said to Moses: "Tell Aaron your brother not to come at *just* any time into the Holy *Place* inside the veil, before the mercy seat which *is* on the ark, lest he die; for I will appear in the cloud above the mercy seat.

3"Thus Aaron shall come into the Holy *Place:* with *the blood of* a young bull as a sin offering, and *of* a ram as a burnt offering. 4He shall put the holy linen tunic and the linen trousers on his body; he shall be girded with a linen sash, and with the linen turban he shall be attired. These *are* holy garments. Therefore he shall wash his body in water, and put them on. 5And he shall take from the congregation of the children of Israel two kids of the goats as a sin offering, and one ram as a burnt offering.

6"Aaron shall offer the bull as a sin offering, which *is* for himself, and make atonement for himself and for his house. 7He shall take the two goats and present them before the LORD *at* the door of the tabernacle of meeting. 8Then Aaron shall cast lots for the two goats: one lot for the LORD and the other lot for the scapegoat. 9And Aaron shall bring the goat on which the LORD's lot fell, and offer it *as* a sin offering. 10But the goat on which the lot fell to be the scapegoat shall be presented alive before the LORD, to make atonement upon it, *and* to let it go as the scapegoat into the wilderness.

11"And Aaron shall bring the bull of the sin offering, which is for himself, and make atonement for himself and for his house, and shall kill the bull as the sin offering which *is* for himself. 12Then he shall take a censer full of burning coals of fire from the altar before the LORD, with his hands full of sweet incense beaten fine, and bring *it* inside the veil. 13And he shall put the incense on the fire before the LORD, that the cloud of incense may cover the mercy seat that *is* on the Testimony, lest he die. 14He shall take some of the blood of the bull and sprinkle *it* with his finger on the mercy seat on the east *side;* and before the mercy seat he shall sprinkle some of the blood with his finger seven times.

15"Then he shall kill the goat of the sin offering, which *is* for the people, bring its blood inside the veil, do with that blood as he did with the blood of the bull, and sprinkle it on the mercy seat and before the mercy seat. 16So he shall make atonement for the Holy *Place,* because of the uncleanness of the children of Israel, and because of their transgressions, for all their sins; and so he shall do for the tabernacle of meeting which remains among them in the midst of their uncleanness. 17There shall be no man in the tabernacle of meeting when he goes in to make atonement in the Holy *Place,* until he comes out, that he may make atonement for himself, for his household, and for all the assembly of Israel. 18And he shall go out to the altar that *is* before the LORD, and make atonement for it, and shall take some of the blood of the bull and some of the blood of the goat, and put it on the horns of the altar all around. 19Then he shall sprinkle some of the blood on it with his finger seven times, cleanse it, and consecrate it from the uncleanness of the children of Israel.

20"And when he has made an end of atoning for the Holy *Place,* the tabernacle of meeting, and the altar, he shall bring the live goat. 21Aaron shall lay both his hands on the head of the live goat, confess over it

---

16:1–34 Chapter 16 and also 23:26–32 describe the Day of Atonement, the most sacred event in the year. Postbiblical Judaism referred to it as "the day" or "the great day." In the NT Paul calls it "the Fast" (Acts 27:9). Today it is usually called *Yom Kippur.*

all the iniquities of the children of Israel,
and all their transgressions, concerning all
their sins, putting them on the head of the
goat, and shall send *it* away into the
wilderness by the hand of a suitable man.
[22]The goat shall bear on itself all their iniq-
uities to an uninhabited land; and he shall
release the goat in the wilderness.

[23]"Then Aaron shall come into the taber-
nacle of meeting, shall take off the linen
garments which he put on when he went
into the Holy *Place,* and shall leave them
there. [24]And he shall wash his body with
water in a holy place, put on his garments,
come out and offer his burnt offering and
the burnt offering of the people, and make
atonement for himself and for the people.
[25]The fat of the sin offering he shall burn on
the altar. [26]And he who released the goat as
the scapegoat shall wash his clothes and
bathe his body in water, and afterward he
may come into the camp. [27]The bull *for* the
sin offering and the goat *for* the sin offer-
ing, whose blood was brought in to make
atonement in the Holy *Place,* shall be car-
ried outside the camp. And they shall burn
in the fire their skins, their flesh, and their
offal. [28]Then he who burns them shall wash
his clothes and bathe his body in water,
and afterward he may come into the camp.

[29]"*This* shall be a statute forever for you:
In the seventh month, on the tenth *day* of
the month, you shall afflict your souls, and
do no work at all, *whether* a native of your
own country or a stranger who dwells
among you. [30]For on that day *the priest*
shall make atonement for you, to cleanse
you, *that* you may be clean from all your
sins before the LORD. [31]It *is* a sabbath of
solemn rest for you, and you shall afflict
your souls. *It is* a statute forever. [32]And the
priest, who is anointed and consecrated to
minister as priest in his father's place, shall
make atonement, and put on the linen
clothes, the holy garments; [33]then he shall
make atonement for the Holy Sanctuary,[a]
and he shall make atonement for the taber-
nacle of meeting and for the altar, and he
shall make atonement for the priests and
for all the people of the assembly. [34]This
shall be an everlasting statute for you, to
make atonement for the children of Israel,
for all their sins, once a year." And he did
as the LORD commanded Moses.

CHAPTER 17

The Sanctity of Blood

And the LORD spoke to Moses, saying,
[2]"Speak to Aaron, to his sons, and to all the
children of Israel, and say to them, 'This *is*
the thing which the LORD has commanded,
saying: [3]"Whatever man of the house of Is-
rael who kills an ox or lamb or goat in the
camp, or who kills *it* outside the camp,
[4]and does not bring it to the door of the
tabernacle of meeting to offer an offering
to the LORD before the tabernacle of the
LORD, the guilt of bloodshed shall be im-
puted to that man. He has shed blood; and
that man shall be cut off from among his
people, [5]to the end that the children of Is-
rael may bring their sacrifices which they
offer in the open field, that they may bring
them to the LORD at the door of the taber-
nacle of meeting, to the priest, and offer
them *as* peace offerings to the LORD. [6]And
the priest shall sprinkle the blood on the al-
tar of the LORD *at* the door of the tabernacle
of meeting, and burn the fat for a sweet
aroma to the LORD. [7]They shall no more of-
fer their sacrifices to demons, after whom
they have played the harlot. This shall be a
statute forever for them throughout their
generations." '

[8]"Also you shall say to them: 'Whatever
man of the house of Israel, or of the
strangers who dwell among you, who

16:33 [a]That is, the Most Holy Place

16:34 The inadequacy of this ceremony to fully deal with sin reverberates in the phrase "once a year." In contrast, Christ's work of atonement occurred only once yet covers all sin.

offers a burnt offering or sacrifice, 9and
does not bring it to the door of the taber-
nacle of meeting, to offer it to the LORD,
that man shall be cut off from among his
people.

10'And whatever man of the house of Is-
rael, or of the strangers who dwell among
you, who eats any blood, I will set My face
against that person who eats blood, and
will cut him off from among his people.
11For the life of the flesh *is* in the blood, and
I have given it to you upon the altar to
make atonement for your souls; for it *is* the
blood *that* makes atonement for the soul.'
12Therefore I said to the children of Israel,
'No one among you shall eat blood, nor
shall any stranger who dwells among you
eat blood.'

13"Whatever man of the children of Is-
rael, or of the strangers who dwell among
you, who hunts and catches any animal or
bird that may be eaten, he shall pour out its
blood and cover it with dust; 14for *it is* the
life of all flesh. Its blood sustains its life.
Therefore I said to the children of Israel,
'You shall not eat the blood of any flesh, for
the life of all flesh is its blood. Whoever
eats it shall be cut off.'

15"And every person who eats what
died *naturally* or what was torn *by beasts,*
whether he is a native of your own country
or a stranger, he shall both wash his clothes
and bathe in water, and be unclean until
evening. Then he shall be clean. 16But if he
does not wash *them* or bathe his body, then
he shall bear his guilt."

CHAPTER 18

Laws of Sexual Morality

Then the LORD spoke to Moses, saying,
2"Speak to the children of Israel, and say to
them: 'I am the LORD your God. 3According
to the doings of the land of Egypt, where
you dwelt, you shall not do; and according
to the doings of the land of Că'naan, where
I am bringing you, you shall not do; nor
shall you walk in their ordinances. 4You
shall observe My judgments and keep My
ordinances, to walk in them: I *am* the LORD
your God. 5You shall therefore keep My
statutes and My judgments, which if a
man does, he shall live by them: I *am* the
LORD.

6'None of you shall approach anyone
who is near of kin to him, to uncover his
nakedness: I *am* the LORD. 7The nakedness
of your father or the nakedness of your
mother you shall not uncover. She *is* your
mother; you shall not uncover her naked-
ness. 8The nakedness of your father's wife
you shall not uncover; it *is* your father's
nakedness. 9The nakedness of your sister,
the daughter of your father, or the daugh-
ter of your mother, *whether* born at home or
elsewhere, their nakedness you shall not
uncover. 10The nakedness of your son's
daughter or your daughter's daughter,
their nakedness you shall not uncover; for
theirs *is* your own nakedness. 11The naked-
ness of your father's wife's daughter, be-
gotten by your father—she *is* your sister—
you shall not uncover her nakedness. 12You
shall not uncover the nakedness of your
father's sister; she *is* near of kin to your
father. 13You shall not uncover the naked-
ness of your mother's sister, for she *is* near
of kin to your mother. 14You shall not un-
cover the nakedness of your father's
brother. You shall not approach his wife;
she *is* your aunt. 15You shall not uncover
the nakedness of your daughter-in-law—
she *is* your son's wife—you shall not un-
cover her nakedness. 16You shall not un-
cover the nakedness of your brother's
wife; it *is* your brother's nakedness. 17You
shall not uncover the nakedness of a
woman and her daughter, nor shall you

17:11 The emphasis on **blood** making **atonement** for the soul serves as the theological basis for a substitutionary theory of sacrifice. Its position here, after the description of the Day of Atonement (ch. 16), serves to reemphasize the truth that all life is a gift from God, never to be taken lightly, and that only life, not some lesser gift, can be given for sin.

take her son's daughter or her daughter's
daughter, to uncover her nakedness. They
are near of kin to her. It *is* wickedness.
18Nor shall you take a woman as a rival to
her sister, to uncover her nakedness while
the other is alive.
19'Also you shall not approach a woman
to uncover her nakedness as long as she is
in her *customary* impurity. 20Moreover you
shall not lie carnally with your neighbor's
wife, to defile yourself with her. 21And you
shall not let any of your descendants pass
through *the fire* to Mō'lech, nor shall you
profane the name of your God: I *am* the
LORD. 22You shall not lie with a male as
with a woman. It *is* an abomination. 23Nor
shall you mate with any animal, to defile
yourself with it. Nor shall any woman
stand before an animal to mate with it. It *is*
perversion.
24'Do not defile yourselves with any of
these things; for by all these the nations are
defiled, which I am casting out before you.
25For the land is defiled; therefore I visit the
punishment of its iniquity upon it, and the
land vomits out its inhabitants. 26You shall
therefore keep My statutes and My judg-
ments, and shall not commit *any* of these
abominations, *either* any of your own na-
tion or any stranger who dwells among
you 27(for all these abominations the men
of the land have done, who *were* before
you, and thus the land is defiled), 28lest the
land vomit you out also when you defile it,
as it vomited out the nations that *were* be-
fore you. 29For whoever commits any of
these abominations, the persons who com-
mit *them* shall be cut off from among their
people.
30'Therefore you shall keep My ordi-
nance, so that *you* do not commit *any* of
these abominable customs which were
committed before you, and that you do not
defile yourselves by them: I *am* the LORD
your God.' "

CHAPTER 19

Moral and Ceremonial Laws

And the LORD spoke to Moses, saying,
2"Speak to all the congregation of the chil-
dren of Israel, and say to them: 'You shall
be holy, for I the LORD your God *am* holy.
3'Every one of you shall revere his
mother and his father, and keep My Sab-
baths: I *am* the LORD your God.
4'Do not turn to idols, nor make for
yourselves molded gods: I *am* the LORD
your God.
5'And if you offer a sacrifice of a peace
offering to the LORD, you shall offer it of
your own free will. 6It shall be eaten the
same day you offer *it*, and on the next day.
And if any remains until the third day, it
shall be burned in the fire. 7And if it is
eaten at all on the third day, it *is* an
abomination. It shall not be accepted.
8Therefore *everyone* who eats it shall bear
his iniquity, because he has profaned the
hallowed *offering* of the LORD; and that per-
son shall be cut off from his people.
9'When you reap the harvest of your
land, you shall not wholly reap the corners
of your field, nor shall you gather the
gleanings of your harvest. 10And you shall
not glean your vineyard, nor shall you
gather *every* grape of your vineyard; you
shall leave them for the poor and the
stranger: I *am* the LORD your God.
11'You shall not steal, nor deal falsely,
nor lie to one another. 12And you shall not
swear by My name falsely, nor shall you
profane the name of your God: I *am* the
LORD.
13'You shall not cheat your neighbor, nor
rob *him*. The wages of him who is hired

18:19–30 These several sexual aberrations, among them adultery (v. 20), homosexuality (v. 22), and bestiality (v. 23), were practiced by the Canaanites (v. 24). Besides blurring the distinction between the believer and the world, indulgence in such immoralities leads to a life that denies all moral boundaries. It makes personal desires supreme, and rejects God's will as irrelevant.

> The rule for all of us is perfectly simple. Do not waste time bothering whether you "love" your neighbor; act as if you did.
>
> C. S. Lewis

shall not remain with you all night until
morning. 14You shall not curse the deaf, nor
put a stumbling block before the blind, but
shall fear your God: I *am* the LORD.

15'You shall do no injustice in judgment.
You shall not be partial to the poor, nor
honor the person of the mighty. In righ-
teousness you shall judge your neighbor.
16You shall not go about *as* a talebearer
among your people; nor shall you take a
stand against the life of your neighbor: I *am*
the LORD.

17'You shall not hate your brother in
your heart. You shall surely rebuke your
neighbor, and not bear sin because of him.
18You shall not take vengeance, nor bear
any grudge against the children of your
people, but you shall love your neighbor
as yourself: I *am* the LORD.

19'You shall keep My statutes. You shall
not let your livestock breed with another
kind. You shall not sow your field with
mixed seed. Nor shall a garment of mixed
linen and wool come upon you.

20'Whoever lies carnally with a woman
who *is* betrothed to a man as a concubine,
and who has not at all been redeemed nor
given her freedom, for this there shall be
scourging; *but* they shall not be put to
death, because she was not free. 21And he
shall bring his trespass offering to the
LORD, to the door of the tabernacle of meet-
ing, a ram as a trespass offering. 22The
priest shall make atonement for him with
the ram of the trespass offering before the
LORD for his sin which he has committed.
And the sin which he has committed shall
be forgiven him.

23'When you come into the land, and
have planted all kinds of trees for food,
then you shall count their fruit as uncir-
cumcised. Three years it shall be as uncir-
cumcised to you. *It* shall not be eaten.
24But in the fourth year all its fruit shall be
holy, a praise to the LORD. 25And in the fifth
year you may eat its fruit, that it may
yield to you its increase: I *am* the LORD your
God.

26'You shall not eat *anything* with the
blood, nor shall you practice divination or
soothsaying. 27You shall not shave around
the sides of your head, nor shall you dis-
figure the edges of your beard. 28You shall
not make any cuttings in your flesh for the
dead, nor tattoo any marks on you: I *am* the
LORD.

29'Do not prostitute your daughter, to
cause her to be a harlot, lest the land fall
into harlotry, and the land become full of
wickedness.

30'You shall keep My Sabbaths and rev-
erence My sanctuary: I *am* the LORD.

31'Give no regard to mediums and famil-
iar spirits; do not seek after them, to be de-
filed by them: I *am* the LORD your God.

32'You shall rise before the gray headed
and honor the presence of an old man, and
fear your God: I *am* the LORD.

33'And if a stranger dwells with you in
your land, you shall not mistreat him.
34The stranger who dwells among you
shall be to you as one born among you,
and you shall love him as yourself; for you

19:17 You shall surely rebuke: Each of us bears a responsibility for trying to curb known sins in the life of another. Today, we often refer to this as "accountability." By openly confronting fellow Christians about their sin, we give them an opportunity to repent and maintain purity within the body of Christ.

19:18 you shall love your neighbor as yourself: Quoted nine times in the NT (Matt. 5:43; 19:19; 22:39; Mark 12:31, 33; Luke 10:27; Rom. 13:9; Gal. 5:14; James 2:8). It is the second half of Jesus' summary of the law (Matt. 22:37–40).

were strangers in the land of Egypt: I *am*
the LORD your God.
[35]'You shall do no injustice in judgment,
in measurement of length, weight, or vol-
ume. [36]You shall have honest scales, honest
weights, an honest ephah, and an honest
hin: I *am* the LORD your God, who brought
you out of the land of Egypt.
[37]'Therefore you shall observe all My
statutes and all My judgments, and per-
form them: I *am* the LORD.' "

CHAPTER 20

Penalties for Breaking the Law

Then the LORD spoke to Moses, saying,
[2]"Again, you shall say to the children of Is-
rael: 'Whoever of the children of Israel, or
of the strangers who dwell in Israel, who
gives *any* of his descendants to Mō'lech, he
shall surely be put to death. The people of
the land shall stone him with stones. [3]I will
set My face against that man, and will cut
him off from his people, because he has
given *some* of his descendants to Mō'lech,
to defile My sanctuary and profane My
holy name. [4]And if the people of the land
should in any way hide their eyes from the
man, when he gives *some* of his descen-
dants to Mō'lech, and they do not kill him,
[5]then I will set My face against that man
and against his family; and I will cut him
off from his people, and all who prostitute
themselves with him to commit harlotry
with Mō'lech.
[6]'And the person who turns to mediums
and familiar spirits, to prostitute himself
with them, I will set My face against that
person and cut him off from his people.
[7]Consecrate yourselves therefore, and be
holy, for I *am* the LORD your God. [8]And you
shall keep My statutes, and perform them:
I *am* the LORD who sanctifies you.

Loving Guidance

Jay Kesler

Our grandchildren today are bombarded by society's standards of "acceptable" sexual behavior. They are much more conscious—and conscious much earlier—of their own sexuality and of society's focus on sex. They are faced with school sex education that often teaches them ideas about sexuality that are in opposition to Christian principles of purity. They see sex on television used to sell perfume, blue jeans, and automobiles; they hear sex in the music that blares from every street corner; they are confronted at every turn by a standard of behavior that encourages exploration and freedom, promiscuity and exploitation.

We cannot change society—at least not quickly or all at once. We cannot control what our young people see and hear and experience when they are away from us.

But what we *can* do, as grandparents, is provide for them a solid moral framework, based on biblical principles, to help them establish their own moral standards. We can seek to understand the world they live in, to empathize with their struggles. We can listen. We can love. We can offer guidelines. We can pull them back from the edge. ✦

20:2–5 Child sacrifice was a fairly common practice among the Canaanites and later Phoenicians, often used in the hope of securing a larger family. God says He will bring the opposite result. The offender **shall . . . be put to death** (v. 2). If the community defaults, God says, **I will cut him off** (v. 5).

9'For everyone who curses his father or his mother shall surely be put to death. He has cursed his father or his mother. His blood *shall be* upon him.

10'The man who commits adultery with *another* man's wife, *he* who commits adultery with his neighbor's wife, the adulterer and the adulteress, shall surely be put to death. 11The man who lies with his father's wife has uncovered his father's nakedness; both of them shall surely be put to death. Their blood *shall be* upon them. 12If a man lies with his daughter-in-law, both of them shall surely be put to death. They have committed perversion. Their blood *shall be* upon them. 13If a man lies with a male as he lies with a woman, both of them have committed an abomination. They shall surely be put to death. Their blood *shall be* upon them. 14If a man marries a woman and her mother, it *is* wickedness. They shall be burned with fire, both he and they, that there may be no wickedness among you. 15If a man mates with an animal, he shall surely be put to death, and you shall kill the animal. 16If a woman approaches any animal and mates with it, you shall kill the woman and the animal. They shall surely be put to death. Their blood *is* upon them.

17'If a man takes his sister, his father's daughter or his mother's daughter, and sees her nakedness and she sees his nakedness, it *is* a wicked thing. And they shall be cut off in the sight of their people. He has uncovered his sister's nakedness. He shall bear his guilt. 18If a man lies with a woman during her sickness and uncovers her nakedness, he has exposed her flow, and she has uncovered the flow of her blood. Both of them shall be cut off from their people.

19'You shall not uncover the nakedness of your mother's sister nor of your father's sister, for that would uncover his near of kin. They shall bear their guilt. 20If a man lies with his uncle's wife, he has uncovered his uncle's nakedness. They shall bear their sin; they shall die childless. 21If a man takes his brother's wife, it *is* an unclean thing. He has uncovered his brother's nakedness. They shall be childless.

22'You shall therefore keep all My statutes and all My judgments, and perform them, that the land where I am bringing you to dwell may not vomit you out. 23And you shall not walk in the statutes of the nation which I am casting out before you; for they commit all these things, and therefore I abhor them. 24But I have said to you, "You shall inherit their land, and I will give it to you to possess, a land flowing with milk and honey." I *am* the LORD your God, who has separated you from the peoples. 25You shall therefore distinguish between clean animals and unclean, between unclean birds and clean, and you shall not make yourselves abominable by beast or by bird, or by any kind of living thing that creeps on the ground, which I have separated from you as unclean. 26And you shall be holy to Me, for I the LORD *am* holy, and have separated you from the peoples, that you should be Mine.

27'A man or a woman who is a medium, or who has familiar spirits, shall surely be put to death; they shall stone them with stones. Their blood *shall be* upon them.' "

CHAPTER 21

Regulations for Conduct of Priests

And the LORD said to Moses, "Speak to the priests, the sons of Aaron, and say to them: 'None shall defile himself for the

20:26 you shall be holy to Me: It is not adequate only to be separated *from* the impure. God's people must be separated *to* Him. This is true holiness.

21:1–4 Since even entering the tent of the dead defiled a person for seven days and would prevent a priest from fulfilling his duties, priests were forbidden to make themselves unclean for any but their nearest relatives.

dead among his people, 2except for his rel-
atives who are nearest to him: his mother,
his father, his son, his daughter, and his
brother; 3also his virgin sister who is near
to him, who has had no husband, for her
he may defile himself. 4*Otherwise* he shall
not defile himself, *being* a chief man among
his people, to profane himself.

5'They shall not make any bald *place* on
their heads, nor shall they shave the edges
of their beards nor make any cuttings in
their flesh. 6They shall be holy to their God
and not profane the name of their God, for
they offer the offerings of the LORD made
by fire, *and* the bread of their God; there-
fore they shall be holy. 7They shall not take
a wife *who is* a harlot or a defiled woman,
nor shall they take a woman divorced from
her husband; for *the priest*[a] is holy to his
God. 8Therefore you shall consecrate him,
for he offers the bread of your God. He
shall be holy to you, for I the LORD, who
sanctify you, *am* holy. 9The daughter of any
priest, if she profanes herself by playing
the harlot, she profanes her father. She
shall be burned with fire.

10'*He who is* the high priest among his
brethren, on whose head the anointing oil
was poured and who is consecrated to
wear the garments, shall not uncover his
head nor tear his clothes; 11nor shall he go
near any dead body, nor defile himself for
his father or his mother; 12nor shall he go
out of the sanctuary, nor profane the sanc-
tuary of his God; for the consecration of
the anointing oil of his God *is* upon him: I
am the LORD. 13And he shall take a wife in
her virginity. 14A widow or a divorced
woman or a defiled woman *or* a harlot—
these he shall not marry; but he shall take a
virgin of his own people as wife. 15Nor
shall he profane his posterity among his
people, for I the LORD sanctify him.' "

16And the LORD spoke to Moses, saying,
17"Speak to Aaron, saying: 'No man of your
descendants in *succeeding* generations,
who has *any* defect, may approach to offer
the bread of his God. 18For any man who
has a defect shall not approach: a man
blind or lame, who has a marred *face* or
any *limb* too long, 19a man who has a bro-
ken foot or broken hand, 20or is a hunch-
back or a dwarf, or *a man* who has a defect
in his eye, or eczema or scab, or is a eu-
nuch. 21No man of the descendants of
Aaron the priest, who has a defect, shall
come near to offer the offerings made by
fire to the LORD. He has a defect; he shall
not come near to offer the bread of his
God. 22He may eat the bread of his God,
both the most holy and the holy; 23only he
shall not go near the veil or approach the
altar, because he has a defect, lest he pro-
fane My sanctuaries; for I the LORD sanctify
them.' "

24And Moses told *it* to Aaron and his
sons, and to all the children of Israel.

CHAPTER 22

Then the LORD spoke to Moses, saying,
2"Speak to Aaron and his sons, that they
separate themselves from the holy things
of the children of Israel, and that they do
not profane My holy name *by* what they
dedicate to Me: I *am* the LORD. 3Say to
them: 'Whoever of all your descendants
throughout your generations, who goes
near the holy things which the children of
Israel dedicate to the LORD, while he has
uncleanness upon him, that person shall
be cut off from My presence: I *am* the LORD.

4'Whatever man of the descendants of
Aaron, who *is* a leper or has a discharge,
shall not eat the holy offerings until he is
clean. And whoever touches anything
made unclean *by* a corpse, or a man who
has had an emission of semen, 5or whoever
touches any creeping thing by which he
would be made unclean, or any person by
whom he would become unclean, what-
ever his uncleanness may be— 6the person
who has touched any such thing shall be
unclean until evening, and shall not eat the
holy *offerings* unless he washes his body
with water. 7And when the sun goes down

21:7 [a]Literally *he*

he shall be clean; and afterward he may eat
the holy *offerings,* because it *is* his food.
8 Whatever dies *naturally* or is torn *by beasts*
he shall not eat, to defile himself with it: I
am the LORD.
9 'They shall therefore keep My ordi-
nance, lest they bear sin for it and die
thereby, if they profane it: I the LORD sanc-
tify them.
10 'No outsider shall eat the holy *offering;*
one who dwells with the priest, or a hired
servant, shall not eat the holy thing. 11 But if
the priest buys a person with his money, he
may eat it; and one who is born in his
house may eat his food. 12 If the priest's
daughter is married to an outsider, she
may not eat of the holy offerings. 13 But if
the priest's daughter is a widow or di-
vorced, and has no child, and has returned
to her father's house as in her youth, she
may eat her father's food; but no outsider
shall eat it.
14 'And if a man eats the holy *offering*
unintentionally, then he shall restore a
holy *offering* to the priest, and add one-fifth
to it. 15 They shall not profane the holy *offer-
ings* of the children of Israel, which they
offer to the LORD, 16 or allow them to bear
the guilt of trespass when they eat their
holy *offerings;* for I the LORD sanctify
them.' "

Offerings Accepted and Not Accepted

17 And the LORD spoke to Moses, saying,
18 "Speak to Aaron and his sons, and to all
the children of Israel, and say to them:
'Whatever man of the house of Israel, or of
the strangers in Israel, who offers his sacri-
fice for any of his vows or for any of his
freewill offerings, which they offer to the
LORD as a burnt offering— 19 *you shall offer*
of your own free will a male without blem-
ish from the cattle, from the sheep, or from
the goats. 20 Whatever has a defect, you
shall not offer, for it shall not be acceptable
on your behalf. 21 And whoever offers a sac-
rifice of a peace offering to the LORD, to ful-
fill *his* vow, or a freewill offering from the
cattle or the sheep, it must be perfect to be
accepted; there shall be no defect in it.
22 Those *that are* blind or broken or maimed,
or have an ulcer or eczema or scabs, you
shall not offer to the LORD, nor make an of-
fering by fire of them on the altar to the
LORD. 23 Either a bull or a lamb that has any
limb too long or too short you may offer *as*
a freewill offering, but for a vow it shall not
be accepted.
24 'You shall not offer to the LORD what is
bruised or crushed, or torn or cut; nor shall
you make *any offering of them* in your land.
25 Nor from a foreigner's hand shall you of-
fer any of these as the bread of your God,
because their corruption *is* in them, *and* de-
fects *are* in them. They shall not be ac-
cepted on your behalf.' "
26 And the LORD spoke to Moses, saying:
27 "When a bull or a sheep or a goat is born,
it shall be seven days with its mother; and
from the eighth day and thereafter it shall
be accepted as an offering made by fire to
the LORD. 28 *Whether it is* a cow or ewe, do
not kill both her and her young on the
same day. 29 And when you offer a sacrifice
of thanksgiving to the LORD, offer *it* of your
own free will. 30 On the same day it shall be
eaten; you shall leave none of it until
morning: I *am* the LORD.
31 "Therefore you shall keep My com-
mandments, and perform them: I *am* the
LORD. 32 You shall not profane My holy
name, but I will be hallowed among the
children of Israel. I *am* the LORD who sanc-
tifies you, 33 who brought you out of the
land of Egypt, to be your God: I *am* the
LORD."

22:17–33 Any physical blemish in an animal disqualified it as a sacrifice. God deserves our very best. It is inconceivable that a believer, whether in OT or NT times, would want to present to God a life with moral **blemish** (v. 19), removable **defect** (v. 20), or less than a **perfect** love (v. 21).

CHAPTER 23

Feasts of the LORD

And the LORD spoke to Moses, saying, 2"Speak to the children of Israel, and say to them: 'The feasts of the LORD, which you shall proclaim *to be* holy convocations, these *are* My feasts.

The Sabbath

3'Six days shall work be done, but the seventh day *is* a Sabbath of solemn rest, a holy convocation. You shall do no work *on it;* it *is* the Sabbath of the LORD in all your dwellings.

The Passover and Unleavened Bread

4'These *are* the feasts of the LORD, holy convocations which you shall proclaim at their appointed times. 5On the fourteenth *day* of the first month at twilight *is* the LORD's Passover. 6And on the fifteenth day of the same month *is* the Feast of Unleavened Bread to the LORD; seven days you must eat unleavened bread. 7On the first day you shall have a holy convocation; you shall do no customary work on it. 8But you shall offer an offering made by fire to the LORD for seven days. The seventh day *shall be* a holy convocation; you shall do no customary work *on it.*' "

The Feast of Firstfruits

9And the LORD spoke to Moses, saying, 10"Speak to the children of Israel, and say to them: 'When you come into the land which I give to you, and reap its harvest, then you shall bring a sheaf of the firstfruits of your harvest to the priest. 11He shall wave the sheaf before the LORD, to be accepted on your behalf; on the day after the Sabbath the priest shall wave it. 12And you shall offer on that day, when you wave the sheaf, a male lamb of the first year, without blemish, as a burnt offering to the LORD. 13Its grain offering *shall be* two-tenths *of an ephah* of fine flour mixed with oil, an offering made by fire to the LORD, for a sweet aroma; and its drink offering *shall be* of wine, one-fourth of a hin. 14You shall eat neither bread nor parched grain nor fresh grain until the same day that you have brought an offering to your God; *it shall be* a statute forever throughout your generations in all your dwellings.

The Feast of Weeks

15'And you shall count for yourselves from the day after the Sabbath, from the day that you brought the sheaf of the wave offering: seven Sabbaths shall be completed. 16Count fifty days to the day after the seventh Sabbath; then you shall offer a new grain offering to the LORD. 17You shall bring from your dwellings two wave *loaves* of two-tenths *of an ephah.* They shall be of fine flour; they shall be baked with leaven. *They are* the firstfruits to the LORD. 18And you shall offer with the bread seven lambs of the first year, without blemish, one young bull, and two rams. They shall be *as* a burnt offering to the LORD, with their

---

23:1–44 Not counting the Sabbath, there are seven sacred festivals in the Hebrew calendar. Leviticus has already spoken of a holy people, holy priests, holy buildings. To that list Lev. 23 adds the concept of holy days.

23:2 Holy convocation appears 11 times in this chapter (vv. 2, 3, 4, 7, 8, 21, 24, 27, 35, 36, 37). The Hebrew word for "convocation" means lit. "a call." These **feasts** were occasions for nationwide gatherings which called the people to public worship.

23:9–14 The barley harvest was consecrated to the Lord on the Feast of Firstfruits, which took place on the day after the Sabbath of Passover Week. The resurrection of Jesus took place on the Feast of Firstfruits.

23:15–21 The feast which occurred fifty days after the seventh Sabbath (v. 16) is referred to as the Feast of Weeks (Ex. 34:22; Num. 28:26), Feast of Harvest (Ex. 23:16), and Pentecost (Acts 2:1). Like the festivals of Passover and Unleavened Bread, this holy day came in the spring. It was an expression of thanks as the Palestinian grain harvest concluded.

grain offering and their drink offerings, an
offering made by fire for a sweet aroma to
the LORD. [19]Then you shall sacrifice one kid
of the goats as a sin offering, and two male
lambs of the first year as a sacrifice of a
peace offering. [20]The priest shall wave
them with the bread of the firstfruits *as* a
wave offering before the LORD, with the
two lambs. They shall be holy to the LORD
for the priest. [21]And you shall proclaim on
the same day *that* it is a holy convocation to
you. You shall do no customary work *on it.*
It shall be a statute forever in all your
dwellings throughout your generations.

[22]'When you reap the harvest of your
land, you shall not wholly reap the corners
of your field when you reap, nor shall you
gather any gleaning from your harvest.
You shall leave them for the poor and for
the stranger: I *am* the LORD your God.' "

The Feast of Trumpets

[23]Then the LORD spoke to Moses, saying,
[24]"Speak to the children of Israel, saying:
'In the seventh month, on the first *day* of
the month, you shall have a sabbath-*rest,* a
memorial of blowing of trumpets, a holy
convocation. [25]You shall do no customary
work *on it;* and you shall offer an offering
made by fire to the LORD.' "

The Day of Atonement

[26]And the LORD spoke to Moses, saying:
[27]"Also the tenth *day* of this seventh month
shall be the Day of Atonement. It shall be a
holy convocation for you; you shall afflict
your souls, and offer an offering made by
fire to the LORD. [28]And you shall do no
work on that same day, for it *is* the Day of
Atonement, to make atonement for you be-
fore the LORD your God. [29]For any person
who is not afflicted *in soul* on that same
day shall be cut off from his people. [30]And
any person who does any work on that
same day, that person I will destroy from
among his people. [31]You shall do no man-
ner of work; *it shall be* a statute forever
throughout your generations in all your
dwellings. [32]It *shall be* to you a sabbath of
solemn rest, and you shall afflict your souls;
on the ninth *day* of the month at evening,
from evening to evening, you shall cele-
brate your sabbath."

The Feast of Tabernacles

[33]Then the LORD spoke to Moses, saying,
[34]"Speak to the children of Israel, saying:
'The fifteenth day of this seventh month
shall be the Feast of Tabernacles *for* seven
days to the LORD. [35]On the first day *there*
shall be a holy convocation. You shall do no
customary work *on it.* [36]*For* seven days you
shall offer an offering made by fire to the
LORD. On the eighth day you shall have a
holy convocation, and you shall offer an
offering made by fire to the LORD. It *is* a sa-
cred assembly, *and* you shall do no custom-
ary work *on it.*

[37]'These *are* the feasts of the LORD which
you shall proclaim *to be* holy convocations,
to offer an offering made by fire to the
LORD, a burnt offering and a grain offering,
a sacrifice and drink offerings, everything
on its day— [38]besides the Sabbaths of the
LORD, besides your gifts, besides all your
vows, and besides all your freewill offer-
ings which you give to the LORD.

[39]'Also on the fifteenth day of the sev-
enth month, when you have gathered in
the fruit of the land, you shall keep the
feast of the LORD *for* seven days; on the first
day *there shall be* a sabbath-*rest,* and on the

23:26–32 The **Day of Atonement** was the only sacred celebration in which the Mosaic law required the Hebrews to "afflict" their souls through fasting (see vv. 27, 32; 16:29, 30). It was also the only time in the year when the high priest entered the Most Holy Place to appear before the mercy seat (see 16:11–17; Heb. 9:7).

23:33–44 Feast of Tabernacles: This festival occurs in the fall, beginning five days after the Day of Atonement (v. 34; 16:29). It commemorated the Exodus, when Israel lived in temporary shelters (tabernacles) while traveling to the land of promise.

eighth day a sabbath-*rest.* 40And you shall
take for yourselves on the first day the fruit
of beautiful trees, branches of palm trees,
the boughs of leafy trees, and willows of
the brook; and you shall rejoice before the
LORD your God for seven days. 41You shall
keep it as a feast to the LORD for seven days
in the year. *It shall be* a statute forever in
your generations. You shall celebrate it in
the seventh month. 42You shall dwell
in booths for seven days. All who are na-
tive Israelites shall dwell in booths, 43that
your generations may know that I made
the children of Israel dwell in booths when
I brought them out of the land of Egypt: I
am the LORD your God.' "

44So Moses declared to the children of Is-
rael the feasts of the LORD.

CHAPTER 24

Care of the Tabernacle Lamps

Then the LORD spoke to Moses, saying:
2"Command the children of Israel that they
bring to you pure oil of pressed olives for
the light, to make the lamps burn continu-
ally. 3Outside the veil of the Testimony, in
the tabernacle of meeting, Aaron shall be in
charge of it from evening until morning be-
fore the LORD continually; *it shall be* a
statute forever in your generations. 4He
shall be in charge of the lamps on the pure
gold lampstand before the LORD continu-
ally.

The Bread of the Tabernacle

5"And you shall take fine flour and bake
twelve cakes with it. Two-tenths *of an ephah*
shall be in each cake. 6You shall set them in
two rows, six in a row, on the pure *gold*
table before the LORD. 7And you shall put
pure frankincense on *each* row, that it may
be on the bread for a memorial, an offering
made by fire to the LORD. 8Every Sabbath
he shall set it in order before the LORD con-
tinually, *being taken* from the children of Is-
rael by an everlasting covenant. 9And it
shall be for Aaron and his sons, and they
shall eat it in a holy place; for it *is* most
holy to him from the offerings of the LORD
made by fire, by a perpetual statute."

The Penalty for Blasphemy

10Now the son of an Israelite woman,
whose father *was* an Egyptian, went out
among the children of Israel; and this Isra-
elite *woman's* son and a man of Israel
fought each other in the camp. 11And the
Israelite woman's son blasphemed the
name *of the LORD* and cursed; and so they
brought him to Moses. (His mother's name
was She·lō'mith the daughter of Dib'rī, of
the tribe of Dan.) 12Then they put him in
custody, that the mind of the LORD might
be shown to them.

13And the LORD spoke to Moses, saying,
14"Take outside the camp him who has
cursed; then let all who heard *him* lay their
hands on his head, and let all the congre-
gation stone him.

15"Then you shall speak to the children
of Israel, saying: 'Whoever curses his God
shall bear his sin. 16And whoever blas-
phemes the name of the LORD shall surely
be put to death. All the congregation shall
certainly stone him, the stranger as well as
him who is born in the land. When he blas-
phemes the name *of the LORD,* he shall be
put to death.

17'Whoever kills any man shall surely be
put to death. 18Whoever kills an animal
shall make it good, animal for animal.

19'If a man causes disfigurement of
his neighbor, as he has done, so shall it
be done to him— 20fracture for fracture,
eye for eye, tooth for tooth; as he has
caused disfigurement of a man, so shall it
be done to him. 21And whoever kills an an-
imal shall restore it; but whoever kills a
man shall be put to death. 22You shall have
the same law for the stranger and for one
from your own country; for I *am* the LORD
your God.' "

23Then Moses spoke to the children of Is-
rael; and they took outside the camp him
who had cursed, and stoned him with
stones. So the children of Israel did as the
LORD commanded Moses.

CHAPTER 25

The Sabbath of the Seventh Year

And the LORD spoke to Moses on Mount
Sinai, saying, 2“Speak to the children of Is-
rael, and say to them: ‘When you come into
the land which I give you, then the land
shall keep a sabbath to the LORD. 3Six years
you shall sow your field, and six years you
shall prune your vineyard, and gather its
fruit; 4but in the seventh year there shall be
a sabbath of solemn rest for the land, a sab-
bath to the LORD. You shall neither sow
your field nor prune your vineyard. 5What
grows of its own accord of your harvest
you shall not reap, nor gather the grapes of
your untended vine, *for* it is a year of rest
for the land. 6And the sabbath *produce* of
the land shall be food for you: for you,
your male and female servants, your hired
man, and the stranger who dwells with
you, 7for your livestock and the beasts that
are in your land—all its produce shall be
for food.

The Year of Jubilee

8‘And you shall count seven sabbaths of
years for yourself, seven times seven years;
and the time of the seven sabbaths of years
shall be to you forty-nine years. 9Then you
shall cause the trumpet of the Jubilee to
sound on the tenth *day* of the seventh
month; on the Day of Atonement you shall
make the trumpet to sound throughout all
your land. 10And you shall consecrate the
fiftieth year, and proclaim liberty through-
out *all* the land to all its inhabitants. It shall
be a Jubilee for you; and each of you shall
return to his possession, and each of you
shall return to his family. 11That fiftieth
year shall be a Jubilee to you; in it you shall
neither sow nor reap what grows of its
own accord, nor gather *the grapes* of your
untended vine. 12For it *is* the Jubilee; it shall
be holy to you; you shall eat its produce
from the field.

13‘In this Year of Jubilee, each of you
shall return to his possession. 14And if you
sell anything to your neighbor or buy from
your neighbor’s hand, you shall not op-
press one another. 15According to the num-
ber of years after the Jubilee you shall buy
from your neighbor, and according to the
number of years of crops he shall sell to
you. 16According to the multitude of years
you shall increase its price, and according
to the fewer number of years you shall di-
minish its price; for he sells to you *accord-
ing* to the number *of the years* of the crops.
17Therefore you shall not oppress one an-
other, but you shall fear your God; for I *am*
the LORD your God.

Provisions for the Seventh Year

18‘So you shall observe My statutes
and keep My judgments, and perform
them; and you will dwell in the land in
safety. 19Then the land will yield its fruit,
and you will eat your fill, and dwell there
in safety.

20‘And if you say, “What shall we eat in
the seventh year, since we shall not sow
nor gather in our produce?” 21Then I
will command My blessing on you in the
sixth year, and it will bring forth pro-
duce enough for three years. 22And you
shall sow in the eighth year, and eat old
produce until the ninth year; until its pro-
duce comes in, you shall eat *of* the old *har-
vest*.

25:8–17 Jubilee (v. 9) came every **fiftieth year** (v. 11). Thus both the 49th and the 50th years were to be Sabbath years. *Jubilee* comes from the Hebrew word meaning “ram’s horn,” the Hebrew trumpet. It is fitting that the trumpet blast inaugurating the Jubilee was sounded on the **Day of Atonement** (v. 9). Reconciliation with God both precedes, and inevitably brings, reconciliation with one’s fellows.

25:18–22 Obedience to God’s directives would not result in shortage but in enough produce for **three years** (v. 21). As we now know the ecological importance of giving the soil a rest, we can see how God always provides for His children.

Redemption of Property

23'The land shall not be sold perma-
nently, for the land *is* Mine; for you *are*
strangers and sojourners with Me. 24And in
all the land of your possession you shall
grant redemption of the land.

25'If one of your brethren becomes poor,
and has sold *some* of his possession, and if
his redeeming relative comes to redeem it,
then he may redeem what his brother sold.
26Or if the man has no one to redeem it, but
he himself becomes able to redeem it,
27then let him count the years since its sale,
and restore the remainder to the man to
whom he sold it, that he may return to his
possession. 28But if he is not able to have *it*
restored to himself, then what was sold
shall remain in the hand of him who
bought it until the Year of Jubilee; and in
the Jubilee it shall be released, and he shall
return to his possession.

29'If a man sells a house in a walled city,
then he may redeem it within a whole year
after it is sold; *within* a full year he may re-
deem it. 30But if it is not redeemed within
the space of a full year, then the house in
the walled city shall belong permanently
to him who bought it, throughout his gen-
erations. It shall not be released in the Ju-
bilee. 31However the houses of villages
which have no wall around them shall be
counted as the fields of the country. They
may be redeemed, and they shall be re-
leased in the Jubilee. 32Nevertheless the
cities of the Lē'vītes, *and* the houses in the
cities of their possession, the Lē'vītes may
redeem at any time. 33And if a man pur-
chases a house from the Lē'vītes, then the
house that was sold in the city of his pos-
session shall be released in the Jubilee; for
the houses in the cities of the Lē'vītes *are*
their possession among the children of Is-
rael. 34But the field of the common-land of
their cities may not be sold, for it *is* their
perpetual possession.

Lending to the Poor

35'If one of your brethren becomes poor,
and falls into poverty among you, then
you shall help him, like a stranger or a so-
journer, that he may live with you. 36Take
no usury or interest from him; but fear
your God, that your brother may live with
you. 37You shall not lend him your money
for usury, nor lend him your food at a
profit. 38I *am* the LORD your God, who
brought you out of the land of Egypt, to
give you the land of Cā'naan *and* to be
your God.

The Law Concerning Slavery

39'And if *one of* your brethren *who dwells*
by you becomes poor, and sells himself to
you, you shall not compel him to serve as a
slave. 40As a hired servant *and* a sojourner
he shall be with you, *and* shall serve you
until the Year of Jubilee. 41And *then* he shall
depart from you—he and his children with
him—and shall return to his own family.
He shall return to the possession of his
fathers. 42For they *are* My servants, whom I
brought out of the land of Egypt; they shall
not be sold as slaves. 43You shall not rule
over him with rigor, but you shall fear
your God. 44And as for your male and fe-
male slaves whom you may have—from
the nations that are around you, from them
you may buy male and female slaves.

25:23 the land is Mine: Here is the theological basis for Jubilee. God owns the land and graciously permits families to live on it. It was not for them to sell in any permanent way, nor was it for someone else to amass in an orgy of possessiveness.

25:35–38 These laws prohibited charging **usury** or **interest** (v. 36) to the poor. Nothing is said here about capital investment. The law sought to prevent taking advantage of the helpless.

25:44–46 Slavery of foreigners was permitted. Although slavery has a long history from ancient times, both the OT and the NT ameliorated it significantly among believers. The whole spirit of Christianity, furthermore, undermined the institution (Gal. 3:28).

45Moreover you may buy the children of
the strangers who dwell among you, and
their families who are with you, which
they beget in your land; and they shall be-
come your property. 46And you may take
them as an inheritance for your children
after you, to inherit *them as* a possession;
they shall be your permanent slaves. But
regarding your brethren, the children of Is-
rael, you shall not rule over one another
with rigor.

47'Now if a sojourner or stranger close to
you becomes rich, and *one of* your brethren
who dwells by him becomes poor, and sells
himself to the stranger *or* sojourner close to
you, or to a member of the stranger's fam-
ily, 48after he is sold he may be redeemed
again. One of his brothers may redeem
him; 49or his uncle or his uncle's son may
redeem him; or *anyone* who is near of kin to
him in his family may redeem him; or if he
is able he may redeem himself. 50Thus he
shall reckon with him who bought him:
The price of his release shall be according
to the number of years, from the year that
he was sold to him until the Year of Jubilee;
it shall be according to the time of a hired
servant for him. 51If *there are* still many
years *remaining,* according to them he shall
repay the price of his redemption from the
money with which he was bought. 52And if
there remain but a few years until the Year
of Jubilee, then he shall reckon with him,
and according to his years he shall repay
him the price of his redemption. 53He shall
be with him as a yearly hired servant, and
he shall not rule with rigor over him in
your sight. 54And if he is not redeemed in
these *years,* then he shall be released in the
Year of Jubilee—he and his children with
him. 55For the children of Israel *are* servants
to Me; they *are* My servants whom I
brought out of the land of Egypt: I *am* the
LORD your God.

CHAPTER 26

Promise of Blessing and Retribution

'You shall not make idols for your-
selves;
neither a carved image nor a *sacred* pil-
lar shall you rear up for yourselves;
nor shall you set up an engraved stone
in your land, to bow down to it;
for I *am* the LORD your God.
2 You shall keep My Sabbaths and rever-
ence My sanctuary:
I *am* the LORD.

3 'If you walk in My statutes and keep
My commandments, and perform
them,
4 then I will give you rain in its season,
the land shall yield its produce, and
the trees of the field shall yield their
fruit.
5 Your threshing shall last till the time of
vintage, and the vintage shall last till
the time of sowing;
you shall eat your bread to the full,
and dwell in your land safely.
6 I will give peace in the land, and you
shall lie down, and none will make
you afraid;
I will rid the land of evil beasts,
and the sword will not go through
your land.
7 You will chase your enemies, and they
shall fall by the sword before you.
8 Five of you shall chase a hundred, and
a hundred of you shall put ten thou-
sand to flight;
your enemies shall fall by the sword
before you.

26:1–46 A section listing the terms of the agreement was a regular part of ancient Near Eastern covenant form. God's laws, if obeyed, brought blessing (vv. 3–13). If disobeyed, they brought judgment (vv. 14–46). These results were not casual, but a direct result of the oath which the Israelites swore at Sinai. They had obligated themselves to obey, as God had obligated Himself to be their God. See also Deut. 27:1—28:68.

9 'For I will look on you favorably and
make you fruitful, multiply you and
confirm My covenant with you.
10 You shall eat the old harvest, and clear
out the old because of the new.
11 I will set My tabernacle among you,
and My soul shall not abhor you.
12 I will walk among you and be your
God, and you shall be My people.
13 I *am* the LORD your God, who brought
you out of the land of Egypt, that
you should not be their slaves;
I have broken the bands of your yoke
and made you walk upright.

14 'But if you do not obey Me, and do not
observe all these commandments,
15 and if you despise My statutes, or if
your soul abhors My judgments, so
that you do not perform all My commandments,
but break My covenant,
16 I also will do this to you:
I will even appoint terror over you,
wasting disease and fever which
shall consume the eyes and cause
sorrow of heart.
And you shall sow your seed in vain,
for your enemies shall eat it.
17 I will set My face against you, and you
shall be defeated by your enemies.
Those who hate you shall reign over
you, and you shall flee when no one
pursues you.

18 'And after all this, if you do not obey
Me, then I will punish you seven
times more for your sins.
19 I will break the pride of your power;
I will make your heavens like iron and
your earth like bronze.
20 And your strength shall be spent in
vain;
for your land shall not yield its produce,
nor shall the trees of the land
yield their fruit.

21 'Then, if you walk contrary to Me, and
are not willing to obey Me, I will
bring on you seven times more
plagues, according to your sins.
22 I will also send wild beasts among
you, which shall rob you of your
children, destroy your livestock, and
make you few in number;
and your highways shall be desolate.

23 'And if by these things you are not reformed
by Me, but walk contrary to
Me,
24 then I also will walk contrary to you,
and I will punish you yet seven
times for your sins.
25 And I will bring a sword against you
that will execute the vengeance of
the covenant;
when you are gathered together
within your cities I will send pestilence
among you;
and you shall be delivered into the
hand of the enemy.
26 When I have cut off your supply of
bread, ten women shall bake your
bread in one oven, and they shall
bring back your bread by weight,
and you shall eat and not be satisfied.

27 'And after all this, if you do not obey
Me, but walk contrary to Me,
28 then I also will walk contrary to you in
fury;
and I, even I, will chastise you seven
times for your sins.
29 You shall eat the flesh of your sons,
and you shall eat the flesh of your
daughters.
30 I will destroy your high places, cut
down your incense altars, and cast
your carcasses on the lifeless forms
of your idols;
and My soul shall abhor you.
31 I will lay your cities waste and bring
your sanctuaries to desolation, and I
will not smell the fragrance of your
sweet aromas.
32 I will bring the land to desolation, and
your enemies who dwell in it shall
be astonished at it.
33 I will scatter you among the nations

and draw out a sword after you;
your land shall be desolate and your
cities waste.
34 Then the land shall enjoy its sabbaths
as long as it lies desolate and you *are*
in your enemies' land;
then the land shall rest and enjoy its
sabbaths.
35 As long as *it* lies desolate it shall rest—
for the time it did not rest on your sab-
baths when you dwelt in it.

36 'And as for those of you who are left, I
will send faintness into their hearts
in the lands of their enemies;
the sound of a shaken leaf shall cause
them to flee;
they shall flee as though fleeing from a
sword, and they shall fall when no
one pursues.
37 They shall stumble over one another,
as it were before a sword, when no
one pursues;
and you shall have no *power* to stand
before your enemies.
38 You shall perish among the nations,
and the land of your enemies shall
eat you up.
39 And those of you who are left shall
waste away in their iniquity in your
enemies' lands;
also in their fathers' iniquities, which
are with them, they shall waste
away.

40 '*But* if they confess their iniquity and
the iniquity of their fathers, with
their unfaithfulness in which they
were unfaithful to Me, and that they
also have walked contrary to Me,
41 and *that* I also have walked contrary to
them and have brought them into
the land of their enemies;
if their uncircumcised hearts are hum-
bled, and they accept their guilt—
42 then I will remember My covenant
with Jacob, and My covenant with
Isaac and My covenant with Abra-
ham I will remember;
I will remember the land.
43 The land also shall be left empty by
them, and will enjoy its sabbaths
while it lies desolate without them;
they will accept their guilt, because
they despised My judgments and
because their soul abhorred My
statutes.
44 Yet for all that, when they are in the
land of their enemies, I will not cast
them away, nor shall I abhor them,
to utterly destroy them and break
My covenant with them;
for I *am* the LORD their God.
45 But for their sake I will remember the
covenant of their ancestors, whom I
brought out of the land of Egypt in
the sight of the nations, that I might
be their God:
I *am* the LORD.' "

46These *are* the statutes and judgments
and laws which the LORD made between
Himself and the children of Israel on
Mount Sinai by the hand of Moses.

CHAPTER 27

Redeeming Persons and Property Dedicated to God

Now the LORD spoke to Moses, saying,
2"Speak to the children of Israel, and say to
them: 'When a man consecrates by a vow
certain persons to the LORD, according to
your valuation, 3if your valuation is of a
male from twenty years old up to sixty
years old, then your valuation shall be fifty
shekels of silver, according to the shekel of

26:40–46 But if they confess their iniquity: The promise of restoration is based on repentance. Under those conditions, God says: **I will remember the covenant** (v. 45). These blessings and curses are all temporal, physical, and immediate.

the sanctuary. [4]If it *is* a female, then your
valuation shall be thirty shekels; [5]and if
from five years old up to twenty years old,
then your valuation for a male shall be
twenty shekels, and for a female ten
shekels; [6]and if from a month old up to five
years old, then your valuation for a male
shall be five shekels of silver, and for a female your valuation shall be three shekels
of silver; [7]and if from sixty years old and
above, if *it is* a male, then your valuation
shall be fifteen shekels, and for a female
ten shekels.

[8]'But if he is too poor to pay your valuation, then he shall present himself before the priest, and the priest shall set a
value for him; according to the ability of
him who vowed, the priest shall value
him.

[9]'If *it is* an animal that men may bring as
an offering to the LORD, all that *anyone*
gives to the LORD shall be holy. [10]He shall
not substitute it or exchange it, good for
bad or bad for good; and if he at all exchanges animal for animal, then both it
and the one exchanged for it shall be holy.
[11]If *it is* an unclean animal which they do
not offer as a sacrifice to the LORD, then he
shall present the animal before the priest;
[12]and the priest shall set a value for it,
whether it is good or bad; as you, the
priest, value it, so it shall be. [13]But if he
wants at all *to* redeem it, then he must add
one-fifth to your valuation.

[14]'And when a man dedicates his house
to be holy to the LORD, then the priest shall
set a value for it, whether it is good or bad;
as the priest values it, so it shall stand. [15]If
he who dedicated it *wants to* redeem his
house, then he must add one-fifth of the
money of your valuation to it, and it shall
be his.

[16]'If a man dedicates to the LORD *part* of
a field of his possession, then your valuation shall be according to the seed for it. A
homer of barley seed *shall be valued* at fifty
shekels of silver. [17]If he dedicates his field
from the Year of Jubilee, according to your
valuation it shall stand. [18]But if he dedicates his field after the Jubilee, then the
priest shall reckon to him the money due
according to the years that remain till the
Year of Jubilee, and it shall be deducted
from your valuation. [19]And if he who dedicates the field ever wishes to redeem it,
then he must add one-fifth of the money of
your valuation to it, and it shall belong to
him. [20]But if he does not want to redeem
the field, or if he has sold the field to another man, it shall not be redeemed anymore; [21]but the field, when it is released in
the Jubilee, shall be holy to the LORD, as a
devoted field; it shall be the possession of
the priest.

[22]'And if a man dedicates to the LORD a
field which he has bought, which is not the
field of his possession, [23]then the priest
shall reckon to him the worth of your valuation, up to the Year of Jubilee, and he shall
give your valuation on that day *as* a holy
offering to the LORD. [24]In the Year of Jubilee
the field shall return to him from whom it
was bought, to the one who *owned* the land
as a possession. [25]And all your valuations
shall be according to the shekel of the sanctuary: twenty gerahs to the shekel.

[26]'But the firstborn of the animals, which
should be the LORD's firstborn, no man
shall dedicate; whether *it is* an ox or sheep,
it *is* the LORD's. [27]And if *it is* an unclean animal, then he shall redeem *it* according to
your valuation, and shall add one-fifth to
it; or if it is not redeemed, then it shall be
sold according to your valuation.

[28]'Nevertheless no devoted *offering* that
a man may devote to the LORD of all that he
has, *both* man and beast, or the field of his
possession, shall be sold or redeemed;
every devoted *offering is* most holy to the
LORD. [29]No person under the ban, who may
become doomed to destruction among
men, shall be redeemed, *but* shall surely be
put to death. [30]And all the tithe of the land,
whether of the seed of the land *or* of the fruit
of the tree, *is* the LORD's. It *is* holy to the
LORD. [31]If a man wants at all to redeem *any*
of his tithes, he shall add one-fifth to it.
[32]And concerning the tithe of the herd or

the flock, of whatever passes under the
rod, the tenth one shall be holy to the LORD.
33He shall not inquire whether it is good or
bad, nor shall he exchange it; and if he ex-
changes it at all, then both it and the one
exchanged for it shall be holy; it shall not
be redeemed.' "

34These *are* the commandments which
the LORD commanded Moses for the chil-
dren of Israel on Mount Sinai.

✦Numbers✦

Numbers was written by Moses (33:2), probably around 1400 B.C., as the Israelites prepared to enter the Promised Land. Covering 1440 to 1400 B.C., Numbers tells how Israel failed to believe in God (chapter 14) and was forced to wander in the wilderness for forty years.

The older generation of Israelites, described by chapters 1—10, witnessed God's protection, His commandments, and His deliverance as the people spiritually prepared to enter Canaan. But in chapters 11—25, Israel refused to trust God to conquer the Promised Land. God's judgment required the nation to wander one year for each day that the twelve spies inspected Canaan. When the second generation replaced the first, Joshua was appointed Moses' successor and Israel made ready to move into the land (chapters 26—36).

Numbers depicts both God's wrath against rebellion and His everlasting mercy. The unbelief of the older generation in breaking the covenant hindered God's blessing, but God did not give up; He blessed them by bringing their children into the Promised Land. ✦

CHAPTER 1

The First Census of Israel

Now the LORD spoke to Moses in the
Wilderness of Sinai, in the tabernacle of
meeting, on the first *day* of the second
month, in the second year after they had
come out of the land of Egypt, saying:
2"Take a census of all the congregation of
the children of Israel, by their families, by
their fathers' houses, according to the
number of names, every male individually,
3from twenty years old and above—all
who *are able to* go to war in Israel. You and
Aaron shall number them by their armies.
4And with you there shall be a man from
every tribe, each one the head of his father's house.
5"These are the names of the men who
shall stand with you: from Reuben,
E·lī'zur the son of Shed'ē·ur; 6from
Sim'ē·on, She·lū'mi·el the son of
Zū·ri·shad'daī; 7from Judah, Nah'shon the
son of Am·min'a·dab; 8from Is'sa·char,
Ne·than'el the son of Zū'ar; 9from
Zeb'ū·lun, E·lī'ab the son of Hē'lon; 10from
the sons of Joseph: from Ē'phra·im,
E·lish'a·ma the son of Am·mī'hud; from
Ma·nas'seh, Ga·mā'li·el the son of
Pe·dah'zur; 11from Benjamin, A·bī'dan the
son of Gid·ē·ō'ni; 12from Dan, Ā·hī·ē'zer
the son of Am·mi·shad'daī; 13from Ash'er,
Pā'gi·el the son of Oc'ran; 14from Gad,
E·lī'a·saph the son of Deū'el;[a] 15from

1:14 [a]Spelled *Reuel* in 2:14

1:2–19 Take a census: Moses was commanded by God to count all males over **twenty years old**. The purpose of the census was to determine how many men were available for war (v. 3).

Naph′ta·lī, A·hī′ra the son of Ē′nan."
16These *were* chosen from the congregation,
leaders of their fathers' tribes, heads of the
divisions in Israel.

17Then Moses and Aaron took these men
who had been mentioned by name, 18and
they assembled all the congregation to-
gether on the first *day* of the second month;
and they recited their ancestry by families,
by their fathers' houses, according to the
number of names, from twenty years old
and above, each one individually. 19As the
LORD commanded Moses, so he numbered
them in the Wilderness of Sinai.

20Now the children of Reuben, Israel's
oldest son, their genealogies by their fami-
lies, by their fathers' house, according to
the number of names, every male individ-
ually, from twenty years old and above, all
who *were able to* go to war: 21those who
were numbered of the tribe of Reuben *were*
forty-six thousand five hundred.

22From the children of Sim′ē·on, their
genealogies by their families, by their fa-
thers' house, of those who were numbered,
according to the number of names, every
male individually, from twenty years old
and above, all who *were able to* go to war:
23those who were numbered of the tribe of
Sim′ē·on *were* fifty-nine thousand three
hundred.

24From the children of Gad, their ge-
nealogies by their families, by their fathers'
house, according to the number of names,
from twenty years old and above, all who
were able to go to war: 25those who were
numbered of the tribe of Gad *were* forty-
five thousand six hundred and fifty.

26From the children of Judah, their ge-
nealogies by their families, by their fathers'
house, according to the number of names,
from twenty years old and above, all who
were able to go to war: 27those who were
numbered of the tribe of Judah *were*
seventy-four thousand six hundred.

28From the children of Is′sa·char, their
genealogies by their families, by their fa-
thers' house, according to the number of
names, from twenty years old and above,
all who *were able to* go to war: 29those who
were numbered of the tribe of Is′sa·char
were fifty-four thousand four hundred.

30From the children of Zeb′ū·lun, their
genealogies by their families, by their fa-
thers' house, according to the number of
names, from twenty years old and above,
all who *were able to* go to war: 31those who
were numbered of the tribe of Zeb′ū·lun
were fifty-seven thousand four hundred.

32From the sons of Joseph, the children
of Ē′phra·im, their genealogies by their
families, by their fathers' house, according
to the number of names, from twenty years
old and above, all who *were able to* go to
war: 33those who were numbered of the
tribe of Ē′phra·im *were* forty thousand five
hundred.

34From the children of Ma·nas′seh, their
genealogies by their families, by their fa-
thers' house, according to the number of
names, from twenty years old and above,
all who *were able to* go to war: 35those who
were numbered of the tribe of Ma·nas′seh
were thirty-two thousand two hundred.

36From the children of Benjamin, their
genealogies by their families, by their fa-
thers' house, according to the number of
names, from twenty years old and above,
all who *were able to* go to war: 37those who
were numbered of the tribe of Benjamin
were thirty-five thousand four hundred.

38From the children of Dan, their ge-
nealogies by their families, by their fathers'
house, according to the number of names,
from twenty years old and above, all who
were able to go to war: 39those who were

1:20–46 The census report, tribe by tribe, giving the name of each tribe and a round number of combat-aged males. Some scholars have disputed the accuracy of the number given, based on previous passages that state only seventy Israelites went into Egypt. However, such rapid growth can be fully explained as God's miraculous fulfillment of His covenant with Abraham.

numbered of the tribe of Dan *were* sixty-two thousand seven hundred.

40From the children of Ash′er, their genealogies by their families, by their fathers′ house, according to the number of names, from twenty years old and above, all who *were able to* go to war: 41those who were numbered of the tribe of Ash′er *were* forty-one thousand five hundred.

42From the children of Naph′ta·lī, their genealogies by their families, by their fathers′ house, according to the number of names, from twenty years old and above, all who *were able to* go to war: 43those who were numbered of the tribe of Naph′ta·lī *were* fifty-three thousand four hundred.

44These are the ones who were numbered, whom Moses and Aaron numbered, with the leaders of Israel, twelve men, each one representing his father′s house. 45So all who were numbered of the children of Israel, by their fathers′ houses, from twenty years old and above, all who *were able to* go to war in Israel— 46all who were numbered were six hundred and three thousand five hundred and fifty.

47But the Lē′vītes were not numbered among them by their fathers′ tribe; 48for the LORD had spoken to Moses, saying: 49"Only the tribe of Levi you shall not number, nor take a census of them among the children of Israel; 50but you shall appoint the Lē′vītes over the tabernacle of the Testimony, over all its furnishings, and over all things that belong to it; they shall carry the tabernacle and all its furnishings; they shall attend to it and camp around the tabernacle. 51And when the tabernacle is to go forward, the Lē′vītes shall take it down; and when the tabernacle is to be set up, the Lē′vītes shall set it up. The outsider who comes near shall be put to death. 52The children of Israel shall pitch their tents, everyone by his own camp, everyone by his own standard, according to their armies; 53but the Lē′vītes shall camp around the tabernacle of the Testimony, that there may be no wrath on the congregation of the children of Israel; and the Lē′vītes shall keep charge of the tabernacle of the Testimony."

54Thus the children of Israel did; according to all that the LORD commanded Moses, so they did.

CHAPTER 2

The Tribes and Leaders by Armies

And the LORD spoke to Moses and Aaron, saying: 2"Everyone of the children of Israel shall camp by his own standard, beside the emblems of his father′s house; they shall camp some distance from the tabernacle of meeting. 3On the east side, toward the rising of the sun, those of the standard of the forces with Judah shall camp according to their armies; and Nah′shon the son of Am·min′a·dab *shall be* the leader of the children of Judah." 4And his army was numbered at seventy-four thousand six hundred.

5"Those who camp next to him *shall be* the tribe of Is′sa·char, and Ne·than′el the son of Zū′ar *shall be* the leader of the children of Is′sa·char." 6And his army was numbered at fifty-four thousand four hundred.

7"Then *comes* the tribe of Zeb′ū·lun, and E·lī′ab the son of Hē′lon *shall be* the leader of the children of Zeb′ū·lun." 8And his army was numbered at fifty-seven thousand four hundred. 9"All who were

1:47–54 The **Levites** were **not numbered** because they were responsible for the **tabernacle** (v. 50) and thus exempt from military service.

2:9–31 break camp first: In camp and on the move, the tabernacle was at the center of Israel. When the Israelites journeyed, the tribes of Judah, Issachar, and Zebulun, who camped eastward of the centrally located tabernacle, marched in front. The southward group—Reuben, Simeon, and Gad—moved out next, followed by the tabernacle entourage in the middle of the line. Then came the westward group, comprised of Ephraim, Manasseh,

numbered according to their armies of the
forces with Judah, one hundred and
eighty-six thousand four hundred—these
shall break camp first.
10"On the south side *shall be* the standard
of the forces with Reuben according to
their armies, and the leader of the children
of Reuben *shall be* E·lī′zur the son of
Shed′ē·ur." 11And his army was numbered
at forty-six thousand five hundred.
12"Those who camp next to him *shall be*
the tribe of Sim′ē·on, and the leader of the
children of Sim′ē·on *shall be* She·lū′mi·el
the son of Zū·ri·shad′daī." 13And his army
was numbered at fifty-nine thousand three
hundred.
14"Then *comes* the tribe of Gad, and the
leader of the children of Gad *shall be*
E·lī′a·saph the son of Reū′el."[a] 15And his
army was numbered at forty-five thou-
sand six hundred and fifty. 16"All who
were numbered according to their armies
of the forces with Reuben, one hundred
and fifty-one thousand four hundred and
fifty—they shall be the second to break
camp.
17"And the tabernacle of meeting shall
move out with the camp of the Lē′vītes in
the middle of the camps; as they camp, so
they shall move out, everyone in his place,
by their standards.
18"On the west side *shall be* the standard
of the forces with Ē′phra·im according to
their armies, and the leader of the child-
ren of Ē′phra·im *shall be* E·lish′a·ma
the son of Am·mī′hud." 19And his army
was numbered at forty thousand five hun-
dred.
20"Next to him *comes* the tribe of
Ma·nas′seh, and the leader of the children
of Ma·nas′seh *shall be* Ga·mā′li·el the son
of Pe·dah′zur." 21And his army was num-
bered at thirty-two thousand two hun-
dred.
22"Then *comes* the tribe of Benjamin, and
the leader of the children of Benjamin *shall
be* A·bī′dan the son of Gid·ē·ō′ni." 23And
his army was numbered at thirty-five
thousand four hundred. 24"All who were
numbered according to their armies of the
forces with Ē′phra·im, one hundred and
eight thousand one hundred—they shall
be the third to break camp.
25"The standard of the forces with
Dan *shall be* on the north side according to
their armies, and the leader of the children
of Dan *shall be* Ā·hī·ē′zer the son of
Am·mi·shad′daī." 26And his army was
numbered at sixty-two thousand seven
hundred.
27"Those who camp next to him *shall be*
the tribe of Ash′er, and the leader of the
children of Ash′er *shall be* Pā′gi·el the son
of Oc′ran." 28And his army was numbered
at forty-one thousand five hundred.
29"Then *comes* the tribe of Naph′ta·lī,
and the leader of the children of Naph′ta·lī
shall be A·hī′ra the son of Ē′nan." 30And his
army was numbered at fifty-three thou-
sand four hundred. 31"All who were num-
bered of the forces with Dan, one hundred
and fifty-seven thousand six hundred—
they shall break camp last, with their stan-
dards."
32These *are* the ones who were num-
bered of the children of Israel by their
fathers′ houses. All who were numbered
according to their armies of the forces
were six hundred and three thousand
five hundred and fifty. 33But the Lē′vītes
were not numbered among the children
of Israel, just as the LORD commanded Mo-
ses.
34Thus the children of Israel did accord-
ing to all that the LORD commanded Moses;
so they camped by their standards and so
they broke camp, each one by his family,
according to their fathers′ houses.

2:14 [a]Spelled *Deuel* in 1:14 and 7:42

and Benjamin. Finally, the tribes of Dan, Asher, and Naphtali, who camped north of the tabernacle, completed the procession.

CHAPTER 3

The Sons of Aaron

Now these *are* the records of Aaron and Moses when the LORD spoke with Moses on Mount Sinai. 2And these *are* the names of the sons of Aaron: Nā'dab, the firstborn, and A·bī'hū, El·ē·ā'zar, and Ith'a·mar. 3These *are* the names of the sons of Aaron, the anointed priests, whom he consecrated to minister as priests. 4Nā'dab and A·bī'hū had died before the LORD when they offered profane fire before the LORD in the Wilderness of Sinai; and they had no children. So El·ē·ā'zar and Ith'a·mar ministered as priests in the presence of Aaron their father.

The Levites Serve in the Tabernacle

5And the LORD spoke to Moses, saying: 6"Bring the tribe of Levi near, and present them before Aaron the priest, that they may serve him. 7And they shall attend to his needs and the needs of the whole congregation before the tabernacle of meeting, to do the work of the tabernacle. 8Also they shall attend to all the furnishings of the tabernacle of meeting, and to the needs of the children of Israel, to do the work of the tabernacle. 9And you shall give the Lē'vītes to Aaron and his sons; they *are* given entirely to him[a] from among the children of Israel. 10So you shall appoint Aaron and his sons, and they shall attend to their priesthood; but the outsider who comes near shall be put to death."

11Then the LORD spoke to Moses, saying: 12"Now behold, I Myself have taken the Lē'vītes from among the children of Israel instead of every firstborn who opens the womb among the children of Israel. Therefore the Lē'vītes shall be Mine, 13because all the firstborn *are* Mine. On the day that I struck all the firstborn in the land of Egypt, I sanctified to Myself all the firstborn in Israel, both man and beast. They shall be Mine: I *am* the LORD."

Census of the Levites Commanded

14Then the LORD spoke to Moses in the Wilderness of Sinai, saying: 15"Number the children of Levi by their fathers' houses, by their families; you shall number every male from a month old and above."

16So Moses numbered them according to the word of the LORD, as he was commanded. 17These were the sons of Levi by their names: Ger'shon, Kō'hath, and Merar'ī. 18And these *are* the names of the sons of Ger'shon by their families: Lib'nī and Shim'ē·ī. 19And the sons of Kō'hath by their families: Am'ram, Iz'e·har, Hē'bron, and Uz'zi·el. 20And the sons of Me·rar'ī by their families: Mah'lī and Mū'shī. These *are* the families of the Lē'vītes by their fathers' houses.

21From Ger'shon *came* the family of the Lib'nītes and the family of the Shim'ītes; these *were* the families of the Ger'shon·ītes. 22Those who were numbered, according to the number of all the males from a month old and above—of those who were numbered *there were* seven thousand five hundred. 23The families of the Ger'shon·ītes were to camp behind the tabernacle westward. 24And the leader of the father's house of the Ger'shon·ītes *was* E·lī'a·saph the son of Lā'el. 25The duties of the children of Ger'shon in the tabernacle of meeting *included* the tabernacle, the tent with its covering, the screen for the door of the tabernacle of meeting, 26the screen for the door of the court, the hangings of the court which *are* around the tabernacle and the altar, and their cords, according to all the work relating to them.

27From Kō'hath *came* the family of the Am'ram·ītes, the family of the Iz'har·ītes,

3:9 [a]Samaritan Pentateuch and Septuagint read *Me*.

3:12 Levites shall be Mine: They were separated to God for a special purpose. This implies the twofold nature of sanctification: out from the world and for God's service.

the family of the Hē′bron·ītes, and the
family of the Uz′zi·el·ītes; these *were* the
families of the Kō′hath·ītes. 28According to
the number of all the males, from a month
old and above, *there were* eight thousand
six[a] hundred keeping charge of the sanctu-
ary. 29The families of the children of
Kō′hath were to camp on the south side of
the tabernacle. 30And the leader of the
fathers′ house of the families of the
Kō′hath·ītes *was* E·li·zā′phan the son of
Uz′zi·el. 31Their duty *included* the ark, the
table, the lampstand, the altars, the uten-
sils of the sanctuary with which they min-
istered, the screen, and all the work relat-
ing to them.

32And El·ē·ā′zar the son of Aaron the
priest *was to be* chief over the leaders of the
Lē′vītes, *with* oversight of those who kept
charge of the sanctuary.

33From Me·rar′ī *came* the family of the
Mah′lītes and the family of the Mū′shītes;
these *were* the families of Me·rar′ī.
34And those who were numbered, accord-
ing to the number of all the males from a
month old and above, *were* six thousand
two hundred. 35The leader of the fathers′
house of the families of Me·rar′ī *was*
Zū′ri·el the son of Ab·i·hā′il. These *were*
to camp on the north side of the taber-
nacle. 36And the appointed duty of the
children of Me·rar′ī *included* the boards of
the tabernacle, its bars, its pillars, its sock-
ets, its utensils, all the work relating to
them, 37and the pillars of the court all
around, with their sockets, their pegs, and
their cords.

38Moreover those who were to camp be-
fore the tabernacle on the east, before the
tabernacle of meeting, *were* Moses, Aaron,
and his sons, keeping charge of the sanctu-
ary, to meet the needs of the children of Is-
rael; but the outsider who came near was
to be put to death. 39All who were num-
bered of the Lē′vītes, whom Moses and
Aaron numbered at the commandment of
the LORD, by their families, all the males
from a month old and above, *were* twenty-
two thousand.

Levites Dedicated Instead of the Firstborn

40Then the LORD said to Moses: "Num-
ber all the firstborn males of the children of
Israel from a month old and above, and
take the number of their names. 41And you
shall take the Lē′vītes for Me—I *am* the
LORD—instead of all the firstborn among
the children of Israel, and the livestock of
the Lē′vītes instead of all the firstborn
among the livestock of the children of Is-
rael." 42So Moses numbered all the first-
born among the children of Israel, as the
LORD commanded him. 43And all the first-
born males, according to the number of
names from a month old and above, of
those who were numbered of them, were
twenty-two thousand two hundred and
seventy-three.

44Then the LORD spoke to Moses, saying:
45"Take the Lē′vītes instead of all the first-
born among the children of Israel, and the
livestock of the Lē′vītes instead of their
livestock. The Lē′vītes shall be Mine: I *am*
the LORD. 46And for the redemption of the
two hundred and seventy-three of the
firstborn of the children of Israel, who are
more than the number of the Lē′vītes,
47you shall take five shekels for each one
individually; you shall take *them* in the
currency of the shekel of the sanctuary, the
shekel of twenty gerahs. 48And you shall
give the money, with which the excess
number of them is redeemed, to Aaron and
his sons."

49So Moses took the redemption money
from those who were over and above those
who were redeemed by the Lē′vītes.
50From the firstborn of the children of Is-
rael he took the money, one thousand
three hundred and sixty-five *shekels*, ac-
cording to the shekel of the sanctuary.
51And Moses gave their redemption money
to Aaron and his sons, according to the
word of the LORD, as the LORD commanded
Moses.

3:28 [a]Some manuscripts of the Septuagint read *three.*

CHAPTER 4

Duties of the Sons of Kohath

Then the LORD spoke to Moses and Aaron, saying: 2"Take a census of the sons of Kō'hath from among the children of Levi, by their families, by their fathers' house, 3from thirty years old and above, even to fifty years old, all who enter the service to do the work in the tabernacle of meeting.

4"This *is* the service of the sons of Kō'hath in the tabernacle of meeting, *relating to* the most holy things: 5When the camp prepares to journey, Aaron and his sons shall come, and they shall take down the covering veil and cover the ark of the Testimony with it. 6Then they shall put on it a covering of badger skins, and spread over *that* a cloth entirely of blue; and they shall insert its poles.

7"On the table of showbread they shall spread a blue cloth, and put on it the dishes, the pans, the bowls, and the pitchers for pouring; and the showbread[a] shall be on it. 8They shall spread over them a scarlet cloth, and cover the same with a covering of badger skins; and they shall insert its poles. 9And they shall take a blue cloth and cover the lampstand of the light, with its lamps, its wick-trimmers, its trays, and all its oil vessels, with which they service it. 10Then they shall put it with all its utensils in a covering of badger skins, and put *it* on a carrying beam.

11"Over the golden altar they shall spread a blue cloth, and cover it with a covering of badger skins; and they shall insert its poles. 12Then they shall take all the utensils of service with which they minister in the sanctuary, put *them* in a blue cloth, cover them with a covering of badger skins, and put *them* on a carrying beam. 13Also they shall take away the ashes from the altar, and spread a purple cloth over it. 14They shall put on it all its implements with which they minister there—the firepans, the forks, the shovels, the basins, and all the utensils of the altar—and they shall spread on it a covering of badger skins, and insert its poles. 15And when Aaron and his sons have finished covering the sanctuary and all the furnishings of the sanctuary, when the camp is set to go, then the sons of Kō'hath shall come to carry *them;* but they shall not touch any holy thing, lest they die.

"These *are* the things in the tabernacle of meeting which the sons of Kō'hath are to carry.

16"The appointed duty of El·ē·ā'zar the son of Aaron the priest *is* the oil for the light, the sweet incense, the daily grain offering, the anointing oil, the oversight of all the tabernacle, of all that *is* in it, with the sanctuary and its furnishings."

17Then the LORD spoke to Moses and Aaron, saying: 18"Do not cut off the tribe of the families of the Kō'hath·ītes from among the Lē'vītes; 19but do this in regard to them, that they may live and not die when they approach the most holy things: Aaron and his sons shall go in and appoint each of them to his service and his task. 20But they shall not go in to watch while the holy things are being covered, lest they die."

4:7 [a]Literally *the continual bread*

4:1–33 These Levites were responsible for moving the tabernacle furnishings. They could do so only after the Aaronic priests had wrapped the items in the tabernacle coverings (vv. 19, 20). Otherwise they would die (see 2 Sam. 6:3–7).

4:16 Eleazar, a priest, was the overseer of transporting and setting up the tabernacle. He was to make sure that all the holy objects were covered before the Kohathites were allowed to enter.

4:19 appoint each . . . his task: The service required of each family in the tribe of Levi was specific. They must fulfill those responsibilities—a reminder that we are responsible to follow God's will as revealed to us.

Duties of the Sons of Gershon

21Then the LORD spoke to Moses, saying:
22"Also take a census of the sons of
Ger'shon, by their fathers' house, by
their families. 23From thirty years old and
above, even to fifty years old, you shall
number them, all who enter to perform the
service, to do the work in the tabernacle of
meeting. 24This *is* the service of the families
of the Ger'shon·ītes, in serving and carry-
ing: 25They shall carry the curtains of the
tabernacle and the tabernacle of meeting
with its covering, the covering of badger
skins that *is* on it, the screen for the door of
the tabernacle of meeting, 26the screen for
the door of the gate of the court, the hang-
ings of the court which *are* around the
tabernacle and altar, and their cords, all
the furnishings for their service and all that
is made for these things: so shall they
serve.

27"Aaron and his sons shall assign all the
service of the sons of the Ger'shon·ītes, all
their tasks and all their service. And you
shall appoint to them all their tasks as their
duty. 28This *is* the service of the families of
the sons of Ger'shon in the tabernacle of
meeting. And their duties *shall be* under the
authority[a] of Ith'a·mar the son of Aaron
the priest.

Duties of the Sons of Merari

29"*As for* the sons of Me·rar'ī, you shall
number them by their families and by their
fathers' house. 30From thirty years old and
above, even to fifty years old, you shall
number them, everyone who enters the
service to do the work of the tabernacle of
meeting. 31And this *is* what they must
carry as all their service for the tabernacle
of meeting: the boards of the tabernacle, its
bars, its pillars, its sockets, 32and the pillars
around the court with their sockets, pegs,
and cords, with all their furnishings and all
their service; and you shall assign *to each*
man by name the items he must carry.
33This *is* the service of the families of the
sons of Me·rar'ī, as all their service for the
tabernacle of meeting, under the authority[a]
of Ith'a·mar the son of Aaron the priest."

Census of the Levites

34And Moses, Aaron, and the leaders of
the congregation numbered the sons of the
Kō'hath·ītes by their families and by their
fathers' house, 35from thirty years old and
above, even to fifty years old, everyone
who entered the service for work in the
tabernacle of meeting; 36and those who
were numbered by their families were two
thousand seven hundred and fifty. 37These
were the ones who were numbered of the
families of the Kō'hath·ītes, all who might
serve in the tabernacle of meeting, whom
Moses and Aaron numbered according to
the commandment of the LORD by the
hand of Moses.

38And those who were numbered of the
sons of Ger'shon, by their families and by
their fathers' house, 39from thirty years old
and above, even to fifty years old, every-
one who entered the service for work in
the tabernacle of meeting— 40those who
were numbered by their families, by their
fathers' house, were two thousand six hun-
dred and thirty. 41These *are* the ones who
were numbered of the families of the sons
of Ger'shon, of all who might serve in the
tabernacle of meeting, whom Moses and
Aaron numbered according to the com-
mandment of the LORD.

42Those of the families of the sons of
Me·rar'ī who were numbered, by their
families, by their fathers' house, 43from
thirty years old and above, even to fifty
years old, everyone who entered the ser-
vice for work in the tabernacle of meet-
ing— 44those who were numbered by their
families were three thousand two hun-
dred. 45These *are* the ones who were num-
bered of the families of the sons of Me-
rar'ī, whom Moses and Aaron numbered
according to the word of the LORD by the
hand of Moses.

46All who were numbered of the Lē'-

4:28 [a]Literally *hand* 4:33 [a]Literally *hand*

vītes, whom Moses, Aaron, and the leaders
of Israel numbered, by their families and
by their fathers' houses, [47]from thirty years
old and above, even to fifty years old,
everyone who came to do the work of ser-
vice and the work of bearing burdens in
the tabernacle of meeting— [48]those who
were numbered were eight thousand five
hundred and eighty.

[49]According to the commandment of the
LORD they were numbered by the hand of
Moses, each according to his service and
according to his task; thus were they num-
bered by him, as the LORD commanded
Moses.

CHAPTER 5

Ceremonially Unclean Persons Isolated

And the LORD spoke to Moses, saying:
[2]"Command the children of Israel that they
put out of the camp every leper, everyone
who has a discharge, and whoever be-
comes defiled by a corpse. [3]You shall put
out both male and female; you shall put
them outside the camp, that they may not
defile their camps in the midst of which I
dwell." [4]And the children of Israel did so,
and put them outside the camp; as the
LORD spoke to Moses, so the children of Is-
rael did.

Confession and Restitution

[5]Then the LORD spoke to Moses, saying,
[6]"Speak to the children of Israel: 'When a
man or woman commits any sin that men
commit in unfaithfulness against the LORD,
and that person is guilty, [7]then he shall
confess the sin which he has committed.
He shall make restitution for his trespass in
full, plus one-fifth of it, and give *it* to the
one he has wronged. [8]But if the man has no
relative to whom restitution may be made
for the wrong, the restitution for the wrong
must go to the LORD for the priest, in addi-
tion to the ram of the atonement with
which atonement is made for him. [9]Every
offering of all the holy things of the chil-
dren of Israel, which they bring to the
priest, shall be his. [10]And every man's holy
things shall be his; whatever any man
gives the priest shall be his.' "

Concerning Unfaithful Wives

[11]And the LORD spoke to Moses, saying,
[12]"Speak to the children of Israel, and say
to them: 'If any man's wife goes astray and
behaves unfaithfully toward him, [13]and a
man lies with her carnally, and it is hidden
from the eyes of her husband, and it is con-
cealed that she has defiled herself, and
there was no witness against her, nor was
she caught— [14]if the spirit of jealousy
comes upon him and he becomes jealous of
his wife, who has defiled herself; or if the
spirit of jealousy comes upon him and he
becomes jealous of his wife, although she
has not defiled herself— [15]then the man
shall bring his wife to the priest. He shall
bring the offering required for her, one-
tenth of an ephah of barley meal; he shall
pour no oil on it and put no frankincense
on it, because it *is* a grain offering of jeal-
ousy, an offering for remembering, for
bringing iniquity to remembrance.

[16]'And the priest shall bring her near,
and set her before the LORD. [17]The priest
shall take holy water in an earthen vessel,
and take some of the dust that is on the
floor of the tabernacle and put *it* into the
water. [18]Then the priest shall stand

5:2 Both a spiritual and a physical significance can be seen here. God desires a thorough attention to purity among His people. Furthermore, the large size of the camp made it necessary to insist upon stringent health regulations involving the separation of those with contagious conditions. A **discharge** from sexual diseases (see Lev. 15) or contact with decayed dead bodies indicated the potential for infection.

5:14 spirit of jealousy: When a man suspected that his wife had been unfaithful, he must bring her to the priest. This protected the wife as well as the husband.

the woman before the LORD, uncover the woman's head, and put the offering for remembering in her hands, which *is* the grain offering of jealousy. And the priest shall have in his hand the bitter water that brings a curse. 19And the priest shall put her under oath, and say to the woman, "If no man has lain with you, and if you have not gone astray to uncleanness *while* under your husband's *authority,* be free from this bitter water that brings a curse. 20But if you have gone astray *while* under your husband's *authority,* and if you have defiled yourself and some man other than your husband has lain with you"— 21then the priest shall put the woman under the oath of the curse, and he shall say to the woman—"the LORD make you a curse and an oath among your people, when the LORD makes your thigh rot and your belly swell; 22and may this water that causes the curse go into your stomach, and make *your* belly swell and *your* thigh rot."

'Then the woman shall say, "Amen, so be it."

23'Then the priest shall write these curses in a book, and he shall scrape *them* off into the bitter water. 24And he shall make the woman drink the bitter water that brings a curse, and the water that brings the curse shall enter her *to become* bitter. 25Then the priest shall take the grain offering of jealousy from the woman's hand, shall wave the offering before the LORD, and bring it to the altar; 26and the priest shall take a handful of the offering, as its memorial portion, burn *it* on the altar, and afterward make the woman drink the water. 27When he has made her drink the water, then it shall be, if she has defiled herself and behaved unfaithfully toward her husband, that the water that brings a curse will enter her *and become* bitter, and her belly will swell, her thigh will rot, and the woman will become a curse among her people. 28But if the woman has not defiled herself, and is clean, then she shall be free and may conceive children.

29'This *is* the law of jealousy, when a wife, *while* under her husband's *authority,* goes astray and defiles herself, 30or when the spirit of jealousy comes upon a man, and he becomes jealous of his wife; then he shall stand the woman before the LORD, and the priest shall execute all this law upon her. 31Then the man shall be free from iniquity, but that woman shall bear her guilt.' "

CHAPTER 6

The Law of the Nazirite

Then the LORD spoke to Moses, saying, 2"Speak to the children of Israel, and say to them: 'When either a man or woman consecrates an offering to take the vow of a Naz'ir·īte, to separate himself to the LORD, 3he shall separate himself from wine and *similar* drink; he shall drink neither vinegar made from wine nor vinegar made from *similar* drink; neither shall he drink any grape juice, nor eat fresh grapes or raisins. 4All the days of his separation he shall eat nothing that is produced by the grapevine, from seed to skin.

5'All the days of the vow of his separation no razor shall come upon his head; until the days are fulfilled for which he separated himself to the LORD, he shall be

---

6:2–8 The **Nazirite** was distinguished primarily by the special consecration that characterized his life and service. As such Nazirites were an example to, and a judgment upon, an Israel which found it very hard to make a real dedication to God (see Amos 2:11, 12). They separated themselves from wine and other strong drink (v. 3), did not cut their hair (v. 5), and did not touch a corpse (v. 6). Nazirites usually took this vow for a specified time (v. 8); Samson, Samuel, and John the Baptist were Nazirites for life. The Rechabites, to whom Jeremiah refers (Jer. 35:1–19), took similar vows for life.

holy. *Then* he shall let the locks of the hair
of his head grow. 6 All the days that he sep-
arates himself to the LORD he shall not go
near a dead body. 7 He shall not make him-
self unclean even for his father or his
mother, for his brother or his sister, when
they die, because his separation to God *is*
on his head. 8 All the days of his separation
he shall be holy to the LORD.
9 'And if anyone dies very suddenly be-
side him, and he defiles his consecrated
head, then he shall shave his head on the
day of his cleansing; on the seventh day
he shall shave it. 10 Then on the eighth
day he shall bring two turtledoves or
two young pigeons to the priest, to the
door of the tabernacle of meeting; 11 and the
priest shall offer one as a sin offering and
the other as a burnt offering, and make
atonement for him, because he sinned in
regard to the corpse; and he shall sanctify
his head that same day. 12 He shall conse-
crate to the LORD the days of his separa-
tion, and bring a male lamb in its first year
as a trespass offering; but the former days
shall be lost, because his separation was
defiled.
13 'Now this *is* the law of the Naz'ir·īte:
When the days of his separation are ful-
filled, he shall be brought to the door of the
tabernacle of meeting. 14 And he shall pre-
sent his offering to the LORD: one male
lamb in its first year without blemish as a
burnt offering, one ewe lamb in its first
year without blemish as a sin offering, one
ram without blemish as a peace offering,
15 a basket of unleavened bread, cakes of
fine flour mixed with oil, unleavened
wafers anointed with oil, and their grain
offering with their drink offerings.
16 'Then the priest shall bring *them* before
the LORD and offer his sin offering and his
burnt offering; 17 and he shall offer the ram
as a sacrifice of a peace offering to the
LORD, with the basket of unleavened
bread; the priest shall also offer its grain of-
fering and its drink offering. 18 Then the
Naz'ir·īte shall shave his consecrated head
at the door of the tabernacle of meeting,
and shall take the hair from his conse-
crated head and put *it* on the fire which is
under the sacrifice of the peace offering.
19 'And the priest shall take the boiled
shoulder of the ram, one unleavened cake
from the basket, and one unleavened
wafer, and put *them* upon the hands of the
Naz'ir·īte after he has shaved his conse-
crated *hair,* 20 and the priest shall wave
them as a wave offering before the LORD;
they *are* holy for the priest, together with
the breast of the wave offering and the
thigh of the heave offering. After that the
Naz'ir·īte may drink wine.'
21 "This is the law of the Naz'ir·īte who
vows to the LORD the offering for his sepa-
ration, and besides that, whatever else his
hand is able to provide; according to the
vow which he takes, so he must do accord-
ing to the law of his separation."

The Priestly Blessing

22 And the LORD spoke to Moses, saying:
23 "Speak to Aaron and his sons, saying,
'This is the way you shall bless the children
of Israel. Say to them:

24 "The LORD bless you and keep you;
25 The LORD make His face shine upon
you,
And be gracious to you;
26 The LORD lift up His countenance
upon you,
And give you peace." '

6:22–27 Chapters 3—6, which relate largely to the activities of the priests, close with a beautiful summation of the priestly role. The priests are to be the persons through whom God's name (v. 27), or character, can be manifested to the people and through whom the blessing of God can rest upon the people. However stern God may sometimes seem, or however rigorous His expectations, His end purpose is blessing and peace. Verses 24–26, the Aaronic blessing, are worth memorizing.

I pray that You, O Lord, will bless and keep my children and grandchildren; that You make Your face shine upon them, and be gracious to them; that You lift up Your countenance upon them, and give them peace.

adapted from Numbers 6:24–26

27"So they shall put My name on the children of Israel, and I will bless them."

CHAPTER 7

Offerings of the Leaders

Now it came to pass, when Moses had finished setting up the tabernacle, that he anointed it and consecrated it and all its furnishings, and the altar and all its utensils; so he anointed them and consecrated them. 2Then the leaders of Israel, the heads of their fathers' houses, who *were* the leaders of the tribes and over those who were numbered, made an offering. 3And they brought their offering before the LORD, six covered carts and twelve oxen, a cart for *every* two of the leaders, and for each one an ox; and they presented them before the tabernacle.

4Then the LORD spoke to Moses, saying, 5"Accept *these* from them, that they may be used in doing the work of the tabernacle of meeting; and you shall give them to the Lē'vītes, *to* every man according to his service." 6So Moses took the carts and the oxen, and gave them to the Lē'vītes. 7Two carts and four oxen he gave to the sons of Ger'shon, according to their service; 8and four carts and eight oxen he gave to the sons of Me·rar'ī, according to their service, under the authority[a] of Ith'a·mar the son of Aaron the priest. 9But to the sons of Kō'hath he gave none, because theirs *was* the service of the holy things, *which* they carried on their shoulders.

10Now the leaders offered the dedication *offering* for the altar when it was anointed; so the leaders offered their offering before the altar. 11For the LORD said to Moses, "They shall offer their offering, one leader each day, for the dedication of the altar."

12And the one who offered his offering on the first day *was* Nah'shon the son of Am·min'a·dab, from the tribe of Judah. 13His offering *was* one silver platter, the weight of which *was* one hundred and thirty *shekels,* and one silver bowl of seventy shekels, according to the shekel of the sanctuary, both of them full of fine flour mixed with oil as a grain offering; 14one gold pan of ten *shekels,* full of incense; 15one young bull, one ram, and one male lamb in its first year, as a burnt offering; 16one kid of the goats as a sin offering; 17and for the sacrifice of peace offerings: two oxen, five rams, five male goats, and five male lambs in their first year. This *was* the offering of Nah'shon the son of Am·min'a·dab.

18On the second day Ne·than'el the son of Zū'ar, leader of Is'sa·char, presented *an offering.* 19*For* his offering he offered one silver platter, the weight of which *was* one hundred and thirty *shekels,* and one silver bowl of seventy shekels, according to the shekel of the sanctuary, both of them full of fine flour mixed with oil as a grain offering; 20one gold pan of ten *shekels,* full of incense; 21one young bull, one ram, and one male lamb in its first year, as a burnt offering; 22one kid of the goats as a sin offering; 23and as the sacrifice of peace offerings: two oxen, five rams, five male goats, and five male lambs in their first year. This *was* the offering of Ne·than'el the son of Zū'ar.

24On the third day E·lī'ab the son of Hē'lon, leader of the children of Zeb'ū·lun, *presented an offering.* 25His offering *was* one

7:8 [a]Literally *hand*

silver platter, the weight of which *was* one hundred and thirty *shekels,* and one silver bowl of seventy shekels, according to the shekel of the sanctuary, both of them full of fine flour mixed with oil as a grain offering; 26 one gold pan of ten *shekels,* full of incense; 27 one young bull, one ram, and one male lamb in its first year, as a burnt offering; 28 one kid of the goats as a sin offering; 29 and for the sacrifice of peace offerings: two oxen, five rams, five male goats, and five male lambs in their first year. This *was* the offering of E·lī′ab the son of Hē′lon.

30 On the fourth day E·lī′zur the son of Shed′ē·ur, leader of the children of Reuben, *presented an offering.* 31 His offering *was* one silver platter, the weight of which *was* one hundred and thirty *shekels,* and one silver bowl of seventy shekels, according to the shekel of the sanctuary, both of them full of fine flour mixed with oil as a grain offering; 32 one gold pan of ten *shekels,* full of incense; 33 one young bull, one ram, and one male lamb in its first year, as a burnt offering; 34 one kid of the goats as a sin offering; 35 and as the sacrifice of peace offerings: two oxen, five rams, five male goats, and five male lambs in their first year. This *was* the offering of E·lī′zur the son of Shed′ē·ur.

36 On the fifth day She·lū′mi·el the son of Zū·ri·shad′daī, leader of the children of Sim′ē·on, *presented an offering.* 37 His offering *was* one silver platter, the weight of which *was* one hundred and thirty *shekels,* and one silver bowl of seventy shekels, according to the shekel of the sanctuary, both of them full of fine flour mixed with oil as a grain offering; 38 one gold pan of ten *shekels,* full of incense; 39 one young bull, one ram, and one male lamb in its first year, as a burnt offering; 40 one kid of the goats as a sin offering; 41 and as the sacrifice of peace offerings: two oxen, five rams, five male goats, and five male lambs in their first year. This *was* the offering of She·lū′mi·el the son of Zū·ri·shad′daī.

42 On the sixth day E·lī′a·saph the son of Deū′el,[a] leader of the children of Gad, *presented an offering.* 43 His offering *was* one silver platter, the weight of which *was* one hundred and thirty *shekels,* and one silver bowl of seventy shekels, according to the shekel of the sanctuary, both of them full of fine flour mixed with oil as a grain offering; 44 one gold pan of ten *shekels,* full of incense; 45 one young bull, one ram, and one male lamb in its first year, as a burnt offering; 46 one kid of the goats as a sin offering; 47 and as the sacrifice of peace offerings: two oxen, five rams, five male goats, and five male lambs in their first year. This *was* the offering of E·lī′a·saph the son of Deū′el.

48 On the seventh day E·lish′a·ma the son of Am·mī′hud, leader of the children of Ē′phra·im, *presented an offering.* 49 His offering *was* one silver platter, the weight of which *was* one hundred and thirty *shekels,* and one silver bowl of seventy shekels, according to the shekel of the sanctuary, both of them full of fine flour mixed with oil as a grain offering; 50 one gold pan of ten *shekels,* full of incense; 51 one young bull, one ram, and one male lamb in its first year, as a burnt offering; 52 one kid of the goats as a sin offering; 53 and as the sacrifice of peace offerings: two oxen, five rams, five male goats, and five male lambs in their first year. This *was* the offering of E·lish′a·ma the son of Am·mī′hud.

54 On the eighth day Ga·mā′li·el the son of Pe·dah′zur, leader of the children of Ma·nas′seh, *presented an offering.* 55 His offering *was* one silver platter, the weight of which *was* one hundred and thirty *shekels,* and one silver bowl of seventy shekels, according to the shekel of the sanctuary, both of them full of fine flour mixed with oil as a grain offering; 56 one gold pan of ten *shekels,* full of incense; 57 one young bull, one ram, and one male lamb in its first

7:42 [a]Spelled *Reuel* in 2:14

year, as a burnt offering; 58one kid of the goats as a sin offering; 59and as the sacrifice of peace offerings: two oxen, five rams, five male goats, and five male lambs in their first year. This *was* the offering of Ga·mā′li·el the son of Pe·dah′zur.

60On the ninth day A·bī′dan the son of Gid·ē·ō′ni, leader of the children of Benjamin, *presented an offering.* 61His offering *was* one silver platter, the weight of which *was* one hundred and thirty *shekels,* and one silver bowl of seventy shekels, according to the shekel of the sanctuary, both of them full of fine flour mixed with oil as a grain offering; 62one gold pan of ten *shekels,* full of incense; 63one young bull, one ram, and one male lamb in its first year, as a burnt offering; 64one kid of the goats as a sin offering; 65and as the sacrifice of peace offerings: two oxen, five rams, five male goats, and five male lambs in their first year. This *was* the offering of A·bī′dan the son of Gid·ē·ō′ni.

66On the tenth day Ā·hī·ē′zer the son of Am·mi·shad′daī, leader of the children of Dan, *presented an offering.* 67His offering *was* one silver platter, the weight of which *was* one hundred and thirty *shekels,* and one silver bowl of seventy shekels, according to the shekel of the sanctuary, both of them full of fine flour mixed with oil as a grain offering; 68one gold pan of ten *shekels,* full of incense; 69one young bull, one ram, and one male lamb in its first year, as a burnt offering; 70one kid of the goats as a sin offering; 71and as the sacrifice of peace offerings: two oxen, five rams, five male goats, and five male lambs in their first year. This *was* the offering of Ā·hī·ē′zer the son of Am·mi·shad′daī.

72On the eleventh day Pā′gi·el the son of Oc′ran, leader of the children of Ash′er, *presented an offering.* 73His offering *was* one silver platter, the weight of which *was* one hundred and thirty *shekels,* and one silver bowl of seventy shekels, according to the shekel of the sanctuary, both of them full of fine flour mixed with oil as a grain offering; 74one gold pan of ten *shekels,* full of incense; 75one young bull, one ram, and one male lamb in its first year, as a burnt offering; 76one kid of the goats as a sin offering; 77and as the sacrifice of peace offerings: two oxen, five rams, five male goats, and five male lambs in their first year. This *was* the offering of Pā′gi·el the son of Oc′ran.

78On the twelfth day A·hī′ra the son of Ē′nan, leader of the children of Naph′ta·lī, *presented an offering.* 79His offering *was* one silver platter, the weight of which *was* one hundred and thirty *shekels,* and one silver bowl of seventy shekels, according to the shekel of the sanctuary, both of them full of fine flour mixed with oil as a grain offering; 80one gold pan of ten *shekels,* full of incense; 81one young bull, one ram, and one male lamb in its first year, as a burnt offering; 82one kid of the goats as a sin offering; 83and as the sacrifice of peace offerings: two oxen, five rams, five male goats, and five male lambs in their first year. This *was* the offering of A·hī′ra the son of Ē′nan.

84This *was* the dedication *offering* for the altar from the leaders of Israel, when it was anointed: twelve silver platters, twelve silver bowls, and twelve gold pans. 85Each silver platter *weighed* one hundred and thirty *shekels* and each bowl seventy *shekels.* All the silver of the vessels *weighed* two thousand four hundred *shekels,* according to the shekel of the sanctuary. 86The twelve gold pans full of incense *weighed* ten *shekels* apiece, according to the shekel of the sanctuary; all the gold of the pans *weighed* one hundred and twenty *shekels.* 87All the oxen for the burnt offering *were* twelve young bulls, the rams twelve, the male lambs in their first year twelve, with their grain offering, and the kids of the goats as a sin offering twelve. 88And all the oxen for the sacrifice of peace offerings were twenty-four bulls, the rams sixty, the male goats sixty, and the lambs in their first year sixty. This *was* the dedication *offering* for the altar after it was anointed.

89Now when Moses went into the taber-
nacle of meeting to speak with Him, he
heard the voice of One speaking to him
from above the mercy seat that *was* on the
ark of the Testimony, from between the
two cherubim; thus He spoke to him.

CHAPTER 8

Arrangement of the Lamps

And the LORD spoke to Moses, saying:
2"Speak to Aaron, and say to him, 'When
you arrange the lamps, the seven lamps
shall give light in front of the lampstand.' "
3And Aaron did so; he arranged the lamps
to face toward the front of the lampstand,
as the LORD commanded Moses. 4Now this
workmanship of the lampstand *was* ham-
mered gold; from its shaft to its flowers it
was hammered work. According to the pat-
tern which the LORD had shown Moses, so
he made the lampstand.

Cleansing and Dedication of the Levites

5Then the LORD spoke to Moses, saying:
6"Take the Lē′vītes from among the chil-
dren of Israel and cleanse them *ceremoni-
ally.* 7Thus you shall do to them to cleanse
them: Sprinkle water of purification on
them, and let them shave all their body,
and let them wash their clothes, and *so*
make themselves clean. 8Then let them
take a young bull with its grain offering of
fine flour mixed with oil, and you shall
take another young bull as a sin offering.
9And you shall bring the Lē′vītes before
the tabernacle of meeting, and you shall
gather together the whole congregation of
the children of Israel. 10So you shall bring
the Lē′vītes before the LORD, and the chil-
dren of Israel shall lay their hands on the
Lē′vītes; 11and Aaron shall offer the
Lē′vītes before the LORD *like* a wave offer-
ing from the children of Israel, that they
may perform the work of the LORD. 12Then
the Lē′vītes shall lay their hands on the
heads of the young bulls, and you shall of-
fer one as a sin offering and the other as a
burnt offering to the LORD, to make atone-
ment for the Lē′vītes.

13"And you shall stand the Lē′vītes be-
fore Aaron and his sons, and then offer
them *like* a wave offering to the LORD.
14Thus you shall separate the Lē′vītes from
among the children of Israel, and the
Lē′vītes shall be Mine. 15After that the
Lē′vītes shall go in to service the taberna-
cle of meeting. So you shall cleanse them
and offer them *like* a wave offering. 16For
they *are* wholly given to Me from among
the children of Israel; I have taken them for
Myself instead of all who open the womb,
the firstborn of all the children of Israel.
17For all the firstborn among the children of
Israel *are* Mine, *both* man and beast; on the
day that I struck all the firstborn in the
land of Egypt I sanctified them to Myself.
18I have taken the Lē′vītes instead of all the
firstborn of the children of Israel. 19And I
have given the Lē′vītes as a gift to Aaron
and his sons from among the children of Is-
rael, to do the work for the children of Is-
rael in the tabernacle of meeting, and to
make atonement for the children of Israel,

7:89 voice of One speaking: The whole purpose of the tabernacle was to make tangible the presence of God among His people. Without that sense of the Presence, religion is a dull affair.

8:2 seven lamps: Seven is a number of deep significance to Israel. Here it is joined with light, which no doubt symbolized the presence of God. These lamps would continue to remind the people of God's power to deliver and sustain.

8:7 Along with their sanitary function, these actions symbolized a break with a past lifestyle and a commitment to purity. For us they illustrate the kind of pure service to which all Christians are called (Heb. 10:22).

8:10, 11 The laying on of hands demonstrated that the Levites were living sacrifices, taking the place of the firstborn of Israel.

that there be no plague among the children
of Israel when the children of Israel come
near the sanctuary."
20 Thus Moses and Aaron and all the con-
gregation of the children of Israel did to
the Lē′vītes; according to all that the LORD
commanded Moses concerning the Lē′-
vītes, so the children of Israel did to them.
21 And the Lē′vītes purified themselves and
washed their clothes; then Aaron pre-
sented them *like* a wave offering before the
LORD, and Aaron made atonement for
them to cleanse them. 22 After that the
Lē′vītes went in to do their work in the
tabernacle of meeting before Aaron and
his sons; as the LORD commanded Moses
concerning the Lē′vītes, so they did to
them.
23 Then the LORD spoke to Moses, saying,
24 "This *is* what *pertains* to the Lē′vītes:
From twenty-five years old and above one
may enter to perform service in the work
of the tabernacle of meeting; 25 and at the
age of fifty years they must cease perform-
ing this work, and shall work no more.
26 They may minister with their brethren in
the tabernacle of meeting, to attend to
needs, but they *themselves* shall do no
work. Thus you shall do to the Lē′vītes re-
garding their duties."

CHAPTER 9

The Second Passover

Now the LORD spoke to Moses in the
Wilderness of Sinai, in the first month of
the second year after they had come out of
the land of Egypt, saying: 2 "Let the chil-
dren of Israel keep the Passover at its ap-
pointed time. 3 On the fourteenth day of
this month, at twilight, you shall keep it at
its appointed time. According to all its rites
and ceremonies you shall keep it." 4 So Mo-
ses told the children of Israel that they
should keep the Passover. 5 And they kept
the Passover on the fourteenth day of the
first month, at twilight, in the Wilderness
of Sinai; according to all that the LORD
commanded Moses, so the children of Is-
rael did.
6 Now there were *certain* men who were
defiled by a human corpse, so that they
could not keep the Passover on that day;
and they came before Moses and Aaron
that day. 7 And those men said to him, "We
became defiled by a human corpse. Why are
we kept from presenting the offering of the
LORD at its appointed time among the chil-
dren of Israel?"
8 And Moses said to them, "Stand still,
that I may hear what the LORD will com-
mand concerning you."
9 Then the LORD spoke to Moses, saying,
10 "Speak to the children of Israel, saying: 'If
anyone of you or your posterity is unclean
because of a corpse, or *is* far away on a
journey, he may still keep the LORD's
Passover. 11 On the fourteenth day of the
second month, at twilight, they may keep
it. They shall eat it with unleavened bread
and bitter herbs. 12 They shall leave none of
it until morning, nor break one of its bones.
According to all the ordinances of the
Passover they shall keep it. 13 But the man
who *is* clean and is not on a journey, and
ceases to keep the Passover, that same per-
son shall be cut off from among his people,
because he did not bring the offering of the
LORD at its appointed time; that man shall
bear his sin.
14 'And if a stranger dwells among you,

9:2–14 Passover: With the camp organized and their religious practices established, only one thing remained before setting out—to celebrate the memorial of God's grace in delivering them from the death angel in Egypt. By it the Israelites were constantly reminded of God's grace in choosing them and His power in delivering them. The Christian is reminded that Jesus, "our Passover, was sacrificed for us" (see 1 Cor. 5:7, 8).

9:14 one ordinance: Believing Gentiles who accepted circumcision (see Ex. 12:48) were not to be forbidden from participating in the Passover.

and would keep the LORD's Passover, he
must do so according to the rite of
the Passover and according to its cere-
mony; you shall have one ordinance, both
for the stranger and the native of the
land.' "

The Cloud and the Fire

15 Now on the day that the tabernacle
was raised up, the cloud covered the taber-
nacle, the tent of the Testimony; from
evening until morning it was above the
tabernacle like the appearance of fire. 16 So
it was always: the cloud covered it *by day,*
and the appearance of fire by night.
17 Whenever the cloud was taken up from
above the tabernacle, after that the chil-
dren of Israel would journey; and in the
place where the cloud settled, there the
children of Israel would pitch their tents.
18 At the command of the LORD the children
of Israel would journey, and at the com-
mand of the LORD they would camp; as
long as the cloud stayed above the taberna-
cle they remained encamped. 19 Even when
the cloud continued long, many days
above the tabernacle, the children of Israel
kept the charge of the LORD and did not
journey. 20 So it was, when the cloud was
above the tabernacle a few days: according
to the command of the LORD they would
remain encamped, and according to the
command of the LORD they would journey.
21 So it was, when the cloud remained only
from evening until morning: when the
cloud was taken up in the morning, then
they would journey; whether by day or by
night, whenever the cloud was taken up,
they would journey. 22 *Whether it was* two
days, a month, or a year that the cloud re-
mained above the tabernacle, the children
of Israel would remain encamped and not
journey; but when it was taken up, they
would journey. 23 At the command of the
LORD they remained encamped, and at the
command of the LORD they journeyed;
they kept the charge of the LORD, at the
command of the LORD by the hand of Mo-
ses.

CHAPTER 10

Two Silver Trumpets

And the LORD spoke to Moses, saying:
2 "Make two silver trumpets for yourself;
you shall make them of hammered work;
you shall use them for calling the congre-
gation and for directing the movement of
the camps. 3 When they blow both of them,
all the congregation shall gather before
you at the door of the tabernacle of meet-
ing. 4 But if they blow *only* one, then the
leaders, the heads of the divisions of Israel,
shall gather to you. 5 When you sound the
advance, the camps that lie on the east side
shall then begin their journey. 6 When you
sound the advance the second time, then
the camps that lie on the south side shall
begin their journey; they shall sound the
call for them to begin their journeys. 7 And
when the assembly is to be gathered to-
gether, you shall blow, but not sound the
advance. 8 The sons of Aaron, the priests,
shall blow the trumpets; and these shall be
to you as an ordinance forever throughout
your generations.

9 "When you go to war in your land
against the enemy who oppresses you,
then you shall sound an alarm with the
trumpets, and you will be remembered be-
fore the LORD your God, and you will be
saved from your enemies. 10 Also in the day
of your gladness, in your appointed feasts,
and at the beginning of your months, you
shall blow the trumpets over your burnt
offerings and over the sacrifices of your
peace offerings; and they shall be a memo-
rial for you before your God: I *am* the LORD
your God."

Departure from Sinai

11 Now it came to pass on the twentieth
day of the second month, in the second
year, that the cloud was taken up from
above the tabernacle of the Testimony.
12 And the children of Israel set out from the
Wilderness of Sinai on their journeys; then
the cloud settled down in the Wilderness
of Par'an. 13 So they started out for the first

time according to the command of the
LORD by the hand of Moses.
14The standard of the camp of the chil-
dren of Judah set out first according to
their armies; over their army was Nah'-
shon the son of Am·min'a·dab. 15Over the
army of the tribe of the children of Is'sa-
char *was* Ne·than'el the son of Zū'ar. 16And
over the army of the tribe of the children of
Zeb'ū·lun *was* E·lī'ab the son of Hē'lon.
17Then the tabernacle was taken down;
and the sons of Ger'shon and the sons of
Me·rar'ī set out, carrying the tabernacle.
18And the standard of the camp of Reu-
ben set out according to their armies; over
their army *was* E·lī'zur the son of Shed'-
ē·ur. 19Over the army of the tribe of the
children of Sim'ē·on *was* She·lū'mi·el the
son of Zū·ri·shad'daī. 20And over the army
of the tribe of the children of Gad *was*
E·lī'a·saph the son of Deū'el.
21Then the Kō'hath·ītes set out, carrying
the holy things. (The tabernacle would be
prepared for their arrival.)
22And the standard of the camp of the
children of Ē'phra·im set out according to
their armies; over their army *was* E·lish'-
a·ma the son of Am·mī'hud. 23Over the
army of the tribe of the children of Ma-
nas'seh *was* Ga·mā'li·el the son of Pe·dah'-
zur. 24And over the army of the tribe of the
children of Benjamin *was* A·bī'dan the son
of Gid·ē·ō'ni.
25Then the standard of the camp of the
children of Dan (the rear guard of all the
camps) set out according to their armies;
over their army *was* Ā·hi·ē'zer the son of
Am·mi·shad'daī. 26Over the army of the
tribe of the children of Ash'er *was* Pā'gi·el
the son of Oc'ran. 27And over the army of
the tribe of the children of Naph'ta·lī *was*
A·hī'ra the son of Ē'nan.
28Thus *was* the order of march of the
children of Israel, according to their
armies, when they began their journey.
29Now Moses said to Hō'bab the son of
Reū'el[a] the Mid'i·an·īte, Moses' father-in-
law, "We are setting out for the place of
which the LORD said, 'I will give it to you.'
Come with us, and we will treat you well;
for the LORD has promised good things to
Israel."
30And he said to him, "I will not go, but
I will depart to my *own* land and to my rel-
atives."
31So *Moses* said, "Please do not leave,
inasmuch as you know how we are to
camp in the wilderness, and you can be
our eyes. 32And it shall be, if you go with
us—indeed it shall be—that whatever
good the LORD will do to us, the same we
will do to you."
33So they departed from the mountain of
the LORD on a journey of three days; and
the ark of the covenant of the LORD went
before them for the three days' journey, to
search out a resting place for them. 34And
the cloud of the LORD *was* above them by
day when they went out from the camp.
35So it was, whenever the ark set out,
that Moses said:

"Rise up, O LORD!
Let Your enemies be scattered,
And let those who hate You flee
before You."

36And when it rested, he said:

"Return, O LORD,
To the many thousands of Israel."

CHAPTER 11

The People Complain

Now *when* the people complained, it
displeased the LORD; for the LORD heard *it*,

10:29 [a]Septuagint reads *Raguel* (compare Exodus 2:18).

11:1–3 His anger: In light of all the people had seen of God's grace and power, God's wrath seems entirely justified. Yet He was willing to relent as a result of Moses' prayer.

and His anger was aroused. So the fire of
the LORD burned among them, and con-
sumed *some* in the outskirts of the camp.
2Then the people cried out to Moses, and
when Moses prayed to the LORD, the fire
was quenched. 3So he called the name of
the place Tab'e·rah,[a] because the fire of the
LORD had burned among them.

4Now the mixed multitude who were
among them yielded to intense craving; so
the children of Israel also wept again and
said: "Who will give us meat to eat? 5We
remember the fish which we ate freely in
Egypt, the cucumbers, the melons, the
leeks, the onions, and the garlic; 6but now
our whole being *is* dried up; *there is* noth-
ing at all except this manna *before* our
eyes!"

7Now the manna *was* like coriander
seed, and its color like the color of bdel-
lium. 8The people went about and gath-
ered *it*, ground *it* on millstones or beat *it* in
the mortar, cooked *it* in pans, and made
cakes of it; and its taste was like the taste of
pastry prepared with oil. 9And when the
dew fell on the camp in the night, the
manna fell on it.

10Then Moses heard the people weeping
throughout their families, everyone at the
door of his tent; and the anger of the LORD
was greatly aroused; Moses also was dis-
pleased. 11So Moses said to the LORD, "Why
have You afflicted Your servant? And why
have I not found favor in Your sight, that
You have laid the burden of all these peo-
ple on me? 12Did I conceive all these peo-
ple? Did I beget them, that You should say
to me, 'Carry them in your bosom, as a
guardian carries a nursing child,' to the
land which You swore to their fathers?
13Where am I to get meat to give to all these
people? For they weep all over me, saying,
'Give us meat, that we may eat.' 14I am not
able to bear all these people alone, because
the burden *is* too heavy for me. 15If You
treat me like this, please kill me here and
now—if I have found favor in Your sight—
and do not let me see my wretchedness!"

The Seventy Elders

16So the LORD said to Moses: "Gather to
Me seventy men of the elders of Israel,
whom you know to be the elders of the
people and officers over them; bring them
to the tabernacle of meeting, that they may
stand there with you. 17Then I will come
down and talk with you there. I will take of
the Spirit that *is* upon you and will put *the
same* upon them; and they shall bear the
burden of the people with you, that you
may not bear *it* yourself alone. 18Then you
shall say to the people, 'Consecrate your-
selves for tomorrow, and you shall eat
meat; for you have wept in the hearing of
the LORD, saying, "Who will give us meat
to eat? For *it was* well with us in Egypt."
Therefore the LORD will give you meat, and
you shall eat. 19You shall eat, not one day,
nor two days, nor five days, nor ten days,
nor twenty days, 20but *for* a whole month,
until it comes out of your nostrils and be-
comes loathsome to you, because you have
despised the LORD who is among you, and
have wept before Him, saying, "Why did
we ever come up out of Egypt?" ' "

21And Moses said, "The people whom I
am among *are* six hundred thousand men
on foot; yet You have said, 'I will give them

11:3 [a]Literally *Burning*

11:10–15 the burden of all these people: This is one of the low moments in the life of Moses. Leaders must always make sacrifices, and there are times of frustration. But here Moses was ready to quit. Like Elijah many years later, he had come to the end of his resources. He felt he would rather die than go on (v. 15; see 1 Kin. 19:4). But our extremity is God's opportunity (see 2 Cor. 12:9, 10). Only when we realize our own helplessness can we truly appreciate God's power.

11:16–25 Delegation is a vital part of godly leadership. While the Lord provides strength to complete the tasks He assigns, He often uses others to supply that strength and help finish the work.

meat, that they may eat *for* a whole month.'
22Shall flocks and herds be slaughtered for
them, to provide enough for them? Or
shall all the fish of the sea be gathered to-
gether for them, to provide enough for
them?"
23And the LORD said to Moses, "Has the
LORD's arm been shortened? Now you
shall see whether what I say will happen to
you or not."
24So Moses went out and told the people
the words of the LORD, and he gathered the
seventy men of the elders of the people
and placed them around the tabernacle.
25Then the LORD came down in the cloud,
and spoke to him, and took of the Spirit
that *was* upon him, and placed *the same*
upon the seventy elders; and it happened,
when the Spirit rested upon them, that
they prophesied, although they never did
so again.[a]
26But two men had remained in the
camp: the name of one *was* El'dad, and the
name of the other Mē'dad. And the Spirit
rested upon them. Now they *were* among
those listed, but who had not gone out to
the tabernacle; yet they prophesied in the
camp. 27And a young man ran and told
Moses, and said, "El'dad and Mē'dad are
prophesying in the camp."
28So Joshua the son of Nun, Moses' as-
sistant, *one* of his choice men, answered
and said, "Moses my lord, forbid them!"
29Then Moses said to him, "Are you
zealous for my sake? Oh, that all the
LORD's people were prophets *and* that the
LORD would put His Spirit upon them!"
30And Moses returned to the camp, he and
the elders of Israel.

The LORD Sends Quail

31Now a wind went out from the LORD,
and it brought quail from the sea and left
them fluttering near the camp, about a
day's journey on this side and about a
day's journey on the other side, all around
the camp, and about two cubits above the
surface of the ground. 32And the people
stayed up all that day, all night, and all the
next day, and gathered the quail (he who
gathered least gathered ten homers); and
they spread *them* out for themselves all
around the camp. 33But while the meat *was*
still between their teeth, before it was
chewed, the wrath of the LORD was
aroused against the people, and the LORD
struck the people with a very great plague.
34So he called the name of that place
Kib'roth Hat·tā'a·vah,[a] because there they
buried the people who had yielded to crav-
ing.
35From Kib'roth Hat·tā'a·vah the people
moved to Ha·zē'roth, and camped at Ha-
zē'roth.

CHAPTER 12

Dissension of Aaron and Miriam

Then Miriam and Aaron spoke against
Moses because of the Ethiopian woman
whom he had married; for he had married
an Ethiopian woman. 2So they said, "Has
the LORD indeed spoken only through Mo-
ses? Has He not spoken through us also?"
And the LORD heard *it*. 3(Now the man Mo-
ses *was* very humble, more than all men
who *were* on the face of the earth.)
4Suddenly the LORD said to Moses,
Aaron, and Miriam, "Come out, you three,
to the tabernacle of meeting!" So the three
came out. 5Then the LORD came down in
the pillar of cloud and stood *in* the door of
the tabernacle, and called Aaron and
Miriam. And they both went forward.
6Then He said,

11:25 [a]Targum and Vulgate read *did not cease.*
11:34 [a]Literally *Graves of Craving*

11:31–34 It might appear that the people were being punished for eating meat, which God had provided, but a deeper problem existed. It was the people's chronic failure to trust God which provoked the **wrath of the LORD** (v. 33; see vv. 4–8). Sin comes from selfish desires (see James 4:1–3).

"Hear now My words:
If there is a prophet among you,
I, the LORD, make Myself known to
him in a vision;
I speak to him in a dream.
7 Not so with My servant Moses;
He *is* faithful in all My house.
8 I speak with him face to face,
Even plainly, and not in dark sayings;
And he sees the form of the LORD.
Why then were you not afraid
To speak against My servant Moses?"

9 So the anger of the LORD was aroused
against them, and He departed. 10 And
when the cloud departed from above the
tabernacle, suddenly Miriam *became* lep-
rous, as *white as* snow. Then Aaron turned
toward Miriam, and there she was, a leper.
11 So Aaron said to Moses, "Oh, my lord!
Please do not lay *this* sin on us, in which
we have done foolishly and in which we
have sinned. 12 Please do not let her be as
one dead, whose flesh is half consumed
when he comes out of his mother's
womb!"

13 So Moses cried out to the LORD, saying,
"Please heal her, O God, I pray!"

14 Then the LORD said to Moses, "If her
father had but spit in her face, would she
not be shamed seven days? Let her be shut
out of the camp seven days, and afterward
she may be received *again*." 15 So Miriam
was shut out of the camp seven days, and
the people did not journey till Miriam was
brought in *again*. 16 And afterward the peo-
ple moved from Ha·zē′roth and camped in
the Wilderness of Par′an.

13:8 [a]Septuagint and Vulgate read *Oshea*.
13:16 [a]Septuagint and Vulgate read *Oshea*.

CHAPTER 13

Spies Sent into Canaan

And the LORD spoke to Moses, saying,
2 "Send men to spy out the land of Cā′naan,
which I am giving to the children of Israel;
from each tribe of their fathers you shall
send a man, every one a leader among
them."

3 So Moses sent them from the Wilder-
ness of Par′an according to the command
of the LORD, all of them men who *were*
heads of the children of Israel. 4 Now these
were their names: from the tribe of Reuben,
Sham′mū·a the son of Zac′cur; 5 from the
tribe of Sim′ē·on, Shā′phat the son of
Hō′rī; 6 from the tribe of Judah, Caleb the
son of Je·phūn′neh; 7 from the tribe of
Is′sa·char, Ī′gal the son of Joseph; 8 from the
tribe of Ē′phra·im, Hō·shē′a[a] the son of
Nun; 9 from the tribe of Benjamin, Pal′tī the
son of Rā′phū; 10 from the tribe of Zeb′-
ū·lun, Gad′di·el the son of Sō′dī; 11 from the
tribe of Joseph, *that is*, from the tribe of
Ma·nas′seh, Gad′dī the son of Sū′sī; 12 from
the tribe of Dan, Am′mi·el the son of Ge-
mal′lī; 13 from the tribe of Ash′er, Seth′ur
the son of Michael; 14 from the tribe of
Naph′ta·lī, Nah′bī the son of Voph′sī;
15 from the tribe of Gad, Ge·ū′el the son of
Mā′chī.

16 These *are* the names of the men whom
Moses sent to spy out the land. And Moses
called Hō·shē′a[a] the son of Nun, Joshua.

17 Then Moses sent them to spy out the
land of Cā′naan, and said to them, "Go up
this *way* into the South, and go up to the
mountains, 18 and see what the land is like:
whether the people who dwell in it *are*

12:9, 10 He departed: The ultimate punishment for Miriam and Aaron's jealousy had taken place; God withdrew His presence. **Miriam became leprous**: Her leprosy had at least two implications: (1) she was unclean and could not serve God, (2) but neither could she remain in the community as part of the people.

12:13 Instead of gloating in God's punishment of Aaron and Miriam, Moses intercedes on their behalf.

13:16 Hoshea means "Salvation"; **Joshua** means "The LORD is Salvation". Appropriately, Joshua is one of only two men who include God in their evaluation of Israel's strategy (14:8, 9).

Caleb: Faith in Action

Often overlooked as one of the Old Testament heroes, Caleb provides an inspiring example of spiritual, physical, and mental excellence. His courage, vigor, and consecration reveal a man truly dedicated to the Lord.

As one of the twelve men sent to spy out the land of Canaan, Caleb had observed the walled cities and the intimidating giants, but he had also seen the fruitfulness of the region, and he knew the promise of God to give the land to the Israelites. So Caleb encouraged the people to proceed with God's plan: "Let us go up at once and take possession, for we are well able to overcome it" (Num. 13:30).

However, his opinion was disregarded as most of the other spies emphasized the difficulty of the task before them and discouraged the people from continuing. Only Caleb and Joshua showed the courage and faith to oppose popular opinion. They understood that, with God on their side, nothing could stop the Israelites except sin and unbelief. "Do not rebel against the LORD, nor fear . . . the LORD is with us" (14:9).

Not only did the Israelites refuse to listen, they wanted to stone the two men. The Lord became angry with the Israelites' lack of faith and condemned them to wander in the wilderness for forty years, one year for each day the spies had searched the land (v. 34). He also decreed that Caleb and Joshua would be the only members of the adult generation to enter the Promised Land (v. 30).

Caleb was further singled out and blessed for his faithfulness; the Lord pledged to give him the portion of the land he had spied out "because he wholly followed the LORD" (Deut. 1:36).

By the time this promise was fulfilled, Caleb was eighty-five years old (Josh. 14), yet his physical strength had not abated, nor had his courage and faith waned (vv. 11–14). He was still eager for the opportunity to drive out the Anakims—the giants who had so intimidated the other spies—and he continued to trust the Lord to give him the victory. He acted on his faith and was duly rewarded (15:13, 14).

Even at this point, Caleb did not rest on his past achievements. Many might have been tempted to say, "I've served the Lord faithfully for years; now it's time to reap the rewards." Yet Caleb relinquished control of much of his hard-won inheritance when Hebron became one of the Levitical cities (21:11, 12). What a testimony to his spiritual integrity!

God continues to use His children as long as we make ourselves available, and He will provide the strength we need to perform our assigned ministry. When your faith and courage wane, remember the invincible Caleb, eighty-five years old and still going strong for the Lord. ✦

strong or weak, few or many; [19]whether the
land they dwell in *is* good or bad; whether
the cities they inhabit *are* like camps or
strongholds; [20]whether the land *is* rich or
poor; and whether there are forests there
or not. Be of good courage. And bring
some of the fruit of the land." Now the
time *was* the season of the first ripe grapes.
[21]So they went up and spied out the land
from the Wilderness of Zin as far as Rē′-
hob, near the entrance of Hā′math. [22]And
they went up through the South and came
to Hē′bron; A·hī′man, Shē′shai, and Tal′-
maī, the descendants of Ā′nak, *were* there.
(Now Hē′bron was built seven years be-
fore Zō′an in Egypt.) [23]Then they came to
the Valley of Esh′col, and there cut down a
branch with one cluster of grapes; they car-
ried it between two of them on a pole. *They*
also *brought* some of the pomegranates and
figs. [24]The place was called the Valley of
Esh′col,[a] because of the cluster which the
men of Israel cut down there. [25]And they
returned from spying out the land after
forty days.
[26]Now they departed and came back to
Moses and Aaron and all the congregation
of the children of Israel in the Wilderness
of Par′an, at Kā′desh; they brought back
word to them and to all the congregation,
and showed them the fruit of the land.
[27]Then they told him, and said: "We went
to the land where you sent us. It truly
flows with milk and honey, and this *is* its
fruit. [28]Nevertheless the people who dwell
in the land *are* strong; the cities *are* fortified
and very large; moreover we saw the de-
scendants of Ā′nak there. [29]The A·mal′-
e·kītes dwell in the land of the South; the
Hit′tītes, the Jeb′ū·sītes, and the Am′o-
rītes dwell in the mountains; and the Cā′-
naan·ītes dwell by the sea and along the
banks of the Jordan."
[30]Then Caleb quieted the people before
Moses, and said, "Let us go up at once and
take possession, for we are well able to
overcome it."
[31]But the men who had gone up with
him said, "We are not able to go up against
the people, for they *are* stronger than we."
[32]And they gave the children of Israel a bad
report of the land which they had spied
out, saying, "The land through which we
have gone as spies *is* a land that devours its
inhabitants, and all the people whom we
saw in it *are* men of *great* stature. [33]There
we saw the giants[a] (the descendants of
Ā′nak came from the giants); and we were
like grasshoppers in our own sight, and so
we were in their sight."

13:24 [a]Literally *Cluster* 13:33 [a]Hebrew *nephilim*

CHAPTER 14

Israel Refuses to Enter Canaan

So all the congregation lifted up their
voices and cried, and the people wept that
night. [2]And all the children of Israel com-
plained against Moses and Aaron, and the
whole congregation said to them, "If only
we had died in the land of Egypt! Or if
only we had died in this wilderness! [3]Why
has the LORD brought us to this land to fall
by the sword, that our wives and children
should become victims? Would it not be
better for us to return to Egypt?" [4]So they
said to one another, "Let us select a leader
and return to Egypt."
[5]Then Moses and Aaron fell on their

13:30, 31 Let us go up at once: Essentially, the facts of the mission's report, both good and bad, were shared by all the spies. The only real difference was that Joshua and Caleb believed God would help Israel to conquer; the others did not. How often do we allow difficult situations to cloud our faith in God?

13:33 like grasshoppers: The 10 spies saw only the magnitude of the task before them. These people lost the battle before it was waged. It is one of the tragic moments in the life of Israel. Because of this failure, none of those who left Egypt except Caleb and Joshua would enter Canaan. The 10 discouragers bear a terrible responsibility.

faces before all the assembly of the congregation of the children of Israel.

6But Joshua the son of Nun and Caleb the son of Je·phū′neh, *who were* among those who had spied out the land, tore their clothes; 7and they spoke to all the congregation of the children of Israel, saying: "The land we passed through to spy out *is* an exceedingly good land. 8If the LORD delights in us, then He will bring us into this land and give it to us, 'a land which flows with milk and honey.'[a] 9Only do not rebel against the LORD, nor fear the people of the land, for they *are* our bread; their protection has departed from them, and the LORD *is* with us. Do not fear them."

10And all the congregation said to stone them with stones. Now the glory of the LORD appeared in the tabernacle of meeting before all the children of Israel.

Moses Intercedes for the People

11Then the LORD said to Moses: "How long will these people reject Me? And how long will they not believe Me, with all the signs which I have performed among them? 12I will strike them with the pestilence and disinherit them, and I will make of you a nation greater and mightier than they."

13And Moses said to the LORD: "Then the Egyptians will hear *it,* for by Your might You brought these people up from among them, 14and they will tell *it* to the inhabitants of this land. They have heard that You, LORD, *are* among these people; that You, LORD, are seen face to face and Your cloud stands above them, and You go before them in a pillar of cloud by day and in a pillar of fire by night. 15Now *if* You kill these people as one man, then the nations which have heard of Your fame will speak, saying, 16'Because the LORD was not able to bring this people to the land which He swore to give them, therefore He killed them in the wilderness.' 17And now, I pray, let the power of my Lord be great, just as You have spoken, saying, 18'The LORD is longsuffering and abundant in mercy, forgiving iniquity and transgression; but He by no means clears *the guilty,* visiting the iniquity of the fathers on the children to the third and fourth *generation.*'[a] 19Pardon the iniquity of this people, I pray, according to the greatness of Your mercy, just as You have forgiven this people, from Egypt even until now."

20Then the LORD said: "I have pardoned, according to your word; 21but truly, as I live, all the earth shall be filled with the glory of the LORD— 22because all these men who have seen My glory and the signs which I did in Egypt and in the wilderness, and have put Me to the test now these ten times, and have not heeded My voice, 23they certainly shall not see the land of which I swore to their fathers, nor shall any of those who rejected Me see it. 24But My servant Caleb, because he has a different spirit in him and has followed Me fully, I will bring into the land where he went, and his descendants shall inherit it. 25Now the A·mal′e·kītes and the Cā′naan·ītes dwell in the valley; tomorrow turn and move out into the wilderness by the Way of the Red Sea."

Death Sentence on the Rebels

26And the LORD spoke to Moses and Aaron, saying, 27"How long *shall I bear with* this evil congregation who complain against Me? I have heard the complaints which the children of Israel make against Me. 28Say to them, 'As I live,' says the LORD, 'just as you have spoken in My hearing, so I will do to you: 29The carcasses of

14:8 [a]Exodus 3:8 14:18 [a]Exodus 34:6, 7

14:20 I have pardoned: This does not mean that there would be no punishment. Unbelief has consequences which cannot be avoided. But the people would not be abandoned.

14:24 Like Caleb, we are to follow the Lord wholeheartedly in an attitude of unwavering belief. Such dedication will be rewarded.

you who have complained against Me
shall fall in this wilderness, all of you who
were numbered, according to your entire
number, from twenty years old and above.
30Except for Caleb the son of Je·phŭn′neh
and Joshua the son of Nun, you shall by no
means enter the land which I swore I
would make you dwell in. 31But your little
ones, whom you said would be victims, I
will bring in, and they shall know the land
which you have despised. 32But *as for* you,
your carcasses shall fall in this wilderness.
33And your sons shall be shepherds in the
wilderness forty years, and bear the brunt
of your infidelity, until your carcasses are
consumed in the wilderness. 34According
to the number of the days in which you
spied out the land, forty days, for each day
you shall bear your guilt one year, *namely*
forty years, and you shall know My re-
jection. 35I the LORD have spoken this. I will
surely do so to all this evil congregation
who are gathered together against Me. In
this wilderness they shall be consumed,
and there they shall die.' "

36Now the men whom Moses sent to spy
out the land, who returned and made all
the congregation complain against him by
bringing a bad report of the land, 37those
very men who brought the evil report
about the land, died by the plague before
the LORD. 38But Joshua the son of Nun and
Caleb the son of Je·phŭn′neh remained
alive, of the men who went to spy out the
land.

A Futile Invasion Attempt

39Then Moses told these words to all the
children of Israel, and the people mourned
greatly. 40And they rose early in the morn-
ing and went up to the top of the moun-
tain, saying, "Here we are, and we will go
up to the place which the LORD has
promised, for we have sinned!"

41And Moses said, "Now why do you
transgress the command of the LORD? For
this will not succeed. 42Do not go up, lest
you be defeated by your enemies, for the
LORD *is* not among you. 43For the A·mal′-
e·kītes and the Cā′naan·ītes *are* there be-
fore you, and you shall fall by the sword;
because you have turned away from the
LORD, the LORD will not be with you."

44But they presumed to go up to the
mountaintop. Nevertheless, neither the
ark of the covenant of the LORD nor Moses
departed from the camp. 45Then the
A·mal′e·kītes and the Cā′naan·ītes who
dwelt in that mountain came down and at-
tacked them, and drove them back as far as
Hor′mah.

CHAPTER 15

Laws of Grain and Drink Offerings

And the LORD spoke to Moses, saying,
2"Speak to the children of Israel, and say to
them: 'When you have come into the land
you are to inhabit, which I am giving to
you, 3and you make an offering by fire to
the LORD, a burnt offering or a sacrifice,
to fulfill a vow or as a freewill offering or
in your appointed feasts, to make a sweet
aroma to the LORD, from the herd or the
flock, 4then he who presents his offering to
the LORD shall bring a grain offering of
one-tenth *of an ephah* of fine flour mixed
with one-fourth of a hin of oil; 5and one-
fourth of a hin of wine as a drink offering
you shall prepare with the burnt offering
or the sacrifice, for each lamb. 6Or for a ram
you shall prepare as a grain offering two-
tenths *of an ephah* of fine flour mixed with
one-third of a hin of oil; 7and as a drink

15:1—20:13 These chapters, covering the 40 years of wandering, contain only two types of material: (1) Laws which relate to the Promised Land (15:1–41; 18:1—19:22). These show that one generation's rebellion cannot defeat God's purposes. (2) Stories about the failure of the leadership, including Moses (16:1—17:13; 20:1–13), which reemphasize that it is God, not the Levites or Moses, who will accomplish God's purpose. None of these leaders would enter the Promised Land.

offering you shall offer one-third of a hin of wine as a sweet aroma to the LORD. [8]And when you prepare a young bull as a burnt offering, or as a sacrifice to fulfill a vow, or as a peace offering to the LORD, [9]then shall be offered with the young bull a grain offering of three-tenths *of an ephah* of fine flour mixed with half a hin of oil; [10]and you shall bring as the drink offering half a hin of wine as an offering made by fire, a sweet aroma to the LORD.

[11]'Thus it shall be done for each young bull, for each ram, or for each lamb or young goat. [12]According to the number that you prepare, so you shall do with everyone according to their number. [13]All who are native-born shall do these things in this manner, in presenting an offering made by fire, a sweet aroma to the LORD. [14]And if a stranger dwells with you, or whoever *is* among you throughout your generations, and would present an offering made by fire, a sweet aroma to the LORD, just as you do, so shall he do. [15]One ordinance *shall be* for you of the assembly and for the stranger who dwells *with you,* an ordinance forever throughout your generations; as you are, so shall the stranger be before the LORD. [16]One law and one custom shall be for you and for the stranger who dwells with you.' "[a]

[17]Again the LORD spoke to Moses, saying, [18]"Speak to the children of Israel, and say to them: 'When you come into the land to which I bring you, [19]then it will be, when you eat of the bread of the land, that you shall offer up a heave offering to the LORD. [20]You shall offer up a cake of the first of your ground meal *as* a heave offering; as a heave offering of the threshing floor, so shall you offer it up. [21]Of the first of your ground meal you shall give to the LORD a heave offering throughout your generations.

Laws Concerning Unintentional Sin

[22]'If you sin unintentionally, and do not observe all these commandments which the LORD has spoken to Moses— [23]all that the LORD has commanded you by the hand of Moses, from the day the LORD gave commandment and onward throughout your generations— [24]then it will be, if it is unintentionally committed, without the knowledge of the congregation, that the whole congregation shall offer one young bull as a burnt offering, as a sweet aroma to the LORD, with its grain offering and its drink offering, according to the ordinance, and one kid of the goats as a sin offering. [25]So the priest shall make atonement for the whole congregation of the children of Israel, and it shall be forgiven them, for it was unintentional; they shall bring their offering, an offering made by fire to the LORD, and their sin offering before the LORD, for their unintended sin. [26]It shall be forgiven the whole congregation of the children of Israel and the stranger who dwells among them, because all the people *did it* unintentionally.

[27]'And if a person sins unintentionally, then he shall bring a female goat in its first year as a sin offering. [28]So the priest shall make atonement for the person who sins unintentionally, when he sins unintentionally before the LORD, to make atonement for him; and it shall be forgiven him. [29]You shall have one law for him who sins unintentionally, *for* him who is native-born

15:16 [a]Compare Exodus 12:49

15:22–31 sin unintentionally: In the law given at Sinai, God was careful to distinguish between willful sin and unintentional breaking of His laws (Lev. 4:1–35). Here Moses is told that this distinction is to be carefully observed in Canaan. God provides a way of escape for the well-intended individual who sins without malice or intent (vv. 22–29). Yet, He is severe with the person who sins flagrantly without regard for God (vv. 30, 31). It is a mistake to equalize all transgression whether it is unintentional or not. The old phrase "sin is sin" is not appropriate to the teaching of Scripture. God looks at the motives of the heart.

among the children of Israel and for the
stranger who dwells among them.

Law Concerning Presumptuous Sin

30'But the person who does *anything* pre-
sumptuously, *whether he is* native-born or a
stranger, that one brings reproach on the
LORD, and he shall be cut off from among
his people. 31Because he has despised the
word of the LORD, and has broken His
commandment, that person shall be com-
pletely cut off; his guilt *shall be* upon
him.' "

Penalty for Violating the Sabbath

32Now while the children of Israel were
in the wilderness, they found a man gath-
ering sticks on the Sabbath day. 33And
those who found him gathering sticks
brought him to Moses and Aaron, and to
all the congregation. 34They put him under
guard, because it had not been explained
what should be done to him.

35Then the LORD said to Moses, "The
man must surely be put to death; all the
congregation shall stone him with stones
outside the camp." 36So, as the LORD com-
manded Moses, all the congregation
brought him outside the camp and stoned
him with stones, and he died.

Tassels on Garments

37Again the LORD spoke to Moses, say-
ing, 38"Speak to the children of Israel: Tell
them to make tassels on the corners of their
garments throughout their generations,
and to put a blue thread in the tassels of the
corners. 39And you shall have the tassel,
that you may look upon it and remember
all the commandments of the LORD and do
them, and that you *may* not follow the har-
lotry to which your own heart and your
own eyes are inclined, 40and that you may
remember and do all My commandments,
and be holy for your God. 41I *am* the LORD
your God, who brought you out of the
land of Egypt, to be your God: I *am* the
LORD your God."

CHAPTER 16

Rebellion Against Moses and Aaron

Now Kō'rah the son of Iz'har, the son of
Kō'hath, the son of Levi, with Dā'than and
A·bī'ram the sons of E·lī'ab, and On the
son of Pē'leth, sons of Reuben, took *men;*
2and they rose up before Moses with some
of the children of Israel, two hundred and
fifty leaders of the congregation, represen-
tatives of the congregation, men of
renown. 3They gathered together against
Moses and Aaron, and said to them, "*You
take* too much upon yourselves, for all the
congregation *is* holy, every one of them,
and the LORD *is* among them. Why then do
you exalt yourselves above the assembly of
the LORD?"

4So when Moses heard *it,* he fell on his
face; 5and he spoke to Kō'rah and all his
company, saying, "Tomorrow morning the
LORD will show who *is* His and *who is* holy,
and will cause *him* to come near to Him.
That one whom He chooses He will cause
to come near to Him. 6Do this: Take
censers, Kō'rah and all your company; 7put
fire in them and put incense in them before

15:37–41 The **tassels** with the blue thread were to serve as a reminder of the holy conduct to which the Israelites were called. The origin of the Jewish *tallit,* or prayer shawl, can be traced to this passage.

16:1–11 Korah was dissatisfied with his position as a Levite, desiring the glory of the priesthood. So he challenged the exclusive right of Aaron and his descendants to hold that office. Dathan, Abiram, and On were more interested in civil power, and they challenged Moses' authority as the leader of Israel. **seeking the priesthood** (v. 10): Moses saw that the real cause of the conflict was not a desire for religious freedom but jealousy. The argument "for all the congregation is holy" (v. 3), as often with such high-flown rhetoric, covered much baser motives. To be jealous and desirous of another position is to scorn the blessing God has already provided.

the LORD tomorrow, and it shall be *that* the
man whom the LORD chooses *is* the holy
one. *You take* too much upon yourselves,
you sons of Levi!"
[8]Then Moses said to Kō'rah, "Hear now,
you sons of Levi: [9]*Is it* a small thing to you
that the God of Israel has separated you
from the congregation of Israel, to bring
you near to Himself, to do the work of the
tabernacle of the LORD, and to stand before
the congregation to serve them; [10]and that
He has brought you near *to Himself,* you
and all your brethren, the sons of Levi,
with you? And are you seeking the priest-
hood also? [11]Therefore you and all your
company *are* gathered together against the
LORD. And what *is* Aaron that you com-
plain against him?"
[12]And Moses sent to call Dā'than and
A·bī'ram the sons of E·lī'ab, but they said,
"We will not come up! [13]*Is it* a small thing
that you have brought us up out of a land
flowing with milk and honey, to kill us in
the wilderness, that you should keep act-
ing like a prince over us? [14]Moreover you
have not brought us into a land flowing
with milk and honey, nor given us inheri-
tance of fields and vineyards. Will you put
out the eyes of these men? We will not
come up!"
[15]Then Moses was very angry, and said
to the LORD, "Do not respect their offering.
I have not taken one donkey from them,
nor have I hurt one of them."
[16]And Moses said to Kō'rah, "Tomor-
row, you and all your company be present
before the LORD—you and they, as well as
Aaron. [17]Let each take his censer and put
incense in it, and each of you bring his
censer before the LORD, two hundred and
fifty censers; both you and Aaron, each
with his censer." [18]So every man took his
censer, put fire in it, laid incense on it, and
stood at the door of the tabernacle of meet-
ing with Moses and Aaron. [19]And Kō'rah
gathered all the congregation against them
at the door of the tabernacle of meeting.
Then the glory of the LORD appeared to all
the congregation.

[20]And the LORD spoke to Moses and
Aaron, saying, [21]"Separate yourselves from
among this congregation, that I may con-
sume them in a moment."
[22]Then they fell on their faces, and said,
"O God, the God of the spirits of all flesh,
shall one man sin, and You be angry with
all the congregation?"
[23]So the LORD spoke to Moses, saying,
[24]"Speak to the congregation, saying, 'Get
away from the tents of Kō'rah, Dā'than,
and A·bī'ram.' "
[25]Then Moses rose and went to Dā'than
and A·bī'ram, and the elders of Israel fol-
lowed him. [26]And he spoke to the congre-
gation, saying, "Depart now from the tents
of these wicked men! Touch nothing of
theirs, lest you be consumed in all their
sins." [27]So they got away from around the
tents of Kō'rah, Dā'than, and A·bī'ram;
and Dā'than and A·bī'ram came out and
stood at the door of their tents, with
their wives, their sons, and their little chil-
dren.
[28]And Moses said: "By this you shall
know that the LORD has sent me to do all
these works, for *I have* not *done them* of my
own will. [29]If these men die naturally like
all men, or if they are visited by the com-
mon fate of all men, *then* the LORD has not
sent me. [30]But if the LORD creates a new
thing, and the earth opens its mouth and
swallows them up with all that belongs to
them, and they go down alive into the pit,
then you will understand that these men
have rejected the LORD."
[31]Now it came to pass, as he finished
speaking all these words, that the ground
split apart under them, [32]and the earth
opened its mouth and swallowed them up,
with their households and all the men with
Kō'rah, with all *their* goods. [33]So they and
all those with them went down alive into
the pit; the earth closed over them, and
they perished from among the assembly.
[34]Then all Israel who *were* around them fled
at their cry, for they said, "Lest the earth
swallow us up *also!*"
[35]And a fire came out from the LORD and

consumed the two hundred and fifty men
who were offering incense.
36Then the LORD spoke to Moses, saying:
37"Tell El·ē·ā′zar, the son of Aaron the
priest, to pick up the censers out of the
blaze, for they are holy, and scatter the fire
some distance away. 38The censers of these
men who sinned against their own souls,
let them be made into hammered plates as
a covering for the altar. Because they pre-
sented them before the LORD, therefore
they are holy; and they shall be a sign to
the children of Israel." 39So El·ē·ā′zar the
priest took the bronze censers, which those
who were burned up had presented, and
they were hammered out as a covering on
the altar, 40*to be* a memorial to the children
of Israel that no outsider, who *is* not a de-
scendant of Aaron, should come near to of-
fer incense before the LORD, that he might
not become like Kō′rah and his compan-
ions, just as the LORD had said to him
through Moses.

Complaints of the People

41On the next day all the congregation of
the children of Israel complained against
Moses and Aaron, saying, "You have killed
the people of the LORD." 42Now it hap-
pened, when the congregation had gath-
ered against Moses and Aaron, that they
turned toward the tabernacle of meeting;
and suddenly the cloud covered it, and the
glory of the LORD appeared. 43Then Moses
and Aaron came before the tabernacle of
meeting.
44And the LORD spoke to Moses, saying,
45"Get away from among this congrega-
tion, that I may consume them in a mo-
ment."
And they fell on their faces.
46So Moses said to Aaron, "Take a censer
and put fire in it from the altar, put incense
on it, and take it quickly to the congrega-
tion and make atonement for them; for
wrath has gone out from the LORD. The
plague has begun." 47Then Aaron took *it* as
Moses commanded, and ran into the midst
of the assembly; and already the plague
had begun among the people. So he put in
the incense and made atonement for the
people. 48And he stood between the dead
and the living; so the plague was stopped.
49Now those who died in the plague were
fourteen thousand seven hundred, besides
those who died in the Kō′rah incident. 50So
Aaron returned to Moses at the door of the
tabernacle of meeting, for the plague had
stopped.

CHAPTER 17

The Budding of Aaron's Rod

And the LORD spoke to Moses, saying:
2"Speak to the children of Israel, and get
from them a rod from each father's house,
all their leaders according to their fathers'
houses—twelve rods. Write each man's
name on his rod. 3And you shall write Aar-
on's name on the rod of Levi. For there
shall be one rod for the head of *each*
father's house. 4Then you shall place them
in the tabernacle of meeting before the Tes-
timony, where I meet with you. 5And it
shall be *that* the rod of the man whom I
choose will blossom; thus I will rid Myself
of the complaints of the children of Israel,
which they make against you."
6So Moses spoke to the children of Is-
rael, and each of their leaders gave him a
rod apiece, for each leader according to
their fathers' houses, twelve rods; and the
rod of Aaron *was* among their rods. 7And
Moses placed the rods before the LORD in
the tabernacle of witness.
8Now it came to pass on the next day
that Moses went into the tabernacle of wit-
ness, and behold, the rod of Aaron, of the
house of Levi, had sprouted and put forth
buds, had produced blossoms and yielded

16:42–50 Again **Moses** and **Aaron** effectively intercede for the very people who so recently maligned them.

ripe almonds. 9Then Moses brought out all the rods from before the LORD to all the children of Israel; and they looked, and each man took his rod.

10And the LORD said to Moses, "Bring Aaron's rod back before the Testimony, to be kept as a sign against the rebels, that you may put their complaints away from Me, lest they die." 11Thus did Moses; just as the LORD had commanded him, so he did.

12So the children of Israel spoke to Moses, saying, "Surely we die, we perish, we all perish! 13Whoever even comes near the tabernacle of the LORD must die. Shall we all utterly die?"

CHAPTER 18

Duties of Priests and Levites

Then the LORD said to Aaron: "You and your sons and your father's house with you shall bear the iniquity *related to* the sanctuary, and you and your sons with you shall bear the iniquity *associated with* your priesthood. 2Also bring with you your brethren of the tribe of Levi, the tribe of your father, that they may be joined with you and serve you while you and your sons *are* with you before the tabernacle of witness. 3They shall attend to your needs and all the needs of the tabernacle; but they shall not come near the articles of the sanctuary and the altar, lest they die—they and you also. 4They shall be joined with you and attend to the needs of the tabernacle of meeting, for all the work of the tabernacle; but an outsider shall not come near you. 5And you shall attend to the duties of the sanctuary and the duties of the altar, that there *may* be no more wrath on the children of Israel. 6Behold, I Myself have taken your brethren the Lē′vītes from among the children of Israel; *they are* a gift to you, given by the LORD, to do the work of the tabernacle of meeting. 7Therefore you and your sons with you shall attend to your priesthood for everything at the altar and behind the veil; and you shall serve. I give your priesthood *to you* as a gift for service, but the outsider who comes near shall be put to death."

Offerings for Support of the Priests

8And the LORD spoke to Aaron: "Here, I Myself have also given you charge of My heave offerings, all the holy gifts of the children of Israel; I have given them as a portion to you and your sons, as an ordinance forever. 9This shall be yours of the most holy things *reserved* from the fire: every offering of theirs, every grain offering and every sin offering and every trespass offering which they render to Me, *shall be* most holy for you and your sons. 10In a most holy *place* you shall eat it; every male shall eat it. It shall be holy to you.

11"This also *is* yours: the heave offering of their gift, with all the wave offerings of the children of Israel; I have given them to you, and your sons and daughters with you, as an ordinance forever. Everyone who is clean in your house may eat it.

12"All the best of the oil, all the best of the new wine and the grain, their firstfruits which they offer to the LORD, I have given them to you. 13Whatever first ripe fruit is in their land, which they bring to the LORD, shall be yours. Everyone who is clean in your house may eat it.

14"Every devoted thing in Israel shall be yours.

15"Everything that first opens the womb of all flesh, which they bring to the LORD, whether man or beast, shall be yours; nevertheless the firstborn of man you shall surely redeem, and the firstborn of unclean animals you shall redeem. 16And those redeemed of the devoted things you shall redeem when one month old, according to your valuation, for five shekels of silver, according to the shekel of the sanctuary, which *is* twenty gerahs. 17But the firstborn of a cow, the firstborn of a sheep, or the firstborn of a goat you shall not redeem; they *are* holy. You shall sprinkle their blood on the altar, and burn their fat *as* an offering made by fire for a sweet aroma to the LORD. 18And their flesh shall be yours, just

as the wave breast and the right thigh are
yours.
19"All the heave offerings of the holy
things, which the children of Israel offer to
the LORD, I have given to you and your
sons and daughters with you as an ordi-
nance forever; it *is* a covenant of salt for-
ever before the LORD with you and your
descendants with you."
20Then the LORD said to Aaron: "You
shall have no inheritance in their land, nor
shall you have any portion among them; I
am your portion and your inheritance
among the children of Israel.

Tithes for Support of the Levites

21"Behold, I have given the children of
Levi all the tithes in Israel as an inheritance
in return for the work which they perform,
the work of the tabernacle of meeting.
22Hereafter the children of Israel shall not
come near the tabernacle of meeting, lest
they bear sin and die. 23But the Lē'vītes
shall perform the work of the tabernacle of
meeting, and they shall bear their iniquity;
it shall be a statute forever, throughout your
generations, that among the children of Is-
rael they shall have no inheritance. 24For
the tithes of the children of Israel, which
they offer up *as* a heave offering to the
LORD, I have given to the Lē'vītes as an in-
heritance; therefore I have said to them,
'Among the children of Israel they shall
have no inheritance.' "

The Tithe of the Levites

25Then the LORD spoke to Moses, saying,
26"Speak thus to the Lē'vītes, and say to
them: 'When you take from the children of
Israel the tithes which I have given you
from them as your inheritance, then you
shall offer up a heave offering of it to the
LORD, a tenth of the tithe. 27And your heave
offering shall be reckoned to you as though
it were the grain of the threshing floor and
as the fullness of the winepress. 28Thus you
shall also offer a heave offering to the LORD
from all your tithes which you receive
from the children of Israel, and you shall
give the LORD's heave offering from it to
Aaron the priest. 29Of all your gifts you
shall offer up every heave offering due to
the LORD, from all the best of them, the
consecrated part of them.' 30Therefore you
shall say to them: 'When you have lifted
up the best of it, then *the rest* shall be ac-
counted to the Lē'vītes as the produce of
the threshing floor and as the produce of
the winepress. 31You may eat it in any
place, you and your households, for it *is*
your reward for your work in the taberna-
cle of meeting. 32And you shall bear no sin
because of it, when you have lifted up the
best of it. But you shall not profane the
holy gifts of the children of Israel, lest you
die.' "

CHAPTER 19

Laws of Purification

Now the LORD spoke to Moses and
Aaron, saying, 2"This *is* the ordinance of
the law which the LORD has commanded,
saying: 'Speak to the children of Israel, that
they bring you a red heifer without blem-
ish, in which there *is* no defect *and* on
which a yoke has never come. 3You shall
give it to El·ē·ā'zar the priest, that he may
take it outside the camp, and it shall be
slaughtered before him; 4and El·ē·ā'zar the

18:19 covenant of salt: Believed to be a type of covenant in which the two parties exchanged salt, a precious commodity.

19:1–22 The ritual described provided purification from uncleanness caused by contact with the dead. As life represents what is holy, so death represents sin. In some aspects this ritual was unique among OT rites: (1) the heifer was **slaughtered** (v. 3) outside the camp, not sacrificed at the altar; (2) the **blood** and **offal** (v. 5) were included in the burning, rather than the blood being poured on the altar; (3) the **ashes** (v. 9), rather than the water, were the cleansing agent (see vv. 17, 18; Heb. 9:13).

priest shall take some of its blood with his
finger, and sprinkle some of its blood
seven times directly in front of the taberna-
cle of meeting. 5Then the heifer shall be
burned in his sight: its hide, its flesh, its
blood, and its offal shall be burned. 6And
the priest shall take cedar wood and hys-
sop and scarlet, and cast *them* into the
midst of the fire burning the heifer. 7Then
the priest shall wash his clothes, he shall
bathe in water, and afterward he shall
come into the camp; the priest shall be un-
clean until evening. 8And the one who
burns it shall wash his clothes in water,
bathe in water, and shall be unclean until
evening. 9Then a man *who is* clean shall
gather up the ashes of the heifer, and store
them outside the camp in a clean place; and
they shall be kept for the congregation of
the children of Israel for the water of puri-
fication;[a] it *is* for purifying from sin. 10And
the one who gathers the ashes of the heifer
shall wash his clothes, and be unclean un-
til evening. It shall be a statute forever to
the children of Israel and to the stranger
who dwells among them.

11'He who touches the dead body of
anyone shall be unclean seven days. 12He
shall purify himself with the water on the
third day and on the seventh day; *then* he
will be clean. But if he does not purify him-
self on the third day and on the seventh
day, he will not be clean. 13Whoever
touches the body of anyone who has died,
and does not purify himself, defiles the
tabernacle of the LORD. That person shall
be cut off from Israel. He shall be unclean,
because the water of purification was not
sprinkled on him; his uncleanness *is* still
on him.

14'This *is* the law when a man dies in a
tent: All who come into the tent and all
who *are* in the tent shall be unclean seven
days; 15and every open vessel, which has
no cover fastened on it, *is* unclean. 16Who-
ever in the open field touches one who is
slain by a sword or who has died, or a bone
of a man, or a grave, shall be unclean seven
days.

17'And for an unclean *person* they shall
take some of the ashes of the heifer burnt
for purification from sin, and running wa-
ter shall be put on them in a vessel. 18A
clean person shall take hyssop and dip *it* in
the water, sprinkle *it* on the tent, on all the
vessels, on the persons who were there, or
on the one who touched a bone, the slain,
the dead, or a grave. 19The clean *person*
shall sprinkle the unclean on the third day
and on the seventh day; and on the sev-
enth day he shall purify himself, wash his
clothes, and bathe in water; and at evening
he shall be clean.

20'But the man who is unclean and does
not purify himself, that person shall be cut
off from among the assembly, because he
has defiled the sanctuary of the LORD. The
water of purification has not been sprin-
kled on him; he *is* unclean. 21It shall be a
perpetual statute for them. He who sprin-
kles the water of purification shall wash
his clothes; and he who touches the water
of purification shall be unclean until
evening. 22Whatever the unclean *person*
touches shall be unclean; and the person
who touches *it* shall be unclean until
evening.' "

CHAPTER 20

Moses' Error at Kadesh

Then the children of Israel, the whole
congregation, came into the Wilderness of
Zin in the first month, and the people

19:9 [a]Literally *impurity*

19:9 purifying from sin: Water was not enough for moral cleansing; a sacrifice must be included.

19:18 hyssop: A special branch used to apply the water of purification to the altar. While the purification here is ceremonial, it prefigures the purification from sin which takes place through the life and death of Christ.

stayed in Kā′desh; and Miriam died there
and was buried there.
2Now there was no water for the congre-
gation; so they gathered together against
Moses and Aaron. 3And the people con-
tended with Moses and spoke, saying: "If
only we had died when our brethren died
before the LORD! 4Why have you brought
up the assembly of the LORD into this
wilderness, that we and our animals
should die here? 5And why have you made
us come up out of Egypt, to bring us to this
evil place? It *is* not a place of grain or figs
or vines or pomegranates; nor *is* there any
water to drink." 6So Moses and Aaron
went from the presence of the assembly to
the door of the tabernacle of meeting, and
they fell on their faces. And the glory of the
LORD appeared to them.
7Then the LORD spoke to Moses, saying,
8"Take the rod; you and your brother
Aaron gather the congregation together.
Speak to the rock before their eyes, and it
will yield its water; thus you shall bring
water for them out of the rock, and give
drink to the congregation and their ani-
mals." 9So Moses took the rod from before
the LORD as He commanded him.
10And Moses and Aaron gathered the as-
sembly together before the rock; and he
said to them, "Hear now, you rebels! Must
we bring water for you out of this rock?"
11Then Moses lifted his hand and struck the
rock twice with his rod; and water came
out abundantly, and the congregation and
their animals drank.
12Then the LORD spoke to Moses and
Aaron, "Because you did not believe Me,
to hallow Me in the eyes of the children of
Israel, therefore you shall not bring this as-
sembly into the land which I have given
them."
13This *was* the water of Mer′i·bah,[a] be-
cause the children of Israel contended with
the LORD, and He was hallowed among
them.

Passage Through Edom Refused

14Now Moses sent messengers from
Kā′desh to the king of Ē′dom. "Thus says
your brother Israel: 'You know all the
hardship that has befallen us, 15how our fa-
thers went down to Egypt, and we dwelt in
Egypt a long time, and the Egyptians af-
flicted us and our fathers. 16When we cried
out to the LORD, He heard our voice and
sent the Angel and brought us up out of
Egypt; now here we are in Kā′desh, a city
on the edge of your border. 17Please let us
pass through your country. We will not
pass through fields or vineyards, nor will
we drink water from wells; we will go
along the King's Highway; we will not
turn aside to the right hand or to the left
until we have passed through your terri-
tory.' "
18Then Ē′dom said to him, "You shall
not pass through my *land*, lest I come out
against you with the sword."
19So the children of Israel said to him,
"We will go by the Highway, and if I or my
livestock drink any of your water, then I
will pay for it; let me only pass through on
foot, nothing *more*."
20Then he said, "You shall not pass
through." So Ē′dom came out against them

20:13 [a]Literally *Contention*

20:10–13 Must we bring water? Moses' sin involved more than his striking the rock instead of speaking to it (v. 8). Striking the rock made it appear that the power to produce water was Moses' own. But God alone is all-powerful; He alone can save. He, not even a Moses, is our hope.

20:14–21 Moses' request for permission for Israel to travel through Edom was rebuffed. This route via the **King's Highway** (v. 17) was the main road from Damascus in the north to the Gulf of Elath in the south. It would have provided the easiest and shortest way to reach Moab. Because Israel was denied the right to travel through any part of Edom, they had to take a long detour to the south and east (21:4) and then north along the edge of the Arabian desert.

with many men and with a strong hand.
21Thus Ē′dom refused to give Israel pas-
sage through his territory; so Israel turned
away from him.

Death of Aaron

22Now the children of Israel, the whole
congregation, journeyed from Kā′desh and
came to Mount Hor. 23And the LORD spoke
to Moses and Aaron in Mount Hor by the
border of the land of Ē′dom, saying:
24"Aaron shall be gathered to his people,
for he shall not enter the land which I have
given to the children of Israel, because you
rebelled against My word at the water of
Mer′i·bah. 25Take Aaron and El·ē·ā′zar his
son, and bring them up to Mount Hor;
26and strip Aaron of his garments and put
them on El·ē·ā′zar his son; for Aaron shall
be gathered *to his people* and die there." 27So
Moses did just as the LORD commanded,
and they went up to Mount Hor in the
sight of all the congregation. 28Moses
stripped Aaron of his garments and put
them on El·ē·ā′zar his son; and Aaron died
there on the top of the mountain. Then Mo-
ses and El·ē·ā′zar came down from the
mountain. 29Now when all the congrega-
tion saw that Aaron was dead, all the
house of Israel mourned for Aaron thirty
days.

CHAPTER 21

Canaanites Defeated at Hormah

The king of Ar′ad, the Cā′naan·īte, who
dwelt in the South, heard that Israel was
coming on the road to Ath′a·rim. Then he
fought against Israel and took *some* of them
prisoners. 2So Israel made a vow to the
LORD, and said, "If You will indeed deliver
this people into my hand, then I will ut-
terly destroy their cities." 3And the LORD
listened to the voice of Israel and delivered
up the Cā′naan·ītes, and they utterly de-
stroyed them and their cities. So the name
of that place was called Hor′mah.[a]

The Bronze Serpent

4Then they journeyed from Mount Hor
by the Way of the Red Sea, to go around
the land of Ē′dom; and the soul of the peo-
ple became very discouraged on the way.
5And the people spoke against God and
against Moses: "Why have you brought us
up out of Egypt to die in the wilderness?
For *there is* no food and no water, and our
soul loathes this worthless bread." 6So the
LORD sent fiery serpents among the people,
and they bit the people; and many of the
people of Israel died.

7Therefore the people came to Moses,
and said, "We have sinned, for we have
spoken against the LORD and against you;
pray to the LORD that He take away the ser-
pents from us." So Moses prayed for the
people.

8Then the LORD said to Moses, "Make a
fiery *serpent*, and set it on a pole; and it
shall be that everyone who is bitten, when
he looks at it, shall live." 9So Moses made a
bronze serpent, and put it on a pole; and so
it was, if a serpent had bitten anyone,
when he looked at the bronze serpent, he
lived.

From Mount Hor to Moab

10Now the children of Israel moved on
and camped in Ō′both. 11And they jour-
neyed from Ō′both and camped at Ī′jē
Ab′a·rim, in the wilderness which *is* east of
Mō′ab, toward the sunrise. 12From there
they moved and camped in the Valley of
Zē′red. 13From there they moved and
camped on the other side of the Ar′non,
which *is* in the wilderness that extends
from the border of the Am′o·rītes; for the
Ar′non *is* the border of Mō′ab, between

21:3 [a]Literally *Utter Destruction*

21:9 made a bronze serpent: The NT teaches that this was a prefiguring of Christ who was lifted up for our sin (see John 3:14, 15).

Mō′ab and the Am′o·rītes. 14Therefore it is
said in the Book of the Wars of the LORD:

"Wa′heb in Sū′phah,[a]
The brooks of the Ar′non,
15 And the slope of the brooks
That reaches to the dwelling of Ar,
And lies on the border of Mō′ab."

16From there *they went* to Bē′er, which *is*
the well where the LORD said to Moses,
"Gather the people together, and I will
give them water." 17Then Israel sang this
song:

"Spring up, O well!
All of you sing to it—
18 The well the leaders sank,
Dug by the nation's nobles,
By the lawgiver, with their staves."

And from the wilderness *they went* to
Mat′ta·nah, 19from Mat′ta·nah to Na·hal′-
i·el, from Na·hal′i·el to Bā′moth, 20and
from Bā′moth, *in* the valley that *is* in the
country of Mō′ab, to the top of Pis′gah
which looks down on the wasteland.[a]

King Sihon Defeated

21Then Israel sent messengers to Sī′hon
king of the Am′o·rītes, saying, 22"Let me
pass through your land. We will not turn
aside into fields or vineyards; we will not
drink water from wells. We will go by the
King's Highway until we have passed
through your territory." 23But Sī′hon
would not allow Israel to pass through his
territory. So Sī′hon gathered all his people
together and went out against Israel in the
wilderness, and he came to Jā′haz and
fought against Israel. 24Then Israel de-
feated him with the edge of the sword, and
took possession of his land from the
Ar′non to the Jab′bok, as far as the people
of Am′mon; for the border of the people of
Am′mon *was* fortified. 25So Israel took all
these cities, and Israel dwelt in all the cities
of the Am′o·rītes, in Hesh′bon and in all its
villages. 26For Hesh′bon *was* the city of
Sī′hon king of the Am′o·rītes, who had
fought against the former king of Mō′ab,
and had taken all his land from his hand as
far as the Ar′non. 27Therefore those who
speak in proverbs say:

"Come to Hesh′bon, let it be built;
Let the city of Sī′hon be repaired.

28 "For fire went out from Hesh′bon,
A flame from the city of Sī′hon;
It consumed Ar of Mō′ab,
The lords of the heights of the
Ar′non.
29 Woe to you, Mō′ab!
You have perished, O people of
Chē′mosh!
He has given his sons as fugitives,
And his daughters into captivity,
To Sī′hon king of the Am′o·rītes.

30 "But we have shot at them;
Hesh′bon has perished as far as
Dī′bon.
Then we laid waste as far as Nō′phah,
Which *reaches* to Med′e·ba."

31Thus Israel dwelt in the land of the
Am′o·rītes. 32Then Moses sent to spy out
Jā′zer; and they took its villages and drove
out the Am′o·rītes who *were* there.

King Og Defeated

33And they turned and went up by the
way to Bā′shan. So Og king of Bā′shan
went out against them, he and all his peo-
ple, to battle at Ed′rē·ī. 34Then the LORD
said to Moses, "Do not fear him, for I have
delivered him into your hand, with all his
people and his land; and you shall do to
him as you did to Sī′hon king of the
Am′o·rītes, who dwelt at Hesh′bon."
35So they defeated him, his sons, and all
his people, until there was no survivor
left him; and they took possession of his
land.

21:14 [a]Ancient unknown places; Vulgate reads *What He did in the Red Sea.* 21:20 [a]Hebrew *Jeshimon*

CHAPTER 22

Balak Sends for Balaam

Then the children of Israel moved, and camped in the plains of Mō′ab on the side of the Jordan *across from* Jericho.

2 Now Bā′lak the son of Zip′por saw all that Israel had done to the Am′o·rītes. 3 And Mō′ab was exceedingly afraid of the people because they *were* many, and Mō′ab was sick with dread because of the children of Israel. 4 So Mō′ab said to the elders of Mid′i·an, "Now this company will lick up everything around us, as an ox licks up the grass of the field." And Bā′lak the son of Zip′por *was* king of the Mō′ab·ītes at that time. 5 Then he sent messengers to Bā′laam the son of Bē′or at Pē′thor, which *is* near the River[a] in the land of the sons of his people,[b] to call him, saying: "Look, a people has come from Egypt. See, they cover the face of the earth, and are settling next to me! 6 Therefore please come at once, curse this people for me, for they *are* too mighty for me. Perhaps I shall be able to defeat them and drive them out of the land, for I know that he whom you bless *is* blessed, and he whom you curse is cursed."

7 So the elders of Mō′ab and the elders of Mid′i·an departed with the diviner's fee in their hand, and they came to Bā′laam and spoke to him the words of Bā′lak. 8 And he said to them, "Lodge here tonight, and I will bring back word to you, as the LORD speaks to me." So the princes of Mō′ab stayed with Bā′laam.

9 Then God came to Bā′laam and said, "Who *are* these men with you?"

10 So Bā′laam said to God, "Bā′lak the son of Zip′por, king of Mō′ab, has sent to me, *saying,* 11 'Look, a people has come out of Egypt, and they cover the face of the earth. Come now, curse them for me; perhaps I shall be able to overpower them and drive them out.' "

12 And God said to Bā′laam, "You shall not go with them; you shall not curse the people, for they *are* blessed."

13 So Bā′laam rose in the morning and said to the princes of Bā′lak, "Go back to your land, for the LORD has refused to give me permission to go with you."

14 And the princes of Mō′ab rose and went to Bā′lak, and said, "Bā′laam refuses to come with us."

15 Then Bā′lak again sent princes, more numerous and more honorable than they. 16 And they came to Bā′laam and said to him, "Thus says Bā′lak the son of Zip′por: 'Please let nothing hinder you from coming to me; 17 for I will certainly honor you greatly, and I will do whatever you say to me. Therefore please come, curse this people for me.' "

18 Then Bā′laam answered and said to the servants of Bā′lak, "Though Bā′lak were to give me his house full of silver and gold, I could not go beyond the word of the LORD my God, to do less or more. 19 Now therefore, please, you also stay here tonight, that I may know what more the LORD will say to me."

20 And God came to Bā′laam at night and said to him, "If the men come to call you, rise *and* go with them; but only the word which I speak to you—that you shall do." 21 So Bā′laam rose in the morning, saddled his donkey, and went with the princes of Mō′ab.

Balaam, the Donkey, and the Angel

22 Then God's anger was aroused because he went, and the Angel of the LORD took His stand in the way as an adversary against him. And he was riding on his don-

22:5 [a]That is, the Euphrates [b]Or *the people of Amau*

22:20, 21 go with them: Sometimes because of our importunity God gives us permission for something He does not really want. In this case, He allowed Balaam to go to teach them, the Moabites, and the Israelites about the powerlessness of pagan divinations beside the strength of the almighty God.

key, and his two servants *were* with him.
23Now the donkey saw the Angel of the
LORD standing in the way with His drawn
sword in His hand, and the donkey turned
aside out of the way and went into the
field. So Bā′laam struck the donkey to turn
her back onto the road. 24Then the Angel of
the LORD stood in a narrow path between
the vineyards, *with* a wall on this side and
a wall on that side. 25And when the donkey
saw the Angel of the LORD, she pushed her-
self against the wall and crushed Bā′laam's
foot against the wall; so he struck her
again. 26Then the Angel of the LORD went
further, and stood in a narrow place where
there *was* no way to turn either to the right
hand or to the left. 27And when the donkey
saw the Angel of the LORD, she lay down
under Bā′laam; so Bā′laam's anger was
aroused, and he struck the donkey with his
staff.

28Then the LORD opened the mouth of
the donkey, and she said to Bā′laam,
"What have I done to you, that you have
struck me these three times?"

29And Bā′laam said to the donkey, "Be-
cause you have abused me. I wish there
were a sword in my hand, for now I would
kill you!"

30So the donkey said to Bā′laam, "*Am* I
not your donkey on which you have rid-
den, ever since *I became* yours, to this day?
Was I ever disposed to do this to you?"

And he said, "No."

31Then the LORD opened Bā′laam's eyes,
and he saw the Angel of the LORD standing
in the way with His drawn sword in His
hand; and he bowed his head and fell flat
on his face. 32And the Angel of the LORD
said to him, "Why have you struck your
donkey these three times? Behold, I have
come out to stand against you, because
your way is perverse before Me. 33The
donkey saw Me and turned aside from Me
these three times. If she had not
turned aside from Me, surely I would
also have killed you by now, and let her
live."

34And Bā′laam said to the Angel of the
LORD, "I have sinned, for I did not know
You stood in the way against me. Now
therefore, if it displeases You, I will turn
back."

35Then the Angel of the LORD said to
Bā′laam, "Go with the men, but only the
word that I speak to you, that you shall
speak." So Bā′laam went with the princes
of Bā′lak.

36Now when Bā′lak heard that Bā′laam
was coming, he went out to meet him at
the city of Mō′ab, which *is* on the border at
the Ar′non, the boundary of the territory.
37Then Bā′lak said to Bā′laam, "Did I not
earnestly send to you, calling for you?
Why did you not come to me? Am I not
able to honor you?"

38And Bā′laam said to Bā′lak, "Look, I
have come to you! Now, have I any power
at all to say anything? The word that God
puts in my mouth, that I must speak." 39So
Bā′laam went with Bā′lak, and they came
to Kir′jath Hu′zoth. 40Then Bā′lak offered
oxen and sheep, and he sent *some* to
Bā′laam and to the princes who *were* with
him.

Balaam's First Prophecy

41So it was, the next day, that Bā′lak took
Bā′laam and brought him up to the high
places of Bā′al, that from there he might
observe the extent of the people.

CHAPTER 23

Then Bā′laam said to Bā′lak, "Build
seven altars for me here, and prepare for
me here seven bulls and seven rams."

22:23 the donkey saw the Angel: A strange story of God's control over human behavior. Though Balaam was determined to reach Moab, the simple donkey was enabled to see that to which the great diviner was blind. Those who try to accomplish good apart from God are blind to His will and presence.

2And Bā′lak did just as Bā′laam had
spoken, and Bā′lak and Bā′laam offered a
bull and a ram on *each* altar. 3Then Bā′laam
said to Bā′lak, "Stand by your burnt offer-
ing, and I will go; perhaps the LORD will
come to meet me, and whatever He shows
me I will tell you." So he went to a desolate
height. 4And God met Bā′laam, and he said
to Him, "I have prepared the seven altars,
and I have offered on *each* altar a bull and a
ram."

5Then the LORD put a word in Bā′laam's
mouth, and said, "Return to Bā′lak, and
thus you shall speak." 6So he returned to
him, and there he was, standing by his
burnt offering, he and all the princes of
Mō′ab.

7And he took up his oracle and said:

"Bā′lak the king of Mō′ab has brought
me from Ar′am,
From the mountains of the east.
'Come, curse Jacob for me,
And come, denounce Israel!'

8 "How shall I curse whom God has not
cursed?
And how shall I denounce *whom* the
LORD has not denounced?
9 For from the top of the rocks I see
him,
And from the hills I behold him;
There! A people dwelling alone,
Not reckoning itself among the
nations.

10 "Who can count the dust[a] of Jacob,
Or number one-fourth of Israel?
Let me die the death of the righteous,
And let my end be like his!"

11Then Bā′lak said to Bā′laam, "What
have you done to me? I took you to curse
my enemies, and look, you have blessed
them bountifully!"

12So he answered and said, "Must I not
take heed to speak what the LORD has put
in my mouth?"

Balaam's Second Prophecy

13Then Bā′lak said to him, "Please come
with me to another place from which you
may see them; you shall see only the outer
part of them, and shall not see them all;
curse them for me from there." 14So he
brought him to the field of Zō′phim, to the
top of Pis′gah, and built seven altars, and
offered a bull and a ram on *each* altar.

15And he said to Bā′lak, "Stand here by
your burnt offering while I meet[a] *the LORD*
over there."

16Then the LORD met Bā′laam, and put a
word in his mouth, and said, "Go back to
Bā′lak, and thus you shall speak." 17So he
came to him, and there he was, standing by
his burnt offering, and the princes of
Mō′ab were with him. And Bā′lak said to
him, "What has the LORD spoken?"

18Then he took up his oracle and
said:

"Rise up, Bā′lak, and hear!
Listen to me, son of Zip′por!

19 "God *is* not a man, that He should lie,
Nor a son of man, that He should
repent.
Has He said, and will He not do?

23:10 [a]Or *dust cloud* 23:15 [a]Following Masoretic Text, Targum, and Vulgate; Syriac reads *call;* Septuagint reads *go and ask God.*

23:7–10 The first of seven prophetic discourses by Balaam, each introduced by the phrase **he took up his oracle and said**. Balaam recognized his own inability to curse those whom God has blessed (v. 8). **The dust of Jacob** (v. 10) refers to the covenant made with Abraham (Gen. 13:16) and proclaims its continuing significance.

23:18–24 The second oracle. Balaam makes a magnificent statement concerning God that is worth remembering (v. 19). He declares that the source of Israel's strength is to be found in God Himself, who is gracious to forgive (v. 21) and strong to deliver (v. 22). Because God never changes, we can still count on Him to fulfill His Word.

Or has He spoken, and will He not
make it good?
20 Behold, I have received *a command* to
bless;
He has blessed, and I cannot reverse
it.

21 "He has not observed iniquity in Jacob,
Nor has He seen wickedness in Israel.
The LORD his God *is* with him,
And the shout of a King *is* among
them.
22 God brings them out of Egypt;
He has strength like a wild ox.

23 "For *there is* no sorcery against Jacob,
Nor any divination against Israel.
It now must be said of Jacob
And of Israel, 'Oh, what God has
done!'
24 Look, a people rises like a lioness,
And lifts itself up like a lion;
It shall not lie down until it devours
the prey,
And drinks the blood of the slain."

25Then Bā'lak said to Bā'laam, "Neither
curse them at all, nor bless them at all!"
26So Bā'laam answered and said to
Bā'lak, "Did I not tell you, saying, 'All that
the LORD speaks, that I must do'?"

Balaam's Third Prophecy

27Then Bā'lak said to Bā'laam, "Please
come, I will take you to another place; per-
haps it will please God that you may curse
them for me from there." 28So Bā'lak took
Bā'laam to the top of Pē'or, that overlooks
the wasteland.[a] 29Then Bā'laam said to
Bā'lak, "Build for me here seven altars, and
prepare for me here seven bulls and seven
rams." 30And Bā'lak did as Bā'laam had
said, and offered a bull and a ram on *every*
altar.

CHAPTER 24

Now when Bā'laam saw that it pleased
the LORD to bless Israel, he did not go as at
other times, to seek to use sorcery, but he
set his face toward the wilderness. 2And
Bā'laam raised his eyes, and saw Israel en-
camped according to their tribes; and the
Spirit of God came upon him.
3Then he took up his oracle and said:

"The utterance of Bā'laam the son of
Bē'or,
The utterance of the man whose eyes
are opened,
4 The utterance of him who hears the
words of God,
Who sees the vision of the Almighty,
Who falls down, with eyes wide
open:

5 "How lovely are your tents, O Jacob!
Your dwellings, O Israel!
6 Like valleys that stretch out,
Like gardens by the riverside,
Like aloes planted by the LORD,
Like cedars beside the waters.
7 He shall pour water from his buckets,
And his seed *shall be* in many waters.

"His king shall be higher than Ā'gag,
And his kingdom shall be exalted.

8 "God brings him out of Egypt;
He has strength like a wild ox;
He shall consume the nations, his
enemies;
He shall break their bones
And pierce *them* with his arrows.
9 'He bows down, he lies down as a
lion;
And as a lion, who shall rouse him?'[a]

23:28 [a]Hebrew *Jeshimon* 24:9 [a]Genesis 49:9

24:3–9 The third oracle. **Agag** (v. 7): Balaam here spoke of the day when the Amalekites who had sought to destroy Israel (Ex. 17:8–16) would themselves be destroyed at the hands of King Saul and Samuel. See 1 Sam. 15:2, 3, 8, 32, 33.

"Blessed *is* he who blesses you,
And cursed *is* he who curses you."

[10]Then Bā'lak's anger was aroused
against Bā'laam, and he struck his hands
together; and Bā'lak said to Bā'laam, "I
called you to curse my enemies, and look,
you have bountifully blessed *them* these
three times! [11]Now therefore, flee to your
place. I said I would greatly honor you, but
in fact, the LORD has kept you back from
honor."

[12]So Bā'laam said to Bā'lak, "Did I not
also speak to your messengers whom you
sent to me, saying, [13]'If Bā'lak were to give
me his house full of silver and gold, I could
not go beyond the word of the LORD, to do
good or bad of my own will. What the
LORD says, that I must speak'? [14]And now,
indeed, I am going to my people. Come, I
will advise you what this people will do to
your people in the latter days."

Balaam's Fourth Prophecy

[15]So he took up his oracle and said:

"The utterance of Bā'laam the son of
Bē'or,
And the utterance of the man whose
eyes are opened;
16 The utterance of him who hears the
words of God,
And has the knowledge of the Most
High,
Who sees the vision of the Almighty,
Who falls down, with eyes wide open:

17 "I see Him, but not now;
I behold Him, but not near;
A Star shall come out of Jacob;
A Scepter shall rise out of Israel,
And batter the brow of Mō'ab,
And destroy all the sons of tumult.[a]

18 "And Ē'dom shall be a possession;
Sē'ir also, his enemies, shall be a
possession,
While Israel does valiantly.
19 Out of Jacob One shall have
dominion,
And destroy the remains of the city."

[20]Then he looked on Am'a·lek, and he
took up his oracle and said:

"Am'a·lek *was* first among the nations,
But *shall be* last until he perishes."

[21]Then he looked on the Ken'ītes, and he
took up his oracle and said:

"Firm is your dwelling place,
And your nest is set in the rock;
22 Nevertheless Kāin shall be burned.
How long until As'shur carries you
away captive?"

[23]Then he took up his oracle and said:

"Alas! Who shall live when God does
this?
24 But ships *shall come* from the coasts of
Cyprus,[a]
And they shall afflict As'shur and
afflict Ē'ber,
And so shall *Am'a·lek*,[b] until he
perishes."

24:17 [a]Hebrew *Sheth* (compare Jeremiah 48:45)
24:24 [a]Hebrew *Kittim* [b]Literally *he* or *that one*

24:15–19 The fourth oracle expands the second in vv. 3–9; both open with the same words (vv. 3, 4, 15, 16). There is a sense of awe. Balaam knew this was more than mere fortune-telling. The **Star** and **Scepter** have clear messianic overtones, speaking of a coming King who would rule all the nations.

24:20–24 Oracles five (v. 20), six (vv. 21, 22), and seven (vv. 23, 24) deal not with Moab, but with other nations probably allied with Moab that would face war and turmoil. **Amalek** was the first to fight with Israel. The **Kenites** would be conquered by **Asshur** (Assyria) who would in turn face conflict with the Greeks from **Cyprus**. Further details of these prophecies are unknown.

25So Bā′laam rose and departed and re-
turned to his place; Bā′lak also went his
way.

CHAPTER 25

Israel's Harlotry in Moab

Now Israel remained in Acacia Grove,[a]
and the people began to commit harlotry
with the women of Mō′ab. 2They invited
the people to the sacrifices of their gods,
and the people ate and bowed down to
their gods. 3So Israel was joined to Bā′al of
Pē′or, and the anger of the LORD was
aroused against Israel.

4Then the LORD said to Moses, "Take all
the leaders of the people and hang the of-
fenders before the LORD, out in the sun,
that the fierce anger of the LORD may turn
away from Israel."

5So Moses said to the judges of Israel,
"Every one of you kill his men who were
joined to Bā′al of Pē′or."

6And indeed, one of the children of Is-
rael came and presented to his brethren a
Mid′i·an·īte woman in the sight of Moses
and in the sight of all the congregation of
the children of Israel, who *were* weeping at
the door of the tabernacle of meeting.
7Now when Phin′e·has the son of El·ē·ā′-
zar, the son of Aaron the priest, saw *it,* he
rose from among the congregation and
took a javelin in his hand; 8and he went af-
ter the man of Israel into the tent and
thrust both of them through, the man of Is-
rael, and the woman through her body. So
the plague was stopped among the chil-
dren of Israel. 9And those who died in the
plague were twenty-four thousand.

10Then the LORD spoke to Moses, saying:
11"Phin′e·has the son of El·ē·ā′zar, the son
of Aaron the priest, has turned back My
wrath from the children of Israel, because
he was zealous with My zeal among them,
so that I did not consume the children of Is-
rael in My zeal. 12Therefore say, 'Behold, I
give to him My covenant of peace; 13and it
shall be to him and his descendants after
him a covenant of an everlasting priest-
hood, because he was zealous for his God,
and made atonement for the children of Is-
rael.' "

14Now the name of the Israelite who was
killed, who was killed with the Mid′i·an-
īte woman, *was* Zim′rī the son of Sa′lū, a
leader of a father's house among the Sim′-
ē·on·ītes. 15And the name of the Mid′-
i·an·īte woman who was killed *was* Cōz′bī
the daughter of Zūr; he *was* head of the
people of a father's house in Mid′i·an.

16Then the LORD spoke to Moses, saying:
17"Harass the Mid′i·an·ītes, and attack
them; 18for they harassed you with their
schemes by which they seduced you in the
matter of Pē′or and in the matter of Cōz′bī,
the daughter of a leader of Mid′i·an, their
sister, who was killed in the day of the
plague because of Pē′or."

CHAPTER 26

The Second Census of Israel

And it came to pass, after the plague,
that the LORD spoke to Moses and El·ē-
ā′zar the son of Aaron the priest, saying:
2"Take a census of all the congregation of
the children of Israel from twenty years old
and above, by their fathers' houses, all
who are able to go to war in Israel." 3So
Moses and El·ē·ā′zar the priest spoke with
them in the plains of Mō′ab by the Jordan,
across from Jericho, saying: 4"*Take a census of*

25:1 [a]Hebrew *Shittim*

25:8 the plague was stopped: An Israelite had brazenly presented a Midianite woman (v. 6) as his wife in the presence of the camp. This was a threat to Israel's life and mission. It was imperative that the Israelites remain separate from the pagan religions if the unique revelation of God was to survive among them.

26:2 Take a census: The second census of Israel recorded in Numbers (see 1:1). Like the first, its purpose was to prepare the people for entering the Promised Land.

the people from twenty years old and above,
just as the LORD commanded Moses and
the children of Israel who came out of the
land of Egypt."
[5]Reuben *was* the firstborn of Israel. The
children of Reuben *were: of* Hā′noch, the
family of the Hā′noch·ītes; *of* Pal′lū,
the family of the Pal′lū·ītes; [6]*of* Hez′-
ron, the family of the Hez′ron·ītes; *of*
Car′mī, the family of the Car′mītes. [7]These
are the families of the Reū′ben·ītes: those
who were numbered of them were forty-
three thousand seven hundred and thirty.
[8]And the son of Pal′lū *was* E·lī′ab. [9]The
sons of E·lī′ab *were* Nem′ū·el, Dā′than,
and A·bī′ram. These *are* the Dā′than and
A·bī′ram, representatives of the congrega-
tion, who contended against Moses and
Aaron in the company of Kō′rah, when
they contended against the LORD; [10]and the
earth opened its mouth and swallowed
them up together with Kō′rah when that
company died, when the fire devoured
two hundred and fifty men; and they be-
came a sign. [11]Nevertheless the children of
Kō′rah did not die.
[12]The sons of Sim′ē·on according to their
families *were: of* Nem′ū·el,[a] the family of
the Nem′ū·el·ītes; *of* Jā′min, the family of
the Jā′min·ītes; *of* Jā′chin,[b] the family of the
Jā′chin·ītes; [13]*of* Zē′rah,[a] the family of the
Zar′hītes; *of* Shā′ūl, the family of
the Shā′u·lītes. [14]These *are* the families of
the Sim′ē·on·ītes: twenty-two thousand
two hundred.
[15]The sons of Gad according to their
families *were: of* Zē′phon,[a] the family of the
Zē′phon·ītes; *of* Hag′gī, the family of the
Hag′gītes; *of* Shū′nī, the family of
the Shū′nītes; [16]*of* Oz′nī,[a] the family of
the Oz′nītes; *of* Ē′rī, the family of the
Ē′rītes; [17]*of* Ar′od,[a] the family of the Ar′od-
ītes; *of* A·rē′lī, the family of the A·rē′lītes.
[18]These *are* the families of the sons of Gad
according to those who were numbered of
them: forty thousand five hundred.
[19]The sons of Judah *were* Er and Ō′nan;
and Er and Ō′nan died in the land of
Cā′naan. [20]And the sons of Judah accord-
ing to their families were: *of* Shē′lah, the
family of the Shē′la·nītes; *of* Per′ez, the
family of the Par′zītes; *of* Zē′rah, the fam-
ily of the Zar′hītes. [21]And the sons of
Per′ez were: *of* Hez′ron, the family of the
Hez′ron·ītes; *of* Hā′mul, the family of the
Hā′mul·ītes. [22]These *are* the families of Ju-
dah according to those who were num-
bered of them: seventy-six thousand five
hundred.
[23]The sons of Is′sa·char according to
their families *were: of* Tō′la, the family of
the Tō′la·ītes; of Pū′ah,[a] the family of the
Pū′nītes;[b] [24]of Jash′ub, the family of the
Jash′ub·ītes; of Shim′ron, the family of
the Shim′ron·ītes. [25]These *are* the families
of Is′sa·char according to those who were
numbered of them: sixty-four thousand
three hundred.
[26]The sons of Zeb′ū·lun according to
their families *were:* of Sē′red, the family of
the Sar′dītes; of Ē′lon, the family of the
Ē′lon·ītes; of Jah′lē·el, the family of the
Jah′lē·el·ītes. [27]These *are* the families of
the Zeb′ū·lun·ītes according to those who
were numbered of them: sixty thousand
five hundred.
[28]The sons of Joseph according to their
families, by Ma·nas′seh and Ē′phra·im,
were: [29]The sons of Ma·nas′seh: of Mā′chir,
the family of the Mā′chir·ītes; and Mā′chir
begot Gil′ē·ad; of Gil′ē·ad, the family of
the Gil′ē·ad·ītes. [30]These *are* the sons of
Gil′ē·ad: *of* Je·ē′zer,[a] the family of the
Je·ē′zer·ītes; of Hē′lek, the family of the
Hē′lek·ītes; [31]*of* As′ri·el, the family of
the As′ri·el·ītes; *of* Shē′chem, the family of
the Shē′chem·ītes; [32]*of* She·mī′da, the fam-
ily of the She·mī′da·ītes; *of* Hē′pher, the
family of the Hē′pher·ītes. [33]Now Ze-

26:12 [a]Spelled *Jemuel* in Genesis 46:10 and Exodus 6:15 [b]Called *Jarib* in 1 Chronicles 4:24
26:13 [a]Called *Zohar* in Genesis 46:10
26:15 [a]Called *Ziphion* in Genesis 46:16
26:16 [a]Called *Ezbon* in Genesis 46:16
26:17 [a]Spelled *Arodi* in Samaritan Pentateuch, Syriac, and Genesis 46:16
26:23 [a]Hebrew *Puvah* (compare Genesis 46:13 and 1 Chronicles 7:1); Samaritan Pentateuch, Septuagint, Syriac, and Vulgate read *Puah.* [b]Samaritan Pentateuch, Septuagint, Syriac, and Vulgate read *Puaites.*
26:30 [a]Called *Abiezer* in Joshua 17:2

loph′e·had the son of Hē′pher had no sons, but daughters; and the names of the daughters of Ze·loph′e·had *were* Mah′lah, Noah, Hog′lah, Mil′cah, and Tir′zah. 34 These *are* the families of Ma·nas′seh; and those who were numbered of them *were* fifty-two thousand seven hundred.

35 These *are* the sons of Ē′phra·im according to their families: of Shū′the·lah, the family of the Shū′thal·hītes; of Bē′cher,[a] the family of the Bach′rītes; of Tā′han, the family of the Tā′han·ītes. 36 And these *are* the sons of Shū′the·lah: of Ē′ran, the family of the Ē′ran·ītes. 37 These *are* the families of the sons of Ē′phra·im according to those who were numbered of them: thirty-two thousand five hundred.

These *are* the sons of Joseph according to their families.

38 The sons of Benjamin according to their families were: of Bē′la, the family of the Bē′la·ītes; of Ash′bel, the family of the Ash′bel·ītes; of A·hī′ram, the family of the A·hī′ram·ītes; 39 of Shū′pham,[a] the family of the Shū′pham·ītes; of Hū′pham,[b] the family of the Hū′pham·ītes. 40 And the sons of Bē′la were Ard[a] and Nā′a·man: *of Ard,* the family of the Ard′ītes; of Nā′a·man, the family of the Nā′a·mītes. 41 These *are* the sons of Benjamin according to their families; and those who were numbered of them *were* forty-five thousand six hundred.

42 These *are* the sons of Dan according to their families: of Shū′ham,[a] the family of the Shū′ham·ītes. These *are* the families of Dan according to their families. 43 All the families of the Shū′ham·ītes, according to those who were numbered of them, *were* sixty-four thousand four hundred.

44 The sons of Ash′er according to their families *were:* of Jim′na, the family of the Jim′nītes; of Jes′ū·ī, the family of the Jes′ū·ītes; of Bē·rī′ah, the family of the Bē·rī′ītes. 45 Of the sons of Bē·rī′ah: of Hē′-ber, the family of the Hē′ber·ītes; of Mal′-chi·el, the family of the Mal′chi-el·ītes. 46 And the name of the daughter of Ash′er *was* Sē′rah. 47 These *are* the families of the sons of Ash′er according to those who were numbered of them: fifty-three thousand four hundred.

48 The sons of Naph′ta·lī according to their families *were:* of Jah′zē·el,[a] the family of the Jah′zē·el·ītes; of Gū′nī, the family of the Gū′nītes; 49 of Jē′zer, the family of the Jē′zer·ītes; of Shil′lem, the family of the Shil′lem·ītes. 50 These *are* the families of Naph′ta·lī according to their families; and those who were numbered of them *were* forty-five thousand four hundred.

51 These *are* those who were numbered of the children of Israel: six hundred and one thousand seven hundred and thirty.

52 Then the LORD spoke to Moses, saying: 53 "To these the land shall be divided as an inheritance, according to the number of names. 54 To a large *tribe* you shall give a larger inheritance, and to a small *tribe* you shall give a smaller inheritance. Each shall be given its inheritance according to those who were numbered of them. 55 But the land shall be divided by lot; they shall inherit according to the names of the tribes of their fathers. 56 According to the lot their inheritance shall be divided between the larger and the smaller."

57 And these *are* those who were numbered of the Lē′vītes according to their families: of Ger′shon, the family of the Ger′shon·ītes; of Kō′hath, the family of the Kō′hath·ītes; of Me·rar′ī, the family of the Me·rar′ītes. 58 These *are* the families of the Lē′vītes: the family of the Lib′nītes, the family of the Hē′bron·ītes, the family of the Mah′lītes, the family of the Mū′shītes, and the family of the Kō′ra·thītes. And Kō′hath begot Am′ram. 59 The name of Am′ram's wife *was* Joch′e·bed the daughter of Levi, who was born to Levi in Egypt; and to Am′ram she bore Aaron and Moses and their sister Miriam. 60 To Aaron were born Nā′dab and A·bī′hū, El·ē·ā′zar and Ith′a·mar. 61 And Nā′dab and A·bī′hū died

26:35 [a]Called *Bered* in 1 Chronicles 7:20
26:39 [a]Masoretic Text reads *Shephupham*, spelled *Shephuphan* in 1 Chronicles 8:5. [b]Called *Huppim* in Genesis 46:21
26:40 [a]Called *Addar* in 1 Chronicles 8:3
26:42 [a]Called *Hushim* in Genesis 46:23
26:48 [a]Spelled *Jahziel* in 1 Chronicles 7:13

when they offered profane fire before the LORD.

[62]Now those who were numbered of them were twenty-three thousand, every male from a month old and above; for they were not numbered among the other children of Israel, because there was no inheritance given to them among the children of Israel.

[63]These *are* those who were numbered by Moses and El·ē·ā′zar the priest, who numbered the children of Israel in the plains of Mō′ab by the Jordan, *across from* Jericho. [64]But among these there was not a man of those who were numbered by Moses and Aaron the priest when they numbered the children of Israel in the Wilderness of Sinai. [65]For the LORD had said of them, "They shall surely die in the wilderness." So there was not left a man of them, except Caleb the son of Je·phūn′neh and Joshua the son of Nun.

CHAPTER 27

Inheritance Laws

Then came the daughters of Ze·loph′e·had the son of Hē′pher, the son of Gil′ē·ad, the son of Mā′chir, the son of Ma·nas′seh, from the families of Ma·nas′seh the son of Joseph; and these *were* the names of his daughters: Mah′lah, Noah, Hog′lah, Mil′cah, and Tir′zah. [2]And they stood before Moses, before El·ē·ā′zar the priest, and before the leaders and all the congregation, *by* the doorway of the tabernacle of meeting, saying: [3]"Our father died in the wilderness; but he was not in the company of those who gathered together against the LORD, in company with Kō′rah, but he died in his own sin; and he had no sons. [4]Why should the name of our father be removed from among his family because he had no son? Give us a possession among our father's brothers."

[5]So Moses brought their case before the LORD.

[6]And the LORD spoke to Moses, saying: [7]"The daughters of Ze·loph′e·had speak *what is* right; you shall surely give them a possession of inheritance among their father's brothers, and cause the inheritance of their father to pass to them. [8]And you shall speak to the children of Israel, saying: 'If a man dies and has no son, then you shall cause his inheritance to pass to his daughter. [9]If he has no daughter, then you shall give his inheritance to his brothers. [10]If he has no brothers, then you shall give his inheritance to his father's brothers. [11]And if his father has no brothers, then you shall give his inheritance to the relative closest to him in his family, and he shall possess it.'[a]" And it shall be to the children of Israel a statute of judgment, just as the LORD commanded Moses.

Joshua the Next Leader of Israel

[12]Now the LORD said to Moses: "Go up into this Mount Ab′a·rim, and see the land which I have given to the children of Israel. [13]And when you have seen it, you also shall be gathered to your people, as Aaron your brother was gathered. [14]For in the Wilderness of Zin, during the strife of the congregation, you rebelled against My command to hallow Me at the waters before their eyes." (These *are* the waters of

---

26:64, 65 there was not left a man: This is one of the saddest statements in Scripture. All of those who had been in the original census were dead except Caleb and Joshua. Just as had been foretold, all the unbelief had been purged; now they could make plans to enter Canaan.

27:1–11 The Promised Land always belonged to God. But He delighted to give it in trust to the Hebrews. Because each family held its land in trust, it could not be sold; God was the true owner. This incident provided for those situations where there was no son to whom the family property could pass. The provisions insured that the land would be retained in the original family name.

Mer′i·bah, at Kā′desh in the Wilderness of Zin.)

15Then Moses spoke to the LORD, saying: 16"Let the LORD, the God of the spirits of all flesh, set a man over the congregation, 17who may go out before them and go in before them, who may lead them out and bring them in, that the congregation of the LORD may not be like sheep which have no shepherd."

18And the LORD said to Moses: "Take Joshua the son of Nun with you, a man in whom *is* the Spirit, and lay your hand on him; 19set him before El·ē·ā′zar the priest and before all the congregation, and inaugurate him in their sight. 20And you shall give *some* of your authority to him, that all the congregation of the children of Israel may be obedient. 21He shall stand before El·ē·ā′zar the priest, who shall inquire before the LORD for him by the judgment of the Ū′rim. At his word they shall go out, and at his word they shall come in, he and all the children of Israel with him—all the congregation."

22So Moses did as the LORD commanded him. He took Joshua and set him before El·ē·ā′zar the priest and before all the congregation. 23And he laid his hands on him and inaugurated him, just as the LORD commanded by the hand of Moses.

CHAPTER 28

Daily Offerings

Now the LORD spoke to Moses, saying, 2"Command the children of Israel, and say to them, 'My offering, My food for My offerings made by fire as a sweet aroma to Me, you shall be careful to offer to Me at their appointed time.'

3"And you shall say to them, 'This *is* the offering made by fire which you shall offer to the LORD: two male lambs in their first year without blemish, day by day, as a regular burnt offering. 4The one lamb you shall offer in the morning, the other lamb you shall offer in the evening, 5and one-tenth of an ephah of fine flour as a grain offering mixed with one-fourth of a hin of pressed oil. 6*It is* a regular burnt offering which was ordained at Mount Sinai for a sweet aroma, an offering made by fire to the LORD. 7And its drink offering *shall be* one-fourth of a hin for each lamb; in a holy *place* you shall pour out the drink to the LORD as an offering. 8The other lamb you shall offer in the evening; as the morning grain offering and its drink offering, you shall offer *it* as an offering made by fire, a sweet aroma to the LORD.

Sabbath Offerings

9'And on the Sabbath day two lambs in their first year, without blemish, and two-tenths *of an ephah* of fine flour as a grain offering, mixed with oil, with its drink offering— 10*this is* the burnt offering for every Sabbath, besides the regular burnt offering with its drink offering.

Monthly Offerings

11'At the beginnings of your months you shall present a burnt offering to the LORD: two young bulls, one ram, and seven lambs in their first year, without blemish; 12three-tenths *of an ephah* of fine flour as a grain offering, mixed with oil, for each

---

27:18–21 Take Joshua: Because of Joshua's obedience, he would now become the leader of Israel. **some of your authority** (v. 20): Joshua would not enjoy the same face-to-face contact with God as Moses had. Instead he would depend upon **Eleazar**, the priest, who would **inquire before the LORD.** Nevertheless, Joshua would lead the people into Canaan. God is always able to use the obedient person in order to accomplish His will.

28:9–11 The **Sabbath** offering was added to the **regular** daily offering, doubling the amount offered on this holy day. The beginning of the month was also marked by a special offering. Each calendar period (day, week, and month) is dedicated to God through an act of worship. We too should follow this model, prayerfully committing each new day, week, and month to the Lord.

bull; two-tenths *of an ephah* of fine flour as a grain offering, mixed with oil, for the one ram; 13and one-tenth *of an ephah* of fine flour, mixed with oil, as a grain offering for each lamb, as a burnt offering of sweet aroma, an offering made by fire to the LORD. 14Their drink offering shall be half a hin of wine for a bull, one-third of a hin for a ram, and one-fourth of a hin for a lamb; this *is* the burnt offering for each month throughout the months of the year. 15Also one kid of the goats as a sin offering to the LORD shall be offered, besides the regular burnt offering and its drink offering.

Offerings at Passover

16'On the fourteenth day of the first month *is* the Passover of the LORD. 17And on the fifteenth day of this month *is* the feast; unleavened bread shall be eaten for seven days. 18On the first day *you shall have* a holy convocation. You shall do no customary work. 19And you shall present an offering made by fire as a burnt offering to the LORD: two young bulls, one ram, and seven lambs in their first year. Be sure they are without blemish. 20Their grain offering shall be of fine flour mixed with oil: three-tenths *of an ephah* you shall offer for a bull, and two-tenths for a ram; 21you shall offer one-tenth *of an ephah* for each of the seven lambs; 22also one goat *as* a sin offering, to make atonement for you. 23You shall offer these besides the burnt offering of the morning, which *is* for a regular burnt offering. 24In this manner you shall offer the food of the offering made by fire daily for seven days, as a sweet aroma to the LORD; it shall be offered besides the regular burnt offering and its drink offering. 25And on the seventh day you shall have a holy convocation. You shall do no customary work.

Offerings at the Feast of Weeks

26'Also on the day of the firstfruits, when you bring a new grain offering to the LORD at your *Feast of* Weeks, you shall have a holy convocation. You shall do no customary work. 27You shall present a burnt offering as a sweet aroma to the LORD: two young bulls, one ram, and seven lambs in their first year, 28with their grain offering of fine flour mixed with oil: three-tenths *of an ephah* for each bull, two-tenths for the one ram, 29and one-tenth for each of the seven lambs; 30*also* one kid of the goats, to make atonement for you. 31Be sure they are without blemish. You shall present *them* with their drink offerings, besides the regular burnt offering with its grain offering.

CHAPTER 29

Offerings at the Feast of Trumpets

'And in the seventh month, on the first *day* of the month, you shall have a holy convocation. You shall do no customary work. For you it is a day of blowing the trumpets. 2You shall offer a burnt offering as a sweet aroma to the LORD: one young bull, one ram, *and* seven lambs in their first year, without blemish. 3Their grain offering *shall be* fine flour mixed with oil: three-tenths *of an ephah* for the bull, two-tenths for the ram, 4and one-tenth for each of the seven lambs; 5also one kid of the goats *as* a sin offering, to make atonement for you; 6besides the burnt offering with its grain offering for the New Moon, the regular burnt offering with its grain offering, and their drink offerings, according to their ordinance, as a sweet aroma, an offering made by fire to the LORD.

Offerings on the Day of Atonement

7'On the tenth *day* of this seventh month you shall have a holy convocation. You shall afflict your souls; you shall not do any work. 8You shall present a burnt offering to the LORD *as* a sweet aroma: one young bull, one ram, *and* seven lambs in their first year. Be sure they are without blemish. 9Their grain offering *shall be of* fine flour mixed with oil: three-tenths *of an ephah* for the bull, two-tenths for the one ram, 10and one-tenth for each of the seven lambs; 11also one kid of the goats *as* a sin offering, besides the sin offering for atone-

ment, the regular burnt offering with its
grain offering, and their drink offerings.

Offerings at the Feast of Tabernacles

12'On the fifteenth day of the seventh
month you shall have a holy convocation.
You shall do no customary work, and you
shall keep a feast to the LORD seven days.
13You shall present a burnt offering, an of-
fering made by fire as a sweet aroma to the
LORD: thirteen young bulls, two rams, *and*
fourteen lambs in their first year. They
shall be without blemish. 14Their grain of-
fering *shall be of* fine flour mixed with oil:
three-tenths *of an ephah* for each of the thir-
teen bulls, two-tenths for each of the two
rams, 15and one-tenth for each of the four-
teen lambs; 16also one kid of the goats *as* a
sin offering, besides the regular burnt of-
fering, its grain offering, and its drink of-
fering.

17'On the second day *present* twelve
young bulls, two rams, fourteen lambs in
their first year without blemish, 18and their
grain offering and their drink offerings for
the bulls, for the rams, and for the lambs,
by their number, according to the ordi-
nance; 19also one kid of the goats *as* a sin of-
fering, besides the regular burnt offering
with its grain offering, and their drink of-
ferings.

20'On the third day *present* eleven bulls,
two rams, fourteen lambs in their first year
without blemish, 21and their grain offering
and their drink offerings for the bulls, for
the rams, and for the lambs, by their num-
ber, according to the ordinance; 22also one
goat *as* a sin offering, besides the regular
burnt offering, its grain offering, and its
drink offering.

23'On the fourth day *present* ten bulls,
two rams, *and* fourteen lambs in their first
year, without blemish, 24and their grain of-
fering and their drink offerings for the
bulls, for the rams, and for the lambs, by
their number, according to the ordinance;
25also one kid of the goats *as* a sin offering,
besides the regular burnt offering, its grain
offering, and its drink offering.

26'On the fifth day *present* nine bulls, two
rams, *and* fourteen lambs in their first year
without blemish, 27and their grain offering
and their drink offerings for the bulls, for
the rams, and for the lambs, by their num-
ber, according to the ordinance; 28also one
goat *as* a sin offering, besides the regular
burnt offering, its grain offering, and its
drink offering.

29'On the sixth day *present* eight bulls,
two rams, *and* fourteen lambs in their first
year without blemish, 30and their grain of-
fering and their drink offerings for the
bulls, for the rams, and for the lambs, by
their number, according to the ordinance;
31also one goat *as* a sin offering, besides the
regular burnt offering, its grain offering,
and its drink offering.

32'On the seventh day *present* seven
bulls, two rams, *and* fourteen lambs in
their first year without blemish, 33and
their grain offering and their drink
offerings for the bulls, for the rams, and
for the lambs, by their number, according
to the ordinance; 34also one goat *as*
a sin offering, besides the regular burnt
offering, its grain offering, and its drink of-
fering.

35'On the eighth day you shall have a sa-
cred assembly. You shall do no customary
work. 36You shall present a burnt offering,
an offering made by fire as a sweet aroma
to the LORD: one bull, one ram, seven lambs
in their first year without blemish, 37and
their grain offering and their drink offer-
ings for the bull, for the ram, and for the
lambs, by their number, according to the
ordinance; 38also one goat *as* a sin offering,
besides the regular burnt offering, its grain
offering, and its drink offering.

39'These you shall present to the LORD at
your appointed feasts (besides your
vowed offerings and your freewill offer-
ings) as your burnt offerings and your
grain offerings, as your drink offerings and
your peace offerings.' "

40So Moses told the children of Israel
everything, just as the LORD commanded
Moses.

CHAPTER 30

The Law Concerning Vows

Then Moses spoke to the heads of the
tribes concerning the children of Israel,
saying, "This *is* the thing which the LORD
has commanded: [2]If a man makes a vow to
the LORD, or swears an oath to bind himself
by some agreement, he shall not break his
word; he shall do according to all that pro-
ceeds out of his mouth.

[3]"Or if a woman makes a vow to the
LORD, and binds *herself* by some agreement
while in her father's house in her youth,
[4]and her father hears her vow and the
agreement by which she has bound her-
self, and her father holds his peace, then all
her vows shall stand, and every agreement
with which she has bound herself shall
stand. [5]But if her father overrules her on
the day that he hears, then none of her
vows nor her agreements by which she has
bound herself shall stand; and the LORD
will release her, because her father over-
ruled her.

[6]"If indeed she takes a husband, while
bound by her vows or by a rash utterance
from her lips by which she bound herself,
[7]and her husband hears *it,* and makes no
response to her on the day that he hears,
then her vows shall stand, and her agree-
ments by which she bound herself shall
stand. [8]But if her husband overrules her on
the day that he hears *it,* he shall make void
her vow which she took and what she ut-
tered with her lips, by which she bound
herself, and the LORD will release her.

[9]"Also any vow of a widow or a di-
vorced woman, by which she has bound
herself, shall stand against her.

[10]"If she vowed in her husband's house,
or bound herself by an agreement with an
oath, [11]and her husband heard *it,* and made
no response to her *and* did not overrule
her, then all her vows shall stand, and
every agreement by which she bound her-
self shall stand. [12]But if her husband truly
made them void on the day he heard *them,*
then whatever proceeded from her lips
concerning her vows or concerning the
agreement binding her, it shall not stand;
her husband has made them void, and the
LORD will release her. [13]Every vow and
every binding oath to afflict her soul, her
husband may confirm it, or her husband
may make it void. [14]Now if her husband
makes no response whatever to her from
day to day, then he confirms all her vows
or all the agreements that bind her; he con-
firms them, because he made no response
to her on the day that he heard *them.* [15]But
if he does make them void after he has
heard *them,* then he shall bear her guilt."

[16]These *are* the statutes which the LORD
commanded Moses, between a man and
his wife, and between a father and his
daughter in her youth in her father's
house.

CHAPTER 31

Vengeance on the Midianites

And the LORD spoke to Moses, saying:
[2]"Take vengeance on the Mid'i·an·ītes for
the children of Israel. Afterward you shall
be gathered to your people."

[3]So Moses spoke to the people, saying,
"Arm some of yourselves for war, and let
them go against the Mid'i·an·ītes to take
vengeance for the LORD on Mid'i·an. [4]A
thousand from each tribe of all the tribes of
Israel you shall send to the war."

[5]So there were recruited from the divi-
sions of Israel one thousand from *each*
tribe, twelve thousand armed for war.
[6]Then Moses sent them to the war, one

30:1–16 A vow to the Lord, meaning a promise to abstain from something or a promise to give something to God, was a serious matter. A man of any age or status and a widow of any age were bound to keep their vows. However, a promise made by a woman under her father's rule or by a married woman could be nullified by a father or husband, if he deemed the vow to be inappropriate.

thousand from *each* tribe; he sent them to
the war with Phin′e·has the son of El·ē-
ā′zar the priest, with the holy articles and
the signal trumpets in his hand. 7And they
warred against the Mid′i·an·ītes, just as
the LORD commanded Moses, and they
killed all the males. 8They killed the kings
of Mid′i·an with *the rest of* those who were
killed—Ē′vī, Rē′kem, Zūr, Hur, and Rē′ba,
the five kings of Mid′i·an. Bā′laam the son
of Bē′or they also killed with the sword.
9And the children of Israel took the
women of Mid′i·an captive, with their lit-
tle ones, and took as spoil all their cattle, all
their flocks, and all their goods. 10They also
burned with fire all the cities where they
dwelt, and all their forts. 11And they took
all the spoil and all the booty—of man and
beast.

Return from the War

12Then they brought the captives, the
booty, and the spoil to Moses, to El·ē·ā′zar
the priest, and to the congregation of the
children of Israel, to the camp in the plains
of Mō′ab by the Jordan, *across from* Jericho.
13And Moses, El·ē·ā′zar the priest, and all
the leaders of the congregation, went to
meet them outside the camp. 14But Moses
was angry with the officers of the army,
with the captains over thousands and cap-
tains over hundreds, who had come from
the battle.
15And Moses said to them: "Have you
kept all the women alive? 16Look, these
women caused the children of Israel,
through the counsel of Bā′laam, to trespass
against the LORD in the incident of Pē′or,
and there was a plague among the congre-
gation of the LORD. 17Now therefore, kill
every male among the little ones, and kill
every woman who has known a man inti-
mately. 18But keep alive for yourselves all
the young girls who have not known a
man intimately. 19And as for you, remain
outside the camp seven days; whoever has
killed any person, and whoever has
touched any slain, purify yourselves and
your captives on the third day and on the
seventh day. 20Purify every garment,
everything made of leather, everything
woven of goats' *hair,* and everything made
of wood."
21Then El·ē·ā′zar the priest said to the
men of war who had gone to the battle,
"This *is* the ordinance of the law which the
LORD commanded Moses: 22"Only the
gold, the silver, the bronze, the iron, the tin,
and the lead, 23everything that can endure
fire, you shall put through the fire, and it
shall be clean; and it shall be purified with
the water of purification. But all that can-
not endure fire you shall put through wa-
ter. 24And you shall wash your clothes on
the seventh day and be clean, and after-
ward you may come into the camp."

Division of the Plunder

25Now the LORD spoke to Moses, saying:
26"Count up the plunder that was taken—
of man and beast—you and El·ē·ā′zar the
priest and the chief fathers of the congre-
gation; 27and divide the plunder into two
parts, between those who took part in the
war, who went out to battle, and all the
congregation. 28And levy a tribute for
the LORD on the men of war who went out
to battle: one of every five hundred of the
persons, the cattle, the donkeys, and the
sheep; 29take *it* from their half, and give *it*
to El·ē·ā′zar the priest as a heave offering
to the LORD. 30And from the children of Is-
rael's half you shall take one of every fifty,
drawn from the persons, the cattle, the
donkeys, and the sheep, from all the live-
stock, and give them to the Lē′vītes who
keep charge of the tabernacle of the LORD."
31So Moses and El·ē·ā′zar the priest did as
the LORD commanded Moses.
32The booty remaining from the plunder,

31:28–54 The emphasis upon **offering** (v. 29) and **tribute** (v. 37) underlines the recognition that God is the true source of Israel's victory.

which the men of war had taken, was six hundred and seventy-five thousand sheep, [33]seventy-two thousand cattle, [34]sixty-one thousand donkeys, [35]and thirty-two thousand persons in all, of women who had not known a man intimately. [36]And the half, the portion for those who had gone out to war, was in number three hundred and thirty-seven thousand five hundred sheep; [37]and the LORD's tribute of the sheep was six hundred and seventy-five. [38]The cattle *were* thirty-six thousand, of which the LORD's tribute *was* seventy-two. [39]The donkeys *were* thirty thousand five hundred, of which the LORD's tribute *was* sixty-one. [40]The persons *were* sixteen thousand, of which the LORD's tribute *was* thirty-two persons. [41]So Moses gave the tribute *which was* the LORD's heave offering to El·ē·ā′zar the priest, as the LORD commanded Moses.

[42]And from the children of Israel's half, which Moses separated from the men who fought— [43]now the half belonging to the congregation was three hundred and thirty-seven thousand five hundred sheep, [44]thirty-six thousand cattle, [45]thirty thousand five hundred donkeys, [46]and sixteen thousand persons— [47]and from the children of Israel's half Moses took one of every fifty, drawn from man and beast, and gave them to the Lē′vītes, who kept charge of the tabernacle of the LORD, as the LORD commanded Moses.

[48]Then the officers who *were* over thousands of the army, the captains of thousands and captains of hundreds, came near to Moses; [49]and they said to Moses, "Your servants have taken a count of the men of war who *are* under our command, and not a man of us is missing. [50]Therefore we have brought an offering for the LORD, what every man found of ornaments of gold: armlets and bracelets and signet rings and earrings and necklaces, to make atonement for ourselves before the LORD." [51]So Moses and El·ē·ā′zar the priest received the gold from them, all the fashioned ornaments. [52]And all the gold of the offering that they offered to the LORD, from the captains of thousands and captains of hundreds, was sixteen thousand seven hundred and fifty shekels. [53](The men of war had taken spoil, every man for himself.) [54]And Moses and El·ē·ā′zar the priest received the gold from the captains of thousands and of hundreds, and brought it into the tabernacle of meeting as a memorial for the children of Israel before the LORD.

CHAPTER 32

The Tribes Settling East of the Jordan

Now the children of Reuben and the children of Gad had a very great multitude of livestock; and when they saw the land of Jā′zer and the land of Gil′ē·ad, that indeed the region *was* a place for livestock, [2]the children of Gad and the children of Reuben came and spoke to Moses, to El·ē·ā′zar the priest, and to the leaders of the congregation, saying, [3]"At′a·roth, Dī′bon, Jā′zer, Nim′rah, Hesh′bon, Ē·le·ā′leh, Shē′bam, Nē′bō, and Bē′on, [4]the country which the LORD defeated before the congregation of Israel, *is* a land for livestock, and your servants have livestock." [5]Therefore they said, "If we have found favor in your sight, let this land be given to your servants as a

32:1–42 This first threat to the unity of the tribes foreshadowed a problem that came into real prominence during the period of the judges and later. Here Moses was concerned that the desire of **Reuben** and **Gad** to settle east of the Jordan (v. 5) would discourage the other tribes from conquering the rest of the promised territory (vv. 6–15). When they assured Moses that they would assist in the whole conquest, he had no further objection. Later, half the tribe of **Manasseh** (vv. 33, 39, 40) joined Reuben and Gad in this Transjordan agreement. On the land of Gilead east of the Jordan being included in the promise, see Deut. 34:1.

possession. Do not take us over the Jordan."

6And Moses said to the children of Gad and to the children of Reuben: "Shall your brethren go to war while you sit here? 7Now why will you discourage the heart of the children of Israel from going over into the land which the LORD has given them? 8Thus your fathers did when I sent them away from Kā′desh Bar·nē′a to see the land. 9For when they went up to the Valley of Esh′col and saw the land, they discouraged the heart of the children of Israel, so that they did not go into the land which the LORD had given them. 10So the LORD's anger was aroused on that day, and He swore an oath, saying, 11'Surely none of the men who came up from Egypt, from twenty years old and above, shall see the land of which I swore to Abraham, Isaac, and Jacob, because they have not wholly followed Me, 12except Caleb the son of Je·phūn′neh, the Kē′niz·zīte, and Joshua the son of Nun, for they have wholly followed the LORD.' 13So the LORD's anger was aroused against Israel, and He made them wander in the wilderness forty years, until all the generation that had done evil in the sight of the LORD was gone. 14And look! You have risen in your fathers' place, a brood of sinful men, to increase still more the fierce anger of the LORD against Israel. 15For if you turn away from following Him, He will once again leave them in the wilderness, and you will destroy all these people."

16Then they came near to him and said: "We will build sheepfolds here for our livestock, and cities for our little ones, 17but we ourselves will be armed, ready *to go* before the children of Israel until we have brought them to their place; and our little ones will dwell in the fortified cities because of the inhabitants of the land. 18We will not return to our homes until every one of the children of Israel has received his inheritance. 19For we will not inherit with them on the other side of the Jordan and beyond, because our inheritance has fallen to us on this eastern side of the Jordan."

20Then Moses said to them: "If you do this thing, if you arm yourselves before the LORD for the war, 21and all your armed men cross over the Jordan before the LORD until He has driven out His enemies from before Him, 22and the land is subdued before the LORD, then afterward you may return and be blameless before the LORD and before Israel; and this land shall be your possession before the LORD. 23But if you do not do so, then take note, you have sinned against the LORD; and be sure your sin will find you out. 24Build cities for your little ones and folds for your sheep, and do what has proceeded out of your mouth."

25And the children of Gad and the children of Reuben spoke to Moses, saying: "Your servants will do as my lord commands. 26Our little ones, our wives, our flocks, and all our livestock will be there in the cities of Gil′ē·ad; 27but your servants will cross over, every man armed for war, before the LORD to battle, just as my lord says."

28So Moses gave command concerning them to El·ē·ā′zar the priest, to Joshua the son of Nun, and to the chief fathers of the tribes of the children of Israel. 29And Moses said to them: "If the children of Gad and the children of Reuben cross over the Jordan with you, every man armed for battle before the LORD, and the land is subdued before you, then you shall give them the land of Gil′ē·ad as a possession. 30But if they do not cross over armed with you, they shall have possessions among you in the land of Cā′naan."

31Then the children of Gad and the children of Reuben answered, saying: "As the LORD has said to your servants, so we will

32:12 God's best is always reserved for those who have wholly followed Him.

do. 32We will cross over armed before the
LORD into the land of Cā′naan, but the pos-
session of our inheritance *shall remain* with
us on this side of the Jordan."
33So Moses gave to the children of Gad,
to the children of Reuben, and to half
the tribe of Ma·nas′seh the son of Joseph,
the kingdom of Sī′hon king of the
Am′o·rītes and the kingdom of Og king of
Bā′shan, the land with its cities within the
borders, the cities of the surrounding
country. 34And the children of Gad built
Dī′bon and At′a·roth and A·rō′er, 35
At′roth and Shō′-phan and Jā′zer and
Jog′be·hah, 36Beth Nim′rah and Beth
Har′an, fortified cities, and folds for sheep.
37And the children of Reuben built
Hesh′bon and Ē·le·ā′leh and Kir·jath′a·im,
38Nē′bō and Bā′al Mē′on (*their* names be-
ing changed) and Shib′mah; and they
gave *other* names to the cities which they
built.
39And the children of Mā′chir the son
of Ma·nas′seh went to Gil′ē·ad and took
it, and dispossessed the Am′o·rītes who
were in it. 40So Moses gave Gil′ē·ad to
Mā′chir the son of Ma·nas′seh, and he
dwelt in it. 41Also Jā′ir the son of
Ma·nas′seh went and took its small towns,
and called them Hā′voth Jā′ir.[a] 42Then
Nō′bah went and took Kē′nath and its vil-
lages, and he called it Nō′bah, after his
own name.

CHAPTER 33

Israel's Journey from Egypt Reviewed

These *are* the journeys of the children of
Israel, who went out of the land of Egypt
by their armies under the hand of Moses
and Aaron. 2Now Moses wrote down the
starting points of their journeys at the
command of the LORD. And these *are*
their journeys according to their starting
points:
3They departed from Ram′e·sēs in the
first month, on the fifteenth day of the first
month; on the day after the Passover the
children of Israel went out with boldness
in the sight of all the Egyptians. 4For the
Egyptians were burying all *their* firstborn,
whom the LORD had killed among them.
Also on their gods the LORD had executed
judgments.

A Journal of Your Journey

Luci Shaw

If you think journaling is just for novelists, poets, or war heroes, think again. A *true* journal is full of seemingly trivial events—the clever things your children and grandchildren say, gifts you and your spouse exchange, books you read, or movies you see, all of which become significant road markers on your life track.

Each day of our lives is a journey, with a beginning (the past) and an end (the future). The present is sandwiched between. A journal helps us follow and chart our life paths, logging our progress.

Your life *is* exciting. You may have lived through a war. You may have traveled to foreign countries. You may have had children and grandchildren. Your life is rich with experience, your mind full of ideas and wisdom, your heart pulled by a spectrum of emotions. Why not record them?

If we keep a record of our past, it may provide us with clues about the future. We need the sense of moving forward to give our lives meaning and purpose. A journal provides proof that a personal history is being formed. Your journal is a process as well as a product. ✦

32:41 [a]Literally *Towns of Jair*

5Then the children of Israel moved from
Ram'e·sēs and camped at Suc'coth. 6They
departed from Suc'coth and camped at
Ē'tham, which *is* on the edge of the wilder-
ness. 7They moved from Ē'tham and
turned back to Pī Ha·hī'roth, which *is*
east of Bā'al Zē'phon; and they
camped near Mig'dōl. 8They departed
from before Ha·hī'roth[a] and passed
through the midst of the sea into the
wilderness, went three days' journey in the
Wilderness of Ē'tham, and camped at
Mar'ah. 9They moved from Mar'ah and
came to Ē'lim. At Ē'lim *were* twelve springs
of water and seventy palm trees; so they
camped there.

10They moved from Ē'lim and camped
by the Red Sea. 11They moved from the
Red Sea and camped in the Wilderness of
Sin. 12They journeyed from the Wilderness
of Sin and camped at Doph'kah. 13They
departed from Doph'kah and camped
at Ā'lush. 14They moved from Ā'lush
and camped at Reph'i·dim, where
there was no water for the people to
drink.

15They departed from Reph'i·dim and
camped in the Wilderness of Sinai. 16They
moved from the Wilderness of Sinai and
camped at Kib'roth Hat·tā'a·vah. 17They
departed from Kib'roth Hat·tā'a·vah and
camped at Ha·zē'roth. 18They departed
from Ha·zē'roth and camped at Rith'mah.
19They departed from Rith'mah and
camped at Rim'mon Per'ez. 20They de-
parted from Rim'mon Per'ez and camped
at Lib'nah. 21They moved from Lib'nah
and camped at Ris'sah. 22They journeyed
from Ris'sah and camped at Kē·he·lā'thah.
23They went from Kē·he·lā'thah and
camped at Mount Shē'pher. 24They moved
from Mount Shē'pher and camped at
Ha·rā'dah. 25They moved from Ha·rā'dah
and camped at Mak·hē'loth. 26They moved
from Mak·hē'loth and camped at Tā'hath.
27They departed from Tā'hath and camped
at Tē'rah. 28They moved from Tē'rah and
camped at Mith'kah. 29They went from
Mith'kah and camped at Hash·mō'nah.
30They departed from Hash·mō'nah and
camped at Mō·sē'roth. 31They departed
from Mō·sē'roth and camped at Ben'ē
Jā'a·kan. 32They moved from Ben'ē Jā'-
a·kan and camped at Hor Ha·gid'gad.
33They went from Hor Ha·gid'gad and
camped at Jot'ba·thah. 34They moved from
Jot'ba·thah and camped at A·brō'nah.
35They departed from A·brō'nah and
camped at Ē'zi·on Gē'ber. 36They moved
from Ē'zi·on Gē'ber and camped in the
Wilderness of Zin, which *is* Kā'desh.
37They moved from Kā'desh and camped
at Mount Hor, on the boundary of the land
of Ē'dom.

38Then Aaron the priest went up to
Mount Hor at the command of the LORD,
and died there in the fortieth year after
the children of Israel had come out of the
land of Egypt, on the first *day* of the fifth
month. 39Aaron *was* one hundred and
twenty-three years old when he died on
Mount Hor.

40Now the king of Ar'ad, the Cā'naan-
īte, who dwelt in the South in the land of
Cā'naan, heard of the coming of the chil-
dren of Israel.

41So they departed from Mount Hor and
camped at Zal·mō'nah. 42They departed
from Zal·mō'nah and camped at Pū'non.
43They departed from Pū'non and camped
at Ō'both. 44They departed from Ō'both
and camped at Ī'jē Ab'a·rim, at the border
of Mō'ab. 45They departed from Ī'jim[a] and
camped at Dī'bon Gad. 46They moved
from Dī'bon Gad and camped at Al'mon
Dib·la·thā'im. 47They moved from Al'mon
Dib·la·thā'im and camped in the moun-
tains of Ab'a·rim, before Nē'bō. 48They de-
parted from the mountains of Ab'a·rim
and camped in the plains of Mō'ab by the
Jordan, *across from* Jericho. 49They camped
by the Jordan, from Beth Jes'i·moth as far
as the Abel Acacia Grove[a] in the plains of
Mō'ab.

33:8 [a]Many Hebrew manuscripts, Samaritan Pentateuch, Syriac, Targum, and Vulgate read *from Pi Hahiroth* (compare verse 7). 33:45 [a]Same as *Ije Abarim*, verse 44 33:49 [a]Hebrew *Abel Shittim*

Instructions for the Conquest of Canaan

[50]Now the LORD spoke to Moses in the plains of Mō'ab by the Jordan, *across from* Jericho, saying, [51]"Speak to the children of Israel, and say to them: 'When you have crossed the Jordan into the land of Cā'naan, [52]then you shall drive out all the inhabitants of the land from before you, destroy all their engraved stones, destroy all their molded images, and demolish all their high places; [53]you shall dispossess *the inhabitants of* the land and dwell in it, for I have given you the land to possess. [54]And you shall divide the land by lot as an inheritance among your families; to the larger you shall give a larger inheritance, and to the smaller you shall give a smaller inheritance; there everyone's *inheritance* shall be whatever falls to him by lot. You shall inherit according to the tribes of your fathers. [55]But if you do not drive out the inhabitants of the land from before you, then it shall be that those whom you let remain *shall be* irritants in your eyes and thorns in your sides, and they shall harass you in the land where you dwell. [56]Moreover it shall be *that* I will do to you as I thought to do to them.' "

CHAPTER 34

The Appointed Boundaries of Canaan

Then the LORD spoke to Moses, saying, [2]"Command the children of Israel, and say to them: 'When you come into the land of Cā'naan, this *is* the land that shall fall to you as an inheritance—the land of Cā'naan to its boundaries. [3]Your southern border shall be from the Wilderness of Zin along the border of Ē'dom; then your southern border shall extend eastward to the end of the Salt Sea; [4]your border shall turn from the southern side of the Ascent of Ak·rab'bim, continue to Zin, and be on the south of Kā'desh Bar·nē'a; then it shall go on to Hā'zar Ad'dar, and continue to Az'mon; [5]the border shall turn from Az'mon to the Brook of Egypt, and it shall end at the Sea.

[6]'As for the western border, you shall have the Great Sea for a border; this shall be your western border.

[7]'And this shall be your northern border: From the Great Sea you shall mark out your *border* line to Mount Hor; [8]from Mount Hor you shall mark out *your border* to the entrance of Hā'math; then the direction of the border shall be toward Zē'dad; [9]the border shall proceed to Ziph'ron, and it shall end at Hā'zar Ē'nan. This shall be your northern border.

[10]'You shall mark out your eastern border from Hā'zar Ē'nan to Shē'pham; [11]the border shall go down from Shē'pham to Rib'lah on the east side of Ā'in; the border shall go down and reach to the eastern side of the Sea of Chin'ne·reth; [12]the border shall go down along the Jordan, and it shall end at the Salt Sea. This shall be your land with its surrounding boundaries.' "

[13]Then Moses commanded the children of Israel, saying: "This *is* the land which you shall inherit by lot, which the LORD has commanded to give to the nine tribes and to the half-tribe. [14]For the tribe of the children of Reuben according to the house of their fathers, and the tribe of the children of Gad according to the house of their fathers, have received *their inheritance;* and the half-tribe of Ma·nas'seh has received its inheritance. [15]The two tribes and the half-tribe have received their inheritance on this side of the Jordan, *across from* Jericho eastward, toward the sunrise."

33:50–56 The command to "drive out" the current inhabitants of Canaan emphasizes that compromise with the pagans was unacceptable. The world's ways are totally incompatible with the ways of God.

The Leaders Appointed to Divide the Land

16And the LORD spoke to Moses, saying, 17"These *are* the names of the men who shall divide the land among you as an inheritance: El·ē·ā'zar the priest and Joshua the son of Nun. 18And you shall take one leader of every tribe to divide the land for the inheritance. 19These *are* the names of the men: from the tribe of Judah, Caleb the son of Je·phŭn'neh; 20from the tribe of the children of Sim'ē·on, She·mū'el the son of Am·mī'hud; 21from the tribe of Benjamin, Ē·lī'dad the son of Chis'lon; 22a leader from the tribe of the children of Dan, Buk'kī the son of Jog'lī; 23from the sons of Joseph: a leader from the tribe of the children of Ma·nas'seh, Han'ni·el the son of Ephod, 24and a leader from the tribe of the children of Ē'phra·im, Ke·mū'el the son of Shiph'tan; 25a leader from the tribe of the children of Zeb'ū·lun, E·li·zā'phan the son of Par'nach; 26a leader from the tribe of the children of Is'sa·char, Pal'ti·el the son of Az'zan; 27a leader from the tribe of the children of Ash'er, A·hī'hud the son of She·lō'mī; 28and a leader from the tribe of the children of Naph'ta·lī, Ped'a·hel the son of Am·mī'hud."

29These *are* the ones the LORD commanded to divide the inheritance among the children of Israel in the land of Cā'naan.

CHAPTER 35

Cities for the Levites

And the LORD spoke to Moses in the plains of Mō'ab by the Jordan *across from* Jericho, saying: 2"Command the children of Israel that they give the Lē'vītes cities to dwell in from the inheritance of their possession, and you shall *also* give the Lē'vītes common-land around the cities. 3They shall have the cities to dwell in; and their common-land shall be for their cattle, for their herds, and for all their animals. 4The common-land of the cities which you will give the Lē'vītes *shall extend* from the wall of the city outward a thousand cubits all around. 5And you shall measure outside the city on the east side two thousand cubits, on the south side two thousand cubits, on the west side two thousand cubits, and on the north side two thousand cubits. The city *shall be* in the middle. This shall belong to them as common-land for the cities.

6"Now among the cities which you will give to the Lē'vītes *you shall appoint* six cities of refuge, to which a manslayer may flee. And to these you shall add forty-two cities. 7So all the cities you will give to the Lē'vītes *shall be* forty-eight; these *you shall give* with their common-land. 8And the cities which you will give *shall be* from the possession of the children of Israel; from the larger *tribe* you shall give many, from the smaller you shall give few. Each shall give some of its cities to the Lē'vītes, in proportion to the inheritance that each receives."

Cities of Refuge

9Then the LORD spoke to Moses, saying, 10"Speak to the children of Israel, and say to them: 'When you cross the Jordan into the land of Cā'naan, 11then you shall appoint cities to be cities of refuge for you, that the manslayer who kills any person

---

35:4 common-land: Grazing lands extending about half a mile in all directions around the towns. This light agriculture would supplement the support they received from their portion of all the offerings.

35:6 cities of refuge: These cities were under the control of the Levites and were intended to stop the emergence of blood feuds. They were places where someone who had killed another by accident (v. 11) could go in order to escape the quick revenge of the dead person's family. These cities were not places where justice could be avoided, but places where further bloodshed could be prevented while an investigation took place (v. 12).

accidentally may flee there. [12]They shall be cities of refuge for you from the avenger, that the manslayer may not die until he stands before the congregation in judgment. [13]And of the cities which you give, you shall have six cities of refuge. [14]You shall appoint three cities on this side of the Jordan, and three cities you shall appoint in the land of Cā'naan, *which* will be cities of refuge. [15]These six cities shall be for refuge for the children of Israel, for the stranger, and for the sojourner among them, that anyone who kills a person accidentally may flee there.

[16]'But if he strikes him with an iron implement, so that he dies, he *is* a murderer; the murderer shall surely be put to death. [17]And if he strikes him with a stone in the hand, by which one could die, and he does die, he *is* a murderer; the murderer shall surely be put to death. [18]Or *if* he strikes him with a wooden hand weapon, by which one could die, and he does die, he *is* a murderer; the murderer shall surely be put to death. [19]The avenger of blood himself shall put the murderer to death; when he meets him, he shall put him to death. [20]If he pushes him out of hatred or, while lying in wait, hurls something at him so that he dies, [21]or in enmity he strikes him with his hand so that he dies, the one who struck *him* shall surely be put to death. He *is* a murderer. The avenger of blood shall put the murderer to death when he meets him.

[22]'However, if he pushes him suddenly without enmity, or throws anything at him without lying in wait, [23]or uses a stone, by which a man could die, throwing *it* at him without seeing *him*, so that he dies, while he was not his enemy or seeking his harm, [24]then the congregation shall judge between the manslayer and the avenger of blood according to these judgments. [25]So the congregation shall deliver the manslayer from the hand of the avenger of blood, and the congregation shall return him to the city of refuge where he had fled, and he shall remain there until the death of the high priest who was anointed with the holy oil. [26]But if the manslayer at any time goes outside the limits of the city of refuge where he fled, [27]and the avenger of blood finds him outside the limits of his city of refuge, and the avenger of blood kills the manslayer, he shall not be guilty of blood, [28]because he should have remained in his city of refuge until the death of the high priest. But after the death of the high priest the manslayer may return to the land of his possession.

[29]'And these *things* shall be a statute of judgment to you throughout your generations in all your dwellings. [30]Whoever kills a person, the murderer shall be put to death on the testimony of witnesses; but one witness is not *sufficient* testimony against a person for the death *penalty*. [31]Moreover you shall take no ransom for the life of a murderer who *is* guilty of death, but he shall surely be put to death. [32]And you shall take no ransom for him who has fled to his city of refuge, that he may return to dwell in the land before the death of the priest. [33]So you shall not pollute the land where you *are;* for blood defiles the land, and no atonement can be

---

35:16–21 if he strikes him: If a person killed another using an iron tool, a stone (v. 17), or a club (v. 18), there was a clear intent to destroy. These people were guilty of murder. Hatred and premeditation (vv. 20, 21) also proved murder.

35:25 The **death of the high priest** brought freedom to the manslayer. Apparently the high priest's death was accepted as a substitutionary atonement.

35:26–28 Any bloodshed was serious enough that extraordinary provisions were made to cover the incident. If the **manslayer** took those provisions lightly, he forfeited his life.

35:30–32 An accused person could not receive the death penalty on the testimony of only **one witness**. God's plan is to protect the innocent while dealing severely with the offender (vv. 31, 32). Also, the value of life cannot be measured in money; thus, neither a murderer nor a manslayer could buy off his sentence.

made for the land, for the blood that is
shed on it, except by the blood of him who
shed it. 34Therefore do not defile the land
which you inhabit, in the midst of which I
dwell; for I the LORD dwell among the chil-
dren of Israel.' "

CHAPTER 36

Marriage of Female Heirs

Now the chief fathers of the families of
the children of Gil'ē·ad the son of Mā'chir,
the son of Ma·nas'seh, of the families of the
sons of Joseph, came near and spoke before
Moses and before the leaders, the chief
fathers of the children of Israel. 2And they
said: "The LORD commanded my lord *Mo-*
ses to give the land as an inheritance by lot
to the children of Israel, and my lord was
commanded by the LORD to give the inher-
itance of our brother Ze·loph'e·had to his
daughters. 3Now if they are married to any
of the sons of the *other* tribes of the children
of Israel, then their inheritance will be
taken from the inheritance of our fathers,
and it will be added to the inheritance of
the tribe into which they marry; so it will
be taken from the lot of our inheritance.
4And when the Jubilee of the children of Is-
rael comes, then their inheritance will be
added to the inheritance of the tribe into
which they marry; so their inheritance will
be taken away from the inheritance of the
tribe of our fathers."
5Then Moses commanded the children
of Israel according to the word of the LORD,
saying: "What the tribe of the sons of Jo-
seph speaks is right. 6This *is* what the LORD
commands concerning the daughters of
Ze·loph'e·had, saying, 'Let them marry
whom they think best, but they may marry
only within the family of their father's
tribe.' 7So the inheritance of the children of
Israel shall not change hands from tribe to
tribe, for every one of the children of Israel
shall keep the inheritance of the tribe of his
fathers. 8And every daughter who pos-
sesses an inheritance in any tribe of the
children of Israel shall be the wife of one
of the family of her father's tribe, so that
the children of Israel each may possess
the inheritance of his fathers. 9Thus no in-
heritance shall change hands from *one*
tribe to another, but every tribe of the chil-
dren of Israel shall keep its own inheri-
tance."
10Just as the LORD commanded Moses,
so did the daughters of Ze·loph'e·had;
11for Mah'lah, Tir'zah, Hog'lah, Mil'cah,
and Noah, the daughters of Ze·loph'e·had,
were married to the sons of their father's
brothers. 12They were married into the
families of the children of Ma·nas'seh the
son of Joseph, and their inheritance re-
mained in the tribe of their father's family.
13These *are* the commandments and the
judgments which the LORD commanded
the children of Israel by the hand of Moses
in the plains of Mō'ab by the Jordan, *across*
from Jericho.

36:1–12 This chapter deals with the law concerning **land as an inheritance** (v. 2). A woman who carried the family inheritance could marry only within the tribe of her birth (v. 6). This would ensure that the land promised by God to a particular tribe would remain in its possession (v. 9).

But God's concern for justice is also reflected. In 27:1–8 Zelophehad's daughters were about to be treated in a manner that was legal, but unfair. Because the law authorized an inheritance to sons only, the family was about to lose its inheritance in the Promised Land. These women asked for special treatment beyond that provided by the law—and God granted it.

✦Deuteronomy✦

Like the first four books of the Bible, Deuteronomy was most likely written around 1400 B.C. by Moses (31:9–13), and Joshua probably wrote chapter 34 as a tribute to Moses after his death. This book marks a turning point for the Israelites after wandering for forty years because of their rebellion.

Deuteronomy tells of Moses' three sermons—reminding the people of God's past judgment and deliverance (chapters 1—4), reviewing the Law (chapters 5—26), and revealing what will happen to the people in the future (chapters 27—33). Although it may seem like a repetition of material in previous books, Deuteronomy is actually a restatement of the law for the benefit of the new generation destined to claim the Promised Land. Moses summarized the past so that future generations could learn from it. In addition, this book is a record of the renewal of the covenant between Israel and God.

Deuteronomy is cited more than eighty times in the New Testament, including Christ's rebuttals to Satan when He was tempted in the wilderness. ✦

CHAPTER 1

The Previous Command to Enter Canaan

These *are* the words which Moses spoke
to all Israel on this side of the Jordan in the
wilderness, in the plain[a] opposite Sūph,[b]
between Par′an, Tō′phel, Lā′ban,
Ha·zē′roth, and Diz′a·hab. 2*It is* eleven
days' *journey* from Hō′reb by way of
Mount Sē′ir to Kā′desh Bar·nē′a. 3Now it
came to pass in the fortieth year, in the
eleventh month, on the first *day* of the
month, *that* Moses spoke to the children of
Israel according to all that the LORD had
given him as commandments to them, 4after he had killed Sī′hon king of the
Am′o·rītes, who dwelt in Hesh′bon, and
Og king of Bā′shan, who dwelt at
Ash′ta·roth in[a] Ed′rē·ī.
5On this side of the Jordan in the land of
Mō′ab, Moses began to explain this law,
saying, 6"The LORD our God spoke to us in

1:1 [a]Hebrew *arabah* [b]One manuscript of the Septuagint, also Targum and Vulgate, read *Red Sea*.
1:4 [a]Septuagint, Syriac, and Vulgate read *and* (compare Joshua 12:4).

1:2, 3 eleven days . . . fortieth year: The wages of sin: an 11-day journey takes 40 years. **Horeb**: Another name for Sinai.

1:4 These victories over **Sihon** and **Og** always loomed large in Israel's memory (Ps. 135:10–12). They were proof of God's renewed blessing on His people after the wilderness wanderings.

1:6—4:43 In his first discourse Moses very carefully prepared his people to obey God and enter the land. He did so by showing what had brought them to this point—both disobedience (1:19–46) and obedience (2:1—3:22). Then he reminded them of the significance of those startling events at Sinai and of God's election of them to be His special people

Hō′reb, saying: 'You have dwelt long enough at this mountain. 7Turn and take your journey, and go to the mountains of the Am′o·rītes, to all the neighboring *places* in the plain,[a] in the mountains and in the lowland, in the South and on the seacoast, to the land of the Cā′naan·ītes and to Lebanon, as far as the great river, the River Eū·phrā′tēs. 8See, I have set the land before you; go in and possess the land which the LORD swore to your fathers—to Abraham, Isaac, and Jacob—to give to them and their descendants after them.'

Tribal Leaders Appointed

9"And I spoke to you at that time, saying: 'I alone am not able to bear you. 10The LORD your God has multiplied you, and here you *are* today, as the stars of heaven in multitude. 11May the LORD God of your fathers make you a thousand times more numerous than you are, and bless you as He has promised you! 12How can I alone bear your problems and your burdens and your complaints? 13Choose wise, understanding, and knowledgeable men from among your tribes, and I will make them heads over you.' 14And you answered me and said, 'The thing which you have told *us* to do *is* good.' 15So I took the heads of your tribes, wise and knowledgeable men, and made them heads over you, leaders of thousands, leaders of hundreds, leaders of fifties, leaders of tens, and officers for your tribes.

16"Then I commanded your judges at that time, saying, 'Hear *the cases* between your brethren, and judge righteously between a man and his brother or the stranger who is with him. 17You shall not show partiality in judgment; you shall hear the small as well as the great; you shall not be afraid in any man's presence, for the judgment *is* God's. The case that is too hard for you, bring to me, and I will hear it.' 18And I commanded you at that time all the things which you should do.

Israel's Refusal to Enter the Land

19"So we departed from Hō′reb, and went through all that great and terrible wilderness which you saw on the way to the mountains of the Am′o·rītes, as the LORD our God had commanded us. Then we came to Kā′desh Bar·nē′a. 20And I said to you, 'You have come to the mountains of the Am′o·rītes, which the LORD our God is giving us. 21Look, the LORD your God has set the land before you; go up *and* possess *it*, as the LORD God of your fathers has spoken to you; do not fear or be discouraged.'

22"And every one of you came near to me and said, 'Let us send men before us, and let them search out the land for us, and bring back word to us of the way by which we should go up, and of the cities into which we shall come.'

23"The plan pleased me well; so I took twelve of your men, one man from *each* tribe. 24And they departed and went up into the mountains, and came to the Valley of Esh′col, and spied it out. 25They also took *some* of the fruit of the land in their hands and brought *it* down to us; and they brought back word to us, saying, '*It is* a good land which the LORD our God is giving us.'

26"Nevertheless you would not go up, but rebelled against the command of the LORD your God; 27and you complained in your tents, and said, 'Because the LORD hates us, He has brought us out of the land of Egypt to deliver us into the hand of the Am′o·rītes, to destroy us. 28Where can we

1:7 [a]Hebrew *arabah*

(4:1–43). We do well to remember that any good in our lives comes from the hand of God, and, while we should not live in the past, it is important to keep in mind the lessons we have learned from past experiences.

1:17 Above all, Israel's judges must not show **partiality**. The Israelites had known oppression in Egypt and their new society must be different because God's nature is different.

go up? Our brethren have discouraged our hearts, saying, "The people *are* greater and taller than we; the cities *are* great and fortified up to heaven; moreover we have seen the sons of the An'a·kim there." '

29"Then I said to you, 'Do not be terrified, or afraid of them. 30The LORD your God, who goes before you, He will fight for you, according to all He did for you in Egypt before your eyes, 31and in the wilderness where you saw how the LORD your God carried you, as a man carries his son, in all the way that you went until you came to this place.' 32Yet, for all that, you did not believe the LORD your God, 33who went in the way before you to search out a place for you to pitch your tents, to show you the way you should go, in the fire by night and in the cloud by day.

The Penalty for Israel's Rebellion

34"And the LORD heard the sound of your words, and was angry, and took an oath, saying, 35'Surely not one of these men of this evil generation shall see that good land of which I swore to give to your fathers, 36except Caleb the son of Je-phūn'neh; he shall see it, and to him and his children I am giving the land on which he walked, because he wholly followed the LORD.' 37The LORD was also angry with me for your sakes, saying, 'Even you shall not go in there. 38Joshua the son of Nun, who stands before you, he shall go in there. Encourage him, for he shall cause Israel to inherit it.

39'Moreover your little ones and your children, who you say will be victims, who today have no knowledge of good and evil, they shall go in there; to them I will give it, and they shall possess it. 40But *as for* you, turn and take your journey into the wilderness by the Way of the Red Sea.'

41"Then you answered and said to me, 'We have sinned against the LORD; we will go up and fight, just as the LORD our God commanded us.' And when everyone of you had girded on his weapons of war, you were ready to go up into the mountain.

42"And the LORD said to me, 'Tell them, "Do not go up nor fight, for I *am* not among you; lest you be defeated before your enemies." ' 43So I spoke to you; yet you would not listen, but rebelled against the command of the LORD, and presumptuously went up into the mountain. 44And the Am'o·rītes who dwelt in that mountain came out against you and chased you as bees do, and drove you back from Sē'ir to Hor'mah. 45Then you returned and wept before the LORD, but the LORD would not listen to your voice nor give ear to you.

46"So you remained in Kā'desh many days, according to the days that you spent *there.*

CHAPTER 2

The Desert Years

"Then we turned and journeyed into the wilderness of the Way of the Red Sea, as the LORD spoke to me, and we skirted Mount Sē'ir for many days.

2"And the LORD spoke to me, saying: 3'You have skirted this mountain long enough; turn northward. 4And command the people, saying, "You *are about to* pass through the territory of your brethren, the descendants of Esau, who live in Sē'ir; and they will be afraid of you. Therefore watch yourselves carefully. 5Do not meddle with them, for I will not give you *any* of their

1:42–44 When we attempt something without God's approval, we set ourselves up for disaster.

2:1—3:22 The results of obedience. God's blessing on the trip from Kadesh Barnea to Moab.

2:5 Do not meddle with them: The age-old rivalry between Jacob and Esau is alluded to here. The Edomites were afraid of the Israelites and refused them passage. But God would not allow the Israelites to attack them; therefore, they obeyed and traveled along

land, no, not so much as one footstep, be-
cause I have given Mount Sē′ir to Esau *as* a
possession. 6You shall buy food from them
with money, that you may eat; and you
shall also buy water from them with
money, that you may drink.
7"For the LORD your God has blessed
you in all the work of your hand. He
knows your trudging through this great
wilderness. These forty years the LORD
your God *has been* with you; you have
lacked nothing." '
8"And when we passed beyond our
brethren, the descendants of Esau who
dwell in Sē′ir, away from the road of the
plain, away from Ē′lath and Ē′zi·on
Gē′ber, we turned and passed by way of
the Wilderness of Mō′ab. 9Then the LORD
said to me, 'Do not harass Mō′ab, nor con-
tend with them in battle, for I will not give
you *any* of their land *as* a possession, be-
cause I have given Ar to the descendants of
Lot *as* a possession.' "
10(The Ē′mim had dwelt there in times
past, a people as great and numerous and
tall as the An′a·kim. 11They were also re-
garded as giants,[a] like the An′a·kim, but
the Mō′ab·ītes call them Ē′mim. 12The
Hor′ītes formerly dwelt in Sē′ir, but the
descendants of Esau dispossessed them
and destroyed them from before them, and
dwelt in their place, just as Israel did to the
land of their possession which the LORD
gave them.)
13" 'Now rise and cross over the Valley
of the Zē′red.' So we crossed over the Val-
ley of the Zē′red. 14And the time we took to
come from Kā′desh Bar·nē′a until we
crossed over the Valley of the Zē′red *was*
thirty-eight years, until all the generation
of the men of war was consumed from the
midst of the camp, just as the LORD had
sworn to them. 15For indeed the hand of
the LORD was against them, to destroy
them from the midst of the camp until they
were consumed.
16"So it was, when all the men of war
had finally perished from among the peo-
ple, 17that the LORD spoke to me, saying:
18'This day you are to cross over at Ar, the
boundary of Mō′ab. 19And *when* you come
near the people of Am′mon, do not harass
them or meddle with them, for I will not
give you *any* of the land of the people of
Am′mon *as* a possession, because I have
given it to the descendants of Lot *as* a pos-
session.' "
20(That was also regarded as a land of gi-
ants;[a] giants formerly dwelt there. But the
Am′mon·ītes call them Zam·zum′mim, 21a
people as great and numerous and tall as
the An′a·kim. But the LORD destroyed
them before them, and they dispossessed
them and dwelt in their place, 22just as He
had done for the descendants of Esau, who
dwelt in Sē′ir, when He destroyed the
Hor′ītes from before them. They dispos-
sessed them and dwelt in their place, even
to this day. 23And the Av′im, who dwelt in
villages as far as Gā′za—the Caph′to·rim,
who came from Caph′tor, destroyed them
and dwelt in their place.)
24" 'Rise, take your journey, and cross
over the River Ar′non. Look, I have given
into your hand Sī′hon the Am′o·rīte, king
of Hesh′bon, and his land. Begin to possess
it, and engage him in battle. 25This day I
will begin to put the dread and fear of you
upon the nations under the whole heaven,
who shall hear the report of you, and shall
tremble and be in anguish because of you.'

King Sihon Defeated

26"And I sent messengers from the
Wilderness of Ked′e·moth to Sī′hon king
of Hesh′bon, with words of peace, saying,

2:11 [a]Hebrew *rephaim* 2:20 [a]Hebrew *rephaim*

Edom's eastern borders. **I have given**: God gave land to other descendants of Abraham as well as Jacob (see also vv. 9, 19). His blessings extend to more than just the covenant people.

2:26–29 And I: Moses is speaking, not God as in vv. 24, 25.

27'Let me pass through your land; I will keep strictly to the road, and I will turn neither to the right nor to the left. 28You shall sell me food for money, that I may eat, and give me water for money, that I may drink; only let me pass through on foot, 29just as the descendants of Esau who dwell in Sē'ir and the Mō'ab·ītes who dwell in Ar did for me, until I cross the Jordan to the land which the LORD our God is giving us.'

30"But Sī'hon king of Hesh'bon would not let us pass through, for the LORD your God hardened his spirit and made his heart obstinate, that He might deliver him into your hand, as *it is* this day.

31"And the LORD said to me, 'See, I have begun to give Sī'hon and his land over to you. Begin to possess *it*, that you may inherit his land.' 32Then Sī'hon and all his people came out against us to fight at Jā'haz. 33And the LORD our God delivered him over to us; so we defeated him, his sons, and all his people. 34We took all his cities at that time, and we utterly destroyed the men, women, and little ones of every city; we left none remaining. 35We took only the livestock as plunder for ourselves, with the spoil of the cities which we took. 36From A·rō'er, which *is* on the bank of the River Ar'non, and *from* the city that *is* in the ravine, as far as Gil'ē·ad, there was not one city too strong for us; the LORD our God delivered all to us. 37Only you did not go near the land of the people of Am'mon—anywhere along the River Jab'bok, or to the cities of the mountains, or wherever the LORD our God had forbidden us.

CHAPTER 3

King Og Defeated

"Then we turned and went up the road to Bā'shan; and Og king of Bā'shan came out against us, he and all his people, to battle at Ed'rē·ī. 2And the LORD said to me, 'Do not fear him, for I have delivered him and all his people and his land into your hand; you shall do to him as you did to Sī'hon king of the Am'o·rītes, who dwelt at Hesh'bon.'

3"So the LORD our God also delivered into our hands Og king of Bā'shan, with all his people, and we attacked him until he had no survivors remaining. 4And we took all his cities at that time; there was not a city which we did not take from them: sixty cities, all the region of Ar'gob, the kingdom of Og in Bā'shan. 5All these cities *were* fortified with high walls, gates, and bars, besides a great many rural towns. 6And we utterly destroyed them, as we did to Sī'hon king of Hesh'bon, utterly destroying the men, women, and children of every city. 7But all the livestock and the spoil of the cities we took as booty for ourselves.

8"And at that time we took the land from the hand of the two kings of the Am'o·rītes who *were* on this side of the Jordan, from the River Ar'non to Mount Her'mon 9(the Sī·dō'ni·ans call Her'mon Sir'i·on, and the Am'o·rītes call it Sē'nir), 10all the cities of the plain, all Gil'ē·ad, and all Bā'shan, as far as Sal'cah and Ed'rē·ī, cities of the kingdom of Og in Bā'shan.

11"For only Og king of Bā'shan remained of the remnant of the giants.[a] Indeed his bedstead *was* an iron bedstead. (*Is* it not in Rab'bah of the people of Am'mon?) Nine cubits *is* its length and four cubits its width, according to the standard cubit.

The Land East of the Jordan Divided

12"And this land, *which* we possessed at that time, from A·rō'er, which *is* by the

3:11 [a]Hebrew *rephaim*

2:34, 35 By utterly destroying the cities of the Canaanites, Israel would put a stop to their false religions and execute God's judgment for their sinfulness.

3:12–22 Moses apportioned the Canaanite territory on the east side of the Jordan to the

River Ar'non, and half the mountains of
Gil'ē·ad and its cities, I gave to the
Reū'ben·ītes and the Gad'ītes. 13The rest of
Gil'ē·ad, and all Bā'shan, the kingdom of
Og, I gave to half the tribe of Ma·nas'seh.
(All the region of Ar'gob, with all Bā'shan,
was called the land of the giants.[a] 14Jā'ir the
son of Ma·nas'seh took all the region of
Ar'gob, as far as the border of the
Gesh'ū·rītes and the Mā'a·cha·thītes, and
called Bā'shan after his own name,
Hā'voth Jā'ir,[a] to this day.)
15"Also I gave Gil'ē·ad to Mā'chir. 16And
to the Reū'ben·ītes and the Gad'ītes I gave
from Gil'ē·ad as far as the River Ar'non,
the middle of the river as *the* border, as far
as the River Jab'bok, the border of the peo-
ple of Am'mon; 17the plain also, with the
Jordan as *the* border, from Chin'ne·reth as
far as the east side of the Sea of the
Ar'a·bah (the Salt Sea), below the slopes of
Pis'gah.
18"Then I commanded you at that time,
saying: 'The LORD your God has given you
this land to possess. All you men of valor
shall cross over armed before your
brethren, the children of Israel. 19But your
wives, your little ones, and your livestock
(I know that you have much livestock)
shall stay in your cities which I have given
you, 20until the LORD has given rest to your
brethren as to you, and they also possess
the land which the LORD your God is giv-
ing them beyond the Jordan. Then each of
you may return to his possession which I
have given you.'

3:13 [a]Hebrew *rephaim* 3:14 [a]Literally *Towns of Jair*

21"And I commanded Joshua at that
time, saying, 'Your eyes have seen all that
the LORD your God has done to these two
kings; so will the LORD do to all the king-
doms through which you pass. 22You must
not fear them, for the LORD your God Him-
self fights for you.'

Moses Forbidden to Enter the Land

23"Then I pleaded with the LORD at that
time, saying: 24'O Lord GOD, You have be-
gun to show Your servant Your greatness
and Your mighty hand, for what god *is*
there in heaven or on earth who can do *any-
thing* like Your works and Your mighty
deeds? 25I pray, let me cross over and see the
good land beyond the Jordan, those pleas-
ant mountains, and Lebanon.'
26"But the LORD was angry with me on
your account, and would not listen to me.
So the LORD said to me: 'Enough of that!
Speak no more to Me of this matter. 27Go
up to the top of Pis'gah, and lift your eyes
toward the west, the north, the south, and
the east; behold *it* with your eyes, for you
shall not cross over this Jordan. 28But com-
mand Joshua, and encourage him and
strengthen him; for he shall go over before
this people, and he shall cause them to in-
herit the land which you will see.'
29"So we stayed in the valley opposite
Beth Pē'or.

CHAPTER 4

Moses Commands Obedience

"Now, O Israel, listen to the statutes and
the judgments which I teach you to

tribes of Reuben, Gad, and half the tribe of Manasseh. **rest to your brethren** (v. 20): These allotments were given on the condition that the three tribes assist the rest of the tribes in conquering their territory.

3:21, 22 When we are on the Lord's side we do not fight in our own strength; the battle is His and He alone can achieve victory.

4:1–9 The Sinai **statutes** and **judgments** distinguished Israel from all other nations. This was not so much because of unique content; there are similar laws from other parts of the ancient Near East. What made Israel unique was that obedience to the laws was made an expression of her faith in God and her commitment to Him. No other nation had **God so near to it**—in a covenant relation with it (v. 7).

> Children today need to be brought up in the church and taught to read and respect God's Word. I tell my children when I see them letting their own children get away with things. It's my responsibility as a grandmother.
>
> Delores "Mom" Winans

observe, that you may live, and go in and
possess the land which the LORD God of
your fathers is giving you. 2You shall not
add to the word which I command you,
nor take from it, that you may keep the
commandments of the LORD your God
which I command you. 3Your eyes have
seen what the LORD did at Bā'al Pē'or; for
the LORD your God has destroyed from
among you all the men who followed Bā'al
of Pē'or. 4But you who held fast to the LORD
your God *are* alive today, every one of you.
5"Surely I have taught you statutes and
judgments, just as the LORD my God com-
manded me, that you should act according
to them in the land which you go to pos-
sess. 6Therefore be careful to observe *them;*
for this *is* your wisdom and your under-
standing in the sight of the peoples who
will hear all these statutes, and say, 'Surely
this great nation *is* a wise and understand-
ing people.'
7"For what great nation *is there* that has
God *so* near to it, as the LORD our God *is* to
us, for whatever *reason* we may call upon
Him? 8And what great nation *is there* that
has *such* statutes and righteous judgments
as are in all this law which I set before you
this day? 9Only take heed to yourself, and
diligently keep yourself, lest you forget the
things your eyes have seen, and lest they
depart from your heart all the days of your
life. And teach them to your children and
your grandchildren, 10*especially concerning*
the day you stood before the LORD your
God in Hō'reb, when the LORD said to me,
'Gather the people to Me, and I will let
them hear My words, that they may learn
to fear Me all the days they live on the
earth, and *that* they may teach their chil-
dren.'
11"Then you came near and stood at the
foot of the mountain, and the mountain
burned with fire to the midst of heaven,
with darkness, cloud, and thick darkness.
12And the LORD spoke to you out of the
midst of the fire. You heard the sound of
the words, but saw no form; *you* only *heard*
a voice. 13So He declared to you His
covenant which He commanded you to
perform, the Ten Commandments; and He
wrote them on two tablets of stone. 14And
the LORD commanded me at that time to
teach you statutes and judgments, that you
might observe them in the land which you
cross over to possess.

Beware of Idolatry

15"Take careful heed to yourselves, for
you saw no form when the LORD spoke to
you at Hō'reb out of the midst of the fire,
16lest you act corruptly and make for your-
selves a carved image in the form of any
figure: the likeness of male or female, 17the
likeness of any animal that *is* on the earth
or the likeness of any winged bird that flies
in the air, 18the likeness of anything that
creeps on the ground or the likeness of any
fish that *is* in the water beneath the earth.
19And *take heed,* lest you lift your eyes to
heaven, and *when* you see the sun, the
moon, and the stars, all the host of heaven,
you feel driven to worship them and serve
them, which the LORD your God has given
to all the peoples under the whole heaven
as a heritage. 20But the LORD has taken you

4:10 Those who **fear** God hold Him in holy reverence, which is expressed in worshipful obedience.

4:15–19 Since the visual symbols at Sinai included no form, the Hebrews were forbidden from trying to capture God in any created shape. God transcends creation and therefore cannot be represented by anything in it.

Teaching the Faith

Jerry and Jack Schreur

Recent research on the role of grandparents has shown that most of us *do not* share our personal faith with our grandchildren, and that we do not have much influence on their beliefs. Many of us have evidently decided that it is *not* our responsibility to share Jesus with our grandchildren. We assume it to be the job of the parents. The primary responsibility for the spiritual education of our grandchildren does fall on the parents, but that does not mean we may neglect our responsibility to do our part.

Many grandparents simply never try to talk to their grandchildren about faith. We may believe that it is important, and we may pray that our precious grandchildren receive Christ, but it just "never comes up." During visits, most of us have difficulty talking about our faith. This holds true whether talking to our friends on the golf course or our grandchildren in the car. It is not easy or natural for us to bring our relationship with Jesus into the conversation.

We must realize that our grandchildren are growing up in a "post-Christian" society. The overriding beliefs today are diametrically opposed to the values of Christianity. Our grandchildren are not going to inherit our faith automatically. All the Christians in a child's life must therefore be committed to passing on their faith to that child. The future of our grandchildren demands that their fathers, mothers, uncles, aunts, and especially their grandparents live out their faith in front of the children. ✦

and brought you out of the iron furnace,
out of Egypt, to be His people, an inheri-
tance, as you are this day. [21]Furthermore
the LORD was angry with me for your
sakes, and swore that I would not cross
over the Jordan, and that I would not enter
the good land which the LORD your God is
giving you as an inheritance. [22]But I must
die in this land, I must not cross over the
Jordan; but you shall cross over and pos-
sess that good land. [23]Take heed to your-
selves, lest you forget the covenant of the
LORD your God which He made with you,
and make for yourselves a carved image in
the form of anything which the LORD your
God has forbidden you. [24]For the LORD
your God *is* a consuming fire, a jealous
God.

[25]"When you beget children and
grandchildren and have grown old in the
land, and act corruptly and make a carved
image in the form of anything, and do evil
in the sight of the LORD your God to pro-
voke Him to anger, [26]I call heaven and
earth to witness against you this day, that
you will soon utterly perish from the land
which you cross over the Jordan to pos-
sess; you will not prolong *your* days in it,
but will be utterly destroyed. [27]And the
LORD will scatter you among the peoples,
and you will be left few in number among
the nations where the LORD will drive you.
[28]And there you will serve gods, the work
of men's hands, wood and stone, which
neither see nor hear nor eat nor smell. [29]But
from there you will seek the LORD your

4:24 Jealousy indicates the zealous righteousness of God, which is intolerant of any interference in His relationship with those He loves.

4:29 The Lord will always respond with mercy toward those who are truly penitent. No

God, and you will find *Him* if you seek
Him with all your heart and with all your
soul. 30 When you are in distress, and all
these things come upon you in the latter
days, when you turn to the LORD your God
and obey His voice 31 (for the LORD your
God *is* a merciful God), He will not forsake
you nor destroy you, nor forget the
covenant of your fathers which He swore
to them.

32 "For ask now concerning the days that
are past, which were before you, since the
day that God created man on the earth,
and *ask* from one end of heaven to the
other, whether *any* great *thing* like this has
happened, or *anything* like it has been
heard. 33 Did *any* people *ever* hear the voice
of God speaking out of the midst of the
fire, as you have heard, and live? 34 Or did
God *ever* try to go *and* take for Himself a
nation from the midst of *another* nation, by
trials, by signs, by wonders, by war, by a
mighty hand and an outstretched arm, and
by great terrors, according to all that the
LORD your God did for you in Egypt before
your eyes? 35 To you it was shown, that you
might know that the LORD Himself *is* God;
there is none other besides Him. 36 Out of
heaven He let you hear His voice, that He
might instruct you; on earth He showed
you His great fire, and you heard His
words out of the midst of the fire. 37 And be-
cause He loved your fathers, therefore He
chose their descendants after them; and He
brought you out of Egypt with His Pres-
ence, with His mighty power, 38 driving out
from before you nations greater and
mightier than you, to bring you in, to give
you their land *as* an inheritance, as *it is* this
day. 39 Therefore know this day, and con-
sider *it* in your heart, that the LORD Him-
self *is* God in heaven above and on the
earth beneath; *there is* no other. 40 You shall
therefore keep His statutes and His com-
mandments which I command you today,
that it may go well with you and with your
children after you, and that you may pro-
long *your* days in the land which the LORD
your God is giving you for all time."

Cities of Refuge East of the Jordan

41 Then Moses set apart three cities on
this side of the Jordan, toward the rising of
the sun, 42 that the manslayer might flee
there, who kills his neighbor unin-
tentionally, without having hated him in
time past, and that by fleeing to one of
these cities he might live: 43 Bē'zer in the
wilderness on the plateau for the
Reū'ben·ītes, Rā'moth in Gil'ē·ad for
the Gad'ītes, and Gō'lan in Bā'shan for
the Ma·nas'sītes.

Introduction to God's Law

44 Now this *is* the law which Moses set
before the children of Israel. 45 These *are* the
testimonies, the statutes, and the judg-
ments which Moses spoke to the children
of Israel after they came out of Egypt, 46 on
this side of the Jordan, in the valley oppo-
site Beth Pē'or, in the land of Sī'hon king of
the Am'o·rītes, who dwelt at Hesh'bon,
whom Moses and the children of Israel de-
feated after they came out of Egypt. 47 And
they took possession of his land and the
land of Og king of Bā'shan, two kings of
the Am'o·rītes, who *were* on this side of the
Jordan, toward the rising of the sun, 48 from
A·rō'er, which *is* on the bank of the River
Ar'non, even to Mount Sī'on[a] (that is,
Her'mon), 49 and all the plain on the east

4:48 [a]Syriac reads *Sirion* (compare 3:9).

matter how far we have wandered, if we return to Him with a "broken and a contrite heart" (Ps. 51:17), He will not turn us away.

4:44—26:19 The second major discourse of the book. Moses reminds the people of their covenant obligations to be kept when they enter the land. It is plain, especially in chs. 6—11, that his purpose was not primarily informational, but motivational. His concern was to ensure that they would obey what they knew.

side of the Jordan as far as the Sea of the
Ar'a·bah, below the slopes of Pis'gah.

CHAPTER 5

The Ten Commandments Reviewed

And Moses called all Israel, and said to
them: "Hear, O Israel, the statutes and
judgments which I speak in your hearing
today, that you may learn them and be
careful to observe them. 2The LORD our
God made a covenant with us in Hō'reb.
3The LORD did not make this covenant with
our fathers, but with us, those who *are* here
today, all of us who *are* alive. 4The LORD
talked with you face to face on the moun-
tain from the midst of the fire. 5I stood be-
tween the LORD and you at that time, to de-
clare to you the word of the LORD; for you
were afraid because of the fire, and you did
not go up the mountain. *He* said:

6 'I *am* the LORD your God who brought
you out of the land of Egypt, out of
the house of bondage.

7 'You shall have no other gods before
Me.

8 'You shall not make for yourself a
carved image—any likeness *of any-
thing* that *is* in heaven above, or
that *is* in the earth beneath, or that
is in the water under the earth; 9you
shall not bow down to them nor
serve them. For I, the LORD your
God, *am* a jealous God, visiting the
iniquity of the fathers upon the
children to the third and fourth
generations of those who hate Me,
10but showing mercy to thousands,
to those who love Me and keep My
commandments.

11 'You shall not take the name of the
LORD your God in vain, for the
LORD will not hold *him* guiltless
who takes His name in vain.

12 'Observe the Sabbath day, to keep it
holy, as the LORD your God com-
manded you. 13Six days you shall
labor and do all your work, 14but
the seventh day *is* the Sabbath of
the LORD your God. *In it* you shall
do no work: you, nor your son, nor
your daughter, nor your male ser-
vant, nor your female servant, nor
your ox, nor your donkey, nor any
of your cattle, nor your stranger
who *is* within your gates, that your
male servant and your female ser-
vant may rest as well as you. 15And
remember that you were a slave in
the land of Egypt, and the LORD
your God brought you out from
there by a mighty hand and by an
outstretched arm; therefore the
LORD your God commanded you to
keep the Sabbath day.

16 'Honor your father and your mother, as
the LORD your God has com-
manded you, that your days may
be long, and that it may be well
with you in the land which the
LORD your God is giving you.

17 'You shall not murder.

18 'You shall not commit adultery.

19 'You shall not steal.

20 'You shall not bear false witness against
your neighbor.

5:2–21 As in Exodus, the Ten Commandments function as a summary of the whole law. They introduce the law and provide a big picture of what it is really about. God requires exclusive loyalty to Himself (vv. 2–15), along with a treatment of other people that demonstrates (1) how God values persons, and (2) how those whose needs are being met by God should treat others. This account expands the Exodus version (Ex. 20:1–17), especially concerning idolatry (vv. 8–10) and Sabbath keeping (vv. 12–15). These issues would be much more troublesome when the people were surrounded by pagan neighbors in the Promised Land.

5:11 in vain: Swearing in God's name to do something but then not doing it. This reduces God to the casual and insignificant. The positive side of this commandment is that our talk of God should be characterized by awe and worship.

21 'You shall not covet your neighbor's
wife; and you shall not desire your
neighbor's house, his field, his
male servant, his female servant,
his ox, his donkey, or anything that
is your neighbor's.'

22 "These words the LORD spoke to all
your assembly, in the mountain from the
midst of the fire, the cloud, and the thick
darkness, with a loud voice; and He added
no more. And He wrote them on two
tablets of stone and gave them to me.

The People Afraid of God's Presence

23 "So it was, when you heard the voice
from the midst of the darkness, while the
mountain was burning with fire, that you
came near to me, all the heads of your
tribes and your elders. 24 And you said:
'Surely the LORD our God has shown us
His glory and His greatness, and we have
heard His voice from the midst of the fire.
We have seen this day that God speaks
with man; yet he *still* lives. 25 Now there-
fore, why should we die? For this great fire
will consume us; if we hear the voice of the
LORD our God anymore, then we shall die.
26 For who *is there* of all flesh who has heard
the voice of the living God speaking from
the midst of the fire, as we *have,* and lived?
27 You go near and hear all that the LORD
our God may say, and tell us all that the
LORD our God says to you, and we will
hear and do *it.*'

28 "Then the LORD heard the voice of
your words when you spoke to me, and
the LORD said to me: 'I have heard the voice
of the words of this people which they
have spoken to you. They are right *in* all
that they have spoken. 29 Oh, that they had
such a heart in them that they would fear
Me and always keep all My command-
ments, that it might be well with them and
with their children forever! 30 Go and say to
them, "Return to your tents." 31 But as for
you, stand here by Me, and I will speak to
you all the commandments, the statutes,
and the judgments which you shall teach
them, that they may observe *them* in the
land which I am giving them to possess.'

32 "Therefore you shall be careful to do as
the LORD your God has commanded you;
you shall not turn aside to the right hand
or to the left. 33 You shall walk in all the
ways which the LORD your God has com-
manded you, that you may live and *that it
may be* well with you, and *that* you may
prolong *your* days in the land which you
shall possess.

CHAPTER 6

The Greatest Commandment

"Now this *is* the commandment, *and
these are* the statutes and judgments which
the LORD your God has commanded to
teach you, that you may observe *them* in
the land which you are crossing over to
possess, 2 that you may fear the LORD your
God, to keep all His statutes and His com-
mandments which I command you, you
and your son and your grandson, all the
days of your life, and that your days may

5:29 The Lord knew that the Israelites would not support their words of reverence with actions of faith because their hearts were not truly dedicated to Him. Those who truly love God will demonstrate that love through consistent holy living, not just with mere words.

5:33 that you may live: This is not to say that keeping the law saves. They had been delivered from Egypt and received the promise of Canaan by God's grace alone. The question is: Can people continue to experience the grace of God if they refuse to manifest His character? The answer is no!

6:1–25 God calls for the covenant obligations to be internalized. They are to become an integral part of the people's conversation and behavior, protecting them in times of temptation, and must be passed on to the coming generation. Our role as Christians is to live holy lives as examples to our children and grandchildren and to share with them the truth of the new covenant we have with God through Christ Jesus.

FREE TO LOVE GOD

Charles R. Swindoll

By making us in His image, God gave us capacities not given to other forms of life. Ideally, He made us to know Him, to love Him, and to obey Him. He did not put rings in our noses to pull us around like oxen, nor did He create us with strings permanently attached to our hands and feet like human marionettes to control and manipulate our every move. What pleasure would He have in the love of a puppet or the obedience of a dumb animal?

No, He gave us freedom to make choices. By His grace we are equipped to understand His plan because we have a mind with which we can know Him. We are also free to love and adore Him because we have emotions. He takes pleasure in our affection and devotion. We can obey His instructions, but we are not pawns on a global chessboard. It is in the voluntary spontaneity of our response that He finds divine pleasure. When His people freely respond in worship and praise, obedience and adoration, God is glorified to the maximum. ✦

"He gave us freedom to make choices."

be prolonged. [3]Therefore hear, O Israel, and be careful to observe *it,* that it may be well with you, and that you may multiply greatly as the LORD God of your fathers has promised you—'a land flowing with milk and honey.'[a]

[4]"Hear, O Israel: The LORD our God, the LORD *is* one![a] [5]You shall love the LORD your God with all your heart, with all your soul, and with all your strength.

[6]"And these words which I command you today shall be in your heart. [7]You shall teach them diligently to your children, and shall talk of them when you sit in your house, when you walk by the way, when you lie down, and when you rise up. [8]You shall bind them as a sign on your hand, and they shall be as frontlets between your eyes. [9]You shall write them on the doorposts of your house and on your gates.

Caution Against Disobedience

[10]"So it shall be, when the LORD your God brings you into the land of which He swore to your fathers, to Abraham, Isaac, and Jacob, to give you large and beautiful cities which you did not build, [11]houses full of all good things, which you did not fill, hewn-out wells which you did not dig, vineyards and olive trees which you did not plant—when you have eaten and are full— [12]*then* beware, lest you forget the LORD who brought you out of the land of

6:3 [a]Exodus 3:8 6:4 [a]Or *The LORD is our God, the LORD alone* (that is, the only one)

6:6–9 A number of expressions underline the importance of God's covenant embracing every moment of life. God's law is to be in the **heart**, not on a **doorpost** or a forehead.

Egypt, from the house of bondage. [13]You shall fear the LORD your God and serve Him, and shall take oaths in His name. [14]You shall not go after other gods, the gods of the peoples who *are* all around you [15](for the LORD your God *is* a jealous God among you), lest the anger of the LORD your God be aroused against you and destroy you from the face of the earth.

[16]"You shall not tempt the LORD your God as you tempted *Him* in Mas'sah. [17]You shall diligently keep the commandments of the LORD your God, His testimonies, and His statutes which He has commanded you. [18]And you shall do *what is* right and good in the sight of the LORD, that it may be well with you, and that you may go in and possess the good land of which the LORD swore to your fathers, [19]to cast out all your enemies from before you, as the LORD has spoken.

[20]"When your son asks you in time to come, saying, 'What *is the meaning of* the testimonies, the statutes, and the judgments which the LORD our God has commanded you?' [21]then you shall say to your son: 'We were slaves of Pharaoh in Egypt, and the LORD brought us out of Egypt with a mighty hand; [22]and the LORD showed signs and wonders before our eyes, great and severe, against Egypt, Pharaoh, and all his household. [23]Then He brought us out from there, that He might bring us in, to give us the land of which He swore to our fathers. [24]And the LORD commanded us to observe all these statutes, to fear the LORD our God, for our good always, that He might preserve us alive, as *it is* this day. [25]Then it will be righteousness for us, if we are careful to observe all these commandments before the LORD our God, as He has commanded us.'

CHAPTER 7

A Chosen People

"When the LORD your God brings you into the land which you go to possess, and has cast out many nations before you, the Hit'tītes and the Gir'ga·shītes and the Am'o·rītes and the Cā'naan·ītes and the Per'iz·zītes and the Hī'vītes and the Jeb'ū·sītes, seven nations greater and mightier than you, [2]and when the LORD your God delivers them over to you, you shall conquer them *and* utterly destroy them. You shall make no covenant with them nor show mercy to them. [3]Nor shall you make marriages with them. You shall not give your daughter to their son, nor take their daughter for your son. [4]For they will turn your sons away from following Me, to serve other gods; so the anger of the LORD will be aroused against you and destroy you suddenly. [5]But thus you shall deal with them: you shall destroy their altars, and break down their *sacred* pillars, and cut down their wooden images,[a] and burn their carved images with fire.

[6]"For you *are* a holy people to the LORD your God; the LORD your God has chosen you to be a people for Himself, a special treasure above all the peoples on the face of the earth. [7]The LORD did not set His love on you nor choose you because you were more in number than any other people, for you were the least of all peoples; [8]but because the LORD loves you, and because He would keep the oath which He swore to your fathers, the LORD has brought you out with a mighty hand, and redeemed you from the house of bondage, from the hand of Pharaoh king of Egypt.

7:5 [a]Hebrew *Asherim*, Canaanite deities

6:16 Jesus quoted this verse to Satan when he tempted Him in the wilderness (Matt. 4:7; Luke 4:12).

7:1–6 they will turn your sons away (v. 4): This was the reason for thoroughly destroying the Canaanite people and culture. To become like them would eventually destroy the plan of salvation (see also v. 16).

9"Therefore know that the LORD your
God, He *is* God, the faithful God who
keeps covenant and mercy for a thousand
generations with those who love Him and
keep His commandments; 10and He repays
those who hate Him to their face, to de-
stroy them. He will not be slack with him
who hates Him; He will repay him to his
face. 11Therefore you shall keep the com-
mandment, the statutes, and the judg-
ments which I command you today, to ob-
serve them.

Blessings of Obedience

12"Then it shall come to pass, because
you listen to these judgments, and keep
and do them, that the LORD your God will
keep with you the covenant and the mercy
which He swore to your fathers. 13And He
will love you and bless you and multiply
you; He will also bless the fruit of your
womb and the fruit of your land, your
grain and your new wine and your oil, the
increase of your cattle and the offspring of
your flock, in the land of which He swore
to your fathers to give you. 14You shall be
blessed above all peoples; there shall not
be a male or female barren among you or
among your livestock. 15And the LORD will
take away from you all sickness, and will
afflict you with none of the terrible dis-
eases of Egypt which you have known, but
will lay *them* on all those who hate you.
16Also you shall destroy all the peoples
whom the LORD your God delivers over to
you; your eye shall have no pity on them;
nor shall you serve their gods, for that *will*
be a snare to you.

17"If you should say in your heart,
'These nations are greater than I; how can I
dispossess them?'— 18you shall not be
afraid of them, *but* you shall remember
well what the LORD your God did to
Pharaoh and to all Egypt: 19the great trials
which your eyes saw, the signs and the
wonders, the mighty hand and the out-
stretched arm, by which the LORD your
God brought you out. So shall the LORD
your God do to all the peoples of whom
you are afraid. 20Moreover the LORD your
God will send the hornet among them un-
til those who are left, who hide themselves
from you, are destroyed. 21You shall not be
terrified of them; for the LORD your God,
the great and awesome God, *is* among you.
22And the LORD your God will drive out
those nations before you little by little; you
will be unable to destroy them at once, lest
the beasts of the field become *too* numer-
ous for you. 23But the LORD your God will
deliver them over to you, and will inflict
defeat upon them until they are destroyed.
24And He will deliver their kings into your
hand, and you will destroy their name
from under heaven; no one shall be able to
stand against you until you have de-
stroyed them. 25You shall burn the carved
images of their gods with fire; you shall
not covet the silver or gold *that is* on them,
nor take *it* for yourselves, lest you be
snared by it; for it *is* an abomination to the
LORD your God. 26Nor shall you bring an
abomination into your house, lest you be
doomed to destruction like it. You shall ut-
terly detest it and utterly abhor it, for it *is*
an accursed thing.

CHAPTER 8

Remember the LORD Your God

"Every commandment which I com-
mand you today you must be careful to

7:9 God noted in 5:9 that He may extend the punishment for sins to three or four generations. When children suffered this judgment it was chiefly temporal, usually deprivation and disease following a parent's evil conduct (note that benefits of wise choices were similarly shared). Children are held personally guilty as regards eternal salvation only if they continue in the parent's sin (Ezek. 18:14–17). And while the physical and social consequences of sin may persist as far as our great-grandchildren, God's spiritual rewards for love, obedience, and faithfulness go on for a **thousand generations**.

observe, that you may live and multiply,
and go in and possess the land of which
the LORD swore to your fathers. 2And you
shall remember that the LORD your God
led you all the way these forty years in the
wilderness, to humble you *and* test you, to
know what *was* in your heart, whether you
would keep His commandments or not.
3So He humbled you, allowed you to
hunger, and fed you with manna which
you did not know nor did your fathers
know, that He might make you know that
man shall not live by bread alone; but
man lives by every *word* that proceeds
from the mouth of the LORD. 4Your gar-
ments did not wear out on you, nor did
your foot swell these forty years. 5You
should know in your heart that as a man
chastens his son, *so* the LORD your God
chastens you.

6"Therefore you shall keep the com-
mandments of the LORD your God, to walk
in His ways and to fear Him. 7For the LORD
your God is bringing you into a good land,
a land of brooks of water, of fountains and
springs, that flow out of valleys and hills;
8a land of wheat and barley, of vines and
fig trees and pomegranates, a land of olive
oil and honey; 9a land in which you will
eat bread without scarcity, in which you
will lack nothing; a land whose stones *are*
iron and out of whose hills you can dig
copper. 10When you have eaten and are
full, then you shall bless the LORD your
God for the good land which He has given
you.

11"Beware that you do not forget the
LORD your God by not keeping His com-
mandments, His judgments, and His
statutes which I command you today,
12lest—*when* you have eaten and are full,
and have built beautiful houses and dwell
in them; 13and *when* your herds and your
flocks multiply, and your silver and your
gold are multiplied, and all that you have
is multiplied; 14when your heart is lifted
up, and you forget the LORD your God who
brought you out of the land of Egypt, from
the house of bondage; 15who led you
through that great and terrible wilderness,
in which were fiery serpents and scorpions
and thirsty land where there was no water;
who brought water for you out of the flinty
rock; 16who fed you in the wilderness with
manna, which your fathers did not know,
that He might humble you and that He
might test you, to do you good in the
end— 17then you say in your heart, 'My
power and the might of my hand have
gained me this wealth.'

18"And you shall remember the LORD
your God, for *it is* He who gives you power
to get wealth, that He may establish His
covenant which He swore to your fathers,
as *it is* this day. 19Then it shall be, if you by
any means forget the LORD your God, and
follow other gods, and serve them and
worship them, I testify against you this
day that you shall surely perish. 20As the
nations which the LORD destroys before
you, so you shall perish, because you
would not be obedient to the voice of the
LORD your God.

CHAPTER 9

Israel's Rebellions Reviewed

"Hear, O Israel: You *are* to cross over the
Jordan today, and go in to dispossess na-
tions greater and mightier than yourself,
cities great and fortified up to heaven, 2a
people great and tall, the descendants of

8:11–20 These verses express the dangers that accompany success. While wealth and prosperity are not in themselves a sin, we must be careful not to let success go to our heads. All we have and are is solely by the grace of God, not by anything we have done of our own power.

8:14 forget: This word, as well as "remember," is not referring merely to mental activity. To forget God is to act as if He did not exist; there is no separation of intellect and behavior. Knowledge or memory that does not change behavior is worthless.

the An′a·kim, whom you know, and *of whom* you heard *it said,* 'Who can stand before the descendants of Ā′nak?' 3Therefore understand today that the LORD your God *is* He who goes over before you *as* a consuming fire. He will destroy them and bring them down before you; so you shall drive them out and destroy them quickly, as the LORD has said to you.

4"Do not think in your heart, after the LORD your God has cast them out before you, saying, 'Because of my righteousness the LORD has brought me in to possess this land'; but *it is* because of the wickedness of these nations *that* the LORD is driving them out from before you. 5*It is* not because of your righteousness or the uprightness of your heart *that* you go in to possess their land, but because of the wickedness of these nations *that* the LORD your God drives them out from before you, and that He may fulfill the word which the LORD swore to your fathers, to Abraham, Isaac, and Jacob. 6Therefore understand that the LORD your God is not giving you this good land to possess because of your righteousness, for you *are* a stiff-necked people.

7"Remember! Do not forget how you provoked the LORD your God to wrath in the wilderness. From the day that you departed from the land of Egypt until you came to this place, you have been rebellious against the LORD. 8Also in Hō′reb you provoked the LORD to wrath, so that the LORD was angry *enough* with you to have destroyed you. 9When I went up into the mountain to receive the tablets of stone, the tablets of the covenant which the LORD made with you, then I stayed on the mountain forty days and forty nights. I neither ate bread nor drank water. 10Then the LORD delivered to me two tablets of stone written with the finger of God, and on them *were* all the words which the LORD had spoken to you on the mountain from the midst of the fire in the day of the assembly. 11And it came to pass, at the end of forty days and forty nights, *that* the LORD gave me the two tablets of stone, the tablets of the covenant.

12"Then the LORD said to me, 'Arise, go down quickly from here, for your people whom you brought out of Egypt have acted corruptly; they have quickly turned aside from the way which I commanded them; they have made themselves a molded image.'

13"Furthermore the LORD spoke to me, saying, 'I have seen this people, and indeed they are a stiff-necked people. 14Let Me alone, that I may destroy them and blot out their name from under heaven; and I will make of you a nation mightier and greater than they.'

15"So I turned and came down from the mountain, and the mountain burned with fire; and the two tablets of the covenant *were* in my two hands. 16And I looked, and behold, you had sinned against the LORD your God—had made for yourselves a molded calf! You had turned aside quickly from the way which the LORD had commanded you. 17Then I took the two tablets and threw them out of my two hands and broke them before your eyes. 18And I fell down before the LORD, as at the first, forty days and forty nights; I neither ate bread nor drank water, because of all your sin which you committed in doing wickedly in the sight of the LORD, to provoke Him to anger. 19For I was afraid of the anger and hot displeasure with which the LORD was angry with you, to destroy you. But the LORD listened to me at that time also. 20And the LORD was very angry with Aaron *and* would have destroyed him; so I prayed for Aaron also at the same time. 21Then I took your sin, the calf which you had made, and burned it with fire and crushed it *and* ground *it* very small, until it was as fine as dust; and I threw its dust into the brook that descended from the mountain.

22"Also at Tab′e·rah and Mas′sah and Kib′roth Hat·tā′a·vah you provoked the LORD to wrath. 23Likewise, when the LORD sent you from Kā′desh Bar·nē′a, saying, 'Go up and possess the land which I have given you,' then you rebelled against the

commandment of the LORD your God, and
you did not believe Him nor obey His
voice. [24]You have been rebellious against
the LORD from the day that I knew you.
[25]"Thus I prostrated myself before the
LORD; forty days and forty nights I kept
prostrating myself, because the LORD had
said He would destroy you. [26]Therefore I
prayed to the LORD, and said: 'O Lord GOD,
do not destroy Your people and Your in-
heritance whom You have redeemed
through Your greatness, whom You have
brought out of Egypt with a mighty hand.
[27]Remember Your servants, Abraham,
Isaac, and Jacob; do not look on the stub-
bornness of this people, or on their
wickedness or their sin, [28]lest the land from
which You brought us should say, "Be-
cause the LORD was not able to bring them
to the land which He promised them, and
because He hated them, He has brought
them out to kill them in the wilderness."
[29]Yet they *are* Your people and Your inheri-
tance, whom You brought out by Your
mighty power and by Your outstretched
arm.'

CHAPTER 10

The Second Pair of Tablets

"At that time the LORD said to me, 'Hew
for yourself two tablets of stone like the
first, and come up to Me on the mountain
and make yourself an ark of wood. [2]And I
will write on the tablets the words that
were on the first tablets, which you broke;
and you shall put them in the ark.'
[3]"So I made an ark of acacia wood,
hewed two tablets of stone like the first,
and went up the mountain, having the two
tablets in my hand. [4]And He wrote on the
tablets according to the first writing, the
Ten Commandments, which the LORD had
spoken to you in the mountain from the
midst of the fire in the day of the assembly;
and the LORD gave them to me. [5]Then I
turned and came down from the moun-
tain, and put the tablets in the ark which I
had made; and there they are, just as the
LORD commanded me."
[6](Now the children of Israel journeyed
from the wells of Ben'ē Jā'a·kan to
Mō·sē'rah, where Aaron died, and where
he was buried; and El·ē·ā'zar his son min-
istered as priest in his stead. [7]From there
they journeyed to Gud'gō·dah, and from
Gud'gō·dah to Jot'ba·thah, a land of rivers
of water. [8]At that time the LORD separated
the tribe of Levi to bear the ark of the
covenant of the LORD, to stand before the
LORD to minister to Him and to bless in His
name, to this day. [9]Therefore Levi has no
portion nor inheritance with his brethren;
the LORD *is* his inheritance, just as the LORD
your God promised him.)
[10]"As at the first time, I stayed in the
mountain forty days and forty nights; the
LORD also heard me at that time, *and*
the LORD chose not to destroy you. [11]Then
the LORD said to me, 'Arise, begin *your*
journey before the people, that they may
go in and possess the land which I swore to
their fathers to give them.'

The Essence of the Law

[12]"And now, Israel, what does the LORD
your God require of you, but to fear the
LORD your God, to walk in all His ways

10:1–11 God's mercy in response to Moses' plea is seen in three ways: (1) the covenant was reinstituted, as symbolized by the giving of the second set of tablets; (2) the covenant was placed in the ark upon which the blood of atonement could be sprinkled (Lev. 16:14); and (3) the Levites were appointed to be intermediaries between the people and God.

10:12—11:21 In view of all the foregoing blessings from God, loving obedience is the only appropriate response. To drive home this logical conclusion Moses says five times, "Therefore."

10:12, 13 See Mic. 6:8; Matt. 22:37. God's requirements are still the same today, and all of His commandments are for our good.

and to love Him, to serve the LORD your God with all your heart and with all your soul, [13]*and* to keep the commandments of the LORD and His statutes which I command you today for your good? [14]Indeed heaven and the highest heavens belong to the LORD your God, *also* the earth with all that *is* in it. [15]The LORD delighted only in your fathers, to love them; and He chose their descendants after them, you above all peoples, as *it is* this day. [16]Therefore circumcise the foreskin of your heart, and be stiff-necked no longer. [17]For the LORD your God *is* God of gods and Lord of lords, the great God, mighty and awesome, who shows no partiality nor takes a bribe. [18]He administers justice for the fatherless and the widow, and loves the stranger, giving him food and clothing. [19]Therefore love the stranger, for you were strangers in the land of Egypt. [20]You shall fear the LORD your God; you shall serve Him, and to Him you shall hold fast, and take oaths in His name. [21]He *is* your praise, and He *is* your God, who has done for you these great and awesome things which your eyes have seen. [22]Your fathers went down to Egypt with seventy persons, and now the LORD your God has made you as the stars of heaven in multitude.

CHAPTER 11

Love and Obedience Rewarded

"Therefore you shall love the LORD your God, and keep His charge, His statutes, His judgments, and His commandments always. [2]Know today that *I do* not *speak* with your children, who have not known and who have not seen the chastening of the LORD your God, His greatness and His mighty hand and His outstretched arm— [3]His signs and His acts which He did in the midst of Egypt, to Pharaoh king of Egypt, and to all his land; [4]what He did to the army of Egypt, to their horses and their chariots: how He made the waters of the Red Sea overflow them as they pursued you, and *how* the LORD has destroyed them to this day; [5]what He did for you in the wilderness until you came to this place; [6]and what He did to Dā′than and A·bī′ram the sons of E·lī′ab, the son of Reuben: how the earth opened its mouth and swallowed them up, their households, their tents, and all the substance that *was* in their possession, in the midst of all Israel— [7]but your eyes have seen every great act of the LORD which He did.

[8]"Therefore you shall keep every commandment which I command you today, that you may be strong, and go in and possess the land which you cross over to possess, [9]and that you may prolong *your* days in the land which the LORD swore to give your fathers, to them and their descendants, 'a land flowing with milk and honey.'[a] [10]For the land which you go to possess *is* not like the land of Egypt from which you have come, where you sowed your seed and watered *it* by foot, as a vegetable garden; [11]but the land which you cross over to possess *is* a land of hills and valleys, which drinks water from the rain of heaven, [12]a land for which the LORD your God cares; the eyes of the LORD your God *are* always on it, from the beginning of the year to the very end of the year.

11:9 [a]Exodus 3:8

10:16 circumcise . . . your heart: circumcision was a physical reminder to the Israelites that they were God's people. Here the meaning of circumcision is deepened to include the heart. Obedience to God is not merely a matter of external conformity but an expression of the deepest attitudes, feelings, and purposes. Ultimately, the bringing of these into submission to God is made possible in the grace provided in Christ. Paul reflects this understanding of circumcision in Rom. 2:28, 29.

11:1 Over and over we see that true love for God is demonstrated by obedience to His commands. True faith will always be accompanied by works.

13'And it shall be that if you earnestly obey My commandments which I command you today, to love the LORD your God and serve Him with all your heart and with all your soul, 14then I[a] will give *you* the rain for your land in its season, the early rain and the latter rain, that you may gather in your grain, your new wine, and your oil. 15And I will send grass in your fields for your livestock, that you may eat and be filled.' 16Take heed to yourselves, lest your heart be deceived, and you turn aside and serve other gods and worship them, 17lest the LORD's anger be aroused against you, and He shut up the heavens so that there be no rain, and the land yield no produce, and you perish quickly from the good land which the LORD is giving you.

18"Therefore you shall lay up these words of mine in your heart and in your soul, and bind them as a sign on your hand, and they shall be as frontlets between your eyes. 19You shall teach them to your children, speaking of them when you sit in your house, when you walk by the way, when you lie down, and when you rise up. 20And you shall write them on the doorposts of your house and on your gates, 21that your days and the days of your children may be multiplied in the land of which the LORD swore to your fathers to give them, like the days of the heavens above the earth.

22"For if you carefully keep all these commandments which I command you to do—to love the LORD your God, to walk in all His ways, and to hold fast to Him—23then the LORD will drive out all these nations from before you, and you will dispossess greater and mightier nations than yourselves. 24Every place on which the sole of your foot treads shall be yours: from the wilderness and Lebanon, from the river, the River Eū·phrā'tēs, even to the Western Sea,[a] shall be your territory. 25No man shall be able to stand against you; the LORD your God will put the dread of you and the fear of you upon all the land where you tread, just as He has said to you.

26"Behold, I set before you today a blessing and a curse: 27the blessing, if you obey the commandments of the LORD your God which I command you today; 28and the curse, if you do not obey the commandments of the LORD your God, but turn aside from the way which I command you today, to go after other gods which you have not known. 29Now it shall be, when the LORD your God has brought you into the land which you go to possess, that you shall put the blessing on Mount Ger'i·zim and the curse on Mount Ē'bal. 30*Are* they not on the other side of the Jordan, toward the setting sun, in the land of the Cā'naan·ītes who dwell in the plain opposite Gil'gal, beside the terebinth trees of Mō'reh? 31For you will cross over the Jordan and go in to possess the land which the LORD your God is giving you, and you will possess it and dwell in it. 32And you shall be careful to observe all the statutes and judgments which I set before you today.

CHAPTER 12

A Prescribed Place of Worship

"These *are* the statutes and judgments which you shall be careful to observe in the land which the LORD God of your fathers is giving you to possess, all the days that you live on the earth. 2You shall utterly destroy all the places where the nations which you shall dispossess served their gods, on the high mountains and on the hills and under every green tree. 3And you shall destroy their altars, break their *sacred* pillars, and burn their wooden images with fire; you shall cut down the carved images of their gods and destroy their names from that place. 4You shall not worship the LORD your God *with* such *things*.

11:14 [a]Following Masoretic Text and Targum; Samaritan Pentateuch, Septuagint, and Vulgate read *He*.
11:24 [a]That is, the Mediterranean

5"But you shall seek the place where the
LORD your God chooses, out of all your
tribes, to put His name for His dwelling
place; and there you shall go. 6There you
shall take your burnt offerings, your sacri-
fices, your tithes, the heave offerings of
your hand, your vowed offerings, your
freewill offerings, and the firstborn of your
herds and flocks. 7And there you shall eat
before the LORD your God, and you shall
rejoice in all to which you have put your
hand, you and your households, in which
the LORD your God has blessed you.

8"You shall not at all do as we are doing
here today—every man doing whatever *is*
right in his own eyes— 9for as yet you have
not come to the rest and the inheritance
which the LORD your God is giving you.
10But *when* you cross over the Jordan and
dwell in the land which the LORD your God
is giving you to inherit, and He gives you
rest from all your enemies round about, so
that you dwell in safety, 11then there will be
the place where the LORD your God
chooses to make His name abide. There
you shall bring all that I command you:
your burnt offerings, your sacrifices, your
tithes, the heave offerings of your hand,
and all your choice offerings which you
vow to the LORD. 12And you shall rejoice
before the LORD your God, you and your
sons and your daughters, your male and
female servants, and the Lē′vīte who *is*
within your gates, since he has no portion
nor inheritance with you. 13Take heed to
yourself that you do not offer your burnt
offerings in every place that you see; 14but
in the place which the LORD chooses, in one
of your tribes, there you shall offer your
burnt offerings, and there you shall do all
that I command you.

15"However, you may slaughter and eat
meat within all your gates, whatever your
heart desires, according to the blessing of
the LORD your God which He has given
you; the unclean and the clean may eat of
it, of the gazelle and the deer alike. 16Only
you shall not eat the blood; you shall pour
it on the earth like water. 17You may not eat
within your gates the tithe of your grain or
your new wine or your oil, of the firstborn
of your herd or your flock, of any of your
offerings which you vow, of your freewill
offerings, or of the heave offering of your
hand. 18But you must eat them before the
LORD your God in the place which the
LORD your God chooses, you and your son
and your daughter, your male servant and
your female servant, and the Lē′vīte who
is within your gates; and you shall rejoice
before the LORD your God in all to which
you put your hands. 19Take heed to your-
self that you do not forsake the Lē′vīte as
long as you live in your land.

20"When the LORD your God enlarges
your border as He has promised you, and
you say, 'Let me eat meat,' because you
long to eat meat, you may eat as much
meat as your heart desires. 21If the place
where the LORD your God chooses to put

12:5–7 seek the place: The central sanctuary. If the people were allowed to build shrines to God everywhere, they would soon forget His Oneness. In fact, that is exactly what happened later (see 1 Kin. 12:28–31). Initially, and until Samuel's day, the tabernacle was at Shiloh, about 20 miles (32 km) north of Jerusalem in the territory of Ephraim. God's final choice was Jerusalem.

12:8 as we are doing: During the years of wandering and conquest the Israelites were not able to observe all the details of their appointed worship activities. We are not to base our behavior on what those around us are doing or even on what we think is right; rather, our conduct should be determined by what God has told us to do.

12:21–25 Evidently during the wilderness years all slaughtering with one exception (Num. 19:2–4) was done in the tabernacle precincts. In Canaan that would no longer be possible, so permission to butcher elsewhere was given, so long as the blood was not eaten. Among primitive peoples, the blood of a particularly strong or swift animal might be drunk in hopes of getting its power. God forbade that, because it was a use of magic and because the blood was sacred to Him.

His name is too far from you, then you may slaughter from your herd and from your flock which the LORD has given you, just as I have commanded you, and you may eat within your gates as much as your heart desires. 22Just as the gazelle and the deer are eaten, so you may eat them; the unclean and the clean alike may eat them. 23Only be sure that you do not eat the blood, for the blood *is* the life; you may not eat the life with the meat. 24You shall not eat it; you shall pour it on the earth like water. 25You shall not eat it, that it may go well with you and your children after you, when you do *what is* right in the sight of the LORD. 26Only the holy things which you have, and your vowed offerings, you shall take and go to the place which the LORD chooses. 27And you shall offer your burnt offerings, the meat and the blood, on the altar of the LORD your God; and the blood of your sacrifices shall be poured out on the altar of the LORD your God, and you shall eat the meat. 28Observe and obey all these words which I command you, that it may go well with you and your children after you forever, when you do *what is* good and right in the sight of the LORD your God.

Beware of False Gods

29"When the LORD your God cuts off from before you the nations which you go to dispossess, and you displace them and dwell in their land, 30take heed to yourself that you are not ensnared to follow them, after they are destroyed from before you, and that you do not inquire after their gods, saying, 'How did these nations serve their gods? I also will do likewise.' 31You shall not worship the LORD your God in that way; for every abomination to the LORD which He hates they have done to their gods; for they burn even their sons and daughters in the fire to their gods.

32"Whatever I command you, be careful to observe it; you shall not add to it nor take away from it.

CHAPTER 13

Punishment of Apostates

"If there arises among you a prophet or a dreamer of dreams, and he gives you a sign or a wonder, 2and the sign or the wonder comes to pass, of which he spoke to you, saying, 'Let us go after other gods'—which you have not known—'and let us serve them,' 3you shall not listen to the words of that prophet or that dreamer of dreams, for the LORD your God is testing you to know whether you love the LORD your God with all your heart and with all your soul. 4You shall walk after the LORD your God and fear Him, and keep His commandments and obey His voice; you shall serve Him and hold fast to Him. 5But that prophet or that dreamer of dreams shall be put to death, because he has spoken in order to turn *you* away from the LORD your God, who brought you out of the land of Egypt and redeemed you from the house of bondage, to entice you from the way in which the LORD your God commanded you to walk. So you shall put away the evil from your midst.

6"If your brother, the son of your mother, your son or your daughter, the wife of your bosom, or your friend who is as your own soul, secretly entices you, say-

---

12:30, 31 The Lord had given the Israelites—and has given to us through the Bible—clear instructions for serving Him. We have no need to look elsewhere for direction.

13:1–5 True prophecy was usually indicated by whether or not the prophesied event actually came to pass (see 18:21, 22 and note). However, if a **prophet** whose prediction comes true teaches false religion, he is still a false prophet. In the same way apparent blessing from God upon an action does not prove the action was right. Wrong is wrong regardless of the outcome. All teaching today should be tested against Scripture; anything that contradicts the Word of God is false and should be put away.

> ***I pray that my children and grandchildren will walk after You, the Lord their God, and fear You, and keep Your commandments and obey Your voice, and that they shall serve You and hold fast to You.***
>
> *adapted from* Deuteronomy 13:4

ing, 'Let us go and serve other gods,' which you have not known, neither you nor your fathers, 7of the gods of the people which *are* all around you, near to you or far off from you, from *one* end of the earth to the *other* end of the earth, 8you shall not consent to him or listen to him, nor shall your eye pity him, nor shall you spare him or conceal him; 9but you shall surely kill him; your hand shall be first against him to put him to death, and afterward the hand of all the people. 10And you shall stone him with stones until he dies, because he sought to entice you away from the LORD your God, who brought you out of the land of Egypt, from the house of bondage. 11So all Israel shall hear and fear, and not again do such wickedness as this among you.

12"If you hear someone in one of your cities, which the LORD your God gives you to dwell in, saying, 13'Corrupt men have gone out from among you and enticed the inhabitants of their city, saying, "Let us go and serve other gods" '—which you have not known— 14then you shall inquire, search out, and ask diligently. And *if it is* indeed true *and* certain *that* such an abomination was committed among you, 15you shall surely strike the inhabitants of that city with the edge of the sword, utterly destroying it, all that is in it and its livestock—with the edge of the sword. 16And you shall gather all its plunder into the middle of the street, and completely burn with fire the city and all its plunder, for the LORD your God. It shall be a heap forever; it shall not be built again. 17So none of the accursed things shall remain in your hand, that the LORD may turn from the fierceness of His anger and show you mercy, have compassion on you and multiply you, just as He swore to your fathers, 18because you have listened to the voice of the LORD your God, to keep all His commandments which I command you today, to do *what is* right in the eyes of the LORD your God.

CHAPTER 14

Improper Mourning

"You *are* the children of the LORD your God; you shall not cut yourselves nor shave the front of your head for the dead. 2For you *are* a holy people to the LORD your God, and the LORD has chosen you to be a people for Himself, a special treasure above all the peoples who *are* on the face of the earth.

Clean and Unclean Meat

3"You shall not eat any detestable thing. 4These *are* the animals which you may eat: the ox, the sheep, the goat, 5the deer, the gazelle, the roe deer, the wild goat, the mountain goat,[a] the antelope, and the mountain sheep. 6And you may eat every animal with cloven hooves, having the hoof split into two parts, *and that* chews the cud, among the animals. 7Nevertheless, of those that chew the cud or have cloven hooves, you shall not eat, *such as* these: the camel, the hare, and the rock hyrax; for they chew the cud but do not have cloven hooves; they *are* unclean for you. 8Also the swine is unclean for you, because it has cloven hooves, yet *does* not *chew* the cud; you shall not eat their flesh or touch their dead carcasses.

9"These you may eat of all that *are* in the waters: you may eat all that have fins and scales. 10And whatever does not have fins

14:5 [a]Or *addax*

and scales you shall not eat; it *is* unclean for you.

11"All clean birds you may eat. 12But these you shall not eat: the eagle, the vulture, the buzzard, 13the red kite, the falcon, and the kite after their kinds; 14every raven after its kind; 15the ostrich, the short-eared owl, the sea gull, and the hawk after their kinds; 16the little owl, the screech owl, the white owl, 17the jackdaw, the carrion vulture, the fisher owl, 18the stork, the heron after its kind, and the hoopoe and the bat.

19"Also every creeping thing that flies is unclean for you; they shall not be eaten.

20"You may eat all clean birds.

21"You shall not eat anything that dies *of itself;* you may give it to the alien who *is* within your gates, that he may eat it, or you may sell it to a foreigner; for you *are* a holy people to the LORD your God.

"You shall not boil a young goat in its mother's milk.

Tithing Principles

22"You shall truly tithe all the increase of your grain that the field produces year by year. 23And you shall eat before the LORD your God, in the place where He chooses to make His name abide, the tithe of your grain and your new wine and your oil, of the firstborn of your herds and your flocks, that you may learn to fear the LORD your God always. 24But if the journey is too long for you, so that you are not able to carry *the tithe, or* if the place where the LORD your God chooses to put His name is too far from you, when the LORD your God has blessed you, 25then you shall exchange *it* for money, take the money in your hand, and go to the place which the LORD your God chooses. 26And you shall spend that money for whatever your heart desires: for oxen or sheep, for wine or similar drink, for whatever your heart desires; you shall eat there before the LORD your God, and you shall rejoice, you and your household. 27You shall not forsake the Lē'vīte who *is* within your gates, for he has no part nor inheritance with you.

28"At the end of *every* third year you shall bring out the tithe of your produce of that year and store *it* up within your gates. 29And the Lē'vīte, because he has no portion nor inheritance with you, and the stranger and the fatherless and the widow who *are* within your gates, may come and eat and be satisfied, that the LORD your God may bless you in all the work of your hand which you do.

CHAPTER 15

Debts Canceled Every Seven Years

"At the end of *every* seven years you shall grant a release *of debts.* 2And this *is* the form of the release: Every creditor who has lent *anything* to his neighbor shall release *it;* he shall not require *it* of his neighbor or his brother, because it is called the LORD's release. 3Of a foreigner you may require *it;* but you shall give up your claim to what is owed by your brother, 4except when there may be no poor among you; for the LORD will greatly bless you in the land which the LORD your God is giving you to possess *as* an inheritance— 5only if you carefully obey the voice of the LORD your God, to observe with care all these commandments which I command you today. 6For the LORD your God will bless you just as He promised you; you shall lend to many nations, but you shall not borrow; you shall reign over many nations, but they shall not reign over you.

Generosity to the Poor

7"If there is among you a poor man of your brethren, within any of the gates in your land which the LORD your God is giving you, you shall not harden your heart

14:22 The **tithe** serves as a reminder that prosperity is a gift of God, who is the Creator and Owner of all.

nor shut your hand from your poor
brother, 8but you shall open your hand
wide to him and willingly lend him suffi-
cient for his need, whatever he needs. 9Be-
ware lest there be a wicked thought in your
heart, saying, 'The seventh year, the year of
release, is at hand,' and your eye be evil
against your poor brother and you give
him nothing, and he cry out to the LORD
against you, and it become sin among you.
10You shall surely give to him, and your
heart should not be grieved when you give
to him, because for this thing the LORD
your God will bless you in all your works
and in all to which you put your hand.
11For the poor will never cease from the
land; therefore I command you, saying,
'You shall open your hand wide to your
brother, to your poor and your needy, in
your land.'

The Law Concerning Bondservants

12"If your brother, a Hebrew man, or a
Hebrew woman, is sold to you and serves
you six years, then in the seventh year you
shall let him go free from you. 13And when
you send him away free from you, you
shall not let him go away empty-handed;
14you shall supply him liberally from your
flock, from your threshing floor, and from
your winepress. *From what* the LORD has
blessed you with, you shall give to him.
15You shall remember that you were a slave
in the land of Egypt, and the LORD your
God redeemed you; therefore I command
you this thing today. 16And if it happens
that he says to you, 'I will not go away
from you,' because he loves you and your
house, since he prospers with you, 17then
you shall take an awl and thrust *it* through
his ear to the door, and he shall be your
servant forever. Also to your female ser-
vant you shall do likewise. 18It shall not
seem hard to you when you send him
away free from you; for he has been worth
a double hired servant in serving you six
years. Then the LORD your God will bless
you in all that you do.

The Law Concerning Firstborn Animals

19"All the firstborn males that come
from your herd and your flock you shall
sanctify to the LORD your God; you shall
do no work with the firstborn of your herd,
nor shear the firstborn of your flock. 20You
and your household shall eat *it* before the
LORD your God year by year in the place
which the LORD chooses. 21But if there is a
defect in it, *if it is* lame or blind *or has* any
serious defect, you shall not sacrifice it to
the LORD your God. 22You may eat it within
your gates; the unclean and the clean *per-*
son alike *may eat it,* as *if it were* a gazelle or
a deer. 23Only you shall not eat its blood;
you shall pour it on the ground like water.

CHAPTER 16

The Passover Reviewed

"Observe the month of Ā'bib, and keep
the Passover to the LORD your God, for in
the month of Ā'bib the LORD your God
brought you out of Egypt by night. 2There-
fore you shall sacrifice the Passover to the
LORD your God, from the flock and the
herd, in the place where the LORD chooses
to put His name. 3You shall eat no leavened
bread with it; seven days you shall eat un-
leavened bread with it, *that is,* the bread of
affliction (for you came out of the land of
Egypt in haste), that you may remember
the day in which you came out of the land
of Egypt all the days of your life. 4And no
leaven shall be seen among you in all your
territory for seven days, nor shall *any* of
the meat which you sacrifice the first day
at twilight remain overnight until morn-
ing.

15:12–15 The indentured servant was not merely to be freed in the seventh year, but to be sent out with gifts. Justice must be accompanied with mercy, remembering the mercy received from God.

5"You may not sacrifice the Passover within any of your gates which the LORD your God gives you; 6but at the place where the LORD your God chooses to make His name abide, there you shall sacrifice the Passover at twilight, at the going down of the sun, at the time you came out of Egypt. 7And you shall roast and eat *it* in the place which the LORD your God chooses, and in the morning you shall turn and go to your tents. 8Six days you shall eat unleavened bread, and on the seventh day there *shall be* a sacred assembly to the LORD your God. You shall do no work *on it.*

The Feast of Weeks Reviewed

9"You shall count seven weeks for yourself; begin to count the seven weeks from *the time* you begin *to put* the sickle to the grain. 10Then you shall keep the Feast of Weeks to the LORD your God with the tribute of a freewill offering from your hand, which you shall give as the LORD your God blesses you. 11You shall rejoice before the LORD your God, you and your son and your daughter, your male servant and your female servant, the Lē′vīte who *is* within your gates, the stranger and the fatherless and the widow who *are* among you, at the place where the LORD your God chooses to make His name abide. 12And you shall remember that you were a slave in Egypt, and you shall be careful to observe these statutes.

The Feast of Tabernacles Reviewed

13"You shall observe the Feast of Tabernacles seven days, when you have gathered from your threshing floor and from your winepress. 14And you shall rejoice in your feast, you and your son and your daughter, your male servant and your female servant and the Lē′vīte, the stranger and the fatherless and the widow, who *are* within your gates. 15Seven days you shall keep a sacred feast to the LORD your God in the place which the LORD chooses, because the LORD your God will bless you in all your produce and in all the work of your hands, so that you surely rejoice.

16"Three times a year all your males shall appear before the LORD your God in the place which He chooses: at the Feast of Unleavened Bread, at the Feast of Weeks, and at the Feast of Tabernacles; and they shall not appear before the LORD emptyhanded. 17Every man *shall give* as he is able, according to the blessing of the LORD your God which He has given you.

Justice Must Be Administered

18"You shall appoint judges and officers in all your gates, which the LORD your God gives you, according to your tribes, and they shall judge the people with just judgment. 19You shall not pervert justice; you shall not show partiality, nor take a bribe, for a bribe blinds the eyes of the wise and twists the words of the righteous. 20You shall follow what is altogether just, that you may live and inherit the land which the LORD your God is giving you.

21"You shall not plant for yourself any tree, as a wooden image, near the altar which you build for yourself to the LORD your God. 22You shall not set up a sacred pillar, which the LORD your God hates.

CHAPTER 17

"You shall not sacrifice to the LORD your God a bull or sheep which has any blemish *or* defect, for that *is* an abomination to the LORD your God.

16:16 Three times: This practice of annual pilgrimage feasts would keep pulling the nation back to the fountainhead of truth and orthodoxy, and away from the blandishments of paganism. Regular worship with God's people is essential to robust faith.

17:1 Not only is paganizing God's worship (16:21, 22) distasteful to Him, so also is trivializing it by giving less than our best. How we worship tells much about what we really think of God.

2“If there is found among you, within
any of your gates which the LORD your
God gives you, a man or a woman who has
been wicked in the sight of the LORD your
God, in transgressing His covenant, 3who
has gone and served other gods and wor-
shiped them, either the sun or moon or any
of the host of heaven, which I have not
commanded, 4and it is told you, and you
hear *of it,* then you shall inquire diligently.
And if *it is* indeed true *and* certain that
such an abomination has been committed
in Israel, 5then you shall bring out to your
gates that man or woman who has com-
mitted that wicked thing, and shall stone
to death that man or woman with stones.
6Whoever is deserving of death shall be
put to death on the testimony of two or
three witnesses; he shall not be put to
death on the testimony of one witness.
7The hands of the witnesses shall be the
first against him to put him to death, and
afterward the hands of all the people. So
you shall put away the evil from among
you.

8“If a matter arises which is too hard for
you to judge, between degrees of guilt for
bloodshed, between one judgment or an-
other, or between one punishment or an-
other, matters of controversy within your
gates, then you shall arise and go up to the
place which the LORD your God chooses.
9And you shall come to the priests, the
Lē′vītes, and to the judge *there* in those
days, and inquire *of them;* they shall pro-
nounce upon you the sentence of judg-
ment. 10You shall do according to the sen-
tence which they pronounce upon you in
that place which the LORD chooses. And
you shall be careful to do according to all
that they order you. 11According to the sen-
tence of the law in which they instruct you,
according to the judgment which they tell
you, you shall do; you shall not turn aside
to the right hand or *to* the left from the sen-
tence which they pronounce upon you.
12Now the man who acts presumptuously
and will not heed the priest who stands to
minister there before the LORD your God,
or the judge, that man shall die. So you
shall put away the evil from Israel. 13And
all the people shall hear and fear, and no
longer act presumptuously.

Principles Governing Kings

14“When you come to the land which the
LORD your God is giving you, and possess
it and dwell in it, and say, ‘I will set a king
over me like all the nations that *are* around
me,’ 15you shall surely set a king over you
whom the LORD your God chooses; *one*
from among your brethren you shall set as
king over you; you may not set a foreigner
over you, who *is* not your brother. 16But he
shall not multiply horses for himself, nor
cause the people to return to Egypt to mul-
tiply horses, for the LORD has said to you,
‘You shall not return that way again.’
17Neither shall he multiply wives for him-
self, lest his heart turn away; nor shall he
greatly multiply silver and gold for him-
self.

18“Also it shall be, when he sits on the
throne of his kingdom, that he shall write
for himself a copy of this law in a book,
from *the one* before the priests, the Lē′vītes.
19And it shall be with him, and he shall
read it all the days of his life, that he may
learn to fear the LORD his God and be care-
ful to observe all the words of this law and
these statutes, 20that his heart may not be
lifted above his brethren, that he may not
turn aside from the commandment *to* the
right hand or *to* the left, and that he may
prolong *his* days in his kingdom, he and
his children in the midst of Israel.

17:8–11 The principle of subjection to authority is repeated throughout Scripture and is vital to maintain order and unity.

17:16, 17 Solomon and other rulers violated every instruction given here, bringing judgment and destruction on the kingdom of Israel.

CHAPTER 18

The Portion of the Priests and Levites

"The priests, the Lē'vītes—all the tribe
of Levi—shall have no part nor inheritance
with Israel; they shall eat the offerings of
the LORD made by fire, and His portion.
2Therefore they shall have no inheritance
among their brethren; the LORD is their in-
heritance, as He said to them.

3"And this shall be the priest's due from
the people, from those who offer a sacri-
fice, whether *it is* bull or sheep: they shall
give to the priest the shoulder, the cheeks,
and the stomach. 4The firstfruits of your
grain and your new wine and your oil, and
the first of the fleece of your sheep, you
shall give him. 5For the LORD your God has
chosen him out of all your tribes to stand to
minister in the name of the LORD, him and
his sons forever.

6"So if a Lē'vīte comes from any of your
gates, from where he dwells among all Is-
rael, and comes with all the desire of his
mind to the place which the LORD chooses,
7then he may serve in the name of the LORD
his God as all his brethren the Lē'vītes *do,*
who stand there before the LORD. 8They
shall have equal portions to eat, besides
what comes from the sale of his inheri-
tance.

Avoid Wicked Customs

9"When you come into the land which
the LORD your God is giving you, you shall
not learn to follow the abominations of
those nations. 10There shall not be found
among you *anyone* who makes his son or
his daughter pass through the fire, *or one*
who practices witchcraft, *or* a soothsayer,
or one who interprets omens, or a sorcerer,
11or one who conjures spells, or a medium,
or a spiritist, or one who calls up the dead.
12For all who do these things *are* an
abomination to the LORD, and because of
these abominations the LORD your God
drives them out from before you. 13You
shall be blameless before the LORD your
God. 14For these nations which you will
dispossess listened to soothsayers and di-
viners; but as for you, the LORD your God
has not appointed such for you.

A New Prophet Like Moses

15"The LORD your God will raise up for
you a Prophet like me from your midst,
from your brethren. Him you shall hear,
16according to all you desired of the LORD
your God in Hō'reb in the day of the as-
sembly, saying, 'Let me not hear again the
voice of the LORD my God, nor let me see
this great fire anymore, lest I die.'

17"And the LORD said to me: 'What they
have spoken is good. 18I will raise up for
them a Prophet like you from among their
brethren, and will put My words in His
mouth, and He shall speak to them all that
I command Him. 19And it shall be *that*
whoever will not hear My words, which
He speaks in My name, I will require *it* of
him. 20But the prophet who presumes to
speak a word in My name, which I have
not commanded him to speak, or who
speaks in the name of other gods, that
prophet shall die.' 21And if you say in your
heart, 'How shall we know the word
which the LORD has not spoken?'— 22when
a prophet speaks in the name of the LORD,
if the thing does not happen or come to
pass, that *is* the thing which the LORD has
not spoken; the prophet has spoken it pre-
sumptuously; you shall not be afraid of
him.

18:1–8 the LORD is their inheritance (v. 2): The final reward for a lifetime of service to the temple and tabernacle. This did not, however, relieve the people from supporting the Levites and priests. Specifically, the Levites were not to be excluded from the offerings made to the Lord.

18:15 The ultimate fulfillment of this prophecy was proclaimed by Peter to be Jesus Christ (Acts 3:22, 23).

CHAPTER 19

Three Cities of Refuge

"When the LORD your God has cut off the nations whose land the LORD your God is giving you, and you dispossess them and dwell in their cities and in their houses, [2]you shall separate three cities for yourself in the midst of your land which the LORD your God is giving you to possess. [3]You shall prepare roads for yourself, and divide into three parts the territory of your land which the LORD your God is giving you to inherit, that any manslayer may flee there.

[4]"And this *is* the case of the manslayer who flees there, that he may live: Whoever kills his neighbor unintentionally, not having hated him in time past— [5]as when *a man* goes to the woods with his neighbor to cut timber, and his hand swings a stroke with the ax to cut down the tree, and the head slips from the handle and strikes his neighbor so that he dies—he shall flee to one of these cities and live; [6]lest the avenger of blood, while his anger is hot, pursue the manslayer and overtake him, because the way is long, and kill him, though he *was* not deserving of death, since he had not hated the victim in time past. [7]Therefore I command you, saying, 'You shall separate three cities for yourself.'

[8]"Now if the LORD your God enlarges your territory, as He swore to your fathers, and gives you the land which He promised to give to your fathers, [9]and if you keep all these commandments and do them, which I command you today, to love the LORD your God and to walk always in His ways, then you shall add three more cities for yourself besides these three, [10]lest innocent blood be shed in the midst of your land which the LORD your God is giving you *as* an inheritance, and *thus* guilt of bloodshed be upon you.

[11]"But if anyone hates his neighbor, lies in wait for him, rises against him and strikes him mortally, so that he dies, and he flees to one of these cities, [12]then the elders of his city shall send and bring him from there, and deliver him over to the hand of the avenger of blood, that he may die. [13]Your eye shall not pity him, but you shall put away *the guilt of* innocent blood from Israel, that it may go well with you.

Property Boundaries

[14]"You shall not remove your neighbor's landmark, which the men of old have set, in your inheritance which you will inherit in the land that the LORD your God is giving you to possess.

The Law Concerning Witnesses

[15]"One witness shall not rise against a man concerning any iniquity or any sin that he commits; by the mouth of two or three witnesses the matter shall be established. [16]If a false witness rises against any man to testify against him of wrongdoing, [17]then both men in the controversy shall stand before the LORD, before the priests and the judges who serve in those days. [18]And the judges shall make careful inquiry, and indeed, *if* the witness *is* a false witness, who has testified falsely against his brother, [19]then you shall do to him as he thought to have done to his brother; so you shall put away the evil from among you.

19:6 The closest male relative of a person who was murdered or accidentally killed was called "the avenger of blood." It was his responsibility to bring the responsible party to court and, if the verdict was "guilty," to take the life of the killer as revenge for the death of the innocent.

19:15–19 The word of one person was not enough to convict someone suspected of wrongdoing; two or three witnesses were required. Anyone caught lying in an attempt to convict another of wrongdoing was to receive whatever punishment would have fallen on the person who was falsely accused.

20And those who remain shall hear and
fear, and hereafter they shall not again
commit such evil among you. 21Your eye
shall not pity: life *shall be* for life, eye for
eye, tooth for tooth, hand for hand, foot for
foot.

CHAPTER 20

Principles Governing Warfare

"When you go out to battle against your
enemies, and see horses and chariots *and*
people more numerous than you, do not be
afraid of them; for the LORD your God *is*
with you, who brought you up from the
land of Egypt. 2So it shall be, when you are
on the verge of battle, that the priest shall
approach and speak to the people. 3And he
shall say to them, 'Hear, O Israel: Today
you are on the verge of battle with your en-
emies. Do not let your heart faint, do not be
afraid, and do not tremble or be terrified
because of them; 4for the LORD your God *is*
He who goes with you, to fight for you
against your enemies, to save you.'

5"Then the officers shall speak to the
people, saying: 'What man *is there* who has
built a new house and has not dedicated it?
Let him go and return to his house, lest he
die in the battle and another man dedicate
it. 6Also what man *is there* who has planted
a vineyard and has not eaten of it? Let him
go and return to his house, lest he die in
the battle and another man eat of it. 7And
what man *is there* who is betrothed to a
woman and has not married her? Let him
go and return to his house, lest he die in
the battle and another man marry her.'

8"The officers shall speak further to the
people, and say, 'What man *is there who is*
fearful and fainthearted? Let him go and
return to his house, lest the heart of his
brethren faint[a] like his heart.' 9And so it
shall be, when the officers have finished
speaking to the people, that they shall
make captains of the armies to lead the
people.

10"When you go near a city to fight
against it, then proclaim an offer of peace
to it. 11And it shall be that if they accept
your offer of peace, and open to you, then
all the people *who are* found in it shall be
placed under tribute to you, and serve you.
12Now if *the city* will not make peace with
you, but war against you, then you shall
besiege it. 13And when the LORD your God
delivers it into your hands, you shall strike
every male in it with the edge of the sword.
14But the women, the little ones, the live-
stock, and all that is in the city, all its spoil,
you shall plunder for yourself; and you
shall eat the enemies' plunder which the
LORD your God gives you. 15Thus you shall
do to all the cities *which are* very far from
you, which *are* not of the cities of these na-
tions.

16"But of the cities of these peoples
which the LORD your God gives you *as* an
inheritance, you shall let nothing that
breathes remain alive, 17but you shall ut-
terly destroy them: the Hit'tīte and the
Am'o·rīte and the Cā'naan·īte and the
Per'iz·zīte and the Hī'vīte and the Jeb'-
ū·sīte, just as the LORD your God has com-
manded you, 18lest they teach you to do ac-
cording to all their abominations which
they have done for their gods, and you sin
against the LORD your God.

20:8 [a]Following Masoretic Text and Targum; Samaritan Pentateuch, Septuagint, Syriac, and Vulgate read *lest he make his brother's heart faint.*

19:21 life . . . for life: Once a person had been judged guilty, justice must be performed with complete impartiality. The rich man must not receive a lesser sentence for the same crime than the poor man.

20:10–18 proclaim an offer of peace: Cities which were not part of Canaan proper (v. 15) were to be given the option of peace. If they accepted, they became servants of Israel. Refusal of this offer would result in the death of all males in the attacked city, but not the utter destruction of the city as was decreed for the Canaanite cities.

19"When you besiege a city for a long
time, while making war against it to take it,
you shall not destroy its trees by wielding
an ax against them; if you can eat of them,
do not cut them down to use in the siege,
for the tree of the field *is* man's *food.* 20Only
the trees which you know *are* not trees for
food you may destroy and cut down, to
build siegeworks against the city that
makes war with you, until it is subdued.

CHAPTER 21

The Law Concerning Unsolved Murder

"If *anyone* is found slain, lying in the
field in the land which the LORD your God
is giving you to possess, *and* it is not
known who killed him, 2then your elders
and your judges shall go out and measure
the distance from the slain man to the sur-
rounding cities. 3And it shall be *that* the el-
ders of the city nearest to the slain man will
take a heifer which has not been worked
and which has not pulled with a yoke. 4The
elders of that city shall bring the heifer
down to a valley with flowing water,
which is neither plowed nor sown, and
they shall break the heifer's neck there in
the valley. 5Then the priests, the sons of
Levi, shall come near, for the LORD your
God has chosen them to minister to Him
and to bless in the name of the LORD; by
their word every controversy and every as-
sault shall be *settled.* 6And all the elders of
that city nearest to the slain *man* shall wash
their hands over the heifer whose neck was
broken in the valley. 7Then they shall an-
swer and say, 'Our hands have not shed
this blood, nor have our eyes seen *it.* 8Pro-
vide atonement, O LORD, for Your people
Israel, whom You have redeemed, and do
not lay innocent blood to the charge of
Your people Israel.' And atonement shall
be provided on their behalf for the blood.
9So you shall put away the *guilt of* innocent
blood from among you when you do *what
is* right in the sight of the LORD.

Female Captives

10"When you go out to war against your
enemies, and the LORD your God delivers
them into your hand, and you take them
captive, 11and you see among the captives a
beautiful woman, and desire her and
would take her for your wife, 12then you
shall bring her home to your house, and
she shall shave her head and trim her nails.
13She shall put off the clothes of her captiv-
ity, remain in your house, and mourn her
father and her mother a full month; after
that you may go in to her and be her hus-
band, and she shall be your wife. 14And it
shall be, if you have no delight in her, then
you shall set her free, but you certainly
shall not sell her for money; you shall not
treat her brutally, because you have hum-
bled her.

Firstborn Inheritance Rights

15"If a man has two wives, one loved
and the other unloved, and they have
borne him children, *both* the loved and the
unloved, and *if* the firstborn son is of her
who is unloved, 16then it shall be, on the
day he bequeaths his possessions to his
sons, *that* he must not bestow firstborn

20:19 When you besiege: The Israelites were not permitted to follow a "scorched-earth" policy. To render the land incapable of supporting life was wrong. The cities themselves were to be destroyed because Canaanite religion thoroughly corrupted life itself. But the fruit trees had done nothing wrong. Respect for nature because God is the Creator must be balanced with the need to thoroughly cleanse a pagan land.

21:1–9 Provide atonement (v. 8): The corporate nature of Israel's life is indicated here. If an innocent person were murdered and no one apprehended, the nation was held responsible. Therefore, a sacrifice must be made for all the people.

21:14 you shall set her free: This whole practice (vv. 10–14) seems barbaric to a developed Christian conscience, but in ancient times this prohibition of mistreatment of a slave wife was a significant expression of the woman's rights as a person.

status on the son of the loved wife in preference to the son of the unloved, the *true* firstborn. 17But he shall acknowledge the son of the unloved wife *as* the firstborn by giving him a double portion of all that he has, for he *is* the beginning of his strength; the right of the firstborn *is* his.

The Rebellious Son

18"If a man has a stubborn and rebellious son who will not obey the voice of his father or the voice of his mother, and *who,* when they have chastened him, will not heed them, 19then his father and his mother shall take hold of him and bring him out to the elders of his city, to the gate of his city. 20And they shall say to the elders of his city, 'This son of ours is stubborn and rebellious; he will not obey our voice; he is a glutton and a drunkard.' 21Then all the men of his city shall stone him to death with stones; so you shall put away the evil from among you, and all Israel shall hear and fear.

Miscellaneous Laws

22"If a man has committed a sin deserving of death, and he is put to death, and you hang him on a tree, 23his body shall not remain overnight on the tree, but you shall surely bury him that day, so that you do not defile the land which the LORD your God is giving you *as* an inheritance; for he who is hanged *is* accursed of God.

CHAPTER 22

"You shall not see your brother's ox or his sheep going astray, and hide yourself from them; you shall certainly bring them back to your brother. 2And if your brother *is* not near you, or if you do not know him, then you shall bring it to your own house, and it shall remain with you until your brother seeks it; then you shall restore it to him. 3You shall do the same with his donkey, and so shall you do with his garment; with any lost thing of your brother's, which he has lost and you have found, you shall do likewise; you must not hide yourself.

4"You shall not see your brother's donkey or his ox fall down along the road, and hide yourself from them; you shall surely help him lift *them* up again.

5"A woman shall not wear anything that pertains to a man, nor shall a man put on a woman's garment, for all who do so *are* an abomination to the LORD your God.

6"If a bird's nest happens to be before you along the way, in any tree or on the ground, with young ones or eggs, with the mother sitting on the young or on the eggs, you shall not take the mother with the young; 7you shall surely let the mother go, and take the young for yourself, that it may be well with you and *that* you may prolong *your* days.

8"When you build a new house, then you shall make a parapet for your roof, that you may not bring guilt of bloodshed on your household if anyone falls from it.

9"You shall not sow your vineyard with different kinds of seed, lest the yield of the seed which you have sown and the fruit of your vineyard be defiled.

10"You shall not plow with an ox and a donkey together.

11"You shall not wear a garment of dif-

21:22, 23 The Israelites did not use hanging as a means of execution. This passage refers to displaying the body of a criminal who had been executed as a warning of the consequences of disobeying God's law.

22:1–4 The human reluctance to get involved must be overcome by Christian love; we cannot justly ignore the problems of those around us.

22:9–11 Object lessons for God's people, who must always keep themselves distinct from a sinful cultural environment, even when such a distinction does not make pragmatic sense. See 2 Cor. 6:14–6.

ferent sorts, *such as* wool and linen mixed
together.
12"You shall make tassels on the four
corners of the clothing with which you
cover *yourself*.

Laws of Sexual Morality

13"If any man takes a wife, and goes in to
her, and detests her, 14and charges her with
shameful conduct, and brings a bad name
on her, and says, 'I took this woman, and
when I came to her I found she *was* not a
virgin,' 15then the father and mother of the
young woman shall take and bring out *the*
evidence of the young woman's virginity to
the elders of the city at the gate. 16And the
young woman's father shall say to the el-
ders, 'I gave my daughter to this man as
wife, and he detests her. 17Now he has
charged her with shameful conduct, say-
ing, "I found your daughter *was* not a vir-
gin," and yet these *are the evidences of* my
daughter's virginity.' And they shall
spread the cloth before the elders of the
city. 18Then the elders of that city shall take
that man and punish him; 19and they shall
fine him one hundred *shekels* of silver and
give *them* to the father of the young
woman, because he has brought a bad
name on a virgin of Israel. And she shall be
his wife; he cannot divorce her all his days.
20"But if the thing is true, *and evidences of*
virginity are not found for the young
woman, 21then they shall bring out the
young woman to the door of her father's
house, and the men of her city shall stone
her to death with stones, because she has
done a disgraceful thing in Israel, to play
the harlot in her father's house. So you
shall put away the evil from among you.
22"If a man is found lying with a woman
married to a husband, then both of them
shall die—the man that lay with the
woman, and the woman; so you shall put
away the evil from Israel.
23"If a young woman *who is* a virgin is
betrothed to a husband, and a man finds
her in the city and lies with her, 24then you
shall bring them both out to the gate of that
city, and you shall stone them to death
with stones, the young woman because
she did not cry out in the city, and the man
because he humbled his neighbor's wife;
so you shall put away the evil from among
you.
25"But if a man finds a betrothed young
woman in the countryside, and the man
forces her and lies with her, then only
the man who lay with her shall die. 26But
you shall do nothing to the young woman;
there is in the young woman no sin *deserv-*
ing of death, for just as when a man rises
against his neighbor and kills him, even so
is this matter. 27For he found her in the
countryside, *and* the betrothed young
woman cried out, but *there was* no one to
save her.
28"If a man finds a young woman *who is*
a virgin, who is not betrothed, and he
seizes her and lies with her, and they are
found out, 29then the man who lay with her
shall give to the young woman's father
fifty *shekels* of silver, and she shall be his
wife because he has humbled her; he shall
not be permitted to divorce her all his
days.
30"A man shall not take his father's wife,
nor uncover his father's bed.

CHAPTER 23

Those Excluded from the Congregation

"He who is emasculated by crushing or
mutilation shall not enter the assembly of
the LORD.
2"One of illegitimate birth shall not en-
ter the assembly of the LORD; even to the
tenth generation none of his *descendants*
shall enter the assembly of the LORD.
3"An Am'mon·īte or Mō'ab·īte shall not
enter the assembly of the LORD; even to the
tenth generation none of his *descendants*
shall enter the assembly of the LORD for-
ever, 4because they did not meet you with
bread and water on the road when you
came out of Egypt, and because they hired
against you Bā'laam the son of Bē'or from

Pē′thor of Mes·o·po·tā′mi·a,[a] to curse you.
5Nevertheless the LORD your God would
not listen to Bā′laam, but the LORD your
God turned the curse into a blessing for
you, because the LORD your God loves you.
6You shall not seek their peace nor their
prosperity all your days forever.

7"You shall not abhor an Ē′dom·īte, for
he *is* your brother. You shall not abhor an
Egyptian, because you were an alien in his
land. 8The children of the third generation
born to them may enter the assembly of the
LORD.

Cleanliness of the Camp Site

9"When the army goes out against your
enemies, then keep yourself from every
wicked thing. 10If there is any man among
you who becomes unclean by some occur-
rence in the night, then he shall go outside
the camp; he shall not come inside the
camp. 11But it shall be, when evening
comes, that he shall wash with water; and
when the sun sets, he may come into the
camp.

12"Also you shall have a place outside
the camp, where you may go out; 13and
you shall have an implement among your
equipment, and when you sit down out-
side, you shall dig with it and turn and
cover your refuse. 14For the LORD your God
walks in the midst of your camp, to deliver
you and give your enemies over to you;
therefore your camp shall be holy, that He
may see no unclean thing among you, and
turn away from you.

Miscellaneous Laws

15"You shall not give back to his master
the slave who has escaped from his master
to you. 16He may dwell with you in your
midst, in the place which he chooses
within one of your gates, where it seems
best to him; you shall not oppress him.

17"There shall be no *ritual* harlot[a] of the
daughters of Israel, or a perverted[b] one of
the sons of Israel. 18You shall not bring the
wages of a harlot or the price of a dog to
the house of the LORD your God for any
vowed offering, for both of these *are* an
abomination to the LORD your God.

19"You shall not charge interest to your
brother—interest on money *or* food *or* any-
thing that is lent out at interest. 20To a for-
eigner you may charge interest, but to your
brother you shall not charge interest, that
the LORD your God may bless you in all to
which you set your hand in the land which
you are entering to possess.

21"When you make a vow to the LORD
your God, you shall not delay to pay it; for
the LORD your God will surely require it of
you, and it would be sin to you. 22But if you
abstain from vowing, it shall not be sin to
you. 23That which has gone from your lips
you shall keep and perform, for you volun-
tarily vowed to the LORD your God what
you have promised with your mouth.

24"When you come into your neighbor's
vineyard, you may eat your fill of grapes at
your pleasure, but you shall not put *any* in
your container. 25When you come into your
neighbor's standing grain, you may pluck
the heads with your hand, but you shall
not use a sickle on your neighbor's stand-
ing grain.

CHAPTER 24

Law Concerning Divorce

"When a man takes a wife and marries
her, and it happens that she finds no favor
in his eyes because he has found some un-

23:4 [a]Hebrew *Aram Naharaim* 23:17 [a]Hebrew *qedeshah*, feminine of *qadesh* (see note *b*) [b]Hebrew *qadesh*, that is, one practicing sodomy and prostitution in religious rituals

24:1–4 As Jesus recognized (Matt. 19:8), this passage does not legitimize divorce. Rather, it attempts to control the tragic result of human hard-heartedness. Specifically, it prohibited remarriage after an intervening marriage had occurred. The plan of God is for a man and woman to be committed to one another for life.

cleanness in her, and he writes her a certif-
icate of divorce, puts *it* in her hand, and
sends her out of his house, 2when she has
departed from his house, and goes and be-
comes another man's *wife,* 3*if* the latter hus-
band detests her and writes her a certifi-
cate of divorce, puts *it* in her hand, and
sends her out of his house, or if the latter
husband dies who took her as his wife,
4*then* her former husband who divorced
her must not take her back to be his wife
after she has been defiled; for that *is* an
abomination before the LORD, and you
shall not bring sin on the land which the
LORD your God is giving you *as* an inheri-
tance.

Miscellaneous Laws

5"When a man has taken a new wife, he
shall not go out to war or be charged with
any business; he shall be free at home one
year, and bring happiness to his wife
whom he has taken.
6"No man shall take the lower or the up-
per millstone in pledge, for he takes *one's*
living in pledge.
7"If a man is found kidnapping any of
his brethren of the children of Israel, and
mistreats him or sells him, then that kid-
napper shall die; and you shall put away
the evil from among you.
8"Take heed in an outbreak of leprosy,
that you carefully observe and do accord-
ing to all that the priests, the Lē′vītes, shall
teach you; just as I commanded them, *so*
you shall be careful to do. 9Remember
what the LORD your God did to Miriam on
the way when you came out of Egypt!
10"When you lend your brother any-
thing, you shall not go into his house to get
his pledge. 11You shall stand outside, and
the man to whom you lend shall bring the
pledge out to you. 12And if the man *is* poor,
you shall not keep his pledge overnight.
13You shall in any case return the pledge to
him again when the sun goes down, that
he may sleep in his own garment and bless
you; and it shall be righteousness to you
before the LORD your God.
14"You shall not oppress a hired servant
who is poor and needy, *whether* one of your
brethren or one of the aliens who *is* in your
land within your gates. 15Each day you
shall give *him* his wages, and not let the
sun go down on it, for he *is* poor and has
set his heart on it; lest he cry out against
you to the LORD, and it be sin to you.
16"Fathers shall not be put to death for
their children, nor shall children be put to
death for *their* fathers; a person shall be put
to death for his own sin.
17"You shall not pervert justice due the
stranger or the fatherless, nor take a
widow's garment as a pledge. 18But you
shall remember that you were a slave in
Egypt, and the LORD your God redeemed
you from there; therefore I command you
to do this thing.
19"When you reap your harvest in your
field, and forget a sheaf in the field, you
shall not go back to get it; it shall be for the
stranger, the fatherless, and the widow,
that the LORD your God may bless you in
all the work of your hands. 20When you
beat your olive trees, you shall not go over
the boughs again; it shall be for the
stranger, the fatherless, and the widow.
21When you gather the grapes of your vine-
yard, you shall not glean *it* afterward; it
shall be for the stranger, the fatherless, and
the widow. 22And you shall remember that
you were a slave in the land of Egypt;
therefore I command you to do this thing.

CHAPTER 25

"If there is a dispute between men, and
they come to court, that *the judges* may

24:6 Every Israelite owned a **millstone**, which was used to prepare bread. The prohibition against requiring the millstone as a **pledge** ensured that everyone would have the equipment necessary to feed a family.

judge them, and they justify the righteous and condemn the wicked, 2then it shall be, if the wicked man deserves to be beaten, that the judge will cause him to lie down and be beaten in his presence, according to his guilt, with a certain number of blows. 3Forty blows he may give him *and* no more, lest he should exceed this and beat him with many blows above these, and your brother be humiliated in your sight.

4"You shall not muzzle an ox while it treads out *the grain.*

Marriage Duty of the Surviving Brother

5"If brothers dwell together, and one of them dies and has no son, the widow of the dead man shall not be *married* to a stranger outside *the family;* her husband's brother shall go in to her, take her as his wife, and perform the duty of a husband's brother to her. 6And it shall be *that* the firstborn son which she bears will succeed to the name of his dead brother, that his name may not be blotted out of Israel. 7But if the man does not want to take his brother's wife, then let his brother's wife go up to the gate to the elders, and say, 'My husband's brother refuses to raise up a name to his brother in Israel; he will not perform the duty of my husband's brother.' 8Then the elders of his city shall call him and speak to him. But *if* he stands firm and says, 'I do not want to take her,' 9then his brother's wife shall come to him in the presence of the elders, remove his sandal from his foot, spit in his face, and answer and say, 'So shall it be done to the man who will not build up his brother's house.' 10And his name shall be called in Israel, 'The house of him who had his sandal removed.'

Miscellaneous Laws

11"If *two* men fight together, and the wife of one draws near to rescue her husband from the hand of the one attacking him, and puts out her hand and seizes him by the genitals, 12then you shall cut off her hand; your eye shall not pity *her.*

13"You shall not have in your bag differing weights, a heavy and a light. 14You shall not have in your house differing measures, a large and a small. 15You shall have a perfect and just weight, a perfect and just measure, that your days may be lengthened in the land which the LORD your God is giving you. 16For all who do such things, all who behave unrighteously, *are* an abomination to the LORD your God.

Destroy the Amalekites

17"Remember what Am'a·lek did to you on the way as you were coming out of Egypt, 18how he met you on the way and attacked your rear ranks, all the stragglers at your rear, when you *were* tired and weary; and he did not fear God. 19Therefore it shall be, when the LORD your God has given you rest from your enemies all around, in the land which the LORD your God is giving you to possess *as* an inheritance, *that* you will blot out the remembrance of Am'a·lek from under heaven. You shall not forget.

25:3 Forty: The purpose was to avoid humiliation. Punishment is meant to preserve justice, not to degrade people. Excessive punishment perverts justice. Often only 39 blows were given to ensure that the limit was not exceeded by miscount (see 2 Cor. 11:24).

25:5 duty of a husband's brother: Preserving the family line was important in Israel (Ruth 4:5, 10; 1 Sam. 24:21). This practice, called levirate marriage, was linked to laws of inheritance. Any offspring from the husband's brother were considered children of the deceased.

25:9, 10 spit in his face: A woman had a right to bear children to her deceased husband. If her brother-in-law refused her that right, she could publicly humiliate him—an indication of the seriousness of God concerning a widow's rights.

25:13–16 differing weights . . . differing measures: See Mic. 6:10, 11. We should conduct all our business according to the highest standards and ethics.

CHAPTER 26

Offerings of Firstfruits and Tithes

"And it shall be, when you come into
the land which the LORD your God is giv-
ing you *as* an inheritance, and you possess
it and dwell in it, 2that you shall take some
of the first of all the produce of the ground,
which you shall bring from your land that
the LORD your God is giving you, and put
it in a basket and go to the place where the
LORD your God chooses to make His name
abide. 3And you shall go to the one who is
priest in those days, and say to him, 'I de-
clare today to the LORD your[a] God that I
have come to the country which the LORD
swore to our fathers to give us.'

4"Then the priest shall take the basket
out of your hand and set it down before the
altar of the LORD your God. 5And you shall
answer and say before the LORD your God:
'My father *was* a Syrian,[a] about to perish,
and he went down to Egypt and dwelt
there, few in number; and there he became
a nation, great, mighty, and populous. 6But
the Egyptians mistreated us, afflicted us,
and laid hard bondage on us. 7Then we
cried out to the LORD God of our fathers,
and the LORD heard our voice and looked
on our affliction and our labor and our op-
pression. 8So the LORD brought us out of
Egypt with a mighty hand and with an
outstretched arm, with great terror and
with signs and wonders. 9He has brought
us to this place and has given us this land,
"a land flowing with milk and honey";[a]
10and now, behold, I have brought the first-
fruits of the land which you, O LORD, have
given me.'

"Then you shall set it before the LORD
your God, and worship before the LORD
your God. 11So you shall rejoice in every
good *thing* which the LORD your God has
given to you and your house, you and the
Lē′vīte and the stranger who *is* among
you.

26:3 [a]Septuagint reads *my.* 26:5 [a]Or *Aramean*
26:9 [a]Exodus 3:8 26:15 [a]Exodus 3:8

> ***I praise You and rejoice in every good thing which You, the Lord my God, have given to me and my house.***
>
> *adapted from* Deuteronomy 26:11

12"When you have finished laying aside
all the tithe of your increase in the third
year—the year of tithing—and have given
it to the Lē′vīte, the stranger, the fatherless,
and the widow, so that they may eat within
your gates and be filled, 13then you shall
say before the LORD your God: 'I have re-
moved the holy *tithe* from *my* house, and
also have given them to the Lē′vīte, the
stranger, the fatherless, and the widow, ac-
cording to all Your commandments which
You have commanded me; I have not
transgressed Your commandments, nor
have I forgotten *them.* 14I have not eaten
any of it when in mourning, nor have I re-
moved *any* of it for an unclean *use,* nor
given *any* of it for the dead. I have obeyed
the voice of the LORD my God, and have
done according to all that You have com-
manded me. 15Look down from Your holy
habitation, from heaven, and bless Your
people Israel and the land which You have
given us, just as You swore to our fathers,
"a land flowing with milk and honey." '[a]

A Special People of God

16"This day the LORD your God com-
mands you to observe these statutes and
judgments; therefore you shall be careful
to observe them with all your heart and
with all your soul. 17Today you have pro-
claimed the LORD to be your God, and that
you will walk in His ways and keep His
statutes, His commandments, and His
judgments, and that you will obey
His voice. 18Also today the LORD has pro-
claimed you to be His special people, just
as He promised you, that *you* should keep
all His commandments, 19and that He will

set you high above all nations which He has made, in praise, in name, and in honor, and that you may be a holy people to the LORD your God, just as He has spoken."

CHAPTER 27

The Law Inscribed on Stones

Now Moses, with the elders of Israel, commanded the people, saying: "Keep all the commandments which I command you today. 2And it shall be, on the day when you cross over the Jordan to the land which the LORD your God is giving you, that you shall set up for yourselves large stones, and whitewash them with lime. 3You shall write on them all the words of this law, when you have crossed over, that you may enter the land which the LORD your God is giving you, 'a land flowing with milk and honey,'[a] just as the LORD God of your fathers promised you. 4Therefore it shall be, when you have crossed over the Jordan, *that* on Mount Ē'bal you shall set up these stones, which I command you today, and you shall whitewash them with lime. 5And there you shall build an altar to the LORD your God, an altar of stones; you shall not use an iron *tool* on them. 6You shall build with whole stones the altar of the LORD your God, and offer burnt offerings on it to the LORD your God. 7You shall offer peace offerings, and shall eat there, and rejoice before the LORD your God. 8And you shall write very plainly on the stones all the words of this law."

9Then Moses and the priests, the Lē'vītes, spoke to all Israel, saying, "Take heed and listen, O Israel: This day you have become the people of the LORD your God. 10Therefore you shall obey the voice of the LORD your God, and observe His commandments and His statutes which I command you today."

Curses Pronounced from Mount Ebal

11And Moses commanded the people on the same day, saying, 12"These shall stand on Mount Ger'i·zim to bless the people, when you have crossed over the Jordan: Sim'ē·on, Levi, Judah, Is'sa·char, Joseph, and Benjamin; 13and these shall stand on Mount Ē'bal to curse: Reuben, Gad, Ash'er, Zeb'ū·lun, Dan, and Naph'ta·lī.

14"And the Lē'vītes shall speak with a loud voice and say to all the men of Israel: 15'Cursed *is* the one who makes a carved or molded image, an abomination to the LORD, the work of the hands of the craftsman, and sets *it* up in secret.'

"And all the people shall answer and say, 'Amen!'

16'Cursed *is* the one who treats his father or his mother with contempt.'

"And all the people shall say, 'Amen!'

17'Cursed *is* the one who moves his neighbor's landmark.'

"And all the people shall say, 'Amen!'

18'Cursed *is* the one who makes the blind to wander off the road.'

"And all the people shall say, 'Amen!'

19'Cursed *is* the one who perverts the justice due the stranger, the fatherless, and widow.'

"And all the people shall say, 'Amen!'

20'Cursed *is* the one who lies with his father's wife, because he has uncovered his father's bed.'

27:3 [a]Exodus 3:8

27:1—33:29 In covenant documents of the ancient Near East, the covenant stipulations were normally followed by several other sections. These covered such matters as where the covenant document should be kept, when it should be read, and the pronouncement of blessings and curses for keeping or breaking the agreement. This final discourse of Moses contains such matters, including a future reading and confirmation (27:1–26), blessings and cursings (28:1–68), a final charge (29:1—31:13), and safekeeping of the document (31:24–29). Also included is an account of the inauguration of Joshua (31:14–23), a hymnic summary (31:30—32:47), and a final blessing (33:1–29).

"And all the people shall say, 'Amen!'
21'Cursed *is* the one who lies with any
kind of animal.'
"And all the people shall say, 'Amen!'
22'Cursed *is* the one who lies with his sis-
ter, the daughter of his father or the daugh-
ter of his mother.'
"And all the people shall say, 'Amen!'
23'Cursed *is* the one who lies with his
mother-in-law.'
"And all the people shall say, 'Amen!'
24'Cursed *is* the one who attacks his
neighbor secretly.'
"And all the people shall say, 'Amen!'
25'Cursed *is* the one who takes a bribe to
slay an innocent person.'
"And all the people shall say, 'Amen!'
26'Cursed *is* the one who does not con-
firm *all* the words of this law.'
"And all the people shall say, 'Amen!' "

CHAPTER 28

Blessings on Obedience

"Now it shall come to pass, if you dili-
gently obey the voice of the LORD your
God, to observe carefully all His com-
mandments which I command you today,
that the LORD your God will set you high
above all nations of the earth. 2And all
these blessings shall come upon you and
overtake you, because you obey the voice
of the LORD your God:
3"Blessed *shall* you *be* in the city, and
blessed *shall* you *be* in the country.
4"Blessed *shall be* the fruit of your body,
the produce of your ground and the in-
crease of your herds, the increase of your
cattle and the offspring of your flocks.

> Daniel Webster, when asked what was the greatest thought that had ever entered his mind, replied: "My accountability to Almighty God."
> *Anonymous*

5"Blessed *shall be* your basket and your
kneading bowl.
6"Blessed *shall* you *be* when you come
in, and blessed *shall* you *be* when you go
out.
7"The LORD will cause your enemies
who rise against you to be defeated before
your face; they shall come out against you
one way and flee before you seven ways.
8"The LORD will command the blessing
on you in your storehouses and in all to
which you set your hand, and He will bless
you in the land which the LORD your God
is giving you.
9"The LORD will establish you as a holy
people to Himself, just as He has sworn to
you, if you keep the commandments of the
LORD your God and walk in His ways.
10Then all peoples of the earth shall see that
you are called by the name of the LORD,
and they shall be afraid of you. 11And the
LORD will grant you plenty of goods, in the
fruit of your body, in the increase of your
livestock, and in the produce of your
ground, in the land of which the LORD
swore to your fathers to give you. 12The
LORD will open to you His good treasure,
the heavens, to give the rain to your land in
its season, and to bless all the work of your
hand. You shall lend to many nations, but
you shall not borrow. 13And the LORD will

28:9, 10 called by . . . the LORD: The people had been called out of all the nations (Gen. 12) and out of slavery (Ex. 12). As the Israelites obeyed God and were blessed, it would become evident that they were a **holy people**, like Him who chose them.

28:12 you shall not borrow: God would provide for His people, and they could share out of their abundance with other people. These blessings were all physical and material; however, they were used as object lessons of spiritual truth in the OT. Our reason for serving God must never be to obtain physical and material wealth. If these come to us, they are gifts, not earnings, and if the possession of these makes us spiritually impoverished, they are a curse, not a blessing (see Luke 6:20–26).

make you the head and not the tail; you shall be above only, and not be beneath, if you heed the commandments of the LORD your God, which I command you today, and are careful to observe *them.* 14So you shall not turn aside from any of the words which I command you this day, *to* the right or the left, to go after other gods to serve them.

Curses on Disobedience

15"But it shall come to pass, if you do not obey the voice of the LORD your God, to observe carefully all His commandments and His statutes which I command you today, that all these curses will come upon you and overtake you:

16"Cursed *shall* you *be* in the city, and cursed *shall* you *be* in the country.

17"Cursed *shall be* your basket and your kneading bowl.

18"Cursed *shall be* the fruit of your body and the produce of your land, the increase of your cattle and the offspring of your flocks.

19"Cursed *shall* you *be* when you come in, and cursed *shall* you *be* when you go out.

20"The LORD will send on you cursing, confusion, and rebuke in all that you set your hand to do, until you are destroyed and until you perish quickly, because of the wickedness of your doings in which you have forsaken Me. 21The LORD will make the plague cling to you until He has consumed you from the land which you are going to possess. 22The LORD will strike you with consumption, with fever, with inflammation, with severe burning fever, with the sword, with scorching, and with mildew; they shall pursue you until you perish. 23And your heavens which *are* over your head shall be bronze, and the earth which is under you *shall be* iron. 24The LORD will change the rain of your land to powder and dust; from the heaven it shall come down on you until you are destroyed.

25"The LORD will cause you to be defeated before your enemies; you shall go out one way against them and flee seven ways before them; and you shall become troublesome to all the kingdoms of the earth. 26Your carcasses shall be food for all the birds of the air and the beasts of the earth, and no one shall frighten *them* away. 27The LORD will strike you with the boils of Egypt, with tumors, with the scab, and with the itch, from which you cannot be healed. 28The LORD will strike you with madness and blindness and confusion of heart. 29And you shall grope at noonday, as a blind man gropes in darkness; you shall not prosper in your ways; you shall be only oppressed and plundered continually, and no one shall save *you.*

30"You shall betroth a wife, but another man shall lie with her; you shall build a house, but you shall not dwell in it; you shall plant a vineyard, but shall not gather its grapes. 31Your ox *shall be* slaughtered before your eyes, but you shall not eat of it; your donkey *shall be* violently taken away from before you, and shall not be restored to you; your sheep *shall be* given to your enemies, and you shall have no one to rescue *them.* 32Your sons and your daughters *shall be* given to another people, and your eyes shall look and fail *with longing* for them all day long; and *there shall be* no strength in your hand. 33A nation whom you have not known shall eat the fruit of your land and the produce of your labor,

---

28:15–68 The solemn message of this passage is that disobedience would not be tolerated in Israel. They could enjoy a land flowing with milk and honey, or they could become the victim of an eagle swooping down (vv. 26, 49). They could know unity in fellowship or be scattered (v. 64). There is no middle ground (v. 63)—the people must choose between God's blessings and His wrath.

28:32 The children of Israel did indeed become enslaved to foreign nations when Israel fell to Assyria in 721 B.C. and Judah was captured by Babylon in 587 B.C.

and you shall be only oppressed and
crushed continually. 34So you shall be
driven mad because of the sight which
your eyes see. 35The LORD will strike you in
the knees and on the legs with severe boils
which cannot be healed, and from the sole
of your foot to the top of your head.

36"The LORD will bring you and the king
whom you set over you to a nation which
neither you nor your fathers have known,
and there you shall serve other gods—
wood and stone. 37And you shall become
an astonishment, a proverb, and a byword
among all nations where the LORD will
drive you.

38"You shall carry much seed out to the
field but gather little in, for the locust shall
consume it. 39You shall plant vineyards
and tend *them,* but you shall neither drink
of the wine nor gather the *grapes;* for the
worms shall eat them. 40You shall have
olive trees throughout all your territory,
but you shall not anoint *yourself* with the
oil; for your olives shall drop off. 41You
shall beget sons and daughters, but they
shall not be yours; for they shall go into
captivity. 42Locusts shall consume all your
trees and the produce of your land.

43"The alien who *is* among you shall rise
higher and higher above you, and you
shall come down lower and lower. 44He
shall lend to you, but you shall not lend to
him; he shall be the head, and you shall be
the tail.

45"Moreover all these curses shall come
upon you and pursue and overtake you,
until you are destroyed, because you did
not obey the voice of the LORD your God, to
keep His commandments and His statutes
which He commanded you. 46And they
shall be upon you for a sign and a wonder,
and on your descendants forever.

47"Because you did not serve the LORD
your God with joy and gladness of heart,
for the abundance of everything, 48there-
fore you shall serve your enemies, whom
the LORD will send against you, in hunger,
in thirst, in nakedness, and in need of
everything; and He will put a yoke of iron
on your neck until He has destroyed you.
49The LORD will bring a nation against you
from afar, from the end of the earth, *as swift*
as the eagle flies, a nation whose language
you will not understand, 50a nation of
fierce countenance, which does not respect
the elderly nor show favor to the young.
51And they shall eat the increase of your
livestock and the produce of your land, un-
til you are destroyed; they shall not leave
you grain or new wine or oil, *or* the in-
crease of your cattle or the offspring of
your flocks, until they have destroyed you.

52"They shall besiege you at all your
gates until your high and fortified walls, in
which you trust, come down throughout
all your land; and they shall besiege you at
all your gates throughout all your land
which the LORD your God has given you.
53You shall eat the fruit of your own body,
the flesh of your sons and your daughters
whom the LORD your God has given you,
in the siege and desperate straits in which
your enemy shall distress you. 54The sensi-
tive and very refined man among you will
be hostile toward his brother, toward the
wife of his bosom, and toward the rest of
his children whom he leaves behind, 55so
that he will not give any of them the flesh
of his children whom he will eat, because
he has nothing left in the siege and desper-
ate straits in which your enemy shall dis-
tress you at all your gates. 56The tender and
delicate woman among you, who would
not venture to set the sole of her foot on the
ground because of her delicateness and
sensitivity, will refuse[a] to the husband of
her bosom, and to her son and her daugh-
ter, 57her placenta which comes out from
between her feet and her children whom
she bears; for she will eat them secretly for

28:56 [a]Literally *her eye shall be evil toward*

28:52 They shall besiege you: A prophecy that was fulfilled (see 2 Kin. 25:1–21).

lack of everything in the siege and desperate straits in which your enemy shall distress you at all your gates.

58"If you do not carefully observe all the words of this law that are written in this book, that you may fear this glorious and awesome name, THE LORD YOUR GOD, 59then the LORD will bring upon you and your descendants extraordinary plagues—great and prolonged plagues—and serious and prolonged sicknesses. 60Moreover He will bring back on you all the diseases of Egypt, of which you were afraid, and they shall cling to you. 61Also every sickness and every plague, which *is* not written in this Book of the Law, will the LORD bring upon you until you are destroyed. 62You shall be left few in number, whereas you were as the stars of heaven in multitude, because you would not obey the voice of the LORD your God. 63And it shall be, *that* just as the LORD rejoiced over you to do you good and multiply you, so the LORD will rejoice over you to destroy you and bring you to nothing; and you shall be plucked from off the land which you go to possess.

64"Then the LORD will scatter you among all peoples, from one end of the earth to the other, and there you shall serve other gods, which neither you nor your fathers have known—wood and stone. 65And among those nations you shall find no rest, nor shall the sole of your foot have a resting place; but there the LORD will give you a trembling heart, failing eyes, and anguish of soul. 66Your life shall hang in doubt before you; you shall fear day and night, and have no assurance of life. 67In the morning you shall say, 'Oh, that it were evening!' And at evening you shall say, 'Oh, that it were morning!' because of the fear which terrifies your heart, and because of the sight which your eyes see.

68"And the LORD will take you back to Egypt in ships, by the way of which I said to you, 'You shall never see it again.' And there you shall be offered for sale to your enemies as male and female slaves, but no one will buy *you.*"

CHAPTER 29

The Covenant Renewed in Moab

These *are* the words of the covenant which the LORD commanded Moses to make with the children of Israel in the land of Mō'ab, besides the covenant which He made with them in Hō'reb.

2Now Moses called all Israel and said to them: "You have seen all that the LORD did before your eyes in the land of Egypt, to Pharaoh and to all his servants and to all his land— 3the great trials which your eyes have seen, the signs, and those great wonders. 4Yet the LORD has not given you a heart to perceive and eyes to see and ears to hear, to this *very* day. 5And I have led you forty years in the wilderness. Your clothes have not worn out on you, and your sandals have not worn out on your feet. 6You have not eaten bread, nor have you drunk wine or *similar* drink, that you may know that I *am* the LORD your God. 7And when you came to this place, Sī'hon king of Hesh'bon and Og king of Bā'shan

---

29:1—31:13 Moses' final charge includes a review of Israel's recent God-given victories over idolatrous nations (29:1–19) and a prediction of their future apostasy (29:20–29), but of God's restoration and cleansing (30:1–10). In light of all of this, Moses calls on them to choose life (30:11—31:6). He concludes with charges to Joshua (31:7, 8) and the priests (31:9–13).

29:1–13 The Israelites must remember God's help in the past to motivate them to keep the covenant in the present. They must keep the **covenant** in the present in order to **prosper** (v. 9) in the future. If they disobeyed, it would be because they had forgotten the wonderful things God had done for them. It was especially important that future generations learn the story.

came out against us to battle, and we conquered them. 8We took their land and gave it as an inheritance to the Reū'ben·ītes, to the Gad'ītes, and to half the tribe of Ma·nas'seh. 9Therefore keep the words of this covenant, and do them, that you may prosper in all that you do.

10"All of you stand today before the LORD your God: your leaders and your tribes and your elders and your officers, all the men of Israel, 11your little ones and your wives—also the stranger who *is* in your camp, from the one who cuts your wood to the one who draws your water— 12that you may enter into covenant with the LORD your God, and into His oath, which the LORD your God makes with you today, 13that He may establish you today as a people for Himself, and *that* He may be God to you, just as He has spoken to you, and just as He has sworn to your fathers, to Abraham, Isaac, and Jacob.

14"I make this covenant and this oath, not with you alone, 15but with *him* who stands here with us today before the LORD our God, as well as with *him* who *is* not here with us today 16(for you know that we dwelt in the land of Egypt and that we came through the nations which you passed by, 17and you saw their abominations and their idols which *were* among them—wood and stone and silver and gold); 18so that there may not be among you man or woman or family or tribe, whose heart turns away today from the LORD our God, to go *and* serve the gods of these nations, and that there may not be among you a root bearing bitterness or wormwood; 19and so it may not happen, when he hears the words of this curse, that he blesses himself in his heart, saying, 'I shall have peace, even though I follow the dictates[a] of my heart'—as though the drunkard could be included with the sober.

20"The LORD would not spare him; for then the anger of the LORD and His jealousy would burn against that man, and every curse that is written in this book would settle on him, and the LORD would blot out his name from under heaven. 21And the LORD would separate him from all the tribes of Israel for adversity, according to all the curses of the covenant that are written in this Book of the Law, 22so that the coming generation of your children who rise up after you, and the foreigner who comes from a far land, would say, when they see the plagues of that land and the sicknesses which the LORD has laid on it:

23'The whole land *is* brimstone, salt, and burning; it is not sown, nor does it bear, nor does any grass grow there, like the overthrow of Sod'om and Go·mor'rah, Ad'mah, and Ze·boi'im, which the LORD overthrew in His anger and His wrath.' 24All nations would say, 'Why has the LORD done so to this land? What does the heat of this great anger mean?' 25Then *people* would say: 'Because they have forsaken the covenant of the LORD God of their fathers, which He made with them when He brought them out of the land of Egypt; 26for they went and served other gods and worshiped them, gods that they did not know and that He had not given to them. 27Then the anger of the LORD was aroused against this land, to bring on it every curse that is written in this book. 28And the LORD uprooted them from their land in anger, in wrath, and in great indignation, and cast them into another land, as *it is* this day.'

29"The secret *things belong* to the LORD our God, but those *things which are* revealed *belong* to us and to our children forever, that *we* may do all the words of this law.

29:19 [a]Or *stubbornness*

29:19 Life's greatest deception is to say, **I shall have peace** if I do what I want. We can never find true peace when we are outside of the will of God.

CHAPTER 30

The Blessing of Returning to God

"Now it shall come to pass, when all
these things come upon you, the blessing
and the curse which I have set before you,
and you call *them* to mind among all the
nations where the LORD your God drives
you, [2]and you return to the LORD your God
and obey His voice, according to all that I
command you today, you and your chil-
dren, with all your heart and with all your
soul, [3]that the LORD your God will bring
you back from captivity, and have compas-
sion on you, and gather you again from all
the nations where the LORD your God has
scattered you. [4]If *any* of you are driven out
to the farthest *parts* under heaven, from
there the LORD your God will gather you,
and from there He will bring you. [5]Then
the LORD your God will bring you to the
land which your fathers possessed, and
you shall possess it. He will prosper you
and multiply you more than your fathers.
[6]And the LORD your God will circumcise
your heart and the heart of your descen-
dants, to love the LORD your God with all
your heart and with all your soul, that you
may live.

[7]"Also the LORD your God will put all
these curses on your enemies and on those
who hate you, who persecuted you. [8]And
you will again obey the voice of the LORD
and do all His commandments which I
command you today. [9]The LORD your God
will make you abound in all the work of
your hand, in the fruit of your body, in the
increase of your livestock, and in the pro-
duce of your land for good. For the
LORD will again rejoice over you for good
as He rejoiced over your fathers, [10]if
you obey the voice of the LORD your God,
to keep His commandments and His
statutes which are written in this Book of
the Law, *and* if you turn to the LORD your
God with all your heart and with all your
soul.

The Choice of Life or Death

[11]"For this commandment which I com-
mand you today *is* not *too* mysterious for
you, nor *is* it far off. [12]It *is* not in heaven,
that you should say, 'Who will ascend into
heaven for us and bring it to us, that we
may hear it and do it?' [13]Nor *is* it beyond
the sea, that you should say, 'Who will go
over the sea for us and bring it to us, that
we may hear it and do it?' [14]But the word *is*
very near you, in your mouth and in your
heart, that you may do it.

[15]"See, I have set before you today life
and good, death and evil, [16]in that I com-
mand you today to love the LORD your
God, to walk in His ways, and to keep His
commandments, His statutes, and His
judgments, that you may live and multi-
ply; and the LORD your God will bless you
in the land which you go to possess. [17]But if
your heart turns away so that you do not
hear, and are drawn away, and worship
other gods and serve them, [18]I announce to
you today that you shall surely perish; you
shall not prolong *your* days in the land
which you cross over the Jordan to go in
and possess. [19]I call heaven and earth as
witnesses today against you, *that* I have set
before you life and death, blessing and
cursing; therefore choose life, that both
you and your descendants may live; [20]that
you may love the LORD your God, that you
may obey His voice, and that you may
cling to Him, for He *is* your life and the
length of your days; and that you may
dwell in the land which the LORD swore to
your fathers, to Abraham, Isaac, and Jacob,
to give them."

30:6 circumcise your heart: This important statement points to the internal dimension of the law. Jesus sums it up with two principles: love God and love people (Mark 12:29–31). This is more than sentimental and emotional love. It is the kind of sacrificial self-giving that arises from a thorough commitment to serve God. Far greater than bearing a mark on your body is to bear God's mark on your spirit.

CHAPTER 31

Joshua the New Leader of Israel

Then Moses went and spoke these
words to all Israel. 2And he said to them: "I
am one hundred and twenty years old to-
day. I can no longer go out and come in.
Also the LORD has said to me, 'You shall
not cross over this Jordan.' 3The LORD your
God Himself crosses over before you; He
will destroy these nations from before you,
and you shall dispossess them. Joshua
himself crosses over before you, just as the
LORD has said. 4And the LORD will do to
them as He did to Sī'hon and Og, the kings
of the Am'o·rītes and their land, when He
destroyed them. 5The LORD will give them
over to you, that you may do to them ac-
cording to every commandment which I
have commanded you. 6Be strong and of
good courage, do not fear nor be afraid of
them; for the LORD your God, He *is* the One
who goes with you. He will not leave you
nor forsake you."

7Then Moses called Joshua and said to
him in the sight of all Israel, "Be strong and
of good courage, for you must go with this
people to the land which the LORD has
sworn to their fathers to give them, and
you shall cause them to inherit it. 8And the
LORD, He *is* the One who goes before you.
He will be with you, He will not leave you
nor forsake you; do not fear nor be dis-
mayed."

The Law to Be Read Every Seven Years

9So Moses wrote this law and delivered
it to the priests, the sons of Levi, who bore
the ark of the covenant of the LORD, and to
all the elders of Israel. 10And Moses com-

> ***I pray that my children and grandchildren will be strong and of good courage and that they do not fear nor be afraid, for You, the Lord their God, are the One who goes with them. I pray that You will not leave them nor forsake them.***
>
> *adapted from* Deuteronomy 31:6

manded them, saying: "At the end of *every*
seven years, at the appointed time in the
year of release, at the Feast of Tabernacles,
11when all Israel comes to appear before
the LORD your God in the place which He
chooses, you shall read this law before all
Israel in their hearing. 12Gather the people
together, men and women and little ones,
and the stranger who *is* within your gates,
that they may hear and that they may learn
to fear the LORD your God and carefully
observe all the words of this law, 13and *that*
their children, who have not known it,
may hear and learn to fear the LORD your
God as long as you live in the land which
you cross the Jordan to possess."

Prediction of Israel's Rebellion

14Then the LORD said to Moses, "Behold,
the days approach when you must die; call
Joshua, and present yourselves in the
tabernacle of meeting, that I may inaugu-
rate him."

So Moses and Joshua went and pre-
sented themselves in the tabernacle of
meeting. 15Now the LORD appeared at the

31:1–29 Moses' final activities included the inauguration of his successor and the provisions for keeping the covenant prominent in the life of the people. He first reminded them that it would be neither he nor **Joshua** (v. 3), but God who would lead them into the land (vv. 3–5). It was precisely because Moses had tried to usurp the place of God (Num. 20:10–13) that God could not permit him to lead Israel's entry. The people would have given all the glory to Moses. In a final exhortation, Moses commanded the regular reading of the law (vv. 9–13) and its safekeeping with the ark (vv. 24–29).

tabernacle in a pillar of cloud, and the pil-
lar of cloud stood above the door of the
tabernacle.
[16]And the LORD said to Moses: "Behold,
you will rest with your fathers; and this
people will rise and play the harlot with
the gods of the foreigners of the land,
where they go *to be* among them, and they
will forsake Me and break My covenant
which I have made with them. [17]Then My
anger shall be aroused against them in that
day, and I will forsake them, and I will hide
My face from them, and they shall be de-
voured. And many evils and troubles shall
befall them, so that they will say in that
day, 'Have not these evils come upon us
because our God *is* not among us?' [18]And I
will surely hide My face in that day be-
cause of all the evil which they have done,
in that they have turned to other gods.
[19]"Now therefore, write down this song
for yourselves, and teach it to the children
of Israel; put it in their mouths, that this
song may be a witness for Me against the
children of Israel. [20]When I have brought
them to the land flowing with milk and
honey, of which I swore to their fathers,
and they have eaten and filled themselves
and grown fat, then they will turn to other
gods and serve them; and they will pro-
voke Me and break My covenant. [21]Then it
shall be, when many evils and troubles
have come upon them, that this song will
testify against them as a witness; for it will
not be forgotten in the mouths of their de-
scendants, for I know the inclination of
their behavior today, even before I have
brought them to the land of which I swore
to give them."
[22]Therefore Moses wrote this song
the same day, and taught it to the children
of Israel. [23]Then He inaugurated Joshua
the son of Nun, and said, "Be strong
and of good courage; for you shall
bring the children of Israel into the land of
which I swore to them, and I will be with
you."
[24]So it was, when Moses had completed
writing the words of this law in a book,
when they were finished, [25]that Moses
commanded the Lē'vītes, who bore the ark
of the covenant of the LORD, saying: [26]"Take
this Book of the Law, and put it beside the
ark of the covenant of the LORD your God,
that it may be there as a witness against
you; [27]for I know your rebellion and your
stiff neck. *If* today, while I am yet alive
with you, you have been rebellious against
the LORD, then how much more after my
death? [28]Gather to me all the elders of your
tribes, and your officers, that I may speak
these words in their hearing and call
heaven and earth to witness against
them. [29]For I know that after my death you
will become utterly corrupt, and turn
aside from the way which I have com-
manded you. And evil will befall you in
the latter days, because you will do evil
in the sight of the LORD, to provoke
Him to anger through the work of your
hands."

The Song of Moses

[30]Then Moses spoke in the hearing of all
the assembly of Israel the words of this
song until they were ended:

CHAPTER 32

"Give ear, O heavens, and I will speak;
And hear, O earth, the words of my
mouth.

31:30—32:43 Moses obeys God's command (31:19) to summarize in a poem or song (31:30) what God had done for the Hebrew people in the past (32:7–14), how they would rebel against Him in the future (32:5, 6, 15–18), how God would punish them (32:19–33) and yet have mercy on them in the end (32:34–43). All of this was designed to motivate Israel towards obedience by teaching them the certainty of judgment on sin (see 31:16–21). Five times in this song the Lord is called "the Rock," expressing the reliable, immutable nature of God.

2 Let my teaching drop as the rain,
My speech distill as the dew,
As raindrops on the tender herb,
And as showers on the grass.
3 For I proclaim the name of the LORD:
Ascribe greatness to our God.
4 *He is* the Rock, His work *is* perfect;
For all His ways *are* justice,
A God of truth and without injustice;
Righteous and upright *is* He.

5 "They have corrupted themselves;
They are not His children,
Because of their blemish:
A perverse and crooked generation.
6 Do you thus deal with the LORD,
O foolish and unwise people?
Is He not your Father, *who* bought
you?
Has He not made you and established
you?

7 "Remember the days of old,
Consider the years of many
generations.
Ask your father, and he will show
you;
Your elders, and they will tell you:
8 When the Most High divided their
inheritance to the nations,
When He separated the sons of
Adam,
He set the boundaries of the peoples
According to the number of the chil-
dren of Israel.
9 For the LORD'S *portion is* His people;
Jacob *is* the place of His inheritance.

10 "He found him in a desert land
And in the wasteland, a howling
wilderness;
He encircled him, He instructed him,
He kept him as the apple of His eye.
11 As an eagle stirs up its nest,
Hovers over its young,
Spreading out its wings, taking them
up,
Carrying them on its wings,
12 *So* the LORD alone led him,
And *there was* no foreign god with
him.

13 "He made him ride in the heights of
the earth,
That he might eat the produce of the
fields;
He made him draw honey from the
rock,
And oil from the flinty rock;
14 Curds from the cattle, and milk of the
flock,
With fat of lambs;
And rams of the breed of Bā'shan,
and goats,
With the choicest wheat;
And you drank wine, the blood of the
grapes.

15 "But Jesh'ū·run grew fat and kicked;
You grew fat, you grew thick,
You are obese!
Then he forsook God *who* made him,
And scornfully esteemed the Rock of
his salvation.
16 They provoked Him to jealousy with
foreign *gods;*
With abominations they provoked
Him to anger.
17 They sacrificed to demons, not to
God,
To gods they did not know,
To new *gods,* new arrivals
That your fathers did not fear.
18 Of the Rock *who* begot you, you are
unmindful,
And have forgotten the God who
fathered you.

19 "And when the LORD saw *it,* He
spurned *them,*
Because of the provocation of His
sons and His daughters.
20 And He said: 'I will hide My face
from them,
I will see what their end *will be,*
For they *are* a perverse generation,
Children in whom *is* no faith.

21 They have provoked Me to jealousy
by *what* is not God;
They have moved Me to anger by
their foolish idols.
But I will provoke them to jealousy
by *those who are* not a nation;
I will move them to anger by a foolish
nation.
22 For a fire is kindled in My anger,
And shall burn to the lowest hell;
It shall consume the earth with her
increase,
And set on fire the foundations of the
mountains.

23 'I will heap disasters on them;
I will spend My arrows on them.
24 *They shall be* wasted with hunger,
Devoured by pestilence and bitter
destruction;
I will also send against them the teeth
of beasts,
With the poison of serpents of the
dust.
25 The sword shall destroy outside;
There shall be terror within
For the young man and virgin,
The nursing child with the man of
gray hairs.
26 I would have said, "I will dash them
in pieces,
I will make the memory of them to
cease from among men,"
27 Had I not feared the wrath of the
enemy,
Lest their adversaries should misun-
derstand,
Lest they should say, "Our hand *is*
high;
And it is not the LORD who has done
all this." '

28 "For they *are* a nation void of counsel,
Nor *is there any* understanding in
them.
29 Oh, that they were wise, *that* they
understood this,
That they would consider their latter
end!
30 How could one chase a thousand,
And two put ten thousand to flight,
Unless their Rock had sold them,
And the LORD had surrendered
them?
31 For their rock *is* not like our Rock,
Even our enemies themselves *being*
judges.
32 For their vine *is* of the vine of Sod'om
And of the fields of Go·mor'rah;
Their grapes *are* grapes of gall,
Their clusters *are* bitter.
33 Their wine *is* the poison of serpents,
And the cruel venom of cobras.

34 '*Is* this not laid up in store with Me,
Sealed up among My treasures?
35 Vengeance is Mine, and recompense;
Their foot shall slip in *due* time;
For the day of their calamity *is* at
hand,
And the things to come hasten upon
them.'

36 "For the LORD will judge His people
And have compassion on His
servants,
When He sees that *their* power is
gone,
And *there is* no one *remaining*, bond or
free.
37 He will say: 'Where *are* their gods,
The rock in which they sought
refuge?
38 Who ate the fat of their sacrifices,

32:22 lowest hell: Lit. "the underworld" or "the grave." This does not refer to eternal punishment. Rather, it is here a poetic expression of God's anger as fire which will consume the earth even to its lowest parts—**the foundations of the mountains**.

32:26, 27 Utter destruction of Israel would cause neighboring nations to misunderstand and believe that Israel was destroyed because God was not strong enough to help them.

And drank the wine of their drink
offering?
Let them rise and help you,
And be your refuge.

39 'Now see that I, *even* I, *am* He,
And *there is* no God besides Me;
I kill and I make alive;
I wound and I heal;
Nor *is there any* who can deliver from
My hand.
40 For I raise My hand to heaven,
And say, "*As* I live forever,
41 If I whet My glittering sword,
And My hand takes hold on
judgment,
I will render vengeance to My
enemies,
And repay those who hate Me.
42 I will make My arrows drunk with
blood,
And My sword shall devour flesh,
With the blood of the slain and the
captives,
From the heads of the leaders of the
enemy." '

43 "Rejoice, O Gentiles, *with* His people;[a]
For He will avenge the blood of His
servants,
And render vengeance to His
adversaries;
He will provide atonement for His
land *and* His people."

44So Moses came with Joshua[a] the son of
Nun and spoke all the words of this song
in the hearing of the people. 45Moses fin-
ished speaking all these words to all Israel,
46and he said to them: "Set your hearts on
all the words which I testify among you to-
day, which you shall command your chil-
dren to be careful to observe—all the
words of this law. 47For it *is* not a futile
thing for you, because it *is* your life, and by
this word you shall prolong *your* days in
the land which you cross over the Jordan
to possess."

Moses to Die on Mount Nebo

48Then the LORD spoke to Moses that
very same day, saying: 49"Go up this
mountain of the Ab'a·rim, Mount Nē'bō,
which *is* in the land of Mō'ab, across from
Jericho; view the land of Cā'naan, which I
give to the children of Israel as a posses-
sion; 50and die on the mountain which you
ascend, and be gathered to your people,
just as Aaron your brother died on Mount
Hor and was gathered to his people; 51be-
cause you trespassed against Me among
the children of Israel at the waters of
Mer'i·bah Kā'desh, in the Wilderness of
Zin, because you did not hallow Me in the
midst of the children of Israel. 52Yet you
shall see the land before *you,* though you
shall not go there, into the land which I am
giving to the children of Israel."

CHAPTER 33

Moses' Final Blessing on Israel

Now this *is* the blessing with which Mo-
ses the man of God blessed the children of
Israel before his death. 2And he said:

"The LORD came from Sinai,
And dawned on them from Sē'ir;
He shone forth from Mount Par'an,
And He came with ten thousands of
saints;

32:43 [a]A Dead Sea Scroll fragment adds *And let all the gods (angels) worship Him* (compare Septuagint and Hebrews 1:6).
32:44 [a]Hebrew *Hoshea* (compare Numbers 13:8, 16)

32:48–52 Moses' sin of glorifying himself rather than God meant that he could not enter the Promised Land (3:23–27), but God gave him some gracious compensations (see 34:1). For various reasons we may not achieve all we would like in this life. Nevertheless, if we continue to walk with the Lord, He offers eternal healing for every heartache. There are no disappointments in heaven. We shall see as God sees and be satisfied.

From His right hand
Came a fiery law for them.
3 Yes, He loves the people;
All His saints *are* in Your hand;
They sit down at Your feet;
Everyone receives Your words.
4 Moses commanded a law for us,
A heritage of the congregation of
Jacob.
5 And He was King in Jesh'ū·run,
When the leaders of the people were
gathered,
All the tribes of Israel together.

6 "Let Reuben live, and not die,
Nor let his men be few."

7 And this he said of Judah:

"Hear, LORD, the voice of Judah,
And bring him to his people;
Let his hands be sufficient for him,
And may You be a help against his
enemies."

8 And of Levi he said:

"*Let* Your Thum'mim and Your Ū'rim
be with Your holy one,
Whom You tested at Mas'sah,
And with whom You contended at
the waters of Mer'i·bah,
9 Who says of his father and mother,
'I have not seen them';
Nor did he acknowledge his brothers,
Or know his own children;
For they have observed Your word
And kept Your covenant.
10 They shall teach Jacob Your
judgments,
And Israel Your law.
They shall put incense before You,
And a whole burnt sacrifice on Your
altar.
11 Bless his substance, LORD,
And accept the work of his hands;
Strike the loins of those who rise
against him,
And of those who hate him, that they
rise not again."

12 Of Benjamin he said:

"The beloved of the LORD shall dwell
in safety by Him,
Who shelters him all the day long;
And he shall dwell between His
shoulders."

13 And of Joseph he said:

"Blessed of the LORD *is* his land,
With the precious things of heaven,
with the dew,
And the deep lying beneath,
14 With the precious fruits of the sun,
With the precious produce of the
months,
15 With the best things of the ancient
mountains,
With the precious things of the
everlasting hills,
16 With the precious things of the earth
and its fullness,
And the favor of Him who dwelt in
the bush.
Let *the blessing* come 'on the head of
Joseph,
And on the crown of the head of him
who was separate from his
brothers.'[a]
17 His glory *is like* a firstborn bull,

33:16 [a]Genesis 49:26

33:8 Thummim and Your Urim: The Urim and Thummim were a device for determining the will of God where other guidance was not available. As such they symbolized Israel's commitment to do the will of God. It is not known exactly how the Urim and Thummim were used, but probably each was marked in some way to signify yes and no. If, when they were thrown, both came up yes or both no, it was understood to indicate God's will for that situation.

And his horns *like* the horns of the
wild ox;
Together with them
He shall push the peoples
To the ends of the earth;
They *are* the ten thousands of
Ē'phra·im,
And they *are* the thousands of
Ma·nas'seh."

18And of Zeb'ū·lun he said:

"Rejoice, Zeb'ū·lun, in your going out,
And Is'sa·char in your tents!
19 They shall call the peoples *to* the
mountain;
There they shall offer sacrifices of
righteousness;
For they shall partake *of* the
abundance of the seas
And *of* treasures hidden in the sand."

20And of Gad he said:

"Blessed *is* he who enlarges Gad;
He dwells as a lion,
And tears the arm and the crown of
his head.
21 He provided the first *part* for
himself,
Because a lawgiver's portion was
reserved there.
He came *with* the heads of the
people;
He administered the justice of the
LORD,
And His judgments with Israel."

22And of Dan he said:

"Dan *is* a lion's whelp;
He shall leap from Bā'shan."

23And of Naph'ta·lī he said:

"O Naph'ta·lī, satisfied with favor,
And full of the blessing of the LORD,
Possess the west and the south."

24And of Ash'er he said:

"Ash'er *is* most blessed of sons;
Let him be favored by his brothers,
And let him dip his foot in oil.
25 Your sandals *shall be* iron and
bronze;
As your days, *so shall* your strength
be.
26 "*There is* no one like the God of
Jesh'ū·run,
Who rides the heavens to help you,
And in His excellency on the clouds.
27 The eternal God *is your* refuge,
And underneath *are* the everlasting
arms;
He will thrust out the enemy from
before you,
And will say, 'Destroy!'
28 Then Israel shall dwell in safety,
The fountain of Jacob alone,
In a land of grain and new wine;
His heavens shall also drop dew.
29 Happy *are* you, O Israel!
Who *is* like you, a people saved by
the LORD,
The shield of your help
And the sword of your majesty!
Your enemies shall submit to you,
And you shall tread down their high
places."

CHAPTER 34

Moses Dies on Mount Nebo

Then Moses went up from the plains of
Mō'ab to Mount Nē'bō, to the top of
Pis'gah, which is across from Jericho. And
the LORD showed him all the land of
Gil'ē·ad as far as Dan, 2all Naph'ta·lī and

34:1 Nebo: Though he could not enter, Moses was allowed to see the new land. This is an indication of the compassion of God for His valiant servant. By looking it over, there is a sense in which Moses actually took possession of it for the Israelites.

USE IT OR LOSE IT

Leslie E. Moser, Ph.D.

Some folks encounter problems with their minds as they grow older. About 5 percent of those over age fifty-five have some problems caused by strokes, organic brain syndromes, and Alzheimer's Disease. Most of these have been lumped together as Alzheimer's patients. Both those who suffer from this terrible disease and their loved ones can take comfort in knowing that one day our earthly bodies will be exchanged for gloriously healthy eternal ones.

However, of the remaining 95 percent of us, many are losing mind power because they believe the myth that the mind decays with age—it gives them a good excuse to "hang it up." And when they do, the myth becomes reality. The myths of fading mentality are really a gaggle of half-truths that will permit people to allow their minds to fade. However, you do not have to let this happen—you can keep your mind sharp by using it.

I have already passed age seventy-four, and I know I have slowed down a little in my ability to handle complex problems. But only a little. For the most part, I only let the younger folk do what I don't really care to do anyway. My intellectual skills have changed, and I'm sure they will change some more. But I wouldn't change places with anyone. Would you? Researchers have shown that mental exercise helps intellectual performance. The more of these intellectual exercises you do, the longer you will maintain your brain power and the more you can accomplish for the cause of Christ. ✦

the land of Ē'phra·im and Ma·nas'seh, all
the land of Judah as far as the Western Sea,[a]
3 the South, and the plain of the Valley of
Jericho, the city of palm trees, as far as
Zō'ar. 4 Then the LORD said to him, "This *is*
the land of which I swore to give Abraham,
Isaac, and Jacob, saying, 'I will give it to
your descendants.' I have caused you to
see *it* with your eyes, but you shall not
cross over there."
5 So Moses the servant of the LORD died
there in the land of Mō'ab, according to the
word of the LORD. 6 And He buried him in a
valley in the land of Mō'ab, opposite Beth
Pē'or; but no one knows his grave to this
day. 7 Moses *was* one hundred and twenty
years old when he died. His eyes were not
dim nor his natural vigor diminished.
8 And the children of Israel wept for Moses
in the plains of Mō'ab thirty days. So the
days of weeping *and* mourning for Moses
ended.
9 Now Joshua the son of Nun was full of
the spirit of wisdom, for Moses had laid
his hands on him; so the children of Israel
heeded him, and did as the LORD had commanded Moses.

34:2 [a]That is, the Mediterranean

[10]But since then there has not arisen in
Israel a prophet like Moses, whom the
LORD knew face to face, [11]in all the signs
and wonders which the LORD sent him to
do in the land of Egypt, before Pharaoh,
before all his servants, and in all his land,
[12]and by all that mighty power and all the
great terror which Moses performed in the
sight of all Israel.

34:10 a prophet like Moses: He had been the great spokesman for God. There would be other prophets in Israel, but no one would ever hold the place of the man who led them out of Egypt to the Promised Land. Nevertheless, One would come (see 18:15, 18, 19), whose sandals Moses was not worthy to unloose. That One, Jesus Christ, would carry the sins of us all, including those of Moses.

✦Joshua✦

While the author of this book is not clearly identified, Joshua probably wrote large sections of it (24:26), as only an eyewitness (5:1, 6) could have recorded the vivid battle scenes. Later, someone else recounted Joshua's death and perhaps organized his writings into this book. The first of the twelve historical books, Joshua covers three major military campaigns involving more than thirty enemy armies, and it was probably completed close to Joshua's death around 1375 B.C.

Joshua accepted God's call to lead Israel when he was more than ninety years old, and the first chapters tell of the Israelites' spiritual, moral, physical, and military preparation for conquering Canaan under his leadership. Chapters 6—13:7 describe their seven-year conquest of the land, while chapters 13:8—21 explain the allocation of the land to the twelve tribes. Through their many battles, God taught them that victory only came through complete dependence upon and obedience to the Lord, and sin brought dire consequences (7:1–26).

After Israel settled in Canaan, Joshua gave a moving farewell speech, warning the Israelites against worshiping idols and urging them to renew their allegiance to the covenant. ✦

CHAPTER 1

God's Commission to Joshua

After the death of Moses the servant of
the LORD, it came to pass that the LORD
spoke to Joshua the son of Nun, Moses' as-
sistant, saying: 2"Moses My servant is
dead. Now therefore, arise, go over this
Jordan, you and all this people, to the land
which I am giving to them—the children of
Israel. 3Every place that the sole of your
foot will tread upon I have given you, as I
said to Moses. 4From the wilderness and
this Lebanon as far as the great river, the
River Eū·phrā'tēs, all the land of the

> The Promised Land always lies on the other side of a wilderness.
>
> Havelock Ellis

Hit'tītes, and to the Great Sea toward
the going down of the sun, shall be your
territory. 5No man shall *be able to* stand be-
fore you all the days of your life; as I was
with Moses, *so* I will be with you. I will not
leave you nor forsake you. 6Be strong and
of good courage, for to this people you
shall divide as an inheritance the land

1:1–9 The Israelites are on the east bank of the **Jordan** (v. 2). **The LORD** encouraged **Joshua** as He does every leader whom He calls. The answer to fear and uncertainty is the presence of God and a determination to follow His guidance.

1:6 Four times in this chapter God encourages Joshua for the task at hand with the phrase "be strong and of good courage."

which I swore to their fathers to give them.
[7]Only be strong and very courageous, that
you may observe to do according to all the
law which Moses My servant commanded
you; do not turn from it to the right hand
or to the left, that you may prosper wher-
ever you go. [8]This Book of the Law shall
not depart from your mouth, but you shall
meditate in it day and night, that you may
observe to do according to all that is writ-
ten in it. For then you will make your way
prosperous, and then you will have good
success. [9]Have I not commanded you? Be
strong and of good courage; do not be
afraid, nor be dismayed, for the LORD your
God *is* with you wherever you go."

> Our grand business in life is not to see what lies dimly at a distance, but to do what lies clearly at hand.
>
> Thomas Carlyle

The Order to Cross the Jordan

[10]Then Joshua commanded the officers
of the people, saying, [11]"Pass through the
camp and command the people, saying,
'Prepare provisions for yourselves, for
within three days you will cross over this
Jordan, to go in to possess the land which
the LORD your God is giving you to pos-
sess.' "

[12]And to the Reū'ben·ītes, the Gad'ītes,
and half the tribe of Ma·nas'seh Joshua
spoke, saying, [13]"Remember the word
which Moses the servant of the LORD com-
manded you, saying, 'The LORD your God
is giving you rest and is giving you this
land.' [14]Your wives, your little ones, and
your livestock shall remain in the land
which Moses gave you on this side of the
Jordan. But you shall pass before your
brethren armed, all your mighty men of
valor, and help them, [15]until the LORD has
given your brethren rest, as He *gave* you,
and they also have taken possession of the
land which the LORD your God is giving
them. Then you shall return to the land of
your possession and enjoy it, which Moses
the LORD's servant gave you on this side of
the Jordan toward the sunrise."

[16]So they answered Joshua, saying, "All
that you command us we will do, and
wherever you send us we will go. [17]Just as
we heeded Moses in all things, so we will
heed you. Only the LORD your God be with
you, as He was with Moses. [18]Whoever
rebels against your command and does not
heed your words, in all that you command
him, shall be put to death. Only be strong
and of good courage."

CHAPTER 2

Rahab Hides the Spies

Now Joshua the son of Nun sent out
two men from Acacia Grove[a] to spy se-
cretly, saying, "Go, view the land, espe-
cially Jericho."

So they went, and came to the house of
a harlot named Rā'hab, and lodged there.
[2]And it was told the king of Jericho, saying,
"Behold, men have come here tonight from
the children of Israel to search out the
country."

[3]So the king of Jericho sent to Rā'hab,
saying, "Bring out the men who have come
to you, who have entered your house, for
they have come to search out all the coun-
try."

[4]Then the woman took the two men and
hid them. So she said, "Yes, the men came

2:1 [a]Hebrew *Shittim*

1:8 This Book of the Law: God's Word is to be our guide—always. **meditate**: the Hebrew word infers an active recitation.

2:1–4 In order to avoid detection, the spies lodged in a brothel which travelers would frequent. Because of the constant traffic, their presence would not arouse suspicion, and they could gain information from others who were there.

JOSHUA: THE WISE WARRIOR

One of the best-known leaders of Israel in the Old Testament, Joshua has long been respected for his faith and courage as Moses' successor; but his training began years earlier, during the early days of the Exodus.

His first battle experience came just a few months into the journey (Ex. 17:9). Joshua probably did not gain any combat experience while serving as a slave to the Egyptians, but he didn't hesitate to respond when Moses called him to command the Israelite army (v. 10). He led Israel to triumph as Moses prayed for the victory (vv. 11–13).

Later, as one of the men sent to spy out Canaan, Joshua sided with Caleb in urging the people to proceed according to the Lord's plan. Overruled by the fearful, faithless people, Joshua and Caleb alone lived to enter the Promised Land (Num. 14:30). Their lives were spared because they "wholly followed the Lord" (32:12).

According to God's command, Moses selected Joshua as his successor (27:22, 23), and the spiritual and mental strength this godly warrior had exhibited in these and other incidents were put to the test.

Although it must have been disconcerting to follow after a leader as outstanding as Moses, Joshua successfully accepted the challenge. Scripture attributes his strong leadership skills to the "spirit of wisdom" that filled him (Deut. 34:9). The Book of Joshua is filled with tales of his exploits in conquering Canaan, including the miraculous defeat of Jericho (Josh. 6).

God never gives His servants an assignment without providing everything they need to complete the task. When He commissioned Joshua to lead His people, the Lord supplied the authority he needed to be successful: "On that day the LORD exalted Joshua in the sight of all Israel; and they feared him, as they had feared Moses, all the days of his life" (Josh. 4:14).

Many Christians find "easy" ways to serve the Lord but fail when they face more difficult challenges. Not so with Joshua. "As the LORD had commanded Moses his servant, so Moses commanded Joshua, and so Joshua did. He left nothing undone of all that the LORD had commanded Moses" (Josh. 11:15).

His thorough dedication influenced the Israelites and inspired them to greater obedience than they had ever shown:

> "So the people served the LORD all the days of Joshua" (Judg. 2:7).

This servant of God, whose faith rarely faltered through his 110 years, should inspire Christians to remain steadfast in the small things as preparation for the larger tasks. As those who have gone before us relinquish the burden of ministry, we must commit ourselves—physically, mentally, and spiritually—to fulfill the tasks left to us and to provide healthy leadership for the next generation. ✦

to me, but I did not know where they *were*
from. [5]And it happened as the gate was
being shut, when it was dark, that the men
went out. Where the men went I do not
know; pursue them quickly, for you may
overtake them." [6](But she had brought
them up to the roof and hidden them
with the stalks of flax, which she had laid
in order on the roof.) [7]Then the men
pursued them by the road to the Jordan, to
the fords. And as soon as those who pur-
sued them had gone out, they shut the
gate.

[8]Now before they lay down, she came
up to them on the roof, [9]and said to the
men: "I know that the LORD has given you
the land, that the terror of you has fallen on
us, and that all the inhabitants of the land
are fainthearted because of you. [10]For we
have heard how the LORD dried up the wa-
ter of the Red Sea for you when you came
out of Egypt, and what you did to the two
kings of the Am'o·rītes who *were* on the
other side of the Jordan, Sī'hon and Og,
whom you utterly destroyed. [11]And as
soon as we heard *these things,* our hearts
melted; neither did there remain any more
courage in anyone because of you, for the
LORD your God, He *is* God in heaven above
and on earth beneath. [12]Now therefore, I
beg you, swear to me by the LORD, since I
have shown you kindness, that you also
will show kindness to my father's house,
and give me a true token, [13]and spare my
father, my mother, my brothers, my sisters,
and all that they have, and deliver our
lives from death."

[14]So the men answered her, "Our lives
for yours, if none of you tell this business
of ours. And it shall be, when the LORD has
given us the land, that we will deal kindly
and truly with you."

[15]Then she let them down by a rope
through the window, for her house *was* on
the city wall; she dwelt on the wall. [16]And
she said to them, "Get to the mountain, lest
the pursuers meet you. Hide there three
days, until the pursuers have returned.
Afterward you may go your way."

[17]So the men said to her: "We *will be*
blameless of this oath of yours which you
have made us swear, [18]unless, *when* we
come into the land, you bind this line of
scarlet cord in the window through which
you let us down, and unless you bring
your father, your mother, your brothers,
and all your father's household to your
own home. [19]So it shall be *that* whoever
goes outside the doors of your house into
the street, his blood *shall be* on his own
head, and we *will be* guiltless. And who-
ever is with you in the house, his blood
shall be on our head if a hand is laid on him.
[20]And if you tell this business of ours, then
we will be free from your oath which you
made us swear."

[21]Then she said, "According to your
words, so *be* it." And she sent them away,
and they departed. And she bound the
scarlet cord in the window.

[22]They departed and went to the moun-
tain, and stayed there three days until the
pursuers returned. The pursuers sought
them all along the way, but did not find
them. [23]So the two men returned, de-
scended from the mountain, and crossed

2:5 I do not know: The NT commends Rahab for her faith, not her falsehood (see Heb. 11:31). James mentions her together with Abraham as an example of good works (see James 2:25).

2:9–11 A response of faith to the evidence of God's power. Rahab's remarkable confession may have been motivated by fear and a desire for self-preservation, but it was nonetheless genuine. God looks at the heart and rewards those who turn to Him in faith whatever their initial motives. See Heb. 11:31. Rahab is one of only four women listed in the messianic genealogy of Matt. 1.

2:12–14 Kindness in Hebrew denotes loyal commitment. **deal kindly . . . with you**: God brings awe to those who know about Him; He is faithful to all who follow Him.

over; and they came to Joshua the son of Nun, and told him all that had befallen them. 24And they said to Joshua, "Truly the LORD has delivered all the land into our hands, for indeed all the inhabitants of the country are fainthearted because of us."

CHAPTER 3

Israel Crosses the Jordan

Then Joshua rose early in the morning; and they set out from Acacia Grove[a] and came to the Jordan, he and all the children of Israel, and lodged there before they crossed over. 2So it was, after three days, that the officers went through the camp; 3and they commanded the people, saying, "When you see the ark of the covenant of the LORD your God, and the priests, the Lē′vītes, bearing it, then you shall set out from your place and go after it. 4Yet there shall be a space between you and it, about two thousand cubits by measure. Do not come near it, that you may know the way by which you must go, for you have not passed *this* way before."

5And Joshua said to the people, "Sanctify yourselves, for tomorrow the LORD will do wonders among you." 6Then Joshua spoke to the priests, saying, "Take up the ark of the covenant and cross over before the people."

So they took up the ark of the covenant and went before the people.

7And the LORD said to Joshua, "This day I will begin to exalt you in the sight of all Israel, that they may know that, as I was with Moses, *so* I will be with you. 8You shall command the priests who bear the ark of the covenant, saying, 'When you have come to the edge of the water of the Jordan, you shall stand in the Jordan.' "

9So Joshua said to the children of Israel, "Come here, and hear the words of the LORD your God." 10And Joshua said, "By this you shall know that the living God *is* among you, and *that* He will without fail drive out from before you the Cā′naan·ītes and the Hit′tītes and the Hī′vītes and the Per′iz·zītes and the Gir′ga·shītes and the Am′o·rītes and the Jeb′ū·sītes: 11Behold, the ark of the covenant of the Lord of all the earth is crossing over before you into the Jordan. 12Now therefore, take for yourselves twelve men from the tribes of Israel, one man from every tribe. 13And it shall come to pass, as soon as the soles of the feet of the priests who bear the ark of the LORD, the Lord of all the earth, shall rest in the waters of the Jordan, *that* the waters of the Jordan shall be cut off, the waters that come down from upstream, and they shall stand as a heap."

14So it was, when the people set out from their camp to cross over the Jordan, with the priests bearing the ark of the covenant before the people, 15and as those who bore the ark came to the Jordan, and the feet of the priests who bore the ark dipped in the edge of the water (for the Jordan overflows all its banks during the whole time of harvest), 16that the waters which came down from upstream stood *still, and* rose in a heap very far away at Adam, the city that *is* beside Zar′e·tan. So the waters that went down into the Sea of the Ar′a·bah, the Salt Sea, failed, *and* were cut off; and the people crossed over opposite Jericho. 17Then the priests who bore the ark of the covenant of the LORD stood firm on dry ground in the midst of the Jordan; and all Israel crossed over on dry ground, until all the people had crossed completely over the Jordan.

3:1 [a]Hebrew *Shittim*

3:3 The **ark of the covenant** led the procession as it did during the wilderness journey (see Num. 10:33–36).

3:7–10 God's actions would make it clear that His hand of approval was on Joshua's leadership. **He will . . . drive out**: This is God's plan; they are to understand it solely as His work.

CHAPTER 4

The Memorial Stones

And it came to pass, when all the people
had completely crossed over the Jordan,
that the LORD spoke to Joshua, saying:
2"Take for yourselves twelve men from the
people, one man from every tribe, 3and
command them, saying, 'Take for yourselves twelve stones from here, out of the
midst of the Jordan, from the place where
the priests' feet stood firm. You shall carry
them over with you and leave them in the
lodging place where you lodge tonight.' "
4Then Joshua called the twelve men
whom he had appointed from the children
of Israel, one man from every tribe; 5and
Joshua said to them: "Cross over before the
ark of the LORD your God into the midst of
the Jordan, and each one of you take up a
stone on his shoulder, according to the
number of the tribes of the children of Israel, 6that this may be a sign among you
when your children ask in time to come,
saying, 'What do these stones *mean* to
you?' 7Then you shall answer them that the
waters of the Jordan were cut off before the
ark of the covenant of the LORD; when it
crossed over the Jordan, the waters of the
Jordan were cut off. And these stones shall
be for a memorial to the children of Israel
forever."
8And the children of Israel did so, just as
Joshua commanded, and took up twelve
stones from the midst of the Jordan, as the
LORD had spoken to Joshua, according to
the number of the tribes of the children of
Israel, and carried them over with them to
the place where they lodged, and laid them
down there. 9Then Joshua set up twelve
stones in the midst of the Jordan, in the
place where the feet of the priests who bore
the ark of the covenant stood; and they are
there to this day.

Keeping the Past Alive

Jay Kesler

After the children of Israel had just crossed over the Jordan River on dry land, Joshua commanded the leader of each tribe to take one stone out of the riverbed and carry it with them (Josh. 4). He then told them to make a monument out of the stones. "When your children ask in time to come, saying, 'What do these stones mean to you?' Then you shall answer them that the waters of the Jordan were cut off before the ark of the covenant of the Lord; when it crossed over the Jordan, the waters of the Jordan were cut off. And these stones shall be for a memorial to the children of Israel forever" (Josh. 4:6, 7).

We, too, set up memorial stones—systems and traditions that remind us of God's faithfulness. But often our children and grandchildren are never really answered when they ask, "What do these stones mean?"

To a large degree, grandparents bear the responsibility of keeping the past alive, reminding others of the faithfulness of God. We can do that, in part, by telling our stories. All ancient people have traditions of storytelling. The stories are preserved from generation to generation, and this combined wisdom provides the foundation on which culture is built. ✦

4:1–9 God's saving acts are unique, once-for-all events in history. Our faith is inspired by recalling these acts. Here **stones** (v. 3) were set up as a visible reminder for generations to come of God's mighty acts on their behalf (v. 7; see also vv. 21–24).

10So the priests who bore the ark stood
in the midst of the Jordan until everything
was finished that the LORD had com-
manded Joshua to speak to the people,
according to all that Moses had com-
manded Joshua; and the people hurried
and crossed over. 11Then it came to pass,
when all the people had completely
crossed over, that the ark of the LORD
and the priests crossed over in the pres-
ence of the people. 12And the men of
Reuben, the men of Gad, and half the tribe
of Ma·nas′seh crossed over armed before
the children of Israel, as Moses had
spoken to them. 13About forty thousand
prepared for war crossed over before the
LORD for battle, to the plains of Jericho.
14On that day the LORD exalted Joshua in
the sight of all Israel; and they feared him,
as they had feared Moses, all the days of
his life.

15Then the LORD spoke to Joshua, say-
ing, 16"Command the priests who bear the
ark of the Testimony to come up from the
Jordan." 17Joshua therefore commanded
the priests, saying, "Come up from the
Jordan." 18And it came to pass, when the
priests who bore the ark of the covenant
of the LORD had come from the midst of
the Jordan, *and* the soles of the priests'
feet touched the dry land, that the
waters of the Jordan returned to their
place and overflowed all its banks as be-
fore.

19Now the people came up from the Jor-
dan on the tenth *day* of the first month, and
they camped in Gil′gal on the east border
of Jericho. 20And those twelve stones
which they took out of the Jordan, Joshua
set up in Gil′gal. 21Then he spoke to the
children of Israel, saying: "When your
children ask their fathers in time to come,
saying, 'What *are* these stones?' 22then
you shall let your children know, saying,
'Israel crossed over this Jordan on dry
land'; 23for the LORD your God dried up
the waters of the Jordan before you until
you had crossed over, as the LORD
your God did to the Red Sea, which He
dried up before us until we had crossed
over, 24that all the peoples of the earth may
know the hand of the LORD, that it *is*
mighty, that you may fear the LORD your
God forever."

CHAPTER 5

The Second Generation Circumcised

So it was, when all the kings of the
Am′o·rītes who *were* on the west side of
the Jordan, and all the kings of the
Cā′naan·ītes who *were* by the sea, heard
that the LORD had dried up the waters of
the Jordan from before the children of Is-
rael until we[a] had crossed over, that their
heart melted; and there was no spirit in
them any longer because of the children of
Israel.

2At that time the LORD said to Joshua,
"Make flint knives for yourself, and cir-
cumcise the sons of Israel again the second
time." 3So Joshua made flint knives for
himself, and circumcised the sons of Israel
at the hill of the foreskins.[a] 4And this *is* the
reason why Joshua circumcised them: All
the people who came out of Egypt *who were*
males, all the men of war, had died in the

5:1 [a]Following Kethib; Qere, some Hebrew manuscripts and editions, Septuagint, Syriac, Targum, and Vulgate read *they*. 5:3 [a]Hebrew *Gibeath Haaraloth*

4:24 Two reasons are given for miracles: (1) **that . . . peoples . . . may know the . . . LORD**; (2) **that you may fear** (reverence) **the LORD**.

5:2–10 This was a circumcision of the second generation (vv. 2–5). Where circumcision was practiced among other ancient Semites, it was usually a puberty rite related to fertility religion. For Israel it signified a separation from Canaanite practices and a "sanctification" of one's sexuality to God as a sign of their covenant relationship (see Gen. 17:9–14). The cutting off of the part was a token of the consecration of the whole person. This spiritual significance was already understood by Joshua's time (see Deut. 30:6).

wilderness on the way, after they had come out of Egypt. 5For all the people who came out had been circumcised, but all the people born in the wilderness, on the way as they came out of Egypt, had not been circumcised. 6For the children of Israel walked forty years in the wilderness, till all the people *who were* men of war, who came out of Egypt, were consumed, because they did not obey the voice of the LORD—to whom the LORD swore that He would not show them the land which the LORD had sworn to their fathers that He would give us, "a land flowing with milk and honey."[a] 7Then Joshua circumcised their sons *whom* He raised up in their place; for they were uncircumcised, because they had not been circumcised on the way.

8So it was, when they had finished circumcising all the people, that they stayed in their places in the camp till they were healed. 9Then the LORD said to Joshua, "This day I have rolled away the reproach of Egypt from you." Therefore the name of the place is called Gil'gal[a] to this day.

10Now the children of Israel camped in Gil'gal, and kept the Passover on the fourteenth day of the month at twilight on the plains of Jericho. 11And they ate of the produce of the land on the day after the Passover, unleavened bread and parched grain, on the very same day. 12Then the manna ceased on the day after they had eaten the produce of the land; and the children of Israel no longer had manna, but they ate the food of the land of Cā'naan that year.

5:6 [a]Exodus 3:8 5:9 [a]Literally *Rolling*

The Commander of the Army of the LORD

13And it came to pass, when Joshua was by Jericho, that he lifted his eyes and looked, and behold, a Man stood opposite him with His sword drawn in His hand. And Joshua went to Him and said to Him, "*Are* You for us or for our adversaries?"

14So He said, "No, but *as* Commander of the army of the LORD I have now come."

And Joshua fell on his face to the earth and worshiped, and said to Him, "What does my Lord say to His servant?"

15Then the Commander of the LORD's army said to Joshua, "Take your sandal off your foot, for the place where you stand *is* holy." And Joshua did so.

CHAPTER 6

The Destruction of Jericho

Now Jericho was securely shut up because of the children of Israel; none went out, and none came in. 2And the LORD said to Joshua: "See! I have given Jericho into your hand, its king, *and* the mighty men of valor. 3You shall march around the city, all *you* men of war; you shall go all around the city once. This you shall do six days. 4And seven priests shall bear seven trumpets of rams' horns before the ark. But the seventh day you shall march around the city seven times, and the priests shall blow the trumpets. 5It shall come to pass, when they make a long *blast* with the ram's horn, *and* when you hear the sound of the trumpet, that all the people shall shout with a great shout; then the wall of the city will fall

5:11, 12 The **manna ceased** on the day after the Israelites first ate of the fruit of the Promised Land, underscoring God's miraculous provision as His work alone, which ceased when no longer needed.

5:14, 15 Commander of the army of the LORD: This "Man" is evidently God, or a representative of God in human form. The encounter with the divine **Commander** validated to Joshua his place as Moses' rightful successor, but Joshua is not in ultimate command; this is God's war. **Joshua fell on his face**: As Christians we need to experience a similar submission if our warfare is to be successful.

6:1 Archeologists estimate Jericho's population to have been about 10,000.

down flat. And the people shall go up
every man straight before him."
6Then Joshua the son of Nun called
the priests and said to them, "Take up
the ark of the covenant, and let seven
priests bear seven trumpets of rams'
horns before the ark of the LORD." 7And
he said to the people, "Proceed, and
march around the city, and let him who is
armed advance before the ark of the
LORD."
8So it was, when Joshua had spoken
to the people, that the seven priests bear-
ing the seven trumpets of rams' horns be-
fore the LORD advanced and blew the
trumpets, and the ark of the covenant of
the LORD followed them. 9The armed men
went before the priests who blew the trum-
pets, and the rear guard came after the ark,
while *the priests* continued blowing the
trumpets. 10Now Joshua had commanded
the people, saying, "You shall not shout or
make any noise with your voice, nor shall a
word proceed out of your mouth, until the
day I say to you, 'Shout!' Then you shall
shout." 11So he had the ark of the LORD cir-
cle the city, going around *it* once. Then
they came into the camp and lodged in the
camp.
12And Joshua rose early in the morning,
and the priests took up the ark of the LORD.
13Then seven priests bearing seven trum-
pets of rams' horns before the ark of the
LORD went on continually and blew with
the trumpets. And the armed men went be-
fore them. But the rear guard came after
the ark of the LORD, while *the priests* contin-
ued blowing the trumpets. 14And the sec-
ond day they marched around the city
once and returned to the camp. So they did
six days.
15But it came to pass on the seventh day
that they rose early, about the dawning of
the day, and marched around the city
seven times in the same manner. On that
day only they marched around the city
seven times. 16And the seventh time it hap-
pened, when the priests blew the trum-
pets, that Joshua said to the people:
"Shout, for the LORD has given you the
city! 17Now the city shall be doomed by the
LORD to destruction, it and all who *are* in it.
Only Rā'hab the harlot shall live, she and
all who *are* with her in the house, because
she hid the messengers that we sent. 18And
you, by all means abstain from the ac-
cursed things, lest you become accursed
when you take of the accursed things, and
make the camp of Israel a curse, and trou-
ble it. 19But all the silver and gold, and ves-
sels of bronze and iron, *are* consecrated to
the LORD; they shall come into the treasury
of the LORD."
20So the people shouted when *the priests*
blew the trumpets. And it happened when
the people heard the sound of the trumpet,
and the people shouted with a great shout,
that the wall fell down flat. Then the peo-
ple went up into the city, every man
straight before him, and they took the city.
21And they utterly destroyed all that *was* in
the city, both man and woman, young and
old, ox and sheep and donkey, with the
edge of the sword.
22But Joshua had said to the two men
who had spied out the country, "Go into
the harlot's house, and from there bring
out the woman and all that she has, as you

6:15 In the Bible, the number **seven** symbolizes completion and perfection.

6:16 Despite the odds against Israel, Joshua took the Lord at His word and moved ahead in faith. When we rely fully on God, we can claim the victory He has promised.

6:17 doomed . . . to destruction: The practice of offering everything in a captured city as a sacrifice to God. The troops were to refrain from taking any plunder; all was to be consecrated to God. This was His battle.

6:21 they utterly destroyed all: The Canaanites were evidently so sinful that their survival threatened God's plan for a holy nation through which the Savior of the world would come. No alternative existed, therefore, but to destroy them.

swore to her." 23And the young men who
had been spies went in and brought out
Rā'hab, her father, her mother, her
brothers, and all that she had. So they
brought out all her relatives and left them
outside the camp of Israel. 24But they
burned the city and all that *was* in it with
fire. Only the silver and gold, and the ves-
sels of bronze and iron, they put into the
treasury of the house of the LORD. 25And
Joshua spared Rā'hab the harlot, her
father's household, and all that she had. So
she dwells in Israel to this day, because she
hid the messengers whom Joshua sent to
spy out Jericho.
26Then Joshua charged *them* at that time,
saying, "Cursed *be* the man before the
LORD who rises up and builds this city Jer-
icho; he shall lay its foundation with his
firstborn, and with his youngest he shall
set up its gates."
27So the LORD was with Joshua, and his
fame spread throughout all the country.

CHAPTER 7

Defeat at Ai

But the children of Israel committed a
trespass regarding the accursed things, for
Ā'chan the son of Car'mī, the son of
Zab'dī,[a] the son of Zē'rah, of the tribe of
Judah, took of the accursed things; so the
anger of the LORD burned against the chil-
dren of Israel.
2Now Joshua sent men from Jericho to
Aī, which *is* beside Beth Ā'ven, on the east
side of Beth'el, and spoke to them, saying,
"Go up and spy out the country." So the
men went up and spied out Aī. 3And they
returned to Joshua and said to him, "Do
not let all the people go up, but let about
two or three thousand men go up and at-
tack Aī. Do not weary all the people there,
for *the people of Aī are* few." 4So about three
thousand men went up there from the peo-
ple, but they fled before the men of Aī.
5And the men of Aī struck down about
thirty-six men, for they chased them *from*
before the gate as far as Sheb'a·rim, and
struck them down on the descent; there-
fore the hearts of the people melted and
became like water.
6Then Joshua tore his clothes, and fell to
the earth on his face before the ark of the
LORD until evening, he and the elders of Is-
rael; and they put dust on their heads.
7And Joshua said, "Alas, Lord GOD, why
have You brought this people over the Jor-
dan at all—to deliver us into the hand of
the Am'o·rītes, to destroy us? Oh, that we
had been content, and dwelt on the other
side of the Jordan! 8O Lord, what shall I say
when Israel turns its back before its ene-
mies? 9For the Cā'naan·ītes and all the in-
habitants of the land will hear *it,* and sur-
round us, and cut off our name from the
earth. Then what will You do for Your
great name?"

The Sin of Achan

10So the LORD said to Joshua: "Get up!
Why do you lie thus on your face? 11Israel
has sinned, and they have also trans-
gressed My covenant which I commanded
them. For they have even taken some of
the accursed things, and have both stolen
and deceived; and they have also put *it*
among their own stuff. 12Therefore the chil-
dren of Israel could not stand before their
enemies, *but* turned *their* backs before their
enemies, because they have become
doomed to destruction. Neither will I be
with you anymore, unless you destroy the

7:1 [a]Called *Zimri* in 1 Chronicles 2:6

6:23 Rahab and her family, as Gentiles, were ceremonially unclean and thus had to stay outside the camp until appropriate procedures were followed.

7:11 **sinned**: God had not forsaken Israel; the people had forsaken God.

7:12 A holy thing must not be defiled. It must be destroyed if it cannot be kept pure. Israel had now become **doomed to destruction** unless the accursed thing was removed from her midst.

accursed from among you. 13Get up, sanc-
tify the people, and say, 'Sanctify your-
selves for tomorrow, because thus says the
LORD God of Israel: "*There is* an accursed
thing in your midst, O Israel; you cannot
stand before your enemies until you take
away the accursed thing from among
you." 14In the morning therefore you shall
be brought according to your tribes. And it
shall be *that* the tribe which the LORD takes
shall come according to families; and the
family which the LORD takes shall come by
households; and the household which the
LORD takes shall come man by man. 15Then
it shall be *that* he who is taken with the ac-
cursed thing shall be burned with fire, he
and all that he has, because he has trans-
gressed the covenant of the LORD, and be-
cause he has done a disgraceful thing in Is-
rael.' "

16So Joshua rose early in the morning
and brought Israel by their tribes, and the
tribe of Judah was taken. 17He brought
the clan of Judah, and he took the family of
the Zar'hītes; and he brought the family
of the Zar'hītes man by man, and Zab'dī
was taken. 18Then he brought his house-
hold man by man, and Ā'chan the son of
Car'mī, the son of Zab'dī, the son of Zē'-
rah, of the tribe of Judah, was taken.

19Now Joshua said to Ā'chan, "My son, I
beg you, give glory to the LORD God of Is-
rael, and make confession to Him, and tell
me now what you have done; do not hide
it from me."

20And Ā'chan answered Joshua and
said, "Indeed I have sinned against the
LORD God of Israel, and this is what I have
done: 21When I saw among the spoils a
beautiful Babylonian garment, two hun-
dred shekels of silver, and a wedge of gold
weighing fifty shekels, I coveted them and
took them. And there they are, hidden in
the earth in the midst of my tent, with the
silver under it."

22So Joshua sent messengers, and they
ran to the tent; and there it was, hidden in
his tent, with the silver under it. 23And they
took them from the midst of the tent,
brought them to Joshua and to all the chil-
dren of Israel, and laid them out before the
LORD. 24Then Joshua, and all Israel with
him, took Ā'chan the son of Zē'rah, the sil-
ver, the garment, the wedge of gold, his
sons, his daughters, his oxen, his donkeys,
his sheep, his tent, and all that he had, and
they brought them to the Valley of Ā'chor.
25And Joshua said, "Why have you trou-
bled us? The LORD will trouble you this
day." So all Israel stoned him with stones;
and they burned them with fire after they
had stoned them with stones.

26Then they raised over him a great heap
of stones, still there to this day. So the LORD
turned from the fierceness of His anger.
Therefore the name of that place has been
called the Valley of Ā'chor[a] to this day.

CHAPTER 8

The Fall of Ai

Now the LORD said to Joshua: "Do not
be afraid, nor be dismayed; take all the
people of war with you, and arise, go up to
Aī. See, I have given into your hand the
king of Aī, his people, his city, and his
land. 2And you shall do to Aī and its king
as you did to Jericho and its king. Only its
spoil and its cattle you shall take as booty
for yourselves. Lay an ambush for the city
behind it."

3So Joshua arose, and all the people of
war, to go up against Aī; and Joshua chose
thirty thousand mighty men of valor and

7:26 [a]Literally *Trouble*

7:24–26 Achor: The Hebrew word meaning "trouble." The place was named "Valley of Trouble" because of the "trouble" Achan brought upon Israel through his sin. **burned them**: An appropriate punishment for violation of the sacred burning of the city.

8:2 Just as sin brings destruction, obedience brings reward. If Achan had been obedient at Jericho, he could have taken all the spoil he wanted at Ai.

sent them away by night. 4And he com-
manded them, saying: "Behold, you shall
lie in ambush against the city, behind the
city. Do not go very far from the city, but all
of you be ready. 5Then I and all the people
who *are* with me will approach the city;
and it will come about, when they come
out against us as at the first, that we shall
flee before them. 6For they will come out
after us till we have drawn them from the
city, for they will say, '*They are* fleeing be-
fore us as at the first.' Therefore we will
flee before them. 7Then you shall rise from
the ambush and seize the city, for the LORD
your God will deliver it into your hand.
8And it will be, when you have taken the
city, *that* you shall set the city on fire. Ac-
cording to the commandment of the LORD
you shall do. See, I have commanded you."

9Joshua therefore sent them out; and
they went to lie in ambush, and stayed be-
tween Beth'el and Aī, on the west side of
Aī; but Joshua lodged that night among
the people. 10Then Joshua rose up early in
the morning and mustered the people, and
went up, he and the elders of Israel, before
the people to Aī. 11And all the people of
war who *were* with him went up and drew
near; and they came before the city and
camped on the north side of Aī. Now a val-
ley *lay* between them and Aī. 12So he took
about five thousand men and set them in
ambush between Beth'el and Aī, on the
west side of the city. 13And when they had
set the people, all the army that *was* on the
north of the city, and its rear guard on the
west of the city, Joshua went that night into
the midst of the valley.

14Now it happened, when the king of Aī
saw *it*, that the men of the city hurried and
rose early and went out against Israel to
battle, he and all his people, at an ap-
pointed place before the plain. But he did
not know that *there was* an ambush against
him behind the city. 15And Joshua and all
Israel made as if they were beaten before
them, and fled by the way of the wilder-
ness. 16So all the people who *were* in Aī
were called together to pursue them. And
they pursued Joshua and were drawn
away from the city. 17There was not a man
left in Aī or Beth'el who did not go out af-
ter Israel. So they left the city open and
pursued Israel.

18Then the LORD said to Joshua, "Stretch
out the spear that *is* in your hand toward
Aī, for I will give it into your hand." And
Joshua stretched out the spear that *was* in
his hand toward the city. 19So *those in* am-
bush arose quickly out of their place; they
ran as soon as he had stretched out his
hand, and they entered the city and took it,
and hurried to set the city on fire. 20And
when the men of Aī looked behind them,
they saw, and behold, the smoke of the city
ascended to heaven. So they had no power
to flee this way or that way, and the people
who had fled to the wilderness turned
back on the pursuers.

21Now when Joshua and all Israel saw
that the ambush had taken the city and
that the smoke of the city ascended, they
turned back and struck down the men of
Aī. 22Then the others came out of the city
against them; so they were *caught* in the
midst of Israel, some on this side and some
on that side. And they struck them down,
so that they let none of them remain or es-
cape. 23But the king of Aī they took alive,
and brought him to Joshua.

24And it came to pass when Israel had
made an end of slaying all the inhabitants
of Aī in the field, in the wilderness where
they pursued them, and when they all had
fallen by the edge of the sword until they
were consumed, that all the Israelites re-
turned to Aī and struck it with the edge of
the sword. 25So it was *that* all who fell that
day, both men and women, *were* twelve
thousand—all the people of Aī. 26For
Joshua did not draw back his hand, with
which he stretched out the spear, until he
had utterly destroyed all the inhabitants of
Aī. 27Only the livestock and the spoil of
that city Israel took as booty for them-
selves, according to the word of the LORD
which He had commanded Joshua. 28So
Joshua burned Aī and made it a heap

forever, a desolation to this day. 29And the king of Aī he hanged on a tree until evening. And as soon as the sun was down, Joshua commanded that they should take his corpse down from the tree, cast it at the entrance of the gate of the city, and raise over it a great heap of stones *that remains* to this day.

Joshua Renews the Covenant

30Now Joshua built an altar to the LORD God of Israel in Mount Ē′bal, 31as Moses the servant of the LORD had commanded the children of Israel, as it is written in the Book of the Law of Moses: "an altar of whole stones over which no man has wielded an iron *tool*."[a] And they offered on it burnt offerings to the LORD, and sacrificed peace offerings. 32And there, in the presence of the children of Israel, he wrote on the stones a copy of the law of Moses, which he had written. 33Then all Israel, with their elders and officers and judges, stood on either side of the ark before the priests, the Lē′vītes, who bore the ark of the covenant of the LORD, the stranger as well as he who was born among them. Half of them *were* in front of Mount Ger′i·zim and half of them in front of Mount Ē′bal, as Moses the servant of the LORD had commanded before, that they should bless the people of Israel. 34And afterward he read all the words of the law, the blessings and the cursings, according to all that is written in the Book of the Law. 35There was not a word of all that Moses had commanded which Joshua did not read before all the assembly of Israel, with the women, the little ones, and the strangers who were living among them.

CHAPTER 9

The Treaty with the Gibeonites

And it came to pass when all the kings who *were* on this side of the Jordan, in the hills and in the lowland and in all the coasts of the Great Sea toward Lebanon—the Hit′tīte, the Am′o·rīte, the Cā′naan·īte, the Per′iz·zīte, the Hī′vīte, and the Jeb′ū·sīte—heard *about it,* 2that they gathered together to fight with Joshua and Israel with one accord.

3But when the inhabitants of Gib′ē·on heard what Joshua had done to Jericho and Aī, 4they worked craftily, and went and pretended to be ambassadors. And they took old sacks on their donkeys, old wineskins torn and mended, 5old and patched sandals on their feet, and old garments on themselves; and all the bread of their provision was dry *and* moldy. 6And they went to Joshua, to the camp at Gil′gal, and said to him and to the men of Israel, "We have come from a far country; now therefore, make a covenant with us."

7Then the men of Israel said to the Hī′vītes, "Perhaps you dwell among us; so how can we make a covenant with you?"

8But they said to Joshua, "We *are* your servants."

And Joshua said to them, "Who *are* you, and where do you come from?"

8:31 [a]Deuteronomy 27:5, 6

8:30–35 The central campaign ends with a covenant ceremony at Shechem, located between **Mount Ebal** (v. 30) and **Mount Gerizim** (v. 33). An altar at Shechem would carry strong reminders of God's promise to Abraham (see Gen. 12:7). It would validate the conquest as a fulfillment of God's promises to him as well as to Isaac and Jacob. The ceremony was also a way of reinforcing in their minds the covenant nature of their relationship to God as required in Deuteronomy (Deut. 27; 28).

9:2 with one accord: Joshua's strategic thrust into central Canaan effectively divided Canaan in half. Unable to unite as a whole, the enemy would have to fight Joshua in smaller coalitions to the south and north.

9:4–15 Israel had been instructed not to make treaties with the inhabitants of Canaan (Deut. 7:2). Therefore, the Gibeonites had to work **craftily** (v. 4) to make it appear they were from another country.

9So they said to him: "From a very far country your servants have come, because of the name of the LORD your God; for we have heard of His fame, and all that He did in Egypt, 10and all that He did to the two kings of the Am′o·rītes who *were* beyond the Jordan—to Sī′hon king of Hesh′bon, and Og king of Bā′shan, who was at Ash′ta·roth. 11Therefore our elders and all the inhabitants of our country spoke to us, saying, 'Take provisions with you for the journey, and go to meet them, and say to them, "We *are* your servants; now therefore, make a covenant with us." ' 12This bread of ours we took hot *for* our provision from our houses on the day we departed to come to you. But now look, it is dry and moldy. 13And these wineskins which we filled *were* new, and see, they are torn; and these our garments and our sandals have become old because of the very long journey."

14Then the men of Israel took some of their provisions; but they did not ask counsel of the LORD. 15So Joshua made peace with them, and made a covenant with them to let them live; and the rulers of the congregation swore to them.

16And it happened at the end of three days, after they had made a covenant with them, that they heard that they *were* their neighbors who dwelt near them. 17Then the children of Israel journeyed and came to their cities on the third day. Now their cities *were* Gib′ē·on, Chē·phī′rah, Be·er′oth, and Kir′jath Jē′a·rim. 18But the children of Israel did not attack them, because the rulers of the congregation had sworn to them by the LORD God of Israel. And all the congregation complained against the rulers.

19Then all the rulers said to all the congregation, "We have sworn to them by the LORD God of Israel; now therefore, we may not touch them. 20This we will do to them: We will let them live, lest wrath be upon us because of the oath which we swore to them." 21And the rulers said to them, "Let them live, but let them be woodcutters and water carriers for all the congregation, as the rulers had promised them."

22Then Joshua called for them, and he spoke to them, saying, "Why have you deceived us, saying, 'We *are* very far from you,' when you dwell near us? 23Now therefore, you *are* cursed, and none of you shall be freed from being slaves—woodcutters and water carriers for the house of my God."

24So they answered Joshua and said, "Because your servants were clearly told that the LORD your God commanded His servant Moses to give you all the land, and to destroy all the inhabitants of the land from before you; therefore we were very much afraid for our lives because of you, and have done this thing. 25And now, here we are, in your hands; do with us as it seems good and right to do to us." 26So he did to them, and delivered them out of the hand of the children of Israel, so that they did not kill them. 27And that day Joshua made them woodcutters and water carriers for the congregation and for the altar of the LORD, in the place which He would choose, even to this day.

CHAPTER 10

The Sun Stands Still

Now it came to pass when A·dō′ni-Zē′dek king of Jerusalem heard how Joshua had taken Aī and had utterly destroyed it—as he had done to Jericho and

9:15 In this type of vassal treaty, Gibeon (the vassal) promised, through their service, to provide support to Israel (the superior nation) in return for protection. It was typical for the culture of that period.

9:16–27 The treaty had been sworn in the Lord's name and thus could not be revoked, even though it had been entered into under false pretenses. If Joshua had gone back on his word, it would have been equal to breaking a promise to God.

its king, so he had done to Aī and its
king—and how the inhabitants of Gib′ē·on
had made peace with Israel and were
among them, 2that they feared greatly, be-
cause Gib′ē·on *was* a great city, like one of
the royal cities, and because it *was* greater
than Aī, and all its men *were* mighty.
3Therefore A·dō′ni-Zē′dek king of Jerusa-
lem sent to Hō′ham king of Hē′bron, Pī′-
ram king of Jar′muth, Ja·phī′a king of Lā′-
chish, and Dē′bir king of Eg′lon, saying,
4"Come up to me and help me, that we
may attack Gib′ē·on, for it has made peace
with Joshua and with the children of Is-
rael." 5Therefore the five kings of the
Am′o·rītes, the king of Jerusalem, the king
of Hē′bron, the king of Jar′muth, the king
of Lā′chish, *and* the king of Eg′lon, gath-
ered together and went up, they and all
their armies, and camped before Gib′ē·on
and made war against it.

6And the men of Gib′ē·on sent to Joshua
at the camp at Gil′gal, saying, "Do not for-
sake your servants; come up to us quickly,
save us and help us, for all the kings of the
Am′o·rītes who dwell in the mountains
have gathered together against us."

7So Joshua ascended from Gil′gal, he
and all the people of war with him, and all
the mighty men of valor. 8And the LORD
said to Joshua, "Do not fear them, for I
have delivered them into your hand; not a
man of them shall stand before you."
9Joshua therefore came upon them sud-
denly, having marched all night from
Gil′gal. 10So the LORD routed them before
Israel, killed them with a great slaughter at
Gib′ē·on, chased them along the road that
goes to Beth Hor′on, and struck them
down as far as A·zē′kah and Mak·kē′dah.
11And it happened, as they fled before Is-
rael *and* were on the descent of Beth
Hor′on, that the LORD cast down large hail-
stones from heaven on them as far as
A·zē′kah, and they died. *There were* more
who died from the hailstones than the chil-
dren of Israel killed with the sword.

12Then Joshua spoke to the LORD in the
day when the LORD delivered up the
Am′o·rītes before the children of Israel,
and he said in the sight of Israel:

"Sun, stand still over Gib′ē·on;
And Moon, in the Valley of
Aī′ja·lon."
13 So the sun stood still,
And the moon stopped,
Till the people had revenge
Upon their enemies.

Is this not written in the Book of Jā′sher? So
the sun stood still in the midst of heaven,
and did not hasten to go *down* for about a
whole day. 14And there has been no day
like that, before it or after it, that the LORD
heeded the voice of a man; for the LORD
fought for Israel.

15Then Joshua returned, and all Israel
with him, to the camp at Gil′gal.

The Amorite Kings Executed

16But these five kings had fled and hid-
den themselves in a cave at Mak·kē′dah.
17And it was told Joshua, saying, "The five
kings have been found hidden in the cave
at Mak·kē′dah."

18So Joshua said, "Roll large stones
against the mouth of the cave, and set men
by it to guard them. 19And do not stay *there*
yourselves, *but* pursue your enemies, and

10:12–14 This is not the only time God caused a celestial miracle for His purposes. The sun retraced its passage as a sign to Hezekiah (2 Kin. 20:9–11), and during Christ's crucifixion it ceased to shine altogether (Matt. 27:45). Such a change in the sun and moon does not mean that the earth's rotation actually altered, however; indeed, God had already said that it would not do so (Gen. 9:22). Just as Hezekiah's sign was not global but local ("in the land," 2 Chr. 21:31), so Joshua's extended day was probably confined to the area of battle.

10:13 The **Book of Jasher** was an uninspired, ancient book that contained poems about Israel's heroes and achievements.

attack their rear *guard*. Do not allow them
to enter their cities, for the LORD your God
has delivered them into your hand."
20 Then it happened, while Joshua and the
children of Israel made an end of slaying
them with a very great slaughter, till they
had finished, that those who escaped en-
tered fortified cities. 21 And all the people
returned to the camp, to Joshua at Mak-
kē'dah, in peace.

No one moved his tongue against any of
the children of Israel.

22 Then Joshua said, "Open the mouth of
the cave, and bring out those five kings to
me from the cave." 23 And they did so, and
brought out those five kings to him from
the cave: the king of Jerusalem, the king of
Hē'bron, the king of Jar'muth, the king of
Lā'chish, *and* the king of Eg'lon.

24 So it was, when they brought out those
kings to Joshua, that Joshua called for all
the men of Israel, and said to the captains
of the men of war who went with him,
"Come near, put your feet on the necks of
these kings." And they drew near and put
their feet on their necks. 25 Then Joshua said
to them, "Do not be afraid, nor be dis-
mayed; be strong and of good courage, for
thus the LORD will do to all your enemies
against whom you fight." 26 And afterward
Joshua struck them and killed them, and
hanged them on five trees; and they were
hanging on the trees until evening. 27 So it
was at the time of the going down of the
sun *that* Joshua commanded, and they
took them down from the trees, cast
them into the cave where they had been
hidden, and laid large stones against the
cave's mouth, *which remain* until this very
day.

Conquest of the Southland

28 On that day Joshua took Mak•kē'dah,
and struck it and its king with the edge of
the sword. He utterly destroyed them[a]—all
the people who *were* in it. He let none re-
main. He also did to the king of Mak-
kē'dah as he had done to the king of Jeri-
cho.

29 Then Joshua passed from Mak•kē'dah,
and all Israel with him, to Lib'nah; and
they fought against Lib'nah. 30 And the
LORD also delivered it and its king into the
hand of Israel; he struck it and all the peo-
ple who *were* in it with the edge of the
sword. He let none remain in it, but did to
its king as he had done to the king of Jeri-
cho.

31 Then Joshua passed from Lib'nah, and
all Israel with him, to Lā'chish; and they
encamped against it and fought against it.
32 And the LORD delivered Lā'chish into the
hand of Israel, who took it on the second
day, and struck it and all the people who
were in it with the edge of the sword, ac-
cording to all that he had done to Lib'nah.
33 Then Hō'ram king of Gē'zer came up to
help Lā'chish; and Joshua struck him and
his people, until he left him none remain-
ing.

34 From Lā'chish Joshua passed to Eg'-
lon, and all Israel with him; and they en-
camped against it and fought against it.
35 They took it on that day and struck it
with the edge of the sword; all the people
who *were* in it he utterly destroyed that
day, according to all that he had done to
Lā'chish.

36 So Joshua went up from Eg'lon, and all
Israel with him, to Hē'bron; and they
fought against it. 37 And they took it and
struck it with the edge of the sword—its
king, all its cities, and all the people who
were in it; he left none remaining, accord-
ing to all that he had done to Eg'lon, but
utterly destroyed it and all the people who
were in it.

38 Then Joshua returned, and all Israel
with him, to Dē'bir; and they fought
against it. 39 And he took it and its king and
all its cities; they struck them with the edge
of the sword and utterly destroyed all the
people who *were* in it. He left none remain-
ing; as he had done to Hē'bron, so he did

10:28 [a]Following Masoretic Text and most authorities; many Hebrew manuscripts, some manuscripts of the Septuagint, and some manuscripts of the Targum read *it*.

to Dē′bir and its king, as he had done also
to Lib′nah and its king.
40So Joshua conquered all the land: the
mountain country and the South[a] and the
lowland and the wilderness slopes, and all
their kings; he left none remaining, but ut-
terly destroyed all that breathed, as the
LORD God of Israel had commanded. 41And
Joshua conquered them from Kā′desh
Bar·nē′a as far as Gā′za, and all the coun-
try of Gō′shen, even as far as Gib′ē·on.
42All these kings and their land Joshua took
at one time, because the LORD God of Israel
fought for Israel. 43Then Joshua returned,
and all Israel with him, to the camp at
Gil′gal.

CHAPTER 11

The Northern Conquest

And it came to pass, when Jā′bin king of
Hā′zor heard *these things,* that he sent to
Jō′bab king of Mā′don, to the king of
Shim′ron, to the king of Ach′shaph, 2and to
the kings who *were* from the north, in the
mountains, in the plain south of Chin′-
ne·roth, in the lowland, and in the heights
of Dor on the west, 3to the Cā′naan·ītes in
the east and in the west, the Am′o·rīte, the
Hit′tīte, the Per′iz·zīte, the Jeb′ū·sīte in the
mountains, and the Hī′vīte below Her′-
mon in the land of Miz′pah. 4So they went
out, they and all their armies with them, *as*
many people *as* the sand that *is* on the
seashore in multitude, with very many
horses and chariots. 5And when all these
kings had met together, they came and
camped together at the waters of Mē′rom
to fight against Israel.
6But the LORD said to Joshua, "Do not be
afraid because of them, for tomorrow
about this time I will deliver all of them
slain before Israel. You shall hamstring
their horses and burn their chariots with
fire." 7So Joshua and all the people of war
with him came against them suddenly by
the waters of Mē′rom, and they attacked
them. 8And the LORD delivered them into
the hand of Israel, who defeated them and
chased them to Greater Sī′don, to the
Brook Mis′re·photh,[a] and to the Valley of
Miz′pah eastward; they attacked them un-
til they left none of them remaining. 9So
Joshua did to them as the LORD had told
him: he hamstrung their horses and
burned their chariots with fire.
10Joshua turned back at that time and
took Hā′zor, and struck its king with the
sword; for Hā′zor was formerly the head
of all those kingdoms. 11And they struck all
the people who *were* in it with the edge of
the sword, utterly destroying *them.* There
was none left breathing. Then he burned
Hā′zor with fire.
12So all the cities of those kings, and all
their kings, Joshua took and struck with
the edge of the sword. He utterly de-
stroyed them, as Moses the servant of the
LORD had commanded. 13But *as for* the
cities that stood on their mounds,[a] Israel
burned none of them, except Hā′zor only,
which Joshua burned. 14And all the spoil of
these cities and the livestock, the children
of Israel took as booty for themselves; but
they struck every man with the edge of the
sword until they had destroyed them, and
they left none breathing. 15As the LORD had
commanded Moses his servant, so Moses
commanded Joshua, and so Joshua did. He
left nothing undone of all that the LORD
had commanded Moses.

10:40 [a]Hebrew *Negev,* and so throughout this book
11:8 [a]Hebrew *Misrephoth Maim*
11:13 [a]Hebrew *tel,* a heap of successive city ruins

11:1–15 Hazor, with a population of some 40,000, was probably the largest city that Joshua conquered. By capturing it, the Israelites broke up the power structure north of the Jezreel Valley and made that territory their own.

11:6 hamstring their horses: At this time the horse-drawn chariot was the "ultimate" weapon. God forbade Joshua's use of these captured weapons because it would lessen Israel's dependence on Him.

Summary of Joshua's Conquests

16 Thus Joshua took all this land: the
mountain country, all the South, all the
land of Gō'shen, the lowland, and the Jor-
dan plain[a]—the mountains of Israel and its
lowlands, 17 from Mount Hā'lak and the as-
cent to Sē'ir, even as far as Bā'al Gad in the
Valley of Lebanon below Mount Her'mon.
He captured all their kings, and struck
them down and killed them. 18 Joshua
made war a long time with all those kings.
19 There was not a city that made peace with
the children of Israel, except the Hī'vītes,
the inhabitants of Gib'ē·on. All *the others*
they took in battle. 20 For it was of the LORD
to harden their hearts, that they should
come against Israel in battle, that He might
utterly destroy them, *and* that they might
receive no mercy, but that He might de-
stroy them, as the LORD had commanded
Moses.

21 And at that time Joshua came and cut
off the An'a·kim from the mountains: from
Hē'bron, from Dē'bir, from Ā'nab, from all
the mountains of Judah, and from all the
mountains of Israel; Joshua utterly de-
stroyed them with their cities. 22 None of
the An'a·kim were left in the land of the
children of Israel; they remained only in
Gā'za, in Gath, and in Ash'dod.

23 So Joshua took the whole land, accord-
ing to all that the LORD had said to Moses;
and Joshua gave it as an inheritance to Is-
rael according to their divisions by their
tribes. Then the land rested from war.

CHAPTER 12

The Kings Conquered by Moses

These *are* the kings of the land whom
the children of Israel defeated, and whose
land they possessed on the other side of
the Jordan toward the rising of the sun,
from the River Ar'non to Mount Her'mon,
and all the eastern Jordan plain: 2 *One king*
was Sī'hon king of the Am'o·rītes, who
dwelt in Hesh'bon *and* ruled half of
Gil'ē·ad, from A·rō'er, which is on the
bank of the River Ar'non, from the middle
of that river, even as far as the River
Jab'bok, *which is* the border of the Am'-
mon·ītes, 3 and the eastern Jordan plain
from the Sea of Chin'ne·roth as far as the
Sea of the Ar'a·bah (the Salt Sea), the road
to Beth Jesh'i·moth, and southward below
the slopes of Pis'gah. 4 *The other king was* Og
king of Bā'shan and his territory, *who was*
of the remnant of the giants, who dwelt at
Ash'ta·roth and at Ed'rē·ī, 5 and reigned
over Mount Her'mon, over Sal'-cah, over
all Bā'shan, as far as the border of the
Gesh'ū·rītes and the Mā'a·cha·thītes, and
over half of Gil'ē·ad *to* the border of Sī'hon
king of Hesh'bon.

6 These Moses the servant of the LORD
and the children of Israel had conquered;
and Moses the servant of the LORD had
given it *as* a possession to the Reū'ben·ītes,
the Gad'ītes, and half the tribe of Ma-
nas'seh.

The Kings Conquered by Joshua

7 And these *are* the kings of the country
which Joshua and the children of Israel
conquered on this side of the Jordan, on
the west, from Bā'al Gad in the Valley of
Lebanon as far as Mount Hā'lak and the
ascent to Sē'ir, which Joshua gave to the
tribes of Israel *as* a possession according to
their divisions, 8 in the mountain country,
in the lowlands, in the *Jordan* plain, in the
slopes, in the wilderness, and in the
South—the Hit'tītes, the Am'o·rītes, the

11:16 [a]Hebrew *arabah*

11:20 harden their hearts: As with Pharaoh (see note on Ex. 4:21), there is no intent to lessen blame on the Canaanites. Rather, God "gave them up" to their evildoing. In this sense, God allows the hard heart of the already wicked Canaanites to run its course unrestrained.

11:23 Whole land does not mean that the conquest was completed (see 13:1); rather, the initial foothold was secured and the settlement of the **tribes** could begin.

Cā′naan·ītes, the Per′iz·zītes, the Hī′vītes,
and the Jeb′ū·sītes: 9the king of Jericho,
one; the king of Aī, which *is* beside Beth′el,
one; 10the king of Jerusalem, one; the king
of Hē′bron, one; 11the king of Jar′muth,
one; the king of Lā′chish, one; 12the king of
Eg′lon, one; the king of Gē′zer, one; 13the
king of Dē′bir, one; the king of Gē′der, one;
14the king of Hor′mah, one; the king of
Ar′ad, one; 15the king of Lib′nah, one; the
king of A·dul′lam, one; 16the king of
Mak·kē′dah, one; the king of Beth′el, one;
17the king of Tap′pū·ah, one; the king
of Hē′pher, one; 18the king of Ā′phek,
one; the king of La·shar′on, one; 19the king
of Mā′don, one; the king of Hā′zor,
one; 20the king of Shim′ron Mē′ron,
one; the king of Ach′shaph, one; 21the king
of Tā′a·nach, one; the king of Me·gid′dō,
one; 22the king of Kē′desh, one; the
king of Jok′nē·am in Car′mel, one; 23the
king of Dor in the heights of Dor, one;
the king of the people of Gil′gal, one;
24the king of Tir′zah, one—all the kings,
thirty-one.

CHAPTER 13

Remaining Land to Be Conquered

Now Joshua was old, advanced in
years. And the LORD said to him: "You are
old, advanced in years, and there remains
very much land yet to be possessed. 2This
is the land that yet remains: all the territory
of the Phi·lis′tines and all *that of* the
Gesh′ū·rītes, 3from Sī′hor, which *is* east of
Egypt, as far as the border of Ek′ron north-
ward (*which* is counted as Cā′naan·īte); the
five lords of the Phi·lis′tines—the Gā′zītes,
the Ash′dod·ītes, the Ash′ke·lon·ītes, the
Git′tītes, and the Ek′ron·ītes; also the
Av′ītes; 4from the south, all the land of
the Cā′naan·ītes, and Me·ar′ah that be-
longs to the Sī·dō′ni·ans as far as Ā′phek,
to the border of the Am′o·rītes; 5the land of
the Gē′bal·ītes,[a] and all Lebanon, toward
the sunrise, from Bā′al Gad below Mount
Her′mon as far as the entrance to Hā′math;
6all the inhabitants of the mountains from
Lebanon as far as the Brook Mis′re·photh,[a]
and all the Sī·dō′ni·ans—them I will drive
out from before the children of Israel; only
divide it by lot to Israel as an inheritance,
as I have commanded you. 7Now there-
fore, divide this land as an inheritance to
the nine tribes and half the tribe of
Ma·nas′seh."

The Land Divided East of the Jordan

8With the other half-tribe the Reū′-
ben·ītes and the Gad′ītes received their in-
heritance, which Moses had given them,
beyond the Jordan eastward, as Moses the
servant of the LORD had given them: 9from
A·rō′er which *is* on the bank of the River
Ar′non, and the town that *is* in the midst of
the ravine, and all the plain of Med′e·ba as
far as Dī′bon; 10all the cities of Sī′hon king
of the Am′o·rītes, who reigned in Hesh′-
bon, as far as the border of the children of
Am′mon; 11Gil′ē·ad, and the border of the
Gesh′ū·rītes and Mā′a·cha·thītes, all
Mount Her′mon, and all Bā′shan as far as
Sal′cah; 12all the kingdom of Og in Bā′shan,
who reigned in Ash′ta·roth and Ed′rē·ī,
who remained of the remnant of the giants;
for Moses had defeated and cast out these.

13Nevertheless the children of Israel did
not drive out the Gesh′ū·rītes or the Mā′-
a·cha·thītes, but the Gesh′ū·rītes and the
Mā′a·cha·thītes dwell among the Israelites
until this day.

13:5 [a]Or *Giblites* 13:6 [a]Hebrew *Misrephoth Maim*

13:1 much land yet to be possessed: Essentially the coastal plains and populous valleys between the key cities remained.

13:7 nine . . . and half: Excluding Reuben, Gad, and half of Manasseh, who had received territories east of the Jordan.

13:13 This failure to obey God's command sets the stage for the Israelites to compromise and intermingle with the pagans.

14 Only to the tribe of Levi he had given no inheritance; the sacrifices of the LORD God of Israel made by fire *are* their inheritance, as He said to them.

The Land of Reuben

15 And Moses had given to the tribe of the children of Reuben *an inheritance* according to their families. 16 Their territory was from A·rō′er, which *is* on the bank of the River Ar′non, and the city that *is* in the midst of the ravine, and all the plain by Med′e·ba; 17 Hesh′bon and all its cities that *are* in the plain: Dī′bon, Bā′moth Bā′al, Beth Bā′al Mē′on, 18 Ja·hā′za, Ked′e·moth, Meph′a·ath, 19 Kir·jath′a·im, Sib′mah, Zē′reth Shā′har on the mountain of the valley, 20 Beth Pē′or, the slopes of Pis′gah, and Beth Jesh′i·moth— 21 all the cities of the plain and all the kingdom of Sī′hon king of the Am′o·rītes, who reigned in Hesh′bon, whom Moses had struck with the princes of Mid′i·an: Ē′vī, Rē′kem, Zūr, Hur, and Rē′ba, who *were* princes of Sī′hon dwelling in the country. 22 The children of Israel also killed with the sword Bā′laam the son of Bē′or, the soothsayer, among those who were killed by them. 23 And the border of the children of Reuben was the bank of the Jordan. This *was* the inheritance of the children of Reuben according to their families, the cities and their villages.

The Land of Gad

24 Moses also had given *an inheritance* to the tribe of Gad, to the children of Gad according to their families. 25 Their territory was Jā′zer, and all the cities of Gil′ē·ad, and half the land of the Am′mon·ītes as far as A·rō′er, which *is* before Rab′bah, 26 and from Hesh′bon to Rā′math Miz′pah and Bet′ō·nim, and from Mā·ha·na′im to the border of Dē′bir, 27 and in the valley Beth Hā′ram, Beth Nim′rah, Suc′coth, and Zā′phon, the rest of the kingdom of Sī′hon king of Hesh′bon, with the Jordan as *its* border, as far as the edge of the Sea of Chin′ne·reth, on the other side of the Jordan eastward. 28 This *is* the inheritance of the children of Gad according to their families, the cities and their villages.

Half the Tribe of Manasseh (East)

29 Moses also had given *an inheritance* to half the tribe of Ma·nas′seh; it was for half the tribe of the children of Ma·nas′seh according to their families: 30 Their territory was from Mā·ha·na′im, all Bā′shan, all the kingdom of Og king of Bā′shan, and all the towns of Jā′ir which are in Bā′shan, sixty cities; 31 half of Gil′ē·ad, and Ash′ta·roth and Ed′rē·ī, cities of the kingdom of Og in Bā′shan, *were* for the children of Mā′chir the son of Ma·nas′seh, for half of the children of Mā′chir according to their families.

32 These *are the areas* which Moses had distributed as an inheritance in the plains of Mō′ab on the other side of the Jordan, by Jericho eastward. 33 But to the tribe of Levi Moses had given no inheritance; the LORD God of Israel *was* their inheritance, as He had said to them.

CHAPTER 14

The Land Divided West of the Jordan

These *are the areas* which the children of Israel inherited in the land of Cā′naan, which El·ē·ā′zar the priest, Joshua the son of Nun, and the heads of the fathers of the tribes of the children of Israel distributed as an inheritance to them. 2 Their inheritance *was* by lot, as the LORD had commanded by the hand of Moses, for the nine tribes and the half-tribe. 3 For Moses had given the inheritance of the two tribes and the half-tribe on the other side of the Jordan; but to the Lē′vītes he had given no

14:1 Eleazar was appointed by Moses to succeed his father Aaron as priest (Num. 20:25–28; Deut. 10:6). As priest he presided over the distribution of the land.

inheritance among them. 4For the children of Joseph were two tribes: Ma·nas′seh and Ē′phra·im. And they gave no part to the Lē′vītes in the land, except cities to dwell *in,* with their common-lands for their livestock and their property. 5As the LORD had commanded Moses, so the children of Israel did; and they divided the land.

Caleb Inherits Hebron

6Then the children of Judah came to Joshua in Gil′gal. And Caleb the son of Je·phūn′neh the Kē′niz·zīte said to him: "You know the word which the LORD said to Moses the man of God concerning you and me in Kā′desh Bar·nē′a. 7I *was* forty years old when Moses the servant of the LORD sent me from Kā′desh Bar·nē′a to spy out the land, and I brought back word to him as *it was* in my heart. 8Nevertheless my brethren who went up with me made the heart of the people melt, but I wholly followed the LORD my God. 9So Moses swore on that day, saying, 'Surely the land where your foot has trodden shall be your inheritance and your children's forever, because you have wholly followed the LORD my God.' 10And now, behold, the LORD has kept me alive, as He said, these forty-five years, ever since the LORD spoke this word to Moses while Israel wandered in the wilderness; and now, here I am this day, eighty-five years old. 11As yet I *am as* strong this day as on the day that Moses sent me; just as my strength *was* then, so now *is* my strength for war, both for going out and for coming in. 12Now therefore, give me this mountain of which the LORD spoke in that day; for you heard in that day how the An′a·kim *were* there, and *that* the cities *were* great *and* fortified. It may be that the LORD *will be* with me, and I shall be able to drive them out as the LORD said."

13And Joshua blessed him, and gave Hē′bron to Caleb the son of Je·phūn′neh as an inheritance. 14Hē′bron therefore became the inheritance of Caleb the son of Je·phūn′neh the Kē′niz·zīte to this day, because he wholly followed the LORD God of Israel. 15And the name of Hē′bron formerly was Kir′jath Ar′ba (*Ar′ba* was the greatest man among the An′a·kim).

Then the land had rest from war.

CHAPTER 15

The Land of Judah

So *this* was the lot of the tribe of the children of Judah according to their families:

The border of Ē′dom at the Wilderness of Zin southward *was* the extreme southern boundary. 2And their southern border began at the shore of the Salt Sea, from the bay that faces southward. 3Then it went out to the southern side of the Ascent of Ak·rab′bim, passed along to Zin, ascended on the south side of Kā′desh Bar·nē′a, passed along to Hez′ron, went up to Ā′dar, and went around to Kar′ka·a. 4*From there* it passed toward Az′mon and went out to the Brook of Egypt; and the border ended

14:4 Manasseh and Ephraim: The tribe of **Joseph** accounted for **two tribes**, thus keeping the total number at 12.

14:6–15 Caleb, as patriarch and the only survivor other than Joshua of those who left Egypt, is given the privilege of choosing his own land.

14:10 Caleb notes that it had been **forty-five years** since the Lord spoke to Moses about his inheritance. That word was spoken (Num. 14:24) in the second year after the Israelites left Egypt (Num. 9:1; 10:11), thus 38 years before they entered the Promised Land. This suggests that the conquest to this point had taken approximately seven years (45 minus 38).

14:11, 12 At age eighty-five, Caleb's strength was unabated and his faith in God stronger than ever. It is a tribute to Caleb's faith that he had chosen territory which would be difficult to conquer.

at the sea. This shall be your southern bor-
der.
5The east border *was* the Salt Sea as far
as the mouth of the Jordan.
And the border on the northern quarter
began at the bay of the sea at the mouth of
the Jordan. 6The border went up to Beth
Hog'lah and passed north of Beth Ar'a-
bah; and the border went up to the stone of
Bō'han the son of Reuben. 7Then the border
went up toward Dē'bir from the Valley of
Ā'chor, and it turned northward toward
Gil'gal, which *is* before the Ascent of
A·dum'mim, which *is* on the south side of
the valley. The border continued toward
the waters of En Shem'esh and ended at En
Rō'gel. 8And the border went up by the
Valley of the Son of Hin'nom to the south-
ern slope of the Jeb'ū·sīte *city* (which *is* Je-
rusalem). The border went up to the top of
the mountain that *lies* before the Valley of
Hin'nom westward, which *is* at the end
of the Valley of Reph'a·im[a] northward.
9Then the border went around from the top
of the hill to the fountain of the water of
Neph-tō'ah, and extended to the cities of
Mount Ē'phron. And the border went
around to Bā'a·lah (which *is* Kir'jath Jē'-
a·rim). 10Then the border turned westward
from Bā'a·lah to Mount Sē'ir, passed
along to the side of Mount Jē'a·rim on
the north (which *is* Ches'a·lon), went
down to Beth Shem'esh, and passed on
to Tim'nah. 11And the border went out to
the side of Ek'ron northward. Then the
border went around to Shic'ron, passed
along to Mount Bā'a·lah, and extended
to Jab'nē·el; and the border ended at the
sea.
12The west border *was* the coastline of
the Great Sea. This *is* the boundary of the
children of Judah all around according to
their families.

15:8 [a]Literally *Giants*

Caleb Occupies Hebron and Debir

13Now to Caleb the son of Je·phūn'neh
he gave a share among the children of Ju-
dah, according to the commandment of the
LORD to Joshua, *namely,* Kir'jath Ar'ba,
which *is* Hē'bron (*Ar'*ba was the father of
Ā'nak). 14Caleb drove out the three sons of
Ā'nak from there: Shē'shai, A·hī'man, and
Tal'maī, the children of Ā'nak. 15Then he
went up from there to the inhabitants of
Dē'bir (formerly the name of Dē'bir *was*
Kir'jath Sē'pher).
16And Caleb said, "He who attacks
Kir'jath Sē'pher and takes it, to him I will
give Ach'sah my daughter as wife." 17So
Oth'ni·el the son of Kē'naz, the brother of
Caleb, took it; and he gave him Ach'sah his
daughter as wife. 18Now it was so, when
she came *to him,* that she persuaded him to
ask her father for a field. So she dis-
mounted from *her* donkey, and Caleb said
to her, "What do you wish?" 19She an-
swered, "Give me a blessing; since you
have given me land in the South, give me
also springs of water." So he gave her the
upper springs and the lower springs.

The Cities of Judah

20This *was* the inheritance of the tribe of
the children of Judah according to their
families:
21The cities at the limits of the tribe of
the children of Judah, toward the border of
Ē'dom in the South, were Kab'zē·el, Ē'der,
Jā'gur, 22Kinah, Di·mō'nah, A·dā'dah,
23Kē'desh, Hā'zor, Ith'nan, 24Ziph, Tē'lem,
Be·ā'loth, 25Hā'zor, Ha·dat'tah, Ker'i·oth,
Hez'ron (which *is* Hā'zor), 26Ā'mam,
Shē'ma, Mō'la·dah, 27Hā'zar Gad'dah,
Hesh'mon, Beth Pē'let, 28Hā'zar Shū'al,
Bē·er·shē'ba, Biz·joth'jah, 29Bā'a·lah, Ī'jim,
Ē'zem, 30El·tō'lad, Chē'sil, Hor'mah,
31Zik'lag, Mad·man'nah, San·san'nah,
32Le·bā'oth, Shil'him, Ā'in, and Rim'mon:

15:17 Othniel: The first deliverer mentioned in the Book of Judges (see Judg. 3:9–11).
15:19 Land in the South was in a more arid region. Access to **water** would be highly desirable.

all the cities *are* twenty-nine, with their villages.

33In the lowland: Esh'tā·ol, Zō'rah, Ash'nah, 34Za·nō'ah, En Gan'nim, Tap'pū·ah, Ē'nam, 35Jar'muth, A·dul'lam, Sō'cōh, A·zē'kah, 36Sha·rā'im, Ad·i·thā'im, Ge·dē'rah, and Ged·e·rō·thā'im: fourteen cities with their villages; 37Zē'nan, Hadash'ah, Migdal Gad, 38Dil'e·an, Miz'pah, Jok'the·el, 39Lā'chish, Boz'kath, Eg'lon, 40Cab'bon, Lah'mas,[a] Kith'lish, 41Ge·dē'roth, Beth Dā'gon, Nā'a·mah, and Mak·kē'dah: sixteen cities with their villages; 42Lib'nah, Ē'ther, Ā'shan, 43Jiph'tah, Ash'nah, Nē'zib, 44Kē·ī'lah, Ach'zib, and Ma·rē'shah: nine cities with their villages; 45Ek'ron, with its towns and villages; 46from Ek'ron to the sea, all that *lay* near Ash'dod, with their villages; 47Ash'dod with its towns and villages, Gā'za with its towns and villages—as far as the Brook of Egypt and the Great Sea with *its* coastline.

48And in the mountain country: Shā'mir, Jat'tir, Sō'chōh, 49Dan'nah, Kir'jath San'nah (which *is* Dē'bir), 50Ā'nab, Esh'te·mōh, Ā'nim, 51Gō'shen, Hō'lon, and Gī'lōh: eleven cities with their villages; 52Arab, Dū'mah, Esh'e·an, 53Jā'num, Beth Tap'pū·ah, A·phē'kah, 54Hum'tah, Kir'jath Ar'ba (which *is* Hē'bron), and Zī'or: nine cities with their villages; 55Mā'on, Car'mel, Ziph, Jut'tah, 56Jez'rē·el, Jok'dē·am, Za·nō'ah, 57Kāin, Gib'ē·ah, and Tim'nah: ten cities with their villages; 58Hal'hul, Beth Zūr, Gē'dor, 59Mā'a·rath, Beth Ā'noth, and El'tē·kon: six cities with their villages; 60Kir'jath Bā'al (which *is* Kir'jath Jē'a·rim) and Rab'bah: two cities with their villages.

61In the wilderness: Beth Ar'a·bah, Mid'din, Se·cā'cah, 62Nib'shan, the City of Salt, and En Ge'di: six cities with their villages.

63As for the Jeb'ū·sītes, the inhabitants of Jerusalem, the children of Judah could not drive them out; but the Jeb'ū·sītes dwell with the children of Judah at Jerusalem to this day.

CHAPTER 16

Ephraim and West Manasseh

The lot fell to the children of Joseph from the Jordan, by Jericho, to the waters of Jericho on the east, to the wilderness that goes up from Jericho through the mountains to Beth'el, 2then went out from Beth'el to Luz,[a] passed along to the border of the Ar'chītes at At'a·roth, 3and went down westward to the boundary of the Japh'let·ītes, as far as the boundary of Lower Beth Hor'on to Gē'zer; and it ended at the sea.

4So the children of Joseph, Ma·nas'seh and Ē'phra·im, took their inheritance.

The Land of Ephraim

5The border of the children of Ē'phra·im, according to their families, was *thus:* The border of their inheritance on the east side was At'a·roth Ad'dar as far as Upper Beth Hor'on.

6And the border went out toward the sea on the north side of Mich·mē'thath; then the border went around eastward to Tā'a·nath Shī'lōh, and passed by it on the east of Ja·nō'hah. 7Then it went down from Ja·nō'hah to At'a·roth and Nā'a·rah,[a] reached to Jericho, and came out at the Jordan.

8The border went out from Tap'pū·ah westward to the Brook Kā'nah, and it ended at the sea. This *was* the inheritance of the tribe of the children of Ē'phra·im according to their families. 9The separate cities for the children of Ē'phra·im *were*

15:40 [a]Or *Lahmam*
16:2 [a]Septuagint reads *Bethel* (that is, Luz).
16:7 [a]Or *Naaran* (compare 1 Chronicles 7:28)

15:63 Jerusalem seems to have lain between Judah and Benjamin (see Judg. 1:21). Despite Judg. 1:8, it seems not to have been actually possessed until the time of David (see 2 Sam. 5:6–9).

among the inheritance of the children of Ma·nas′seh, all the cities with their villages.

10And they did not drive out the Cā′naan·ītes who dwelt in Gē′zer; but the Cā′naan·ītes dwell among the Ē′phra·im·ītes to this day and have become forced laborers.

CHAPTER 17

The Other Half-Tribe of Manasseh (West)

There was also a lot for the tribe of Ma·nas′seh, for he *was* the firstborn of Joseph: *namely* for Mā′chir the firstborn of Ma·nas′seh, the father of Gil′ē·ad, because he was a man of war; therefore he was given Gil′ē·ad and Bā′shan. 2And there was *a lot* for the rest of the children of Ma·nas′seh according to their families: for the children of Ā·bi·ē′zer,[a] the children of Hē′lek, the children of As′ri·el, the children of Shē′chem, the children of Hē′pher, and the children of She·mī′da; these *were* the male children of Ma·nas′seh the son of Joseph according to their families.

3But Ze·loph′e·had the son of Hē′pher, the son of Gil′ē·ad, the son of Mā′chir, the son of Ma·nas′seh, had no sons, but only daughters. And these *are* the names of his daughters: Mah′lah, Noah, Hog′lah, Mil′cah, and Tir′zah. 4And they came near before El·ē·ā′zar the priest, before Joshua the son of Nun, and before the rulers, saying, "The LORD commanded Moses to give us an inheritance among our brothers." Therefore, according to the commandment of the LORD, he gave them an inheritance among their father's brothers. 5Ten shares fell to Ma·nas′seh, besides the land of Gil′ē·ad and Bā′shan, which *were* on the other side of the Jordan, 6because the daughters of Ma·nas′seh received an inheritance among his sons; and the rest of Ma·nas′seh's sons had the land of Gil′ē·ad.

7And the territory of Ma·nas′seh was from Ash′er to Mich·mē′thath, that *lies* east of Shē′chem; and the border went along south to the inhabitants of En Tap′pū·ah. 8Ma·nas′seh had the land of Tap′pū·ah, but Tap′pū·ah on the border of Ma·nas′seh *belonged* to the children of Ē′phra·im. 9And the border descended to the Brook Kā′nah, southward to the brook. These cities of Ē′phra·im *are* among the cities of Ma·nas′seh. The border of Ma·nas′seh *was* on the north side of the brook; and it ended at the sea.

10Southward *it was* Ē′phra·im's, northward *it was* Ma·nas′seh's, and the sea was its border. Ma·nas′seh's territory was adjoining Ash′er on the north and Is′sa·char on the east. 11And in Is′sa·char and in Ash′er, Ma·nas′seh had Beth Shē′an and its towns, Ib′lē·am and its towns, the inhabitants of Dor and its towns, the inhabitants of En Dor and its towns, the inhabitants of Tā′a·nach and its towns, and the inhabitants of Me·gid′dō and its towns—three hilly regions. 12Yet the children of Ma·nas′seh could not drive out *the inhabitants of* those cities, but the Cā′naan·ītes were determined to dwell in that land. 13And it happened, when the children of Israel grew strong, that they put the Cā′naan·ītes to forced labor, but did not utterly drive them out.

More Land for Ephraim and Manasseh

14Then the children of Joseph spoke to Joshua, saying, "Why have you given us *only* one lot and one share to inherit, since we *are* a great people, inasmuch as the LORD has blessed us until now?"

17:2 [a]Called *Jeezer* in Numbers 26:30

16:10 Gezer was a major city in central Palestine. It was strategically located in the hills between the mountains and the coast. It only came to the Israelites when the Egyptian pharaoh captured it and gave it to Solomon as a wedding present (1 Kin. 9:16).

15So Joshua answered them, "If you *are* a
great people, *then* go up to the forest *coun-*
try and clear a place for yourself there in
the land of the Per'iz·zītes and the giants,
since the mountains of Ē'phra·im are too
confined for you."
16But the children of Joseph said, "The
mountain country is not enough for us;
and all the Cā'naan·ītes who dwell in the
land of the valley have chariots of iron,
both those who *are* of Beth Shē'an and its
towns and *those* who *are* of the Valley of
Jez'rē·el."
17And Joshua spoke to the house of Jo-
seph—to Ē'phra·im and Ma·nas'seh—say-
ing, "You *are* a great people and have great
power; you shall not have *only* one lot,
18but the mountain country shall be yours.
Although it *is* wooded, you shall cut it
down, and its farthest extent shall be
yours; for you shall drive out the Cā'-
naan·ītes, though they have iron chariots
and are strong."

CHAPTER 18

The Remainder of the Land Divided

Now the whole congregation of the
children of Israel assembled together
at Shī'lōh, and set up the tabernacle
of meeting there. And the land was sub-
dued before them. 2But there remained
among the children of Israel seven tribes
which had not yet received their inheri-
tance.
3Then Joshua said to the children of Is-
rael: "How long will you neglect to go and
possess the land which the LORD God of
your fathers has given you? 4Pick out from
among you three men for *each* tribe, and I
will send them; they shall rise and go
through the land, survey it according to
their inheritance, and come *back* to me.
5And they shall divide it into seven parts.
Judah shall remain in their territory on the
south, and the house of Joseph shall re-
main in their territory on the north. 6You
shall therefore survey the land in seven
parts and bring *the survey* here to me, that I
may cast lots for you here before the LORD
our God. 7But the Lē'vītes have no part
among you, for the priesthood of the LORD
is their inheritance. And Gad, Reuben, and
half the tribe of Ma·nas'seh have received
their inheritance beyond the Jordan on the
east, which Moses the servant of the LORD
gave them."
8Then the men arose to go away; and
Joshua charged those who went to survey
the land, saying, "Go, walk through the
land, survey it, and come back to me, that I
may cast lots for you here before the LORD
in Shī'lōh." 9So the men went, passed
through the land, and wrote the survey in
a book in seven parts by cities; and they
came to Joshua at the camp in Shī'lōh.
10Then Joshua cast lots for them in Shī'lōh
before the LORD, and there Joshua divided
the land to the children of Israel according
to their divisions.

The Land of Benjamin

11Now the lot of the tribe of the children
of Benjamin came up according to their

17:15 A challenge is extended to the discontented.

17:16 This lack of faith among the tribes of Ephraim and Manasseh is appalling. The **Valley of Jezreel** was not conquered until the time of Deborah and Barak (Judg. 4; 5).

18:1–10 After the main tribes of Ephraim, Manasseh, and Judah had received their allotments, the remainder of the land was apportioned by lot to the other seven tribes.

18:1 Shiloh was located about 20 miles north of Jerusalem. Although the tabernacle is not mentioned in the Book of Judges, that it was still at Shiloh in Samuel's day (1 Sam. 1:3; 2:22) suggests it was permanently located there until Shiloh's destruction by the Philistines. Excavations reveal that Shiloh was destroyed about 1050 B.C. This would have been at the time when the Philistines captured the ark (1 Sam. 4:11). Evidently the original tabernacle was destroyed at that time, although the Bible does not say so specifically. See Jer. 7:12.

18:11–28 Benjamin's allotment of land was relatively small, but it was in the heart of the

families, and the territory of their lot came out between the children of Judah and the children of Joseph. [12]Their border on the north side began at the Jordan, and the border went up to the side of Jericho on the north, and went up through the mountains westward; it ended at the Wilderness of Beth Ā′ven. [13]The border went over from there toward Luz, to the side of Luz (which *is* Beth′el) southward; and the border descended to At′a·roth Ad′dar, near the hill that *lies* on the south side of Lower Beth Hor′on.

[14]Then the border extended around the west side to the south, from the hill that *lies* before Beth Hor′on southward; and it ended at Kir′jath Bā′al (which *is* Kir′jath Jē′a·rim), a city of the children of Judah. This *was* the west side.

[15]The south side *began* at the end of Kir′jath Jē′a·rim, and the border extended on the west and went out to the spring of the waters of Neph·tō′ah. [16]Then the border came down to the end of the mountain that *lies* before the Valley of the Son of Hin′nom, which *is* in the Valley of the Reph′a·im[a] on the north, descended to the Valley of Hin′nom, to the side of the Jeb′ū·sīte *city* on the south, and descended to En Rō′gel. [17]And it went around from the north, went out to En Shem′esh, and extended toward Ge·lī′loth, which is before the Ascent of A·dum′mim, and descended to the stone of Bō′han the son of Reuben. [18]Then it passed along toward the north side of Ar′a·bah,[a] and went down to Ar′a·bah. [19]And the border passed along to the north side of Beth Hog′lah; then the border ended at the north bay at the Salt Sea, at the south end of the Jordan. This *was* the southern boundary.

[20]The Jordan was its border on the east side. This *was* the inheritance of the children of Benjamin, according to its boundaries all around, according to their families.

[21]Now the cities of the tribe of the children of Benjamin, according to their families, were Jericho, Beth Hog′lah, Ē′mek Kē′ziz, [22]Beth Ar′a·bah, Zem·a·rā′im, Beth′el, [23]Av′im, Par′ah, Oph′rah, [24]Chē′phar Ha·am′mo·nī, Oph′nī, and Gā′ba: twelve cities with their villages; [25]Gib′ē·on, Rā′mah, Be·er′oth, [26]Miz′pah, Chē·phī′rah, Mō′zah, [27]Rē′kem, Ir′pē·el, Tar′a·lah, [28]Zē′lah, Ē′leph, Jē′bus (which *is* Jerusalem), Gib′ē·ath, *and* Kir′jath: fourteen cities with their villages. This was the inheritance of the children of Benjamin according to their families.

CHAPTER 19

Simeon's Inheritance with Judah

The second lot came out for Sim′ē·on, for the tribe of the children of Sim′ē·on according to their families. And their inheritance was within the inheritance of the children of Judah. [2]They had in their inheritance Bē·er·shē′ba (Shē′ba), Mō′la·dah, [3]Hā′zar Shū′al, Bā′lah, Ē′zem, [4]El·tō′lad, Bē′thul, Hor′mah, [5]Zik′lag, Beth Mar′ca·both, Hā′zar Sū′sah, [6]Beth Le·bā′oth, and Sha·rū′hen: thirteen cities and their villages; [7]Ā′in, Rim′mon, Ē′ther, and Ā′shan: four cities and their villages; [8]and all the villages that *were* all around these cities as far as Bā′a·lath Bē′er, Rā′mah of the South. This *was* the inheritance of the tribe of the children of Sim′ē·on according to their families.

[9]The inheritance of the children of Sim′ē·on *was included* in the share of the children of Judah, for the share of the children of Judah was too much for them.

18:16 [a]Literally *Giants* 18:18 [a]Or *Beth Arabah* (compare 15:6 and 18:22)

Promised Land and encompassed such spiritually important places as Gilgal, the ruins of Jericho, and the city of Jerusalem.

19:1–9 Simeon had little influence on the subsequent history of Israel. Here they were allotted an inheritance (v. 1) within the territory of **Judah** (v. 9).

Therefore the children of Sim′ē·on had
their inheritance within the inheritance of
that people.

The Land of Zebulun

[10]The third lot came out for the children
of Zeb′ū·lun according to their families,
and the border of their inheritance was as
far as Sā′rid. [11]Their border went toward
the west and to Mar′a·lah, went to
Dab′ba·sheth, and extended along the
brook that is east of Jok′nē·am. [12]Then
from Sā′rid it went eastward toward the
sunrise along the border of Chis′loth
Tā′bor, and went out toward Dab′e·rath,
bypassing Ja·phī′a. [13]And from there it
passed along on the east of Gath Hē′pher,
toward Eth Kā′zin, and extended to
Rim′mon, which borders on Nē′ah. [14]Then
the border went around it on the north side
of Han·na′thon, and it ended in the Valley
of Jiph′thah El. [15]Included were Kat′tath,
Na·hal′lal, Shim′ron, I′da·lah, and Bethle-
hem: twelve cities with their villages.
[16]This *was* the inheritance of the children of
Zeb′ū·lun according to their families, these
cities with their villages.

The Land of Issachar

[17]The fourth lot came out to Is′sa·char,
for the children of Is′sa·char according to
their families. [18]And their territory went to
Jez′rē·el, and *included* Che·sul′loth,
Shū′nem, [19]Haph·rā′im, Shī′on, A·nā′-
ha·rath, [20]Rab′bith, Kish′i·on, Ā′bez,
[21]Rē′meth, En Gan′nim, En Had′dah, and
Beth Paz′zez. [22]And the border reached to
Tā′bor, Shā·ha·zi′mah, and Beth Shem′esh;
their border ended at the Jordan: sixteen
cities with their villages. [23]This *was* the in-
heritance of the tribe of the children of
Is′sa·char according to their families, the
cities and their villages.

The Land of Asher

[24]The fifth lot came out for the tribe of
the children of Ash′er according to their
families. [25]And their territory included
Hel′kath, Hā′lī, Bē′ten, Ach′shaph,
[26]A·lam′me·lech, Ā′mad, and Mī′shal; it
reached to Mount Car′mel westward,
along *the Brook* Shī′hor Lib′nath. [27]It turned
toward the sunrise to Beth Dā′gon; and it
reached to Zeb′ū·lun and to the Valley of
Jiph′thah El, then northward beyond Beth
Ē′mek and Nē·ī′el, bypassing Cā′bul *which*
was on the left, [28]including Ē′bron,[a] Rē′hob,
Ham′mon, and Kā′nah, as far as Greater
Sī′don. [29]And the border turned to Rā′mah
and to the fortified city of Tȳre; then the
border turned to Hō′sah, and ended at the
sea by the region of Ach′zib. [30]Also
Um′mah, Ā′phek, and Rē′hob *were in-*
cluded: twenty-two cities with their vil-
lages. [31]This *was* the inheritance of the tribe
of the children of Ash′er according to their
families, these cities with their villages.

The Land of Naphtali

[32]The sixth lot came out to the children
of Naph′ta·lī, for the children of Naph′ta·lī
according to their families. [33]And their bor-
der began at Hē′leph, enclosing the terri-
tory from the terebinth tree in Zā·a-
nan′nim, Ad′a·mī Nē′keb, and Jab′nē·el,
as far as Lak′kum; it ended at the Jordan.
[34]From Hē′leph the border extended west-

19:28 [a]Following Masoretic Text, Targum, and Vulgate; a few Hebrew manuscripts read *Abdon* (compare 21:30 and 1 Chronicles 6:74).

19:10–16 Zebulun (v. 10) was the land of Jesus' boyhood (Is. 9:1). **Gath Hepher** (v. 13) was the home of the prophet Jonah (2 Kin. 14:25).

19:17–23 Issachar included **Jezreel** (v. 18), summer home of the kings of Israel and site of Jehu's slaughter of Jezebel and her son King Joram (see 2 Kin. 9:14–37).

19:24–31 Asher, site of **Mount Carmel** (v. 26) where Elijah confronted the prophets of Baal (1 Kin. 18:19–40).

19:32–39 Part of the eastern boundary of **Naphtali** was the western shore of the Sea of Galilee.

ward to Az′noth Tā′bor, and went out from
there toward Huk′kok; it adjoined
Zeb′ū·lun on the south side and Ash′er on
the west side, and ended at Judah by the
Jordan toward the sunrise. 35And the forti-
fied cities *are* Zid′dim, Zer, Ham′math,
Rak′kath, Chin′ne·reth, 36Ad′a·mah,
Rā′mah, Hā′zor, 37Kē′desh, Ed′rē·ī, En
Hā′zor, 38Iron, Migdal El, Hō′rem, Beth
Ā′nath, and Beth Shem′esh: nineteen cities
with their villages. 39This *was* the inheri-
tance of the tribe of the children of
Naph′ta·lī according to their families, the
cities and their villages.

The Land of Dan

40The seventh lot came out for the tribe
of the children of Dan according to their
families. 41And the territory of their inheri-
tance was Zō′rah, Esh′tā·ol, Ir Shem′esh,
42Shā·a·lab′bin, Aī′ja·lon, Jeth′lah, 43Ē′lon,
Tim′nah, Ek′ron, 44El′tē·keh, Gib′be·thon,
Bā′a·lath, 45Jē′hud, Ben′ē Be′rak, Gath
Rim′mon, 46Me Jar′kon, and Rak′kon, with
the region near Jop′pa. 47And the border of
the children of Dan went beyond these, be-
cause the children of Dan went up to fight
against Lē′shem and took it; and they
struck it with the edge of the sword, took
possession of it, and dwelt in it. They
called Lē′shem, Dan, after the name of Dan
their father. 48This *is* the inheritance of the
tribe of the children of Dan according to
their families, these cities with their vil-
lages.

Joshua's Inheritance

49When they had made an end of divid-
ing the land as an inheritance according to
their borders, the children of Israel gave an
inheritance among them to Joshua the son
of Nun. 50According to the word of the
LORD they gave him the city which he
asked for, Tim′nath Sē′rah in the moun-
tains of Ē′phra·im; and he built the city
and dwelt in it.

51These *were* the inheritances which
El·ē·ā′zar the priest, Joshua the son of
Nun, and the heads of the fathers of the
tribes of the children of Israel divided as an
inheritance by lot in Shī′lōh before the
LORD, at the door of the tabernacle of meet-
ing. So they made an end of dividing the
country.

CHAPTER 20

The Cities of Refuge

The LORD also spoke to Joshua, saying,
2"Speak to the children of Israel, saying:
'Appoint for yourselves cities of refuge, of
which I spoke to you through Moses, 3that
the slayer who kills a person accidentally
or unintentionally may flee there; and they
shall be your refuge from the avenger of
blood. 4And when he flees to one of those
cities, and stands at the entrance of the gate
of the city, and declares his case in the
hearing of the elders of that city, they shall
take him into the city as one of them, and
give him a place, that he may dwell among
them. 5Then if the avenger of blood pur-
sues him, they shall not deliver the slayer
into his hand, because he struck his neigh-
bor unintentionally, but did not hate him
beforehand. 6And he shall dwell in that
city until he stands before the congregation

19:40–48 The original territory of Dan bordered on the Mediterranean Sea and included the city of Joppa. For their migration to a new territory see Judg. 18.

19:49, 50 Joshua did not choose his own inheritance until all the others had received their allotments.

20:1–9 The custom of blood revenge was of long standing (see Gen. 9:6). The **cities of refuge** (v. 2) were established to give asylum to those who had **unintentionally** (v. 5) killed another (see Deut. 19:1–10). This institution prevented blood feud excesses.

20:4 Frequently the **gate of the city** was the place where arbitration was conducted (see 2 Sam. 15:2; Amos 5:10–15).

for judgment, *and* until the death of the one who is high priest in those days. Then the slayer may return and come to his own city and his own house, to the city from which he fled.' "

[7]So they appointed Kē′desh in Galilee, in the mountains of Naph′ta·lī, Shē′chem in the mountains of Ē′phra·im, and Kir′jath Ar′ba (which *is* Hē′bron) in the mountains of Judah. [8]And on the other side of the Jordan, by Jericho eastward, they assigned Bē′zer in the wilderness on the plain, from the tribe of Reuben, Rā′moth in Gil′ē·ad, from the tribe of Gad, and Gō′lan in Bā′shan, from the tribe of Ma·nas′seh. [9]These were the cities appointed for all the children of Israel and for the stranger who dwelt among them, that whoever killed a person accidentally might flee there, and not die by the hand of the avenger of blood until he stood before the congregation.

A Place of Refuge

Jerry and Jack Schreur

As creative grandparents, we want to befriend and help our grandchildren through the teenage years. One thing we can do is turn our house into a "city of refuge" for them. We can provide a place for them out of harm's way. We can protect them and offer them safekeeping.

Creative grandparents are sanctuaries; our homes are cities of refuge to our adolescent grandchildren. We offer them a place to which they can flee when it feels as though the world is crashing down around them. I have an image of myself standing at the city gate and telling my granddaughter's pursuers, "Stop! I have her now. She is safe here. You cannot harm her anymore." Then those seeking to harm my granddaughter turn away empty-handed.

Creating a safe atmosphere will endear your teenage grandchildren to you forever. They need a place of refuge, a sanctuary. You can provide it. And in so doing you can teach them about God, who is their fortress and strength through all of life (2 Sam. 22:2, 3). ✦

CHAPTER 21

Cities of the Levites

Then the heads of the fathers' *houses* of the Lē′vītes came near to El·ē·ā′zar the priest, to Joshua the son of Nun, and to the heads of the fathers' *houses* of the tribes of the children of Israel. [2]And they spoke to them at Shī′lōh in the land of Cā′naan, saying, "The LORD commanded through Moses to give us cities to dwell in, with their common-lands for our livestock." [3]So the children of Israel gave to the Lē′vītes from their inheritance, at the commandment of the LORD, these cities and their common-lands:

[4]Now the lot came out for the families of the Kō′hath·ītes. And the children of Aaron the priest, *who were* of the Lē′vītes, had thirteen cities by lot from the tribe of Judah, from the tribe of Sim′ē·on, and from the tribe of Benjamin. [5]The rest of the chil-

21:1–45 The tribe of Levi received no territory as an **inheritance** (v. 3) other than the 48 cities named here. The Levites were to be custodians of Israel's spiritual life, and their cities were distributed throughout the tribal territories: 13 in the south (v. 4), 10 in central Palestine (v. 5), 13 in the north (v. 6), and 12 east of the Jordan (v. 7). The cities of refuge (20:1–9) were often priestly cities as well (see note on Num. 35:6).

dren of Kō′hath had ten cities by lot from
the families of the tribe of Ē′phra·im, from
the tribe of Dan, and from the half-tribe of
Ma·nas′seh.
6And the children of Ger′shon had thir-
teen cities by lot from the families of the
tribe of Is′sa·char, from the tribe of Ash′er,
from the tribe of Naph′ta·lī, and from the
half-tribe of Ma·nas′seh in Bā′shan.
7The children of Me·rar′ī according to
their families had twelve cities from the
tribe of Reuben, from the tribe of Gad, and
from the tribe of Zeb′ū·lun.
8And the children of Israel gave these
cities with their common-lands by lot to
the Lē′vītes, as the LORD had commanded
by the hand of Moses.
9So they gave from the tribe of the chil-
dren of Judah and from the tribe of the
children of Sim′ē·on these cities which are
designated by name, 10which were for the
children of Aaron, one of the families of the
Kō′hath·ītes, *who were* of the children of
Levi; for the lot was theirs first. 11And they
gave them Kir′jath Ar′ba (*Ar′ba* was the fa-
ther of Ā′nak), which *is* Hē′bron, in the
mountains of Judah, with the common-
land surrounding it. 12But the fields of the
city and its villages they gave to Caleb the
son of Je·phūn′neh as his possession.
13Thus to the children of Aaron the
priest they gave Hē′bron with its common-
land (a city of refuge for the slayer),
Lib′nah with its common-land, 14Jat′tir
with its common-land, Esh·te·mō′a with
its common-land, 15Hō′lon with its com-
mon-land, Dē′bir with its common-land,
16Ā′in with its common-land, Jut′tah with
its common-land, and Beth Shem′esh with
its common-land: nine cities from those
two tribes; 17and from the tribe of Benja-
min, Gib′ē·on with its common-land,
Gē′ba with its common-land, 18An′a·thoth
with its common-land, and Al′mon with
its common-land: four cities. 19All the cities
of the children of Aaron, the priests, *were*
thirteen cities with their common-lands.
20And the families of the children of
Kō′hath, the Lē′vītes, the rest of the chil-
dren of Kō′hath, even they had the cities of
their lot from the tribe of Ē′phra·im. 21For
they gave them Shē′chem with its com-
mon-land in the mountains of Ē′phra·im (a
city of refuge for the slayer), Gē′zer with
its common-land, 22Kib′zā·im with its com-
mon-land, and Beth Hor′on with its com-
mon-land: four cities; 23and from the tribe
of Dan, El′tē·keh with its common-land,
Gib′be·thon with its common-land,
24Aī′ja·lon with its common-land, *and* Gath
Rim′mon with its common-land: four
cities; 25and from the half-tribe of Ma-
nas′seh, Tā′nach with its common-land
and Gath Rim′mon with its common-land:
two cities. 26All the ten cities with their
common-lands were for the rest of the fam-
ilies of the children of Kō′hath.
27Also to the children of Ger′shon, of the
families of the Lē′vītes, from the *other* half-
tribe of Ma·nas′seh, *they gave* Gō′lan in
Bā′shan with its common-land (a city of
refuge for the slayer), and Be Esh′te·rah
with its common-land: two cities; 28and
from the tribe of Is′sa·char, Kish′i·on with
its common-land, Dab′e·rath with its com-
mon-land, 29Jar′muth with its common-
land, *and* En Gan′nim with its common-
land: four cities; 30and from the tribe of
Ash′er, Mī′shal with its common-land,
Ab′don with its common-land, 31Hel′kath
with its common-land, and Rē′hob with its
common-land: four cities; 32and from the
tribe of Naph′ta·lī, Kē′desh in Galilee with
its common-land (a city of refuge for the
slayer), Ham′moth Dor with its common-
land, and Kar′tan with its common-land:
three cities. 33All the cities of the Ger′-
shon·ītes according to their families *were*
thirteen cities with their common-lands.
34And to the families of the children of
Me·rar′ī, the rest of the Lē′vītes, from the
tribe of Zeb′ū·lun, Jok′nē·am with its com-
mon-land, Kar′tah with its common-land,
35Dim′nah with its common-land, *and*
Na·hal′al with its common-land: four
cities; 36and from the tribe of Reuben,
Bē′zer with its common-land, Jā′haz with
its common-land, 37Ked′e·moth with its

common-land, and Meph'a·ath with its common-land: four cities;[a] 38and from the tribe of Gad, Rā'moth in Gil'ē·ad with its common-land (a city of refuge for the slayer), Mā·ha·na'im with its common-land, 39Hesh'bon with its common-land, *and* Jā'zer with its common-land: four cities in all. 40So all the cities for the children of Me·rar'ī according to their families, the rest of the families of the Lē'vītes, were *by* their lot twelve cities.

41All the cities of the Lē'vītes within the possession of the children of Israel *were* forty-eight cities with their common-lands. 42Every one of these cities had its common-land surrounding it; thus *were* all these cities.

The Promise Fulfilled

43So the LORD gave to Israel all the land of which He had sworn to give to their fathers, and they took possession of it and dwelt in it. 44The LORD gave them rest all around, according to all that He had sworn to their fathers. And not a man of all their enemies stood against them; the LORD delivered all their enemies into their hand. 45Not a word failed of any good thing which the LORD had spoken to the house of Israel. All came to pass.

CHAPTER 22

Eastern Tribes Return to Their Lands

Then Joshua called the Reū'ben·ītes, the Gad'ītes, and half the tribe of Ma·nas'seh, 2and said to them: "You have kept all that Moses the servant of the LORD commanded you, and have obeyed my voice in all that I commanded you. 3You have not left your brethren these many days, up to this day, but have kept the charge of the commandment of the LORD your God. 4And now the LORD your God has given rest to your brethren, as He promised them; now therefore, return and go to your tents *and* to the land of your possession, which Moses the servant of the LORD gave you on the other side of the Jordan. 5But take careful heed to do the commandment and the law which Moses the servant of the LORD commanded you, to love the LORD your God, to walk in all His ways, to keep His commandments, to hold fast to Him, and to serve Him with all your heart and with all your soul." 6So Joshua blessed them and sent them away, and they went to their tents.

> ***I pray that my children will love You, the Lord their God, and walk in all Your ways, keep Your commandments, and hold fast to You, and that they will serve You with all their hearts and with all their souls.***
>
> *adapted from* Joshua 22:5

7Now to half the tribe of Ma·nas'seh Moses had given a possession in Bā'shan, but to the *other* half of it Joshua gave *a possession* among their brethren on this side of the Jordan, westward. And indeed, when Joshua sent them away to their tents, he blessed them, 8and spoke to them, saying, "Return with much riches to your tents, with very much livestock, with silver, with gold, with bronze, with iron, and with very much clothing. Divide the spoil of your enemies with your brethren."

9So the children of Reuben, the children

21:37 [a]Following Septuagint and Vulgate (compare 1 Chronicles 6:78, 79); Masoretic Text, Bomberg, and Targum omit verses 36 and 37.

21:45 The Lord has never failed to fulfill His promise—and He never will!
22:5 Joshua's command follows faithfully the instructions given to him when he assumed leadership (1:7, 8).

of Gad, and half the tribe of Ma•nas'seh re-
turned, and departed from the children of
Israel at Shī'lōh, which *is* in the land of
Cā'naan, to go to the country of Gil'ē•ad,
to the land of their possession, which they
had obtained according to the word of the
LORD by the hand of Moses.

An Altar by the Jordan

10And when they came to the region of
the Jordan which *is* in the land of Cā'naan,
the children of Reuben, the children of
Gad, and half the tribe of Ma•nas'seh built
an altar there by the Jordan—a great, im-
pressive altar. 11Now the children of Israel
heard *someone* say, "Behold, the children of
Reuben, the children of Gad, and half the
tribe of Ma•nas'seh have built an altar on
the frontier of the land of Cā'naan, in the
region of the Jordan—on the children of Is-
rael's side." 12And when the children of Is-
rael heard *of it,* the whole congregation of
the children of Israel gathered together at
Shī'lōh to go to war against them.
13Then the children of Israel sent
Phin'e•has the son of El•ē•ā'zar the priest
to the children of Reuben, to the children of
Gad, and to half the tribe of Ma•nas'seh,
into the land of Gil'ē•ad, 14and with him
ten rulers, one ruler each from the chief
house of every tribe of Israel; and each one
was the head of the house of his father
among the divisions[a] of Israel. 15Then they
came to the children of Reuben, to the chil-
dren of Gad, and to half the tribe of
Ma•nas'seh, to the land of Gil'ē•ad, and
they spoke with them, saying, 16"Thus says
the whole congregation of the LORD: 'What
treachery *is* this that you have committed
against the God of Israel, to turn away this
day from following the LORD, in that you
have built for yourselves an altar, that you
might rebel this day against the LORD? 17*Is*
the iniquity of Pē'or not enough for us,
from which we are not cleansed till this
day, although there was a plague in the
congregation of the LORD, 18but that you
must turn away this day from following
the LORD? And it shall be, if you rebel to-
day against the LORD, that tomorrow He
will be angry with the whole congregation
of Israel. 19Nevertheless, if the land of your
possession *is* unclean, *then* cross over to the
land of the possession of the LORD, where
the LORD's tabernacle stands, and take pos-
session among us; but do not rebel against
the LORD, nor rebel against us, by building
yourselves an altar besides the altar of the
LORD our God. 20Did not Ā'chan the son of
Zē'rah commit a trespass in the accursed
thing, and wrath fell on all the congrega-
tion of Israel? And that man did not perish
alone in his iniquity.' "
21Then the children of Reuben, the chil-
dren of Gad, and half the tribe of Ma-
nas'seh answered and said to the heads of
the divisions[a] of Israel: 22"The LORD God of
gods, the LORD God of gods, He knows,
and let Israel itself know—if *it is* in rebel-
lion, or if in treachery against the LORD, do
not save us this day. 23If we have built our-
selves an altar to turn from following the
LORD, or if to offer on it burnt offerings or
grain offerings, or if to offer peace offer-
ings on it, let the LORD Himself require *an*
account. 24But in fact we have done it for
fear, for a reason, saying, 'In time to come
your descendants may speak to our de-
scendants, saying, "What have you to do
with the LORD God of Israel? 25For the LORD
has made the Jordan a border between you
and us, *you* children of Reuben and chil-
dren of Gad. You have no part in the
LORD." So your descendants would make
our descendants cease fearing the LORD.'
26Therefore we said, 'Let us now prepare to

22:14 [a]Literally *thousands*

22:21 [a]Literally *thousands*

22:11–20 The western tribes apparently thought the three tribes had built a rival **altar**, contrary to the law (Deut. 12:5–14). Afraid that God's judgment might come upon them all (v. 18), they marched against the eastern tribes prepared for **war**. A delegation was sent to determine the facts.

build ourselves an altar, not for burnt of-
fering nor for sacrifice, 27but *that* it *may be* a
witness between you and us and our gen-
erations after us, that we may perform the
service of the LORD before Him with our
burnt offerings, with our sacrifices, and
with our peace offerings; that your descen-
dants may not say to our descendants in
time to come, "You have no part in the
LORD." ' 28Therefore we said that it will be,
when they say *this* to us or to our genera-
tions in time to come, that we may say,
'Here is the replica of the altar of the LORD
which our fathers made, though not for
burnt offerings nor for sacrifices; but it *is* a
witness between you and us.' 29Far be it
from us that we should rebel against the
LORD, and turn from following the LORD
this day, to build an altar for burnt offer-
ings, for grain offerings, or for sacrifices,
besides the altar of the LORD our God
which *is* before His tabernacle."

30Now when Phin'e·has the priest and
the rulers of the congregation, the heads of
the divisions[a] of Israel who *were* with him,
heard the words that the children of Reu-
ben, the children of Gad, and the children
of Ma·nas'seh spoke, it pleased them.
31Then Phin'e·has the son of El·ē·ā'zar the
priest said to the children of Reuben, the
children of Gad, and the children of
Ma·nas'seh, "This day we perceive that the
LORD *is* among us, because you have not
committed this treachery against the LORD.
Now you have delivered the children of Is-
rael out of the hand of the LORD."

32And Phin'e·has the son of El·ē·ā'zar
the priest, and the rulers, returned from
the children of Reuben and the children of
Gad, from the land of Gil'ē·ad to the land
of Cā'naan, to the children of Israel, and
brought back word to them. 33So the thing
pleased the children of Israel, and the chil-
dren of Israel blessed God; they spoke no
more of going against them in battle, to de-
stroy the land where the children of Reu-
ben and Gad dwelt.

34The children of Reuben and the chil-
dren of Gad[a] called the altar, *Witness*, "For
it is a witness between us that the LORD *is*
God."

CHAPTER 23

Joshua's Farewell Address

Now it came to pass, a long time after
the LORD had given rest to Israel from all
their enemies round about, that Joshua
was old, advanced in age. 2And Joshua
called for all Israel, for their elders, for
their heads, for their judges, and for their
officers, and said to them:

"I am old, advanced in age. 3You have
seen all that the LORD your God has done
to all these nations because of you, for the
LORD your God *is* He who has fought for
you. 4See, I have divided to you by lot
these nations that remain, to be an inheri-
tance for your tribes, from the Jordan, with
all the nations that I have cut off, as far as
the Great Sea westward. 5And the LORD
your God will expel them from before you
and drive them out of your sight. So you
shall possess their land, as the LORD your
God promised you. 6Therefore be very
courageous to keep and to do all that is
written in the Book of the Law of Moses,
lest you turn aside from it to the right hand
or to the left, 7*and* lest you go among these
nations, these who remain among you. You
shall not make mention of the name of
their gods, nor cause *anyone* to swear *by
them;* you shall not serve them nor bow
down to them, 8but you shall hold fast to
the LORD your God, as you have done to

22:30 [a]Literally *thousands* 22:34 [a]Septuagint adds *and half the tribe of Manasseh*

23:1–11 The essence of Joshua's address: (1) God's part—His past performance and future promises (vv. 3–5); (2) the people's part—obedience (v. 6), separation (v. 7), loyalty (v. 8), and love (v. 11).

this day. 9 For the LORD has driven out from
before you great and strong nations; but *as
for* you, no one has been able to stand
against you to this day. 10 One man of you
shall chase a thousand, for the LORD your
God *is* He who fights for you, as He
promised you. 11 Therefore take careful
heed to yourselves, that you love the LORD
your God. 12 Or else, if indeed you do go
back, and cling to the remnant of these na-
tions—these that remain among you—and
make marriages with them, and go in to
them and they to you, 13 know for certain
that the LORD your God will no longer
drive out these nations from before you.
But they shall be snares and traps to you,
and scourges on your sides and thorns in
your eyes, until you perish from this good
land which the LORD your God has given
you.
14 "Behold, this day I *am* going the way of
all the earth. And you know in all your
hearts and in all your souls that not one
thing has failed of all the good things
which the LORD your God spoke concern-
ing you. All have come to pass for you; not
one word of them has failed. 15 Therefore it
shall come to pass, that as all the good
things have come upon you which the
LORD your God promised you, so the LORD
will bring upon you all harmful things, un-
til He has destroyed you from this good
land which the LORD your God has given
you. 16 When you have transgressed the
covenant of the LORD your God, which He
commanded you, and have gone and
served other gods, and bowed down to
them, then the anger of the LORD will burn
against you, and you shall perish quickly
from the good land which He has given
you."

CHAPTER 24

The Covenant at Shechem

Then Joshua gathered all the tribes of Is-
rael to Shē′chem and called for the elders
of Israel, for their heads, for their judges,
and for their officers; and they presented
themselves before God. 2 And Joshua said
to all the people, "Thus says the LORD God
of Israel: 'Your fathers, *including* Tē′rah, the
father of Abraham and the father of
Nā′hor, dwelt on the other side of the
River[a] in old times; and they served other
gods. 3 Then I took your father Abraham
from the other side of the River, led him
throughout all the land of Cā′naan, and
multiplied his descendants and gave him
Isaac. 4 To Isaac I gave Jacob and Esau. To
Esau I gave the mountains of Sē′ir to pos-
sess, but Jacob and his children went down
to Egypt. 5 Also I sent Moses and Aaron,
and I plagued Egypt, according to what I
did among them. Afterward I brought you
out.
6 'Then I brought your fathers out of
Egypt, and you came to the sea; and the
Egyptians pursued your fathers with char-
iots and horsemen to the Red Sea. 7 So they
cried out to the LORD; and He put darkness
between you and the Egyptians, brought

24:2 [a]Hebrew *Nahar,* the Euphrates, and so in verses 3, 14, and 15

23:12–16 A reminder of the covenant: obedience means blessing, disobedience means curse. **if indeed you . . . make marriages with them**: Joshua repeats the warning given earlier by Moses (see Deut. 7:3, 4 and note on Deut. 7:1–6).

23:14 the way of all the earth: An idiom for death.

23:15, 16 God's wonderful grace is balanced by His awesome righteousness. Ignoring either of these holy characteristics is a grave mistake.

24:1–28 The form of the covenant here, as well as in Deuteronomy, has been recognized as based upon a common ancient treaty formula. The formula contains a preamble ("Thus says the LORD God of Israel"); a historical prologue ("Your fathers," vv. 2–13); stipulations (vv. 14, 15); warnings (vv. 19, 20); witnesses (v. 22); and a depositing of the document (v. 26).

the sea upon them, and covered them. And
your eyes saw what I did in Egypt. Then
you dwelt in the wilderness a long time.
8And I brought you into the land of the
Am'o·rītes, who dwelt on the other side of
the Jordan, and they fought with you. But I
gave them into your hand, that you might
possess their land, and I destroyed them
from before you. 9Then Bā'lak the son of
Zip'por, king of Mō'ab, arose to make war
against Israel, and sent and called Bā'laam
the son of Bē'or to curse you. 10But I would
not listen to Bā'laam; therefore he contin-
ued to bless you. So I delivered you out of
his hand. 11Then you went over the Jordan
and came to Jericho. And the men of Jeri-
cho fought against you—*also* the Am'o-
rītes, the Per'iz·zītes, the Cā'-naan·ītes,
the Hit'tītes, the Gir'ga·shītes, the Hī'-
vītes, and the Jeb'ū·sītes. But I delivered
them into your hand. 12I sent the hornet be-
fore you which drove them out from before
you, *also* the two kings of the Am'o·rītes,
but not with your sword or with your bow.
13I have given you a land for which you did
not labor, and cities which you did not
build, and you dwell in them; you eat of
the vineyards and olive groves which you
did not plant.'

14"Now therefore, fear the LORD, serve
Him in sincerity and in truth, and put
away the gods which your fathers served
on the other side of the River and in Egypt.
Serve the LORD! 15And if it seems evil to
you to serve the LORD, choose for your-
selves this day whom you will serve,
whether the gods which your fathers
served that *were* on the other side of the
River, or the gods of the Am'o·rītes, in
whose land you dwell. But as for me and
my house, we will serve the LORD."

16So the people answered and said: "Far
be it from us that we should forsake the
LORD to serve other gods; 17for the LORD
our God *is* He who brought us and our fa-
thers up out of the land of Egypt, from the
house of bondage, who did those great
signs in our sight, and preserved us in all
the way that we went and among all the
people through whom we passed. 18And
the LORD drove out from before us all the
people, including the Am'o·rītes who
dwelt in the land. We also will serve the
LORD, for He *is* our God."

19But Joshua said to the people, "You
cannot serve the LORD, for He *is* a holy
God. He *is* a jealous God; He will not for-
give your transgressions nor your sins. 20If
you forsake the LORD and serve foreign
gods, then He will turn and do you harm
and consume you, after He has done you
good."

21And the people said to Joshua, "No,
but we will serve the LORD!"

22So Joshua said to the people, "You *are*
witnesses against yourselves that you have
chosen the LORD for yourselves, to serve
Him."

And they said, "*We are* witnesses!"

23"Now therefore," *he said,* "put away
the foreign gods which *are* among you, and
incline your heart to the LORD God of Is-
rael."

24And the people said to Joshua, "The

24:14 The former generations had practiced idolatry **on the other side of the River** (in Syria) and in Egypt. The temptations to serve the gods of Canaan were ever present.

24:15 While few today are tempted to serve graven images, we must guard against the idolatry of worshiping money, fame, beauty, or any of the other gods of present society. The Lord alone must be the focus of our adoration and obedience.

24:19 **You cannot serve** unless you experience a radical change of heart. **He will not forgive** refers to Israel's actual violation of the covenant and practicing of idolatry. The sense evident in v. 20 is "will not tolerate." Commitment is not just lip service; it demands a way of life.

24:21–25 These verses represent ancient Israel's greatest hour spiritually. In our lives also there is no greater hour than when we make the commitment: **The LORD our God we will serve, and His voice we will obey** (v. 24).

LORD our God we will serve, and His voice
we will obey!"
25So Joshua made a covenant with the
people that day, and made for them a
statute and an ordinance in Shē′chem.
26Then Joshua wrote these words in the
Book of the Law of God. And he took a
large stone, and set it up there under the
oak that *was* by the sanctuary of the LORD.
27And Joshua said to all the people, "Be-
hold, this stone shall be a witness to us, for
it has heard all the words of the LORD
which He spoke to us. It shall therefore be
a witness to you, lest you deny your God."
28So Joshua let the people depart, each to
his own inheritance.

Death of Joshua and Eleazar

29Now it came to pass after these things
that Joshua the son of Nun, the servant of
the LORD, died, *being* one hundred and ten
years old. 30And they buried him within
the border of his inheritance at Tim′nath
Sē′rah, which *is* in the mountains of
Ē′phra·im, on the north side of Mount
Gā′ash.
31Israel served the LORD all the days of
Joshua, and all the days of the elders who
outlived Joshua, who had known all the
works of the LORD which He had done for
Israel.
32The bones of Joseph, which the chil-
dren of Israel had brought up out of Egypt,
they buried at Shē′chem, in the plot of
ground which Jacob had bought from the
sons of Hā′mor the father of Shē′chem for
one hundred pieces of silver, and which
had become an inheritance of the children
of Joseph.
33And El·ē·ā′zar the son of Aaron died.
They buried him in a hill *belonging to*
Phin′e·has his son, which was given to him
in the mountains of Ē′phra·im.

24:32 The burial of the **bones of Joseph** in Canaan underscored the fulfillment of God's promise. The patriarch is laid to rest in the Promised Land.

✦Judges✦

The author of Judges is unknown, but the book was most likely written around 1050 or 1000 B.C., during the reign of King Saul or King David. The events, which took place after Joshua's generation had died, show that, rather than driving out the Canaanites, Israel had mingled with them and was practicing idolatry.

Judges is written thematically instead of chronologically, and it illustrates the depravity of Israel most effectively in the last verse: "Everyone did what was right in his own eyes" (21:25). The author uses a cycle involving sin, servitude, supplication, salvation, and silence to show the repeated results of disobedience. Chapters 1 and 2 detail the deterioration of Israel due to the people's lack of faith and obedience. Chapters 3—16 describe various deliverances through the efforts of twelve judges raised up by God after the people repented. Some of the judges God elected were courageous people who simply made themselves available for the Lord's work.

Chapters 17—21 show the depravity of the nation during this time. This depravity proves that human deliverance is never complete. Judges tells of the need for an eternal Savior and points to Jesus Christ, the ultimate Judge. ✦

CHAPTER 1

The Continuing Conquest of Canaan

Now after the death of Joshua it came to
pass that the children of Israel asked the
LORD, saying, "Who shall be first to go up
for us against the Cā′naan·ītes to fight
against them?"
2And the LORD said, "Judah shall go up.
Indeed I have delivered the land into his
hand."
3So Judah said to Sim′ē·on his brother,
"Come up with me to my allotted territory,
that we may fight against the Cā′naan·ītes;
and I will likewise go with you to your allotted territory." And Sim′ē·on went with
him. 4Then Judah went up, and the LORD
delivered the Cā′naan·ītes and the
Per′iz·zītes into their hand; and they killed
ten thousand men at Bē′zek. 5And they
found A·dō′ni-Bē′zek in Bē′zek, and
fought against him; and they defeated the
Cā′naan·ītes and the Per′iz·zītes. 6Then
A·dō′ni-Bē′zek fled, and they pursued him
and caught him and cut off his thumbs and
big toes. 7And A·dō′ni-Bē′zek said, "Seventy kings with their thumbs and big toes
cut off used to gather *scraps* under my

1:6, 7 The Hebrew punishment of **Adoni-Bezek** reflects the law of retaliation. Kings who had received such treatment would be unable to lead their soldiers in battle; without thumbs they could not hold their weapons and without big toes they would not be able to keep their balance during battle.

table; as I have done, so God has repaid me." Then they brought him to Jerusalem, and there he died.

8 Now the children of Judah fought against Jerusalem and took it; they struck it with the edge of the sword and set the city on fire. 9 And afterward the children of Judah went down to fight against the Cā'naan·ītes who dwelt in the mountains, in the South,[a] and in the lowland. 10 Then Judah went against the Cā'naan·ītes who dwelt in Hē'bron. (Now the name of Hē'bron *was* formerly Kir'jath Ar'ba.) And they killed Shē'shai, A·hī'man, and Tal'maī.

11 From there they went against the inhabitants of Dē'bir. (The name of Dē'bir *was* formerly Kir'jath Sē'pher.)

12 Then Caleb said, "Whoever attacks Kir'jath Sē'pher and takes it, to him I will give my daughter Ach'sah as wife." 13 And Oth'ni·el the son of Kē'naz, Caleb's younger brother, took it; so he gave him his daughter Ach'sah as wife. 14 Now it happened, when she came *to him,* that she urged him[a] to ask her father for a field. And she dismounted from *her* donkey, and Caleb said to her, "What do you wish?" 15 So she said to him, "Give me a blessing; since you have given me land in the South, give me also springs of water."

And Caleb gave her the upper springs and the lower springs.

16 Now the children of the Ken'īte, Moses' father-in-law, went up from the City of Palms with the children of Judah into the Wilderness of Judah, which *lies* in the South *near* Ar'ad; and they went and dwelt among the people. 17 And Judah went with his brother Sim'ē·on, and they attacked the Cā'naan·ītes who inhabited Zē'phath, and utterly destroyed it. So the name of the city was called Hor'mah. 18 Also Judah took Gā'za with its territory, Ash'ke·lon with its territory, and Ek'ron with its territory. 19 So the LORD was with Judah. And they drove out the mountaineers, but they could not drive out the inhabitants of the lowland, because they had chariots of iron. 20 And they gave Hē'bron to Caleb, as Moses had said. Then he expelled from there the three sons of Ā'nak. 21 But the children of Benjamin did not drive out the Jeb'ū·sītes who inhabited Jerusalem; so the Jeb'ū·sītes dwell with the children of Benjamin in Jerusalem to this day.

22 And the house of Joseph also went up against Beth'el, and the LORD *was* with them. 23 So the house of Joseph sent men to spy out Beth'el. (The name of the city *was* formerly Luz.) 24 And when the spies saw a man coming out of the city, they said to him, "Please show us the entrance to the city, and we will show you mercy." 25 So he showed them the entrance to the city, and they struck the city with the edge of the sword; but they let the man and all his family go. 26 And the man went to the land of the Hit'tītes, built a city, and called its name Luz, which *is* its name to this day.

Incomplete Conquest of the Land

27 However, Ma·nas'seh did not drive out *the inhabitants of* Beth Shē'an and its villages, or Tā'a·nach and its villages, or the inhabitants of Dor and its villages, or the inhabitants of Ib'lē·am and its villages, or the inhabitants of Me·gid'dō and its

1:9 [a]Hebrew *Negev,* and so throughout this book
1:14 [a]Septuagint and Vulgate read *he urged her.*

1:8 The Jebusites controlled **Jerusalem** at the time of King David (see 2 Sam. 5:6–10). Evidently they regained power at a time after the event of this verse (see v. 21). Such a situation would not have occurred if the Israelites had driven out the Jebusites completely, as God had instructed.

1:22–36 In direct disobedience to the Lord's command, the Israelites failed to dislodge the Canaanites who lived in the Jezreel Valley (v. 28) and in key cities on the coastal edge of the mountains, such as **Gezer** (v. 29) and **Acco** (v. 31). This failure incurred God's wrath and led to disaster (see 2:1–3).

villages; for the Cā′naan·ītes were deter-
mined to dwell in that land. 28And it came
to pass, when Israel was strong, that they
put the Cā′naan·ītes under tribute, but did
not completely drive them out.
29Nor did Ē′phra·im drive out the Cā′-
naan·ītes who dwelt in Gē′zer; so the
Cā′naan·ītes dwelt in Gē′zer among them.
30Nor did Zeb′ū·lun drive out the inhab-
itants of Kit′ron or the inhabitants of
Na·hal′ol; so the Cā′naan·ītes dwelt
among them, and were put under tribute.
31Nor did Ash′er drive out the inhab-
itants of Ac′cō or the inhabitants of Sī′don,
or of Ah′lab, Ach′zib, Hel′bah, Ā′phik, or
Rē′hob. 32So the Ash′er·ītes dwelt among
the Cā′naan·ītes, the inhabitants of the
land; for they did not drive them out.
33Nor did Naph′ta·lī drive out the in-
habitants of Beth Shem′esh or the inhab-
itants of Beth Ā′nath; but they dwelt
among the Cā′naan·ītes, the inhabitants of
the land. Nevertheless the inhabitants of
Beth Shem′esh and Beth Ā′nath were put
under tribute to them.
34And the Am′o·rītes forced the children
of Dan into the mountains, for they would
not allow them to come down to the valley;
35and the Am′o·rītes were determined to
dwell in Mount Hē′res, in Aī′ja·lon, and in
Shā·al′bim;[a] yet when the strength of the
house of Joseph became greater, they were
put under tribute.
36Now the boundary of the Am′o·rītes
was from the Ascent of Ak·rab′bim, from
Sē′la, and upward.

CHAPTER 2

Israel's Disobedience

Then the Angel of the LORD came up
from Gil′gal to Bō′chim, and said: "I led
you up from Egypt and brought you to the
land of which I swore to your fathers; and
I said, 'I will never break My covenant
with you. 2And you shall make no
covenant with the inhabitants of this land;
you shall tear down their altars.' But you
have not obeyed My voice. Why have you
done this? 3Therefore I also said, 'I will not
drive them out before you; but they shall
be *thorns* in your side,[a] and their gods shall
be a snare to you.' " 4So it was, when the
Angel of the LORD spoke these words to all
the children of Israel, that the people lifted
up their voices and wept.
5Then they called the name of that place
Bō′chim;[a] and they sacrificed there to the
LORD. 6And when Joshua had dismissed
the people, the children of Israel went each
to his own inheritance to possess the land.

Death of Joshua

7So the people served the LORD all the
days of Joshua, and all the days of the el-
ders who outlived Joshua, who had seen
all the great works of the LORD which He
had done for Israel. 8Now Joshua the son of
Nun, the servant of the LORD, died *when he
was* one hundred and ten years old. 9And
they buried him within the border of his
inheritance at Tim′nath Hē′res, in the
mountains of Ē′phra·im, on the north side
of Mount Gā′ash. 10When all that genera-
tion had been gathered to their fathers, an-
other generation arose after them who did
not know the LORD nor the work which He
had done for Israel.

Israel's Unfaithfulness

11Then the children of Israel did evil in
the sight of the LORD, and served the
Bā′als; 12and they forsook the LORD God of
their fathers, who had brought them out of
the land of Egypt; and they followed other
gods from *among* the gods of the people

1:35 [a]Spelled *Shaalabbin* in Joshua 19:42
2:3 [a]Septuagint, Targum, and Vulgate read *enemies to you.* 2:5 [a]Literally *Weeping*

2:11–19 A description of the recurring cycle of apostasy, oppression, supplication, and deliverance.

who *were* all around them, and they bowed down to them; and they provoked the LORD to anger. 13They forsook the LORD and served Bā'al and the Ash'to·reths.[a] 14And the anger of the LORD was hot against Israel. So He delivered them into the hands of plunderers who despoiled them; and He sold them into the hands of their enemies all around, so that they could no longer stand before their enemies. 15Wherever they went out, the hand of the LORD was against them for calamity, as the LORD had said, and as the LORD had sworn to them. And they were greatly distressed.

16Nevertheless, the LORD raised up judges who delivered them out of the hand of those who plundered them. 17Yet they would not listen to their judges, but they played the harlot with other gods, and bowed down to them. They turned quickly from the way in which their fathers walked, in obeying the commandments of the LORD; they did not do so. 18And when the LORD raised up judges for them, the LORD was with the judge and delivered them out of the hand of their enemies all the days of the judge; for the LORD was moved to pity by their groaning because of those who oppressed them and harassed them. 19And it came to pass, when the judge was dead, that they reverted and behaved more corruptly than their fathers, by following other gods, to serve them and bow down to them. They did not cease from their own doings nor from their stubborn way.

20Then the anger of the LORD was hot against Israel; and He said, "Because this nation has transgressed My covenant which I commanded their fathers, and has not heeded My voice, 21I also will no longer drive out before them any of the nations which Joshua left when he died, 22so that through them I may test Israel, whether they will keep the ways of the LORD, to walk in them as their fathers kept *them*, or not." 23Therefore the LORD left those nations, without driving them out immediately; nor did He deliver them into the hand of Joshua.

CHAPTER 3

The Nations Remaining in the Land

Now these *are* the nations which the LORD left, that He might test Israel by them, *that is*, all who had not known any of the wars in Cā'naan 2(*this was* only so that the generations of the children of Israel might be taught to know war, at least those who had not formerly known it), 3*namely*, five lords of the Phi·lis'tines, all the Cā'naan·ītes, the Sī·dō'ni·ans, and the Hī'vītes who dwelt in Mount Lebanon, from Mount Bā'al Her'mon to the entrance of Hā'math. 4And they were *left, that He might* test Israel by them, to know whether they would obey the commandments of the LORD, which He had commanded their fathers by the hand of Moses.

5Thus the children of Israel dwelt among the Cā'naan·ītes, the Hit'tītes, the Am'o·rītes, the Per'iz·zītes, the Hī'vītes, and the Jeb'ū·sītes. 6And they took their daughters to be their wives, and gave their daughters to their sons; and they served their gods.

Othniel

7So the children of Israel did evil in the sight of the LORD. They forgot the LORD their God, and served the Bā'als and A·shē'rahs.[a] 8Therefore the anger of the

2:13 [a]Canaanite goddesses for Canaanite goddesses

3:7 [a]Name or symbol

3:4 that He might test: God does not tempt His children to do evil. Rather, He allows opportunity for them to exercise their resolve to do His will (see James 1:12, 13). God knows whether we will **obey the commandments of the LORD** but He permits us to demonstrate it for ourselves.

LORD was hot against Israel, and He sold
them into the hand of Cū'shan-Rish·a-
thā'im king of Mes·o·po·tā'mi·a; and the
children of Israel served Cū'shan-Rish·a-
thā'im eight years. 9When the children of
Israel cried out to the LORD, the LORD
raised up a deliverer for the children of Is-
rael, who delivered them: Oth'ni·el the son
of Kē'naz, Caleb's younger brother. 10The
Spirit of the LORD came upon him, and he
judged Israel. He went out to war, and the
LORD delivered Cū'shan-Rish·a·thā'im
king of Mes·o·po·tā'mi·a into his hand;
and his hand prevailed over Cū'shan-
Rish·a·thā'im. 11So the land had rest for
forty years. Then Oth'ni·el the son of
Kē'naz died.

Ehud

12And the children of Israel again did
evil in the sight of the LORD. So the LORD
strengthened Eg'lon king of Mō'ab against
Israel, because they had done evil in the
sight of the LORD. 13Then he gathered to
himself the people of Am'mon and Am'-
a·lek, went and defeated Israel, and took
possession of the City of Palms. 14So the
children of Israel served Eg'lon king of
Mō'ab eighteen years.

15But when the children of Israel cried
out to the LORD, the LORD raised up a de-
liverer for them: Ē'hud the son of Gē'ra,
the Ben'ja·mīte, a left-handed man. By him
the children of Israel sent tribute to Eg'lon
king of Mō'ab. 16Now Ē'hud made himself
a dagger (it was double-edged and a cubit
in length) and fastened it under his clothes
on his right thigh. 17So he brought the trib-
ute to Eg'lon king of Mō'ab. (Now Eg'lon
was a very fat man.) 18And when he had
finished presenting the tribute, he sent
away the people who had carried the trib-
ute. 19But he himself turned back from the
stone images that *were* at Gil'gal, and said,
"I have a secret message for you, O king."

He said, "Keep silence!" And all who at-
tended him went out from him.

20So Ē'hud came to him (now he was sit-
ting upstairs in his cool private chamber).
Then Ē'hud said, "I have a message from
God for you." So he arose from *his* seat.
21Then Ē'hud reached with his left hand,
took the dagger from his right thigh, and
thrust it into his belly. 22Even the hilt went
in after the blade, and the fat closed over
the blade, for he did not draw the dagger
out of his belly; and his entrails came out.
23Then Ē'hud went out through the porch
and shut the doors of the upper room be-
hind him and locked them.

24When he had gone out, *Eg'lon's*[a] ser-
vants came to look, and *to their* surprise,
the doors of the upper room were locked.
So they said, "He is probably attending to
his needs in the cool chamber." 25So they
waited till they were embarrassed, and still
he had not opened the doors of the upper
room. Therefore they took the key and
opened *them*. And there was their master,
fallen dead on the floor.

26But Ē'hud had escaped while they de-
layed, and passed beyond the stone im-
ages and escaped to Sē·ī'rah. 27And it hap-
pened, when he arrived, that he blew the
trumpet in the mountains of Ē'phra·im,
and the children of Israel went down with
him from the mountains; and he led them.
28Then he said to them, "Follow *me,* for the
LORD has delivered your enemies the
Mō'ab·ītes into your hand." So they went
down after him, seized the fords of the Jor-
dan leading to Mō'ab, and did not allow

3:24 [a]Literally *his*

3:15–21 Being **left-handed** (v. 15), Ehud was able to hide a dagger on the opposite side of his garment (v. 16) and, consequently, make unexpected use of the weapon with the left hand (v. 21).

3:28, 29 fords of the Jordan: Eglon and his army of occupation were apparently located on Israel's territory in Jericho, west of the Jordan. Ehud and the Israelites cut off Eglon's retreat to Moab.

anyone to cross over. 29And at that time
they killed about ten thousand men of
Mō′ab, all stout men of valor; not a man es-
caped. 30So Mō′ab was subdued that day
under the hand of Israel. And the land had
rest for eighty years.

Shamgar

31After him was Sham′gar the son of
Ā′nath, who killed six hundred men of the
Phi·lis′tines with an ox goad; and he also
delivered Israel.

CHAPTER 4

Deborah

When Ē′hud was dead, the children of
Israel again did evil in the sight of the
LORD. 2So the LORD sold them into the hand
of Jā′bin king of Cā′naan, who reigned in
Hā′zor. The commander of his army *was*
Sis′e·ra, who dwelt in Ha·rō′sheth Ha-
goy′im. 3And the children of Israel cried
out to the LORD; for Jā′bin had nine hun-
dred chariots of iron, and for twenty years
he had harshly oppressed the children of
Israel.

4Now Deb′or·ah, a prophetess, the wife
of Lap′i·doth, was judging Israel at that
time. 5And she would sit under the palm
tree of Deb′or·ah between Rā′mah and
Beth′el in the mountains of Ē′phra·im. And
the children of Israel came up to her for
judgment. 6Then she sent and called for
Bar′ak the son of A·bin′ō·am from Kē′desh
in Naph′ta·lī, and said to him, "Has not
the LORD God of Israel commanded, 'Go
and deploy *troops* at Mount Tā′bor; take
with you ten thousand men of the sons of
Naph′ta·lī and of the sons of Zeb′ū·lun;
7and against you I will deploy Sis′e·ra, the
commander of Jā′bin's army, with his char-
iots and his multitude at the River Kī′shon;
and I will deliver him into your hand'?"

8And Bar′ak said to her, "If you will go
with me, then I will go; but if you will not
go with me, I will not go!"

9So she said, "I will surely go with you;
nevertheless there will be no glory for you
in the journey you are taking, for the LORD
will sell Sis′e·ra into the hand of a
woman." Then Deb′or·ah arose and went
with Bar′ak to Kē′desh. 10And Bar′ak
called Zeb′ū·lun and Naph′ta·lī to Kē′-
desh; he went up with ten thousand men
under his command,[a] and Deb′or·ah went
up with him.

11Now Hē′ber the Ken′īte, of the chil-
dren of Hō′bab the father-in-law of Moses,
had separated himself from the Ken′ītes
and pitched his tent near the terebinth tree
at Zā·a·nā′im, which *is* beside Kē′desh.

12And they reported to Sis′e·ra that
Bar′ak the son of A·bin′ō·am had gone up
to Mount Tā′bor. 13So Sis′e·ra gathered to-
gether all his chariots, nine hundred chari-
ots of iron, and all the people who *were*
with him, from Ha·rō′sheth Ha·goy′im to
the River Kī′shon.

14Then Deb′or·ah said to Bar′ak, "Up!
For this *is* the day in which the LORD has
delivered Sis′e·ra into your hand. Has not
the LORD gone out before you?" So Bar′ak
went down from Mount Tā′bor with ten
thousand men following him. 15And the
LORD routed Sis′e·ra and all *his* chariots
and all *his* army with the edge of the sword
before Bar′ak; and Sis′e·ra alighted from
his chariot and fled away on foot. 16But
Bar′ak pursued the chariots and the army
as far as Ha·rō′sheth Ha·goy′im, and all

4:10 [a]Literally *at his feet*

4:9 In the culture of the day, it would be a disgrace for a woman to receive greater military glory than the commander, perhaps a rebuke for Barak's timidity.

4:12–15 Barak and his army had camped near **Mount Tabor** (v. 12). **Sisera** and his army came from the north and camped near the Kishon River. Barak's forces moved down and met them there.

the army of Sis′e·ra fell by the edge of the
sword; not a man was left.
17 However, Sis′e·ra had fled away on
foot to the tent of Jā′el, the wife of Hē′ber
the Ken′īte; for *there was* peace between
Jā′bin king of Hā′zor and the house of
Hē′ber the Ken′īte. 18 And Jā′el went out to
meet Sis′e·ra, and said to him, "Turn aside,
my lord, turn aside to me; do not fear."
And when he had turned aside with her
into the tent, she covered him with a blan-
ket.
19 Then he said to her, "Please give me a
little water to drink, for I am thirsty." So
she opened a jug of milk, gave him a drink,
and covered him. 20 And he said to her,
"Stand at the door of the tent, and if
any man comes and inquires of you, and
says, 'Is there any man here?' you shall
say, 'No.' "
21 Then Jā′el, Hē′ber's wife, took a tent
peg and took a hammer in her hand, and
went softly to him and drove the peg into
his temple, and it went down into the
ground; for he was fast asleep and weary.
So he died. 22 And then, as Bar′ak pursued
Sis′e·ra, Jā′el came out to meet him, and
said to him, "Come, I will show you the
man whom you seek." And when he went
into her *tent,* there lay Sis′e·ra, dead with
the peg in his temple.
23 So on that day God subdued Jā′bin
king of Cā′naan in the presence of the chil-
dren of Israel. 24 And the hand of the chil-
dren of Israel grew stronger and stronger
against Jā′bin king of Cā′naan, until they
had destroyed Jā′bin king of Cā′naan.

CHAPTER 5

The Song of Deborah

Then Deb′or·ah and Bar′ak the son of
A·bin′ō·am sang on that day, saying:

2 "When leaders lead in Israel,
When the people willingly offer
themselves,
Bless the LORD!

3 "Hear, O kings! Give ear, O princes!
I, *even* I, will sing to the LORD;
I will sing praise to the LORD God of
Israel.

4 "LORD, when You went out from Sē′ir,
When You marched from the field of
Ē′dom,
The earth trembled and the heavens
poured,
The clouds also poured water;
5 The mountains gushed before the
LORD,
This Sinai, before the LORD God of
Israel.

6 "In the days of Sham′gar, son of
Ā′nath,
In the days of Jā′el,
The highways were deserted,
And the travelers walked along the
byways.
7 Village life ceased, it ceased in Israel,
Until I, Deb′or·ah, arose,
Arose a mother in Israel.
8 They chose new gods;
Then *there was* war in the gates;
Not a shield or spear was seen among
forty thousand in Israel.
9 My heart *is* with the rulers of Israel
Who offered themselves willingly
with the people.
Bless the LORD!

10 "Speak, you who ride on white
donkeys,
Who sit in judges' attire,
And who walk along the road.

4:17–21 Verse 11 explains the geography of vv. 17–22. **Heber the Kenite** had relocated from the ancestral home of the Kenites in the south to the far north of Canaan. Thus as **Sisera** fled the battle, he passed the tent of Heber's wife Jael.

5:1–31 Known as the "Song of Deborah," this poem is typical of the many songs written to celebrate national victories and is one of the oldest examples in biblical literature.

11 Far from the noise of the archers,
among the watering places,
There they shall recount the righteous acts of the LORD,
The righteous acts *for* His villagers in Israel;
Then the people of the LORD shall go down to the gates.

12 "Awake, awake, Deb'or·ah!
Awake, awake, sing a song!
Arise, Bar'ak, and lead your captives away,
O son of A·bin'ō·am!
13 "Then the survivors came down, the people against the nobles;
The LORD came down for me against the mighty.
14 From Ē'phra·im *were* those whose roots were in Am'a·lek.
After you, Benjamin, with your peoples,
From Mā'chir rulers came down,
And from Zeb'ū·lun those who bear the recruiter's staff.
15 And the princes of Is'sa·char[a] *were* with Deb'or·ah;
As Is'sa·char, so *was* Bar'ak
Sent into the valley under his command;[b]
Among the divisions of Reuben
There were great resolves of heart.
16 Why did you sit among the sheepfolds,
To hear the pipings for the flocks?
The divisions of Reuben have great searchings of heart.
17 Gil'ē·ad stayed beyond the Jordan,
And why did Dan remain on ships?[a]
Ash'er continued at the seashore,
And stayed by his inlets.
18 Zeb'ū·lun *is* a people *who* jeopardized their lives to the point of death,
Naph'ta·lī also, on the heights of the battlefield.

19 "The kings came *and* fought,
Then the kings of Cā'naan fought
In Tā'a·nach, by the waters of Me·gid'dō;
They took no spoils of silver.
20 They fought from the heavens;
The stars from their courses fought against Sis'e·ra.
21 The torrent of Kī'shon swept them away,
That ancient torrent, the torrent of Kī'shon.
O my soul, march on in strength!
22 Then the horses' hooves pounded,
The galloping, galloping of his steeds.
23 'Curse Mē'roz,' said the angel[a] of the LORD,
'Curse its inhabitants bitterly,
Because they did not come to the help of the LORD,
To the help of the LORD against the mighty.'

24 "Most blessed among women is Jā'el,
The wife of Hē'ber the Ken'īte;
Blessed is she among women in tents.

5:15 [a]Following Septuagint, Syriac, Targum, and Vulgate; Masoretic Text reads *And my princes in Issachar.* [b]Literally *at his feet* 5:17 [a]Or *at ease* 5:23 [a]Or *Angel*

5:20, 21 A poetic description of a miracle of weather on Israel's behalf. Out of the **heavens** came torrential rains causing flash floods that swept Sisera away.

5:23 Meroz was a community in northern Palestine. Its people failed to **come to the help of the LORD** when He needed them. There is no greater failure than this. When troubles arise, Christians should actively respond to help their brothers and sisters in Christ. If we are unwilling to risk our comfort and safety for the Lord's work, then our priorities are out of order.

5:24–27 A poetic description of events related in 4:17–21. If Jael's decisively brutal act grates on our sensibilities, we must remember the brutal nature of the times. The delicate and indecisive did not survive.

25 He asked for water, she gave milk;
She brought out cream in a lordly bowl.
26 She stretched her hand to the tent peg,
Her right hand to the workmen's hammer;
She pounded Sis'e·ra, she pierced his head,
She split and struck through his temple.
27 At her feet he sank, he fell, he lay still;
At her feet he sank, he fell;
Where he sank, there he fell dead.

28 "The mother of Sis'e·ra looked through the window,
And cried out through the lattice,
'Why is his chariot *so* long in coming?
Why tarries the clatter of his chariots?'
29 Her wisest ladies answered her,
Yes, she answered herself,
30 'Are they not finding and dividing the spoil:
To every man a girl *or* two;
For Sis'e·ra, plunder of dyed garments,
Plunder of garments embroidered and dyed,
Two pieces of dyed embroidery for the neck of the looter?'

31 "Thus let all Your enemies perish, O LORD!
But *let* those who love Him *be* like the sun
When it comes out in full strength."

So the land had rest for forty years.

CHAPTER 6

Midianites Oppress Israel

Then the children of Israel did evil in the
sight of the LORD. So the LORD delivered
them into the hand of Mid'i·an for seven
years, 2and the hand of Mid'i·an prevailed
against Israel. Because of the Mid'i·an·ītes,
the children of Israel made for themselves
the dens, the caves, and the strongholds
which *are* in the mountains. 3So it was,
whenever Israel had sown, Mid'i·an·ītes
would come up; also A·mal'e·kītes and the
people of the East would come up against
them. 4Then they would encamp against
them and destroy the produce of the earth
as far as Gā'za, and leave no sustenance for
Israel, neither sheep nor ox nor donkey.
5For they would come up with their live-
stock and their tents, coming in as numer-
ous as locusts; both they and their camels
were without number; and they would en-
ter the land to destroy it. 6So Israel was
greatly impoverished because of the
Mid'i·an·ītes, and the children of Israel
cried out to the LORD.

7And it came to pass, when the children
of Israel cried out to the LORD because of
the Mid'i·an·ītes, 8that the LORD sent a
prophet to the children of Israel, who said
to them, "Thus says the LORD God of Israel:
'I brought you up from Egypt and brought
you out of the house of bondage; 9and I de-
livered you out of the hand of the Egyp-
tians and out of the hand of all who op-
pressed you, and drove them out before
you and gave you their land. 10Also I said
to you, "I *am* the LORD your God; do not
fear the gods of the Am'o·rītes, in whose
land you dwell." But you have not obeyed
My voice.' "

Gideon

11Now the Angel of the LORD came and
sat under the terebinth tree which *was* in

6:11 winepress: A large vat for crushing grapes, located not on a hilltop like a threshing floor, but in a valley. Gideon was threshing in small quantities in an inconspicuous place, hoping to finish quickly and avoid detection by marauding bands.

Oph'rah, which *belonged* to Jō'ash the Ā·bi·ez'rīte, while his son Gideon threshed wheat in the winepress, in order to hide *it* from the Mid'i·an·ītes. 12And the Angel of the LORD appeared to him, and said to him, "The LORD *is* with you, you mighty man of valor!"

13Gideon said to Him, "O my lord,[a] if the LORD is with us, why then has all this happened to us? And where *are* all His miracles which our fathers told us about, saying, 'Did not the LORD bring us up from Egypt?' But now the LORD has forsaken us and delivered us into the hands of the Mid'i·an·ītes."

14Then the LORD turned to him and said, "Go in this might of yours, and you shall save Israel from the hand of the Mid'i·an·ītes. Have I not sent you?"

15So he said to Him, "O my Lord,[a] how can I save Israel? Indeed my clan *is* the weakest in Ma·nas'seh, and I *am* the least in my father's house."

16And the LORD said to him, "Surely I will be with you, and you shall defeat the Mid'i·an·ītes as one man."

17Then he said to Him, "If now I have found favor in Your sight, then show me a sign that it is You who talk with me. 18Do not depart from here, I pray, until I come to You and bring out my offering and set *it* before You."

And He said, "I will wait until you come back."

19So Gideon went in and prepared a young goat, and unleavened bread from an ephah of flour. The meat he put in a basket, and he put the broth in a pot; and he brought *them* out to Him under the terebinth tree and presented *them*. 20The Angel of God said to him, "Take the meat and the unleavened bread and lay *them* on this rock, and pour out the broth." And he did so.

21Then the Angel of the LORD put out the end of the staff that *was* in His hand, and touched the meat and the unleavened bread; and fire rose out of the rock and consumed the meat and the unleavened bread. And the Angel of the LORD departed out of his sight.

22Now Gideon perceived that He *was* the Angel of the LORD. So Gideon said, "Alas, O Lord GOD! For I have seen the Angel of the LORD face to face."

23Then the LORD said to him, "Peace *be* with you; do not fear, you shall not die." 24So Gideon built an altar there to the LORD, and called it The-LORD-*Is*-Peace.[a] To this day it *is* still in Oph'rah of the Ā·bi·ez'rītes.

25Now it came to pass the same night that the LORD said to him, "Take your father's young bull, the second bull of seven years old, and tear down the altar of Bā'al that your father has, and cut down the wooden image[a] that *is* beside it; 26and build an altar to the LORD your God on top of this rock in the proper arrangement, and take the second bull and offer a burnt sacrifice with the wood of the image which you shall cut down." 27So Gideon took ten men from among his servants and did as the LORD had said to him. But because he feared his father's household and the men of the city too much to do *it* by day, he did *it* by night.

Gideon Destroys the Altar of Baal

28And when the men of the city arose early in the morning, there was the altar of Bā'al, torn down; and the wooden image that *was* beside it was cut down, and the

6:13 [a]Hebrew *adoni,* used of man 6:15 [a]Hebrew *Adonai,* used of God 6:24 [a]Hebrew *YHWH Shalom* 6:25 [a]Hebrew *Asherah,* a Canaanite goddess

6:15 The choice of one who appears to be **the least** is a pattern throughout the OT (see 1 Sam. 16:10, 11). By using relatively insignificant people to fulfill His plans, God demonstrates His wondrous power. If He used powerful men, victories could easily be attributed to their strength rather than to the presence of God.

second bull was being offered on the altar
which had been built. 29So they said to one
another, "Who has done this thing?" And
when they had inquired and asked, they
said, "Gideon the son of Jō'ash has done
this thing." 30Then the men of the city said
to Jō'ash, "Bring out your son, that he may
die, because he has torn down the altar of
Bā'al, and because he has cut down the
wooden image that *was* beside it."
31But Jō'ash said to all who stood against
him, "Would you plead for Bā'al? Would
you save him? Let the one who would
plead for him be put to death by morning!
If he *is* a god, let him plead for himself, be-
cause his altar has been torn down!"
32Therefore on that day he called him
Jer·ub·bā'al,[a] saying, "Let Bā'al plead
against him, because he has torn down his
altar."
33Then all the Mid'i·an·ītes and
A·mal'e·kītes, the people of the East, gath-
ered together; and they crossed over and
encamped in the Valley of Jez'rē·el. 34But
the Spirit of the LORD came upon Gideon;
then he blew the trumpet, and the
Ā·bi·ez'rītes gathered behind him. 35And
he sent messengers throughout all Ma-
nas'seh, who also gathered behind him. He
also sent messengers to Ash'er, Zeb'ū·lun,
and Naph'ta·lī; and they came up to meet
them.

The Sign of the Fleece

36So Gideon said to God, "If You will
save Israel by my hand as You have said—
37look, I shall put a fleece of wool on the
threshing floor; if there is dew on the fleece
only, and *it is* dry on all the ground, then I
shall know that You will save Israel by my
hand, as You have said." 38And it was so.
When he rose early the next morning and
squeezed the fleece together, he wrung the
dew out of the fleece, a bowlful of water.
39Then Gideon said to God, "Do not be an-
gry with me, but let me speak just once
more: Let me test, I pray, just once more
with the fleece; let it now be dry only on
the fleece, but on all the ground let there be
dew." 40And God did so that night. It was
dry on the fleece only, but there was dew
on all the ground.

CHAPTER 7

Gideon's Valiant Three Hundred

Then Jer·ub·bā'al (that *is,* Gideon) and
all the people who *were* with him rose early
and encamped beside the well of Har'od,
so that the camp of the Mid'i·an·ītes was
on the north side of them by the hill of
Mō'reh in the valley.
2And the LORD said to Gideon, "The
people who *are* with you *are* too many for
Me to give the Mid'i·an·ītes into their
hands, lest Israel claim glory for itself
against Me, saying, 'My own hand has
saved me.' 3Now therefore, proclaim in the
hearing of the people, saying, 'Whoever *is*
fearful and afraid, let him turn and depart
at once from Mount Gil'ē·ad.' " And
twenty-two thousand of the people re-
turned, and ten thousand remained.
4But the LORD said to Gideon, "The peo-
ple *are* still *too* many; bring them down to
the water, and I will test them for you
there. Then it will be, *that* of whom I say to
you, 'This one shall go with you,' the same

6:32 [a]Literally *Let Baal Plead*

6:31 An adroit response. Let Baal take care of himself, if he is real, by striking dead the one who profaned his shrine. A son's faith can encourage his father to be faithful.

6:36–40 Gideon already knew God's will, but he sought assurance to strengthen his faith. **test**: God does not object to being tested by one who intends to obey. But those who test Him to reinforce their doubt earn His anger (Ps. 95:8–11).

7:4–7 Apparently the ones who remained in an upright position and lapped water from the palm of their hand showed correct military alertness. The others put down their weapons and bent carelessly on hands and knees.

shall go with you; and of whomever I say to you, 'This one shall not go with you,' the same shall not go." 5So he brought the people down to the water. And the LORD said to Gideon, "Everyone who laps from the water with his tongue, as a dog laps, you shall set apart by himself; likewise everyone who gets down on his knees to drink." 6And the number of those who lapped, *putting* their hand to their mouth, was three hundred men; but all the rest of the people got down on their knees to drink water. 7Then the LORD said to Gideon, "By the three hundred men who lapped I will save you, and deliver the Mid′i·an·ītes into your hand. Let all the *other* people go, every man to his place." 8So the people took provisions and their trumpets in their hands. And he sent away all *the rest of* Israel, every man to his tent, and retained those three hundred men. Now the camp of Mid′i·an was below him in the valley.

9It happened on the same night that the LORD said to him, "Arise, go down against the camp, for I have delivered it into your hand. 10But if you are afraid to go down, go down to the camp with Pū′rah your servant, 11and you shall hear what they say; and afterward your hands shall be strengthened to go down against the camp." Then he went down with Pū′rah his servant to the outpost of the armed men who *were* in the camp. 12Now the Mid′i·an·ītes and A·mal′e·kītes, all the people of the East, were lying in the valley as numerous as locusts; and their camels *were* without number, as the sand by the seashore in multitude.

13And when Gideon had come, there was a man telling a dream to his companion. He said, "I have had a dream: *To my surprise,* a loaf of barley bread tumbled into the camp of Mid′i·an; it came to a tent and struck it so that it fell and overturned, and the tent collapsed."

14Then his companion answered and said, "This *is* nothing else but the sword of Gideon the son of Jō′ash, a man of Israel! Into his hand God has delivered Mid′i·an and the whole camp."

15And so it was, when Gideon heard the telling of the dream and its interpretation, that he worshiped. He returned to the camp of Israel, and said, "Arise, for the LORD has delivered the camp of Mid′i·an into your hand." 16Then he divided the three hundred men *into* three companies, and he put a trumpet into every man's hand, with empty pitchers, and torches inside the pitchers. 17And he said to them, "Look at me and do likewise; watch, and when I come to the edge of the camp you shall do as I do: 18When I blow the trumpet, I and all who *are* with me, then you also blow the trumpets on every side of the whole camp, and say, *'The sword of* the LORD and of Gideon!' "

19So Gideon and the hundred men who *were* with him came to the outpost of the camp at the beginning of the middle watch, just as they had posted the watch; and they blew the trumpets and broke the pitchers that *were* in their hands. 20Then the three companies blew the trumpets and broke the pitchers—they held the torches in their left hands and the trumpets in their right hands for blowing—and they cried, "The sword of the LORD and of Gideon!" 21And every man stood in his place all around the camp; and the whole army ran and cried out and fled. 22When the three hundred blew the trumpets, the LORD set every man's sword against his companion throughout the whole camp; and the army fled to Beth Acacia,[a] toward Zer′e·rah, as far as the border of Abel Me·hō′lah, by Tab′bath.

23And the men of Israel gathered together from Naph′ta·lī, Ash′er, and all Ma·nas′seh, and pursued the Mid′i·an·ītes.

24Then Gideon sent messengers throughout all the mountains of Ē′phra·im, saying, "Come down against the Mid′i·an·ītes, and seize from them the watering places as far as Beth Ba′rah and the

7:22 aHebrew *Beth Shittah*

Jordan." Then all the men of Ē'phra·im gathered together and seized the watering places as far as Beth Ba'rah and the Jordan. 25And they captured two princes of the Mid'i·an·ītes, Or'eb and Zē'eb. They killed Or'eb at the rock of Or'eb, and Zē'eb they killed at the winepress of Zē'eb. They pursued Mid'i·an and brought the heads of Or'eb and Zē'eb to Gideon on the other side of the Jordan.

CHAPTER 8

Gideon Subdues the Midianites

Now the men of Ē'phra·im said to him, "Why have you done this to us by not calling us when you went to fight with the Mid'i·an·ītes?" And they reprimanded him sharply.

2So he said to them, "What have I done now in comparison with you? *Is* not the gleaning *of the grapes* of Ē'phra·im better than the vintage of Ā·bi·ē'zer? 3God has delivered into your hands the princes of Mid'i·an, Or'eb and Zē'eb. And what was I able to do in comparison with you?" Then their anger toward him subsided when he said that.

4When Gideon came to the Jordan, he and the three hundred men who *were* with him crossed over, exhausted but still in pursuit. 5Then he said to the men of Suc'coth, "Please give loaves of bread to the people who follow me, for they are exhausted, and I am pursuing Zē'bah and Zal·mun'na, kings of Mid'i·an."

6And the leaders of Suc'coth said, "*Are* the hands of Zē'bah and Zal·mun'na now in your hand, that we should give bread to your army?"

7So Gideon said, "For this cause, when the LORD has delivered Zē'bah and Zal·mun'na into my hand, then I will tear your flesh with the thorns of the wilderness and with briers!" 8Then he went up from there to Pe·nū'el and spoke to them in the same way. And the men of Pe·nū'el answered him as the men of Suc'coth had answered. 9So he also spoke to the men of Pe·nū'el, saying, "When I come back in peace, I will tear down this tower!"

10Now Zē'bah and Zal·mun'na *were* at Kar'kor, and their armies with them, about fifteen thousand, all who were left of all the army of the people of the East; for one hundred and twenty thousand men who drew the sword had fallen. 11Then Gideon went up by the road of those who dwell in tents on the east of Nō'bah and Jog'be·hah; and he attacked the army while the camp felt secure. 12When Zē'bah and Zal·mun'na fled, he pursued them; and he took the two kings of Mid'i·an, Zē'bah and Zal·mun'na, and routed the whole army.

13Then Gideon the son of Jō'ash returned from battle, from the Ascent of Hē'res. 14And he caught a young man of the men of Suc'coth and interrogated him; and he wrote down for him the leaders of Suc'coth and its elders, seventy-seven men. 15Then he came to the men of Suc'coth and said, "Here are Zē'bah and Zal·mun'na, about whom you ridiculed me, saying, '*Are* the hands of Zē'bah and Zal·mun'na now in your hand, that we should give bread to your weary men?' " 16And he took the elders of the city, and thorns of the wilderness and briers, and with them he taught the men of Suc'coth. 17Then he tore down the tower of Pe·nū'el and killed the men of the city.

18And he said to Zē'bah and Zal·mun'na, "What kind of men *were they* whom you killed at Tā'bor?"

8:1–3 Probably the **men of Ephraim** were really angry because they were sent to guard the fords and missed the looting of the Midianite camp. Gideon handled the situation adroitly by praising **Ephraim** and playing down **Abiezer** (a clan representing Manasseh; see Josh. 17:2).

8:18, 19 Tabor: A mountain in the Jezreel Valley. Gideon seems to be referring to atrocities committed against Israelites while the Midianites occupied the valley.

So they answered, "As you *are,* so *were*
they; each one resembled the son of a
king."
19Then he said, "They *were* my brothers,
the sons of my mother. *As* the LORD lives, if
you had let them live, I would not kill
you." 20And he said to Jē'ther his firstborn,
"Rise, kill them!" But the youth would not
draw his sword; for he was afraid, because
he *was* still a youth.
21So Zē'bah and Zal·mun'na said, "Rise
yourself, and kill us; for as a man *is, so is*
his strength." So Gideon arose and killed
Zē'bah and Zal·mun'na, and took the cres-
cent ornaments that *were* on their camels'
necks.

Gideon's Ephod

22Then the men of Israel said to Gideon,
"Rule over us, both you and your son, and
your grandson also; for you have delivered
us from the hand of Mid'i·an."
23But Gideon said to them, "I will not
rule over you, nor shall my son rule over
you; the LORD shall rule over you." 24Then
Gideon said to them, "I would like to make
a request of you, that each of you would
give me the earrings from his plunder."
For they had golden earrings, because they
were Ish'ma·el·ītes.
25So they answered, "We will gladly
give *them.*" And they spread out a gar-
ment, and each man threw into it the ear-
rings from his plunder. 26Now the weight
of the gold earrings that he requested was
one thousand seven hundred *shekels* of
gold, besides the crescent ornaments, pen-
dants, and purple robes which *were* on the
kings of Mid'i·an, and besides the chains
that *were* around their camels' necks.
27Then Gideon made it into an ephod and
set it up in his city, Oph'rah. And all Israel
played the harlot with it there. It became a
snare to Gideon and to his house.
28Thus Mid'i·an was subdued before the
children of Israel, so that they lifted their
heads no more. And the country was quiet
for forty years in the days of Gideon.

Death of Gideon

29Then Jer·ub·bā'al the son of Jō'ash
went and dwelt in his own house. 30Gideon
had seventy sons who were his own off-
spring, for he had many wives. 31And his
concubine who *was* in Shē'chem also bore
him a son, whose name he called
A·bim'e·lech. 32Now Gideon the son of
Jō'ash died at a good old age, and was
buried in the tomb of Jō'ash his father, in
Oph'rah of the Ā·bi·ez'rītes.
33So it was, as soon as Gideon was dead,
that the children of Israel again played the
harlot with the Bā'als, and made Bā'al-
Be'rith their god. 34Thus the children of Is-
rael did not remember the LORD their God,
who had delivered them from the hands of
all their enemies on every side; 35nor did
they show kindness to the house of
Jer·ub·bā'al (Gideon) in accordance with
the good he had done for Israel.

CHAPTER 9

Abimelech's Conspiracy

Then A·bim'e·lech the son of Jer-
ub·bā'al went to Shē'chem, to his mother's
brothers, and spoke with them and with all
the family of the house of his mother's fa-
ther, saying, 2"Please speak in the hearing
of all the men of Shē'chem: 'Which is better
for you, that all seventy of the sons of
Jer·ub·bā'al reign over you, or that one

8:22, 23 Rule over us: Gideon rightly turned down Israel's offer to make him king; the Lord was to be Israel's Ruler (see 1 Sam. 8:6, 7).

8:27 ephod: Apparently a replica in gold of the high priest's ephod (see Ex. 28:31). Since an ephod appears again in 18:14–20 in a context of idolatry, it may have been used as an instrument of divination because of its connection with the Urim and Thummim. **a snare**: Even a Gideon may be misled unless he is careful (see 2:3).

8:29 Jerubbaal: An alternate name for Gideon (see 6:32; 7:1).

reign over you?' Remember that I *am* your
own flesh and bone."
3And his mother's brothers spoke all
these words concerning him in the hearing
of all the men of Shē'chem; and their heart
was inclined to follow A·bim'e·lech, for
they said, "He is our brother." 4So they
gave him seventy *shekels* of silver from the
temple of Bā'al-Be'rith, with which
A·bim'e·lech hired worthless and reckless
men; and they followed him. 5Then he
went to his father's house at Oph'rah and
killed his brothers, the seventy sons of
Jer·ub·bā'al, on one stone. But Jō'tham the
youngest son of Jer·ub·bā'al was left, be-
cause he hid himself. 6And all the men of
Shē'chem gathered together, all of Beth
Mil'lō, and they went and made
A·bim'e·lech king beside the terebinth tree
at the pillar that *was* in Shē'chem.

The Parable of the Trees

7Now when they told Jō'tham, he went
and stood on top of Mount Ger'i·zim, and
lifted his voice and cried out. And he said
to them:

"Listen to me, you men of Shē'chem,
That God may listen to you!

8 "The trees once went forth to anoint a
king over them.
And they said to the olive tree,
'Reign over us!'
9 But the olive tree said to them,
'Should I cease giving my oil,
With which they honor God and men,
And go to sway over trees?'
10 "Then the trees said to the fig tree,
'You come *and* reign over us!'
11 But the fig tree said to them,
'Should I cease my sweetness and my
good fruit,
And go to sway over trees?'
12 "Then the trees said to the vine,
'You come *and* reign over us!'
13 But the vine said to them,
'Should I cease my new wine,
Which cheers *both* God and men,
And go to sway over trees?'
14 "Then all the trees said to the bramble,
'You come *and* reign over us!'
15 And the bramble said to the trees,
'If in truth you anoint me as king over
you,
Then come *and* take shelter in my
shade;
But if not, let fire come out of the
bramble
And devour the cedars of Lebanon!'

16"Now therefore, if you have acted in
truth and sincerity in making A·bim'e·lech
king, and if you have dealt well with
Jer·ub·bā'al and his house, and have done
to him as he deserves— 17for my father
fought for you, risked his life, and deliv-
ered you out of the hand of Mid'i·an; 18but
you have risen up against my father's
house this day, and killed his seventy sons
on one stone, and made A·bim'e·lech, the
son of his female servant, king over the
men of Shē'chem, because he is your
brother— 19if then you have acted in truth
and sincerity with Jer·ub·bā'al and with
his house this day, *then* rejoice in
A·bim'e·lech, and let him also rejoice in
you. 20But if not, let fire come from
A·bim'e·lech and devour the men of
Shē'chem and Beth Mil'lō; and let fire

9:7–21 Mount Gerizim rises directly south of **Shechem**. The point of the complaint by **Jotham** was obvious to the hearers: Abimelech, as son of a concubine (v. 18; 8:31), was the least worthy of Gideon's sons to be king. He was only a **bramble** (v. 14) compared to them. And like the bramble bushes spread a brushfire to the forest, so Abimelech would be the source of their destruction.

come from the men of Shē′chem and from
Beth Mil′lō and devour A·bim′e·lech!"
[21]And Jō′tham ran away and fled; and he
went to Bē′er and dwelt there, for fear of
A·bim′e·lech his brother.

Downfall of Abimelech

[22]After A·bim′e·lech had reigned over
Israel three years, [23]God sent a spirit of ill
will between A·bim′e·lech and the men of
Shē′chem; and the men of Shē′chem dealt
treacherously with A·bim′e·lech, [24]that the
crime *done* to the seventy sons of Jer-
ub·bā′al might be settled and their blood
be laid on A·bim′e·lech their brother, who
killed them, and on the men of Shē′chem,
who aided him in the killing of his
brothers. [25]And the men of Shē′chem set
men in ambush against him on the tops of
the mountains, and they robbed all who
passed by them along that way; and it was
told A·bim′e·lech.

[26]Now Gā′al the son of Ē′bed came with
his brothers and went over to Shē′chem;
and the men of Shē′chem put their confi-
dence in him. [27]So they went out into the
fields, and gathered *grapes* from their vine-
yards and trod *them,* and made merry. And
they went into the house of their god, and
ate and drank, and cursed A·bim′e·lech.
[28]Then Gā′al the son of Ē′bed said, "Who *is*
A·bim′e·lech, and who *is* Shē′chem, that
we should serve him? *Is he* not the son of
Jer·ub·bā′al, and *is not* Zē′bul his officer?
Serve the men of Hā′mor the father of
Shē′chem; but why should we serve him?
[29]If only this people were under my au-
thority![a] Then I would remove A·bim′-
e·lech." So he[b] said to A·bim′e·lech, "In-
crease your army and come out!"

[30]When Zē′bul, the ruler of the city,
heard the words of Gā′al the son of Ē′bed,
his anger was aroused. [31]And he sent mes-
sengers to A·bim′e·lech secretly, saying,
"Take note! Gā′al the son of Ē′bed and his
brothers have come to Shē′chem; and here
they are, fortifying the city against you.
[32]Now therefore, get up by night, you and
the people who *are* with you, and lie in
wait in the field. [33]And it shall be, as soon
as the sun is up in the morning, *that* you
shall rise early and rush upon the city; and
when he and the people who are with him
come out against you, you may then do to
them as you find opportunity."

[34]So A·bim′e·lech and all the people
who *were* with him rose by night, and lay
in wait against Shē′chem in four compa-
nies. [35]When Gā′al the son of Ē′bed went
out and stood in the entrance to the city
gate, A·bim′e·lech and the people who
were with him rose from lying in wait.
[36]And when Gā′al saw the people, he said
to Zē′bul, "Look, people are coming down
from the tops of the mountains!"

But Zē′bul said to him, "You see the
shadows of the mountains as *if they were*
men."

[37]So Gā′al spoke again and said, "See,
people are coming down from the center of
the land, and another company is coming
from the Diviners′[a] Terebinth Tree."

[38]Then Zē′bul said to him, "Where in-
deed *is* your mouth now, with which you
said, 'Who is A·bim′e·lech, that we should
serve him?' *Are* not these the people whom
you despised? Go out, if you will, and fight
with them now."

[39]So Gā′al went out, leading the men of
Shē′chem, and fought with A·bim′e·lech.
[40]And A·bim′e·lech chased him, and he
fled from him; and many fell wounded, to
the *very* entrance of the gate. [41]Then

9:29 [a]Literally *hand* [b]Following Masoretic Text and Targum; Dead Sea Scrolls read *they;* Septuagint reads *I.*
9:37 [a]Hebrew *Meonenim*

9:22 reigned over Israel: Not a king over all Israel, but over the Israelites around Shechem who made Abimelech a local ruler.

9:36 You see the shadows: Zebul, Abimelech's chief officer and appointed ruler (vv. 28, 30), keeps Gaal off his guard, then openly opposes him (vv. 38, 41).

A·bim′e·lech dwelt at A·rū′mah, and
Zē′bul drove out Gā′al and his brothers, so
that they would not dwell in Shē′chem.
42 And it came about on the next day that
the people went out into the field, and they
told A·bim′e·lech. 43 So he took his people,
divided them into three companies, and
lay in wait in the field. And he looked, and
there were the people, coming out of the
city; and he rose against them and attacked
them. 44 Then A·bim′e·lech and the com-
pany that *was* with him rushed forward
and stood at the entrance of the gate of the
city; and the *other* two companies rushed
upon all who *were* in the fields and killed
them. 45 So A·bim′e·lech fought against the
city all that day; he took the city and killed
the people who *were* in it; and he demol-
ished the city and sowed it with salt.
46 Now when all the men of the tower of
Shē′chem had heard *that*, they entered the
stronghold of the temple of the god Be′rith.
47 And it was told A·bim′e·lech that all the
men of the tower of Shē′chem were gath-
ered together. 48 Then A·bim′e·lech went up
to Mount Zal′mon, he and all the people
who *were* with him. And A·bim′e·lech took
an ax in his hand and cut down a bough
from the trees, and took it and laid *it* on his
shoulder; then he said to the people who
were with him, "What you have seen me
do, make haste *and* do as I *have done*." 49 So
each of the people likewise cut down his
own bough and followed A·bim′e·lech,
put *them* against the stronghold, and set
the stronghold on fire above them, so that
all the people of the tower of Shē′chem
died, about a thousand men and women.
50 Then A·bim′e·lech went to Thē′bez,
and he encamped against Thē′bez and
took it. 51 But there was a strong tower in
the city, and all the men and women—all
the people of the city—fled there and shut
themselves in; then they went up to the top
of the tower. 52 So A·bim′e·lech came as far
as the tower and fought against it; and he
drew near the door of the tower to burn it
with fire. 53 But a certain woman dropped
an upper millstone on A·bim′e·lech's head
and crushed his skull. 54 Then he called
quickly to the young man, his armorbearer,
and said to him, "Draw your sword and
kill me, lest men say of me, 'A woman
killed him.' " So his young man thrust him
through, and he died. 55 And when the men
of Israel saw that A·bim′e·lech was dead,
they departed, every man to his place.
56 Thus God repaid the wickedness of
A·bim′e·lech, which he had done to his fa-
ther by killing his seventy brothers. 57 And
all the evil of the men of Shē′chem God re-
turned on their own heads, and on them
came the curse of Jō′tham the son of
Jer·ub·bā′al.

CHAPTER 10

Tola

After A·bim′e·lech there arose to save
Israel Tō′la the son of Pū′ah, the son of
Dodo, a man of Is′sa·char; and he dwelt in
Shā′mir in the mountains of Ē′phra·im.
2 He judged Israel twenty-three years; and
he died and was buried in Shā′mir.

Jair

3 After him arose Jā′ir, a Gil′ē·ad·īte; and
he judged Israel twenty-two years. 4 Now
he had thirty sons who rode on thirty don-
keys; they also had thirty towns, which are

9:45 The scattering of salt indicated a curse of barrenness.

9:46 tower of Shechem: The innermost fortress of the city, which was still intact after the rest of the city had been destroyed (v. 45).

9:56, 57 evil . . . God returned on their own heads: Abimelech was judged for a prior sin while the men of Shechem were judged for their own more recent sins. God's moral justice will be done, though not always right away. We can be confident that although the wicked may seem to prosper for a time, God will not forget to judge them appropriately when He sees fit to do so.

called "Hā′voth Jā′ir"[a] to this day, which
are in the land of Gil′ē·ad. 5 And Jā′ir died
and was buried in Cā′mon.

Israel Oppressed Again

6 Then the children of Israel again did
evil in the sight of the LORD, and served the
Bā′als and the Ash′to·reths, the gods of
Syria, the gods of Sī′don, the gods of
Mō′ab, the gods of the people of Am′mon,
and the gods of the Phi·lis′tines; and they
forsook the LORD and did not serve Him.
7 So the anger of the LORD was hot against
Israel; and He sold them into the hands of
the Phi·lis′tines and into the hands of the
people of Am′mon. 8 From that year they
harassed and oppressed the children of Is-
rael for eighteen years—all the children of
Israel who *were* on the other side of the Jor-
dan in the land of the Am′o·rītes, in
Gil′ē·ad. 9 Moreover the people of Am′mon
crossed over the Jordan to fight against Ju-
dah also, against Benjamin, and against the
house of Ē′phra·im, so that Israel was se-
verely distressed.
10 And the children of Israel cried out to
the LORD, saying, "We have sinned against
You, because we have both forsaken our
God and served the Bā′als!"
11 So the LORD said to the children of Is-
rael, "*Did I* not *deliver you* from the Egyp-
tians and from the Am′o·rītes and from
the people of Am′mon and from the
Phi·lis′tines? 12 Also the Sī·dō′ni·ans and
A·mal′e·kītes and Mā′on·ītes[a] oppressed
you; and you cried out to Me, and I deliv-
ered you from their hand. 13 Yet you have
forsaken Me and served other gods. There-
fore I will deliver you no more. 14 Go and
cry out to the gods which you have chosen;
let them deliver you in your time of dis-
tress."
15 And the children of Israel said to the
LORD, "We have sinned! Do to us whatever
seems best to You; only deliver us this day,
we pray." 16 So they put away the foreign
gods from among them and served the
LORD. And His soul could no longer en-
dure the misery of Israel.
17 Then the people of Am′mon gathered
together and encamped in Gil′ē·ad. And
the children of Israel assembled together
and encamped in Miz′pah. 18 And the peo-
ple, the leaders of Gil′ē·ad, said to one an-
other, "Who *is* the man who will begin the
fight against the people of Am′mon? He
shall be head over all the inhabitants of
Gil′ē·ad."

CHAPTER 11

Jephthah

Now Jeph′thah the Gil′ē·ad·īte was a
mighty man of valor, but he *was* the son of
a harlot; and Gil′ē·ad begot Jeph′thah.
2 Gil′ē·ad's wife bore sons; and when his
wife's sons grew up, they drove Jeph′thah
out, and said to him, "You shall have no in-
heritance in our father's house, for you *are*
the son of another woman." 3 Then Jeph′-
thah fled from his brothers and dwelt in
the land of Tob; and worthless men banded
together with Jeph′thah and went out *raid-
ing* with him.
4 It came to pass after a time that the peo-
ple of Am′mon made war against Israel.
5 And so it was, when the people of Am′-
mon made war against Israel, that the el-
ders of Gil′ē·ad went to get Jeph′thah from
the land of Tob. 6 Then they said to
Jeph′thah, "Come and be our commander,
that we may fight against the people of
Am′mon."
7 So Jeph′thah said to the elders of

10:4 [a]Literally *Towns of Jair* (compare Numbers 32:41 and Deuteronomy 3:14) 10:12 [a]Some Septuagint manuscripts read *Midianites.*

10:7 Philistines: Apparently an introduction to chs. 10—16, with the Ammonites oppressing from the east and the Philistines from the west. Jephthah and Samson may have been living and working at the same time.

Gil′-ē·ad, "Did you not hate me, and expel
me from my father's house? Why have you
come to me now when you are in dis-
tress?"
8And the elders of Gil′ē·ad said to
Jeph′thah, "That is why we have turned
again to you now, that you may go with us
and fight against the people of Am′mon,
and be our head over all the inhabitants of
Gil′ē·ad."
9So Jeph′thah said to the elders of Gil′-
ē·ad, "If you take me back home to fight
against the people of Am′mon, and the
LORD delivers them to me, shall I be your
head?"
10And the elders of Gil′ē·ad said to
Jeph′thah, "The LORD will be a witness be-
tween us, if we do not do according to
your words." 11Then Jeph′thah went with
the elders of Gil′ē·ad, and the people made
him head and commander over them; and
Jeph′thah spoke all his words before the
LORD in Miz′pah.
12Now Jeph′thah sent messengers to the
king of the people of Am′mon, saying,
"What do you have against me, that you
have come to fight against me in my
land?"
13And the king of the people of Am′mon
answered the messengers of Jeph′thah,
"Because Israel took away my land when
they came up out of Egypt, from the
Ar′non as far as the Jab′bok, and to the Jor-
dan. Now therefore, restore those *lands*
peaceably."
14So Jeph′thah again sent messengers to
the king of the people of Am′mon, 15and
said to him, "Thus says Jeph′thah: 'Israel
did not take away the land of Mō′ab, nor
the land of the people of Am′mon; 16for
when Israel came up from Egypt, they
walked through the wilderness as far as
the Red Sea and came to Kā′desh. 17Then
Israel sent messengers to the king of
Ē′dom, saying, "Please let me pass through
your land." But the king of Ē′dom would
not heed. And in like manner they sent to
the king of Mō′ab, but he would not *con-
sent*. So Israel remained in Kā′desh. 18And
they went along through the wilderness
and bypassed the land of Ē′dom and the
land of Mō′ab, came to the east side of the
land of Mō′ab, and encamped on the other
side of the Ar′non. But they did not enter
the border of Mō′ab, for the Ar′non *was* the
border of Mō′ab. 19Then Israel sent messen-
gers to Sī′hon king of the Am′o·rītes, king
of Hesh′bon; and Israel said to him,
"Please let us pass through your land into
our place." 20But Sī′hon did not trust Israel
to pass through his territory. So Sī′hon
gathered all his people together, encamped
in Jā′haz, and fought against Israel. 21And
the LORD God of Israel delivered Sī′hon
and all his people into the hand of Israel,
and they defeated them. Thus Israel
gained possession of all the land of the
Am′o·rītes, who inhabited that country.
22They took possession of all the territory
of the Am′o·rītes, from the Ar′non to the
Jab′bok and from the wilderness to the Jor-
dan.
23'And now the LORD God of Israel has
dispossessed the Am′o·rītes from before
His people Israel; should you then possess
it? 24Will you not possess whatever
Chē′mosh your god gives you to possess?
So whatever the LORD our God takes pos-
session of before us, we will possess. 25And
now, *are* you any better than Bā′lak the son
of Zip′por, king of Mō′ab? Did he ever
strive against Israel? Did he ever fight
against them? 26While Israel dwelt in
Hesh′bon and its villages, in A·rō′er and its
villages, and in all the cities along the
banks of the Ar′non, for three hundred
years, why did you not recover *them*
within that time? 27Therefore I have not

11:12–28 Jephthah asserts that Ammon has permitted Israel to live in Gilead unmolested since the conquest (vv. 26, 27). The present attack is unwarranted. Israel had not taken the land from Ammon or Moab. Rather, Israel's God had given her the territory of the Amorite king Sihon (vv. 15–24).

sinned against you, but you wronged me
by fighting against me. May the LORD, the
Judge, render judgment this day between
the children of Israel and the people of
Am'mon.' " 28However, the king of the
people of Am'mon did not heed the words
which Jeph'thah sent him.

Jephthah's Vow and Victory

29Then the Spirit of the LORD came upon
Jeph'thah, and he passed through Gil'ē·ad
and Ma·nas'seh, and passed through
Miz'pah of Gil'ē·ad; and from Miz'pah of
Gil'ē·ad he advanced *toward* the people of
Am'mon. 30And Jeph'thah made a vow to
the LORD, and said, "If You will indeed de-
liver the people of Am'mon into my hands,
31then it will be that whatever comes out of
the doors of my house to meet me, when I
return in peace from the people of
Am'mon, shall surely be the LORD's, and I
will offer it up as a burnt offering."
32So Jeph'thah advanced toward the
people of Am'mon to fight against them,
and the LORD delivered them into his
hands. 33And he defeated them from
A·rō'er as far as Min'nith—twenty cities—
and to Abel Ker'a·mim,[a] with a very great
slaughter. Thus the people of Am'mon
were subdued before the children of Israel.

Jephthah's Daughter

34When Jeph'thah came to his house at
Miz'pah, there was his daughter, coming
out to meet him with timbrels and danc-
ing; and she *was his* only child. Besides her
he had neither son nor daughter. 35And it
came to pass, when he saw her, that he tore
his clothes, and said, "Alas, my daughter!
You have brought me very low! You are
among those who trouble me! For I have
given my word to the LORD, and I cannot
go back on it."
36So she said to him, "My father, *if* you
have given your word to the LORD, do to
me according to what has gone out of your
mouth, because the LORD has avenged you
of your enemies, the people of Am'mon."
37Then she said to her father, "Let this thing
be done for me: let me alone for two
months, that I may go and wander on the
mountains and bewail my virginity, my
friends and I."
38So he said, "Go." And he sent her
away *for* two months; and she went with
her friends, and bewailed her virginity on
the mountains. 39And it was so at the end
of two months that she returned to her fa-
ther, and he carried out his vow with her
which he had vowed. She knew no man.
And it became a custom in Israel 40*that*
the daughters of Israel went four days each
year to lament the daughter of Jeph'thah
the Gil'ē·ad·īte.

CHAPTER 12

Jephthah's Conflict with Ephraim

Then the men of Ē'phra·im gathered to-
gether, crossed over toward Zā'phon, and
said to Jeph'thah, "Why did you cross over
to fight against the people of Am'mon, and

11:33 [a]Literally *Plain of Vineyards*

11:30, 31 He did not have to make this vow. The Spirit of the Lord had already empowered him; victory was already his.

11:35 Because of his rash vow (v. 30), his daughter had unwittingly become the source of his agony. Later the Israelites were to prevent King Saul from carrying out a similar vow (1 Sam. 14:24–46).

11:37 bewail my virginity: She would die having no husband or child, a condition considered a great tragedy in ancient times.

11:39 The biblical writer does not condone what Jephthah did; he only reports it. This behavior is one more indication of the loss of moral sensitivity in Israel during this period. The **custom** is explained in v. 40.

12:1 The Ephraimites had reacted in the same way in Gideon's time (see 8:1). These incidents reflect the growing sectional tension in Israel.

did not call us to go with you? We will burn your house down on you with fire!"

2And Jeph'thah said to them, "My people and I were in a great struggle with the people of Am'mon; and when I called you, you did not deliver me out of their hands. 3So when I saw that you would not deliver *me,* I took my life in my hands and crossed over against the people of Am'mon; and the LORD delivered them into my hand. Why then have you come up to me this day to fight against me?" 4Now Jeph'thah gathered together all the men of Gil'ē·ad and fought against Ē'phra·im. And the men of Gil'ē·ad defeated Ē'phra·im, because they said, "You Gil'ē·ad·ītes *are* fugitives of Ē'phra·im among the Ē'phra·im·ītes *and* among the Ma·nas'sītes." 5The Gil'ē·ad·ītes seized the fords of the Jordan before the Ē'phra·im·ītes *arrived.* And when *any* Ē'phra·im·īte who escaped said, "Let me cross over," the men of Gil'ē·ad would say to him, "*Are* you an Ē'phra·im·īte?" If he said, "No," 6then they would say to him, "Then say, 'Shib'bo·leth'!" And he would say, "Sib'bo·leth," for he could not pronounce *it* right. Then they would take him and kill him at the fords of the Jordan. There fell at that time forty-two thousand Ē'phra·im·ītes.

7And Jeph'thah judged Israel six years. Then Jeph'thah the Gil'ē·ad·īte died and was buried among the cities of Gil'ē·ad.

Ibzan, Elon, and Abdon

8After him, Ib'zan of Bethlehem judged Israel. 9He had thirty sons. And he gave away thirty daughters in marriage, and brought in thirty daughters from elsewhere for his sons. He judged Israel seven years. 10Then Ib'zan died and was buried at Bethlehem.

11After him, Ē'lon the Zeb'ū·lun·īte judged Israel. He judged Israel ten years. 12And Ē'lon the Zeb'ū·lun·īte died and was buried at Aī'ja·lon in the country of Zeb'ū·lun.

13After him, Ab'don the son of Hil'lel the Pir'a·thon·īte judged Israel. 14He had forty sons and thirty grandsons, who rode on seventy young donkeys. He judged Israel eight years. 15Then Ab'don the son of Hil'lel the Pir'a·thon·īte died and was buried in Pir'a·thon in the land of Ē'phra·im, in the mountains of the A·mal'e·kītes.

CHAPTER 13

The Birth of Samson

Again the children of Israel did evil in the sight of the LORD, and the LORD delivered them into the hand of the Phi·lis'tines for forty years.

2Now there was a certain man from Zō'rah, of the family of the Dan'ītes, whose name *was* Ma·nō'ah; and his wife *was* barren and had no children. 3And the Angel of the LORD appeared to the woman and said to her, "Indeed now, you are barren and have borne no children, but you shall conceive and bear a son. 4Now therefore, please be careful not to drink wine or *similar* drink, and not to eat anything unclean. 5For behold, you shall conceive and bear a son. And no razor shall come upon his head, for the child shall be a Naz'ir·īte to God from the womb; and he shall begin to deliver Israel out of the hand of the Phi·lis'tines."

6So the woman came and told her husband, saying, "A Man of God came to me, and His countenance *was* like the countenance of the Angel of God, very awesome;

12:6 Shibboleth . . . Sibboleth: Differences in dialect between major sections of Israel were now noticeable, a sign of increasing isolation from one another.

13:2 The announcement of conception, especially to a woman previously barren, is a favorite biblical theme from Sarah (Gen. 17:15, 16) to Elizabeth (Luke 1:13). In all the cases the child is important to God's revelation (see Luke 1:15; Judg. 13:4, 5).

but I did not ask Him where He *was* from,
and He did not tell me His name. 7And He
said to me, 'Behold, you shall conceive and
bear a son. Now drink no wine or *similar*
drink, nor eat anything unclean, for the
child shall be a Naz'ir·īte to God from the
womb to the day of his death.' "

8Then Ma·nō'ah prayed to the LORD, and
said, "O my Lord, please let the Man of
God whom You sent come to us again and
teach us what we shall do for the child who
will be born."

9And God listened to the voice of Ma-
nō'ah, and the Angel of God came to the
woman again as she was sitting in the
field; but Ma·nō'ah her husband *was* not
with her. 10Then the woman ran in haste
and told her husband, and said to him,
"Look, the Man who came to me the *other*
day has just now appeared to me!"

11So Ma·nō'ah arose and followed his
wife. When he came to the Man, he said to
Him, "Are You the Man who spoke to this
woman?"

And He said, "I *am*."

12Ma·nō'ah said, "Now let Your words
come *to pass!* What will be the boy's rule of
life, and his work?"

13So the Angel of the LORD said to
Ma·nō'ah, "Of all that I said to the woman
let her be careful. 14She may not eat any-
thing that comes from the vine, nor may
she drink wine or *similar* drink, nor eat
anything unclean. All that I commanded
her let her observe."

15Then Ma·nō'ah said to the Angel of the
LORD, "Please let us detain You, and we
will prepare a young goat for You."

16And the Angel of the LORD said to
Ma·nō'ah, "Though you detain Me, I will
not eat your food. But if you offer a burnt
offering, you must offer it to the LORD."
(For Ma·nō'ah did not know He *was* the
Angel of the LORD.)

17Then Ma·nō'ah said to the Angel of the
LORD, "What *is* Your name, that when Your
words come *to pass* we may honor You?"

18And the Angel of the LORD said to him,
"Why do you ask My name, seeing it *is*
wonderful?"

19So Ma·nō'ah took the young goat with
the grain offering, and offered it upon the
rock to the LORD. And He did a wondrous
thing while Ma·nō'ah and his wife looked
on— 20it happened as the flame went up to-
ward heaven from the altar—the Angel of
the LORD ascended in the flame of the altar!
When Ma·nō'ah and his wife saw *this*, they
fell on their faces to the ground. 21When the
Angel of the LORD appeared no more to
Ma·nō'ah and his wife, then Ma·nō'ah
knew that He *was* the Angel of the LORD.

22And Ma·nō'ah said to his wife, "We
shall surely die, because we have seen
God!"

23But his wife said to him, "If the LORD
had desired to kill us, He would not have
accepted a burnt offering and a grain offer-
ing from our hands, nor would He have
shown us all these *things*, nor would He
have told us *such things* as these at this
time."

24So the woman bore a son and called
his name Samson; and the child grew, and
the LORD blessed him. 25And the Spirit of
the LORD began to move upon him at
Mā'ha·neh Dan[a] between Zō'rah and
Esh'tā·ol.

CHAPTER 14

Samson's Philistine Wife

Now Samson went down to Tim'nah,
and saw a woman in Tim'nah of the
daughters of the Phi·lis'tines. 2So he went
up and told his father and mother, saying,

13:25 [a]Literally *Camp of Dan* (compare 18:12)

14:1 The **Philistines** were a warlike people, apparently from the Aegean region, who had developed a monopoly on casting iron. They settled on the southern coast of Canaan in five principal cities, each with its own ruler (see 16:5).

"I have seen a woman in Tim′nah of the
daughters of the Phi·lis′tines; now there-
fore, get her for me as a wife."
3Then his father and mother said to him,
"*Is there* no woman among the daughters
of your brethren, or among all my people,
that you must go and get a wife from the
uncircumcised Phi·lis′tines?"
And Samson said to his father, "Get her
for me, for she pleases me well."
4But his father and mother did not know
that it was of the LORD—that He was seek-
ing an occasion to move against the Phi-
lis′tines. For at that time the Phi·lis′tines
had dominion over Israel.
5So Samson went down to Tim′nah with
his father and mother, and came to the
vineyards of Tim′nah.
Now *to his* surprise, a young lion *came*
roaring against him. 6And the Spirit of the
LORD came mightily upon him, and he tore
the lion apart as one would have torn apart
a young goat, though *he had* nothing in his
hand. But he did not tell his father or his
mother what he had done.
7Then he went down and talked with
the woman; and she pleased Samson well.
8After some time, when he returned to get
her, he turned aside to see the carcass of
the lion. And behold, a swarm of bees and
honey *were* in the carcass of the lion. 9He
took some of it in his hands and went
along, eating. When he came to his father
and mother, he gave *some* to them, and
they also ate. But he did not tell them that
he had taken the honey out of the carcass
of the lion.
10So his father went down to the
woman. And Samson gave a feast there,
for young men used to do so. 11And it hap-
pened, when they saw him, that they
brought thirty companions to be with him.
12Then Samson said to them, "Let me
pose a riddle to you. If you can correctly
solve and explain it to me within the seven
days of the feast, then I will give you thirty
linen garments and thirty changes of cloth-
ing. 13But if you cannot explain *it* to me,
then you shall give me thirty linen gar-
ments and thirty changes of clothing."
And they said to him, "Pose your riddle,
that we may hear it."
14So he said to them:

"Out of the eater came something to
eat,
And out of the strong came
something sweet."

Now for three days they could not explain
the riddle.
15But it came to pass on the seventh[a] day
that they said to Samson's wife, "Entice
your husband, that he may explain the rid-
dle to us, or else we will burn you and your
father's house with fire. Have you invited
us in order to take what is ours? *Is that* not
so?"
16Then Samson's wife wept on him, and
said, "You only hate me! You do not love
me! You have posed a riddle to the sons of
my people, but you have not explained *it*
to me."
And he said to her, "Look, I have not ex-
plained *it* to my father or my mother; so
should I explain *it* to you?" 17Now she had
wept on him the seven days while their
feast lasted. And it happened on the sev-

14:15 [a]Following Masoretic Text, Targum, and Vulgate; Septuagint and Syriac read *fourth.*

14:4 an occasion to move against the Philistines: This may be the key to understanding Samson's role. On previous occasions the Israelites had repented of their sin and cried to the Lord for help. Now there was no cry; they had become content to live under pagan domination. God's purpose for Samson was to cause a breach between Israel and Philistia, and to reestablish Israel's sense of separateness and covenant identity.

14:8, 9 In touching the **carcass** of the lion, Samson had broken the Nazirite vow and become ceremonially unclean.

enth day that he told her, because she
pressed him so much. Then she explained
the riddle to the sons of her people. 18So the
men of the city said to him on the seventh
day before the sun went down:

"What *is* sweeter than honey?
And what *is* stronger than a lion?"

And he said to them:

"If you had not plowed with my
heifer,
You would not have solved my
riddle!"

19Then the Spirit of the LORD came upon
him mightily, and he went down to
Ash'ke·lon and killed thirty of their men,
took their apparel, and gave the changes *of*
clothing to those who had explained the
riddle. So his anger was aroused, and he
went back up to his father's house. 20And
Samson's wife was *given* to his companion,
who had been his best man.

CHAPTER 15

Samson Defeats the Philistines

After a while, in the time of wheat har-
vest, it happened that Samson visited his
wife with a young goat. And he said, "Let
me go in to my wife, into *her* room." But
her father would not permit him to go in.
2Her father said, "I really thought that
you thoroughly hated her; therefore I gave
her to your companion. *Is* not her younger
sister better than she? Please, take her in-
stead."
3And Samson said to them, "This time I
shall be blameless regarding the Phi·lis'-
tines if I harm them!" 4Then Samson went
and caught three hundred foxes; and he
took torches, turned *the foxes* tail to tail,
and put a torch between each pair of tails.
5When he had set the torches on fire, he let
the foxes go into the standing grain of the
Phi·lis'tines, and burned up both the
shocks and the standing grain, as well as
the vineyards *and* olive groves.
6Then the Phi·lis'tines said, "Who has
done this?"
And they answered, "Samson, the son-
in-law of the Tim'nīte, because he has
taken his wife and given her to his com-
panion." So the Phi·lis'tines came up and
burned her and her father with fire.
7Samson said to them, "Since you would
do a thing like this, I will surely take re-
venge on you, and after that I will cease."
8So he attacked them hip and thigh with a
great slaughter; then he went down and
dwelt in the cleft of the rock of Ē'tam.
9Now the Phi·lis'tines went up, en-
camped in Judah, and deployed them-
selves against Lē'hi. 10And the men of Ju-
dah said, "Why have you come up against
us?"
So they answered, "We have come up to
arrest Samson, to do to him as he has done
to us."
11Then three thousand men of Judah
went down to the cleft of the rock of Ē'tam,
and said to Samson, "Do you not know
that the Phi·lis'tines rule over us? What *is*
this you have done to us?"
And he said to them, "As they did to
me, so I have done to them."
12But they said to him, "We have come
down to arrest you, that we may deliver
you into the hand of the Phi·lis'tines."
Then Samson said to them, "Swear to
me that you will not kill me yourselves."
13So they spoke to him, saying, "No, but
we will tie you securely and deliver you
into their hand; but we will surely not kill
you." And they bound him with two new
ropes and brought him up from the rock.
14When he came to Lē'hi, the Phi·lis'-
tines came shouting against him. Then the

15:8 hip and thigh: An expression from wrestling terminology indicating a complete victory.

SAMSON: HOW EVEN THE MIGHTY CAN FALL

As a Nazirite, Samson had been singled out by God to serve as an example to Israel. From birth he was to be committed wholly to the Lord, forbidden to drink wine or strong drink or to eat any unclean thing. In addition, he was never to have his hair cut.

Samson, one of the last of the judges of Israel, was given unparalleled physical strength, which he used against the Philistines. His heroic deeds included killing a young lion, murdering one thousand Philistines with the jawbone of a donkey, and removing the immense city gate of Gaza (Judg. 14:6; 15:15; 16:3). He also caught three hundred foxes, tied them tail to tail, put a torch between each pair, and let them loose in the fields and vineyards of the Philistines (15:4, 5).

Unfortunately, Samson refused to acknowledge the Lord's claim on his life. He broke two aspects of the Nazirite vow: he touched the body of a dead lion (14:8, 9), and he attended a drinking feast (v. 10). This lack of depth in his spiritual life impacted Samson's judgment. He violated the Mosaic law regarding mixed marriages (see Deut. 7:3; Judg. 14:3), and he participated in promiscuous sex (Judg. 16:1). His faith in Delilah was misplaced, and he failed to perceive her treacherous nature.

In addition to the problems of a shallow spiritual life and hampered judgment, Samson's lack of emotional control contributed to his failure as an effective leader. He treated his parents with contempt (14:3), and his pride knew no bounds. He baited the Philistines, seeking opportunities to flaunt his incredible strength.

Eventually his pride and weakness for women led to Samson's downfall. Although the Bible clearly states that the Spirit of the Lord enabled Samson to carry out his feats of strength (13:25; 14:6; 14:19; 15:14), he told Delilah that the secret lay in his uncut hair. When she cut his hair, the third aspect of his Nazirite vow was broken and the Spirit of the Lord departed from him (16:20).

With his physical strength gone, his self-reliance came to an abrupt end. The Philistines effectively destroyed every vestige of Samson's pride. Slaving in the mill apparently gave him time to reconsider his relationship with God and get his priorities back in order.

When the Philistines brought him out as entertainment for their pagan feast, Samson called upon God to restore his strength "just this once" (v. 28).

The Lord answered his plea and provided him with one final victory —the greatest triumph of his career. But it cost Samson his life.

Imagine what God could have accomplished through a warrior like Samson, if he had yielded his strength to the Lord. Today, God desires to use every Christian for His glory, if only we will surrender ourselves to Him—body, mind, and soul. ✦

Spirit of the LORD came mightily upon him; and the ropes that *were* on his arms became like flax that is burned with fire, and his bonds broke loose from his hands. 15He found a fresh jawbone of a donkey, reached out his hand and took it, and killed a thousand men with it. 16Then Samson said:

"With the jawbone of a donkey,
Heaps upon heaps,
With the jawbone of a donkey
I have slain a thousand men!"

17And so it was, when he had finished speaking, that he threw the jawbone from his hand, and called that place Rā′math Lē′hi.[a]

18Then he became very thirsty; so he cried out to the LORD and said, "You have given this great deliverance by the hand of Your servant; and now shall I die of thirst and fall into the hand of the uncircumcised?" 19So God split the hollow place that *is* in Lē′hi,[a] and water came out, and he drank; and his spirit returned, and he revived. Therefore he called its name En Hak′ko·rē,[b] which is in Lē′hi to this day. 20And he judged Israel twenty years in the days of the Phi·lis′tines.

CHAPTER 16

Samson and Delilah

Now Samson went to Gā′za and saw a harlot there, and went in to her. 2*When* the Gā′zītes *were told,* "Samson has come here!" they surrounded *the place* and lay in wait for him all night at the gate of the city. They were quiet all night, saying, "In the morning, when it is daylight, we will kill him." 3And Samson lay *low* till midnight; then he arose at midnight, took hold of the doors of the gate of the city and the two gateposts, pulled them up, bar and all, put *them* on his shoulders, and carried them to the top of the hill that faces Hē′bron.

4Afterward it happened that he loved a woman in the Valley of Sō′rek, whose name *was* Dē·lī′lah. 5And the lords of the Phi·lis′tines came up to her and said to her, "Entice him, and find out where his great strength *lies,* and by what *means* we may overpower him, that we may bind him to afflict him; and every one of us will give you eleven hundred *pieces* of silver."

6So Dē·lī′lah said to Samson, "Please tell me where your great strength *lies,* and with what you may be bound to afflict you."

7And Samson said to her, "If they bind me with seven fresh bowstrings, not yet dried, then I shall become weak, and be like any *other* man."

8So the lords of the Phi·lis′tines brought up to her seven fresh bowstrings, not yet dried, and she bound him with them. 9Now *men were* lying in wait, staying with her in the room. And she said to him, "The Phi·lis′tines *are* upon you, Samson!" But he broke the bowstrings as a strand of yarn breaks when it touches fire. So the secret of his strength was not known.

10Then Dē·lī′lah said to Samson, "Look, you have mocked me and told me lies. Now, please tell me what you may be bound with."

11So he said to her, "If they bind me securely with new ropes that have never

15:17 [a]Literally *Jawbone Height* 15:19 [a]Literally *Jawbone* (compare verse 14) [b]Literally *Spring of the Caller*

15:18, 19 Another indication of Samson's impetuous nature. But in v. 19 there is a reflection of his appreciation for God's help. Having cried to the Lord, he named the place of his help **En Hakkore**, "Spring of the Caller."

16:1 Gaza: Another of the chief Philistine cities. Again the biblical writer neither condemns nor approves. He simply reports and, in so doing, gives a powerful picture of the low level of moral sensitivity in those times.

been used, then I shall become weak, and
be like any *other* man."
12 Therefore Dē·lī'lah took new ropes
and bound him with them, and said to
him, "The Phi·lis'tines *are* upon you, Sam-
son!" And *men were* lying in wait, staying
in the room. But he broke them off his arms
like a thread.
13 Dē·lī'lah said to Samson, "Until now
you have mocked me and told me lies. Tell
me what you may be bound with."
And he said to her, "If you weave the
seven locks of my head into the web of the
loom"—
14 So she wove *it* tightly with the batten
of the loom, and said to him, "The
Phi·lis'tines *are* upon you, Samson!" But he
awoke from his sleep, and pulled out the
batten and the web from the loom.
15 Then she said to him, "How can you
say, 'I love you,' when your heart *is* not
with me? You have mocked me these three
times, and have not told me where your
great strength *lies*." 16 And it came to pass,
when she pestered him daily with her
words and pressed him, *so* that his soul
was vexed to death, 17 that he told her all
his heart, and said to her, "No razor has
ever come upon my head, for I *have been* a
Naz'ir·īte to God from my mother's
womb. If I am shaven, then my strength
will leave me, and I shall become weak,
and be like any *other* man."
18 When Dē·lī'lah saw that he had told
her all his heart, she sent and called for the
lords of the Phi·lis'tines, saying, "Come up
once more, for he has told me all his heart."
So the lords of the Phi·lis'tines came up to
her and brought the money in their hand.
19 Then she lulled him to sleep on her knees,
and called for a man and had him shave off
the seven locks of his head. Then she began
to torment him,[a] and his strength left him.
20 And she said, "The Phi·lis'tines *are* upon
you, Samson!" So he awoke from his sleep,
and said, "I will go out as before, at other
times, and shake myself free!" But he did
not know that the LORD had departed from
him.
21 Then the Phi·lis'tines took him and
put out his eyes, and brought him down to
Gā'za. They bound him with bronze fet-
ters, and he became a grinder in the prison.
22 However, the hair of his head began to
grow again after it had been shaven.

Samson Dies with the Philistines

23 Now the lords of the Phi·lis'tines gath-
ered together to offer a great sacrifice to
Dā'gon their god, and to rejoice. And they
said:

"Our god has delivered into our hands
Samson our enemy!"

24 When the people saw him, they praised
their god; for they said:

"Our god has delivered into our hands
our enemy,
The destroyer of our land,
And the one who multiplied our
dead."

25 So it happened, when their hearts were
merry, that they said, "Call for Samson,
that he may perform for us." So they called
for Samson from the prison, and he per-
formed for them. And they stationed him
between the pillars. 26 Then Samson said to
the lad who held him by the hand, "Let me
feel the pillars which support the temple,
so that I can lean on them." 27 Now the tem-
ple was full of men and women. All the
lords of the Phi·lis'tines *were* there—about

16:19 [a]Following Masoretic Text, Targum, and Vulgate; Septuagint reads *he began to be weak.*

16:20 the LORD had departed: Samson forgot that his strength was not some magical power in his hair; it rather lay in the empowering of the Spirit, which he had lost through disobedience.

three thousand men and women on the
roof watching while Samson performed.
28 Then Samson called to the LORD, say-
ing, "O Lord GOD, remember me, I pray!
Strengthen me, I pray, just this once, O
God, that I may with one *blow* take
vengeance on the Phi·lis′tines for my two
eyes!" 29 And Samson took hold of the two
middle pillars which supported the tem-
ple, and he braced himself against them,
one on his right and the other on his left.
30 Then Samson said, "Let me die with the
Phi·lis′tines!" And he pushed with *all his*
might, and the temple fell on the lords and
all the people who *were* in it. So the dead
that he killed at his death were more than
he had killed in his life.
31 And his brothers and all his father's
household came down and took him, and
brought *him* up and buried him between
Zō′rah and Esh′tā·ol in the tomb of his fa-
ther Ma·nō′ah. He had judged Israel
twenty years.

CHAPTER 17

Micah's Idolatry

Now there was a man from the moun-
tains of Ē′phra·im, whose name *was*
Mī′cah. 2 And he said to his mother, "The
eleven hundred *shekels* of silver that were
taken from you, and on which you put a
curse, even saying it in my ears—here *is*
the silver with me; I took it."
And his mother said, "*May you be*
blessed by the LORD, my son!" 3 So when he
had returned the eleven hundred *shekels* of
silver to his mother, his mother said, "I had
wholly dedicated the silver from my hand
to the LORD for my son, to make a carved
image and a molded image; now therefore,
I will return it to you." 4 Thus he returned
the silver to his mother. Then his mother
took two hundred *shekels* of silver and
gave them to the silversmith, and he made
it into a carved image and a molded image;
and they were in the house of Mī′cah.
5 The man Mī′cah had a shrine, and
made an ephod and household idols;[a] and
he consecrated one of his sons, who be-
came his priest. 6 In those days *there was* no
king in Israel; everyone did *what was* right
in his own eyes.
7 Now there was a young man from
Bethlehem in Judah, of the family of Judah;
he *was* a Lē′vīte, and was staying there.
8 The man departed from the city of Bethle-
hem in Judah to stay wherever he could
find *a place.* Then he came to the mountains
of Ē′phra·im, to the house of Mī′cah, as he
journeyed. 9 And Mī′cah said to him,
"Where do you come from?"
So he said to him, "I *am* a Lē′vīte from
Bethlehem in Judah, and I am on my way
to find *a place* to stay."
10 Mī′cah said to him, "Dwell with me,
and be a father and a priest to me, and I
will give you ten *shekels* of silver per year, a
suit of clothes, and your sustenance." So
the Lē′vīte went in. 11 Then the Lē′vīte was
content to dwell with the man; and the
young man became like one of his sons to
him. 12 So Mī′cah consecrated the Lē′vīte,
and the young man became his priest, and
lived in the house of Mī′cah. 13 Then Mī′cah
said, "Now I know that the LORD will be
good to me, since I have a Lē′vīte as
priest!"

17:5 [a]Hebrew *teraphim*

17:2–4 The silver was dedicated for religious purpose (v. 3), and a curse was invoked against anyone who used it for himself. The son stole the money, but later returned it. **blessed**: The mother altered the effects of the curse so as not to condemn her son. In irony she said, "I dedicated the silver so my son could make an idol." **carved . . . molded**: Idols were frequently carved from wood and heavily overlaid with melted silver.

17:7–13 An illustration of the corruption of the Levites. That a true Levite could set up worship somewhere other than the tabernacle, and furthermore serve an idol, is unthinkable and indicates how deeply the Israelites had fallen into sin.

CHAPTER 18

The Danites Adopt Micah's Idolatry

In those days *there was* no king in Israel. And in those days the tribe of the Dan′ītes was seeking an inheritance for itself to dwell in; for until that day *their* inheritance among the tribes of Israel had not fallen to them. [2]So the children of Dan sent five men of their family from their territory, men of valor from Zō′rah and Esh′tā·ol, to spy out the land and search it. They said to them, "Go, search the land." So they went to the mountains of Ē′phra·im, to the house of Mī′cah, and lodged there. [3]While they *were* at the house of Mī′cah, they recognized the voice of the young Lē′vīte. They turned aside and said to him, "Who brought you here? What are you doing in this *place?* What do you have here?"

[4]He said to them, "Thus and so Mī′cah did for me. He has hired me, and I have become his priest."

[5]So they said to him, "Please inquire of God, that we may know whether the journey on which we go will be prosperous."

[6]And the priest said to them, "Go in peace. The presence of the LORD *be* with you on your way."

[7]So the five men departed and went to Lā′ish. They saw the people who *were* there, how they dwelt safely, in the manner of the Sī·dō′ni·ans, quiet and secure. *There were* no rulers in the land who might put *them* to shame for anything. They *were* far from the Sī·dō′ni·ans, and they had no ties with anyone.[a]

[8]Then *the spies* came back to their brethren at Zō′rah and Esh′tā·ol, and their brethren said to them, "What *is* your *report?"*

[9]So they said, "Arise, let us go up against them. For we have seen the land, and indeed it *is* very good. *Would* you *do* nothing? Do not hesitate to go, *and* enter to possess the land. [10]When you go, you will come to a secure people and a large land. For God has given it into your hands, a place where *there is* no lack of anything that *is* on the earth."

[11]And six hundred men of the family of the Dan′ītes went from there, from Zō′rah and Esh′tā·ol, armed with weapons of war. [12]Then they went up and encamped in Kir′jath Jē′a·rim in Judah. (Therefore they call that place Mā′ha·neh Dan[a] to this day. There *it is,* west of Kir′jath Jē′a·rim.) [13]And they passed from there to the mountains of Ē′phra·im, and came to the house of Mī′cah.

[14]Then the five men who had gone to spy out the country of Lā′ish answered and said to their brethren, "Do you know that there are in these houses an ephod, household idols, a carved image, and a molded image? Now therefore, consider what you should do." [15]So they turned aside there, and came to the house of the young Lē′vīte man—to the house of Mī′cah—and greeted him. [16]The six hundred men armed with their weapons of war, who *were* of the children of Dan, stood by the entrance of the gate. [17]Then the five men who had gone to spy out the land went up. Entering there, they took the carved image, the ephod, the household idols, and the molded image. The priest stood at the entrance of the gate with the six hundred men *who were* armed with weapons of war.

[18]When these went into Mī′cah's house and took the carved image, the ephod, the household idols, and the molded image, the priest said to them, "What are you doing?"

18:7 [a]Following Masoretic Text, Targum, and Vulgate; Septuagint reads *with Syria.* 18:12 [a]Literally *Camp of Dan*

18:3 Voice here means "accent." These Danites did not know the Levite personally but recognized his southern dialect in that northern territory.

19 And they said to him, "Be quiet, put
your hand over your mouth, and come
with us; be a father and a priest to us. *Is it*
better for you to be a priest to the house-
hold of one man, or that you be a priest to
a tribe and a family in Israel?" 20 So the
priest's heart was glad; and he took
the ephod, the household idols, and the
carved image, and took his place among
the people.
21 Then they turned and departed, and
put the little ones, the livestock, and the
goods in front of them. 22 When they were a
good way from the house of Mī'cah, the
men who *were* in the houses near Mī'cah's
house gathered together and overtook the
children of Dan. 23 And they called out to
the children of Dan. So they turned around
and said to Mī'cah, "What ails you, that
you have gathered such a company?"
24 So he said, "You have taken away my
gods which I made, and the priest, and you
have gone away. Now what more do I
have? How can you say to me, 'What ails
you?' "
25 And the children of Dan said to him,
"Do not let your voice be heard among us,
lest angry men fall upon you, and you lose
your life, with the lives of your house-
hold!" 26 Then the children of Dan went
their way. And when Mī'cah saw that they
were too strong for him, he turned and
went back to his house.

Danites Settle in Laish

27 So they took *the things* Mī'cah had
made, and the priest who had belonged to
him, and went to Lā'ish, to a people quiet
and secure; and they struck them with the
edge of the sword and burned the city with
fire. 28 *There was* no deliverer, because it *was*
far from Sī'don, and they had no ties with
anyone. It was in the valley that belongs to
Beth Rē'hob. So they rebuilt the city and
dwelt there. 29 And they called the name of
the city Dan, after the name of Dan their fa-
ther, who was born to Israel. However, the
name of the city formerly *was* Lā'ish.
30 Then the children of Dan set up for
themselves the carved image; and Jona-
than the son of Ger'shom, the son of
Ma·nas'seh,[a] and his sons were priests to
the tribe of Dan until the day of the captiv-
ity of the land. 31 So they set up for them-
selves Mī'cah's carved image which he
made, all the time that the house of God
was in Shī'lōh.

CHAPTER 19

The Levite's Concubine

1 And it came to pass in those days, when
there was no king in Israel, that there was a
certain Lē'vīte staying in the remote
mountains of Ē'phra·im. He took for him-
self a concubine from Bethlehem in Judah.
2 But his concubine played the harlot
against him, and went away from him to
her father's house at Bethlehem in Judah,
and was there four whole months. 3 Then
her husband arose and went after her, to
speak kindly to her *and* bring her back,
having his servant and a couple of don-
keys with him. So she brought him into her
father's house; and when the father of the
young woman saw him, he was glad to
meet him. 4 Now his father-in-law, the
young woman's father, detained him; and
he stayed with him three days. So they ate
and drank and lodged there.
5 Then it came to pass on the fourth day
that they arose early in the morning, and
he stood to depart; but the young woman's
father said to his son-in-law, "Refresh your
heart with a morsel of bread, and after-
ward go your way."

18:30 [a]Septuagint and Vulgate read *Moses*.

18:19 The title **father** was given to important persons to convey honor and respect. In this sense it is used of Joseph (Gen. 45:8), the prophets (2 Kin. 2:12; 6:21), Naaman the Syrian commander (2 Kin. 5:1, 13), and in 17:10 and here of a priest.

19:5–9 A very believable picture of the niceties of oriental hospitality.

6So they sat down, and the two of them
ate and drank together. Then the young
woman's father said to the man, "Please be
content to stay all night, and let your heart
be merry." 7And when the man stood to
depart, his father-in-law urged him; so he
lodged there again. 8Then he arose early in
the morning on the fifth day to depart, but
the young woman's father said, "Please re-
fresh your heart." So they delayed until af-
ternoon; and both of them ate.
9And when the man stood to depart—he
and his concubine and his servant—his fa-
ther-in-law, the young woman's father,
said to him, "Look, the day is now draw-
ing toward evening; please spend the
night. See, the day is coming to an end;
lodge here, that your heart may be merry.
Tomorrow go your way early, so that you
may get home."
10However, the man was not willing to
spend that night; so he rose and departed,
and came opposite Jē'bus (that *is,* Jerusa-
lem). With him were the two saddled don-
keys; his concubine *was* also with him.
11They *were* near Jē'bus, and the day was
far spent; and the servant said to his mas-
ter, "Come, please, and let us turn aside
into this city of the Jeb'ū·sītes and lodge in
it."
12But his master said to him, "We will
not turn aside here into a city of foreigners,
who *are* not of the children of Israel; we
will go on to Gib'ē·ah." 13So he said to his
servant, "Come, let us draw near to one of
these places, and spend the night in
Gib'ē·ah or in Rā'mah." 14And they passed
by and went their way; and the sun went
down on them near Gib'ē·ah, which be-
longs to Benjamin. 15They turned aside
there to go in to lodge in Gib'ē·ah. And
when he went in, he sat down in the open
square of the city, for no one would take
them into *his* house to spend the night.
16Just then an old man came in from his
work in the field at evening, who also *was*
from the mountains of Ē'phra·im; he was
staying in Gib'ē·ah, whereas the men of
the place *were* Ben'ja·mītes. 17And when he
raised his eyes, he saw the traveler in the
open square of the city; and the old man
said, "Where are you going, and where do
you come from?"
18So he said to him, "We *are* passing
from Bethlehem in Judah toward the re-
mote mountains of Ē'phra·im; I *am* from
there. I went to Bethlehem in Judah; *now* I
am going to the house of the LORD. But
there *is* no one who will take me into his
house, 19although we have both straw and
fodder for our donkeys, and bread and
wine for myself, for your female servant,
and for the young man *who is* with your
servant; *there is* no lack of anything."
20And the old man said, "Peace *be* with
you! However, *let* all your needs *be* my re-
sponsibility; only do not spend the night in
the open square." 21So he brought him into
his house, and gave fodder to the donkeys.
And they washed their feet, and ate and
drank.

Gibeah's Crime

22As they were enjoying themselves,
suddenly certain men of the city, perverted
men,[a] surrounded the house *and* beat on
the door. They spoke to the master of the
house, the old man, saying, "Bring out the
man who came to your house, that we may
know him *carnally!*"
23But the man, the master of the house,
went out to them and said to them, "No,
my brethren! I beg you, do not act *so*
wickedly! Seeing this man has come into
my house, do not commit this outrage.
24Look, *here is* my virgin daughter and *the
man's*[a] concubine; let me bring them out

19:22 [a]Literally *sons of Belial* 19:24 [a]Literally *his*

19:15 A serious breach of oriental hospitality. This treatment contrasts with that of vv. 5, 6.

19:24 Surely a difficult offer to understand, even in that paganized society. The similarity between this situation and that of Lot in Sodom (Gen. 19:5–8) suggests that the writer of

now. Humble them, and do with them as
you please; but to this man do not do such
a vile thing!" 25But the men would not heed
him. So the man took his concubine and
brought *her* out to them. And they knew
her and abused her all night until morning;
and when the day began to break, they let
her go.

26Then the woman came as the day was
dawning, and fell down at the door of the
man's house where her master *was,* till it
was light.

27When her master arose in the morning,
and opened the doors of the house and
went out to go his way, there was his con-
cubine, fallen *at* the door of the house with
her hands on the threshold. 28And he said
to her, "Get up and let us be going." But
there was no answer. So the man lifted her
onto the donkey; and the man got up and
went to his place.

29When he entered his house he took a
knife, laid hold of his concubine, and di-
vided her into twelve pieces, limb by
limb,[a] and sent her throughout all the terri-
tory of Israel. 30And so it was that all who
saw it said, "No such deed has been done
or seen from the day that the children
of Israel came up from the land of Egypt
until this day. Consider it, confer, and
speak up!"

CHAPTER 20

Israel's War with the Benjamites

So all the children of Israel came out,
from Dan to Bē·er·shē'ba, as well as from
the land of Gil'ē·ad, and the congregation
gathered together as one man before the
LORD at Miz'pah. 2And the leaders of all
the people, all the tribes of Israel, pre-
sented themselves in the assembly of the
people of God, four hundred thousand
foot soldiers who drew the sword. 3(Now
the children of Benjamin heard that the
children of Israel had gone up to Miz'pah.)

Then the children of Israel said, "Tell *us,*
how did this wicked deed happen?"

4So the Lē'vīte, the husband of the
woman who was murdered, answered and
said, "My concubine and I went into
Gib'ē·ah, which belongs to Benjamin, to
spend the night. 5And the men of Gib'ē·ah
rose against me, and surrounded the house
at night because of me. They intended to
kill me, but instead they ravished my con-
cubine so that she died. 6So I took hold of
my concubine, cut her in pieces, and sent
her throughout all the territory of the in-
heritance of Israel, because they commit-
ted lewdness and outrage in Israel. 7Look!
All of you *are* children of Israel; give your
advice and counsel here and now!"

8So all the people arose as one man, say-
ing, "None *of us* will go to his tent, nor will
any turn back to his house; 9but now this *is*
the thing which we will do to Gib'ē·ah: *We
will go up* against it by lot. 10We will take
ten men out of *every* hundred throughout
all the tribes of Israel, a hundred out of
every thousand, and a thousand out of
every ten thousand, to make provisions for
the people, that when they come to
Gib'ē·ah in Benjamin, they may repay all
the vileness that they have done in Israel."
11So all the men of Israel were gathered
against the city, united together as one
man.

12Then the tribes of Israel sent men

19:29 [a]Literally *with her bones*

Judges intended to make a connection between the two with all of the terrible implications for Israel's true condition.

19:29, 30 This strange act seems to have been a ritual call to the tribes to join in war against Benjamin. Saul followed a similar action in 1 Sam. 11:7. The horrific nature of the message seems to have been designed to galvanize even the most callous to action. The success of the ploy is indicated in 20:1.

20:9–11 Not all would be needed in the battle—only one out of **ten**. But it was a united effort.

through all the tribe of Benjamin, saying, "What *is* this wickedness that has occurred among you? 13 Now therefore, deliver up the men, the perverted men[a] who *are* in Gib'ē·ah, that we may put them to death and remove the evil from Israel!" But the children of Benjamin would not listen to the voice of their brethren, the children of Israel. 14 Instead, the children of Benjamin gathered together from their cities to Gib'ē·ah, to go to battle against the children of Israel. 15 And from their cities at that time the children of Benjamin numbered twenty-six thousand men who drew the sword, besides the inhabitants of Gib'ē·ah, who numbered seven hundred select men. 16 Among all this people *were* seven hundred select men *who were* left-handed; every one could sling a stone at a hair's *breadth* and not miss. 17 Now besides Benjamin, the men of Israel numbered four hundred thousand men who drew the sword; all of these *were* men of war.

18 Then the children of Israel arose and went up to the house of God[a] to inquire of God. They said, "Which of us shall go up first to battle against the children of Benjamin?"

The LORD said, "Judah first!"

19 So the children of Israel rose in the morning and encamped against Gib'ē·ah. 20 And the men of Israel went out to battle against Benjamin, and the men of Israel put themselves in battle array to fight against them at Gib'ē·ah. 21 Then the children of Benjamin came out of Gib'ē·ah, and on that day cut down to the ground twenty-two thousand men of the Israelites. 22 And the people, that is, the men of Israel, encouraged themselves and again formed the battle line at the place where they had put themselves in array on the first day. 23 Then the children of Israel went up and wept before the LORD until evening, and asked counsel of the LORD, saying, "Shall I again draw near for battle against the children of my brother Benjamin?"

And the LORD said, "Go up against him."

24 So the children of Israel approached the children of Benjamin on the second day. 25 And Benjamin went out against them from Gib'ē·ah on the second day, and cut down to the ground eighteen thousand more of the children of Israel; all these drew the sword.

26 Then all the children of Israel, that is, all the people, went up and came to the house of God[a] and wept. They sat there before the LORD and fasted that day until evening; and they offered burnt offerings and peace offerings before the LORD. 27 So the children of Israel inquired of the LORD (the ark of the covenant of God *was* there in those days, 28 and Phin'e·has the son of El·ē·ā'zar, the son of Aaron, stood before it in those days), saying, "Shall I yet again go out to battle against the children of my brother Benjamin, or shall I cease?"

And the LORD said, "Go up, for tomorrow I will deliver them into your hand."

29 Then Israel set men in ambush all around Gib'ē·ah. 30 And the children of Israel went up against the children of Benjamin on the third day, and put themselves in battle array against Gib'ē·ah as at the other times. 31 So the children of Benjamin went out against the people, *and* were drawn away from the city. They began to strike down *and* kill some of the people, as at the other times, in the highways (one of which goes up to Beth'el and the other to Gib'ē·ah) and in the field, about thirty men of Israel. 32 And the children of Benjamin said, "They *are* defeated before us, as at first."

But the children of Israel said, "Let us flee and draw them away from the city to the highways." 33 So all the men of Israel rose from their place and put themselves in battle array at Bā'al Tā'mar. Then Israel's men in ambush burst forth from their position in the plain of Gē'ba. 34 And ten thousand select men from all Israel came against Gib'ē·ah, and the battle was fierce.

20:13 [a]Literally *sons of Belial* 20:18 [a]Or *Bethel*
20:26 [a]Or *Bethel*

But *the Ben'ja·mītes*[a] did not know that di-
saster *was* upon them. 35The LORD defeated
Benjamin before Israel. And the children of
Israel destroyed that day twenty-five thou-
sand one hundred Ben'ja·mītes; all these
drew the sword.
36So the children of Benjamin saw that
they were defeated. The men of Israel had
given ground to the Ben'ja·mītes, because
they relied on the men in ambush whom
they had set against Gib'ē·ah. 37And the
men in ambush quickly rushed upon
Gib'ē·ah; the men in ambush spread out
and struck the whole city with the edge of
the sword. 38Now the appointed signal be-
tween the men of Israel and the men in am-
bush was that they would make a great
cloud of smoke rise up from the city,
39whereupon the men of Israel would turn
in battle. Now Benjamin had begun to
strike *and* kill about thirty of the men of Is-
rael. For they said, "Surely they are de-
feated before us, as *in* the first battle." 40But
when the cloud began to rise from the city
in a column of smoke, the Ben'ja·mītes
looked behind them, and there was the
whole city going up *in smoke* to heaven.
41And when the men of Israel turned back,
the men of Benjamin panicked, for they
saw that disaster had come upon them.
42Therefore they turned *their backs* before
the men of Israel in the direction of the
wilderness; but the battle overtook them,
and whoever *came* out of the cities they de-
stroyed in their midst. 43They surrounded
the Ben'ja·mītes, chased them, *and* easily
trampled them down as far as the front of
Gib'ē·ah toward the east. 44And eighteen
thousand men of Benjamin fell; all these
were men of valor. 45Then they[a] turned and
fled toward the wilderness to the rock of
Rim'mon; and they cut down five thou-
sand of them on the highways. Then they
pursued them relentlessly up to Gī'dom,
and killed two thousand of them. 46So all
who fell of Benjamin that day were twenty-
five thousand men who drew the sword;
all these *were* men of valor.
47But six hundred men turned and fled
toward the wilderness to the rock of
Rim'mon, and they stayed at the rock of
Rim'mon for four months. 48And the men
of Israel turned back against the children
of Benjamin, and struck them down with
the edge of the sword—from *every* city,
men and beasts, all who were found. They
also set fire to all the cities they came to.

CHAPTER 21

Wives Provided for the Benjamites

Now the men of Israel had sworn an
oath at Miz'pah, saying, "None of us shall
give his daughter to Benjamin as a wife."
2Then the people came to the house of
God,[a] and remained there before God till
evening. They lifted up their voices and
wept bitterly, 3and said, "O LORD God of Is-
rael, why has this come to pass in Israel,
that today there should be one tribe *miss-
ing* in Israel?"
4So it was, on the next morning, that the
people rose early and built an altar there,
and offered burnt offerings and peace of-
ferings. 5The children of Israel said, "Who
is there among all the tribes of Israel who
did not come up with the assembly to the
LORD?" For they had made a great oath
concerning anyone who had not come up
to the LORD at Miz'pah, saying, "He shall

20:34 [a]Literally *they* 20:45 [a]Septuagint reads *the rest.* 21:2 [a]Or *Bethel*

20:36 The men of Israel: These words begin a retelling of the portion of the battle described in vv. 29–36. Thus, vv. 36–46 provide additional details of Israel's victory.

21:1–25 In their zeal to punish Benjamin, the other tribes all but destroyed one of the 12, a number of great importance to their heritage (v. 6). Furthermore, they made a foolish vow which could not be taken back. It only complicated the matter.

21:5 did not come up with the assembly: Hence had not taken the vow to refuse to let their daughters marry men of Benjamin.

surely be put to death." 6And the children
of Israel grieved for Benjamin their
brother, and said, "One tribe is cut off from
Israel today. 7What shall we do for wives
for those who remain, seeing we have
sworn by the LORD that we will not give
them our daughters as wives?"

8And they said, "What one *is there* from
the tribes of Israel who did not come up to
Miz'pah to the LORD?" And, in fact, no one
had come to the camp from Jā'besh Gil'-
ē·ad to the assembly. 9For when the people
were counted, indeed, not one of the in-
habitants of Jā'besh Gil'ē·ad *was* there. 10So
the congregation sent out there twelve
thousand of their most valiant men, and
commanded them, saying, "Go and strike
the inhabitants of Jā'besh Gil'ē·ad with the
edge of the sword, including the women
and children. 11And this *is* the thing that
you shall do: You shall utterly destroy
every male, and every woman who has
known a man intimately." 12So they found
among the inhabitants of Jā'besh Gil'ē·ad
four hundred young virgins who had not
known a man intimately; and they brought
them to the camp at Shī'lōh, which is in the
land of Cā'naan.

13Then the whole congregation sent
word to the children of Benjamin who *were*
at the rock of Rim'mon, and announced
peace to them. 14So Benjamin came back at
that time, and they gave them the women
whom they had saved alive of the women
of Jā'besh Gil'ē·ad; and yet they had not
found enough for them.

15And the people grieved for Benjamin,
because the LORD had made a void in the
tribes of Israel.

16Then the elders of the congregation
said, "What shall we do for wives for those
who remain, since the women of Benjamin
have been destroyed?" 17And they said,
"*There must be* an inheritance for the sur-
vivors of Benjamin, that a tribe may not be
destroyed from Israel. 18However, we can-
not give them wives from our daughters,
for the children of Israel have sworn an
oath, saying, 'Cursed *be* the one who gives
a wife to Benjamin.' " 19Then they said, "In
fact, *there is* a yearly feast of the LORD in
Shī'lōh, which *is* north of Beth'el, on the
east side of the highway that goes up from
Beth'el to Shē'chem, and south of Le·bō'-
nah."

20Therefore they instructed the children
of Benjamin, saying, "Go, lie in wait in the
vineyards, 21and watch; and just when the
daughters of Shī'lōh come out to perform
their dances, then come out from the vine-
yards, and every man catch a wife for him-
self from the daughters of Shī'lōh; then go
to the land of Benjamin. 22Then it shall be,
when their fathers or their brothers come
to us to complain, that we will say to them,
'Be kind to them for our sakes, because we
did not take a wife for any of them in the
war; for *it is* not *as though* you have given
the *women* to them at this time, making
yourselves guilty of your oath.' "

23And the children of Benjamin did so;
they took enough wives for their number
from those who danced, whom they
caught. Then they went and returned to
their inheritance, and they rebuilt the cities
and dwelt in them. 24So the children of Is-
rael departed from there at that time, every
man to his tribe and family; they went out
from there, every man to his inheritance.

25In those days *there was* no king in Is-
rael; everyone did *what was* right in his
own eyes.

21:25 The preceding events and this verse demonstrate the depravity of the Israelites at this time. How quickly they abandoned their covenant vow. Yet, while we are tempted to condemn their inconsistency, we must acknowlege how frequently and easily we allow ourselves to be drawn away from the things of God.

✦Ruth✦

Ruth lived during the period of the judges (1:1), a dark time in Israel's history when the people repeatedly turned to false gods. Although the author is not mentioned, many scholars believe that Samuel wrote the book.

Chapters 1 and 2 demonstrate Ruth's love for her mother-in-law, Naomi. Ruth gave up her homeland and people to follow Naomi back to Israel after a terrible famine. Chapters 3 and 4 tell how God rewarded Ruth's love by giving her Boaz as a husband and providing her with a son, Obed, the grandfather of David.

The book is a beautiful illustration of God's provision for those who love Him. The Hebrew word for kinsman *(goel)* appears thirteen times and means "one who redeems"; Boaz acted as a redeemer by bringing Ruth from poverty to riches and from her Moabite heritage to the line of David.

In addition to the theme of redemption, the Book of Ruth shows Naomi's faith and selflessness in the face of grief, providing a godly example for anyone coping with the loss of a loved one. ✦

CHAPTER 1

Elimelech's Family Goes to Moab

Now it came to pass, in the days when
the judges ruled, that there was a famine in
the land. And a certain man of Bethlehem,
Judah, went to dwell in the country of
Mō'ab, he and his wife and his two sons.
[2]The name of the man *was* Ē·lim'e·lech, the
name of his wife *was* Nā'o·mī, and the
names of his two sons *were* Mah'lon and
Chil'i·on—Eph'ra·thītes of Bethlehem, Ju-
dah. And they went to the country of
Mō'ab and remained there. [3]Then Ē·lim'-
e·lech, Nā'o·mī's husband, died; and she
was left, and her two sons. [4]Now they took
wives of the women of Mō'ab: the name of
the one *was* Or'pah, and the name of the
other Ruth. And they dwelt there about ten
years. [5]Then both Mah'lon and Chil'i·on
also died; so the woman survived her two
sons and her husband.

Naomi Returns with Ruth

[6]Then she arose with her daughters-in-
law that she might return from the country
of Mō'ab, for she had heard in the country
of Mō'ab that the LORD had visited His
people by giving them bread. [7]Therefore
she went out from the place where she
was, and her two daughters-in-law with
her; and they went on the way to return to
the land of Judah. [8]And Nā'o·mī said to
her two daughters-in-law, "Go, return each
to her mother's house. The LORD deal
kindly with you, as you have dealt with

1:2 Ephrathites: Ephrath or Ephrathah was an earlier name for Bethlehem.

1:6 visited: A frequent expression of divine activity, whether in punishment or, as here, in blessing.

NAOMI: ACCEPTING THE HAND OF THE LORD

During the period of the judges, "everyone did what was right in his own eyes" (Judg. 21:25). Against this dark background we find Naomi, a woman who experienced great tragedy yet clung to her faith in God.

When a famine struck her homeland, Naomi and her husband fled to Moab. While Naomi lived in exile, her husband and her two sons died, leaving her and their two Moabite widows to fend for themselves.

Naomi decided to return to Judah, and encouraged her daughters-in-law to return to their homes. When they insisted on going with her, Naomi reminded Ruth and Orpah that she had no sons to carry out the Israelite custom of levirate marriage and thus could offer them nothing. Naomi also told them that the hand of the Lord was against her, indicating that she may have viewed her tragic experiences as punishment for having left Judah in the first place (Ruth 1:13).

Although Orpah decided to leave Naomi, Ruth pledged herself to accompany her mother-in-law and adopt her homeland. Further, she committed herself to embracing Naomi's God, a decision that speaks volumes about Naomi's testimony.

Many people who endure extreme heartache either accuse God of cruelty or abandon their faith altogether. While Naomi attributed her misery to God, she accepted it as punishment for her own faithlessness (1:21). She clung to her faith in the Lord, and her circumstances slowly began to change. Naomi also credited Him for her blessings. When the kindness of Boaz enabled Ruth to take home some barley, Naomi praised the Lord for providing for their needs (2:20).

Her love for her daughter-in-law prompted Naomi to assume the role of Ruth's mother in arranging for a possible marriage with Boaz. She explained the Israelite tradition of a redeeming relative and gave Ruth specific instructions for proposing marriage to Boaz.

The Lord used Boaz to reward Naomi for her consistent faith. Boaz redeemed the field her poverty had forced her to sell, and he and Ruth provided her with a grandson, Obed. Although Obed could not replace Naomi's dead sons, to her he signified the end of God's judgment on her life and brought joy to her old age.

When we stray from the Lord, we can expect to suffer the consequences. Then we must choose whether to repent and learn from our experience or to turn away from Him in bitterness. Naomi shows us that we can be restored to fellowship with the Lord through sincere repentance. Only when we accept the hand of the Lord in both tragedy and blessing can we truly achieve spiritual and emotional health. ✦

the dead and with me. 9The LORD grant
that you may find rest, each in the house of
her husband."

So she kissed them, and they lifted up
their voices and wept. 10And they said to
her, "Surely we will return with you to
your people."

11But Nā'o·mī said, "Turn back, my
daughters; why will you go with me? *Are*
there still sons in my womb, that they may
be your husbands? 12Turn back, my daugh-
ters, go—for I am too old to have a hus-
band. If I should say I have hope, *if* I
should have a husband tonight and should
also bear sons, 13would you wait for them
till they were grown? Would you restrain
yourselves from having husbands? No, my
daughters; for it grieves me very much for
your sakes that the hand of the LORD has
gone out against me!"

14Then they lifted up their voices and
wept again; and Or'pah kissed her mother-
in-law, but Ruth clung to her.

15And she said, "Look, your sister-in-
law has gone back to her people and to her
gods; return after your sister-in-law."

16But Ruth said:

"Entreat me not to leave you,
Or to turn back from following after
you;
For wherever you go, I will go;
And wherever you lodge, I will
lodge;
Your people *shall be* my people,
And your God, my God.
17 Where you die, I will die,
And there will I be buried.
The LORD do so to me, and more also,
If *anything but* death parts you and
me."

18When she saw that she was determined
to go with her, she stopped speaking to her.

19Now the two of them went until they
came to Bethlehem. And it happened,
when they had come to Bethlehem, that all
the city was excited because of them; and
the women said, "*Is* this Nā'o·mī?"

20But she said to them, "Do not call me
Nā'o·mī;[a] call me Mar'a,[b] for the Almighty
has dealt very bitterly with me. 21I went out
full, and the LORD has brought me home
again empty. Why do you call me Nā'o·mī,
since the LORD has testified against me,
and the Almighty has afflicted me?"

22So Nā'o·mī returned, and Ruth the
Mō'ab·ī·tess her daughter-in-law with her,
who returned from the country of Mō'ab.
Now they came to Bethlehem at the begin-
ning of barley harvest.

CHAPTER 2

Ruth Meets Boaz

There was a relative of Nā'o·mī's hus-
band, a man of great wealth, of the family
of Ē·lim'e·lech. His name *was* Bō'az. 2So
Ruth the Mō'ab·ī·tess said to Nā'o·mī,
"Please let me go to the field, and glean
heads of grain after *him* in whose sight I
may find favor."

And she said to her, "Go, my daughter."
3Then she left, and went and gleaned in
the field after the reapers. And she hap-
pened to come to the part of the field *be-
longing* to Bō'az, who *was* of the family of
Ē·lim'e·lech.

1:20 [a]Literally *Pleasant* [b]Literally *Bitter*

1:9 Naomi gives them her blessing to seek new husbands. **Rest** implies stability and security.

1:16, 17 Ruth's mention of the Lord indicates that her commitment is based on faith in God, of whom Naomi has taught her.

2:2 glean: A landowner was required by Hebrew law (see Lev. 19:9) to leave behind some stalks of grain at harvest time so that the poor could go through the fields after the reapers and gather what was left.

2:3 she happened to come: What seemed a coincidence to Ruth is seen by the writer of the book as God's gracious providence (2:20).

4 Now behold, Bō'az came from Bethlehem, and said to the reapers, "The LORD *be* with you!"

And they answered him, "The LORD bless you!"

5 Then Bō'az said to his servant who was in charge of the reapers, "Whose young woman *is* this?"

6 So the servant who was in charge of the reapers answered and said, "It *is* the young Mō'ab·īte woman who came back with Nā'o·mī from the country of Mō'ab. 7 And she said, 'Please let me glean and gather after the reapers among the sheaves.' So she came and has continued from morning until now, though she rested a little in the house."

8 Then Bō'az said to Ruth, "You will listen, my daughter, will you not? Do not go to glean in another field, nor go from here, but stay close by my young women. 9 *Let* your eyes *be* on the field which they reap, and go after them. Have I not commanded the young men not to touch you? And when you are thirsty, go to the vessels and drink from what the young men have drawn."

10 So she fell on her face, bowed down to the ground, and said to him, "Why have I found favor in your eyes, that you should take notice of me, since I *am* a foreigner?"

11 And Bō'az answered and said to her, "It has been fully reported to me, all that you have done for your mother-in-law since the death of your husband, and *how* you have left your father and your mother and the land of your birth, and have come to a people whom you did not know before. 12 The LORD repay your work, and a full reward be given you by the LORD God of Israel, under whose wings you have come for refuge."

13 Then she said, "Let me find favor in your sight, my lord; for you have comforted me, and have spoken kindly to your maidservant, though I am not like one of your maidservants."

14 Now Bō'az said to her at mealtime, "Come here, and eat of the bread, and dip your piece of bread in the vinegar." So she sat beside the reapers, and he passed parched *grain* to her; and she ate and was satisfied, and kept some back. 15 And when she rose up to glean, Bō'az commanded his young men, saying, "Let her glean even among the sheaves, and do not reproach her. 16 Also let *grain* from the bundles fall purposely for her; leave *it* that she may glean, and do not rebuke her."

17 So she gleaned in the field until evening, and beat out what she had gleaned, and it was about an ephah of barley. 18 Then she took *it* up and went into the city, and her mother-in-law saw what she had gleaned. So she brought out and gave to her what she had kept back after she had been satisfied.

19 And her mother-in-law said to her, "Where have you gleaned today? And where did you work? Blessed be the one who took notice of you."

So she told her mother-in-law with whom she had worked, and said, "The man's name with whom I worked today *is* Bō'az."

20 Then Nā'o·mī said to her daughter-in-law, "Blessed *be* he of the LORD, who has not forsaken His kindness to the living and the dead!" And Nā'o·mī said to her, "This man *is* a relation of ours, one of our close relatives."

2:4 The faithful conversation of these people contrasts strongly with the evil that pervaded most of Israel at this time.

2:20 Though it is Boaz who has acted in kindness, Naomi, who had been bitter (1:20), now recognizes God's covenant love (a theme throughout the book). If He had brought evil into her life temporarily, He could also be depended upon for good. **close relatives**: Lit. "redeemers," a reference to the legal obligation of redeeming or buying back the property of destitute relatives from foreclosure (see Lev. 25:25–28).

21 Ruth the Mō′ab·ī·tess said, "He also said to me, 'You shall stay close by my young men until they have finished all my harvest.' "

22 And Nā′o·mī said to Ruth her daughter-in-law, "*It is* good, my daughter, that you go out with his young women, and that people do not meet you in any other field." 23 So she stayed close by the young women of Bō′az, to glean until the end of barley harvest and wheat harvest; and she dwelt with her mother-in-law.

CHAPTER 3

Ruth's Redemption Assured

Then Nā′o·mī her mother-in-law said to her, "My daughter, shall I not seek security for you, that it may be well with you? 2 Now Bō′az, whose young women you were with, *is he* not our relative? In fact, he is winnowing barley tonight at the threshing floor. 3 Therefore wash yourself and anoint yourself, put on your *best* garment and go down to the threshing floor; *but* do not make yourself known to the man until he has finished eating and drinking. 4 Then it shall be, when he lies down, that you shall notice the place where he lies; and you shall go in, uncover his feet, and lie down; and he will tell you what you should do."

5 And she said to her, "All that you say to me I will do."

6 So she went down to the threshing floor and did according to all that her mother-in-law instructed her. 7 And after Bō′az had eaten and drunk, and his heart was cheerful, he went to lie down at the end of the heap of grain; and she came softly, uncovered his feet, and lay down.

8 Now it happened at midnight that the man was startled, and turned himself; and there, a woman was lying at his feet. 9 And he said, "Who *are* you?"

So she answered, "I *am* Ruth, your maidservant. Take your maidservant under your wing,[a] for you are a close relative."

10 Then he said, "Blessed *are* you of the LORD, my daughter! For you have shown more kindness at the end than at the beginning, in that you did not go after young men, whether poor or rich. 11 And now, my daughter, do not fear. I will do for you all that you request, for all the people of my town know that you *are* a virtuous woman. 12 Now it is true that I *am* a close relative; however, there is a relative closer than I. 13 Stay this night, and in the morning it shall be *that* if he will perform the duty of a close relative for you—good; let him do it. But if he does not want to perform the duty for you, then I will perform the duty for you, *as* the LORD lives! Lie down until morning."

14 So she lay at his feet until morning, and she arose before one could recognize another. Then he said, "Do not let it be known that the woman came to the threshing floor." 15 Also he said, "Bring the shawl that *is* on you and hold it." And when she held it, he measured six *ephahs* of barley, and laid *it* on her. Then she[a] went into the city.

16 When she came to her mother-in-law, she said, "*Is* that you, my daughter?"

Then she told her all that the man had done for her. 17 And she said, "These six *ephahs* of barley he gave me; for he said to me, 'Do not go empty-handed to your mother-in-law.' "

18 Then she said, "Sit still, my daughter, until you know how the matter will turn out; for the man will not rest until he has concluded the matter this day."

3:9 [a]Or *Spread the corner of your garment over your maidservant* 3:15 [a]Many Hebrew manuscripts, Syriac, and Vulgate read *she;* Masoretic Text, Septuagint, and Targum read *he.*

3:1 Naomi shows genuine concern for Ruth, desiring her daughter-in-law to have a husband and home.

Ruth: God Shall Supply All Our Needs

Ruth, one of the strongest female characters in the Old Testament, shows how God's love extends to every aspect of our lives. When we surrender fully to Him, He not only blesses us spiritually but physically and emotionally as well.

Having grown up in Moab, Ruth did not have the advantage of a rich spiritual heritage, but she apparently learned from her mother-in-law Naomi the importance of giving spiritual matters priority in her life. When she decided to accompany Naomi to Judah, Ruth also determined to leave behind her family and her pagan gods and embrace the God of Israel. Once committed to this course of action, she never looked back.

We do not know much of Ruth's pre-conversion personality, but she clearly exemplified godly love in her concerned and caring attitude toward Naomi after her declaration of faith. In contrast to many Christians today who limit their kindness to superficial gestures or comments, this new believer put her thoughtfulness into action.

Ruth took the initiative in finding food for herself and Naomi. Her willingness to labor in the fields with other impoverished people illustrates her lack of pride or self-consciousness. This humility is further demonstrated by her obedience to Naomi's suggestions for proposing marriage to Boaz.

Ruth's righteous behavior did not go unnoticed by God—or by the townspeople, who brought her virtue to the attention of Boaz (Ruth 3:11). The Lord had already softened the heart of Boaz toward Ruth, so fulfilling the duty of levirate marriage became a joy rather than just a responsibility. God rewarded Ruth's faithfulness by supplying her physical and emotional needs. Her marriage to Boaz provided the love and security for which she must have yearned.

Our relationship with God should always be our primary concern, and we learn from the story of Ruth and Boaz that He cares about our physical and emotional needs as well as our spiritual health. When we limit our interaction with God to the spiritual realm, we forego the blessings He longs to give us in so many other areas. ✦

CHAPTER 4

Boaz Redeems Ruth

Now Bō'az went up to the gate and sat
down there; and behold, the close relative
of whom Bō'az had spoken came by. So
Bō'az said, "Come aside, friend,[a] sit down
here." So he came aside and sat down.

4:1 [a]Hebrew *peloni almoni;* literally *so and so*

[2]And he took ten men of the elders of the
city, and said, "Sit down here." So they sat
down. [3]Then he said to the close relative,
"Nā'o·mī, who has come back from the
country of Mō'ab, sold the piece of land
which *belonged* to our brother Ē·lim'e·lech.
[4]And I thought to inform you, saying, 'Buy
it back in the presence of the inhabitants
and the elders of my people. If you will
redeem *it*, redeem *it*; but if you[a] will not redeem
it, *then* tell me, that I may know; for
there is no one but you to redeem *it*, and I
am next after you.' "

And he said, "I will redeem *it*."

[5]Then Bō'az said, "On the day you buy
the field from the hand of Nā'o·mī, you
must also buy *it* from Ruth the Mō'ab-ī·tess, the wife of the dead, to perpetuate[a]
the name of the dead through his inheritance."

[6]And the close relative said, "I cannot
redeem *it* for myself, lest I ruin my own inheritance.
You redeem my right of redemption for yourself, for I cannot redeem *it*."

[7]Now this *was the custom* in former times
in Israel concerning redeeming and
exchanging, to confirm anything: one man
took off his sandal and gave *it* to the other,
and this *was* a confirmation in Israel.

[8]Therefore the close relative said to
Bō'az, "Buy *it* for yourself." So he took off
his sandal. [9]And Bō'az said to the elders
and all the people, "You *are* witnesses this
day that I have bought all that was
Ē·lim'e·lech's, and all that *was* Chil'i·on's
and Mah'lon's, from the hand of Nā'o·mī.
[10]Moreover, Ruth the Mō'ab·ī·tess, the
widow of Mah'lon, I have acquired as my
wife, to perpetuate the name of the dead
through his inheritance, that the name of

4:4 [a]Following many Hebrew manuscripts, Septuagint, Syriac, Targum, and Vulgate; Masoretic Text reads *he*.
4:5 [a]Literally *raise up*

History in the Making

Gloria Gaither

One of the things that bruises my heart most is that so many people don't enjoy the benefits of an extended family. I don't see how parents in their twenties cope without the help of others. We live in a town where our kids have grown up with aunts and uncles and grandparents, and each relative has helped contribute to my children's sense of identity.

I think it's important to remember that we are all building a history. Maybe you don't like where you've come from, but it's not a one-way thing. Each day you are building a history in your relationships, and it's hard to believe how quickly it happens. People begin to know you for certain qualities and characteristics. They know if they can trust you, if you are consistent. Histories are built one day at a time. You aren't aware of them until they're built. ✦

4:3, 4 Sold suggests a foreclosure when Naomi's family was destitute. The nearest relative was obligated to **buy . . . back** the land and thus secure it within the family (Lev. 25:25–28). **I will redeem it**: The nearer kinsman was willing to do this in order to expand his property.

4:5, 6 Boaz adroitly brings up the added responsibility of the levirate. According to this law (Deut. 25:5–10), Naomi's brother-in-law was to marry her, but their offspring would carry the name and inheritance of her former husband. In Naomi's case the law applied to more distant male relatives. Furthermore, since she was beyond childbearing age, the levirate marriage would be to her widowed daughter-in-law Ruth. The closest relative was not willing to assume this obligation, thus he could not redeem the land either.

the dead may not be cut off from among
his brethren and from his position at the
gate.[a] You *are* witnesses this day."
11And all the people who *were* at the
gate, and the elders, said, "*We are* wit-
nesses. The LORD make the woman who is
coming to your house like Rachel and
Leah, the two who built the house of Israel;
and may you prosper in Eph'ra·thah and
be famous in Bethlehem. 12May your house
be like the house of Per'ez, whom Tā'mar
bore to Judah, because of the offspring
which the LORD will give you from this
young woman."

Descendants of Boaz and Ruth

13So Bō'az took Ruth and she became his
wife; and when he went in to her, the LORD
gave her conception, and she bore a son.
14Then the women said to Nā'o·mī,
"Blessed *be* the LORD, who has not left you
this day without a close relative; and may
his name be famous in Israel! 15And may
he be to you a restorer of life and a nour-
isher of your old age; for your daughter-in-
law, who loves you, who is better to
you than seven sons, has borne him."
16Then Nā'o·mī took the child and laid him
on her bosom, and became a nurse to him.
17Also the neighbor women gave him a
name, saying, "There is a son born to
Nā'o·mī." And they called his name
Ō'bed. He *is* the father of Jesse, the father
of David.

18Now this *is* the genealogy of Per'ez:
Per'ez begot Hez'ron; 19Hez'ron begot
Ram, and Ram begot Am·min'a·dab;
20Am·min'a·dab begot Nah'shon, and
Nah'shon begot Sal'mon;[a] 21Sal'mon begot
Bō'az, and Bō'az begot Ō'bed; 22Ō'bed be-
got Jesse, and Jesse begot David.

4:10 [a]Probably his civic office

4:20 [a]Hebrew *Salmah*

4:18 This genealogy links Ruth, a Gentile, with the messianic line, while the book itself provides information on the family background of King David.

✦1 Samuel✦

Most people assume that Samuel wrote these two books named after him, yet some of the later text covers events after his death during the reign of David. Abiathar the priest may have written these later parts, since he had access to court records. First Samuel describes the period when Israel demanded a king to unite the nation. Samuel anointed King Saul in 1050 B.C. and David ascended the throne in 1010 B.C.; each ruled for forty years (2 Sam. 5:4; Acts 13:21).

The early chapters of First Samuel record events during the chaotic period of the judges and focus on Eli, the judge-priest whose leadership was corrupted by his two evil sons. When Eli died, Samuel became the last judge and the first of the prophets in this period, and he led the Israelites through a revival. However, Samuel's sons, who had hoped to succeed him, proved to be unjust and wicked judges, and the people cried out for a king "like all the nations" (8:5).

Through Saul's kingship recorded in First Samuel, God shows the consequences that Israel faced in rejecting God's rule. Saul was so stubborn that even after God rejected him as king and anointed David as His next choice, Saul refused to give up his crown. His reign ended abruptly when he was wounded in battle and, soon after, took his own life.

First Samuel records three transitions of power: Eli to Samuel, Samuel to Saul, and Saul to David. In each case, God transferred His blessing from one man to another because of sin. The examples of Eli, Samuel, and Saul demonstrate the need for diligence in matters of holiness, no matter how long we have been serving the Lord. ✦

CHAPTER 1

The Family of Elkanah

Now there was a certain man of
Rā·ma·thā'im Zō'phim, of the mountains
of Ē'phra·im, and his name *was* El·kā'nah
the son of Je·rō'ham, the son of E·lī'hū,[a] the
son of Tō'hū,[b] the son of Zuph, an
Ē'phra·im·īte. 2And he had two wives: the
name of one *was* Hannah, and the name of
the other Pe·nin'nah. Pe·nin'nah had chil-
dren, but Hannah had no children. 3This

1:1 [a]Spelled *Eliel* in 1 Chronicles 6:34 [b]Spelled *Toah* in 1 Chronicles 6:34

1:1 Ramathaim Zophim, usually called Ramah (1:19; 2:11), was not only Samuel's ancestral home but became his official residence and burial place.

1:2 two wives: Polygamy was permitted, but was not sanctioned by God and it usually caused problems, as in the case of Elkanah's family. To have **no children** was a source of great disgrace for a woman in OT times. See also Gen. 29:31—30:24.

1:3 The LORD of hosts (armies) is a phrase used here for the first time in the OT. It refers to God's almighty power. God is the Lord of all earthly and heavenly forces, Israel's invisible Leader fighting for His people.

HANNAH: FROM SORROW TO SONG

Hannah's situation reflects the suffering of many people today. Even though their basic needs are provided, they struggle with one overwhelming desire that goes unanswered for years. Some long for restored eyesight or hearing, some wish for a close friend, and others pray for the salvation of a child or spouse.

The overpowering longing of Hannah's heart was to provide her husband with a son. Her spiritual life was in order, and she experienced a loving relationship with her husband, Elkanah; yet she felt unfulfilled. The heartless taunts of Peninnah—Elkanah's other wife and Hannah's rival—contributed to her misery.

Elkanah loved Hannah deeply, but he could not understand her yearning for motherhood. His failed attempt to console his wife is mirrored in the platitudes many would-be comforters use today: "It's probably all for the best," or "You'll soon get over it," or "Your life is great. What more could you want?"

No amount of love or concern can enable someone to understand another person's pain. Rather than trying to explain away their grief, we must be satisfied to listen and to pray. Our presence alone is the comfort they need, not the trite truisms on which so many "comforters" rely.

After her conversation with Elkanah, Hannah realized that only the Lord could truly understand her desire. "In bitterness of soul," she prayed and poured her heart out to the Lord in tears (1 Sam. 1:10).

When her encounter in the tabernacle with Eli the priest brought assurance that her petition would be granted, Hannah did not pursue the matter any further. She simply trusted the Lord to answer her prayer. The Bible tells us that she "went her way and ate, and her face was no longer sad" (vv. 17, 18).

The Lord rewarded Hannah's faith through the birth of Samuel, and she remembered her vow to dedicate the child to God. While many people make rash promises to God out of desperation, few remember to fulfill them once the sense of urgency is gone. Hannah not only kept her vow without complaint, she composed a song of praise to the Lord for giving her victory over her barrenness (2:1–10).

Hannah's story gives an inspiring example of the blessed joy of surrendering our desires to the Lord. He can fill the gaps in our lives, just as He did for Hannah. While God may not always grant our requests in the way we expect, we can be certain He will satisfy our desires, if we let Him. ✦

man went up from his city yearly to wor-
ship and sacrifice to the LORD of hosts in
Shī'lōh. Also the two sons of Ē'lī, Hoph'nī
and Phin'e·has, the priests of the LORD,
were there. 4And whenever the time came
for El·kā'nah to make an offering, he
would give portions to Pe·nin'nah his wife
and to all her sons and daughters. 5But to
Hannah he would give a double portion,
for he loved Hannah, although the LORD
had closed her womb. 6And her rival also
provoked her severely, to make her miser-
able, because the LORD had closed her
womb. 7So it was, year by year, when she
went up to the house of the LORD, that she
provoked her; therefore she wept and did
not eat.

Hannah's Vow

8Then El·kā'nah her husband said to
her, "Hannah, why do you weep? Why do
you not eat? And why is your heart
grieved? *Am* I not better to you than ten
sons?"
9So Hannah arose after they had fin-
ished eating and drinking in Shī'lōh. Now
Ē'lī the priest was sitting on the seat by the
doorpost of the tabernacle[a] of the LORD.
10And she *was* in bitterness of soul, and
prayed to the LORD and wept in anguish.
11Then she made a vow and said, "O LORD
of hosts, if You will indeed look on the af-
fliction of Your maidservant and remem-
ber me, and not forget Your maidservant,
but will give Your maidservant a male
child, then I will give him to the LORD all
the days of his life, and no razor shall come
upon his head."
12And it happened, as she continued
praying before the LORD, that Ē'lī watched
her mouth. 13Now Hannah spoke in her
heart; only her lips moved, but her voice
was not heard. Therefore Ē'lī thought she
was drunk. 14So Ē'lī said to her, "How long
will you be drunk? Put your wine away
from you!"
15But Hannah answered and said, "No,
my lord, I *am* a woman of sorrowful spirit.
I have drunk neither wine nor intoxicating
drink, but have poured out my soul before
the LORD. 16Do not consider your maidser-
vant a wicked woman,[a] for out of the abun-
dance of my complaint and grief I have
spoken until now."
17Then Ē'lī answered and said, "Go in
peace, and the God of Israel grant your pe-
tition which you have asked of Him."
18And she said, "Let your maidservant
find favor in your sight." So the woman
went her way and ate, and her face was no
longer *sad*.

Samuel Is Born and Dedicated

19Then they rose early in the morning
and worshiped before the LORD, and re-
turned and came to their house at Rā'mah.
And El·kā'nah knew Hannah his wife, and
the LORD remembered her. 20So it came to
pass in the process of time that Hannah
conceived and bore a son, and called his
name Samuel,[a] *saying,* "Because I have
asked for him from the LORD."
21Now the man El·kā'nah and all his
house went up to offer to the LORD the
yearly sacrifice and his vow. 22But Hannah
did not go up, for she said to her husband,
"*Not* until the child is weaned; then I will
take him, that he may appear before the
LORD and remain there forever."
23So El·kā'nah her husband said to her,
"Do what seems best to you; wait until you
have weaned him. Only let the LORD estab-
lish His[a] word." Then the woman stayed
and nursed her son until she had weaned
him.
24Now when she had weaned him, she

1:9 [a]Hebrew *heykal,* palace or temple 1:16 [a]Literally *daughter of Belial* 1:20 [a]Literally *Heard by God* 1:23 [a]Following Masoretic Text, Targum, and Vulgate; Dead Sea Scrolls, Septuagint, and Syriac read *your.*

1:11 Hannah promised to consecrate her child to God's service as a Nazirite (Num. 6:2–5) whose hair would never be cut and who would drink no strong drink.

took him up with her, with three bulls,[a] one
ephah of flour, and a skin of wine, and
brought him to the house of the LORD in
Shī′lōh. And the child *was* young. 25Then
they slaughtered a bull, and brought the
child to Ē′lī. 26And she said, "O my lord! As
your soul lives, my lord, I *am* the woman
who stood by you here, praying to the
LORD. 27For this child I prayed, and the
LORD has granted me my petition which I
asked of Him. 28Therefore I also have lent
him to the LORD; as long as he lives he shall
be lent to the LORD." So they worshiped the
LORD there.

CHAPTER 2

Hannah's Prayer

And Hannah prayed and said:

"My heart rejoices in the LORD;
My horn[a] is exalted in the LORD.
I smile at my enemies,
Because I rejoice in Your salvation.

2 "No one is holy like the LORD,
For *there is* none besides You,
Nor *is there* any rock like our God.

3 "Talk no more so very proudly;
Let no arrogance come from your
mouth,
For the LORD *is* the God of knowledge;
And by Him actions are weighed.

4 "The bows of the mighty men *are*
broken,
And those who stumbled are girded
with strength.
5 *Those who were* full have hired
themselves out for bread,
And the hungry have ceased *to
hunger.*
Even the barren has borne seven,
And she who has many children has
become feeble.

6 "The LORD kills and makes alive;
He brings down to the grave and
brings up.
7 The LORD makes poor and makes
rich;
He brings low and lifts up.
8 He raises the poor from the dust
And lifts the beggar from the ash
heap,
To set *them* among princes
And make them inherit the throne of
glory.

"For the pillars of the earth *are* the
LORD's,
And He has set the world upon them.
9 He will guard the feet of His saints,
But the wicked shall be silent in
darkness.

"For by strength no man shall prevail.
10 The adversaries of the LORD shall be
broken in pieces;
From heaven He will thunder against
them.
The LORD will judge the ends of the
earth.

"He will give strength to His king,
And exalt the horn of His anointed."

11Then El·kā′nah went to his house at Rā′-
mah. But the child ministered to the LORD
before Ē′lī the priest.

The Wicked Sons of Eli

12Now the sons of Ē′lī *were* corrupt;[a]
they did not know the LORD. 13And the

1:24 [a]Dead Sea Scrolls, Septuagint, and Syriac read *a three-year-old bull.* 2:1 [a]That is, strength
2:12 [a]Literally *sons of Belial*

2:10 His king and **His anointed** refer not only to the earthly ruler but also to Christ. *Messiah*, translated "Christ" in the NT, comes from a Hebrew term meaning "the anointed one."

2:12–17 The sins of Eli's sons were symptomatic of their heart condition. They wanted the best parts of the meat offered in sacrifice rather than those assigned them in the

priests' custom with the people *was that* when any man offered a sacrifice, the priest's servant would come with a three-pronged fleshhook in his hand while the meat was boiling. 14Then he would thrust *it* into the pan, or kettle, or caldron, or pot; and the priest would take for himself all that the fleshhook brought up. So they did in Shī'lōh to all the Israelites who came there. 15Also, before they burned the fat, the priest's servant would come and say to the man who sacrificed, "Give meat for roasting to the priest, for he will not take boiled meat from you, but raw."

16And *if* the man said to him, "They should really burn the fat first; *then* you may take *as much* as your heart desires," he would then answer him, "*No,* but you must give *it* now; and if not, I will take *it* by force."

17Therefore the sin of the young men was very great before the LORD, for men abhorred the offering of the LORD.

Samuel's Childhood Ministry

18But Samuel ministered before the LORD, *even as* a child, wearing a linen ephod. 19Moreover his mother used to make him a little robe, and bring *it* to him year by year when she came up with her husband to offer the yearly sacrifice. 20And Ē'lī would bless El·kā'nah and his wife, and say, "The LORD give you descendants from this woman for the loan that was given to the LORD." Then they would go to their own home.

21And the LORD visited Hannah, so that she conceived and bore three sons and two daughters. Meanwhile the child Samuel grew before the LORD.

Prophecy Against Eli's Household

22Now Ē'lī was very old; and he heard everything his sons did to all Israel,[a] and how they lay with the women who assembled at the door of the tabernacle of meeting. 23So he said to them, "Why do you do such things? For I hear of your evil dealings from all the people. 24No, my sons! For *it is* not a good report that I hear. You make the LORD's people transgress. 25If one man sins against another, God will judge him. But if a man sins against the LORD, who will intercede for him?" Nevertheless they did not heed the voice of their father, because the LORD desired to kill them.

26And the child Samuel grew in stature, and in favor both with the LORD and men.

27Then a man of God came to Ē'lī and said to him, "Thus says the LORD: 'Did I not clearly reveal Myself to the house of your father when they were in Egypt in Pharaoh's house? 28Did I not choose him out of all the tribes of Israel *to be* My priest, to offer upon My altar, to burn incense, and to wear an ephod before Me? And did I not give to the house of your father all the offerings of the children of Israel made by fire? 29Why do you kick at My sacrifice and My offering which I have commanded *in My* dwelling place, and honor your sons more than Me, to make yourselves fat with the best of all the offerings of Israel My people?' 30Therefore the LORD God of Israel says: 'I said indeed *that* your house and the house of your father would walk before Me forever.' But now the LORD says: 'Far be it from Me; for those who honor Me I will honor, and those who despise Me shall be lightly esteemed. 31Behold, the days are

2:22 [a]Following Masoretic Text, Targum, and Vulgate; Dead Sea Scrolls and Septuagint omit the rest of this verse.

covenant. They were not looking on their positions as places of solemn responsibility but as positions of privilege and self-serving opportunity. **did not know the LORD**: This was not an intellectual lack, but a moral and spiritual deficiency. In the Bible "knowing God" does not mean having information about Him, but rather having personal acquaintance with Him (John 17:3). There is a contrast throughout these first four chapters between the evil of Eli's natural sons and the flowering spirituality of Samuel, Eli's foster son.

coming that I will cut off your arm and the
arm of your father's house, so that there
will not be an old man in your house.
32And you will see an enemy *in My*
dwelling place, *despite* all the good which
God does for Israel. And there shall not be
an old man in your house forever. 33But
any of your men *whom* I do not cut off from
My altar shall consume your eyes and
grieve your heart. And all the descendants
of your house shall die in the flower of
their age. 34Now this *shall be* a sign to you
that will come upon your two sons, on
Hoph'nī and Phin'e·has: in one day they
shall die, both of them. 35Then I will raise
up for Myself a faithful priest *who* shall do
according to what *is* in My heart and in My
mind. I will build him a sure house, and he
shall walk before My anointed forever.
36And it shall come to pass that everyone
who is left in your house will come *and*
bow down to him for a piece of silver and
a morsel of bread, and say, "Please, put me
in one of the priestly positions, that I may
eat a piece of bread." ' "

CHAPTER 3

Samuel's First Prophecy

Now the boy Samuel ministered to the
LORD before Ē'lī. And the word of the LORD
was rare in those days; *there was* no wide-
spread revelation. 2And it came to pass at
that time, while Ē'lī *was* lying down in his
place, and when his eyes had begun to
grow so dim that he could not see, 3and be-
fore the lamp of God went out in the taber-
nacle[a] of the LORD where the ark of God
was, and while Samuel was lying down,
4that the LORD called Samuel. And he an-
swered, "Here I am!" 5So he ran to Ē'lī and
said, "Here I am, for you called me."

And he said, "I did not call; lie down
again." And he went and lay down.

6Then the LORD called yet again, "Sam-
uel!"

So Samuel arose and went to Ē'lī, and
said, "Here I am, for you called me." He
answered, "I did not call, my son; lie down
again." 7(Now Samuel did not yet know
the LORD, nor was the word of the LORD yet
revealed to him.)

8And the LORD called Samuel again the
third time. So he arose and went to Ē'lī,
and said, "Here I am, for you did call me."

Then Ē'lī perceived that the LORD had
called the boy. 9Therefore Ē'lī said to Sam-
uel, "Go, lie down; and it shall be, if He
calls you, that you must say, 'Speak, LORD,
for Your servant hears.' " So Samuel went
and lay down in his place.

10Now the LORD came and stood and
called as at other times, "Samuel! Samuel!"

And Samuel answered, "Speak, for Your
servant hears."

11Then the LORD said to Samuel: "Be-
hold, I will do something in Israel at which
both ears of everyone who hears it will tin-
gle. 12In that day I will perform against Ē'lī
all that I have spoken concerning his
house, from beginning to end. 13For I have
told him that I will judge his house forever
for the iniquity which he knows, because
his sons made themselves vile, and he did
not restrain them. 14And therefore I have
sworn to the house of Ē'lī that the iniquity
of Ē'lī's house shall not be atoned for by
sacrifice or offering forever."

15So Samuel lay down until morning,[a]
and opened the doors of the house of the
LORD. And Samuel was afraid to tell Ē'lī
the vision. 16Then Ē'lī called Samuel and
said, "Samuel, my son!"

He answered, "Here I am."

17And he said, "What *is* the word that *the*

3:3 [a]Hebrew *heykal,* palace or temple
3:15 [a]Following Masoretic Text, Targum, and Vulgate; Septuagint adds *and he arose in the morning.*

3:1 The spiritual degradation of the Israelites greatly hindered their fellowship with the Lord. Since so few were receptive to God's Word, it rarely came.

3:17 God do so to you, and more also: A form of oath used in the books of Samuel and Kings. It invoked the most dire consequences for failure to speak the truth.

LORD spoke to you? Please do not hide *it* from me. God do so to you, and more also, if you hide anything from me of all the things that He said to you." 18Then Samuel told him everything, and hid nothing from him. And he said, "It *is* the LORD. Let Him do what seems good to Him."

19So Samuel grew, and the LORD was with him and let none of his words fall to the ground. 20And all Israel from Dan to Bē·er·shē'ba knew that Samuel *had been* established as a prophet of the LORD. 21Then the LORD appeared again in Shī'lōh. For the LORD revealed Himself to Samuel in Shī'lōh by the word of the LORD.

CHAPTER 4

And the word of Samuel came to all Israel.[a]

The Ark of God Captured

Now Israel went out to battle against the Phi·lis'tines, and encamped beside Eb·e·nē'zer; and the Phi·lis'tines encamped in Ā'phek. 2Then the Phi·lis'tines put themselves in battle array against Israel. And when they joined battle, Israel was defeated by the Phi·lis'tines, who killed about four thousand men of the army in the field. 3And when the people had come into the camp, the elders of Israel said, "Why has the LORD defeated us today before the Phi·lis'tines? Let us bring the ark of the covenant of the LORD from Shī'lōh to us, that when it comes among us it may save us from the hand of our enemies." 4So the people sent to Shī'lōh, that they might bring from there the ark of the covenant of the LORD of hosts, who dwells *between* the cherubim. And the two sons of Ē'lī, Hoph'nī and Phin'e·has, *were* there with the ark of the covenant of God.

5And when the ark of the covenant of the LORD came into the camp, all Israel shouted so loudly that the earth shook. 6Now when the Phi·lis'tines heard the noise of the shout, they said, "What *does* the sound of this great shout in the camp of the Hebrews *mean?*" Then they understood that the ark of the LORD had come into the camp. 7So the Phi·lis'tines were afraid, for they said, "God has come into the camp!" And they said, "Woe to us! For such a thing has never happened before. 8Woe to us! Who will deliver us from the hand of these mighty gods? These *are* the gods who struck the Egyptians with all the plagues in the wilderness. 9Be strong and conduct yourselves like men, you Phi·lis'tines, that you do not become servants of the Hebrews, as they have been to you. Conduct yourselves like men, and fight!"

10So the Phi·lis'tines fought, and Israel was defeated, and every man fled to his tent. There was a very great slaughter, and there fell of Israel thirty thousand foot soldiers. 11Also the ark of God was captured; and the two sons of Ē'lī, Hoph'nī and Phin'e·has, died.

Death of Eli

12Then a man of Benjamin ran from the battle line the same day, and came to Shī'lōh with his clothes torn and dirt on his head. 13Now when he came, there was Ē'lī,

4:1 [a]Following Masoretic Text and Targum; Septuagint and Vulgate add *And it came to pass in those days that the Philistines gathered themselves together to fight;* Septuagint adds further *against Israel.*

4:3 The Israelites were trying to use the **ark** as a magic charm, rather than as a focus for obedient living. But trying to use God magically never works (v. 10). He would not protect them because they had broken the covenant and did not honor Him.

4:4 That God **dwells between the cherubim** (the plural form of "cherub") is a frequent statement in the OT (Num. 7:89; 2 Sam. 6:2). The cherubim were two angel-like figures facing each other with wings extended over the mercy seat, the covering of **the ark of the covenant**. The ark symbolized the presence of the Lord in a special way.

4:8 Although their remark demonstrates a lack of understanding about the nature of God, the Philistines regard Him with more respect than do the Israelites.

sitting on a seat by the wayside watching,[a] for his heart trembled for the ark of God. And when the man came into the city and told *it,* all the city cried out. 14When Ē′lī heard the noise of the outcry, he said, "What *does* the sound of this tumult *mean?*" And the man came quickly and told Ē′lī. 15Ē′lī was ninety-eight years old, and his eyes were so dim that he could not see.

16Then the man said to Ē′lī, "I *am* he who came from the battle. And I fled today from the battle line."

And he said, "What happened, my son?"

17So the messenger answered and said, "Israel has fled before the Phi·lis′tines, and there has been a great slaughter among the people. Also your two sons, Hoph′nī and Phin′e·has, are dead; and the ark of God has been captured."

18Then it happened, when he made mention of the ark of God, that Ē′lī fell off the seat backward by the side of the gate; and his neck was broken and he died, for the man was old and heavy. And he had judged Israel forty years.

Ichabod

19Now his daughter-in-law, Phin′e·has′ wife, was with child, *due* to be delivered; and when she heard the news that the ark of God was captured, and that her father-in-law and her husband were dead, she bowed herself and gave birth, for her labor pains came upon her. 20And about the time of her death the women who stood by her said to her, "Do not fear, for you have borne a son." But she did not answer, nor did she regard *it.* 21Then she named the child Ich′a·bod,[a] saying, "The glory has departed from Israel!" because the ark of God had been captured and because of her father-in-law and her husband. 22And she said, "The glory has departed from Israel, for the ark of God has been captured."

CHAPTER 5

The Philistines and the Ark

Then the Phi·lis′tines took the ark of God and brought it from Eb·e·nē′zer to Ash′dod. 2When the Phi·lis′tines took the ark of God, they brought it into the house of Dā′gon[a] and set it by Dā′gon. 3And when the people of Ash′dod arose early in the morning, there was Dā′gon, fallen on its face to the earth before the ark of the LORD. So they took Dā′gon and set it in its place again. 4And when they arose early the next morning, there was Dā′gon, fallen on its face to the ground before the ark of the LORD. The head of Dā′gon and both the palms of its hands *were* broken off on the threshold; only Dā′gon's torso[a] was left of it. 5Therefore neither the priests of Dā′gon nor any who come into Dā′gon's house tread on the threshold of Dā′gon in Ash′dod to this day.

6But the hand of the LORD was heavy on the people of Ash′dod, and He ravaged

4:13 [a]Following Masoretic Text and Vulgate; Septuagint reads *beside the gate watching the road.*
4:21 [a]Literally *Inglorious* 5:2 [a]A Philistine idol
5:4 [a]Following Septuagint, Syriac, Targum, and Vulgate; Masoretic Text reads *Dagon.*

4:21, 22 The glory has departed: This was a significant defeat for Israel which was remembered as the time when God "forsook the tabernacle of Shiloh" (see Ps. 78:60, 61 and note).

5:1–5 Although God would not allow the Israelites to use the **ark** in a magical way, neither would He allow it to appear that the Philistine gods had defeated Him.

5:2 Dagon: The Philistine idol-god. He was probably thought of as a deity who controlled vegetation since the name appears to be derived from a term meaning "grain." The Israelites made no distinction between the idol and the god it was supposed to represent. When the idol was shattered (vv. 4, 5), it was Dagon who was defeated.

them and struck them with tumors,[a] *both*
Ash'dod and its territory. 7And when the
men of Ash'dod saw how *it was,* they said,
"The ark of the God of Israel must not re-
main with us, for His hand is harsh toward
us and Dā'gon our god." 8Therefore they
sent and gathered to themselves all the
lords of the Phi·lis'tines, and said, "What
shall we do with the ark of the God of Is-
rael?"

And they answered, "Let the ark of the
God of Israel be carried away to Gath." So
they carried the ark of the God of Israel
away. 9So it was, after they had carried it
away, that the hand of the LORD was
against the city with a very great destruc-
tion; and He struck the men of the city,
both small and great, and tumors broke
out on them.

10Therefore they sent the ark of God to
Ek'ron. So it was, as the ark of God came to
Ek'ron, that the Ek'ron·ītes cried out, say-
ing, "They have brought the ark of the God
of Israel to us, to kill us and our people!"
11So they sent and gathered together all the
lords of the Phi·lis'tines, and said, "Send
away the ark of the God of Israel, and let it
go back to its own place, so that it does not
kill us and our people." For there was a
deadly destruction throughout all the city;
the hand of God was very heavy there.
12And the men who did not die were
stricken with the tumors, and the cry of the
city went up to heaven.

CHAPTER 6

The Ark Returned to Israel

Now the ark of the LORD was in the
country of the Phi·lis'tines seven months.
2And the Phi·lis'tines called for the priests
and the diviners, saying, "What shall we
do with the ark of the LORD? Tell us how
we should send it to its place."

3So they said, "If you send away the ark
of the God of Israel, do not send it empty;
but by all means return *it* to Him *with* a
trespass offering. Then you will be healed,
and it will be known to you why His hand
is not removed from you."

4Then they said, "What *is* the trespass
offering which we shall return to Him?"

They answered, "Five golden tumors
and five golden rats, *according to* the num-
ber of the lords of the Phi·lis'tines. For the
same plague *was* on all of you and on your
lords. 5Therefore you shall make images of
your tumors and images of your rats that
ravage the land, and you shall give glory
to the God of Israel; perhaps He will
lighten His hand from you, from your
gods, and from your land. 6Why then do
you harden your hearts as the Egyptians
and Pharaoh hardened their hearts? When
He did mighty things among them, did
they not let the people go, that they might
depart? 7Now therefore, make a new cart,
take two milk cows which have never been
yoked, and hitch the cows to the cart; and
take their calves home, away from them.
8Then take the ark of the LORD and set it on
the cart; and put the articles of gold which
you are returning to Him *as* a trespass of-
fering in a chest by its side. Then send it
away, and let it go. 9And watch: if it goes
up the road to its own territory, to Beth
Shem'esh, *then* He has done us this great
evil. But if not, then we shall know that *it is*
not His hand *that* struck us—it happened
to us by chance."

10Then the men did so; they took two
milk cows and hitched them to the cart,
and shut up their calves at home. 11And
they set the ark of the LORD on the cart, and
the chest with the gold rats and the images
of their tumors. 12Then the cows headed
straight for the road to Beth Shem'esh, *and*

5:6 [a]Probably bubonic plague. Septuagint and Vulgate add here *And in the midst of their land rats sprang up, and there was a great death panic in the city.*

6:7–9 This would provide clear evidence of the supernatural because a cow would never willingly leave her calf.

went along the highway, lowing as they
went, and did not turn aside to the right
hand or the left. And the lords of the Phi-
lis'tines went after them to the border of
Beth Shem'esh.

13 Now *the people of* Beth Shem'esh *were*
reaping their wheat harvest in the valley;
and they lifted their eyes and saw the ark,
and rejoiced to see *it*. 14 Then the cart came
into the field of Joshua of Beth Shem'esh,
and stood there; a large stone *was* there. So
they split the wood of the cart and offered
the cows as a burnt offering to the LORD.
15 The Lē'vītes took down the ark of the
LORD and the chest that *was* with it, in
which *were* the articles of gold, and put
them on the large stone. Then the men of
Beth Shem'esh offered burnt offerings and
made sacrifices the same day to the LORD.
16 So when the five lords of the Phi·lis'tines
had seen *it*, they returned to Ek'ron the
same day.

17 These *are* the golden tumors which the
Phi·lis'tines returned *as* a trespass offering
to the LORD: one for Ash'dod, one for
Gā'za, one for Ash'ke·lon, one for Gath,
one for Ek'ron; 18 and the golden rats, *ac-*
cording to the number of all the cities of the
Phi·lis'tines *belonging* to the five lords, *both*
fortified cities and country villages, even
as far as the large *stone of* Abel on which
they set the ark of the LORD, *which stone re-*
mains to this day in the field of Joshua of
Beth Shem'esh.

19 Then He struck the men of Beth
Shem'esh, because they had looked into
the ark of the LORD. He struck fifty thou-
sand and seventy men[a] of the people, and
the people lamented because the LORD had
struck the people with a great slaughter.

The Ark at Kirjath Jearim

20 And the men of Beth Shem'esh said,
"Who is able to stand before this holy LORD
God? And to whom shall it go up from
us?" 21 So they sent messengers to the in-
habitants of Kir'jath Jē'a·rim, saying, "The
Phi·lis'tines have brought back the ark of
the LORD; come down *and* take it up with
you."

CHAPTER 7

Then the men of Kir'jath Jē'a·rim came
and took the ark of the LORD, and brought
it into the house of A·bin'a·dab on the hill,
and consecrated El·ē·ā'zar his son to keep
the ark of the LORD.

Samuel Judges Israel

2 So it was that the ark remained in
Kir'jath Jē'a·rim a long time; it was there
twenty years. And all the house of Israel
lamented after the LORD.

3 Then Samuel spoke to all the house of
Israel, saying, "If you return to the LORD
with all your hearts, *then* put away the for-
eign gods and the Ash'to·reths[a] from
among you, and prepare your hearts for
the LORD, and serve Him only; and He
will deliver you from the hand of the
Phi·lis'tines." 4 So the children of Israel put
away the Bā'als and the Ash'to·reths,[a] and
served the LORD only.

5 And Samuel said, "Gather all Israel to
Miz'pah, and I will pray to the LORD for
you." 6 So they gathered together at
Miz'pah, drew water, and poured *it* out be-

6:19 [a]Or *He struck seventy men of the people and fifty oxen of a man* 7:3 [a]Canaanite goddesses
7:4 [a]Canaanite goddesses

6:19 looked into the ark: They actually "looked with profane curiosity," an act forbidden under penalty of death in Num. 4:19, 20. Men of the Levitical tribe would certainly have been aware of the law in this regard.

7:2 At last the Israelites were turning their hearts back to God. However, the ark remained at Kirjath Jearim until David retrieved it nearly 100 years after its capture.

7:3, 4 with all your hearts: Complete commitment. **Ashtoreths** were images of Astarte, the Canaanite goddess of fertility and sex. The foreign gods included the Baals, the male gods of the pagan fertility cults.

SAMUEL: A LIFE OF SERVICE

The prophet Samuel, the last of the Old Testament judges, exercised every ounce of his spiritual, emotional, and physical energy in the work of the Lord. Having been dedicated to the Lord even before his birth, Samuel served the Lord in the temple from the time he was a small child (1 Sam. 2:18). Under the direction of Eli the priest, he learned to listen for and respond to God's call at an early age (3:9, 10), and as he matured, he walked closely with his Lord (v. 19).

This spiritual intimacy prepared Samuel to be a man of prayer throughout his ministry, frequently interceding with God on behalf of the children of Israel. Even when they sinfully asked for a king so they could be like "all the nations," Samuel's rebuke was tempered with a commitment to pray on their behalf: "Far be it from me that I should sin against the LORD in ceasing to pray for you" (12:23).

Through his close fellowship with God, Samuel also learned to love Israel deeply. When he discovered Saul's sin in failing to utterly destroy the Amalekites and their possessions as the Lord had commanded, "it grieved Samuel, and he cried out to the LORD all night" (15:11). He mourned when God determined to end Saul's reign over Israel because of his sin (15:35).

In addition to being a man of spiritual and emotional sensitivity, Samuel was a physically active man. He worked throughout the year as a judge, traveling from his home in Ramah to Bethel, Gilgal, and Mizpah. He apparently maintained excellent health even throughout his old age, for he "judged Israel all the days of his life" (7:15).

Today, we can follow Samuel's example in serving the Lord in every area of our lives. Fellowship with the Lord and intercessory prayer should be a regular part of each day. As we achieve spiritual intimacy with God, our hearts will become sensitive to the sin and pain in the world around us, and we will be motivated to act as the Lord directs. ✦

fore the LORD. And they fasted that day,
and said there, "We have sinned against
the LORD." And Samuel judged the chil-
dren of Israel at Miz'pah.
7Now when the Phi·lis'tines heard that
the children of Israel had gathered to-
gether at Miz'pah, the lords of the Phi-
lis'tines went up against Israel. And when
the children of Israel heard *of it,* they were
afraid of the Phi·lis'tines. 8So the children
of Israel said to Samuel, "Do not cease to
cry out to the LORD our God for us, that He
may save us from the hand of the Phi-
lis'tines."

9And Samuel took a suckling lamb and offered *it as* a whole burnt offering to the LORD. Then Samuel cried out to the LORD for Israel, and the LORD answered him. 10Now as Samuel was offering up the burnt offering, the Phi·lis'tines drew near to battle against Israel. But the LORD thundered with a loud thunder upon the Phi·lis'tines that day, and so confused them that they were overcome before Israel. 11And the men of Israel went out of Miz'pah and pursued the Phi·lis'tines, and drove them back as far as below Beth Car. 12Then Samuel took a stone and set *it* up between Miz'pah and Shen, and called its name Eb·e·nē'zer,[a] saying, "Thus far the LORD has helped us."

13So the Phi·lis'tines were subdued, and they did not come anymore into the territory of Israel. And the hand of the LORD was against the Phi·lis'tines all the days of Samuel. 14Then the cities which the Phi·lis'tines had taken from Israel were restored to Israel, from Ek'ron to Gath; and Israel recovered its territory from the hands of the Phi·lis'tines. Also there was peace between Israel and the Am'o·rītes.

15And Samuel judged Israel all the days of his life. 16He went from year to year on a circuit to Beth'el, Gil'gal, and Miz'pah, and judged Israel in all those places. 17But he always returned to Rā'mah, for his home *was* there. There he judged Israel, and there he built an altar to the LORD.

CHAPTER 8

Israel Demands a King

Now it came to pass when Samuel was old that he made his sons judges over Israel. 2The name of his firstborn was Jō'el, and the name of his second, A·bī'jah; *they were* judges in Bē·er·shē'ba. 3But his sons did not walk in his ways; they turned aside after dishonest gain, took bribes, and perverted justice.

4Then all the elders of Israel gathered together and came to Samuel at Rā'mah, 5and said to him, "Look, you are old, and your sons do not walk in your ways. Now make us a king to judge us like all the nations."

6But the thing displeased Samuel when they said, "Give us a king to judge us." So Samuel prayed to the LORD. 7And the LORD said to Samuel, "Heed the voice of the people in all that they say to you; for they have not rejected you, but they have rejected Me, that I should not reign over them. 8According to all the works which they have done since the day that I brought them up out of Egypt, even to this day—with which they have forsaken Me and served other gods—so they are doing to you also. 9Now therefore, heed their voice. However, you shall solemnly forewarn them, and show them the behavior of the king who will reign over them."

10So Samuel told all the words of the LORD to the people who asked him for a king. 11And he said, "This will be the behavior of the king who will reign over you: He will take your sons and appoint *them* for his own chariots and *to be* his horsemen, and *some* will run before his chariots. 12He will appoint captains over his thousands and captains over his fifties, *will set*

7:12 [a]Literally *Stone of Help*

7:10 The thunder is especially significant since it was Baal whom the Canaanites thought to be the god of the thunderstorm. Only the LORD is God!

8:1–5 Samuel's **sons** (v. 3), as Eli's before him, were unworthy of their father. Although Samuel (unlike Eli) is not blamed for his sons' ways, as a father he was probably grieved that their behavior provided the excuse for the people's sinful demand.

8:6, 7 A faithful religious leader prays to **the LORD** and listens to the concerns of the people. In this case, the deeper motive of the people in seeking a king (vv. 19, 20) amounted to a rejection of God's direct authority.

8:10–18 The picture Samuel gave was typical of Near Eastern kings: oppressive, greedy,

some to plow his ground and reap his har-
vest, and *some* to make his weapons of war
and equipment for his chariots. 13He will
take your daughters *to be* perfumers,
cooks, and bakers. 14And he will take the
best of your fields, your vineyards, and
your olive groves, and give *them* to his ser-
vants. 15He will take a tenth of your grain
and your vintage, and give it to his officers
and servants. 16And he will take your male
servants, your female servants, your finest
young men,[a] and your donkeys, and put
them to his work. 17He will take a tenth of
your sheep. And you will be his servants.
18And you will cry out in that day because
of your king whom you have chosen for
yourselves, and the LORD will not hear you
in that day."

19Nevertheless the people refused to
obey the voice of Samuel; and they said,
"No, but we will have a king over us, 20that
we also may be like all the nations, and
that our king may judge us and go out be-
fore us and fight our battles."

21And Samuel heard all the words of the
people, and he repeated them in the hear-
ing of the LORD. 22So the LORD said to Sam-
uel, "Heed their voice, and make them a
king."

And Samuel said to the men of Israel,
"Every man go to his city."

CHAPTER 9

Saul Chosen to Be King

There was a man of Benjamin whose
name *was* Kish the son of A·bī'el, the son of
Zē'ror, the son of Be·chō'rath, the son of
A·phī'ah, a Ben'ja·mīte, a mighty man of
power. 2And he had a choice and hand-
some son whose name *was* Saul. *There was*
not a more handsome person than he
among the children of Israel. From his
shoulders upward *he was* taller than any of
the people.

3Now the donkeys of Kish, Saul's father,
were lost. And Kish said to his son Saul,
"Please take one of the servants with you,
and arise, go and look for the donkeys."
4So he passed through the mountains of
Ē'phra·im and through the land of Shal'-
i·sha, but they did not find *them*. Then they
passed through the land of Shā'a·lim, and
they were not *there*. Then he passed through
the land of the Ben'ja·mītes, but they did
not find *them*.

5When they had come to the land of
Zuph, Saul said to his servant who *was*
with him, "Come, let us return, lest my fa-
ther cease *caring* about the donkeys and
become worried about us."

6And he said to him, "Look now, *there is*
in this city a man of God, and *he is* an hon-
orable man; all that he says surely comes to
pass. So let us go there; perhaps he can
show us the way that we should go."

7Then Saul said to his servant, "But
look, *if* we go, what shall we bring the
man? For the bread in our vessels is all
gone, and *there is* no present to bring to the
man of God. What do we have?"

8And the servant answered Saul again
and said, "Look, I have here at hand one-
fourth of a shekel of silver. I will give *that*
to the man of God, to tell us our way."
9(Formerly in Israel, when a man went to
inquire of God, he spoke thus: "Come, let
us go to the seer"; for *he who is* now *called* a
prophet was formerly called a seer.)

10Then Saul said to his servant, "Well
said; come, let us go." So they went to the
city where the man of God *was*.

11As they went up the hill to the city,
they met some young women going out to
draw water, and said to them, "Is the seer
here?"

12And they answered them and said,

8:16 [a]Septuagint reads *cattle*.

---

and self-serving. This compares to descriptions of the end of Solomon's reign (1 Kin. 10:14—11:13), but contrasts with prophecies of the Messiah's kingdom in Is. 9; 11; 61.

9:12 sacrifice . . . on the high place: An indication of the decline in adherence to the

"Yes, there he is, just ahead of you. Hurry now; for today he came to this city, because there is a sacrifice of the people today on the high place. [13]As soon as you come into the city, you will surely find him before he goes up to the high place to eat. For the people will not eat until he comes, because he must bless the sacrifice; afterward those who are invited will eat. Now therefore, go up, for about this time you will find him."
[14]So they went up to the city. As they were coming into the city, there was Samuel, coming out toward them on his way up to the high place.

[15]Now the LORD had told Samuel in his ear the day before Saul came, saying, [16]"Tomorrow about this time I will send you a man from the land of Benjamin, and you shall anoint him commander over My people Israel, that he may save My people from the hand of the Phi·lis′tines; for I have looked upon My people, because their cry has come to Me."

[17]So when Samuel saw Saul, the LORD said to him, "There he is, the man of whom I spoke to you. This one shall reign over My people." [18]Then Saul drew near to Samuel in the gate, and said, "Please tell me, where *is* the seer's house?"

[19]Samuel answered Saul and said, "I *am* the seer. Go up before me to the high place, for you shall eat with me today; and tomorrow I will let you go and will tell you all that *is* in your heart. [20]But as for your donkeys that were lost three days ago, do not be anxious about them, for they have been found. And on whom *is* all the desire of Israel? *Is it* not on you and on all your father's house?"

[21]And Saul answered and said, "*Am* I not a Ben′ja·mīte, of the smallest of the tribes of Israel, and my family the least of all the families of the tribe[a] of Benjamin? Why then do you speak like this to me?"

[22]Now Samuel took Saul and his servant and brought them into the hall, and had them sit in the place of honor among those who were invited; there *were* about thirty persons. [23]And Samuel said to the cook, "Bring the portion which I gave you, of which I said to you, 'Set it apart.' " [24]So the cook took up the thigh with its upper part and set *it* before Saul. And *Samuel* said, "Here it is, what was kept back. *It* was set apart for you. Eat; for until this time it has been kept for you, since I said I invited the people." So Saul ate with Samuel that day.

[25]When they had come down from the high place into the city, *Samuel* spoke with Saul on the top of the house.[a] [26]They arose early; and it was about the dawning of the day that Samuel called to Saul on the top of the house, saying, "Get up, that I may send you on your way." And Saul arose, and both of them went outside, he and Samuel.

Saul Anointed King

[27]As they were going down to the outskirts of the city, Samuel said to Saul, "Tell the servant to go on ahead of us." And he went on. "But you stand here awhile, that I may announce to you the word of God."

CHAPTER 10

Then Samuel took a flask of oil and poured *it* on his head, and kissed him and

9:21 [a]Literally *tribes* 9:25 [a]Following Masoretic Text and Targum; Septuagint omits *He spoke with Saul on the top of the house;* Septuagint and Vulgate add *And he prepared a bed for Saul on the top of the house, and he slept.*

Mosaic covenant during and after the judges period. Sacrifice was supposed to be performed only at the tabernacle (Deut. 12:2–7). If, as seems probable, the Philistines destroyed Moses' tabernacle at Shiloh when they captured the ark, this irregularity would have increased as a consequence.

9:23, 24 Saul was honored by being served the thigh, one of the portions normally reserved for the priest (see Lev. 7:31–35).

10:1 Anointing with oil was a religious rite used in the consecration of priests (Ex. 29:7),

Saul: Pride Goes Before Destruction

As the first king of Israel, Saul brought many admirable qualities to his role, but he failed to live up to his full potential.

When Samuel anointed Saul to be king, he found a tall and handsome young man who responded to the call with humility (1 Sam. 9:2, 21; 10:22). Soon after, Samuel presented Saul to the people as their king. Some people rebelled against his choice, but Saul did not respond to their insolence.

As a handsome and courageous warrior, Saul led his people in battle against the Ammonites, and his victory confirmed his fitness for the role. Some called for the deaths of those who had objected to his assumption of the throne, but Saul showed great restraint. "Not a man shall be put to death this day, for today the LORD has accomplished salvation in Israel" (11:13).

Unfortunately, Saul's humility soon gave way to pride in himself and his own exalted position. He usurped the office of the priest (13:9) and disobeyed the Lord's command to utterly destroy the Amalekites (15:9). In each instance, he tried to excuse his actions rather than accept responsibility for his sin.

Samuel confronted Saul about his sin and told him of the Lord's judgment: "Because you have rejected the word of the LORD, He also has rejected you from being king" (v. 23).

Yet even in the face of this punishment, Saul did not repent. For years he refused to surrender his throne and tried to destroy his successor. As he repeatedly failed in his attempts to rid himself of David, Saul became increasingly bitter. His hatred and jealousy ruined his relationship with his son Jonathan (20:30–34) and drove him to murder the priests of the Lord (22:17).

Saul's spiritual perception eventually deteriorated so drastically that he consulted a medium at En-Dor. He wanted to communicate with Samuel, who had died some time ago. He admitted to the prophet his miserable state: "God has departed from me and does not answer me anymore" (28:15).

Samuel responded by reminding the rebellious king of his sin and predicting the death of Saul and his sons in battle the following day. True to Samuel's prophecy, Saul's sons died in battle and Saul committed suicide, a fitting end to his years of self-destruction.

The story of Saul is certainly not a happy one, but it serves to remind us that we must be ever vigilant against sin in our lives. Saul's downward slide began when he started to regard his strength and position as more important than his relationship with God.

Like Saul, we may have strength, intelligence, and courage, but none of these mean anything without the power of God behind them. In seeking physical and mental success, we must never neglect our spiritual health. ✦

said: "*Is it* not because the LORD has
anointed you commander over His inheri-
tance?[a] 2 When you have departed from me
today, you will find two men by Rachel's
tomb in the territory of Benjamin at
Zel'zah; and they will say to you, 'The
donkeys which you went to look for have
been found. And now your father has
ceased caring about the donkeys and is
worrying about you, saying, "What shall I
do about my son?" ' 3 Then you shall go on
forward from there and come to the tere-
binth tree of Tā'bor. There three men going
up to God at Beth'el will meet you, one car-
rying three young goats, another carrying
three loaves of bread, and another carrying
a skin of wine. 4 And they will greet you
and give you two *loaves* of bread, which
you shall receive from their hands. 5 After
that you shall come to the hill of God
where the Phi·lis'tine garrison *is*. And it
will happen, when you have come there to
the city, that you will meet a group of
prophets coming down from the high
place with a stringed instrument, a tam-
bourine, a flute, and a harp before them;
and they will be prophesying. 6 Then the
Spirit of the LORD will come upon you, and
you will prophesy with them and be
turned into another man. 7 And let it be,
when these signs come to you, *that* you do
as the occasion demands; for God *is* with
you. 8 You shall go down before me to
Gil'gal; and surely I will come down to you
to offer burnt offerings *and* make sacrifices
of peace offerings. Seven days you shall
wait, till I come to you and show you what
you should do."
9 So it was, when he had turned his back
to go from Samuel, that God gave him an-
other heart; and all those signs came to
pass that day. 10 When they came there to
the hill, there was a group of prophets to
meet him; then the Spirit of God came
upon him, and he prophesied among
them. 11 And it happened, when all who
knew him formerly saw that he indeed
prophesied among the prophets, that the
people said to one another, "What *is* this
that has come upon the son of Kish? *Is* Saul
also among the prophets?" 12 Then a man
from there answered and said, "But who *is*
their father?" Therefore it became a
proverb: "*Is* Saul also among the
prophets?" 13 And when he had finished
prophesying, he went to the high place.
14 Then Saul's uncle said to him and his
servant, "Where did you go?"
So he said, "To look for the donkeys.
When we saw that *they were* nowhere *to be
found*, we went to Samuel."
15 And Saul's uncle said, "Tell me, please,
what Samuel said to you."
16 So Saul said to his uncle, "He told us
plainly that the donkeys had been found."
But about the matter of the kingdom, he
did not tell him what Samuel had said.

Saul Proclaimed King

17 Then Samuel called the people to-
gether to the LORD at Miz'pah, 18 and said to
the children of Israel, "Thus says the LORD
God of Israel: 'I brought up Israel out of
Egypt, and delivered you from the hand of

10:1 [a]Following Masoretic Text, Targum, and Vulgate; Septuagint reads *His people Israel; and you shall rule the people of the Lord;* Septuagint and Vulgate add *And you shall deliver His people from the hands of their enemies all around them. And this shall be a sign to you, that God has anointed you to be a prince.*

---

prophets, and kings (1 Kin. 19:16). The king, as well as the prophet and the priest, was to serve under God's direction.

10:9, 10 another heart: The earliest direct biblical reference to the inner changes God makes in those who serve Him. **the Spirit of God came upon him**: God gave Saul an inner unction validating the external anointing with oil. This was primarily an enduement of the Spirit for skill, understanding, or power as elsewhere in the OT rather than the inner cleansing as at Pentecost (Acts 15:8, 9) and elsewere in the NT. However, the element of cleansing was present in a measure even in the OT (v. 9).

the Egyptians *and* from the hand of all
kingdoms and from those who oppressed
you.' 19But you have today rejected your
God, who Himself saved you from all your
adversities and your tribulations; and you
have said to Him, 'No, set a king over us!'
Now therefore, present yourselves before
the LORD by your tribes and by your
clans."[a]

20And when Samuel had caused all the
tribes of Israel to come near, the tribe of
Benjamin was chosen. 21When he had
caused the tribe of Benjamin to come near
by their families, the family of Mā'trī was
chosen. And Saul the son of Kish was cho-
sen. But when they sought him, he could
not be found. 22Therefore they inquired of
the LORD further, "Has the man come here
yet?"

And the LORD answered, "There he is,
hidden among the equipment."

23So they ran and brought him from
there; and when he stood among the peo-
ple, he was taller than any of the people
from his shoulders upward. 24And Samuel
said to all the people, "Do you see him
whom the LORD has chosen, that *there is* no
one like him among all the people?"

So all the people shouted and said,
"Long live the king!"

25Then Samuel explained to the people
the behavior of royalty, and wrote *it* in a
book and laid *it* up before the LORD. And
Samuel sent all the people away, every
man to his house. 26And Saul also went
home to Gib'ē·ah; and valiant *men* went
with him, whose hearts God had touched.
27But some rebels said, "How can this man
save us?" So they despised him, and
brought him no presents. But he held his
peace.

CHAPTER 11

Saul Saves Jabesh Gilead

Then Nā'hash the Am'mon·īte came up
and encamped against Jā'besh Gil'ē·ad;
and all the men of Jā'besh said to Nā'hash,
"Make a covenant with us, and we will
serve you."

2And Nā'hash the Am'mon·īte an-
swered them, "On this *condition* I will
make *a covenant* with you, that I may put
out all your right eyes, and bring reproach
on all Israel."

3Then the elders of Jā'besh said to him,
"Hold off for seven days, that we may send
messengers to all the territory of Israel.
And then, if *there is* no one to save us, we
will come out to you."

4So the messengers came to Gib'ē·ah of
Saul and told the news in the hearing of the
people. And all the people lifted up their
voices and wept. 5Now there was Saul,
coming behind the herd from the field; and
Saul said, "What *troubles* the people, that
they weep?" And they told him the words
of the men of Jā'besh. 6Then the Spirit of
God came upon Saul when he heard this
news, and his anger was greatly aroused.
7So he took a yoke of oxen and cut them in
pieces, and sent *them* throughout all the
territory of Israel by the hands of messen-
gers, saying, "Whoever does not go out
with Saul and Samuel to battle, so it shall
be done to his oxen."

And the fear of the LORD fell on the peo-
ple, and they came out with one consent.
8When he numbered them in Bē'zek, the
children of Israel were three hundred

10:19 [a]Literally *thousands*

10:20 Although Samuel had already anointed Saul, his appointment as king was confirmed publicly through the casting of lots so the people could see for themselves who had been chosen.

11:6 The **Spirit of God** came upon Saul in supernatural empowerment just as He did upon the earlier judges. Saul was still functioning much as the earlier judges, supporting himself and having no standing army. Although he had the title of king, he had not as yet taken a king's prerogatives.

thousand, and the men of Judah thirty thousand. 9And they said to the messengers who came, "Thus you shall say to the men of Jā′besh Gil′ē·ad: 'Tomorrow, by *the time* the sun is hot, you shall have help.' " Then the messengers came and reported *it* to the men of Jā′besh, and they were glad. 10Therefore the men of Jā′besh said, "Tomorrow we will come out to you, and you may do with us whatever seems good to you."

11So it was, on the next day, that Saul put the people in three companies; and they came into the midst of the camp in the morning watch, and killed Am′mon·ītes until the heat of the day. And it happened that those who survived were scattered, so that no two of them were left together.

12Then the people said to Samuel, "Who *is* he who said, 'Shall Saul reign over us?' Bring the men, that we may put them to death."

13But Saul said, "Not a man shall be put to death this day, for today the LORD has accomplished salvation in Israel."

14Then Samuel said to the people, "Come, let us go to Gil′gal and renew the kingdom there." 15So all the people went to Gil′gal, and there they made Saul king before the LORD in Gil′gal. There they made sacrifices of peace offerings before the LORD, and there Saul and all the men of Israel rejoiced greatly.

CHAPTER 12

Samuel's Address at Saul's Coronation

Now Samuel said to all Israel: "Indeed I have heeded your voice in all that you said to me, and have made a king over you. 2And now here is the king, walking before you; and I am old and gray headed, and look, my sons *are* with you. I have walked before you from my childhood to this day. 3Here I am. Witness against me before the LORD and before His anointed: Whose ox have I taken, or whose donkey have I taken, or whom have I cheated? Whom have I oppressed, or from whose hand have I received *any* bribe with which to blind my eyes? I will restore *it* to you."

4And they said, "You have not cheated us or oppressed us, nor have you taken anything from any man's hand."

5Then he said to them, "The LORD *is* witness against you, and His anointed *is* witness this day, that you have not found anything in my hand."

And they answered, "*He is* witness."

6Then Samuel said to the people, "*It is* the LORD who raised up Moses and Aaron, and who brought your fathers up from the land of Egypt. 7Now therefore, stand still, that I may reason with you before the LORD concerning all the righteous acts of the LORD which He did to you and your fathers: 8When Jacob had gone into Egypt,[a] and your fathers cried out to the LORD, then the LORD sent Moses and Aaron, who brought your fathers out of Egypt and made them dwell in this place. 9And when they forgot the LORD their God, He sold them into the hand of Sis′e·ra, commander of the army of Hā′zor, into the hand of the Phi·lis′tines, and into the hand of the king of Mō′ab; and they fought against them. 10Then they cried out to the LORD, and said, 'We have sinned, because we have forsaken the LORD and served the Bā′als and Ash′to·reths;[a] but now deliver us from the hand of our enemies, and we will serve You.' 11And the LORD sent Jer·ub·bā′al,[a] Bē′dan,[b] Jeph′thah, and Samuel,[c] and de-

12:8 [a]Following Masoretic Text, Targum, and Vulgate; Septuagint adds *and the Egyptians afflicted them.* 12:10 [a]Canaanite goddesses 12:11 [a]Syriac reads *Deborah;* Targum reads *Gideon.* [b]Septuagint and Syriac read *Barak;* Targum reads *Simson.* [c]Syriac reads *Simson.*

11:13 Salvation is the work of the Lord both in the OT and the NT. Here it is used to describe deliverance from physical danger.

12:1–25 This passage marks the conclusion of the time of the judges; now the Israelites would look to a king for leadership.

livered you out of the hand of your enemies on every side; and you dwelt in safety. 12And when you saw that Nā'hash king of the Am'mon·ītes came against you, you said to me, 'No, but a king shall reign over us,' when the LORD your God *was* your king.

13"Now therefore, here is the king whom you have chosen *and* whom you have desired. And take note, the LORD has set a king over you. 14If you fear the LORD and serve Him and obey His voice, and do not rebel against the commandment of the LORD, then both you and the king who reigns over you will continue following the LORD your God. 15However, if you do not obey the voice of the LORD, but rebel against the commandment of the LORD, then the hand of the LORD will be against you, as *it was* against your fathers.

16"Now therefore, stand and see this great thing which the LORD will do before your eyes: 17*Is* today not the wheat harvest? I will call to the LORD, and He will send thunder and rain, that you may perceive and see that your wickedness *is* great, which you have done in the sight of the LORD, in asking a king for yourselves."

18So Samuel called to the LORD, and the LORD sent thunder and rain that day; and all the people greatly feared the LORD and Samuel.

19And all the people said to Samuel, "Pray for your servants to the LORD your God, that we may not die; for we have added to all our sins the evil of asking a king for ourselves."

20Then Samuel said to the people, "Do not fear. You have done all this wickedness; yet do not turn aside from following the LORD, but serve the LORD with all your heart. 21And do not turn aside; for *then you* *would go* after empty things which cannot profit or deliver, for they *are* nothing. 22For the LORD will not forsake His people, for His great name's sake, because it has pleased the LORD to make you His people. 23Moreover, as for me, far be it from me that I should sin against the LORD in ceasing to pray for you; but I will teach you the good and the right way. 24Only fear the LORD, and serve Him in truth with all your heart; for consider what great things He has done for you. 25But if you still do wickedly, you shall be swept away, both you and your king."

I pray that my child does not turn aside from following You, Lord, but serves You with all his heart. I pray that he does not turn aside, for then he would go after empty things which cannot profit or deliver, for they are nothing. For You will not forsake him, for Your great name's sake, because it has pleased You to make him Yours.

adapted from 1 Samuel 12:20–22

CHAPTER 13

Saul's Unlawful Sacrifice

Saul reigned one year; and when he had reigned two years over Israel,[a] 2Saul chose for himself three thousand *men* of Israel. Two thousand were with Saul in Mich'mash and in the mountains of Beth'el, and a thousand were with Jonathan in Gib'ē·ah

13:1 [a]The Hebrew is difficult (compare 2 Samuel 5:4; 2 Kings 14:2; see also 2 Samuel 2:10; Acts 13:21).

12:23 Despite the people's rejection of him, Samuel continued steadfastly to pray for them and urge them to follow the Lord. He did not give up his work simply because Saul had entered the picture.

of Benjamin. The rest of the people he sent
away, every man to his tent.
3And Jonathan attacked the garrison of
the Phi·lis'tines that *was* in Gē'ba, and the
Phi·lis'tines heard *of it*. Then Saul blew the
trumpet throughout all the land, saying,
"Let the Hebrews hear!" 4Now all Israel
heard it said *that* Saul had attacked a garri-
son of the Phi·lis'tines, and *that* Israel had
also become an abomination to the Phi-
lis'tines. And the people were called to-
gether to Saul at Gil'gal.
5Then the Phi·lis'tines gathered together
to fight with Israel, thirty[a] thousand chari-
ots and six thousand horsemen, and peo-
ple as the sand which *is* on the seashore in
multitude. And they came up and en-
camped in Mich'mash, to the east of Beth
Ā'ven. 6When the men of Israel saw that
they were in danger (for the people were
distressed), then the people hid in caves, in
thickets, in rocks, in holes, and in pits.
7And *some of* the Hebrews crossed over the
Jordan to the land of Gad and Gil'ē·ad.
As for Saul, he *was* still in Gil'gal, and all
the people followed him trembling. 8Then
he waited seven days, according to the
time set by Samuel. But Samuel did not
come to Gil'gal; and the people were scat-
tered from him. 9So Saul said, "Bring a
burnt offering and peace offerings here to
me." And he offered the burnt offering.
10Now it happened, as soon as he had fin-
ished presenting the burnt offering, that
Samuel came; and Saul went out to meet
him, that he might greet him.
11And Samuel said, "What have you
done?"
Saul said, "When I saw that the people
were scattered from me, and *that* you did
not come within the days appointed, and
that the Phi·lis'tines gathered together at
Mich'mash, 12then I said, 'The Phi·lis'tines
will now come down on me at Gil'gal, and
I have not made supplication to the LORD.'
Therefore I felt compelled, and offered a
burnt offering."
13And Samuel said to Saul, "You have
done foolishly. You have not kept the com-
mandment of the LORD your God, which
He commanded you. For now the LORD
would have established your kingdom
over Israel forever. 14But now your king-
dom shall not continue. The LORD has
sought for Himself a man after His own
heart, and the LORD has commanded him
to be commander over His people, because
you have not kept what the LORD com-
manded you."
15Then Samuel arose and went up from
Gil'gal to Gib'ē·ah of Benjamin.[a] And Saul
numbered the people present with him,
about six hundred men.

No Weapons for the Army

16Saul, Jonathan his son, and the people
present with them remained in Gib'ē·ah of
Benjamin. But the Phi·lis'tines encamped
in Mich'mash. 17Then raiders came out of
the camp of the Phi·lis'tines in three com-
panies. One company turned onto the road
to Oph'rah, to the land of Shū'al, 18another
company turned to the road *to* Beth
Hor'on, and another company turned *to*
the road of the border that overlooks the
Valley of Ze·bō'im toward the wilderness.

13:5 [a]Following Masoretic Text, Septuagint, Targum, and Vulgate; Syriac and some manuscripts of the Septuagint read *three.* 13:15 [a]Following Masoretic Text and Targum; Septuagint and Vulgate add *And the rest of the people went up after Saul to meet the people who fought against them, going from Gilgal to Gibeah in the hill of Benjamin.*

13:9 Saul presumed to offer a sacrifice that should have been offered by Samuel. Sacrifice was the province of the priest alone (v. 13; Num. 3:10; 18:7; see 2 Chr. 26:16–21). The king who took the part of priest would soon feel himself to be God.

13:11 Clear signs of Saul's drift away from God. At each critical point in his growing alienation from the Lord, Saul's excuse is the people.

13:17, 18 The places named indicate that Saul's men were surrounded by the enemy to the north, the west, and the south. The **Valley of Zeboim** was a ravine near Michmash.

19 Now there was no blacksmith to be
found throughout all the land of Israel, for
the Phi·lis'tines said, "Lest the Hebrews
make swords or spears." 20 But all the Isra-
elites would go down to the Phi·lis'tines to
sharpen each man's plowshare, his mat-
tock, his ax, and his sickle; 21 and the charge
for a sharpening was a pim[a] for the plow-
shares, the mattocks, the forks, and the
axes, and to set the points of the goads. 22 So
it came about, on the day of battle, that
there was neither sword nor spear found in
the hand of any of the people who *were*
with Saul and Jonathan. But they were
found with Saul and Jonathan his son.
23 And the garrison of the Phi·lis'tines
went out to the pass of Mich'mash.

CHAPTER 14

Jonathan Defeats the Philistines

Now it happened one day that Jonathan
the son of Saul said to the young man who
bore his armor, "Come, let us go over to the
Phi·lis'tines' garrison that *is* on the other
side." But he did not tell his father. 2 And
Saul was sitting in the outskirts of Gib'ē·ah
under a pomegranate tree which *is* in
Mig'ron. The people who *were* with him
were about six hundred men. 3 A·hī'jah the
son of A·hī'tub, Ich'a·bod's brother, the
son of Phin'e·has, the son of Ē'lī,
the LORD's priest in Shī'lōh, was wearing
an ephod. But the people did not know
that Jonathan had gone.
4 Between the passes, by which Jonathan
sought to go over to the Phi·lis'tines' garri-
son, *there was* a sharp rock on one side and
a sharp rock on the other side. And the
name of one *was* Bō'zez, and the name of
the other Sē'neh. 5 The front of one faced
northward opposite Mich'mash, and the
other southward opposite Gib'ē·ah.
6 Then Jonathan said to the young man
who bore his armor, "Come, let us go over
to the garrison of these uncircumcised; it
may be that the LORD will work for us. For
nothing restrains the LORD from saving by
many or by few."
7 So his armorbearer said to him, "Do all
that is in your heart. Go then; here I am
with you, according to your heart."
8 Then Jonathan said, "Very well, let us
cross over to *these* men, and we will show
ourselves to them. 9 If they say thus to us,
'Wait until we come to you,' then we will
stand still in our place and not go up to
them. 10 But if they say thus, 'Come up to
us,' then we will go up. For the LORD has
delivered them into our hand, and this *will
be* a sign to us."
11 So both of them showed themselves to
the garrison of the Phi·lis'tines. And the
Phi·lis'tines said, "Look, the Hebrews are
coming out of the holes where they have
hidden." 12 Then the men of the garrison
called to Jonathan and his armorbearer,
and said, "Come up to us, and we will
show you something."
Jonathan said to his armorbearer,
"Come up after me, for the LORD has deliv-
ered them into the hand of Israel." 13 And
Jonathan climbed up on his hands and
knees with his armorbearer after him; and
they fell before Jonathan. And as he came
after him, his armorbearer killed them.

13:21 [a]About two-thirds shekel weight

13:22 Saul's army had **neither sword nor spear** made of iron. Undoubtedly the Hebrews still had bronze weapons, but only Saul and Jonathan had the new iron ones.

14:6 these uncircumcised: An expression of contempt. The Philistines, whose origin was in the west, did not practice circumcision as did the eastern Semitic people. **nothing restrains the LORD**: A wonderful statement of faith.

14:13 on his hands and knees: The ravines leading down to the Jordan Valley are deep and steep-sided. Jonathan and his armorbearer had to go down from the ridge on which they were camped and crawl up the other side to get at the Philistines. Hardly an advantageous position for attack! But "nothing restrains" God! See v. 6.

14 That first slaughter which Jonathan and
his armorbearer made was about twenty
men within about half an acre of land.[a]
15 And there was trembling in the camp,
in the field, and among all the people. The
garrison and the raiders also trembled; and
the earth quaked, so that it was a very
great trembling. 16 Now the watchmen of
Saul in Gib′ē·ah of Benjamin looked, and
there was the multitude, melting away; and
they went here and there. 17 Then Saul said
to the people who *were* with him, "Now
call the roll and see who has gone from
us." And when they had called the roll,
surprisingly, Jonathan and his armorbearer
were not *there*. 18 And Saul said to A·hī′jah,
"Bring the ark[a] of God here" (for at that
time the ark[b] of God was with the children
of Israel). 19 Now it happened, while Saul
talked to the priest, that the noise which
was in the camp of the Phi·lis′tines contin-
ued to increase; so Saul said to the priest,
"Withdraw your hand." 20 Then Saul and
all the people who *were* with him assem-
bled, and they went to the battle; and in-
deed every man's sword was against his
neighbor, *and there was* very great confu-
sion. 21 Moreover the Hebrews *who* were
with the Phi·lis′tines before that time, who
went up with them into the camp *from the*
surrounding *country*, they also joined the
Israelites who *were* with Saul and Jona-
than. 22 Likewise all the men of Israel who
had hidden in the mountains of Ē′phra·im,
when they heard that the Phi·lis′tines fled,
they also followed hard after them in the
battle. 23 So the LORD saved Israel that day,
and the battle shifted to Beth Ā′ven.

Saul's Rash Oath

24 And the men of Israel were distressed
that day, for Saul had placed the people
under oath, saying, "Cursed *is* the man
who eats *any* food until evening, before I
have taken vengeance on my enemies." So
none of the people tasted food. 25 Now all
the people of the land came to a forest; and
there was honey on the ground. 26 And
when the people had come into the woods,
there was the honey, dripping; but no one
put his hand to his mouth, for the people
feared the oath. 27 But Jonathan had not
heard his father charge the people with the
oath; therefore he stretched out the end of
the rod that *was* in his hand and dipped it
in a honeycomb, and put his hand to his
mouth; and his countenance brightened.
28 Then one of the people said, "Your father
strictly charged the people with an oath,
saying, 'Cursed *is* the man who eats food
this day.' " And the people were faint.

29 But Jonathan said, "My father has
troubled the land. Look now, how my
countenance has brightened because I
tasted a little of this honey. 30 How much
better if the people had eaten freely today
of the spoil of their enemies which they
found! For now would there not have been
a much greater slaughter among the
Phi·lis′tines?"

31 Now they had driven back the
Phi·lis′tines that day from Mich′mash to
Aī′ja·lon. So the people were very faint.
32 And the people rushed on the spoil, and
took sheep, oxen, and calves, and slaugh-
tered *them* on the ground; and the people
ate *them* with the blood. 33 Then they told
Saul, saying, "Look, the people are sinning
against the LORD by eating with the
blood!"

So he said, "You have dealt treacher-

14:14 [a]Literally *half the area plowed by a yoke* (of oxen in a day) 14:18 [a]Following Masoretic Text, Targum, and Vulgate; Septuagint reads *ephod*. [b]Following Masoretic Text, Targum, and Vulgate; Septuagint reads *ephod*.

14:14, 15 The Philistines, thinking Jonathan and his companion were deserters (v. 11), were taken completely by surprise. Their confusion was heightened by an earthquake.

14:19 Withdraw your hand: Probably means not to go any farther with the ceremony. Saul was too impatient to wait for the Lord's guidance.

14:24–30 Saul's rash **oath** limited the victory that would otherwise have been won (v. 30)

ously; roll a large stone to me this day."
34Then Saul said, "Disperse yourselves
among the people, and say to them, 'Bring
me here every man's ox and every man's
sheep, slaughter *them* here, and eat; and do
not sin against the LORD by eating with the
blood.' " So every one of the people
brought his ox with him that night, and
slaughtered *it* there. 35Then Saul built an al-
tar to the LORD. This was the first altar that
he built to the LORD.

36Now Saul said, "Let us go down after
the Phi·lis'tines by night, and plunder
them until the morning light; and let us not
leave a man of them."

And they said, "Do whatever seems
good to you."

Then the priest said, "Let us draw near
to God here."

37So Saul asked counsel of God, "Shall I
go down after the Phi·lis'tines? Will You
deliver them into the hand of Israel?" But
He did not answer him that day. 38And
Saul said, "Come over here, all you chiefs
of the people, and know and see what this
sin was today. 39For *as* the LORD lives, who
saves Israel, though it be in Jonathan my
son, he shall surely die." But not a man
among all the people answered him.
40Then he said to all Israel, "You be on one
side, and my son Jonathan and I will be on
the other side."

And the people said to Saul, "Do what
seems good to you."

41Therefore Saul said to the LORD God of
Israel, "Give a perfect *lot*."[a] So Saul and
Jonathan were taken, but the people es-
caped. 42And Saul said, "Cast *lots* between
my son Jonathan and me." So Jonathan
was taken. 43Then Saul said to Jonathan,
"Tell me what you have done."

And Jonathan told him, and said, "I
only tasted a little honey with the end of
the rod that *was* in my hand. So now I must
die!"

44Saul answered, "God do so and more
also; for you shall surely die, Jonathan."

45But the people said to Saul, "Shall Jon-
athan die, who has accomplished this great
deliverance in Israel? Certainly not! *As* the
LORD lives, not one hair of his head shall
fall to the ground, for he has worked with
God this day." So the people rescued Jona-
than, and he did not die.

46Then Saul returned from pursuing the
Phi·lis'tines, and the Phi·lis'tines went to
their own place.

Saul's Continuing Wars

47So Saul established his sovereignty
over Israel, and fought against all his ene-
mies on every side, against Mō'ab, against
the people of Am'mon, against Ē'dom,
against the kings of Zō'bah, and against
the Phi·lis'tines. Wherever he turned, he
harassed *them*.[a] 48And he gathered an army
and attacked the A·mal'e·kītes, and deliv-
ered Israel from the hands of those who
plundered them.

49The sons of Saul were Jonathan,
Jish'ū·ī,[a] and Mal·chī·shū'a. And the
names of his two daughters *were these:* the
name of the firstborn Mē'rab, and
the name of the younger Mī'chal. 50The
name of Saul's wife *was* A·hin'ō·am the
daughter of A·him'a·az. And the name of
the commander of his army *was* Abner the
son of Ner, Saul's uncle. 51Kish *was* the fa-
ther of Saul, and Ner the father of Abner
was the son of A·bī'el.

52Now there was fierce war with the

14:41 [a]Following Masoretic Text and Targum; Septuagint and Vulgate read *Why do You not answer Your servant today? If the injustice is with me or Jonathan my son, O LORD God of Israel, give proof; and if You say it is with Your people Israel, give holiness.*
14:47 [a]Septuagint and Vulgate read *prospered.*
14:49 [a]Called *Abinadab* in 1 Chronicles 8:33 and 9:39

and imperiled the life of his son. The prominence of **I** in the vow (v. 24) points to Saul's self-centered pride.

14:52 This confirms Samuel's prophecy that a king would take the Israelites' sons to be his soldiers (1 Sam. 8:11).

Phi·lis′tines all the days of Saul. And when
Saul saw any strong man or any valiant
man, he took him for himself.

CHAPTER 15

Saul Spares King Agag

Samuel also said to Saul, "The LORD sent
me to anoint you king over His people,
over Israel. Now therefore, heed the voice
of the words of the LORD. 2Thus says the
LORD of hosts: 'I will punish Am′a·lek *for*
what he did to Israel, how he ambushed
him on the way when he came up from
Egypt. 3Now go and attack Am′a·lek, and
utterly destroy all that they have, and do
not spare them. But kill both man and
woman, infant and nursing child, ox and
sheep, camel and donkey.' "

4So Saul gathered the people together
and numbered them in Te·lā′im, two hun-
dred thousand foot soldiers and ten thou-
sand men of Judah. 5And Saul came to a
city of Am′a·lek, and lay in wait in the val-
ley.

6Then Saul said to the Ken′ītes, "Go, de-
part, get down from among the A·mal′-
e·kītes, lest I destroy you with them. For
you showed kindness to all the children of
Israel when they came up out of Egypt." So
the Ken′ītes departed from among the
A·mal′e·kītes. 7And Saul attacked the
A·mal′e·kītes, from Hav′i·lah all the way
to Shūr, which is east of Egypt. 8He also
took Ā′gag king of the A·mal′e·kītes alive,
and utterly destroyed all the people with
the edge of the sword. 9But Saul and the
people spared Ā′gag and the best of the
sheep, the oxen, the fatlings, the lambs,
and all *that was* good, and were unwilling
to utterly destroy them. But everything de-
spised and worthless, that they utterly de-
stroyed.

Saul Rejected as King

10Now the word of the LORD came to
Samuel, saying, 11"I greatly regret that I
have set up Saul *as* king, for he has turned
back from following Me, and has not per-
formed My commandments." And it
grieved Samuel, and he cried out to the
LORD all night. 12So when Samuel rose
early in the morning to meet Saul, it was
told Samuel, saying, "Saul went to Car′-
mel, and indeed, he set up a monument for
himself; and he has gone on around,
passed by, and gone down to Gil′gal."
13Then Samuel went to Saul, and Saul said
to him, "Blessed *are* you of the LORD! I have
performed the commandment of the
LORD."

14But Samuel said, "What then *is* this
bleating of the sheep in my ears, and the
lowing of the oxen which I hear?"

15And Saul said, "They have brought
them from the A·mal′e·kītes; for the peo-
ple spared the best of the sheep and the
oxen, to sacrifice to the LORD your God;
and the rest we have utterly destroyed."

16Then Samuel said to Saul, "Be quiet!
And I will tell you what the LORD said to
me last night."

And he said to him, "Speak on."

17So Samuel said, "When you *were* little
in your own eyes, *were* you not head of the
tribes of Israel? And did not the LORD
anoint you king over Israel? 18Now the
LORD sent you on a mission, and said, 'Go,
and utterly destroy the sinners, the
A·mal′e·kītes, and fight against them until
they are consumed.' 19Why then did you
not obey the voice of the LORD? Why did

15:3 utterly destroy: Lit. "to put under the ban," used of persons or objects under the judgment of God. Since this was no ordinary war of plunder, Israel was to take no booty.

15:13–15 Saul compounded the sin of disobedience with an outright lie. Again he blamed his failure on the people (v. 15, but see v. 9). Saul's reference to God as **the LORD your God** (vv. 15, 21, 30) possibly underlies Saul's personal understanding that the Lord was no longer *his* God.

you swoop down on the spoil, and do evil
in the sight of the LORD?"
[20]And Saul said to Samuel, "But I have
obeyed the voice of the LORD, and gone on
the mission on which the LORD sent me,
and brought back Ā'gag king of Am'a·lek; I
have utterly destroyed the A·mal'e·kītes.
[21]But the people took of the plunder, sheep
and oxen, the best of the things which
should have been utterly destroyed, to sac-
rifice to the LORD your God in Gil'gal."
[22]So Samuel said:

"Has the LORD *as great* delight in burnt
offerings and sacrifices,
As in obeying the voice of the LORD?
Behold, to obey is better than
sacrifice,
And to heed than the fat of rams.
23 For rebellion *is as* the sin of
witchcraft,
And stubbornness *is as* iniquity and
idolatry.
Because you have rejected the word
of the LORD,
He also has rejected you from *being*
king."

[24]Then Saul said to Samuel, "I have
sinned, for I have transgressed the com-
mandment of the LORD and your words,
because I feared the people and obeyed
their voice. [25]Now therefore, please pardon
my sin, and return with me, that I may
worship the LORD."
[26]But Samuel said to Saul, "I will not re-
turn with you, for you have rejected the
word of the LORD, and the LORD has re-
jected you from being king over Israel."
[27]And as Samuel turned around to go
away, *Saul* seized the edge of his robe, and
it tore. [28]So Samuel said to him, "The LORD
has torn the kingdom of Israel from you to-
day, and has given it to a neighbor of
yours, *who is* better than you. [29]And also
the Strength of Israel will not lie nor relent.
For He *is* not a man, that He should re-
lent."
[30]Then he said, "I have sinned; *yet* honor
me now, please, before the elders of my
people and before Israel, and return with
me, that I may worship the LORD your
God." [31]So Samuel turned back after Saul,
and Saul worshiped the LORD.
[32]Then Samuel said, "Bring Ā'gag king
of the A·mal'e·kītes here to me." So Ā'gag
came to him cautiously.
And Ā'gag said, "Surely the bitterness
of death is past."
[33]But Samuel said, "As your sword has
made women childless, so shall your
mother be childless among women." And
Samuel hacked Ā'gag in pieces before the
LORD in Gil'gal.
[34]Then Samuel went to Rā'mah, and
Saul went up to his house at Gib'ē·ah
of Saul. [35]And Samuel went no more to
see Saul until the day of his death. Never-
theless Samuel mourned for Saul, and the
LORD regretted that He had made Saul
king over Israel.

CHAPTER 16

David Anointed King

Now the LORD said to Samuel, "How
long will you mourn for Saul, seeing I have
rejected him from reigning over Israel? Fill
your horn with oil, and go; I am sending
you to Jesse the Beth'le·hem·īte. For I have
provided Myself a king among his sons."
[2]And Samuel said, "How can I go? If
Saul hears *it*, he will kill me."
But the LORD said, "Take a heifer with
you, and say, 'I have come to sacrifice to
the LORD.' [3]Then invite Jesse to the sacri-
fice, and I will show you what you shall

15:30 Even after his disobedience is revealed, Saul shows more concern about his reputation among men than his relationship with the Lord. He asks Samuel to stay with him so that the people won't suspect anything is wrong.

Only God Knows

Gloria Gaither

What each of us *really* is surfaces when we are truly alone with ourselves. When all the opinions and impressions others have of us are dismissed, when all the conjecture and suppositions are peeled away, when all the surface appearances are discarded—when we stand without defense or pretense alone before God—that is when what we really are stands up. If we don't like what we see then, no amount of deception can sell us a bill of goods about ourselves. No matter how well we have fooled others, when we close the door and are alone with our decisions, our motives will outshout any good impression we might have made on others.

"We stand without defense or pretense alone before God."

Actually, no one else really knows whether a decision we have made was a right one or not. At times a decision seems to be a big mistake to those who don't know our motives. At other times people may be very complimentary of a decision that, deep inside, we know wasn't particularly noble. In each of our lives there are decisions that we alone can make. In the final analysis, we make those decisions out of the resources we have at our disposal. Only God truly knows our deepest needs and our deepest motives. ✦

do; you shall anoint for Me the one I name to you."

4So Samuel did what the LORD said, and went to Bethlehem. And the elders of the town trembled at his coming, and said, "Do you come peaceably?"

5And he said, "Peaceably; I have come to sacrifice to the LORD. Sanctify yourselves, and come with me to the sacrifice." Then he consecrated Jesse and his sons, and invited them to the sacrifice.

6So it was, when they came, that he looked at E·lī'ab and said, "Surely the LORD's anointed *is* before Him!"

7But the LORD said to Samuel, "Do not look at his appearance or at his physical stature, because I have refused him. For *the* LORD *does* not *see* as man sees;[a] for man looks at the outward appearance, but the LORD looks at the heart."

16:7 [a]Septuagint reads *For God does not see as man sees;* Targum reads *It is not by the appearance of a man;* Vulgate reads *Nor do I judge according to the looks of a man.*

16:5 Sanctify yourselves: The typical OT use of the term sanctify in the sense of consecration or setting oneself apart for a divine purpose. It is an essential part of sanctification. The NT further develops the concept of moral and spiritual purity to the idea of sanctification (Eph. 5:25–27; 1 Thess. 5:22–24).

8So Jesse called A·bin′a·dab, and made him pass before Samuel. And he said, "Neither has the LORD chosen this one." 9Then Jesse made Sham′mah pass by. And he said, "Neither has the LORD chosen this one." 10Thus Jesse made seven of his sons pass before Samuel. And Samuel said to Jesse, "The LORD has not chosen these." 11And Samuel said to Jesse, "Are all the young men here?" Then he said, "There remains yet the youngest, and there he is, keeping the sheep."

And Samuel said to Jesse, "Send and bring him. For we will not sit down[a] till he comes here." 12So he sent and brought him in. Now he *was* ruddy, with bright eyes, and good-looking. And the LORD said, "Arise, anoint him; for this *is* the one!" 13Then Samuel took the horn of oil and anointed him in the midst of his brothers; and the Spirit of the LORD came upon David from that day forward. So Samuel arose and went to Rā′mah.

A Distressing Spirit Troubles Saul

14But the Spirit of the LORD departed from Saul, and a distressing spirit from the LORD troubled him. 15And Saul's servants said to him, "Surely, a distressing spirit from God is troubling you. 16Let our master now command your servants, *who are* before you, to seek out a man *who is* a skillful player on the harp. And it shall be that he will play it with his hand when the distressing spirit from God is upon you, and you shall be well."

17So Saul said to his servants, "Provide me now a man who can play well, and bring *him* to me."

18Then one of the servants answered and said, "Look, I have seen a son of Jesse the Beth′le·hem·īte, *who is* skillful in playing, a mighty man of valor, a man of war, prudent in speech, and a handsome person; and the LORD *is* with him."

19Therefore Saul sent messengers to Jesse, and said, "Send me your son David, who *is* with the sheep." 20And Jesse took a donkey *loaded with* bread, a skin of wine, and a young goat, and sent *them* by his son David to Saul. 21So David came to Saul and stood before him. And he loved him greatly, and he became his armorbearer. 22Then Saul sent to Jesse, saying, "Please let David stand before me, for he has found favor in my sight." 23And so it was, whenever the spirit from God was upon Saul, that David would take a harp and play *it* with his hand. Then Saul would become refreshed and well, and the distressing spirit would depart from him.

16:11 [a]Following Septuagint and Vulgate; Masoretic Text reads *turn around;* Targum and Syriac read *turn away.*

CHAPTER 17

David and Goliath

Now the Phi·lis′tines gathered their armies together to battle, and were gathered at Sō′chōh, which *belongs* to Judah; they encamped between Sō′chōh and A·zē′kah, in Ē′phes Dam′mim. 2And Saul and the men of Israel were gathered together, and they encamped in the Valley of Ē′lah, and drew up in battle array against the Phi·lis′tines. 3The Phi·lis′tines stood on a mountain on one side, and Israel stood on a mountain on the other side, with a valley between them.

4And a champion went out from the camp of the Phi·lis′tines, named Goliath, from Gath, whose height *was* six cubits and a span. 5*He had* a bronze helmet on his head, and he *was* armed with a coat of

17:1 If chs. 16 and 17 are in chronological order, probably several years elapsed between the events of ch. 16 and the renewal of the Philistine invasion reported here. The invasion this time came through the southwestern lowlands of Judah.

17:4–7 Goliath was a little over nine feet (2.7 m) tall. His armor weighed about 150 pounds (68 kg); the head of his spear, 20 pounds (9 kg).

DAVID: THE VERSATILE KING

Most people, while competent at many things, excel primarily at one specific talent. For some, their gift may be music, while others prevail in sports. Many prove to be brilliant with the written word, whereas others who cannot write a grammatical sentence have a flair for touching hearts through speech. Yet one man in Scripture excelled in all these areas and more.

Even before he became king, with all the advantages of that position, David proved himself to be one of the most talented men of all time, and his lifestyle revealed an individual who had discovered the secret to balanced living: trusting the Lord in every situation (see 1 Sam. 17:32–37).

A poet, shepherd, and musician, he was undoubtedly in good physical health when Samuel first encountered the youth (16:12). The Lord's selection of David to be Israel's next king demonstrated the strength of his spiritual walk, and the beauty of his many psalms indicates he did not waste his time on idle or foolish thoughts while tending his father's sheep. He sharpened his talents and mental skills.

The servant who suggested Saul hire David as his musician provided an apt description of the young man as "skillful in playing, a mighty man of valor, a man of war, prudent in speech, and a handsome person; and the LORD *is* with him" (v. 18). What better recommendation could a king desire?

Through years of persecution by Saul, David maintained his relationship with the Lord and continued to exercise his talent for words and music. The Psalms give a poignant glimpse into the closeness of his walk with God and the strength of his faith in the midst of adversity.

As happens with so many other godly people, however, success opened the door for David's downfall. After making a name for himself as a brilliant, courageous warrior and king, David apparently decided he deserved a rest. When all the other kings went forth to battle, he sent Joab in his place (2 Sam. 11:1).

During this time of idleness, he committed adultery with Bathsheba. When she announced her pregnancy, he sought to cover up his sin instead of facing the consequences. He used his God-given intelligence for deceit and—when that did not work—for murder.

Not only had he severed his relationship with God, but David also lied to himself in thinking all was well once the evidence of his sin was destroyed. In other words, the deficit in his spiritual life threw his mental health out of balance. The old David would have looked at the situation clearly and honestly, rather than deceiving himself into thinking no one would know.

So far had he wandered from God that David refused to acknowledge his guilt until the prophet Nathan

confronted him. But years of sweet fellowship had built a strong foundation, and David immediately admitted his sin and set to work to resolve the situation. Psalm 51 demonstrates his eagerness to restore his relationship with God.

While he was not a perfect man, David exhibited a spiritual sensitivity that very few experience. He pled for cleansing and forgiveness, and he accepted the consequences of his sin.

Instead of covering up the failures of its heroes, the Bible gives us an honest picture so that we can learn how to handle sin in our own lives. David's example clearly shows that, while balance comes from a consistent walk with God, even a wonderfully talented man after God's own heart can fall prey to temptation. When we fail, sincere repentance will restore our relationship with God and bring balance back to our lives. ✦

mail, and the weight of the coat *was* five
thousand shekels of bronze. 6And *he had*
bronze armor on his legs and a bronze
javelin between his shoulders. 7Now the
staff of his spear *was* like a weaver's beam,
and his iron spearhead *weighed* six hundred shekels; and a shield-bearer went before him. 8Then he stood and cried out to
the armies of Israel, and said to them,
"Why have you come out to line up for battle? *Am* I not a Phi·lis'tine, and you the servants of Saul? Choose a man for yourselves, and let him come down to me. 9If he
is able to fight with me and kill me, then
we will be your servants. But if I prevail
against him and kill him, then you shall be
our servants and serve us." 10And the
Phi·lis'tine said, "I defy the armies of Israel
this day; give me a man, that we may fight
together." 11When Saul and all Israel heard
these words of the Phi·lis'tine, they were dismayed and greatly afraid.
12Now David *was* the son of that Eph'ra·thīte of Bethlehem Judah, whose name
was Jesse, and who had eight sons. And the
man was old, advanced *in years,* in the
days of Saul. 13The three oldest sons of
Jesse had gone to follow Saul to the battle.
The names of his three sons who went to
the battle *were* E·lī'ab the firstborn, next to
him A·bin'a·dab, and the third Sham'mah.
14David *was* the youngest. And the three
oldest followed Saul. 15But David occasionally went and returned from Saul to feed
his father's sheep at Bethlehem.
16And the Phi·lis'tine drew near and
presented himself forty days, morning and evening.
17Then Jesse said to his son David, "Take
now for your brothers an ephah of this
dried *grain* and these ten loaves, and run to
your brothers at the camp. 18And carry
these ten cheeses to the captain of *their*
thousand, and see how your brothers fare,
and bring back news of them." 19Now Saul
and they and all the men of Israel *were* in
the Valley of Ē'lah, fighting with the Phi·lis'tines.
20So David rose early in the morning,
left the sheep with a keeper, and took *the things* and went as Jesse had commanded
him. And he came to the camp as the army
was going out to the fight and shouting for
the battle. 21For Israel and the Phi·lis'tines
had drawn up in battle array, army against
army. 22And David left his supplies in the

17:9–11 In those times, a challenge so issued could not be ignored. Honor demanded that it be met. If Israel refused, they would suffer a moral defeat.

hand of the supply keeper, ran to the army,
and came and greeted his brothers. 23Then
as he talked with them, there was the
champion, the Phi·lis′tine of Gath, Goliath
by name, coming up from the armies of the
Phi·lis′tines; and he spoke according to the
same words. So David heard *them.* 24And
all the men of Israel, when they saw the
man, fled from him and were dreadfully
afraid. 25So the men of Israel said, "Have
you seen this man who has come up?
Surely he has come up to defy Israel; and it
shall be *that* the man who kills him the
king will enrich with great riches, will give
him his daughter, and give his father's
house exemption *from taxes* in Israel."

26Then David spoke to the men who
stood by him, saying, "What shall be done
for the man who kills this Phi·lis′tine and
takes away the reproach from Israel? For
who *is* this uncircumcised Phi·lis′tine, that
he should defy the armies of the living
God?"

27And the people answered him in this
manner, saying, "So shall it be done for the
man who kills him."

28Now E·lī′ab his oldest brother heard
when he spoke to the men; and E·lī′ab's
anger was aroused against David, and he
said, "Why did you come down here? And
with whom have you left those few sheep
in the wilderness? I know your pride and
the insolence of your heart, for you have
come down to see the battle."

29And David said, "What have I done
now? *Is there* not a cause?" 30Then he
turned from him toward another and said
the same thing; and these people answered
him as the first ones *did.*

31Now when the words which David
spoke were heard, they reported *them* to
Saul; and he sent for him. 32Then David
said to Saul, "Let no man's heart fail be-
cause of him; your servant will go and
fight with this Phi·lis′tine."

33And Saul said to David, "You are not
able to go against this Phi·lis′tine to fight
with him; for you *are* a youth, and he a
man of war from his youth."

34But David said to Saul, "Your servant
used to keep his father's sheep, and when
a lion or a bear came and took a lamb out
of the flock, 35I went out after it and struck
it, and delivered *the lamb* from its mouth;
and when it arose against me, I caught *it* by
its beard, and struck and killed it. 36Your
servant has killed both lion and bear; and
this uncircumcised Phi·lis′tine will be like
one of them, seeing he has defied the
armies of the living God." 37Moreover Da-
vid said, "The LORD, who delivered me
from the paw of the lion and from the paw
of the bear, He will deliver me from the
hand of this Phi·lis′tine."

And Saul said to David, "Go, and the
LORD be with you!"

38So Saul clothed David with his armor,
and he put a bronze helmet on his head; he
also clothed him with a coat of mail. 39Da-
vid fastened his sword to his armor and
tried to walk, for he had not tested *them.*
And David said to Saul, "I cannot walk
with these, for I have not tested *them.*" So
David took them off.

40Then he took his staff in his hand; and
he chose for himself five smooth stones
from the brook, and put them in a shep-
herd's bag, in a pouch which he had, and
his sling was in his hand. And he drew
near to the Phi·lis′tine. 41So the Phi·lis′tine
came, and began drawing near to David,
and the man who bore the shield *went* be-
fore him. 42And when the Phi·lis′tine
looked about and saw David, he disdained
him; for he was *only* a youth, ruddy and
good-looking. 43So the Phi·lis′tine said to

17:26 The living God is in total contrast to the lifeless idols of the Philistine (v. 36). David feels deeply the reproach upon God which Israel's helplessness brings about.

17:34–37 Having experienced God's deliverance before, David trusted Him in this new situation. When we allow God to use us in relatively unimportant tasks, we grow in faith and He prepares us for greater things.

David, "*Am* I a dog, that you come to me
with sticks?" And the Phi·lis'tine cursed
David by his gods. 44And the Phi·lis'tine
said to David, "Come to me, and I will give
your flesh to the birds of the air and the
beasts of the field!"

45Then David said to the Phi·lis'tine,
"You come to me with a sword, with a
spear, and with a javelin. But I come to you
in the name of the LORD of hosts, the God
of the armies of Israel, whom you have de-
fied. 46This day the LORD will deliver you
into my hand, and I will strike you and
take your head from you. And this day I
will give the carcasses of the camp of the
Phi·lis'tines to the birds of the air and the
wild beasts of the earth, that all the earth
may know that there is a God in Israel.
47Then all this assembly shall know that the
LORD does not save with sword and spear;
for the battle *is* the LORD's, and He will
give you into our hands."

48So it was, when the Phi·lis'tine arose
and came and drew near to meet David,
that David hurried and ran toward the
army to meet the Phi·lis'tine. 49Then David
put his hand in his bag and took out a
stone; and he slung *it* and struck the
Phi·lis'tine in his forehead, so that the
stone sank into his forehead, and he fell on
his face to the earth. 50So David prevailed
over the Phi·lis'tine with a sling and a
stone, and struck the Phi·lis'tine and killed
him. But *there was* no sword in the hand of
David. 51Therefore David ran and stood
over the Phi·lis'tine, took his sword and
drew it out of its sheath and killed him,
and cut off his head with it.

And when the Phi·lis'tines saw that
their champion was dead, they fled. 52Now
the men of Israel and Judah arose and
shouted, and pursued the Phi·lis'tines as
far as the entrance of the valley[a] and to the
gates of Ek'ron. And the wounded of the
Phi·lis'tines fell along the road to Shā-
a·rā'im, even as far as Gath and Ek'ron.
53Then the children of Israel returned from
chasing the Phi·lis'tines, and they plun-
dered their tents. 54And David took the
head of the Phi·lis'tine and brought it to Je-
rusalem, but he put his armor in his tent.

55When Saul saw David going out
against the Phi·lis'tine, he said to Abner,
the commander of the army, "Abner,
whose son *is* this youth?"

And Abner said, "As your soul lives,
O king, I do not know."

56So the king said, "Inquire whose son
this young man *is*."

57Then, as David returned from the
slaughter of the Phi·lis'tine, Abner took
him and brought him before Saul with the
head of the Phi·lis'tine in his hand. 58And
Saul said to him, "Whose son *are* you,
young man?"

So David answered, "*I am* the son of
your servant Jesse the Beth'le·hem·īte."

CHAPTER 18

Saul Resents David

Now when he had finished speaking to
Saul, the soul of Jonathan was knit to the
soul of David, and Jonathan loved him as
his own soul. 2Saul took him that day, and

17:52 [a]Following Masoretic Text, Syriac, Targum, and Vulgate; Septuagint reads *Gath*.

17:45–47 David's faith was in **the LORD of hosts**. He confidently predicted victory for God's sake, so that all the earth may know that God reigns in Israel (v. 46). David's faith was strong enough for him literally to lay his life on the line.

17:55–58 That David was not recognized by Saul and Abner could be accounted for by a lapse of time between the youth's appearance as a musician in Saul's court and the Philistine war described here.

18:1–4 Jonathan recognized a kindred spirit in David. Their relationship is one of the classic friendships of all time. Jonathan's lack of jealousy of David is in sharp contrast to the spirit of Saul which began to emerge at once.

would not let him go home to his father's
house anymore. 3Then Jonathan and David
made a covenant, because he loved him as
his own soul. 4And Jonathan took off the
robe that *was* on him and gave it to David,
with his armor, even to his sword and his
bow and his belt.

5So David went out wherever Saul sent
him, *and* behaved wisely. And Saul set him
over the men of war, and he was accepted
in the sight of all the people and also in the
sight of Saul's servants. 6Now it had hap-
pened as they were coming *home,* when
David was returning from the slaughter of
the Phi·lis'tine, that the women had come
out of all the cities of Israel, singing and
dancing, to meet King Saul, with tam-
bourines, with joy, and with musical in-
struments. 7So the women sang as they
danced, and said:

"Saul has slain his thousands,
And David his ten thousands."

8Then Saul was very angry, and the saying
displeased him; and he said, "They have
ascribed to David ten thousands, and to
me they have ascribed *only* thousands.
Now *what* more can he have but the king-
dom?" 9So Saul eyed David from that day
forward.

10And it happened on the next day that
the distressing spirit from God came upon
Saul, and he prophesied inside the house.
So David played *music* with his hand, as at
other times; but *there was* a spear in Saul's
hand. 11And Saul cast the spear, for he said,
"I will pin David to the wall!" But David
escaped his presence twice.

12Now Saul was afraid of David, be-
cause the LORD was with him, but had de-
parted from Saul. 13Therefore Saul re-
moved him from his presence, and made
him his captain over a thousand; and he
went out and came in before the people.
14And David behaved wisely in all his
ways, and the LORD *was* with him. 15There-
fore, when Saul saw that he behaved very
wisely, he was afraid of him. 16But all Israel
and Judah loved David, because he went
out and came in before them.

David Marries Michal

17Then Saul said to David, "Here is my
older daughter Mē'rab; I will give her to
you as a wife. Only be valiant for me, and
fight the LORD's battles." For Saul thought,
"Let my hand not be against him, but let
the hand of the Phi·lis'tines be against
him."

18So David said to Saul, "Who *am* I, and
what *is* my life *or* my father's family in Is-
rael, that I should be son-in-law to the
king?" 19But it happened at the time when
Mē'rab, Saul's daughter, should have been
given to David, that she was given to
Ā'dri·el the Me·hō'la·thīte as a wife.

20Now Mī'chal, Saul's daughter, loved
David. And they told Saul, and the thing
pleased him. 21So Saul said, "I will give her
to him, that she may be a snare to him, and
that the hand of the Phi·lis'tines may be
against him." Therefore Saul said to David
a second time, "You shall be my son-in-law
today."

22And Saul commanded his servants,
"Communicate with David secretly, and
say, 'Look, the king has delight in you, and
all his servants love you. Now therefore,
become the king's son-in-law.' "

18:13 A demotion for David. He was removed from Saul's counselors and made captain over a smaller unit of the army.

18:16 all Israel and Judah: The disastrous division which was eventually to tear the nation in two was already well advanced.

18:17–27 David demonstrates a becoming modesty (vv. 18, 23) which was intertwined with his inability to pay a **dowry** (bride-price, v. 25) appropriate to a king's daughter. But Saul's trap becomes David's opportunity. **foreskins**: Proof of compliance with the king's demand; these could only come from the bodies of uncircumcised Philistines.

23So Saul's servants spoke those words
in the hearing of David. And David said,
"Does it seem to you *a* light *thing* to be a
king's son-in-law, seeing I *am* a poor and
lightly esteemed man?" 24And the servants
of Saul told him, saying, "In this manner
David spoke."

25Then Saul said, "Thus you shall say to
David: 'The king does not desire any
dowry but one hundred foreskins of the
Phi·lis'tines, to take vengeance on the
king's enemies.' " But Saul thought to
make David fall by the hand of the
Phi·lis'tines. 26So when his servants told
David these words, it pleased David well
to become the king's son-in-law. Now the
days had not expired; 27therefore David
arose and went, he and his men, and killed
two hundred men of the Phi·lis'tines. And
David brought their foreskins, and they
gave them in full count to the king, that he
might become the king's son-in-law. Then
Saul gave him Mī'chal his daughter as a
wife.

28Thus Saul saw and knew that the LORD
was with David, and *that* Mī'chal, Saul's
daughter, loved him; 29and Saul was still
more afraid of David. So Saul became Da-
vid's enemy continually. 30Then the princes
of the Phi·lis'tines went out *to war.* And so
it was, whenever they went out, *that* David
behaved more wisely than all the servants
of Saul, so that his name became highly es-
teemed.

CHAPTER 19

Saul Persecutes David

Now Saul spoke to Jonathan his son and
to all his servants, that they should kill Da-
vid; but Jonathan, Saul's son, delighted
greatly in David. 2So Jonathan told David,
saying, "My father Saul seeks to kill you.
Therefore please be on your guard until
morning, and stay in a secret *place* and
hide. 3And I will go out and stand beside
my father in the field where you *are,* and I
will speak with my father about you. Then
what I observe, I will tell you."

4Thus Jonathan spoke well of David to
Saul his father, and said to him, "Let not
the king sin against his servant, against
David, because he has not sinned against
you, and because his works *have been* very
good toward you. 5For he took his life in
his hands and killed the Phi·lis'tine, and
the LORD brought about a great deliverance
for all Israel. You saw *it* and rejoiced. Why
then will you sin against innocent blood, to
kill David without a cause?"

6So Saul heeded the voice of Jonathan,
and Saul swore, "*As* the LORD lives, he
shall not be killed." 7Then Jonathan called
David, and Jonathan told him all these
things. So Jonathan brought David to Saul,
and he was in his presence as in times past.

8And there was war again; and David
went out and fought with the Phi·lis'tines,
and struck them with a mighty blow, and
they fled from him.

9Now the distressing spirit from the
LORD came upon Saul as he sat in his house
with his spear in his hand. And David was
playing *music* with *his* hand. 10Then Saul
sought to pin David to the wall with the
spear, but he slipped away from Saul's
presence; and he drove the spear into the
wall. So David fled and escaped that night.

11Saul also sent messengers to David's
house to watch him and to kill him in the
morning. And Mī'chal, David's wife, told
him, saying, "If you do not save your life
tonight, tomorrow you will be killed." 12So
Mī'chal let David down through a win-
dow. And he went and fled and escaped.
13And Mī'chal took an image and laid *it* in
the bed, put a cover of goats' *hair* for his
head, and covered *it* with clothes. 14So

19:1–10 Jonathan was able to bring about a brief reconciliation between his father and his friend (vv. 1–7), but a new victory won by David (v. 8) again touched off Saul's jealous rage.

when Saul sent messengers to take David, she said, "He *is* sick."

[15]Then Saul sent the messengers *back* to see David, saying, "Bring him up to me in the bed, that I may kill him." [16]And when the messengers had come in, there was the image in the bed, with a cover of goats' *hair* for his head. [17]Then Saul said to Mī'chal, "Why have you deceived me like this, and sent my enemy away, so that he has escaped?"

And Mī'chal answered Saul, "He said to me, 'Let me go! Why should I kill you?' "

[18]So David fled and escaped, and went to Samuel at Rā'mah, and told him all that Saul had done to him. And he and Samuel went and stayed in Naī'oth. [19]Now it was told Saul, saying, "Take note, David *is* at Naī'oth in Rā'mah!" [20]Then Saul sent messengers to take David. And when they saw the group of prophets prophesying, and Samuel standing *as* leader over them, the Spirit of God came upon the messengers of Saul, and they also prophesied. [21]And when Saul was told, he sent other messengers, and they prophesied likewise. Then Saul sent messengers again the third time, and they prophesied also. [22]Then he also went to Rā'mah, and came to the great well that *is* at Sē'chu. So he asked, and said, "Where *are* Samuel and David?"

And *someone* said, "Indeed *they are* at Naī'oth in Rā'mah." [23]So he went there to Naī'oth in Rā'mah. Then the Spirit of God was upon him also, and he went on and prophesied until he came to Naī'oth in Rā'mah. [24]And he also stripped off his clothes and prophesied before Samuel in like manner, and lay down naked all that day and all that night. Therefore they say, "*Is* Saul also among the prophets?"[a]

CHAPTER 20

Jonathan's Loyalty to David

Then David fled from Naī'oth in Rā'mah, and went and said to Jonathan, "What have I done? What *is* my iniquity, and what *is* my sin before your father, that he seeks my life?"

[2]So Jonathan said to him, "By no means! You shall not die! Indeed, my father will do nothing either great or small without first telling me. And why should my father hide this thing from me? It *is* not *so!*"

[3]Then David took an oath again, and said, "Your father certainly knows that I have found favor in your eyes, and he has said, 'Do not let Jonathan know this, lest he be grieved.' But truly, *as* the LORD lives and *as* your soul lives, *there is* but a step between me and death."

[4]So Jonathan said to David, "Whatever you yourself desire, I will do *it* for you."

[5]And David said to Jonathan, "Indeed tomorrow *is* the New Moon, and I should not fail to sit with the king to eat. But let me go, that I may hide in the field until the third *day* at evening. [6]If your father misses me at all, then say, 'David earnestly asked *permission* of me that he might run over to Bethlehem, his city, for *there is* a yearly sacrifice there for all the family.' [7]If he says thus: '*It is* well,' your servant will be safe. But if he is very angry, be sure that evil is determined by him. [8]Therefore you shall

19:24 [a]Compare 1 Samuel 10:12

19:18 In times of trouble we should always turn immediately to God. While David went to Samuel, God's messenger, we have direct access to our Lord through the presence of the Holy Spirit.

19:23, 24 The Spirit of God came upon Saul in prostrating power to prevent him from capturing David. Saul's second instance of prophesying (see 10:10, 11) again provoked the question, **Is Saul also among the prophets**?

20:1–42 A remarkable story of a crown prince's willing surrender of his future kingdom to another whom God had chosen.

deal kindly with your servant, for you
have brought your servant into a covenant
of the LORD with you. Nevertheless, if
there is iniquity in me, kill me yourself, for
why should you bring me to your father?"
9But Jonathan said, "Far be it from you!
For if I knew certainly that evil was deter-
mined by my father to come upon you,
then would I not tell you?"
10Then David said to Jonathan, "Who
will tell me, or what *if* your father answers
you roughly?"
11And Jonathan said to David, "Come,
let us go out into the field." So both of
them went out into the field. 12Then Jona-
than said to David: "The LORD God of Is-
rael *is witness!* When I have sounded out
my father sometime tomorrow, *or* the third
day, and indeed *there is* good toward Da-
vid, and I do not send to you and tell you,
13may the LORD do so and much more to
Jonathan. But if it pleases my father *to do*
you evil, then I will report it to you and
send you away, that you may go in safety.
And the LORD be with you as He has been
with my father. 14And you shall not only
show me the kindness of the LORD while I
still live, that I may not die; 15but you shall
not cut off your kindness from my house
forever, no, not when the LORD has cut off
every one of the enemies of David from the
face of the earth." 16So Jonathan made *a
covenant* with the house of David, *saying,*
"Let the LORD require *it* at the hand of Da-
vid's enemies."
17Now Jonathan again caused David to
vow, because he loved him; for he loved
him as he loved his own soul. 18Then Jona-
than said to David, "Tomorrow *is* the New
Moon; and you will be missed, because
your seat will be empty. 19And *when* you
have stayed three days, go down quickly
and come to the place where you hid on
the day of the deed; and remain by the
stone Ē'zel. 20Then I will shoot three arrows
to the side, as though I shot at a target;
21and there I will send a lad, *saying,* 'Go,
find the arrows.' If I expressly say to the
lad, 'Look, the arrows *are* on this side of
you; get them and come'—then, as the
LORD lives, *there is* safety for you and no
harm. 22But if I say thus to the young man,
'Look, the arrows *are* beyond you'—go
your way, for the LORD has sent you away.
23And as for the matter which you and I
have spoken of, indeed the LORD *be* be-
tween you and me forever."
24Then David hid in the field. And when
the New Moon had come, the king sat
down to eat the feast. 25Now the king sat
on his seat, as at other times, on a seat by
the wall. And Jonathan arose,[a] and Abner
sat by Saul's side, but David's place was
empty. 26Nevertheless Saul did not say
anything that day, for he thought, "Some-
thing has happened to him; he *is* unclean,
surely he *is* unclean." 27And it happened
the next day, the second *day* of the month,
that David's place was empty. And Saul
said to Jonathan his son, "Why has the son
of Jesse not come to eat, either yesterday or
today?"
28So Jonathan answered Saul, "David
earnestly asked *permission* of me *to go* to
Bethlehem. 29And he said, 'Please let me
go, for our family has a sacrifice in the city,
and my brother has commanded me *to be
there.* And now, if I have found favor in
your eyes, please let me get away and see
my brothers.' Therefore he has not come to
the king's table."
30Then Saul's anger was aroused against
Jonathan, and he said to him, "You son of a
perverse, rebellious *woman!* Do I not know

20:25 [a]Following Masoretic Text, Syriac, Targum, and Vulgate; Septuagint reads *he sat across from Jonathan.*

20:30–34 Jonathan at last realized that no reconciliation between Saul and David was possible. Saul revealed his awareness that David would succeed him as king, but he stubbornly refuses to accept God's will, attempting to change the course of history in his own power.

that you have chosen the son of Jesse to
your own shame and to the shame of your
mother's nakedness? 31For as long as the
son of Jesse lives on the earth, you shall not
be established, nor your kingdom. Now
therefore, send and bring him to me, for he
shall surely die."
32And Jonathan answered Saul his fa-
ther, and said to him, "Why should he be
killed? What has he done?" 33Then Saul
cast a spear at him to kill him, by which
Jonathan knew that it was determined by
his father to kill David.
34So Jonathan arose from the table in
fierce anger, and ate no food the second
day of the month, for he was grieved for
David, because his father had treated him
shamefully.
35And so it was, in the morning, that
Jonathan went out into the field at the time
appointed with David, and a little lad *was*
with him. 36Then he said to his lad, "Now
run, find the arrows which I shoot." As the
lad ran, he shot an arrow beyond him.
37When the lad had come to the place
where the arrow was which Jonathan had
shot, Jonathan cried out after the lad and
said, "*Is* not the arrow beyond you?" 38And
Jonathan cried out after the lad, "Make
haste, hurry, do not delay!" So Jonathan's
lad gathered up the arrows and came back
to his master. 39But the lad did not know
anything. Only Jonathan and David knew
of the matter. 40Then Jonathan gave his
weapons to his lad, and said to him, "Go,
carry *them* to the city."
41As soon as the lad had gone, David
arose from *a place* toward the south, fell on
his face to the ground, and bowed down
three times. And they kissed one another;
and they wept together, but David more
so. 42Then Jonathan said to David, "Go in
peace, since we have both sworn in the
name of the LORD, saying, 'May the LORD
be between you and me, and between your
descendants and my descendants, for-
ever.' " So he arose and departed, and Jon-
athan went into the city.

CHAPTER 21

David and the Holy Bread

Now David came to Nob, to A·him'-
e·lech the priest. And A·him'e·lech was
afraid when he met David, and said to
him, "Why *are* you alone, and no one is
with you?"
2So David said to A·him'e·lech the
priest, "The king has ordered me on some
business, and said to me, 'Do not let any-
one know anything about the business on
which I send you, or what I have com-
manded you.' And I have directed *my*
young men to such and such a place. 3Now
therefore, what have you on hand? Give
me five *loaves of* bread in my hand, or what-
ever can be found."
4And the priest answered David and
said, "*There is* no common bread on hand;
but there is holy bread, if the young men
have at least kept themselves from
women."
5Then David answered the priest, and
said to him, "Truly, women *have been* kept
from us about three days since I came out.
And the vessels of the young men are holy,
and *the bread is* in effect common, even
though it was consecrated in the vessel this
day."
6So the priest gave him holy *bread;* for
there was no bread there but the show-
bread which had been taken from before
the LORD, in order to put hot bread *in its
place* on the day when it was taken away.

21:1 Nob, a community of priests, was just northeast of Jerusalem. After the destruction of the original tabernacle at Shiloh (see note on Josh. 18:1), the successor seems to have been located at several different places for periods of time.

21:3–6 Holy bread refers to the showbread (Ex. 25:30) that was specially consecrated to be eaten in "a holy place" only by the priests (Lev. 24:5–9).

[7]Now a certain man of the servants of
Saul *was* there that day, detained before the
LORD. And his name *was* Dō'eg, an Ē'dom-
īte, the chief of the herdsmen who *belonged*
to Saul.
[8]And David said to A·him'e·lech, "Is
there not here on hand a spear or a sword?
For I have brought neither my sword nor
my weapons with me, because the king's
business required haste."
[9]So the priest said, "The sword of Goli-
ath the Phi·lis'tine, whom you killed in the
Valley of Ē'lah, there it is, wrapped in a
cloth behind the ephod. If you will take
that, take *it*. For *there is* no other except that
one here."
And David said, "*There is* none like it;
give it to me."

David Flees to Gath

[10]Then David arose and fled that day
from before Saul, and went to Ā'chish the
king of Gath. [11]And the servants of Ā'chish
said to him, "*Is* this not David the king of
the land? Did they not sing of him to one
another in dances, saying:

'Saul has slain his thousands,
And David his ten thousands'?"[a]

[12]Now David took these words to heart,
and was very much afraid of Ā'chish the
king of Gath. [13]So he changed his behavior
before them, pretended madness in their
hands, scratched on the doors of the gate,
and let his saliva fall down on his beard.
[14]Then Ā'chish said to his servants, "Look,
you see the man is insane. Why have you
brought him to me? [15]Have I need of mad-
men, that you have brought this *fellow* to
play the madman in my presence? Shall
this *fellow* come into my house?"

21:11 [a]Compare 1 Samuel 18:7

CHAPTER 22

David's Four Hundred Men

David therefore departed from there
and escaped to the cave of A·dul'lam. So
when his brothers and all his father's
house heard *it*, they went down there to
him. [2]And everyone *who was* in distress,
everyone who *was* in debt, and everyone
who was discontented gathered to him. So
he became captain over them. And there
were about four hundred men with him.
[3]Then David went from there to
Miz'pah of Mō'ab; and he said to the king
of Mō'ab, "Please let my father and mother
come here with you, till I know what God
will do for me." [4]So he brought them be-
fore the king of Mō'ab, and they dwelt
with him all the time that David was in the
stronghold.
[5]Now the prophet Gad said to David,
"Do not stay in the stronghold; depart, and
go to the land of Judah." So David de-
parted and went into the forest of Hē'reth.

Saul Murders the Priests

[6]When Saul heard that David and the
men who *were* with him had been discov-
ered—now Saul was staying in Gib'ē·ah
under a tamarisk tree in Rā'mah, with his
spear in his hand, and all his servants
standing about him— [7]then Saul said to his
servants who stood about him, "Hear now,
you Ben'ja·mītes! Will the son of Jesse give
every one of you fields and vineyards, *and*
make you all captains of thousands and
captains of hundreds? [8]All of you have
conspired against me, and *there is* no one
who reveals to me that my son has made a

22:1, 2 The **cave of Adullam** was in the lowland country of Judah some 16 miles (26 km) southwest of Jerusalem and about 12 miles (19 km) northeast of Gath. **Four hundred men** (v. 2; later 600, 23:13) gathered around David. Many were probably refugees from Saul's misguided and erratic rule, but others merely discontented—not a particularly savory group.

covenant with the son of Jesse; and *there is*
not one of you who is sorry for me or re-
veals to me that my son has stirred up my
servant against me, to lie in wait, as *it is*
this day."

9Then answered Dō'eg the Ē'dom·īte,
who was set over the servants of Saul, and
said, "I saw the son of Jesse going to Nob,
to A·him'e·lech the son of A·hī'tub. 10And
he inquired of the LORD for him, gave him
provisions, and gave him the sword of Go-
liath the Phi·lis'tine."

11So the king sent to call A·him'e·lech
the priest, the son of A·hī'tub, and all his
father's house, the priests who *were* in
Nob. And they all came to the king. 12And
Saul said, "Hear now, son of A·hī'tub!"

He answered, "Here I am, my lord."

13Then Saul said to him, "Why have you
conspired against me, you and the son of
Jesse, in that you have given him bread
and a sword, and have inquired of God for
him, that he should rise against me, to lie
in wait, as it is this day?"

14So A·him'e·lech answered the king
and said, "And who among all your ser-
vants *is as* faithful as David, who is the
king's son-in-law, who goes at your bid-
ding, and is honorable in your house?
15Did I then begin to inquire of God
for him? Far be it from me! Let not the
king impute anything to his servant, *or* to
any in the house of my father. For your ser-
vant knew nothing of all this, little or
much."

16And the king said, "You shall surely
die, A·him'e·lech, you and all your father's
house!" 17Then the king said to the guards
who stood about him, "Turn and kill the
priests of the LORD, because their hand also
is with David, and because they knew
when he fled and did not tell it to me." But
the servants of the king would not lift their
hands to strike the priests of the LORD.
18And the king said to Dō'eg, "You turn
and kill the priests!" So Dō'eg the
Ē'dom·īte turned and struck the priests,
and killed on that day eighty-five men
who wore a linen ephod. 19Also Nob, the
city of the priests, he struck with the edge
of the sword, both men and women, chil-
dren and nursing infants, oxen and don-
keys and sheep—with the edge of the
sword.

20Now one of the sons of A·him'e·lech
the son of A·hī'tub, named A·bī'a·thar, es-
caped and fled after David. 21And A·bī'-
a·thar told David that Saul had killed the
LORD's priests. 22So David said to A·bī'-
a·thar, "I knew that day, when Dō'eg the
Ē'dom·īte *was* there, that he would surely
tell Saul. I have caused *the death* of all the
persons of your father's house. 23Stay with
me; do not fear. For he who seeks my life
seeks your life, but with me you *shall be*
safe."

CHAPTER 23

David Saves the City of Keilah

Then they told David, saying, "Look,
the Phi·lis'tines are fighting against
Kē·ī'lah, and they are robbing the thresh-
ing floors."

2Therefore David inquired of the LORD,
saying, "Shall I go and attack these
Phi·lis'tines?"

And the LORD said to David, "Go and at-
tack the Phi·lis'tines, and save Kē·ī'lah."

3But David's men said to him, "Look,
we are afraid here in Judah. How much
more then if we go to Kē·ī'lah against the
armies of the Phi·lis'tines?" 4Then David
inquired of the LORD once again.

And the LORD answered him and said,
"Arise, go down to Kē·ī'lah. For I will de-
liver the Phi·lis'tines into your hand."
5And David and his men went to Kē·ī'lah
and fought with the Phi·lis'tines, struck
them with a mighty blow, and took away

22:20–23 Abiathar later became high priest under David and was his counselor on a number of occasions.

their livestock. So David saved the inhab-
itants of Kē·ī′lah.
[6]Now it happened, when A·bī′a·thar
the son of A·him′e·lech fled to David at
Kē·ī′lah, *that* he went down *with* an ephod
in his hand.
[7]And Saul was told that David had
gone to Kē·ī′lah. So Saul said, "God has
delivered him into my hand, for he has
shut himself in by entering a town that
has gates and bars." [8]Then Saul called
all the people together for war, to go
down to Kē·ī′lah to besiege David and his
men.
[9]When David knew that Saul plotted
evil against him, he said to A·bī′a·thar
the priest, "Bring the ephod here." [10]Then
David said, "O LORD God of Israel,
Your servant has certainly heard that Saul
seeks to come to Kē·ī′lah to destroy
the city for my sake. [11]Will the men of
Kē·ī′lah deliver me into his hand? Will
Saul come down, as Your servant has
heard? O LORD God of Israel, I pray, tell
Your servant."

And the LORD said, "He will come
down."
[12]Then David said, "Will the men of
Kē·ī′lah deliver me and my men into the
hand of Saul?"

And the LORD said, "They will deliver
you."
[13]So David and his men, about six
hundred, arose and departed from
Kē·ī′lah and went wherever they could go.
Then it was told Saul that David had es-
caped from Kē·ī′lah; so he halted the expe-
dition.

David in Wilderness Strongholds

[14]And David stayed in strongholds in
the wilderness, and remained in the moun-
tains in the Wilderness of Ziph. Saul
sought him every day, but God did not de-
liver him into his hand. [15]So David saw
that Saul had come out to seek his life. And
David *was* in the Wilderness of Ziph in a
forest.[a] [16]Then Jonathan, Saul's son, arose
and went to David in the woods and
strengthened his hand in God. [17]And he
said to him, "Do not fear, for the hand of
Saul my father shall not find you. You shall
be king over Israel, and I shall be next to
you. Even my father Saul knows that." [18]So
the two of them made a covenant before
the LORD. And David stayed in the woods,
and Jonathan went to his own house.
[19]Then the Ziph′ītes came up to Saul at
Gib′ē·ah, saying, "Is David not hiding
with us in strongholds in the woods, in the
hill of Ha·chī′lah, which *is* on the south of
Jē·shī′mon? [20]Now therefore, O king, come
down according to all the desire of your
soul to come down; and our part *shall be* to
deliver him into the king's hand."
[21]And Saul said, "Blessed *are* you of the
LORD, for you have compassion on me.
[22]Please go and find out for sure, and see
the place where his hideout is, *and* who has
seen him there. For I am told he is very
crafty. [23]See therefore, and take knowledge
of all the lurking places where he hides;
and come back to me with certainty, and I
will go with you. And it shall be, if he is in
the land, that I will search for him through-
out all the clans[a] of Judah."
[24]So they arose and went to Ziph before
Saul. But David and his men *were* in the

23:15 [a]Or *in Horesh* 23:23 [a]Literally *thousands*

23:9–12 The call for **the ephod**, the linen apron worn by the priest, probably indicates the method of seeking God's guidance in that day. It is supposed that a pocket in the ephod contained two counters, called Urim and Thummim (Ex. 28:30), each of which was marked affirmative on one side and negative on the other. Probably two affirmatives meant "yes," two negatives meant "no," and one of each indicated no answer.

23:14–29 David moved on farther south into the **Wilderness of Ziph**. This territory east and southeast of Hebron is a jumble of arid hills where there is little rainfall and almost no habitation. There are no roads and few vantage points. Thus Saul's difficulty in tracking down David is easily understood.

Wilderness of Mā′on, in the plain on the south of Jē·shī′mon. 25When Saul and his men went to seek *him,* they told David. Therefore he went down to the rock, and stayed in the Wilderness of Mā′on. And when Saul heard *that,* he pursued David in the Wilderness of Mā′on. 26Then Saul went on one side of the mountain, and David and his men on the other side of the mountain. So David made haste to get away from Saul, for Saul and his men were encircling David and his men to take them.

27But a messenger came to Saul, saying, "Hurry and come, for the Phi·lis′tines have invaded the land!" 28Therefore Saul returned from pursuing David, and went against the Phi·lis′tines; so they called that place the Rock of Escape.[a] 29Then David went up from there and dwelt in strongholds at En Ge′di.

CHAPTER 24

David Spares Saul

Now it happened, when Saul had returned from following the Phi·lis′tines, that it was told him, saying, "Take note! David *is* in the Wilderness of En Ge′di." 2Then Saul took three thousand chosen men from all Israel, and went to seek David and his men on the Rocks of the Wild Goats. 3So he came to the sheepfolds by the road, where there *was* a cave; and Saul went in to attend to his needs. (David and his men were staying in the recesses of the cave.) 4Then the men of David said to him, "This is the day of which the LORD said to you, 'Behold, I will deliver your enemy into your hand, that you may do to him as it seems good to you.' " And David arose and secretly cut off a corner of Saul's robe. 5Now it happened afterward that David's heart troubled him because he had cut Saul's *robe.* 6And he said to his men, "The LORD forbid that I should do this thing to my master, the LORD's anointed, to stretch out my hand against him, seeing he *is* the anointed of the LORD." 7So David restrained his servants with *these* words, and did not allow them to rise against Saul. And Saul got up from the cave and went on *his* way.

8David also arose afterward, went out of the cave, and called out to Saul, saying, "My lord the king!" And when Saul looked behind him, David stooped with his face to the earth, and bowed down. 9And David said to Saul: "Why do you listen to the words of men who say, 'Indeed David seeks your harm'? 10Look, this day your eyes have seen that the LORD delivered you today into my hand in the cave, and *someone* urged *me* to kill you. But *my eye* spared you, and I said, 'I will not stretch out my hand against my lord, for he *is* the LORD's anointed.' 11Moreover, my father, see! Yes, see the corner of your robe in my hand! For in that I cut off the corner of your robe, and did not kill you, know and see that *there is* neither evil nor rebellion in my hand, and I have not sinned against you. Yet you hunt my life to take it. 12Let the LORD judge between you and me, and let the LORD avenge me on you. But my hand shall not be against you. 13As the proverb of the ancients says, 'Wickedness proceeds from the wicked.' But my hand shall not be against you. 14After whom has the king of Israel come out? Whom do you pursue? A dead dog? A flea? 15Therefore let the LORD be judge, and judge between you and me, and see and plead my case, and deliver me out of your hand."

16So it was, when David had finished

23:28 [a]Hebrew *Sela Hammahlekoth*

24:3–22 David's deep respect for God's anointing compelled him to spare Saul's life when the king was within his power. David's decision to allow the Lord to deal with Saul rather than taking revenge himself indicates his growing wisdom. Saul's change of attitude (vv. 16, 17), unfortunately, was only temporary.

speaking these words to Saul, that Saul
said, "*Is* this your voice, my son David?"
And Saul lifted up his voice and wept.
[17]Then he said to David: "You *are* more
righteous than I; for you have rewarded
me with good, whereas I have rewarded
you with evil. [18]And you have shown this
day how you have dealt well with me; for
when the LORD delivered me into your
hand, you did not kill me. [19]For if a man
finds his enemy, will he let him get away
safely? Therefore may the LORD reward
you with good for what you have done to
me this day. [20]And now I know indeed that
you shall surely be king, and that the king-
dom of Israel shall be established in your
hand. [21]Therefore swear now to me by the
LORD that you will not cut off my descen-
dants after me, and that you will not de-
stroy my name from my father's house."
[22]So David swore to Saul. And Saul went
home, but David and his men went up to
the stronghold.

CHAPTER 25

Death of Samuel

Then Samuel died; and the Israelites
gathered together and lamented for him,
and buried him at his home in Rā'mah.
And David arose and went down to the
Wilderness of Par'an.[a]

David and the Wife of Nabal

[2]Now *there was* a man in Mā'on whose
business *was* in Car'mel, and the man *was*
very rich. He had three thousand sheep
and a thousand goats. And he was shear-
ing his sheep in Car'mel. [3]The name of the
man *was* Nā'bal, and the name of his wife
Ab'i·gāil. And *she was* a woman of good
understanding and beautiful appearance;
but the man *was* harsh and evil in *his* do-
ings. He *was of the house of* Caleb.
[4]When David heard in the wilderness
that Nā'bal was shearing his sheep, [5]David
sent ten young men; and David said to the
young men, "Go up to Car'mel, go to Nā'-
bal, and greet him in my name. [6]And thus
you shall say to him who lives *in prosperity:*
'Peace *be* to you, peace to your house, and
peace to all that you have! [7]Now I have
heard that you have shearers. Your shep-
herds were with us, and we did not hurt
them, nor was there anything missing
from them all the while they were in
Car'mel. [8]Ask your young men, and they
will tell you. Therefore let *my* young men
find favor in your eyes, for we come on a
feast day. Please give whatever comes to
your hand to your servants and to your
son David.'"
[9]So when David's young men came,
they spoke to Nā'bal according to all these
words in the name of David, and waited.
[10]Then Nā'bal answered David's ser-
vants, and said, "Who *is* David, and who *is*
the son of Jesse? There are many servants
nowadays who break away each one from
his master. [11]Shall I then take my bread and
my water and my meat that I have killed
for my shearers, and give *it* to men when I
do not know where they *are* from?"
[12]So David's young men turned on their
heels and went back; and they came and
told him all these words. [13]Then David said
to his men, "Every man gird on his
sword." So every man girded on his
sword, and David also girded on
his sword. And about four hundred men

25:1 [a]Following Masoretic Text, Syriac, Targum, and Vulgate; Septuagint reads *Maon.*

24:21 Saul, clearly aware that David would become his successor, extracted a promise that his family would be spared the usual fate of the families of displaced dynasties.

25:1 The death of Samuel is related at this point. The prophet had been in retirement since his farewell address (see ch. 12) except for the private anointing of David (ch. 16). It is a tribute to this godly man that the entire nation rallied for his funeral.

25:2, 3 Nabal means "fool" (v. 25) and his reply to David's request (vv. 10, 11) shows the appropriateness of the name.

went with David, and two hundred stayed with the supplies.

14Now one of the young men told Ab'i·gāil, Nā'bal's wife, saying, "Look, David sent messengers from the wilderness to greet our master; and he reviled them. 15But the men *were* very good to us, and we were not hurt, nor did we miss anything as long as we accompanied them, when we were in the fields. 16They were a wall to us both by night and day, all the time we were with them keeping the sheep. 17Now therefore, know and consider what you will do, for harm is determined against our master and against all his household. For he *is such* a scoundrel[a] that *one* cannot speak to him."

18Then Ab'i·gāil made haste and took two hundred *loaves* of bread, two skins of wine, five sheep already dressed, five seahs of roasted *grain,* one hundred clusters of raisins, and two hundred cakes of figs, and loaded *them* on donkeys. 19And she said to her servants, "Go on before me; see, I am coming after you." But she did not tell her husband Nā'bal.

20So it was, *as* she rode on the donkey, that she went down under cover of the hill; and there were David and his men, coming down toward her, and she met them. 21Now David had said, "Surely in vain I have protected all that this *fellow* has in the wilderness, so that nothing was missed of all that *belongs* to him. And he has repaid me evil for good. 22May God do so, and more also, to the enemies of David, if I leave one male of all who *belong* to him by morning light."

23Now when Ab'i·gāil saw David, she dismounted quickly from the donkey, fell on her face before David, and bowed down to the ground. 24So she fell at his feet and said: "On me, my lord, *on* me *let* this iniquity *be!* And please let your maidservant speak in your ears, and hear the words of your maidservant. 25Please, let not my lord regard this scoundrel Nā'bal. For as his name *is,* so *is* he: Nā'bal[a] *is* his name, and folly *is* with him! But I, your maidservant, did not see the young men of my lord whom you sent. 26Now therefore, my lord, *as* the LORD lives and *as* your soul lives, since the LORD has held you back from coming to bloodshed and from avenging yourself with your own hand, now then, let your enemies and those who seek harm for my lord be as Nā'bal. 27And now this present which your maidservant has brought to my lord, let it be given to the young men who follow my lord. 28Please forgive the trespass of your maidservant. For the LORD will certainly make for my lord an enduring house, because my lord fights the battles of the LORD, and evil is not found in you throughout your days. 29Yet a man has risen to pursue you and seek your life, but the life of my lord shall be bound in the bundle of the living with the LORD your God; and the lives of your enemies He shall sling out, *as from* the pocket of a sling. 30And it shall come to pass, when the LORD has done for my lord according to all the good that He has spoken concerning you, and has appointed you ruler over Israel, 31that this will be no grief to you, nor offense of heart to my lord, either that you have shed blood without cause, or that my lord has avenged himself. But when the LORD has dealt well

25:17 [a]Literally *son of Belial* 25:25 [a]Literally *Fool*

25:18 While some may interpret Abigail's actions as a rebellion against her husband, the context shows that, knowing Nabal had rudely denied David's request, she wanted to save her husband from certain disaster.

25:23–31 The plea of **Abigail** (her name means "My Father Redeems") is a masterpiece of wisdom. **Bound in the bundle of the living** (v. 29) describes one whose life is in the safekeeping of the Lord.

25:31 Through all his life, David's impulsiveness was to be his strength and his weakness. Here Abigail's quick thinking and well-chosen words prevented him from doing something he would later regret.

with my lord, then remember your maidservant."
[32]Then David said to Ab'i·gāil: "Blessed *is* the LORD God of Israel, who sent you this day to meet me! [33]And blessed *is* your advice and blessed *are* you, because you have kept me this day from coming to bloodshed and from avenging myself with my own hand. [34]For indeed, *as* the LORD God of Israel lives, who has kept me back from hurting you, unless you had hurried and come to meet me, surely by morning light no males would have been left to Nā'bal!"
[35]So David received from her hand what she had brought him, and said to her, "Go up in peace to your house. See, I have heeded your voice and respected your person."

[36]Now Ab'i·gāil went to Nā'bal, and there he was, holding a feast in his house, like the feast of a king. And Nā'bal's heart *was* merry within him, for he *was* very drunk; therefore she told him nothing, little or much, until morning light. [37]So it was, in the morning, when the wine had gone from Nā'bal, and his wife had told him these things, that his heart died within him, and he became *like* a stone. [38]Then it happened, *after* about ten days, that the LORD struck Nā'bal, and he died.

[39]So when David heard that Nā'bal was dead, he said, "Blessed *be* the LORD, who has pleaded the cause of my reproach from the hand of Nā'bal, and has kept His servant from evil! For the LORD has returned the wickedness of Nā'bal on his own head."

And David sent and proposed to Ab'i·gāil, to take her as his wife. [40]When the servants of David had come to Ab'i·gāil at Car'mel, they spoke to her saying, "David sent us to you, to ask you to become his wife."

[41]Then she arose, bowed her face to the earth, and said, "Here is your maidservant, a servant to wash the feet of the servants of my lord." [42]So Ab'i·gāil rose in haste and rode on a donkey, attended by five of her maidens; and she followed the messengers of David, and became his wife. [43]David also took A·hin'ō·am of Jez'rē·el, and so both of them were his wives.

[44]But Saul had given Mī'chal his daughter, David's wife, to Pal'tī[a] the son of Lā'ish, who *was* from Gal'lim.

CHAPTER 26

David Spares Saul a Second Time

Now the Ziph'ītes came to Saul at Gib'ē·ah, saying, "Is David not hiding in the hill of Ha·chī'lah, opposite Jē·shī'mon?" [2]Then Saul arose and went down to the Wilderness of Ziph, having three thousand chosen men of Israel with him, to seek David in the Wilderness of Ziph. [3]And Saul encamped in the hill of Ha·chī'lah, which *is* opposite Jē·shī'mon, by the road. But David stayed in the wilderness, and he saw that Saul came after him into the wilderness. [4]David therefore sent out spies, and understood that Saul had indeed come.

[5]So David arose and came to the place where Saul had encamped. And David saw the place where Saul lay, and Abner the son of Ner, the commander of his army. Now Saul lay within the camp, with the people encamped all around him. [6]Then David answered, and said to A·him'e·lech the Hit'tīte and to A·bi'shaī the son of Ze·rū'i·ah, brother of Jō'ab, saying, "Who will go down with me to Saul in the camp?"

And A·bi'shaī said, "I will go down with you."

[7]So David and A·bi'shaī came to the

25:44 [a]Spelled *Paltiel* in 2 Samuel 3:15

26:1–25 David spares Saul's life a second time (see ch. 24), resulting in Saul's second expression of remorse—an expression David did not trust, as shown by his response in 27:1.

people by night; and there Saul lay sleep-
ing within the camp, with his spear stuck
in the ground by his head. And Abner and
the people lay all around him. 8Then
A·bi'shaī said to David, "God has deliv-
ered your enemy into your hand this day.
Now therefore, please, let me strike him at
once with the spear, right to the earth; and
I will not *have to strike* him a second time!"
9But David said to A·bi'shaī, "Do not
destroy him; for who can stretch out his
hand against the LORD's anointed, and be
guiltless?" 10David said furthermore, "*As*
the LORD lives, the LORD shall strike him, or
his day shall come to die, or he shall go out
to battle and perish. 11The LORD forbid that
I should stretch out my hand against the
LORD's anointed. But please, take now the
spear and the jug of water that *are* by his
head, and let us go." 12So David took the
spear and the jug of water *by* Saul's head,
and they got away; and no man saw or
knew *it* or awoke. For they *were* all asleep,
because a deep sleep from the LORD had
fallen on them.
13Now David went over to the other
side, and stood on the top of a hill afar off,
a great distance *being* between them. 14And
David called out to the people and to Ab-
ner the son of Ner, saying, "Do you not an-
swer, Abner?"
Then Abner answered and said, "Who
are you, calling out to the king?"
15So David said to Abner, "*Are* you not a
man? And who *is* like you in Israel? Why
then have you not guarded your lord the
king? For one of the people came in to de-
stroy your lord the king. 16This thing that
you have done *is* not good. *As* the LORD
lives, you deserve to die, because you have
not guarded your master, the LORD's
anointed. And now see where the king's
spear *is,* and the jug of water that *was* by
his head."
17Then Saul knew David's voice, and
said, "*Is* that your voice, my son David?"
David said, "*It is* my voice, my lord, O
king." 18And he said, "Why does my lord
thus pursue his servant? For what have I
done, or what evil *is* in my hand? 19Now
therefore, please, let my lord the king hear
the words of his servant: If the LORD has
stirred you up against me, let Him accept
an offering. But if *it is* the children of men,
may they *be* cursed before the LORD, for
they have driven me out this day from
sharing in the inheritance of the LORD, say-
ing, 'Go, serve other gods.' 20So now, do
not let my blood fall to the earth before the
face of the LORD. For the king of Israel has
come out to seek a flea, as when one hunts
a partridge in the mountains."
21Then Saul said, "I have sinned. Return,
my son David. For I will harm you no
more, because my life was precious in your
eyes this day. Indeed I have played the fool
and erred exceedingly."
22And David answered and said, "Here
is the king's spear. Let one of the young
men come over and get it. 23May the LORD
repay every man *for* his righteousness and
his faithfulness; for the LORD delivered you
into *my* hand today, but I would not stretch
out my hand against the LORD's anointed.
24And indeed, as your life was valued
much this day in my eyes, so let my life
be valued much in the eyes of the LORD,
and let Him deliver me out of all tribula-
tion."
25Then Saul said to David, "*May* you *be*
blessed, my son David! You shall both do
great things and also still prevail."
So David went on his way, and Saul re-
turned to his place.

CHAPTER 27

David Allied with the Philistines

And David said in his heart, "Now I
shall perish someday by the hand of Saul.

26:19 the inheritance of the LORD: The Israelite people. Because of Saul's hatred David could not participate in the life of his people, especially their worship. Evidently he was already contemplating going over to the Philistines, the step he takes in ch. 27.

There is nothing better for me than that I should speedily escape to the land of the Phi·lis′tines; and Saul will despair of me, to seek me anymore in any part of Israel. So I shall escape out of his hand." 2Then David arose and went over with the six hundred men who *were* with him to Ā′chish the son of Mā′och, king of Gath. 3So David dwelt with Ā′chish at Gath, he and his men, each man with his household, *and* David with his two wives, A·hin′ō·am the Jez′rē·el·ī·tess, and Ab′i·gāil the Car′mel·ī·tess, Nā′bal's widow. 4And it was told Saul that David had fled to Gath; so he sought him no more.

5Then David said to Ā′chish, "If I have now found favor in your eyes, let them give me a place in some town in the country, that I may dwell there. For why should your servant dwell in the royal city with you?" 6So Ā′chish gave him Zik′lag that day. Therefore Zik′lag has belonged to the kings of Judah to this day. 7Now the time that David dwelt in the country of the Phi·lis′tines was one full year and four months.

8And David and his men went up and raided the Gesh′ū·rītes, the Gir′zītes,[a] and the A·mal′e·kītes. For those nations were the inhabitants of the land from of old, as you go to Shūr, even as far as the land of Egypt. 9Whenever David attacked the land, he left neither man nor woman alive, but took away the sheep, the oxen, the donkeys, the camels, and the apparel, and returned and came to Ā′chish. 10Then Ā′chish would say, "Where have you made a raid today?" And David would say, "Against the southern *area* of Judah, or against the southern *area* of the Je·rah′mē·el·ītes, or against the southern *area* of the Ken′ītes." 11David would save neither man nor woman alive, to bring *news* to Gath, saying, "Lest they should inform on us, saying, 'Thus David did.' " And thus *was* his behavior all the time he dwelt in the country of the Phi·lis′tines. 12So Ā′chish believed David, saying, "He has made his people Israel utterly abhor him; therefore he will be my servant forever."

CHAPTER 28

Now it happened in those days that the Phi·lis′tines gathered their armies together for war, to fight with Israel. And Ā′chish said to David, "You assuredly know that you will go out with me to battle, you and your men."

2So David said to Ā′chish, "Surely you know what your servant can do."

And Ā′chish said to David, "Therefore I will make you one of my chief guardians forever."

Saul Consults a Medium

3Now Samuel had died, and all Israel had lamented for him and buried him in Rā′mah, in his own city. And Saul had put the mediums and the spiritists out of the land.

4Then the Phi·lis′tines gathered together, and came and encamped at Shū′nem. So Saul gathered all Israel together, and they encamped at Gil·bō′a. 5When Saul saw the army of the Phi·lis′tines, he was afraid, and his heart trembled greatly. 6And when Saul inquired of the LORD, the LORD did not answer him, either by dreams or by Ū′rim or by the prophets.

7Then Saul said to his servants, "Find me a woman who is a medium, that I may go to her and inquire of her."

27:8 [a]Or *Gezrites*

27:6 Ziklag was a city about 22 miles (35 km) southeast of Gath, then under Philistine control. **to this day**: Reference to the kings of Judah indicates that this portion of the account was either written or edited after Solomon's death in about 930 B.C. but before the Babylonian exile of 586 B.C.

28:3 the mediums and the spiritists: All forms of spiritualism and necromancy were forbidden in the law. Before his break with Samuel, Saul had vigorously enforced this law.

And his servants said to him, "In fact,
there is a woman who is a medium at En
Dor."
8So Saul disguised himself and put on
other clothes, and he went, and two men
with him; and they came to the woman by
night. And he said, "Please conduct a
séance for me, and bring up for me the one
I shall name to you."
9Then the woman said to him, "Look,
you know what Saul has done, how he has
cut off the mediums and the spiritists from
the land. Why then do you lay a snare for
my life, to cause me to die?"
10And Saul swore to her by the LORD,
saying, "*As* the LORD lives, no punishment
shall come upon you for this thing."
11Then the woman said, "Whom shall I
bring up for you?"
And he said, "Bring up Samuel for me."
12When the woman saw Samuel, she
cried out with a loud voice. And the
woman spoke to Saul, saying, "Why have
you deceived me? For you *are* Saul!"
13And the king said to her, "Do not be
afraid. What did you see?"
And the woman said to Saul, "I saw a
spirit[a] ascending out of the earth."
14So he said to her, "What *is* his form?"
And she said, "An old man is coming
up, and he *is* covered with a mantle." And
Saul perceived that it *was* Samuel, and he
stooped with *his* face to the ground and
bowed down.
15Now Samuel said to Saul, "Why have
you disturbed me by bringing me up?"
And Saul answered, "I am deeply dis-
tressed; for the Phi·lis'tines make war
against me, and God has departed from
me and does not answer me anymore, nei-
ther by prophets nor by dreams. Therefore
I have called you, that you may reveal to
me what I should do."
16Then Samuel said: "So why do you ask
me, seeing the LORD has departed from
you and has become your enemy? 17And
the LORD has done for Himself[a] as He
spoke by me. For the LORD has torn the
kingdom out of your hand and given it to
your neighbor, David. 18Because you did
not obey the voice of the LORD nor execute
His fierce wrath upon Am'a·lek, therefore
the LORD has done this thing to you this
day. 19Moreover the LORD will also deliver
Israel with you into the hand of the
Phi·lis'tines. And tomorrow you and your
sons *will be* with me. The LORD will also de-
liver the army of Israel into the hand of the
Phi·lis'tines."
20Immediately Saul fell full length on the
ground, and was dreadfully afraid because
of the words of Samuel. And there was no
strength in him, for he had eaten no food
all day or all night.
21And the woman came to Saul and saw
that he was severely troubled, and said to
him, "Look, your maidservant has obeyed
your voice, and I have put my life in my
hands and heeded the words which you
spoke to me. 22Now therefore, please, heed
also the voice of your maidservant, and let
me set a piece of bread before you; and eat,
that you may have strength when you go
on *your* way."
23But he refused and said, "I will not
eat."
So his servants, together with the
woman, urged him; and he heeded their
voice. Then he arose from the ground and
sat on the bed. 24Now the woman had a fat-
ted calf in the house, and she hastened to
kill it. And she took flour and kneaded *it,*
and baked unleavened bread from it. 25So
she brought *it* before Saul and his servants,

28:13 [a]Hebrew *elohim* 28:17 [a]Or *him,* that is, David

28:15 God has departed from me: A pathetic confession from one who had started out with everything in his favor. It was Saul who departed from God.

28:19 will be with me: In Sheol, the abode of the dead. The OT understanding of existence after death was limited (with no clear differentiation, for example, between the fates of the righteous and the wicked). The emphasis was instead upon life on earth.

and they ate. Then they rose and went away that night.

CHAPTER 29

The Philistines Reject David

Then the Phi·lis'tines gathered together all their armies at Ā'phek, and the Israelites encamped by a fountain which *is* in Jez'-rē·el. [2]And the lords of the Phi·lis'tines passed in review by hundreds and by thousands, but David and his men passed in review at the rear with Ā'chish. [3]Then the princes of the Phi·lis'tines said, "What *are* these Hebrews *doing here?*"

And Ā'chish said to the princes of the Phi·lis'tines, "*Is* this not David, the servant of Saul king of Israel, who has been with me these days, or these years? And to this day I have found no fault in him since he defected *to me.*"

[4]But the princes of the Phi·lis'tines were angry with him; so the princes of the Phi·lis'tines said to him, "Make this fellow return, that he may go back to the place which you have appointed for him, and do not let him go down with us to battle, lest in the battle he become our adversary. For with what could he reconcile himself to his master, if not with the heads of these men? [5]*Is* this not David, of whom they sang to one another in dances, saying:

'Saul has slain his thousands,
And David his ten thousands'?"[a]

[6]Then Ā'chish called David and said to him, "Surely, *as* the LORD lives, you have been upright, and your going out and your coming in with me in the army *is* good in my sight. For to this day I have not found evil in you since the day of your coming to me. Nevertheless the lords do not favor you. [7]Therefore return now, and go in peace, that you may not displease the lords of the Phi·lis'tines."

[8]So David said to Ā'chish, "But what have I done? And to this day what have you found in your servant as long as I have been with you, that I may not go and fight against the enemies of my lord the king?"

[9]Then Ā'chish answered and said to David, "I know that you *are* as good in my sight as an angel of God; nevertheless the princes of the Phi·lis'tines have said, 'He shall not go up with us to the battle.' [10]Now therefore, rise early in the morning with your master's servants who have come with you.[a] And as soon as you are up early in the morning and have light, depart."

[11]So David and his men rose early to depart in the morning, to return to the land of the Phi·lis'tines. And the Phi·lis'tines went up to Jez'rē·el.

CHAPTER 30

David's Conflict with the Amalekites

Now it happened, when David and his men came to Zik'lag, on the third day, that the A·mal'e·kītes had invaded the South and Zik'lag, attacked Zik'lag and burned it with fire, [2]and had taken captive the women and those who *were* there, from small to great; they did not kill anyone, but carried *them* away and went their way. [3]So

29:5 [a]Compare 1 Samuel 18:7 29:10 [a]Following Masoretic Text, Targum, and Vulgate; Septuagint adds *and go to the place which I have selected for you there; and set no bothersome word in your heart, for you are good before me. And rise on your way.*

29:9 an angel of God: That is, esteemed as a messenger of the gods. Achish, a worshiper of many gods, does not use the covenant name of the Lord but a term that in this context could be translated "the gods."

30:1–20 David's return to Ziklag was both tragic and timely. Encouraged by a leading from the Lord (v. 8), David overtook the marauding Amalekites and, in a surprise attack (v. 17), recovered the captives and plunder that had been taken. While Saul was losing his kingdom in death, David was being harassed by, and harassing, the Amalekites whose incomplete destruction was the cause of Saul's rejection.

David and his men came to the city, and there it was, burned with fire; and their wives, their sons, and their daughters had been taken captive. 4Then David and the people who *were* with him lifted up their voices and wept, until they had no more power to weep. 5And David's two wives, A·hin'ō·am the Jez'rē·el·ī·tess, and Ab'-i·gāil the widow of Nā'bal the Car'mel·īte, had been taken captive. 6Now David was greatly distressed, for the people spoke of stoning him, because the soul of all the people was grieved, every man for his sons and his daughters. But David strengthened himself in the LORD his God.

7Then David said to A·bī'a·thar the priest, A·him'e·lech's son, "Please bring the ephod here to me." And A·bī'a·thar brought the ephod to David. 8So David inquired of the LORD, saying, "Shall I pursue this troop? Shall I overtake them?"

And He answered him, "Pursue, for you shall surely overtake *them* and without fail recover *all*."

9So David went, he and the six hundred men who *were* with him, and came to the Brook Bē'sor, where those stayed who were left behind. 10But David pursued, he and four hundred men; for two hundred stayed *behind,* who were so weary that they could not cross the Brook Bē'sor.

11Then they found an Egyptian in the field, and brought him to David; and they gave him bread and he ate, and they let him drink water. 12And they gave him a piece of a cake of figs and two clusters of raisins. So when he had eaten, his strength came back to him; for he had eaten no bread nor drunk water for three days and three nights. 13Then David said to him, "To whom do you *belong,* and where *are* you from?"

And he said, "I *am* a young man from Egypt, servant of an A·mal'e·kīte; and my master left me behind, because three days ago I fell sick. 14We made an invasion of the southern *area* of the Cher'e·thītes, in the *territory* which *belongs* to Judah, and of the southern *area* of Caleb; and we burned Zik'lag with fire."

15And David said to him, "Can you take me down to this troop?"

So he said, "Swear to me by God that you will neither kill me nor deliver me into the hands of my master, and I will take you down to this troop."

16And when he had brought him down, there they were, spread out over all the land, eating and drinking and dancing, because of all the great spoil which they had taken from the land of the Phi·lis'tines and from the land of Judah. 17Then David attacked them from twilight until the evening of the next day. Not a man of them escaped, except four hundred young men who rode on camels and fled. 18So David recovered all that the A·mal'e·kītes had carried away, and David rescued his two wives. 19And nothing of theirs was lacking, either small or great, sons or daughters, spoil or anything which they had taken from them; David recovered all. 20Then David took all the flocks and herds they had driven before those *other* livestock, and said, "This *is* David's spoil."

21Now David came to the two hundred men who had been so weary that they could not follow David, whom they also had made to stay at the Brook Bē'sor. So they went out to meet David and to meet the people who *were* with him. And when David came near the people, he greeted them. 22Then all the wicked and worthless men[a] of those who went with David answered and said, "Because they did not go with us, we will not give them *any* of the spoil that we have recovered, except for every man's wife and children, that they may lead *them* away and depart."

30:22 [a]Literally *men of Belial*

30:21–25 A just and compassionate rule became general policy for the armies of Israel. Surely this instinct for fairness was a part of what made David so beloved by his men.

23But David said, "My brethren, you
shall not do so with what the LORD has
given us, who has preserved us and deliv-
ered into our hand the troop that came
against us. 24For who will heed you in this
matter? But as his part *is* who goes down
to the battle, so *shall* his part *be* who stays
by the supplies; they shall share alike." 25So
it was, from that day forward; he made it a
statute and an ordinance for Israel to this
day.

26Now when David came to Zik′lag, he
sent *some* of the spoil to the elders of Judah,
to his friends, saying, "Here is a present for
you from the spoil of the enemies of the
LORD"— 27to *those* who *were* in Beth′el, *those*
who *were* in Rā′moth of the South, *those*
who *were* in Jat′tir, 28*those* who *were* in
A·rō′er, *those* who *were* in Siph′moth, *those*
who *were* in Esh·te·mō′a, 29*those* who *were*
in Rā′chal, *those* who *were* in the cities of
the Je·rah′mē·el·ītes, *those* who *were* in the
cities of the Ken′ītes, 30*those* who *were* in
Hor′mah, *those* who *were* in Chor·ash′an,[a]
those who *were* in Ā′thach, 31*those* who *were*
in Hē′bron, and to all the places where Da-
vid himself and his men were accustomed
to rove.

CHAPTER 31

The Tragic End of Saul and His Sons

Now the Phi·lis′tines fought against Is-
rael; and the men of Israel fled from before
the Phi·lis′tines, and fell slain on Mount
Gil·bō′a. 2Then the Phi·lis′tines followed
hard after Saul and his sons. And the
Phi·lis′tines killed Jonathan, A·bin′a·dab,
and Mal·chī·shū′a, Saul's sons. 3The battle
became fierce against Saul. The archers hit
him, and he was severely wounded by the
archers.

4Then Saul said to his armorbearer,
"Draw your sword, and thrust me through
with it, lest these uncircumcised men come
and thrust me through and abuse me."

But his armorbearer would not, for he
was greatly afraid. Therefore Saul took a
sword and fell on it. 5And when his armor-
bearer saw that Saul was dead, he also fell
on his sword, and died with him. 6So Saul,
his three sons, his armorbearer, and all his
men died together that same day.

7And when the men of Israel who *were*
on the other side of the valley, and *those*
who *were* on the other side of the Jordan,
saw that the men of Israel had fled and that
Saul and his sons were dead, they forsook
the cities and fled; and the Phi·lis′tines
came and dwelt in them. 8So it happened
the next day, when the Phi·lis′tines came to
strip the slain, that they found Saul and his
three sons fallen on Mount Gil·bō′a. 9And
they cut off his head and stripped off his
armor, and sent *word* throughout the land
of the Phi·lis′tines, to proclaim *it in* the
temple of their idols and among the peo-
ple. 10Then they put his armor in the tem-
ple of the Ash′to·reths, and they fastened
his body to the wall of Beth Shan.[a]

11Now when the inhabitants of Jā′besh
Gil′ē·ad heard what the Phi·lis′tines had
done to Saul, 12all the valiant men arose
and traveled all night, and took the body
of Saul and the bodies of his sons from the
wall of Beth Shan; and they came to
Jā′besh and burned them there. 13Then
they took their bones and buried *them* un-
der the tamarisk tree at Jā′besh, and fasted
seven days.

30:30 [a]Or *Borashan* 31:10 [a]Spelled *Beth Shean* in Joshua 17:11 and elsewhere

30:23 what the LORD has given us: Recognizing that God is the Giver makes us generous with others. We have no right to be selfish with what does not really belong to us.

31:7 A very significant defeat. The Philistines gained control of the Jezreel Valley all the way to the Jordan. Not only did they split off the northern tribes, but they also gained the vast agricultural and commercial wealth of the valley.

31:11–13 A last grim service for the fallen king and his sons was performed in memory of the deliverance of Jabesh Gilead by Saul many years before (ch. 11).

✦2 Samuel✦

The events of Second Samuel, which center around David, were probably recorded by Abiathar the priest. David ruled from 1010 to 971 B.C.

Chapters 1—10 describe David's seven years of triumph in battle and his prosperous reign. However, chapter 11 marks the pivotal point in his life when he committed adultery with Bathsheba and had her husband murdered. The rest of the book shows how, despite his repentance, David had to suffer the consequences of his sin. David and Bathsheba's baby died, David's son Amnon raped his sister Tamar, his son Absalom murdered Amnon and rebelled against David, and David was forced to flee Jerusalem.

God protected David and soon brought him back to the throne, only to encounter conflict and division in Israel until his death. However, despite the tragic events at the end of his reign, David continued to praise God until his death, including his official last words (2 Sam. 23:1–7).

Second Samuel shows how God formed and protected the messianic line of David, and it also demonstrates that the nation's health clearly depended upon the integrity and morality of its leader. ✦

CHAPTER 1

The Report of Saul's Death

Now it came to pass after the death of Saul, when David had returned from the slaughter of the A·mal'e·kītes, and David had stayed two days in Zik'lag, [2]on the third day, behold, it happened that a man came from Saul's camp with his clothes torn and dust on his head. So it was, when he came to David, that he fell to the ground and prostrated himself.

[3]And David said to him, "Where have you come from?"

So he said to him, "I have escaped from the camp of Israel."

[4]Then David said to him, "How did the matter go? Please tell me."

And he answered, "The people have fled from the battle, many of the people are fallen and dead, and Saul and Jonathan his son are dead also."

[5]So David said to the young man who told him, "How do you know that Saul and Jonathan his son are dead?"

[6]Then the young man who told him said, "As I happened by chance *to be* on Mount Gil·bō'a, there was Saul, leaning on his spear; and indeed the chariots and horsemen followed hard after him. [7]Now when he looked behind him, he saw me and called to me. And I answered, 'Here I

1:2–16 A comparison with 1 Sam. 31:4 would indicate that the young **Amalekite** (v. 8) fabricated the story (vv. 6–10) to curry favor with David. He probably found Saul dead on the battlefield, took his **crown** and **bracelet** (v. 10), and brought them to David. His misjudgment of David's character cost him his life.

am.' [8]And he said to me, 'Who *are* you?' So
I answered him, 'I *am* an A·mal'e·kīte.' [9]He
said to me again, 'Please stand over me
and kill me, for anguish has come upon
me, but my life still *remains* in me.' [10]So I
stood over him and killed him, because I
was sure that he could not live after he had
fallen. And I took the crown that *was* on his
head and the bracelet that *was* on his arm,
and have brought them here to my lord."

[11]Therefore David took hold of his own
clothes and tore them, and *so did* all the
men who *were* with him. [12]And they
mourned and wept and fasted until
evening for Saul and for Jonathan his son,
for the people of the LORD and for the
house of Israel, because they had fallen by
the sword.

[13]Then David said to the young man
who told him, "Where *are* you from?"

And he answered, "I *am* the son of an
alien, an A·mal'e·kīte."

[14]So David said to him, "How was it you
were not afraid to put forth your hand to
destroy the LORD's anointed?" [15]Then Da-
vid called one of the young men and said,
"Go near, *and* execute him!" And he struck
him so that he died. [16]So David said to him,
"Your blood *is* on your own head, for your
own mouth has testified against you, say-
ing, 'I have killed the LORD's anointed.' "

The Song of the Bow

[17]Then David lamented with this lamen-
tation over Saul and over Jonathan his son,
[18]and he told *them* to teach the children of
Judah *the Song of* the Bow; indeed *it is* writ-
ten in the Book of Jā'sher:

19 "The beauty of Israel is slain on your
high places!
How the mighty have fallen!
20 Tell *it* not in Gath,
Proclaim *it* not in the streets of
Ash'ke·lon—
Lest the daughters of the Phi·lis'tines
rejoice,
Lest the daughters of the
uncircumcised triumph.

21 "O mountains of Gil·bō'a,
Let there be no dew nor rain upon you,
Nor fields of offerings.
For the shield of the mighty is cast
away there!
The shield of Saul, not anointed with
oil.
22 From the blood of the slain,
From the fat of the mighty,
The bow of Jonathan did not turn
back,
And the sword of Saul did not return
empty.

23 "Saul and Jonathan *were* beloved and
pleasant in their lives,
And in their death they were not
divided;
They were swifter than eagles,
They were stronger than lions.

24 "O daughters of Israel, weep over
Saul,
Who clothed you in scarlet, with
luxury;
Who put ornaments of gold on your
apparel.

25 "How the mighty have fallen in the
midst of the battle!
Jonathan *was* slain in your high
places.
26 I am distressed for you, my brother
Jonathan;

1:13–16 Modern sensitivities are repulsed at David's action; nonetheless, there is every reason to believe he was acting in integrity. Believing the Amalekite's report that he had killed Saul, David, far from rewarding the man, executed him for his wanton act. David himself had twice refused to kill Saul. He refused to allow his men to kill the king. Even if it would give him the throne, David would not approve the murder of his predecessor.

1:18 The Book of Jasher contained records of Israel's heroes and achievements in the form of poems.

You have been very pleasant to me;
Your love to me was wonderful,
Surpassing the love of women.

27 "How the mighty have fallen,
And the weapons of war perished!"

CHAPTER 2

David Anointed King of Judah

It happened after this that David in-
quired of the LORD, saying, "Shall I go up
to any of the cities of Judah?"
And the LORD said to him, "Go up."
David said, "Where shall I go up?"
And He said, "To Hē′bron."
2So David went up there, and his two
wives also, A·hin′ō·am the Jez′rē·el·ī·tess,
and Ab′i·gāil the widow of Nā′bal the
Car′mel·īte. 3And David brought up the
men who *were* with him, every man with
his household. So they dwelt in the cities of
Hē′bron.
4Then the men of Judah came, and there
they anointed David king over the house
of Judah. And they told David, saying,
"The men of Jā′besh Gil′ē·ad *were the ones*
who buried Saul." 5So David sent messen-
gers to the men of Jā′besh Gil′ē·ad, and
said to them, "You *are* blessed of the LORD,
for you have shown this kindness to your
lord, to Saul, and have buried him. 6And
now may the LORD show kindness and
truth to you. I also will repay you this
kindness, because you have done this
thing. 7Now therefore, let your hands be
strengthened, and be valiant; for your mas-
ter Saul is dead, and also the house of Ju-
dah has anointed me king over them."

Ishbosheth Made King of Israel

8But Abner the son of Ner, commander
of Saul's army, took Ish·bō′sheth[a] the son
of Saul and brought him over to Mā-
ha·na′im; 9and he made him king over
Gil′-ē·ad, over the Ash′ur·ītes, over Jez′-
rē·el, over Ē′phra·im, over Benjamin, and
over all Israel. 10Ish·bō′sheth, Saul's son,
was forty years old when he began to reign
over Israel, and he reigned two years. Only
the house of Judah followed David. 11And
the time that David was king in Hē′bron
over the house of Judah was seven years
and six months.

Israel and Judah at War

12Now Abner the son of Ner, and the ser-
vants of Ish·bō′sheth the son of Saul, went
out from Mā·ha·na′im to Gib′ē·on. 13And
Jō′ab the son of Ze·rū′i·ah, and the ser-
vants of David, went out and met them by
the pool of Gib′ē·on. So they sat down, one
on one side of the pool and the other on the
other side of the pool. 14Then Abner said to
Jō′ab, "Let the young men now arise and
compete before us."

2:8 [a]Called *Esh-Baal* in 1 Chronicles 8:33 and 9:39

2:3 The cities of Hebron became David's capital during his seven-and-one-half year reign over Judah. **cities**: Four closely associated towns were known by the name Hebron. They were located about 19 miles (31 km) southwest of Jerusalem near the southern border of Judah's tribal territory.

2:4–7 A witness to David's thoughtfulness, but also his alertness to all opportunities to advance his own cause. His compliment to **Jabesh Gilead** is also a request for them to accept him as their king in place of their deceased master Saul (v. 7). Shrewdness and sincerity are not incompatible.

2:9–11 Ishbosheth's reign of two years appears to contradict David's seven years and six months. The impression of 4:12—5:5 is that David assumed kingship **over all Israel** immediately after Ishbosheth's death. The answer may lie in the expression *all Israel* (v. 9). Ishbosheth reigned in Mahanaim for five and a half years over Gilead, the Ashurites, Jezreel, Benjamin and Ephraim but only over all Israel the last two years before he was assassinated. *All Israel* is a term which excludes Judah and predates the division after Solomon's death.

And Jō′ab said, "Let them arise."
15So they arose and went over by num-
ber, twelve from Benjamin, *followers* of
Ish·bō′sheth the son of Saul, and twelve
from the servants of David. 16And each
one grasped his opponent by the head
and *thrust* his sword in his opponent's
side; so they fell down together. There-
fore that place was called the Field
of Sharp Swords,[a] which *is* in Gib′ē·
on. 17So there was a very fierce battle
that day, and Abner and the men of
Israel were beaten before the servants of
David.

18Now the three sons of Ze·rū′i·ah were
there: Jō′ab and A·bi′shaī and As′a·hel.
And As′a·hel *was* as fleet of foot as a wild
gazelle. 19So As′a·hel pursued Abner, and
in going he did not turn to the right hand
or to the left from following Abner.

20Then Abner looked behind him and
said, "*Are* you As′a·hel?"

He answered, "I *am*."

21And Abner said to him, "Turn aside to
your right hand or to your left, and lay
hold on one of the young men and take his
armor for yourself." But As′a·hel would
not turn aside from following him. 22So Ab-
ner said again to As′a·hel, "Turn aside
from following me. Why should I strike
you to the ground? How then could I face
your brother Jō′ab?" 23However, he refused
to turn aside. Therefore Abner struck him
in the stomach with the blunt end of the
spear, so that the spear came out of his
back; and he fell down there and died on
the spot. So it was *that* as many as came to
the place where As′a·hel fell down and
died, stood still.

24Jō′ab and A·bi′shaī also pursued Ab-
ner. And the sun was going down when
they came to the hill of Am′mah, which *is*
before Gī′ah by the road to the Wilderness
of Gib′ē·on. 25Now the children of Benja-
min gathered together behind Abner and
became a unit, and took their stand on top
of a hill. 26Then Abner called to Jō′ab and
said, "Shall the sword devour forever? Do
you not know that it will be bitter in the
latter end? How long will it be then until
you tell the people to return from pursuing
their brethren?"

27And Jō′ab said, "*As* God lives, unless
you had spoken, surely then by morning
all the people would have given up pursu-
ing their brethren." 28So Jō′ab blew a trum-
pet; and all the people stood still and did
not pursue Israel anymore, nor did they
fight anymore. 29Then Abner and his men
went on all that night through the plain,
crossed over the Jordan, and went through
all Bith′ron; and they came to Mā·ha-
na′im.

30So Jō′ab returned from pursuing Ab-
ner. And when he had gathered all the peo-
ple together, there were missing of David's
servants nineteen men and As′a·hel. 31But
the servants of David had struck down, of
Benjamin and Abner's men, three hundred
and sixty men who died. 32Then they took
up As′a·hel and buried him in his father's
tomb, which *was in* Bethlehem. And Jō′ab
and his men went all night, and they came
to Hē′bron at daybreak.

CHAPTER 3

Now there was a long war between the
house of Saul and the house of David. But
David grew stronger and stronger, and the
house of Saul grew weaker and weaker.

Sons of David

2Sons were born to David in Hē′bron:
His firstborn was Am′non by A·hin′ō·am
the Jez′rē·el·ī·tess; 3his second, Chil′ē·ab,
by Ab′i·gā il the widow of Nā′bal the
Car′mel·īte; the third, Ab′sa·lom the son of
Mā′a·cah, the daughter of Tal′maī, king of
Gē′shur; 4the fourth, Ad·o·nī′jah the son of
Hag′gith; the fifth, Sheph·a·tī′ah the son
of A·bī′tal; 5and the sixth, Ith′rē·am, by
David's wife Eg′lah. These were born to
David in Hē′bron.

2:16 [a]Hebrew *Helkath Hazzurim*

Abner Joins Forces with David

6 Now it was so, while there was war be-
tween the house of Saul and the house of
David, that Abner was strengthening *his*
hold on the house of Saul.

7 And Saul had a concubine, whose
name *was* Riz′pah, the daughter of Ā′i·ah.
So *Ish·bō′sheth* said to Abner, "Why have
you gone in to my father's concubine?"

8 Then Abner became very angry at the
words of Ish·bō′sheth, and said, "*Am* I a
dog's head that belongs to Judah? Today I
show loyalty to the house of Saul your fa-
ther, to his brothers, and to his friends, and
have not delivered you into the hand of
David; and you charge me today with a
fault concerning this woman? 9 May God
do so to Abner, and more also, if I do not
do for David as the LORD has sworn to
him— 10 to transfer the kingdom from the
house of Saul, and set up the throne of Da-
vid over Israel and over Judah, from Dan
to Bē·er·shē′ba." 11 And he could not an-
swer Abner another word, because he
feared him.

12 Then Abner sent messengers on his be-
half to David, saying, "Whose *is* the land?"
saying *also*, "Make your covenant with me,
and indeed my hand *shall be* with you to
bring all Israel to you."

13 And *David* said, "Good, I will make a
covenant with you. But one thing I require
of you: you shall not see my face unless
you first bring Mī′chal, Saul's daughter,
when you come to see my face." 14 So David
sent messengers to Ish·bō′sheth, Saul's
son, saying, "Give *me* my wife Mī′chal,
whom I betrothed to myself for a hundred
foreskins of the Phi·lis′tines." 15 And
Ish·bō′sheth sent and took her from *her*
husband, from Pal′ti·el[a] the son of Lā′ish.
16 Then her husband went along with her to
Ba·hū′rim, weeping behind her. So Abner
said to him, "Go, return!" And he returned.

17 Now Abner had communicated with
the elders of Israel, saying, "In time past
you were seeking for David *to be* king over
you. 18 Now then, do *it!* For the LORD has
spoken of David, saying, 'By the hand of
My servant David, I[a] will save My people
Israel from the hand of the Phi·lis′tines and
the hand of all their enemies.' " 19 And Ab-
ner also spoke in the hearing of Benjamin.
Then Abner also went to speak in the hear-
ing of David in Hē′bron all that seemed
good to Israel and the whole house of Ben-
jamin.

20 So Abner and twenty men with him
came to David at Hē′bron. And David
made a feast for Abner and the men who
were with him. 21 Then Abner said to David,
"I will arise and go, and gather all Israel to
my lord the king, that they may make a
covenant with you, and that you may reign
over all that your heart desires." So David
sent Abner away, and he went in peace.

Joab Murders Abner

22 At that moment the servants of David
and Jō′ab came from a raid and brought
much spoil with them. But Abner *was* not
with David in Hē′bron, for he had sent him
away, and he had gone in peace. 23 When
Jō′ab and all the troops that *were* with him
had come, they told Jō′ab, saying, "Abner
the son of Ner came to the king, and he
sent him away, and he has gone in peace."
24 Then Jō′ab came to the king and said,
"What have you done? Look, Abner came
to you; why *is* it *that* you sent him away,
and he has already gone? 25 Surely you real-

3:15 [a]Spelled *Palti* in 1 Samuel 25:44 3:18 [a]Following many Hebrew manuscripts, Septuagint, Syriac, and Targum; Masoretic Text reads *he*.

3:6 The balance of this chapter and all of ch. 4 deal with events summarized in 3:1. Ishbosheth's position was steadily weakening, being propped up chiefly by Abner's ability.

3:9–11 Abner was clearly the power behind Ishbosheth's shaky kingship. Once Abner was alienated, Ishbosheth's strength was eroded and his doom sealed.

3:13–16 David's desire for the restoration of Michal as his wife may have been partly political since it would strengthen his position with remnants of the house of Saul.

ize that Abner the son of Ner came to de-
ceive you, to know your going out and
your coming in, and to know all that you
are doing."
26And when Jō′ab had gone from Da-
vid's presence, he sent messengers after
Abner, who brought him back from the
well of Sī′rah. But David did not know *it.*
27Now when Abner had returned to
Hē′bron, Jō′ab took him aside in the gate to
speak with him privately, and there
stabbed him in the stomach, so that he died
for the blood of As′a·hel his brother.
28Afterward, when David heard *it,* he
said, "My kingdom and I *are* guiltless be-
fore the LORD forever of the blood of Abner
the son of Ner. 29Let it rest on the head of
Jō′ab and on all his father's house; and let
there never fail to be in the house of Jō′ab
one who has a discharge or is a leper, who
leans on a staff or falls by the sword, or
who lacks bread." 30So Jō′ab and A·bi′shaī
his brother killed Abner, because he had
killed their brother As′a·hel at Gib′ē·on in
the battle.

David's Mourning for Abner

31Then David said to Jō′ab and to all the
people who were with him, "Tear your
clothes, gird yourselves with sackcloth,
and mourn for Abner." And King David
followed the coffin. 32So they buried Abner
in Hē′bron; and the king lifted up his voice
and wept at the grave of Abner, and all the
people wept. 33And the king sang *a lament*
over Abner and said:

"Should Abner die as a fool dies?
34 Your hands were not bound
Nor your feet put into fetters;
As a man falls before wicked men, *so*
you fell."

Then all the people wept over him again.
35And when all the people came to per-
suade David to eat food while it was still
day, David took an oath, saying, "God do
so to me, and more also, if I taste bread or
anything else till the sun goes down!"
36Now all the people took note *of it,* and it
pleased them, since whatever the king did
pleased all the people. 37For all the people
and all Israel understood that day that it
had not been the king's *intent* to kill Abner
the son of Ner. 38Then the king said to his
servants, "Do you not know that a prince
and a great man has fallen this day in Is-
rael? 39And I *am* weak today, though
anointed king; and these men, the sons of
Ze·rū′i·ah, *are* too harsh for me. The LORD
shall repay the evildoer according to his
wickedness."

CHAPTER 4

Ishbosheth Is Murdered

When Saul's son[a] heard that Abner had
died in Hē′bron, he lost heart, and all Israel
was troubled. 2Now Saul's son *had* two
men *who were* captains of troops. The name
of one *was* Bā′a·nah and the name of the
other Rē′chab, the sons of Rim′mon the
Be·er′oth·īte, of the children of Benjamin.
(For Be·er′oth also was *part* of Benjamin,
3because the Be·er′oth·ītes fled to Git′ta·im
and have been sojourners there until this
day.)
4Jonathan, Saul's son, had a son *who was*
lame in *his* feet. He was five years old
when the news about Saul and Jonathan
came from Jez′rē·el; and his nurse took

4:1 [a]That is, Ishbosheth

3:27 Joab's motive was not only revenge for his brother's death (see 2:22, 23), but the elimination of a potential rival. Joab, who had accused Abner of treachery, himself used treachery. We often suspect others of our own sins.

3:28–36 David's sorrow seems genuine, although he stood to gain by the death of Abner. **die as a fool dies** (v. 33): That is, die the kind of death a fool deserves, not that of a brave and honorable man.

4:1–7 Without Abner's support, Ishbosheth (v. 5) was vulnerable and soon perished.

him up and fled. And it happened, as she made haste to flee, that he fell and became lame. His name *was* Me·phib′o·sheth.[a]

[5]Then the sons of Rim′mon the Be·er′-oth·īte, Rē′chab and Bā′a·nah, set out and came at about the heat of the day to the house of Ish·bō′sheth, who was lying on his bed at noon. [6]And they came there, all the way into the house, *as though* to get wheat, and they stabbed him in the stomach. Then Rē′chab and Bā′a·nah his brother escaped. [7]For when they came into the house, he was lying on his bed in his bedroom; then they struck him and killed him, beheaded him and took his head, and were all night escaping through the plain. [8]And they brought the head of Ish·bō′sheth to David at Hē′bron, and said to the king, "Here is the head of Ish·bō′sheth, the son of Saul your enemy, who sought your life; and the LORD has avenged my lord the king this day of Saul and his descendants."

[9]But David answered Rē′chab and Bā′a·nah his brother, the sons of Rim′mon the Be·er′oth·īte, and said to them, "*As* the LORD lives, who has redeemed my life from all adversity, [10]when someone told me, saying, 'Look, Saul is dead,' thinking to have brought good news, I arrested him and had him executed in Zik′lag—the one who *thought* I would give him a reward for *his* news. [11]How much more, when wicked men have killed a righteous person in his own house on his bed? Therefore, shall I not now require his blood at your hand and remove you from the earth?" [12]So David commanded his young men, and they executed them, cut off their hands and feet, and hanged *them* by the pool in Hē′bron. But they took the head of Ish·bō′sheth and buried *it* in the tomb of Abner in Hē′bron.

CHAPTER 5

David Reigns over All Israel

Then all the tribes of Israel came to David at Hē′bron and spoke, saying, "Indeed we *are* your bone and your flesh. [2]Also, in time past, when Saul was king over us, you were the one who led Israel out and brought them in; and the LORD said to you, 'You shall shepherd My people Israel, and be ruler over Israel.' " [3]Therefore all the elders of Israel came to the king at Hē′bron, and King David made a covenant with them at Hē′bron before the LORD. And they anointed David king over Israel. [4]David *was* thirty years old when he began to reign, *and* he reigned forty years. [5]In Hē′bron he reigned over Judah seven years and six months, and in Jerusalem he reigned thirty-three years over all Israel and Judah.

The Conquest of Jerusalem

[6]And the king and his men went to Jerusalem against the Jeb′ū·sītes, the inhabitants of the land, who spoke to David, saying, "You shall not come in here; but the blind and the lame will repel you," thinking, "David cannot come in here." [7]Nevertheless David took the stronghold of Zion (that *is*, the City of David).

[8]Now David said on that day, "Whoever climbs up by way of the water shaft and

4:4 [a]Called *Merib-Baal* in 1 Chronicles 8:34 and 9:40

4:12 David's response to the murders of Abner and Ishbosheth demonstrate to the northern tribes his respect for Saul and his tribe.

5:6–9 David's capture of **Jerusalem** and the transfer of his capital was a judicious move. Neither Hebron in the extreme south nor Mahanaim east of the Jordan, where Ishbosheth had his capital, was suited to be the capital of the united nation. Jerusalem was located near the center of the united kingdom, in Benjamin, Saul's tribal territory. The terrain allowed the city to be easily fortified and defended. Also because it was not previously an Israelite city, it had no association with either North or South.

5:7 Zion, a name familiar throughout the balance of the OT, is first mentioned here. It was the hill on which the Jebusites had their fortification.

defeats the Jeb′ū·sītes (the lame and the blind, *who are* hated by David's soul), *he shall be chief and captain.*"[a] Therefore they say, "The blind and the lame shall not come into the house."

9 Then David dwelt in the stronghold, and called it the City of David. And David built all around from the Mil′lō[a] and inward. 10 So David went on and became great, and the LORD God of hosts *was* with him.

11 Then Hī′ram king of Tȳre sent messengers to David, and cedar trees, and carpenters and masons. And they built David a house. 12 So David knew that the LORD had established him as king over Israel, and that He had exalted His kingdom for the sake of His people Israel.

13 And David took more concubines and wives from Jerusalem, after he had come from Hē′bron. Also more sons and daughters were born to David. 14 Now these *are* the names of those who were born to him in Jerusalem: Sham′mū·a,[a] Shō′bab, Nathan, Solomon, 15 Ib′har, E·lish′ū·a,[a] Nē′pheg, Ja·phī′a, 16 E·lish′a·ma, E·lī′a·da, and E·liph′e·let.

The Philistines Defeated

17 Now when the Phi·lis′tines heard that they had anointed David king over Israel, all the Phi·lis′tines went up to search for David. And David heard *of it* and went down to the stronghold. 18 The Phi·lis′tines also went and deployed themselves in the Valley of Reph′a·im. 19 So David inquired of the LORD, saying, "Shall I go up against the Phi·lis′tines? Will You deliver them into my hand?"

And the LORD said to David, "Go up, for I will doubtless deliver the Phi·lis′tines into your hand."

20 So David went to Bā′al Pe·rā′zim, and David defeated them there; and he said, "The LORD has broken through my enemies before me, like a breakthrough of water." Therefore he called the name of that place Bā′al Pe·rā′zim.[a] 21 And they left their images there, and David and his men carried them away.

22 Then the Phi·lis′tines went up once again and deployed themselves in the Valley of Reph′a·im. 23 Therefore David inquired of the LORD, and He said, "You shall not go up; circle around behind them, and come upon them in front of the mulberry trees. 24 And it shall be, when you hear the sound of marching in the tops of the mulberry trees, then you shall advance quickly. For then the LORD will go out before you to strike the camp of the Phi·lis′tines." 25 And David did so, as the LORD commanded him; and he drove back the Phi·lis′tines from Gē′ba[a] as far as Gē′zer.

CHAPTER 6

The Ark Brought to Jerusalem

Again David gathered all *the* choice *men* of Israel, thirty thousand. 2 And David arose and went with all the people who *were* with him from Bā′a·lē Judah to bring up from there the ark of God, whose name is called by the Name,[a] the LORD of Hosts, who dwells *between* the cherubim. 3 So they set the ark of God on a new cart, and brought it out of the house of A·bin′a·dab, which *was* on the hill; and Uz′zah and

5:8 [a]Compare 1 Chronicles 11:6 5:9 [a]Literally *The Landfill* 5:14 [a]Spelled *Shimea* in 1 Chronicles 3:5 5:15 [a]Spelled *Elishama* in 1 Chronicles 3:6 5:20 [a]Literally *Master of Breakthroughs* 5:25 [a]Following Masoretic Text, Targum, and Vulgate; Septuagint reads *Gibeon.* 6:2 [a]Septuagint, Targum, and Vulgate omit *by the Name;* many Hebrew manuscripts and Syriac read *there.*

6:2 Jerusalem was to be not only the military and political capital of the nation but its religious center as well. This was accomplished by bringing **the ark of God** from Baale Judah, that is, Kirjath Jearim, where it had been centered for more than 20 years (1 Sam. 7:1; 14:18). It especially symbolized the presence of **the LORD of Hosts, who dwells between the cherubim**.

A·hī′ō, the sons of A·bin′a·dab, drove the new cart.[a] 4And they brought it out of the house of A·bin′a·dab, which *was* on the hill, accompanying the ark of God; and A·hī′ō went before the ark. 5Then David and all the house of Israel played *music* before the LORD on all kinds of *instruments of* fir wood, on harps, on stringed instruments, on tambourines, on sistrums, and on cymbals.

6And when they came to Nā′chon′s threshing floor, Uz′zah put out *his* hand to the ark of God and took hold of it, for the oxen stumbled. 7Then the anger of the LORD was aroused against Uz′zah, and God struck him there for *his* error; and he died there by the ark of God. 8And David became angry because of the LORD′s outbreak against Uz′zah; and he called the name of the place Per′ez Uz′zah[a] to this day.

9David was afraid of the LORD that day; and he said, "How can the ark of the LORD come to me?" 10So David would not move the ark of the LORD with him into the City of David; but David took it aside into the house of Ō′bed-Ē′dom the Git′tīte. 11The ark of the LORD remained in the house of Ō′bed-Ē′dom the Git′tīte three months. And the LORD blessed Ō′bed-Ē′dom and all his household.

12Now it was told King David, saying, "The LORD has blessed the house of Ō′bed-Ē′dom and all that *belongs* to him, because of the ark of God." So David went and brought up the ark of God from the house of Ō′bed-Ē′dom to the City of David with gladness. 13And so it was, when those bearing the ark of the LORD had gone six paces, that he sacrificed oxen and fatted sheep. 14Then David danced before the LORD with all *his* might; and David *was* wearing a linen ephod. 15So David and all the house of Israel brought up the ark of the LORD with shouting and with the sound of the trumpet.

16Now as the ark of the LORD came into the City of David, Mī′chal, Saul′s daughter, looked through a window and saw King David leaping and whirling before the LORD; and she despised him in her heart. 17So they brought the ark of the LORD, and set it in its place in the midst of the tabernacle that David had erected for it. Then David offered burnt offerings and peace offerings before the LORD. 18And when David had finished offering burnt offerings and peace offerings, he blessed the people in the name of the LORD of hosts. 19Then he distributed among all the people, among the whole multitude of Israel, both the women and the men, to everyone a loaf of bread, a piece *of meat*, and a cake of raisins. So all the people departed, everyone to his house.

20Then David returned to bless his household. And Mī′chal the daughter of Saul came out to meet David, and said, "How glorious was the king of Israel today, uncovering himself today in the eyes of the maids of his servants, as one of the base fellows shamelessly uncovers himself!"

21So David said to Mī′chal, "*It was* before the LORD, who chose me instead of your father and all his house, to appoint me ruler over the people of the LORD, over Israel. Therefore I will play *music* before the LORD. 22And I will be even more undignified than this, and will be humble in my own sight. But as for the maidservants of

6:3 [a]Septuagint adds *with the ark.* 6:8 [a]Literally *Outburst Against Uzzah*

6:6–15 Irreverence is a better rendering than error. There were specific instructions for moving the ark (Ex. 25:14, 15; Num. 4:15). When these instructions were followed (v. 13), the ark was moved with no further trouble.

6:14 Expressing joy through dancing was customary at major victories; David's dance demonstrated his joy in the Lord. From Michal's response (v. 20), it appears that David had little else on but the linen ephod, or apron. David was not concerned with his image!

whom you have spoken, by them I will be
held in honor."
23Therefore Mī´chal the daughter of Saul
had no children to the day of her death.

CHAPTER 7

God's Covenant with David

Now it came to pass when the king was
dwelling in his house, and the LORD had
given him rest from all his enemies all
around, 2that the king said to Nathan the
prophet, "See now, I dwell in a house of
cedar, but the ark of God dwells inside tent
curtains."
3Then Nathan said to the king, "Go, do
all that *is* in your heart, for the LORD *is* with
you."
4But it happened that night that the
word of the LORD came to Nathan, saying,
5"Go and tell My servant David, 'Thus says
the LORD: "Would you build a house for
Me to dwell in? 6For I have not dwelt in a
house since the time that I brought the chil-
dren of Israel up from Egypt, even to this
day, but have moved about in a tent and in
a tabernacle. 7Wherever I have moved
about with all the children of Israel, have I
ever spoken a word to anyone from the
tribes of Israel, whom I commanded to
shepherd My people Israel, saying, 'Why
have you not built Me a house of
cedar?' " ' 8Now therefore, thus shall you
say to My servant David, 'Thus says the
LORD of hosts: "I took you from the sheep-
fold, from following the sheep, to be ruler
over My people, over Israel. 9And I have
been with you wherever you have gone,
and have cut off all your enemies from be-
fore you, and have made you a great name,
like the name of the great men who *are* on
the earth. 10Moreover I will appoint a place
for My people Israel, and will plant them,
that they may dwell in a place of their own
and move no more; nor shall the sons of
wickedness oppress them anymore, as pre-
viously, 11since the time that I commanded
judges *to be* over My people Israel, and
have caused you to rest from all your ene-
mies. Also the LORD tells you that He will
make you a house.[a]
12"When your days are fulfilled and you
rest with your fathers, I will set up your
seed after you, who will come from your
body, and I will establish his kingdom.
13He shall build a house for My name, and
I will establish the throne of his kingdom
forever. 14I will be his Father, and he shall
be My son. If he commits iniquity, I will
chasten him with the rod of men and with
the blows of the sons of men. 15But My
mercy shall not depart from him, as I took
it from Saul, whom I removed from before
you. 16And your house and your kingdom
shall be established forever before you.[a]
Your throne shall be established
forever." ' "
17According to all these words and ac-
cording to all this vision, so Nathan spoke
to David.

David's Thanksgiving to God

18Then King David went in and sat be-
fore the LORD; and he said: "Who *am* I, O
Lord GOD? And what is my house, that You
have brought me this far? 19And yet this
was a small thing in Your sight, O Lord

7:11 [a]That is, a royal dynasty 7:16 [a]Septuagint reads *Me.*

7:1–16 David was not permitted to build a temple since he had been "a man of war and [had] shed blood" (1 Chr. 28:3). The honor and responsibility for building the temple would go to his son.

7:5–16 More important for the human race than any house (v. 5) David could build is what God was going to make of David's **house** (family, v. 11). In this Davidic covenant, God's promises are unconditional; the Lord would bless David as part of His eternal plan. **forever**: No earthly dynasty or kingdom could endure forever. This part of the prophecy was fulfilled in "David's greater Son," the Lord Jesus Christ (Luke 1:31–33).

GOD; and You have also spoken of Your
servant's house for a great while to come.
Is this the manner of man, O Lord GOD?
20Now what more can David say to You?
For You, Lord GOD, know Your servant.
21For Your word's sake, and according to
Your own heart, You have done all these
great things, to make Your servant know
them. 22Therefore You are great, O Lord
GOD.[a] For *there is* none like You, nor *is there*
any God besides You, according to all that
we have heard with our ears. 23And who *is*
like Your people, like Israel, the one nation
on the earth whom God went to redeem
for Himself as a people, to make for Him-
self a name—and to do for Yourself great
and awesome deeds for Your land—before
Your people whom You redeemed for
Yourself from Egypt, the nations, and their
gods? 24For You have made Your people Is-
rael Your very own people forever; and
You, LORD, have become their God.
25"Now, O LORD God, the word which
You have spoken concerning Your servant
and concerning his house, establish *it* for-
ever and do as You have said. 26So let Your
name be magnified forever, saying, 'The
LORD of hosts *is* the God over Israel.' And
let the house of Your servant David be es-
tablished before You. 27For You, O LORD of
hosts, God of Israel, have revealed *this* to
Your servant, saying, 'I will build you a
house.' Therefore Your servant has found it
in his heart to pray this prayer to You.
28"And now, O Lord GOD, You are God,
and Your words are true, and You have
promised this goodness to Your servant.
29Now therefore, let it please You to bless
the house of Your servant, that it may con-
tinue before You forever; for You, O Lord
GOD, have spoken *it*, and with Your bless-
ing let the house of Your servant be blessed
forever."

CHAPTER 8

David's Further Conquests

After this it came to pass that David at-
tacked the Phi·lis′tines and subdued them.
And David took Meth′eg Am′mah from
the hand of the Phi·lis′tines.
2Then he defeated Mō′ab. Forcing them
down to the ground, he measured them off
with a line. With two lines he measured off
those to be put to death, and with one full
line those to be kept alive. So the Mō′-
ab·ītes became David's servants, *and*
brought tribute.
3David also defeated Had·a·dē′zer the
son of Rē′hob, king of Zō′bah, as he went
to recover his territory at the River Eū-
phrā′tēs. 4David took from him one thou-
sand *chariots*, seven hundred[a] horsemen,
and twenty thousand foot soldiers. Also
David hamstrung all the chariot horses, ex-
cept that he spared *enough* of them for one
hundred chariots.
5When the Syrians of Damascus came
to help Had·a·dē′zer king of Zō′bah,
David killed twenty-two thousand of
the Syrians. 6Then David put garrisons
in Syria of Damascus; and the Syrians
became David's servants, *and* brought
tribute. So the LORD preserved David
wherever he went. 7And David took
the shields of gold that had belonged to
the servants of Had·a·dē′zer, and brought
them to Jerusalem. 8Also from Bē′tah[a]
and from Berothai, cities of Had-a·dē′zer,
King David took a large amount of
bronze.
9When Tō′ī[a] king of Hā′math heard that
David had defeated all the army of

7:22 [a]Targum and Syriac read *O LORD God.*
8:4 [a]Or *seven thousand* (compare 1 Chronicles 18:4)
8:8 [a]Spelled *Tibhath* in 1 Chronicles 18:8
8:9 [a]Spelled *Tou* in 1 Chronicles 18:9

8:4 hamstrung . . . horses: Horse-drawn chariots were the ultimate weapon of that day. God had forbidden Israel to use them lest His people come to trust in them (Josh. 11:6; Ps. 20:7). David qualified his obedience by keeping one hundred, probably an encouragement to Solomon to go much further (1 Kin. 10:26).

Had·a·dē′zer, [10]then Tō′ī sent Jō′ram[a] his son to King David, to greet him and bless him, because he had fought against Had·a·dē′zer and defeated him (for Had·a·dē′zer had been at war with Tō′ī); and Jō′ram brought with him articles of silver, articles of gold, and articles of bronze. [11]King David also dedicated these to the LORD, along with the silver and gold that he had dedicated from all the nations which he had subdued—[12]from Syria,[a] from Mō′ab, from the people of Am′mon, from the Phi·lis′tines, from Am′a·lek, and from the spoil of Had·a·dē′zer the son of Rē′hob, king of Zō′bah.

[13]And David made *himself* a name when he returned from killing eighteen thousand Syrians[a] in the Valley of Salt. [14]He also put garrisons in Ē′dom; throughout all Ē′dom he put garrisons, and all the Ē′dom·ītes became David's servants. And the LORD preserved David wherever he went.

David's Administration

[15]So David reigned over all Israel; and David administered judgment and justice to all his people. [16]Jō′ab the son of Ze·rū′i·ah *was* over the army; Je·hosh′a·phat the son of A·hī′lud *was* recorder; [17]Zā′dok the son of A·hī′tub and A·him′e·lech the son of A·bī′a·thar *were* the priests; Se·rāi′ah[a] *was* the scribe; [18]Be·nā′i·ah the son of Je·hoi′a·da *was over* both the Cher′e·thītes and the Pel′eth·ītes; and David's sons were chief ministers.

8:10 [a]Spelled *Hadoram* in 1 Chronicles 18:10
8:12 [a]Septuagint, Syriac, and some Hebrew manuscripts read *Edom*. 8:13 [a]Septuagint, Syriac, and some Hebrew manuscripts read *Edomites* (compare 1 Chronicles 18:12). 8:17 [a]Spelled *Shavsha* in 1 Chronicles 18:16

CHAPTER 9

David's Kindness to Mephibosheth

Now David said, "Is there still anyone who is left of the house of Saul, that I may show him kindness for Jonathan's sake?"

[2]And *there was* a servant of the house of Saul whose name *was* Zī′ba. So when they had called him to David, the king said to him, "*Are* you Zī′ba?"

He said, "At your service!"

[3]Then the king said, "*Is* there not still someone of the house of Saul, to whom I may show the kindness of God?"

And Zī′ba said to the king, "There is still a son of Jonathan *who is* lame in *his* feet."

[4]So the king said to him, "Where *is* he?"

And Zī′ba said to the king, "Indeed he *is* in the house of Mā′chir the son of Am′mi·el, in Lo Dē′bar."

[5]Then King David sent and brought him out of the house of Mā′chir the son of Am′mi·el, from Lo Dē′bar.

[6]Now when Me·phib′o·sheth the son of Jonathan, the son of Saul, had come to David, he fell on his face and prostrated himself. Then David said, "Me·phib′o·sheth?"

And he answered, "Here is your servant!"

[7]So David said to him, "Do not fear, for I will surely show you kindness for Jonathan your father's sake, and will restore to you all the land of Saul your grandfather; and you shall eat bread at my table continually."

[8]Then he bowed himself, and said, "What *is* your servant, that you should look upon such a dead dog as I?"

[9]And the king called to Zī′ba, Saul's servant, and said to him, "I have given to your master's son all that belonged to Saul and to all his house. [10]You therefore, and

9:1–13 Instead of destroying the last helpless representative of the house of Saul (v. 1), David honored him and thus honored his covenant with Jonathan (see 1 Sam. 20:14–17). **Mephibosheth** (v. 6) was five years old when his father was killed (4:4). He now had a young son of his own (v. 12), which indicates that this event took place about midway in David's reign.

your sons and your servants, shall work
the land for him, and you shall bring in *the
harvest,* that your master's son may have
food to eat. But Me·phib'o·sheth your
master's son shall eat bread at my table al-
ways." Now Zī'ba had fifteen sons and
twenty servants.
11 Then Zī'ba said to the king, "Ac-
cording to all that my lord the king has
commanded his servant, so will your ser-
vant do."
"As for Me·phib'o·sheth," *said the king,*
"he shall eat at my table[a] like one of the
king's sons." 12 Me·phib'o·sheth had a
young son whose name *was* Mī'cha. And
all who dwelt in the house of Zī'ba *were*
servants of Me·phib'o·sheth. 13 So Me-
phib'o·sheth dwelt in Jerusalem, for he ate
continually at the king's table. And he was
lame in both his feet.

CHAPTER 10

The Ammonites and Syrians Defeated

It happened after this that the king of
the people of Am'mon died, and Hā'nun
his son reigned in his place. 2 Then David
said, "I will show kindness to Hā'nun the
son of Nā'hash, as his father showed kind-
ness to me."
So David sent by the hand of his ser-
vants to comfort him concerning his father.
And David's servants came into the land
of the people of Am'mon. 3 And the princes
of the people of Am'mon said to Hā'nun
their lord, "Do you think that David really
honors your father because he has sent
comforters to you? Has David not *rather*
sent his servants to you to search the city,
to spy it out, and to overthrow it?"
4 Therefore Hā'nun took David's ser-
vants, shaved off half of their beards, cut
off their garments in the middle, at their
buttocks, and sent them away. 5 When they
told David, he sent to meet them, because
the men were greatly ashamed. And the
king said, "Wait at Jericho until your
beards have grown, and *then* return."
6 When the people of Am'mon saw that
they had made themselves repulsive to
David, the people of Am'mon sent and
hired the Syrians of Beth Rē'hob and the
Syrians of Zō'ba, twenty thousand foot sol-
diers; and from the king of Mā'a·cah one
thousand men, and from Ish-Tob twelve
thousand men. 7 Now when David heard *of
it,* he sent Jō'ab and all the army of the
mighty men. 8 Then the people of Am'mon
came out and put themselves in battle
array at the entrance of the gate. And the
Syrians of Zō'ba, Beth Rē'hob, Ish-Tob,
and Mā'a·cah *were* by themselves in the
field.
9 When Jō'ab saw that the battle line was
against him before and behind, he chose
some of Israel's best and put *them* in battle
array against the Syrians. 10 And the rest of
the people he put under the command of
A·bi'shaī his brother, that he might set
them in battle array against the people of
Am'mon. 11 Then he said, "If the Syrians are
too strong for me, then you shall help me;
but if the people of Am'mon are too strong
for you, then I will come and help you. 12 Be
of good courage, and let us be strong for
our people and for the cities of our God.
And may the LORD do *what is* good in His
sight."
13 So Jō'ab and the people who *were* with
him drew near for the battle against the
Syrians, and they fled before him. 14 When
the people of Am'mon saw that the Syrians
were fleeing, they also fled before
A·bi'shaī, and entered the city. So Jō'ab re-

9:11 [a]Septuagint reads *David's table.*

10:4, 5 Insult to the messengers was intended as an affront to David who had sent them. **Beards** were accepted symbols of maturity and dignity.

10:9–11 Only an unusually confident commander divides his forces.

10:12 be strong: Our best effort plus complete trust in God.

turned from the people of Am′mon and
went to Jerusalem.
15When the Syrians saw that they had
been defeated by Israel, they gathered to-
gether. 16Then Had·a·dē′zer[a] sent and
brought out the Syrians who *were* beyond
the River,[b] and they came to Hē′lam. And
Shō′bach the commander of Had·a·dē′-
zer's army *went* before them. 17When it was
told David, he gathered all Israel, crossed
over the Jordan, and came to Hē′lam. And
the Syrians set themselves in battle array
against David and fought with him. 18Then
the Syrians fled before Israel; and David
killed seven hundred charioteers and forty
thousand horsemen of the Syrians, and
struck Shō′bach the commander of their
army, who died there. 19And when all the
kings *who were* servants to Had·a·dē′zer[a]
saw that they were defeated by Israel, they
made peace with Israel and served them.
So the Syrians were afraid to help the peo-
ple of Am′mon anymore.

CHAPTER 11

David, Bathsheba, and Uriah

It happened in the spring of the year, at
the time when kings go out *to battle,* that
David sent Jō′ab and his servants with
him, and all Israel; and they destroyed the
people of Am′mon and besieged Rab′bah.
But David remained at Jerusalem.
2Then it happened one evening that Da-
vid arose from his bed and walked on the
roof of the king's house. And from the roof
he saw a woman bathing, and the woman
was very beautiful to behold. 3So David
sent and inquired about the woman. And
someone said, "*Is* this not Bath·shē′ba, the
daughter of E·lī′am, the wife of Ū·rī′ah the
Hit′tīte?" 4Then David sent messengers,
and took her; and she came to him, and he
lay with her, for she was cleansed from her
impurity; and she returned to her house.
5And the woman conceived; so she sent
and told David, and said, "I *am* with
child."
6Then David sent to Jō′ab, *saying,* "Send
me Ū·rī′ah the Hit′tīte." And Jō′ab sent
Ū·rī′ah to David. 7When Ū·rī′ah had come
to him, David asked how Jō′ab was doing,
and how the people were doing, and how
the war prospered. 8And David said to
Ū·rī′ah, "Go down to your house and
wash your feet." So Ū·rī′ah departed from
the king's house, and a gift *of food* from the
king followed him. 9But Ū·rī′ah slept at the
door of the king's house with all the ser-
vants of his lord, and did not go down to
his house. 10So when they told David, say-
ing, "Ū·rī′ah did not go down to his
house," David said to Ū·rī′ah, "Did you

10:16 [a]Hebrew *Hadarezer* [b]That is, the Euphrates
10:19 [a]Hebrew *Hadarezer*

11:1–27 The stark realism of the Bible is seen in this dispassionate account of David's terrible sins. Sin is sin whether committed by hero or wretch, and the Bible treats it so. Much of the book that follows describes direct and indirect consequences of this adultery and murder. As we mature in faith, we should realize that no one is immune from temptation. We must be ever vigilant, knowing that Satan is most likely to attack when we feel most confident.

11:1 remained at Jerusalem: How much better if David had gone with his army into the field! Idleness opens the door to temptation. Any lifestyle change may leave us with time on our hands. A little planning can help us maintain active schedules that prevent the pitfalls of idleness.

11:3 the wife of Uriah: David acted with full knowledge that the woman he desired was another man's wife. In fact, Uriah was a member of David's elite bodyguard, one of the mighty men listed in 23:39. This makes David's duplicity even more appalling.

11:4 cleansed from her impurity: He did not want to have relations with a woman during her period, but whether she was married or not was immaterial.

11:6–11 Go down to your house: Beginning a frantic but futile effort at coverup. **Uriah** was more honorable than his king (vv. 9–11).

not come from a journey? Why did you not go down to your house?"

11And Ū·rī'ah said to David, "The ark and Israel and Judah are dwelling in tents, and my lord Jō'ab and the servants of my lord are encamped in the open fields. Shall I then go to my house to eat and drink, and to lie with my wife? *As* you live, and *as* your soul lives, I will not do this thing."

12Then David said to Ū·rī'ah, "Wait here today also, and tomorrow I will let you depart." So Ū·rī'ah remained in Jerusalem that day and the next. 13Now when David called him, he ate and drank before him; and he made him drunk. And at evening he went out to lie on his bed with the servants of his lord, but he did not go down to his house.

14In the morning it happened that David wrote a letter to Jō'ab and sent *it* by the hand of Ū·rī'ah. 15And he wrote in the letter, saying, "Set Ū·rī'ah in the forefront of the hottest battle, and retreat from him, that he may be struck down and die." 16So it was, while Jō'ab besieged the city, that he assigned Ū·rī'ah to a place where he knew there *were* valiant men. 17Then the men of the city came out and fought with Jō'ab. And *some* of the people of the servants of David fell; and Ū·rī'ah the Hit'tīte died also.

18Then Jō'ab sent and told David all the things concerning the war, 19and charged the messenger, saying, "When you have finished telling the matters of the war to the king, 20if it happens that the king's wrath rises, and he says to you: 'Why did you approach so near to the city when you fought? Did you not know that they would shoot from the wall? 21Who struck A·bim'e·lech the son of Je·rub'be·sheth?[a] Was it not a woman who cast a piece of a millstone on him from the wall, so that he died in Thē'bez? Why did you go near the wall?'—then you shall say, 'Your servant Ū·rī'ah the Hit'tīte is dead also.' "

22So the messenger went, and came and told David all that Jō'ab had sent by him. 23And the messenger said to David, "Surely the men prevailed against us and came out to us in the field; then we drove them back as far as the entrance of the gate. 24The archers shot from the wall at your servants; and *some* of the king's servants are dead, and your servant Ū·rī'ah the Hit'tīte is dead also."

25Then David said to the messenger, "Thus you shall say to Jō'ab: 'Do not let this thing displease you, for the sword devours one as well as another. Strengthen your attack against the city, and overthrow it.' So encourage him."

26When the wife of Ū·rī'ah heard that Ū·rī'ah her husband was dead, she mourned for her husband. 27And when her mourning was over, David sent and brought her to his house, and she became his wife and bore him a son. But the thing that David had done displeased the LORD.

CHAPTER 12

Nathan's Parable and David's Confession

Then the LORD sent Nathan to David. And he came to him, and said to him: "There were two men in one city, one rich and the other poor. 2The rich *man* had exceedingly many flocks and herds. 3But the poor *man* had nothing, except one little ewe lamb which he had bought and nourished; and it grew up together with him and with his children. It ate of his own food and drank from his own cup and lay in his bosom; and it was like a daughter to him. 4And a traveler came to the rich man, who refused to take from his own flock

11:21 [a]Same as *Jerubbaal* (Gideon), Judges 6:32ff

12:1–4 Each aspect of Nathan's parable was designed to arouse the king's sympathy. This way he condemned himself.

and from his own herd to prepare one for the wayfaring man who had come to him; but he took the poor man's lamb and prepared it for the man who had come to him."

5So David's anger was greatly aroused against the man, and he said to Nathan, "*As* the LORD lives, the man who has done this shall surely die! 6And he shall restore fourfold for the lamb, because he did this thing and because he had no pity."

7Then Nathan said to David, "You *are* the man! Thus says the LORD God of Israel: 'I anointed you king over Israel, and I delivered you from the hand of Saul. 8I gave you your master's house and your master's wives into your keeping, and gave you the house of Israel and Judah. And if *that had been* too little, I also would have given you much more! 9Why have you despised the commandment of the LORD, to do evil in His sight? You have killed Ū·rī'ah the Hit'tīte with the sword; you have taken his wife *to be* your wife, and have killed him with the sword of the people of Am'mon. 10Now therefore, the sword shall never depart from your house, because you have despised Me, and have taken the wife of Ū·rī'ah the Hit'tīte to be your wife.' 11Thus says the LORD: 'Behold, I will raise up adversity against you from your own house; and I will take your wives before your eyes and give *them* to your neighbor, and he shall lie with your wives in the sight of this sun. 12For you did *it* secretly, but I will do this thing before all Israel, before the sun.' "

13So David said to Nathan, "I have sinned against the LORD."

And Nathan said to David, "The LORD also has put away your sin; you shall not die. 14However, because by this deed you have given great occasion to the enemies of the LORD to blaspheme, the child also *who is* born to you shall surely die." 15Then Nathan departed to his house.

The Death of David's Son

And the LORD struck the child that Ū·rī'ah's wife bore to David, and it became ill. 16David therefore pleaded with God for the child, and David fasted and went in and lay all night on the ground. 17So the elders of his house arose *and went* to him, to raise him up from the ground. But he would not, nor did he eat food with them. 18Then on the seventh day it came to pass that the child died. And the servants of David were afraid to tell him that the child was dead. For they said, "Indeed, while the child was alive, we spoke to him, and he would not heed our voice. How can we tell him that the child is dead? He may do some harm!"

19When David saw that his servants were whispering, David perceived that the child was dead. Therefore David said to his servants, "Is the child dead?"

And they said, "He is dead."

20So David arose from the ground, washed and anointed himself, and changed his clothes; and he went into the house of the LORD and worshiped. Then he went to his own house; and when he requested, they set food before him, and he ate. 21Then his servants said to him, "What *is* this that you have done? You fasted and wept for the child *while he was* alive, but when the child died, you arose and ate food."

22And he said, "While the child was alive, I fasted and wept; for I said, 'Who

---

12:10–12 David's sins would be forgiven, but their temporal consequences would follow him the rest of his life. Forgiveness removes guilt before God, but does not necessarily cancel the physical or social results of evil.

12:13 David's repentance was utterly sincere, quite different from the mood of Saul even though three times he also confessed **I have sinned** (1 Sam. 15:24, 30; 26:21). Although David's sin had defiled Bathsheba and cost Uriah his life, all sin is ultimately **against the LORD** (see Ps. 51:4, thought to have reference to this occasion).

can tell *whether* the LORD[a] will be gracious to me, that the child may live?' 23But now he is dead; why should I fast? Can I bring him back again? I shall go to him, but he shall not return to me."

Solomon Is Born

24Then David comforted Bath·shē'ba his wife, and went in to her and lay with her. So she bore a son, and he[a] called his name Solomon. Now the LORD loved him, 25and He sent *word* by the hand of Nathan the prophet: So he[a] called his name Jed·i·dī'ah,[b] because of the LORD.

Rabbah Is Captured

26Now Jō'ab fought against Rab'bah of the people of Am'mon, and took the royal city. 27And Jō'ab sent messengers to David, and said, "I have fought against Rab'bah, and I have taken the city's water *supply*. 28Now therefore, gather the rest of the people together and encamp against the city and take it, lest I take the city and it be called after my name." 29So David gathered all the people together and went to Rab'bah, fought against it, and took it. 30Then he took their king's crown from his head. Its weight *was* a talent of gold, with precious stones. And it was *set* on David's head. Also he brought out the spoil of the city in great abundance. 31And he brought out the people who *were* in it, and put *them to work* with saws and iron picks and iron axes, and made them cross over to the brick works. So he did to all the cities of the people of Am'mon. Then David and all the people returned to Jerusalem.

CHAPTER 13

Amnon and Tamar

After this Ab'sa·lom the son of David had a lovely sister, whose name *was* Tā'mar; and Am'non the son of David loved her. 2Am'non was so distressed over his sister Tā'mar that he became sick; for she *was* a virgin. And it was improper for Am'non to do anything to her. 3But Am'non had a friend whose name *was* Jon'a·dab the son of Shim'ē·ah, David's brother. Now Jon'a·dab *was* a very crafty man. 4And he said to him, "Why *are* you, the king's son, becoming thinner day after day? Will you not tell me?"

Am'non said to him, "I love Tā'mar, my brother Ab'sa·lom's sister."

5So Jon'a·dab said to him, "Lie down on your bed and pretend to be ill. And when your father comes to see you, say to him, 'Please let my sister Tā'mar come and give me food, and prepare the food in my sight, that I may see *it* and eat it from her hand.' " 6Then Am'non lay down and pretended to be ill; and when the king came to see him, Am'non said to the king, "Please let Tā'mar my sister come and make a couple of cakes for me in my sight, that I may eat from her hand."

7And David sent home to Tā'mar, saying, "Now go to your brother Am'non's house, and prepare food for him." 8So Tā'mar went to her brother Am'non's house; and he was lying down. Then she took flour and kneaded *it*, made cakes in his sight, and baked the cakes. 9And she took the pan and placed *them* out before him, but he refused to eat. Then Am'non said, "Have everyone go out from me." And they all went out from him. 10Then Am'non said to Tā'mar, "Bring the food

12:22 [a]A few Hebrew manuscripts and Syriac read *God*. 12:24 [a]Following Kethib, Septuagint, and Vulgate; Qere, a few Hebrew manuscripts, Syriac, and Targum read *she*. 12:25 [a]Qere, some Hebrew manuscripts, Syriac, and Targum read *she*. [b]Literally *Beloved of the LORD*

12:25 The birth of Solomon—the first surviving son of David's union with Bathsheba—is evidence of God's ability to bring about good in spite of our sin. Since God knew the end from the beginning, He was not stymied by David's sin.

12:31 To recognize the sincerity of David's love for God does not require us to endorse everything he did. He was a child of his own day.

into the bedroom, that I may eat from
your hand." And Tā'mar took the
cakes which she had made, and brought
them to Am'non her brother in the bed-
room. [11]Now when she had brought
them to him to eat, he took hold of her
and said to her, "Come, lie with me, my
sister."

[12]But she answered him, "No, my
brother, do not force me, for no such thing
should be done in Israel. Do not do this
disgraceful thing! [13]And I, where could I
take my shame? And as for you, you
would be like one of the fools in Israel.
Now therefore, please speak to the king;
for he will not withhold me from you."
[14]However, he would not heed her voice;
and being stronger than she, he forced her
and lay with her.

[15]Then Am'non hated her exceedingly,
so that the hatred with which he hated her
was greater than the love with which he
had loved her. And Am'non said to her,
"Arise, be gone!"

[16]So she said to him, "No, indeed! This
evil of sending me away *is* worse than the
other that you did to me."

But he would not listen to her. [17]Then he
called his servant who attended him, and
said, "Here! Put this *woman* out, away from
me, and bolt the door behind her." [18]Now
she had on a robe of many colors, for the
king's virgin daughters wore such apparel.
And his servant put her out and bolted the
door behind her.

[19]Then Tā'mar put ashes on her head,
and tore her robe of many colors that *was*
on her, and laid her hand on her head and
went away crying bitterly. [20]And Ab'sa-
lom her brother said to her, "Has Am'non
your brother been with you? But now hold
your peace, my sister. He *is* your brother;
do not take this thing to heart." So Tā'mar
remained desolate in her brother Ab'sa-
lom's house.

[21]But when King David heard of all
these things, he was very angry. [22]And
Ab'sa·lom spoke to his brother Am'non
neither good nor bad. For Ab'sa·lom hated
Am'non, because he had forced his sister
Tā'mar.

Absalom Murders Amnon

[23]And it came to pass, after two
full years, that Ab'sa·lom had sheepshear-
ers in Bā'al Hā'zor, which *is* near
Ē'phra·im; so Ab'sa·lom invited all
the king's sons. [24]Then Ab'sa·lom came
to the king and said, "Kindly note, your
servant has sheepshearers; please, let the
king and his servants go with your ser-
vant."

[25]But the king said to Ab'sa·lom, "No,
my son, let us not all go now, lest we be a
burden to you." Then he urged him, but he
would not go; and he blessed him.

[26]Then Ab'sa·lom said, "If not, please let
my brother Am'non go with us."

And the king said to him, "Why should
he go with you?" [27]But Ab'sa·lom urged
him; so he let Am'non and all the king's
sons go with him.

[28]Now Ab'sa·lom had commanded his
servants, saying, "Watch now, when
Am'non's heart is merry with wine, and
when I say to you, 'Strike Am'non!' then
kill him. Do not be afraid. Have I not com-
manded you? Be courageous and valiant."
[29]So the servants of Ab'sa·lom did to
Am'non as Ab'sa·lom had commanded.

13:15, 16 In taking Tamar's virginity, Amnon had acted abominably; however, his refusal to marry her compounded the tragedy and broke the Law, which required him to take her as wife and never divorce her (Deut. 22:29).

13:21 David was very angry at Amnon's evil, but as far as the record goes, did nothing about it. His inability to be decisive in family matters became a major source of difficulty (see 1 Kin. 1:6). Sometimes a consciousness of our own sins makes us unable to deal forthrightly with the sins of others, especially those close to us.

Then all the king's sons arose, and each one got on his mule and fled.

[30]And it came to pass, while they were on the way, that news came to David, saying, "Ab'sa·lom has killed all the king's sons, and not one of them is left!" [31]So the king arose and tore his garments and lay on the ground, and all his servants stood by with their clothes torn. [32]Then Jon'a·dab the son of Shim'ē·ah, David's brother, answered and said, "Let not my lord suppose they have killed all the young men, the king's sons, for only Am'non is dead. For by the command of Ab'sa·lom this has been determined from the day that he forced his sister Tā'mar. [33]Now therefore, let not my lord the king take the thing to his heart, to think that all the king's sons are dead. For only Am'non is dead."

Absalom Flees to Geshur

[34]Then Ab'sa·lom fled. And the young man who was keeping watch lifted his eyes and looked, and there, many people were coming from the road on the hillside behind him.[a] [35]And Jon'a·dab said to the king, "Look, the king's sons are coming; as your servant said, so it is." [36]So it was, as soon as he had finished speaking, that the king's sons indeed came, and they lifted up their voice and wept. Also the king and all his servants wept very bitterly.

[37]But Ab'sa·lom fled and went to Tal'maī the son of Am·mī'hud, king of Gē'shur. And *David* mourned for his son every day. [38]So Ab'sa·lom fled and went to Gē'shur, and was there three years. [39]And King David[a] longed to go to[b] Ab'sa·lom. For he had been comforted concerning Am'non, because he was dead.

CHAPTER 14

Absalom Returns to Jerusalem

So Jō'ab the son of Ze·rū'i·ah perceived that the king's heart *was* concerned about Ab'sa·lom. [2]And Jō'ab sent to Te·kō'a and brought from there a wise woman, and said to her, "Please pretend to be a mourner, and put on mourning apparel; do not anoint yourself with oil, but act like a woman who has been mourning a long time for the dead. [3]Go to the king and speak to him in this manner." So Jō'ab put the words in her mouth.

[4]And when the woman of Te·kō'a spoke[a] to the king, she fell on her face to the ground and prostrated herself, and said, "Help, O king!"

[5]Then the king said to her, "What troubles you?"

And she answered, "Indeed I *am* a widow, my husband is dead. [6]Now your maidservant had two sons; and the two fought with each other in the field, and *there was* no one to part them, but the one struck the other and killed him. [7]And now the whole family has risen up against your maidservant, and they said, 'Deliver him who struck his brother, that we may execute him for the life of his brother whom he killed; and we will destroy the heir also.' So they would extinguish my ember that is left, and leave to my husband *neither* name nor remnant on the earth."

13:34 [a]Septuagint adds *And the watchman went and told the king, and said, "I see men from the way of Horonaim, from the regions of the mountains."* 13:39 [a]Following Masoretic Text, Syriac, and Vulgate; Septuagint reads *the spirit of the king;* Targum reads *the soul of King David.* [b]Following Masoretic Text and Targum; Septuagint and Vulgate read *ceased to pursue after.* 14:4 [a]Many Hebrew manuscripts, Septuagint, Syriac, and Vulgate read *came.*

13:30–33 The report that **all the king's sons** were killed may have been planned so that instead of being irate at Amnon's death, the king would be relieved at discovering only Amnon was dead. Jonadab's presence (v. 32) both here and in the tragic affair of Tamar (v. 3) suggests a court intriguer.

13:37–39 David was glad that Amnon had been punished, yet his own horror of treachery would not permit him to forgive the punisher, Absalom.

8 Then the king said to the woman, "Go
to your house, and I will give orders con-
cerning you."
9 And the woman of Te·kō'a said to the
king, "My lord, O king, *let* the iniquity *be*
on me and on my father's house, and the
king and his throne *be* guiltless."
10 So the king said, "Whoever says *any-*
thing to you, bring him to me, and he shall
not touch you anymore."
11 Then she said, "Please let the king re-
member the LORD your God, and do not
permit the avenger of blood to destroy
anymore, lest they destroy my son."
And he said, "*As* the LORD lives, not
one hair of your son shall fall to the
ground."
12 Therefore the woman said, "Please, let
your maidservant speak *another* word to
my lord the king."
And he said, "Say on."
13 So the woman said: "Why then have
you schemed such a thing against the peo-
ple of God? For the king speaks this thing
as one who is guilty, *in that* the king does
not bring his banished one home again.
14 For we will surely die and *become* like wa-
ter spilled on the ground, which cannot be
gathered up again. Yet God does not take
away a life; but He devises means, so that
His banished ones are not expelled from
Him. 15 Now therefore, I have come to
speak of this thing to my lord the king be-
cause the people have made me afraid.
And your maidservant said, 'I will now
speak to the king; it may be that the king
will perform the request of his maidser-
vant. 16 For the king will hear and deliver
his maidservant from the hand of the man
who would destroy me and my son together
from the inheritance of God.' 17 Your
maidservant said, 'The word of my lord
the king will now be comforting; for as the
angel of God, so *is* my lord the king in dis-
cerning good and evil. And may the LORD
your God be with you.' "
18 Then the king answered and said to
the woman, "Please do not hide from me
anything that I ask you."
And the woman said, "Please, let my
lord the king speak."
19 So the king said, "*Is* the hand of Jō'ab
with you in all this?" And the woman an-
swered and said, "*As* you live, my lord the
king, no one can turn to the right hand or
to the left from anything that my lord the
king has spoken. For your servant Jō'ab
commanded me, and he put all these
words in the mouth of your maidservant.
20 To bring about this change of affairs your
servant Jō'ab has done this thing; but my
lord *is* wise, according to the wisdom of
the angel of God, to know everything that
is in the earth."
21 And the king said to Jō'ab, "All right,
I have granted this thing. Go there-
fore, bring back the young man
Ab'sa·lom."
22 Then Jō'ab fell to the ground on his
face and bowed himself, and thanked the
king. And Jō'ab said, "Today your servant
knows that I have found favor in your
sight, my lord, O king, in that the king has
fulfilled the request of his servant." 23 So
Jō'ab arose and went to Gē'shur, and
brought Ab'sa·lom to Jerusalem. 24 And the
king said, "Let him return to his own
house, but do not let him see my face." So
Ab'sa·lom returned to his own house, but
did not see the king's face.

14:11 The law required that vengeance for the murder be limited to the life of the murderer.

14:13, 14 Evidently Chileab, next in line for the throne after Amnon (3:3), had died at some previous point. Absalom was third in line, thus David, by his actions, was depriving the nation of the heir to the throne.

14:24 David still could not bring himself to forgive treachery. When bitterness mars a relationship, it affects everyone in the family, as is seen in subsequent events in David's family. Such problems need to be resolved immediately if tragedy is to be averted.

David Forgives Absalom

25Now in all Israel there was no one who was praised as much as Ab′sa·lom for his good looks. From the sole of his foot to the crown of his head there was no blemish in him. 26And when he cut the hair of his head—at the end of every year he cut *it* because it was heavy on him—when he cut it, he weighed the hair of his head at two hundred shekels according to the king's standard. 27To Ab′sa·lom were born three sons, and one daughter whose name *was* Tā′mar. She was a woman of beautiful appearance.

28And Ab′sa·lom dwelt two full years in Jerusalem, but did not see the king's face. 29Therefore Ab′sa·lom sent for Jō′ab, to send him to the king, but he would not come to him. And when he sent again the second time, he would not come. 30So he said to his servants, "See, Jō′ab's field is near mine, and he has barley there; go and set it on fire." And Ab′sa·lom's servants set the field on fire.

31Then Jō′ab arose and came to Ab′sa·lom's house, and said to him, "Why have your servants set my field on fire?"

32And Ab′sa·lom answered Jō′ab, "Look, I sent to you, saying, 'Come here, so that I may send you to the king, to say, "Why have I come from Gē′shur? *It would be* better for me *to be* there still."' Now therefore, let me see the king's face; but if there is iniquity in me, let him execute me."

33So Jō′ab went to the king and told him. And when he had called for Ab′sa·lom, he came to the king and bowed himself on his face to the ground before the king. Then the king kissed Ab′sa·lom.

CHAPTER 15

Absalom's Treason

After this it happened that Ab′sa·lom provided himself with chariots and horses, and fifty men to run before him. 2Now Ab′sa·lom would rise early and stand beside the way to the gate. *So* it was, whenever anyone who had a lawsuit came to the king for a decision, that Ab′sa·lom would call to him and say, "What city *are* you from?" And he would say, "Your servant *is* from such and such a tribe of Israel." 3Then Ab′sa·lom would say to him, "Look, your case *is* good and right; but *there is* no deputy of the king to hear you." 4Moreover Ab′sa·lom would say, "Oh, that I were made judge in the land, and everyone who has any suit or cause would come to me; then I would give him justice." 5And *so* it was, whenever anyone came near to bow down to him, that he would put out his hand and take him and kiss him. 6In this manner Ab′sa·lom acted toward all Israel who came to the king for judgment. So Ab′sa·lom stole the hearts of the men of Israel.

7Now it came to pass after forty[a] years that Ab′sa·lom said to the king, "Please, let me go to Hē′bron and pay the vow which I made to the LORD. 8For your servant took a vow while I dwelt at Gē′shur in Syria, saying, 'If the LORD indeed brings me back to Jerusalem, then I will serve the LORD.'"

9And the king said to him, "Go in peace." So he arose and went to Hē′bron.

10Then Ab′sa·lom sent spies throughout all the tribes of Israel, saying, "As soon as you hear the sound of the trumpet, then

15:7 [a]Septuagint manuscripts, Syriac, and Josephus read *four.*

15:1–6 David's advancing years and his preoccupation with war and his family problems may have delayed the administration of justice. In this Absalom (v. 1) saw the opportunity to work his way into the good graces of the men of Israel (v. 6).

15:1 After this: An indeterminate time. Chapters 15—18 record Absalom's response to all that had happened to him.

15:2 the gate . . . a lawsuit: The gate of a city was where legal and commercial transactions took place. See Ruth 4:1, 2.

you shall say, 'Ab′sa·lom reigns in
Hē′bron!' " 11And with Ab′sa·lom went
two hundred men invited from Jerusalem,
and they went along innocently and did
not know anything. 12Then Ab′sa·lom sent
for A·hith′o·phel the Gī′lo·nīte, David's
counselor, from his city—from Gī′lōh—
while he offered sacrifices. And the con-
spiracy grew strong, for the people with
Ab′sa·lom continually increased in num-
ber.

David Escapes from Jerusalem

13Now a messenger came to David, say-
ing, "The hearts of the men of Israel are
with Ab′sa·lom."

14So David said to all his servants who
were with him at Jerusalem, "Arise, and let
us flee, or we shall not escape from
Ab′sa·lom. Make haste to depart, lest he
overtake us suddenly and bring disaster
upon us, and strike the city with the edge
of the sword."

15And the king's servants said to the
king, "We *are* your servants, *ready to do*
whatever my lord the king commands."
16Then the king went out with all his
household after him. But the king left ten
women, concubines, to keep the house.
17And the king went out with all the people
after him, and stopped at the outskirts.
18Then all his servants passed before him;
and all the Cher′e·thītes, all the Pel′-
eth·ītes, and all the Git′tītes, six hundred
men who had followed him from Gath,
passed before the king.

19Then the king said to It′taī the Git′tīte,
"Why are you also going with us? Return
and remain with the king. For you *are* a
foreigner and also an exile from your own
place. 20In fact, you came *only* yesterday.
Should I make you wander up and down
with us today, since I go I know not where?
Return, and take your brethren back.
Mercy and truth *be* with you."

21But It′taī answered the king and
said, "*As* the LORD lives, and *as* my lord the
king lives, surely in whatever place my
lord the king shall be, whether in death or
life, even there also your servant will be."

22So David said to It′taī, "Go, and cross
over." Then It′taī the Git′tīte and all his
men and all the little ones who *were* with
him crossed over. 23And all the country
wept with a loud voice, and all the people
crossed over. The king himself also crossed
over the Brook Kid′ron, and all the people
crossed over toward the way of the wilder-
ness.

24There was Zā′dok also, and all the
Lē′vītes with him, bearing the ark of the
covenant of God. And they set down
the ark of God, and A·bī′a·thar went up
until all the people had finished crossing
over from the city. 25Then the king said to
Zā′dok, "Carry the ark of God back into
the city. If I find favor in the eyes of the
LORD, He will bring me back and show me
both it and His dwelling place. 26But if He
says thus: 'I have no delight in you,' here I
am, let Him do to me as seems good to
Him." 27The king also said to Zā′dok the
priest, "*Are* you *not* a seer? Return to the
city in peace, and your two sons with you,

15:18 The **Cherethites, Pelethites,** and **Gittites** were seasoned professional soldiers, David's "mighty men" (16:6; 20:7), and his military escort whose personal loyalty to him was unquestioned.

15:21 What better response of dedication than this could we make to the King of kings! Just as Ittai devoted himself to David during the king's exile, we should give ourselves fully to God, despite the world's rejection of Him.

15:24, 25 David sent the Levites, led by **Zadok** and **Abiathar**, together with the ark of the covenant back to the tabernacle in Jerusalem (see 6:17). He expressed the conviction that if God favored his cause, he would return and see it again. Also the priests could send him information from the city (v. 28). Zadok was to become the father of a new priestly line. He was a descendant of Aaron through Eleazar, whereas Eli and his family (including Abiathar) were descended through Ithamar (see 1 Chr. 6:1–12).

A·him′a·az your son, and Jonathan the son of A·bī′a·thar. 28See, I will wait in the plains of the wilderness until word comes from you to inform me." 29Therefore Zā′dok and A·bī′a·thar carried the ark of God back to Jerusalem. And they remained there.

30So David went up by the Ascent of the *Mount of* Olives, and wept as he went up; and he had his head covered and went barefoot. And all the people who *were* with him covered their heads and went up, weeping as they went up. 31Then *someone* told David, saying, "A·hith′o·phel *is* among the conspirators with Ab′sa·lom." And David said, "O LORD, I pray, turn the counsel of A·hith′o·phel into foolishness!"

32Now it happened when David had come to the top *of the mountain,* where he worshiped God—there was Hū′shai the Ar′chīte coming to meet him with his robe torn and dust on his head. 33David said to him, "If you go on with me, then you will become a burden to me. 34But if you return to the city, and say to Ab′sa·lom, 'I will be your servant, O king; *as* I *was* your father's servant previously, so I *will* now also *be* your servant,' then you may defeat the counsel of A·hith′o·phel for me. 35And *do* you not *have* Zā′dok and A·bī′a·thar the priests with you there? Therefore it will be *that* whatever you hear from the king's house, you shall tell to Zā′dok and A·bī′a·thar the priests. 36Indeed *they have* there with them their two sons, A·him′a·az, Zā′dok's *son,* and Jonathan, A·bī′a·thar's *son;* and by them you shall send me everything you hear."

37So Hū′shai, David's friend, went into the city. And Ab′sa·lom came into Jerusalem.

CHAPTER 16

Mephibosheth's Servant

When David was a little past the top *of the mountain,* there was Zī′ba the servant of Me·phib′o·sheth, who met him with a couple of saddled donkeys, and on them two hundred *loaves* of bread, one hundred clusters of raisins, one hundred summer fruits, and a skin of wine. 2And the king said to Zī′ba, "What do you mean to do with these?"

So Zī′ba said, "The donkeys *are* for the king's household to ride on, the bread and summer fruit for the young men to eat, and the wine for those who are faint in the wilderness to drink."

3Then the king said, "And where *is* your master's son?"

And Zī′ba said to the king, "Indeed he is staying in Jerusalem, for he said, 'Today the house of Israel will restore the kingdom of my father to me.' "

4So the king said to Zī′ba, "Here, all that *belongs* to Me·phib′o·sheth *is* yours."

And Zī′ba said, "I humbly bow before you, *that* I may find favor in your sight, my lord, O king!"

Shimei Curses David

5Now when King David came to Ba·hū′rim, there was a man from the family of the house of Saul, whose name *was* Shim′ē·ī the son of Gē′ra, coming from there. He came out, cursing continuously as he came. 6And he threw stones at David and at all the servants of King David. And all the people and all the mighty men *were* on his right hand and on his left. 7Also Shim′ē·ī said thus when he cursed: "Come out! Come out! You bloodthirsty man, you rogue! 8The LORD has brought upon you all the blood of the house of Saul, in whose place you have reigned; and the LORD has delivered the kingdom into the hand of Ab′sa·lom your son. So now you *are caught* in your own evil, because you are a bloodthirsty man!"

9Then A·bi′shaī the son of Ze·rū′i·ah

16:9–14 David's magnanimity is seen again. **Because** (v. 10) is better understood as "If the LORD has said to him."

said to the king, "Why should this dead
dog curse my lord the king? Please, let me
go over and take off his head!"
10But the king said, "What have I to do
with you, you sons of Ze·rū'i·ah? So let
him curse, because the LORD has said to
him, 'Curse David.' Who then shall say,
'Why have you done so?' "
11And David said to A·bi'shaī and all his
servants, "See how my son who came from
my own body seeks my life. How much
more now *may this* Ben'ja·mīte? Let him
alone, and let him curse; for so the LORD
has ordered him. 12It may be that the LORD
will look on my affliction,[a] and that the
LORD will repay me with good for his curs-
ing this day." 13And as David and his men
went along the road, Shim'ē·ī went along
the hillside opposite him and cursed as he
went, threw stones at him and kicked up
dust. 14Now the king and all the people
who *were* with him became weary; so they
refreshed themselves there.

The Advice of Ahithophel

15Meanwhile Ab'sa·lom and all the peo-
ple, the men of Israel, came to Jerusalem;
and A·hith'o·phel *was* with him. 16And so
it was, when Hū'shai the Ar'chīte, David's
friend, came to Ab'sa·lom, that Hū'shai
said to Ab'sa·lom, "*Long* live the king!
Long live the king!"
17So Ab'sa·lom said to Hū'shai, "*Is* this
your loyalty to your friend? Why did you
not go with your friend?"
18And Hū'shai said to Ab'sa·lom, "No,
but whom the LORD and this people and all
the men of Israel choose, his I will be, and
with him I will remain. 19"Furthermore,
whom should I serve? *Should I* not *serve* in
the presence of his son? As I have served in
your father's presence, so will I be in your
presence."
20Then Ab'sa·lom said to A·hith'o·phel,
"Give advice as to what we should do."
21And A·hith'o·phel said to Ab'sa·lom,
"Go in to your father's concubines, whom
he has left to keep the house; and all Israel
will hear that you are abhorred by your fa-
ther. Then the hands of all who are with
you will be strong." 22So they pitched a tent
for Ab'sa·lom on the top of the house, and
Ab'sa·lom went in to his father's concu-
bines in the sight of all Israel.
23Now the advice of A·hith'o·phel,
which he gave in those days, *was* as if one
had inquired at the oracle of God. So *was*
all the advice of A·hith'o·phel both with
David and with Ab'sa·lom.

CHAPTER 17

Moreover A·hith'o·phel said to Ab'-
sa·lom, "Now let me choose twelve thou-
sand men, and I will arise and pursue Da-
vid tonight. 2I will come upon him while
he *is* weary and weak, and make him
afraid. And all the people who *are* with
him will flee, and I will strike only the
king. 3Then I will bring back all the people
to you. When all return except the man
whom you seek, all the people will be at
peace." 4And the saying pleased Ab'sa·lom
and all the elders of Israel.

The Advice of Hushai

5Then Ab'sa·lom said, "Now call Hū'-
shai the Ar'chīte also, and let us hear what
he says too." 6And when Hū'shai came to
Ab'sa·lom, Ab'sa·lom spoke to him, say-
ing, "A·hith'o·phel has spoken in this
manner. Shall we do as he says? If not,
speak up."
7So Hū'shai said to Ab'sa·lom: "The ad-
vice that A·hith'o·phel has given *is* not

16:12 [a]Following Kethib, Septuagint, Syriac, and Vulgate; Qere reads *my eyes;* Targum reads *tears of my eyes.*

16:20–23 This shameful act would both publicly claim royal authority and make reconciliation with David virtually impossible. Absalom's followers would know that he was fully committed to usurping the throne from his father. Absalom's action fulfilled Nathan's prophecy (12:11, 12).

good at this time. 8For," said Hū'shai, "you
know your father and his men, that they
are mighty men, and they *are* enraged in
their minds, like a bear robbed of her cubs
in the field; and your father *is* a man of
war, and will not camp with the people.
9Surely by now he is hidden in some pit, or
in some *other* place. And it will be, when
some of them are overthrown at the first,
that whoever hears *it* will say, 'There is a
slaughter among the people who follow
Ab'sa·lom.' 10And even he *who is* valiant,
whose heart *is* like the heart of a lion, will
melt completely. For all Israel knows that
your father *is* a mighty man, and *those* who
are with him *are* valiant men. 11Therefore I
advise that all Israel be fully gathered to
you, from Dan to Bē·er·shē'ba, like the
sand that *is* by the sea for multitude, and
that you go to battle in person. 12So we will
come upon him in some place where he
may be found, and we will fall on him
as the dew falls on the ground. And of
him and all the men who *are* with him
there shall not be left so much as one.
13Moreover, if he has withdrawn into
a city, then all Israel shall bring ropes to
that city; and we will pull it into the river,
until there is not one small stone found
there."

14So Ab'sa·lom and all the men of Israel
said, "The advice of Hū'shai the Ar'chīte *is*
better than the advice of A·hith'o·phel."
For the LORD had purposed to defeat the
good advice of A·hith'o·phel, to the intent
that the LORD might bring disaster on
Ab'sa·lom.

Hushai Warns David to Escape

15Then Hū'shai said to Zā'dok and
A·bī'a·thar the priests, "Thus and so
A·hith'o·phel advised Ab'sa·lom and the
elders of Israel, and thus and so I have ad-
vised. 16Now therefore, send quickly and
tell David, saying, 'Do not spend this night
in the plains of the wilderness, but speed-
ily cross over, lest the king and all the peo-
ple who *are* with him be swallowed up.' "
17Now Jonathan and A·him'a·az stayed at
En Rō'gel, for they dared not be seen com-
ing into the city; so a female servant would
come and tell them, and they would go
and tell King David. 18Nevertheless a lad
saw them, and told Ab'sa·lom. But both of
them went away quickly and came to a
man's house in Ba·hū'rim, who had a well
in his court; and they went down into it.
19Then the woman took and spread a
covering over the well's mouth, and
spread ground grain on it; and the thing
was not known. 20And when Ab'sa·lom's
servants came to the woman at the house,
they said, "Where *are* A·him'a·az and Jon-
athan?"

So the woman said to them, "They have
gone over the water brook."

And when they had searched and could
not find *them,* they returned to Jerusalem.
21Now it came to pass, after they had de-
parted, that they came up out of the well
and went and told King David, and said to
David, "Arise and cross over the water
quickly. For thus has A·hith'o·phel ad-
vised against you." 22So David and all the
people who *were* with him arose and
crossed over the Jordan. By morning light
not one of them was left who had not gone
over the Jordan.

23Now when A·hith'o·phel saw that his
advice was not followed, he saddled a
donkey, and arose and went home to his
house, to his city. Then he put his house-

17:14 the LORD had purposed: God worked through Hushai to overthrow the rebels. Had they followed the advice of Ahithophel, they would have triumphed. His judgment in v. 2 was right, as shown by 16:14.

17:21–23 Suicide is extremely rare in Scripture. Besides **Ahithophel**, only Samson (Judg. 16:28–30), Saul and his armorbearer (1 Sam. 31:4, 5), and Zimri (1 Kin. 16:18) are recorded in the OT, and only Judas (Matt. 27:3–5) in the NT. Ahithophel knew that he would receive a traitor's reward because he could clearly foresee that David would win.

hold in order, and hanged himself, and
died; and he was buried in his father's
tomb.
[24]Then David went to Mā·ha·na'im.
And Ab'sa·lom crossed over the Jordan, he
and all the men of Israel with him. [25]And
Ab'sa·lom made A·mā'sa captain of the
army instead of Jō'ab. This A·mā'sa *was* the
son of a man whose name *was* Jith'ra,[a] an
Israelite,[b] who had gone in to Ab'i·gāil the
daughter of Nā'hash, sister of Ze·rū'i·ah,
Jō'ab's mother. [26]So Israel and Ab'sa·lom
encamped in the land of Gil'ē·ad.
[27]Now it happened, when David had
come to Mā·ha·na'im, that Shō'bī the son
of Nā'hash from Rab'bah of the people of
Am'mon, Mā'chir the son of Am'mi·el
from Lo Dē'bar, and Bar·zil'laī the Gil'-
ē·ad·īte from Rō'ge·lim, [28]brought beds
and basins, earthen vessels and wheat, bar-
ley and flour, parched *grain* and beans,
lentils and parched *seeds*, [29]honey and
curds, sheep and cheese of the herd, for
David and the people who *were* with him
to eat. For they said, "The people are hun-
gry and weary and thirsty in the wilder-
ness."

CHAPTER 18

Absalom's Defeat and Death

And David numbered the people who
were with him, and set captains of thou-
sands and captains of hundreds over them.
[2]Then David sent out one third of the peo-
ple under the hand of Jō'ab, one third un-
der the hand of A·bi'shaī the son of Ze-
rū'i·ah, Jō'ab's brother, and one third
under the hand of It'taī the Git'tīte. And
the king said to the people, "I also will
surely go out with you myself."
[3]But the people answered, "You shall
not go out! For if we flee away, they will
not care about us; nor if half of us die, will
they care about us. But *you are* worth ten
thousand of us now. For you are now more
help to us in the city."
[4]Then the king said to them, "Whatever
seems best to you I will do." So the king
stood beside the gate, and all the people
went out by hundreds and by thousands.
[5]Now the king had commanded Jō'ab,
A·bi'shaī, and It'taī, saying, "*Deal* gently
for my sake with the young man Ab'-
sa·lom." And all the people heard when
the king gave all the captains orders con-
cerning Ab'sa·lom.
[6]So the people went out into the field of
battle against Israel. And the battle was in
the woods of Ē'phra·im. [7]The people of Is-
rael were overthrown there before the ser-
vants of David, and a great slaughter of
twenty thousand took place there that day.
[8]For the battle there was scattered over the
face of the whole countryside, and the
woods devoured more people that day
than the sword devoured.
[9]Then Ab'sa·lom met the servants of Da-
vid. Ab'sa·lom rode on a mule. The mule
went under the thick boughs of a great
terebinth tree, and his head caught in the
terebinth; so he was left hanging between
heaven and earth. And the mule which *was*
under him went on. [10]Now a certain man
saw *it* and told Jō'ab, and said, "I just saw
Ab'sa·lom hanging in a terebinth tree!"
[11]So Jō'ab said to the man who told him,
"You just saw *him!* And why did you not
strike him there to the ground? I would
have given you ten *shekels* of silver and a
belt."
[12]But the man said to Jō'ab, "Though I

17:25 [a]Spelled *Jether* in 1 Chronicles 2:17 and elsewhere [b]Following Masoretic Text, some manuscripts of the Septuagint, and Targum; some manuscripts of the Septuagint read *Ishmaelite* (compare 1 Chronicles 2:17); Vulgate reads *of Jezrael.*

17:27–29 Machir is identified as the man who had provided for Mephibosheth after the death of Saul (9:4, 5) and **Barzillai** was later invited to return to Jerusalem with David (19:31–40). The supplies provided were of vital importance to the fugitives.

18:8 the woods devoured: The wild environment caused more injuries than the battle.

were to receive a thousand *shekels* of silver in my hand, I would not raise my hand against the king's son. For in our hearing the king commanded you and A·bi′shaī and It′taī, saying, 'Beware lest anyone *touch* the young man Ab′sa·lom!'[a] 13 Otherwise I would have dealt falsely against my own life. For there is nothing hidden from the king, and you yourself would have set yourself against *me*."

14 Then Jō′ab said, "I cannot linger with you." And he took three spears in his hand and thrust them through Ab′sa·lom's heart, while he was *still* alive in the midst of the terebinth tree. 15 And ten young men who bore Jō′ab's armor surrounded Ab′sa·lom, and struck and killed him.

16 So Jō′ab blew the trumpet, and the people returned from pursuing Israel. For Jō′ab held back the people. 17 And they took Ab′sa·lom and cast him into a large pit in the woods, and laid a very large heap of stones over him. Then all Israel fled, everyone to his tent.

18 Now Ab′sa·lom in his lifetime had taken and set up a pillar for himself, which *is* in the King's Valley. For he said, "I have no son to keep my name in remembrance." He called the pillar after his own name. And to this day it is called Ab′sa·lom's Monument.

David Hears of Absalom's Death

19 Then A·him′a·az the son of Zā′dok said, "Let me run now and take the news to the king, how the LORD has avenged him of his enemies."

20 And Jō′ab said to him, "You shall not take the news this day, for you shall take the news another day. But today you shall take no news, because the king's son is dead." 21 Then Jō′ab said to the Cū′shīte, "Go, tell the king what you have seen." So the Cū′shīte bowed himself to Jō′ab and ran.

22 And A·him′a·az the son of Zā′dok said again to Jō′ab, "But whatever happens, please let me also run after the Cū′shīte."

So Jō′ab said, "Why will you run, my son, since you have no news ready?"

23 "But whatever happens," *he said*, "let me run."

So he said to him, "Run." Then A·him′a·az ran by way of the plain, and outran the Cū′shīte.

24 Now David was sitting between the two gates. And the watchman went up to the roof over the gate, to the wall, lifted his eyes and looked, and there was a man, running alone. 25 Then the watchman cried out and told the king. And the king said, "If he *is* alone, *there is* news in his mouth." And he came rapidly and drew near.

26 Then the watchman saw *another* man running, and the watchman called to the gatekeeper and said, "There is *another* man, running alone!"

And the king said, "He also brings news."

27 So the watchman said, "I think the running of the first is like the running of A·him′a·az the son of Zā′dok."

And the king said, "He *is* a good man, and comes with good news."

28 So A·him′a·az called out and said to the king, "All is well!" Then he bowed down with his face to the earth before the king, and said, "Blessed *be* the LORD your God, who has delivered up the men who raised their hand against my lord the king!"

29 The king said, "Is the young man Ab′sa·lom safe?"

A·him′a·az answered, "When Jō′ab sent the king's servant and *me* your servant, I saw a great tumult, but I did not know what *it was about*."

30 And the king said, "Turn aside *and*

18:12 [a]The ancient versions read *'Protect the young man Absalom for me!'*

18:14 Joab knew there could be no peace while Absalom lived, whatever David might sentimentally believe.

stand here." So he turned aside and stood
still.
31 Just then the Cū'shīte came, and the
Cū'shīte said, "There is good news, my
lord the king! For the LORD has avenged
you this day of all those who rose against
you."
32 And the king said to the Cū'shīte, "Is
the young man Ab'sa·lom safe?"
So the Cū'shīte answered, "May the en-
emies of my lord the king, and all who rise
against you to do harm, be like *that* young
man!"

David's Mourning for Absalom

33 Then the king was deeply moved, and
went up to the chamber over the gate, and
wept. And as he went, he said thus: "O my
son Ab'sa·lom—my son, my son Ab'sa-
lom—if only I had died in your place! O
Ab'sa·lom my son, my son!"

CHAPTER 19

And Jō'ab was told, "Behold, the king is
weeping and mourning for Ab'sa·lom."
2 So the victory that day was *turned* into
mourning for all the people. For the people
heard it said that day, "The king is grieved
for his son." 3 And the people stole back
into the city that day, as people who are
ashamed steal away when they flee in bat-
tle. 4 But the king covered his face, and the
king cried out with a loud voice, "O my
son Ab'sa·lom! O Ab'sa·lom, my son, my
son!"
5 Then Jō'ab came into the house to the
king, and said, "Today you have disgraced
all your servants who today have saved
your life, the lives of your sons and daugh-
ters, the lives of your wives and the lives of
your concubines, 6 in that you love your en-
emies and hate your friends. For you have
declared today that you regard neither
princes nor servants; for today I perceive
that if Ab'sa·lom had lived and all of us
had died today, then it would have pleased
you well. 7 Now therefore, arise, go out and
speak comfort to your servants. For I
swear by the LORD, if you do not go out,
not one will stay with you this night. And
that will be worse for you than all the evil
that has befallen you from your youth un-
til now." 8 Then the king arose and sat in the
gate. And they told all the people, saying,
"There is the king, sitting in the gate." So
all the people came before the king.
For everyone of Israel had fled to his
tent.

David Returns to Jerusalem

9 Now all the people were in a dispute
throughout all the tribes of Israel, saying,
"The king saved us from the hand of our
enemies, he delivered us from the hand of
the Phi·lis'tines, and now he has fled from
the land because of Ab'sa·lom. 10 But
Ab'sa·lom, whom we anointed over us,
has died in battle. Now therefore, why do
you say nothing about bringing back the
king?"
11 So King David sent to Zā'dok and

18:33 David's weakness and strength. When Absalom was alive, David had not done what he could to reconcile the crown prince because of his treachery. Now when he is dead, David is moved with compassion for him.

19:5–8 Joab, ever ruthless, makes his king face reality.

19:8 By **sitting in the gate**, David indicated his intention to resume his reign now that the rebellion was over.

19:9, 10 The people were thrown into confusion by their lingering loyalty to David and the news of Absalom's death.

19:11–14 David made two moves to secure his return to the throne: (1) He sent word to the priests Zadok and Abiathar to rally the elders of Judah. Since Judah had rallied to Absalom first (15:10), David wanted to be sure that they were the first to officially welcome him back. (2) He made Absalom's general **Amasa**, who was his nephew (v. 13), general in place of Joab. David apparently blamed Joab for the death of Absalom as well as for the earlier murder of Abner (3:27).

A·bī′a·thar the priests, saying, "Speak to the elders of Judah, saying, 'Why are you the last to bring the king back to his house, since the words of all Israel have come to the king, to his *very* house? 12You *are* my brethren, you *are* my bone and my flesh. Why then are you the last to bring back the king?' 13And say to A·mā′sa, '*Are* you not my bone and my flesh? God do so to me, and more also, if you are not commander of the army before me continually in place of Jō′ab.' " 14So he swayed the hearts of all the men of Judah, just as *the heart of* one man, so that they sent *this word* to the king: "Return, you and all your servants!"

15Then the king returned and came to the Jordan. And Judah came to Gil′gal, to go to meet the king, to escort the king across the Jordan. 16And Shim′ē·ī the son of Gē′ra, a Ben′ja·mīte, who *was* from Ba·hū′rim, hurried and came down with the men of Judah to meet King David. 17*There were* a thousand men of Benjamin with him, and Zī′ba the servant of the house of Saul, and his fifteen sons and his twenty servants with him; and they went over the Jordan before the king. 18Then a ferryboat went across to carry over the king's household, and to do what he thought good.

David's Mercy to Shimei

Now Shim′ē·ī the son of Gē′ra fell down before the king when he had crossed the Jordan. 19Then he said to the king, "Do not let my lord impute iniquity to me, or remember what wrong your servant did on the day that my lord the king left Jerusalem, that the king should take *it* to heart. 20For I, your servant, know that I have sinned. Therefore here I am, the first to come today of all the house of Joseph to go down to meet my lord the king."

21But A·bi′shaī the son of Ze·rū′i·ah answered and said, "Shall not Shim′ē·ī be put to death for this, because he cursed the LORD's anointed?"

22And David said, "What have I to do with you, you sons of Ze·rū′i·ah, that you should be adversaries to me today? Shall any man be put to death today in Israel? For do I not know that today I *am* king over Israel?" 23Therefore the king said to Shim′ē·ī, "You shall not die." And the king swore to him.

David and Mephibosheth Meet

24Now Me·phib′o·sheth the son of Saul came down to meet the king. And he had not cared for his feet, nor trimmed his mustache, nor washed his clothes, from the day the king departed until the day he returned in peace. 25So it was, when he had come to Jerusalem to meet the king, that the king said to him, "Why did you not go with me, Me·phib′o·sheth?"

26And he answered, "My lord, O king, my servant deceived me. For your servant said, 'I will saddle a donkey for myself, that I may ride on it and go to the king,' because your servant *is* lame. 27And he has slandered your servant to my lord the king, but my lord the king *is* like the angel of God. Therefore do *what is* good in your eyes. 28For all my father's house were but dead men before my lord the king. Yet you set your servant among those who eat at your own table. Therefore what right have I still to cry out anymore to the king?"

29So the king said to him, "Why do you speak anymore of your matters? I have said, 'You and Zī′ba divide the land.' "

30Then Me·phib′o·sheth said to the king, "Rather, let him take it all, inasmuch as my lord the king has come back in peace to his own house."

David's Kindness to Barzillai

31And Bar·zil′laī the Gil′ē·ad·īte came down from Rō′ge·lim and went across the

---

19:29 divide the land: A reversal of David's previous decision (16:4). He was unwilling to adjudicate the matter further. At this point too many other issues demanded attention.

Jordan with the king, to escort him across
the Jordan. 32Now Bar·zil'laī was a very
aged man, eighty years old. And he had
provided the king with supplies while he
stayed at Mā·ha·na'im, for he *was* a very
rich man. 33And the king said to Bar·zil'laī,
"Come across with me, and I will provide
for you while you are with me in Jerusa-
lem."

34But Bar·zil'laī said to the king, "How
long have I to live, that I should go up with
the king to Jerusalem? 35I *am* today eighty
years old. Can I discern between the good
and bad? Can your servant taste what I eat
or what I drink? Can I hear any longer the
voice of singing men and singing women?
Why then should your servant be a further
burden to my lord the king? 36Your servant
will go a little way across the Jordan with
the king. And why should the king repay
me *with* such a reward? 37Please let your
servant turn back again, that I may die in
my own city, near the grave of my father
and mother. But here is your servant
Chim'ham; let him cross over with my lord
the king, and do for him what seems good
to you."

38And the king answered, "Chim'ham
shall cross over with me, and I will do for
him what seems good to you. Now what-
ever you request of me, I will do for you."
39Then all the people went over the Jordan.
And when the king had crossed over, the
king kissed Bar·zil'laī and blessed him,
and he returned to his own place.

The Quarrel About the King

40Now the king went on to Gil'gal, and
Chim'ham[a] went on with him. And all the
people of Judah escorted the king, and also
half the people of Israel. 41Just then all the
men of Israel came to the king, and said to
the king, "Why have our brethren, the men
of Judah, stolen you away and brought the
king, his household, and all David's men
with him across the Jordan?"

42So all the men of Judah answered the
men of Israel, "Because the king *is* a close
relative of ours. Why then are you angry
over this matter? Have we ever eaten at the
king's *expense?* Or has he given us any
gift?"

43And the men of Israel answered the
men of Judah, and said, "We have ten
shares in the king; therefore we also have
more *right* to David than you. Why then do
you despise us—were we not the first to
advise bringing back our king?"

Yet the words of the men of Judah were fiercer than the words of the men of Israel.

CHAPTER 20

The Rebellion of Sheba

And there happened to be there a rebel,[a]
whose name *was* Shē'ba the son of Bich'rī,
a Ben'ja·mīte. And he blew a trumpet, and
said:

"We have no share in David,
Nor do we have inheritance in the
son of Jesse;
Every man to his tents, O Israel!"

2So every man of Israel deserted David,
and followed Shē'ba the son of Bich'rī. But
the men of Judah, from the Jordan as far as
Jerusalem, remained loyal to their king.

3Now David came to his house at Jeru-
salem. And the king took the ten women,
his concubines whom he had left to keep
the house, and put them in seclusion and
supported them, but did not go in to them.

19:40 [a]Masoretic Text reads *Chimhan.* 20:1 [a]Literally *man of Belial*

19:35 good and bad: Not a reference to moral issues, but to matters of taste and enjoyment. He was too old to be able to appreciate the delights of court life.

20:1, 2 The revolt of **Sheba** was still another demonstration of the long-standing, but growing, tension between North and South. **Every man to his tents** apparently became a rallying cry for northern dissidents (see 1 Kin. 12:16).

So they were shut up to the day of their death, living in widowhood.

4And the king said to A·mā′sa, "Assemble the men of Judah for me within three days, and be present here yourself." 5So A·mā′sa went to assemble *the men of* Judah. But he delayed longer than the set time which David had appointed him. 6And David said to A·bi′shaī, "Now Shē′ba the son of Bich′rī will do us more harm than Ab′sa·lom. Take your lord's servants and pursue him, lest he find for himself fortified cities, and escape us." 7So Jō′ab's men, with the Cher′e·thītes, the Pel′eth·ītes, and all the mighty men, went out after him. And they went out of Jerusalem to pursue Shē′ba the son of Bich′rī. 8When they *were* at the large stone which *is* in Gib′ē·on, A·mā′sa came before them. Now Jō′ab was dressed in battle armor; on it was a belt *with* a sword fastened in its sheath at his hips; and as he was going forward, it fell out. 9Then Jō′ab said to A·mā′sa, "*Are* you in health, my brother?" And Jō′ab took A·mā′sa by the beard with his right hand to kiss him. 10But A·mā′sa did not notice the sword that *was* in Jō′ab's hand. And he struck him with it in the stomach, and his entrails poured out on the ground; and he did not *strike* him again. Thus he died.

Then Jō′ab and A·bi′shaī his brother pursued Shē′ba the son of Bich′rī. 11Meanwhile one of Jō′ab's men stood near A·mā′sa, and said, "Whoever favors Jō′ab and whoever *is* for David—follow Jō′ab!" 12But A·mā′sa wallowed in *his* blood in the middle of the highway. And when the man saw that all the people stood still, he moved A·mā′sa from the highway to the field and threw a garment over him, when he saw that everyone who came upon him halted. 13When he was removed from the highway, all the people went on after Jō′ab to pursue Shē′ba the son of Bich′rī.

14And he went through all the tribes of Israel to Abel and Beth Mā′a·chah and all the Be′rītes. So they were gathered together and also went after *Shē′ba*.[a] 15Then they came and besieged him in Abel of Beth Mā′a·chah; and they cast up a siege mound against the city, and it stood by the rampart. And all the people who *were* with Jō′ab battered the wall to throw it down.

16Then a wise woman cried out from the city, "Hear, hear! Please say to Jō′ab, 'Come nearby, that I may speak with you.' " 17When he had come near to her, the woman said, "*Are* you Jō′ab?"

He answered, "I *am*."

Then she said to him, "Hear the words of your maidservant."

And he answered, "I am listening."

18So she spoke, saying, "They used to talk in former times, saying, 'They shall surely seek *guidance* at Abel,' and so they would end *disputes*. 19I *am among the* peaceable *and* faithful in Israel. You seek to destroy a city and a mother in Israel. Why would you swallow up the inheritance of the LORD?"

20And Jō′ab answered and said, "Far be it, far be it from me, that I should swallow up or destroy! 21That *is* not so. But a man from the mountains of Ē′phra·im, Shē′ba the son of Bich′rī by name, has raised his hand against the king, against David. Deliver him only, and I will depart from the city."

So the woman said to Jō′ab, "Watch, his head will be thrown to you over the wall." 22Then the woman in her wisdom went to all the people. And they cut off the head of Shē′ba the son of Bich′rī, and threw *it* out to Jō′ab. Then he blew a trumpet, and they

20:14 [a]Literally *him*

20:19 A mother in Israel could refer either to the woman who spoke, or to the city as a center for a group of villages clustered around it.

20:20 Ironic in view of Joab's recent treatment of Amasa.

withdrew from the city, every man to his
tent. So Jō'ab returned to the king at Jerusalem.

David's Government Officers

[23]And Jō'ab *was* over all the army of Israel; Be·nā'i·ah the son of Je·hoi'a·da *was*
over the Cher'e·thītes and the Pel'eth·ītes;
[24]A·dor'am *was* in charge of revenue;
Je·hosh'a·phat the son of A·hī'lud *was*
recorder; [25]Shē'va *was* scribe; Zā'dok and
A·bī'a·thar *were* the priests; [26]and Ī'ra the
Jā'i·rīte was a chief minister under David.

CHAPTER 21

David Avenges the Gibeonites

Now there was a famine in the days of
David for three years, year after year; and
David inquired of the LORD. And the LORD
answered, "*It is* because of Saul and *his*
bloodthirsty house, because he killed the
Gib'ē·on·ītes." [2]So the king called the
Gib'ē·on·ītes and spoke to them. Now
the Gib'ē·on·ītes *were* not of the children of
Israel, but of the remnant of the Am'o·rītes; the children of Israel had sworn protection to them, but Saul had sought to kill
them in his zeal for the children of Israel
and Judah.

[3]Therefore David said to the Gib'ē·on·ītes, "What shall I do for you? And with
what shall I make atonement, that you
may bless the inheritance of the LORD?"

[4]And the Gib'ē·on·ītes said to him, "We
will have no silver or gold from Saul or
from his house, nor shall you kill any man
in Israel for us."

So he said, "Whatever you say, I will do
for you."

[5]Then they answered the king, "As for
the man who consumed us and plotted
against us, *that* we should be destroyed
from remaining in any of the territories of
Israel, [6]let seven men of his descendants be
delivered to us, and we will hang them before the LORD in Gib'ē·ah of Saul, *whom* the
LORD chose."

And the king said, "I will give *them*."

[7]But the king spared Me·phib'o·sheth
the son of Jonathan, the son of Saul, because of the LORD's oath that *was* between
them, between David and Jonathan the son
of Saul. [8]So the king took Ar·mō'nī and
Me·phib'o·sheth, the two sons of Riz'pah
the daughter of Ā'i·ah, whom she bore to
Saul, and the five sons of Mī'chal[a] the
daughter of Saul, whom she brought up
for Ā'dri·el the son of Bar·zil'laī the
Me·hō'la·thīte; [9]and he delivered them
into the hands of the Gib'ē·on·ītes, and
they hanged them on the hill before the
LORD. So they fell, *all* seven together, and
were put to death in the days of harvest, in
the first *days*, in the beginning of barley
harvest.

[10]Now Riz'pah the daughter of Ā'i·ah
took sackcloth and spread it for herself on
the rock, from the beginning of harvest until the late rains poured on them from
heaven. And she did not allow the birds of
the air to rest on them by day nor the
beasts of the field by night.

[11]And David was told what Riz'pah the
daughter of Ā'i·ah, the concubine of Saul,

21:8 [a]Or *Merab* (compare 1 Samuel 18:19 and 25:44; 2 Samuel 3:14 and 6:23)

21:1–14 The precise time when this gruesome episode occurred is unknown, but it must have been some time after David brought Mephibosheth to Jerusalem (v. 7; 9:13). Some scholars relate this killing of Saul's descendants to the curse of Shimei against David as a bloodthirsty man (16:7, 8). If so, it would have occurred before the revolt of Absalom.

21:8 The name **Michal** should be corrected to *Merab*, Saul's oldest daughter (1 Sam. 18:19; 25:44). Michal was childless (2 Sam. 6:23).

21:10 **Rizpah** prevented the corpses from being ravaged by birds, considered the greatest insult possible. Her devotion prompted David to provide burial places for the family of Saul, in one last act of kindness toward the man who had so abused him.

had done. 12Then David went and took the
bones of Saul, and the bones of Jonathan
his son, from the men of Jā′besh Gil′ē·ad
who had stolen them from the street of
Beth Shan,[a] where the Phi·lis′tines had
hung them up, after the Phi·lis′tines had
struck down Saul in Gil·bō′a. 13So he
brought up the bones of Saul and the bones
of Jonathan his son from there; and they
gathered the bones of those who had been
hanged. 14They buried the bones of Saul
and Jonathan his son in the country of Ben-
jamin in Zē′lah, in the tomb of Kish his fa-
ther. So they performed all that the king
commanded. And after that God heeded
the prayer for the land.

Philistine Giants Destroyed

15When the Phi·lis′tines were at war
again with Israel, David and his servants
with him went down and fought against
the Phi·lis′tines; and David grew faint.
16Then Ish′bi-Bē′nob, who *was* one of the
sons of the giant, the weight of whose
bronze spear *was* three hundred *shekels*,
who was bearing a new *sword*, thought he
could kill David. 17But A·bi′shaī the son of
Ze·rū′i·ah came to his aid, and struck the
Phi·lis′tine and killed him. Then the men
of David swore to him, saying, "You shall
go out no more with us to battle, lest you
quench the lamp of Israel."

18Now it happened afterward that there
was again a battle with the Phi·lis′tines at
Gob. Then Sib′be·chaī the Hū′sha·thīte
killed Saph,[a] who *was* one of the sons of the
giant. 19Again there was war at Gob with
the Phi·lis′tines, where El·hā′nan the son
of Jā′a·rē-Or′e·gim[a] the Beth′le·hem·īte
killed *the brother of* Goliath the Git′tīte, the
shaft of whose spear *was* like a weaver's
beam.

20Yet again there was war at Gath, where
there was a man of *great* stature, who had
six fingers on each hand and six toes on
each foot, twenty-four in number; and he
also was born to the giant. 21So when he de-
fied Israel, Jonathan the son of Shim′ē·a,[a]
David's brother, killed him.

22These four were born to the giant in
Gath, and fell by the hand of David and by
the hand of his servants.

CHAPTER 22

Praise for God's Deliverance

Then David spoke to the LORD the
words of this song, on the day when the
LORD had delivered him from the hand of
all his enemies, and from the hand of Saul.
2And he said:[a]

"The LORD *is* my rock and my fortress
and my deliverer;
3 The God of my strength, in whom I
will trust;
My shield and the horn of my
salvation,

I praise you, Lord, because You are my rock, my fortress, and my deliverer; the God of my strength. I will trust in You, for You are my shield and the horn of my salvation, my stronghold, and my refuge; my Savior, You save me from violence.

adapted from 2 Samuel 22:2, 3

21:12 [a]Spelled *Beth Shean* in Joshua 17:11 and elsewhere 21:18 [a]Spelled *Sippai* in 1 Chronicles 20:4 21:19 [a]Spelled *Jair* in 1 Chronicles 20:5 21:21 [a]Spelled *Shammah* in 1 Samuel 16:9 and elsewhere 22:2 [a]Compare Psalm 18

21:15–22 Four examples of courage on the part of David's warriors are given without indication of when they occurred. All took place during battles with the Philistines (v. 15).

22:3 David's song of deliverance (vv. 2–51) is preserved in Ps. 18. We learn from the title preceding the psalm that it was composed shortly after David became king.

My stronghold and my refuge;
My Savior, You save me from
violence.
4 I will call upon the LORD, *who is*
worthy to be praised;
So shall I be saved from my enemies.

5 "When the waves of death surrounded
me,
The floods of ungodliness made me
afraid.
6 The sorrows of Shē′ōl surrounded
me;
The snares of death confronted me.
7 In my distress I called upon the LORD,
And cried out to my God;
He heard my voice from His temple,
And my cry *entered* His ears.

8 "Then the earth shook and trembled;
The foundations of heaven[a] quaked
and were shaken,
Because He was angry.
9 Smoke went up from His nostrils,
And devouring fire from His mouth;
Coals were kindled by it.
10 He bowed the heavens also, and came
down
With darkness under His feet.
11 He rode upon a cherub, and flew;
And He was seen[a] upon the wings of
the wind.
12 He made darkness canopies around
Him,
Dark waters *and* thick clouds of the
skies.

22:8 [a]Following Masoretic Text, Septuagint, and Targum; Syriac and Vulgate read *hills* (compare Psalm 18:7).
22:11 [a]Following Masoretic Text and Septuagint; many Hebrew manuscripts, Syriac, and Vulgate read *He flew* (compare Psalm 18:10); Targum reads *He spoke with power.*

13 From the brightness before Him
Coals of fire were kindled.

14 "The LORD thundered from heaven,
And the Most High uttered His voice.
15 He sent out arrows and scattered
them;
Lightning bolts, and He vanquished
them.
16 Then the channels of the sea were
seen,
The foundations of the world were
uncovered,
At the rebuke of the LORD,
At the blast of the breath of His
nostrils.

17 "He sent from above, He took me,
He drew me out of many waters.
18 He delivered me from my strong
enemy,
From those who hated me;
For they were too strong for me.
19 They confronted me in the day of my
calamity,
But the LORD was my support.
20 He also brought me out into a broad
place;
He delivered me because He
delighted in me.

21 "The LORD rewarded me according to
my righteousness;
According to the cleanness of my
hands
He has recompensed me.
22 For I have kept the ways of the LORD,
And have not wickedly departed
from my God.
23 For all His judgments *were* before me;
And *as for* His statutes, I did not
depart from them.

22:8–20 A vivid description of God's deliverance, perhaps by means of the storm that broke out during a previous battle with the Philistines (1 Sam. 7:10). God's interventions are often described in terms of earthquake and storm (1 Kin. 19:11, 12; Job 38:1).

22:21–25 These words are not to be taken by themselves and used as proof that salvation is by works even in the OT. They must be interpreted in the light of such other statements as Ps. 38:15–22.

24 I was also blameless before Him,
And I kept myself from my iniquity.
25 Therefore the LORD has recompensed
me according to my righteousness,
According to my cleanness in His
eyes.[a]

26 "With the merciful You will show
Yourself merciful;
With a blameless man You will show
Yourself blameless;
27 With the pure You will show Yourself
pure;
And with the devious You will show
Yourself shrewd.
28 You will save the humble people;
But Your eyes *are* on the haughty, *that*
You may bring *them* down.

29 "For You *are* my lamp, O LORD;
The LORD shall enlighten my
darkness.
30 For by You I can run against a troop;
By my God I can leap over a wall.
31 *As for* God, His way *is* perfect;
The word of the LORD *is* proven;
He *is* a shield to all who trust in Him.

32 "For who *is* God, except the LORD?
And who *is* a rock, except our God?
33 God *is* my strength *and* power,[a]
And He makes my[b] way perfect.
34 He makes my[a] feet like the *feet* of
deer,
And sets me on my high places.
35 He teaches my hands to make war,
So that my arms can bend a bow of
bronze.

36 "You have also given me the shield of
Your salvation;
Your gentleness has made me great.
37 You enlarged my path under me;
So my feet did not slip.

38 "I have pursued my enemies and
destroyed them;
Neither did I turn back again till they
were destroyed.
39 And I have destroyed them and
wounded them,
So that they could not rise;
They have fallen under my feet.
40 For You have armed me with strength
for the battle;
You have subdued under me those
who rose against me.
41 You have also given me the necks of
my enemies,
So that I destroyed those who hated
me.
42 They looked, but *there was* none to
save;
Even to the LORD, but He did not
answer them.
43 Then I beat them as fine as the dust of
the earth;
I trod them like dirt in the streets,
And I spread them out.

44 "You have also delivered me from the
strivings of my people;
You have kept me as the head of the
nations.
A people I have not known shall
serve me.

22:25 [a]Septuagint, Syriac, and Vulgate read *the cleanness of my hands in His sight* (compare Psalm 18:24); Targum reads *my cleanness before His word.*
22:33 [a]Dead Sea Scrolls, Septuagint, Syriac, and Vulgate read *It is God who arms me with strength* (compare Psalm 18:32); Targum reads *It is God who sustains me with strength.* [b]Following Qere, Septuagint, Syriac, Targum, and Vulgate (compare Psalm 18:32); Kethib reads *His.* 22:34 [a]Following Qere, Septuagint, Syriac, Targum, and Vulgate (compare Psalm 18:33); Kethib reads *His.*

22:38–51 David attributes his victories to God, not, as some might, to their own power and craftiness. If such militaristic statements fall harshly upon our modern ears, we must remember David's situation in which it was either destroy or be destroyed, and God's requirement that various peoples be exterminated because of their sin and for the sake of His plan.

45 The foreigners submit to me;
As soon as they hear, they obey me.
46 The foreigners fade away,
And come frightened[a] from their
hideouts.

47 "The LORD lives!
Blessed *be* my Rock!
Let God be exalted,
The Rock of my salvation!
48 *It is* God who avenges me,
And subdues the peoples under me;
49 He delivers me from my enemies.
You also lift me up above those who
rise against me;
You have delivered me from the
violent man.
50 Therefore I will give thanks to You,
O LORD, among the Gentiles,
And sing praises to Your name.

51 *He is* the tower of salvation to His
king,
And shows mercy to His anointed,
To David and his descendants
forevermore."

CHAPTER 23

David's Last Words

Now these *are* the last words of David.

Thus says David the son of Jesse;
Thus says the man raised up on high,
The anointed of the God of Jacob,
And the sweet psalmist of Israel:

2 "The Spirit of the LORD spoke by me,
And His word *was* on my tongue.
3 The God of Israel said,
The Rock of Israel spoke to me:
'He who rules over men *must be* just,
Ruling in the fear of God.
4 And *he shall be* like the light of the
morning *when* the sun rises,
A morning without clouds,
Like the tender grass *springing* out of
the earth,
By clear shining after rain.'

> The only sure way to keep fear out of living is to keep a respectful fear of God in our lives, which means to maintain a reverent attitude toward His place and influence in the scheme of things. This brand of fear is a healthy ingredient, a deterrent to want, a spur to courage and confidence, an insurance against loss, a source of comfort and understanding at any age.
>
> Eugene Asa Carr

5 "Although my house *is* not so with
God,
Yet He has made with me an
everlasting covenant,
Ordered in all *things* and secure.
For *this is* all my salvation and all *my*
desire;
Will He not make *it* increase?
6 But *the sons* of rebellion *shall* all *be* as
thorns thrust away,
Because they cannot be taken with
hands.
7 But the man *who* touches them
Must be armed with iron and the
shaft of a spear,
And they shall be utterly burned with
fire in *their* place."

22:46 [a]Following Septuagint, Targum, and Vulgate (compare Psalm 18:45); Masoretic Text reads *gird themselves.*

23:2 The 73 psalms attributed to David by their titles, as well as vv. 1–7 preserved here, testify to the truth that the **Spirit of the LORD** spoke by David.

23:5 my house is not so: Although my family is not prominent. **everlasting covenant**: Fulfilled in "David's greater Son," the Lord Jesus Christ.

David's Mighty Men

[8]These *are* the names of the mighty men
whom David had: Jō'sheb-Bas·shē'beth[a]
the Tach'mo·nīte, chief among the cap-
tains.[b] He was called Ad'i·nō the Ez'nīte,
because he had killed eight hundred men
at one time. [9]And after him *was* El·ē·ā'zar
the son of Dodo,[a] the A·hō'hīte, *one* of the
three mighty men with David when they
defied the Phi·lis'tines *who* were gathered
there for battle, and the men of Israel had
retreated. [10]He arose and attacked the
Phi·lis'tines until his hand was weary, and
his hand stuck to the sword. The LORD
brought about a great victory that day; and
the people returned after him only to plun-
der. [11]And after him *was* Sham'mah the son
of Ā'gee the Har'a·rīte. The Phi·lis'tines
had gathered together into a troop where
there was a piece of ground full of lentils.
So the people fled from the Phi·lis'tines.
[12]But he stationed himself in the middle of
the field, defended it, and killed the
Phi·lis'tines. So the LORD brought about a
great victory.

[13]Then three of the thirty chief men went
down at harvest time and came to David at
the cave of A·dul'lam. And the troop of
Phi·lis'tines encamped in the Valley of
Reph'a·im. [14]David *was* then in the strong-
hold, and the garrison of the Phi·lis'tines
was then *in* Bethlehem. [15]And David said
with longing, "Oh, that someone would
give me a drink of the water from the well
of Bethlehem, which *is* by the gate!" [16]So
the three mighty men broke through the
camp of the Phi·lis'tines, drew water from
the well of Bethlehem that *was* by the gate,
and took it and brought *it* to David. Never-
theless he would not drink it, but poured it
out to the LORD. [17]And he said, "Far be it
from me, O LORD, that I should do this! Is
this not the blood of the men who went in
jeopardy of their lives?" Therefore he would
not drink it.

These things were done by the three
mighty men.

[18]Now A·bi'shaī the brother of Jō'ab, the
son of Ze·rū'i·ah, was chief of *another*
three.[a] He lifted his spear against three
hundred *men,* killed *them,* and won a name
among *these* three. [19]Was he not the most
honored of three? Therefore he became
their captain. However, he did not attain to
the *first* three.

[20]Be·nā'i·ah *was* the son of Je·hoi'a·da,
the son of a valiant man from Kab'zē·el,
who had done many deeds. He had killed
two lion-like heroes of Mō'ab. He also had
gone down and killed a lion in the midst of
a pit on a snowy day. [21]And he killed an
Egyptian, a spectacular man. The Egyptian
had a spear in his hand; so he went down to
him with a staff, wrested the spear out of
the Egyptian's hand, and killed him with
his own spear. [22]These *things* Be·nā'i·ah the
son of Je·hoi'a·da did, and won a name
among three mighty men. [23]He was more
honored than the thirty, but he did not at-
tain to the *first* three. And David appointed
him over his guard.

[24]As'a·hel the brother of Jō'ab *was* one of
the thirty; El·hā'nan the son of Dodo of
Bethlehem, [25]Sham'mah the Har'od·īte,

23:8 [a]Literally *One Who Sits in the Seat* (compare 1 Chronicles 11:11) [b]Following Masoretic Text and Targum; Septuagint and Vulgate read *the three.*
23:9 [a]Spelled *Dodai* in 1 Chronicles 27:4
23:18 [a]Following Masoretic Text, Septuagint, and Vulgate; some Hebrew manuscripts and Syriac read *thirty;* Targum reads *the mighty men.*

23:8–23 The differences between this passage and its parallel in 1 Chr. 11:11–25 are explained on the basis of variation in copying, Chronicles from Samuel or both from other sources. None of the differences are significant for doctrine.

23:13–17 A touching description of the love and loyalty inspired by David in his men. David **poured it out to the LORD** (v. 16) as an act of sacrifice and worship.

23:24–39 A listing of the men who constituted David's elite corps of warriors and leaders. The differences in order and names from the parallel in 1 Chr. 11:26–47 may result because the group changed from time to time.

E·lī′ka the Har′od·īte, 26Hē′lez the Pal′tīte,
Ī′ra the son of Ik′kesh the Te·kō′īte,
27Ā·bi·ē′zer the An′a·thoth·īte, Me·bun′nai
the Hū′sha·thīte, 28Zal′mon the A·hō′hīte,
Mā′ha·raī the Ne·toph′a·thīte, 29Hē′leb the
son of Bā′a·nah (the Ne·toph′a·thīte), It′taī
the son of Rī′baī from Gib′ē·ah of the chil-
dren of Benjamin, 30Be·nā′i·ah a Pir′a-
thon·īte, Hid′daī from the brooks of
Gā′·ash, 31Ā′bi·Al′bon the Ar′ba·thīte,
Az′ma·veth the Bar·hū′mīte, 32Ē·lī′ah·ba
the Shā·al′bon·īte (of the sons of Jā′shen),
Jonathan, 33Sham′mah the Har′a·rīte,
A·hī′am the son of Shar′ar the Har′a·rīte,
34E·liph′e·let the son of A·has′baī, the son
of the Mā′a·cha·thīte, E·lī′am the son of
A·hith′o·phel the Gī′lo·nīte, 35Hez′raī[a] the
Car′mel·īte, Pā′a·raī the Ar′bīte, 36Ī′gal the
son of Nathan of Zō′bah, Bā′nī the Gad′īte,
37Zē′lek the Am′mon·īte, Nā′ha·raī the
Be·er′oth·īte (armorbearer of Jō′ab the son
of Ze·rū′i·ah), 38Ī′ra the Ith′rīte, Gā′reb the
Ith′rīte, 39*and* Ū·rī′ah the Hit′tīte: thirty-
seven in all.

CHAPTER 24

David's Census of Israel and Judah

Again the anger of the LORD was
aroused against Israel, and He moved Da-
vid against them to say, "Go, number Israel
and Judah."
2So the king said to Jō′ab the comman-
der of the army who *was* with him, "Now
go throughout all the tribes of Israel, from
Dan to Bē·er·shē′ba, and count the people,
that I may know the number of the peo-
ple."
3And Jō′ab said to the king, "Now may
the LORD your God add to the people a
hundred times more than there are, and
may the eyes of my lord the king see *it*. But
why does my lord the king desire this
thing?" 4Nevertheless the king's word pre-
vailed against Jō′ab and against the cap-
tains of the army. Therefore Jō′ab and the
captains of the army went out from the
presence of the king to count the people of
Israel.
5And they crossed over the Jordan and
camped in A·rō′er, on the right side of the
town which *is* in the midst of the ravine of
Gad, and toward Jā′zer. 6Then they came to
Gil′ē·ad and to the land of Tah′tim Hod′-
shī; they came to Dan Jā′an and around to
Sī′don; 7and they came to the stronghold of
Tȳre and to all the cities of the Hī′vītes and
the Cā′naan·ītes. Then they went out to
South Judah *as far as* Bē·er·shē′ba. 8So
when they had gone through all the land,
they came to Jerusalem at the end of nine
months and twenty days. 9Then Jō′ab gave
the sum of the number of the people to the
king. And there were in Israel eight hun-
dred thousand valiant men who drew the
sword, and the men of Judah were five
hundred thousand men.

The Judgment on David's Sin

10And David's heart condemned him af-
ter he had numbered the people. So David
said to the LORD, "I have sinned greatly in
what I have done; but now, I pray, O LORD,
take away the iniquity of Your servant, for
I have done very foolishly."
11Now when David arose in the morn-
ing, the word of the LORD came to the
prophet Gad, David's seer, saying, 12"Go
and tell David, 'Thus says the LORD: "I of-
fer you three *things;* choose one of them for

23:35 [a]Spelled *Hezro* in 1 Chronicles 11:37

24:1–25 It is not clear in what sense the taking of a census should be considered sinful. Since the numbering was obviously in terms of military strength (v. 9), it could have been motivated by sinful pride and a spirit of self-sufficiency on the king's part. Or Joab's resistance may indicate popular disapproval of a plan to further taxation or forced labor.

24:9 The differences in numbers given here from those in 1 Chr. 21:5, 6 may be explained on the basis of slightly different methods of reckoning. **Israel**: Not the entire nation, but only the northern tribes distinct from **Judah**.

yourself, that I may do *it* to you." ' " 13So Gad came to David and told him; and he said to him, "Shall seven[a] years of famine come to you in your land? Or shall you flee three months before your enemies, while they pursue you? Or shall there be three days' plague in your land? Now consider and see what answer I should take back to Him who sent me."

14And David said to Gad, "I am in great distress. Please let us fall into the hand of the LORD, for His mercies *are* great; but do not let me fall into the hand of man."

15So the LORD sent a plague upon Israel from the morning till the appointed time. From Dan to Bē·er·shē'ba seventy thousand men of the people died. 16And when the angel[a] stretched out His hand over Jerusalem to destroy it, the LORD relented from the destruction, and said to the angel who was destroying the people, "It is enough; now restrain your hand." And the angel of the LORD was by the threshing floor of A·rau'nah[b] the Jeb'ū·sīte.

17Then David spoke to the LORD when he saw the angel who was striking the people, and said, "Surely I have sinned, and I have done wickedly; but these sheep, what have they done? Let Your hand, I pray, be against me and against my father's house."

The Altar on the Threshing Floor

18And Gad came that day to David and said to him, "Go up, erect an altar to the LORD on the threshing floor of A·rau'nah the Jeb'ū·sīte." 19So David, according to the word of Gad, went up as the LORD commanded. 20Now A·rau'nah looked, and saw the king and his servants coming toward him. So A·rau'nah went out and bowed before the king with his face to the ground.

21Then A·rau'nah said, "Why has my lord the king come to his servant?"

And David said, "To buy the threshing floor from you, to build an altar to the LORD, that the plague may be withdrawn from the people."

22Now A·rau'nah said to David, "Let my lord the king take and offer up whatever *seems* good to him. Look, *here are* oxen for burnt sacrifice, and threshing implements and the yokes of the oxen for wood. 23All these, O king, A·rau'nah has given to the king."

And A·rau'nah said to the king, "May the LORD your God accept you."

24Then the king said to A·rau'nah, "No, but I will surely buy *it* from you for a price; nor will I offer burnt offerings to the LORD my God with that which costs me nothing." So David bought the threshing floor and the oxen for fifty shekels of silver. 25And David built there an altar to the LORD, and offered burnt offerings and peace offerings. So the LORD heeded the prayers for the land, and the plague was withdrawn from Israel.

24:13 [a]Following Masoretic Text, Syriac, Targum, and Vulgate; Septuagint reads *three* (compare 1 Chronicles 21:12). 24:16 [a]Or *Angel* [b]Spelled *Ornan* in 1 Chronicles 21:15

24:17 David's immediate acknowledgment of his sin and readiness to repent stand in stark contrast to Saul's consistent excuses. When we are made aware of sin in our own lives, we must resist the temptation to offer alibis; the Lord simply wants us to offer broken and contrite hearts.

24:24 **Sacrifices that cost nothing** are worth nothing. The difference between the **fifty shekels of silver** here and the "six hundred shekels of gold" in 1 Chr. 21:25 is probably to be explained on the basis that 50 shekels represented the price of the immediate spot for the altar. The much larger 600 shekels of gold represented what David paid for the land surrounding the threshing floor itself.

24:25 **Burnt offerings** in general in the OT were sin offerings related to forgiveness. The entire carcass of the sacrificial animal was burned. **Peace offerings** were usually related to renewal of the covenant and reconciliation with God. After the blood of the sacrificial animal was offered on the altar, the meat was eaten in joyous celebration of worship and fellowship with God.

✦1 Kings✦

1 Kings reviews a time of disobedience, idolatry, and ungodliness that resulted in the eventual defeat of Israel by Assyria and Babylon, which is recorded in 2 Kings. Evidence points to an unknown prophet as the author who compiled these historical events around 570 B.C.

1 Kings covers the reign of Solomon and other kings who led Israel into moral decline. Solomon began with a true love for God, but later he fell astray through ungodly marriages and idol worship. Solomon's departure from righteousness shows that believers must remain vigilant throughout their lives.

Under the reign of Solomon's son, Rehoboam, the kingdom split into two nations—Judah and Israel. The two nations were headed separately by a series of kings, nearly all of whom were idolaters, usurpers, and murderers. Elijah ministered to Israel during this time of darkness.

1 Kings demonstrates that the welfare of Israel and Judah depended on the people's obedience and their kings' godliness. Following the Lord brought wealth and prosperity; idol worship and other sins brought destruction. ✦

CHAPTER 1

Adonijah Presumes to Be King

Now King David was old, advanced in
years; and they put covers on him, but he
could not get warm. 2Therefore his ser-
vants said to him, "Let a young woman, a
virgin, be sought for our lord the king, and
let her stand before the king, and let her
care for him; and let her lie in your bosom,
that our lord the king may be warm." 3So
they sought for a lovely young woman
throughout all the territory of Israel, and
found Ab'i·shag the Shū'nam·mīte, and
brought her to the king. 4The young
woman *was* very lovely; and she cared for
the king, and served him; but the king did
not know her.
5Then Ad·o·nī'jah the son of Hag'gith
exalted himself, saying, "I will be king";
and he prepared for himself chariots and
horsemen, and fifty men to run before him.
6(And his father had not rebuked him at
any time by saying, "Why have you done
so?" He *was* also very good-looking. *His
mother* had borne him after Ab'sa·lom.)
7Then he conferred with Jō'ab the son of
Ze·rū'i·ah and with A·bī'a·thar the priest,
and they followed and helped Ad·o·nī'jah.
8But Zā'dok the priest, Be·nā'i·ah the son

1:5 Adonijah, the fourth son of David (see 2 Sam. 3:2–4), was the heir apparent. The deaths of two of his older brothers are recorded in 2 Sam. 13:28, 29; 18:14. Although no cause of death is reported, it is apparent that Chileab, the remaining brother in line for the throne, was also dead by this time. **exalted himself**: Pride often ends in personal humiliation (see v. 50).

of Je·hoi'a·da, Nathan the prophet, Shim'ē·ī, Rē'ī, and the mighty men who *belonged* to David were not with Ad·o-nī'jah.

9And Ad·o·nī'jah sacrificed sheep and oxen and fattened cattle by the stone of Zō'he·leth, which *is* by En Rō'gel; he also invited all his brothers, the king's sons, and all the men of Judah, the king's servants. 10But he did not invite Nathan the prophet, Be·nā'i·ah, the mighty men, or Solomon his brother.

11So Nathan spoke to Bath·shē'ba the mother of Solomon, saying, "Have you not heard that Ad·o·nī'jah the son of Hag'gith has become king, and David our lord does not know *it?* 12Come, please, let me now give you advice, that you may save your own life and the life of your son Solomon. 13Go immediately to King David and say to him, 'Did you not, my lord, O king, swear to your maidservant, saying, "Assuredly your son Solomon shall reign after me, and he shall sit on my throne"? Why then has Ad·o·nī'jah become king?' 14Then, while you are still talking there with the king, I also will come in after you and confirm your words."

15So Bath·shē'ba went into the chamber to the king. (Now the king was very old, and Ab'i·shag the Shū'nam·mīte was serving the king.) 16And Bath·shē'ba bowed and did homage to the king. Then the king said, "What is your wish?"

17Then she said to him, "My lord, you swore by the LORD your God to your maidservant, *saying,* 'Assuredly Solomon your son shall reign after me, and he shall sit on my throne.' 18So now, look! Ad·o-nī'jah has become king; and now, my lord the king, you do not know about *it.* 19He has sacrificed oxen and fattened cattle and sheep in abundance, and has invited all the sons of the king, A·bī'a·thar the priest, and Jō'ab the commander of the army; but Solomon your servant he has not invited. 20And as for you, my lord, O king, the eyes of all Israel *are* on you, that you should tell them who will sit on the throne of my lord the king after him. 21Otherwise it will happen, when my lord the king rests with his fathers, that I and my son Solomon will be counted as offenders."

22And just then, while she was still talking with the king, Nathan the prophet also came in. 23So they told the king, saying, "Here is Nathan the prophet." And when he came in before the king, he bowed down before the king with his face to the ground. 24And Nathan said, "My lord, O king, have you said, 'Ad·o·nī'jah shall reign after me, and he shall sit on my throne'? 25For he has gone down today, and has sacrificed oxen and fattened cattle and sheep in abundance, and has invited all the king's sons, and the commanders of the army, and A·bī'a·thar the priest; and look! They are eating and drinking before him; and they say, *'Long* live King Ad·o·nī'jah!' 26But he has not invited me—me your servant—nor Zā'dok the priest, nor Be·nā'-i·ah the son of Je·hoi'a·da, nor your servant Solomon. 27Has this thing been done by my lord the king, and you have not told your servant who should sit on the throne of my lord the king after him?"

David Proclaims Solomon King

28Then King David answered and said, "Call Bath·shē'ba to me." So she came into the king's presence and stood before the

---

1:9 The sacrifice was meant to provide an extravagant feast for Adonijah's guests as much as for religious significance. A rebellious Absalom sponsored a similar festive meal (2 Sam. 15:11, 12).

1:11 has become king: is attempting to take the throne.

1:26 Nathan lists David's most ardent and powerful supporters who have been spurned by Adonijah.

king. 29And the king took an oath and
said, "*As* the LORD lives, who has re-
deemed my life from every distress, 30just
as I swore to you by the LORD God of Israel,
saying, 'Assuredly Solomon your son shall
be king after me, and he shall sit on my
throne in my place,' so I certainly will do
this day."

31Then Bath·shē′ba bowed with *her* face
to the earth, and paid homage to the king,
and said, "Let my lord King David live for-
ever!"

32And King David said, "Call to me
Zā′dok the priest, Nathan the prophet, and
Be·nā′i·ah the son of Je·hoi′a·da." So they
came before the king. 33The king also said
to them, "Take with you the servants of
your lord, and have Solomon my son ride
on my own mule, and take him down to
Gī′hon. 34There let Zā′dok the priest and
Nathan the prophet anoint him king over
Israel; and blow the horn, and say, '*Long*
live King Solomon!' 35Then you shall come
up after him, and he shall come and sit on
my throne, and he shall be king in my
place. For I have appointed him to be ruler
over Israel and Judah."

36Be·nā′i·ah the son of Je·hoi′a·da an-
swered the king and said, "Amen! May the
LORD God of my lord the king say so *too*.
37As the LORD has been with my lord the
king, even so may He be with Solomon,
and make his throne greater than the
throne of my lord King David."

38So Zā′dok the priest, Nathan the
prophet, Be·nā′i·ah the son of Je·hoi′a·da,
the Cher′e·thītes, and the Pel′eth·ītes went
down and had Solomon ride on King Da-
vid's mule, and took him to Gī′hon. 39Then
Zā′dok the priest took a horn of oil from
the tabernacle and anointed Solomon. And
they blew the horn, and all the people said,
"*Long* live King Solomon!" 40And all the
people went up after him; and the people
played the flutes and rejoiced with great
joy, so that the earth *seemed to* split with
their sound.

41Now Ad·o·nī′jah and all the guests
who *were* with him heard *it* as they
finished eating. And when Jō′ab heard
the sound of the horn, he said, "Why *is* the
city in such a noisy uproar?" 42While he
was still speaking, there came Jonathan,
the son of A·bī′a·thar the priest. And
Ad·o·nī′jah said to him, "Come in, for you
are a prominent man, and bring good
news."

43Then Jonathan answered and said to
Ad·o·nī′jah, "No! Our lord King David has
made Solomon king. 44The king has sent
with him Zā′dok the priest, Nathan the
prophet, Be·nā′i·ah the son of Je·hoi′a·da,
the Cher′e·thītes, and the Pel′eth·ītes; and
they have made him ride on the king's
mule. 45So Zā′dok the priest and Nathan
the prophet have anointed him king at
Gī′hon; and they have gone up from there
rejoicing, so that the city is in an uproar.
This *is* the noise that you have heard.
46Also Solomon sits on the throne of the
kingdom. 47And moreover the king's ser-
vants have gone to bless our lord King Da-
vid, saying, 'May God make the name of
Solomon better than your name, and may
He make his throne greater than your
throne.' Then the king bowed himself on

1:29 David had seen his share of **distress**, but he affirmed the Lord as a God of redemption.

1:33 Placing **Solomon** on King David's **mule** was a powerful symbol of royalty.

1:36 **Amen**: Lit. "truly!" An expression of affirmation saying, "May the king's decision please the LORD."

1:38 **Benaiah** was in charge of the **Cherethites** and **Pelethites**, David's faithful, personal troops. They were foreigners (possibly from Crete by way of Philistia) who had fiercely supported David in his early years (2 Sam. 8:18; 15:18 and note). They constituted a serious hurdle for any opponent of Solomon.

1:46 Many believe Solomon ruled as co-regent with David for about two years.

the bed. [48]Also the king said thus, 'Blessed *be* the LORD God of Israel, who has given *one* to sit on my throne this day, while my eyes see *it!*' "

[49]So all the guests who were with Ad·o·nī′jah were afraid, and arose, and each one went his way.

[50]Now Ad·o·nī′jah was afraid of Solomon; so he arose, and went and took hold of the horns of the altar. [51]And it was told Solomon, saying, "Indeed Ad·o·nī′jah is afraid of King Solomon; for look, he has taken hold of the horns of the altar, saying, 'Let King Solomon swear to me today that he will not put his servant to death with the sword.' "

[52]Then Solomon said, "If he proves himself a worthy man, not one hair of him shall fall to the earth; but if wickedness is found in him, he shall die." [53]So King Solomon sent them to bring him down from the altar. And he came and fell down before King Solomon; and Solomon said to him, "Go to your house."

CHAPTER 2

David's Instructions to Solomon

Now the days of David drew near that he should die, and he charged Solomon his son, saying: [2]"I go the way of all the earth; be strong, therefore, and prove yourself a man. [3]And keep the charge of the LORD your God: to walk in His ways, to keep His statutes, His commandments, His judgments, and His testimonies, as it is written in the Law of Moses, that you may prosper in all that you do and wherever you turn; [4]that the LORD may fulfill His word which He spoke concerning me, saying, 'If your sons take heed to their way, to walk before Me in truth with all their heart and with all their soul,' He said, 'you shall not lack a man on the throne of Israel.'

[5]"Moreover you know also what Jō′ab the son of Ze·rū′i·ah did to me, *and* what he did to the two commanders of the armies of Israel, to Abner the son of Ner and A·mā′sa the son of Jē′ther, whom he killed. And he shed the blood of war in peacetime, and put the blood of war on his belt that *was* around his waist, and on his sandals that *were* on his feet. [6]Therefore do according to your wisdom, and do not let his gray hair go down to the grave in peace.

[7]"But show kindness to the sons of Bar·zil′laī the Gil′ē·ad·īte, and let them be among those who eat at your table, for so they came to me when I fled from Ab′sa·lom your brother.

[8]"And see, *you have* with you Shim′ē·ī the son of Gē′ra, a Ben′ja·mīte from Ba·hū′rim, who cursed me with a malicious curse in the day when I went to Mā·ha·na′im. But he came down to meet me at the Jordan, and I swore to him by the LORD, saying, 'I will not put you to death with the sword.' [9]Now therefore, do not hold him guiltless, for you *are* a wise man and know what you ought to do to him; but bring his gray hair down to the grave with blood."

Death of David

[10]So David rested with his fathers, and was buried in the City of David. [11]The pe-

---

1:48 Blessed be the LORD: The king's reaction suggests submission to God's will. The man who was anointed by other men was nonetheless **given** by God. See 2 Sam. 7:12–16.

1:50 horns of the altar: Israel considered the altar to be a sanctuary only in cases of unintentional murder (see Ex. 21:12–14). The horns were projections at the four corners of the altar (see Ex. 27:2).

2:3, 4 Success always depends on obedience to God's Word. While the wicked may prosper financially for a time, true success is measured in the realm of eternity and only those who are faithful will achieve it.

2:5, 6 David had never been able to bring himself to punish his old friend for his acts of vengeance.

riod that David reigned over Israel *was* forty years; seven years he reigned in Hē'bron, and in Jerusalem he reigned thirty-three years. 12Then Solomon sat on the throne of his father David; and his kingdom was firmly established.

Solomon Executes Adonijah

13Now Ad·o·nī'jah the son of Hag'gith came to Bath·shē'ba the mother of Solomon. So she said, "Do you come peaceably?"

And he said, "Peaceably." 14Moreover he said, "I have something *to say* to you."

And she said, "Say it."

15Then he said, "You know that the kingdom was mine, and all Israel had set their expectations on me, that I should reign. However, the kingdom has been turned over, and has become my brother's; for it was his from the LORD. 16Now I ask one petition of you; do not deny me."

And she said to him, "Say it."

17Then he said, "Please speak to King Solomon, for he will not refuse you, that he may give me Ab'i·shag the Shū'nam·mīte as wife."

18So Bath·shē'ba said, "Very well, I will speak for you to the king."

19Bath·shē'ba therefore went to King Solomon, to speak to him for Ad·o·nī'jah. And the king rose up to meet her and bowed down to her, and sat down on his throne and had a throne set for the king's mother; so she sat at his right hand. 20Then she said, "I desire one small petition of you; do not refuse me."

And the king said to her, "Ask it, my mother, for I will not refuse you."

21So she said, "Let Ab'i·shag the Shū'nam·mīte be given to Ad·o·nī'jah your brother as wife."

22And King Solomon answered and said to his mother, "Now why do you ask Ab'i·shag the Shū'nam·mīte for Ad·o·nī'jah? Ask for him the kingdom also—for he *is* my older brother—for him, and for A·bī'a·thar the priest, and for Jō'ab the son of Ze·rū'i·ah." 23Then King Solomon swore by the LORD, saying, "May God do so to me, and more also, if Ad·o·nī'jah has not spoken this word against his own life! 24Now therefore, *as* the LORD lives, who has confirmed me and set me on the throne of David my father, and who has established a house[a] for me, as He promised, Ad·o·nī'jah shall be put to death today!"

25So King Solomon sent by the hand of Be·nā'i·ah the son of Je·hoi'a·da; and he struck him down, and he died.

Abiathar Exiled, Joab Executed

26And to A·bī'a·thar the priest the king said, "Go to An'a·thoth, to your own fields, for you *are* deserving of death; but I will not put you to death at this time, because you carried the ark of the Lord GOD before my father David, and because you were afflicted every time my father was afflicted." 27So Solomon removed A·bī'a·thar from being priest to the LORD, that he might fulfill the word of the LORD which He spoke concerning the house of Ē'lī at Shī'lōh.

28Then news came to Jō'ab, for Jō'ab had defected to Ad·o·nī'jah, though he had not

2:24 [a]That is, a royal dynasty

2:13–25 Although Adonijah's request seems innocent enough, Abishag was a member of the royal harem, and claiming a deceased king's harem was equivalent to claiming his kingdom. Adonijah was insinuating that he had a right to the king's possessions, including the throne.

2:26, 27 By stripping **Abiathar** of his priestly office, Solomon distanced himself from religious opposition (see 1:7) and prepared the way for a priesthood loyal to himself (see 1:8; 2:35).

2:28–35 Executing Joab fulfilled David's dying request (vv. 5, 6). It also freed Solomon of a dangerous military opponent and made it possible to unite the army under Benaiah (v. 35).

defected to Ab′sa·lom. So Jō′ab fled to the
tabernacle of the LORD, and took hold of
the horns of the altar. 29And King Solomon
was told, "Jō′ab has fled to the tabernacle
of the LORD; there *he is,* by the altar." Then
Solomon sent Be·nā′i·ah the son of Je-
hoi′a·da, saying, "Go, strike him down."
30So Be·nā′i·ah went to the tabernacle of
the LORD, and said to him, "Thus says the
king, 'Come out!' "

And he said, "No, but I will die here."
And Be·nā′i·ah brought back word to the
king, saying, "Thus said Jō′ab, and thus he
answered me."

31Then the king said to him, "Do as he
has said, and strike him down and bury
him, that you may take away from me and
from the house of my father the innocent
blood which Jō′ab shed. 32So the LORD will
return his blood on his head, because he
struck down two men more righteous and
better than he, and killed them with the
sword—Abner the son of Ner, the com-
mander of the army of Israel, and A·mā′sa
the son of Jē′ther, the commander of the
army of Judah—though my father David
did not know *it.* 33Their blood shall there-
fore return upon the head of Jō′ab and
upon the head of his descendants forever.
But upon David and his descendants,
upon his house and his throne, there shall
be peace forever from the LORD."

34So Be·nā′i·ah the son of Je·hoi′a·da
went up and struck and killed him; and he
was buried in his own house in the wilder-
ness. 35The king put Be·nā′i·ah the son of
Je·hoi′a·da in his place over the army, and
the king put Zā′dok the priest in the place
of A·bī′a·thar.

Shimei Executed

36Then the king sent and called for
Shim′ē·ī, and said to him, "Build yourself
a house in Jerusalem and dwell there, and
do not go out from there anywhere. 37For it
shall be, on the day you go out and cross
the Brook Kid′ron, know for certain you
shall surely die; your blood shall be on
your own head."

38And Shim′ē·ī said to the king, "The
saying *is* good. As my lord the king has
said, so your servant will do." So Shim′ē·ī
dwelt in Jerusalem many days.

39Now it happened at the end of three
years, that two slaves of Shim′ē·ī ran away
to Ā′chish the son of Mā′a·chah, king of
Gath. And they told Shim′ē·ī, saying,
"Look, your slaves *are* in Gath!" 40So
Shim′ē·ī arose, saddled his donkey, and
went to Ā′chish at Gath to seek his slaves.
And Shim′ē·ī went and brought his slaves
from Gath. 41And Solomon was told that
Shim′ē·ī had gone from Jerusalem to Gath
and had come back. 42Then the king sent
and called for Shim′ē·ī, and said to him,
"Did I not make you swear by the LORD,
and warn you, saying, 'Know for certain
that on the day you go out and travel any-
where, you shall surely die'? And you said
to me, 'The word I have heard *is* good.'
43Why then have you not kept the oath of
the LORD and the commandment that I
gave you?" 44The king said moreover to
Shim′ē·ī, "You know, as your heart
acknowledges, all the wickedness that you
did to my father David; therefore the LORD
will return your wickedness on your own
head. 45But King Solomon *shall be* blessed,
and the throne of David shall be estab-
lished before the LORD forever."

46So the king commanded Be·nā′i·ah the
son of Je·hoi′a·da; and he went out and
struck him down, and he died. Thus the
kingdom was established in the hand of
Solomon.

CHAPTER 3

Solomon Requests Wisdom

Now Solomon made a treaty with
Pharaoh king of Egypt, and married

3:1 treaty: The first of Solomon's many marriage alliances which eventually led to his ruin (see 11:3). This particular marriage brought Solomon the city of Gezer (see 9:16).

The Meaning of Wisdom

Sherwood Eliot Wirt

What is wisdom? I didn't pay much attention to it when I was younger. If I thought about it at all, I thought of wisdom as something out of the past—dignified, profound, and rather awesome, like the Gettysburg Address or the Ten Commandments.

Now that I am older, I do have a definition: Wisdom is knowing how to live. It is not just knowing how to use your time, or how to figure the square root, or make right decisions, or deal with people, or judge the future, or even memorize all the verses in the Bible. All such matters are connected with knowledge, but knowledge is not necessarily wisdom. Wisdom is knowing how to live—not going on lecture tours to tell others how to live or writing books or recording videotapes about it, but just knowing how to live.

The entire Book of Proverbs is devoted to this subject, providing a guide to living righteously before God. Through its teaching, we learn that the secret of obtaining true wisdom is reverence for the Lord. No matter how long we live, we cannot find wisdom apart from obedience to God. ✦

Pharaoh's daughter; then he brought her
to the City of David until he had finished
building his own house, and the house of
the LORD, and the wall all around Jerusa-
lem. 2Meanwhile the people sacrificed at
the high places, because there was no
house built for the name of the LORD until
those days. 3And Solomon loved the LORD,
walking in the statutes of his father David,
except that he sacrificed and burned in-
cense at the high places.

4Now the king went to Gib′ē·on to sacri-
fice there, for that *was* the great high place:
Solomon offered a thousand burnt offer-
ings on that altar. 5At Gib′ē·on the LORD
appeared to Solomon in a dream by night;
and God said, "Ask! What shall I give
you?"

6And Solomon said: "You have shown
great mercy to Your servant David my fa-
ther, because he walked before You in
truth, in righteousness, and in uprightness
of heart with You; You have continued this
great kindness for him, and You have
given him a son to sit on his throne, as *it is*
this day. 7Now, O LORD my God, You have

3:2 high places: Elevated, open-air sanctuaries patterned after Canaanite practices but forbidden by Hebrew law (see Num. 33:52). Allowance was made here because the temple had not yet been constructed and the tabernacle had apparently been destroyed (see notes on 8:16 and Josh. 18:1).

3:3 Solomon's early reign was marked by love and obedience. The one flaw mentioned could be rectified when the temple was built.

3:7–14 A sincere petition that conforms to God's will pleases Him and gets results. Solomon's humble request reminds us to lean on the Lord daily for the wisdom needed for the tasks He has given to us. We invite tragedy when we forget to depend wholly upon the Lord.

made Your servant king instead of my fa-
ther David, but I *am* a little child; I do not
know *how* to go out or come in. 8And Your
servant *is* in the midst of Your people
whom You have chosen, a great people, too
numerous to be numbered or counted.
9Therefore give to Your servant an under-
standing heart to judge Your people, that I
may discern between good and evil. For
who is able to judge this great people of
Yours?"

10The speech pleased the LORD, that Sol-
omon had asked this thing. 11Then God
said to him: "Because you have asked this
thing, and have not asked long life for
yourself, nor have asked riches for your-
self, nor have asked the life of your ene-
mies, but have asked for yourself under-
standing to discern justice, 12behold, I have
done according to your words; see, I have
given you a wise and understanding heart,
so that there has not been anyone like you
before you, nor shall any like you arise af-
ter you. 13And I have also given you what
you have not asked: both riches and honor,
so that there shall not be anyone like you
among the kings all your days. 14So if you
walk in My ways, to keep My statutes and
My commandments, as your father David
walked, then I will lengthen your days."

> ***I pray that my children will walk in Your ways, God, to keep Your statutes and Your commandments, and that You will lengthen their days.***
>
> *adapted from* 1 Kings 3:14

15Then Solomon awoke; and indeed it
had been a dream. And he came to Jerusa-
lem and stood before the ark of the
covenant of the LORD, offered up burnt of-
ferings, offered peace offerings, and made
a feast for all his servants.

Solomon's Wise Judgment

16Now two women *who were* harlots
came to the king, and stood before him.
17And one woman said, "O my lord, this
woman and I dwell in the same house; and
I gave birth while she *was* in the house.
18Then it happened, the third day after I
had given birth, that this woman also gave
birth. And we *were* together; no one *was*
with us in the house, except the two of us
in the house. 19And this woman's son died
in the night, because she lay on him. 20So
she arose in the middle of the night and
took my son from my side, while your
maidservant slept, and laid him in her bo-
som, and laid her dead child in my bosom.
21And when I rose in the morning to nurse
my son, there he was, dead. But when I
had examined him in the morning, indeed,
he was not my son whom I had borne."

22Then the other woman said, "No! But
the living one *is* my son, and the dead one
is your son."

And the first woman said, "No! But the
dead one *is* your son, and the living one *is*
my son."

Thus they spoke before the king.

23And the king said, "The one says, 'This
is my son, who lives, and your son *is* the
dead one'; and the other says, 'No! But
your son *is* the dead one, and my son *is* the
living one.' " 24Then the king said, "Bring
me a sword." So they brought a sword be-
fore the king. 25And the king said, "Divide
the living child in two, and give half to
one, and half to the other."

26Then the woman whose son *was* living
spoke to the king, for she yearned with
compassion for her son; and she said, "O
my lord, give her the living child, and by
no means kill him!"

But the other said, "Let him be neither
mine nor yours, *but* divide *him*."

3:14 if you walk: Even divinely granted wisdom is no substitute for obedience.

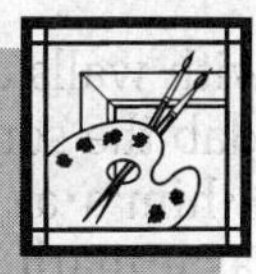

SOLOMON: THE UNDOING OF A KING

King Solomon, although the wisest man in history, illustrates the danger of allowing physical desires to take control to the detriment of spiritual, physical, and mental health.

Early in Solomon's reign, the Lord appeared to him and offered to give him whatever he asked (1 Kin. 3:5). Recognizing his own lack of experience and desiring to follow in his father's footsteps, Solomon requested an understanding heart.

His desire for wisdom rather than riches or power pleased the Lord. God not only granted Solomon's request but blessed him with riches and honor as well. He promised the king a long life, if he would continue to observe the Lord's commands.

Over the next several years, Solomon's wisdom and wealth brought him great fame and honor. People from all over the known world, including the Queen of Sheba, came to witness his wisdom and prosperity for themselves.

He built the temple for the Lord and a palace for himself. He extended the kingdom to its greatest geographical limits and brought it to the height of material prosperity.

Unfortunately, Solomon lost sight of the source of his success. Although the attention he received was due to the blessing of God, he apparently allowed pride to alter his judgment. In direct disobedience to the law, he married not one, but many foreign women who persuaded him to worship their pagan gods (11:3).

Solomon's forty-year reign, which began so auspiciously, eventually ended in idolatry and oppression (12:4). The man who had once loved God wholeheartedly had allowed fleshly desire and personal pride to destroy his spiritual discernment. His sinful behavior invoked the wrath of God upon himself and the kingdom of Israel.

Like Solomon, each of us has been given intellectual capacity, an appreciation for beauty, and the desire for sexual expression. However, God expects us to use each of these gifts within the guidelines He has set. When any one of these areas becomes overly important to us, we endanger our spiritual, mental, and physical health.

We should exercise our brains without allowing our intelligence to hinder our faith. We should glory in the beauty of His creation and enjoy the material blessings He provides, but we should not place more importance on them than on the Creator and Giver. ✦

27 So the king answered and said, "Give the first woman the living child, and by no means kill him; she *is* his mother."

28 And all Israel heard of the judgment which the king had rendered; and they feared the king, for they saw that the wisdom of God *was* in him to administer justice.

CHAPTER 4

Solomon's Administration

So King Solomon was king over all Israel. 2 And these *were* his officials: Az·a·rī'ah the son of Zā'dok, the priest; 3 El·i·hor'eph and A·hī'jah, the sons of Shī'sha, scribes; Je·hosh'a·phat the son of A·hī'lud, the recorder; 4 Be·nā'i·ah the son of Je·hoi'a·da, over the army; Zā'dok and A·bī'a·thar, the priests; 5 Az·a·rī'ah the son of Nathan, over the officers; Zā'bud the son of Nathan, a priest *and* the king's friend; 6 A·hī'shar, over the household; and Ad·o·nī'ram the son of Ab'da, over the labor force.

7 And Solomon had twelve governors over all Israel, who provided food for the king and his household; each one made provision for one month of the year. 8 These *are* their names: Ben-Hur,[a] in the mountains of Ē'phra·im; 9 Ben-Dē'ker,[a] in Mā'kaz, Shā·al'bim, Beth Shem'esh, and Ē'lon Beth Hā'nan; 10 Ben-Hē'sed,[a] in A·rūb'both; to him *belonged* Sō'chōh and all the land of Hē'pher; 11 Ben-A·bin'a·dab,[a] *in* all the regions of Dor; he had Tā'phath the daughter of Solomon as wife; 12 Bā'a·na the son of A·hī'lud, *in* Tā'a·nach, Me·gid'dō, and all Beth Shē'an, which *is* beside Zar'e·tan below Jez'rē·el, from Beth Shē'an to Abel Me·hō'lah, as far as the other side of Jok'nē·am; 13 Ben-Gē'ber,[a] in Rā'moth Gil'ē·ad; to him *belonged* the towns of Jā'ir the son of Ma·nas'seh, in Gil'ē·ad; to him *also belonged* the region of Ar'gob in Bā'shan—sixty large cities with walls and bronze gate-bars; 14 A·hin'a·dab the son of Id'dō, *in* Mā·ha·na'im; 15 A·him'a·az, in Naph'ta·lī; he also took Bas'e·math the daughter of Solomon as wife; 16 Bā'a·nah the son of Hū'shai, in Ash'er and Ā'loth; 17 Je·hosh'a·phat the son of Pa·rū'ah, in Is'sa·char; 18 Shim'ē·ī the son of Ē'lah, in Benjamin; 19 Gē'ber the son of Ū'rī, in the land of Gil'ē·ad, *in* the country of Sī'hon king of the Am'o·rītes, and of Og king of Bā'shan. *He was* the only governor who *was* in the land.

Prosperity and Wisdom of Solomon's Reign

20 Judah and Israel *were* as numerous as the sand by the sea in multitude, eating and drinking and rejoicing. 21 So Solomon reigned over all kingdoms from the River[a] *to* the land of the Phi·lis'tines, as far as the border of Egypt. *They* brought tribute and served Solomon all the days of his life.

22 Now Solomon's provision for one day was thirty kors of fine flour, sixty kors of meal, 23 ten fatted oxen, twenty oxen from the pastures, and one hundred sheep, besides deer, gazelles, roebucks, and fatted fowl.

24 For he had dominion over all *the region* on this side of the River[a] from Tiph'sah even to Gā'za, namely over all the kings on this side of the River; and he had peace on every side all around him. 25 And Judah and Israel dwelt safely, each man under his vine and his fig tree, from Dan as far as Bē·er·shē'ba, all the days of Solomon.

26 Solomon had forty[a] thousand stalls of horses for his chariots, and twelve thou-

4:8 [a]Literally *Son of Hur* 4:9 [a]Literally *Son of Deker* 4:10 [a]Literally *Son of Hesed* 4:11 [a]Literally *Son of Abinadab* 4:13 [a]Literally *Son of Geber* 4:21 [a]That is, the Euphrates 4:24 [a]That is, the Euphrates 4:26 [a]Following Masoretic Text and most other authorities; some manuscripts of the Septuagint read *four* (compare 2 Chronicles 9:25).

4:26 The keeping of horses and chariots violated God's command (see Deut. 17:16).

sand horsemen. 27And these governors,
each man in his month, provided food for
King Solomon and for all who came to
King Solomon's table. There was no lack in
their supply. 28They also brought barley
and straw to the proper place, for the
horses and steeds, each man according to
his charge.

29And God gave Solomon wisdom and
exceedingly great understanding, and
largeness of heart like the sand on the
seashore. 30Thus Solomon's wisdom ex-
celled the wisdom of all the men of the East
and all the wisdom of Egypt. 31For he was
wiser than all men—than Ē'than the Ez'-
ra·hīte, and Hē'man, Chal'col, and Dar'da,
the sons of Mā'hol; and his fame was in all
the surrounding nations. 32He spoke three
thousand proverbs, and his songs were
one thousand and five. 33Also he spoke of
trees, from the cedar tree of Lebanon even
to the hyssop that springs out of the wall;
he spoke also of animals, of birds, of creep-
ing things, and of fish. 34And men of all na-
tions, from all the kings of the earth who
had heard of his wisdom, came to hear the
wisdom of Solomon.

CHAPTER 5

Solomon Prepares to Build the Temple

Now Hī'ram king of Tȳre sent his ser-
vants to Solomon, because he heard that
they had anointed him king in place of his
father, for Hī'ram had always loved Da-
vid. 2Then Solomon sent to Hī'ram, saying:

3 You know how my father David could
not build a house for the name of the
LORD his God because of the wars
which were fought against him on
every side, until the LORD put *his foes*[a]
under the soles of his feet.
4 But now the LORD my God has given
me rest on every side; *there is* neither
adversary nor evil occurrence.
5 And behold, I propose to build a
house for the name of the LORD my
God, as the LORD spoke to my father
David, saying, "Your son, whom I will
set on your throne in your place, he
shall build the house for My name."
6 Now therefore, command that they
cut down cedars for me from Leba-
non; and my servants will be with
your servants, and I will pay you
wages for your servants according to
whatever you say. For you know *there
is* none among us who has skill to cut
timber like the Sī·dō'ni·ans.

7So it was, when Hī'ram heard the
words of Solomon, that he rejoiced greatly
and said,

Blessed *be* the LORD this day, for He
has given David a wise son over this
great people!

8Then Hī'ram sent to Solomon, saying:

I have considered *the message* which
you sent me, *and* I will do all you de-
sire concerning the cedar and cypress
logs.
9 My servants shall bring *them* down
from Lebanon to the sea; I will float
them in rafts by sea to the place you
indicate to me, and will have them

5:3 [a]Literally *them*

4:31 Ethan and **Heman** were famous in Canaan for their great wisdom and are connected with the Psalms (see titles to Ps. 88; 89).

4:33 Probably the use of nature to illustrate proverbial wisdom (see Prov. 6:6).

5:1 The relationship of **Solomon** with **Hiram** (c. 970–936 B.C.) was mutually beneficial. Solomon lacked the artisans and material for his buildings, and Hiram lacked agricultural produce (see v. 9). Although the Bible makes no comment on this arrangement with a Canaanite king, it is still to be wondered how much this affected Solomon's later apostasy.

broken apart there; then you can take
them away. And you shall fulfill my
desire by giving food for my house-
hold.

10Then Hī'ram gave Solomon cedar
and cypress logs *according to* all his de-
sire. 11And Solomon gave Hī'ram twenty
thousand kors of wheat *as* food for his
household, and twenty[a] kors of pressed oil.
Thus Solomon gave to Hī'ram year by
year.

12So the LORD gave Solomon wisdom,
as He had promised him; and there
was peace between Hī'ram and Solomon,
and the two of them made a treaty to-
gether.

13Then King Solomon raised up a labor
force out of all Israel; and the labor force
was thirty thousand men. 14And he sent
them to Lebanon, ten thousand a month in
shifts: they were one month in Lebanon
and two months at home; Ad·o·nī'ram *was*
in charge of the labor force. 15Solomon had
seventy thousand who carried burdens,
and eighty thousand who quarried *stone* in
the mountains, 16besides three thousand
three hundred[a] from the chiefs of Sol-
omon's deputies, who supervised the peo-
ple who labored in the work. 17And the
king commanded them to quarry large
stones, costly stones, *and* hewn stones, to
lay the foundation of the temple.[a] 18So Sol-
omon's builders, Hī'ram's builders, and
the Gē'bal·ītes quarried *them;* and they
prepared timber and stones to build the
temple.

CHAPTER 6

Solomon Builds the Temple

And it came to pass in the four hundred
and eightieth[a] year after the children of Is-
rael had come out of the land of Egypt, in
the fourth year of Solomon's reign over Is-
rael, in the month of Ziv, which *is* the sec-
ond month, that he began to build the
house of the LORD. 2Now the house which
King Solomon built for the LORD, its length
was sixty cubits, its width twenty, and its
height thirty cubits. 3The vestibule in front
of the sanctuary[a] of the house *was* twenty
cubits long across the width of the house,
and the width of *the vestibule*[b] extended ten
cubits from the front of the house. 4And he
made for the house windows with beveled
frames.

5Against the wall of the temple he built
chambers all around, *against* the walls of
the temple, all around the sanctuary and
the inner sanctuary.[a] Thus he made side
chambers all around it. 6The lowest cham-
ber *was* five cubits wide, the middle *was* six
cubits wide, and the third *was* seven cubits
wide; for he made narrow ledges around

5:11 [a]Following Masoretic Text, Targum, and Vulgate; Septuagint and Syriac read *twenty thousand.*
5:16 [a]Following Masoretic Text, Targum, and Vulgate; Septuagint reads *three thousand six hundred.*
5:17 [a]Literally *house,* and so frequently throughout this book 6:1 [a]Following Masoretic Text, Targum, and Vulgate; Septuagint reads *fortieth.* 6:3 [a]Hebrew *heykal;* here the main room of the temple, elsewhere called the holy place (compare Exodus 26:33 and Ezekiel 41:1) [b]Literally *it* 6:5 [a]Hebrew *debir;* here the inner room of the temple, elsewhere called the Most Holy Place (compare verse 16)

5:12 peace: The Hebrew word *shalom* indicates more than the absence of conflict. It is a harmonious relationship resulting in security and wholeness of life.

5:13–18 Solomon's **labor force** amounted to a draft of people for work on building projects. The prophet Samuel had warned Israel that the future kings would oppress them in this manner (see 1 Sam. 8:10).

6:1 The 480 years are sometimes interpreted as figurative—namely the result of multiplying the 12 tribes by the standard length of a generation (i.e., 40 years). But taken literally, a simple calculation from the fourth year of Solomon (966 B.C.) would date the Israelite exodus from Egypt at 1446 B.C.

6:2, 3 The temple was built according to David's plans (see 1 Chr. 28:11–19). These plans included many details which are now known to have been common in temple designs of that time.

the outside of the temple, so that *the support beams* would not be fastened into the walls of the temple. [7]And the temple, when it was being built, was built with stone finished at the quarry, so that no hammer or chisel *or* any iron tool was heard in the temple while it was being built. [8]The doorway for the middle story[a] *was* on the right side of the temple. They went up by stairs to the middle *story*, and from the middle to the third.

[9]So he built the temple and finished it, and he paneled the temple with beams and boards of cedar. [10]And he built side chambers against the entire temple, each five cubits high; they were attached to the temple with cedar beams.

[11]Then the word of the LORD came to Solomon, saying: [12]"*Concerning* this temple which you are building, if you walk in My statutes, execute My judgments, keep all My commandments, and walk in them, then I will perform My word with you, which I spoke to your father David. [13]And I will dwell among the children of Israel, and will not forsake My people Israel."

[14]So Solomon built the temple and finished it. [15]And he built the inside walls of the temple with cedar boards; from the floor of the temple to the ceiling he paneled the inside with wood; and he covered the floor of the temple with planks of cypress. [16]Then he built the twenty-cubit room at the rear of the temple, from floor to ceiling, with cedar boards; he built *it* inside as the inner sanctuary, as the Most Holy *Place*. [17]And in front of it the temple sanctuary was forty cubits *long*. [18]The inside of the temple was cedar, carved with ornamental buds and open flowers. All *was* cedar; there was no stone *to be* seen.

[19]And he prepared the inner sanctuary inside the temple, to set the ark of the covenant of the LORD there. [20]The inner sanctuary *was* twenty cubits long, twenty cubits wide, and twenty cubits high. He overlaid it with pure gold, and overlaid the altar of cedar. [21]So Solomon overlaid the inside of the temple with pure gold. He stretched gold chains across the front of the inner sanctuary, and overlaid it with gold. [22]The whole temple he overlaid with gold, until he had finished all the temple; also he overlaid with gold the entire altar that *was* by the inner sanctuary.

[23]Inside the inner sanctuary he made two cherubim *of* olive wood, *each* ten cubits high. [24]One wing of the cherub *was* five cubits, and the other wing of the cherub five cubits: ten cubits from the tip of one wing to the tip of the other. [25]And the other cherub *was* ten cubits; both cherubim *were* of the same size and shape. [26]The height of one cherub *was* ten cubits, and so *was* the other cherub. [27]Then he set the cherubim inside the inner room;[a] and they stretched out the wings of the cherubim so that the wing of the one touched *one* wall, and the wing of the other cherub touched the other wall. And their wings touched each other in the middle of the room. [28]Also he overlaid the cherubim with gold.

[29]Then he carved all the walls of the temple all around, both the inner and outer *sanctuaries*, with carved figures of cherubim, palm trees, and open flowers. [30]And the floor of the temple he overlaid with gold, both the inner and outer *sanctuaries*.

[31]For the entrance of the inner sanctuary he made doors *of* olive wood; the lintel *and* doorposts *were* one-fifth *of the wall*. [32]The two doors *were of* olive wood; and he

6:8 [a]Following Masoretic Text and Vulgate; Septuagint reads *upper story;* Targum reads *ground story.*
6:27 [a]Literally *house*

6:16 The interior of the temple corresponded to the plan of the tabernacle, being divided into the holy place and the Most Holy Place (see note on Ex. 26:31–35).

6:22 The **altar . . . by the inner sanctuary** corresponds to the altar of incense which stood in the holy place of the tabernacle.

carved on them figures of cherubim, palm
trees, and open flowers, and overlaid *them*
with gold; and he spread gold on the
cherubim and on the palm trees. 33So for
the door of the sanctuary he also made
doorposts *of* olive wood, one-fourth *of the*
wall. 34And the two doors *were of* cypress
wood; two panels *comprised* one folding
door, and two panels *comprised* the other
folding door. 35Then he carved cherubim,
palm trees, and open flowers *on them,* and
overlaid *them* with gold applied evenly on
the carved work.

36And he built the inner court with three
rows of hewn stone and a row of cedar
beams.

37In the fourth year the foundation of the
house of the LORD was laid, in the month of
Ziv. 38And in the eleventh year, in the
month of Bul, which is the eighth month,
the house was finished in all its details and
according to all its plans. So he was seven
years in building it.

CHAPTER 7

Solomon's Other Buildings

But Solomon took thirteen years to
build his own house; so he finished all his
house.

2He also built the House of the Forest of
Lebanon; its length *was* one hundred cu-
bits, its width fifty cubits, and its height
thirty cubits, with four rows of cedar pil-
lars, and cedar beams on the pillars. 3And
it was paneled with cedar above the beams
that *were* on forty-five pillars, fifteen *to* a
row. 4*There were* windows *with beveled*
frames in three rows, and window *was* op-
posite window *in* three tiers. 5And all the
doorways and doorposts *had* rectangular
frames; and window *was* opposite window
in three tiers.

6He also made the Hall of Pillars: its
length *was* fifty cubits, and its width thirty
cubits; and in front of them *was* a portico
with pillars, and a canopy *was* in front of
them.

7Then he made a hall for the throne, the
Hall of Judgment, where he might judge;
and *it was* paneled with cedar from floor to
ceiling.[a]

8And the house where he dwelt *had* an-
other court inside the hall, of like work-
manship. Solomon also made a house like
this hall for Pharaoh's daughter, whom he
had taken *as wife.*

9All these *were of* costly stones cut to
size, trimmed with saws, inside and out,
from the foundation to the eaves, and also
on the outside to the great court. 10The
foundation *was of* costly stones, large
stones, some ten cubits and some eight cu-
bits. 11And above *were* costly stones, hewn
to size, and cedar wood. 12The great court
was enclosed with three rows of hewn
stones and a row of cedar beams. So were
the inner court of the house of the LORD
and the vestibule of the temple.

Hiram the Craftsman

13Now King Solomon sent and brought
Hū'ram[a] from Tȳre. 14He *was* the son of a
widow from the tribe of Naph'ta·lī, and
his father *was* a man of Tȳre, a bronze
worker; he was filled with wisdom and un-

7:7 [a]Literally *floor,* that is, of the upper level
7:13 [a]Hebrew *Hiram* (compare 2 Chronicles 2:13, 14)

6:36 All the people had access to an outer court called the "great court" (7:12). Since the **inner court** was reserved for priests, it was also called the "court of the priests" (2 Chr. 4:9).

7:1–51 The chapter is arranged according to the types of materials used: wood (vv. 2–8); stone (vv. 9–12); bronze (vv. 13–47); and gold (vv. 48–50).

7:1–8 The palace complex took longer to complete because it included several buildings south of the temple. **The House of the Forest of Lebanon** (vv. 2–5) served as a treasury (see 10:17) and armory (see Is. 22:8). Other buildings were the **Hall of Pillars** (v. 6), the **Hall of Judgment** (v. 7), and residences for Solomon and Pharaoh's daughter (v. 8).

7:13, 14 Huram: The same Hebrew word elsewhere rendered *Hiram*, but a different person than King Hiram of Tyre in 5:1.

derstanding and skill in working with all
kinds of bronze work. So he came to King
Solomon and did all his work.

The Bronze Pillars for the Temple

15 And he cast two pillars of bronze, each
one eighteen cubits high, and a line of
twelve cubits measured the circumference
of each. 16 Then he made two capitals *of* cast
bronze, to set on the tops of the pillars. The
height of one capital *was* five cubits, and
the height of the other capital *was* five cu-
bits. 17 *He made* a lattice network, with
wreaths of chainwork, for the capitals
which *were* on top of the pillars: seven
chains for one capital and seven for the
other capital. 18 So he made the pillars, and
two rows of pomegranates above the net-
work all around to cover the capitals that
were on top; and thus he did for the other
capital.

19 The capitals which *were* on top of the
pillars in the hall *were* in the shape of lilies,
four cubits. 20 The capitals on the two pil-
lars also *had pomegranates* above, by the
convex surface which *was* next to the net-
work; and there *were* two hundred such
pomegranates in rows on each of the capi-
tals all around.

21 Then he set up the pillars by the
vestibule of the temple; he set up the pillar
on the right and called its name Jā′chin,
and he set up the pillar on the left and
called its name Bō′az. 22 The tops of the pil-
lars were in the shape of lilies. So the work
of the pillars was finished.

The Sea and the Oxen

23 And he made the Sea of cast bronze,
ten cubits from one brim to the other; *it was*
completely round. Its height *was* five cu-
bits, and a line of thirty cubits measured its
circumference.

24 Below its brim *were* ornamental buds
encircling it all around, ten to a cubit, all
the way around the Sea. The ornamental
buds *were* cast in two rows when it was
cast. 25 It stood on twelve oxen: three look-
ing toward the north, three looking toward
the west, three looking toward the south,
and three looking toward the east; the Sea
was set upon them, and all their back parts
pointed inward. 26 It *was* a handbreadth
thick; and its brim was shaped like the
brim of a cup, *like* a lily blossom. It con-
tained two thousand[a] baths.

The Carts and the Lavers

27 He also made ten carts of bronze; four
cubits *was* the length of each cart, four cu-
bits its width, and three cubits its height.
28 And this *was* the design of the carts: They
had panels, and the panels *were* between
frames; 29 on the panels that *were* between
the frames *were* lions, oxen, and cherubim.
And on the frames *was* a pedestal on top.
Below the lions and oxen *were* wreaths of
plaited work. 30 Every cart had four bronze
wheels and axles of bronze, and its four
feet had supports. Under the laver *were*
supports of cast *bronze* beside each wreath.
31 Its opening inside the crown at the top
was one cubit in diameter; and the opening
was round, shaped *like* a pedestal, one and
a half cubits in outside diameter; and also
on the opening *were* engravings, but the
panels were square, not round. 32 Under the
panels *were* the four wheels, and the axles
of the wheels *were joined* to the cart. The
height of a wheel *was* one and a half cubits.
33 The workmanship of the wheels *was* like
the workmanship of a chariot wheel; their
axle pins, their rims, their spokes, and their
hubs *were* all of cast *bronze*. 34 And *there were*

7:26 [a]Or *three thousand* (compare 2 Chronicles 4:5)

7:21 These **pillars** were symbolic of stability and strength. *Stability* and *strength* may have been the first words of praise sung traditionally at the temple.

7:23–26 Used for ceremonial washings, this bronze **Sea** replaced the laver of the tabernacle (see Ex. 30:18). The bath was equal to six gallons (27 l).

four supports at the four corners of each cart; its supports *were* part of the cart itself. 35On the top of the cart, at the height of half a cubit, *it was* perfectly round. And on the top of the cart, its flanges and its panels *were* of the same casting. 36On the plates of its flanges and on its panels he engraved cherubim, lions, and palm trees, wherever there was a clear space on each, with wreaths all around. 37Thus he made the ten carts. All of them were of the same mold, one measure, *and* one shape.

38Then he made ten lavers of bronze; each laver contained forty baths, *and* each laver *was* four cubits. On each of the ten carts *was* a laver. 39And he put five carts on the right side of the house, and five on the left side of the house. He set the Sea on the right side of the house, toward the southeast.

Furnishings of the Temple

40Hū'ram[a] made the lavers and the shovels and the bowls. So Hū'ram finished doing all the work that he was to do for King Solomon *for* the house of the LORD: 41the two pillars, the *two* bowl-shaped capitals that *were* on top of the two pillars; the two networks covering the two bowl-shaped capitals which *were* on top of the pillars; 42four hundred pomegranates for the two networks (two rows of pomegranates for each network, to cover the two bowl-shaped capitals that *were* on top of the pillars); 43the ten carts, and ten lavers on the carts; 44one Sea, and twelve oxen under the Sea; 45the pots, the shovels, and the bowls.

All these articles which Hū'ram[a] made for King Solomon *for* the house of the LORD *were of* burnished bronze. 46In the plain of Jordan the king had them cast in clay molds, between Suc'coth and Zar'e·tan. 47And Solomon did not weigh all the articles, because *there were* so many; the weight of the bronze was not determined.

48Thus Solomon had all the furnishings made for the house of the LORD: the altar of gold, and the table of gold on which *was* the showbread; 49the lampstands of pure gold, five on the right *side* and five on the left in front of the inner sanctuary, with the flowers and the lamps and the wick-trimmers of gold; 50the basins, the trimmers, the bowls, the ladles, and the censers of pure gold; and the hinges of gold, *both* for the doors of the inner room (the Most Holy *Place*) *and* for the doors of the main hall of the temple.

51So all the work that King Solomon had done for the house of the LORD was finished; and Solomon brought in the things which his father David had dedicated: the silver and the gold and the furnishings. He put them in the treasuries of the house of the LORD.

CHAPTER 8

The Ark Brought into the Temple

Now Solomon assembled the elders of Israel and all the heads of the tribes, the chief fathers of the children of Israel, to King Solomon in Jerusalem, that they might bring up the ark of the covenant of the LORD from the City of David, which *is* Zion. 2Therefore all the men of Israel assembled with King Solomon at the feast in the month of Eth'a·nim, which *is* the seventh month. 3So all the elders of Israel came, and the priests took up the ark. 4Then they brought up the ark of the LORD, the tabernacle of meeting, and all the holy furnishings that *were* in the tabernacle. The priests and the Lē'vītes brought them up. 5Also King Solomon, and all the congrega-

7:40 [a]Hebrew *Hiram* (compare 2 Chronicles 2:13, 14)
7:45 [a]Hebrew *Hiram* (compare 2 Chronicles 2:13, 14)

7:38, 39 The water in the **lavers** was used to cleanse the worshipers, the altar, and the court (2 Chr. 4:6). But the Sea of cast bronze (vv. 23–26) was reserved for the priests.

8:2 Israel held three celebrations in the **seventh month** (see Lev. 23:23–43). This assembly was probably the Feast of Tabernacles, one of Israel's three major feasts.

tion of Israel who were assembled with
him, *were* with him before the ark, sacrific-
ing sheep and oxen that could not be
counted or numbered for multitude. 6Then
the priests brought in the ark of the
covenant of the LORD to its place, into the
inner sanctuary of the temple, to the Most
Holy *Place,* under the wings of the cheru-
bim. 7For the cherubim spread *their* two
wings over the place of the ark, and the
cherubim overshadowed the ark and its
poles. 8The poles extended so that the ends
of the poles could be seen from the holy
place, in front of the inner sanctuary; but
they could not be seen from outside. And
they are there to this day. 9Nothing *was* in
the ark except the two tablets of stone
which Moses put there at Hō'reb, when the
LORD made *a covenant* with the children of
Israel, when they came out of the land of
Egypt.

10And it came to pass, when the priests
came out of the holy *place,* that the cloud
filled the house of the LORD, 11so that the
priests could not continue ministering be-
cause of the cloud; for the glory of the
LORD filled the house of the LORD.

12Then Solomon spoke:

"The LORD said He would dwell in the
dark cloud.
13 I have surely built You an exalted
house,
And a place for You to dwell in
forever."

8:17 [a]Literally *house,* and so in verses 18–20

Solomon's Speech at Completion of the Work

14Then the king turned around and
blessed the whole assembly of Israel, while
all the assembly of Israel was standing.
15And he said: "Blessed *be* the LORD God of
Israel, who spoke with His mouth to my
father David, and with His hand has ful-
filled *it,* saying, 16'Since the day that I
brought My people Israel out of Egypt, I
have chosen no city from any tribe of Israel
in which to build a house, that My name
might be there; but I chose David to be
over My people Israel.' 17Now it was in the
heart of my father David to build a temple[a]
for the name of the LORD God of Israel.
18But the LORD said to my father David,
'Whereas it was in your heart to build a
temple for My name, you did well that it
was in your heart. 19Nevertheless you shall
not build the temple, but your son who
will come from your body, he shall build
the temple for My name.' 20So the LORD has
fulfilled His word which He spoke; and I
have filled the position of my father David,
and sit on the throne of Israel, as the LORD
promised; and I have built a temple for the
name of the LORD God of Israel. 21And
there I have made a place for the ark, in
which *is* the covenant of the LORD which
He made with our fathers, when He
brought them out of the land of Egypt."

Solomon's Prayer of Dedication

22Then Solomon stood before the altar
of the LORD in the presence of all the

8:8 there to this day: An indication that the original edition of the book was written before the destruction of the temple in 586 B.C.

8:9 Evidently the pot of manna and Aaron's budding rod were not always kept in the ark itself. See Heb. 9:4; Ex. 16:33; Num. 17:10.

8:16 chosen no city: The tabernacle, however, had remained at Shiloh in the territory of Ephraim from about 1400 B.C. until its apparent destruction by the Philistines around 1050 B.C. (see Josh. 18:1; 1 Sam. 1:3; Jer. 7:12–14).

8:22–53 After beginning his prayer with praise (vv. 23, 24), Solomon entreats the Lord to completely fulfill His promises to David (vv. 25, 26). He then calls for God to be attentive to the prayers offered in the new **temple** and to forgive sinners who worship there (vv. 27–30). From here the prayer lists seven concerns: sacred oaths (vv. 31, 32); military defeat (vv. 33, 34); drought (vv. 35, 36); other natural catastrophies (vv. 37–40); protection of foreigners (vv. 41–43); holy war (vv. 44, 45); and return from exile (vv. 46–53).

assembly of Israel, and spread out his hands toward heaven; [23]and he said: "LORD God of Israel, *there is* no God in heaven above or on earth below like You, who keep *Your* covenant and mercy with Your servants who walk before You with all their hearts. [24]You have kept what You promised Your servant David my father; You have both spoken with Your mouth and fulfilled *it* with Your hand, as *it is* this day. [25]Therefore, LORD God of Israel, now keep what You promised Your servant David my father, saying, 'You shall not fail to have a man sit before Me on the throne of Israel, only if your sons take heed to their way, that they walk before Me as you have walked before Me.' [26]And now I pray, O God of Israel, let Your word come true, which You have spoken to Your servant David my father.

[27]"But will God indeed dwell on the earth? Behold, heaven and the heaven of heavens cannot contain You. How much less this temple which I have built! [28]Yet regard the prayer of Your servant and his supplication, O LORD my God, and listen to the cry and the prayer which Your servant is praying before You today: [29]that Your eyes may be open toward this temple night and day, toward the place of which You said, 'My name shall be there,' that You may hear the prayer which Your servant makes toward this place. [30]And may You hear the supplication of Your servant and of Your people Israel, when they pray toward this place. Hear in heaven Your dwelling place; and when You hear, forgive.

[31]"When anyone sins against his neighbor, and is forced to take an oath, and comes *and* takes an oath before Your altar in this temple, [32]then hear in heaven, and act, and judge Your servants, condemning the wicked, bringing his way on his head, and justifying the righteous by giving him according to his righteousness.

[33]"When Your people Israel are defeated before an enemy because they have sinned against You, and when they turn back to You and confess Your name, and pray and make supplication to You in this temple, [34]then hear in heaven, and forgive the sin of Your people Israel, and bring them back to the land which You gave to their fathers.

[35]"When the heavens are shut up and there is no rain because they have sinned against You, when they pray toward this place and confess Your name, and turn from their sin because You afflict them, [36]then hear in heaven, and forgive the sin of Your servants, Your people Israel, that You may teach them the good way in which they should walk; and send rain on Your land which You have given to Your people as an inheritance.

[37]"When there is famine in the land, pestilence *or* blight *or* mildew, locusts *or* grasshoppers; when their enemy besieges them in the land of their cities; whatever plague or whatever sickness *there is;* [38]whatever prayer, whatever supplication is made by anyone, *or* by all Your people Israel, when each one knows the plague of his own heart, and spreads out his hands toward this temple: [39]then hear in heaven Your dwelling place, and forgive, and act, and give to everyone according to all his ways, whose heart You know (for You alone know the hearts of all the sons of men), [40]that they may fear You all the days that they live in the land which You gave to our fathers.

[41]"Moreover, concerning a foreigner, who *is* not of Your people Israel, but has come from a far country for Your name's sake [42](for they will hear of Your great

---

8:25 God's continued blessings are always contingent upon our faithfulness.

8:27 Solomon understood that no man-made thing can ever be truly worthy of God. Sometimes we become so caught up in our own importance that we fail to realize how incapable we are of grasping the fullness of God's glory.

name and Your strong hand and Your out-
stretched arm), when he comes and prays
toward this temple, [43]hear in heaven Your
dwelling place, and do according to all for
which the foreigner calls to You, that all
peoples of the earth may know Your name
and fear You, as *do* Your people Israel, and
that they may know that this temple which
I have built is called by Your name.

[44]"When Your people go out to battle
against their enemy, wherever You send
them, and when they pray to the LORD to-
ward the city which You have chosen and
the temple which I have built for Your
name, [45]then hear in heaven their prayer
and their supplication, and maintain their
cause.

[46]"When they sin against You (for *there is*
no one who does not sin), and You become
angry with them and deliver them to the
enemy, and they take them captive to the
land of the enemy, far or near; [47]*yet* when
they come to themselves in the land where
they were carried captive, and repent, and
make supplication to You in the land of
those who took them captive, saying, 'We
have sinned and done wrong, we have
committed wickedness'; [48]and *when* they
return to You with all their heart and with
all their soul in the land of their enemies
who led them away captive, and pray to
You toward their land which You gave to
their fathers, the city which You have cho-
sen and the temple which I have built for
Your name: [49]then hear in heaven Your
dwelling place their prayer and their sup-
plication, and maintain their cause, [50]and
forgive Your people who have sinned
against You, and all their transgressions
which they have transgressed against You;
and grant them compassion before those
who took them captive, that they may
have compassion on them [51](for they *are*
Your people and Your inheritance, whom
You brought out of Egypt, out of the iron
furnace), [52]that Your eyes may be open to
the supplication of Your servant and the
supplication of Your people Israel, to listen
to them whenever they call to You. [53]For
You separated them from among all the
peoples of the earth *to be* Your inheritance,
as You spoke by Your servant Moses, when
You brought our fathers out of Egypt, O
Lord GOD."

Solomon Blesses the Assembly

[54]And so it was, when Solomon had fin-
ished praying all this prayer and supplica-
tion to the LORD, that he arose from before
the altar of the LORD, from kneeling on his
knees with his hands spread up to heaven.
[55]Then he stood and blessed all the assem-
bly of Israel with a loud voice, saying:
[56]"Blessed *be* the LORD, who has given rest
to His people Israel, according to all that
He promised. There has not failed one
word of all His good promise, which He
promised through His servant Moses.
[57]May the LORD our God be with us, as He
was with our fathers. May He not leave us
nor forsake us, [58]that He may incline our
hearts to Himself, to walk in all His ways,
and to keep His commandments and His
statutes and His judgments, which He
commanded our fathers. [59]And may these
words of mine, with which I have made
supplication before the LORD, be near the
LORD our God day and night, that He may
maintain the cause of His servant and the
cause of His people Israel, as each day may
require, [60]that all the peoples of the earth
may know that the LORD *is* God; *there is* no

8:46 no one who does not sin: That is, no one can live up to the absolute perfection of God.

8:56 The prosperity of Solomon's reign was a result of God's promises to faithful servants like **Moses** and David. But each generation has its own covenant responsibility, which led Solomon to the exhortation in v. 61. The church is never more than one generation from extinction.

other. 61 Let your heart therefore be loyal to the LORD our God, to walk in His statutes and keep His commandments, as at this day."

Solomon Dedicates the Temple

62 Then the king and all Israel with him offered sacrifices before the LORD. 63 And Solomon offered a sacrifice of peace offerings, which he offered to the LORD, twenty-two thousand bulls and one hundred and twenty thousand sheep. So the king and all the children of Israel dedicated the house of the LORD. 64 On the same day the king consecrated the middle of the court that *was* in front of the house of the LORD; for there he offered burnt offerings, grain offerings, and the fat of the peace offerings, because the bronze altar that *was* before the LORD *was* too small to receive the burnt offerings, the grain offerings, and the fat of the peace offerings.

65 At that time Solomon held a feast, and all Israel with him, a great assembly from the entrance of Hā′math to the Brook of Egypt, before the LORD our God, seven days and seven *more* days—fourteen days. 66 On the eighth day he sent the people away; and they blessed the king, and went to their tents joyful and glad of heart for all the good that the LORD had done for His servant David, and for Israel His people.

CHAPTER 9

God's Second Appearance to Solomon

And it came to pass, when Solomon had finished building the house of the LORD and the king's house, and all Solomon's desire which he wanted to do, 2 that the LORD appeared to Solomon the second time, as He had appeared to him at Gib′ē·on. 3 And the LORD said to him: "I have heard your prayer and your supplication that you have made before Me; I have consecrated this house which you have built to put My name there forever, and My eyes and My heart will be there perpetually. 4 Now if you walk before Me as your father David walked, in integrity of heart and in uprightness, to do according to all that I have commanded you, *and* if you keep My statutes and My judgments, 5 then I will establish the throne of your kingdom over Israel forever, as I promised David your father, saying, 'You shall not fail to have a man on the throne of Israel.' 6 *But* if you or your sons at all turn from following Me, and do not keep My commandments *and* My statutes which I have set before you, but go and serve other gods and worship them, 7 then I will cut off Israel from the land which I have given them; and this house which I have consecrated for My name I will cast out of My sight. Israel will be a proverb and a byword among all peoples. 8 And *as for* this house, *which* is exalted, everyone who passes by it will be astonished and will hiss, and say, 'Why has the LORD done thus to this land and to this house?' 9 Then they will answer, 'Because they forsook the LORD their God, who brought their fathers out of the land of Egypt, and have embraced other gods, and worshiped them and served them; therefore the LORD has brought all this calamity on them.' "

Solomon and Hiram Exchange Gifts

10 Now it happened at the end of twenty years, when Solomon had built the two houses, the house of the LORD and the king's house 11 (Hī′ram the king of Tȳre had supplied Solomon with cedar and cy-

---

8:61 We need to examine ourselves daily for any sign of complacency or apathy to the things of God. How easily our feet can stray from His statutes, almost without our realizing it.

9:4–9 if you walk . . . I will establish: God's promise of a perpetual Davidic line did not guarantee the success of a disobedient Israel. His sovereignty never abrogates human accountability.

press and gold, as much as he desired), *that* King Solomon then gave Hī′ram twenty cities in the land of Galilee. [12]Then Hī′ram went from Tȳre to see the cities which Solomon had given him, but they did not please him. [13]So he said, "What *kind of* cities *are* these which you have given me, my brother?" And he called them the land of Cā′bul,[a] as they are to this day. [14]Then Hī′ram sent the king one hundred and twenty talents of gold.

Solomon's Additional Achievements

[15]And this *is* the reason for the labor force which King Solomon raised: to build the house of the LORD, his own house, the Mil′lō,[a] the wall of Jerusalem, Hā′zor, Me·gid′dō, and Gē′zer. [16](Pharaoh king of Egypt had gone up and taken Gē′zer and burned it with fire, had killed the Cā′naan·ītes who dwelt in the city, and had given it *as* a dowry to his daughter, Solomon's wife.) [17]And Solomon built Gē′zer, Lower Beth Hor′on, [18]Bā′a·lath, and Tad′mor in the wilderness, in the land *of Judah,* [19]all the storage cities that Solomon had, cities for his chariots and cities for his cavalry, and whatever Solomon desired to build in Jerusalem, in Lebanon, and in all the land of his dominion.

[20]All the people *who were* left of the Am′o·rītes, Hit′tītes, Per′iz·zītes, Hī′vītes, and Jeb′ū·sītes, who *were* not of the children of Israel— [21]that is, their descendants who were left in the land after them, whom the children of Israel had not been able to destroy completely—from these Solomon raised forced labor, as it is to this day. [22]But of the children of Israel Solomon made no forced laborers, because they *were* men of war and his servants: his officers, his captains, commanders of his chariots, and his cavalry.

[23]Others *were* chiefs of the officials who *were* over Solomon's work: five hundred and fifty, who ruled over the people who did the work.

[24]But Pharaoh's daughter came up from the City of David to her house which *Solomon*[a] had built for her. Then he built the Mil′lō.

[25]Now three times a year Solomon offered burnt offerings and peace offerings on the altar which he had built for the LORD, and he burned incense with them *on the altar* that *was* before the LORD. So he finished the temple.

[26]King Solomon also built a fleet of ships at Ē′zi·on Gē′ber, which *is* near Ē′lath[a] on the shore of the Red Sea, in the land of Ē′dom. [27]Then Hī′ram sent his servants with the fleet, seamen who knew the sea, to work with the servants of Solomon. [28]And they went to Ō′phir, and acquired four hundred and twenty talents of gold from there, and brought *it* to King Solomon.

CHAPTER 10

The Queen of Sheba's Praise of Solomon

Now when the queen of Shē′ba heard of the fame of Solomon concerning the name

9:13 [a]Literally *Good for Nothing*
9:15 [a]Literally *The Landfill*
9:24 [a]Literally *he* (compare 2 Chronicles 8:11)
9:26 [a]Hebrew *Eloth* (compare 2 Kings 14:22)

9:15–19 the Millo: A rampart of two walls with a space between them filled in. The one at Jerusalem was an old fortification perhaps built by the Jebusites (see 2 Sam. 5:9). The cities listed were important for Israel's defense. Archeology has confirmed Solomon's fortification of **Hazor, Megiddo**, and **Gezer**, all of which lay on a critical international highway. **Lower Beth Horon** and **Baalath** protected the central hills from the west, and **Tadmor** guarded Solomon's southern border.

10:1 Sheba was a kingdom of southwestern Arabia encompassing most of modern Yemen. Archeology has verified the existence of an advanced Arabian culture built on trade between Africa and Asia during the period. One purpose for the visit of the queen was commerce (see vv. 10 and 13).

of the LORD, she came to test him with hard questions. 2She came to Jerusalem with a very great retinue, with camels that bore spices, very much gold, and precious stones; and when she came to Solomon, she spoke with him about all that was in her heart. 3So Solomon answered all her questions; there was nothing so difficult for the king that he could not explain *it* to her. 4And when the queen of Shē´ba had seen all the wisdom of Solomon, the house that he had built, 5the food on his table, the seating of his servants, the service of his waiters and their apparel, his cupbearers, and his entryway by which he went up to the house of the LORD, there was no more spirit in her. 6Then she said to the king: "It was a true report which I heard in my own land about your words and your wisdom. 7However I did not believe the words until I came and saw with my own eyes; and indeed the half was not told me. Your wisdom and prosperity exceed the fame of which I heard. 8Happy *are* your men and happy *are* these your servants, who stand continually before you *and* hear your wisdom! 9Blessed be the LORD your God, who delighted in you, setting you on the throne of Israel! Because the LORD has loved Israel forever, therefore He made you king, to do justice and righteousness."

10Then she gave the king one hundred and twenty talents of gold, spices in great quantity, and precious stones. There never again came such abundance of spices as the queen of Shē´ba gave to King Solomon. 11Also, the ships of Hī´ram, which brought gold from Ō´phir, brought great *quantities* of almug[a] wood and precious stones from Ō´phir. 12And the king made steps of the almug wood for the house of the LORD and for the king's house, also harps and stringed instruments for singers. There never again came such almug wood, nor has the like been seen to this day.

13Now King Solomon gave the queen of Shē´ba all she desired, whatever she asked, besides what Solomon had given her according to the royal generosity. So she turned and went to her own country, she and her servants.

Solomon's Great Wealth

14The weight of gold that came to Solomon yearly was six hundred and sixty-six talents of gold, 15besides *that* from the traveling merchants, from the income of traders, from all the kings of Arabia, and from the governors of the country.

16And King Solomon made two hundred large shields *of* hammered gold; six hundred *shekels* of gold went into each shield. 17He also *made* three hundred shields *of* hammered gold; three minas of gold went into each shield. The king put them in the House of the Forest of Lebanon.

18Moreover the king made a great throne of ivory, and overlaid it with pure gold. 19The throne had six steps, and the top of the throne *was* round at the back; *there were* armrests on either side of the place of the seat, and two lions stood beside the armrests. 20Twelve lions stood there, one on each side of the six steps; nothing like *this* had been made for any *other* kingdom.

21All King Solomon's drinking vessels *were* gold, and all the vessels of the House of the Forest of Lebanon *were* pure gold. Not *one was* silver, for this was accounted as nothing in the days of Solomon. 22For the king had merchant ships[a] at sea with the fleet of Hī´ram. Once every three years the merchant ships came bringing gold, silver, ivory, apes, and monkeys.[b] 23So King Solomon surpassed all the kings of the earth in riches and wisdom.

24Now all the earth sought the presence of Solomon to hear his wisdom, which God had put in his heart. 25Each man brought his present: articles of silver and gold, garments, armor, spices, horses, and mules, at a set rate year by year.

10:11 [a]Or *algum* (compare 2 Chronicles 9:10, 11)
10:22 [a]Literally *ships of Tarshish,* deep-sea vessels
[b]Or *peacocks*

26And Solomon gathered chariots and
horsemen; he had one thousand four hun-
dred chariots and twelve thousand horse-
men, whom he stationed[a] in the chariot
cities and with the king at Jerusalem. 27The
king made silver *as common* in Jerusalem as
stones, and he made cedar trees as abun-
dant as the sycamores which *are* in the low-
land.

28Also Solomon had horses imported
from Egypt and Ke·veh'; the king's mer-
chants bought them in Ke·veh' at the *cur-
rent* price. 29Now a chariot that was im-
ported from Egypt cost six hundred *shekels*
of silver, and a horse one hundred and
fifty; and thus, through their agents,[a] they
exported *them* to all the kings of the
Hit'tītes and the kings of Syria.

CHAPTER 11

Solomon's Heart Turns from the LORD

But King Solomon loved many foreign
women, as well as the daughter of
Pharaoh: women of the Mō'ab·ītes,
Am'mon·ītes, Ē'dom·ītes, Sī·dō'ni·ans,
and Hit'tītes— 2from the nations of whom
the LORD had said to the children of Israel,
"You shall not intermarry with them, nor
they with you. Surely they will turn away
your hearts after their gods." Solomon
clung to these in love. 3And he had seven
hundred wives, princesses, and three hun-
dred concubines; and his wives turned
away his heart. 4For it was so, when Sol-
omon was old, that his wives turned his
heart after other gods; and his heart was
not loyal to the LORD his God, as *was* the
heart of his father David. 5For Solomon
went after Ash'to·reth the goddess of the
Sī·dō'ni·ans, and after Mil'com the
abomination of the Am'mon·ītes. 6Sol-
omon did evil in the sight of the LORD, and
did not fully follow the LORD, as *did* his fa-
ther David. 7Then Solomon built a high
place for Chē'mosh the abomination of
Mō'ab, on the hill that *is* east of Jerusalem,
and for Mō'lech the abomination of the
people of Am'mon. 8And he did likewise
for all his foreign wives, who burned in-
cense and sacrificed to their gods.

9So the LORD became angry with Sol-
omon, because his heart had turned from
the LORD God of Israel, who had appeared
to him twice, 10and had commanded him
concerning this thing, that he should not
go after other gods; but he did not keep
what the LORD had commanded. 11There-
fore the LORD said to Solomon, "Because
you have done this, and have not kept My
covenant and My statutes, which I have
commanded you, I will surely tear the
kingdom away from you and give it to
your servant. 12Nevertheless I will not do it
in your days, for the sake of your father
David; I will tear it out of the hand of your
son. 13However I will not tear away the
whole kingdom; I will give one tribe to
your son for the sake of My servant David,
and for the sake of Jerusalem which I have
chosen."

Adversaries of Solomon

14Now the LORD raised up an adversary
against Solomon, Hā'dad the Ē'dom·īte;

10:26 [a]Following Septuagint, Syriac, Targum, and Vulgate (compare 2 Chronicles 9:25); Masoretic Text reads *led*. 10:29 [a]Literally *by their hands*

10:26–29 Solomon had broken God's solemn warning against an Israelite king returning to Egypt "to multiply horses," or against multiplying "silver and gold for himself" (see Deut. 17:16, 17). Dependence on material possessions automatically takes our focus away from God and leads to disaster.

11:1–8 Solomon's politically motivated marriages left him with many **foreign** wives who adversely affected his faith. He gradually shifted from an exclusive monotheism (see 8:23) to the worship of many gods, although he probably still recognized the Lord as supreme (11:5–8). The change in Solomon demonstrates how we can deceive ourselves little by little and eventually find ourselves fully enslaved by evil.

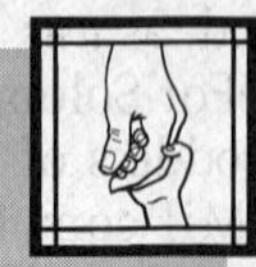

Walk with Integrity

Ron Lee Davis

Despite all his wisdom and achievements for God, Solomon began to compromise and flirt with the evil of the world. His magnificent reign came under a cloud. Seduced by his own baser instincts and the attentions of foreign women who worshiped other gods, Solomon wandered in his heart from the laws of God. The wise man who had built the temple of God now became a fool, building altars to false gods. Tragically, King Solomon reinstated the idolatry his father, David, had driven out of Israel.

Solomon's lack of integrity contaminated his son Rehoboam, whom Solomon was mentoring and training to succeed him as king. Although Solomon had spent many hours with Rehoboam—teaching him wisdom, faith, obedience to God, and the duties of leadership—when Rehoboam took up the crown of Israel following Solomon's apostasy and death, he led Israel even deeper into error and idolatry. The promising young prince became a cruel and hated despot. The once-prosperous nation of Israel fell into poverty, turmoil, and war. Only five years into Rehoboam's reign, the once-glorious temple built by his father Solomon was plundered and desecrated (1 Kin. 14:26).

That is a lesson that all of us—not only as parents but as mentors and leaders—should take to heart: When we fail to walk with integrity, we contaminate the generations that follow us. ✦

he *was* a descendant of the king in Ē'dom.
15For it happened, when David was in
Ē'dom, and Jō'ab the commander of the
army had gone up to bury the slain, after
he had killed every male in Ē'dom 16(be-
cause for six months Jō'ab remained there
with all Israel, until he had cut down every
male in Ē'dom), 17that Hā'dad fled to go to
Egypt, he and certain Ē'dom·ītes of his fa-
ther's servants with him. Hā'dad *was* still a
little child. 18Then they arose from Mid'i·an
and came to Par'an; and they took men
with them from Par'an and came to Egypt,
to Pharaoh king of Egypt, who gave him a
house, apportioned food for him, and gave
him land. 19And Hā'dad found great favor
in the sight of Pharaoh, so that he gave him
as wife the sister of his own wife, that is,
the sister of Queen Tah'pe·nēs. 20Then the
sister of Tah'pe·nēs bore him Ge·nū'bath
his son, whom Tah'pe·nēs weaned in
Pharaoh's house. And Ge·nū'bath was in
Pharaoh's household among the sons
of Pharaoh.

21So when Hā'dad heard in Egypt that
David rested with his fathers, and that
Jō'ab the commander of the army was
dead, Hā'dad said to Pharaoh, "Let me de-
part, that I may go to my own country."

22Then Pharaoh said to him, "But what
have you lacked with me, that suddenly
you seek to go to your own country?"

So he answered, "Nothing, but do let
me go anyway."

23And God raised up *another* adversary
against him, Rē'zon the son of E·lī'a·dah,
who had fled from his lord, Had·a·dē'zer
king of Zō'bah. 24So he gathered men to

him and became captain over a band *of*
raiders, when David killed those *of Zō′bah.*
And they went to Damascus and dwelt
there, and reigned in Damascus. 25He was
an adversary of Israel all the days of Sol-
omon (besides the trouble that Hā′dad
caused); and he abhorred Israel, and
reigned over Syria.

Jeroboam's Rebellion

26Then Solomon's servant, Jer·o·bō′am
the son of Nē′bat, an Ē′phra·im·īte from
Zer′e·da, whose mother's name *was*
Ze·rū′ah, a widow, also rebelled against
the king.

27And this *is* what caused him to rebel
against the king: Solomon had built the
Mil′lō *and* repaired the damages to the
City of David his father. 28The man Jer·o-
bō′am *was* a mighty man of valor; and Sol-
omon, seeing that the young man was in-
dustrious, made him the officer over all
the labor force of the house of Joseph.

29Now it happened at that time, when
Jer·o·bō′am went out of Jerusalem, that the
prophet A·hī′jah the Shī′lo·nīte met him
on the way; and he had clothed himself
with a new garment, and the two *were*
alone in the field. 30Then A·hī′jah took
hold of the new garment that *was* on him,
and tore it *into* twelve pieces. 31And he said
to Jer·o·bō′am, "Take for yourself ten
pieces, for thus says the LORD, the God of
Israel: 'Behold, I will tear the kingdom out
of the hand of Solomon and will give ten
tribes to you 32(but he shall have one tribe
for the sake of My servant David, and for
the sake of Jerusalem, the city which I have
chosen out of all the tribes of Israel), 33be-
cause they have[a] forsaken Me, and wor-
shiped Ash′to·reth the goddess of the
Sī·dō′ni·ans, Chē′mosh the god of the

11:33 [a]Following Masoretic Text and Targum; Septuagint, Syriac, and Vulgate read *he has.*

Mō′ab·ītes, and Mil′com the god of
the people of Am′mon, and have not
walked in My ways to do *what is* right in
My eyes and *keep* My statutes and My
judgments, as *did* his father David. 34How-
ever I will not take the whole kingdom out
of his hand, because I have made him ruler
all the days of his life for the sake of My
servant David, whom I chose because he
kept My commandments and My statutes.
35But I will take the kingdom out of his
son's hand and give it to you—ten tribes.
36And to his son I will give one tribe, that
My servant David may always have a
lamp before Me in Jerusalem, the city
which I have chosen for Myself, to put My
name there. 37So I will take you, and you
shall reign over all your heart desires, and
you shall be king over Israel. 38Then it shall
be, if you heed all that I command you,
walk in My ways, and do *what is* right in
My sight, to keep My statutes and My
commandments, as My servant David did,
then I will be with you and build for you
an enduring house, as I built for David,
and will give Israel to you. 39And I will af-
flict the descendants of David because of
this, but not forever.' "

40Solomon therefore sought to kill
Jer·o·bō′am. But Jer·o·bō′am arose and
fled to Egypt, to Shī′shak king of Egypt,
and was in Egypt until the death of Sol-
omon.

Death of Solomon

41Now the rest of the acts of Solomon, all
that he did, and his wisdom, *are* they not
written in the book of the acts of Solomon?
42And the period that Solomon reigned in
Jerusalem over all Israel *was* forty years.
43Then Solomon rested with his fathers,
and was buried in the City of David his
father. And Rē·ho·bō′am his son reigned
in his place.

11:40 Despite his heritage and the promising start of his reign, Solomon succumbed to the temptations of pride and glory just as Saul had. He even followed Saul's lead in attempting to kill God's chosen successor to the throne.

CHAPTER 12

The Revolt Against Rehoboam

And Rē·ho·bō′am went to Shē′chem, for all Israel had gone to Shē′chem to make him king. 2So it happened, when Jer·o·bō′am the son of Nē′bat heard *it* (he was still in Egypt, for he had fled from the presence of King Solomon and had been dwelling in Egypt), 3that they sent and called him. Then Jer·o·bō′am and the whole assembly of Israel came and spoke to Rē·ho·bō′am, saying, 4"Your father made our yoke heavy; now therefore, lighten the burdensome service of your father, and his heavy yoke which he put on us, and we will serve you."

5So he said to them, "Depart *for* three days, then come back to me." And the people departed.

6Then King Rē·ho·bō′am consulted the elders who stood before his father Solomon while he still lived, and he said, "How do you advise *me* to answer these people?"

7And they spoke to him, saying, "If you will be a servant to these people today, and serve them, and answer them, and speak good words to them, then they will be your servants forever."

8But he rejected the advice which the elders had given him, and consulted the young men who had grown up with him, who stood before him. 9And he said to them, "What advice do you give? How should we answer this people who have spoken to me, saying, 'Lighten the yoke which your father put on us'?"

10Then the young men who had grown up with him spoke to him, saying, "Thus you should speak to this people who have spoken to you, saying, 'Your father made our yoke heavy, but you make *it* lighter on us'—thus you shall say to them: 'My little *finger* shall be thicker than my father's waist! 11And now, whereas my father put a heavy yoke on you, I will add to your yoke; my father chastised you with whips, but I will chastise you with scourges!' "[a]

12So Jer·o·bō′am and all the people came to Rē·ho·bō′am the third day, as the king had directed, saying, "Come back to me the third day." 13Then the king answered the people roughly, and rejected the advice which the elders had given him; 14and he spoke to them according to the advice of the young men, saying, "My father made your yoke heavy, but I will add to your yoke; my father chastised you with whips, but I will chastise you with scourges!"[a] 15So the king did not listen to the people; for the turn *of events* was from the LORD, that He might fulfill His word, which the LORD had spoken by A·hī′jah the Shī′lo·nīte to Jer·o·bō′am the son of Nē′bat.

16Now when all Israel saw that the king did not listen to them, the people answered the king, saying:

"What share have we in David?
We have no inheritance in the son of
Jesse.
To your tents, O Israel!
Now, see to your own house,
O David!"

So Israel departed to their tents. 17But Rē·ho·bō′am reigned over the children of Israel who dwelt in the cities of Judah.

18Then King Rē·ho·bō′am sent A·dor′am, who *was* in charge of the revenue; but all Israel stoned him with stones, and he died. Therefore King Rē·ho·bō′am mounted his chariot in haste to flee to Jerusalem. 19So Israel has been in rebellion against the house of David to this day.

20Now it came to pass when all Israel

12:11 [a]Literally *scorpions* 12:14 [a]Literally *scorpions*

12:16–20 The unity between North (Israel) and South (Judah) under Saul, David, and Solomon had never been firmly established (see 2 Sam. 19:9–15). The kingdom had been held together by the charisma and strength of its leaders.

heard that Jer•o•bō′am had come back, they sent for him and called him to the congregation, and made him king over all Israel. There was none who followed the house of David, but the tribe of Judah only.

21And when Rē•ho•bō′am came to Jerusalem, he assembled all the house of Judah with the tribe of Benjamin, one hundred and eighty thousand chosen *men* who were warriors, to fight against the house of Israel, that he might restore the kingdom to Rē•ho•bō′am the son of Solomon. 22But the word of God came to She•māi′ah the man of God, saying, 23"Speak to Rē•ho•bō′am the son of Solomon, king of Judah, to all the house of Judah and Benjamin, and to the rest of the people, saying, 24'Thus says the LORD: "You shall not go up nor fight against your brethren the children of Israel. Let every man return to his house, for this thing is from Me." ' " Therefore they obeyed the word of the LORD, and turned back, according to the word of the LORD.

Jeroboam's Gold Calves

25Then Jer•o•bō′am built Shē′chem in the mountains of Ē′phra•im, and dwelt there. Also he went out from there and built Pe•nū′el. 26And Jer•o•bō′am said in his heart, "Now the kingdom may return to the house of David: 27If these people go up to offer sacrifices in the house of the LORD at Jerusalem, then the heart of this people will turn back to their lord, Rē•ho•bō′am king of Judah, and they will kill me and go back to Rē•ho•bō′am king of Judah."

28Therefore the king asked advice, made two calves of gold, and said to the people, "It is too much for you to go up to Jerusalem. Here are your gods, O Israel, which brought you up from the land of Egypt!" 29And he set up one in Beth′el, and the other he put in Dan. 30Now this thing became a sin, for the people went *to worship* before the one as far as Dan. 31He made shrines[a] on the high places, and made priests from every class of people, who were not of the sons of Levi.

32Jer•o•bō′am ordained a feast on the fifteenth day of the eighth month, like the feast that *was* in Judah, and offered sacrifices on the altar. So he did at Beth′el, sacrificing to the calves that he had made. And at Beth′el he installed the priests of the high places which he had made. 33So he made offerings on the altar which he had made at Beth′el on the fifteenth day of the eighth month, in the month which he had devised in his own heart. And he ordained a feast for the children of Israel, and offered sacrifices on the altar and burned incense.

CHAPTER 13

The Message of the Man of God

And behold, a man of God went from Judah to Beth′el by the word of the LORD, and Jer•o•bō′am stood by the altar to burn incense. 2Then he cried out against the altar by the word of the LORD, and said,

12:31 [a]Literally *a house*

12:27 The methods by which Jereboam sought to keep his people from defecting to Judah were in obvious contradiction to God's commands and ensured his downfall. The lack of protest from the people indicates how corrupt they had become.

12:28–31 The **two calves** may have been perceived as pedestals upon which the invisible Yahweh rode in victory. However, that this was genuine idolatry is suggested by the use of bulls in Egyptian religious practices and by Jeroboam's words **here are your gods**—the same words uttered hundreds of years earlier of Aaron's golden calf (see Ex. 32:3, 4). **Bethel . . . Dan**: Important cities with long histories, serving as the southern and northern extremities of Jeroboam's kingdom. Jeroboam's appointment of priests from non-Levitical tribes was in violation of God's covenant with Levi (see Num. 25:10–13; Mal. 2:4, 5). As a result, the Levitical priests fled from Jeroboam to Judah (see 2 Chr. 11:13–15).

"O altar, altar! Thus says the LORD: 'Behold, a child, Jō·sī'ah by name, shall be born to the house of David; and on you he shall sacrifice the priests of the high places who burn incense on you, and men's bones shall be burned on you.' "
[3]And he gave a sign the same day, saying, "This *is* the sign which the LORD has spoken: Surely the altar shall split apart, and the ashes on it shall be poured out."

[4]So it came to pass when King Jer·o·bō'am heard the saying of the man of God, who cried out against the altar in Beth'el, that he stretched out his hand from the altar, saying, "Arrest him!" Then his hand, which he stretched out toward him, withered, so that he could not pull it back to himself.
[5]The altar also was split apart, and the ashes poured out from the altar, according to the sign which the man of God had given by the word of the LORD.
[6]Then the king answered and said to the man of God, "Please entreat the favor of the LORD your God, and pray for me, that my hand may be restored to me."

So the man of God entreated the LORD, and the king's hand was restored to him, and became as before.
[7]Then the king said to the man of God, "Come home with me and refresh yourself, and I will give you a reward."

[8]But the man of God said to the king, "If you were to give me half your house, I would not go in with you; nor would I eat bread nor drink water in this place.
[9]For so it was commanded me by the word of the LORD, saying, 'You shall not eat bread, nor drink water, nor return by the same way you came.' "
[10]So he went another way and did not return by the way he came to Beth'el.

Death of the Man of God

[11]Now an old prophet dwelt in Beth'el, and his sons came and told him all the works that the man of God had done that day in Beth'el; they also told their father the words which he had spoken to the king.
[12]And their father said to them, "Which way did he go?" For his sons had seen[a] which way the man of God went who came from Judah.
[13]Then he said to his sons, "Saddle the donkey for me." So they saddled the donkey for him; and he rode on it,
[14]and went after the man of God, and found him sitting under an oak. Then he said to him, "*Are* you the man of God who came from Judah?"

And he said, "I *am*."

[15]Then he said to him, "Come home with me and eat bread."

[16]And he said, "I cannot return with you nor go in with you; neither can I eat bread nor drink water with you in this place.
[17]For I have been told by the word of the LORD, 'You shall not eat bread nor drink water there, nor return by going the way you came.' "

[18]He said to him, "I too *am* a prophet as you *are*, and an angel spoke to me by the word of the LORD, saying, 'Bring him back with you to your house, that he may eat bread and drink water.' " (He was lying to him.)

[19]So he went back with him, and ate bread in his house, and drank water.

[20]Now it happened, as they sat at the table, that the word of the LORD came to the prophet who had brought him back;
[21]and he cried out to the man of God who came from Judah, saying, "Thus says the LORD: 'Because you have disobeyed the word of the LORD, and have not kept the commandment which the LORD your God commanded you,
[22]but you came back, ate bread, and drank water in the place of which *the LORD* said to you, "Eat no bread and drink no water," your corpse shall not come to the tomb of your fathers.' "

[23]So it was, after he had eaten bread and after he had drunk, that he saddled the donkey for him, the prophet whom he had brought back.
[24]When he was gone, a lion met him on the road and killed him. And his corpse was thrown on the road, and the donkey stood by it. The lion also stood by

13:12 [a]Septuagint, Syriac, Targum, and Vulgate read *showed him.*

the corpse. 25And there, men passed by and
saw the corpse thrown on the road, and the
lion standing by the corpse. Then they
went and told *it* in the city where the old
prophet dwelt.
26Now when the prophet who had
brought him back from the way heard *it,*
he said, "It *is* the man of God who was
disobedient to the word of the LORD.
Therefore the LORD has delivered him to
the lion, which has torn him and killed
him, according to the word of the LORD
which He spoke to him." 27And he spoke to
his sons, saying, "Saddle the donkey for
me." So they saddled *it.* 28Then he went
and found his corpse thrown on the road,
and the donkey and the lion standing by
the corpse. The lion had not eaten the
corpse nor torn the donkey. 29And the
prophet took up the corpse of the man of
God, laid it on the donkey, and brought it
back. So the old prophet came to the city to
mourn, and to bury him. 30Then he laid the
corpse in his own tomb; and they mourned
over him, *saying,* "Alas, my brother!" 31So
it was, after he had buried him, that he
spoke to his sons, saying, "When I am
dead, then bury me in the tomb where the
man of God *is* buried; lay my bones beside
his bones. 32For the saying which he cried
out by the word of the LORD against the al-
tar in Beth'el, and against all the shrines[a]
on the high places which *are* in the cities of
Samaria, will surely come to pass."
33After this event Jer·o·bō'am did not
turn from his evil way, but again he made
priests from every class of people for the
high places; whoever wished, he conse-
crated him, and he became *one* of the
priests of the high places. 34And this thing
was the sin of the house of Jer·o·bō'am, so
as to exterminate and destroy *it* from the
face of the earth.

13:32 [a]Literally *houses*

CHAPTER 14

Judgment on the House of Jeroboam

At that time A·bī'jah the son of Jer-
o·bō'am became sick. 2And Jer·o·bō'am
said to his wife, "Please arise, and disguise
yourself, that they may not recognize you
as the wife of Jer·o·bō'am, and go to
Shī'lōh. Indeed, A·hī'jah the prophet *is*
there, who told me that *I would be* king over
this people. 3Also take with you ten loaves,
some cakes, and a jar of honey, and go to
him; he will tell you what will become of
the child." 4And Jer·o·bō'am's wife did so;
she arose and went to Shī'lōh, and came to
the house of A·hī'jah. But A·hī'jah could
not see, for his eyes were glazed by reason
of his age.
5Now the LORD had said to A·hī'jah,
"Here is the wife of Jer·o·bō'am, coming to
ask you something about her son, for he *is*
sick. Thus and thus you shall say to her; for
it will be, when she comes in, that she will
pretend *to be* another *woman.*"
6And so it was, when A·hī'jah heard the
sound of her footsteps as she came through
the door, he said, "Come in, wife of Jer-
o·bō'am. Why do you pretend *to be* another
person? For I *have been* sent to you *with* bad
news. 7Go, tell Jer·o·bō'am, 'Thus says the
LORD God of Israel: "Because I exalted you
from among the people, and made you
ruler over My people Israel, 8and tore the
kingdom away from the house of David,
and gave it to you; and *yet* you have not
been as My servant David, who kept My
commandments and who followed Me
with all his heart, to do only *what was* right
in My eyes; 9but you have done more evil
than all who were before you, for you have

13:33, 34 Even after the warnings from this prophet, Jeroboam refused to turn from **his evil way**. His dynasty lasted only two years after his death (15:25–28), and he became the stereotype of the sinful king.

gone and made for yourself other gods and
molded images to provoke Me to anger,
and have cast Me behind your back—
10therefore behold! I will bring disaster on
the house of Jer·o·bō'am, and will cut off
from Jer·o·bō'am every male in Israel,
bond and free; I will take away the rem-
nant of the house of Jer·o·bō'am, as one
takes away refuse until it is all gone. 11The
dogs shall eat whoever belongs to Jer-
o·bō'am and dies in the city, and the birds
of the air shall eat whoever dies in the
field; for the LORD has spoken!"' 12Arise
therefore, go to your own house. When
your feet enter the city, the child shall die.
13And all Israel shall mourn for him and
bury him, for he is the only one of Jer-
o·bō'am who shall come to the grave, be-
cause in him there is found something
good toward the LORD God of Israel in the
house of Jer·o·bō'am.

14"Moreover the LORD will raise up for
Himself a king over Israel who shall cut off
the house of Jer·o·bō'am; this is the day.
What? Even now! 15For the LORD will strike
Israel, as a reed is shaken in the water. He
will uproot Israel from this good land
which He gave to their fathers, and will
scatter them beyond the River,[a] because
they have made their wooden images,[b]
provoking the LORD to anger. 16And He
will give Israel up because of the sins of
Jer·o·bō'am, who sinned and who made Is-
rael sin."

17Then Jer·o·bō'am's wife arose and de-
parted, and came to Tir'zah. When she
came to the threshold of the house, the
child died. 18And they buried him; and all
Israel mourned for him, according to the
word of the LORD which He spoke through
His servant A·hī'jah the prophet.

Death of Jeroboam

19Now the rest of the acts of Jer·o·bō'am,
how he made war and how he reigned, in-
deed they *are* written in the book of the
chronicles of the kings of Israel. 20The pe-
riod that Jer·o·bō'am reigned *was* twenty-
two years. So he rested with his fathers.
Then Nā'dab his son reigned in his place.

Rehoboam Reigns in Judah

21And Rē·ho·bō'am the son of Solomon
reigned in Judah. Rē·ho·bō'am *was* forty-
one years old when he became king. He
reigned seventeen years in Jerusalem, the
city which the LORD had chosen out of all
the tribes of Israel, to put His name there.
His mother's name *was* Nā'a·mah, an
Am'mon·ī·tess. 22Now Judah did evil in
the sight of the LORD, and they provoked
Him to jealousy with their sins which they
committed, more than all that their fathers
had done. 23For they also built for them-
selves high places, *sacred* pillars, and
wooden images on every high hill and un-
der every green tree. 24And there were also
perverted persons[a] in the land. They did
according to all the abominations of the na-
tions which the LORD had cast out before
the children of Israel.

25It happened in the fifth year of King
Rē·ho·bō'am *that* Shī'shak king of Egypt

14:15 [a]That is, the Euphrates [b]Hebrew *Asherim*, Canaanite deities 14:24 [a]Hebrew *qadesh*, that is, one practicing sodomy and prostitution in religious rituals

14:13 Ahijah prophesied that all male descendants of Jeroboam, with the exception of Abijah, would die and their bodies would not be buried.

14:19, 29 the book of the chronicles of the kings: Not a reference to the OT books of 1 and 2 Chronicles but probably some sort of official journal kept by a member of the royal court (see 4:3).

14:24 perverted persons: Male prostitutes designated by a word meaning "separated ones." Certain pagan religions "separated" or "set apart" practitioners of imitative magic to promote fertility in nature. But biblical faith consistently argued that holiness involved an ethical and moral separateness. Children of God naturally manifest His character, i.e., ethical holiness.

came up against Jerusalem. [26]And he took
away the treasures of the house of the
LORD and the treasures of the king's house;
he took away everything. He also took
away all the gold shields which Solomon
had made. [27]Then King Rē·ho·bō'am made
bronze shields in their place, and commit-
ted *them* to the hands of the captains of the
guard, who guarded the doorway of the
king's house. [28]And whenever the king en-
tered the house of the LORD, the guards
carried them, then brought them back into
the guardroom.

[29]Now the rest of the acts of
Rē·ho·bō'am, and all that he did, *are* they
not written in the book of the chronicles of
the kings of Judah? [30]And there was war
between Rē·ho·bō'am and Jer·o·bō'am all
their days. [31]So Rē·ho·bō'am rested with
his fathers, and was buried with his fathers
in the City of David. His mother's name
was Nā'a·mah, an Am'mon·ī·tess. Then
A·bī'jam[a] his son reigned in his place.

CHAPTER 15

Abijam Reigns in Judah

In the eighteenth year of King Jer-
o·bō'am the son of Nē'bat, A·bī'jam be-
came king over Judah. [2]He reigned three
years in Jerusalem. His mother's name *was*
Mā'a·chah the granddaughter of A·bish'-
a·lom. [3]And he walked in all the sins of his
father, which he had done before him; his
heart was not loyal to the LORD his God, as
was the heart of his father David. [4]Never-
theless for David's sake the LORD his God
gave him a lamp in Jerusalem, by setting
up his son after him and by establishing Je-
rusalem; [5]because David did *what was* right
in the eyes of the LORD, and had not turned
aside from anything that He commanded
him all the days of his life, except in the
matter of Ū·rī'ah the Hit'tīte. [6]And there
was war between Rē·ho·bō'am[a] and
Jer·o·bō'am all the days of his life. [7]Now
the rest of the acts of A·bī'jam, and all that
he did, *are* they not written in the book of
the chronicles of the kings of Judah? And
there was war between A·bī'jam and
Jer·o·bō'am.

[8]So A·bī'jam rested with his fathers, and
they buried him in the City of David. Then
Ā'sa his son reigned in his place.

Asa Reigns in Judah

[9]In the twentieth year of Jer·o·bō'am
king of Israel, Ā'sa became king over Ju-
dah. [10]And he reigned forty-one years in
Jerusalem. His grandmother's name *was*
Mā'a·chah the granddaughter of A·bish'-
a·lom. [11]Ā'sa did *what was* right in the eyes
of the LORD, as *did* his father David. [12]And
he banished the perverted persons[a] from
the land, and removed all the idols that his
fathers had made. [13]Also he removed
Mā'a·chah his grandmother from *being*
queen mother, because she had made an
obscene image of A·shē'rah.[a] And Ā'sa cut
down her obscene image and burned *it* by
the Brook Kid'ron. [14]But the high places
were not removed. Nevertheless Ā'sa's
heart was loyal to the LORD all his days.
[15]He also brought into the house of the
LORD the things which his father had dedi-
cated, and the things which he himself had
dedicated: silver and gold and utensils.

[16]Now there was war between Ā'sa and
Bā'a·sha king of Israel all their days. [17]And

14:31 [a]Spelled *Abijah* in 2 Chronicles 12:16ff
15:6 [a]Following Masoretic Text, Septuagint, Targum, and Vulgate; some Hebrew manuscripts and Syriac read *Abijam.* 15:12 [a]Hebrew *qedeshim,* that is, those practicing sodomy and prostitution in religious rituals
15:13 [a]A Canaanite goddess

15:17–22 A border dispute over districts in Benjamin, which Israel claimed. Under **Baasha**, Israel was able to press south and claim **Ramah**, just five miles (8 km) north of Jerusalem. He **built** (fortified) Ramah because of its strategic location on a main highway between north and south. This allowed him to safeguard the new border and prohibit his subjects from worshiping in Jerusalem.

Bā′a·sha king of Israel came up against
Judah, and built Rā′mah, that he might
let none go out or come in to Ā′sa king
of Judah. 18Then Ā′sa took all the silver
and gold *that was* left in the treasuries of
the house of the LORD and the treasuries
of the king's house, and delivered
them into the hand of his servants.
And King Ā′sa sent them to Ben-Hā′dad
the son of Tabrim′mon, the son of
Hē′zi·on, king of Syria, who dwelt in
Damascus, saying, 19"*Let there be* a treaty
between you and me, as there was between
my father and your father. See, I have
sent you a present of silver and gold. Come
and break your treaty with Bā′a·sha king
of Israel, so that he will withdraw from
me."
20So Ben-Hā′dad heeded King Ā′sa, and
sent the captains of his armies against the
cities of Israel. He attacked Ī′jon, Dan, Abel
Beth Mā′a·chah, and all Chin′ne·roth, with
all the land of Naph′ta·lī. 21Now it hap-
pened, when Bā′a·sha heard *it,* that he
stopped building Rā′mah, and remained
in Tir′zah.
22Then King Ā′sa made a proclamation
throughout all Judah; none *was* exempted.
And they took away the stones and timber
of Rā′mah, which Bā′a·sha had used for
building; and with them King Ā′sa built
Gē′ba of Benjamin, and Miz′pah.
23The rest of all the acts of Ā′sa, all
his might, all that he did, and the cities
which he built, *are* they not written in
the book of the chronicles of the kings of
Judah? But in the time of his old age
he was diseased in his feet. 24So Ā′sa
rested with his fathers, and was buried
with his fathers in the City of David his fa-
ther. Then Je·hosh′a·phat his son reigned
in his place.

Nadab Reigns in Israel

25Now Nā′dab the son of Jer·o·bō′am
became king over Israel in the second year
of Ā′sa king of Judah, and he reigned over
Israel two years. 26And he did evil in the
sight of the LORD, and walked in the way of
his father, and in his sin by which he had
made Israel sin.
27Then Bā′a·sha the son of A·hī′jah, of
the house of Is′sa·char, conspired against
him. And Bā′a·sha killed him at Gib′-
be·thon, which *belonged* to the Phi·lis′tines,
while Nā′dab and all Israel laid siege to
Gib′be·thon. 28Bā′a·sha killed him in the
third year of Ā′sa king of Judah, and
reigned in his place. 29And it was so, when
he became king, *that* he killed all the house
of Jer·o·bō′am. He did not leave to
Jer·o·bō′am anyone that breathed, until he
had destroyed him, according to the word
of the LORD which He had spoken by His
servant A·hī′jah the Shī′lo·nīte, 30because
of the sins of Jer·o·bō′am, which he had
sinned and by which he had made Israel
sin, because of his provocation with which
he had provoked the LORD God of Israel to
anger.
31Now the rest of the acts of Nā′dab,
and all that he did, *are* they not written
in the book of the chronicles of the kings of
Israel? 32And there was war between
Ā′sa and Bā′a·sha king of Israel all their
days.

Baasha Reigns in Israel

33In the third year of Ā′sa king of Judah,
Bā′a·sha the son of A·hī′jah became king
over all Israel in Tir′zah, and *reigned*
twenty-four years. 34He did evil in the sight
of the LORD, and walked in the way of
Jer·o·bō′am, and in his sin by which he had
made Israel sin.

15:18, 19 During the ninth century B.C. **Damascus** (Syria) allied itself with various Aramean kingdoms and became a serious threat to Israel's northeast. The kings of Damascus were frequently named **Ben-Hadad** (meaning "Son of Hadad," the Syrian god). Asa enticed the first Ben-Hadad, king of Syria, to invade Israel from the northeast, hoping to relieve military pressure on Jerusalem in the south.

CHAPTER 16

Then the word of the LORD came to Jē'hū the son of Ha·nā'nī, against Bā'a·sha, saying: 2"Inasmuch as I lifted you out of the dust and made you ruler over My people Israel, and you have walked in the way of Jer·o·bō'am, and have made My people Israel sin, to provoke Me to anger with their sins, 3surely I will take away the posterity of Bā'a·sha and the posterity of his house, and I will make your house like the house of Jer·o·bō'am the son of Nē'bat. 4The dogs shall eat whoever belongs to Bā'a·sha and dies in the city, and the birds of the air shall eat whoever dies in the fields."

5Now the rest of the acts of Bā'a·sha, what he did, and his might, *are* they not written in the book of the chronicles of the kings of Israel? 6So Bā'a·sha rested with his fathers and was buried in Tir'zah. Then Ē'lah his son reigned in his place.

7And also the word of the LORD came by the prophet Jē'hū the son of Ha·nā'nī against Bā'a·sha and his house, because of all the evil that he did in the sight of the LORD in provoking Him to anger with the work of his hands, in being like the house of Jer·o·bō'am, and because he killed them.

Elah Reigns in Israel

8In the twenty-sixth year of Ā'sa king of Judah, Ē'lah the son of Bā'a·sha became king over Israel, *and reigned* two years in Tir'zah. 9Now his servant Zim'rī, commander of half *his* chariots, conspired against him as he was in Tir'zah drinking himself drunk in the house of Ar'za, steward of *his* house in Tir'zah. 10And Zim'rī went in and struck him and killed him in the twenty-seventh year of Ā'sa king of Judah, and reigned in his place.

11Then it came to pass, when he began to reign, as soon as he was seated on his throne, *that* he killed all the household of Bā'a·sha; he did not leave him one male, neither of his relatives nor of his friends. 12Thus Zim'rī destroyed all the household of Bā'a·sha, according to the word of the LORD, which He spoke against Bā'a·sha by Jē'hū the prophet, 13for all the sins of Bā'a·sha and the sins of Ē'lah his son, by which they had sinned and by which they had made Israel sin, in provoking the LORD God of Israel to anger with their idols.

14Now the rest of the acts of Ē'lah, and all that he did, *are* they not written in the book of the chronicles of the kings of Israel?

Zimri Reigns in Israel

15In the twenty-seventh year of Ā'sa king of Judah, Zim'rī had reigned in Tir'zah seven days. And the people *were* encamped against Gib'be·thon, which *belonged* to the Phi·lis'tines. 16Now the people *who were* encamped heard it said, "Zim'rī has conspired and also has killed the king." So all Israel made Om'rī, the commander of the army, king over Israel that day in the camp. 17Then Om'rī and all Israel with him went up from Gib'be·thon, and they besieged Tir'zah. 18And it happened, when Zim'rī saw that the city was taken, that he went into the citadel of the king's house and burned the king's house down upon himself with fire, and died, 19because of the sins which he had committed in doing evil in the sight of the LORD, in walking in the way of Jer·o·bō'am, and in his sin which he had committed to make Israel sin.

20Now the rest of the acts of Zim'rī, and the treason he committed, *are* they not written in the book of the chronicles of the kings of Israel?

16:1 Jehu: A prophet. Not to be confused with Jehu, the 10th king of Israel (see 19:16, 17). It seems likely that **Hanani**, Jehu's father, was the seer who prophesied against King Asa's alliance with Syria (see also 2 Chr. 16:7–10).

Omri Reigns in Israel

21Then the people of Israel were divided into two parts: half of the people followed Tib′nī the son of Gī′nath, to make him king, and half followed Om′rī. 22But the people who followed Om′rī prevailed over the people who followed Tib′nī the son of Gī′nath. So Tib′nī died and Om′rī reigned. 23In the thirty-first year of Ā′sa king of Judah, Om′rī became king over Israel, *and reigned* twelve years. Six years he reigned in Tir′zah. 24And he bought the hill of Samaria from Shē′mer for two talents of silver; then he built on the hill, and called the name of the city which he built, Samaria, after the name of Shē′mer, owner of the hill. 25Om′rī did evil in the eyes of the LORD, and did worse than all who *were* before him. 26For he walked in all the ways of Jer·o·bō′am the son of Nē′bat, and in his sin by which he had made Israel sin, provoking the LORD God of Israel to anger with their idols.

27Now the rest of the acts of Om′rī which he did, and the might that he showed, *are* they not written in the book of the chronicles of the kings of Israel?

28So Om′rī rested with his fathers and was buried in Samaria. Then Ā′hab his son reigned in his place.

Ahab Reigns in Israel

29In the thirty-eighth year of Ā′sa king of Judah, Ā′hab the son of Om′rī became king over Israel; and Ā′hab the son of Om′rī reigned over Israel in Samaria twenty-two years. 30Now Ā′hab the son of Om′rī did evil in the sight of the LORD, more than all who *were* before him. 31And it came to pass, as though it had been a trivial thing for him to walk in the sins of Jer·o·bō′am the son of Nē′bat, that he took as wife Jez′e·bel the daughter of Eth·bā′al, king of the Sī·dō′ni·ans; and he went and served Bā′al and worshiped him. 32Then he set up an altar for Bā′al in the temple of Bā′al, which he had built in Samaria. 33And Ā′hab made a wooden image.[a] Ā′hab did more to provoke the LORD God of Israel to anger than all the kings of Israel who were before him. 34In his days Hī′el of Beth′el built Jericho. He laid its foundation with A·bī′ram his firstborn, and with his youngest *son* Sē′gub he set up its gates, according to the word of the LORD, which He had spoken through Joshua the son of Nun.[a]

CHAPTER 17

Elijah Proclaims a Drought

And E·lī′jah the Tish′bīte, of the inhabitants of Gil′ē·ad, said to Ā′hab, "*As* the LORD God of Israel lives, before whom I stand, there shall not be dew nor rain these years, except at my word."

2Then the word of the LORD came to

16:33 [a]Hebrew *Asherah,* a Canaanite goddess
16:34 [a]Compare Joshua 6:26

16:24 Samaria: An excellent capital city because it was militarily defensible and close to a major international highway. It remained the capital of the northern kingdom until its fall to the Assyrians in 722 B.C.

16:25–28 worse than all: Politically, **Omri** accomplished much during his brief reign. But the author of the Book of Kings is less impressed by political sagacity than by covenant faithfulness.

16:29 Asa's reign in Judah continued through the reigns of Jeroboam, Nadab, Baasha, Elah, Zimri, and Omri.

17:1 Without any introduction **Elijah** appears in the narrative. He reminds **Ahab** that Yahweh, not Baal, is **God of Israel** (see 16:31). Significantly, Elijah means "The LORD Is My God." His announcement that **dew** and **rain** would end was a direct challenge to Baal, the Canaanite god of storm and rain.

him, saying, 3"Get away from here and
turn eastward, and hide by the Brook
Chē'rith, which flows into the Jordan.
4And it will be *that* you shall drink from the
brook, and I have commanded the ravens
to feed you there."
5So he went and did according to the
word of the LORD, for he went and stayed
by the Brook Chē'rith, which flows into the
Jordan. 6The ravens brought him bread
and meat in the morning, and bread and
meat in the evening; and he drank from the
brook. 7And it happened after a while that
the brook dried up, because there had been
no rain in the land.

Elijah and the Widow

8Then the word of the LORD came to
him, saying, 9"Arise, go to Zar'e·phath,
which *belongs* to Sī'don, and dwell there.
See, I have commanded a widow there to
provide for you." 10So he arose and went to
Zar'e·phath. And when he came to the
gate of the city, indeed a widow *was* there
gathering sticks. And he called to her and
said, "Please bring me a little water in a
cup, that I may drink." 11And as she was
going to get *it*, he called to her and said,
"Please bring me a morsel of bread in your
hand."
12So she said, "As the LORD your God
lives, I do not have bread, only a handful of
flour in a bin, and a little oil in a jar; and
see, I *am* gathering a couple of sticks that I
may go in and prepare it for myself and
my son, that we may eat it, and die."
13And E·lī'jah said to her, "Do not fear;
go *and* do as you have said, but make me a
small cake from it first, and bring *it* to me;
and afterward make *some* for yourself and
your son. 14For thus says the LORD God of
Israel: 'The bin of flour shall not be used
up, nor shall the jar of oil run dry, until the
day the LORD sends rain on the earth.' "
15So she went away and did according to
the word of E·lī'jah; and she and he and
her household ate for *many* days. 16The bin
of flour was not used up, nor did the jar of
oil run dry, according to the word of the
LORD which He spoke by E·lī'jah.

Elijah Revives the Widow's Son

17Now it happened after these things
that the son of the woman who owned the
house became sick. And his sickness was
so serious that there was no breath left in
him. 18So she said to E·lī'jah, "What have I
to do with you, O man of God? Have you
come to me to bring my sin to remem-
brance, and to kill my son?"
19And he said to her, "Give me your
son." So he took him out of her arms and
carried him to the upper room where he
was staying, and laid him on his own bed.
20Then he cried out to the LORD and said,
"O LORD my God, have You also brought
tragedy on the widow with whom I lodge,
by killing her son?" 21And he stretched
himself out on the child three times, and
cried out to the LORD and said, "O LORD
my God, I pray, let this child's soul come
back to him." 22Then the LORD heard the
voice of E·lī'jah; and the soul of the child
came back to him, and he revived.
23And E·lī'jah took the child and
brought him down from the upper room
into the house, and gave him to his mother.
And E·lī'jah said, "See, your son lives!"
24Then the woman said to E·lī'jah,
"Now by this I know that you *are* a man of
God, *and* that the word of the LORD in your
mouth *is* the truth."

17:8–15 Elijah's first miracle provided an endless supply of flour and oil to a widow who, in faith, had given Elijah the last of her food. God will always provide for our needs when we respond to the needs of others.

17:9 Zarephath . . . Sidon: God was in command of nature, people, and circumstances, not only in Israel, but even in Jezebel's home region—the heart of Baal country.

17:23 This is the first biblical record of an individual's being raised from the dead.

ELIJAH: MAN OF FAITH AND FEELINGS

As one of the great Old Testament prophets, Elijah performed many miracles under the power of God. His ministry spanned the reigns of Ahab and Ahaziah in the northern kingdom of Israel, each of whom he confronted about their sin.

His courageous actions leave no doubt about the depth of Elijah's spiritual life, and his close fellowship with God was demonstrated through his power in prayer (1 Kin. 17:20–22; 18:36–38; James 5:17). Elijah is described as a "man of God" (1 Kin. 17:24). This phrase, one of several terms used to denote a prophet, stresses the nature of the prophet's relationship with the Lord. So Elijah was, above all else, God's man.

In this role he proclaimed a drought in Israel as punishment for Ahab's extreme wickedness (17:1). For three years and six months no rain or dew fell in the land. During this time the Lord hid Elijah and provided him sustenance, first by means of ravens who carried bread and meat to the prophet twice a day (v. 6) and later by the miraculously increased stores of a generous widow (vv. 15, 16).

In the third year of the drought Elijah emerged from hiding to publicly challenge the false prophets (18:24). His wise handling of the confrontation clearly revealed the weakness of Baal in contrast with the mighty power of God, and the people who witnessed Elijah's victory acknowledged the Lord as the one true God (v. 39).

Yet for all his faith and courage, Elijah was just as vulnerable to human weakness as anyone else (James 5:17). Soon after his miraculous triumph against the false prophets, Elijah's courage failed, and he allowed his emotions to overrule his judgment. At the most opportune moment for revival in years, he fled to the wilderness, intimidated by Jezebel's threats on his life. He fell into a deep depression, even asking the Lord to take his life (19:4).

Rather than immediately rebuking Elijah for his lack of faith, the Lord allowed the emotionally exhausted prophet to rest. He then sent an angel to minister to Elijah's physical needs (v. 5).

The food provided by the angel gave Elijah the strength to travel forty days and forty nights to Horeb, also known as Sinai. This journey, which may have been symbolic of the Israelites' wandering in the wilderness for forty years, probably served to remind Elijah of the spiritual lessons of the past and prepare him for the challenges to come.

After Elijah arrived at his destination, the Lord allowed him to express his feelings. The prophet's complaint reveals a man whose courage has given way to pride and self-pity: "I have been very zealous for the LORD God of hosts. . . . I alone am left; and they seek to take my life" (vv. 10, 14).

The Lord prescribes action as an antidote for Elijah's depression, and He reminds the prophet that things are not as bad as they seem: "Go. . . . I have reserved seven thousand in Israel, all whose knees have not bowed to Baal, and every mouth that has not kissed him" (vv. 15–18).

Elijah promptly departed and acted according to the Lord's instructions. His life was preserved, his enemies destroyed, and no further complaints from him are recorded in Scripture.

This man of God shows us that even the most dedicated servant will occasionally succumb to the weakness of human nature. But our forgiving God, who has supplied our physical needs in the past, can and will provide for our emotional needs as well.

We need never be afraid to tell Him what is in our hearts; He already knows and understands. ✦

CHAPTER 18

Elijah's Message to Ahab

And it came to pass *after* many days that
the word of the LORD came to E·lī'jah, in
the third year, saying, "Go, present your-
self to Ā'hab, and I will send rain on the
earth."
2So E·lī'jah went to present himself to
Ā'hab; and *there was* a severe famine in Sa-
maria. 3And Ā'hab had called Ō·ba·dī'ah,
who *was* in charge of *his* house. (Now
Ō·ba·dī'ah feared the LORD greatly. 4For so
it was, while Jez'e·bel massacred the
prophets of the LORD, that Ō·ba·dī'ah had
taken one hundred prophets and hidden
them, fifty to a cave, and had fed them
with bread and water.) 5And Ā'hab had
said to Ō·ba·dī'ah, "Go into the land to all
the springs of water and to all the brooks;
perhaps we may find grass to keep the
horses and mules alive, so that we will not
have to kill any livestock." 6So they di-
vided the land between them to explore it;
Ā'hab went one way by himself, and
Ō·ba·dī'ah went another way by himself.
7Now as Ō·ba·dī'ah was on his way,
suddenly E·lī'jah met him; and he recog-
nized him, and fell on his face, and said, "*Is*
that you, my lord E·lī'jah?"
8And he answered him, "*It is* I. Go, tell
your master, 'E·lī'jah *is here.*' "
9So he said, "How have I sinned, that
you are delivering your servant into the
hand of Ā'hab, to kill me? 10*As* the LORD
your God lives, there is no nation or king-
dom where my master has not sent some-
one to hunt for you; and when they said,
'*He is* not *here*,' he took an oath from the
kingdom or nation that they could not find
you. 11And now you say, 'Go, tell your
master, "E·lī'jah *is here*" '! 12And it shall
come to pass, *as soon as* I am gone from
you, that the Spirit of the LORD will carry
you to a place I do not know; so when I go
and tell Ā'hab, and he cannot find you, he

18:3 Obadiah: The officer in charge of Ahab's property. He was not the same person as the prophet by that name.

18:12 the Spirit of the LORD will carry you: It was known that the Lord was protecting Elijah, and it was thought He might put him in a place of safety (see 17:3). The Jericho prophets had the same response (2 Kin. 2:15, 16).

will kill me. But I your servant have feared
the LORD from my youth. 13Was it not re-
ported to my lord what I did when
Jez'e·bel killed the prophets of the LORD,
how I hid one hundred men of the LORD's
prophets, fifty to a cave, and fed them with
bread and water? 14And now you say, 'Go,
tell your master, "E·lī'jah *is here.*" ' He will
kill me!"

15Then E·lī'jah said, "*As* the LORD of
hosts lives, before whom I stand, I will
surely present myself to him today."

16So Ō·ba·dī'ah went to meet Ā'hab, and
told him; and Ā'hab went to meet E·lī'jah.

17Then it happened, when Ā'hab saw
E·lī'jah, that Ā'hab said to him, "*Is that*
you, O troubler of Israel?"

18And he answered, "I have not troubled
Israel, but you and your father's house
have, in that you have forsaken the com-
mandments of the LORD and have followed
the Bā'als. 19Now therefore, send *and*
gather all Israel to me on Mount Car'mel,
the four hundred and fifty prophets of
Bā'al, and the four hundred prophets
of A·shē'rah,[a] who eat at Jez'e·bel's
table."

Elijah's Mount Carmel Victory

20So Ā'hab sent for all the children of Is-
rael, and gathered the prophets together
on Mount Car'mel. 21And E·lī'jah came to
all the people, and said, "How long will
you falter between two opinions? If the
LORD *is* God, follow Him; but if Bā'al, fol-
low him." But the people answered him
not a word. 22Then E·lī'jah said to the peo-
ple, "I alone am left a prophet of the
LORD; but Bā'al's prophets *are* four hun-
dred and fifty men. 23Therefore let them
give us two bulls; and let them choose
one bull for themselves, cut it in pieces,
and lay *it* on the wood, but put no fire
under it; and I will prepare the other bull,
and lay *it* on the wood, but put no fire *un-
der it.* 24Then you call on the name of your
gods, and I will call on the name of the
LORD; and the God who answers by fire,
He is God."

So all the people answered and said, "It
is well spoken."

25Now E·lī'jah said to the prophets of
Bā'al, "Choose one bull for yourselves and
prepare *it* first, for you *are* many; and call
on the name of your god, but put no fire
under it."

26So they took the bull which was given
them, and they prepared *it,* and called on
the name of Bā'al from morning even till
noon, saying, "O Bā'al, hear us!" But *there
was* no voice; no one answered. Then they
leaped about the altar which they had
made.

27And so it was, at noon, that E·lī'jah
mocked them and said, "Cry aloud, for he
is a god; either he is meditating, or he is
busy, or he is on a journey, *or* perhaps he is
sleeping and must be awakened." 28So they
cried aloud, and cut themselves, as was
their custom, with knives and lances, until
the blood gushed out on them. 29And when
midday was past, they prophesied until
the *time* of the offering of the *evening* sacri-

18:19 [a]A Canaanite goddess

18:17 Ahab refused to accept responsibility for bringing God's judgment on Israel. Sometimes when we suffer from the consequences of our sin, pride prevents us from repenting and renewing our fellowship with God.

18:19 **Mount Carmel** was believed by ancient worshipers to be sacred to Baal, so that Elijah challenged Baal and Asherah on their own turf. Asherah was the mother-goddess of the fertility cult.

18:27 Elijah's sarcastic **he is a god** sets the stage for his scathing ridicule. Meditating and busy are probably euphemistic for defecation.

18:28 **cut themselves**: The action of mourners at a funeral. Each fall the fertility god was given a respectful burial so that he would arise in the spring. Perhaps this was the basis for these actions: trying to get Baal to rise from the dead and act. See Deut. 14:1.

fice. But *there was* no voice; no one an-
swered, no one paid attention.
30 Then E·lī′jah said to all the people,
"Come near to me." So all the people came
near to him. And he repaired the altar of
the LORD *that was* broken down. 31 And
E·lī′jah took twelve stones, according to
the number of the tribes of the sons of Ja-
cob, to whom the word of the LORD had
come, saying, "Israel shall be your name."[a]
32 Then with the stones he built an altar in
the name of the LORD; and he made a
trench around the altar large enough to
hold two seahs of seed. 33 And he put the
wood in order, cut the bull in pieces, and
laid *it* on the wood, and said, "Fill four wa-
terpots with water, and pour *it* on the
burnt sacrifice and on the wood." 34 Then
he said, "Do *it* a second time," and they
did *it* a second time; and he said, "Do *it* a
third time," and they did *it* a third time.
35 So the water ran all around the altar; and
he also filled the trench with water.
36 And it came to pass, at *the time of* the
offering of the *evening* sacrifice, that
E·lī′jah the prophet came near and said,
"LORD God of Abraham, Isaac, and Israel,
let it be known this day that You *are* God in
Israel and I *am* Your servant, and *that* I
have done all these things at Your word.
37 Hear me, O LORD, hear me, that this peo-
ple may know that You *are* the LORD God,
and *that* You have turned their hearts back
to You again."
38 Then the fire of the LORD fell and con-
sumed the burnt sacrifice, and the wood
and the stones and the dust, and it licked
up the water that *was* in the trench. 39 Now
when all the people saw *it,* they fell on
their faces; and they said, "The LORD, He *is*
God! The LORD, He *is* God!"
40 And E·lī′jah said to them, "Seize the
prophets of Bā′al! Do not let one of them
escape!" So they seized them; and E·lī′jah
brought them down to the Brook Kī′shon
and executed them there.

The Drought Ends

41 Then E·lī′jah said to Ā′hab, "Go up, eat
and drink; for *there is* the sound of abun-
dance of rain." 42 So Ā′hab went up to eat
and drink. And E·lī′jah went up to the top
of Car′mel; then he bowed down on the
ground, and put his face between his
knees, 43 and said to his servant, "Go up
now, look toward the sea."
So he went up and looked, and said,
"*There is* nothing." And seven times he
said, "Go again."
44 Then it came to pass the seventh *time,*
that he said, "There is a cloud, as small as a
man's hand, rising out of the sea!" So he
said, "Go up, say to Ā′hab, 'Prepare *your*
chariot, and go down before the rain stops
you.' "
45 Now it happened in the meantime that
the sky became black with clouds and
wind, and there was a heavy rain. So Ā′hab
rode away and went to Jez′rē·el. 46 Then the
hand of the LORD came upon E·lī′jah; and
he girded up his loins and ran ahead of
Ā′hab to the entrance of Jez′rē·el.

CHAPTER 19

Elijah Escapes from Jezebel

And Ā′hab told Jez′e·bel all that E·lī′jah
had done, also how he had executed all the
prophets with the sword. 2 Then Jez′e·bel
sent a messenger to E·lī′jah, saying, "So let
the gods do *to me,* and more also, if I do not
make your life as the life of one of them by
tomorrow about this time." 3 And when he
saw *that,* he arose and ran for his life, and

18:31 [a]Genesis 32:28

18:30 altar of the LORD: An ancient one ruined by lack of attention, or destroyed during Jezebel's tyranny (see 19:10).

18:46 Only by the miraculous hand of God could Elijah have successfully outrun Ahab's chariot over this distance, about 25 miles.

GOD'S STILL, SMALL VOICE

Claire Cloninger

To see the glorious in the commonplace, to find the holy in the everyday is the challenge at the heart of our lives as Christ-conscious believers. The perfect light of Jesus is *always* there, shining through the imperfect events and people in our lives. The exquisite patterns of His love are being formed and reformed, shifted and rearranged like jewels before our eyes in the small particulars of our lives every single day. The problem is that we aren't always able to see them.

How many Christians wait for that one hour on Sunday morning to hear from God, when He's been trying to whisper in our ears all week long? How many of us wait for that once-a-year retreat or seminar to give us the super-spiritual uplift, when God has been riding around in our cars with us, eating bacon and eggs with us, and working at our jobs with us every day of the year?

The perfect light of Jesus is *always* there.

went to Bē·er·shē'ba, which *belongs* to Judah, and left his servant there.
[4]But he himself went a day's journey into the wilderness, and came and sat down under a broom tree. And he prayed that he might die, and said, "It is enough! Now, LORD, take my life, for I *am* no better than my fathers!"
[5]Then as he lay and slept under a broom tree, suddenly an angel[a] touched him, and said to him, "Arise *and* eat." [6]Then he looked, and there by his head *was* a cake baked on coals, and a jar of water. So he ate and drank, and lay down again. [7]And the angel[a] of the LORD came back the second time, and touched him, and said, "Arise *and* eat, because the journey *is* too great for you." [8]So he arose, and ate and drank; and he went in the strength of that food forty days and forty nights as far as Hō'reb, the mountain of God.
[9]And there he went into a cave, and spent the night in that place; and behold, the word of the LORD *came* to him, and He said to him, "What are you doing here, E·lī'jah?"
[10]So he said, "I have been very zealous for the LORD God of hosts; for the children of Israel have forsaken Your covenant, torn down Your altars, and killed Your

19:5 [a]Or *Angel* 19:7 [a]Or *Angel*

19:8, 9 Horeb: A range of mountains, of which Mt. Sinai is the highest. It was the site of the covenant between God and Israel, to which Elijah's ministry was committed. The cave here and "the cleft of the rock" in Ex. 33:22 form one of the many parallels between Elijah's experience on this mountain and that of Moses. **What are you doing here?** A tender invitation for Elijah to verbalize his emotions.

prophets with the sword. I alone am left;
and they seek to take my life."

God's Revelation to Elijah

11Then He said, "Go out, and stand on
the mountain before the LORD." And be-
hold, the LORD passed by, and a great and
strong wind tore into the mountains and
broke the rocks in pieces before the LORD,
but the LORD *was* not in the wind; and after
the wind an earthquake, *but* the LORD *was*
not in the earthquake; 12and after the earth-
quake a fire, *but* the LORD *was* not in the
fire; and after the fire a still small voice.
13So it was, when E·lī'jah heard *it*, that
he wrapped his face in his mantle and
went out and stood in the entrance of the
cave. Suddenly a voice *came* to him, and
said, "What are you doing here, E·lī'jah?"
14And he said, "I have been very zealous
for the LORD God of hosts; because the
children of Israel have forsaken Your
covenant, torn down Your altars, and
killed Your prophets with the sword. I
alone am left; and they seek to take my
life."
15Then the LORD said to him: "Go, return
on your way to the Wilderness of Damas-
cus; and when you arrive, anoint Haz'a·el
as king over Syria. 16Also you shall anoint
Jē'hū the son of Nim'shī *as* king over Is-
rael. And E·lī'sha the son of Shā'phat of
Abel Me·hō'lah you shall anoint *as* prophet
in your place. 17It shall be *that* whoever es-
capes the sword of Haz'a·el, Jē'hū will kill;
and whoever escapes the sword of Jē'hū,
E·lī'sha will kill. 18Yet I have reserved
seven thousand in Israel, all whose knees
have not bowed to Bā'al, and every mouth
that has not kissed him."

Elisha Follows Elijah

19So he departed from there, and found
E·lī'sha the son of Shā'phat, who *was*
plowing *with* twelve yoke *of oxen* before
him, and he was with the twelfth. Then
E·lī'jah passed by him and threw his man-
tle on him. 20And he left the oxen and ran
after E·lī'jah, and said, "Please let me kiss
my father and my mother, and *then* I will
follow you."
And he said to him, "Go back again, for
what have I done to you?"
21So *E·lī'sha* turned back from him, and
took a yoke of oxen and slaughtered them
and boiled their flesh, using the oxen's
equipment, and gave it to the people, and
they ate. Then he arose and followed
E·lī'jah, and became his servant.

CHAPTER 20

Ahab Defeats the Syrians

Now Ben-Hā'dad the king of Syria
gathered all his forces together; thirty-two
kings *were* with him, with horses and char-
iots. And he went up and besieged Sa-
maria, and made war against it. 2Then he
sent messengers into the city to Ā'hab king
of Israel, and said to him, "Thus says Ben-
Hā'dad: 3'Your silver and your gold *are*
mine; your loveliest wives and children are
mine.' "
4And the king of Israel answered and
said, "My lord, O king, just as you say, I
and all that I have *are* yours."

19:15–18 Although there was no longer a threat that Baalism would become the official religion of Israel, it was still necessary to destroy the dynasty of Omri and the paganizing tendencies of that royal family. Elijah received instructions to anoint three persons who would have a vital role in this task. He would select Elisha (vv. 19–21), who would in turn anoint **Hazael** (2 Kin. 8:13) and **Jehu** (2 Kin. 9:1–3). Hazael later became the king of Syria (see also 2 Kin. 8:13–15); Jehu, the 10th king of Israel (see 2 Kin. 9; 10). Through the prophet Hosea God would pronounce judgment on Jehu for his excessive violence (see Hos. 1:3–5 and note).

19:19 By throwing his **mantle** on Elisha, the prophet Elijah was saying that he elected the young farmer to receive the authority and power of the prophet's office and to become his successor.

5 Then the messengers came back and
said, "Thus speaks Ben-Hā'dad, saying,
'Indeed I have sent to you, saying, "You
shall deliver to me your silver and your
gold, your wives and your children"; 6 but I
will send my servants to you tomorrow
about this time, and they shall search your
house and the houses of your servants.
And it shall be, *that* whatever is pleasant in
your eyes, they will put *it* in their hands
and take *it*.' "
7 So the king of Israel called all the elders
of the land, and said, "Notice, please, and
see how this *man* seeks trouble, for he sent
to me for my wives, my children, my silver,
and my gold; and I did not deny him."
8 And all the elders and all the people
said to him, "Do not listen or consent."
9 Therefore he said to the messengers of
Ben-Hā'dad, "Tell my lord the king, 'All
that you sent for to your servant the first
time I will do, but this thing I cannot do.' "

And the messengers departed and
brought back word to him.
10 Then Ben-Hā'dad sent to him and
said, "The gods do so to me, and more also,
if enough dust is left of Samaria for a hand-
ful for each of the people who follow me."
11 So the king of Israel answered and
said, "Tell *him*, 'Let not the one who puts
on *his armor* boast like the one who takes *it*
off.' "
12 And it happened when *Ben-Hā'dad*
heard this message, as he and the kings
were drinking at the command post, that he
said to his servants, "Get ready." And they
got ready to attack the city.
13 Suddenly a prophet approached Ā'hab
king of Israel, saying, "Thus says the LORD:
'Have you seen all this great multitude?
Behold, I will deliver it into your hand to-
day, and you shall know that I *am* the
LORD.' "
14 So Ā'hab said, "By whom?"

And he said, "Thus says the LORD: 'By
the young leaders of the provinces.' "

Then he said, "Who will set the battle in
order?"

And he answered, "You."
15 Then he mustered the young leaders of
the provinces, and there were two hundred
and thirty-two; and after them he mus-
tered all the people, all the children of Is-
rael—seven thousand.
16 So they went out at noon. Meanwhile
Ben-Hā'dad and the thirty-two kings help-
ing him were getting drunk at the com-
mand post. 17 The young leaders of the
provinces went out first. And Ben-Hā'dad
sent out *a patrol*, and they told him, saying,
"Men are coming out of Samaria!" 18 So he
said, "If they have come out for peace, take
them alive; and if they have come out for
war, take them alive."
19 Then these young leaders of the
provinces went out of the city with the
army which followed them. 20 And each
one killed his man; so the Syrians fled, and
Israel pursued them; and Ben-Hā'dad the
king of Syria escaped on a horse with the
cavalry. 21 Then the king of Israel went out
and attacked the horses and chariots, and
killed the Syrians with a great slaughter.
22 And the prophet came to the king of Is-
rael and said to him, "Go, strengthen your-
self; take note, and see what you should
do, for in the spring of the year the king of
Syria will come up against you."

The Syrians Again Defeated

23 Then the servants of the king of Syria
said to him, "Their gods *are* gods of the

20:11 Ahab's response to Ben-Hadad's threat essentially means that he should not declare victory before he has fought the battle.

20:23–25 The Syrian advisors identified two tactics that they thought would bring them victory in another battle: (1) Fight on the plains of Transjordan where the mountain gods of Israel would be helpless (v. 23). (2) Use military men, not (halfhearted) vassal kings as generals (v. 24). But the Syrians were to learn that the Lord of Israel was not limited by geography.

hills. Therefore they were stronger than
we; but if we fight against them in the
plain, surely we will be stronger than
they. 24So do this thing: Dismiss the kings,
each from his position, and put captains in
their places; 25and you shall muster an
army like the army that you have lost,
horse for horse and chariot for chariot.
Then we will fight against them in the
plain; surely we will be stronger than
they."

And he listened to their voice and did
so.

26So it was, in the spring of the year, that
Ben-Hā'dad mustered the Syrians and
went up to Ā'phek to fight against Israel.
27And the children of Israel were mustered
and given provisions, and they went
against them. Now the children of Israel
encamped before them like two little flocks
of goats, while the Syrians filled the coun-
tryside.

28Then a man of God came and spoke
to the king of Israel, and said, "Thus
says the LORD: 'Because the Syrians have
said, "The LORD *is* God of the hills, but He
is not God of the valleys," therefore I
will deliver all this great multitude into
your hand, and you shall know that I *am*
the LORD.' " 29And they encamped oppo-
site each other for seven days. So it was
that on the seventh day the battle was
joined; and the children of Israel killed one
hundred thousand foot soldiers *of* the Syr-
ians in one day. 30But the rest fled to
Ā'phek, into the city; then a wall fell on
twenty-seven thousand of the men *who
were* left.

And Ben-Hā'dad fled and went into the
city, into an inner chamber.

Ahab's Treaty with Ben-Hadad

31Then his servants said to him, "Look
now, we have heard that the kings of the
house of Israel *are* merciful kings. Please,
let us put sackcloth around our waists
and ropes around our heads, and go
out to the king of Israel; perhaps he
will spare your life." 32So they wore sack-
cloth around their waists and *put* ropes
around their heads, and came to the
king of Israel and said, "Your serv-
ant Ben-Hā'dad says, 'Please let me
live.' "

And he said, "*Is* he still alive? He *is* my
brother."

33Now the men were watching closely to
see whether *any sign of mercy would come*
from him; and they quickly grasped *at this
word* and said, "Your brother Ben-Hā'-
dad."

So he said, "Go, bring him." Then Ben-
Hā'dad came out to him; and he had him
come up into the chariot.

34So *Ben-Hā'dad* said to him, "The cities
which my father took from your father I
will restore; and you may set up market-
places for yourself in Damascus, as my fa-
ther did in Samaria."

Then *Āhab* said, "I will send you away
with this treaty." So he made a treaty with
him and sent him away.

Ahab Condemned

35Now a certain man of the sons of the
prophets said to his neighbor by the word
of the LORD, "Strike me, please." And the
man refused to strike him. 36Then he said
to him, "Because you have not obeyed the
voice of the LORD, surely, as soon as you
depart from me, a lion shall kill you." And

20:28 God gave the victory to Ahab not because of any righteousness on his part, but so the Syrians could know the power of God.

20:32 By calling Ben-Hadad **my brother**, Ahab showed his willingness to make a treaty with the defeated Syrian king (see v. 34).

20:35, 36 Any opposition to God's command through the prophets was opposition to God Himself. **Sons of the prophets** refers to the disciples of the prophetical schools which sought to preserve and promote the Law of Moses.

as soon as he left him, a lion found him and
killed him.
37And he found another man, and said,
"Strike me, please." So the man struck him,
inflicting a wound. 38Then the prophet de-
parted and waited for the king by the road,
and disguised himself with a bandage over
his eyes. 39Now as the king passed by, he
cried out to the king and said, "Your ser-
vant went out into the midst of the battle;
and there, a man came over and brought a
man to me, and said, 'Guard this man; if by
any means he is missing, your life shall be
for his life, or else you shall pay a talent of
silver.' 40While your servant was busy here
and there, he was gone."

Then the king of Israel said to him, "So
shall your judgment *be;* you yourself have
decided *it.*"
41And he hastened to take the bandage
away from his eyes; and the king of Israel
recognized him as one of the prophets.
42Then he said to him, "Thus says the LORD:
'Because you have let slip out of *your* hand
a man whom I appointed to utter destruc-
tion, therefore your life shall go for his life,
and your people for his people.' "
43So the king of Israel went to his house
sullen and displeased, and came to Sa-
maria.

CHAPTER 21

Naboth Is Murdered for His Vineyard

And it came to pass after these things
that Nā′both the Jez′rē·el·īte had a vine-
yard which *was* in Jez′rē·el, next to the
palace of Ā′hab king of Samaria. 2So
Ā′hab spoke to Nā′both, saying, "Give
me your vineyard, that I may have it for
a vegetable garden, because it *is* near, next
to my house; and for it I will give you
a vineyard better than it. *Or,* if it seems
good to you, I will give you its worth in
money."
3But Nā′both said to Ā′hab, "The LORD
forbid that I should give the inheritance of
my fathers to you!"
4So Ā′hab went into his house sullen and
displeased because of the word which
Nā′both the Jez′rē·el·īte had spoken to
him; for he had said, "I will not give you
the inheritance of my fathers." And he lay
down on his bed, and turned away his
face, and would eat no food. 5But Jez′e·bel
his wife came to him, and said to him,
"Why is your spirit so sullen that you eat
no food?"
6He said to her, "Because I spoke to
Nā′both the Jez′rē·el·īte, and said to him,
'Give me your vineyard for money; or else,
if it pleases you, I will give you *another*
vineyard for it.' And he answered, 'I will
not give you my vineyard.' "
7Then Jez′e·bel his wife said to him,
"You now exercise authority over Israel!
Arise, eat food, and let your heart be cheer-
ful; I will give you the vineyard of Nā′both
the Jez′rē·el·īte."
8And she wrote letters in Ā′hab's name,
sealed *them* with his seal, and sent the let-
ters to the elders and the nobles who *were*
dwelling in the city with Nā′both. 9She
wrote in the letters, saying,

20:43 Notice that instead of repenting of his guilt, Ahab became "sullen and displeased." Rather than resenting corrections, mature Christians are happy to take the opportunity to set things right.

21:3–7 The ancient prohibition against the sale of one's inheritance may no longer have been practiced during the monarchy, but the idea still seemed appalling to Naboth. **sullen and displeased**: Ahab still had enough respect for the law to know he was helpless before it. As the daughter of the king of Sidon (see 16:31), Jezebel assumed the king was a law to himself—an absolute monarch.

21:4, 5 Ahab's behavior was certainly not worthy of a king. He apparently had abdicated some of his authority to Jezebel and the chain of command seems to have been reversed, with Jezebel giving orders to her husband.

Proclaim a fast, and seat Nā′both with high honor among the people; [10]and seat two men, scoundrels, before him to bear witness against him, saying, You have blasphemed God and the king. *Then* take him out, and stone him, that he may die.

[11]So the men of his city, the elders and nobles who were inhabitants of his city, did as Jez′e•bel had sent to them, as it *was* written in the letters which she had sent to them. [12]They proclaimed a fast, and seated Nā′both with high honor among the people. [13]And two men, scoundrels, came in and sat before him; and the scoundrels witnessed against him, against Nā′both, in the presence of the people, saying, "Nā′both has blasphemed God and the king!" Then they took him outside the city and stoned him with stones, so that he died. [14]Then they sent to Jez′e•bel, saying, "Nā′both has been stoned and is dead."

[15]And it came to pass, when Jez′e•bel heard that Nā′both had been stoned and was dead, that Jez′e•bel said to Ā′hab, "Arise, take possession of the vineyard of Nā′both the Jez′rē•el•īte, which he refused to give you for money; for Nā′both is not alive, but dead." [16]So it was, when Ā′hab heard that Nā′both was dead, that Ā′hab got up and went down to take possession of the vineyard of Nā′both the Jez′rē•el•īte.

The LORD Condemns Ahab

[17]Then the word of the LORD came to E•lī′jah the Tish′bīte, saying, [18]"Arise, go down to meet Ā′hab king of Israel, who *lives* in Samaria. There *he is,* in the vineyard of Nā′both, where he has gone down to take possession of it. [19]You shall speak to him, saying, 'Thus says the LORD: "Have you murdered and also taken possession?" ' And you shall speak to him, saying, 'Thus says the LORD: "In the place where dogs licked the blood of Nā′both, dogs shall lick your blood, even yours." ' "

[20]So Ā′hab said to E•lī′jah, "Have you found me, O my enemy?"

And he answered, "I have found *you,* because you have sold yourself to do evil in the sight of the LORD: [21]'Behold, I will bring calamity on you. I will take away your posterity, and will cut off from Ā′hab every male in Israel, both bond and free. [22]I will make your house like the house of Jer•o•bō′am the son of Nē′bat, and like the house of Bā′a•sha the son of A•hī′jah, because of the provocation with which you have provoked *Me* to anger, and made Israel sin.' [23]And concerning Jez′e•bel the LORD also spoke, saying, 'The dogs shall eat Jez′e•bel by the wall[a] of Jez′rē•el.' [24]The dogs shall eat whoever belongs to Ā′hab and dies in the city, and the birds of the air shall eat whoever dies in the field."

[25]But there was no one like Ā′hab who sold himself to do wickedness in the sight of the LORD, because Jez′e•bel his wife stirred him up. [26]And he behaved very abominably in following idols, according to all *that* the Am′o•rītes had done, whom the LORD had cast out before the children of Israel.

[27]So it was, when Ā′hab heard those words, that he tore his clothes and put sackcloth on his body, and fasted and lay in sackcloth, and went about mourning.

21:23 [a]Following Masoretic Text and Septuagint; some Hebrew manuscripts, Syriac, Targum, and Vulgate read *plot of ground* (compare 2 Kings 9:36).

21:10 two men . . . to bear witness: Two reprobates (lit. "worthless men") acting as witnesses to lend credence to the legal proceedings (see Deut. 17:6, 7; 19:15 and note on Num. 35:30–32).

21:15 take possession: Property of public criminals reverted to the crown.

21:20–24 The prophet delivered his terrible message not because of his personal perception, but because Ahab had done a great **evil in the sight of the LORD**. The phrase **sold yourself** indicates the power of sin. See also v. 25.

28 And the word of the LORD came to E·lī′jah the Tish′bīte, saying, 29 "See how Ā′hab has humbled himself before Me? Because he has humbled himself before Me, I will not bring the calamity in his days. In the days of his son I will bring the calamity on his house."

CHAPTER 22

Micaiah Warns Ahab

Now three years passed without war between Syria and Israel. 2 Then it came to pass, in the third year, that Je·hosh′a·phat the king of Judah went down to *visit* the king of Israel.

3 And the king of Israel said to his servants, "Do you know that Rā′moth in Gil′ē·ad *is* ours, but we hesitate to take it out of the hand of the king of Syria?" 4 So he said to Je·hosh′a·phat, "Will you go with me to fight at Rā′moth Gil′ē·ad?"

Je·hosh′a·phat said to the king of Israel, "I *am* as you *are,* my people as your people, my horses as your horses." 5 Also Je·hosh′a·phat said to the king of Israel, "Please inquire for the word of the LORD today."

6 Then the king of Israel gathered the prophets together, about four hundred men, and said to them, "Shall I go against Rā′moth Gil′ē·ad to fight, or shall I refrain?"

So they said, "Go up, for the Lord will deliver *it* into the hand of the king."

7 And Je·hosh′a·phat said, "*Is there* not still a prophet of the LORD here, that we may inquire of Him?"[a]

8 So the king of Israel said to Je·hosh′a·phat, "*There is* still one man, Mī·cāi′ah the son of Im′lah, by whom we may inquire of the LORD; but I hate him, because he does not prophesy good concerning me, but evil."

And Je·hosh′a·phat said, "Let not the king say such things!"

9 Then the king of Israel called an officer and said, "Bring Mī·cāi′ah the son of Im′lah quickly!"

10 The king of Israel and Je·hosh′a·phat the king of Judah, having put on *their* robes, sat each on his throne, at a threshing floor at the entrance of the gate of Samaria; and all the prophets prophesied before them. 11 Now Zed·e·kī′ah the son of Che·nā′a·nah had made horns of iron for himself; and he said, "Thus says the LORD: 'With these you shall gore the Syrians until they are destroyed.' " 12 And all the prophets prophesied so, saying, "Go up to Rā′moth Gil′ē·ad and prosper, for the LORD will deliver *it* into the king's hand."

13 Then the messenger who had gone to call Mī·cāi′ah spoke to him, saying, "Now listen, the words of the prophets with one accord encourage the king. Please, let your word be like the word of one of them, and speak encouragement."

14 And Mī·cāi′ah said, "*As* the LORD lives, whatever the LORD says to me, that I will speak."

15 Then he came to the king; and the king said to him, "Mī·cāi′ah, shall we go to war against Rā′moth Gil′ē·ad, or shall we refrain?"

And he answered him, "Go and prosper, for the LORD will deliver *it* into the hand of the king!"

22:7 [a]Or *him*

22:1 Jehoshaphat succeeded Asa on the throne of Judah.

22:8 For Ahab, prophecy was a form of magic in which the prophet manipulated God. For **Jehoshaphat**, the prophet was a mouthpiece for God through whom His will was made known to man.

22:15–17 Micaiah's first prophecy was a sarcastic repetition of the advice given by the false prophets (see vv. 12, 13). **tell me nothing but the truth**: To this Micaiah responded, "if you want to know the truth, I saw all Israel scattered" (v. 17). **no shepherd . . . no master**: Ahab could not have escaped the meaning that he would be killed in the campaign.

✦2 Kings✦

Written by the same unknown prophet as 1 Kings, 2 Kings shows that the collapse of Israel and Judah occurred because the nations worshiped idols and committed other sins instead of following God.

2 Kings describes several corrupt kings—including Ahaziah, Hoshea, and Manasseh—and a few righteous kings like Jeroboam II, Hezekiah, and Josiah. God led the divided kingdom through both defeat and prosperity, depending on the morality of the kings.

The mentoring relationship between Elijah and Elisha, which began in 1 Kings, comes to a dramatic conclusion (2 Kin. 2). Their example demonstrates the importance of "passing the mantle" to the next generation. Elisha took on Elijah's responsibilities in ministering to the northern kingdom of Israel, but the nation did not respond. Ultimately, the sins of the leaders and the nation resulted in judgment, deportation, and the destruction of the temple. Assyria conquered Israel in 722 B.C.; Babylon conquered Judah in 586 B.C. ✦

CHAPTER 1

God Judges Ahaziah

Moab rebelled against Israel after the
death of Ā'hab.
2Now Ā·ha·zī'ah fell through the lattice
of his upper room in Samaria, and was in-
jured; so he sent messengers and said to
them, "Go, inquire of Bā'al-Zebub, the god
of Ek'ron, whether I shall recover from this
injury." 3But the angel[a] of the LORD said to
E·lī'jah the Tish'bīte, "Arise, go up to meet
the messengers of the king of Samaria, and
say to them, '*Is it* because *there is* no God in
Israel *that* you are going to inquire of Bā'al-
Zebub, the god of Ek'ron?' 4Now therefore,
thus says the LORD: 'You shall not come
down from the bed to which you have
gone up, but you shall surely die.' " So
E·lī'jah departed.
5And when the messengers returned to
him, he said to them, "Why have you come
back?"
6So they said to him, "A man came up to
meet us, and said to us, 'Go, return to the
king who sent you, and say to him, "Thus
says the LORD: '*Is it* because *there is* no God
in Israel *that* you are sending to inquire of
Bā'al-Zebub, the god of Ek'ron? Therefore
you shall not come down from the bed to
which you have gone up, but you shall
surely die.' " ' "
7Then he said to them, "What kind of

1:3 [a]Or *Angel*

1:2 Baal-Zebub: A form of Baal worshiped at the Philistine city of Ekron. His name may imply he was the producer and controller of disease-bearing flies, or it may be a derisive play on the name Baal-Zebul, "Baal the Prince" or "Exalted Prince."

man *was it* who came up to meet you and
told you these words?"
8So they answered him, "A hairy man
wearing a leather belt around his waist."
And he said, "It *is* E·lī'jah the Tish'bīte."
9Then the king sent to him a captain of
fifty with his fifty men. So he went up to
him; and there he was, sitting on the top of
a hill. And he spoke to him: "Man of God,
the king has said, 'Come down!' "
10So E·lī'jah answered and said to the
captain of fifty, "If I *am* a man of God, then
let fire come down from heaven and con-
sume you and your fifty men." And fire
came down from heaven and consumed
him and his fifty. 11Then he sent to him an-
other captain of fifty with his fifty men.
And he answered and said to him:
"Man of God, thus has the king said,
'Come down quickly!' "
12So E·lī'jah answered and said to them,
"If I *am* a man of God, let fire come down
from heaven and consume you and your
fifty men." And the fire of God came down
from heaven and consumed him and his
fifty.
13Again, he sent a third captain of fifty
with his fifty men. And the third captain of
fifty went up, and came and fell on his
knees before E·lī'jah, and pleaded with
him, and said to him: "Man of God, please
let my life and the life of these fifty ser-
vants of yours be precious in your sight.
14Look, fire has come down from heaven
and burned up the first two captains of
fifties with their fifties. But let my life now
be precious in your sight."
15And the angel[a] of the LORD said to
E·lī'jah, "Go down with him; do not be
afraid of him." So he arose and went down
with him to the king. 16Then he said to him,
"Thus says the LORD: 'Because you have
sent messengers to inquire of Bā'al-Zebub,
the god of Ek'ron, *is it* because *there is* no
God in Israel to inquire of His word?
Therefore you shall not come down from
the bed to which you have gone up, but
you shall surely die.' "
17So *Ā·ha·zī'ah* died according to the
word of the LORD which E·lī'jah had spo-
ken. Because he had no son, Je·hō'ram[a] be-
came king in his place, in the second year
of Je·hō'ram the son of Je·hosh'a·phat,
king of Judah.
18Now the rest of the acts of Ā·ha·zī'ah
which he did, *are* they not written in the
book of the chronicles of the kings of Is-
rael?

CHAPTER 2

Elijah Ascends to Heaven

And it came to pass, when the LORD was
about to take up E·lī'jah into heaven by a
whirlwind, that E·lī'jah went with E·lī'sha
from Gil'gal. 2Then E·lī'jah said to E·lī'sha,
"Stay here, please, for the LORD has sent
me on to Beth'el."
But E·lī'sha said, "*As* the LORD lives,
and *as* your soul lives, I will not leave
you!" So they went down to Beth'el.

1:15 [a]Or *Angel* 1:17 [a]The son of Ahab king of Israel (compare 3:1)

1:8 A hairy man: The messengers probably refer to the "robe of coarse hair" (see Zech. 13:4; Matt. 3:4) which distinguished the attire of the prophets. From the description Ahaziah knew it was Elijah.

1:9–12 The command **come down** called for the prophet of the Lord to be submissive to the idolatrous king, Ahaziah.

1:17 Both Jehoshaphat and Ahab had sons named Jehoram.

2:1–8 Gilgal . . . Bethel . . . Jericho . . . Jordan: Elijah was directed to take this route in order to visit and encourage the local prophetic schools one last time before his departure. Of several cities named Gilgal, this was probably the one located seven miles (11 km) northeast of Bethel. Jericho had been recently rebuilt (see 1 Kin. 16:34).

3 Now the sons of the prophets who *were*
at Beth′el came out to E·lī′sha, and said to
him, "Do you know that the LORD will take
away your master from over you today?"
And he said, "Yes, I know; keep silent!"
4 Then E·lī′jah said to him, "E·lī′sha,
stay here, please, for the LORD has sent me
on to Jericho."
But he said, "*As* the LORD lives, and *as*
your soul lives, I will not leave you!" So
they came to Jericho.
5 Now the sons of the prophets who *were*
at Jericho came to E·lī′sha and said to him,
"Do you know that the LORD will take
away your master from over you today?"
So he answered, "Yes, I know; keep
silent!"
6 Then E·lī′jah said to him, "Stay here,
please, for the LORD has sent me on to the
Jordan."
But he said, "*As* the LORD lives, and *as*
your soul lives, I will not leave you!" So
the two of them went on. 7 And fifty men of
the sons of the prophets went and stood
facing *them* at a distance, while the two of
them stood by the Jordan. 8 Now E·lī′jah
took his mantle, rolled *it* up, and struck the
water; and it was divided this way and
that, so that the two of them crossed over
on dry ground.
9 And so it was, when they had crossed
over, that E·lī′jah said to E·lī′sha, "Ask!
What may I do for you, before I am taken
away from you?"
E·lī′sha said, "Please let a double por-
tion of your spirit be upon me."
10 So he said, "You have asked a hard
thing. *Nevertheless,* if you see me *when I am*
taken from you, it shall be so for you; but if
not, it shall not be *so.*" 11 Then it happened,
as they continued on and talked, that sud-
denly a chariot of fire *appeared* with horses
of fire, and separated the two of them; and
E·lī′jah went up by a whirlwind into
heaven.
12 And E·lī′sha saw *it,* and he cried out,
"My father, my father, the chariot of Israel
and its horsemen!" So he saw him no more.
And he took hold of his own clothes and
tore them into two pieces. 13 He also took
up the mantle of E·lī′jah that had fallen
from him, and went back and stood by the
bank of the Jordan. 14 Then he took the
mantle of E·lī′jah that had fallen from him,
and struck the water, and said, "Where *is*
the LORD God of E·lī′jah?" And when he
also had struck the water, it was divided
this way and that; and E·lī′sha crossed
over.
15 Now when the sons of the prophets
who *were* from Jericho saw him, they said,
"The spirit of E·lī′jah rests on E·lī′sha."
And they came to meet him, and bowed to
the ground before him. 16 Then they said to
him, "Look now, there are fifty strong men
with your servants. Please let them go and
search for your master, lest perhaps the
Spirit of the LORD has taken him up and
cast him upon some mountain or into
some valley."
And he said, "You shall not send any-
one."
17 But when they urged him till he was
ashamed, he said, "Send *them!*" Therefore

2:3 sons of the prophets: A school for the training and preparation of young prophets. Samuel may have established the first school at Ramah (see 1 Sam. 19:20). They provided worship of God as an alternative for those who rejected Jeroboam's idolatrous state church. See also 4:38; 6:1.

2:8 Elijah is seen here as a second Moses, initiating a new stage in Israel's history (see Ex. 14:21, 22).

2:9 Elisha's request for a **double portion** is based on OT inheritance laws in which the firstborn son received two shares of the estate (see Deut. 21:17 and note on Deut. 21:14, 17). Elisha was asking to become Elijah's successor.

2:11 Elijah and Enoch are the only individuals recorded in the Bible who went to be with the Lord without dying.

2:12 the chariot of Israel: Elijah, not Ahab's armies, had been the defender of Israel.

they sent fifty men, and they searched for
three days but did not find him. 18And
when they came back to him, for he had
stayed in Jericho, he said to them, "Did I
not say to you, 'Do not go'?"

Elisha Performs Miracles

19Then the men of the city said to
E·lī'sha, "Please notice, the situation of
this city *is* pleasant, as my lord sees; but the
water *is* bad, and the ground barren."
20And he said, "Bring me a new bowl,
and put salt in it." So they brought *it* to
him. 21Then he went out to the source of
the water, and cast in the salt there, and
said, "Thus says the LORD: 'I have healed
this water; from it there shall be no more
death or barrenness.' " 22So the water re-
mains healed to this day, according to the
word of E·lī'sha which he spoke.
23Then he went up from there to Beth'el;
and as he was going up the road, some
youths came from the city and mocked
him, and said to him, "Go up, you bald-
head! Go up, you baldhead!"
24So he turned around and looked at
them, and pronounced a curse on them in
the name of the LORD. And two female
bears came out of the woods and mauled
forty-two of the youths.
25Then he went from there to Mount
Car'mel, and from there he returned to Sa-
maria.

CHAPTER 3

Moab Rebels Against Israel

Now Je·hō'ram the son of Ā'hab became
king over Israel at Samaria in the eigh-
teenth year of Je·hosh'a·phat king of Ju-
dah, and reigned twelve years. 2And he
did evil in the sight of the LORD, but not
like his father and mother; for he put away
the *sacred* pillar of Bā'al that his father had
made. 3Nevertheless he persisted in the
sins of Jer·o·bō'am the son of Nē'bat, who
had made Israel sin; he did not depart
from them.
4Now Mē'sha king of Mō'ab was a
sheepbreeder, and he regularly paid the
king of Israel one hundred thousand lambs
and the wool of one hundred thousand
rams. 5But it happened, when Ā'hab died,
that the king of Mō'ab rebelled against the
king of Israel.
6So King Je·hō'ram went out of Samaria
at that time and mustered all Israel. 7Then
he went and sent to Je·hosh'a·phat king of
Judah, saying, "The king of Mō'ab has re-
belled against me. Will you go with me to
fight against Mō'ab?"
And he said, "I will go up; I *am* as you
are, my people as your people, my horses
as your horses." 8Then he said, "Which
way shall we go up?"
And he answered, "By way of the
Wilderness of Ē'dom."
9So the king of Israel went with the king
of Judah and the king of Ē'dom, and they
marched on that roundabout route seven
days; and there was no water for the army,
nor for the animals that followed them.
10And the king of Israel said, "Alas! For the
LORD has called these three kings together
to deliver them into the hand of Mō'ab."
11But Je·hosh'a·phat said, "*Is there* no
prophet of the LORD here, that we may in-
quire of the LORD by him?"

3:2, 3 Half-hearted dedication to the Lord does not qualify as pleasing to God. Jehoram's faith was split between the gods of his parents and the One true God. Such behavior will not be rewarded.

3:4 This account of Israel's wars with **Mesha king of Moab** was supported by the Moabite Stone discovered in 1868. In this inscription, Mesha narrates Omri's conquest of northern Moab and the tribute that he required.

3:10, 11 Jehoshaphat's quiet sincere faith in the presence of the blaspheming Jehoram provides an example for us to courageously maintain our Christian testimonies no matter how those around us are acting.

today? *It is* neither the New Moon nor the
Sabbath."

And she said, "*It is* well." 24 Then she
saddled a donkey, and said to her servant,
"Drive, and go forward; do not slacken the
pace for me unless I tell you." 25 And so she
departed, and went to the man of God at
Mount Car'mel.

So it was, when the man of God saw her
afar off, that he said to his servant Ge-
hā'zī, "Look, the Shū'nam·mīte woman!
26 Please run now to meet her, and say to
her, '*Is it* well with you? *Is it* well with your
husband? *Is it* well with the child?' "

And she answered, "*It is* well." 27 Now
when she came to the man of God at the
hill, she caught him by the feet, but
Ge·hā'zī came near to push her away. But
the man of God said, "Let her alone; for her
soul *is* in deep distress, and the LORD has
hidden *it* from me, and has not told me."

28 So she said, "Did I ask a son of my
lord? Did I not say, 'Do not deceive me'?"

29 Then he said to Ge·hā'zī, "Get your-
self ready, and take my staff in your hand,
and be on your way. If you meet anyone,
do not greet him; and if anyone greets you,
do not answer him; but lay my staff on the
face of the child."

30 And the mother of the child said, "*As*
the LORD lives, and *as* your soul lives, I will
not leave you." So he arose and followed
her. 31 Now Ge·hā'zī went on ahead of
them, and laid the staff on the face of the
child; but *there was* neither voice nor hear-
ing. Therefore he went back to meet him,
and told him, saying, "The child has not
awakened."

32 When E·lī'sha came into the house,
there was the child, lying dead on his bed.
33 He went in therefore, shut the door be-
hind the two of them, and prayed to the
LORD. 34 And he went up and lay on the
child, and put his mouth on his mouth, his
eyes on his eyes, and his hands on his
hands; and he stretched himself out on the
child, and the flesh of the child became
warm. 35 He returned and walked back and
forth in the house, and again went up and
stretched himself out on him; then the
child sneezed seven times, and the child
opened his eyes. 36 And he called Ge·hā'zī
and said, "Call this Shū'nam·mīte
woman." So he called her. And when she
came in to him, he said, "Pick up your
son." 37 So she went in, fell at his feet, and
bowed to the ground; then she picked up
her son and went out.

Elisha Purifies the Pot of Stew

38 And E·lī'sha returned to Gil'gal, and
there was a famine in the land. Now the
sons of the prophets *were* sitting before
him; and he said to his servant, "Put on the
large pot, and boil stew for the sons of the
prophets." 39 So one went out into the field
to gather herbs, and found a wild vine, and
gathered from it a lapful of wild gourds,
and came and sliced *them* into the pot of
stew, though they did not know *what they
were*. 40 Then they served it to the men to
eat. Now it happened, as they were eating
the stew, that they cried out and said,
"Man of God, *there is* death in the pot!"
And they could not eat *it*.

41 So he said, "Then bring some flour."
And he put *it* into the pot, and said, "Serve
it to the people, that they may eat." And
there was nothing harmful in the pot.

Elisha Feeds One Hundred Men

42 Then a man came from Bā'al Shal'i-
sha, and brought the man of God bread of
the firstfruits, twenty loaves of barley

4:27 the LORD has hidden it: Prophets did not always receive special revelation; they sometimes awaited the unfolding of events.

4:40 The gourds in the stew, while harmless in small amounts, were fatal when ingested in large quantities.

4:42 firstfruits: Normally donated to the priesthood (see Deut. 18:3–5), but in the north-

bread, and newly ripened grain in his
knapsack. And he said, "Give *it* to the peo-
ple, that they may eat."
43But his servant said, "What? Shall I set
this before one hundred men?"
He said again, "Give it to the people,
that they may eat; for thus says the LORD:
'They shall eat and have *some* left over.' "
44So he set *it* before them; and they ate and
had *some* left over, according to the word of
the LORD.

CHAPTER 5

Naaman's Leprosy Healed

Now Nā′a·man, commander of the
army of the king of Syria, was a great and
honorable man in the eyes of his master,
because by him the LORD had given victory
to Syria. He was also a mighty man of
valor, *but* a leper. 2And the Syrians had
gone out on raids, and had brought back
captive a young girl from the land of Israel.
She waited on Nā′a·man's wife. 3Then she
said to her mistress, "If only my master
were with the prophet who *is* in Samaria!
For he would heal him of his leprosy."
4And *Nā′a·man* went in and told his mas-
ter, saying, "Thus and thus said the girl
who *is* from the land of Israel."
5Then the king of Syria said, "Go now,
and I will send a letter to the king of Is-
rael."
So he departed and took with him ten
talents of silver, six thousand *shekels* of
gold, and ten changes of clothing. 6Then he
brought the letter to the king of Israel,
which said,

> Now be advised, when this letter
> comes to you, that I have sent
> Nā′a·man my servant to you, that you
> may heal him of his leprosy.

7And it happened, when the king of Israel
read the letter, that he tore his clothes and
said, "*Am* I God, to kill and make alive,
that this man sends a man to me to heal
him of his leprosy? Therefore please con-
sider, and see how he seeks a quarrel with
me."
8So it was, when E·lī′sha the man of
God heard that the king of Israel had torn
his clothes, that he sent to the king, saying,
"Why have you torn your clothes? Please
let him come to me, and he shall know that
there is a prophet in Israel."
9Then Nā′a·man went with his horses
and chariot, and he stood at the door of
E·lī′sha's house. 10And E·lī′sha sent a mes-
senger to him, saying, "Go and wash in the
Jordan seven times, and your flesh shall be
restored to you, and *you shall* be clean."
11But Nā′a·man became furious, and went
away and said, "Indeed, I said to myself,
'He will surely come out *to me,* and stand
and call on the name of the LORD his God,
and wave his hand over the place, and heal
the leprosy.' 12*Are* not the A·bā′nah[a] and
the Phar′par, the rivers of Damascus, bet-

5:12 [a]Following Kethib, Septuagint, and Vulgate; Qere, Syriac, and Targum read *Amanah.*

---

ern kingdom, pious Israelites may have supported the groups of prophets rather than Jeroboam's idolatrous state church. **he**: Elisha.

5:1 leper: Leprosy was a skin disease controlled with utmost care to prevent infection of others (see Lev. 13; 14). But in Syria, **Naaman** was still able to hold high office.

5:2 The concern expressed by this little maid for her captor's welfare exemplifies for us the true Christian attitude of love toward those society says we should despise.

5:7 Jehoram thought the Syrian king was looking for a reason to fight.

5:10–13 Naaman, conscious of his self-importance, came to Elisha's house in full military gear (v. 9). It was humiliating enough for a Syrian commander to seek help from his Israelite enemies, and then to be sent to this eccentric prophet. But to be dealt with by messenger and sent on a 25-mile (40 km) trip to the muddy Jordan River was a critical test of Naaman's faith. Pride is often the obstacle to faith and cleansing.

ter than all the waters of Israel? Could I not
wash in them and be clean?" So he turned
and went away in a rage. 13And his ser-
vants came near and spoke to him, and
said, "My father, *if* the prophet had told
you *to do* something great, would you not
have done *it*? How much more then, when
he says to you, 'Wash, and be clean'?" 14So
he went down and dipped seven times in
the Jordan, according to the saying of the
man of God; and his flesh was restored like
the flesh of a little child, and he was clean.

15And he returned to the man of God, he
and all his aides, and came and stood be-
fore him; and he said, "Indeed, now I
know that *there is* no God in all the earth,
except in Israel; now therefore, please take
a gift from your servant."

16But he said, "*As* the LORD lives, before
whom I stand, I will receive nothing." And
he urged him to take *it*, but he refused.

17So Nā'a·man said, "Then, if not, please
let your servant be given two mule-loads
of earth; for your servant will no longer of-
fer either burnt offering or sacrifice to
other gods, but to the LORD. 18Yet in this
thing may the LORD pardon your servant:
when my master goes into the temple of
Rim'mon to worship there, and he leans on
my hand, and I bow down in the temple of
Rim'mon—when I bow down in the tem-
ple of Rim'mon, may the LORD please par-
don your servant in this thing."

19Then he said to him, "Go in peace." So
he departed from him a short distance.

Gehazi's Greed

20But Ge·hā'zī, the servant of E·lī'sha
the man of God, said, "Look, my master
has spared Nā'a·man this Syrian, while
not receiving from his hands what he
brought; but *as* the LORD lives, I will run af-
ter him and take something from him."
21So Ge·hā'zī pursued Nā'a·man. When
Nā'a·man saw *him* running after him, he
got down from the chariot to meet him,
and said, "*Is* all well?"

22And he said, "All *is* well. My master
has sent me, saying, 'Indeed, just now
two young men of the sons of the prophets
have come to me from the mountains
of Ē'phra·im. Please give them a talent
of silver and two changes of gar-
ments.' "

23So Nā'a·man said, "Please, take two
talents." And he urged him, and bound
two talents of silver in two bags, with two
changes of garments, and handed *them* to
two of his servants; and they carried *them*
on ahead of him. 24When he came to the
citadel, he took *them* from their hand, and
stored *them* away in the house; then he let
the men go, and they departed. 25Now he
went in and stood before his master.
E·lī'sha said to him, "Where *did you go*,
Ge·hā'zī?"

And he said, "Your servant did not go
anywhere."

26Then he said to him, "Did not my heart
go *with you* when the man turned back
from his chariot to meet you? *Is it* time to
receive money and to receive clothing,
olive groves and vineyards, sheep and
oxen, male and female servants? 27There-
fore the leprosy of Nā'a·man shall cling to
you and your descendants forever." And
he went out from his presence leprous, *as
white* as snow.

5:17 sacrifice . . . to the LORD: Naaman was still limited by his pagan roots to a localized concept of God and thought the Lord could be worshiped only on soil from Israel.

5:20 this Syrian: May reflect some bitter emotions on the part of Gehazi. He did not share the unselfish attitude of his master, who may have wanted to avoid any resemblance to the professional prophets who prophesied for gain (see 1 Kin. 22:5–28).

5:24 citadel: Lit. "hill." Probably the place where Elisha lived.

5:26 Did not my heart go with you? Has not God shown me what you did? Are greed and selfishness appropriate for His servants?

CHAPTER 6

The Floating Ax Head

And the sons of the prophets said to E•lī′sha, "See now, the place where we dwell with you is too small for us. 2Please, let us go to the Jordan, and let every man take a beam from there, and let us make there a place where we may dwell."

So he answered, "Go."

3Then one said, "Please consent to go with your servants."

And he answered, "I will go." 4So he went with them. And when they came to the Jordan, they cut down trees. 5But as one was cutting down a tree, the iron *ax head* fell into the water; and he cried out and said, "Alas, master! For it was borrowed."

6So the man of God said, "Where did it fall?" And he showed him the place. So he cut off a stick, and threw *it* in there; and he made the iron float. 7Therefore he said, "Pick *it* up for yourself." So he reached out his hand and took it.

The Blinded Syrians Captured

8Now the king of Syria was making war against Israel; and he consulted with his servants, saying, "My camp *will be* in such and such a place." 9And the man of God sent to the king of Israel, saying, "Beware that you do not pass this place, for the Syrians are coming down there." 10Then the king of Israel sent *someone* to the place of which the man of God had told him. Thus he warned him, and he was watchful there, not just once or twice.

11Therefore the heart of the king of Syria was greatly troubled by this thing; and he called his servants and said to them, "Will you not show me which of us *is* for the king of Israel?"

12And one of his servants said, "None, my lord, O king; but E•lī′sha, the prophet who *is* in Israel, tells the king of Israel the words that you speak in your bedroom."

13So he said, "Go and see where he *is*, that I may send and get him."

And it was told him, saying, "Surely *he is* in Dō′than."

14Therefore he sent horses and chariots and a great army there, and they came by night and surrounded the city. 15And when the servant of the man of God arose early and went out, there was an army, surrounding the city with horses and chariots. And his servant said to him, "Alas, my master! What shall we do?"

16So he answered, "Do not fear, for those who *are* with us *are* more than those who *are* with them." 17And E•lī′sha prayed, and said, "LORD, I pray, open his eyes that he may see." Then the LORD opened the eyes of the young man, and he saw. And behold, the mountain *was* full of horses and chariots of fire all around E•lī′sha. 18So when *the Syrians* came down to him, E•lī′sha prayed to the LORD, and said, "Strike this people, I pray, with blindness." And He struck them with blindness according to the word of E•lī′sha.

19Now E•lī′sha said to them, "This *is* not the way, nor *is* this the city. Follow me, and I will bring you to the man whom you seek." But he led them to Samaria.

20So it was, when they had come to Samaria, that E•lī′sha said, "LORD, open the eyes of these *men*, that they may see." And the LORD opened their eyes, and they saw; and there *they were*, inside Samaria!

21Now when the king of Israel saw them, he said to E•lī′sha, "My father, shall I kill *them*? Shall I kill *them*?"

22But he answered, "You shall not kill *them*. Would you kill those whom you have taken captive with your sword and your bow? Set food and water before them, that they may eat and drink and go to their master." 23Then he prepared a great feast

---

6:16 This verse is a wonderful source of comfort when we find ourselves surrounded by sin or discouragement.

for them; and after they ate and drank, he sent them away and they went to their master. So the bands of Syrian *raiders* came no more into the land of Israel.

Syria Besieges Samaria in Famine

[24]And it happened after this that Ben-Hā′dad king of Syria gathered all his army, and went up and besieged Samaria. [25]And there was a great famine in Samaria; and indeed they besieged it until a donkey's head was *sold* for eighty *shekels* of silver, and one-fourth of a kab of dove droppings for five *shekels* of silver.

[26]Then, as the king of Israel was passing by on the wall, a woman cried out to him, saying, "Help, my lord, O king!"

[27]And he said, "If the LORD does not help you, where can I find help for you? From the threshing floor or from the winepress?" [28]Then the king said to her, "What is troubling you?"

And she answered, "This woman said to me, 'Give your son, that we may eat him today, and we will eat my son tomorrow.' [29]So we boiled my son, and ate him. And I said to her on the next day, 'Give your son, that we may eat him'; but she has hidden her son."

[30]Now it happened, when the king heard the words of the woman, that he tore his clothes; and as he passed by on the wall, the people looked, and there underneath *he had* sackcloth on his body. [31]Then he said, "God do so to me and more also, if the head of E·lī′sha the son of Shā′phat remains on him today!"

[32]But E·lī′sha was sitting in his house, and the elders were sitting with him. And *the king* sent a man ahead of him, but before the messenger came to him, he said to the elders, "Do you see how this son of a murderer has sent someone to take away my head? Look, when the messenger comes, shut the door, and hold him fast at the door. *Is* not the sound of his master's feet behind him?" [33]And while he was still talking with them, there was the messenger, coming down to him; and then *the king* said, "Surely this calamity *is* from the LORD; why should I wait for the LORD any longer?"

CHAPTER 7

Then E·lī′sha said, "Hear the word of the LORD. Thus says the LORD: 'Tomorrow about this time a seah of fine flour *shall be sold* for a shekel, and two seahs of barley for a shekel, at the gate of Samaria.' "

[2]So an officer on whose hand the king leaned answered the man of God and said, "Look, *if* the LORD would make windows in heaven, could this thing be?"

And he said, "In fact, you shall see *it* with your eyes, but you shall not eat of it."

The Syrians Flee

[3]Now there were four leprous men at the entrance of the gate; and they said to one another, "Why are we sitting here until we die? [4]If we say, 'We will enter the city,' the famine *is* in the city, and we shall die there. And if we sit here, we die also. Now therefore, come, let us surrender to the army of the Syrians. If they keep us alive, we shall live; and if they kill us, we shall only die." [5]And they rose at twilight to go to the camp of the Syrians; and when they had come to the outskirts of the Syrian camp, to their surprise no one *was* there. [6]For the LORD had caused the army of the

6:28, 29 Cannibalism during times of famine was common in ancient history.

6:30 sackcloth on his body: In sympathy with his people's suffering.

6:31–33 Elisha had probably encouraged the king not to surrender, but to **wait for the LORD** to deliver them (v. 33). The king blamed Elisha for Israel's trouble, but acknowledged the Lord's hand in the situation.

7:6 Hittites: Inhabitants of northern Syria and southern Asia Minor. Enlisting foreign armies to campaign against one's enemies was widely practiced (see 16:7).

Syrians to hear the noise of chariots and the noise of horses—the noise of a great army; so they said to one another, "Look, the king of Israel has hired against us the kings of the Hit'tītes and the kings of the Egyptians to attack us!" 7Therefore they arose and fled at twilight, and left the camp intact—their tents, their horses, and their donkeys—and they fled for their lives. 8And when these lepers came to the outskirts of the camp, they went into one tent and ate and drank, and carried from it silver and gold and clothing, and went and hid *them;* then they came back and entered another tent, and carried *some* from there *also,* and went and hid *it.*

9Then they said to one another, "We are not doing right. This day *is* a day of good news, and we remain silent. If we wait until morning light, some punishment will come upon us. Now therefore, come, let us go and tell the king's household." 10So they went and called to the gatekeepers of the city, and told them, saying, "We went to the Syrian camp, and surprisingly no one *was* there, not a human sound—only horses and donkeys tied, and the tents intact." 11And the gatekeepers called out, and they told *it* to the king's household inside.

12So the king arose in the night and said to his servants, "Let me now tell you what the Syrians have done to us. They know that we *are* hungry; therefore they have gone out of the camp to hide themselves in the field, saying, 'When they come out of the city, we shall catch them alive, and get into the city.' "

13And one of his servants answered and said, "Please, let several *men* take five of the remaining horses which are left in the city. Look, they *may either become* like all the multitude of Israel that are left in it; or indeed, *I say,* they *may become* like all the multitude of Israel left from those who are consumed; so let us send them and see." 14Therefore they took two chariots with horses; and the king sent them in the direction of the Syrian army, saying, "Go and see." 15And they went after them to the Jordan; and indeed all the road *was* full of garments and weapons which the Syrians had thrown away in their haste. So the messengers returned and told the king. 16Then the people went out and plundered the tents of the Syrians. So a seah of fine flour was *sold* for a shekel, and two seahs of barley for a shekel, according to the word of the LORD.

17Now the king had appointed the officer on whose hand he leaned to have charge of the gate. But the people trampled him in the gate, and he died, just as the man of God had said, who spoke when the king came down to him. 18So it happened just as the man of God had spoken to the king, saying, "Two seahs of barley for a shekel, and a seah of fine flour for a shekel, shall be *sold* tomorrow about this time in the gate of Samaria."

19Then that officer had answered the man of God, and said, "Now look, *if* the LORD would make windows in heaven, could such a thing be?"

And he had said, "In fact, you shall see *it* with your eyes, but you shall not eat of it." 20And so it happened to him, for the people trampled him in the gate, and he died.

CHAPTER 8

The King Restores the Shunammite's Land

Then E·lī'sha spoke to the woman whose son he had restored to life, saying, "Arise and go, you and your household, and stay wherever you can; for the LORD has called for a famine, and furthermore, it

---

7:9 The words of the lepers should remind us to share the good news of the gospel; to remain silent about something of such importance is not right.

8:1 famine: Not the siege famine of 6:25. This was a general famine of the land.

will come upon the land for seven years."
2So the woman arose and did according to
the saying of the man of God, and she went
with her household and dwelt in the land
of the Phi·lis'tines seven years.

3It came to pass, at the end of seven
years, that the woman returned from the
land of the Phi·lis'tines; and she went to
make an appeal to the king for her house
and for her land. 4Then the king talked
with Ge·hā'zī, the servant of the man of
God, saying, "Tell me, please, all the great
things E·lī'sha has done." 5Now it hap-
pened, as he was telling the king how he
had restored the dead to life, that there was
the woman whose son he had restored to
life, appealing to the king for her house
and for her land. And Ge·hā'zī said, "My
lord, O king, this *is* the woman, and this *is*
her son whom E·lī'sha restored to life."
6And when the king asked the woman, she
told him.

So the king appointed a certain officer
for her, saying, "Restore all that *was* hers,
and all the proceeds of the field from the
day that she left the land until now."

Death of Ben-Hadad

7Then E·lī'sha went to Damascus, and
Ben-Hā'dad king of Syria was sick; and it
was told him, saying, "The man of God has
come here." 8And the king said to Haz'a·el,
"Take a present in your hand, and go to
meet the man of God, and inquire of the
LORD by him, saying, 'Shall I recover from
this disease?' " 9So Haz'a·el went to meet
him and took a present with him, of every
good thing of Damascus, forty camel-
loads; and he came and stood before him,
and said, "Your son Ben-Hā'dad king of
Syria has sent me to you, saying, 'Shall I re-
cover from this disease?' "

10And E·lī'sha said to him, "Go, say to
him, 'You shall certainly recover.' How-
ever the LORD has shown me that he will
really die." 11Then he set his countenance
in a stare until he was ashamed; and the
man of God wept. 12And Haz'a·el said,
"Why is my lord weeping?"

He answered, "Because I know the evil
that you will do to the children of Israel:
Their strongholds you will set on fire, and
their young men you will kill with the
sword; and you will dash their children,
and rip open their women with child."

13So Haz'a·el said, "But what *is* your ser-
vant—a dog, that he should do this gross
thing?"

And E·lī'sha answered, "The LORD has
shown me that you *will become* king over
Syria."

14Then he departed from E·lī'sha, and
came to his master, who said to him,
"What did E·lī'sha say to you?" And he
answered, "He told me you would surely
recover." 15But it happened on the next day

8:3 During her absence, her estate had become crown property. Her elderly husband (4:14) had apparently died, and she was forced to act on her own behalf.

8:5 **Now it happened**: A case of God's timing.

8:7–9 At that time, consulting another's god concerning one's fate was a common practice; this passage does not mean **Ben-Hadad** had turned to the Lord.

8:8 **Hazael**: A Syrian officer. The instructions given Elijah to anoint Hazael king of Syria would be completed in this meeting of Hazael with Elisha (see 1 Kin. 19:15 and note on 1 Kin. 19:15–18).

8:9 **Your son**: A way of expressing deference to another.

8:10 The king's illness was not fatal, but **Elisha** knew he would soon die from other causes (v. 15).

8:11, 12 Elisha stared at Hazael until Hazael became embarrassed. The prophet wept because of the destruction Hazael would bring (see 2 Kin. 10:32, 33; 12:17, 18; 13:22).

8:13 Elijah had been commanded by God to anoint Hazael as king of Syria (1 Kin. 19:15). At his leaving, the assignment was passed on to Elisha.

8:15 Hazael murdered Ben-Hadad by suffocating him.

that he took a thick cloth and dipped *it* in water, and spread *it* over his face so that he died; and Haz'a·el reigned in his place.

Jehoram Reigns in Judah

16 Now in the fifth year of Jō'ram the son of Ā'hab, king of Israel, Je·hosh'a·phat *having been* king of Judah, Je·hō'ram the son of Je·hosh'a·phat began to reign as king of Judah. 17 He was thirty-two years old when he became king, and he reigned eight years in Jerusalem. 18 And he walked in the way of the kings of Israel, just as the house of Ā'hab had done, for the daughter of Ā'hab was his wife; and he did evil in the sight of the LORD. 19 Yet the LORD would not destroy Judah, for the sake of His servant David, as He promised him to give a lamp to him *and* his sons forever.

20 In his days Ē'dom revolted against Judah's authority, and made a king over themselves. 21 So Jō'ram[a] went to Zā'ir, and all his chariots with him. Then he rose by night and attacked the Ē'dom·ītes who had surrounded him and the captains of the chariots; and the troops fled to their tents. 22 Thus Ē'dom has been in revolt against Judah's authority to this day. And Lib'nah revolted at that time.

23 Now the rest of the acts of Jō'ram, and all that he did, *are* they not written in the book of the chronicles of the kings of Judah? 24 So Jō'ram rested with his fathers, and was buried with his fathers in the City of David. Then Ā·ha·zī'ah his son reigned in his place.

Ahaziah Reigns in Judah

25 In the twelfth year of Jō'ram the son of Ā'hab, king of Israel, Ā·ha·zī'ah the son of Je·hō'ram, king of Judah, began to reign. 26 Ā·ha·zī'ah *was* twenty-two years old when he became king, and he reigned one year in Jerusalem. His mother's name *was* Ath·a·lī'ah the granddaughter of Om'rī, king of Israel. 27 And he walked in the way of the house of Ā'hab, and did evil in the sight of the LORD, like the house of Ā'hab, for he *was* the son-in-law of the house of Ā'hab.

28 Now he went with Jō'ram the son of Ā'hab to war against Haz'a·el king of Syria at Rā'moth Gil'ē·ad; and the Syrians wounded Jō'ram. 29 Then King Jō'ram went back to Jez'rē·el to recover from the wounds which the Syrians had inflicted on him at Rā'mah, when he fought against Haz'a·el king of Syria. And Ā·ha·zī'ah the son of Je·hō'ram, king of Judah, went down to see Jō'ram the son of Ā'hab in Jez'rē·el, because he was sick.

CHAPTER 9

Jehu Anointed King of Israel

And E·lī'sha the prophet called one of the sons of the prophets, and said to him, "Get yourself ready, take this flask of oil in

8:21 [a]Spelled *Jehoram* in verse 16

8:19 give a lamp: God's promise to David to preserve his dynasty. **forever**: Ultimately fulfilled in Christ (see 2 Sam. 7:13, 16 and note on 2 Sam. 7:5–16).

8:25 Ahaziah: sometimes called "Jehoahaz" (2 Chr. 21) or "Azariah" (2 Chr. 22:6).

8:26, 27 Athaliah, the king's mother, was a daughter of Ahab (see v. 18), and the king's wife was also related to Ahab's family. These family ties contributed to Ahaziah's evil ways (see 2 Chr. 22:3–5).

8:28, 29 Hazael: See vv. 7–15. **Ahaziah . . . went down to see Joram**: The nephew visits his wounded uncle (see v. 16).

9:1—10:36 Jehu's bloody purge was the judgment of God against Baalism (see 1 Kin. 19:17, 18). Although he completed the destruction of official Baalism (10:28) begun by Elijah, Jehu was unable to mount a serious military recovery. His persecution of the royal family estranged both Phoenicia to the north and Athaliah's Judah to the south. Furthermore, Syria under Hazael succeeded in capturing much Israelite territory (10:32, 33). And in it all, a resurgent Assyria compelled him to pay tribute, an event recorded on the Black Obelisk of the Assyrian king Shalmaneser III.

your hand, and go to Rā'moth Gil'ē·ad.
2Now when you arrive at that place, look
there for Jē'hū the son of Je·hosh'a·phat,
the son of Nim'shī, and go in and make
him rise up from among his associates, and
take him to an inner room. 3Then take the
flask of oil, and pour *it* on his head, and
say, 'Thus says the LORD: "I have anointed
you king over Israel." ' Then open the door
and flee, and do not delay."
4So the young man, the servant of the
prophet, went to Rā'moth Gil'ē·ad. 5And
when he arrived, there *were* the captains of
the army sitting; and he said, "I have a
message for you, Commander."
Jē'hū said, "For which *one* of us?"
And he said, "For you, Commander."
6Then he arose and went into the house.
And he poured the oil on his head, and
said to him, "Thus says the LORD God of Is-
rael: 'I have anointed you king over the
people of the LORD, over Israel. 7You shall
strike down the house of Ā'hab your mas-
ter, that I may avenge the blood of My ser-
vants the prophets, and the blood of all the
servants of the LORD, at the hand of
Jez'e·bel. 8For the whole house of Ā'hab
shall perish; and I will cut off from Ā'hab
all the males in Israel, both bond and free.
9So I will make the house of Ā'hab like the
house of Jer·o·bō'am the son of Nē'bat,
and like the house of Bā'a·sha the son of
A·hī'jah. 10The dogs shall eat Jez'e·bel on
the plot *of ground* at Jez'rē·el, and *there shall
be* none to bury *her*.' " And he opened the
door and fled.
11Then Jē'hū came out to the servants of
his master, and *one* said to him, "*Is* all well?
Why did this madman come to you?"
And he said to them, "You know the
man and his babble."
12And they said, "A lie! Tell us now."
So he said, "Thus and thus he spoke to
me, saying, 'Thus says the LORD: "I have
anointed you king over Israel." ' "
13Then each man hastened to take his
garment and put *it* under him on the top of
the steps; and they blew trumpets, saying,
"Jē'hū is king!"

Joram of Israel Killed

14So Jē'hū the son of Je·hosh'a·phat, the
son of Nim'shī, conspired against Jō'ram.
(Now Jō'ram had been defending Rā'moth
Gil'ē·ad, he and all Israel, against Haz'a·el
king of Syria. 15But King Jō'ram had re-
turned to Jez'rē·el to recover from the
wounds which the Syrians had inflicted on
him when he fought with Haz'a·el king of
Syria.) And Jē'hū said, "If you are so
minded, let no one leave *or* escape from the
city to go and tell *it* in Jez'rē·el." 16So Jē'hū
rode in a chariot and went to Jez'rē·el, for
Jō'ram was laid up there; and Ā·ha·zī'ah
king of Judah had come down to see
Jō'ram.
17Now a watchman stood on the tower
in Jez'rē·el, and he saw the company of Jē'-
hū as he came, and said, "I see a company
of men."
And Jō'ram said, "Get a horseman and
send him to meet them, and let him say, '*Is
it* peace?' "
18So the horseman went to meet him,
and said, "Thus says the king: '*Is it*
peace?' "
And Jē'hū said, "What have you to do
with peace? Turn around and follow me."

9:7–9 Ahab's would be the fourth dynasty destroyed by God, following the eradication of the houses of Jeroboam (1 Kin. 14:10), of Baasha (1 Kin. 16:3), and of Zimri (1 Kin. 16:16).

9:11 madman: Ridiculing the young man's odd behavior or his unusual prophetic appearance (see 1:8 and note). Jehu's evasive response may have been equivalent to "You know what prophets are like!"

9:13 A man's **garment** was assumed to be imbued with his personality and represented the man himself. Placing their garments under Jehu indicated submission to his authority. In the same way, the people of Jerusalem acknowledged the royal authority of Jesus at His triumphal entry (see Matt. 21:7, 8).

So the watchman reported, saying, "The
messenger went to them, but is not coming
back."
19Then he sent out a second horseman
who came to them, and said, "Thus says
the king: '*Is it* peace?' "
And Jē'hū answered, "What have you
to do with peace? Turn around and follow
me."
20So the watchman reported, saying,
"He went up to them and is not coming
back; and the driving *is* like the driving of
Jē'hū the son of Nim'shī, for he drives furi-
ously!"
21Then Jō'ram said, "Make ready." And
his chariot was made ready. Then Jō'ram
king of Israel and Ā·ha·zī'ah king of Judah
went out, each in his chariot; and they
went out to meet Jē'hū, and met him on the
property of Nā'both the Jez'rē·el·īte.
22Now it happened, when Jō'ram saw
Jē'hū, that he said, "*Is it* peace, Jē'hū?"
So he answered, "What peace, as long as
the harlotries of your mother Jez'e·bel and
her witchcraft *are so* many?"
23Then Jō'ram turned around and fled,
and said to Ā·ha·zī'ah, "Treachery, Ā·ha-
zī'ah!" 24Now Jē'hū drew his bow with full
strength and shot Je·hō'ram between his
arms; and the arrow came out at his heart,
and he sank down in his chariot. 25Then
Jē'hū said to Bid'kar his captain, "Pick *him*
up, *and* throw him into the tract of the field
of Nā'both the Jez'rē·el·īte; for remember,
when you and I were riding together be-
hind Ā'hab his father, that the LORD laid
this burden upon him: 26'Surely I saw yes-
terday the blood of Nā'both and the blood
of his sons,' says the LORD, 'and I will re-
pay you in this plot,' says the LORD. Now
therefore, take *and* throw him on the plot *of
ground*, according to the word of the
LORD."

Ahaziah of Judah Killed

27But when Ā·ha·zī'ah king of Judah
saw *this*, he fled by the road to Beth
Hag'gan.[a] So Jē'hū pursued him, and said,
"Shoot him also in the chariot." *And they
shot him* at the Ascent of Gur, which is by
Ib'lē·am. Then he fled to Me·gid'dō, and
died there. 28And his servants carried him
in the chariot to Jerusalem, and buried him
in his tomb with his fathers in the City of
David. 29In the eleventh year of Jō'ram the
son of Ā'hab, Ā·ha·zī'ah had become king
over Judah.

Jezebel's Violent Death

30Now when Jē'hū had come to Jez'rē·el,
Jez'e·bel heard *of it;* and she put paint on
her eyes and adorned her head, and
looked through a window. 31Then, as Jē'hū
entered at the gate, she said, "*Is it* peace,
Zim'rī, murderer of your master?"
32And he looked up at the window, and
said, "Who *is* on my side? Who?" So two *or*
three eunuchs looked out at him. 33Then he
said, "Throw her down." So they threw her
down, and *some* of her blood spattered on
the wall and on the horses; and he tram-
pled her underfoot. 34And when he had
gone in, he ate and drank. Then he said,
"Go now, see to this accursed *woman*, and
bury her, for she was a king's daughter."
35So they went to bury her, but they found
no more of her than the skull and the feet
and the palms of *her* hands. 36Therefore
they came back and told him. And he said,
"This *is* the word of the LORD, which He

9:27 [a]Literally *The Garden House*

9:25, 26 the LORD laid this burden upon him: Elijah had prophesied to Ahab that his blood would be required "in the place" where Naboth's blood had been spilled (see 1 Kin. 21:17–19). Jehu considered that prophecy now fulfilled in disposing of Joram's dead body on Naboth's property.

9:31 Calling Jehu **Zimri** was an acute insult because Zimri was also an army commander who had usurped the throne. He ruled only seven days (see 1 Kin. 16:9–18).

9:36, 37 Elijah predicted Jezebel's fate in 1 Kin. 21:23.

spoke by His servant E·lī′jah the Tish′bīte,
saying, ‘On the plot *of ground* at Jez′rē·el
dogs shall eat the flesh of Jez′e·bel;[a] [37]and
the corpse of Jez′e·bel shall be as refuse on
the surface of the field, in the plot at
Jez′rē·el, so that they shall not say, “Here
lies Jez′e·bel.” ’ ”

CHAPTER 10

Ahab's Seventy Sons Killed

Now Ā′hab had seventy sons in Samaria. And Jē′hū wrote and sent letters to Samaria, to the rulers of Jez′rē·el,[a] to the elders, and to those who reared Ā′hab's *sons*, saying:

2 Now as soon as this letter comes to
you, since your master's sons *are* with
you, and you have chariots and
horses, a fortified city also, and
weapons, [3]choose the best qualified of
your master's sons, set *him* on his father's throne, and fight for your master's house.

[4]But they were exceedingly afraid, and
said, “Look, two kings could not stand up
to him; how then can we stand?” [5]And he
who *was* in charge of the house, and he
who *was* in charge of the city, the elders
also, and those who reared *the sons,* sent to
Jē′hū, saying, “We *are* your servants, we
will do all you tell us; but we will not make
anyone king. Do *what is* good in your
sight.” [6]Then he wrote a second letter to
them, saying:

If you *are* for me and will obey my
voice, take the heads of the men, your
master's sons, and come to me at
Jez′rē·el by this time tomorrow.

Now the king's sons, seventy persons,
were with the great men of the city, *who*
were rearing them. [7]So it was, when the letter came to them, that they took the king's
sons and slaughtered seventy persons, put
their heads in baskets and sent *them* to him
at Jez′rē·el.
[8]Then a messenger came and told him,
saying, “They have brought the heads of
the king's sons.”

And he said, “Lay them in two heaps at
the entrance of the gate until morning.”
[9]So it was, in the morning, that he went
out and stood, and said to all the people,
“You *are* righteous. Indeed I conspired
against my master and killed him; but who
killed all these? [10]Know now that nothing
shall fall to the earth of the word of the
LORD which the LORD spoke concerning the
house of Ā′hab; for the LORD has done
what He spoke by His servant E·lī′jah.”
[11]So Jē′hū killed all who remained of the
house of Ā′hab in Jez′rē·el, and all his
great men and his close acquaintances and
his priests, until he left him none remaining.

Ahaziah's Forty-two Brothers Killed

[12]And he arose and departed and went
to Samaria. On the way, at Beth Ē′ked[a] of
the Shepherds, [13]Jē′hū met with the brothers of Ā·ha·zī′ah king of Judah, and said,
“Who *are* you?”

So they answered, “We *are* the brothers
of Ā·ha·zī′ah; we have come down to greet

9:36 [a]1 Kings 21:23 10:1 [a]Following Masoretic Text, Syriac, and Targum; Septuagint reads *Samaria;* Vulgate reads *city.* 10:12 [a]Or *The Shearing House*

10:9, 10 who killed all these? Implying his innocence, and suggesting that divine providence was supporting his cause (v. 10).

10:11 Everyone remotely associated with Ahab's reign was massacred. It is probably this unbridled bloodthirstiness to which Hosea refers (see Hos. 1:3–5 and note), and which brought judgment on Jehu's dynasty.

10:13 brothers: Relatives or close associates of Ahaziah, and thus friendly to King Joram, whom Jehu had killed.

the sons of the king and the sons of the queen mother."

14 And he said, "Take them alive!" So they took them alive, and killed them at the well of Beth Ē'ked, forty-two men; and he left none of them.

The Rest of Ahab's Family Killed

15 Now when he departed from there, he met Je·hon'a·dab the son of Rē'chab, *coming* to meet him; and he greeted him and said to him, "Is your heart right, as my heart *is* toward your heart?"

And Je·hon'a·dab answered, "It is."

Jē'hū said, "If it is, give *me* your hand." So he gave *him* his hand, and he took him up to him into the chariot. 16 Then he said, "Come with me, and see my zeal for the LORD." So they had him ride in his chariot. 17 And when he came to Samaria, he killed all who remained to Ā'hab in Samaria, till he had destroyed them, according to the word of the LORD which He spoke to E·lī'jah.

Worshipers of Baal Killed

18 Then Jē'hū gathered all the people together, and said to them, "Ā'hab served Bā'al a little, Jē'hū will serve him much. 19 Now therefore, call to me all the prophets of Bā'al, all his servants, and all his priests. Let no one be missing, for I have a great sacrifice for Bā'al. Whoever is missing shall not live." But Jē'hū acted deceptively, with the intent of destroying the worshipers of Bā'al. 20 And Jē'hū said, "Proclaim a solemn assembly for Bā'al." So they proclaimed *it.* 21 Then Jē'hū sent throughout all Israel; and all the worshipers of Bā'al came, so that there was not a man left who did not come. So they came into the temple[a] of Bā'al, and the temple of Bā'al was full from one end to the other. 22 And he said to the one in charge of the wardrobe, "Bring out vestments for all the worshipers of Bā'al." So he brought out vestments for them. 23 Then Jē'hū and Je·hon'a·dab the son of Rē'chab went into the temple of Bā'al, and said to the worshipers of Bā'al, "Search and see that no servants of the LORD are here with you, but only the worshipers of Bā'al." 24 So they went in to offer sacrifices and burnt offerings. Now Jē'hū had appointed for himself eighty men on the outside, and had said, "*If* any of the men whom I have brought into your hands escapes, *whoever lets him escape, it shall be* his life for the life of the other."

25 Now it happened, as soon as he had made an end of offering the burnt offering, that Jē'hū said to the guard and to the captains, "Go in *and* kill them; let no one come out!" And they killed them with the edge of the sword; then the guards and the officers threw *them* out, and went into the inner room of the temple of Bā'al. 26 And they brought the *sacred* pillars out of the temple of Bā'al and burned them. 27 Then they broke down the *sacred* pillar of Bā'al, and tore down the temple of Bā'al and made it a refuse dump to this day. 28 Thus Jē'hū destroyed Bā'al from Israel.

29 However Jē'hū did not turn away from the sins of Jer·o·bō'am the son of Nē'bat, who had made Israel sin, *that is,* from the golden calves that *were* at Beth'el and Dan. 30 And the LORD said to Jē'hū, "Because you have done well in doing *what is* right in My sight, *and* have done to the house of Ā'hab all that *was* in My heart, your sons shall sit on the throne of Israel to

10:21 [a]Literally *house,* and so elsewhere in this chapter

10:15 son of Rechab: The Rechabites were a tribal group who as a vow to God practiced the strictest nomadic life-style, denouncing all agricultural pursuits. Jehu was probably hoping to gain the support of the more conservative members of society by displaying **Jehonadab** as his ally in the chariot.

10:30 to the fourth generation: Four descendants of Jehu ruled Israel: Jehoahaz, Jehoash, Jeroboam II, Zechariah.

the fourth *generation*." 31But Jē'hū took no
heed to walk in the law of the LORD God of
Israel with all his heart; for he did not de-
part from the sins of Jer·o·bō'am, who had
made Israel sin.

Death of Jehu

32In those days the LORD began to cut off
parts of Israel; and Haz'a·el conquered
them in all the territory of Israel 33from the
Jordan eastward: all the land of Gil'ē·ad—
Gad, Reuben, and Ma·nas'seh—from
A·rō'er, which *is* by the River Ar'non, in-
cluding Gil'ē·ad and Bā'shan.
34Now the rest of the acts of Jē'hū, all that he
did, and all his might, *are* they not written
in the book of the chronicles of the kings of
Israel? 35So Jē'hū rested with his fathers,
and they buried him in Samaria. Then
Je·hō'a·haz his son reigned in his place.
36And the period that Jē'hū reigned over Is-
rael in Samaria *was* twenty-eight years.

CHAPTER 11

Athaliah Reigns in Judah

When Ath·a·lī'ah the mother of
Ā·ha·zī'ah saw that her son was dead, she
arose and destroyed all the royal heirs.
2But Je·hosh'e·ba, the daughter of King
Jō'ram, sister of Ā·ha·zī'ah, took Jō'ash the
son of Ā·ha·zī'ah, and stole him away from
among the king's sons *who were* being mur-
dered; and they hid him and his nurse in
the bedroom, from Ath·a·lī'ah, so that he
was not killed. 3So he was hidden with her
in the house of the LORD for six years,
while Ath·a·lī'ah reigned over the land.

Joash Crowned King of Judah

4In the seventh year Je·hoi'a·da sent and
brought the captains of hundreds—of the
bodyguards and the escorts—and brought
them into the house of the LORD to him.
And he made a covenant with them and
took an oath from them in the house of the
LORD, and showed them the king's son.
5Then he commanded them, saying, "This
is what you shall do: One-third of you who
come on duty on the Sabbath shall be keep-
ing watch over the king's house, 6one-third
shall be at the gate of Sūr, and one-third at
the gate behind the escorts. You shall keep
the watch of the house, lest it be broken
down. 7The two contingents of you who go
off duty on the Sabbath shall keep the
watch of the house of the LORD for the
king. 8But you shall surround the king on
all sides, every man with his weapons in
his hand; and whoever comes within
range, let him be put to death. You are to be
with the king as he goes out and as he
comes in."
9So the captains of the hundreds did ac-
cording to all that Je·hoi'a·da the priest
commanded. Each of them took his men
who were to be on duty on the Sabbath,
with those who were going off duty on the
Sabbath, and came to Je·hoi'a·da the
priest. 10And the priest gave the captains of
hundreds the spears and shields which *had
belonged* to King David, that were in the
temple of the LORD. 11Then the escorts
stood, every man with his weapons in his
hand, all around the king, from the right
side of the temple to the left side of the
temple, by the altar and the house. 12And

10:31 No matter how much good we do, if our hearts are not fully dedicated to God, our works are meaningless. We cannot reserve even a tiny corner of our hearts for ourselves if we desire God's fullest blessing.

11:1 Athaliah, the daughter of Ahab, nearly exterminated the Davidic line, perhaps out of revenge for Jehu's slaughter of her family in the northern kingdom.

11:5–9 Jehoiada chose the **Sabbath** as the occasion for the enthronement of Jehoash. All three divisions of the temple and palace guards would be available, and their regular changing of the posts would attract little attention.

11:12 Testimony: A copy of the law (Deut. 17:18–20) by which the king was to be reminded of his accountability to the King of the universe. But within 200 years the law would have been forgotten (see 22:11).

he brought out the king's son, put the crown on him, and *gave him* the Testimony;[a] they made him king and anointed him, and they clapped their hands and said, "Long live the king!"

Death of Athaliah

[13]Now when Ath·a·lī'ah heard the noise of the escorts *and* the people, she came to the people *in* the temple of the LORD. [14]When she looked, there was the king standing by a pillar according to custom; and the leaders and the trumpeters were by the king. All the people of the land were rejoicing and blowing trumpets. So Ath·a·lī'ah tore her clothes and cried out, "Treason! Treason!"

[15]And Je·hoi'a·da the priest commanded the captains of the hundreds, the officers of the army, and said to them, "Take her outside under guard, and slay with the sword whoever follows her." For the priest had said, "Do not let her be killed in the house of the LORD." [16]So they seized her; and she went by way of the horses' entrance *into* the king's house, and there she was killed.

[17]Then Je·hoi'a·da made a covenant between the LORD, the king, and the people, that they should be the LORD's people, and *also* between the king and the people. [18]And all the people of the land went to the temple of Bā'al, and tore it down. They thoroughly broke in pieces its altars and images, and killed Mat'tan the priest of Bā'al before the altars. And the priest appointed officers over the house of the LORD. [19]Then he took the captains of hundreds, the bodyguards, the escorts, and all the people of the land; and they brought the king down from the house of the LORD, and went by way of the gate of the escorts to the king's house. Then he sat on the throne of the kings. [20]So all the people of the land rejoiced; and the city was quiet, for they had slain Ath·a·lī'ah with the sword *in* the king's house. [21]Je·hō'ash *was* seven years old when he became king.

CHAPTER 12

Jehoash Repairs the Temple

In the seventh year of Jē'hū, Je·hō'ash[a] became king, and he reigned forty years in Jerusalem. His mother's name *was* Zib'i·ah of Bē·er·shē'ba. [2]Je·hō'ash did *what was* right in the sight of the LORD all the days in which Je·hoi'a·da the priest instructed him. [3]But the high places were not taken away; the people still sacrificed and burned incense on the high places.

[4]And Je·hō'ash said to the priests, "All

11:12 [a]That is, the Law (compare Exodus 25:16, 21 and Deuteronomy 31:9)
12:1 [a]Spelled *Joash* in 11:2ff

11:14 a pillar: One of the pillars set up by Solomon in the vestibule of the temple (see 1 Kin. 7:21 and note). **according to custom**: At a coronation. **People of the land** refers to landowning countrymen. Their presence in Jerusalem indicates that the coronation coincided with a festival occasion.

11:17 The **covenant** between **the LORD** and His **people** had to be reestablished because under Athaliah it had been expressly broken (see Ex. 19:6 and note).

11:18 True repentance calls for zeal in eradicating from our lives everything that takes our focus away from God. Clinging to even the smallest remnant indicates rebellion that will prevent us from following the Lord wholeheartedly.

12:2, 3 Unfortunately, after Jehoiada's death, his godly influence over Jehoash was soon forgotten, and the nation fell into severe apostasy under the young king (see 2 Chr. 24:17–25).

12:4, 5 The dedicated gifts were of three types: a **census** or poll tax (see Ex. 30:11–16 and note); an **assessment** or offering made in connection with thanksgiving or a vow (see Lev. 27:2, 3); and the freewill offerings (see Deut. 16:10). The temple was now over 140 years old, hence natural deterioration would be expected. But 2 Chr. 24:7 implies the temple had also been ill-treated by Athaliah and her sons.

the money of the dedicated gifts that are
brought into the house of the LORD—each
man's census money, each man's assess-
ment money[a]—*and* all the money that a
man purposes in his heart to bring into the
house of the LORD, 5let the priests take *it*
themselves, each from his constituency;
and let them repair the damages of the
temple, wherever any dilapidation is
found."
6Now it was so, by the twenty-third year
of King Je·hō'ash, *that* the priests had not
repaired the damages of the temple. 7So
King Je·hō'ash called Je·hoi'a·da the priest
and the *other* priests, and said to them,
"Why have you not repaired the damages
of the temple? Now therefore, do not take
more money from your constituency, but
deliver it for repairing the damages of the
temple." 8And the priests agreed that they
would neither receive *more* money from
the people, nor repair the damages of the
temple.
9Then Je·hoi'a·da the priest took a chest,
bored a hole in its lid, and set it beside the
altar, on the right side as one comes into
the house of the LORD; and the priests who
kept the door put there all the money
brought into the house of the LORD. 10So it
was, whenever they saw that *there was*
much money in the chest, that the king's
scribe and the high priest came up and put
it in bags, and counted the money that was
found in the house of the LORD. 11Then they
gave the money, which had been appor-
tioned, into the hands of those who did the
work, who had the oversight of the house
of the LORD; and they paid it out to the
carpenters and builders who worked on
the house of the LORD, 12and to masons and
stonecutters, and for buying timber and
hewn stone, to repair the damage of the
house of the LORD, and for all that was paid
out to repair the temple. 13However there
were not made for the house of the LORD
basins of silver, trimmers, sprinkling-
bowls, trumpets, any articles of gold or ar-
ticles of silver, from the money brought
into the house of the LORD. 14But they gave
that to the workmen, and they repaired the
house of the LORD with it. 15Moreover they
did not require an account from the men
into whose hand they delivered the money
to be paid to workmen, for they dealt faith-
fully. 16The money from the trespass offer-
ings and the money from the sin offerings
was not brought into the house of the
LORD. It belonged to the priests.

Hazael Threatens Jerusalem

17Haz'a·el king of Syria went up and
fought against Gath, and took it; then
Haz'a·el set his face to go up to Jerusalem.
18And Je·hō'ash king of Judah took all the
sacred things that his fathers, Je·hosh'-
a·phat and Je·hō'ram and Ā·ha·zī'ah,
kings of Judah, had dedicated, and his
own sacred things, and all the gold found
in the treasuries of the house of the LORD
and in the king's house, and sent *them* to
Haz'a·el king of Syria. Then he went away
from Jerusalem.

Death of Joash

19Now the rest of the acts of Jō'ash,[a] and
all that he did, *are* they not written in the
book of the chronicles of the kings of Ju-
dah?
20And his servants arose and formed a
conspiracy, and killed Jō'ash in the house
of the Mil'lō,[a] which goes down to Sil'la.

12:4 [a]Compare Leviticus 27:2ff
12:19 [a]Spelled *Jehoash* in 12:1ff
12:20 [a]Literally *The Landfill*

12:17, 18 Hazael: The perennial foe of the northern kingdom (10:32, 33) now threatened the South as well. But Hazael had his own threat in the rising strength of Assyria, and he was easily bought off (v. 18). However, Jehoash robbed God by giving Hazael gold from the temple treasury and other sacred valuables. Gath was located just 30 miles (48 km) from Jerusalem.

21For Joz′a•char[a] the son of Shim′ē•ath and
Je•hō′za•bad the son of Shō′mer,[b] his ser-
vants, struck him. So he died, and they
buried him with his fathers in the City of
David. Then Am•a•zī′ah his son reigned in
his place.

CHAPTER 13

Jehoahaz Reigns in Israel

In the twenty-third year of Jō′ash[a] the
son of Ā•ha•zī′ah, king of Judah, Je•hō′-
a•haz the son of Jē′hū became king over Is-
rael in Samaria, *and reigned* seventeen
years. 2And he did evil in the sight of the
LORD, and followed the sins of Jer•o•bō′am
the son of Nē′bat, who had made Israel sin.
He did not depart from them.

3Then the anger of the LORD was
aroused against Israel, and He delivered
them into the hand of Haz′a•el king of
Syria, and into the hand of Ben-Hā′dad the
son of Haz′a•el, all *their* days. 4So Je-
hō′a•haz pleaded with the LORD, and the
LORD listened to him; for He saw the op-
pression of Israel, because the king of Syria
oppressed them. 5Then the LORD gave Is-
rael a deliverer, so that they escaped from
under the hand of the Syrians; and the chil-
dren of Israel dwelt in their tents as before.
6Nevertheless they did not depart from the
sins of the house of Jer•o•bō′am, who had
made Israel sin, *but* walked in them; and
the wooden image[a] also remained in Sa-
maria. 7For He left of the army of Je•hō′-
a•haz only fifty horsemen, ten chariots,
and ten thousand foot soldiers; for the king
of Syria had destroyed them and made
them like the dust at threshing.

8Now the rest of the acts of Je•hō′a•haz,
all that he did, and his might, *are* they not
written in the book of the chronicles of the
kings of Israel? 9So Je•hō′a•haz rested with
his fathers, and they buried him in Sa-
maria. Then Jō′ash his son reigned in his
place.

Jehoash Reigns in Israel

10In the thirty-seventh year of Jō′ash
king of Judah, Je•hō′ash[a] the son of Je-
hō′a•haz became king over Israel in Sa-
maria, *and reigned* sixteen years. 11And he
did evil in the sight of the LORD. He did not
depart from all the sins of Jer•o•bō′am the
son of Nē′bat, who made Israel sin, *but*
walked in them.

12Now the rest of the acts of Jō′ash, all
that he did, and his might with which he
fought against Am•a•zī′ah king of Judah,
are they not written in the book of the
chronicles of the kings of Israel? 13So Jō′ash
rested with his fathers. Then Jer•o•bō′am
sat on his throne. And Jō′ash was buried in
Samaria with the kings of Israel.

Death of Elisha

14E•lī′sha had become sick with the ill-
ness of which he would die. Then Jō′ash
the king of Israel came down to him, and
wept over his face, and said, "O my father,
my father, the chariots of Israel and their
horsemen!"

15And E•lī′sha said to him, "Take a bow
and some arrows." So he took himself a
bow and some arrows. 16Then he said to
the king of Israel, "Put your hand on the
bow." So he put his hand *on it,* and E•lī′sha
put his hands on the king's hands. 17And

12:21 [a]Called *Zabad* in 2 Chronicles 24:26 [b]Called *Shimrith* in 2 Chronicles 24:26 13:1 [a]Spelled *Jehoash* in 12:1ff 13:6 [a]Hebrew *Asherah,* a Canaanite goddess 13:10 [a]Spelled *Joash* in verse 9

13:5 The identity of this **deliverer** is not clear. Perhaps it is Jehoahaz's successors, Jehoash (v. 25) and Jeroboam II (see 14:25, 27), or even Assyria, which besieged Damascus under Adad-nirari III (c. 806 B.C.). It might also be Elisha because of the inclusion of vv. 14–19. **dwelt in their tents**: Farmers felt secure enough to leave the protection of the walled cities and dwell in the open country.

13:14 wept over his face: Leaned over the dying prophet. **the chariots of Israel . . . horsemen**: Recalling the national loss at Elijah's departure (see 2:12).

he said, "Open the east window"; and he
opened *it*. Then E·lī'sha said, "Shoot"; and
he shot. And he said, "The arrow of the
LORD's deliverance and the arrow of deliv-
erance from Syria; for you must strike the
Syrians at Ā'phek till you have destroyed
them." 18Then he said, "Take the arrows";
so he took *them*. And he said to the king of
Israel, "Strike the ground"; so he struck
three times, and stopped. 19And the man of
God was angry with him, and said, "You
should have struck five or six times; then
you would have struck Syria till you had
destroyed *it*! But now you will strike Syria
only three times."

20Then E·lī'sha died, and they buried
him. And the *raiding* bands from Mō'ab in-
vaded the land in the spring of the year.
21So it was, as they were burying a man,
that suddenly they spied a band *of raiders*;
and they put the man in the tomb of
E·lī'sha; and when the man was let down
and touched the bones of E·lī'sha, he re-
vived and stood on his feet.

Israel Recaptures Cities from Syria

22And Haz'a·el king of Syria oppressed
Israel all the days of Je·hō'a·haz. 23But the
LORD was gracious to them, had compas-
sion on them, and regarded them, because
of His covenant with Abraham, Isaac, and
Jacob, and would not yet destroy them or
cast them from His presence.

24Now Haz'a·el king of Syria died. Then
Ben-Hā'dad his son reigned in his place.
25And Je·hō'ash[a] the son of Je·hō'a·haz
recaptured from the hand of Ben-Hā'dad,
the son of Haz'a·el, the cities which he had
taken out of the hand of Je·hō'a·haz his fa-
ther by war. Three times Jō'ash defeated
him and recaptured the cities of Israel.

CHAPTER 14

Amaziah Reigns in Judah

In the second year of Jō'ash the son of
Je·hō'a·haz, king of Israel, Am·a·zī'ah the
son of Jō'ash, king of Judah, became king.
2He was twenty-five years old when he be-
came king, and he reigned twenty-nine
years in Jerusalem. His mother's name was
Jē·hō·ad'dan of Jerusalem. 3And he did
what was right in the sight of the LORD, yet
not like his father David; he did everything
as his father Jō'ash had done. 4However
the high places were not taken away, and
the people still sacrificed and burned in-
cense on the high places.

5Now it happened, as soon as the king-
dom was established in his hand, that he
executed his servants who had murdered
his father the king. 6But the children of the
murderers he did not execute, according to
what is written in the Book of the Law of
Moses, in which the LORD commanded,
saying, "Fathers shall not be put to death
for their children, nor shall children be put
to death for their fathers; but a person shall
be put to death for his own sin."[a]

7He killed ten thousand Ē'dom·ītes in
the Valley of Salt, and took Sē'la by war,
and called its name Jok'the·el to this day.
8Then Am·a·zī'ah sent messengers to

13:25 [a]Spelled *Joash* in verses 12–14, 25
14:6 [a]Deuteronomy 24:16

13:21 Elisha's departure was as spectacular in its own way as was Elijah's (2:11).

13:23 Despite the idolatry and half-hearted worship of Israel's king and his people, the Lord held back His full judgment and kept His covenants with Abraham, Isaac, and Jacob.

13:24 Ben-Hadad: Apparently the third Syrian king of this name (see 1 Kin. 15:18, 19).

13:25 Three times: In fulfillment of Elisha's prophecy (see v. 19).

14:4 high places . . . not taken away: Worship was still allowed at places other than Jerusalem.

14:7 Sela: The name means "The Rock." The city, later called Petra, was the capital of Edom and was known for its strong defenses (see Ps. 60:9).

14:8 Amaziah's lack of wisdom in challenging **Israel** to war with Judah is depicted as a judgment because of his idolatrous acceptance of the gods of Edom (see 2 Chr. 25:14–20).

Je·hō'ash[a] the son of Je·hō'a·haz, the son of Jē'hū, king of Israel, saying, "Come, let us face one another *in battle*." 9And Je·hō'ash king of Israel sent to Am·a·zī'ah king of Judah, saying, "The thistle that *was* in Lebanon sent to the cedar that *was* in Lebanon, saying, 'Give your daughter to my son as wife'; and a wild beast that *was* in Lebanon passed by and trampled the thistle. 10You have indeed defeated Ē'dom, and your heart has lifted you up. Glory *in that*, and stay at home; for why should you meddle with trouble so that you fall—you and Judah with you?"

11But Am·a·zī'ah would not heed. Therefore Je·hō'ash king of Israel went out; so he and Am·a·zī'ah king of Judah faced one another at Beth Shem'esh, which *belongs* to Judah. 12And Judah was defeated by Israel, and every man fled to his tent. 13Then Je·hō'ash king of Israel captured Am·a·zī'ah king of Judah, the son of Je·hō'ash, the son of Ā·ha·zī'ah, at Beth Shem'esh; and he went to Jerusalem, and broke down the wall of Jerusalem from the Gate of Ē'phra·im to the Corner Gate—four hundred cubits. 14And he took all the gold and silver, all the articles that were found in the house of the LORD and in the treasuries of the king's house, and hostages, and returned to Samaria.

15Now the rest of the acts of Je·hō'ash which he did—his might, and how he fought with Am·a·zī'ah king of Judah—*are* they not written in the book of the chronicles of the kings of Israel? 16So Je·hō'ash rested with his fathers, and was buried in Samaria with the kings of Israel. Then Jer·o·bō'am his son reigned in his place.

17Am·a·zī'ah the son of Jō'ash, king of Judah, lived fifteen years after the death of Je·hō'ash the son of Je·hō'a·haz, king of Israel. 18Now the rest of the acts of Am·a·zī'ah, *are* they not written in the book of the chronicles of the kings of Judah? 19And they formed a conspiracy against him in Jerusalem, and he fled to Lā'chish; but they sent after him to Lā'chish and killed him there. 20Then they brought him on horses, and he was buried at Jerusalem with his fathers in the City of David.

21And all the people of Judah took Az·a·rī'ah,[a] who *was* sixteen years old, and made him king instead of his father Am·a·zī'ah. 22He built Ē'lath and restored it to Judah, after the king rested with his fathers.

Jeroboam II Reigns in Israel

23In the fifteenth year of Am·a·zī'ah the son of Jō'ash, king of Judah, Jer·o·bō'am the son of Jō'ash, king of Israel, became king in Samaria, *and reigned* forty-one years. 24And he did evil in the sight of the LORD; he did not depart from all the sins of Jer·o·bō'am the son of Nē'bat, who had made Israel sin. 25He restored the territory of Israel from the entrance of Hā'math to the Sea of the Ar'a·bah, according to the word of the LORD God of Israel, which He had spoken through His servant Jonah the son of A·mit'taī, the prophet who *was* from Gath Hē'pher. 26For the LORD saw *that* the affliction of Israel *was* very bitter; and whether bond or free, there was no helper for Israel. 27And the LORD did not say that He would blot out the name of Israel from under heaven; but He saved them by the hand of Jer·o·bō'am the son of Jō'ash.

28Now the rest of the acts of Jer·o·bō'am, and all that he did—his might, how he

14:8 [a]Spelled *Joash* in 13:12ff and 2 Chronicles 25:17ff
14:21 [a]Called *Uzziah* in 2 Chronicles 26:1ff, Isaiah 6:1, and elsewhere

14:21 The prophets Isaiah, Amos, and Hosea began ministering during the reign of Azariah (also called Uzziah) in Judah.

14:23–29 King Jeroboam II and the people of Israel persisted in their sinful lifestyle of idolatry; however, God continued to show them mercy and enabled Jeroboam II to claim several military victories and prevent Israel from being utterly destroyed.

14:25 Jonah . . . the prophet: Author of the Book of Jonah.

made war, and how he recaptured for Is-
rael, from Damascus and Hā'math, *what*
had belonged to Judah—*are* they not written
in the book of the chronicles of the kings of
Israel? 29So Jer·o·bō'am rested with his fa-
thers, the kings of Israel. Then Zech·a·rī'ah
his son reigned in his place.

CHAPTER 15

Azariah Reigns in Judah

In the twenty-seventh year of Jer·o-
bō'am king of Israel, Az·a·rī'ah the son of
Am·a·zī'ah, king of Judah, became king.
2He was sixteen years old when he became
king, and he reigned fifty-two years in Je-
rusalem. His mother's name *was* Jech-
o·lī'ah of Jerusalem. 3And he did *what was*
right in the sight of the LORD, according to
all that his father Am·a·zī'ah had done,
4except that the high places were not re-
moved; the people still sacrificed and
burned incense on the high places. 5Then
the LORD struck the king, so that he was a
leper until the day of his death; so he dwelt
in an isolated house. And Jō'tham the
king's son *was* over the *royal* house, judg-
ing the people of the land.
6Now the rest of the acts of Az·a·rī'ah,
and all that he did, *are* they not written in
the book of the chronicles of the kings of
Judah? 7So Az·a·rī'ah rested with his fa-
thers, and they buried him with his fathers
in the City of David. Then Jō'tham his son
reigned in his place.

Zechariah Reigns in Israel

8In the thirty-eighth year of Az·a·rī'ah
king of Judah, Zech·a·rī'ah the son of
Jer·o·bō'am reigned over Israel in Samaria
six months. 9And he did evil in the sight of
the LORD, as his fathers had done; he did
not depart from the sins of Jer·o·bō'am the
son of Nē'bat, who had made Israel sin.
10Then Shal'lum the son of Jā'besh con-
spired against him, and struck and killed
him in front of the people; and he reigned
in his place.
11Now the rest of the acts of Zech-
a·rī'ah, indeed they *are* written in the book
of the chronicles of the kings of Israel.
12This *was* the word of the LORD which
He spoke to Jē'hū, saying, "Your sons shall
sit on the throne of Israel to the fourth *gen-*
eration."[a] And so it was.

Shallum Reigns in Israel

13Shal'lum the son of Jā'besh became
king in the thirty-ninth year of Uz·zī'ah[a]
king of Judah; and he reigned a full month
in Samaria. 14For Men'a·hem the son of
Gā'dī went up from Tir'zah, came to Sa-
maria, and struck Shal'lum the son of
Jā'besh in Samaria and killed him; and he
reigned in his place.
15Now the rest of the acts of Shal'lum,
and the conspiracy which he led, indeed
they *are* written in the book of the chroni-
cles of the kings of Israel. 16Then from
Tir'zah, Men'a·hem attacked Tiph'sah, all
who *were* there, and its territory. Because
they did not surrender, therefore he at-
tacked *it*. All the women there who were
with child he ripped open.

Menahem Reigns in Israel

17In the thirty-ninth year of Az·a·rī'ah
king of Judah, Men'a·hem the son of Gā'dī
became king over Israel, *and reigned* ten
years in Samaria. 18And he did evil in the

15:12 [a]2 Kings 10:30
15:13 [a]Called *Azariah* in 14:21ff and 15:1ff

15:1 Azariah: Probably his birth name; Uzziah was his coronation name (see 2 Chr. 26:1).

15:5 the LORD struck the king: The result of Uzziah's usurping the place of the priest by burning incense on the altar (see Ex. 30:7, 8; 2 Chr. 26:16–21). **an isolated house**: See Lev. 13:45, 46.

15:10 Shallum's assassination of Zechariah fulfilled the prophecy of Amos (Amos 7:9).

15:12 to the fourth generation: See 10:30.

sight of the LORD; he did not depart all his
days from the sins of Jer·o·bō′am the son of
Nē′bat, who had made Israel sin. 19Pūl[a]
king of Assyria came against the land; and
Men′a·hem gave Pūl a thousand talents of
silver, that his hand might be with him to
strengthen the kingdom under his control.
20And Men′a·hem exacted the money from
Israel, from all the very wealthy, from each
man fifty shekels of silver, to give to the
king of Assyria. So the king of Assyria
turned back, and did not stay there in the
land.

21Now the rest of the acts of Men′a·hem,
and all that he did, *are* they not written in
the book of the chronicles of the kings of Is-
rael? 22So Men′a·hem rested with his fa-
thers. Then Pek·a·hī′ah his son reigned in
his place.

Pekahiah Reigns in Israel

23In the fiftieth year of Az·a·rī′ah king
of Judah, Pek·a·hī′ah the son of
Men′a·hem became king over Israel in
Samaria, *and reigned* two years. 24And he
did evil in the sight of the LORD; he did not
depart from the sins of Jer·o·bō′am the
son of Nē′bat, who had made Israel sin.
25Then Pē′kah the son of Rem·a·lī′ah, an
officer of his, conspired against him and
killed him in Samaria, in the citadel of the
king's house, along with Ar′gob and
A·ri′eh; and with him were fifty men of
Gil′ē·ad. He killed him and reigned in his
place.

26Now the rest of the acts of Pek·a·hī′ah,
and all that he did, indeed they *are* written
in the book of the chronicles of the kings of
Israel.

Pekah Reigns in Israel

27In the fifty-second year of Az·a·rī′ah
king of Judah, Pē′kah the son of Rem-
a·lī′ah became king over Israel in Samaria,
and reigned twenty years. 28And he did evil
in the sight of the LORD; he did not depart
from the sins of Jer·o·bō′am the son of
Nē′bat, who had made Israel sin. 29In the
days of Pē′kah king of Israel, Tig′lath-
Pī·lē′ser king of Assyria came and took
Ī′jon, Abel Beth Mā′a·chah, Ja·nō′ah,
Kē′desh, Hā′zor, Gil′ē·ad, and Galilee, all
the land of Naph′ta·lī; and he carried them
captive to Assyria. 30Then Hō·shē′a the son
of Ē′lah led a conspiracy against Pē′kah
the son of Rem·a·lī′ah, and struck and
killed him; so he reigned in his place in the
twentieth year of Jō′tham the son of
Uz·zī′ah.

31Now the rest of the acts of Pē′kah, and
all that he did, indeed they *are* written in
the book of the chronicles of the kings of Is-
rael.

Jotham Reigns in Judah

32In the second year of Pē′kah the son of
Rem·a·lī′ah, king of Israel, Jō′tham the son
of Uz·zī′ah, king of Judah, began to reign.
33He was twenty-five years old when he
became king, and he reigned sixteen years
in Jerusalem. His mother's name *was*
Je·rū′sha[a] the daughter of Zā′dok. 34And
he did *what was* right in the sight of the
LORD; he did according to all that his father
Uz·zī′ah had done. 35However the high
places were not removed; the people still

15:19 [a]That is, Tiglath-Pileser III (compare verse 29)
15:33 [a]Spelled *Jerushah* in 2 Chronicles 27:1

15:19, 20 Pul is the Babylonian throne name assumed by Tiglath-Pileser III of Assyria (745–727 B.C.) when he captured Babylon in 729 B.C. This energetic king revived Assyrian might and brutally extended the empire to the west. The bribery paid by Menahem was only a temporary respite; the new Assyrian presence in Syria-Palestine eventually led to Israel's destruction.

15:28, 29 This event—the invasion by Assyria and the taking of Israelite captives—was a warning of things to come. Unfortunately, Israel did not heed the admonition and continued in idolatry until the kingdom was destroyed around 722 B.C.

15:32 The ministry of the prophet Micah began during Jotham's reign.

I pray that I will do what is right in the sight of the Lord.

adapted from 2 Kings 15:34

sacrificed and burned incense on the high places. He built the Upper Gate of the house of the LORD.

36Now the rest of the acts of Jō'tham, and all that he did, *are* they not written in the book of the chronicles of the kings of Judah? 37In those days the LORD began to send Rē'zin king of Syria and Pē'kah the son of Rem·a·lī'ah against Judah. 38So Jō'tham rested with his fathers, and was buried with his fathers in the City of David his father. Then Ā'haz his son reigned in his place.

CHAPTER 16

Ahaz Reigns in Judah

In the seventeenth year of Pē'kah the son of Rem·a·lī'ah, Ā'haz the son of Jō'tham, king of Judah, began to reign. 2Ā'haz *was* twenty years old when he became king, and he reigned sixteen years in Jerusalem; and he did not do *what was* right in the sight of the LORD his God, as his father David *had done*. 3But he walked in the way of the kings of Israel; indeed he made his son pass through the fire, according to the abominations of the nations whom the LORD had cast out from before the children of Israel. 4And he sacrificed and burned incense on the high places, on the hills, and under every green tree.

5Then Rē'zin king of Syria and Pē'kah the son of Rem·a·lī'ah, king of Israel, came up to Jerusalem to *make* war; and they besieged Ā'haz but could not overcome *him*. 6At that time Rē'zin king of Syria captured Ē'lath for Syria, and drove the men of Judah from Ē'lath. Then the Ē'dom·ītes[a] went to Ē'lath, and dwell there to this day.

7So Ā'haz sent messengers to Tig'lath-Pī·lē'ser king of Assyria, saying, "I *am* your servant and your son. Come up and save me from the hand of the king of Syria and from the hand of the king of Israel, who rise up against me." 8And Ā'haz took the silver and gold that was found in the house of the LORD, and in the treasuries of the king's house, and sent *it as* a present to the king of Assyria. 9So the king of Assyria heeded him; for the king of Assyria went up against Damascus and took it, carried *its people* captive to Kir, and killed Rē'zin.

10Now King Ā'haz went to Damascus to meet Tig'lath-Pī·lē'ser king of Assyria, and saw an altar that *was* at Damascus; and King Ā'haz sent to Ū·rī'jah the priest the design of the altar and its pattern, according to all its workmanship. 11Then Ū·rī'jah the priest built an altar according to all that King Ā'haz had sent from Damascus. So Ū·rī'jah the priest made *it* before King Ā'haz came back from Damascus. 12And when the king came back from Damascus, the king saw the altar; and the king approached the altar and made offerings on it. 13So he burned his burnt offering and his grain offering; and he poured his drink of-

16:6 [a]Some ancient authorities read *Syrians*.

16:3 pass through the fire: Child sacrifice was a deplorable form of worship practiced by the Phoenicians, the Moabites (3:27), and others (see Jer. 19:5).

16:5 Rezin: The last king of Syria. He and **Pekah** desired to place a puppet ruler, the son of Tabel (see Is. 7:5, 6), in Jerusalem to join them in defiance of Assyria. **Ahaz**, however, was pro-Assyrian (v. 7). The details of the war are given in 2 Chr. 28:5–21.

16:7 Ahaz decided to trust Assyria rather than God for protection from Israel and Syria. These events prompted the first public phase of Isaiah's ministry (see Is. 7:1—8:8). **your son**: An expression meaning "subservient to you."

16:9 Amos had prophesied this captivity (see Amos 1:5).

16:13 The offerings prescribed for worshiping the Lord were made on an alien altar.

fering and sprinkled the blood of his peace offerings on the altar. 14He also brought the bronze altar which *was* before the LORD, from the front of the temple—from between the *new* altar and the house of the LORD—and put it on the north side of the *new* altar. 15Then King Ā′haz commanded Ū·rī′jah the priest, saying, "On the great *new* altar burn the morning burnt offering, the evening grain offering, the king's burnt sacrifice, and his grain offering, with the burnt offering of all the people of the land, their grain offering, and their drink offerings; and sprinkle on it all the blood of the burnt offering and all the blood of the sacrifice. And the bronze altar shall be for me to inquire *by.*" 16Thus did Ū·rī′jah the priest, according to all that King Ā′haz commanded.

17And King Ā′haz cut off the panels of the carts, and removed the lavers from them; and he took down the Sea from the bronze oxen that *were* under it, and put it on a pavement of stones. 18Also he removed the Sabbath pavilion which they had built in the temple, and he removed the king's outer entrance from the house of the LORD, on account of the king of Assyria.

19Now the rest of the acts of Ā′haz which he did, *are* they not written in the book of the chronicles of the kings of Judah? 20So Ā′haz rested with his fathers, and was buried with his fathers in the City of David. Then Hez·e·kī′ah his son reigned in his place.

CHAPTER 17

Hoshea Reigns in Israel

In the twelfth year of Ā′haz king of Judah, Hō·shē′a the son of Ē′lah became king of Israel in Samaria, *and he reigned* nine years. 2And he did evil in the sight of the LORD, but not as the kings of Israel who were before him. 3Shal·man·ē′ser king of Assyria came up against him; and Hō·shē′a became his vassal, and paid him tribute money. 4And the king of Assyria uncovered a conspiracy by Hō·shē′a; for he had sent messengers to So, king of Egypt, and brought no tribute to the king of Assyria, as *he had done* year by year. Therefore the king of Assyria shut him up, and bound him in prison.

Israel Carried Captive to Assyria

5Now the king of Assyria went throughout all the land, and went up to Samaria and besieged it for three years. 6In the ninth year of Hō·shē′a, the king of Assyria took Samaria and carried Israel away to Assyria, and placed them in Hā′lah and by the Hā′bor, the River of Gō′zan, and in the cities of the Mēdes.

7For so it was that the children of Israel had sinned against the LORD their God,

16:15 for me to inquire by: The **bronze altar** was relegated to divination, an Assyrian practice.

16:17, 18 Alterations in the temple and palace were made to conform to Judah's new role as a vassal state and to raise tribute to pay off Assyria. **Sea**: see 1 Kin. 7:23–26.

17:1 Hoshea was the last of the 19 kings who ruled Israel over a period of about 200 years.

17:3 Shalmaneser V was king of Assyria from 727 to 722 B.C.

17:4 No Egyptian pharaoh by the name of **So** is known. The reference may be to the Egyptian commander with a similar-sounding name who is listed in the Assyrian inscriptions.

17:6 The king of Assyria who **took Samaria** was not the Shalmaneser V who began the three-year siege (see v. 3). Sargon II (722–705 B.C.) took the throne shortly before Samaria fell in 722 B.C. In an inscription Sargon claims credit for deporting 27,290 captives. This marked the end of the northern kingdom.

17:7–23 The reasons for Israel's destruction. The nation did not fall simply because it had a smaller army. **Israel** had broken the **statutes** and **commandments** of the Lord (vv. 15, 16). Ultimately it was the Lord who was responsible for Israel's fall (vv. 18, 20, 23). To continue in sin is to mock God; He will not allow evil to go unpunished.

who had brought them up out of the land of Egypt, from under the hand of Pharaoh king of Egypt; and they had feared other gods, [8]and had walked in the statutes of the nations whom the LORD had cast out from before the children of Israel, and of the kings of Israel, which they had made. [9]Also the children of Israel secretly did against the LORD their God things that *were* not right, and they built for themselves high places in all their cities, from watchtower to fortified city. [10]They set up for themselves *sacred* pillars and wooden images[a] on every high hill and under every green tree. [11]There they burned incense on all the high places, like the nations whom the LORD had carried away before them; and they did wicked things to provoke the LORD to anger, [12]for they served idols, of which the LORD had said to them, "You shall not do this thing."

[13]Yet the LORD testified against Israel and against Judah, by all of His prophets, every seer, saying, "Turn from your evil ways, and keep My commandments *and* My statutes, according to all the law which I commanded your fathers, and which I sent to you by My servants the prophets." [14]Nevertheless they would not hear, but stiffened their necks, like the necks of their fathers, who did not believe in the LORD their God. [15]And they rejected His statutes and His covenant that He had made with their fathers, and His testimonies which He had testified against them; they followed idols, became idolaters, and *went* after the nations who *were* all around them, *concerning* whom the LORD had charged them that they should not do like them. [16]So they left all the commandments of the LORD their God, made for themselves a molded image *and* two calves, made a wooden image and worshiped all the host of heaven, and served Bā'al. [17]And they caused their sons and daughters to pass through the fire, practiced witchcraft and soothsaying, and sold themselves to do evil in the sight of the LORD, to provoke Him to anger. [18]Therefore the LORD was very angry with Israel, and removed them from His sight; there was none left but the tribe of Judah alone.

[19]Also Judah did not keep the commandments of the LORD their God, but walked in the statutes of Israel which they made. [20]And the LORD rejected all the descendants of Israel, afflicted them, and delivered them into the hand of plunderers, until He had cast them from His sight. [21]For He tore Israel from the house of David, and they made Jer·o·bō'am the son of Nē'bat king. Then Jer·o·bō'am drove Israel from following the LORD, and made them commit a great sin. [22]For the children of Israel walked in all the sins of Jer·o·bō'am which he did; they did not depart from them, [23]until the LORD removed Israel out of His sight, as He had said by all His servants the prophets. So Israel was carried away from their own land to Assyria, *as it is* to this day.

Assyria Resettles Samaria

[24]Then the king of Assyria brought *people* from Babylon, Cū'thah, Ā'va, Hā'math, and from Seph·ar·vā'im, and placed *them* in the cities of Samaria instead of the children of Israel; and they took possession of Samaria and dwelt in its cities. [25]And it was so, at the beginning of their dwelling there, *that* they did not fear the LORD; therefore the LORD sent lions among them, which

17:10 [a]Hebrew *Asherim*, Canaanite deities

17:16 host of heaven: Assyrian star worship, perhaps imposed on Israel as a symbol of subjection.

17:17 pass through the fire: Sacrificed them to the god Molech (see Ezek. 23:37).

17:24 The custom of many Assyrian kings was to replace the deported captives with inhabitants from other conquered areas. The mixture of races broke rebellious tendencies, and blended religious practices as recorded in vv. 29–41.

killed *some* of them. 26So they spoke to the king of Assyria, saying, "The nations whom you have removed and placed in the cities of Samaria do not know the rituals of the God of the land; therefore He has sent lions among them, and indeed, they are killing them because they do not know the rituals of the God of the land." 27Then the king of Assyria commanded, saying, "Send there one of the priests whom you brought from there; let him go and dwell there, and let him teach them the rituals of the God of the land." 28Then one of the priests whom they had carried away from Samaria came and dwelt in Beth'el, and taught them how they should fear the LORD.

29However every nation continued to make gods of its own, and put *them* in the shrines on the high places which the Samaritans had made, *every* nation in the cities where they dwelt. 30The men of Babylon made Suc'coth Be·noth', the men of Cūth made Ner'gal, the men of Hā'math made A·shī'ma, 31and the Av'ītes made Nib'haz and Tar'tak; and the Se·phar'vītes burned their children in fire to A·dram'me·lech and A·nam'me·lech, the gods of Seph·ar·vā'im. 32So they feared the LORD, and from every class they appointed for themselves priests of the high places, who sacrificed for them in the shrines of the high places. 33They feared the LORD, yet served their own gods—according to the rituals of the nations from among whom they were carried away.

34To this day they continue practicing the former rituals; they do not fear the LORD, nor do they follow their statutes or their ordinances, or the law and commandment which the LORD had commanded the children of Jacob, whom He named Israel, 35with whom the LORD had made a covenant and charged them, saying: "You shall not fear other gods, nor bow down to them nor serve them nor sacrifice to them; 36but the LORD, who brought you up from the land of Egypt with great power and an outstretched arm, Him you shall fear, Him you shall worship, and to Him you shall offer sacrifice. 37And the statutes, the ordinances, the law, and the commandment which He wrote for you, you shall be careful to observe forever; you shall not fear other gods. 38And the covenant that I have made with you, you shall not forget, nor shall you fear other gods. 39But the LORD your God you shall fear; and He will deliver you from the hand of all your enemies." 40However they did not obey, but they followed their former rituals. 41So these nations feared the LORD, yet served their carved images; also their children and their children's children have continued doing as their fathers did, even to this day.

CHAPTER 18

Hezekiah Reigns in Judah

Now it came to pass in the third year of Hō·shē'a the son of Ē'lah, king of Israel, *that* Hez·e·kī'ah the son of Ā'haz, king of Judah, began to reign. 2He was twenty-five years old when he became king, and he reigned twenty-nine years in Jerusalem. His mother's name *was* Ā'bī[a] the daughter of Zech·a·rī'ah. 3And he did *what was* right in the sight of the LORD, according to all that his father David had done.

4He removed the high places and broke the *sacred* pillars, cut down the wooden im-

18:2 [a]Called *Abijah* in 2 Chronicles 29:1ff

17:28, 29 The origin of the divergent Samaritan religion in the time of Jesus (see John 4:9, 19, 20). The descendants of mixed marriages between foreigners and Israelites left in the land came to be known as Samaritans, and they followed a religion that mixed worship of Yahweh with worship of foreign gods.

18:4 the bronze serpent: What had originally been a symbol of faith in God's promise had become an object of worship (Num. 21:6–9).

age[a] and broke in pieces the bronze serpent that Moses had made; for until those days the children of Israel burned incense to it, and called it Ne·hush'tan.[b] 5He trusted in the LORD God of Israel, so that after him was none like him among all the kings of Judah, nor who were before him. 6For he held fast to the LORD; he did not depart from following Him, but kept His commandments, which the LORD had commanded Moses. 7The LORD was with him; he prospered wherever he went. And he rebelled against the king of Assyria and did not serve him. 8He subdued the Phi·lis'tines, as far as Gā'za and its territory, from watchtower to fortified city.

9Now it came to pass in the fourth year of King Hez·e·kī'ah, which *was* the seventh year of Hō·shē'a the son of Ē'lah, king of Israel, *that* Shal·man·ē'ser king of Assyria came up against Samaria and besieged it. 10And at the end of three years they took it. In the sixth year of Hez·e·kī'ah, that *is,* the ninth year of Hō·shē'a king of Israel, Samaria was taken. 11Then the king of Assyria carried Israel away captive to Assyria, and put them in Hā'lah and by the Hā'bor, the River of Gō'zan, and in the cities of the Mēdes, 12because they did not obey the voice of the LORD their God, but transgressed His covenant *and* all that Moses the servant of the LORD had commanded; and they would neither hear nor do *them.*

13And in the fourteenth year of King Hez·e·kī'ah, Sen·nach'e·rib king of Assyria came up against all the fortified cities of Judah and took them. 14Then Hez·e·kī'ah king of Judah sent to the king of Assyria at Lā'chish, saying, "I have done wrong; turn away from me; whatever you impose on me I will pay." And the king of Assyria assessed Hez·e·kī'ah king of Judah three hundred talents of silver and thirty talents of gold. 15So Hez·e·kī'ah gave *him* all the silver that was found in the house of the LORD and in the treasuries of the king's house. 16At that time Hez·e·kī'ah stripped *the gold from* the doors of the temple of the LORD, and *from* the pillars which Hez·e·kī'ah king of Judah had overlaid, and gave it to the king of Assyria.

Sennacherib Boasts Against the LORD

17Then the king of Assyria sent *the* Tartan,[a] *the* Rab·sar'is,[b] *and the* Rab'sha·keh[c] from Lā'chish, with a great army against Jerusalem, to King Hez·e·kī'ah. And they went up and came to Jerusalem. When they had come up, they went and stood by the aqueduct from the upper pool, which *was* on the highway to the Fuller's Field. 18And when they had called to the king, E·lī'a·kim the son of Hil·kī'ah, who *was* over the household, Sheb'na the scribe, and Jō'ah the son of Ā'saph, the recorder, came out to them. 19Then *the* Rab'sha·keh said to them, "Say now to Hez·e·kī'ah, 'Thus says the great king, the king of Assyria: "What confidence *is* this in which you trust? 20You speak of *having* plans and power for war; but *they are* mere words.

18:4 [a]Hebrew *Asherah,* a Canaanite goddess [b]Literally *Bronze Thing* 18:17 [a]A title, probably *Commander in Chief* [b]A title, probably *Chief Officer* [c]A title, probably *Chief of Staff* or *Governor*

18:5–8 A comparison between Hezekiah's accomplishments during this time and the victories of his predecessors demonstrates how much more God can do with someone fully dedicated to Him.

18:14–16 The conquest of **Lachish** is well attested in Assyrian sources. Hezekiah's admission that he had **done wrong** acknowledged that he had rebelled against Assyrian rule. He was undoubtedly hoping that upon receiving the demanded tribute Sennacherib would go home. That was not the case. The Assyrian wanted nothing less than total surrender (vv. 17–35).

18:15 Hezekiah's previously strong faith faltered, and he followed his father's sinful example of robbing God's temple to pay tribute to Assyria.

And in whom do you trust, that you rebel against me? 21Now look! You are trusting in the staff of this broken reed, Egypt, on which if a man leans, it will go into his hand and pierce it. So *is* Pharaoh king of Egypt to all who trust in him. 22But if you say to me, 'We trust in the LORD our God,' *is* it not He whose high places and whose altars Hez·e·kī'ah has taken away, and said to Judah and Jerusalem, 'You shall worship before this altar in Jerusalem'?" ' 23Now therefore, I urge you, give a pledge to my master the king of Assyria, and I will give you two thousand horses—if you are able on your part to put riders on them! 24How then will you repel one captain of the least of my master's servants, and put your trust in Egypt for chariots and horsemen? 25Have I now come up without the LORD against this place to destroy it? The LORD said to me, 'Go up against this land, and destroy it.' "

26Then E·lī'a·kim the son of Hil·kī'ah, Sheb'na, and Jō'ah said to *the* Rab'sha·keh, "Please speak to your servants in Ar·a·mā'ic, for we understand *it;* and do not speak to us in Hebrew[a] in the hearing of the people who *are* on the wall."

27But *the* Rab'sha·keh said to them, "Has my master sent me to your master and to you to speak these words, and not to the men who sit on the wall, who will eat and drink their own waste with you?"

28Then *the* Rab'sha·keh stood and called out with a loud voice in Hebrew, and spoke, saying, "Hear the word of the great king, the king of Assyria! 29Thus says the king: 'Do not let Hez·e·kī'ah deceive you, for he shall not be able to deliver you from his hand; 30nor let Hez·e·kī'ah make you trust in the LORD, saying, "The LORD will surely deliver us; this city shall not be given into the hand of the king of Assyria." ' 31Do not listen to Hez·e·kī'ah; for thus says the king of Assyria: 'Make *peace* with me by a present and come out to me; and every one of you eat from his own vine and every one from his own fig tree, and every one of you drink the waters of his own cistern; 32until I come and take you away to a land like your own land, a land of grain and new wine, a land of bread and vineyards, a land of olive groves and honey, that you may live and not die. But do not listen to Hez·e·kī'ah, lest he persuade you, saying, "The LORD will deliver us." 33Has any of the gods of the nations at all delivered its land from the hand of the king of Assyria? 34Where *are* the gods of Hā'math and Ar'pad? Where *are* the gods of Seph·ar·vā'im and Hē'na and Ī'vah? Indeed, have they delivered Samaria from my hand? 35Who among all the gods of the lands have delivered their countries from my hand, that the LORD should deliver Jerusalem from my hand?' "

36But the people held their peace and answered him not a word; for the king's commandment was, "Do not answer him." 37Then E·lī'a·kim the son of Hil·kī'ah, who *was* over the household, Sheb'na the scribe, and Jō'ah the son of Ā'saph, the recorder, came to Hez·e·kī'ah with *their* clothes torn, and told him the words of *the* Rab'sha·keh.

8:26 [a]Literally *Judean*

18:25 In claiming God's authority to **go up against this land**, the Rabshakeh spoke more truthfully than he knew (see Is. 10:5–11).

18:26 Aramaic: The diplomatic language understood by government officials. **Hebrew**: The common language of the people.

18:33–35 Hamath . . . Arpad . . . Ivah: Strong cities Assyria had already conquered. If their gods had not been able to save these lands and cities, why should the Jews expect **the LORD** to deliver them?

18:37 clothes torn: As a sign of grief and terror.

CHAPTER 19

Isaiah Assures Deliverance

And so it was, when King Hez·e·kī′ah
heard *it,* that he tore his clothes, covered
himself with sackcloth, and went into the
house of the LORD. 2Then he sent E·lī′-
a·kim, who *was* over the household,
Sheb′na the scribe, and the elders of the
priests, covered with sackcloth, to Ī·sāi′ah
the prophet, the son of Ā′moz. 3And they
said to him, "Thus says Hez·e·kī′ah: 'This
day *is* a day of trouble, and rebuke, and
blasphemy; for the children have come to
birth, but *there is* no strength to bring them
forth. 4It may be that the LORD your God
will hear all the words of *the* Rab′sha·keh,
whom his master the king of Assyria has
sent to reproach the living God, and will
rebuke the words which the LORD your
God has heard. Therefore lift up *your*
prayer for the remnant that is left.' "
5So the servants of King Hez·e·kī′ah
came to Ī·sāi′ah. 6And Ī·sāi′ah said to
them, "Thus you shall say to your master,
'Thus says the LORD: "Do not be afraid of
the words which you have heard, with
which the servants of the king of Assyria
have blasphemed Me. 7Surely I will send a
spirit upon him, and he shall hear a rumor
and return to his own land; and I will
cause him to fall by the sword in his own
land." ' "

Sennacherib's Threat and Hezekiah's Prayer

8Then *the* Rab′sha·keh returned and
found the king of Assyria warring against
Lib′nah, for he heard that he had departed
from Lā′chish. 9And the king heard con-
cerning Tir·hā′kah king of Ethiopia,
"Look, he has come out to make war with
you." So he again sent messengers to
Hez·e·kī′ah, saying, 10"Thus you shall
speak to Hez·e·kī′ah king of Judah, saying:
'Do not let your God in whom you trust
deceive you, saying, "Jerusalem shall not
be given into the hand of the king of As-
syria." 11Look! You have heard what the
kings of Assyria have done to all lands by
utterly destroying them; and shall you be
delivered? 12Have the gods of the nations
delivered those whom my fathers have de-
stroyed, Gō′zan and Har′an and Rē′zeph,
and the people of Eden who *were* in
Te·las′sar? 13Where *is* the king of Hā′math,
the king of Ar′pad, and the king of the city
of Seph·ar·vā′im, Hē′na, and Ī′vah?' "
14And Hez·e·kī′ah received the letter
from the hand of the messengers, and read
it; and Hez·e·kī′ah went up to the house of
the LORD, and spread it before the LORD.
15Then Hez·e·kī′ah prayed before the
LORD, and said: "O LORD God of Israel, *the
One* who dwells *between* the cherubim, You
are God, You alone, of all the kingdoms of
the earth. You have made heaven and
earth. 16Incline Your ear, O LORD, and hear;
open Your eyes, O LORD, and see; and hear
the words of Sen·nach′e·rib, which he has
sent to reproach the living God. 17Truly,
LORD, the kings of Assyria have laid waste
the nations and their lands, 18and have cast
their gods into the fire; for they *were* not
gods, but the work of men's hands—wood
and stone. Therefore they destroyed them.
19Now therefore, O LORD our God, I pray,
save us from his hand, that all the king-
doms of the earth may know that You *are*
the LORD God, You alone."

The Word of the LORD Concerning Sennacherib

20Then Ī·sāi′ah the son of Ā′moz sent to
Hez·e·kī′ah, saying, "Thus says the LORD
God of Israel: 'Because you have prayed to

19:1 Hezekiah turned directly to the Lord for help—always the wisest course of action.
19:7 This prophecy of Isaiah found its fulfillment in vv. 36, 37.
19:14–19 Hezekiah's prayer provides a model for Christians who find themselves in desperate straits: he acknowledged God's power and position as the One true God, he pled his case before the Lord, and He asked that his request be answered for the glory of God.

Me against Sen·nach'e·rib king of Assyria,
I have heard.' 21This *is* the word which the
LORD has spoken concerning him:

'The virgin, the daughter of Zion,
Has despised you, laughed you to
scorn;
The daughter of Jerusalem
Has shaken *her* head behind your
back!

22 'Whom have you reproached and
blasphemed?
Against whom have you raised *your*
voice,
And lifted up your eyes on high?
Against the Holy *One* of Israel.
23 By your messengers you have
reproached the Lord,
And said: "By the multitude of my
chariots
I have come up to the height of the
mountains,
To the limits of Lebanon;
I will cut down its tall cedars
And its choice cypress trees;
I will enter the extremity of its
borders,
To its fruitful forest.
24 I have dug and drunk strange water,
And with the soles of my feet I have
dried up
All the brooks of defense."

25 'Did you not hear long ago
How I made it,
From ancient times that I formed it?
Now I have brought it to pass,
That you should be
For crushing fortified cities *into* heaps
of ruins.
26 Therefore their inhabitants had little
power;
They were dismayed and
confounded;
They were *as* the grass of the field
And the green herb,
As the grass on the housetops
And *grain* blighted before it is grown.

27 'But I know your dwelling place,
Your going out and your coming in,
And your rage against Me.
28 Because your rage against Me and
your tumult
Have come up to My ears,
Therefore I will put My hook in your
nose
And My bridle in your lips,
And I will turn you back
By the way which you came.

29'This *shall be* a sign to you:

You shall eat this year such as grows
of itself,
And in the second year what springs
from the same;
Also in the third year sow and reap,
Plant vineyards and eat the fruit of
them.
30 And the remnant who have escaped
of the house of Judah
Shall again take root downward,
And bear fruit upward.

19:21 The beginning of a "taunt song" in which the smallest and weakest in Jerusalem mock the mighty king of Assyria.

19:25, 26 The Assyrian thinks his accomplishments are the result of his own efforts. Little does he know that he is merely fulfilling the plan of Judah's God (see Is. 10:15 and note). **grass on the housetops**: Grass seed could sprout in the mud plaster or in pockets of dust blown on the flat roofs. But it soon died.

19:28 hook in your nose . . . bridle in your lips: Because Assyria led away conquered kings in this way (see 2 Chr. 33:11), this was a fitting judgment.

19:29, 31 No more than two harvests would be lost, after which the nation would again see normal growth of field and family.

31 For out of Jerusalem shall go a
remnant,
And those who escape from Mount
Zion.
The zeal of the LORD of hosts[a] will do
this.'

[32]"Therefore thus says the LORD con-
cerning the king of Assyria:

'He shall not come into this city,
Nor shoot an arrow there,
Nor come before it with shield,
Nor build a siege mound against it.
33 By the way that he came,
By the same shall he return;
And he shall not come into this city,'
Says the LORD.
34 'For I will defend this city, to save it
For My own sake and for My servant
David's sake.' "

Sennacherib's Defeat and Death

[35]And it came to pass on a certain night
that the angel[a] of the LORD went out, and
killed in the camp of the Assyrians one
hundred and eighty-five thousand; and
when *people* arose early in the morning,
there were the corpses—all dead. [36]So
Sen·nach'e·rib king of Assyria departed
and went away, returned *home,* and re-
mained at Nin'e·veh. [37]Now it came to
pass, as he was worshiping in the temple
of Nis'roch his god, that his sons
A·dram'me·lech and Sha·rē'zer struck him
down with the sword; and they escaped
into the land of Ar'a·rat. Then Ē·sar-
had'don his son reigned in his place.

19:31 [a]Following many Hebrew manuscripts and ancient versions (compare Isaiah 37:32); Masoretic Text omits *of hosts.* 19:35 [a]Or *Angel*

CHAPTER 20

Hezekiah's Life Extended

In those days Hez·e·kī'ah was sick and
near death. And Ī·sāi'ah the prophet, the
son of Ā'moz, went to him and said to him,
"Thus says the LORD: 'Set your house in or-
der, for you shall die, and not live.' "
[2]Then he turned his face toward the
wall, and prayed to the LORD, saying, [3]"Re-
member now, O LORD, I pray, how I have
walked before You in truth and with a
loyal heart, and have done *what was* good
in Your sight." And Hez·e·kī'ah wept bit-
terly.
[4]And it happened, before Ī·sāi'ah had
gone out into the middle court, that the
word of the LORD came to him, saying,
[5]"Return and tell Hez·e·kī'ah the leader of
My people, 'Thus says the LORD, the God
of David your father: "I have heard your
prayer, I have seen your tears; surely I will
heal you. On the third day you shall go up
to the house of the LORD. [6]And I will add to
your days fifteen years. I will deliver you
and this city from the hand of the king of
Assyria; and I will defend this city for My
own sake, and for the sake of My servant
David." ' "
[7]Then Ī·sāi'ah said, "Take a lump of
figs." So they took and laid *it* on the boil,
and he recovered.
[8]And Hez·e·kī'ah said to Ī·sāi'ah,
"What *is* the sign that the LORD will heal
me, and that I shall go up to the house of
the LORD the third day?"
[9]Then Ī·sāi'ah said, "This is the sign to

19:35 The number **one hundred and eighty-five thousand** is no exaggeration, given the size of the armies attested in Assyrian records.

19:36, 37 Sennacherib, who had mocked God, was cut down in the temple of his own god. **Esarhaddon** reigned from 681 to 669 B.C.

20:8 sign: Normally a miracle which validates a prophetic statement. Ahaz unwisely rejected a sign, but Hezekiah sought such confirmation (see Is. 7:11, 12).

20:9–11 sundial of Ahaz: Probably a stepped building or altar erected by Ahaz for worship of the stars, and located somewhere in the temple complex (23:12). The **shadow** would ordinarily lengthen **down** the eastern steps during the afternoon.

you from the LORD, that the LORD will do
the thing which He has spoken: *shall* the
shadow go forward ten degrees or go
backward ten degrees?"
10And Hez·e·kī'ah answered, "It is an
easy thing for the shadow to go down ten
degrees; no, but let the shadow go back-
ward ten degrees."
11So Ī·sāi'ah the prophet cried out to the
LORD, and He brought the shadow ten de-
grees backward, by which it had gone
down on the sundial of Ā'haz.

The Babylonian Envoys

12At that time Be·rō'dach-Bal'a·dan[a] the
son of Bal'a·dan, king of Babylon, sent let-
ters and a present to Hez·e·kī'ah, for he
heard that Hez·e·kī'ah had been sick.
13And Hez·e·kī'ah was attentive to them,
and showed them all the house of his trea-
sures—the silver and gold, the spices and
precious ointment, and all[a] his armory—all
that was found among his treasures. There
was nothing in his house or in all his do-
minion that Hez·e·kī'ah did not show
them.
14Then Ī·sāi'ah the prophet went to King
Hez·e·kī'ah, and said to him, "What did
these men say, and from where did they
come to you?"
So Hez·e·kī'ah said, "They came from a
far country, from Babylon."
15And he said, "What have they seen in
your house?"
So Hez·e·kī'ah answered, "They have
seen all that *is* in my house; there is noth-
ing among my treasures that I have not
shown them."
16Then Ī·sāi'ah said to Hez·e·kī'ah,
"Hear the word of the LORD: 17'Behold, the
days are coming when all that *is* in your
house, and what your fathers have accu-
mulated until this day, shall be carried to
Babylon; nothing shall be left,' says the
LORD. 18'And they shall take away some of
your sons who will descend from you,
whom you will beget; and they shall be eu-
nuchs in the palace of the king of Bab-
ylon.' "
19So Hez·e·kī'ah said to Ī·sāi'ah, "The
word of the LORD which you have spoken
is good!" For he said, "Will there not be
peace and truth at least in my days?"

Death of Hezekiah

20Now the rest of the acts of Hez·e-
kī'ah—all his might, and how he made a
pool and a tunnel and brought water into
the city—*are* they not written in the book of
the chronicles of the kings of Judah? 21So
Hez·e·kī'ah rested with his fathers. Then
Ma·nas'seh his son reigned in his place.

CHAPTER 21

Manasseh Reigns in Judah

Ma·nas'seh *was* twelve years old when
he became king, and he reigned fifty-five
years in Jerusalem. His mother's name *was*
Heph'zi·bah. 2And he did evil in the sight
of the LORD, according to the abominations
of the nations whom the LORD had cast out

20:12 [a]Spelled *Merodach-Baladan* in Isaiah 39:1
20:13 [a]Following many Hebrew manuscripts, Syriac, and Targum; Masoretic Text omits *all*.

20:17 This prophecy was fulfilled one century later when Nebuchadnezzar II captured Judah.

20:20 As a defensive measure, Hezekiah built a **tunnel** which would bring water from the Spring of Gihon outside the walls of Jerusalem for storage in the **pool** of Siloam within the city (see 2 Chr. 32:30). Thus the water supply of Jerusalem would be secure during a siege by an invading army. A Hebrew inscription, now called the Siloam Inscription, at the end of the tunnel describes how the workmen dug the tunnel from two sides and met in the middle.

21:1–18 Manasseh's reign is presented as the worst period in Judah's history; she was more sinful than the pagan nations driven out of Canaan during the Israelite conquest (v. 9).

before the children of Israel. 3For he rebuilt the high places which Hez·e·kī'ah his father had destroyed; he raised up altars for Bā'al, and made a wooden image,[a] as Ā'hab king of Israel had done; and he worshiped all the host of heaven[b] and served them. 4He also built altars in the house of the LORD, of which the LORD had said, "In Jerusalem I will put My name." 5And he built altars for all the host of heaven in the two courts of the house of the LORD. 6Also he made his son pass through the fire, practiced soothsaying, used witchcraft, and consulted spiritists and mediums. He did much evil in the sight of the LORD, to provoke *Him* to anger. 7He even set a carved image of A·shē'rah[a] that he had made, in the house of which the LORD had said to David and to Solomon his son, "In this house and in Jerusalem, which I have chosen out of all the tribes of Israel, I will put My name forever; 8and I will not make the feet of Israel wander anymore from the land which I gave their fathers—only if they are careful to do according to all that I have commanded them, and according to all the law that My servant Moses commanded them." 9But they paid no attention, and Ma·nas'seh seduced them to do more evil than the nations whom the LORD had destroyed before the children of Israel.

10And the LORD spoke by His servants the prophets, saying, 11"Because Ma·nas'seh king of Judah has done these abominations (he has acted more wickedly than all the Am'o·rītes who *were* before him, and has also made Judah sin with his idols), 12therefore thus says the LORD God of Israel: 'Behold, *I* am bringing *such* calamity upon Jerusalem and Judah, that whoever hears of it, both his ears will tingle. 13And I will stretch over Jerusalem the measuring line of Samaria and the plummet of the house of Ā'hab; I will wipe Jerusalem as *one* wipes a dish, wiping *it* and turning *it* upside down. 14So I will forsake the remnant of My inheritance and deliver them into the hand of their enemies; and they shall become victims of plunder to all their enemies, 15because they have done evil in My sight, and have provoked Me to anger since the day their fathers came out of Egypt, even to this day.' "

16Moreover Ma·nas'seh shed very much innocent blood, till he had filled Jerusalem from one end to another, besides his sin by which he made Judah sin, in doing evil in the sight of the LORD.

17Now the rest of the acts of Ma·nas'seh—all that he did, and the sin that he committed—*are* they not written in the book of the chronicles of the kings of Judah? 18So Ma·nas'seh rested with his fathers, and was buried in the garden of his own house, in the garden of Uz'za. Then his son Ā'mon reigned in his place.

Amon's Reign and Death

19Ā'mon *was* twenty-two years old when he became king, and he reigned two years in Jerusalem. His mother's name *was* Me·shul'le·meth the daughter of Ha'ruz of Jot'bah. 20And he did evil in the sight of the LORD, as his father Ma·nas'seh had done. 21So he walked in all the ways that his father had walked; and he served the idols that his father had served, and worshiped

21:3 [a]Hebrew *Asherah*, a Canaanite goddess [b]The gods of the Assryians 21:7 [a]A Canaanite goddess

21:3 high places . . . wooden image: Practices of Canaanite religion condemned by God (see Deut. 12:1–3).

21:7 Asherah: An image of the mother-goddess of the Canaanite fertility cult was set up in the temple.

21:17 2 Chronicles further records Manasseh's captivity and exile in Babylon; his repentance and return to Jerusalem; and his acts of reform and restoration after his return (2 Chr. 33:11–16). Though he himself could repent and experience God's grace, his influence on the national course had been set.

them. [22]He forsook the LORD God of his fathers, and did not walk in the way of the LORD.

[23]Then the servants of Ā'mon conspired against him, and killed the king in his own house. [24]But the people of the land executed all those who had conspired against King Ā'mon. Then the people of the land made his son Jō·sī'ah king in his place.

[25]Now the rest of the acts of Ā'mon which he did, *are* they not written in the book of the chronicles of the kings of Judah? [26]And he was buried in his tomb in the garden of Uz'za. Then Jō·sī'ah his son reigned in his place.

CHAPTER 22

Josiah Reigns in Judah

Josiah *was* eight years old when he became king, and he reigned thirty-one years in Jerusalem. His mother's name *was* Je·dī'dah the daughter of A·dāi'ah of Boz'kath. [2]And he did *what was* right in the sight of the LORD, and walked in all the ways of his father David; he did not turn aside to the right hand or to the left.

Hilkiah Finds the Book of the Law

[3]Now it came to pass, in the eighteenth year of King Jō·sī'ah, *that* the king sent Shā'phan the scribe, the son of Az·a·lī'ah, the son of Me·shul'lam, to the house of the LORD, saying: [4]"Go up to Hil·kī'ah the high priest, that he may count the money which has been brought into the house of the LORD, which the doorkeepers have gathered from the people. [5]And let them deliver it into the hand of those doing the work, who are the overseers in the house of the LORD; let them give it to those who *are* in the house of the LORD doing the work, to repair the damages of the house— [6]to carpenters and builders and masons—and to buy timber and hewn stone to repair the house. [7]However there need be no accounting made with them of the money delivered into their hand, because they deal faithfully."

[8]Then Hil·kī'ah the high priest said to Shā'phan the scribe, "I have found the Book of the Law in the house of the LORD." And Hil·kī'ah gave the book to Shā'phan, and he read it. [9]So Shā'phan the scribe went to the king, bringing the king word, saying, "Your servants have gathered the money that was found in the house, and have delivered it into the hand of those who do the work, who oversee the house of the LORD." [10]Then Shā'phan the scribe showed the king, saying, "Hil·kī'ah the priest has given me a book." And Shā'phan read it before the king.

[11]Now it happened, when the king heard the words of the Book of the Law, that he tore his clothes. [12]Then the king commanded Hil·kī'ah the priest, A·hī'kam the son of Shā'phan, Ach'bor[a] the son of Mī·chaī'ah, Shā'phan the scribe, and A·sāi'ah a servant of the king, saying, [13]"Go, inquire of the LORD for me, for the people and for all Judah, concerning the words of this book that has been found; for

22:12 [a]*Abdon the son of Micah* in 2 Chronicles 34:20

21:24 The conspiracy was probably a palace intrigue and not a popular revolt since **the people of the land** enacted vengeance upon the conspirators.

22:1—23:30 Josiah was a religious reformer of the highest order. The discovery of **the Book of the Law** (22:8) greatly affected the young king (22:19), and he quickly purged pagan worship from the country, reestablished the covenant with the Lord, and reinstituted the Passover feast which had been neglected since the time of the judges (23:22). See Jer. 22:15–17.

22:8 the Book of the Law: Probably part or all of Deuteronomy which had been deposited in the temple at Solomon's dedication (see 1 Kin. 8:1–4; Deut. 31:26). This temple copy had been neglected during the reigns of Manasseh and Amon.

22:11 tore his clothes: In alarm that his nation had been so unfaithful to the Lord (v. 13).

great *is* the wrath of the LORD that is
aroused against us, because our fathers
have not obeyed the words of this book, to
do according to all that is written concern-
ing us."
14 So Hil·kī'ah the priest, A·hī'kam,
Ach'bor, Shā'phan, and A·sāi'ah went to
Hul'dah the prophetess, the wife of
Shal'lum the son of Tik'vah, the son of
Har'has, keeper of the wardrobe. (She
dwelt in Jerusalem in the Second Quarter.)
And they spoke with her.
15 Then she said
to them, "Thus says the LORD God of Israel,
'Tell the man who sent you to Me,
16 "Thus
says the LORD: 'Behold, I will bring
calamity on this place and on its inhab-
itants—all the words of the book which the
king of Judah has read—
17 because they
have forsaken Me and burned incense to
other gods, that they might provoke Me to
anger with all the works of their hands.
Therefore My wrath shall be aroused
against this place and shall not be
quenched.' " '
18 But as for the king of Ju-
dah, who sent you to inquire of the LORD,
in this manner you shall speak to him,
'Thus says the LORD God of Israel: "*Con-
cerning* the words which you have heard—
19 because your heart was tender, and you
humbled yourself before the LORD when
you heard what I spoke against this place
and against its inhabitants, that they
would become a desolation and a curse,
and you tore your clothes and wept before
Me, I also have heard *you*," says the LORD.
20 Surely, therefore, I will gather you to your
fathers, and you shall be gathered to your
grave in peace; and your eyes shall not see
all the calamity which I will bring on this
place." ' " So they brought back word to
the king.

CHAPTER 23

Josiah Restores True Worship

Now the king sent them to gather all the
elders of Judah and Jerusalem to him.
2 The
king went up to the house of the LORD with
all the men of Judah, and with him all the
inhabitants of Jerusalem—the priests and
the prophets and all the people, both small
and great. And he read in their hearing all
the words of the Book of the Covenant
which had been found in the house of the
LORD.

3 Then the king stood by a pillar and
made a covenant before the LORD, to follow
the LORD and to keep His commandments
and His testimonies and His statutes, with
all *his* heart and all *his* soul, to perform the
words of this covenant that were written in
this book. And all the people took a stand
for the covenant.
4 And the king com-
manded Hil·kī'ah the high priest, the
priests of the second order, and the door-
keepers, to bring out of the temple of the
LORD all the articles that were made for
Bā'al, for A·shē'rah,[a] and for all the host of
heaven;[b] and he burned them outside Jeru-
salem in the fields of Kid'ron, and carried
their ashes to Beth'el.
5 Then he removed
the idolatrous priests whom the kings of
Judah had ordained to burn incense on the
high places in the cities of Judah and in the
places all around Jerusalem, and those
who burned incense to Bā'al, to the sun, to

23:4 [a]A Canaanite goddess [b]The gods of the Assyrians

22:20 The fact that Josiah died in battle (23:29) does not neccessarily contradict Huldah's prediction that he would "be gathered to [his] grave in peace." She probably meant that Josiah would be at peace with God or that his death would occur before the promised judgment.

23:4, 5 Destruction of the **articles . . . for all the host of heaven** represented both a revival of true religion and also a rebellion against Assyrian rule. Among the **kings of Judah,** Manasseh (21:3–5, 7) and Amon (21:20, 21) were particularly involved in idolatry.

23:4–14 Josiah's immediate action to reform the nation's religious practices shows a tenderness and reverence for the Lord that very few have today.

the moon, to the constellations, and to all the host of heaven. 6And he brought out the wooden image[a] from the house of the LORD, to the Brook Kid'ron outside Jerusalem, burned it at the Brook Kid'ron and ground *it* to ashes, and threw its ashes on the graves of the common people. 7Then he tore down the *ritual* booths of the perverted persons[a] that *were* in the house of the LORD, where the women wove hangings for the wooden image. 8And he brought all the priests from the cities of Judah, and defiled the high places where the priests had burned incense, from Gē'ba to Bē·er·shē'ba; also he broke down the high places at the gates which *were* at the entrance of the Gate of Joshua the governor of the city, which *were* to the left of the city gate. 9Nevertheless the priests of the high places did not come up to the altar of the LORD in Jerusalem, but they ate unleavened bread among their brethren.

10And he defiled Tō'pheth, which *is* in the Valley of the Son[a] of Hin'nom, that no man might make his son or his daughter pass through the fire to Mō'lech. 11Then he removed the horses that the kings of Judah had dedicated to the sun, at the entrance to the house of the LORD, by the chamber of Nā'than-Mē'lech, the officer who *was* in the court; and he burned the chariots of the sun with fire. 12The altars that *were* on the roof, the upper chamber of Ā'haz, which the kings of Judah had made, and the altars which Ma·nas'seh had made in the two courts of the house of the LORD, the king broke down and pulverized there, and threw their dust into the Brook Kid'ron. 13Then the king defiled the high places that *were* east of Jerusalem, which *were* on the south of the Mount of Corruption, which Solomon king of Israel had built for Ash'to·reth the abomination of the Sī·dō'ni·ans, for Chē'mosh the abomination of the Mō'ab·ītes, and for Mil'com the abomination of the people of Am'mon. 14And he broke in pieces the *sacred* pillars and cut down the wooden images, and filled their places with the bones of men.

15Moreover the altar that *was* at Beth'el, *and* the high place which Jer·o·bō'am the son of Nē'bat, who made Israel sin, had made, both that altar and the high place he broke down; and he burned the high place *and* crushed *it* to powder, and burned the wooden image. 16As Jō·sī'ah turned, he saw the tombs that *were* there on the mountain. And he sent and took the bones out of the tombs and burned *them* on the altar, and defiled it according to the word of the LORD which the man of God proclaimed, who proclaimed these words. 17Then he said, "What gravestone *is* this that I see?"

So the men of the city told him, "*It is* the tomb of the man of God who came from Judah and proclaimed these things which you have done against the altar of Beth'el."

18And he said, "Let him alone; let no one move his bones." So they let his bones

23:6 [a]Hebrew *Asherah,* a Canaanite goddess
23:7 [a]Hebrew *qedeshim,* that is, those practicing sodomy and prostitution in religious rituals
23:10 [a]Kethib reads *Sons.*

23:10 Topheth: A fire pit for the purpose of child sacrifice, first introduced in Judah by Ahaz (16:3). **Molech**: The Ammonite god, Milcom (see v. 13).

23:11 horses . . . chariots: Possibly idol figures dedicated to sun worship. Pagans sometimes envisioned the sun as crossing the sky in a chariot.

23:13 Mount of Corruption: The hill to the east of Jerusalem (the Mount of Olives) where Solomon built worship centers for the gods of his foreign wives (see 1 Kin. 11:7, 8).

23:14 bones of men: The use of human bones desecrated a shrine and prohibited its further use.

23:16, 20 bones out of the tombs: Josiah burned the remains of the priests of the Bethel high places, as prophesied in the days of Jeroboam I (see 1 Kin. 13:2).

23:17 More than 300 years before, a man had prophesied about Josiah and the actions he would take to reform Judah. He even mentioned Josiah by name! See 1 Kin. 13:2.

alone, with the bones of the prophet who came from Samaria.

19Now Jō·sī′ah also took away all the shrines of the high places that *were* in the cities of Samaria, which the kings of Israel had made to provoke the LORD[a] to anger; and he did to them according to all the deeds he had done in Beth′el. 20He executed all the priests of the high places who *were* there, on the altars, and burned men's bones on them; and he returned to Jerusalem.

21Then the king commanded all the people, saying, "Keep the Passover to the LORD your God, as *it is* written in this Book of the Covenant." 22Such a Passover surely had never been held since the days of the judges who judged Israel, nor in all the days of the kings of Israel and the kings of Judah. 23But in the eighteenth year of King Jō·sī′ah this Passover was held before the LORD in Jerusalem. 24Moreover Jō·sī′ah put away those who consulted mediums and spiritists, the household gods and idols, all the abominations that were seen in the land of Judah and in Jerusalem, that he might perform the words of the law which were written in the book that Hil·kī′ah the priest found in the house of the LORD. 25Now before him there was no king like him, who turned to the LORD with all his heart, with all his soul, and with all his might, according to all the Law of Moses; nor after him did *any* arise like him.

Impending Judgment on Judah

26Nevertheless the LORD did not turn from the fierceness of His great wrath, with which His anger was aroused against Judah, because of all the provocations with which Ma·nas′seh had provoked Him. 27And the LORD said, "I will also remove Judah from My sight, as I have removed Israel, and will cast off this city Jerusalem which I have chosen, and the house of which I said, 'My name shall be there.' "[a]

Josiah Dies in Battle

28Now the rest of the acts of Jō·sī′ah, and all that he did, *are* they not written in the book of the chronicles of the kings of Judah? 29In his days Pharaoh Nē′cho king of Egypt went to the aid of the king of Assyria, to the River Eū·phrā′tēs; and King Jō·sī′ah went against him. And *Pharaoh* *Nē′*cho killed him at Me·gid′dō when he confronted him. 30Then his servants moved his body in a chariot from Me·gid′dō, brought him to Jerusalem, and buried him in his own tomb. And the people of the land took Je·hō′a·haz the son of Jō·sī′ah, anointed him, and made him king in his father's place.

The Reign and Captivity of Jehoahaz

31Je·hō′a·haz *was* twenty-three years old when he became king, and he reigned three months in Jerusalem. His mother's name *was* Ha·mū′tal the daughter of Jer·e·mī′ah of Lib′nah. 32And he did evil in the sight of the LORD, according to all that his fathers had done. 33Now Pharaoh Nē′cho put him in prison at Rib′lah in the land of Hā′math, that he might not reign in Jerusalem; and he imposed on the land a tribute of one hundred talents of silver and a talent of gold. 34Then Pharaoh Nē′cho made E·lī′a·kim the son of Jō·sī′ah king in

23:19 [a]Following Septuagint, Syriac, and Vulgate; Masoretic Text and Targum omit *the LORD*.
23:27 [a]1 Kings 8:29

23:29 Nineveh had fallen to the Babylonians and Medes in 612 B.C. But a remnant of Assyrian forces were embedded near the **Euphrates** to the northeast of Judah. **Necho** supported the Assyrians in order to prevent Babylon from gaining sole control of Mesopotamia and succeeding Assyria as the next great world empire.

23:31 Jeremiah: the prophet Jeremiah

23:33, 34 Necho returned from **Riblah** to Egypt, taking with him the young King **Jehoahaz**, whom he had held in temporary custody in Riblah (v. 33). He made **Jehoiakim** a puppet ruler and put Judah under tribute to Egypt.

place of his father Jō·sī′ah, and changed
his name to Je·hoi′a·kim. And *Pharaoh* took
Je·hō′a·haz and went to Egypt, and he[a]
died there.

Jehoiakim Reigns in Judah

35So Je·hoi′a·kim gave the silver and
gold to Pharaoh; but he taxed the land to
give money according to the command of
Pharaoh; he exacted the silver and gold
from the people of the land, from every
one according to his assessment, to give *it*
to Pharaoh Nē′cho. 36Je·hoi′a·kim *was*
twenty-five years old when he became
king, and he reigned eleven years in Jeru-
salem. His mother's name *was* Ze·bū′dah
the daughter of Pe·dāi′ah of Rū′mah.
37And he did evil in the sight of the LORD,
according to all that his fathers had done.

CHAPTER 24

Judah Overrun by Enemies

In his days Ne·bū·chad·nez′zar king of
Babylon came up, and Je·hoi′a·kim be-
came his vassal *for* three years. Then he
turned and rebelled against him. 2And the
LORD sent against him *raiding* bands of
Chal·dē′ans, bands of Syrians, bands of
Mō′ab·ītes, and bands of the people
of Am′mon; He sent them against Judah
to destroy it, according to the word of the
LORD which He had spoken by His ser-
vants the prophets. 3Surely at the com-
mandment of the LORD *this* came upon Ju-
dah, to remove *them* from His sight
because of the sins of Ma·nas′seh, accord-
ing to all that he had done, 4and also be-
cause of the innocent blood that he had
shed; for he had filled Jerusalem with in-
nocent blood, which the LORD would not
pardon.
5Now the rest of the acts of Je·hoi′a·kim,
and all that he did, *are* they not written in
the book of the chronicles of the kings of
Judah? 6So Je·hoi′a·kim rested with his fa-
thers. Then Je·hoi′a·chin his son reigned in
his place.
7And the king of Egypt did not come out
of his land anymore, for the king of Bab-
ylon had taken all that belonged to the
king of Egypt from the Brook of Egypt to
the River Eū·phrā′tēs.

The Reign and Captivity of Jehoiachin

8Je·hoi′a·chin *was* eighteen years old
when he became king, and he reigned in
Jerusalem three months. His mother's
name *was* Ne·hush′ta the daughter of
El·nā′than of Jerusalem. 9And he did evil
in the sight of the LORD, according to all
that his father had done.
10At that time the servants of Ne·bū-
chad·nez′zar king of Babylon came up
against Jerusalem, and the city was be-
sieged. 11And Ne·bū·chad·nez′zar king of
Babylon came against the city, as his ser-
vants were besieging it. 12Then Je·hoi′-
a·chin king of Judah, his mother, his ser-
vants, his princes, and his officers went out
to the king of Babylon; and the king of
Babylon, in the eighth year of his reign,
took him prisoner.

23:34 [a]That is, Jehoahaz

24:1, 2 As commander of the Babylonian army, **Nebuchadnezzar** defeated the Egyptians at Carchemish on the Euphrates in 605 B.C., thus ending Egyptian dominance of Judah. After this victory, he moved south to force the submission of **Jehoiakim**. It is probable that hostages, among them Daniel, were taken. When Nebuchadnezzar's father, King Nabopolassar, died unexpectedly, Nebuchadnezzar rushed home to assume the throne of Babylon which he held until 562 B.C. After Jehoiakim's rebellion, Nebuchadnezzar sent troops from neighboring vassal countries to harass Judah. But the Babylonian king was merely an agent for **the LORD** who was finally responsible for Jerusalem's punishment (vv. 3, 4).

24:10–12 The siege in 597 B.C. was a delayed reaction to the rebellion of v. 1. **Jehoiakim** died before the fall of the city, and **Jehoiachin** wisely surrendered (v. 12).

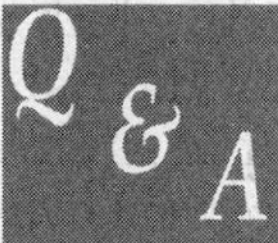

Is it possible to break the chain of family dysfunction?

Gary Rosberg, Ed. D.

Yes! And necessary if the next generation is going to survive an often hostile culture. It starts with you. I believe in leaving healthy legacies. Webster defines "legacy" as "anything handed down as from an ancestor." We all have two legacies: the one we inherited from our parents and the one we will leave to our children.

Confronting any unresolved conflict in our lives is crucial. By doing so we learn how to restore broken relationships and strengthen healthy ones. This means we need to learn to deal with the hurt and anger in our lives and to communicate effectively and forgive so that our relationships can experience the vitality they once had. Your adult children need and may be quietly screaming for a healthy relationship with you and your spouse.

I encourage you to take the risk to tell your adult children that you realize you may have passed on a few unhealthy patterns. Also, share that you would like to deal with them in a healthier way. This may create some anxiety, but it could lead to significant growth in your relationships. Perhaps share a painful experience you had with your own parents and how it impacted your own parenting style. A little humility goes a long way in restoring a relationship.

If you need encouragement or counsel, share your concerns with God and with a friend you trust. Turn also to the Bible for advice, which speaks directly to conflicts among family members as well as among believers. Wisdom for dealing with such situations comes "from above" (James 3:17).

Remember that you cannot change the legacy you inherited, but you can impact the legacy you leave behind. Start today! ✦

The Captivity of Jerusalem

13And he carried out from there all the
treasures of the house of the LORD and the
treasures of the king's house, and he cut in
pieces all the articles of gold which Sol-
omon king of Israel had made in the tem-
ple of the LORD, as the LORD had said.
14Also he carried into captivity all Jerusa-
lem: all the captains and all the mighty
men of valor, ten thousand captives, and
all the craftsmen and smiths. None re-
mained except the poorest people of the
land. 15And he carried Je·hoi'a·chin captive
to Babylon. The king's mother, the king's
wives, his officers, and the mighty of the
land he carried into captivity from Jerusa-
lem to Babylon. 16All the valiant men,
seven thousand, and craftsmen and
smiths, one thousand, all *who were* strong
and fit for war, these the king of Babylon
brought captive to Babylon.

24:14 Ezekiel was among those taken captive at this time.

Zedekiah Reigns in Judah

17Then the king of Babylon made Mat-
ta·nī'ah, *Je·hoi'a·chin's*[a] uncle, king in his
place, and changed his name to Zed-
e·kī'ah.
18Zed·e·kī'ah *was* twenty-one years old
when he became king, and he reigned
eleven years in Jerusalem. His mother's
name *was* Ha·mū'tal the daughter of
Jer·e·mī'ah of Lib'nah. 19He also did evil
in the sight of the LORD, according to all
that Je·hoi'a·kim had done. 20For because
of the anger of the LORD *this* happened in
Jerusalem and Judah, that He finally cast
them out from His presence. Then
Zed·e·kī'ah rebelled against the king of
Babylon.

CHAPTER 25

The Fall and Captivity of Judah

Now it came to pass in the ninth year of
his reign, in the tenth month, on the tenth
day of the month, *that* Ne·bū·chad·nez'zar
king of Babylon and all his army came
against Jerusalem and encamped against
it; and they built a siege wall against it
all around. 2So the city was besieged until
the eleventh year of King Zed·e·kī'ah. 3By
the ninth *day* of the *fourth* month the
famine had become so severe in the city
that there was no food for the people of the
land.
4Then the city wall was broken through,
and all the men of war *fled* at night by way
of the gate between two walls, which was
by the king's garden, even though the
Chal·dē'ans *were* still encamped all around
against the city. And *the king*[a] went by way
of the plain.[b] 5But the army of the Chal-
dē'ans pursued the king, and they over-
took him in the plains of Jericho. All his
army was scattered from him. 6So they
took the king and brought him up to the
king of Babylon at Rib'lah, and they pro-
nounced judgment on him. 7Then they
killed the sons of Zed·e·kī'ah before his
eyes, put out the eyes of Zed·e·kī'ah,
bound him with bronze fetters, and took
him to Babylon.
8And in the fifth month, on the seventh
day of the month (which *was* the nineteenth
year of King Ne·bū·chad·nez'zar king of
Babylon), Ne·bū·za·rad'an the captain of
the guard, a servant of the king of Babylon,
came to Jerusalem. 9He burned the house
of the LORD and the king's house; all the
houses of Jerusalem, that is, all the houses
of the great, he burned with fire. 10And all
the army of the Chal·dē'ans who *were with*
the captain of the guard broke down the
walls of Jerusalem all around.
11Then Ne·bū·za·rad'an the captain of
the guard carried away captive the rest of
the people *who* remained in the city
and the defectors who had deserted to the

24:17 [a]Literally *his* 25:4 [a]Literally *he* [b]Or *Arabah*, that is, the Jordan Valley

24:17 The change of name from **Mattaniah** implies Nebuchadnezzar's absolute authority over Judah (see also 23:34). **Zedekiah** was his puppet king.

24:20 **Zedekiah rebelled** in spite of Jeremiah's warnings (Jer. 27:12–15). Zedekiah's associates likewise were guilty of ignoring and mocking God's prophets (see 2 Chr. 36:14–16).

25:1–3 **ninth year . . . eleventh year**: The siege lasted from early in 588 until the summer of 586 B.C.

25:4 When Zedekiah knew Jerusalem's defense was hopeless, he and his army tried to desert the city (see Ezek. 12:12–14). **the Chaldeans**: The ethnic identity of the people who had conquered Babylon and now ruled.

25:6 **Riblah**: Convenient military headquarters for foreign conquerors in Palestine (see 23:33).

25:7 **Zedekiah** was the last of Judah's twenty kings.

25:8 **Nebuzaradan**: Nebuchadnezzar's official deputy.

king of Babylon, with the rest of the multi-
tude. 12But the captain of the guard left
some of the poor of the land as vinedressers
and farmers. 13The bronze pillars that *were*
in the house of the LORD, and the carts and
the bronze Sea that *were* in the house of the
LORD, the Chal·dē'ans broke in pieces, and
carried their bronze to Babylon. 14They also
took away the pots, the shovels, the trim-
mers, the spoons, and all the bronze uten-
sils with which the priests ministered.
15The firepans and the basins, the things of
solid gold and solid silver, the captain of
the guard took away. 16The two pillars, one
Sea, and the carts, which Solomon had
made for the house of the LORD, the bronze
of all these articles was beyond measure.
17The height of one pillar *was* eighteen cu-
bits, and the capital on it *was* of bronze.
The height of the capital was three cubits,
and the network and pomegranates all
around the capital were all of bronze. The
second pillar was the same, with a net-
work.

18And the captain of the guard took
Se·rāi'ah the chief priest, Zeph·a·nī'ah the
second priest, and the three doorkeepers.
19He also took out of the city an officer who
had charge of the men of war, five men of
the king's close associates who were found
in the city, the chief recruiting officer of the
army, who mustered the people of the
land, and sixty men of the people of
the land *who were* found in the city. 20So
Ne·bū·za·rad'an, captain of the guard,
took these and brought them to the king of
Babylon at Rib'lah. 21Then the king of
Babylon struck them and put them to
death at Rib'lah in the land of Hā'math.
Thus Judah was carried away captive from
its own land.

Gedaliah Made Governor of Judah

22Then he made Ged·a·lī'ah the son of
A·hī'kam, the son of Shā'phan, governor
over the people who remained in the land
of Judah, whom Ne·bū·chad·nez'zar king
of Babylon had left. 23Now when all the
captains of the armies, they and *their* men,
heard that the king of Babylon had made
Ged·a·lī'ah governor, they came to
Ged·a·lī'ah at Miz'pah—Ish'ma·el the son
of Neth·a·nī'ah, Jō·hā'nan the son of
Ca·rē'ah, Se·rāi'ah the son of Tan'hu·meth
the Ne·toph'a·thīte, and Jā·az·a·nī'ah[a] the
son of a Mā'a·cha·thīte, they and their
men. 24And Ged·a·lī'ah took an oath be-
fore them and their men, and said to them,
"Do not be afraid of the servants of the
Chal·dē'ans. Dwell in the land and serve
the king of Babylon, and it shall be well
with you."

25But it happened in the seventh month
that Ish'ma·el the son of Neth·a·nī'ah, the
son of E·lish'a·ma, of the royal family,
came with ten men and struck and killed
Ged·a·lī'ah, the Jews, as well as the
Chal·dē'ans who were with him at Miz'-
pah. 26And all the people, small and great,
and the captains of the armies, arose and
went to Egypt; for they were afraid of the
Chal·dē'ans.

Jehoiachin Released from Prison

27Now it came to pass in the thirty-sev-
enth year of the captivity of Je·hoi'a·chin

25:23 [a]Spelled *Jezaniah* in Jeremiah 40:8
25:27 [a]Literally *Man of Marduk*

25:13–17 The last vestiges of Solomon's splendor were taken as spoils of war. **carts**: (see 1 Kin. 7:27–37).

25:22 governor: The tragic story of the Hebrew monarchy is officially over.

25:24 Ahikam, the father of **Gedaliah**, had befriended the prophet Jeremiah (see Jer. 26:24). Now Gedaliah himself would offer similar advice to that given by Jeremiah: Judah would find peace only by submitting to the Babylonians (see Jer. 38:17, 18).

25:26 went to Egypt: The Exodus reversed.

25:27 thirty-seventh year: The date was March or April, 561 B.C. **Evil-Merodach**: Nebuchadnezzar's son who followed him as **king of Babylon**. The books of Kings end on the

king of Judah, in the twelfth month, on the
twenty-seventh *day* of the month, *that*
Ē'vil-Me·rō'dach[a] king of Babylon, in the
year that he began to reign, released
Je·hoi'a·chin king of Judah from prison.
28He spoke kindly to him, and gave him a
more prominent seat than those of the
kings who *were* with him in Babylon. 29So
Je·hoi'a·chin changed from his prison gar-
ments, and he ate bread regularly before
the king all the days of his life. 30And as for
his provisions, *there was* a regular ration
given him by the king, a portion for each
day, all the days of his life.

---

hopeful assertion that a son of David was alive and well. Whatever the human motives behind Jehoiachin's release, God's decree was that the family of David, though severely chastened, would not be exterminated (see Matt. 1:1–16). Though humans break their covenants, God keeps His.

✦1 Chronicles✦

1 and 2 Chronicles were most likely written by Ezra between 450 and 430 B.C. The last two verses of 2 Chronicles are repeated in the first few verses of Ezra, and both books cover the time period between the founding of Israel as a nation and the end of its captivity in Babylon (about 538 B.C.).

The first nine chapters of 1 Chronicles give a detailed genealogy of David and Israel to show God's intricate plan to preserve the messianic line. The genealogies show the importance of tradition, ancestry, and the spiritual integrity of each generation.

The rest of the book focuses on David's life, but it omits his struggles with Saul, his adultery with Bathsheba, and Absalom's rebellion. Instead, it tells of David's preparations to build the temple—a task Solomon would later complete.

Although 1 Chronicles covers the same period as 1 and 2 Samuel, the perspective is different, emphasizing items of spiritual, rather than historical, importance. It shows God's faithfulness to keep His covenant with Israel. For Christians today, it demonstrates that God always keeps His promises. His ultimate purpose for their lives will prevail throughout time. ✦

CHAPTER 1

The Family of Adam—Seth to Abraham

Adam, Seth, Ē'nosh, [2]Cā·ī'nan,[a] Ma-
hal'a·lel, Jar'ed, [3]Ē'noch, Me·thū'-se·lah,
Lā'mech, [4]Noah,[a] Shem, Ham, and Jā'-
pheth.

[5]The sons of Jā'pheth *were* Gō'mer,
Mā'gog, Mā'daī, Jā'van, Tū'bal, Mē'shech,
and Tī'ras. [6]The sons of Gō'mer *were*
Ash'ke·naz, Dī'phath,[a] and Tō·gar'mah.
[7]The sons of Jā'van *were* E·li'shah, Tar-
shish'ah,[a] Kit'tim, and Rod'a·nim.[b]

[8]The sons of Ham *were* Cush, Miz'ra·im,
Put, and Cā'naan. [9]The sons of Cush *were*
Sē'ba, Hav'i·lah, Sab'ta,[a] Rā'a·ma,[b] and
Sab'te·cha. The sons of Rā'a·ma *were*

1:2 [a]Hebrew *Qenan* 1:4 [a]Following Masoretic Text and Vulgate; Septuagint adds *the sons of Noah.* 1:6 [a]Spelled *Riphath* in Genesis 10:3 1:7 [a]Spelled *Tarshish* in Genesis 10:4 [b]Spelled *Dodanim* in Genesis 10:4 1:9 [a]Spelled *Sabtah* in Genesis 10:7 [b]Spelled *Raamah* in Genesis 10:7

1:1–28 This passage provides a general list of Adam's descendants through Abraham. From there the chronicler narrows his focus indicating his primary concern with the line of David, from which the Messiah would come.

1:1–4 For the parallel genealogy covering the period from creation to the Flood, see Gen. 5:1–32.

1:5–27 **Japheth** was the ancestor of the Indo-Europeans (vv. 5–7; Gen. 10:2–5); **Ham**, the father of Arabians, Egyptians, Libyans, and Canaanites (vv. 8–16; Gen. 10:6–20); and **Shem**, the ancestor of the Semites of western Asia and Eastern Africa (vv. 17–27; Gen. 10:21–31).

Shē'ba and Dē'dan. 10 Cush begot Nim'rod; he began to be a mighty one on the earth. 11 Miz'ra·im begot Lū'dim, An'a·mim, Le·hā'bim, Naph'tū·him, 12 Path·rū'sim, Cas·lū'him (from whom came the Philis'tines and the Caph'to·rim). 13 Cā'naan begot Sī'don, his firstborn, and Heth; 14 the Jeb'ū·sīte, the Am'o·rīte, and the Gir'ga·shīte; 15 the Hī'vīte, the Ar'kīte, and the Sī'nīte; 16 the Ar'vad·īte, the Zem'a·rīte, and the Hā'math·īte.

17 The sons of Shem *were* Ē'lam, As'shur, Ar·phā'xad, Lud, Ar'am, Uz, Hul, Gē'ther, and Mē'shech.[a] 18 Ar·phā'xad begot Shē'lah, and Shē'lah begot Ē'ber. 19 To Ē'ber were born two sons: the name of one *was* Pē'leg,[a] for in his days the earth was divided; and his brother's name *was* Jok'tan. 20 Jok'tan begot Al·mō'dad, Shē'leph, Hā·zar·mā'veth, Jē'rah, 21 Ha·dor'am, Ū'zal, Dik'lah, 22 Ē'bal,[a] A·bim'a·el, Shē'ba, 23 Ō'phir, Hav'i·lah, and Jō'bab. All these *were* the sons of Jok'tan.

24 Shem, Ar·phā'xad, Shē'lah, 25 Ē'ber, Pē'leg, Rē'ū, 26 Sē'rug, Nā'hor, Tē'rah, 27 and Abram, who *is* Abraham. 28 The sons of Abraham *were* Isaac and Ish'ma·el.

The Family of Ishmael

29 These *are* their genealogies: The firstborn of Ish'ma·el *was* Ne·bā'joth; then Kē'dar, Ad'be·el, Mib'sam, 30 Mish'ma, Dū'mah, Mas'sa, Hā'dad,[a] Tē'ma, 31 Jē'tur, Nā'phish, and Ked'e·mah. These *were* the sons of Ish'ma·el.

The Family of Keturah

32 Now the sons born to Ke·tū'rah, Abraham's concubine, *were* Zim'ran, Jok'shan, Mē'dan, Mid'i·an, Ish'bak, and Shū'ah. The sons of Jok'shan *were* Shē'ba and Dē'dan. 33 The sons of Mid'i·an *were* Ē'phah, Ē'pher, Hā'noch, A·bī'da, and El·dā'ah. All these were the children of Ke·tū'rah.

The Family of Isaac

34 And Abraham begot Isaac. The sons of Isaac *were* Esau and Israel. 35 The sons of Esau *were* E·lī'phaz, Reū'el, Jē'ush, Jā'a·lam, and Kō'rah. 36 And the sons of E·lī'phaz *were* Tē'man, Ō'mar, Zē'phī,[a] Gā'tam, *and* Kē'naz; and *by* Tim'na,[b] Am'a·lek. 37 The sons of Reū'el *were* Nā'hath, Zē'rah, Sham'mah, and Miz'zah.

The Family of Seir

38 The sons of Sē'ir *were* Lō'tan, Shō'bal, Zib'ē·on, An'ah, Dī'shon, Ē'zer, and Dī'shan. 39 And the sons of Lō'tan *were* Hō'rī and Hō'mam; Lō'tan's sister *was* Tim'na. 40 The sons of Shō'bal *were* Al'i·an,[a] Man'a·hath, Ē'bal, Shē'phī,[b] and Ō'nam. The sons of Zib'ē·on *were* Ā'jah and An'ah. 41 The son of An'ah *was* Dī'shon. The sons of Dī'shon *were* Ham'ran,[a] Esh'ban, Ith'ran, and Chē'ran. 42 The sons of Ē'zer *were* Bil'han, Zā'a·van, *and* Jā'a·kan.[a] The sons of Dī'shan *were* Uz and Ar'an.

1:17 [a]Spelled *Mash* in Genesis 10:23 1:19 [a]Literally *Division* 1:22 [a]Spelled *Obal* in Genesis 10:28 1:30 [a]Spelled *Hadar* in Genesis 25:15 1:36 [a]Spelled *Zepho* in Genesis 36:11 [b]Compare Genesis 36:12 1:40 [a]Spelled *Alvan* in Genesis 36:23 [b]Spelled *Shepho* in Genesis 36:23 1:41 [a]Spelled *Hemdan* in Genesis 36:26 1:42 [a]Spelled *Akan* in Genesis 36:27

1:10 Nimrod . . . mighty one: In the sense of a political leader. He was the patriarch of the Assyrians and the Babylonians. Some identify him with Sargon I (the Great), in the 24th century B.C. See Gen. 10:8, where Nimrod is portrayed as a "hunter," most likely of men, and thus a conqueror.

1:12 Philistines . . . Caphtorim: See Amos 9:7.

1:28–54 The descendants of Abraham are listed briefly as a prelude to Jacob, God's chosen line (ch. 2).

1:28–33 For the descendants of Abraham through his wife Keturah, see Gen. 25:1–4.

1:29–31 For the genealogy of Ishmael, see Gen. 25:12–16.

1:35–54 For an earlier genealogy of Esau, see Gen. 36:9–43.

The Kings of Edom

43Now these *were* the kings who reigned
in the land of Ē′dom before a king reigned
over the children of Israel: Bē′la the son of
Bē′or, and the name of his city was
Din′ha·bah. 44And when Bē′la died, Jō′bab
the son of Zē′rah of Boz′rah reigned in his
place. 45When Jō′bab died, Hū′sham of the
land of the Tē′man·ītes reigned in his
place. 46And when Hū′sham died, Hā′dad
the son of Bē′dad, who attacked Mid′i·an
in the field of Mō′ab, reigned in his place.
The name of his city *was* Ā′vith. 47When
Hā′dad died, Sam′lah of Mas·rē′kah
reigned in his place. 48And when Sam′lah
died, Saul of Re·hō′both-by-the-River
reigned in his place. 49When Saul died,
Bā′al-Hā′nan the son of Ach′bor reigned
in his place. 50And when Bā′al-Hā′nan
died, Hā′dad[a] reigned in his place; and the
name of his city was Pā′ī.[b] His wife's
name was Me·het′a·bel the daughter of
Mā′tred, the daughter of Mez′a·hab.
51Hā′dad died also. And the chiefs of
Ē′dom were Chief Tim′nah, Chief Al′i·ah,[a]
Chief Jē′theth, 52Chief A·hol·i·bā′mah,
Chief Ē′lah, Chief Pī′non, 53Chief Kē′-
naz, Chief Tē′man, Chief Mib′zar,
54Chief Mag′di·el, and Chief Ī′ram. These
were the chiefs of Ē′dom.

1:50 [a]Spelled *Hadar* in Genesis 36:39 [b]Spelled *Pau* in Genesis 36:39 1:51 [a]Spelled *Alvah* in Genesis 36:40 2:7 [a]Spelled *Achan* in Joshua 7:1 and elsewhere 2:9 [a]Spelled *Caleb* in 2:18, 42
2:11 [a]Spelled *Salmon* in Ruth 4:21 and Luke 3:32
2:13 [a]Spelled *Shammah* in 1 Samuel 16:9 and elsewhere

CHAPTER 2

The Family of Israel

These *were* the sons of Israel: Reuben,
Sim′ē·on, Levi, Judah, Is′sa·char, Zeb′-
ū·lun, 2Dan, Joseph, Benjamin, Naph′ta·lī,
Gad, and Ash′er.

From Judah to David

3The sons of Judah *were* Er, Ō′nan, and
Shē′lah. *These* three were born to him by
the daughter of Shū′a, the Cā′naan·ī·tess.
Er, the firstborn of Judah, was wicked in
the sight of the LORD; so He killed him.
4And Tā′mar, his daughter-in-law, bore
him Per′ez and Zē′rah. All the sons of Ju-
dah *were* five.

5The sons of Per′ez *were* Hez′ron and
Hā′mul. 6The sons of Zē′rah *were* Zim′rī,
Ē′than, Hē′man, Cal′col, and Dar′a—five
of them in all.

7The son of Car′mī *was* Ā′char,[a] the trou-
bler of Israel, who transgressed in the ac-
cursed thing.

8The son of Ē′than *was* Az·a·rī′ah.

9Also the sons of Hez′ron who were
born to him *were* Je·rah′mē·el, Ram, and
Che·lū′baī.[a] 10Ram begot Am·min′a·dab,
and Am·min′a·dab begot Nah′shon,
leader of the children of Judah; 11Nah′shon
begot Sal′ma,[a] and Sal′ma begot Bō′az;
12Bō′az begot Ō′bed, and Ō′bed begot Jesse;
13Jesse begot E·lī′ab his firstborn, A·bin′-
a·dab the second, Shim′ē·a[a] the third,
14Ne·than′el the fourth, Rad′daī the fifth,
15Ō′zem the sixth, *and* David the seventh.

16Now their sisters *were* Ze·rū′i·ah and

1:43–54 For a parallel list of the kings and chiefs of Edom, the territory of Esau's descendants, see Gen. 36:31–43.

2:1 The name **Israel** rather than Jacob stresses the uniqueness of this child of Abraham as the son of promise (see Gen. 32:28).

2:3 Although we don't know what Er's sin was, we can learn from him that our actions have far-reaching effects. For his sin, Er lost his life and his place in the messianic line. In addition, this blot on the family records has been viewed by all generations since the Chronicles were written. What a warning to us to consider the consequences of our actions!

2:3–15 The preeminence given to **Judah** (v. 3) and the lineage of **David** (v. 15) reflects the author's conviction that David's line was to be God's instrument of blessing for all humankind.

2:7 Achar: Elsewhere spelled Achan. **the troubler of Israel**: See Josh. 7:24–26 and note.

Ab'i·gāil. And the sons of Ze·rū'i·ah *were* A·bi'shaī, Jō'ab, and As'a·hel—three. 17Ab'i·gāil bore A·mā'sa; and the father of A·mā'sa *was* Jē'ther the Ish'ma·el·īte.[a]

The Family of Hezron

18Caleb the son of Hez'ron had children by A·zū'bah, *his* wife, and by Jer'i·oth. Now these were her sons: Jē'sher, Shō'bab, and Ar'don. 19When A·zū'bah died, Caleb took Eph'rath[a] as his wife, who bore him Hur. 20And Hur begot Ū'rī, and Ū'rī begot Bez'a·lel.

21Now afterward Hez'ron went in to the daughter of Mā'chir the father of Gil'ē·ad, whom he married when he *was* sixty years old; and she bore him Sē'gub. 22Sē'gub begot Jā'ir, who had twenty-three cities in the land of Gil'ē·ad. 23(Gē'shur and Syria took from them the towns of Jā'ir, with Kē'nath and its towns—sixty towns.) All these *belonged to* the sons of Mā'chir the father of Gil'ē·ad. 24After Hez'ron died in Caleb Eph'ra·thah, Hez'ron's wife A·bī'jah bore him Ash'hur the father of Te·kō'a.

The Family of Jerahmeel

25The sons of Je·rah'mē·el, the firstborn of Hez'ron, *were* Ram, the firstborn, and Bū'nah, Ō'ren, Ō'zem, *and* A·hī'jah. 26Je·rah'mē·el had another wife, whose name was At'a·rah; she was the mother of Ō'nam. 27The sons of Ram, the firstborn of Je·rah'mē·el, were Mā'az, Jā'min, and Ē'ker. 28The sons of Ō'nam were Sham'maī and Jā'da. The sons of Sham'maī *were* Nā'dab and A·bī'shur.

29And the name of the wife of A·bī'shur *was* Ab·i·hā'il, and she bore him Ah'ban and Mō'lid. 30The sons of Nā'dab *were* Sē'led and Ap'pa·im; Sē'led died without children. 31The son of Ap'pa·im *was* Ish'ī, the son of Ish'ī *was* Shē'shan, and Shē'shan's son *was* Ah'laī. 32The sons of Jā'da, the brother of Sham'maī, *were* Jē'ther and Jonathan; Jē'ther died without children. 33The sons of Jonathan *were* Pē'leth and Zā'za. These were the sons of Je·rah'mē·el.

34Now Shē'shan had no sons, only daughters. And Shē'shan had an Egyptian servant whose name *was* Jar'ha. 35Shē'shan gave his daughter to Jar'ha his servant as wife, and she bore him At'taī. 36At'taī begot Nathan, and Nathan begot Zā'bad; 37Zā'bad begot Eph'lal, and Eph'lal begot Ō'bed; 38Ō'bed begot Jē'hū, and Jē'hū begot Az·a·rī'ah; 39Az·a·rī'ah begot Hē'lez, and Hē'lez begot El·e·ā'sah; 40El·e·ā'sah begot Sis'maī, and Sis'maī begot Shal'lum; 41Shal'lum begot Jek·a·mī'ah, and Jek·a·mī'ah begot E·lish'a·ma.

The Family of Caleb

42The descendants of Caleb the brother of Je·rah'mē·el *were* Mē'sha, his firstborn, who was the father of Ziph, and the sons of Ma·rē'shah the father of Hē'bron. 43The sons of Hē'bron *were* Kō'rah, Tap'pū·ah, Rē'kem, and Shē'ma. 44Shē'ma begot Rā'ham the father of Jor·kō'am, and Rē'kem begot Sham'maī. 45And the son of Sham'maī *was* Mā'on, and Mā'on *was* the father of Beth Zūr.

46Ē'phah, Caleb's concubine, bore Har'an, Mō'za, and Gā'zez; and Har'an begot Gā'zez. 47And the sons of Jah'daī *were* Rē'gem, Jō'tham, Gē'shan, Pē'let, Ē'phah, and Shā'aph.

48Mā'a·chah, Caleb's concubine, bore Shē'ber and Tir'hā·nah. 49She also bore

2:17 [a]Compare 2 Samuel 17:25
2:19 [a]Spelled *Ephrathah* elsewhere

2:18–20 The genealogy of **Caleb the son of Hezron** continues in vv. 42–55. He is apparently not the "Caleb the son of Jephunneh" who served with Joshua (see 4:15; Num. 14:38). Though both claim a daughter named Achsah (v. 49; Josh. 15:16), none of the sons of 4:15 are mentioned in the genealogy of 2:18–20, 42–55.

2:21–24 Machir was a descendant of Manasseh, and **Gilead** was a part of that tribe's holdings on the east side of the Jordan River (7:14).

2:25–41 The genealogy of **Jerahmeel**. David encountered the Jerahmeelites during his military raids in southern Judah (see 1 Sam. 27:10; 30:29).

Shā'aph the father of Mad·man'nah,
Shē'va the father of Mach·bē'nah and the
father of Gib'ē·a. And the daughter of Ca-
leb *was* Ach'sah.
50These were the descendants of Caleb:
The sons of Hur, the firstborn of Eph'-
ra·thah, *were* Shō'bal the father of Kir'jath
Jē'a·rim, 51Sal'ma the father of Bethlehem,
and Har'eph the father of Beth Gā'der.
52And Shō'bal the father of Kir'jath
Jē'a·rim had descendants: Ha·rō'eh, *and*
half of the *families of* Ma·nū'hoth.[a] 53The
families of Kir'jath Jē'a·rim *were* the
Ith'rītes, the Pū'thītes, the Shū'ma·thītes,
and the Mish'ra·ītes. From these came the
Zō'ra·thītes and the Esh'ta·o·lītes.
54The sons of Sal'ma *were* Bethlehem, the
Ne·toph'a·thītes, At'roth Beth Jō'ab, half of
the Ma·nā'heth·ītes, and the Zō'rītes.
55And the families of the scribes who
dwelt at Jā'bez *were* the Tī'ra·thītes, the
Shim'ē·a·thītes, *and* the Sū'cha·thītes. These
were the Ken'ītes who came from Ham'math,
the father of the house of Rē'chab.

CHAPTER 3

The Family of David

Now these were the sons of David who
were born to him in Hē'bron: The firstborn
was Am'non, by A·hin'ō·am the Jez'rē-
el·ī·tess; the second, Daniel,[a] by Ab'i·gāil
the Car'mel·ī·tess; 2the third, Ab'sa·lom
the son of Mā'a·cah, the daughter of Tal'-
maī, king of Gē'shur; the fourth, Ad·o-
nī'jah the son of Hag'gith; 3the fifth,
Sheph·a·tī'ah, by A·bī'tal; the sixth,
Ith'rē·am, by his wife Eg'lah.
4*These* six were born to him in Hē'bron.
There he reigned seven years and six
months, and in Jerusalem he reigned
thirty-three years. 5And these were born
to him in Jerusalem: Shim'ē·a,[a] Shō'-
bab, Nathan, and Solomon—four by
Bath·shū'a[b] the daughter of Am'mi·el.[c]
6Also *there* were Ib'har, E·lish'a·ma,[a]
E·liph'e·let,[b] 7Nō'gah, Nē'pheg, Ja·phī'a,
8E·lish'a·ma, E·lī'a·da,[a] and E·liph'e·let—
nine *in all.* 9*These were* all the sons of David,
besides the sons of the concubines, and
Tā'mar their sister.

The Family of Solomon

10Solomon's son *was* Rē·ho·bō'am;
A·bī'jah[a] *was* his son, Ā'sa his son, Je-
hosh'a·phat his son, 11Jō'ram[a] his son,
Ā·ha·zī'ah his son, Jō'ash[b] his son, 12Am-
a·zī'ah his son, Az·a·rī'ah[a] his son, Jō'tham
his son, 13Ā'haz his son, Hez·e·kī'ah his
son, Ma·nas'seh his son, 14Ā'mon his son,
and Jō·sī'ah his son. 15The sons of Jō·sī'ah
were Jō·hā'nan the firstborn, the second
Je·hoi'a·kim, the third Zed·e·kī'ah, and the
fourth Shal'lum.[a] 16The sons of Je·hoi'-
a·kim *were* Jec·o·nī'ah his son *and* Zed-
e·kī'ah[a] his son.

The Family of Jeconiah

17And the sons of Jec·o·nī'ah[a] *were*
As'sir,[b] She·al'ti·el his son, 18*and* Mal-

2:52 [a]Same as *the Manahethites,* verse 54
3:1 [a]Called *Chileab* in 2 Samuel 3:3 3:5 [a]Spelled *Shammua* in 14:4 and 2 Samuel 5:14 [b]Spelled *Bathsheba* in 2 Samuel 11:3 [c]Called *Eliam* in 2 Samuel 11:3 3:6 [a]Spelled *Elishua* in 14:5 and 2 Samuel 5:15 [b]Spelled *Elpelet* in 14:5
3:8 [a]Spelled *Beeliada* in 14:7 3:10 [a]Spelled *Abijam* in 1 Kings 15:1 3:11 [a]Spelled *Jehoram* in 2 Kings 1:17 and 8:16 [b]Spelled *Jehoash* in 2 Kings 12:1
3:12 [a]Called *Uzziah* in Isaiah 6:1 3:15 [a]Called *Jehoahaz* in 2 Kings 23:31 3:16 [a]Compare 2 Kings 24:17 3:17 [a]Also called *Coniah* in Jeremiah 22:24 and *Jehoiachin* in 2 Kings 24:8 [b]Or *Jeconiah the captive were*

3:1–9 The descendants of **David** are divided between those born in **Hebron** (vv. 1–4) and those born in **Jerusalem** (vv. 5–9).

3:10–16 The kings of Judah from the reign of Solomon to the fall of Jerusalem.

3:17–24 The genealogy of **Jeconiah** contains names of persons who were important during Judah's postexilic period, such as **Shealtiel** and **Zerubbabel** (see note on v. 19). **Shenazzar** (v. 18) may be a variant spelling of Sheshbazzar, the first governor of postexilic Judah (Ezra 5:14). Being a descendant of Jeconiah would explain why he is called a "prince of Judah" (Ezra 1:8).

chī′ram, Pe·dāi′ah, Shen·az′zar, Jec·a-mī′ah, Hosh′a·ma, and Ned·a·bī′ah. 19The sons of Pe·dāi′ah *were* Ze·rub′ba·bel and Shim′ē·ī. The sons of Ze·rub′ba·bel *were* Me·shul′lam, Han·a·nī′ah, She·lō′mith their sister, 20and Ha·shū′bah, Ō′hel, Ber·e·chī′ah, Has·a·dī′ah, and Jū′shab-Hē′sed—five *in all.*

21The sons of Han·a·nī′ah *were* Pel-a·tī′ah and Je·shā′i·ah, the sons of Reph-āi′ah, the sons of Ar′nan, the sons of Ō·ba·dī′ah, and the sons of Shech·a·nī′ah. 22The son of Shech·a·nī′ah was She-māi′ah. The sons of She·māi′ah *were* Hat′tush, Ī′gal, Ba·rī′ah, Nē·a·rī′ah, and Shā′phat—six *in all.* 23The sons of Nē·a-rī′ah *were* El·i·ō·ē′naī, Hez·e·kī′ah, and Az·rī′kam—three *in all.* 24The sons of El·i-ō·ē′naī *were* Hod·a·vī′ah, E·lī′a·shib, Pe·lāi′ah, Ak′kub, Jō·hā′nan, De·laī′ah, and A·nā′nī—seven *in all.*

CHAPTER 4

The Family of Judah

The sons of Judah *were* Per′ez, Hez′ron, Car′mī, Hur, and Shō′bal. 2And Rē·āi′ah the son of Shō′bal begot Jā′hath, and Jā′hath begot A·hū′māi and Lā′had. These *were* the families of the Zō′ra·thītes. 3These *were* the sons *of the father* of Ē′tam: Jez′rē·el, Ish′ma, and Id′bash; and the name of their sister *was* Haz·e·lel·pō′ni; 4and Pe·nū′el *was* the father of Gē′dor, and Ē′zer *was the* father of Hū′shah.

These *were* the sons of Hur, the firstborn of Eph′ra·thah the father of Bethlehem.

5And Ash′hur the father of Te·kō′a had two wives, Hē′lah and Nā′a·rah. 6Nā′a·rah bore him A·huz′zam, Hē′pher, Tē′me·nī, and Hā·a·hash′ta·rī. These *were* the sons of Nā′a·rah. 7The sons of Hē′lah *were* Zē′reth, Zō′har, and Eth′nan; 8and Koz begot Ā′nub, Zō·bē′bah, and the families of A·har′hel the son of Har′um.

9Now Jā′bez was more honorable than his brothers, and his mother called his name Jā′bez,[a] saying, "Because I bore *him* in pain." 10And Jā′bez called on the God of Israel saying, "Oh, that You would bless me indeed, and enlarge my territory, that Your hand would be with me, and that You would keep *me* from evil, that I may not cause pain!" So God granted him what he requested.

11Chē′lub the brother of Shū′hah begot Mē′hir, who *was* the father of Esh′ton. 12And Esh′ton begot Beth-Rā′pha, Pa-sē′ah, and Te·hin′nah the father of Ir-Nā′hash. These *were* the men of Rē′chah.

13The sons of Kē′naz *were* Oth′ni·el and Se·rāi′ah. The sons of Oth′ni·el *were* Hā′-thath,[a] 14and Me·on′o·thaī *who* begot Oph′rah. Se·rāi′ah begot Jō′ab the father of Ge Ha·ra′shim,[a] for they were craftsmen. 15The sons of Caleb the son of Je·phūn′neh *were* Ī′rū, Ē′lah, and Nā′am. The son of Ē′lah *was* Kē′naz. 16The sons of Je·hal′le·lel

4:9 [a]Literally *He Will Cause Pain* 4:13 [a]Septuagint and Vulgate add *and Meonothai.* 4:14 [a]Literally *Valley of Craftsmen*

3:19 The father of **Zerubbabel** is identified elsewhere not as **Pedaiah** but as his brother Shealtiel (see Hag. 1:1). If Shealtiel died early, his younger brother Pedaiah would have married the childless widow according to levirate marriage (see Deut. 25:5–10 and note on Deut. 25:5). So Pedaiah would be Zerubbabel's biological father, but Shealtiel his legal father. Zerubbabel was governor of the province of Judah for more than 20 years during the restoration (see Ezra 3:2).

4:1–23 The genealogy of **Judah** is listed before the other tribes (4:24—8:40) because Judah was to be the instrument of the promised blessing (see Gen. 49:8–12).

4:9,10 Just as Er's wickedness was recorded for all generations to see (2:3), the faith of Jabez was proclaimed so that he would be honored for his righteousness. Our actions today will affect our children and grandchildren tomorrow.

4:15 **Caleb**: The spy sent out by Moses in Num. 13:6. He should not be confused with the Caleb in 2:18. See note on 2:18–20.

were Ziph, Zī′phah, Tir′i·a, and As′a·rel.
17The sons of Ez′rah *were* Jē′ther, Mē′red,
Ē′pher, and Jā′lon. And *Mē′red's wife*[a]
bore Miriam, Sham′maī, and Ish′bah the
father of Esh·te·mō′a. 18(His wife
Jē·hu·dī′jah[a] bore Jē′red the father of
Gē′dor, Hē′ber the father of Sō′chōh, and
Je·kū′thi·el the father of Za·nō′ah.)
And these were the sons of Bith′i·ah
the daughter of Pharaoh, whom Mē′red
took.

19The sons of Hō·dī′ah's wife, the sister
of Nā′ham, *were* the fathers of Kē·ī′lah the
Gar′mīte and of Esh·te·mō′a the Mā′-
a·cha·thīte. 20And the sons of Shī′mon *were*
Am′non, Rin′nah, Ben-Hā′nan, and Tī′lon.
And the sons of Ish′ī *were* Zō′heth and Ben-
Zō′heth.

21The sons of Shē′lah the son of Judah
were Er the father of Lē′cah, Lā′a·dah
the father of Ma·rē′shah, and the families
of the house of the linen workers of
the house of Ash′bē·a; 22also Jō′kim, the
men of Cho·zē′ba, and Jō′ash; Sar′aph,
who ruled in Mō′ab, and Ja·shū′bī-
Lē′hem. Now the records are ancient.
23These *were* the potters and those
who dwell at Ne·tā′im[a] and Ge·dē′rah;[b]
there they dwelt with the king for his
work.

The Family of Simeon

24The sons of Sim′ē·on *were* Nem′ū·el,
Jā′min, Jā′rib,[a] Zē′rah,[b] *and* Shā′ūl,
25Shal′lum his son, Mib′sam his son, and
Mish′ma his son. 26And the sons of
Mish′ma *were* Ham′ū·el his son, Zac′chur
his son, and Shim′ē·ī his son. 27Shim′ē·ī
had sixteen sons and six daughters; but his
brothers did not have many children, nor
did any of their families multiply as much
as the children of Judah.

28They dwelt at Bē·er·shē′ba, Mō′la·dah,
Hā′zar Shū′al, 29Bil′hah, Ē′zem, Tō′lad,
30Be·thū′el, Hor′mah, Zik′lag, 31Beth
Mar′ca·both, Hā′zar Sū′sim, Beth Bi′ri, and
at Shā·a·rā′im. These *were* their cities until
the reign of David. 32And their villages
were Ē′tam, Ā′in, Rim′mon, Tō′chen, and
Ā′shan—five cities— 33and all the villages
that *were* around these cities as far as
Bā′al.[a] These *were* their dwelling places,
and they maintained their genealogy:
34Me·shō′bab, Jam′lech, and Jō′shah the
son of Am·a·zī′ah; 35Jō′el, and Jē′hū the son
of Josh·i·bī′ah, the son of Se·rāi′ah, the son
of As′i·el; 36El·i·ō·ē′naī, Jā·a·kō′bah,
Jesh·ō·hāi′ah, A·sāi′ah, Ad′i·el, Je·sim′i·el,
and Be·nā′i·ah; 37Zī′za the son of Shī′phī,
the son of Al′lon, the son of Je·daī′ah, the
son of Shim′rī, the son of She·māi′ah—
38these mentioned by name *were* leaders in
their families, and their father's house in-
creased greatly.

39So they went to the entrance of Gē′dor,
as far as the east side of the valley, to seek
pasture for their flocks. 40And they found
rich, good pasture, and the land *was* broad,
quiet, and peaceful; for some Ham′ītes for-
merly lived there.

41These recorded by name came in the
days of Hez·e·kī′ah king of Judah; and
they attacked their tents and the Me-
ū′nītes who were found there, and utterly
destroyed them, as it is to this day. So they
dwelt in their place, because *there was* pas-
ture for their flocks there. 42Now *some* of
them, five hundred men of the sons of
Sim′ē·on, went to Mount Sē′ir, having as
their captains Pel·a·tī′ah, Nē·a·rī′ah,
Reph·āi′ah, and Uz′zi·el, the sons of Ish′ī.
43And they defeated the rest of the
A·mal′e·kītes who had escaped. They
have dwelt there to this day.

4:17 [a]Literally *she* 4:18 [a]Or *His Judean wife*
4:23 [a]Literally *Plants* [b]Literally *Hedges*
4:24 [a]Called *Jachin* in Genesis 46:10 [b]Called *Zohar* in Genesis 46:10 4:33 [a]Or *Baalath Beer* (compare Joshua 19:8)

4:39–43 The territorial conquests of the Simeonites. A small tribe, Simeon had settled within the southern border of Judah. **Mount Seir** (v. 42): Apparently some of the tribe of Simeon conquered territory south and east of the Dead Sea.

CHAPTER 5

The Family of Reuben

Now the sons of Reuben the firstborn of
Israel—he *was* indeed the firstborn, but
because he defiled his father's bed, his
birthright was given to the sons of Joseph,
the son of Israel, so that the genealogy is
not listed according to the birthright; 2yet
Judah prevailed over his brothers, and
from him *came* a ruler, although the
birthright was Joseph's— 3the sons of Reu-
ben the firstborn of Israel were Hā′noch,
Pal′lū, Hez′ron, and Car′mī.

4The sons of Jō′el *were* She·māi′ah his
son, Gog his son, Shim′ē·ī his son, 5Mī′cah
his son, Rē·āi′ah his son, Bā′al his son,
6and Be·er′ah his son, whom Tig′lath-
Pī·lē′ser[a] king of Assyria carried into
captivity. He *was* leader of the
Reū′ben·ītes. 7And his brethren by their
families, when the genealogy of their gen-
erations was registered: the chief, Je·ī′el,
and Zech·a·rī′ah, 8and Bē′la the son of
Ā′zaz, the son of Shē′ma, the son of Jō′el,
who dwelt in A·rō′er, as far as Nē′bō
and Bā′al Mē′on. 9Eastward they settled as
far as the entrance of the wilderness this
side of the River Eū·phrā′tēs, because their
cattle had multiplied in the land of
Gil′ē·ad.

10Now in the days of Saul they made
war with the Hag′rītes, who fell by their
hand; and they dwelt in their tents
throughout the entire *area* east of
Gil′ē·ad.

The Family of Gad

11And the children of Gad dwelt next to
them in the land of Bā′shan as far as
Sal′cah: 12Jō′el *was* the chief, Shā′pham the
next, then Jā′a·naī and Shā′phat in
Bā′shan, 13and their brethren of their
father's house: Michael, Me·shul′lam,
Shē′ba, Jō′raī, Jā′chan, Zī′a, and Ē′ber—
seven *in all.* 14These *were* the children of
Ab·i·hā′il the son of Hū′rī, the son of
Ja·rō′ah, the son of Gil′ē·ad, the son of Mi-
chael, the son of Je·shish′aī, the son of
Jah′dō, the son of Buz; 15Ā′hī the son of
Ab′di·el, the son of Gū′nī, *was* chief of their
father's house. 16And *the Gad′ītes* dwelt in
Gil′ē·ad, in Bā′shan and in its villages, and
in all the common-lands of Sharon within
their borders. 17All these were registered
by genealogies in the days of Jō′tham king
of Judah, and in the days of Jer·o·bō′am
king of Israel.

18The sons of Reuben, the Gad′ītes, and
half the tribe of Ma·nas′seh *had* forty-four
thousand seven hundred and sixty valiant
men, men able to bear shield and sword, to
shoot with the bow, and skillful in war,
who went to war. 19They made war with
the Hag′rītes, Jē′tur, Nā′phish, and
Nō′dab. 20And they were helped against
them, and the Hag′rītes were delivered
into their hand, and all who *were* with
them, for they cried out to God in the bat-
tle. He heeded their prayer, because they
put their trust in Him. 21Then they took

5:6 [a]Hebrew *Tilgath-Pilneser*

5:1–26 Three tribes—Reuben, Gad, and half of Manasseh—remained on the east side of the Jordan when Israel settled in Canaan (see Num. 32; Josh. 13:8–32). Their territory had been annexed by Assyria in 734 B.C. (v. 6). According to v. 17, the author is here relying on royal records made several centuries earlier.

5:1, 2 The sequence of the genealogies is intended to illustrate God's choices. Because of Reuben's sin, possession of the **birthright** was given to the sons of Joseph. But Judah's was the line from which the **ruler** should come. It was a gift determined by God's grace, rather than by the merit of natural rights. See note on Gen. 49:3–12.

5:10 Hagrites: Arabs living in the vicinity of Moab (see Ps. 83:6), descendants of the Egyptian mother of Ishmael.

5:11 Bashan: Region east and southeast of the Sea of Galilee.

5:20 because they put their trust in Him: The purpose of the chronicler was to emphasize that Judah's salvation was linked to trust in God.

away their livestock—fifty thousand of
their camels, two hundred and fifty thou-
sand of their sheep, and two thousand of
their donkeys—also one hundred thou-
sand of their men; 22for many fell dead, be-
cause the war *was* God's. And they dwelt
in their place until the captivity.

The Family of Manasseh (East)

23So the children of the half-tribe of
Ma·nas'seh dwelt in the land. Their *num-
bers* increased from Bā'shan to Bā'al
Her'mon, that is, to Sē'nir, or Mount Her'-
mon. 24These *were* the heads of their
fathers' houses: Ē'pher, Ish'ī, E·lī'el, Az'-
ri·el, Jer·e·mī'ah, Hod·a·vī'ah, and Jah'-
di·el. They were mighty men of valor, famous
men, *and* heads of their fathers' houses.
25And they were unfaithful to the God of
their fathers, and played the harlot after
the gods of the peoples of the land, whom
God had destroyed before them. 26So the
God of Israel stirred up the spirit of Pūl
king of Assyria, that is, Tig'lath-Pī·lē'ser[a]
king of Assyria. He carried the Reū'-
ben·ītes, the Gad'ītes, and the half-tribe of
Ma·nas'seh into captivity. He took them to
Hā'lah, Hā'bor, Hā'ra, and the river of
Gō'zan to this day.

CHAPTER 6

The Family of Levi

The sons of Levi *were* Ger'shon, Kō'hath,
and Me·rar'ī. 2The sons of Kō'hath *were*
Am'ram, Iz'har, Hē'bron, and Uz'zi·el.
3The children of Am'ram *were* Aaron, Mo-
ses, and Miriam. And the sons of Aaron
were Nā'dab, A·bī'hū, El·ē·ā'zar, and
Ith'a·mar. 4El·ē·ā'zar begot Phin'e·has, *and*
Phin'e·has begot Ab·i·shū'a; 5Ab·i·shū'a
begot Buk'kī, and Buk'kī begot Uz'zī;
6Uz'zī begot Zer·a·hī'ah, and Zer·a·hī'ah
begot Me·rā'i·oth; 7Me·rā'i·oth begot
Am·a·rī'ah, and Am·a·rī'ah begot
A·hī'tub; 8A·hī'tub begot Zā'dok, and
Zā'dok begot A·him'a·az; 9A·him'a·az be-
got Az·a·rī'ah, and Az·a·rī'ah begot
Jō·hā'nan; 10Jō·hā'nan begot Az·a·rī'ah (it
was he who ministered as priest in the
temple that Solomon built in Jerusalem);
11Az·a·rī'ah begot Am·a·rī'ah, and
Am·a·rī'ah begot A·hī'tub; 12A·hī'tub be-
got Zā'dok, and Zā'dok begot Shal'lum;
13Shal'lum begot Hil·kī'ah, and Hil·kī'ah
begot Az·a·rī'ah; 14Az·a·rī'ah begot Se-
rāi'ah, and Se·rāi'ah begot Je·hoz'a·dak.
15Je·hoz'a·dak went *into captivity* when the
LORD carried Judah and Jerusalem into
captivity by the hand of Ne·bū·chad-
nez'zar.

16The sons of Levi *were* Ger'shon,[a]
Kō'hath, and Me·rar'ī. 17These are the
names of the sons of Ger'shon: Lib'nī and
Shim'ē·ī. 18The sons of Kō'hath *were*
Am'ram, Iz'har, Hē'bron, and Uz'zi·el.
19The sons of Me·rar'ī *were* Mah'lī and
Mū'shī. Now these *are* the families of the
Lē'vītes according to their fathers: 20Of
Ger'shon *were* Lib'nī his son, Jā'hath his
son, Zim'mah his son, 21Jō'ah his son, Id'dō
his son, Zē'rah his son, *and* Jē·ath'e·raī his

5:26 [a]Hebrew *Tilgath-Pilneser* 6:16 [a]Hebrew *Gershom* (alternate spelling of *Gershon,* as in verses 1, 17, 20, 43, 62, and 71)

5:25, 26 unfaithful to . . . God: Because they rejected God, He rejected them and used His servant **Tiglath-Pileser** as a tool to carry out His punishment of Israel (see notes on Deut. 28:15–68; 2 Kin. 15:19, 20).

6:1–15 Only those Levites who were direct descendants of Aaron, the great grandson of Levi, could serve as priests at the temple (see Num. 3:5–38). In order to determine who could legitimately serve as priests after the Exile, this first list of the chapter traces the Levitical line from Aaron, the first priest, through Eleazar, his third son, to his descendants in the captivity. The branch through Ithamar was rejected because of the sins of Eli's sons (see 1 Sam. 3:10–14; 1 Chr. 24:3–6 and note on 24:3).

6:16–53 The second Levitical list traces the descendants of Levi in general. These persons assisted in tabernacle and temple worship, but did not themselves offer sacrifices (vv. 48, 49).

son. 22The sons of Kō'hath *were* Am·min'a·dab his son, Kō'rah his son, As'sir his son, 23El·kā'nah his son, E·bī'a·saph his son, As'sir his son, 24Tā'hath his son, Ū·rī'el his son, Uz·zī'ah his son, and Shā'ŭl his son. 25The sons of El·kā'nah *were* A·mā'saī and A·hī'moth. 26*As for* El·kā'nah,[a] the sons of El·kā'nah *were* Zō'phaī[b] his son, Nā'hath[c] his son, 27E·lī'ab[a] his son, Je-rō'ham his son, *and* El·kā'nah his son. 28The sons of Samuel *were* *Jō'el*[a] the first-born, and A·bī'jah the second.[b] 29The sons of Me·rar'ī *were* Mah'lī, Lib'nī his son, Shim'ē·ī his son, Uz'zah his son, 30Shim'ē·a his son, Hag·gī'ah his son, *and* A·sāi'ah his son.

Musicians in the House of the LORD

31Now these are the men whom David appointed over the service of song in the house of the LORD, after the ark came to rest. 32They were ministering with music before the dwelling place of the tabernacle of meeting, until Solomon had built the house of the LORD in Jerusalem, and they served in their office according to their order.

33And these *are* the ones who ministered with their sons: Of the sons of the Kō'hath·ītes *were* Hē'man the singer, the son of Jō'el, the son of Samuel, 34the son of El·kā'nah, the son of Je·rō'ham, the son of E·lī'el,[a] the son of Tō'ah,[b] 35the son of Zuph, the son of El·kā'nah, the son of Mā'hath, the son of A·mā'saī, 36the son of El·kā'nah, the son of Jō'el, the son of Az·a·rī'ah, the son of Zeph·a·nī'ah, 37the son of Tā'hath, the son of As'sir, the son of E·bī'a·saph, the son of Kō'rah, 38the son of Iz'har, the son of Kō'hath, the son of Levi, the son of Israel. 39And his brother Ā'saph, who stood at his right hand, *was* Ā'saph the son of Ber·a-chī'ah, the son of Shim'ē·a, 40the son of Mi-chael, the son of Bā·a·sē'i·ah, the son of Mal·chī'jah, 41the son of Eth'nī, the son of Zē'rah, the son of A·dāi'ah, 42the son of Ē'than, the son of Zim'mah, the son of Shim'ē·ī, 43the son of Jā'hath, the son of Ger'shon, the son of Levi.

44Their brethren, the sons of Me·rar'ī, on the left hand, *were* Ē'than the son of Kish'ī, the son of Ab'dī, the son of Mal'luch, 45the son of Hash·a·bī'ah, the son of Am·a-zī'ah, the son of Hil·kī'ah, 46the son of Am'zī, the son of Bā'nī, the son of Shā'mer, 47the son of Mah'lī, the son of Mū'shī, the son of Me·rar'ī, the son of Levi.

48And their brethren, the Lē'vītes, *were* appointed to every kind of service of the tabernacle of the house of God.

The Family of Aaron

49But Aaron and his sons offered sacrifices on the altar of burnt offering and on the altar of incense, for all the work of the Most Holy *Place,* and to make atonement for Israel, according to all that Moses the servant of God had commanded. 50Now these *are* the sons of Aaron: El·ē·ā'zar his son, Phin'e·has his son, Ab·i·shū'a his son, 51Buk'kī his son, Uz'zī his son, Zer·a·hī'ah his son, 52Me·rā'i·oth his son, Am·a·rī'ah his son, A·hī'tub his son, 53Zā'dok his son, *and* A·him'a·az his son.

Dwelling Places of the Levites

54Now these *are* their dwelling places throughout their settlements in their terri-

6:26 [a]Compare verse 35 [b]Spelled *Zuph* in verse 35 and 1 Samuel 1:1 [c]Compare verse 34 6:27 [a]Compare verse 34 6:28 [a]Following Septuagint, Syriac, and Arabic (compare verse 33 and 1 Samuel 8:2) [b]Hebrew *Vasheni* 6:34 [a]Spelled *Elihu* in 1 Samuel 1:1 [b]Spelled *Tohu* in 1 Samuel 1:1

6:31–48 The list of those who led the music in the temple. David, who apparently had a great talent for and love of music, incorporated music into the worship of the Lord. Heman, Asaph, and Ethan were in charge of the choirs and orchestras, and each has been associated with the Psalms. Heman probably wrote Psalm 88, and Ethan may be the author of Psalm 89. Asaph is credited with Psalm 50 and Psalms 73–83.

6:54–81 The locations of the Levitical cities (see Josh. 21:1–45 and note).

tory, for they were *given* by lot to the sons
of Aaron, of the family of the Kō'hath·ītes:
55They gave them Hē'bron in the land of
Judah, with its surrounding common-
lands. 56But the fields of the city and its
villages they gave to Caleb the son
of Je·phū'neh. 57And to the sons of
Aaron they gave *one of* the cities of
refuge, Hē'bron; also Lib'nah with
its common-lands, Jat'tir, Esh·te·mō'a
with its common-lands, 58Hī'len[a] with
its common-lands, Dē'bir with its
common-lands, 59Ā'shan[a] with its
common-lands, and Beth Shem'esh with
its common-lands. 60And from the tribe of
Benjamin: Gē'ba with its common-lands,
Al'e·meth[a] with its common-lands, and
An'a·thoth with its common-lands. All
their cities among their families *were* thir-
teen.

61To the rest of the family of the tribe of
the Kō'hath·ītes *they gave* by lot ten cities
from half the tribe of Ma·nas'seh. 62And to
the sons of Ger'shon, throughout their
families, *they gave* thirteen cities from the
tribe of Is'sa·char, from the tribe of Ash'er,
from the tribe of Naph'ta·lī, and from the
tribe of Ma·nas'seh in Bā'shan. 63To the
sons of Me·rar'ī, throughout their families,
they gave twelve cities from the tribe of
Reuben, from the tribe of Gad, and from
the tribe of Zeb'ū·lun. 64So the children of
Israel gave *these* cities with their common-
lands to the Lē'vītes. 65And they gave by
lot from the tribe of the children of Judah,
from the tribe of the children of Sim'ē·on,
and from the tribe of the children of Benja-
min these cities which are called by *their*
names.

66Now some of the families of the sons
of Kō'hath *were given* cities as their terri-
tory from the tribe of Ē'phra·im. 67And
they gave them *one of* the cities of refuge,
Shē'chem with its common-lands, in the
mountains of Ē'phra·im, also Gē'zer with
its common-lands, 68Jok'mē·am with
its common-lands, Beth Hor'on with its
common-lands, 69Aī'ja·lon with its
common-lands, and Gath Rim'mon with
its common-lands. 70And from the half-
tribe of Ma·nas'seh: Ā'ner with its
common-lands and Bil'ē·am with its
common-lands, for the rest of the family of
the sons of Kō'hath.

71From the family of the half-tribe of
Ma·nas'seh the sons of Ger'shon *were given*
Gō'lan in Bā'shan with its common-lands
and Ash'ta·roth with its common-lands.
72And from the tribe of Is'sa·char: Kē'desh
with its common-lands, Dab'e·rath
with its common-lands, 73Rā'moth with
its common-lands, and Ā'nem with
its common-lands. 74And from the tribe
of Ash'er: Mā'shal with its common-
lands, Ab'don with its common-lands,
75Hū'kok with its common-lands, and
Rē'hob with its common-lands. 76And
from the tribe of Naph'ta·lī: Kē'desh
in Galilee with its common-lands,
Ham'mon with its common-lands,
and Kir·jath'a·im with its common-
lands.

77From the tribe of Zeb'ū·lun the rest of
the children of Me·rar'ī *were given*
Rim'mon[a] with its common-lands and
Tā'bor with its common-lands. 78And on
the other side of the Jordan, across from
Jericho, on the east side of the Jordan, *they
were given* from the tribe of Reuben: Bē'zer
in the wilderness with its common-lands,
Jah'zah with its common-lands, 79Ked'-
e·moth with its common-lands, and
Meph'a·ath with its common-lands. 80And
from the tribe of Gad: Rā'moth in Gil'ē·ad
with its common-lands, Mā·ha·na'im with
its common-lands, 81Hesh'bon with its

6:58 [a]Spelled *Holon* in Joshua 21:15 6:59 [a]Spelled *Ain* in Joshua 21:16 6:60 [a]Spelled *Almon* in Joshua 21:18 6:77 [a]Hebrew *Rimmono,* alternate spelling of *Rimmon;* see 4:32

6:55 common-lands: See Num. 35:1–5.
6:57 cities of refuge: See Num. 35:6 and note.

common-lands, and Jā′zer with its common-lands.

CHAPTER 7

The Family of Issachar

The sons of Is′sa·char *were* Tō′la, Pū′ah,[a] Jash′ub, and Shim′ron—four *in all.* 2The sons of Tō′la *were* Uz′zī, Reph·āi′ah, Jē′ri·el, Jah′maī, Jib′sam, and She·mū′el, heads of their father′s house. *The sons* of Tō′la *were* mighty men of valor in their generations; their number in the days of David *was* twenty-two thousand six hundred. 3The son of Uz′zī *was* Iz·ra·hī′ah, and the sons of Iz·ra·hī′ah *were* Michael, Ō·ba·dī′ah, Jō′el, and Ish·ī′ah. All five of them *were* chief men. 4And with them, by their generations, according to their fathers′ houses, *were* thirty-six thousand troops ready for war; for they had many wives and sons.

5Now their brethren among all the families of Is′sa·char *were* mighty men of valor, listed by their genealogies, eighty-seven thousand in all.

The Family of Benjamin

6*The sons* of Benjamin *were* Bē′la, Bē′cher, and Je·dī′a·el—three *in all.* 7The sons of Bē′la were Ez′bon, Uz′zī, Uz′zi·el, Jer′i·moth, and Iri—five *in all.* They *were* heads of *their* fathers′ houses, and they were listed by their genealogies, twenty-two thousand and thirty-four mighty men of valor.

8The sons of Bē′cher *were* Ze·mī′rah, Jō′ash, El·i·ē′zer, El·i·ō·ē′naī, Om′rī, Jer′i·moth, A·bī′jah, An′a·thoth, and Al′e·meth. All these *are* the sons of Bē′cher. 9And they were recorded by genealogy according to their generations, heads of their fathers′ houses, twenty thousand two hundred mighty men of valor. 10The son of Je·dī′a·el *was* Bil′han, and the sons of Bil′han *were* Jē′ush, Benjamin, Ē′hud, Che·nā′a·nah, Zē′than, Thar′shish, and A·hish′a·har.

11All these sons of Je·dī′a·el *were* heads of their fathers′ houses; *there were* seventeen thousand two hundred mighty men of valor fit to go out for war *and* battle. 12Shup′pim and Hup′pim[a] *were* the sons of Ir, *and* Hū′shim *was* the son of Ā′her.

The Family of Naphtali

13The sons of Naph′ta·lī *were* Jah′zi·el,[a] Gū′nī, Jē′zer, and Shal′lum,[b] the sons of Bil′hah.

The Family of Manasseh (West)

14The descendants of Ma·nas′seh: his Syrian concubine bore him Mā′chir the father of Gil′ē·ad, the father of As′ri·el.[a] 15Mā′chir took as his wife *the sister* of Hup′pim and Shup′pim,[a] whose name *was* Mā′a·chah. The name of *Gil′ē·ad′s* grandson[b] *was* Ze·loph′e·had,[c] but Ze·loph′e·had begot only daughters. 16(Mā′a·chah the wife of Mā′chir bore a son, and she called his name Pē′resh. The name of his brother *was* Shē′resh, and his sons *were* Ū′lam and Rā′kem. 17The son of Ū′lam *was* Bē′dan.) These *were* the descendants of

7:1 [a]Spelled *Puvah* in Genesis 46:13 7:12 [a]Called *Hupham* in Numbers 26:39 7:13 [a]Spelled *Jahzeel* in Genesis 46:24 [b]Spelled *Shillem* in Genesis 46:24 7:14 [a]The son of Gilead (compare Numbers 26:30, 31) 7:15 [a]Compare verse 12 [b]Literally *the second* [c]Compare Numbers 26:30–33

7:1–40 The genealogical survey of Israel's families ends with lists of Issachar (vv. 1–5), Benjamin (vv. 6–12), Naphtali (v. 13), West Manasseh (vv. 14–19), Ephraim (vv. 20–29), and Asher (vv. 30–40).

7:12 Some scholars feel the reference to **Hushim** is an indirect allusion to the tribe of Dan (see Gen. 46:23) which together with Zebulun is otherwise omitted from the genealogies of chs. 4—8. The reason for this omission is unknown.

7:14–19 The genealogy of the half-tribe of Manasseh living east of the Jordan. Those living on the west side are listed in 5:23, 24.

Gil′ē·ad the son of Mā′chir, the son of
Ma·nas′seh.
18His sister Ham·mo′le·keth bore
Ish′hod, Ā·bi·ē′zer, and Mah′lah.
19And the sons of She·mī′da were
A·hī′an, Shē′chem, Lik′hī, and A·nī′am.

The Family of Ephraim

20The sons of Ē′phra·im *were* Shū′-
the·lah, Bē′red his son, Tā′hath his son,
El′a·dah his son, Tā′hath his son, 21Zā′bad
his son, Shū′the·lah his son, and Ē′zer and
Ē′lē·ad. The men of Gath who were born in
that land killed *them* because they came
down to take away their cattle. 22Then
Ē′phra·im their father mourned many
days, and his brethren came to comfort
him.
23And when he went in to his wife, she
conceived and bore a son; and he called his
name Bē·rī′ah,[a] because tragedy had come
upon his house. 24Now his daughter *was*
Shē′e·rah, who built Lower and Upper
Beth Hor′on and Uz′zen Shē′e·rah; 25and
Rē′phah *was* his son, *as well* as Rē′sheph,
and Tē′lah his son, Tā′han his son, 26Lā′-
a·dan his son, Am·mī′hud his son,
E·lish′a·ma his son, 27Nun[a] his son, and
Joshua his son.
28Now their possessions and dwelling
places *were* Beth′el and its towns: to the
east Nā′a·ran, to the west Gē′zer and its
towns, and Shē′chem and its towns, as far
as Āy′yah[a] and its towns; 29and by the bor-
ders of the children of Ma·nas′seh *were*
Beth Shē′an and its towns, Tā′a·nach and
its towns, Me·gid′dō and its towns, Dor
and its towns. In these dwelt the children
of Joseph, the son of Israel.

The Family of Asher

30The sons of Ash′er *were* Im′nah,
Ish′vah, Ish′vī, Bē·rī′ah, and their sister
Sē′rah. 31The sons of Bē·rī′ah *were* Hē′ber
and Mal′chi·el, who was the father of
Bir′zā·ith.[a] 32And Hē′ber begot Japh′let,
Shō′mer,[a] Hō′tham,[b] and their sister Shū′a.
33The sons of Japh′let *were* Pā′sach,
Bim′hal, and Ash′vath. These *were*
the children of Japh′let. 34The sons of
Shē′mer *were* Ā′hī, Rōh′gah, Je·hub′bah,
and Ar′am. 35And the sons of his brother
Hē′lem *were* Zō′phah, Im′na, Shē′lesh,
and Ā′mal. 36The sons of Zō′phah *were*
Sū′ah, Har′ne·pher, Shū′al, Bē′rī, Im′rah,
37Bē′zer, Hod, Sham′ma, Shil′shah,
Jith′ran,[a] and Be·ē′ra. 38The sons of Jē′ther
were Je·phūn′neh, Pis′pah, and Ar′a. 39The
sons of Ul′la *were* Ā′rah, Han′i·el, and
Rī·zī′a.
40All these *were* the children of Ash′er,
heads of *their* fathers′ houses, choice men,
mighty men of valor, chief leaders. And
they were recorded by genealogies among
the army fit for battle; their number *was*
twenty-six thousand.

CHAPTER 8

The Family Tree of King Saul of Benjamin

Now Benjamin begot Bē′la his firstborn,
Ash′bel the second, A′har·ah[a] the third,
2Nō′hah the fourth, and Rā′pha the fifth.
3The sons of Bē′la *were* Ad′dar,[a] Gē′ra,
A·bī′hud, 4Ab·i·shū′a, Nā′a·man, A·hō′ah,
5Gē′ra, She·phū′phan, and Hū′ram.
6These *are* the sons of Ē′hud, who were

7:23 [a]Literally *In Tragedy* 7:27 [a]Hebrew *Non*
7:28 [a]Many Hebrew manuscripts, Bomberg, Septuagint, Targum, and Vulgate read *Gazza.* 7:31 [a]Or *Birzavith* or *Birzoth* 7:32 [a]Spelled *Shemer* in verse 34 [b]Spelled *Helem* in verse 35 7:37 [a]Spelled *Jether* in verse 38 8:1 [a]Spelled *Ahiram* in Numbers 26:38
8:3 [a]Called *Ard* in Numbers 26:40

7:30–39 The tribe of Asher does not stand out in Israel's history for any specific achievement; in fact, the tribe is omitted altogether from the list of David's chief officers (27:16–22). However, the NT prophetess Anna shows Asher's role in the messianic agenda (Luke 2:36–38).

8:1–40 This list of the tribe and family of Saul serves as a transition to the first narrative section of Chronicles—the death of Saul and the coronation of David (10:1—11:3).

the heads of the fathers′ *houses* of the
inhabitants of Gē′ba, and who forced them
to move to Man′a·hath: 7Nā′a·man,
A·hī′jah, and Gē′ra who forced them to
move. He begot Uz′za and A·hī′hud.

8Also Shā·ha·rā′im had children in the
country of Mō′ab, after he had sent away
Hū′shim and Bā′a·ra his wives. 9By
Hō′desh his wife he begot Jō′bab, Zib′i·a,
Mē′sha, Mal′cam, 10Jē′uz, Sa·chī′ah, and
Mir′mah. These *were* his sons, heads of
their fathers′ *houses*.

11And by Hū′shim he begot A·bī′tub
and El·pā′al. 12The sons of El·pā′al *were*
Ē′ber, Mī′sham, and Shē′med, who built
Ō′nō and Lod with its towns; 13and
Bē·rī′ah and Shē′ma, who *were* heads of
their fathers′ *houses* of the inhabitants of
Aī′ja·lon, who drove out the inhabitants
of Gath. 14A·hī′ō, Shā′shak, Jer′e·moth,
15Zeb·a·dī′ah, Ar′ad, Ē′der, 16Michael,
Is′pah, and Jō′ha *were* the sons of
Bē·rī′ah. 17Zeb·a·dī′ah, Me·shul′lam,
Hiz′kī, Hē′ber, 18Ish′me·raī, Jiz·lī′ah, and
Jō′bab *were* the sons of El·pā′al. 19Jā′kim,
Zich′rī, Zab′dī, 20E·li·ē′naī, Zil′le·thaī,
E·lī′el, 21A·dāi′ah, Be·rā′i·ah, and
Shim′rath *were* the sons of Shim′ē·ī.
22Ish′pan, Ē′ber, E·lī′el, 23Ab′don, Zich′rī,
Hā′nan, 24Han·a·nī′ah, Ē′lam, An·to-
thī′jah, 25Iph·dē′i·ah, and Pe·nū′el *were*
the sons of Shā′shak. 26Sham′she·raī,
Shē·ha·rī′ah, Ath·a·lī′ah, 27Jā·ar·e·shī′ah,
E·lī′jah, and Zich′rī *were* the sons of Je-
rō′ham.

28These *were* heads of the fathers′ *houses*
by their generations, chief men. These
dwelt in Jerusalem.

29Now the father of Gib′ē·on, whose
wife′s name *was* Mā′a·cah, dwelt at
Gib′ē·on. 30And his firstborn son *was* Ab′-
don, then Zūr, Kish, Bā′al, Nā′dab,
31Gē′dor, A·hī′ō, Zē′cher, 32and Mik′loth,
who begot Shim′ē·ah.[a] They also dwelt
alongside their relatives in Jerusalem, with
their brethren. 33Ner[a] begot Kish, Kish be-
got Saul, and Saul begot Jonathan, Mal-
chī·shū′a, A·bin′a·dab,[b] and Esh-Bā′al.[c]
34The son of Jonathan *was* Mer′ib-Bā′al,[a]
and Mer′ib-Bā′al begot Mī′cah. 35The sons
of Mī′cah *were* Pī′thon, Mē′lech, Ta·rē′a,
and Ā′haz. 36And Ā′haz begot Je·hō′-
ad·dah;[a] Je·hō′ad·dah begot Al′e·meth,
Az′ma·veth, and Zim′rī; and Zim′rī begot
Mō′za. 37Mō′za begot Bin′ē·a, Rā′phah[a] his
son, El·e·ā′sah his son, *and* Ā′zel his son.

38Ā′zel had six sons whose names *were*
these: Az·rī′kam, Bō′che·rū, Ish′ma·el,
Shē·a·rī′ah, Ō·ba·dī′ah, and Hā′nan. All
these *were* the sons of Ā′zel. 39And the sons
of Ē′shek his brother *were* Ū′lam his first-
born, Jē′ush the second, and E·liph′e·let
the third.

40The sons of Ū′lam were mighty men of
valor—archers. *They* had many sons and
grandsons, one hundred and fifty *in all*.
These *were* all sons of Benjamin.

CHAPTER 9

So all Israel was recorded by genealo-
gies, and indeed, they *were* inscribed in the
book of the kings of Israel. But Judah was
carried away captive to Babylon because of

8:32 [a]Spelled *Shimeam* in 9:38 8:33 [a]Also the son of Gibeon (compare 9:36, 39) [b]Called *Jishui* in 1 Samuel 14:49 [c]Called *Ishbosheth* in 2 Samuel 2:8 and elsewhere 8:34 [a]Called *Mephibosheth* in 2 Samuel 4:4 8:36 [a]Spelled *Jarah* in 9:42 8:37 [a]Spelled *Rephaiah* in 9:43

8:28, 29 There seems to be an intentional contrast here between **Gibeon** (the site of the tabernacle in Saul's time, 16:39) and **Jerusalem**, God's choice in David's time. See also 9:34, 35.

9:1 Similarities to Neh. 11 suggest to some that ch. 9 deals with the postexilic inhabitants of Jerusalem. Thus the "first inhabitants" (v. 2) would refer to the first Jews to return after the Exile. However, the differences between 1 Chr. 9 and Neh. 11 are as great as the similarities, which has caused others to take "first inhabitants" as those who dwelt in Judah before the Exile, and 9:3 as beginning a list of preexilic citizens in Jerusalem.

their unfaithfulness. 2And the first inhabitants who *dwelt* in their possessions in their cities *were* Israelites, priests, Lē'vītes, and the Neth'i·nim.

Dwellers in Jerusalem

3Now in Jerusalem the children of Judah dwelt, and some of the children of Benjamin, and of the children of Ē'phra·im and Ma·nas'seh: 4Ū'thaī the son of Am·mī'hud, the son of Om'rī, the son of Im'rī, the son of Bā'nī, of the descendants of Per'ez, the son of Judah. 5Of the Shī'lo·nītes: A·sāi'ah the firstborn and his sons. 6Of the sons of Zē'rah: Je·ū'el, and their brethren—six hundred and ninety. 7Of the sons of Benjamin: Sal'lū the son of Me·shul'lam, the son of Hod·a·vī'ah, the son of Has·se·nū'ah; 8Ib·nē'i·ah the son of Je·rō'ham; Ē'lah the son of Uz'zī, the son of Mich'rī; Me·shul'lam the son of Sheph·a·tī'ah, the son of Reū'el, the son of Ib·nī'jah; 9and their brethren, according to their generations—nine hundred and fifty-six. All these men *were* heads of a father's *house* in their fathers' houses.

The Priests at Jerusalem

10Of the priests: Je·daī'ah, Je·hoi'a·rib, and Jā'chin; 11Az·a·rī'ah the son of Hil·kī'ah, the son of Me·shul'lam, the son of Zā'dok, the son of Me·rā'i·oth, the son of A·hī'tub, the officer over the house of God; 12A·dāi'ah the son of Je·rō'ham, the son of Pash'ur, the son of Mal·chī'jah; Mā'a·saī the son of Ad'i·el, the son of Jah'ze·rah, the son of Me·shul'lam, the son of Me·shil'le·mith, the son of Im'mer; 13and their brethren, heads of their fathers' *houses*—one thousand seven hundred and sixty. *They were* very able men for the work of the service of the house of God.

The Levites at Jerusalem

14Of the Lē'vītes: She·māi'ah the son of Has'shub, the son of Az·rī'kam, the son of Hash·a·bī'ah, of the sons of Me·rar'ī; 15Bak·bak'kar, Hē'resh, Gā'lal, and Mat·ta·nī'ah the son of Mī'cah, the son of Zich'rī, the son of Ā'saph; 16Ō·ba·dī'ah the son of She·māi'ah, the son of Gā'lal, the son of Je·dū'thun; and Ber·e·chī'ah the son of Ā'sa, the son of El·kā'nah, who lived in the villages of the Ne·toph'a·thītes.

The Levite Gatekeepers

17And the gatekeepers *were* Shal'lum, Ak'kub, Tal'mon, A·hī'man, and their brethren. Shal'lum *was* the chief. 18Until then *they had been* gatekeepers for the camps of the children of Levi at the King's Gate on the east.

19Shal'lum the son of Kō're, the son of E·bī'a·saph, the son of Kō'rah, and his brethren, from his father's house, the Kō'ra·hītes, *were* in charge of the work of the service, gatekeepers of the tabernacle. Their fathers had been keepers of the

---

9:2–9 The first families to return from the Exile.

9:2 first inhabitants: After returning from Babylon. **Israelites** would include returnees from both the southern tribes (Judah and Benjamin, v. 3) and the northern tribes (Ephraim and Manasseh, v. 3). **Nethinim**, meaning "those given," probably refers to prisoners of war who were given to the menial tasks in the temple.

9:10–34 The priestly and Levitical families. Some were assigned as gatekeepers at the temple (vv. 17–27); others were responsible for the furnishings, implements and supplies connected with temple worship (vv. 28–32); still others were involved in the temple music (v. 33).

9:18 Until then indicates gatekeepers who were stationed at the King's Gate until the Exile. However, if vv. 17, 18 discuss postexilic gatekeepers (see note on v. 1), the translation should read "Until now," referring to the time of the writing. **they**: The family of Shallum, since all the gatekeepers were not at the eastern gate (see v. 24). **camps of the children of Levi**: The temple, recalling the wilderness years when the Levites encamped around the tabernacle (see Num. 3:23, 29, 35).

entrance to the camp of the LORD. [20]And Phin′e·has the son of El·ē·ā′zar had been the officer over them in time past; the LORD *was* with him. [21]Zech·a·rī′ah the son of Me·shel·e·mī′ah *was* keeper of the door of the tabernacle of meeting.

[22]All those chosen as gatekeepers *were* two hundred and twelve. They were recorded by their genealogy, in their villages. David and Samuel the seer had appointed them to their trusted office. [23]So they and their children *were* in charge of the gates of the house of the LORD, the house of the tabernacle, by assignment. [24]The gatekeepers were assigned to the four directions: the east, west, north, and south. [25]And their brethren in their villages *had* to come with them from time to time for seven days. [26]For in this trusted office *were* four chief gatekeepers; they were Lē′vītes. And they had charge over the chambers and treasuries of the house of God. [27]And they lodged *all* around the house of God because they *had* the responsibility, and they *were* in charge of opening *it* every morning.

Other Levite Responsibilities

[28]Now *some* of them were in charge of the serving vessels, for they brought them in and took them out by count. [29]*Some* of them *were* appointed over the furnishings and over all the implements of the sanctuary, and over the fine flour and the wine and the oil and the incense and the spices. [30]And *some* of the sons of the priests made the ointment of the spices.

[31]Mat·ti·thī′ah of the Lē′vītes, the firstborn of Shal′lum the Kō′ra·hīte, had the trusted office over the things that were baked in the pans. [32]And some of their brethren of the sons of the Kō′hath·ītes *were* in charge of preparing the showbread for every Sabbath.

[33]These are the singers, heads of the fathers′ *houses* of the Lē′vītes, *who lodged* in the chambers, *and were* free *from other duties;* for they were employed in *that* work day and night. [34]These heads of the fathers′ *houses* of the Lē′vītes *were* heads throughout their generations. They dwelt at Jerusalem.

The Family of King Saul

[35]Je·ī′el the father of Gib′ē·on, whose wife′s name *was* Mā′a·cah, dwelt at Gib′ē·on. [36]His firstborn son *was* Ab′don, then Zūr, Kish, Bā′al, Ner, Nā′dab, [37]Gē′dor, A·hī′ō, Zech·a·rī′ah,[a] and Mik′loth. [38]And Mik′loth begot Shim′ē·am.[a] They also dwelt alongside their relatives in Jerusalem, with their brethren. [39]Ner begot Kish, Kish begot Saul, and Saul begot Jonathan, Mal·chī·shū′a, A·bin′a·dab, and Esh-Bā′al. [40]The son of Jonathan *was* Mer′ib-Bā′al, and Mer′ib-Bā′al begot Mī′cah. [41]The sons of Mī′cah *were* Pī′thon, Mē′lech, Tah′rē·a,[a] *and Ā′haz.*[b] [42]And *Ā′haz* begot Jar′ah;[a] Jar′ah begot Al′e·meth, Az′ma-veth, and Zim′rī; and Zim′rī begot Mō′za; [43]Mō′za begot Bin′ē·a, Reph·āi′ah[a] his son, El·e·ā′sah his son, and Ā′zel his son.

[44]And Ā′zel had six sons whose names *were* these: Az·rī′kam, Bō′che·rū, Ish′ma·el, Shē·a·rī′ah, Ō·ba·dī′ah, and Hā′nan; these *were* the sons of Ā′zel.

9:37 [a]Called *Zecher* in 8:31 9:38 [a]Spelled *Shimeah* in 8:32 9:41 [a]Spelled *Tarea* in 8:35 [b]Following Arabic, Syriac, Targum, and Vulgate (compare 8:35); Masoretic Text and Septuagint omit *and Ahaz.* 9:42 [a]Spelled *Jehoaddah* in 8:36 9:43 [a]Spelled *Raphah* in 8:37

9:25 come . . . for seven days: The normal rotations of service for the Levites who served as gatekeepers at the temple.

9:34, 35 On the distinction between **Jerusalem** and **Gibeon** see note on 8:28, 29.

9:35–44 These verses repeat the list of 8:29–38 and set the stage for the narrative of ch. 10.

CHAPTER 10

Tragic End of Saul and His Sons

Now the Phi·lis'tines fought against Is-
rael; and the men of Israel fled from before
the Phi·lis'tines, and fell slain on Mount
Gil·bō'a. [2]Then the Phi·lis'tines followed
hard after Saul and his sons. And the
Phi·lis'tines killed Jonathan, A·bin'a·dab,
and Mal·chī·shū'a, Saul's sons. [3]The battle
became fierce against Saul. The archers hit
him, and he was wounded by the archers.
[4]Then Saul said to his armorbearer, "Draw
your sword, and thrust me through with it,
lest these uncircumcised men come and
abuse me." But his armorbearer would not,
for he was greatly afraid. Therefore Saul
took a sword and fell on it. [5]And when his
armorbearer saw that Saul was dead, he
also fell on his sword and died. [6]So Saul
and his three sons died, and all his house
died together. [7]And when all the men of Is-
rael who *were* in the valley saw that they
had fled and that Saul and his sons were
dead, they forsook their cities and fled;
then the Phi·lis'tines came and dwelt in
them.

[8]So it happened the next day, when the
Phi·lis'tines came to strip the slain, that
they found Saul and his sons fallen on
Mount Gil·bō'a. [9]And they stripped him
and took his head and his armor, and sent
word *throughout* the land of the Phi-
lis'tines to proclaim the news *in the temple*
of their idols and among the people. [10]Then
they put his armor in the temple of their
gods, and fastened his head in the temple
of Dā'gon.

[11]And when all Jā'besh Gil'ē·ad heard
all that the Phi·lis'tines had done to Saul,
[12]all the valiant men arose and took the
body of Saul and the bodies of his sons;
and they brought them to Jā'besh, and
buried their bones under the tamarisk tree
at Jā'besh, and fasted seven days.

[13]So Saul died for his unfaithfulness
which he had committed against the LORD,
because he did not keep the word of the
LORD, and also because he consulted a
medium for guidance. [14]But *he* did not in-
quire of the LORD; therefore He killed him,
and turned the kingdom over to David the
son of Jesse.

CHAPTER 11

David Made King over All Israel

Then all Israel came together to David at
Hē'bron, saying, "Indeed we *are* your bone
and your flesh. [2]Also, in time past, even
when Saul was king, you *were* the one who
led Israel out and brought them in; and the
LORD your God said to you, 'You shall
shepherd My people Israel, and be ruler
over My people Israel.' " [3]Therefore all the
elders of Israel came to the king at
Hē'bron, and David made a covenant with
them at Hē'bron before the LORD. And they
anointed David king over Israel, according
to the word of the LORD by Samuel.

The City of David

[4]And David and all Israel went to Jeru-
salem, which is Jē'bus, where the Jeb'-
ū·sītes *were,* the inhabitants of the land.
[5]But the inhabitants of Jē'bus said to Da-
vid, "You shall not come in here!" Never-
theless David took the stronghold of Zion
(that is, the City of David). [6]Now David
said, "Whoever attacks the Jeb'ū·sītes first
shall be chief and captain." And Jō'ab the
son of Ze·rū'i·ah went up first, and became
chief. [7]Then David dwelt in the stronghold;
therefore they called it the City of David.

10:1–14 The chronicler is mainly interested in the Davidic kingship, Jerusalem, and the temple as God's chosen instruments of salvation. Thus, Saul's life is passed over, and only his ignominious end is recorded as background to David's rise to the throne.

10:6 all his house died: A reference to those who fought with Saul, his armorbearer and his men (see 1 Sam. 31:6). Some of Saul's descendants, including Ishbosheth, survived into David's reign (2 Sam. 2:8; see also 2 Sam. 21:5, 6 and note on 2 Sam. 21:1–14).

[8]And he built the city around it, from the Mil'lō[a] to the surrounding area. Jō'ab repaired the rest of the city. [9]So David went on and became great, and the LORD of hosts *was* with him.

The Mighty Men of David

[10]Now these *were* the heads of the mighty men whom David had, who strengthened themselves with him in his kingdom, with all Israel, to make him king, according to the word of the LORD concerning Israel.

[11]And this *is* the number of the mighty men whom David had: Ja·shō'bē·am the son of a Hach'mo·nīte, chief of the captains;[a] he had lifted up his spear against three hundred, killed *by him* at one time.

[12]After him *was* El·ē·ā'zar the son of Dodo, the A·hō'hīte, who *was one* of the three mighty men. [13]He was with David at Pas·dam'mim. Now there the Phi·lis'tines were gathered for battle, and there was a piece of ground full of barley. So the people fled from the Phi·lis'tines. [14]But they stationed themselves in the middle of *that* field, defended it, and killed the Phi·lis'tines. So the LORD brought about a great victory.

[15]Now three of the thirty chief men went down to the rock to David, into the cave of A·dul'lam; and the army of the Phi·lis'tines encamped in the Valley of Reph'a·im. [16]David *was* then in the stronghold, and the garrison of the Phi·lis'tines *was* then in Bethlehem. [17]And David said with longing, "Oh, that someone would give me a drink of water from the well of Bethlehem, which is by the gate!" [18]So the three broke through the camp of the Phi·lis'tines, drew water from the well of Bethlehem that *was* by the gate, and took *it* and brought *it* to David. Nevertheless David would not drink it, but poured it out to the LORD. [19]And he said, "Far be it from me, O my God, that I should do this! Shall I drink the blood of these men *who have put* their lives *in jeopardy?* For at the risk of their lives they brought it." Therefore he would not drink it. These things were done by the three mighty men.

[20]A·bi'shaī the brother of Jō'ab was chief of *another* three.[a] He had lifted up his spear against three hundred *men,* killed *them,* and won a name among *these* three. [21]Of the three he was more honored than the other two men. Therefore he became their captain. However he did not attain to the *first* three.

[22]Be·nā'i·ah was the son of Je·hoi'a·da, the son of a valiant man from Kab'zē·el, who had done many deeds. He had killed two lion-like heroes of Mō'ab. He also had gone down and killed a lion in the midst of a pit on a snowy day. [23]And he killed an Egyptian, a man of *great* height, five cubits tall. In the Egyptian's hand *there was* a spear like a weaver's beam; and he went down to him with a staff, wrested the spear out of the Egyptian's hand, and killed him with his own spear. [24]These *things* Be·nā'i·ah the son of Je·hoi'a·da did, and won a name among three mighty men. [25]Indeed he was more honored than the thirty, but he did not attain to the *first* three. And David appointed him over his guard.

11:8 [a]Literally *The Landfill* 11:11 [a]Following Qere; Kethib, Septuagint, and Vulgate read *the thirty* (compare 2 Samuel 23:8). 11:20 [a]Following Masoretic Text, Septuagint, and Vulgate; Syriac reads *thirty.*

11:10–47 The organization of David's mighty men in these verses and the parallel passage in 2 Sam. 23:8–39 reveals some difficulties which are not capable of being solved with the biblical information alone. For instance, Abishai is said to be "chief" of the three yet "did not attain" to the three (vv. 20, 21). Attempts to resolve the textual problems have included: (1) suggesting two or more groups of three (indicated by the NKJV supplied words in vv. 20, 21, 25); or (2) accepting the Syriac variant readings of "thirty" for "three." In any case, we may be confident that if we had enough information the truth of the details would be confirmed.

26Also the mighty warriors *were* As′a·hel
the brother of Jō′ab, El·hā′nan the son of
Dodo of Bethlehem, 27Sham′moth the
Ha′rō·rīte,[a] Hē′lez the Pel′o·nīte,[b] 28Ī′ra the
son of Ik′kesh the Te·kō′īte, Ā·bi·ē′zer the
An′a·thoth·īte, 29Sib′be·chaī the Hū′-
sha·thīte, Ī′lāi the A·hō′hīte, 30Mā′ha·raī
the Ne·toph′a·thīte, Hē′led[a] the son of
Bā′a·nah the Ne·toph′a·thīte, 31Ith′aī[a] the
son of Rī′baī of Gib′ē·ah, of the sons of
Benjamin, Be·nā′i·ah the Pir′a·thon·īte,
32Hū′raī[a] of the brooks of Gā′ash, A·bī′el[b]
the Ar′ba·thīte, 33Az′ma·veth the Ba-
har′um·īte,[a] Ē·lī′ah·ba the Shā·al′bon·īte,
34the sons of Hā′shem the Gī′zō·nīte, Jona-
than the son of Shā′geh the Har′a·rīte,
35A·hī′am the son of Sā′car the Har′a·rīte,
E·lī′phal the son of Ūr, 36Hē′pher the
Me·chē′ra·thīte, A·hī′jah the Pel′o·nīte,
37Hez′rō the Car′mel·īte, Nā′a·raī the son
of Ez′baī, 38Jō′el the brother of Nathan,
Mib′har the son of Hag′rī, 39Zē′lek the
Am′mon·īte, Nā′ha·raī the Be·rō′thīte[a]
(the armorbearer of Jō′ab the son of
Ze·rū′i·ah), 40Ī′ra the Ith′rīte, Gā′reb the
Ith′rīte, 41Ū·rī′ah the Hit′tīte, Zā′bad the
son of Ah′laī, 42Ad′i·na the son of Shī′za
the Reū′ben·īte (a chief of the Reū′-
ben·ītes) and thirty with him, 43Hā′nan the
son of Mā′a·chah, Josh′a·phat the Mith′-
nīte, 44Uz·zī′a the Ash′te·ra·thīte, Shā′ma
and Je·ī′el the sons of Hō′tham the
A·rō′er·īte, 45Je·dī′a·el the son of Shim′rī,
and Jō′ha his brother, the Tī′zīte, 46E·lī′el
the Mā′ha·vīte, Jer′i·baī and Josh·a·vī′ah
the sons of El′nā·am, Ith′mah the Mō′-
ab·īte, 47E·lī′el, Ō′bed, and Jā·a·sī′el the
Me·zō′ba·īte.

11:27 [a]Spelled *Harodite* in 2 Samuel 23:25 [b]Called *Paltite* in 2 Samuel 23:26 11:30 [a]Spelled *Heleb* in 2 Samuel 23:29 and *Heldai* in 1 Chronicles 27:15
11:31 [a]Spelled *Ittai* in 2 Samuel 23:29
11:32 [a]Spelled *Hiddai* in 2 Samuel 23:30 [b]Spelled *Abi-Albon* in 2 Samuel 23:31 11:33 [a]Spelled *Bar-humite* in 2 Samuel 23:31 11:39 [a]Spelled *Beerothite* in 2 Samuel 23:37

CHAPTER 12

The Growth of David's Army

Now these *were* the men who came to
David at Zik′lag while he was still a
fugitive from Saul the son of Kish;
and they *were* among the mighty men,
helpers in the war, 2armed with bows, us-
ing both the right hand and the left in *hurl-
ing* stones and *shooting* arrows with the
bow. *They were* of Benjamin, Saul's
brethren.

3The chief *was* Ā·hī·ē′zer, then Jō′ash,
the sons of She·mā′ah the Gib′ē·a·thīte;
Jē′zi·el and Pē′let the sons of Az′ma·veth;
Ber′a·chah, and Jē′hū the An′a·thoth·īte;
4Ish·mā′i·ah the Gib′ē·on·īte, a mighty
man among the thirty, and over the thirty;
Jer·e·mī′ah, Ja·hā′zi·el, Jō·hā′nan, and
Joz′a·bad the Ge·dē′ra·thīte; 5E·lū′zaī,
Jer′i·moth, Bē·a·lī′ah, Shem·a·rī′ah, and
Sheph·a·tī′ah the Ha·rū′phīte; 6El·kā′nah,
Jis·shī′ah, Az′a·rel, Jō·ē′zer, and Ja·shō′-
bē·am, the Kō′ra·hītes; 7and Jō·ē′lah and
Zeb·a·dī′ah the sons of Je·rō′ham of
Gē′dor.

8*Some* Gad′ītes joined David at the
stronghold in the wilderness, mighty men
of valor, men trained for battle, who could
handle shield and spear, whose faces *were
like* the faces of lions, and *were* as swift as
gazelles on the mountains: 9Ē′zer the first,
Ō·ba·dī′ah the second, E·lī′ab the third,
10Mish·man′nah the fourth, Jer·e·mī′ah the
fifth, 11At′taī the sixth, E·lī′el the seventh,
12Jō·hā′nan the eighth, El·zā′bad the ninth,
13Jer·e·mī′ah the tenth, and Mach′ba·naī
the eleventh. 14These *were* from the sons of
Gad, captains of the army; the least was
over a hundred, and the greatest was over

12:1 Ziklag in the extreme south of Judah was given to David by Achish, the Philistine king (see 1 Sam. 27:5, 6). It became David's "stronghold" (vv. 8, 16) and military headquarters.
12:2 Some of Saul's relatives joined David even before Saul was dead, and while the struggle between them was going on (see also v. 29).

a thousand. [15]These *are* the ones who crossed the Jordan in the first month, when it had overflowed all its banks; and they put to flight all *those* in the valleys, to the east and to the west.

[16]Then some of the sons of Benjamin and Judah came to David at the stronghold. [17]And David went out to meet them, and answered and said to them, "If you have come peaceably to me to help me, my heart will be united with you; but if to betray me to my enemies, since *there is* no wrong in my hands, may the God of our fathers look and bring judgment." [18]Then the Spirit came upon A·mā′saī, chief of the captains, *and he said:*

"*We are* yours, O David;
We *are* on your side, O son of Jesse!
Peace, peace to you,
And peace to your helpers!
For your God helps you."

So David received them, and made them captains of the troop.

[19]And *some* from Ma·nas′seh defected to David when he was going with the Phi·lis′tines to battle against Saul; but they did not help them, for the lords of the Phi·lis′tines sent him away by agreement, saying, "He may defect to his master Saul *and endanger* our heads." [20]When he went to Zik′lag, those of Ma·nas′seh who defected to him were Ad′nah, Joz′a·bad, Je·dī′a·el, Michael, Joz′a·bad, E·lī′hū, and Zil′le·thaī, captains of the thousands who *were* from Ma·nas′seh. [21]And they helped David against the bands *of raiders,* for they *were* all mighty men of valor, and they were captains in the army. [22]For at *that* time they came to David day by day to help him, until *it was* a great army, like the army of God.

David's Army at Hebron

[23]Now these *were* the numbers of the divisions *that were* equipped for war, *and* came to David at Hē′bron to turn *over* the kingdom of Saul to him, according to the word of the LORD: [24]of the sons of Judah bearing shield and spear, six thousand eight hundred armed for war; [25]of the sons of Sim′ē·on, mighty men of valor fit for war, seven thousand one hundred; [26]of the sons of Levi four thousand six hundred; [27]Je·hoi′a·da, the leader of the Aaronites, and with him three thousand seven hundred; [28]Zā′dok, a young man, a valiant warrior, and from his father's house twenty-two captains; [29]of the sons of Benjamin, relatives of Saul, three thousand (until then the greatest part of them had remained loyal to the house of Saul); [30]of the sons of Ē′phra·im twenty thousand eight hundred, mighty men of valor, famous men throughout their father's house; [31]of the half-tribe of Ma·nas′seh eighteen thousand, who were designated by name to come and make David king; [32]of the sons of Is′sa·char who had understanding of the times, to know what Israel ought to do, their chiefs were two hundred; and all their brethren were at their command; [33]of Zeb′ū·lun there were fifty thousand who went out to battle, expert in war with all weapons of war, stouthearted men who could keep ranks; [34]of Naph′ta·lī one thousand captains, and with them thirty-seven thousand with shield and spear; [35]of the Dan′ītes who could keep battle formation,

12:15 This victory is not recorded elsewhere. **first month**: March-April, when melting snows from Mt. Hermon would cause overflowing of the **Jordan**.

12:18 the Spirit came upon Amasai: The song of Amasai was of more than human inspiration. *Came upon* is literally "clothed," an idea moving in the direction of indwelling, which finds its ultimate meaning in the experience of being filled with the Spirit (see Ezek. 36:27; Eph. 5:18 and notes).

12:23 to turn over the kingdom: Verses 23–40 report the strength of David's armies and the celebration when he was crowned king of all Israel (see 11:1–3).

twenty-eight thousand six hundred; [36]of Ash'er, those who could go out to war, able to keep battle formation, forty thousand; [37]of the Reū'ben·ītes and the Gad'ītes and the half-tribe of Ma·nas'seh, from the other side of the Jordan, one hundred and twenty thousand armed for battle with every *kind* of weapon of war.

[38]All these men of war, who could keep ranks, came to Hē'bron with a loyal heart, to make David king over all Israel; and all the rest of Israel *were* of one mind to make David king. [39]And they were there with David three days, eating and drinking, for their brethren had prepared for them. [40]Moreover those who were near to them, from as far away as Is'sa·char and Zeb'ū·lun and Naph'ta·lī, were bringing food on donkeys and camels, on mules and oxen—provisions of flour and cakes of figs and cakes of raisins, wine and oil and oxen and sheep abundantly, for *there was* joy in Israel.

CHAPTER 13

The Ark Brought from Kirjath Jearim

Then David consulted with the captains of thousands and hundreds, *and* with every leader. [2]And David said to all the assembly of Israel, "If *it seems* good to you, and if it is of the LORD our God, let us send out to our brethren everywhere *who are* left in all the land of Israel, and with them to the priests and Lē'vītes *who are* in their cities *and* their common-lands, that they may gather together to us; [3]and let us bring the ark of our God back to us, for we have not inquired at it since the days of Saul." [4]Then all the assembly said that they would do so, for the thing was right in the eyes of all the people.

[5]So David gathered all Israel together, from Shī'hor in Egypt to as far as the entrance of Hā'math, to bring the ark of God from Kir'jath Jē'a·rim. [6]And David and all Israel went up to Bā'a·lah,[a] to Kir'jath Jē'a·rim, which belonged to Judah, to bring up from there the ark of God the LORD, who dwells *between* the cherubim, where *His* name is proclaimed. [7]So they carried the ark of God on a new cart from the house of A·bin'a·dab, and Uz'za and A·hī'ō drove the cart. [8]Then David and all Israel played *music* before God with all *their* might, with singing, on harps, on stringed instruments, on tambourines, on cymbals, and with trumpets.

[9]And when they came to Chī'don's[a] threshing floor, Uz'za put out his hand to hold the ark, for the oxen stumbled. [10]Then the anger of the LORD was aroused against Uz'za, and He struck him because he put his hand to the ark; and he died there before God. [11]And David became angry because of the LORD's outbreak against Uz'za; therefore that place is called Per'ez Uz'za[a] to this day. [12]David was afraid of God that day, saying, "How can I bring the ark of God to me?"

13:6 [a]Called *Baale Judah* in 2 Samuel 6:2
13:9 [a]Called *Nachon* in 2 Samuel 6:6
13:11 [a]Literally *Outburst Against Uzza*

13:5, 6 Shihor . . . Hamath: The ideal southern and northern boundaries of Israel. **Kirjath Jearim** was earlier known by its Canaanite name Kirjath Baal and the shortened form **Baalah** (see Josh. 15:9, 60). The ark had remained there since its return by the Philistines in Samuel's day (1 Sam. 6:1–16).

13:7, 8 A **cart** pulled by oxen was a suitable way for the Philistines to move the ark (see 1 Sam. 6:7), but God's people had been given a specific command in this matter (see Num. 4:11–15). Though they celebrated the ark's presence, they disobeyed God's instructions and thus failed to acknowledge the presence of a holy God in their midst.

13:9–12 The chronicler probably highlights this episode to underline the importance of the Levites, who should have been appointed to transport the ark (see 15:11–15). David's desire was commendable, but his method was flawed. See 2 Sam. 6:6–15. How arrogant we would be to think we have a better solution than God! But isn't that what our actions say when we ignore His leading and do things "our way"?

13So David would not move the ark with
him into the City of David, but took it
aside into the house of Ō'bed-Ē'dom the
Git'tīte. 14The ark of God remained with
the family of Ō'bed-Ē'dom in his house
three months. And the LORD blessed the
house of Ō'bed-Ē'dom and all that he had.

CHAPTER 14

David Established at Jerusalem

Now Hī'ram king of Tȳre sent messen-
gers to David, and cedar trees, with ma-
sons and carpenters, to build him a house.
2So David knew that the LORD had estab-
lished him as king over Israel, for his king-
dom was highly exalted for the sake of His
people Israel.
3Then David took more wives in Jerusa-
lem, and David begot more sons and
daughters. 4And these are the names of his
children whom he had in Jerusalem:
Sham'mū·a,[a] Shō'bab, Nathan, Solomon,
5Ib'har, E·lish'ū·a,[a] El'pe·let,[b] 6Nō'gah,
Nē'pheg, Ja·phī'a, 7E·lish'a·ma, Bē·e-
lī'a·da,[a] and E·liph'e·let.

The Philistines Defeated

8Now when the Phi·lis'tines heard that
David had been anointed king over all Is-
rael, all the Phi·lis'tines went up to search
for David. And David heard *of it* and went out
against them. 9Then the Phi·lis'tines went
and made a raid on the Valley of Reph'a·im.
10And David inquired of God, saying,
"Shall I go up against the Phi-lis'tines?
Will You deliver them into my hand?"
The LORD said to him, "Go up, for I will
deliver them into your hand."
11So they went up to Bā'al Pe·rā'zim,
and David defeated them there. Then Da-
vid said, "God has broken through my en-
emies by my hand like a breakthrough of
water." Therefore they called the name of
that place Bā'al Pe·rā'zim.[a] 12And when
they left their gods there, David gave a
commandment, and they were burned
with fire.
13Then the Phi·lis'tines once again made
a raid on the valley. 14Therefore David in-
quired again of God, and God said to him,
"You shall not go up after them; circle
around them, and come upon them in
front of the mulberry trees. 15And it shall
be, when you hear a sound of marching in
the tops of the mulberry trees, then you
shall go out to battle, for God has gone out
before you to strike the camp of the
Phi·lis'tines." 16So David did as God com-
manded him, and they drove back the
army of the Phi·lis'tines from Gib'ē·on as
far as Gē'zer. 17Then the fame of David
went out into all lands, and the LORD
brought the fear of him upon all nations.

CHAPTER 15

The Ark Brought to Jerusalem

David built houses for himself in the
City of David; and he prepared a place for
the ark of God, and pitched a tent for it.
2Then David said, "No one may carry the
ark of God but the Lē'vītes, for the LORD
has chosen them to carry the ark of God
and to minister before Him forever." 3And

14:4 [a]Spelled *Shimea* in 3:5 14:5 [a]Spelled *Elishama* in 3:6 [b]Spelled *Eliphelet* in 3:6 14:7 [a]Spelled *Eliada* in 3:8 14:11 [a]Literally *Master of Breakthroughs*

14:8 Since the defeat of Saul at Mt. Gilboa (see 10:1–14), the **Philistines** had been in possession of the main northeast trade routes on the coast and in the Jezreel Valley. The rise of David posed an economic and military threat to this monopoly.

14:14 Note that David didn't assume God's answer would be the same as in the previous incident. God is not limited to specific methods in fulfilling His plan. Christians who try to predict God's actions in a given situation do not have a true grasp of the awesomeness of God; our human minds can never fully comprehend His ways.

15:1–24 David corrects his earlier mistake. **The first time** (v. 13) the ark was moved was a disaster because the Levites were not in charge (see ch. 13 and note on 13:9–12).

David gathered all Israel together at Jerusalem, to bring up the ark of the LORD to its place, which he had prepared for it. [4]Then David assembled the children of Aaron and the Lē′vītes: [5]of the sons of Kō′hath, Ū·rī′el the chief, and one hundred and twenty of his brethren; [6]of the sons of Me·rar′ī, A·sāi′ah the chief, and two hundred and twenty of his brethren; [7]of the sons of Ger′shom, Jō′el the chief, and one hundred and thirty of his brethren; [8]of the sons of E·li·zā′phan, She·māi′ah the chief, and two hundred of his brethren; [9]of the sons of Hē′bron, E·lī′el the chief, and eighty of his brethren; [10]of the sons of Uz′zi·el, Am·min′a·dab the chief, and one hundred and twelve of his brethren.

[11]And David called for Zā′dok and A·bī′a·thar the priests, and for the Lē′vītes: for Ū·rī′el, A·sāi′ah, Jō′el, She·māi′ah, E·lī′el, and Am·min′a·dab. [12]He said to them, "You *are* the heads of the fathers′ *houses* of the Lē′vītes; sanctify yourselves, you and your brethren, that you may bring up the ark of the LORD God of Israel to *the place* I have prepared for it. [13]For because you *did* not *do it* the first *time,* the LORD our God broke out against us, because we did not consult Him about the proper order."

[14]So the priests and the Lē′vītes sanctified themselves to bring up the ark of the LORD God of Israel. [15]And the children of the Lē′vītes bore the ark of God on their shoulders, by its poles, as Moses had commanded according to the word of the LORD.

[16]Then David spoke to the leaders of the Lē′vītes to appoint their brethren *to be* the singers accompanied by instruments of music, stringed instruments, harps, and cymbals, by raising the voice with resounding joy. [17]So the Lē′vītes appointed Hē′man the son of Jō′el; and of his brethren, Ā′saph the son of Ber·e·chī′ah; and of their brethren, the sons of Me·rar′ī, Ē′than the son of Kū·shā′i·ah; [18]and with them their brethren of the second *rank:* Zech·a·rī′ah, Ben,[a] Ja·ā′zi·el, She·mir′a·moth, Je·hī′el, Un′nī, E·lī′ab, Be·nā′i·ah, Mā·a·sēi′ah, Mat·ti·thī′ah, E·liph′e·leh, Mik·nē′i·ah, Ō′bed-Ē′dom, and Je·ī′el, the gatekeepers; [19]the singers, Hē′man, Ā′saph, and Ē′than, *were* to sound the cymbals of bronze; [20]Zech·a·rī′ah, Ā′zi·el, She·mir′a·moth, Je·hī′el, Un′nī, E·lī′ab, Mā·a·sēi′ah, and Be·nā′i·ah, with strings according to Al′a·moth; [21]Mat·ti·thī′ah, E·liph′e·leh, Mik·nē′i·ah, Ō′bed-Ē′dom, Je·ī′el, and Az·a·zī′ah, to direct with harps on the Shem′i·nith; [22]Chen·a·nī′ah, leader of the Lē′vītes, was instructor *in charge of* the music, because he *was* skillful; [23]Ber·e·chī′ah and El·kā′nah *were* doorkeepers for the ark; [24]Sheb·a·nī′ah, Josh′a·phat, Ne·than′el, A·mā′saī, Zech·a·rī′ah, Be·nā′i·ah, and El·i·ē′zer, the priests, were to blow the trumpets before the ark of God; and Ō′bed-Ē′dom and Je·hī′ah, doorkeepers for the ark.

[25]So David, the elders of Israel, and the captains over thousands went to bring up the ark of the covenant of the LORD from the house of Ō′bed-Ē′dom with joy. [26]And so it was, when God helped the Lē′vītes who bore the ark of the covenant of the LORD, that they offered seven bulls and seven rams. [27]David was clothed with a robe of fine linen, as were all the Lē′vītes who bore the ark, the singers, and Chen·a·nī′ah the music master *with* the singers. David also wore a linen ephod. [28]Thus all Israel brought up the ark of the covenant of the LORD with shouting and with the

15:18 [a]Following Masoretic Text and Vulgate; Septuagint omits *Ben.*

15:19 These **singers** are associated with the psalms: **Heman** (Ps. 88:title), **Asaph** (Ps. 73—83:titles), **Ethan** (Ps. 89:title).

15:27 David was dressed in a **robe of fine linen**, as well as the **linen ephod**. The reaction of Michal in 2 Sam. 6:20 may suggest that he discarded the robe during the dancing (see 2 Sam. 6:14 and note).

sound of the horn, with trumpets and with cymbals, making music with stringed instruments and harps.

[29]And it happened, *as* the ark of the covenant of the LORD came to the City of David, that Mī′chal, Saul's daughter, looked through a window and saw King David whirling and playing music; and she despised him in her heart.

CHAPTER 16

The Ark Placed in the Tabernacle

So they brought the ark of God, and set it in the midst of the tabernacle that David had erected for it. Then they offered burnt offerings and peace offerings before God.
[2]And when David had finished offering the burnt offerings and the peace offerings, he blessed the people in the name of the
LORD. [3]Then he distributed to everyone of Israel, both man and woman, to everyone a loaf of bread, a piece *of meat,* and a cake of raisins.

[4]And he appointed some of the Lē′vītes to minister before the ark of the LORD, to commemorate, to thank, and to praise the LORD God of Israel: [5]Ā′saph the chief, and next to him Zech·a·rī′ah, *then* Je·ī′el, She·mir′a·moth, Je·hī′el, Mat·ti·thī′ah, E·lī′ab, Be·nā′i·ah, and Ō′bed-Ē′dom: Je·ī′el with stringed instruments and harps, but Ā′saph made music with cymbals; [6]Be·nā′i·ah and Ja·hā′zi·el the priests regularly *blew* the trumpets before the ark of the covenant of God.

David's Song of Thanksgiving

[7]On that day David first delivered *this psalm* into the hand of Ā′saph and his brethren, to thank the LORD:

8 Oh, give thanks to the LORD!
Call upon His name;
Make known His deeds among the
peoples!
9 Sing to Him, sing psalms to Him;
Talk of all His wondrous works!
10 Glory in His holy name;
Let the hearts of those rejoice who
seek the LORD!
11 Seek the LORD and His strength;
Seek His face evermore!
12 Remember His marvelous works
which He has done,
His wonders, and the judgments of
His mouth,
13 O seed of Israel His servant,
You children of Jacob, His chosen
ones!

14 He *is* the LORD our God;
His judgments *are* in all the earth.
15 Remember His covenant forever,
The word which He commanded, for
a thousand generations,
16 *The covenant which* He made with
Abraham,
And His oath to Isaac,
17 And confirmed it to Jacob for a
statute,
To Israel *for* an everlasting covenant,
18 Saying, "To you I will give the land
of Cā′naan

16:1 tabernacle: A center for worship in David's new capital city, Jerusalem. Gibeon began to decline as Israel's religious center (see v. 39; 1 Kin. 3:4) and was eventually replaced by Jerusalem after the temple was built. There was possibly no outcry against this new tabernacle because the tabernacle at Gibeon was also a copy, the original having been destroyed (by the Philistines?) at Shiloh (see Jer. 7:12, 14 and notes on Josh 18:1 and 2 Chr. 1:3).

16:4–6 The arrangements made in 15:16–24 for the celebration were so satisfactory that David established certain Levitical families to be permanently in charge of worship (v. 37).

16:7–36 Parts of this song appear in three others found in the Book of Psalms: (vv. 8–22 in Ps. 105:1–15; vv. 23–33 in Ps. 96:1–13; vv. 34–36 in Ps. 106:1, 47, 48; see notes there). Israel's worship was evangelical in that it was directed outward to all people of all lands as well as upward toward God.

As the allotment of your inheritance,"
19 When you were few in number,
Indeed very few, and strangers in it.
20 When they went from one nation to
another,
And from *one* kingdom to another
people,
21 He permitted no man to do them
wrong;
Yes, He rebuked kings for their sakes,
22 *Saying,* "Do not touch My anointed
ones,
And do My prophets no harm."[a]

23 Sing to the LORD, all the earth;
Proclaim the good news of His
salvation from day to day.
24 Declare His glory among the nations,
His wonders among all peoples.
25 For the LORD *is* great and greatly to be
praised;
He *is* also to be feared above all gods.

I praise You, Lord, for You are great and greatly to be praised.

adapted from 1 Chronicles 16:25

26 For all the gods of the peoples *are*
idols,
But the LORD made the heavens.
27 Honor and majesty *are* before Him;
Strength and gladness are in His
place.

28 Give to the LORD, O families of the
peoples,
Give to the LORD glory and strength.
29 Give to the LORD the glory *due* His
name;
Bring an offering, and come before
Him.
Oh, worship the LORD in the beauty
of holiness!
30 Tremble before Him, all the earth.
The world also is firmly established,
It shall not be moved.
31 Let the heavens rejoice, and let the
earth be glad;
And let them say among the nations,
"The LORD reigns."
32 Let the sea roar, and all its fullness;
Let the field rejoice, and all that *is* in
it.
33 Then the trees of the woods shall
rejoice before the LORD,
For He is coming to judge the earth.[a]

34 Oh, give thanks to the LORD, for *He is*
good!
For His mercy *endures* forever.[a]
35 And say, "Save us, O God of our
salvation;
Gather us together, and deliver us
from the Gentiles,
To give thanks to Your holy name,
To triumph in Your praise."
36 Blessed *be* the LORD God of Israel
From everlasting to everlasting![a]

And all the people said, "Amen!" and praised the LORD.

Regular Worship Maintained

37So he left Ā'saph and his brothers there
before the ark of the covenant of the LORD
to minister before the ark regularly, as
every day's work required; 38and O'bed-
Ē'dom with his sixty-eight brethren, in-
cluding Ō'bed-Ē'dom the son of Je·dū'-

16:22 [a]Compare verses 8–22 with Psalm 105:1–15
16:33 [a]Compare verses 23–33 with Psalm 96:1–13
16:34 [a]Compare verse 34 with Psalm 106:1
16:36 [a]Compare verses 35, 36 with Psalm 106:47, 48

16:37–39 Apparently David established two places of worship: the ark of the Lord in Jerusalem and the altar with its vessels in Gibeon.

thun, and Hō'sah, *to be* gatekeepers; 39and
Zā'dok the priest and his brethren the
priests, before the tabernacle of the LORD at
the high place that *was* at Gib'ē·on, 40to of-
fer burnt offerings to the LORD on the altar
of burnt offering regularly morning and
evening, and *to do* according to all that is
written in the Law of the LORD which He
commanded Israel; 41and with them
Hē'man and Je·dū'thun and the rest who
were chosen, who were designated by
name, to give thanks to the LORD, because
His mercy *endures* forever; 42and with them
Hē'man and Je·dū'thun, to sound aloud
with trumpets and cymbals and the musi-
cal instruments of God. Now the sons of
Je·dū'thun *were* gatekeepers.
43Then all the people departed, every
man to his house; and David returned to
bless his house.

CHAPTER 17

God's Covenant with David

Now it came to pass, when David was
dwelling in his house, that David said to
Nathan the prophet, "See now, I dwell in a
house of cedar, but the ark of the covenant
of the LORD *is* under tent curtains."
2Then Nathan said to David, "Do all that
is in your heart, for God *is* with you."
3But it happened that night that the
word of God came to Nathan, saying, 4"Go
and tell My servant David, 'Thus says the
LORD: "You shall not build Me a house to
dwell in. 5For I have not dwelt in a house
since the time that I brought up Israel, even
to this day, but have gone from tent to tent,
and from *one* tabernacle *to another.* 6Wher-
ever I have moved about with all Israel,
have I ever spoken a word to any of the
judges of Israel, whom I commanded to
shepherd My people, saying, 'Why have
you not built Me a house of cedar?' " '
7Now therefore, thus shall you say to My
servant David, 'Thus says the LORD of
hosts: "I took you from the sheepfold, from
following the sheep, to be ruler over My
people Israel. 8And I have been with you
wherever you have gone, and have cut off
all your enemies from before you, and
have made you a name like the name of the
great men who *are* on the earth. 9Moreover
I will appoint a place for My people Israel,
and will plant them, that they may dwell
in a place of their own and move no more;
nor shall the sons of wickedness oppress
them anymore, as previously, 10since the
time that I commanded judges *to be* over
My people Israel. Also I will subdue all
your enemies. Furthermore I tell you that
the LORD will build you a house.[a] 11And it
shall be, when your days are fulfilled,
when you must go *to be* with your fathers,
that I will set up your seed after you, who
will be of your sons; and I will establish his
kingdom. 12He shall build Me a house, and
I will establish his throne forever. 13I will be
his Father, and he shall be My son; and I
will not take My mercy away from him, as
I took *it* from *him* who was before you.
14And I will establish him in My house and
in My kingdom forever; and his throne
shall be established forever." ' "

17:10 [a]That is, a royal dynasty

16:41 For the connection of **Jeduthun** to the psalms, see titles to Ps. 39; 77.

17:5, 6 David's request was denied because (1) God had not required such a house, and (2) David was primarily a king of warfare (see 22:8; 28:3). Solomon would build the temple during peacetime, while Israel enjoyed the results of David's conquests.

17:10 God responds to David's sincere desire to build a house (temple) for God by promising to **build** David **a house** (royal dynasty).

17:12–14 forever: See note on 2 Sam. 7:5–16.

17:13, 14 The parallel account in 2 Sam. 7:14 recognizes the possibility of sin and punishment for David's descendants. But the chronicler's concern is not with the failure of David's sons. His eye is on the Christ who will fulfill this promise perfectly (see John 4:34). **him who was before you**: Saul (see 2 Sam. 7:15).

[15]According to all these words and ac-
cording to all this vision, so Nathan spoke
to David.

[16]Then King David went in and sat be-
fore the LORD; and he said: "Who *am* I, O
LORD God? And what is my house, that
You have brought me this far? [17]And *yet*
this was a small thing in Your sight, O God;
and You have *also* spoken of Your servant's
house for a great while to come, and have
regarded me according to the rank of a
man of high degree, O LORD God. [18]What
more can David *say* to You for the honor of
Your servant? For You know Your servant.
[19]O LORD, for Your servant's sake, and ac-
cording to Your own heart, You have done
all this greatness, in making known all
these great things. [20]O LORD, *there is* none
like You, nor *is there any* God besides You,
according to all that we have heard with
our ears. [21]And who *is* like Your people Is-
rael, the one nation on the earth whom
God went to redeem for Himself *as* a peo-
ple—to make for Yourself a name by great
and awesome deeds, by driving out na-
tions from before Your people whom You
redeemed from Egypt? [22]For You have
made Your people Israel Your very own
people forever; and You, LORD, have be-
come their God.

[23]"And now, O LORD, the word which
You have spoken concerning Your servant
and concerning his house, *let it* be estab-
lished forever, and do as You have said.
[24]So let it be established, that Your
name may be magnified forever, saying,
'The LORD of hosts, the God of Israel, *is* Is-
rael's God.' And let the house of Your ser-
vant David be established before You.
[25]For You, O my God, have revealed to
Your servant that You will build him a
house. Therefore Your servant has found
it *in his heart* to pray before You. [26]And
now, LORD, You are God, and have
promised this goodness to Your servant.
[27]Now You have been pleased to bless
the house of Your servant, that it may con-
tinue before You forever; for You have
blessed it, O LORD, and *it shall be* blessed
forever."

CHAPTER 18

David's Further Conquests

After this it came to pass that David
attacked the Phi·lis'tines, subdued
them, and took Gath and its towns from
the hand of the Phi·lis'tines. [2]Then he
defeated Mō'ab, and the Mō'ab·ītes be-
came David's servants, *and* brought trib-
ute.

[3]And David defeated Had·a·dē'zer[a]
king of Zō'bah *as far as* Hā'math, as
he went to establish his power by the
River Eū·phrā'tēs. [4]David took from
him one thousand chariots, seven thou-
sand[a] horsemen, and twenty thousand
foot soldiers. Also David hamstrung
all the chariot *horses,* except that he
spared enough of them for one hundred
chariots.

[5]When the Syrians of Damascus came to
help Had·a·dē'zer king of Zō'bah, David
killed twenty-two thousand of the Syrians.
[6]Then David put *garrisons* in Syria of

18:3 [a]Hebrew *Hadarezer,* and so throughout chapters 18 and 19 18:4 [a]Or *seven hundred* (compare 2 Samuel 8:4)

17:16 before the LORD: Before the ark in the newly established worship center in Jerusalem. **Who am I?** Humility and trust permeate this prayer.

17:23–27 The recurrence of the words **established** and **forever** reach a climax of certainty in v. 27.

18:1 David's victories over the **Philistines** in 14:8–16 were purely defensive measures. Here he launched an offensive in order to win greater security from his toughest enemy.

18:3 Hadadezer: A king in Syria. **Zobah**: Strongest of the Aramean states northeast of Israel at this time.

18:4 On the **seven thousand** horsemen and **hamstrung** horses see note on 2 Sam. 8:4.

Damascus; and the Syrians became David's servants, *and* brought tribute. So the LORD preserved David wherever he went.
7And David took the shields of gold that were on the servants of Had·a·dē'zer, and brought them to Jerusalem. 8Also from Tib'hath[a] and from Chun, cities of Had·a·dē'zer, David brought a large amount of bronze, with which Solomon made the bronze Sea, the pillars, and the articles of bronze.

9Now when Tō'ū[a] king of Hā'math heard that David had defeated all the army of Had·a·dē'zer king of Zō'bah, 10he sent Ha·dor'am[a] his son to King David, to greet him and bless him, because he had fought against Had·a·dē'zer and defeated him (for Had·a·dē'zer had been at war with Tō'ū); and *Ha*·dor'am brought with him all kinds of articles of gold, silver, and bronze.
11King David also dedicated these to the LORD, along with the silver and gold that he had brought from all *these* nations—from Ē'dom, from Mō'ab, from the people of Am'mon, from the Phi·lis'tines, and from Am'a·lek.

12Moreover A·bi'shaī the son of Ze-rū'i·ah killed eighteen thousand Ē'dom-ītes[a] in the Valley of Salt. 13He also put garrisons in Ē'dom, and all the Ē'dom·ītes became David's servants. And the LORD preserved David wherever he went.

David's Administration

14So David reigned over all Israel, and administered judgment and justice to all his people. 15Jō'ab the son of Ze·rū'i·ah *was* over the army; Je·hosh'a·phat the son of A·hī'lud *was* recorder; 16Zā'dok the son of A·hī'tub and A·bim'e·lech the son of A·bī'a·thar *were* the priests; Shav'sha[a] *was* the scribe; 17Be·nā'i·ah the son of Je-hoi'a·da *was* over the Cher'e·thītes and the Pel'eth·ītes; and David's sons *were* chief ministers at the king's side.

CHAPTER 19

The Ammonites and Syrians Defeated

It happened after this that Nā'hash the king of the people of Am'mon died, and his son reigned in his place. 2Then David said, "I will show kindness to Hā'nun the son of Nā'hash, because his father showed kindness to me." So David sent messengers to comfort him concerning his father. And David's servants came to Hā'nun in the land of the people of Am'mon to comfort him.

3And the princes of the people of Am'-mon said to Hā'nun, "Do you think that David really honors your father because he has sent comforters to you? Did his servants not come to you to search and to overthrow and to spy out the land?"

4Therefore Hā'nun took David's servants, shaved them, and cut off their garments in the middle, at their buttocks, and sent them away. 5Then *some* went and told David about the men; and he sent to meet them, because the men were greatly ashamed. And the king said, "Wait at Jericho until your beards have grown, and *then* return."

6When the people of Am'mon saw that

18:8 [a]Spelled *Betah* in 2 Samuel 8:8
18:9 [a]Spelled *Toi* in 2 Samuel 8:9, 10
18:10 [a]Spelled *Joram* in 2 Samuel 8:10
18:12 [a]Or *Syrians* (compare 2 Samuel 8:13)
18:16 [a]Spelled *Seraiah* in 2 Samuel 8:17

18:8–11 dedicated these to the LORD: David maintained a complete commitment to God's work. He was not permitted to build the temple (17:3), but he was ready to help **Solomon** (v. 8) who would have that honor. See 29:2–5.
18:17 Cherethites . . . Pelethites: See note on 1 Kin. 1:38.
19:2–5 kindness: Hebrew *hesed*, a covenant term reflecting devotion and obligation. In this light, Hanun's actions (v. 4) could only mean war.

they had made themselves repulsive to David, Hā'nun and the people of Am'mon sent a thousand talents of silver to hire for themselves chariots and horsemen from Mes·o·po·tā'mi·a,[a] from Syrian Mā'a·cah, and from Zō'bah.[b] 7So they hired for themselves thirty-two thousand chariots, with the king of Mā'a·cah and his people, who came and encamped before Med'e·ba. Also the people of Am'mon gathered together from their cities, and came to battle.

8Now when David heard *of it,* he sent Jō'ab and all the army of the mighty men. 9Then the people of Am'mon came out and put themselves in battle array before the gate of the city, and the kings who had come *were* by themselves in the field.

10When Jō'ab saw that the battle line was against him before and behind, he chose some of Israel's best, and put *them* in battle array against the Syrians. 11And the rest of the people he put under the command of A·bi'shaī his brother, and they set *themselves* in battle array against the people of Am'mon. 12Then he said, "If the Syrians are too strong for me, then you shall help me; but if the people of Am'mon are too strong for you, then I will help you. 13Be of good courage, and let us be strong for our people and for the cities of our God. And may the LORD do *what is* good in His sight."

14So Jō'ab and the people who *were* with him drew near for the battle against the Syrians, and they fled before him. 15When the people of Am'mon saw that the Syrians were fleeing, they also fled before A·bi'shaī his brother, and entered the city. So Jō'ab went to Jerusalem.

16Now when the Syrians saw that they had been defeated by Israel, they sent messengers and brought the Syrians who were beyond the River,[a] and Shō'phach[b] the commander of Had·a·dē'zer's army *went* before them. 17When it was told David, he gathered all Israel, crossed over the Jordan and came upon them, and set up in battle array against them. So when David had set up in *battle* array against the Syrians, they fought with him. 18Then the Syrians fled before Israel; and David killed seven thousand[a] charioteers and forty thousand foot soldiers[b] of the Syrians, and killed Shō'phach the commander of the army. 19And when the servants of Had·a·dē'zer saw that they were defeated by Israel, they made peace with David and became his servants. So the Syrians were not willing to help the people of Am'mon anymore.

CHAPTER 20

Rabbah Is Conquered

It happened in the spring of the year, at the time kings go out *to battle,* that Jō'ab led out the armed forces and ravaged the country of the people of Am'mon, and came and besieged Rab'bah. But David stayed at Jerusalem. And Jō'ab defeated Rab'bah and overthrew it. 2Then David took their king's crown from his head, and found it to weigh a talent of gold, and *there were* precious stones in it. And it was set on David's head. Also he brought out the spoil of the city in great abundance. 3And he brought out the people who *were* in it, and put *them* to work[a] with saws, with iron picks, and with axes. So David did to all the cities of the people of Am'mon. Then David and all the people returned *to* Jerusalem.

19:6 [a]Hebrew *Aram Naharaim* [b]Spelled *Zoba* in 2 Samuel 10:6 19:16 [a]That is, the Euphrates [b]Spelled *Shobach* in 2 Samuel 10:16 19:18 [a]Or *seven hundred* (compare 2 Samuel 10:18) [b]Or *horsemen* (compare 2 Samuel 10:18) 20:3 [a]Septuagint reads *cut them.*

20:1 The chronicler avoids any mention of the Bathsheba incident which is recorded at this point in the Samuel narrative (see 2 Sam. 11:2—12:24). From the author's postexilic standpoint he did not need to repeat the well-known failures of the past.

Philistine Giants Destroyed

4Now it happened afterward that war
broke out at Gē′zer with the Phi·lis′tines,
at which time Sib′be·chai̅ the Hū′sha·thīte
killed Sip′pai̅,[a] *who was one* of the sons of
the giant. And they were subdued.
5Again there was war with the Phi-
lis′tines, and El·hā′nan the son of Jā′ir[a]
killed Lah′mī the brother of Goliath the
Git′tīte, the shaft of whose spear *was* like a
weaver's beam.
6Yet again there was war at Gath, where
there was a man of *great* stature, with
twenty-four fingers and toes, six *on each
hand* and six *on each foot;* and he also was
born to the giant. 7So when he defied Is-
rael, Jonathan the son of Shim′ē·a,[a] Da-
vid's brother, killed him.
8These were born to the giant in Gath,
and they fell by the hand of David and by
the hand of his servants.

CHAPTER 21

The Census of Israel and Judah

Now Satan stood up against Israel, and
moved David to number Israel. 2So David
said to Jō′ab and to the leaders of the peo-
ple, "Go, number Israel from Bē·er·shē′ba
to Dan, and bring the number of them to
me that I may know *it.*"
3And Jō′ab answered, "May the LORD
make His people a hundred times more
than they are. But, my lord the king, *are*
they not all my lord's servants? Why then
does my lord require this thing? Why
should he be a cause of guilt in Israel?"
4Nevertheless the king's word prevailed
against Jō′ab. Therefore Jō′ab departed and
went throughout all Israel and came to Je-
rusalem. 5Then Jō′ab gave the sum of the
number of the people to David. All Israel
had one million one hundred thousand
men who drew the sword, and Judah *had*
four hundred and seventy thousand men
who drew the sword. 6But he did not count
Levi and Benjamin among them, for the
king's word was abominable to Jō′ab.
7And God was displeased with this
thing; therefore He struck Israel. 8So David
said to God, "I have sinned greatly, be-
cause I have done this thing; but now, I
pray, take away the iniquity of Your ser-
vant, for I have done very foolishly."
9Then the LORD spoke to Gad, David's
seer, saying, 10"Go and tell David, saying,
'Thus says the LORD: "I offer you three
things; choose one of them for yourself,
that I may do *it* to you." ' "
11So Gad came to David and said to him,
"Thus says the LORD: 'Choose for yourself,
12either three[a] years of famine, or three
months to be defeated by your foes with
the sword of your enemies overtaking *you,*

20:4 [a]Spelled *Saph* in 2 Samuel 21:18 20:5 [a]Spelled *Jaare-Oregim* in 2 Samuel 21:19 20:7 [a]Spelled *Shimeah* in 2 Samuel 21:21 and *Shammah* in 1 Samuel 16:9 21:12 [a]Or *seven* (compare 2 Samuel 24:13)

20:4 the giant: Hebrew *rephaim*, a reference to ancient people of Palestine who were renowned for their gigantic stature. They were also called the Emim and Zamzummim (Deut. 2:11, 20), and are described as being as tall as the Anakim (see Deut. 2:10, 11).

21:1 In the parallel account in 2 Sam. 24:1, "the anger of the LORD," rather than Satan, motivated David. The difference presents no theological conflict because Satan "the adversary" is here perceived as an agent of God. However, there is some development in the understanding of causation: Satan's enticement accounts for David's persistence against Joab's objection (v. 4). See notes on 2 Sam. 24:1–25; Job 1:6, 7.

21:2 Beersheba . . . Dan: National boundaries in the south and north respectively.

21:3 a cause of guilt: David's purpose was probably to determine the strength of his armies (v. 5), which implied trust in military might rather than in God.

21:12 David's options underline the awesome responsibility of the leader: his people suffer because of his sinful choices. This was not directly so in the more personal sin with Bathsheba, but here the sin of pride involved David's status as the national leader. The punishments would diminish the very numbers that were the source of his pride.

or else for three days the sword of the
LORD—the plague in the land, with the an-
gel[b] of the LORD destroying throughout all
the territory of Israel.' Now consider what
answer I should take back to Him who sent
me."
13 And David said to Gad, "I am in great
distress. Please let me fall into the hand of
the LORD, for His mercies *are* very great;
but do not let me fall into the hand of
man."
14 So the LORD sent a plague upon Israel,
and seventy thousand men of Israel fell.
15 And God sent an angel to Jerusalem to
destroy it. As he[a] was destroying, the LORD
looked and relented of the disaster, and
said to the angel who was destroying, "It is
enough; now restrain your[b] hand." And
the angel of the LORD stood by the thresh-
ing floor of Or'nan[c] the Jeb'ū·sīte.
16 Then David lifted his eyes and saw the
angel of the LORD standing between earth
and heaven, having in his hand a drawn
sword stretched out over Jerusalem. So
David and the elders, clothed in sackcloth,
fell on their faces. 17 And David said to God,
"Was it not I who commanded the people
to be numbered? I am the one who has
sinned and done evil indeed; but these
sheep, what have they done? Let Your
hand, I pray, O LORD my God, be against
me and my father's house, but not against
Your people that they should be plagued."
18 Therefore, the angel of the LORD com-
manded Gad to say to David that David
should go and erect an altar to the LORD on
the threshing floor of Or'nan the Jeb'ū·sīte.
19 So David went up at the word of Gad,
which he had spoken in the name of the
LORD. 20 Now Or'nan turned and saw the
angel; and his four sons *who were* with him
hid themselves, but Or'nan continued
threshing wheat. 21 So David came to
Or'nan, and Or'nan looked and saw Da-
vid. And he went out from the threshing
floor, and bowed before David with *his*
face to the ground. 22 Then David said to
Or'nan, "Grant me the place of *this* thresh-
ing floor, that I may build an altar on it to
the LORD. You shall grant it to me at the full
price, that the plague may be withdrawn
from the people."
23 But Or'nan said to David, "Take *it* to
yourself, and let my lord the king do *what
is* good in his eyes. Look, I *also* give *you* the
oxen for burnt offerings, the threshing im-
plements for wood, and the wheat for the
grain offering; I give *it* all."
24 Then King David said to Or'nan, "No,
but I will surely buy *it* for the full price, for
I will not take what is yours for the LORD,
nor offer burnt offerings with *that which*
costs *me* nothing." 25 So David gave Or'nan
six hundred shekels of gold by weight for
the place. 26 And David built there an altar
to the LORD, and offered burnt offerings
and peace offerings, and called on the
LORD; and He answered him from heaven
by fire on the altar of burnt offering.
27 So the LORD commanded the angel,
and he returned his sword to its sheath.
28 At that time, when David saw that the
LORD had answered him on the threshing
floor of Or'nan the Jeb'ū·sīte, he sacrificed
there. 29 For the tabernacle of the LORD and
the altar of the burnt offering, which Mo-
ses had made in the wilderness, *were* at
that time at the high place in Gib'ē·on.
30 But David could not go before it to

21:12 [b]Or *Angel*, and so elsewhere in this chapter
21:15 [a]Or *He* [b]Or *Your* [c]Spelled *Araunah* in 2 Samuel 24:16

21:15, 16 the threshing floor of Ornan: The exact spot where the Lord's angel stopped and the future site of the temple.

21:26 The **fire** from God was an immediate confirmation that David's sin was forgiven and God was well pleased.

21:30 David no longer went to Gibeon because he was convinced that the threshing floor of Ornan was God's choice for the future site of the temple (22:1). **it**: The altar of v. 26 (see 2 Kin. 16:15; 2 Chr. 1:5).

inquire of God, for he was afraid of the sword of the angel of the LORD.

CHAPTER 22

David Prepares to Build the Temple

Then David said, "This *is* the house of the LORD God, and this *is* the altar of burnt offering for Israel." 2So David commanded to gather the aliens who *were* in the land of Israel; and he appointed masons to cut hewn stones to build the house of God. 3And David prepared iron in abundance for the nails of the doors of the gates and for the joints, and bronze in abundance beyond measure, 4and cedar trees in abundance; for the Sī·dō′ni·ans and those from Tȳre brought much cedar wood to David.

5Now David said, "Solomon my son *is* young and inexperienced, and the house to be built for the LORD *must be* exceedingly magnificent, famous and glorious throughout all countries. I will now make preparation for it." So David made abundant preparations before his death.

6Then he called for his son Solomon, and charged him to build a house for the LORD God of Israel. 7And David said to Solomon: "My son, as for me, it was in my mind to build a house to the name of the LORD my God; 8but the word of the LORD came to me, saying, 'You have shed much blood and have made great wars; you shall not build a house for My name, because you have shed much blood on the earth in My sight. 9Behold, a son shall be born to you, who shall be a man of rest; and I will give him rest from all his enemies all around. His name shall be Solomon,[a] for I will give peace and quietness to Israel in his days. 10He shall build a house for My name, and he shall be My son, and I *will be* his Father; and I will establish the throne of his kingdom over Israel forever.' 11Now, my son, may the LORD be with you; and may you prosper, and build the house of the LORD your God, as He has said to you. 12Only may the LORD give you wisdom and understanding, and give you charge concerning Israel, that you may keep the law of the LORD your God. 13Then you will prosper, if you take care to fulfill the statutes and judgments with which the LORD charged Moses concerning Israel. Be strong and of good courage; do not fear nor be dismayed. 14Indeed I have taken much trouble to prepare for the house of the LORD one hundred thousand talents of gold and one million talents of silver, and bronze and iron beyond measure, for it is so abundant. I have prepared timber and stone also, and you may add to them. 15Moreover *there are* workmen with you in abundance: woodsmen and stonecutters, and all types of skillful men for every kind of work. 16Of gold and silver and bronze and iron *there is* no limit. Arise and begin working, and the LORD be with you."

17David also commanded all the leaders of Israel to help Solomon his son, *saying,* 18"*Is* not the LORD your God with you? And has He *not* given you rest on every side? For He has given the inhabitants of the land into my hand, and the land is subdued before the LORD and before His people. 19Now set your heart and your soul to seek the LORD your God. Therefore arise and build the sanctuary of the LORD God, to bring the ark of the covenant of the LORD and the holy articles of God into the house

22:9 [a]Literally *Peaceful*

22:1 David's statement could also have a future sense: "This *will be* (the site of) the house . . . . and this *will be* (the site of) the altar." The rest of 1 Chronicles is largely devoted to David's preparations for the temple.

22:2 gather the aliens: David conscripted foreigners into a labor force, but his son Solomon would draft even fellow Israelites (see 1 Kin. 5:13–18 and note).

22:8, 9 As a man of war, David was unfit to build the house of God. The task was reserved for **Solomon**, whose name means "Peaceful."

I pray that my grandchild will set her heart and her soul to seek the Lord her God.

adapted from 1 Chronicles 22:19

that is to be built for the name of the LORD."

CHAPTER 23

The Divisions of the Levites

So when David was old and full of days, he made his son Solomon king over Israel.
[2]And he gathered together all the lead-
ers of Israel, with the priests and the
Lē′vītes. [3]Now the Lē′vītes were num-
bered from the age of thirty years and above; and the number of individual males was thirty-eight thousand. [4]Of these,
twenty-four thousand *were* to look after the work of the house of the LORD, six thousand *were* officers and judges, [5]four thou-
sand *were* gatekeepers, and four thousand praised the LORD with *musical* instruments, "which I made," *said David*, "for giving praise."
[6]Also David separated them into divi-
sions among the sons of Levi: Ger′shon, Kō′hath, and Me·rar′ī.
[7]Of the Ger′shon·ītes: Lā′a·dan[a] and
Shim′ē·ī. [8]The sons of Lā′a·dan: the first Je·hī′el, then Zē′tham and Jō′el—three *in*
all. [9]The sons of Shim′ē·ī: She·lō′mith, Hā′zi·el, and Har′an—three *in all.* These were the heads of the fathers' *houses* of
Lā′a·dan. [10]And the sons of Shim′ē·ī: Jā′hath, Zī′na,[a] Jē′ush, and Bē·rī′ah. These
were the four sons of Shim′ē·ī. [11]Jā′hath
was the first and Zī′zah the second. But Jē′ush and Bē·rī′ah did not have many sons; therefore they were assigned as one father's house.
[12]The sons of Kō′hath: Am′ram, Iz′har,
Hē′bron, and Uz′zi·el—four *in all.* [13]The
sons of Am′ram: Aaron and Moses; and Aaron was set apart, he and his sons forever, that he should sanctify the most holy things, to burn incense before the LORD, to minister to Him, and to give the blessing in His name forever. [14]Now the sons of Moses
the man of God were reckoned to the tribe of Levi. [15]The sons of Moses *were* Ger′shon[a]
and El·i·ē′zer. [16]Of the sons of Ger′shon,
She·bū′el[a] *was* the first. [17]Of the descen-
dants of El·i·ē′zer, Rē·ha·bī′ah was the first. And El·i·ē′zer had no other sons, but the sons of Rē·ha·bī′ah were very many.
[18]Of the sons of Iz′har, She·lō′mith *was* the
first. [19]Of the sons of Hē′bron, Je·rī′ah *was*
the first, Am·a·rī′ah the second, Ja·hā′zi·el the third, and Jek·a·mē′am the fourth. [20]Of
the sons of Uz′zi·el, Mī′chah *was* the first and Jes·shī′ah the second.

23:7 [a]Spelled *Libni* in Exodus 6:17 23:10 [a]Septuagint and Vulgate read *Zizah* (compare verse 11).
23:15 [a]Hebrew *Gershom* (compare 6:16)
23:16 [a]Spelled *Shubael* in 24:20

23:1—27:34 During the closing days of his life David called a national convocation to affirm Israel's governmental organization, and to arrange for transfer of leadership from himself to his son Solomon.

David had become king of a scattered, unorganized people. After 40 years of leadership he was leaving them greatly enlarged, and well organized in religious life, military power, and civil government. Six hundred years later, seeking to raise the morale of the nation after the Exile, the chronicler made his people aware of this structure: religious life (23:1—26:19); military and governmental organization (27:1–34).

23:3–32 After the heads of the Levites are listed (vv. 3–24), their duties are redefined in light of the transition from the portable tabernacle to the permanent temple (see v. 26). The sources for this information were likely the temple archives.

23:3–5 From the total of 38,000 Levites, 14,000 were given special appointments as leaders (v. 4), gatekeepers, and singers (v. 5).

21The sons of Me·rar′ī *were* Mah′lī and Mū′shī. The sons of Mah′lī *were* El·ē·ā′zar and Kish. 22And El·ē·ā′zar died, and had no sons, but only daughters; and their brethren, the sons of Kish, took them *as wives*. 23The sons of Mū′shī *were* Mah′lī, Ē′der, and Jer′e·moth—three *in all*.

24These *were* the sons of Levi by their fathers' houses—the heads of the fathers' *houses* as they were counted individually by the number of their names, who did the work for the service of the house of the LORD, from the age of twenty years and above.

25For David said, "The LORD God of Israel has given rest to His people, that they may dwell in Jerusalem forever"; 26and also to the Lē′vītes, "They shall no longer carry the tabernacle, or any of the articles for its service." 27For by the last words of David the Lē′vītes *were* numbered from twenty years old and above; 28because their duty *was* to help the sons of Aaron in the service of the house of the LORD, in the courts and in the chambers, in the purifying of all holy things and the work of the service of the house of God, 29both with the showbread and the fine flour for the grain offering, with the unleavened cakes and *what is baked in* the pan, with what is mixed and with all kinds of measures and sizes; 30to stand every morning to thank and praise the LORD, and likewise at evening; 31and at every presentation of a burnt offering to the LORD on the Sabbaths and on the New Moons and on the set feasts, by number according to the ordinance governing them, regularly before the LORD; 32and that they should attend to the needs of the tabernacle of meeting, the needs of the holy *place*, and the needs of the sons of Aaron their brethren in the work of the house of the LORD.

CHAPTER 24

The Divisions of the Priests

Now *these are* the divisions of the sons of Aaron. The sons of Aaron *were* Nā′dab, A·bī′hū, El·ē·ā′zar, and Ith′a·mar. 2And Nā′dab and A·bī′hū died before their father, and had no children; therefore El·ē·ā′zar and Ith′a·mar ministered as priests. 3Then David with Zā′dok of the sons of El·ē·ā′zar, and A·him′e·lech of the sons of Ith′a·mar, divided them according to the schedule of their service.

4There were more leaders found of the sons of El·ē·ā′zar than of the sons of Ith′a·mar, and *thus* they were divided. Among the sons of El·ē·ā′zar *were* sixteen heads of *their* fathers' houses, and eight heads of their fathers' houses among the sons of Ith′a·mar. 5Thus they were divided by lot, one group as another, for there were officials of the sanctuary and officials *of the house* of God, from the sons of El·ē·ā′zar and from the sons of Ith′a·mar. 6And the scribe, She·māi′ah the son of Ne·than′el, *one of* the Lē′vītes, wrote them down be-

23:28–32 the work of the service of the house of God: See note on 9:10–34.

24:1–19 The Aaronic priesthood was divided into 24 families. Each family would thus come from its ancestral city to minister in the temple for 15 days each year (see Luke 1:5, 8, 9). Apparently the Levites were divided in the same way (v. 31).

24:3 Ahimelech of the sons of Ithamar: Ithamar was the youngest son of Aaron, the first high priest (Ex. 6:23). Since the Bible does not give specific information about the priesthood during the years of the judges, we can only speculate about the situation. However, this verse suggests that there may have been two priestly lines functioning at the same time: the descendants of Eleazar, the older son, and those of Ithamar, the younger. Furthermore, for some unknown reason, the Ithamarites were the high priests during the early monarchy. The line can be traced backward through various Scripture references: Abiathar, son of Ahimelech, son of Ahitub (1 Sam. 22:20); Ahitub, son of Phinehas (1 Sam. 14:3); Phinehas, son of Eli (1 Sam. 4:11; see also 1 Kin. 2:27). No genealogy can be found which covers the gap between Eli and Ithamar.

fore the king, the leaders, Zā′dok the priest, A·him′e·lech the son of A·bī′a·thar, and the heads of the fathers′ *houses* of the priests and Lē′vītes, one father′s house taken for El·ē·ā′zar and *one* for Ith′a·mar.

7Now the first lot fell to Je·hoi′a·rib, the second to Je·daī′ah, 8the third to Hā′rim, the fourth to Sē·ō′rim, 9the fifth to Mal·chī′jah, the sixth to Mij′a·min, 10the seventh to Hak′koz, the eighth to A·bī′jah, 11the ninth to Jesh′ū·a, the tenth to Shec·a·nī′ah, 12the eleventh to E·lī′a·shib, the twelfth to Jā′kim, 13the thirteenth to Hup′pah, the fourteenth to Je·sheb′e·ab, 14the fifteenth to Bil′gah, the sixteenth to Im′mer, 15the seventeenth to Hē′zir, the eighteenth to Hap′piz·zez,[a] 16the nineteenth to Peth·a·hī′ah, the twentieth to Je·hez′e·kel,[a] 17the twenty-first to Jā′chin, the twenty-second to Gā′mūl, 18the twenty-third to De·laī′ah, the twenty-fourth to Mā·a·zī′ah.

19This *was* the schedule of their service for coming into the house of the LORD according to their ordinance by the hand of Aaron their father, as the LORD God of Israel had commanded him.

Other Levites

20And the rest of the sons of Levi: of the sons of Am′ram, Shū′ba·el;[a] of the sons of Shū′ba·el, Jeh·dē′i·ah. 21Concerning Rē·ha·bī′ah, of the sons of Rē·ha·bī′ah, the first *was* Is·shī′ah. 22Of the Iz′har·ītes, She·lō′moth;[a] of the sons of She·lō′moth, Jā′hath. 23Of the sons *of Hē′bron,*[a] Je·rī′ah *was the first,*[b] Am·a·rī′ah the second, Ja·hā′zi·el the third, *and* Jek·a·mē′am the fourth. 24*Of* the sons of Uz′zi·el, Mī′chah; of the sons of Mī′chah, Shā′mir. 25The brother of Mī′chah, Is·shī′ah; of the sons of Is·shī′ah, Zech·a·rī′ah. 26The sons of Me·rar′ī *were* Mah′lī and Mū′shī; the son of Jā·a·zī′ah, Bē′no. 27The sons of Me·rar′ī by Jā·a·zī′ah *were* Bē′no, Shō′ham, Zac′cur, and Ib′rī. 28Of Mah′lī: El·ē·ā′zar, who had no sons. 29Of Kish: the son of Kish, Je-rah′mē·el.

30Also the sons of Mū′shī *were* Mah′lī, Ē′der, and Jer′i·moth. These *were* the sons of the Lē′vītes according to their fathers′ houses.

31These also cast lots just as their brothers the sons of Aaron did, in the presence of King David, Zā′dok, A·him′e·lech, and the heads of the fathers′ *houses* of the priests and Lē′vītes. The chief fathers *did* just as their younger brethren.

CHAPTER 25

The Musicians

Moreover David and the captains of the army separated for the service *some* of the sons of Ā′saph, of Hē′man, and of Je·dū′thun, who *should* prophesy with harps, stringed instruments, and cymbals. And the number of the skilled men performing their service was: 2Of the sons of Ā′saph: Zac′cur, Joseph, Neth·a·nī′ah, and Ash·a·rē′lah;[a] the sons of Ā′saph *were* under the direction of Ā′saph, who prophesied according to the order of the king. 3Of Je·dū′thun, the sons of Je·dū′thun: Ged·a·lī′ah, Zē′rī,[a] Je·shā′i·ah, Shim′ē·ī, Hash·a·bī′ah, and Mat·ti·thī′ah, six,[b] under the direction of their father Je·dū′thun, who prophesied with a harp to give thanks and to praise the LORD. 4Of Hē′man, the sons of Hē′man: Buk·kī′ah, Mat·ta·nī′ah,

24:15 [a]Septuagint and Vulgate read *Aphses.*
24:16 [a]Masoretic Text reads *Jehezkel.*
24:20 [a]Spelled *Shebuel* in 23:16 24:22 [a]Spelled *Shelomith* in 23:18 24:23 [a]Supplied from 23:19 (following some Hebrew manuscripts and Septuagint manuscripts) [b]Supplied from 23:19 (following some Hebrew manuscripts and Septuagint manuscripts)
25:2 [a]Spelled *Jesharelah* in verse 14 25:3 [a]Spelled *Jizri* in verse 11 [b]*Shimei,* appearing in one Hebrew and several Septuagint manuscripts, completes the total of six sons (compare verse 17).

25:1 Asaph . . . Heman: See note on 15:19. **prophesy with harps**: Declare the word of God with praise and thanksgiving (see v. 3) through the medium of music.

Uz′zi·el,[a] She·bū′el,[b] Jer′i·moth,[c] Han·a·nī′ah, Ha·nā′nī, E·lī′a·thah, Gid·dal′tī, Rō·mam′ti-Ē′zer, Josh·be·kash′ah, Mal·lō′thī, Hō′thir, *and* Ma·hā′zi·oth. 5All these *were* the sons of Hē′man the king's seer in the words of God, to exalt his horn.[a] For God gave Hē′man fourteen sons and three daughters.

6All these *were* under the direction of their father for the music *in* the house of the LORD, with cymbals, stringed instruments, and harps, for the service of the house of God. Ā′saph, Je·dū′thun, and Hē′man *were* under the authority of the king. 7So the number of them, with their brethren who were instructed in the songs of the LORD, all who were skillful, *was* two hundred and eighty-eight.

8And they cast lots for their duty, the small as well as the great, the teacher with the student.

9Now the first lot for Ā′saph came out for Joseph; the second for Ged·a·lī′ah, him with his brethren and sons, twelve; 10the third for Zac′cur, his sons and his brethren, twelve; 11the fourth for Jiz′rī,[a] his sons and his brethren, twelve; 12the fifth for Neth·a·nī′ah, his sons and his brethren, twelve; 13the sixth for Buk·kī′ah, his sons and his brethren, twelve; 14the seventh for Jesh·a·rē′lah,[a] his sons and his brethren, twelve; 15the eighth for Je·shā′i·ah, his sons and his brethren, twelve; 16the ninth for Mat·ta·nī′ah, his sons and his brethren, twelve; 17the tenth for Shim′ē·ī, his sons and his brethren, twelve; 18the eleventh for Az′a·rel,[a] his sons and his brethren, twelve; 19the twelfth for Hash·a·bī′ah, his sons and his brethren, twelve; 20the thirteenth for Shū′ba·el,[a] his sons and his brethren, twelve; 21the fourteenth for Mat·ti·thī′ah, his sons and his brethren, twelve; 22the fifteenth for Jer′e·moth,[a] his sons and his brethren, twelve; 23the sixteenth for Han·a·nī′ah, his sons and his brethren, twelve; 24the seventeenth for Josh·be·kash′ah, his sons and his brethren, twelve; 25the eighteenth for Ha·nā′nī, his sons and his brethren, twelve; 26the nineteenth for Mal·lō′thī, his sons and his brethren, twelve; 27the twentieth for E·lī′a·thah, his sons and his brethren, twelve; 28the twenty-first for Hō′thir, his sons and his brethren, twelve; 29the twenty-second for Gid·dal′tī, his sons and his brethren, twelve; 30the twenty-third for Ma·hā′zi·oth, his sons and his brethren, twelve; 31the twenty-fourth for Rō·mam′ti-Ē′zer, his sons and his brethren, twelve.

CHAPTER 26

The Gatekeepers

Concerning the divisions of the gatekeepers: of the Kō′ra·hītes, Me·shel·e·mī′ah the son of Kō′re, of the sons of Ā′saph. 2And the sons of Me·shel·e·mī′ah *were* Zech·a·rī′ah the firstborn, Je·dī′a·el the second, Zeb·a·dī′ah the third, Jath′ni·el the fourth, 3Ē′lam the fifth, Jē·hō·hā′nan the sixth, El·i·ē·hō·ē′naī the seventh.

4Moreover the sons of Ō′bed-Ē′dom *were* She·māi′ah the firstborn, Je·hō′za·bad the second, Jō′ah the third, Sā′car the fourth, Ne·than′el the fifth, 5Am′mi·el the sixth, Is′sa·char the seventh, Pē·ul′thaī the eighth; for God blessed him.

6Also to She·māi′ah his son were sons born who governed their fathers' houses, because they *were* men of great ability. 7The sons of She·māi′ah *were* Oth′nī, Reph′a·el,

25:4 [a]Spelled *Azarel* in verse 18 [b]Spelled *Shubael* in verse 20 [c]Spelled *Jeremoth* in verse 22
25:5 [a]That is, to increase his power or influence
25:11 [a]Spelled *Zeri* in verse 3
25:14 [a]Spelled *Asharelah* in verse 2
25:18 [a]Spelled *Uzziel* in verse 4
25:20 [a]Spelled *Shebuel* in verse 4
25:22 [a]Spelled *Jerimoth* in verse 4

25:9–31 Like the priests and Levites (see note on 24:1–19), the musicians were divided into 24 groups (v. 31). Each group served 15 days a year in the temple.

26:1 gatekeepers: Temple guards were necessary because of the costly materials used to build the temple and the valuables stored in its treasury (vv. 27, 28).

Ō′bed, and El·zā′bad, whose brothers
E·lī′hū and Sem·a·chī′ah *were* able men.
[8]All these *were* of the sons of Ō′bed-
Ē′dom, they and their sons and their
brethren, able men with strength for the
work: sixty-two of Ō′bed-Ē′dom.
[9]And Me·shel·e·mī′ah had sons and
brethren, eighteen able men.
[10]Also Hō′sah, of the children of Me-
rar′ī, had sons: Shim′rī the first (for *though*
he was not the firstborn, his father made
him the first), [11]Hil·kī′ah the second,
Teb·a·lī′ah the third, Zech·a·rī′ah the
fourth; all the sons and brethren of Hō′sah
were thirteen.
[12]Among these *were* the divisions of the
gatekeepers, among the chief men, *having*
duties just like their brethren, to serve in
the house of the LORD. [13]And they cast lots
for each gate, the small as well as the great,
according to their father's house. [14]The lot
for the East *Gate* fell to Shel·e·mī′ah. Then
they cast lots *for* his son Zech·a·rī′ah, a
wise counselor, and his lot came out for the
North Gate; [15]to Ō′bed-Ē′dom the South
Gate, and to his sons the storehouse.[a] [16]To
Shup′pim and Hō′sah *the lot came out* for
the West Gate, with the Shal′le·cheth Gate
on the ascending highway—watchman
opposite watchman. [17]On the east were *six*
Lē′vītes, on the north four each day, on the
south four each day, and for the store-
house[a] two by two. [18]As for the Par′bar[a] on
the west, *there were* four on the highway
and two at the Par′bar. [19]These were the
divisions of the gatekeepers among the
sons of Kō′rah and among the sons of
Me·rar′ī.

26:15 [a]Hebrew *asuppim* 26:17 [a]Hebrew *asuppim*
26:18 [a]Probably a court or colonnade extending west of the temple

The Treasuries and Other Duties

[20]Of the Lē′vītes, A·hī′jah *was* over the
treasuries of the house of God and over
the treasuries of the dedicated things. [21]The
sons of Lā′a·dan, the descendants of the
Ger′shon·ītes of Lā′a·dan, heads of their
fathers' *houses,* of Lā′a·dan the Ger′-
shon·īte: Je·hī′e·lī. [22]The sons of Je·hī′e·lī,
Zē′tham and Jō′el his brother, *were* over the
treasuries of the house of the LORD. [23]Of the
Am′ram·ītes, the Iz′har·ītes, the Hē′-
bron·ītes, and the Uz′zi·el·ītes: [24]She·bū′el
the son of Ger′shom, the son of Moses, *was*
overseer of the treasuries. [25]And his
brethren by El·i·ē′zer *were* Rē·ha·bī′ah his
son, Je·shā′i·ah his son, Jō′ram his son,
Zich′rī his son, and She·lō′mith his son.
[26]This She·lō′mith and his brethren *were*
over all the treasuries of the dedicated
things which King David and the heads of
fathers' *houses,* the captains over thou-
sands and hundreds, and the captains of
the army, had dedicated. [27]Some of the
spoils won in battles they dedicated to
maintain the house of the LORD. [28]And all
that Samuel the seer, Saul the son of Kish,
Abner the son of Ner, and Jō′ab the son of
Ze·rū′i·ah had dedicated, every dedicated
thing, was under the hand of She·lō′mith
and his brethren.
[29]Of the Iz′har·ītes, Chen·a·nī′ah and
his sons *performed* duties as officials and
judges over Israel outside Jerusalem.
[30]Of the Hē′bron·ītes, Hash·a·bī′ah and
his brethren, one thousand seven hundred
able men, had the oversight of Israel on the
west side of the Jordan for all the business
of the LORD, and in the service of the king.
[31]Among the Hē′bron·ītes, Je·rī′jah *was*
head of the Hē′bron·ītes according to his
genealogy of the fathers. In the fortieth
year of the reign of David they were

26:29—27:34 The organization of David's kingdom concludes with lists of judicial officers (26:29–32); military captains and officers (27:1–15); tribal officers (27:16–22); administrators (27:25–31); and counselors (27:32–34).

26:29–32 Only 1,700 officers on the **west side of the Jordan**, in light of 2,700 on the east side among Reuben, Gad, and Manasseh, gives some idea of the significance of the Transjordanian tribes in the early days of the kingdom.

sought, and there were found among them capable men at Jā′zer of Gil′ē·ad. 32And his brethren *were* two thousand seven hundred able men, heads of fathers′ *houses,* whom King David made officials over the Reū′ben·ītes, the Gad′ītes, and the half-tribe of Ma·nas′seh, for every matter pertaining to God and the affairs of the king.

CHAPTER 27

The Military Divisions

And the children of Israel, according to their number, the heads of fathers′ *houses,* the captains of thousands and hundreds and their officers, served the king in every matter of the *military* divisions. *These divisions* came in and went out month by month throughout all the months of the year, each division *having* twenty-four thousand.

2Over the first division for the first month *was* Ja·shō′bē·am the son of Zab′di·el, and in his division *were* twenty-four thousand; 3*he was* of the children of Per′ez, and the chief of all the captains of the army for the first month. 4Over the division of the second month *was* Dō′daī[a] an A·hō′hīte, and of his division Mik′loth also *was* the leader; in his division *were* twenty-four thousand. 5The third captain of the army for the third month *was* Be·nā′i·ah, the son of Je·hoi′a·da the priest, who was chief; in his division *were* twenty-four thousand. 6This was the Be·nā′i·ah *who was* mighty *among* the thirty, and was over the thirty; in his division *was* Am·miz′a·bad his son. 7The fourth *captain* for the fourth month *was* As′a·hel the brother of Jō′ab, and Zeb·a·dī′ah his son after him; in his division *were* twenty-four thousand. 8The fifth *captain* for the fifth month *was* Sham′huth[a] the Iz′ra·hīte; in his division were twenty-four thousand. 9The sixth *captain* for the sixth month *was* Ī′ra the son of Ik′kesh the Te·kō′īte; in his division *were* twenty-four thousand. 10The seventh *captain* for the seventh month *was* Hē′lez the Pel′o·nīte, of the children of Ē′phra·im; in his division *were* twenty-four thousand. 11The eighth *captain* for the eighth month *was* Sib′be·chaī the Hū′sha·thīte, of the Zar′hītes; in his division *were* twenty-four thousand. 12The ninth *captain* for the ninth month *was* Ā·bi·ē′zer the An′a·thoth·īte, of the Ben′ja·mītes; in his division *were* twenty-four thousand. 13The tenth *captain* for the tenth month *was* Mā′ha·raī the Ne-toph′a·thīte, of the Zar′hītes; in his division *were* twenty-four thousand. 14The eleventh *captain* for the eleventh month *was* Be·nā′i·ah the Pir′a·thon·īte, of the children of Ē′phra·im; in his division *were* twenty-four thousand. 15The twelfth *captain* for the twelfth month *was* Hel′daī[a] the Ne·toph′a·thīte, of Oth′ni·el; in his division *were* twenty-four thousand.

Leaders of Tribes

16Furthermore, over the tribes of Israel: the officer over the Reū′ben·ītes *was* El·i·ē′zer the son of Zich′rī; over the Sim′ē·on·ītes, Sheph·a·tī′ah the son of Mā′a·chah; 17*over* the Lē′vītes, Hash·a-bī′ah the son of Ke·mū′el; over the Aaronites, Zā′dok; 18*over* Judah, E·lī′hū, *one* of David′s brothers; *over* Is′sa·char, Om′rī the son of Michael; 19*over* Zeb′ū·lun, Ish-mā′i·ah the son of Ō·ba·dī′ah; *over* Naph′ta·lī, Jer′i·moth the son of Az′ri·el; 20*over* the children of Ē′phra·im, Hō·shē′a the son of Az·a·zī′ah; *over* the half-tribe of

27:4 [a]Hebrew *Dodai,* usually spelled *Dodo* (compare 2 Samuel 23:9) 27:8 [a]Spelled *Shammoth* in 11:27 and *Shammah* in 2 Samuel 23:11 27:15 [a]Spelled *Heled* in 11:30 and *Heleb* in 2 Samuel 23:29

27:1–15 David's **military** organization consisted of 12 armies of 24,000 men, each army serving one month of the year.

27:16–22 over the tribes: These men were civil administrators comparable to state governors.

Ma·nas′seh, Jō′el the son of Pe·dāi′ah;
21*over* the half-*tribe* of Ma·nas′seh in
Gil′ē·ad, Id′dō the son of Zech·a·rī′ah; *over*
Benjamin, Jā·a·sī′el the son of Abner; 22*over*
Dan, Az′a·rel the son of Je·rō′ham. These
were the leaders of the tribes of Israel.
23But David did not take the number of
those twenty years old and under, because
the LORD had said He would multiply Is-
rael like the stars of the heavens. 24Jō′ab the
son of Ze·rū′i·ah began a census, but he
did not finish, for wrath came upon Israel
because of this census; nor was the number
recorded in the account of the chronicles of
King David.

Other State Officials

25And Az′ma·veth the son of Ad′i·el *was*
over the king's treasuries; and Je·hon′-
a·than the son of Uz·zī′ah was over the
storehouses in the field, in the cities, in the
villages, and in the fortresses. 26Ez′rī
the son of Chē′lub was over those who did
the work of the field for tilling the ground.
27And Shim′ē·ī the Rā′ma·thīte *was* over
the vineyards, and Zab′dī the Shiph′mīte
was over the produce of the vineyards for
the supply of wine. 28Bā′al-Hā′nan the
Ge·dē′rīte was over the olive trees and the
sycamore trees that *were* in the lowlands,
and Jō′ash *was* over the store of oil. 29And
Shit′raī the Shar′on·īte *was* over the herds
that fed in Sharon, and Shā′phat the son of
Ad′lā·ī was over the herds *that were* in the
valleys. 30Ō′bil the Ish′ma·el·īte *was* over
the camels, Jeh·dē′i·ah the Me·ron′o·thīte
was over the donkeys, 31and Jā′ziz the
Hag′rīte *was* over the flocks. All these *were*
the officials over King David's property.
32Also Je·hon′a·than, David's uncle, *was*
a counselor, a wise man, and a scribe; and
Je·hī′el the son of Hach′mo·nī *was* with the
king's sons. 33A·hith′o·phel *was* the king's
counselor, and Hū′shai the Ar′chīte *was*
the king's companion. 34After A·hith′-
o·phel *was* Je·hoi′a·da the son of Be-
nā′i·ah, then A·bī′a·thar. And the general
of the king's army *was* Jō′ab.

CHAPTER 28

Solomon Instructed to Build the Temple

Now David assembled at Jerusalem all
the leaders of Israel: the officers of the
tribes and the captains of the divisions
who served the king, the captains over
thousands and captains over hundreds,
and the stewards over all the substance
and possessions of the king and of his sons,
with the officials, the valiant men, and all
the mighty men of valor.
2Then King David rose to his feet and
said, "Hear me, my brethren and my peo-
ple: I *had* it in my heart to build a house of
rest for the ark of the covenant of the LORD,
and for the footstool of our God, and had
made preparations to build it. 3But God
said to me, 'You shall not build a house for
My name, because you *have been* a man of
war and have shed blood.' 4However the
LORD God of Israel chose me above all the
house of my father to be king over Israel
forever, for He has chosen Judah *to be* the
ruler. And of the house of Judah, the house
of my father, and among the sons of my
father, He was pleased with me to make *me*
king over all Israel. 5And of all my sons (for

27:24 did not finish: See 21:1–8 and notes. **chronicles of King David**: Royal annals which may have been the source for this material.

27:25–34 These administrators and counselors were personally responsible to King David—perhaps comparable to a president's cabinet.

28:1—29:25 The narrative continues the theme of 23:1: "David . . . made his son Solomon king over Israel."

28:2 The **ark** was God's **footstool** because He symbolically resided between the cherubim above it.

28:3 You shall not build: See 22:7–10 and note on 22:8, 9.

the LORD has given me many sons) He has chosen my son Solomon to sit on the throne of the kingdom of the LORD over Israel. [6]Now He said to me, 'It is your son Solomon *who* shall build My house and My courts; for I have chosen him *to be* My son, and I will be his Father. [7]Moreover I will establish his kingdom forever, if he is steadfast to observe My commandments and My judgments, as it is this day.' [8]Now therefore, in the sight of all Israel, the assembly of the LORD, and in the hearing of our God, be careful to seek out all the commandments of the LORD your God, that you may possess this good land, and leave *it* as an inheritance for your children after you forever.

[9]"As for you, my son Solomon, know the God of your father, and serve Him with a loyal heart and with a willing mind; for the LORD searches all hearts and understands all the intent of the thoughts. If you seek Him, He will be found by you; but if you forsake Him, He will cast you off forever. [10]Consider now, for the LORD has chosen you to build a house for the sanctuary; be strong, and do it."

[11]Then David gave his son Solomon the plans for the vestibule, its houses, its treasuries, its upper chambers, its inner chambers, and the place of the mercy seat; [12]and the plans for all that he had by the Spirit, of the courts of the house of the LORD, of all the chambers all around, of the treasuries of the house of God, and of the treasuries for the dedicated things; [13]also for the division of the priests and the Lē'vītes, for all the work of the service of the house of the LORD, and for all the articles of service in the house of the LORD. [14]*He gave* gold by weight for *things* of gold, for all articles used in every kind of service; also *silver* for all articles of silver by weight, for all articles used in every kind of service; [15]the weight for the lampstands of gold, and their lamps of gold, by weight for each lampstand and its lamps; for the lampstands of silver by weight, for the lampstand and its lamps, according to the use of each lampstand. [16]And by weight *he gave* gold for the tables of the showbread, for each table, and silver for the tables of silver; [17]also pure gold for the forks, the basins, the pitchers of pure gold, and the golden bowls—*he gave gold* by weight for every bowl; and for the silver bowls, *silver* by weight for every bowl; [18]and refined gold by weight for the altar of incense, and for the construction of the chariot, that is, the gold cherubim that spread *their wings* and overshadowed the ark of the covenant of the LORD. [19]"All *this,*" *said David,* "the LORD made me understand in writing, by *His* hand upon me, all the works of these plans."

[20]And David said to his son Solomon, "Be strong and of good courage, and do *it;* do not fear nor be dismayed, for the LORD God—my God—*will be* with you. He will not leave you nor forsake you, until you have finished all the work for the service of the house of the LORD. [21]*Here are* the divisions of the priests and the Lē'vītes for all the service of the house of God; and every willing craftsman *will be* with you for all manner of workmanship, for every kind of

---

28:7 forever: David believed God's promise for a lasting kingdom (17:11–14) was soon to be fulfilled in Solomon. Centuries later, the chronicler was also hoping for an imminent fulfillment. Hope characterizes God's people in every generation, but alongside our hopes God places His condition: **if he is steadfast to observe My commandments**. For the ultimate fulfillment see note on 2 Sam. 7:5–16.

28:9 the LORD searches all hearts: Although public worship is essential for God's people, it is no substitute for a personal sincerity in our relationship with God. This was the burden of all the prophets. **loyal heart**: Lit. "whole (undivided) heart." **willing mind**: Lit. "a delighting soul."

28:12 by the Spirit: David's **plans** were the outcome of direct divine guidance (v. 19).

service; also the leaders and all the people
will be completely at your command."

CHAPTER 29

Offerings for Building the Temple

Furthermore King David said to all the
assembly: "My son Solomon, whom alone
God has chosen, *is* young and inexperi-
enced; and the work *is* great, because the
temple[a] *is* not for man but for the LORD
God. 2 Now for the house of my God I have
prepared with all my might: gold for *things*
to be made of gold, silver for *things of* silver,
bronze for *things of* bronze, iron for *things*
of iron, wood for *things of* wood, onyx
stones, *stones* to be set, glistening stones of
various colors, all kinds of precious stones,
and marble slabs in abundance. 3 Moreover,
because I have set my affection on the
house of my God, I have given to the house
of my God, over and above all that I have
prepared for the holy house, my own spe-
cial treasure of gold and silver: 4 three thou-
sand talents of gold, of the gold of Ō'phir,
and seven thousand talents of refined sil-
ver, to overlay the walls of the houses; 5 the
gold for *things of* gold and the silver for
things of silver, and for all kinds of work *to*
be done by the hands of craftsmen. Who
then is willing to consecrate himself this
day to the LORD?"

6 Then the leaders of the fathers' *houses,*
leaders of the tribes of Israel, the captains
of thousands and of hundreds, with the of-
ficers over the king's work, offered will-
ingly. 7 They gave for the work of the house
of God five thousand talents and ten thou-
sand darics of gold, ten thousand talents of
silver, eighteen thousand talents of bronze,
and one hundred thousand talents of iron.
8 And whoever had *precious* stones gave
them to the treasury of the house of the
LORD, into the hand of Je·hī'el[a] the Ger'-
shon·īte. 9 Then the people rejoiced, for
they had offered willingly, because with a
loyal heart they had offered willingly to
the LORD; and King David also rejoiced
greatly.

David's Praise to God

10 Therefore David blessed the LORD be-
fore all the assembly; and David said:

"Blessed are You, LORD God of Israel,
our Father, forever and ever.
11 Yours, O LORD, *is* the greatness,
The power and the glory,
The victory and the majesty;
For all *that is* in heaven and in earth *is*
Yours;
Yours *is* the kingdom, O LORD,
And You are exalted as head over all.
12 Both riches and honor *come* from You,
And You reign over all.
In Your hand *is* power and might;
In Your hand *it is* to make great
And to give strength to all.

13 "Now therefore, our God,
We thank You
And praise Your glorious name.
14 But who *am* I, and who *are* my
people,
That we should be able to offer so
willingly as this?
For all things *come* from You,
And of Your own we have given You.
15 For we *are* aliens and pilgrims before
You,
As *were* all our fathers;
Our days on earth *are* as a shadow,
And without hope.

29:1 [a]Literally *palace*
29:8 [a]Possibly the same as *Jehieli* (compare 26:21, 22)

29:3 David's testimony **I have set my affection** gives us a glimpse of the man who was after God's own heart (see 1 Sam. 13:14).
29:9 loyal heart: See Ex. 35:5, 21, 22 and note on 1 Chr. 28:9.
29:14 all things come from You: The cheerful giver recognizes the source of his gift.
29:15 without hope: Apart from God.

16"O LORD our God, all this abundance that we have prepared to build You a house for Your holy name is from Your hand, and *is* all Your own. 17I know also, my God, that You test the heart and have pleasure in uprightness. As for me, in the uprightness of my heart I have willingly offered all these *things;* and now with joy I have seen Your people, who are present here to offer willingly to You. 18O LORD God of Abraham, Isaac, and Israel, our fathers, keep this forever in the intent of the thoughts of the heart of Your people, and fix their heart toward You. 19And give my son Solomon a loyal heart to keep Your commandments and Your testimonies and Your statutes, to do all *these things,* and to build the temple[a] for which I have made provision."

20Then David said to all the assembly, "Now bless the LORD your God." So all the assembly blessed the LORD God of their fathers, and bowed their heads and prostrated themselves before the LORD and the king.

Solomon Anointed King

21And they made sacrifices to the LORD and offered burnt offerings to the LORD on the next day: a thousand bulls, a thousand rams, a thousand lambs, with their drink offerings, and sacrifices in abundance for all Israel. 22So they ate and drank before the LORD with great gladness on that day. And they made Solomon the son of David king the second time, and anointed *him* before the LORD *to be* the leader, and Zā'dok *to be* priest. 23Then Solomon sat on the throne of the LORD as king instead of David his father, and prospered; and all Israel obeyed him. 24All the leaders and the mighty men, and also all the sons of King David, submitted themselves to King Solomon. 25So the LORD exalted Solomon exceedingly in the sight of all Israel, and bestowed on him *such* royal majesty as had not been on any king before him in Israel.

The Close of David's Reign

26Thus David the son of Jesse reigned over all Israel. 27And the period that he reigned over Israel *was* forty years; seven years he reigned in Hē'bron, and thirty-three *years* he reigned in Jerusalem. 28So he died in a good old age, full of days and riches and honor; and Solomon his son reigned in his place. 29Now the acts of King David, first and last, indeed they *are* written in the book of Samuel the seer, in the book of Nathan the prophet, and in the book of Gad the seer, 30with all his reign and his might, and the events that happened to him, to Israel, and to all the kingdoms of the lands.

29:19 [a]Literally *palace*

29:20 To **bless the LORD** is to give to Him. There are at least five reasons to give to God: (1) because it is for God's work (v. 1); (2) because we love God (v. 3); (3) because we have consecrated ourselves (v. 5); (4) because when we offer willingly, we rejoice greatly (v. 9); (5) because God has given to us (v. 14).

29:22 the second time: Probably to be taken as a public confirmation of the hasty and private first coronation (see 1 Kin. 1:32–40). There only David's entourage attended. Here "all the leaders of Israel" are present (28:1).

✦2 Chronicles✦

2 Chronicles, written by Ezra, covers Solomon's reign and the kings who followed. Although it parallels 1 and 2 Kings, this book centers around the temple, which symbolized God's presence among His people.

Following David's reign, which ended in division and conflict, Solomon brought a period of prosperity to the nation, and six of the first nine chapters cover the process of building the temple. Soon after Solomon's death, however, the kingdom began a downward spiral and split into two nations: Judah and Israel. Chapters 10—36 tell of godly kings of Judah who implemented reforms, attempting to pull the people out of sin and false worship. The faithfulness of righteous leaders like Jehoshaphat and Jotham obtained God's blessing for the entire nation. The writer focuses on Judah rather than Israel because the latter refused to acknowledge the temple, turning to idolatry.

2 Chronicles provides a topical account of the end of the united kingdom and the kingdom of Judah, and it also highlights the spiritual characteristics of David's line. The book ends on a positive note, setting the stage for the return of the people to Jerusalem after Persia defeated Babylon. ✦

CHAPTER 1

Solomon Requests Wisdom

Now Solomon the son of David was
strengthened in his kingdom, and the
LORD his God *was* with him and exalted
him exceedingly.
2And Solomon spoke to all Israel, to the
captains of thousands and of hundreds, to
the judges, and to every leader in all Israel,
the heads of the fathers' *houses*. 3Then Sol-
omon, and all the assembly with him, went
to the high place that *was* at Gib'ē·on; for
the tabernacle of meeting with God was
there, which Moses the servant of the LORD
had made in the wilderness. 4But David
had brought up the ark of God from
Kir'jath Jē'a·rim to *the place* David had pre-
pared for it, for he had pitched a tent for it
at Jerusalem. 5Now the bronze altar that
Bez'a·lel the son of Ū'rī, the son of Hur,
had made, he put[a] before the tabernacle of
the LORD; Solomon and the assembly
sought Him *there*. 6And Solomon went up
there to the bronze altar before the LORD,
which *was* at the tabernacle of meeting, and
offered a thousand burnt offerings on it.

1:5 [a]Some authorities read *it was there.*

1:1—9:31 The Chronicles account of Solomon's reign is shorter than its parallel passages in 1 Kin. 1—11 and includes only events that reflect the chronicler's concern for the temple. Chapter 1 relates the gathering of the wealth and skills needed to build the temple.

1:3 Gibeon: Still the approved site for sacrificing to God (vv. 5, 6). If this is the actual **tabernacle** made by **Moses**, then there seems to be a conflict with Jer. 7:12, 14, which at least imply that the first tabernacle was destroyed. Either it was only profaned at Shiloh, or the Gibeon tabernacle was a copy of the original. See Jer. 7:12.

7On that night God appeared to Sol-
omon, and said to him, "Ask! What shall I
give you?"
8And Solomon said to God: "You have
shown great mercy to David my father,
and have made me king in his place. 9Now,
O LORD God, let Your promise to David my
father be established, for You have made
me king over a people like the dust of the
earth in multitude. 10Now give me wisdom
and knowledge, that I may go out and
come in before this people; for who can
judge this great people of Yours?"
11Then God said to Solomon: "Because
this was in your heart, and you have not
asked riches or wealth or honor or the life
of your enemies, nor have you asked long
life—but have asked wisdom and knowl-
edge for yourself, that you may judge My
people over whom I have made you
king— 12wisdom and knowledge *are*
granted to you; and I will give you riches
and wealth and honor, such as none of the
kings have had who *were* before you, nor
shall any after you have the like."

Solomon's Military and Economic Power

13So Solomon came to Jerusalem from
the high place that *was* at Gib'ē·on, from
before the tabernacle of meeting, and
reigned over Israel. 14And Solomon gath-
ered chariots and horsemen; he had one
thousand four hundred chariots and
twelve thousand horsemen, whom he sta-
tioned in the chariot cities and with the
king in Jerusalem. 15Also the king made sil-
ver and gold as common in Jerusalem as
stones, and he made cedars as abundant
as the sycamores which *are* in the low-
land. 16And Solomon had horses imported
from Egypt and Ke·veh'; the king's
merchants bought them in Ke·veh' at the
current price. 17They also acquired and
imported from Egypt a chariot for six
hundred *shekels* of silver, and a horse
for one hundred and fifty; thus, through
their agents,[a] they exported them to all the
kings of the Hit'tītes and the kings of
Syria.

CHAPTER 2

Solomon Prepares to Build the Temple

Then Solomon determined to build a
temple for the name of the LORD, and a
royal house for himself. 2Solomon selected
seventy thousand men to bear burdens,
eighty thousand to quarry *stone* in the
mountains, and three thousand six hun-
dred to oversee them.
3Then Solomon sent to Hī'ram[a] king of
Tȳre, saying:

As you have dealt with David my
father, and sent him cedars to build
himself a house to dwell in, *so deal
with me.* 4Behold, I am building a tem-
ple for the name of the LORD my God,
to dedicate *it* to Him, to burn before
Him sweet incense, for the continual
showbread, for the burnt offerings
morning and evening, on the Sab-
baths, on the New Moons, and on the
set feasts of the LORD our God. This *is
an ordinance* forever to Israel.

5 And the temple which I build *will be*
great, for our God is greater than all

1:17 [a]Literally *by their hands* (compare 1 Kings 5:1)

2:3 [a]Hebrew *Huram*

1:11, 12 Because . . . you have not asked riches: The Lord always honors those who depend on Him for wisdom and guidance. As we face the many decisions regarding our future finances, retirement, family situations, and more, we can rely on God to give us the wisdom we need, if only we will ask.

1:13–17 While Solomon's wealth was a gift from God, his decision to use it acquiring horses and chariots was contrary to God's command in Deut. 17:16. How we handle God's blessings should demonstrate our gratitude to the Giver.

gods. 6But who is able to build Him a
temple, since heaven and the heaven
of heavens cannot contain Him? Who
am I then, that I should build Him a
temple, except to burn sacrifice before
Him?

7 Therefore send me at once a man skill-
ful to work in gold and silver, in
bronze and iron, in purple and crim-
son and blue, who has skill to engrave
with the skillful men who are with me
in Judah and Jerusalem, whom David
my father provided. 8Also send me
cedar and cypress and algum logs
from Lebanon, for I know that your
servants have skill to cut timber in
Lebanon; and indeed my servants *will*
be with your servants, 9to prepare tim-
ber for me in abundance, for the tem-
ple which I am about to build *shall be*
great and wonderful.

10 And indeed I will give to your ser-
vants, the woodsmen who cut timber,
twenty thousand kors of ground
wheat, twenty thousand kors of bar-
ley, twenty thousand baths of wine,
and twenty thousand baths of oil.

11Then Hī′ram king of Tȳre answered in
writing, which he sent to Solomon:

Because the LORD loves His people,
He has made you king over them.
12 Hī′ram[a] also said:

Blessed *be* the LORD God of Israel,
who made heaven and earth, for He
has given King David a wise son, en-
dowed with prudence and under-
standing, who will build a temple for
the LORD and a royal house for him-
self!

13 And now I have sent a skillful man,
endowed with understanding,
Hū′ram[a] my master[b] *craftsman* 14(the
son of a woman of the daughters of
Dan, and his father was a man of
Tȳre), skilled to work in gold and sil-
ver, bronze and iron, stone and wood,
purple and blue, fine linen and crim-
son, and to make any engraving and
to accomplish any plan which may be
given to him, with your skillful men
and with the skillful men of my lord
David your father.

15 Now therefore, the wheat, the barley,
the oil, and the wine which my lord
has spoken of, let him send to his ser-
vants. 16And we will cut wood from
Lebanon, as much as you need; we
will bring it to you in rafts by sea to
Jop′pa, and you will carry it up to Je-
rusalem.

17Then Solomon numbered all the aliens
who *were* in the land of Israel, after the cen-
sus in which David his father had num-
bered them; and there were found to be
one hundred and fifty-three thousand six
hundred. 18And he made seventy thousand
of them bearers of burdens, eighty thou-
sand stonecutters in the mountain, and
three thousand six hundred overseers to
make the people work.

2:12 [a]Hebrew *Huram* (compare 1 Kings 5:1)
2:13 [a]Spelled *Hiram* in 1 Kings 7:13 [b]Literally *father* (compare 1 Kings 7:13, 14)

2:6 Solomon's understanding of God's transcendant omnipresence reflects an important, but often neglected, aspect of Christianity: Our God defies human limitations and exceeds our imagination. When we try to define and compartmentalize Him, we forget His indescribable greatness.

2:13, 14 Huram is described as the son of a Danite woman and Tyrian father. In 1 Kin. 7:14 his mother is "a widow from the tribe of Naphtali." It is possible that the woman was born in the tribe of Dan but married into the tribe of Naphtali. After becoming a widow from her Naphtalite husband, she married a man from Tyre. See also note on 1 Kin. 7:13, 14.

CHAPTER 3

Solomon Builds the Temple

Now Solomon began to build the house of the LORD at Jerusalem on Mount Mō-rī′ah, where *the LORD*[a] had appeared to his father David, at the place that David had prepared on the threshing floor of Or′nan[b] the Jeb′ū·sīte. 2And he began to build on the second *day* of the second month in the fourth year of his reign.

3This is the foundation which Solomon laid for building the house of God: The length *was* sixty cubits (by cubits according to the former measure) and the width twenty cubits. 4And the vestibule that *was* in front *of the sanctuary*[a] was twenty cubits long across the width of the house, and the height *was* one hundred and[b] twenty. He overlaid the inside with pure gold. 5The larger room[a] he paneled with cypress which he overlaid with fine gold, and he carved palm trees and chainwork on it. 6And he decorated the house with precious stones for beauty, and the gold *was* gold from Par·vā′im. 7He also overlaid the house—the beams and doorposts, its walls and doors—with gold; and he carved cherubim on the walls.

8And he made the Most Holy Place. Its length was according to the width of the house, twenty cubits, and its width twenty cubits. He overlaid it with six hundred talents of fine gold. 9The weight of the nails *was* fifty shekels of gold; and he overlaid the upper area with gold. 10In the Most Holy Place he made two cherubim, fashioned by carving, and overlaid them with gold. 11The wings of the cherubim *were* twenty cubits in *overall* length: one wing *of the one cherub was* five cubits, touching the wall of the room, and the other wing *was* five cubits, touching the wing of the other cherub; 12*one* wing of the other cherub *was* five cubits, touching the wall of the room, and the other wing *also was* five cubits, touching the wing of the other cherub. 13The wings of these cherubim spanned twenty cubits overall. They stood on their feet, and they faced inward. 14And he made the veil of blue, purple, crimson, and fine linen, and wove cherubim into it.

15Also he made in front of the temple[a] two pillars thirty-five[b] cubits high, and the capital that *was* on the top of each of *them* was five cubits. 16He made wreaths of chainwork, as in the inner sanctuary, and put *them* on top of the pillars; and he made one hundred pomegranates, and put *them* on the wreaths of chainwork. 17Then he set up the pillars before the temple, one on the right hand and the other on the left; he called the name of the one on the right hand Jā′chin, and the name of the one on the left Bō′az.

CHAPTER 4

Furnishings of the Temple

Moreover he made a bronze altar: twenty cubits was its length, twenty cubits its width, and ten cubits its height.

3:1 [a]Literally *He,* following Masoretic Text and Vulgate; Septuagint reads *the LORD;* Targum reads *the Angel of the LORD.* [b]Spelled *Araunah* in 2 Samuel 24:16ff
3:4 [a]The main room of the temple; elsewhere called the holy place (compare 1 Kings 6:3) [b]Following Masoretic Text, Septuagint, and Vulgate; Arabic, some manuscripts of the Septuagint, and Syriac omit *one hundred and.*
3:5 [a]Literally *house* 3:15 [a]Literally *house* [b]Or *eighteen* (compare 1 Kings 7:15; 2 Kings 25:17; and Jeremiah 52:21)

3:1—4:22 The chronicler shortens the Kings account of the construction of the temple. His main interest was in the institutions and worship connected with the building. For further discussion on the details see 1 Kin. 6; 7 and notes.

3:1 Mount Moriah: Thus the chronicler associates the temple site with "the Mount of the LORD" on which Abraham was asked to sacrifice Isaac (see Gen. 22:2, 14).

3:3 the former measure: A reference to the "standard cubit" (Deut. 3:11) which was about 18 inches (45 cm). By exilic times the cubit seems to have been extended by a handbreadth to approximately 21 inches (53 cm). See Ezek. 40:5; 43:13.

2Then he made the Sea of cast *bronze,* ten
cubits from one brim to the other; *it was*
completely round. Its height *was* five cu-
bits, and a line of thirty cubits measured its
circumference. 3And under it *was* the like-
ness of oxen encircling it all around, ten to
a cubit, all the way around the Sea. The
oxen *were* cast in two rows, when it was
cast. 4It stood on twelve oxen: three look-
ing toward the north, three looking toward
the west, three looking toward the south,
and three looking toward the east; the Sea
was set upon them, and all their back parts
pointed inward. 5It *was* a handbreadth
thick; and its brim was shaped like the
brim of a cup, *like* a lily blossom. It con-
tained three thousand[a] baths.

6He also made ten lavers, and put five
on the right side and five on the left, to
wash in them; such things as they offered
for the burnt offering they would wash in
them, but the Sea *was* for the priests to
wash in. 7And he made ten lampstands of
gold according to their design, and set
them in the temple, five on the right side
and five on the left. 8He also made ten ta-
bles, and placed *them* in the temple, five on
the right side and five on the left. And he
made one hundred bowls of gold.

9Furthermore he made the court of the
priests, and the great court and doors for
the court; and he overlaid these doors with
bronze. 10He set the Sea on the right side,
toward the southeast.

11Then Hū'ram made the pots and the
shovels and the bowls. So Hū'ram finished
doing the work that he was to do for King
Solomon for the house of God: 12the two
pillars and the bowl-shaped capitals *that*
were on top of the two pillars; the two net-
works covering the two bowl-shaped capi-
tals which *were* on top of the pillars; 13four
hundred pomegranates for the two net-
works (two rows of pomegranates for each
network, to cover the two bowl-shaped
capitals that *were* on the pillars); 14he also
made carts and the lavers on the carts;
15one Sea and twelve oxen under it; 16also
the pots, the shovels, the forks—and all
their articles Hū'ram his master[a] *craftsman*
made of burnished bronze for King Sol-
omon for the house of the LORD.

17In the plain of Jordan the king had
them cast in clay molds, between Suc'coth
and Zer'e·dah.[a] 18And Solomon had all
these articles made in such great abun-
dance that the weight of the bronze was
not determined.

19Thus Solomon had all the furnishings
made for the house of God: the altar of
gold and the tables on which *was* the show-
bread; 20the lampstands with their lamps of
pure gold, to burn in the prescribed man-
ner in front of the inner sanctuary, 21with
the flowers and the lamps and the wick-
trimmers of gold, of purest gold; 22the trim-
mers, the bowls, the ladles, and the censers
of pure gold. As for the entry of the sanctu-
ary, its inner doors to the Most Holy *Place,*
and the doors of the main hall of the tem-
ple, *were* gold.

CHAPTER 5

So all the work that Solomon had done
for the house of the LORD was finished; and
Solomon brought in the things which his
father David had dedicated: the silver and
the gold and all the furnishings. And he
put *them* in the treasuries of the house of
God.

The Ark Brought into the Temple

2Now Solomon assembled the elders of
Israel and all the heads of the tribes, the

4:5 [a]Or *two thousand* (compare 1 Kings 7:26)
4:16 [a]Literally *father* 4:17 [a]Spelled *Zaretan* in 1 Kings 7:46

5:2 The temple was built on a mound (Mt. Moriah) north of the ancient **City of David** (Mt. Zion). The city limits were then extended to include the temple area. Thus, it was necessary to **bring the ark . . . up** from its former resting place.

chief fathers of the children of Israel, in Je-
rusalem, that they might bring the ark of
the covenant of the LORD up from the City
of David, which *is* Zion. 3Therefore all the
men of Israel assembled with the king at
the feast, which *was* in the seventh month.
4So all the elders of Israel came, and the
Lē'vītes took up the ark. 5Then they
brought up the ark, the tabernacle of meet-
ing, and all the holy furnishings that *were*
in the tabernacle. The priests and the
Lē'vītes brought them up. 6Also King Sol-
omon, and all the congregation of Israel
who were assembled with him before the
ark, were sacrificing sheep and oxen that
could not be counted or numbered for
multitude. 7Then the priests brought in the
ark of the covenant of the LORD to its place,
into the inner sanctuary of the temple,[a] to
the Most Holy *Place,* under the wings of
the cherubim. 8For the cherubim spread
their wings over the place of the ark, and
the cherubim overshadowed the ark and
its poles. 9The poles extended so that the
ends of the poles of the ark could be seen
from *the holy place,* in front of the inner
sanctuary; but they could not be seen from
outside. And they are there to this day.
10Nothing was in the ark except the two
tablets which Moses put *there* at Hō'reb,
when the LORD made *a covenant* with the
children of Israel, when they had come out
of Egypt.

11And it came to pass when the priests
came out of the *Most* Holy *Place* (for all the
priests who *were* present had sanctified
themselves, without keeping to their divi-
sions), 12and the Lē'vītes *who were* the
singers, all those of Ā'saph and Hē'man
and Je·dū'thun, with their sons and their
brethren, stood at the east end of the altar,
clothed in white linen, having cymbals,
stringed instruments and harps, and with
them one hundred and twenty priests
sounding with trumpets—13indeed it
came to pass, when the trumpeters and
singers *were* as one, to make one sound to
be heard in praising and thanking the
LORD, and when they lifted up their voice
with the trumpets and cymbals and instru-
ments of music, and praised the LORD, *say-
ing:*

"For He is good,
For His mercy *endures* forever,"[a]

that the house, the house of the LORD, was
filled with a cloud, 14so that the priests
could not continue ministering because of
the cloud; for the glory of the LORD filled
the house of God.

CHAPTER 6

Then Solomon spoke:
"The LORD said He would dwell in the
dark cloud.
2 I have surely built You an exalted
house,
And a place for You to dwell in
forever."

Solomon's Speech upon Completion of the Work

3Then the king turned around and
blessed the whole assembly of Israel, while
all the assembly of Israel was standing.
4And he said: "Blessed *be* the LORD God of

5:7 [a]Literally *house* 5:13 [a]Compare Psalm 106:1

5:3 The time of three feasts: the Feast of Trumpets, the Day of Atonement, and the Feast of Tabernacles. The **feast** here was probably Tabernacles which lasted seven days (see 7:8, 9).

5:10 Nothing . . . except the two tablets: Apparently the pot of manna and Aaron's rod had been lost by this time. See Heb. 9:4; Ex. 16:32–34; Num. 17:10, 11.

5:11, 12 all the priests: Normally the priests and **singers** took turns serving 15 days out of each year (see 1 Chr. 24; 25). On this important occasion all 24 **divisions** were represented.

5:14 the glory of the LORD: A visible manifestation of God's presence. Thus did God honor the obedience of both Moses (see Ex. 40:34) and Solomon.

Israel, who has fulfilled with His hands *what* He spoke with His mouth to my father David, saying, 5'Since the day that I brought My people out of the land of Egypt, I have chosen no city from any tribe of Israel *in which* to build a house, that My name might be there, nor did I choose any man to be a ruler over My people Israel. 6Yet I have chosen Jerusalem, that My name may be there, and I have chosen David to be over My people Israel.' 7Now it was in the heart of my father David to build a temple[a] for the name of the LORD God of Israel. 8But the LORD said to my father David, 'Whereas it was in your heart to build a temple for My name, you did well in that it was in your heart. 9Nevertheless you shall not build the temple, but your son who will come from your body, he shall build the temple for My name.' 10So the LORD has fulfilled His word which He spoke, and I have filled the position of my father David, and sit on the throne of Israel, as the LORD promised; and I have built the temple for the name of the LORD God of Israel. 11And there I have put the ark, in which *is* the covenant of the LORD which He made with the children of Israel."

Solomon's Prayer of Dedication

12Then *Solomon*[a] stood before the altar of the LORD in the presence of all the assembly of Israel, and spread out his hands 13(for Solomon had made a bronze platform five cubits long, five cubits wide, and three cubits high, and had set it in the midst of the court; and he stood on it, knelt down on his knees before all the assembly of Israel, and spread out his hands toward heaven); 14and he said: "LORD God of Israel, *there is* no God in heaven or on earth like You, who keep *Your* covenant and mercy with Your servants who walk before You with all their hearts. 15You have kept what You promised Your servant David my father; You have both spoken with Your mouth and fulfilled *it* with Your hand, as *it is* this day. 16Therefore, LORD God of Israel, now keep what You promised Your servant David my father, saying, 'You shall not fail to have a man sit before Me on the throne of Israel, only if your sons take heed to their way, that they walk in My law as you have walked before Me.' 17And now, O LORD God of Israel, let Your word come true, which You have spoken to Your servant David.

18"But will God indeed dwell with men on the earth? Behold, heaven and the heaven of heavens cannot contain You. How much less this temple[a] which I have built! 19Yet regard the prayer of Your servant and his supplication, O LORD my God, and listen to the cry and the prayer which Your servant is praying before You: 20that Your eyes may be open toward this temple day and night, toward the place where *You* said *You would* put Your name, that You may hear the prayer which Your servant makes toward this place. 21And may You hear the supplications of Your servant and of Your people Israel, when they pray toward this place. Hear from heaven Your dwelling place, and when You hear, forgive.

22"If anyone sins against his neighbor,

6:7 [a]Literally *house,* and so in verses 8–10 6:12 [a]Literally *he* (compare 1 Kings 8:22) 6:18 [a]Literally *house*

6:5 that My name might be there: That I might reveal Myself there (see v. 20).

6:13 Leaders were not known to publicly prostrate themselves in a position of humility, yet Solomon built a platform specifically for the purpose of bowing down before God in the sight of the people.

6:20 Your name: The God of the universe (v. 18) made His presence especially accessible at the place of worship; He still does.

6:22 forced to take an oath: By the judges who were charged with determining the guilt or innocence of accused persons (see Ex. 22:8–15).

and is forced to take an oath, and comes
and takes an oath before Your altar in this
temple, [23]then hear from heaven, and act,
and judge Your servants, bringing retribu-
tion on the wicked by bringing his way on
his own head, and justifying the righteous
by giving him according to his righteous-
ness.

[24]"Or if Your people Israel are defeated
before an enemy because they have sinned
against You, and return and confess Your
name, and pray and make supplication
before You in this temple, [25]then hear
from heaven and forgive the sin of Your
people Israel, and bring them back to the
land which You gave to them and their
fathers.

[26]"When the heavens are shut up and
there is no rain because they have sinned
against You, when they pray toward this
place and confess Your name, and turn
from their sin because You afflict them,
[27]then hear *in* heaven, and forgive the sin of
Your servants, Your people Israel, that You
may teach them the good way in which
they should walk; and send rain on Your
land which You have given to Your people
as an inheritance.

[28]"When there is famine in the land,
pestilence or blight or mildew, locusts or
grasshoppers; when their enemies besiege
them in the land of their cities; whatever
plague or whatever sickness *there is;*
[29]whatever prayer, whatever supplication
is *made* by anyone, or by all Your people Is-
rael, when each one knows his own bur-
den and his own grief, and spreads out his
hands to this temple: [30]then hear from
heaven Your dwelling place, and forgive,
and give to everyone according to all his
ways, whose heart You know (for You
alone know the hearts of the sons of men),
[31]that they may fear You, to walk in Your
ways as long as they live in the land which
You gave to our fathers.

[32]"Moreover, concerning a foreigner,
who is not of Your people Israel, but has
come from a far country for the sake of
Your great name and Your mighty hand
and Your outstretched arm, when they
come and pray in this temple; [33]then hear
from heaven Your dwelling place, and do
according to all for which the foreigner
calls to You, that all peoples of the earth
may know Your name and fear You, as *do*
Your people Israel, and that they may
know that this temple which I have built is
called by Your name.

[34]"When Your people go out to battle
against their enemies, wherever You send
them, and when they pray to You toward
this city which You have chosen and the
temple which I have built for Your name,
[35]then hear from heaven their prayer and
their supplication, and maintain their
cause.

[36]"When they sin against You (for *there is*
no one who does not sin), and You become
angry with them and deliver them to the
enemy, and they take them captive to a
land far or near; [37]*yet* when they come to
themselves in the land where they were
carried captive, and repent, and make sup-
plication to You in the land of their captiv-
ity, saying, 'We have sinned, we have done
wrong, and have committed wickedness';
[38]and *when* they return to You with all their
heart and with all their soul in the land of
their captivity, where they have been car-
ried captive, and pray toward their land
which You gave to their fathers, the city
which You have chosen, and toward the
temple which I have built for Your name:
[39]then hear from heaven Your dwelling
place their prayer and their supplications,
and maintain their cause, and forgive Your
people who have sinned against You.
[40]Now, my God, I pray, let Your eyes be
open and *let* Your ears *be* attentive to the
prayer *made* in this place.

6:23 Maintain moral order in Your world.
6:33 know Your name: Answer prayer so that those who pray may know that You are God.

41 "Now therefore,
Arise, O LORD God, to Your resting
place,
You and the ark of Your strength.
Let Your priests, O LORD God, be
clothed with salvation,
And let Your saints rejoice in
goodness.

42 "O LORD God, do not turn away the
face of Your Anointed;
Remember the mercies of Your
servant David."[a]

CHAPTER 7

Solomon Dedicates the Temple

When Solomon had finished praying,
fire came down from heaven and con-
sumed the burnt offering and the sacri-
fices; and the glory of the LORD filled the
temple.[a] 2And the priests could not enter
the house of the LORD, because the glory of
the LORD had filled the LORD's house.
3When all the children of Israel saw how
the fire came down, and the glory of the
LORD on the temple, they bowed their faces
to the ground on the pavement, and wor-
shiped and praised the LORD, *saying:*

"For *He is* good,
For His mercy *endures* forever."[a]

6:42 [a]Compare Psalm 132:8–10 7:1 [a]Literally *house* 7:3 [a]Compare Psalm 106:1 7:6 [a]Compare Psalm 106:1 7:8 [a]That is, the Shihor (compare 1 Chronicles 13:5)

4Then the king and all the people of-
fered sacrifices before the LORD. 5King Sol-
omon offered a sacrifice of twenty-two
thousand bulls and one hundred and
twenty thousand sheep. So the king and all
the people dedicated the house of God.
6And the priests attended to their services;
the Lē'vītes also with instruments of the
music of the LORD, which King David had
made to praise the LORD, saying, "For His
mercy *endures* forever,"[a] whenever David
offered praise by their ministry. The priests
sounded trumpets opposite them, while all
Israel stood.
7Furthermore Solomon consecrated the
middle of the court that *was* in front of the
house of the LORD; for there he offered
burnt offerings and the fat of the peace of-
ferings, because the bronze altar which
Solomon had made was not able to receive
the burnt offerings, the grain offerings, and
the fat.
8At that time Solomon kept the feast
seven days, and all Israel with him, a very
great assembly from the entrance of Hā'-
math to the Brook of Egypt.[a] 9And on the
eighth day they held a sacred assembly, for
they observed the dedication of the altar
seven days, and the feast seven days. 10On
the twenty-third day of the seventh month
he sent the people away to their tents, joy-
ful and glad of heart for the good that the
LORD had done for David, for Solomon,
and for His people Israel. 11Thus Solomon
finished the house of the LORD and the
king's house; and Solomon successfully ac-
complished all that came into his heart to

6:41, 42 The chronicler's version of Solomon's prayer closes slightly differently than that of 1 Kin. 8:50–53. Here Solomon is reported to have closed with a portion of Ps. 132, a psalm that concerns the movement of the ark of the covenant to Jerusalem (see Ps. 132:8–10).

7:1 The **fire** from heaven and the fullness of God's **glory** indicated that He was well pleased (see Ex. 40:34–38).

7:6 For His mercy endures forever: A refrain which is repeated in every verse of Ps. 136.

7:7 middle of the court: Perhaps the original rock threshing floor on which David offered sacrifice (see 1 Chr. 21:18–27).

7:9 the eighth day: The holy convocation held in connection with the Feast of Tabernacles (see Lev. 23:33–36).

WE NEED EACH OTHER

David R. Enlow

One great product of seeing urgent needs met through prayer involves realizing our interdependence upon others, especially brothers and sisters in Christ. Do we really understand how much we need each other? Besides our prayers, we must share with others our time, our encouragement, our availability, our sympathy, and our empathy.

"Recognizing our interdependence is humbling but necessary."

Recognizing our interdependence is humbling but necessary; through it we learn to pray at every stage of life, especially as we grow older. Humility is a virtue, for without it, we cannot grow closer to God. It is also a prime key to revival, the subject of many earnest prayers by people of all ages. God says: "If My people who are called by My name will humble themselves, and pray and seek My face, and turn from their wicked ways, then I will hear from heaven, and will forgive their sin and heal their land" (2 Chr. 7:14). ✦

make in the house of the LORD and in his
own house.

God's Second Appearance to Solomon

12Then the LORD appeared to Solomon
by night, and said to him: "I have heard
your prayer, and have chosen this place for
Myself as a house of sacrifice. 13When I
shut up heaven and there is no rain, or
command the locusts to devour the land,
or send pestilence among My people, 14if
My people who are called by My name will
humble themselves, and pray and seek My
face, and turn from their wicked ways,
then I will hear from heaven, and will forgive their sin and heal their land. 15Now
My eyes will be open and My ears attentive to prayer *made* in this place. 16For now
I have chosen and sanctified this house,
that My name may be there forever; and
My eyes and My heart will be there perpetually. 17As for you, if you walk before Me
as your father David walked, and do according to all that I have commanded you,
and if you keep My statutes and My judgments, 18then I will establish the throne of

7:12–22 Like the fire from heaven and the glory-cloud in the temple, this appearance confirmed God's approval of **Solomon**. But the most conspicuous element in the message is the conditionality of God's blessings: **if you walk before Me . . . But if you turn away** (vv. 17, 19).

7:14 The fate of every nation rests with its individual citizens. As each of us takes responsibility for his or her own walk with the Lord, we do our part in changing the course of the country.

7:16 While this verse seems to indicate the temple would stand forever, vv. 21, 22 explain that such preservation was conditional. If the people turned their hearts from God, He would reject the temple.

your kingdom, as I covenanted with David your father, saying, 'You shall not fail *to have* a man as ruler in Israel.'

19"But if you turn away and forsake My statutes and My commandments which I have set before you, and go and serve other gods, and worship them, 20then I will uproot them from My land which I have given them; and this house which I have sanctified for My name I will cast out of My sight, and will make it a proverb and a byword among all peoples.

21"And *as for* this house, which is exalted, everyone who passes by it will be astonished and say, 'Why has the LORD done thus to this land and this house?' 22Then they will answer, 'Because they forsook the LORD God of their fathers, who brought them out of the land of Egypt, and embraced other gods, and worshiped them and served them; therefore He has brought all this calamity on them.' "

CHAPTER 8

Solomon's Additional Achievements

It came to pass at the end of twenty years, when Solomon had built the house of the LORD and his own house, 2that the cities which Hī'ram[a] had given to Solomon, Solomon built them; and he settled the children of Israel there. 3And Solomon went to Hā'math Zō'bah and seized it. 4He also built Tad'mor in the wilderness, and all the storage cities which he built in Hā'math. 5He built Upper Beth Hor'on and Lower Beth Hor'on, fortified cities *with* walls, gates, and bars, 6also Bā'a·lath and all the storage cities that Solomon had, and all the chariot cities and the cities of the cavalry, and all that Solomon desired to build in Jerusalem, in Lebanon, and in all the land of his dominion.

7All the people *who were* left of the Hit'tītes, Am'o·rītes, Per'iz·zītes, Hī'vītes, and Jeb'ū·sītes, who *were* not of Israel—8that is, their descendants who were left in the land after them, whom the children of Israel did not destroy—from these Solomon raised forced labor, as it is to this day. 9But Solomon did not make the children of Israel servants for his work. Some *were* men of war, captains of his officers, captains of his chariots, and his cavalry. 10And others *were* chiefs of the officials of King Solomon: two hundred and fifty, who ruled over the people.

11Now Solomon brought the daughter of Pharaoh up from the City of David to the house he had built for her, for he said, "My wife shall not dwell in the house of David king of Israel, because *the places* to which the ark of the LORD has come are holy."

12Then Solomon offered burnt offerings to the LORD on the altar of the LORD which he had built before the vestibule, 13according to the daily rate, offering according to the commandment of Moses, for the Sabbaths, the New Moons, and the three appointed yearly feasts—the Feast of Unleavened Bread, the Feast of Weeks, and the Feast of Tabernacles. 14And, according to the order of David his father, he appointed the divisions of the priests for their service, the Lē'vītes for their duties (to praise and serve before the priests) as the duty of each day required, and the gatekeepers by their divisions at each gate; for so David the man of God had commanded. 15They did not depart from the command of the king to the priests and Lē'vītes concerning any matter or concerning the treasuries.

16Now all the work of Solomon was well-ordered from[a] the day of the foundation of the house of the LORD until it was

8:2 [a]Hebrew *Huram* (compare 2 Chronicles 2:3)
8:16 [a]Following Septuagint, Syriac, and Vulgate; Masoretic Text reads *as far as.*

8:1—9:31 The great extent to which the Lord established Solomon's kingdom (7:18).
8:11 Apparently it did not occur to Solomon to turn Pharaoh's daughter to the worship of the true God. He left her to her pagan ways, but removed her from the temple precincts.

finished. So the house of the LORD was
completed.
[17]Then Solomon went to Ē′zi·on Gē′ber
and Ē′lath[a] on the seacoast, in the land of
Ē′dom. [18]And Hī′ram sent him ships by the
hand of his servants, and servants who
knew the sea. They went with the servants
of Solomon to Ō′phir, and acquired four
hundred and fifty talents of gold from
there, and brought it to King Solomon.

CHAPTER 9

The Queen of Sheba's Praise of Solomon

Now when the queen of Shē′ba heard of
the fame of Solomon, she came to Jerusa-
lem to test Solomon with hard questions,
having a very great retinue, camels that
bore spices, gold in abundance, and pre-
cious stones; and when she came to Sol-
omon, she spoke with him about all that
was in her heart. [2]So Solomon answered all
her questions; there was nothing so diffi-
cult for Solomon that he could not explain
it to her. [3]And when the queen of Shē′ba
had seen the wisdom of Solomon, the
house that he had built, [4]the food on his
table, the seating of his servants, the ser-
vice of his waiters and their apparel, his
cupbearers and their apparel, and his
entryway by which he went up to the
house of the LORD, there was no more
spirit in her.
[5]Then she said to the king: "*It was* a true
report which I heard in my own land about
your words and your wisdom. [6]However I
did not believe their words until I came
and saw with my own eyes; and indeed
the half of the greatness of your wisdom
was not told me. You exceed the fame of
which I heard. [7]Happy *are* your men and
happy *are* these your servants, who stand
continually before you and hear your wis-
dom! [8]Blessed be the LORD your God, who
delighted in you, setting you on His throne
to be king for the LORD your God! Because
your God has loved Israel, to establish
them forever, therefore He made you king
over them, to do justice and righteous-
ness."
[9]And she gave the king one hundred
and twenty talents of gold, spices in
great abundance, and precious stones;
there never were any spices such as
those the queen of Shē′ba gave to King Sol-
omon.
[10]Also, the servants of Hī′ram and the
servants of Solomon, who brought gold
from Ō′phir, brought algum[a] wood and
precious stones. [11]And the king made
walkways *of* the algum[a] wood for the
house of the LORD and for the king's house,
also harps and stringed instruments for
singers; and there were none such *as these*
seen before in the land of Judah.
[12]Now King Solomon gave to the queen
of Shē′ba all she desired, whatever she
asked, *much more* than she had brought to
the king. So she turned and went to her
own country, she and her servants.

Solomon's Great Wealth

[13]The weight of gold that came to Sol-
omon yearly was six hundred and sixty-six
talents of gold, [14]besides *what* the traveling
merchants and traders brought. And all
the kings of Arabia and governors of the
country brought gold and silver to Sol-
omon. [15]And King Solomon made two
hundred large shields of hammered gold;
six hundred *shekels* of hammered gold
went into each shield. [16]*He* also *made* three
hundred shields of hammered gold; three
hundred *shekels*[a] of gold went into each

8:17 [a]Hebrew *Eloth* (compare 2 Kings 14:22)
9:10 [a]Or *almug* (compare 1 Kings 10:11, 12)
9:11 [a]Or *almug* (compare 1 Kings 10:11, 12)
9:16 [a]Or *three minas* (compare 1 Kings 10:17)

9:8 In 1 Kin. 10:9 the queen blesses the Lord for setting Solomon on "the throne of Israel." But here she calls it **His throne**, recognizing God as the true King of Israel.

9:13 gold that came . . . yearly: Tribute from vassal peoples (see also v. 24).

shield. The king put them in the House of the Forest of Lebanon.

17 Moreover the king made a great throne of ivory, and overlaid it with pure gold. 18 The throne *had* six steps, with a footstool of gold, *which were* fastened to the throne; there were armrests on either side of the place of the seat, and two lions stood beside the armrests. 19 Twelve lions stood there, one on each side of the six steps; nothing like *this* had been made for any *other* kingdom.

20 All King Solomon's drinking vessels *were* gold, and all the vessels of the House of the Forest of Lebanon *were* pure gold. Not *one was* silver, for this was accounted as nothing in the days of Solomon. 21 For the king's ships went to Tar'shish with the servants of Hī'ram.[a] Once every three years the merchant ships[b] came, bringing gold, silver, ivory, apes, and monkeys.[c]

22 So King Solomon surpassed all the kings of the earth in riches and wisdom. 23 And all the kings of the earth sought the presence of Solomon to hear his wisdom, which God had put in his heart. 24 Each man brought his present: articles of silver and gold, garments, armor, spices, horses, and mules, at a set rate year by year.

25 Solomon had four thousand stalls for horses and chariots, and twelve thousand horsemen whom he stationed in the chariot cities and with the king at Jerusalem.

26 So he reigned over all the kings from the River[a] to the land of the Phi·lis'tines, as far as the border of Egypt. 27 The king made silver *as common* in Jerusalem as stones, and he made cedar trees as abundant as the sycamores which *are* in the lowland.

28 And they brought horses to Solomon from Egypt and from all lands.

Death of Solomon

29 Now the rest of the acts of Solomon, first and last, *are* they not written in the book of Nathan the prophet, in the prophecy of A·hī'jah the Shī'lo·nīte, and in the visions of Id'dō the seer concerning Jer·o·bō'am the son of Nē'bat? 30 Solomon reigned in Jerusalem over all Israel forty years. 31 Then Solomon rested with his fathers, and was buried in the City of David his father. And Rē·ho·bō'am his son reigned in his place.

CHAPTER 10

The Revolt Against Rehoboam

And Rē·ho·bō'am went to Shē'chem, for all Israel had gone to Shē'chem to make him king. 2 So it happened, when Jer·o·bō'am the son of Nē'bat heard *it* (he was in Egypt, where he had fled from the presence of King Solomon), that Jer·o·bō'am returned from Egypt. 3 Then they sent for him and called him. And Jer·o·bō'am and all Israel came and spoke to Rē·ho·bō'am, saying, 4 "Your father made our yoke heavy; now therefore, lighten the burdensome service of your father and his heavy yoke which he put on us, and we will serve you."

5 So he said to them, "Come back to me after three days." And the people departed.

6 Then King Rē·ho·bō'am consulted the elders who stood before his father Solomon while he still lived, saying, "How do you advise *me* to answer these people?"

7 And they spoke to him, saying, "If you

9:21 [a]Hebrew *Huram* (compare 1 Kings 10:22) [b]Literally *ships of Tarshish* (deep-sea vessels) [c]Or *peacocks*
9:26 [a]That is, the Euphrates

9:29 The books mentioned here may have been used by the chronicler as resources; however, they are not part of the canon and seem to have disappeared.

10:1—36:23 The remainder of Chronicles enumerates the descendants of David who ruled Judah until it fell into the hands of the Babylonians. The purpose is not to demonstrate the failure of God's promise to David (1 Chr. 17), but to show that the promise still awaits fulfillment. The One who would reign as the perfect Son of David was yet to come.

are kind to these people, and please them, and speak good words to them, they will be your servants forever."

8But he rejected the advice which the el-
ders had given him, and consulted the
young men who had grown up with him,
who stood before him. 9And he said to
them, "What advice do you give? How
should we answer this people who have
spoken to me, saying, 'Lighten the yoke
which your father put on us'?"

10Then the young men who had grown
up with him spoke to him, saying,
"Thus you should speak to the people
who have spoken to you, saying, 'Your
father made our yoke heavy, but you make
it lighter on us'—thus you shall say to
them: 'My little *finger* shall be thicker than
my father's waist! 11And now, whereas my
father put a heavy yoke on you, I will add
to your yoke; my father chastised you with
whips, but I *will chastise you* with
scourges!' "[a]

12So Jer•o•bō'am and all the people came
to Rē•ho•bō'am on the third day, as the
king had directed, saying, "Come back to
me the third day." 13Then the king an-
swered them roughly. King Rē•ho•bō'am
rejected the advice of the elders, 14and
he spoke to them according to the advice
of the young men, saying, "My father[a]
made your yoke heavy, but I will add to
it; my father chastised you with whips,
but I *will chastise you* with scourges!"[b]
15So the king did not listen to the people;
for the turn *of events* was from God, that
the LORD might fulfill His word, which
He had spoken by the hand of A•hī'jah
the Shī'lo•nīte to Jer•o•bō'am the son of
Nē'bat.

16Now when all Israel *saw* that the king
did not listen to them, the people an-
swered the king, saying:

"What share have we in David?
We have no inheritance in the son of
Jesse.
Every man to your tents, O Israel!
Now see to your own house, O Da-
vid!"

So all Israel departed to their tents. 17But
Rē•ho•bō'am reigned over the children of
Israel who dwelt in the cities of Judah.

18Then King Rē•ho•bō'am sent Ha-
dor'am, who *was* in charge of revenue; but
the children of Israel stoned him with
stones, and he died. Therefore King
Rē•ho•bō'am mounted *his* chariot in haste
to flee to Jerusalem. 19So Israel has been in
rebellion against the house of David to this
day.

CHAPTER 11

Now when Rē•ho•bō'am came to
Jerusalem, he assembled from the
house of Judah and Benjamin one
hundred and eighty thousand chosen *men*
who were warriors, to fight against Israel,
that he might restore the kingdom to
Rē•ho•bō'am.

2But the word of the LORD came to
She•māi'ah the man of God, saying,
3"Speak to Rē•ho•bō'am the son of Sol-
omon, king of Judah, and to all Israel in Ju-
dah and Benjamin, saying, 4'Thus says the
LORD: "You shall not go up or fight against
your brethren! Let every man return to
his house, for this thing is from Me." ' "
Therefore they obeyed the words of the
LORD, and turned back from attacking
Jer•o•bō'am.

10:11 [a]Literally *scorpions* 10:14 [a]Following many Hebrew manuscripts, Septuagint, Syriac, and Vulgate (compare verse 10 and 1 Kings 12:14); Masoretic Text reads *I.* [b]Literally *scorpions*

10:15 the turn of events was from God: Both Rehoboam and the northern tribes made their own free choices. Yet through those choices God brought about the fulfillment of the prophecy to divide Israel for Solomon's apostasy. See 11:4 and 1 Kin. 11:30–32.

11:2–4 they obeyed: Rehoboam at least listened and accepted God's will spoken by the prophet.

Rehoboam Fortifies the Cities

[5]So Rē·ho·bō′am dwelt in Jerusalem, and built cities for defense in Judah. [6]And he built Bethlehem, Ē′tam, Te·kō′a, [7]Beth Zūr, Sō′chōh, A·dul′lam, [8]Gath, Ma·rē′-shah, Ziph, [9]Ad·o·rā′im, Lā′chish, A·zē′-kah, [10]Zō′rah, Aī′ja·lon, and Hē′bron, which are in Judah and Benjamin, fortified cities. [11]And he fortified the strongholds, and put captains in them, and stores of food, oil, and wine. [12]Also in every city *he put* shields and spears, and made them very strong, having Judah and Benjamin on his side.

Priests and Levites Move to Judah

[13]And from all their territories the priests and the Lē′vītes who *were* in all Israel took their stand with him. [14]For the Lē′vītes left their common-lands and their possessions and came to Judah and Jerusalem, for Jer·o·bō′am and his sons had rejected them from serving as priests to the LORD. [15]Then he appointed for himself priests for the high places, for the demons, and the calf idols which he had made. [16]And after *the Lē′vītes* left,[a] those from all the tribes of Israel, such as set their heart to seek the LORD God of Israel, came to Jerusalem to sacrifice to the LORD God of their fathers. [17]So they strengthened the kingdom of Judah, and made Rē·ho·bō′am the son of Solomon strong for three years, because they walked in the way of David and Solomon for three years.

The Family of Rehoboam

[18]Then Rē·ho·bō′am took for himself as wife Mā′ha·lath the daughter of Jer′i·moth the son of David, *and of* Ab·i·hā′il the daughter of E·lī′ah the son of Jesse. [19]And she bore him children: Jē′ush, Sham·a·rī′ah, and Zā′ham. [20]After her he took Mā′a·chah the granddaughter[a] of Ab′sa·lom; and she bore him A·bī′jah, At′taī, Zī′za, and She·lō′mith. [21]Now Rē·ho·bō′am loved Mā′a·chah the granddaughter of Ab′sa·lom more than all his wives and his concubines; for he took eighteen wives and sixty concubines, and begot twenty-eight sons and sixty daughters. [22]And Rē·ho·bō′am appointed A·bī′jah the son of Mā′a·chah as chief, *to be* leader among his brothers; for he *intended* to make him king. [23]He dealt wisely, and dispersed some of his sons throughout all the territories of Judah and Benjamin, to every fortified city; and he gave them provisions in abundance. He also sought many wives *for them.*

CHAPTER 12

Egypt Attacks Judah

Now it came to pass, when Rē·ho·bō′am had established the kingdom and had strengthened himself, that he forsook the law of the LORD, and all Israel along with him. [2]And it happened in the fifth year of

11:16 [a]Literally *after them* 11:20 [a]Literally *daughter,* but in the broader sense of granddaughter (compare 2 Chronicles 13:2)

11:5–10 Bethlehem . . . Hebron: Rehoboam left only his northern border with no fortification. He probably hoped for reconciliation with the rebellious northern tribes.

11:13–15 The **Levites** must have protested violently against the idolatrous worship established at Bethel and Dan by Jeroboam (see 1 Kin. 12:28–31).

11:16, 17 strengthened . . . Judah: Besides the Levites there were others from the northern tribes who chose to follow Israel's true God. They moved from their homes to Judah.

11:22 intended to make him king: Rehoboam violated the instructions of Deut. 21:15–17 by favoring **Abijah**, the son of his most loved wife Maachah, over his true firstborn son, which was probably Jeush, the son of Mahalath (vv. 18, 19; see also 21:3).

12:2 Shishak: Reigned about 940 to 915 B.C. **because they had transgressed**: This explanation is not found in the parallel account in 1 Kin. 14:25. The chronicler emphasizes the consequences of disobedience. See v. 5.

King Rē·ho·bō′am *that* Shī′shak king of
Egypt came up against Jerusalem, because
they had transgressed against the LORD,
3with twelve hundred chariots, sixty thou-
sand horsemen, and people without num-
ber who came with him out of Egypt—the
Lū′bim and the Suk′ki·im and the Ethio-
pians. 4And he took the fortified cities of
Judah and came to Jerusalem.

5Then She·māi′ah the prophet came to
Rē·ho·bō′am and the leaders of Judah,
who were gathered together in Jerusalem
because of Shī′shak, and said to them,
"Thus says the LORD: 'You have forsaken
Me, and therefore I also have left you in the
hand of Shī′shak.' "

6So the leaders of Israel and the king
humbled themselves; and they said, "The
LORD *is* righteous."

7Now when the LORD saw that they
humbled themselves, the word of the LORD
came to She·māi′ah, saying, "They have
humbled themselves; *therefore* I will not de-
stroy them, but I will grant them some de-
liverance. My wrath shall not be poured
out on Jerusalem by the hand of Shī′shak.
8Nevertheless they will be his servants,
that they may distinguish My service from
the service of the kingdoms of the na-
tions."

9So Shī′shak king of Egypt came up
against Jerusalem, and took away the trea-
sures of the house of the LORD and the trea-
sures of the king's house; he took every-
thing. He also carried away the gold
shields which Solomon had made. 10Then
King Rē·ho·bō′am made bronze shields in
their place, and committed *them* to the
hands of the captains of the guard, who
guarded the doorway of the king's house.
11And whenever the king entered the
house of the LORD, the guard would go and
bring them out; then they would take them
back into the guardroom. 12When he hum-
bled himself, the wrath of the LORD turned
from him, so as not to destroy *him* com-
pletely; and things also went well in Judah.

The End of Rehoboam's Reign

13Thus King Rē·ho·bō′am strengthened
himself in Jerusalem and reigned. Now
Rē·ho·bō′am *was* forty-one years old when
he became king; and he reigned seventeen
years in Jerusalem, the city which the LORD
had chosen out of all the tribes of Israel, to
put His name there. His mother's name
was Nā′a·mah, an Am′mon·ī·tess. 14And
he did evil, because he did not prepare his
heart to seek the LORD.

15The acts of Rē·ho·bō′am, first and last,
are they not written in the book of
She·māi′ah the prophet, and of Id′dō the
seer concerning genealogies? And *there
were* wars between Rē·ho·bō′am and
Jer·o·bō′am all their days. 16So Rē·ho-
bō′am rested with his fathers, and was
buried in the City of David. Then A·bī′jah[a]
his son reigned in his place.

CHAPTER 13

Abijah Reigns in Judah

In the eighteenth year of King Jer·o-
bō′am, A·bī′jah became king over Judah.
2He reigned three years in Jerusalem. His

12:16 [a]Spelled *Abijam* in 1 Kings 14:31

12:5 The underlying cause of this invasion was Judah's sin. The nation had abandoned God, so He abandoned them. See v. 2.

12:6 While the author of Kings refers to the northern kingdom as "Israel" and the southern kingdom as "Judah," the chronicler frequently refers to Judah as "Israel." This is because the people of Judah considered the descendants of David to be the only true kings of Israel and they regarded themselves as the only true Israelites because they remained loyal.

12:7–12 When Rehoboam and the leaders of Israel humbled themselves in repentance for their sin, the Lord forgave them and prevented Shishak from destroying the nation. However, God used the opportunity to teach Israel the consequences of turning from His loving rule to sin's painful enslavement.

mother's name *was* Mī·chaī′ah[a] the daugh-
ter of Ū·rī′el of Gib′ē·ah.
And there was war between A·bī′jah
and Jer·o·bō′am. 3A·bī′jah set the battle in
order with an army of valiant warriors,
four hundred thousand choice men.
Jer·o·bō′am also drew up in battle forma-
tion against him with eight hundred thou-
sand choice men, mighty men of valor.
4Then A·bī′jah stood on Mount
Zem·a·rā′im, which *is* in the mountains of
Ē′phra·im, and said, "Hear me, Jer·o-
bō′am and all Israel: 5Should you not know
that the LORD God of Israel gave the do-
minion over Israel to David forever, to him
and his sons, by a covenant of salt? 6Yet
Jer·o·bō′am the son of Nē′bat, the servant
of Solomon the son of David, rose up and
rebelled against his lord. 7Then worthless
rogues gathered to him, and strengthened
themselves against Rē·ho·bō′am the son of
Solomon, when Rē·ho·bō′am was young
and inexperienced and could not with-
stand them. 8And now you think to with-
stand the kingdom of the LORD, which is in
the hand of the sons of David; and you *are*
a great multitude, and with you are the
gold calves which Jer·o·bō′am made for
you as gods. 9Have you not cast out the
priests of the LORD, the sons of Aaron, and
the Lē′vītes, and made for yourselves
priests, like the peoples of *other* lands, so
that whoever comes to consecrate himself
with a young bull and seven rams may be
a priest of *things that are* not gods? 10But as
for us, the LORD *is* our God, and we have
not forsaken Him; and the priests who
minister to the LORD *are* the sons of Aaron,
and the Lē′vītes *attend* to *their* duties.
11And they burn to the LORD every morn-
ing and every evening burnt sacrifices and
sweet incense; *they* also *set* the showbread
in order on the pure *gold* table, and the
lampstand of gold with its lamps to burn
every evening; for we keep the command
of the LORD our God, but you have for-
saken Him. 12Now look, God Himself is
with us as *our* head, and His priests with
sounding trumpets to sound the alarm
against you. O children of Israel, do not
fight against the LORD God of your fathers,
for you shall not prosper!"
13But Jer·o·bō′am caused an ambush to
go around behind them; so they were in front
of Judah, and the ambush *was* behind them.
14And when Judah looked around, to their
surprise the battle line *was* at both front
and rear; and they cried out to the LORD,
and the priests sounded the trumpets.
15Then the men of Judah gave a shout; and as
the men of Judah shouted, it happened
that God struck Jer·o·bō′am and all Israel be-
fore A·bī′jah and Judah. 16And the children
of Israel fled before Judah, and God deliv-
ered them into their hand. 17Then A·bī′jah
and his people struck them with a great
slaughter; so five hundred thousand choice
men of Israel fell slain. 18Thus the children of
Israel were subdued at that time; and the
children of Judah prevailed, because they
relied on the LORD God of their fathers.
19And A·bī′jah pursued Jer·o·bō′am and
took cities from him: Beth′el with its vil-
lages, Je·shā′nah with its villages, and
Ē′phra·in[a] with its villages. 20So Jer·o-
bō′am did not recover strength again in the
days of A·bī′jah; and the LORD struck him,
and he died.
21But A·bī′jah grew mighty, married
fourteen wives, and begot twenty-two
sons and sixteen daughters. 22Now the rest
of the acts of A·bī′jah, his ways, and his
sayings *are* written in the annals of the
prophet Id′dō.

13:2 [a]Spelled *Maachah* in 11:20, 21 and 1 Kings 15:2
13:19 [a]Or *Ephron*

13:5 covenant of salt: A perpetual covenant that could not be broken (see Lev. 2:13; Num. 18:19). The figure of salt was employed probably because salt was used to preserve foods for long periods.

13:15 Israel's superior numbers (v. 3) and strategy (vv. 13, 14) were to no avail because the victory was divine in origin.

CHAPTER 14

So A·bī'jah rested with his fathers, and they buried him in the City of David. Then Ā'sa his son reigned in his place. In his days the land was quiet for ten years.

Asa Reigns in Judah

2Ā'sa did *what was* good and right in the eyes of the LORD his God, 3for he removed the altars of the foreign *gods* and the high places, and broke down the *sacred* pillars and cut down the wooden images. 4He commanded Judah to seek the LORD God of their fathers, and to observe the law and the commandment. 5He also removed the high places and the incense altars from all the cities of Judah, and the kingdom was quiet under him. 6And he built fortified cities in Judah, for the land had rest; he had no war in those years, because the LORD had given him rest. 7Therefore he said to Judah, "Let us build these cities and make walls around *them,* and towers, gates, and bars, *while* the land *is* yet before us, because we have sought the LORD our God; we have sought *Him,* and He has given us rest on every side." So they built and prospered. 8And Ā'sa had an army of three hundred thousand from Judah who carried shields and spears, and from Benjamin two hundred and eighty thousand men who carried shields and drew bows; all these *were* mighty men of valor.

9Then Zē'rah the Ethiopian came out against them with an army of a million men and three hundred chariots, and he came to Ma·rē'shah. 10So Ā'sa went out against him, and they set the troops in battle array in the Valley of Zeph'a·thah at Ma·rē'shah. 11And Ā'sa cried out to the LORD his God, and said, "LORD, *it is* nothing for You to help, whether with many or with those who have no power; help us, O LORD our God, for we rest on You, and in Your name we go against this multitude. O LORD, You *are* our God; do not let man prevail against You!"

12So the LORD struck the Ethiopians before Ā'sa and Judah, and the Ethiopians fled. 13And Ā'sa and the people who *were* with him pursued them to Gē'rar. So the Ethiopians were overthrown, and they could not recover, for they were broken before the LORD and His army. And they carried away very much spoil. 14Then they defeated all the cities around Gē'rar, for the fear of the LORD came upon them; and they plundered all the cities, for there was exceedingly much spoil in them. 15They also attacked the livestock enclosures, and carried off sheep and camels in abundance, and returned to Jerusalem.

CHAPTER 15

The Reforms of Asa

Now the Spirit of God came upon Az·a·rī'ah the son of Ō'ded. 2And he went

---

14:3 sacred pillars . . . wooden images: Shrines of Canaanite nature religions condemned in Deut. 12:1–3. While Asa's intentions were good, he was unable to completely rid the land of the pagan **high places** (see 15:17).

14:5 from all the cities of Judah: Thus concentrating worship in Jerusalem.

14:9 Zerah: Often identified as Osorkon I (924–895 B.C.), successor of Shishak as pharaoh of Egypt. His is the largest army recorded in the Old Testament.

14:11 in Your name we go: If we are on God's side, He is on our side (see 15:2). Asa's prayer, though born of desperation, expresses great confidence in the Lord. He had nothing to fear because he served the Lord faithfully in peace as well as in war. Today we must carefully avoid the temptation of becoming too busy when all is well, then suddenly remembering God when we face a crisis. Through faithful, consistent fellowship in the Lord, we can depend on Him in time of need.

15:1–19 A more detailed account of Asa's reform mentioned in 14:3–5.

15:1 the Spirit of God came upon Azariah: Most great revivals begin with Spirit-filled individuals who speak on God's behalf.

out to meet Ā'sa, and said to him: "Hear
me, Ā'sa, and all Judah and Benjamin. The
LORD *is* with you while you are with Him.
If you seek Him, He will be found by you;
but if you forsake Him, He will forsake
you. 3For a long time Israel *has been* with-
out the true God, without a teaching priest,
and without law; 4but when in their trou-
ble they turned to the LORD God of Israel,
and sought Him, He was found by them.
5And in those times *there was* no peace to
the one who went out, nor to the one who
came in, but great turmoil *was* on all the
inhabitants of the lands. 6So nation was de-
stroyed by nation, and city by city, for God
troubled them with every adversity. 7But
you, be strong and do not let your hands
be weak, for your work shall be re-
warded!"

8And when Ā'sa heard these words and
the prophecy of Ō'ded[a] the prophet, he
took courage, and removed the abom-
inable idols from all the land of Judah and
Benjamin and from the cities which he had
taken in the mountains of Ē'phra·im; and
he restored the altar of the LORD that *was*
before the vestibule of the LORD. 9Then he
gathered all Judah and Benjamin, and
those who dwelt with them from
Ē'phra·im, Ma·nas'seh, and Sim'ē·on, for
they came over to him in great numbers
from Israel when they saw that the LORD
his God was with him.

10So they gathered together at Jerusalem
in the third month, in the fifteenth year of
the reign of Ā'sa. 11And they offered to the
LORD at that time seven hundred bulls and
seven thousand sheep from the spoil they
had brought. 12Then they entered into a
covenant to seek the LORD God of their
fathers with all their heart and with all
their soul; 13and whoever would not seek
the LORD God of Israel was to be put to
death, whether small or great, whether
man or woman. 14Then they took an oath
before the LORD with a loud voice, with
shouting and trumpets and rams' horns.
15And all Judah rejoiced at the oath, for
they had sworn with all their heart and
sought Him with all their soul; and He was
found by them, and the LORD gave them
rest all around.

16Also he removed Mā'a·chah, the
mother of Ā'sa the king, from *being* queen
mother, because she had made an obscene
image of A·shē'rah;[a] and Ā'sa cut down
her obscene image, then crushed and
burned *it* by the Brook Kid'ron. 17But the
high places were not removed from Israel.
Nevertheless the heart of Ā'sa was loyal all
his days.

18He also brought into the house of God
the things that his father had dedicated
and that he himself had dedicated: silver
and gold and utensils. 19And there was no
war until the thirty-fifth year of the reign
of Ā'sa.

CHAPTER 16

Asa's Treaty with Syria

In the thirty-sixth year of the reign of
Ā'sa, Bā'a·sha king of Israel came up
against Judah and built Rā'mah, that he
might let none go out or come in to Ā'sa

15:8 [a]Following Masoretic Text and Septuagint; Syriac and Vulgate read *Azariah the son of Oded* (compare verse 1). 15:16 [a]A Canaanite deity

15:3 a teaching priest: Both Asa and his son Jehoshaphat placed much importance on instruction in "the Book of the Law of the LORD" (see 17:7–9).

15:8 the prophecy of Oded the prophet: Through Azariah his son (see v. 1).

15:10 The Feast of Weeks was a one-day celebration held in the **third month**, and may have been the occasion for this renewing of their "covenant" (v. 12) obligations.

15:17 high places: It is probable that the Lord was worshiped on these hilltops (contrary to the law), as well as pagan gods. You do not have to be pagan to be disobedient.

king of Judah. 2Then Ā'sa brought silver
and gold from the treasuries of the
house of the LORD and of the king's
house, and sent to Ben-Hā'dad king of
Syria, who dwelt in Damascus, saying,
3"*Let there be* a treaty between you and me,
as there was between my father and your
father. See, I have sent you silver and gold;
come, break your treaty with Bā'a·sha king
of Israel, so that he will withdraw from
me."

4So Ben-Hā'dad heeded King Ā'sa, and
sent the captains of his armies against
the cities of Israel. They attacked Ī'jon,
Dan, Abel Mā'im, and all the storage
cities of Naph'ta·lī. 5Now it happened,
when Bā'a·sha heard *it,* that he stopped
building Rā'mah and ceased his work.
6Then King Ā'sa took all Judah, and they
carried away the stones and timber of
Rā'mah, which Bā'a·sha had used for
building; and with them he built Gē'ba
and Miz'pah.

Hanani's Message to Asa

7And at that time Ha·nā'nī the seer
came to Ā'sa king of Judah, and said to
him: "Because you have relied on the king
of Syria, and have not relied on the LORD
your God, therefore the army of the king of
Syria has escaped from your hand. 8Were
the Ethiopians and the Lū'bim not a huge
army with very many chariots and horse-
men? Yet, because you relied on the LORD,
He delivered them into your hand. 9For the
eyes of the LORD run to and fro throughout
the whole earth, to show Himself strong on
behalf of *those* whose heart *is* loyal to Him.
In this you have done foolishly; therefore
from now on you shall have wars." 10Then
Ā'sa was angry with the seer, and put him
in prison, for *he was* enraged at him be-
cause of this. And Ā'sa oppressed *some* of
the people at that time.

Illness and Death of Asa

11Note that the acts of Ā'sa, first and last,
are indeed written in the book of the kings
of Judah and Israel. 12And in the thirty-
ninth year of his reign, Ā'sa became dis-
eased in his feet, and his malady was se-
vere; yet in his disease he did not seek the
LORD, but the physicians.

13So Ā'sa rested with his fathers; he died
in the forty-first year of his reign. 14They
buried him in his own tomb, which he had
made for himself in the City of David; and
they laid him in the bed which was filled
with spices and various ingredients pre-
pared in a mixture of ointments. They
made a very great burning for him.

CHAPTER 17

Jehoshaphat Reigns in Judah

Then Je·hosh'a·phat his son reigned in
his place, and strengthened himself
against Israel. 2And he placed troops in all
the fortified cities of Judah, and set gar-
risons in the land of Judah and in the cities
of Ē'phra·im which Ā'sa his father had
taken. 3Now the LORD was with Je·hosh'-
a·phat, because he walked in the former
ways of his father David; he did not seek
the Bā'als, 4but sought the God[a] of his
father, and walked in His commandments
and not according to the acts of Israel.
5Therefore the LORD established the king-
dom in his hand; and all Judah gave pres-
ents to Je·hosh'a·phat, and he had riches
and honor in abundance. 6And his heart
took delight in the ways of the LORD; more-
over he removed the high places and
wooden images from Judah.

7Also in the third year of his reign he
sent his leaders, Ben-Hā'il, Ō·ba·dī'ah,
Zech·a·rī'ah, Ne·than'el, and Mī·chaī'ah,
to teach in the cities of Judah. 8And with

17:4 [a]Septuagint reads *LORD God.*

16:7 Hanani the seer: Probably the son of Jehu the prophet (see 19:2).
16:14 a very great burning: Burning of spices as a rite of mourning (see Jer. 34:5).
17:8, 9 Recognizing the necessity of constant vigilance against idolatry and other sin,

them *he sent* Lē′vītes: She·māi′ah,
Neth·a·nī′ah, Zeb·a·dī′ah, As′a·hel,
She·mir′a·moth, Je·hon′a·than, Ad-
o·nī′jah, Tō·bī′jah, and Tob·ad·o·nī′jah—
the Lē′vītes; and with them E·lish′a·ma
and Je·hō′ram, the priests. 9So they taught
in Judah, and *had* the Book of the Law of
the LORD with them; they went throughout
all the cities of Judah and taught the peo-
ple.
10And the fear of the LORD fell on all the
kingdoms of the lands that *were* around Ju-
dah, so that they did not make war against
Je·hosh′a·phat. 11Also *some* of the Phi-
lis′tines brought Je·hosh′a·phat presents
and silver as tribute; and the Arabians
brought him flocks, seven thousand seven
hundred rams and seven thousand seven
hundred male goats.
12So Je·hosh′a·phat became increasingly
powerful, and he built fortresses and stor-
age cities in Judah. 13He had much prop-
erty in the cities of Judah; and the men of
war, mighty men of valor, *were* in Jerusa-
lem.
14These *are* their numbers, according to
their fathers′ houses. Of Judah, the cap-
tains of thousands: Ad′nah the captain,
and with him three hundred thousand
mighty men of valor; 15and next to him *was*
Jē·hō·hā′nan the captain, and with him
two hundred and eighty thousand; 16and
next to him *was* Am·a·sī′ah the son of
Zich′rī, who willingly offered himself to
the LORD, and with him two hundred thou-
sand mighty men of valor. 17Of Benjamin:
E·lī′a·da a mighty man of valor, and with
him two hundred thousand men armed
with bow and shield; 18and next to him *was*
Je·hō′za·bad, and with him one hundred
and eighty thousand prepared for war.
19These served the king, besides those the
king put in the fortified cities throughout
all Judah.

CHAPTER 18

Micaiah Warns Ahab

Je·hosh′a·phat had riches and honor in
abundance; and by marriage he allied him-
self with Ā′hab. 2After some years he went
down to *visit* Ā′hab in Samaria; and Ā′hab
killed sheep and oxen in abundance for
him and the people who were with him,
and persuaded him to go up *with him* to
Rā′moth Gil′ē·ad. 3So Ā′hab king of Israel
said to Je·hosh′a·phat king of Judah, "Will
you go with me *against* Rā′moth Gil′ē·ad?"
And he answered him, "I *am* as you *are*,
and my people as your people; *we will be*
with you in the war."
4Also Je·hosh′a·phat said to the king of
Israel, "Please inquire for the word of the
LORD today."
5Then the king of Israel gathered the
prophets together, four hundred men, and
said to them, "Shall we go to war against
Rā′moth Gil′ē·ad, or shall I refrain?"

Jehoshaphat instituted "traveling Sunday schools"—teams of teachers who instructed the people of Judah in the Law.

18:1 The **marriage** of Jehoshaphat's son Jehoram and Ahab's daughter Athaliah resulted in an alliance between Judah and Israel (see 2 Kin. 8:18), which later brought disaster on the house of David.

18:2 persuaded him: By the great feast made in his honor. The feast and the abundance of the occasion are not mentioned in 1 Kin. 22:2. The chronicler possibly wants to show that Ahab was primarily responsible for the unsuccessful campaign against Ramoth Gilead.

18:5–27 The struggle between the professional prophets of false idols and the true **prophet of the LORD** is portrayed in the clash of **Micaiah** and **Zedekiah** (see vv. 23, 24). At stake was the validity and credibility of the prophet's message: Which prophet spoke the true word from the Lord (v. 13)? This same struggle would be waged nearly 300 years later between the prophets Jeremiah and Hananiah (see Jer. 28:1–17).

So they said, "Go up, for God will de-
liver it into the king's hand."
6But Je·hosh'a·phat said, "*Is there* not
still a prophet of the LORD here, that we
may inquire of Him?"[a]
7So the king of Israel said to Je·hosh'-
a·phat, "*There is* still one man by whom we
may inquire of the LORD; but I hate him, be-
cause he never prophesies good concern-
ing me, but always evil. He *is* Mī·cāi'ah the
son of Im'la."

And Je·hosh'a·phat said, "Let not the
king say such things!"
8Then the king of Israel called one *of his*
officers and said, "Bring Mī·cāi'ah the son
of Im'la quickly!"
9The king of Israel and Je·hosh'a·phat
king of Judah, clothed in *their* robes, sat
each on his throne; and they sat at a thresh-
ing floor at the entrance of the gate of Sa-
maria; and all the prophets prophesied be-
fore them. 10Now Zed·e·kī'ah the son of
Che·nā'a·nah had made horns of iron for
himself; and he said, "Thus says the LORD:
'With these you shall gore the Syrians until
they are destroyed.' "
11And all the prophets prophesied so,
saying, "Go up to Rā'moth Gil'ē·ad and
prosper, for the LORD will deliver *it* into the
king's hand."
12Then the messenger who had gone to
call Mī·cāi'ah spoke to him, saying, "Now
listen, the words of the prophets with one
accord encourage the king. Therefore
please let your word be like *the word of* one
of them, and speak encouragement."
13And Mī·cāi'ah said, "*As* the LORD
lives, whatever my God says, that I will
speak."
14Then he came to the king; and the king
said to him, "Mī·cāi'ah, shall we go to war
against Rā'moth Gil'ē·ad, or shall I re-
frain?"

And he said, "Go and prosper, and they
shall be delivered into your hand!"
15So the king said to him, "How many
times shall I make you swear that you tell
me nothing but the truth in the name of the
LORD?"
16Then he said, "I saw all Israel scattered
on the mountains, as sheep that have no
shepherd. And the LORD said, 'These have
no master. Let each return to his house in
peace.' "
17And the king of Israel said to Je-
hosh'a·phat, "Did I not tell you he would
not prophesy good concerning me, but
evil?"
18Then *Mī*·cāi'ah said, "Therefore hear
the word of the LORD: I saw the LORD sit-
ting on His throne, and all the host of
heaven standing on His right hand and His
left. 19And the LORD said, 'Who will per-
suade Ā'hab king of Israel to go up, that he
may fall at Rā'moth Gil'ē·ad?' So one
spoke in this manner, and another spoke in
that manner. 20Then a spirit came forward
and stood before the LORD, and said, 'I will
persuade him.' The LORD said to him, 'In
what way?' 21So he said, 'I will go out and
be a lying spirit in the mouth of all his
prophets.' And *the LORD* said, 'You shall
persuade *him* and also prevail; go out and
do so.' 22Therefore look! The LORD has put
a lying spirit in the mouth of these
prophets of yours, and the LORD has de-
clared disaster against you."
23Then Zed·e·kī'ah the son of Che-
nā'a·nah went near and struck Mī·cāi'ah
on the cheek, and said, "Which way did
the spirit from the LORD go from me to
speak to you?"
24And Mī·cāi'ah said, "Indeed you shall
see on that day when you go into an inner
chamber to hide!"
25Then the king of Israel said, "Take
Mī·cāi'ah, and return him to Ā'mon the
governor of the city and to Jō'ash the king's
son; 26and say, 'Thus says the king: "Put
this *fellow* in prison, and feed him with
bread of affliction and water of affliction,
until I return in peace." ' "
27But Mī·cāi'ah said, "If you ever re-
turn in peace, the LORD has not spoken by
me." And he said, "Take heed, all you peo-
ple!"

18:6 [a]Or *him*

Ahab Dies in Battle

28So the king of Israel and Je·hosh′-
a·phat the king of Judah went up to
Rā′moth Gil′ē·ad. 29And the king of Israel
said to Je·hosh′a·phat, "I will disguise my-
self and go into battle; but you put on your
robes." So the king of Israel disguised him-
self, and they went into battle.
30Now the king of Syria had com-
manded the captains of the chariots who
were with him, saying, "Fight with no one
small or great, but only with the king of Is-
rael."
31So it was, when the captains of the
chariots saw Je·hosh′a·phat, that they
said, "It *is* the king of Israel!" Therefore
they surrounded him to attack; but
Je·hosh′·a·phat cried out, and the LORD
helped him, and God diverted them
from him. 32For so it was, when the cap-
tains of the chariots saw that it was not the
king of Israel, that they turned back from
pursuing him. 33Now a certain man drew a
bow at random, and struck the king of Is-
rael between the joints of his armor. So he
said to the driver of his chariot, "Turn
around and take me out of the battle, for I
am wounded." 34The battle increased that
day, and the king of Israel propped *himself*
up in *his* chariot facing the Syrians until
evening; and about the time of sunset he
died.

CHAPTER 19

Then Je·hosh′a·phat the king of Judah
returned safely to his house in Jerusalem.
2And Jē′hū the son of Ha·nā′nī the seer
went out to meet him, and said to King
Je·hosh′a·phat, "Should you help the
wicked and love those who hate the LORD?
Therefore the wrath of the LORD *is* upon
you. 3Nevertheless good things are found
in you, in that you have removed the
wooden images from the land, and have
prepared your heart to seek God."

The Reforms of Jehoshaphat

4So Je·hosh′a·phat dwelt at Jerusalem;
and he went out again among the people
from Bē·er·shē′ba to the mountains of
Ē′phra·im, and brought them back to the
LORD God of their fathers. 5Then he set
judges in the land throughout all the forti-
fied cities of Judah, city by city, 6and said to
the judges, "Take heed to what you are do-
ing, for you do not judge for man but for
the LORD, who *is* with you in the judgment.
7Now therefore, let the fear of the LORD be
upon you; take care and do *it*, for *there is* no
iniquity with the LORD our God, no partial-
ity, nor taking of bribes."
8Moreover in Jerusalem, for the judg-
ment of the LORD and for controversies,
Je·hosh′a·phat appointed some of the

18:31 the LORD helped him: Jehoshaphat's alliance with Ahab was a mistake, but he was saved by God's intervention. 1 Kings emphasizes the fulfillment of prophecy against Ahab (1 Kin. 22:38), but the message here is that God will deliver the king who seeks to do His will.

19:2 the wicked . . . who hate the LORD: Ahab and his followers. As God's holy people, Christians are not to support the evil in attaining their goals. While it is necessary for us to mingle with unbelievers in order to share the gospel message, we must guard against showing support for their unrighteous actions.

19:6 Working not for **man**, but for the Lord makes all human endeavors sacred. Every judgment rendered by the judges was sacred in this sense, whether it was religious cases dealing with "matters of the LORD" or civil cases concerning "the king's matters" (see v. 11). Even so, everything we do, whether at work, at home, or elsewhere, should be done as unto the Lord. While not everyone is called to the mission field or the pastorate, every believer should be dedicated to full-time Christian service.

19:7 no partiality . . . bribes: Jehoshaphat calls Judah back to the high level of justice God had outlined to Moses (see Deut. 1:17; 16:19). Honesty in the workplace is founded on the character of God, which we His people are expected to share.

Lē′vītes and priests, and some of the chief fathers of Israel, when they returned to Jerusalem.[a] 9And he commanded them, saying, "Thus you shall act in the fear of the LORD, faithfully and with a loyal heart: 10Whatever case comes to you from your brethren who dwell in their cities, whether of bloodshed or offenses against law or commandment, against statutes or ordinances, you shall warn them, lest they trespass against the LORD and wrath come upon you and your brethren. Do this, and you will not be guilty. 11And take notice: Am·a·rī′ah the chief priest *is* over you in all matters of the LORD; and Zeb·a·dī′ah the son of Ish′ma·el, the ruler of the house of Judah, for all the king's matters; also the Lē′vītes *will be* officials before you. Behave courageously, and the LORD will be with the good."

CHAPTER 20

Ammon, Moab, and Mount Seir Defeated

It happened after this *that* the people of Mō′ab with the people of Am′mon, and *others* with them besides the Am′monītes,[a] came to battle against Je·hosh′a·phat. 2Then some came and told Je·hosh′a·phat, saying, "A great multitude is coming against you from beyond the sea, from Syria;[a] and they are in Haz′a·zon Tā′mar" (which *is* En Ge′di). 3And Je·hosh′a·phat feared, and set himself to seek the LORD, and proclaimed a fast throughout all Judah. 4So Judah gathered together to ask *help* from the LORD; and from all the cities of Judah they came to seek the LORD.

5Then Je·hosh′a·phat stood in the assembly of Judah and Jerusalem, in the house of the LORD, before the new court, 6and said: "O LORD God of our fathers, *are* You not God in heaven, and do You *not* rule over all the kingdoms of the nations, and in Your hand *is there not* power and might, so that no one is able to withstand You? 7*Are* You not our God, *who* drove out the inhabitants of this land before Your people Israel, and gave it to the descendants of Abraham Your friend forever? 8And they dwell in it, and have built You a sanctuary in it for Your name, saying, 9'If disaster comes upon us—sword, judgment, pestilence, or famine—we will stand before this temple and in Your presence (for Your name *is* in this temple), and cry out to You in our affliction, and You will hear and save.' 10And now, here are the people of Am′mon, Mō′ab, and Mount Sē′ir—whom You would not let Israel invade when they came out of the land of Egypt, but they turned from them and did not destroy them— 11here they are, rewarding us by coming to throw us out of Your possession which You have given us to inherit. 12O our God, will You not judge them? For we have no power against this great multitude that is coming against us; nor do we know what to do, but our eyes *are* upon You."

13Now all Judah, with their little ones, their wives, and their children, stood before the LORD.

14Then the Spirit of the LORD came upon Ja·hā′zi·el the son of Zech·a·rī′ah, the son of Be·nā′i·ah, the son of Je·ī′el, the son of Mat·ta·nī′ah, a Lē′vīte of the sons of Ā′saph, in the midst of the assembly. 15And he said, "Listen, all you of Judah and you

19:8 [a]Septuagint and Vulgate read *for the inhabitants of Jerusalem.* 20:1 [a]Following Masoretic Text and Vulgate; Septuagint reads *Meunites* (compare 26:7). 20:2 [a]Following Masoretic Text, Septuagint, and Vulgate; some Hebrew manuscripts and Old Latin read *Edom.*

20:3, 4 Here **Jehoshaphat** and **Judah** humbled themselves and prayed, as God instructed Solomon (see 7:14).

20:12 When we acknowledge our helplessness and put our faith solely in the Lord, He will be faithful to see us through.

20:15, 17 the battle is . . . God's: A theme of the chronicler. See 1 Chr. 5:20.

inhabitants of Jerusalem, and you, King
Je·hosh'a·phat! Thus says the LORD to you:
'Do not be afraid nor dismayed because of
this great multitude, for the battle *is* not
yours, but God's. 16Tomorrow go down
against them. They will surely come up by
the Ascent of Ziz, and you will find them at
the end of the brook before the Wilderness
of Je·rū'el. 17You will not *need* to fight in
this *battle*. Position yourselves, stand still
and see the salvation of the LORD, who is
with you, O Judah and Jerusalem!' Do not
fear or be dismayed; tomorrow go out
against them, for the LORD *is* with you."

18And Je·hosh'a·phat bowed his head
with *his* face to the ground, and all Judah
and the inhabitants of Jerusalem bowed
before the LORD, worshiping the LORD.
19Then the Lē'vītes of the children of the
Kō'hath·ītes and of the children of the
Kō'ra·hītes stood up to praise the LORD
God of Israel with voices loud and high.

20So they rose early in the morning and
went out into the Wilderness of Te·kō'a;
and as they went out, Je·hosh'a·phat stood
and said, "Hear me, O Judah and you
inhabitants of Jerusalem: Believe in the
LORD your God, and you shall be estab-
lished; believe His prophets, and you shall
prosper." 21And when he had consulted
with the people, he appointed those who
should sing to the LORD, and who should
praise the beauty of holiness, as they went
out before the army and were saying:

"Praise the LORD,
For His mercy *endures* forever."[a]

22Now when they began to sing and to
praise, the LORD set ambushes against the
people of Am'mon, Mō'ab, and Mount
Sē'ir, who had come against Judah; and
they were defeated. 23For the people of
Am'mon and Mō'ab stood up against the
inhabitants of Mount Sē'ir to utterly kill
and destroy *them*. And when they had
made an end of the inhabitants of Sē'ir,
they helped to destroy one another.

24So when Judah came to a place over-
looking the wilderness, they looked to-
ward the multitude; and there *were* their
dead bodies, fallen on the earth. No one
had escaped.

25When Je·hosh'a·phat and his people
came to take away their spoil, they found
among them an abundance of valuables on
the dead bodies,[a] and precious jewelry,
which they stripped off for themselves,
more than they could carry away; and they
were three days gathering the spoil be-
cause there was so much. 26And on the
fourth day they assembled in the Valley of
Ber'a·chah, for there they blessed the
LORD; therefore the name of that place was
called The Valley of Ber'a·chah[a] until this
day. 27Then they returned, every man of Ju-
dah and Jerusalem, with Je·hosh'a·phat in
front of them, to go back to Jerusalem with
joy, for the LORD had made them rejoice
over their enemies. 28So they came to Jeru-
salem, with stringed instruments and
harps and trumpets, to the house of the
LORD. 29And the fear of God was on all the
kingdoms of *those* countries when they
heard that the LORD had fought against the
enemies of Israel. 30Then the realm of
Je·hosh'a·phat was quiet, for his God gave
him rest all around.

The End of Jehoshaphat's Reign

31So Je·hosh'a·phat was king over Ju-
dah. *He was* thirty-five years old when he
became king, and he reigned twenty-five
years in Jerusalem. His mother's name *was*

20:21 [a]Compare Psalm 106:1 20:25 [a]A few Hebrew manuscripts, Old Latin, and Vulgate read *garments;* Septuagint reads *armor.* 20:26 [a]Literally *Blessing*

20:21 The musicians advancing **before the army** demonstrated Jehoshaphat's reliance upon God. **beauty of holiness**: Synonymous with the Lord.

20:22, 23 ambushes: It is not specified whether local inhabitants or supernatural forces were used. In either case, Judah's allied enemies fell out and destroyed each other.

A·zū'bah the daughter of Shil'hī. 32And he
walked in the way of his father Ā'sa, and
did not turn aside from it, doing *what was*
right in the sight of the LORD. 33Neverthe-
less the high places were not taken away,
for as yet the people had not directed their
hearts to the God of their fathers.

34Now the rest of the acts of Je·hosh'-
a·phat, first and last, indeed they *are* writ-
ten in the book of Jē'hū the son of Ha-
nā'nī, which *is* mentioned in the book of
the kings of Israel.

35After this Je·hosh'a·phat king of Judah
allied himself with Ā·ha·zī'ah king of Is-
rael, who acted very wickedly. 36And he al-
lied himself with him to make ships to go
to Tar'shish, and they made the ships in
Ē'zi·on Gē'ber. 37But El·i·ē'zer the son of
Dō'da·vah of Ma·rē'shah prophesied
against Je·hosh'a·phat, saying, "Because
you have allied yourself with Ā·ha·zī'ah,
the LORD has destroyed your works." Then
the ships were wrecked, so that they were
not able to go to Tar'shish.

CHAPTER 21

Jehoram Reigns in Judah

And Je·hosh'a·phat rested with his
fathers, and was buried with his fathers in
the City of David. Then Je·hō'ram his son
reigned in his place. 2He had brothers, the
sons of Je·hosh'a·phat: Az·a·rī'ah, Je·hī'el,
Zech·a·rī'ah, Az'ar·ya·hu, Michael, and
Sheph·a·tī'ah; all these *were* the sons of
Je·hosh'a·phat king of Israel. 3Their father
gave them great gifts of silver and gold
and precious things, with fortified cities in
Judah; but he gave the kingdom to Je-
hō'ram, because he *was* the firstborn.

4Now when Je·hō'ram was established
over the kingdom of his father, he
strengthened himself and killed all his
brothers with the sword, and also *others* of
the princes of Israel.

5Je·hō'ram *was* thirty-two years old
when he became king, and he reigned
eight years in Jerusalem. 6And he walked
in the way of the kings of Israel, just as the
house of Ā'hab had done, for he had the
daughter of Ā'hab as a wife; and he did evil
in the sight of the LORD. 7Yet the LORD
would not destroy the house of David, be-
cause of the covenant that He had made
with David, and since He had promised to
give a lamp to him and to his sons forever.
8In his days Ē'dom revolted against Ju-
dah's authority, and made a king over
themselves. 9So Je·hō'ram went out with
his officers, and all his chariots with him.
And he rose by night and attacked the
Ē'dom·ītes who had surrounded him and
the captains of the chariots. 10Thus Ē'dom
has been in revolt against Judah's author-
ity to this day. At that time Lib'nah re-
volted against his rule, because he had
forsaken the LORD God of his fathers.
11Moreover he made high places in the
mountains of Judah, and caused the inhab-
itants of Jerusalem to commit harlotry, and
led Judah astray.

12And a letter came to him from E·lī'jah
the prophet, saying,

> Thus says the LORD God of your
> father David:
> Because you have not walked in the
> ways of Je·hosh'a·phat your father, or
> in the ways of Ā'sa king of Judah,
> 13but have walked in the way of the

20:33 A contrast to Jehoshaphat's earlier reform attempts (17:6). Although he had attempted to obliterate worship at these **high places**, the people were persistent in sin. His father, Asa, had a similar experience.

21:4–7 killed . . . princes: Eight years later, Jehoram's wife, Athaliah (v. 6), attempted to complete what Jehoram had begun. But they were unable to wipe out the Davidic line. God had given His promise (v. 7). a **lamp**: A dynasty.

21:12–15 The letter was evidently written before Elijah's death during the reign of Jehoshaphat (2 Kin. 3:11). It would come to Jehoram as a voice from the dead.

kings of Israel, and have made Judah
and the inhabitants of Jerusalem to
play the harlot like the harlotry of the
house of Ā′hab, and also have killed
your brothers, those of your father's
household, *who were* better than your-
self, 14behold, the LORD will strike
your people with a serious affliction—
your children, your wives, and all
your possessions; 15and you *will be-
come* very sick with a disease of your
intestines, until your intestines come
out by reason of the sickness, day by
day.

16Moreover the LORD stirred up against
Je·hō′ram the spirit of the Phi·lis′tines and
the Arabians who *were* near the Ethiopians.
17And they came up into Judah and in-
vaded it, and carried away all the posses-
sions that were found in the king's house,
and also his sons and his wives, so that
there was not a son left to him except
Je·hō′a·haz,[a] the youngest of his sons.
18After all this the LORD struck him in his
intestines with an incurable disease. 19Then
it happened in the course of time, after the
end of two years, that his intestines came
out because of his sickness; so he died in
severe pain. And his people made no burn-
ing for him, like the burning for his fathers.
20He was thirty-two years old when he
became king. He reigned in Jerusalem
eight years and, to no one's sorrow, de-
parted. However they buried him in the
City of David, but not in the tombs of the
kings.

CHAPTER 22

Ahaziah Reigns in Judah

Then the inhabitants of Jerusalem made
Ā·ha·zī′ah his youngest son king in his
place, for the raiders who came with the
Arabians into the camp had killed all the
older *sons*. So Ā·ha·zī′ah the son of Je-
hō′ram, king of Judah, reigned. 2Ā·ha·zī′ah
was forty-two[a] years old when he became
king, and he reigned one year in Jerusalem.
His mother's name *was* Ath·a·lī′ah the
granddaughter of Om′rī. 3He also walked
in the ways of the house of Ā′hab, for his
mother advised him to do wickedly.
4Therefore he did evil in the sight of the
LORD, like the house of Ā′hab; for they
were his counselors after the death of his
father, to his destruction. 5He also followed
their advice, and went with Je·hō′ram[a] the
son of Ā′hab king of Israel to war against
Haz′a·el king of Syria at Rā′moth Gil′ē·ad;
and the Syrians wounded Jō′ram. 6Then he
returned to Jez′rē·el to recover from the
wounds which he had received at Rā′mah,
when he fought against Haz′a·el king of
Syria. And Az·a·rī′ah[a] the son of Je·hō′-
ram, king of Judah, went down to see
Je·hō′ram the son of Ā′hab in Jez′rē·el, be-
cause he was sick.

7His going to Jō′ram was God's occasion
for Ā·ha·zī′ah's downfall; for when he

21:17 [a]Elsewhere called *Ahaziah* (compare 2 Chronicles 22:1) 22:2 [a]Or *twenty-two* (compare 2 Kings 8:26) 22:5 [a]Also spelled *Joram* (compare verses 5 and 7; 2 Kings 8:28; and elsewhere) 22:6 [a]Some Hebrew manuscripts, Septuagint, Syriac, Vulgate, and 2 Kings 8:29 read *Ahaziah*.

21:16, 17 Just as Jehoram had ruthlessly murdered his father's family, his own family was taken away.

21:20 No one was sorry to see Jehoram die. Many of us wonder what lasting effect our lives will have and whether we will be mourned at death. For the Christian who is faithfully serving the Lord, there is no need to worry. As we act toward others in brotherly love and seek to spread the gospel, we can't help but impact the lives of everyone around us.

22:7 God's occasion: He often accomplishes His will through human circumstances and human choices. Jehu, who was **anointed** by the Lord to destroy **the house of Ahab**, chose to exceed the role he was to fill. His actions were denounced by the prophet Hosea. When we deviate from the Lord's plan, we are essentially challenging His wisdom and authority. We need to seek His will and carefully follow it to the letter.

arrived, he went out with Je·hō′ram against Jē′hū the son of Nim′shī, whom the LORD had anointed to cut off the house of Ā′hab. 8And it happened, when Jē′hū was executing judgment on the house of Ā′hab, and found the princes of Judah and the sons of Ā·ha·zī′ah's brothers who served Ā·ha-zī′ah, that he killed them. 9Then he searched for Ā·ha·zī′ah; and they caught him (he was hiding in Samaria), and brought him to Jē′hū. When they had killed him, they buried him, "because," they said, "he is the son of Je·hosh′a·phat, who sought the LORD with all his heart."

So the house of Ā·ha·zī′ah had no one to assume power over the kingdom.

Athaliah Reigns in Judah

10Now when Ath·a·lī′ah the mother of Ā·ha·zī′ah saw that her son was dead, she arose and destroyed all the royal heirs of the house of Judah. 11But Jē·hō·shab′e·ath,[a] the daughter of the king, took Jō′ash the son of Ā·ha·zī′ah, and stole him away from among the king's sons who were being murdered, and put him and his nurse in a bedroom. So Jē·hō·shab′e·ath, the daughter of King Je·hō′ram, the wife of Je·hoi′a·da the priest (for she was the sister of Ā·ha·zī′ah), hid him from Ath·a·lī′ah so that she did not kill him. 12And he was hidden with them in the house of God for six years, while Ath·a·lī′ah reigned over the land.

CHAPTER 23

Joash Crowned King of Judah

In the seventh year Je·hoi′a·da strengthened himself, *and made a* covenant with the captains of hundreds: Az·a·rī′ah the son of Je·rō′ham, Ish′ma·el the son of Jē·hō·hā′nan, Az·a·rī′ah the son of Ō′bed, Mā·a·sēi′ah the son of A·dāi′ah, and El·i·shā′phat the son of Zich′rī. 2And they went throughout Judah and gathered the Lē′vītes from all the cities of Judah, and the chief fathers of Israel, and they came to Jerusalem.

3Then all the assembly made a covenant with the king in the house of God. And he said to them, "Behold, the king's son shall reign, as the LORD has said of the sons of David. 4This *is* what you shall do: One-third of you entering on the Sabbath, of the priests and the Lē′vītes, *shall be* keeping watch over the doors; 5one-third *shall be* at the king's house; and one-third at the Gate of the Foundation. All the people *shall be* in the courts of the house of the LORD. 6But let no one come into the house of the LORD except the priests and those of the Lē′vītes who serve. They may go in, for they *are* holy; but all the people shall keep the watch of the LORD. 7And the Lē′vītes shall surround the king on all sides, every man with his weapons in his hand; and whoever comes into the house, let him be put to death. You are to be with the king when he comes in and when he goes out."

8So the Lē′vītes and all Judah did according to all that Je·hoi′a·da the priest commanded. And each man took his men who were to be on duty on the Sabbath, with those who were going *off duty* on the Sabbath; for Je·hoi′a·da the priest had not dismissed the divisions. 9And Je·hoi′a·da the priest gave to the captains of hundreds the spears and the large and small shields which *had belonged* to King David, that *were*

22:11 [a]Spelled *Jehosheba* in 2 Kings 11:2

22:9 they buried him: To lack a proper burial was a disgrace (see Jer. 22:18, 19). **Ahaziah** was spared this dishonor because his father had followed the Lord faithfully (see 20:31, 32).

23:4–7 priests . . . Levites: While Kings gives Jehoiada's instructions to the temple and palace guards (2 Kin. 11:5–9), the chronicler is concerned to highlight the part played by the religious personnel. Even though a revolution was about to take place, it was yet crucial that only the holy (v. 6), and not the "unclean" (v. 19), should enter the temple.

in the temple of God. 10Then he set all the
people, every man with his weapon in his
hand, from the right side of the temple to
the left side of the temple, along by the al-
tar and by the temple, all around the king.
11And they brought out the king's son, put
the crown on him, *gave him* the Testimony,[a]
and made him king. Then Je·hoi'a·da and
his sons anointed him, and said, "*Long* live
the king!"

Death of Athaliah

12Now when Ath·a·lī'ah heard the noise
of the people running and praising the
king, she came to the people *in* the temple
of the LORD. 13*When* she looked, there was
the king standing by his pillar at the en-
trance; and the leaders and the trumpeters
were by the king. All the people of the land
were rejoicing and blowing trumpets, also
the singers with musical instruments, and
those who led in praise. So Ath·a·lī'ah tore
her clothes and said, "Treason! Treason!"
14And Je·hoi'a·da the priest brought out
the captains of hundreds who were set
over the army, and said to them, "Take her
outside under guard, and slay with the
sword whoever follows her." For the priest
had said, "Do not kill her in the house of
the LORD."
15So they seized her; and she went by
way of the entrance of the Horse Gate *into*
the king's house, and they killed her there.
16Then Je·hoi'a·da made a covenant be-
tween himself, the people, and the king,
that they should be the LORD's people.
17And all the people went to the temple[a] of
Bā'al, and tore it down. They broke in
pieces its altars and images, and killed
Mat'tan the priest of Bā'al before the altars.
18Also Je·hoi'a·da appointed the oversight
of the house of the LORD to the hand of the
priests, the Lē'vītes, whom David had as-
signed in the house of the LORD, to offer the
burnt offerings of the LORD, as *it is* written
in the Law of Moses, with rejoicing and
with singing, *as it was established* by David.
19And he set the gatekeepers at the gates of
the house of the LORD, so that no one *who*
was in any way unclean should enter.
20Then he took the captains of hundreds,
the nobles, the governors of the people,
and all the people of the land, and brought
the king down from the house of the LORD;
and they went through the Upper Gate to
the king's house, and set the king on the
throne of the kingdom. 21So all the people
of the land rejoiced; and the city was quiet,
for they had slain Ath·a·lī'ah with the
sword.

CHAPTER 24

Joash Repairs the Temple

Jō'ash *was* seven years old when he be-
came king, and he reigned forty years in Je-
rusalem. His mother's name *was* Zib'i·ah
of Bē·er·shē'ba. 2Jō'ash did *what was* right
in the sight of the LORD all the days of
Je·hoi'a·da the priest. 3And Je·hoi'a·da
took two wives for him, and he had sons
and daughters.
4Now it happened after this *that* Jō'ash
set his heart on repairing the house of the
LORD. 5Then he gathered the priests and
the Lē'vītes, and said to them, "Go out to
the cities of Judah, and gather from all Is-
rael money to repair the house of your God
from year to year, and see that you do it
quickly."

However the Lē'vītes did not do it
quickly. 6So the king called Je·hoi'a·da the
chief *priest*, and said to him, "Why have
you not required the Lē'vītes to bring in
from Judah and from Jerusalem the collec-
tion, *according to the commandment* of Moses

23:11 [a]That is, the Law (compare Exodus 25:16, 21; 31:18) 23:17 [a]Literally *house*

23:16, 17 The **people** must make a decisive break from Baal and all that represented Baal worship; they must renew their commitment to **the LORD**.

23:18, 19 These verses are not found in the parallel account of 2 Kin. 11:17–20. The chronicler emphasizes that all was restored in accordance with the **Law of Moses**.

the servant of the LORD and of the assem-
bly of Israel, for the tabernacle of witness?"
7For the sons of Ath·a·lī′ah, that wicked
woman, had broken into the house of God,
and had also presented all the dedicated
things of the house of the LORD to the
Bā′als.

8Then at the king's command they
made a chest, and set it outside at the
gate of the house of the LORD. 9And
they made a proclamation throughout
Judah and Jerusalem to bring to the LORD
the collection *that* Moses the servant of
God *had imposed* on Israel in the wilder-
ness. 10Then all the leaders and all the peo-
ple rejoiced, brought their contributions,
and put *them* into the chest until all had
given. 11So it was, at that time, when the
chest was brought to the king's official by
the hand of the Lē′vītes, and when they
saw that *there was* much money, that the
king's scribe and the high priest's officer
came and emptied the chest, and took it
and returned it to its place. Thus they did
day by day, and gathered money in abun-
dance.

12The king and Je·hoi′a·da gave it to
those who did the work of the service of
the house of the LORD; and they hired ma-
sons and carpenters to repair the house of
the LORD, and also those who worked in
iron and bronze to restore the house of the
LORD. 13So the workmen labored, and the
work was completed by them; they re-
stored the house of God to its original con-
dition and reinforced it. 14When they had
finished, they brought the rest of the
money before the king and Je·hoi′a·da;
they made from it articles for the house of
the LORD, articles for serving and offering,
spoons and vessels of gold and silver. And
they offered burnt offerings in the house of
the LORD continually all the days of
Je·hoi′a·da.

Apostasy of Joash

15But Je·hoi′a·da grew old and was full
of days, and he died; *he was* one hundred
and thirty years old when he died. 16And
they buried him in the City of David
among the kings, because he had done
good in Israel, both toward God and His
house.

17Now after the death of Je·hoi′a·da the
leaders of Judah came and bowed down to
the king. And the king listened to them.
18Therefore they left the house of the LORD
God of their fathers, and served wooden
images and idols; and wrath came upon
Judah and Jerusalem because of their tres-
pass. 19Yet He sent prophets to them, to
bring them back to the LORD; and they tes-
tified against them, but they would not lis-
ten.

20Then the Spirit of God came upon
Zech·a·rī′ah the son of Je·hoi′a·da the
priest, who stood above the people, and
said to them, "Thus says God: 'Why do
you transgress the commandments of the
LORD, so that you cannot prosper? Because
you have forsaken the LORD, He also has
forsaken you.' " 21So they conspired
against him, and at the command of the
king they stoned him with stones in the

24:12–14 gave it to . . . the work: Initially the temple funds were not available for replacing articles used by the priests in their temple duties (see 2 Kin. 12:13, 14). But when the repair work was complete, the excess money was applied to needs not previously met by the priests' normal offerings (see 2 Kin. 12:16).

24:17–19 The reign of Joash illustrates the chronicler's major themes: (1) In order to fulfill God's great promises to David, the king must be obedient to God's will. Obedience is usually measured by the king's concern for true worship at the temple. (2) When the nation falls into apostasy, rather than completely forsake His people, God sends His prophets to warn of the inevitable consequences of their action (v. 19). **bowed down**: Put pressure on the king to change his policies. Today the Lord will bless us as we abide in His will. When we stray from the truth, our fellow believers are charged with the responsibility of confronting us and leading us back to the fold.

court of the house of the LORD. 22Thus Jō′ash the king did not remember the kindness which Je·hoi′a·da his father had done to him, but killed his son; and as he died, he said, "The LORD look on *it,* and repay!"

Death of Joash

23So it happened in the spring of the year *that* the army of Syria came up against him; and they came to Judah and Jerusalem, and destroyed all the leaders of the people from among the people, and sent all their spoil to the king of Damascus. 24For the army of the Syrians came with a small company of men; but the LORD delivered a very great army into their hand, because they had forsaken the LORD God of their fathers. So they executed judgment against Jō′ash. 25And when they had withdrawn from him (for they left him severely wounded), his own servants conspired against him because of the blood of the sons[a] of Je·hoi′a·da the priest, and killed him on his bed. So he died. And they buried him in the City of David, but they did not bury him in the tombs of the kings.

26These are the ones who conspired against him: Zā′bad[a] the son of Shim′ē·ath the Am′mon·ī·tess, and Je·hō′za·bad the son of Shim′rith[b] the Mō′ab·ī·tess. 27Now *concerning* his sons, and the many oracles about him, and the repairing of the house of God, indeed they *are* written in the annals of the book of the kings. Then Am·a·zī′ah his son reigned in his place.

CHAPTER 25

Amaziah Reigns in Judah

Am·a·zī′ah *was* twenty-five years old *when* he became king, and he reigned twenty-nine years in Jerusalem. His mother's name *was* Jē·hō·ad′dan of Jerusalem. 2And he did *what was* right in the sight of the LORD, but not with a loyal heart.

3Now it happened, as soon as the kingdom was established for him, that he executed his servants who had murdered his father the king. 4However he did not execute their children, but *did* as *it is* written in the Law in the Book of Moses, where the LORD commanded, saying, "The fathers shall not be put to death for their children, nor shall the children be put to death for their fathers; but a person shall die for his own sin."[a]

The War Against Edom

5Moreover Am·a·zī′ah gathered Judah together and set over them captains of thousands and captains of hundreds, according to *their* fathers' houses, throughout all Judah and Benjamin; and he numbered them from twenty years old and above, and found them to be three hundred thousand choice *men, able* to go to war, who could handle spear and shield. 6He also hired one hundred thousand mighty men of valor from Israel for one hundred talents of silver. 7But a man of God came to him, saying, "O king, do not let the army of Israel go with you, for the

24:25 [a]Septuagint and Vulgate read *son* (compare verses 20–22). 24:26 [a]Or *Jozachar* (compare 2 Kings 12:21) [b]Or *Shomer* (compare 2 Kings 12:21)
25:4 [a]Deuteronomy 24:16

24:22 killed his son: The murder was still remembered in Jesus' time (see Matt. 23:35).

24:25 not . . . in the tombs of the kings: A sign of dishonor which contrasts Joash's burial with that of a good king such as Hezekiah (see 32:33). Although Joash had a promising start to his kingdom, in the end he turned away from the Lord. This is a solemn warning to us to be consistently vigilant against temptation. Wisdom does not automatically come with age, nor do we become immune to the wiles of the devil.

25:2 not with a loyal heart: That is, a whole heart. His obedience was only partial.

25:4 Human judgment must not go beyond the guilty individual. There is no contradiction between this instruction of Deut. 24:16 and divine judgment extending to following generations.

LORD *is* not with Israel—*not with* any of the
children of Ē′phra·im. 8But if you go, be
gone! Be strong in battle! *Even so,* God shall
make you fall before the enemy; for God
has power to help and to overthrow."
9Then Am·a·zī′ah said to the man of
God, "But what *shall we* do about the hun-
dred talents which I have given to the
troops of Israel?"
And the man of God answered, "The
LORD is able to give you much more than
this." 10So Am·a·zī′ah discharged the
troops that had come to him from
Ē′phra·im, to go back home. Therefore
their anger was greatly aroused against Ju-
dah, and they returned home in great
anger.
11Then Am·a·zī′ah strengthened him-
self, and leading his people, he went to the
Valley of Salt and killed ten thousand of
the people of Sē′ir. 12Also the children of
Judah took captive ten thousand alive,
brought them to the top of the rock, and
cast them down from the top of the rock, so
that they all were dashed in pieces.
13But as for the soldiers of the army
which Am·a·zī′ah had discharged, so that
they would not go with him to battle, they
raided the cities of Judah from Samaria to
Beth Hor′on, killed three thousand in
them, and took much spoil.
14Now it was so, after Am·a·zī′ah came
from the slaughter of the Ē′dom·ītes, that
he brought the gods of the people of Sē′ir,
set them up *to be* his gods, and bowed
down before them and burned incense to
them. 15Therefore the anger of the LORD
was aroused against Am·a·zī′ah, and He
sent him a prophet who said to him, "Why
have you sought the gods of the people,
which could not rescue their own people
from your hand?"
16So it was, as he talked with him, that
the king said to him, "Have we made you
the king's counselor? Cease! Why should
you be killed?"
Then the prophet ceased, and said, "I
know that God has determined to destroy
you, because you have done this and have
not heeded my advice."

Israel Defeats Judah

17Now Am·a·zī′ah king of Judah asked
advice and sent to Jō′ash[a] the son of Je-
hō′a·haz, the son of Jē′hū, king of Israel,
saying, "Come, let us face one another *in
battle."*
18And Jō′ash king of Israel sent to Am-
a·zī′ah king of Judah, saying, "The thistle
that *was* in Lebanon sent to the cedar that
was in Lebanon, saying, 'Give your daugh-
ter to my son as wife'; and a wild beast that
was in Lebanon passed by and trampled
the thistle. 19Indeed you say that you have
defeated the Ē′dom·ītes, and your heart is
lifted up to boast. Stay at home now; why
should you meddle with trouble, that you
should fall—you and Judah with you?"
20But Am·a·zī′ah would not heed, for it
came from God, that He might give them
into the hand *of their enemies,* because they
sought the gods of Ē′dom. 21So Jō′ash king
of Israel went out; and he and Am·a·zī′ah
king of Judah faced one another at Beth
Shem′esh, which *belongs* to Judah. 22And
Judah was defeated by Israel, and every
man fled to his tent. 23Then Jō′ash the king
of Israel captured Am·a·zī′ah king of Ju-

25:17 [a]Spelled *Jehoash* in 2 Kings 14:8ff

25:8 God has power: A source of comfort for believers, but a cause of concern for others, as Amaziah was to discover (vv. 22–24).

25:9 Although a mature Christian is a good steward of money, finances should never be the determining factor in our relationship with God. He will supply all our need; all we are required to do is obey Him.

25:14 Amaziah's actions were typical of the heathen kings of the ancient world in that he sought to incorporate the captured gods into his own religion. He is the only Hebrew king guilty of such behavior.

dah, the son of Jō'ash, the son of Je·hō'-
a·haz, at Beth Shem'esh; and he brought
him to Jerusalem, and broke down the wall
of Jerusalem from the Gate of Ē'phra·im to
the Corner Gate—four hundred cubits.
24And *he took* all the gold and silver, all the
articles that were found in the house of
God with Ō-bed-Ē'dom, the treasures of
the king's house, and hostages, and re-
turned to Samaria.

Death of Amaziah

25Am·a·zī'ah the son of Jō'ash, king of
Judah, lived fifteen years after the death of
Jō'ash the son of Je·hō'a·haz, king of Israel.
26Now the rest of the acts of Am·a·zī'ah,
from first to last, indeed *are* they not writ-
ten in the book of the kings of Judah and
Israel? 27After the time that Am·a·zī'ah
turned away from following the LORD,
they made a conspiracy against him in Je-
rusalem, and he fled to Lā'chish; but they
sent after him to Lā'chish and killed him
there. 28Then they brought him on horses
and buried him with his fathers in the City
of Judah.

CHAPTER 26

Uzziah Reigns in Judah

Now all the people of Judah took
Uz·zī'ah,[a] who *was* sixteen years old, and
made him king instead of his father
Am·a·zī'ah. 2He built Ē'lath[a] and restored
it to Judah, after the king rested with his
fathers.

3Uz·zī'ah *was* sixteen years old when he
became king, and he reigned fifty-two
years in Jerusalem. His mother's name was
Jech·o·lī'ah of Jerusalem. 4And he did *what
was* right in the sight of the LORD, accord-
ing to all that his father Am·a·zī'ah had
done. 5He sought God in the days of
Zech·a·rī'ah, who had understanding in
the visions[a] of God; and as long as he
sought the LORD, God made him prosper.

6Now he went out and made war
against the Phi·lis'tines, and broke down
the wall of Gath, the wall of Jab'neh, and
the wall of Ash'dod; and he built cities
around Ash'dod and among the Phi-
lis'tines. 7God helped him against the Phi-
lis'tines, against the Arabians who lived in
Gur Bā'al, and against the Me·ū'nītes.
8Also the Am'mon·ītes brought tribute to
Uz·zī'ah. His fame spread as far as the en-
trance of Egypt, for he became exceedingly
strong.

9And Uz·zī'ah built towers in Jerusalem
at the Corner Gate, at the Valley Gate, and
at the corner buttress of the wall; then he
fortified them. 10Also he built towers in the
desert. He dug many wells, for he had
much livestock, both in the lowlands and
in the plains; *he also had* farmers and vine-
dressers in the mountains and in Car'mel,
for he loved the soil.

11Moreover Uz·zī'ah had an army of
fighting men who went out to war by com-
panies, according to the number on their
roll as prepared by Je·ī'el the scribe and
Mā·a·sēi'ah the officer, under the hand of
Han·a·nī'ah, *one* of the king's captains.
12The total number of chief officers[a] of the
mighty men of valor *was* two thousand six
hundred. 13And under their authority *was*
an army of three hundred and seven thou-
sand five hundred, that made war with
mighty power, to help the king against the
enemy. 14Then Uz·zī'ah prepared for them,
for the entire army, shields, spears, hel-
mets, body armor, bows, and slings *to cast*

26:1 [a]Called *Azariah* in 2 Kings 14:21ff
26:2 [a]Hebrew *Eloth* 26:5 [a]Several Hebrew manuscripts, Septuagint, Syriac, Targum, and Arabic read *fear.* 26:12 [a]Literally *chief fathers*

26:1 Uzziah was the coronation name for this king whose birth name was Azariah (see 2 Kin. 14:21).

26:5 This prophet **Zechariah** is not the same person as Jehoiada's son who was killed by Uzziah's grandfather Joash (see 24:20–22). **sought the LORD.** Seeking God meant tenaciously guarding the worship of the Lord at the temple.

stones. 15And he made devices in Jerusalem, invented by skillful men, to be on the towers and the corners, to shoot arrows and large stones. So his fame spread far and wide, for he was marvelously helped till he became strong.

The Penalty for Uzziah's Pride

16But when he was strong his heart was lifted up, to *his* destruction, for he transgressed against the LORD his God by entering the temple of the LORD to burn incense on the altar of incense. 17So Az·a·rī'ah the priest went in after him, and with him were eighty priests of the LORD—valiant men. 18And they withstood King Uz·zī'ah, and said to him, "*It* is not for you, Uz·zī'ah, to burn incense to the LORD, but for the priests, the sons of Aaron, who are consecrated to burn incense. Get out of the sanctuary, for you have trespassed! You *shall have* no honor from the LORD God."

19Then Uz·zī'ah became furious; and he *had* a censer in his hand to burn incense. And while he was angry with the priests, leprosy broke out on his forehead, before the priests in the house of the LORD, beside the incense altar. 20And Az·a·rī'ah the chief priest and all the priests looked at him, and there, on his forehead, he *was* leprous; so they thrust him out of that place. Indeed he also hurried to get out, because the LORD had struck him.

21King Uz·zī'ah was a leper until the day of his death. He dwelt in an isolated house, because he was a leper; for he was cut off from the house of the LORD. Then Jō'tham his son *was* over the king's house, judging the people of the land.

22Now the rest of the acts of Uz·zī'ah, from first to last, the prophet Ī·sāi'ah the son of Ā'moz wrote. 23So Uz·zī'ah rested with his fathers, and they buried him with his fathers in the field of burial which *belonged* to the kings, for they said, "He is a leper." Then Jō'tham his son reigned in his place.

CHAPTER 27

Jotham Reigns in Judah

Jō'tham *was* twenty-five years old when he became king, and he reigned sixteen years in Jerusalem. His mother's name *was* Je·rū'shah[a] the daughter of Zā'dok. 2And he did *what was* right in the sight of the LORD, according to all that his father Uz·zī'ah had done (although he did not enter the temple of the LORD). But still the people acted corruptly.

3He built the Upper Gate of the house of the LORD, and he built extensively on the wall of Ō'phel. 4Moreover he built cities in the mountains of Judah, and in the forests he built fortresses and towers. 5He also fought with the king of the Am'mon·ītes and defeated them. And the people of Am'mon gave him in that year one hundred talents of silver, ten thousand kors of wheat, and ten thousand of barley. The people of Am'mon paid this to him in the second and third years also. 6So Jō'tham became mighty, because he prepared his ways before the LORD his God.

7Now the rest of the acts of Jō'tham, and all his wars and his ways, indeed they *are* written in the book of the kings of Israel and Judah. 8He was twenty-five years old when he became king, and he reigned sixteen years in Jerusalem. 9So Jō'tham rested with his fathers, and they buried him in the

27:1 [a]Spelled *Jerusha* in 2 Kings 15:33

26:16 heart was lifted up: "Pride goes before destruction, and a haughty spirit before a fall" (Prov. 16:18).

26:18 no honor from . . . God: When the roles of king and priest were combined, the king soon assumed that he was divine.

27:2 Although Jotham was basically loyal to the Lord, he apparently did little to encourage his people to walk uprightly. He was a strong military leader but a weak spiritual guide.

City of David. Then Ā′haz his son reigned in his place.

CHAPTER 28

Ahaz Reigns in Judah

Ā′haz *was* twenty years old when he became king, and he reigned sixteen years in Jerusalem; and he did not do *what was* right in the sight of the LORD, as his father David *had done*. 2For he walked in the ways of the kings of Israel, and made molded images for the Bā′als. 3He burned incense in the Valley of the Son of Hin′nom, and burned his children in the fire, according to the abominations of the nations whom the LORD had cast out before the children of Israel. 4And he sacrificed and burned incense on the high places, on the hills, and under every green tree.

Syria and Israel Defeat Judah

5Therefore the LORD his God delivered him into the hand of the king of Syria. They defeated him, and carried away a great multitude of them as captives, and brought *them* to Damascus. Then he was also delivered into the hand of the king of Israel, who defeated him with a great slaughter. 6For Pē′kah the son of Rem·a·lī′ah killed one hundred and twenty thousand in Judah in one day, all valiant men, because they had forsaken the LORD God of their fathers. 7Zich′rī, a mighty man of Ē′phra·im, killed Mā·a·sēi′ah the king's son, Az·rī′kam the officer over the house, and El·kā′nah *who was* second to the king. 8And the children of Israel carried away captive of their brethren two hundred thousand women, sons, and daughters; and they also took away much spoil from them, and brought the spoil to Samaria.

> Aim at heaven and you will get earth "thrown in"; aim at earth and you will get neither.
>
> C. S. Lewis

Israel Returns the Captives

9But a prophet of the LORD was there, whose name *was* Ō′ded; and he went out before the army that came to Samaria, and said to them: "Look, because the LORD God of your fathers was angry with Judah, He has delivered them into your hand; but you have killed them in a rage *that* reaches up to heaven. 10And now you propose to force the children of Judah and Jerusalem to be your male and female slaves; *but are* you not also guilty before the LORD your God? 11Now hear me, therefore, and return the captives, whom you have taken captive from your brethren, for the fierce wrath of the LORD *is* upon you."

12Then some of the heads of the children of Ē′phra·im, Az·a·rī′ah the son of Jō·hā′nan, Ber·e·chī′ah the son of Me·shil′le·moth, Jē·hiz·kī′ah the son of Shal′lum, and A·mā′sa the son of Had′laī, stood up against those who came from the war, 13and said to them, "You shall not bring the captives here, for we *already* have offended the LORD. You intend to add to our sins and to our guilt; for our guilt is great, and *there is* fierce wrath against Israel." 14So the armed men left the captives and the spoil

---

28:1–27 King Ahaz, defeated by his two northern neighbors, Syria and Israel (v. 5), sent to his ultimate enemy, Assyria, for help (v. 16). In his attempt to obtain that help, he had to strip the temple in Jerusalem of many of its treasures (v. 21). What he did not do was turn to God; in fact, he turned farther from Him (vv. 22–25).

28:2–4 Wholesale reversion to pagan religious practices prominent in Canaan.

28:9–15 For Israel to have enslaved their **brethren** (v. 11) from Judah would have been in violation of the Mosaic law (see Lev. 25:39–43), and thus brought them the **wrath of the LORD**. The Israelites of Ephraim were sensitive to the **guilt** involved (v. 13) and influenced the kind treatment of the Judahite captives (v. 15).

before the leaders and all the assembly.
15Then the men who were designated by
name rose up and took the captives, and
from the spoil they clothed all who were
naked among them, dressed them and
gave them sandals, gave them food and
drink, and anointed them; and they let all
the feeble ones ride on donkeys. So they
brought them to their brethren at Jericho,
the city of palm trees. Then they returned
to Samaria.

Assyria Refuses to Help Judah

16At the same time King Ā'haz sent to
the kings[a] of Assyria to help him. 17For
again the Ē'dom·ītes had come, attacked
Judah, and carried away captives. 18The
Phi·lis'tines also had invaded the cities of
the lowland and of the South of Judah, and
had taken Beth Shem'esh, Aī'ja·lon,
Ge·dē'roth, Sō'chōh with its villages,
Tim'nah with its villages, and Gim'zō with
its villages; and they dwelt there. 19For the
LORD brought Judah low because of Ā'haz
king of Israel, for he had encouraged moral
decline in Judah and had been continually
unfaithful to the LORD. 20Also Tig'lath-
Pī·lē'ser[a] king of Assyria came to him and
distressed him, and did not assist him.
21For Ā'haz took part *of the treasures* from
the house of the LORD, from the house of
the king, and from the leaders, and he gave
it to the king of Assyria; but he did not help
him.

Apostasy and Death of Ahaz

22Now in the time of his distress King
Ā'haz became increasingly unfaithful to
the LORD. This *is that* King Ā'haz. 23For he
sacrificed to the gods of Damascus which
had defeated him, saying, "Because the
gods of the kings of Syria help them, I will
sacrifice to them that they may help me."
But they were the ruin of him and of all Is-
rael. 24So Ā'haz gathered the articles of the
house of God, cut in pieces the articles of
the house of God, shut up the doors of the
house of the LORD, and made for himself
altars in every corner of Jerusalem. 25And
in every single city of Judah he made high
places to burn incense to other gods, and
provoked to anger the LORD God of his
fathers.

26Now the rest of his acts and all his
ways, from first to last, indeed they *are*
written in the book of the kings of Judah
and Israel. 27So Ā'haz rested with his
fathers, and they buried him in the city,
in Jerusalem; but they did not bring
him into the tombs of the kings of Israel.
Then Hez·e·kī'ah his son reigned in his
place.

CHAPTER 29

Hezekiah Reigns in Judah

Hez·e·kī'ah became king *when he was*
twenty-five years old, and he reigned
twenty-nine years in Jerusalem. His
mother's name *was* A·bī'jah[a] the daughter
of Zech·a·rī'ah. 2And he did *what was* right
in the sight of the LORD, according to all
that his father David had done.

28:16 [a]Septuagint, Syriac, and Vulgate read *king* (compare verse 20). 28:20 [a]Hebrew *Tilgath-Pilneser*
29:1 [a]Spelled *Abi* in 2 Kings 18:2

28:20, 21 did not assist him: The Assyrian king turned Edom and Philistia into Assyrian provinces rather than returning them to Judah as Ahaz had hoped he would (v. 16). Judah's ransom payment depleted her resources but did not make Assyria her ally. While Tiglath-Pileser did attack Damascus (2 Kin. 16:9), and possibly also deported many Israelites at this time (1 Chr. 5:25, 26), Judah was forced to become a vassal of Assyria at a high cost (see 2 Kin. 16:17, 18). To the chronicler this was not true assistance.

28:27 not . . . into the tombs of the kings: A sign of dishonor.

29:1—32:33 The author of Kings covered Hezekiah's religious reforms in one verse (2 Kin. 18:4) and devoted three chapters to his political achievements. But the chronicler details the reforms in chs. 29—31 in order to illustrate that when the son of David cared for God's house and provided for genuine worship, God brought peace to his kingdom (ch. 32).

Hezekiah Cleanses the Temple

[3]In the first year of his reign, in the first
month, he opened the doors of the house
of the LORD and repaired them. [4]Then he
brought in the priests and the Lē′vītes, and
gathered them in the East Square, [5]and
said to them: "Hear me, Lē′vītes! Now
sanctify yourselves, sanctify the house of
the LORD God of your fathers, and carry
out the rubbish from the holy *place*. [6]For
our fathers have trespassed and done evil
in the eyes of the LORD our God; they have
forsaken Him, have turned their faces
away from the dwelling place of the LORD,
and turned *their* backs *on Him*. [7]They have
also shut up the doors of the vestibule, put
out the lamps, and have not burned in-
cense or offered burnt offerings in the holy
place to the God of Israel. [8]Therefore the
wrath of the LORD fell upon Judah and Je-
rusalem, and He has given them up to
trouble, to desolation, and to jeering, as
you see with your eyes. [9]For indeed, be-
cause of this our fathers have fallen by the
sword; and our sons, our daughters, and
our wives *are* in captivity.

[10]"Now *it is* in my heart to make a
covenant with the LORD God of Israel, that
His fierce wrath may turn away from us.
[11]My sons, do not be negligent now, for the
LORD has chosen you to stand before Him,
to serve Him, and that you should minister
to Him and burn incense."

[12]Then these Lē′vītes arose: Mā′hath the
son of A·mā′saī and Jō′el the son of Az-
a·rī′ah, of the sons of the Kō′hath·ītes; of
the sons of Me·rar′ī, Kish the son of Ab′dī
and Az·a·rī′ah the son of Je·hal′le·lel; of
the Ger′shon·ītes, Jō′ah the son of Zim′-
mah and Eden the son of Jō′ah; [13]of the
sons of E·li·zā′phan, Shim′rī and Je·ī′el; of
the sons of Ā′saph, Zech·a·rī′ah and
Mat·ta·nī′ah; [14]of the sons of Hē′man,
Je·hī′el and Shim′ē·ī; and of the sons of
Je·dū′thun, She·māi′ah and Uz′zi·el.

[15]And they gathered their brethren,
sanctified themselves, and went according
to the commandment of the king, at the
words of the LORD, to cleanse the house of
the LORD. [16]Then the priests went into the
inner part of the house of the LORD to
cleanse *it*, and brought out all the debris
that they found in the temple of the LORD
to the court of the house of the LORD. And
the Lē′vītes took *it* out and carried *it* to the
Brook Kid′ron.

[17]Now they began to sanctify on the first
day of the first month, and on the eighth
day of the month they came to the
vestibule of the LORD. So they sanctified
the house of the LORD in eight days, and on
the sixteenth day of the first month they
finished.

[18]Then they went in to King Hez·e·kī′ah
and said, "We have cleansed all the house
of the LORD, the altar of burnt offerings
with all its articles, and the table of the
showbread with all its articles. [19]Moreover
all the articles which King Ā′haz in his
reign had cast aside in his transgression
we have prepared and sanctified;
and there they *are*, before the altar of the
LORD."

Hezekiah Restores Temple Worship

[20]Then King Hez·e·kī′ah rose early,
gathered the rulers of the city, and went up
to the house of the LORD. [21]And they
brought seven bulls, seven rams, seven
lambs, and seven male goats for a sin offer-
ing for the kingdom, for the sanctuary, and
for Judah. Then he commanded the priests,
the sons of Aaron, to offer *them* on the altar
of the LORD. [22]So they killed the bulls, and
the priests received the blood and sprin-
kled *it* on the altar. Likewise they killed the

29:3 opened . . . the house of the LORD: It had been closed and desecrated (28:21, 24) during the reign of Ahaz.
29:4 East Square: The open space before the temple entrance.
29:17 first month: March-April, the time of Passover.

rams and sprinkled the blood on the altar.
They also killed the lambs and sprinkled
the blood on the altar. [23]Then they brought
out the male goats *for* the sin offering be-
fore the king and the assembly, and they
laid their hands on them. [24]And the priests
killed them; and they presented their
blood on the altar as a sin offering to make
an atonement for all Israel, for the king
commanded *that* the burnt offering and the
sin offering *be made* for all Israel.

[25]And he stationed the Lē′vītes in the
house of the LORD with cymbals, with
stringed instruments, and with harps, ac-
cording to the commandment of David, of
Gad the king's seer, and of Nathan the
prophet; for thus *was* the commandment of
the LORD by His prophets. [26]The Lē′vītes
stood with the instruments of David, and
the priests with the trumpets. [27]Then
Hez·e·kī′ah commanded *them* to offer the
burnt offering on the altar. And when the
burnt offering began, the song of the LORD
also began, with the trumpets and with the
instruments of David king of Israel. [28]So all
the assembly worshiped, the singers sang,
and the trumpeters sounded; all *this contin-
ued* until the burnt offering was finished.
[29]And when they had finished offering, the
king and all who were present with him
bowed and worshiped. [30]Moreover King
Hez·e·kī′ah and the leaders commanded
the Lē′vītes to sing praise to the LORD with
the words of David and of Ā′saph the seer.
So they sang praises with gladness, and
they bowed their heads and worshiped.

[31]Then Hez·e·kī′ah answered and said,
"Now *that* you have consecrated your-
selves to the LORD, come near, and bring
sacrifices and thank offerings into the
house of the LORD." So the assembly
brought in sacrifices and thank offerings,
and as many as were of a willing heart
brought burnt offerings. [32]And the number
of the burnt offerings which the assembly
brought was seventy bulls, one hundred
rams, *and* two hundred lambs; all these
were for a burnt offering to the LORD. [33]The
consecrated things *were* six hundred bulls
and three thousand sheep. [34]But the priests
were too few, so that they could not skin all
the burnt offerings; therefore their
brethren the Lē′vītes helped them until the
work was ended and until the *other* priests
had sanctified themselves, for the Lē′vītes
were more diligent in sanctifying them-
selves than the priests. [35]Also the burnt of-
ferings *were* in abundance, with the fat of
the peace offerings and *with* the drink of-
ferings for *every* burnt offering.

So the service of the house of the LORD
was set in order. [36]Then Hez·e·kī′ah and all
the people rejoiced that God had prepared
the people, since the events took place so
suddenly.

CHAPTER 30

Hezekiah Keeps the Passover

And Hez·e·kī′ah sent to all Israel and
Judah, and also wrote letters to Ē′phra·im
and Ma·nas′seh, that they should come to
the house of the LORD at Jerusalem, to keep
the Passover to the LORD God of Israel. [2]For
the king and his leaders and all the assem-
bly in Jerusalem had agreed to keep the

29:24 all Israel: See "Judah" in v. 21. Hezekiah was also concerned for his kinsmen in the north.

29:30 the words of David and of Asaph: Probably includes some of the 73 psalms attributed to David or the 12 to Asaph.

30:1 Ephraim and Manasseh: Hezekiah was especially concerned for the remnant of the northern kingdom destroyed by Assyria.

30:2–4 While Hezekiah restored the Passover celebration, he was not able to observe it fully as prescribed in the Mosaic law. The first irregularity was the time of the **second month**. The first month was the **regular time** for the feast (see Lev. 23:5). The second irregularity involved some who were not properly "cleansed" (vv. 18, 19; see Ex. 9:5–14). Partly because of these deficiencies, the chronicler would report of Josiah's later Passover:

Passover in the second month. [3]For they
could not keep it at the regular time,[a] be-
cause a sufficient number of priests had
not consecrated themselves, nor had the
people gathered together at Jerusalem.
[4]And the matter pleased the king and all
the assembly. [5]So they resolved to make a
proclamation throughout all Israel, from
Bē·er·shē'ba to Dan, that they should come
to keep the Passover to the LORD God of Is-
rael at Jerusalem, since they had not done
it for a long *time* in the *prescribed* manner.

[6]Then the runners went throughout all
Israel and Judah with the letters from the
king and his leaders, and spoke according
to the command of the king: "Children of
Israel, return to the LORD God of Abraham,
Isaac, and Israel; then He will return to the
remnant of you who have escaped from
the hand of the kings of Assyria. [7]And do
not be like your fathers and your brethren,
who trespassed against the LORD God of
their fathers, so that He gave them up to
desolation, as you see. [8]Now do not be
stiff-necked, as your fathers *were, but* yield
yourselves to the LORD; and enter His sanc-
tuary, which He has sanctified forever, and
serve the LORD your God, that the fierce-
ness of His wrath may turn away from
you. [9]For if you return to the LORD, your
brethren and your children *will be treated*
with compassion by those who lead them
captive, so that they may come back to this
land; for the LORD your God *is* gracious
and merciful, and will not turn *His* face
from you if you return to Him."

[10]So the runners passed from city to city
through the country of Ē'phra·im and
Ma·nas'seh, as far as Zeb'ū·lun; but
they laughed at them and mocked them.
[11]Nevertheless some from Ash'er, Ma-
nas'seh, and Zeb'ū·lun humbled them-
selves and came to Jerusalem. [12]Also the
hand of God was on Judah to give them
singleness of heart to obey the command
of the king and the leaders, at the word of
the LORD.

[13]Now many people, a very great assem-
bly, gathered at Jerusalem to keep the Feast
of Unleavened Bread in the second month.
[14]They arose and took away the altars that
were in Jerusalem, and they took away all
the incense altars and cast *them* into the
Brook Kid'ron. [15]Then they slaughtered the
Passover *lambs* on the fourteenth *day* of
the second month. The priests and the Lē'-
vītes were ashamed, and sanctified them-
selves, and brought the burnt offerings to
the house of the LORD. [16]They stood in their
place according to their custom, according
to the Law of Moses the man of God; the
priests sprinkled the blood *received* from
the hand of the Lē'vītes. [17]For *there were*
many in the assembly who had not sancti-
fied themselves; therefore the Lē'vītes had
charge of the slaughter of the Passover
lambs for everyone *who was* not clean, to
sanctify *them* to the LORD. [18]For a multitude
of the people, many from Ē'phra·im, Ma-
nas'seh, Is'sa·char, and Zeb'ū·lun, had not
cleansed themselves, yet they ate the
Passover contrary to what was written. But
Hez·e·kī'ah prayed for them, saying,

I praise You because You, the Lord my God, are gracious and merciful, and will not turn Your face from me if I return to you.

adapted from 2 Chronicles 30:9

30:3 [a]That is, the first month (compare Leviticus 23:5); literally *at that time*

"There had been no Passover kept in Israel like that since the days of Samuel the prophet" (2 Chr. 35:18).

30:5 Beersheba to Dan: The traditional southern and northern borders of old Israel before the divided monarchy.

30:12 singleness of heart: Complete commitment to the word of the LORD.

"May the good LORD provide atonement
for everyone [19]*who* prepares his heart to
seek God, the LORD God of his fathers,
though *he is* not *cleansed* according to the
purification of the sanctuary." [20]And the
LORD listened to Hez·e·kī'ah and healed
the people.

[21]So the children of Israel who were pre-
sent at Jerusalem kept the Feast of Unleav-
ened Bread seven days with great glad-
ness; and the Lē'vītes and the priests
praised the LORD day by day, *singing* to the
LORD, accompanied by loud instruments.
[22]And Hez·e·kī'ah gave encouragement to
all the Lē'vītes who taught the good
knowledge of the LORD; and they ate
throughout the feast seven days, offering
peace offerings and making confession to
the LORD God of their fathers.

[23]Then the whole assembly agreed to
keep *the feast* another seven days, and they
kept it *another* seven days with gladness.
[24]For Hez·e·kī'ah king of Judah gave to the
assembly a thousand bulls and seven thou-
sand sheep, and the leaders gave to the as-
sembly a thousand bulls and ten thousand
sheep; and a great number of priests sanc-
tified themselves. [25]The whole assembly of
Judah rejoiced, also the priests and
Lē'vītes, all the assembly that came from
Israel, the sojourners who came from the
land of Israel, and those who dwelt in Ju-
dah. [26]So there was great joy in Jerusalem,
for since the time of Solomon the son of
David, king of Israel, *there had* been noth-
ing like this in Jerusalem. [27]Then the
priests, the Lē'vītes, arose and blessed the
people, and their voice was heard; and
their prayer came *up* to His holy dwelling
place, to heaven.

CHAPTER 31

The Reforms of Hezekiah

Now when all this was finished, all Is-
rael who were present went out to the
cities of Judah and broke the sacred pillars
in pieces, cut down the wooden images,
and threw down the high places and
the altars—from all Judah, Benjamin,
Ē'phra·im, and Ma·nas'seh—until they
had utterly destroyed them all. Then all the
children of Israel returned to their own
cities, every man to his possession.

[2]And Hez·e·kī'ah appointed the divi-
sions of the priests and the Lē'vītes accord-
ing to their divisions, each man according
to his service, the priests and Lē'vītes for
burnt offerings and peace offerings, to
serve, to give thanks, and to praise in the
gates of the camp[a] of the LORD. [3]The king
also *appointed* a portion of his possessions
for the burnt offerings: for the morning
and evening burnt offerings, the burnt of-
ferings for the Sabbaths and the New
Moons and the set feasts, as *it is* written in
the Law of the LORD.

[4]Moreover he commanded the people
who dwelt in Jerusalem to contribute sup-

31:2 [a]That is, the temple

30:19, 20 God desires a seeking heart rather than mere formal worship (see Ps. 51:9, 10; Luke 18:13, 14). **not . . . according to the purification of the sanctuary**: See 30:2–4. Although the Lord expects us to follow His instructions precisely, in situations like this one He is more concerned with the state of our hearts. Rituals mean nothing when performed with an empty heart.

30:23 the whole assembly: The revival that began in the heart of Hezekiah spread to his people.

30:26 nothing like this: However, Hezekiah's Passover would later be surpassed by the observance of Josiah (see 35:18).

31:1 sacred pillars: Forms of Canaanite worship forbidden by God (Deut. 12:1–3). The Feast of Unleavened Bread (30:21) was one of Israel's three pilgrim feasts in which males were required to journey to Jerusalem (see Ex. 23:17). Having renewed this pilgrimage observation, the attendees returned to their own cities.

31:4–10 The **tithe** (v. 5) from the people was God's plan to support the Levites who would serve Him full-time (see Deut. 14:22–29). Likewise, Christians are to support full-time

port for the priests and the Lē′vītes, that they might devote themselves to the Law of the LORD.

[5]As soon as the commandment was circulated, the children of Israel brought in abundance the firstfruits of grain and wine, oil and honey, and of all the produce of the field; and they brought in abundantly the tithe of everything. [6]And the children of Israel and Judah, who dwelt in the cities of Judah, brought the tithe of oxen and sheep; also the tithe of holy things which were consecrated to the LORD their God they laid in heaps.

[7]In the third month they began laying them in heaps, and they finished in the seventh month. [8]And when Hez·e·kī′ah and the leaders came and saw the heaps, they blessed the LORD and His people Israel. [9]Then Hez·e·kī′ah questioned the priests and the Lē′vītes concerning the heaps. [10]And Az·a·rī′ah the chief priest, from the house of Zā′dok, answered him and said, "Since *the people* began to bring the offerings into the house of the LORD, we have had enough to eat and have plenty left, for the LORD has blessed His people; and what is left *is* this great abundance."

[11]Now Hez·e·kī′ah commanded *them* to prepare rooms in the house of the LORD, and they prepared them. [12]Then they faithfully brought in the offerings, the tithes, and the dedicated things; Con·o·nī′ah the Lē′vīte had charge of them, and Shim′ē·ī his brother *was* the next. [13]Je·hī′el, Az·a·zī′ah, Nā′hath, As′a·hel, Jer′i·moth, Joz′a·bad, E·lī′el, Is·ma·chī′ah, Mā′hath, and Be·nā′i·ah *were* overseers under the hand of Con·o·nī′ah and Shim′ē·ī his brother, at the commandment of Hez·e·kī′ah the king and Az·a·rī′ah the ruler of the house of God. [14]Kō′re the son of Im′nah the Lē′vīte, the keeper of the East Gate, *was* over the freewill offerings to God, to distribute the offerings of the LORD and the most holy things. [15]And under him *were* Eden, Min′ia·min, Jesh′ū·a, She·māi′ah, Am·a·rī′ah, and Shec·a·nī′ah, *his* faithful assistants in the cities of the priests, to distribute allotments to their brethren by divisions, to the great as well as the small.

[16]Besides those males from three years old and up who were written in the genealogy, they distributed to everyone who entered the house of the LORD his daily portion for the work of his service, by his division, [17]and to the priests who were written in the genealogy according to their father's house, and to the Lē′vītes from twenty years old and up according to their work, by their divisions, [18]and to all who were written in the genealogy—their little ones and their wives, their sons and daughters, the whole company of them—for in their faithfulness they sanctified themselves in holiness.

[19]Also for the sons of Aaron the priests, *who were* in the fields of the common-lands of their cities, in every single city, *there were* men who were designated by name to distribute portions to all the males among the priests and to all who were listed by genealogies among the Lē′vītes.

[20]Thus Hez·e·kī′ah did throughout all Judah, and he did what *was* good and right and true before the LORD his God. [21]And in every work that he began in the service of the house of God, in the law and in the

workers in the NT church (see 1 Tim. 5:17, 18). **enough to eat and . . . plenty left**: In response to Hezekiah's command, the people gave abundantly to the Lord's service, but after the Exile they would have to be stirred again (see Mal. 3:8–10).

31:18 Sanctified themselves in holiness evidently means that after a period of laxness concerning God's commands the priestly families once again took these commands seriously. See Lev. 21:1—22:16.

31:21 This key verse introduces ch. 32 and links the defeat of the Assyrian army to Hezekiah's wholehearted devotion to the **house of God**. The phrase **with all his heart** expresses the key to Hezekiah's service to God—and the requirement for ours (see Matt. 22:37).

commandment, to seek his God, he did *it* with all his heart. So he prospered.

CHAPTER 32

Sennacherib Boasts Against the LORD

After these deeds of faithfulness, Sen·nach′e·rib king of Assyria came and entered Judah; he encamped against the fortified cities, thinking to win them over to himself. [2]And when Hez·e·kī′ah saw that Sen·nach′e·rib had come, and that his purpose was to make war against Jerusalem, [3]he consulted with his leaders and commanders[a] to stop the water from the springs which *were* outside the city; and they helped him. [4]Thus many people gathered together who stopped all the springs and the brook that ran through the land, saying, "Why should the kings[a] of Assyria come and find much water?" [5]And he strengthened himself, built up all the wall that was broken, raised *it* up to the towers, and *built* another wall outside; also he repaired the Mil′lō[a] *in* the City of David, and made weapons and shields in abundance. [6]Then he set military captains over the people, gathered them together to him in the open square of the city gate, and gave them encouragement, saying, [7]"Be strong and courageous; do not be afraid nor dismayed before the king of Assyria, nor before all the multitude that *is* with him; for *there are* more with us than with him. [8]With him *is* an arm of flesh; but with us *is* the LORD our God, to help us and to fight our battles." And the people were strengthened by the words of Hez·e·kī′ah king of Judah.

[9]After this Sen·nach′e·rib king of Assyria sent his servants to Jerusalem (but he and all the forces with him *laid siege* against Lā′chish), to Hez·e·kī′ah king of Judah, and to all Judah who *were* in Jerusalem, saying, [10]"Thus says Sen·nach′e·rib king of Assyria: 'In what do you trust, that you remain under siege in Jerusalem? [11]Does not Hez·e·kī′ah persuade you to give yourselves over to die by famine and by thirst, saying, "The LORD our God will deliver us from the hand of the king of Assyria"? [12]Has not the same Hez·e·kī′ah taken away His high places and His altars, and commanded Judah and Jerusalem, saying, "You shall worship before one altar and burn incense on it"? [13]Do you not know what I and my fathers have done to all the peoples of *other* lands? Were the gods of the nations of those lands in any way able to deliver their lands out of my hand? [14]Who *was there* among all the gods of those nations that my fathers utterly destroyed that could deliver his people from my hand, that your God should be able to deliver you from my hand? [15]Now therefore, do not let Hez·e·kī′ah deceive you or persuade you like this, and do not believe him; for no god of any nation or kingdom was able to deliver his people from my hand or the hand of my fathers. How much less will your God deliver you from my hand?' "

[16]Furthermore, his servants spoke against the LORD God and against His servant Hez·e·kī′ah.

[17]He also wrote letters to revile the LORD God of Israel, and to speak against Him, saying, "As the gods of the nations of *other* lands have not delivered their people from

32:3 [a]Literally *mighty men* 32:4 [a]Following Masoretic Text and Vulgate; Arabic, Septuagint, and Syriac read *king*. 32:5 [a]Literally *The Landfill*

32:7, 8 Finite man can never prevail against our all-powerful God. When we are on the Lord's side, victory is assured.

32:9 sent his servants: See 2 Kin. 18:17.

32:12 taken away His high places: Actually, Hezekiah's purge of the high places (see v. 1) had been pleasing to the Lord.

32:13–15 will your God deliver you? (v. 15): See 2 Kin. 18:33–35.

32:14 Who . . . among all the gods? In Dan. 3:15 a similar taunt is hurled by Nebuchadnezzar: "Who is the god who will deliver you from my hands?"

my hand, so the God of Hez·e·kī′ah will not deliver His people from my hand." 18Then they called out with a loud voice in Hebrew[a] to the people of Jerusalem who *were* on the wall, to frighten them and trouble them, that they might take the city. 19And they spoke against the God of Jerusalem, as against the gods of the people of the earth—the work of men's hands.

Sennacherib's Defeat and Death

20Now because of this King Hez·e·kī′ah and the prophet Ī·sāi′ah, the son of Ā′moz, prayed and cried out to heaven. 21Then the LORD sent an angel who cut down every mighty man of valor, leader, and captain in the camp of the king of Assyria. So he returned shamefaced to his own land. And when he had gone into the temple of his god, some of his own offspring struck him down with the sword there.

22Thus the LORD saved Hez·e·kī′ah and the inhabitants of Jerusalem from the hand of Sen·nach′e·rib the king of Assyria, and from the hand of all *others,* and guided them[a] on every side. 23And many brought gifts to the LORD at Jerusalem, and presents to Hez·e·kī′ah king of Judah, so that he was exalted in the sight of all nations thereafter.

Hezekiah Humbles Himself

24In those days Hez·e·kī′ah was sick and near death, and he prayed to the LORD; and He spoke to him and gave him a sign. 25But Hez·e·kī′ah did not repay according to the favor *shown* him, for his heart was lifted up; therefore wrath was looming over him and over Judah and Jerusalem. 26Then Hez·e·kī′ah humbled himself for the pride of his heart, he and the inhabitants of Jerusalem, so that the wrath of the LORD did not come upon them in the days of Hez·e·kī′ah.

Hezekiah's Wealth and Honor

27Hez·e·kī′ah had very great riches and honor. And he made himself treasuries for silver, for gold, for precious stones, for spices, for shields, and for all kinds of desirable items; 28storehouses for the harvest of grain, wine, and oil; and stalls for all kinds of livestock, and folds for flocks.[a] 29Moreover he provided cities for himself, and possessions of flocks and herds in abundance; for God had given him very much property. 30This same Hez·e·kī′ah also stopped the water outlet of Upper Gī′hon, and brought the water by tunnel[a] to the west side of the City of David. Hez·e·kī′ah prospered in all his works.

31However, *regarding* the ambassadors of the princes of Babylon, whom they sent to him to inquire about the wonder that was *done* in the land, God withdrew from him, in order to test him, that He might know all *that was* in his heart.

Death of Hezekiah

32Now the rest of the acts of Hez·e·kī′ah, and his goodness, indeed they *are* written in the vision of Ī·sāi′ah the prophet, the son of Ā′moz, *and* in the book of the kings

32:18 [a]Literally *Judean* 32:22 [a]Septuagint reads *gave them rest;* Vulgate reads *gave them treasures.* 32:28 [a]Following Septuagint and Vulgate; Arabic and Syriac omit *folds for flocks;* Masoretic Text reads *flocks for sheepfolds.* 32:30 [a]Literally *brought it straight* (compare 2 Kings 20:20)

32:18 in Hebrew: So that the common people would understand (see 2 Kin. 18:26 and note).

32:20–22 For details see 2 Kin. 19:1–7, 35–37.

32:25 Hezekiah's pride nearly brought destruction on his kingdom. We must constantly guard against this insidious sin, which often tempts us at the times we are closest to God.

32:27–29 Because the chronicler wanted to remind Judah of the high points of her past, he reports that Hezekiah had great riches and honor, and was "exalted" before "all nations" (v. 23). These statements are not found in the account in 2 Kings.

32:30 tunnel: See vv. 3, 4 and note on 2 Kin. 20:20.

32:31 princes of Babylon: See 2 Kin. 20:14–19.

of Judah and Israel. 33So Hez·e·kī'ah rested with his fathers, and they buried him in the upper tombs of the sons of David; and all Judah and the inhabitants of Jerusalem honored him at his death. Then Ma·nas'seh his son reigned in his place.

CHAPTER 33

Manasseh Reigns in Judah

Ma·nas'seh *was* twelve years old when he became king, and he reigned fifty-five years in Jerusalem. 2But he did evil in the sight of the LORD, according to the abominations of the nations whom the LORD had cast out before the children of Israel. 3For he rebuilt the high places which Hez·e·kī'ah his father had broken down; he raised up altars for the Bā'als, and made wooden images; and he worshiped all the host of heaven[a] and served them. 4He also built altars in the house of the LORD, of which the LORD had said, "In Jerusalem shall My name be forever." 5And he built altars for all the host of heaven in the two courts of the house of the LORD. 6Also he caused his sons to pass through the fire in the Valley of the Son of Hin'nom; he practiced soothsaying, used witchcraft and sorcery, and consulted mediums and spiritists. He did much evil in the sight of the LORD, to provoke Him to anger. 7He even set a carved image, the idol which he had made, in the house of God, of which God had said to David and to Solomon his son, "In this house and in Jerusalem, which I have chosen out of all the tribes of Israel, I will put My name forever; 8and I will not again remove the foot of Israel from the land which I have appointed for your fathers—only if they are careful to do all that I have commanded them, according to the whole law and the statutes and the ordinances by the hand of Moses." 9So Ma·nas'seh seduced Judah and the inhabitants of Jerusalem to do more evil than the nations whom the LORD had destroyed before the children of Israel.

Manasseh Restored After Repentance

10And the LORD spoke to Ma·nas'seh and his people, but they would not listen. 11Therefore the LORD brought upon them the captains of the army of the king of Assyria, who took Ma·nas'seh with hooks,[a] bound him with bronze *fetters,* and carried him off to Babylon. 12Now when he was in affliction, he implored the LORD his God, and humbled himself greatly before the God of his fathers, 13and prayed to Him; and He received his entreaty, heard his supplication, and brought him back to Jerusalem into his kingdom. Then Ma·nas'seh knew that the LORD *was* God.

14After this he built a wall outside the City of David on the west side of Gī'hon, in the valley, as far as the entrance of the Fish Gate; and *it* enclosed Ō'phel, and he raised it to a very great height. Then he put military captains in all the fortified cities of Judah. 15He took away the foreign gods and the idol from the house of the LORD, and all the altars that he had built in the mount of the house of the LORD and in Jerusalem; and he cast *them* out of the city. 16He also repaired the altar of the LORD, sacrificed peace offerings and thank offerings on it, and commanded Judah to serve the LORD God of Israel. 17Nevertheless the

33:3 [a]The gods of the Assyrians 33:11 [a]That is, nose hooks (compare 2 Kings 19:28)

33:11 The city of Babylon was under the control of Assyria at this time.

33:13 The chronicler probably includes the account of Manasseh's repentance and restoration to show the mercy of God to the people in exile. Just as the king who was most responsible for the Babylonian exile (2 Kin. 23:26) could turn from his sin and find grace, so could the people. See 7:14.

33:14–17 The chronicler records both Manasseh's repentance (see v. 13 and note) and the good things which he accomplished, such as his building, military, and reform activities. The writer of Kings mentions neither.

people still sacrificed on the high places,
but only to the LORD their God.

Death of Manasseh

18Now the rest of the acts of Ma·nas′seh,
his prayer to his God, and the words of the
seers who spoke to him in the name of the
LORD God of Israel, indeed they *are written*
in the book[a] of the kings of Israel. 19Also his
prayer and *how God* received his entreaty,
and all his sin and trespass, and the sites
where he built high places and set up
wooden images and carved images, before
he was humbled, indeed they *are* written
among the sayings of Hō′zā·ī.[a] 20So Ma-
nas′seh rested with his fathers, and they
buried him in his own house. Then his son
Ā′mon reigned in his place.

Amon's Reign and Death

21Ā′mon *was* twenty-two years old when
he became king, and he reigned two years
in Jerusalem. 22But he did evil in the sight
of the LORD, as his father Ma·nas′seh had
done; for Ā′mon sacrificed to all the carved
images which his father Ma·nas′seh had
made, and served them. 23And he did not
humble himself before the LORD, as his
father Ma·nas′seh had humbled himself;
but Ā′mon trespassed more and more.
24Then his servants conspired against
him, and killed him in his own house. 25But
the people of the land executed all those
who had conspired against King Ā′mon.
Then the people of the land made his son
Jō·sī′ah king in his place.

CHAPTER 34

Josiah Reigns in Judah

Jō·sī′ah *was* eight years old when he be-
came king, and he reigned thirty-one years
in Jerusalem. 2And he did *what was* right in
the sight of the LORD, and walked in the
ways of his father David; *he* did *not* turn
aside to the right hand or to the left.
3For in the eighth year of his reign, while
he was still young, he began to seek the
God of his father David; and in the twelfth
year he began to purge Judah and Jerusa-
lem of the high places, the wooden images,
the carved images, and the molded im-
ages. 4They broke down the altars of the
Bā′als in his presence, and the incense al-
tars which *were* above them he cut down;
and the wooden images, the carved im-
ages, and the molded images he broke in
pieces, and made dust of them and scat-
tered *it* on the graves of those who had sac-
rificed to them. 5He also burned the bones
of the priests on their altars, and cleansed
Judah and Jerusalem. 6And *so he did* in the
cities of Ma·nas′seh, Ē′phra·im, and
Sim′ē·on, as far as Naph′ta·lī and all
around, with axes.[a] 7When he had broken
down the altars and the wooden images,
had beaten the carved images into powder,
and cut down all the incense altars
throughout all the land of Israel, he re-
turned to Jerusalem.

Hilkiah Finds the Book of the Law

8In the eighteenth year of his reign,
when he had purged the land and the tem-
ple,[a] he sent Shā′phan the son of Az·a-
lī′ah, Mā·a·sēi′ah the governor of the city,

33:18 [a]Literally *words* 33:19 [a]Septuagint reads *the seers.* 34:6 [a]Literally *swords* 34:8 [a]Literally *house*

33:23 did not humble himself . . . as his father: The evil which Manasseh committed had a greater influence on his son Amon than Manasseh's later entreaty of God for forgiveness. This should be a warning to parents who would take their own sin lightly.

34:3–7 eighth year: 16 years old. **twelfth year**: Age 20. The writer of Kings did not mention the early reform efforts of Josiah recorded here. Instead, he began with the finding of the Book of the Law in Josiah's 18th year when he was 26 (see v. 8).

34:4, 5 Josiah's actions fulfilled the prophecy of the Judahite prophet to King Jeroboam 300 years before. **those who had sacrificed**: The priests of the high places.

34:8–13 Almost 200 years had passed since the last temple restoration project during the reign of Joash (see 24:4–14).

and Jō'ah the son of Jō'a·haz the recorder,
to repair the house of the LORD his God.
[9]When they came to Hil·kī'ah the high
priest, they delivered the money that was
brought into the house of God, which the
Lē'vītes who kept the doors had gathered
from the hand of Ma·nas'seh and
Ē'phra·im, from all the remnant of Israel,
from all Judah and Benjamin, and *which*
they had brought back to Jerusalem. [10]Then
they put *it* in the hand of the foremen who
had the oversight of the house of the LORD;
and they gave it to the workmen who
worked in the house of the LORD, to repair
and restore the house. [11]They gave *it* to the
craftsmen and builders to buy hewn stone
and timber for beams, and to floor the
houses which the kings of Judah had de-
stroyed. [12]And the men did the work faith-
fully. Their overseers *were* Jā'hath and
Ō·ba·dī'ah the Lē'vītes, of the sons of
Me·rar'ī, and Zech·a·rī'ah and Me·shul'-
lam, of the sons of the Kō'hath·ītes, to su-
pervise. *Others of* the Lē'vītes, all of whom
were skillful with instruments of music,
[13]*were* over the burden bearers and *were*
overseers of all who did work in any kind
of service. And *some* of the Lē'vītes *were*
scribes, officers, and gatekeepers.

[14]Now when they brought out the
money that was brought into the house of
the LORD, Hil·kī'ah the priest found the
Book of the Law of the LORD *given* by Mo-
ses. [15]Then Hil·kī'ah answered and said to
Shā'phan the scribe, "I have found the
Book of the Law in the house of the LORD."
And Hil·kī'ah gave the book to Shā'phan.
[16]So Shā'phan carried the book to the king,
bringing the king word, saying, "All that
was committed to your servants they are
doing. [17]And they have gathered the
money that was found in the house of
the LORD, and have delivered it into the
hand of the overseers and the workmen."
[18]Then Shā'phan the scribe told the king,
saying, "Hil·kī'ah the priest has given me
a book." And Shā'phan read it before the
king.

[19]Thus it happened, when the king
heard the words of the Law, that he tore his
clothes. [20]Then the king commanded
Hil·kī'ah, A·hī'kam the son of Shā'phan,
Ab'don[a] the son of Mī'cah, Shā'phan the
scribe, and A·sāi'ah a servant of the king,
saying, [21]"Go, inquire of the LORD for me,
and for those who are left in Israel and Ju-
dah, concerning the words of the book that
is found; for great *is* the wrath of the LORD
that is poured out on us, because our
fathers have not kept the word of the LORD,
to do according to all that is written in this
book."

[22]So Hil·kī'ah and those the king *had ap-
pointed* went to Hul'dah the prophetess,
the wife of Shal'lum the son of Tok'hath,[a]
the son of Has'rah,[b] keeper of the
wardrobe. (She dwelt in Jerusalem in the
Second Quarter.) And they spoke to her to
that *effect*.

[23]Then she answered them, "Thus says
the LORD God of Israel, 'Tell the man who
sent you to Me, [24]"Thus says the LORD: 'Be-
hold, I will bring calamity on this place
and on its inhabitants, all the curses that
are written in the book which they have
read before the king of Judah, [25]because
they have forsaken Me and burned incense
to other gods, that they might provoke Me
to anger with all the works of their hands.
Therefore My wrath will be poured out on
this place, and not be quenched.' " ' [26]But
as for the king of Judah, who sent you to
inquire of the LORD, in this manner you
shall speak to him, 'Thus says the LORD
God of Israel: "*Concerning* the words
which you have heard— [27]because your
heart was tender, and you humbled your-
self before God when you heard His words
against this place and against its inhab-
itants, and you humbled yourself before
Me, and you tore your clothes and wept
before Me, I also have heard *you*," says the
LORD. [28]"Surely I will gather you to your
fathers, and you shall be gathered to your
grave in peace; and your eyes shall not see

34:20 [a]*Achbor the son of Michaiah* in 2 Kings 22:12
34:22 [a]Spelled *Tikvah* in 2 Kings 22:14 [b]Spelled *Harhas* in 2 Kings 22:14

all the calamity which I will bring on this place and its inhabitants." ' " So they brought back word to the king.

Josiah Restores True Worship

29Then the king sent and gathered all the elders of Judah and Jerusalem. 30The king went up to the house of the LORD, with all the men of Judah and the inhabitants of Jerusalem—the priests and the Lē′vītes, and all the people, great and small. And he read in their hearing all the words of the Book of the Covenant which had been found in the house of the LORD. 31Then the king stood in his place and made a covenant before the LORD, to follow the LORD, and to keep His commandments and His testimonies and His statutes with all his heart and all his soul, to perform the words of the covenant that were written in this book. 32And he made all who were present in Jerusalem and Benjamin take a stand. So the inhabitants of Jerusalem did according to the covenant of God, the God of their fathers. 33Thus Jō·sī′ah removed all the abominations from all the country that *belonged* to the children of Israel, and made all who were present in Israel diligently serve the LORD their God. All his days they did not depart from following the LORD God of their fathers.

CHAPTER 35

Josiah Keeps the Passover

Now Jō·sī′ah kept a Passover to the LORD in Jerusalem, and they slaughtered the Passover *lambs* on the fourteenth *day* of the first month. 2And he set the priests in their duties and encouraged them for the service of the house of the LORD. 3Then he said to the Lē′vītes who taught all Israel, who were holy to the LORD: "Put the holy ark in the house which Solomon the son of David, king of Israel, built. *It shall* no longer *be* a burden on *your* shoulders. Now serve the LORD your God and His people Israel. 4Prepare *yourselves* according to your fathers' houses, according to your divisions, following the written instruction of David king of Israel and the written instruction of Solomon his son. 5And stand in the holy *place* according to the divisions of the fathers' houses of your brethren the *lay* people, and *according to* the division of the father's house of the Lē′vītes. 6So slaughter the Passover *offerings,* consecrate yourselves, and prepare *them* for your brethren, that *they* may do according to the word of the LORD by the hand of Moses."

7Then Jō·sī′ah gave the *lay* people lambs and young goats from the flock, all for Passover *offerings* for all who were present, to the number of thirty thousand, as well as three thousand cattle; these *were* from the king's possessions. 8And his leaders gave willingly to the people, to the priests, and to the Lē′vītes. Hil·kī′ah, Zech·a·rī′ah, and Je·hī′el, rulers of the house of God, gave to the priests for the Passover *offerings* two thousand six hundred *from the flock,* and three hundred cattle. 9Also Con·a·nī′ah, his brothers She·māi′ah and Ne·than′el, and Hash·a·bī′ah and Je·ī′el and Joz′a·bad, chief of the Lē′vītes, gave to the Lē′vītes for Passover *offerings* five thousand *from the flock* and five hundred cattle.

10So the service was prepared, and the priests stood in their places, and the

35:1–19 Celebration of the Passover had been neglected. There is no record of this feast since it had been observed by Hezekiah perhaps 80 years earlier. See 30:1–27.

35:3 Put the . . . ark in the house: Perhaps it had been removed during the repairs on the temple (34:8–13). **burden on your shoulders**: It was the Levites' task to carry the ark whenever it moved, a responsibility that had been violated in the past with tragic consequences (see notes on 2 Sam. 6:6–15; 1 Chr. 15:1–24). They would be relieved of this task when the ark rested again in the temple.

Lē'vītes in their divisions, according to the king's command. [11]And they slaughtered the Passover *offerings;* and the priests sprinkled *the blood* with their hands, while the Lē'vītes skinned *the animals.* [12]Then they removed the burnt offerings that *they* might give them to the divisions of the fathers' houses of the *lay* people, to offer to the LORD, as *it is* written in the Book of Moses. And so *they did* with the cattle. [13]Also they roasted the Passover *offerings* with fire according to the ordinance; but the *other* holy *offerings* they boiled in pots, in caldrons, and in pans, and divided *them* quickly among all the *lay* people. [14]Then afterward they prepared portions for themselves and for the priests, because the priests, the sons of Aaron, *were busy* in offering burnt offerings and fat until night; therefore the Lē'vītes prepared portions for themselves and for the priests, the sons of Aaron. [15]And the singers, the sons of Ā'saph, *were* in their places, according to the command of David, Ā'saph, Hē'man, and Je·dū'thun the king's seer. Also the gatekeepers were at each gate; they did not have to leave their position, because their brethren the Lē'vītes prepared portions for them.

[16]So all the service of the LORD was prepared the same day, to keep the Passover and to offer burnt offerings on the altar of the LORD, according to the command of King Jō·sī'ah. [17]And the children of Israel who were present kept the Passover at that time, and the Feast of Unleavened Bread for seven days. [18]There had been no Passover kept in Israel like that since the days of Samuel the prophet; and none of the kings of Israel had kept such a Passover as Jō·sī'ah kept, with the priests and the Lē'vītes, all Judah and Israel who were present, and the inhabitants of Jerusalem. [19]In the eighteenth year of the reign of Jō·sī'ah this Passover was kept.

Josiah Dies in Battle

[20]After all this, when Jō·sī'ah had prepared the temple, Nē'cho king of Egypt came up to fight against Car'chem·ish by the Eū·phrā'tēs; and Jō·sī'ah went out against him. [21]But he sent messengers to him, saying, "What have I to do with you, king of Judah? *I have* not *come* against you this day, but against the house with which I have war; for God commanded me to make haste. Refrain *from meddling with* God, who *is* with me, lest He destroy you." [22]Nevertheless Jō·sī'ah would not turn his face from him, but disguised himself so that he might fight with him, and did not heed the words of Nē'cho from the mouth of God. So he came to fight in the Valley of Me·gid'dō.

[23]And the archers shot King Jō·sī'ah; and the king said to his servants, "Take me away, for I am severely wounded." [24]His servants therefore took him out of that chariot and put him in the second chariot that he had, and they brought him to Jerusalem. So he died, and was buried in *one of* the tombs of his fathers. And all Judah and Jerusalem mourned for Jō·sī'ah.

[25]Jer·e·mī'ah also lamented for Jō·sī'ah. And to this day all the singing men and the singing women speak of Jō·sī'ah in their lamentations. They made it a custom in Israel; and indeed they *are* written in the Laments.

[26]Now the rest of the acts of Jō·sī'ah and his goodness, according to *what was* written in the Law of the LORD, [27]and his deeds from first to last, indeed they *are* written in the book of the kings of Israel and Judah.

35:21, 22 God commanded me . . . is with me: The chronicler reports that God accomplishes His purposes even through the foreign Egyptian Pharaoh Necho (see 36:22; Is. 45:1 and note). **Megiddo**: The location of many OT battles and the future site of Armageddon.

35:25 Jeremiah . . . lamented: If this lament was recorded in writing, it has since been lost.

CHAPTER 36

The Reign and Captivity of Jehoahaz

Then the people of the land took
Je·hō'a·haz the son of Jō·sī'ah, and made
him king in his father's place in Jerusalem.
[2]Je·hō'a·haz[a] *was* twenty-three years old
when he became king, and he reigned
three months in Jerusalem. [3]Now the king
of Egypt deposed him at Jerusalem; and he
imposed on the land a tribute of one hundred talents of silver and a talent of gold.
[4]Then the king of Egypt made *Je·hō'a·haz's*[a] brother E·lī'a·kim king over Judah
and Jerusalem, and changed his name to
Je·hoi'a·kim. And Nē'cho took Je·hō'a·haz[b] his brother and carried him off to
Egypt.

The Reign and Captivity of Jehoiakim

[5]Je·hoi'a·kim *was* twenty-five years old
when he became king, and he reigned
eleven years in Jerusalem. And he did evil
in the sight of the LORD his God. [6]Ne·bū·chad·nez'zar king of Babylon came up
against him, and bound him in bronze *fetters* to carry him off to Babylon. [7]Ne·bū·chad·nez'zar also carried off *some* of the articles from the house of the LORD to
Babylon, and put them in his temple at
Babylon. [8]Now the rest of the acts of
Je·hoi'a·kim, the abominations which he
did, and what was found against him, indeed they *are* written in the book of the
kings of Israel and Judah. Then Je·hoi'a·chin his son reigned in his place.

The Reign and Captivity of Jehoiachin

[9]Je·hoi'a·chin *was* eight[a] years old when
he became king, and he reigned in Jerusalem three months and ten days. And he did
evil in the sight of the LORD. [10]At the turn of
the year King Ne·bū·chad·nez'zar summoned *him* and took him to Babylon, with
the costly articles from the house of the
LORD, and made Zed·e·kī'ah, *Je·hoi'a·kim's*[a] brother, king over Judah and Jerusalem.

Zedekiah Reigns in Judah

[11]Zed·e·kī'ah *was* twenty-one years old
when he became king, and he reigned
eleven years in Jerusalem. [12]He did evil in
the sight of the LORD his God, *and* did not
humble himself before Jer·e·mī'ah the
prophet, *who spoke* from the mouth of the
LORD. [13]And he also rebelled against King
Ne·bū·chad·nez'zar, who had made him
swear *an oath* by God; but he stiffened his
neck and hardened his heart against turning to the LORD God of Israel. [14]Moreover
all the leaders of the priests and the people
transgressed more and more, *according* to
all the abominations of the nations, and defiled the house of the LORD which He had
consecrated in Jerusalem.

36:2 [a]Masoretic Text reads *Joahaz.* 36:4 [a]Literally *his* [b]Masoretic Text reads *Joahaz.* 36:9 [a]Some Hebrew manuscripts, Septuagint, Syriac, and 2 Kings 24:8 read *eighteen.* 36:10 [a]Literally *his* (compare 2 Kings 24:17)

36:6–10 The failure of Jehoiakim's rebellion against Nebuchadnezzar in 598/7 (see 2 Kin. 24:1–12). This account makes it appear that Jehoiakim died after Jerusalem had surrendered, but before the Babylonians could carry him into captivity (vv. 6–8). It was his 18-year-old son, Jehoiachin, who had the unhappy fate of being exiled in the place of his dead father.

36:9 eight years old: A part of the Hebrew number is missing here. The mention of Jehoiachin's wives (2 Kin. 24:15) and 2 Kin. 24:8 indicate his correct age to be 18.

36:11–21 Zedekiah's reign and the final revolt against Babylon, culminating in Jerusalem's capture and destruction in 586 B.C. See 2 Kin. 24:17—25:21.

36:12 Jeremiah was God's voice to the kings and people of Judah in the last years of the nation. He told them of the futility of revolting against the Babylonians, God's chosen instrument of punishment, and instead called them to return to God. But they refused (see Jer. 32:1–5).

The Fall of Jerusalem

[15]And the LORD God of their fathers sent
warnings to them by His messengers, rising
up early and sending *them,* because He had
compassion on His people and on His
dwelling place. [16]But they mocked the mes-
sengers of God, despised His words, and
scoffed at His prophets, until the wrath of
the LORD arose against His people, till *there*
was no remedy.
[17]Therefore He brought against them the
king of the Chal·dē′ans, who killed their
young men with the sword in the house of
their sanctuary, and had no compassion on
young man or virgin, on the aged or the
weak; He gave *them* all into his hand.
[18]And all the articles from the house of
God, great and small, the treasures of the
house of the LORD, and the treasures of the
king and of his leaders, all *these* he took to
Babylon. [19]Then they burned the house of
God, broke down the wall of Jerusalem,
burned all its palaces with fire, and de-
stroyed all its precious possessions. [20]And
those who escaped from the sword he car-
ried away to Babylon, where they became
servants to him and his sons until the rule
of the kingdom of Persia, [21]to fulfill the
word of the LORD by the mouth of
Jer·e·mī′ah, until the land had enjoyed her
Sabbaths. As long as she lay desolate she
kept Sabbath, to fulfill seventy years.

The Proclamation of Cyrus

[22]Now in the first year of Cyrus king of
Persia, that the word of the LORD by the
mouth of Jer·e·mī′ah might be fulfilled,
the LORD stirred up the spirit of Cyrus king
of Persia, so that he made a proclamation
throughout all his kingdom, and also *put it*
in writing, saying,

23 Thus says Cyrus king of Persia:
All the kingdoms of the earth the
LORD God of heaven has given me.
And He has commanded me to build
Him a house at Jerusalem which is in
Judah. Who *is* among you of all His
people? May the LORD his God *be* with
him, and let him go up!

36:15, 16 God in His mercy does not want to send judgment, and He provides every opportunity for repentance.

36:20–22 The kingdom of Persia conquered Babylon during the reign of the Babylonian king Belshazzar (Dan. 5:25–30). The new Persian emperor, **Cyrus**, adopted a policy of amnesty and permitted the conquered Jews to return to Jerusalem.

36:23 For 490 years, God's people refused to observe the sabbatic year as commanded; now the land would rest in a forced Sabbath for seventy years. The closing of 2 Chronicles parallels Ezra 1:2, 3. By ending on this note, the chronicler sheds a ray of hope across both 1 and 2 Chronicles. Although the temple was in ruins, God had already begun to "hear from heaven" and to "heal their land" (7:14). If they would follow the good examples of David, Solomon, Asa, Jehoshaphat, Hezekiah, and Josiah in their devotion to God, He would bless them again.

✦Ezra✦

In the Hebrew text, Ezra and Nehemiah appeared as one book, similar in theme and style to 1 and 2 Chronicles. As a result, most scholars agree that Ezra wrote all four books (except for some of the material in Nehemiah) during the fifth century B.C. Ezra covers the years just after the Jews returned to their land from Babylon. When they defeated Babylon, the Persians let all captive people return to their homeland and live under a ruling governor; however, only a small portion of the Jews chose to take advantage of the opportunity.

The first six chapters describe the rebuilding of the temple under Zerubbabel's direction. Another group of Jews, led by Ezra, made the journey from Babylon to Jerusalem about sixty years after the first return under Zerubbabel. Chapters 7—10 show how God used Ezra to encourage the people to turn from their sin and honor God. Ezra reminded the people of their spiritual heritage, just as each generation is responsible for teaching spiritual truths to following generations. Many of the Jews had married foreign women, and Ezra told them to divorce these women because this had contributed to the previous spiritual downfall of the nation.

Restoration is the theme of Ezra, from the people's worship practices to their temple to their moral lives. In the tenth chapter, the people repent of their sin and make a covenant to live in accordance with God's law. ✦

CHAPTER 1

End of the Babylonian Captivity

Now in the first year of Cyrus king of Persia, that the word of the LORD by the mouth of Jer·e·mī'ah might be fulfilled, the LORD stirred up the spirit of Cyrus king of Persia, so that he made a proclamation throughout all his kingdom, and also *put it* in writing, saying,

2 Thus says Cyrus king of Persia:
All the kingdoms of the earth the
LORD God of heaven has given me.
And He has commanded me to build
Him a house at Jerusalem which *is* in
Judah. 3Who *is* among you of all His
people? May his God be with him,
and let him go up to Jerusalem which
is in Judah, and build the house of the
LORD God of Israel (He *is* God), which
is in Jerusalem. 4And whoever is left
in any place where he dwells, let the
men of his place help him with silver
and gold, with goods and livestock,

1:1 first year of Cyrus: 538 B.C. **Jeremiah**: What the Persian emperor did was a fulfillment of God's plan in history, already announced through the prophets. Cyrus's **proclamation** came approximately 70 years after Jeremiah's 70-year prophecy given in 605 B.C. (see Jer. 25:1, 8–12).

1:2–4 2 Chr. 36:23 is a condensed version of this decree which here appears in a fuller form. Archeological evidence suggests that Cyrus made a similar decree for each of the captive peoples he inherited when he conquered the Babylonian empire.

besides the freewill offerings for the house of God which *is* in Jerusalem.

5Then the heads of the fathers' *houses* of Judah and Benjamin, and the priests and the Lē′vītes, with all whose spirits God had moved, arose to go up and build the house of the LORD which *is* in Jerusalem. 6And all those who *were* around them encouraged them with articles of silver and gold, with goods and livestock, and with precious things, besides all *that* was willingly offered.

7King Cyrus also brought out the articles of the house of the LORD, which Ne·bū·chad·nez′zar had taken from Jerusalem and put in the temple of his gods; 8and Cyrus king of Persia brought them out by the hand of Mith′re·dath the treasurer, and counted them out to Shesh·baz′zar the prince of Judah. 9This *is* the number of them: thirty gold platters, one thousand silver platters, twenty-nine knives, 10thirty gold basins, four hundred and ten silver basins of a similar *kind, and* one thousand other articles. 11All the articles of gold and silver *were* five thousand four hundred. All *these* Shesh·baz′zar took with the captives who were brought from Babylon to Jerusalem.

CHAPTER 2

The Captives Who Returned to Jerusalem

Now[a] these *are* the people of the province who came back from the captivity, of those who had been carried away, whom Ne·bū·chad·nez′zar the king of Babylon had carried away to Babylon, and who returned to Jerusalem and Judah, everyone to his *own* city.

2*Those* who came with Ze·rub′ba·bel *were* Jesh′ū·a, Nē·he·mī′ah, Se·rāi′ah, Rē·el·āi′ah, Mor′de·caī, Bil′shan, Mis′par,[a] Big′vaī, Rē′hum,[b] *and* Bā′a·nah. The number of the men of the people of Israel: 3the people of Pā′rosh, two thousand one hundred and seventy-two; 4the people of Sheph·a·tī′ah, three hundred and seventy-two; 5the people of Ā′rah, seven hundred and seventy-five; 6the people of Pā′hath-Mō′ab, of the people of Jesh′ū·a *and* Jō′ab, two thousand eight hundred and twelve; 7the people of Ē′lam, one thousand two hundred and fifty-four; 8the people of Zat′tū, nine hundred and forty-five; 9the people of Zac′caī, seven hundred and sixty; 10the people of Bā′nī,[a] six hundred and forty-two; 11the people of Bē′baī, six hundred and twenty-three; 12the people of Az′gad, one thousand two hundred and twenty-two; 13the people of Ad·o·nī′kam, six hundred and sixty-six; 14the people of Big′vaī, two thousand and fifty-six; 15the people of Ā′din, four hundred and fifty-four; 16the people of Ā′ter of Hez·e·kī′ah, ninety-eight; 17the people of Bē′zaī, three hundred and twenty-three; 18the people of Jō′rah,[a] one hundred and twelve; 19the people of Hā′shum, two hundred and twenty-three; 20the people of Gib′bar,[a] ninety-five; 21the people of Bethlehem, one hundred and twenty-three; 22the men of Ne·toph′ah,

2:1 [a]Compare this chapter with Nehemiah 7:6–73.
2:2 [a]Spelled *Mispereth* in Nehemiah 7:7 [b]Spelled *Nehum* in Nehemiah 7:7 2:10 [a]Spelled *Binnui* in Nehemiah 7:15 2:18 [a]Called *Hariph* in Nehemiah 7:24 2:20 [a]Called *Gibeon* in Nehemiah 7:25

1:8 Sheshbazaar may be a Babylonian name for Zerubbabel, or he may be a totally different person, perhaps an official assisted by Zerubbabel.

2:1–70 The importance of these lists was to establish the continuity of the covenant people, especially in the priesthood (v. 62).

2:2 Jeshua: A variant spelling of Joshua, the high priest who served with Zerubbabel (see Hag. 1:1; Zech. 4:14). **Nehemiah**: not to be confused with the book by the same name.

2:21–35 The new Judah would not be as large as preexilic Judah under Uzziah and Hezekiah had been.

fifty-six; 23the men of An′a•thoth, one hundred and twenty-eight; 24the people of Az′ma•veth,[a] forty-two; 25the people of Kir′jath Ar′im,[a] Chē•phī′rah, and Be-er′oth, seven hundred and forty-three; 26the people of Rā′mah and Gē′ba, six hundred and twenty-one; 27the men of Mich′-mas, one hundred and twenty-two; 28the men of Beth′el and Aī, two hundred and twenty-three; 29the people of Nē′bō, fifty-two; 30the people of Mag′bish, one hundred and fifty-six; 31the people of the other Ē′lam, one thousand two hundred and fifty-four; 32the people of Hā′rim, three hundred and twenty; 33the people of Lod, Hā′did, and Ō′nō, seven hundred and twenty-five; 34the people of Jericho, three hundred and forty-five; 35the people of Se•nā′ah, three thousand six hundred and thirty.

36The priests: the sons of Je•daī′ah, of the house of Jesh′ū•a, nine hundred and seventy-three; 37the sons of Im′mer, one thousand and fifty-two; 38the sons of Pash′hur, one thousand two hundred and forty-seven; 39the sons of Hā′rim, one thousand and seventeen.

40The Lē′vītes: the sons of Jesh′ū•a and Kad′mi•el, of the sons of Hod•a•vī′ah,[a] seventy-four.

41The singers: the sons of Ā′saph, one hundred and twenty-eight.

42The sons of the gatekeepers: the sons of Shal′lum, the sons of Ā′ter, the sons of Tal′mon, the sons of Ak′kub, the sons of Ha•tī′ta, and the sons of Shō′baī, one hundred and thirty-nine *in* all.

43The Neth′i•nim: the sons of Zī′ha, the sons of Ha•sū′pha, the sons of Tab•bā′oth, 44the sons of Kē′ros, the sons of Sī′a•ha,[a] the sons of Pā′don, 45the sons of Le•bā′nah, the sons of Hag′a•bah, the sons of Ak′kub, 46the sons of Hā′gab, the sons of Shal′maī, the sons of Hā′nan, 47the sons of Gid′del, the sons of Gā′har, the sons of Rē•āi′ah, 48the sons of Rē′zin, the sons of Ne•kō′da, the sons of Gaz′zam, 49the sons of Uz′za, the sons of Pa•sē′ah, the sons of Bē′saī, 50the sons of As′nah, the sons of Me•ū′nim, the sons of Ne•phū′sim,[a] 51the sons of Bak′buk, the sons of Ha•kū′pha, the sons of Har′hur, 52the sons of Baz′luth,[a] the sons of Me•hī′da, the sons of Har′sha, 53the sons of Bar′kos, the sons of Sis′e•ra, the sons of Tam′ah, 54the sons of Ne•zī′ah, and the sons of Ha•tī′pha.

55The sons of Solomon's servants: the sons of Sō′taī, the sons of Sō′phe•reth, the sons of Pe•rū′da,[a] 56the sons of Jā′a•la, the sons of Dar′kon, the sons of Gid′del, 57the sons of Sheph•a•tī′ah, the sons of Hat′til, the sons of Poch′e•reth of Ze•bā′im, and the sons of Ā′mī.[a] 58All the Neth′i•nim and the children of Solomon's servants were three hundred and ninety-two.

59And these *were* the ones who came up from Tel Mē′lah, Tel Har′sha, Chē′rub, Ad′dan,[a] and Im′mer; but they could not identify their father's house or their genealogy,[b] whether they *were* of Israel: 60the sons of De•laī′ah, the sons of Tō•bī′ah, and the sons of Ne•kō′da, six hundred and fifty-two; 61and of the sons of the priests:

2:24 [a]Called *Beth Azmaveth* in Nehemiah 7:28
2:25 [a]Called *Kirjath Jearim* in Nehemiah 7:29
2:40 [a]Spelled *Hodevah* in Nehemiah 7:43
2:44 [a]Spelled *Sia* in Nehemiah 7:47 2:50 [a]Spelled *Nephishesim* in Nehemiah 7:52 2:52 [a]Spelled *Bazlith* in Nehemiah 7:54 2:55 [a]Spelled *Perida* in Nehemiah 7:57 2:57 [a]Spelled *Amon* in Nehemiah 7:59 2:59 [a]Spelled *Addon* in Nehemiah 7:61 [b]Literally *seed*

2:23 Some of those returning to **Anathoth** possibly could recall how their townsmen had rejected the prophet Jeremiah's warning of the coming exile (see Jer. 11:21–23; see also Jer. 32:8 and note on Jer. 32:1–44).

2:28, 34 Bethel . . . Ai . . . Jericho: It was at these cities that God enabled Joshua and the Hebrews to first enter the Promised Land (see Josh. 6—8). Here God enables them to return to the place where they began.

2:55 sons of Solomon's servants: Probably descendants of the foreigners who were conscripted into Solomon's labor force (see 2 Chr. 2:17, 18).

the sons of Ha·bai'ah, the sons of Koz,[a] and the sons of Bar·zil'lai, who took a wife of the daughters of Bar·zil'lai the Gil'ē·ad·īte, and was called by their name. 62These sought their listing *among* those who were registered by genealogy, but they were not found; therefore they *were excluded* from the priesthood as defiled. 63And the governor[a] said to them that they should not eat of the most holy things till a priest could consult with the Ū'rim and Thum'mim.

64The whole assembly together *was* forty-two thousand three hundred *and* sixty, 65besides their male and female servants, of whom *there were* seven thousand three hundred and thirty-seven; and they had two hundred men and women singers. 66Their horses *were* seven hundred and thirty-six, their mules two hundred and forty-five, 67their camels four hundred and thirty-five, and *their* donkeys six thousand seven hundred and twenty.

68*Some* of the heads of the fathers' *houses,* when they came to the house of the LORD which *is* in Jerusalem, offered freely for the house of God, to erect it in its place: 69According to their ability, they gave to the treasury for the work sixty-one thousand gold drachmas, five thousand minas of silver, and one hundred priestly garments.

70So the priests and the Lē'vītes, *some* of the people, the singers, the gatekeepers, and the Neth'i·nim, dwelt in their cities, and all Israel in their cities.

CHAPTER 3

Worship Restored at Jerusalem

And when the seventh month had come, and the children of Israel *were* in the cities, the people gathered together as one man to Jerusalem. 2Then Jesh'ū·a the son of Jō'za·dak[a] and his brethren the priests, and Ze·rub'ba·bel the son of She·al'ti·el and his brethren, arose and built the altar of the God of Israel, to offer burnt offerings on it, as *it is* written in the Law of Moses the man of God. 3Though fear *had come* upon them because of the people of those countries, they set the altar on its bases; and they offered burnt offerings on it to the LORD, *both* the morning and evening burnt offerings. 4They also kept the Feast of Tabernacles, as *it is* written, and *offered* the daily burnt offerings in the number required by ordinance for each day. 5Afterwards *they offered* the regular burnt offering, and *those* for New Moons and for all the appointed feasts of the LORD that were consecrated, and *those* of everyone who willingly offered a freewill offering to the LORD. 6From the first day of the seventh month they began to offer burnt offerings to the LORD, although the foundation of the temple of the LORD had not been laid. 7They also gave money to the masons and the carpenters, and food, drink, and oil to the people of Sī'don and Tȳre to bring cedar logs from Lebanon to the sea, to Jop'pa, according to the permission which they had from Cyrus king of Persia.

Restoration of the Temple Begins

8Now in the second month of the second year of their coming to the house of God at Jerusalem, Ze·rub'ba·bel the son of She·al'ti·el, Jesh'ū·a the son of Jō'za·dak,[a] and

2:61 [a]Or *Hakkoz* 2:63 [a]Hebrew *Tirshatha*
3:2 [a]Spelled *Jehozadak* in 1 Chronicles 6:14
3:8 [a]Spelled *Jehozadak* in 1 Chronicles 6:14

2:63 The **governor** of Judah was appointed by the Persians (see Hag. 1:1). Here it probably refers to either Sheshbazzar (5:14) or Zerubbabel (5:2; 6:7).

2:64 The number returning from exile was only a fraction of those taken captive.

3:1—6:22 Rebuilding the temple. If the Jews were now to find their identity as a nation of priests to reveal God to the world, it was imperative that the temple be rebuilt.

3:2, 3 The **altar** was erected as the first step in the restoration of the sacrificial system. By acting in faith despite hostile opposition, the returned captives set the tone for their future relationship with God.

the rest of their brethren the priests and the Lē′vītes, and all those who had come out of the captivity to Jerusalem, began *work* and appointed the Lē′vītes from twenty years old and above to oversee the work of the house of the LORD. [9]Then Jesh′ū·a *with* his sons and brothers, Kad′mi·el *with* his sons, and the sons of Judah,[a] arose as one to oversee those working on the house of God: the sons of Hen′a·dad *with* their sons and their brethren the Lē′vītes.

[10]When the builders laid the foundation of the temple of the LORD, the priests stood[a] in their apparel with trumpets, and the Lē′vītes, the sons of Ā′saph, with cymbals, to praise the LORD, according to the ordinance of David king of Israel. [11]And they sang responsively, praising and giving thanks to the LORD:

"For *He is* good,
For His mercy *endures* forever toward Israel."[a]

Then all the people shouted with a great shout, when they praised the LORD, because the foundation of the house of the LORD was laid.

[12]But many of the priests and Lē′vītes and heads of the fathers′ *houses,* old men who had seen the first temple, wept with a loud voice when the foundation of this temple was laid before their eyes. Yet many shouted aloud for joy, [13]so that the people could not discern the noise of the shout of joy from the noise of the weeping of the people, for the people shouted with a loud shout, and the sound was heard afar off.

CHAPTER 4

Resistance to Rebuilding the Temple

Now when the adversaries of Judah and Benjamin heard that the descendants of the captivity were building the temple of the LORD God of Israel, [2]they came to Ze-rub′ba·bel and the heads of the fathers′ *houses,* and said to them, "Let us build with you, for we seek your God as you *do;* and we have sacrificed to Him since the days of Ē·sar·had′don king of Assyria, who brought us here." [3]But Ze·rub′ba·bel and Jesh′ū·a and the rest of the heads of the fathers′ *houses* of Israel said to them, "You may do nothing with us to build a house for our God; but we alone will build to the LORD God of Israel, as King Cyrus the king of Persia has commanded us." [4]Then the people of the land tried to discourage the people of Judah. They troubled them in building, [5]and hired counselors against them to frustrate their purpose all the days of Cyrus king of Persia, even until the reign of Da·rī′us king of Persia.

Rebuilding of Jerusalem Opposed

[6]In the reign of A·has·ū·ē′rus, in the beginning of his reign, they wrote an accusa-

3:9 [a]Or *Hodaviah* (compare 2:40) 3:10 [a]Following Septuagint, Syriac, and Vulgate; Masoretic Text reads *they stationed the priests.* 3:11 [a]Compare Psalm 136:1

3:12, 13 The joy of the people was diminished by the remembrance of the temple's former glory. While the Lord is merciful when we repent, how much better if we had not sinned in the first place! The lost opportunities of that time of broken fellowship can never be regained. However, we must not allow ourselves to be discouraged by looking back at prior failures.

4:2 The "adversaries of Judah and Benjamin" were the descendants of mixed marriages between Israelites who remained in the land and the foreigners who were moved into the land by the Assyrians. They had combined the worship of Jehovah with idolatrous religions and thus were not considered by Zerubbabel to be genuine children of God. This group of people later became known as Samaritans.

4:5 Work on the temple ceased from 536 until 520 B.C., partly because of opposition (see v. 24).

4:6–23 In the reign of Ahasuerus: The events described here took place some 50 years later between 486 and 465 B.C. The writer probably included them here to illustrate the kinds

tion against the inhabitants of Judah and
Jerusalem.
7In the days of Ar·ta·xerx′ēs also, Bish′-
lam, Mith′re·dath, Tā′bel, and the rest of
their companions wrote to Ar·ta·xerx′ēs
king of Persia; and the letter *was* written in
Ar·a·mā′ic script, and translated into the
Ar·a·mā′ic language. 8Rē′hum[a] the com-
mander and Shim′shaī the scribe wrote a
letter against Jerusalem to King Ar·ta-
xerx′ēs in this fashion:

9 From[a] Rē′hum the commander,
Shim′shaī the scribe, and the rest of
their companions—*representatives* of
the Dī′na·ītes, the A·phar′sath·chītes,
the Tar′pel·ītes, the people of Persia
and Ē′rech and Babylon and
Shū′shan,[b] the De·hā′vītes, the
Ē′lam·ītes, 10and the rest of the na-
tions whom the great and noble
Os·nap′per took captive and settled in
the cities of Samaria and the remain-
der beyond the River[a]—and so forth.[b]

11(This *is* a copy of the letter that they
sent him)

To King Ar·ta·xerx′ēs from your ser-
vants, the men *of the region* beyond the
River, and so forth:[a]

12 Let it be known to the king that the
Jews who came up from you have
come to us at Jerusalem, and are
building the rebellious and evil city,
and are finishing *its* walls and repair-
ing the foundations. 13Let it now be
known to the king that, if this city is
built and the walls completed, they
will not pay tax, tribute, or custom,
and the king′s treasury will be dimin-
ished. 14Now because we receive sup-
port from the palace, it was not
proper for us to see the king′s dis-
honor; therefore we have sent and in-
formed the king, 15that search may be
made in the book of the records of
your fathers. And you will find in the
book of the records and know that
this city *is* a rebellious city, harmful to
kings and provinces, and that they
have incited sedition within the city in
former times, for which cause this city
was destroyed.

16 We inform the king that if this city is
rebuilt and its walls are completed,
the result will be that you will have
no dominion beyond the River.

17The king sent an answer:

To Rē′hum the commander, *to*
Shim′shaī the scribe, *to* the rest of
their companions who dwell in Sa-
maria, and *to* the remainder beyond
the River:

Peace, and so forth.[a]

18 The letter which you sent to us has
been clearly read before me. 19And I
gave the command, and a search has
been made, and it was found that this
city in former times has revolted
against kings, and rebellion and sedi-
tion have been fostered in it. 20There

4:8 [a]The original language of Ezra 4:8 through 6:18 is Aramaic. 4:9 [a]Literally *Then* [b]Or *Susa*
4:10 [a]That is, the Euphrates [b]Literally *and now*
4:11 [a]Literally *and now* 4:17 [a]Literally *and now*

of hostility the Jews faced. This letter (vv. 9–16) and the king′s response (vv. 17–22) also explain why Jerusalem′s **walls** had still not been rebuilt in 444 B.C. (vv. 12, 16).

4:6, 7 Ahasuerus is considered to be the same ruler as Xerxes the Great, king of Persia from 486 to 465 B.C. There were three kings of Persia named **Artaxerxes**. The reference here is to Artaxerxes I (465–424 B.C.), the son of Xerxes.

4:9, 10 Osnapper is usually identified with the Assyrian king Ashurbanipal who is known to have conquered **the Elamites** around 640 B.C.

have also been mighty kings over Je-
rusalem, who have ruled over all *the*
region beyond the River; and tax, trib-
ute, and custom were paid to them.
21Now give the command to make
these men cease, that this city may not
be built until the command is given
by me.

22 Take heed now that you do not fail to
do this. Why should damage increase
to the hurt of the kings?

23Now when the copy of King Ar·ta-
xerx'ēs' letter *was* read before Rē'hum,
Shim'shaī the scribe, and their compan-
ions, they went up in haste to Jerusalem
against the Jews, and by force of arms
made them cease. 24Thus the work of the
house of God which *is* at Jerusalem ceased,
and it was discontinued until the second
year of the reign of Da·rī'us king of Persia.

CHAPTER 5

Restoration of the Temple Resumed

Then the prophet Hag'gaī and Zech-
a·rī'ah the son of Id'dō, prophets, prophe-
sied to the Jews who *were* in Judah and Je-
rusalem, in the name of the God of Israel,
who was over them. 2So Ze·rub'ba·bel the
son of She·al'ti·el and Jesh'ū·a the son of
Jō'za·dak[a] rose up and began to build the
house of God which *is* in Jerusalem; and
the prophets of God *were* with them, help-
ing them.

5:2 [a]Spelled *Jehozadak* in 1 Chronicles 6:14
5:3 [a]That is, the Euphrates

3At the same time Tat'te·naī the gover-
nor of *the region* beyond the River[a] and
Shē'thar-Boz'nai and their companions
came to them and spoke thus to them:
"Who has commanded you to build this
temple and finish this wall?" 4Then, ac-
cordingly, we told them the names of the
men who were constructing this building.
5But the eye of their God was upon the el-
ders of the Jews, so that they could not
make them cease till a report could go to
Da·rī'us. Then a written answer was re-
turned concerning this *matter*. 6This is a
copy of the letter that Tat'te·naī sent:

The governor of *the region* beyond the
River, and Shē'thar-Boz'nai, and his
companions, the Persians who *were in*
the region beyond the River, to
Da·rī'us the king.

7(They sent a letter to him, in which was
written thus)

To Da·rī'us the king:

All peace.

8 Let it be known to the king that we
went into the province of Judea, to the
temple of the great God, which is be-
ing built with heavy stones, and tim-
ber is being laid in the walls; and this
work goes on diligently and prospers
in their hands.

9 Then we asked those elders,
and spoke thus to them: "Who

4:24 the work . . . ceased: The focus returns to 537/536 B.C. **until the second year . . . of Darius**: Until 520 B.C.

5:1 The prophets, **Haggai** and **Zechariah**, encourage the people to finish their task (520–516 B.C.). These two represented the two groups among the Jews. The older ones, with Haggai, had worshiped in Solomon's temple before its destruction in 586 B.C. Zechariah in some measure represented the younger generation who were born after 586. Haggai challenged the people to pay as much attention to God's house as they were paying to their own houses, while Zechariah excited them with visions of a blessed future for those who obeyed.

5:5 cease: The Jews would not stop working while the appeal was going to the Persian king.

commanded you to build this temple
and to finish these walls?" [10]We also
asked them their names to inform
you, that we might write the names
of the men who *were* chief among
them.

11 And thus they returned us an answer,
saying: "We are the servants of the
God of heaven and earth, and we are
rebuilding the temple that was built
many years ago, which a great king of
Israel built and completed. [12]But be-
cause our fathers provoked the God of
heaven to wrath, He gave them into
the hand of Ne·bū·chad·nez'zar king
of Babylon, the Chal·dē'an, *who* de-
stroyed this temple and carried the
people away to Babylon. [13]However,
in the first year of Cyrus king of Bab-
ylon, King Cyrus issued a decree to
build this house of God. [14]Also, the
gold and silver articles of the house of
God, which Ne·bū·chad·nez'zar had
taken from the temple that *was* in Je-
rusalem and carried into the temple of
Babylon—those King Cyrus took from
the temple of Babylon, and they were
given to one named Shesh·baz'zar,
whom he had made governor. [15]And
he said to him, 'Take these articles; go,
carry them to the temple *site* that *is* in
Jerusalem, and let the house of God
be rebuilt on its former site.' [16]Then
the same Shesh·baz'zar came *and* laid
the foundation of the house of God
which *is* in Jerusalem; but from that
time even until now it has been under
construction, and it is not finished."

17 Now therefore, if *it seems* good to the
king, let a search be made in the
king's treasure house, which *is* there
in Babylon, whether it is *so* that a de-
cree was issued by King Cyrus to
build this house of God at Jerusalem,
and let the king send us his pleasure
concerning this *matter*.

CHAPTER 6

The Decree of Darius

Then King Da·rī'us issued a decree, and
a search was made in the archives,[a] where
the treasures were stored in Babylon. [2]And
at Ach'me·tha,[a] in the palace that *is* in the
province of Media, a scroll was found, and
in it a record *was* written thus:

3 In the first year of King Cyrus, King
Cyrus issued a decree *concerning* the
house of God at Jerusalem: "Let the
house be rebuilt, the place where they
offered sacrifices; and let the founda-
tions of it be firmly laid, its height
sixty cubits *and* its width sixty cubits,
[4]*with* three rows of heavy stones and
one row of new timber. Let the ex-
penses be paid from the king's trea-
sury. [5]Also let the gold and silver arti-
cles of the house of God, which
Ne·bū·chad·nez'zar took from the

6:1 [a]Literally *house of the scrolls*
6:2 [a]Probably *Ecbatana*, the ancient capital of Media

5:11 This verse demonstrates the change that had taken place in the hearts of the people since their captivity: no longer is their loyalty split among many gods, but they willingly served the Lord alone and dedicated themselves to His work.

5:16 Sheshbazzar . . . laid the foundation: As David's descendant, Zerubbabel could be the "prince of Judah" of 1:8; if not, then Sheshbazzar must have made plans for the temple building that Zerubbabel later initiated (see 3:8).

6:2 the palace . . . of Media: Cyrus conquered the Medes in 549 B.C.; however, Media was not merely absorbed into the Persian empire. This is indicated by its capital city continuing as a dual capital with Persian Susa (Esth. 1:2) in the south, as well as by such phrases as "Persia and Media" (Esth. 1:18) and "the Persians and the Medes" (Esth. 1:19).

6:3–5 The original decree of Cyrus (v. 3). It was possibly an Aramaic documentation of the public "proclamation" in 1:2–4.

temple which *is* in Jerusalem and
brought to Babylon, be restored and
taken back to the temple which *is* in
Jerusalem, *each* to its place; and de-
posit *them* in the house of God"—

6 Now *therefore,* Tat′te·naī, governor of
the region beyond the River, and
Shē′thar-Boz′nai, and your compan-
ions the Persians who *are* beyond the
River, keep yourselves far from there.
[7]Let the work of this house of God
alone; let the governor of the Jews and
the elders of the Jews build this house
of God on its site.

8 Moreover I issue a decree *as to* what
you shall do for the elders of these
Jews, for the building of this house of
God: Let the cost be paid at the king's
expense from taxes *on the region* be-
yond the River; this is to be given im-
mediately to these men, so that they
are not hindered. [9]And whatever they
need—young bulls, rams, and lambs
for the burnt offerings of the God of
heaven, wheat, salt, wine, and oil, ac-
cording to the request of the priests
who *are* in Jerusalem—let it be given
them day by day without fail, [10]that
they may offer sacrifices of sweet
aroma to the God of heaven, and pray
for the life of the king and his sons.

11 Also I issue a decree that whoever al-
ters this edict, let a timber be pulled
from his house and erected, and let
him be hanged on it; and let his house
be made a refuse heap because of this.
[12]And may the God who causes His
name to dwell there destroy any king
or people who put their hand to alter
it, or to destroy this house of God
which is in Jerusalem. I Da·rī′us issue
a decree; let it be done diligently.

The Temple Completed and Dedicated

[13]Then Tat′te·naī, governor of *the region* beyond the River, Shē′thar-Boz′nai, and their companions diligently did according to what King Da·rī′us had sent. [14]So the elders of the Jews built, and they prospered through the prophesying of Hag′gaī the prophet and Zech·a·rī′ah the son of Id′dō. And they built and finished *it,* according to the commandment of the God of Israel, and according to the command of Cyrus, Da·rī′us, and Ar·ta·xerx′ēs king of Persia. [15]Now the temple was finished on the third day of the month of Ā′dar, which was in the sixth year of the reign of King Da·rī′us. [16]Then the children of Israel, the priests and the Lē′vītes and the rest of the descendants of the captivity, celebrated the dedication of this house of God with joy. [17]And they offered sacrifices at the dedication of this house of God, one hundred bulls, two hundred rams, four hundred lambs, and as a sin offering for all Israel twelve male goats, according to the number of the tribes of Israel. [18]They assigned the priests to their divisions and the Lē′vītes to their divisions, over the service of God in Jerusalem, as it is written in the Book of Moses.

The Passover Celebrated

[19]And the descendants of the captivity kept the Passover on the fourteenth *day* of the first month. [20]For the priests and the Lē′vītes had purified themselves; all of them *were ritually* clean. And they slaughtered the Passover *lambs* for all the descendants of the captivity, for their brethren the priests, and for themselves. [21]Then the children of Israel who had returned from the captivity ate together with all who had separated themselves from the filth of the

6:14 Artaxerxes: His commands had to do with rebuilding the city later during the times of Ezra and Nehemiah.

6:15 The construction of the temple was completed about 72 years after the destruction of Solomon's temple.

nations of the land in order to seek the LORD God of Israel. 22And they kept the Feast of Unleavened Bread seven days with joy; for the LORD made them joyful, and turned the heart of the king of Assyria toward them, to strengthen their hands in the work of the house of God, the God of Israel.

CHAPTER 7

The Arrival of Ezra

Now after these things, in the reign of Ar·ta·xerx'ēs king of Persia, Ezra the son of Se·rāi'ah, the son of Az·a·rī'ah, the son of Hil·kī'ah, 2the son of Shal'lum, the son of Zā'dok, the son of A·hī'tub, 3the son of Am·a·rī'ah, the son of Az·a·rī'ah, the son of Me·rā'i·oth, 4the son of Zer·a·hī'ah, the son of Uz'zī, the son of Buk'kī, 5the son of Ab·i·shū'a, the son of Phin'e·has, the son of El·ē·ā'zar, the son of Aaron the chief priest— 6this Ezra came up from Babylon; and he *was* a skilled scribe in the Law of Moses, which the LORD God of Israel had given. The king granted him all his request, according to the hand of the LORD his God upon him. 7*Some* of the children of Israel, the priests, the Lē'vītes, the singers, the gatekeepers, and the Neth'i·nim came up to Jerusalem in the seventh year of King Ar·ta·xerx'ēs. 8And Ezra came to Jerusalem in the fifth month, which *was* in the seventh year of the king. 9On the first *day* of the first month he began *his* journey from Babylon, and on the first *day* of the fifth month he came to Jerusalem, according to the good hand of his God upon him. 10For Ezra had prepared his heart to seek the Law of the LORD, and to do *it*, and to teach statutes and ordinances in Israel.

The Letter of Artaxerxes to Ezra

11This *is* a copy of the letter that King Ar·ta·xerx'ēs gave Ezra the priest, the scribe, expert in the words of the commandments of the LORD, and of His statutes to Israel:

12 Ar·ta·xerx'ēs,[a] king of kings,

To Ezra the priest, a scribe of the Law of the God of heaven:

Perfect *peace*, and so forth.[b]

13 I issue a decree that all those of the people of Israel and the priests and Lē'vītes in my realm, who volunteer to go up to Jerusalem, may go with you. 14And whereas you are being sent by the king and his seven counselors to inquire concerning Judah and Jerusalem, with regard to the Law of your God which *is* in your hand; 15and *whereas you are* to carry the silver and gold which the king and his counselors have freely offered to the God of Israel, whose dwelling *is* in Jerusalem; 16and *whereas* all the silver

7:12 [a]The original language of Ezra 7:12–26 is Aramaic. [b]Literally *and now*

6:22 king of Assyria: Darius was the Persian king, but the term Assyria still referred to territories once ruled by Assyria. God still controls world leaders and uses them to fulfill His plan.

7:1–5 The genealogy of Ezra, the priest/scribe, is traced back to **Aaron** (v. 5), the chief priest. This validated Ezra's right to teach the law and enforce it among his people. **in the reign of Artaxerxes**: Dating ch. 7 in the seventh year of Artaxerxes I (see vv. 7, 8), places Ezra's journey to Jerusalem in 458 B.C.

7:6 skilled scribe: Not merely a copyist, but a student of the law in all its aspects.

7:9 first day: Preparations for the trip delayed the actual departure until the "twelfth day" (8:31; see also 8:15, 21).

7:10 Ezra, with a significant group of Jews, went from Babylon to Jerusalem to **seek**, to **do**, and to **teach** the law. This journey, the second return of the Jews, occurred in 458 B.C., approximately 79 years after the first return.

and gold that you may find in all the
province of Babylon, along with the
freewill offering of the people and the
priests, *are to be* freely offered for the
house of their God in Jerusalem—
17now therefore, be careful to buy with
this money bulls, rams, and lambs,
with their grain offerings and their
drink offerings, and offer them on the
altar of the house of your God in Jeru-
salem.

18 And whatever seems good to you and
your brethren to do with the rest of
the silver and the gold, do it accord-
ing to the will of your God. 19Also the
articles that are given to you for the
service of the house of your God, de-
liver in full before the God of Jerusa-
lem. 20And whatever more may be
needed for the house of your God,
which you may have occasion to pro-
vide, pay *for it* from the king's trea-
sury.

21 And I, *even* I, Ar·ta·xerx'ēs the king,
issue a decree to all the treasurers
who *are in the region* beyond the River,
that whatever Ezra the priest, the
scribe of the Law of the God of
heaven, may require of you, let it be
done diligently, 22up to one hundred
talents of silver, one hundred kors of
wheat, one hundred baths of wine,
one hundred baths of oil, and salt
without prescribed limit. 23Whatever
is commanded by the God of heaven,
let it diligently be done for the house
of the God of heaven. For why should
there be wrath against the realm of
the king and his sons?

24 Also we inform you that it shall not
be lawful to impose tax, tribute, or
custom *on* any of the priests, Lē'vītes,
singers, gatekeepers, Neth'i·nim, or
servants of this house of God. 25And
you, Ezra, according to your God-
given wisdom, set magistrates and
judges who may judge all the people
who *are in the region* beyond the River,
all such as know the laws of your
God; and teach those who do not
know *them*. 26Whoever will not ob-
serve the law of your God and the law
of the king, let judgment be executed
speedily on him, whether *it be* death,
or banishment, or confiscation of
goods, or imprisonment.

27Blessed *be* the LORD God of our fathers,
who has put *such a thing* as this in the
king's heart, to beautify the house of the
LORD which *is* in Jerusalem, 28and has ex-
tended mercy to me before the king and his
counselors, and before all the king's
mighty princes.

So I was encouraged, as the hand of the
LORD my God *was* upon me; and I gathered
leading men of Israel to go up with me.

CHAPTER 8

Heads of Families Who Returned with Ezra

These *are* the heads of their fathers'
houses, and *this is* the genealogy of those
who went up with me from Babylon, in the

7:17–20 The instructions of the king repeatedly emphasize that the money is to be used solely for religious purposes related to the temple.

7:23–26 The king evidently believed it was in his best interests to keep the **God of heaven** (v. 23), whose house was in Jerusalem, happy with him. If this God was characterized by a set of laws, then His people should keep those laws (vv. 25, 26).

7:23 wrath against the realm: The king operated under the ancient Near Eastern thought that the god of any land would execute vengeance if his worship rituals were disrupted. Similarly, Sargon of Assyria was willing to restore the proper worship of Israel's God in Samaria after its fall in 722 B.C. (see 2 Kin. 17:24–28).

7:24 Tax exemption of churches is a time-honored custom.

reign of King Ar·ta·xerx′ēs: 2of the sons of
Phin′e·has, Ger′shom; of the sons of Ith′a-
mar, Daniel; of the sons of David, Hat′-
tush; 3of the sons of Shec·a·nī′ah, of the
sons of Pā′rosh, Zech·a·rī′ah; and regis-
tered with him *were* one hundred and fifty
males; 4of the sons of Pā′hath-Mō′ab,
El·i·ē·hō·ē′naī the son of Zer·a·hī′ah, and
with him two hundred males; 5of the sons
of Shech·a·nī′ah,[a] Ben-Ja·hā′zi·el, and
with him three hundred males; 6of the sons
of Ā′din, Ē′bed the son of Jonathan, and
with him fifty males; 7of the sons of Ē′lam,
Je·shā′i·ah the son of Ath·a·lī′ah, and with
him seventy males; 8of the sons of
Sheph·a·tī′ah, Zeb·a·dī′ah the son of Mi-
chael, and with him eighty males; 9of the
sons of Jō′ab, Ō·ba·dī′ah the son of Je·hī′el,
and with him two hundred and eighteen
males; 10of the sons of She·lō′mith,[a] Ben-
Jō·si·phī′ah, and with him one hundred
and sixty males; 11of the sons of Bē′baī,
Zech·a·rī′ah the son of Bē′baī, and with
him twenty-eight males; 12of the sons of
Az′gad, Jō·hā′nan the son of Hak′ka·tan,
and with him one hundred and ten males;
13of the last sons of Ad·o·nī′kam, whose
names *are* these—E·liph′e·let, Je·ī′el,
and She·māi′ah—and with them sixty
males; 14also of the sons of Big′vaī, Ū′thaī
and Zab′bud, and with them seventy
males.

Servants for the Temple

15Now I gathered them by the river that
flows to A·hā′va, and we camped there
three days. And I looked among the people
and the priests, and found none of the sons
of Levi there. 16Then I sent for El·i·ē′zer,
Ar′i·el, She·māi′ah, El·nā′than, Jā′rib,
El·nā′than, Nathan, Zech·a·rī′ah, and
Me·shul′lam, leaders; also for Joi′ā·rib and
El·nā′than, men of understanding. 17And I
gave them a command for Id′dō the chief
man at the place Cas·i·phī′a, and I told
them what they should say to Id′dō *and* his
brethren[a] the Neth′i·nim at the place
Cas·i·phī′a—that they should bring us ser-
vants for the house of our God. 18Then, by
the good hand of our God upon us, they
brought us a man of understanding, of the
sons of Mah′lī the son of Levi, the son of Is-
rael, namely Sher·e·bī′ah, with his sons
and brothers, eighteen men; 19and Hash-
a·bī′ah, and with him Je·shā′i·ah of the
sons of Me·rar′ī, his brothers and their
sons, twenty men; 20also of the Neth′i·nim,
whom David and the leaders had ap-
pointed for the service of the Lē′vītes, two
hundred and twenty Neth′i·nim. All of
them were designated by name.

Fasting and Prayer for Protection

21Then I proclaimed a fast there at the
river of A·hā′va, that we might humble
ourselves before our God, to seek from
Him the right way for us and our little
ones and all our possessions. 22For I was
ashamed to request of the king an escort of
soldiers and horsemen to help us against
the enemy on the road, because we had
spoken to the king, saying, "The hand of
our God *is* upon all those for good who
seek Him, but His power and His wrath *are*
against all those who forsake Him." 23So
we fasted and entreated our God for this,
and He answered our prayer.

8:5 [a]Following Masoretic Text and Vulgate; Septuagint reads *the sons of Zatho, Shechaniah.* 8:10 [a]Following Masoretic Text and Vulgate; Septuagint reads *the sons of Banni, Shelomith.* 8:17 [a]Following Vulgate; Masoretic Text reads *to Iddo his brother;* Septuagint reads *to their brethren.*

8:15–20 The reason the Levites were reluctant to return is not stated. Probably they were quite comfortable in Babylon by this time.

8:16 men of understanding: So called because of their function to help the people understand the sense of the Law (see Neh. 8:7, 8). Sherebiah (v. 18) served in this capacity under Nehemiah and Ezra (Neh. 8:7).

8:21 Fasting is not a method to manipulate God but an outward indication of one's sincerity and dedication in seeking the will and blessing of the Lord.

Gifts for the Temple

[24]And I separated twelve of the leaders of the priests—Sher·e·bī′ah, Hash·a·bī′ah, and ten of their brethren with them— [25]and weighed out to them the silver, the gold, and the articles, the offering for the house of our God which the king and his counselors and his princes, and all Israel *who were* present, had offered. [26]I weighed into their hand six hundred and fifty talents of silver, silver articles *weighing* one hundred talents, one hundred talents of gold, [27]twenty gold basins *worth* a thousand drachmas, and two vessels of fine polished bronze, precious as gold. [28]And I said to them, "You *are* holy to the LORD; the articles *are* holy also; and the silver and the gold *are* a freewill offering to the LORD God of your fathers. [29]Watch and keep *them* until you weigh *them* before the leaders of the priests and the Lē′vītes and heads of the fathers' *houses* of Israel in Jerusalem, *in* the chambers of the house of the LORD." [30]So the priests and the Lē′vītes received the silver and the gold and the articles by weight, to bring *them* to Jerusalem to the house of our God.

The Return to Jerusalem

[31]Then we departed from the river of A·hā′va on the twelfth *day* of the first month, to go to Jerusalem. And the hand of our God was upon us, and He delivered us from the hand of the enemy and from ambush along the road. [32]So we came to Jerusalem, and stayed there three days.

[33]Now on the fourth day the silver and the gold and the articles were weighed in the house of our God by the hand of Mer′e·moth the son of Ū·rī′ah the priest, and with him *was* El·ē·ā′zar the son of Phin′e·has; with them *were* the Lē′vītes, Joz′a·bad the son of Jesh′ū·a and Nō·a·dī′ah the son of Bin′nū·ī, [34]with the number *and* weight of everything. All the weight was written down at that time.

[35]The children of those who had been carried away captive, who had come from the captivity, offered burnt offerings to the God of Israel: twelve bulls for all Israel, ninety-six rams, seventy-seven lambs, and twelve male goats *as* a sin offering. All *this was* a burnt offering to the LORD.

[36]And they delivered the king's orders to the king's satraps and the governors *in the region* beyond the River. So they gave support to the people and the house of God.

CHAPTER 9

Intermarriage with Pagans

When these things were done, the leaders came to me, saying, "The people of Israel and the priests and the Lē′vītes have not separated themselves from the peoples of the lands, with respect to the abominations of the Cā′naan·ītes, the Hit′tītes, the Per′iz·zītes, the Jeb′ū·sītes, the Am′mon·ītes, the Mō′ab·ītes, the Egyptians, and the Am′o·rītes. [2]For they have taken some of their daughters *as wives* for themselves and their sons, so that the holy seed is mixed with the peoples of *those* lands. Indeed, the hand of the leaders and rulers has been foremost in this trespass." [3]So

---

8:34 All . . . was written down: Perhaps Ezra was required to send a receipt to Artaxerxes (see note on 7:17–20).

9:1–4 Ezra was horrified when he learned of the mixed marriages, especially since both **leaders** and **rulers** (v. 2) were involved.

9:1 The listing of foreign peoples from the **Canaanites** to the **Amorites** signifies all the nations that threatened to corrupt Israel's holiness from her first experiences in the Promised Land (see v. 11; Deut. 20:17). In Ezra's time the **Ammonites, Moabites**, and **Egyptians** were the current cause of defilement.

9:3 tore . . . plucked out: Ezra's actions were typical Near Eastern customs of mourning (see Jer. 41:5). We should be equally disturbed by sin, realizing its destructive power. As we grow older, we must guard against becoming callous to the sin and evil around us.

when I heard this thing, I tore my garment
and my robe, and plucked out some of the
hair of my head and beard, and sat down
astonished. 4Then everyone who trembled
at the words of the God of Israel assembled
to me, because of the transgression of those
who had been carried away captive, and I
sat astonished until the evening sacrifice.

5At the evening sacrifice I arose from my
fasting; and having torn my garment and
my robe, I fell on my knees and spread out
my hands to the LORD my God. 6And I said:
"O my God, I am too ashamed and humil-
iated to lift up my face to You, my God; for
our iniquities have risen higher than *our*
heads, and our guilt has grown up to the
heavens. 7Since the days of our fathers to
this day we *have been* very guilty, and for
our iniquities we, our kings, *and* our
priests have been delivered into the hand
of the kings of the lands, to the sword, to
captivity, to plunder, and to humiliation, as
it is this day. 8And now for a little while
grace has been *shown* from the LORD our
God, to leave us a remnant to escape, and
to give us a peg in His holy place, that our
God may enlighten our eyes and give us a
measure of revival in our bondage. 9For we
were slaves. Yet our God did not forsake us
in our bondage; but He extended mercy to
us in the sight of the kings of Persia, to re-
vive us, to repair the house of our God, to
rebuild its ruins, and to give us a wall in
Judah and Jerusalem. 10And now, O our
God, what shall we say after this? For we
have forsaken Your commandments,
11which You commanded by Your servants
the prophets, saying, 'The land which you
are entering to possess is an unclean land,
with the uncleanness of the peoples of the
lands, with their abominations which have
filled it from one end to another with their
impurity. 12Now therefore, do not give
your daughters as wives for their sons, nor
take their daughters to your sons; and
never seek their peace or prosperity, that
you may be strong and eat the good of the
land, and leave *it* as an inheritance to your
children forever.' 13And after all that has
come upon us for our evil deeds and for
our great guilt, since You our God have
punished us less than our iniquities *de-
serve*, and have given us *such* deliverance
as this, 14should we again break Your com-
mandments, and join in marriage with the
people *committing* these abominations?
Would You not be angry with us until You
had consumed *us*, so that *there would be* no
remnant or survivor? 15O LORD God of Is-
rael, You *are* righteous, for we are left as a
remnant, as *it is* this day. Here we *are* be-
fore You, in our guilt, though no one can
stand before You because of this!"

CHAPTER 10

Confession of Improper Marriages

Now while Ezra was praying, and while
he was confessing, weeping, and bowing
down before the house of God, a very large
assembly of men, women, and children
gathered to him from Israel; for the people
wept very bitterly. 2And Shech·a·nī′ah the
son of Je·hī′el, *one* of the sons of Ē′lam,
spoke up and said to Ezra, "We have tres-
passed against our God, and have taken
pagan wives from the peoples of the land;
yet now there is hope in Israel in spite
of this. 3Now therefore, let us make
a covenant with our God to put away

9:4 who trembled: Who took the commandments of God seriously.

9:8 a peg: A time of peace.

9:9 a wall: Representing protection in **Judah**.

9:11, 12 Marriage between believers and unbelievers almost always results in a dilution of faith. This was Solomon's error (1 Kin. 11:1–8).

10:2–4 Shechaniah encouraged Ezra to correct the evil of mixed marriages. Reformation must follow repentance. Ezra already had legal authority to dissolve the marriages, but that authority would be useless unless he had been given moral authority in the eyes of the people.

all these wives and those who have been born to them, according to the advice of my master and of those who tremble at the commandment of our God; and let it be done according to the law. [4]Arise, for *this* matter *is* your *responsibility*. We also *are* with you. Be of good courage, and do *it*."

[5]Then Ezra arose, and made the leaders of the priests, the Lē'vītes, and all Israel swear an oath that they would do according to this word. So they swore an oath. [6]Then Ezra rose up from before the house of God, and went into the chamber of Jē·hō·hā'nan the son of E·lī'a·shib; and *when* he came there, he ate no bread and drank no water, for he mourned because of the guilt of those from the captivity.

[7]And they issued a proclamation throughout Judah and Jerusalem to all the descendants of the captivity, that they must gather at Jerusalem, [8]and that whoever would not come within three days, according to the instructions of the leaders and elders, all his property would be confiscated, and he himself would be separated from the assembly of those from the captivity.

[9]So all the men of Judah and Benjamin gathered at Jerusalem within three days. It *was* the ninth month, on the twentieth of the month; and all the people sat in the open square of the house of God, trembling because of *this* matter and because of heavy rain. [10]Then Ezra the priest stood up and said to them, "You have transgressed and have taken pagan wives, adding to the guilt of Israel. [11]Now therefore, make confession to the LORD God of your fathers, and do His will; separate yourselves from the peoples of the land, and from the pagan wives."

[12]Then all the assembly answered and said with a loud voice, "Yes! As you have said, so we must do. [13]But *there are* many people; *it is* the season for heavy rain, and we are not able to stand outside. Nor *is this* the work of one or two days, for *there are* many of us who have transgressed in this matter. [14]Please, let the leaders of our entire assembly stand; and let all those in our cities who have taken pagan wives come at appointed times, together with the elders and judges of their cities, until the fierce wrath of our God is turned away from us in this matter." [15]Only Jonathan the son of As'a·hel and Jā·ha·zī'ah the son of Tik'vah opposed this, and Me·shul'lam and Shab'be·thaī the Lē'vīte gave them support.

[16]Then the descendants of the captivity did so. And Ezra the priest, *with* certain heads of the fathers' *households*, were set apart by the fathers' *households*, each of them by name; and they sat down on the first day of the tenth month to examine the matter. [17]By the first day of the first month they finished *questioning* all the men who had taken pagan wives.

Pagan Wives Put Away

[18]And among the sons of the priests who had taken pagan wives *the following* were found of the sons of Jesh'ū·a the son of Jō'za·dak,[a] and his brothers: Mā·a·sēi'ah, El·i·ē'zer, Jā'rib, and Ged·a·lī'ah. [19]And they gave their promise that they would put away their wives; and *being* guilty, *they*

10:18 [a]Spelled *Jehozadak* in 1 Chronicles 6:14

10:9 Heavy rain was characteristic in the **ninth month** of the sacred year (November-December) during the time of the former rains.

10:14–17 Systematically by households over a period of three months (vv. 16, 17) everyone who was guilty confessed, offered sacrifice, and sent their pagan wives back to their homes. These actions were radical, but necessary if the revelation of God was not to be dissolved into paganism. Then as now, it is the religion of the mother which is usually passed on to the children.

10:18–44 A terribly long list of offenders.

presented a ram of the flock as their trespass
offering.
20 Also of the sons of Im′mer: Ha·nā′nī
and Zeb·a·dī′ah; 21 of the sons of Hā′rim:
Mā·a·sēi′ah, E·lī′jah, She·māi′ah, Je·hī′el,
and Uz·zī′ah; 22 of the sons of Pash′hur:
El·i·ō·ē′naī, Mā·a·sēi′ah, Ish′ma·el, Ne-
than′el, Joz′a·bad, and El·ā′sah.
23 Also of the Lē′vītes: Joz′a·bad,
Shim′ē·ī, Ke·lāi′ah (the same *is* Ke·lī′ta),
Peth·a·hī′ah, Judah, and El·i·ē′zer.
24 Also of the singers: E·lī′a·shib; and of
the gatekeepers: Shal′lum, Tē′lem, and
Ū′rī.
25 And others of Israel: of the sons of
Pā′rosh: Ra·mī′ah, Je·zī′ah, Mal·chī′ah,
Mij′a·min, El·ē·ā′zar, Mal·chī′jah, and
Be·nā′i·ah; 26 of the sons of Ē′lam: Mat-
ta·nī′ah, Zech·a·rī′ah, Je·hī′el, Ab′dī,
Jer′e·moth, and E·lī′ah; 27 of the sons of
Zat′tū: El·i·ō·ē′naī, E·lī′a·shib, Mat-
ta·nī′ah, Jer′e·moth, Zā′bad, and A·zī′za;
28 of the sons of Bē′baī: Jē·hō·hā′nan,
Han·a·nī′ah, Zab′baī, *and* Ath′laī; 29 of the
sons of Bā′nī: Me·shul′lam, Mal′luch,
A·dāi′ah, Jash′ub, Shē′al, *and* Rā′moth;[a]
30 of the sons of Pā′hath-Mō′ab: Ad′na,
Chē′lal, Be·nā′i·ah, Mā·a·sēi′ah, Mat-
ta·nī′ah, Bez′a·lel, Bin′nū·ī, and Ma-
nas′seh; 31 *of* the sons of Hā′rim: El·i·ē′zer,
Ish·ī′jah, Mal·chī′jah, She·māi′ah, Shim′-
ē·on, 32 Benjamin, Mal′luch, *and* Shem-
a·rī′ah; 33 of the sons of Hā′shum: Mat-
tē′naī, Mat·tat′tah, Zā′bad, E·liph′e·let,
Jer′e·maī, Ma·nas′seh, *and* Shim′ē·ī; 34 of
the sons of Bā′nī: Mā·a·dā′ī, Am′ram, Ū′el,
35 Be·nā′i·ah, Bē·dēi′ah, Chel′ūh,[a] 36 Va-
nī′ah, Mer′e·moth, E·lī′a·shib, 37 Mat-
ta·nī′ah, Mat·tē′naī, Jā′a·sai,[a] 38 Bā′nī,
Bin′nū·ī, Shim′ē·ī, 39 Shel·e·mī′ah, Nathan,
A·dāi′ah, 40 Mach·nad′e·baī, Shā′shaī,
Shā′raī, 41 Az′a·rel, Shel·e·mī′ah, Shem-
a·rī′ah, 42 Shal′lum, Am·a·rī′ah, *and* Joseph;
43 of the sons of Nē′bō: Je·ī′el, Mat·ti·thī′ah,
Zā′bad, Ze·bī′na, Jad′daī,[a] Jō′el, *and*
Be·nā′i·ah.
44 All these had taken pagan wives, and
some of them had wives *by whom* they had
children.

10:29 [a]Or *Jeremoth* 10:35 [a]Or *Cheluhi*, or *Cheluhu*
10:37 [a]Or *Jaasu* 10:43 [a]Or *Jaddu*

10:44 Marriage outside the will of God creates hazards for **children**.

✦Nehemiah✦

Although Ezra probably compiled this book, Nehemiah apparently wrote some of the material in chapters 1—7 and 11—13. This book covers events between 444 and 425 B.C., after the Jews had returned from captivity in Babylon.

While the Book of Ezra focuses on the spiritual renewal of the nation, Nehemiah concentrates on the political and geographical restoration. Chapters 1—7 describe the rebuilding of the walls of Jerusalem to strengthen the city. The task was accomplished in fifty-two days and was followed by a renewed dedication to God's covenant by the citizens of Jerusalem.

The Book of Nehemiah also emphasizes the power of prayer. The Jews faced overwhelming odds in building the temple, yet in God's strength, they completed the job in a short time. This can encourage Christians today as they encounter challenges that seem overwhelming or impossible. Nehemiah, a man of prayer and action, shows what can be accomplished by a person wholly dedicated to God, no matter what age. ✦

CHAPTER 1

Nehemiah Prays for His People

The words of Nē·he·mī'ah the son of
Ha·cha·lī'ah.
It came to pass in the month of Chis'lev,
in the twentieth year, as I was in Shū'shan[a]
the citadel, 2that Ha·nā'nī one of my
brethren came with men from Judah; and I
asked them concerning the Jews who had
escaped, who had survived the captivity,
and concerning Jerusalem. 3And they said
to me, "The survivors who are left from the
captivity in the province *are* there in great
distress and reproach. The wall of Jerusa-
lem *is* also broken down, and its gates *are*
burned with fire."
4So it was, when I heard these words,
that I sat down and wept, and mourned *for*
many days; I was fasting and praying be-
fore the God of heaven.
5And I said: "I pray, LORD God of
heaven, O great and awesome God, *You*
who keep *Your* covenant and mercy with
those who love You[a] and observe Your[b]
commandments, 6please let Your ear be at-
tentive and Your eyes open, that You may
hear the prayer of Your servant which I
pray before You now, day and night, for
the children of Israel Your servants, and
confess the sins of the children of Israel
which we have sinned against You. Both

1:1 [a]Or *Susa* 1:5 [a]Literally *Him* [b]Literally *His*

1:1 Nehemiah means "The LORD Comforts." **Chislev**: Babylonian name for the ninth month in the Jewish calendar (November-December). **the twentieth year**: Of the reign of Artaxerxes I (465–424 B.C.), thus 445 B.C. (see 2:1).

1:5–11 A prayer of confession in which Nehemiah, like Ezra (see Ezra 9:5–15), identified with his people's sin, although he was not personally guilty. We, too, should be burdened for God's people and pray for them regularly.

my father's house and I have sinned. 7We
have acted very corruptly against You, and
have not kept the commandments, the
statutes, nor the ordinances which You
commanded Your servant Moses. 8Remem-
ber, I pray, the word that You commanded
Your servant Moses, saying, '*If* you are
unfaithful, I will scatter you among the na-
tions;[a] 9but *if* you return to Me, and keep
My commandments and do them, though
some of you were cast out to the farthest
part of the heavens, *yet* I will gather them
from there, and bring them to the place
which I have chosen as a dwelling for My
name.'[a] 10Now these *are* Your servants and
Your people, whom You have redeemed by
Your great power, and by Your strong
hand. 11O Lord, I pray, please let Your
ear be attentive to the prayer of Your ser-
vant, and to the prayer of Your servants
who desire to fear Your name; and let
Your servant prosper this day, I pray,
and grant him mercy in the sight of this
man."

For I was the king's cupbearer.

CHAPTER 2

Nehemiah Sent to Judah

And it came to pass in the month of
Nī'san, in the twentieth year of King
Ar·ta·xerx'ēs, *when* wine *was* before him,
that I took the wine and gave it to the
king. Now I had never been sad in his pres-
ence before. 2Therefore the king said to
me, "Why *is* your face sad, since you *are*
not sick? This *is* nothing but sorrow of
heart."

So I became dreadfully afraid, 3and said
to the king, "May the king live forever!
Why should my face not be sad, when the
city, the place of my fathers' tombs, *lies*
waste, and its gates are burned with fire?"

4Then the king said to me, "What do
you request?"

So I prayed to the God of heaven. 5And I
said to the king, "If it pleases the king, and
if your servant has found favor in your
sight, I ask that you send me to Judah, to
the city of my fathers' tombs, that I may re-
build it."

6Then the king said to me (the queen
also sitting beside him), "How long will
your journey be? And when will you re-
turn?" So it pleased the king to send me;
and I set him a time.

7Furthermore I said to the king, "If it
pleases the king, let letters be given to me
for the governors *of the region* beyond the
River,[a] that they must permit me to pass
through till I come to Judah, 8and a letter to
Ā'saph the keeper of the king's forest, that
he must give me timber to make beams for
the gates of the citadel which *pertains* to the
temple,[a] for the city wall, and for the house
that I will occupy." And the king granted
them to me according to the good hand of
my God upon me.

9Then I went to the governors *in the re-
gion* beyond the River, and gave them the
king's letters. Now the king had sent cap-
tains of the army and horsemen with me.
10When San·bal'lat the Hor'o·nīte and
Tō·bī'ah the Am'mon·īte official[a] heard *of
it*, they were deeply disturbed that a man
had come to seek the well-being of the chil-
dren of Israel.

1:8 [a]Leviticus 26:33 1:9 [a]Deuteronomy 30:2–5
2:7 [a]That is, the Euphrates, and so elsewhere in this book 2:8 [a]Literally *house* 2:10 [a]Literally *servant*, and so elsewhere in this book

1:11 this man: The Persian emperor. Unless he gave permission for the rebuilding of Jerusalem, nothing could be done. Nehemiah knew that his success with the emperor rested in God's hands. **the king's cupbearer**: Evidently a kind of personal adviser.

2:4 Before answering the king, Nehemiah wisely paused to pray. His example should prompt us to exercise similar caution when we find ourselves in uncertain or stressful situations; such prudence will prevent us from answering impetuously and will guard our tongues from evil.

Nehemiah Views the Wall of Jerusalem

11So I came to Jerusalem and was there
three days. 12Then I arose in the night, I and
a few men with me; I told no one what my
God had put in my heart to do at Jerusa-
lem; nor was there any animal with me, ex-
cept the one on which I rode. 13And I went
out by night through the Valley Gate to the
Serpent Well and the Refuse Gate, and
viewed the walls of Jerusalem which were
broken down and its gates which were
burned with fire. 14Then I went on to the
Fountain Gate and to the King's Pool, but
there was no room for the animal under me
to pass. 15So I went up in the night by the
valley, and viewed the wall; then I turned
back and entered by the Valley Gate, and
so returned. 16And the officials did not
know where I had gone or what I had
done; I had not yet told the Jews, the
priests, the nobles, the officials, or the oth-
ers who did the work.
17Then I said to them, "You see the dis-
tress that we *are* in, how Jerusalem *lies*
waste, and its gates are burned with fire.
Come and let us build the wall of Jerusa-
lem, that we may no longer be a reproach."
18And I told them of the hand of my
God which had been good upon me, and
also of the king's words that he had spoken
to me.
So they said, "Let us rise up and build."
Then they set their hands to *this* good *work.*
19But when San·bal'lat the Hor'o·nīte,
Tō·bī'ah the Am'mon·īte official, and
Gē'shem the Arab heard *of it,* they laughed
at us and despised us, and said, "What *is*
this thing that you are doing? Will you
rebel against the king?"
20So I answered them, and said to them,
"The God of heaven Himself will prosper
us; therefore we His servants will arise and
build, but you have no heritage or right or
memorial in Jerusalem."

CHAPTER 3

Rebuilding the Wall

Then E·lī'a·shib the high priest rose up
with his brethren the priests and built the
Sheep Gate; they consecrated it and hung
its doors. They built as far as the Tower of
the Hundred,[a] *and* consecrated it, then as
far as the Tower of Ha·nan'el. 2Next to
E·lī'a·shib[a] the men of Jericho built. And
next to them Zac'cur the son of Im'rī built.
3Also the sons of Has·se·nā'ah built the
Fish Gate; they laid its beams and hung its
doors with its bolts and bars. 4And next to
them Mer'e·moth the son of Ū·rī'jah, the
son of Koz,[a] made repairs. Next to them
Me·shul'lam the son of Ber·e·chī'ah, the
son of Me·shez'a·bel, made repairs. Next
to them Zā'dok the son of Bā'a·na made re-
pairs. 5Next to them the Te·kō'ītes made

3:1 [a]Hebrew *Hammeah,* also at 12:39 3:2 [a]Literally *On his hand* 3:4 [a]Or *Hakkoz*

2:13–15 The journey probably went counterclockwise around the city beginning at the southwest corner in the **Valley** of Hinnom and proceeding around into the Kidron Valley where the **Fountain** of Gihon and the **Pool** of Shiloah (later, Siloam) were located. He then proceeded northward up the narrow valley on foot since the fallen walls made it impossible for his horse to cross. The text is not clear as to whether he **turned back** (v. 15) without completing the circuit of the city or turned at the northeast corner and continued west and south to return to the Valley Gate.

3:1–32 Each of 42 groups and guilds from within the city, beginning with the priests, accepted responsibility for a section of the wall. The plan certainly seems an inspired way of overcoming apathy. Everyone had ownership in the project, and no doubt some competitiveness emerged both to speed and improve the work. Recent archeological work in Jerusalem indicates that the territory enclosed within the repaired walls was not as extensive as it had been before 586 B.C. This undoubtedly reflected both the straitened circumstances of the postexilic community and the desire to "pull in the lines" to increase the defensibility of the citadel.

repairs; but their nobles did not put their
shoulders[a] to the work of their Lord.
6Moreover Je·hoi′a·da the son of Pa-
sē′ah and Me·shul′lam the son of Bes-
o·dēi′ah repaired the Old Gate; they laid
its beams and hung its doors, with its bolts
and bars. 7And next to them Me·la·tī′ah
the Gib′ē·on·īte, Jā′don the Me·ron′-
o·thīte, the men of Gib′ē·on and Miz′pah,
repaired the residence[a] of the governor *of
the region* beyond the River. 8Next to him
Uz′zi·el the son of Har·haī′ah, one of the
goldsmiths, made repairs. Also next to him
Han·a·nī′ah, one[a] of the perfumers, made
repairs; and they fortified Jerusalem as far
as the Broad Wall. 9And next to them
Reph·āi′ah the son of Hur, leader of half
the district of Jerusalem, made repairs.
10Next to them Je·daī′ah the son of
Har·ū′maph made repairs in front of his
house. And next to him Hat′tush the son of
Ha·shab·nī′ah made repairs.

11Mal·chī′jah the son of Hā′rim and
Hash′ub the son of Pā′hath-Mō′ab re-
paired another section, as well as the
Tower of the Ovens. 12And next to him was
Shal′lum the son of Hal·lō′hesh, leader of
half the district of Jerusalem; he and his
daughters made repairs.

13Hā′nun and the inhabitants of
Za·nō′ah repaired the Valley Gate. They
built it, hung its doors with its bolts and
bars, and *repaired* a thousand cubits of the
wall as far as the Refuse Gate.

14Mal·chī′jah the son of Rē′chab, leader
of the district of Beth Hac′ce·rem, repaired
the Refuse Gate; he built it and hung its
doors with its bolts and bars.

15Shal′lun the son of Col-Hō′zeh, leader
of the district of Miz′pah, repaired the
Fountain Gate; he built it, covered it, hung
its doors with its bolts and bars, and re-
paired the wall of the Pool of Shē′lah by
the King's Garden, as far as the stairs that
go down from the City of David. 16After
him Nē·he·mī′ah the son of Az′buk, leader
of half the district of Beth Zūr, made re-
pairs as far as *the place* in front of the
tombs[a] of David, to the man-made pool,
and as far as the House of the Mighty.

17After him the Lē′vītes, *under* Rē′hum
the son of Bā′nī, made repairs. Next to him
Hash·a·bī′ah, leader of half the district of
Kē·ī′lah, made repairs for his district. 18Af-
ter him their brethren, *under* Bav′a·ī[a] the
son of Hen′a·dad, leader of the *other* half of
the district of Kē·ī′lah, made repairs. 19And
next to him Ē′zer the son of Jesh′ū·a, the
leader of Miz′pah, repaired another sec-
tion in front of the Ascent to the Armory at
the buttress. 20After him Bar′uch the son of
Zab′baī[a] carefully repaired the other sec-
tion, from the buttress to the door of the
house of E·lī′a·shib the high priest. 21After
him Mer′e·moth the son of Ū·rī′jah, the
son of Koz,[a] repaired another section, from
the door of the house of E·lī′a·shib to the
end of the house of E·lī′a·shib.

22And after him the priests, the men of
the plain, made repairs. 23After him Benja-
min and Has′shub made repairs opposite
their house. After them Az·a·rī′ah the son
of Mā·a·sēi′ah, the son of An·a·nī′ah,
made repairs by his house. 24After him
Bin′nū·ī the son of Hen′a·dad repaired an-
other section, from the house of Az·a·rī′ah
to the buttress, even as far as the corner.
25Pā′lal the son of Ū′zaī *made repairs* oppo-
site the buttress, and on the tower which
projects from the king's upper house that
was by the court of the prison. After him
Pe·dāi′ah the son of Pā′rosh *made repairs.*

3:5 [a]Literally *necks* 3:7 [a]Literally *throne* 3:8 [a]Literally *the son* 3:16 [a]Septuagint, Syriac, and Vulgate read *tomb.* 3:18 [a]Following Masoretic Text and Vulgate; some Hebrew manuscripts, Septuagint, and Syriac read *Binnui* (compare verse 24). 3:20 [a]A few Hebrew manuscripts, Syriac, and Vulgate read *Zaccai.* 3:21 [a]Or *Hakkoz*

3:5 This is the only mention of resistance to unity in rebuilding Jerusalem. The harmony among the people in their work is an example for today's church. If each of us works wholeheartedly on the task at hand, we'll have no time for quarrelling or gossip.

26Moreover the Neth'i·nim who dwelt in
Ō'phel *made repairs* as far as *the place* in
front of the Water Gate toward the east,
and on the projecting tower. 27After them
the Te·kō'ītes repaired another section,
next to the great projecting tower, and as
far as the wall of Ō'phel.

28Beyond the Horse Gate the priests
made repairs, each in front of his *own*
house. 29After them Zā'dok the son of
Im'mer made repairs in front of his *own*
house. After him She·māi'ah the son of
Shech·a·nī'ah, the keeper of the East Gate,
made repairs. 30After him Han·a·nī'ah the
son of Shel·e·mī'ah, and Hā'nun, the sixth
son of Zā'laph, repaired another section.
After him Me·shul'lam the son of Ber-
e·chī'ah made repairs in front of his dwell-
ing. 31After him Mal·chī'jah, one of the
goldsmiths, made repairs as far as the
house of the Neth'i·nim and of the mer-
chants, in front of the Miph'kad[a] Gate, and
as far as the upper room at the corner.
32And between the upper room at the cor-
ner, as far as the Sheep Gate, the gold-
smiths and the merchants made repairs.

CHAPTER 4

The Wall Defended Against Enemies

But it so happened, when San·bal'lat
heard that we were rebuilding the wall,
that he was furious and very indignant,
and mocked the Jews. 2And he spoke be-
fore his brethren and the army of Samaria,
and said, "What are these feeble Jews do-
ing? Will they fortify themselves? Will they
offer sacrifices? Will they complete it in a
day? Will they revive the stones from the
heaps of rubbish—*stones* that are burned?"

3Now Tō·bī'ah the Am'mon·īte *was* be-
side him, and he said, "Whatever they
build, if even a fox goes up *on it*, he will
break down their stone wall."

4Hear, O our God, for we are despised;
turn their reproach on their own heads,
and give them as plunder to a land of cap-
tivity! 5Do not cover their iniquity, and do
not let their sin be blotted out from before
You; for they have provoked *You* to anger
before the builders.

6So we built the wall, and the entire wall
was joined together up to half its *height*, for
the people had a mind to work.

7Now it happened, when San·bal'lat,
Tō·bī'ah, the Arabs, the Am'mon·ītes, and
the Ash'dod·ītes heard that the walls of Je-
rusalem were being restored and the gaps
were beginning to be closed, that they be-
came very angry, 8and all of them con-
spired together to come *and* attack Jerusa-
lem and create confusion. 9Nevertheless
we made our prayer to our God, and be-
cause of them we set a watch against them
day and night.

10Then Judah said, "The strength of the
laborers is failing, and *there is* so much rub-
bish that we are not able to build the wall."

11And our adversaries said, "They will
neither know nor see anything, till we
come into their midst and kill them and
cause the work to cease."

12So it was, when the Jews who dwelt
near them came, that they told us ten
times, "From whatever place you turn, *they
will be* upon us."

3:31 [a]Literally *Inspection* or *Recruiting*

4:6 a mind to work: As in so many tasks, and as Judah's enemies understood, attitude is often the major ingredient for success. We must ignore those who discourage us from the Lord's work, confident that He will reward us for our dedication to Him.

4:9, 17 The strategy of Nehemiah and the people was to pray, watch, and wait in preparedness. While they took steps to protect themselves, they allowed neither outside pressures nor inner discouragement to hinder the work of the Lord.

4:10–15 The continuing crisis of attitude. If the people could be delivered from discouragement (v. 10) and fear (vv. 11–14), the work itself would not be a problem. This is true with most of our challenges. **near them** (v. 12): Near Judah's enemies. **ten times**: Reflects irrational terror.

[13]Therefore I positioned *men* behind the
lower parts of the wall, at the openings;
and I set the people according to their fam-
ilies, with their swords, their spears, and
their bows. [14]And I looked, and arose and
said to the nobles, to the leaders, and to the
rest of the people, "Do not be afraid of
them. Remember the Lord, great and awe-
some, and fight for your brethren, your
sons, your daughters, your wives, and
your houses."
[15]And it happened, when our enemies
heard that it was known to us, and *that*
God had brought their plot to nothing, that
all of us returned to the wall, everyone to
his work. [16]So it was, from that time on,
that half of my servants worked at con-
struction, while the other half held the
spears, the shields, the bows, and *wore* ar-
mor; and the leaders *were* behind all the
house of Judah. [17]Those who built on the
wall, and those who carried burdens,
loaded themselves so that with one hand
they worked at construction, and with the
other held a weapon. [18]Every one of the
builders had his sword girded at his side
as he built. And the one who sounded the
trumpet *was* beside me.
[19]Then I said to the nobles, the rulers,
and the rest of the people, "The work *is*
great and extensive, and we are separated
far from one another on the wall. [20]Wher-
ever you hear the sound of the trumpet,
rally to us there. Our God will fight for us."
[21]So we labored in the work, and half of
the men[a] held the spears from daybreak un-
til the stars appeared. [22]At the same time I
also said to the people, "Let each man and
his servant stay at night in Jerusalem, that
they may be our guard by night and a
working party by day." [23]So neither I, my
brethren, my servants, nor the men of the
guard who followed me took off our
clothes, *except* that everyone took them off
for washing.

CHAPTER 5

Nehemiah Deals with Oppression

And there was a great outcry of the peo-
ple and their wives against their Jewish
brethren. [2]For there were those who said,
"We, our sons, and our daughters *are*
many; therefore let us get grain, that we
may eat and live."
[3]There were also *some* who said, "We
have mortgaged our lands and vineyards
and houses, that we might buy grain be-
cause of the famine."
[4]There were also those who said, "We
have borrowed money for the king's tax *on*
our lands and vineyards. [5]Yet now our
flesh *is* as the flesh of our brethren, our
children as their children; and indeed we
are forcing our sons and our daughters to
be slaves, and *some* of our daughters have
been brought into slavery. *It is* not in our
power *to redeem them,* for other men have
our lands and vineyards."
[6]And I became very angry when I heard
their outcry and these words. [7]After seri-
ous thought, I rebuked the nobles and
rulers, and said to them, "Each of you is ex-
acting usury from his brother." So I called a
great assembly against them. [8]And I said to
them, "According to our ability we have

4:21 [a]Literally *them*

4:17 Probably not a literal statement, but a figurative picture of the total work force as though it functioned as one person (see v. 21).

5:1–19 Nehemiah's chief concern was not with Jerusalem's defenses. He sought a restoration of the Judeans' sense of themselves as the chosen people of God. That could not happen if Jerusalem was not livable, but it also could not happen if the people were not one with each other.

5:5 our flesh . . . our brethren: The Jewish brethren should have been treating each other as equals, not as potential slaves.

5:8 redeemed our Jewish brethren: After all the effort to make possible the return from

redeemed our Jewish brethren who were
sold to the nations. Now indeed, will you
even sell your brethren? Or should they be
sold to us?"

Then they were silenced and found
nothing *to say*. 9Then I said, "What you are
doing *is* not good. Should you not walk in
the fear of our God because of the reproach
of the nations, our enemies? 10I also, *with*
my brethren and my servants, am lending
them money and grain. Please, let us stop
this usury! 11Restore now to them, even
this day, their lands, their vineyards, their
olive groves, and their houses, also a hun-
dredth of the money and the grain, the
new wine and the oil, that you have
charged them."

12So they said, "We will restore *it*, and
will require nothing from them; we will do
as you say."

Then I called the priests, and required
an oath from them that they would do ac-
cording to this promise. 13Then I shook out
the fold of my garment[a] and said, "So may
God shake out each man from his house,
and from his property, who does not per-
form this promise. Even thus may he be
shaken out and emptied."

And all the assembly said, "Amen!" and
praised the LORD. Then the people did ac-
cording to this promise.

The Generosity of Nehemiah

14Moreover, from the time that I was ap-
pointed to be their governor in the land of
Judah, from the twentieth year until the
thirty-second year of King Ar·ta·xerx'ēs,
twelve years, neither I nor my brothers ate
the governor's provisions. 15But the former
governors who *were* before me laid bur-
dens on the people, and took from them
bread and wine, besides forty shekels of
silver. Yes, even their servants bore rule
over the people, but I did not do so, be-
cause of the fear of God. 16Indeed, I also
continued the work on this wall, and we[a]
did not buy any land. All my servants *were*
gathered there for the work.

17And at my table *were* one hundred and
fifty Jews and rulers, besides those who
came to us from the nations around us.
18Now *that* which was prepared daily *was*
one ox *and* six choice sheep. Also fowl were
prepared for me, and once every ten days
an abundance of all kinds of wine. Yet in
spite of this I did not demand the gover-
nor's provisions, because the bondage was
heavy on this people.

19Remember me, my God, for good, *ac-
cording to* all that I have done for this peo-
ple.

CHAPTER 6

Conspiracy Against Nehemiah

Now it happened when San·bal'lat,
Tō·bī'ah, Gē'shem the Arab, and the rest of
our enemies heard that I had rebuilt the
wall, and *that* there were no breaks left in it
(though at that time I had not hung the
doors in the gates), 2that San·bal'lat and
Gē'shem sent to me, saying, "Come, let us
meet together among the villages in the
plain of Ō'nō." But they thought to do me
harm.

3So I sent messengers to them, saying, "I
am doing a great work, so that I cannot

5:13 [a]Literally *my lap* 5:16 [a]Following Masoretic Text; Septuagint, Syriac, and Vulgate read *I*.

exile, would the rich now destroy it? By charging interest and foreclosing mortgages, they were forcing their fellow Jews into tenancy and then slavery.

5:9 Such flaunting of God's law (see Lev. 25:39–43) made Him appear insignificant, just as their pagan neighbors believed.

5:14 twentieth year . . . thirty-second year: 445 to 433 B.C. During his 12-year tenure as governor Nehemiah paid all of his own expenses.

6:3 Rather than openly accusing Sanballat of plotting against him, Nehemiah politely rejected his offer and allowed God to expose Sanballat's motives (vv.6–9). His wise plan of action protected him from the plot while enabling him to continue with the work.

come down. Why should the work cease
while I leave it and go down to you?"
[4]But they sent me this message four
times, and I answered them in the same
manner.
[5]Then San·bal′lat sent his servant to me
as before, the fifth time, with an open letter
in his hand. [6]In it *was* written:

> It is reported among the nations, and
> Gē′shem[a] says, *that* you and the Jews
> plan to rebel; therefore, according to
> these rumors, you are rebuilding the
> wall, that you may be their king. [7]And
> you have also appointed prophets to
> proclaim concerning you at Jerusalem,
> saying, "*There is* a king in Judah!"
> Now these matters will be reported to
> the king. So come, therefore, and let
> us consult together.

[8]Then I sent to him, saying, "No such
things as you say are being done, but you
invent them in your own heart."
[9]For they all *were trying to* make us
afraid, saying, "Their hands will be weak-
ened in the work, and it will not be done."
Now therefore, *O God,* strengthen my
hands.
[10]Afterward I came to the house of
She·māi′ah the son of De·laī′ah, the son of
Me·het′a·bel, who *was* a secret informer;
and he said, "Let us meet together in the
house of God, within the temple, and let us
close the doors of the temple, for they are
coming to kill you; indeed, at night they
will come to kill you."
[11]And I said, "Should such a man as I
flee? And who *is there* such as I who would
go into the temple to save his life? I will not
go in!" [12]Then I perceived that God had not
sent him at all, but that he pronounced *this*
prophecy against me because Tō·bī′ah and
San·bal′lat had hired him. [13]For this reason
he *was* hired, that I should be afraid and act
that way and sin, so *that* they might have
cause for an evil report, that they might re-
proach me.
[14]My God, remember Tō·bī′ah and
San·bal′lat, according to these their works,
and the prophetess Nō·a·dī′ah and the rest
of the prophets who would have made me
afraid.

The Wall Completed

[15]So the wall was finished on the
twenty-fifth *day* of Ē′lul, in fifty-two days.
[16]And it happened, when all our enemies
heard *of it,* and all the nations around us
saw *these things,* that they were very dis-
heartened in their own eyes; for they per-
ceived that this work was done by our
God.
[17]Also in those days the nobles of Judah
sent many letters to Tō·bī′ah, and *the letters
of* Tō·bī′ah came to them. [18]For many in Ju-
dah were pledged to him, because he was
the son-in-law of Shech·a·nī′ah the son of
Ā′rah, and his son Jē·hō·hā′nan had mar-
ried the daughter of Me·shul′lam the son
of Ber·e·chī′ah. [19]Also they reported his
good deeds before me, and reported my
words to him. Tō·bī′ah sent letters to
frighten me.

CHAPTER 7

Then it was, when the wall was built
and I had hung the doors, when the gate-
keepers, the singers, and the Lē′vītes had
been appointed, [2]that I gave the charge of
Jerusalem to my brother Ha·nā′nī, and
Han·a·nī′ah the leader of the citadel, for he

6:6 [a]Hebrew *Gashmu*

7:1—13:30 After rebuilding the wall, Nehemiah's next task was to help reestablish Judah's distinctive identity as a people under God. To accomplish this he did three things: regularized worship (7:1; 10:32–39; 12:27–47); organized the society along original family lines (7:4–73; 11:1—12:26); and brought about a recommitment to the Mosaic law (8:1—10:31). Examples of the impact of these policies are given in ch. 13.

was a faithful man and feared God more
than many.
3 And I said to them, "Do not let the
gates of Jerusalem be opened until the sun
is hot; and while they stand *guard,* let them
shut and bar the doors; and appoint
guards from among the inhabitants of Je-
rusalem, one at his watch station and an-
other in front of his own house."

The Captives Who Returned to Jerusalem

4 Now the city *was* large and spacious,
but the people in it *were* few, and the
houses *were* not rebuilt. 5 Then my God put
it into my heart to gather the nobles, the
rulers, and the people, that they might be
registered by genealogy. And I found a reg-
ister of the genealogy of those who had
come up in the first *return,* and found writ-
ten in it:

6 These[a] *are* the people of the province
who came back from the captivity, of
those who had been carried away,
whom Ne·bū·chad·nez'zar the king of
Babylon had carried away, and who
returned to Jerusalem and Judah,
everyone to his city.

7 Those who came with Ze·rub'ba·bel
were Jesh'ū·a, Nē·he·mī'ah,
Az·a·rī'ah, Rā·a·mī'ah, Nā·ham'a·nī,
Mor'de·caī, Bil'shan, Mis'pe·reth,[a]
Big'vaī, Nē'hum, and Bā'a·nah.

The number of the men of the people
of Israel: 8 the sons of Pā'rosh, two
thousand one hundred and seventy-
two;
9 the sons of Sheph·a·tī'ah, three hun-
dred and seventy-two;
10 the sons of Ā'rah, six hundred and
fifty-two;
11 the sons of Pā'hath-Mō'ab, of the
sons of Jesh'ū·a and Jō'ab, two thou-
sand eight hundred and eighteen;
12 the sons of Ē'lam, one thousand two
hundred and fifty-four;
13 the sons of Zat'tū, eight hundred
and forty-five;
14 the sons of Zac'caī, seven hundred
and sixty;
15 the sons of Bin'nū·ī,[a] six hundred
and forty-eight;
16 the sons of Bē'baī, six hundred and
twenty-eight;
17 the sons of Az'gad, two thousand
three hundred and twenty-two;
18 the sons of Ad·o·nī'kam, six hun-
dred and sixty-seven;
19 the sons of Big'vaī, two thousand
and sixty-seven;
20 the sons of Ā'din, six hundred and
fifty-five;
21 the sons of Ā'ter of Hez·e·kī'ah,
ninety-eight;
22 the sons of Hā'shum, three hundred
and twenty-eight;
23 the sons of Bē'zaī, three hundred
and twenty-four;
24 the sons of Hā'riph,[a] one hundred
and twelve;
25 the sons of Gib'ē·on,[a] ninety-five;
26 the men of Bethlehem and

7:6 [a]Compare verses 6–72 with Ezra 2:1–70
7:7 [a]Spelled *Mispar* in Ezra 2:2 7:15 [a]Spelled *Bani* in Ezra 2:10 7:24 [a]Called *Jorah* in Ezra 2:18
7:25 [a]Called *Gibbar* in Ezra 2:20

7:4–60 Because the society was so disorganized, the population was still small 100 years after the return. Nehemiah sought to reestablish a sense of family identity and solidarity. To do this, he began with the original report (vv. 5–73) of those who returned from Babylon with **Zerubbabel** (v. 7). To us, these lists of names make boring reading. But for the Hebrews they were of vital importance. By these memories they reminded themselves of their position as a chosen people, and of God's faithfulness to them across the centuries. In moments when God's providence and love might be doubted or in moments when they questioned whether their stern laws really were of eternal significance, these lists provided an anchor for them—an anchor which many of us sorely lack.

Ne·toph′ah, one hundred and eighty-eight;
[27]the men of An′a·thoth, one hundred and twenty-eight;
[28]the men of Beth Az′ma·veth,[a] forty-two;
[29]the men of Kir′jath Jē′a·rim, Chē·phī′rah, and Be·er′oth, seven hundred and forty-three;
[30]the men of Rā′mah and Gē′ba, six hundred and twenty-one;
[31]the men of Mich′mas, one hundred and twenty-two;
[32]the men of Beth′el and Aī, one hundred and twenty-three;
[33]the men of the other Nē′bō, fifty-two;
[34]the sons of the other Ē′lam, one thousand two hundred and fifty-four;
[35]the sons of Hā′rim, three hundred and twenty;
[36]the sons of Jericho, three hundred and forty-five;
[37]the sons of Lod, Hā′did, and Ō′nō, seven hundred and twenty-one;
[38]the sons of Se·nā′ah, three thousand nine hundred and thirty.

39 The priests: the sons of Je·daī′ah, of the house of Jesh′ū·a, nine hundred and seventy-three;
[40]the sons of Im′mer, one thousand and fifty-two;
[41]the sons of Pash′hur, one thousand two hundred and forty-seven;
[42]the sons of Hā′rim, one thousand and seventeen.

43 The Lē′vītes: the sons of Jesh′ū·a, of Kad′mi·el,
and of the sons of Hō′de·vah,[a] seventy-four.

44 The singers: the sons of Ā′saph, one hundred and forty-eight.

45 The gatekeepers: the sons of Shal′lum,
the sons of Ā′ter,
the sons of Tal′mon,
the sons of Ak′kub,
the sons of Ha·tī′ta,
the sons of Shō′baī, one hundred and thirty-eight.

46 The Neth′i·nim: the sons of Zī′ha,
the sons of Ha·sū′pha,
the sons of Tab·bā′oth,
[47]the sons of Kē′ros,
the sons of Sī′a,[a]
the sons of Pā′don,
[48]the sons of Le·bā′na,[a]
the sons of Hag′a·ba,[b]
the sons of Sal′maī,[c]
[49]the sons of Hā′nan,
the sons of Gid′del,
the sons of Gā′har,
[50]the sons of Rē·āi′ah,
the sons of Rē′zin,
the sons of Ne·kō′da,
[51]the sons of Gaz′zam,
the sons of Uz′za,
the sons of Pa·sē′ah,
[52]the sons of Bē′saī,
the sons of Me·ū′nim,
the sons of Ne·phish′e·sim,[a]
[53]the sons of Bak′buk,
the sons of Ha·kū′pha,
the sons of Har′hur,
[54]the sons of Baz′lith,[a]
the sons of Me·hī′da,
the sons of Har′sha,

7:28 [a]Called *Azmaveth* in Ezra 2:24 7:43 [a]Spelled *Hodaviah* in Ezra 2:40 7:47 [a]Spelled *Siaha* in Ezra 2:44 7:48 [a]Masoretic Text reads *Lebanah.* [b]Masoretic Text reads *Hogabah.* [c]Or *Shalmai*, or *Shamlai* 7:52 [a]Spelled *Nephusim* in Ezra 2:50 7:54 [a]Spelled *Bazluth* in Ezra 2:52

7:39–56 The list makes special note of persons involved in the religious life of Israel: **priests** (vv. 39–42), **Levites** (v. 43), **singers** (v. 44), and **gatekeepers** for the temple (v. 45). The **Nethinim** (vv. 46–56) were special temple servants, perhaps foreign slaves assigned to the more menial tasks.

[55]the sons of Bar′kos,
the sons of Sis′e·ra,
the sons of Tam′ah,
[56]the sons of Ne·zī′ah,
and the sons of Ha·tī′pha.

57 The sons of Solomon's servants: the
sons of Sō′taī,
the sons of Sō′phe·reth,
the sons of Pe·rī′da,[a]
[58]the sons of Jā′a·la,
the sons of Dar′kon,
the sons of Gid′del,
[59]the sons of Sheph·a·tī′ah,
the sons of Hat′til,
the sons of Poch′e·reth of Ze·bā′im,
and the sons of Ā′mon.[a]
[60]All the Neth′i·nim, and the sons of
Solomon's servants, *were* three hun-
dred and ninety-two.

61 And these *were* the ones who came up
from Tel Mē′lah, Tel Har′sha,
Chē′rub, Ad′don,[a] and Im′mer, but
they could not identify their father's
house nor their lineage, whether they
were of Israel: [62]the sons of De·laī′ah,
the sons of Tō·bī′ah,
the sons of Ne·kō′da, six hundred and
forty-two;
[63]and of the priests: the sons of
Ha·baī′ah,
the sons of Koz,[a]
the sons of Bar·zil′laī, who took a wife
of the daughters of Bar·zil′laī the
Gil′ē·ad·īte, and was called by their
name.
[64]These sought their listing *among*
those who were registered by geneal-
ogy, but it was not found; therefore
they were excluded from the priest-
hood as defiled. [65]And the governor[a]
said to them that they should not eat
of the most holy things till a priest
could consult with the Ū′rim and
Thum′mim.

66 Altogether the whole assembly *was*
forty-two thousand three hundred
and sixty, [67]besides their male and fe-
male servants, of whom *there were*
seven thousand three hundred and
thirty-seven; and they had two hun-
dred and forty-five men and women
singers. [68]Their horses were seven
hundred and thirty-six, their mules
two hundred and forty-five, [69]*their*
camels four hundred and thirty-five,
and donkeys six thousand seven hun-
dred and twenty.

70 And some of the heads of the fathers'
houses gave to the work. The gover-
nor[a] gave to the treasury one thou-
sand gold drachmas, fifty basins, and
five hundred and thirty priestly gar-
ments. [71]Some of the heads of the
fathers' *houses* gave to the treasury of
the work twenty thousand gold
drachmas, and two thousand two
hundred silver minas. [72]And that
which the rest of the people gave *was*

7:57 [a]Spelled *Peruda* in Ezra 2:55 7:59 [a]Spelled *Ami* in Ezra 2:57 7:61 [a]Spelled *Addan* in Ezra 2:59 7:63 [a]Or *Hakkoz* 7:65 [a]Hebrew *Tirshatha* 7:70 [a]Hebrew *Tirshatha*

7:57 sons of Solomon's servants: This group, like the Nethinim, was a hereditary guild of temple servants, originally appointed by Solomon.

7:61–65 Unless **priests** (v. 63) could show that they were indeed from the priestly line, their theology was questioned. Of course being from Aaron's line did not guarantee a right theology, which was important for the priest's teaching function (see 2 Chr. 15:3; 30:22; Ezek. 44:23). But the test provided one minimal guard against the ever-present threat of apostasy.

7:65 The priests who could not prove their descent from Aaron were forbidden to participate in the ceremonies. However, a favorable response from the **Urim and Thummim** (see note on Deut 33:8) would allow them to continue receiving the priestly food allowance.

twenty thousand gold drachmas, two
thousand silver minas, and sixty-
seven priestly garments.

[73]So the priests, the Lē′vītes, the gate-
keepers, the singers, *some* of the people, the
Neth′i·nim, and all Israel dwelt in their
cities.

Ezra Reads the Law

When the seventh month came, the chil-
dren of Israel *were* in their cities.

CHAPTER 8

Now all the people gathered together as
one man in the open square that *was* in
front of the Water Gate; and they told Ezra
the scribe to bring the Book of the Law of
Moses, which the LORD had commanded
Israel. [2]So Ezra the priest brought the Law
before the assembly of men and women
and all who *could* hear with understanding
on the first day of the seventh month.
[3]Then he read from it in the open square
that *was* in front of the Water Gate from
morning until midday, before the men and
women and those who could understand;
and the ears of all the people *were attentive*
to the Book of the Law.
[4]So Ezra the scribe stood on a platform
of wood which they had made for the pur-
pose; and beside him, at his right hand,
stood Mat·ti·thī′ah, Shē′ma, A·naī′ah,
Ū·rī′jah, Hil·kī′ah, and Mā·a·sēi′ah; and at
his left hand Pe·dāi′ah, Mish′a·el, Mal-
chī′jah, Hā′shum, Hash·ba·da′na, Zech-
a·rī′ah, *and* Me·shul′lam. [5]And Ezra
opened the book in the sight of all the peo-
ple, for he was *standing* above all the peo-
ple; and when he opened it, all the people
stood up. [6]And Ezra blessed the LORD, the
great God.
Then all the people answered, "Amen,
Amen!" while lifting up their hands. And
they bowed their heads and worshiped the
LORD with *their* faces to the ground.
[7]Also Jesh′ū·a, Bā′nī, Sher·e·bī′ah,
Jā′min, Ak′kub, Shab′be·thaī, Hō·dī′jah,
Mā·a·sēi′ah, Ke·lī′ta, Az·a·rī′ah, Joz′-
a·bad, Hā′nan, Pe·lāi′ah, and the Lē′vītes,
helped the people to understand the Law;
and the people *stood* in their place. [8]So they
read distinctly from the book, in the Law of
God; and they gave the sense, and helped
them to understand the reading.
[9]And Nē·he·mī′ah, who *was* the gover-
nor,[a] Ezra the priest *and* scribe, and the
Lē′vītes who taught the people said to all
the people, "This day *is* holy to the LORD
your God; do not mourn nor weep." For all
the people wept, when they heard the
words of the Law.
[10]Then he said to them, "Go your way,
eat the fat, drink the sweet, and send por-
tions to those for whom nothing is pre-
pared; for *this* day *is* holy to our Lord. Do
not sorrow, for the joy of the LORD is your
strength."
[11]So the Lē′vītes quieted all the people,
saying, "Be still, for the day *is* holy; do not
be grieved." [12]And all the people went
their way to eat and drink, to send portions
and rejoice greatly, because they under-
stood the words that were declared to
them.

The Feast of Tabernacles

[13]Now on the second day the heads of
the fathers' *houses* of all the people, with

8:9 [a]Hebrew *Tirshatha*

7:73 It is important that people were settled in **their cities** by the **seventh month** (Tishri), the month of sacred assemblies. The walls had been completed in the preceding month of Elul. The timing was now right to gather in Jerusalem for festival celebration and covenant renewal.

8:7, 8 The Law was read from the Hebrew and explained immediately, perhaps in the dialect of the people.

8:13–18 The command to live in booths was given so that the Hebrews would remember

the priests and Lē′vītes, were gathered to Ezra the scribe, in order to understand the words of the Law. [14]And they found written in the Law, which the LORD had commanded by Moses, that the children of Israel should dwell in booths during the feast of the seventh month, [15]and that they should announce and proclaim in all their cities and in Jerusalem, saying, "Go out to the mountain, and bring olive branches, branches of oil trees, myrtle branches, palm branches, and branches of leafy trees, to make booths, as *it is* written."

[16]Then the people went out and brought *them* and made themselves booths, each one on the roof of his house, or in their courtyards or the courts of the house of God, and in the open square of the Water Gate and in the open square of the Gate of Ē′phra·im. [17]So the whole assembly of those who had returned from the captivity made booths and sat under the booths; for since the days of Joshua the son of Nun until that day the children of Israel had not done so. And there was very great gladness. [18]Also day by day, from the first day until the last day, he read from the Book of the Law of God. And they kept the feast seven days; and on the eighth day *there was* a sacred assembly, according to the *prescribed* manner.

CHAPTER 9

The People Confess Their Sins

Now on the twenty-fourth day of this month the children of Israel were assembled with fasting, in sackcloth, and with dust on their heads.[a] [2]Then those of Israelite lineage separated themselves from all foreigners; and they stood and confessed their sins and the iniquities of their fathers. [3]And they stood up in their place and read from the Book of the Law of the LORD their God *for one*-fourth of the day; and *for another* fourth they confessed and worshiped the LORD their God.

[4]Then Jesh′ū·a, Bā′nī, Kad′mi·el, Sheb·a·nī′ah, Bun′nī, Sher·e·bī′ah, Bā′nī, *and* Che·nā′nī stood on the stairs of the Lē′vītes and cried out with a loud voice to the LORD their God. [5]And the Lē′vītes, Jesh′ū·a, Kad′mi·el, Bā′nī, Ha·shab·nī′ah, Sher·e·bī′ah, Hō·dī′jah, Sheb·a·nī′ah, *and* Peth·a·hī′ah, said:

"Stand up *and* bless the LORD your God
Forever and ever!

"Blessed be Your glorious name,
Which is exalted above all blessing and praise!

9:1 [a]Literally *earth on them*

how their ancestors had lived in such dwellings for 40 years. During this time, despite their sin, they experienced the faithfulness of God (Lev. 23:42, 43).

8:17 Although the Feast of Tabernacles had been observed occasionally since Joshua's time, it had been celebrated merely as a harvest festival rather than an occasion to recall both the "Ingathering" (Ex. 34:22) and God's provision for Israel in the wilderness (Lev. 23:43).

9:1–38 God's gift of the Law as His guide for living is a cause for joy, but our failure to live up to that guide must be a source of grief. Admission of that failure is the first step to hope. Here, led by the Levites, the Israelites recall their history, emphasizing both God's unfailing faithfulness to them, and their continual unfaithfulness to God. The heavy emphasis upon those portions of the history found in the books of the Law (Genesis through Deuteronomy; vv. 1–25) is undoubtedly because that story was still fresh in their minds from the recent reading (8:1–3).

9:1–15 The story of God's election love: how the Creator God chose to bless Abraham and his descendants and kept faith with them by delivering them from Egypt and giving them the Sinai covenant.

9:5 The poetic form is often used to recite Israel's history (see Ps. 106; 107; 136).

I praise you, O God, because You alone are the Lord; You have made heaven, the heaven of heavens, with all their host, the earth and everything on it, the seas and all that is in them, and You preserve them all.

adapted from Nehemiah 9:6

6 You alone *are* the LORD;
You have made heaven,
The heaven of heavens, with all their
host,
The earth and everything on it,
The seas and all that is in them,
And You preserve them all.
The host of heaven worships You.

7 "You *are* the LORD God,
Who chose Abram,
And brought him out of Ūr of the
Chal·dē′ans,
And gave him the name Abraham;
8 You found his heart faithful before
You,
And made a covenant with him
To give the land of the Cā′naan·ītes,
The Hit′tītes, the Am′o·rītes,
The Per′iz·zītes, the Jeb′ū·sītes,
And the Gir′ga·shītes—
To give *it* to his descendants.
You have performed Your words,
For You *are* righteous.

9 "You saw the affliction of our fathers
in Egypt,
And heard their cry by the Red Sea.
10 You showed signs and wonders
against Pharaoh,
Against all his servants,
And against all the people of his land.
For You knew that they acted proudly
against them.
So You made a name for Yourself, as
it is this day.
11 And You divided the sea before them,
So that they went through the midst
of the sea on the dry land;
And their persecutors You threw into
the deep,
As a stone into the mighty waters.
12 Moreover You led them by day with a
cloudy pillar,
And by night with a pillar of fire,
To give them light on the road
Which they should travel.

13 "You came down also on Mount Sinai,
And spoke with them from heaven,
And gave them just ordinances and
true laws,
Good statutes and commandments.
14 You made known to them Your holy
Sabbath,
And commanded them precepts,
statutes and laws,
By the hand of Moses Your servant.
15 You gave them bread from heaven for
their hunger,
And brought them water out of the
rock for their thirst,
And told them to go in to possess the
land
Which You had sworn to give them.

16 "But they and our fathers acted
proudly,
Hardened their necks,
And did not heed Your
commandments.
17 They refused to obey,
And they were not mindful of Your
wonders
That You did among them.
But they hardened their necks,

9:16–25 God's forgiving love. In spite of Israel's rebellion and idolatry in the desert, God delivered His people and brought them into Canaan.

And in their rebellion[a]
They appointed a leader
To return to their bondage.
But You *are* God,
Ready to pardon,
Gracious and merciful,
Slow to anger,
Abundant in kindness,
And did not forsake them.

18 "Even when they made a molded calf
for themselves,
And said, 'This *is* your god
That brought you up out of Egypt,'
And worked great provocations,
19 Yet in Your manifold mercies
You did not forsake them in the
wilderness.
The pillar of the cloud did not depart
from them by day,
To lead them on the road;
Nor the pillar of fire by night,
To show them light,
And the way they should go.
20 You also gave Your good Spirit to
instruct them,
And did not withhold Your manna
from their mouth,
And gave them water for their thirst.
21 Forty years You sustained them in the
wilderness;
They lacked nothing;
Their clothes did not wear out[a]
And their feet did not swell.

22 "Moreover You gave them kingdoms
and nations,
And divided them into districts.[a]
So they took possession of the land of
Sī'hon,
The land of[b] the king of Hesh'bon,
And the land of Og king of Bā'shan.

9:17 [a]Following Masoretic Text and Vulgate; Septuagint reads *in Egypt.* 9:21 [a]Compare Deuteronomy 29:5 9:22 [a]Literally *corners* [b]Following Masoretic Text and Vulgate; Septuagint omits *The land of.*

23 You also multiplied their children as
the stars of heaven,
And brought them into the land
Which You had told their fathers
To go in and possess.
24 So the people went in
And possessed the land;
You subdued before them the
inhabitants of the land,
The Cā'naan·ītes,
And gave them into their hands,
With their kings
And the people of the land,
That they might do with them as they
wished.
25 And they took strong cities and a rich
land,
And possessed houses full of all
goods,
Cisterns *already* dug, vineyards, olive
groves,
And fruit trees in abundance.
So they ate and were filled and grew
fat,
And delighted themselves in Your
great goodness.

26 "Nevertheless they were disobedient
And rebelled against You,
Cast Your law behind their backs
And killed Your prophets, who testi-
fied against them
To turn them to Yourself;
And they worked great provocations.
27 Therefore You delivered them into the
hand of their enemies,
Who oppressed them;
And in the time of their trouble,
When they cried to You,
You heard from heaven;
And according to Your abundant
mercies
You gave them deliverers who saved
them
From the hand of their enemies.

9:26–31 God's chastening love. God allowed His people to experience the results of their sin in oppression and domination, but He did not permit them to be consumed.

28 "But after they had rest,
They again did evil before You.
Therefore You left them in the hand
of their enemies,
So that they had dominion over
them;
Yet when they returned and cried out
to You,
You heard from heaven;
And many times You delivered them
according to Your mercies,
29 And testified against them,
That You might bring them back to
Your law.
Yet they acted proudly,
And did not heed Your
commandments,
But sinned against Your judgments,
'Which if a man does, he shall live by
them.'[a]
And they shrugged their shoulders,
Stiffened their necks,
And would not hear.
30 Yet for many years You had patience
with them,
And testified against them by Your
Spirit in Your prophets.
Yet they would not listen;
Therefore You gave them into the
hand of the peoples of the lands.
31 Nevertheless in Your great mercy
You did not utterly consume them
nor forsake them;
For You *are* God, gracious and
merciful.

32 "Now therefore, our God,
The great, the mighty, and awesome
God,
Who keeps covenant and mercy:
Do not let all the trouble seem small
before You
That has come upon us,
Our kings and our princes,
Our priests and our prophets,
Our fathers and on all Your people,
From the days of the kings of Assyria
until this day.
33 However You *are* just in all that has
befallen us;
For You have dealt faithfully,
But we have done wickedly.
34 Neither our kings nor our princes,
Our priests nor our fathers,
Have kept Your law,
Nor heeded Your commandments
and Your testimonies,
With which You testified against
them.
35 For they have not served You in their
kingdom,
Or in the many good *things* that You
gave them,
Or in the large and rich land which
You set before them;
Nor did they turn from their wicked
works.

36 "Here we *are,* servants today!
And the land that You gave to our
fathers,
To eat its fruit and its bounty,
Here we *are,* servants in it!
37 And it yields much increase to the
kings
You have set over us,
Because of our sins;
Also they have dominion over our
bodies and our cattle
At their pleasure;
And we *are* in great distress.

38 "And because of all this,
We make a sure *covenant* and write *it;*
Our leaders, our Lē'vītes, *and* our
priests seal *it.*"

CHAPTER 10

The People Who Sealed the Covenant

Now those who placed *their* seal on *the document were:*

9:29 [a]Leviticus 18:5

10:1–27 The individuals who signed the covenant on behalf of the people.

Nē·he·mī′ah the governor, the son of
Hac·a·lī′ah, and Zed·e·kī′ah,
2Se·rāi′ah, Az·a·rī′ah, Jer·e·mī′ah,
3Pash′hur, Am·a·rī′ah, Mal·chī′jah,
4Hat′tush, Sheb·a·nī′ah, Mal′luch,
5Hā′rim, Mer′e·moth, Ō·ba·dī′ah,
6Daniel, Gin′ne·thon, Bar′uch,
7Me·shul′lam, A·bī′jah, Mij′a·min,
8Mā·a·zī′ah, Bil′gaī, *and* She·māi′ah.
These *were* the priests.

9 The Lē′vītes: Jesh′ū·a the son of
Az·a·nī′ah, Bin′nū·ī of the sons of
Hen′a·dad, *and* Kad′mi·el.

10Their brethren: Sheb·a·nī′ah,
Hō·dī′jah, Ke·lī′ta, Pe·lāi′ah, Hā′nan,
11Mī′cha, Rē′hob, Hash·a·bī′ah,
12Zac′cur, Sher·e·bī′ah, Sheb·a·nī′ah,
13Hō·dī′jah, Bā′nī, *and* Be·nī′nū.

14The leaders of the people:
Pā′rosh, Pā′hath-Mō′ab, Ē′lam, Zat′tū,
Bā′nī, 15Bun′nī, Az′gad, Bē′baī,
16Ad·o·nī′jah, Big′vaī, Ā′din, 17Ā′ter,
Hez·e·kī′ah, Az′zur, 18Hō·dī′jah,
Hā′shum, Bē′zaī, 19Hā′riph,
An′a·thoth, Nē′baī, 20Mag′pi·ash,
Me·shul′lam, Hē′zir, 21Me·shez′a·bel,
Zā′dok, Jad′dū·a, 22Pel·a·tī′ah,
Hā′nan, A·naī′ah, 23Hō·shē′a,
Han·a·nī′ah, Has′shub, 24Hal·lō′hesh,
Pil′ha, Shō′bek, 25Rē′hum,
Ha·shab′nah, Mā·a·sēi′ah, 26A·hī′jah,
Hā′nan, Ā′nan, 27Mal′luch, Hā′rim,
and Bā′a·nah.

The Covenant That Was Sealed

28Now the rest of the people—the
priests, the Lē′vītes, the gatekeepers, the
singers, the Neth′i·nim, and all those who
had separated themselves from the peo-
ples of the lands to the Law of God, their
wives, their sons, and their daughters,
everyone who had knowledge and under-
standing— 29these joined with their
brethren, their nobles, and entered into a
curse and an oath to walk in God's Law,
which was given by Moses the servant of
God, and to observe and do all the com-
mandments of the LORD our Lord, and His
ordinances and His statutes: 30We would
not give our daughters as wives to the peo-
ples of the land, nor take their daughters
for our sons; 31*if* the peoples of the land
brought wares or any grain to sell on the
Sabbath day, we would not buy it from
them on the Sabbath, or on a holy day; and
we would forego the seventh year's *pro-
duce* and the exacting of every debt.

32Also we made ordinances for our-
selves, to exact from ourselves yearly one-
third of a shekel for the service of the
house of our God: 33for the showbread, for
the regular grain offering, for the regular
burnt offering of the Sabbaths, the New
Moons, and the set feasts; for the holy
things, for the sin offerings to make atone-
ment for Israel, and all the work of the
house of our God. 34We cast lots among the
priests, the Lē′vītes, and the people, for
bringing the wood offering into the house
of our God, according to our fathers'
houses, at the appointed times year by
year, to burn on the altar of the LORD our
God as *it is* written in the Law.

35And *we made ordinances* to bring the
firstfruits of our ground and the firstfruits
of all fruit of all trees, year by year, to the

10:28, 29 Following the public example of their leaders, **the people**, beginning with the priesthood, joined the covenant.

10:30, 31 The commands mentioned relate to the particular problems of the postexilic community—intermarriage, Sabbath observance, and their treatment of the poor. These areas indicated the lack of separation from their pagan neighbors; they were representative of the general lack of commitment to God's plan.

10:32–39 How we treat the **house of our God** (v. 39) and His ministers speaks volumes about the real nature of our commitment to Him.

10:32 **Made ordinances** may imply that they felt free to make some amplifications of the Law to suit their particular circumstances. **exact from ourselves**: Serving God requires self-discipline.

house of the LORD; 36to bring the firstborn of our sons and our cattle, as *it is* written in the Law, and the firstborn of our herds and our flocks, to the house of our God, to the priests who minister in the house of our God; 37to bring the firstfruits of our dough, our offerings, the fruit from all kinds of trees, *the* new wine and oil, to the priests, to the storerooms of the house of our God; and to bring the tithes of our land to the Lē′vītes, for the Lē′vītes should receive the tithes in all our farming communities. 38And the priest, the descendant of Aaron, shall be with the Lē′vītes when the Lē′vītes receive tithes; and the Lē′vītes shall bring up a tenth of the tithes to the house of our God, to the rooms of the storehouse.

39For the children of Israel and the children of Levi shall bring the offering of the grain, of the new wine and the oil, to the storerooms where the articles of the sanctuary *are, where* the priests who minister and the gatekeepers and the singers *are;* and we will not neglect the house of our God.

CHAPTER 11

The People Dwelling in Jerusalem

Now the leaders of the people dwelt at Jerusalem; the rest of the people cast lots to bring one out of ten to dwell in Jerusalem, the holy city, and nine-tenths *were to dwell* in *other* cities. 2And the people blessed all the men who willingly offered themselves to dwell at Jerusalem.

3These *are* the heads of the province who dwelt in Jerusalem. (But in the cities of Judah everyone dwelt in his own possession in their cities—Israelites, priests, Lē′vītes, Neth′i·nim, and descendants of Solomon's servants.) 4Also in Jerusalem dwelt *some* of the children of Judah and of the children of Benjamin.

The children of Judah: A·thaī′ah the son of Uz·zī′ah, the son of Zech·a·rī′ah, the son of Am·a·rī′ah, the son of Sheph·a·tī′ah, the son of Ma·hal′a·lel, of the children of Per′ez; 5and Mā·a·sēi′ah the son of Bar′uch, the son of Col-Hō′zeh, the son of Ha·zaī′ah, the son of A·dāi′ah, the son of Joi′ā·rib, the son of Zech·a·rī′ah, the son of Shi·lō′nī. 6All the sons of Per′ez who dwelt at Jerusalem *were* four hundred and sixty-eight valiant men.

7And these are the sons of Benjamin: Sal′lū the son of Me·shul′lam, the son of Jō′ed, the son of Pe·dāi′ah, the son of Kō·laī′ah, the son of Mā·a·sēi′ah, the son of Ith′i·el, the son of Je·shā′i·ah; 8and after him Gab·bā′ī *and* Sal′laī, nine hundred and twenty-eight. 9Jō′el the son of Zich′rī *was* their overseer, and Judah the son of Se·nū′ah[a] *was* second over the city.

10Of the priests: Je·daī′ah the son of Joi′ā·rib, and Jā′chin; 11Se·rāi′ah the son of Hil·kī′ah, the son of Me·shul′lam, the son of Zā′dok, the son of Me·rā′i·oth, the son of A·hī′tub, *was* the leader of the house of God. 12Their brethren who did the work of the house *were* eight hundred and twenty-two; and A·dāi′ah the son of Je·rō′ham, the son of Pel·a·lī′ah, the son of Am′zī, the son of Zech·a·rī′ah, the son of Pash′hur, the son of Mal·chī′jah, 13and his brethren, heads of the fathers' *houses, were* two hundred and forty-two; and A·mash′aī the son of Az′a·rel, the son of Ah′zaī, the son of Me·shil′le·moth, the son of Im′mer, 14and their brethren, mighty men of valor, *were* one hundred and twenty-eight. Their overseer *was* Zab′di·el the son of *one of* the great men.[a]

11:9 [a]Or *Hassenuah* 11:14 [a]Or *the son of Haggedolim*

11:1–24 A list of those who took up residence in Jerusalem, either as a result of casting **lots** (v. 1) or voluntarily (v. 2). Evidently the restored city was capable of handling a larger population than it had previously sustained. The list includes **heads of the province** (nobles, vv. 3–9), **priests** (vv. 10–14), **Levites** (vv. 15–18), temple guards (v. 19). Verses 20–24 offer further notes on the location of the priests.

[15]Also of the Lē′vītes: She·māi′ah the son of Has′shub, the son of Az·rī′kam, the son of Hash·a·bī′ah, the son of Bun′nī; [16]Shab′be·thaī and Joz′a·bad, of the heads of the Lē′vītes, *had* the oversight of the business outside of the house of God; [17]Mat·ta·nī′ah the son of Mī′cha,[a] the son of Zab′dī, the son of Ā′saph, the leader *who* began the thanksgiving with prayer; Bak·bū·kī′ah, the second among his brethren; and Ab′da the son of Sham′mū·a, the son of Gā′lal, the son of Je·dū′thun. [18]All the Lē′vītes in the holy city *were* two hundred and eighty-four.

[19]Moreover the gatekeepers, Ak′kub, Tal′mon, and their brethren who kept the gates, *were* one hundred and seventy-two.

[20]And the rest of Israel, of the priests *and* Lē′vītes, *were* in all the cities of Judah, everyone in his inheritance. [21]But the Neth′i·nim dwelt in Ō′phel. And Zī′ha and Gish′pa *were* over the Neth′i·nim.

[22]Also the overseer of the Lē′vītes at Jerusalem *was* Uz′zī the son of Bā′nī, the son of Hash·a·bī′ah, the son of Mat·ta·nī′ah, the son of Mī′cha, of the sons of Ā′saph, the singers in charge of the service of the house of God. [23]For *it was* the king's command concerning them that a certain portion should be for the singers, a quota day by day. [24]Peth·a·hī′ah the son of Me·shez′a·bel, of the children of Zē′rah the son of Judah, *was* the king's deputy[a] in all matters concerning the people.

The People Dwelling Outside Jerusalem

[25]And as for the villages with their fields, *some* of the children of Judah dwelt in Kir′jath Ar′ba and its villages, Dī′bon and its villages, Je·kab′zē·el and its villages; [26]in Jesh′ū·a, Mō′la·dah, Beth Pē′let, [27]Hā′zar Shū′al, and Bē·er·shē′ba and its villages; [28]in Zik′lag and Mē·cō′nah and its villages; [29]in En Rim′mon, Zō′rah, Jar′muth, [30]Za·nō′ah, A·dul′lam, and their villages; in Lā′chish and its fields; in A·zē′kah and its villages. They dwelt from Bē·er·shē′ba to the Valley of Hin′nom.

[31]Also the children of Benjamin from Gē′ba *dwelt* in Mich′mash, Āi′ja, and Beth′el, and their villages; [32]in An′a·thoth, Nob, An·a·nī′ah; [33]in Hā′zor, Rā′mah, Git′ta·im; [34]in Hā′did, Ze·bō′im, Ne·bal′lat; [35]in Lod, Ō′nō, *and* the Valley of Craftsmen. [36]Some of the Judean divisions of Lē′vītes *were* in Benjamin.

CHAPTER 12

The Priests and Levites

Now these *are* the priests and the Lē′vītes who came up with Ze·rub′ba·bel the son of She·al′ti·el, and Jesh′ū·a: Se·rāi′ah, Jer·e·mī′ah, Ezra, [2]Am·a·rī′ah, Mal′luch, Hat′tush, [3]Shech·a·nī′ah, Rē′hum, Mer′e·moth, [4]Id′dō, Gin′ne·thoi,[a] A·bī′jah, [5]Mij′a·min, Mā·a·dī′ah, Bil′gah, [6]She·māi′ah, Joi′ā·rib, Je·daī′ah, [7]Sal′lū, A′mok, Hil·kī′ah, *and* Je·daī′ah.

These *were* the heads of the priests and their brethren in the days of Jesh′ū·a.

[8]Moreover the Lē′vītes *were* Jesh′ū·a, Bin′nū·ī, Kad′mi·el, Sher·e·bī′ah, Judah, *and* Mat·ta·nī′ah *who led* the thanksgiving *psalms,* he and his brethren. [9]Also Bak·bū·kī′ah and Un′nī, their brethren, *stood* across from them in *their* duties.

[10]Jesh′ū·a begot Joi′a·kim, Joi′a·kim begot E·lī′a·shib, E·lī′a·shib begot Joi′a·da, [11]Joi′a·da begot Jonathan, and Jonathan begot Jad′dū·a.

[12]Now in the days of Joi′a·kim, the priests, the heads of the fathers' *houses were:* of Se·rāi′ah, Me·raī′ah; of

11:17 [a]Or *Michah* 11:24 [a]Literally *at the king's hand*
12:4 [a]Or *Ginnethon* (compare verse 16)

11:23 The king's command may refer to the instructions of Darius (Ezra 6:8, 9) or more probably of Artaxerxes I (Ezra 7:20). Both commanded that the daily temple worship be supported; that support would include a daily provision for the **singers**.

12:9 stood across from them: Sang antiphonally.

Jer·e·mī′ah, Han·a·nī′ah; 13of Ezra, Me·shul′lam; of Am·a·rī′ah, Jē·hō·hā′nan; 14of Mel′i·chū,[a] Jonathan; of Sheb·a·nī′ah,[b] Joseph; 15of Hā′rim,[a] Ad′na; of Me·rā′i·oth,[b] Hel′kaī; 16of Id′dō, Zech·a·rī′ah; of Gin′ne·thon, Me·shul′lam; 17of A·bī′jah, Zich′rī; *the son* of Min′ja·min;[a] of Mō·a·dī′ah,[b] Pil′taī; 18of Bil′gah, Sham′mū·a; of She·māi′ah, Je·hon′a·than; 19of Joi′ā·rib, Mat·tē′naī; of Je·daī′ah, Uz′zī; 20of Sal′laī,[a] Kal′laī; of A′mok, Ē′ber; 21of Hil·kī′ah, Hash·a·bī′ah; *and* of Je·daī′ah, Ne·than′el.

22During the reign of Da·rī′us the Persian, a record *was also kept* of the Lē′vītes and priests *who had been* heads of their fathers′ *houses* in the days of E·lī′a·shib, Joi′a·da, Jō·hā′nan, and Jad′dū·a. 23The sons of Levi, the heads of the fathers′ *houses* until the days of Jō·hā′nan the son of E·lī′a·shib, *were* written in the book of the chronicles.

24And the heads of the Lē′vītes *were* Hash·a·bī′ah, Sher·e·bī′ah, and Jesh′ū·a the son of Kad′mi·el, with their brothers across from them, to praise *and* give thanks, group alternating with group, according to the command of David the man of God. 25Mat·ta·nī′ah, Bak·bū·kī′ah, Ō·ba·dī′ah, Me·shul′lam, Tal′mon, and Ak′kub *were* gatekeepers keeping the watch at the storerooms of the gates. 26These *lived* in the days of Joi′a·kim the son of Jesh′ū·a, the son of Jō′za·dak,[a] and in the days of Nē·he·mī′ah the governor, and of Ezra the priest, the scribe.

Nehemiah Dedicates the Wall

27Now at the dedication of the wall of Jerusalem they sought out the Lē′vītes in all their places, to bring them to Jerusalem to celebrate the dedication with gladness, both with thanksgivings and singing, *with* cymbals and stringed instruments and harps. 28And the sons of the singers gathered together from the countryside around Jerusalem, from the villages of the Ne·toph′a·thītes, 29from the house of Gil′gal, and from the fields of Gē′ba and Az′ma·veth; for the singers had built themselves villages all around Jerusalem. 30Then the priests and Lē′vītes purified themselves, and purified the people, the gates, and the wall.

31So I brought the leaders of Judah up on the wall, and appointed two large thanksgiving choirs. *One* went to the right hand on the wall toward the Refuse Gate. 32After them went Hō·shaī′ah and half of the leaders of Judah, 33and Az·a·rī′ah, Ezra, Me·shul′lam, 34Judah, Benjamin, She·māi′ah, Jer·e·mī′ah, 35and some of the priests′ sons with trumpets—Zech·a·rī′ah the son of Jonathan, the son of She·māi′ah, the son of Mat·ta·nī′ah, the son of Mī·chaī′ah, the son of Zac′cur, the son of Ā′saph, 36and his brethren, She·māi′ah, Az′a·rel, Mil′a·laī, Gil′a·laī, Mā′aī, Ne·than′el, Judah, *and* Ha·nā′nī, with the musical instruments of David the man of God. And Ezra the scribe *went* before them. 37By the Fountain Gate, in front of them, they went up the stairs of the City of David, on the stairway of the wall, beyond the house of David, as far as the Water Gate eastward.

12:14 [a]Or *Malluch* (compare verse 2) [b]Or *Shechaniah* (compare verse 3) 12:15 [a]Or *Rehum* (compare verse 3) [b]Or *Meremoth* (compare verse 3) 12:17 [a]Or *Mijamin* (compare verse 5) [b]Or *Maadiah* (compare verse 5) 12:20 [a]Or *Sallu* (compare verse 7) 12:26 [a]Spelled *Jehozadak* in 1 Chronicles 6:14

12:22 Darius the Persian does not refer to the king of Persia mentioned in the Book of Ezra (see Ezra 4:5, 24; 6:13–15). Two later kings had the same name: Darius II (423–404 B.C.) and Darius III (336–331 B.C.).

12:24 The context suggests that responsive or antiphonal singing is intended (see Ezra 3:10, 11). Instructions for such singing were probably recorded in some noncanonical writing of David.

12:36 musical instruments of David: cymbals, psaltries, and harps.

38 The other thanksgiving choir went the opposite *way,* and I *was* behind them with half of the people on the wall, going past the Tower of the Ovens as far as the Broad Wall, 39 and above the Gate of Ē'phra·im, above the Old Gate, above the Fish Gate, the Tower of Ha·nan'el, the Tower of the Hundred, as far as the Sheep Gate; and they stopped by the Gate of the Prison.

40 So the two thanksgiving choirs stood in the house of God, likewise I and the half of the rulers with me; 41 and the priests, E·lī'a·kim, Mā·a·sēi'ah, Min'ja·min,[a] Mī·chaī'ah, El·i·ō·ē'naī, Zech·a·rī'ah, *and* Han·a·nī'ah, with trumpets; 42 also Mā·a·sēi'ah, She·māi'ah, El·ē·ā'zar, Uz'zī, Jē·hō·hā'nan, Mal·chī'jah, Ē'lam, and Ē'zer. The singers sang loudly with Jez·ra·hī'ah the director.

43 Also that day they offered great sacrifices, and rejoiced, for God had made them rejoice with great joy; the women and the children also rejoiced, so that the joy of Jerusalem was heard afar off.

Temple Responsibilities

44 And at the same time some were appointed over the rooms of the storehouse for the offerings, the firstfruits, and the tithes, to gather into them from the fields of the cities the portions specified by the Law for the priests and Lē'vītes; for Judah rejoiced over the priests and Lē'vītes who ministered. 45 Both the singers and the gatekeepers kept the charge of their God and the charge of the purification, according to the command of David *and* Solomon his son. 46 For in the days of David and Ā'saph of old *there were* chiefs of the singers, and songs of praise and thanksgiving to God. 47 In the days of Ze·rub'ba·bel and in the days of Nē·he·mī'ah all Israel gave the portions for the singers and the gatekeepers, a portion for each day. They also consecrated *holy things* for the Lē'vītes, and the Lē'vītes consecrated *them* for the children of Aaron.

CHAPTER 13

Principles of Separation

On that day they read from the Book of Moses in the hearing of the people, and in it was found written that no Am'mon·īte or Mō'ab·īte should ever come into the assembly of God, 2 because they had not met the children of Israel with bread and water, but hired Bā'laam against them to curse them. However, our God turned the curse into a blessing. 3 So it was, when they had heard the Law, that they separated all the mixed multitude from Israel.

The Reforms of Nehemiah

4 Now before this, E·lī'a·shib the priest, having authority over the storerooms of the house of our God, *was* allied with Tō·bī'ah. 5 And he had prepared for him a large room, where previously they had stored the grain offerings, the frankincense, the articles, the tithes of grain, the new wine and oil, which were commanded *to be given* to the Lē'vītes and singers and gatekeepers, and the offerings for the priests. 6 But during all this I was not in Jerusalem, for in the thirty-second year of

12:41 [a]Or *Mijamin* (compare verse 5)

12:44–47 This use of the choirs seems to have further established the roles and prerogatives of the **singers** and **gatekeepers** (v. 45) among the Levites. **consecrated holy things** (v. 47): The people gave their tithes to the Levites who in turn gave a tithe of the tithe to the priests (vv. 44, 47; see 10:38, 39).

13:4 Eliashib: Almost certainly the high priest himself (see 3:1). **Tobiah**: Judah's mortal enemy (4:3) had wormed his way into the temple itself. Corrupt the religious leadership of a nation and the very fountainhead of its possible redemption is perverted.

13:6 thirty-second year: See 1:1; Nehemiah was in Jerusalem for 12 years before returning to the Persian court for an unknown period of time. When he returned to Jerusalem,

Ar·ta·xerx'ēs king of Babylon I had returned to the king. Then after certain days I obtained leave from the king, 7and I came to Jerusalem and discovered the evil that E·lī'a·shib had done for Tō·bī'ah, in preparing a room for him in the courts of the house of God. 8And it grieved me bitterly; therefore I threw all the household goods of Tō·bī'ah out of the room. 9Then I commanded them to cleanse the rooms; and I brought back into them the articles of the house of God, with the grain offering and the frankincense.

10I also realized that the portions for the Lē'vītes had not been given *them;* for each of the Lē'vītes and the singers who did the work had gone back to his field. 11So I contended with the rulers, and said, "Why is the house of God forsaken?" And I gathered them together and set them in their place. 12Then all Judah brought the tithe of the grain and the new wine and the oil to the storehouse. 13And I appointed as treasurers over the storehouse Shel·e·mī'ah the priest and Zā'dok the scribe, and of the Lē'vītes, Pe·dāi'ah; and next to them *was* Hā'nan the son of Zac'cur, the son of Mat·ta·nī'ah; for they were considered faithful, and their task *was* to distribute to their brethren.

14Remember me, O my God, concerning this, and do not wipe out my good deeds that I have done for the house of my God, and for its services!

15In those days I saw *people* in Judah treading wine presses on the Sabbath, and bringing in sheaves, and loading donkeys with wine, grapes, figs, and all *kinds of* burdens, which they brought into Jerusalem on the Sabbath day. And I warned *them* about the day on which they were selling provisions. 16Men of Tȳre dwelt there also, who brought in fish and all kinds of goods, and sold *them* on the Sabbath to the children of Judah, and in Jerusalem.

17Then I contended with the nobles of Judah, and said to them, "What evil thing *is* this that you do, by which you profane the Sabbath day? 18Did not your fathers do thus, and did not our God bring all this disaster on us and on this city? Yet you bring added wrath on Israel by profaning the Sabbath."

19So it was, at the gates of Jerusalem, as it began to be dark before the Sabbath, that I commanded the gates to be shut, and charged that they must not be opened till after the Sabbath. Then I posted *some* of my servants at the gates, *so that* no burdens would be brought in on the Sabbath day. 20Now the merchants and sellers of all kinds of wares lodged outside Jerusalem once or twice.

21Then I warned them, and said to them, "Why do you spend the night around the wall? If you do *so* again, I will lay hands on you!" From that time on they came no *more* on the Sabbath. 22And I commanded the Lē'vītes that they should cleanse themselves, and that they should go and guard the gates, to sanctify the Sabbath day.

Remember me, O my God, *concerning* this also, and spare me according to the greatness of Your mercy!

23In those days I also saw Jews *who* had married women of Ash'dod, Am'mon, *and*

---

he discovered that the high priest was not only consorting with the enemy but in so doing had taken an Ammonite into the temple, something forbidden in the Law (13:1).

13:10, 11 The purpose of the guaranteed income for the priesthood was to allow priests to give full time to the service of God. Because the tithes were not being paid, the Levites had gone back to their villages to make a living. **gathered them**: The Levites.

13:19–22 began to be dark: The Sabbath began at sundown on Friday and extended until sundown on Saturday. Evidently some merchants reasoned that if they were not inside the holy city they did not have to keep the Sabbath—a good example of evading the intent of the law. **sanctify the Sabbath**: Keep the day wholly consecrated to God's purposes.

Mō′ab. [24]And half of their children spoke
the language of Ash′dod, and could not
speak the language of Judah, but spoke ac-
cording to the language of one or the other
people.
[25]So I contended with them and cursed
them, struck some of them and pulled out
their hair, and made them swear by God,
saying, "You shall not give your daughters
as wives to their sons, nor take their
daughters for your sons or yourselves.
[26]Did not Solomon king of Israel sin by
these things? Yet among many nations
there was no king like him, who was
beloved of his God; and God made him
king over all Israel. Nevertheless pagan
women caused even him to sin. [27]Should
we then hear of your doing all this great
evil, transgressing against our God by
marrying pagan women?"
[28]And *one* of the sons of Joi′a·da, the son
of E·lī′a·shib the high priest, *was* a son-in-
law of San·bal′lat the Hor′o·nīte; therefore
I drove him from me.
[29]Remember them, O my God, because
they have defiled the priesthood and the
covenant of the priesthood and the Lē′-
vītes.
[30]Thus I cleansed them of everything pa-
gan. I also assigned duties to the priests
and the Lē′vītes, each to his service, [31]and
to bringing the wood offering and the first-
fruits at appointed times.

Remember me, O my God, for good!

13:24 When children no longer speak the **language** of their culture, the culture itself cannot long survive.

13:26, 27 Had the Exile taught Israel nothing about God's punishment for disobedience? **pagan women caused even him to sin**: See 1 Kin. 11:5–8.

13:28 The problem of intermarriage (vv. 23–27) had become so serious as to reach the family of the **high priest**. The law specifically forbade marriage between the high priest and a foreign woman (Lev. 21:10, 14). **Sanballat**, another enemy (see 2:10 and note on 13:4), had wormed himself into Jewish society. How easily we let down the bars against those who are not friends of God.

INVEST IN A FEW

Ron Lee Davis

Moses mentored Joshua. Naomi mentored her daughter-in-law Ruth. Ezra mentored Nehemiah. Elijah mentored Elisha. Elizabeth mentored her cousin Mary. Barnabas mentored Paul and John Mark. Paul mentored his spiritual son Timothy. Paul also mentored Priscilla and Aquila, who, in turn, mentored Apollos.

Jesus transformed the world because He poured His life into the Twelve. Though He preached to the masses, He invested Himself in a few, knowing that those few would invest themselves in still others and thus transform the world. If we want to transform our families, our churches, our businesses, our communities, and ultimately our world, then we must discover what it means to pour our lives into individuals. We must learn to spend more time with the few. We must learn to live for the next generation. We must become mentors. ✦

✦Esther✦

Scholars are still debating the author of Esther, which was written around 465 B.C. It covers events in Persia under King Ahasuerus (also known as Xerxes), and it tells of Jews who were scattered after their release from Babylon. Although the Jews were allowed to return to their homeland, many chose to stay in Persia.

The story of one such Jew, Mordecai, and his cousin, Esther, is related in this book. Esther was made queen because of her beauty, and she kept her Jewish ancestry a secret. When Haman convinced the king to order the execution of all Jews in the land, Esther revealed her heritage, uncovered Haman's wicked plot, and thereby saved her people.

The Book of Esther shows that God protects His chosen people; bringing Esther into the palace was His way of saving the Jews from execution. This fulfills the promise in Genesis 12:1, 3, which says that God will bless His covenant people and curse those who try to harm them. Esther and Mordecai prove that God uses ordinary women and men to accomplish His purposes. ✦

CHAPTER 1

The King Dethrones Queen Vashti

Now it came to pass in the days of
A·has·ū·ē'rus[a] (this *was* the A·has·ū·ē'rus
who reigned over one hundred and
twenty-seven provinces, from India to
Ethiopia), [2]in those days when King
A·has·ū·ē'rus sat on the throne of his king-
dom, which *was* in Shū'shan[a] the citadel,
[3]*that* in the third year of his reign he made
a feast for all his officials and servants—
the powers of Persia and Media, the no-
bles, and the princes of the provinces *being*
before him— [4]when he showed the riches
of his glorious kingdom and the splendor
of his excellent majesty for many days, one
hundred and eighty days *in all*.
[5]And when these days were completed,
the king made a feast lasting seven days
for all the people who were present in
Shū'shan the citadel, from great to small,
in the court of the garden of the king's
palace. [6]*There were* white and blue linen
curtains fastened with cords of fine linen
and purple on silver rods and marble pil-
lars; *and the* couches *were* of gold and silver
on a *mosaic* pavement of alabaster,
turquoise, and white and black marble.

1:1 [a]Generally identified with Xerxes I (485–464 B.C.)
1:2 [a]Or *Susa*, and so throughout this book

1:1, 2 Ahasuerus: Xerxes I (486–465 B.C.). **Shushan**: Susa, located in what is today extreme southwestern Iran. It was the winter capitol of the Persian empire.

1:3–7 third year: 483 B.C. The magnificence and abundance were undoubtedly calculated to impress the leaders of the empire that the emperor had the power and wealth to rule as he wished.

[7]And they served drinks in golden vessels,
each vessel being different from the other,
with royal wine in abundance, according
to the generosity of the king. [8]In accor-
dance with the law, the drinking was not
compulsory; for so the king had ordered
all the officers of his household, that they
should do according to each man's plea-
sure.

[9]Queen Vash'tī also made a feast for the
women *in* the royal palace which *belonged*
to King A·has·ū·ē'rus.

[10]On the seventh day, when the heart of
the king was merry with wine, he com-
manded Me·hū'man, Biz'tha, Har·bō'na,
Big'tha, A·bag'tha, Zē'thar, and Car'cas,
seven eunuchs who served in the presence
of King A·has·ū·ē'rus, [11]to bring Queen
Vash'tī before the king, *wearing* her royal
crown, in order to show her beauty to the
people and the officials, for she *was* beauti-
ful to behold. [12]But Queen Vash'tī refused
to come at the king's command *brought* by
his eunuchs; therefore the king was furi-
ous, and his anger burned within him.

[13]Then the king said to the wise men
who understood the times (for this *was* the
king's manner toward all who knew law
and justice, [14]those closest to him *being*
Car·shē'na, Shē'thar, Ad·mā'tha, Tar'-
shish, Mē'rēs, Mar·sē'na, and Mē·mū'can,
the seven princes of Persia and Media,
who had access to the king's presence, *and*
who ranked highest in the kingdom):
[15]"What *shall we* do to Queen Vash'tī, ac-
cording to law, because she did not obey
the command of King A·has·ū·ē'rus
brought to her by the eunuchs?"

[16]And Mē·mū'can answered before the
king and the princes: "Queen Vash'tī has
not only wronged the king, but also all the
princes, and all the people who *are* in all
the provinces of King A·has·ū·ē'rus. [17]For
the queen's behavior will become known
to all women, so that they will despise
their husbands in their eyes, when they re-
port, 'King A·has·ū·ē'rus commanded
Queen Vash'tī to be brought in before him,
but she did not come.' [18]This very day the
noble ladies of Persia and Media will say to
all the king's officials that they have heard
of the behavior of the queen. Thus *there will
be* excessive contempt and wrath. [19]If it
pleases the king, let a royal decree go out
from him, and let it be recorded in the laws
of the Persians and the Mēdes, so that it
will not be altered, that Vash'tī shall come
no more before King A·has·ū·ē'rus; and let
the king give her royal position to another
who is better than she. [20]When the king's
decree which he will make is proclaimed
throughout all his empire (for it is great),
all wives will honor their husbands, both
great and small."

[21]And the reply pleased the king and the
princes, and the king did according to the
word of Mē·mū'can. [22]Then he sent letters
to all the king's provinces, to each province
in its own script, and to every people in
their own language, that each man should
be master in his own house, and speak in
the language of his own people.

CHAPTER 2

Esther Becomes Queen

After these things, when the wrath of
King A·has·ū·ē'rus subsided, he remem-
bered Vash'tī, what she had done, and
what had been decreed against her. [2]Then

1:10–12 The queen **refused** to be made the object of drunken stares. Such might be conceivable for a concubine or a dancing girl, but not for the first woman in the empire.

1:14 seven princes: These were the closest advisors to the king. Their position is also referred to as "seven counselors" (see Ezra 7:14).

1:19 Once a ruling of the king became Persian law, it could **not be altered** or revoked (see 8:8). **come no more**: For the rest of her life Vashti would be confined to the harem, never seeing the king again and having no royal prerogatives. Under Persian law she could not be killed, but her punishment might be almost as bad.

the king's servants who attended him said: "Let beautiful young virgins be sought for the king; 3and let the king appoint officers in all the provinces of his kingdom, that they may gather all the beautiful young virgins to Shū'shan the citadel, into the women's quarters, under the custody of Heg'aī[a] the king's eunuch, custodian of the women. And let beauty preparations be given *them.* 4Then let the young woman who pleases the king be queen instead of Vash'tī."

This thing pleased the king, and he did so.

5In Shū'shan the citadel there was a certain Jew whose name *was* Mor'de·caī the son of Jā'ir, the son of Shim'ē·ī, the son of Kish, a Ben'ja·mīte. 6*Kish*[a] had been carried away from Jerusalem with the captives who had been captured with Jec·o·nī'ah[b] king of Judah, whom Ne·bū·chad·nez'zar the king of Babylon had carried away. 7And *Mor'*de·caī had brought up Ha·das'sah, that *is,* Esther, his uncle's daughter, for she had neither father nor mother. The young woman *was* lovely and beautiful. When her father and mother died, Mor'de·caī took her as his own daughter.

8So it was, when the king's command and decree were heard, and when many young women were gathered at Shū'shan the citadel, *under* the custody of Heg'aī, that Esther also was taken to the king's palace, into the care of Heg'aī the custodian of the women. 9Now the young woman pleased him, and she obtained his favor; so he readily gave beauty preparations to her, besides her allowance. Then seven choice maidservants were provided for her from the king's palace, and he moved her and her maidservants to the best *place* in the house of the women.

10Esther had not revealed her people or family, for Mor'de·caī had charged her not to reveal *it.* 11And every day Mor'de·caī paced in front of the court of the women's quarters, to learn of Esther's welfare and what was happening to her.

12Each young woman's turn came to go in to King A·has·ū·ē'rus after she had completed twelve months' preparation, according to the regulations for the women, for thus were the days of their preparation apportioned: six months with oil of myrrh, and six months with perfumes and preparations for beautifying women. 13Thus *prepared, each* young woman went to the king, and she was given whatever she desired to take with her from the women's quarters to the king's palace. 14In the evening she went, and in the morning she returned to the second house of the women, to the custody of Sha·ash'gaz, the king's eunuch who kept the concubines. She would not go in to the king again unless the king delighted in her and called for her by name.

15Now when the turn came for Esther the daughter of Ab·i·hā'il the uncle of Mor'de·caī, who had taken her as his daughter, to go in to the king, she requested nothing but what Heg'aī the

2:3 [a]Hebrew *Hege* 2:6 [a]Literally *Who* [b]Same as *Jehoiachin,* 2 Kings 24:6 and elsewhere

2:5–7 uncle's daughter: Mordecai and Esther were cousins, but her response as a daughter (v. 15) to him suggests that there may have been a considerable age difference between them.

2:8–14 The **twelve months' preparation** (v. 12) indicates the great pains taken to prepare a woman for one night with the emperor.

2:10 not revealed her people: So as not to arouse suspicion of disloyalty to the Persian Empire. In that inclusive culture, the Jews' insistence that theirs was the only true God, and that they were His distinct people, was anomalous at best. See 3:8.

2:14 second house: Now that these women were no longer virgins, they would be kept in a separate place for royal **concubines**. They were doomed to splendid isolation for the rest of their lives. They could not have relations with any other man, and unless the king called for them **by name**, they would never see him again.

king's eunuch, the custodian of the women, advised. And Esther obtained favor in the sight of all who saw her. [16]So Esther was taken to King A·has·ū·ē'rus, into his royal palace, in the tenth month, which *is* the month of Tē'beth, in the seventh year of his reign. [17]The king loved Esther more than all the *other* women, and she obtained grace and favor in his sight more than all the virgins; so he set the royal crown upon her head and made her queen instead of Vash'tī. [18]Then the king made a great feast, the Feast of Esther, for all his officials and servants; and he proclaimed a holiday in the provinces and gave gifts according to the generosity of a king.

Mordecai Discovers a Plot

[19]When virgins were gathered together a second time, Mor'de·caī sat within the king's gate. [20]*Now* Esther had not revealed her family and her people, just as Mor'de·caī had charged her, for Esther obeyed the command of Mor'de·caī as when she was brought up by him.

[21]In those days, while Mor'de·caī sat within the king's gate, two of the king's eunuchs, Big'than and Tē'resh, doorkeepers, became furious and sought to lay hands on King A·has·ū·ē'rus. [22]So the matter became known to Mor'de·caī, who told Queen Esther, and Esther informed the king in Mor'de·caī's name. [23]And when an inquiry was made into the matter, it was confirmed, and both were hanged on a gallows; and it was written in the book of the chronicles in the presence of the king.

CHAPTER 3

Haman's Conspiracy Against the Jews

After these things King A·has·ū·ē'rus promoted Hā'man, the son of Ham-me·dā'tha the Ag'ag·īte, and advanced him and set his seat above all the princes who *were* with him. [2]And all the king's servants who *were* within the king's gate bowed and paid homage to Hā'man, for so the king had commanded concerning him. But Mor'de·caī would not bow or pay homage. [3]Then the king's servants who *were* within the king's gate said to Mor'de·caī, "Why do you transgress the king's command?" [4]Now it happened, when they spoke to him daily and he would not listen to them, that they told *it* to Hā'man, to see whether Mor'de·caī's words would stand; for *Mor'de·caī* had told them that he *was* a Jew. [5]When Hā'man saw that Mor'de·caī did not bow or pay him homage, Hā'man was filled with wrath. [6]But he disdained to lay hands on Mor'de·caī alone, for they had told him of the people of Mor'de·caī. Instead, Hā'man sought to destroy all the Jews who *were* throughout the whole kingdom of A·has·ū·ē'rus—the people of Mor'de·caī.

[7]In the first month, which is the month of Nī'san, in the twelfth year of King A·has·ū·ē'rus, they cast Pūr (that *is,* the lot), before Hā'man to determine the day and the month,[a] until *it fell on the* twelfth *month,*[b] which *is* the month of Ā'dar.

3:7 [a]Septuagint adds *to destroy the people of Mordecai in one day;* Vulgate adds *the nation of the Jews should be destroyed.* [b]Following Masoretic Text and Vulgate; Septuagint reads *and the lot fell on the fourteenth of the month.*

2:16 seventh year: 479 B.C. Four years had elapsed since Vashti's offense (see 1:3). During this time the king had been fighting an unsuccessful war against Greece.

2:21–23 the book of the chronicles: Not to be confused with the OT books, this deed and record were to play a large role in saving the Jews (see 6:1–10).

3:1 An interval of approximately five years passed between chapters 2 and 3.

3:4 told them that he was a Jew: Although Mordecai gave no answer to the question why he would not bow down, the questioners knew the answer: as a Jew he worshiped God alone (see Rev. 22:8, 9). Mordecai was evidently concerned about Esther's safety and had told her not to reveal her identity (2:10, 20), but he obviously disdained such precautions for himself.

[8]Then Hā'man said to King A·has-ū·ē'rus, "There is a certain people scattered and dispersed among the people in all the provinces of your kingdom; their laws *are* different from all *other* people's, and they do not keep the king's laws. Therefore it *is* not fitting for the king to let them remain. [9]If it pleases the king, let *a decree* be written that they be destroyed, and I will pay ten thousand talents of silver into the hands of those who do the work, to bring *it* into the king's treasuries."

[10]So the king took his signet ring from his hand and gave it to Hā'man, the son of Ham·me·dā'tha the Ag'ag·īte, the enemy of the Jews. [11]And the king said to Hā'man, "The money and the people *are* given to you, to do with them as seems good to you."

[12]Then the king's scribes were called on the thirteenth day of the first month, and *a decree* was written according to all that Hā'man commanded—to the king's satraps, to the governors who *were* over each province, to the officials of all people, to every province according to its script, and to every people in their language. In the name of King A·has·ū·ē'rus it was written, and sealed with the king's signet ring. [13]And the letters were sent by couriers into all the king's provinces, to destroy, to kill, and to annihilate all the Jews, both young and old, little children and women, in one day, on the thirteenth *day* of the twelfth *month*, which *is* the month of Ā'dar, and to plunder their possessions.[a] [14]A copy of the document was to be issued as law in every province, being published for all people, that they should be ready for that day. [15]The couriers went out, hastened by the king's command; and the decree was proclaimed in Shū'shan the citadel. So the king and Hā'man sat down to drink, but the city of Shū'shan was perplexed.

CHAPTER 4

Esther Agrees to Help the Jews

When Mor'de·caī learned all that had happened, he tore his clothes and put on sackcloth and ashes, and went out into the midst of the city. He cried out with a loud and bitter cry. [2]He went as far as the front of the king's gate, for no one *might* enter the king's gate clothed with sackcloth. [3]And in every province where the king's command and decree arrived, *there was* great mourning among the Jews, with fasting, weeping, and wailing; and many lay in sackcloth and ashes.

[4]So Esther's maids and eunuchs came and told her, and the queen was deeply distressed. Then she sent garments to clothe Mor'de·caī and take his sackcloth away from him, but he would not accept *them*. [5]Then Esther called Hā'thach, *one* of the king's eunuchs whom he had appointed to attend her, and she gave him a command concerning Mor'de·caī, to learn what and why this *was*. [6]So Hā'thach went out to Mor'de·caī in the city square that *was* in front of the king's gate. [7]And Mor'de·caī told him all that had happened to him, and the sum of money that Hā'man had promised to pay into the king's treasuries to destroy the Jews. [8]He also gave him a copy of the written decree for their destruction, which was given at Shū'shan, that he might show it to Esther and explain it to her, and that he might command her to go in to the king to make supplication to him and plead before him for her people.

3:13 [a]Septuagint adds the text of the letter here.

3:8 laws are different: This has been the basis of anti-Semitism through the ages: Jews insist upon being different. Whenever we choose to be different from the world, we invite its derision, and eventually its hatred.

3:10 his signet ring: The king was giving Haman the right to make any orders he wished and to put the royal seal upon them (see 8:8).

> Do all the good you can,
> By all the means you can,
> In all the ways you can,
> In all the places you can,
> At all the times you can,
> To all the people you can,
> As long as ever you can.
> John Wesley

9So Hā'thach returned and told Esther the
words of Mor'de·caī.
10Then Esther spoke to Hā'thach, and
gave him a command for Mor'de·caī:
11"All the king's servants and the people of
the king's provinces know that any man or
woman who goes into the inner court to
the king, who has not been called, *he has*
but one law: put *all* to death, except the one
to whom the king holds out the golden
scepter, that he may live. Yet I myself have
not been called to go in to the king these
thirty days." 12So they told Mor'de·caī Es-
ther's words.
13And Mor'de·caī told *them* to answer
Esther: "Do not think in your heart that
you will escape in the king's palace any
more than all the other Jews. 14For if you re-
main completely silent at this time, relief
and deliverance will arise for the Jews
from another place, but you and your fa-
ther's house will perish. Yet who knows
whether you have come to the kingdom
for *such* a time as this?"
15Then Esther told *them* to reply to
Mor'de·caī: 16"Go, gather all the Jews
who are present in Shū'shan, and fast for
me; neither eat nor drink for three days,
night or day. My maids and I will fast
likewise. And so I will go to the king,
which *is* against the law; and if I perish, I
perish!"
17So Mor'de·caī went his way and did
according to all that Esther commanded
him.[a]

CHAPTER 5

Esther's Banquet

Now it happened on the third day that
Esther put on *her* royal *robes* and stood in
the inner court of the king's palace, across
from the king's house, while the king sat
on his royal throne in the royal house, fac-
ing the entrance of the house.[a] 2So it was,
when the king saw Queen Esther standing
in the court, *that* she found favor in his
sight, and the king held out to Esther the
golden scepter that *was* in his hand. Then
Esther went near and touched the top of
the scepter.
3And the king said to her, "What do you
wish, Queen Esther? What *is* your request?
It shall be given to you—up to half the
kingdom!"
4So Esther answered, "If it pleases the
king, let the king and Hā'man come today
to the banquet that I have prepared for
him."
5Then the king said, "Bring Hā'man
quickly, that he may do as Esther has said."

4:17 [a]Septuagint adds a prayer of Mordecai here.
5:1 [a]Septuagint adds many extra details in verses 1 and 2.

4:11 inner court: Evidently the king's private apartments. **thirty days**: Her request for an audience might fail because she did not seem to be in any special favor at that time.

4:13, 14 Mordecai offers two reasons that this is not the time for caution: (1) Esther cannot save herself in the long run; (2) failure to act may frustrate the purpose for which she had been brought to the queenship. She has everything to gain and nothing to lose. One cannot righteously ignore personal responsibility for the sake of self-preservation. Each believer has been assigned a role in God's eternal plan, and we must faithfully complete our task.

5:1–8 An authentic report of the intricate social conventions typical of some societies even today: (1) the king's offer of half his kingdom (v. 3); (2) Esther's request to attend one banquet (v. 4) as the basis to request attendance at a second banquet (vv. 6–8) at which the real request will be presented!

So the king and Hā′man went to the ban-
quet that Esther had prepared.
6At the banquet of wine the king said to
Esther, "What *is* your petition? It shall be
granted you. What *is* your request, up to
half the kingdom? It shall be done!"
7Then Esther answered and said, "My
petition and request *is this:* 8If I have found
favor in the sight of the king, and if it
pleases the king to grant my petition and
fulfill my request, then let the king and
Hā′man come to the banquet which I will
prepare for them, and tomorrow I will do
as the king has said."

Haman's Plot Against Mordecai

9So Hā′man went out that day joyful
and with a glad heart; but when Hā′man
saw Mor′de·caī in the king's gate, and that
he did not stand or tremble before him, he
was filled with indignation against
Mor′de·caī. 10Nevertheless Hā′man re-
strained himself and went home, and he
sent and called for his friends and his wife
Zē′resh. 11Then Hā′man told them of his
great riches, the multitude of his children,
everything in which the king had pro-
moted him, and how he had advanced him
above the officials and servants of the king.
12Moreover Hā′man said, "Besides,
Queen Esther invited no one but me to
come in with the king to the banquet that
she prepared; and tomorrow I am again in-
vited by her, along with the king. 13Yet all
this avails me nothing, so long as I see
Mor′de·caī the Jew sitting at the king's
gate."
14Then his wife Zē′resh and all his
friends said to him, "Let a gallows be
made, fifty cubits high, and in the morning
suggest to the king that Mor′de·caī be
hanged on it; then go merrily with the king
to the banquet."
And the thing pleased Hā′man; so he
had the gallows made.

CHAPTER 6

The King Honors Mordecai

That night the king could not sleep. So
one was commanded to bring the book of
the records of the chronicles; and they
were read before the king. 2And it was
found written that Mor′de·caī had told of
Big·thā′na and Tē′resh, two of the king's
eunuchs, the doorkeepers who had sought
to lay hands on King A·has·ū·ē′rus. 3Then
the king said, "What honor or dignity has
been bestowed on Mor′de·caī for this?"
And the king's servants who attended
him said, "Nothing has been done for
him."
4So the king said, "Who *is* in the court?"
Now Hā′man had *just* entered the outer
court of the king's palace to suggest that
the king hang Mor′de·caī on the gallows
that he had prepared for him.
5The king's servants said to him,
"Hā′man is there, standing in the court."
And the king said, "Let him come in."
6So Hā′man came in, and the king asked
him, "What shall be done for the man
whom the king delights to honor?"
Now Hā′man thought in his heart,
"Whom would the king delight to honor
more than me?" 7And Hā′man answered
the king, "*For* the man whom the king de-
lights to honor, 8let a royal robe be brought

6:1 That night: That the king's sleeplessness should occur on this night is an indication that it was not by chance but by God's design.

6:2, 3 it was found written: Although Mordecai's Jewish convictions prevented him from bowing down to a human overlord, nevertheless he was now proven faithful to the king. His Judaism did not make him disloyal. See 2:21–23.

6:4–6 A classic use of irony. At the moment Haman plans to ask for Mordecai's death, circumstances (God) contrive for him to recommend the terms of Mordecai's honor. That honor was made greater because Haman thought he was prescribing it for himself. So will pride always be humbled, either in this life or the one to come.

which the king has worn, and a horse on which the king has ridden, which has a royal crest placed on its head. 9Then let this robe and horse be delivered to the hand of one of the king's most noble princes, that he may array the man whom the king delights to honor. Then parade him on horseback through the city square, and proclaim before him: 'Thus shall it be done to the man whom the king delights to honor!' "

10Then the king said to Hā'man, "Hurry, take the robe and the horse, as you have suggested, and do so for Mor'de·caī the Jew who sits within the king's gate! Leave nothing undone of all that you have spoken."

11So Hā'man took the robe and the horse, arrayed Mor'de·caī and led him on horseback through the city square, and proclaimed before him, "Thus shall it be done to the man whom the king delights to honor!"

12Afterward Mor'de·caī went back to the king's gate. But Hā'man hurried to his house, mourning and with his head covered. 13When Hā'man told his wife Zē'resh and all his friends everything that had happened to him, his wise men and his wife Zē'resh said to him, "If Mor'de·caī, before whom you have begun to fall, is of Jewish descent, you will not prevail against him but will surely fall before him."

14While they *were* still talking with him, the king's eunuchs came, and hastened to bring Hā'man to the banquet which Esther had prepared.

CHAPTER 7

Haman Hanged Instead of Mordecai

So the king and Hā'man went to dine with Queen Esther. 2And on the second day, at the banquet of wine, the king again said to Esther, "What *is* your petition, Queen Esther? It shall be granted you. And what *is* your request, up to half the kingdom? It shall be done!"

3Then Queen Esther answered and said, "If I have found favor in your sight, O king, and if it pleases the king, let my life be given me at my petition, and my people at my request. 4For we have been sold, my people and I, to be destroyed, to be killed, and to be annihilated. Had we been sold as male and female slaves, I would have held my tongue, although the enemy could never compensate for the king's loss."

5So King A·has·ū·ē'rus answered and said to Queen Esther, "Who is he, and where is he, who would dare presume in his heart to do such a thing?"

6And Esther said, "The adversary and enemy *is* this wicked Hā'man!"

So Hā'man was terrified before the king and queen.

7Then the king arose in his wrath from the banquet of wine *and went* into the palace garden; but Hā'man stood before Queen Esther, pleading for his life, for he saw that evil was determined against him by the king. 8When the king returned from the palace garden to the place of the banquet of wine, Hā'man had fallen across the

---

7:2, 3 At the second banquet during the time of relaxation following the meal, Esther sensed the time was right.

7:3, 4 After the careful preparation, Esther is finally ready to state her request. By destroying the many talents of the Jewish subjects, Haman's plot would result in the **king's loss**.

7:5 who would dare presume? Evidently the king did not yet realize that Esther was a Jewess, one of those whom Haman had vowed to kill.

7:7 The king faced a serious dilemma. **Haman** was his prime minister, and he had proclaimed a law that could not now be erased (see 8:8). Perhaps part of the king's anger was because Haman had deceived him.

7:8 In his concern over his own fate, Haman violated palace etiquette by going too close to Esther. The covering of Haman's face indicated his being sentenced to death.

couch where Esther *was*. Then the king
said, "Will he also assault the queen while
I *am* in the house?"
As the word left the king's mouth, they
covered Hā'man's face. [9]Now Har·bō'nah,
one of the eunuchs, said to the king, "Look!
The gallows, fifty cubits high, which
Hā'man made for Mor'de·caī, who spoke
good on the king's behalf, is standing at
the house of Hā'man."
Then the king said, "Hang him on it!"
[10]So they hanged Hā'man on the gal-
lows that he had prepared for Mor'de·caī.
Then the king's wrath subsided.

CHAPTER 8

Esther Saves the Jews

On that day King A·has·ū·ē'rus gave
Queen Esther the house of Hā'man, the en-
emy of the Jews. And Mor'de·caī came be-
fore the king, for Esther had told how he
was related to her. [2]So the king took off his
signet ring, which he had taken from
Hā'man, and gave it to Mor'de·caī; and Es-
ther appointed Mor'de·caī over the house
of Hā'man.
[3]Now Esther spoke again to the king,
fell down at his feet, and implored him
with tears to counteract the evil of Hā'man
the Ag'ag·īte, and the scheme which he
had devised against the Jews. [4]And the
king held out the golden scepter toward
Esther. So Esther arose and stood before
the king, [5]and said, "If it pleases the king,
and if I have found favor in his sight and
the thing *seems* right to the king and I am
pleasing in his eyes, let it be written to re-
voke the letters devised by Hā'man, the
son of Ham·me·dā'tha the Ag'ag·īte,
which he wrote to annihilate the Jews who
are in all the king's provinces. [6]For how can
I endure to see the evil that will come to
my people? Or how can I endure to see the
destruction of my countrymen?"
[7]Then King A·has·ū·ē'rus said to Queen
Esther and Mor'de·caī the Jew, "Indeed, I
have given Esther the house of Hā'man,
and they have hanged him on the gallows
because he *tried to* lay his hand on the Jews.
[8]You yourselves write *a decree* concerning
the Jews, as you please, in the king's name,
and seal *it* with the king's signet ring; for
whatever is written in the king's name and
sealed with the king's signet ring no one
can revoke."
[9]So the king's scribes were called at that
time, in the third month, which *is* the
month of Sī'van, on the twenty-third *day*;
and it was written, according to all that
Mor'de·caī commanded, to the Jews, the
satraps, the governors, and the princes of
the provinces from India to Ethiopia, one
hundred and twenty-seven provinces *in
all*, to every province in its own script, to
every people in their own language, and to
the Jews in their own script and language.
[10]And he wrote in the name of King A·has-
ū·ē'rus, sealed *it* with the king's signet
ring, and sent letters by couriers on horse-
back, riding on royal horses bred from
swift steeds.[a]
[11]By these letters the king permitted the
Jews who *were* in every city to gather to-
gether and protect their lives—to destroy,
kill, and annihilate all the forces of any
people or province that would assault
them, *both* little children and women, and
to plunder their possessions, [12]on one day
in all the provinces of King A·has·ū·ē'rus,
on the thirteenth *day* of the twelfth month,
which *is* the month of Ā'dar.[a] [13]A copy of
the document was to be issued as a decree
in every province and published for all

8:10 [a]Literally *sons of the swift horses*
8:12 [a]Septuagint adds the text of the letter here.

8:1–14 Because the law giving the enemies of the Jews the right to kill them could not be revoked, another law had to be announced that would nullify the first. This second law gave the Jews the right to retaliate against any who would assault them (v. 11).

8:6 how can I endure? A selfless plea for others (see Gen. 44:33, 34; Rom. 9:3).

people, so that the Jews would be ready on
that day to avenge themselves on their en-
emies. [14]The couriers who rode on royal
horses went out, hastened and pressed on
by the king's command. And the decree
was issued in Shū'shan the citadel.
[15]So Mor'de·caī went out from the pres-
ence of the king in royal apparel of blue
and white, with a great crown of gold and
a garment of fine linen and purple; and the
city of Shū'shan rejoiced and was glad.
[16]The Jews had light and gladness, joy and
honor. [17]And in every province and city,
wherever the king's command and decree
came, the Jews had joy and gladness, a
feast and a holiday. Then many of the peo-
ple of the land became Jews, because fear
of the Jews fell upon them.

CHAPTER 9

The Jews Destroy Their Tormentors

Now in the twelfth month, that *is,* the
month of Ā'dar, on the thirteenth day, *the
time* came for the king's command and his
decree to be executed. On the day that the
enemies of the Jews had hoped to over-
power them, the opposite occurred, in that
the Jews themselves overpowered those
who hated them. [2]The Jews gathered to-
gether in their cities throughout all the
provinces of King A·has·ū·ē'rus to lay
hands on those who sought their harm.
And no one could withstand them, be-
cause fear of them fell upon all people.
[3]And all the officials of the provinces, the
satraps, the governors, and all those doing
the king's work, helped the Jews, because
the fear of Mor'de·caī fell upon them. [4]For
Mor'de·caī *was* great in the king's palace,
and his fame spread throughout all the
provinces; for this man Mor'de·caī became
increasingly prominent. [5]Thus the Jews de-
feated all their enemies with the stroke of
the sword, with slaughter and destruction,
and did what they pleased with those who
hated them.
[6]And in Shū'shan the citadel the Jews
killed and destroyed five hundred men.
[7]Also Par·shan·dā'tha, Dal'phon, As-
pā'tha, [8]Pō·rā'tha, A·dā'li·a, Ar·i·dā'tha,
[9]Par·mash'ta, Ar'i·saī, Ar'i·daī, and Va-
jez'a·tha— [10]the ten sons of Hā'man the
son of Ham·me·dā'tha, the enemy of the
Jews—they killed; but they did not lay a
hand on the plunder.
[11]On that day the number of those who
were killed in Shū'shan the citadel was
brought to the king. [12]And the king said to
Queen Esther, "The Jews have killed and
destroyed five hundred men in Shū'shan
the citadel, and the ten sons of Hā'man.
What have they done in the rest of the
king's provinces? Now what *is* your peti-
tion? It shall be granted to you. Or what *is*
your further request? It shall be done."
[13]Then Esther said, "If it pleases the
king, let it be granted to the Jews who *are* in
Shū'shan to do again tomorrow according
to today's decree, and let Hā'man's ten
sons be hanged on the gallows."
[14]So the king commanded this to be
done; the decree was issued in Shū'shan,
and they hanged Hā'man's ten sons.
[15]And the Jews who *were* in Shū'shan
gathered together again on the fourteenth

8:17 many . . . became Jews: Instead of being destroyed, as Haman had planned, the Jews were actually increased. God makes even the wrath of evil persons to praise Him.

9:1 those who hated them: As evidenced either by attacks at that time, or by previous action.

9:3, 4 The fear of Mordecai marks the climax of an amazing change in fortunes: from the descendant of an exiled Jew (2:5, 6), to an attendant in the king's court (2:19), to possessor of the king's signet ring (8:2), to a man who was prominent throughout the Persian kingdom. God accomplished the care of His people through the rise of one who had faith in God's providential activity (see 4:14).

9:10, 15 did not lay a hand on the plunder: The actions of the Jews were not motivated by greed or covetousness but by the desire for self-protection and justice.

day of the month of Ā′dar and killed three hundred men at Shū′shan; but they did not lay a hand on the plunder.

16The remainder of the Jews in the king's provinces gathered together and protected their lives, had rest from their enemies, and killed seventy-five thousand of their enemies; but they did not lay a hand on the plunder. 17*This was* on the thirteenth day of the month of Ā′dar. And on the fourteenth of *the month*[a] they rested and made it a day of feasting and gladness.

The Feast of Purim

18But the Jews who *were* at Shū′shan assembled together on the thirteenth *day,* as well as on the fourteenth; and on the fifteenth of *the month*[a] they rested, and made it a day of feasting and gladness. 19Therefore the Jews of the villages who dwelt in the unwalled towns celebrated the fourteenth day of the month of Ā′dar *with* gladness and feasting, as a holiday, and for sending presents to one another.

20And Mor′de·caī wrote these things and sent letters to all the Jews, near and far, who *were* in all the provinces of King A·has·ū·ē′rus, 21to establish among them that they should celebrate yearly the fourteenth and fifteenth days of the month of Ā′dar, 22as the days on which the Jews had rest from their enemies, as the month which was turned from sorrow to joy for them, and from mourning to a holiday; that they should make them days of feasting and joy, of sending presents to one another and gifts to the poor. 23So the Jews accepted the custom which they had begun, as Mor′de·caī had written to them, 24because Hā′man, the son of Ham·me·dā′tha the Ag′ag·īte, the enemy of all the Jews, had plotted against the Jews to annihilate them, and had cast Pūr (that *is,* the lot), to consume them and destroy them; 25but when *Esther*[a] came before the king, he commanded by letter that this wicked[b] plot which *Hā′man* had devised against the Jews should return on his own head, and that he and his sons should be hanged on the gallows.

26So they called these days Pūr′im, after the name Pūr. Therefore, because of all the words of this letter, what they had seen concerning this matter, and what had happened to them, 27the Jews established and imposed it upon themselves and their descendants and all who would join them, that without fail they should celebrate these two days every year, according to the written *instructions* and according to the *prescribed* time, 28*that* these days *should be* remembered and kept throughout every generation, every family, every province, and every city, that these days of Pūr′im should not fail *to be observed* among the Jews, and *that* the memory of them should not perish among their descendants.

29Then Queen Esther, the daughter of Ab·i·hā′il, with Mor′de·caī the Jew, wrote with full authority to confirm this second letter about Pūr′im. 30And *Mor′*de·caī sent

9:17 [a]Literally *it* 9:18 [a]Literally *it* 9:25 [a]Literally *she* or *it* [b]Literally *his*

9:16 seventy-five thousand: The Greek OT (the Septuagint) reads only 15,000. Either way, the high numbers killed in the provinces, along with the 800 in Shushan alone (vv. 6, 15), indicate the tremendous size of the forces as well as the immense evil Haman had sought to bring upon the Jews throughout the empire. By abstaining from taking any plunder, the Jews demonstrated that they desired only to protect themselves, not to become rich at the expense of others.

9:17–19 The one day of feasting at Purim is now observed on two separate days because it was first celebrated in the villages on the fourteenth, but in the city of Shushan on the **fifteenth**.

9:22 from sorrow to joy: God often gives His people "beauty for ashes, the oil of joy for mourning, the garment of praise for the spirit of heaviness" (Is. 61:3).

letters to all the Jews, to the one hundred
and twenty-seven provinces of the king-
dom of A·has·ū·ē′rus, *with* words of peace
and truth, [31]to confirm these days of
Pūr′im at their *appointed* time, as
Mor′de·caī the Jew and Queen Esther had
prescribed for them, and as they had de-
creed for themselves and their descen-
dants concerning matters of their fasting
and lamenting. [32]So the decree of Esther
confirmed these matters of Pūr′im, and it
was written in the book.

CHAPTER 10

Mordecai's Advancement

And King A·has·ū·ē′rus imposed trib-
ute on the land and *on* the islands of the
sea. [2]Now all the acts of his power and his
might, and the account of the greatness of
Mor′de·caī, to which the king advanced
him, *are* they not written in the book of the
chronicles of the kings of Media and Per-
sia? [3]For Mor′de·caī the Jew *was* second to
King A·has·ū·ē′rus, and was great among
the Jews and well received by the multi-
tude of his brethren, seeking the good of
his people and speaking peace to all his
countrymen.[a]

10:3 [a]Literally *seed.* Septuagint and Vulgate add a dream of Mordecai here; Vulgate adds six more chapters.

10:1 That King Ahasuerus **imposed tribute** may show that the king who dealt faithfully with God's people gained even greater power and strength for his kingdom. Had he followed Haman's lead, the result would have been to his loss.

✦Job✦

Since Job's wealth was measured in livestock and flocks, he probably lived around the time of Abraham, about 2000 B.C. Although the author is unknown, most evidence points to a Gentile writer who compiled the book around 950 B.C. during the golden age of the poetical books (Job, Psalms, Proverbs, Ecclesiastes, and the Song of Solomon).

Job was a righteous man, yet the Lord allowed Satan to test his devotion by taking away his flocks, his wealth, his family, and even his health. Faced with utter sorrow, Job was confronted by three "friends" and encouraged by his wife to curse the Lord for allowing his suffering.

The Book of Job poses a basic question: Why do the righteous suffer? After God revealed His power, wisdom, and sovereign authority in chapters 38—42, Job realized that he must not question God but accept His sovereignty. Job learned the importance of trusting God, even through inexplicable trials. Like this faithful man, some Christians suffer without knowing why, yet they must trust God through everything and submit to Him. ✦

CHAPTER 1

Job and His Family in Uz

There was a man in the land of Uz,
whose name *was* Job; and that man was
blameless and upright, and one who
feared God and shunned evil. [2]And seven
sons and three daughters were born to
him. [3]Also, his possessions were seven
thousand sheep, three thousand camels,
five hundred yoke of oxen, five hundred
female donkeys, and a very large household, so that this man was the greatest of
all the people of the East.
[4]And his sons would go and feast *in
their* houses, each on his *appointed* day, and
would send and invite their three sisters to
eat and drink with them. [5]So it was, when
the days of feasting had run their course,
that Job would send and sanctify them,
and he would rise early in the morning
and offer burnt offerings *according to* the
number of them all. For Job said, "It may
be that my sons have sinned and cursed[a]
God in their hearts." Thus Job did regularly.

1:5 [a]Literally *blessed,* but used here in the evil sense, and so in verse 11 and 2:5, 9

1:1—2:13 The prologue's repeated concern about cursing God focuses the entire book's concern on righteousness. Job fears that his children may have cursed God (1:4, 5); Satan argues that if Job suffers, he will curse God (1:11); and Job's wife encourages him to curse God and die (2:9). The issue is Job's motive for serving God. We confront the same issue today. Do we serve God because He is God or because it profits us?

1:5 Job recognized the human tendency to slip into sinful talk, especially during social gatherings, which encouraged light-hearted conversation. We should immediately confess when we sin through idle talk or unholy conversation.

Satan Attacks Job's Character

[6]Now there was a day when the sons of
God came to present themselves before the
LORD, and Satan[a] also came among them.
[7]And the LORD said to Satan, "From where
do you come?"

So Satan answered the LORD and said,
"From going to and fro on the earth, and
from walking back and forth on it."

[8]Then the LORD said to Satan, "Have you
considered My servant Job, that *there is*
none like him on the earth, a blameless and
upright man, one who fears God and
shuns evil?"

[9]So Satan answered the LORD and
said, "Does Job fear God for nothing?
[10]Have You not made a hedge around him,
around his household, and around all that
he has on every side? You have blessed the
work of his hands, and his possessions
have increased in the land. [11]But now,
stretch out Your hand and touch all that he
has, and he will surely curse You to Your
face!"

[12]And the LORD said to Satan, "Behold,
all that he has *is* in your power; only do not
lay a hand on his *person*."

So Satan went out from the presence of
the LORD.

Job Loses His Property and Children

[13]Now there was a day when his sons
and daughters *were* eating and drinking
wine in their oldest brother's house; [14]and
a messenger came to Job and said, "The
oxen were plowing and the donkeys feed-
ing beside them, [15]when the Sa·bē′ans[a]
raided *them* and took them away—indeed
they have killed the servants with the edge
of the sword; and I alone have escaped to
tell you!"

[16]While he *was* still speaking, another
also came and said, "The fire of God fell
from heaven and burned up the sheep and
the servants, and consumed them; and I
alone have escaped to tell you!"

[17]While he *was* still speaking, another
also came and said, "The Chal·dē′ans
formed three bands, raided the camels and
took them away, yes, and killed the ser-
vants with the edge of the sword; and I
alone have escaped to tell you!"

[18]While he *was* still speaking, another
also came and said, "Your sons and daugh-
ters *were* eating and drinking wine in their
oldest brother's house, [19]and suddenly a
great wind came from across[a] the wilder-
ness and struck the four corners of the
house, and it fell on the young people, and
they are dead; and I alone have escaped to
tell you!"

[20]Then Job arose, tore his robe, and
shaved his head; and he fell to the ground
and worshiped. [21]And he said:

"Naked I came from my mother's
womb,
And naked shall I return there.
The LORD gave, and the LORD has
taken away;
Blessed be the name of the LORD."

1:6 [a]Literally *the Adversary,* and so throughout this book
1:15 [a]Literally *Sheba* (compare 6:19)
1:19 [a]Septuagint omits *across.*

1:6, 7 sons of God: Here celestial beings or angels created by God as His servants. **Satan**: The adversary here means someone who opposes God and accuses His people. Satan instigates trouble by challenging God's confidence in Job.

1:13–19 Four disasters suddenly wiped out Job's wealth and family. The number *four* symbolizes totality. It seemed as if heaven and earth had turned against Job—the **fire of God** and the wind bring devastation; earthly marauding bands attack.

1:15 Sabeans: a nomadic Arabian tribe.

1:17 Chaldeans: a wandering tribe noted for their plundering raids.

1:20, 21 Job mourned his losses in traditional expressions of sorrow (see 2:12, 13). But he acknowledged God's control over every earthly possession, and sought consolation from God. Thus he took the proper attitude toward possessions that enables one to rebuild a life devastated by loss of material wealth. To question God's motives is to blaspheme His name.

22In all this Job did not sin nor charge
God with wrong.

CHAPTER 2

Satan Attacks Job's Health

Again there was a day when the sons of
God came to present themselves before the
LORD, and Satan came also among them to
present himself before the LORD. 2And the
LORD said to Satan, "From where do you
come?"
Satan answered the LORD and said,
"From going to and fro on the earth, and
from walking back and forth on it."
3Then the LORD said to Satan, "Have
you considered My servant Job, that *there*
is none like him on the earth, a blame-
less and upright man, one who fears God
and shuns evil? And still he holds fast to
his integrity, although you incited Me
against him, to destroy him without
cause."
4So Satan answered the LORD and said,
"Skin for skin! Yes, all that a man has he
will give for his life. 5But stretch out Your
hand now, and touch his bone and his
flesh, and he will surely curse You to Your
face!"
6And the LORD said to Satan, "Behold,
he *is* in your hand, but spare his life."
7So Satan went out from the presence of
the LORD, and struck Job with painful boils
from the sole of his foot to the crown of his
head. 8And he took for himself a potsherd
with which to scrape himself while he sat
in the midst of the ashes.
9Then his wife said to him, "Do you still
hold fast to your integrity? Curse God and
die!"
10But he said to her, "You speak as one of
the foolish women speaks. Shall we indeed
accept good from God, and shall we not ac-
cept adversity?" In all this Job did not sin
with his lips.

Job's Three Friends

11Now when Job's three friends heard of
all this adversity that had come upon him,
each one came from his own place—E·lī'-
phaz the Tē'man·īte, Bil'dad the Shū'hīte,
and Zō'phar the Nā'a·ma·thīte. For they
had made an appointment together to
come and mourn with him, and to comfort
him. 12And when they raised their eyes
from afar, and did not recognize him, they
lifted their voices and wept; and each one
tore his robe and sprinkled dust on his
head toward heaven. 13So they sat down
with him on the ground seven days and
seven nights, and no one spoke a word to
him, for they saw that *his* grief was very
great.

CHAPTER 3

Job Deplores His Birth

After this Job opened his mouth and
cursed the day of his *birth*. 2And Job spoke,
and said:

2:6 Although God may allow Satan to persecute us, He ultimately holds the power and limits of Satan's actions.

2:11 The Hebrew word translated **friends** has a wide range of meanings including "intimate counselor" and "close friend." Their love and commitment to Job led them to come **to comfort him**. The name **Eliphaz** means "God Is Fine Gold." **Temanite**: From the northern region of Edom which was well known for its excellent wisdom. **Bildad**: Possibly "Son of Hadad." **Shuhite**: From a location on the Middle Euphrates River between Carchemish and Mari, or somewhat farther to the south. **Zophar**: Meaning "Young Bird." **Naamathite**: Perhaps a native of Naameh in northwest Arabia.

2:12, 13 did not recognize him: Because of Job's disfiguring affliction. **sprinkled dust . . . toward heaven**: Threw dirt into the air and let it fall on them. This action together with the tearing of the robes was a sign of grief. **seven days**: The period of mourning for an important person (see Gen. 50:10). Their concern for Job was genuine.

3:1 Here we see that Job's attitude began to change; although he did not curse God, his earlier patience and trust are noticeably missing.

JOB: TRUST AMID TRAGEDY

Are you currently experiencing a major valley in your life? Perhaps tragedy has struck in the form of unemployment or financial setbacks, a serious quarrel with your best friend, or even the death of a spouse or family member.

Whatever your present crisis, Job would certainly understand. In a matter of a few days, this man, who once had everything the world holds dear, lost it all.

His possessions—seven thousand sheep, three thousand camels, five hundred yoke of oxen, five hundred female donkeys, and hundreds of servants—were all taken from him in a matter of hours by plundering marauders and fire from heaven.

All of his children died the same day when a sudden windstorm brought their house crashing down on top of them. Soon after, Job's health deteriorated. Painful boils covered his body from head to toe.

He had lost his wealth, family, and health. His wife urged him to "curse God and die" (Job 2:9), but Job held firm to his faith in God's wisdom: "Shall we indeed accept good from God, and shall we not accept adversity?" (v. 10). In the midst of such disaster, his wife's negative attitude was just one more vexation with which Job had to cope.

Job found himself at the lowest possible point in life. Physically, he had absolutely nothing left, and no one could provide the emotional support he desperately needed. The only thing remaining intact in Job's life was his faith in God: "Though He slay me, yet will I trust Him" (13:15). Even when it seemed as if God had turned his back on a steadfast servant, Job's faith stood firm.

Then along came three friends to comfort Job in his misery. Perhaps you have had "friends" like these before, people who feel the need to constantly express their personal opinions regarding your problems or who come to comfort and stay to criticize.

In the end, the Lord rebuked the three disparaging "comforters" and demonstrated His approval of Job in front of them. When they offered a sacrifice according to God's commands, Job prayed on their behalf. Following that unselfish petition, God restored Job's losses, doubling his earlier wealth and blessing him with ten more children.

When tragedy brings discouragement to your life, consider the faithful servant Job. He came to understand that one must humbly submit to God's authority when it comes to the mystery of suffering. Remember that, although circumstances may damage and even destroy your physical or emotional balance, you can protect your spiritual health by choosing to trust God. ✦

3 "May the day perish on which I was
born,
And the night *in which* it was said,
'A male child is conceived.'
4 May that day be darkness;
May God above not seek it,
Nor the light shine upon it.
5 May darkness and the shadow of
death claim it;
May a cloud settle on it;
May the blackness of the day terrify it.
6 *As for* that night, may darkness seize
it;
May it not rejoice[a] among the days of
the year,
May it not come into the number of
the months.
7 Oh, may that night be barren!
May no joyful shout come into it!
8 May those curse it who curse the day,
Those who are ready to arouse
Le·vī'a·than.
9 May the stars of its morning be dark;
May it look for light, but *have* none,
And not see the dawning of the day;
10 Because it did not shut up the doors
of my *mother's* womb,
Nor hide sorrow from my eyes.

11 "Why did I not die at birth?
Why did I *not* perish when I came
from the womb?
12 Why did the knees receive me?
Or why the breasts, that I should
nurse?
13 For now I would have lain still and
been quiet,
I would have been asleep;
Then I would have been at rest
14 With kings and counselors of the
earth,
Who built ruins for themselves,
15 Or with princes who had gold,
Who filled their houses *with* silver;
16 Or *why* was I not hidden like a
stillborn child,
Like infants who never saw light?
17 There the wicked cease *from*
troubling,
And there the weary are at rest.
18 *There* the prisoners rest together;
They do not hear the voice of the
oppressor.
19 The small and great are there,
And the servant *is* free from his
master.

20 "Why is light given to him who is in
misery,
And life to the bitter of soul,
21 Who long for death, but it does not
come,
And search for it more than hidden
treasures;
22 Who rejoice exceedingly,
And are glad when they can find the
grave?
23 *Why is light given* to a man whose
way is hidden,
And whom God has hedged in?
24 For my sighing comes before I eat,[a]
And my groanings pour out like
water.
25 For the thing I greatly feared has
come upon me,
And what I dreaded has happened to
me.
26 I am not at ease, nor am I quiet;
I have no rest, for trouble comes."

CHAPTER 4

Eliphaz: Job Has Sinned

Then E·lī'phaz the Tē'man·īte answered and said:

3:6 [a]Septuagint, Syriac, Targum, and Vulgate read *be joined.* 3:24 [a]Literally *my bread*

4:1—5:27 After Job has spoken, his friends join the conversation, each expressing a similar view of God's rewards and punishments. According to their doctrine, a righteous person received material blessings and long life (4:7). In contrast, a wicked person suffered hardships in this life and came to a premature death (4:8, 9). **Eliphaz** stresses that no human or angel is pure before God the Creator (4:17). Furthermore, God is absolutely fair, and

2 "*If* one attempts a word with you, will
you become weary?
But who can withhold himself from
speaking?
3 Surely you have instructed many,
And you have strengthened weak
hands.
4 Your words have upheld him who
was stumbling,
And you have strengthened the feeble
knees;
5 But now it comes upon you, and you
are weary;
It touches you, and you are troubled.
6 *Is* not your reverence your
confidence?
And the integrity of your ways your
hope?

7 "Remember now, who *ever* perished
being innocent?
Or where were the upright *ever* cut
off?
8 Even as I have seen,
Those who plow iniquity
And sow trouble reap the same.
9 By the blast of God they perish,
And by the breath of His anger they
are consumed.
10 The roaring of the lion,
The voice of the fierce lion,
And the teeth of the young lions are
broken.
11 The old lion perishes for lack of prey,
And the cubs of the lioness are
scattered.

12 "Now a word was secretly brought to
me,
And my ear received a whisper of it.
13 In disquieting thoughts from the
visions of the night,
When deep sleep falls on men,
14 Fear came upon me, and trembling,
Which made all my bones shake.
15 Then a spirit passed before my face;
The hair on my body stood up.
16 It stood still,
But I could not discern its
appearance.
A form *was* before my eyes;
There was silence;
Then I heard a voice *saying:*
17 'Can a mortal be more righteous than
God?
Can a man be more pure than his
Maker?
18 If He puts no trust in His servants,
If He charges His angels with error,
19 How much more those who dwell in
houses of clay,
Whose foundation is in the dust,
Who are crushed before a moth?
20 They are broken in pieces from
morning till evening;
They perish forever, with no one
regarding.
21 Does not their own excellence go
away?
They die, even without wisdom.'

CHAPTER 5

Eliphaz: Job Is Chastened by God

"Call out now;
Is there anyone who will answer you?
And to which of the holy ones will
you turn?

any hardship the righteous may experience is God's effort to discipline us. Overall, this is true, but there is a hazard in applying it too rigidly to every situation.

4:8 Eliphaz consistently bases his judgments on his own experience. He fails to recognize that his limited knowledge could not possibly encompass all truth or that his opinions might need to be adjusted in certain situations.

4:10, 11 The **lion** is a metaphor for the wicked who abuse God's people (see Ps. 10:9). Even the lion cannot resist God. God's most powerful enemies will suffer His punishment.

5:1 holy ones: Angels. Eliphaz thinks Job's lament accuses God. In order to have his charge heard in the divine court, Job needs an angel as an intermediary. That, however, will not succeed because even angels make errors (4:18).

2 For wrath kills a foolish man,
And envy slays a simple one.
3 I have seen the foolish taking root,
But suddenly I cursed his dwelling
place.
4 His sons are far from safety,
They are crushed in the gate,
And *there is* no deliverer.
5 Because the hungry eat up his
harvest,
Taking it even from the thorns,[a]
And a snare snatches their substance.[b]
6 For affliction does not come from the
dust,
Nor does trouble spring from the
ground;
7 Yet man is born to trouble,
As the sparks fly upward.

8 "But as for me, I would seek God,
And to God I would commit my
cause—
9 Who does great things, and
unsearchable,
Marvelous things without number.
10 He gives rain on the earth,
And sends waters on the fields.
11 He sets on high those who are lowly,
And those who mourn are lifted to
safety.
12 He frustrates the devices of the crafty,
So that their hands cannot carry out
their plans.
13 He catches the wise in their own
craftiness,
And the counsel of the cunning
comes quickly upon them.
14 They meet with darkness in the
daytime,
And grope at noontime as in the
night.
15 But He saves the needy from the
sword,
From the mouth of the mighty,
And from their hand.
16 So the poor have hope,
And injustice shuts her mouth.

17 "Behold, happy *is* the man whom God
corrects;
Therefore do not despise the
chastening of the Almighty.
18 For He bruises, but He binds up;
He wounds, but His hands make
whole.
19 He shall deliver you in six troubles,
Yes, in seven no evil shall touch you.
20 In famine He shall redeem you from
death,
And in war from the power of the
sword.
21 You shall be hidden from the scourge
of the tongue,
And you shall not be afraid of
destruction when it comes.
22 You shall laugh at destruction and
famine,
And you shall not be afraid of the
beasts of the earth.
23 For you shall have a covenant with
the stones of the field,
And the beasts of the field shall be at
peace with you.
24 You shall know that your tent *is* in
peace;
You shall visit your dwelling and find
nothing amiss.
25 You shall also know that your
descendants *shall be* many,
And your offspring like the grass of
the earth.

5:5 [a]Septuagint reads *They shall not be taken from evil men;* Vulgate reads *And the armed man shall take him by violence.* [b]Septuagint reads *The might shall draw them off;* Vulgate reads *And the thirsty shall drink up their riches.*

5:13 Paul quotes this verse in 1 Cor. 3:19.

5:19 six troubles: God's power to deliver is greater than any single calamity or series of tragedies. **Seven** suggests completeness, the very worst that can come to us. God allows us to pass through suffering, but He will deliver us from all kinds of troubles. Nothing can ultimately harm us while we are in His care.

Likened to Grain

John Gilmore

Job was an expert farmer. The Lord had blessed him with acres and acres of crops, seven thousand sheep, three thousand camels, five hundred donkeys, and much more (1:3). No doubt he took great care of his crops and animals, being a good steward of the riches God had given him.

How appropriate, then, that an interesting crop analogy was used to describe Job. Eliphaz, one of Job's three friends, said, "You shall come to the grave at a full age, as a sheaf of grain ripens in its season" (5:26). This seems to be a wonderful blessing of longevity for Job, except for a subtle sarcasm in Eliphaz's comparison. In the context of the chapter, Eliphaz's poetic moralizing was heartless, detached, and insensitive.

Underneath Eliphaz's statement lies an element of gloom rather than elation. A full age is like full grain, yet death is the final harvest. Once matured, single grains were bundled with others ready for threshing. So in spite of Job's rich blessings from God and his righteous living, his lot would be no different from anyone else's.

"Those who are planted in the house of the Lord shall flourish in the courts of our God."

On the surface these thoughts seemed to have simple objectivity, a friendly optimism. But in fact they contained cold realism without reference to God's personal interest in Job's loyalty or acknowledgment of Job's fidelity to God in his public statements (1:21; 2:10). Much kinder was the statement in Ps. 92:13, 14: "Those who are planted in the house of the Lord shall flourish in the courts of our God. They shall still bear fruit in old age; they shall be fresh and flourishing." ✦

26 You shall come to the grave at a full
age,
As a sheaf of grain ripens in its
season.
27 Behold, this we have searched out;
It *is* true.
Hear it, and know for yourself."

CHAPTER 6

Job: My Complaint Is Just

Then Job answered and said:

2 "Oh, that my grief were fully weighed,
And my calamity laid with it on the
scales!

6:1—7:21 Job defends his right to complain (6:1–13), laments the treachery of his friends (6:14–30), and accuses God of being unusually cruel (7:1–21). But he is less caustic than in his first lament and moves away from self-pity. He longs for God to leave him alone and to stop tormenting him.

3 For then it would be heavier than the
sand of the sea—
Therefore my words have been rash.
4 For the arrows of the Almighty *are*
within me;
My spirit drinks in their poison;
The terrors of God are arrayed
against me.
5 Does the wild donkey bray when it
has grass,
Or does the ox low over its fodder?
6 Can flavorless food be eaten without
salt?
Or is there *any* taste in the white of an
egg?
7 My soul refuses to touch them;
They *are* as loathsome food to me.

8 "Oh, that I might have my request,
That God would grant *me* the thing
that I long for!
9 That it would please God to crush
me,
That He would loose His hand and
cut me off!
10 Then I would still have comfort;
Though in anguish I would exult,
He will not spare;
For I have not concealed the words of
the Holy One.

11 "What strength do I have, that I should
hope?
And what *is* my end, that I should
prolong my life?
12 *Is* my strength the strength of stones?
Or is my flesh bronze?
13 *Is* my help not within me?
And is success driven from me?

14 "To him who is afflicted, kindness
should be shown by his friend,
Even though he forsakes the fear of
the Almighty.
15 My brothers have dealt deceitfully
like a brook,
Like the streams of the brooks that
pass away,
16 Which are dark because of the ice,
And into which the snow vanishes.
17 When it is warm, they cease to flow;
When it is hot, they vanish from their
place.
18 The paths of their way turn aside,
They go nowhere and perish.
19 The caravans of Tē′ma look,
The travelers of Shē′ba hope for them.
20 They are disappointed because they
were confident;
They come there and are confused.
21 For now you are nothing,
You see terror and are afraid.
22 Did I ever say, 'Bring *something* to
me'?
Or, 'Offer a bribe for me from your
wealth'?
23 Or, 'Deliver me from the enemy's
hand'?
Or, 'Redeem me from the hand of
oppressors'?

24 "Teach me, and I will hold my tongue;
Cause me to understand wherein I
have erred.

6:8–13 Sarcastically, Job asserts that real **comfort** (v. 10) would come from God crushing him. That would be preferable to Eliphaz's urging him to trust in an upright life (4:6) or the assurance that God delivers a person from troubles (5:15–18). Eliphaz's high-toned challenges for Job to suffer manfully while God disciplines him seem worse than useless to a man whose life was simply unbearable.

6:14–23 Job does not need intellectual rationalization, especially when that reasoning is completely irrelevant to this particular situation. What he needs is simple human caring. Even a person who does not acknowledge God can offer that. The Hebrew word translated **kindness** is often used in a covenant context and may indicate that a covenant relationship existed between Job and his friends. Because of this relationship, Job expected support from them.

6:24–30 **Teach me**: Job requests that his friends be supportive teachers rather than prosecuting attorneys (v. 25). **erred**: Unintentional sins. Job does not deny the possibility

25 How forceful are right words!
But what does your arguing prove?
26 Do you intend to rebuke *my* words,
And the speeches of a desperate one, *which are* as wind?
27 Yes, you overwhelm the fatherless,
And you undermine your friend.
28 Now therefore, be pleased to look at me;
For I would never lie to your face.
29 Yield now, let there be no injustice!
Yes, concede, my righteousness still stands!
30 Is there injustice on my tongue?
Cannot my taste discern the unsavory?

CHAPTER 7

Job: My Suffering Is Comfortless

"Is *there* not a time of hard service for man on earth?
Are not his days also like the days of a hired man?
2 Like a servant who earnestly desires the shade,
And like a hired man who eagerly looks for his wages,
3 So I have been allotted months of futility,
And wearisome nights have been appointed to me.
4 When I lie down, I say, 'When shall I arise,
And the night be ended?'
For I have had my fill of tossing till dawn.
5 My flesh is caked with worms and dust,
My skin is cracked and breaks out afresh.

6 "My days are swifter than a weaver's shuttle,
And are spent without hope.
7 Oh, remember that my life *is* a breath!
My eye will never again see good.
8 The eye of him who sees me will see me no *more;*
While your *eyes* are upon me, I shall no longer *be.*
9 *As* the cloud disappears and vanishes away,
So he who goes down to the grave does not come up.
10 He shall never return to his house,
Nor shall his place know him anymore.

11 "Therefore I will not restrain my mouth;
I will speak in the anguish of my spirit;
I will complain in the bitterness of my soul.
12 *Am* I a sea, or a sea serpent,
That You set a guard over me?
13 When I say, 'My bed will comfort me,
My couch will ease my complaint,'
14 Then You scare me with dreams
And terrify me with visions,
15 So that my soul chooses strangling
And death rather than my body.[a]
16 I loathe *my life;*
I would not live forever.
Let me alone,
For my days *are but* a breath.

17 "What *is* man, that You should exalt him,
That You should set Your heart on him,
18 That You should visit him every morning,
And test him every moment?
19 How long?

7:15 [a]Literally *my bones*

that he has sinned. He denies that he has sinned as consciously and willfully as his suffering seems to indicate.

7:1–21 Job now addresses his questions and comments to God.

7:19 till I swallow: A proverbial term for "a short time." Job asks for a brief moment of relief (see 9:18).

Will You not look away from me,
And let me alone till I swallow my saliva?
20 Have I sinned?
What have I done to You, O watcher of men?
Why have You set me as Your target,
So that I am a burden to myself?[a]
21 Why then do You not pardon my transgression,
And take away my iniquity?
For now I will lie down in the dust,
And You will seek me diligently,
But I *will* no longer *be*."

CHAPTER 8

Bildad: Job Should Repent

Then Bil'dad the Shū'hīte answered and said:

2 "How long will you speak these *things*,
And the words of your mouth *be like* a strong wind?
3 Does God subvert judgment?
Or does the Almighty pervert justice?
4 If your sons have sinned against Him,
He has cast them away for their transgression.
5 If you would earnestly seek God
And make your supplication to the Almighty,
6 If you *were* pure and upright,
Surely now He would awake for you,
And prosper your rightful dwelling place.
7 Though your beginning was small,
Yet your latter end would increase abundantly.

8 "For inquire, please, of the former age,
And consider the things discovered by their fathers;
9 For we *were born* yesterday, and know nothing,
Because our days on earth *are* a shadow.
10 Will they not teach you and tell you,
And utter words from their heart?

11 "Can the papyrus grow up without a marsh?
Can the reeds flourish without water?
12 While it *is* yet green *and* not cut down,
It withers before any *other* plant.
13 So *are* the paths of all who forget God;
And the hope of the hypocrite shall perish,
14 Whose confidence shall be cut off,
And whose trust *is* a spider's web.
15 He leans on his house, but it does not stand.
He holds it fast, but it does not endure.
16 He grows green in the sun,
And his branches spread out in his garden.
17 His roots wrap around the rock heap,
And look for a place in the stones.
18 If he is destroyed from his place,
Then *it* will deny him, *saying*, 'I have not seen you.'

19 "Behold, this is the joy of His way,
And out of the earth others will grow.
20 Behold, God will not cast away the blameless,
Nor will He uphold the evildoers.
21 He will yet fill your mouth with laughing,
And your lips with rejoicing.
22 Those who hate you will be clothed with shame,
And the dwelling place of the wicked will come to nothing."[a]

7:20 [a]Following Masoretic Text, Targum, and Vulgate; Septuagint and Jewish tradition read *to You.*
8:22 [a]Literally *will not be*

8:1–22 Bildad states his position in a question: Does God subvert justice (v. 3)? He thinks that Job is foolish to accuse God of being unjust. Using nature as a model (vv. 11–18), he insists that evil must fail, and righteousness must prosper. Like Eliphaz, he does not allow room for exceptions or alterations, or even for delays in the timetable of just rewards.

CHAPTER 9

Job: There Is No Mediator

Then Job answered and said:

2 "Truly I know *it is* so,
But how can a man be righteous
before God?
3 If one wished to contend with Him,
He could not answer Him one time
out of a thousand.
4 God is wise in heart and mighty in
strength.
Who has hardened *himself* against
Him and prospered?
5 He removes the mountains, and they
do not know
When He overturns them in His
anger;
6 He shakes the earth out of its place,
And its pillars tremble;
7 He commands the sun, and it does
not rise;
He seals off the stars;
8 He alone spreads out the heavens,
And treads on the waves of the sea;
9 He made the Bear, Ō·rī′on, and the
Plēi′a·dēs,
And the chambers of the south;
10 He does great things past finding out,
Yes, wonders without number.
11 If He goes by me, I do not see *Him;*
If He moves past, I do not perceive
Him;
12 If He takes away, who can hinder
Him?
Who can say to Him, 'What are You
doing?'
13 God will not withdraw His anger,
The allies of the proud[a] lie prostrate
beneath Him.

14 "How then can I answer Him,
And choose my words *to reason* with
Him?
15 For though I were righteous, I could
not answer Him;
I would beg mercy of my Judge.
16 If I called and He answered me,
I would not believe that He was
listening to my voice.
17 For He crushes me with a tempest,
And multiplies my wounds without
cause.
18 He will not allow me to catch my
breath,
But fills me with bitterness.
19 If *it is a matter* of strength, indeed *He
is* strong;
And if of justice, who will appoint
my day *in court?*

9:13 [a]Hebrew *rahab*

9:1—10:22 Job considers taking God to court because of God's actions toward him. But aware of God's power, Job knows he could not win (9:1–20, 32–35), so he laments God's hostility toward him (9:21–31; 10:1–22).

9:2 I know it is so: Job accepts Bildad's point that God never perverts justice (8:3). But he rejects the idea that his suffering results because he is unrighteous (8:6). No one can be **righteous** in comparison to God (4:17).

9:3 contend: Legal language for going to court. **one . . . of a thousand**: Job acknowledges that he faces impossible odds in his dispute with God.

9:9 This verse refers to ancient astronomy.

9:14–20 Even though innocent, Job knows that he cannot defend himself against God. He is outwardly righteous, but he suspects that this all-wise and all-powerful Judge would find some hidden perversity in him (v. 20) to justify His actions. Job's only option is to beg **mercy** of his **Judge** (v. 15). This foreshadows the direction of the drama. Job will continue to press for a legal solution. But, when God answers (chs. 38—41), Job will abandon his case and beg for mercy (42:1–6).

9:17 without cause: Job's feeling that his sufferings are meaningless threatens his faith that God is just. This is the most serious test any faithful servant of God can face. At the same time, God's confidence in Job is so great that He is not afraid to let His actions appear to be unjust.

20 Though I were righteous, my own mouth would condemn me;
Though I *were* blameless, it would prove me perverse.

21 "I am blameless, yet I do not know myself;
I despise my life.
22 It *is* all one *thing;*
Therefore I say, 'He destroys the blameless and the wicked.'
23 If the scourge slays suddenly,
He laughs at the plight of the innocent.
24 The earth is given into the hand of the wicked.
He covers the faces of its judges.
If it is not *He,* who else could it be?

25 "Now my days are swifter than a runner;
They flee away, they see no good.
26 They pass by like swift ships,
Like an eagle swooping on its prey.
27 If I say, 'I will forget my complaint,
I will put off my sad face and wear a smile,'
28 I am afraid of all my sufferings;
I know that You will not hold me innocent.
29 *If* I am condemned,
Why then do I labor in vain?
30 If I wash myself with snow water,
And cleanse my hands with soap,
31 Yet You will plunge me into the pit,
And my own clothes will abhor me.

32 "For *He is* not a man, as I *am,*
That I may answer Him,
And that we should go to court together.
33 Nor is there any mediator between us,
Who may lay his hand on us both.
34 Let Him take His rod away from me,
And do not let dread of Him terrify me.
35 *Then* I would speak and not fear Him,
But it is not so with me.

CHAPTER 10

Job: I Would Plead with God

"My soul loathes my life;
I will give free course to my complaint,
I will speak in the bitterness of my soul.
2 I will say to God, 'Do not condemn me;
Show me why You contend with me.
3 *Does it* seem good to You that You should oppress,
That You should despise the work of Your hands,
And smile on the counsel of the wicked?
4 Do You have eyes of flesh?
Or do You see as man sees?
5 *Are* Your days like the days of a mortal man?
Are Your years like the days of a mighty man,
6 That You should seek for my iniquity
And search out my sin,
7 Although You know that I am not wicked,
And *there is* no one who can deliver from Your hand?

8 'Your hands have made me and fashioned me,
An intricate unity;
Yet You would destroy me.
9 Remember, I pray, that You have made me like clay.
And will You turn me into dust again?

9:32, 33 Since Job cannot hope to win in court and cannot prove his innocence in a trial by ordeal, he longs for a **mediator** who could arbitrate his dispute with God. Today we can no longer complain that there is no mediator. Jesus Christ now mediates between heaven and earth; to Him the Father has committed all judgment.

10 Did You not pour me out like milk,
And curdle me like cheese,
11 Clothe me with skin and flesh,
And knit me together with bones and sinews?
12 You have granted me life and favor,
And Your care has preserved my spirit.

13 'And these *things* You have hidden in Your heart;
I know that this *was* with You:
14 If I sin, then You mark me,
And will not acquit me of my iniquity.
15 If I am wicked, woe to me;
Even *if* I am righteous, I cannot lift up my head.
I am full of disgrace;
See my misery!
16 If *my head* is exalted,
You hunt me like a fierce lion,
And again You show Yourself awesome against me.
17 You renew Your witnesses against me,
And increase Your indignation toward me;
Changes and war are *ever* with me.

18 'Why then have You brought me out of the womb?
Oh, that I had perished and no eye had seen me!
19 I would have been as though I had not been.
I would have been carried from the womb to the grave.
20 Are not my days few?
Cease! Leave me alone, that I may take a little comfort,
21 Before I go *to the place from which* I shall not return,
To the land of darkness and the shadow of death,
22 A land as dark as darkness *itself*,
As the shadow of death, without any order,
Where even the light *is* like darkness.' "

CHAPTER 11

Zophar Urges Job to Repent

Then Zō'phar the Nā'a·ma·thīte answered and said:

2 "Should not the multitude of words be answered?
And should a man full of talk be vindicated?
3 Should your empty talk make men hold their peace?
And when you mock, should no one rebuke you?
4 For you have said,
'My doctrine *is* pure,
And I am clean in your eyes.'
5 But oh, that God would speak,
And open His lips against you,
6 That He would show you the secrets of wisdom!
For *they would* double *your* prudence.
Know therefore that God exacts from you
Less than your iniquity *deserves*.

7 "Can you search out the deep things of God?
Can you find out the limits of the Almighty?
8 *They are* higher than heaven—what can you do?
Deeper than Shē'ōl—what can you know?
9 Their measure *is* longer than the earth
And broader than the sea.

11:1–20 Zophar reasons that there are only two classes of people: contrite worshipers and arrogant sinners. Job's rash words bid fair to put him in the latter class. In fact, he deserves worse suffering than he is getting (v. 6). Because of God's mercy, Job's misery is limited. He can prosper again if only he will repent (vv. 13–19).

10 "If He passes by, imprisons, and
gathers *to judgment,*
Then who can hinder Him?
11 For He knows deceitful men;
He sees wickedness also.
Will He not then consider *it?*
12 For an empty-headed man will be
wise,
When a wild donkey's colt is born a
man.

13 "If you would prepare your heart,
And stretch out your hands toward
Him;
14 If iniquity *were* in your hand, *and you*
put it far away,
And would not let wickedness dwell
in your tents;
15 Then surely you could lift up your
face without spot;
Yes, you could be steadfast, and not
fear;
16 Because you would forget *your*
misery,
And remember *it* as waters *that have*
passed away,
17 And *your* life would be brighter than
noonday.
Though you were dark, you would be
like the morning.
18 And you would be secure, because
there is hope;
Yes, you would dig *around you, and*
take your rest in safety.
19 You would also lie down, and no one
would make *you* afraid;
Yes, many would court your favor.
20 But the eyes of the wicked will fail,
And they shall not escape,
And their hope—loss of life!"

CHAPTER 12

Job Answers His Critics

Then Job answered and said:

2 "No doubt you *are* the people,
And wisdom will die with you!
3 But I have understanding as well as
you;
I *am* not inferior to you.
Indeed, who does not *know* such
things as these?

4 "I am one mocked by his friends,
Who called on God, and He answered
him,
The just and blameless *who is*
ridiculed.
5 A lamp[a] is despised in the thought of
one who is at ease;
It is made ready for those whose feet
slip.
6 The tents of robbers prosper,
And those who provoke God are
secure—
In what God provides by His hand.

7 "But now ask the beasts, and they will
teach you;

12:5 [a]Or *disaster*

11:11 Zophar views suffering as a direct result of sin.

12:1—14:22 Job's longest discourse comes at the end of the first round of speeches. It has two parts: an address to his friends (12:1—13:19) and an address to God (13:20—14:22). To his friends, Job insists that a study of life (12:7–12) does not yield nearly as consistent a set of principles as his comforters suggest (12:13–25). Their simplistic defense of God does Him no honor (13:1–19). To God, he begins by asking that He not overpower him with deity (13:21, 22) but show him his wrong (13:23, 24). From that point he moves into a meditation on the brevity of life (13:28—14:22). His realization of how fleeting and futile this life can be leads him to wonder poignantly whether there might be new life with God—after this one (14:7–17).

12:7–11 Job says that nature itself would **teach** his friends the truth that both good and bad come from the **hand of the LORD** (v. 9; see also v. 6). Not all suffering is due to iniquity. As **words** and **food** (v. 11) are tested for their quality, so Job would test the viewpoints of his friends for their truthfulness.

And the birds of the air, and they will tell you;
8 Or speak to the earth, and it will teach you;
And the fish of the sea will explain to you.
9 Who among all these does not know
That the hand of the LORD has done this,
10 In whose hand *is* the life of every living thing,
And the breath of all mankind?
11 Does not the ear test words
And the mouth taste its food?
12 Wisdom *is* with aged men,
And with length of days, understanding.

> Age in a virtuous person, of either sex, carries in it an authority which makes it preferable to all the pleasures of youth.
> Sir Richard Steele

13 "With Him *are* wisdom and strength,
He has counsel and understanding.
14 If He breaks *a thing* down, it cannot be rebuilt;
If He imprisons a man, there can be no release.
15 If He withholds the waters, they dry up;
If He sends them out, they overwhelm the earth.
16 With Him *are* strength and prudence.
The deceived and the deceiver *are* His.
17 He leads counselors away plundered,
And makes fools of the judges.
18 He loosens the bonds of kings,
And binds their waist with a belt.
19 He leads princes[a] away plundered,
And overthrows the mighty.

12:19 [a]Literally *priests*, but not in a technical sense

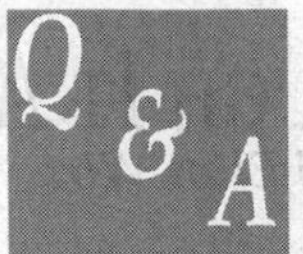

Do people get wiser with age?

Elmer L. Gray

Wisdom should come with age. Job said, "Wisdom is with aged men, and with length of days, understanding" (Job 12:12).

The problem with getting wiser is that many people have no idea what wisdom is. Wisdom is not the same as knowledge, but a wise person will seek knowledge. In a practical sense it is having good judgment. It looks for the cause behind things, anticipates what things will lead to, evaluates the good or bad in things, and discovers how to effect those causes and results.

Much wisdom happens because people have experiences that teach lessons, yet wisdom can be more deliberate than that. Be alert to causes and results and also to value and effective actions, and you will grow in wisdom and help others.

The Bible is useful in gaining wisdom. "The testimony of the Lord is sure, making wise the simple" (Ps. 19:7). True wisdom responds to the lovingkindness of God. "Whoever is wise will observe these things, and they will understand the lovingkindness of the Lord" (Ps. 107:43).

Remember that only in Christ do we find real wisdom (Luke 21:15; James 3:17). Ask God to help you to understand causes and effects and also to know what is good. ✦

12:18 bonds of kings: The bands with which they fasten their robes. They are led away captive in only a **belt** (loincloth).

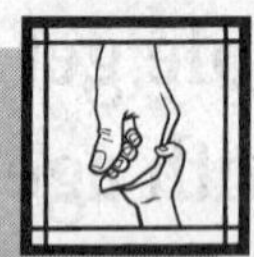

Through It All

Sherwood Eliot Wirt

Christians of any age should reach out as mentors to younger men and women. We can grasp their hands in ours and give them the mature assurance they seem to want so keenly, even as they reject it from their own parents. We can instill confidence in them, tell them that we are praying for them and that we believe God is going to give their lives new meaning. We can show them that they need to reach across the bridge to their own children and assure them of their love. God Himself will open up ways to do it! Sometimes plain words have to be spoken. Hurts and griefs must be aired. But the real movement off dead center may come when our own voices speak love and good cheer, and our own faces shine with reassurance as the younger ones receive the hope that God has promised in His Word.

We have been through it all! We know about it. We know that, while there is no way over or under or around or back, there is a way through, for we have taken that route, and here we are. ✦

20 He deprives the trusted ones of speech,
And takes away the discernment of the elders.
21 He pours contempt on princes,
And disarms the mighty.
22 He uncovers deep things out of darkness,
And brings the shadow of death to light.
23 He makes nations great, and destroys them;
He enlarges nations, and guides them.
24 He takes away the understanding[a] of the chiefs of the people of the earth,
And makes them wander in a pathless wilderness.
25 They grope in the dark without light,
And He makes them stagger like a drunken *man*.

CHAPTER 13

"Behold, my eye has seen all *this*,
My ear has heard and understood it.
2 What you know, I also know;
I *am* not inferior to you.
3 But I would speak to the Almighty,
And I desire to reason with God.
4 But you forgers of lies,
You *are* all worthless physicians.
5 Oh, that you would be silent,
And it would be your wisdom!
6 Now hear my reasoning,
And heed the pleadings of my lips.
7 Will you speak wickedly for God,

12:24 [a]Literally *heart*

13:7–11 This series of questions warns Job's friends that their simplistic defense of God violates justice. **when He searches you out** (v. 9): They conceitedly assume that God will honor them because they break Job on the rock of their own inadequate concepts of God. They may be surprised when He examines their conduct. This warning could apply to many

And talk deceitfully for Him?
8 Will you show partiality for Him?
Will you contend for God?
9 Will it be well when He searches you out?
Or can you mock Him as one mocks a man?
10 He will surely rebuke you
If you secretly show partiality.
11 Will not His excellence make you afraid,
And the dread of Him fall upon you?
12 Your platitudes *are* proverbs of ashes,
Your defenses are defenses of clay.

13 "Hold your peace with me, and let me speak,
Then let come on me what *may!*
14 Why do I take my flesh in my teeth,
And put my life in my hands?
15 Though He slay me, yet will I trust Him.
Even so, I will defend my own ways before Him.
16 He also *shall* be my salvation,
For a hypocrite could not come before Him.
17 Listen carefully to my speech,
And to my declaration with your ears.
18 See now, I have prepared *my* case,
I know that I shall be vindicated.
19 Who *is* he *who* will contend with me?
If now I hold my tongue, I perish.

Job's Despondent Prayer

20 "Only two *things* do not do to me,
Then I will not hide myself from You:
21 Withdraw Your hand far from me,
And let not the dread of You make me afraid.
22 Then call, and I will answer;
Or let me speak, then You respond to me.
23 How many *are* my iniquities and sins?
Make me know my transgression and my sin.
24 Why do You hide Your face,
And regard me as Your enemy?
25 Will You frighten a leaf driven to and fro?
And will You pursue dry stubble?
26 For You write bitter things against me,
And make me inherit the iniquities of my youth.
27 You put my feet in the stocks,
And watch closely all my paths.
You set a limit[a] for the soles of my feet.

28 "*Man*[a] decays like a rotten thing,
Like a garment that is moth-eaten.

CHAPTER 14

"Man *who is* born of woman
Is of few days and full of trouble.
2 He comes forth like a flower and fades away;

13:27 [a]Literally *inscribe a print* 13:28 [a]Literally *He*

---

of us today as we try to explain God in a way that will satisfy us. We need to understand that when we reduce God to the human level we deny the greatness of who He is. We can never fully define or explain God and His ways. To put Him in a box that fits our preconceptions is sheer arrogance.

13:15–19 Though He slay me: People believed that the awesome splendor of God's presence would so overwhelm any human being that he would die. But a hearing with God is Job's only hope to prove his innocence. Earlier (9:1–3) he could not even think of asking for such a hearing. **I shall be vindicated** (v. 18): Job's strongest statement of confidence yet that God will declare him innocent.

13:20, 21 Job requests **only two things** as pretrial concessions from God: (1) that God withdraw His hand and end Job's physical suffering, and (2) that God not frighten him so much that he cannot present his case.

He flees like a shadow and does not
continue.
3 And do You open Your eyes on such a
one,
And bring me[a] to judgment with
Yourself?
4 Who can bring a clean *thing* out of an
unclean?
No one!
5 Since his days *are* determined,
The number of his months *is* with You;
You have appointed his limits, so that
he cannot pass.
6 Look away from him that he may rest,
Till like a hired man he finishes his
day.

7 "For there is hope for a tree,
If it is cut down, that it will sprout
again,
And that its tender shoots will not
cease.
8 Though its root may grow old in the
earth,
And its stump may die in the ground,
9 *Yet* at the scent of water it will bud
And bring forth branches like a plant.
10 But man dies and is laid away;
Indeed he breathes his last
And where *is* he?
11 *As* water disappears from the sea,
And a river becomes parched and
dries up,
12 So man lies down and does not rise.
Till the heavens *are* no more,
They will not awake
Nor be roused from their sleep.

13 "Oh, that You would hide me in the
grave,
That You would conceal me until
Your wrath is past,
That You would appoint me a set
time, and remember me!
14 If a man dies, shall he live *again?*
All the days of my hard service I will
wait,
Till my change comes.
15 You shall call, and I will answer You;
You shall desire the work of Your
hands.
16 For now You number my steps,
But do not watch over my sin.
17 My transgression *is* sealed up in a
bag,
And You cover[a] my iniquity.

18 "But *as* a mountain falls *and* crumbles
away,
And *as* a rock is moved from its place;
19 *As* water wears away stones,
And as torrents wash away the soil of
the earth;
So You destroy the hope of man.
20 You prevail forever against him, and
he passes on;
You change his countenance and send
him away.
21 His sons come to honor, and he does
not know *it;*
They are brought low, and he does
not perceive *it.*
22 But his flesh will be in pain over it,
And his soul will mourn over it."

CHAPTER 15

Eliphaz Accuses Job of Folly

Then E·lī′phaz the Tē′man·īte answered and said:

14:3 [a]Septuagint, Syriac, and Vulgate read *him.*
14:17 [a]Literally *plaster over*

14:5, 6 Look away: Because God has so completely **determined** a human's **limits**, He should relent in His persistent punishment and let a person find at least the satisfaction that a **hired man** finds in his work.

14:17 sealed up: In the courts, charges against a lawbreaker were kept in a sealed **bag** so that none would be lost; all would be held against him when he faced the judge. **cover**: The meaning of the Hebrew word indicates that God will preserve Job's sins with plaster until judgment day. Job accuses God of this same unrelenting prosecution.

2 "Should a wise man answer with
empty knowledge,
And fill himself with the east wind?
3 Should he reason with unprofitable
talk,
Or by speeches with which he can do
no good?
4 Yes, you cast off fear,
And restrain prayer before God.
5 For your iniquity teaches your mouth,
And you choose the tongue of the
crafty.
6 Your own mouth condemns you, and
not I;
Yes, your own lips testify against you.

7 "*Are* you the first man *who* was born?
Or were you made before the hills?
8 Have you heard the counsel of God?
Do you limit wisdom to yourself?
9 What do you know that we do not
know?
What do you understand that *is* not in
us?
10 Both the gray-haired and the aged *are*
among us,
Much older than your father.
11 *Are* the consolations of God too small
for you,
And the word *spoken* gently[a] with
you?
12 Why does your heart carry you away,
And what do your eyes wink at,
13 That you turn your spirit against
God,
And let *such* words go out of your
mouth?

14 "What *is* man, that he could be pure?
And *he who is* born of a woman, that
he could be righteous?
15 If *God* puts no trust in His saints,
And the heavens are not pure in His
sight,
16 How much less man, *who is*
abominable and filthy,
Who drinks iniquity like water!

17 "I will tell you, hear me;
What I have seen I will declare,
18 What wise men have told,
Not hiding *anything received* from
their fathers,
19 To whom alone the land was given,
And no alien passed among them:
20 The wicked man writhes with pain all
his days,
And the number of years is hidden
from the oppressor.
21 Dreadful sounds *are* in his ears;
In prosperity the destroyer comes
upon him.
22 He does not believe that he will
return from darkness,
For a sword is waiting for him.
23 He wanders about for bread, *saying,*
'Where *is it?*'
He knows that a day of darkness is
ready at his hand.
24 Trouble and anguish make him
afraid;
They overpower him, like a king
ready for battle.
25 For he stretches out his hand against
God,
And acts defiantly against the
Almighty,

15:11 [a]Septuagint reads *a secret thing.*

15:2, 3 Wise man refers to Job and his claims to be as wise as his friends (12:3; 13:2). The **east wind** coming from the desert brought irritation because of its extreme heat. **himself**: The lower abdomen, one's innermost being (see Prov. 18:8; 20:27). This may be a pun meaning that Job's words are full of hot air and come from his belly, not from his reason.

15:11 Apparently Eliphaz arrogantly considers himself a messenger of God and rebukes Job for not accepting His words.

15:14, 15 Eliphaz is correct in saying that man cannot be righteous in and of himself. Like many of the statements in the Book of Job, this is a correct concept but the application is inappropriate.

26 Running stubbornly against Him
With his strong, embossed shield.

27 "Though he has covered his face with
his fatness,
And made *his* waist heavy with fat,
28 He dwells in desolate cities,
In houses which no one inhabits,
Which are destined to become ruins.
29 He will not be rich,
Nor will his wealth continue,
Nor will his possessions overspread
the earth.
30 He will not depart from darkness;
The flame will dry out his branches,
And by the breath of His mouth he
will go away.
31 Let him not trust in futile *things*,
deceiving himself,
For futility will be his reward.
32 It will be accomplished before his
time,
And his branch will not be green.
33 He will shake off his unripe grape
like a vine,
And cast off his blossom like an olive
tree.
34 For the company of hypocrites *will be*
barren,
And fire will consume the tents of
bribery.
35 They conceive trouble and bring forth
futility;
Their womb prepares deceit."

CHAPTER 16

Job Reproaches His Pitiless Friends

Then Job answered and said:

2 "I have heard many such things;
Miserable comforters *are* you all!
3 Shall words of wind have an end?
Or what provokes you that you
answer?
4 I also could speak as you *do*,
If your soul were in my soul's place.
I could heap up words against you,
And shake my head at you;
5 *But* I would strengthen you with my
mouth,
And the comfort of my lips would
relieve *your grief*.

6 "Though I speak, my grief is not
relieved;
And *if* I remain silent, how am I
eased?
7 But now He has worn me out;
You have made desolate all my
company.
8 You have shriveled me up,
And it is a witness *against me*;
My leanness rises up against me
And bears witness to my face.
9 He tears *me* in His wrath, and hates
me;
He gnashes at me with His teeth;
My adversary sharpens His gaze on
me.
10 They gape at me with their mouth,
They strike me reproachfully on the
cheek,
They gather together against me.
11 God has delivered me to the ungodly,
And turned me over to the hands of
the wicked.
12 I was at ease, but He has shattered
me;

15:27–35 In a series of word pictures Eliphaz describes how a sinful life will be disappointing. **fatness . . . fat**: An OT figure for wealth and earthly success.

16:1—17:16 Job both laments God's treatment and affirms that God will be the witness in his defense. He closes with a lament on the hopelessness of his life and his prospects.

16:2–5 How easy it is for us to offer platitudes and explanations when someone else is suffering! True comfort is not found in empty words but in having a comforter identify with one's own pain. Loving silence is often better medicine than futile talk.

16:8 My leanness: The marks of illness on Job's body provided conclusive evidence to others that he had sinned. No matter how strongly his conscience asserted his innocence, his body was a **witness** against him.

He also has taken *me* by my neck, and
shaken me to pieces;
He has set me up for His target,
13 His archers surround me.
He pierces my heart[a] and does not
pity;
He pours out my gall on the ground.
14 He breaks me with wound upon
wound;
He runs at me like a warrior.[a]

15 "I have sewn sackcloth over my skin,
And laid my head[a] in the dust.
16 My face is flushed from weeping,
And on my eyelids *is* the shadow of
death;
17 Although no violence *is* in my hands,
And my prayer *is* pure.

18 "O earth, do not cover my blood,
And let my cry have no *resting* place!
19 Surely even now my witness *is* in
heaven,
And my evidence *is* on high.
20 My friends scorn me;
My eyes pour out *tears* to God.
21 Oh, that one might plead for a man
with God,
As a man *pleads* for his neighbor!
22 For when a few years are finished,
I shall go the way of no return.

CHAPTER 17

Job Prays for Relief

"My spirit is broken,
My days are extinguished,
The grave *is ready* for me.
2 *Are* not mockers with me?
And does not my eye dwell on their
provocation?

3 "Now put down a pledge for me with
Yourself.
Who *is* he *who* will shake hands with
me?
4 For You have hidden their heart from
understanding;
Therefore You will not exalt *them*.
5 He who speaks flattery to *his* friends,
Even the eyes of his children will fail.

6 "But He has made me a byword of the
people,
And I have become one in whose face
men spit.
7 My eye has also grown dim because
of sorrow,
And all my members *are* like
shadows.
8 Upright *men* are astonished at this,
And the innocent stirs himself up
against the hypocrite.
9 Yet the righteous will hold to his way,
And he who has clean hands will be
stronger and stronger.

10 "But please, come back again, all of
you,[a]
For I shall not find *one* wise *man*
among you.
11 My days are past,
My purposes are broken off,
Even the thoughts of my heart.
12 They change the night into day;
'The light *is* near,' *they say*, in the face
of darkness.
13 If I wait *for* the grave *as* my house,
If I make my bed in the darkness,
14 If I say to corruption, 'You *are* my
father,'

16:13 [a]Literally *kidneys* 16:14 [a]Vulgate reads *giant.* 16:15 [a]Literally *horn* 17:10 [a]Following some Hebrew manuscripts, Septuagint, Syriac, and Vulgate; Masoretic Text and Targum read *all of them.*

16:19 Job's cry for vindication arouses hope, and he declares **my witness is in heaven**. In Christian redemption we see the drama of God the Savior witnessing for the sinner before the bar of God the Judge. Job trusts God in spite of how God appears to treat him.

17:10–16 My days are past (v. 11): After his burst of faith (vv. 8, 9), Job once more subsides into gloom: I only **wait for the grave** (v. 13).

And to the worm, 'You *are* my mother
and my sister,'
15 Where then *is* my hope?
As for my hope, who can see it?
16 *Will* they go down to the gates of
Shē'ōl?
Shall *we have* rest together in the
dust?"

CHAPTER 18

Bildad: The Wicked Are Punished

Then Bil'dad the Shū'hīte answered and
said:

2 "How long *till* you put an end to
words?
Gain understanding, and afterward
we will speak.
3 Why are we counted as beasts,
And regarded as stupid in your sight?
4 You who tear yourself in anger,
Shall the earth be forsaken for you?
Or shall the rock be removed from its
place?

5 "The light of the wicked indeed goes
out,
And the flame of his fire does not
shine.
6 The light is dark in his tent,
And his lamp beside him is put out.
7 The steps of his strength are
shortened,
And his own counsel casts him down.
8 For he is cast into a net by his own
feet,
And he walks into a snare.
9 The net takes *him* by the heel,
And a snare lays hold of him.
10 A noose *is* hidden for him on the
ground,
And a trap for him in the road.
11 Terrors frighten him on every side,
And drive him to his feet.
12 His strength is starved,
And destruction *is* ready at his side.
13 It devours patches of his skin;
The firstborn of death devours his
limbs.
14 He is uprooted from the shelter of his
tent,
And they parade him before the king
of terrors.
15 They dwell in his tent *who are* none of
his;
Brimstone is scattered on his
dwelling.
16 His roots are dried out below,
And his branch withers above.
17 The memory of him perishes from the
earth,
And he has no name among the
renowned.[a]
18 He is driven from light into darkness,
And chased out of the world.
19 He has neither son nor posterity
among his people,
Nor any remaining in his dwellings.
20 Those in the west are astonished at
his day,
As those in the east are frightened.
21 Surely such *are* the dwellings of the
wicked,
And this *is* the place *of him who* does
not know God."

CHAPTER 19

Job Trusts in His Redeemer

Then Job answered and said:

18:17 [a]Literally *before the outside,* meaning distinguished, famous

18:1–21 Bildad rails against Job with a graphic picture of the terrible fate of the wicked. All of this is true. God holds us accountable for our actions. But Bildad's fault, as with the others, is threatening an innocent sufferer with God's judgments against evil persons. Not all suffering is a direct result of personal sin.

18:13 firstborn of death: Death in its fullest, most powerful spiritual form.

19:1–29 Job pleads with his friends to change their attitude toward him. They need to realize that his misfortune comes from God's action, not from some sin that he has committed

2 "How long will you torment my soul,
And break me in pieces with words?
3 These ten times you have reproached me;
You are not ashamed *that* you have wronged me.[a]
4 And if indeed I have erred,
My error remains with me.
5 If indeed you exalt *yourselves* against me,
And plead my disgrace against me,
6 Know then that God has wronged me,
And has surrounded me with His net.

7 "If I cry out concerning wrong, I am not heard.
If I cry aloud, *there is* no justice.
8 He has fenced up my way, so that I cannot pass;
And He has set darkness in my paths.
9 He has stripped me of my glory,
And taken the crown *from* my head.
10 He breaks me down on every side,
And I am gone;
My hope He has uprooted like a tree.
11 He has also kindled His wrath against me,
And He counts me as *one of* His enemies.
12 His troops come together
And build up their road against me;
They encamp all around my tent.

13 "He has removed my brothers far from me,
And my acquaintances are completely estranged from me.
14 My relatives have failed,
And my close friends have forgotten me.
15 Those who dwell in my house, and my maidservants,
Count me as a stranger;
I am an alien in their sight.
16 I call my servant, but he gives no answer;
I beg him with my mouth.
17 My breath is offensive to my wife,
And I am repulsive to the children of my own body.
18 Even young children despise me;
I arise, and they speak against me.
19 All my close friends abhor me,
And those whom I love have turned against me.
20 My bone clings to my skin and to my flesh,
And I have escaped by the skin of my teeth.

21 "Have pity on me, have pity on me,
O you my friends,
For the hand of God has struck me!
22 Why do you persecute me as God *does*,
And are not satisfied with my flesh?

23 "Oh, that my words were written!
Oh, that they were inscribed in a book!
24 That they were engraved on a rock
With an iron pen and lead, forever!
25 For I know *that* my Redeemer lives,
And He shall stand at last on the earth;

19:3 [a]A Jewish tradition reads *make yourselves strange to me.*

(vv. 6–12). Despairing of support from his friends and loved ones (vv. 13–22), Job makes his strongest statements yet that God Himself will one day declare Job's righteousness, if not in this life, then in the next (vv. 25–27). He does not know how this will happen, but he does not doubt that God, the Redeemer, will act on his behalf.

19:13–20 In patriarchal societies, the bond between members of a tribe was very strong. Each member was responsible for every other member. But in Job's troubles God seemed to have separated him from both family and close friends.

19:25–27 In the final analysis, Job does not place his trust in an inscribed monument. He trusts in a **Redeemer** who **lives**. Even though abandoned, he asserts confidently that God will deliver him and vindicate his honor. "Redeemer" was a title for God as Israel's deliverer

26 And after my skin is destroyed, this *I know,*
That in my flesh I shall see God,
27 Whom I shall see for myself,
And my eyes shall behold, and not another.
How my heart yearns within me!
28 If you should say, 'How shall we persecute him?'—
Since the root of the matter is found in me,
29 Be afraid of the sword for yourselves;
For wrath *brings* the punishment of the sword,
That you may know *there is* a judgment."

CHAPTER 20

Zophar's Sermon on the Wicked Man

Then Zō′phar the Nā′a·ma·thīte answered and said:

2 "Therefore my anxious thoughts make me answer,
Because of the turmoil within me.
3 I have heard the rebuke that reproaches me,
And the spirit of my understanding causes me to answer.

4 "Do you *not* know this of old,
Since man was placed on earth,
5 That the triumphing of the wicked is short,
And the joy of the hypocrite is *but* for a moment?
6 Though his haughtiness mounts up to the heavens,
And his head reaches to the clouds,
7 *Yet* he will perish forever like his own refuse;
Those who have seen him will say, 'Where is he?'
8 He will fly away like a dream, and not be found;
Yes, he will be chased away like a vision of the night.
9 The eye *that* saw him will *see him* no more,
Nor will his place behold him anymore.
10 His children will seek the favor of the poor,
And his hands will restore his wealth.
11 His bones are full of his youthful vigor,
But it will lie down with him in the dust.

12 "Though evil is sweet in his mouth,
And he hides it under his tongue,
13 *Though* he spares it and does not forsake it,
But still keeps it in his mouth,
14 *Yet* his food in his stomach turns sour;
It becomes cobra venom within him.
15 He swallows down riches
And vomits them up again;
God casts them out of his belly.
16 He will suck the poison of cobras;
The viper's tongue will slay him.
17 He will not see the streams,
The rivers flowing with honey and cream.
18 He will restore that for which he labored,
And will not swallow *it* down;
From the proceeds of business
He will get no enjoyment.
19 For he has oppressed *and* forsaken the poor,
He has violently seized a house which he did not build.

from Egyptian bondage (see Ex. 6:6; Ps. 74:2; Is. 41:14). Job was sure that this Redeemer would testify to his faithfulness. Similarly, Christians today confidently affirm that God in Christ cares for them.

20:12–15 Zophar's description of sin is quite accurate. While at first deceptively sweet, sin eventually becomes bitter and poisonous. This is the secret to Satan's success; he distracts us with promises of pleasure while ensnaring us with evil.

20 "Because he knows no quietness in his
heart,[a]
He will not save anything he desires.
21 Nothing is left for him to eat;
Therefore his well-being will not last.
22 In his self-sufficiency he will be in
distress;
Every hand of misery will come
against him.
23 *When* he is about to fill his stomach,
God will cast on him the fury of His
wrath,
And will rain *it* on him while he is
eating.
24 He will flee from the iron weapon;
A bronze bow will pierce him
through.
25 It is drawn, and comes out of the
body;
Yes, the glittering *point comes* out of
his gall.
Terrors *come* upon him;
26 Total darkness *is* reserved for his
treasures.
An unfanned fire will consume him;
It shall go ill with him who is left in
his tent.
27 The heavens will reveal his iniquity,
And the earth will rise up against
him.
28 The increase of his house will depart,
And his goods will flow away in the
day of His wrath.
29 This *is* the portion from God for a
wicked man,
The heritage appointed to him by
God."

20:20 [a]Literally *belly*

CHAPTER 21

Job's Discourse on the Wicked

Then Job answered and said:

2 "Listen carefully to my speech,
And let this be your consolation.
3 Bear with me that I may speak,
And after I have spoken, keep
mocking.

4 "As for me, *is* my complaint against
man?
And if *it were,* why should I not be
impatient?
5 Look at me and be astonished;
Put *your* hand over *your* mouth.
6 Even when I remember I am terrified,
And trembling takes hold of my flesh.
7 Why do the wicked live *and* become
old,
Yes, become mighty in power?
8 Their descendants are established
with them in their sight,
And their offspring before their eyes.
9 Their houses *are* safe from fear,
Neither *is* the rod of God upon them.
10 Their bull breeds without failure;
Their cow calves without miscarriage.
11 They send forth their little ones like a
flock,
And their children dance.
12 They sing to the tambourine and
harp,
And rejoice to the sound of the flute.

20:20–23 he knows no quietness: The wicked person is so consumed by desires that he cannot enjoy their fulfillment. Faddishness is an expression of this principle: quickly taken up and quickly discarded.

21:1–34 Job completely rejects the simplified doctrine of retribution which his friends have expressed. Observation shows that there are wicked people who do prosper (vv. 7–16). Further, the claim that the wicked who prosper will die a horrible death at the prime of life is not supported by experience (vv. 17–21). Many wicked people live and die without suffering. If the doctrine of retribution does not always apply to the wicked, it may not always apply to those who suffer. Death is no more a friend to the righteous than an enemy to the wicked (vv. 22–34).

21:4 Job's **complaint** is not against **man**, but against God.

13 They spend their days in wealth,
And in a moment go down to the
grave.[a]
14 Yet they say to God, 'Depart from us,
For we do not desire the knowledge
of Your ways.
15 Who *is* the Almighty, that we should
serve Him?
And what profit do we have if we
pray to Him?'
16 Indeed their prosperity *is* not in their
hand;
The counsel of the wicked is far from
me.

17 "How often is the lamp of the wicked
put out?
How often does their destruction come
upon them,
The sorrows *God* distributes in His
anger?
18 They are like straw before the wind,
And like chaff that a storm carries
away.
19 *They say,* 'God lays up one's[a] iniquity
for his children';
Let Him recompense him, that he
may know *it*.
20 Let his eyes see his destruction,
And let him drink of the wrath of the
Almighty.
21 For what does he care about his
household after him,
When the number of his months is
cut in half?

22 "Can *anyone* teach God knowledge,
Since He judges those on high?
23 One dies in his full strength,
Being wholly at ease and secure;
24 His pails[a] are full of milk,
And the marrow of his bones is
moist.
25 Another man dies in the bitterness of
his soul,
Never having eaten with pleasure.
26 They lie down alike in the dust,
And worms cover them.

27 "Look, I know your thoughts,
And the schemes *with which* you
would wrong me.
28 For you say,
'Where *is* the house of the prince?
And where *is* the tent,[a]
The dwelling place of the wicked?'
29 Have you not asked those who travel
the road?
And do you not know their signs?
30 For the wicked are reserved for the
day of doom;
They shall be brought out on the day
of wrath.
31 Who condemns his way to his face?
And who repays him *for what* he has
done?
32 Yet he shall be brought to the grave,
And a vigil kept over the tomb.
33 The clods of the valley shall be sweet
to him;
Everyone shall follow him,
As countless *have gone* before him.
34 How then can you comfort me with
empty words,
Since falsehood remains in your
answers?"

CHAPTER 22

Eliphaz Accuses Job of Wickedness

Then E·lī′phaz the Tē′man·īte answered and said:

21:13 [a]Or *Sheol* 21:19 [a]Literally *his*
21:24 [a]Septuagint and Vulgate read *bowels;* Syriac reads *sides;* Targum reads *breasts.* 21:28 [a]Vulgate omits *the tent.*

21:13–15 Unlike Job, the wicked do not suffer severely; they die in a moment. Their lives are comfortable even though they pay no attention to God (v. 14).

21:33 The clods are **sweet** because he rests peacefully in the grave.

22:1—31:40 The third round of speeches (chs. 22—26) is followed by Job's lengthy defense (chs. 27—31). Of the comforters only Eliphaz and Bildad speak. They bluntly assert that Job's claims of righteousness are false. Job reflects on God's power (26:1–14) and

2 "Can a man be profitable to God,
Though he who is wise may be
profitable to himself?
3 *Is it* any pleasure to the Almighty that
you are righteous?
Or *is it* gain *to Him* that you make
your ways blameless?

4 "Is it because of your fear of Him that
He corrects you,
And enters into judgment with you?
5 *Is* not your wickedness great,
And your iniquity without end?
6 For you have taken pledges from
your brother for no reason,
And stripped the naked of their
clothing.
7 You have not given the weary water
to drink,
And you have withheld bread from
the hungry.
8 But the mighty man possessed the
land,
And the honorable man dwelt in it.
9 You have sent widows away empty,
And the strength of the fatherless was
crushed.
10 Therefore snares *are* all around you,
And sudden fear troubles you,
11 Or darkness *so that* you cannot see;
And an abundance of water covers
you.

12 "Is not God in the height of heaven?
And see the highest stars, how lofty
they are!
13 And you say, 'What does God know?
Can He judge through the deep
darkness?
14 Thick clouds cover Him, so that He
cannot see,
And He walks above the circle of
heaven.'
15 Will you keep to the old way
Which wicked men have trod,
16 Who were cut down before their time,
Whose foundations were swept away
by a flood?
17 They said to God, 'Depart from us!
What can the Almighty do to them?'[a]
18 Yet He filled their houses with good
things;
But the counsel of the wicked is far
from me.

19 "The righteous see *it* and are glad,
And the innocent laugh at them:
20 'Surely our adversaries[a] are cut down,
And the fire consumes their remnant.'

21 "Now acquaint yourself with Him, and
be at peace;
Thereby good will come to you.
22 Receive, please, instruction from His
mouth,
And lay up His words in your heart.
23 If you return to the Almighty, you
will be built up;
You will remove iniquity far from
your tents.

22:17 [a]Septuagint and Syriac read *us.* 22:20 [a]Septuagint reads *substance.*

then launches into his final statement lamenting his condition, insisting on his righteousness, and questioning the operation of justice in the world.

22:1–30 Because Job refuses to surrender his claim of innocence in the face of God's continuing punishment, Eliphaz accuses Job of specific sins he has committed. Eliphaz hopes to help Job by exalting God. But, in fact, his limited concept of God forces him to make Job a liar.

22:16 This verse is probably referring to the wicked people of Noah's day whom God judged with a flood.

22:21–30 This is a beautiful charge to the sinner to repent of his unrighteousness; however, it is wasted on Job, who has not been living in sin. While we are to exhort and confront fellow believers who have fallen, we should carefully pray that the Lord will open our eyes to the truth and prevent us from making false accusations.

24 Then you will lay your gold in the
dust,
And the *gold* of Ō'phir among the
stones of the brooks.
25 Yes, the Almighty will be your gold[a]
And your precious silver;
26 For then you will have your delight
in the Almighty,
And lift up your face to God.
27 You will make your prayer to Him,
He will hear you,
And you will pay your vows.
28 You will also declare a thing,
And it will be established for you;
So light will shine on your ways.
29 When they cast *you* down, and you
say, 'Exaltation *will come!*'
Then He will save the humble *person.*
30 He will *even* deliver one who is not
innocent;
Yes, he will be delivered by the purity
of your hands."

CHAPTER 23

Job Proclaims God's Righteous Judgments

Then Job answered and said:

2 "Even today my complaint is bitter;
My[a] hand is listless because of my
groaning.
3 Oh, that I knew where I might find
Him,
That I might come to His seat!
4 I would present *my* case before Him,
And fill my mouth with arguments.
5 I would know the words *which* He
would answer me,
And understand what He would say
to me.
6 Would He contend with me in His
great power?
No! But He would take *note* of me.
7 There the upright could reason with
Him,
And I would be delivered forever
from my Judge.

8 "Look, I go forward, but He is not
there,
And backward, but I cannot perceive
Him;
9 When He works on the left hand, I
cannot behold *Him;*
When He turns to the right hand, I
cannot see *Him.*
10 But He knows the way that I take;
When He has tested me, I shall come
forth as gold.
11 My foot has held fast to His steps;
I have kept His way and not turned
aside.
12 I have not departed from the com-
mandment of His lips;

I pray, O Lord, that when You have tested me, I shall come forth as gold.

adapted from Job 23:10

22:25 [a]The ancient versions suggest *defense;* Hebrew reads *gold* as in verse 24. 23:2 [a]Following Masoretic Text, Targum, and Vulgate; Septuagint and Syriac read *His.*

23:1—24:25 Rather than respond to his friends, Job expresses his determination to find God. The only way he can improve his situation is to argue his case before the Almighty. The advice of his friends is to appease God by repenting of imaginary sins. This Job will not do. But he confesses that he cannot figure out what God is doing.

23:2–7 Job is confident that he could present a good case to which God would courteously listen if he could only find God. Note that his primary concern is not to be healed but to find God and talk with Him.

23:10 God allows adversity in our lives to purify our faith.

I have treasured the words of His mouth
More than my necessary *food*.

13 "But He *is* unique, and who can make Him change?
And *whatever* His soul desires, *that* He does.
14 For He performs *what is* appointed for me,
And many such *things are* with Him.
15 Therefore I am terrified at His presence;
When I consider *this*, I am afraid of Him.
16 For God made my heart weak,
And the Almighty terrifies me;
17 Because I was not cut off from the presence of darkness,
And He did *not* hide deep darkness from my face.

CHAPTER 24

Job Complains of Violence on the Earth

"Since times are not hidden from the Almighty,
Why do those who know Him see not His days?
2 "*Some* remove landmarks;
They seize flocks violently and feed *on them;*
3 They drive away the donkey of the fatherless;
They take the widow's ox as a pledge.
4 They push the needy off the road;
All the poor of the land are forced to hide.
5 Indeed, *like* wild donkeys in the desert,
They go out to their work, searching for food.
The wilderness *yields* food for them
and for *their* children.
6 They gather their fodder in the field
And glean in the vineyard of the wicked.
7 They spend the night naked, without clothing,
And have no covering in the cold.
8 They are wet with the showers of the mountains,
And huddle around the rock for want of shelter.

9 "*Some* snatch the fatherless from the breast,
And take a pledge from the poor.
10 They cause *the poor* to go naked, without clothing;
And they take away the sheaves from the hungry.
11 They press out oil within their walls,
And tread winepresses, yet suffer thirst.
12 The dying groan in the city,
And the souls of the wounded cry out;
Yet God does not charge *them* with wrong.

13 "There are those who rebel against the light;
They do not know its ways
Nor abide in its paths.
14 The murderer rises with the light;
He kills the poor and needy;
And in the night he is like a thief.
15 The eye of the adulterer waits for the twilight,

23:13–17 He is unique: God does not have to explain all of His actions to us. Job's problem is not hidden sin as his friends thought, but understanding God's actions toward him. He believes he could find peace if he only understood what God was doing. But the terrifying gulf between human limitations and the **Almighty** (v. 16) makes Job wonder whether that is possible.

24:1 times . . . days: The time set by God to judge oppressors and rightly reward all earthly events.

Saying, 'No eye will see me';
And he disguises *his* face.
16 In the dark they break into houses
Which they marked for themselves in the daytime;
They do not know the light.
17 For the morning is the same to them as the shadow of death;
If *someone* recognizes *them,*
They are in the terrors of the shadow of death.

18 "They *should be* swift on the face of the waters,
Their portion *should be* cursed in the earth,
So that no *one would* turn into the way of their vineyards.
19 As drought and heat consume the snow waters,
So the grave[a] *consumes those who* have sinned.
20 The womb *should* forget him,
The worm *should* feed sweetly on him;
He *should* be remembered no more,
And wickedness *should* be broken like a tree.
21 For he preys on the barren *who* do not bear,
And does no good for the widow.

22 "But *God* draws the mighty away with His power;
He rises up, but no *man* is sure of life.
23 He gives them security, and they rely *on it;*
Yet His eyes *are* on their ways.
24 They are exalted for a little while,
Then they are gone.
They are brought low;
They are taken out of the way like all *others;*
They dry out like the heads of grain.

25 "Now if *it is* not *so,* who will prove me a liar,
And make my speech worth nothing?"

CHAPTER 25

Bildad: How Can Man Be Righteous?

Then Bil'dad the Shū'hīte answered and said:

2 "Dominion and fear *belong* to Him;
He makes peace in His high places.
3 Is there any number to His armies?
Upon whom does His light not rise?
4 How then can man be righteous before God?
Or how can he be pure *who is* born of a woman?
5 If even the moon does not shine,
And the stars are not pure in His sight,
6 How much less man, *who is* a maggot,
And a son of man, *who is* a worm?"

CHAPTER 26

Job: Man's Frailty and God's Majesty

But Job answered and said:

24:19 [a]Or *Sheol*

24:18–21 A description of what should happen to the wicked, but all too often does not.

24:22–24 Job is coming closer to a right understanding of God's actions. The wicked ought to suffer (vv. 18–21), but God in mercy **gives them security . . . for a little while** (vv. 23, 24). Nevertheless, His eyes are **on their ways**, and if they presume on His mercy, they are soon **brought low**. Death is the great leveler.

26:1—31:40 Job's final words to his friends reveal his exasperation with their faulty application of the doctrine of retribution. Instead of helping Job, they have tempted him to confess when he had nothing to confess. He asserts God's power (26:5–14), but stubbornly insists on his own innocence (27:1–10). He knows the doctrine of retribution as well as they (27:11–23), but questions whether life is as simple as optimistic wisdom claims (28:1–28). He weeps over the honor he once knew (29:1–25) and the human dishonor (30:1–19) and

2 "How have you helped *him who is* without power?
How have you saved the arm *that has* no strength?
3 How have you counseled *one who has* no wisdom?
And *how* have you declared sound advice to many?
4 To whom have you uttered words?
And whose spirit came from you?

5 "The dead tremble,
Those under the waters and those inhabiting them.
6 Shē'ōl *is* naked before Him,
And Destruction has no covering.
7 He stretches out the north over empty space;
He hangs the earth on nothing.
8 He binds up the water in His thick clouds,
Yet the clouds are not broken under it.
9 He covers the face of *His* throne,
And spreads His cloud over it.
10 He drew a circular horizon on the face of the waters,
At the boundary of light and darkness.
11 The pillars of heaven tremble,
And are astonished at His rebuke.
12 He stirs up the sea with His power,
And by His understanding He breaks up the storm.
13 By His Spirit He adorned the heavens;
His hand pierced the fleeing serpent.
14 Indeed these *are* the mere edges of His ways,
And how small a whisper we hear of Him!
But the thunder of His power who can understand?"

CHAPTER 27

Job Maintains His Integrity

Moreover Job continued his discourse, and said:

2 "*As* God lives, *who* has taken away my justice,
And the Almighty, *who* has made my soul bitter,
3 As long as my breath *is* in me,
And the breath of God in my nostrils,
4 My lips will not speak wickedness,
Nor my tongue utter deceit.
5 Far be it from me
That I should say you are right;
Till I die I will not put away my integrity from me.
6 My righteousness I hold fast, and will not let it go;
My heart shall not reproach *me* as long as I live.

7 "May my enemy be like the wicked,
And he who rises up against me like the unrighteous.
8 For what is the hope of the hypocrite,
Though he may gain *much*,
If God takes away his life?
9 Will God hear his cry
When trouble comes upon him?
10 Will he delight himself in the Almighty?
Will he always call on God?

11 "I will teach you about the hand of God;
What *is* with the Almighty I will not conceal.
12 Surely all of you have seen *it;*
Why then do you behave with complete nonsense?

divine silence (30:20–31) he now knows. Finally, he insists again in the most emphatic terms that he has done no wrong (31:1–40).

26:6 destruction: may be translated "Abaddon," or "the grave."

26:11 pillars of heaven: probably a metaphor referring to the high mountains.

13 "This is the portion of a wicked man
with God,
And the heritage of oppressors,
received from the Almighty:
14 If his children are multiplied, *it is* for
the sword;
And his offspring shall not be
satisfied with bread.
15 Those who survive him shall be
buried in death,
And their[a] widows shall not weep,
16 Though he heaps up silver like dust,
And piles up clothing like clay—
17 He may pile *it* up, but the just will
wear *it*,
And the innocent will divide the
silver.
18 He builds his house like a moth,[a]
Like a booth *which* a watchman
makes.
19 The rich man will lie down,
But not be gathered *up*;[a]
He opens his eyes,
And he *is* no more.
20 Terrors overtake him like a flood;
A tempest steals him away in the
night.
21 The east wind carries him away, and
he is gone;
It sweeps him out of his place.
22 It hurls against him and does not
spare;
He flees desperately from its power.
23 *Men* shall clap their hands at him,
And shall hiss him out of his place.

CHAPTER 28

Job's Discourse on Wisdom

"Surely there is a mine for silver,
And a place *where* gold is refined.
2 Iron is taken from the earth,
And copper *is* smelted *from* ore.
3 *Man* puts an end to darkness,
And searches every recess
For ore in the darkness and the
shadow of death.
4 He breaks open a shaft away from
people;
In places forgotten by feet
They hang far away from men;
They swing to and fro.
5 *As for* the earth, from it comes bread,
But underneath it is turned up as by
fire;
6 Its stones *are* the source of sapphires,
And it contains gold dust.
7 *That* path no bird knows,
Nor has the falcon's eye seen it.
8 The proud lions[a] have not trodden it,
Nor has the fierce lion passed over it.
9 He puts his hand on the flint;
He overturns the mountains at the
roots.
10 He cuts out channels in the rocks,
And his eye sees every precious
thing.
11 He dams up the streams from
trickling;
What is hidden he brings forth to
light.

12 "But where can wisdom be found?
And where *is* the place of
understanding?

27:15 [a]Literally *his* 27:18 [a]Following Masoretic Text and Vulgate; Septuagint and Syriac read *spider* (compare 8:14); Targum reads *decay.* 27:19 [a]Following Masoretic Text and Targum; Septuagint and Syriac read *But shall not add* (that is, do it again); Vulgate reads *But take away nothing.* 28:8 [a]Literally *sons of pride,* figurative of the great lions

28:1–28 Job follows his discourse on retribution (27:7–23) with the assertion that ultimate wisdom belongs only to God (vv. 23–28). All human attempts to categorize it neatly must fail. This is the message of the book. Whenever we try to force all human experience into our categories, however generally true those categories may be, we are going to injure humans and defame God.

28:3 Man puts an end to darkness by digging mine shafts and descending with his lamps to uncover the ore.

28:12–19 **Man does not know** (v. 13): Humans seek **wisdom** in order to control the

13 Man does not know its value,
Nor is it found in the land of the living.
14 The deep says, '*It is* not in me';
And the sea says, '*It is* not with me.'
15 It cannot be purchased for gold,
Nor can silver be weighed *for* its price.
16 It cannot be valued in the gold of Ōphir,
In precious onyx or sapphire.
17 Neither gold nor crystal can equal it,
Nor can it be exchanged for jewelry of fine gold.
18 No mention shall be made of coral or quartz,
For the price of wisdom *is* above rubies.
19 The topaz of Ethiopia cannot equal it,
Nor can it be valued in pure gold.

20 "From where then does wisdom come?
And where *is* the place of understanding?
21 It is hidden from the eyes of all living,
And concealed from the birds of the air.

I pray that my children will remember that the price of wisdom is above rubies.

adapted from Job 28:18

22 Destruction and Death say,
'We have heard a report about it with our ears.'
23 God understands its way,
And He knows its place.
24 For He looks to the ends of the earth,
And sees under the whole heavens,
25 To establish a weight for the wind,
And apportion the waters by measure.
26 When He made a law for the rain,
And a path for the thunderbolt,
27 Then He saw *wisdom*[a] and declared it;
He prepared it, indeed, He searched it out.
28 And to man He said,
'Behold, the fear of the Lord, that *is* wisdom,
And to depart from evil *is* understanding.' "

CHAPTER 29

Job's Summary Defense

Job further continued his discourse, and said:

2 "Oh, that I were as *in* months past,
As *in* the days *when* God watched over me;
3 When His lamp shone upon my head,
And when by His light I walked *through* darkness;
4 Just as I was in the days of my prime,
When the friendly counsel of God *was* over my tent;

28:27 [a]Literally *it*

world. But wisdom is never completely in our grasp. We are not so successful at finding what is spiritually hidden, even though it is infinitely more valuable than any mineral or gem.

28:20–28 Wisdom, the understanding of reality, belongs to God alone. Thus the essence of wisdom is submission to Him and obedience to His revealed principles (v. 28). In this, both Proverbs and Ecclesiastes agree.

28:28 Humans cannot fully explain existence. What they can do is live in submission to the Lord of existence. True religion has two branches: to do good, expressed here as the **fear of the Lord**, and to **depart from evil**.

29:2–25 Job remembers the position of honor he once enjoyed (see vv. 7–17, 21–25). He acknowledges that prosperity came from God watching over him (v. 2), not from his own efforts. When experiencing difficulties, we too should remember those times when God has blessed us.

LET GO OF THE PAST

Leslie E. Moser, Ph.D.

Letting go of things that are no more is not an all-or-nothing proposition, but in a very real way, we do have to let go of the past to reach forward to the future. We must lean forward, ready to move ahead even before we fully know what we are reaching out to embrace.

For each of us, the future is mysterious, but it will be a puzzle never solved unless we join with Paul in an attitude of forward movement and forward intent: "But one thing I do, forgetting those things which are behind and reaching forward to those things which are ahead, I press toward the goal for the prize of the upward call of God in Christ Jesus" (Phil. 3:13, 14). Thankfully, it is not necessary for us to clearly see the entire road ahead before we launch ourselves into the unseen and unknown. Our God goes before us and beside us (Ex. 14:19; Is. 52:12).

With that assurance, each of us—regardless of our age—must reach out to our world and to the people around us. Our capacity for reaching out must be halted only temporarily by our painful losses and the winds of change in our lives. Then we once again must offer the touch of a caring hand, which is always an expression of love. After all, love unexpressed is love lost. If ours was a serving profession, we must now reach out and serve in new and fresh ways. Never looking back is not a Christian virtue, and never looking forward is certain death for our Christian witness and to our wellness of mind and body. We learn from the past, but we must then look forward and reach out. That's what we are called to do. ✦

5 When the Almighty *was* yet with me,
When my children *were* around me;
6 When my steps were bathed with
cream,[a]
And the rock poured out rivers of oil
for me!

7 "When I went out to the gate by the
city,
When I took my seat in the open
square,
8 The young men saw me and hid,
And the aged arose *and* stood;
9 The princes refrained from talking,
And put *their* hand on their mouth;
10 The voice of nobles was hushed,
And their tongue stuck to the roof of
their mouth.
11 When the ear heard, then it blessed
me,
And when the eye saw, then it
approved me;

29:6 [a]Masoretic Text reads *wrath;* ancient versions and some Hebrew manuscripts read *cream* (compare 20:17).

29:7–10 gate by the city: Where people gathered for the elders to settle disputes (see Ruth 4:1, 2). **the aged arose**: Job's position of honor was much like a judge today. People stand and are quiet when he enters the court.

12 Because I delivered the poor who
cried out,
The fatherless and *the one who* had no
helper.
13 The blessing of a perishing *man* came
upon me,
And I caused the widow's heart to
sing for joy.
14 I put on righteousness, and it clothed
me;
My justice *was* like a robe and a
turban.
15 I *was* eyes to the blind,
And I *was* feet to the lame.
16 I *was* a father to the poor,
And I searched out the case *that* I did
not know.
17 I broke the fangs of the wicked,
And plucked the victim from his
teeth.

18 "Then I said, 'I shall die in my nest,
And multiply *my* days as the sand.
19 My root *is* spread out to the waters,
And the dew lies all night on my
branch.
20 My glory *is* fresh within me,
And my bow is renewed in my hand.'

21 "*Men* listened to me and waited,
And kept silence for my counsel.
22 After my words they did not speak
again,
And my speech settled on them *as*
dew.
23 They waited for me *as* for the rain,
And they opened their mouth wide *as*
for the spring rain.
24 *If* I mocked at them, they did not
believe *it*,
And the light of my countenance they
did not cast down.
25 I chose the way for them, and sat as
chief;

Blessed is the man who, having nothing to say, abstains from giving in words evidence of the fact.

George Eliot

So I dwelt as a king in the army,
As one *who* comforts mourners.

CHAPTER 30

"But now they mock at me, *men*
younger than I,
Whose fathers I disdained to put with
the dogs of my flock.
2 Indeed, what *profit* is the strength of
their hands to me?
Their vigor has perished.
3 *They are* gaunt from want and famine,
Fleeing late to the wilderness,
desolate and waste,
4 Who pluck mallow by the bushes,
And broom tree roots *for* their food.
5 They were driven out from among
men,
They shouted at them as *at* a thief.
6 *They had* to live in the clefts of the
valleys,
In caves of the earth and the rocks.
7 Among the bushes they brayed,
Under the nettles they nestled.
8 *They were* sons of fools,
Yes, sons of vile men;
They were scourged from the land.

9 "And now I am their taunting song;
Yes, I am their byword.
10 They abhor me, they keep far from
me;
They do not hesitate to spit in my
face.

29:12–17 While it may at first seem that Job is boasting, he is simply defending his character against the attack of his friends. Job's acts of kindness set the pace for Christians today. We are not called only to receive God's blessings but to share them with those around us. Christian love does not ignore the cries of the needy.

11 Because He has loosed my[a] bowstring
and afflicted me,
They have cast off restraint before me.
12 At *my* right *hand* the rabble arises;
They push away my feet,
And they raise against me their ways
of destruction.
13 They break up my path,
They promote my calamity;
They have no helper.
14 They come as broad breakers;
Under the ruinous storm they roll
along.
15 Terrors are turned upon me;
They pursue my honor as the wind,
And my prosperity has passed like a
cloud.

16 "And now my soul is poured out
because of my *plight;*
The days of affliction take hold of me.
17 My bones are pierced in me at night,
And my gnawing pains take no rest.
18 By great force my garment is
disfigured;
It binds me about as the collar of my
coat.
19 He has cast me into the mire,
And I have become like dust and
ashes.

20 "I cry out to You, but You do not
answer me;
I stand up, and You regard me.
21 *But* You have become cruel to me;
With the strength of Your hand You
oppose me.
22 You lift me up to the wind and cause
me to ride *on it;*
You spoil my success.
23 For I know *that* You will bring me *to*
death,
And *to* the house appointed for all
living.

24 "Surely He would not stretch out *His*
hand against a heap of ruins,
If they cry out when He destroys *it.*
25 Have I not wept for him who was in
trouble?
Has *not* my soul grieved for the poor?
26 But when I looked for good, evil
came *to me;*
And when I waited for light, then
came darkness.
27 My heart is in turmoil and cannot
rest;
Days of affliction confront me.
28 I go about mourning, but not in the
sun;
I stand up in the assembly *and* cry out
for help.
29 I am a brother of jackals,
And a companion of ostriches.
30 My skin grows black and falls from
me;
My bones burn with fever.
31 My harp is *turned* to mourning,
And my flute to the voice of those
who weep.

CHAPTER 31

"I have made a covenant with my eyes;
Why then should I look upon a
young woman?

30:11 [a]Following Masoretic Text, Syriac, and Targum; Septuagint and Vulgate read *His.*

30:11 Job compares his body to a bow. Because God had loosened the string, the disrespectful did not hesitate to attack him. This situation was the opposite of Job's expectations that his bow would be supple and strong (see 29:20).

30:20–31 I cry . . . to You: Job addresses God directly. Why has this terrible fall from honor occurred? Because of God, who refuses to answer. Job will not curse God nor give up his hope in God. But neither will he absolve God of responsibility.

31:1–40 Job swears that his fall from honor (chs. 29; 30) was not because of sin. Chapter 31 constitutes an oath of innocence that lists the sins which a person has not committed. Job's list is exemplary because he penetrates behind the act to the motives of the heart. He

2 For what *is* the allotment of God from above,
And the inheritance of the Almighty from on high?
3 *Is* it not destruction for the wicked,
And disaster for the workers of iniquity?
4 Does He not see my ways,
And count all my steps?

5 "If I have walked with falsehood,
Or if my foot has hastened to deceit,
6 Let me be weighed on honest scales,
That God may know my integrity.
7 If my step has turned from the way,
Or my heart walked after my eyes,
Or if any spot adheres to my hands,
8 *Then* let me sow, and another eat;
Yes, let my harvest be rooted out.

9 "If my heart has been enticed by a woman,
Or *if* I have lurked at my neighbor's door,
10 *Then* let my wife grind for another,
And let others bow down over her.
11 For that *would be* wickedness;
Yes, it *would be* iniquity *deserving of* judgment.
12 For that *would be* a fire *that* consumes to destruction,
And would root out all my increase.

13 "If I have despised the cause of my male or female servant
When they complained against me,
14 What then shall I do when God rises up?
When He punishes, how shall I answer Him?

15 Did not He who made me in the womb make them?
Did not the same One fashion us in the womb?

16 "If I have kept the poor from *their* desire,
Or caused the eyes of the widow to fail,
17 Or eaten my morsel by myself,
So that the fatherless could not eat of it
18 (But from my youth I reared him as a father,
And from my mother's womb I guided *the widow*[a]);
19 If I have seen anyone perish for lack of clothing,
Or any poor *man* without covering;
20 If his heart[a] has not blessed me,
And *if* he was *not* warmed with the fleece of my sheep;
21 If I have raised my hand against the fatherless,
When I saw I had help in the gate;
22 *Then* let my arm fall from my shoulder,
Let my arm be torn from the socket.
23 For destruction *from* God *is* a terror to me,
And because of His magnificence I cannot endure.

24 "If I have made gold my hope,
Or said to fine gold, '*You are* my confidence';
25 If I have rejoiced because my wealth *was* great,
And because my hand had gained much;
26 If I have observed the sun[a] when it shines,
Or the moon moving *in* brightness,

31:18 [a]Literally *her* (compare verse 16) 31:20 [a]Literally *loins* 31:26 [a]Literally *light*

is so confident as to specify four times what should happen to him if he has sinned (31:8, 10, 22, 40). It was assumed that such an oath of innocence obligated God to carry out the curses or to clear the one being charged.

31:21 help in the gate: Job had not oppressed the needy even when the legal system was on his side.

27 So that my heart has been secretly
enticed,
And my mouth has kissed my hand;
28 This also *would be* an iniquity
deserving of judgment,
For I would have denied God *who is*
above.

29 "If I have rejoiced at the destruction of
him who hated me,
Or lifted myself up when evil found
him
30 (Indeed I have not allowed my mouth
to sin
By asking for a curse on his soul);
31 If the men of my tent have not said,
'Who is there that has not been
satisfied with his meat?'
32 (*But* no sojourner had to lodge in the
street,
For I have opened my doors to the
traveler[a]);
33 If I have covered my transgressions as
Adam,
By hiding my iniquity in my bosom,
34 Because I feared the great multitude,
And dreaded the contempt of
families,
So that I kept silence
And did not go out of the door—
35 Oh, that I had one to hear me!
Here is my mark.
Oh, that the Almighty would answer
me,
That my Prosecutor had written a
book!
36 Surely I would carry it on my
shoulder,
And bind it on me *like* a crown;
37 I would declare to Him the number of
my steps;
Like a prince I would approach Him.

38 "If my land cries out against me,
And its furrows weep together;
39 If I have eaten its fruit[a] without
money,
Or caused its owners to lose their
lives;
40 *Then* let thistles grow instead of
wheat,
And weeds instead of barley."

The words of Job are ended.

CHAPTER 32

Elihu Contradicts Job's Friends

So these three men ceased answering
Job, because he *was* righteous in his own
eyes. 2Then the wrath of E·lī'hū, the son of
Bar'a·chel the Būz'īte, of the family of
Ram, was aroused against Job; his wrath
was aroused because he justified himself
rather than God. 3Also against his three
friends his wrath was aroused, because
they had found no answer, and *yet* had
condemned Job.
4Now because they *were* years older

31:32 [a]Following Septuagint, Syriac, Targum, and Vulgate; Masoretic Text reads *road.* 31:39 [a]Literally *its strength*

31:35 Job's **mark** is his signature; it makes his oath of innocence an official document. He begs **the Almighty** to respond to his oath. God may either carry out the curses or write a book to confirm Job's innocence.

32:1—37:24 Job's oath of innocence has left his friends speechless. They wait in terror for God to answer. But God remains silent. Elihu speaks in an attempt to break the impasse. He is horrified at Job's presumption in questioning God's justice, but he is also incensed at the comforters' simplistic answers. His four speeches offer some other possible reasons for suffering than merely punishment for sin. Suffering may show a person a hidden error or keep him from taking a wrong course of action. As an instrument for training, suffering may be an expression of God's mercy.

32:3 In ancient legal practice finding no **answer** meant Job's friends must concede that he was right about his suffering.

32:4, 5 Customarily, only older men spoke. Others could speak only when the elders recognized them. Elihu **waited** until he felt they had conceded by not speaking (see v. 16).

than he, E·lī'hū had waited to speak to
Job.[a] 5When E·lī'hū saw that *there was* no
answer in the mouth of these three men,
his wrath was aroused.
6So E·lī'hū, the son of Bar'a·chel the
Būz'īte, answered and said:

"I *am* young in years, and you *are* very old;
Therefore I was afraid,
And dared not declare my opinion to you.
7 I said, 'Age[a] should speak,
And multitude of years should teach wisdom.'
8 But *there is* a spirit in man,
And the breath of the Almighty gives him understanding.
9 Great men[a] are not *always* wise,
Nor do the aged *always* understand justice.

10 "Therefore I say, 'Listen to me,
I also will declare my opinion.'
11 Indeed I waited for your words,
I listened to your reasonings, while you searched out what to say.
12 I paid close attention to you;
And surely not one of you convinced Job,
Or answered his words—
13 Lest you say,
'We have found wisdom';
God will vanquish him, not man.

32:4 [a]Vulgate reads *till Job had spoken.* 32:7 [a]Literally *Days,* that is, years 32:9 [a]Or *Men of many years*

14 Now he has not directed *his* words against me;
So I will not answer him with your words.

15 "They are dismayed and answer no more;
Words escape them.
16 And I have waited, because they did not speak,
Because they stood still *and* answered no more.
17 I also will answer my part,
I too will declare my opinion.
18 For I am full of words;
The spirit within me compels me.
19 Indeed my belly *is* like wine *that* has no vent;
It is ready to burst like new wineskins.
20 I will speak, that I may find relief;
I must open my lips and answer.
21 Let me not, I pray, show partiality to anyone;
Nor let me flatter any man.
22 For I do not know how to flatter,
Else my Maker would soon take me away.

CHAPTER 33

Elihu Contradicts Job

"But please, Job, hear my speech,
And listen to all my words.
2 Now, I open my mouth;
My tongue speaks in my mouth.
3 My words *come* from my upright heart;

32:6 the Buzite: Elihu was from Buz; the location is unknown.

32:8 The **breath of the Almighty**, the Spirit of God, gives insight to a man. Elihu's wisdom can be trusted because it comes from God (see 1 Kin. 3:9, 12; 4:29; see also Jesus' NT promise in John 16:12–15).

32:9 In our dealings with younger generations, we need to acknowledge that, despite our experience, we do not have all the answers. While we should expect young people to give us due respect, we ought also to listen to them, realizing that their perspective may provide valid insights.

33:1–33 Unlike Job's three friends, Elihu confronts Job about his complaints against God rather than for any suspected past sins. Elihu defends God's honor by explaining how He uses suffering to direct people.

My lips utter pure knowledge.
4 The Spirit of God has made me,
And the breath of the Almighty gives me life.
5 If you can answer me,
Set *your words* in order before me;
Take your stand.
6 Truly I *am* as your spokesman[a] before God;
I also have been formed out of clay.
7 Surely no fear of me will terrify you,
Nor will my hand be heavy on you.

8 "Surely you have spoken in my hearing,
And I have heard the sound of *your* words, *saying,*
9 'I *am* pure, without transgression;
I *am* innocent, and *there is* no iniquity in me.
10 Yet He finds occasions against me,
He counts me as His enemy;
11 He puts my feet in the stocks,
He watches all my paths.'

12 "Look, *in* this you are not righteous.
I will answer you,
For God is greater than man.
13 Why do you contend with Him?
For He does not give an accounting of any of His words.
14 For God may speak in one way, or in another,
Yet man does not perceive it.
15 In a dream, in a vision of the night,
When deep sleep falls upon men,
While slumbering on their beds,
16 Then He opens the ears of men,
And seals their instruction.
17 In order to turn man *from his* deed,
And conceal pride from man,
18 He keeps back his soul from the Pit,
And his life from perishing by the sword.

19 "*Man* is also chastened with pain on his bed,
And with strong *pain* in many of his bones,
20 So that his life abhors bread,
And his soul succulent food.
21 His flesh wastes away from sight,
And his bones stick out *which once* were not seen.
22 Yes, his soul draws near the Pit,
And his life to the executioners.

23 "If there is a messenger for him,
A mediator, one among a thousand,
To show man His uprightness,
24 Then He is gracious to him, and says,
'Deliver him from going down to the Pit;
I have found a ransom';
25 His flesh shall be young like a child's,
He shall return to the days of his youth.
26 He shall pray to God, and He will delight in him,
He shall see His face with joy,
For He restores to man His righteousness.
27 Then he looks at men and says,
'I have sinned, and perverted *what was* right,
And it did not profit me.'
28 He will redeem his[a] soul from going down to the Pit,
And his[a] life shall see the light.

33:6 [a]Literally *as your mouth* 33:28 [a]Or *my* (Kethib)

33:15–18 Dreams were not very important in Israel, but occasionally God spoke through them (see Gen. 20:3; 28:11–16). Elihu may be telling Job that his troubling dreams (7:14) were God's attempts to teach him.

33:23, 24 A mediator works for the restoration of those who have strayed from God. He tells them what is right and what **ransom** is necessary so they will not be judged. The NT reveals that our Mediator is the Lord Jesus Christ (1 Tim. 2:5, 6).

29 "Behold, God works all these *things,*
Twice, *in fact,* three *times* with a man,
30 To bring back his soul from the Pit,
That he may be enlightened with the light of life.

31 "Give ear, Job, listen to me;
Hold your peace, and I will speak.
32 If you have anything to say, answer me;
Speak, for I desire to justify you.
33 If not, listen to me;
Hold your peace, and I will teach you wisdom."

CHAPTER 34

Elihu Proclaims God's Justice

Elihu further answered and said:

2 "Hear my words, you wise *men;*
Give ear to me, you who have knowledge.
3 For the ear tests words
As the palate tastes food.
4 Let us choose justice for ourselves;
Let us know among ourselves what *is* good.

5 "For Job has said, 'I am righteous,
But God has taken away my justice;
6 Should I lie concerning my right?
My wound *is* incurable, *though I am* without transgression.'
7 What man *is* like Job,
Who drinks scorn like water,
8 Who goes in company with the workers of iniquity,
And walks with wicked men?
9 For he has said, 'It profits a man nothing
That he should delight in God.'

10 "Therefore listen to me, you men of understanding:
Far be it from God *to do* wickedness,
And *from* the Almighty to *commit* iniquity.
11 For He repays man *according to* his work,
And makes man to find a reward according to *his* way.
12 Surely God will never do wickedly,
Nor will the Almighty pervert justice.
13 Who gave Him charge over the earth?
Or who appointed *Him over* the whole world?
14 If He should set His heart on it,
If He should gather to Himself His Spirit and His breath,
15 All flesh would perish together,
And man would return to dust.

16 "If *you have* understanding, hear this;
Listen to the sound of my words:
17 Should one who hates justice govern?
Will you condemn *Him who is* most just?
18 *Is it fitting* to say to a king, *'You are* worthless,'
And to nobles, *'You are* wicked'?
19 Yet He is not partial to princes,
Nor does He regard the rich more than the poor;
For they *are* all the work of His hands.
20 In a moment they die, in the middle of the night;
The people are shaken and pass away;
The mighty are taken away without a hand.

33:29, 30 Twice . . . three times: God does not try just once to redeem us. No matter how desperate our situation, He is working to bring us to Himself. God's justice will bring judgment, but not before repeated expressions of love (Hos. 11:3, 4; Matt. 11:28–30).

34:10–12 Although we may not understand God's ways, we can be certain that He is always righteous and just.

34:19–30 Elihu insists that the sovereign God deals justly. He does not favor the **rich** over the **poor** (v. 19). Workers of **iniquity** cannot hide from His **judgment** (v. 22, 23). He **strikes** only when we turn **back from Him** (vv. 26, 27).

21 "For His eyes *are* on the ways of man,
And He sees all his steps.
22 There is no darkness nor shadow of death
Where the workers of iniquity may hide themselves.
23 For He need not further consider a man,
That he should go before God in judgment.
24 He breaks in pieces mighty men without inquiry,
And sets others in their place.
25 Therefore He knows their works;
He overthrows *them* in the night,
And they are crushed.
26 He strikes them as wicked *men*
In the open sight of others,
27 Because they turned back from Him,
And would not consider any of His ways,
28 So that they caused the cry of the poor to come to Him;
For He hears the cry of the afflicted.
29 When He gives quietness, who then can make trouble?
And when He hides *His* face, who then can see Him,
Whether *it is* against a nation or a man alone?—
30 That the hypocrite should not reign,
Lest the people be ensnared.

31 "For has *anyone* said to God,
'I have borne *chastening;*
I will offend no more;
32 Teach me *what* I do not see;
If I have done iniquity, I will do no more'?
33 Should He repay *it* according to your *terms,*
Just because you disavow it?
You must choose, and not I;
Therefore speak what you know.

34 "Men of understanding say to me,
Wise men who listen to me:
35 'Job speaks without knowledge,
His words *are* without wisdom.'
36 Oh, that Job were tried to the utmost,
Because *his* answers *are like* those of wicked men!
37 For he adds rebellion to his sin;
He claps *his hands* among us,
And multiplies his words against God."

CHAPTER 35

Elihu Condemns Self-Righteousness

Moreover E·lī′hū answered and said:

2 "Do you think this is right?
Do you say,
'My righteousness is more than God's'?
3 For you say,
'What advantage will it be to You?
What profit shall I have, more than *if* I had sinned?'

4 "I will answer you,
And your companions with you.
5 Look to the heavens and see;
And behold the clouds—
They are higher than you.
6 If you sin, what do you accomplish against Him?

34:31–33 Elihu, by questioning if **anyone** has sought God's instruction, claims that Job has not spoken sincerely. Rather, Job has challenged God to prove that he has been wrong. In v. 33 Elihu warns Job that we cannot command God to handle our situation on our **terms**.

35:1–16 My righteousness: Elihu says that Job cannot obligate God by demanding that He acknowledge Job's past righteous acts. In comparison to God, "all our righteousnesses are like filthy rags" (Is. 64:6). See Jesus' statement in Luke 17:10.

35:6–8 Elihu incorrectly maintains that Job's behavior doesn't affect God, one way or the other. Yet we know that God is grieved when we sin (Gen. 6:6; Eph. 4:30) and He is pleased when we obey (1:8; 2 Cor. 9:7).

Or, *if* your transgressions are
multiplied, what do you do to
Him?
7 If you are righteous, what do you
give Him?
Or what does He receive from your
hand?
8 Your wickedness affects a man such
as you,
And your righteousness a son of man.

9 "Because of the multitude of
oppressions they cry out;
They cry out for help because of the
arm of the mighty.
10 But no one says, 'Where *is* God my
Maker,
Who gives songs in the night,
11 Who teaches us more than the beasts
of the earth,
And makes us wiser than the birds of
heaven?'
12 There they cry out, but He does not
answer,
Because of the pride of evil men.
13 Surely God will not listen to empty
talk,
Nor will the Almighty regard it.
14 Although you say you do not see
Him,
Yet justice *is* before Him, and you
must wait for Him.
15 And now, because He has not pun-
ished in His anger,
Nor taken much notice of folly,
16 Therefore Job opens his mouth in
vain;
He multiplies words without
knowledge."

CHAPTER 36

Elihu Proclaims God's Goodness

Elihu also proceeded and said:

2 "Bear with me a little, and I will show
you
That *there are* yet words to speak on
God's behalf.
3 I will fetch my knowledge from afar;
I will ascribe righteousness to my
Maker.
4 For truly my words *are* not false;
One who is perfect in knowledge *is*
with you.

5 "Behold, God *is* mighty, but despises
no one;
He is mighty in strength of
understanding.
6 He does not preserve the life of the
wicked,
But gives justice to the oppressed.
7 He does not withdraw His eyes from
the righteous;
But *they are* on the throne with kings,
For He has seated them forever,
And they are exalted.
8 And if *they are* bound in fetters,
Held in the cords of affliction,
9 Then He tells them their work and
their transgressions—
That they have acted defiantly.
10 He also opens their ear to instruction,
And commands that they turn from
iniquity.
11 If they obey and serve *Him*,
They shall spend their days in
prosperity,
And their years in pleasures.

God is good. Our retirement years can be our most productive by drawing on our past experiences, gifts, and talents, and His faithful guidance.
Barbara Hanrahan

36:1—37:24 The Sovereign disciplines everyone, even the mightiest. This speech prepares the way for what follows as it hymns the transcendent greatness of God.

36:7–12 God knows the **righteous** and rewards them. But He disciplines them if they have acted **defiantly**. Elihu had already charged Job with rebellion (34:34–37).

12 But if they do not obey,
They shall perish by the sword,
And they shall die without
knowledge.[a]
13 "But the hypocrites in heart store up
wrath;
They do not cry for help when He
binds them.
14 They die in youth,
And their life *ends* among the
perverted persons.[a]
15 He delivers the poor in their
affliction,
And opens their ears in oppression.

16 "Indeed He would have brought you
out of dire distress,
Into a broad place where *there is* no
restraint;
And what is set on your table *would
be* full of richness.
17 But you are filled with the judgment
due the wicked;
Judgment and justice take hold *of
you.*
18 Because *there is* wrath, *beware* lest He
take you away with *one* blow;
For a large ransom would not help
you avoid *it.*
19 Will your riches,
Or all the mighty forces,
Keep you from distress?
20 Do not desire the night,
When people are cut off in their place.
21 Take heed, do not turn to iniquity,
For you have chosen this rather than
affliction.

22 "Behold, God is exalted by His power;
Who teaches like Him?
23 Who has assigned Him His way,
Or who has said, 'You have done
wrong'?

Elihu Proclaims God's Majesty

24 "Remember to magnify His work,
Of which men have sung.
25 Everyone has seen it;
Man looks on *it* from afar.

26 "Behold, God *is* great, and we do not
know *Him;*
Nor can the number of His years *be*
discovered.
27 For He draws up drops of water,
Which distill as rain from the mist,
28 Which the clouds drop down
And pour abundantly on man.
29 Indeed, can *anyone* understand the
spreading of clouds,
The thunder from His canopy?
30 Look, He scatters His light upon it,
And covers the depths of the sea.
31 For by these He judges the peoples;
He gives food in abundance.
32 He covers *His* hands with lightning,
And commands it to strike.
33 His thunder declares it,
The cattle also, concerning the rising
storm.

CHAPTER 37

"At this also my heart trembles,

36:12 [a]Masoretic Text reads *as one without knowledge.*
36:14 [a]Hebrew *qedeshim,* that is, those practicing sodomy and prostitution in religious rituals

36:13–15 when He binds: God's punishment is for discipline, not destruction. But those who resist His discipline **store up wrath** for themselves. **opens their ears**: God causes those who respond to Him to hear good news of deliverance from their oppression.

36:16–21 Instead of asking to die (v. 20; see 3:11), Job should have asked what he could learn from his affliction. A good point, but one manifesting little compassion in Elihu.

36:24 The proper attitude toward God is to **magnify His work**, not to challenge His justice.

36:26—37:18 God's might is manifested in the storm. He **causes** them to come, and He can adapt them to our needs (37:13). Who are we to challenge the wisdom of Him who does such **wondrous works** (37:14–16), and whose works are so far beyond our comprehension (36:29; 37:5)?

And leaps from its place.
2 Hear attentively the thunder of His voice,
And the rumbling *that* comes from His mouth.
3 He sends it forth under the whole heaven,
His lightning to the ends of the earth.
4 After it a voice roars;
He thunders with His majestic voice,
And He does not restrain them when His voice is heard.
5 God thunders marvelously with His voice;
He does great things which we cannot comprehend.
6 For He says to the snow, 'Fall *on* the earth';
Likewise to the gentle rain and the heavy rain of His strength.
7 He seals the hand of every man,
That all men may know His work.
8 The beasts go into dens,
And remain in their lairs.
9 From the chamber *of the south* comes the whirlwind,
And cold from the scattering winds *of the north.*
10 By the breath of God ice is given,
And the broad waters are frozen.
11 Also with moisture He saturates the thick clouds;
He scatters His bright clouds.
12 And they swirl about, being turned by His guidance,
That they may do whatever He commands them
On the face of the whole earth.[a]
13 He causes it to come,
Whether for correction,
Or for His land,
Or for mercy.

14 "Listen to this, O Job;
Stand still and consider the wondrous works of God.
15 Do you know when God dispatches them,
And causes the light of His cloud to shine?
16 Do you know how the clouds are balanced,
Those wondrous works of Him who is perfect in knowledge?
17 Why *are* your garments hot,
When He quiets the earth by the south *wind?*
18 With Him, have you spread out the skies,
Strong as a cast metal mirror?

19 "Teach us what we should say to Him,
For we can prepare nothing because of the darkness.
20 Should He be told that I *wish to* speak?
If a man were to speak, surely he would be swallowed up.
21 Even now *men* cannot look at the light *when it is* bright in the skies,
When the wind has passed and cleared them.
22 He comes from the north *as* golden *splendor;*
With God *is* awesome majesty.
23 *As for* the Almighty, we cannot find Him;
He is excellent in power,
In judgment and abundant justice;
He does not oppress.
24 Therefore men fear Him;
He shows no partiality to any *who are* wise of heart."

37:12 [a]Literally *the world of the earth*

37:6, 7 He seals the hand: Men cease their work in the face of God's elements, snow and rain.

37:23, 24 Elihu's conclusion parallels the conclusion to the hymn of wisdom (28:28). Since we cannot understand all that God does in nature, the wise thing is to submit to Him and to consider carefully "what we should say to Him" (v. 19).

CHAPTER 38

The LORD Reveals His Omnipotence to Job

Then the LORD answered Job out of the
whirlwind, and said:

2 "Who *is* this who darkens counsel
By words without knowledge?
3 Now prepare yourself like a man;
I will question you, and you shall
answer Me.

4 "Where were you when I laid the
foundations of the earth?
Tell *Me,* if you have understanding.
5 Who determined its measurements?
Surely you know!
Or who stretched the line upon it?
6 To what were its foundations
fastened?
Or who laid its cornerstone,
7 When the morning stars sang
together,
And all the sons of God shouted for
joy?

8 "Or *who* shut in the sea with doors,
When it burst forth *and* issued from
the womb;
9 When I made the clouds its garment,
And thick darkness its swaddling
band;
10 When I fixed My limit for it,
And set bars and doors;
11 When I said,
'This far you may come, but no
farther,
And here your proud waves must
stop!'

12 "Have you commanded the morning
since your days *began,*
And caused the dawn to know its
place,
13 That it might take hold of the ends of
the earth,
And the wicked be shaken out of it?
14 It takes on form like clay *under* a seal,
And stands out like a garment.
15 From the wicked their light is
withheld,
And the upraised arm is broken.

16 "Have you entered the springs of the
sea?
Or have you walked in search of the
depths?
17 Have the gates of death been revealed
to you?
Or have you seen the doors of the
shadow of death?
18 Have you comprehended the breadth
of the earth?
Tell *Me,* if you know all this.

19 "Where *is* the way *to* the dwelling of
light?
And darkness, where *is* its place,
20 That you may take it to its territory,
That you may know the paths *to* its
home?
21 Do you know *it,* because you were
born then,
Or *because* the number of your days *is*
great?

38:1—42:6 God speaks out of concern for Job, not because Job's demand has forced Him. Everyone is startled that God speaks to a mere man. He ignores Job's complaints and does not reprove him. Using rhetorical questions, God teaches Job that he cannot dispute with the Almighty. At the same time, He gives Job a word of insight and hope.

38:1 the LORD answered: God revealed Himself. The **whirlwind** may have been the storm that Elihu had seen developing in the north (37:22).

38:7 sons of God: Angels.

38:18–30 Job is challenged to explain the size of the **earth** (v. 18), the origin of **light** and **darkness** (vv. 19–21), the functions of **snow, hail**, and **wind** (vv. 22–24). Verses 25–28 show the providence of God in giving **water** in streams and rain on the land even where **no man** lives.

22 "Have you entered the treasury of snow,
Or have you seen the treasury of hail,
23 Which I have reserved for the time of trouble,
For the day of battle and war?
24 By what way is light diffused,
Or the east wind scattered over the earth?

25 "Who has divided a channel for the overflowing *water,*
Or a path for the thunderbolt,
26 To cause it to rain on a land *where there is* no one,
A wilderness in which *there is* no man;
27 To satisfy the desolate waste,
And cause to spring forth the growth of tender grass?
28 Has the rain a father?
Or who has begotten the drops of dew?
29 From whose womb comes the ice?
And the frost of heaven, who gives it birth?
30 The waters harden like stone,
And the surface of the deep is frozen.

31 "Can you bind the cluster of the Plēi′a·dēs,
Or loose the belt of Ō·rī′on?
32 Can you bring out Maz′za·roth[a] in its season?
Or can you guide the Great Bear with its cubs?
33 Do you know the ordinances of the heavens?
Can you set their dominion over the earth?

34 "Can you lift up your voice to the clouds,
That an abundance of water may cover you?
35 Can you send out lightnings, that they may go,
And say to you, 'Here we *are!*'?
36 Who has put wisdom in the mind?[a]
Or who has given understanding to the heart?
37 Who can number the clouds by wisdom?
Or who can pour out the bottles of heaven,
38 When the dust hardens in clumps,
And the clods cling together?

39 "Can you hunt the prey for the lion,
Or satisfy the appetite of the young lions,
40 When they crouch in *their* dens,
Or lurk in their lairs to lie in wait?
41 Who provides food for the raven,
When its young ones cry to God,
And wander about for lack of food?

CHAPTER 39

"Do you know the time when the wild mountain goats bear young?
Or can you mark when the deer gives birth?
2 Can you number the months *that* they fulfill?
Or do you know the time when they bear young?
3 They bow down,
They bring forth their young,
They deliver their offspring.[a]
4 Their young ones are healthy,
They grow strong with grain;
They depart and do not return to them.

5 "Who set the wild donkey free?
Who loosed the bonds of the onager,

38:32 [a]Literally *Constellations* 38:36 [a]Literally *inward parts* 39:3 [a]Literally *pangs,* figurative of offspring

38:39—39:30 God illustrates His sovereignty with pictures of His care for wild animals. He governs the world for the well-being of all creatures: the lion and the **raven** (38:39–41).

> Can a mortal ask questions which God finds unanswerable? Quite easily, I should think. All nonsense questions are unanswerable. How many hours are there in a mile? Is yellow square or round? Probably half the questions we ask—half our great theological and metaphysical problems—are like that.
> C. S. Lewis

6 Whose home I have made the wilderness,
And the barren land his dwelling?
7 He scorns the tumult of the city;
He does not heed the shouts of the driver.
8 The range of the mountains *is* his pasture,
And he searches after every green thing.

9 "Will the wild ox be willing to serve you?
Will he bed by your manger?
10 Can you bind the wild ox in the furrow with ropes?
Or will he plow the valleys behind you?
11 Will you trust him because his strength *is* great?
Or will you leave your labor to him?
12 Will you trust him to bring home your grain,
And gather it to your threshing floor?

13 "The wings of the ostrich wave proudly,
But are her wings and pinions *like the* kindly stork's?
14 For she leaves her eggs on the ground,
And warms them in the dust;
15 She forgets that a foot may crush them,
Or that a wild beast may break them.
16 She treats her young harshly, as though *they were* not hers;
Her labor is in vain, without concern,
17 Because God deprived her of wisdom,
And did not endow her with understanding.
18 When she lifts herself on high,
She scorns the horse and its rider.

19 "Have you given the horse strength?
Have you clothed his neck with thunder?[a]
20 Can you frighten him like a locust?
His majestic snorting strikes terror.
21 He paws in the valley, and rejoices in *his* strength;
He gallops into the clash of arms.
22 He mocks at fear, and is not frightened;
Nor does he turn back from the sword.
23 The quiver rattles against him,
The glittering spear and javelin.
24 He devours the distance with fierceness and rage;
Nor does he come to a halt because the trumpet *has* sounded.
25 At *the blast of* the trumpet he says, 'Aha!'
He smells the battle from afar,
The thunder of captains and shouting.

26 "Does the hawk fly by your wisdom,
And spread its wings toward the south?
27 Does the eagle mount up at your command,
And make its nest on high?

39:19 [a]Or *a mane*

39:5–8 The wild donkey is also called an **onager**.
39:9–12 The wild ox cannot be tamed and harnessed.

28 On the rock it dwells and resides,
On the crag of the rock and the stronghold.
29 From there it spies out the prey;
Its eyes observe from afar.
30 Its young ones suck up blood;
And where the slain *are,* there it *is.*"

CHAPTER 40

Moreover the LORD answered Job, and said:

2 "Shall the one who contends with the Almighty correct *Him?*
He who rebukes God, let him answer it."

Job's Response to God

3Then Job answered the LORD and said:

4 "Behold, I am vile;
What shall I answer You?
I lay my hand over my mouth.
5 Once I have spoken, but I will not answer;
Yes, twice, but I will proceed no further."

God's Challenge to Job

6Then the LORD answered Job out of the whirlwind, and said:

7 "Now prepare yourself like a man;
I will question you, and you shall answer Me:

> We cannot avoid suffering, but we can determine our response to it.
> Billy Graham

8 "Would you indeed annul My judgment?
Would you condemn Me that you may be justified?
9 Have you an arm like God?
Or can you thunder with a voice like His?
10 Then adorn yourself *with* majesty and splendor,
And array yourself with glory and beauty.
11 Disperse the rage of your wrath;
Look on everyone *who is* proud, and humble him.
12 Look on everyone *who is* proud, *and* bring him low;
Tread down the wicked in their place.
13 Hide them in the dust together,
Bind their faces in hidden *darkness.*
14 Then I will also confess to you
That your own right hand can save you.

15 "Look now at the behemoth,[a] which I made *along* with you;
He eats grass like an ox.
16 See now, his strength *is* in his hips,
And his power *is* in his stomach muscles.
17 He moves his tail like a cedar;

40:15 [a]A large animal, exact identity unknown

40:2 Can Job correct the **Almighty**? His complaints implied that God needed correction. Since God has responded to Job's challenge, Job must answer God or lose his claim to innocence. But, if he continues to argue, he will risk being rebuked by God.

40:3–5 Job's brief answer indicates that he has nothing to add to his claim of innocence. God's questions, not His power (see 9:12, 14, 15), have ended Job's arguments.

40:5 While Job holds back from saying more, he will not give up his position which he has stated **once**, and even **twice**. God must continue the dialogue in order to convince Job completely.

40:6—41:34 After an opening challenge (40:6–14), God uses two great animals, the behemoth (40:15–24) and Leviathan (41:1–34), to symbolize His total control of creation and Job's complete helplessness.

The sinews of his thighs are tightly
knit.
18 His bones *are like* beams of bronze,
His ribs like bars of iron.
19 He *is* the first of the ways of God;
Only He who made him can bring
near His sword.
20 Surely the mountains yield food for
him,
And all the beasts of the field play
there.
21 He lies under the lotus trees,
In a covert of reeds and marsh.
22 The lotus trees cover him *with* their
shade;
The willows by the brook surround
him.
23 Indeed the river may rage,
Yet he is not disturbed;
He is confident, though the Jordan
gushes into his mouth,
24 *Though* he takes it in his eyes,
Or one pierces *his* nose with a snare.

CHAPTER 41

"Can you draw out Le·vī′a·than[a] with a
hook,
Or *snare* his tongue with a line *which*
you lower?
2 Can you put a reed through his nose,
Or pierce his jaw with a hook?
3 Will he make many supplications to
you?
Will he speak softly to you?
4 Will he make a covenant with you?
Will you take him as a servant
forever?
5 Will you play with him as *with* a bird,
Or will you leash him for your
maidens?
6 Will *your* companions make a
banquet[a] of him?
Will they apportion him among the
merchants?
7 Can you fill his skin with harpoons,
Or his head with fishing spears?
8 Lay your hand on him;
Remember the battle—
Never do it again!
9 Indeed, *any* hope of *overcoming* him is
false;
Shall *one not* be overwhelmed at the
sight of him?
10 No one *is so* fierce that he would dare
stir him up.
Who then is able to stand against Me?
11 Who has preceded Me, that I should
pay *him?*
Everything under heaven is Mine.

12 "I will not conceal[a] his limbs,
His mighty power, or his graceful
proportions.
13 Who can remove his outer coat?
Who can approach *him* with a double
bridle?
14 Who can open the doors of his face,
With his terrible teeth all around?

41:1 [a]A large sea creature, exact identity unknown
41:6 [a]Or *bargain over him* 41:12 [a]Literally *keep silent about*

40:19 first of the ways of God: The behemoth (perhaps "hippopotamus") is the crown of the animal creation, but he is created by God and therefore under God's control. Likewise God has created everything in the universe; therefore, He can control all the forces of chaos and injustice.

41:1 Leviathan: Here, a large sea creature, perhaps a crocodile (see Ps. 3:8; 104:24–26 and note). In ancient Near Eastern mythology, the chaos monster which God defeated at creation was also called Leviathan. The OT occasionally uses this image without endorsing the myth (see 26:13; see also notes on Ps. 74:13–17; Is. 27:1).

41:10, 11 Who . . . is able to stand? God confronts Job about the audacity of arguing his case directly with the Almighty, when he cannot master the created world. **Who has preceded?** Who has put Me under obligation to him? I have created **everything**.

41:14 doors of his face: His jaws.

15 *His* rows of scales are *his* pride,
Shut up tightly *as with* a seal;
16 One is so near another
That no air can come between them;
17 They are joined one to another,
They stick together and cannot be
parted.
18 His sneezings flash forth light,
And his eyes *are* like the eyelids of
the morning.
19 Out of his mouth go burning lights;
Sparks of fire shoot out.
20 Smoke goes out of his nostrils,
As *from* a boiling pot and burning
rushes.
21 His breath kindles coals,
And a flame goes out of his mouth.
22 Strength dwells in his neck,
And sorrow dances before him.
23 The folds of his flesh are joined
together;
They are firm on him and cannot be
moved.
24 His heart is as hard as stone,
Even as hard as the lower *millstone.*
25 When he raises himself up, the
mighty are afraid;
Because of his crashings they are
beside[a] themselves.
26 *Though* the sword reaches him, it
cannot avail;
Nor does spear, dart, or javelin.
27 He regards iron as straw,
And bronze as rotten wood.
28 The arrow cannot make him flee;
Slingstones become like stubble to
him.

41:25 [a]Or *purify themselves*

29 Darts are regarded as straw;
He laughs at the threat of javelins.
30 His undersides *are* like sharp
potsherds;
He spreads pointed *marks* in the mire.
31 He makes the deep boil like a pot;
He makes the sea like a pot of
ointment.
32 He leaves a shining wake behind him;
One would think the deep had white
hair.
33 On earth there is nothing like him,
Which is made without fear.
34 He beholds every high *thing;*
He *is* king over all the children of
pride."

CHAPTER 42

Job's Repentance and Restoration

Then Job answered the LORD and said:

2 "I know that You can do everything,
And that no purpose *of Yours* can be
withheld from You.
3 *You asked,* 'Who *is* this who hides
counsel without knowledge?'
Therefore I have uttered what I did
not understand,
Things too wonderful for me, which I
did not know.
4 Listen, please, and let me speak;
You said, 'I will question you, and you
shall answer Me.'

5 "I have heard of You by the hearing of
the ear,
But now my eye sees You.

41:33, 34 Leviathan as **king** fears no human. If none can control him, then none can successfully challenge God, the Creator of Leviathan.

42:1–6 Job accepts God's opening accusation (38:2) and confesses, I have **uttered what I did not understand**. He had not sinned in his complaints to God, but he came close to the sin of pride. When made aware of this wrong attitude, Job humbled himself before God.

42:5, 6 Job had **heard** of God through the tradition, but now his deepest longing (19:25–27), to see his Redeemer, has been fulfilled. All of our pressing complaints evaporate in the vision of God. Job repents, but not of the imaginary sins charged against him by his comforters. Rather he repents of demanding that God justify His actions. The change in

GLORY IN PAIN
Billy Graham

Pain can drive us in two directions. Either it can make us curse God for allowing our misery or it can draw us to Him for relief. There is the expression, "God helps those who help themselves." I think a saying like "God helps us when we are helpless" is infinitely more comforting (2 Cor. 12:10).

Sickness teaches us that activity is not the only way to serve God. "They also serve who only stand and wait." Man seems to judge active duty, but God shows us that He is also glorified through suffering.

Jesus said, "Whatever I tell you in the dark, speak in the light" (Matt. 10:27). What does this mean to us? It means be quiet, listen to God when things are their worst, and you will be able to talk to others when you are better.

"To resist God's hand in our lives is to miss one of the greatest spiritual blessings."

To resist and resist God's hand in our lives is to miss one of the greatest spiritual blessings we Christians can enjoy this side of heaven. Though Job suffered as few others have, he never lost sight of God's presence with Him in the midst of suffering. He emerged victorious on the other side of sorrow because he never allowed resentment to cloud his relationship with God. ✦

6 Therefore I abhor *myself*,
And repent in dust and ashes."

[7]And so it was, after the LORD had spo-
ken these words to Job, that the LORD said
to E·lī'phaz the Tē'man·īte, "My wrath is
aroused against you and your two friends,
for you have not spoken of Me *what is*
right, as My servant Job *has.* [8]Now there-
fore, take for yourselves seven bulls and
seven rams, go to My servant Job, and offer
up for yourselves a burnt offering; and My
servant Job shall pray for you. For I will ac-
cept him, lest I deal with you *according to
your* folly; because you have not spoken of
Me *what is* right, as My servant Job *has.*"
[9]So E·lī'phaz the Tē'man·īte and Bil'dad
the Shū'hīte *and* Zō'phar the Nā'a·ma-
thīte went and did as the LORD com-
manded them; for the LORD had accepted
Job. [10]And the LORD restored Job's losses[a]

42:10 [a]Literally *Job's captivity,* that is, what was captured from Job

Job's attitude reflects a discovery made daily by maturing Christians: The more we learn about the greatness of God, the less we think of ourselves.

42:8, 9 seven bulls . . . seven rams: A very expensive offering. **I will accept him**: The effectiveness of Job's intercession demonstrates his restoration to God's favor. God accepts genuine questioning more than we often do because we, like the comforters, do not want our simple systems upset.

when he prayed for his friends. Indeed the
LORD gave Job twice as much as he had be-
fore. 11 Then all his brothers, all his sisters,
and all those who had been his acquain-
tances before, came to him and ate food
with him in his house; and they consoled
him and comforted him for all the adver-
sity that the LORD had brought upon him.
Each one gave him a piece of silver and
each a ring of gold.
12 Now the LORD blessed the latter *days* of
Job more than his beginning; for he had
fourteen thousand sheep, six thousand
camels, one thousand yoke of oxen, and
one thousand female donkeys. 13 He also
had seven sons and three daughters. 14 And
he called the name of the first Je·mī′mah,
the name of the second Ke·zī′ah, and the
name of the third Ker′en-Hap′puch. 15 In all
the land were found no women *so* beauti-
ful as the daughters of Job; and their father
gave them an inheritance among their
brothers.
16 After this Job lived one hundred and
forty years, and saw his children and
grandchildren *for* four generations. 17 So Job
died, old and full of days.

42:15 It was unusual in patriarchal society for daughters to receive an **inheritance** (see Num. 27:8).

42:16 A lifetime exceeding **one hundred and forty years** was long even during the patriarchal period. It is more than double that indicated in the psalms (see Ps. 90:10). That Job died **full of days** is evidence of God's favor on him.

✦Psalms✦

David, known as "the sweet psalmist of Israel," wrote most of this book, but other authors contributed as well. Solomon wrote Psalm 72 and 127, and Moses wrote Psalm 90. About twenty-five other psalms are attributed to various priests or Levites during David's reign, and about fifty psalms contain no author references. Because of the various authors, the book spans a period between 1400 and 400 B.C.

The psalms fall into various categories: Lament, Thanksgiving, Praise, Enthronement (of Yahweh), Pilgrimage, Royal, and Wisdom. The verses reflect the parallelism between lines that is characteristic of Hebrew poetry. Worship and praise are central to Psalms, showing the majesty, power, and character of God; His faithfulness extends through time. Some of the most-loved psalms include 1, 22, 23, 24, 37, 72, 100, 101, 119, 121, and 150. ✦

Book One: Psalms 1—41

PSALM 1

The Way of the Righteous and the End of the Ungodly

Blessed *is* the man
Who walks not in the counsel of the ungodly,
Nor stands in the path of sinners,
Nor sits in the seat of the scornful;
2 But his delight *is* in the law of the LORD,
And in His law he meditates day and night.

3 He shall be like a tree
Planted by the rivers of water,
That brings forth its fruit in its season,
Whose leaf also shall not wither;
And whatever he does shall prosper.

4 The ungodly *are* not so,
But *are* like the chaff which the wind drives away.
5 Therefore the ungodly shall not stand in the judgment,
Nor sinners in the congregation of the righteous.

1:1 Blessed introduces a beatitude. It is a word of congratulation upon one's prospects. This is the single best word for describing the righteous. **walks not**: He chooses another path. We are to keep ourselves distinct from the world and avoid compromising situations in both our work and our social activities. The people with whom we associate regularly have a strong impact on our lives, and we need to be sure they influence us for the better. However, this verse does not imply that we should completely sequester ourselves from unbelievers. Rather, as we seek to lead them to Christ, we must not give approval to their sin, even through silence. We can befriend the ungodly in their time of need, but we cannot become their partners.

1:3 shall prosper: This does not promise material prosperity, but rather suggests that the righteous will always achieve what is worthwhile (see Josh. 1:8).

Choose Friends Wisely

Gloria Gaither

All of us are influenced by the people we are with. Perhaps we don't think of our friends as "advisors" or "counselors," but it is very likely that they are helping to shape our thinking and outlook if we spend much time with them. Coleridge said, "Advice is like snow; the softer it falls, the longer it dwells upon, and the deeper it sinks into the mind." Most of us would pick a professional counselor carefully, yet sometimes we don't give much thought at all to the relationships that mold our thinking. Most of us have at one time or another taken advice from chance acquaintances and happenstance peers for no better reason than our secret hunch that they will tell us what we want to hear or confirm the course we want to take. This spells danger.

"Our own lives will be enriched as we surround ourselves with Christian friends."

Just as children come home from school with the walk, the talk, the slang, and the mannerism of the latest "best friend," so we adults, more often than we like to admit, pick up the thought processes, the values, and the standards of those with whom we choose to spend our time. Paul told Timothy to surround himself with people and experiences that would exert influence on him for doing right. This is sound advice for us. Our own lives will be enriched as we surround ourselves with Christian friends committed to spiritual growth. ✦

6 For the LORD knows the way of the
righteous,
But the way of the ungodly shall
perish.

PSALM 2

The Messiah's Triumph and Kingdom

Why do the nations rage,
And the people plot a vain thing?
2 The kings of the earth set themselves,
And the rulers take counsel together,
Against the LORD and against His
Anointed, *saying*,
3 "Let us break Their bonds in pieces
And cast away Their cords from us."

4 He who sits in the heavens shall
laugh;
The LORD shall hold them in derision.

Psalm 2 The first of the "royal messianic psalms." It may have been read at the coronation of a new king in Judah, but is clearly prophetic of the Messiah, as seen from NT quotations of this psalm.

5 Then He shall speak to them in His wrath,
And distress them in His deep displeasure:
6 "Yet I have set My King
On My holy hill of Zion."

7 "I will declare the decree:
The LORD has said to Me,
'You *are* My Son,
Today I have begotten You.
8 Ask of Me, and I will give *You*
The nations *for* Your inheritance,
And the ends of the earth *for* Your possession.
9 You shall break[a] them with a rod of iron;
You shall dash them to pieces like a potter's vessel.' "

10 Now therefore, be wise, O kings;
Be instructed, you judges of the earth.
11 Serve the LORD with fear,
And rejoice with trembling.
12 Kiss the Son,[a] lest He[b] be angry,
And you perish *in* the way,
When His wrath is kindled but a little.
Blessed *are* all those who put their trust in Him.

PSALM 3

The LORD Helps His Troubled People

A Psalm of David when he fled from Absalom his son.

LORD, how they have increased who trouble me!
Many *are* they who rise up against me.
2 Many *are* they who say of me,
"*There is* no help for him in God." Sē'lah

3 But You, O LORD, *are* a shield for me,
My glory and the One who lifts up my head.
4 I cried to the LORD with my voice,
And He heard me from His holy hill. Sē'lah

5 I lay down and slept;
I awoke, for the LORD sustained me.
6 I will not be afraid of ten thousands of people
Who have set *themselves* against me all around.

7 Arise, O LORD;
Save me, O my God!
For You have struck all my enemies on the cheekbone;
You have broken the teeth of the ungodly.
8 Salvation *belongs* to the LORD.
Your blessing *is* upon Your people. Sē'lah

2:9 [a]Following Masoretic Text and Targum; Septuagint, Syriac, and Vulgate read *rule* (compare Revelation 2:27). 2:12 [a]Septuagint and Vulgate read *Embrace discipline;* Targum reads *Receive instruction.* [b]Septuagint reads *the LORD.*

2:7–9 decree: The testimony concerning the Messiah as the divine Son. The privileges and extent of the Messiah's **inheritance** (v. 8) and **possession** will be unlimited. His power over **nations** will be complete. This could not refer only to a human king.

2:7 My Son: Probably refers to the Messiah, but **the LORD** also called the Davidic king His "son" (see reference to King Solomon in 2 Sam. 7:12–14).

2:12 kiss: give homage to.

Psalm 3 An individual lament which contains elements of both petition and praise. Many of the laments end on a note of praise, signifying that the psalmist had prayed through his problem and realized God's presence, care, and eventual resolution of the difficulty.

3:4, 5 The inveterate worrier should follow David's example: After he took his problem to the Lord, he went to sleep, confident in the Lord's divine protection.

PSALM 4

The Safety of the Faithful

To the Chief Musician. With stringed instruments. A Psalm of David.

Hear me when I call, O God of my
righteousness!
You have relieved me in *my* distress;
Have mercy on me, and hear my
prayer.

2 How long, O you sons of men,
Will you turn my glory to shame?
How long will you love worthlessness
And seek falsehood? Sē′lah
3 But know that the LORD has set apart[a]
for Himself him who is godly;
The LORD will hear when I call to
Him.

4 Be angry, and do not sin.
Meditate within your heart on your
bed, and be still. Sē′lah
5 Offer the sacrifices of righteousness,
And put your trust in the LORD.

6 *There are* many who say,
"Who will show us *any* good?"
LORD, lift up the light of Your
countenance upon us.
7 You have put gladness in my heart,
More than in the season that their
grain and wine increased.
8 I will both lie down in peace, and
sleep;
For You alone, O LORD, make me
dwell in safety.

4:3 [a]Many Hebrew manuscripts, Septuagint, Targum, and Vulgate read *made wonderful.* 5:title [a]Hebrew *nehiloth*

> ***I pray that my grandchildren will lie down in peace, and sleep; for You alone, O Lord, make them dwell in safety.***
>
> *adapted from* Psalm 4:8

PSALM 5

A Prayer for Guidance

To the Chief Musician. With flutes.[a] A Psalm of David.

Give ear to my words, O LORD,
Consider my meditation.
2 Give heed to the voice of my cry,
My King and my God,
For to You I will pray.
3 My voice You shall hear in the
morning, O LORD;
In the morning I will direct *it* to You,
And I will look up.

4 For You *are* not a God who takes
pleasure in wickedness,
Nor shall evil dwell with You.
5 The boastful shall not stand in Your
sight;
You hate all workers of iniquity.
6 You shall destroy those who speak
falsehood;
The LORD abhors the bloodthirsty and
deceitful man.

4:2 my glory: God. By mocking David, his enemies mock God. In so doing they are choosing their own **shame. Selah**: Lit. "pause." In some cases this word marks the end of a poetic stanza. However, this is not always the case. It may be an exhortation to reflect on what was just said.

4:4 There is a proper anger which is not sinful. To master wrong anger, the psalmist's counsel is to **meditate** on God's word and **be still**.

5:3 As we pray daily during a time set apart for fellowship with God, we should look to Him, expecting Him to speak to us. Prayer should not be one-sided; we should be alert to God's responses during our devotional time and throughout the day.

7 But as for me, I will come into Your
house in the multitude of Your
mercy;
In fear of You I will worship toward
Your holy temple.
8 Lead me, O LORD, in Your
righteousness because of my
enemies;
Make Your way straight before my
face.

9 For *there is* no faithfulness in their
mouth;
Their inward part *is* destruction;
Their throat *is* an open tomb;
They flatter with their tongue.
10 Pronounce them guilty, O God!
Let them fall by their own counsels;
Cast them out in the multitude of
their transgressions,
For they have rebelled against You.

11 But let all those rejoice who put their
trust in You;
Let them ever shout for joy, because
You defend them;
Let those also who love Your name
Be joyful in You.
12 For You, O LORD, will bless the
righteous;
With favor You will surround him as
with a shield.

PSALM 6

A Prayer of Faith in Time of Distress

To the Chief Musician. With stringed instruments. On an eight-stringed harp.[a] *A Psalm of David.*

O LORD, do not rebuke me in Your
anger,
Nor chasten me in Your hot
displeasure.
2 Have mercy on me, O LORD, for I *am*
weak;
O LORD, heal me, for my bones are
troubled.
3 My soul also is greatly troubled;
But You, O LORD—how long?

4 Return, O LORD, deliver me!
Oh, save me for Your mercies' sake!
5 For in death *there is* no remembrance
of You;
In the grave who will give You
thanks?

6 I am weary with my groaning;
All night I make my bed swim;
I drench my couch with my tears.
7 My eye wastes away because of
grief;
It grows old because of all my
enemies.

8 Depart from me, all you workers of
iniquity;
For the LORD has heard the voice of
my weeping.
9 The LORD has heard my supplication;
The LORD will receive my prayer.
10 Let all my enemies be ashamed and
greatly troubled;
Let them turn back *and* be ashamed
suddenly.

6:title [a]Hebrew *sheminith*

Psalm 6 The first of seven penitential psalms (Ps. 6; 32; 38; 51; 102; 130; 143). Ps. 6 contains no explicit confession of sin, but it is implied. The prayer and lament are found in vv. 1–7, while vv. 8–10 express David's confidence that God has heard his prayer.

6:2, 3 my bones . . . My soul: OT people did not think of their souls as being separate from their bodies or housed inside their bodies. Rather "soul" and "body" both refer to the whole person. The psalmist knows that sin has weakened him completely, physically and emotionally.

PSALM 7
Prayer and Praise for Deliverance from Enemies

A Meditation[a] *of David, which he sang to the* LORD *concerning the words of Cush, a Benjamīte.*

O LORD my God, in You I put my trust;
Save me from all those who
persecute me;
And deliver me,
2 Lest they tear me like a lion,
Rending *me* in pieces, while *there is*
none to deliver.

3 O LORD my God, if I have done this:
If there is iniquity in my hands,
4 If I have repaid evil to him who was
at peace with me,
Or have plundered my enemy
without cause,
5 Let the enemy pursue me and
overtake *me;*
Yes, let him trample my life to the
earth,
And lay my honor in the dust. Sē′lah

6 Arise, O LORD, in Your anger;
Lift Yourself up because of the rage of
my enemies;
Rise up for me[a] *to* the judgment You
have commanded!
7 So the congregation of the peoples
shall surround You;
For their sakes, therefore, return on
high.
8 The LORD shall judge the peoples;
Judge me, O LORD, according to my
righteousness,
And according to my integrity within
me.

9 Oh, let the wickedness of the wicked
come to an end,
But establish the just;
For the righteous God tests the hearts
and minds.
10 My defense *is* of God,
Who saves the upright in heart.

11 God *is* a just judge,
And God is angry *with the wicked*
every day.
12 If he does not turn back,
He will sharpen His sword;
He bends His bow and makes it
ready.
13 He also prepares for Himself
instruments of death;
He makes His arrows into fiery
shafts.

14 Behold, *the wicked* brings forth
iniquity;
Yes, he conceives trouble and brings
forth falsehood.
15 He made a pit and dug it out,
And has fallen into the ditch *which* he
made.
16 His trouble shall return upon his own
head,

7:title [a]Hebrew *Shiggaion* 7:6 [a]Following Masoretic Text, Targum, and Vulgate; Septuagint reads *O LORD my God.*

Psalm 7 Another lament in which a man calls for God's just judgment upon his own life (vv. 1–5) and upon the wicked (vv. 6–8). Verses 9–13 extol God's fairness; vv. 14–16 speak of sin's retribution; v. 17 is a closing note of praise. The man Cush is mentioned only here in the Bible. The content of Ps. 7 suggests that he was an enemy of David; his affiliation with the tribe of Benjamin makes it likely he followed Saul.

7:8 my righteousness: David is here speaking only relatively. In comparison with his enemies he has acted with **integrity**, but in comparison to God "there is none righteous, no, not one" (Rom. 3:10; see Ps. 14:3).

7:14–16 This passage demonstrates the confidence we all can have that the wicked will be punished if they refuse to repent. When we find ourselves frustrated by the apparent success of sinners, we can rely on God to bring them to justice in His time.

And his violent dealing shall come
down on his own crown.

17 I will praise the LORD according to
His righteousness,
And will sing praise to the name of
the LORD Most High.

PSALM 8

The Glory of the LORD in Creation

To the Chief Musician. On the instrument of Gath.[a] A Psalm of David.

O LORD, our Lord,
How excellent *is* Your name in all
the earth,
Who have set Your glory above the
heavens!

2 Out of the mouth of babes and
nursing infants
You have ordained strength,
Because of Your enemies,
That You may silence the enemy and
the avenger.

3 When I consider Your heavens, the
work of Your fingers,
The moon and the stars, which You
have ordained,
4 What is man that You are mindful of
him,
And the son of man that You visit
him?
5 For You have made him a little lower
than the angels,[a]
And You have crowned him with
glory and honor.
6 You have made him to have
dominion over the works of Your
hands;
You have put all *things* under his feet,
7 All sheep and oxen—
Even the beasts of the field,
8 The birds of the air,
And the fish of the sea
That pass through the paths of the
seas.

9 O LORD, our Lord,
How excellent *is* Your name in all the
earth!

PSALM 9

Prayer and Thanksgiving for the LORD's Righteous Judgments

To the Chief Musician. To the tune of "Death of the Son."[a] A Psalm of David.

I will praise *You*, O LORD, with my whole
heart;
I will tell of all Your marvelous
works.
2 I will be glad and rejoice in You;
I will sing praise to Your name, O
Most High.

3 When my enemies turn back,
They shall fall and perish at Your
presence.
4 For You have maintained my right
and my cause;
You sat on the throne judging in
righteousness.

8:title [a]Hebrew *Al Gittith* 8:5 [a]Hebrew *Elohim, God;* Septuagint, Syriac, Targum, and Jewish tradition translate as *angels.* 9:title [a]Hebrew *Muth Labben*

8:2 Jesus quoted the opening phrase of this verse at His triumphal entry into Jerusalem (Matt. 21:16).

8:5–8 Lower than the angels implies man's mortal and earthbound existence. **crowned . . . with glory and honor**: What marvelous grace on God's part. **dominion**: What daring faith in humanity by God! What an awesome trust committed to humankind! Whatever honor belongs to humanity is only a reflection of the greater glory of God.

9:1 I will tell: Here David's praise of God is a public declaration of God's saving deeds to others. He praises God among the people (v. 11) and in the gates of the city (v. 14).

5 You have rebuked the nations,
You have destroyed the wicked;
You have blotted out their name
forever and ever.

6 O enemy, destructions are finished
forever!
And you have destroyed cities;
Even their memory has perished.
7 But the LORD shall endure forever;
He has prepared His throne for
judgment.
8 He shall judge the world in
righteousness,
And He shall administer judgment
for the peoples in uprightness.

9 The LORD also will be a refuge for the
oppressed,
A refuge in times of trouble.
10 And those who know Your name will
put their trust in You;
For You, LORD, have not forsaken
those who seek You.

11 Sing praises to the LORD, who dwells
in Zion!
Declare His deeds among the people.
12 When He avenges blood, He
remembers them;
He does not forget the cry of the
humble.

13 Have mercy on me, O LORD!
Consider my trouble from those who
hate me,
You who lift me up from the gates of
death,
14 That I may tell of all Your praise
In the gates of the daughter of Zion.
I will rejoice in Your salvation.

15 The nations have sunk down in the
pit *which* they made;
In the net which they hid, their own
foot is caught.
16 The LORD is known *by* the judgment
He executes;
The wicked is snared in the work of
his own hands.
Meditation.[a] Sē′lah

17 The wicked shall be turned into hell,
And all the nations that forget God.
18 For the needy shall not always be
forgotten;
The expectation of the poor shall *not*
perish forever.

19 Arise, O LORD,
Do not let man prevail;
Let the nations be judged in Your
sight.
20 Put them in fear, O LORD,
That the nations may know
themselves *to be but* men. Sē′lah

PSALM 10

A Song of Confidence in God's Triumph over Evil

Why do You stand afar off, O LORD?
Why do You hide in times of
trouble?
2 The wicked in *his* pride persecutes the
poor;
Let them be caught in the plots which
they have devised.

9:16 [a]Hebrew *Higgaion*

9:13, 14 You who lift me up: Enemies have plotted to kill David, but the faithful God frustrates their plots.

9:19, 20 Do not let man prevail: The Hebrew word *man*, here and in v. 20, emphasizes human frailty. It stands in contrast to the power and right of the Lord to judge humankind.

10:1 Why do You hide? A typical complaint of the righteous sufferer. For example, Job cried out, "Why do You hide Your face?" (see Job 13:23, 24). God's seeming absence in the midst of suffering always adds to our anxiety. But we must remember that the feeling of aloneness is due to our blindness, not to God's absence.

3 For the wicked boasts of his heart's
desire;
He blesses the greedy *and* renounces
the LORD.
4 The wicked in his proud countenance
does not seek *God;*
God *is* in none of his thoughts.

5 His ways are always prospering;
Your judgments *are* far above, out of
his sight;
As for all his enemies, he sneers at
them.
6 He has said in his heart, "I shall not
be moved;
I shall never be in adversity."
7 His mouth is full of cursing and
deceit and oppression;
Under his tongue *is* trouble and
iniquity.

8 He sits in the lurking places of the
villages;
In the secret places he murders the
innocent;
His eyes are secretly fixed on the
helpless.
9 He lies in wait secretly, as a lion in his
den;
He lies in wait to catch the poor;
He catches the poor when he draws
him into his net.
10 So he crouches, he lies low,
That the helpless may fall by his
strength.
11 He has said in his heart,
"God has forgotten;
He hides His face;
He will never see."

12 Arise, O LORD!
O God, lift up Your hand!
Do not forget the humble.
13 Why do the wicked renounce God?
He has said in his heart,
"You will not require *an account.*"

14 But You have seen, for You observe
trouble and grief,
To repay *it* by Your hand.
The helpless commits himself to You;
You are the helper of the fatherless.
15 Break the arm of the wicked and the
evil *man;*
Seek out his wickedness *until* You
find none.

16 The LORD *is* King forever and ever;
The nations have perished out of His
land.
17 LORD, You have heard the desire of
the humble;
You will prepare their heart;
You will cause Your ear to hear,
18 To do justice to the fatherless and the
oppressed,
That the man of the earth may op-
press no more.

PSALM 11

Faith in the LORD's Righteousness

To the Chief Musician. A Psalm of David.

In the LORD I put my trust;
How can you say to my soul,
"Flee *as* a bird to your mountain"?
2 For look! The wicked bend *their*
bow,
They make ready their arrow on the
string,
That they may shoot secretly at the
upright in heart.
3 If the foundations are destroyed,
What can the righteous do?

Psalm 11 This psalm reflects some crisis in which David was advised to flee because of the attack of the wicked (vv. 1–3). His response (vv. 4–7) is to declare that the Lord is greater than the dangers from men.

11:3 foundations: The first principles of life. If they are destroyed, we are left without hope or direction.

4 The LORD *is* in His holy temple,
The LORD's throne *is* in heaven;
His eyes behold,
His eyelids test the sons of men.
5 The LORD tests the righteous,
But the wicked and the one who
loves violence His soul hates.
6 Upon the wicked He will rain coals;
Fire and brimstone and a burning
wind
Shall be the portion of their cup.

7 For the LORD *is* righteous,
He loves righteousness;
His countenance beholds the upright.[a]

PSALM 12

Man's Treachery and God's Constancy

To the Chief Musician. On an eight-stringed harp.[a] A Psalm of David.

Help, LORD, for the godly man
ceases!
For the faithful disappear from
among the sons of men.
2 They speak idly everyone with his
neighbor;
With flattering lips *and* a double heart
they speak.

3 May the LORD cut off all flattering
lips,
And the tongue that speaks proud
things,
4 Who have said,
"With our tongue we will prevail;
Our lips *are* our own;
Who *is* lord over us?"

5 "For the oppression of the poor, for the
sighing of the needy,
Now I will arise," says the LORD;
"I will set *him* in the safety for which
he yearns."

6 The words of the LORD *are* pure
words,
Like silver tried in a furnace of earth,
Purified seven times.
7 You shall keep them, O LORD,
You shall preserve them from this
generation forever.

8 The wicked prowl on every side,
When vileness is exalted among the
sons of men.

PSALM 13

Trust in the Salvation of the LORD

To the Chief Musician. A Psalm of David.

How long, O LORD? Will You forget me
forever?
How long will You hide Your face
from me?
2 How long shall I take counsel in my
soul,
Having sorrow in my heart daily?
How long will my enemy be exalted
over me?

3 Consider *and* hear me, O LORD my
God;

11:7 [a]Or *The upright beholds His countenance*
12:title [a]Hebrew *sheminith*

11:4 The eye of faith sees **the LORD . . . in heaven**. This vision of God's eternal reality lifts us above every earthly threat.

11:5, 6 The Lord **tests** the **righteous** to determine the quality of their faith (see 7:9). But such testing does not indicate displeasure. On the other hand, the often easy road of the **wicked** must not blind us to God's fundamental hatred of their ways. See Gen. 22:1.

12:6, 7 Pure words characterize God's speech in contrast to that of the wicked described in vv. 2–4. For the Israelites **seven times** symbolized complete purity. **Keep them** refers to the poor and needy of v. 5.

Psalm 13 In the midst of a terrible crisis, the psalmist wonders when the Lord will intervene on his behalf. Note that he never questions the outcome—he knows the Lord will deliver him, he's simply asking when.

Enlighten my eyes,
Lest I sleep the *sleep of* death;
4 Lest my enemy say,
"I have prevailed against him";
Lest those who trouble me rejoice
when I am moved.

5 But I have trusted in Your mercy;
My heart shall rejoice in Your
salvation.
6 I will sing to the LORD,
Because He has dealt bountifully with
me.

PSALM 14

Folly of the Godless, and God's Final Triumph

To the Chief Musician. A Psalm of David.

The fool has said in his heart,
"*There is* no God."
They are corrupt,
They have done abominable works,
There is none who does good.

2 The LORD looks down from heaven
upon the children of men,
To see if there are any who
understand, who seek God.
3 They have all turned aside,
They have together become corrupt;
There is none who does good,
No, not one.

4 Have all the workers of iniquity no
knowledge,
Who eat up my people *as* they eat
bread,
And do not call on the LORD?
5 There they are in great fear,
For God *is* with the generation of the
righteous.
6 You shame the counsel of the poor,
But the LORD *is* his refuge.

7 Oh, that the salvation of Israel *would*
come out of Zion!
When the LORD brings back the
captivity of His people,
Let Jacob rejoice *and* Israel be glad.

PSALM 15

The Character of Those Who May Dwell with the LORD

A Psalm of David.

LORD, who may abide in Your
tabernacle?
Who may dwell in Your holy hill?

2 He who walks uprightly,
And works righteousness,
And speaks the truth in his heart;
3 He *who* does not backbite with his
tongue,
Nor does evil to his neighbor,
Nor does he take up a reproach
against his friend;
4 In whose eyes a vile person is
despised,
But he honors those who fear the
LORD;

14:1 There is no God is not so much a philosophical statement as a practical one. Many people who would not claim God does not exist still live as though He did not. Although it is impossible to elude God and His moral demands, the foolish person tries both.

14:3 none who does good: Aside from divine grace everyone is by nature and practice corrupt and sinful (see Rom. 3:23).

14:4 Eat up my people indicates the absence of social conscience on the part of the wicked. Their treatment of the poor is like cannibalism (see Mic. 3:1–3).

Psalm 15 The question (v. 1) and answer (vv. 2–5) may reflect the ancient practice in which the worshiper inquired about conditions of entrance to the sanctuary, and a priest responded. As a poem of David, it may simply reflect his meditation. This psalm provides an excellent description of the life that pleases God.

15:4, 5 swears to his own hurt: Keeps his word even when it is not to his advantage. To

He *who* swears to his own hurt and
does not change;
5 He *who* does not put out his money at
usury,
Nor does he take a bribe against
the innocent.

He who does these *things* shall never
be moved.

PSALM 16

The Hope of the Faithful, and the Messiah's Victory

A Michtam of David.

Preserve me, O God, for in You I put
my trust.

2 *O my soul,* you have said to the LORD,
"You *are* my Lord,
My goodness is nothing apart from
You."
3 As for the saints who *are* on the earth,
"They are the excellent ones, in whom
is all my delight."

4 Their sorrows shall be multiplied
who hasten *after* another *god;*
Their drink offerings of blood I will
not offer,
Nor take up their names on my lips.

5 O LORD, *You are* the portion of my
inheritance and my cup;
You maintain my lot.
6 The lines have fallen to me in
pleasant *places;*
Yes, I have a good inheritance.

7 I will bless the LORD who has given
me counsel;
My heart also instructs me in the
night seasons.
8 I have set the LORD always before me;
Because *He is* at my right hand I shall
not be moved.

9 Therefore my heart is glad, and my
glory rejoices;
My flesh also will rest in hope.
10 For You will not leave my soul in
Shē'ōl,
Nor will You allow Your Holy One to
see corruption.
11 You will show me the path of life;
In Your presence *is* fullness of joy;
At Your right hand *are* pleasures
forevermore.

PSALM 17

Prayer with Confidence in Final Salvation

A Prayer of David.

Hear a just cause, O LORD,
Attend to my cry;
Give ear to my prayer *which is* not
from deceitful lips.
2 Let my vindication come from Your
presence;
Let Your eyes look on the things that
are upright.

3 You have tested my heart;
You have visited *me* in the night;
You have tried me and have found
nothing;

---

maintain a pure testimony before the world, we must always honor our commitments. **never be moved**: The person described in this psalm has learned the secret of abiding in God. No trouble will be able to move him or her out of that sheltering presence (see 91:1, 2).

16:8–11 In Acts 2:25–28 Peter quotes these verses in reference to the resurrection of Christ.

16:9 my glory: my soul.

17:3 Knowing the power the tongue has for good or for evil, each of us, like David, should make a special commitment to guard our tongues from unholy conversation.

I have purposed that my mouth shall
not transgress.
4 Concerning the works of men,
By the word of Your lips,
I have kept away from the paths of
the destroyer.
5 Uphold my steps in Your paths,
That my footsteps may not slip.

6 I have called upon You, for You will
hear me, O God;
Incline Your ear to me, *and* hear my
speech.
7 Show Your marvelous lovingkindness
by Your right hand,
O You who save those who trust *in
You*
From those who rise up *against them.*
8 Keep me as the apple of Your eye;
Hide me under the shadow of Your
wings,
9 From the wicked who oppress me,
From my deadly enemies who
surround me.

10 They have closed up their fat *hearts;*
With their mouths they speak proudly.
11 They have now surrounded us in our
steps;
They have set their eyes, crouching
down to the earth,
12 As a lion is eager to tear his prey,
And like a young lion lurking in
secret places.

13 Arise, O LORD,
Confront him, cast him down;
Deliver my life from the wicked with
Your sword,
14 With Your hand from men, O LORD,
From men of the world *who have* their
portion in *this* life,
And whose belly You fill with Your
hidden treasure.
They are satisfied with children,
And leave the rest of their *possession*
for their babes.

15 As for me, I will see Your face in
righteousness;
I shall be satisfied when I awake in
Your likeness.

PSALM 18

God the Sovereign Savior

To the Chief Musician. A Psalm of David the servant of the LORD, who spoke to the LORD the words of this song on the day that the LORD delivered him from the hand of all his enemies and from the hand of Saul. And he said:

I will love You, O LORD, my strength.
2 The LORD is my rock and my fortress
and my deliverer;
My God, my strength, in whom I will
trust;
My shield and the horn of my
salvation, my stronghold.
3 I will call upon the LORD, *who is
worthy* to be praised;
So shall I be saved from my enemies.

4 The pangs of death surrounded me,
And the floods of ungodliness made
me afraid.

17:14 their portion in this life: To be worldly is to live as though physical gratification, many possessions, and power are all that matter. But there is a life to come (see 1 John 2:15–17). **Your hidden treasure**: Whatever good things the wicked enjoy on earth are from God, but they do not recognize Him.

17:15 see Your face: The goal of every child of God; it is the ultimate expression of spiritual joy (see Job 19:26, 27; Rev. 22:4). **when I awake**: Used here of the resurrection (see 1 John 3:2).

18:title All his enemies suggests that **Saul** is understood as being included in a total grouping. Thus some such situation as described in 2 Sam. 8:14, 15 may be the setting for the psalm.

5 The sorrows of Shē'ōl surrounded me;
The snares of death confronted me.
6 In my distress I called upon the LORD,
And cried out to my God;
He heard my voice from His temple,
And my cry came before Him, *even* to
His ears.

7 Then the earth shook and trembled;
The foundations of the hills also
quaked and were shaken,
Because He was angry.
8 Smoke went up from His nostrils,
And devouring fire from His mouth;
Coals were kindled by it.
9 He bowed the heavens also, and came
down
With darkness under His feet.
10 And He rode upon a cherub, and
flew;
He flew upon the wings of the wind.
11 He made darkness His secret place;
His canopy around Him *was* dark
waters
And thick clouds of the skies.
12 From the brightness before Him,
His thick clouds passed with
hailstones and coals of fire.

13 The LORD thundered from heaven,
And the Most High uttered His voice,
Hailstones and coals of fire.[a]

18:13 [a]Following Masoretic Text, Targum, and Vulgate; a few Hebrew manuscripts and Septuagint omit *Hailstones and coals of fire.*

14 He sent out His arrows and scattered
the foe,
Lightnings in abundance, and He
vanquished them.
15 Then the channels of the sea were
seen,
The foundations of the world were
uncovered
At Your rebuke, O LORD,
At the blast of the breath of Your
nostrils.

16 He sent from above, He took me;
He drew me out of many waters.
17 He delivered me from my strong
enemy,
From those who hated me,
For they were too strong for me.
18 They confronted me in the day of my
calamity,
But the LORD was my support.
19 He also brought me out into a broad
place;
He delivered me because He
delighted in me.

20 The LORD rewarded me according to
my righteousness;
According to the cleanness of my
hands
He has recompensed me.
21 For I have kept the ways of the LORD,
And have not wickedly departed
from my God.

18:6 Rather than turning to earthly friends or wasting time in complaining, David turned directly to the Lord for help. We can always trust Him to hear our pleas and respond in loving wisdom.

18:7–15 The coming of God to rescue the king is described in figures similar to His appearance at Mt. Sinai (see Ex. 19:16–19). We see the awful majesty and power of God (see Is. 6:1–4). **Channels of the sea** (v. 15) could refer to the miracle at the Red Sea.

18:14 sent out His arrows: God's deliverance is often described by depicting Him as the Divine Warrior. See 7:11–13; 35:1–3.

18:16, 17 The personal deliverance accomplished by God is emphasized by the fourfold use of *He*.

18:19 He delighted in me: The Lord described David as one "who kept My commandments and who followed Me with all his heart, to do only what was right in My eyes" (1 Kin. 14:8). It was this wholehearted obedience that won for David God's favor, and which David confidently notes in vv. 20–24.

22 For all His judgments *were* before me,
And I did not put away His statutes
from me.
23 I was also blameless before Him,
And I kept myself from my iniquity.
24 Therefore the LORD has recompensed
me according to my righteousness,
According to the cleanness of my
hands in His sight.

25 With the merciful You will show
Yourself merciful;
With a blameless man You will show
Yourself blameless;
26 With the pure You will show Yourself
pure;
And with the devious You will show
Yourself shrewd.
27 For You will save the humble people,
But will bring down haughty looks.

28 For You will light my lamp;
The LORD my God will enlighten my
darkness.
29 For by You I can run against a troop,
By my God I can leap over a wall.
30 *As for* God, His way *is* perfect;
The word of the LORD is proven;
He *is* a shield to all who trust in
Him.

31 For who *is* God, except the LORD?
And who *is* a rock, except our God?
32 *It is* God who arms me with strength,
And makes my way perfect.
33 He makes my feet like the *feet of* deer,
And sets me on my high places.
34 He teaches my hands to make war,
So that my arms can bend a bow of
bronze.
35 You have also given me the shield of
Your salvation;
Your right hand has held me up,
Your gentleness has made me great.
36 You enlarged my path under me,
So my feet did not slip.

37 I have pursued my enemies and
overtaken them;
Neither did I turn back again till they
were destroyed.
38 I have wounded them,
So that they could not rise;
They have fallen under my feet.
39 For You have armed me with strength
for the battle;
You have subdued under me those
who rose up against me.
40 You have also given me the necks of
my enemies,
So that I destroyed those who hated
me.
41 They cried out, but *there was* none to
save;
Even to the LORD, but He did not
answer them.
42 Then I beat them as fine as the dust
before the wind;
I cast them out like dirt in the
streets.

43 You have delivered me from the
strivings of the people;
You have made me the head of the
nations;
A people I have not known shall
serve me.
44 As soon as they hear of me they obey
me;
The foreigners submit to me.

18:28 Light my lamp is an idiom for the new vitality of life that comes from God's enabling grace.

18:32–42 It is God: Here a king and general of the armies confesses his dependence on God. He recounts his victories with various terms which indicate complete triumphs: **overtaken, destroyed, wounded, subdued**. The credit is given completely to God (vv. 39, 40). A lesser person might say, "Because of my righteousness I triumphed over my enemies." Not David.

45 The foreigners fade away,
And come frightened from their hideouts.

46 The LORD lives!
Blessed *be* my Rock!
Let the God of my salvation be exalted.
47 *It is* God who avenges me,
And subdues the peoples under me;
48 He delivers me from my enemies.
You also lift me up above those who rise against me;
You have delivered me from the violent man.
49 Therefore I will give thanks to You, O LORD, among the Gentiles,
And sing praises to Your name.

50 Great deliverance He gives to His king,
And shows mercy to His anointed,
To David and his descendants forevermore.

PSALM 19

The Perfect Revelation of the LORD

To the Chief Musician. A Psalm of David.

The heavens declare the glory of God;
And the firmament shows His handiwork.
2 Day unto day utters speech,
And night unto night reveals knowledge.
3 *There is* no speech nor language
Where their voice is not heard.
4 Their line[a] has gone out through all the earth,
And their words to the end of the world.

In them He has set a tabernacle for the sun,
5 Which *is* like a bridegroom coming out of his chamber,
And rejoices like a strong man to run its race.
6 Its rising *is* from one end of heaven,
And its circuit to the other end;
And there is nothing hidden from its heat.

7 The law of the LORD *is* perfect, converting the soul;
The testimony of the LORD *is* sure, making wise the simple;
8 The statutes of the LORD *are* right, rejoicing the heart;
The commandment of the LORD *is* pure, enlightening the eyes;
9 The fear of the LORD *is* clean, enduring forever;
The judgments of the LORD *are* true *and* righteous altogether.
10 More to be desired *are they* than gold,
Yea, than much fine gold;

19:4 [a]Septuagint, Syriac, and Vulgate read *sound;* Targum reads *business.*

19:1 The purpose of creation is to **declare the glory of God**. The OT is never interested in merely the beauties of nature (see 8:1).

19:4–6 The eloquence of nature extends to the **end of the world**. David singles out the sun as an example of nature's testimony. Other nations might worship the sun, but God had shown the Hebrews that it only pointed to One infinitely greater than itself.

19:7–9 The law of the LORD: The psalmist moves from general revelation in nature to special revelation in the Bible, which goes beyond general revelation to demonstrate the moral nature of God's holiness. The English word law translates Hebrew *torah*, "guidance, teaching, instruction." In the following verses several synonyms occur, stating characteristics of the law. These indicate the godliness which is intended to result from God's revelation. His work is **converting**; it changes and saves. His revelation is **clean**, cleansing the human spirit from sin.

19:10 While the value of God's Word cannot be estimated in terms of gold or money, the

I pray that the words of my mouth and the meditation of my heart will be acceptable in Your sight, O Lord, my strength and my Redeemer.

adapted from Psalm 19:14

Sweeter also than honey and the
honeycomb.
11 Moreover by them Your servant is
warned,
And in keeping them *there is* great
reward.

12 Who can understand *his* errors?
Cleanse me from secret *faults.*
13 Keep back Your servant also from
presumptuous *sins;*
Let them not have dominion over me.
Then I shall be blameless,
And I shall be innocent of great
transgression.

14 Let the words of my mouth and the
meditation of my heart
Be acceptable in Your sight,
O LORD, my strength and my
Redeemer.

PSALM 20

The Assurance of God's Saving Work

To the Chief Musician. A Psalm of David.

May the LORD answer you in the day
of trouble;
May the name of the God of Jacob
defend you;
2 May He send you help from the
sanctuary,
And strengthen you out of Zion;
3 May He remember all your offerings,
And accept your burnt sacrifice.
Sē'lah

4 May He grant you according to your
heart's *desire,*
And fulfill all your purpose.
5 We will rejoice in your salvation,
And in the name of our God we will
set up *our* banners!
May the LORD fulfill all your
petitions.

6 Now I know that the LORD saves His
anointed;
He will answer him from His holy
heaven
With the saving strength of His right
hand.

7 Some *trust* in chariots, and some in
horses;
But we will remember the name of
the LORD our God.
8 They have bowed down and fallen;
But we have risen and stand upright.

9 Save, LORD!
May the King answer us when we
call.

PSALM 21

Joy in the Salvation of the LORD

To the Chief Musician. A Psalm of David.

The king shall have joy in Your
strength, O LORD;

comparison with gold holds true in that both miners and seekers of God's treasure must dig for their hearts' desire. We can never know the true value of Scripture until we delve into its contents with all our hearts.

20:7 Just as many in David's time believed **horses** and **chariots** provided true strength, many today try to achieve power by acquiring money, power, or popularity. But we know that genuine power can only be found in the Lord.

And in Your salvation how greatly
shall he rejoice!
2 You have given him his heart's desire,
And have not withheld the request of
his lips. Sē'lah

3 For You meet him with the blessings
of goodness;
You set a crown of pure gold upon
his head.
4 He asked life from You, *and* You gave
it to him—
Length of days forever and ever.
5 His glory *is* great in Your salvation;
Honor and majesty You have placed
upon him.
6 For You have made him most blessed
forever;
You have made him exceedingly glad
with Your presence.
7 For the king trusts in the LORD,
And through the mercy of the Most
High he shall not be moved.

8 Your hand will find all Your enemies;
Your right hand will find those who
hate You.
9 You shall make them as a fiery oven
in the time of Your anger;
The LORD shall swallow them up in
His wrath,
And the fire shall devour them.
10 Their offspring You shall destroy
from the earth,
And their descendants from among
the sons of men.
11 For they intended evil against You;
They devised a plot *which* they are
not able *to perform*.
12 Therefore You will make them turn
their back;
You will make ready *Your arrows* on
Your string toward their faces.

13 Be exalted, O LORD, in Your own
strength!
We will sing and praise Your power.

PSALM 22

The Suffering, Praise, and Posterity of the Messiah

To the Chief Musician. Set to "The Deer of the Dawn."[a] *A Psalm of David.*

My God, My God, why have You
forsaken Me?
Why are You so far from helping Me,
And from the words of My groaning?
2 O My God, I cry in the daytime, but
You do not hear;
And in the night season, and am not
silent.

3 But You *are* holy,
Enthroned in the praises of Israel.
4 Our fathers trusted in You;
They trusted, and You delivered
them.
5 They cried to You, and were
delivered;
They trusted in You, and were not
ashamed.

6 But I *am* a worm, and no man;
A reproach of men, and despised by
the people.

22:title [a]Hebrew *Aijeleth Hashahar*

21:10 Middle Eastern culture regarded the inability to pass on the family name as a terrible curse.

Psalm 22 An individual lament which follows directly after two royal messianic poems. Ps. 20; 21 celebrate the reign and dominion of the Messiah, but Ps. 22 introduces the theme of the Suffering Servant. Both themes come together in the Person of Jesus. Pronouns in the NKJV reflect the messianic interpretation; those of the notes, the lament of the psalmist. Both interpretations are possible.

22:6 I am a worm: This is the psalmist's own assessment of his condition, and accurately expresses how we often feel in times of despair. But it is not a part of the biblical

7 All those who see Me ridicule Me;
They shoot out the lip, they shake the head, *saying*,
8 "He trusted[a] in the LORD, let Him rescue Him;
Let Him deliver Him, since He delights in Him!"

9 But You *are* He who took Me out of the womb;
You made Me trust *while* on My mother's breasts.
10 I was cast upon You from birth.
From My mother's womb
You *have been* My God.
11 Be not far from Me,
For trouble *is* near;
For *there is* none to help.

12 Many bulls have surrounded Me;
Strong *bulls* of Bā'shan have encircled Me.
13 They gape at Me *with* their mouths,
Like a raging and roaring lion.

14 I am poured out like water,
And all My bones are out of joint;
My heart is like wax;
It has melted within Me.
15 My strength is dried up like a potsherd,
And My tongue clings to My jaws;
You have brought Me to the dust of death.

16 For dogs have surrounded Me;
The congregation of the wicked has enclosed Me.
They pierced[a] My hands and My feet;
17 I can count all My bones.
They look *and* stare at Me.
18 They divide My garments among them,
And for My clothing they cast lots.

19 But You, O LORD, do not be far from Me;
O My Strength, hasten to help Me!
20 Deliver Me from the sword,
My precious *life* from the power of the dog.
21 Save Me from the lion's mouth
And from the horns of the wild oxen!

You have answered Me.

22 I will declare Your name to My brethren;
In the midst of the assembly I will praise You.
23 You who fear the LORD, praise Him!
All you descendants of Jacob, glorify Him,
And fear Him, all you offspring of Israel!
24 For He has not despised nor abhorred the affliction of the afflicted;
Nor has He hidden His face from Him;
But when He cried to Him, He heard.

25 My praise *shall be* of You in the great assembly;
I will pay My vows before those who fear Him.

22:8 [a]Septuagint, Syriac, and Vulgate read *hoped;* Targum reads *praised.* 22:16 [a]Following some Hebrew manuscripts, Septuagint, Syriac, Vulgate; Masoretic Text reads *Like a lion.*

doctrine of humanity. In God's sight we are only a little less than God Himself (8:5). **despised**: Onlookers scornfully added to his misery by confirming his original thought that he was forsaken by God.

22:16 dogs: frequently used to refer to evil men.

22:25, 26 pay My vows: Probably a promise to offer a special sacrifice because God had delivered him. **The poor shall eat** the meat of this sacrifice (v. 25; see Deut. 14:29).

26 The poor shall eat and be satisfied;
Those who seek Him will praise the LORD.
Let your heart live forever!

27 All the ends of the world
Shall remember and turn to the LORD,
And all the families of the nations
Shall worship before You.[a]
28 For the kingdom *is* the LORD's,
And He rules over the nations.

29 All the prosperous of the earth
Shall eat and worship;
All those who go down to the dust
Shall bow before Him,
Even he who cannot keep himself alive.

30 A posterity shall serve Him.
It will be recounted of the Lord to the *next* generation,
31 They will come and declare His righteousness to a people who will be born,
That He has done *this*.

PSALM 23

The LORD the Shepherd of His People

A Psalm of David.

The LORD *is* my shepherd;
I shall not want.

22:27 [a]Following Masoretic Text, Septuagint, and Targum; Arabic, Syriac, and Vulgate read *Him*.
23:6 [a]Following Septuagint, Syriac, Targum, and Vulgate; Masoretic Text reads *return*.

I praise you, O Lord, that although I may walk through the valley of the shadow of death, I will fear no evil; for You, God, are with me and Your rod and Your staff comfort me.

adapted from Psalm 23:4

2 He makes me to lie down in green pastures;
He leads me beside the still waters.
3 He restores my soul;
He leads me in the paths of righteousness
For His name's sake.

4 Yea, though I walk through the valley of the shadow of death,
I will fear no evil;
For You *are* with me;
Your rod and Your staff, they comfort me.

5 You prepare a table before me in the presence of my enemies;
You anoint my head with oil;
My cup runs over.
6 Surely goodness and mercy shall follow me
All the days of my life;
And I will dwell[a] in the house of the LORD
Forever.

23:1 The LORD is my shepherd: This imagery casts the divine-human relationship into the most intimate and personal terms.

23:4 The shepherd's **rod** was a short club used to fend off wild animals while the **staff** with its crook was used to direct the sheep. One represents protection, the other guidance. Just like the shepherd, the Lord protects and guides us, His sheep.

23:5 You prepare a table: As the Host, God has made complete provision for our every need. **in the presence of my enemies**: The sheep/Shepherd imagery cannot convey all that needs to be said about God's grace and mercy to His people. The Near Eastern host who would lay down his life for the guest adds the deeper dimension.

MERELY A SHADOW

Ron Mehl

David wrote, "Though I walk through the valley of the shadow of death, I will fear no evil; for You are with me" (Ps. 23:4). As a shepherd, David knew what it was like to walk alone through the dangers that lurk in the shadows. But David knew something that you and I must also realize: "shadows" can cause no harm. The shadow of a bear cannot bite, the shadow of a lion cannot scratch, and the shadow of death cannot conquer. In fact, a shadow can only harm us when *we are afraid of it*, and our fear leads us to react in such a way that *we harm ourselves.*

When you know the Lord, death *is* only a shadow. It holds no power; it is nothing to fear. One of my friends once said, "I'd rather walk through the valley of the shadow of death with the Shepherd than in the lush green pastures without Him." For those who know the Lord, death is truly just a shadow. It is a defeated foe, a doorway to heaven. ✦

"A shadow can only harm us when we are afraid of it."

PSALM 24

The King of Glory and His Kingdom

A Psalm of David.

The earth *is* the LORD's, and all its
fullness,
The world and those who dwell
therein.
2 For He has founded it upon the seas,
And established it upon the waters.

3 Who may ascend into the hill of the
LORD?
Or who may stand in His holy
place?
4 He who has clean hands and a pure
heart,
Who has not lifted up his soul to an
idol,
Nor sworn deceitfully.
5 He shall receive blessing from the
LORD,

Psalm 24 This majestic hymn begins with the recognition of God's dominion over all the earth (vv. 1, 2). Instructions for coming into the sanctuary and the presence of God (vv. 3–6) are followed by a celebration of God entering into His prepared dwelling place (vv. 7–10). The psalm may have been sung originally when the ark was brought to Jerusalem (see 1 Chr. 16:1–6).

24:1 the LORD's: God owns the whole creation. We enjoy it simply by His permission. **Fullness** refers to the earth's wealth, fertility, and inhabitants.

24:3 Who may ascend? Fellowship with God is not automatic. Only the righteous are accorded that privilege. See introduction to Ps. 15.

24:4 To maintain fellowship with God, we must conduct ourselves righteously (**clean hands**), act on sincere motives (**pure heart**), keep the Lord our top priority, and uphold honesty and integrity.

And righteousness from the God of
his salvation.
6 This *is* Jacob, the generation of those
who seek Him,
Who seek Your face. Sē′lah

7 Lift up your heads, O you gates!
And be lifted up, you everlasting
doors!
And the King of glory shall come in.
8 Who *is* this King of glory?
The LORD strong and mighty,
The LORD mighty in battle.
9 Lift up your heads, O you gates!
Lift up, you everlasting doors!
And the King of glory shall come in.
10 Who is this King of glory?
The LORD of hosts,
He *is* the King of glory. Sē′lah

PSALM 25

A Plea for Deliverance and Forgiveness

A Psalm of David.

To You, O LORD, I lift up my soul.
2 O my God, I trust in You;
Let me not be ashamed;
Let not my enemies triumph over me.
3 Indeed, let no one who waits on You
be ashamed;
Let those be ashamed who deal
treacherously without cause.

4 Show me Your ways, O LORD;
Teach me Your paths.
5 Lead me in Your truth and teach me,
For You *are* the God of my salvation;
On You I wait all the day.

6 Remember, O LORD, Your tender
mercies and Your lovingkindnesses,
For they *are* from of old.
7 Do not remember the sins of my
youth, nor my transgressions;
According to Your mercy remember
me,
For Your goodness' sake, O LORD.

8 Good and upright *is* the LORD;
Therefore He teaches sinners in the
way.
9 The humble He guides in justice,
And the humble He teaches His way.
10 All the paths of the LORD *are* mercy
and truth,
To such as keep His covenant and His
testimonies.
11 For Your name's sake, O LORD,
Pardon my iniquity, for it *is* great.

12 Who *is* the man that fears the LORD?
Him shall He[a] teach in the way He[b]
chooses.
13 He himself shall dwell in prosperity,
And his descendants shall inherit the
earth.
14 The secret of the LORD *is* with those
who fear Him,
And He will show them His
covenant.
15 My eyes *are* ever toward the LORD,
For He shall pluck my feet out of the
net.

25:12 [a]Or *he* [b]Or *he*

24:10 LORD of hosts: Lit. "LORD of armies." God has infinite numbers of angels at His command. Thus He is sovereign over all that exists (see Matt. 26:53).

Psalm 25 A lament which uses the acrostic form—each verse begins with a succeeding letter of the Hebrew alphabet—with a few irregularities. The psalm contains a personal prayer (vv. 1–7); general truths in the form of wisdom statements (vv. 8–15); a second personal prayer (vv. 16–21); and an application to the nation (v. 22).

25:4, 5 Teach me Your paths: Spiritual life is more than the initial experience of trust in God; we must learn to walk in His ways. To **wait** on God is to live in utter dependence upon Him.

25:11 David recognizes his guilt and unworthiness and asks the Lord for forgiveness based not on anything he has done but solely on the Lord's merciful character.

16 Turn Yourself to me, and have mercy
on me,
For I *am* desolate and afflicted.
17 The troubles of my heart have
enlarged;
Bring me out of my distresses!
18 Look on my affliction and my pain,
And forgive all my sins.
19 Consider my enemies, for they are
many;
And they hate me with cruel hatred.
20 Keep my soul, and deliver me;
Let me not be ashamed, for I put my
trust in You.
21 Let integrity and uprightness
preserve me,
For I wait for You.

22 Redeem Israel, O God,
Out of all their troubles!

PSALM 26

A Prayer for Divine Scrutiny and Redemption

A Psalm of David.

Vindicate me, O LORD,
For I have walked in my integrity.
I have also trusted in the LORD;
I shall not slip.
2 Examine me, O LORD, and prove me;
Try my mind and my heart.
3 For Your lovingkindness *is* before my
eyes,
And I have walked in Your truth.
4 I have not sat with idolatrous mortals,
Nor will I go in with hypocrites.
5 I have hated the assembly of
evildoers,
And will not sit with the wicked.

6 I will wash my hands in innocence;
So I will go about Your altar, O LORD,
7 That I may proclaim with the voice of
thanksgiving,
And tell of all Your wondrous works.
8 LORD, I have loved the habitation of
Your house,
And the place where Your glory
dwells.

9 Do not gather my soul with sinners,
Nor my life with bloodthirsty men,
10 In whose hands *is* a sinister scheme,
And whose right hand is full of
bribes.

11 But as for me, I will walk in my
integrity;
Redeem me and be merciful to me.
12 My foot stands in an even place;
In the congregations I will bless the
LORD.

PSALM 27

An Exuberant Declaration of Faith

A Psalm of David.

The LORD *is* my light and my salvation;
Whom shall I fear?
The LORD *is* the strength of my life;
Of whom shall I be afraid?
2 When the wicked came against me
To eat up my flesh,

26:2, 3 Try means to test. It is used in Hebrew for the refining of metals (see Mal. 3:3). **walked in Your truth**: The confession of one who has found the grace of God; it is not to be interpreted as the self-righteous boasting of the Pharisee (see Luke 18:9–14).

26:6–8 Wash my hands may refer to the priestly custom of washing before coming to the altar.

26:11, 12 The **integrity** that David professed in v. 1 is his way of life, but he does not depend upon it in lieu of redemption and mercy. Based on these he can testify, **My foot stands in an even place**. The OT believer often describes his salvation in terms of God giving him a flat place to stand where his feet will not slip (see 18:33; 31:8; 40:2).

27:2 eat up my flesh: A graphic portrayal of the destruction caused by the wicked. It is a phrase used especially of slander.

My enemies and foes,
They stumbled and fell.
3 Though an army may encamp against me,
My heart shall not fear;
Though war may rise against me,
In this I *will be* confident.

4 One *thing* I have desired of the LORD,
That will I seek:
That I may dwell in the house of the LORD
All the days of my life,
To behold the beauty of the LORD,
And to inquire in His temple.
5 For in the time of trouble
He shall hide me in His pavilion;
In the secret place of His tabernacle
He shall hide me;
He shall set me high upon a rock.

6 And now my head shall be lifted up above my enemies all around me;
Therefore I will offer sacrifices of joy in His tabernacle;
I will sing, yes, I will sing praises to the LORD.

7 Hear, O LORD, *when* I cry with my voice!
Have mercy also upon me, and answer me.
8 *When You said,* "Seek My face,"
My heart said to You, "Your face, LORD, I will seek."
9 Do not hide Your face from me;
Do not turn Your servant away in anger;
You have been my help;
Do not leave me nor forsake me,
O God of my salvation.
10 When my father and my mother forsake me,
Then the LORD will take care of me.

11 Teach me Your way, O LORD,
And lead me in a smooth path, because of my enemies.
12 Do not deliver me to the will of my adversaries;
For false witnesses have risen against me,
And such as breathe out violence.
13 *I would have lost heart,* unless I had believed
That I would see the goodness of the LORD
In the land of the living.

14 Wait on the LORD;
Be of good courage,
And He shall strengthen your heart;
Wait, I say, on the LORD!

PSALM 28

Rejoicing in Answered Prayer

A Psalm of David.

To You I will cry, O LORD my Rock:
Do not be silent to me,
Lest, if You *are* silent to me,
I become like those who go down to the pit.
2 Hear the voice of my supplications
When I cry to You,

27:4 One thing I have desired: This puts God's will first in my life. See Phil. 3:13, 14 for a similar desire expressed by Paul. The perfect heart is unified with a single desire: God and His fullness. **inquire in His temple**: Direct communion with God.

27:8 Seek My face: An OT command meaning to come into the presence of God. The **heart** is understood in the OT to be the seat of not only the affections but also the thoughts and the will. He made a complete response.

27:14 What a challenge to us in the hectic pace of today's world! While we are seething with impatience and feeling pressured to act, God is viewing our lives from an eternal, unrushed perspective. His timing is perfect, and we need to learn to wait on Him.

When I lift up my hands toward Your
holy sanctuary.

3 Do not take me away with the wicked
And with the workers of iniquity,
Who speak peace to their neighbors,
But evil *is* in their hearts.
4 Give them according to their deeds,
And according to the wickedness of
their endeavors;
Give them according to the work of
their hands;
Render to them what they deserve.
5 Because they do not regard the works
of the LORD,
Nor the operation of His hands,
He shall destroy them
And not build them up.

6 Blessed *be* the LORD,
Because He has heard the voice of my
supplications!
7 The LORD *is* my strength and my
shield;
My heart trusted in Him, and I am
helped;
Therefore my heart greatly rejoices,
And with my song I will praise Him.

8 The LORD *is* their strength,[a]
And He *is* the saving refuge of His
anointed.
9 Save Your people,
And bless Your inheritance;
Shepherd them also,
And bear them up forever.

PSALM 29

Praise to God in His Holiness and Majesty

A Psalm of David.

Give unto the LORD, O you mighty
ones,
Give unto the LORD glory and
strength.
2 Give unto the LORD the glory due to
His name;
Worship the LORD in the beauty of
holiness.

3 The voice of the LORD *is* over the
waters;
The God of glory thunders;
The LORD *is* over many waters.
4 The voice of the LORD *is* powerful;
The voice of the LORD *is* full of
majesty.

5 The voice of the LORD breaks the
cedars,
Yes, the LORD splinters the cedars of
Lebanon.
6 He makes them also skip like a calf,
Lebanon and Sir'i·on like a young
wild ox.
7 The voice of the LORD divides the
flames of fire.

28:8 [a]Following Masoretic Text and Targum; Septuagint, Syriac, and Vulgate read *the strength of His people.*

28:4 In OT thought God brings justice to everyone in this life. Thus David prays, **Give them . . . what they deserve**.

29:1, 2 We should make worship a regular part of our personal devotions, and we should tell others of God's goodness. **beauty of holiness**: The OT usually portrays God's holiness as causing fear and trembling, but here it recognizes the attractiveness of a holy life in contrast to the ugliness of sin.

29:3–9 Seven times the **voice of the LORD** is mentioned in these seven verses. It is identified with the thunder of a raging storm, moving eastward from the **waters** of the Mediterranean, across **Lebanon**, and through the **wilderness**. Humanity joins in this praise by the angels and the elements: **everyone says, "Glory!"** (v. 9).

29:6 **Sirion**, Mt. Hermon, stands across the Beqa Valley from the Lebanon mountains north of Israel. Here the psalmist declares that the Lord has power to make these great mountains **skip like a calf**.

8 The voice of the LORD shakes the
wilderness;
The LORD shakes the Wilderness of
Kā'desh.
9 The voice of the LORD makes the deer
give birth,
And strips the forests bare;
And in His temple everyone says,
"Glory!"

10 The LORD sat *enthroned* at the Flood,
And the LORD sits as King forever.
11 The LORD will give strength to His
people;
The LORD will bless His people with
peace.

PSALM 30

The Blessedness of Answered Prayer

A Psalm. A Song at the dedication of the house of David.

I will extol You, O LORD, for You have
lifted me up,
And have not let my foes rejoice over
me.
2 O LORD my God, I cried out to You,
And You healed me.
3 O LORD, You brought my soul up
from the grave;
You have kept me alive, that I should
not go down to the pit.[a]

4 Sing praise to the LORD, you saints of
His,
And give thanks at the remembrance
of His holy name.[a]
5 For His anger *is but for* a moment,
His favor *is for* life;
Weeping may endure for a night,
But joy *comes* in the morning.

6 Now in my prosperity I said,
"I shall never be moved."
7 LORD, by Your favor You have made
my mountain stand strong;
You hid Your face, *and* I was troubled.

8 I cried out to You, O LORD;
And to the LORD I made supplication:
9 "What profit *is there* in my blood,
When I go down to the pit?
Will the dust praise You?
Will it declare Your truth?
10 Hear, O LORD, and have mercy on me;
LORD, be my helper!"

11 You have turned for me my
mourning into dancing;
You have put off my sackcloth and
clothed me with gladness,
12 To the end that *my* glory may sing
praise to You and not be silent.
O LORD my God, I will give thanks to
You forever.

PSALM 31

The LORD a Fortress in Adversity

To the Chief Musician. A Psalm of David.

In You, O LORD, I put my trust;
Let me never be ashamed;
Deliver me in Your righteousness.
2 Bow down Your ear to me,
Deliver me speedily;

30:3 [a]Following Qere and Targum; Kethib, Septuagint, Syriac, and Vulgate read *from those who descend to the pit.* 30:4 [a]Or *His holiness*

30:1 Lifted me up translates the Hebrew word used to describe pulling a bucket from a well. It is typical of all that the psalms say of the deliverance of the Lord. Every person needs this saving experience.

30:6 David's sinful pride and self-glorification greatly displeased the Lord. This may refer to the forbidden census described in 1 Chr. 21:1–3. Any prosperity we experience is from the Lord, and He alone should receive the glory.

30:9 Three questions concerning the **profit** or value of a person's death. Much of the OT has a very limited view of life beyond the grave.

Be my rock of refuge,
A fortress of defense to save me.

3 For You *are* my rock and my fortress;
Therefore, for Your name's sake,
Lead me and guide me.
4 Pull me out of the net which they
have secretly laid for me,
For You *are* my strength.
5 Into Your hand I commit my spirit;
You have redeemed me, O LORD God
of truth.

6 I have hated those who regard useless
idols;
But I trust in the LORD.
7 I will be glad and rejoice in Your
mercy,
For You have considered my trouble;
You have known my soul in adversities,
8 And have not shut me up into the
hand of the enemy;
You have set my feet in a wide place.

9 Have mercy on me, O LORD, for I am
in trouble;
My eye wastes away with grief,
Yes, my soul and my body!
10 For my life is spent with grief,
And my years with sighing;
My strength fails because of my
iniquity,
And my bones waste away.
11 I am a reproach among all my
enemies,
But especially among my neighbors,
And *am* repulsive to my
acquaintances;
Those who see me outside flee from
me.
12 I am forgotten like a dead man, out of
mind;
I am like a broken vessel.
13 For I hear the slander of many;
Fear *is* on every side;
While they take counsel together
against me,
They scheme to take away my life.

14 But as for me, I trust in You, O
LORD;
I say, "You *are* my God."
15 My times *are* in Your hand;
Deliver me from the hand of my
enemies,
And from those who persecute me.
16 Make Your face shine upon Your
servant;
Save me for Your mercies' sake.
17 Do not let me be ashamed, O LORD,
for I have called upon You;
Let the wicked be ashamed;
Let them be silent in the grave.
18 Let the lying lips be put to silence,
Which speak insolent things proudly
and contemptuously against the
righteous.

19 Oh, how great *is* Your goodness,
Which You have laid up for those
who fear You,
Which You have prepared for those
who trust in You
In the presence of the sons of
men!
20 You shall hide them in the secret
place of Your presence
From the plots of man;
You shall keep them secretly in a
pavilion
From the strife of tongues.

31:5 This statement of trust was quoted by Jesus on the cross (Luke 23:46) and a similar declaration was made by the martyr Stephen (Acts 7:59).

31:8 set my feet in a wide place: Set me free from the enemies' traps, giving me a number of pleasant choices.

31:15 My times are in Your hand: Not a statement of resignation, but a strong affirmation of faith, as in Rom. 8:28.

21 Blessed *be* the LORD,
For He has shown me His marvelous
kindness in a strong city!
22 For I said in my haste,
"I am cut off from before Your eyes";
Nevertheless You heard the voice of
my supplications
When I cried out to You.

23 Oh, love the LORD, all you His saints!
For the LORD preserves the faithful,
And fully repays the proud person.
24 Be of good courage,
And He shall strengthen your heart,
All you who hope in the LORD.

PSALM 32

The Joy of Forgiveness

A Psalm of David. A Contemplation.[a]

Blessed *is he whose* transgression *is*
forgiven,
Whose sin *is* covered.
2 Blessed *is* the man to whom the LORD
does not impute iniquity,
And in whose spirit *there is* no deceit.

3 When I kept silent, my bones grew
old
Through my groaning all the day
long.
4 For day and night Your hand was
heavy upon me;
My vitality was turned into the
drought of summer. Sē′lah
5 I acknowledged my sin to You,

32:title [a]Hebrew *Maschil*

Hide me, O my Savior, hide,
Till the storm of life be past;
Safe into the haven guide,
O receive my soul at last.
Charles Wesley

And my iniquity I have not hidden.
I said, "I will confess my
transgressions to the LORD,"
And You forgave the iniquity of my
sin. Sē′lah

6 For this cause everyone who is godly
shall pray to You
In a time when You may be found;
Surely in a flood of great waters
They shall not come near him.
7 You *are* my hiding place;
You shall preserve me from trouble;
You shall surround me with songs of
deliverance. Sē′lah

8 I will instruct you and teach you in
the way you should go;
I will guide you with My eye.
9 Do not be like the horse *or* like the
mule,
Which have no understanding,
Which must be harnessed with bit
and bridle,
Else they will not come near you.

10 Many sorrows *shall be* to the wicked;
But he who trusts in the LORD, mercy
shall surround him.

31:21, 22 The Hebrew word here translated **kindness** speaks of God's passionate, and wholly undeserved, loyalty to His own. It is too impetuous to say **I am cut off** from God.

32:3–5 The confession of David is the experience of everyone. When he **kept silent** in resistance to God, the inner struggle of conscience and conviction drained away the very **vitality** of life. But when he said, **I will confess my transgressions**, then God **forgave**. See 1 John 1:9. This passage confirms the principle that physical and emotional health are greatly impacted by spiritual well-being.

32:10, 11 mercy shall surround him: This is not to say that the righteous will never have trouble, but that by God's gracious provision, they may come through the trouble in triumph (see 34:19).

11 Be glad in the LORD and rejoice, you righteous;
And shout for joy, all *you* upright in heart!

PSALM 33

The Sovereignty of the LORD in Creation and History

Rejoice in the LORD, O you righteous!
For praise from the upright is beautiful.
2 Praise the LORD with the harp;
Make melody to Him with an instrument of ten strings.
3 Sing to Him a new song;
Play skillfully with a shout of joy.

4 For the word of the LORD *is* right,
And all His work *is done* in truth.
5 He loves righteousness and justice;
The earth is full of the goodness of the LORD.

6 By the word of the LORD the heavens were made,
And all the host of them by the breath of His mouth.
7 He gathers the waters of the sea together as a heap;[a]
He lays up the deep in storehouses.

8 Let all the earth fear the LORD;
Let all the inhabitants of the world stand in awe of Him.
9 For He spoke, and it was *done;*
He commanded, and it stood fast.

10 The LORD brings the counsel of the nations to nothing;
He makes the plans of the peoples of no effect.
11 The counsel of the LORD stands forever,
The plans of His heart to all generations.
12 Blessed *is* the nation whose God *is* the LORD,
The people He has chosen as His own inheritance.

13 The LORD looks from heaven;
He sees all the sons of men.
14 From the place of His dwelling He looks
On all the inhabitants of the earth;
15 He fashions their hearts individually;
He considers all their works.

16 No king *is* saved by the multitude of an army;
A mighty man is not delivered by great strength.
17 A horse *is* a vain hope for safety;
Neither shall it deliver *any* by its great strength.

18 Behold, the eye of the LORD *is* on those who fear Him,
On those who hope in His mercy,
19 To deliver their soul from death,
And to keep them alive in famine.

20 Our soul waits for the LORD;
He *is* our help and our shield.
21 For our heart shall rejoice in Him,
Because we have trusted in His holy name.

33:7 [a]Septuagint, Targum, and Vulgate read *in a vessel.*

33:6–9 He spoke, and it was (v. 9): God spoke the universe into existence as the expression of His divine will. See Gen. 1:3.

33:14, 15 The Lord knows where I am and what I am doing. **fashions their hearts individually**: In Hebrew, "The One who forms their hearts together." The sense is that because God created human personality, He understands exactly why we do what we do and is thus able to judge rightly.

33:16, 17 No human measure of strength is accurate unless it takes the Lord into account. Time and time again, the Israelites conquered armies much greater than theirs by earthly standards. God was their secret weapon and, if we're on His side, He'll be ours, too.

22 Let Your mercy, O LORD, be upon us,
Just as we hope in You.

PSALM 34

The Happiness of Those Who Trust in God

A Psalm of David when he pretended madness before Abimelech, who drove him away, and he departed.

I will bless the LORD at all times;
His praise *shall* continually *be* in my mouth.
2 My soul shall make its boast in the LORD;
The humble shall hear *of it* and be glad.
3 Oh, magnify the LORD with me,
And let us exalt His name together.

4 I sought the LORD, and He heard me,
And delivered me from all my fears.
5 They looked to Him and were radiant,
And their faces were not ashamed.
6 This poor man cried out, and the LORD heard *him,*
And saved him out of all his troubles.
7 The angel[a] of the LORD encamps all around those who fear Him,
And delivers them.

8 Oh, taste and see that the LORD *is* good;
Blessed *is* the man *who* trusts in Him!
9 Oh, fear the LORD, you His saints!
There is no want to those who fear Him.

34:7 [a]Or *Angel*

10 The young lions lack and suffer hunger;
But those who seek the LORD shall not lack any good *thing.*

11 Come, you children, listen to me;
I will teach you the fear of the LORD.
12 Who *is* the man *who* desires life,
And loves *many* days, that he may see good?
13 Keep your tongue from evil,
And your lips from speaking deceit.
14 Depart from evil and do good;
Seek peace and pursue it.

15 The eyes of the LORD *are* on the righteous,
And His ears *are open* to their cry.
16 The face of the LORD *is* against those who do evil,
To cut off the remembrance of them from the earth.

17 *The righteous* cry out, and the LORD hears,
And delivers them out of all their troubles.
18 The LORD *is* near to those who have a broken heart,
And saves such as have a contrite spirit.

19 Many *are* the afflictions of the righteous,
But the LORD delivers him out of them all.
20 He guards all his bones;
Not one of them is broken.

34:title before Abimelech: In 1 Sam. 21:10–15, where this incident is reported, the king's name is given as Achish. Possibly "Abimelech" was a title for kings of the Philistine regions (see Gen. 20:2; 26:1) as Pharaoh was for Egypt.

34:8 Anyone who has truly experienced the Lord's grace longs to have others share in the joy.

34:13 Keep your tongue: Again and again in the Bible, it is our mouth that shows our true relationship to God (see Job 5:21; Ps. 120:2; Is. 6:5; James 3:5).

34:18 broken heart . . . contrite spirit: The conditions for approaching God and receiving His grace and help. These are the sacrifices God will not consider worthless (see 51:17).

21 Evil shall slay the wicked,
And those who hate the righteous
shall be condemned.
22 The LORD redeems the soul of His
servants,
And none of those who trust in Him
shall be condemned.

PSALM 35

The LORD the Avenger of His People

A Psalm of David.

Plead *my cause,* O LORD, with those who
strive with me;
Fight against those who fight against
me.
2 Take hold of shield and buckler,
And stand up for my help.
3 Also draw out the spear,
And stop those who pursue me.
Say to my soul,
"I *am* your salvation."

4 Let those be put to shame and
brought to dishonor
Who seek after my life;
Let those be turned back and brought
to confusion
Who plot my hurt.
5 Let them be like chaff before the
wind,
And let the angel[a] of the LORD chase
them.
6 Let their way be dark and slippery,
And let the angel of the LORD pursue
them.
7 For without cause they have hidden
their net for me *in* a pit,
Which they have dug without cause
for my life.
8 Let destruction come upon him
unexpectedly,
And let his net that he has hidden
catch himself;
Into that very destruction let him fall.

9 And my soul shall be joyful in the
LORD;
It shall rejoice in His salvation.
10 All my bones shall say,
"LORD, who *is* like You,
Delivering the poor from him who is
too strong for him,
Yes, the poor and the needy from him
who plunders him?"

11 Fierce witnesses rise up;
They ask me *things* that I do not
know.
12 They reward me evil for good,
To the sorrow of my soul.
13 But as for me, when they were sick,
My clothing *was* sackcloth;
I humbled myself with fasting;
And my prayer would return to my
own heart.
14 I paced about as though *he were* my
friend *or* brother;
I bowed down heavily, as one who
mourns *for his* mother.

15 But in my adversity they rejoiced
And gathered together;
Attackers gathered against me,
And I did not know *it;*
They tore *at me* and did not cease;

35:5 [a]Or *Angel*

35:1 Plead my cause is language of the legal system. David sees the Lord as his Advocate (see 1 John 2:1), the One who will **fight** his foes.

35:4–8 David prays against his enemies. Because he sees his persecution as being **without cause**, he prays for the **destruction** of the persecutors.

35:9, 10 In full expectation of divine deliverance, **my soul** can break forth in praise. **All my bones**: His total being is involved in praising God. The opposite experience is in view in 38:3.

35:13, 14 But as for me: These people to whom he once had shown compassion now show none to him. **my prayer would return**: It went unanswered.

35:15, 16 They tore at me: As is frequent in laments, persecutors are compared to wild beasts. In Semitic languages slander is often referred to by such figures.

16 With ungodly mockers at feasts
They gnashed at me with their teeth.

17 Lord, how long will You look on?
Rescue me from their destructions,
My precious *life* from the lions.
18 I will give You thanks in the great
assembly;
I will praise You among many people.

19 Let them not rejoice over me who are
wrongfully my enemies;
Nor let them wink with the eye who
hate me without a cause.
20 For they do not speak peace,
But they devise deceitful matters
Against *the* quiet ones in the land.
21 They also opened their mouth wide
against me,
And said, "Aha, aha!
Our eyes have seen *it*."

22 *This* You have seen, O LORD;
Do not keep silence.
O Lord, do not be far from me.
23 Stir up Yourself, and awake to my
vindication,
To my cause, my God and my Lord.
24 Vindicate me, O LORD my God,
according to Your righteousness;
And let them not rejoice over me.
25 Let them not say in their hearts, "Ah,
so we would have it!"
Let them not say, "We have
swallowed him up."

26 Let them be ashamed and brought to
mutual confusion
Who rejoice at my hurt;
Let them be clothed with shame and
dishonor
Who exalt themselves against me.

27 Let them shout for joy and be glad,
Who favor my righteous cause;
And let them say continually,
"Let the LORD be magnified,
Who has pleasure in the prosperity of
His servant."
28 And my tongue shall speak of Your
righteousness
And of Your praise all the day long.

PSALM 36

Man's Wickedness and God's Perfections

To the Chief Musician. A Psalm of David the servant of the LORD.

An oracle within my heart concerning
the transgression of the wicked:
There is no fear of God before his
eyes.
2 For he flatters himself in his own
eyes,
When he finds out his iniquity *and*
when he hates.
3 The words of his mouth *are*
wickedness and deceit;
He has ceased to be wise *and* to do
good.
4 He devises wickedness on his bed;
He sets himself in a way *that is* not
good;
He does not abhor evil.

5 Your mercy, O LORD, *is* in the
heavens;
Your faithfulness *reaches* to the clouds.
6 Your righteousness *is* like the great
mountains;
Your judgments *are* a great deep;
O LORD, You preserve man and beast.

36:1 no fear of God: A characteristic of the sinner. In contrast the proper fear of God—living as accountable to an all-knowing, all-powerful, all-righteous Creator—is the typical OT description of right religion. The description of the wicked (vv. 2–4) follows logically from no fear of God. Failure to acknowledge God's holy lordship leaves the apparent attractions of evil without check.

36:5–9 The character of the Lord is described in contrast to the depravity of the wicked (vv.1–4).

7 How precious *is* Your lovingkindness, O God!
Therefore the children of men put their trust under the shadow of Your wings.
8 They are abundantly satisfied with the fullness of Your house,
And You give them drink from the river of Your pleasures.
9 For with You *is* the fountain of life;
In Your light we see light.

10 Oh, continue Your lovingkindness to those who know You,
And Your righteousness to the upright in heart.
11 Let not the foot of pride come against me,
And let not the hand of the wicked drive me away.
12 There the workers of iniquity have fallen;
They have been cast down and are not able to rise.

PSALM 37

The Heritage of the Righteous and the Calamity of the Wicked

A Psalm of David.

Do not fret because of evildoers,
Nor be envious of the workers of iniquity.
2 For they shall soon be cut down like the grass,
And wither as the green herb.

3 Trust in the LORD, and do good;
Dwell in the land, and feed on His faithfulness.
4 Delight yourself also in the LORD,
And He shall give you the desires of your heart.

5 Commit your way to the LORD,
Trust also in Him,
And He shall bring *it* to pass.
6 He shall bring forth your righteousness as the light,
And your justice as the noonday.

7 Rest in the LORD, and wait patiently for Him;
Do not fret because of him who prospers in his way,
Because of the man who brings wicked schemes to pass.
8 Cease from anger, and forsake wrath;
Do not fret—*it* only *causes* harm.

9 For evildoers shall be cut off;
But those who wait on the LORD,
They shall inherit the earth.
10 For yet a little while and the wicked *shall be* no *more;*
Indeed, you will look carefully for his place,
But it *shall be* no *more.*

36:9 fountain of life: God not only has life, He is its source (see John 4:7–15). God is also the source of **light** (see 1 John 1:5–7; 2:8–11).

36:11 The foot of pride is placed on the necks of those forced to submit; **the hand of the wicked** is clenched into a fist to make others obey an evil purpose.

Psalm 37 This collection of wise sayings is often compared to the Book of Proverbs. Its basic theme is to commend trust in God for everyday living in the face of wickedness and temptation, because despite temporary prosperity, the wicked must ultimately fail. Each section of the psalm contains some reference to the failure of the wicked and the ultimate triumph of the righteous. It is an alphabetic acrostic in which every opening word of every other verse begins with a succeeding letter of the Hebrew alphabet.

37:3–6 A clear four-part prescription for the diseases of anxiety and envy: **trust, dwell, delight, commit**.

37:5 As we approach or begin retirement, we're faced with many difficult decisions regarding the future. By taking this verse to heart and relying on the Lord, we can set aside our worries and leave the navigating to Him!

11 But the meek shall inherit the earth,
And shall delight themselves in the abundance of peace.

12 The wicked plots against the just,
And gnashes at him with his teeth.
13 The Lord laughs at him,
For He sees that his day is coming.
14 The wicked have drawn the sword
And have bent their bow,
To cast down the poor and needy,
To slay those who are of upright conduct.
15 Their sword shall enter their own heart,
And their bows shall be broken.

16 A little that a righteous man has
Is better than the riches of many wicked.
17 For the arms of the wicked shall be broken,
But the LORD upholds the righteous.

18 The LORD knows the days of the upright,
And their inheritance shall be forever.
19 They shall not be ashamed in the evil time,
And in the days of famine they shall be satisfied.
20 But the wicked shall perish;
And the enemies of the LORD,
Like the splendor of the meadows, shall vanish.
Into smoke they shall vanish away.

21 The wicked borrows and does not repay,
But the righteous shows mercy and gives.
22 For *those* blessed by Him shall inherit the earth,
But *those* cursed by Him shall be cut off.

23 The steps of a *good* man are ordered by the LORD,
And He delights in his way.
24 Though he fall, he shall not be utterly cast down;
For the LORD upholds *him with* His hand.

25 I have been young, and *now* am old;
Yet I have not seen the righteous forsaken,
Nor his descendants begging bread.
26 *He is* ever merciful, and lends;
And his descendants *are* blessed.

27 Depart from evil, and do good;
And dwell forevermore.
28 For the LORD loves justice,
And does not forsake His saints;
They are preserved forever,
But the descendants of the wicked shall be cut off.
29 The righteous shall inherit the land,
And dwell in it forever.

30 The mouth of the righteous speaks wisdom,
And his tongue talks of justice.
31 The law of his God *is* in his heart;
None of his steps shall slide.

32 The wicked watches the righteous,
And seeks to slay him.
33 The LORD will not leave him in his hand,
Nor condemn him when he is judged.

37:27–29 A summary of the basic teaching of the OT. Fundamental to this teaching is the command: **Depart from evil . . . do good**. The consequence which follows is to **dwell forevermore**. God's love of **justice** is our perfect assurance that His **saints . . . are preserved**, but the **wicked** are **cut off**.

37:31 The law . . . is in his heart: The inward nature of true religion (see Jer. 31:33). The law is then no longer an external burden, but becomes a delight to the soul. Ps. 119 is a celebration of this delight in God's law.

> The great thing in this world is not so much where we are, but in what direction we are moving.
> Oliver Wendell Holmes

34 Wait on the LORD,
And keep His way,
And He shall exalt you to inherit the land;
When the wicked are cut off, you shall see *it*.
35 I have seen the wicked in great power,
And spreading himself like a native green tree.
36 Yet he passed away,[a] and behold, he *was* no *more;*
Indeed I sought him, but he could not be found.

37 Mark the blameless *man,* and observe the upright;
For the future of *that* man *is* peace.
38 But the transgressors shall be destroyed together;
The future of the wicked shall be cut off.

39 But the salvation of the righteous *is* from the LORD;
He is their strength in the time of trouble.
40 And the LORD shall help them and deliver them;
He shall deliver them from the wicked,
And save them,
Because they trust in Him.

PSALM 38

Prayer in Time of Chastening

A Psalm of David. To bring to remembrance.

O LORD, do not rebuke me in Your wrath,
Nor chasten me in Your hot displeasure!
2 For Your arrows pierce me deeply,
And Your hand presses me down.

3 *There is* no soundness in my flesh
Because of Your anger,
Nor *any* health in my bones
Because of my sin.
4 For my iniquities have gone over my head;
Like a heavy burden they are too heavy for me.
5 My wounds are foul *and* festering
Because of my foolishness.

6 I am troubled, I am bowed down greatly;
I go mourning all the day long.
7 For my loins are full of inflammation,
And *there is* no soundness in my flesh.
8 I am feeble and severely broken;
I groan because of the turmoil of my heart.

9 Lord, all my desire *is* before You;
And my sighing is not hidden from You.
10 My heart pants, my strength fails me;
As for the light of my eyes, it also has gone from me.

11 My loved ones and my friends stand aloof from my plague,

37:36 [a]Following Masoretic Text, Septuagint, and Targum; Syriac and Vulgate read *I passed by.*

37:34 To **wait on the LORD** is a patient dependence with expectant faith, not fretting and anxious. It is difficult to practice, but absolutely essential.

38:3–5 While there is often a close connection between conviction for **sin** and physical suffering, the language here may also be figurative of his soul's condition (see 32:3; 35:10).

And my relatives stand afar off.
12 Those also who seek my life lay
snares *for me;*
Those who seek my hurt speak of
destruction,
And plan deception all the day long.

13 But I, like a deaf *man,* do not hear;
And *I am* like a mute *who* does not
open his mouth.
14 Thus I am like a man who does not
hear,
And in whose mouth *is* no response.

15 For in You, O LORD, I hope;
You will hear, O Lord my God.
16 For I said, "*Hear me,* lest they rejoice
over me,
Lest, when my foot slips, they exalt
themselves against me."

17 For I *am* ready to fall,
And my sorrow *is* continually before
me.
18 For I will declare my iniquity;
I will be in anguish over my sin.
19 But my enemies *are* vigorous, *and*
they are strong;
And those who hate me wrongfully
have multiplied.
20 Those also who render evil for good,
They are my adversaries, because I
follow *what is* good.

21 Do not forsake me, O LORD;
O my God, be not far from me!
22 Make haste to help me,
O Lord, my salvation!

PSALM 39

Prayer for Wisdom and Forgiveness

To the Chief Musician. To Jedūthun. A Psalm of David.

I said, "I will guard my ways,
Lest I sin with my tongue;
I will restrain my mouth with a
muzzle,
While the wicked are before me."
2 I was mute with silence,
I held my peace *even* from good;
And my sorrow was stirred up.
3 My heart was hot within me;
While I was musing, the fire burned.
Then I spoke with my tongue:

4 "LORD, make me to know my end,
And what *is* the measure of my days,
That I may know how frail I *am.*
5 Indeed, You have made my days *as*
handbreadths,
And my age *is* as nothing before You;
Certainly every man at his best state
is but vapor. Sē'lah
6 Surely every man walks about like a
shadow;
Surely they busy themselves in vain;
He heaps up *riches,*
And does not know who will gather
them.

7 "And now, Lord, what do I wait for?
My hope *is* in You.

38:17 I am ready to fall speaks of weakness that is a result of his sin, freely confessed in v. 18. Sin weakens our character, willpower, and resolve for constructive action.

38:18 Rather than glossing over his "mistakes," as we often tend to do, David humbly acknowledged his error as "sin" and "iniquity." The Lord knows our hearts and it's foolish to attempt to cover up our transgressions or disguise them as simple "mistakes." We're only deceiving ourselves.

39:title 1 Chr. 15:17–19 tells us that Jeduthun is another name for Ethan, one of David's musicians.

39:1–3 Though suffering from God's discipline (vv. 9, 10), David recognizes the power of the **tongue** for evil as expressed in James 3:1–12. The temptation to sin in this way is especially prevalent in the presence of the **wicked**. Self-control and restraint are marks of grace. **My heart was hot** speaks of strong agitation of spirit which eventually led him to break his vow of v. 1. Evidently what disturbed him was the apparent futility of life reflected in vv. 4–6.

39:7–11 what do I wait for? The question is answered by the hope and expectation of the child of God, which is not disappointed. **You who did it**: He recognized that God had

8 Deliver me from all my
transgressions;
Do not make me the reproach of the
foolish.
9 I was mute, I did not open my mouth,
Because it was You who did *it.*
10 Remove Your plague from me;
I am consumed by the blow of Your
hand.
11 When with rebukes You correct man
for iniquity,
You make his beauty melt away like a
moth;
Surely every man *is* vapor. Sē'lah

12 "Hear my prayer, O LORD,
And give ear to my cry;
Do not be silent at my tears;
For I *am* a stranger with You,
A sojourner, as all my fathers *were.*
13 Remove Your gaze from me, that I
may regain strength,
Before I go away and am no more."

PSALM 40

Faith Persevering in Trial

To the Chief Musician. A Psalm of David.

I waited patiently for the LORD;
And He inclined to me,
And heard my cry.
2 He also brought me up out of a
horrible pit,
Out of the miry clay,
And set my feet upon a rock,
And established my steps.
3 He has put a new song in my
mouth—
Praise to our God;
Many will see *it* and fear,
And will trust in the LORD.

I pray that my friend will wait patiently for You, Lord, and that You will incline Yourself to her and hear her cry.

adapted from Psalm 40:1

4 Blessed *is* that man who makes the
LORD his trust,
And does not respect the proud, nor
such as turn aside to lies.
5 Many, O LORD my God, *are* Your
wonderful works
Which You have done;
And Your thoughts toward us
Cannot be recounted to You in order;
If I would declare and speak *of them,*
They are more than can be numbered.

6 Sacrifice and offering You did not
desire;
My ears You have opened.
Burnt offering and sin offering You
did not require.
7 Then I said, "Behold, I come;
In the scroll of the book *it is* written
of me.
8 I delight to do Your will, O my God,
And Your law *is* within my heart."

9 I have proclaimed the good news of
righteousness
In the great assembly;
Indeed, I do not restrain my lips,
O LORD, You Yourself know.
10 I have not hidden Your righteousness
within my heart;

permitted his trouble in order to discipline him. **consumed by . . . Your hand**: He felt almost destroyed by the discipline of God. **You correct man for iniquity**: God disciplines us "that we may be partakers of His holiness" (Heb. 12:10). The heavenly Father loves us too much to allow us to blindly follow the ways of sin. Yet His correction often seems too much for the fragility of life (see 90:9). **beauty**: Man's sense of well-being.

40:5 Your thoughts: We are never out of God's consciousness; He never forgets us.

40:6–8 The author of Hebrews quotes these verses in reference to Jesus.

I have declared Your faithfulness and
Your salvation;
I have not concealed Your
lovingkindness and Your truth
From the great assembly.

11 Do not withhold Your tender mercies
from me, O LORD;
Let Your lovingkindness and Your
truth continually preserve me.
12 For innumerable evils have
surrounded me;
My iniquities have overtaken me, so
that I am not able to look up;
They are more than the hairs of my
head;
Therefore my heart fails me.

13 Be pleased, O LORD, to deliver
me;
O LORD, make haste to help me!
14 Let them be ashamed and brought to
mutual confusion
Who seek to destroy my life;
Let them be driven backward and
brought to dishonor
Who wish me evil.
15 Let them be confounded because of
their shame,
Who say to me, "Aha, aha!"

16 Let all those who seek You rejoice and
be glad in You;
Let such as love Your salvation say
continually,
"The LORD be magnified!"
17 But I *am* poor and needy;
Yet the LORD thinks upon me.
You *are* my help and my deliverer;
Do not delay, O my God.

PSALM 41

The Blessing and Suffering of the Godly

To the Chief Musician. A Psalm of David.

Blessed *is* he who considers the poor;
The LORD will deliver him in time of
trouble.
2 The LORD will preserve him and keep
him alive,
And he will be blessed on the earth;
You will not deliver him to the will of
his enemies.
3 The LORD will strengthen him on his
bed of illness;
You will sustain him on his sickbed.

4 I said, "LORD, be merciful to me;
Heal my soul, for I have sinned
against You."
5 My enemies speak evil of me:
"When will he die, and his name
perish?"
6 And if he comes to see *me,* he speaks
lies;
His heart gathers iniquity to itself;
When he goes out, he tells *it.*

7 All who hate me whisper together
against me;
Against me they devise my hurt.
8 "An evil disease," *they say,* "clings to
him.
And *now* that he lies down, he will
rise up no more."
9 Even my own familiar friend in
whom I trusted,
Who ate my bread,
Has lifted up *his* heel against me.

10 But You, O LORD, be merciful to me,
and raise me up,
That I may repay them.

41:1–3 Blessed: This opening beatitude is close to the words of Jesus, "Blessed are the merciful" (Matt. 5:7). It is followed by four glowing terms describing God's faithfulness: **deliver, preserve, strengthen,** and **sustain**.

41:8 An evil disease: A terminal illness.

41:9 lifted up his heel: An expression of enmity.

41:10 Rather than dwelling on the treachery of his one-time friend, David turns to the Lord for help and comfort.

11 By this I know that You are well
pleased with me,
Because my enemy does not triumph
over me.
12 As for me, You uphold me in my
integrity,
And set me before Your face forever.

13 Blessed *be* the LORD God of Israel
From everlasting to everlasting!
Amen and Amen.

Book Two: Psalms 42—72

PSALM 42

Yearning for God in the Midst of Distresses

To the Chief Musician. A Contemplation[a] *of the sons of Kōrah.*

As the deer pants for the water brooks,
So pants my soul for You, O God.
2 My soul thirsts for God, for the living
God.
When shall I come and appear before
God?[a]
3 My tears have been my food day and
night,
While they continually say to me,
"Where *is* your God?"

4 When I remember these *things,*
I pour out my soul within me.
For I used to go with the multitude;
I went with them to the house of God,
With the voice of joy and praise,
With a multitude that kept a pilgrim
feast.

5 Why are you cast down, O my soul?
And *why* are you disquieted within
me?
Hope in God, for I shall yet praise
Him
For the help of His countenance.[a]

6 O my God,[a] my soul is cast down
within me;
Therefore I will remember You from
the land of the Jordan,
And from the heights of Her'mon,
From the Hill Mī'zar.
7 Deep calls unto deep at the noise of
Your waterfalls;
All Your waves and billows have
gone over me.
8 The LORD will command His
lovingkindness in the daytime,
And in the night His song *shall be*
with me—
A prayer to the God of my life.

9 I will say to God my Rock,
"Why have You forgotten me?
Why do I go mourning because of the
oppression of the enemy?"
10 *As* with a breaking of my bones,
My enemies reproach me,
While they say to me all day long,
"Where *is* your God?"

42:title [a]Hebrew *Maschil* 42:2 [a]Following Masoretic Text and Vulgate; some Hebrew manuscripts, Septuagint, Syriac, and Targum read *I see the face of God.* 42:5 [a]Following Masoretic Text and Targum; a few Hebrew manuscripts, Septuagint, Syriac, and Vulgate read *The help of my countenance, my God.* 42:6 [a]Following Masoretic Text and Targum; a few Hebrew manuscripts, Septuagint, Syriac, and Vulgate put *my God* at the end of verse 5.

41:13 This doxology indicates the end of the first book of the Psalms (see also 72:18, 19; 89:52; 106:48; 150).

Psalm 42 The psalmist eloquently expresses the suffering he endured away from God and the temple. In vv. 1–5 he tells of his spiritual thirst during a sad experience of exile; in vv. 6–11 the agony continues as he prays. Both sections end with the psalmist encouraging himself to trust God (vv. 5, 11). See introduction to Ps. 43.

42:2 My soul thirsts: For one who had known God, to be cut off from His presence brings spiritual desire as real as physical thirst. A truly mature Christian should be so in tune to the presence of God that any breach in fellowship will be immediately noticed so reparation can be sought.

Hope in God

Barbara Johnson

No matter what the pain and problems may be like, everybody is looking for the answers to two basic questions: Why? and How? Folks who write to me often ask, "Why me?" "Why us?" "Why our family?" But just as often they also want to know, "how." "How can I deal with this?" "How do I learn to live with pain?"

I do not have all the answers. Frankly, sometimes I am not even sure I fully understand the questions. I wish I could always have something to say that would make everything all right right now, but I don't. I do know one thing, though: Whatever comes to any of us is sent or allowed by God.

"Whatever comes to any of us is sent or allowed by God."

To some people, that may make God sound weak, uncaring, or even sadistic, but when you are facing the real world, it helps to remember that God is in control. He is still at work, even when we feel that our suffering will never end. As the psalmist commanded, we must "hope in God." ✦

11 Why are you cast down, O my soul?
And why are you disquieted within me?
Hope in God;
For I shall yet praise Him,
The help of my countenance and my God.

PSALM 43

Prayer to God in Time of Trouble

Vindicate me, O God,
And plead my cause against an ungodly nation;
Oh, deliver me from the deceitful and unjust man!
2 For You *are* the God of my strength;
Why do You cast me off?
Why do I go mourning because of the oppression of the enemy?

3 Oh, send out Your light and Your truth!
Let them lead me;
Let them bring me to Your holy hill
And to Your tabernacle.
4 Then I will go to the altar of God,
To God my exceeding joy;
And on the harp I will praise You,
O God, my God.

5 Why are you cast down, O my soul?

Psalm 43 Some consider this psalm to be the conclusion of Ps. 42, noting a parallel progression of thought and the similar wording of 42:5, 11 and 43:5. This might explain why Ps. 43 has no superscription. In any case, the psalm stands independently as a prayer.

And why are you disquieted within me?
Hope in God;
For I shall yet praise Him,
The help of my countenance and my God.

PSALM 44

Redemption Remembered in Present Dishonor

To the Chief Musician. A Contemplation[a] *of the sons of Kōrah.*

We have heard with our ears, O God,
Our fathers have told us,
The deeds You did in their days,
In days of old:
2 You drove out the nations with Your hand,
But them You planted;
You afflicted the peoples, and cast them out.
3 For they did not gain possession of the land by their own sword,
Nor did their own arm save them;
But it was Your right hand, Your arm, and the light of Your countenance,
Because You favored them.

4 You are my King, O God;[a]
Command[b] victories for Jacob.
5 Through You we will push down our enemies;
Through Your name we will trample those who rise up against us.
6 For I will not trust in my bow,
Nor shall my sword save me.
7 But You have saved us from our enemies,
And have put to shame those who hated us.
8 In God we boast all day long,
And praise Your name forever. Sē′lah

9 But You have cast *us* off and put us to shame,
And You do not go out with our armies.
10 You make us turn back from the enemy,
And those who hate us have taken spoil for themselves.
11 You have given us up like sheep *intended* for food,
And have scattered us among the nations.
12 You sell Your people for *next to* nothing,
And are not enriched by selling them.

13 You make us a reproach to our neighbors,
A scorn and a derision to those all around us.
14 You make us a byword among the nations,
A shaking of the head among the peoples.
15 My dishonor *is* continually before me,
And the shame of my face has covered me,

44:title [a]Hebrew *Maschil* 44:4 [a]Following Masoretic Text and Targum; Septuagint and Vulgate read *and my God.* [b]Following Masoretic Text and Targum; Septuagint, Syriac, and Vulgate read *Who commands.*

44:1–3 In days of old: The glorious history of Israel is recalled. They believed that God was then in control; their successes came because the Lord Himself fought for them (Deut. 3:22). Today God is still in control not only of the world in general, but of each of our lives individually. Thus, while we continue to work at the tasks He has assigned us, we don't need to waste energy worrying about the outcome; the battle—and the victory—belong to the Lord.

44:4–8 The psalmist expresses confidence that God will continue to fight for Israel. He affirms, **You are my King**. This affirmation is doubly significant if the psalmist himself was the ruling king or commander of the army.

44:6 not . . . my bow, Nor . . . my sword: The Lord's angel would later deliver the same message to the prophet Zechariah about accomplishing God's work: "Not by might nor by power, but by My Spirit" (Zech. 4:6).

16 Because of the voice of him who
reproaches and reviles,
Because of the enemy and the
avenger.

17 All this has come upon us;
But we have not forgotten You,
Nor have we dealt falsely with Your
covenant.
18 Our heart has not turned back,
Nor have our steps departed from
Your way;
19 But You have severely broken us in
the place of jackals,
And covered us with the shadow of
death.

20 If we had forgotten the name of our
God,
Or stretched out our hands to a
foreign god,
21 Would not God search this out?
For He knows the secrets of the heart.
22 Yet for Your sake we are killed all day
long;
We are accounted as sheep for the
slaughter.

23 Awake! Why do You sleep, O Lord?
Arise! Do not cast *us* off forever.
24 Why do You hide Your face,
And forget our affliction and our
oppression?
25 For our soul is bowed down to the
dust;
Our body clings to the ground.
26 Arise for our help,
And redeem us for Your mercies'
sake.

PSALM 45

The Glories of the Messiah and His Bride

To the Chief Musician. Set to "The Lilies."[a] *A Contemplation*[b] *of the sons of Kōrah. A Song of Love.*

My heart is overflowing with a good
theme;
I recite my composition concerning
the King;
My tongue *is* the pen of a ready
writer.

2 You are fairer than the sons of men;
Grace is poured upon Your lips;
Therefore God has blessed You
forever.
3 Gird Your sword upon *Your* thigh, O
Mighty One,
With Your glory and Your majesty.
4 And in Your majesty ride
prosperously because of truth,
humility, *and* righteousness;
And Your right hand shall teach You
awesome things.
5 Your arrows *are* sharp in the heart of
the King's enemies;
The peoples fall under You.

6 Your throne, O God, *is* forever and
ever;
A scepter of righteousness *is* the
scepter of Your kingdom.
7 You love righteousness and hate
wickedness;
Therefore God, Your God, has
anointed You
With the oil of gladness more than
Your companions.
8 All Your garments are scented with
myrrh and aloes *and* cassia,

45:title [a]Hebrew *Shoshannim* [b]Hebrew *Maschil*

44:17–22 This protest of righteousness certainly cannot describe either Israel or Judah before their respective exiles. The denunciations of all the prophets concerning Israel's pre-exilic breaking of the **covenant** are too clear. Perhaps these verses are the words of the righteous remnant during the exile. They have not surrendered their faith despite suffering and deprivation.

Psalm 45 This psalm describes the crown prince, or the king, marrying a princess. The psalm is also messianic, as it is interpreted in the NT (see Heb. 1:8, 9). The king is addressed in vv. 1–9, 16, 17, while the princess is addressed in vv. 10–15.

Out of the ivory palaces, by which
they have made You glad.
9 Kings' daughters *are* among Your
honorable women;
At Your right hand stands the queen
in gold from Ō'phir.

10 Listen, O daughter,
Consider and incline your ear;
Forget your own people also, and
your father's house;
11 So the King will greatly desire your
beauty;
Because He *is* your Lord, worship
Him.
12 And the daughter of Tȳre *will come*
with a gift;
The rich among the people will seek
your favor.

13 The royal daughter *is* all glorious
within *the palace;*
Her clothing *is* woven with gold.
14 She shall be brought to the King in
robes of many colors;
The virgins, her companions who
follow her, shall be brought to You.
15 With gladness and rejoicing they shall
be brought;
They shall enter the King's palace.

16 Instead of Your fathers shall be Your
sons,
Whom You shall make princes in all
the earth.
17 I will make Your name to be
remembered in all generations;

I praise you, O God, because You are my refuge and strength and a very present help in trouble.

adapted from Psalm 46:1

Therefore the people shall praise You
forever and ever.

PSALM 46

God the Refuge of His People and Conqueror of the Nations

To the Chief Musician. A Psalm of the sons of Kōrah. A Song for Alamoth.

God *is* our refuge and strength,
A very present help in trouble.
2 Therefore we will not fear,
Even though the earth be removed,
And though the mountains be carried
into the midst of the sea;
3 *Though* its waters roar *and* be
troubled,
Though the mountains shake with its
swelling. Sē'lah

4 *There is* a river whose streams shall
make glad the city of God,
The holy *place* of the tabernacle of the
Most High.
5 God *is* in the midst of her, she shall
not be moved;
God shall help her, just at the break of
dawn.

45:10 Just as a bride is required to break with her family and culture when she marries, so Christians are to sever all ties to the world and commit themselves wholly to the Lord.

45:16, 17 in all generations: The Messiah is promised an everlasting kingdom. This was partly accomplished by preserving the succession of family members in the Davidic royal dynasty. The kings' **sons** would sit on the thrones their **fathers** once occupied. It is completely fulfilled in Christ, "the greater Son of David."

46:1–3 No matter what tragedies befall us, as God's children we can find our refuge in Him. Nothing that can possibly happen has the power to overcome His protective care.

46:4, 5 The **river** symbolizes the constant flow of the gracious blessings of God in the **midst** of His people. See 36:8. **city of God**: Jerusalem, Mt. Zion, the earthly dwelling of God (see 48:2, 3 and note).

6 The nations raged, the kingdoms
were moved;
He uttered His voice, the earth
melted.

7 The LORD of hosts *is* with us;
The God of Jacob *is* our refuge.
Sē'lah

8 Come, behold the works of the LORD,
Who has made desolations in the
earth.
9 He makes wars cease to the end of
the earth;
He breaks the bow and cuts the spear
in two;
He burns the chariot in the fire.

10 Be still, and know that I *am* God;
I will be exalted among the nations,
I will be exalted in the earth!

11 The LORD of hosts *is* with us;
The God of Jacob *is* our refuge.
Sē'lah

PSALM 47

Praise to God, the Ruler of the Earth

To the Chief Musician. A Psalm of the sons of Kōrah.

Oh, clap your hands, all you peoples!
Shout to God with the voice of
triumph!
2 For the LORD Most High *is* awesome;
He is a great King over all the earth.
3 He will subdue the peoples under us,
And the nations under our feet.
4 He will choose our inheritance for us,
The excellence of Jacob whom He
loves. Sē'lah

5 God has gone up with a shout,
The LORD with the sound of a
trumpet.
6 Sing praises to God, sing praises!
Sing praises to our King, sing praises!
7 For God *is* the King of all the earth;
Sing praises with understanding.

8 God reigns over the nations;
God sits on His holy throne.
9 The princes of the people have
gathered together,
The people of the God of Abraham.
For the shields of the earth *belong* to
God;
He is greatly exalted.

PSALM 48

The Glory of God in Zion

A Song. A Psalm of the sons of Kōrah.

Great *is* the LORD, and greatly to be
praised
In the city of our God,
In His holy mountain.
2 Beautiful in elevation,
The joy of the whole earth,
Is Mount Zion *on* the sides of the
north,
The city of the great King.
3 God *is* in her palaces;
He is known as her refuge.

4 For behold, the kings assembled,
They passed by together.
5 They saw *it, and* so they marveled;

46:10, 11 Be still is a rebuke, a call to cease from personal efforts and submit to God. When we do, the Lord is with us, and God is our **refuge**.

47:7 With understanding translates the Hebrew word *maschil*, which may also refer to a type of psalm called "A Contemplation" (see 45:title).

47:9 shields of the earth: protective rulers.

48:2, 3 sides of the north: In ancient Near Eastern thought the gods were believed to rule the earth from some high mountain in the far north. Here the psalmist uses that language to say that Jerusalem is the place from which the one God rules (see also Is. 2:2–4).

They were troubled, they hastened
away.
6 Fear took hold of them there,
And pain, as of a woman in birth
pangs,
7 *As when* You break the ships of
Tar'shish
With an east wind.

8 As we have heard,
So we have seen
In the city of the LORD of hosts,
In the city of our God:
God will establish it forever. Sē'lah

9 We have thought, O God, on Your
lovingkindness,
In the midst of Your temple.
10 According to Your name, O God,
So *is* Your praise to the ends of the
earth;
Your right hand is full of
righteousness.
11 Let Mount Zion rejoice,
Let the daughters of Judah be glad,
Because of Your judgments.

12 Walk about Zion,
And go all around her.
Count her towers;
13 Mark well her bulwarks;
Consider her palaces;
That you may tell *it* to the generation
following.
14 For this *is* God,
Our God forever and ever;
He will be our guide
Even to death.[a]

PSALM 49

The Confidence of the Foolish

To the Chief Musician. A Psalm of the sons of Kōrah.

Hear this, all peoples;
Give ear, all inhabitants of the world,
2 Both low and high,
Rich and poor together.
3 My mouth shall speak wisdom,
And the meditation of my heart *shall
give* understanding.
4 I will incline my ear to a proverb;
I will disclose my dark saying on the
harp.

5 Why should I fear in the days of evil,
When the iniquity at my heels
surrounds me?
6 Those who trust in their wealth
And boast in the multitude of their
riches,
7 None *of them* can by any means
redeem *his* brother,
Nor give to God a ransom for him—
8 For the redemption of their souls *is*
costly,
And it shall cease forever—
9 That he should continue to live
eternally,
And not see the Pit.

10 For he sees wise men die;
Likewise the fool and the senseless
person perish,
And leave their wealth to others.

48:14 [a]Following Masoretic Text and Syriac; Septuagint and Vulgate read *Forever.*

48:12, 13 towers . . . bulwarks . . . palaces: The people were to boast of Zion's defenses to the next generation, but only with the understanding that their true strength was found in God Himself (see v. 3; Is. 26:1). We, too, are responsible to tell succeeding generations about the power of God and share specific instances of His blessing us.

49:4 dark saying: A universal mystery. **on the harp**: Poetry set to music is the easiest material to memorize. Ideas considered especially important to remember were often treated in this way (see Deut. 31:19).

49:6–9 No one can buy off death and thus avoid it. The **ransom** for the eternal soul of a fellow human being is too costly for any mortal, and cannot be weighed in earthly treasures (see 1 Pet. 1:18, 19).

11 Their inner thought *is that* their
houses *will last* forever,[a]
Their dwelling places to all
generations;
They call *their* lands after their own
names.
12 Nevertheless man, *though* in honor,
does not remain;[a]
He is like the beasts *that* perish.

13 This is the way of those who *are*
foolish,
And of their posterity who approve
their sayings. Sē′lah
14 Like sheep they are laid in the grave;
Death shall feed on them;
The upright shall have dominion over
them in the morning;
And their beauty shall be consumed
in the grave, far from their
dwelling.
15 But God will redeem my soul from
the power of the grave,
For He shall receive me. Sē′lah

16 Do not be afraid when one becomes
rich,
When the glory of his house is
increased;
17 For when he dies he shall carry
nothing away;
His glory shall not descend after him.
18 Though while he lives he blesses
himself
(For *men* will praise you when you do
well for yourself),
19 He shall go to the generation of his
fathers;
They shall never see light.
20 A man *who is* in honor, yet does not
understand,
Is like the beasts *that* perish.

PSALM 50

God the Righteous Judge

A Psalm of Āsaph.

The Mighty One, God the LORD,
Has spoken and called the earth
From the rising of the sun to its going
down.
2 Out of Zion, the perfection of beauty,
God will shine forth.
3 Our God shall come, and shall not
keep silent;
A fire shall devour before Him,
And it shall be very tempestuous all
around Him.

4 He shall call to the heavens from
above,
And to the earth, that He may judge
His people:
5 "Gather My saints together to Me,
Those who have made a covenant
with Me by sacrifice."
6 Let the heavens declare His
righteousness,
For God Himself *is* Judge. Sē′lah

7 "Hear, O My people, and I will speak,
O Israel, and I will testify against you;
I *am* God, your God!
8 I will not rebuke you for your
sacrifices

49:11 [a]Septuagint, Syriac, Targum, and Vulgate read *Their graves shall be their houses forever.*
49:12 [a]Following Masoretic Text and Targum; Septuagint, Syriac, and Vulgate read *understand* (compare verse 20).

49:15 He shall receive me: A strong assertion of faith in a blessed afterlife for the righteous. The same Hebrew word translated *receive* here is used also of Enoch where it is said that "God took him" (Gen. 5:24; see also 73:24 and note).
49:17 Death touches people in all walks of life without regard for wealth or power.
49:19 They shall never see light: The influential rich who die without hope. The idea of eternal punishment for the wicked had not yet been fully revealed to Hebrew thought.
50:8–15 I will not rebuke . . . for your sacrifices: It was not the **offerings** as such that brought reproof, but the wrong attitude and understanding that God was **hungry** (v. 12) and

Or your burnt offerings,
Which are continually before Me.
9 I will not take a bull from your house,
Nor goats out of your folds.
10 For every beast of the forest *is* Mine,
And the cattle on a thousand hills.
11 I know all the birds of the mountains,
And the wild beasts of the field *are*
Mine.

12 "If I were hungry, I would not tell you;
For the world *is* Mine, and all its
fullness.
13 Will I eat the flesh of bulls,
Or drink the blood of goats?
14 Offer to God thanksgiving,
And pay your vows to the Most
High.
15 Call upon Me in the day of trouble;
I will deliver you, and you shall
glorify Me."

16 But to the wicked God says:
"What *right* have you to declare My
statutes,
Or take My covenant in your mouth,
17 Seeing you hate instruction
And cast My words behind you?
18 When you saw a thief, you
consented[a] with him,
And have been a partaker with
adulterers.
19 You give your mouth to evil,
And your tongue frames deceit.
20 You sit *and* speak against your
brother;
You slander your own mother's son.
21 These *things* you have done, and I
kept silent;
You thought that I was altogether like
you;
But I will rebuke you,
And set *them* in order before your
eyes.

22 "Now consider this, you who forget
God,
Lest I tear *you* in pieces,
And *there be* none to deliver:
23 Whoever offers praise glorifies Me;
And to him who orders *his* conduct
aright
I will show the salvation of God."

PSALM 51

A Prayer of Repentance

To the Chief Musician. A Psalm of David when Nathan the prophet went to him, after he had gone in to Bathshēba.

Have mercy upon me, O God,
According to Your lovingkindness;
According to the multitude of Your
tender mercies,
Blot out my transgressions.
2 Wash me thoroughly from my
iniquity,
And cleanse me from my sin.

3 For I acknowledge my transgressions,
And my sin *is* always before me.
4 Against You, You only, have I sinned,
And done *this* evil in Your sight—
That You may be found just when
You speak,[a]
And blameless when You judge.

5 Behold, I was brought forth in
iniquity,
And in sin my mother conceived me.

50:18 [a]Septuagint, Syriac, Targum, and Vulgate read *ran.* 51:4 [a]Septuagint, Targum, and Vulgate read *in Your words.*

dependent on humans. True worship recognizes God as Lord and ourselves as dependent on Him.

51:3 David does not attempt to justify his sin. True repentance always begins with acknowledgment of one's sin, without excuse.

51:5 brought forth in iniquity: Refusal to do right is an integral part of human character from birth onward. That David described his conception as **in sin** does not mean that procreation is sinful. Rather, the sin problem is endemic to us from the first moment of our existence.

6 Behold, You desire truth in the
inward parts,
And in the hidden *part* You will make
me to know wisdom.
7 Purge me with hyssop, and I shall be
clean;
Wash me, and I shall be whiter than
snow.
8 Make me hear joy and gladness,
That the bones You have broken may
rejoice.
9 Hide Your face from my sins,
And blot out all my iniquities.

10 Create in me a clean heart, O God,
And renew a steadfast spirit within me.
11 Do not cast me away from Your
presence,
And do not take Your Holy Spirit
from me.

12 Restore to me the joy of Your
salvation,
And uphold me *by Your* generous
Spirit.
13 *Then* I will teach transgressors Your
ways,
And sinners shall be converted to You.

14 Deliver me from the guilt of
bloodshed, O God,
The God of my salvation,
And my tongue shall sing aloud of
Your righteousness.
15 O Lord, open my lips,
And my mouth shall show forth Your
praise.
16 For You do not desire sacrifice, or else
I would give *it;*
You do not delight in burnt offering.
17 The sacrifices of God *are* a broken
spirit,
A broken and a contrite heart—
These, O God, You will not despise.

18 Do good in Your good pleasure to
Zion;
Build the walls of Jerusalem.
19 Then You shall be pleased with the
sacrifices of righteousness,
With burnt offering and whole burnt
offering;
Then they shall offer bulls on Your
altar.

PSALM 52

The End of the Wicked and the Peace of the Godly

To the Chief Musician. A Contemplation[a] *of David when Dōeg the Ēdomīte went and told Saul, and said to him, "David has gone to the house of Ahimelech."*

Why do you boast in evil, O mighty
man?
The goodness of God *endures*
continually.

52:title [a]Hebrew *Maschil*

51:6 inward parts: David recognizes that sin is primarily a matter of attitude, and this must be dealt with before the problem of wrong actions can be resolved.

51:7 Hyssop branches were used to sprinkle blood on the doorways of the Israelites in Egypt to prevent death by the destroyer (see Ex. 12:22, 23). It was also used in the same manner to pronounce a leper cleansed (see Lev. 14:1–7).

51:8 When a Christian turns from God's will, sweet fellowship is destroyed and the song of joy departs from the heart, leaving the transgressor feeling broken and empty. Repentance leads to a return of that fellowship and joy.

51:11 While the Holy Spirit is always with NT Christians, He was taken from some in the OT, like Saul, as a result of their sin.

51:16–19 Outward worship, such as OT sacrifice, is pleasing to God only if it expresses the inward spiritual conditions of a **broken spirit** and **contrite heart**. Formal worship in the absence of these conditions accomplishes nothing; however, if it is offered as a result of them, God is pleased (v. 19).

51:18, 19 Build . . . Jerusalem: David recognizes that his sin has injured not only himself but his city and nation as well. He therefore asks God to deal with those broader damages.

2 Your tongue devises destruction,
Like a sharp razor, working
deceitfully.
3 You love evil more than good,
Lying rather than speaking
righteousness. Sē′lah

4 You love all devouring words,
You deceitful tongue.

5 God shall likewise destroy you
forever;
He shall take you away, and pluck
you out of *your* dwelling place,
And uproot you from the land of the
living. Sē′lah
6 The righteous also shall see and fear,
And shall laugh at him, *saying,*
7 "Here is the man *who* did not make
God his strength,
But trusted in the abundance of his
riches,
And strengthened himself in his
wickedness."

8 But I *am* like a green olive tree in the
house of God;
I trust in the mercy of God forever
and ever.
9 I will praise You forever,
Because You have done *it;*
And in the presence of Your saints
I will wait on Your name, for *it is*
good.

PSALM 53

Folly of the Godless, and the Restoration of Israel

To the Chief Musician. Set to "Māhalath." A Contemplation[a] of David.

The fool has said in his heart,
"*There is* no God."
They are corrupt, and have done
abominable iniquity;
There is none who does good.

2 God looks down from heaven upon
the children of men,
To see if there are *any* who
understand, who seek God.
3 Every one of them has turned aside;
They have together become corrupt;
There is none who does good,
No, not one.

4 Have the workers of iniquity no
knowledge,
Who eat up my people *as* they eat
bread,
And do not call upon God?
5 There they are in great fear
Where no fear was,
For God has scattered the bones of
him who encamps against you;
You have put *them* to shame,
Because God has despised them.

6 Oh, that the salvation of Israel would
come out of Zion!
When God brings back the captivity
of His people,
Let Jacob rejoice *and* Israel be glad.

PSALM 54

Answered Prayer for Deliverance from Adversaries

To the Chief Musician. With stringed instruments.[a] A Contemplation[b] of David when the Ziphites went and said to Saul, "Is David not hiding with us?"

Save me, O God, by Your name,
And vindicate me by Your strength.
2 Hear my prayer, O God;

53:title [a]Hebrew *Maschil* 54:title [a]Hebrew *neginoth* [b]Hebrew *Maschil*

52:8 green olive tree: Full of vitality and with prospects of many productive years.

Psalm 53 This psalm is almost identical with Ps. 14 except for v. 5, which compares to 14:5, 6. In addition, Ps. 14 uses "the LORD" as opposed to the exclusive use of "God" in Ps. 53 (see 14:2, 4, 7; 53:2, 4, 6). See the notes to Ps. 14.

53:3 none who does good: Aside from divine grace everyone is by nature and practice corrupt and sinful (see Rom. 3:23).

Give ear to the words of my mouth.
3 For strangers have risen up against me,
And oppressors have sought after my life;
They have not set God before them. Sē'lah

4 Behold, God *is* my helper;
The Lord *is* with those who uphold my life.
5 He will repay my enemies for their evil.
Cut them off in Your truth.

6 I will freely sacrifice to You;
I will praise Your name, O LORD, for *it is* good.
7 For He has delivered me out of all trouble;
And my eye has seen *its desire* upon my enemies.

PSALM 55

Trust in God Concerning the Treachery of Friends

To the Chief Musician. With stringed instruments.[a] *A Contemplation*[b] *of David.*

Give ear to my prayer, O God,
And do not hide Yourself from my supplication.
2 Attend to me, and hear me;
I am restless in my complaint, and moan noisily,
3 Because of the voice of the enemy,
Because of the oppression of the wicked;
For they bring down trouble upon me,
And in wrath they hate me.

4 My heart is severely pained within me,
And the terrors of death have fallen upon me.
5 Fearfulness and trembling have come upon me,
And horror has overwhelmed me.
6 So I said, "Oh, that I had wings like a dove!
I would fly away and be at rest.
7 Indeed, I would wander far off,
And remain in the wilderness. Sē'lah
8 I would hasten my escape
From the windy storm *and* tempest."

9 Destroy, O Lord, *and* divide their tongues,
For I have seen violence and strife in the city.
10 Day and night they go around it on its walls;
Iniquity and trouble *are* also in the midst of it.
11 Destruction *is* in its midst;
Oppression and deceit do not depart from its streets.

12 For *it is* not an enemy *who* reproaches me;
Then I could bear *it*.
Nor *is it* one *who* hates me who has exalted *himself* against me;
Then I could hide from him.
13 But *it was* you, a man my equal,
My companion and my acquaintance.
14 We took sweet counsel together,
And walked to the house of God in the throng.

55:title [a]Hebrew *neginoth* [b]Hebrew *Maschil*

54:7 David's confidence in the Lord's deliverance sets an inspiring example for us to follow as we present our requests in prayer.

55:9–11 Destroy . . . divide their tongues: As David began his petition against the enemies, he may have had in mind the incident at the Tower of Babel. As God defeated the plans of those in that day by confusing their languages (see Gen. 11:1–9), so He is called to confuse the evil plans of David's oppressors.

55:12–14 The betrayer is identified as a **companion** with whom he visited the **house of God** in public worship. A friend turned enemy is devastating.

15 Let death seize them;
Let them go down alive into hell,
For wickedness *is* in their dwellings
and among them.

16 As for me, I will call upon God,
And the LORD shall save me.
17 Evening and morning and at noon
I will pray, and cry aloud,
And He shall hear my voice.
18 He has redeemed my soul in peace
from the battle *that was* against me,
For there were many against me.
19 God will hear, and afflict them,
Even He who abides from of old.
Sē'lah
Because they do not change,
Therefore they do not fear God.

20 He has put forth his hands against
those who were at peace with him;
He has broken his covenant.
21 *The words* of his mouth were
smoother than butter,
But war *was* in his heart;
His words were softer than oil,
Yet they *were* drawn swords.

22 Cast your burden on the LORD,
And He shall sustain you;
He shall never permit the righteous to
be moved.

23 But You, O God, shall bring them
down to the pit of destruction;
Bloodthirsty and deceitful men shall
not live out half their days;
But I will trust in You.

PSALM 56

Prayer for Relief from Tormentors

To the Chief Musician. Set to "The Silent Dove in Distant Lands."[a] A Michtam of David when the Philistines captured him in Gath.

Be merciful to me, O God, for man
would swallow me up;
Fighting all day he oppresses me.
2 My enemies would hound *me* all day,
For *there are* many who fight against
me, O Most High.

3 Whenever I am afraid,
I will trust in You.
4 In God (I will praise His word),
In God I have put my trust;
I will not fear.
What can flesh do to me?

5 All day they twist my words;
All their thoughts *are* against me for
evil.
6 They gather together,
They hide, they mark my steps,
When they lie in wait for my life.
7 Shall they escape by iniquity?
In anger cast down the peoples,
O God!

8 You number my wanderings;
Put my tears into Your bottle;
Are they not in Your book?
9 When I cry out *to You,*
Then my enemies will turn back;
This I know, because God *is* for me.

56:title [a]Hebrew *Jonath Elem Rechokim*

55:20, 21 Broken his covenant speaks of the crime of the friend turned enemy (see vv. 12–14 and note). Breaking a covenant is always a serious matter in the OT and characterizes human sin against God. The treachery is vividly portrayed in v. 21.

55:22 A comforting promise of God's sustaining hand. **burden**: A broad word meaning our lot in life, our total circumstances. We can trust God to this extent because He is in total control.

56:3 In times of crisis, rather than acting on our tumultuous emotions we need to put our faith in the Lord and draw strength from Him.

56:8 David is certain that nothing which he is undergoing is insignificant to God. He sees every tear that falls and lists them in His book; not one is lost. The person who is surrendered to God can know that every facet of life has meaning.

10 In God (I will praise *His* word),
In the LORD (I will praise *His* word),
11 In God I have put my trust;
I will not be afraid.
What can man do to me?

12 Vows *made* to You *are binding* upon me, O God;
I will render praises to You,
13 For You have delivered my soul from death.
Have You not *kept* my feet from falling,
That I may walk before God
In the light of the living?

PSALM 57

Prayer for Safety from Enemies

To the Chief Musician. Set to "Do Not Destroy."[a] A Michtam of David when he fled from Saul into the cave.

Be merciful to me, O God, be merciful to me!
For my soul trusts in You;
And in the shadow of Your wings I will make my refuge,
Until *these* calamities have passed by.

2 I will cry out to God Most High,
To God who performs *all things* for me.
3 He shall send from heaven and save me;
He reproaches the one who would swallow me up. Sē'lah
God shall send forth His mercy and His truth.

4 My soul *is* among lions;
I lie *among* the sons of men
Who are set on fire,
Whose teeth *are* spears and arrows,
And their tongue a sharp sword.
5 Be exalted, O God, above the heavens;
Let Your glory *be* above all the earth.

6 They have prepared a net for my steps;
My soul is bowed down;
They have dug a pit before me;
Into the midst of it they *themselves* have fallen. Sē'lah

7 My heart is steadfast, O God, my heart is steadfast;
I will sing and give praise.
8 Awake, my glory!
Awake, lute and harp!
I will awaken the dawn.

9 I will praise You, O Lord, among the peoples;
I will sing to You among the nations.
10 For Your mercy reaches unto the heavens,
And Your truth unto the clouds.

11 Be exalted, O God, above the heavens;
Let Your glory *be* above all the earth.

PSALM 58

The Just Judgment of the Wicked

To the Chief Musician. Set to "Do Not Destroy."[a] A Michtam of David.

Do you indeed speak righteousness, you silent ones?
Do you judge uprightly, you sons of men?

57:title [a]Hebrew *Al Tashcheth* 58:title [a]Hebrew *Al Tashcheth*

56:11 No matter what tragedy threatens us, we can find comfort in knowing that nothing can happen without God's knowledge and we will not die until our work here is done.

57:8 awaken the dawn: David's praise of the Lord begins early in the morning, the first order of the day. **my glory:** my soul.

2 No, in heart you work wickedness;
You weigh out the violence of your hands in the earth.

3 The wicked are estranged from the womb;
They go astray as soon as they are born, speaking lies.
4 Their poison *is* like the poison of a serpent;
They are like the deaf cobra *that* stops its ear,
5 Which will not heed the voice of charmers,
Charming ever so skillfully.

6 Break their teeth in their mouth, O God!
Break out the fangs of the young lions, O LORD!
7 Let them flow away as waters *which* run continually;
When he bends *his bow,*
Let his arrows be as if cut in pieces.
8 *Let them be* like a snail which melts away as it goes,
Like a stillborn child of a woman, that they may not see the sun.

9 Before your pots can feel *the burning* thorns,
He shall take them away as with a whirlwind,
As in His living and burning wrath.
10 The righteous shall rejoice when he sees the vengeance;
He shall wash his feet in the blood of the wicked,
11 So that men will say,
"Surely *there is* a reward for the righteous;
Surely He is God who judges in the earth."

PSALM 59

The Assured Judgment of the Wicked

To the Chief Musician. Set to "Do Not Destroy."[a] *A Michtam of David when Saul sent men, and they watched the house in order to kill him.*

Deliver me from my enemies, O my God;
Defend me from those who rise up against me.
2 Deliver me from the workers of iniquity,
And save me from bloodthirsty men.

3 For look, they lie in wait for my life;
The mighty gather against me,
Not *for* my transgression nor *for* my sin, O LORD.
4 They run and prepare themselves through no fault *of mine.*

Awake to help me, and behold!
5 You therefore, O LORD God of hosts, the God of Israel,
Awake to punish all the nations;
Do not be merciful to any wicked transgressors. Sē′lah

6 At evening they return,
They growl like a dog,
And go all around the city.
7 Indeed, they belch with their mouth;
Swords *are* in their lips;
For *they say,* "Who hears?"

8 But You, O LORD, shall laugh at them;

59:title [a]Hebrew *Al Tashcheth*

58:6–9 An imprecatory prayer for judgment on the wicked, including removing their capacity for harm (v. 6) and destroying their significance (vv. 7, 8). See introduction to Ps. 109. **Thorns** (v. 9) were a quick-burning fuel for cooking fires. Before the kettle could get hot, God would **take . . . away** the wicked.

58:10 wash . . . in the blood of the wicked: This is a strong statement of judgment which may offend our sensibilities. But it appropriately reflects God's attitude toward sin and the tragic fate of the wicked (see Rev. 14:18–20).

You shall have all the nations in
derision.
9 I will wait for You, O You his
Strength;[a]
For God *is* my defense.
10 My God of mercy[a] shall come to meet
me;
God shall let me see *my desire* on my
enemies.

11 Do not slay them, lest my people
forget;
Scatter them by Your power,
And bring them down,
O Lord our shield.
12 *For* the sin of their mouth *and* the
words of their lips,
Let them even be taken in their pride,
And for the cursing and lying *which*
they speak.
13 Consume *them* in wrath, consume
them,
That they *may* not *be;*
And let them know that God rules in
Jacob
To the ends of the earth. Sē'lah

14 And at evening they return,
They growl like a dog,
And go all around the city.
15 They wander up and down for food,
And howl[a] if they are not satisfied.

16 But I will sing of Your power;
Yes, I will sing aloud of Your mercy in
the morning;
For You have been my defense
And refuge in the day of my trouble.
17 To You, O my Strength, I will sing
praises;
For God *is* my defense,
My God of mercy.

PSALM 60

Urgent Prayer for the Restored Favor of God

To the Chief Musician. Set to "Lily of the Testimony."[a] A Michtam of David. For teaching. When he fought against Mesopotāmia and Syria of Zōbah, and Jōab returned and killed twelve thousand Edomītes in the Valley of Salt.

O God, You have cast us off;
You have broken us down;
You have been displeased;
Oh, restore us again!
2 You have made the earth tremble;
You have broken it;
Heal its breaches, for it is shaking.
3 You have shown Your people hard
things;
You have made us drink the wine of
confusion.

4 You have given a banner to those
who fear You,
That it may be displayed because of
the truth. Sē'lah
5 That Your beloved may be delivered,
Save *with* Your right hand, and hear
me.

59:9 [a]Following Masoretic Text and Syriac; some Hebrew manuscripts, Septuagint, Targum, and Vulgate read *my Strength.* 59:10 [a]Following Qere; some Hebrew manuscripts, Septuagint, and Vulgate read *My God, His mercy;* Kethib, some Hebrew manuscripts and Targum read *O God, my mercy;* Syriac reads *O God, Your mercy.* 59:15 [a]Following Septuagint and Vulgate; Masoretic Text, Syriac, and Targum read *spend the night.* 60:title [a]Hebrew *Shushan Eduth*

59:11 Do not slay them: Thus, the prayer is for a more drawn out punishment—**scatter them**. Presumably instant death would remove the wicked from the scene too quickly so that David's **people** would **forget** the salutary lessons to be learned from a long-term decline.

59:13 Consume them: This does not contradict the previous statement on the fate of the wicked. A people scattered among the nations is a people consumed.

60:3 wine of confusion: An idiom reflecting one of the worst effects of alcoholic beverages.

60:4 A banner is a battle flag used to identify different troops. Here it identifies those who follow truth.

6 God has spoken in His holiness:
"I will rejoice;
I will divide Shē′chem
And measure out the Valley of
Suc′coth.
7 Gil′ē·ad *is* Mine, and Ma·nas′seh *is*
Mine;
Ē′phra·im also *is* the helmet for My
head;
Judah *is* My lawgiver.
8 Mō′ab *is* My washpot;
Over Ē′dom I will cast My shoe;
Phi·lis′ti·a, shout in triumph because
of Me."

9 Who will bring me *to* the strong city?
Who will lead me to Ē′dom?
10 *Is it* not You, O God, *who* cast us off?
And You, O God, *who* did not go out
with our armies?
11 Give us help from trouble,
For the help of man *is* useless.
12 Through God we will do valiantly,
For *it is* He *who* shall tread down our
enemies.[a]

PSALM 61

Assurance of God's Eternal Protection

To the Chief Musician. On a stringed instrument.[a] A Psalm of David.

Hear my cry, O God;
Attend to my prayer.
2 From the end of the earth I will cry to
You,
When my heart is overwhelmed;
Lead me to the rock that is higher
than I.
3 For You have been a shelter for me,
A strong tower from the enemy.
4 I will abide in Your tabernacle
forever;
I will trust in the shelter of Your
wings. Sē′lah

5 For You, O God, have heard my
vows;
You have given *me* the heritage of
those who fear Your name.
6 You will prolong the king's life,
His years as many generations.
7 He shall abide before God forever.
Oh, prepare mercy and truth, *which*
may preserve him!

8 So I will sing praise to Your name
forever,
That I may daily perform my vows.

PSALM 62

A Calm Resolve to Wait for the Salvation of God

To the Chief Musician. To Jedūthun. A Psalm of David.

Truly my soul silently *waits* for God;
From Him *comes* my salvation.
2 He only *is* my rock and my salvation;
He is my defense;
I shall not be greatly moved.

3 How long will you attack a man?
You shall be slain, all of you,
Like a leaning wall and a tottering
fence.
4 They only consult to cast *him* down
from his high position;

60:12 [a]Compare verses 5–12 with 108:6–13
61:title [a]Hebrew *neginah*

60:6–8 in His holiness: Here referring to God's power and absolute sovereignty. The warfare of the nations is incidental; God determines destinies. All the nations listed highlight God's sovereign control. **My washpot** (v. 8): My menial servant. **Cast My shoe** (v. 8) means to claim a property (see Ruth 4:7).

60:11, 12 In our own strength we are powerless against the onslaught of the devil and the temptations of the flesh. But through His death and resurrection, Jesus Christ obtained the victory for us; we need only to trust in Him.

61:2 end of the earth: A metaphorical expression for a personal extremity. **The rock that is higher than I** describes a place of safety in God's care above earthly turmoil.

They delight in lies;
They bless with their mouth,
But they curse inwardly. Sē′lah

5 My soul, wait silently for God alone,
For my expectation *is* from Him.
6 He only *is* my rock and my salvation;
He is my defense;
I shall not be moved.
7 In God *is* my salvation and my glory;
The rock of my strength,
And my refuge, *is* in God.

8 Trust in Him at all times, you people;
Pour out your heart before Him;
God *is* a refuge for us. Sē′lah

9 Surely men of low degree *are* a vapor,
Men of high degree *are* a lie;
If they are weighed on the scales,
They *are* altogether *lighter* than vapor.
10 Do not trust in oppression,
Nor vainly hope in robbery;
If riches increase,
Do not set *your* heart *on them.*

11 God has spoken once,
Twice I have heard this:
That power *belongs* to God.
12 Also to You, O Lord, *belongs* mercy;
For You render to each one according
to his work.

PSALM 63

Joy in the Fellowship of God

A Psalm of David when he was in the wilderness of Judah.

O God, You *are* my God;
Early will I seek You;
My soul thirsts for You;
My flesh longs for You
In a dry and thirsty land
Where there is no water.
2 So I have looked for You in the
sanctuary,
To see Your power and Your glory.

3 Because Your lovingkindness *is* better
than life,
My lips shall praise You.
4 Thus I will bless You while I live;
I will lift up my hands in Your name.
5 My soul shall be satisfied as with
marrow and fatness,
And my mouth shall praise You with
joyful lips.

6 When I remember You on my bed,
I meditate on You in the *night*
watches.
7 Because You have been my help,
Therefore in the shadow of Your
wings I will rejoice.
8 My soul follows close behind You;
Your right hand upholds me.

9 But those *who* seek my life, to destroy
it,
Shall go into the lower parts of the
earth.
10 They shall fall by the sword;
They shall be a portion for jackals.

11 But the king shall rejoice in God;
Everyone who swears by Him shall
glory;

62:11, 12 once, Twice: The ascending number emphasizes the truth of the following statement.

63:1, 2 You are my God: The key theme of this psalm. He is found by those who seek Him. He satisfies the **thirsty**. His **power** and **glory** are discovered when we worship in His **sanctuary**.

63:2–6 This is no half-hearted expression of praise! The psalmist worships God with His eyes (v. 2), **lips** (v. 3), **hands** (v. 4), **soul** (v. 5), **mouth** (v. 5), and mind (v. 6). Every Christian would do well to follow his example.

63:5 Marrow and fatness were considered the choicest of delicacies. For all of life's rich blessings, our **lips** sing the **praise** of our hearts.

63:9–11 If God be for us, our enemies fall under His righteous judgment (vv. 9, 10). But **everyone** who trusts in Him **shall rejoice**.

But the mouth of those who speak
lies shall be stopped.

PSALM 64

Oppressed by the Wicked but Rejoicing in the LORD

To the Chief Musician. A Psalm of David.

Hear my voice, O God, in my
meditation;
Preserve my life from fear of the
enemy.
2 Hide me from the secret plots of the
wicked,
From the rebellion of the workers of
iniquity,
3 Who sharpen their tongue like a
sword,
And bend *their bows to shoot* their
arrows—bitter words,
4 That they may shoot in secret at the
blameless;
Suddenly they shoot at him and do
not fear.

5 They encourage themselves *in* an evil
matter;
They talk of laying snares secretly;
They say, "Who will see them?"
6 They devise iniquities:
"We have perfected a shrewd scheme."
Both the inward thought and the
heart of man are deep.

7 But God shall shoot at them *with* an
arrow;
Suddenly they shall be wounded.
8 So He will make them stumble over
their own tongue;
All who see them shall flee away.
9 All men shall fear,
And shall declare the work of God;
For they shall wisely consider His
doing.

10 The righteous shall be glad in the
LORD, and trust in Him.
And all the upright in heart shall
glory.

PSALM 65

Praise to God for His Salvation and Providence

To the Chief Musician. A Psalm of David. A Song.

Praise is awaiting You, O God, in
Zion;
And to You the vow shall be
performed.
2 O You who hear prayer,
To You all flesh will come.
3 Iniquities prevail against me;
As for our transgressions,
You will provide atonement for them.

4 Blessed *is the man* You choose,
And cause to approach *You*,
That he may dwell in Your courts.
We shall be satisfied with the
goodness of Your house,
Of Your holy temple.

5 *By* awesome deeds in righteousness
You will answer us,
O God of our salvation,
You who are the confidence of all the
ends of the earth,
And of the far-off seas;

64:6 In fallen humanity, the **inward thought** and the **heart** represent inner motives which lean towards evil activities. The prophet Jeremiah described this condition: "The heart is deceitful above all things, and desperately wicked" (Jer. 17:9).

64:7 God shall shoot: Divine judgment corresponds to the acts of the wicked (v. 3). It is swift and appropriate.

65:5–7 awesome deeds: Acts of God that arouse respect and fear of people. **confidence of all . . . the earth**: An evidence of God's universal power and work. His power to control the **peoples** is based on His **power** as Creator to control the natural elements of the universe. See 19:1–4.

6 Who established the mountains by
His strength,
Being clothed with power;
7 You who still the noise of the seas,
The noise of their waves,
And the tumult of the peoples.
8 They also who dwell in the farthest
parts are afraid of Your signs;
You make the outgoings of the
morning and evening rejoice.

9 You visit the earth and water it,
You greatly enrich it;
The river of God is full of water;
You provide their grain,
For so You have prepared it.
10 You water its ridges abundantly,
You settle its furrows;
You make it soft with showers,
You bless its growth.

11 You crown the year with Your
goodness,
And Your paths drip *with* abundance.
12 They drop *on* the pastures of the
wilderness,
And the little hills rejoice on every
side.
13 The pastures are clothed with flocks;
The valleys also are covered with
grain;
They shout for joy, they also sing.

PSALM 66

Praise to God for His Awesome Works

To the Chief Musician. A Song. A Psalm.

Make a joyful shout to God, all the
earth!
2 Sing out the honor of His name;
Make His praise glorious.
3 Say to God,
"How awesome are Your works!
Through the greatness of Your power
Your enemies shall submit themselves
to You.
4 All the earth shall worship You
And sing praises to You;
They shall sing praises *to* Your
name." Sē'lah

5 Come and see the works of God;
He is awesome *in His* doing toward
the sons of men.
6 He turned the sea into dry *land;*
They went through the river on foot.
There we will rejoice in Him.
7 He rules by His power forever;
His eyes observe the nations;
Do not let the rebellious exalt
themselves. Sē'lah

8 Oh, bless our God, you peoples!
And make the voice of His praise to
be heard,
9 Who keeps our soul among the
living,
And does not allow our feet to be
moved.
10 For You, O God, have tested us;
You have refined us as silver is
refined.
11 You brought us into the net;
You laid affliction on our backs.
12 You have caused men to ride over our
heads;
We went through fire and through
water;

65:8 Morning and **evening** here refer to the whole expanse of the world, from east to west.

65:9 You visit the earth: A typical biblical expression to say that God is present and active in His world.

66:6, 7 The sea is a reference to the Exodus, Israel's national deliverance, which culminated in Israel's crossing the dried-up river Jordan into Canaan (see Josh. 3:14–16). All this was by the **power** of God.

66:10–12 The concept of adversity as an instrument of strengthening our faith is consistent with various passages throughout the Bible, including the Book of Job.

But You brought us out to rich
fulfillment.

13 I will go into Your house with burnt
offerings;
I will pay You my vows,
14 Which my lips have uttered
And my mouth has spoken when I
was in trouble.
15 I will offer You burnt sacrifices of fat
animals,
With the sweet aroma of rams;
I will offer bulls with goats. Sē′lah

16 Come *and* hear, all you who fear
God,
And I will declare what He has done
for my soul.
17 I cried to Him with my mouth,
And He was extolled with my
tongue.
18 If I regard iniquity in my heart,
The Lord will not hear.
19 *But* certainly God has heard *me;*
He has attended to the voice of my
prayer.

20 Blessed *be* God,
Who has not turned away my prayer,
Nor His mercy from me!

PSALM 67

An Invocation and a Doxology

To the Chief Musician. On stringed instruments.[a] *A Psalm. A Song.*

God be merciful to us and bless us,
And cause His face to shine upon us,
Sē′lah
2 That Your way may be known on
earth,
Your salvation among all nations.

3 Let the peoples praise You, O God;
Let all the peoples praise You.
4 Oh, let the nations be glad and sing
for joy!
For You shall judge the people
righteously,
And govern the nations on earth.
Sē′lah

5 Let the peoples praise You, O God;
Let all the peoples praise You.
6 *Then* the earth shall yield her increase;
God, our own God, shall bless us.
7 God shall bless us,
And all the ends of the earth shall
fear Him.

PSALM 68

The Glory of God in His Goodness to Israel

To the Chief Musician. A Psalm of David. A Song.

Let God arise,
Let His enemies be scattered;
Let those also who hate Him flee
before Him.
2 As smoke is driven away,
So drive *them* away;
As wax melts before the fire,
So let the wicked perish at the
presence of God.
3 But let the righteous be glad;
Let them rejoice before God;
Yes, let them rejoice exceedingly.

67:title [a]Hebrew *neginoth*

66:18–20 Iniquity in my heart is the only barrier to my fellowship with God. But the psalmist testifies that for him this barrier has been removed. **God has heard me** (v. 19): The sin has been forgiven, and I walk again with God.

67:1, 2 The invocation borrows from the blessing of Aaron (Num. 6:24–26). But here, the **salvation** is for **all nations**, fulfilling the promise to Abraham (Gen. 12:3).

68:1–3 Let God arise: This ancient cry originated during the wilderness wanderings when Israel broke camp and the ark of the covenant moved ahead of the people (see Num. 10:35). The ark was the sign of God's presence. In that presence the **wicked perish**, but the **righteous . . . rejoice.**

4 Sing to God, sing praises to His name;
Extol Him who rides on the clouds,[a]
By His name YAH,
And rejoice before Him.

5 A father of the fatherless, a defender
of widows,
Is God in His holy habitation.
6 God sets the solitary in families;
He brings out those who are bound
into prosperity;
But the rebellious dwell in a dry *land*.

7 O God, when You went out before
Your people,
When You marched through the
wilderness, Sē'lah
8 The earth shook;
The heavens also dropped *rain* at the
presence of God;
Sinai itself *was moved* at the presence
of God, the God of Israel.
9 You, O God, sent a plentiful rain,
Whereby You confirmed Your
inheritance,
When it was weary.
10 Your congregation dwelt in it;
You, O God, provided from Your
goodness for the poor.

11 The Lord gave the word;
Great *was* the company of those who
proclaimed *it:*
12 "Kings of armies flee, they flee,
And she who remains at home
divides the spoil.

68:4 [a]Masoretic Text reads *deserts;* Targum reads *heavens* (compare verse 34 and Isaiah 19:1).

13 Though you lie down among the
sheepfolds,
You will be like the wings of a dove
covered with silver,
And her feathers with yellow gold."
14 When the Almighty scattered kings in
it,
It was *white* as snow in Zal'mon.

15 A mountain of God *is* the mountain
of Bā'shan;
A mountain *of many* peaks *is* the
mountain of Bā'shan.
16 Why do you fume with envy, you
mountains of *many* peaks?
This is the mountain *which* God
desires to dwell in;
Yes, the LORD will dwell *in it* forever.

17 The chariots of God *are* twenty
thousand,
Even thousands of thousands;
The Lord is among them *as in* Sinai,
in the Holy *Place*.
18 You have ascended on high,
You have led captivity captive;
You have received gifts among men,
Even *from* the rebellious,
That the LORD God might dwell *there*.

19 Blessed *be* the Lord,
Who daily loads us *with benefits,*
The God of our salvation! Sē'lah
20 Our God *is* the God of salvation;
And to GOD the Lord *belong* escapes
from death.

21 But God will wound the head of His
enemies,

68:4 YAH is an abbreviation for Yahweh, the Hebrews' personal name for God. It is a form of the Hebrew verb "to be," meaning "I AM" (see Ex. 3:14).

68:5, 6 These verses provide comfort when we feel lonely or defenseless; God truly does care!

68:9 plentiful rain: bountiful provision, perhaps a reference to the manna from heaven.

68:17, 18 The chariots of God: He has all the resources He needs. The triumph begun in the Exodus is now completed as God **ascended on high**, possibly referring to the moment when the ark reached its destination in the procession. The imagery pictures God as a victorious king leading a line of captive prisoners and enjoying the **gifts** of booty taken in battle.

The hairy scalp of the one who still
goes on in his trespasses.
22 The Lord said, "I will bring back from
Bā'shan,
I will bring *them* back from the depths
of the sea,
23 That your foot may crush *them*[a] in
blood,
And the tongues of your dogs *may
have* their portion from *your*
enemies."

24 They have seen Your procession, O
God,
The procession of my God, my King,
into the sanctuary.
25 The singers went before, the players
on instruments *followed* after;
Among *them were* the maidens
playing timbrels.
26 Bless God in the congregations,
The Lord, from the fountain of
Israel.
27 There *is* little Benjamin, their leader,
The princes of Judah *and* their com-
pany,
The princes of Zeb'ū·lun *and* the
princes of Naph'ta·lī.

28 Your God has commanded[a] your
strength;
Strengthen, O God, what You have
done for us.
29 Because of Your temple at Jerusalem,
Kings will bring presents to You.
30 Rebuke the beasts of the reeds,
The herd of bulls with the calves of
the peoples,
Till everyone submits himself with
pieces of silver.
Scatter the peoples *who* delight in
war.
31 Envoys will come out of Egypt;
Ethiopia will quickly stretch out her
hands to God.

32 Sing to God, you kingdoms of the
earth;
Oh, sing praises to the Lord, Sē'lah
33 To Him who rides on the heaven of
heavens, *which were* of old!
Indeed, He sends out His voice, a
mighty voice.
34 Ascribe strength to God;
His excellence *is* over Israel,
And His strength *is* in the clouds.
35 O God, *You are* more awesome than
Your holy places.
The God of Israel *is* He who gives
strength and power to *His* people.

Blessed *be* God!

PSALM 69

An Urgent Plea for Help in Trouble

To the Chief Musician. Set to "The Lilies."[a] *A Psalm of David.*

Save me, O God!
For the waters have come up to *my*
neck.
2 I sink in deep mire,
Where *there is* no standing;

68:23 [a]Septuagint, Syriac, Targum, and Vulgate read *you may dip your foot.* 68:28 [a]Septuagint, Syriac, Targum, and Vulgate read *Command, O God.* 69:title [a]Hebrew *Shoshannim*

68:22, 23 back from Bashan: Perhaps a reference to the victory over Og, king of Bashan (Num. 21:33–35).

68:28–31 Kings will bring presents (v. 29): The subjugation of nations and peoples to the Lord is a theme that is common in OT teaching about the end days. See Is. 2:1–4; Mic. 4:1–3.

68:30 beasts of the reeds: The hippopotamus, which symbolized Egypt. **bulls:** Rulers of other neighboring nations.

Psalm 69 An individual lament including a variety of themes connected with suffering. Only Ps. 22 is quoted more often in the NT. Both have a number of passages that are applicable to Christ.

I have come into deep waters,
Where the floods overflow me.
3 I am weary with my crying;
My throat is dry;
My eyes fail while I wait for my
God.

4 Those who hate me without a cause
Are more than the hairs of my head;
They are mighty who would destroy
me,
Being my enemies wrongfully;
Though I have stolen nothing,
I *still* must restore *it*.

5 O God, You know my foolishness;
And my sins are not hidden from
You.
6 Let not those who wait for You, O
Lord GOD of hosts, be ashamed
because of me;
Let not those who seek You be
confounded because of me, O God
of Israel.
7 Because for Your sake I have borne
reproach;
Shame has covered my face.
8 I have become a stranger to my
brothers,
And an alien to my mother's
children;
9 Because zeal for Your house has eaten
me up,
And the reproaches of those who
reproach You have fallen on me.
10 When I wept *and chastened* my soul
with fasting,
That became my reproach.
11 I also made sackcloth my garment;
I became a byword to them.
12 Those who sit in the gate speak
against me,
And I *am* the song of the drunkards.

13 But as for me, my prayer *is* to You,
O LORD, *in* the acceptable time;
O God, in the multitude of Your
mercy,
Hear me in the truth of Your
salvation.
14 Deliver me out of the mire,
And let me not sink;
Let me be delivered from those who
hate me,
And out of the deep waters.
15 Let not the floodwater overflow me,
Nor let the deep swallow me up;
And let not the pit shut its mouth on
me.

16 Hear me, O LORD, for Your
lovingkindness *is* good;
Turn to me according to the
multitude of Your tender mercies.
17 And do not hide Your face from Your
servant,
For I am in trouble;
Hear me speedily.
18 Draw near to my soul, *and* redeem it;
Deliver me because of my enemies.

19 You know my reproach, my shame,
and my dishonor;
My adversaries *are* all before You.
20 Reproach has broken my heart,
And I am full of heaviness;
I looked *for someone* to take pity, but
there was none;
And for comforters, but I found none.
21 They also gave me gall for my food,

69:4 Jesus quoted this verse in reference to Himself (John 15:25).

69:7–9 for Your sake: He is suffering because of his identification with God. **Zeal for Your house** reflects the intensity of his devotion and service. The thought of anyone dishonoring God or God's house is terrible to him.

69:19 reproach . . . shame . . . dishonor: An expression of the depth of David's suffering. Public disgrace would be especially damaging to a public leader.

69:21 A messianic passage represented in the reports of all four Gospels on Jesus' crucifixion.

And for my thirst they gave me
vinegar to drink.
22 Let their table become a snare before
them,
And their well-being a trap.
23 Let their eyes be darkened, so that
they do not see;
And make their loins shake
continually.
24 Pour out Your indignation upon
them,
And let Your wrathful anger take
hold of them.
25 Let their dwelling place be desolate;
Let no one live in their tents.
26 For they persecute the *ones* You have
struck,
And talk of the grief of those You
have wounded.
27 Add iniquity to their iniquity,
And let them not come into Your
righteousness.
28 Let them be blotted out of the book of
the living,
And not be written with the
righteous.

29 But I *am* poor and sorrowful;
Let Your salvation, O God, set me up
on high.
30 I will praise the name of God with a
song,
And will magnify Him with
thanksgiving.
31 *This* also shall please the LORD better
than an ox *or* bull,
Which has horns and hooves.
32 The humble shall see *this and* be
glad;
And you who seek God, your hearts
shall live.
33 For the LORD hears the poor,
And does not despise His prisoners.

34 Let heaven and earth praise Him,
The seas and everything that moves
in them.
35 For God will save Zion
And build the cities of Judah,
That they may dwell there and
possess it.
36 Also, the descendants of His servants
shall inherit it,
And those who love His name shall
dwell in it.

PSALM 70

Prayer for Relief from Adversaries

To the Chief Musician. A Psalm of David. To bring to remembrance.

Make haste, O God, to deliver me!
Make haste to help me, O LORD!

2 Let them be ashamed and
confounded
Who seek my life;
Let them be turned back[a] and
confused
Who desire my hurt.
3 Let them be turned back because of
their shame,
Who say, "Aha, aha!"

4 Let all those who seek You rejoice and
be glad in You;

70:2 [a]Following Masoretic Text, Septuagint, Targum, and Vulgate; some Hebrew manuscripts and Syriac read *be appalled* (compare 40:15).

69:35, 36 This last declaration of praise indicates that David's suffering was not merely personal; his people suffered also. The psalm was possibly written some time after an attack upon Judah and thus the praise that God would **build the cities** that were damaged or destroyed by the enemies. David is confident that God will **save Zion** so that His people may **dwell there**. Zion represents God's purposes and blessings for all His people on earth.

Psalm 70 A petition to God for His deliverance from enemies. This psalm is almost identical with 40:13–17. One difference is that Ps. 40 uses "the LORD" as opposed to the use of "God" in Ps. 70.

FINDING FELLOWSHIP

John Gilmore

Isolation—and feeling lonely—can ruin a fulfilling retirement. Yet friends can encourage and stimulate us as we work through transitions. They make adjustments less painful. The company of fellow Christians is especially important for interpreting life, getting acclimated, and regaining a positive outlook (see Heb. 10:24, 25).

In addition, the best way to beat loneliness is to focus on the presence of God (Deut. 31:6). Fellowship with God means that, though we are physically alone, we are not lonely. Personal and group Bible study renews and refreshes. Christians who share similar trying circumstances can neutralize debilitating self-pity; insights from Scripture and encouragement from others help banish loneliness. ✦

And let those who love Your
salvation say continually,
"Let God be magnified!"

5 But I *am* poor and needy;
Make haste to me, O God!
You *are* my help and my deliverer;
O LORD, do not delay.

PSALM 71

God the Rock of Salvation

In You, O LORD, I put my trust;
Let me never be put to shame.
2 Deliver me in Your righteousness,
and cause me to escape;
Incline Your ear to me, and save me.
3 Be my strong refuge,
To which I may resort continually;
You have given the commandment to
save me,
For You *are* my rock and my fortress.
4 Deliver me, O my God, out of the
hand of the wicked,
Out of the hand of the unrighteous
and cruel man.
5 For You are my hope, O Lord GOD;
You are my trust from my youth.
6 By You I have been upheld from
birth;
You are He who took me out of my
mother's womb.
My praise *shall be* continually of You.

7 I have become as a wonder to many,
But You *are* my strong refuge.
8 Let my mouth be filled *with* Your
praise
And with Your glory all the day.

9 Do not cast me off in the time of old
age;

Psalm 71 Verse 9 indicates this psalm was written by an older man with great faith; his faithful memorization of Scripture, as quoted throughout the psalm, reflects a heart fully dedicated to the Lord. As we face the uncertainty of coming years, this psalm of trust, prayer, and praise can become a meaningful part of our personal devotions.

71:9 The psalmist echoes the fears many of us have about growing older, but rather than brooding over his concerns he takes them directly to the Lord. He doesn't plead for eternal youth but for continual fellowship with God.

Do not forsake me when my strength
fails.
10 For my enemies speak against me;
And those who lie in wait for my life
take counsel together,
11 Saying, "God has forsaken him;
Pursue and take him, for *there is* none
to deliver *him*."

12 O God, do not be far from me;
O my God, make haste to help me!
13 Let them be confounded *and*
consumed
Who are adversaries of my life;
Let them be covered *with* reproach
and dishonor
Who seek my hurt.

14 But I will hope continually,
And will praise You yet more and
more.
15 My mouth shall tell of Your
righteousness
And Your salvation all the day,
For I do not know *their* limits.
16 I will go in the strength of the Lord
GOD;
I will make mention of Your
righteousness, of Yours only.

17 O God, You have taught me from my
youth;
And to this *day* I declare Your
wondrous works.
18 Now also when *I am* old and
grayheaded,
O God, do not forsake me,
Until I declare Your strength to *this*
generation,
Your power to everyone *who* is to
come.

19 Also Your righteousness, O God, *is*
very high,
You who have done great things;
O God, who *is* like You?
20 *You*, who have shown me great and
severe troubles,
Shall revive me again,
And bring me up again from the
depths of the earth.
21 You shall increase my greatness,
And comfort me on every side.

22 Also with the lute I will praise You—
And Your faithfulness, O my God!
To You I will sing with the harp,
O Holy One of Israel.
23 My lips shall greatly rejoice when I
sing to You,
And my soul, which You have
redeemed.
24 My tongue also shall talk of Your
righteousness all the day long;
For they are confounded,
For they are brought to shame
Who seek my hurt.

PSALM 72

Glory and Universality of the Messiah's Reign

A Psalm of Solomon.

Give the king Your judgments, O God,
And Your righteousness to the king's
Son.
2 He will judge Your people with
righteousness,

71:22 Holy One of Israel is a frequent title for God in Isaiah, but rare elsewhere. It emphasizes both God's divine perfection and His special choice of Israel to be His representative to the nations.

Psalm 72 This psalm is clearly messianic, but it is also a prayer for the ruling monarch in Judah, using the extravagant court language of that day.

72:1–4 Righteousness, justice, and **peace** describe the expected rule of the king. They were, however, often sadly lacking in the leadership of Israel's kings and thus came to be especially looked for in the rule of Messiah. See Jer. 23:5.

And Your poor with justice.
3 The mountains will bring peace to the people,
And the little hills, by righteousness.
4 He will bring justice to the poor of the people;
He will save the children of the needy,
And will break in pieces the oppressor.

5 They shall fear You[a]
As long as the sun and moon endure,
Throughout all generations.
6 He shall come down like rain upon the grass before mowing,
Like showers *that* water the earth.
7 In His days the righteous shall flourish,
And abundance of peace,
Until the moon is no more.

8 He shall have dominion also from sea to sea,
And from the River to the ends of the earth.
9 Those who dwell in the wilderness will bow before Him,
And His enemies will lick the dust.
10 The kings of Tar'shish and of the isles
Will bring presents;
The kings of Shē'ba and Sē'ba
Will offer gifts.
11 Yes, all kings shall fall down before Him;
All nations shall serve Him.

12 For He will deliver the needy when he cries,
The poor also, and *him* who has no helper.
13 He will spare the poor and needy,
And will save the souls of the needy.
14 He will redeem their life from oppression and violence;
And precious shall be their blood in His sight.

15 And He shall live;
And the gold of Shē'ba will be given to Him;
Prayer also will be made for Him continually,
And daily He shall be praised.

16 There will be an abundance of grain in the earth,
On the top of the mountains;
Its fruit shall wave like Lebanon;
And *those* of the city shall flourish like grass of the earth.

17 His name shall endure forever;
His name shall continue as long as the sun.
And *men* shall be blessed in Him;
All nations shall call Him blessed.

18 Blessed *be* the LORD God, the God of Israel,
Who only does wondrous things!
19 And blessed *be* His glorious name forever!
And let the whole earth be filled *with* His glory.
Amen and Amen.

20 The prayers of David the son of Jesse are ended.

72:5 [a]Following Masoretic Text and Targum; Septuagint and Vulgate read *They shall continue.*

72:14 precious shall be their blood: Because life is in the blood (Lev. 17:11). This is an OT way of saying that life is of supreme worth.

72:18, 19 These verses comprise the closing doxology for Book Two.

72:20 Since seventeen psalms are attributed to David in the remaining three books, the probable explanation is that this subscription closed a smaller collection of psalms that were incorporated into Book Two.

Book Three: Psalms 73—89

PSALM 73

The Tragedy of the Wicked, and the Blessedness of Trust in God

A Psalm of Āsaph.

Truly God *is* good to Israel,
To such as are pure in heart.
2 But as for me, my feet had almost
stumbled;
My steps had nearly slipped.
3 For I *was* envious of the boastful,
When I saw the prosperity of the
wicked.

4 For *there are* no pangs in their death,
But their strength *is* firm.
5 They *are* not in trouble *as other* men,
Nor are they plagued like *other* men.
6 Therefore pride serves as their
necklace;
Violence covers them *like* a garment.
7 Their eyes bulge[a] with abundance;
They have more than heart could
wish.
8 They scoff and speak wickedly
concerning oppression;
They speak loftily.
9 They set their mouth against the
heavens,
And their tongue walks through the
earth.

10 Therefore his people return here,
And waters of a full *cup* are drained
by them.
11 And they say, "How does God know?
And is there knowledge in the Most
High?"
12 Behold, these *are* the ungodly,
Who are always at ease;
They increase *in* riches.
13 Surely I have cleansed my heart *in*
vain,
And washed my hands in innocence.
14 For all day long I have been plagued,
And chastened every morning.

15 If I had said, "I will speak thus,"
Behold, I would have been untrue to
the generation of Your children.
16 When I thought *how* to understand
this,
It *was* too painful for me—
17 Until I went into the sanctuary of
God;
Then I understood their end.

18 Surely You set them in slippery
places;
You cast them down to destruction.
19 Oh, how they are *brought* to
desolation, as in a moment!
They are utterly consumed with
terrors.
20 As a dream when *one* awakes,
So, Lord, when You awake,
You shall despise their image.

21 Thus my heart was grieved,
And I was vexed in my mind.
22 I *was* so foolish and ignorant;
I was *like* a beast before You.
23 Nevertheless I *am* continually with
You;

73:7 [a]Targum reads *face bulges;* Septuagint, Syriac, and Vulgate read *iniquity bulges.*

73:title Asaph was one of David's chief musicians (1 Chr. 16:4–7). Eleven psalms (73–83) of this third book have the name Asaph in their titles (as does also Ps. 50), suggesting that these psalms were associated with the Asaphite musical guild.

73:16, 17 When we find ourselves bewildered by the seeming inconsistencies of life or confused about the ways of God, we need to turn to Him with our questions. While not all of our questions will be answered during this life on earth, as our fellowship deepens we will begin to see things more clearly from His perspective.

73:23 by my right hand: To be grasped by the right hand is symbolic of being honored. God does not reject people merely because they sometimes fall prey to doubts.

Finding Rest and Counsel

Dale Evans Rogers

God made us truly unique as human beings. He built into us specific levels of energy for physical activity, intellectual activity, emotional activity, and spiritual activity. When we are, for example, involved in heavy physical activity, we talk about being "drained" and too tired to do anything until we regain some energy. We do not like to talk, read, or even pray.

"Nothing happens outside the love of God."

Similarly, when we experience severe emotional trauma we become "drained" of energy as well. During that time our physical energy may be almost zero—we have used up so much emotional energy that just getting out of bed requires a huge effort. Our intellectual energy may be extremely low; we don't even want to think about what we will make for supper, much less read a book. Similarly, our spiritual energy may be so low we cannot even pray. We may read the Bible but remember nothing—and the truths that normally leap off the pages of the Bible don't mean anything to us.

No wonder Satan approaches us at such time of extreme emotional distress. We cannot think straight, so his simple, direct suggestions seem to make sense. Repeated, they begin to wear a groove in our brains, enjoying a life of their own. This would never happen if we were not experiencing emotional trauma.

Notice how the psalmist Asaph describes his emotional upheaval from distress over the success of the unrighteous and the struggles of the righteous: "Thus my heart was grieved, and I was vexed in my mind. I was so foolish and ignorant; I was like a beast before You" (Ps. 73:21, 22).

That certainly sounds like someone whose emotions were using so much of his intellectual energy that he could not think clearly. Until, of course, he entered the place of worship, the sanctuary of God. That calmed his heart and his spirit, letting him begin to think clearly. Then he saw what God really meant to him: "Nevertheless I am continually with You; You hold me by my right hand. You will guide me with Your counsel, and afterward receive me to glory" (vv. 23, 24).

He recognized that the Master Potter's plan is truly the best, that nothing happens outside the love of God. Once you have your head on straight about God, your emotional healing also accelerates. So the last verse of the psalm reveals Asaph's renewed commitment to the Master Potter: "But it is good for me to draw near to God; I have put my trust in the Lord God, that I may declare all Your works" (v. 28).

We will not fully understand God this side of heaven, but if we release what is bothering us to Him, He may give us understanding in other ways—usually much later, after He has been able to shape us more into His image. ✦

You hold *me* by my right hand.
24 You will guide me with Your counsel,
And afterward receive me *to* glory.

25 Whom have I in heaven *but You?*
And *there is* none upon earth *that* I
desire besides You.
26 My flesh and my heart fail;
But God *is* the strength of my heart
and my portion forever.

27 For indeed, those who are far from
You shall perish;
You have destroyed all those who
desert You for harlotry.
28 But *it is* good for me to draw near to
God;
I have put my trust in the Lord
GOD,
That I may declare all Your works.

> I come to the office each morning and stay for long hours doing what has to be done to the best of my ability. And when you've done the best you can, you can't do any better. So when I go to sleep I turn everything over to the Lord and forget it.
>
> Harry S. Truman

PSALM 74

A Plea for Relief from Oppressors

A Contemplation[a] *of Āsaph.*

O God, why have You cast *us* off
forever?
Why does Your anger smoke against
the sheep of Your pasture?
2 Remember Your congregation, *which*
You have purchased of old,
The tribe of Your inheritance, *which*
You have redeemed—
This Mount Zion where You have
dwelt.
3 Lift up Your feet to the perpetual
desolations.
The enemy has damaged everything
in the sanctuary.
4 Your enemies roar in the midst of
Your meeting place;
They set up their banners *for* signs.
5 They seem like men who lift up
Axes among the thick trees.
6 And now they break down its carved
work, all at once,
With axes and hammers.
7 They have set fire to Your
sanctuary;
They have defiled the dwelling place
of Your name to the ground.
8 They said in their hearts,
"Let us destroy them altogether."
They have burned up all the meeting
places of God in the land.

9 We do not see our signs;
There is no longer any prophet;
Nor *is there* any among us who knows
how long.
10 O God, how long will the adversary
reproach?
Will the enemy blaspheme Your name
forever?
11 Why do You withdraw Your hand,
even Your right hand?
Take it out of Your bosom and destroy
them.

74:title [a]Hebrew *Maschil*

73:24 Afterward suggests a climax, either in this life or in the next. **Receive** translates the same Hebrew verb used in the story of Enoch (Gen. 5:24). Given this allusion to Enoch's ascension, **glory** may well designate some heavenly bliss (see 49:15).

Psalm 74 A community lament over the destruction of the temple, most likely in 586 B.C. by the Babylonians.

74:7 Jerusalem and the temple were burned by the Babylonians in 586 B.C. (see 2 Kin. 25:9).

12 For God *is* my King from old,
Working salvation in the midst of the earth.
13 You divided the sea by Your strength;
You broke the heads of the sea serpents in the waters.
14 You broke the heads of Le•vi'a•than in pieces,
And gave him *as* food to the people inhabiting the wilderness.
15 You broke open the fountain and the flood;
You dried up mighty rivers.
16 The day *is* Yours, the night also *is* Yours;
You have prepared the light and the sun.
17 You have set all the borders of the earth;
You have made summer and winter.

18 Remember this, *that* the enemy has reproached, O LORD,
And *that* a foolish people has blasphemed Your name.
19 Oh, do not deliver the life of Your turtledove to the wild beast!
Do not forget the life of Your poor forever.
20 Have respect to the covenant;
For the dark places of the earth are full of the haunts of cruelty.
21 Oh, do not let the oppressed return ashamed!
Let the poor and needy praise Your name.

22 Arise, O God, plead Your own cause;
Remember how the foolish man reproaches You daily.
23 Do not forget the voice of Your enemies;
The tumult of those who rise up against You increases continually.

PSALM 75

Thanksgiving for God's Righteous Judgment

To the Chief Musician. Set to "Do Not Destroy."[a] A Psalm of Asaph. A Song.

We give thanks to You, O God, we give thanks!
For Your wondrous works declare *that* Your name is near.

2 "When I choose the proper time,
I will judge uprightly.
3 The earth and all its inhabitants are dissolved;
I set up its pillars firmly. Se'lah

4 "I said to the boastful, 'Do not deal boastfully,'
And to the wicked, 'Do not lift up the horn.
5 Do not lift up your horn on high;
Do *not* speak with a stiff neck.' "

6 For exaltation *comes* neither from the east

75:title [a]Hebrew *Al Tashcheth*

74:12 The enemy has wrought great havoc, but it is not to be compared with the **salvation** (deliverance) that God had previously given.

74:13, 14 The writer uses some of the language of an ancient myth to depict how great God was as Redeemer when in the Exodus He **divided the sea** (v. 13). **Leviathan** (v. 14) is a sea monster, symbolizing the waters of chaos which threaten life. God, having no difficulty with "Leviathan," will have no problem with the present enemy, no matter how strong he may appear.

74:22, 23 Israel's **cause** is God's also. The same is true for the modern believer. God has a stake in those who carry His name.

75:6, 7 When our lives are characterized by humility, we recognize that any honor accorded to us comes only because of the Lord. Rather than drinking in the praise, we will glorify God for His blessings and grace.

Nor from the west nor from the
south.
7 But God *is* the Judge:
He puts down one,
And exalts another.
8 For in the hand of the LORD *there is* a
cup,
And the wine is red;
It is fully mixed, and He pours it out;
Surely its dregs shall all the wicked of
the earth
Drain *and* drink down.

9 But I will declare forever,
I will sing praises to the God of Jacob.

10 "All the horns of the wicked I will also
cut off,
But the horns of the righteous shall be
exalted."

PSALM 76

The Majesty of God in Judgment

To the Chief Musician. On stringed instruments.[a] A Psalm of Āsaph. A Song.

In Judah God *is* known;
His name *is* great in Israel.
2 In Sā'lem[a] also is His tabernacle,
And His dwelling place in Zion.
3 There He broke the arrows of the
bow,
The shield and sword of battle.
Sē'lah

4 You *are* more glorious and excellent
Than the mountains of prey.
5 The stouthearted were plundered;
They have sunk into their sleep;
And none of the mighty men have
found the use of their hands.
6 At Your rebuke, O God of Jacob,
Both the chariot and horse were cast
into a dead sleep.

7 You, Yourself, *are* to be feared;
And who may stand in Your presence
When once You are angry?
8 You caused judgment to be heard
from heaven;
The earth feared and was still,
9 When God arose to judgment,
To deliver all the oppressed of the
earth. Sē'lah

10 Surely the wrath of man shall praise
You;
With the remainder of wrath You
shall gird Yourself.

11 Make vows to the LORD your God,
and pay *them;*
Let all who are around Him bring
presents to Him who ought to be
feared.
12 He shall cut off the spirit of princes;
He is awesome to the kings of the
earth.

PSALM 77

The Consoling Memory of God's Redemptive Works

To the Chief Musician. To Jedūthun. A Psalm of Āsaph.

I cried out to God with my voice—
To God with my voice;
And He gave ear to me.
2 In the day of my trouble I sought the
Lord;

76:title [a]Hebrew *neginoth* 76:2 [a]That is, Jerusalem

75:8 Cup is used figuratively of divine judgment (see Is. 51:17).
76:4 more glorious: God elicits awe. **mountains of prey**: Mt. Zion or mountains in general. The Greek OT translation (the Septuagint) reads "the everlasting mountains."
76:5, 6 sleep: Death. This may refer to the defeat of the Assyrian army (2 Kin. 19:35).
77:2 stretched out: The posture of prayer. **Without ceasing** suggests that the ordeal was a long one. **Refused to be comforted** indicates commendable persistence until God intervenes to resolve the problem.

My hand was stretched out in the
night without ceasing;
My soul refused to be comforted.
3 I remembered God, and was troubled;
I complained, and my spirit was
overwhelmed. Sē′lah

4 You hold my eyelids *open;*
I am so troubled that I cannot speak.
5 I have considered the days of old,
The years of ancient times.
6 I call to remembrance my song in the
night;
I meditate within my heart,
And my spirit makes diligent search.

7 Will the Lord cast off forever?
And will He be favorable no more?
8 Has His mercy ceased forever?
Has *His* promise failed forevermore?
9 Has God forgotten to be gracious?
Has He in anger shut up His tender
mercies? Sē′lah

10 And I said, "This *is* my anguish;
But I will remember the years of the
right hand of the Most High."
11 I will remember the works of the
LORD;
Surely I will remember Your wonders
of old.
12 I will also meditate on all Your work,
And talk of Your deeds.

13 Your way, O God, *is* in the sanctuary;
Who *is* so great a God as *our* God?
14 You *are* the God who does wonders;
You have declared Your strength
among the peoples.
15 You have with *Your* arm redeemed
Your people,
The sons of Jacob and Joseph. Sē′lah

16 The waters saw You, O God;
The waters saw You, they were afraid;
The depths also trembled.
17 The clouds poured out water;
The skies sent out a sound;
Your arrows also flashed about.
18 The voice of Your thunder *was* in the
whirlwind;
The lightnings lit up the world;
The earth trembled and shook.
19 Your way *was* in the sea,
Your path in the great waters,
And Your footsteps were not known.
20 You led Your people like a flock
By the hand of Moses and Aaron.

PSALM 78

God's Kindness to Rebellious Israel

A Contemplation[a] *of Āsaph.*

Give ear, O my people, *to* my law;
Incline your ears to the words of my
mouth.
2 I will open my mouth in a parable;
I will utter dark sayings of old,

78:title [a]Hebrew *Maschil*

77:4 eyelids open: Sleeplessness.

77:5, 6 considered the days of old: He reflects upon God's earlier gracious help. **Song in the night** refers to happier days that he now recalls in the present darkness. He resolutely refuses to allow present troubles to erase the reality of God's grace in the past.

77:10–20 Looking back on God's past blessings will give us courage, and sharing our testimony with younger generations will strengthen our faith.

77:13, 14 Your way . . . is in the sanctuary can be seen as a counterpart to "Your way was in the sea" (v. 19). As God's saving presence was evident in the Exodus deliverance, so it is now in His holy temple. The word here translated "sanctuary" is lit. "holiness." It thus may characterize God's goodness in dealing with Israel.

77:19, 20 God's grace as revealed in the Exodus. **By the hand of Moses and Aaron**: God uses human leadership to accomplish His redemptive purposes.

Psalm 78 In a song of praise this psalm reviews the sacred history of Israel from enslavement in Egypt to the reign of David. Beginning with a statement of purpose (vv. 1–8), it

3 Which we have heard and known,
And our fathers have told us.
4 We will not hide *them* from their
children,
Telling to the generation to come the
praises of the LORD,
And His strength and His wonderful
works that He has done.

5 For He established a testimony in
Jacob,
And appointed a law in Israel,
Which He commanded our fathers,
That they should make them known
to their children;
6 That the generation to come might
know *them*,
The children *who* would be born,
That they may arise and declare *them*
to their children,
7 That they may set their hope in
God,
And not forget the works of God,
But keep His commandments;
8 And may not be like their fathers,
A stubborn and rebellious generation,
A generation *that* did not set its heart
aright,
And whose spirit was not faithful to
God.

9 The children of Ē′phra·im, *being*
armed *and* carrying bows,
Turned back in the day of battle.
10 They did not keep the covenant of
God;
They refused to walk in His law,
11 And forgot His works
And His wonders that He had shown
them.

12 Marvelous things He did in the sight
of their fathers,
In the land of Egypt, *in* the field of
Zō′an.
13 He divided the sea and caused them
to pass through;
And He made the waters stand up
like a heap.
14 In the daytime also He led them with
the cloud,
And all the night with a light of fire.
15 He split the rocks in the wilderness,
And gave *them* drink in abundance
like the depths.
16 He also brought streams out of the
rock,
And caused waters to run down like
rivers.

17 But they sinned even more against
Him
By rebelling against the Most High in
the wilderness.
18 And they tested God in their heart
By asking for the food of their fancy.
19 Yes, they spoke against God:
They said, "Can God prepare a table
in the wilderness?
20 Behold, He struck the rock,
So that the waters gushed out,
And the streams overflowed.
Can He give bread also?
Can He provide meat for His
people?"

21 Therefore the LORD heard *this* and
was furious;
So a fire was kindled against Jacob,
And anger also came up against
Israel,

---

moves to a rehearsal of God's care in the wilderness (vv. 9–41), a reminder of the Egyptian plagues (vv. 42–53), and a summary of the judges period (vv. 54–72), culminating in the choice of David. Its purpose is to serve as a warning against rebellion and a reminder of God's promises.

78:4–8 The principle of providing a legacy of faith for our children and grandchildren has been enforced by God since OT times. Each of us shares this responsibility of training younger generations in biblical precepts, and with the pressures of the world today, children and their parents need all the support they can get in this area.

22 Because they did not believe in God,
And did not trust in His salvation.
23 Yet He had commanded the clouds above,
And opened the doors of heaven,
24 Had rained down manna on them to eat,
And given them of the bread of heaven.
25 Men ate angels' food;
He sent them food to the full.

26 He caused an east wind to blow in the heavens;
And by His power He brought in the south wind.
27 He also rained meat on them like the dust,
Feathered fowl like the sand of the seas;
28 And He let *them* fall in the midst of their camp,
All around their dwellings.
29 So they ate and were well filled,
For He gave them their own desire.
30 They were not deprived of their craving;
But while their food *was* still in their mouths,
31 The wrath of God came against them,
And slew the stoutest of them,
And struck down the choice *men* of Israel.

32 In spite of this they still sinned,
And did not believe in His wondrous works.
33 Therefore their days He consumed in futility,
And their years in fear.
34 When He slew them, then they sought Him;
And they returned and sought earnestly for God.
35 Then they remembered that God *was* their rock,
And the Most High God their Redeemer.
36 Nevertheless they flattered Him with their mouth,
And they lied to Him with their tongue;
37 For their heart was not steadfast with Him,
Nor were they faithful in His covenant.
38 But He, *being* full of compassion, forgave *their* iniquity,
And did not destroy *them*.
Yes, many a time He turned His anger away,
And did not stir up all His wrath;
39 For He remembered that they *were but* flesh,
A breath that passes away and does not come again.

40 How often they provoked Him in the wilderness,
And grieved Him in the desert!
41 Yes, again and again they tempted God,
And limited the Holy One of Israel.

78:22 did not believe in God: Not an intellectual problem, but refusal to trust. Unbelief is at the very heart of rebellion.

78:29 He gave them their own desire: God gave them their demand, but they died in the midst of their satisfaction. It is better not to get what we want in these circumstances (see 106:15).

78:34 they returned: Repented. But their repentance was hasty and superficial. It was only a passing mood.

78:38 Although it's easy to become exasperated by the fickleness of the nation of Israel, we should not be overly critical. If we examine our lives honestly, we'll realize how inconsistent we have been in our own spiritual walks and that we have grieved the Lord innumerable times.

42 They did not remember His power:
The day when He redeemed them
from the enemy,
43 When He worked His signs in Egypt,
And His wonders in the field of
Zō'an;
44 Turned their rivers into blood,
And their streams, that they could not
drink.
45 He sent swarms of flies among them,
which devoured them,
And frogs, which destroyed them.
46 He also gave their crops to the
caterpillar,
And their labor to the locust.
47 He destroyed their vines with hail,
And their sycamore trees with frost.
48 He also gave up their cattle to the
hail,
And their flocks to fiery lightning.
49 He cast on them the fierceness of His
anger,
Wrath, indignation, and trouble,
By sending angels of destruction
among them.
50 He made a path for His anger;
He did not spare their soul from
death,
But gave their life over to the
plague,
51 And destroyed all the firstborn in
Egypt,
The first of *their* strength in the tents
of Ham.
52 But He made His own people go
forth like sheep,
And guided them in the wilderness
like a flock;
53 And He led them on safely, so that
they did not fear;
But the sea overwhelmed their
enemies.
54 And He brought them to His holy
border,
This mountain *which* His right hand
had acquired.
55 He also drove out the nations before
them,
Allotted them an inheritance by
survey,
And made the tribes of Israel dwell in
their tents.

56 Yet they tested and provoked the
Most High God,
And did not keep His testimonies,
57 But turned back and acted unfaith-
fully like their fathers;
They were turned aside like a
deceitful bow.
58 For they provoked Him to anger with
their high places,
And moved Him to jealousy with
their carved images.
59 When God heard *this,* He was
furious,
And greatly abhorred Israel,
60 So that He forsook the tabernacle of
Shī'lōh,
The tent He had placed among men,
61 And delivered His strength into
captivity,
And His glory into the enemy's hand.
62 He also gave His people over to the
sword,
And was furious with His
inheritance.
63 The fire consumed their young men,
And their maidens were not given in
marriage.

78:43–51 All of the **signs** (plagues on Egypt) are alluded to here except the flies, the boils, and the darkness.

78:49 angels of destruction: The messengers of the Lord who carry out His sentence of judgment. In the OT, administering God's punishment is sometimes the task of the Angel of the Lord (see 35:5; 2 Sam. 24:15, 16).

78:61 His strength may refer to the ark, captured by the Philistines (1 Sam. 4:10, 11). Neither the tabernacle nor the ark could save Israel from the punishment due her sins (see vv. 58, 59; also Jer. 7:3–7 and note).

64 Their priests fell by the sword,
And their widows made no lamentation.

65 Then the Lord awoke as *from* sleep,
Like a mighty man who shouts because of wine.
66 And He beat back His enemies;
He put them to a perpetual reproach.

67 Moreover He rejected the tent of Joseph,
And did not choose the tribe of Ē'phra·im,
68 But chose the tribe of Judah,
Mount Zion which He loved.
69 And He built His sanctuary like the heights,
Like the earth which He has established forever.
70 He also chose David His servant,
And took him from the sheepfolds;
71 From following the ewes that had young He brought him,
To shepherd Jacob His people,
And Israel His inheritance.
72 So he shepherded them according to the integrity of his heart,
And guided them by the skillfulness of his hands.

PSALM 79

A Dirge and a Prayer for Israel, Destroyed by Enemies

A Psalm of Āsaph.

O God, the nations have come into Your inheritance;
Your holy temple they have defiled;
They have laid Jerusalem in heaps.
2 The dead bodies of Your servants
They have given *as* food for the birds of the heavens,
The flesh of Your saints to the beasts of the earth.
3 Their blood they have shed like water all around Jerusalem,
And *there was* no one to bury *them*.
4 We have become a reproach to our neighbors,
A scorn and derision to those who are around us.

5 How long, LORD?
Will You be angry forever?
Will Your jealousy burn like fire?
6 Pour out Your wrath on the nations that do not know You,
And on the kingdoms that do not call on Your name.
7 For they have devoured Jacob,
And laid waste his dwelling place.

8 Oh, do not remember former iniquities against us!
Let Your tender mercies come speedily to meet us,
For we have been brought very low.
9 Help us, O God of our salvation,
For the glory of Your name;
And deliver us, and provide atonement for our sins,
For Your name's sake!
10 Why should the nations say,
"Where *is* their God?"

78:64 priests fell: A reference to the death of Eli and his two sons. The widow of Phinehas was so stunned that she did not speak (1 Sam. 4:20).

78:67–72 God rejected the northern kingdom represented here by the tribe of **Ephraim** from the house of **Joseph**. Instead He chose Judah as the tribe and Mount Zion as the place where His sanctuary should be located, and He chose David to **shepherd . . . His people** (v. 71).

78:71 shepherd: A common title of the king in the ancient Near East. It was also a biblical figure for leaders charged with the care of God's people (see Ezek. 34:1–10).

79:8 do not remember: Do not hold us accountable for the sins of our fathers. Yet the pleas for mercy and forgiveness show that the people were aware of their own sins.

79:9 We must always make our requests of God on the basis of His glory. His blessings

Let there be known among the
nations in our sight
The avenging of the blood of Your
servants *which has been* shed.

11 Let the groaning of the prisoner come
before You;
According to the greatness of Your
power
Preserve those who are appointed to
die;
12 And return to our neighbors seven-
fold into their bosom
Their reproach with which they have
reproached You, O Lord.

13 So we, Your people and sheep of Your
pasture,
Will give You thanks forever;
We will show forth Your praise to all
generations.

PSALM 80

Prayer for Israel's Restoration

To the Chief Musician. Set to "The Lilies."[a] A Testimony[b] of Āsaph. A Psalm.

Give ear, O Shepherd of Israel,
You who lead Joseph like a flock;
You who dwell *between* the cherubim,
shine forth!
2 Before Ē'phra·im, Benjamin, and
Ma·nas'seh,
Stir up Your strength,
And come *and* save us!

3 Restore us, O God;
Cause Your face to shine,
And we shall be saved!

4 O LORD God of hosts,
How long will You be angry
Against the prayer of Your people?
5 You have fed them with the bread of
tears,
And given them tears to drink in
great measure.
6 You have made us a strife to our
neighbors,
And our enemies laugh among
themselves.

7 Restore us, O God of hosts;
Cause Your face to shine,
And we shall be saved!

8 You have brought a vine out of Egypt;
You have cast out the nations, and
planted it.
9 You prepared *room* for it,
And caused it to take deep root,
And it filled the land.
10 The hills were covered with its
shadow,
And the mighty cedars with its
boughs.
11 She sent out her boughs to the Sea,[a]
And her branches to the River.[b]

12 Why have You broken down her
hedges,

80:title [a]Hebrew *Shoshannim* [b]Hebrew *Eduth*
80:11 [a]That is, the Mediterranean [b]That is, the Euphrates

are given only because of His character and for His honor, not because of any righteousness or worthiness on our part.

80:1 Shepherd of Israel: The concept is a familiar one (see 23:1 and note), but this particular phrase appears only here in the OT. **dwell between the cherubim**: Reference is to the cherubim of the mercy seat where God met with His people (Num. 7:89). The Hebrew word translated "dwell" is lit. "to sit," picturing God as a King sitting on His throne in His audience chamber.

80:8–11 God's relationship to Israel is compared to that which exists between the vinedresser and the vine which he plants and cares for (Is. 5:1, 2; see John 15:1–5). The vine's overshadowing the **mighty cedars** probably refers to Israel's ascendance over the Canaanites.

So that all who pass by the way pluck
her *fruit?*
13 The boar out of the woods uproots it,
And the wild beast of the field
devours it.

14 Return, we beseech You, O God of
hosts;
Look down from heaven and see,
And visit this vine
15 And the vineyard which Your right
hand has planted,
And the branch *that* You made strong
for Yourself.
16 *It is* burned with fire, *it is* cut down;
They perish at the rebuke of Your
countenance.
17 Let Your hand be upon the man of
Your right hand,
Upon the son of man *whom* You made
strong for Yourself.
18 Then we will not turn back from You;
Revive us, and we will call upon Your
name.

19 Restore us, O LORD God of hosts;
Cause Your face to shine,
And we shall be saved!

PSALM 81

An Appeal for Israel's Repentance

To the Chief Musician. On an instrument of Gath.[a] *A Psalm of Āsaph.*

Sing aloud to God our strength;
Make a joyful shout to the God of
Jacob.
2 Raise a song and strike the timbrel,
The pleasant harp with the lute.

3 Blow the trumpet at the time of the
New Moon,
At the full moon, on our solemn feast
day.
4 For this *is* a statute for Israel,
A law of the God of Jacob.
5 This He established in Joseph *as* a
testimony,
When He went throughout the land
of Egypt,
Where I heard a language I did not
understand.

6 "I removed his shoulder from the
burden;
His hands were freed from the
baskets.
7 You called in trouble, and I delivered
you;
I answered you in the secret place of
thunder;
I tested you at the waters of
Mer'i·bah. Sē'lah

8 "Hear, O My people, and I will
admonish you!
O Israel, if you will listen to Me!
9 There shall be no foreign god among
you;
Nor shall you worship any foreign
god.
10 I *am* the LORD your God,
Who brought you out of the land of
Egypt;
Open your mouth wide, and I will fill
it.

11 "But My people would not heed My
voice,
And Israel would *have* none of Me.

81:title [a]Hebrew *Al Gittith*

80:17 Son of man is probably a reference to Israel who is God's right-hand man.

81:3 trumpet: Its use here is not for making music, but the sounding of a signal to mark the beginning of the month. **New Moon** probably refers to the beginning of the seventh month; **full moon** to the 15th day of that month, the first day of the Feast of Tabernacles.

81:11–15 Often we are our own worst enemies in the spiritual battle. We stubbornly cling to our disobedient attitudes, all the while wondering why God is not helping us. Only when we surrender every corner of our hearts to Him can we expect to win the victory.

12 So I gave them over to their own
stubborn heart,
To walk in their own counsels.

13 "Oh, that My people would listen to
Me,
That Israel would walk in My ways!
14 I would soon subdue their enemies,
And turn My hand against their
adversaries.
15 The haters of the LORD would pretend
submission to Him,
But their fate would endure forever.
16 He would have fed them also with
the finest of wheat;
And with honey from the rock I
would have satisfied you."

PSALM 82

A Plea for Justice

A Psalm of Āsaph.

God stands in the congregation of the
mighty;
He judges among the gods.[a]
2 How long will you judge unjustly,
And show partiality to the wicked?
Sē'lah
3 Defend the poor and fatherless;
Do justice to the afflicted and needy.
4 Deliver the poor and needy;
Free *them* from the hand of the
wicked.

5 They do not know, nor do they
understand;
They walk about in darkness;
All the foundations of the earth are
unstable.

6 I said, "You *are* gods,[a]
And all of you *are* children of the
Most High.
7 But you shall die like men,
And fall like one of the princes."

8 Arise, O God, judge the earth;
For You shall inherit all nations.

PSALM 83

Prayer to Frustrate Conspiracy Against Israel

A Song. A Psalm of Āsaph.

Do not keep silent, O God!
Do not hold Your peace,
And do not be still, O God!
2 For behold, Your enemies make a
tumult;
And those who hate You have lifted
up their head.
3 They have taken crafty counsel
against Your people,
And consulted together against Your
sheltered ones.
4 They have said, "Come, and let us cut
them off from *being* a nation,
That the name of Israel may be
remembered no more."

5 For they have consulted together with
one consent;
They form a confederacy against You:

82:1 [a]Hebrew *elohim*, mighty *ones;* that is, the judges
82:6 [a]Hebrew *elohim*, mighty *ones;* that is, the judges

82:1 congregation of the mighty: A heavenly assembly (see 1 Kin. 22:19–22) gathered for judgment. The gods have been identified both as heavenly beings (see 29:1) and as earthly judges (see Ex. 21:6). In this case, God the Judge will judge those who would judge others.

82:2 How long? The patience of God is exhausted with judges who have not executed justice among the people.

82:6 Jesus quoted part of this verse as He defended His claim to be the Son of God.

83:5–8 Ten nations are identified here as forming a coalition against Israel. No such conspiracy is recorded in the OT. Perhaps the psalmist is speaking figuratively to show the strength of the opposition experienced by Israel.

6 The tents of Ē′dom and the
Ish′ma•el•ītes;
Mō′ab and the Hag′rītes;
7 Gē′bal, Am′mon, and Am′a•lek;
Phi•lis′ti•a with the inhabitants of
Tȳre;
8 Assyria also has joined with them;
They have helped the children of Lot.
Sē′lah

9 Deal with them as *with* Mid′i•an,
As *with* Sis′e•ra,
As *with* Jā′bin at the Brook Kī′shon,
10 Who perished at En Dor,
Who became *as* refuse on the earth.
11 Make their nobles like Or′eb and like
Zē′eb,
Yes, all their princes like Zē′bah and
Zal•mun′na,
12 Who said, "Let us take for ourselves
The pastures of God for a
possession."

13 O my God, make them like the
whirling dust,
Like the chaff before the wind!
14 As the fire burns the woods,
And as the flame sets the mountains
on fire,
15 So pursue them with Your tempest,
And frighten them with Your storm.
16 Fill their faces with shame,
That they may seek Your name, O
LORD.
17 Let them be confounded and
dismayed forever;
Yes, let them be put to shame and
perish,
18 That they may know that You, whose
name alone *is* the LORD,
Are the Most High over all the earth.

PSALM 84

The Blessedness of Dwelling in the House of God

To the Chief Musician. On an instrument of Gath.[a] A Psalm of the sons of Kōrah.

How lovely *is* Your tabernacle,
O LORD of hosts!
2 My soul longs, yes, even faints
For the courts of the LORD;
My heart and my flesh cry out for the
living God.

3 Even the sparrow has found a home,
And the swallow a nest for herself,
Where she may lay her young—
Even Your altars, O LORD of hosts,
My King and my God.
4 Blessed *are* those who dwell in Your
house;
They will still be praising You.
Sē′lah

5 Blessed *is* the man whose strength *is*
in You,
Whose heart *is* set on pilgrimage.

84:title [a]Hebrew *Al Gittith*

83:11, 12 Gideon's victory over Midian, represented by the princes and kings **Oreb, Zeeb, Zebah**, and **Zalmunna**, was so significant that the names of these enemies and the battle are recalled here, as well as in Israel's other writings (see Is. 9:4; 10:26). **pastures of God:** The land of Canaan.

84:2 The true object of the pilgrim's longing is not so much the physical **courts** of the temple (see note on 1 Kin. 6:36) as it is a Person, the living God.

84:3, 4 He desires to reside permanently in God's presence, just as the birds nest about the temple complex. **My King and my God**: Not just his nation's God, but his personal Sovereign.

84:5, 6 The **pilgrimage** to the temple could be arduous, but seeking God is always worth the effort—and God gives **strength**. The location of the **Valley of Baca** is unknown. Perhaps it was an arid spot explaining the allusion to the autumn rains which end the summer drought and revive the parched land. The meaning of the Hebrew name may indicate wordplay in which "weeping" becomes "springs."

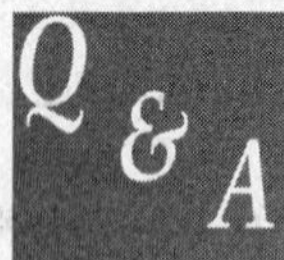

How can I adjust to life in a retirement home?

Elmer L. Gray

If you are planning to move into a retirement home, a few simple steps can ease your adjustment.

Find out what is available in your area or where you would like to live. Visit some of the places. Like anything else, these facilities range from inadequate to four-star ratings. Your family might be able to work with you in surveying the possibilities.

Such housing ranges from complete independence for residents to complete care. Some facilities have graduated provisions where residents first move into an apartment and take care of themselves, coming and going as they please. When needs change, they move to another area where they receive limited care. Then, as needed, they move to another room where they can get complete care.

Recognize your own needs and the love of your family. Work with them and express your appreciation for their love and care.

These suggestions will help you adjust:

✦ Get acquainted with your space and furnishings.

✦ Learn the regulations and the schedule of the facility.

✦ Make friends with the attendants and other residents.

✦ Keep in contact with family and friends.

✦ Remember Jesus promised to be with you everywhere.

Think about Paul's statement: "I have learned in whatever state I am, to be content" (Phil. 4:11).✦

6 *As they* pass through the Valley of
Bā'ca,
They make it a spring;
The rain also covers it with pools.
7 They go from strength to strength;
Each one appears before God in Zion.[a]

8 O LORD God of hosts, hear my prayer;
Give ear, O God of Jacob! Sē'lah
9 O God, behold our shield,
And look upon the face of Your
anointed.

10 For a day in Your courts *is* better than
a thousand.
I would rather be a doorkeeper in the
house of my God
Than dwell in the tents of
wickedness.
11 For the LORD God *is* a sun and shield;
The LORD will give grace and glory;

84:7 [a]Septuagint, Syriac, and Vulgate read *The God of gods shall be seen.*

84:10 The **doorkeeper** refers not to some official of the temple, but rather to any person who stands at the door, perhaps a worshiper or even a beggar (see Acts 3:1, 2).

84:11 This verse does not say that God will fulfill our every desire but that He will not deny us anything that He judges from His eternal perspective to be good.

No good *thing* will He withhold
From those who walk uprightly.

12 O LORD of hosts,
Blessed *is* the man who trusts in You!

PSALM 85

Prayer that the LORD Will Restore Favor to the Land

To the Chief Musician. A Psalm of the sons of Kōrah.

LORD, You have been favorable to Your land;
You have brought back the captivity of Jacob.
2 You have forgiven the iniquity of Your people;
You have covered all their sin. Sē'lah
3 You have taken away all Your wrath;
You have turned from the fierceness of Your anger.

4 Restore us, O God of our salvation,
And cause Your anger toward us to cease.
5 Will You be angry with us forever?
Will You prolong Your anger to all generations?
6 Will You not revive us again,
That Your people may rejoice in You?
7 Show us Your mercy, LORD,
And grant us Your salvation.

8 I will hear what God the LORD will speak,
For He will speak peace
To His people and to His saints;
But let them not turn back to folly.
9 Surely His salvation *is* near to those who fear Him,
That glory may dwell in our land.

10 Mercy and truth have met together;
Righteousness and peace have kissed.
11 Truth shall spring out of the earth,
And righteousness shall look down from heaven.
12 Yes, the LORD will give *what is* good;
And our land will yield its increase.
13 Righteousness will go before Him,
And shall make His footsteps *our* pathway.

PSALM 86

Prayer for Mercy, with Meditation on the Excellencies of the LORD

A Prayer of David.

Bow down Your ear, O LORD, hear me;
For I *am* poor and needy.
2 Preserve my life, for I *am* holy;
You are my God;
Save Your servant who trusts in You!
3 Be merciful to me, O Lord,
For I cry to You all day long.
4 Rejoice the soul of Your servant,
For to You, O Lord, I lift up my soul.
5 For You, Lord, *are* good, and ready to forgive,
And abundant in mercy to all those who call upon You.

6 Give ear, O LORD, to my prayer;
And attend to the voice of my supplications.
7 In the day of my trouble I will call upon You,
For You will answer me.

8 Among the gods *there is* none like You, O Lord;
Nor *are there any works* like Your works.

85:1 This psalm of gratitude may have been written after the Babylonian captivity.
85:9 The **glory** that had departed when the temple was destroyed would now return and **dwell** in the **land**.
Psalm 86 This is the only psalm in Book Three ascribed to David.

9 All nations whom You have made
Shall come and worship before You,
O Lord,
And shall glorify Your name.
10 For You *are* great, and do wondrous
things;
You alone *are* God.

11 Teach me Your way, O LORD;
I will walk in Your truth;
Unite my heart to fear Your name.
12 I will praise You, O Lord my God,
with all my heart,
And I will glorify Your name
forevermore.
13 For great *is* Your mercy toward me,
And You have delivered my soul
from the depths of Shē'ōl.

14 O God, the proud have risen against
me,
And a mob of violent *men* have
sought my life,
And have not set You before them.
15 But You, O Lord, *are* a God full of
compassion, and gracious,
Longsuffering and abundant in mercy
and truth.

16 Oh, turn to me, and have mercy on
me!
Give Your strength to Your servant,
And save the son of Your maidser-
vant.
17 Show me a sign for good,
That those who hate me may see *it*
and be ashamed,
Because You, LORD, have helped me
and comforted me.

PSALM 87

The Glories of the City of God

A Psalm of the sons of Kōrah. A Song.

His foundation *is* in the holy
mountains.
2 The LORD loves the gates of Zion
More than all the dwellings of Jacob.
3 Glorious things are spoken of you,
O city of God! Sē'lah

4 "I will make mention of Rā'hab and
Babylon to those who know Me;
Behold, O Phi·lis'ti·a and Tȳre, with
Ethiopia:
'This *one* was born there.' "

5 And of Zion it will be said,
"This *one* and that *one* were born in
her;
And the Most High Himself shall
establish her."
6 The LORD will record,
When He registers the peoples:
"This *one* was born there." Sē'lah

7 Both the singers and the players on
instruments *say,*
"All my springs *are* in you."

86:11 Unite my heart: The united heart is one totally committed to God's will. A closer relationship with God can only be achieved as we actively seek Him and dedicate ourselves continually to obedience to His Word.

Psalm 87 A song about Zion, establishing Jerusalem's preeminence over all the great cities of the world.

87:2 gates of Zion: City gates represent the whole city. God loves Zion more than any other Israelite sanctuary.

87:4 Rahab: Egypt (see Is. 30:7).

87:6 This verse reminds us of that future day, when the register of heaven—the Book of Life—will be opened, and the true citizens of the city allowed to enter eternal life. We each need to ask ourselves if on that day the statement will be made of us, "This one was born again in such and such a place."

PSALM 88

A Prayer for Help in Despondency

A Song. A Psalm of the sons of Kōrah. To the Chief Musician. Set to "Māhalath Leannoth." A Contemplation[a] *of Hēman the Ezrahīte.*

O LORD, God of my salvation,
I have cried out day and night
before You.
2 Let my prayer come before You;
Incline Your ear to my cry.

3 For my soul is full of troubles,
And my life draws near to the grave.
4 I am counted with those who go
down to the pit;
I am like a man *who has* no strength,
5 Adrift among the dead,
Like the slain who lie in the grave,
Whom You remember no more,
And who are cut off from Your hand.

6 You have laid me in the lowest pit,
In darkness, in the depths.
7 Your wrath lies heavy upon me,
And You have afflicted *me* with all
Your waves. Sē'lah
8 You have put away my acquaintances
far from me;
You have made me an abomination to
them;
I am shut up, and I cannot get out;
9 My eye wastes away because of
affliction.

LORD, I have called daily upon You;
I have stretched out my hands to You.
10 Will You work wonders for the dead?
Shall the dead arise *and* praise You?
Sē'lah
11 Shall Your lovingkindness be declared
in the grave?
Or Your faithfulness in the place of
destruction?
12 Shall Your wonders be known in the
dark?
And Your righteousness in the land of
forgetfulness?

13 But to You I have cried out, O LORD,
And in the morning my prayer comes
before You.
14 LORD, why do You cast off my soul?
Why do You hide Your face from me?
15 I *have been* afflicted and ready to die
from *my* youth;
I suffer Your terrors;
I am distraught.
16 Your fierce wrath has gone over me;
Your terrors have cut me off.
17 They came around me all day long
like water;
They engulfed me altogether.
18 Loved one and friend You have put
far from me,
And my acquaintances into darkness.

PSALM 89

Remembering the Covenant with David, and Sorrow for Lost Blessings

A Contemplation[a] *of Ēthan the Ezrahīte.*

I will sing of the mercies of the LORD
forever;

88:title [a]Hebrew *Maschil* 89:title [a]Hebrew *Maschil*

Psalm 88 An individual lament, yet lacking the customary expressions of trust and praise, this psalm is generally recognized as the saddest of the entire book. The double title may be explained by considering Heman the Ezrahite as the leader of the guild of Korah (1 Chr. 6:33, 37).

88:11 The expected answer to the questions in vv. 10–12 is no. It is among the living that God's covenant love is expressed, that His praises are sung, and that His miracles are done. Other passages in the OT (see Job 19:26, 27), however, as well as the NT doctrine of the resurrection, show that the redeemed will praise God after death.

Psalm 89 A royal lament either by, or on behalf of, a Davidic king, whose identity is uncertain. The foundation of the poem is the promise of a throne for David's dynasty forever (2 Sam. 7:13–16).

With my mouth will I make known
Your faithfulness to all generations.
2 For I have said, "Mercy shall be built
up forever;
Your faithfulness You shall establish
in the very heavens."

3 "I have made a covenant with My
chosen,
I have sworn to My servant David:
4 'Your seed I will establish forever,
And build up your throne to all
generations.' " Sē'lah

5 And the heavens will praise Your
wonders, O LORD;
Your faithfulness also in the assembly
of the saints.
6 For who in the heavens can be
compared to the LORD?
Who among the sons of the mighty
can be likened to the LORD?
7 God is greatly to be feared in the
assembly of the saints,
And to be held in reverence by all
those around Him.
8 O LORD God of hosts,
Who *is* mighty like You, O LORD?
Your faithfulness also surrounds You.
9 You rule the raging of the sea;
When its waves rise, You still them.
10 You have broken Rā'hab in pieces, as
one who is slain;
You have scattered Your enemies with
Your mighty arm.

11 The heavens *are* Yours, the earth also
is Yours;
The world and all its fullness, You
have founded them.
12 The north and the south, You have
created them;
Tā'bor and Her'mon rejoice in Your
name.
13 You have a mighty arm;
Strong is Your hand, *and* high is Your
right hand.
14 Righteousness and justice *are* the
foundation of Your throne;
Mercy and truth go before Your face.
15 Blessed *are* the people who know the
joyful sound!
They walk, O LORD, in the light of
Your countenance.
16 In Your name they rejoice all day
long,
And in Your righteousness they are
exalted.
17 For You *are* the glory of their strength,
And in Your favor our horn is ex-
alted.
18 For our shield *belongs* to the LORD,
And our king to the Holy One of
Israel.

19 Then You spoke in a vision to Your
holy one,[a]
And said: "I have given help to *one*
who is mighty;
I have exalted one chosen from the
people.
20 I have found My servant David;
With My holy oil I have anointed
him,
21 With whom My hand shall be
established;
Also My arm shall strengthen him.
22 The enemy shall not outwit him,

89:19 [a]Following many Hebrew manuscripts; Masoretic Text, Septuagint, Targum, and Vulgate read *holy ones*.

89:9 Only God can control **the sea**. The disciples, recognizing this, were awed when Jesus stilled the waters. "Who can this be!" was their amazed response (Mark 4:41).

89:11, 12 Even the mountains praise Him. Mt. **Tabor** in the northeast corner of the Jezreel Valley is paired with the much higher Mt. **Hermon** in Syria.

89:15–18 We can find true peace by walking with the Lord and praising His name. Few people fail to find encouragement and strength by glorifying God in worshipful song. As we focus on His strength in an attitude of worship, we forget about our own troubles and inadequacies.

Nor the son of wickedness afflict him.
23 I will beat down his foes before his face,
And plague those who hate him.

24 "But My faithfulness and My mercy *shall be* with him,
And in My name his horn shall be exalted.
25 Also I will set his hand over the sea,
And his right hand over the rivers.
26 He shall cry to Me, 'You *are* my Father,
My God, and the rock of my salvation.'
27 Also I will make him *My* firstborn,
The highest of the kings of the earth.
28 My mercy I will keep for him forever,
And My covenant shall stand firm with him.
29 His seed also I will make *to endure* forever,
And his throne as the days of heaven.

30 "If his sons forsake My law
And do not walk in My judgments,
31 If they break My statutes
And do not keep My commandments,
32 Then I will punish their transgression with the rod,
And their iniquity with stripes.
33 Nevertheless My lovingkindness I will not utterly take from him,
Nor allow My faithfulness to fail.
34 My covenant I will not break,
Nor alter the word that has gone out of My lips.
35 Once I have sworn by My holiness;
I will not lie to David:
36 His seed shall endure forever,
And his throne as the sun before Me;
37 It shall be established forever like the moon,
Even *like* the faithful witness in the sky." Sē'lah

38 But You have cast off and abhorred,
You have been furious with Your anointed.
39 You have renounced the covenant of Your servant;
You have profaned his crown *by casting it* to the ground.
40 You have broken down all his hedges;
You have brought his strongholds to ruin.
41 All who pass by the way plunder him;
He is a reproach to his neighbors.
42 You have exalted the right hand of his adversaries;
You have made all his enemies rejoice.
43 You have also turned back the edge of his sword,
And have not sustained him in the battle.
44 You have made his glory cease,
And cast his throne down to the ground.
45 The days of his youth You have shortened;
You have covered him with shame. Sē'lah

46 How long, LORD?
Will You hide Yourself forever?
Will Your wrath burn like fire?
47 Remember how short my time is;
For what futility have You created all the children of men?

89:26, 27 The decree of 2:7 is in mind here: "You are My Son, today I have begotten You." **My firstborn**: Language used first of Israel (Ex. 4:22) is now applied to David or to one from his line. **The highest**: David's relationship to earthly powers is the same as God's to heavenly powers.

89:28–37 The covenant is conditional with individual kings (vv. 30–32), but unconditional with David's family (vv. 28, 29, 33–37). This is similar to God's covenant with Abraham.

89:38–45 These verses describe a successor to David who was defeated and deposed—perhaps Jehoiachin (2 Kin. 24:8–16) or Zedekiah (2 Kin. 25:4–7).

48 What man can live and not see death?
Can he deliver his life from the power
of the grave? Sē′lah

49 Lord, where *are* Your former
lovingkindnesses,
Which You swore to David in Your
truth?
50 Remember, Lord, the reproach of
Your servants—
How I bear in my bosom *the reproach*
of all the many peoples,
51 With which Your enemies have
reproached, O LORD,
With which they have reproached the
footsteps of Your anointed.

52 Blessed *be* the LORD forevermore!
Amen and Amen.

Book Four: Psalms 90—106

PSALM 90

The Eternity of God, and Man's Frailty

A Prayer of Moses the man of God.

LORD, You have been our dwelling
place[a] in all generations.
2 Before the mountains were brought
forth,
Or ever You had formed the earth
and the world,
Even from everlasting to everlasting,
You *are* God.

3 You turn man to destruction,
And say, "Return, O children of men."
4 For a thousand years in Your sight
Are like yesterday when it is past,
And *like* a watch in the night.
5 You carry them away *like* a flood;
They are like a sleep.
In the morning they are like grass
which grows up:
6 In the morning it flourishes and
grows up;
In the evening it is cut down and
withers.

7 For we have been consumed by Your
anger,
And by Your wrath we are terrified.
8 You have set our iniquities before You,
Our secret *sins* in the light of Your
countenance.
9 For all our days have passed away in
Your wrath;
We finish our years like a sigh.
10 The days of our lives *are* seventy
years;
And if by reason of strength *they are*
eighty years,
Yet their boast *is* only labor and
sorrow;

90:1 [a]Septuagint, Targum, and Vulgate read *refuge*.

89:52 A doxology, most likely added to mark the end of the third book of the Psalms. Each of the five books ends in a similar way (see 41:13; 72:18–20; 106:48; 150:1–6).

Psalm 90 A community lament, yet characterized by faith and hope.

90:2 The mountains are mentioned because they were regarded as the oldest parts of the earth. The psalmist reaffirms that God is not part of creation. In the midst of an ever-changing world and the constant shifting of our lives we can find comfort in the steadfast refuge of our Lord.

90:4 A thousand years represents a very short time to God—no more than a four-hour **watch in the night** (see Lam. 2:19). Thus our life span is put into the context of eternity.

90:9 like a sigh: The end of life is not dramatic, but simply a last exhalation of breath.

90:10 seventy . . . eighty: The life span is in contrast to those who lived before the Flood (see Gen. 5:1–31; 11:10–26). Note that those who lived longer lives at this time were miserable because they knew they would not live to see the Promised Land. Today we have every reason to rejoice at the prospect of longer life, knowing each day is an opportunity to serve God and lay up treasures in heaven.

WORDS OF COMFORT

Victor M. Parachin

The main theme of at least a dozen psalms is trusting God for all that we need. Consider the example of actor Jimmy Stewart, who left show business at the peak of his Hollywood career to join the army during World War II. The night before Stewart left America to serve as a combat pilot in Europe, his father came to visit. Both father and son were deeply distressed about the future. Stewart's father knew this might be the last time he would ever see his son alive. After they embraced, the father slipped a handwritten note into Jimmy Stewart's palm.

When his father left, the actor opened the note. His father had written sections of Psalm 91: "Surely He shall deliver you from the snare of the fowler. . . . He shall cover you with his feathers, and under His wings you shall take refuge; His truth shall be your shield and buckler. You shall not be afraid of the terror by night, nor of the arrow that flies by day . . . A thousand may fall at your side, and ten thousand at your right hand; but it shall not come near you." That psalm emphasizing trust in God for safety was meaningful and comforting to both the father and the young man. ✦

"That psalm emphasizing trust in God for safety was meaningful and comforting."

For it is soon cut off, and we fly away.
11 Who knows the power of Your anger?
For as the fear of You, *so is* Your wrath.
12 So teach *us* to number our days,
That we may gain a heart of wisdom.

13 Return, O LORD!
How long?
And have compassion on Your servants.
14 Oh, satisfy us early with Your mercy,
That we may rejoice and be glad all our days!
15 Make us glad according to the days *in which* You have afflicted us,
The years *in which* we have seen evil.
16 Let Your work appear to Your servants,
And Your glory to their children.
17 And let the beauty of the LORD our God be upon us,

90:11, 12 Since sin has made our days few, we ought to use them the more carefully. A good steward does not waste time but makes the most of each and every moment. We are to live life to the fullest so that we do not hinder the work of the Lord.

90:16, 17 Your work . . . the work of our hands: Just as God's work will endure, so His blessings on our works will cause them to endure. Though our days are few, they can be lived in God and thus take on eternal significance.

I pray that You, God, will give Your angels charge over my grandchild to keep her in all her ways.

adapted from Psalm 91:11

And establish the work of our hands
for us;
Yes, establish the work of our hands.

PSALM 91

Safety of Abiding in the Presence of God

He who dwells in the secret place of
the Most High
Shall abide under the shadow of the
Almighty.
2 I will say of the LORD, "*He is* my
refuge and my fortress;
My God, in Him I will trust."

3 Surely He shall deliver you from the
snare of the fowler[a]
And from the perilous pestilence.
4 He shall cover you with His feathers,
And under His wings you shall take
refuge;
His truth *shall be your* shield and
buckler.
5 You shall not be afraid of the terror
by night,
Nor of the arrow *that* flies by day,
6 *Nor* of the pestilence *that* walks in
darkness,
Nor of the destruction *that* lays waste
at noonday.

7 A thousand may fall at your side,
And ten thousand at your right hand;
But it shall not come near you.
8 Only with your eyes shall you look,
And see the reward of the wicked.

9 Because you have made the LORD,
who is my refuge,
Even the Most High, your dwelling
place,
10 No evil shall befall you,
Nor shall any plague come near your
dwelling;
11 For He shall give His angels charge
over you,
To keep you in all your ways.
12 In *their* hands they shall bear you
up,
Lest you dash your foot against a
stone.
13 You shall tread upon the lion and the
cobra,
The young lion and the serpent you
shall trample underfoot.

14 "Because he has set his love upon Me,
therefore I will deliver him;
I will set him on high, because he has
known My name.

91:3 [a]That is, one who catches birds in a trap or snare

Psalm 91 This psalm appears to be a composite of a wisdom poem (vv. 1–13) and a divine oracle (vv. 14–16). It speaks of the security that the Messiah and His followers may find in God.

91:5, 6 God's protection is continuous **night** and **day**. The ills mentioned here are personified. In the ancient world each of these was thought to be a god.

91:11, 12 These verses indicate that God has assigned angels to protect His children. Thus, nothing will befall us that is not part of His eternal plan.

92:2 morning . . . night: Regular worship deepens fellowship with God. **Lovingkindness** and **faithfulness** distinguish God from the pagan deities, who do not manifest these virtues.

92:14 Christians who draw their strength from the Lord will not wilt in their later years but will continue to grow spiritually, and their dynamic spiritual lives will not cease to bear fruit.

15 He shall call upon Me, and I will
answer him;
I *will be* with him in trouble;
I will deliver him and honor him.
16 With long life I will satisfy him,
And show him My salvation."

PSALM 92

Praise to the LORD for His Love and Faithfulness

A Psalm. A Song for the Sabbath day.

It is good to give thanks to the LORD,
And to sing praises to Your name,
O Most High;
2 To declare Your lovingkindness in the
morning,
And Your faithfulness every night,
3 On an instrument of ten strings,
On the lute,
And on the harp,
With harmonious sound.
4 For You, LORD, have made me glad
through Your work;
I will triumph in the works of Your
hands.

5 O LORD, how great are Your works!
Your thoughts are very deep.
6 A senseless man does not know,
Nor does a fool understand this.
7 When the wicked spring up like
grass,
And when all the workers of iniquity
flourish,
It is that they may be destroyed
forever.

8 But You, LORD, *are* on high
forevermore.
9 For behold, Your enemies, O LORD,
For behold, Your enemies shall
perish;
All the workers of iniquity shall be
scattered.
10 But my horn You have exalted like a
wild ox;
I have been anointed with fresh oil.
11 My eye also has seen *my desire* on my
enemies;
My ears hear *my desire* on the wicked
Who rise up against me.

12 The righteous shall flourish like a
palm tree,
He shall grow like a cedar in
Lebanon.
13 Those who are planted in the house
of the LORD
Shall flourish in the courts of our
God.
14 They shall still bear fruit in old age;
They shall be fresh and flourishing,
15 To declare that the LORD is upright;
He is my rock, and *there is* no
unrighteousness in Him.

PSALM 93

The Eternal Reign of the LORD

The LORD reigns, He is clothed with
majesty;
The LORD is clothed,
He has girded Himself with strength.
Surely the world is established, so
that it cannot be moved.
2 Your throne *is* established from of old;
You *are* from everlasting.

3 The floods have lifted up, O LORD,
The floods have lifted up their voice;
The floods lift up their waves.
4 The LORD on high *is* mightier
Than the noise of many waters,
Than the mighty waves of the sea.

Psalm 93 All of Ps. 93—99 celebrate the rule of God the divine King and thus are known as enthronement psalms. They especially celebrate His establishment of justice on the earth. Ps. 93 rejoices over the kingship of the Lord.

93:3, 4 The floods: Perhaps an allusion to the theme of pagan creation accounts where the primeval deep was conquered by a deity. Or it may refer to the hostile nations that are sometimes likened to "the rushing of mighty waters" (Is. 17:12).

ALWAYS FRUITFUL

Carolyn Koons with John Archer

Resistance to change is natural, but no one is exempt. At no age does change miraculously disappear from the landscape. In fact, studies show that its pace accelerates as we move further into adulthood, even though we are not prepared for the rapid and continuous shifts that mark our adult lives. Many older adults call themselves "chronologically gifted." This apt phrase describes people who enjoy longer, healthier lives—additional decades to explore life's dynamic potential.

New research has shown that many traditional assumptions about adult human development seem to have been conceived in reverse. For example, IQ peaks at around age fifty-five, not eighteen, and intelligence continues to mature and deepen well past the biblical allotment of "threescore and ten." The time of greatest productivity, when we can expect to make our most significant contributions, *begins* at age forty-five. Did you know, for example, that George Bernard Shaw won the Nobel prize for literature at age seventy? There is no age at which we should just stop and watch the world go by! ✦

5 Your testimonies are very sure;
Holiness adorns Your house,
O LORD, forever.

PSALM 94

God the Refuge of the Righteous

O LORD God, to whom vengeance
belongs—
O God, to whom vengeance belongs,
shine forth!
2 Rise up, O Judge of the earth;
Render punishment to the proud.
3 LORD, how long will the wicked,
How long will the wicked triumph?

4 They utter speech, *and* speak insolent
things;
All the workers of iniquity boast in
themselves.
5 They break in pieces Your people, O
LORD,
And afflict Your heritage.
6 They slay the widow and the
stranger,
And murder the fatherless.
7 Yet they say, "The LORD does not see,
Nor does the God of Jacob
understand."

8 Understand, you senseless among the
people;
And *you* fools, when will you be
wise?
9 He who planted the ear, shall He not
hear?
He who formed the eye, shall He not
see?

94:9 ear . . . eye: How senseless to believe that God who has made hearing and seeing should not Himself possess the capacities.

10 He who instructs the nations, shall
He not correct,
He who teaches man knowledge?
11 The LORD knows the thoughts of man,
That they *are* futile.

12 Blessed *is* the man whom You instruct, O LORD,
And teach out of Your law,
13 That You may give him rest from the
days of adversity,
Until the pit is dug for the wicked.
14 For the LORD will not cast off His
people,
Nor will He forsake His inheritance.
15 But judgment will return to
righteousness,
And all the upright in heart will
follow it.

16 Who will rise up for me against the
evildoers?
Who will stand up for me against the
workers of iniquity?
17 Unless the LORD *had been* my help,
My soul would soon have settled in
silence.
18 If I say, "My foot slips,"
Your mercy, O LORD, will hold me up.
19 In the multitude of my anxieties
within me,
Your comforts delight my soul.

20 Shall the throne of iniquity, which
devises evil by law,
Have fellowship with You?
21 They gather together against the life
of the righteous,
And condemn innocent blood.
22 But the LORD has been my defense,
And my God the rock of my refuge.
23 He has brought on them their own
iniquity,
And shall cut them off in their own
wickedness;
The LORD our God shall cut them off.

PSALM 95

A Call to Worship and Obedience

Oh come, let us sing to the LORD!
Let us shout joyfully to the Rock of
our salvation.
2 Let us come before His presence with
thanksgiving;
Let us shout joyfully to Him with
psalms.
3 For the LORD *is* the great God,
And the great King above all gods.
4 In His hand *are* the deep places of the
earth;
The heights of the hills *are* His also.
5 The sea *is* His, for He made it;
And His hands formed the dry *land*.

6 Oh come, let us worship and bow
down;
Let us kneel before the LORD our
Maker.
7 For He *is* our God,
And we *are* the people of His pasture,
And the sheep of His hand.

Today, if you will hear His voice:
8 "Do not harden your hearts, as in the
rebellion,[a]

95:8 [a]Or *Meribah*

94:12–15 Discipline is a tool of a wise and loving God and, as such, should be a cause for gratitude.

94:17 settled in silence: Gone to the realm of the dead, which was often described as a place of silence.

94:19 Turning to the Lord for comfort is the only sure cure for worrying.

95:8–11 Worship must be more than vocal and formal. **Do not harden** means do not be disobedient. We must not repeat the stubbornness and unbelief of Israel's **fathers** during their **forty years** in the **wilderness** (Ex. 17:1–7). There was no excuse for their disobedience and unbelief—God says, **they saw My work** (the miracles performed on Israel's behalf).

As *in* the day of trial[b] in the
wilderness,
9 When your fathers tested Me;
They tried Me, though they saw My
work.
10 For forty years I was grieved with
that generation,
And said, 'It *is* a people who go
astray in their hearts,
And they do not know My ways.'
11 So I swore in My wrath,
'They shall not enter My rest.' "

PSALM 96

A Song of Praise to God Coming in Judgment

Oh, sing to the LORD a new song!
Sing to the LORD, all the earth.
2 Sing to the LORD, bless His name;
Proclaim the good news of His
salvation from day to day.
3 Declare His glory among the nations,
His wonders among all peoples.

4 For the LORD *is* great and greatly to be
praised;
He *is* to be feared above all gods.
5 For all the gods of the peoples *are*
idols,
But the LORD made the heavens.
6 Honor and majesty *are* before Him;
Strength and beauty *are* in His
sanctuary.

7 Give to the LORD, O families of the
peoples,
Give to the LORD glory and strength.
8 Give to the LORD the glory *due* His
name;
Bring an offering, and come into His
courts.
9 Oh, worship the LORD in the beauty
of holiness!
Tremble before Him, all the earth.

10 Say among the nations, "The LORD
reigns;
The world also is firmly established,
It shall not be moved;
He shall judge the peoples
righteously."
11 Let the heavens rejoice, and let the
earth be glad;
Let the sea roar, and all its fullness;
12 Let the field be joyful, and all that *is*
in it.
Then all the trees of the woods will
rejoice before the LORD.
13 For He is coming, for He is coming to
judge the earth.
He shall judge the world with
righteousness,
And the peoples with His truth.

PSALM 97

A Song of Praise to the Sovereign LORD

The LORD reigns;
Let the earth rejoice;
Let the multitude of isles be glad!

2 Clouds and darkness surround Him;
Righteousness and justice *are* the
foundation of His throne.

95:8 [b]Or *Massah*

96:7–9 the glory due His name: The call here is for more than holy array. The worship most worthy is the **beauty of holiness** (v. 9), the manifestation of God's holy character in the lives of the worshipers.

96:11–13 The **heavens** and the **earth** are called to glorify God. His coming kingdom will be a blessing to nature as well as to human nature. As at creation the "morning stars sang together" (Job 38:7), so at the consummation all nature will render praise to God. This is because He will **judge . . . with righteousness** and set all things right.

97:2–6 Clouds and **darkness** recall Sinai (Ex. 19:16, 18) and emphasize God's unapproachable presence. **Fire** and **lightnings** suggest a divine revelation with emphasis on the awesome aspects of His appearance. But ultimately, it is God's **righteousness** (vv. 2, 6) which most distinguishes Him from all else.

3 A fire goes before Him,
And burns up His enemies round
about.
4 His lightnings light the world;
The earth sees and trembles.
5 The mountains melt like wax at the
presence of the LORD,
At the presence of the Lord of the
whole earth.
6 The heavens declare His
righteousness,
And all the peoples see His glory.

7 Let all be put to shame who serve
carved images,
Who boast of idols.
Worship Him, all *you* gods.
8 Zion hears and is glad,
And the daughters of Judah rejoice
Because of Your judgments, O LORD.
9 For You, LORD, *are* most high above
all the earth;
You are exalted far above all gods.

10 You who love the LORD, hate evil!
He preserves the souls of His saints;
He delivers them out of the hand of
the wicked.
11 Light is sown for the righteous,
And gladness for the upright in heart.
12 Rejoice in the LORD, you righteous,
And give thanks at the remembrance
of His holy name.[a]

PSALM 98

A Song of Praise to the LORD for His Salvation and Judgment

A Psalm.

Oh, sing to the LORD a new song!
For He has done marvelous things;
His right hand and His holy arm
have gained Him the victory.
2 The LORD has made known His
salvation;
His righteousness He has revealed in
the sight of the nations.
3 He has remembered His mercy and
His faithfulness to the house of
Israel;
All the ends of the earth have seen
the salvation of our God.

4 Shout joyfully to the LORD, all the
earth;
Break forth in song, rejoice, and sing
praises.
5 Sing to the LORD with the harp,
With the harp and the sound of a
psalm,
6 With trumpets and the sound of a
horn;
Shout joyfully before the LORD, the
King.

7 Let the sea roar, and all its fullness,
The world and those who dwell in it;
8 Let the rivers clap *their* hands;
Let the hills be joyful together before
the LORD,
9 For He is coming to judge the earth.
With righteousness He shall judge the
world,
And the peoples with equity.

PSALM 99

Praise to the LORD for His Holiness

The LORD reigns;
Let the peoples tremble!
He dwells *between* the cherubim;
Let the earth be moved!
2 The LORD *is* great in Zion,
And He *is* high above all the peoples.

97:12 [a]Or *His holiness*

97:10 This verse demonstrates that love for God and a sinful life are mutually exclusive. One cannot continue in sin and honestly claim to love the Lord. See 1 John 2:5.

98:2, 3 God's character is shown in what He does for His people. Here perhaps the psalmist refers to the restoration from Babylonian captivity (see Ezek. 36:23, 24).

98:7, 8 Here the scene seems to shift to the end times.

3 Let them praise Your great and
awesome name—
He *is* holy.

4 The King's strength also loves justice;
You have established equity;
You have executed justice and
righteousness in Jacob.
5 Exalt the LORD our God,
And worship at His footstool—
He *is* holy.

6 Moses and Aaron were among His
priests,
And Samuel was among those who
called upon His name;
They called upon the LORD, and He
answered them.
7 He spoke to them in the cloudy pillar;
They kept His testimonies and the
ordinance He gave them.

8 You answered them, O LORD our God;
You were to them God-Who-Forgives,
Though You took vengeance on their
deeds.
9 Exalt the LORD our God,
And worship at His holy hill;
For the LORD our God *is* holy.

PSALM 100

A Song of Praise for the LORD'S Faithfulness to His People

A Psalm of Thanksgiving.

Make a joyful shout to the LORD, all
you lands!
2 Serve the LORD with gladness;
Come before His presence with
singing.
3 Know that the LORD, He *is* God;
It is He *who* has made us, and not we
ourselves;[a]
We are His people and the sheep of
His pasture.

4 Enter into His gates with
thanksgiving,
And into His courts with praise.
Be thankful to Him, *and* bless His
name.
5 For the LORD *is* good;
His mercy *is* everlasting,
And His truth *endures* to all
generations.

PSALM 101

Promised Faithfulness to the LORD

A Psalm of David.

I will sing of mercy and justice;
To You, O LORD, I will sing praises.

2 I will behave wisely in a perfect
way.
Oh, when will You come to me?
I will walk within my house with a
perfect heart.

100:3 [a]Following Kethib, Septuagint, and Vulgate; Qere, many Hebrew manuscripts, and Targum read *we are His.*

99:5 footstool: A term applied to the temple (Is. 60:13), the ark (1 Chr. 28:2), Jerusalem (Lam. 2:1), and the whole earth (Is. 66:1). When we truly worship God, we automatically humble ourselves. As we lift Him up and acknowledge His greatness, we are reminded of our own frailty, and we have no reason to glory in ourselves. Beside the greatness of God, the universe is but a lowly footstool from which we offer our praise.

99:8 answered them: Probably the three mentioned in v. 6. The second **them** likely refers to the nation in general who experienced the **God-Who-Forgives. vengeance on their deeds**: Forgiveness does not cancel all the consequences of sin.

99:9 holy hill: temple mount at Jerusalem.

100:3 Know here means more than an intellectual consent. It is to incorporate God and His character into the practices of life.

100:5 This verse lists just three of the many reasons to praise God.

Psalm 101 A royal psalm, reflecting the principles that the king vows to keep.

3 I will set nothing wicked before my
eyes;
I hate the work of those who fall
away;
It shall not cling to me.
4 A perverse heart shall depart from
me;
I will not know wickedness.

5 Whoever secretly slanders his
neighbor,
Him I will destroy;
The one who has a haughty look and
a proud heart,
Him I will not endure.

6 My eyes *shall be* on the faithful of the
land,
That they may dwell with me;
He who walks in a perfect way,
He shall serve me.
7 He who works deceit shall not dwell
within my house;
He who tells lies shall not continue in
my presence.
8 Early I will destroy all the wicked of
the land,
That I may cut off all the evildoers
from the city of the LORD.

PSALM 102

The LORD's Eternal Love

A Prayer of the afflicted, when he is overwhelmed and pours out his complaint before the LORD.

Hear my prayer, O LORD,
And let my cry come to You.
2 Do not hide Your face from me in the
day of my trouble;
Incline Your ear to me;
In the day that I call, answer me
speedily.

3 For my days are consumed like
smoke,
And my bones are burned like a
hearth.
4 My heart is stricken and withered like
grass,
So that I forget to eat my bread.
5 Because of the sound of my groaning
My bones cling to my skin.
6 I am like a pelican of the wilderness;
I am like an owl of the desert.
7 I lie awake,
And am like a sparrow alone on the
housetop.

8 My enemies reproach me all day
long;
Those who deride me swear an oath
against me.
9 For I have eaten ashes like bread,
And mingled my drink with
weeping,
10 Because of Your indignation and Your
wrath;
For You have lifted me up and cast
me away.
11 My days *are* like a shadow that
lengthens,
And I wither away like grass.

12 But You, O LORD, shall endure
forever,
And the remembrance of Your name
to all generations.

101:3 Because our thought life and actions are determined to a great extent by that which we focus on, we must carefully screen the items we read, the programs and movies we watch, and the activities in which we participate.

101:6, 7 Dwell with me indicates the associates of the king.

102:6, 7 These ceremonially unclean birds stress the psalmist's sense of uncleanness and separation from God.

102:11 Through the Bible, **grass** is used to symbolize the brevity of life.

102:12, 13 But You is emphatic, expressing a sharp contrast between the nature of the psalmist and the Lord. God's last word to His people is always **mercy**.

13 You will arise *and* have mercy on
Zion;
For the time to favor her,
Yes, the set time, has come.
14 For Your servants take pleasure in her
stones,
And show favor to her dust.
15 So the nations shall fear the name of
the LORD,
And all the kings of the earth Your
glory.
16 For the LORD shall build up Zion;
He shall appear in His glory.
17 He shall regard the prayer of the
destitute,
And shall not despise their prayer.

18 This will be written for the generation
to come,
That a people yet to be created may
praise the LORD.
19 For He looked down from the height
of His sanctuary;
From heaven the LORD viewed the
earth,
20 To hear the groaning of the prisoner,
To release those appointed to death,
21 To declare the name of the LORD in
Zion,
And His praise in Jerusalem,
22 When the peoples are gathered
together,
And the kingdoms, to serve the LORD.

23 He weakened my strength in the way;
He shortened my days.
24 I said, "O my God,
Do not take me away in the midst of
my days;
Your years *are* throughout all
generations.
25 Of old You laid the foundation of the
earth,
And the heavens *are* the work of Your
hands.
26 They will perish, but You will endure;
Yes, they will all grow old like a
garment;
Like a cloak You will change them,
And they will be changed.
27 But You *are* the same,
And Your years will have no end.
28 The children of Your servants will
continue,
And their descendants will be
established before You."

PSALM 103

Praise for the LORD's Mercies

A Psalm of David.

Bless the LORD, O my soul;
And all that is within me, *bless* His
holy name!
2 Bless the LORD, O my soul,
And forget not all His benefits:
3 Who forgives all your iniquities,
Who heals all your diseases,
4 Who redeems your life from
destruction,
Who crowns you with lovingkindness
and tender mercies,
5 Who satisfies your mouth with good
things,

102:25–27 Even the **earth** and **heavens** are like a **garment** that will wear out and **be changed** when compared to God's eternity. These verses are cited in Heb. 1:10–12 where Christ is viewed as the agent of creation. **You are the same**: Applied to Christ in Heb. 13:8.

102:28 In the OT posterity was regarded as a sign of divine favor (37:37, 38). Though the righteous person may die, yet God will keep faith with him through his children.

103:1 O my soul: whole being.

103:2 Benefits are the blessings of the Lord mentioned in vv. 3–5, all of which have to do with redemption and renewal. By remembering His past goodness, we strengthen our faith to face the troubles of today.

103:5 The eagle is long-lived and is known for its swiftness and strength (see Is. 40:31).

How can I overcome bouts of self-pity?

Elmer L. Gray

Do not get into the habit of enjoying self-pity. That can become a way of life. Feeling sorry for yourself can happen to you before you realize it. Anybody can get "down in the dumps," and, without realizing it, a person can sink into self-pity because it may attract attention and win some concern. Do not let feeling blue become a daily pastime.

Do something about your depressed feeling. Seek to identify the cause, especially if the cause is negative emotion. Talking with a close Christian friend about the matter can ventilate the problem. Improve your feelings through devotional reading of the Bible, listening to or singing happy music, fellowshiping with Christian friends, thinking of good times, and counting your blessings.

Take charge of yourself and do as David in these words: "Bless the Lord, O my soul; and all that is within me, bless His holy name!" (Ps. 103:1).

Pray to the Lord about your problem and ask for His help.

So that your youth is renewed like the
eagle's.

6 The LORD executes righteousness
And justice for all who are oppressed.
7 He made known His ways to Moses,
His acts to the children of Israel.
8 The LORD *is* merciful and gracious,
Slow to anger, and abounding in
mercy.
9 He will not always strive *with us,*
Nor will He keep *His anger* forever.
10 He has not dealt with us according to
our sins,
Nor punished us according to our
iniquities.

11 For as the heavens are high above the
earth,
So great is His mercy toward those
who fear Him;
12 As far as the east is from the west,
So far has He removed our
transgressions from us.
13 As a father pities *his* children,
So the LORD pities those who fear
Him.
14 For He knows our frame;
He remembers that we *are* dust.

15 *As for* man, his days *are* like grass;
As a flower of the field, so he
flourishes.
16 For the wind passes over it, and it is
gone,
And its place remembers it no more.[a]
17 But the mercy of the LORD *is* from
everlasting to everlasting
On those who fear Him,
And His righteousness to children's
children,
18 To such as keep His covenant,
And to those who remember His
commandments to do them.

103:16 [a]Compare Job 7:10

103:13, 14 The image of a father and his children is one way in which God's covenant is expressed. Children of God are those who fear Him, that is, obey Him (see vv. 17, 18). God has both affection and compassion for His children. **we are dust**: See Gen. 2:7; Job 10:9.

19 The LORD has established His throne
in heaven,
And His kingdom rules over all.

20 Bless the LORD, you His angels,
Who excel in strength, who do His
word,
Heeding the voice of His word.
21 Bless the LORD, all *you* His hosts,
You ministers of His, who do His
pleasure.
22 Bless the LORD, all His works,
In all places of His dominion.

Bless the LORD, O my soul!

PSALM 104

Praise to the Sovereign LORD for His Creation and Providence

Bless the LORD, O my soul!

O LORD my God, You are very great:
You are clothed with honor and
majesty,
2 Who cover *Yourself* with light as *with*
a garment,
Who stretch out the heavens like a
curtain.

3 He lays the beams of His upper
chambers in the waters,
Who makes the clouds His chariot,
Who walks on the wings of the wind,
4 Who makes His angels spirits,
His ministers a flame of fire.

5 *You who* laid the foundations of the
earth,
So *that* it should not be moved
forever,
6 You covered it with the deep as *with* a
garment;
The waters stood above the
mountains.
7 At Your rebuke they fled;
At the voice of Your thunder they
hastened away.
8 They went up over the mountains;
They went down into the valleys,
To the place which You founded for
them.
9 You have set a boundary that they
may not pass over,
That they may not return to cover the
earth.

10 He sends the springs into the valleys;
They flow among the hills.
11 They give drink to every beast of the
field;
The wild donkeys quench their thirst.
12 By them the birds of the heavens
have their home;
They sing among the branches.
13 He waters the hills from His upper
chambers;
The earth is satisfied with the fruit of
Your works.

14 He causes the grass to grow for the
cattle,
And vegetation for the service of
man,
That he may bring forth food from
the earth,
15 And wine *that* makes glad the heart
of man,

Psalm 104 The psalm is a hymn about creation. All of the elements of God's creative work are mentioned: creation of the heavens (vv. 1–4), division of waters and land (vv. 5–9), provisions for animals and humans (vv. 10–18), the luminaries (vv. 19–23), and sea creatures (vv. 24–26). The dependence of all creatures on God (vv. 27–32) leads to a closing note of praise (vv. 33–35).

104:3 Chambers in the waters envisions the sky as the source of rain and the place of God's abode (see 29:10). Making the clouds His chariot stresses that it is the Lord who gives rain. This phrase was used of the Canaanite storm-god, Baal, but the psalmist is here claiming that it really applies only to God.

104:15 Wine, olive oil, and bread were the three staples of the Israelite diet.

Oil to make *his* face shine,
And bread *which* strengthens man's heart.
16 The trees of the LORD are full *of sap,*
The cedars of Lebanon which He planted,
17 Where the birds make their nests;
The stork has her home in the fir trees.
18 The high hills *are* for the wild goats;
The cliffs are a refuge for the rock badgers.[a]

19 He appointed the moon for seasons;
The sun knows its going down.
20 You make darkness, and it is night,
In which all the beasts of the forest creep about.
21 The young lions roar after their prey,
And seek their food from God.
22 *When* the sun rises, they gather together
And lie down in their dens.
23 Man goes out to his work
And to his labor until the evening.

24 O LORD, how manifold are Your works!
In wisdom You have made them all.
The earth is full of Your possessions—
25 This great and wide sea,
In which *are* innumerable teeming things,
Living things both small and great.
26 There the ships sail about;
There is that Le·vī'a·than
Which You have made to play there.

104:18 [a]Or *rock hyrax* (compare Leviticus 11:5)

27 These all wait for You,
That You may give *them* their food in due season.
28 *What* You give them they gather in;
You open Your hand, they are filled with good.
29 You hide Your face, they are troubled;
You take away their breath, they die and return to their dust.
30 You send forth Your Spirit, they are created;
And You renew the face of the earth.

31 May the glory of the LORD endure forever;
May the LORD rejoice in His works.
32 He looks on the earth, and it trembles;
He touches the hills, and they smoke.

33 I will sing to the LORD as long as I live;
I will sing praise to my God while I have my being.
34 May my meditation be sweet to Him;
I will be glad in the LORD.
35 May sinners be consumed from the earth,
And the wicked be no more.

Bless the LORD, O my soul!
Praise the LORD!

PSALM 105

The Eternal Faithfulness of the LORD

Oh, give thanks to the LORD!
Call upon His name;

104:24–26 While at creation "God created great sea creatures and every living thing that moves" (Gen. 1:21), the psalmist recognizes that God is also at work in the man-made **ships**.

104:34 We should not allow our thoughts to dwell on things that are not pleasing to God.

104:35 The psalmist finds sin and wickedness to be a jarring discord in such a well-ordered world.

Psalm 105 This psalm is a hymn reviewing Israel's history, beginning with Abraham (vv. 5–15), continuing with Joseph (vv. 16–22), the deliverance from Egypt (vv. 23–36), provision in the wilderness (vv. 37–41), and concluding with the occupation of Canaan (vv. 42–45).

Make known His deeds among the
peoples!
2 Sing to Him, sing psalms to Him;
Talk of all His wondrous works!
3 Glory in His holy name;
Let the hearts of those rejoice who
seek the LORD!
4 Seek the LORD and His strength;
Seek His face evermore!
5 Remember His marvelous works
which He has done,
His wonders, and the judgments of
His mouth,
6 O seed of Abraham His servant,
You children of Jacob, His chosen
ones!

7 He *is* the LORD our God;
His judgments *are* in all the earth.
8 He remembers His covenant forever,
The word *which* He commanded, for a
thousand generations,
9 *The covenant* which He made with
Abraham,
And His oath to Isaac,
10 And confirmed it to Jacob for a
statute,
To Israel *as* an everlasting covenant,
11 Saying, "To you I will give the land of
Cā'naan
As the allotment of your inheritance,"
12 When they were few in number,
Indeed very few, and strangers in it.

13 When they went from one nation to
another,
From *one* kingdom to another people,
14 He permitted no one to do them
wrong;
Yes, He rebuked kings for their sakes,
15 *Saying,* "Do not touch My anointed
ones,
And do My prophets no harm."

16 Moreover He called for a famine in
the land;
He destroyed all the provision of
bread.
17 He sent a man before them—
Joseph—*who* was sold as a slave.
18 They hurt his feet with fetters,
He was laid in irons.
19 Until the time that his word came to
pass,
The word of the LORD tested him.
20 The king sent and released him,
The ruler of the people let him go
free.
21 He made him lord of his house,
And ruler of all his possessions,
22 To bind his princes at his pleasure,
And teach his elders wisdom.

23 Israel also came into Egypt,
And Jacob dwelt in the land of Ham.
24 He increased His people greatly,
And made them stronger than their
enemies.
25 He turned their heart to hate His
people,
To deal craftily with His servants.

26 He sent Moses His servant,
And Aaron whom He had chosen.

105:3 His holy name refers to God's character, the very essence of His being.

105:7 The words "He" and "His" in reference to God are repeated nearly fifty times in this psalm, demonstrating that the psalmist is more concerned with demonstrating God's hand in Israel's history than with simply reciting past events.

105:8 remembers: Not simply recollection, but fulfillment of His promises.

105:9, 10 The **covenant** with **Abraham** was later confirmed to **Isaac** (Gen. 26:3) and to **Jacob** (Gen. 28:13, 14).

105:15 My anointed ones: Usually used of kings and priests, but here of the patriarchs to show God's choice of them. Abraham is the only patriarch to be called a prophet (Gen. 20:7).

105:16–22 Reference here is to the famine of Canaan in Jacob's time, which ultimately led to Joseph's elevation as prime minister of Egypt (see Gen. 37: 39–41).

27 They performed His signs among them,
And wonders in the land of Ham.
28 He sent darkness, and made *it* dark;
And they did not rebel against His word.
29 He turned their waters into blood,
And killed their fish.
30 Their land abounded with frogs,
Even in the chambers of their kings.
31 He spoke, and there came swarms of flies,
And lice in all their territory.
32 He gave them hail for rain,
And flaming fire in their land.
33 He struck their vines also, and their fig trees,
And splintered the trees of their territory.
34 He spoke, and locusts came,
Young locusts without number,
35 And ate up all the vegetation in their land,
And devoured the fruit of their ground.
36 He also destroyed all the firstborn in their land,
The first of all their strength.

37 He also brought them out with silver and gold,
And *there was* none feeble among His tribes.
38 Egypt was glad when they departed,
For the fear of them had fallen upon them.
39 He spread a cloud for a covering,
And fire to give light in the night.

106:3 [a]Septuagint, Syriac, Targum, and Vulgate read *those who do.*

40 *The people* asked, and He brought quail,
And satisfied them with the bread of heaven.
41 He opened the rock, and water gushed out;
It ran in the dry places *like* a river.

42 For He remembered His holy promise,
And Abraham His servant.
43 He brought out His people with joy,
His chosen ones with gladness.
44 He gave them the lands of the Gentiles,
And they inherited the labor of the nations,
45 That they might observe His statutes
And keep His laws.

Praise the LORD!

PSALM 106

Joy in Forgiveness of Israel's Sins

Praise the LORD!

Oh, give thanks to the LORD, for *He is* good!
For His mercy *endures* forever.
2 Who can utter the mighty acts of the LORD?
Who can declare all His praise?
3 Blessed *are* those who keep justice,
And he who does[a] righteousness at all times!

4 Remember me, O LORD, with the favor *You have toward* Your people.
Oh, visit me with Your salvation,

105:37 When the Exodus occurred, God moved the Egyptians to give Israel silver and **gold** (Ex. 12:35, 36).

Psalm 106 This psalm has elements of a lament and a hymn, reciting the rebellion of Israel. After a brief introduction (vv. 1–6), the rebellion in the wilderness is recounted (vv. 7–33). The following discussion concerns Israel's succumbing to the Canaanite gods (vv. 34–39) and the ensuing Exile (vv. 40–46). In all of these God's faithfulness endures.

106:1 The cause for thanks is always the **good** character of God.

FORGETFULNESS IS NOT ALWAYS FUNNY

John Gilmore

It's natural to forget sometimes. In fact, some memory mix-ups may have mild ramifications and can allow us to laugh at ourselves.

On the other hand, the psalmist refers to a form of forgetfulness that is reprehensible and tragic. "They forgot God their Savior, who had done great things in Egypt, wondrous works in the land of Ham, awesome things by the Red Sea" (106:21, 22). Forgetting to give thanks to God is tragic. God said through the psalmist what Shakespeare said through King Lear: "Sharper than a serpent's tooth is a thankless child."

Isaiah also sensed tears in God's eyes over human neglect: "I have nourished and brought up children, and they have rebelled against Me; the ox knows its owner and the donkey its master's crib; but Israel does not know, My people do not consider" (Is. 1:2, 3).

"We must always be sure to thank the One who gives us all things."

We must always be sure to thank the One who gives us all things, remembering that "every good gift and every perfect gift is from above" (James 1:17). ✦

5 That I may see the benefit of Your
chosen ones,
That I may rejoice in the gladness of
Your nation,
That I may glory with Your
inheritance.

6 We have sinned with our fathers,
We have committed iniquity,
We have done wickedly.
7 Our fathers in Egypt did not
understand Your wonders;
They did not remember the multitude
of Your mercies,
But rebelled by the sea—the Red Sea.

8 Nevertheless He saved them for His
name's sake,
That He might make His mighty
power known.
9 He rebuked the Red Sea also, and it
dried up;
So He led them through the depths,
As through the wilderness.
10 He saved them from the hand of him
who hated *them,*
And redeemed them from the hand of
the enemy.
11 The waters covered their enemies;
There was not one of them left.
12 Then they believed His words;
They sang His praise.

13 They soon forgot His works;
They did not wait for His counsel,
14 But lusted exceedingly in the
wilderness,
And tested God in the desert.
15 And He gave them their request,
But sent leanness into their soul.

16 When they envied Moses in the camp,
And Aaron the saint of the LORD,
17 The earth opened up and swallowed
Dā'than,
And covered the faction of A·bī'ram.
18 A fire was kindled in their company;
The flame burned up the wicked.

19 They made a calf in Hō'reb,
And worshiped the molded image.
20 Thus they changed their glory
Into the image of an ox that eats
grass.
21 They forgot God their Savior,
Who had done great things in Egypt,
22 Wondrous works in the land of Ham,
Awesome things by the Red Sea.
23 Therefore He said that He would
destroy them,
Had not Moses His chosen one stood
before Him in the breach,
To turn away His wrath, lest He
destroy *them.*

24 Then they despised the pleasant land;
They did not believe His word,
25 But complained in their tents,
And did not heed the voice of the
LORD.
26 Therefore He raised His hand *in an
oath* against them,
To overthrow them in the wilderness,
27 To overthrow their descendants
among the nations,
And to scatter them in the lands.

28 They joined themselves also to Bā'al
of Pē'or,
And ate sacrifices made to the dead.
29 Thus they provoked *Him* to anger
with their deeds,
And the plague broke out among
them.
30 Then Phin'e·has stood up and
intervened,
And the plague was stopped.
31 And that was accounted to him for
righteousness
To all generations forevermore.

32 They angered *Him* also at the waters
of strife,[a]
So that it went ill with Moses on
account of them;
33 Because they rebelled against His
Spirit,
So that he spoke rashly with his lips.

34 They did not destroy the peoples,
Concerning whom the LORD had
commanded them,
35 But they mingled with the Gentiles
And learned their works;
36 They served their idols,
Which became a snare to them.
37 They even sacrificed their sons
And their daughters to demons,
38 And shed innocent blood,
The blood of their sons and
daughters,
Whom they sacrificed to the idols of
Cā'naan;
And the land was polluted with
blood.
39 Thus they were defiled by their own
works,
And played the harlot by their own
deeds.

106:32 [a]Or *Meribah*

106:16 saint: Aaron was consecrated to the Lord and therefore not to be lightly pushed aside.

106:23 Moses demonstrated for us the power of the intercessory prayer of a righteous individual.

106:27 This same kind of unbelief would ultimately lead to exile from the land.

106:28–31 Baal of Peor: The reference is to Israel's harlotry with Moab with stress upon involvement in Moabite worship (Num. 25). The zeal that **Phinehas** showed for God was **accounted . . . for righteousness** and resulted in God's covenant with his descendants for "an everlasting priesthood" (see Num. 25:10–13; Mal. 2:5).

40 Therefore the wrath of the LORD was
kindled against His people,
So that He abhorred His own
inheritance.
41 And He gave them into the hand of
the Gentiles,
And those who hated them ruled
over them.
42 Their enemies also oppressed them,
And they were brought into
subjection under their hand.
43 Many times He delivered them;
But they rebelled in their counsel,
And were brought low for their
iniquity.

44 Nevertheless He regarded their
affliction,
When He heard their cry;
45 And for their sake He remembered
His covenant,
And relented according to the
multitude of His mercies.
46 He also made them to be pitied
By all those who carried them away
captive.

47 Save us, O LORD our God,
And gather us from among the
Gentiles,
To give thanks to Your holy name,
To triumph in Your praise.

48 Blessed *be* the LORD God of Israel
From everlasting to everlasting!
And let all the people say, "Amen!"

Praise the LORD!

Book Five: Psalms 107—150

PSALM 107

Thanksgiving to the LORD for His Great Works of Deliverance

Oh, give thanks to the LORD, for *He is*
good!
For His mercy *endures* forever.
2 Let the redeemed of the LORD say *so,*
Whom He has redeemed from the
hand of the enemy,
3 And gathered out of the lands,
From the east and from the west,
From the north and from the south.

4 They wandered in the wilderness in a
desolate way;
They found no city to dwell in.
5 Hungry and thirsty,
Their soul fainted in them.
6 Then they cried out to the LORD in
their trouble,
And He delivered them out of their
distresses.
7 And He led them forth by the right
way,
That they might go to a city for a
dwelling place.
8 Oh, that *men* would give thanks to
the LORD *for* His goodness,
And *for* His wonderful works to the
children of men!
9 For He satisfies the longing soul,
And fills the hungry soul with
goodness.

10 Those who sat in darkness and in the
shadow of death,

106:46 The prime example of the Israelite exiles being **pitied** by their captors is the decree of Cyrus allowing their release and return (see Ezra 1:1–4).

106:47 No claims upon God can be advanced. Only pure mercy and concern for His **holy name** could motivate Him to restore such a persistently rebellious people. The phrase "gather us" indicates this psalm was written during the period of Israel's exile.

106:48 The doxology marking the close of the fourth book of the Psalms (see note on 89:52).

107:8 A refrain which recurs at the close of each stanza (vv. 15, 21, 31). Verses 8, 9 are worthy of memorizing as a reminder for us to offer proper thanks to God for the wonderful blessings He bestows on His people.

107:10–16 It is evident that the distress of imprisonment and bondage described here re-

Bound in affliction and irons—
11 Because they rebelled against the
words of God,
And despised the counsel of the Most
High,
12 Therefore He brought down their
heart with labor;
They fell down, and *there was* none to
help.
13 Then they cried out to the LORD in
their trouble,
And He saved them out of their
distresses.
14 He brought them out of darkness and
the shadow of death,
And broke their chains in pieces.
15 Oh, that *men* would give thanks to
the LORD *for* His goodness,
And *for* His wonderful works to the
children of men!
16 For He has broken the gates of
bronze,
And cut the bars of iron in two.

17 Fools, because of their transgression,
And because of their iniquities, were
afflicted.
18 Their soul abhorred all manner of
food,
And they drew near to the gates of
death.
19 Then they cried out to the LORD in
their trouble,
And He saved them out of their
distresses.
20 He sent His word and healed them,
And delivered *them* from their
destructions.
21 Oh, that *men* would give thanks to
the LORD *for* His goodness,
And *for* His wonderful works to the
children of men!
22 Let them sacrifice the sacrifices of
thanksgiving,
And declare His works with rejoicing.

23 Those who go down to the sea in ships,
Who do business on great waters,
24 They see the works of the LORD,
And His wonders in the deep.
25 For He commands and raises the
stormy wind,
Which lifts up the waves of the sea.
26 They mount up to the heavens,
They go down again to the depths;
Their soul melts because of trouble.
27 They reel to and fro, and stagger like
a drunken man,
And are at their wits' end.
28 Then they cry out to the LORD in their
trouble,
And He brings them out of their
distresses.
29 He calms the storm,
So that its waves are still.
30 Then they are glad because they are
quiet;
So He guides them to their desired
haven.
31 Oh, that *men* would give thanks to
the LORD *for* His goodness,
And *for* His wonderful works to the
children of men!
32 Let them exalt Him also in the
assembly of the people,
And praise Him in the company of
the elders.

33 He turns rivers into a wilderness,
And the watersprings into dry
ground;

sulted from Israel's own sin against God's will (vv. 11, 12). Yet God answered their cry for help (vv. 13, 14). Those who are delivered are called to praise God.

107:17, 18 Sickness is featured here, emphasizing the connection between illness and sin, perhaps dissipation.

107:22 Israelites often gave sacrifices specifically as thank offerings to express gratitude to the Lord. This verse may also refer to offering verbal sacrifices of worship and praise.

107:33–43 A description of the Lord's ability to turn abundance into barrenness (vv. 33, 34) and poverty into exaltation (vv. 35–42). He does the first because of human **wickedness**; the second because of His **lovingkindness** (v. 43).

34 A fruitful land into barrenness,
For the wickedness of those who
dwell in it.
35 He turns a wilderness into pools of
water,
And dry land into watersprings.
36 There He makes the hungry dwell,
That they may establish a city for a
dwelling place,
37 And sow fields and plant vineyards,
That they may yield a fruitful harvest.
38 He also blesses them, and they
multiply greatly;
And He does not let their cattle
decrease.

39 When they are diminished and
brought low
Through oppression, affliction and
sorrow,
40 He pours contempt on princes,
And causes them to wander in the
wilderness *where there is* no way;
41 Yet He sets the poor on high, far from
affliction,
And makes *their* families like a flock.
42 The righteous see *it* and rejoice,
And all iniquity stops its mouth.

43 Whoever *is* wise will observe these
things,
And they will understand the
lovingkindness of the LORD.

PSALM 108

Assurance of God's Victory over Enemies

A Song. A Psalm of David.

O God, my heart is steadfast;
I will sing and give praise, even with
my glory.
2 Awake, lute and harp!
I will awaken the dawn.
3 I will praise You, O LORD, among the
peoples,
And I will sing praises to You among
the nations.
4 For Your mercy *is* great above the
heavens,
And Your truth *reaches* to the clouds.

5 Be exalted, O God, above the
heavens,
And Your glory above all the earth;
6 That Your beloved may be delivered,
Save *with* Your right hand, and hear
me.

7 God has spoken in His holiness:
"I will rejoice;
I will divide Shē'chem
And measure out the Valley of
Suc'coth.
8 Gil'ē·ad *is* Mine; Ma·nas'seh *is* Mine;
Ē'phra·im also *is* the helmet for My
head;
Judah *is* My lawgiver.
9 Mō'ab *is* My washpot;
Over Ē'dom I will cast My shoe;
Over Phi·lis'ti·a I will triumph."

10 Who will bring me *into* the strong
city?
Who will lead me to Ē'dom?
11 *Is it* not *You*, O God, *who* cast us off?
And *You*, O God, *who* did not go out
with our armies?
12 Give us help from trouble,
For the help of man is useless.
13 Through God we will do valiantly,
For *it is* He *who* shall tread down our
enemies.[a]

108:13 [a]Compare verses 6–13 with 60:5–12

107:43 Whoever is wise: The scenes of this psalm are descriptive of the plight of all sinners. Perhaps the emphasis of v. 43 is that the reader should recognize his own need and his own salvation as being described in the four scenes of the chapter.

Psalm 108 The first part of this psalm (vv. 1–5) is nearly identical with 57:7–11, and the second part (vv. 6–13) with 60:6–12. See notes on those passages.

PSALM 109

Plea for Judgment of False Accusers

To the Chief Musician. A Psalm of David.

Do not keep silent,
O God of my praise!
2 For the mouth of the wicked and the mouth of the deceitful
Have opened against me;
They have spoken against me with a lying tongue.
3 They have also surrounded me with words of hatred,
And fought against me without a cause.
4 In return for my love they are my accusers,
But I *give myself to* prayer.
5 Thus they have rewarded me evil for good,
And hatred for my love.

6 Set a wicked man over him,
And let an accuser[a] stand at his right hand.
7 When he is judged, let him be found guilty,
And let his prayer become sin.
8 Let his days be few,
And let another take his office.
9 Let his children be fatherless,
And his wife a widow.
10 Let his children continually be vagabonds, and beg;
Let them seek *their bread*[a] also from their desolate places.
11 Let the creditor seize all that he has,
And let strangers plunder his labor.
12 Let there be none to extend mercy to him,
Nor let there be any to favor his fatherless children.
13 Let his posterity be cut off,
And in the generation following let their name be blotted out.

14 Let the iniquity of his fathers be remembered before the LORD,
And let not the sin of his mother be blotted out.
15 Let them be continually before the LORD,
That He may cut off the memory of them from the earth;
16 Because he did not remember to show mercy,
But persecuted the poor and needy man,
That he might even slay the broken in heart.
17 As he loved cursing, so let it come to him;
As he did not delight in blessing, so let it be far from him.
18 As he clothed himself with cursing as with his garment,
So let it enter his body like water,
And like oil into his bones.

109:6 [a]Hebrew *satan* 109:10 [a]Following Masoretic Text and Targum; Septuagint and Vulgate read *be cast out.*

Psalm 109 This is the best known of the "imprecatory" or "cursing" psalms. In considering the harsh, often vindictive nature of these psalms, we would remember that they are fundamental pleas for God to administer justice—which the Hebrews believed would happen in this life. Furthermore, strong emotions in poetry are expressed by strong language; while to us that language seems harsh, its theme of God's righteous judgment is entirely proper. Perhaps these psalms are included in Scripture to express God's approval of a passionate hatred of evil and evil deeds.

109:6, 7 Satan gets his name from the Hebrew word translated **accuser**. Here the request is for a dishonest judge to try the enemy and find him guilty as has happened too often to the righteous.

109:8 The apostles applied this to Judas Iscariot following His death (Acts 1:20).

109:13 In Middle Eastern culture this is the greatest shame that could ever befall a family.

19 Let it be to him like the garment
which covers him,
And for a belt with which he girds
himself continually.
20 *Let* this *be* the LORD's reward to my
accusers,
And to those who speak evil against
my person.

21 But You, O GOD the Lord,
Deal with me for Your name's sake;
Because Your mercy *is* good, deliver
me.
22 For I *am* poor and needy,
And my heart is wounded within me.
23 I am gone like a shadow when it
lengthens;
I am shaken off like a locust.
24 My knees are weak through fasting,
And my flesh is feeble from lack of
fatness.
25 I also have become a reproach to
them;
When they look at me, they shake
their heads.

26 Help me, O LORD my God!
Oh, save me according to Your mercy,
27 That they may know that this *is* Your
hand—
That You, LORD, have done it!
28 Let them curse, but You bless;
When they arise, let them be
ashamed,
But let Your servant rejoice.
29 Let my accusers be clothed with
shame,
And let them cover themselves with
their own disgrace as with a
mantle.

30 I will greatly praise the LORD with my
mouth;
Yes, I will praise Him among the
multitude.
31 For He shall stand at the right hand
of the poor,
To save *him* from those who condemn
him.

PSALM 110

Announcement of the Messiah's Reign

A Psalm of David.

The LORD said to my Lord,
"Sit at My right hand,
Till I make Your enemies Your
footstool."
2 The LORD shall send the rod of Your
strength out of Zion.
Rule in the midst of Your enemies!

3 Your people *shall be* volunteers
In the day of Your power;
In the beauties of holiness, from the
womb of the morning,
You have the dew of Your youth.
4 The LORD has sworn
And will not relent,
"You *are* a priest forever
According to the order of
Mel·chiz'e·dek."

109:20 the LORD's reward: Jesus brought a fuller understanding of God's plan for forgiveness. For us to receive forgiveness from God, we must be willing to forgive others their transgressions against us (Matt. 6:14, 15).

Psalm 110 This psalm is classified as a royal psalm, but is widely understood as messianic. It is the psalm most frequently quoted or alluded to in the NT.

110:2 rod: royal scepter, a symbol of power.

110:4 Verse 4 begins a section of the psalm which seems clearly messianic. It identifies the King as a perpetual priest **according to the order of Melchizedek**. In Gen. 14:18 Melchizedek is identified as "king of Salem" and "priest of God Most High." No king of Israel was ever permitted to usurp the role of priest (1 Sam. 13:9–13; 2 Chr. 26:16–20).

5 The Lord *is* at Your right hand;
He shall execute kings in the day of
His wrath.
6 He shall judge among the nations,
He shall fill *the places* with dead
bodies,
He shall execute the heads of many
countries.
7 He shall drink of the brook by the
wayside;
Therefore He shall lift up the head.

PSALM 111

Praise to God for His Faithfulness and Justice

Praise the LORD!

I will praise the LORD with *my* whole
heart,
In the assembly of the upright and *in*
the congregation.

2 The works of the LORD *are* great,
Studied by all who have pleasure in
them.
3 His work *is* honorable and glorious,
And His righteousness endures
forever.
4 He has made His wonderful works to
be remembered;
The LORD *is* gracious and full of
compassion.
5 He has given food to those who fear
Him;
He will ever be mindful of His
covenant.

6 He has declared to His people the
power of His works,
In giving them the heritage of the
nations.

7 The works of His hands *are* verity and
justice;
All His precepts *are* sure.
8 They stand fast forever and ever,
And are done in truth and
uprightness.
9 He has sent redemption to His
people;
He has commanded His covenant
forever:
Holy and awesome *is* His name.

10 The fear of the LORD *is* the beginning
of wisdom;
A good understanding have all those
who do *His commandments*.
His praise endures forever.

PSALM 112

The Blessed State of the Righteous

Praise the LORD!

Blessed *is* the man *who* fears the LORD,
Who delights greatly in His
commandments.

2 His descendants will be mighty on
earth;
The generation of the upright will be
blessed.
3 Wealth and riches *will be* in his house,
And his righteousness endures
forever.

Psalm 111 A hymn in praise of God, this psalm is an acrostic having 22 lines, each succeeding line beginning with the next letter of the Hebrew alphabet.

111:10 fear of the LORD: True religion, that is, a life which expresses its accountability to God. This awareness of accountability to God is seen as the foundation of wisdom.

112:1 Blessed: A formula of congratulations which in the OT usually places primary emphasis upon material blessing (see 1:1).

112:2 Obedience to God's commandments not only brings blessings to the righteous but also builds a foundation for the spiritual lives of their children and grandchildren.

112:3 In the light of other Scripture, this verse clearly refers to the rewards laid up in heaven.

4 Unto the upright there arises light in
the darkness;
He is gracious, and full of
compassion, and righteous.
5 A good man deals graciously and
lends;
He will guide his affairs with
discretion.
6 Surely he will never be shaken;
The righteous will be in everlasting
remembrance.
7 He will not be afraid of evil tidings;
His heart is steadfast, trusting in the
LORD.
8 His heart *is* established;
He will not be afraid,
Until he sees *his desire* upon his
enemies.

9 He has dispersed abroad,
He has given to the poor;
His righteousness endures forever;
His horn will be exalted with honor.
10 The wicked will see *it* and be grieved;
He will gnash his teeth and melt
away;
The desire of the wicked shall perish.

PSALM 113

The Majesty and Condescension of God

Praise the LORD!

Praise, O servants of the LORD,
Praise the name of the LORD!
2 Blessed be the name of the LORD
From this time forth and forevermore!
3 From the rising of the sun to its going
down
The LORD's name *is* to be praised.
4 The LORD *is* high above all nations,
His glory above the heavens.
5 Who *is* like the LORD our God,
Who dwells on high,
6 Who humbles Himself to behold
The things that are in the heavens and
in the earth?

7 He raises the poor out of the dust,
And lifts the needy out of the ash
heap,
8 That He may seat *him* with princes—
With the princes of His people.
9 He grants the barren woman a home,
Like a joyful mother of children.

Praise the LORD!

PSALM 114

The Power of God in His Deliverance of Israel

When Israel went out of Egypt,
The house of Jacob from a people of
strange language,
2 Judah became His sanctuary,
And Israel His dominion.

3 The sea saw *it* and fled;
Jordan turned back.
4 The mountains skipped like rams,
The little hills like lambs.
5 What ails you, O sea, that you fled?
O Jordan, *that* you turned back?
6 O mountains, *that* you skipped like
rams?
O little hills, like lambs?

7 Tremble, O earth, at the presence of
the Lord,
At the presence of the God of Jacob,

Psalm 113 This is the first of six psalms (Ps. 113—118) known as the Egyptian Hallel (Egyptian Praise; see 114:1). Ps. 113 and 114 were customarily sung before the Passover meal, while 115—118 were sung after it (see Matt. 26:30). The call to offer praise (vv. 1–3) precedes a recital of the characteristics of God that are worthy of such praise (vv. 4–9).

113:9 The barren woman in Israel felt despised and rejected, but God offers her security. The person the world rejects, God receives.

Psalm 114 The second psalm of the Egyptian Hallel (Ps. 113—118), a hymn of praise to God who delivered Israel from Egypt in the Exodus.

8 Who turned the rock *into* a pool of
water,
The flint into a fountain of waters.

PSALM 115

The Futility of Idols and the Trustworthiness of God

Not unto us, O LORD, not unto us,
But to Your name give glory,
Because of Your mercy,
Because of Your truth.
2 Why should the Gentiles say,
"So where *is* their God?"

3 But our God *is* in heaven;
He does whatever He pleases.
4 Their idols *are* silver and gold,
The work of men's hands.
5 They have mouths, but they do not
speak;
Eyes they have, but they do not see;
6 They have ears, but they do not hear;
Noses they have, but they do not
smell;
7 They have hands, but they do not
handle;
Feet they have, but they do not walk;
Nor do they mutter through their
throat.
8 Those who make them are like them;
So is everyone who trusts in them.

9 O Israel, trust in the LORD;
He *is* their help and their shield.
10 O house of Aaron, trust in the LORD;
He *is* their help and their shield.
11 You who fear the LORD, trust in the
LORD;
He *is* their help and their shield.

12 The LORD has been mindful of *us;*
He will bless us;
He will bless the house of Israel;
He will bless the house of Aaron.
13 He will bless those who fear the
LORD,
Both small and great.

14 May the LORD give you increase more
and more,
You and your children.
15 *May* you *be* blessed by the LORD,
Who made heaven and earth.

16 The heaven, *even* the heavens, *are* the
LORD's;
But the earth He has given to the
children of men.
17 The dead do not praise the LORD,
Nor any who go down into silence.
18 But we will bless the LORD
From this time forth and forevermore.

Praise the LORD!

PSALM 116

Thanksgiving for Deliverance from Death

I love the LORD, because He has heard
My voice *and* my supplications.

115:2–8 This passage reflects the inadequacy of pagan gods—or today's objects of worship—to meet the needs of those who serve them.

115:3 The Christian can be assured that, in doing "whatever He pleases," God is always merciful and just.

115:3–7 Like other OT references to idolatry (Is. 46:1–7; Jer. 10:3–5), the lifelessness of the idol is the chief point. **In heaven** (v. 3) suggests a contrast between **God** and the earth-bound idols.

115:8 To trust in an idol is to become like it—powerless and false.

115:16 God is the Lord of the **heavens**, while **men** are the stewards of the **earth**.

Psalm 116 A psalm of individual thanksgiving which is part of the Egyptian Hallel (Ps. 113—118). The psalmist recounts his deliverance by the Lord (vv. 1–11) and vows to praise Him publicly before all of His people (vv. 12–19).

2 Because He has inclined His ear to
me,
Therefore I will call *upon Him* as long
as I live.

3 The pains of death surrounded me,
And the pangs of Shē'ōl laid hold of
me;
I found trouble and sorrow.
4 Then I called upon the name of the
LORD:
"O LORD, I implore You, deliver my
soul!"

5 Gracious *is* the LORD, and righteous;
Yes, our God *is* merciful.
6 The LORD preserves the simple;
I was brought low, and He saved
me.
7 Return to your rest, O my soul,
For the LORD has dealt bountifully
with you.

8 For You have delivered my soul from
death,
My eyes from tears,
And my feet from falling.
9 I will walk before the LORD
In the land of the living.
10 I believed, therefore I spoke,
"I am greatly afflicted."
11 I said in my haste,
"All men *are* liars."

12 What shall I render to the LORD
For all His benefits toward me?
13 I will take up the cup of salvation,
And call upon the name of the LORD.
14 I will pay my vows to the LORD
Now in the presence of all His
people.

15 Precious in the sight of the LORD
Is the death of His saints.

16 O LORD, truly I *am* Your servant;
I *am* Your servant, the son of Your
maidservant;
You have loosed my bonds.
17 I will offer to You the sacrifice of
thanksgiving,
And will call upon the name of the
LORD.

18 I will pay my vows to the LORD
Now in the presence of all His
people,
19 In the courts of the LORD's house,
In the midst of you, O Jerusalem.

Praise the LORD!

PSALM 117

Let All Peoples Praise the LORD

Praise the LORD, all you Gentiles!
Laud Him, all you peoples!
2 For His merciful kindness is great
toward us,
And the truth of the LORD *endures*
forever.

Praise the LORD!

116:9 walk before the LORD: Live in obedience (see Gen. 17:1).

116:12–14 cup of salvation: Probably the drink offering, thus an expression of gratitude. The offering most appreciated by God is sincere praise. **pay my vows**: Perhaps promises made during his illness. The peace offering was associated with discharged vows (Lev. 7:16).

116:15 Precious: In the sense of costly, indicating that the life of the saint is valuable.

117:1 This verse is cited by Paul (Rom. 15:11) to show that the **Gentiles** are a part of the divine plan.

117:2 God's mercy and **truth** are constant themes of the Bible and characteristics worthy of continual praise.

PSALM 118

Praise to God for His Everlasting Mercy

Oh, give thanks to the LORD, for *He is* good!
For His mercy *endures* forever.

2 Let Israel now say,
"His mercy *endures* forever."
3 Let the house of Aaron now say,
"His mercy *endures* forever."
4 Let those who fear the LORD now say,
"His mercy *endures* forever."

5 I called on the LORD in distress;
The LORD answered me *and set me* in a broad place.
6 The LORD *is* on my side;
I will not fear.
What can man do to me?
7 The LORD is for me among those who help me;
Therefore I shall see *my desire* on those who hate me.
8 *It is* better to trust in the LORD
Than to put confidence in man.
9 *It is* better to trust in the LORD
Than to put confidence in princes.

10 All nations surrounded me,
But in the name of the LORD I will destroy them.
11 They surrounded me,
Yes, they surrounded me;
But in the name of the LORD I will destroy them.
12 They surrounded me like bees;
They were quenched like a fire of thorns;
For in the name of the LORD I will destroy them.
13 You pushed me violently, that I might fall,
But the LORD helped me.
14 The LORD *is* my strength and song,
And He has become my salvation.[a]

15 The voice of rejoicing and salvation
Is in the tents of the righteous;
The right hand of the LORD does valiantly.
16 The right hand of the LORD is exalted;
The right hand of the LORD does valiantly.
17 I shall not die, but live,
And declare the works of the LORD.
18 The LORD has chastened me severely,
But He has not given me over to death.

19 Open to me the gates of righteousness;
I will go through them,
And I will praise the LORD.
20 This is the gate of the LORD,
Through which the righteous shall enter.

21 I will praise You,
For You have answered me,
And have become my salvation.

22 The stone *which* the builders rejected
Has become the chief cornerstone.
23 This was the LORD's doing;
It *is* marvelous in our eyes.
24 This *is* the day the LORD has made;
We will rejoice and be glad in it.

118:14 [a]Compare Exodus 15:2

Psalm 118 The last of the Egyptian Hallel psalms (Ps. 113—118).

118:10–13 I will destroy them: The representative of the nation, perhaps the king, speaks for all Israel. He refers to the surrounding nations, expressing their hostility towards the city of God. But acting **in the name of the LORD** (in God's behalf), he has triumphed and will continue to do so.

118:22, 23 Five times these verses are quoted in the NT regarding the rejection of Jesus by the Jewish leadership. What a demonstration of God's power to use the evil of men to accomplish His plan.

25 Save now, I pray, O LORD;
O LORD, I pray, send now prosperity.
26 Blessed *is* he who comes in the name
of the LORD!
We have blessed you from the house
of the LORD.
27 God *is* the LORD,
And He has given us light;
Bind the sacrifice with cords to the
horns of the altar.
28 You *are* my God, and I will praise
You;
You are my God, I will exalt You.

29 Oh, give thanks to the LORD, for *He is*
good!
For His mercy *endures* forever.

PSALM 119

Meditations on the Excellencies of the Word of God

א ALEPH

Blessed *are* the undefiled in the way,
Who walk in the law of the LORD!
2 Blessed *are* those who keep His
testimonies,
Who seek Him with the whole heart!
3 They also do no iniquity;
They walk in His ways.
4 You have commanded *us*
To keep Your precepts diligently.
5 Oh, that my ways were directed
To keep Your statutes!
6 Then I would not be ashamed,
When I look into all Your
commandments.
7 I will praise You with uprightness of
heart,
When I learn Your righteous
judgments.
8 I will keep Your statutes;
Oh, do not forsake me utterly!

ב BETH

9 How can a young man cleanse his
way?
By taking heed according to Your
word.
10 With my whole heart I have sought
You;
Oh, let me not wander from Your
commandments!
11 Your word I have hidden in my heart,
That I might not sin against You.
12 Blessed *are* You, O LORD!
Teach me Your statutes.
13 With my lips I have declared
All the judgments of Your mouth.
14 I have rejoiced in the way of Your
testimonies,
As *much as* in all riches.

118:25, 26 These verses were shouted at Jesus' triumphal entry, as the people praised Him for fulfilling the prophecy of the Messiah.

Psalm 119 This, the longest psalm, is an acrostic with 22 stanzas, each of which has eight pairs of lines. Each verse within a given stanza begins with the same letter of the Hebrew alphabet. Almost every one of the 176 verses refers in some way to the Word of God.

119:1 Law of the LORD can refer both to the Pentateuch and to the Scripture as a whole. The key to happiness is obedience to God's will.

119:2 testimonies: The first of eight synonyms for the law used in this psalm. It emphasizes both the outspokenness and the dependability of God's law. The use of eight verses per stanza and eight synonyms for law may be to stress completeness (7 + 1). The righteous desire to please God completely, "with the whole heart."

119:9 Word is another of the eight synonyms for law. It indicates either a specific message from the Lord or all of Scripture. Only through obedience to God's will expressed in His word can our **way** be pure.

119:11 Scripture memorization keeps our minds occupied with the pure Word of God, allowing little room to harbor sinful thoughts.

119:13 judgments: Another synonym for law, expressing God's righteous governing. As we discover the treasures of God's Word, we naturally want to share them with others.

15 I will meditate on Your precepts,
And contemplate Your ways.
16 I will delight myself in Your statutes;
I will not forget Your word.

ג GIMEL

17 Deal bountifully with Your servant,
That I may live and keep Your word.
18 Open my eyes, that I may see
Wondrous things from Your law.
19 I *am* a stranger in the earth;
Do not hide Your commandments
from me.
20 My soul breaks with longing
For Your judgments at all times.
21 You rebuke the proud—the cursed,
Who stray from Your
commandments.
22 Remove from me reproach and
contempt,
For I have kept Your testimonies.
23 Princes also sit *and* speak against me,
But Your servant meditates on Your
statutes.
24 Your testimonies also *are* my delight
And my counselors.

ד DALEPH

25 My soul clings to the dust;
Revive me according to Your word.
26 I have declared my ways, and You
answered me;
Teach me Your statutes.
27 Make me understand the way of Your
precepts;
So shall I meditate on Your wonderful
works.
28 My soul melts from heaviness;
Strengthen me according to Your
word.
29 Remove from me the way of lying,
And grant me Your law graciously.
30 I have chosen the way of truth;
Your judgments I have laid *before me.*
31 I cling to Your testimonies;
O LORD, do not put me to shame!
32 I will run the course of Your
commandments,
For You shall enlarge my heart.

ה HE

33 Teach me, O LORD, the way of Your
statutes,
And I shall keep it *to* the end.
34 Give me understanding, and I shall
keep Your law;
Indeed, I shall observe it with *my*
whole heart.
35 Make me walk in the path of Your
commandments,
For I delight in it.
36 Incline my heart to Your testimonies,
And not to covetousness.
37 Turn away my eyes from looking at
worthless things,
And revive me in Your way.[a]
38 Establish Your word to Your servant,
Who *is devoted* to fearing You.
39 Turn away my reproach which I
dread,
For Your judgments *are* good.
40 Behold, I long for Your precepts;
Revive me in Your righteousness.

ו WAW

41 Let Your mercies come also to me,
O LORD—

119:37 [a]Following Masoretic Text, Septuagint, and Vulgate; Targum reads *Your words.*

119:18 As we read God's Word, we should pray that He will use it to soften our hearts and reveal His will for our lives.

119:24 The Hebrew word translated **delight** is seldom used in the OT, and is different from that used in v. 16. It emphasizes that God's law is not something bad, but something good.

119:27 Knowledge of God's Word is ineffective until we understand its practical application for our lives.

119:30 To live a holy life, we must consciously choose to do so; it will not come about by mere chance. We make the decision to follow God's holy principles or rebel against them.

Your salvation according to Your word.
42 So shall I have an answer for him
who reproaches me,
For I trust in Your word.
43 And take not the word of truth
utterly out of my mouth,
For I have hoped in Your ordinances.
44 So shall I keep Your law continually,
Forever and ever.
45 And I will walk at liberty,
For I seek Your precepts.
46 I will speak of Your testimonies also
before kings,
And will not be ashamed.
47 And I will delight myself in Your
commandments,
Which I love.
48 My hands also I will lift up to Your
commandments,
Which I love,
And I will meditate on Your statutes.

ז ZAYIN

49 Remember the word to Your servant,
Upon which You have caused me to
hope.
50 This *is* my comfort in my affliction,
For Your word has given me life.
51 The proud have me in great derision,
Yet I do not turn aside from Your law.
52 I remembered Your judgments of old,
O LORD,
And have comforted myself.
53 Indignation has taken hold of me
Because of the wicked, who forsake
Your law.
54 Your statutes have been my songs
In the house of my pilgrimage.
55 I remember Your name in the night,
O LORD,
And I keep Your law.
56 This has become mine,
Because I kept Your precepts.

ח HETH

57 *You are* my portion, O LORD;
I have said that I would keep Your
words.
58 I entreated Your favor with *my* whole
heart;
Be merciful to me according to Your
word.
59 I thought about my ways,
And turned my feet to Your
testimonies.
60 I made haste, and did not delay
To keep Your commandments.
61 The cords of the wicked have bound
me,
But I have not forgotten Your law.
62 At midnight I will rise to give thanks
to You,
Because of Your righteous judgments.
63 I *am* a companion of all who fear You,
And of those who keep Your
precepts.
64 The earth, O LORD, is full of Your
mercy;
Teach me Your statutes.

ט TETH

65 You have dealt well with Your
servant,
O LORD, according to Your word.
66 Teach me good judgment and
knowledge,
For I believe Your commandments.
67 Before I was afflicted I went astray,
But now I keep Your word.
68 You *are* good, and do good;

119:47 The **delight** of God's people is not in material things but in obedience to His **commandments**. Love is more than an emotion; it includes obedience.

119:50 During agonizing trials the attempts people make to comfort us often succeed only in adding to our pain, but God's Word is a faithful source of consolation.

119:57 The Lord is seen as the portion of His people (73:26), while Israel is seen as "the LORD's portion" (Deut. 32:9).

119:65–72 Affliction is seen here as having a positive influence in teaching the reliability of what God says.

I pray that You, God, will teach my child good judgment and knowledge, for he believes Your commandments.

adapted from Psalm 119:66

Teach me Your statutes.
69 The proud have forged a lie against me,
But I will keep Your precepts with *my* whole heart.
70 Their heart is as fat as grease,
But I delight in Your law.
71 *It is* good for me that I have been afflicted,
That I may learn Your statutes.
72 The law of Your mouth *is* better to me
Than thousands of *coins of* gold and silver.

 י YOD

73 Your hands have made me and fashioned me;
Give me understanding, that I may learn Your commandments.
74 Those who fear You will be glad when they see me,
Because I have hoped in Your word.
75 I know, O LORD, that Your judgments *are* right,
And *that* in faithfulness You have afflicted me.
76 Let, I pray, Your merciful kindness be for my comfort,
According to Your word to Your servant.
77 Let Your tender mercies come to me, that I may live;
For Your law *is* my delight.
78 Let the proud be ashamed,
For they treated me wrongfully with falsehood;
But I will meditate on Your precepts.
79 Let those who fear You turn to me,
Those who know Your testimonies.
80 Let my heart be blameless regarding Your statutes,
That I may not be ashamed.

כ KAPH

81 My soul faints for Your salvation,
But I hope in Your word.
82 My eyes fail *from searching* Your word,
Saying, "When will You comfort me?"
83 For I have become like a wineskin in smoke,
Yet I do not forget Your statutes.
84 How many *are* the days of Your servant?
When will You execute judgment on those who persecute me?
85 The proud have dug pits for me,
Which *is* not according to Your law.
86 All Your commandments *are* faithful;
They persecute me wrongfully;
Help me!
87 They almost made an end of me on earth,
But I did not forsake Your precepts.
88 Revive me according to Your lovingkindness,
So that I may keep the testimony of Your mouth.

ל LAMED

89 Forever, O LORD,
Your word is settled in heaven.

119:73–80 Your judgments are right (v. 75): In keeping with the covenant, God must both chastise and bless.

119:83 A wineskin would shrivel up and become black from the smoke of the house.

119:87 When crises and trials cause you to become discouraged about serving God, do not falter. He will take care of you if you continue to keep His precepts.

119:89–96 Destruction is near, but the eternal God is nearer.

119:89, 90 God's **word** is one of the great certainties of life. His care for the world is evidence of His **faithfulness**.

90 Your faithfulness *endures* to all
generations;
You established the earth, and it
abides.
91 They continue this day according to
Your ordinances,
For all *are* Your servants.
92 Unless Your law *had been* my delight,
I would then have perished in my
affliction.
93 I will never forget Your precepts,
For by them You have given me life.
94 I *am* Yours, save me;
For I have sought Your precepts.
95 The wicked wait for me to destroy
me,
But I will consider Your testimonies.
96 I have seen the consummation of all
perfection,
But Your commandment *is*
exceedingly broad.

מ MEM

97 Oh, how I love Your law!
It *is* my meditation all the day.
98 You, through Your commandments,
make me wiser than my enemies;
For they *are* ever with me.
99 I have more understanding than all
my teachers,
For Your testimonies *are* my
meditation.
100 I understand more than the ancients,
Because I keep Your precepts.
101 I have restrained my feet from every
evil way,
That I may keep Your word.
102 I have not departed from Your
judgments,
For You Yourself have taught me.

> To keep a lamp burning we have to keep putting oil in it.
>
> Mother Teresa of Calcutta

103 How sweet are Your words to my
taste,
Sweeter than honey to my mouth!
104 Through Your precepts I get
understanding;
Therefore I hate every false way.

נ NUN

105 Your word *is* a lamp to my feet
And a light to my path.
106 I have sworn and confirmed
That I will keep Your righteous
judgments.
107 I am afflicted very much;
Revive me, O LORD, according to Your
word.
108 Accept, I pray, the freewill offerings
of my mouth, O LORD,
And teach me Your judgments.
109 My life *is* continually in my hand,
Yet I do not forget Your law.
110 The wicked have laid a snare for me,
Yet I have not strayed from Your
precepts.
111 Your testimonies I have taken as a
heritage forever,
For they *are* the rejoicing of my heart.
112 I have inclined my heart to perform
Your statutes
Forever, to the very end.

ס SAMEK

113 I hate the double-minded,
But I love Your law.

119:97–104 Scripture gives true wisdom that far outweighs the value of secular knowledge.

119:105–112 In the midst of afflictions, God's word is a light. As we follow it, He will provide guidance one step at a time.

119:108 Prayers of praise are the **freewill offerings** in mind here.

119:109, 110 The psalmist clings to God's law even though he is in continual danger.

119:113–120 The law discloses wickedness.

119:113 Double-minded people may equivocate, but God's law does not (see James 1:8).

114 You *are* my hiding place and my
shield;
I hope in Your word.
115 Depart from me, you evildoers,
For I will keep the commandments of
my God!
116 Uphold me according to Your word,
that I may live;
And do not let me be ashamed of my
hope.
117 Hold me up, and I shall be safe,
And I shall observe Your statutes
continually.
118 You reject all those who stray from
Your statutes,
For their deceit *is* falsehood.
119 You put away all the wicked of the
earth *like* dross;
Therefore I love Your testimonies.
120 My flesh trembles for fear of You,
And I am afraid of Your judgments.

ע AYIN

121 I have done justice and righteousness;
Do not leave me to my oppressors.
122 Be surety for Your servant for good;
Do not let the proud oppress me.
123 My eyes fail *from seeking* Your
salvation
And Your righteous word.
124 Deal with Your servant according to
Your mercy,
And teach me Your statutes.
125 I *am* Your servant;
Give me understanding,
That I may know Your testimonies.
126 *It is* time for *You* to act, O LORD,
For they have regarded Your law as
void.
127 Therefore I love Your commandments
More than gold, yes, than fine gold!
128 Therefore all *Your* precepts *concerning*
all *things*
I consider *to be* right;
I hate every false way.

פ PE

129 Your testimonies are wonderful;
Therefore my soul keeps them.
130 The entrance of Your words gives
light;
It gives understanding to the simple.
131 I opened my mouth and panted,
For I longed for Your
commandments.
132 Look upon me and be merciful to me,
As Your custom *is* toward those who
love Your name.
133 Direct my steps by Your word,
And let no iniquity have dominion
over me.
134 Redeem me from the oppression of
man,
That I may keep Your precepts.
135 Make Your face shine upon Your
servant,
And teach me Your statutes.
136 Rivers of water run down from my
eyes,
Because *men* do not keep Your law.

צ TSADDE

137 Righteous *are* You, O LORD,
And upright *are* Your judgments.
138 Your testimonies, *which* You have
commanded,
Are righteous and very faithful.
139 My zeal has consumed me,
Because my enemies have forgotten
Your words.
140 Your word *is* very pure;
Therefore Your servant loves it.

119:116 my hope: My trust in God.

119:129–136 A prayer that God will translate love for the law into righteous behavior.

119:131 If our hearts are right before God, we will crave fellowship with Him through His Word, "as the deer pants for the water brooks" (Ps. 42:1).

119:139 The psalmist is eager to maintain the honor of God (see the attitude of young David in 1 Sam. 17:26).

141 I *am* small and despised,
Yet I do not forget Your precepts.
142 Your righteousness *is* an everlasting
righteousness,
And Your law *is* truth.
143 Trouble and anguish have overtaken
me,
Yet Your commandments *are* my
delights.
144 The righteousness of Your testimonies
is everlasting;
Give me understanding, and I shall
live.

ק QOPH

145 I cry out with *my* whole heart;
Hear me, O LORD!
I will keep Your statutes.
146 I cry out to You;
Save me, and I will keep Your
testimonies.
147 I rise before the dawning of the
morning,
And cry for help;
I hope in Your word.
148 My eyes are awake through the *night*
watches,
That I may meditate on Your
word.
149 Hear my voice according to Your
lovingkindness;
O LORD, revive me according to Your
justice.
150 They draw near who follow after
wickedness;
They are far from Your law.
151 You *are* near, O LORD,
And all Your commandments *are*
truth.
152 Concerning Your testimonies,
I have known of old that You have
founded them forever.

ר RESH

153 Consider my affliction and deliver
me,
For I do not forget Your law.
154 Plead my cause and redeem me;
Revive me according to Your word.
155 Salvation *is* far from the wicked,
For they do not seek Your statutes.
156 Great *are* Your tender mercies, O
LORD;
Revive me according to Your
judgments.
157 Many *are* my persecutors and my
enemies,
Yet I do not turn from Your
testimonies.
158 I see the treacherous, and am
disgusted,
Because they do not keep Your word.
159 Consider how I love Your precepts;
Revive me, O LORD, according to Your
lovingkindness.
160 The entirety of Your word *is* truth,
And every one of Your righteous
judgments *endures* forever.

ש SHIN

161 Princes persecute me without a cause,
But my heart stands in awe of Your
word.
162 I rejoice at Your word
As one who finds great treasure.
163 I hate and abhor lying,
But I love Your law.
164 Seven times a day I praise You,
Because of Your righteous judgments.
165 Great peace have those who love
Your law,
And nothing causes them to stumble.
166 LORD, I hope for Your salvation,
And I do Your commandments.
167 My soul keeps Your testimonies,
And I love them exceedingly.

119:145–152 A cry in **the night** in view of God's previous faithfulness.
119:148 During the hours of the night the psalmist will **meditate** on God's **word** (promises), another synonym for law.
119:153–160 God's word teaches His faithfulness to **redeem** and **revive** (v. 154).
119:161–168 Despite adverse pressure the psalmist will not forsake his commitments.

168 I keep Your precepts and Your
testimonies,
For all my ways *are* before You.

ת TAU

169 Let my cry come before You, O LORD;
Give me understanding according to
Your word.
170 Let my supplication come before You;
Deliver me according to Your word.
171 My lips shall utter praise,
For You teach me Your statutes.
172 My tongue shall speak of Your word,
For all Your commandments *are*
righteousness.
173 Let Your hand become my help,
For I have chosen Your precepts.
174 I long for Your salvation, O LORD,
And Your law *is* my delight.
175 Let my soul live, and it shall praise
You;
And let Your judgments help me.
176 I have gone astray like a lost sheep;
Seek Your servant,
For I do not forget Your
commandments.

PSALM 120

Plea for Relief from Bitter Foes

A Song of Ascents.

In my distress I cried to the LORD,
And He heard me.
2 Deliver my soul, O LORD, from lying
lips
And from a deceitful tongue.
3 What shall be given to you,
Or what shall be done to you,
You false tongue?
4 Sharp arrows of the warrior,
With coals of the broom tree!

5 Woe is me, that I dwell in Mē'shech,
That I dwell among the tents of
Kē'dar!
6 My soul has dwelt too long
With one who hates peace.
7 I *am for* peace;
But when I speak, they *are* for war.

PSALM 121

God the Help of Those Who Seek Him

A Song of Ascents.

I will lift up my eyes to the hills—
From whence comes my help?
2 My help *comes* from the LORD,
Who made heaven and earth.

3 He will not allow your foot to be
moved;
He who keeps you will not slumber.
4 Behold, He who keeps Israel
Shall neither slumber nor sleep.

5 The LORD *is* your keeper;
The LORD *is* your shade at your right
hand.
6 The sun shall not strike you by day,
Nor the moon by night.

7 The LORD shall preserve you from all
evil;

Psalm 120 The first of a group of psalms labeled as Songs of Ascents (Ps. 120—134). The precise meaning of this term is uncertain, but there is some support to understand these psalms as songs sung by pilgrims as they went up to Jerusalem to celebrate the great feasts. Thus these psalms accompanied the ascent to the city of God.

Psalm 121 A pilgrim song in the form of a dialogue, possibly between the worshipers and a priest. It has been called the traveler's psalm.

121:1, 2 The psalmist speaks either of **the hills** he had to cross on his return home, or those hills surrounding Jerusalem. His help does not come from the hills, but from the Lord, the Creator of the hills.

121:7 This promise of a preservation does not mean we will never face adversity but that through every situation He is in control and will help us emerge victorious. Nothing can enter our lives that He cannot use for good (Rom.8:28).

He shall preserve your soul.
8 The LORD shall preserve your going
out and your coming in
From this time forth, and even
forevermore.

PSALM 122

The Joy of Going to the House of the LORD

A Song of Ascents. Of David.

I was glad when they said to me,
"Let us go into the house of the
LORD."
2 Our feet have been standing
Within your gates, O Jerusalem!

3 Jerusalem is built
As a city that is compact together,
4 Where the tribes go up,
The tribes of the LORD,
To the Testimony of Israel,
To give thanks to the name of the
LORD.
5 For thrones are set there for
judgment,
The thrones of the house of David.

6 Pray for the peace of Jerusalem:
"May they prosper who love you.
7 Peace be within your walls,
Prosperity within your palaces."
8 For the sake of my brethren and
companions,
I will now say, "Peace *be* within you."
9 Because of the house of the LORD our
God
I will seek your good.

PSALM 123

Prayer for Relief from Contempt

A Song of Ascents.

Unto You I lift up my eyes,
O You who dwell in the heavens.
2 Behold, as the eyes of servants *look* to
the hand of their masters,
As the eyes of a maid to the hand of
her mistress,
So our eyes *look* to the LORD our God,
Until He has mercy on us.

3 Have mercy on us, O LORD, have
mercy on us!
For we are exceedingly filled with
contempt.
4 Our soul is exceedingly filled
With the scorn of those who are at
ease,
With the contempt of the proud.

PSALM 124

The LORD the Defense of His People

A Song of Ascents. Of David.

"If it had not been the LORD who was
on our side,"
Let Israel now say—
2 "If it had not been the LORD who was
on our side,
When men rose up against us,
3 Then they would have swallowed us
alive,
When their wrath was kindled
against us;

122: title Of David: Since the "house of the LORD" (vv. 1, 9) was not built until King Solomon's time (1 Kin. 6:1), the psalm title must mean "in memory of David" rather than "written by David."

122:3, 4 compact: Bound firmly together. Not so much the physical properties of Jerusalem, as the unity of the worshipers who came together to celebrate the festivals. **Testimony of Israel**: The ark of the covenant (see Ex. 16:34).

122:6–8 This prayer is that Jerusalem, whose final two syllables sound like the Hebrew word *shalom*, meaning "peace," may actually know peace. When weeping over Jerusalem (Luke 19:42), Jesus may have had this psalm in mind. But the peace Christ gives is more than the world can imagine.

4 Then the waters would have
overwhelmed us,
The stream would have gone over
our soul;
5 Then the swollen waters
Would have gone over our soul."

6 Blessed *be* the LORD,
Who has not given us *as* prey to their
teeth.
7 Our soul has escaped as a bird from
the snare of the fowlers;[a]
The snare is broken, and we have
escaped.
8 Our help *is* in the name of the LORD,
Who made heaven and earth.

PSALM 125

The LORD the Strength of His People

A Song of Ascents.

Those who trust in the LORD
Are like Mount Zion,
Which cannot be moved, *but* abides
forever.
2 As the mountains surround
Jerusalem,
So the LORD surrounds His people
From this time forth and forever.

3 For the scepter of wickedness shall
not rest
On the land allotted to the righteous,
Lest the righteous reach out their
hands to iniquity.

4 Do good, O LORD, to *those who are*
good,

124:7 [a]That is, persons who catch birds in a trap or snare

Grow old along with me!
The best is yet to be,
The last of life, for which the first was
made:
Our times are in His hand
Who saith "A whole I planned,
Youth shows but half; trust God: see
all, nor be afraid!"
Robert Browning

And to *those who are* upright in their
hearts.

5 As for such as turn aside to their
crooked ways,
The LORD shall lead them away
With the workers of iniquity.

Peace *be* upon Israel!

PSALM 126

A Joyful Return to Zion

A Song of Ascents.

When the LORD brought back the
captivity of Zion,
We were like those who dream.
2 Then our mouth was filled with
laughter,
And our tongue with singing.
Then they said among the nations,
"The LORD has done great things for
them."
3 The LORD has done great things for
us,
And we are glad.

4 Bring back our captivity, O LORD,
As the streams in the South.

125:1 When we place our faith in God, the storms of life cannot move us. See Matt. 7:25.

125:2 Just as the Lord put a protective hedge around Job (Job 1:1), so we are secure in His arms; nothing can reach us except by His permissive will.

Psalm 126 This psalm is a request for God to extend the benefits of the return from exile to more than the initial few who returned from Babylon. The psalmist recounts the joy of those who have returned (vv. 1–3) and offers a prayer and a blessing for those yet to return (vv. 4–6).

5 Those who sow in tears
Shall reap in joy.
6 He who continually goes forth
weeping,
Bearing seed for sowing,
Shall doubtless come again with
rejoicing,
Bringing his sheaves *with him*.

PSALM 127

Laboring and Prospering with the LORD

A Song of Ascents. Of Solomon.

Unless the LORD builds the house,
They labor in vain who build it;
Unless the LORD guards the city,
The watchman stays awake in vain.
2 *It is* vain for you to rise up early,
To sit up late,
To eat the bread of sorrows;
For so He gives His beloved sleep.

3 Behold, children *are* a heritage from
the LORD,
The fruit of the womb *is* a reward.
4 Like arrows in the hand of a warrior,
So *are* the children of one's youth.
5 Happy *is* the man who has his quiver
full of them;
They shall not be ashamed,
But shall speak with their enemies in
the gate.

PSALM 128

Blessings of Those Who Fear the LORD

A Song of Ascents.

Blessed *is* every one who fears the
LORD,
Who walks in His ways.
2 When you eat the labor of your
hands,
You *shall be* happy, and *it shall be* well
with you.
3 Your wife *shall be* like a fruitful vine
In the very heart of your house,
Your children like olive plants
All around your table.
4 Behold, thus shall the man be blessed
Who fears the LORD.

5 The LORD bless you out of Zion,
And may you see the good of
Jerusalem
All the days of your life.
6 Yes, may you see your children's
children.

Peace *be* upon Israel!

PSALM 129

Song of Victory over Zion's Enemies

A Song of Ascents.

"Many a time they have afflicted me
from my youth,"
Let Israel now say—
2 "Many a time they have afflicted me
from my youth;
Yet they have not prevailed against
me.
3 The plowers plowed on my back;
They made their furrows long."
4 The LORD *is* righteous;
He has cut in pieces the cords of the
wicked.

5 Let all those who hate Zion
Be put to shame and turned back.

126:6 The spiritual application for today's Christian is that any suffering we experience for the sake of the gospel cannot compare to the joy of seeing those we've led to Christ join us in heaven.

127:1 the house: This word can refer both to the building and to the family itself. **in vain**: Efforts to develop a family or community apart from God will lead nowhere.

127:2 This verse does not endorse idleness. It means that apart from God even hard work will not prove finally satisfying. **Sleep** is a gift from God.

129:5–7 After a rain, grass would spring up in the mud brick roofs of Palestinian houses

6 Let them be as the grass *on* the housetops,
Which withers before it grows up,
7 With which the reaper does not fill his hand,
Nor he who binds sheaves, his arms.
8 Neither let those who pass by them say,
"The blessing of the LORD *be* upon you;
We bless you in the name of the LORD!"

PSALM 130

Waiting for the Redemption of the LORD

A Song of Ascents.

Out of the depths I have cried to You, O LORD;
2 Lord, hear my voice!
Let Your ears be attentive
To the voice of my supplications.

3 If You, LORD, should mark iniquities,
O Lord, who could stand?
4 But *there is* forgiveness with You,
That You may be feared.

5 I wait for the LORD, my soul waits,
And in His word I do hope.
6 My soul *waits* for the Lord
More than those who watch for the morning—
Yes, more than those who watch for the morning.

7 O Israel, hope in the LORD;
For with the LORD *there is* mercy,
And with Him *is* abundant redemption.
8 And He shall redeem Israel
From all his iniquities.

PSALM 131

Simple Trust in the LORD

A Song of Ascents. Of David.

LORD, my heart is not haughty,
Nor my eyes lofty.
Neither do I concern myself with great matters,
Nor with things too profound for me.

2 Surely I have calmed and quieted my soul,
Like a weaned child with his mother;
Like a weaned child *is* my soul within me.

3 O Israel, hope in the LORD
From this time forth and forever.

PSALM 132

The Eternal Dwelling of God in Zion

A Song of Ascents.

LORD, remember David
And all his afflictions;
2 How he swore to the LORD,
And vowed to the Mighty One of Jacob:
3 "Surely I will not go into the chamber of my house,
Or go up to the comfort of my bed;

---

only to be withered quickly by the wind and sun. Such plants never produced **sheaves** to bind or grain for the **reaper**.

Psalm 130 This is an individual lament, known as one of the seven penitential psalms (Ps. 6; 32; 38; 51; 102; 130; 143).

130:5, 6 These verses express the longing every Christian should feel in anticipation of the Second Coming of Christ.

131:1 Rather than being distracted by curiosity or confusion about matters God has not yet chosen to reveal, Christians should calmly trust in the Lord's wisdom and act according to what He has shown us.

Psalm 132 This is a royal psalm with an emphasis upon the Davidic covenant and the ark of the covenant. The first part (vv. 2–9) concerns the moving of the ark to Jerusalem; the second part covers God's promises to David and choice of Zion (vv. 11–18).

4 I will not give sleep to my eyes
Or slumber to my eyelids,
5 Until I find a place for the LORD,
A dwelling place for the Mighty One of Jacob."

6 Behold, we heard of it in Eph'ra·thah;
We found it in the fields of the woods.[a]
7 Let us go into His tabernacle;
Let us worship at His footstool.
8 Arise, O LORD, to Your resting place,
You and the ark of Your strength.
9 Let Your priests be clothed with righteousness,
And let Your saints shout for joy.

10 For Your servant David's sake,
Do not turn away the face of Your Anointed.

11 The LORD has sworn *in* truth to David;
He will not turn from it:
"I will set upon your throne the fruit of your body.
12 If your sons will keep My covenant
And My testimony which I shall teach them,
Their sons also shall sit upon your throne forevermore."

13 For the LORD has chosen Zion;
He has desired *it* for His dwelling place:
14 "This *is* My resting place forever;
Here I will dwell, for I have desired it.
15 I will abundantly bless her provision;
I will satisfy her poor with bread.
16 I will also clothe her priests with salvation,
And her saints shall shout aloud for joy.
17 There I will make the horn of David grow;
I will prepare a lamp for My Anointed.
18 His enemies I will clothe with shame,
But upon Himself His crown shall flourish."

PSALM 133

Blessed Unity of the People of God

A Song of Ascents. Of David.

Behold, how good and how pleasant *it is*
For brethren to dwell together in unity!

2 *It is* like the precious oil upon the head,
Running down on the beard,
The beard of Aaron,
Running down on the edge of his garments.
3 *It is* like the dew of Her'mon,
Descending upon the mountains of Zion;
For there the LORD commanded the blessing—
Life forevermore.

132:6 [a]Hebrew *Jaar*

132:5 a place for the Lord: a suitable temple for the ark of the covenant.

132:7 Let us go: This call to worship is addressed to the pilgrims taking part in the festive procession which reenacted the moving of the ark to Jerusalem.

132:8–10 Used to close Solomon's prayer for the dedication of the temple (see 2 Chr. 6:41, 42). **Arise, O LORD**: This invocation was first used when the ark was moved during the wilderness wanderings (Num. 10:35, 36). It is now sung as the ark goes before the worshipers approaching the tabernacle (temple).

133:1 Unity is vital to the success of the church in spreading the message of the gospel. This does not require us to agree on every detail of theology, as long as we agree on the basics and act toward each other with a spirit of love.

PSALM 134

Praising the LORD in His House at Night

A Song of Ascents.

Behold, bless the LORD,
All *you* servants of the LORD,
Who by night stand in the house of the LORD!
2 Lift up your hands *in* the sanctuary,
And bless the LORD.

3 The LORD who made heaven and earth
Bless you from Zion!

PSALM 135

Praise to God in Creation and Redemption

Praise the LORD!

Praise the name of the LORD;
Praise *Him,* O you servants of the LORD!
2 You who stand in the house of the LORD,
In the courts of the house of our God,
3 Praise the LORD, for the LORD *is* good;
Sing praises to His name, for *it is* pleasant.
4 For the LORD has chosen Jacob for Himself,
Israel for His special treasure.

5 For I know that the LORD *is* great,
And our Lord *is* above all gods.
6 Whatever the LORD pleases He does,
In heaven and in earth,
In the seas and in all deep places.
7 He causes the vapors to ascend from the ends of the earth;
He makes lightning for the rain;
He brings the wind out of His treasuries.
8 He destroyed the firstborn of Egypt,
Both of man and beast.
9 He sent signs and wonders into the midst of you, O Egypt,
Upon Pharaoh and all his servants.
10 He defeated many nations
And slew mighty kings—
11 Sī'hon king of the Am'o·rītes,
Og king of Bā'shan,
And all the kingdoms of Cā'naan—
12 And gave their land *as* a heritage,
A heritage to Israel His people.

13 Your name, O LORD, *endures* forever,
Your fame, O LORD, throughout all generations.
14 For the LORD will judge His people,
And He will have compassion on His servants.

15 The idols of the nations *are* silver and gold,
The work of men's hands.
16 They have mouths, but they do not speak;
Eyes they have, but they do not see;
17 They have ears, but they do not hear;
Nor is there *any* breath in their mouths.
18 Those who make them are like them;
So is everyone who trusts in them.

19 Bless the LORD, O house of Israel!
Bless the LORD, O house of Aaron!
20 Bless the LORD, O house of Levi!
You who fear the LORD, bless the LORD!
21 Blessed be the LORD out of Zion,
Who dwells in Jerusalem!

Praise the LORD!

134:1 Here **stand** means to minister. **night**: The Levitical singers "were employed in that work day and night" (1 Chr. 9:33). Night services were held during the fall festivals.

135:1–4 The call to **praise the LORD** is directed to the ministering priests and perhaps to all Israel.

135:4 **Jacob**: the nation of Israel.

PSALM 136

Thanksgiving to God for His Enduring Mercy

Oh, give thanks to the LORD, for *He is* good!
For His mercy *endures* forever.
2 Oh, give thanks to the God of gods!
For His mercy *endures* forever.
3 Oh, give thanks to the Lord of lords!
For His mercy *endures* forever:

4 To Him who alone does great wonders,
For His mercy *endures* forever;
5 To Him who by wisdom made the heavens,
For His mercy *endures* forever;
6 To Him who laid out the earth above the waters,
For His mercy *endures* forever;
7 To Him who made great lights,
For His mercy *endures* forever—
8 The sun to rule by day,
For His mercy *endures* forever;
9 The moon and stars to rule by night,
For His mercy *endures* forever.

10 To Him who struck Egypt in their firstborn,
For His mercy *endures* forever;
11 And brought out Israel from among them,
For His mercy *endures* forever;
12 With a strong hand, and with an outstretched arm,
For His mercy *endures* forever;
13 To Him who divided the Red Sea in two,
For His mercy *endures* forever;
14 And made Israel pass through the midst of it,
For His mercy *endures* forever;
15 But overthrew Pharaoh and his army in the Red Sea,
For His mercy *endures* forever;
16 To Him who led His people through the wilderness,
For His mercy *endures* forever;
17 To Him who struck down great kings,
For His mercy *endures* forever;
18 And slew famous kings,
For His mercy *endures* forever—
19 Sī'hon king of the Am'o·rītes,
For His mercy *endures* forever;
20 And Og king of Bā'shan,
For His mercy *endures* forever—
21 And gave their land as a heritage,
For His mercy *endures* forever;
22 A heritage to Israel His servant,
For His mercy *endures* forever.

23 Who remembered us in our lowly state,
For His mercy *endures* forever;
24 And rescued us from our enemies,
For His mercy *endures* forever;
25 Who gives food to all flesh,
For His mercy *endures* forever.

26 Oh, give thanks to the God of heaven!
For His mercy *endures* forever.

PSALM 137

Longing for Zion in a Foreign Land

By the rivers of Babylon,
There we sat down, yea, we wept
When we remembered Zion.
2 We hung our harps
Upon the willows in the midst of it.

Psalm 136 This is a hymn of thanksgiving and is commonly known as the Great Hallel (Praise). Its unique feature is the recurrence of the same refrain in each verse with the stress upon God's mercy (covenant loyalty).

136:10–15 The deliverance of Israel from Egypt is the revelation of God's **mercy**.

136:23–25 Beyond specific miracles for Israel (v. 23) God's **mercy** is revealed in giving **food to all flesh** (v. 25).

137:2 We hung our harps: The exiles were too sad for any expression of joy.

3 For there those who carried us away
captive asked of us a song,
And those who plundered us
requested mirth,
Saying, "Sing us *one* of the songs of
Zion!"

4 How shall we sing the LORD's song
In a foreign land?
5 If I forget you, O Jerusalem,
Let my right hand forget *its skill!*
6 If I do not remember you,
Let my tongue cling to the roof of my
mouth—
If I do not exalt Jerusalem
Above my chief joy.

7 Remember, O LORD, against the sons
of Ē'dom
The day of Jerusalem,
Who said, "Raze *it,* raze *it,*
To its very foundation!"
8 O daughter of Babylon, who are to be
destroyed,
Happy the one who repays you as
you have served us!
9 Happy the one who takes and dashes
Your little ones against the rock!

PSALM 138

The LORD's Goodness to the Faithful

A Psalm of David.

I will praise You with my whole heart;
Before the gods I will sing praises to
You.
2 I will worship toward Your holy
temple,
And praise Your name
For Your lovingkindness and Your
truth;
For You have magnified Your word
above all Your name.
3 In the day when I cried out, You
answered me,
And made me bold *with* strength in
my soul.

4 All the kings of the earth shall praise
You, O LORD,
When they hear the words of Your
mouth.
5 Yes, they shall sing of the ways of the
LORD,
For great *is* the glory of the LORD.
6 Though the LORD *is* on high,
Yet He regards the lowly;
But the proud He knows from afar.

7 Though I walk in the midst of
trouble, You will revive me;
You will stretch out Your hand
Against the wrath of my enemies,
And Your right hand will save me.
8 The LORD will perfect *that which*
concerns me;
Your mercy, O LORD, *endures* forever;
Do not forsake the works of Your
hands.

PSALM 139

God's Perfect Knowledge of Man

For the Chief Musician. A Psalm of David.

O LORD, You have searched me and
known *me.*
2 You know my sitting down and my
rising up;
You understand my thought afar off.
3 You comprehend my path and my
lying down,
And are acquainted with all my ways.

138:6 Although highly exalted, God is near the **lowly**. But He is far removed from the **proud** (see Is. 57:15).

138:8 perfect that which concerns me: Here is great confidence. God will execute completely His plans for those who walk with Him.

139:3, 4 comprehend: The Hebrew word means "to sift or winnow." He sorts out both our words and thoughts, knowing what is wheat and what is chaff.

4 For *there is* not a word on my tongue,
But behold, O LORD, You know it altogether.
5 You have hedged me behind and before,
And laid Your hand upon me.
6 *Such* knowledge *is* too wonderful for me;
It is high, I cannot *attain* it.

7 Where can I go from Your Spirit?
Or where can I flee from Your presence?
8 If I ascend into heaven, You *are* there;
If I make my bed in hell, behold, You *are there.*
9 *If* I take the wings of the morning,
And dwell in the uttermost parts of the sea,
10 Even there Your hand shall lead me,
And Your right hand shall hold me.
11 If I say, "Surely the darkness shall fall[a] on me,"
Even the night shall be light about me;
12 Indeed, the darkness shall not hide from You,
But the night shines as the day;
The darkness and the light *are* both alike *to You.*

13 For You formed my inward parts;
You covered me in my mother's womb.
14 I will praise You, for I am fearfully *and* wonderfully made;[a]
Marvelous are Your works,
And *that* my soul knows very well.
15 My frame was not hidden from You,
When I was made in secret,
And skillfully wrought in the lowest parts of the earth.
16 Your eyes saw my substance, being yet unformed.
And in Your book they all were written,
The days fashioned for me,
When *as yet there were* none of them.

17 How precious also are Your thoughts to me, O God!
How great is the sum of them!
18 *If* I should count them, they would be more in number than the sand;
When I awake, I am still with You.

19 Oh, that You would slay the wicked, O God!
Depart from me, therefore, you bloodthirsty men.
20 For they speak against You wickedly;
Your enemies take *Your name* in vain.[a]
21 Do I not hate them, O LORD, who hate You?
And do I not loathe those who rise up against You?
22 I hate them with perfect hatred;
I count them my enemies.

23 Search me, O God, and know my heart;
Try me, and know my anxieties;
24 And see if *there is any* wicked way in me,
And lead me in the way everlasting.

139:11 [a]Vulgate and Symmachus read *cover.*
139:14 [a]Following Masoretic Text and Targum; Septuagint, Syriac, and Vulgate read *You are fearfully wonderful.* 139:20 [a]Septuagint and Vulgate read *They take your cities in vain.*

139:7–12 God is always present with me regardless of where I am.
139:9, 10 wings of the morning: A poetic expression for the swift spreading of light at dawn.
139:13–16 God made me as an individual physical being.
139:18 Awake or asleep, we are still in His care.
139:23, 24 As we discipline ourselves to abide in God's way, we must diligently guard against sin in our lives. By daily asking God to search our hearts, we can root out sinful tendencies before they take hold and grow into something more difficult to get rid of.

LITTLE THINGS MEAN A LOT

Claire Cloninger

Coming to grips with the fact of my smallness in relation to God's enormity is destined to be depressing unless I also grasp, as David did, that God does care for me—very much. I am small, yes. But I am assured all through the Scripture that small things matter tremendously to God.

Even the most minute details of my life are of enormous importance to Him. He carefully chose and assembled every part of my being in my mother's womb (Ps. 139:13), and He even knows the number of hairs on my head (Matt. 10:30). He calls me to come to Him as a little child, cautioning that any other spiritual condition will result in my failure to gain the kingdom (Matt. 18:3). He invites me to cast every single concern of my heart (even the small ones) upon Him, because He cares for me so intimately (1 Pet. 5:7). He is a God who knows when even a sparrow falls (Matt. 10:29) and who sees the essence of the kingdom in a tiny mustard seed (Matt. 13:31). Understanding these things about God helps me to realize that smallness cannot be equated with unimportance in His sight, for small things matter greatly to Him. ✦

"Small things matter tremendously to God."

PSALM 140

Prayer for Deliverance from Evil Men

To the Chief Musician. A Psalm of David.

Deliver me, O LORD, from evil men;
Preserve me from violent men,
2 Who plan evil things in *their* hearts;
They continually gather together *for* war.
3 They sharpen their tongues like a serpent;
The poison of asps *is* under their lips. Sē'lah

4 Keep me, O LORD, from the hands of the wicked;
Preserve me from violent men,
Who have purposed to make my steps stumble.
5 The proud have hidden a snare for me, and cords;
They have spread a net by the wayside;
They have set traps for me. Sē'lah

6 I said to the LORD: "You *are* my God;
Hear the voice of my supplications, O LORD.
7 O GOD the Lord, the strength of my salvation,
You have covered my head in the day of battle.
8 Do not grant, O LORD, the desires of the wicked;
Do not further his *wicked* scheme,
Lest they be exalted. Sē'lah

9 "*As for* the head of those who
surround me,
Let the evil of their lips cover them;
10 Let burning coals fall upon them;
Let them be cast into the fire,
Into deep pits, that they rise not up
again.
11 Let not a slanderer be established in
the earth;
Let evil hunt the violent man to
overthrow *him*."

12 I know that the LORD will maintain
The cause of the afflicted,
And justice for the poor.
13 Surely the righteous shall give thanks
to Your name;
The upright shall dwell in Your
presence.

PSALM 141

Prayer for Safekeeping from Wickedness

A Psalm of David.

LORD, I cry out to You;
Make haste to me!
Give ear to my voice when I cry out
to You.
2 Let my prayer be set before You *as*
incense,
The lifting up of my hands *as* the
evening sacrifice.

3 Set a guard, O LORD, over my mouth;
Keep watch over the door of my lips.
4 Do not incline my heart to any evil
thing,
To practice wicked works
With men who work iniquity;
And do not let me eat of their
delicacies.

5 Let the righteous strike me;
It shall be a kindness.
And let him rebuke me;
It shall be as excellent oil;
Let my head not refuse it.

For still my prayer *is* against the
deeds of the wicked.
6 Their judges are overthrown by the
sides of the cliff,
And they hear my words, for they are
sweet.
7 Our bones are scattered at the mouth
of the grave,
As when one plows and breaks up
the earth.

8 But my eyes *are* upon You, O GOD the
Lord;
In You I take refuge;
Do not leave my soul destitute.
9 Keep me from the snares they have
laid for me,
And from the traps of the workers of
iniquity.
10 Let the wicked fall into their own
nets,
While I escape safely.

PSALM 142

A Plea for Relief from Persecutors

A Contemplation[a] of David. A Prayer when he was in the cave.

I cry out to the LORD with my voice;
With my voice to the LORD I make my
supplication.
2 I pour out my complaint before Him;
I declare before Him my trouble.

3 When my spirit was overwhelmed
within me,
Then You knew my path.
In the way in which I walk

142:title [a]Hebrew *Maschil*

140:9, 10 The curse calls for the **head** of his enemies to be exposed to **burning coals**. The **pits** (v. 10) are an indication of divine judgment (see Num. 16:31–33). On the imprecations, see introduction to Ps. 109.

They have secretly set a snare for me.
4 Look on *my* right hand and see,
For *there is* no one who acknowledges me;
Refuge has failed me;
No one cares for my soul.

5 I cried out to You, O LORD:
I said, "You *are* my refuge,
My portion in the land of the living.
6 Attend to my cry,
For I am brought very low;
Deliver me from my persecutors,
For they are stronger than I.
7 Bring my soul out of prison,
That I may praise Your name;
The righteous shall surround me,
For You shall deal bountifully with me."

PSALM 143

An Earnest Appeal for Guidance and Deliverance

A Psalm of David.

Hear my prayer, O LORD,
Give ear to my supplications!
In Your faithfulness answer me,
And in Your righteousness.
2 Do not enter into judgment with Your servant,
For in Your sight no one living is righteous.

3 For the enemy has persecuted my soul;
He has crushed my life to the ground;
He has made me dwell in darkness,
Like those who have long been dead.
4 Therefore my spirit is overwhelmed within me;
My heart within me is distressed.

5 I remember the days of old;
I meditate on all Your works;
I muse on the work of Your hands.
6 I spread out my hands to You;
My soul *longs* for You like a thirsty land. Sē'lah

7 Answer me speedily, O LORD;
My spirit fails!
Do not hide Your face from me,
Lest I be like those who go down into the pit.
8 Cause me to hear Your lovingkindness in the morning,
For in You do I trust;
Cause me to know the way in which I should walk,
For I lift up my soul to You.

9 Deliver me, O LORD, from my enemies;
In You I take shelter.[a]
10 Teach me to do Your will,
For You *are* my God;
Your Spirit *is* good.
Lead me in the land of uprightness.

11 Revive me, O LORD, for Your name's sake!
For Your righteousness' sake bring my soul out of trouble.
12 In Your mercy cut off my enemies,
And destroy all those who afflict my soul;
For I *am* Your servant.

143:9 [a]Septuagint and Vulgate read *To You I flee.*

142:4 There was no one on his right hand where a helper would normally stand. **my soul**: The psalmist himself.

142:5 My portion: The Levites who received no land inheritance recognized God as their portion (Deut. 10:9). The psalmist either was a Levite or put himself in their place of total dependence on God.

142:7 prison: Possibly an actual imprisonment, but more likely a figure of speech for a distressing emotion.

143:8 Requesting divine guidance should be the first step in every major decision we make. Only when we follow God's will can we be assured of true peace and success.

PSALM 144

A Song to the LORD Who Preserves and Prospers His People

A Psalm of David.

Blessed *be* the LORD my Rock,
Who trains my hands for war,
And my fingers for battle—
2 My lovingkindness and my fortress,
My high tower and my deliverer,
My shield and *the One* in whom I take refuge,
Who subdues my people[a] under me.

3 LORD, what *is* man, that You take knowledge of him?
Or the son of man, that You are mindful of him?
4 Man is like a breath;
His days *are* like a passing shadow.

5 Bow down Your heavens, O LORD, and come down;
Touch the mountains, and they shall smoke.
6 Flash forth lightning and scatter them;
Shoot out Your arrows and destroy them.
7 Stretch out Your hand from above;
Rescue me and deliver me out of great waters,
From the hand of foreigners,
8 Whose mouth speaks lying words,
And whose right hand *is* a right hand of falsehood.

9 I will sing a new song to You, O God;
On a harp of ten strings I will sing praises to You,
10 *The One* who gives salvation to kings,
Who delivers David His servant
From the deadly sword.

11 Rescue me and deliver me from the hand of foreigners,
Whose mouth speaks lying words,
And whose right hand *is* a right hand of falsehood—

12 That our sons *may be* as plants grown up in their youth;
That our daughters *may be* as pillars,
Sculptured in palace style;
13 *That* our barns *may be* full,
Supplying all kinds of produce;
That our sheep may bring forth thousands
And ten thousands in our fields;
14 *That* our oxen *may be* well laden;
That there be no breaking in or going out;
That there be no outcry in our streets.
15 Happy *are* the people who are in such a state;
Happy *are* the people whose God *is* the LORD!

PSALM 145

A Song of God's Majesty and Love

A Praise of David.

I will extol You, my God, O King;
And I will bless Your name forever and ever.

> ***I pray that every day my children will bless You, God, and will praise Your name forever and ever.***
>
> *adapted from* Psalm 145:2

144:2 [a]Following Masoretic Text, Septuagint, and Vulgate; Syriac and Targum read *the peoples* (compare 18:47).

144:5, 6 The Lord is asked to manifest Himself as He did at Sinai (Ex. 19:18).

144:10 The name **David** here refers to the reigning king. If King David did not write this psalm, then one of his descendants on the throne stresses that God's deliverance of David is fulfilled in his successor's victory. But God is **the One** who gives the deliverance.

144:15 **Happy** is the nation that enjoys the blessings of vv. 11–14. But the crowning blessing is to be a **people whose God is the LORD**.

Psalm 145 This acrostic poem, comprising twenty-two couplets beginning with successive letters of the Hebrew alphabet, covers nearly every possible form of verbal praise (extol, bless, praise, etc.).

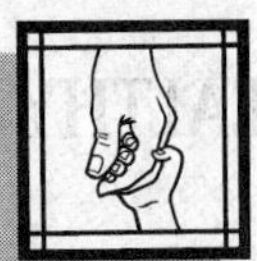

Committing to the Future

Lucibel Van Atta

We who are older (and we're all older than someone else!) have a beautiful opportunity to encourage our younger friends in developing and cultivating ministries of their own, to gently push them into new situations—slightly beyond their present depth—which enable them to trust God totally. How sad if any young person should stub a toe on our indifference!

Commitment to God requires commitment to God's people because God's plan—past, present, future—is always wrapped around people. "One generation shall praise Your works to another, and shall declare Your mighty acts" (Ps. 145:4).

Mentoring is not just another activity to scrunch into our already overcrowded calendars. It is a relationship, a commitment, and a step of faith—a faith defined as giving God the opportunity to fulfill His promise through our lives. This is indeed what pleases God. ✦

2 Every day I will bless You,
And I will praise Your name forever and ever.
3 Great *is* the LORD, and greatly to be praised;
And His greatness *is* unsearchable.

4 One generation shall praise Your works to another,
And shall declare Your mighty acts.
5 I[a] will meditate on the glorious splendor of Your majesty,
And on Your wondrous works.[b]
6 *Men* shall speak of the might of Your awesome acts,
And I will declare Your greatness.
7 They shall utter the memory of Your great goodness,
And shall sing of Your righteousness.

8 The LORD *is* gracious and full of compassion,
Slow to anger and great in mercy.
9 The LORD *is* good to all,
And His tender mercies *are* over all His works.

10 All Your works shall praise You, O LORD,
And Your saints shall bless You.
11 They shall speak of the glory of Your kingdom,
And talk of Your power,
12 To make known to the sons of men His mighty acts,
And the glorious majesty of His kingdom.
13 Your kingdom *is* an everlasting kingdom,
And Your dominion *endures* throughout all generations.[a]

145:5 [a]Following Masoretic Text and Targum; Dead Sea Scrolls, Septuagint, Syriac, and Vulgate read *They.* [b]Literally *on the words of Your wondrous works*
145:13 [a]Following Masoretic Text and Targum; Dead Sea Scrolls, Septuagint, Syriac, and Vulgate add *The LORD is faithful in all His words, And holy in all His works.*

Materialism: Not Just for the Wealthy

Anne Ortlund

Our family has lived for several months at a time overseas. Before we went the first time, we thought Americans were worldly and materialistic because they have so much.

Then we discovered that Christians overseas can be worldly and materialistic, even though they have little. Their focus can be on what they do not have—talking constantly about their high taxes, their low wages, how wonderful America must be, their frustrations over lacking this and lacking that.

"Christians can be worldly and materialistic, even though they have little."

Then we began thinking about Christians we know, American or otherwise, who are wealthy but not worldly, material-rich but not materialistic. They are responsible or even lavish in their giving: Their eyes are on Jesus.

And we know "poor" Christians who are the same!

And we thought, *being materialistic means being too aware of the material, whether you have much or little.* ✦

14 The LORD upholds all who fall,
And raises up all *who are* bowed down.
15 The eyes of all look expectantly to You,
And You give them their food in due season.
16 You open Your hand
And satisfy the desire of every living thing.

17 The LORD *is* righteous in all His ways,
Gracious in all His works.
18 The LORD *is* near to all who call upon Him,
To all who call upon Him in truth.
19 He will fulfill the desire of those who fear Him;
He also will hear their cry and save them.
20 The LORD preserves all who love Him,
But all the wicked He will destroy.
21 My mouth shall speak the praise of the LORD,
And all flesh shall bless His holy name
Forever and ever.

PSALM 146

The Happiness of Those Whose Help Is the LORD

Praise the LORD!

Praise the LORD, O my soul!
2 While I live I will praise the LORD;
I will sing praises to my God while I have my being.

3 Do not put your trust in princes,
Nor in a son of man, in whom *there is* no help.
4 His spirit departs, he returns to his earth;
In that very day his plans perish.

5 Happy *is he* who *has* the God of Jacob for his help,
Whose hope *is* in the LORD his God,
6 Who made heaven and earth,
The sea, and all that *is* in them;
Who keeps truth forever,
7 Who executes justice for the oppressed,
Who gives food to the hungry.
The LORD gives freedom to the prisoners.

8 The LORD opens *the eyes of* the blind;
The LORD raises those who are bowed down;
The LORD loves the righteous.
9 The LORD watches over the strangers;
He relieves the fatherless and widow;
But the way of the wicked He turns upside down.

10 The LORD shall reign forever—
Your God, O Zion, to all generations.

Praise the LORD!

PSALM 147

Praise to God for His Word and Providence

Praise the LORD!
For *it is* good to sing praises to our God;
For *it is* pleasant, *and* praise is beautiful.

2 The LORD builds up Jerusalem;
He gathers together the outcasts of Israel.
3 He heals the brokenhearted
And binds up their wounds.
4 He counts the number of the stars;
He calls them all by name.
5 Great *is* our Lord, and mighty in power;
His understanding *is* infinite.
6 The LORD lifts up the humble;
He casts the wicked down to the ground.

7 Sing to the LORD with thanksgiving;
Sing praises on the harp to our God,
8 Who covers the heavens with clouds,
Who prepares rain for the earth,
Who makes grass to grow on the mountains.
9 He gives to the beast its food,
And to the young ravens that cry.
10 He does not delight in the strength of the horse;

146:7–9 These words, similar to Is. 61:1–3, reflect the mission Jesus saw as His own when He claimed to fulfill the words of Isaiah "to preach the gospel to the poor . . . to heal the brokenhearted . . . to set at liberty those who are oppressed" (Luke 4:17, 18, 21), and when He described His ministry to the disciples of John the Baptist (see Luke 7:19, 22, 23). But, the other side of the gospel is God's judgment on **the wicked**.

Psalm 147 This psalm is a composite of three hymns. The first (vv. 1–6), mentioning the **outcasts of Israel** (v. 2), would seem to concern God's care of the returning exiles. The second (vv. 7–11) stresses God's provisions for creation. The third (vv. 12–20) notes God's dealings with Israel and Jerusalem through His word.

147:2 Builds up Jerusalem could refer to a particular instance, such as Nehemiah rebuilding the walls (Neh. 6; 7), or to the continuous expansion of Jerusalem with increasing population.

147:8, 9 If our great and awesome God takes time to arrange the weather and feed baby birds, how much more interest does He take in the people for whom He sent His son to die? We need never feel lonely or neglected; God cares—actively—for each of us.

He takes no pleasure in the legs of a
man.
11 The LORD takes pleasure in those who
fear Him,
In those who hope in His mercy.
12 Praise the LORD, O Jerusalem!
Praise your God, O Zion!
13 For He has strengthened the bars of
your gates;
He has blessed your children within
you.
14 He makes peace *in* your borders,
And fills you with the finest wheat.

15 He sends out His command *to the*
earth;
His word runs very swiftly.
16 He gives snow like wool;
He scatters the frost like ashes;
17 He casts out His hail like morsels;
Who can stand before His cold?
18 He sends out His word and melts
them;
He causes His wind to blow, *and* the
waters flow.

19 He declares His word to Jacob,
His statutes and His judgments to
Israel.
20 He has not dealt thus with any
nation;
And *as for His* judgments, they have
not known them.

Praise the LORD!

PSALM 148

Praise to the LORD from Creation

Praise the LORD!

Praise the LORD from the heavens;
Praise Him in the heights!
2 Praise Him, all His angels;
Praise Him, all His hosts!
3 Praise Him, sun and moon;
Praise Him, all you stars of light!
4 Praise Him, you heavens of heavens,
And you waters above the heavens!

5 Let them praise the name of the LORD,
For He commanded and they were
created.
6 He also established them forever and
ever;
He made a decree which shall not
pass away.

7 Praise the LORD from the earth,
You great sea creatures and all the
depths;
8 Fire and hail, snow and clouds;
Stormy wind, fulfilling His word;
9 Mountains and all hills;
Fruitful trees and all cedars;
10 Beasts and all cattle;
Creeping things and flying fowl;
11 Kings of the earth and all peoples;
Princes and all judges of the earth;
12 Both young men and maidens;
Old men and children.

13 Let them praise the name of the LORD,
For His name alone is exalted;
His glory *is* above the earth and
heaven.
14 And He has exalted the horn of His
people,
The praise of all His saints—
Of the children of Israel,
A people near to Him.

Praise the LORD!

147:19, 20 God's creative word becomes His redeeming Word. He reveals Himself in Israel's Scriptures as to no other nation. This revelation of truth brings special responsibility.

148:7–12 The call now shifts to the **earth**. All that depend on God's care are charged to **praise** Him. The list of those called moves from nature (vv. 7–10) to find its climax in humankind (vv. 11, 12; see 8:5–8 and note). All people may praise Him: all ages from **children** to the **young** and **old**.

Q & A I am widowed. How can I keep from feeling so lonely?

Dr. Frank Minirth and Dr. Paul Meier

You will always miss your "best friend" and treasure the happy moments you shared. But surely your mate would have wanted you to get back into life. Several things may help your loneliness:

✦ *Be active.* Many lonely people passively wait for someone interesting to come along or for something spectacular to happen. Whenever you feel lonely, get up and go! Join a club, take up a new hobby, or do volunteer work. These are simplistic solutions, but they often work. Of course, activity is only one step in the process, since many very busy people are lonely. But give yourself a chance to fellowship with others, especially those who have shared your grief.

✦ *Walk closely with God.* An intimate friendship with God offers the ultimate solution to loneliness. Many find comfort in Psalm 27: "When my father and my mother forsake me, then the Lord will take care of me" (v. 10). This step in overcoming loneliness—developing a close walk with God—leads to the next suggestion.

✦ *Develop the fruit of the Spirit.* "But the fruit of the Spirit is love, joy, peace, longsuffering, kindness, goodness, faithfulness, gentleness, self-control. Against such there is no law" (Gal. 5:22, 23). When we exhibit these beautiful qualities of the Holy Spirit, others want to be with us. A critical and judgmental attitude drives others away.

✦ *Realize the love of Christ.* Being grounded in God's love is probably the best remedy for any emotional problem; accepting that love is vital for coping with loneliness. So is sharing that love with others. Offering love from a heart filled with God's love usually results in receiving more love in return.

✦ *Dwell on your belonging to God.* Even tiny infants need a sense of belonging—the assurance that their parents will never forsake them.

Lonely people need to remind themselves that—as children of God—they can place all their confidence in their heavenly Father. ✦

PSALM 149

Praise to God for His Salvation and Judgment

Praise the LORD!

Sing to the LORD a new song,
And His praise in the assembly of saints.

2 Let Israel rejoice in their Maker;
Let the children of Zion be joyful in their King.

3 Let them praise His name with the
dance;
Let them sing praises to Him with the
timbrel and harp.
4 For the LORD takes pleasure in His
people;
He will beautify the humble with
salvation.

5 Let the saints be joyful in glory;
Let them sing aloud on their beds.
6 *Let* the high praises of God *be* in their
mouth,
And a two-edged sword in their
hand,
7 To execute vengeance on the nations,
And punishments on the peoples;
8 To bind their kings with chains,
And their nobles with fetters of iron;
9 To execute on them the written
judgment—
This honor have all His saints.

Praise the LORD!

PSALM 150

Let All Things Praise the LORD

Praise the LORD!

Praise God in His sanctuary;
Praise Him in His mighty firmament!

2 Praise Him for His mighty acts;
Praise Him according to His excellent
greatness!

3 Praise Him with the sound of the
trumpet;
Praise Him with the lute and harp!
4 Praise Him with the timbrel and
dance;
Praise Him with stringed instruments
and flutes!
5 Praise Him with loud cymbals;
Praise Him with clashing cymbals!

6 Let everything that has breath praise
the LORD.

Praise the LORD!

149:3, 4 Celebration included not only singing, but dancing to the accompaniment of **timbrel** and **harp**. The sacred **dance** was a significant element of Israelite worship.

149:6–8 A dance, featuring swords, anticipated future judgment on **the nations** and **their kings**.

149:9 **The written judgment** may refer to the heavenly books in which the deeds of humans were recorded, or to the words of Scripture in the Law and the Prophets.

Psalm 150 This passage serves as the doxology for both Book Five and the entire collection of Psalms. It defines the where, what, how, and who of praise.

150:1 God is to be praised inside and out—everywhere.

150:2 God is to be praised for what He has done and for who He is.

150:3–5 Here is the ministry of instrumental music. God is to be praised with **trumpet, harp**, and **cymbals**—with brass, strings, and percussion instruments.

150:6 God is to be praised by every living creature on earth and in heaven.

✦Proverbs✦

Solomon wrote a great majority of Proverbs; chapters 10—22:16 and 25—29 identify his authorship. Some portions, however, are attributed to other people, such as "the wise" (22:17), Agur (30:1), and King Lemuel (31:1). Solomon probably used their words and properly named the sources. He most likely wrote the book between 970 and 931 B.C.

Proverbs clearly names its dual purpose: wisdom and instruction (1:2). The Hebrew word for wisdom also means skill, and the word for instruction also means discipline. Discipline allows for the proper use of skills, and Proverbs emphasizes the most important skill—living righteously before God. It tells us that a long life is a reward for righteous living (Prov. 16:31). True wisdom is based on following God's ultimate plan and purpose for everything. ✦

CHAPTER 1

The Beginning of Knowledge

The proverbs of Solomon the son of David, king of Israel:

2 To know wisdom and instruction,
To perceive the words of understanding,
3 To receive the instruction of wisdom,
Justice, judgment, and equity;
4 To give prudence to the simple,
To the young man knowledge and discretion—
5 A wise *man* will hear and increase learning,
And a man of understanding will attain wise counsel,
6 To understand a proverb and an enigma,
The words of the wise and their riddles.
7 The fear of the LORD *is* the beginning of knowledge,
But fools despise wisdom and instruction.

1:1–7 These verses form an introduction to the entire Book of Proverbs. The rest of the book is designed to fulfill the purposes set out here. It is offered to provide its readers with **wisdom** and **instruction** (v. 2). Similar words emphasize this purpose: **judgment** and **equity** (v. 3), **prudence, knowledge**, and **discretion** (v. 4), **learning** and **wise counsel** (v. 5). All these are related to knowing how to live well and deciding to live that way. **proverbs of Solomon**: The great wisdom of this king made a deep impression on the visiting queen of Sheba (see 2 Chr. 9:1–12).

1:2 Wisdom is skill for living and comes from **instruction** and **understanding**.

1:6 The **proverb** was a short statement of truth concerning some aspect of human life. The **enigma**, as well as **riddles**, presented a principle of truth through a puzzle or problem to be solved.

1:7 Fear of the LORD is the sort of reverence and respect that results in obedience. **Knowledge** in the moral and religious sense of Proverbs is possible only if one has a proper regard for God. **Fools** are contrasted to the wise man throughout the book.

> I grew up in a tiny little house with big lessons. Today we have great big houses and little tiny lessons.
> Margaret Jensen

Shun Evil Counsel

8 My son, hear the instruction of your
father,
And do not forsake the law of your
mother;
9 For they *will be* a graceful ornament
on your head,
And chains about your neck.

10 My son, if sinners entice you,
Do not consent.
11 If they say, "Come with us,
Let us lie in wait to *shed* blood;
Let us lurk secretly for the innocent
without cause;
12 Let us swallow them alive like
Shē'ōl,[a]
And whole, like those who go down
to the Pit;
13 We shall find all *kinds* of precious
possessions,
We shall fill our houses with spoil;
14 Cast in your lot among us,
Let us all have one purse"—
15 My son, do not walk in the way with
them,
Keep your foot from their path;
16 For their feet run to evil,
And they make haste to shed blood.
17 Surely, in vain the net is spread
In the sight of any bird;
18 But they lie in wait for their *own*
blood,
They lurk secretly for their *own* lives.
19 So *are* the ways of everyone who is
greedy for gain;
It takes away the life of its owners.

The Call of Wisdom

20 Wisdom calls aloud outside;
She raises her voice in the open
squares.
21 She cries out in the chief concourses,[a]
At the openings of the gates in the
city
She speaks her words:
22 "How long, you simple ones, will you
love simplicity?
For scorners delight in their
scorning,
And fools hate knowledge.
23 Turn at my rebuke;
Surely I will pour out my spirit on
you;
I will make my words known to you.
24 Because I have called and you
refused,
I have stretched out my hand and no
one regarded,
25 Because you disdained all my
counsel,
And would have none of my rebuke,
26 I also will laugh at your calamity;
I will mock when your terror comes,
27 When your terror comes like a
storm,
And your destruction comes like a
whirlwind,

1:12 [a]Or *the grave* 1:21 [a]Septuagint, Syriac, and Targum read *top of the walls;* Vulgate reads *the head of multitudes.*

1:10 Being tempted is not a sin, but yielding to temptation is. Each of us bears the responsibility of deciding how we will respond to the lure of evil. We cannot put the blame on those around us, nor can we honestly claim, "The devil made me do it." God gave each of us the capacity to choose, and we prove our love for Him by choosing obedience.

1:20—2:20 **Wisdom** is pictured as a woman who calls to everyone passing by the gates. As wisdom is symbolized by a woman (1:20, 21), so is folly. But these are not merely symbols. A woman who embodies wisdom can help a man (31:10–31), while one who embodies folly may destroy him (7:6–23).

When distress and anguish come
upon you.

28 "Then they will call on me, but I will
not answer;
They will seek me diligently, but they
will not find me.
29 Because they hated knowledge
And did not choose the fear of the
LORD,
30 They would have none of my counsel
And despised my every rebuke.
31 Therefore they shall eat the fruit of
their own way,
And be filled to the full with their
own fancies.
32 For the turning away of the simple
will slay them,
And the complacency of fools will
destroy them;
33 But whoever listens to me will dwell
safely,
And will be secure, without fear of
evil."

CHAPTER 2

The Value of Wisdom

My son, if you receive my words,
And treasure my commands within
you,
2 So that you incline your ear to
wisdom,
And apply your heart to
understanding;
3 Yes, if you cry out for discernment,
And lift up your voice for
understanding,
4 If you seek her as silver,
And search for her as *for* hidden
treasures;
5 Then you will understand the fear of
the LORD,
And find the knowledge of God.
6 For the LORD gives wisdom;
From His mouth *come* knowledge and
understanding;
7 He stores up sound wisdom for the
upright;
He is a shield to those who walk
uprightly;
8 He guards the paths of justice,
And preserves the way of His
saints.
9 Then you will understand
righteousness and justice,
Equity *and* every good path.

10 When wisdom enters your heart,
And knowledge is pleasant to your
soul,
11 Discretion will preserve you;
Understanding will keep you,
12 To deliver you from the way of
evil,
From the man who speaks perverse
things,
13 From those who leave the paths of
uprightness
To walk in the ways of darkness;
14 Who rejoice in doing evil,
And delight in the perversity of the
wicked;
15 Whose ways *are* crooked,
And *who are* devious in their paths;
16 To deliver you from the immoral
woman,
From the seductress *who* flatters with
her words,
17 Who forsakes the companion of her
youth,
And forgets the covenant of her
God.
18 For her house leads down to death,
And her paths to the dead;
19 None who go to her return,
Nor do they regain the paths of life—
20 So you may walk in the way of
goodness,
And keep *to* the paths of
righteousness.
21 For the upright will dwell in the
land,
And the blameless will remain in it;
22 But the wicked will be cut off from
the earth,
And the unfaithful will be uprooted
from it.

CHAPTER 3

Guidance for the Young

My son, do not forget my law,
But let your heart keep my
commands;
2 For length of days and long life
And peace they will add to you.

3 Let not mercy and truth forsake you;
Bind them around your neck,
Write them on the tablet of your
heart,
4 *And* so find favor and high esteem
In the sight of God and man.

5 Trust in the LORD with all your heart,
And lean not on your own
understanding;
6 In all your ways acknowledge Him,
And He shall direct[a] your paths.

7 Do not be wise in your own eyes;
Fear the LORD and depart from evil.
8 It will be health to your flesh,[a]
And strength[b] to your bones.

9 Honor the LORD with your
possessions,
And with the firstfruits of all your
increase;
10 So your barns will be filled with
plenty,
And your vats will overflow with
new wine.

11 My son, do not despise the
chastening of the LORD,
Nor detest His correction;
12 For whom the LORD loves He corrects,
Just as a father the son *in whom* he
delights.

13 Happy *is* the man *who* finds wisdom,
And the man *who* gains
understanding;
14 For her proceeds *are* better than the
profits of silver,
And her gain than fine gold.
15 She *is* more precious than rubies,
And all the things you may desire
cannot compare with her.
16 Length of days *is* in her right hand,
In her left hand riches and honor.
17 Her ways *are* ways of pleasantness,
And all her paths *are* peace.
18 She *is* a tree of life to those who take
hold of her,
And happy *are all* who retain her.

19 The LORD by wisdom founded the
earth;
By understanding He established the
heavens;
20 By His knowledge the depths were
broken up,
And clouds drop down the dew.

21 My son, let them not depart from
your eyes—
Keep sound wisdom and discretion;
22 So they will be life to your soul
And grace to your neck.
23 Then you will walk safely in your
way,
And your foot will not stumble.

3:6 [a]Or *make smooth* or *straight* 3:8 [a]Literally *navel,* figurative of the body [b]Literally *drink* or *refreshment*

3:1, 2 The connection between keeping God's commands and enjoying long life is supported by the fifth commandment (see Ex. 20:12).

3:5, 6 Verses, worthy of being memorized, which sum up the biblical approach to life. Wisdom is not the result of mere human insight, but of learning God's unchanging ways. As we seek His guidance in the small decisions we make each day He will supply direction for the bigger issues we face in the future.

3:9, 10 To honor the LORD meant giving Him the portion of material goods that He required. **Firstfruits** were the first items harvested, and often the best.

3:11, 12 God shows His love for us by correcting us when we sin. Rather than rejecting such treatment, we should be thankful for His loving care and take appropriate action.

I pray, Lord, that when my grandchild lies down, he will not be afraid. I pray that he will lie down and his sleep will be sweet.

adapted from Proverbs 3:24

24 When you lie down, you will not be
afraid;
Yes, you will lie down and your sleep
will be sweet.
25 Do not be afraid of sudden terror,
Nor of trouble from the wicked when
it comes;
26 For the LORD will be your
confidence,
And will keep your foot from being
caught.

27 Do not withhold good from those to
whom it is due,
When it is in the power of your hand
to do *so.*
28 Do not say to your neighbor,
"Go, and come back,
And tomorrow I will give *it,"*
When *you have* it with you.
29 Do not devise evil against your
neighbor,
For he dwells by you for safety's
sake.
30 Do not strive with a man without
cause,
If he has done you no harm.

31 Do not envy the oppressor,
And choose none of his ways;
32 For the perverse *person is* an
abomination to the LORD,
But His secret counsel *is* with the
upright.
33 The curse of the LORD *is* on the house
of the wicked,
But He blesses the home of the just.
34 Surely He scorns the scornful,
But gives grace to the humble.
35 The wise shall inherit glory,
But shame shall be the legacy of fools.

CHAPTER 4

Security in Wisdom

Hear, *my* children, the instruction of a
father,
And give attention to know
understanding;
2 For I give you good doctrine:
Do not forsake my law.
3 When I was my father's son,
Tender and the only one in the sight
of my mother,
4 He also taught me, and said to me:
"Let your heart retain my words;
Keep my commands, and live.
5 Get wisdom! Get understanding!
Do not forget, nor turn away from the
words of my mouth.
6 Do not forsake her, and she will
preserve you;
Love her, and she will keep you.
7 Wisdom *is* the principal thing;
Therefore get wisdom.
And in all your getting, get
understanding.

3:24–26 Serving God saves us from many fears.

3:27–30 The wise person does not delay payment—delay may lead to misunderstanding and strife.

4:1–13 Wisdom is the principal thing (v. 7) because it is not merely an intellectual activity; wisdom leads to a full life. It is a life skillfully lived (v. 13).

4:3, 4 Each generation is responsible to instruct succeeding generations in the way of the Lord. God expects us to pass our legacy of faith on to our children. We should also seek to be mentors to young people who do not come from Christian backgrounds but desire to walk in God's way.

4:5–7 Learning without the gain of **wisdom** is a waste.

THE VALUE OF WISDOM

Leslie E. Moser, Ph.D.

Wisdom was valued in Old Testament days. Is it valued as much today? Maybe we have come to place too much emphasis on intelligence and IQ scores, but we could never place too much emphasis on wisdom. For, you see, "The fear of the Lord is the beginning of knowledge" (Prov. 1:7), and "The fear of the Lord is the beginning of wisdom" (Prov. 9:10). Wisdom is a God-given, precious treasure that we acquire by walking through life with the Lord.

Wisdom is something you get, and you get it by knowing who the Lord is and by making Him Lord over your life. Only then can you and I receive wisdom and greater understanding. Wisdom and understanding come from your efforts, and keeping your wisdom and knowledge will also come from your efforts. You and I will, of course, give them up to some extent before God calls us home. Before we die, within the providence of God, you may have to give up some wisdom and knowledge as your body fails. But do not give them up out of laziness or because of a myth that says you should be less intelligent because you are growing old. You must ignore the voices of the world and continue to grow in wisdom and knowledge. ✦

8 Exalt her, and she will promote you;
She will bring you honor, when you embrace her.
9 She will place on your head an ornament of grace;
A crown of glory she will deliver to you."

10 Hear, my son, and receive my sayings,
And the years of your life will be many.
11 I have taught you in the way of wisdom;
I have led you in right paths.
12 When you walk, your steps will not be hindered,
And when you run, you will not stumble.
13 Take firm hold of instruction, do not let go;
Keep her, for she *is* your life.

14 Do not enter the path of the wicked,
And do not walk in the way of evil.
15 Avoid it, do not travel on it;
Turn away from it and pass on.
16 For they do not sleep unless they have done evil;
And their sleep is taken away unless they make *someone* fall.
17 For they eat the bread of wickedness,
And drink the wine of violence.

18 But the path of the just *is* like the shining sun,[a]

4:18 [a]Literally *light*

4:18 Walking with God becomes better as we travel farther on. The thought is well worth

That shines ever brighter unto the
perfect day.
19 The way of the wicked *is* like
darkness;
They do not know what makes them
stumble.

20 My son, give attention to my words;
Incline your ear to my sayings.
21 Do not let them depart from your
eyes;
Keep them in the midst of your heart;
22 For they *are* life to those who find
them,
And health to all their flesh.
23 Keep your heart with all diligence,
For out of it *spring* the issues of life.
24 Put away from you a deceitful mouth,
And put perverse lips far from you.
25 Let your eyes look straight ahead,
And your eyelids look right before
you.
26 Ponder the path of your feet,
And let all your ways be established.
27 Do not turn to the right or the left;
Remove your foot from evil.

I pray that my grandchild will give attention to Your words, O God, that he will incline his ear to Your sayings. Do not let them depart from his eyes and may he keep them in the midst of his heart. They will be life to him when he finds them and health to his flesh.

adapted from Proverbs 4:20–22

CHAPTER 5

The Peril of Adultery

My son, pay attention to my wisdom;
Lend your ear to my understanding,
2 That you may preserve discretion,
And your lips may keep knowledge.
3 For the lips of an immoral woman
drip honey,
And her mouth *is* smoother than oil;
4 But in the end she is bitter as
wormwood,
Sharp as a two-edged sword.
5 Her feet go down to death,
Her steps lay hold of hell.[a]
6 Lest you ponder *her* path of life—
Her ways are unstable;
You do not know *them*.

7 Therefore hear me now, *my* children,
And do not depart from the words of
my mouth.
8 Remove your way far from her,
And do not go near the door of her
house,
9 Lest you give your honor to others,
And your years to the cruel *one;*
10 Lest aliens be filled with your wealth,
And your labors *go* to the house of a
foreigner;
11 And you mourn at last,
When your flesh and your body are
consumed,
12 And say:
"How I have hated instruction,
And my heart despised correction!
13 I have not obeyed the voice of my
teachers,

5:5 [a]Or *Sheol*

remembering as we encounter the circumstances of life. **the perfect day**: Noon. The time when the light of day is at its fullest.

4:24 Perverse lips utter lies instead of truth.

5:1–14 An **immoral woman** (v. 3) promises much but delivers little. Evil is never as satisfying as it appears.

5:4 Wormwood, a shrub that has a bitter taste, is a symbol for sorrow and pain.

SPIRITUAL FENCES

Dr. Henry Cloud

Boundaries ensure that we can say who is and is not welcome on our property. We can invite friends into our home, but we also use locks and fences to keep out unwelcome people. In the same manner, we cannot walk into someone else's house uninvited.

Spiritual boundaries define the perimeters of our souls. They tell us where our spiritual ownership extends. As a result, they tell where our responsibility begins and ends. The Bible says to "keep your heart with all diligence" (Prov. 4:23), looking after your heart and soul.

"Spiritual boundaries define the perimeters of our souls."

The Bible consistently says we must take responsibility for our souls. One day we will be accountable for developing this eternal "property." Listen to the warning from Jesus to a man who did not develop his own soul: "But God said to him, 'Fool! This night your soul will be required of you; then whose will those things be which you have provided?'" (Luke 12:20).

This is one reason boundaries are so important: stewardship. As we define what is on our property, we can take responsibility for ourselves. ✦

Nor inclined my ear to those who
instructed me!
14 I was on the verge of total ruin,
In the midst of the assembly and
congregation."

15 Drink water from your own cistern,
And running water from your own
well.
16 Should your fountains be dispersed
abroad,
Streams of water in the streets?
17 Let them be only your own,
And not for strangers with you.
18 Let your fountain be blessed,
And rejoice with the wife of your
youth.
19 *As a* loving deer and a graceful doe,
Let her breasts satisfy you at all times;
And always be enraptured with her
love.
20 For why should you, my son, be
enraptured by an immoral woman,
And be embraced in the arms of a
seductress?
21 For the ways of man *are* before the
eyes of the LORD,
And He ponders all his paths.
22 His own iniquities entrap the wicked
man,
And he is caught in the cords of his
sin.
23 He shall die for lack of instruction,

5:21 "We cannot hide from God" (Ps. 139:3).

And in the greatness of his folly he
shall go astray.

CHAPTER 6

Dangerous Promises

My son, if you become surety for
your friend,
If you have shaken hands in pledge
for a stranger,
2 You are snared by the words of your
mouth;
You are taken by the words of your
mouth.
3 So do this, my son, and deliver
yourself;
For you have come into the hand of
your friend:
Go and humble yourself;
Plead with your friend.
4 Give no sleep to your eyes,
Nor slumber to your eyelids.
5 Deliver yourself like a gazelle from
the hand *of the hunter,*
And like a bird from the hand of the
fowler.[a]

The Folly of Indolence

6 Go to the ant, you sluggard!
Consider her ways and be wise,
7 Which, having no captain,
Overseer or ruler,
8 Provides her supplies in the summer,
And gathers her food in the harvest.
9 How long will you slumber, O
sluggard?
When will you rise from your sleep?
10 A little sleep, a little slumber,
A little folding of the hands to sleep—
11 So shall your poverty come on you
like a prowler,
And your need like an armed man.

The Wicked Man

12 A worthless person, a wicked man,
Walks with a perverse mouth;
13 He winks with his eyes,
He shuffles his feet,
He points with his fingers;
14 Perversity *is* in his heart,
He devises evil continually,
He sows discord.
15 Therefore his calamity shall come
suddenly;
Suddenly he shall be broken without
remedy.

16 These six *things* the LORD hates,
Yes, seven *are* an abomination to Him:
17 A proud look,
A lying tongue,
Hands that shed innocent blood,
18 A heart that devises wicked plans,
Feet that are swift in running to evil,
19 A false witness *who* speaks lies,
And one who sows discord among
brethren.

Beware of Adultery

20 My son, keep your father's command,
And do not forsake the law of your
mother.

6:5 [a]That is, one who catches birds in a trap or snare

6:1–5 Surety means to cosign or pledge to pay someone else's debt.

6:6–8 The **ant**, a diligent worker and provider, is a model for the **sluggard** to observe. But this verse should not be used to justify sacrificing one's family relationships in order to be financially secure.

6:9–11 Poverty is not avoided by chance. It must be diligently guarded against, as against a **prowler** or an **armed man**.

6:12–15 worthless person: A troublemaker who uses all kinds of subtle, deceitful methods to sow **discord**. In God's providence such a person is certain to face **calamity**.

6:16–19 These seven . . . abominations expand upon the description of the troublemaker of vv. 12–15. They are sins of both action and attitude (v. 12); they involve private life and public **evil** (v. 18).

6:20–23 Observing both a good **father's command** and the law of a loving **mother** will keep us from many an evil.

21 Bind them continually upon your
heart;
Tie them around your neck.
22 When you roam, they[a] will lead you;
When you sleep, they will keep you;
And *when* you awake, they will speak
with you.
23 For the commandment *is* a lamp,
And the law a light;
Reproofs of instruction *are* the way of
life,
24 To keep you from the evil woman,
From the flattering tongue of a
seductress.
25 Do not lust after her beauty in your
heart,
Nor let her allure you with her eyelids.
26 For by means of a harlot
A man is reduced to a crust of bread;
And an adulteress[a] will prey upon his
precious life.
27 Can a man take fire to his bosom,
And his clothes not be burned?
28 Can one walk on hot coals,
And his feet not be seared?
29 So *is* he who goes in to his neighbor's
wife;
Whoever touches her shall not be
innocent.

30 *People* do not despise a thief
If he steals to satisfy himself when he
is starving.
31 Yet *when* he is found, he must restore
sevenfold;
He may have to give up all the
substance of his house.
32 Whoever commits adultery with a
woman lacks understanding;
He *who* does so destroys his own soul.
33 Wounds and dishonor he will get,
And his reproach will not be wiped
away.
34 For jealousy *is* a husband's fury;
Therefore he will not spare in the day
of vengeance.
35 He will accept no recompense,
Nor will he be appeased though you
give many gifts.

CHAPTER 7

My son, keep my words,
And treasure my commands within
you.
2 Keep my commands and live,
And my law as the apple of your eye.
3 Bind them on your fingers;
Write them on the tablet of your
heart.
4 Say to wisdom, "You *are* my sister,"
And call understanding *your* nearest
kin,
5 That they may keep you from the
immoral woman,
From the seductress *who* flatters with
her words.

The Crafty Harlot

6 For at the window of my house
I looked through my lattice,
7 And saw among the simple,
I perceived among the youths,
A young man devoid of
understanding,
8 Passing along the street near her
corner;
And he took the path to her house
9 In the twilight, in the evening,
In the black and dark night.

10 And there a woman met him,
With the attire of a harlot, and a
crafty heart.
11 She *was* loud and rebellious,
Her feet would not stay at home.

6:22 [a]Literally *it* 6:26 [a]Literally *a man's wife,* that is, of another

6:30–35 A thief will have to pay dearly to assuage the anger of the householder he has robbed. But what is taken in adultery can never be restored.

7:4 Wisdom and understanding through obeying God's words and commands are the keys to moral and spiritual success.

12 At times *she was* outside, at times in
the open square,
Lurking at every corner.
13 So she caught him and kissed him;
With an impudent face she said to
him:
14 "*I have* peace offerings with me;
Today I have paid my vows.
15 So I came out to meet you,
Diligently to seek your face,
And I have found you.
16 I have spread my bed with tapestry,
Colored coverings of Egyptian linen.
17 I have perfumed my bed
With myrrh, aloes, and cinnamon.
18 Come, let us take our fill of love until
morning;
Let us delight ourselves with love.
19 For my husband *is* not at home;
He has gone on a long journey;
20 He has taken a bag of money with
him,
And will come home on the
appointed day."

21 With her enticing speech she caused
him to yield,
With her flattering lips she seduced
him.
22 Immediately he went after her, as an
ox goes to the slaughter,
Or as a fool to the correction of the
stocks,[a]
23 Till an arrow struck his liver.
As a bird hastens to the snare,
He did not know it *would cost* his life.

24 Now therefore, listen to me, *my*
children;
Pay attention to the words of my
mouth:
25 Do not let your heart turn aside to her
ways,
Do not stray into her paths;
26 For she has cast down many
wounded,
And all who were slain by her were
strong *men*.
27 Her house *is* the way to hell,[a]
Descending to the chambers of death.

CHAPTER 8

The Excellence of Wisdom

Does not wisdom cry out,
And understanding lift up her voice?
2 She takes her stand on the top of the
high hill,
Beside the way, where the paths meet.
3 She cries out by the gates, at the entry
of the city,
At the entrance of the doors:
4 "To you, O men, I call,
And my voice *is* to the sons of men.
5 O you simple ones, understand
prudence,
And you fools, be of an
understanding heart.
6 Listen, for I will speak of excellent
things,
And from the opening of my lips *will
come* right things;
7 For my mouth will speak truth;
Wickedness *is* an abomination to my
lips.
8 All the words of my mouth *are* with
righteousness;
Nothing crooked or perverse *is* in
them.
9 They *are* all plain to him who
understands,
And right to those who find
knowledge.

7:22 [a]Septuagint, Syriac, and Targum read *as a dog to bonds;* Vulgate reads *as a lamb . . . to bonds.*
7:27 [a]Or *Sheol*

8:5 Even **simple ones** and **fools** can choose to gain prudence and understanding through wisdom, or they can go to destruction (7:21, 22).

8:6–11 Following wisdom is much more than mere pragmatism. Wisdom is ethical and moral, associated with **excellent things** (v. 6), **truth** (v. 7), **righteousness** (v. 8), and **knowledge** (v. 9).

10 Receive my instruction, and not
silver,
And knowledge rather than choice
gold;
11 For wisdom *is* better than rubies,
And all the things one may desire
cannot be compared with her.

12 "I, wisdom, dwell with prudence,
And find out knowledge *and*
discretion.
13 The fear of the LORD *is* to hate evil;
Pride and arrogance and the evil
way
And the perverse mouth I hate.
14 Counsel *is* mine, and sound wisdom;
I *am* understanding, I have strength.
15 By me kings reign,
And rulers decree justice.
16 By me princes rule, and nobles,
All the judges of the earth.[a]
17 I love those who love me,
And those who seek me diligently
will find me.
18 Riches and honor *are* with me,
Enduring riches and righteousness.
19 My fruit *is* better than gold, yes, than
fine gold,
And my revenue than choice silver.
20 I traverse the way of righteousness,
In the midst of the paths of justice,
21 That I may cause those who love me
to inherit wealth,
That I may fill their treasuries.

22 "The LORD possessed me at the
beginning of His way,
Before His works of old.
23 I have been established from
everlasting,
From the beginning, before there was
ever an earth.
24 When *there were* no depths I was
brought forth,
When *there were* no fountains
abounding with water.
25 Before the mountains were settled,
Before the hills, I was brought forth;
26 While as yet He had not made the
earth or the fields,
Or the primal dust of the world.
27 When He prepared the heavens, I *was*
there,
When He drew a circle on the face of
the deep,
28 When He established the clouds
above,
When He strengthened the fountains
of the deep,
29 When He assigned to the sea its limit,
So that the waters would not
transgress His command,
When He marked out the foundations
of the earth,
30 Then I was beside Him *as* a master
craftsman;[a]
And I was daily *His* delight,
Rejoicing always before Him,
31 Rejoicing in His inhabited world,
And my delight *was* with the sons of
men.

32 "Now therefore, listen to me, *my*
children,
For blessed *are those who* keep my
ways.
33 Hear instruction and be wise,
And do not disdain *it*.
34 Blessed is the man who listens to me,
Watching daily at my gates,

8:16 [a]Masoretic Text, Syriac, Targum, and Vulgate read *righteousness;* Septuagint, Bomberg, and some manuscripts and editions read *earth.* 8:30 [a]A Jewish tradition reads *one brought up.*

8:13 To hate evil is one way to demonstrate the **fear of the LORD**.

8:18–21 Wisdom is **better** than money and is to be preferred to it, although wisdom often leads to wealth.

8:27 drew a circle: Determined the boundaries (v. 29).

8:30, 31 master craftsman: Wisdom is personified as a skillful craftsman active in each day of creation culminating with the creation of man.

Waiting at the posts of my doors.
35 For whoever finds me finds life,
And obtains favor from the LORD;
36 But he who sins against me wrongs his own soul;
All those who hate me love death."

CHAPTER 9

The Way of Wisdom

Wisdom has built her house,
She has hewn out her seven pillars;
2 She has slaughtered her meat,
She has mixed her wine,
She has also furnished her table.
3 She has sent out her maidens,
She cries out from the highest places of the city,
4 "Whoever *is* simple, let him turn in here!"
As for him who lacks understanding, she says to him,
5 "Come, eat of my bread
And drink of the wine I have mixed.
6 Forsake foolishness and live,
And go in the way of understanding.

7 "He who corrects a scoffer gets shame for himself,
And he who rebukes a wicked *man* *only* harms himself.
8 Do not correct a scoffer, lest he hate you;
Rebuke a wise *man,* and he will love you.
9 Give *instruction* to a wise *man,* and he will be still wiser;
Teach a just *man,* and he will increase in learning.
10 "The fear of the LORD *is* the beginning of wisdom,
And the knowledge of the Holy One *is* understanding.
11 For by me your days will be multiplied,
And years of life will be added to you.
12 If you are wise, you are wise for yourself,
And *if* you scoff, you will bear *it* alone."

The Way of Folly

13 A foolish woman is clamorous;
She is simple, and knows nothing.
14 For she sits at the door of her house,
On a seat *by* the highest places of the city,
15 To call to those who pass by,
Who go straight on their way:
16 "Whoever *is* simple, let him turn in here";
And *as for* him who lacks understanding, she says to him,
17 "Stolen water is sweet,
And bread *eaten* in secret is pleasant."
18 But he does not know that the dead *are* there,
That her guests *are* in the depths of hell.[a]

CHAPTER 10

Wise Sayings of Solomon

The proverbs of Solomon:

A wise son makes a glad father,
But a foolish son *is* the grief of his mother.

9:18 [a]Or *Sheol*

9:4–6 Wisdom and folly issue similar calls (see vv. 14–16). Both profess to help a young person "grow up." But wisdom brings maturity while folly deteriorates life. The one calls for open commitment; the other offers illicit secret pleasures (v. 17).

9:7–9 The **scoffer** mocks the very principles of morality. He cannot be instructed and hurls his **shame** back upon the one who would correct him. The wise man accepts correction and grows wiser. Our response to a loving rebuke is a measure of our character.

9:12 Here again we see that each individual bears the responsibility to choose wisdom or folly.

PLAN FOR A BETTER TOMORROW

Ron Blue

Having just turned fifty-one, I feel that life just gets better and better. The primary reason, I believe, is that the maturity and wisdom that come with age allow us to maintain a better perspective on life. As I have gotten older, I realize that the age I am doesn't feel as old as what I thought it would. I do not know what age fifty *should* feel like, but I certainly feel better than I ever thought possible. Many people today are leading active lives in their seventies, eighties, and even nineties.

Nevertheless, as they get older, many people fear managing their finances. Americans are living longer. This is good news. But it can also be fearful news when we consider the economic resources a longer life requires.

However, establishing clear financial goals as we grow older can help alleviate these fears. I find five specific goals to be most helpful: meeting retirement income needs, providing adequate healthcare protection, planning estate distribution, planning for the financial implications of the death of a spouse, and planning for the major lifestyle changes likely to occur at retirement.

Once you determine your goals, planning for them becomes logical. Begin planning for your better tomorrow today! ✦

2 Treasures of wickedness profit
nothing,
But righteousness delivers from
death.
3 The LORD will not allow the righteous
soul to famish,
But He casts away the desire of the
wicked.

4 He who has a slack hand becomes
poor,
But the hand of the diligent makes
rich.
5 He who gathers in summer *is* a wise
son;
He who sleeps in harvest *is* a son
who causes shame.

6 Blessings *are* on the head of the
righteous,
But violence covers the mouth of the
wicked.
7 The memory of the righteous *is*
blessed,
But the name of the wicked will rot.

8 The wise in heart will receive
commands,
But a prating fool will fall.

9 He who walks with integrity walks
securely,
But he who perverts his ways will
become known.

10:2 Treasures of wickedness are acquired by unjust or immoral means. **Righteousness** is our security against the ultimate threat of death.

10:8 A wise person accepts direction but a **prating fool** acts like a know-it-all and fails.

I pray that my children remember that hatred stirs up strife, but love covers all sins.

adapted from Proverbs 10:12

10 He who winks with the eye causes
trouble,
But a prating fool will fall.

11 The mouth of the righteous *is* a well
of life,
But violence covers the mouth of the
wicked.

12 Hatred stirs up strife,
But love covers all sins.

13 Wisdom is found on the lips of him
who has understanding,
But a rod *is* for the back of him who
is devoid of understanding.

14 Wise *people* store up knowledge,
But the mouth of the foolish *is* near
destruction.

15 The rich man's wealth *is* his strong
city;
The destruction of the poor *is* their
poverty.

16 The labor of the righteous *leads* to life,
The wages of the wicked to sin.

17 He who keeps instruction *is in* the
way of life,
But he who refuses correction goes
astray.

18 Whoever hides hatred *has* lying lips,
And whoever spreads slander *is* a
fool.

19 In the multitude of words sin is not
lacking,
But he who restrains his lips *is* wise.
20 The tongue of the righteous *is* choice
silver;
The heart of the wicked *is worth*
little.
21 The lips of the righteous feed many,
But fools die for lack of wisdom.[a]

22 The blessing of the LORD makes *one*
rich,
And He adds no sorrow with it.

23 To do evil *is* like sport to a fool,
But a man of understanding has
wisdom.
24 The fear of the wicked will come
upon him,
And the desire of the righteous will
be granted.
25 When the whirlwind passes by, the
wicked *is* no *more,*
But the righteous *has* an everlasting
foundation.

26 As vinegar to the teeth and smoke to
the eyes,
So *is* the lazy *man* to those who send
him.

27 The fear of the LORD prolongs days,
But the years of the wicked will be
shortened.

10:21 [a]Literally *heart*

10:10 winks with the eye: A sign of insincerity (see 16:30).

10:14 mouth . . . near destruction: In contrast to the wise man, the foolish talk before they understand.

10:14–21 The wise Christian does not speak carelessly but weighs each word to be certain it will properly build up the body of Christ.

10:22 The Lord gives riches that bring no regrets.

10:26 The lazy man is trouble, not help, to those who would employ him.

28 The hope of the righteous *will be*
gladness,
But the expectation of the wicked will
perish.
29 The way of the LORD *is* strength for
the upright,
But destruction *will come* to the
workers of iniquity.

30 The righteous will never be removed,
But the wicked will not inhabit the
earth.
31 The mouth of the righteous brings
forth wisdom,
But the perverse tongue will be cut
out.
32 The lips of the righteous know what
is acceptable,
But the mouth of the wicked *what is*
perverse.

CHAPTER 11

Dishonest scales *are* an abomination to
the LORD,
But a just weight *is* His delight.

2 When pride comes, then comes
shame;
But with the humble *is* wisdom.

3 The integrity of the upright will guide
them,
But the perversity of the unfaithful
will destroy them.
4 Riches do not profit in the day of
wrath,
But righteousness delivers from death.
5 The righteousness of the blameless
will direct[a] his way aright,
But the wicked will fall by his own
wickedness.
6 The righteousness of the upright will
deliver them,
But the unfaithful will be caught by
their lust.

7 When a wicked man dies, *his*
expectation will perish,
And the hope of the unjust perishes.
8 The righteous is delivered from
trouble,
And it comes to the wicked instead.
9 The hypocrite with *his* mouth
destroys his neighbor,
But through knowledge the righteous
will be delivered.
10 When it goes well with the righteous,
the city rejoices;
And when the wicked perish, *there is*
jubilation.
11 By the blessing of the upright the city
is exalted,
But it is overthrown by the mouth of
the wicked.

12 He who is devoid of wisdom despises
his neighbor,
But a man of understanding holds his
peace.

13 A talebearer reveals secrets,
But he who is of a faithful spirit
conceals a matter.

14 Where *there is* no counsel, the people
fall;
But in the multitude of counselors
there is safety.

15 He who is surety for a stranger will
suffer,
But one who hates being surety is
secure.

16 A gracious woman retains honor,
But ruthless *men* retain riches.

11:5 [a]Or *make smooth* or *straight*

11:1 Dishonest scales did not show true weight.

11:11 A city prospers, is exalted, when the upright make their voices heard, speaking wisdom. A city falls when wicked voices become dominant.

11:13 A talebearer deliberately betrays others.

17 The merciful man does good for his
own soul,
But *he who is* cruel troubles his own
flesh.
18 The wicked *man* does deceptive
work,
But he who sows righteousness *will
have* a sure reward.
19 As righteousness *leads* to life,
So he who pursues evil *pursues it* to
his own death.
20 Those who are of a perverse heart *are*
an abomination to the LORD,
But *the* blameless in their ways *are*
His delight.
21 *Though they join* forces,[a] the wicked
will not go unpunished;
But the posterity of the righteous will
be delivered.

22 *As* a ring of gold in a swine's snout,
So is a lovely woman who lacks dis-
cretion.

23 The desire of the righteous *is* only
good,
But the expectation of the wicked *is*
wrath.

24 There is *one* who scatters, yet
increases more;
And there is *one* who withholds more
than is right,
But it *leads* to poverty.
25 The generous soul will be made rich,
And he who waters will also be
watered himself.
26 The people will curse him who
withholds grain,
But blessing *will be* on the head of
him who sells *it*.

27 He who earnestly seeks good finds
favor,
But trouble will come to him who
seeks *evil*.

28 He who trusts in his riches will fall,
But the righteous will flourish like
foliage.

29 He who troubles his own house will
inherit the wind,
And the fool *will be* servant to the
wise of heart.

30 The fruit of the righteous *is a* tree of
life,
And he who wins souls *is* wise.

31 If the righteous will be recompensed
on the earth,
How much more the ungodly and the
sinner.

CHAPTER 12

Whoever loves instruction loves
knowledge,
But he who hates correction *is* stupid.

2 A good *man* obtains favor from the
LORD,
But a man of wicked intentions He
will condemn.

3 A man is not established by
wickedness,
But the root of the righteous cannot
be moved.

4 An excellent[a] wife *is* the crown of her
husband,
But she who causes shame *is* like
rottenness in his bones.

11:21 [a]Literally *hand to hand*

12:4 [a]Literally *A wife of valor*

11:24–26 The more we give of ourselves to others, the more we receive. In contrast, one who does not share with others finds that others will not share with him.

11:31 The **righteous** usually live to see their good deeds rewarded. The ungodly and sinners are even more likely to "reap what they sow."

5 The thoughts of the righteous *are* right,
But the counsels of the wicked *are* deceitful.
6 The words of the wicked *are,* "Lie in wait for blood,"
But the mouth of the upright will deliver them.

7 The wicked are overthrown and *are* no more,
But the house of the righteous will stand.

8 A man will be commended according to his wisdom,
But he who is of a perverse heart will be despised.

9 Better *is the one* who is slighted but has a servant,
Than he who honors himself but lacks bread.

10 A righteous *man* regards the life of his animal,
But the tender mercies of the wicked *are* cruel.

11 He who tills his land will be satisfied with bread,
But he who follows frivolity *is* devoid of understanding.[a]

12 The wicked covet the catch of evil *men,*
But the root of the righteous yields *fruit.*
13 The wicked is ensnared by the transgression of *his* lips,
But the righteous will come through trouble.
14 A man will be satisfied with good by the fruit of *his* mouth,
And the recompense of a man's hands will be rendered to him.

15 The way of a fool *is* right in his own eyes,
But he who heeds counsel *is* wise.
16 A fool's wrath is known at once,
But a prudent *man* covers shame.

17 He *who* speaks truth declares righteousness,
But a false witness, deceit.
18 There is one who speaks like the piercings of a sword,
But the tongue of the wise *promotes* health.
19 The truthful lip shall be established forever,
But a lying tongue *is* but for a moment.
20 Deceit is in the heart of those who devise evil,
But counselors of peace have joy.
21 No grave trouble will overtake the righteous,
But the wicked shall be filled with evil.
22 Lying lips *are* an abomination to the LORD,
But those who deal truthfully *are* His delight.

23 A prudent man conceals knowledge,
But the heart of fools proclaims foolishness.

24 The hand of the diligent will rule,
But the lazy *man* will be put to forced labor.

12:11 [a]Literally *heart*

12:9 slighted: Receives no attention. It is better to say too little about yourself than too much.
12:14 The **mouth** and **hands** are our most productive members; success or failure depends on their proper use.
12:23 Blurting out all we know is not necessary or helpful.

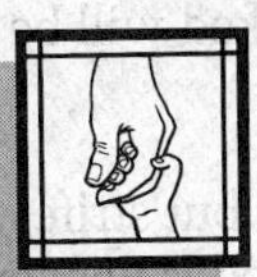

A Friend in Deed

Dr. Richard Meier

In this busy world where many women work and also care for a family, taking the time to be a friend can seem like a luxury. But how can women model Christ to one another if they don't spend moments listening, offering help, or simply sharing pain and joy?

In days gone by, friendships between women were important ways to share concerns, seek solutions, and support one another. Today women put a great deal of pressure on their spouses to fulfill all their needs. In the past, friends played a more important part in women's lives.

Friendship as a place for ministry and support is an important addition to our busy lives. But to have a friend you have to be a friend and that takes time and commitment. Try to add these elements to your life:

• Pray. Ask God to direct you to women who need you and women who could support you. Then begin to pray for the women you know in your neighborhood or at work. If appropriate, let the person know that you are praying for her.

• Listen. Open your heart and your mind to the needs of people around you. Go beyond "How are you?" and ask specific questions without being nosy. Then let the person talk. Many women have no one to listen to them.

• Offer. Try to find specific ways to help. "I'm on my way to the grocery store. Can I pick up anything for you?" can be a godsend on a busy day. If your children have left home and you are willing, why not offer to take the after-school shift for a neighbor, entertaining her children while she fixes dinner?

• Share. Friendships are two-way streets. From time to time call someone just to give some good news or share a story about your grandchild. Then tell the person that you appreciate the opportunity to share your story with a friend.

• Affirm. In this often brutal world, giving a sincere compliment can really brighten someone's day. "Mary, you have the nicest laugh," is wonderful to hear and will make Mary smile more often. Affirmation is contagious. Try it and you will have more friends than you can count. ✦

25 Anxiety in the heart of man causes
depression,
But a good word makes it glad.

26 The righteous should choose his
friends carefully,
For the way of the wicked leads them
astray.

27 The lazy *man* does not roast what he
took in hunting,
But diligence *is* man's precious
possession.

28 In the way of righteousness *is* life,
And in *its* pathway *there is* no
death.

12:25 A verse to be memorized and remembered when encountering those who are prone to worry. **A good word** is a word of encouragement, faith, or hope.

> Four steps to achievement: plan purposefully, prepare prayerfully, proceed positively, pursue persistently.
> William A. Ward

CHAPTER 13

A wise son *heeds* his father's
instruction,
But a scoffer does not listen to rebuke.

2 A man shall eat well by the fruit of *his*
mouth,
But the soul of the unfaithful feeds on
violence.
3 He who guards his mouth preserves
his life,
But he who opens wide his lips shall
have destruction.

4 The soul of a lazy *man* desires, and
has nothing;
But the soul of the diligent shall be
made rich.

5 A righteous *man* hates lying,
But a wicked *man* is loathsome and
comes to shame.
6 Righteousness guards *him whose* way
is blameless,
But wickedness overthrows the
sinner.

7 There is one who makes himself rich,
yet *has* nothing;
And one who makes himself poor, yet
has great riches.

8 The ransom of a man's life *is* his
riches,
But the poor does not hear rebuke.

9 The light of the righteous rejoices,
But the lamp of the wicked will be
put out.

10 By pride comes nothing but strife,
But with the well-advised *is* wisdom.

11 Wealth *gained by* dishonesty will be
diminished,
But he who gathers by labor will
increase.

12 Hope deferred makes the heart sick,
But *when* the desire comes, *it is* a tree
of life.

13 He who despises the word will be
destroyed,
But he who fears the commandment
will be rewarded.
14 The law of the wise *is* a fountain of
life,
To turn *one* away from the snares of
death.

15 Good understanding gains favor,
But the way of the unfaithful *is*
hard.
16 Every prudent *man* acts with
knowledge,
But a fool lays open *his* folly.

17 A wicked messenger falls into
trouble,
But a faithful ambassador *brings*
health.

18 Poverty and shame *will come* to him
who disdains correction,
But he who regards a rebuke will be
honored.

19 A desire accomplished is sweet to the
soul,

13:1 A **scoffer** will ignore correction, indeed they will hate it. It is not an act of love to withhold discipline, including physical punishment for wrongdoing (see Eph. 6:4). Lack of discipline can result in destruction for the child. A disciplined child can bring honor to a family; but an undisciplined child, shame.

FRIENDSHIP: A TWO-WAY STREET

Dr. Frank Minirth, Dr. Paul Meier, and Don Hawkins

Not all friendships are healthy. Some actually can *cause* anxiety instead of relieve it. If you feel some doubt as to whether or not a relationship is positive, ask yourself this question: "Is this friendship developing me?" If the relationship is one-way, with one partner always giving and the other partner always receiving, the answer is probably no. If it is a dependency relationship in which one person feels slighted if she isn't in her friend's company every day, the answer is no. If it is a fair-weather relationship that withers when one of the partners endures a period of adversity, the answer is no. If it is an ego-boosting relationship in which one person merely strokes the ego of the other person without giving honest—even negative—feedback, the answer is no.

Just as happiness and forgiveness are choices, so is friendship. Each of us has to choose to develop friendships, and each of us must decide what kind of and how many friends we want. A few well-chosen, deep friendships are generally more beneficial to us than a wide circle of superficial acquaintances.

The Book of Proverbs offers good advice on how to select friends. Perhaps the most important verse is the one that states, "He who walks with wise men will be wise, but the companion of fools will be destroyed" (13:20). Our friends influence us, and in a nurturing two-way relationship, each participant often takes on certain characteristics of the other. Friendships can change us for the better or for the worse. The person who frequently is in the company of a wise friend is likely to become wiser because of it. The person who surrounds himself with fools risks becoming a fool. ✦

But *it is* an abomination to fools to
depart from evil.

20 He who walks with wise *men* will be
wise,
But the companion of fools will be
destroyed.

21 Evil pursues sinners,
But to the righteous, good shall be
repaid.

22 A good *man* leaves an inheritance to
his children's children,
But the wealth of the sinner is stored
up for the righteous.

23 Much food *is in* the fallow *ground* of
the poor,
And for lack of justice there is waste.[a]

24 He who spares his rod hates his son,
But he who loves him disciplines him
promptly.

13:23 [a]Literally *what is swept away*

25 The righteous eats to the satisfying of his soul,
But the stomach of the wicked shall be in want.

CHAPTER 14

The wise woman builds her house,
But the foolish pulls it down with her hands.

2 He who walks in his uprightness fears the LORD,
But *he who is* perverse in his ways despises Him.

3 In the mouth of a fool *is* a rod of pride,
But the lips of the wise will preserve them.

4 Where no oxen *are*, the trough *is* clean;
But much increase *comes* by the strength of an ox.

5 A faithful witness does not lie,
But a false witness will utter lies.

6 A scoffer seeks wisdom and does not *find it*,
But knowledge *is* easy to him who understands.

7 Go from the presence of a foolish man,
When you do not perceive *in him* the lips of knowledge.

8 The wisdom of the prudent *is* to understand his way,
But the folly of fools *is* deceit.

9 Fools mock at sin,
But among the upright *there is* favor.

10 The heart knows its own bitterness,
And a stranger does not share its joy.

11 The house of the wicked will be overthrown,
But the tent of the upright will flourish.

12 There is a way *that seems* right to a man,
But its end *is* the way of death.

13 Even in laughter the heart may sorrow,
And the end of mirth *may be* grief.

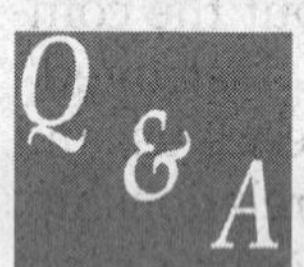

Is insurance scriptural?

Charles Ross

Insurance deals with *restitution*, which literally means "to restore." In the area of finances, this term normally refers to replacing a material possession. In the books of Exodus, Leviticus, and Deuteronomy, verses touch on subjects as diverse as payment for theft and responsibility for borrowed goods. And the Book of Proverbs discusses leaving an inheritance for your children. Not only does the Bible advise that we leave money to our children, but it goes further to imply that we should give some of the inheritance while we are still alive to teach the children how to manage it.

14:1 pulls it down: She acts in ways which will harm the family.
14:6 The **scoffer** does not find wisdom because he cannot recognize its source—fear of the Lord (1:7).
14:10 No one but the Lord can fully understand how we feel in times of tragedy. Wise friends know that their loving presence best expresses sympathy.

14 The backslider in heart will be filled
with his own ways,
But a good man *will be satisfied* from
above.[a]

15 The simple believes every word,
But the prudent considers well his
steps.
16 A wise *man* fears and departs from
evil,
But a fool rages and is self-confident.
17 A quick-tempered *man* acts foolishly,
And a man of wicked intentions is
hated.
18 The simple inherit folly,
But the prudent are crowned with
knowledge.
19 The evil will bow before the good,
And the wicked at the gates of the
righteous.

20 The poor *man* is hated even by his
own neighbor,
But the rich *has* many friends.
21 He who despises his neighbor sins;
But he who has mercy on the poor,
happy *is* he.

22 Do they not go astray who devise
evil?
But mercy and truth *belong* to those
who devise good.

23 In all labor there is profit,
But idle chatter[a] *leads* only to poverty.

24 The crown of the wise is their riches,
But the foolishness of fools *is* folly.

25 A true witness delivers souls,
But a deceitful *witness* speaks lies.

26 In the fear of the LORD *there is* strong
confidence,
And His children will have a place of
refuge.
27 The fear of the LORD *is* a fountain of
life,
To turn *one* away from the snares of
death.

28 In a multitude of people *is* a king's
honor,
But in the lack of people *is* the
downfall of a prince.

29 *He who is* slow to wrath has great
understanding,
But *he who is* impulsive[a] exalts folly.

30 A sound heart *is* life to the body,
But envy *is* rottenness to the bones.

31 He who oppresses the poor
reproaches his Maker,
But he who honors Him has mercy on
the needy.

32 The wicked is banished in his
wickedness,
But the righteous has a refuge in his
death.

33 Wisdom rests in the heart of him who
has understanding,
But *what is* in the heart of fools is
made known.

34 Righteousness exalts a nation,
But sin *is* a reproach to *any* people.

35 The king's favor *is* toward a wise
servant,

14:14 [a]Literally *from above himself* 14:23 [a]Literally *talk of the lips* 14:29 [a]Literally *short of spirit*

14:15–17 Three ways to play the fool: (1) be gullible (v. 15), (2) be arrogant (v. 16), (3) be quick-tempered (v. 17).

14:30 Even in OT time people recognized the connection between attitude and physical health.

14:34 National welfare is tied to **righteousness**.

But his wrath *is against* him who
causes shame.

CHAPTER 15

A soft answer turns away wrath,
But a harsh word stirs up anger.
2 The tongue of the wise uses
knowledge rightly,
But the mouth of fools pours forth
foolishness.

3 The eyes of the LORD *are* in every
place,
Keeping watch on the evil and the
good.

4 A wholesome tongue *is* a tree of life,
But perverseness in it breaks the
spirit.

5 A fool despises his father's
instruction,
But he who receives correction is
prudent.

6 *In* the house of the righteous *there is*
much treasure,
But in the revenue of the wicked is
trouble.

7 The lips of the wise disperse
knowledge,
But the heart of the fool *does* not *do*
so.

8 The sacrifice of the wicked *is* an
abomination to the LORD,
But the prayer of the upright *is* His
delight.
9 The way of the wicked *is* an
abomination to the LORD,
But He loves him who follows
righteousness.

10 Harsh discipline *is* for him who
forsakes the way,
And he who hates correction will die.

11 Hell[a] and Destruction[b] *are* before the
LORD;
So how much more the hearts of the
sons of men.

12 A scoffer does not love one who
corrects him,
Nor will he go to the wise.

13 A merry heart makes a cheerful
countenance,
But by sorrow of the heart the spirit is
broken.

14 The heart of him who has
understanding seeks knowledge,
But the mouth of fools feeds on
foolishness.

15 All the days of the afflicted *are* evil,
But he who is of a merry heart *has* a
continual feast.

16 Better *is* a little with the fear of the
LORD,
Than great treasure with trouble.
17 Better *is* a dinner of herbs[a] where love
is,
Than a fatted calf with hatred.

18 A wrathful man stirs up strife,
But *he who is* slow to anger allays
contention.

15:11 [a]Or *Sheol* [b]Hebrew *Abaddon* 15:17 [a]Or *vegetables*

15:3 We may be able to deceive others about the state of our hearts, but no sinful action or thought can be hidden from God.

15:4 Words have the power to heal or to crush the spirit of another.

15:9 The Lord is concerned with the pattern of our lives. Are we in the way of the **wicked**, or do we follow **righteousness?**

15:10 There is no hope of improvement for one who is wrong, yet rejects **correction** (also v. 12).

ADJUST YOUR ATTITUDE!

Gloria Gaither

When we get up in the morning, we have just so much energy. We can spend that energy creatively, seeking positive solutions, or we can spend it dragging ourselves down with negative thinking. Either way, we may still be tired at the end of the day. But in the first instance, we will have accomplished something and made progress. In the other, we will have plodded along and managed to make ourselves not only tired, but depressed as well!

Half the battle in solving problems is our attitude. We are not just pumping ourselves full of sunshine when we say, "Think YES!" How we think about a situation usually dictates the course we will take—and sometimes, when we get bogged down in all the tangle of detail, we need a friend who will help us think clearly about all aspects of the situation, refocusing our attention from the obstacles to the possibilities in striving for proper choices and desired goals. ✦

"Half the battle in solving problems is our attitude."

19 The way of the lazy *man is* like a
hedge of thorns,
But the way of the upright *is* a
highway.

20 A wise son makes a father glad,
But a foolish man despises his
mother.

21 Folly *is* joy *to him who is* destitute of
discernment,
But a man of understanding walks
uprightly.

22 Without counsel, plans go awry,
But in the multitude of counselors
they are established.

23 A man has joy by the answer of his
mouth,
And a word *spoken* in due season,
how good *it is!*

24 The way of life *winds* upward for the
wise,
That he may turn away from hell[a]
below.

25 The LORD will destroy the house of
the proud,
But He will establish the boundary of
the widow.

26 The thoughts of the wicked *are* an
abomination to the LORD,
But *the words* of the pure *are* pleasant.

27 He who is greedy for gain troubles
his own house,
But he who hates bribes will live.

28 The heart of the righteous studies
how to answer,
But the mouth of the wicked pours
forth evil.

15:24 [a]Or *Sheol*

29 The LORD *is* far from the wicked,
But He hears the prayer of the righteous.

30 The light of the eyes rejoices the heart,
And a good report makes the bones healthy.[a]

31 The ear that hears the rebukes of life
Will abide among the wise.
32 He who disdains instruction despises his own soul,
But he who heeds rebuke gets understanding.
33 The fear of the LORD *is* the instruction of wisdom,
And before honor *is* humility.

CHAPTER 16

The preparations of the heart *belong* to man,
But the answer of the tongue *is* from the LORD.

2 All the ways of a man *are* pure in his own eyes,
But the LORD weighs the spirits.

3 Commit your works to the LORD,
And your thoughts will be established.

4 The LORD has made all for Himself,
Yes, even the wicked for the day of doom.

5 Everyone proud in heart *is* an abomination to the LORD;
Though they join forces,[a] none will go unpunished.

6 In mercy and truth
Atonement is provided for iniquity;
And by the fear of the LORD *one* departs from evil.

7 When a man's ways please the LORD,
He makes even his enemies to be at peace with him.

8 Better *is* a little with righteousness,
Than vast revenues without justice.

9 A man's heart plans his way,
But the LORD directs his steps.

10 Divination *is* on the lips of the king;
His mouth must not transgress in judgment.
11 Honest weights and scales *are* the LORD's;
All the weights in the bag *are* His work.
12 *It is* an abomination for kings to commit wickedness,
For a throne is established by righteousness.
13 Righteous lips *are* the delight of kings,
And they love him who speaks *what is* right.
14 As messengers of death *is* the king's wrath,
But a wise man will appease it.
15 In the light of the king's face *is* life,
And his favor *is* like a cloud of the latter rain.

16 How much better to get wisdom than gold!
And to get understanding is to be chosen rather than silver.

17 The highway of the upright *is* to depart from evil;
He who keeps his way preserves his soul.

18 Pride *goes* before destruction,
And a haughty spirit before a fall.
19 Better *to be* of a humble spirit with the lowly,

15:30 [a]Literally *fat* 16:5 [a]Literally *hand to hand*

15:33 Humility before the Lord opens the way for Him to honor us.

Than to divide the spoil with the
proud.

20 He who heeds the word wisely will
find good,
And whoever trusts in the LORD,
happy *is* he.

21 The wise in heart will be called
prudent,
And sweetness of the lips increases
learning.

22 Understanding *is* a wellspring of life
to him who has it.
But the correction of fools *is* folly.

23 The heart of the wise teaches his
mouth,
And adds learning to his lips.

24 Pleasant words *are like* a honeycomb,
Sweetness to the soul and health to
the bones.

25 There is a way *that seems* right to a
man,
But its end *is* the way of death.

26 The person who labors, labors for
himself,
For his *hungry* mouth drives him *on.*

27 An ungodly man digs up evil,
And *it is* on his lips like a burning
fire.

28 A perverse man sows strife,
And a whisperer separates the best of
friends.

29 A violent man entices his neighbor,
And leads him in a way *that is* not
good.

30 He winks his eye to devise perverse
things;
He purses his lips *and* brings about
evil.

31 The silver-haired head *is* a crown of
glory,
If it is found in the way of
righteousness.

32 *He who is* slow to anger *is* better than
the mighty,
And he who rules his spirit than he
who takes a city.

33 The lot is cast into the lap,
But its every decision *is* from the
LORD.

CHAPTER 17

Better *is* a dry morsel with quietness,
Than a house full of feasting[a] *with*
strife.

2 A wise servant will rule over a son
who causes shame,
And will share an inheritance among
the brothers.

3 The refining pot *is* for silver and the
furnace for gold,
But the LORD tests the hearts.

4 An evildoer gives heed to false lips;
A liar listens eagerly to a spiteful
tongue.

5 He who mocks the poor reproaches
his Maker;

17:1 [a]Or *sacrificial meals*

16:24 We can make such a difference in the lives of others by offering a simple word of encouragement.

16:25 This way **seems right** to fallen man whose mind is alienated from God.

16:33 lot is cast: Even the apparently random is under the Lord's control.

17:3 A holy, ethical God purifies a person's heart just as a refiner purifies **silver** and **gold**.

He who is glad at calamity will not
go unpunished.

6 Children's children *are* the crown of
old men,
And the glory of children *is* their
father.

7 Excellent speech is not becoming to a
fool,
Much less lying lips to a prince.

8 A present *is* a precious stone in the
eyes of its possessor;
Wherever he turns, he prospers.

9 He who covers a transgression seeks
love,
But he who repeats a matter separates
friends.

10 Rebuke is more effective for a wise
man
Than a hundred blows on a fool.

11 An evil *man* seeks only rebellion;
Therefore a cruel messenger will be
sent against him.

12 Let a man meet a bear robbed of her
cubs,
Rather than a fool in his folly.

13 Whoever rewards evil for good,
Evil will not depart from his house.

14 The beginning of strife *is like* releasing
water;
Therefore stop contention before a
quarrel starts.

15 He who justifies the wicked, and he
who condemns the just,
Both of them alike *are* an abomination
to the LORD.

16 Why *is there* in the hand of a fool the
purchase price of wisdom,
Since *he has* no heart *for it?*

17 A friend loves at all times,
And a brother is born for adversity.

18 A man devoid of understanding
shakes hands in a pledge,
And becomes surety for his friend.

19 He who loves transgression loves
strife,
And he who exalts his gate seeks
destruction.

20 He who has a deceitful heart finds no
good,
And he who has a perverse tongue
falls into evil.

21 He who begets a scoffer *does so* to his
sorrow,
And the father of a fool has no joy.

22 A merry heart does good, *like*
medicine,[a]
But a broken spirit dries the bones.

17:22 [a]Or *makes medicine even better*

17:8 A present: In the ancient Near East giving someone a gift to encourage them to do the right thing was commended.

17:9 covers: Forgives and forgets. Forgiveness is an act worthy of praise. It imitates God (see 10:12).

17:13 The wise do not return **evil for good**. The NT teaches us to go beyond this, even to return good for evil (Rom. 12:17, 21).

17:16 Wisdom cannot be bought; you must internalize it.

17:17 Our true **friend** and **brother** becomes known when trouble comes.

17:20 deceitful heart: The prophet Jeremiah warned that the human heart was morally depraved (see Jer. 17:9).

23 A wicked *man* accepts a bribe behind
the back[a]
To pervert the ways of justice.

24 Wisdom *is* in the sight of him who
has understanding,
But the eyes of a fool *are* on the ends
of the earth.

25 A foolish son *is* a grief to his father,
And bitterness to her who bore him.

17:23 [a]Literally *from the bosom*

26 Also, to punish the righteous *is* not
good,
Nor to strike princes for *their*
uprightness.

27 He who has knowledge spares his
words,
And a man of understanding is of a
calm spirit.

28 Even a fool is counted wise when he
holds his peace;
When he shuts his lips, *he is considered*
perceptive.

LAUGH A LITTLE

Barbara Johnson

In recent years, grants have been awarded to 125 hospitals, nursing homes, and other agencies to start humor programs for their patients. Specifically, here's what a little laughter can do for you:

Laughter helps you relax and unwind. Just try lifting anything heavy when you are enjoying a good belly laugh. You cannot do it because your large muscles are totally relaxed. The only ones working are some muscles in your face and your abdomen.

Laughter strengthens the immune system. Research shows that when you have a really good laugh, the body produces more immunoglobulin A, the body's warrior against upper respiratory infections.

Laughter improves your circulation by increasing the heart rate and boosting the oxygen supply to the brain. This is part of what helps you relax and calm down.

Laughter is a way to live an enriched life instead of just maintaining your existence, getting through each day somehow. Laughter is a key to finding pleasure, and when you have to endure mental and emotional pain, you need all the pleasure you can get. I am not talking about being "lovers of pleasure rather than lovers of God" (2 Tim. 3:4), or "enjoy[ing] the passing pleasures of sin" (Heb. 11:25). Those verses describe the kind of hedonism that leaves God out, but there are unlimited legitimate pleasures you can enjoy by letting God in. For example: enjoying a tasty meal, listening to favorite music, watching the embers of a fire, marveling at the leaves turning color in the fall, and *seeing the humor that is all around us.*

All of these are pleasure-moments God wants us to enjoy, and we can do so if we learn to fine-tune the pleasure channels of our lives to His frequency. ✦

CHAPTER 18

A man who isolates himself seeks his
own desire;

He rages against all wise judgment.

2 A fool has no delight in
understanding,
But in expressing his own heart.

3 When the wicked comes, contempt
comes also;
And with dishonor *comes* reproach.

4 The words of a man's mouth *are* deep
waters;
The wellspring of wisdom *is* a
flowing brook.

5 *It is* not good to show partiality to the
wicked,
Or to overthrow the righteous in
judgment.

6 A fool's lips enter into contention,
And his mouth calls for blows.

7 A fool's mouth *is* his destruction,
And his lips *are* the snare of his soul.

8 The words of a talebearer *are* like
tasty trifles,[a]
And they go down into the inmost
body.

9 He who is slothful in his work
Is a brother to him who is a great
destroyer.

10 The name of the LORD *is* a strong
tower;
The righteous run to it and are safe.

11 The rich man's wealth *is* his strong
city,
And like a high wall in his own
esteem.

12 Before destruction the heart of a man
is haughty,
And before honor *is* humility.

13 He who answers a matter before he
hears *it*,
It *is* folly and shame to him.

14 The spirit of a man will sustain him
in sickness,
But who can bear a broken spirit?

15 The heart of the prudent acquires
knowledge,
And the ear of the wise seeks
knowledge.

16 A man's gift makes room for him,
And brings him before great men.

17 The first *one* to plead his cause *seems*
right,
Until his neighbor comes and
examines him.

18 Casting lots causes contentions to
cease,
And keeps the mighty apart.

19 A brother offended *is harder to win*
than a strong city,
And contentions *are* like the bars of a
castle.

20 A man's stomach shall be satisfied
from the fruit of his mouth;

18:8 [a]A Jewish tradition reads *wounds.*

18:1 isolates himself: One who always insists on his own way will break with his friends and companions.

18:2 More can be learned by listening than by talking.

18:13 before he hears it: Shows prejudice in his decision.

18:16 Gift in this context means a legitimate contribution. Thus, it contrasts with the bribe of 15:27 and Deut. 16:19.

18:17 Both sides of a story must be heard.

From the produce of his lips he shall
be filled.

21 Death and life *are* in the power of the
tongue,
And those who love it will eat its
fruit.

22 *He who* finds a wife finds a good
thing,
And obtains favor from the LORD.

23 The poor *man* uses entreaties,
But the rich answers roughly.

24 A man *who has* friends must himself
be friendly,[a]
But there is a friend *who* sticks closer
than a brother.

CHAPTER 19

Better *is* the poor who walks in his
integrity
Than *one who is* perverse in his lips,
and is a fool.

2 Also it is not good *for* a soul *to be*
without knowledge,
And he sins who hastens with *his*
feet.

3 The foolishness of a man twists his
way,
And his heart frets against the LORD.

4 Wealth makes many friends,
But the poor is separated from his
friend.

5 A false witness will not go unpun-
ished,
And *he who* speaks lies will not
escape.

6 Many entreat the favor of the nobility,
And every man *is* a friend to one who
gives gifts.

7 All the brothers of the poor hate him;
How much more do his friends go far
from him!
He may pursue *them with* words, *yet*
they abandon *him.*

8 He who gets wisdom loves his own
soul;
He who keeps understanding will
find good.

9 A false witness will not go unpun-
ished,
And *he who* speaks lies shall perish.

10 Luxury is not fitting for a fool,
Much less for a servant to rule over
princes.

11 The discretion of a man makes him
slow to anger,
And his glory *is* to overlook a
transgression.

12 The king's wrath *is* like the roaring of
a lion,
But his favor *is* like dew on the grass.

13 A foolish son *is* the ruin of his father,
And the contentions of a wife *are* a
continual dripping.

14 Houses and riches *are* an inheritance
from fathers,
But a prudent wife *is* from the LORD.

15 Laziness casts *one* into a deep sleep,
And an idle person will suffer
hunger.

18:24 [a]Following Greek manuscripts, Syriac, Targum, and Vulgate; Masoretic Text reads *may come to ruin.*

18:24 This verse instructs us about how to attain friends and points out that some friends are closer than family.
19:1 Poverty is preferable to moral corruption.
19:11 No attitude is more godly than to forgive or to **overlook** a wrong.

16 He who keeps the commandment
keeps his soul,
But he who is careless[a] of his ways
will die.

17 He who has pity on the poor lends to
the LORD,
And He will pay back what he has
given.

18 Chasten your son while there is hope,
And do not set your heart on his
destruction.[a]

19 *A man of* great wrath will suffer
punishment;
For if you rescue *him,* you will have
to do it again.

20 Listen to counsel and receive
instruction,
That you may be wise in your latter
days.

21 There are many plans in a man's
heart,
Nevertheless the LORD's counsel—
that will stand.

22 What is desired in a man is kindness,
And a poor man is better than a liar.

23 The fear of the LORD *leads* to life,
And *he who has it* will abide in
satisfaction;
He will not be visited with evil.

24 A lazy *man* buries his hand in the
bowl,[a]
And will not so much as bring it to
his mouth again.

25 Strike a scoffer, and the simple will
become wary;
Rebuke one who has understanding,
and he will discern knowledge.

26 He who mistreats *his* father *and*
chases away *his* mother
Is a son who causes shame and brings
reproach.

27 Cease listening to instruction, my son,
And you will stray from the words of
knowledge.

28 A disreputable witness scorns justice,
And the mouth of the wicked
devours iniquity.

29 Judgments are prepared for scoffers,
And beatings for the backs of fools.

CHAPTER 20

Wine *is* a mocker,
Strong drink *is* a brawler,
And whoever is led astray by it is not
wise.

2 The wrath[a] of a king *is* like the
roaring of a lion;
Whoever provokes him to anger sins
against his own life.

3 *It is* honorable for a man to stop
striving,
Since any fool can start a quarrel.

4 The lazy *man* will not plow because
of winter;
He will beg during harvest and *have*
nothing.

19:16 [a]Literally *despises,* figurative of recklessness or carelessness 19:18 [a]Literally *to put him to death;* a Jewish tradition reads *on his crying.* 19:24 [a]Septuagint and Syriac read *bosom;* Targum and Vulgate read *armpit.* 20:2 [a]Literally *fear* or *terror* which is produced by the king's wrath

19:18 To fail to discipline a child is to destroy him.
19:19 An unmastered temper is a source of unending grief.
19:21 Plans made without considering God's will lead only to disappointment.
20:3 Anyone can **start a quarrel**; to refuse to continue one takes courage and brings honor.

5 Counsel in the heart of man *is like* deep water,
But a man of understanding will draw it out.

6 Most men will proclaim each his own goodness,
But who can find a faithful man?

7 The righteous *man* walks in his integrity;
His children *are* blessed after him.

8 A king who sits on the throne of judgment
Scatters all evil with his eyes.

9 Who can say, "I have made my heart clean,
I am pure from my sin"?

10 Diverse weights *and* diverse measures,
They *are* both alike, an abomination to the LORD.

11 Even a child is known by his deeds,
Whether what he does *is* pure and right.

12 The hearing ear and the seeing eye,
The LORD has made them both.

13 Do not love sleep, lest you come to poverty;
Open your eyes, *and* you will be satisfied with bread.

14 "*It is* good for nothing,"[a] cries the buyer;
But when he has gone his way, then he boasts.

15 There is gold and a multitude of rubies,
But the lips of knowledge *are* a precious jewel.

16 Take the garment of one who is surety *for* a stranger,
And hold it as a pledge *when it* is for a seductress.

17 Bread gained by deceit *is* sweet to a man,
But afterward his mouth will be filled with gravel.

18 Plans are established by counsel;
By wise counsel wage war.

19 He who goes about *as* a talebearer reveals secrets;
Therefore do not associate with one who flatters with his lips.

20 Whoever curses his father or his mother,
His lamp will be put out in deep darkness.

21 An inheritance gained hastily at the beginning
Will not be blessed at the end.

22 Do not say, "I will recompense evil";
Wait for the LORD, and He will save you.

23 Diverse weights *are* an abomination to the LORD,
And dishonest scales *are* not good.

20:14 [a]Literally *evil, evil*

20:7 Remembering that our decisions and manner of living will affect our children and grandchildren—either for good or bad—should encourage us to make wise and godly choices.

20:9 While this is impossible for us to do for ourselves, God wants to do it for us.

20:15 gold . . . rubies: knowledge is another sort of treasure.

20:19 Flattery and gossip often accompany each other. One who is quick to tell "juicy" gossip *to* us will as surely gossip to others *about* us. Do not use your ears to hear tales or your lips to tell them.

24 A man's steps *are* of the LORD;
How then can a man understand his own way?

25 *It is* a snare for a man to devote rashly *something as* holy,
And afterward to reconsider *his* vows.

26 A wise king sifts out the wicked,
And brings the threshing wheel over them.

27 The spirit of a man *is* the lamp of the LORD,
Searching all the inner depths of his heart.[a]

28 Mercy and truth preserve the king,
And by lovingkindness he upholds his throne.

29 The glory of young men *is* their strength,
And the splendor of old men *is* their gray head.

30 Blows that hurt cleanse away evil,
As *do* stripes the inner depths of the heart.[a]

CHAPTER 21

The king's heart *is* in the hand of the LORD,
Like the rivers of water; He turns it wherever He wishes.

2 Every way of a man *is* right in his own eyes,
But the LORD weighs the hearts.

3 To do righteousness and justice
Is more acceptable to the LORD than sacrifice.

4 A haughty look, a proud heart,
And the plowing[a] of the wicked *are* sin.

5 The plans of the diligent *lead* surely to plenty,
But *those of* everyone *who is* hasty, surely to poverty.

6 Getting treasures by a lying tongue
Is the fleeting fantasy of those who seek death.[a]

7 The violence of the wicked will destroy them,[a]
Because they refuse to do justice.

8 The way of a guilty man *is* perverse;[a]
But *as for* the pure, his work *is* right.

9 Better to dwell in a corner of a housetop,
Than in a house shared with a contentious woman.

10 The soul of the wicked desires evil;
His neighbor finds no favor in his eyes.

11 When the scoffer is punished, the simple is made wise;

20:27 [a]Literally *the rooms of the belly* 20:30 [a]Literally *the rooms of the belly* 21:4 [a]Or *lamp* 21:6 [a]Septuagint reads *Pursue vanity on the snares of death;* Vulgate reads *Is vain and foolish, and shall stumble on the snares of death;* Targum reads *They shall be destroyed, and they shall fall who seek death.* 21:7 [a]Literally *drag them away* 21:8 [a]Or *The way of a man is perverse and strange*

20:25 to devote rashly . . . to reconsider: The importance of considering carefully the vows one would make to the Lord is illustrated clearly in the experience of Jephthah (see Judg. 11:34, 35).

20:29 Both the energy of youth and the wisdom of experience are needed in the Lord's work. These two working together accomplish much for God.

21:11 The mind of the **scoffer** is closed; the mind of the **simple** is empty, but he is teachable. The mind of the **wise** is open and accepts instruction.

But when the wise is instructed, he
receives knowledge.

12 The righteous *God* wisely considers
the house of the wicked,
Overthrowing the wicked for *their*
wickedness.

13 Whoever shuts his ears to the cry of
the poor
Will also cry himself and not be heard.

14 A gift in secret pacifies anger,
And a bribe behind the back,[a] strong
wrath.

15 *It is* a joy for the just to do justice,
But destruction *will come* to the
workers of iniquity.

16 A man who wanders from the way of
understanding
Will rest in the assembly of the dead.

17 He who loves pleasure *will be* a poor
man;
He who loves wine and oil will not be
rich.

18 The wicked *shall be* a ransom for the
righteous,
And the unfaithful for the upright.

19 Better to dwell in the wilderness,
Than with a contentious and angry
woman.

20 *There is* desirable treasure,
And oil in the dwelling of the wise,
But a foolish man squanders it.

21 He who follows righteousness and
mercy
Finds life, righteousness and honor.

22 A wise *man* scales the city of the
mighty,
And brings down the trusted
stronghold.

23 Whoever guards his mouth and
tongue
Keeps his soul from troubles.

24 A proud *and* haughty *man*—"Scoffer"
is his name;
He acts with arrogant pride.

25 The desire of the lazy *man* kills him,
For his hands refuse to labor.
26 He covets greedily all day long,
But the righteous gives and does not
spare.

27 The sacrifice of the wicked *is* an
abomination;
How much more *when* he brings it
with wicked intent!

28 A false witness shall perish,
But the man who hears *him* will speak
endlessly.
29 A wicked man hardens his face,
But *as for* the upright, he establishes[a]
his way.

30 *There is* no wisdom or understanding
Or counsel against the LORD.

31 The horse *is* prepared for the day of
battle,
But deliverance *is* of the LORD.

CHAPTER 22

A *good* name is to be chosen rather than
great riches,
Loving favor rather than silver and
gold.

21:14 [a]Literally *in the bosom* 21:29 [a]Qere and Septuagint read *understands.*

21:30, 31 We may, and should, make preparations and plans (22:3). But we should not believe our efforts guarantee the outcome.

Q & A

Is it fair to set some rules of my own when I babysit for my grandchildren?

Gary Rosberg, Ed.D.

Setting some basic rules when you are caring for your grandchildren is entirely fair. But keep in mind that if they tend to behave without boundaries, you may all be in for an experience. These few tips will make a positive visit:

✦ Tell the parents that you are delighted to be with the kids while they are gone. Explain that you enjoy making memories with your grandkids, but you need some freedom to set ground rules of respect and responsibility.

✦ When you are with the kids, try to present the boundaries in an upbeat way, making as much of a game of it as possible. Remember Mary Poppins and the "spoonful of sugar" approach? It also works in the nineties. Lighten up the approach but set firm boundaries. The kids may bristle at first, but they will most likely respond if you stick to your rules. Boundaries are an expression of love, and we all need them. Some of those boundaries may even stick after your visit is over.

✦ Keep in mind the different ages of your grandchildren. What works for a three-year-old may not work with a teen.

Most of all, have a great visit and make memories that will last a lifetime!✦

2 The rich and the poor have this in
common,
The LORD *is* the maker of them all.

3 A prudent *man* foresees evil and hides
himself,
But the simple pass on and are
punished.

4 By humility *and* the fear of the LORD
Are riches and honor and life.

5 Thorns *and* snares *are* in the way of
the perverse;
He who guards his soul will be far
from them.

6 Train up a child in the way he should
go,
And when he is old he will not
depart from it.

7 The rich rules over the poor,
And the borrower *is* servant to the
lender.
8 He who sows iniquity will reap sorrow,
And the rod of his anger will fail.

9 He who has a generous eye will be
blessed,
For he gives of his bread to the poor.

✦ **22:2** Therefore, both **rich** and **poor** are equal before their **maker**. ✦

Make Time to Take Time

Irene M. Endicott

What does spending quality time with your grandchildren mean to you? Is it taking them to a special place? On a long trip? Is it spending quiet hours together, talking and listening? Do you have to plan this time, or can it happen spontaneously as only the Lord can plan it?

Whatever form it takes, make opportunities to teach the children something or to learn something together. The smallest or seemingly insignificant times with your grandchildren might be the most memorable to them as they grow older. ✦

10 Cast out the scoffer, and contention
will leave;
Yes, strife and reproach will cease.

11 He who loves purity of heart
And has grace on his lips,
The king *will be* his friend.

12 The eyes of the LORD preserve
knowledge,
But He overthrows the words of the
faithless.

13 The lazy *man* says, "*There is* a lion
outside!
I shall be slain in the streets!"

14 The mouth of an immoral woman *is* a
deep pit;
He who is abhorred by the LORD will
fall there.

15 Foolishness *is* bound up in the heart
of a child;
The rod of correction will drive it far
from him.

16 He who oppresses the poor to
increase his *riches*,
And he who gives to the rich, *will*
surely *come* to poverty.

Sayings of the Wise

17 Incline your ear and hear the words
of the wise,
And apply your heart to my
knowledge;
18 For *it is* a pleasant thing if you keep
them within you;
Let them all be fixed upon your lips,
19 So that your trust may be in the LORD;
I have instructed you today, even
you.
20 Have I not written to you excellent
things
Of counsels and knowledge,
21 That I may make you know the
certainty of the words of truth,
That you may answer words of truth
To those who send to you?

22 Do not rob the poor because he *is*
poor,
Nor oppress the afflicted at the gate;
23 For the LORD will plead their cause,
And plunder the soul of those who
plunder them.

24 Make no friendship with an angry
man,

22:10 The **scoffer**, by mocking God's principles of living, creates **strife** and **reproach** that will destroy many relationships. It is better to remove him from places of influence.

22:13 How easily we find excuses for not doing what we should.

22:16 The one who seeks to further his own cause by whatever means necessary is condemned ultimately to fail.

22:22, 23 The Lord is concerned for those who cannot defend themselves.

And with a furious man do not go,
25 Lest you learn his ways
And set a snare for your soul.

26 Do not be one of those who shakes
hands in a pledge,
One of those who is surety for debts;
27 If you have nothing *with which* to pay,
Why should he take away your bed
from under you?

28 Do not remove the ancient landmark
Which your fathers have set.

29 Do you see a man *who* excels in his
work?
He will stand before kings;
He will not stand before unknown
men.

CHAPTER 23

When you sit down to eat with a ruler,
Consider carefully what *is* before you;
2 And put a knife to your throat
If you *are* a man given to appetite.
3 Do not desire his delicacies,
For they *are* deceptive food.

4 Do not overwork to be rich;
Because of your own understanding,
cease!
5 Will you set your eyes on that which
is not?
For *riches* certainly make themselves
wings;
They fly away like an eagle *toward*
heaven.

6 Do not eat the bread of a miser,[a]
Nor desire his delicacies;
7 For as he thinks in his heart, so *is* he.
"Eat and drink!" he says to you,
But his heart is not with you.
8 The morsel you have eaten, you will
vomit up,
And waste your pleasant words.

9 Do not speak in the hearing of a fool,
For he will despise the wisdom of
your words.

10 Do not remove the ancient landmark,
Nor enter the fields of the fatherless;
11 For their Redeemer *is* mighty;
He will plead their cause against you.

12 Apply your heart to instruction,
And your ears to words of
knowledge.

13 Do not withhold correction from a
child,
For *if* you beat him with a rod, he will
not die.
14 You shall beat him with a rod,
And deliver his soul from hell.[a]

15 My son, if your heart is wise,
My heart will rejoice—indeed, I
myself;
16 Yes, my inmost being will rejoice
When your lips speak right things.

17 Do not let your heart envy sinners,
But *be zealous* for the fear of the LORD
all the day;
18 For surely there is a hereafter,
And your hope will not be cut off.

19 Hear, my son, and be wise;
And guide your heart in the way.

23:6 [a]Literally *one who has an evil eye* 23:14 [a]Or *Sheol*

22:28 Ancient landmark refers to a boundary marker. Land in Israel was to be held by each family in perpetuity as a trust from God.

23:10, 11 their Redeemer: In Israel the close relative of a financially troubled landowner could buy the land back, and thus redeem it. The Lord will be the close relative of the fatherless.

23:13, 14 Correction and wise physical punishment have an impact for good.

SUBDUING MIDDLE-AGE SPREAD

Dr. Sharon Sneed and Dr. David Sneed

Too much of a good thing can definitely create problems (Prov. 23:20, 21), and this certainly applies to our diets. As a rule of thumb, adults must consume fewer calories as they age to maintain their weight. One of the primary reasons for this is that after age twenty, the basal metabolic rate (i.e., the rate at which your body burns calories) decreases by 2 percent every decade. Thus, you would require caloric decreases at each subsequent decade of life, assuming you maintained your weight with an intake of two thousand calories per day at age twenty.

These changes may not seem very significant to you since the calorie difference between what you need at age twenty and at age forty accounts for no more than the calorie equivalent of one large slice of bread. However, this does seem to be one of the main reasons that body weight increases with age. So one would do well to keep in mind the nutrition axiom: It takes only one hundred calories per day of extra food eaten and stored as fat to gain ten pounds in one year. Based on this, it is easy to see how those extra pounds accumulate, even when you are eating the same amount of food (or less) than you always have.

Your personal health goal should include a plan for decreasing the fuel storage tanks (fat) and increasing the number of operating engines in your body (muscles). ✦

20 Do not mix with winebibbers,
Or with gluttonous eaters of meat;
21 For the drunkard and the glutton will
come to poverty,
And drowsiness will clothe *a man*
with rags.

22 Listen to your father who begot you,
And do not despise your mother
when she is old.

23 Buy the truth, and do not sell *it,*
Also wisdom and instruction and
understanding.

24 The father of the righteous will
greatly rejoice,
And he who begets a wise *child* will
delight in him.
25 Let your father and your mother be
glad,
And let her who bore you rejoice.

26 My son, give me your heart,
And let your eyes observe my ways.
27 For a harlot *is* a deep pit,
And a seductress *is* a narrow well.
28 She also lies in wait as *for* a victim,
And increases the unfaithful among
men.

29 Who has woe?
Who has sorrow?
Who has contentions?

23:29–35 A classic statement on the dangers of alcohol consumption. Look beyond short-term pleasure (v. 31) to long-term consequences.

Who has complaints?
Who has wounds without cause?
Who has redness of eyes?
30 Those who linger long at the wine,
Those who go in search of mixed wine.
31 Do not look on the wine when it is red,
When it sparkles in the cup,
When it swirls around smoothly;
32 At the last it bites like a serpent,
And stings like a viper.
33 Your eyes will see strange things,
And your heart will utter perverse things.
34 Yes, you will be like one who lies down in the midst of the sea,
Or like one who lies at the top of the mast, *saying:*
35 "They have struck me, *but* I was not hurt;
They have beaten me, but I did not feel *it*.
When shall I awake, that I may seek another *drink?"*

CHAPTER 24

Do not be envious of evil men,
Nor desire to be with them;
2 For their heart devises violence,
And their lips talk of troublemaking.

3 Through wisdom a house is built,
And by understanding it is established;
4 By knowledge the rooms are filled
With all precious and pleasant riches.

5 A wise man *is* strong,
Yes, a man of knowledge increases strength;
6 For by wise counsel you will wage your own war,
And in a multitude of counselors *there is* safety.

A Different Point of View

Jay Kesler

There is a myth afoot that says that moderns know things that people did not know before. Yes, they can probably program their calendar watches quicker than we can and do things with a VCR that we haven't yet attempted. But when it comes to the basic issues of right and wrong, good and bad, respect and disrespect, instant gratification and making do, cause and effect, reaping what you sow, the costliness of shortcuts, and the heartache connected with breaking God's moral law, no new rules have been invented. The grandparent's experience is still valid and needs to be shared.

As we open our hearts, our minds, and our homes, we find that grandchildren move toward us and welcome our participation and involvement in their lives. After all, we do live at the same moment in history in the same world—and it is our world as well as theirs. We have just been here longer. We have seen a little more and made our own mistakes, and we can share a perspective from a little higher vantage point—even if it is through trifocals! ✦

7 Wisdom *is* too lofty for a fool;
He does not open his mouth in the gate.

8 He who plots to do evil
Will be called a schemer.

24:1, 2 The corrupt character and speech of evil men are the real reasons why they should be shunned.

9 The devising of foolishness *is* sin,
And the scoffer *is* an abomination to men.

10 *If* you faint in the day of adversity,
Your strength *is* small.

11 Deliver *those who* are drawn toward death,
And hold back *those* stumbling to the slaughter.
12 If you say, "Surely we did not know this,"
Does not He who weighs the hearts consider *it?*
He who keeps your soul, does He *not* know *it?*
And will He *not* render to *each* man according to his deeds?

13 My son, eat honey because *it is* good,
And the honeycomb *which is* sweet to your taste;
14 So *shall* the knowledge of wisdom *be* to your soul;
If you have found *it,* there is a prospect,
And your hope will not be cut off.

15 Do not lie in wait, O wicked *man,* against the dwelling of the righteous;
Do not plunder his resting place;
16 For a righteous *man* may fall seven times
And rise again,
But the wicked shall fall by calamity.

17 Do not rejoice when your enemy falls,
And do not let your heart be glad when he stumbles;
18 Lest the LORD see *it,* and it displease Him,
And He turn away His wrath from him.

19 Do not fret because of evildoers,
Nor be envious of the wicked;
20 For there will be no prospect for the evil *man;*
The lamp of the wicked will be put out.

21 My son, fear the LORD and the king;
Do not associate with those given to change;
22 For their calamity will rise suddenly,
And who knows the ruin those two can bring?

Further Sayings of the Wise

23 These *things* also *belong* to the wise:

It is not good to show partiality in judgment.
24 He who says to the wicked, "You *are* righteous,"
Him the people will curse;
Nations will abhor him.
25 But those who rebuke *the wicked* will have delight,
And a good blessing will come upon them.

26 He who gives a right answer kisses the lips.

27 Prepare your outside work,
Make it fit for yourself in the field;
And afterward build your house.

24:9 Here, foolishness is not foolish behavior, but ignoring God and scoffing at godly living.

24:19–22 Two important life principles: Do not envy the wicked, and do not be a slave of fads (v. 21).

24:27 The work of the field should be given priority over comfort.

28 Do not be a witness against your
neighbor without cause,
For would you deceive[a] with your
lips?
29 Do not say, "I will do to him just as
he has done to me;
I will render to the man according to
his work."

30 I went by the field of the lazy *man*,
And by the vineyard of the man
devoid of understanding;
31 And there it was, all overgrown with
thorns;
Its surface was covered with nettles;
Its stone wall was broken down.
32 When I saw *it*, I considered *it* well;
I looked on *it and* received
instruction:
33 A little sleep, a little slumber,
A little folding of the hands to rest;
34 So shall your poverty come *like* a
prowler,
And your need like an armed man.

CHAPTER 25

Further Wise Sayings of Solomon

These also *are* proverbs of Solomon which the men of Hez·e·ki'ah king of Judah copied:

2 *It is* the glory of God to conceal a
matter,
But the glory of kings *is* to search out
a matter.

3 *As* the heavens for height and the
earth for depth,
So the heart of kings *is* unsearchable.

4 Take away the dross from silver,
And it will go to the silversmith *for*
jewelry.
5 Take away the wicked from before the
king,
And his throne will be established in
righteousness.

6 Do not exalt yourself in the presence
of the king,
And do not stand in the place of the
great;
7 For *it is* better that he say to you,
"Come up here,"
Than that you should be put lower in
the presence of the prince,
Whom your eyes have seen.
8 Do not go hastily to court;
For what will you do in the end,
When your neighbor has put you to
shame?
9 Debate your case with your neighbor,
And do not disclose the secret to
another;
10 Lest he who hears *it* expose your
shame,
And your reputation be ruined.

11 A word fitly spoken *is like* apples of
gold
In settings of silver.
12 *Like* an earring of gold and an
ornament of fine gold
Is a wise rebuker to an obedient ear.

13 Like the cold of snow in time of
harvest
Is a faithful messenger to those who
send him,
For he refreshes the soul of his
masters.

14 Whoever falsely boasts of giving
Is like clouds and wind without rain.

24:28 [a]Septuagint and Vulgate read *Do not deceive.*

24:28, 29 Vengeance was reserved for God.

25:1—29:27 Proverbs copied out at Hezekiah's instructions. The message of the proverbs would be of much interest to this king who led a great religious reform in Judah.

25:6, 7 In God's kingdom, and in human affairs, humility is the key to promotion before the Great King (see Luke 14:7–11).

15 By long forbearance a ruler is persuaded,
And a gentle tongue breaks a bone.

16 Have you found honey?
Eat only as much as you need,
Lest you be filled with it and vomit.

17 Seldom set foot in your neighbor's house,
Lest he become weary of you and hate you.

18 A man who bears false witness against his neighbor
Is like a club, a sword, and a sharp arrow.

19 Confidence in an unfaithful *man* in time of trouble
Is like a bad tooth and a foot out of joint.

20 *Like* one who takes away a garment in cold weather,
And like vinegar on soda,
Is one who sings songs to a heavy heart.

21 If your enemy is hungry, give him bread to eat;
And if he is thirsty, give him water to drink;
22 For *so* you will heap coals of fire on his head,
And the LORD will reward you.

23 The north wind brings forth rain,
And a backbiting tongue an angry countenance.

24 *It is* better to dwell in a corner of a housetop,
Than in a house shared with a contentious woman.

25 *As* cold water to a weary soul,
So *is* good news from a far country.

26 A righteous *man* who falters before the wicked
Is like a murky spring and a polluted well.

27 *It is* not good to eat much honey;
So to seek one's own glory *is not* glory.
28 Whoever *has* no rule over his own spirit
Is like a city broken down, without walls.

CHAPTER 26

As snow in summer and rain in harvest,
So honor is not fitting for a fool.

2 Like a flitting sparrow, like a flying swallow,
So a curse without cause shall not alight.

3 A whip for the horse,
A bridle for the donkey,
And a rod for the fool's back.
4 Do not answer a fool according to his folly,
Lest you also be like him.
5 Answer a fool according to his folly,
Lest he be wise in his own eyes.
6 He who sends a message by the hand of a fool
Cuts off *his own* feet *and* drinks violence.

25:16 Excess, even in that which is good, leads to disappointment.

25:28 Like a city . . . without walls, the person who cannot control himself is defenseless against outside forces.

26:3–12 All proverbs about fools. Here the **fool** seems to be a person who lacks tact; he is thoughtless or indifferent.

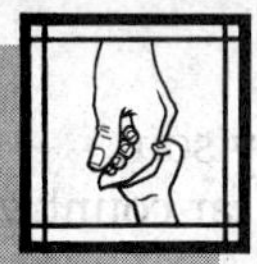

THE FREEDOM OF ACCOUNTABILITY

Dr. Richard Meier

"As iron sharpens iron, so a man sharpens the countenance of his friend" (Prov. 27:17). We all need to be accountable to someone. Surrounding yourself with people who only tell you what you want to hear is asking for trouble. We need trusted individuals to confront us when necessary and make suggestions as we make decisions.

Men need other men. They can encourage each other in ways women cannot. Having faced similar struggles, men can more easily identify with the issues and feelings involved. Sadly, though, many men feel that to be dependent on anyone, especially another man, is contrary to the macho image they're trying to project.

Men can find strength and freedom in confiding in someone who is committed to our growth and who has experienced the same struggles and demonstrated a spirit of perseverance. What a relief to know that we don't have to have all of life's answers. We can learn from each other! ✦

7 *Like* the legs of the lame that hang limp
Is a proverb in the mouth of fools.
8 Like one who binds a stone in a sling
Is he who gives honor to a fool.
9 *Like* a thorn *that* goes into the hand of a drunkard
Is a proverb in the mouth of fools.
10 The great *God* who formed everything
Gives the fool *his* hire and the transgressor *his* wages.[a]
11 As a dog returns to his own vomit,
So a fool repeats his folly.
12 Do you see a man wise in his own eyes?
There is more hope for a fool than for him.

13 The lazy *man* says, *"There is* a lion in the road!
A fierce lion *is* in the streets!"
14 *As* a door turns on its hinges,
So *does* the lazy *man* on his bed.
15 The lazy *man* buries his hand in the bowl;[a]
It wearies him to bring it back to his mouth.
16 The lazy *man is* wiser in his own eyes
Than seven men who can answer sensibly.

17 He who passes by *and* meddles in a quarrel not his own
Is like one who takes a dog by the ears.

18 Like a madman who throws firebrands, arrows, and death,
19 *Is* the man *who* deceives his neighbor,
And says, "I was only joking!"

20 Where *there is* no wood, the fire goes out;
And where *there is* no talebearer, strife ceases.
21 *As* charcoal *is* to burning coals, and wood to fire,
So *is* a contentious man to kindle strife.

26:10 [a]The Hebrew is difficult; ancient and modern translators differ greatly. 26:15 [a]Compare 19:24

22 The words of a talebearer *are* like
tasty trifles,
And they go down into the inmost
body.

23 Fervent lips with a wicked heart
Are like earthenware covered with
silver dross.
24 He who hates, disguises *it* with his
lips,
And lays up deceit within himself;
25 When he speaks kindly, do not
believe him,
For *there are* seven abominations in
his heart;
26 *Though his* hatred is covered by
deceit,
His wickedness will be revealed
before the assembly.

27 Whoever digs a pit will fall into it,
And he who rolls a stone will have it
roll back on him.
28 A lying tongue hates *those who are*
crushed by it,
And a flattering mouth works ruin.

CHAPTER 27

Do not boast about tomorrow,
For you do not know what a day may
bring forth.

2 Let another man praise you, and not
your own mouth;
A stranger, and not your own lips.

3 A stone *is* heavy and sand *is* weighty,
But a fool's wrath *is* heavier than both
of them.
4 Wrath *is* cruel and anger a torrent,
But who *is* able to stand before
jealousy?

5 Open rebuke *is* better
Than love carefully concealed.

6 Faithful *are* the wounds of a friend,
But the kisses of an enemy *are*
deceitful.
7 A satisfied soul loathes the
honeycomb,
But to a hungry soul every bitter
thing *is* sweet.

8 Like a bird that wanders from its
nest
Is a man who wanders from his
place.

9 Ointment and perfume delight the
heart,
And the sweetness of a man's friend
gives delight by hearty counsel.

10 Do not forsake your own friend or
your father's friend,
Nor go to your brother's house in the
day of your calamity;
Better *is* a neighbor nearby than a
brother far away.
11 My son, be wise, and make my heart
glad,
That I may answer him who
reproaches me.

12 A prudent *man* foresees evil *and*
hides himself;
The simple pass on *and* are punished.

26:25 seven abominations: The number seven symbolized completeness. His character and plans are thoroughly wicked.

27:7 hungry soul: A person who is desperate will accept even bitter things and think they are good.

27:10 The proverb does not forbid our turning to family members for support in times of need. Rather, it emphasizes the importance of developing close, dependable friendships.

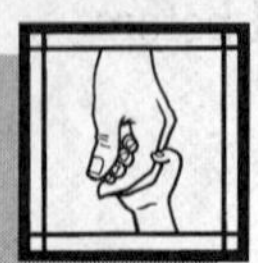

TENDING OUR FRIENDSHIPS

Sherwood Eliot Wirt

Friendship—what a priceless possession! Yet it is not a possession at all; rather, it is a gift of God, and it is to be received with thanksgiving. Some friends are naturally closer than others. Our Lord had many friends, but three—Peter, James, and John—seem to have had a special place in His heart. We also find we have more in common with certain friends than with others, but that does not mean that the others are not our friends! Sometimes after we have befriended one of the others in a crisis, we learn that he or she had more in common with us than we realized. Friendship demands time and effort, just as a plant requires watering. Without it, our lives can become like deserts. ✦

13 Take the garment of him who is
surety for a stranger,
And hold it in pledge *when* he is
surety for a seductress.

14 He who blesses his friend with a loud
voice, rising early in the morning,
It will be counted a curse to him.

15 A continual dripping on a very rainy
day
And a contentious woman are alike;
16 Whoever restrains her restrains the
wind,
And grasps oil with his right hand.

17 *As* iron sharpens iron,
So a man sharpens the countenance
of his friend.

18 Whoever keeps the fig tree will eat its
fruit;
So he who waits on his master will be
honored.

19 As in water face *reflects* face,
So a man's heart *reveals* the man.

20 Hell[a] and Destruction[b] are never full;
So the eyes of man are never satisfied.

21 The refining pot *is* for silver and the
furnace for gold,
And a man *is valued* by what others
say of him.

22 Though you grind a fool in a mortar
with a pestle along with crushed
grain,
Yet his foolishness will not depart
from him.

23 Be diligent to know the state of your
flocks,
And attend to your herds;
24 For riches *are* not forever,
Nor does a crown *endure* to all
generations.

27:20 [a]Or *Sheol* [b]Hebrew *Abaddon*

27:14 Wisdom has a good sense of timing.

27:15, 16 contentious woman: Five times Proverbs speaks of the difficulty of living with such a person (19:13; 21:9, 19; 25:24).

27:21 valued by what others say: A principle to be remembered and applied to our lives.

25 *When* the hay is removed, and the
tender grass shows itself,
And the herbs of the mountains are
gathered in,
26 The lambs *will provide* your clothing,
And the goats the price of a field;
27 *You shall have* enough goats' milk for
your food,
For the food of your household,
And the nourishment of your
maidservants.

CHAPTER 28

The wicked flee when no one pursues,
But the righteous are bold as a lion.

2 Because of the transgression of a land,
many *are* its princes;
But by a man of understanding *and*
knowledge
Right will be prolonged.

3 A poor man who oppresses the poor
Is like a driving rain which leaves no
food.

4 Those who forsake the law praise the
wicked,
But such as keep the law contend
with them.

5 Evil men do not understand justice,
But those who seek the LORD
understand all.

6 Better *is* the poor who walks in his
integrity
Than one perverse *in his* ways,
though he *be* rich.

7 Whoever keeps the law *is* a
discerning son,
But a companion of gluttons shames
his father.

8 One who increases his possessions by
usury and extortion
Gathers it for him who will pity the
poor.

9 One who turns away his ear from
hearing the law,
Even his prayer *is* an abomination.

10 Whoever causes the upright to go
astray in an evil way,
He himself will fall into his own pit;
But the blameless will inherit good.

11 The rich man *is* wise in his own eyes,
But the poor who has understanding
searches him out.

12 When the righteous rejoice, *there is*
great glory;
But when the wicked arise, men hide
themselves.

13 He who covers his sins will not
prosper,
But whoever confesses and forsakes
them will have mercy.

14 Happy *is* the man who is always
reverent,
But he who hardens his heart will fall
into calamity.

15 *Like* a roaring lion and a charging
bear
Is a wicked ruler over poor people.

28:1 The godly person can face life boldly; the wicked can only fear.

28:4, 5, 7 The law is used by God to help curb evil.

28:9 Refusing to do God's will, but expecting His approval.

28:13 He who covers (hides or denies) sin will not prosper. The best way to handle sin is to confess and forsake it.

28:14 always reverent: To have a proper sense of awe and worship for God, which results in an appreciation for God's truth and a desire to live by it.

16 A ruler who lacks understanding *is* a
great oppressor,
But he who hates covetousness will
prolong *his* days.
17 A man burdened with bloodshed will
flee into a pit;
Let no one help him.

18 Whoever walks blamelessly will be
saved,
But *he who is* perverse *in his* ways will
suddenly fall.

19 He who tills his land will have plenty
of bread,
But he who follows frivolity will have
poverty enough!

20 A faithful man will abound with
blessings,
But he who hastens to be rich will not
go unpunished.

21 To show partiality *is* not good,
Because for a piece of bread a man
will transgress.

22 A man with an evil eye hastens after
riches,
And does not consider that poverty
will come upon him.

23 He who rebukes a man will find more
favor afterward
Than he who flatters with the tongue.
24 Whoever robs his father or his
mother,
And says, "*It is* no transgression,"
The same *is* companion to a destroyer.

25 He who is of a proud heart stirs up
strife,
But he who trusts in the LORD will be
prospered.

Our job in life is not to be successful, but to be faithful. Many Christians would prefer to hear "What a great guy" from the crowd rather than "Well done, good and faithful servant" from the Master.
Billy Graham

26 He who trusts in his own heart is a
fool,
But whoever walks wisely will be
delivered.

27 He who gives to the poor will not
lack,
But he who hides his eyes will have
many curses.

28 When the wicked arise, men hide
themselves;
But when they perish, the righteous
increase.

CHAPTER 29

He who is often rebuked, *and* hardens
his neck,
Will suddenly be destroyed, and that
without remedy.

2 When the righteous are in authority,
the people rejoice;
But when a wicked *man* rules, the
people groan.

3 Whoever loves wisdom makes his
father rejoice,
But a companion of harlots wastes *his*
wealth.

4 The king establishes the land by
justice,

28:16 covetousness: The obsessive desire to possess is a critical defect whether in a ruler or in the people.
28:23 Rebuke sometimes shows more love for another than soothing words.
28:25, 26 Trust in self (pride) is a source of **strife**, hatred, and war.

But he who receives bribes
overthrows it.
5 A man who flatters his neighbor
Spreads a net for his feet.

6 By transgression an evil man is
snared,
But the righteous sings and rejoices.

7 The righteous considers the cause of
the poor,
But the wicked does not understand
such knowledge.
8 Scoffers set a city aflame,
But wise *men* turn away wrath.

9 *If* a wise man contends with a foolish
man,
Whether *the fool* rages or laughs, *there
is* no peace.

10 The bloodthirsty hate the blameless,
But the upright seek his well-being.[a]

11 A fool vents all his feelings,[a]
But a wise *man* holds them back.

12 If a ruler pays attention to lies,
All his servants *become* wicked.

13 The poor *man* and the oppressor have
this in common:
The LORD gives light to the eyes of
both.

14 The king who judges the poor with
truth,
His throne will be established forever.

Q & A What does the Bible say about giving to the poor?

Charles Ross

You probably remember from Sunday school the verse, "It is more blessed to give than to receive" (Acts 20:35). In the biblical sense, giving is recognized as an admission that a higher authority governs the universe. Giving to support the work of the church and those who are less fortunate acknowledges that divine influence.

In addition, when we give, we receive a blessing equal to or greater than the gift. Stewardship over finances is a constant theme in the Bible, and a closer examination will reveal principles that you can apply to your financial life today. ✦

15 The rod and rebuke give wisdom,
But a child left *to himself* brings shame
to his mother.

16 When the wicked are multiplied,
transgression increases;
But the righteous will see their fall.

17 Correct your son, and he will give
you rest;
Yes, he will give delight to your soul.

29:10 [a]Literally *soul* 29:11 [a]Literally *spirit*

29:15, 17 Children need wise discipline in order to form good character. Let no parent forget it.

18 Where *there is* no revelation,[a] the
people cast off restraint;
But happy *is* he who keeps the law.
19 A servant will not be corrected by
mere words;
For though he understands, he will
not respond.

20 Do you see a man hasty in his words?
There is more hope for a fool than for
him.

21 He who pampers his servant from
childhood
Will have him as a son in the end.

22 An angry man stirs up strife,
And a furious man abounds in
transgression.

23 A man's pride will bring him low,
But the humble in spirit will retain
honor.

24 Whoever is a partner with a thief
hates his own life;
He swears to tell the truth,[a] but
reveals nothing.

25 The fear of man brings a snare,
But whoever trusts in the LORD shall
be safe.

26 Many seek the ruler's favor,
But justice for man *comes* from the
LORD.

27 An unjust man *is* an abomination to
the righteous,
And *he who is* upright in the way *is* an
abomination to the wicked.

CHAPTER 30

The Wisdom of Agur

The words of Ā'gur the son of Jā'keh, *his*
utterance. This man declared to Ith'i·el—to
Ith'i·el and Ū'cal:

2 Surely I *am* more stupid than *any*
man,
And do not have the understanding
of a man.
3 I neither learned wisdom
Nor have knowledge of the Holy
One.

4 Who has ascended into heaven, or
descended?
Who has gathered the wind in His
fists?
Who has bound the waters in a
garment?
Who has established all the ends of
the earth?
What *is* His name, and what *is* His
Son's name,
If you know?

5 Every word of God *is* pure;
He *is* a shield to those who put their
trust in Him.
6 Do not add to His words,
Lest He rebuke you, and you be
found a liar.

7 Two *things* I request of You
(Deprive me not before I die):

29:18 [a]Or *prophetic vision* 29:24 [a]Literally *hears the adjuration*

29:18 The law shows us God's unchanging principles; a **revelation** or prophetic vision shows us how those principles should work out in life. Both the law and the vision are revealed.

29:20 hasty in . . . words: The problem is words spoken without careful thought.

29:21 The pampered one will not be content to remain a servant.

30:2, 3 A humble, but rhetorical denial of wisdom by Agur sets the scene for his display of wisdom, a fairly common practice in Wisdom Literature of the ancient world.

30:7–9 neither poverty nor riches: An amazing understanding of material blessings—that he be allotted his fair portion, but no more. More may lead to pride; less may lead to theft.

8 Remove falsehood and lies far from
me;
Give me neither poverty nor riches—
Feed me with the food allotted to me;
9 Lest I be full and deny *You*,
And say, "Who *is* the LORD?"
Or lest I be poor and steal,
And profane the name of my God.

10 Do not malign a servant to his master,
Lest he curse you, and you be found
guilty.

11 *There is* a generation *that* curses its
father,
And does not bless its mother.
12 *There is* a generation *that is* pure in its
own eyes,
Yet is not washed from its filthiness.
13 *There is* a generation— oh, how lofty
are their eyes!
And their eyelids are lifted up.
14 *There is* a generation whose teeth *are
like* swords,
And whose fangs *are like* knives,
To devour the poor from off the earth,
And the needy from *among* men.

15 The leech has two daughters—
Give *and* Give!

There are three *things that* are never
satisfied,
Four never say, "Enough!":
16 The grave,[a]
The barren womb,
The earth *that* is not satisfied with
water—
And the fire never says, "Enough!"

17 The eye *that* mocks *his* father,
And scorns obedience to *his* mother,
The ravens of the valley will pick it
out,
And the young eagles will eat it.

18 There are three *things which* are too
wonderful for me,
Yes, four *which* I do not understand:
19 The way of an eagle in the air,
The way of a serpent on a rock,
The way of a ship in the midst of the
sea,
And the way of a man with a virgin.

20 This *is* the way of an adulterous
woman:
She eats and wipes her mouth,
And says, "I have done no
wickedness."

21 For three *things* the earth is
perturbed,
Yes, for four it cannot bear up:
22 For a servant when he reigns,
A fool when he is filled with food,
23 A hateful *woman* when she is married,
And a maidservant who succeeds her
mistress.

24 There are four *things which* are little
on the earth,
But they *are* exceedingly wise:
25 The ants *are* a people not strong,
Yet they prepare their food in the
summer;
26 The rock badgers[a] are a feeble folk,
Yet they make their homes in the
crags;

30:16 [a]Or *Sheol* 30:26 [a]Or *hyraxes*

30:11–14 Generation here represents a class of people with certain corrupt characteristics. There are such people, now as well as then, who display four evils: Disrespectful to parents (v. 11), self-righteous (v. 12), proud (v. 13), ruthless (v. 14).

30:15, 16 The **leech** which is never satisfied symbolizes the grave, the **barren womb**, dry earth, and fire.

30:18, 19 The writer marvels at natural activities which have a beauty and a grace beyond rational explanation. **three . . . Yes, four**: A Semitic expression for completeness.

30:24–28 The stress is on the mysterious wisdom and orderliness found in the Creator's work.

27 The locusts have no king,
Yet they all advance in ranks;
28 The spider[a] skillfully grasps with its hands,
And it is in kings' palaces.
29 There are three *things which* are majestic in pace,
Yes, four *which* are stately in walk:
30 A lion, *which is* mighty among beasts
And does not turn away from any;
31 A greyhound,[a]
A male goat also,
And a king *whose* troops *are* with him.[a]

32 If you have been foolish in exalting yourself,
Or if you have devised evil, *put your* hand on *your* mouth.
33 For *as* the churning of milk produces butter,
And wringing the nose produces blood,
So the forcing of wrath produces strife.

CHAPTER 31

The Words of King Lemuel's Mother

The words of King Lem'ū·el, the utterance which his mother taught him:

2 What, my son?
And what, son of my womb?
And what, son of my vows?
3 Do not give your strength to women,
Nor your ways to that which destroys kings.

4 *It is* not for kings, O Lem'ū·el,
It is not for kings to drink wine,
Nor for princes intoxicating drink;
5 Lest they drink and forget the law,
And pervert the justice of all the afflicted.
6 Give strong drink to him who is perishing,
And wine to those who are bitter of heart.
7 Let him drink and forget his poverty,
And remember his misery no more.

8 Open your mouth for the speechless,
In the cause of all *who are* appointed to die.[a]
9 Open your mouth, judge righteously,
And plead the cause of the poor and needy.

The Virtuous Wife

10 Who[a] can find a virtuous[b] wife?
For her worth *is* far above rubies.
11 The heart of her husband safely trusts her;
So he will have no lack of gain.
12 She does him good and not evil
All the days of her life.
13 She seeks wool and flax,
And willingly works with her hands.
14 She is like the merchant ships,
She brings her food from afar.
15 She also rises while it is yet night,
And provides food for her household,
And a portion for her maidservants.
16 She considers a field and buys it;
From her profits she plants a vineyard.
17 She girds herself with strength,
And strengthens her arms.

30:28 [a]Or *lizard* 30:31 [a]Exact identity unknown [b]A Jewish tradition reads *a king against whom there is no uprising.* 31:8 [a]Literally *sons of passing away* 31:10 [a]Verses 10 through 31 are an alphabetic acrostic in Hebrew (compare Psalm 119). [b]Literally *a wife of valor,* in the sense of all forms of excellence

31:10–31 It is significant that the Book of Proverbs ends with a description of a virtuous wife.

We see here that such a woman is trustworthy (vv. 11, 12), industrious (vv. 13–15), resourceful (vv. 16–19), compassionate (v. 20), prudent (vv. 21–24), and well-spoken (v. 26). All of these are an expression of her obedience to God (v. 30).

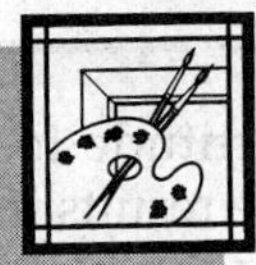

The Virtuous Woman

The woman described in Proverbs 31:10–31 embraces life wholeheartedly. Among other things, she is trustworthy (v. 11), an early riser (v. 15), willing to do hard work (v. 17), compassionate (v. 20), wise and kind (v. 26), and godly (v. 30). She successfully meets the physical, spiritual, and mental health needs of herself and her family.

Many women find this passage intimidating, yet the virtues for which the Proverbs woman is praised are within the reach of any woman who dedicates herself to the task of making her house a home, no matter what her current circumstances.

Societal norms have changed since Old Testament times, but human nature has not. With so many women working outside the home, more importance than ever can be placed on wives giving their husbands reason to trust them. Trustworthiness goes beyond major things like relationships with other men to such responsibilities as respecting marital privacy in conversations with friends and abiding by the family budget.

Although an early morning schedule works for some women, rising at 5:30 A.M. does not automatically constitute virtue. In fact, many people find maintaining a positive Christian attitude difficult when they don't get their full eight hours of sleep. A woman seeking to be virtuous takes care of her own health, but her many obligations do not leave time for idleness or laziness. Each must create a balanced, personalized schedule that enables her to operate effectively.

Similarly, weaving clothes by hand and shipping in food from afar are no longer prerequisites for the godly woman, but she can still fulfill her responsibilities simply by helping to clothe and feed her family with love and care.

Verse 18 reinforces the need for women to take pride in their work, whether for their family or for an employer. The godly woman recognizes the impact of inferior workmanship on both herself and those around her, and she strives to do her very best at each task to which she lays her hands or mind.

The Virtuous Woman provides material assistance to the needy, just as many do today through donations to their churches and favorite charities. However, she takes compassion one step further. Verse 20 indicates that she does not shrink from face-to-face contact with the poor and needy. If she were living today would she satisfy her conscience with a weekly tithe, or would she offer her services at a local soup kitchen or shelter?

Although her hectic schedule does not allow for leisurely gossip, the Virtuous Woman is a wise and kind counselor (vv. 26, 27). She does not have time to nit-pick her husband and children about minor problems,

but she watches over them and makes time for their spiritual and emotional needs (v. 27).

And in all this, she does not neglect her relationship with God (v. 30). In fact, her faithfulness toward her family reflects her reverence for the Lord. Her balanced attitude toward various aspects of life results in a loving family, children who bless her, a husband who praises her, and self-fulfillment that could never be achieved solely by pursuing her own desires. ✦

18 She perceives that her merchandise *is* good,
And her lamp does not go out by night.
19 She stretches out her hands to the distaff,
And her hand holds the spindle.
20 She extends her hand to the poor,
Yes, she reaches out her hands to the needy.
21 She is not afraid of snow for her household,
For all her household *is* clothed with scarlet.
22 She makes tapestry for herself;
Her clothing *is* fine linen and purple.
23 Her husband is known in the gates,
When he sits among the elders of the land.
24 She makes linen garments and sells *them,*
And supplies sashes for the merchants.
25 Strength and honor *are* her clothing;
She shall rejoice in time to come.
26 She opens her mouth with wisdom,
And on her tongue *is* the law of kindness.
27 She watches over the ways of her household,
And does not eat the bread of idleness.
28 Her children rise up and call her blessed;
Her husband *also,* and he praises her:
29 "Many daughters have done well,
But you excel them all."
30 Charm *is* deceitful and beauty *is* passing,
But a woman *who* fears the LORD, she shall be praised.
31 Give her of the fruit of her hands,
And let her own works praise her in the gates.

31:30, 31 As the book opened with a call to the wise man (1:5) to fear the Lord (1:7), it closes with this beautiful description of the wise woman who also **fears the LORD** (v. 30).

✦Ecclesiastes✦

Most scholars agree that Ecclesiastes was written by King Solomon during the same time as the other poetic books (970 to 931 B.C.). Ecclesiastes details the search for purpose and satisfaction in life. The word "vanity" appears thirty-seven times as the author explores the futility of trying to be happy apart from God. When man sees life from God's perspective, however, he discovers the secret to a meaningful life: "Fear God and keep His commandments, for this is man's all" (12:13).

The revelations in Ecclesiastes are important to Christians living in a materialistic society. Solomon discovered that the key to a fulfilling life at any age is a personal relationship with God. Hard work, many possessions, and great accomplishments bring little reward; we will find true happiness only in serving God and following His will. ✦

CHAPTER 1

The Vanity of Life

The words of the Preacher, the son of David, king in Jerusalem.

2 "Vanity[a] of vanities," says the Preacher;
"Vanity of vanities, all *is* vanity."

3 What profit has a man from all his labor
In which he toils under the sun?
4 *One* generation passes away, and *another* generation comes;
But the earth abides forever.
5 The sun also rises, and the sun goes down,
And hastens to the place where it arose.
6 The wind goes toward the south,
And turns around to the north;
The wind whirls about continually,
And comes again on its circuit.
7 All the rivers run into the sea,
Yet the sea *is* not full;
To the place from which the rivers come,
There they return again.
8 All things *are* full of labor;
Man cannot express *it*.
The eye is not satisfied with seeing,
Nor the ear filled with hearing.

9 That which has been *is* what will be,
That which *is* done is what will be done,

1:2 [a]Or *Absurdity, Frustration, Futility,* Nonsense; and so throughout this book

1:2 The thesis of the Preacher is that life lived without regard for God is of no value. It is indeed vanity (emptiness). The phrase **vanity of vanities** is the Hebrew way of describing the most vain thing imaginable.

1:3—3:22 Human attainments and accomplishments are worthless, thus they are referred to as **labor** in these verses.

And *there is* nothing new under the
sun.
10 Is there anything of which it may be
said,
"See, this *is* new"?
It has already been in ancient times
before us.
11 *There is* no remembrance of former
things,
Nor will there be any remembrance of
things that are to come
By *those* who will come after.

The Grief of Wisdom

[12]I, the Preacher, was king over Israel in
Jerusalem. [13]And I set my heart to seek and
search out by wisdom concerning all that
is done under heaven; this burdensome
task God has given to the sons of man, by
which they may be exercised. [14]I have seen
all the works that are done under the sun;
and indeed, all *is* vanity and grasping for
the wind.

15 *What is* crooked cannot be made
straight,
And what is lacking cannot be
numbered.

[16]I communed with my heart, saying,
"Look, I have attained greatness, and have
gained more wisdom than all who were
before me in Jerusalem. My heart has understood great wisdom and knowledge."
[17]And I set my heart to know wisdom and
to know madness and folly. I perceived
that this also is grasping for the wind.

18 For in much wisdom *is* much grief,
And he who increases knowledge
increases sorrow.

CHAPTER 2

The Vanity of Pleasure

I said in my heart, "Come now, I will
test you with mirth; therefore enjoy pleasure"; but surely, this also *was* vanity. [2]I
said of laughter—"Madness!"; and of
mirth, "What does it accomplish?" [3]I
searched in my heart *how* to gratify my
flesh with wine, while guiding my heart
with wisdom, and how to lay hold on folly,
till I might see what *was* good for the sons
of men to do under heaven all the days of
their lives.

[4]I made my works great, I built myself
houses, and planted myself vineyards. [5]I
made myself gardens and orchards, and
I planted all *kinds* of fruit trees in them. [6]I
made myself water pools from which to
water the growing trees of the grove. [7]I acquired male and female servants, and had
servants born in my house. Yes, I had
greater possessions of herds and flocks
than all who were in Jerusalem before me.
[8]I also gathered for myself silver and gold
and the special treasures of kings and of
the provinces. I acquired male and female
singers, the delights of the sons of men, *and*
musical instruments[a] of all kinds.

[9]So I became great and excelled more
than all who were before me in Jerusalem.
Also my wisdom remained with me.

10 Whatever my eyes desired I did not
keep from them.
I did not withhold my heart from any
pleasure,
For my heart rejoiced in all my labor;
And this was my reward from all my
labor.
11 Then I looked on all the works that
my hands had done

2:8 [a]Exact meaning unknown

1:12—2:23 The accomplishments of a great king: **wisdom** (1:13–18); **pleasure** (2:1–3, 10); great works (2:4–9). But because all of these bring no satisfaction, he is plunged into despair (2:17–23).

1:15 What is crooked: He despairs of straightening out the world's problems.

And on the labor in which I had
toiled;
And indeed all *was* vanity and
grasping for the wind.
There was no profit under the sun.

The End of the Wise and the Fool

12 Then I turned myself to consider
wisdom and madness and folly;
For what *can* the man *do* who
succeeds the king?—
Only what he has already done.
13 Then I saw that wisdom excels folly
As light excels darkness.
14 The wise man's eyes *are* in his head,
But the fool walks in darkness.
Yet I myself perceived
That the same event happens to them
all.

15 So I said in my heart,
"As it happens to the fool,
It also happens to me,
And why was I then more wise?"
Then I said in my heart,
"This also *is* vanity."
16 For *there is* no more remembrance of
the wise than of the fool forever,
Since all that now *is* will be forgotten
in the days to come.
And how does a wise *man* die?
As the fool!

17Therefore I hated life because the work
that was done under the sun *was* distress-
ing to me, for all *is* vanity and grasping for
the wind.
18Then I hated all my labor in which I
had toiled under the sun, because I must
leave it to the man who will come after me.
19And who knows whether he will be wise
or a fool? Yet he will rule over all my labor
in which I toiled and in which I have
shown myself wise under the sun. This
also *is* vanity. 20Therefore I turned my heart
and despaired of all the labor in which I
had toiled under the sun. 21For there is a
man whose labor *is* with wisdom, knowl-
edge, and skill; yet he must leave his heri-
tage to a man who has not labored for it.
This also *is* vanity and a great evil. 22For
what has man for all his labor, and for the
striving of his heart with which he has
toiled under the sun? 23For all his days *are*
sorrowful, and his work burdensome;
even in the night his heart takes no rest.
This also is vanity.
24Nothing *is* better for a man *than* that he
should eat and drink, and *that* his soul
should enjoy good in his labor. This also, I
saw, was from the hand of God. 25For who
can eat, or who can have enjoyment, more
than I?[a] 26For *God* gives wisdom and
knowledge and joy to a man who *is* good
in His sight; but to the sinner He gives the
work of gathering and collecting, that he
may give to *him who is* good before God.
This also *is* vanity and grasping for the
wind.

2:25 [a]Following Masoretic Text, Targum, and Vulgate; some Hebrew manuscripts, Septuagint, and Syriac read *without Him.*

I pray, God, that you will give wisdom and knowledge and joy to my mate who is good in Your sight.

adapted from Ecclesiastes 2:26

2:14 eyes . . . in his head: The knowledge, discretion, and understanding from God which keep the wise man from the ways of darkness.

2:17–23 One of the bitterest thoughts for a person of great material accomplishments: Some fool will get this after I die.

2:24–26 This is one of several conclusions that assert the best way to approach life. It calls for us to (1) enjoy the simple things of life; food, drink, work, (2) recognize God as the source of all benefits, and (3) recognize that the good things from His hand are designed for our enjoyment.

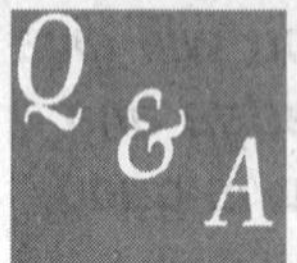

What should I do about a "living will"?

Gary Rosberg, Ed. D.

One of the hardest things for everyone, both maturing parents and adult children, is discussing anticipated loss. Your family may be premature in talking about losing you. On the other hand, they may just be trying to discern what your desires would be, should you become unable to make decisions due to a medical crisis. Ironically, your "perfect health" makes this the perfect time to decide how to deal with potential problems.

Living wills allow both parents and their children to clarify the needs of everyone while they are able to discuss these issues honestly. A living will can direct the family to remove all life-support systems if a patient is dying, and it speaks for the patient if he or she cannot express his or her views.

Discussing a living will with your family is very important, so try these suggestions to make it easier. First, after you think it over, initiate the discussion. That way, you can set the pace and timing of the discussion. Second, admit that it is scary to talk about death because you want to enjoy your current health, and explain that anticipating separation from your family is painful.

Be honest with family members about your feelings so you can enjoy your time together. ✦

CHAPTER 3

Everything Has Its Time

To everything *there is* a season,
A time for every purpose under heaven:

2 A time to be born,
And a time to die;
A time to plant,
And a time to pluck *what is* planted;
3 A time to kill,
And a time to heal;
A time to break down,
And a time to build up;
4 A time to weep,
And a time to laugh;
A time to mourn,
And a time to dance;
5 A time to cast away stones,
And a time to gather stones;
A time to embrace,
And a time to refrain from embracing;
6 A time to gain,
And a time to lose;
A time to keep,
And a time to throw away;
7 A time to tear,
And a time to sew;
A time to keep silence,
And a time to speak;
8 A time to love,
And a time to hate;
A time of war,
And a time of peace.

3:1–22 God has established the patterns of life, and all our **labors** (v. 9) cannot change them (vv. 11, 14). Therefore we should stop straining against these limits and find the real joy (vv. 12, 13, 22) and beauty (v. 11) which exist in the daily round.

The God-Given Task

9What profit has the worker from that in which he labors? 10I have seen the God-given task with which the sons of men are to be occupied. 11He has made everything beautiful in its time. Also He has put eternity in their hearts, except that no one can find out the work that God does from beginning to end.

12I know that nothing *is* better for them than to rejoice, and to do good in their lives, 13and also that every man should eat and drink and enjoy the good of all his labor—it *is* the gift of God.

14 I know that whatever God does,
It shall be forever.
Nothing can be added to it,
And nothing taken from it.
God does *it*, that men should fear
before Him.
15 That which is has already been,
And what is to be has already been;
And God requires an account of what
is past.

Injustice Seems to Prevail

16Moreover I saw under the sun:

In the place of judgment,
Wickedness *was* there;
And *in* the place of righteousness,
Iniquity *was* there.

17I said in my heart,

"God shall judge the righteous and the
wicked,
For *there is* a time there for every purpose and for every work."

18I said in my heart, "Concerning the condition of the sons of men, God tests them, that they may see that they themselves are *like* animals." 19For what happens to the sons of men also happens to animals; one thing befalls them: as one dies, so dies the other. Surely, they all have one breath; man has no advantage over animals, for all *is* vanity. 20All go to one place: all are from the dust, and all return to dust. 21Who knows the spirit of the sons of men, which goes upward, and the spirit of the animal, which goes down to the earth?[a] 22So I perceived that nothing *is* better than that a man should rejoice in his own works, for that *is* his heritage. For who can bring him to see what will happen after him?

CHAPTER 4

Then I returned and considered all the oppression that is done under the sun:

And look! The tears of the oppressed,
But they have no comforter—
On the side of their oppressors *there is*
power,
But they have no comforter.
2 Therefore I praised the dead who
were already dead,
More than the living who are still
alive.
3 Yet, better than both *is he* who has
never existed,
Who has not seen the evil work that
is done under the sun.

3:21 [a]Septuagint, Syriac, Targum, and Vulgate read *Who knows whether the spirit . . . goes upward, and whether . . . goes downward to the earth?*

3:11 Eternity may refer to the desire people have to discover and understand God. The Preacher does not question whether there is a God, or that His ways, though often strange, are right.

3:14–22 God's decisions for His world stand secure and complete. The world is constructed to lead men to fear (acknowledge and respect) Him. The fear of God is the basis for a correct approach to life.

The Vanity of Selfish Toil

4 Again, I saw that for all toil and every skillful work a man is envied by his neighbor. This also *is* vanity and grasping for the wind.

5 The fool folds his hands
And consumes his own flesh.
6 Better a handful *with* quietness
Than both hands full, *together with* toil
and grasping for the wind.

7 Then I returned, and I saw vanity under the sun:

8 There is one alone, without companion:
He has neither son nor brother.
Yet *there is* no end to all his labors,
Nor is his eye satisfied with riches.
But he never asks,
"For whom do I toil and deprive
myself of good?"
This also *is* vanity and a grave
misfortune.

The Value of a Friend

9 Two *are* better than one,
Because they have a good reward for
their labor.
10 For if they fall, one will lift up his
companion.
But woe to him *who is* alone when he
falls,
For *he has* no one to help him up.
11 Again, if two lie down together, they
will keep warm;
But how can one be warm *alone?*
12 Though one may be overpowered by
another, two can withstand him.
And a threefold cord is not quickly
broken.

Popularity Passes Away

13 Better a poor and wise youth
Than an old and foolish king who
will be admonished no more.
14 For he comes out of prison to be king,
Although he was born poor in his
kingdom.
15 I saw all the living who walk under
the sun;
They were with the second youth
who stands in his place.
16 *There was* no end of all the people
over whom he was made king;
Yet those who come afterward will
not rejoice in him.
Surely this also *is* vanity and grasping
for the wind.

CHAPTER 5

Fear God, Keep Your Vows

Walk prudently when you go to the house of God; and draw near to hear rather than to give the sacrifice of fools, for they do not know that they do evil.

2 Do not be rash with your mouth,
And let not your heart utter anything
hastily before God.
For God *is* in heaven, and you on
earth;
Therefore let your words be few.
3 For a dream comes through much
activity,
And a fool's voice *is known* by *his*
many words.

4 When you make a vow to God, do
not delay to pay it;
For *He has* no pleasure in fools.
Pay what you have vowed—
5 Better not to vow than to vow and
not pay.

4:4–8 The foolishness of incessant labor beyond that necessary to satisfy daily needs.

4:13–16 Even the glory of having become king, after being poor and obscure, finally ends in being replaced by a second youth (v. 15) and forgotten. It is vain to grasp even for power.

5:4, 5 Better not to vow: It is always dangerous to make a vow since we cannot be absolutely sure we can fulfill it.

> Of the Seven Deadly Sins, anger is possibly the most fun. To lick your wounds, to smack your lips over grievances long past, to roll over your tongue the prospect of bitter confrontations still to come, to savor the last toothsome morsel both of the pain you are given and the pain you are giving back—in many ways it is a feast fit for a king. The chief drawback is that what you are wolfing down is yourself. The skeleton at the feast is you.
>
> Frederick Buechner

6Do not let your mouth cause your flesh to
sin, nor say before the messenger *of God*
that it *was* an error. Why should God be an-
gry at your excuse[a] and destroy the work
of your hands? 7For in the multitude of
dreams and many words *there is* also van-
ity. But fear God.

The Vanity of Gain and Honor

8If you see the oppression of the poor, and the violent perversion of justice and righteousness in a province, do not marvel at the matter; for high official watches over high official, and higher officials are over them.

9Moreover the profit of the land is for all; *even* the king is served from the field.

10 He who loves silver will not be
satisfied with silver;
Nor he who loves abundance, with
increase.
This also *is* vanity.

11 When goods increase,
They increase who eat them;
So what profit have the owners
Except to see *them* with their eyes?

12 The sleep of a laboring man *is* sweet,
Whether he eats little or much;
But the abundance of the rich will not
permit him to sleep.

13 There is a severe evil *which* I have
seen under the sun:
Riches kept for their owner to his
hurt.
14 But those riches perish through
misfortune;
When he begets a son, *there is* nothing
in his hand.
15 As he came from his mother's womb,
naked shall he return,
To go as he came;
And he shall take nothing from his
labor
Which he may carry away in his
hand.

16 And this also *is* a severe evil—
Just exactly as he came, so shall he
go.
And what profit has he who has
labored for the wind?
17 All his days he also eats in darkness,
And *he has* much sorrow and sickness
and anger.

18Here is what I have seen: *It is* good and
fitting *for one* to eat and drink, and to enjoy
the good of all his labor in which he toils
under the sun all the days of his life which
God gives him; for it *is* his heritage. 19As
for every man to whom God has given
riches and wealth, and given him power to
eat of it, to receive his heritage and rejoice
in his labor—this *is* the gift of God. 20For he
will not dwell unduly on the days of his
life, because God keeps *him* busy with the
joy of his heart.

5:6 [a]Literally *voice*

5:10 loves silver: Setting your sights on money will never bring satisfaction (1 Tim. 6:9, 10).

5:12 Money, valued too highly, corrodes life with worry. We will leave all our material wealth behind when we die.

SET YOUR OWN PACE

Pam Smith

Exercise is a vital part of healthful living. It can speed up slowed metabolism, which helps control weight and cholesterol; improve muscle tone; help reduce blood pressure; and lift simple depression. Exercise is also considered God's best tranquilizer: just thirty minutes a day releases tension.

You don't have to take up the latest exercise craze to become fit. Instead, forge your own path at your own pace in your own direction. The frequency, intensity, and duration of your workouts will influence the health benefits you reap. Choose a type and time of exercise that you can maintain.

Frequency: Four to six days a week.

Intensity: A level where you feel slightly out of breath, without gasping.

Time: Thirty to sixty minutes, when you feel good and can build a schedule.

Type: Whatever type of aerobic exercise you enjoy and can do regularly. ✦

CHAPTER 6

There is an evil which I have seen under
the sun, and it *is* common among men: [2]A
man to whom God has given riches and
wealth and honor, so that he lacks nothing
for himself of all he desires; yet God does
not give him power to eat of it, but a foreigner consumes it. This *is* vanity, and it *is*
an evil affliction.

[3]If a man begets a hundred *children* and
lives many years, so that the days of his
years are many, but his soul is not satisfied
with goodness, or indeed he has no burial,
I say *that* a stillborn child *is* better than
he— [4]for it comes in vanity and departs in
darkness, and its name is covered with
darkness. [5]Though it has not seen the sun
or known *anything,* this has more rest than
that man, [6]even if he lives a thousand years
twice—but has not seen goodness. Do not
all go to one place?

7 All the labor of man *is* for his mouth,
And yet the soul is not satisfied.
8 For what more has the wise *man* than
the fool?
What does the poor man have,
Who knows *how* to walk before the
living?
9 Better *is* the sight of the eyes than the
wandering of desire.
This also *is* vanity and grasping for
the wind.

10 Whatever one is, he has been named
already,
For it is known that he *is* man;

6:2–4 foreigner consumes it: Possibly the results of war. **no burial**: To come to the end of one's life without proper respect and honor was regarded with horror all across the ancient Near East.

6:7 A profound insight. What can satisfy our souls? (see Matt. 6:33).

And he cannot contend with Him
who is mightier than he.
11 Since there are many things that
increase vanity,
How *is* man the better?

12For who knows what *is* good for man
in life, all the days of his vain life which
he passes like a shadow? Who can tell a
man what will happen after him under the
sun?

CHAPTER 7

The Value of Practical Wisdom

A good name *is* better than precious
ointment,
And the day of death than the day of
one's birth;
2 Better to go to the house of
mourning
Than to go to the house of feasting,
For that *is* the end of all men;
And the living will take *it* to heart.
3 Sorrow *is* better than laughter,
For by a sad countenance the heart is
made better.
4 The heart of the wise *is* in the house
of mourning,
But the heart of fools *is* in the house
of mirth.

5 *It is* better to hear the rebuke of the
wise
Than for a man to hear the song of
fools.
6 For like the crackling of thorns under
a pot,
So *is* the laughter of the fool.
This also is vanity.
7 Surely oppression destroys a wise
man's reason,
And a bribe debases the heart.
8 The end of a thing *is* better than its
beginning;
The patient in spirit *is* better than the
proud in spirit.
9 Do not hasten in your spirit to be
angry,
For anger rests in the bosom of
fools.
10 Do not say,
"Why were the former days better
than these?"
For you do not inquire wisely
concerning this.

11 Wisdom *is* good with an inheritance,
And profitable to those who see the
sun.
12 For wisdom *is* a defense *as* money *is* a
defense,
But the excellence of knowledge *is*
that wisdom gives life to those who
have it.

13 Consider the work of God;
For who can make straight what He
has made crooked?
14 In the day of prosperity be joyful,
But in the day of adversity consider:
Surely God has appointed the one as
well as the other,
So that man can find out nothing *that*
will come after him.

15I have seen everything in my days of
vanity:

There is a just *man* who perishes in
his righteousness,
And there is a wicked *man* who
prolongs *life* in his wickedness.

16 Do not be overly righteous,
Nor be overly wise:
Why should you destroy yourself?

7:6 thorns under a pot: Thorns burn hot and make a crackling sound but the fire does not last long.

7:10 It is wise to put the past behind us and to concentrate on the future. The "good old days" were not really better.

17 Do not be overly wicked,
Nor be foolish:
Why should you die before your time?
18 *It is* good that you grasp this,
And also not remove your hand from the other;
For he who fears God will escape them all.

19 Wisdom strengthens the wise
More than ten rulers of the city.

20 For *there is* not a just man on earth who does good
And does not sin.

21 Also do not take to heart everything people say,
Lest you hear your servant cursing you.
22 For many times, also, your own heart has known
That even you have cursed others.

23 All this I have proved by wisdom.
I said, "I will be wise";
But it *was* far from me.
24 As for that which is far off and exceedingly deep,
Who can find it out?
25 I applied my heart to know,
To search and seek out wisdom and the reason *of things*,
To know the wickedness of folly,
Even of foolishness *and* madness.
26 And I find more bitter than death
The woman whose heart *is* snares and nets,
Whose hands *are* fetters.
He who pleases God shall escape from her,
But the sinner shall be trapped by her.

27 "Here is what I have found," says the Preacher,
"*Adding* one thing to the other to find out the reason,
28 Which my soul still seeks but I cannot find:
One man among a thousand I have found,
But a woman among all these I have not found.
29 Truly, this only I have found:
That God made man upright,
But they have sought out many schemes."

CHAPTER 8

Who *is* like a wise *man?*
And who knows the interpretation of a thing?
A man's wisdom makes his face shine,
And the sternness of his face is changed.

Obey Authorities for God's Sake

2I *say*, "Keep the king's commandment
for the sake of your oath to God. 3Do not be
hasty to go from his presence. Do not take
your stand for an evil thing, for he does
whatever pleases him."

4 Where the word of a king *is, there is* power;
And who may say to him, "What are you doing?"
5 He who keeps his command will experience nothing harmful;
And a wise man's heart discerns both time and judgment,
6 Because for every matter there is a time and judgment,

7:23–29 The limits of wisdom. It can show us how to conduct ourselves; it cannot show us what is **exceedingly deep** (v. 24), the explanations of existence.
8:1–9 Adjusting to the inevitable appears to be the theme of these verses.
8:2–6 It is wise to obey authority.

Though the misery of man increases
greatly.
7 For he does not know what will
happen;
So who can tell him when it will
occur?
8 No one has power over the spirit to
retain the spirit,
And no one has power in the day of
death.
There is no release from that war,
And wickedness will not deliver
those who are given to it.

9All this I have seen, and applied my
heart to every work that is done under the
sun: *There is* a time in which one man rules
over another to his own hurt.

Death Comes to All

10Then I saw the wicked buried, who
had come and gone from the place of holi-
ness, and they were forgotten[a] in the city
where they had so done. This also *is* vanity.
11Because the sentence against an evil work
is not executed speedily, therefore the
heart of the sons of men is fully set in them
to do evil. 12Though a sinner does evil a
hundred *times,* and his *days* are prolonged,
yet I surely know that it will be well with
those who fear God, who fear before Him.
13But it will not be well with the wicked;
nor will he prolong *his* days, *which are* as a
shadow, because he does not fear before
God.

14There is a vanity which occurs on
earth, that there are just *men* to whom it
happens according to the work of the
wicked; again, there are wicked *men* to
whom it happens according to the work of
the righteous. I said that this also *is* vanity.
15So I commended enjoyment, because a
man has nothing better under the sun than
to eat, drink, and be merry; for this will re-
main with him in his labor *all* the days of
his life which God gives him under the
sun.

16When I applied my heart to know wis-
dom and to see the business that is done on
earth, even though one sees no sleep day
or night, 17then I saw all the work of God,
that a man cannot find out the work that is
done under the sun. For though a man
labors to discover *it,* yet he will not find *it;*
moreover, though a wise *man* attempts to
know *it,* he will not be able to find *it.*

CHAPTER 9

For I considered all this in my heart, so
that I could declare it all: that the righteous
and the wise and their works *are* in the
hand of God. People know neither love nor
hatred *by* anything *they see* before them.
2All things *come* alike to all:

One event *happens* to the righteous
and the wicked;
To the good,[a] the clean, and the
unclean;
To him who sacrifices and him who
does not sacrifice.
As is the good, so *is* the sinner;
He who takes an oath as *he* who fears
an oath.

3This *is* an evil in all that is done under the
sun: that one thing *happens* to all. Truly the
hearts of the sons of men are full of evil;
madness *is* in their hearts while they live,
and after that *they go* to the dead. 4But for
him who is joined to all the living there is
hope, for a living dog is better than a dead
lion.

5 For the living know that they will die;
But the dead know nothing,

8:10 [a]Some Hebrew manuscripts, Septuagint, and Vulgate read *praised.* 9:2 [a]Septuagint, Syriac, and Vulgate read *good and bad.*

8:16, 17 The writer concludes again that the meaning of life and its labor cannot be fully grasped.

9:5, 6 the dead know nothing: Certainly true from a secular perspective. It remained for Jesus to bring "life and immortality to light through the gospel" (2 Tim. 1:10).

Give the Gift of Grace

Bill Gaither

Part of a good, happy, fulfilling life is the ability to make and maintain friendships and keep good relationships. I appreciate so much my friends who honestly understand that, because there are no perfect people, neither are there any perfect friends. I want to be a good friend, but I don't want anyone to expect me to be perfect. That's not friendship; that's pressure.

"On a given day, any of us can be bad guys and disappoint one another."

We human beings can be wonderful; we can also be jerks. Once we understand that, we are free to develop friendships that can last years. Too many of us were raised in the church in a manner that makes us tend to categorize people. There are the believers and the unbelievers, the Christians and the non-Christians. But also within the church are the good people and the bad, the trustworthy and the not. Some people are considered *in* because they have stayed married and raised a family. Other people are treated as outcasts because even though they are Christians, they are divorced or were once caught in some "big" sin.

I believe in and advocate holy living, but something bad happens if we draw too fine a line and demand perfection from people. What we have done is to disparage the forgiveness and restoration God Himself offers. When we become so black and white in this area, our list of good guys shrinks. Someone disappoints you, shows some selfishness or anger or pride, and he's out. The problem is, on a given day, any of us can be bad guys and disappoint one another. ✦

And they have no more reward,
For the memory of them is forgotten.
6 Also their love, their hatred, and their
envy have now perished;
Nevermore will they have a share
In anything done under the sun.

7 Go, eat your bread with joy,
And drink your wine with a merry
heart;
For God has already accepted your
works.
8 Let your garments always be white,
And let your head lack no oil.

9 Live joyfully with the wife whom you
love all the days of your vain life which He
has given you under the sun, all your days
of vanity; for that *is* your portion in life,
and in the labor which you perform under
the sun.

9:7–10 God the Creator has made a world in which joy is to be found in the daily rounds of life. Our unanswered questions should not prevent us from finding that joy.

[10]Whatever your hand finds to do, do *it*
with your might; for *there is* no work or de-
vice or knowledge or wisdom in the grave
where you are going.
[11]I returned and saw under the sun
that—

The race *is* not to the swift,
Nor the battle to the strong,
Nor bread to the wise,
Nor riches to men of understanding,
Nor favor to men of skill;
But time and chance happen to them
all.
12 For man also does not know his time:
Like fish taken in a cruel net,
Like birds caught in a snare,
So the sons of men *are* snared in an
evil time,
When it falls suddenly upon them.

Wisdom Superior to Folly

[13]This wisdom I have also seen under
the sun, and it *seemed* great to me: [14]*There
was* a little city with few men in it; and a
great king came against it, besieged it, and
built great snares[a] around it. [15]Now there
was found in it a poor wise man, and he by
his wisdom delivered the city. Yet no one
remembered that same poor man.
[16]Then I said:

"Wisdom *is* better than strength.
Nevertheless the poor man's wisdom
is despised,
And his words are not heard.
17 Words of the wise, *spoken* quietly,
should be heard
Rather than the shout of a ruler of
fools.
18 Wisdom *is* better than weapons of
war;
But one sinner destroys much good."

CHAPTER 10

Dead flies putrefy[a] the perfumer's
ointment,
And cause it to give off a foul odor;
So does a little folly to one respected
for wisdom *and* honor.
2 A wise man's heart *is* at his right
hand,
But a fool's heart at his left.
3 Even when a fool walks along the
way,
He lacks wisdom,
And he shows everyone *that* he *is* a
fool.
4 If the spirit of the ruler rises against
you,
Do not leave your post;
For conciliation pacifies great
offenses.

5 There is an evil I have seen under the
sun,
As an error proceeding from the
ruler:
6 Folly is set in great dignity,
While the rich sit in a lowly place.
7 I have seen servants on horses,
While princes walk on the ground
like servants.

9:14 [a]Septuagint, Syriac, and Vulgate read *bulwarks.*
10:1 [a]Targum and Vulgate omit *putrefy.*

9:13–18 Wisdom is better than strength (v. 16) because wise strategy saved the city. Nevertheless, we should not be surprised if wisdom does not always receive its due reward here **under the sun** (v. 13).

9:18 one sinner destroys much good: We must not think that good will automatically triumph.

10:1 One moral failure can destroy the influence of a lifetime of wisdom and honor.

10:2 At his right hand means to be in the place of honor (see Ps. 110:1). It was also a place of power (see Ps. 20:6) and a place of righteousness (see Is. 41:10). **Heart** in this context, implies the place decisions are made.

8 He who digs a pit will fall into it,
And whoever breaks through a wall
will be bitten by a serpent.
9 He who quarries stones may be hurt
by them,
And he who splits wood may be
endangered by it.
10 If the ax is dull,
And one does not sharpen the edge,
Then he must use more strength;
But wisdom brings success.

11 A serpent may bite when *it is* not
charmed;
The babbler is no different.
12 The words of a wise man's mouth *are*
gracious,
But the lips of a fool shall swallow
him up;
13 The words of his mouth begin with
foolishness,
And the end of his talk *is* raving
madness.
14 A fool also multiplies words.
No man knows what is to be;
Who can tell him what will be after
him?
15 The labor of fools wearies them,
For they do not even know how to go
to the city!

16 Woe to you, O land, when your king
is a child,
And your princes feast in the
morning!
17 Blessed *are* you, O land, when your
king *is* the son of nobles,
And your princes feast at the proper
time—
For strength and not for
drunkenness!
18 Because of laziness the building
decays,
And through idleness of hands the
house leaks.
19 A feast is made for laughter,
And wine makes merry;
But money answers everything.

20 Do not curse the king, even in your
thought;
Do not curse the rich, even in your
bedroom;
For a bird of the air may carry your
voice,
And a bird in flight may tell the
matter.

CHAPTER 11

The Value of Diligence

Cast your bread upon the waters,
For you will find it after many days.
2 Give a serving to seven, and also to
eight,
For you do not know what evil will
be on the earth.

3 If the clouds are full of rain,
They empty *themselves* upon the
earth;
And if a tree falls to the south or the
north,
In the place where the tree falls, there
it shall lie.
4 He who observes the wind will not
sow,
And he who regards the clouds will
not reap.

5 As you do not know what *is* the way
of the wind,[a]

11:5 [a]Or *spirit*

10:8–10 These verses teach the need to think ahead about consequences and be prepared.

10:11–14 One mark of a fool is endless babbling.

10:16 feast in the morning: Early drinking and carousing is considered a sure sign of debauchery, and who could prosper with rulers like that?

11:4–6 Be diligent in spite of obstacles, even if it "looks like rain."

From Generation to Generation

Una McManus

Healthy, strong families share their stories. When children know their roots, they develop a strong sense of identity. Because they know where they came from, they know better who they are today. Keeping secrets is a sign of an unhealthy family.

Your autobiography is a gift of love to your family. It is a priceless, irreplaceable offering that will help your stories last longer than your lifetime. Recording memories entails some work, but the Bible says, "Cast your bread upon the waters, for you will find it after many days" (Eccl. 11:1). This labor of love will blossom, maybe in your lifetime, maybe beyond. But God will honor your gift, and your descendants will cherish it. ✦

Or how the bones *grow* in the womb
of her who is with child,
So you do not know the works of
God who makes everything.
6 In the morning sow your seed,
And in the evening do not withhold
your hand;
For you do not know which will
prosper,
Either this or that,
Or whether both alike *will be* good.

7 Truly the light is sweet,
And *it is* pleasant for the eyes to
behold the sun;
8 But if a man lives many years
And rejoices in them all,
Yet let him remember the days of
darkness,
For they will be many.
All that is coming *is* vanity.

Seek God in Early Life

9 Rejoice, O young man, in your youth,
And let your heart cheer you in the
days of your youth;
Walk in the ways of your heart,
And in the sight of your eyes;
But know that for all these
God will bring you into judgment.
10 Therefore remove sorrow from your
heart,
And put away evil from your flesh,
For childhood and youth *are* vanity.

CHAPTER 12

Remember now your Creator in the
days of your youth,
Before the difficult days come,
And the years draw near when you
say,
"I have no pleasure in them":
2 While the sun and the light,
The moon and the stars,
Are not darkened,

11:7, 8 Love life, but hold it with a light hand, so you will not be devastated if things do not turn out as you wished.

12:1–7 This beautiful poem describing old age develops from the ideas in 11:8. We cannot be sure what the figures are meant to convey, but an interpretation is given for some of them. Together they depict the physical weaknesses of the different members of an aging body (12:1). **difficult days**: Of old age. **keepers of the house**: The arms. **strong men**: The legs. **grinders**: The teeth. **those that look**: The eyes. **doors**: The ears. **almond tree blossoms**: White hair. Even a **grasshopper** is too heavy to carry. **For man goes to his eternal home**: dies.

A Balanced Life

John Gilmore

Elevation can sometimes disorient us and throw us off balance, especially as we get older. The Bible even mentions a fear of heights (Eccl. 12:5).

Yet keeping our balance is essential to enjoying life. That principle is true physically, emotionally, and spiritually. We should try to maintain balance, but that does not mean we should stay forever in one place. What can become out of balance in our lives? These situations may lead to spiritual falls and injuries:

"The Bible challenges and counteracts our natural spiritual imbalances."

- ✦ too much emphasis on mystical encounters with God and too little emphasis on the biblical text;
- ✦ too much emphasis on a favorite doctrine and too little on other equally important Bible teachings;
- ✦ too much stress on Christian social action and too little involvement with Christian evangelism;
- ✦ too much occupation with our needs and too little interest in the needs of others;
- ✦ too much time spent watching television and not enough time spent reading the Word of God;
- ✦ too much dwelling on our hurts, aches, pains, and troubles and too little time rejoicing in the goodness and mercy of God.

The Bible challenges and counteracts our natural spiritual imbalances. Our sinful selves destabilize us, but Scripture rights us. ✦

And the clouds do not return after the
rain;
3 In the day when the keepers of the
house tremble,
And the strong men bow down;
When the grinders cease because they
are few,
And those that look through the
windows grow dim;
4 When the doors are shut in the
streets,
And the sound of grinding is low;
When one rises up at the sound of a
bird,
And all the daughters of music are
brought low.
5 Also they are afraid of height,
And of terrors in the way;
When the almond tree blossoms,
The grasshopper is a burden,
And desire fails.
For man goes to his eternal home,
And the mourners go about the
streets.

6 *Remember your Creator* before the
silver cord is loosed,[a]
Or the golden bowl is broken,
Or the pitcher shattered at the
fountain,
Or the wheel broken at the well.
7 Then the dust will return to the earth
as it was,
And the spirit will return to God who
gave it.

8 "Vanity of vanities," says the Preacher,
"All *is* vanity."

The Whole Duty of Man

9 And moreover, because the Preacher
was wise, he still taught the people knowl-
edge; yes, he pondered and sought out
and set in order many proverbs. 10 The
Preacher sought to find acceptable words;
and *what was* written *was* upright—words
of truth. 11 The words of the wise are like
goads, and the words of scholars[a] are like
well-driven nails, given by one Shepherd.
12 And further, my son, be admonished by
these. Of making many books *there is* no
end, and much study *is* wearisome to the
flesh.
13 Let us hear the conclusion of the whole
matter:

Fear God and keep His
commandments,
For this is man's all.
14 For God will bring every work into
judgment,
Including every secret thing,
Whether good or evil.

12:6 [a]Following Qere and Targum; Kethib reads *removed;* Septuagint and Vulgate read *broken.*
12:11 [a]Literally *masters of the assemblies*

Be a Cheerleader!

As we age, perhaps what we need more than anything is the grace of God to live each chapter of our lives without regret, to discover the charm and blessing each phase of life offers to us. We cannot relive the past. We live in the present. But the past serves as a prologue, preparing us for the calling of the present.

We have had our shot at parenting. We tried to do the best we could, and our children are the product of our work. Even our failures provide experience that makes us wiser, more patient, and more forgiving. Now, as grandparents, we become a support to our children as they attempt the confusing and demanding task of parenting.

I believe one of the major roles of the grandparent is to be cheerleader—that is, to encourage our children in their own parenting. We have already given advice in the form of our own theory of parenting and our own conduct over their entire lifetimes. Now is the time for encouragement and support.✦

12:6, 7 These verses refer to the death of the elderly person. The **silver cord**, the **golden bowl**, the **pitcher**, and the **wheel** are all metaphors of life, now broken in death. **spirit will return to God**: A hint at an eternal perspective.

12:13 The fear of God is shown by keeping His commandments. **this is man's all**: Fulfillment in God's teachings that lead to a loving relationship with Him.

12:14 Knowing God will judge motivates us to obey His commandments now. **every secret thing**: Even the inner motives of our hearts and the thoughts of our minds are known to God. We seek to be like Him here, and trust in His promise of life eternal there.

✦Song of Solomon✦

Written by King Solomon around 965 B.C., the Song of Solomon is the last of the poetic books. Solomon had seven hundred wives and three hundred concubines. Most of them were probably political arrangements. However, this book seems to be written about only one of his wives—the Shulamite woman, a lowly vineyard keeper—probably early in his reign, before he wandered from the Lord. Allegorically, this book symbolizes God's love for the nation of Israel and Christ's love for His bride, the church, and we can take heart in knowing that Christ's love for His bride, the church, exceeds even the greatest expression of human love.

Historically, the Song details the romance and marriage between Solomon and the Shulamite woman, and it glorifies the natural love between a man and a woman. With poetic language and metaphors, it exemplifies physical attraction within the sanctity of marriage as part of God's purpose, and it portrays the natural stages of love in marriage—falling in love, uniting in love, struggling through life, and growing from experience. It also points to the initiator of love between men and women—God Himself—and shows that the deep love shared between two people results from God working in their lives. ✦

CHAPTER 1

The song of songs, which *is* Solomon's.

The Banquet

THE SHULAMITE[a]

2 Let him kiss me with the kisses of his mouth—
For your[b] love *is* better than wine.
3 Because of the fragrance of your good ointments,
Your name *is* ointment poured forth;
Therefore the virgins love you.
4 Draw me away!

THE DAUGHTERS OF JERUSALEM

We will run after you.[a]

THE SHULAMITE

The king has brought me into his chambers.

1:2 [a]A Palestinian young woman (compare 6:13). The speaker and audience are identified according to the number, gender, and person of the Hebrew words. Occasionally the identity is not certain. [b]Masculine singular, that is, the Beloved 1:4 [a]Masculine

1:2—2:7 The "Shulamite" maiden (see 6:13) praises her beloved and he responds.

THE DAUGHTERS OF JERUSALEM

We will be glad and rejoice in you.[b]
We will remember your[c] love more
than wine.

THE SHULAMITE

Rightly do they love you.[d]

5 I *am* dark, but lovely,
O daughters of Jerusalem,
Like the tents of Kē′dar,
Like the curtains of Solomon.
6 Do not look upon me, because I *am*
dark,
Because the sun has tanned me.
My mother's sons were angry with
me;
They made me the keeper of the
vineyards,
But my own vineyard I have not kept.

(TO HER BELOVED)

7 Tell me, O you whom I love,
Where you feed *your flock,*
Where you make *it* rest at noon.
For why should I be as one who veils
herself[a]
By the flocks of your companions?

THE BELOVED

8 If you do not know, O fairest among
women,
Follow in the footsteps of the flock,
And feed your little goats
Beside the shepherds' tents.

singular, that is, the Beloved [b]Feminine singular, that is, the Shulamite [c]Masculine singular, that is, the Beloved [d]Masculine singular, that is, the Beloved
1:7 [a]Septuagint, Syriac, and Vulgate read *wanders.*
1:11 [a]Feminine singular, that is, the Shulamite

9 I have compared you, my love,
To my filly among Pharaoh's chariots.
10 Your cheeks are lovely with
ornaments,
Your neck with chains *of gold.*

THE DAUGHTERS OF JERUSALEM

11 We will make you[a] ornaments of gold
With studs of silver.

THE SHULAMITE

12 While the king *is* at his table,
My spikenard sends forth its
fragrance.
13 A bundle of myrrh *is* my beloved to
me,
That lies all night between my
breasts.
14 My beloved *is* to me a cluster of
henna *blooms*
In the vineyards of En Ge′di.

THE BELOVED

15 Behold, you *are* fair, my love!
Behold, you *are* fair!
You *have* dove's eyes.

THE SHULAMITE

16 Behold, you *are* handsome, my
beloved!
Yes, pleasant!
Also our bed *is* green.
17 The beams of our houses *are* cedar,
And our rafters of fir.

CHAPTER 2

I *am* the rose of Sharon,
And the lily of the valleys.

1:5 dark: Suntanned, unlike a woman from the city.

1:6 This is a key verse for understanding the progression of the love poems (1:1—2:7; 2:8—3:5; 3:6—5:1; 5:2—6:3; 6:4—8:14). Here the girl's physical charm is barely suggested. In 8:8–12 her maturing is celebrated. The Shulamite's chagrin slowly turns to joy. **my own vineyard**: Personal appearance and charm.

1:12–14 Spikenard was a fragrant ointment used in ancient times. **Henna blooms** (v. 14) were small red or white flowers with an odor like roses. **En Gedi** (v. 14): A fertile oasis near the Dead Sea.

2:1 rose of Sharon: A medium-sized bush that bears rose-like flowers, found especially

THE BELOVED

2 Like a lily among thorns,
So is my love among the daughters.

THE SHULAMITE

3 Like an apple tree among the trees of
the woods,
So *is* my beloved among the sons.
I sat down in his shade with great
delight,
And his fruit *was* sweet to my taste.

THE SHULAMITE TO THE DAUGHTERS OF JERUSALEM

4 He brought me to the banqueting
house,
And his banner over me *was* love.
5 Sustain me with cakes of raisins,
Refresh me with apples,
For I *am* lovesick.

6 His left hand *is* under my head,
And his right hand embraces me.
7 I charge you, O daughters of
Jerusalem,
By the gazelles or by the does of the
field,
Do not stir up nor awaken love
Until it pleases.

The Beloved's Request

THE SHULAMITE

8 The voice of my beloved!
Behold, he comes
Leaping upon the mountains,
Skipping upon the hills.
9 My beloved is like a gazelle or a
young stag.
Behold, he stands behind our wall;
He is looking through the windows,
Gazing through the lattice.

10 My beloved spoke, and said to me:
"Rise up, my love, my fair one,
And come away.
11 For lo, the winter is past,
The rain is over *and* gone.
12 The flowers appear on the earth;
The time of singing has come,
And the voice of the turtledove
Is heard in our land.
13 The fig tree puts forth her green
figs,
And the vines *with* the tender grapes
Give a good smell.
Rise up, my love, my fair one,
And come away!

14 "O my dove, in the clefts of the rock,
In the secret *places* of the cliff,
Let me see your face,
Let me hear your voice;
For your voice *is* sweet,
And your face *is* lovely."

HER BROTHERS

15 Catch us the foxes,
The little foxes that spoil the vines,
For our vines *have* tender grapes.

THE SHULAMITE

16 My beloved *is* mine, and I *am* his.
He feeds *his flock* among the lilies.

---

in the coastal Plain of Sharon. **lily of the valleys**: A perennial that grows in shade. These beautiful metaphors became famous as descriptions of Christ.

2:4 His banner is an attempt to translate a difficult Hebrew word. Perhaps it means "he looked upon me with love."

2:7 The Shulamite determines to experience love only when the time is right. She was careful to guard her purity in thought and deed.

2:15 Possibly a precautionary measure: keep the things that could spoil budding love from destroying it. Perhaps this is also a demand from her brothers not to allow small distractions to jeopardize her marriage to the king.

2:16, 17 An assertion of devotion between the Shulamite and the beloved (v. 16). **mountains of Bether**: Lit. "mountains of separation," perhaps the obstacles that separate us.

(TO HER BELOVED)

17 Until the day breaks
And the shadows flee away,
Turn, my beloved,
And be like a gazelle
Or a young stag
Upon the mountains of Bē′ther.[a]

CHAPTER 3

A Troubled Night

THE SHULAMITE

By night on my bed I sought the one I love;
I sought him, but I did not find him.
2 "I will rise now," *I said,*
"And go about the city;
In the streets and in the squares
I will seek the one I love."
I sought him, but I did not find him.
3 The watchmen who go about the city found me;
I said,
"Have you seen the one I love?"

4 Scarcely had I passed by them,
When I found the one I love.
I held him and would not let him go,
Until I had brought him to the house of my mother,
And into the chamber of her who conceived me.

5 I charge you, O daughters of Jerusalem,
By the gazelles or by the does of the field,
Do not stir up nor awaken love
Until it pleases.

The Coming of Solomon

THE SHULAMITE

6 Who *is* this coming out of the wilderness
Like pillars of smoke,
Perfumed with myrrh and frankincense,
With all the merchant's fragrant powders?
7 Behold, it *is* Solomon's couch,
With sixty valiant men around it,
Of the valiant of Israel.
8 They all hold swords,
Being expert in war.
Every man *has* his sword on his thigh
Because of fear in the night.

9 Of the wood of Lebanon
Solomon the King
Made himself a palanquin:[a]
10 He made its pillars *of* silver,
Its support *of* gold,
Its seat *of* purple,
Its interior paved *with* love
By the daughters of Jerusalem.
11 Go forth, O daughters of Zion,
And see King Solomon with the crown
With which his mother crowned him
On the day of his wedding,
The day of the gladness of his heart.

CHAPTER 4

THE BELOVED

Behold, you *are* fair, my love!
Behold, you *are* fair!
You *have* dove's eyes behind your veil.
Your hair *is* like a flock of goats,
Going down from Mount Gil′ē·ad.

2:17 [a]Literally *Separation* 3:9 [a]A portable enclosed chair

3:4 House of my mother indicates that the love affair was not to be clandestine, but one carrying the full blessing of the family.

3:7, 9 A couch is a covered litter on a canopied framework carried by bearers. Thus the king could recline in splendor while being carried.

4:1—5:1 The beloved praises the Shulamite; she responds with her whole heart.

2 Your teeth *are* like a flock of shorn
sheep
Which have come up from the
washing,
Every one of which bears twins,
And none *is* barren among them.
3 Your lips *are* like a strand of scarlet,
And your mouth is lovely.
Your temples behind your veil
Are like a piece of pomegranate.
4 Your neck *is* like the tower of David,
Built for an armory,
On which hang a thousand bucklers,
All shields of mighty men.
5 Your two breasts *are* like two fawns,
Twins of a gazelle,
Which feed among the lilies.

6 Until the day breaks
And the shadows flee away,
I will go my way to the mountain of
myrrh
And to the hill of frankincense.

7 You *are* all fair, my love,
And *there is* no spot in you.
8 Come with me from Lebanon, *my*
spouse,
With me from Lebanon.
Look from the top of A·ma′na,
From the top of Sē′nir and Her′mon,
From the lions' dens,
From the mountains of the leopards.

9 You have ravished my heart,
My sister, *my* spouse;
You have ravished my heart
With one *look* of your eyes,
With one link of your necklace.
10 How fair is your love,
My sister, *my* spouse!
How much better than wine is your
love,
And the scent of your perfumes
Than all spices!
11 Your lips, O *my* spouse,
Drip as the honeycomb;
Honey and milk *are* under your
tongue;
And the fragrance of your garments
Is like the fragrance of Lebanon.

12 A garden enclosed
Is my sister, *my* spouse,
A spring shut up,
A fountain sealed.
13 Your plants *are* an orchard of
pomegranates
With pleasant fruits,
Fragrant henna with spikenard,
14 Spikenard and saffron,
Calamus and cinnamon,
With all trees of frankincense,
Myrrh and aloes,
With all the chief spices—
15 A fountain of gardens,
A well of living waters,
And streams from Lebanon.

THE SHULAMITE

16 Awake, O north *wind*,
And come, O south!
Blow upon my garden,
That its spices may flow out.
Let my beloved come to his garden
And eat its pleasant fruits.

CHAPTER 5

THE BELOVED

I have come to my garden, my sister,
my spouse;

4:3 pomegranate: Smooth and unlined.

4:9 My sister, my spouse: A common oriental way of referring to one's bride or wife.

4:11 Ancient people associated milk with **honey** in describing that which was very desirable (see Ex. 3:8).

4:12–15 These lines revel in the private beauty of the future bride. She is shut up or sealed, that is, reserved for her beloved (6:3). Like a **well of living waters** (v. 15) she is constantly fresh and wholesome.

I have gathered my myrrh with my spice;
I have eaten my honeycomb with my honey;
I have drunk my wine with my milk.

(TO HIS FRIENDS)

Eat, O friends!
Drink, yes, drink deeply,
O beloved ones!

The Shulamite's Troubled Evening

THE SHULAMITE

2 I sleep, but my heart is awake;
It is the voice of my beloved!
He knocks, *saying,*
"Open for me, my sister, my love,
My dove, my perfect one;
For my head is covered with dew,
My locks with the drops of the night."

3 I have taken off my robe;
How can I put it on *again?*
I have washed my feet;
How can I defile them?
4 My beloved put his hand
By the latch *of the door,*
And my heart yearned for him.
5 I arose to open for my beloved,
And my hands dripped *with* myrrh,
My fingers with liquid myrrh,
On the handles of the lock.

6 I opened for my beloved,
But my beloved had turned away *and* was gone.
My heart leaped up when he spoke.
I sought him, but I could not find him;
I called him, but he gave me no answer.
7 The watchmen who went about the city found me.
They struck me, they wounded me;
The keepers of the walls
Took my veil away from me.
8 I charge you, O daughters of Jerusalem,
If you find my beloved,
That you tell him I *am* lovesick!

THE DAUGHTERS OF JERUSALEM

9 What *is* your beloved
More than *another* beloved,
O fairest among women?
What *is* your beloved
More than *another* beloved,
That you so charge us?

THE SHULAMITE

10 My beloved *is* white and ruddy,
Chief among ten thousand.
11 His head *is like* the finest gold;
His locks *are* wavy,
And black as a raven.
12 His eyes *are* like doves
By the rivers of waters,
Washed with milk,
And fitly set.
13 His cheeks *are* like a bed of spices,
Banks of scented herbs.
His lips *are* lilies,
Dripping liquid myrrh.

14 His hands *are* rods of gold
Set with beryl.
His body *is* carved ivory
Inlaid *with* sapphires.
15 His legs *are* pillars of marble
Set on bases of fine gold.
His countenance *is* like Lebanon,
Excellent as the cedars.
16 His mouth *is* most sweet,
Yes, he *is* altogether lovely.

5:2 covered with dew: He has come in the middle of the night. Love is importunate.

5:7 Perhaps reflecting outsiders who misunderstood the actions of those in love.

5:9–16 An amazing flow of oriental imagery. **my friend** (v. 16): Another common oriental way of describing one's beloved. At least two of these figures, **chief among ten thousand** (v. 10) and **altogether lovely** (v. 16), have been applied to Christ.

This *is* my beloved,
And this *is* my friend,
O daughters of Jerusalem!

CHAPTER 6

THE DAUGHTERS OF JERUSALEM

Where has your beloved gone,
O fairest among women?
Where has your beloved turned aside,
That we may seek him with you?

THE SHULAMITE

2 My beloved has gone to his garden,
To the beds of spices,
To feed *his flock* in the gardens,
And to gather lilies.
3 I *am* my beloved's,
And my beloved *is* mine.
He feeds *his flock* among the lilies.

Praise of the Shulamite's Beauty

THE BELOVED

4 O my love, you *are as* beautiful as Tir'zah,
Lovely as Jerusalem,
Awesome as *an army* with banners!
5 Turn your eyes away from me,
For they have overcome me.
Your hair *is* like a flock of goats
Going down from Gil'ē·ad.
6 Your teeth *are* like a flock of sheep
Which have come up from the washing;
Every one bears twins,
And none *is* barren among them.
7 Like a piece of pomegranate
Are your temples behind your veil.

8 There are sixty queens
And eighty concubines,
And virgins without number.
9 My dove, my perfect one,
Is the only one,
The only one of her mother,
The favorite of the one who bore her.
The daughters saw her
And called her blessed,
The queens and the concubines,
And they praised her.

10 Who is she who looks forth as the morning,
Fair as the moon,
Clear as the sun,
Awesome as *an army* with banners?

THE SHULAMITE

11 I went down to the garden of nuts
To see the verdure of the valley,
To see whether the vine had budded
And the pomegranates had bloomed.
12 Before I was even aware,
My soul had made me
As the chariots of my noble people.[a]

THE BELOVED AND HIS FRIENDS

13 Return, return, O Shū'lam·īte;
Return, return, that we may look upon you!

THE SHULAMITE

What would you see in the Shū'lam·īte—
As it were, the dance of the two camps?[a]

CHAPTER 7

Expressions of Praise

THE BELOVED

How beautiful are your feet in sandals,
O prince's daughter!
The curves of your thighs *are* like jewels,

6:12 [a]Hebrew *Ammi Nadib* 6:13 [a]Hebrew *Mahanaim*

6:1–3 The beloved had left. In the ancient Near East his garden represented a place of love and beauty. But the Shulamite is the true garden of love for her beloved (4:16; 5:1).

7:1 prince's daughter: A reference to the maiden who married the king.

The work of the hands of a skillful
workman.
2 Your navel *is* a rounded goblet;
It lacks no blended beverage.
Your waist *is* a heap of wheat
Set about with lilies.
3 Your two breasts *are* like two fawns,
Twins of a gazelle.
4 Your neck *is* like an ivory tower,
Your eyes *like* the pools in Hesh'bon
By the gate of Bath Rab'bim.
Your nose *is* like the tower of Lebanon
Which looks toward Damascus.
5 Your head *crowns* you like *Mount* Car'mel,
And the hair of your head *is* like purple;
A king *is* held captive by *your* tresses.

6 How fair and how pleasant you are,
O love, with your delights!
7 This stature of yours is like a palm tree,
And your breasts *like* its clusters.
8 I said, "I will go up to the palm tree,
I will take hold of its branches."
Let now your breasts be like clusters of the vine,
The fragrance of your breath like apples,
9 And the roof of your mouth like the best wine.

THE SHULAMITE

The wine goes *down* smoothly for my beloved,
Moving gently the lips of sleepers.[a]
10 I *am* my beloved's,
And his desire *is* toward me.

7:9 [a]Septuagint, Syriac, and Vulgate read *lips and teeth.*

11 Come, my beloved,
Let us go forth to the field;
Let us lodge in the villages.
12 Let us get up early to the vineyards;
Let us see if the vine has budded,
Whether the grape blossoms are open,
And the pomegranates are in bloom.
There I will give you my love.
13 The mandrakes give off a fragrance,
And at our gates *are* pleasant *fruits,*
All manner, new and old,
Which I have laid up for you, my beloved.

CHAPTER 8

Oh, that you were like my brother,
Who nursed at my mother's breasts!
If I should find you outside,
I would kiss you;
I would not be despised.
2 I would lead you *and* bring you
Into the house of my mother,
She *who* used to instruct me.
I would cause you to drink of spiced wine,
Of the juice of my pomegranate.

(TO THE DAUGHTERS OF JERUSALEM)
3 His left hand *is* under my head,
And his right hand embraces me.
4 I charge you, O daughters of Jerusalem,
Do not stir up nor awaken love
Until it pleases.

Love Renewed in Lebanon

A RELATIVE
5 Who *is* this coming up from the wilderness,
Leaning upon her beloved?

7:13 pleasant fruits: The figures of this verse suggest the fruitfulness of her love. The ancient oriental woman was praised for her fertility.

8:5–14 The priceless value, permanence, and satisfaction of love completed in union between the Shulamite and her beloved is stressed. The unpromising Shulamite has now matured. She attains love and fulfillment.

I awakened you under the apple tree.
There your mother brought you forth;
There she *who* bore you brought *you*
forth.

THE SHULAMITE TO HER BELOVED

6 Set me as a seal upon your heart,
As a seal upon your arm;
For love *is as* strong as death,
Jealousy *as* cruel as the grave;[a]
Its flames *are* flames of fire,
A most vehement[b] flame.

7 Many waters cannot quench love,
Nor can the floods drown it.
If a man would give for love
All the wealth of his house,
It would be utterly despised.

THE SHULAMITE'S BROTHERS

8 We have a little sister,
And she has no breasts.
What shall we do for our sister
In the day when she is spoken for?
9 If she *is* a wall,
We will build upon her
A battlement of silver;
And if she *is* a door,
We will enclose her
With boards of cedar.

THE SHULAMITE

10 I *am* a wall,
And my breasts like towers;
Then I became in his eyes
As one who found peace.
11 Solomon had a vineyard at Bā'al
Hā'mon;
He leased the vineyard to keepers;
Everyone was to bring for its fruit
A thousand silver coins.

(TO SOLOMON)

12 My own vineyard *is* before me.
You, O Solomon, *may have* a
thousand,
And those who tend its fruit two
hundred.

THE BELOVED

13 You who dwell in the gardens,
The companions listen for your
voice—
Let me hear it!

THE SHULAMITE

14 Make haste, my beloved,
And be like a gazelle
Or a young stag
On the mountains of spices.

8:6 [a]Or *Sheol* [b]Literally *A flame of* YAH (a poetic form of *YHWH, the* LORD)

8:8–12 A flashback and a response to the sorry plight of the **little siste**r who had **no breasts** and no vineyard (1:6). She now has peace (v. 10), love, maturity, and fertility (vv. 10, 12).

8:9 Brothers had responsibility for the welfare of their sister in marital arrangements, as seen in Laban's concerns for Rebekah (Gen. 24:55–59) and the concerns of Dinah's brothers for her (Gen. 34:13–17).

8:13, 14 The beloved calls and the Shulamite responds (see 2:8, 17). She represents every true chaste maiden. The way to fulfillment in love is to be found in the Shulamite's sterling character. And so closes this strange book which is different from any other in the Bible. It is a book about love between a man and a woman—one of God's most mysterious and satisfying gifts to us.

✦Isaiah✦

The first of the prophetic books, Isaiah is recognized as the work of Isaiah, son of Amoz, by most conservative scholars. In about 740 B.C., Isaiah was called to be a prophet through a vision as he worshiped in the temple. While his call came late in life, he ministered for more than forty years during a chaotic time in Judah's history.

At that time, Judah was full of sin and defiance against God. Isaiah warned of God's coming judgment as he condemned Judah and pronounced oracles against surrounding countries in chapters 1—35. He then reviewed the events of the earlier Assyrian invasion in chapters 36—39 and prophesied the coming Babylonian invasion. Chapters 40—66, however, proclaim hope for Judah in the eventual destruction of Babylon and the coming of the Messiah, the ultimate Savior who will pay for their sins and establish a kingdom of peace.

Sometimes called "the fifth Gospel," the Book of Isaiah concentrates on salvation from the Lord. In fact, Isaiah means "Yahweh is salvation." It also describes God in greater detail than any other book in the Old Testament, highlighting His holiness and glory in the temple, His concern for our salvation, and His sovereignty. During His New Testament ministry, Jesus often quoted from Isaiah to show that the prophecies were being fulfilled. ✦

CHAPTER 1

The vision of Ī·sāi'ah the son of Ā'moz, which he saw concerning Judah and Jerusalem in the days of Uz·zī'ah, Jō'tham, Ā'haz, *and* Hez·e·kī'ah, kings of Judah.

The Wickedness of Judah

2 Hear, O heavens, and give ear,
O earth!
For the LORD has spoken:
"I have nourished and brought up
children,
And they have rebelled against Me;
3 The ox knows its owner
And the donkey its master's crib;
But Israel does not know,
My people do not consider."

4 Alas, sinful nation,
A people laden with iniquity,
A brood of evildoers,
Children who are corrupters!
They have forsaken the LORD,
They have provoked to anger
The Holy One of Israel,
They have turned away backward.

5 Why should you be stricken again?
You will revolt more and more.
The whole head is sick,
And the whole heart faints.

1:1 Uzziah . . . Hezekiah: From about 740 B.C. to about 695 B.C.
1:5–9 The results of sin: spiritual sickness and desolation.

6 From the sole of the foot even to the
head,
There is no soundness in it,
But wounds and bruises and
putrefying sores;
They have not been closed or bound
up,
Or soothed with ointment.

7 Your country *is* desolate,
Your cities *are* burned with fire;
Strangers devour your land in your
presence;
And *it is* desolate, as overthrown by
strangers.
8 So the daughter of Zion is left as a
booth in a vineyard,
As a hut in a garden of cucumbers,
As a besieged city.
9 Unless the LORD of hosts
Had left to us a very small remnant,
We would have become like Sod'om,
We would have been made like
Go·mor'rah.

10 Hear the word of the LORD,
You rulers of Sod'om;
Give ear to the law of our God,
You people of Go·mor'rah:
11 "To what purpose *is* the multitude of
your sacrifices to Me?"
Says the LORD.
"I have had enough of burnt offerings
of rams
And the fat of fed cattle.
I do not delight in the blood of bulls,
Or of lambs or goats.

12 "When you come to appear before Me,
Who has required this from your
hand,
To trample My courts?
13 Bring no more futile sacrifices;
Incense is an abomination to Me.
The New Moons, the Sabbaths, and
the calling of assemblies—
I cannot endure iniquity and the
sacred meeting.
14 Your New Moons and your ap-
pointed feasts
My soul hates;
They are a trouble to Me,
I am weary of bearing *them.*
15 When you spread out your hands,
I will hide My eyes from you;
Even though you make many
prayers,
I will not hear.
Your hands are full of blood.

16 "Wash yourselves, make yourselves
clean;
Put away the evil of your doings from
before My eyes.
Cease to do evil,
17 Learn to do good;
Seek justice,
Rebuke the oppressor;[a]
Defend the fatherless,
Plead for the widow.

18 "Come now, and let us reason
together,"
Says the LORD,
"Though your sins are like scarlet,
They shall be as white as snow;
Though they are red like crimson,
They shall be as wool.
19 If you are willing and obedient,
You shall eat the good of the land;

1:17 [a]Some ancient versions read *the oppressed.*

1:8 a booth in a vineyard: A temporary shelter for harvesters. After the harvest these flimsy structures were abandoned and forlorn.

1:10 Despite all their religious pretensions, the Hebrews are no different at heart from the people of Sodom and Gomorrah (see Gen. 13:13; 18:20, 21).

1:13 iniquity and the sacred meeting: A reference to iniquitous assemblies. As far as God is concerned, their religious meetings are actually sinful because they are attempting to substitute formal religion for godly lives.

1:18, 19 Here is the heartbeat of God. He longs to free us from sin.

20 But if you refuse and rebel,
You shall be devoured by the sword";
For the mouth of the LORD has
spoken.

The Degenerate City

21 How the faithful city has become a
harlot!
It was full of justice;
Righteousness lodged in it,
But now murderers.
22 Your silver has become dross,
Your wine mixed with water.
23 Your princes *are* rebellious,
And companions of thieves;
Everyone loves bribes,
And follows after rewards.
They do not defend the fatherless,
Nor does the cause of the widow
come before them.

24 Therefore the Lord says,
The LORD of hosts, the Mighty One of
Israel,
"Ah, I will rid Myself of My
adversaries,
And take vengeance on My enemies.
25 I will turn My hand against you,
And thoroughly purge away your
dross,
And take away all your alloy.
26 I will restore your judges as at the
first,
And your counselors as at the
beginning.
Afterward you shall be called the city
of righteousness, the faithful city."

27 Zion shall be redeemed with justice,
And her penitents with
righteousness.
28 The destruction of transgressors and
of sinners *shall be* together,
And those who forsake the LORD shall
be consumed.
29 For they[a] shall be ashamed of the
terebinth trees
Which you have desired;
And you shall be embarrassed
because of the gardens
Which you have chosen.
30 For you shall be as a terebinth whose
leaf fades,
And as a garden that has no water.
31 The strong shall be as tinder,
And the work of it as a spark;
Both will burn together,
And no one shall quench *them*.

CHAPTER 2

The Future House of God

The word that Ī·sāi'ah the son of Ā'moz saw concerning Judah and Jerusalem.

2 Now it shall come to pass in the latter
days
That the mountain of the LORD's
house
Shall be established on the top of the
mountains,
And shall be exalted above the
hills;
And all nations shall flow to it.
3 Many people shall come and say,
"Come, and let us go up to the
mountain of the LORD,
To the house of the God of Jacob;
He will teach us His ways,
And we shall walk in His paths."
For out of Zion shall go forth the law,
And the word of the LORD from
Jerusalem.

1:29 [a]Following Masoretic Text, Septuagint, and Vulgate; some Hebrew manuscripts and Targum read *you.*

1:21–31 Because Judah has refused to listen, her doom is certain. But God's purpose in judgment is restoration through cleansing of dross (what is sinful) to a true state of righteousness (vv. 25–27).

2:2 the mountain of the LORD's house: Pagans believed that gods lived on mountains, so this is a way of saying that God will be recognized as being superior to the gods of all the other nations.

4 He shall judge between the nations,
And rebuke many people;
They shall beat their swords into
plowshares,
And their spears into pruning hooks;
Nation shall not lift up sword against
nation,
Neither shall they learn war anymore.

The Day of the LORD

5 O house of Jacob, come and let us
walk
In the light of the LORD.

6 For You have forsaken Your people,
the house of Jacob,
Because they are filled with eastern
ways;
They *are* soothsayers like the
Phi·lis'tines,
And they are pleased with the
children of foreigners.
7 Their land is also full of silver and
gold,
And there is no end to their treasures;
Their land is also full of horses,
And there is no end to their chariots.
8 Their land is also full of idols;
They worship the work of their own
hands,
That which their own fingers have
made.
9 People bow down,
And each man humbles himself;
Therefore do not forgive them.

10 Enter into the rock, and hide in the
dust,
From the terror of the LORD
And the glory of His majesty.
11 The lofty looks of man shall be
humbled,
The haughtiness of men shall be
bowed down,
And the LORD alone shall be exalted
in that day.

12 For the day of the LORD of hosts
Shall come upon everything proud
and lofty,
Upon everything lifted up—
And it shall be brought low—
13 Upon all the cedars of Lebanon *that*
are high and lifted up,
And upon all the oaks of Bā'shan;
14 Upon all the high mountains,
And upon all the hills *that are* lifted
up;
15 Upon every high tower,
And upon every fortified wall;
16 Upon all the ships of Tar'shish,
And upon all the beautiful sloops.
17 The loftiness of man shall be bowed
down,
And the haughtiness of men shall be
brought low;
The LORD alone will be exalted in that
day,
18 But the idols He shall utterly abolish.

19 They shall go into the holes of the
rocks,
And into the caves of the earth,
From the terror of the LORD
And the glory of His majesty,
When He arises to shake the earth
mightily.

20 In that day a man will cast away his
idols of silver
And his idols of gold,
Which they made, *each* for himself to
worship,
To the moles and bats,
21 To go into the clefts of the rocks,
And into the crags of the rugged
rocks,
From the terror of the LORD
And the glory of His majesty,
When He arises to shake the earth
mightily.

2:6–22 The foolishness of exalting humanity, as typified in the practice of idolatry.
2:9 do not forgive: The prophet is jealous for God.

22 Sever yourselves from such a man,
Whose breath *is* in his nostrils;
For of what account is he?

CHAPTER 3

Judgment on Judah and Jerusalem

For behold, the Lord, the LORD of hosts,
Takes away from Jerusalem and from Judah
The stock and the store,
The whole supply of bread and the whole supply of water;
2 The mighty man and the man of war,
The judge and the prophet,
And the diviner and the elder;
3 The captain of fifty and the honorable man,
The counselor and the skillful artisan,
And the expert enchanter.

4 "I will give children *to be* their princes,
And babes shall rule over them.
5 The people will be oppressed,
Every one by another and every one by his neighbor;
The child will be insolent toward the elder,
And the base toward the honorable."

6 When a man takes hold of his brother
In the house of his father, *saying*,
"You have clothing;
You be our ruler,
And *let* these ruins *be* under your power,"[a]
7 In that day he will protest, saying,
"I cannot cure *your* ills,
For in my house *is* neither food nor clothing;
Do not make me a ruler of the people."

8 For Jerusalem stumbled,
And Judah is fallen,
Because their tongue and their doings
Are against the LORD,
To provoke the eyes of His glory.
9 The look on their countenance witnesses against them,
And they declare their sin as Sod'om;
They do not hide *it*.
Woe to their soul!
For they have brought evil upon themselves.

10 "Say to the righteous that *it shall be* well *with them*,
For they shall eat the fruit of their doings.
11 Woe to the wicked! *It shall be* ill *with him*,
For the reward of his hands shall be given him.
12 *As for* My people, children *are* their oppressors,
And women rule over them.
O My people! Those who lead you cause *you* to err,
And destroy the way of your paths."

Oppression and Luxury Condemned

13 The LORD stands up to plead,
And stands to judge the people.
14 The LORD will enter into judgment
With the elders of His people
And His princes:
"For you have eaten up the vineyard;
The plunder of the poor *is* in your houses.
15 What do you mean by crushing My people

3:6 [a]Literally *hand*

3:4 Because Judah has placed her faith in human leadership instead of in God, she is doomed to experience weaker and weaker leadership. This was literally fulfilled from Josiah's death until the fall of Jerusalem in 586 B.C.

3:6 You have clothing: In the coming days the lack of leadership in Judah will be so severe that even the most insignificant qualifications will be enough to propel a person into a place of prominence.

And grinding the faces of the poor?"
Says the Lord GOD of hosts.

16Moreover the LORD says:

"Because the daughters of Zion are haughty,
And walk with outstretched necks
And wanton eyes,
Walking and mincing *as* they go,
Making a jingling with their feet,
17 Therefore the Lord will strike with a scab
The crown of the head of the daughters of Zion,
And the LORD will uncover their secret parts."

18 In that day the Lord will take away the finery:
The jingling anklets, the scarves, and the crescents;
19 The pendants, the bracelets, and the veils;
20 The headdresses, the leg ornaments, and the headbands;
The perfume boxes, the charms,
21 and the rings;
The nose jewels,
22 the festal apparel, and the mantles;
The outer garments, the purses,
23 and the mirrors;
The fine linen, the turbans, and the robes.

24And so it shall be:

Instead of a sweet smell there will be a stench;
Instead of a sash, a rope;
Instead of well-set hair, baldness;
Instead of a rich robe, a girding of sackcloth;
And branding instead of beauty.
25 Your men shall fall by the sword,
And your mighty in the war.

26 Her gates shall lament and mourn,
And she *being* desolate shall sit on the ground.

CHAPTER 4

And in that day seven women shall take hold of one man, saying,

"We will eat our own food and wear our own apparel;
Only let us be called by your name,
To take away our reproach."

The Renewal of Zion

2 In that day the Branch of the LORD shall be beautiful and glorious;
And the fruit of the earth *shall be* excellent and appealing
For those of Israel who have escaped.

3And it shall come to pass that *he who is*
left in Zion and remains in Jerusalem will
be called holy—everyone who is recorded
among the living in Jerusalem. 4When the
Lord has washed away the filth of the
daughters of Zion, and purged the blood
of Jerusalem from her midst, by the spirit
of judgment and by the spirit of burning,
5then the LORD will create above every
dwelling place of Mount Zion, and above
her assemblies, a cloud and smoke by day
and the shining of a flaming fire by night.

3:18–24 the finery: The prophet seems to be extending the list in order to emphasize Judah's excessive concern with external matters.

4:1 in that day: When the Lord's judgment will have fallen and Jerusalem will have been destroyed by Babylon. The siege will have so depleted the male population that women will compete for a husband.

4:3 holy: means "set apart" or "special." Anyone left in Zion will be "special."

4:5, 6 God means to dwell in the midst of a sanctified people with protection, fellowship, and glory.

For over all the glory there *will be* a covering. 6And there will be a tabernacle for shade in the daytime from the heat, for a place of refuge, and for a shelter from storm and rain.

CHAPTER 5

God's Disappointing Vineyard

Now let me sing to my Well-beloved
A song of my Beloved regarding His vineyard:

My Well-beloved has a vineyard
On a very fruitful hill.
2 He dug it up and cleared out its stones,
And planted it with the choicest vine.
He built a tower in its midst,
And also made a winepress in it;
So He expected *it* to bring forth *good* grapes,
But it brought forth wild grapes.

3 "And now, O inhabitants of Jerusalem and men of Judah,
Judge, please, between Me and My vineyard.
4 What more could have been done to My vineyard
That I have not done in it?
Why then, when I expected *it* to bring forth *good* grapes,
Did it bring forth wild grapes?
5 And now, please let Me tell you what I will do to My vineyard:
I will take away its hedge, and it shall be burned;
And break down its wall, and it shall be trampled down.
6 I will lay it waste;
It shall not be pruned or dug,
But there shall come up briers and thorns.
I will also command the clouds
That they rain no rain on it."

7 For the vineyard of the LORD of hosts *is* the house of Israel,
And the men of Judah are His pleasant plant.
He looked for justice, but behold, oppression;
For righteousness, but behold, a cry *for help*.

Impending Judgment on Excesses

8 Woe to those who join house to house;
They add field to field,
Till *there is* no place
Where they may dwell alone in the midst of the land!
9 In my hearing the LORD of hosts *said*,
"Truly, many houses shall be desolate,
Great and beautiful ones, without inhabitant.
10 For ten acres of vineyard shall yield one bath,
And a homer of seed shall yield one ephah."

11 Woe to those who rise early in the morning,
That they may follow intoxicating drink;
Who continue until night, *till* wine inflames them!
12 The harp and the strings,
The tambourine and flute,
And wine are in their feasts;

5:2 cleared out its stones: The soil of Palestine is very rocky. The farmer had to laboriously clear his fields of stones before he could even begin to plow and plant. Often these stones were used to build a wall around the field and a tower from which to watch for marauders.

5:12 do not regard the work of the LORD: They are so concerned with their own pleasure that they pay no attention to God's righteous laws or what God is doing.

But they do not regard the work of the LORD,
Nor consider the operation of His hands.

13 Therefore my people have gone into captivity,
Because *they have* no knowledge;
Their honorable men *are* famished,
And their multitude dried up with thirst.
14 Therefore Shē'ōl has enlarged itself
And opened its mouth beyond measure;
Their glory and their multitude and their pomp,
And he who is jubilant, shall descend into it.
15 People shall be brought down,
Each man shall be humbled,
And the eyes of the lofty shall be humbled.
16 But the LORD of hosts shall be exalted in judgment,
And God who is holy shall be hallowed in righteousness.
17 Then the lambs shall feed in their pasture,
And in the waste places of the fat ones strangers shall eat.

18 Woe to those who draw iniquity with cords of vanity,
And sin as if with a cart rope;
19 That say, "Let Him make speed *and* hasten His work,
That we may see *it;*
And let the counsel of the Holy One of Israel draw near and come,
That we may know *it.*"

20 Woe to those who call evil good, and good evil;
Who put darkness for light, and light for darkness;
Who put bitter for sweet, and sweet for bitter!

21 Woe to *those who are* wise in their own eyes,
And prudent in their own sight!

22 Woe to men mighty at drinking wine,
Woe to men valiant for mixing intoxicating drink,
23 Who justify the wicked for a bribe,
And take away justice from the righteous man!

24 Therefore, as the fire devours the stubble,
And the flame consumes the chaff,
So their root will be as rottenness,
And their blossom will ascend like dust;
Because they have rejected the law of the LORD of hosts,
And despised the word of the Holy One of Israel.
25 Therefore the anger of the LORD is aroused against His people;
He has stretched out His hand against them
And stricken them,
And the hills trembled.
Their carcasses *were* as refuse in the midst of the streets.

For all this His anger is not turned away,
But His hand *is* stretched out still.

26 He will lift up a banner to the nations from afar,

5:13 have gone into captivity: The prophet regards the coming exile as a settled fact.

5:19 They demand evidence: If God is sending judgment, let Him prove it by sending it now. **the Holy One**: They have never seen Him as Isaiah has, or they would not so lightly mock Him.

5:26 nations from afar: Assyria and Babylon were bent upon empire for their own glory, but actually were only tools in the hand of God.

A Compass for Life

Gloria Gaither

I find the Bible is truly the "operations manual" for the construction and maintenance of my life. In our home, in our marriage, in our professional life, and in our businesses, Bill and I are constantly faced with increasingly difficult choices. The Bible speaks again and again to give us direction and help.

The need for that kind of direction is especially acute in the mixed-up world we live in today. Our own resources often are simply not enough to make sense out of the confusion that confronts us. Instincts can be faulty, good intentions lack power, and the day has passed when we can find in the society around us any clear-cut principles that are ethically dependable. Instead, we live in a world that seems to be endorsing a crazy reverse morality, calling good bad, and right wrong.

"The Bible offers direction, hope, and certainty."

In my life I have found the Bible to be the only trustworthy compass from which to chart any accurate course through such a world. It has been for me a teacher, a critic, a censor, an encourager, a defender, and a guide. When the society around me staggers from a lack of direction, the Bible offers direction, hope, and certainty.

And will whistle to them from the
end of the earth;
Surely they shall come with speed,
swiftly.
27 No one will be weary or stumble
among them,
No one will slumber or sleep;
Nor will the belt on their loins be
loosed,
Nor the strap of their sandals be
broken;
28 Whose arrows *are* sharp,
And all their bows bent;
Their horses' hooves will seem like
flint,
And their wheels like a whirlwind.
29 Their roaring *will be* like a lion,
They will roar like young lions;
Yes, they will roar
And lay hold of the prey;
They will carry *it* away safely,
And no one will deliver.
30 In that day they will roar against
them
Like the roaring of the sea.
And if *one* looks to the land,
Behold, darkness *and* sorrow;
And the light is darkened by the
clouds.

CHAPTER 6

Isaiah Called to Be a Prophet

In the year that King Uz·zī'ah died, I
saw the Lord sitting on a throne, high and
lifted up, and the train of His *robe* filled the

temple. [2]Above it stood seraphim; each one had six wings: with two he covered his face, with two he covered his feet, and with two he flew. [3]And one cried to another and said:

"Holy, holy, holy *is* the LORD of hosts;
The whole earth *is* full of His glory!"

[4]And the posts of the door were shaken by the voice of him who cried out, and the house was filled with smoke.

[5]So I said:

"Woe *is* me, for I am undone!
Because I *am* a man of unclean lips,
And I dwell in the midst of a people
of unclean lips;
For my eyes have seen the King,
The LORD of hosts."

[6]Then one of the seraphim flew to me, having in his hand a live coal *which* he had taken with the tongs from the altar. [7]And he touched my mouth *with it*, and said:

"Behold, this has touched your lips;
Your iniquity is taken away,
And your sin purged."

[8]Also I heard the voice of the Lord, saying:

"Whom shall I send,
And who will go for Us?"

Then I said, "Here *am* I! Send me."
[9]And He said, "Go, and tell this people:

> God does not search for the young, beautiful, slender, talented, wealthy, experienced, courageous, worldly wise, well-equipped, or those who know how to defend themselves. Rather, He searches for the humble and willing like Isaiah, who simply say, "Here am I; send me" (Is. 6:8). We are never too young or too old, never too fat or too thin, never too rich or too poor to obey God.
>
> Carolyn Sundseth

'Keep on hearing, but do not
understand;
Keep on seeing, but do not perceive.'

10 "Make the heart of this people dull,
And their ears heavy,
And shut their eyes;
Lest they see with their eyes,
And hear with their ears,
And understand with their heart,
And return and be healed."

[11]Then I said, "Lord, how long?"
And He answered:

"Until the cities are laid waste and
without inhabitant,
The houses are without a man,
The land is utterly desolate,
12 The LORD has removed men far away,
And the forsaken places *are* many in
the midst of the land.
13 But yet a tenth *will be* in it,
And will return and be for
consuming,

6:2 seraphim: Lit. "burning ones." God's holiness is often associated with fire (4:4). Even these holy beings do not presume to look upon His face. The **feet** represent the most humble part of the body. Their "body language" proclaims that they are unworthy.

6:3 Holy, holy, holy: Threefold repetition is a Hebrew way of expressing the superlative. God is holiest of all.

6:9, 10 Keep on hearing . . . do not perceive: Isaiah is to preach God's message even though the people "will not get it."

6:13 Everything in the land will be destroyed. Like a cut-down forest, only the stumps will remain. Yet out of the stump of the tribe of Jesse a shoot will spring up.

As a terebinth tree or as an oak,
Whose stump *remains* when it is cut
down.
So the holy seed *shall be* its stump."

CHAPTER 7

Isaiah Sent to King Ahaz

Now it came to pass in the days of Ā'haz
the son of Jō'tham, the son of Uz·zī'ah,
king of Judah, *that* Rē'zin king of Syria and
Pē'kah the son of Rem·a·lī'ah, king of Is-
rael, went up to Jerusalem to *make* war
against it, but could not prevail against it.
2And it was told to the house of David, say-
ing, "Syria's forces are deployed in
Ē'phra·im." So his heart and the heart of
his people were moved as the trees of the
woods are moved with the wind.
3Then the LORD said to Ī·sāi'ah, "Go out
now to meet Ā'haz, you and Shē'ar-
Jā'shub[a] your son, at the end of the aque-
duct from the upper pool, on the highway
to the Fuller's Field, 4and say to him: 'Take
heed, and be quiet; do not fear or be faint-
hearted for these two stubs of smoking
firebrands, for the fierce anger of Rē'zin
and Syria, and the son of Rem·a·lī'ah. 5Be-
cause Syria, Ē'phra·im, and the son of
Rem·a·lī'ah have plotted evil against you,
saying, 6"Let us go up against Judah and
trouble it, and let us make a gap in its wall
for ourselves, and set a king over them, the
son of Tā'bel"— 7thus says the Lord GOD:

"It shall not stand,
Nor shall it come to pass.
8 For the head of Syria *is* Damascus,
And the head of Damascus *is* Rē'zin.
Within sixty-five years Ē'phra·im will
be broken,
So that it will not *be* a people.
9 The head of Ē'phra·im *is* Samaria,
And the head of Samaria *is*
Rem·a·lī'ah's son.
If you will not believe,
Surely you shall not be
established." ' "

The Immanuel Prophecy

10Moreover the LORD spoke again to
Ā'haz, saying, 11"Ask a sign for yourself
from the LORD your God; ask it either in the
depth or in the height above."
12But Ā'haz said, "I will not ask, nor will
I test the LORD!"
13Then he said, "Hear now, O house of
David! *Is it* a small thing for you to weary
men, but will you weary my God also?
14Therefore the Lord Himself will give you
a sign: Behold, the virgin shall conceive
and bear a Son, and shall call His name
Im·man'ū·el.[a] 15Curds and honey He shall
eat, that He may know to refuse the evil
and choose the good. 16For before the Child
shall know to refuse the evil and choose
the good, the land that you dread will be
forsaken by both her kings. 17The LORD will
bring the king of Assyria upon you and
your people and your father's house—
days that have not come since the day that
Ē'phra·im departed from Judah."

18 And it shall come to pass in that day
That the LORD will whistle for the fly
That *is* in the farthest part of the
rivers of Egypt,
And for the bee that *is* in the land of
Assyria.

7:3 [a]Literally *A Remnant Shall Return* 7:14 [a]Literally *God-With-Us*

7:3 Shear-Jashub: This name, meaning "A Remnant Shall Return," was both an ominous and a hopeful sign. On the one hand, only a bit of Ahaz's proud kingdom would eventually survive, but on the other, it would survive.

7:12 Nor will I test the LORD sounds like a pious response, but it was a cover-up for Ahaz's lack of faith. He had already committed himself to Assyria (2 Kin. 16:7–9). He would trust his worst enemy before he would trust God.

19 They will come, and all of them will rest
In the desolate valleys and in the clefts of the rocks,
And on all thorns and in all pastures.

20 In the same day the Lord will shave with a hired razor,
With those from beyond the River,[a] with the king of Assyria,
The head and the hair of the legs,
And will also remove the beard.

21 It shall be in that day
That a man will keep alive a young cow and two sheep;
22 So it shall be, from the abundance of milk they give,
That he will eat curds;
For curds and honey everyone will eat who is left in the land.

23 It shall happen in that day,
That wherever there could be a thousand vines
Worth a thousand *shekels* of silver,
It will be for briers and thorns.
24 With arrows and bows men will come there,
Because all the land will become briers and thorns.

25 And to any hill which could be dug with the hoe,
You will not go there for fear of briers and thorns;
But it will become a range for oxen
And a place for sheep to roam.

CHAPTER 8

Assyria Will Invade the Land

Moreover the LORD said to me, "Take a
large scroll, and write on it with a man's
pen concerning Mā'her-Shal'al-Hash-Baz.[a]
2And I will take for Myself faithful wit-
nesses to record, Ū·rī'ah the priest and
Zech·a·rī'ah the son of Je·ber·e·chī'ah."
3Then I went to the prophetess, and she
conceived and bore a son. Then the LORD
said to me, "Call his name Mā'her-Shal'al-
Hash-Baz; 4for before the child shall have
knowledge to cry 'My father' and 'My
mother,' the riches of Damascus and the
spoil of Samaria will be taken away before
the king of Assyria."
5The LORD also spoke to me again, say-
ing:

6 "Inasmuch as these people refused
The waters of Shī·lō'ah that flow softly,
And rejoice in Rē'zin and in Rem·a·lī'ah's son;
7 Now therefore, behold, the Lord brings up over them
The waters of the River,[a] strong and mighty—
The king of Assyria and all his glory;
He will go up over all his channels
And go over all his banks.
8 He will pass through Judah,
He will overflow and pass over,
He will reach up to the neck;
And the stretching out of his wings
Will fill the breadth of Your land,
O Im·man'ū·el.[a]

9 "Be shattered, O you peoples, and be broken in pieces!
Give ear, all you from far countries.
Gird yourselves, but be broken in pieces;
Gird yourselves, but be broken in pieces.

7:20 [a]That is, the Euphrates 8:1 [a]Literally *Speed the Spoil, Hasten the Booty* 8:7 [a]That is, the Euphrates 8:8 [a]Literally *God-With-Us*

8:9, 10 Although Judah would be severely threatened, God would not allow the enemy peoples to destroy her. **God is with us** are Isaiah's words of confidence. Because it is God who sends the Assyrians, it is He who will be able to deliver a repentant Judah.

10 Take counsel together, but it will
come to nothing;
Speak the word, but it will not stand,
For God *is* with us."[a]

Fear God, Heed His Word

11For the LORD spoke thus to me with a
strong hand, and instructed me that I
should not walk in the way of this people,
saying:

12 "Do not say, 'A conspiracy,'
Concerning all that this people call a
conspiracy,
Nor be afraid of their threats, nor be
troubled.
13 The LORD of hosts, Him you shall
hallow;
Let Him *be* your fear,
And *let* Him *be* your dread.
14 He will be as a sanctuary,
But a stone of stumbling and a rock of
offense
To both the houses of Israel,
As a trap and a snare to the
inhabitants of Jerusalem.
15 And many among them shall
stumble;
They shall fall and be broken,
Be snared and taken."

16 Bind up the testimony,
Seal the law among my disciples.
17 And I will wait on the LORD,
Who hides His face from the house of
Jacob;
And I will hope in Him.
18 Here am I and the children whom the
LORD has given me!
We are for signs and wonders in
Israel
From the LORD of hosts,
Who dwells in Mount Zion.

19And when they say to you, "Seek those
who are mediums and wizards, who whis-
per and mutter," should not a people seek
their God? *Should they* seek the dead on be-
half of the living? 20To the law and to the
testimony! If they do not speak according
to this word, *it is* because *there* is no light in
them.

21They will pass through it hard-pressed
and hungry; and it shall happen, when
they are hungry, that they will be enraged
and curse their king and their God, and
look upward. 22Then they will look to the
earth, and see trouble and darkness, gloom
of anguish; and *they will be* driven into
darkness.

CHAPTER 9

The Government of the Promised Son

Nevertheless the gloom *will* not *be*
upon her who *is* distressed,
As when at first He lightly esteemed
The land of Zeb'ū·lun and the land of
Naph'ta·lī,
And afterward more heavily
oppressed *her*,
By the way of the sea, beyond the
Jordan,
In Galilee of the Gentiles.
2 The people who walked in darkness
Have seen a great light;
Those who dwelt in the land of the
shadow of death,
Upon them a light has shined.

8:10 [a]Hebrew *Immanuel*

8:16 Bind up the testimony refers to God's word by Isaiah, meaning to keep it until there are those who are ready to listen (see 30:18).

8:18 Isaiah, along with his children Shear-Jashub and Maher-Shalal-Hash-Baz, are living witnesses to God's faithfulness. When Isaiah's prophecies have come to pass, people will know that his message, as symbolized in his children's names, was true.

8:19, 20 To reject God's word for spiritism is to choose darkness rather than light.

9:1 Despite the people's lack of trust, still God will send them the Messiah.

3 You have multiplied the nation
And increased its joy;[a]
They rejoice before You
According to the joy of harvest,
As *men* rejoice when they divide the spoil.
4 For You have broken the yoke of his burden
And the staff of his shoulder,
The rod of his oppressor,
As in the day of Mid′i·an.
5 For every warrior's sandal from the noisy battle,
And garments rolled in blood,
Will be used for burning *and* fuel of fire.

6 For unto us a Child is born,
Unto us a Son is given;
And the government will be upon His shoulder.
And His name will be called
Wonderful, Counselor, Mighty God,
Everlasting Father, Prince of Peace.
7 Of the increase of *His* government and peace
There will be no end,
Upon the throne of David and over His kingdom,
To order it and establish it with judgment and justice
From that time forward, even forever.
The zeal of the Lord of hosts will perform this.

The Punishment of Samaria

8 The LORD sent a word against Jacob,
And it has fallen on Israel.
9 All the people will know—
Ē′phra·im and the inhabitant of Samaria—
Who say in pride and arrogance of heart:
10 "The bricks have fallen down,
But we will rebuild with hewn stones;
The sycamores are cut down,
But we will replace *them* with cedars."
11 Therefore the LORD shall set up
The adversaries of Rē′zin against him,
And spur his enemies on,
12 The Syrians before and the Phi·lis′tines behind;
And they shall devour Israel with an open mouth.

For all this His anger is not turned away,
But His hand *is* stretched out still.

13 For the people do not turn to Him who strikes them,
Nor do they seek the LORD of hosts.
14 Therefore the LORD will cut off head and tail from Israel,
Palm branch and bulrush in one day.
15 The elder and honorable, he *is* the head;
The prophet who teaches lies, he *is* the tail.
16 For the leaders of this people cause *them* to err,
And *those who are* led by them are destroyed.
17 Therefore the Lord will have no joy in their young men,
Nor have mercy on their fatherless and widows;

9:3 [a]Following Qere and Targum; Kethib and Vulgate read *not increased joy;* Septuagint reads *Most of the people You brought down in Your joy.*

9:6 God's answer to the arrogance of the world is a Child, His own Son. He will be what Judah's kings have not been. Because He is the **Mighty God**, He can be a true **Father** to His people, He can bring lasting **peace**, and He can give counsel which is truly **wonderful**.

9:13–15 The people do not rely on the Lord but on their foolish human leaders. Therefore He will deprive them of every leader, both the one who is honorable and the one who teaches lies.

For everyone *is* a hypocrite and an evildoer,
And every mouth speaks folly.

For all this His anger is not turned away,
But His hand *is* stretched out still.

18 For wickedness burns as the fire;
It shall devour the briers and thorns,
And kindle in the thickets of the forest;
They shall mount up *like* rising smoke.
19 Through the wrath of the LORD of hosts
The land is burned up,
And the people shall be as fuel for the fire;
No man shall spare his brother.
20 And he shall snatch on the right hand
And be hungry;
He shall devour on the left hand
And not be satisfied;
Every man shall eat the flesh of his own arm.
21 Ma·nas′seh *shall devour* Ē′phra·im, and Ē′phra·im Ma·nas′seh;
Together they *shall be* against Judah.

For all this His anger is not turned away,
But His hand *is* stretched out still.

CHAPTER 10

"Woe to those who decree unrighteous decrees,
Who write misfortune,
Which they have prescribed
2 To rob the needy of justice,
And to take what is right from the poor of My people,
That widows may be their prey,
And *that* they may rob the fatherless.
3 What will you do in the day of punishment,
And in the desolation *which* will come from afar?
To whom will you flee for help?
And where will you leave your glory?
4 Without Me they shall bow down among the prisoners,
And they shall fall among the slain."

For all this His anger is not turned away,
But His hand *is* stretched out still.

Arrogant Assyria Also Judged

5 "Woe to Assyria, the rod of My anger
And the staff in whose hand is My indignation.
6 I will send him against an ungodly nation,
And against the people of My wrath
I will give him charge,
To seize the spoil, to take the prey,
And to tread them down like the mire of the streets.
7 Yet he does not mean so,
Nor does his heart think so;
But *it is* in his heart to destroy,
And cut off not a few nations.
8 For he says,
'*Are* not my princes altogether kings?
9 *Is* not Cal′nō like Car′chem·ish?
Is not Hā′math like Ar′pad?
Is not Samaria like Damascus?
10 As my hand has found the kingdoms of the idols,
Whose carved images excelled those of Jerusalem and Samaria,
11 As I have done to Samaria and her idols,
Shall I not do also to Jerusalem and her idols?' "

9:18–21 Wickedness will be allowed to run its natural course like a fire. So brother will destroy brother in Israel.

10:1 write misfortune: To write legal judgments that would create hardship and trouble.

10:11 The Assyrians made the fatal mistake of assuming that Jerusalem's God was no

12Therefore it shall come to pass, when the Lord has performed all His work on Mount Zion and on Jerusalem, *that He will say,* "I will punish the fruit of the arrogant heart of the king of Assyria, and the glory of his haughty looks."

13For he says:

"By the strength of my hand I have
done *it,*
And by my wisdom, for I am
prudent;
Also I have removed the boundaries
of the people,
And have robbed their treasuries;
So I have put down the inhabitants
like a valiant *man.*
14 My hand has found like a nest the
riches of the people,
And as one gathers eggs *that are* left,
I have gathered all the earth;
And there was no one who moved *his*
wing,
Nor opened *his* mouth with even a
peep."

15 Shall the ax boast itself against him
who chops with it?
Or shall the saw exalt itself against
him who saws with it?
As if a rod could wield *itself* against
those who lift it up,
Or as if a staff could lift up, *as if it
were* not wood!
16 Therefore the Lord, the Lord[a] of hosts,
Will send leanness among his fat
ones;
And under his glory
He will kindle a burning
Like the burning of a fire.
17 So the Light of Israel will be for a fire,
And his Holy One for a flame;

God designed the human machine to run on Himself.

C. S. Lewis

It will burn and devour
His thorns and his briers in one day.
18 And it will consume the glory of his
forest and of his fruitful field,
Both soul and body;
And they will be as when a sick man
wastes away.
19 Then the rest of the trees of his forest
Will be so few in number
That a child may write them.

The Returning Remnant of Israel

20 And it shall come to pass in that day
That the remnant of Israel,
And such as have escaped of the
house of Jacob,
Will never again depend on him who
defeated them,
But will depend on the LORD, the
Holy One of Israel, in truth.
21 The remnant will return, the remnant
of Jacob,
To the Mighty God.
22 For though your people, O Israel, be
as the sand of the sea,
A remnant of them will return;
The destruction decreed shall
overflow with righteousness.
23 For the Lord GOD of hosts
Will make a determined end
In the midst of all the land.

10:16 [a]Following Bomberg; Masoretic Text and Dead Sea Scrolls read *YHWH* (*the LORD*).

different from the gods of all their other victims. **her idols**: The bull images of the northern kingdom located at Bethel and Dan.

10:15 the ax: Despite her boasting Assyria was nothing but a tool in the hand of Judah's God.

10:20–27 The remnant will return (v. 21): Because Assyria is God's tool, He will not permit her to destroy Israel utterly.

24Therefore thus says the Lord GOD of
hosts: "O My people, who dwell in Zion,
do not be afraid of the Assyrian. He shall
strike you with a rod and lift up his staff
against you, in the manner of Egypt. 25For
yet a very little while and the indignation
will cease, as will My anger in their de-
struction." 26And the LORD of hosts will stir
up a scourge for him like the slaughter of
Mid'i·an at the rock of Or'eb; *as* His rod
was on the sea, so will He lift it up in the
manner of Egypt.

27 It shall come to pass in that day
That his burden will be taken away
from your shoulder,
And his yoke from your neck,
And the yoke will be destroyed
because of the anointing oil.

28 He has come to Aī'ath,
He has passed Mig'ron;
At Mich'mash he has attended to his
equipment.
29 They have gone along the ridge,
They have taken up lodging at Gē'ba.
Rā'mah is afraid,
Gib'ē·ah of Saul has fled.
30 Lift up your voice,
O daughter of Gal'lim!
Cause it to be heard as far as Lā'ish—
O poor An'a·thoth![a]
31 Mad·mē'nah has fled,
The inhabitants of Gē'bim seek
refuge.
32 As yet he will remain at Nob that
day;
He will shake his fist at the mount of
the daughter of Zion,
The hill of Jerusalem.

10:30 [a]Following Masoretic Text, Targum, and Vulgate; Septuagint and Syriac read *Listen to her, O Anathoth.*

33 Behold, the Lord,
The LORD of hosts,
Will lop off the bough with terror;
Those of high stature *will be* hewn
down,
And the haughty will be humbled.
34 He will cut down the thickets of the
forest with iron,
And Lebanon will fall by the Mighty
One.

CHAPTER 11

The Reign of Jesse's Offspring

There shall come forth a Rod from the
stem of Jesse,
And a Branch shall grow out of his
roots.
2 The Spirit of the LORD shall rest upon
Him,
The Spirit of wisdom and
understanding,
The Spirit of counsel and might,
The Spirit of knowledge and of the
fear of the LORD.

3 His delight *is* in the fear of the LORD,
And He shall not judge by the sight
of His eyes,
Nor decide by the hearing of His
ears;
4 But with righteousness He shall judge
the poor,
And decide with equity for the meek
of the earth;
He shall strike the earth with the rod
of His mouth,
And with the breath of His lips He
shall slay the wicked.
5 Righteousness shall be the belt of His
loins,
And faithfulness the belt of His
waist.

10:27 yoke: The Assyrians were fond of saying that they had made people submit to their "heavy yoke." **anointing oil**: Perhaps a reference to those set aside to serve God.

11:1 Rod: A shoot that springs up from a burned-out or cut-down stump (6:13). **Jesse**: David's father.

6 "The wolf also shall dwell with the
lamb,
The leopard shall lie down with the
young goat,
The calf and the young lion and the
fatling together;
And a little child shall lead them.
7 The cow and the bear shall graze;
Their young ones shall lie down
together;
And the lion shall eat straw like the
ox.
8 The nursing child shall play by the
cobra's hole,
And the weaned child shall put his
hand in the viper's den.
9 They shall not hurt nor destroy in all
My holy mountain,
For the earth shall be full of the
knowledge of the LORD
As the waters cover the sea.

10 "And in that day there shall be a Root
of Jesse,
Who shall stand as a banner to the
people;
For the Gentiles shall seek Him,
And His resting place shall be
glorious."

11 It shall come to pass in that day
That the Lord shall set His hand again
the second time
To recover the remnant of His people
who are left,
From Assyria and Egypt,
From Path'ros and Cush,
From Ē'lam and Shī'nar,
From Hā'math and the islands of the
sea.

12 He will set up a banner for the
nations,
And will assemble the outcasts of
Israel,
And gather together the dispersed of
Judah
From the four corners of the earth.
13 Also the envy of Ē'phra·im shall
depart,
And the adversaries of Judah shall be
cut off;
Ē'phra·im shall not envy Judah,
And Judah shall not harass
Ē'phra·im.
14 But they shall fly down upon the
shoulder of the Phi·lis'tines toward
the west;
Together they shall plunder the
people of the East;
They shall lay their hand on Ē'dom
and Mō'ab;
And the people of Am'mon shall
obey them.
15 The LORD will utterly destroy[a] the
tongue of the Sea of Egypt;
With His mighty wind He will shake
His fist over the River,[b]
And strike it in the seven streams,
And make *men* cross over dryshod.
16 There will be a highway for the
remnant of His people
Who will be left from Assyria,
As it was for Israel
In the day that he came up from the
land of Egypt.

CHAPTER 12

A Hymn of Praise

And in that day you will say:

11:15 [a]Following Masoretic Text and Vulgate; Septuagint, Syriac, and Targum read *dry up.* [b]That is, the Euphrates

11:13 In the second return, connected with the messianic kingdom, the regional rivalry between Israel and Judah will have been erased.

11:14 The neighboring countries, the Philistines, Edom, Moab, and Ammon, will come under the dominion of a united Israel.

11:16 The highway will make it easy to get "home."

"O LORD, I will praise You;
Though You were angry with me,
Your anger is turned away, and You comfort me.
2 Behold, God *is* my salvation,
I will trust and not be afraid;
'For YAH, the LORD, *is* my strength and song;
He also has become my salvation.' "[a]

3 Therefore with joy you will draw water
From the wells of salvation.

4 And in that day you will say:

"Praise the LORD, call upon His name;
Declare His deeds among the peoples,
Make mention that His name is exalted.
5 Sing to the LORD,
For He has done excellent things;
This *is* known in all the earth.
6 Cry out and shout, O inhabitant of Zion,
For great *is* the Holy One of Israel in your midst!"

CHAPTER 13

Proclamation Against Babylon

The burden against Babylon which Ī·sāi'ah the son of Ā'moz saw.

2 "Lift up a banner on the high mountain,
Raise your voice to them;
Wave your hand, that they may enter the gates of the nobles.
3 I have commanded My sanctified ones;
I have also called My mighty ones for My anger—
Those who rejoice in My exaltation."

4 The noise of a multitude in the mountains,
Like that of many people!
A tumultuous noise of the kingdoms of nations gathered together!
The LORD of hosts musters
The army for battle.
5 They come from a far country,
From the end of heaven—
The LORD and His weapons of indignation,
To destroy the whole land.

6 Wail, for the day of the LORD *is* at hand!
It will come as destruction from the Almighty.
7 Therefore all hands will be limp,
Every man's heart will melt,
8 And they will be afraid.
Pangs and sorrows will take hold of *them;*
They will be in pain as a woman in childbirth;
They will be amazed at one another;
Their faces *will be like* flames.

9 Behold, the day of the LORD comes,
Cruel, with both wrath and fierce anger,
To lay the land desolate;
And He will destroy its sinners from it.
10 For the stars of heaven and their constellations
Will not give their light;

12:2 [a]Exodus 15:2

12:2 trust: The great question of the first part of the book is whether we will trust God or human resources. **YAH**: The short form of God's personal name.

12:4–6 Declare: When Israel has experienced God's grace and power, she must become His servant to proclaim His true nature to the world.

13:2 banner: Usually army insignia.

13:3 sanctified ones: Set apart by God for the task of punishing Judah.

The sun will be darkened in its going forth,
And the moon will not cause its light to shine.

11 "I will punish the world for *its* evil,
And the wicked for their iniquity;
I will halt the arrogance of the proud,
And will lay low the haughtiness of the terrible.
12 I will make a mortal more rare than fine gold,
A man more than the golden wedge of Ō′phir.
13 Therefore I will shake the heavens,
And the earth will move out of her place,
In the wrath of the LORD of hosts
And in the day of His fierce anger.
14 It shall be as the hunted gazelle,
And as a sheep that no man takes up;
Every man will turn to his own people,
And everyone will flee to his own land.
15 Everyone who is found will be thrust through,
And everyone who is captured will fall by the sword.
16 Their children also will be dashed to pieces before their eyes;
Their houses will be plundered
And their wives ravished.

17 "Behold, I will stir up the Mēdes against them,
Who will not regard silver;
And *as for* gold, they will not delight in it.
18 Also *their* bows will dash the young men to pieces,
And they will have no pity on the fruit of the womb;
Their eye will not spare children.
19 And Babylon, the glory of kingdoms,
The beauty of the Chal·dē′ans' pride,
Will be as when God overthrew Sod′om and Go·mor′rah.
20 It will never be inhabited,
Nor will it be settled from generation to generation;
Nor will the Arabian pitch tents there,
Nor will the shepherds make their sheepfolds there.
21 But wild beasts of the desert will lie there,
And their houses will be full of owls;
Ostriches will dwell there,
And wild goats will caper there.
22 The hyenas will howl in their citadels,
And jackals in their pleasant palaces.
Her time *is* near to come,
And her days will not be prolonged."

CHAPTER 14

Mercy on Jacob

For the LORD will have mercy on Jacob,
and will still choose Israel, and settle them
in their own land. The strangers will be
joined with them, and they will cling to the
house of Jacob. 2Then people will take
them and bring them to their place, and the
house of Israel will possess them for ser-
vants and maids in the land of the LORD;
they will take them captive whose captives
they were, and rule over their oppressors.

Fall of the King of Babylon

3It shall come to pass in the day the
LORD gives you rest from your sorrow, and
from your fear and the hard bondage in

13:17 Medes: People from the mountains east of Mesopotamia. Isaiah's prophecy was fulfilled 200 years later when the Medes and the Persians destroyed Nebuchadnezzar's Babylon.

13:20–22 never be inhabited: God's word is sure. The day will come when **Babylon** is totally destroyed. Yet God's city, Jerusalem, will thrive forever.

14:1–3 Babylon will not be able to keep her captives.

which you were made to serve, [4]that you will take up this proverb against the king of Babylon, and say:

"How the oppressor has ceased,
The golden[a] city ceased!
5 The LORD has broken the staff of the wicked,
The scepter of the rulers;
6 He who struck the people in wrath with a continual stroke,
He who ruled the nations in anger,
Is persecuted *and* no one hinders.
7 The whole earth is at rest *and* quiet;
They break forth into singing.
8 Indeed the cypress trees rejoice over you,
And the cedars of Lebanon,
Saying, 'Since you were cut down,
No woodsman has come up against us.'

9 "Hell from beneath is excited about you,
To meet *you* at your coming;
It stirs up the dead for you,
All the chief ones of the earth;
It has raised up from their thrones
All the kings of the nations.
10 They all shall speak and say to you:
'Have you also become as weak as we?
Have you become like us?
11 Your pomp is brought down to Shē'ōl,
And the sound of your stringed instruments;
The maggot is spread under you,
And worms cover you.'

14:4 [a]Or *insolent* 14:12 [a]Literally *Day Star*

The Fall of Lucifer

12 "How you are fallen from heaven,
O Lū'ci·fer,[a] son of the morning!
How you are cut down to the ground,
You who weakened the nations!
13 For you have said in your heart:
'I will ascend into heaven,
I will exalt my throne above the stars of God;
I will also sit on the mount of the congregation
On the farthest sides of the north;
14 I will ascend above the heights of the clouds,
I will be like the Most High.'
15 Yet you shall be brought down to Shē'ōl,
To the lowest depths of the Pit.

16 "Those who see you will gaze at you,
And consider you, *saying:*
'*Is* this the man who made the earth tremble,
Who shook kingdoms,
17 Who made the world as a wilderness
And destroyed its cities,
Who did not open the house of his prisoners?'

18 "All the kings of the nations,
All of them, sleep in glory,
Everyone in his own house;
19 But you are cast out of your grave
Like an abominable branch,
Like the garment of those who are slain,
Thrust through with a sword,
Who go down to the stones of the pit,
Like a corpse trodden underfoot.
20 You will not be joined with them in burial,

14:4–23 A mocking lament celebrating the death of the Mesopotamian oppressor.
14:12–15 The description of the king of Babylon's fall is often said to be referring to the fall of Satan. The pride which makes a created being think that it can take the place of God will eventually land that creature in hell.
14:20 His pride which led him to try to conquer the world has only brought the world against him and destroyed his own land.

Because you have destroyed your land
And slain your people.
The brood of evildoers shall never be named.
21 Prepare slaughter for his children
Because of the iniquity of their fathers,
Lest they rise up and possess the land,
And fill the face of the world with cities."

Babylon Destroyed

22 "For I will rise up against them," says the LORD of hosts,
"And cut off from Babylon the name and remnant,
And offspring and posterity," says the LORD.
23 "I will also make it a possession for the porcupine,
And marshes of muddy water;
I will sweep it with the broom of destruction," says the LORD of hosts.

Assyria Destroyed

24 The LORD of hosts has sworn, saying,
"Surely, as I have thought, so it shall come to pass,
And as I have purposed, *so* it shall stand:
25 That I will break the Assyrian in My land,
And on My mountains tread him underfoot.
Then his yoke shall be removed from them,
And his burden removed from their shoulders.
26 This *is* the purpose that is purposed against the whole earth,
And this *is* the hand that is stretched out over all the nations.
27 For the LORD of hosts has purposed,
And who will annul *it?*
His hand *is* stretched out,
And who will turn it back?"

Philistia Destroyed

28This is the burden which came in the year that King Ā'haz died.

29 "Do not rejoice, all you of Phi·lis'ti·a,
Because the rod that struck you is broken;
For out of the serpent's roots will come forth a viper,
And its offspring *will be* a fiery flying serpent.
30 The firstborn of the poor will feed,
And the needy will lie down in safety;
I will kill your roots with famine,
And it will slay your remnant.
31 Wail, O gate! Cry, O city!
All you of Phi·lis'ti·a *are* dissolved;
For smoke will come from the north,
And no one *will be* alone in his appointed times."

32 What will they answer the messengers of the nation?
That the LORD has founded Zion,
And the poor of His people shall take refuge in it.

CHAPTER 15

Proclamation Against Moab

The burden against Mō'ab.

14:24–27 Assyria will be broken in God's land according to God's purpose. Verse 27 is a worthy tribute to God's power.

14:28–32 Prophecies against **Philistia**. The serpent (v. 29) probably refers to Assyria against whom Philistia was planning to revolt. The poor (v. 30) of Judea would survive, but the warriors of Philistia (v. 31) would perish (see 40:30, 31).

Because in the night Ar of Mō′ab is
laid waste
And destroyed,
Because in the night Kir of Mō′ab is
laid waste
And destroyed,
2 He has gone up to the temple[a] and
Dī′bon,
To the high places to weep.
Mō′ab will wail over Nē′bō and over
Med′e·ba;
On all their heads *will be* baldness,
And every beard cut off.
3 In their streets they will clothe
themselves with sackcloth;
On the tops of their houses
And in their streets
Everyone will wail, weeping bitterly.
4 Hesh′bon and Ē·le·ā′leh will cry out,
Their voice shall be heard as far as
Jā′haz;
Therefore the armed soldiers[a] of
Mō′ab will cry out;
His life will be burdensome to him.

5 "My heart will cry out for Mō′ab;
His fugitives *shall flee* to Zō′ar,
Like a three-year-old heifer.[a]
For by the Ascent of Lū′hith
They will go up with weeping;
For in the way of Hor·ō·nā′īm
They will raise up a cry of
destruction,
6 For the waters of Nim′rim will be
desolate,
For the green grass has withered
away;
The grass fails, there is nothing green.
7 Therefore the abundance they have
gained,
And what they have laid up,
They will carry away to the Brook of
the Willows.
8 For the cry has gone all around the
borders of Mō′ab,
Its wailing to Eg·lā′im
And its wailing to Bē′er Ē′lim.
9 For the waters of Dī′mon[a] will be full
of blood;
Because I will bring more upon
Dī′mon,[b]
Lions upon him who escapes from
Mō′ab,
And on the remnant of the land."

CHAPTER 16

Moab Destroyed

Send the lamb to the ruler of the
land,
From Sē′la to the wilderness,
To the mount of the daughter of Zion.
2 For it shall be as a wandering bird
thrown out of the nest;
So shall be the daughters of Mō′ab at
the fords of the Ar′non.

3 "Take counsel, execute judgment;
Make your shadow like the night in
the middle of the day;
Hide the outcasts,
Do not betray him who escapes.
4 Let My outcasts dwell with you,
O Mō′ab;
Be a shelter to them from the face of
the spoiler.
For the extortioner is at an end,
Devastation ceases,

15:2 [a]Hebrew *bayith,* literally *house* 15:4 [a]Following Masoretic Text, Targum, and Vulgate; Septuagint and Syriac read *loins.* 15:5 [a]Or *The Third Eglath,* an unknown city (compare Jeremiah 48:34)
15:9 [a]Following Masoretic Text and Targum; Dead Sea Scrolls and Vulgate read *Dibon;* Septuagint reads *Rimon.* [b]Following Masoretic Text and Targum; Dead Sea Scrolls and Vulgate read *Dibon;* Septuagint reads *Rimon.*

15:2, 3 baldness . . . cut off . . . sackcloth: Signs of mourning over the sudden destruction of their country.
15:5 The direction of flight is southward, as would be the case if the attacker were from the north or northeast.
16:1 Send the lamb is perhaps a reference to a peace offering (Lev. 3:6, 7).

The oppressors are consumed out of
the land.
5 In mercy the throne will be
established;
And One will sit on it in truth, in the
tabernacle of David,
Judging and seeking justice and
hastening righteousness."

6 We have heard of the pride of
Mō'ab—
He is very proud—
Of his haughtiness and his pride and
his wrath;
But his lies *shall* not *be* so.
7 Therefore Mō'ab shall wail for Mō'ab;
Everyone shall wail.
For the foundations of Kir Har'e·seth
you shall mourn;
Surely *they are* stricken.

8 For the fields of Hesh'bon languish,
And the vine of Sib'mah;
The lords of the nations have broken
down its choice plants,
Which have reached to Jā'zer
And wandered through the
wilderness.
Her branches are stretched out,
They are gone over the sea.
9 Therefore I will bewail the vine of
Sib'mah,
With the weeping of Jā'zer;
I will drench you with my tears,
O Hesh'bon and Ē·le·ā'leh;
For battle cries have fallen
Over your summer fruits and your
harvest.

10 Gladness is taken away,
And joy from the plentiful field;
In the vineyards there will be no
singing,
Nor will there be shouting;
No treaders will tread out wine in the
presses;
I have made their shouting cease.
11 Therefore my heart shall resound like
a harp for Mō'ab,
And my inner being for Kir Hē'res.

12 And it shall come to pass,
When it is seen that Mō'ab is weary
on the high place,
That he will come to his sanctuary to
pray;
But he will not prevail.

13 This *is* the word which the LORD has
spoken concerning Mō'ab since that time.
14 But now the LORD has spoken, saying,
"Within three years, as the years of a hired
man, the glory of Mō'ab will be despised
with all that great multitude, and the rem-
nant *will be* very small *and* feeble."

CHAPTER 17

Proclamation Against Syria and Israel

The burden against Damascus.

"Behold, Damascus will cease from
being a city,
And it will be a ruinous heap.
2 The cities of A·rō'er *are* forsaken;[a]
They will be for flocks

17:2 [a]Following Masoretic Text and Vulgate; Septuagint reads *It shall be forsaken forever;* Targum reads *Its cities shall be forsaken and desolate.*

16:5 God will establish Israel's rule over Moab (see 11:14) through One who is a descendant of David (see 11:3–5; 61:1; Luke 4:18–20).

16:8–12 Moab is compared to a spreading vine which is now trampled.

16:14 Within three years, as carefully calculated as a hired man (perhaps an indentured servant) would count the days until his independence, Moab will fall.

17:1–11 Prophecies against Damascus and Ephraim, since the two were allies (see 7:1, 2).

Which lie down, and no one will
make *them* afraid.
3 The fortress also will cease from
Ē′phra·im,
The kingdom from Damascus,
And the remnant of Syria;
They will be as the glory of the
children of Israel,"
Says the LORD of hosts.

4 "In that day it shall come to pass
That the glory of Jacob will wane,
And the fatness of his flesh grow
lean.
5 It shall be as when the harvester
gathers the grain,
And reaps the heads with his arm;
It shall be as he who gathers heads of
grain
In the Valley of Reph′a·im.
6 Yet gleaning grapes will be left in it,
Like the shaking of an olive tree,
Two *or* three olives at the top of the
uppermost bough,
Four *or* five in its most fruitful
branches,"
Says the LORD God of Israel.

7 In that day a man will look to his
Maker,
And his eyes will have respect for the
Holy One of Israel.
8 He will not look to the altars,
The work of his hands;
He will not respect what his fingers
have made,
Nor the wooden images[a] nor the
incense altars.

9 In that day his strong cities will be as
a forsaken bough[a]
And an uppermost branch,[b]
Which they left because of the
children of Israel;
And there will be desolation.

10 Because you have forgotten the God
of your salvation,
And have not been mindful of the
Rock of your stronghold,
Therefore you will plant pleasant
plants
And set out foreign seedlings;
11 In the day you will make your plant
to grow,
And in the morning you will make
your seed to flourish;
But the harvest *will be* a heap of ruins
In the day of grief and desperate
sorrow.

12 Woe to the multitude of many people
Who make a noise like the roar of the
seas,
And to the rushing of nations
That make a rushing like the rushing
of mighty waters!
13 The nations will rush like the rushing
of many waters;
But *God* will rebuke them and they
will flee far away,
And be chased like the chaff of the
mountains before the wind,
Like a rolling thing before the
whirlwind.
14 Then behold, at eventide, trouble!
And before the morning, he *is* no
more.
This *is* the portion of those who
plunder us,
And the lot of those who rob us.

17:8 [a]Hebrew *Asherim,* Canaanite deities
17:9 [a]Septuagint reads *Hivites;* Targum reads *laid waste;* Vulgate reads *as the plows.* [b]Septuagint reads *Amorites;* Targum reads *in ruins;* Vulgate reads *corn.*

17:4–6 Like a harvested field or olive tree, Israel will have only a few scraps left.
17:7, 8 Since their idols could not deliver them, the people of northern Israel will be prompted to turn back to God. Often it is only after some disaster that we realize how far we have drifted from God.

CHAPTER 18

Proclamation Against Ethiopia

Woe to the land shadowed with
buzzing wings,
Which *is* beyond the rivers of
Ethiopia,
2 Which sends ambassadors by sea,
Even in vessels of reed on the waters,
saying,
"Go, swift messengers, to a nation tall
and smooth *of skin,*
To a people terrible from their
beginning onward,
A nation powerful and treading
down,
Whose land the rivers divide."

3 All inhabitants of the world and
dwellers on the earth:
When he lifts up a banner on the
mountains, you see *it;*
And when he blows a trumpet, you
hear *it.*
4 For so the LORD said to me,
"I will take My rest,
And I will look from My dwelling
place
Like clear heat in sunshine,
Like a cloud of dew in the heat of
harvest."
5 For before the harvest, when the bud
is perfect
And the sour grape is ripening in the
flower,
He will both cut off the sprigs with
pruning hooks
And take away *and* cut down the
branches.
6 They will be left together for the
mountain birds of prey
And for the beasts of the earth;
The birds of prey will summer on
them,
And all the beasts of the earth will
winter on them.

7 In that time a present will be brought
to the LORD of hosts
From[a] a people tall and smooth *of
skin,*
And from a people terrible from their
beginning onward,
A nation powerful and treading
down,
Whose land the rivers divide—
To the place of the name of the LORD
of hosts,
To Mount Zion.

CHAPTER 19

Proclamation Against Egypt

The burden against Egypt.

Behold, the LORD rides on a swift
cloud,
And will come into Egypt;
The idols of Egypt will totter at His
presence,
And the heart of Egypt will melt in its
midst.

2 "I will set Egyptians against Egyptians;
Everyone will fight against his
brother,
And everyone against his neighbor,
City against city, kingdom against
kingdom.
3 The spirit of Egypt will fail in its
midst;
I will destroy their counsel,
And they will consult the idols and
the charmers,
The mediums and the sorcerers.
4 And the Egyptians I will give
Into the hand of a cruel master,

18:7 [a]Following Dead Sea Scrolls, Septuagint, and Vulgate; Masoretic Text omits *From;* Targum reads *To.*

18:1, 2 Buzzing wings may refer to the flies or mosquitoes of Africa.
19:1–4 The inadequacy of Egypt's ancient religion.

And a fierce king will rule over
them,"
Says the Lord, the LORD of hosts.

5 The waters will fail from the sea,
And the river will be wasted and
dried up.
6 The rivers will turn foul;
The brooks of defense will be emptied
and dried up;
The reeds and rushes will wither.
7 The papyrus reeds by the River,[a] by
the mouth of the River,
And everything sown by the River,
Will wither, be driven away, and be
no more.
8 The fishermen also will mourn;
All those will lament who cast hooks
into the River,
And they will languish who spread
nets on the waters.
9 Moreover those who work in fine flax
And those who weave fine fabric will
be ashamed;
10 And its foundations will be broken.
All who make wages *will be* troubled
of soul.

11 Surely the princes of Zō'an *are* fools;
Pharaoh's wise counselors give
foolish counsel.
How do you say to Pharaoh, "I *am*
the son of the wise,
The son of ancient kings?"
12 Where *are* they?
Where are your wise men?
Let them tell you now,
And let them know what the LORD of
hosts has purposed against Egypt.
13 The princes of Zō'an have become
fools;
The princes of Noph[a] are deceived;
They have also deluded Egypt,
Those who are the mainstay of its
tribes.
14 The LORD has mingled a perverse
spirit in her midst;
And they have caused Egypt to err in
all her work,
As a drunken man staggers in his
vomit.
15 Neither will there be *any* work for
Egypt,
Which the head or tail,
Palm branch or bulrush, may do.[a]

16In that day Egypt will be like women,
and will be afraid and fear because of the
waving of the hand of the LORD of hosts,
which He waves over it. 17And the land of
Judah will be a terror to Egypt; everyone
who makes mention of it will be afraid in
himself, because of the counsel of the LORD
of hosts which He has determined against
it.

Egypt, Assyria, and Israel Blessed

18In that day five cities in the land of
Egypt will speak the language of Cā'naan
and swear by the LORD of hosts; one will be
called the City of Destruction.[a]
19In that day there will be an altar to the
LORD in the midst of the land of Egypt, and
a pillar to the LORD at its border. 20And it
will be for a sign and for a witness to the
LORD of hosts in the land of Egypt; for they

19:7 [a]That is, the Nile 19:13 [a]That is, ancient Memphis 19:15 [a]Compare Isaiah 9:14–16
19:18 [a]Some Hebrew manuscripts, Arabic, Dead Sea Scrolls, Targum, and Vulgate read *Sun;* Septuagint reads *Asedek* (literally *Righteousness*).

19:5–10 The waters will fail: A symbolic statement of the inadequacy of the most reliable thing in Egypt, the Nile, Egypt's source of life. The prophet envisions the Nile drying up and the results of such a catastrophe.

19:15 Egypt cannot be saved by anything that any human can do.

19:16–25 Instead of Judah going to Egypt for help against Assyria, as some were counseling (30:1, 2; 31:1–3), Isaiah sees a day when Egypt will come to Judah to seek God.

19:18 Egypt's conversion will be so complete that some cities will even adopt Hebrew as their language.

will cry to the LORD because of the oppressors, and He will send them a Savior and a Mighty One, and He will deliver them. 21Then the LORD will be known to Egypt, and the Egyptians will know the LORD in that day, and will make sacrifice and offering; yes, they will make a vow to the LORD and perform *it*. 22And the LORD will strike Egypt, He will strike and heal *it;* they will return to the LORD, and He will be entreated by them and heal them.

23In that day there will be a highway from Egypt to Assyria, and the Assyrian will come into Egypt and the Egyptian into Assyria, and the Egyptians will serve with the Assyrians.

24In that day Israel will be one of three with Egypt and Assyria—a blessing in the midst of the land, 25whom the LORD of hosts shall bless, saying, "Blessed *is* Egypt My people, and Assyria the work of My hands, and Israel My inheritance."

CHAPTER 20

The Sign Against Egypt and Ethiopia

In the year that Tartan[a] came to Ash'dod, when Sar'gon the king of Assyria sent him, and he fought against Ash'dod and took it, 2at the same time the LORD spoke by Ī·sāi'ah the son of Ā'moz, saying, "Go, and remove the sackcloth from your body, and take your sandals off your feet." And he did so, walking naked and barefoot.

3Then the LORD said, "Just as My servant Ī·sāi'ah has walked naked and barefoot three years *for* a sign and a wonder against Egypt and Ethiopia, 4so shall the king of Assyria lead away the Egyptians as prisoners and the Ethiopians as captives, young and old, naked and barefoot, with their buttocks uncovered, to the shame of Egypt. 5Then they shall be afraid and ashamed of Ethiopia their expectation and Egypt their glory. 6And the inhabitant of this territory will say in that day, 'Surely such *is* our expectation, wherever we flee for help to be delivered from the king of Assyria; and how shall we escape?' "

CHAPTER 21

The Fall of Babylon Proclaimed

The burden against the Wilderness of the Sea.

As whirlwinds in the South pass
through,
So it comes from the desert, from a
terrible land.
2 A distressing vision is declared to me;
The treacherous dealer deals
treacherously,
And the plunderer plunders.
Go up, O Ē'lam!
Besiege, O Media!
All its sighing I have made to cease.

3 Therefore my loins are filled with
pain;
Pangs have taken hold of me, like the
pangs of a woman in labor.
I was distressed when *I* heard *it;*
I was dismayed when *I* saw *it.*
4 My heart wavered, fearfulness
frightened me;
The night for which I longed He
turned into fear for me.
5 Prepare the table,
Set a watchman in the tower,

20:1 [a]Or *the Commander in Chief*

19:23–25 Instead of looking to Egypt for deliverance from Assyria, Israel should look to God so that she might become a mediator for both Assyria and Egypt to find Him and have fellowship with each other.

20:1–6 Isaiah acts out Egypt's fate of being taken naked into Assyrian captivity.

21:1 Wilderness of the Sea is probably an ironic description of Babylon, apparently lush but truly barren.

21:2 Elam . . . Media: Babylon was captured by a coalition of Persians (from Elam) and Medians.

Eat and drink.
Arise, you princes,
Anoint the shield!

6 For thus has the Lord said to me:
"Go, set a watchman,
Let him declare what he sees."
7 And he saw a chariot *with* a pair of horsemen,
A chariot of donkeys, *and* a chariot of camels,
And he listened earnestly with great care.
8 Then he cried, "A lion,[a] my Lord!
I stand continually on the watchtower in the daytime;
I have sat at my post every night.
9 And look, here comes a chariot of men *with* a pair of horsemen!"
Then he answered and said,
"Babylon is fallen, is fallen!
And all the carved images of her gods
He has broken to the ground."

10 Oh, my threshing and the grain of my floor!
That which I have heard from the LORD of hosts,
The God of Israel,
I have declared to you.

Proclamation Against Edom

11The burden against Dū'mah.

He calls to me out of Sē'ir,
"Watchman, what of the night?
Watchman, what of the night?"
12 The watchman said,
"The morning comes, and also the night.
If you will inquire, inquire;
Return! Come back!"

21:8 [a]Dead Sea Scrolls read *Then the observer cried.*

Proclamation Against Arabia

13The burden against Arabia.

In the forest in Arabia you will lodge,
O you traveling companies of Ded'an·ītes.
14 O inhabitants of the land of Tē'ma,
Bring water to him who is thirsty;
With their bread they met him who fled.
15 For they fled from the swords, from the drawn sword,
From the bent bow, and from the distress of war.

16For thus the LORD has said to me:
"Within a year, according to the year of a
hired man, all the glory of Kē'dar will fail;
17and the remainder of the number of
archers, the mighty men of the people of
Kē'dar, will be diminished; for the LORD
God of Israel has spoken *it*."

CHAPTER 22

Proclamation Against Jerusalem

The burden against the Valley of Vision.

What ails you now, that you have all gone up to the housetops,
2 You who are full of noise,
A tumultuous city, a joyous city?
Your slain *men are* not slain with the sword,
Nor dead in battle.
3 All your rulers have fled together;
They are captured by the archers.
All who are found in you are bound together;
They have fled from afar.
4 Therefore I said, "Look away from me,
I will weep bitterly;

22:1–7 Valley of Vision: An ironic description. Very little can be seen from a valley. Jerusalem is blind.

22:2–5 Probably prophetic, perhaps referring to Zedekiah's abortive flight to escape Nebuchadnezzar in 586 B.C. (2 Kin. 25:4, 5).

Do not labor to comfort me
Because of the plundering of the
daughter of my people."

5 For *it is* a day of trouble and treading
down and perplexity
By the Lord GOD of hosts
In the Valley of Vision—
Breaking down the walls
And of crying to the mountain.
6 Ē′lam bore the quiver
With chariots of men *and* horsemen,
And Kir uncovered the shield.
7 It shall come to pass *that* your
choicest valleys
Shall be full of chariots,
And the horsemen shall set
themselves in array at the gate.
8 He removed the protection of Judah.
You looked in that day to the armor
of the House of the Forest;
9 You also saw the damage to the city
of David,
That it was great;
And you gathered together the waters
of the lower pool.
10 You numbered the houses of
Jerusalem,
And the houses you broke down
To fortify the wall.
11 You also made a reservoir between
the two walls
For the water of the old pool.
But you did not look to its Maker,
Nor did you have respect for Him
who fashioned it long ago.

12 And in that day the Lord GOD of
hosts
Called for weeping and for
mourning,
For baldness and for girding with
sackcloth.
13 But instead, joy and gladness,
Slaying oxen and killing sheep,
Eating meat and drinking wine:
"Let us eat and drink, for tomorrow
we die!"

14 Then it was revealed in my hearing
by the LORD of hosts,
"Surely for this iniquity there will be
no atonement for you,
Even to your death," says the Lord
GOD of hosts.

The Judgment on Shebna

15 Thus says the Lord GOD of hosts:

"Go, proceed to this steward,
To Sheb′na, who *is* over the house,
and say:
16 'What have you here, and whom have
you here,
That you have hewn a sepulcher here,
As he who hews himself a sepulcher
on high,
Who carves a tomb for himself in a
rock?
17 Indeed, the LORD will throw you
away violently,
O mighty man,
And will surely seize you.
18 He will surely turn violently and toss
you like a ball
Into a large country;
There you shall die, and there your
glorious chariots
Shall be the shame of your master's
house.
19 So I will drive you out of your office,
And from your position he will pull
you down.[a]

20 'Then it shall be in that day,
That I will call My servant E·lī′a·kim
the son of Hil·kī′ah;
21 I will clothe him with your robe
And strengthen him with your belt;

22:19 [a]Septuagint omits *he will pull you down;* Syriac, Targum, and Vulgate read *I will pull you down.*

22:20–25 Eliakim, a more faithful man, will replace Shebna. What an honor to be called **My servant** by God.

I will commit your responsibility into his hand.
He shall be a father to the inhabitants of Jerusalem
And to the house of Judah.
22 The key of the house of David
I will lay on his shoulder;
So he shall open, and no one shall shut;
And he shall shut, and no one shall open.
23 I will fasten him *as* a peg in a secure place,
And he will become a glorious throne to his father's house.

24 'They will hang on him all the glory of
his father's house, the offspring and the
posterity, all vessels of small quantity, from
the cups to all the pitchers. 25 In that day,'
says the LORD of hosts, 'the peg that is fas-
tened in the secure place will be removed
and be cut down and fall, and the burden
that *was* on it will be cut off; for the LORD
has spoken.' "

CHAPTER 23

Proclamation Against Tyre

The burden against Tȳre.

Wail, you ships of Tar'shish!
For it is laid waste,
So that there is no house, no harbor;
From the land of Cyprus[a] it is revealed to them.

2 Be still, you inhabitants of the coastland,
You merchants of Sī'don,
Whom those who cross the sea have filled.[a]
3 And on great waters the grain of Shī'hor,
The harvest of the River,[a] *is* her revenue;
And she is a marketplace for the nations.

4 Be ashamed, O Sī'don;
For the sea has spoken,
The strength of the sea, saying,
"I do not labor, nor bring forth children;
Neither do I rear young men,
Nor bring up virgins."
5 When the report *reaches* Egypt,
They also will be in agony at the report of Tȳre.

6 Cross over to Tar'shish;
Wail, you inhabitants of the coastland!
7 *Is* this your joyous *city,*
Whose antiquity *is* from ancient days,
Whose feet carried her far off to dwell?
8 Who has taken this counsel against Tȳre, the crowning *city,*
Whose merchants *are* princes,
Whose traders *are* the honorable of the earth?
9 The LORD of hosts has purposed it,
To bring to dishonor the pride of all glory,
To bring into contempt all the honorable of the earth.

10 Overflow through your land like the River,[a]
O daughter of Tar'shish;
There is no more strength.
11 He stretched out His hand over the sea,

23:1 [a]Hebrew *Kittim,* western lands, especially Cyprus
23:2 [a]Following Masoretic Text and Vulgate; Septuagint and Targum read *Passing over the water;* Dead Sea Scrolls read *Your messengers passing over the sea.*
23:3 [a]That is, the Nile 23:10 [a]That is, the Nile

23:1–18 The Phoenician seaport of **Tyre** was the western commercial giant as Babylon was in the east.
23:1 Tarshish: Probably somewhere in Spain.
23:2 Sidon: Sister city of Tyre.

He shook the kingdoms;
The LORD has given a commandment
against Cā'naan
To destroy its strongholds.
12 And He said, "You will rejoice no
more,
O you oppressed virgin daughter of
Sī'don.
Arise, cross over to Cyprus;
There also you will have no rest."

13 Behold, the land of the Chal·dē'ans,
This people *which* was not;
Assyria founded it for wild beasts of
the desert.
They set up its towers,
They raised up its palaces,
And brought it to ruin.

14 Wail, you ships of Tar'shish!
For your strength is laid waste.

15Now it shall come to pass in that day
that Tȳre will be forgotten seventy years,
according to the days of one king. At the
end of seventy years it will happen to Tȳre
as *in* the song of the harlot:

16 "Take a harp, go about the city,
You forgotten harlot;
Make sweet melody, sing many
songs,
That you may be remembered."

17And it shall be, at the end of seventy
years, that the LORD will deal with Tȳre.
She will return to her hire, and commit for-
nication with all the kingdoms of the
world on the face of the earth. 18Her gain
and her pay will be set apart for the LORD;
it will not be treasured nor laid up, for her
gain will be for those who dwell before the
LORD, to eat sufficiently, and for fine cloth-
ing.

CHAPTER 24

Impending Judgment on the Earth

Behold, the LORD makes the earth
empty and makes it waste,
Distorts its surface
And scatters abroad its inhabitants.
2 And it shall be:
As with the people, so with the priest;
As with the servant, so with his
master;
As with the maid, so with her
mistress;
As with the buyer, so with the seller;
As with the lender, so with the
borrower;
As with the creditor, so with the
debtor.
3 The land shall be entirely emptied
and utterly plundered,
For the LORD has spoken this word.

4 The earth mourns *and* fades away,
The world languishes *and* fades away;
The haughty people of the earth
languish.
5 The earth is also defiled under its
inhabitants,
Because they have transgressed the
laws,
Changed the ordinance,
Broken the everlasting covenant.
6 Therefore the curse has devoured the
earth,
And those who dwell in it are
desolate.
Therefore the inhabitants of the earth
are burned,
And few men *are* left.

23:13 Chaldeans: In Isaiah's day Babylon was not a military power, but he prophesies that it is Babylon, not Assyria, which will overthrow Tyre. He was correct.

24:1–23 Human sin has brought divine judgment, and the earth is laid waste.

24:5, 6 The spiritual laws of God's universe are as immutable as its physical laws. We do not break them; we only break ourselves upon them.

7 The new wine fails, the vine
languishes,
All the merry-hearted sigh.
8 The mirth of the tambourine ceases,
The noise of the jubilant ends,
The joy of the harp ceases.
9 They shall not drink wine with a
song;
Strong drink is bitter to those who
drink it.
10 The city of confusion is broken down;
Every house is shut up, so that none
may go in.
11 *There is* a cry for wine in the streets,
All joy is darkened,
The mirth of the land is gone.
12 In the city desolation is left,
And the gate is stricken with
destruction.
13 When it shall be thus in the midst of
the land among the people,
It shall be like the shaking of an olive
tree,
Like the gleaning of grapes when the
vintage is done.

14 They shall lift up their voice, they
shall sing;
For the majesty of the LORD
They shall cry aloud from the sea.
15 Therefore glorify the LORD in the
dawning light,
The name of the LORD God of Israel in
the coastlands of the sea.
16 From the ends of the earth we have
heard songs:
"Glory to the righteous!"
But I said, "I am ruined, ruined!
Woe to me!
The treacherous dealers have dealt
treacherously,
Indeed, the treacherous dealers have
dealt very treacherously."

17 Fear and the pit and the snare
Are upon you, O inhabitant of the
earth.
18 And it shall be
That he who flees from the noise of
the fear
Shall fall into the pit,
And he who comes up from the midst
of the pit
Shall be caught in the snare;
For the windows from on high are
open,
And the foundations of the earth are
shaken.

19 The earth is violently broken,
The earth is split open,
The earth is shaken exceedingly.
20 The earth shall reel to and fro like a
drunkard,
And shall totter like a hut;
Its transgression shall be heavy upon
it,
And it will fall, and not rise again.

21 It shall come to pass in that day
That the LORD will punish on high the
host of exalted ones,
And on the earth the kings of the
earth.
22 They will be gathered together,
As prisoners are gathered in the
pit,
And will be shut up in the
prison;
After many days they will be
punished.
23 Then the moon will be disgraced
And the sun ashamed;
For the LORD of hosts will reign
On Mount Zion and in Jerusalem
And before His elders, gloriously.

24:14–18 Those who trust God will see His hand in the cataclysms and will know that His dawning light is near. At the same time, sensitive persons like Isaiah will be appalled at the human tragedy accompanying the disasters.

24:21–23 Earth's sin is human pride, the belief that somehow humanity is ultimate, when in fact only God is.

CHAPTER 25

Praise to God

O LORD, You *are* my God.
I will exalt You,
I will praise Your name,
For You have done wonderful *things;*
Your counsels of old *are* faithfulness
and truth.
2 For You have made a city a ruin,
A fortified city a ruin,
A palace of foreigners to be a city no
more;
It will never be rebuilt.
3 Therefore the strong people will
glorify You;
The city of the terrible nations will
fear You.
4 For You have been a strength to the
poor,
A strength to the needy in his
distress,
A refuge from the storm,
A shade from the heat;
For the blast of the terrible ones *is* as
a storm *against* the wall.
5 You will reduce the noise of aliens,
As heat in a dry place;
As heat in the shadow of a cloud,
The song of the terrible ones will be
diminished.

6 And in this mountain
The LORD of hosts will make for all
people
A feast of choice pieces,
A feast of wines on the lees,
Of fat things full of marrow,
Of well-refined wines on the lees.
7 And He will destroy on this
mountain
The surface of the covering cast over
all people,
And the veil that is spread over all
nations.
8 He will swallow up death forever,
And the Lord GOD will wipe away
tears from all faces;
The rebuke of His people
He will take away from all the earth;
For the LORD has spoken.

9 And it will be said in that day:
"Behold, this *is* our God;
We have waited for Him, and He will
save us.
This *is* the LORD;
We have waited for Him;
We will be glad and rejoice in His
salvation."

10 For on this mountain the hand of the
LORD will rest,
And Mō'ab shall be trampled down
under Him,
As straw is trampled down for the
refuse heap.
11 And He will spread out His hands in
their midst
As a swimmer reaches out to swim,
And He will bring down their pride
Together with the trickery of their
hands.
12 The fortress of the high fort of your
walls
He will bring down, lay low,
And bring to the ground, down to the
dust.

> Faith according to the Bible is confidence in God when He is inscrutable and apparently contradictory in His providences.
>
> Oswald Chambers

25:1–12 The city of God. In contrast to the destroyed city of confusion (24:10; 25:2), God's city knows joy and feasting because it has submitted to His rule.

25:6–9 A great feast of joy because God will have vanquished death once and for all.

CHAPTER 26

A Song of Salvation

In that day this song will be sung in the land of Judah:

"We have a strong city;
God will appoint salvation *for* walls
and bulwarks.
2 Open the gates,
That the righteous nation which
keeps the truth may enter in.
3 You will keep *him* in perfect peace,
Whose mind *is* stayed *on You,*
Because he trusts in You.

I pray, God, that You will keep my wife in perfect peace, whose mind is stayed on You, because she trusts in You.

adapted from Isaiah 26:3

4 Trust in the LORD forever,
For in YAH, the LORD, *is* everlasting
strength.[a]
5 For He brings down those who dwell
on high,
The lofty city;
He lays it low,
He lays it low to the ground,
He brings it down to the dust.
6 The foot shall tread it down—
The feet of the poor
And the steps of the needy."

7 The way of the just *is* uprightness;
O Most Upright,
You weigh the path of the just.
8 Yes, in the way of Your judgments,
O LORD, we have waited for You;
The desire of *our* soul *is* for Your
name
And for the remembrance of You.
9 With my soul I have desired You in
the night,
Yes, by my spirit within me I will
seek You early;
For when Your judgments *are* in the
earth,
The inhabitants of the world will
learn righteousness.

10 Let grace be shown to the wicked,
Yet he will not learn righteousness;
In the land of uprightness he will
deal unjustly,
And will not behold the majesty of
the LORD.
11 LORD, *when* Your hand is lifted up,
they will not see.
But they will see and be ashamed
For *their* envy of people;
Yes, the fire of Your enemies shall
devour them.

12 LORD, You will establish peace for us,
For You have also done all our works
in us.
13 O LORD our God, masters besides You
Have had dominion over us;
But by You only we make mention of
Your name.
14 *They are* dead, they will not live;
They are deceased, they will not rise.
Therefore You have punished and
destroyed them,
And made all their memory to perish.
15 You have increased the nation,
O LORD,
You have increased the nation;
You are glorified;
You have expanded all the borders of
the land.

26:4 [a]Or *Rock of Ages*

26:1–6 The song of the righteous. The theme of this song is the trustworthiness of God and the peace and joy that come from dependence upon Him.

16 LORD, in trouble they have visited You,
They poured out a prayer *when* Your chastening *was* upon them.
17 As a woman with child
Is in pain and cries out in her pangs,
When she draws near the time of her delivery,
So have we been in Your sight,
O LORD.
18 We have been with child, we have been in pain;
We have, as it were, brought forth wind;
We have not accomplished any deliverance in the earth,
Nor have the inhabitants of the world fallen.

19 Your dead shall live;
Together with my dead body[a] they shall arise.
Awake and sing, you who dwell in dust;
For your dew *is like* the dew of herbs,
And the earth shall cast out the dead.

Take Refuge from the Coming Judgment

20 Come, my people, enter your chambers,
And shut your doors behind you;
Hide yourself, as it were, for a little moment,
Until the indignation is past.
21 For behold, the LORD comes out of His place
To punish the inhabitants of the earth for their iniquity;
The earth will also disclose her blood,
And will no more cover her slain.

CHAPTER 27

In that day the LORD with His severe sword, great and strong,
Will punish Le·vī'a·than the fleeing serpent,
Le·vī'a·than that twisted serpent;
And He will slay the reptile that *is* in the sea.

The Restoration of Israel

2 In that day sing to her,
"A vineyard of red wine![a]
3 I, the LORD, keep it,
I water it every moment;
Lest any hurt it,
I keep it night and day.
4 Fury *is* not in Me.
Who would set briers *and* thorns
Against Me in battle?
I would go through them,
I would burn them together.
5 Or let him take hold of My strength,
That he may make peace with Me;
And he shall make peace with Me."

6 Those who come He shall cause to take root in Jacob;
Israel shall blossom and bud,
And fill the face of the world with fruit.

7 Has He struck Israel as He struck those who struck him?

26:19 [a]Following Masoretic Text and Vulgate; Syriac and Targum read *their dead bodies;* Septuagint reads *those in the tombs.* 27:2 [a]Following Masoretic Text (Kittel's *Biblia Hebraica*), Bomberg, and Vulgate; Masoretic Text (*Biblia Hebraica Stuttgartensia*), some Hebrew manuscripts, and Septuagint read *delight;* Targum reads *choice vineyard.*

26:19 An OT affirmation of the Resurrection.

26:21 Although God's judgment upon sin often seems slow in coming, it will come.

27:2–6 Israel is again compared to a vineyard. But here God speaks of His desire to protect His people from marauders. His anger is only for the moment; His desire to bless is unchanging (Ps. 30:5).

27:7–11 Isaiah contrasts the punishment of Israel's sin with the fate of her attackers. Israel cannot escape punishment for sin, but will yet find atonement.

Or has He been slain according to the
slaughter of those who were slain
by Him?
8 In measure, by sending it away,
You contended with it.
He removes *it* by His rough wind
In the day of the east wind.
9 Therefore by this the iniquity of Jacob
will be covered;
And this *is* all the fruit of taking away
his sin:
When he makes all the stones of the
altar
Like chalkstones that are beaten to
dust,
Wooden images[a] and incense altars
shall not stand.

10 Yet the fortified city *will be* desolate,
The habitation forsaken and left like a
wilderness;
There the calf will feed, and there it
will lie down
And consume its branches.
11 When its boughs are withered, they
will be broken off;
The women come *and* set them on
fire.
For it *is* a people of no understanding;
Therefore He who made them will
not have mercy on them,
And He who formed them will show
them no favor.

12 And it shall come to pass in that day
That the LORD will thresh,
From the channel of the River[a] to the
Brook of Egypt;
And you will be gathered one by one,
O you children of Israel.

27:9 [a]Hebrew *Asherim*, Canaanite deities
27:12 [a]That is, the Euphrates

13 So it shall be in that day:
The great trumpet will be blown;
They will come, who are about to
perish in the land of Assyria,
And they who are outcasts in the land
of Egypt,
And shall worship the LORD in the
holy mount at Jerusalem.

CHAPTER 28

Woe to Ephraim and Jerusalem

Woe to the crown of pride, to the
drunkards of Ē'phra·im,
Whose glorious beauty *is* a fading
flower
Which *is* at the head of the verdant
valleys,
To those who are overcome with
wine!
2 Behold, the Lord has a mighty and
strong one,
Like a tempest of hail and a
destroying storm,
Like a flood of mighty waters
overflowing,
Who will bring *them* down to the
earth with *His* hand.
3 The crown of pride, the drunkards of
Ē'phra·im,
Will be trampled underfoot;
4 And the glorious beauty is a fading
flower
Which *is* at the head of the verdant
valley,
Like the first fruit before the summer,
Which an observer sees;
He eats it up while it is still in his
hand.

5 In that day the LORD of hosts will be
For a crown of glory and a diadem of
beauty
To the remnant of His people,

27:12 the channel . . . to the Brook of Egypt: The ideal boundaries of Israel, extending from the Euphrates to a point midway along the Mediterranean coast between Gaza and Suez.

6 For a spirit of justice to him who sits in judgment,
And for strength to those who turn back the battle at the gate.

7 But they also have erred through wine,
And through intoxicating drink are out of the way;
The priest and the prophet have erred through intoxicating drink,
They are swallowed up by wine,
They are out of the way through intoxicating drink;
They err in vision, they stumble *in* judgment.
8 For all tables are full of vomit *and* filth;
No place *is clean*.

9 "Whom will he teach knowledge?
And whom will he make to understand the message?
Those *just* weaned from milk?
Those *just* drawn from the breasts?
10 For precept *must be* upon precept, precept upon precept,
Line upon line, line upon line,
Here a little, there a little."

11 For with stammering lips and another tongue
He will speak to this people,
12 To whom He said, "This *is* the rest *with which*
You may cause the weary to rest,"
And, "This *is* the refreshing";
Yet they would not hear.
13 But the word of the LORD was to them,
"Precept upon precept, precept upon precept,
Line upon line, line upon line,
Here a little, there a little,"
That they might go and fall backward, and be broken
And snared and caught.

14 Therefore hear the word of the LORD, you scornful men,
Who rule this people who *are* in Jerusalem,
15 Because you have said, "We have made a covenant with death,
And with Shē'ōl we are in agreement.
When the overflowing scourge passes through,
It will not come to us,
For we have made lies our refuge,
And under falsehood we have hidden ourselves."

A Cornerstone in Zion

16 Therefore thus says the Lord GOD:

"Behold, I lay in Zion a stone for a foundation,
A tried stone, a precious cornerstone, a sure foundation;
Whoever believes will not act hastily.
17 Also I will make justice the measuring line,
And righteousness the plummet;
The hail will sweep away the refuge of lies,
And the waters will overflow the hiding place.
18 Your covenant with death will be annulled,
And your agreement with Shē'ōl will not stand;
When the overflowing scourge passes through,
Then you will be trampled down by it.

28:10 precept . . . line: Possibly refers to methods used to teach a child.

28:14–22 The rulers of Jerusalem are mockers who do not believe Isaiah's prophecies of judgment. Isaiah answers that God will test their fabrication of lies according to the true cornerstone. He will test people with the line of justice and the plummet (plumb bob) of righteousness.

19 As often as it goes out it will take
you;
For morning by morning it will pass
over,
And by day and by night;
It will be a terror just to understand
the report."

20 For the bed is too short to stretch out
on,
And the covering so narrow that one
cannot wrap himself *in it.*
21 For the LORD will rise up as *at* Mount
Pe·rā′zim,
He will be angry as in the Valley of
Gib′ē·on—
That He may do His work, His
awesome work,
And bring to pass His act, His
unusual act.
22 Now therefore, do not be mockers,
Lest your bonds be made strong;
For I have heard from the Lord GOD
of hosts,
A destruction determined even upon
the whole earth.

Listen to the Teaching of God

23 Give ear and hear my voice,
Listen and hear my speech.
24 Does the plowman keep plowing all
day to sow?
Does he keep turning his soil and
breaking the clods?
25 When he has leveled its surface,
Does he not sow the black cummin
And scatter the cummin,
Plant the wheat in rows,
The barley in the appointed place,
And the spelt in its place?
26 For He instructs him in right
judgment,
His God teaches him.

27 For the black cummin is not threshed
with a threshing sledge,
Nor is a cartwheel rolled over the
cummin;
But the black cummin is beaten out
with a stick,
And the cummin with a rod.
28 Bread *flour* must be ground;
Therefore he does not thresh it
forever,
Break *it with* his cartwheel,
Or crush it *with* his horsemen.
29 This also comes from the LORD of
hosts,
Who is wonderful in counsel *and*
excellent in guidance.

CHAPTER 29

Woe to Jerusalem

"Woe to Ar′i·el,[a] to Ar′i·el, the city
where David dwelt!
Add year to year;
Let feasts come around.
2 Yet I will distress Ar′i·el;
There shall be heaviness and sorrow,
And it shall be to Me as Ar′i·el.
3 I will encamp against you all around,
I will lay siege against you with a
mound,
And I will raise siegeworks against
you.
4 You shall be brought down,
You shall speak out of the ground;
Your speech shall be low, out of the
dust;
Your voice shall be like a medium's,
out of the ground;

29:1 [a]That is, Jerusalem

28:23–29 Farmers understand the laws of sowing and reaping. Why do the leaders of Judah not understand as much about God's spiritual principles?
29:1 Ariel: meaning "lion of God," refers to Jerusalem, the City of David. **feasts**: Of themselves religious rites are of no avail.

And your speech shall whisper out of
the dust.

5 "Moreover the multitude of your foes
Shall be like fine dust,
And the multitude of the terrible ones
Like chaff that passes away;
Yes, it shall be in an instant, suddenly.
6 You will be punished by the LORD of
hosts
With thunder and earthquake and
great noise,
With storm and tempest
And the flame of devouring fire.
7 The multitude of all the nations who
fight against Ar'i·el,
Even all who fight against her and
her fortress,
And distress her,
Shall be as a dream of a night vision.
8 It shall even be as when a hungry
man dreams,
And look—he eats;
But he awakes, and his soul is still
empty;
Or as when a thirsty man dreams,
And look—he drinks;
But he awakes, and indeed *he is* faint,
And his soul still craves:
So the multitude of all the nations
shall be,
Who fight against Mount Zion."

The Blindness of Disobedience

9 Pause and wonder!
Blind yourselves and be blind!
They are drunk, but not with wine;
They stagger, but not with
intoxicating drink.
10 For the LORD has poured out on you
The spirit of deep sleep,
And has closed your eyes, namely,
the prophets;
And He has covered your heads,
namely, the seers.

11The whole vision has become to you
like the words of a book that is sealed,
which *men* deliver to one who is literate,
saying, "Read this, please."
And he says, "I cannot, for it *is* sealed."
12Then the book is delivered to one who
is illiterate, saying, "Read this, please."
And he says, "I am not literate."
13Therefore the Lord said:

"Inasmuch as these people draw near
with their mouths
And honor Me with their lips,
But have removed their hearts far
from Me,
And their fear toward Me is taught
by the commandment of men,
14 Therefore, behold, I will again do a
marvelous work
Among this people,
A marvelous work and a wonder;
For the wisdom of their wise *men*
shall perish,
And the understanding of their
prudent *men* shall be hidden."

15 Woe to those who seek deep to hide
their counsel far from the LORD,
And their works are in the dark;
They say, "Who sees us?" and, "Who
knows us?"
16 Surely you have things turned
around!
Shall the potter be esteemed as the
clay;
For shall the thing made say of him
who made it,
"He did not make me"?
Or shall the thing formed say of him
who formed it,
"He has no understanding"?

29:11 What should be perfectly plain is a sealed book to these blind guides, Judah's prophets.

29:15, 16 Probably a denunciation of royal counselors who were saying that Judah's only hope was an alliance with Egypt.

Cleaning Out the Clutter

John Gilmore

Is nostalgia a problem or a solution? When the present is tense, should we consider the past perfect? Some nostalgia may hide a fear of moving forward, a dread of what is down the road. Reminiscing may be a form of regression, of going back to a stage of life when we were happier and handled life better. Job was nostalgic over what he had lost (Job 29:2–4), as was Isaiah, who found nostalgia disappointingly shallow and counterproductive. He knew the past mired the present and obliterated the future (Is. 43:18, 19).

Likewise, we may experience nostalgia, but we must not allow a pleasant association from our memories to become a crippling obsession, a crutch against coping. Sometimes we attach too much value and sentiment to our possessions. Old photographs, clothes we no longer wear, and other collected clutter from decades ago may just take up storage space and get in the way of more important things—things we use daily.

Even Christ's message may not be able to get through to us because we are encased in clutter. The ministry of John the Baptist was to clear the way for Jesus by acknowledging and removing the obstacles of sin. Just as clinging to useless objects is pointless, clinging to sinful clutter is harmful. God wants to get through to us, but He cannot when we hold on to sinful things.

Why is that true? Just as memorabilia may clutter our homes and pleasant memories may fill our minds, sin can block God from entering our hearts. Much of our mental baggage is trash wrapped up as treasure. What we see is temporal, but what is unseen is eternal, according to Paul. We should hold dearest the intangible spiritual gains we have in Christ.

"We should hold dearest the intangible spiritual gains we have in Christ."

Scripture sifts through our blocked passageways and barricaded living space. It discerns broken relationships, damaged feelings, outlandish peeves, destructive habits, and unforgiven hurts. These grudges, resentments, and anxieties need to be confessed and cleared. Heaped-up unconfessed sins and interpersonal rubbish should be promptly discarded and tossed in the trash. Don't cling to what blocks a close relationship with God.

God wants us to be realistic in the present. We should value the past and build upon it, but we must not worship it or dwell on it to the point that we are unable to think of God in the present and future. Look forward—God is as much ahead as behind.

Future Recovery of Wisdom

17 *Is* it not yet a very little while
Till Lebanon shall be turned into a fruitful field,
And the fruitful field be esteemed as a forest?
18 In that day the deaf shall hear the words of the book,
And the eyes of the blind shall see out of obscurity and out of darkness.
19 The humble also shall increase *their* joy in the LORD,
And the poor among men shall rejoice
In the Holy One of Israel.
20 For the terrible one is brought to nothing,
The scornful one is consumed,
And all who watch for iniquity are cut off—
21 Who make a man an offender by a word,
And lay a snare for him who reproves in the gate,
And turn aside the just by empty words.

22Therefore thus says the LORD, who redeemed Abraham, concerning the house of Jacob:

"Jacob shall not now be ashamed,
Nor shall his face now grow pale;
23 But when he sees his children,
The work of My hands, in his midst,
They will hallow My name,
And hallow the Holy One of Jacob,
And fear the God of Israel.
24 These also who erred in spirit will come to understanding,
And those who complained will learn doctrine."

CHAPTER 30

Futile Confidence in Egypt

"Woe to the rebellious children," says the LORD,
"Who take counsel, but not of Me,
And who devise plans, but not of My Spirit,
That they may add sin to sin;
2 Who walk to go down to Egypt,
And have not asked My advice,
To strengthen themselves in the strength of Pharaoh,
And to trust in the shadow of Egypt!
3 Therefore the strength of Pharaoh
Shall be your shame,
And trust in the shadow of Egypt
Shall be *your* humiliation.
4 For his princes were at Zō'an,
And his ambassadors came to Hā'nēs.
5 They were all ashamed of a people *who* could not benefit them,
Or be help or benefit,
But a shame and also a reproach."

6The burden against the beasts of the South.

Through a land of trouble and anguish,
From which *came* the lioness and lion,
The viper and fiery flying serpent,
They will carry their riches on the backs of young donkeys,
And their treasures on the humps of camels,
To a people *who* shall not profit;

29:17–24 The Messiah comes to redeem. Mountainous Lebanon will become a level field, and the field will be as lush as a rain forest. The powerless in society, the deaf, blind, humble, poor, whom the leaders have oppressed, will have their day.

30:6, 7 Verse 6 describes taking tribute to Egypt across the Sinai desert. Rahab was the woman who helped save the spies in Joshua 2:1–21. Here Isaiah is sarcastically calling Egypt the one who could have helped but sat idle.

7 For the Egyptians shall help in vain
and to no purpose.
Therefore I have called her
Rā'hab-Hem-Shē'beth.[a]

A Rebellious People

8 Now go, write it before them on a
tablet,
And note it on a scroll,
That it may be for time to come,
Forever and ever:
9 That this *is* a rebellious people,
Lying children,
Children *who* will not hear the law of
the LORD;
10 Who say to the seers, "Do not see,"
And to the prophets, "Do not
prophesy to us right things;
Speak to us smooth things, prophesy
deceits.
11 Get out of the way,
Turn aside from the path,
Cause the Holy One of Israel
To cease from before us."

12Therefore thus says the Holy One of Is-
rael:

"Because you despise this word,
And trust in oppression and
perversity,
And rely on them,
13 Therefore this iniquity shall be to you
Like a breach ready to fall,
A bulge in a high wall,
Whose breaking comes suddenly, in
an instant.
14 And He shall break it like the
breaking of the potter's vessel,
Which is broken in pieces;
He shall not spare.
So there shall not be found among its
fragments
A shard to take fire from the hearth,
Or to take water from the cistern."

15For thus says the Lord GOD, the Holy
One of Israel:

"In returning and rest you shall be
saved;
In quietness and confidence shall be
your strength."
But you would not,
16 And you said, "No, for we will flee
on horses"—
Therefore you shall flee!
And, "We will ride on swift *horses*"—
Therefore those who pursue you shall
be swift!

17 One thousand *shall flee* at the threat of
one,
At the threat of five you shall flee,
Till you are left as a pole on top of a
mountain
And as a banner on a hill.

God Will Be Gracious

18 Therefore the LORD will wait, that He
may be gracious to you;
And therefore He will be exalted, that
He may have mercy on you.
For the LORD *is* a God of justice;
Blessed *are* all those who wait for
Him.

19 For the people shall dwell in Zion at
Jerusalem;
You shall weep no more.

30:7 [a]Literally *Rahab Sits Idle*

30:8–11 They do not want to hear that their chosen human help is helpless and that they must rely on the **Holy One of Israel** (v. 11).

30:12–14 To despise God's word brings a life that is broken in pieces.

30:18 When we will not wait for Him, God must wait for us to come to our senses. He will be exalted, that He may have mercy: He will conquer the world in order to bless His people.

30:19–33 A series of promises are made here to those who, through judgment, have learned to wait on the Lord.

He will be very gracious to you at the
sound of your cry;
When He hears it, He will answer
you.
20 And *though* the Lord gives you
The bread of adversity and the water
of affliction,
Yet your teachers will not be moved
into a corner anymore,
But your eyes shall see your teachers.
21 Your ears shall hear a word behind
you, saying,
"This *is* the way, walk in it,"
Whenever you turn to the right hand
Or whenever you turn to the left.
22 You will also defile the covering of
your images of silver,
And the ornament of your molded
images of gold.
You will throw them away as an
unclean thing;
You will say to them, "Get away!"

23 Then He will give the rain for your
seed
With which you sow the ground,
And bread of the increase of the
earth;
It will be fat and plentiful.
In that day your cattle will feed
In large pastures.
24 Likewise the oxen and the young
donkeys that work the ground
Will eat cured fodder,
Which has been winnowed with the
shovel and fan.
25 There will be on every high mountain
And on every high hill
Rivers *and* streams of waters,
In the day of the great slaughter,
When the towers fall.
26 Moreover the light of the moon will
be as the light of the sun,
And the light of the sun will be
sevenfold,
As the light of seven days,
In the day that the LORD binds up the
bruise of His people
And heals the stroke of their wound.

Judgment on Assyria

27 Behold, the name of the LORD comes
from afar,
Burning *with* His anger,
And *His* burden *is* heavy;
His lips are full of indignation,
And His tongue like a devouring
fire.
28 His breath is like an overflowing
stream,
Which reaches up to the neck,
To sift the nations with the sieve of
futility;
And *there shall be* a bridle in the jaws
of the people,
Causing *them* to err.

29 You shall have a song
As in the night *when* a holy festival is
kept,
And gladness of heart as when one
goes with a flute,
To come into the mountain of the
LORD,
To the Mighty One of Israel.
30 The LORD will cause His glorious
voice to be heard,
And show the descent of His arm,
With the indignation of *His* anger
And the flame of a devouring fire,
With scattering, tempest, and
hailstones.
31 For through the voice of the LORD
Assyria will be beaten down,
As He strikes with the rod.
32 And *in* every place where the staff of
punishment passes,
Which the LORD lays on him,
It will be with tambourines and
harps;

30:20, 21 No more false teachers, but instead, clear guidance.
30:27–32 The **name of the LORD** emphasizes God in His unique revelation as Creator and Redeemer, the only trustworthy One. He comes to bless His people.

And in battles of brandishing He will
fight with it.
33 For To'phet *was* established of old,
Yes, for the king it is prepared.
He has made *it* deep and large;
Its pyre *is* fire with much wood;
The breath of the LORD, like a stream
of brimstone,
Kindles it.

CHAPTER 31

The Folly of Not Trusting God

Woe to those who go down to Egypt
for help,
And rely on horses,
Who trust in chariots because *they are*
many,
And in horsemen because they are
very strong,
But who do not look to the Holy One
of Israel,
Nor seek the LORD!
2 Yet He also *is* wise and will bring
disaster,
And will not call back His words,
But will arise against the house of
evildoers,
And against the help of those who
work iniquity.
3 Now the Egyptians *are* men, and not
God;
And their horses are flesh, and not
spirit.
When the LORD stretches out His
hand,
Both he who helps will fall,
And he who is helped will fall down;
They all will perish together.

God Will Deliver Jerusalem

4For thus the LORD has spoken to me:

"As a lion roars,
And a young lion over his prey
(When a multitude of shepherds is
summoned against him,
He will not be afraid of their voice
Nor be disturbed by their noise),
So the LORD of hosts will come down
To fight for Mount Zion and for its
hill.
5 Like birds flying about,
So will the LORD of hosts defend
Jerusalem.
Defending, He will also deliver *it;*
Passing over, He will preserve *it.*"

6Return *to Him* against whom the chil-
dren of Israel have deeply revolted. 7For in
that day every man shall throw away his
idols of silver and his idols of gold—sin,
which your own hands have made for
yourselves.

8 "Then Assyria shall fall by a sword not
of man,
And a sword not of mankind shall
devour him.
But he shall flee from the sword,
And his young men shall become
forced labor.
9 He shall cross over to his stronghold
for fear,
And his princes shall be afraid of the
banner,"
Says the LORD,
Whose fire *is* in Zion
And whose furnace *is* in Jerusalem.

CHAPTER 32

A Reign of Righteousness

Behold, a king will reign in
righteousness,
And princes will rule with justice.
2 A man will be as a hiding place from
the wind,

31:5 Like birds defending their nest, so the Lord will defend His people.
32:1–8 In God's kingdom people will be known for what they are: no longer will the wicked be praised and the righteous called fools.

And a cover from the tempest,
As rivers of water in a dry place,
As the shadow of a great rock in a weary land.
3 The eyes of those who see will not be dim,
And the ears of those who hear will listen.
4 Also the heart of the rash will understand knowledge,
And the tongue of the stammerers will be ready to speak plainly.

5 The foolish person will no longer be called generous,
Nor the miser said *to be* bountiful;
6 For the foolish person will speak foolishness,
And his heart will work iniquity:
To practice ungodliness,
To utter error against the LORD,
To keep the hungry unsatisfied,
And he will cause the drink of the thirsty to fail.
7 Also the schemes of the schemer *are* evil;
He devises wicked plans
To destroy the poor with lying words,
Even when the needy speaks justice.
8 But a generous man devises generous things,
And by generosity he shall stand.

Consequences of Complacency

9 Rise up, you women who are at ease,
Hear my voice;
You complacent daughters,
Give ear to my speech.
10 In a year and *some* days
You will be troubled, you complacent women;
For the vintage will fail,
The gathering will not come.
11 Tremble, you *women* who are at ease;
Be troubled, you complacent ones;
Strip yourselves, make yourselves bare,
And gird *sackcloth* on *your* waists.
12 People shall mourn upon their breasts
For the pleasant fields, for the fruitful vine.
13 On the land of my people will come up thorns *and* briers,
Yes, on all the happy homes *in* the joyous city;
14 Because the palaces will be forsaken,
The bustling city will be deserted.
The forts and towers will become lairs forever,
A joy of wild donkeys, a pasture of flocks—
15 Until the Spirit is poured upon us from on high,
And the wilderness becomes a fruitful field,
And the fruitful field is counted as a forest.

The Peace of God's Reign

16 Then justice will dwell in the wilderness,
And righteousness remain in the fruitful field.
17 The work of righteousness will be peace,

As we get older, I think we do get somewhat more secure. We have less to prove. I don't think anyone could say he'd lived his life with nothing to prove. All of us dress up a little bit nicer when we are going to be with people so they won't think we're slovenly. I think as we get older we feel more comfortable about ourselves and so we are willing to let some of those things out.

Charles R. Swindoll

32:15–17 The work of the Spirit of God is profoundly ethical: justice and righteousness result in peace.

And the effect of righteousness,
quietness and assurance forever.
18 My people will dwell in a peaceful
habitation,
In secure dwellings, and in quiet
resting places,
19 Though hail comes down on the
forest,
And the city is brought low in
humiliation.

20 Blessed *are* you who sow beside all
waters,
Who send out freely the feet of the ox
and the donkey.

CHAPTER 33

A Prayer in Deep Distress

Woe to you who plunder, though you
have not *been* plundered;
And you who deal treacherously,
though they have not dealt
treacherously with you!
When you cease plundering,
You will be plundered;
When you make an end of dealing
treacherously,
They will deal treacherously with
you.

2 O LORD, be gracious to us;
We have waited for You.
Be their[a] arm every morning,
Our salvation also in the time of
trouble.
3 At the noise of the tumult the people
shall flee;
When You lift Yourself up, the nations
shall be scattered;
4 And Your plunder shall be gathered
Like the gathering of the caterpillar;
As the running to and fro of locusts,
He shall run upon them.

5 The LORD is exalted, for He dwells on
high;
He has filled Zion with justice and
righteousness.
6 Wisdom and knowledge will be the
stability of your times,
And the strength of salvation;
The fear of the LORD *is* His treasure.

7 Surely their valiant ones shall cry
outside,
The ambassadors of peace shall weep
bitterly.
8 The highways lie waste,
The traveling man ceases.
He has broken the covenant,
He has despised the cities,[a]
He regards no man.
9 The earth mourns *and* languishes,
Lebanon is shamed *and* shriveled;
Sharon is like a wilderness,
And Bā'shan and Car'mel shake off
their fruits.

Impending Judgment on Zion

10 "Now I will rise," says the LORD;
"Now I will be exalted,
Now I will lift Myself up.
11 You shall conceive chaff,
You shall bring forth stubble;
Your breath, *as* fire, shall devour
you.

33:2 [a]Septuagint omits *their;* Syriac, Targum, and Vulgate read *our.* 33:8 [a]Following Masoretic Text and Vulgate; Dead Sea Scrolls read *witnesses;* Septuagint omits *cities;* Targum reads *They have been removed from their cities.*

33:2–6 The people are now depicted as willing to wait for the Lord. This attitude came perhaps after Sennacherib's challenge.

33:2 Be their arm: Be the strength of Your people.

33:7–9 Perhaps the situation when Sennacherib remained on the attack, although Hezekiah had paid him tribute.

33:10–16 Judah has admitted her weakness and the futility of all human assistance. Now God's power can be demonstrated.

12 And the people shall be *like* the
burnings of lime;
Like thorns cut up they shall be
burned in the fire.
13 Hear, you *who are* afar off, what I
have done;
And you *who are* near, acknowledge
My might."

14 The sinners in Zion are afraid;
Fearfulness has seized the hypocrites:
"Who among us shall dwell with the
devouring fire?
Who among us shall dwell with
everlasting burnings?"
15 He who walks righteously and speaks
uprightly,
He who despises the gain of
oppressions,
Who gestures with his hands,
refusing bribes,
Who stops his ears from hearing of
bloodshed,
And shuts his eyes from seeing evil:
16 He will dwell on high;
His place of defense *will be* the
fortress of rocks;
Bread will be given him,
His water *will be* sure.

The Land of the Majestic King

17 Your eyes will see the King in His
beauty;
They will see the land that is very far
off.
18 Your heart will meditate on terror:
"Where *is* the scribe?
Where *is* he who weighs?
Where *is* he who counts the towers?"
19 You will not see a fierce people,
A people of obscure speech, beyond
perception,
Of a stammering tongue *that you*
cannot understand.

20 Look upon Zion, the city of our
appointed feasts;
Your eyes will see Jerusalem, a quiet
home,
A tabernacle *that* will not be taken
down;
Not one of its stakes will ever be
removed,
Nor will any of its cords be broken.
21 But there the majestic LORD *will be* for
us
A place of broad rivers *and* streams,
In which no galley with oars will sail,
Nor majestic ships pass by
22 (For the LORD *is* our Judge,
The LORD *is* our Lawgiver,
The LORD *is* our King;
He will save us);
23 Your tackle is loosed,
They could not strengthen their mast,
They could not spread the sail.

Then the prey of great plunder is
divided;
The lame take the prey.
24 And the inhabitant will not say, "I am
sick";
The people who dwell in it *will be*
forgiven *their* iniquity.

CHAPTER 34

Judgment on the Nations

Come near, you nations, to hear;
And heed, you people!
Let the earth hear, and all that is in it,
The world and all things that come
forth from it.

33:14 Now that the people know they must rely on God, there is a new sense of His awesome holiness and of their own sinfulness. The mood is humility; why should He help us?

33:17–23 The promise of the King. All that their human kings should have done, God will do for His people.

33:18, 19 Assyria's tax collectors will be gone.

33:24 forgiven: Best of all, God offers healing from sin through His Messiah.

2 For the indignation of the LORD *is*
against all nations,
And *His* fury against all their armies;
He has utterly destroyed them,
He has given them over to the
slaughter.
3 Also their slain shall be thrown out;
Their stench shall rise from their
corpses,
And the mountains shall be melted
with their blood.
4 All the host of heaven shall be
dissolved,
And the heavens shall be rolled up
like a scroll;
All their host shall fall down
As the leaf falls from the vine,
And as *fruit* falling from a fig tree.

5 "For My sword shall be bathed in
heaven;
Indeed it shall come down on Ē'dom,
And on the people of My curse, for
judgment.
6 The sword of the LORD is filled with
blood,
It is made overflowing with fatness,
With the blood of lambs and goats,
With the fat of the kidneys of rams.
For the LORD has a sacrifice in
Boz'rah,
And a great slaughter in the land of
Ē'dom.
7 The wild oxen shall come down with
them,
And the young bulls with the mighty
bulls;
Their land shall be soaked with
blood,
And their dust saturated with
fatness."
8 For *it is* the day of the LORD's
vengeance,
The year of recompense for the cause
of Zion.
9 Its streams shall be turned into pitch,
And its dust into brimstone;
Its land shall become burning pitch.
10 It shall not be quenched night or day;
Its smoke shall ascend forever.
From generation to generation it shall
lie waste;
No one shall pass through it forever
and ever.
11 But the pelican and the porcupine
shall possess it,
Also the owl and the raven shall
dwell in it.
And He shall stretch out over it
The line of confusion and the stones
of emptiness.
12 They shall call its nobles to the
kingdom,
But none *shall be* there, and all its
princes shall be nothing.
13 And thorns shall come up in its
palaces,
Nettles and brambles in its fortresses;
It shall be a habitation of jackals,
A courtyard for ostriches.
14 The wild beasts of the desert shall
also meet with the jackals,
And the wild goat shall bleat to its
companion;
Also the night creature shall rest
there,
And find for herself a place of rest.

34:6 The sword of the LORD: Judgment from whatever source is still the judgment of God. The blood of lambs and goats is the language of sacrifice for sins.
34:8 the day of the LORD's vengeance: A general term here rather than a reference to any specific day.
34:11 The birds and animals in this and the succeeding verses are those which inhabit waste and desert places. The palaces through which arrogant humans have strutted will shortly be the haunt of jackal and **porcupine. The line of confusion and the stones of emptiness**: Normally constructive instruments (a builder's measuring line and plumb bob) are turned to destruction by our arrogant pride.

15 There the arrow snake shall make her nest and lay *eggs*
And hatch, and gather *them* under her shadow;
There also shall the hawks be gathered,
Every one with her mate.

16 "Search from the book of the LORD, and read:
Not one of these shall fail;
Not one shall lack her mate.
For My mouth has commanded it, and His Spirit has gathered them.
17 He has cast the lot for them,
And His hand has divided it among them with a measuring line.
They shall possess it forever;
From generation to generation they shall dwell in it."

CHAPTER 35

The Future Glory of Zion

The wilderness and the wasteland shall be glad for them,
And the desert shall rejoice and blossom as the rose;
2 It shall blossom abundantly and rejoice,
Even with joy and singing.
The glory of Lebanon shall be given to it,
The excellence of Car'mel and Sharon.
They shall see the glory of the LORD,
The excellency of our God.

3 Strengthen the weak hands,
And make firm the feeble knees.
4 Say to those *who are* fearful-hearted,
"Be strong, do not fear!
Behold, your God will come *with* vengeance,
With the recompense of God;
He will come and save you."
5 Then the eyes of the blind shall be opened,
And the ears of the deaf shall be unstopped.
6 Then the lame shall leap like a deer,
And the tongue of the dumb sing.
For waters shall burst forth in the wilderness,
And streams in the desert.
7 The parched ground shall become a pool,
And the thirsty land springs of water;
In the habitation of jackals, where each lay,
There shall be grass with reeds and rushes.

8 A highway shall be there, and a road,
And it shall be called the Highway of Holiness.
The unclean shall not pass over it,
But it *shall be* for others.
Whoever walks the road, although a fool,
Shall not go astray.
9 No lion shall be there,
Nor shall *any* ravenous beast go up on it;
It shall not be found there.
But the redeemed shall walk *there*,
10 And the ransomed of the LORD shall return,
And come to Zion with singing,
With everlasting joy on their heads.
They shall obtain joy and gladness,
And sorrow and sighing shall flee away.

CHAPTER 36

Sennacherib Boasts Against the LORD

Now it came to pass in the fourteenth
year of King Hez·e·ki'ah *that* Sen·nach'-
e·rib king of Assyria came up against all

35:3 weak hands . . . feeble knees: Complete helplessness brought on by fear (see Jer. 50:43).

the fortified cities of Judah and took them.
2Then the king of Assyria sent *the* Rab'-
sha·keh[a] with a great army from Lā'chish
to King Hez·e·kī'ah at Jerusalem. And he
stood by the aqueduct from the upper
pool, on the highway to the Fuller's
Field. 3And E·lī'a·kim the son of Hil-
kī'ah, who was over the household,
Sheb'na the scribe, and Jō'ah the
son of Ā'saph, the recorder, came out to
him.

4Then *the* Rab'sha·keh said to them,
"Say now to Hez·e·kī'ah, 'Thus says the
great king, the king of Assyria: "What con-
fidence is this in which you trust? 5I say
you speak of having plans and power for
war; but *they are* mere words. Now in
whom do you trust, that you rebel against
me? 6Look! You are trusting in the staff of
this broken reed, Egypt, on which if a man
leans, it will go into his hand and pierce it.
So *is* Pharaoh king of Egypt to all who trust
in him.

7"But if you say to me, 'We trust in the
LORD our God,' *is it* not He whose high
places and whose altars Hez·e·kī'ah has
taken away, and said to Judah and Jerusa-
lem, 'You shall worship before this al-
tar'?" ' 8Now therefore, I urge you, give a
pledge to my master the king of Assyria,
and I will give you two thousand horses—
if you are able on your part to put riders on
them! 9How then will you repel one cap-
tain of the least of my master's servants,
and put your trust in Egypt for chariots
and horsemen? 10Have I now come up
without the LORD against this land to de-
stroy it? The LORD said to me, 'Go up
against this land, and destroy it.' "

11Then E·lī'a·kim, Sheb'na, and Jō'ah
said to *the* Rab'sha·keh, "Please speak to
your servants in Ar·a·mā'ic, for we under-
stand *it;* and do not speak to us in Hebrew[a]
in the hearing of the people who *are* on the
wall."

12But *the* Rab'sha·keh said, "Has my
master sent me to your master and to you
to speak these words, and not to the men
who sit on the wall, who will eat and drink
their own waste with you?"

13Then *the* Rab'sha·keh stood and called
out with a loud voice in Hebrew, and said,
"Hear the words of the great king, the king
of Assyria! 14Thus says the king: 'Do not let
Hez·e·kī'ah deceive you, for he will not be
able to deliver you; 15nor let Hez·e·kī'ah
make you trust in the LORD, saying, "The
LORD will surely deliver us; this city will
not be given into the hand of the king of
Assyria." ' 16Do not listen to Hez·e·kī'ah;
for thus says the king of Assyria: 'Make
peace with me *by a* present and come out to
me; and every one of you eat from his own
vine and every one from his own fig tree,
and every one of you drink the waters of
his own cistern; 17until I come and take you
away to a land like your own land, a land
of grain and new wine, a land of bread and
vineyards. 18*Beware* lest Hez·e·kī'ah per-
suade you, saying, "The LORD will deliver
us." Has any one of the gods of the nations
delivered its land from the hand of the
king of Assyria? 19Where *are* the gods of
Hā'math and Ar'pad? Where *are* the gods
of Seph·ar·vā'im? Indeed, have they deliv-
ered Samaria from my hand? 20Who
among all the gods of these lands have de-
livered their countries from my hand, that
the LORD should deliver Jerusalem from
my hand?' "

21But they held their peace and an-
swered him not a word; for the king's com-

36:2 [a]A title, probably *Chief of Staff* or *Governor*
36:11 [a]Literally *Judean*

36:2 Rabshakeh: One of the three chief officers in the Assyrian army.

36:7 The Assyrian, with his pagan mindset, could not understand that Hezekiah's destruction of Judah's paganized worship centers pleased the Lord.

36:17 take you away: Assyrian policy was to deport all those inhabitants of a conquered land who were considered a problem for the new Assyrian administration.

mandment was, "Do not answer him."
22Then E·lī'a·kim the son of Hil·kī'ah, who
was over the household, Sheb'na the scribe,
and Jō'ah the son of Ā'saph, the recorder,
came to Hez·e·kī'ah with *their* clothes torn,
and told him the words of *the* Rab'sha·keh.

CHAPTER 37

Isaiah Assures Deliverance

And so it was, when King Hez·e·kī'ah
heard *it,* that he tore his clothes, covered
himself with sackcloth, and went into the
house of the LORD. 2Then he sent E·lī'-
a·kim, who *was* over the household,
Sheb'na the scribe, and the elders of the
priests, covered with sackcloth, to Ī·sāi'ah
the prophet, the son of Ā'moz. 3And they
said to him, "Thus says Hez·e·kī'ah: 'This
day *is* a day of trouble and rebuke and
blasphemy; for the children have come to
birth, but *there is* no strength to bring them
forth. 4It may be that the LORD your God
will hear the words of *the* Rab'sha·keh,
whom his master the king of Assyria has
sent to reproach the living God, and will
rebuke the words which the LORD your
God has heard. Therefore lift up *your*
prayer for the remnant that is left.' "
5So the servants of King Hez·e·kī'ah
came to Ī·sāi'ah. 6And Ī·sāi'ah said to
them, "Thus you shall say to your master,
'Thus says the LORD: "Do not be afraid of
the words which you have heard, with
which the servants of the king of Assyria
have blasphemed Me. 7Surely I will send a
spirit upon him, and he shall hear a rumor
and return to his own land; and I will
cause him to fall by the sword in his own
land." ' "

Sennacherib's Threat and Hezekiah's Prayer

8Then *the* Rab'sha·keh returned, and
found the king of Assyria warring against
Lib'nah, for he heard that he had departed
from Lā'chish. 9And the king heard con-
cerning Tir·hā'kah king of Ethiopia, "He
has come out to make war with you." So
when he heard *it,* he sent messengers to
Hez·e·kī'ah, saying, 10"Thus you shall
speak to Hez·e·kī'ah king of Judah, saying:
'Do not let your God in whom you trust
deceive you, saying, "Jerusalem shall not
be given into the hand of the king of As-
syria." 11Look! You have heard what the
kings of Assyria have done to all lands by
utterly destroying them; and shall you be
delivered? 12Have the gods of the nations
delivered those whom my fathers have de-
stroyed, Gō'zan and Har'an and Rē'zeph,
and the people of Eden who *were* in
Te·las'sar? 13Where *is* the king of Hā'math,
the king of Ar'pad, and the king of the city
of Seph·ar·vā'im, Hē'na, and Ī'vah?' "
14And Hez·e·kī'ah received the letter
from the hand of the messengers, and read
it; and Hez·e·kī'ah went up to the house of
the LORD, and spread it before the LORD.
15Then Hez·e·kī'ah prayed to the LORD,
saying: 16"O LORD of hosts, God of Israel,
the One who dwells *between* the cherubim,
You *are* God, You alone, of all the king-
doms of the earth. You have made heaven
and earth. 17Incline Your ear, O LORD, and
hear; open Your eyes, O LORD, and see; and
hear all the words of Sen·nach'e·rib, which

> God moves in mysterious ways
> His wonders to perform;
> He plants His footsteps in the sea,
> And rides upon the storm.
> William Cowper

37:3 No strength in childbirth expresses complete helplessness, unable to even birth the future. Unless God intervenes there is no hope.

37:4 the living God: Hezekiah's conviction is that there is only one true Deity in the universe.

37:9 king of Ethiopia: Egypt was ruled by Ethiopians at this time.

he has sent to reproach the living God.
[18]Truly, LORD, the kings of Assyria have
laid waste all the nations and their lands,
[19]and have cast their gods into the fire; for
they *were* not gods, but the work of men's
hands—wood and stone. Therefore they
destroyed them. [20]Now therefore, O LORD
our God, save us from his hand, that all the
kingdoms of the earth may know that You
are the LORD, You alone."

The Word of the LORD Concerning Sennacherib

[21]Then Ī·sāi'ah the son of Ā'moz sent to
Hez·e·kī'ah, saying, "Thus says the LORD
God of Israel, 'Because you have prayed to
Me against Sen·nach'e·rib king of Assyria,
[22]this *is* the word which the LORD has spo-
ken concerning him:

"The virgin, the daughter of Zion,
Has despised you, laughed you to scorn;
The daughter of Jerusalem
Has shaken *her* head behind your back!

23 "Whom have you reproached and blasphemed?
Against whom have you raised *your* voice,
And lifted up your eyes on high?
Against the Holy One of Israel.
24 By your servants you have reproached the Lord,
And said, 'By the multitude of my chariots
I have come up to the height of the mountains,
To the limits of Lebanon;
I will cut down its tall cedars
And its choice cypress trees;
I will enter its farthest height,
To its fruitful forest.
25 I have dug and drunk water,
And with the soles of my feet I have dried up
All the brooks of defense.'

26 "Did you not hear long ago
How I made it,
From ancient times that I formed it?
Now I have brought it to pass,
That you should be
For crushing fortified cities *into* heaps of ruins.
27 Therefore their inhabitants *had* little power;
They were dismayed and confounded;
They were *as* the grass of the field
And the green herb,
As the grass on the housetops
And grain blighted before it is grown.

28 "But I know your dwelling place,
Your going out and your coming in,
And your rage against Me.
29 Because your rage against Me and your tumult
Have come up to My ears,
Therefore I will put My hook in your nose
And My bridle in your lips,
And I will turn you back
By the way which you came." '

[30]"This *shall be* a sign to you:

You shall eat this year such as grows of itself,
And the second year what springs from the same;
Also in the third year sow and reap,
Plant vineyards and eat the fruit of them.

37:20 Reveals Hezekiah's level of commitment. His first concern was not for his own safety but for God's glory.

31 And the remnant who have escaped
of the house of Judah
Shall again take root downward,
And bear fruit upward.
32 For out of Jerusalem shall go a
remnant,
And those who escape from Mount
Zion.
The zeal of the LORD of hosts will do
this.

33"Therefore thus says the LORD con-
cerning the king of Assyria:

'He shall not come into this city,
Nor shoot an arrow there,
Nor come before it with shield,
Nor build a siege mound against it.
34 By the way that he came,
By the same shall he return;
And he shall not come into this city,'
Says the LORD.
35 'For I will defend this city, to save it
For My own sake and for My servant
David's sake.' "

Sennacherib's Defeat and Death

36Then the angel[a] of the LORD went out,
and killed in the camp of the Assyrians one
hundred and eighty-five thousand; and
when *people* arose early in the morning,
there were the corpses—all dead. 37So
Sen·nach'e·rib king of Assyria departed
and went away, returned *home,* and re-
mained at Nin'e·veh. 38Now it came to
pass, as he was worshiping in the house of
Nis'roch his god, that his sons A·dram'-
me·lech and Sha·rē'zer struck him down
with the sword; and they escaped into the
land of Ar'a·rat. Then Ē·sar·had'don his
son reigned in his place.

CHAPTER 38

Hezekiah's Life Extended

In those days Hez·e·kī'ah was sick and
near death. And Ī·sāi'ah the prophet, the
son of Ā'moz, went to him and said to him,
"Thus says the LORD: 'Set your house in or-
der, for you shall die and not live.' "
2Then Hez·e·kī'ah turned his face to-
ward the wall, and prayed to the LORD,
3and said, "Remember now, O LORD, I pray,
how I have walked before You in truth and
with a loyal heart, and have done *what is*
good in Your sight." And Hez·e·kī'ah
wept bitterly.
4And the word of the LORD came to
Ī·sāi'ah, saying, 5"Go and tell Hez·e·kī'ah,
'Thus says the LORD, the God of David
your father: "I have heard your prayer, I
have seen your tears; surely I will add to
your days fifteen years. 6I will deliver you
and this city from the hand of the king of
Assyria, and I will defend this city." ' 7And
this *is* the sign to you from the LORD, that
the LORD will do this thing which He has
spoken: 8Behold, I will bring the shadow
on the sundial, which has gone down with
the sun on the sundial of Ā'haz, ten degrees
backward." So the sun returned ten degrees
on the dial by which it had gone down.
9This is the writing of Hez·e·kī'ah king
of Judah, when he had been sick and had
recovered from his sickness:

10 I said,
"In the prime of my life
I shall go to the gates of Shē'ōl;
I am deprived of the remainder of my
years."
11 I said,
"I shall not see YAH,

37:36 [a]Or *Angel*

37:38 The assassination occurred some 20 years after the departure of the preceding verse. It is evident that the writer, while still speaking of Sennacherib, wished to show the fulfillment of the prophecy contained in v. 7.

38:8 The sundial of Ahaz was probably a stepped structure with a pillar on the top. The shadow of the pillar normally lengthened down the eastern steps during the afternoon. God causes the shadow to return up the steps.

Not until each loom is silent
And the shuttles cease to fly,
Will God unroll the pattern
And explain the reason why
The dark threads are as needful
In the Weaver's skillful hand
As the threads of gold and silver
For the pattern which He planned.

The LORD[a] in the land of the living;
I shall observe man no more among
the inhabitants of the world.[b]
12 My life span is gone,
Taken from me like a shepherd's tent;
I have cut off my life like a weaver.
He cuts me off from the loom;
From day until night You make an
end of me.
13 I have considered until morning—
Like a lion,
So He breaks all my bones;
From day until night You make an
end of me.
14 Like a crane *or* a swallow, so I
chattered;
I mourned like a dove;
My eyes fail *from looking* upward.
O LORD,[a] I am oppressed;
Undertake for me!

15 "What shall I say?
He has both spoken to me,[a]
And He Himself has done *it*.

38:11 [a]Hebrew *YAH, YAH* [b]Following some Hebrew manuscripts; Masoretic Text and Vulgate read *rest;* Septuagint omits *among the inhabitants of the world;* Targum reads *land.* 38:14 [a]Following Bomberg; Masoretic Text and Dead Sea Scrolls read *Lord.* 38:15 [a]Following Masoretic Text and Vulgate; Dead Sea Scrolls and Targum read *And shall I say to Him;* Septuagint omits first half of this verse. 39:1 [a]Spelled *Berodach-Baladan* in 2 Kings 20:12

I shall walk carefully all my years
In the bitterness of my soul.
16 O Lord, by these *things men* live;
And in all these *things is* the life of
my spirit;
So You will restore me and make me
live.
17 Indeed *it was* for *my own* peace
That I had great bitterness;
But You have lovingly *delivered* my
soul from the pit of corruption,
For You have cast all my sins behind
Your back.
18 For Shē'ōl cannot thank You,
Death cannot praise You;
Those who go down to the pit cannot
hope for Your truth.
19 The living, the living man, he shall
praise You,
As I *do* this day;
The father shall make known Your
truth to the children.

20 "The LORD *was ready* to save me;
Therefore we will sing my songs with
stringed instruments
All the days of our life, in the house
of the LORD."

21 Now Ī·sāi'ah had said, "Let them take
a lump of figs, and apply *it* as a poultice on
the boil, and he shall recover."
22 And Hez·e·kī'ah had said, "What *is*
the sign that I shall go up to the house of
the LORD?"

CHAPTER 39

The Babylonian Envoys

At that time Mer'o·dach-Bal'a·dan[a] the
son of Bal'a·dan, king of Babylon, sent letters and a present to Hez·e·kī'ah, for he
heard that he had been sick and had recov-

38:13 The Hebrews had little interest in secondary causes; all things were considered to have their ultimate cause in God. But if God like a lion sometimes crushes their bones, He also can deliver them like a lion according to His settled purpose to do them good (v. 17).

ered. [2]And Hez·e·kī′ah was pleased with
them, and showed them the house of his
treasures—the silver and gold, the spices
and precious ointment, and all his ar-
mory—all that was found among his trea-
sures. There was nothing in his house or in
all his dominion that Hez·e·kī′ah did not
show them.

[3]Then Ī·sāi′ah the prophet went to King
Hez·e·kī′ah, and said to him, "What did
these men say, and from where did they
come to you?"

So Hez·e·kī′ah said, "They came to me
from a far country, from Babylon."

[4]And he said, "What have they seen in
your house?"

So Hez·e·kī′ah answered, "They have
seen all that *is* in my house; there is noth-
ing among my treasures that I have not
shown them."

[5]Then Ī·sāi′ah said to Hez·e·kī′ah,
"Hear the word of the LORD of hosts: [6]'Be-
hold, the days are coming when all that *is*
in your house, and what your fathers have
accumulated until this day, shall be carried
to Babylon; nothing shall be left,' says the
LORD. [7]'And they shall take away *some* of
your sons who will descend from you,
whom you will beget; and they shall be
eunuchs in the palace of the king of Bab-
ylon.' "

[8]So Hez·e·kī′ah said to Ī·sāi′ah, "The
word of the LORD which you have spoken
is good!" For he said, "At least there will be
peace and truth in my days."

CHAPTER 40

God's People Are Comforted

"Comfort, yes, comfort My people!"
Says your God.

2 "Speak comfort to Jerusalem, and cry
out to her,
That her warfare is ended,
That her iniquity is pardoned;
For she has received from the LORD's
hand
Double for all her sins."

3 The voice of one crying in the
wilderness:
"Prepare the way of the LORD;
Make straight in the desert[a]
A highway for our God.
4 Every valley shall be exalted
And every mountain and hill brought
low;
The crooked places shall be made
straight
And the rough places smooth;
5 The glory of the LORD shall be
revealed,
And all flesh shall see *it* together;
For the mouth of the LORD has
spoken."

6 The voice said, "Cry out!"
And he[a] said, "What shall I cry?"

"All flesh *is* grass,
And all its loveliness *is* like the flower
of the field.
7 The grass withers, the flower fades,
Because the breath of the LORD blows
upon it;
Surely the people *are* grass.
8 The grass withers, the flower fades,

40:3 [a]Following Masoretic Text, Targum, and Vulgate; Septuagint omits *in the desert.* 40:6 [a]Following Masoretic Text and Targum; Dead Sea Scrolls, Septuagint, and Vulgate read *I.*

39:2 The **house** was probably the temple. Any reference to divine assistance is conspicuously absent. Rather it appears that Hezekiah succumbed to the temptation to parade the trappings of his own power and success.

40:1 Comfort: Encourage or strengthen.

40:6–8 Since the people of Babylon (v. 8), Judah's captors, are merely flesh, they are no match for God.

40:8 word of our God: His promise to deliver.

But the word of our God stands
forever."

9 O Zion,
You who bring good tidings,
Get up into the high mountain;
O Jerusalem,
You who bring good tidings,
Lift up your voice with strength,
Lift *it* up, be not afraid;
Say to the cities of Judah, "Behold
your God!"

10 Behold, the Lord GOD shall come with
a strong *hand*,
And His arm shall rule for Him;
Behold, His reward *is* with Him,
And His work before Him.
11 He will feed His flock like a
shepherd;
He will gather the lambs with His
arm,
And carry *them* in His bosom,
And gently lead those who are with
young.

12 Who has measured the waters[a] in the
hollow of His hand,
Measured heaven with a span
And calculated the dust of the earth
in a measure?
Weighed the mountains in scales
And the hills in a balance?
13 Who has directed the Spirit of the
LORD,
Or *as* His counselor has taught Him?
14 With whom did He take counsel, and
who instructed Him,
And taught Him in the path of
justice?
Who taught Him knowledge,
And showed Him the way of
understanding?

15 Behold, the nations *are* as a drop in a
bucket,
And are counted as the small dust on
the scales;
Look, He lifts up the isles as a very
little thing.
16 And Lebanon *is* not sufficient to burn,
Nor its beasts sufficient for a burnt
offering.
17 All nations before Him *are* as nothing,
And they are counted by Him less
than nothing and worthless.

18 To whom then will you liken God?
Or what likeness will you compare to
Him?
19 The workman molds an image,
The goldsmith overspreads it with
gold,
And the silversmith casts silver
chains.
20 Whoever *is* too impoverished for *such*
a contribution
Chooses a tree *that* will not rot;
He seeks for himself a skillful
workman
To prepare a carved image *that* will
not totter.

21 Have you not known?
Have you not heard?
Has it not been told you from the
beginning?
Have you not understood from the
foundations of the earth?

40:12 [a]Following Masoretic Text, Septuagint, and Vulgate; Dead Sea Scrolls read *waters of the sea;* Targum reads *waters of the world.*

40:9–11 The tenderness of the Shepherd-God. He intends to deliver.

40:12–26 The incomparable greatness of the Creator-God. He is able to deliver.

40:16, 17 All the forests of **Lebanon** would not be fuel enough, nor all of its beasts sacrifice enough, for an offering worthy of God.

40:18–20 God is too great to be captured in any craftsman's handiwork. If He could be adequately portrayed in that way, He would not be worthy of worship.

22 *It is* He who sits above the circle of the earth,
And its inhabitants *are* like grasshoppers,
Who stretches out the heavens like a curtain,
And spreads them out like a tent to dwell in.
23 He brings the princes to nothing;
He makes the judges of the earth useless.

24 Scarcely shall they be planted,
Scarcely shall they be sown,
Scarcely shall their stock take root in the earth,
When He will also blow on them,
And they will wither,
And the whirlwind will take them away like stubble.

25 "To whom then will you liken Me,
Or *to whom* shall I be equal?" says the Holy One.
26 Lift up your eyes on high,
And see who has created these *things*,
Who brings out their host by number;
He calls them all by name,
By the greatness of His might
And the strength of *His* power;
Not one is missing.

27 Why do you say, O Jacob,
And speak, O Israel:
"My way is hidden from the LORD,
And my just claim is passed over by my God"?
28 Have you not known?
Have you not heard?
The everlasting God, the LORD,
The Creator of the ends of the earth,
Neither faints nor is weary.
His understanding is unsearchable.
29 He gives power to the weak,

I pray, God, that You give power to my friend, who is weak, and that You increase her strength.

adapted from Isaiah 40:29

God gives us always strength enough, and sense enough, for every thing He wants us to do.

John Ruskin

And to *those who have* no might He increases strength.
30 Even the youths shall faint and be weary,
And the young men shall utterly fall,
31 But those who wait on the LORD
Shall renew *their* strength;
They shall mount up with wings like eagles,
They shall run and not be weary,
They shall walk and not faint.

CHAPTER 41

Israel Assured of God's Help

"Keep silence before Me, O coastlands,
And let the people renew *their* strength!
Let them come near, then let them speak;
Let us come near together for judgment.

2 "Who raised up one from the east?
Who in righteousness called him to His feet?

40:26 their host: The stars. Angels are sometimes referred to as "stars," but Isaiah knows they are merely the creations of One who is incomparably greater than they.

41:2 one from the east: Cyrus, king of Persia, who would destroy the Neo-Babylonian Empire built by Nebuchadnezzar.

Who gave the nations before him,
And made *him* rule over kings?
Who gave *them* as the dust *to* his
sword,
As driven stubble to his bow?
3 Who pursued them, *and* passed safely
By the way *that* he had not gone with
his feet?
4 Who has performed and done *it,*
Calling the generations from the
beginning?
'I, the LORD, am the first;
And with the last I *am* He.'"

5 The coastlands saw *it* and feared,
The ends of the earth were afraid;
They drew near and came.
6 Everyone helped his neighbor,
And said to his brother,
"Be of good courage!"
7 So the craftsman encouraged the
goldsmith;
He who smooths *with* the hammer
inspired him who strikes the anvil,
Saying, "It *is* ready for the soldering";
Then he fastened it with pegs,
That it might not totter.

8 "But you, Israel, *are* My servant,
Jacob whom I have chosen,
The descendants of Abraham My
friend.
9 *You* whom I have taken from the ends
of the earth,
And called from its farthest regions,
And said to you,
'You *are* My servant,
I have chosen you and have not cast
you away:
10 Fear not, for I *am* with you;
Be not dismayed, for I *am* your God.
I will strengthen you,
Yes, I will help you,
I will uphold you with My righteous
right hand.'

11 "Behold, all those who were incensed
against you
Shall be ashamed and disgraced;
They shall be as nothing,
And those who strive with you shall
perish.
12 You shall seek them and not find
them—
Those who contended with you.
Those who war against you
Shall be as nothing,
As a nonexistent thing.
13 For I, the LORD your God, will hold
your right hand,
Saying to you, 'Fear not, I will help
you.'

14 "Fear not, you worm Jacob,
You men of Israel!
I will help you," says the LORD
And your Redeemer, the Holy One of
Israel.
15 "Behold, I will make you into a new
threshing sledge with sharp teeth;
You shall thresh the mountains and
beat *them* small,
And make the hills like chaff.
16 You shall winnow them, the wind
shall carry them away,
And the whirlwind shall scatter them;
You shall rejoice in the LORD,
And glory in the Holy One of Israel.

17 "The poor and needy seek water, but
there is none,
Their tongues fail for thirst.
I, the LORD, will hear them;
I, the God of Israel, will not forsake
them.

41:15, 16 threshing sledge: A heavy drag with stones or pieces of metal protruding from the bottom. It was pulled by an ox or a donkey over piles of cut grain to separate the kernels from the husks. Far from being weak or cast off, Israel is God's chosen tool to level the hills in preparation for His coming (40:3–5).

18 I will open rivers in desolate heights,
And fountains in the midst of the valleys;
I will make the wilderness a pool of water,
And the dry land springs of water.
19 I will plant in the wilderness the cedar and the acacia tree,
The myrtle and the oil tree;
I will set in the desert the cypress tree *and* the pine
And the box tree together,
20 That they may see and know,
And consider and understand together,
That the hand of the LORD has done this,
And the Holy One of Israel has created it.

The Futility of Idols

21 "Present your case," says the LORD.
"Bring forth your strong *reasons*," says the King of Jacob.
22 "Let them bring forth and show us what will happen;
Let them show the former things, what they *were*,
That we may consider them,
And know the latter end of them;
Or declare to us things to come.
23 Show the things that are to come hereafter,
That we may know that you *are* gods;
Yes, do good or do evil,
That we may be dismayed and see *it* together.
24 Indeed you *are* nothing,
And your work *is* nothing;
He who chooses you *is* an abomination.

25 "I have raised up one from the north,
And he shall come;
From the rising of the sun he shall call on My name;
And he shall come against princes as *though* mortar,
As the potter treads clay.
26 Who has declared from the beginning, that we may know?
And former times, that we may say, '*He is* righteous'?
Surely *there is* no one who shows,
Surely *there is* no one who declares,
Surely *there is* no one who hears your words.
27 The first time *I said* to Zion,
'Look, there they are!'
And I will give to Jerusalem one who brings good tidings.
28 For I looked, and *there was* no man;
I looked among them, but *there was* no counselor,
Who, when I asked of them, could answer a word.
29 Indeed they *are* all worthless;[a]
Their works *are* nothing;
Their molded images *are* wind and confusion.

CHAPTER 42

The Servant of the LORD

"Behold! My Servant whom I uphold,

41:29 [a]Following Masoretic Text and Vulgate; Dead Sea Scrolls, Syriac, and Targum read *nothing;* Septuagint omits the first line.

41:22 Let **them**, the idols, predict the future or explain the past.

41:25 The prophets frequently describe the direction from which the Assyrian and Babylonian hordes would come as from the **north**. This may seem confusing because the Assyrian, Babylonian, and Median empires were east and northeast of Israel. Since the deserts east of Israel were impassable for large armies, invaders had to travel north and west along the Euphrates River before they could turn south to attack the various countries on the east coast of the Mediterranean.

42:1–9 The Messiah, as the ideal Israel, manifests the Spirit of God. This One will be what Israel ought to be, but cannot.

My Elect One *in whom* My soul
delights!
I have put My Spirit upon Him;
He will bring forth justice to the
Gentiles.
2 He will not cry out, nor raise *His*
voice,
Nor cause His voice to be heard in
the street.
3 A bruised reed He will not break,
And smoking flax He will not
quench;
He will bring forth justice for truth.
4 He will not fail nor be discouraged,
Till He has established justice in the
earth;
And the coastlands shall wait for His
law."

5 Thus says God the LORD,
Who created the heavens and
stretched them out,
Who spread forth the earth and that
which comes from it,
Who gives breath to the people on it,
And spirit to those who walk on it:
6 "I, the LORD, have called You in
righteousness,
And will hold Your hand;
I will keep You and give You as a
covenant to the people,
As a light to the Gentiles,
7 To open blind eyes,
To bring out prisoners from the
prison,
Those who sit in darkness from the
prison house.
8 I *am* the LORD, that *is* My name;
And My glory I will not give to
another,
Nor My praise to carved images.
9 Behold, the former things have come
to pass,
And new things I declare;
Before they spring forth I tell you of
them."

Praise to the LORD

10 Sing to the LORD a new song,
And His praise from the ends of the
earth,
You who go down to the sea, and all
that is in it,
You coastlands and you inhabitants of
them!
11 Let the wilderness and its cities lift up
their voice,
The villages *that* Kē'dar inhabits.
Let the inhabitants of Sē'la sing,
Let them shout from the top of the
mountains.
12 Let them give glory to the LORD,
And declare His praise in the
coastlands.
13 The LORD shall go forth like a mighty
man;
He shall stir up *His* zeal like a man of
war.
He shall cry out, yes, shout aloud;
He shall prevail against His enemies.

Promise of the LORD's Help

14 "I have held My peace a long time,
I have been still and restrained
Myself.
Now I will cry like a woman in labor,
I will pant and gasp at once.
15 I will lay waste the mountains and
hills,
And dry up all their vegetation;
I will make the rivers coastlands,
And I will dry up the pools.
16 I will bring the blind by a way they
did not know;
I will lead them in paths they have
not known.
I will make darkness light before
them,

42:9 former things: The predicted exile. **new things**: The promised return.
42:10–17 The Lord delivers the helpless. The ideal Servant (vv. 1–9) and God are identified as doing the same things, pointing to the deity of the Messiah.

And crooked places straight.
These things I will do for them,
And not forsake them.
17 They shall be turned back,
They shall be greatly ashamed,
Who trust in carved images,
Who say to the molded images,
'You *are* our gods.'

18 "Hear, you deaf;
And look, you blind, that you may see.
19 Who *is* blind but My servant,
Or deaf as My messenger *whom* I send?
Who *is* blind as *he who is* perfect,
And blind as the LORD's servant?
20 Seeing many things, but you do not observe;
Opening the ears, but he does not hear."

Israel's Obstinate Disobedience

21 The LORD is well pleased for His righteousness' sake;
He will exalt the law and make *it* honorable.
22 But this *is* a people robbed and plundered;
All of them are snared in holes,
And they are hidden in prison houses;
They are for prey, and no one delivers;
For plunder, and no one says, "Restore!"

23 Who among you will give ear to this?
Who will listen and hear for the time to come?
24 Who gave Jacob for plunder, and Israel to the robbers?
Was it not the LORD,
He against whom we have sinned?
For they would not walk in His ways,
Nor were they obedient to His law.
25 Therefore He has poured on him the fury of His anger
And the strength of battle;
It has set him on fire all around,
Yet he did not know;
And it burned him,
Yet he did not take *it* to heart.

CHAPTER 43

The Redeemer of Israel

But now, thus says the LORD, who created you, O Jacob,
And He who formed you, O Israel:
"Fear not, for I have redeemed you;
I have called *you* by your name;
You *are* Mine.
2 When you pass through the waters, I *will be* with you;
And through the rivers, they shall not overflow you.
When you walk through the fire, you shall not be burned,
Nor shall the flame scorch you.
3 For I *am* the LORD your God,
The Holy One of Israel, your Savior;

I praise You for Your promise that when I pass through the waters, You will be with me; and through the rivers, they shall not overflow me. When I walk through the fire, I shall not be burned, nor shall the flame scorch me.

adapted from Isaiah 43:2

43:1–7 Despite the condition described in 42:21–25, God has not given up on His people. In His intent they are **now** (already) **redeemed** (v. 1).

> If you wait for the perfect moment when all is safe and assured, it may never arrive. Mountains will not be climbed, races won, or lasting happiness achieved.
>
> Maurice Chevalier

I gave Egypt for your ransom,
Ethiopia and Sē'ba in your place.
4 Since you were precious in My sight,
You have been honored,
And I have loved you;
Therefore I will give men for you,
And people for your life.
5 Fear not, for I *am* with you;
I will bring your descendants from the east,
And gather you from the west;
6 I will say to the north, 'Give them up!'
And to the south, 'Do not keep them back!'
Bring My sons from afar,
And My daughters from the ends of the earth—
7 Everyone who is called by My name,
Whom I have created for My glory;
I have formed him, yes, I have made him."

8 Bring out the blind people who have eyes,
And the deaf who have ears.
9 Let all the nations be gathered together,
And let the people be assembled.
Who among them can declare this,
And show us former things?
Let them bring out their witnesses, that they may be justified;
Or let them hear and say, "*It is* truth."
10 "You *are* My witnesses," says the LORD,
"And My servant whom I have chosen,
That you may know and believe Me,
And understand that I *am* He.
Before Me there was no God formed,
Nor shall there be after Me.
11 I, *even* I, *am* the LORD,
And besides Me *there is* no savior.
12 I have declared and saved,
I have proclaimed,
And *there was* no foreign *god* among you;
Therefore you *are* My witnesses,"
Says the LORD, "that I *am* God.
13 Indeed before the day *was*, I *am* He;
And *there is* no one who can deliver out of My hand;
I work, and who will reverse it?"

14 Thus says the LORD, your Redeemer,
The Holy One of Israel:
"For your sake I will send to Babylon,
And bring them all down as fugitives—
The Chal·dē'ans, who rejoice in their ships.
15 I *am* the LORD, your Holy One,
The Creator of Israel, your King."

16 Thus says the LORD, who makes a way in the sea
And a path through the mighty waters,
17 Who brings forth the chariot and horse,
The army and the power
(They shall lie down together, they shall not rise;
They are extinguished, they are quenched like a wick):
18 "Do not remember the former things,
Nor consider the things of old.
19 Behold, I will do a new thing,
Now it shall spring forth;

43:10 My witnesses: God will make Israel the evidence of His greatness in spite of their present broken condition.

43:19–21 a new thing: God's people should not live in the past as though the only deliv-

> Don't try to go back to yesterday; go back to the Bible.
>
> Anne Ortlund

Shall you not know it?
I will even make a road in the wilderness
And rivers in the desert.
20 The beast of the field will honor Me,
The jackals and the ostriches,
Because I give waters in the wilderness
And rivers in the desert,
To give drink to My people, My chosen.
21 This people I have formed for Myself;
They shall declare My praise.

Pleading with Unfaithful Israel

22 "But you have not called upon Me, O Jacob;
And you have been weary of Me, O Israel.
23 You have not brought Me the sheep for your burnt offerings,
Nor have you honored Me with your sacrifices.
I have not caused you to serve with grain offerings,
Nor wearied you with incense.
24 You have bought Me no sweet cane with money,
Nor have you satisfied Me with the fat of your sacrifices;
But you have burdened Me with your sins,
You have wearied Me with your iniquities.

25 "I, *even* I, *am* He who blots out your transgressions for My own sake;
And I will not remember your sins.
26 Put Me in remembrance;
Let us contend together;
State your *case,* that you may be acquitted.
27 Your first father sinned,
And your mediators have transgressed against Me.
28 Therefore I will profane the princes of the sanctuary;
I will give Jacob to the curse,
And Israel to reproaches.

CHAPTER 44

God's Blessing on Israel

"Yet hear me now, O Jacob My servant,
And Israel whom I have chosen.
2 Thus says the LORD who made you
And formed you from the womb, *who* will help you:
'Fear not, O Jacob My servant;
And you, Jesh'ū·run, whom I have chosen.
3 For I will pour water on him who is thirsty,
And floods on the dry ground;

erance He could produce was from Egypt. He is not like the idols, locked into doing the same thing over and over again. He will deliver in new ways.

43:22–24 Irony. Israel had indeed offered all these things, but not from the heart. **You have burdened Me with your sins**.

43:27 The identity of the first **father** is unclear. Suggestions range from Adam to King Manasseh. The point is that Israel did not start to sin recently. Her sinning is a long-term problem.

44:1–5 God's promise to pour out His Spirit upon His servants. Beyond forgiveness for their sins, beyond deliverance from Babylon, what the people really need is the fullness of God's Spirit. Then they can be holy people; then they can truly say **I am the LORD's** (v. 5).

44:2 Jeshurun: An affectionate name for Israel.

44:3 him who is thirsty: Isaiah promises this invaluable blessing to those who thirst for God (see Matt. 5:6).

SPLASH IN THE RIVER OF CHANGE

Carolyn Koons with John Archer

Rivers are fascinating. As water flows through a riverbed, it crashes over rocks, spills over falls, and rests in slow-moving pools; yet it continues toward its final destination—the sea. Many older adults are tempted to sit down by the side of the river of time, refusing to be bumped or bruised by waves of exhilaration or pain. If the years of our lives can be likened to a river, then change is inevitable.

Comparing the present moment with "the way we were" thirty years ago certainly brings us face-to-face with how we have changed. Yet change is constant in our lives. Each of us, no matter what our age and situation, can continue to change and grow. And we need to be open to the new people and circumstances God brings into our lives.

"To experience life as a full gift, we need to break free from things that hold us back."

Even when we know better, we lean toward inertia—staying stuck in a predictable routine, oblivious to opportunities and obstacles. Rather than change the way we act or think, we sometimes prefer a more quiet walk along a comfortable path on the river bank with little room to turn, much less to dance. How comfortable, we think, to simply put one foot in front of the other, day after day!

However, to thrive, to experience life as a full gift, we need to break free from things that hold us back. In other words, we need to become unstuck and change our ways of thinking, doing, and being. To joyfully embrace that expectation is the first step toward braving the river and living a more satisfying life.

I will pour My Spirit on your
descendants,
And My blessing on your offspring;
4 They will spring up among the grass
Like willows by the watercourses.'
5 One will say, 'I *am* the LORD's';
Another will call *himself* by the name
of Jacob;
Another will write *with* his hand, 'The
LORD's,'
And name *himself* by the name of
Israel.

There Is No Other God

6 "Thus says the LORD, the King of
Israel,
And his Redeemer, the LORD of hosts:
'I *am* the First and I *am* the Last;
Besides Me *there is* no God.
7 And who can proclaim as I do?

44:6–8 who can proclaim as I do? Only God can foretell the future.

Then let him declare it and set it in
order for Me,
Since I appointed the ancient people.
And the things that are coming and
shall come,
Let them show these to them.
8 Do not fear, nor be afraid;
Have I not told you from that time,
and declared *it?*
You *are* My witnesses.
Is there a God besides Me?
Indeed *there is* no other Rock;
I know not *one.*' "

Idolatry Is Foolishness

9 Those who make an image, all of
them *are* useless,
And their precious things shall not
profit;
They *are* their own witnesses;
They neither see nor know, that they
may be ashamed.
10 Who would form a god or mold an
image
That profits him nothing?
11 Surely all his companions would be
ashamed;
And the workmen, they *are* mere
men.
Let them all be gathered together,
Let them stand up;
Yet they shall fear,
They shall be ashamed together.

12 The blacksmith with the tongs works
one in the coals,
Fashions it with hammers,
And works it with the strength of his
arms.
Even so, he is hungry, and his
strength fails;
He drinks no water and is faint.
13 The craftsman stretches out *his* rule,
He marks one out with chalk;
He fashions it with a plane,
He marks it out with the compass,
And makes it like the figure of a man,
According to the beauty of a man,
that it may remain in the house.
14 He cuts down cedars for himself,
And takes the cypress and the oak;
He secures *it* for himself among the
trees of the forest.
He plants a pine, and the rain
nourishes *it.*

15 Then it shall be for a man to burn,
For he will take some of it and warm
himself;
Yes, he kindles *it* and bakes bread;
Indeed he makes a god and worships
it;
He makes it a carved image, and falls
down to it.
16 He burns half of it in the fire;
With this half he eats meat;
He roasts a roast, and is satisfied.
He even warms *himself* and says,
"Ah! I am warm,
I have seen the fire."
17 And the rest of it he makes into a
god,
His carved image.
He falls down before it and worships
it,
Prays to it and says,
"Deliver me, for you *are* my god!"

18 They do not know nor understand;
For He has shut their eyes, so that
they cannot see,
And their hearts, so that they cannot
understand.
19 And no one considers in his heart,

44:9–20 Idols are the work of **men** (v. 11), made in the image of a **man** (v. 13). They are just wood, clay, or metal and are thus unable to do anything (vv. 19, 20).

44:15–17 A powerful summary of the foolishness of creating a god from any created thing.

Nor *is there* knowledge nor
understanding to say,
"I have burned half of it in the fire,
Yes, I have also baked bread on its
coals;
I have roasted meat and eaten *it;*
And shall I make the rest of it an
abomination?
Shall I fall down before a block of
wood?"
20 He feeds on ashes;
A deceived heart has turned him
aside;
And he cannot deliver his soul,
Nor say, "*Is there* not a lie in my right
hand?"

Israel Is Not Forgotten

21 "Remember these, O Jacob,
And Israel, for you *are* My servant;
I have formed you, you *are* My
servant;
O Israel, you will not be forgotten by
Me!
22 I have blotted out, like a thick cloud,
your transgressions,
And like a cloud, your sins.
Return to Me, for I have redeemed
you."

23 Sing, O heavens, for the LORD has
done *it!*
Shout, you lower parts of the earth;
Break forth into singing, you
mountains,
O forest, and every tree in it!
For the LORD has redeemed Jacob,
And glorified Himself in Israel.

Judah Will Be Restored

24 Thus says the LORD, your Redeemer,
And He who formed you from the
womb:
"I *am* the LORD, who makes all *things,*
Who stretches out the heavens all
alone,
Who spreads abroad the earth by
Myself;
25 Who frustrates the signs of the
babblers,
And drives diviners mad;
Who turns wise men backward,
And makes their knowledge
foolishness;
26 Who confirms the word of His
servant,
And performs the counsel of His
messengers;
Who says to Jerusalem, 'You shall be
inhabited,'
To the cities of Judah, 'You shall be
built,'
And I will raise up her waste places;
27 Who says to the deep, 'Be dry!
And I will dry up your rivers';
28 Who says of Cyrus, '*He is* My
shepherd,
And he shall perform all My pleasure,
Saying to Jerusalem, "You shall be
built,"
And to the temple, "Your foundation
shall be laid." ' "

CHAPTER 45

Cyrus, God's Instrument

"Thus says the LORD to His anointed,
To Cyrus, whose right hand I have
held—
To subdue nations before him
And loose the armor of kings,
To open before him the double
doors,
So that the gates will not be shut:
2 'I will go before you

44:21–28 God, who is infinitely creative, is able to redeem Israel, His servant. He will do something unheard of: setting an exiled people free to go home. He will do so through the mighty Persian emperor Cyrus, whom Isaiah boldly designates as the Lord's shepherd.

45:1–8 Cyrus is named as God's servant to accomplish the deliverance of His people. God has given the Persian emperor his victories so that he can set God's people free.

And make the crooked places[a]
straight;
I will break in pieces the gates of
bronze
And cut the bars of iron.
3 I will give you the treasures of
darkness
And hidden riches of secret places,
That you may know that I, the LORD,
Who call *you* by your name,
Am the God of Israel.
4 For Jacob My servant's sake,
And Israel My elect,
I have even called you by your name;
I have named you, though you have
not known Me.
5 I *am* the LORD, and *there is* no other;
There is no God besides Me.
I will gird you, though you have not
known Me,
6 That they may know from the rising
of the sun to its setting
That *there is* none besides Me.
I *am* the LORD, and *there is* no other;
7 I form the light and create darkness,
I make peace and create calamity;
I, the LORD, do all these *things*.'

8 "Rain down, you heavens, from above,
And let the skies pour down
righteousness;
Let the earth open, let them bring
forth salvation,
And let righteousness spring up
together.
I, the LORD, have created it.

9 "Woe to him who strives with his
Maker!
Let the potsherd *strive* with the
potsherds of the earth!
Shall the clay say to him who forms
it, 'What are you making?'
Or shall your handiwork *say*, 'He has
no hands'?
10 Woe to him who says to *his* father,
'What are you begetting?'
Or to the woman, 'What have you
brought forth?' "
11 Thus says the LORD,
The Holy One of Israel, and his
Maker:
"Ask Me of things to come concerning
My sons;
And concerning the work of My
hands, you command Me.
12 I have made the earth,
And created man on it.
I—My hands—stretched out the
heavens,
And all their host I have commanded.
13 I have raised him up in
righteousness,
And I will direct all his ways;
He shall build My city
And let My exiles go free,
Not for price nor reward,"
Says the LORD of hosts.

The LORD, the Only Savior

14 Thus says the LORD:

"The labor of Egypt and merchandise
of Cush
And of the Sa·bē'ans, men of stature,
Shall come over to you, and they shall
be yours;
They shall walk behind you,
They shall come over in chains;
And they shall bow down to you.
They will make supplication to you,
saying, 'Surely God *is* in you,

45:2 [a]Dead Sea Scrolls and Septuagint read *mountains;* Targum reads *I will trample down the walls;* Vulgate reads *I will humble the great ones of the earth.*

45:9–13 Since God is the **Maker** (v. 9), He can do as He wishes. Perhaps some responded with shock to God's announcement that He would use the pagan Cyrus as His shepherd to bring Israel home.

45:14–25 The threefold repetition of the phrase **there is no other** emphasizes God's unique character.

And *there is* no other;
There is no other God.' "

15 Truly You *are* God, who hide Yourself,
O God of Israel, the Savior!
16 They shall be ashamed
And also disgraced, all of them;
They shall go in confusion together,
Who are makers of idols.
17 *But* Israel shall be saved by the LORD
With an everlasting salvation;
You shall not be ashamed or
disgraced
Forever and ever.

18 For thus says the LORD,
Who created the heavens,
Who is God,
Who formed the earth and made it,
Who has established it,
Who did not create it in vain,
Who formed it to be inhabited:
"I *am* the LORD, and *there is* no other.
19 I have not spoken in secret,
In a dark place of the earth;
I did not say to the seed of Jacob,
'Seek Me in vain';
I, the LORD, speak righteousness,
I declare things that are right.

20 "Assemble yourselves and come;
Draw near together,
You *who have* escaped from the
nations.
They have no knowledge,
Who carry the wood of their carved
image,
And pray to a god *that* cannot save.
21 Tell and bring forth *your case;*
Yes, let them take counsel together.
Who has declared this from ancient
time?
Who has told it from that time?
Have not I, the LORD?
And *there is* no other God besides Me,
A just God and a Savior;
There is none besides Me.

22 "Look to Me, and be saved,
All you ends of the earth!
For I *am* God, and *there is* no other.
23 I have sworn by Myself;
The word has gone out of My mouth
in righteousness,
And shall not return,
That to Me every knee shall bow,
Every tongue shall take an oath.
24 He shall say,
'Surely in the LORD I have
righteousness and strength.
To Him *men* shall come,
And all shall be ashamed
Who are incensed against Him.
25 In the LORD all the descendants of
Israel
Shall be justified, and shall glory.' "

CHAPTER 46

Dead Idols and the Living God

Bel bows down, Nē'bō stoops;
Their idols were on the beasts and on
the cattle.
Your carriages *were* heavily loaded,
A burden to the weary *beast*.
2 They stoop, they bow down together;
They could not deliver the burden,
But have themselves gone into
captivity.

3 "Listen to Me, O house of Jacob,
And all the remnant of the house of
Israel,
Who have been upheld *by Me* from
birth,
Who have been carried from the
womb:

45:19 I did not say . . . Seek Me in vain: God has revealed Himself to us in ways that anyone who so desires may understand. Seeking is rewarded.

46:1–7 God will carry His people (v. 4), but the idolators must bear their gods (vv. 1, 7).

4 Even to *your* old age, I *am* He,
And *even* to gray hairs I will carry
you!
I have made, and I will bear;
Even I will carry, and will deliver *you.*

5 "To whom will you liken Me, and
make *Me* equal
And compare Me, that we should be
alike?
6 They lavish gold out of the bag,
And weigh silver on the scales;
They hire a goldsmith, and he makes
it a god;
They prostrate themselves, yes, they
worship.
7 They bear it on the shoulder, they
carry it
And set it in its place, and it stands;
From its place it shall not move.
Though *one* cries out to it, yet it
cannot answer
Nor save him out of his trouble.

8 "Remember this, and show yourselves
men;
Recall to mind, O you transgressors.
9 Remember the former things of
old,
For I *am* God, and *there is* no other;
I am God, and *there is* none like Me,
10 Declaring the end from the beginning,
And from ancient times *things* that
are not *yet* done,
Saying, 'My counsel shall stand,
And I will do all My pleasure,'
11 Calling a bird of prey from the
east,
The man who executes My counsel,
from a far country.
Indeed I have spoken *it;*
I will also bring it to pass.
I have purposed *it;*
I will also do it.

12 "Listen to Me, you stubborn-hearted,
Who *are* far from righteousness:
13 I bring My righteousness near, it shall
not be far off;
My salvation shall not linger.
And I will place salvation in Zion,
For Israel My glory.

CHAPTER 47

The Humiliation of Babylon

"Come down and sit in the dust,
O virgin daughter of Babylon;
Sit on the ground without a throne,
O daughter of the Chal·dē′ans!
For you shall no more be called
Tender and delicate.
2 Take the millstones and grind meal.
Remove your veil,
Take off the skirt,
Uncover the thigh,
Pass through the rivers.
3 Your nakedness shall be uncovered,
Yes, your shame will be seen;
I will take vengeance,
And I will not arbitrate with a man."

4 *As for* our Redeemer, the LORD of
hosts *is* His name,
The Holy One of Israel.

5 "Sit in silence, and go into darkness,
O daughter of the Chal·dē′ans;
For you shall no longer be called
The Lady of Kingdoms.
6 I was angry with My people;
I have profaned My inheritance,
And given them into your hand.
You showed them no mercy;
On the elderly you laid your yoke
very heavily.
7 And you said, 'I shall be a lady
forever,'

46:12, 13 stubborn-hearted: Those who would not believe that God could deliver His people from Babylon.

47:1–15 The disgrace of Babylon, the **daughter of the Chaldeans** (vv. 1, 5). She will be like a beautiful lady reduced to slavery (vv. 1–3, 9).

So that you did not take these *things*
to heart,
Nor remember the latter end of them.

8 "Therefore hear this now, *you who are*
given to pleasures,
Who dwell securely,
Who say in your heart, 'I *am*, and
there is no one else besides me;
I shall not sit *as* a widow,
Nor shall I know the loss of children';
9 But these two *things* shall come to you
In a moment, in one day:
The loss of children, and widowhood.
They shall come upon you in their
fullness
Because of the multitude of your
sorceries,
For the great abundance of your
enchantments.

10 "For you have trusted in your
wickedness;
You have said, 'No one sees me';
Your wisdom and your knowledge
have warped you;
And you have said in your heart,
'I *am*, and *there is* no one else besides me.'
11 Therefore evil shall come upon you;
You shall not know from where it
arises.
And trouble shall fall upon you;
You will not be able to put it off.
And desolation shall come upon you
suddenly,
Which you shall not know.

12 "Stand now with your enchantments
And the multitude of your sorceries,
In which you have labored from your
youth—
Perhaps you will be able to profit,
Perhaps you will prevail.
13 You are wearied in the multitude of
your counsels;
Let now the astrologers, the
stargazers,
And the monthly prognosticators
Stand up and save you
From what shall come upon you.
14 Behold, they shall be as stubble,
The fire shall burn them;
They shall not deliver themselves
From the power of the flame;
It shall not *be* a coal to be warmed by,
Nor a fire to sit before!
15 Thus shall they be to you
With whom you have labored,
Your merchants from your youth;
They shall wander each one to his
quarter.
No one shall save you.

CHAPTER 48

Israel Refined for God's Glory

"Hear this, O house of Jacob,
Who are called by the name of Israel,
And have come forth from the
wellsprings of Judah;
Who swear by the name of the LORD,
And make mention of the God of
Israel,
But not in truth or in righteousness;
2 For they call themselves after the holy
city,
And lean on the God of Israel;
The LORD of hosts *is* His name:

3 "I have declared the former things
from the beginning;

47:8 Babylon's, and humanity's, great sin is the pride which says, **I am, and there is no one else besides me** (also v. 10). Such arrogance must always issue in disaster (v. 11) because it is a lie. Only God can truthfully make such a statement.

48:3–8 Israel's perverseness. Some things were revealed to them from the beginning because otherwise they would have ascribed to an idol the work of God (vv. 3–5). Other things were hidden from them until Isaiah's day because otherwise they would have forgotten, or simply dismissed, them (vv. 6–8).

They went forth from My mouth, and
I caused them to hear it.
Suddenly I did *them,* and they came
to pass.
4 Because I knew that you *were*
obstinate,
And your neck *was* an iron sinew,
And your brow bronze,
5 Even from the beginning I have
declared *it* to you;
Before it came to pass I proclaimed *it*
to you,
Lest you should say, 'My idol has
done them,
And my carved image and my
molded image
Have commanded them.'

6 "You have heard;
See all this.
And will you not declare *it?*
I have made you hear new things
from this time,
Even hidden things, and you did not
know them.
7 They are created now and not from
the beginning;
And before this day you have not
heard them,
Lest you should say, 'Of course I
knew them.'
8 Surely you did not hear,
Surely you did not know;
Surely from long ago your ear was
not opened.
For I knew that you would deal very
treacherously,
And were called a transgressor from
the womb.

9 "For My name's sake I will defer My
anger,
And *for* My praise I will restrain it
from you,
So that I do not cut you off.
10 Behold, I have refined you, but not as
silver;
I have tested you in the furnace of
affliction.
11 For My own sake, for My own sake, I
will do *it;*
For how should *My name* be
profaned?
And I will not give My glory to
another.

God's Ancient Plan to Redeem Israel

12 "Listen to Me, O Jacob,
And Israel, My called:
I *am* He, I *am* the First,
I *am* also the Last.
13 Indeed My hand has laid the
foundation of the earth,
And My right hand has stretched out
the heavens;
When I call to them,
They stand up together.

14 "All of you, assemble yourselves, and
hear!
Who among them has declared these
things?
The LORD loves him;

He shall do His pleasure on Babylon,
And His arm *shall be against* the
Chal·dē'ans.
15 I, *even* I, have spoken;
Yes, I have called him,
I have brought him, and his way will
prosper.

16 "Come near to Me, hear this:
I have not spoken in secret from the
beginning;
From the time that it was, I *was*
there.

48:7 now . . . not from the beginning: Redemption, as Isaiah is describing it, is a new creation, not something implicit in the world as it was at first.

48:9–11 Despite the people's perverseness, God seeks to refine them, not cut them off.

48:16 Come near to Me: God's Servant, the Messiah.

And now the Lord GOD and His Spirit
Have[a] sent Me."

17 Thus says the LORD, your Redeemer,
The Holy One of Israel:
"I *am* the LORD your God,
Who teaches you to profit,
Who leads you by the way you should go.
18 Oh, that you had heeded My commandments!
Then your peace would have been like a river,
And your righteousness like the waves of the sea.
19 Your descendants also would have been like the sand,
And the offspring of your body like the grains of sand;
His name would not have been cut off
Nor destroyed from before Me."

20 Go forth from Babylon!
Flee from the Chal·dē'ans!
With a voice of singing,
Declare, proclaim this,
Utter it to the end of the earth;
Say, "The LORD has redeemed
His servant Jacob!"
21 And they did not thirst
When He led them through the deserts;
He caused the waters to flow from the rock for them;
He also split the rock, and the waters gushed out.

22 "*There* is no peace," says the LORD, "for the wicked."

CHAPTER 49

The Servant, the Light to the Gentiles

"Listen, O coastlands, to Me,
And take heed, you peoples from afar!
The LORD has called Me from the womb;
From the matrix of My mother He has made mention of My name.
2 And He has made My mouth like a sharp sword;
In the shadow of His hand He has hidden Me,
And made Me a polished shaft;
In His quiver He has hidden Me."

3 "And He said to me,
'You *are* My servant, O Israel,
In whom I will be glorified.'
4 Then I said, 'I have labored in vain,
I have spent my strength for nothing and in vain;
Yet surely my just reward *is* with the LORD,
And my work with my God.' "

5 "And now the LORD says,
Who formed Me from the womb *to be* His Servant,
To bring Jacob back to Him,
So that Israel is gathered to Him[a]
(For I shall be glorious in the eyes of the LORD,
And My God shall be My strength),

48:16 [a]The Hebrew verb is singular. 49:5 [a]Qere, Dead Sea Scrolls, and Septuagint read *is gathered to Him;* Kethib reads *is not gathered.*

49:1—55:13 The means by which the Lord will accomplish an even greater deliverance than that from Babylon. He will deliver His people from the sin which brought them into bondage. God's instrument is the Messiah, the ideal Servant.

49:1 Called Me from the womb indicates that this mission was not an afterthought; the Servant was called from the beginning.

49:3 Israel: This Person is the ideal Israel, One who incarnates what Israel should have been.

6 Indeed He says,
'It is too small a thing that You should be My Servant
To raise up the tribes of Jacob,
And to restore the preserved ones of Israel;
I will also give You as a light to the Gentiles,
That You should be My salvation to the ends of the earth.' "

7 Thus says the LORD,
The Redeemer of Israel, their Holy One,
To Him whom man despises,
To Him whom the nation abhors,
To the Servant of rulers:
"Kings shall see and arise,
Princes also shall worship,
Because of the LORD who is faithful,
The Holy One of Israel;
And He has chosen You."

8Thus says the LORD:

"In an acceptable time I have heard You,
And in the day of salvation I have helped You;
I will preserve You and give You
As a covenant to the people,
To restore the earth,
To cause them to inherit the desolate heritages;
9 That You may say to the prisoners, 'Go forth,'
To those who *are* in darkness, 'Show yourselves.'

"They shall feed along the roads,
And their pastures *shall be* on all desolate heights.
10 They shall neither hunger nor thirst,
Neither heat nor sun shall strike them;
For He who has mercy on them will lead them,
Even by the springs of water He will guide them.
11 I will make each of My mountains a road,
And My highways shall be elevated.
12 Surely these shall come from afar;
Look! Those from the north and the west,
And these from the land of Sin'im."

13 Sing, O heavens!
Be joyful, O earth!
And break out in singing, O mountains!
For the LORD has comforted His people,
And will have mercy on His afflicted.

God Will Remember Zion

14 But Zion said, "The LORD has forsaken me,
And my Lord has forgotten me."

15 "Can a woman forget her nursing child,
And not have compassion on the son of her womb?
Surely they may forget,
Yet I will not forget you.
16 See, I have inscribed you on the palms *of My hands;*
Your walls *are* continually before Me.
17 Your sons[a] shall make haste;
Your destroyers and those who laid you waste
Shall go away from you.
18 Lift up your eyes, look around and see;
All these gather together *and* come to you.
As I live," says the LORD,

49:17 [a]Dead Sea Scrolls, Septuagint, Targum, and Vulgate read *builders.*

49:6 light to the Gentiles: The Servant's ministry will encompass not only the Jews, but the entire human race.

"You shall surely clothe yourselves
with them all as an ornament,
And bind them *on you* as a bride *does*.

19 "For your waste and desolate places,
And the land of your destruction,
Will even now be too small for the
inhabitants;
And those who swallowed you up
will be far away.
20 The children you will have,
After you have lost the others,
Will say again in your ears,
'The place *is* too small for me;
Give me a place where I may dwell.'
21 Then you will say in your heart,
'Who has begotten these for me,
Since I have lost my children and am
desolate,
A captive, and wandering to and fro?
And who has brought these up?
There I was, left alone;
But these, where *were* they?' "

22 Thus says the Lord GOD:

"Behold, I will lift My hand in an oath
to the nations,
And set up My standard for the
peoples;
They shall bring your sons in *their*
arms,
And your daughters shall be carried
on *their* shoulders;
23 Kings shall be your foster fathers,
And their queens your nursing
mothers;
They shall bow down to you with
their faces to the earth,
And lick up the dust of your feet.
Then you will know that I *am* the
LORD,
For they shall not be ashamed who
wait for Me."

24 Shall the prey be taken from the
mighty,
Or the captives of the righteous[a] be
delivered?

25 But thus says the LORD:

"Even the captives of the mighty shall
be taken away,
And the prey of the terrible be
delivered;
For I will contend with him who
contends with you,
And I will save your children.
26 I will feed those who oppress you
with their own flesh,
And they shall be drunk with their
own blood as with sweet wine.
All flesh shall know
That I, the LORD, *am* your Savior,
And your Redeemer, the Mighty One
of Jacob."

CHAPTER 50

The Servant, Israel's Hope

Thus says the LORD:

"Where *is* the certificate of your
mother's divorce,
Whom I have put away?
Or which of My creditors *is it* to
whom I have sold you?
For your iniquities you have sold
yourselves,
And for your transgressions your
mother has been put away.
2 Why, when I came, *was there* no man?
Why, when I called, *was there* none to
answer?
Is My hand shortened at all that it
cannot redeem?

49:24 [a]Following Masoretic Text and Targum; Dead Sea Scrolls, Syriac, and Vulgate read *the mighty;* Septuagint reads *unjustly*.

49:22 Just as the Lord used a "banner" (5:26) to call the nations to come and destroy, so He will raise His **standard** (same Hebrew word) commanding them to bring back the captives.

Or have I no power to deliver?
Indeed with My rebuke I dry up the
sea,
I make the rivers a wilderness;
Their fish stink because *there is* no
water,
And die of thirst.
3 I clothe the heavens with blackness,
And I make sackcloth their covering."

4 "The Lord GOD has given Me
The tongue of the learned,
That I should know how to speak
A word in season to *him who is* weary.
He awakens Me morning by
morning,
He awakens My ear
To hear as the learned.
5 The Lord GOD has opened My ear;
And I was not rebellious,
Nor did I turn away.
6 I gave My back to those who struck
Me,
And My cheeks to those who plucked
out the beard;
I did not hide My face from shame
and spitting.

7 "For the Lord GOD will help Me;
Therefore I will not be disgraced;
Therefore I have set My face like a
flint,
And I know that I will not be
ashamed.
8 *He is* near who justifies Me;
Who will contend with Me?
Let us stand together.
Who *is* My adversary?
Let him come near Me.
9 Surely the Lord GOD will help Me;
Who *is* he *who* will condemn Me?
Indeed they will all grow old like a
garment;
The moth will eat them up.

10 "Who among you fears the LORD?
Who obeys the voice of His Servant?
Who walks in darkness
And has no light?
Let him trust in the name of the LORD
And rely upon his God.
11 Look, all you who kindle a fire,
Who encircle *yourselves* with sparks:
Walk in the light of your fire and in
the sparks you have kindled—
This you shall have from My hand:
You shall lie down in torment.

CHAPTER 51

The LORD Comforts Zion

"Listen to Me, you who follow after
righteousness,
You who seek the LORD:
Look to the rock *from which* you were
hewn,
And to the hole of the pit *from which*
you were dug.
2 Look to Abraham your father,
And to Sarah *who* bore you;
For I called him alone,
And blessed him and increased him."

3 For the LORD will comfort Zion,
He will comfort all her waste places;

50:4–9 The Servant expresses His confidence in God which made Him able to submit Himself to the abuse of the world. Again, this is clearly not the nation of Israel.

50:4 tongue . . . ear: The ideal Israel is not blind and deaf and hard-hearted (6:9, 10); He is alert to all that God wants to say and do through Him.

50:5, 6 This Servant is not rebellious (contrast with Israel, 1:2). He submits to abuse, not for His own sins, as did the nation, but for the sins of others (53:4–7).

50:10, 11 The hearers are challenged to listen to the Servant. The Hebrew sentence structure here identifies Him as being the same as the **LORD**. People can trust Him and find their light in Him, or they must walk in their own fire and find torment.

51:1, 2 Abraham is referred to here because of his having been justified by faith when he believed God (see Gen. 15:6). Israel is challenged to follow his example.

He will make her wilderness like
Eden,
And her desert like the garden of the
LORD;
Joy and gladness will be found in it,
Thanksgiving and the voice of
melody.

4 "Listen to Me, My people;
And give ear to Me, O My nation:
For law will proceed from Me,
And I will make My justice rest
As a light of the peoples.
5 My righteousness *is* near,
My salvation has gone forth,
And My arms will judge the peoples;
The coastlands will wait upon Me,
And on My arm they will trust.
6 Lift up your eyes to the heavens,
And look on the earth beneath.
For the heavens will vanish away like
smoke,
The earth will grow old like a
garment,
And those who dwell in it will die in
like manner;
But My salvation will be forever,
And My righteousness will not be
abolished.

7 "Listen to Me, you who know
righteousness,
You people in whose heart *is* My law:
Do not fear the reproach of men,
Nor be afraid of their insults.
8 For the moth will eat them up like a
garment,
And the worm will eat them like
wool;
But My righteousness will be forever,
And My salvation from generation to
generation."

9 Awake, awake, put on strength,
O arm of the LORD!
Awake as in the ancient days,
In the generations of old.
Are You not *the arm* that cut Rā'hab
apart,
And wounded the serpent?

10 *Are* You not *the One* who dried up the
sea,
The waters of the great deep;
That made the depths of the sea a
road
For the redeemed to cross over?
11 So the ransomed of the LORD shall
return,
And come to Zion with singing,
With everlasting joy on their heads.
They shall obtain joy and gladness;
Sorrow and sighing shall flee away.

12 "I, *even* I, *am* He who comforts you.
Who *are* you that you should be
afraid
Of a man *who* will die,
And of the son of a man *who* will be
made like grass?
13 And you forget the LORD your Maker,
Who stretched out the heavens
And laid the foundations of the
earth;
You have feared continually every
day
Because of the fury of the oppressor,
When *he has* prepared to destroy.
And where *is* the fury of the
oppressor?
14 The captive exile hastens, that he may
be loosed,
That he should not die in the pit,
And that his bread should not fail.
15 But I *am* the LORD your God,
Who divided the sea whose waves
roared—
The LORD of hosts *is* His name.
16 And I have put My words in your
mouth;

51:9, 10 Rahab was a name for Egypt (Ps. 87:4), which revered serpents. This is underscored when he identifies the time of God's action as being at the Red Sea.

I have covered you with the shadow
of My hand,
That I may plant the heavens,
Lay the foundations of the earth,
And say to Zion, 'You *are* My
people.' "

God's Fury Removed

17 Awake, awake!
Stand up, O Jerusalem,
You who have drunk at the hand of
the LORD
The cup of His fury;
You have drunk the dregs of the cup
of trembling,
And drained *it* out.
18 *There is* no one to guide her
Among all the sons she has brought
forth;
Nor *is there any* who takes her by the
hand
Among all the sons she has brought
up.
19 These two *things* have come to you;
Who will be sorry for you?—
Desolation and destruction, famine
and sword—
By whom will I comfort you?
20 Your sons have fainted,
They lie at the head of all the streets,
Like an antelope in a net;
They are full of the fury of the LORD,
The rebuke of your God.

21 Therefore please hear this, you
afflicted,
And drunk but not with wine.
22 Thus says your Lord,
The LORD and your God,
Who pleads the cause of His people:
"See, I have taken out of your hand
The cup of trembling,
The dregs of the cup of My fury;
You shall no longer drink it.
23 But I will put it into the hand of those
who afflict you,
Who have said to you,[a]
'Lie down, that we may walk over
you.'
And you have laid your body like the
ground,
And as the street, for those who walk
over."

CHAPTER 52

God Redeems Jerusalem

Awake, awake!
Put on your strength, O Zion;
Put on your beautiful garments,
O Jerusalem, the holy city!
For the uncircumcised and the
unclean
Shall no longer come to you.
2 Shake yourself from the dust, arise;
Sit down, O Jerusalem!
Loose yourself from the bonds of
your neck,
O captive daughter of Zion!

3For thus says the LORD:

"You have sold yourselves for nothing,
And you shall be redeemed without
money."

4For thus says the Lord GOD:

"My people went down at first
Into Egypt to dwell there;
Then the Assyrian oppressed them
without cause.

51:23 [a]Literally *your soul*

51:17–23 Awake! The Lord calls Jerusalem (the Judeans) to wake up (v. 9) and to recognize what an amazing thing is going to happen. The cup of God's fury which they have drunk because of their sins (v. 17) will be taken out of their hand (v. 22).

52:3 without money: Who can pay enough to redeem themselves from sin? (see 55:1, 2).

5 Now therefore, what have I here,"
says the LORD,
"That My people are taken away for
nothing?
Those who rule over them
Make them wail,"[a] says the LORD,
"And My name *is* blasphemed
continually every day.
6 Therefore My people shall know My
name;
Therefore *they shall know* in that day
That I *am* He who speaks:
'Behold, *it is* I.' "

7 How beautiful upon the mountains
Are the feet of him who brings good
news,
Who proclaims peace,
Who brings glad tidings of good
things,
Who proclaims salvation,
Who says to Zion,
"Your God reigns!"
8 Your watchmen shall lift up *their*
voices,
With their voices they shall sing
together;
For they shall see eye to eye
When the LORD brings back Zion.
9 Break forth into joy, sing together,
You waste places of Jerusalem!
For the LORD has comforted His
people,
He has redeemed Jerusalem.
10 The LORD has made bare His holy
arm
In the eyes of all the nations;
And all the ends of the earth shall see
The salvation of our God.

11 Depart! Depart! Go out from there,
Touch no unclean *thing;*
Go out from the midst of her,
Be clean,
You who bear the vessels of the LORD.
12 For you shall not go out with haste,
Nor go by flight;
For the LORD will go before you,
And the God of Israel *will* be your
rear guard.

The Sin-Bearing Servant

13 Behold, My Servant shall deal
prudently;
He shall be exalted and extolled and
be very high.
14 Just as many were astonished at you,
So His visage was marred more than
any man,
And His form more than the sons of
men;
15 So shall He sprinkle[a] many nations.
Kings shall shut their mouths at Him;
For what had not been told them they
shall see,
And what they had not heard they
shall consider.

CHAPTER 53

Who has believed our report?
And to whom has the arm of the
LORD been revealed?
2 For He shall grow up before Him as a
tender plant,
And as a root out of dry ground.
He has no form or comeliness;

52:5 [a]Dead Sea Scrolls read *Mock;* Septuagint reads *Marvel and wail;* Targum reads *Boast themselves;* Vulgate reads *Treat them unjustly.*
52:15 [a]Or *startle*

52:7–12 The watchmen (v. 8) announce the coming of messengers with the good news (v. 7) that **the LORD has made bare His holy arm** (v. 10) and delivered Jerusalem (v. 9). As a result, the Jews are commanded to leave their bondage.

52:14—53:1 astonished: No one expected that the all-powerful **arm of the LORD** would be revealed in the form of a servant. No one believed Isaiah's report that the Messiah would be quiet, unassuming, and suffering. We humans have a difficult time envisioning greatness in any form other than majesty and popularity.

And when we see Him,
There is no beauty that we should desire Him.
3 He is despised and rejected by men,
A Man of sorrows and acquainted with grief.
And we hid, as it were, *our* faces from Him;
He was despised, and we did not esteem Him.

4 Surely He has borne our griefs
And carried our sorrows;
Yet we esteemed Him stricken,
Smitten by God, and afflicted.
5 But He *was* wounded for our transgressions,
He was bruised for our iniquities;
The chastisement for our peace *was* upon Him,
And by His stripes we are healed.
6 All we like sheep have gone astray;
We have turned, every one, to his own way;
And the LORD has laid on Him the iniquity of us all.

7 He was oppressed and He was afflicted,
Yet He opened not His mouth;
He was led as a lamb to the slaughter,
And as a sheep before its shearers is silent,
So He opened not His mouth.
8 He was taken from prison and from judgment,
And who will declare His generation?
For He was cut off from the land of the living;
For the transgressions of My people He was stricken.
9 And they[a] made His grave with the wicked—
But with the rich at His death,
Because He had done no violence,
Nor *was any* deceit in His mouth.

10 Yet it pleased the LORD to bruise Him;
He has put *Him* to grief.
When You make His soul an offering for sin,
He shall see *His* seed, He shall prolong *His* days,
And the pleasure of the LORD shall prosper in His hand.
11 He shall see the labor of His soul,[a] *and* be satisfied.
By His knowledge My righteous Servant shall justify many,
For He shall bear their iniquities.
12 Therefore I will divide Him a portion with the great,
And He shall divide the spoil with the strong,
Because He poured out His soul unto death,
And He was numbered with the transgressors,
And He bore the sin of many,
And made intercession for the transgressors.

53:9 [a]Literally *he* or *He* 53:11 [a]Following Masoretic Text, Targum, and Vulgate; Dead Sea Scrolls and Septuagint read *From the labor of His soul He shall see light.*

53:4–7 Probably the clearest statement of substitutionary atonement in the Bible. Though He was a Man of griefs and sorrows, they were not His, but ours. He **has borne** them for us.

53:8 His generation: For a person in that part of the world to die without children was to be under a curse from God. It meant that your name died with you. But because Jesus trusted His future to the Father, children belonging to Him come from all over the globe, and His name is above every name (Phil. 2:9).

53:10, 11 The only reason a good father would choose to bruise (lit. "crush") his son would be for some immensely greater good. In the Lord's plan, that greater good is our deliverance from sin.

CHAPTER 54

A Perpetual Covenant of Peace

"Sing, O barren,
You *who* have not borne!
Break forth into singing, and cry
aloud,
You *who* have not labored with
child!
For more *are* the children of the
desolate
Than the children of the married
woman," says the LORD.
2 "Enlarge the place of your tent,
And let them stretch out the curtains
of your dwellings;
Do not spare;
Lengthen your cords,
And strengthen your stakes.
3 For you shall expand to the right and
to the left,
And your descendants will inherit the
nations,
And make the desolate cities
inhabited.

4 "Do not fear, for you will not be
ashamed;
Neither be disgraced, for you will not
be put to shame;
For you will forget the shame of your
youth,
And will not remember the reproach
of your widowhood anymore.
5 For your Maker *is* your husband,
The LORD of hosts *is* His name;
And your Redeemer *is* the Holy One
of Israel;
He is called the God of the whole
earth.
6 For the LORD has called you
Like a woman forsaken and grieved
in spirit,
Like a youthful wife when you were
refused,"
Says your God.
7 "For a mere moment I have forsaken
you,
But with great mercies I will gather
you.
8 With a little wrath I hid My face from
you for a moment;
But with everlasting kindness I will
have mercy on you,"
Says the LORD, your Redeemer.

9 "For this *is* like the waters of Noah to
Me;
For as I have sworn
That the waters of Noah would no
longer cover the earth,
So have I sworn
That I would not be angry with you,
nor rebuke you.
10 For the mountains shall depart
And the hills be removed,
But My kindness shall not depart
from you,
Nor shall My covenant of peace be
removed,"
Says the LORD, who has mercy on
you.

11 "O you afflicted one,
Tossed with tempest, *and* not
comforted,
Behold, I will lay your stones with
colorful gems,
And lay your foundations with
sapphires.
12 I will make your pinnacles of rubies,
Your gates of crystal,
And all your walls of precious
stones.
13 All your children *shall be* taught by
the LORD,

54:1–17 Israel is like that barren woman who throws herself upon the Lord. In herself she cannot meet her need, but God promises that if she will trust Him (see 55:3–7; 56:4–7), she will be unimaginably fruitful. This important theme in the Bible illustrates the NT concept of the flesh and the Spirit: what is accomplished in our own strength and what is accomplished through reliance upon the Lord (see Gal. 4:21–31).

And great *shall be* the peace of your children.
14 In righteousness you shall be established;
You shall be far from oppression, for you shall not fear;
And from terror, for it shall not come near you.
15 Indeed they shall surely assemble, *but* not because of Me.
Whoever assembles against you shall fall for your sake.

16 "Behold, I have created the blacksmith
Who blows the coals in the fire,
Who brings forth an instrument for his work;
And I have created the spoiler to destroy.
17 No weapon formed against you shall prosper,
And every tongue *which* rises against you in judgment
You shall condemn.
This *is* the heritage of the servants of the LORD,
And their righteousness *is* from Me,"
Says the LORD.

CHAPTER 55

An Invitation to Abundant Life

"Ho! Everyone who thirsts,
Come to the waters;
And you who have no money,
Come, buy and eat.

55:1–3 Everyone: Salvation is offered to all. It can never be earned, only received with gratitude. How easily we spend our lives trying to obtain what will not last even as long as earthly life and, in so doing, miss what will last forever.

LIVING WATER

God created water (Gen. 1:2) even before He created light—that's how vital water is to both our physical and spiritual existence. The significance of water runs throughout our lives, from our physical birth through our spiritual birth waters at baptism to the need for the spirit-filled "living waters" offered by Jesus.

Physically, our overall body weight is 70 percent water, and the human body needs water to aid digestion, keep its temperature under control, and circulate nutrients. Your system must be regularly cleansed by drinking water; otherwise, toxins build up in fat cells that can cause a variety of health problems, including kidney stones, headaches, and joint pain. Water may be one of the oldest of God's creations, but it is still plentiful, still inexpensive, and still good for us.

Spiritually, we must recognize the vital role of the "living water" offered to us by the Lord in the person of the Holy Spirit (John 7:38, 39). His presence in our lives is vital to our spiritual health, and we must not allow the fountain of living water to become muddied by sin and indifference. ✦

Yes, come, buy wine and milk
Without money and without price.
2 Why do you spend money for *what is* not bread,
And your wages for *what* does not satisfy?
Listen carefully to Me, and eat *what is* good,
And let your soul delight itself in abundance.
3 Incline your ear, and come to Me.
Hear, and your soul shall live;
And I will make an everlasting covenant with you—
The sure mercies of David.
4 Indeed I have given him *as* a witness to the people,
A leader and commander for the people.
5 Surely you shall call a nation you do not know,
And nations *who* do not know you shall run to you,
Because of the LORD your God,
And the Holy One of Israel;
For He has glorified you."

6 Seek the LORD while He may be found,
Call upon Him while He is near.
7 Let the wicked forsake his way,
And the unrighteous man his thoughts;
Let him return to the LORD,
And He will have mercy on him;
And to our God,
For He will abundantly pardon.

8 "For My thoughts *are* not your thoughts,
Nor *are* your ways My ways," says the LORD.
9 "For *as* the heavens are higher than the earth,
So are My ways higher than your ways,
And My thoughts than your thoughts.
10 "For as the rain comes down, and the snow from heaven,
And do not return there,
But water the earth,
And make it bring forth and bud,
That it may give seed to the sower
And bread to the eater,
11 So shall My word be that goes forth from My mouth;
It shall not return to Me void,
But it shall accomplish what I please,
And it shall prosper *in the thing* for which I sent it.

12 "For you shall go out with joy,
And be led out with peace;
The mountains and the hills
Shall break forth into singing before you,
And all the trees of the field shall clap *their* hands.
13 Instead of the thorn shall come up the cypress tree,
And instead of the brier shall come up the myrtle tree;
And it shall be to the LORD for a name,
For an everlasting sign *that* shall not be cut off."

CHAPTER 56

Salvation for the Gentiles

Thus says the LORD:

"Keep justice, and do righteousness,
For My salvation *is* about to come,
And My righteousness to be revealed.
2 Blessed *is* the man *who* does this,
And the son of man *who* lays hold on it;
Who keeps from defiling the Sabbath,
And keeps his hand from doing any evil."

3 Do not let the son of the foreigner
Who has joined himself to the LORD
Speak, saying,
"The LORD has utterly separated me from His people";

Nor let the eunuch say,
"Here I am, a dry tree."
4 For thus says the LORD:
"To the eunuchs who keep My Sabbaths,
And choose what pleases Me,
And hold fast My covenant,
5 Even to them I will give in My house
And within My walls a place and a name
Better than that of sons and daughters;
I will give them[a] an everlasting name
That shall not be cut off.

6 "Also the sons of the foreigner
Who join themselves to the LORD, to serve Him,
And to love the name of the LORD, to be His servants—
Everyone who keeps from defiling the Sabbath,
And holds fast My covenant—
7 Even them I will bring to My holy mountain,
And make them joyful in My house of prayer.
Their burnt offerings and their sacrifices
Will be accepted on My altar;
For My house shall be called a house of prayer for all nations."
8 The Lord GOD, who gathers the outcasts of Israel, says,
"Yet I will gather to him
Others besides those who are gathered to him."

Israel's Irresponsible Leaders

9 All you beasts of the field, come to devour,
All you beasts in the forest.
10 His watchmen *are* blind,
They are all ignorant;
They *are* all dumb dogs,
They cannot bark;
Sleeping, lying down, loving to slumber.
11 Yes, *they are* greedy dogs
Which never have enough.
And they *are* shepherds
Who cannot understand;
They all look to their own way,
Every one for his own gain,
From his *own* territory.
12 "Come," *one says,* "I will bring wine,
And we will fill ourselves with intoxicating drink;
Tomorrow will be as today,
And much more abundant."

CHAPTER 57

Israel's Futile Idolatry

The righteous perishes,
And no man takes *it* to heart;
Merciful men *are* taken away,
While no one considers
That the righteous is taken away from evil.
2 He shall enter into peace;
They shall rest in their beds,
Each one walking *in* his uprightness.

3 "But come here,
You sons of the sorceress,
You offspring of the adulterer and the harlot!
4 Whom do you ridicule?
Against whom do you make a wide mouth
And stick out the tongue?
Are you not children of transgression,

56:5 [a]Literally *him*

56:6–8 Israel's mission was to be a vehicle whereby salvation could come to all nations. In the light of 52:13—53:12 that mission can now be fulfilled. Foreigners too can become God's servants. Both the foreigner and the eunuch (v. 3) were forbidden to enter the temple. But Isaiah says that if they keep the Sabbath in spirit they are more pleasing to God than Jews who are depending upon their status as His chosen people.

Offspring of falsehood,
5 Inflaming yourselves with gods
under every green tree,
Slaying the children in the valleys,
Under the clefts of the rocks?
6 Among the smooth *stones* of the stream
Is your portion;
They, they, *are* your lot!
Even to them you have poured a
drink offering,
You have offered a grain offering.
Should I receive comfort in these?

7 "On a lofty and high mountain
You have set your bed;
Even there you went up
To offer sacrifice.
8 Also behind the doors and their posts
You have set up your remembrance;
For you have uncovered yourself *to*
those other than Me,
And have gone up to them;
You have enlarged your bed
And made *a covenant* with them;
You have loved their bed,
Where you saw *their* nudity.[a]
9 You went to the king with ointment,
And increased your perfumes;
You sent your messengers far off,
And *even* descended to Shē'ōl.
10 You are wearied in the length of your
way;
Yet you did not say, 'There is no
hope.'
You have found the life of your hand;
Therefore you were not grieved.

11 "And of whom have you been afraid,
or feared,

That you have lied
And not remembered Me,
Nor taken *it* to your heart?
Is it not because I have held My peace
from of old
That you do not fear Me?
12 I will declare your righteousness
And your works,
For they will not profit you.
13 When you cry out,
Let your collection *of idols* deliver
you.
But the wind will carry them all
away,
A breath will take *them.*
But he who puts his trust in Me shall
possess the land,
And shall inherit My holy
mountain."

Healing for the Backslider

14 And one shall say,
"Heap it up! Heap it up!
Prepare the way,
Take the stumbling block out of the
way of My people."

15 For thus says the High and Lofty
One
Who inhabits eternity, whose name *is*
Holy:
"I dwell in the high and holy *place,*
With him *who* has a contrite and
humble spirit,
To revive the spirit of the humble,
And to revive the heart of the contrite
ones.
16 For I will not contend forever,
Nor will I always be angry;
For the spirit would fail before Me,
And the souls *which* I have made.

57:8 [a]Literally *hand,* a euphemism

57:5 Pagan worship was frequently carried on in groves where the upright trees represented the Canaanite fertility goddess, Asherah. Child sacrifice was another frequent aspect of fertility worship.

57:6 While orthodox Hebrew religion used stones only as historical markers, pagan religions used them to represent gods.

57:7–9 Not only did the worship of the fertility deities involve spiritual adultery, but also literal sexual sin as well.

17 For the iniquity of his covetousness
I was angry and struck him;
I hid and was angry,
And he went on backsliding in the way of his heart.
18 I have seen his ways, and will heal him;
I will also lead him,
And restore comforts to him
And to his mourners.

19 "I create the fruit of the lips:
Peace, peace to *him who is* far off and to *him who is* near,"
Says the LORD,
"And I will heal him."
20 But the wicked *are* like the troubled sea,
When it cannot rest,
Whose waters cast up mire and dirt.

21 "*There* is no peace,"
Says my God, "for the wicked."

CHAPTER 58

Fasting that Pleases God

"Cry aloud, spare not;
Lift up your voice like a trumpet;
Tell My people their transgression,
And the house of Jacob their sins.
2 Yet they seek Me daily,
And delight to know My ways,
As a nation that did righteousness,
And did not forsake the ordinance of their God.
They ask of Me the ordinances of justice;
They take delight in approaching God.
3 'Why have we fasted,' *they say,* 'and You have not seen?
Why have we afflicted our souls, and You take no notice?'

"In fact, in the day of your fast you find pleasure,
And exploit all your laborers.
4 Indeed you fast for strife and debate,
And to strike with the fist of wickedness.
You will not fast as *you do* this day,
To make your voice heard on high.
5 Is it a fast that I have chosen,
A day for a man to afflict his soul?
Is it to bow down his head like a bulrush,
And to spread out sackcloth and ashes?
Would you call this a fast,
And an acceptable day to the LORD?

6 "*Is* this not the fast that I have chosen:
To loose the bonds of wickedness,
To undo the heavy burdens,
To let the oppressed go free,
And that you break every yoke?
7 *Is it* not to share your bread with the hungry,
And that you bring to your house the poor who are cast out;
When you see the naked, that you cover him,
And not hide yourself from your own flesh?
8 Then your light shall break forth like the morning,
Your healing shall spring forth speedily,

57:17 At the heart of idolatry is covetousness. An inordinate desire to possess and control is at the root of our refusal to submit ourselves to God in trust and obedience.
58:1–5 The people feel that their careful attention to religious fasting has brought them no special favors from God. The Lord replies that their fasts are only outward forms, not an expression of their hearts.
58:5 The fast and other spiritual disciplines are not ends in themselves, but are intended to result in greater godliness in all our relationships. If they do not have that result, God has no interest in them.

And your righteousness shall go
before you;
The glory of the LORD shall be your
rear guard.
9 Then you shall call, and the LORD will
answer;
You shall cry, and He will say, 'Here I
am.'

"If you take away the yoke from your
midst,
The pointing of the finger, and
speaking wickedness,
10 *If* you extend your soul to the hungry
And satisfy the afflicted soul,
Then your light shall dawn in the
darkness,
And your darkness shall *be* as the
noonday.
11 The LORD will guide you continually,
And satisfy your soul in drought,
And strengthen your bones;
You shall be like a watered garden,
And like a spring of water, whose
waters do not fail.
12 Those from among you
Shall build the old waste places;
You shall raise up the foundations of
many generations;
And you shall be called the Repairer
of the Breach,
The Restorer of Streets to Dwell In.

13 "If you turn away your foot from the
Sabbath,
From doing your pleasure on My holy
day,
And call the Sabbath a delight,
The holy *day* of the LORD honorable,
And shall honor Him, not doing your
own ways,
Nor finding your own pleasure,
Nor speaking *your own* words,
14 Then you shall delight yourself in the
LORD;
And I will cause you to ride on the
high hills of the earth,
And feed you with the heritage of
Jacob your father.
The mouth of the LORD has spoken."

CHAPTER 59

Separated from God

Behold, the LORD's hand is not
shortened,
That it cannot save;
Nor His ear heavy,
That it cannot hear.
2 But your iniquities have separated
you from your God;
And your sins have hidden *His* face
from you,
So that He will not hear.
3 For your hands are defiled with
blood,
And your fingers with iniquity;
Your lips have spoken lies,
Your tongue has muttered
perversity.
4 No one calls for justice,
Nor does *any* plead for truth.
They trust in empty words and speak
lies;
They conceive evil and bring forth
iniquity.
5 They hatch vipers' eggs and weave
the spider's web;
He who eats of their eggs dies,
And *from* that which is crushed a
viper breaks out.

58:9–12 A heart that is pure toward God cannot be indifferent toward other human beings.

59:1–15 The people have been accusing God of not responding to their pleas for help. He replies that His willingness or ability to respond is not the issue. Their **iniquities** (v. 2) have made it impossible for Him to help them as He would like. If they will not do **justice** (vv. 3, 4) to one another, they can hardly expect God to bring them protection from their enemies.

TRUST AND OBEY

Evelyn Christenson

After God has answered our prayer, whether exciting, mind-boggling, or difficult, the next step is obedience. When God answers our prayer with a command, instruction, or an open door, He fully expects us to obey. We must put into practice what God has told us in His answer. And our obedience to His answer to our prayer opens the curtain on the next act of our lives. "So shall My word be that goes forth from My mouth; it shall not return to Me void, but it shall accomplish what I please, and it shall prosper in the thing for which I sent it" (Is. 55:11).

"After God has answered our prayer, the next step is obedience."

This is the God of the universe speaking, the One whom all the stars, planets, weather, and seasons obey. The One who spoke, and the universe came into being. The One who spoke, and the sea was calm. Who spoke, and the dead came alive. The One who expects obedience to His words.

However, God does not coerce us into obeying His answers to our prayers. He has given each of us a free will, with the privilege of responding as we choose. And, astoundingly, we humans frequently ignore, rebel, make excuses, refuse to obey, or even laugh at a certain answer from Him. This is amazing in light of the fact that it is the omniscient God of the universe who has answered us. God is all-knowing and all-caring, and He has given us the choice of obeying freely. We should trust Him enough to obey.

6 Their webs will not become garments,
Nor will they cover themselves with
their works;
Their works *are* works of iniquity,
And the act of violence *is* in their
hands.
7 Their feet run to evil,
And they make haste to shed
innocent blood;
Their thoughts *are* thoughts of
iniquity;
Wasting and destruction *are* in their
paths.
8 The way of peace they have not
known,
And *there is* no justice in their
ways;
They have made themselves crooked
paths;
Whoever takes that way shall not
know peace.

Sin Confessed

9 Therefore justice is far from us,
Nor does righteousness overtake
us;
We look for light, but there is
darkness!
For brightness, *but* we walk in
blackness!

10 We grope for the wall like the blind,
And we grope as if *we had* no eyes;
We stumble at noonday as at twilight;
We are as dead *men* in desolate places.
11 We all growl like bears,
And moan sadly like doves;
We look for justice, but *there is* none;
For salvation, *but* it is far from us.
12 For our transgressions are multiplied
before You,
And our sins testify against us;
For our transgressions *are* with us,
And *as for* our iniquities, we know
them:
13 In transgressing and lying against the
LORD,
And departing from our God,
Speaking oppression and revolt,
Conceiving and uttering from the
heart words of falsehood.
14 Justice is turned back,
And righteousness stands afar off;
For truth is fallen in the street,
And equity cannot enter.
15 So truth fails,
And he *who* departs from evil makes
himself a prey.

The Redeemer of Zion

Then the LORD saw *it*, and it
displeased Him
That *there was* no justice.
16 He saw that *there was* no man,
And wondered that *there was* no
intercessor;
Therefore His own arm brought
salvation for Him;
And His own righteousness, it
sustained Him.
17 For He put on righteousness as a
breastplate,
And a helmet of salvation on His
head;
He put on the garments of vengeance
for clothing,
And was clad with zeal as a cloak.
18 According to *their* deeds, accordingly
He will repay,
Fury to His adversaries,
Recompense to His enemies;
The coastlands He will fully repay.
19 So shall they fear
The name of the LORD from the
west,
And His glory from the rising of the
sun;
When the enemy comes in like a
flood,
The Spirit of the LORD will lift up a
standard against him.

20 "The Redeemer will come to Zion,
And to those who turn from
transgression in Jacob,"
Says the LORD.

21 "As for Me," says the LORD, "this *is* My
covenant with them: My Spirit who *is*
upon you, and My words which I have put
in your mouth, shall not depart from your
mouth, nor from the mouth of your de-
scendants, nor from the mouth of your de-
scendants' descendants," says the LORD,
"from this time and forevermore."

59:10, 11 A tragic picture of those who do not know God.

59:15–21 Neither conversion nor sanctification can be achieved by human effort. If we are to live the righteous lives that God demands, His own arm must bring the deliverance, and His Spirit must empower us.

59:19, 20 Name and glory are synonyms. They refer to God's changeless character as Creator and Redeemer. The **Spirit of the LORD** is the manifestation of God in His dynamic power in this present world. **Standard** is a military flag. God the Redeemer will take up arms against our enemies.

59:21 them . . . you: The people of God. **My Spirit . . . upon you**: The promise of Pentecost. **mouth**: Note the emphasis on witnessing. The people of unclean lips (6:5) will be enabled to bear a holy word.

CHAPTER 60

The Gentiles Bless Zion

Arise, shine;
For your light has come!
And the glory of the LORD is risen
upon you.
2 For behold, the darkness shall cover
the earth,
And deep darkness the people;
But the LORD will arise over you,
And His glory will be seen upon you.
3 The Gentiles shall come to your
light,
And kings to the brightness of your
rising.

4 "Lift up your eyes all around, and see:
They all gather together, they come to
you;
Your sons shall come from afar,
And your daughters shall be nursed
at *your* side.
5 Then you shall see and become
radiant,
And your heart shall swell with joy;
Because the abundance of the sea
shall be turned to you,
The wealth of the Gentiles shall come
to you.
6 The multitude of camels shall cover
your *land,*
The dromedaries of Mid'i·an and
Ē'phah;
All those from Shē'ba shall come;
They shall bring gold and incense,
And they shall proclaim the praises of
the LORD.
7 All the flocks of Kē'dar shall be
gathered together to you,
The rams of Ne·bā'i·oth shall minister
to you;
They shall ascend with acceptance on
My altar,
And I will glorify the house of My
glory.

8 "Who *are* these *who* fly like a cloud,
And like doves to their roosts?
9 Surely the coastlands shall wait for
Me;
And the ships of Tar'shish *will come*
first,
To bring your sons from afar,
Their silver and their gold with them,
To the name of the LORD your God,
And to the Holy One of Israel,
Because He has glorified you.

10 "The sons of foreigners shall build up
your walls,
And their kings shall minister to you;
For in My wrath I struck you,
But in My favor I have had mercy on
you.
11 Therefore your gates shall be open
continually;
They shall not be shut day or night,
That *men* may bring to you the wealth
of the Gentiles,
And their kings in procession.
12 For the nation and kingdom which
will not serve you shall perish,
And *those* nations shall be utterly
ruined.

13 "The glory of Lebanon shall come to
you,
The cypress, the pine, and the box
tree together,
To beautify the place of My
sanctuary;
And I will make the place of My feet
glorious.
14 Also the sons of those who afflicted
you
Shall come bowing to you,
And all those who despised you shall
fall prostrate at the soles of your
feet;
And they shall call you The City of
the LORD,
Zion of the Holy One of Israel.

60:2 The **LORD will arise** compares His coming to the sunrise.

15 "Whereas you have been forsaken and hated,
So that no one went through *you,*
I will make you an eternal excellence,
A joy of many generations.
16 You shall drink the milk of the Gentiles,
And milk the breast of kings;
You shall know that I, the LORD, *am* your Savior
And your Redeemer, the Mighty One of Jacob.

17 "Instead of bronze I will bring gold,
Instead of iron I will bring silver,
Instead of wood, bronze,
And instead of stones, iron.
I will also make your officers peace,
And your magistrates righteousness.
18 Violence shall no longer be heard in your land,
Neither wasting nor destruction within your borders;
But you shall call your walls Salvation,
And your gates Praise.

God the Glory of His People

19 "The sun shall no longer be your light by day,
Nor for brightness shall the moon give light to you;
But the LORD will be to you an everlasting light,
And your God your glory.
20 Your sun shall no longer go down,
Nor shall your moon withdraw itself;
For the LORD will be your everlasting light,
And the days of your mourning shall be ended.
21 Also your people *shall* all *be* righteous;
They shall inherit the land forever,
The branch of My planting,
The work of My hands,
That I may be glorified.
22 A little one shall become a thousand,
And a small one a strong nation.
I, the LORD, will hasten it in its time."

CHAPTER 61

The Good News of Salvation

"The Spirit of the Lord GOD *is* upon Me,
Because the LORD has anointed Me
To preach good tidings to the poor;
He has sent Me to heal the brokenhearted,
To proclaim liberty to the captives,
And the opening of the prison to *those who are* bound;
2 To proclaim the acceptable year of the LORD,
And the day of vengeance of our God;
To comfort all who mourn,
3 To console those who mourn in Zion,
To give them beauty for ashes,

I pray that You, God, will comfort my friend who mourns and give her beauty for ashes, the oil of joy for mourning, the garment of praise for the spirit of heaviness, so that she may be called a tree of righteousness.

adapted from Isaiah 61:2, 3

61:1–11 This chapter makes it clear that the righteousness (v. 10) which the people will possess will not be of their own doing, but will come from the Messiah upon whom is the **Spirit of the Lord GOD** (v. 1).

61:1 Me: The Messiah, the anointed One.

61:2, 3 the acceptable year: The year of the Lord's favor.

The oil of joy for mourning,
The garment of praise for the spirit of heaviness;
That they may be called trees of righteousness,
The planting of the LORD, that He may be glorified."

4 And they shall rebuild the old ruins,
They shall raise up the former desolations,
And they shall repair the ruined cities,
The desolations of many generations.
5 Strangers shall stand and feed your flocks,
And the sons of the foreigner
Shall be your plowmen and your vinedressers.
6 But you shall be named the priests of the LORD,
They shall call you the servants of our God.
You shall eat the riches of the Gentiles,
And in their glory you shall boast.
7 Instead of your shame *you shall have* double *honor,*
And *instead of* confusion they shall rejoice in their portion.
Therefore in their land they shall possess double;
Everlasting joy shall be theirs.

8 "For I, the LORD, love justice;
I hate robbery for burnt offering;
I will direct their work in truth,
And will make with them an everlasting covenant.
9 Their descendants shall be known among the Gentiles,
And their offspring among the people.
All who see them shall acknowledge them,
That they *are* the posterity *whom* the LORD has blessed."

10 I will greatly rejoice in the LORD,
My soul shall be joyful in my God;
For He has clothed me with the garments of salvation,
He has covered me with the robe of righteousness,
As a bridegroom decks *himself* with ornaments,
And as a bride adorns *herself* with her jewels.
11 For as the earth brings forth its bud,
As the garden causes the things that are sown in it to spring forth,
So the Lord GOD will cause righteousness and praise to spring forth before all the nations.

CHAPTER 62

Assurance of Zion's Salvation

For Zion's sake I will not hold My peace,
And for Jerusalem's sake I will not rest,
Until her righteousness goes forth as brightness,
And her salvation as a lamp *that* burns.
2 The Gentiles shall see your righteousness,
And all kings your glory.
You shall be called by a new name,
Which the mouth of the LORD will name.
3 You shall also be a crown of glory
In the hand of the LORD,

61:4–7 The nation will be freed, both from want and from sin, in order to become **priests of the LORD** (v. 6), in fulfillment of the Exodus promises.

62:2 The new name indicates a changed relationship to God (v. 4), as occurred with Jacob at Peniel.

And a royal diadem
In the hand of your God.
4 You shall no longer be termed
Forsaken,
Nor shall your land any more be
termed Desolate;
But you shall be called Heph′zi·bah,[a]
and your land Beū′lah;[b]
For the LORD delights in you,
And your land shall be married.
5 For *as* a young man marries a virgin,
So shall your sons marry you;
And *as* the bridegroom rejoices over
the bride,
So shall your God rejoice over you.

6 I have set watchmen on your walls,
O Jerusalem;
They shall never hold their peace day
or night.
You who make mention of the LORD,
do not keep silent,
7 And give Him no rest till He
establishes
And till He makes Jerusalem a praise
in the earth.

8 The LORD has sworn by His right
hand
And by the arm of His strength:
"Surely I will no longer give your
grain
As food for your enemies;
And the sons of the foreigner shall
not drink your new wine,
For which you have labored.
9 But those who have gathered it shall
eat it,
And praise the LORD;
Those who have brought it together
shall drink it in My holy courts."

10 Go through,
Go through the gates!
Prepare the way for the people;
Build up,
Build up the highway!
Take out the stones,
Lift up a banner for the peoples!

11 Indeed the LORD has proclaimed
To the end of the world:
"Say to the daughter of Zion,
'Surely your salvation is coming;
Behold, His reward *is* with Him,
And His work before Him.' "
12 And they shall call them The Holy
People,
The Redeemed of the LORD;
And you shall be called Sought Out,
A City Not Forsaken.

62:4 [a]Literally *My Delight Is in Her* [b]Literally *Married*

CHAPTER 63

The LORD in Judgment and Salvation

Who *is* this who comes from Ē′dom,
With dyed garments from Boz′rah,
This *One who is* glorious in His
apparel,
Traveling in the greatness of His
strength?—

"I who speak in righteousness, mighty
to save."

2 Why *is* Your apparel red,
And Your garments like one who
treads in the winepress?

3 "I have trodden the winepress alone,

62:6, 7 watchmen: Those who look for the coming of the Lord victorious over Jerusalem's enemies (see 21:6, 11, 12). **do not keep silent . . . give Him no rest**: Persistent prayer.

63:1–6 These verses explain how God can make the promises of 62:11, 12: "They shall call them The Holy People, the Redeemed of the LORD." The people could not save themselves either from their captors or from their sin. God alone could do it.

63:3–6 Their blood . . . drunk in My fury: A grim passage of final judgment, probably at the Second Coming.

And from the peoples no one *was*
with Me.
For I have trodden them in My anger,
And trampled them in My fury;
Their blood is sprinkled upon My
garments,
And I have stained all My robes.
4 For the day of vengeance *is* in My
heart,
And the year of My redeemed has
come.
5 I looked, but *there was* no one to help,
And I wondered
That *there was* no one to uphold;
Therefore My own arm brought
salvation for Me;
And My own fury, it sustained Me.
6 I have trodden down the peoples in
My anger,
Made them drunk in My fury,
And brought down their strength to
the earth."

God's Mercy Remembered

7 I will mention the lovingkindnesses
of the LORD
And the praises of the LORD,
According to all that the LORD has
bestowed on us,
And the great goodness toward the
house of Israel,
Which He has bestowed on them
according to His mercies,
According to the multitude of His
lovingkindnesses.
8 For He said, "Surely they *are* My
people,
Children *who* will not lie."
So He became their Savior.
9 In all their affliction He was afflicted,
And the Angel of His Presence saved
them;
In His love and in His pity He
redeemed them;
And He bore them and carried them
All the days of old.
10 But they rebelled and grieved His
Holy Spirit;
So He turned Himself against them as
an enemy,
And He fought against them.

11 Then he remembered the days of old,
Moses *and* his people, *saying:*
"Where *is* He who brought them up
out of the sea
With the shepherd of His flock?
Where *is* He who put His Holy Spirit
within them,
12 Who led *them* by the right hand of
Moses,
With His glorious arm,
Dividing the water before them
To make for Himself an everlasting
name,
13 Who led them through the deep,
As a horse in the wilderness,
That they might not stumble?"

14 As a beast goes down into the valley,
And the Spirit of the LORD causes him
to rest,
So You lead Your people,
To make Yourself a glorious name.

A Prayer of Penitence

15 Look down from heaven,
And see from Your habitation, holy
and glorious.
Where *are* Your zeal and Your
strength,
The yearning of Your heart and Your
mercies toward me?
Are they restrained?

63:7–14 the lovingkindnesses of the LORD: The loyal love promised in the previous chapters does not represent something new on God's part. He has kept faith with His people in these ways from the time that He chose them.

63:11–13 Here Isaiah is saying that the God who had led them by His Holy Spirit so long ago could once again meet their needs by that same Spirit.

16 Doubtless You *are* our Father,
Though Abraham was ignorant of us,
And Israel does not acknowledge us.
You, O LORD, *are* our Father;
Our Redeemer from Everlasting *is* Your name.
17 O LORD, why have You made us stray from Your ways,
And hardened our heart from Your fear?
Return for Your servants' sake,
The tribes of Your inheritance.
18 Your holy people have possessed *it* but a little while;
Our adversaries have trodden down Your sanctuary.
19 We have become *like* those of old, over whom You never ruled,
Those who were never called by Your name.

CHAPTER 64

Oh, that You would rend the heavens!
That You would come down!
That the mountains might shake at Your presence—
2 As fire burns brushwood,
As fire causes water to boil—
To make Your name known to Your adversaries,
That the nations may tremble at Your presence!
3 When You did awesome things *for which* we did not look,
You came down,
The mountains shook at Your presence.
4 For since the beginning of the world
Men have not heard nor perceived by the ear,
Nor has the eye seen any God besides You,
Who acts for the one who waits for Him.
5 You meet him who rejoices and does righteousness,
Who remembers You in Your ways.
You are indeed angry, for we have sinned—
In these ways we continue;
And we need to be saved.

6 But we are all like an unclean *thing*,
And all our righteousnesses *are* like filthy rags;
We all fade as a leaf,
And our iniquities, like the wind,
Have taken us away.
7 And *there is* no one who calls on Your name,
Who stirs himself up to take hold of You;
For You have hidden Your face from us,
And have consumed us because of our iniquities.

8 But now, O LORD,
You *are* our Father;
We *are* the clay, and You our potter;
And all we *are* the work of Your hand.
9 Do not be furious, O LORD,
Nor remember iniquity forever;
Indeed, please look—we all *are* Your people!
10 Your holy cities are a wilderness,
Zion is a wilderness,
Jerusalem a desolation.
11 Our holy and beautiful temple,
Where our fathers praised You,
Is burned up with fire;
And all our pleasant things are laid waste.
12 Will You restrain Yourself because of these *things*, O LORD?
Will You hold Your peace, and afflict us very severely?

64:6, 7 Not only are we helpless to save ourselves, we do not even have the desire to take hold of God in faith unless He somehow gives us this ability (see Eph. 2:8, 9).

CHAPTER 65

The Righteousness of God's Judgment

"I was sought by *those who* did not ask
for Me;
I was found by *those who* did not seek
Me.
I said, 'Here I am, here I am,'
To a nation *that* was not called by My
name.
2 I have stretched out My hands all day
long to a rebellious people,
Who walk in a way *that is* not
good,
According to their own thoughts;
3 A people who provoke Me to anger
continually to My face;
Who sacrifice in gardens,
And burn incense on altars of
brick;
4 Who sit among the graves,
And spend the night in the tombs;
Who eat swine's flesh,
And the broth of abominable things is
in their vessels;
5 Who say, 'Keep to yourself,
Do not come near me,
For I am holier than you!'
These *are* smoke in My nostrils,
A fire that burns all the day.

6 "Behold, *it is* written before Me:
I will not keep silence, but will
repay—
Even repay into their bosom—
7 Your iniquities and the iniquities of
your fathers together,"
Says the LORD,
"Who have burned incense on the
mountains
And blasphemed Me on the hills;
Therefore I will measure their former
work into their bosom."

8 Thus says the LORD:

"As the new wine is found in the
cluster,
And *one* says, 'Do not destroy it,
For a blessing *is* in it,'
So will I do for My servants' sake,
That I may not destroy them all.
9 I will bring forth descendants from
Jacob,
And from Judah an heir of My
mountains;
My elect shall inherit it,
And My servants shall dwell there.
10 Sharon shall be a fold of flocks,
And the Valley of Ā'chor a place for
herds to lie down,
For My people who have sought Me.

11 "But you *are* those who forsake the
LORD,
Who forget My holy mountain,
Who prepare a table for Gad,[a]
And who furnish a drink offering for
Menī.[b]
12 Therefore I will number you for the
sword,

65:11 [a]Literally *Troop* or *Fortune*, a pagan deity [b]Literally *Number* or *Destiny*, a pagan deity

65:1–16 God does not waste any honeyed words in His answer. He *will* act on behalf of those whose repentance and obedience is pure. But when our religion is as thoroughly contaminated with paganism as was theirs, God can do little for us.

65:2 stretched out My hands: Far from causing them to sin (63:17), or being insensitive to their cries for help (64:7), God has been reaching out to them, but they have been rebellious.

65:8–16 not destroy them all: Here the remnant theme emerges again. Even after Judah has returned from exile, not all of them will truly be servants (v. 9) of the Lord. Here the contrast is clearly drawn: those who believe God have a glorious hope; those who insist on tailoring their own religion to their supposed needs face judgment. A question to ponder: Are we part of today's believing remnant?

And you shall all bow down to the
slaughter;
Because, when I called, you did not
answer;
When I spoke, you did not hear,
But did evil before My eyes,
And chose *that* in which I do not
delight."

13 Therefore thus says the Lord GOD:

"Behold, My servants shall eat,
But you shall be hungry;
Behold, My servants shall drink,
But you shall be thirsty;
Behold, My servants shall rejoice,
But you shall be ashamed;
14 Behold, My servants shall sing for joy
of heart,
But you shall cry for sorrow of heart,
And wail for grief of spirit.
15 You shall leave your name as a curse
to My chosen;
For the Lord GOD will slay you,
And call His servants by another
name;
16 So that he who blesses himself in the
earth
Shall bless himself in the God of
truth;
And he who swears in the earth
Shall swear by the God of truth;
Because the former troubles are
forgotten,
And because they are hidden from
My eyes.

The Glorious New Creation

17 "For behold, I create new heavens and
a new earth;
And the former shall not be
remembered or come to mind.
18 But be glad and rejoice forever in
what I create;
For behold, I create Jerusalem *as* a
rejoicing,
And her people a joy.
19 I will rejoice in Jerusalem,
And joy in My people;
The voice of weeping shall no longer
be heard in her,
Nor the voice of crying.

20 "No more shall an infant from there
live but a few days,
Nor an old man who has not fulfilled
his days;
For the child shall die one hundred
years old,
But the sinner *being* one hundred
years old shall be accursed.
21 They shall build houses and inhabit
them;
They shall plant vineyards and eat
their fruit.
22 They shall not build and another
inhabit;
They shall not plant and another eat;
For as the days of a tree, *so shall be* the
days of My people,
And My elect shall long enjoy the
work of their hands.
23 They shall not labor in vain,
Nor bring forth children for
trouble;
For they *shall be* the descendants of
the blessed of the LORD,
And their offspring with them.

24 "It shall come to pass
That before they call, I will answer;
And while they are still speaking, I
will hear.
25 The wolf and the lamb shall feed
together,
The lion shall eat straw like the ox,
And dust *shall be* the serpent's
food.

65:17–25 new heavens . . . new earth: The reward for God's servants is a new creation where the effects of sin will no longer be known.

They shall not hurt nor destroy in all
My holy mountain,"
Says the LORD.

CHAPTER 66

True Worship and False

Thus says the LORD:

"Heaven *is* My throne,
And earth *is* My footstool.
Where *is* the house that you will
build Me?
And where *is* the place of My rest?
2 For all those *things* My hand has
made,
And all those *things* exist,"
Says the LORD.
"But on this *one* will I look:
On *him who is* poor and of a contrite
spirit,
And who trembles at My word.

3 "He who kills a bull *is as if* he slays a
man;
He who sacrifices a lamb, *as if* he
breaks a dog's neck;
He who offers a grain offering, *as if he
offers* swine's blood;
He who burns incense, *as if* he blesses
an idol.
Just as they have chosen their own
ways,
And their soul delights in their
abominations,
4 So will I choose their delusions,
And bring their fears on them;
Because, when I called, no one
answered,
When I spoke they did not hear;
But they did evil before My eyes,
And chose *that* in which I do not
delight."

The LORD Vindicates Zion

5 Hear the word of the LORD,
You who tremble at His word:
"Your brethren who hated you,
Who cast you out for My name's
sake, said,
'Let the LORD be glorified,
That we may see your joy.'
But they shall be ashamed."

6 The sound of noise from the city!
A voice from the temple!
The voice of the LORD,
Who fully repays His enemies!

7 "Before she was in labor, she gave
birth;
Before her pain came,
She delivered a male child.
8 Who has heard such a thing?
Who has seen such things?
Shall the earth be made to give birth
in one day?
Or shall a nation be born at once?
For as soon as Zion was in labor,
She gave birth to her children.
9 Shall I bring to the time of birth, and
not cause delivery?" says the
LORD.
"Shall I who cause delivery shut up *the
womb?*" says your God.
10 "Rejoice with Jerusalem,
And be glad with her, all you who
love her;
Rejoice for joy with her, all you who
mourn for her;

66:1, 2 those things: God does not need our religion; He gets no benefit out of our religious behavior. It is a sincere and contrite spirit that He wants.

66:4 To try to use God merely as a way of protecting ourselves from our fears is to be delivered over to those fears. God cannot bless those who try to manipulate Him.

66:5–13 Jerusalem is depicted as a mother with many children. Now she is no longer barren, no longer a widow deprived of her children by war and pestilence. Because of God's blessing she gathers all her children about her and nourishes each one. God will never forget Jerusalem.

11 That you may feed and be satisfied
With the consolation of her bosom,
That you may drink deeply and be delighted
With the abundance of her glory."

12For thus says the LORD:

"Behold, I will extend peace to her like a river,
And the glory of the Gentiles like a flowing stream.
Then you shall feed;
On *her* sides shall you be carried,
And be dandled on *her* knees.
13 As one whom his mother comforts,
So I will comfort you;
And you shall be comforted in Jerusalem."

The Reign and Indignation of God

14 When you see *this,* your heart shall rejoice,
And your bones shall flourish like grass;
The hand of the LORD shall be known to His servants,
And *His* indignation to His enemies.
15 For behold, the LORD will come with fire
And with His chariots, like a whirlwind,
To render His anger with fury,
And His rebuke with flames of fire.
16 For by fire and by His sword
The LORD will judge all flesh;
And the slain of the LORD shall be many.

17 "Those who sanctify themselves and purify themselves,
To go to the gardens
After an *idol* in the midst,
Eating swine's flesh and the abomination and the mouse,
Shall be consumed together," says the LORD.

18"For I *know* their works and their
thoughts. It shall be that I will gather all
nations and tongues; and they shall come
and see My glory. 19I will set a sign among
them; and those among them who escape I
will send to the nations: *to* Tar'shish and
Pūl[a] and Lud, who draw the bow, and
Tū'bal and Jā'van, *to* the coastlands afar off
who have not heard My fame nor seen My
glory. And they shall declare My glory
among the Gentiles. 20Then they shall bring
all your brethren for an offering to the
LORD out of all nations, on horses and in
chariots and in litters, on mules and on
camels, to My holy mountain Jerusalem,"
says the LORD, "as the children of Israel
bring an offering in a clean vessel into the
house of the LORD. 21And I will also take
some of them for priests *and* Lē'vītes,"
says the LORD.

22 "For as the new heavens and the new earth
Which I will make shall remain before Me," says the LORD,
"So shall your descendants and your name remain.
23 And it shall come to pass
That from one New Moon to another,
And from one Sabbath to another,
All flesh shall come to worship before Me," says the LORD.

66:19 [a]Following Masoretic Text and Targum; Septuagint reads *Put* (compare Jeremiah 46:9).

66:14–24 The prophet promises that however long God may seem to delay, He will come and set things right.

66:17 Irony. Our attempts to sanctify ourselves only result in greater unholiness.

66:18–23 The task of the Jewish people as God's servants is to make His glory known to the Gentiles (2:1–5), who will then come to the Lord's house to learn His ways. When Christ came, this occurred, but it will also occur again in the last days.

24 "And they shall go forth and look
Upon the corpses of the men
Who have transgressed against
Me.
For their worm does not die,
And their fire is not quenched.
They shall be an abhorrence to all
flesh."

66:24 God never intends His last word to be judgment, but this does not mean there will be some universal amnesty at the end of the world. Cause and effect will still be in force. Those who have refused to avail themselves of God's provision in Christ, who have insisted on their own ways and transgressed God's ways, will face eternal judgment.

✦Jeremiah✦

Jeremiah, known as "the weeping prophet," wrote this book during his years of ministry, about 640 to 585 B.C. He dictated his message to his faithful scribe, Baruch, who brought the scroll to King Jehoiakim, since Jeremiah had been banned from the king's court. The king threw the message into the fire, so Jeremiah again dictated the message to Baruch. Such persistence provides encouragement for modern-day Christians facing resistance to the Lord's work. Jeremiah's warning of impending judgment came to Judah while the country was caught in a power squeeze between Egypt, Assyria, and Babylon.

Jeremiah often used metaphors to communicate his messages: He carried a yoke around his neck to symbolize submission to the Babylonians, he used a potter and clay to show that the future of Judah was in God's hands, and he bought a plot of land before the Exile to demonstrate Judah's hope of one day returning to its homeland.

Amid his prophecies of judgment, Jeremiah showed God to be forgiving and patient. God delayed Judah's punishment and gave the nation more than ample time to repent. Most important, the Book of Jeremiah contains God's promise to make a new covenant, a covenant of grace, with Israel and Judah (31:31–34). This new covenant was instituted with the death and Resurrection of the Messiah.✦

CHAPTER 1

The words of Jer·e·mī′ah the son of
Hil·kī′ah, of the priests who *were* in
An′a·thoth in the land of Benjamin, [2]to
whom the word of the LORD came in the
days of Jō·sī′ah the son of Ā′mon, king of
Judah, in the thirteenth year of his reign. [3]It
came also in the days of Je·hoi′a·kim the
son of Jō·sī′ah, king of Judah, until the end
of the eleventh year of Zed·e·kī′ah the son
of Jō·sī′ah, king of Judah, until the carrying
away of Jerusalem captive in the fifth
month.

The Prophet Is Called

[4]Then the word of the LORD came to me,
saying:

5 "Before I formed you in the womb I
knew you;
Before you were born I sanctified you;
I ordained you a prophet to the
nations."

1:2 According to presently accepted dating the thirteenth year would indicate Jeremiah received his prophetic call in 626 B.C. during the reign of Josiah. The timing was God's, coming only one year after the king began his reforms (see 2 Chr. 34:3) and five years before he discovered the Book of the Law (see 2 Kin. 22:3, 4, 8).

6Then said I:

"Ah, Lord GOD!
Behold, I cannot speak, for I *am* a
youth."

7But the LORD said to me:

"Do not say, 'I *am* a youth,'
For you shall go to all to whom I send
you,
And whatever I command you, you
shall speak.
8 Do not be afraid of their faces,
For I *am* with you to deliver you,"
says the LORD.

9Then the LORD put forth His hand and
touched my mouth, and the LORD said to
me:

"Behold, I have put My words in your
mouth.
10 See, I have this day set you over the
nations and over the kingdoms,
To root out and to pull down,
To destroy and to throw down,
To build and to plant."

11Moreover the word of the LORD came
to me, saying, "Jer·e·mī'ah, what do you
see?"

And I said, "I see a branch of an almond
tree."

12Then the LORD said to me, "You have
seen well, for I am ready to perform My
word."

13And the word of the LORD came to me
the second time, saying, "What do you
see?"

And I said, "I see a boiling pot, and it is
facing away from the north."

14Then the LORD said to me:

"Out of the north calamity shall break
forth
On all the inhabitants of the land.
15 For behold, I am calling
All the families of the kingdoms of
the north," says the LORD;
"They shall come and each one set his
throne
At the entrance of the gates of
Jerusalem,
Against all its walls all around,
And against all the cities of Judah.
16 I will utter My judgments
Against them concerning all their
wickedness,
Because they have forsaken Me,
Burned incense to other gods,
And worshiped the works of their
own hands.

17 "Therefore prepare yourself and arise,
And speak to them all that I
command you.
Do not be dismayed before their
faces,
Lest I dismay you before them.
18 For behold, I have made you this day
A fortified city and an iron pillar,
And bronze walls against the whole
land—
Against the kings of Judah,
Against its princes,
Against its priests,
And against the people of the land.
19 They will fight against you,
But they shall not prevail against you.

1:6 Jeremiah was probably only in his late teens at the time. But youth was not a valid excuse to reject the call.

1:11, 12 branch of an almond tree: An object lesson using a play on words. The Hebrew name for almond branch is *shaqed*. The similar word *shoqed* means "awake and ready for action." The almond tree is the first to blossom in Israel, normally in late January or early February. The message is that the Lord is always awake and on the job to accomplish His purpose.

For I *am* with you," says the LORD, "to
deliver you."

CHAPTER 2

God's Case Against Israel

Moreover the word of the LORD came to
me, saying, 2"Go and cry in the hearing of
Jerusalem, saying, 'Thus says the LORD:

"I remember you,
The kindness of your youth,
The love of your betrothal,
When you went after Me in the
wilderness,
In a land not sown.
3 Israel *was* holiness to the LORD,
The firstfruits of His increase.
All that devour him will offend;
Disaster will come upon them," says
the LORD.' "

4Hear the word of the LORD, O house of
Jacob and all the families of the house of Is-
rael. 5Thus says the LORD:

"What injustice have your fathers
found in Me,
That they have gone far from Me,
Have followed idols,
And have become idolaters?
6 Neither did they say, 'Where *is* the
LORD,
Who brought us up out of the land of
Egypt,
Who led us through the wilderness,
Through a land of deserts and pits,
Through a land of drought and the
shadow of death,
Through a land that no one
crossed
And where no one dwelt?'
7 I brought you into a bountiful
country,
To eat its fruit and its goodness.
But when you entered, you defiled
My land
And made My heritage an
abomination.
8 The priests did not say, 'Where *is* the
LORD?'
And those who handle the law did
not know Me;
The rulers also transgressed against
Me;
The prophets prophesied by Bā'al,
And walked after *things that* do not
profit.

9 "Therefore I will yet bring charges
against you," says the LORD,
"And against your children's children I
will bring charges.
10 For pass beyond the coasts of Cyprus[a]
and see,
Send to Kē'dar[b] and consider
diligently,
And see if there has been such *a*
thing.
11 Has a nation changed *its* gods,
Which *are* not gods?
But My people have changed their
Glory
For *what* does not profit.
12 Be astonished, O heavens, at this,
And be horribly afraid;
Be very desolate," says the LORD.
13 "For My people have committed two
evils:
They have forsaken Me, the fountain
of living waters,

2:10 [a]Hebrew *Kittim*, western lands, especially Cyprus [b]In the northern Arabian desert, representative of the eastern cultures

2:9–13 will bring charges: The Lord announces a lawsuit against His people. He expresses shock that they had turned from Him, the fountain of living waters, pictured here as a flowing source of water, for idols which were unreal. **their Glory** (v. 11): Their God. **does not profit**: No spiritual benefit. The idols were like **broken cisterns** (v. 13) from which the water would leak out.

And hewn themselves cisterns—
broken cisterns that can hold no water.

14 "*Is* Israel a servant?
Is he a homeborn *slave?*
Why is he plundered?
15 The young lions roared at him, *and* growled;
They made his land waste;
His cities are burned, without inhabitant.
16 Also the people of Noph[a] and Tah'pan·hēs
Have broken the crown of your head.
17 Have you not brought this on yourself,
In that you have forsaken the LORD your God
When He led you in the way?
18 And now why take the road to Egypt,
To drink the waters of Sī'hor?
Or why take the road to Assyria,
To drink the waters of the River?[a]
19 Your own wickedness will correct you,
And your backslidings will rebuke you.
Know therefore and see that *it is* an evil and bitter *thing*
That you have forsaken the LORD your God,
And the fear of Me *is* not in you,"
Says the Lord GOD of hosts.

20 "For of old I have broken your yoke *and* burst your bonds;
And you said, 'I will not transgress,'
When on every high hill and under every green tree
You lay down, playing the harlot.
21 Yet I had planted you a noble vine, a seed of highest quality.
How then have you turned before Me
Into the degenerate plant of an alien vine?
22 For though you wash yourself with lye, and use much soap,
Yet your iniquity is marked before Me," says the Lord GOD.

23 "How can you say, 'I am not polluted,
I have not gone after the Bā'als'?
See your way in the valley;
Know what you have done:
You are a swift dromedary breaking loose in her ways,
24 A wild donkey used to the wilderness,
That sniffs at the wind in her desire;
In her time of mating, who can turn her away?
All those who seek her will not weary themselves;
In her month they will find her.
25 Withhold your foot from being unshod, and your throat from thirst.
But you said, 'There is no hope.
No! For I have loved aliens, and after them I will go.'

26 "As the thief is ashamed when he is found out,
So is the house of Israel ashamed;
They and their kings and their princes, and their priests and their prophets,

2:16 [a]That is, Memphis in ancient Egypt 2:18 [a]That is, the Euphrates

2:18 To drink the waters: To seek help from the lands where these rivers are located. **Sihor**: A body of water representing Egypt. **the River**: The Euphrates representing Assyria.

2:20 broken your yoke: God had often delivered Israel.

2:23–25 The people claimed immorality had not polluted them, but lacking self-control they were acting worse than animals.

2:26–28 a tree (v. 27): A symbol of a fertility goddess. **a stone**: A symbol of a male god of the Canaanites. These gods could not help in trouble, so those who worshiped them would be ashamed of having trusted something so foolish.

27 Saying to a tree, 'You *are* my father,'
And to a stone, 'You gave birth to
me.'
For they have turned *their* back to Me,
and not *their* face.
But in the time of their trouble
They will say, 'Arise and save us.'
28 But where *are* your gods that you
have made for yourselves?
Let them arise,
If they can save you in the time of
your trouble;
For *according to* the number of your
cities
Are your gods, O Judah.

29 "Why will you plead with Me?
You all have transgressed against
Me," says the LORD.
30 "In vain I have chastened your
children;
They received no correction.
Your sword has devoured your
prophets
Like a destroying lion.

31 "O generation, see the word of the
LORD!
Have I been a wilderness to Israel,
Or a land of darkness?
Why do My people say, 'We are lords;
We will come no more to You'?
32 Can a virgin forget her ornaments,
Or a bride her attire?
Yet My people have forgotten Me
days without number.

33 "Why do you beautify your way to
seek love?
Therefore you have also taught
The wicked women your ways.
34 Also on your skirts is found
The blood of the lives of the poor
innocents.
I have not found it by secret search,
But plainly on all these things.
35 Yet you say, 'Because I am innocent,
Surely His anger shall turn from me.'
Behold, I will plead My case against
you,
Because you say, 'I have not sinned.'
36 Why do you gad about so much to
change your way?
Also you shall be ashamed of Egypt
as you were ashamed of Assyria.
37 Indeed you will go forth from him
With your hands on your head;
For the LORD has rejected your
trusted allies,
And you will not prosper by them.

CHAPTER 3

Israel Is Shameless

"They say, 'If a man divorces his wife,
And she goes from him
And becomes another man's,
May he return to her again?'
Would not that land be greatly
polluted?
But you have played the harlot with
many lovers;
Yet return to Me," says the LORD.

2 "Lift up your eyes to the desolate
heights and see:
Where have you not lain *with men?*
By the road you have sat for them
Like an Arabian in the wilderness;
And you have polluted the land
With your harlotries and your
wickedness.

2:29–37 With five questions (vv. 29, 31, 32, 33, 36) the Lord expressed deep sorrow and frustration that He had been rejected by His bride (see 2:2) who mocked His concern. The Judge would bring her to court and exile her. But the people did not recognize their sin. They still believed God would deliver them (vv. 29, 35).

3:2–5 A description of Israel's adulterous behavior, and yet God offers grace to meet her evil.

3 Therefore the showers have been
withheld,
And there has been no latter rain.
You have had a harlot's forehead;
You refuse to be ashamed.
4 Will you not from this time cry to
Me,
'My Father, You *are* the guide of my
youth?
5 Will He remain angry forever?
Will He keep it to the end?'
Behold, you have spoken and done
evil things,
As you were able."

A Call to Repentance

6 The LORD said also to me in the days of
Jō·sī'ah the king: "Have you seen what
backsliding Israel has done? She has gone
up on every high mountain and under
every green tree, and there played the har-
lot. 7 And I said, after she had done all these
things, 'Return to Me.' But she did not re-
turn. And her treacherous sister Judah saw
it. 8 Then I saw that for all the causes for
which backsliding Israel had committed
adultery, I had put her away and given her
a certificate of divorce; yet her treacherous
sister Judah did not fear, but went and
played the harlot also. 9 So it came to pass,
through her casual harlotry, that she de-
filed the land and committed adultery
with stones and trees. 10 And yet for all this
her treacherous sister Judah has not turned
to Me with her whole heart, but in pre-
tense," says the LORD.
11 Then the LORD said to me, "Backslid-
ing Israel has shown herself more righ-
teous than treacherous Judah. 12 Go and
proclaim these words toward the north,
and say:

'Return, backsliding Israel,' says the
LORD;
'I will not cause My anger to fall on
you.
For I *am* merciful,' says the LORD;
'I will not remain angry forever.
13 Only acknowledge your iniquity,
That you have transgressed against
the LORD your God,
And have scattered your charms
To alien deities under every green
tree,
And you have not obeyed My voice,'
says the LORD.

14 "Return, O backsliding children," says
the LORD; "for I am married to you. I will
take you, one from a city and two from a
family, and I will bring you to Zion. 15 And
I will give you shepherds according to My
heart, who will feed you with knowledge
and understanding.
16 "Then it shall come to pass, when you
are multiplied and increased in the land in
those days," says the LORD, "that they will
say no more, 'The ark of the covenant of
the LORD.' It shall not come to mind, nor
shall they remember it, nor shall they visit
it, nor shall it be made anymore.
17 "At that time Jerusalem shall be called
The Throne of the LORD, and all the nations
shall be gathered to it, to the name of the
LORD, to Jerusalem. No more shall they fol-
low the dictates of their evil hearts.
18 "In those days the house of Judah shall
walk with the house of Israel, and they
shall come together out of the land of the
north to the land that I have given as an in-
heritance to your fathers.
19 "But I said:

3:6–10 The northern kingdom of **Israel** had turned from the Lord. Their destruction about 20 years earlier was a **divorce** (v. 8). They too had been invited to repent before that final tragedy, but would not (v. 7). Unfortunately, **Judah** had not learned from this disaster and was sinning more blatantly than had Israel (v. 10).

3:19–25 The Lord wanted the **house of Israel** (v. 20, referring to both Israel and Judah) to repent and cry for help. A prayer of confession is provided to assist them (vv. 22–25).

'How can I put you among the
children
And give you a pleasant land,
A beautiful heritage of the hosts of
nations?'

"And I said:

'You shall call Me, "My Father,"
And not turn away from Me.'
20 Surely, *as* a wife treacherously departs
from her husband,
So have you dealt treacherously with
Me,
O house of Israel," says the LORD.

21 A voice was heard on the desolate
heights,
Weeping *and* supplications of the
children of Israel.
For they have perverted their way;
They have forgotten the LORD their
God.

22 "Return, you backsliding children,
And I will heal your backslidings."

"Indeed we do come to You,
For You are the LORD our God.
23 Truly, in vain *is salvation hoped for*
from the hills,
And from the multitude of mountains;
Truly, in the LORD our God
Is the salvation of Israel.
24 For shame has devoured
The labor of our fathers from our
youth—
Their flocks and their herds,
Their sons and their daughters.
25 We lie down in our shame,
And our reproach covers us.
For we have sinned against the LORD
our God,
We and our fathers,
From our youth even to this day,
And have not obeyed the voice of the
LORD our God."

CHAPTER 4

"If you will return, O Israel," says the
LORD,
"Return to Me;
And if you will put away your
abominations out of My sight,
Then you shall not be moved.
2 And you shall swear, 'The LORD
lives,'
In truth, in judgment, and in
righteousness;
The nations shall bless themselves in
Him,
And in Him they shall glory."

3For thus says the LORD to the men of Ju-
dah and Jerusalem:

"Break up your fallow ground,
And do not sow among thorns.
4 Circumcise yourselves to the LORD,
And take away the foreskins of your
hearts,
You men of Judah and inhabitants of
Jerusalem,
Lest My fury come forth like fire,
And burn so that no one can quench
it,
Because of the evil of your doings."

An Imminent Invasion

5Declare in Judah and proclaim in Jeru-
salem, and say:

4:3 fallow ground: Unplowed fields. A figure of speech standing for hard, rebellious attitudes toward God.

4:4 Circumcise yourselves to the LORD: The symbol of the covenant bond with God. They could show they really belonged to the Lord by doing away with pride, stubbornness, and other **evil . . . doings** (Deut. 10:16–19). Refusal would result in the fire of judgment.

4:5, 6 Blow the trumpet . . . Set up the standard: Preparations for the battle to come.

"Blow the trumpet in the land;
Cry, 'Gather together,'
And say, 'Assemble yourselves,
And let us go into the fortified cities.'
6 Set up the standard toward Zion.
Take refuge! Do not delay!
For I will bring disaster from the north,
And great destruction."

7 The lion has come up from his thicket,
And the destroyer of nations is on his way.
He has gone forth from his place
To make your land desolate.
Your cities will be laid waste,
Without inhabitant.
8 For this, clothe yourself with sackcloth,
Lament and wail.
For the fierce anger of the LORD
Has not turned back from us.

9 "And it shall come to pass in that day," says the LORD,
"*That* the heart of the king shall perish,
And the heart of the princes;
The priests shall be astonished,
And the prophets shall wonder."

10 Then I said, "Ah, Lord GOD!
Surely You have greatly deceived this people and Jerusalem,
Saying, 'You shall have peace,'
Whereas the sword reaches to the heart."

11 At that time it will be said
To this people and to Jerusalem,
"A dry wind of the desolate heights *blows* in the wilderness
Toward the daughter of My people—
Not to fan or to cleanse—
12 A wind too strong for these will come for Me;
Now I will also speak judgment against them."

13 "Behold, he shall come up like clouds,
And his chariots like a whirlwind.
His horses are swifter than eagles.
Woe to us, for we are plundered!"

14 O Jerusalem, wash your heart from wickedness,
That you may be saved.
How long shall your evil thoughts lodge within you?
15 For a voice declares from Dan
And proclaims affliction from Mount Ē′phra·im:
16 "Make mention to the nations,
Yes, proclaim against Jerusalem,
That watchers come from a far country
And raise their voice against the cities of Judah.
17 Like keepers of a field they are against her all around,
Because she has been rebellious against Me," says the LORD.
18 "Your ways and your doings
Have procured these *things* for you.
This *is* your wickedness,
Because it is bitter,
Because it reaches to your heart."

Sorrow for the Doomed Nation

19 O my soul, my soul!
I am pained in my very heart!
My heart makes a noise in me;
I cannot hold my peace,
Because you have heard, O my soul,
The sound of the trumpet,
The alarm of war.
20 Destruction upon destruction is cried,
For the whole land is plundered.
Suddenly my tents are plundered,
And my curtains in a moment.
21 How long will I see the standard,
And hear the sound of the trumpet?

22 "For My people *are* foolish,
They have not known Me.
They *are* silly children,
And they have no understanding.
They *are* wise to do evil,

But to do good they have no
knowledge."

23 I beheld the earth, and indeed *it was*
without form, and void;
And the heavens, they *had* no light.
24 I beheld the mountains, and indeed
they trembled,
And all the hills moved back and
forth.
25 I beheld, and indeed *there was* no
man,
And all the birds of the heavens had
fled.
26 I beheld, and indeed the fruitful land
was a wilderness,
And all its cities were broken down
At the presence of the LORD,
By His fierce anger.

27For thus says the LORD:

"The whole land shall be desolate;
Yet I will not make a full end.
28 For this shall the earth mourn,
And the heavens above be black,
Because I have spoken.
I have purposed and will not
relent,
Nor will I turn back from it.
29 The whole city shall flee from the
noise of the horsemen and
bowmen.
They shall go into thickets and climb
up on the rocks.
Every city *shall be* forsaken,
And not a man shall dwell in it.

30 "And *when* you *are* plundered,
What will you do?
Though you clothe yourself with
crimson,
Though you adorn *yourself* with
ornaments of gold,
Though you enlarge your eyes with
paint,
In vain you will make yourself fair;
Your lovers will despise you;
They will seek your life.

31 "For I have heard a voice as of a
woman in labor,
The anguish as of her who brings
forth her first child,
The voice of the daughter of Zion
bewailing herself;
She spreads her hands, *saying,*
'Woe *is* me now, for my soul is weary
Because of murderers!'

CHAPTER 5

The Justice of God's Judgment

"Run to and fro through the streets of Je-
rusalem;

See now and know;
And seek in her open places
If you can find a man,
If there is *anyone* who executes
judgment,
Who seeks the truth,
And I will pardon her.
2 Though they say, '*As* the LORD lives,'
Surely they swear falsely."

3 O LORD, *are* not Your eyes on the
truth?
You have stricken them,
But they have not grieved;
You have consumed them,
But they have refused to receive
correction.
They have made their faces harder
than rock;
They have refused to return.

4:23–26 without form, and void: Jeremiah saw Judah being returned to a state of chaos like the earth at the beginning of creation.

4:30 crimson . . . ornaments . . . paint: As a harlot prepares herself to impress a lover, so Judah would attempt to appease the invading Babylonians. The tactic would not work.

4 Therefore I said, "Surely these *are* poor.
They are foolish;
For they do not know the way of the LORD,
The judgment of their God.
5 I will go to the great men and speak to them,
For they have known the way of the LORD,
The judgment of their God."

But these have altogether broken the yoke
And burst the bonds.
6 Therefore a lion from the forest shall slay them,
A wolf of the deserts shall destroy them;
A leopard will watch over their cities.
Everyone who goes out from there shall be torn in pieces,
Because their transgressions are many;
Their backslidings have increased.

7 "How shall I pardon you for this?
Your children have forsaken Me
And sworn by *those that are* not gods.
When I had fed them to the full,
Then they committed adultery
And assembled themselves by troops in the harlots' houses.
8 They were *like* well-fed lusty stallions;
Every one neighed after his neighbor's wife.
9 Shall I not punish *them* for these *things?*" says the LORD.
"And shall I not avenge Myself on such a nation as this?

10 "Go up on her walls and destroy,
But do not make a complete end.
Take away her branches,
For they *are* not the LORD's.
11 For the house of Israel and the house of Judah
Have dealt very treacherously with Me," says the LORD.

12 They have lied about the LORD,
And said, "*It is* not He.
Neither will evil come upon us,
Nor shall we see sword or famine.
13 And the prophets become wind,
For the word *is* not in them.
Thus shall it be done to them."

14 Therefore thus says the LORD God of hosts:

"Because you speak this word,
Behold, I will make My words in your mouth fire,
And this people wood,
And it shall devour them.
15 Behold, I will bring a nation against you from afar,
O house of Israel," says the LORD.
"It *is* a mighty nation,
It *is* an ancient nation,
A nation whose language you do not know,
Nor can you understand what they say.
16 Their quiver *is* like an open tomb;
They *are* all mighty men.
17 And they shall eat up your harvest and your bread,
Which your sons and daughters should eat.
They shall eat up your flocks and your herds;
They shall eat up your vines and your fig trees;
They shall destroy your fortified cities,
In which you trust, with the sword.

5:7–11 forsaken Me: Judah's deep sin against God.
5:12–17 A contrast between false prophecy (vv. 12, 13) and true (vv. 14–17).
5:14–17 Jeremiah's words would be powerful like a fire because they were God's words of judgment, fulfilled in the Babylonian invasion of Judah.

18"Nevertheless in those days," says the
LORD, "I will not make a complete end of
you. 19And it will be when you say, 'Why
does the LORD our God do all these *things*
to us?' then you shall answer them, 'Just as
you have forsaken Me and served foreign
gods in your land, so you shall serve aliens
in a land *that is* not yours.'

20 "Declare this in the house of Jacob
And proclaim it in Judah, saying,
21 'Hear this now, O foolish people,
Without understanding,
Who have eyes and see not,
And who have ears and hear not:
22 Do you not fear Me?' says the LORD.
'Will you not tremble at My presence,
Who have placed the sand as the bound of the sea,
By a perpetual decree, that it cannot pass beyond it?
And though its waves toss to and fro,
Yet they cannot prevail;
Though they roar, yet they cannot pass over it.
23 But this people has a defiant and rebellious heart;
They have revolted and departed.
24 They do not say in their heart,
"Let us now fear the LORD our God,
Who gives rain, both the former and the latter, in its season.
He reserves for us the appointed weeks of the harvest."
25 Your iniquities have turned these *things* away,
And your sins have withheld good from you.

26 'For among My people are found wicked *men;*
They lie in wait as one who sets snares;
They set a trap;
They catch men.
27 As a cage is full of birds,
So their houses *are* full of deceit.
Therefore they have become great and grown rich.
28 They have grown fat, they are sleek;
Yes, they surpass the deeds of the wicked;
They do not plead the cause,
The cause of the fatherless;
Yet they prosper,
And the right of the needy they do not defend.
29 Shall I not punish *them* for these *things?'* says the LORD.
'Shall I not avenge Myself on such a nation as this?'

30 "An astonishing and horrible thing
Has been committed in the land:
31 The prophets prophesy falsely,
And the priests rule by their *own* power;
And My people love *to have it* so.
But what will you do in the end?

CHAPTER 6

Impending Destruction from the North

"O you children of Benjamin,
Gather yourselves to flee from the midst of Jerusalem!
Blow the trumpet in Te·kō'a,
And set up a signal-fire in Beth Hac'ce·rem;
For disaster appears out of the north,
And great destruction.
2 I have likened the daughter of Zion
To a lovely and delicate woman.

5:20–31 The Lord's distress was intense. His own covenant people were sinners; they lacked reverence and loyalty to Him. This godlessness stemmed from the religious leaders themselves.

6:1–30 This section, which began with the call to repent (4:1–4), now ends on a note of inescapable doom. The people refuse to repent (see 5:24, 25).

6:1 The children of Benjamin lived on a narrow strip of land extending from east to west, just north of Jerusalem. Jeremiah's home was in this territory.

3 The shepherds with their flocks shall come to her.
They shall pitch *their* tents against her all around.
Each one shall pasture in his own place."

4 "Prepare war against her;
Arise, and let us go up at noon.
Woe to us, for the day goes away,
For the shadows of the evening are lengthening.
5 Arise, and let us go by night,
And let us destroy her palaces."

6 For thus has the LORD of hosts said:

"Cut down trees,
And build a mound against Jerusalem.
This *is* the city to be punished.
She *is* full of oppression in her midst.
7 As a fountain wells up with water,
So she wells up with her wickedness.
Violence and plundering are heard in her.
Before Me continually *are* grief and wounds.
8 Be instructed, O Jerusalem,
Lest My soul depart from you;
Lest I make you desolate,
A land not inhabited."

9 Thus says the LORD of hosts:

"They shall thoroughly glean as a vine the remnant of Israel;
As a grape-gatherer, put your hand back into the branches."

10 To whom shall I speak and give warning,
That they may hear?
Indeed their ear *is* uncircumcised,
And they cannot give heed.
Behold, the word of the LORD is a reproach to them;
They have no delight in it.
11 Therefore I am full of the fury of the LORD.
I am weary of holding *it* in.
"I will pour it out on the children outside,
And on the assembly of young men together;
For even the husband shall be taken with the wife,
The aged with *him who is* full of days.
12 And their houses shall be turned over to others,
Fields and wives together;
For I will stretch out My hand
Against the inhabitants of the land,"
says the LORD.
13 "Because from the least of them even to the greatest of them,
Everyone *is* given to covetousness;
And from the prophet even to the priest,
Everyone deals falsely.
14 They have also healed the hurt of My people slightly,
Saying, 'Peace, peace!'
When *there is* no peace.
15 Were they ashamed when they had committed abomination?
No! They were not at all ashamed;
Nor did they know how to blush.
Therefore they shall fall among those who fall;
At the time I punish them,
They shall be cast down," says the LORD.

6:3 The shepherds: Here, foreign rulers. **flocks**: Their armies.

6:6–8 mound: An earthen ramp up which wooden towers could be pushed to assault the walls of Jerusalem. The city should learn from these preparations that judgment was imminent.

6:10 The description of the ear or the heart as uncircumcised depicts a rebellious attitude toward God's will.

What can I do when I have difficulty sleeping?

Elmer L. Gray

Adults differ in their sleep needs. Some require little while others need a long night's sleep plus an afternoon nap.

A woman who has trouble going to sleep at night tried several things and finally found one that helped. After she tells her husband good night, she closes her eyes and begins to sing silently in her mind. No, she is not a singer and even hesitates to participate in congregational singing at church, but she loves music. Her silent singing works nearly 100 percent of the time. She sings mostly devotional hymns. This helps her go to sleep, blesses her soul, and improves her attitude.

Here are some other suggestions:

✦ Keep a regular sleep schedule as much as possible.

✦ Be active during the day, particularly in the late afternoon.

✦ Try snacking before bedtime, particularly on carbohydrates such as cookies. Avoid coffee late in the day.

✦ Develop some pre-bedtime habits, such as watching the late news, reading your Bible, checking the doors and windows, and praying.

✦ Occupy your mind and spirit with pleasant thoughts and happy feelings.

If these simple things do not help, see your doctor.

Listen to the Lord's advice to Israel: "Ask . . . where the good way is, and walk in it; then you will find rest for your souls" (Jer. 6:16).

16 Thus says the LORD:

"Stand in the ways and see,
And ask for the old paths, where the good way *is,*
And walk in it;
Then you will find rest for your souls.
But they said, 'We will not walk *in it.*'
17 Also, I set watchmen over you, *saying,*
'Listen to the sound of the trumpet!'
But they said, 'We will not listen.'
18 Therefore hear, you nations,
And know, O congregation, what *is* among them.
19 Hear, O earth!
Behold, I will certainly bring calamity on this people—
The fruit of their thoughts,
Because they have not heeded My words
Nor My law, but rejected it.
20 For what purpose to Me
Comes frankincense from Shē′ba,

6:17 watchmen: The prophets, of whom Jeremiah was one (see Ezek. 3:17). They had faithfully blown the trumpet, delivering messages of warning, but they were ignored.

And sweet cane from a far country?
Your burnt offerings *are* not
acceptable,
Nor your sacrifices sweet to Me."

21 Therefore thus says the LORD:

"Behold, I will lay stumbling blocks
before this people,
And the fathers and the sons together
shall fall on them.
The neighbor and his friend shall
perish."

22 Thus says the LORD:

"Behold, a people comes from the
north country,
And a great nation will be raised
from the farthest parts of the earth.
23 They will lay hold on bow and spear;
They *are* cruel and have no mercy;
Their voice roars like the sea;
And they ride on horses,
As men of war set in array against
you, O daughter of Zion."

24 We have heard the report of it;
Our hands grow feeble.
Anguish has taken hold of us,
Pain as of a woman in labor.
25 Do not go out into the field,
Nor walk by the way.
Because of the sword of the enemy,
Fear *is* on every side.
26 O daughter of my people,
Dress in sackcloth
And roll about in ashes!
Make mourning *as for* an only son,
most bitter lamentation;
For the plunderer will suddenly come
upon us.

27 "I have set you *as* an assayer *and* a
fortress among My people,
That you may know and test their
way.
28 They *are* all stubborn rebels, walking
as slanderers.
They are bronze and iron,
They *are* all corrupters;
29 The bellows blow fiercely,
The lead is consumed by the fire;
The smelter refines in vain,
For the wicked are not drawn off.
30 *People* will call them rejected silver,
Because the LORD has rejected them."

CHAPTER 7

Trusting in Lying Words

The word that came to Jer·e·mī'ah from
the LORD, saying, 2 "Stand in the gate of the
LORD's house, and proclaim there this
word, and say, 'Hear the word of the LORD,
all *you of* Judah who enter in at these gates
to worship the LORD!' " 3 Thus says the
LORD of hosts, the God of Israel: "Amend
your ways and your doings, and I will
cause you to dwell in this place. 4 Do not
trust in these lying words, saying, 'The
temple of the LORD, the temple of the LORD,
the temple of the LORD *are* these.'
5 "For if you thoroughly amend your
ways and your doings, if you thoroughly
execute judgment between a man and his
neighbor, 6 *if* you do not oppress the
stranger, the fatherless, and the widow,
and do not shed innocent blood in this
place, or walk after other gods to your
hurt, 7 then I will cause you to dwell in this
place, in the land that I gave to your fathers
forever and ever.
8 "Behold, you trust in lying words that
cannot profit. 9 Will you steal, murder, com-

6:27 assayer: One who determines the amount of precious metal in ore.
6:28 bronze and iron: Not gold or silver.
7:3–7 Amend your ways: The people must quit placing ultimate trust in the temple. No building, however sacred, would save from God's judgment those who were oppressing the helpless, murdering the innocent, and worshiping other gods (v. 6).

mit adultery, swear falsely, burn incense to
Bā'al, and walk after other gods whom you
do not know, 10and *then* come and stand
before Me in this house which is called by
My name, and say, 'We are delivered to do
all these abominations'? 11Has this house,
which is called by My name, become a den
of thieves in your eyes? Behold, I, even I,
have seen *it*," says the LORD.

12"But go now to My place which *was* in
Shī'lōh, where I set My name at the first,
and see what I did to it because of the
wickedness of My people Israel. 13And
now, because you have done all these
works," says the LORD, "and I spoke to
you, rising up early and speaking, but you
did not hear, and I called you, but you did
not answer, 14therefore I will do to the
house which is called by My name, in
which you trust, and to this place which I
gave to you and your fathers, as I have
done to Shī'lōh. 15And I will cast you out
of My sight, as I have cast out all
your brethren—the whole posterity of
Ē'phra·im.

16"Therefore do not pray for this people,
nor lift up a cry or prayer for them, nor
make intercession to Me; for I will not hear
you. 17Do you not see what they do in the
cities of Judah and in the streets of Jerusa-
lem? 18The children gather wood, the
fathers kindle the fire, and the women
knead dough, to make cakes for the queen
of heaven; and *they* pour out drink offer-
ings to other gods, that they may provoke
Me to anger. 19Do they provoke Me to
anger?" says the LORD. "*Do they* not *provoke*
themselves, to the shame of their own
faces?"

20Therefore thus says the Lord GOD: "Be-
hold, My anger and My fury will be
poured out on this place—on man and on
beast, on the trees of the field and on the
fruit of the ground. And it will burn and
not be quenched."

21Thus says the LORD of hosts, the God
of Israel: "Add your burnt offerings to
your sacrifices and eat meat. 22For I did not
speak to your fathers, or command them in
the day that I brought them out of the land
of Egypt, concerning burnt offerings or
sacrifices. 23But this is what I commanded
them, saying, 'Obey My voice, and I will be
your God, and you shall be My people.
And walk in all the ways that I have com-
manded you, that it may be well with you.'
24Yet they did not obey or incline their ear,
but followed the counsels *and* the dictates
of their evil hearts, and went backward
and not forward. 25Since the day that your
fathers came out of the land of Egypt until
this day, I have even sent to you all My ser-
vants the prophets, daily rising up early
and sending *them*. 26Yet they did not obey
Me or incline their ear, but stiffened their
neck. They did worse than their fathers.

27"Therefore you shall speak all these
words to them, but they will not obey you.

I pray, O God, that my grandchildren will obey Your voice, and You will be their God, and they shall be Your children. And that they will walk in all the ways that You have commanded them, that it may be well with them.

adapted from Jeremiah 7:23

7:13 rising up early and speaking: A figure of speech meaning to do something continuously and often. God had been persistent in His efforts to reach Judah; now He must punish (vv. 14, 20).

7:18 children . . . fathers . . . women: Worshiping idols had become a family affair. **queen of heaven**: A pagan goddess.

You shall also call to them, but they will
not answer you.

Judgment on Obscene Religion

28"So you shall say to them, 'This *is* a na-
tion that does not obey the voice of the
LORD their God nor receive correction.
Truth has perished and has been cut off
from their mouth. 29Cut off your hair and
cast *it* away, and take up a lamentation on
the desolate heights; for the LORD has re-
jected and forsaken the generation of His
wrath.' 30For the children of Judah have
done evil in My sight," says the LORD.
"They have set their abominations in the
house which is called by My name, to pol-
lute it. 31And they have built the high
places of Tō'phet, which *is* in the Valley of
the Son of Hin'nom, to burn their sons and
their daughters in the fire, which I did not
command, nor did it come into My heart.
32"Therefore behold, the days are com-
ing," says the LORD, "when it will no more
be called Tō'phet, or the Valley of the Son
of Hin'nom, but the Valley of Slaughter;
for they will bury in Tō'phet until there is
no room. 33The corpses of this people will
be food for the birds of the heaven and for
the beasts of the earth. And no one will
frighten *them away.* 34Then I will cause to
cease from the cities of Judah and from the
streets of Jerusalem the voice of mirth and
the voice of gladness, the voice of the
bridegroom and the voice of the bride. For
the land shall be desolate.

CHAPTER 8

"At that time," says the LORD, "they
shall bring out the bones of the kings of Ju-
dah, and the bones of its princes, and the
bones of the priests, and the bones of the
prophets, and the bones of the inhabitants
of Jerusalem, out of their graves. 2They
shall spread them before the sun and the
moon and all the host of heaven, which
they have loved and which they have
served and after which they have walked,
which they have sought and which they
have worshiped. They shall not be gath-
ered nor buried; they shall be like refuse on
the face of the earth. 3Then death shall be
chosen rather than life by all the residue of
those who remain of this evil family,
who remain in all the places where I have
driven them," says the LORD of hosts.

The Peril of False Teaching

4"Moreover you shall say to them, 'Thus
says the LORD:

"Will they fall and not rise?
Will one turn away and not return?
5 Why has this people slidden back,
Jerusalem, in a perpetual backsliding?
They hold fast to deceit,
They refuse to return.
6 I listened and heard,
But they do not speak aright.
No man repented of his wickedness,
Saying, 'What have I done?'
Everyone turned to his own course,
As the horse rushes into the battle.

7 "Even the stork in the heavens
Knows her appointed times;
And the turtledove, the swift, and the
swallow
Observe the time of their coming.
But My people do not know the
judgment of the LORD.

7:29 Cut off your hair: The action of one in mourning.
7:30—8:3 The people were unclean because of their idolatry and the sacrifice of their sons and daughters. These children were thrown into a firepit, called Tophet, located in the Valley of Hinnom which curves around the west and south side of Jerusalem.
7:30 The ultimate judgment upon Jerusalem and the temple would come as a result of their abominations in God's house.

8 "How can you say, 'We *are* wise,
And the law of the LORD *is* with us'?
Look, the false pen of the scribe
certainly works falsehood.
9 The wise men are ashamed,
They are dismayed and taken.
Behold, they have rejected the word
of the LORD;
So what wisdom do they have?
10 Therefore I will give their wives to
others,
And their fields to those who will
inherit *them;*
Because from the least even to the
greatest
Everyone is given to covetousness;
From the prophet even to the
priest
Everyone deals falsely.
11 For they have healed the hurt of the
daughter of My people slightly,
Saying, 'Peace, peace!'
When *there is* no peace.
12 Were they ashamed when they had
committed abomination?
No! They were not at all ashamed,
Nor did they know how to blush.
Therefore they shall fall among those
who fall;
In the time of their punishment
They shall be cast down," says the
LORD.

13 "I will surely consume them," says the
LORD.
"No grapes *shall be* on the vine,
Nor figs on the fig tree,
And the leaf shall fade;
And *the things* I have given them shall
pass away from them." ' "

14 "Why do we sit still?
Assemble yourselves,
And let us enter the fortified cities,
And let us be silent there.
For the LORD our God has put us to
silence
And given us water of gall to
drink,
Because we have sinned against the
LORD.

15 "*We* looked for peace, but no good
came;
And for a time of health, and there
was trouble!
16 The snorting of His horses was heard
from Dan.
The whole land trembled at the
sound of the neighing of His strong
ones;
For they have come and devoured the
land and all that is in it,
The city and those who dwell in it."

17 "For behold, I will send serpents
among you,
Vipers which cannot be charmed,
And they shall bite you," says the
LORD.

The Prophet Mourns for the People

18 I would comfort myself in sorrow;
My heart *is* faint in me.
19 Listen! The voice,
The cry of the daughter of my people
From a far country:
"*Is* not the LORD in Zion?
Is not her King in her?"

"Why have they provoked Me to anger
With their carved images—
With foreign idols?"

20 "The harvest is past,
The summer is ended,
And we are not saved!"

21 For the hurt of the daughter of my
people I am hurt.
I am mourning;
Astonishment has taken hold of me.
22 *Is there* no balm in Gil'ē·ad,
Is there no physician there?
Why then is there no recovery
For the health of the daughter of my
people?

CHAPTER 9

Oh, that my head were waters,
And my eyes a fountain of tears,
That I might weep day and night
For the slain of the daughter of my people!
2 Oh, that I had in the wilderness
A lodging place for travelers;
That I might leave my people,
And go from them!
For they *are* all adulterers,
An assembly of treacherous men.

3 "And *like* their bow they have bent their tongues *for* lies.
They are not valiant for the truth on the earth.
For they proceed from evil to evil,
And they do not know Me," says the LORD.
4 "Everyone take heed to his neighbor,
And do not trust any brother;
For every brother will utterly supplant,
And every neighbor will walk with slanderers.
5 Everyone will deceive his neighbor,
And will not speak the truth;
They have taught their tongue to speak lies;
They weary themselves to commit iniquity.
6 Your dwelling place *is* in the midst of deceit;
Through deceit they refuse to know Me," says the LORD.

7Therefore thus says the LORD of hosts:

"Behold, I will refine them and try them;
For how shall I deal with the daughter of My people?
8 Their tongue *is* an arrow shot out;
It speaks deceit;
One speaks peaceably to his neighbor with his mouth,
But in his heart he lies in wait.
9 Shall I not punish them for these *things?*" says the LORD.
"Shall I not avenge Myself on such a nation as this?"

10 I will take up a weeping and wailing for the mountains,
And for the dwelling places of the wilderness a lamentation,
Because they are burned up,
So that no one can pass through;
Nor can *men* hear the voice of the cattle.
Both the birds of the heavens and the beasts have fled;
They are gone.

11 "I will make Jerusalem a heap of ruins, a den of jackals.
I will make the cities of Judah desolate, without an inhabitant."

12Who *is* the wise man who may under-
stand this? And *who is he* to whom the
mouth of the LORD has spoken, that he may
declare it? Why does the land perish *and*
burn up like a wilderness, so that no one
can pass through?
13And the LORD said, "Because they
have forsaken My law which I set before
them, and have not obeyed My voice, nor
walked according to it, 14but they have

9:1, 2 In prayer Jeremiah alternates between two moods. Looking at the slaughter caused by the invader, he desires to weep without ceasing (v. 1). Remembering the immorality of the people, he longs to flee **from them** (v. 2).

9:3–6 The Lord confirmed the wickedness of Judah but not Jeremiah's solution of escape (v. 2). His **dwelling place** was to be among these sinners (v. 6). This is often the believer's place in God's redemptive plan.

9:14 Baals: The Canaanites worshiped a storm god called Baal. They also worshiped idols of Baal (Baals) at many local shrines. Many Israelites had mixed the worship of God with this kind of idolatry.

walked according to the dictates of their
own hearts and after the Bā'als, which
their fathers taught them," [15]therefore thus
says the LORD of hosts, the God of Israel:
"Behold, I will feed them, this people, with
wormwood, and give them water of gall to
drink. [16]I will scatter them also among the
Gentiles, whom neither they nor their
fathers have known. And I will send a
sword after them until I have consumed
them."

The People Mourn in Judgment

[17]Thus says the LORD of hosts:

"Consider and call for the mourning
women,
That they may come;
And send for skillful wailing women,
That they may come.
18 Let them make haste
And take up a wailing for us,
That our eyes may run with tears,
And our eyelids gush with water.
19 For a voice of wailing is heard from
Zion:
'How we are plundered!
We are greatly ashamed,
Because we have forsaken the land,
Because we have been cast out of our
dwellings.' "

20 Yet hear the word of the LORD,
O women,
And let your ear receive the word of
His mouth;
Teach your daughters wailing,
And everyone her neighbor a
lamentation.
21 For death has come through our
windows,
Has entered our palaces,
To kill off the children—*no longer to be*
outside!
And the young men—*no longer* on the
streets!

22 Speak, "Thus says the LORD:

'Even the carcasses of men shall fall as
refuse on the open field,
Like cuttings after the harvester,
And no one shall gather *them*.' "

[23]Thus says the LORD:

"Let not the wise *man* glory in his
wisdom,
Let not the mighty *man* glory in his
might,
Nor let the rich *man* glory in his
riches;
24 But let him who glories glory in this,
That he understands and knows Me,
That I *am* the LORD, exercising
lovingkindness, judgment, and
righteousness in the earth.
For in these I delight," says the LORD.

[25]"Behold, the days are coming," says
the LORD, "that I will punish all *who are*
circumcised with the uncircumcised—
[26]Egypt, Judah, Ē'dom, the people of
Am'mon, Mō'ab, and all *who are* in the far-
thest corners, who dwell in the wilderness.
For all *these* nations *are* uncircumcised, and
all the house of Israel *are* uncircumcised in
the heart."

9:17–22 mourning women: The haughty Israelites would be so shattered by the death toll of war that their women would wail with grief.

9:23—10:25 Judah's hope is not in humanity's glory, the attitude that is at the heart of idolatry. If she goes that way, she is simply one more of the nations.

9:23, 24 Words worthy to be memorized. Humans strive for wisdom, might, and riches, while God delights in lovingkindness, judgment (justice), and righteousness. Blessed is the one who understands the Lord so as to delight in what He delights.

CHAPTER 10

Idols and the True God

Hear the word which the LORD speaks to you, O house of Israel.
2Thus says the LORD:

"Do not learn the way of the Gentiles;
Do not be dismayed at the signs of heaven,
For the Gentiles are dismayed at them.
3 For the customs of the peoples *are* futile;
For *one* cuts a tree from the forest,
The work of the hands of the workman, with the ax.
4 They decorate it with silver and gold;
They fasten it with nails and hammers
So that it will not topple.
5 They *are* upright, like a palm tree,
And they cannot speak;
They must be carried,
Because they cannot go *by themselves.*
Do not be afraid of them,
For they cannot do evil,
Nor can they do any good."

6 Inasmuch as *there is* none like You, O LORD
(You *are* great, and Your name *is* great in might),
7 Who would not fear You, O King of the nations?
For this is Your rightful due.
For among all the wise *men* of the nations,
And in all their kingdoms,
There is none like You.

8 But they are altogether dull-hearted and foolish;
A wooden idol *is* a worthless doctrine.
9 Silver is beaten into plates;
It is brought from Tar'shish,
And gold from Ū'phaz,
The work of the craftsman
And of the hands of the metalsmith;
Blue and purple *are* their clothing;
They *are* all the work of skillful *men.*
10 But the LORD *is* the true God;
He *is* the living God and the everlasting King.
At His wrath the earth will tremble,
And the nations will not be able to endure His indignation.

11Thus you shall say to them: "The gods that have not made the heavens and the earth shall perish from the earth and from under these heavens."

12 He has made the earth by His power,
He has established the world by His wisdom,
And has stretched out the heavens at His discretion.
13 When He utters His voice,
There is a multitude of waters in the heavens:
"And He causes the vapors to ascend from the ends of the earth.
He makes lightning for the rain,
He brings the wind out of His treasuries."[a]

14 Everyone is dull-hearted, without knowledge;

10:13 [a]Psalm 135:7

10:1–5 The folly of idolatry is displayed by showing step-by-step how idols are made by human craftsmen (vv. 3–5).

10:2 signs of heaven: The Gentile nations worshiped the various celestial bodies. Judah was not to follow their example.

10:14, 15 Idols are without breath, the product of errors, and make their worshipers dull-hearted (ignorant) and filled with shame. All idols and those who worship them shall perish.

Every metalsmith is put to shame by
an image;
For his molded image *is* falsehood,
And *there is* no breath in them.
15 They *are* futile, a work of errors;
In the time of their punishment they
shall perish.
16 The Portion of Jacob *is* not like them,
For He *is* the Maker of all *things*,
And Israel *is* the tribe of His
inheritance;
The LORD of hosts *is* His name.

The Coming Captivity of Judah

17 Gather up your wares from the land,
O inhabitant of the fortress!

18For thus says the LORD:

"Behold, I will throw out at this time
The inhabitants of the land,
And will distress them,
That they may find *it so*."

19 Woe is me for my hurt!
My wound is severe.
But I say, "Truly this *is* an infirmity,
And I must bear it."
20 My tent is plundered,
And all my cords are broken;
My children have gone from me,
And they *are* no more.
There is no one to pitch my tent
anymore,
Or set up my curtains.

21 For the shepherds have become dull-
hearted,
And have not sought the LORD;
Therefore they shall not prosper,
And all their flocks shall be scattered.

22 Behold, the noise of the report has
come,
And a great commotion out of the
north country,
To make the cities of Judah desolate, a
den of jackals.

23 O LORD, I know the way of man *is* not
in himself;
It is not in man who walks to direct
his own steps.
24 O LORD, correct me, but with justice;
Not in Your anger, lest You bring me
to nothing.
25 Pour out Your fury on the Gentiles,
who do not know You,
And on the families who do not call
on Your name;
For they have eaten up Jacob,
Devoured him and consumed him,
And made his dwelling place
desolate.

CHAPTER 11

The Broken Covenant

The word that came to Jer·e·mi'ah from
the LORD, saying, 2"Hear the words of this
covenant, and speak to the men of Judah
and to the inhabitants of Jerusalem; 3and
say to them, 'Thus says the LORD God of Is-
rael: "Cursed *is* the man who does not
obey the words of this covenant 4which I
commanded your fathers in the day I
brought them out of the land of Egypt,
from the iron furnace, saying, 'Obey My
voice, and do according to all that I com-
mand you; so shall you be My people, and
I will be your God,' 5that I may establish
the oath which I have sworn to your fa-
thers, to give them 'a land flowing with
milk and honey,'[a] as *it is* this day." ' "

11:5 [a]Exodus 3:8

10:19–22 An imagined cry of despair from someone in Judah, due to the predicted invasion from the **north** (v. 22; see note on Is. 41:25).

11:2–5 you . . . My people . . . I . . . your God: The essence of the covenant was the mutual bonding of the Israelites and the Lord in which each freely chose the other at Mt. Sinai.

And I answered and said, "So be it,
LORD."
6Then the LORD said to me, "Proclaim all
these words in the cities of Judah and in
the streets of Jerusalem, saying: 'Hear the
words of this covenant and do them. 7For I
earnestly exhorted your fathers in the day I
brought them up out of the land of Egypt,
until this day, rising early and exhorting,
saying, "Obey My voice." 8Yet they did
not obey or incline their ear, but everyone
followed the dictates of his evil heart;
therefore I will bring upon them all the
words of this covenant, which I com-
manded *them* to do, but *which* they have
not done.' "
9And the LORD said to me, "A conspir-
acy has been found among the men of Ju-
dah and among the inhabitants of Jerusa-
lem. 10They have turned back to the
iniquities of their forefathers who refused
to hear My words, and they have gone af-
ter other gods to serve them; the house of
Israel and the house of Judah have broken
My covenant which I made with their
fathers."
11Therefore thus says the LORD: "Behold,
I will surely bring calamity on them which
they will not be able to escape; and though
they cry out to Me, I will not listen to them.
12Then the cities of Judah and the inhab-
itants of Jerusalem will go and cry out to
the gods to whom they offer incense, but
they will not save them at all in the time of
their trouble. 13For *according to* the number
of your cities were your gods, O Judah;
and *according to* the number of the streets
of Jerusalem you have set up altars to *that*
shameful thing, altars to burn incense to
Bā'al.
14"So do not pray for this people, or lift
up a cry or prayer for them; for I will not
hear *them* in the time that they cry out to
Me because of their trouble.

15 "What has My beloved to do in My
house,
Having done lewd deeds with many?
And the holy flesh has passed from
you.
When you do evil, then you rejoice.
16 The LORD called your name,
Green Olive Tree, Lovely *and* of Good
Fruit.
With the noise of a great tumult
He has kindled fire on it,
And its branches are broken.

17"For the LORD of hosts, who planted
you, has pronounced doom against you for
the evil of the house of Israel and of the
house of Judah, which they have done
against themselves to provoke Me to anger
in offering incense to Bā'al."

Jeremiah's Life Threatened

18Now the LORD gave me knowledge *of
it*, and I know *it;* for You showed me their
doings. 19But I *was* like a docile lamb
brought to the slaughter; and I did not
know that they had devised schemes
against me, *saying*, "Let us destroy the tree
with its fruit, and let us cut him off from
the land of the living, that his name may be
remembered no more."

20 But, O LORD of hosts,
You who judge righteously,
Testing the mind and the heart,
Let me see Your vengeance on them,
For to You I have revealed my cause.

21"Therefore thus says the LORD con-
cerning the men of An'a·thoth who seek

11:18, 19 The Lord reveals to Jeremiah the plot of his own townsmen to kill him. **destroy the tree**: Here applied to Jeremiah; his fellow townsmen of Anathoth (v. 21) would seek his demise.

11:21–23 men of Anathoth . . . The young men: Surely including Jeremiah's close relatives (see 12:6). The Lord's judgment would thus wipe out the prophet's extended family.

your life, saying, 'Do not prophesy in the name of the LORD, lest you die by our hand'— [22]therefore thus says the LORD of hosts: 'Behold, I will punish them. The young men shall die by the sword, their sons and their daughters shall die by famine; [23]and there shall be no remnant of them, for I will bring catastrophe on the men of An'a·thoth, *even* the year of their punishment.' "

CHAPTER 12

Jeremiah's Question

Righteous *are* You, O LORD, when I
plead with You;
Yet let me talk with You about *Your*
judgments.
Why does the way of the wicked
prosper?
Why are those happy who deal so
treacherously?
2 You have planted them, yes, they
have taken root;
They grow, yes, they bear fruit.
You *are* near in their mouth
But far from their mind.

3 But You, O LORD, know me;
You have seen me,
And You have tested my heart
toward You.
Pull them out like sheep for the
slaughter,
And prepare them for the day of
slaughter.

4 How long will the land mourn,
And the herbs of every field wither?
The beasts and birds are consumed,
For the wickedness of those who
dwell there,
Because they said, "He will not see
our final end."

The LORD Answers Jeremiah

5 "If you have run with the footmen,
and they have wearied you,
Then how can you contend with
horses?
And *if* in the land of peace,
In which you trusted, *they wearied you,*
Then how will you do in the flood-
plain[a] of the Jordan?
6 For even your brothers, the house of
your father,
Even they have dealt treacherously
with you;
Yes, they have called a multitude
after you.
Do not believe them,
Even though they speak smooth
words to you.

7 "I have forsaken My house, I have left
My heritage;
I have given the dearly beloved of My
soul into the hand of her enemies.
8 My heritage is to Me like a lion in the
forest;
It cries out against Me;
Therefore I have hated it.
9 My heritage *is* to Me *like* a speckled
vulture;
The vultures all around *are* against
her.

12:5 [a]Or *thicket*

12:1–4 Why . . . the wicked prosper? is a question that made praying often painful for Jeremiah. He saw clearly the approaching punishment of his beloved people. At the same time, the contradiction that allowed sinners to prosper filled him with sorrow.

12:5, 6 God's response to Jeremiah's cry. **footmen** symbolized family members who opposed him; **horses**, the invading army. Jeremiah's relationship to both is likened to a race. **floodplain of the Jordan** symbolized the invaders. The Lord was saying, "The worst is yet to come. Do not give up now."

12:7–13 I: God. **dearly beloved**: The people of Judah. My heritage indicates their value in God's sight. Yet Judah cries out against God. The Judge's heart bled while He punished them.

Come, assemble all the beasts of the
field,
Bring them to devour!

10 "Many rulers[a] have destroyed My
vineyard,
They have trodden My portion
underfoot;
They have made My pleasant portion
a desolate wilderness.
11 They have made it desolate;
Desolate, it mourns to Me;
The whole land is made desolate,
Because no one takes *it* to heart.
12 The plunderers have come
On all the desolate heights in the
wilderness,
For the sword of the LORD shall
devour
From *one* end of the land to the *other*
end of the land;
No flesh shall have peace.
13 They have sown wheat but reaped
thorns;
They have put themselves to pain *but*
do not profit.
But be ashamed of your harvest
Because of the fierce anger of the
LORD."

14Thus says the LORD: "Against all My
evil neighbors who touch the inheritance
which I have caused My people Israel to
inherit—behold, I will pluck them out of
their land and pluck out the house of Ju-
dah from among them. 15Then it shall be,
after I have plucked them out, that I will
return and have compassion on them and
bring them back, everyone to his heritage
and everyone to his land. 16And it shall be,
if they will learn carefully the ways of My
people, to swear by My name, 'As the
LORD lives,' as they taught My people to
swear by Bā'al, then they shall be estab-
lished in the midst of My people. 17But if
they do not obey, I will utterly pluck up
and destroy that nation," says the LORD.

CHAPTER 13

Symbol of the Linen Sash

Thus the LORD said to me: "Go and get
yourself a linen sash, and put it around
your waist, but do not put it in water." 2So
I got a sash according to the word of the
LORD, and put *it* around my waist.

3And the word of the LORD came to me
the second time, saying, 4"Take the sash
that you acquired, which *is* around your
waist, and arise, go to the Eū·phrā'tēs,[a]
and hide it there in a hole in the rock." 5So
I went and hid it by the Eū·phrā'tēs, as the
LORD commanded me.

6Now it came to pass after many days
that the LORD said to me, "Arise, go to the
Eū·phrā'tēs, and take from there the sash
which I commanded you to hide there."
7Then I went to the Eū·phrā'tēs and dug,
and I took the sash from the place where I
had hidden it; and there was the sash,
ruined. It was profitable for nothing.

8Then the word of the LORD came to me,
saying, 9"Thus says the LORD: 'In this man-
ner I will ruin the pride of Judah and the
great pride of Jerusalem. 10This evil people,
who refuse to hear My words, who follow
the dictates of their hearts, and walk after
other gods to serve them and worship
them, shall be just like this sash which is
profitable for nothing. 11For as the sash
clings to the waist of a man, so I have
caused the whole house of Israel and the
whole house of Judah to cling to Me,' says
the LORD, 'that they may become My peo-

12:10 [a]Literally *shepherds* or *pastors* 13:4 [a]Hebrew *Perath*

13:1–11 The Hebrew word here translated sash is actually the loincloth worn next to the skin. After it has rotted (v. 7), the thought of putting it on again is particularly disgusting. This expresses the Lord's feelings about Judah.

13:7 Rotting from the frequent soakings by rain, the sash was ruined.

ple, for renown, for praise, and for glory; but they would not hear.'

Symbol of the Wine Bottles

12"Therefore you shall speak to them this word: 'Thus says the LORD God of Israel: "Every bottle shall be filled with wine."' '

"And they will say to you, 'Do we not certainly know that every bottle will be filled with wine?'

13"Then you shall say to them, 'Thus says the LORD: "Behold, I will fill all the inhabitants of this land—even the kings who sit on David's throne, the priests, the prophets, and all the inhabitants of Jerusalem—with drunkenness!
14And I will dash them one against another, even the fathers and the sons together," says the LORD. "I will not pity nor spare nor have mercy, but will destroy them."' ' "

Pride Precedes Captivity

15 Hear and give ear:
Do not be proud,
For the LORD has spoken.
16 Give glory to the LORD your God
Before He causes darkness,
And before your feet stumble
On the dark mountains,
And while you are looking for light,
He turns it into the shadow of death
And makes *it* dense darkness.
17 But if you will not hear it,
My soul will weep in secret for *your* pride;
My eyes will weep bitterly
And run down with tears,
Because the LORD's flock has been taken captive.

18 Say to the king and to the queen mother,
"Humble yourselves;
Sit down,
For your rule shall collapse, the crown of your glory."
19 The cities of the South shall be shut up,
And no one shall open *them;*
Judah shall be carried away captive, all of it;
It shall be wholly carried away captive.

20 Lift up your eyes and see
Those who come from the north.
Where *is* the flock *that* was given to you,
Your beautiful sheep?
21 What will you say when He punishes you?
For you have taught them
To be chieftains, to be head over you.
Will not pangs seize you,
Like a woman in labor?
22 And if you say in your heart,
"Why have these things come upon me?"
For the greatness of your iniquity
Your skirts have been uncovered,
Your heels made bare.
23 Can the Ethiopian change his skin or the leopard its spots?
Then may you also do good who are accustomed to do evil.

24 "Therefore I will scatter them like stubble
That passes away by the wind of the wilderness.
25 This is your lot,
The portion of your measures from Me," says the LORD,
"Because you have forgotten Me
And trusted in falsehood.
26 Therefore I will uncover your skirts over your face,
That your shame may appear.

13:12–14 Another object lesson. A clay **bottle . . . filled with wine** was displayed. The curious bystanders were told that Judah's judgment would destroy them as surely as drunkenness.

27 I have seen your adulteries
And your *lustful* neighings,
The lewdness of your harlotry,
Your abominations on the hills in the fields.
Woe to you, O Jerusalem!
Will you still not be made clean?"

CHAPTER 14

Sword, Famine, and Pestilence

The word of the LORD that came to Jer·e·mī'ah concerning the droughts.

2 "Judah mourns,
And her gates languish;
They mourn for the land,
And the cry of Jerusalem has gone up.
3 Their nobles have sent their lads for water;
They went to the cisterns *and* found no water.
They returned with their vessels empty;
They were ashamed and confounded
And covered their heads.
4 Because the ground is parched,
For there was no rain in the land,
The plowmen were ashamed;
They covered their heads.
5 Yes, the deer also gave birth in the field,
But left because there was no grass.
6 And the wild donkeys stood in the desolate heights;
They sniffed at the wind like jackals;
Their eyes failed because *there was* no grass."

7 O LORD, though our iniquities testify against us,
Do it for Your name's sake;
For our backslidings are many,
We have sinned against You.
8 O the Hope of Israel, his Savior in time of trouble,
Why should You be like a stranger in the land,
And like a traveler *who* turns aside to tarry for a night?
9 Why should You be like a man astonished,
Like a mighty one *who* cannot save?
Yet You, O LORD, *are* in our midst,
And we are called by Your name;
Do not leave us!

10Thus says the LORD to this people:

"Thus they have loved to wander;
They have not restrained their feet.
Therefore the LORD does not accept them;
He will remember their iniquity now,
And punish their sins."

11Then the LORD said to me, "Do not
pray for this people, for *their* good. 12When
they fast, I will not hear their cry; and
when they offer burnt offering and grain
offering, I will not accept them. But I will
consume them by the sword, by the
famine, and by the pestilence."
13Then I said, "Ah, Lord GOD! Behold,
the prophets say to them, 'You shall not see
the sword, nor shall you have famine, but I
will give you assured peace in this place.' "
14And the LORD said to me, "The
prophets prophesy lies in My name. I have

14:11, 12 For the third time, the Lord told Jeremiah not to pray for the people. They were stubbornly committed to their own sinful ways.

14:13–16 Other prophets were strongly supporting the cause of peace. Jeremiah asks why he should not do the same? For the first time, the Lord clearly exposed the falsehoods of the other prophets: (1) they had no commission from the Lord; (2) they were using pagan divination; and (3) their message sprang from the deceit of their heart. These prophets would be punished the same as the wicked people.

not sent them, commanded them, nor spo-
ken to them; they prophesy to you a false
vision, divination, a worthless thing, and
the deceit of their heart. 15Therefore thus
says the LORD concerning the prophets
who prophesy in My name, whom I did
not send, and who say, 'Sword and famine
shall not be in this land'—'By sword and
famine those prophets shall be consumed!
16And the people to whom they prophesy
shall be cast out in the streets of Jerusalem
because of the famine and the sword; they
will have no one to bury them—them nor
their wives, their sons nor their daugh-
ters—for I will pour their wickedness on
them.'

17"Therefore you shall say this word to
them:

'Let my eyes flow with tears night and day,
And let them not cease;
For the virgin daughter of my people
Has been broken with a mighty stroke, with a very severe blow.
18 If I go out to the field,
Then behold, those slain with the sword!
And if I enter the city,
Then behold, those sick from famine!
Yes, both prophet and priest go about in a land they do not know.' "

The People Plead for Mercy

19 Have You utterly rejected Judah?
Has Your soul loathed Zion?
Why have You stricken us so that *there is* no healing for us?
We looked for peace, but *there was* no good;
And for the time of healing, and there was trouble.
20 We acknowledge, O LORD, our wickedness
And the iniquity of our fathers,
For we have sinned against You.
21 Do not abhor *us*, for Your name's sake;
Do not disgrace the throne of Your glory.
Remember, do not break Your covenant with us.
22 Are there any among the idols of the nations that can cause rain?
Or can the heavens give showers?
Are You not He, O LORD our God?
Therefore we will wait for You,
Since You have made all these.

CHAPTER 15

The LORD Will Not Relent

Then the LORD said to me, "*Even* if Mo-
ses and Samuel stood before Me, My mind
would not *be* favorable toward this people.
Cast *them* out of My sight, and let them go
forth. 2And it shall be, if they say to you,
'Where should we go?' then you shall tell
them, 'Thus says the LORD:

"Such as *are* for death, to death;
And such as *are* for the sword, to the sword;
And such as *are* for the famine, to the famine;
And such as *are* for the captivity, to the captivity." '

3"And I will appoint over them four
forms *of destruction*," says the LORD: "the
sword to slay, the dogs to drag, the birds of
the heavens and the beasts of the earth to
devour and destroy. 4I will hand them over
to trouble, to all kingdoms of the earth,
because of Ma·nas'seh the son of Hez-
e·kī'ah, king of Judah, for what he did in
Jerusalem.

5 "For who will have pity on you, O Jerusalem?
Or who will bemoan you?

15:3 The **four forms of destruction** were typical of battles in those times. Scavengers feasted on the dead bodies.

Or who will turn aside to ask how
you are doing?
6 You have forsaken Me," says the
LORD,
"You have gone backward.
Therefore I will stretch out My hand
against you and destroy you;
I am weary of relenting!
7 And I will winnow them with a
winnowing fan in the gates of the
land;
I will bereave *them* of children;
I will destroy My people,
Since they do not return from their
ways.
8 Their widows will be increased to Me
more than the sand of the seas;
I will bring against them,
Against the mother of the young
men,
A plunderer at noonday;
I will cause anguish and terror to fall
on them suddenly.

9 "She languishes who has borne
seven;
She has breathed her last;
Her sun has gone down
While *it was* yet day;
She has been ashamed and
confounded.
And the remnant of them I will
deliver to the sword
Before their enemies," says the LORD.

Jeremiah's Dejection

10 Woe is me, my mother,
That you have borne me,
A man of strife and a man of
contention to the whole earth!
I have neither lent for interest,
Nor have men lent to me for interest.
Every one of them curses me.

11 The LORD said:

"Surely it will be well with your
remnant;
Surely I will cause the enemy to
intercede with you
In the time of adversity and in the
time of affliction.
12 Can anyone break iron,
The northern iron and the bronze?
13 Your wealth and your treasures
I will give as plunder without price,
Because of all your sins,
Throughout your territories.
14 And I will make *you* cross over with[a]
your enemies
Into a land *which* you do not know;
For a fire is kindled in My anger,
Which shall burn upon you."

15 O LORD, You know;
Remember me and visit me,
And take vengeance for me on my
persecutors.
In Your enduring patience, do not
take me away.
Know that for Your sake I have
suffered rebuke.
16 Your words were found, and I ate
them,
And Your word was to me the joy
and rejoicing of my heart;
For I am called by Your name,
O LORD God of hosts.
17 I did not sit in the assembly of the
mockers,
Nor did I rejoice;
I sat alone because of Your hand,
For You have filled me with
indignation.

15:14 [a]Following Masoretic Text and Vulgate; Septuagint, Syriac, and Targum read *cause you to serve* (compare 17:4).

15:11–14 The Lord confirms that destruction will not be total; there will be a **remnant**.
15:15–18 This is one of the most pain-filled of Jeremiah's prayers; he had hit bottom. Faith and doubt wrestled for control.
15:15, 16 called by Your name: Jeremiah belonged to the Lord and to no other.

18 Why is my pain perpetual
And my wound incurable,
Which refuses to be healed?
Will You surely be to me like an
unreliable stream,
As waters *that* fail?

The LORD Reassures Jeremiah

[19]Therefore thus says the LORD:

"If you return,
Then I will bring you back;
You shall stand before Me;
If you take out the precious from the
vile,
You shall be as My mouth.
Let them return to you,
But you must not return to them.
20 And I will make you to this people a
fortified bronze wall;
And they will fight against you,
But they shall not prevail against you;
For I *am* with you to save you
And deliver you," says the LORD.
21 "I will deliver you from the hand of
the wicked,
And I will redeem you from the grip
of the terrible."

CHAPTER 16

Jeremiah's Life-Style and Message

The word of the LORD also came to me,
saying, [2]"You shall not take a wife, nor
shall you have sons or daughters in this
place." [3]For thus says the LORD concerning
the sons and daughters who are born in
this place, and concerning their mothers
who bore them and their fathers who be-
got them in this land: [4]"They shall die
gruesome deaths; they shall not be la-
mented nor shall they be buried, *but* they
shall be like refuse on the face of the earth.
They shall be consumed by the sword and
by famine, and their corpses shall be meat
for the birds of heaven and for the beasts of
the earth."

[5]For thus says the LORD: "Do not enter
the house of mourning, nor go to lament or
bemoan them; for I have taken away My
peace from this people," says the LORD,
"lovingkindness and mercies. [6]Both the
great and the small shall die in this land.
They shall not be buried; neither shall men
lament for them, cut themselves, nor make
themselves bald for them. [7]Nor shall *men*
break *bread* in mourning for them, to com-
fort them for the dead; nor shall *men* give
them the cup of consolation to drink for
their father or their mother. [8]Also you shall
not go into the house of feasting to sit with
them, to eat and drink."

[9]For thus says the LORD of hosts, the
God of Israel: "Behold, I will cause to cease
from this place, before your eyes and in
your days, the voice of mirth and the voice
of gladness, the voice of the bridegroom
and the voice of the bride.

[10]"And it shall be, when you show this
people all these words, and they say to
you, 'Why has the LORD pronounced all
this great disaster against us? Or what *is*
our iniquity? Or what *is* our sin that we
have committed against the LORD our
God?' [11]then you shall say to them, 'Be-
cause your fathers have forsaken Me,' says
the LORD; 'they have walked after other
gods and have served them and wor-
shiped them, and have forsaken Me and
not kept My law. [12]And you have done

15:18 Jeremiah's tolerance of inner pain was exhausted; he accused the Lord of being an unreliable stream and waters that fail.

15:20, 21 I am with you: When we have failed, God must confront us (v. 19), but He will also encourage us.

16:1–9 The prophet's lifestyle is made an object lesson to Judah. It would be better not to bring children into the world, so they would not experience those tragedies.

16:6, 7 There would be so many deaths that the normal expressions of grieving would be impossible.

worse than your fathers, for behold, each one follows the dictates of his own evil heart, so that no one listens to Me. 13Therefore I will cast you out of this land into a land that you do not know, neither you nor your fathers; and there you shall serve other gods day and night, where I will not show you favor.'

God Will Restore Israel

14"Therefore behold, the days are coming," says the LORD, "that it shall no more be said, 'The LORD lives who brought up the children of Israel from the land of Egypt,' 15but, 'The LORD lives who brought up the children of Israel from the land of the north and from all the lands where He had driven them.' For I will bring them back into their land which I gave to their fathers.

16"Behold, I will send for many fishermen," says the LORD, "and they shall fish them; and afterward I will send for many hunters, and they shall hunt them from every mountain and every hill, and out of the holes of the rocks. 17For My eyes *are* on all their ways; they are not hidden from My face, nor is their iniquity hidden from My eyes. 18And first I will repay double for their iniquity and their sin, because they have defiled My land; they have filled My inheritance with the carcasses of their detestable and abominable idols."

19 O LORD, my strength and my fortress,
My refuge in the day of affliction,
The Gentiles shall come to You
From the ends of the earth and say,
"Surely our fathers have inherited lies,
Worthlessness and unprofitable
things."
20 Will a man make gods for himself,
Which *are* not gods?
21 "Therefore behold, I will this once
cause them to know,
I will cause them to know
My hand and My might;
And they shall know that My name *is*
the LORD.

CHAPTER 17

Judah's Sin and Punishment

"The sin of Judah *is* written with a pen
of iron;
With the point of a diamond *it is*
engraved
On the tablet of their heart,
And on the horns of your altars,
2 While their children remember
Their altars and their wooden images[a]
By the green trees on the high hills.
3 O My mountain in the field,
I will give as plunder your wealth, all
your treasures,
And your high places of sin within all
your borders.
4 And you, even yourself,
Shall let go of your heritage which I
gave you;
And I will cause you to serve your
enemies
In the land which you do not know;
For you have kindled a fire in My
anger *which* shall burn forever."

5Thus says the LORD:

"Cursed *is* the man who trusts in man
And makes flesh his strength,
Whose heart departs from the LORD.
6 For he shall be like a shrub in the
desert,
And shall not see when good comes,

17:2 [a]Hebrew *Asherim,* Canaanite deities

17:1 pen of iron: A chisel. The evil inscription on their hearts would mock the worshipers when they pretended to worship God.

But shall inhabit the parched places in
the wilderness,
In a salt land *which is* not inhabited.

7 "Blessed *is* the man who trusts in the
LORD,
And whose hope is the LORD.
8 For he shall be like a tree planted by
the waters,
Which spreads out its roots by the
river,
And will not fear[a] when heat comes;
But its leaf will be green,
And will not be anxious in the year of
drought,
Nor will cease from yielding fruit.

9 "The heart *is* deceitful above all *things,*
And desperately wicked;
Who can know it?
10 I, the LORD, search the heart,
I test the mind,
Even to give every man according to
his ways,
According to the fruit of his doings.

11 "*As* a partridge that broods but does
not hatch,
So is he who gets riches, but not by
right;
It will leave him in the midst of his
days,
And at his end he will be a fool."

12 A glorious high throne from the
beginning
Is the place of our sanctuary.
13 O LORD, the hope of Israel,
All who forsake You shall be
ashamed.

17:8 [a]Qere and Targum read *see.*

"Those who depart from Me
Shall be written in the earth,
Because they have forsaken the LORD,
The fountain of living waters."

Jeremiah Prays for Deliverance

14 Heal me, O LORD, and I shall be
healed;
Save me, and I shall be saved,
For You *are* my praise.
15 Indeed they say to me,
"Where *is* the word of the LORD?
Let it come now!"
16 As for me, I have not hurried away
from *being* a shepherd *who* follows
You,
Nor have I desired the woeful day;
You know what came out of my lips;
It was right there before You.
17 Do not be a terror to me;
You *are* my hope in the day of doom.
18 Let them be ashamed who persecute
me,
But do not let me be put to shame;
Let them be dismayed,
But do not let me be dismayed.
Bring on them the day of doom,
And destroy them with double
destruction!

Hallow the Sabbath Day

19Thus the LORD said to me: "Go and
stand in the gate of the children of the peo-
ple, by which the kings of Judah come in
and by which they go out, and in all the
gates of Jerusalem; 20and say to them,
'Hear the word of the LORD, you kings of
Judah, and all Judah, and all the inhab-
itants of Jerusalem, who enter by these
gates. 21Thus says the LORD: "Take heed to
yourselves, and bear no burden on the

17:9 A key verse. Humanity is totally depraved; there is no spark of goodness innate in us. Any goodness that may exist is given by God's grace.

17:12, 13 Israel's only hope is to find sanctuary in obedience to God's glorious high throne, His eternal rule. To do otherwise is to forsake life and to choose shame and death. **Written in the earth** seems to mean that apart from God we have no hope beyond this earthly life.

Sabbath day, nor bring *it* in by the gates of Jerusalem; [22]nor carry a burden out of your houses on the Sabbath day, nor do any work, but hallow the Sabbath day, as I commanded your fathers. [23]But they did not obey nor incline their ear, but made their neck stiff, that they might not hear nor receive instruction.

[24]"And it shall be, if you heed Me carefully," says the LORD, "to bring no burden through the gates of this city on the Sabbath day, but hallow the Sabbath day, to do no work in it, [25]then shall enter the gates of this city kings and princes sitting on the throne of David, riding in chariots and on horses, they and their princes, accompanied by the men of Judah and the inhabitants of Jerusalem; and this city shall remain forever. [26]And they shall come from the cities of Judah and from the places around Jerusalem, from the land of Benjamin and from the lowland, from the mountains and from the South, bringing burnt offerings and sacrifices, grain offerings and incense, bringing sacrifices of praise to the house of the LORD.

[27]"But if you will not heed Me to hallow the Sabbath day, such as not carrying a burden when entering the gates of Jerusalem on the Sabbath day, then I will kindle a fire in its gates, and it shall devour the palaces of Jerusalem, and it shall not be quenched." ' "

CHAPTER 18

The Potter and the Clay

The word which came to Jer·e·mī'ah from the LORD, saying: [2]"Arise and go down to the potter's house, and there I will cause you to hear My words." [3]Then I went down to the potter's house, and there he was, making something at the wheel. [4]And the vessel that he made of clay was marred in the hand of the potter; so he made it again into another vessel, as it seemed good to the potter to make.

[5]Then the word of the LORD came to me, saying: [6]"O house of Israel, can I not do with you as this potter?" says the LORD. "Look, as the clay *is* in the potter's hand, so *are* you in My hand, O house of Israel! [7]The instant I speak concerning a nation and concerning a kingdom, to pluck up, to pull down, and to destroy *it,* [8]if that nation against whom I have spoken turns from its evil, I will relent of the disaster that I thought to bring upon it. [9]And the instant I speak concerning a nation and concerning a kingdom, to build and to plant *it,* [10]if it does evil in My sight so that it does not obey My voice, then I will relent concerning the good with which I said I would benefit it.

[11]"Now therefore, speak to the men of Judah and to the inhabitants of Jerusalem, saying, 'Thus says the LORD: "Behold, I am fashioning a disaster and devising a plan against you. Return now every one from his evil way, and make your ways and your doings good." ' "

God's Warning Rejected

[12]And they said, "That is hopeless! So we will walk according to our own plans, and we will every one obey the dictates of his evil heart."

[13]Therefore thus says the LORD:

"Ask now among the Gentiles,
Who has heard such things?
The virgin of Israel has done a very
horrible thing.
14 Will *a man* leave the snow water of
Lebanon,
Which comes from the rock of the
field?
Will the cold flowing waters be
forsaken for strange waters?

17:23 made their neck stiff: Rebelled.
18:1–3 The Lord uses the potter to teach Jeremiah a profound lesson about His sovereignty and His right to discipline Judah until she conformed to His plan.

Surrender to the Master Potter

Dale Evans Rogers

Have you ever asked yourself, "Why should I turn over control of my life to God?"

Strong-willed and determined people like me feel we must be in charge. We are not going to let anyone else run our lives, unless, of course, we run into a brick wall and discover we are at a potential dead end and need help.

"We have to be humble before God and know that only He can make our lives really count."

Does that describe you? Surveys reveal that more people than ever are determined to be the masters of their fate. That is true even among Christians who have attended church regularly for years.

God recognized this tendency in man and spoke to the prophet Jeremiah about it some five hundred years before the birth of Christ. First God told Jeremiah to go to a potter's house. The potter was a key artisan in ancient villages. He or she shaped what people wrote on; stored food, water, and wine in; and ate and drank from. Of course, not all potters were equally skilled, but all had a measure of control over the lump of clay in their hands.

Unfortunately, having an onlooker must have rattled the potter, for the object he was making did not turn out right. So he reworked the clay and shaped it into another vessel. Jeremiah uses a key phrase to describe that process: "So he made it again into another vessel, as it seemed good to the potter to make" (Jer. 18:4).

That description sets the stage for God's words: " 'O house of Israel, can I not do with you as this potter?' says the Lord. 'Look, as the clay *is* in the potter's hand, so *are* you in My hand, O house of Israel!' " (v. 6)

The idea of our being clay and God's being the Master Potter shows up in New Testament writings as well. The apostle Paul made clear reference to it in his letter to the Romans: "But indeed, O man, who are you to reply against God? . . . Does not the potter have power over the clay, from the same lump to make one vessel for honor and another for dishonor?" (9:20, 21).

Recognizing the right of the Master Potter to shape our lives according to His design is a humbling experience. We have to be humble before God, know that He is God, and know that only He can make our lives really count for His glory before we will be willing to accept His shaping. For Christians, it means accepting our weakness, our earthiness, our mistakes, and letting the Master Potter have His way, tough as it may sometimes seem.

15 "Because My people have forgotten
Me,
They have burned incense to
worthless idols.
And they have caused themselves to
stumble in their ways,
From the ancient paths,
To walk in pathways and not on a
highway,
16 To make their land desolate *and* a
perpetual hissing;
Everyone who passes by it will be
astonished
And shake his head.
17 I will scatter them as with an east
wind before the enemy;
I will show them[a] the back and not
the face
In the day of their calamity."

Jeremiah Persecuted

18Then they said, "Come and let us de-
vise plans against Jer·e·mī′ah; for the law
shall not perish from the priest, nor coun-
sel from the wise, nor the word from the
prophet. Come and let us attack him with
the tongue, and let us not give heed to any
of his words."

19 Give heed to me, O LORD,
And listen to the voice of those who
contend with me!
20 Shall evil be repaid for good?
For they have dug a pit for my life.
Remember that I stood before You
To speak good for them,
To turn away Your wrath from them.
21 Therefore deliver up their children to
the famine,
And pour out their *blood*
By the force of the sword;
Let their wives *become* widows
And bereaved of their children.
Let their men be put to death,
Their young men *be* slain
By the sword in battle.
22 Let a cry be heard from their houses,
When You bring a troop suddenly
upon them;
For they have dug a pit to take me,
And hidden snares for my feet.
23 Yet, LORD, You know all their counsel
Which is against me, to slay *me*.
Provide no atonement for their
iniquity,
Nor blot out their sin from Your sight;
But let them be overthrown before
You.
Deal *thus* with them
In the time of Your anger.

CHAPTER 19

The Sign of the Broken Flask

Thus says the LORD: "Go and get a pot-
ter's earthen flask, and *take* some of the el-
ders of the people and some of the elders
of the priests. 2And go out to the Valley of
the Son of Hin′nom, which *is* by the entry
of the Potsherd Gate; and proclaim there
the words that I will tell you, 3and say,
'Hear the word of the LORD, O kings of Ju-
dah and inhabitants of Jerusalem. Thus
says the LORD of hosts, the God of Israel:
"Behold, I will bring such a catastrophe on
this place, that whoever hears of it, his ears
will tingle.
4"Because they have forsaken Me and
made this an alien place, because they
have burned incense in it to other gods
whom neither they, their fathers, nor the
kings of Judah have known, and have

18:17 [a]Following Septuagint, Syriac, Targum, and Vulgate; Masoretic Text reads *look them in.*

18:19–23 Jeremiah's prayer reveals he was frightened and frustrated. He had sought to do good and lead his people to repentance. When they refused, he demanded that the Lord administer justice severely and immediately.

19:3–5 The flask was to represent Jerusalem, and its smashing (v. 10) the destruction of the city. The reasons for the destruction given in vv. 4, 5 would not be new to Jerusalem's people (7:30, 31).

filled this place with the blood of the innocents 5(they have also built the high places of Bā'al, to burn their sons with fire *for* burnt offerings to Bā'al, which I did not command or speak, nor did it come into My mind), 6therefore behold, the days are coming," says the LORD, "that this place shall no more be called Tō'phet or the Valley of the Son of Hin'nom, but the Valley of Slaughter. 7And I will make void the counsel of Judah and Jerusalem in this place, and I will cause them to fall by the sword before their enemies and by the hands of those who seek their lives; their corpses I will give as meat for the birds of the heaven and for the beasts of the earth. 8I will make this city desolate and a hissing; everyone who passes by it will be astonished and hiss because of all its plagues. 9And I will cause them to eat the flesh of their sons and the flesh of their daughters, and everyone shall eat the flesh of his friend in the siege and in the desperation with which their enemies and those who seek their lives shall drive them to despair." '

10"Then you shall break the flask in the sight of the men who go with you, 11and say to them, 'Thus says the LORD of hosts: "Even so I will break this people and this city, as *one* breaks a potter's vessel, which cannot be made whole again; and they shall bury *them* in Tō'phet till *there is* no place to bury. 12Thus I will do to this place," says the LORD, "and to its inhabitants, and make this city like Tō'phet. 13And the houses of Jerusalem and the houses of the kings of Judah shall be defiled like the place of Tō'phet, because of all the houses on whose roofs they have burned incense to all the host of heaven, and poured out drink offerings to other gods." ' "

14Then Jer·e·mī'ah came from Tō'phet, where the LORD had sent him to prophesy; and he stood in the court of the Lord's house and said to all the people, 15"Thus says the LORD of hosts, the God of Israel: 'Behold, I will bring on this city and on all her towns all the doom that I have pronounced against it, because they have stiffened their necks that they might not hear My words.' "

CHAPTER 20

The Word of God to Pashhur

Now Pash'hur the son of Im'mer, the priest who *was* also chief governor in the house of the LORD, heard that Jer·e·mī'ah prophesied these things. 2Then Pash'hur struck Jer·e·mī'ah the prophet, and put him in the stocks that *were* in the high gate of Benjamin, which *was* by the house of the LORD.

3And it happened on the next day that Pash'hur brought Jer·e·mī'ah out of the stocks. Then Jer·e·mī'ah said to him, "The LORD has not called your name Pash'hur, but Mā'gor-Mis·sā'bib.[a] 4For thus says the LORD: 'Behold, I will make you a terror to yourself and to all your friends; and they shall fall by the sword of their enemies, and your eyes shall see *it*. I will give all Judah into the hand of the king of Babylon, and he shall carry them captive to Babylon and slay them with the sword. 5Moreover I will deliver all the wealth of this city, all its produce, and all its precious things; all the treasures of the kings of Judah I will give into the hand of their enemies, who will plunder them, seize them, and carry them to Babylon. 6And you, Pash'hur, and all who dwell in your house, shall go into captivity. You shall go to Babylon, and there you shall die, and be buried there, you and all your friends, to whom you have prophesied lies.' "

20:3 [a]Literally *Fear on Every Side*

20:2 stocks: His hands and feet were bound in a restraining device in the prison.

Jeremiah's Unpopular Ministry

7 O LORD, You induced me, and I was persuaded;
You are stronger than I, and have prevailed.
I am in derision daily;
Everyone mocks me.
8 For when I spoke, I cried out;
I shouted, "Violence and plunder!"
Because the word of the LORD was made to me
A reproach and a derision daily.
9 Then I said, "I will not make mention of Him,
Nor speak anymore in His name."
But *His word* was in my heart like a burning fire
Shut up in my bones;
I was weary of holding *it* back,
And I could not.
10 For I heard many mocking:
"Fear on every side!"
"Report," *they say,* "and we will report it!"
All my acquaintances watched for my stumbling, *saying,*
"Perhaps he can be induced;
Then we will prevail against him,
And we will take our revenge on him."

11 But the LORD *is* with me as a mighty, awesome One.
Therefore my persecutors will stumble, and will not prevail.
They will be greatly ashamed, for they will not prosper.
Their everlasting confusion will never be forgotten.
12 But, O LORD of hosts,
You who test the righteous,
And see the mind and heart,
Let me see Your vengeance on them;
For I have pleaded my cause before You.

13 Sing to the LORD! Praise the LORD!
For He has delivered the life of the poor
From the hand of evildoers.

14 Cursed *be* the day in which I was born!
Let the day not be blessed in which my mother bore me!
15 Let the man *be* cursed
Who brought news to my father, saying,
"A male child has been born to you!"
Making him very glad.
16 And let that man be like the cities
Which the LORD overthrew, and did not relent;
Let him hear the cry in the morning
And the shouting at noon,
17 Because he did not kill me from the womb,
That my mother might have been my grave,
And her womb always enlarged *with me.*
18 Why did I come forth from the womb to see labor and sorrow,
That my days should be consumed with shame?

CHAPTER 21

Jerusalem's Doom Is Sealed

The word which came to Jer·e·mī′ah
from the LORD when King Zed·e·kī′ah sent
to him Pash′hur the son of Mel·chī′ah, and

20:10 The people were throwing back at him his message of fear on every side. Because Jeremiah had said Judah would fall to Babylon, he was considered a traitor, although he had not said anything overtly traitorous.

20:11–13 Sing to the LORD (v. 13): This swing from despair to faith is similar to prayers in Ps. 6; 10. The prophets were fully human, subject to the same emotions, and shifts of emotion, as the rest of us.

Zeph·a·nī′ah the son of Mā·a·sēi′ah, the
priest, saying, 2"Please inquire of the LORD
for us, for Ne·bū·chad·nez′zar[a] king of
Babylon makes war against us. Perhaps
the LORD will deal with us according to all
His wonderful works, that *the king* may go
away from us."

3Then Jer·e·mī′ah said to them, "Thus
you shall say to Zed·e·kī′ah, 4'Thus says
the LORD God of Israel: "Behold, I will turn
back the weapons of war that *are* in your
hands, with which you fight against the
king of Babylon and the Chal·dē′ans[a] who
besiege you outside the walls; and I will
assemble them in the midst of this city. 5I
Myself will fight against you with an out-
stretched hand and with a strong arm,
even in anger and fury and great wrath. 6I
will strike the inhabitants of this city, both
man and beast; they shall die of a great
pestilence. 7And afterward," says the
LORD, "I will deliver Zed·e·kī′ah king of
Judah, his servants and the people, and
such as are left in this city from the pesti-
lence and the sword and the famine, into
the hand of Ne·bū·chad·nez′zar king of
Babylon, into the hand of their enemies,
and into the hand of those who seek their
life; and he shall strike them with the edge
of the sword. He shall not spare them, or
have pity or mercy." '

8"Now you shall say to this people,
'Thus says the LORD: "Behold, I set before
you the way of life and the way of death.
9He who remains in this city shall die by
the sword, by famine, and by pestilence;
but he who goes out and defects to the
Chal·dē′ans who besiege you, he shall live,
and his life shall be as a prize to him. 10For
I have set My face against this city for ad-
versity and not for good," says the LORD.
"It shall be given into the hand of the king
of Babylon, and he shall burn it with fire." '

21:2 [a]Hebrew *Nebuchadrezzar,* and so elsewhere
21:4 [a]Or *Babylonians*

Message to the House of David

11"And concerning the house of the king
of Judah, *say,* 'Hear the word of the LORD,
12O house of David! Thus says the LORD:

"Execute judgment in the morning;
And deliver *him who is* plundered
Out of the hand of the oppressor,
Lest My fury go forth like fire
And burn so that no one can quench
it,
Because of the evil of your doings.

13 "Behold, I *am* against you,
O inhabitant of the valley,
And rock of the plain," says the LORD,
"Who say, 'Who shall come down
against us?
Or who shall enter our dwellings?'
14 But I will punish you according to the
fruit of your doings," says the
LORD;
"I will kindle a fire in its forest,
And it shall devour all things around
it." ' "

CHAPTER 22

Thus says the LORD: "Go down to the
house of the king of Judah, and there speak
this word, 2and say, 'Hear the word of the
LORD, O king of Judah, you who sit on the
throne of David, you and your servants
and your people who enter these gates!
3Thus says the LORD: "Execute judgment
and righteousness, and deliver the plun-
dered out of the hand of the oppressor.
Do no wrong and do no violence to the
stranger, the fatherless, or the widow, nor
shed innocent blood in this place. 4For if
you indeed do this thing, then shall enter
the gates of this house, riding on horses
and in chariots, accompanied by servants
and people, kings who sit on the throne of
David. 5But if you will not hear these

21:13, 14 rock of the plain may be a sarcastic reference to Jerusalem's tendency to rely on its location on a hill for protection from enemies.

words, I swear by Myself," says the LORD, "that this house shall become a desolation." ' "

6For thus says the LORD to the house of the king of Judah:

"You *are* Gil'ē·ad to Me,
The head of Lebanon;
Yet I surely will make you a wilderness,
Cities *which* are not inhabited.
7 I will prepare destroyers against you,
Everyone with his weapons;
They shall cut down your choice cedars
And cast *them* into the fire.

8And many nations will pass by this city; and everyone will say to his neighbor, 'Why has the LORD done so to this great city?' 9Then they will answer, 'Because they have forsaken the covenant of the LORD their God, and worshiped other gods and served them.' "

10 Weep not for the dead, nor bemoan him;
Weep bitterly for him who goes away,
For he shall return no more,
Nor see his native country.

Message to the Sons of Josiah

11For thus says the LORD concerning
Shal'lum[a] the son of Jō·sī'ah, king of Ju-
dah, who reigned instead of Jō·sī'ah his
father, who went from this place: "He shall
not return here anymore, 12but he shall die
in the place where they have led him cap-
tive, and shall see this land no more.

13 "Woe to him who builds his house by unrighteousness
And his chambers by injustice,
Who uses his neighbor's service without wages
And gives him nothing for his work,
14 Who says, 'I will build myself a wide house with spacious chambers,
And cut out windows for it,
Paneling *it* with cedar
And painting *it* with vermilion.'

15 "Shall you reign because you enclose *yourself* in cedar?
Did not your father eat and drink,
And do justice and righteousness?
Then *it was* well with him.
16 He judged the cause of the poor and needy;
Then *it was* well.
Was not this knowing Me?" says the LORD.
17 "Yet your eyes and your heart *are* for nothing but your covetousness,
For shedding innocent blood,
And practicing oppression and violence."

18Therefore thus says the LORD concerning Je·hoi'a·kim the son of Jō·sī'ah, king of Judah:

"They shall not lament for him,
Saying, 'Alas, my brother!' or 'Alas, my sister!'
They shall not lament for him,
Saying, 'Alas, master!' or 'Alas, his glory!'
19 He shall be buried with the burial of a donkey,
Dragged and cast out beyond the gates of Jerusalem.

20 "Go up to Lebanon, and cry out,
And lift up your voice in Bā'shan;

22:11 [a]Also called *Jehoahaz*

22:6, 7 Gilead . . . Lebanon: Some of the choicest areas of Palestine. God had the highest regard for the royal line of Judah, yet they would be cut down.

22:15–17 The model for kingly justice and righteousness was Jehoiakim's father, King Josiah. His care of the poor and needy exemplifies knowing the Lord.

Cry from Ab′a·rim,
For all your lovers are destroyed.
21 I spoke to you in your prosperity,
But you said, 'I will not hear.'
This *has been* your manner from your youth,
That you did not obey My voice.
22 The wind shall eat up all your rulers,
And your lovers shall go into captivity;
Surely then you will be ashamed and humiliated
For all your wickedness.
23 O inhabitant of Lebanon,
Making your nest in the cedars,
How gracious will you be when pangs come upon you,
Like the pain of a woman in labor?

Message to Coniah

[24]"*As* I live," says the LORD, "though
Cō·nī′ah[a] the son of Je·hoi′a·kim, king of
Judah, were the signet on My right hand,
yet I would pluck you off; [25]and I will give
you into the hand of those who seek your
life, and into the hand *of those* whose face
you fear—the hand of Ne·bū·chad·nez′zar
king of Babylon and the hand of the
Chal·dē′ans. [26]So I will cast you out, and
your mother who bore you, into another
country where you were not born; and
there you shall die. [27]But to the land to
which they desire to return, there they
shall not return.

28 "Is this man Cō·nī′ah a despised, broken idol—
A vessel in which *is* no pleasure?
Why are they cast out, he and his descendants,
And cast into a land which they do not know?
29 O earth, earth, earth,
Hear the word of the LORD!
30 Thus says the LORD:
'Write this man down as childless,
A man *who* shall not prosper in his days;
For none of his descendants shall prosper,
Sitting on the throne of David,
And ruling anymore in Judah.' "

CHAPTER 23

The Branch of Righteousness

"Woe to the shepherds who destroy and
scatter the sheep of My pasture!" says the
LORD. [2]Therefore thus says the LORD God of
Israel against the shepherds who feed My
people: "You have scattered My flock,
driven them away, and not attended to
them. Behold, I will attend to you for the
evil of your doings," says the LORD. [3]"But I
will gather the remnant of My flock out of
all countries where I have driven them,
and bring them back to their folds; and
they shall be fruitful and increase. [4]I will
set up shepherds over them who will feed
them; and they shall fear no more, nor be
dismayed, nor shall they be lacking," says
the LORD.

5 "Behold, *the* days are coming," says the LORD,
"That I will raise to David a Branch of righteousness;
A King shall reign and prosper,
And execute judgment and righteousness in the earth.
6 In His days Judah will be saved,
And Israel will dwell safely;

22:24 [a]Also called *Jeconiah* and *Jehoiachin*

22:29, 30 Write this man down as childless: Whether Jehoiachin was personally good or bad, there was to be no reprieve from his destiny of captivity.

23:5, 6 Branch of righteousness: The expected Messiah (33:15; Zech. 3:8). His name will be **THE LORD OUR RIGHTEOUSNESS**. The name indicates that the Messiah will be the model ruler and "the good shepherd" (John 10:11).

Now this *is* His name by which He
will be called:

THE LORD OUR RIGHTEOUSNESS.[a]

7"Therefore, behold, *the* days are com-
ing," says the LORD, "that they shall no
longer say, 'As the LORD lives who brought
up the children of Israel from the land of
Egypt,' 8but, 'As the LORD lives who
brought up and led the descendants of the
house of Israel from the north country and
from all the countries where I had driven
them.' And they shall dwell in their own
land."

False Prophets and Empty Oracles

9 My heart within me is broken
Because of the prophets;
All my bones shake.
I am like a drunken man,
And like a man whom wine has
overcome,
Because of the LORD,
And because of His holy words.
10 For the land is full of adulterers;
For because of a curse the land
mourns.
The pleasant places of the wilderness
are dried up.
Their course of life is evil,
And their might *is* not right.

11 "For both prophet and priest are
profane;
Yes, in My house I have found their
wickedness," says the LORD.
12 "Therefore their way shall be to them
Like slippery *ways;*
In the darkness they shall be driven
on
And fall in them;
For I will bring disaster on them,
The year of their punishment," says
the LORD.
13 "And I have seen folly in the prophets
of Samaria:
They prophesied by Bā'al
And caused My people Israel to err.
14 Also I have seen a horrible thing in
the prophets of Jerusalem:
They commit adultery and walk in
lies;
They also strengthen the hands of
evildoers,
So that no one turns back from his
wickedness.
All of them are like Sod'om to Me,
And her inhabitants like Go·mor'rah.

15"Therefore thus says the LORD of hosts
concerning the prophets:

'Behold, I will feed them with
wormwood,
And make them drink the water of
gall;
For from the prophets of Jerusalem
Profaneness has gone out into all the
land.' "

16Thus says the LORD of hosts:

"Do not listen to the words of the
prophets who prophesy to you.
They make you worthless;
They speak a vision of their own
heart,
Not from the mouth of the LORD.
17 They continually say to those who
despise Me,

23:6 [a]Hebrew *YHWH Tsidkenu*

23:11–14 The **prophets of Jerusalem** (v. 14) are shown to be essentially the same as those of Samaria, the kingdom of northern Israel destroyed in 721 B.C. By bearing false messages of **peace** (v. 17), the prophets of Judah confirmed the people in their sinful ways (v. 14).

23:15 Profaneness: Far from promoting holiness in the land, whether they intended to or not, these religious leaders promoted unholiness.

'The LORD has said, "You shall have peace" ';
And *to* everyone who walks according to the dictates of his own heart, they say,
'No evil shall come upon you.' "

18 For who has stood in the counsel of the LORD,
And has perceived and heard His word?
Who has marked His word and heard *it?*
19 Behold, a whirlwind of the LORD has gone forth in fury—
A violent whirlwind!
It will fall violently on the head of the wicked.
20 The anger of the LORD will not turn back
Until He has executed and performed the thoughts of His heart.
In the latter days you will understand it perfectly.

21 "I have not sent these prophets, yet they ran.
I have not spoken to them, yet they prophesied.
22 But if they had stood in My counsel,
And had caused My people to hear My words,
Then they would have turned them from their evil way
And from the evil of their doings.

23 "*Am* I a God near at hand," says the LORD,
"And not a God afar off?
24 Can anyone hide himself in secret places,
So I shall not see him?" says the LORD;
"Do I not fill heaven and earth?" says the LORD.

25"I have heard what the prophets have
said who prophesy lies in My name, say-
ing, 'I have dreamed, I have dreamed!'
26How long will *this* be in the heart of the
prophets who prophesy lies? Indeed *they*
are prophets of the deceit of their own
heart, 27who try to make My people forget
My name by their dreams which everyone
tells his neighbor, as their fathers forgot
My name for Bā'al.

28 "The prophet who has a dream, let him tell a dream;
And he who has My word, let him speak My word faithfully.
What *is* the chaff to the wheat?" says the LORD.
29 "*Is* not My word like a fire?" says the LORD,
"And like a hammer *that* breaks the rock in pieces?

30"Therefore behold, I *am* against the
prophets," says the LORD, "who steal My
words every one from his neighbor. 31Be-
hold, I *am* against the prophets," says the
LORD, "who use their tongues and say, 'He
says.' 32Behold, I *am* against those who
prophesy false dreams," says the LORD,
"and tell them, and cause My people to err
by their lies and by their recklessness. Yet I
did not send them or command them;
therefore they shall not profit this people at
all," says the LORD.
33"So when these people or the prophet
or the priest ask you, saying, 'What is the
oracle of the LORD?' you shall then say to
them, 'What oracle?'[a] I will even forsake
you," says the LORD. 34"And *as for* the
prophet and the priest and the people who
say, 'The oracle of the LORD!' I will even
punish that man and his house. 35Thus

23:33 [a]Septuagint, Targum, and Vulgate read '*You are the burden.*'

23:29 The penetrating nature of God's word, revealing our human dependence on and responsibility to God, is depicted here by the images of a fire and a hammer.

every one of you shall say to his neighbor,
and every one to his brother, 'What has the
LORD answered?' and, 'What has the LORD
spoken?' 36And the oracle of the LORD you
shall mention no more. For every man's
word will be his oracle, for you have per-
verted the words of the living God, the
LORD of hosts, our God. 37Thus you shall
say to the prophet, 'What has the LORD an-
swered you?' and, 'What has the LORD spo-
ken?' 38But since you say, 'The oracle of the
LORD!' therefore thus says the LORD: 'Be-
cause you say this word, "The oracle of the
LORD!" and I have sent to you, saying, "Do
not say, 'The oracle of the LORD!' " 39there-
fore behold, I, even I, will utterly forget
you and forsake you, and the city that I
gave you and your fathers, and *will cast
you* out of My presence. 40And I will bring
an everlasting reproach upon you, and a
perpetual shame, which shall not be for-
gotten.' "

CHAPTER 24

The Sign of Two Baskets of Figs

The LORD showed me, and there were
two baskets of figs set before the temple
of the LORD, after Ne·bū·chad·nez'zar king
of Babylon had carried away captive
Jec·o·nī'ah the son of Je·hoi'a·kim, king of
Judah, and the princes of Judah with the
craftsmen and smiths, from Jerusalem, and
had brought them to Babylon. 2One basket
had very good figs, like the figs *that are* first
ripe; and the other basket *had* very bad figs
which could not be eaten, they were so
bad. 3Then the LORD said to me, "What do
you see, Jer·e·mī'ah?"

And I said, "Figs, the good figs, very
good; and the bad, very bad, which cannot
be eaten, they are so bad."

4Again the word of the LORD came to
me, saying, 5"Thus says the LORD, the God
of Israel: 'Like these good figs, so will I ac-
knowledge those who are carried away
captive from Judah, whom I have sent out
of this place for *their own* good, into the
land of the Chal·dē'ans. 6For I will set My
eyes on them for good, and I will bring
them back to this land; I will build them
and not pull *them* down, and I will plant
them and not pluck *them* up. 7Then I will
give them a heart to know Me, that I *am* the
LORD; and they shall be My people, and I
will be their God, for they shall return to
Me with their whole heart.

8'And as the bad figs which cannot be
eaten, they are so bad'—surely thus says
the LORD—'so will I give up Zed·e·kī'ah
the king of Judah, his princes, the residue
of Jerusalem who remain in this land, and
those who dwell in the land of Egypt. 9I
will deliver them to trouble into all the
kingdoms of the earth, for *their* harm, *to be*
a reproach and a byword, a taunt and a
curse, in all places where I shall drive
them. 10And I will send the sword, the
famine, and the pestilence among them, till
they are consumed from the land that I
gave to them and their fathers.' "

CHAPTER 25

Seventy Years of Desolation

The word that came to Jer·e·mī'ah con-
cerning all the people of Judah, in the
fourth year of Je·hoi'a·kim the son of
Jō·sī'ah, king of Judah (which *was* the first
year of Ne·bū·chad·nez'zar king of Bab-
ylon), 2which Jer·e·mī'ah the prophet
spoke to all the people of Judah and to all
the inhabitants of Jerusalem, saying:
3"From the thirteenth year of Jō·sī'ah the
son of Ā'mon, king of Judah, even to this
day, this *is* the twenty-third year in which
the word of the LORD has come to me; and
I have spoken to you, rising early and

24:1–10 The people who were taken into exile with Jehoiachin (Jeconiah) in 597 B.C. were evidently considered to be offscourings by those who remained in Judah. They were apparently compared to rotten figs that fell off the tree of their own accord.

speaking, but you have not listened. 4And
the LORD has sent to you all His servants
the prophets, rising early and sending
them, but you have not listened nor in-
clined your ear to hear. 5They said, 'Repent
now everyone of his evil way and his evil
doings, and dwell in the land that the LORD
has given to you and your fathers forever
and ever. 6Do not go after other gods to
serve them and worship them, and do not
provoke Me to anger with the works of
your hands; and I will not harm you.' 7Yet
you have not listened to Me," says the
LORD, "that you might provoke Me to
anger with the works of your hands to
your own hurt.

8"Therefore thus says the LORD of hosts:
'Because you have not heard My words,
9behold, I will send and take all the fami-
lies of the north,' says the LORD, 'and
Ne·bū·chad·nez'zar the king of Babylon,
My servant, and will bring them against
this land, against its inhabitants, and
against these nations all around, and will
utterly destroy them, and make them an
astonishment, a hissing, and perpetual
desolations. 10Moreover I will take from
them the voice of mirth and the voice of
gladness, the voice of the bridegroom and
the voice of the bride, the sound of the
millstones and the light of the lamp. 11And
this whole land shall be a desolation *and* an
astonishment, and these nations shall
serve the king of Babylon seventy years.

12'Then it will come to pass, when sev-
enty years are completed, *that* I will punish
the king of Babylon and that nation, the
land of the Chal·dē'ans, for their iniquity,'
says the LORD; 'and I will make it a perpet-
ual desolation. 13So I will bring on that land
all My words which I have pronounced
against it, all that is written in this book,
which Jer·e·mī'ah has prophesied con-
cerning all the nations. 14(For many nations
and great kings shall be served by them
also; and I will repay them according to
their deeds and according to the works of
their own hands.)' "

Judgment on the Nations

15For thus says the LORD God of Israel to
me: "Take this wine cup of fury from My
hand, and cause all the nations, to whom I
send you, to drink it. 16And they will drink
and stagger and go mad because of the
sword that I will send among them."

17Then I took the cup from the LORD's
hand, and made all the nations drink, to
whom the LORD had sent me: 18Jerusalem
and the cities of Judah, its kings and its
princes, to make them a desolation, an as-
tonishment, a hissing, and a curse, as *it is*
this day; 19Pharaoh king of Egypt, his ser-
vants, his princes, and all his people; 20all
the mixed multitude, all the kings of the
land of Uz, all the kings of the land of the
Phi·lis'tines (namely, Ash'ke·lon, Gā'za,
Ek'ron, and the remnant of Ash'dod);
21Ē'dom, Mō'ab, and the people of
Am'mon; 22all the kings of Tȳre, all the
kings of Sī'don, and the kings of the coast-
lands which *are* across the sea; 23Dē'dan,
Tē'ma, Buz, and all *who are* in the farthest
corners; 24all the kings of Arabia and all the
kings of the mixed multitude who dwell in
the desert; 25all the kings of Zim'rī, all the
kings of Ē'lam, and all the kings of the
Mēdes; 26all the kings of the north, far and
near, one with another; and all the king-
doms of the world which *are* on the face of
the earth. Also the king of Shē'shach[a] shall
drink after them.

25:26 [a]A code word for Babylon (compare 51:41)

25:8–11 My servant: Though Nebuchadnezzar worshiped idols, the Lord had selected him as His instrument to carry out the decreed judgment. This is the first prophecy that the Exile would last seventy years.

25:12–14 At the end of the allotted time, God would punish the king of Babylon and his nation.

[27]"Therefore you shall say to them,
'Thus says the LORD of hosts, the God of Is-
rael: "Drink, be drunk, and vomit! Fall and
rise no more, because of the sword which I
will send among you." ' [28]And it shall be, if
they refuse to take the cup from your hand
to drink, then you shall say to them, 'Thus
says the LORD of hosts: "You shall certainly
drink! [29]For behold, I begin to bring
calamity on the city which is called by My
name, and should you be utterly unpun-
ished? You shall not be unpunished, for I
will call for a sword on all the inhabitants
of the earth," says the LORD of hosts.'
[30]"Therefore prophesy against them all
these words, and say to them:

'The LORD will roar from on high,
And utter His voice from His holy habitation;
He will roar mightily against His fold.
He will give a shout, as those who tread *the grapes*,
Against all the inhabitants of the earth.
31 A noise will come to the ends of the earth—
For the LORD has a controversy with the nations;
He will plead His case with all flesh.
He will give those *who are* wicked to the sword,' says the LORD."

[32]Thus says the LORD of hosts:

"Behold, disaster shall go forth
From nation to nation,
And a great whirlwind shall be raised up
From the farthest parts of the earth.

[33]"And at that day the slain of the LORD
shall be from *one* end of the earth even to
the *other* end of the earth. They shall not be
lamented, or gathered, or buried; they
shall become refuse on the ground.

34 "Wail, shepherds, and cry!
Roll about *in the ashes*,
You leaders of the flock!
For the days of your slaughter and your dispersions are fulfilled;
You shall fall like a precious vessel.
35 And the shepherds will have no way to flee,
Nor the leaders of the flock to escape.
36 A voice of the cry of the shepherds,
And a wailing of the leaders to the flock *will be heard*.
For the LORD has plundered their pasture,
37 And the peaceful dwellings are cut down
Because of the fierce anger of the LORD.
38 He has left His lair like the lion;
For their land is desolate
Because of the fierceness of the Oppressor,
And because of His fierce anger."

CHAPTER 26

Jeremiah Saved from Death

In the beginning of the reign of
Je·hoi'a·kim the son of Jō·sī'ah, king of Ju-
dah, this word came from the LORD, say-
ing, [2]"Thus says the LORD: 'Stand in the
court of the LORD's house, and speak to all
the cities of Judah, which come to worship
in the LORD's house, all the words that I
command you to speak to them. Do not di-
minish a word. [3]Perhaps everyone will lis-
ten and turn from his evil way, that I may
relent concerning the calamity which I
purpose to bring on them because of the
evil of their doings.' [4]And you shall say to
them, 'Thus says the LORD: "If you will not
listen to Me, to walk in My law which I

26:4–6 If you will not listen: Refusal to obey God's law is the basis for punishment.

have set before you, [5]to heed the words of My servants the prophets whom I sent to you, both rising up early and sending *them* (but you have not heeded), [6]then I will make this house like Shī′lōh, and will make this city a curse to all the nations of the earth." ' "

[7]So the priests and the prophets and all the people heard Jer·e·mī′ah speaking these words in the house of the LORD.
[8]Now it happened, when Jer·e·mī′ah had made an end of speaking all that the LORD had commanded *him* to speak to all the people, that the priests and the prophets and all the people seized him, saying, "You will surely die!
[9]Why have you prophesied in the name of the LORD, saying, 'This house shall be like Shī′lōh, and this city shall be desolate, without an inhabitant'?" And all the people were gathered against Jer·e·mī′ah in the house of the LORD.

[10]When the princes of Judah heard these things, they came up from the king's house to the house of the LORD and sat down in the entry of the New Gate of the LORD's *house.*
[11]And the priests and the prophets spoke to the princes and all the people, saying, "This man deserves to die! For he has prophesied against this city, as you have heard with your ears."

[12]Then Jer·e·mī′ah spoke to all the princes and all the people, saying: "The LORD sent me to prophesy against this house and against this city with all the words that you have heard.
[13]Now therefore, amend your ways and your doings, and obey the voice of the LORD your God; then the LORD will relent concerning the doom that He has pronounced against you.
[14]As for me, here I am, in your hand; do with me as seems good and proper to you.
[15]But know for certain that if you put me to death, you will surely bring innocent blood on yourselves, on this city, and on its inhabitants; for truly the LORD has sent me to you to speak all these words in your hearing."

[16]So the princes and all the people said to the priests and the prophets, "This man does not deserve to die. For he has spoken to us in the name of the LORD our God."

[17]Then certain of the elders of the land rose up and spoke to all the assembly of the people, saying:
[18]"Mī′cah of Mō′re·sheth prophesied in the days of Hez·e·kī′ah king of Judah, and spoke to all the people of Judah, saying, 'Thus says the LORD of hosts:

"Zion shall be plowed *like* a field,
Jerusalem shall become heaps of
ruins,
And the mountain of the temple[a]
Like the bare hills of the forest." '[b]

[19]Did Hez·e·kī′ah king of Judah and all Judah ever put him to death? Did he not fear the LORD and seek the LORD's favor? And the LORD relented concerning the doom which He had pronounced against them. But we are doing great evil against ourselves."

26:18 [a]Literally *house* [b]Compare Micah 3:12

26:10 princes of Judah: Members of the royal family who governed Jerusalem. They wanted to change the mob scene into a legal trial. **entry of the New Gate**: The place where trials were held.

26:11 prophesied against this city: They regarded the Holy City as immune from divine judgment.

26:14 here I am: Jeremiah's calmness is a sharp contrast to his extreme distress in 15:18. Why the difference? Jeremiah had repented of his attitude of self-pity, and God had restored him.

26:17–19 Thoughtful elders reminded the people that **Micah**, a true prophet, had spoken against the temple. How could they condemn Jeremiah?

20Now there was also a man who prophesied in the name of the LORD, Ū·rī′jah the son of She·māi′ah of Kir′jath Jē′a·rim, who prophesied against this city and against this land according to all the words of Jer·e·mī′ah. 21And when Je·hoi′a·kim the king, with all his mighty men and all the princes, heard his words, the king sought to put him to death; but when Ū·rī′jah heard *it,* he was afraid and fled, and went to Egypt. 22Then Je·hoi′a·kim the king sent men to Egypt: El·nā′than the son of Ach′bor, and *other* men *who went* with him to Egypt. 23And they brought Ū·rī′jah from Egypt and brought him to Je·hoi′a·kim the king, who killed him with the sword and cast his dead body into the graves of the common people.

24Nevertheless the hand of A·hī′kam the son of Shā′phan was with Jer·e·mī′ah, so that they should not give him into the hand of the people to put him to death.

CHAPTER 27

Symbol of the Bonds and Yokes

In the beginning of the reign of Je·hoi′a·kim[a] the son of Jō·sī′ah, king of Judah, this word came to Jer·e·mī′ah from the LORD, saying,[b] 2"Thus says the LORD to me: 'Make for yourselves bonds and yokes, and put them on your neck, 3and send them to the king of Ē′dom, the king of Mō′ab, the king of the Am′mon·ītes, the king of Tȳre, and the king of Sī′don, by the hand of the messengers who come to Jerusalem to Zed·e·kī′ah king of Judah. 4And command them to say to their masters, "Thus says the LORD of hosts, the God of Israel—thus you shall say to your masters: 5'I have made the earth, the man and the beast that *are* on the ground, by My great power and by My outstretched arm, and have given it to whom it seemed proper to Me. 6And now I have given all these lands into the hand of Ne·bū·chad·nez′zar the king of Babylon, My servant; and the beasts of the field I have also given him to serve him. 7So all nations shall serve him and his son and his son's son, until the time of his land comes; and then many nations and great kings shall make him serve them. 8And it shall be, *that* the nation and kingdom which will not serve Ne·bū·chad·nez′zar the king of Babylon, and which will not put its neck under the yoke of the king of Babylon, that nation I will punish,' says the LORD, 'with the sword, the famine, and the pestilence, until I have consumed them by his hand. 9Therefore do not listen to your prophets, your diviners, your dreamers, your soothsayers, or your sorcerers, who speak to you, saying, "You shall not serve the king of Babylon." 10For they prophesy a lie to you, to remove you far from your land; and I will drive you out, and you will perish. 11But the nations that bring their necks under the yoke of the king of Babylon and serve him, I will let them remain in their own land,' says the LORD, 'and they shall till it and dwell in it.' " ' "

12I also spoke to Zed·e·kī′ah king of Judah according to all these words, saying,

27:1 [a]Following Masoretic Text, Targum, and Vulgate; some Hebrew manuscripts, Arabic, and Syriac read *Zedekiah* (compare 27:3, 12; 28:1). [b]Septuagint omits verse 1.

26:20–23 An incident that shows how dangerous Jeremiah's situation really was. Wise heads do not always prevail.

26:24 Ahikam was a high official in King Josiah's government (2 Kin. 22:12–14). One of Jeremiah's few friends in high places.

27:6–8 I have given . . . Nebuchadnezzar: God had decided that for a period of years all nations in the ancient Near East would be under the king of Babylon. **My servant**: Not from love or choice, but under God's sovereign plan.

27:9, 10 The listing of prophets, diviners, dreamers, soothsayers, sorcerers gives some indication of the variety of fortune-tellers used by people who would not follow Israel's God.

"Bring your necks under the yoke of the king of Babylon, and serve him and his people, and live! 13Why will you die, you and your people, by the sword, by the famine, and by the pestilence, as the LORD has spoken against the nation that will not serve the king of Babylon? 14Therefore do not listen to the words of the prophets who speak to you, saying, 'You shall not serve the king of Babylon,' for they prophesy a lie to you; 15for I have not sent them," says the LORD, "yet they prophesy a lie in My name, that I may drive you out, and that you may perish, you and the prophets who prophesy to you."

16Also I spoke to the priests and to all this people, saying, "Thus says the LORD: 'Do not listen to the words of your prophets who prophesy to you, saying, "Behold, the vessels of the LORD's house will now shortly be brought back from Babylon"; for they prophesy a lie to you. 17Do not listen to them; serve the king of Babylon, and live! Why should this city be laid waste? 18But if they *are* prophets, and if the word of the LORD is with them, let them now make intercession to the LORD of hosts, that the vessels which are left in the house of the LORD, *in* the house of the king of Judah, and at Jerusalem, do not go to Babylon.'

19"For thus says the LORD of hosts concerning the pillars, concerning the Sea, concerning the carts, and concerning the remainder of the vessels that remain in this city, 20which Ne·bū·chad·nez'zar king of Babylon did not take, when he carried away captive Jec·o·nī'ah the son of Je·hoi'a·kim, king of Judah, from Jerusalem to Babylon, and all the nobles of Judah and Jerusalem— 21yes, thus says the LORD of hosts, the God of Israel, concerning the vessels that remain in the house of the LORD, and in the house of the king of Judah and of Jerusalem: 22'They shall be carried to Babylon, and there they shall be until the day that I visit them,' says the LORD. 'Then I will bring them up and restore them to this place.' "

CHAPTER 28

Hananiah's Falsehood and Doom

And it happened in the same year, at the beginning of the reign of Zed·e·kī'ah king of Judah, in the fourth year *and* in the fifth month, *that* Han·a·nī'ah the son of Ā'zur the prophet, who *was* from Gib'ē·on, spoke to me in the house of the LORD in the presence of the priests and of all the people, saying, 2"Thus speaks the LORD of hosts, the God of Israel, saying: 'I have broken the yoke of the king of Babylon. 3Within two full years I will bring back to this place all the vessels of the LORD's house, that Ne·bū·chad·nez'zar king of Babylon took away from this place and carried to Babylon. 4And I will bring back to this place Jec·o·nī'ah the son of Je·hoi'a·kim, king of Judah, with all the captives of Judah who went to Babylon,' says the LORD, 'for I will break the yoke of the king of Babylon.' "

5Then the prophet Jer·e·mī'ah spoke to the prophet Han·a·nī'ah in the presence of the priests and in the presence of all the people who stood in the house of the LORD, 6and the prophet Jer·e·mī'ah said, "Amen! The LORD do so; the LORD perform your words which you have prophesied, to bring back the vessels of the LORD's house and all who were carried away captive, from Babylon to this place. 7Nevertheless hear now this word that I speak in your hearing and in the hearing of all the people: 8The prophets who have been before

---

27:22 I will . . . restore them: God would use a foreign king, Cyrus of Persia, to return the temple treasures to Jerusalem in 537 B.C. (see Ezra 1:7–11; 5:13–15).

28:5, 6 Amen! The LORD do so: Jeremiah expresses, "I wish that were true," although he knows it is not.

me and before you of old prophesied
against many countries and great
kingdoms—of war and disaster and
pestilence. 9As for the prophet who proph-
esies of peace, when the word of the
prophet comes to pass, the prophet will be
known *as* one whom the LORD has truly
sent."

10Then Han·a·nī'ah the prophet took the
yoke off the prophet Jer·e·mī'ah's neck
and broke it. 11And Han·a·nī'ah spoke in
the presence of all the people, saying,
"Thus says the LORD: 'Even so I will break
the yoke of Ne·bū·chad·nez'zar king of
Babylon from the neck of all nations within
the space of two full years.' " And the
prophet Jer·e·mī'ah went his way.

12Now the word of the LORD came to
Jer·e·mī'ah, after Han·a·nī'ah the prophet
had broken the yoke from the neck of the
prophet Jer·e·mī'ah, saying, 13"Go and tell
Han·a·nī'ah, saying, 'Thus says the LORD:
"You have broken the yokes of wood, but
you have made in their place yokes of
iron." 14For thus says the LORD of hosts, the
God of Israel: "I have put a yoke of iron on
the neck of all these nations, that they may
serve Ne·bū·chad·nez'zar king of Babylon;
and they shall serve him. I have given him
the beasts of the field also." ' "

15Then the prophet Jer·e·mī'ah said to
Han·a·nī'ah the prophet, "Hear now,
Han·a·nī'ah, the LORD has not sent you,
but you make this people trust in a lie.
16Therefore thus says the LORD: 'Behold, I
will cast you from the face of the earth.
This year you shall die, because you have
taught rebellion against the LORD.' "

17So Han·a·nī'ah the prophet died the
same year in the seventh month.

CHAPTER 29

Jeremiah's Letter to the Captives

Now these *are* the words of the letter
that Jer·e·mī'ah the prophet sent from Je-
rusalem to the remainder of the elders who
were carried away captive—to the priests,
the prophets, and all the people whom
Ne·bū·chad·nez'zar had carried away cap-
tive from Jerusalem to Babylon. 2(This hap-
pened after Jec·o·nī'ah the king, the queen
mother, the eunuchs, the princes of Judah
and Jerusalem, the craftsmen, and the
smiths had departed from Jerusalem.) 3*The
letter was sent* by the hand of El·ā'sah
the son of Shā'phan, and Gem·a·rī'ah
the son of Hil·kī'ah, whom Zed·e·kī'ah
king of Judah sent to Babylon, to
Ne·bū·chad·nez'zar king of Babylon, say-
ing,

4 Thus says the LORD of hosts, the God
of Israel, to all who were carried away
captive, whom I have caused to be
carried away from Jerusalem to
Babylon:

5 Build houses and dwell *in them;* plant
gardens and eat their fruit. 6Take
wives and beget sons and daughters;
and take wives for your sons and give
your daughters to husbands, so that
they may bear sons and daughters—
that you may be increased there, and
not diminished. 7And seek the peace
of the city where I have caused you to
be carried away captive, and pray to
the LORD for it; for in its peace you
will have peace. 8For thus says the
LORD of hosts, the God of Israel: Do

28:12–14 The Lord strengthened His prophet by providing a more impressive symbol; Hananiah could not break the **yokes of iron** (v. 13). Likewise, the subjection of nations to Babylon could not be changed before the Lord permitted it.

28:17 Hananiah's death in the seventh month, just two months after these events (see 28:1), confirmed to the people the validity of Jeremiah's message.

29:1 the letter: This was not the first letter Jeremiah had written to the exiles on this subject. Verses 24–32 challenge Shemaiah for an earlier rejection of God's message from Jeremiah instructing the exiles to plan for a long stay in Babylon.

not let your prophets and your divin-
ers who are in your midst deceive
you, nor listen to your dreams which
you cause to be dreamed. [9]For they
prophesy falsely to you in My name; I
have not sent them, says the LORD.

10 For thus says the LORD: After seventy
years are completed at Babylon, I will
visit you and perform My good word
toward you, and cause you to return
to this place. [11]For I know the
thoughts that I think toward you, says
the LORD, thoughts of peace and not
of evil, to give you a future and a
hope. [12]Then you will call upon Me
and go and pray to Me, and I will lis-
ten to you. [13]And you will seek Me
and find *Me,* when you search for Me
with all your heart. [14]I will be found
by you, says the LORD, and I will bring
you back from your captivity; I will
gather you from all the nations and
from all the places where I have
driven you, says the LORD, and I will
bring you to the place from which I
cause you to be carried away captive.

15 Because you have said, "The LORD has
raised up prophets for us in Bab-
ylon"— [16]therefore thus says the LORD
concerning the king who sits on the
throne of David, concerning all the
people who dwell in this city, and
concerning your brethren who have
not gone out with you into captivity—
[17]thus says the LORD of hosts: Behold, I
will send on them the sword, the
famine, and the pestilence, and will
make them like rotten figs that cannot
be eaten, they are so bad. [18]And I will
pursue them with the sword, with
famine, and with pestilence; and I will

> Prayer is for every moment of our lives, not just for times of suffering or joy. Prayer is really a place; a place where you meet God in genuine conversation.
> Billy Graham

deliver them to trouble among all the
kingdoms of the earth—to be a curse,
an astonishment, a hissing, and a re-
proach among all the nations where I
have driven them, [19]because they have
not heeded My words, says the LORD,
which I sent to them by My servants
the prophets, rising up early and
sending *them;* neither would you
heed, says the LORD. [20]Therefore hear
the word of the LORD, all you of the
captivity, whom I have sent from Jeru-
salem to Babylon.

21 Thus says the LORD of hosts, the God
of Israel, concerning Ā'hab the son of
Kō·laī'ah, and Zed·e·kī'ah the son of
Mā·a·sēi'ah, who prophesy a lie to
you in My name: Behold, I will de-
liver them into the hand of
Ne·bū·chad·nez'zar king of Babylon,
and he shall slay them before your
eyes. [22]And because of them a curse
shall be taken up by all the captivity
of Judah who *are* in Babylon, saying,
"The LORD make you like Zed·e·kī'ah
and Ā'hab, whom the king of Babylon
roasted in the fire"; [23]because they
have done disgraceful things in Israel,
have committed adultery with their
neighbors' wives, and have spoken ly-
ing words in My name, which I have
not commanded them. Indeed I know,
and *am* a witness, says the LORD.

29:21 Ahab and **Zedekiah** were false prophets among the exiles in Babylon. They were misleading the exiled people as Hananiah had been misleading the people in Jerusalem (see 28:1–4).

29:22 The fate of these men was so terrible that it would be used as a curse when calling down evil on an enemy.

24 You shall also speak to She·māi′ah the
Ne·hel′a·mīte, saying, 25Thus speaks
the LORD of hosts, the God of Israel,
saying: You have sent letters in your
name to all the people who *are* at Jeru-
salem, to Zeph·a·nī′ah the son of
Mā·a·sēi′ah the priest, and to all the
priests, saying, 26"The LORD has made
you priest instead of Je·hoi′a·da the
priest, so that there should be officers
in the house of the LORD over every
man *who* is demented and considers
himself a prophet, that you should
put him in prison and in the stocks.
27Now therefore, why have you not re-
buked Jer·e·mī′ah of An′a·thoth who
makes himself a prophet to you? 28For
he has sent to us *in* Babylon, saying,
'This *captivity is* long; build houses
and dwell *in them,* and plant gardens
and eat their fruit.' "

29 Now Zeph·a·nī′ah the priest read this
letter in the hearing of Jer·e·mī′ah the
prophet. 30Then the word of the LORD
came to Jer·e·mī′ah, saying: 31Send to
all those in captivity, saying, Thus
says the LORD concerning She·māi′ah
the Ne·hel′a·mīte: Because
She·māi′ah has prophesied to you,
and I have not sent him, and he has
caused you to trust in a lie— 32there-
fore thus says the LORD: Behold, I will
punish She·māi′ah the Ne·hel′a·mīte
and his family: he shall not have any-
one to dwell among this people, nor
shall he see the good that I will do for
My people, says the LORD, because he
has taught rebellion against the LORD.

CHAPTER 30

Restoration of Israel and Judah

The word that came to Jer·e·mī′ah from
the LORD, saying, 2"Thus speaks the LORD
God of Israel, saying: 'Write in a book for
yourself all the words that I have spoken to
you. 3For behold, the days are coming,'
says the LORD, 'that I will bring back from
captivity My people Israel and Judah,' says
the LORD. 'And I will cause them to return
to the land that I gave to their fathers, and
they shall possess it.' "

4Now these *are* the words that the LORD
spoke concerning Israel and Judah.

5"For thus says the LORD:

'We have heard a voice of trembling,
Of fear, and not of peace.
6 Ask now, and see,
Whether a man is ever in labor with
child?
So why do I see every man *with* his
hands on his loins
Like a woman in labor,
And all faces turned pale?
7 Alas! For that day *is* great,
So that none *is* like it;
And it *is* the time of Jacob's trouble,
But he shall be saved out of it.

8 'For it shall come to pass in that day,'
Says the LORD of hosts,

29:24–32 The last part of Jeremiah's letter is a pronouncement against **Shemaiah**, a false prophet in exile.

29:29–32 Jeremiah's response to Shemaiah's action was to announce punishment due to **rebellion**. Shemaiah and his family would not live to see the **good** that God planned for Judah after the Exile.

30:1—33:26 This section is called the Book of Consolation, because of its positive messages of hope concerning the future.

30:2 Write in a book: The first command that Jeremiah preserve his prophecies in written form (see 36:1–19, 27, 28).

30:3 Both **Israel**, the captives from the northern 10 tribes exiled in 721 B.C. by the Assyrians, and **Judah**, those exiled by the Babylonians, would be returned to the Promised Land.

30:4–7 Jacob's trouble (v. 7): The focus moves beyond the Babylonian captivity to a future time of trial for Israel and Judah, again scattered among the nations.

'*That* I will break his yoke from your neck,
And will burst your bonds;
Foreigners shall no more enslave them.
9 But they shall serve the LORD their God,
And David their king,
Whom I will raise up for them.

10 'Therefore do not fear, O My servant Jacob,' says the LORD,
'Nor be dismayed, O Israel;
For behold, I will save you from afar,
And your seed from the land of their captivity.
Jacob shall return, have rest and be quiet,
And no one shall make *him* afraid.
11 For I *am* with you,' says the LORD, 'to save you;
Though I make a full end of all nations where I have scattered you,
Yet I will not make a complete end of you.
But I will correct you in justice,
And will not let you go altogether unpunished.'

12"For thus says the LORD:

'Your affliction *is* incurable,
Your wound *is* severe.
13 *There is* no one to plead your cause,
That you may be bound up;
You have no healing medicines.
14 All your lovers have forgotten you;
They do not seek you;
For I have wounded you with the wound of an enemy,
With the chastisement of a cruel one,
For the multitude of your iniquities,
Because your sins have increased.
15 Why do you cry about your affliction?
Your sorrow *is* incurable.
Because of the multitude of your iniquities,
Because your sins have increased,
I have done these things to you.

16 'Therefore all those who devour you shall be devoured;
And all your adversaries, every one of them, shall go into captivity;
Those who plunder you shall become plunder,
And all who prey upon you I will make a prey.
17 For I will restore health to you
And heal you of your wounds,' says the LORD,
'Because they called you an outcast saying:
"This *is* Zion;
No one seeks her." '

18"Thus says the LORD:

'Behold, I will bring back the captivity of Jacob's tents,
And have mercy on his dwelling places;
The city shall be built upon its own mound,
And the palace shall remain according to its own plan.
19 Then out of them shall proceed thanksgiving
And the voice of those who make merry;
I will multiply them, and they shall not diminish;
I will also glorify them, and they shall not be small.
20 Their children also shall be as before,
And their congregation shall be established before Me;

30:9 serve the LORD: The returned people would worship only one God. **David their king**: Although the house of David had been judged, somehow Judah would yet be ruled by a descendant of David.

And I will punish all who oppress
them.
21 Their nobles shall be from among
them,
And their governor shall come from
their midst;
Then I will cause him to draw near,
And he shall approach Me;
For who *is* this who pledged his heart
to approach Me?' says the LORD.
22 'You shall be My people,
And I will be your God.' "

23 Behold, the whirlwind of the LORD
Goes forth with fury,
A continuing whirlwind;
It will fall violently on the head of the
wicked.
24 The fierce anger of the LORD will not
return until He has done it,
And until He has performed the
intents of His heart.

In the latter days you will consider it.

CHAPTER 31

The Remnant of Israel Saved

"At the same time," says the LORD, "I
will be the God of all the families of Israel,
and they shall be My people."
2Thus says the LORD:

"The people who survived the sword
Found grace in the wilderness—
Israel, when I went to give him rest."

3 The LORD has appeared of old to me,
saying:
"Yes, I have loved you with an
everlasting love;

> ***I pray that my friend knows that You, God, have loved him with an everlasting love and with lovingkindness You have drawn him.***
>
> *adapted from* Jeremiah 31:3

Therefore with lovingkindness I have
drawn you.
4 Again I will build you, and you shall
be rebuilt,
O virgin of Israel!
You shall again be adorned with your
tambourines,
And shall go forth in the dances of
those who rejoice.
5 You shall yet plant vines on the
mountains of Samaria;
The planters shall plant and eat *them*
as ordinary food.
6 For there shall be a day
When the watchmen will cry on
Mount Ē'phra·im,
'Arise, and let us go up *to* Zion,
To the LORD our God.' "

7For thus says the LORD:

"Sing with gladness for Jacob,
And shout among the chief of the
nations;
Proclaim, give praise, and say,
'O LORD, save Your people,
The remnant of Israel!'
8 Behold, I will bring them from the
north country,

30:23, 24 God's fierce anger is here directed against Judah's captors.
31:1–3 My people: Just as the Lord led Israel into the wilderness, protecting them from the sword of the Egyptian armies, so His lovingkindness will support His people in the Exile.
31:4–6 virgin of Israel: The exiled people. After the return people from Ephraim (the northern region) would once again come to Jerusalem to worship (Ezek. 37:19–22; Zech. 10:6).
31:8–11 bring . . . gather: The restoration to the Promised Land. **I am a Father to**

LOVING LIKE JESUS

Lucibel Van Atta

Women have an urgent need to learn how to love according to God's pattern. Rather than a feeling, love is always a choice, an act of our will in which special feelings *follow*. As our sovereign role model, the Lord demonstrated the direction—the active giving and accepting and caring—our love should take: "God so loved the world that He gave His only begotten Son" (John 3:16).

This brand of love neither keeps books nor requires repayment with interest next month; it ignores measuring cups and computers and calendars and digital watches. This love will never be wasted—even the tiniest shredded remnant lives on long after we do.

Loving others with God's kind of love means taking on the characteristics we observe in Jesus' life, in the unselfish love He illustrated in the parable of the Good Samaritan (Luke 10:30–37). Instead of stuffing gospel tracts into the folds of the injured man's robes, the Good Samaritan tended to his wounds before taking him to the inn for recovery. He paid in advance for the care of the stranger, asking to be billed for any balance due. This is not the kind of love we see much of these days. ✦

And gather them from the ends of the earth,
Among them the blind and the lame,
The woman with child
And the one who labors with child, together;
A great throng shall return there.
9 They shall come with weeping,
And with supplications I will lead them.
I will cause them to walk by the rivers of waters,
In a straight way in which they shall not stumble;
For I am a Father to Israel,
And Ē'phra·im *is* My firstborn.

10 "Hear the word of the LORD, O nations,
And declare *it* in the isles afar off, and say,
'He who scattered Israel will gather him,
And keep him as a shepherd *does* his flock.'
11 For the LORD has redeemed Jacob,
And ransomed him from the hand of one stronger than he.
12 Therefore they shall come and sing in the height of Zion,
Streaming to the goodness of the LORD—
For wheat and new wine and oil,
For the young of the flock and the herd;

Israel (v.9): God restores because He loves with the love of a parent (see note on Hos. 11:1–12).

31:12–14 My people shall be satisfied (v. 14): In place of the droughts (14:1), famines (8:13; 11:22), and pestilences (14:12) used by God to get a sinful people's attention, there is to be abundance (v. 12) with accompanying **joy** (v. 13) and satisfaction (v. 14).

Their souls shall be like a well-
watered garden,
And they shall sorrow no more at all.

13 "Then shall the virgin rejoice in the
dance,
And the young men and the old,
together;
For I will turn their mourning to joy,
Will comfort them,
And make them rejoice rather than
sorrow.
14 I will satiate the soul of the priests
with abundance,
And My people shall be satisfied with
My goodness, says the LORD."

Mercy on Ephraim

15Thus says the LORD:

"A voice was heard in Rā'mah,
Lamentation *and* bitter weeping,
Rachel weeping for her children,
Refusing to be comforted for her
children,
Because they *are* no more."

16Thus says the LORD:

"Refrain your voice from weeping,
And your eyes from tears;
For your work shall be rewarded,
says the LORD,
And they shall come back from the
land of the enemy.
17 There is hope in your future, says the
LORD,
That *your* children shall come back to
their own border.

18 "I have surely heard Ē'phra·im
bemoaning himself:
'You have chastised me, and I was
chastised,
Like an untrained bull;
Restore me, and I will return,
For You *are* the LORD my God.
19 Surely, after my turning, I repented;
And after I was instructed, I struck
myself on the thigh;
I was ashamed, yes, even humiliated,
Because I bore the reproach of my
youth.'
20 *Is* Ē'phra·im My dear son?
Is he a pleasant child?
For though I spoke against him,
I earnestly remember him still;
Therefore My heart yearns for him;
I will surely have mercy on him, says
the LORD.

21 "Set up signposts,
Make landmarks;
Set your heart toward the highway,
The way in *which* you went.
Turn back, O virgin of Israel,
Turn back to these your cities.
22 How long will you gad about,
O you backsliding daughter?
For the LORD has created a new thing
in the earth—
A woman shall encompass a man."

Future Prosperity of Judah

23Thus says the LORD of hosts, the God
of Israel: "They shall again use this speech
in the land of Judah and in its cities, when
I bring back their captivity: 'The LORD bless
you, O home of justice, *and* mountain of
holiness!' 24And there shall dwell in Judah
itself, and in all its cities together, farmers
and those going out with flocks. 25For I
have satiated the weary soul, and I have re-
plenished every sorrowful soul."
26After this I awoke and looked around,
and my sleep was sweet to me.
27"Behold, the days are coming, says the
LORD, that I will sow the house of Israel
and the house of Judah with the seed of
man and the seed of beast. 28And it shall
come to pass, *that* as I have watched over
them to pluck up, to break down, to throw
down, to destroy, and to afflict, so I will
watch over them to build and to plant, says
the LORD. 29In those days they shall say no
more:

'The fathers have eaten sour grapes,
And the children's teeth are set on edge.'

[30]But every one shall die for his own iniquity; every man who eats the sour grapes, his teeth shall be set on edge.

A New Covenant

[31]"Behold, the days are coming, says the
LORD, when I will make a new covenant
with the house of Israel and with the house
of Judah— [32]not according to the covenant
that I made with their fathers in the day
that I took them by the hand to lead them
out of the land of Egypt, My covenant
which they broke, though I was a husband
to them,[a] says the LORD. [33]But this *is* the
covenant that I will make with the house of
Israel after those days, says the LORD: I will
put My law in their minds, and write it on
their hearts; and I will be their God, and
they shall be My people. [34]No more shall
every man teach his neighbor, and every
man his brother, saying, 'Know the LORD,'
for they all shall know Me, from the least of
them to the greatest of them, says the
LORD. For I will forgive their iniquity, and
their sin I will remember no more."

35 Thus says the LORD,
Who gives the sun for a light by day,

31:32 [a]Following Masoretic Text, Targum, and Vulgate; Septuagint and Syriac read *and I turned away from them.*

> For us God is eternal discovery and eternal growth. The more we think we understand Him, the more He reveals Himself otherwise. The more we think we hold Him, the further He withdraws, drawing us into the depths of Himself.
> Pierre Teilhard de Chardin

The ordinances of the moon and the stars for a light by night,
Who disturbs the sea,
And its waves roar
(The LORD of hosts *is* His name):

36 "If those ordinances depart
From before Me, says the LORD,
Then the seed of Israel shall also cease
From being a nation before Me forever."

[37]Thus says the LORD:

"If heaven above can be measured,
And the foundations of the earth searched out beneath,
I will also cast off all the seed of Israel
For all that they have done, says the LORD.

[38]"Behold, the days are coming, says
the LORD, that the city shall be built for the
LORD from the Tower of Ha·nan'el to the
Corner Gate. [39]The surveyor's line shall

31:31, 32 new covenant: The first instance where the Lord reveals that the covenant of Mt. Sinai would be set aside by a new covenant (Matt. 26:28). When the curse of the broken old covenant was taken by the Son of God on the Cross, a new relationship became possible.

31:33, 34 The traits of the new covenant. **put My law in their minds**: What is most radically new in this covenant is that human nature is to be transformed by the power of God. **write it on their hearts** (v. 33): Impress God's law on the very seat of the personality. There is hope for a new day when God works in the minds and hearts of individuals to make them His **people**. Knowing **the LORD** comes from a personal relationship, not by instruction (v. 34). **all shall know Me**: This personal fellowship can be the privilege of anyone. **I will forgive**: The promise is offered to all who will hear and respond. The difference between the two covenants is not in the behavior expected under each, but in the differing relationship with God. Both require obedience, but the old being external cannot be kept; the new being internal can be a reality.

again extend straight forward over the hill Gā'reb; then it shall turn toward Gō'ath. [40]And the whole valley of the dead bodies and of the ashes, and all the fields as far as the Brook Kid'ron, to the corner of the Horse Gate toward the east, *shall be* holy to the LORD. It shall not be plucked up or thrown down anymore forever."

CHAPTER 32

Jeremiah Buys a Field

The word that came to Jer·e·mī'ah from the LORD in the tenth year of Zed·e·kī'ah king of Judah, which was the eighteenth year of Ne·bū·chad·nez'zar. [2]For then the king of Babylon's army besieged Jerusalem, and Jer·e·mī'ah the prophet was shut up in the court of the prison, which *was in* the king of Judah's house. [3]For Zed·e·kī'ah king of Judah had shut him up, saying, "Why do you prophesy and say, 'Thus says the LORD: "Behold, I will give this city into the hand of the king of Babylon, and he shall take it; [4]and Zed·e·kī'ah king of Judah shall not escape from the hand of the Chal·dē'ans, but shall surely be delivered into the hand of the king of Babylon, and shall speak with him face to face,[a] and see him eye to eye; [5]then he shall lead Zed·e·kī'ah to Babylon, and there he shall be until I visit him," says the LORD; "though you fight with the Chal·dē'ans, you shall not succeed" '?"

[6]And Jer·e·mī'ah said, "The word of the LORD came to me, saying, [7]'Behold, Han'a·mel the son of Shal'lum your uncle will come to you, saying, "Buy my field which *is* in An'a·thoth, for the right of redemption *is* yours to buy *it*." ' [8]Then Han'a·mel my uncle's son came to me in the court of the prison according to the word of the LORD, and said to me, 'Please buy my field that *is* in An'a·thoth, which *is* in the country of Benjamin; for the right of inheritance *is* yours, and the redemption yours; buy *it* for yourself.' Then I knew that this was the word of the LORD. [9]So I bought the field from Han'a·mel, the son of my uncle who *was* in An'a·thoth, and weighed *out to* him the money—seventeen shekels of silver. [10]And I signed the deed and sealed *it*, took witnesses, and weighed the money on the scales. [11]So I took the purchase deed, *both* that which was sealed *according* to the law and custom, and that which was open; [12]and I gave the purchase deed to Bar'uch the son of Ne·rī'ah, son of Mah'sēi·ah, in the presence of Han'a·mel my uncle's *son*, and in the presence of the witnesses who signed the purchase deed, before all the Jews who sat in the court of the prison.

[13]"Then I charged Bar'uch before them, saying, [14]'Thus says the LORD of hosts, the God of Israel: "Take these deeds, both this

32:4 [a]Literally *mouth to mouth*

32:1–44 God asks Jeremiah to buy some land in his hometown. On the surface this seems a strange act because the Babylonians would soon destroy everything (vv. 24, 25). But God insists that judgment is not final and that the scattered people will dwell in their land again (vv. 36–38). In that light, buying the land would be a great step of faith.

32:1 tenth year: 587 B.C., while Jerusalem was under siege but before the city was captured.

32:6–8 right of redemption: See Lev. 25:23–25; Ruth 4:1–4 and note on Ruth 4:3, 4. Perhaps Jeremiah's relatives had been impoverished by the war and were heavily in debt. Obviously Jeremiah still had money.

32:9 I bought: Jeremiah obeyed the Lord though the land at that time was virtually worthless. **money**: Coins were not used at that time, so precious metals were weighed.

32:10–12 both: Two copies were prepared from the same sheet. One copy was folded and **sealed** with wax, probably impressed with Jeremiah's personal seal. The unsealed copy was left **open** for anyone to read; the sealed copy could be opened only in a legal court. Impressed seals of **Baruch** have recently been found in Israel; the surface of a papyrus sheet was impressed on the backside.

purchase deed which is sealed and this deed which is open, and put them in an earthen vessel, that they may last many days." 15For thus says the LORD of hosts, the God of Israel: "Houses and fields and vineyards shall be possessed again in this land." '

Jeremiah Prays for Understanding

16"Now when I had delivered the purchase deed to Bar'uch the son of Ne·rī'ah, I prayed to the LORD, saying: 17'Ah, Lord GOD! Behold, You have made the heavens and the earth by Your great power and outstretched arm. There is nothing too hard for You. 18*You* show lovingkindness to thousands, and repay the iniquity of the fathers into the bosom of their children after them—the Great, the Mighty God, whose name *is* the LORD of hosts. 19*You are* great in counsel and mighty in work, for your eyes *are* open to all the ways of the sons of men, to give everyone according to his ways and according to the fruit of his doings. 20You have set signs and wonders in the land of Egypt, to this day, and in Israel and among *other* men; and You have made Yourself a name, as it is this day. 21You have brought Your people Israel out of the land of Egypt with signs and wonders, with a strong hand and an outstretched arm, and with great terror; 22You have given them this land, of which You swore to their fathers to give them—"a land flowing with milk and honey."[a] 23And they came in and took possession of it, but they have not obeyed Your voice or walked in Your law. They have done nothing of all that You commanded them to do; therefore You have caused all this calamity to come upon them.

24'Look, the siege mounds! They have come to the city to take it; and the city has been given into the hand of the Chal·dē'ans who fight against it, because of the sword and famine and pestilence. What You have spoken has happened; there You see *it!* 25And You have said to me, O Lord GOD, "Buy the field for money, and take witnesses"!—yet the city has been given into the hand of the Chal·dē'ans.' "

God's Assurance of the People's Return

26Then the word of the LORD came to Jer·e·mī'ah, saying, 27"Behold, I *am* the LORD, the God of all flesh. Is there anything too hard for Me? 28Therefore thus says the LORD: 'Behold, I will give this city into the hand of the Chal·dē'ans, into the hand of Ne·bū·chad·nez'zar king of Babylon, and he shall take it. 29And the Chal·dē'ans who fight against this city shall come and set fire to this city and burn it, with the houses on whose roofs they have offered incense to Bā'al and poured out drink offerings to other gods, to provoke Me to anger; 30because the children of Israel and the children of Judah have done only evil before Me from their youth. For the children of Israel have provoked Me only to anger with the work of their hands,' says the LORD. 31'For this city has been to Me *a provocation of* My anger and My fury from the day that they built it, even to this day; so I will remove it from before My face 32because of all the evil of the children of Israel and the children of Judah, which they have done to provoke Me to anger—they, their kings, their princes, their priests, their prophets, the men of Judah, and the inhabitants of Jerusalem. 33And they have turned to Me the back, and not the face; though I taught them, rising up early and teaching *them*, yet they have not listened to receive instruction. 34But they set their abominations

32:22 [a]Exodus 3:8

32:24, 25 Look, the siege mounds! Jeremiah's faith was buffeted by Jerusalem's frightful situation.

32:28–35 The promises are to be fulfilled after judgment, not before.

32:34 set their abominations in the house: See 7:30 and note.

in the house which is called by My name,
to defile it. 35And they built the high places
of Bā′al which *are* in the Valley of the Son
of Hin′nom, to cause their sons and their
daughters to pass through *the fire* to
Mō′lech, which I did not command them,
nor did it come into My mind that they
should do this abomination, to cause Ju-
dah to sin.′

36"Now therefore, thus says the LORD,
the God of Israel, concerning this city of
which you say, 'It shall be delivered into
the hand of the king of Babylon by the
sword, by the famine, and by the pesti-
lence: 37Behold, I will gather them out of all
countries where I have driven them in My
anger, in My fury, and in great wrath; I will
bring them back to this place, and I will
cause them to dwell safely. 38They shall be
My people, and I will be their God; 39then I
will give them one heart and one way, that
they may fear Me forever, for the good of
them and their children after them. 40And I
will make an everlasting covenant with
them, that I will not turn away from doing
them good; but I will put My fear in their
hearts so that they will not depart from
Me. 41Yes, I will rejoice over them to do
them good, and I will assuredly plant them
in this land, with all My heart and with all
My soul.'

42"For thus says the LORD: 'Just as I have
brought all this great calamity on this peo-
ple, so I will bring on them all the good
that I have promised them. 43And fields
will be bought in this land of which you
say, "*It is* desolate, without man or beast; it
has been given into the hand of the
Chal·dē′ans." 44Men will buy fields for
money, sign deeds and seal *them,* and take
witnesses, in the land of Benjamin, in the
places around Jerusalem, in the cities of Ju-
dah, in the cities of the mountains, in the
cities of the lowland, and in the cities of the
South; for I will cause their captives to re-
turn,' says the LORD."

CHAPTER 33

Excellence of the Restored Nation

Moreover the word of the LORD came to
Jer·e·mī′ah a second time, while he was
still shut up in the court of the prison, say-
ing, 2"Thus says the LORD who made it, the
LORD who formed it to establish it (the
LORD *is* His name): 3'Call to Me, and I will
answer you, and show you great and
mighty things, which you do not know.'

4"For thus says the LORD, the God of Is-
rael, concerning the houses of this city and
the houses of the kings of Judah, which
have been pulled down *to fortify*[a] against
the siege mounds and the sword: 5'They
come to fight with the Chal·dē′ans, but
only to fill their places[a] with the dead bod-
ies of men whom I will slay in My anger
and My fury, all for whose wickedness I

33:4 [a]Compare Isaiah 22:10 33:5 [a]Compare 2 Kings 23:14

32:35 pass through the fire: See note on 7:30—8:3.

32:36–41 therefore: God's promise is repeated and confirmed. There will be an eventual release from exile and resettlement in Judah.

32:40 an everlasting covenant: The new covenant (see 31:31–34 and notes).

32:42, 43 fields will be bought: Jeremiah's faith in redeeming his uncle's field (paying off a debt against it) is rewarded by the Lord's promise to resettle the land.

33:1–26 As the final defeat became clearer, some in Jerusalem began to accuse God of having broken His covenant to protect His people (v. 24). God insists this is not so. Despite their breaking of the covenant, He will keep it.

33:1 second time: The first message during Jeremiah's imprisonment is introduced in 32:1, 2.

33:2 made it: A reference to creation (Gen. 1:1).

33:3 great and mighty things: One of God's promises that He will answer prayer.

33:4–9 The houses which were **pulled down** will be rebuilt (v. 7).

have hidden My face from this city. 6Be-
hold, I will bring it health and healing; I
will heal them and reveal to them the
abundance of peace and truth. 7And I will
cause the captives of Judah and the cap-
tives of Israel to return, and will rebuild
those places as at the first. 8I will cleanse
them from all their iniquity by which they
have sinned against Me, and I will pardon
all their iniquities by which they have
sinned and by which they have trans-
gressed against Me. 9Then it shall be to Me
a name of joy, a praise, and an honor before
all nations of the earth, who shall hear all
the good that I do to them; they shall fear
and tremble for all the goodness and all the
prosperity that I provide for it.'

10"Thus says the LORD: 'Again there
shall be heard in this place—of which you
say, "It *is* desolate, without man and with-
out beast"—in the cities of Judah, in the
streets of Jerusalem that are desolate, with-
out man and without inhabitant and with-
out beast, 11the voice of joy and the voice of
gladness, the voice of the bridegroom and
the voice of the bride, the voice of those
who will say:

"Praise the LORD of hosts,
For the LORD *is* good,
For His mercy *endures* forever"—

and of those *who will* bring the sacrifice of
praise into the house of the LORD. For I will
cause the captives of the land to return as
at the first,' says the LORD.

12"Thus says the LORD of hosts: 'In this
place which is desolate, without man and
without beast, and in all its cities, there
shall again be a dwelling place of shep-
herds causing *their* flocks to lie down. 13In
the cities of the mountains, in the cities of
the lowland, in the cities of the South, in
the land of Benjamin, in the places around
Jerusalem, and in the cities of Judah, the
flocks shall again pass under the hands of
him who counts *them*,' says the LORD.

14'Behold, the days are coming,' says the
LORD, 'that I will perform that good thing
which I have promised to the house of Is-
rael and to the house of Judah:

15 'In those days and at that time
I will cause to grow up to David
A Branch of righteousness;
He shall execute judgment and
righteousness in the earth.
16 In those days Judah will be saved,
And Jerusalem will dwell safely.
And this *is the name* by which she will
be called:

THE LORD OUR RIGHTEOUSNESS.'[a]

17"For thus says the LORD: 'David shall
never lack a man to sit on the throne of the
house of Israel; 18nor shall the priests, the
Lē'vītes, lack a man to offer burnt offerings
before Me, to kindle grain offerings, and to
sacrifice continually.' "

33:16 [a]Compare 23:5, 6

33:6, 7 I will heal them: In due time **peace** and **truth** as well as rebuilding (1:10) will become a reality.

33:8, 9 I will cleanse . . . I will pardon: A clear statement of the complete spiritual salvation that God provides.

33:10–13 They say, **It is desolate**, hopeless. However, God insists there will be the **voice of joy**. He will keep His covenant.

33:14–18 perform that good thing: God's ultimate gift and the ultimate proof of His faithfulness would be the Messiah (see note on 23:5, 6). **shall never lack a man** (v. 17): Fulfilled in Jesus who in Himself combined the individual roles of the king and the priest into one.

33:16 she will be called: Jerusalem is to have the same name given the Messiah in 23:6. This is another indication of the unity that will be established between God and His people (see note on 11:2–5).

The Permanence of God's Covenant

19And the word of the LORD came to Jer·e·mī′ah, saying, 20"Thus says the LORD: 'If you can break My covenant with the day and My covenant with the night, so that there will not be day and night in their season, 21then My covenant may also be broken with David My servant, so that he shall not have a son to reign on his throne, and with the Lē′vītes, the priests, My ministers. 22As the host of heaven cannot be numbered, nor the sand of the sea measured, so will I multiply the descendants of David My servant and the Lē′vītes who minister to Me.' "

23Moreover the word of the LORD came to Jer·e·mī′ah, saying, 24"Have you not considered what these people have spoken, saying, 'The two families which the LORD has chosen, He has also cast them off'? Thus they have despised My people, as if they should no more be a nation before them.

25"Thus says the LORD: 'If My covenant *is* not with day and night, *and if* I have not appointed the ordinances of heaven and earth, 26then I will cast away the descendants of Jacob and David My servant, *so* that I will not take *any* of his descendants *to be* rulers over the descendants of Abraham, Isaac, and Jacob. For I will cause their captives to return, and will have mercy on them.' "

CHAPTER 34

Zedekiah Warned by God

The word which came to Jer·e·mī′ah from the LORD, when Ne·bū·chad·nez′zar king of Babylon and all his army, all the kingdoms of the earth under his dominion, and all the people, fought against Jerusalem and all its cities, saying, 2"Thus says the LORD, the God of Israel: 'Go and speak to Zed·e·kī′ah king of Judah and tell him, "Thus says the LORD: 'Behold, I will give this city into the hand of the king of Babylon, and he shall burn it with fire. 3And you shall not escape from his hand, but shall surely be taken and delivered into his hand; your eyes shall see the eyes of the king of Babylon, he shall speak with you face to face,[a] and you shall go to Babylon.' " ' 4Yet hear the word of the LORD, O Zed·e·kī′ah king of Judah! Thus says the LORD concerning you: 'You shall not die by the sword. 5You shall die in peace; as in the ceremonies of your fathers, the former kings who were before you, so they shall burn incense for you and lament for you, *saying,* "Alas, lord!" For I have pronounced the word, says the LORD.' "

6Then Jer·e·mī′ah the prophet spoke all these words to Zed·e·kī′ah king of Judah in Jerusalem, 7when the king of Babylon's army fought against Jerusalem and all the cities of Judah that were left, against Lā′chish and A·zē′kah; for *only* these fortified cities remained of the cities of Judah.

Treacherous Treatment of Slaves

8*This is* the word that came to Jer·e·mī′ah from the LORD, after King Zed·e·kī′ah had made a covenant with all the people who *were* at Jerusalem to proclaim liberty to them: 9that every man should set free his male and female slave—a Hebrew man or woman—that no one should keep a Jewish brother in bondage. 10Now when all the princes and all the people, who had entered into the covenant, heard that every-

34:3 [a]Literally *mouth to mouth*

33:19–26 The firmness of God's **covenant . . . with David** (v. 26; see 2 Sam. 7:12–16) is compared to the stability of God's created world. **host of heaven** (v. 22): The stars in the sky. **two families**: Israel and Judah.

34:8–11 made a covenant: Evidently a well-meaning attempt to encourage some sort of revival. **changed their minds**: Perhaps because they thought the Egyptian army would save Jerusalem from defeat, and Judah would not need God's help.

one should set free his male and female
slaves, that no one should keep them in
bondage anymore, they obeyed and let
them go. 11But afterward they changed their
minds and made the male and female
slaves return, whom they had set free, and
brought them into subjection as male and
female slaves.

12Therefore the word of the LORD came
to Jer·e·mī′ah from the LORD, saying,
13"Thus says the LORD, the God of Israel: 'I
made a covenant with your fathers in the
day that I brought them out of the land of
Egypt, out of the house of bondage, saying,
14"At the end of seven years let every man
set free his Hebrew brother, who has been
sold to him; and when he has served you
six years, you shall let him go free from
you." But your fathers did not obey Me nor
incline their ear. 15Then you recently
turned and did what was right in My
sight—every man proclaiming liberty to
his neighbor; and you made a covenant be-
fore Me in the house which is called by My
name. 16Then you turned around and pro-
faned My name, and every one of you
brought back his male and female slaves,
whom he had set at liberty, at their plea-
sure, and brought them back into subjec-
tion, to be your male and female slaves.'

17"Therefore thus says the LORD: 'You
have not obeyed Me in proclaiming liberty,
every one to his brother and every one to
his neighbor. Behold, I proclaim liberty
to you,' says the LORD—'to the sword, to
pestilence, and to famine! And I will de-
liver you to trouble among all the king-
doms of the earth. 18And I will give the
men who have transgressed My covenant,
who have not performed the words of the
covenant which they made before Me,
when they cut the calf in two and passed
between the parts of it— 19the princes of
Judah, the princes of Jerusalem, the eu-
nuchs, the priests, and all the people of the
land who passed between the parts of the
calf— 20I will give them into the hand of
their enemies and into the hand of those
who seek their life. Their dead bodies shall
be for meat for the birds of the heaven and
the beasts of the earth. 21And I will give
Zed·e·kī′ah king of Judah and his princes
into the hand of their enemies, into the
hand of those who seek their life, and into
the hand of the king of Babylon's army
which has gone back from you. 22Behold, I
will command,' says the LORD, 'and cause
them to return to this city. They will fight
against it and take it and burn it with fire;
and I will make the cities of Judah a deso-
lation without inhabitant.' "

CHAPTER 35

The Obedient Rechabites

The word which came to Jer·e·mī′ah
from the LORD in the days of Je·hoi′a·kim
the son of Jō·sī′ah, king of Judah, saying,
2"Go to the house of the Rē′chab·ītes,
speak to them, and bring them into the
house of the LORD, into one of the cham-
bers, and give them wine to drink."

3Then I took Jā·az·a·nī′ah the son of
Jer·e·mī′ah, the son of Ha·baz·zi·nī′ah, his
brothers and all his sons, and the whole
house of the Rē′chab·ītes, 4and I brought
them into the house of the LORD, into the
chamber of the sons of Hā′nan the son of
Ig·da·lī′ah, a man of God, which *was* by
the chamber of the princes, above the
chamber of Mā·a·sēi′ah the son of Shal′-
lum, the keeper of the door. 5Then I set be-
fore the sons of the house of the Rē′-
chab·ītes bowls full of wine, and cups; and
I said to them, "Drink wine."

6But they said, "We will drink no wine,
for Jon′a·dab the son of Rē′chab, our fa-
ther, commanded us, saying, 'You shall
drink no wine, you nor your sons, forever.
7You shall not build a house, sow seed,

34:18 cut the calf in two: In the covenant oath, participants called upon God to treat them in like manner should they violate the covenant.

plant a vineyard, nor have *any of these;* but all your days you shall dwell in tents, that you may live many days in the land where you are sojourners.' [8]Thus we have obeyed the voice of Jon'a·dab the son of Rē'chab, our father, in all that he charged us, to drink no wine all our days, we, our wives, our sons, or our daughters, [9]nor to build ourselves houses to dwell in; nor do we have vineyard, field, or seed. [10]But we have dwelt in tents, and have obeyed and done according to all that Jon'a·dab our father commanded us. [11]But it came to pass, when Ne·bū·chad·nez'zar king of Babylon came up into the land, that we said, 'Come, let us go to Jerusalem for fear of the army of the Chal·dē'ans and for fear of the army of the Syrians.' So we dwell at Jerusalem."

[12]Then came the word of the LORD to Jer·e·mī'ah, saying, [13]"Thus says the LORD of hosts, the God of Israel: 'Go and tell the men of Judah and the inhabitants of Jerusalem, "Will you not receive instruction to obey My words?" says the LORD. [14]"The words of Jon'a·dab the son of Rē'chab, which he commanded his sons, not to drink wine, are performed; for to this day they drink none, and obey their father's commandment. But although I have spoken to you, rising early and speaking, you did not obey Me. [15]I have also sent to you all My servants the prophets, rising up early and sending *them,* saying, 'Turn now everyone from his evil way, amend your doings, and do not go after other gods to serve them; then you will dwell in the land which I have given you and your fathers.' But you have not inclined your ear, nor obeyed Me. [16]Surely the sons of Jon'a·dab the son of Rē'chab have performed the commandment of their father, which he commanded them, but this people has not obeyed Me." '

[17]"Therefore thus says the LORD God of hosts, the God of Israel: 'Behold, I will bring on Judah and on all the inhabitants of Jerusalem all the doom that I have pronounced against them; because I have spoken to them but they have not heard, and I have called to them but they have not answered.' "

[18]And Jer·e·mī'ah said to the house of the Rē'chab·ītes, "Thus says the LORD of hosts, the God of Israel: 'Because you have obeyed the commandment of Jon'a·dab your father, and kept all his precepts and done according to all that he commanded you, [19]therefore thus says the LORD of hosts, the God of Israel: "Jon'a·dab the son of Rē'chab shall not lack a man to stand before Me forever." ' "

CHAPTER 36

The Scroll Read in the Temple

Now it came to pass in the fourth year of Je·hoi'a·kim the son of Jō·sī'ah, king of Judah, *that* this word came to Jer·e·mī'ah from the LORD, saying: [2]"Take a scroll of a book and write on it all the words that I have spoken to you against Israel, against Judah, and against all the nations, from the day I spoke to you, from the days of Jō·sī'ah even to this day. [3]It may be that the house of Judah will hear all the adversities which I purpose to bring upon them, that everyone may turn from his evil way, that I may forgive their iniquity and their sin."

[4]Then Jer·e·mī'ah called Bar'uch the son of Ne·rī'ah; and Bar'uch wrote on a scroll of a book, at the instruction of Jer·e·mī'ah,[a]

36:4 [a]Literally *from Jeremiah's mouth*

35:18, 19 Because you have obeyed: Obedience was rewarded with a promise.

Chapter 36, like ch. 35, is out of chronological sequence with the events in the reign of Zedekiah recorded in chs. 32—39.

36:2 write: The mode of evangelism shifted from verbal to written communication. **the day I spoke to you**: About 20 years earlier.

36:4 Baruch: Jeremiah's faithful servant and scribe.

all the words of the LORD which He had
spoken to him. [5]And Jer·e·mī′ah com-
manded Bar′uch, saying, "I *am* confined, I
cannot go into the house of the LORD. [6]You
go, therefore, and read from the scroll
which you have written at my instruction,[a]
the words of the LORD, in the hearing of the
people in the LORD's house on the day of
fasting. And you shall also read them in
the hearing of all Judah who come from
their cities. [7]It may be that they will present
their supplication before the LORD, and
everyone will turn from his evil way. For
great *is* the anger and the fury that the
LORD has pronounced against this people."
[8]And Bar′uch the son of Ne·rī′ah did ac-
cording to all that Jer·e·mī′ah the prophet
commanded him, reading from the book
the words of the LORD in the LORD's house.
[9]Now it came to pass in the fifth year of
Je·hoi′a·kim the son of Jō·sī′ah, king of Ju-
dah, in the ninth month, *that* they pro-
claimed a fast before the LORD to all the
people in Jerusalem, and to all the people
who came from the cities of Judah to Jeru-
salem. [10]Then Bar′uch read from the book
the words of Jer·e·mī′ah in the house of
the LORD, in the chamber of Gem·a·rī′ah
the son of Shā′phan the scribe, in the upper
court at the entry of the New Gate of
the LORD's house, in the hearing of all the
people.

The Scroll Read in the Palace

[11]When Mī·chaī′ah the son of
Gem·a·rī′ah, the son of Shā′phan, heard all
the words of the LORD from the book, [12]he
then went down to the king's house, into
the scribe's chamber; and there all the
princes were sitting—E·lish′a·ma the
scribe, De·laī′ah the son of She·māi′ah,
El·nā′than the son of Ach′bor, Gem·a·rī′ah
the son of Shā′phan, Zed·e·kī′ah the son of
Han·a·nī′ah, and all the princes. [13]Then
Mī·chaī′ah declared to them all the words
that he had heard when Bar′uch read the
book in the hearing of the people. [14]There-
fore all the princes sent Je·hū′dī the son of
Neth·a·nī′ah, the son of Shel·e·mī′ah, the
son of Cū′shī, to Bar′uch, saying, "Take in
your hand the scroll from which you have
read in the hearing of the people, and
come." So Bar′uch the son of Ne·rī′ah took
the scroll in his hand and came to them.
[15]And they said to him, "Sit down now,
and read it in our hearing." So Bar′uch
read *it* in their hearing.

[16]Now it happened, when they had
heard all the words, that they looked in
fear from one to another, and said to
Bar′uch, "We will surely tell the king of all
these words." [17]And they asked Bar′uch,
saying, "Tell us now, how did you write all
these words—at his instruction?"[a]

[18]So Bar′uch answered them, "He pro-
claimed with his mouth all these words to
me, and I wrote *them* with ink in the book."

[19]Then the princes said to Bar′uch, "Go
and hide, you and Jer·e·mī′ah; and let no
one know where you are."

The King Destroys Jeremiah's Scroll

[20]And they went to the king, into the
court; but they stored the scroll in the
chamber of E·lish′a·ma the scribe, and told
all the words in the hearing of the king.
[21]So the king sent Je·hū′dī to bring the
scroll, and he took it from E·lish′a·ma the
scribe's chamber. And Je·hū′dī read it in
the hearing of the king and in the hearing
of all the princes who stood beside the
king. [22]Now the king was sitting in the
winter house in the ninth month, with *a fire*
burning on the hearth before him. [23]And it

36:6 [a]Literally *from my mouth* 36:17 [a]Literally *with his mouth*

36:19 Go and hide: It is evident that Jeremiah's denunciations came as a bombshell to these officials, and they feared for the lives of the two men.

36:23, 24 cut it . . . cast it: This chilling disregard for what had so frightened others (v. 16) shows how far gone from God the royal house was by this time.

happened, when Je·hū'dī had read three or four columns, *that the king* cut it with the scribe's knife and cast *it* into the fire that *was* on the hearth, until all the scroll was consumed in the fire that *was* on the hearth. 24Yet they were not afraid, nor did they tear their garments, the king nor any of his servants who heard all these words. 25Nevertheless El·nā'than, De·laī'ah, and Gem·a·rī'ah implored the king not to burn the scroll; but he would not listen to them. 26And the king commanded Je·rah'mē·el the king's[a] son, Se·rāi'ah the son of Az'ri·el, and Shel·e·mī'ah the son of Ab·dē'el, to seize Bar'uch the scribe and Jer·e·mī'ah the prophet, but the LORD hid them.

Jeremiah Rewrites the Scroll

27Now after the king had burned the scroll with the words which Bar'uch had written at the instruction of Jer·e·mī'ah,[a] the word of the LORD came to Jer·e·mī'ah, saying: 28"Take yet another scroll, and write on it all the former words that were in the first scroll which Je·hoi'a·kim the king of Judah has burned. 29And you shall say to Je·hoi'a·kim king of Judah, 'Thus says the LORD: "You have burned this scroll, saying, 'Why have you written in it that the king of Babylon will certainly come and destroy this land, and cause man and beast to cease from here?' " 30Therefore thus says the LORD concerning Je·hoi'a·kim king of Judah: "He shall have no one to sit on the throne of David, and his dead body shall be cast out to the heat of the day and the frost of the night. 31I will punish him, his family, and his servants for their iniquity; and I will bring on them, on the inhabitants of Jerusalem, and on the men of Judah all the doom that I have pronounced against them; but they did not heed." ' "

32Then Jer·e·mī'ah took another scroll and gave it to Bar'uch the scribe, the son of Ne·rī'ah, who wrote on it at the instruction of Jer·e·mī'ah[a] all the words of the book which Je·hoi'a·kim king of Judah had burned in the fire. And besides, there were added to them many similar words.

CHAPTER 37

Zedekiah's Vain Hope

Now King Zed·e·kī'ah the son of Jō·sī'ah reigned instead of Cō·nī'ah the son of Je·hoi'a·kim, whom Ne·bū·chad·nez'zar king of Babylon made king in the land of Judah. 2But neither he nor his servants nor the people of the land gave heed to the words of the LORD which He spoke by the prophet Jer·e·mī'ah.

3And Zed·e·kī'ah the king sent Je·hū'cal the son of Shel·e·mī'ah, and Zeph·a·nī'ah the son of Mā·a·sēi'ah, the priest, to the prophet Jer·e·mī'ah, saying, "Pray now to the LORD our God for us." 4Now Jer·e·mī'ah was coming and going among the people, for they had not *yet* put him in prison. 5Then Pharaoh's army came up from Egypt; and when the Chal·dē'ans who were besieging Jerusalem heard news of them, they departed from Jerusalem.

6Then the word of the LORD came to the prophet Jer·e·mī'ah, saying, 7"Thus says

36:26 [a]Hebrew *Hammelech* 36:27 [a]Literally *from Jeremiah's mouth* 36:32 [a]Literally *from Jeremiah's mouth*

36:25 implored: At least some of the princes were sensitive to the significance of what the king was doing.

36:26 Because **the LORD hid them**, no one could find them. Without this divine help, Jeremiah and Baruch would have been killed as was Urijah.

36:31 I will punish him: To refuse to listen to God does not lessen our responsibility; it increases it.

37:1–4 The time is the early phase of the siege of Jerusalem in 587 B.C. during the reign of Zedekiah. **Coniah** (Jehoiachin), his nephew and predecessor, had been taken into exile and Zedekiah had been appointed in his place.

the LORD, the God of Israel, 'Thus you shall say to the king of Judah, who sent you to Me to inquire of Me: "Behold, Pharaoh's army which has come up to help you will return to Egypt, to their own land. 8And the Chal·dē'ans shall come back and fight against this city, and take it and burn it with fire." ' 9Thus says the LORD: 'Do not deceive yourselves, saying, "The Chal·dē'ans will surely depart from us," for they will not depart. 10For though you had defeated the whole army of the Chal·dē'ans who fight against you, and there remained *only* wounded men among them, they would rise up, every man in his tent, and burn the city with fire.' "

Jeremiah Imprisoned

11And it happened, when the army of the Chal·dē'ans left *the siege* of Jerusalem for fear of Pharaoh's army, 12that Jer·e·mī'ah went out of Jerusalem to go into the land of Benjamin to claim his property there among the people. 13And when he was in the Gate of Benjamin, a captain of the guard *was* there whose name *was* I·rī'jah the son of Shel·e·mī'ah, the son of Han·a·nī'ah; and he seized Jer·e·mī'ah the prophet, saying, "You are defecting to the Chal·dē'ans!"

14Then Jer·e·mī'ah said, "False! I am not defecting to the Chal·dē'ans." But he did not listen to him.

So I·rī'jah seized Jer·e·mī'ah and brought him to the princes. 15Therefore the princes were angry with Jer·e·mī'ah, and they struck him and put him in prison in the house of Jonathan the scribe. For they had made that the prison.

16When Jer·e·mī'ah entered the dungeon and the cells, and Jer·e·mī'ah had remained there many days, 17then Zed·e·kī'ah the king sent and took him *out*. The king asked him secretly in his house, and said, "Is there *any* word from the LORD?"

And Jer·e·mī'ah said, "There is." Then he said, "You shall be delivered into the hand of the king of Babylon!"

18Moreover Jer·e·mī'ah said to King Zed·e·kī'ah, "What offense have I committed against you, against your servants, or against this people, that you have put me in prison? 19Where now *are* your prophets who prophesied to you, saying, 'The king of Babylon will not come against you or against this land'? 20Therefore please hear now, O my lord the king. Please, let my petition be accepted before you, and do not make me return to the house of Jonathan the scribe, lest I die there."

21Then Zed·e·kī'ah the king commanded that they should commit Jer·e·mī'ah to the court of the prison, and that they should give him daily a piece of bread from the bakers' street, until all the bread in the city was gone. Thus Jer·e·mī'ah remained in the court of the prison.

CHAPTER 38

Jeremiah in the Dungeon

Now Sheph·a·tī'ah the son of Mat'tan, Ged·a·lī'ah the son of Pash'hur, Jū'cal[a] the son of Shel·e·mī'ah, and Pash'hur the son of Mal·chī'ah heard the words that Jer·e·mī'ah had spoken to all the people, saying, 2"Thus says the LORD: 'He who remains in this city shall die by the sword, by famine, and by pestilence; but he who goes over to the Chal·dē'ans shall live; his life shall be as a prize to him, and he shall live.'[a] 3Thus says the LORD: 'This city shall surely be given into the hand of the king of Babylon's army, which shall take it.' "

4Therefore the princes said to the king, "Please, let this man be put to death, for thus he weakens the hands of the men of war who remain in this city, and the hands of all the people, by speaking such words

38:1 aSame as *Jehucal* (compare 37:3) 38:2 aCompare 21:9

37:17 secretly: The king was not in full control.

to them. For this man does not seek the welfare of this people, but their harm."

5 Then Zed·e·kī'ah the king said, "Look, he *is* in your hand. For the king can *do* nothing against you." 6 So they took Jer·e·mī'ah and cast him into the dungeon of Mal·chī'ah the king's[a] son, which *was* in the court of the prison, and they let Jer·e·mī'ah down with ropes. And in the dungeon *there was* no water, but mire. So Jer·e·mī'ah sank in the mire.

7 Now Ē'bed-Mē'lech the Ethiopian, one of the eunuchs, who was in the king's house, heard that they had put Jer·e·mī'ah in the dungeon. When the king was sitting at the Gate of Benjamin, 8 Ē'bed-Mē'lech went out of the king's house and spoke to the king, saying: 9 "My lord the king, these men have done evil in all that they have done to Jer·e·mī'ah the prophet, whom they have cast into the dungeon, and he is likely to die from hunger in the place where he is. For *there is* no more bread in the city." 10 Then the king commanded Ē'bed-Mē'lech the Ethiopian, saying, "Take from here thirty men with you, and lift Jer·e·mī'ah the prophet out of the dungeon before he dies." 11 So Ē'bed-Mē'lech took the men with him and went into the house of the king under the treasury, and took from there old clothes and old rags, and let them down by ropes into the dungeon to Jer·e·mī'ah. 12 Then Ē'bed-Mē'lech the Ethiopian said to Jer·e·mī'ah, "Please put these old clothes and rags under your armpits, under the ropes." And Jer·e·mī'ah did so. 13 So they pulled Jer·e·mī'ah up with ropes and lifted him out of the dungeon. And Jer·e·mī'ah remained in the court of the prison.

Zedekiah's Fears and Jeremiah's Advice

14 Then Zed·e·kī'ah the king sent and had Jer·e·mī'ah the prophet brought to him at the third entrance of the house of the LORD. And the king said to Jer·e·mī'ah, "I will ask you something. Hide nothing from me."

15 Jer·e·mī'ah said to Zed·e·kī'ah, "If I declare *it* to you, will you not surely put me to death? And if I give you advice, you will not listen to me."

16 So Zed·e·kī'ah the king swore secretly to Jer·e·mī'ah, saying, "*As* the LORD lives, who made our very souls, I will not put you to death, nor will I give you into the hand of these men who seek your life."

17 Then Jer·e·mī'ah said to Zed·e·kī'ah, "Thus says the LORD, the God of hosts, the God of Israel: 'If you surely surrender to the king of Babylon's princes, then your soul shall live; this city shall not be burned with fire, and you and your house shall live. 18 But if you do not surrender to the king of Babylon's princes, then this city shall be given into the hand of the Chal·dē'ans; they shall burn it with fire, and you shall not escape from their hand.' "

19 And Zed·e·kī'ah the king said to Jer·e·mī'ah, "I am afraid of the Jews who have defected to the Chal·dē'ans, lest they deliver me into their hand, and they abuse me."

38:6 [a]Hebrew *Hammelech*

38:6 dungeon: This cistern had **mire**, several feet of soggy mud, in the bottom. When Jeremiah grew tired of standing, he would slowly sink into it and die, thus his death could not be blamed on the princes.

38:7 Ethiopian: How ironic that Jeremiah had to be rescued by a foreigner. Rulers customarily served as judges for the complaints of the common citizens while sitting at a gateway, a location easily accessible to all.

38:11, 12 rags: Interesting details that support the authenticity of the account. Shows their care and concern for Jeremiah.

38:17–23 A pathetic story. The king receives a word from God that is not wholly negative, but he does not have the courage to act upon it.

20But Jer·e·mī′ah said, "They shall not
deliver *you.* Please, obey the voice of the
LORD which I speak to you. So it shall be
well with you, and your soul shall live.
21But if you refuse to surrender, this *is* the
word that the LORD has shown me: 22'Now
behold, all the women who are left in the
king of Judah's house *shall be* surrendered
to the king of Babylon's princes, and those
women shall say:

"Your close friends have set upon you
And prevailed against you;
Your feet have sunk in the mire,
And they have turned away again."

23'So they shall surrender all your wives
and children to the Chal·dē′ans. You shall
not escape from their hand, but shall be
taken by the hand of the king of Babylon.
And you shall cause this city to be burned
with fire.' "
24Then Zed·e·kī′ah said to Jer·e·mī′ah,
"Let no one know of these words, and you
shall not die. 25But if the princes hear that I
have talked with you, and they come to
you and say to you, 'Declare to us now
what you have said to the king, and also
what the king said to you; do not hide *it*
from us, and we will not put you to death,'
26then you shall say to them, 'I presented
my request before the king, that he would
not make me return to Jonathan's house to
die there.' "
27Then all the princes came to
Jer·e·mī′ah and asked him. And he told
them according to all these words that the
king had commanded. So they stopped
speaking with him, for the conversation
had not been heard. 28Now Jer·e·mī′ah re-
mained in the court of the prison until the
day that Jerusalem was taken. And he was
there when Jerusalem was taken.

CHAPTER 39

The Fall of Jerusalem

In the ninth year of Zed·e·kī′ah king of
Judah, in the tenth month, Ne·bū-
chad·nez′zar king of Babylon and all his
army came against Jerusalem, and be-
sieged it. 2In the eleventh year of
Zed·e·kī′ah, in the fourth month, on the
ninth *day* of the month, the city was pene-
trated.
3Then all the princes of the king of Bab-
ylon came in and sat in the Middle Gate:
Ner′gal-Sha·rē′zer, Sam′gar-Nē′bō,
Sar′se·chim, Rab·sar′is,[a] Ner′gal-Sa·rē′zer,
Rab′mag,[b] with the rest of the princes of
the king of Babylon.
4So it was, when Zed·e·kī′ah the king of
Judah and all the men of war saw them,
that they fled and went out of the city by
night, by way of the king's garden, by the
gate between the two walls. And he went
out by way of the plain.[a] 5But the
Chal·dē′an army pursued them and over-
took Zed·e·kī′ah in the plains of Jericho.
And when they had captured him, they
brought him up to Ne·bū·chad·nez′zar
king of Babylon, to Rib′lah in the land of
Hā′math, where he pronounced judgment
on him. 6Then the king of Babylon killed
the sons of Zed·e·kī′ah before his eyes in
Rib′lah; the king of Babylon also killed all
the nobles of Judah. 7Moreover he put out

39:3 [a]A title, probably *Chief Officer;* also verse 13 [b]A title, probably *Troop Commander;* also verse 13
39:4 [a]Or *the Arabah,* that is, the Jordan Valley

38:20, 21 Jeremiah insisted that King Zedekiah had a choice. Everyone does when obedience to the Lord is involved.

38:22, 23 Although obedience is sometimes hard, the consequences of disobedience are worse. **you shall cause**: Our wrong choices often injure other people.

39:3–5 While the Babylonians were entering the northern part of the city, **Zedekiah** and his court fled through a southern gate toward the **plain**, meaning the Jordan valley.

39:6–9 The words of the Lord through Jeremiah were fulfilled in these horrible days after the fall of Jerusalem.

Zed·e·kī'ah's eyes, and bound him with
bronze fetters to carry him off to Babylon.
8And the Chal·dē'ans burned the king's
house and the houses of the people with
fire, and broke down the walls of Jerusa-
lem. 9Then Ne·bū·za·rad'an the captain of
the guard carried away captive to Babylon
the remnant of the people who remained
in the city and those who defected to him,
with the rest of the people who remained.
10But Ne·bū·za·rad'an the captain of the
guard left in the land of Judah the poor
people, who had nothing, and gave them
vineyards and fields at the same time.

Jeremiah Goes Free

11Now Ne·bū·chad·nez'zar king of
Babylon gave charge concerning Jer·e-
mī'ah to Ne·bū·za·rad'an the captain of
the guard, saying, 12"Take him and look af-
ter him, and do him no harm; but do to
him just as he says to you." 13So Ne·bū-
za·rad'an the captain of the guard sent
Ne·bū·shas'ban, Rab·sar'is, Ner'gal-
Sha·rē'zer, Rab'mag, and all the king of
Babylon's chief officers; 14then they sent
someone to take Jer·e·mī'ah from the court
of the prison, and committed him to
Ged·a·lī'ah the son of A·hī'kam, the son of
Shā'phan, that he should take him home.
So he dwelt among the people.
15Meanwhile the word of the LORD had
come to Jer·e·mī'ah while he was shut up
in the court of the prison, saying, 16"Go and
speak to Ē'bed-Mē'lech the Ethiopian, say-
ing, 'Thus says the LORD of hosts, the God
of Israel: "Behold, I will bring My words
upon this city for adversity and not for
good, and they shall be *performed* in that
day before you. 17But I will deliver you in
that day," says the LORD, "and you shall
not be given into the hand of the men of
whom you *are* afraid. 18For I will surely de-
liver you, and you shall not fall by the
sword; but your life shall be as a prize to
you, because you have put your trust in
Me," says the LORD.' "

CHAPTER 40

Jeremiah with Gedaliah the Governor

The word that came to Jer·e·mī'ah from
the LORD after Ne·bū·za·rad'an the captain
of the guard had let him go from Rā'mah,
when he had taken him bound in chains
among all who were carried away captive
from Jerusalem and Judah, who were car-
ried away captive to Babylon.
2And the captain of the guard took
Jer·e·mī'ah and said to him: "The LORD
your God has pronounced this doom on
this place. 3Now the LORD has brought *it*,
and has done just as He said. Because you
people have sinned against the LORD, and
not obeyed His voice, therefore this thing
has come upon you. 4And now look, I free
you this day from the chains that *were* on
your hand. If it seems good to you to come
with me to Babylon, come, and I will look
after you. But if it seems wrong for you to
come with me to Babylon, remain here.
See, all the land *is* before you; wherever it
seems good and convenient for you to go,
go there."
5Now while Jer·e·mī'ah had not yet
gone back, *Ne·bū·za·rad'an said,* "Go back
to Ged·a·lī'ah the son of A·hī'kam, the son
of Shā'phan, whom the king of Babylon

39:11–14 look after him: King **Nebuchadnezzar**, recognizing that Jeremiah had been his ally, granted a special favor to him—freedom and provisions. **Gedaliah**: This newly appointed governor as well as his father, **Ahikam**, were close friends of Jeremiah.

40:1—44:30 This account of events after the fall of Jerusalem shows that the stubborn rebelliousness of the people did not end with the fall of the city.

40:1 In the confusion of rounding up captives, it seems Jeremiah was arrested by mistake.

40:4–6 Jeremiah had a choice: he could leave his people and have full provisions, or stay with the poor survivors and help them. He chose the latter.

has made governor over the cities of Ju-
dah, and dwell with him among the peo-
ple. Or go wherever it seems convenient
for you to go." So the captain of the guard
gave him rations and a gift and let him go.
6Then Jer·e·mī'ah went to Ged·a·lī'ah the
son of A·hī'kam, to Miz'pah, and dwelt
with him among the people who were left
in the land.
7And when all the captains of the armies
who *were* in the fields, they and their men,
heard that the king of Babylon had made
Ged·a·lī'ah the son of A·hī'kam governor
in the land, and had committed to him
men, women, children, and the poorest of
the land who had not been carried away
captive to Babylon, 8then they came to
Ged·a·lī'ah at Miz'pah—Ish'ma·el the son
of Neth·a·nī'ah, Jō·hā'nan and Jonathan
the sons of Ka·rē'ah, Se·rāi'ah the son of
Tan'hu·meth, the sons of Ē'phaī the
Ne·toph'a·thīte, and Jez·a·nī'ah[a] the son
of a Mā'a·cha·thīte, they and their men.
9And Ged·a·lī'ah the son of A·hī'kam, the
son of Shā'phan, took an oath before them
and their men, saying, "Do not be afraid to
serve the Chal·dē'ans. Dwell in the land
and serve the king of Babylon, and it shall
be well with you. 10As for me, I will indeed
dwell at Miz'pah and serve the Chal-
dē'ans who come to us. But you, gather
wine and summer fruit and oil, put *them* in
your vessels, and dwell in your cities that
you have taken." 11Likewise, when all the
Jews who *were* in Mō'ab, among the
Am'mon·ītes, in Ē'dom, and who *were* in
all the countries, heard that the king of
Babylon had left a remnant of Judah, and
that he had set over them Ged·a·lī'ah the
son of A·hī'kam, the son of Shā'phan,
12then all the Jews returned out of all places
where they had been driven, and came to
the land of Judah, to Ged·a·lī'ah at
Miz'pah, and gathered wine and summer
fruit in abundance.
13Moreover Jō·hā'nan the son of
Ka·rē'ah and all the captains of the forces
that *were* in the fields came to Ged·a·lī'ah
at Miz'pah, 14and said to him, "Do you cer-
tainly know that Bā'a·lis the king of the
Am'mon·ītes has sent Ish'ma·el the son of
Neth·a·nī'ah to murder you?" But
Ged·a·lī'ah the son of A·hī'kam did not
believe them.
15Then Jō·hā'nan the son of Ka·rē'ah
spoke secretly to Ged·a·lī'ah in Miz'pah,
saying, "Let me go, please, and I will kill
Ish'ma·el the son of Neth·a·nī'ah, and no
one will know *it*. Why should he murder
you, so that all the Jews who are gathered
to you would be scattered, and the rem-
nant in Judah perish?"
16But Ged·a·lī'ah the son of A·hī'kam
said to Jō·hā'nan the son of Ka·rē'ah, "You
shall not do this thing, for you speak
falsely concerning Ish'ma·el."

CHAPTER 41

Insurrection Against Gedaliah

Now it came to pass in the seventh
month *that* Ish'ma·el the son of Neth-
a·nī'ah, the son of E·lish'a·ma, of the royal
family and of the officers of the king, came
with ten men to Ged·a·lī'ah the son of
A·hī'kam, at Miz'pah. And there they ate
bread together in Miz'pah. 2Then Ish'ma·el
the son of Neth·a·nī'ah, and the ten men
who were with him, arose and struck
Ged·a·lī'ah the son of A·hī'kam, the son of
Shā'phan, with the sword, and killed him
whom the king of Babylon had made gov-
ernor over the land. 3Ish'ma·el also struck
down all the Jews who were with him, *that
is,* with Ged·a·lī'ah at Miz'pah, and the

40:8 [a]Spelled *Jaazaniah* in 2 Kings 25:23

40:9, 10 Gedaliah . . . took an oath: He granted amnesty to the soldiers who had fought the Babylonians and gave them fields for crops.
41:2, 3 Ishmael . . . struck: A flagrant violation of hospitality taking everyone, including Johanan (40:15, 16; 41:11), by surprise.

Chal·dē′ans who were found there, the men of war.

4And it happened, on the second day after he had killed Ged·a·lī′ah, when as yet no one knew *it,* 5that certain men came from Shē′chem, from Shī′lōh, and from Samaria, eighty men with their beards shaved and their clothes torn, having cut themselves, with offerings and incense in their hand, to bring *them* to the house of the LORD. 6Now Ish′ma·el the son of Neth·a·nī′ah went out from Miz′pah to meet them, weeping as he went along; and it happened as he met them that he said to them, "Come to Ged·a·lī′ah the son of A·hī′kam!" 7So it was, when they came into the midst of the city, that Ish′ma·el the son of Neth·a·nī′ah killed them *and cast them* into the midst of a pit, he and the men who were with him. 8But ten men were found among them who said to Ish′ma·el, "Do not kill us, for we have treasures of wheat, barley, oil, and honey in the field." So he desisted and did not kill them among their brethren. 9Now the pit into which Ish′ma·el had cast all the dead bodies of the men whom he had slain, because of Ged·a·lī′ah, *was* the same one Ā′sa the king had made for fear of Bā′a-sha king of Israel. Ish′ma·el the son of Neth·a·nī′ah filled it with *the* slain. 10Then Ish′ma·el carried away captive all the rest of the people who *were* in Miz′-pah, the king's daughters and all the people who remained in Miz′pah, whom Ne·bū·za·rad′an the captain of the guard had committed to Ged·a·lī′ah the son of A·hī′kam. And Ish′ma·el the son of Neth·a·nī′ah carried them away captive and departed to go over to the Am′-mon·ītes.

11But when Jō·hā′nan the son of Ka·rē′ah and all the captains of the forces that *were* with him heard of all the evil that Ish′ma·el the son of Neth·a·nī′ah had done, 12they took all the men and went to fight with Ish′ma·el the son of Neth·a·nī′ah; and they found him by the great pool that *is* in Gib′ē·on. 13So it was, when all the people who *were* with Ish′ma·el saw Jō·hā′nan the son of Ka·rē′ah, and all the captains of the forces who *were* with him, that they were glad. 14Then all the people whom Ish′ma·el had carried away captive from Miz′pah turned around and came back, and went to Jō·hā′nan the son of Ka·rē′ah. 15But Ish′ma·el the son of Neth·a·nī′ah escaped from Jō·hā′nan with eight men and went to the Am′mon·ītes.

16Then Jō·hā′nan the son of Ka·rē′ah, and all the captains of the forces that were with him, took from Miz′pah all the rest of the people whom he had recovered from Ish′ma·el the son of Neth·a·nī′ah after he had murdered Ged·a·lī′ah the son of A·hī′kam—the mighty men of war and the women and the children and the eunuchs, whom he had brought back from Gib′ē·on. 17And they departed and dwelt in the habitation of Chim′ham, which is near Bethlehem, as they went on their way to Egypt, 18because of the Chal·dē′ans; for they were afraid of them, because Ish′ma·el the son of Neth·a·nī′ah had murdered Ged·a·lī′ah the son of A·hī′kam, whom the king of Babylon had made governor in the land.

CHAPTER 42

The Flight to Egypt Forbidden

Now all the captains of the forces, Jō·hā′nan the son of Ka·rē′ah, Jez·a·nī′ah the son of Hō·shaī′ah, and all the people,

41:4–9 The reason for this atrocity is not given. It is perhaps recounted here to illustrate Ishmael's pointless blood lust.

42:1–6 pray for us: At that time the people seemed sincere. But it is apparent from their response (43:2–4) that all they really wanted was confirmation for a course of action already chosen.

from the least to the greatest, came near
[2]and said to Jer•e•mī′ah the prophet,
"Please, let our petition be acceptable to
you, and pray for us to the LORD your God,
for all this remnant (since we are left *but* a
few of many, as you can see), [3]that the
LORD your God may show us the way in
which we should walk and the thing we
should do."

[4]Then Jer•e•mī′ah the prophet said to
them, "I have heard. Indeed, I will pray to
the LORD your God according to your
words, and it shall be, *that* whatever the
LORD answers you, I will declare *it* to you.
I will keep nothing back from you."

[5]So they said to Jer•e•mī′ah, "Let the
LORD be a true and faithful witness be-
tween us, if we do not do according to
everything which the LORD your God
sends us by you. [6]Whether *it is* pleasing or
displeasing, we will obey the voice of the
LORD our God to whom we send you, that
it may be well with us when we obey the
voice of the LORD our God."

[7]And it happened after ten days that the
word of the LORD came to Jer•e•mī′ah.
[8]Then he called Jō•hā′nan the son of
Ka•rē′ah, all the captains of the forces
which *were* with him, and all the people
from the least even to the greatest, [9]and
said to them, "Thus says the LORD, the God
of Israel, to whom you sent me to present
your petition before Him: [10]'If you will still
remain in this land, then I will build you
and not pull *you* down, and I will plant you
and not pluck *you* up. For I relent concern-
ing the disaster that I have brought upon
you. [11]Do not be afraid of the king of Bab-
ylon, of whom you are afraid; do not be
afraid of him,' says the LORD, 'for I *am* with
you, to save you and deliver you from his
hand. [12]And I will show you mercy, that he
may have mercy on you and cause you to
return to your own land.'

[13]"But if you say, 'We will not dwell in
this land,' disobeying the voice of the LORD
your God, [14]saying, 'No, but we will go to
the land of Egypt where we shall see no
war, nor hear the sound of the trumpet, nor
be hungry for bread, and there we will
dwell'— [15]Then hear now the word of the
LORD, O remnant of Judah! Thus says the
LORD of hosts, the God of Israel: 'If you
wholly set your faces to enter Egypt, and
go to dwell there, [16]then it shall be *that* the
sword which you feared shall overtake
you there in the land of Egypt; the famine
of which you were afraid shall follow close
after you there *in* Egypt; and there you
shall die. [17]So shall it be with all the men
who set their faces to go to Egypt to dwell
there. They shall die by the sword, by
famine, and by pestilence. And none of
them shall remain or escape from the dis-
aster that I will bring upon them.'

[18]"For thus says the LORD of hosts, the
God of Israel: 'As My anger and My fury
have been poured out on the inhabitants of
Jerusalem, so will My fury be poured out
on you when you enter Egypt. And you
shall be an oath, an astonishment, a curse,
and a reproach; and you shall see this place
no more.'

[19]"The LORD has said concerning you, O
remnant of Judah, 'Do not go to Egypt!'
Know certainly that I have admonished
you this day. [20]For you were hypocrites in
your hearts when you sent me to the LORD
your God, saying, 'Pray for us to the LORD
our God, and according to all that the
LORD your God says, so declare to us and
we will do *it*.' [21]And I have this day de-
clared *it* to you, but you have not obeyed
the voice of the LORD your God, or

42:7–18 If (v. 10): The people had a choice amounting to a dilemma. If they trusted the Lord and stayed where they were, they would have to cope with their fear of the Babylonians. If they fled to Egypt, which seemed the reasonable thing to do, they would have to face the anger of the Lord.

42:11 The Lord still assures us, when **I am with you**, you do not need to be afraid of the things of which **you are afraid**.

anything which He has sent you by me.
22Now therefore, know certainly that you
shall die by the sword, by famine, and by
pestilence in the place where you desire to
go to dwell."

CHAPTER 43

Jeremiah Taken to Egypt

Now it happened, when Jer·e·mī'ah
had stopped speaking to all the people all
the words of the LORD their God, for which
the LORD their God had sent him to them,
all these words, 2that Az·a·rī'ah the son of
Hō·shaī'ah, Jō·hā'nan the son of Ka·rē'ah,
and all the proud men spoke, saying to
Jer·e·mī'ah, "You speak falsely! The LORD
our God has not sent you to say, 'Do not go
to Egypt to dwell there.' 3But Bar'uch the
son of Ne·rī'ah has set you against us, to
deliver us into the hand of the Chal·dē'ans,
that they may put us to death or carry us
away captive to Babylon." 4So Jō·hā'nan
the son of Ka·rē'ah, all the captains of the
forces, and all the people would not obey
the voice of the LORD, to remain in the land
of Judah. 5But Jō·hā'nan the son of
Ka·rē'ah and all the captains of the forces
took all the remnant of Judah who had re-
turned to dwell in the land of Judah, from
all nations where they had been driven—
6men, women, children, the king's daugh-
ters, and every person whom Ne·bū-
za·rad'an the captain of the guard had left
with Ged·a·lī'ah the son of A·hī'kam, the
son of Shā'phan, and Jer·e·mī'ah the
prophet and Bar'uch the son of Ne·rī'ah.
7So they went to the land of Egypt, for they
did not obey the voice of the LORD. And
they went as far as Tah'pan·hēs.

8Then the word of the LORD came to
Jer·e·mī'ah in Tah'pan·hēs, saying, 9"Take
large stones in your hand, and hide them
in the sight of the men of Judah, in the clay
in the brick courtyard which *is* at the en-
trance to Pharaoh's house in Tah'pan·hēs;
10and say to them, 'Thus says the LORD of
hosts, the God of Israel: "Behold, I will
send and bring Ne·bū·chad·nez'zar the
king of Babylon, My servant, and will set
his throne above these stones that I have
hidden. And he will spread his royal pavil-
ion over them. 11When he comes, he shall
strike the land of Egypt *and deliver* to death
those appointed for death, and to captivity
those appointed for captivity, and to the
sword *those appointed* for the sword. 12I[a]
will kindle a fire in the houses of the gods
of Egypt, and he shall burn them and carry
them away captive. And he shall array
himself with the land of Egypt, as a shep-
herd puts on his garment, and he shall go
out from there in peace. 13He shall also
break the sacred pillars of Beth Shem'esh[a]
that *are* in the land of Egypt; and the
houses of the gods of the Egyptians he
shall burn with fire." ' "

CHAPTER 44

Israelites Will Be Punished in Egypt

The word that came to Jer·e·mī'ah con-
cerning all the Jews who dwell in the land
of Egypt, who dwell at Mig'dōl, at
Tah'pan·hēs, at Noph,[a] and in the country
of Path'ros, saying, 2"Thus says the LORD
of hosts, the God of Israel: 'You have seen
all the calamity that I have brought on Je-
rusalem and on all the cities of Judah; and

43:12 [a]Following Masoretic Text and Targum; Septuagint, Syriac, and Vulgate read *He*. 43:13 [a]Literally *House of the Sun*, ancient On; later called Heliopolis
44:1 [a]That is, ancient Memphis

42:22 For the fulfillment of these predictions see 43:10–13.

43:2 Azariah and others held that surely the Lord's word would not be different from the popular will of the group.

43:10–13 The fugitives from Judah would not escape the Babylonians; the Lord would allow Babylon to rule Egypt also. The Babylonian invasion of Egypt in 568–67 B.C. would be ruthless.

44:1–30 The last recorded messages of the Lord through Jeremiah.

behold, this day they *are* a desolation, and
no one dwells in them, 3because of their
wickedness which they have committed to
provoke Me to anger, in that they went to
burn incense *and* to serve other gods
whom they did not know, they nor you nor
your fathers. 4However I have sent to you
all My servants the prophets, rising early
and sending *them,* saying, "Oh, do not do
this abominable thing that I hate!" 5But
they did not listen or incline their ear to
turn from their wickedness, to burn no in-
cense to other gods. 6So My fury and My
anger were poured out and kindled in the
cities of Judah and in the streets of Jerusa-
lem; and they are wasted *and* desolate, as it
is this day.'

7"Now therefore, thus says the LORD, the
God of hosts, the God of Israel: 'Why do
you commit *this* great evil against your-
selves, to cut off from you man and
woman, child and infant, out of Judah,
leaving none to remain, 8in that you pro-
voke Me to wrath with the works of your
hands, burning incense to other gods in the
land of Egypt where you have gone to
dwell, that you may cut yourselves off and
be a curse and a reproach among all the na-
tions of the earth? 9Have you forgotten the
wickedness of your fathers, the wicked-
ness of the kings of Judah, the wickedness
of their wives, your own wickedness, and
the wickedness of your wives, which they
committed in the land of Judah and in the
streets of Jerusalem? 10They have not been
humbled, to this day, nor have they feared;
they have not walked in My law or in My
statutes that I set before you and your
fathers.'

11"Therefore thus says the LORD of hosts,
the God of Israel: 'Behold, I will set My
face against you for catastrophe and for
cutting off all Judah. 12And I will take the
remnant of Judah who have set their faces
to go into the land of Egypt to dwell there,
and they shall all be consumed *and* fall in
the land of Egypt. They shall be consumed
by the sword *and* by famine. They shall
die, from the least to the greatest, by the
sword and by famine; and they shall be an
oath, an astonishment, a curse and a re-
proach! 13For I will punish those who dwell
in the land of Egypt, as I have punished Je-
rusalem, by the sword, by famine, and by
pestilence, 14so that none of the remnant of
Judah who have gone into the land of
Egypt to dwell there shall escape or sur-
vive, lest they return to the land of Judah,
to which they desire to return and dwell.
For none shall return except those who es-
cape.' "

15Then all the men who knew that their
wives had burned incense to other gods,
with all the women who stood by, a great
multitude, and all the people who dwelt in
the land of Egypt, in Path'ros, answered
Jer·e·mī'ah, saying: 16"*As for* the word that
you have spoken to us in the name of the
LORD, we will not listen to you! 17But we
will certainly do whatever has gone out of
our own mouth, to burn incense to the
queen of heaven and pour out drink offer-
ings to her, as we have done, we and our
fathers, our kings and our princes, in the
cities of Judah and in the streets of Jerusa-
lem. For *then* we had plenty of food, were
well-off, and saw no trouble. 18But since we
stopped burning incense to the queen of
heaven and pouring out drink offerings to
her, we have lacked everything and have
been consumed by the sword and by
famine."

19*The women also said,* "And when we
burned incense to the queen of heaven and
poured out drink offerings to her, did we
make cakes for her, to worship her, and

44:17 queen of heaven: The mother-goddess of the Canaanites known as Asherah or Ishtar. **then we had plenty**: Evidently referring to the time before King Josiah.

44:18 But since we stopped: A reference to Josiah's reforms. After Josiah's death Judah had been defeated by the Egyptians and invaded by the Babylonians.

pour out drink offerings to her without our
husbands' *permission?*"
20 Then Jer·e·mi'ah spoke to all the peo-
ple—the men, the women, and all the peo-
ple who had given him *that* answer—say-
ing: 21 "The incense that you burned in the
cities of Judah and in the streets of Jerusa-
lem, you and your fathers, your kings and
your princes, and the people of the land,
did not the LORD remember them, and did
it *not* come into His mind? 22 So the LORD
could no longer bear *it*, because of the evil
of your doings *and* because of the
abominations which you committed.
Therefore your land is a desolation, an as-
tonishment, a curse, and without an inhab-
itant, as *it is* this day. 23 Because you have
burned incense and because you have
sinned against the LORD, and have not
obeyed the voice of the LORD or walked in
His law, in His statutes or in His testi-
monies, therefore this calamity has hap-
pened to you, as *at* this day."
24 Moreover Jer·e·mi'ah said to all the
people and to all the women, "Hear the
word of the LORD, all Judah who *are* in
the land of Egypt! 25 Thus says the LORD of
hosts, the God of Israel, saying: 'You and
your wives have spoken with your mouths
and fulfilled with your hands, saying, "We
will surely keep our vows that we have
made, to burn incense to the queen of
heaven and pour out drink offerings to
her." You will surely keep your vows and
perform your vows!' 26 Therefore hear the
word of the LORD, all Judah who dwell in
the land of Egypt: 'Behold, I have sworn by
My great name,' says the LORD, 'that My
name shall no more be named in the
mouth of any man of Judah in all the land
of Egypt, saying, "The Lord GOD lives."
27 Behold, I will watch over them for adver-
sity and not for good. And all the men of
Judah who *are* in the land of Egypt shall be
consumed by the sword and by famine,
until there is an end to them. 28 Yet a small
number who escape the sword shall return
from the land of Egypt to the land of Ju-
dah; and all the remnant of Judah, who
have gone to the land of Egypt to dwell
there, shall know whose words will stand,
Mine or theirs. 29 And this *shall be* a sign to
you,' says the LORD, 'that I will punish you
in this place, that you may know that My
words will surely stand against you for ad-
versity.'
30 "Thus says the LORD: 'Behold, I will
give Pharaoh Hoph'ra king of Egypt into
the hand of his enemies and into the hand
of those who seek his life, as I gave
Zed·e·ki'ah king of Judah into the hand of
Ne·bu·chad·nez'zar king of Babylon, his
enemy who sought his life.' "

CHAPTER 45

Assurance to Baruch

The word that Jer·e·mi'ah the prophet
spoke to Bar'uch the son of Ne·ri'ah, when
he had written these words in a book at the
instruction of Jer·e·mi'ah,[a] in the fourth
year of Je·hoi'a·kim the son of Jo·si'ah,
king of Judah, saying, 2 "Thus says the
LORD, the God of Israel, to you, O Bar'uch:

45:1 [a]Literally *from Jeremiah's mouth*

44:20–23 Jeremiah had to repeat what he had said many times: the cause of their calamity was the wicked worship of idols instead of worshiping the one true God.

44:29, 30 this shall be a sign: Historical events would be a testimony that made clear the truth of God's word. **Pharaoh Hophra**, ruler of Egypt from 589 to 570 B.C., died in a coup led by his rivals.

45:1–5 A flashback to the events recorded in 36:1–19. **great things for yourself** (v. 5): Baruch's brother, Seraiah (both were sons of Neriah, 32:12; 51:59), served as a high official under King Zedekiah (51:59–64). Baruch had good reason to believe that he, too, could have gained a responsible position in Judah's court. He forfeited that dream by siding with Jeremiah and alienating Judah's rulers. **I will give your life to you**: God rewarded a man for his faithfulness.

[3]'You said, "Woe is me now! For the LORD
has added grief to my sorrow. I fainted in
my sighing, and I find no rest." '

[4]"Thus you shall say to him, 'Thus says
the LORD: "Behold, what I have built I will
break down, and what I have planted I will
pluck up, that is, this whole land. [5]And do
you seek great things for yourself? Do not
seek *them;* for behold, I will bring adversity
on all flesh," says the LORD. "But I will give
your life to you as a prize in all places,
wherever you go." ' "

CHAPTER 46

Judgment on Egypt

The word of the LORD which came to
Jer·e·mī'ah the prophet against the na-
tions. [2]Against Egypt.

Concerning the army of Pharaoh Nē'cho, king of Egypt, which was by the River Eū·phrā'tēs in Car'chem·ish, and which Ne·bū·chad·nez'zar king of Babylon defeated in the fourth year of Je·hoi'a·kim the son of Jō·sī'ah, king of Judah:

3 "Order the buckler and shield,
And draw near to battle!
4 Harness the horses,
And mount up, you horsemen!
Stand forth with *your* helmets,
Polish the spears,
Put on the armor!
5 Why have I seen them dismayed *and*
turned back?
Their mighty ones are beaten down;
They have speedily fled,
And did not look back,
For fear *was* all around," says the
LORD.
6 "Do not let the swift flee away,
Nor the mighty man escape;
They will stumble and fall
Toward the north, by the River
Eū·phrā'tēs.

7 "Who *is* this coming up like a flood,
Whose waters move like the rivers?
8 Egypt rises up like a flood,
And *its* waters move like the
rivers;
And he says, 'I will go up *and* cover
the earth,
I will destroy the city and its
inhabitants.'
9 Come up, O horses, and rage,
O chariots!
And let the mighty men come forth:
The Ethiopians and the Lib'yans who
handle the shield,
And the Lyd'i·ans who handle *and*
bend the bow.
10 For this *is* the day of the Lord GOD of
hosts,
A day of vengeance,
That He may avenge Himself on His
adversaries.
The sword shall devour;
It shall be satiated and made drunk
with their blood;
For the Lord GOD of hosts has a
sacrifice
In the north country by the River
Eū·phrā'tēs.

11 "Go up to Gil'ē·ad and take balm,
O virgin, the daughter of Egypt;
In vain you will use many medicines;
You shall not be cured.
12 The nations have heard of your
shame,
And your cry has filled the land;
For the mighty man has stumbled
against the mighty;
They both have fallen together."

46:1—51:64 A series of messages which Jeremiah spoke at various times in his life against pagan nations. Although God would judge His people through these nations, this did not mean that their evils would go unpunished.

46:10–12 The defeat was an incurable wound after which Egypt would never recover her power over Syria and Palestine.

Babylonia Will Strike Egypt

[13]The word that the LORD spoke to Jer·e·mi'ah the prophet, how Ne·bū-chad·nez'zar king of Babylon would come *and* strike the land of Egypt.

14 "Declare in Egypt, and proclaim in Mig'dōl;
Proclaim in Noph[a] and in Tah'pan·hēs;
Say, 'Stand fast and prepare yourselves,
For the sword devours all around you.'
15 Why are your valiant *men* swept away?
They did not stand
Because the LORD drove them away.
16 He made many fall;
Yes, one fell upon another.
And they said, 'Arise!
Let us go back to our own people
And to the land of our nativity
From the oppressing sword.'
17 They cried there,
'Pharaoh, king of Egypt, *is but* a noise.
He has passed by the appointed time!'

18 "*As* I live," says the King,
Whose name *is* the LORD of hosts,
"Surely as Tā'bor *is* among the mountains
And as Car'mel by the sea, *so* he shall come.
19 O you daughter dwelling in Egypt,
Prepare yourself to go into captivity!
For Noph[a] shall be waste and desolate, without inhabitant.

20 "Egypt *is* a very pretty heifer,
But destruction comes, it comes from the north.
21 Also her mercenaries are in her midst like fat bulls,
For they also are turned back,
They have fled away together.
They did not stand,
For the day of their calamity had come upon them,
The time of their punishment.
22 Her noise shall go like a serpent,
For they shall march with an army
And come against her with axes,
Like those who chop wood.

23 "They shall cut down her forest," says the LORD,
"Though it cannot be searched,
Because they *are* innumerable,
And more numerous than grasshoppers.
24 The daughter of Egypt shall be ashamed;
She shall be delivered into the hand
Of the people of the north."

[25]The LORD of hosts, the God of Israel, says: "Behold, I will bring punishment on Ā'mon[a] of No,[b] and Pharaoh and Egypt, with their gods and their kings—Pharaoh and those who trust in him. [26]And I will deliver them into the hand of those who seek their lives, into the hand of Ne·bū-chad·nez'zar king of Babylon and the hand of his servants. Afterward it shall be inhabited as in the days of old," says the LORD.

God Will Preserve Israel

27 "But do not fear, O My servant Jacob,
And do not be dismayed, O Israel!
For behold, I will save you from afar,

46:14 [a]That is, ancient Memphis 46:19 [a]That is, ancient Memphis 46:25 [a]A sun god [b]That is, ancient Thebes

46:13–17 Jeremiah made other similar prophecies against Egypt (43:8–13; 44:30). **go back** (v. 16): Those who survived and fled to Egypt would be left comfortless.

46:23, 24 They: **the people of the north**, the Babylonians.

46:25 Amon: The main god of Egypt who was especially worshiped at the temple of Karnak in Thebes. The city of **No** was Thebes, an ancient capital of Egypt in the south.

46:27, 28 In the midst of international chaos, Israel had a sure promise of the presence

And your offspring from the land of
their captivity;
Jacob shall return, have rest and be at
ease;
No one shall make *him* afraid.
28 Do not fear, O Jacob My servant,"
says the LORD,
"For I *am* with you;
For I will make a complete end of all
the nations
To which I have driven you,
But I will not make a complete end of
you.
I will rightly correct you,
For I will not leave you wholly
unpunished."

CHAPTER 47

Judgment on Philistia

The word of the LORD that came to
Jer·e·mī'ah the prophet against the
Phi·lis'tines, before Pharaoh attacked
Gā'za.
2Thus says the LORD:

"Behold, waters rise out of the north,
And shall be an overflowing flood;
They shall overflow the land and all
that is in it,
The city and those who dwell within;
Then the men shall cry,
And all the inhabitants of the land
shall wail.
3 At the noise of the stamping hooves
of his strong horses,
At the rushing of his chariots,
At the rumbling of his wheels,
The fathers will not look back for *their*
children,
Lacking courage,
4 Because of the day that comes to
plunder all the Phi·lis'tines,
To cut off from Tȳre and Sī'don every
helper who remains;
For the LORD shall plunder the
Phi·lis'tines,
The remnant of the country of
Caph'tor.
5 Baldness has come upon Gā'za,
Ash'ke·lon is cut off
With the remnant of their valley.
How long will you cut yourself?

6 "O you sword of the LORD,
How long until you are quiet?
Put yourself up into your scabbard,
Rest and be still!
7 How can it be quiet,
Seeing the LORD has given it a charge
Against Ash'ke·lon and against the
seashore?
There He has appointed it."

CHAPTER 48

Judgment on Moab

Against Mō'ab.
Thus says the LORD of hosts, the God of
Israel:

"Woe to Nē'bō!
For it is plundered,
Kir·jath'a·im is shamed *and* taken;
The high stronghold[a] is shamed and
dismayed—
2 No more praise of Mō'ab.
In Hesh'bon they have devised evil
against her:
'Come, and let us cut her off as a
nation.'
You also shall be cut down,
O Madmen![a]
The sword shall pursue you;
3 A voice of crying *shall be* from
Hor·ō·nā'im:
'Plundering and great destruction!'

48:1 [a]Hebrew *Misgab* 48:2 [a]A city of Moab

of the Lord, and of survival. The destroyers will themselves be destroyed, but God will have compassion on His own.

47:5 Baldness: A self-imposed expression of grief or an enforced mark of servitude. **cut yourself**: A sign of mourning.

4 "Mō′ab is destroyed;
Her little ones have caused a cry to be heard;[a]
5 For in the Ascent of Lū′hith they ascend with continual weeping;
For in the descent of Hor·ō·nā′īm the enemies have heard a cry of destruction.

6 "Flee, save your lives!
And be like the juniper[a] in the wilderness.
7 For because you have trusted in your works and your treasures,
You also shall be taken.
And Chē′mosh shall go forth into captivity,
His priests and his princes together.
8 And the plunderer shall come against every city;
No one shall escape.
The valley also shall perish,
And the plain shall be destroyed,
As the LORD has spoken.

9 "Give wings to Mō′ab,
That she may flee and get away;
For her cities shall be desolate,
Without any to dwell in them.
10 Cursed *is* he who does the work of the LORD deceitfully,
And cursed *is* he who keeps back his sword from blood.

11 "Mō′ab has been at ease from his[a] youth;
He has settled on his dregs,
And has not been emptied from vessel to vessel,
Nor has he gone into captivity.
Therefore his taste remained in him,
And his scent has not changed.

12 "Therefore behold, the days are coming," says the LORD,
"That I shall send him wine-workers
Who will tip him over
And empty his vessels
And break the bottles.
13 Mō′ab shall be ashamed of Chē′mosh,
As the house of Israel was ashamed of Beth′el, their confidence.

14 "How can you say, 'We *are* mighty
And strong men for the war'?
15 Mō′ab is plundered and gone up *from* her cities;
Her chosen young men have gone down to the slaughter," says the King,
Whose name *is* the LORD of hosts.

16 "The calamity of Mō′ab *is* near at hand,
And his affliction comes quickly.
17 Bemoan him, all you who are around him;
And all you who know his name,
Say, 'How the strong staff is broken,
The beautiful rod!'

18 "O daughter inhabiting Dī′bon,
Come down from *your* glory,
And sit in thirst;
For the plunderer of Mō′ab has come against you,
He has destroyed your strongholds.
19 O inhabitant of A·rō′er,
Stand by the way and watch;
Ask him who flees
And her who escapes;
Say, 'What has happened?'
20 Mō′ab is shamed, for he is broken down.
Wail and cry!
Tell it in Ar′non, that Mō′ab is plundered.

48:4 [a]Following Masoretic Text, Targum, and Vulgate; Septuagint reads *Proclaim it in Zoar.* 48:6 [a]Or *Aroer,* a city of Moab 48:11 [a]The Hebrew uses masculine and feminine pronouns interchangeably in this chapter.

48:18, 19 daughter: A metaphor for the inhabitants of **Dibon**.

21 "And judgment has come on the plain
country:
On Hō′lon and Jah′zah and
Meph′a·ath,
22 On Dī′bon and Nē′bō and Beth
Dib·la·thā′im,
23 On Kir·jath′a·im and Beth Gā′mūl
and Beth Mē′on,
24 On Ker′i·oth and Boz′rah,
On all the cities of the land of Mō′ab,
Far or near.
25 The horn of Mō′ab is cut off,
And his arm is broken," says the
LORD.

26 "Make him drunk,
Because he exalted *himself* against the
LORD.
Mō′ab shall wallow in his vomit,
And he shall also be in derision.
27 For was not Israel a derision to you?
Was he found among thieves?
For whenever you speak of him,
You shake *your head in scorn.*
28 You who dwell in Mō′ab,
Leave the cities and dwell in the rock,
And be like the dove *which* makes her
nest
In the sides of the cave's mouth.

29 "We have heard the pride of Mō′ab
(He *is* exceedingly proud),
Of his loftiness and arrogance and
pride,
And of the haughtiness of his heart."

30 "I know his wrath," says the LORD,
"But it *is* not right;
His lies have made nothing right.
31 Therefore I will wail for Mō′ab,
And I will cry out for all Mō′ab;
I[a] will mourn for the men of Kir
Hē′res.
32 O vine of Sib′mah! I will weep for
you with the weeping of Jā′zer.
Your plants have gone over the sea,
They reach to the sea of Jā′zer.
The plunderer has fallen on your
summer fruit and your vintage.
33 Joy and gladness are taken
From the plentiful field
And from the land of Mō′ab;
I have caused wine to fail from the
winepresses;
No one will tread with joyous
shouting—
Not joyous shouting!

34 "From the cry of Hesh′bon to
Ē·le·ā′leh and to Jā′haz
They have uttered their voice,
From Zō′ar to Hor·ō·nā′im,
Like a three-year-old heifer;[a]
For the waters of Nim′rim also shall
be desolate.

35 "Moreover," says the LORD,
"I will cause to cease in Mō′ab
The one who offers *sacrifices* in the
high places
And burns incense to his gods.
36 Therefore My heart shall wail like
flutes for Mō′ab,
And like flutes My heart shall wail
For the men of Kir Hē′res.
Therefore the riches they have
acquired have perished.

37 "For every head *shall be* bald, and
every beard clipped;
On all the hands *shall be* cuts, and on
the loins sackcloth—
38 A general lamentation
On all the housetops of Mō′ab,
And in its streets;
For I have broken Mō′ab like a vessel
in which *is* no pleasure," says the
LORD.

48:31 [a]Following Dead Sea Scrolls, Septuagint, and Vulgate; Masoretic Text reads *He.* 48:34 [a]Or *The Third Eglath,* an unknown city (compare Isaiah 15:5)

48:30–36 The divine Judge is not hard-hearted; He weeps for those He must punish.

39 "They shall wail:
'How she is broken down!
How Mō'ab has turned her back with
shame!'
So Mō'ab shall be a derision
And a dismay to all those about her."

40For thus says the LORD:

"Behold, one shall fly like an eagle,
And spread his wings over Mō'ab.
41 Ker'i·oth is taken,
And the strongholds are surprised;
The mighty men's hearts in Mō'ab on
that day shall be
Like the heart of a woman in birth
pangs.
42 And Mō'ab shall be destroyed as a
people,
Because he exalted *himself* against the
LORD.
43 Fear and the pit and the snare *shall be*
upon you,
O inhabitant of Mō'ab," says the
LORD.
44 "He who flees from the fear shall fall
into the pit,
And he who gets out of the pit shall
be caught in the snare.
For upon Mō'ab, upon it I will bring
The year of their punishment," says
the LORD.

45 "Those who fled stood under the
shadow of Hesh'bon
Because of exhaustion.
But a fire shall come out of Hesh'bon,
A flame from the midst of Sī'hon,
And shall devour the brow of Mō'ab,
The crown of the head of the sons of
tumult.
46 Woe to you, O Mō'ab!
The people of Chē'mosh perish;
For your sons have been taken
captive,
And your daughters captive.

47 "Yet I will bring back the captives of
Mō'ab
In the latter days," says the LORD.

Thus far *is* the judgment of Mō'ab.

CHAPTER 49

Judgment on Ammon

Against the Am'mon·ītes.
Thus says the LORD:

"Has Israel no sons?
Has he no heir?
Why *then* does Mil'com[a] inherit Gad,
And his people dwell in its cities?
2 Therefore behold, the days are
coming," says the LORD,
"That I will cause to be heard an alarm
of war
In Rab'bah of the Am'mon·ītes;
It shall be a desolate mound,
And her villages shall be burned with
fire.
Then Israel shall take possession of
his inheritance," says the LORD.

3 "Wail, O Hesh'bon, for Aī is
plundered!
Cry, you daughters of Rab'bah,

49:1 [a]Hebrew *Malcam*, literally *their king*, a god of the Ammonites; also called *Molech* (compare verse 3)

48:40 eagle: A metaphor for the invading Babylonians and Nebuchadnezzar (see 49:22; Ezek. 17:3).

48:47 Yet I will bring back: A future for Moab is promised.

49:1 Ammonites: Descendants of Lot (Gen. 19:36–38). Judg. 11:12–28 provides the background to v. 1 and the continuing tension between the Ammonites and the Israelite tribes of Gad, Reuben, and Manasseh who lived on the east side of the Jordan. **Milcom**: The god of the Ammonites (see 1 Kin. 11:5).

49:2 Rabbah: Capital of the Ammonites, now known as Amman.

49:3 The location of this **Ai** is unknown; it is not the Ai as in Josh. 8:1.

Gird yourselves with sackcloth!
Lament and run to and fro by the walls;
For Mil'com shall go into captivity
With his priests and his princes together.
4 Why do you boast in the valleys,
Your flowing valley, O backsliding daughter?
Who trusted in her treasures, *saying,*
'Who will come against me?'
5 Behold, I will bring fear upon you,"
Says the Lord GOD of hosts,
"From all those who are around you;
You shall be driven out, everyone headlong,
And no one will gather those who wander off.
6 But afterward I will bring back
The captives of the people of Am'mon," says the LORD.

Judgment on Edom

7 Against Ē'dom.
Thus says the LORD of hosts:

"*Is* wisdom no more in Tē'man?
Has counsel perished from the prudent?
Has their wisdom vanished?
8 Flee, turn back, dwell in the depths,
O inhabitants of Dē'dan!
For I will bring the calamity of Esau upon him,
The time *that* I will punish him.
9 If grape-gatherers came to you,
Would they not leave *some* gleaning grapes?
If thieves by night,
Would they not destroy until they have enough?
10 But I have made Esau bare;
I have uncovered his secret places,[a]
And he shall not be able to hide himself.
His descendants are plundered,
His brethren and his neighbors,
And he *is* no more.
11 Leave your fatherless children,
I will preserve *them* alive;
And let your widows trust in Me."

12 For thus says the LORD: "Behold, those
whose judgment *was* not to drink of the
cup have assuredly drunk. And *are* you the
one who will altogether go unpunished?
You shall not go unpunished, but you shall
surely drink *of it.* 13 For I have sworn by
Myself," says the LORD, "that Boz'rah shall
become a desolation, a reproach, a waste,
and a curse. And all its cities shall be per-
petual wastes."

14 I have heard a message from the LORD,
And an ambassador has been sent to the nations:
"Gather together, come against her,
And rise up to battle!

15 "For indeed, I will make you small among nations,
Despised among men.
16 Your fierceness has deceived you,
The pride of your heart,
O you who dwell in the clefts of the rock,
Who hold the height of the hill!
Though you make your nest as high as the eagle,
I will bring you down from there,"
says the LORD.[a]

17 "Ē'dom also shall be an astonishment;
Everyone who goes by it will be astonished
And will hiss at all its plagues.

49:10 [a]Compare Obadiah 5, 6 49:16 [a]Compare Obadiah 3, 4

49:7, 8 Edom: Descendants of **Esau**, brother of Jacob (Gen. 32:3).
49:16 clefts of the rock: The place now known as Petra, a city built at the end of a long narrow canyon.

18 As in the overthrow of Sod′om and
Go·mor′rah
And their neighbors," says the LORD,
"No one shall remain there,
Nor shall a son of man dwell in it.

19 "Behold, he shall come up like a lion
from the floodplain[a] of the Jordan
Against the dwelling place of the
strong;
But I will suddenly make him run
away from her.
And who *is* a chosen *man that* I may
appoint over her?
For who *is* like Me?
Who will arraign Me?
And who *is* that shepherd
Who will withstand Me?"

20 Therefore hear the counsel of the
LORD that He has taken against
Ē′dom,
And His purposes that He has
proposed against the inhabitants of
Tē′man:
Surely the least of the flock shall
draw them out;
Surely He shall make their dwelling
places desolate with them.
21 The earth shakes at the noise of their
fall;
At the cry its noise is heard at the Red
Sea.
22 Behold, He shall come up and fly like
the eagle,
And spread His wings over Boz′rah;
The heart of the mighty men of
Ē′dom in that day shall be
Like the heart of a woman in birth
pangs.

Judgment on Damascus

23 Against Damascus.

"Hā′math and Ar′pad are shamed,
For they have heard bad news.
They are fainthearted;
There is trouble on the sea;
It cannot be quiet.
24 Damascus has grown feeble;
She turns to flee,
And fear has seized *her*.
Anguish and sorrows have taken her
like a woman in labor.
25 Why is the city of praise not deserted,
the city of My joy?
26 Therefore her young men shall fall in
her streets,
And all the men of war shall be cut
off in that day," says the LORD of
hosts.
27 "I will kindle a fire in the wall of
Damascus,
And it shall consume the palaces of
Ben-Hā′dad."[a]

Judgment on Kedar and Hazor

28 Against Kē′dar and against the king-
doms of Hā′zor, which Ne·bū·cha·nez′zar
king of Babylon shall strike.
Thus says the LORD:

"Arise, go up to Kē′dar,
And devastate the men of the East!
29 Their tents and their flocks they shall
take away.
They shall take for themselves their
curtains,
All their vessels and their camels;
And they shall cry out to them,
'Fear *is* on every side!'

49:19 [a]Or *thicket* 49:27 [a]Compare Amos 1:4

49:20 flock: The people of Edom, ravaged by the lion of Babylon.
49:21 heard at the Red Sea: Far to the south of Edom.
49:22 eagle: A simile for the Babylonians or for the Lord's presence with them as they accomplish His purpose in punishing Edom (see 48:40).
49:23 Damascus, the capital, is named as a symbol for all of Syria on which judgment is coming.
49:27 Ben-Hadad: The name of several rulers of Syria during Israel's kingdom period.

30 "Flee, get far away! Dwell in the
depths,
O inhabitants of Hā′zor!" says the
LORD.
"For Ne·bū·chad·nez′zar king of
Babylon has taken counsel against
you,
And has conceived a plan against
you.
31 "Arise, go up to the wealthy nation
that dwells securely," says the
LORD,
"Which has neither gates nor bars,
Dwelling alone.
32 Their camels shall be for booty,
And the multitude of their cattle for
plunder.
I will scatter to all winds those in the
farthest corners,
And I will bring their calamity from
all its sides," says the LORD.
33 "Hā′zor shall be a dwelling for jackals,
a desolation forever;
No one shall reside there,
Nor son of man dwell in it."

Judgment on Elam

34The word of the LORD that came to
Jer·e·mī′ah the prophet against Ē′lam, in
the beginning of the reign of Zed·e·kī′ah
king of Judah, saying, 35"Thus says the
LORD of hosts:

'Behold, I will break the bow of Ē′lam,
The foremost of their might.
36 Against Ē′lam I will bring the four
winds
From the four quarters of heaven,
And scatter them toward all those
winds;
There shall be no nations where the
outcasts of Ē′lam will not go.
37 For I will cause Ē′lam to be dismayed
before their enemies
And before those who seek their life.
I will bring disaster upon them,
My fierce anger,' says the LORD;
'And I will send the sword after them
Until I have consumed them.
38 I will set My throne in Ē′lam,
And will destroy from there the king
and the princes,' says the LORD.
39 'But it shall come to pass in the latter
days:
I will bring back the captives of
Ē′lam,' says the LORD."

CHAPTER 50

Judgment on Babylon and Babylonia

The word that the LORD spoke against
Babylon *and* against the land of the
Chal·dē′ans by Jer·e·mī′ah the prophet.

2 "Declare among the nations,
Proclaim, and set up a standard;
Proclaim—do not conceal *it*—
Say, 'Babylon is taken, Bel is shamed.
Mer′o·dach[a] is broken in pieces;
Her idols are humiliated,
Her images are broken in pieces.'

50:2 [a]A Babylonian god; sometimes spelled *Marduk*

49:34–39 Elam: A region in the southwest corner of Iran. **beginning of the reign of Zedekiah**: About 597 B.C. **My throne** (v. 38): God would show His control by punishing Elam.

50:1—51:64 God intends that ruthless power shall not long prevail. Babylon's might devastated Palestine and neighboring countries, but the Lord showed Jeremiah that in the end the powerfully wicked would themselves be destroyed. Thus the dominant theme is the overthrow of Babylon, but following almost every message of destruction for Babylon is an encouraging word for the exiles.

50:2 Bel is the title of Marduk, the chief god of the Babylonians. As the god who "defeated the chaotic waters," he was the counterpart of the Canaanite god Baal. **Her**: The city Babylon.

3 For out of the north a nation comes
up against her,
Which shall make her land desolate,
And no one shall dwell therein.
They shall move, they shall depart,
Both man and beast.

4 "In those days and in that time," says
the LORD,
"The children of Israel shall come,
They and the children of Judah
together;
With continual weeping they shall
come,
And seek the LORD their God.
5 They shall ask the way to Zion,
With their faces toward it, *saying,*
'Come and let us join ourselves to the
LORD
In a perpetual covenant
That will not be forgotten.'

6 "My people have been lost sheep.
Their shepherds have led them
astray;
They have turned them away *on* the
mountains.
They have gone from mountain to
hill;
They have forgotten their resting
place.
7 All who found them have devoured
them;
And their adversaries said, 'We have
not offended,
Because they have sinned against the
LORD, the habitation of justice,
The LORD, the hope of their fathers.'

8 "Move from the midst of Babylon,
Go out of the land of the Chal·dē'ans;
And be like the rams before the
flocks.
9 For behold, I will raise and cause to
come up against Babylon
An assembly of great nations from
the north country,
And they shall array themselves
against her;
From there she shall be captured.
Their arrows *shall be* like *those* of an
expert warrior;[a]
None shall return in vain.
10 And Chal·dē'a shall become plunder;
All who plunder her shall be
satisfied," says the LORD.

11 "Because you were glad, because you
rejoiced,
You destroyers of My heritage,
Because you have grown fat like a
heifer threshing grain,
And you bellow like bulls,
12 Your mother shall be deeply
ashamed;
She who bore you shall be ashamed.
Behold, the least of the nations *shall be*
a wilderness,
A dry land and a desert.
13 Because of the wrath of the LORD
She shall not be inhabited,
But she shall be wholly desolate.
Everyone who goes by Babylon shall
be horrified
And hiss at all her plagues.

14 "Put yourselves in array against
Babylon all around,
All you who bend the bow;

50:9 [a]Following some Hebrew manuscripts, Septuagint, and Syriac; Masoretic Text, Targum, and Vulgate read *a warrior who makes childless.*

50:4, 5 Cyrus, the king of Persia, released **the children of Judah** to return to **Zion**, their Promised Land.

50:11–16 you were glad: Though an instrument of the Lord to punish Judah, Babylon was arrogant and must be punished.

50:12 the least: Lit. "the last." Instead of being at the head of any list of the great nations, Babylon comes at the end.

Shoot at her, spare no arrows,
For she has sinned against the LORD.
15 Shout against her all around;
She has given her hand,
Her foundations have fallen,
Her walls are thrown down;
For it *is* the vengeance of the LORD.
Take vengeance on her.
As she has done, so do to her.
16 Cut off the sower from Babylon,
And him who handles the sickle at harvest time.
For fear of the oppressing sword
Everyone shall turn to his own people,
And everyone shall flee to his own land.

17 "Israel *is* like scattered sheep;
The lions have driven *him* away.
First the king of Assyria devoured him;
Now at last this Ne·bū·chad·nez′zar king of Babylon has broken his bones."

18 Therefore thus says the LORD of hosts, the God of Israel:

"Behold, I will punish the king of Babylon and his land,
As I have punished the king of Assyria.
19 But I will bring back Israel to his home,
And he shall feed on Car′mel and Bā′shan;
His soul shall be satisfied on Mount Ē′phra·im and Gil′ē·ad.
20 In those days and in that time," says the LORD,
"The iniquity of Israel shall be sought, but *there shall be* none;
And the sins of Judah, but they shall not be found;
For I will pardon those whom I preserve.

21 "Go up against the land of Mer·a·thā′im, against it,
And against the inhabitants of Pē′kod.
Waste and utterly destroy them," says the LORD,
"And do according to all that I have commanded you.
22 A sound of battle *is* in the land,
And of great destruction.
23 How the hammer of the whole earth has been cut apart and broken!
How Babylon has become a desolation among the nations!
I have laid a snare for you;
24 You have indeed been trapped, O Babylon,
And you were not aware;
You have been found and also caught,
Because you have contended against the LORD.
25 The LORD has opened His armory,
And has brought out the weapons of His indignation;
For this *is* the work of the Lord GOD of hosts
In the land of the Chal·dē′ans.
26 Come against her from the farthest border;
Open her storehouses;
Cast her up as heaps of ruins,
And destroy her utterly;
Let nothing of her be left.
27 Slay all her bulls,
Let them go down to the slaughter.
Woe to them!
For their day has come, the time of their punishment.

50:17 Assyria wiped out **Israel** in 722 B.C. **Babylon** first invaded the land in 605 B.C. and finally destroyed Jerusalem in 586 B.C.

50:19 These locations are all in Northern Israel, indicating that God intended to restore representatives of all the tribes, not merely the Judeans.

28 The voice of those who flee and
escape from the land of Babylon
Declares in Zion the vengeance of the
LORD our God,
The vengeance of His temple.

29 "Call together the archers against
Babylon.
All you who bend the bow, encamp
against it all around;
Let none of them escape.[a]
Repay her according to her work;
According to all she has done, do to
her;
For she has been proud against the
LORD,
Against the Holy One of Israel.
30 Therefore her young men shall fall in
the streets,
And all her men of war shall be cut
off in that day," says the LORD.
31 "Behold, I *am* against you,
O most haughty one!" says the Lord
GOD of hosts;
"For your day has come,
The time *that* I will punish you.[a]
32 The most proud shall stumble and
fall,
And no one will raise him up;
I will kindle a fire in his cities,
And it will devour all around him."

33 Thus says the LORD of hosts:

"The children of Israel *were* oppressed,
Along with the children of Judah;
All who took them captive have held
them fast;
They have refused to let them go.
34 Their Redeemer *is* strong;
The LORD of hosts *is* His name.
He will thoroughly plead their case,
That He may give rest to the land,
And disquiet the inhabitants of
Babylon.

35 "A sword *is* against the Chal·dē′ans,"
says the LORD,
"Against the inhabitants of Babylon,
And against her princes and her wise
men.
36 A sword *is* against the soothsayers,
and they will be fools.
A sword *is* against her mighty men,
and they will be dismayed.
37 A sword *is* against their horses,
Against their chariots,
And against all the mixed peoples
who *are* in her midst;
And they will become like women.
A sword *is* against her treasures, and
they will be robbed.
38 A drought[a] *is* against her waters, and
they will be dried up.
For it *is* the land of carved images,
And they are insane with *their* idols.

39 "Therefore the wild desert beasts shall
dwell *there* with the jackals,
And the ostriches shall dwell in it.
It shall be inhabited no more forever,
Nor shall it be dwelt in from
generation to generation.
40 As God overthrew Sod′om and
Go·mor′rah
And their neighbors," says the LORD,
"*So* no one shall reside there,
Nor son of man dwell in it.

41 "Behold, a people shall come from the
north,

50:29 [a]Qere, some Hebrew manuscripts, Septuagint, and Targum add *to her.* 50:31 [a]Following Masoretic Text and Targum; Septuagint and Vulgate read *The time of your punishment.* 50:38 [a]Following Masoretic Text, Targum, and Vulgate; Syriac reads *sword;* Septuagint omits *A drought is.*

50:28–32 The people in exile are to regard this event as a means of **escape** for them and as vengeance upon Babylon for what she did to the **temple**. Babylon, the **most proud** (v. 32), would be brought down.

50:35–37 The sword was Persia's military power conquering Babylon.

50:41–43 a people shall come: See 6:22–24. What was first prophesied against Jerusalem is now proclaimed against Babylon.

And a great nation and many kings
Shall be raised up from the ends of
the earth.
42 They shall hold the bow and the
lance;
They *are* cruel and shall not show
mercy.
Their voice shall roar like the sea;
They shall ride on horses,
Set in array, like a man for the battle,
Against you, O daughter of Babylon.

43 "The king of Babylon has heard the
report about them,
And his hands grow feeble;
Anguish has taken hold of him,
Pangs as of a woman in childbirth.

44 "Behold, he shall come up like a lion
from the floodplain[a] of the Jordan
Against the dwelling place of the
strong;
But I will make them suddenly run
away from her.
And who *is* a chosen *man that* I may
appoint over her?
For who *is* like Me?
Who will arraign Me?
And who *is* that shepherd
Who will withstand Me?"

45 Therefore hear the counsel of the
LORD that He has taken against
Babylon,
And His purposes that He has
proposed against the land of the
Chal·dē′ans:
Surely the least of the flock shall
draw them out;
Surely He will make their dwelling
place desolate with them.
46 At the noise of the taking of Babylon
The earth trembles,
And the cry is heard among the
nations.

CHAPTER 51

The Utter Destruction of Babylon

Thus says the LORD:

"Behold, I will raise up against
Babylon,
Against those who dwell in Leb
Kā′maī,[a]
A destroying wind.
2 And I will send winnowers to
Babylon,
Who shall winnow her and empty her
land.
For in the day of doom
They shall be against her all around.
3 Against *her* let the archer bend his
bow,
And lift himself up against *her* in his
armor.
Do not spare her young men;
Utterly destroy all her army.
4 Thus the slain shall fall in the land of
the Chal·dē′ans,

50:44 [a]Or *thicket* 51:1 [a]A code word for Chaldea (Babylonia); may be translated *The Midst of Those Who Rise Up Against Me*

50:43 hands grow feeble: An ancient Near Eastern idiom for helplessness resulting from fear.

50:44–46 A repeat of the prophecy against Edom in 49:19–21, only now directed against Babylon. This suggests that there were certain stock forms and sayings which prophets used in judgment messages, such as the similarities between Is. 15; 16 and Jer. 48 (compare Is. 16:6 and Jer. 48:29; 16:9 and 48:32; 16:10 and 48:33; 15:4 and 48:34; 16:11 and 48:36). The Babylonians would be forced to **run away** from their city. **shepherd . . . flock**: Imagery for the ruler and his people.

51:1 A destroying wind . . . winnowers: Figures of speech for the Persians. To winnow is to throw grain and chaff into a strong breeze so that the wind may blow the chaff away.

51:3, 4 A literal description of the Persian assault against the **Chaldeans**.

And *those* thrust through in her
streets.
5 For Israel is not forsaken, nor Judah,
By his God, the LORD of hosts,
Though their land was filled with sin
against the Holy One of Israel."

6 Flee from the midst of Babylon,
And every one save his life!
Do not be cut off in her iniquity,
For this *is* the time of the LORD's
vengeance;
He shall recompense her.
7 Babylon *was* a golden cup in the
LORD's hand,
That made all the earth drunk.
The nations drank her wine;
Therefore the nations are deranged.
8 Babylon has suddenly fallen and been
destroyed.
Wail for her!
Take balm for her pain;
Perhaps she may be healed.

9 We would have healed Babylon,
But she is not healed.
Forsake her, and let us go everyone to
his own country;
For her judgment reaches to heaven
and is lifted up to the skies.
10 The LORD has revealed our
righteousness.
Come and let us declare in Zion the
work of the LORD our God.

11 Make the arrows bright!
Gather the shields!
The LORD has raised up the spirit of
the kings of the Mēdes.
For His plan *is* against Babylon to
destroy it,
Because it *is* the vengeance of the
LORD,
The vengeance for His temple.
12 Set up the standard on the walls of
Babylon;
Make the guard strong,
Set up the watchmen,
Prepare the ambushes.
For the LORD has both devised and
done
What He spoke against the
inhabitants of Babylon.
13 O you who dwell by many waters,
Abundant in treasures,
Your end has come,
The measure of your covetousness.
14 The LORD of hosts has sworn by
Himself:
"Surely I will fill you with men, as
with locusts,
And they shall lift up a shout against
you."

15 He has made the earth by His power;
He has established the world by His
wisdom,
And stretched out the heaven by His
understanding.
16 When He utters *His* voice—
There is a multitude of waters in the
heavens:
"He causes the vapors to ascend from
the ends of the earth;
He makes lightnings for the rain;
He brings the wind out of His
treasuries."[a]

17 Everyone is dull-hearted, without
knowledge;
Every metalsmith is put to shame by
the carved image;
For his molded image *is* falsehood,
And *there is* no breath in them.

51:16 [a]Psalm 135:7

51:5, 6 not forsaken: The Lord is still supporting the exiles. Two things are clear in this statement of God's grace: (1) His support is undeserved, and (2) this is the Lord's **time**.

51:7 golden cup: Represents Babylon's role as God's instrument to punish the nations.

51:9 We would have healed: The witness of exiles who served the Lord (Daniel and Ezekiel) could have led Babylon out of idol worship, but she rejected this witness.

18 They *are* futile, a work of errors;
In the time of their punishment they shall perish.
19 The Portion of Jacob *is* not like them,
For He *is* the Maker of all things;
And *Israel is* the tribe of His inheritance.
The LORD of hosts *is* His name.

20 "You *are* My battle-ax *and* weapons of war:
For with you I will break the nation in pieces;
With you I will destroy kingdoms;
21 With you I will break in pieces the horse and its rider;
With you I will break in pieces the chariot and its rider;
22 With you also I will break in pieces man and woman;
With you I will break in pieces old and young;
With you I will break in pieces the young man and the maiden;
23 With you also I will break in pieces the shepherd and his flock;
With you I will break in pieces the farmer and his yoke of oxen;
And with you I will break in pieces governors and rulers.

24 "And I will repay Babylon
And all the inhabitants of Chal·dē′a
For all the evil they have done
In Zion in your sight," says the LORD.

25 "Behold, I *am* against you,
O destroying mountain,
Who destroys all the earth," says the LORD.
"And I will stretch out My hand against you,
Roll you down from the rocks,
And make you a burnt mountain.
26 They shall not take from you a stone for a corner
Nor a stone for a foundation,
But you shall be desolate forever," says the LORD.

27 Set up a banner in the land,
Blow the trumpet among the nations!
Prepare the nations against her,
Call the kingdoms together against her:
Ar′a·rat, Min′nī, and Ash′ke·naz.
Appoint a general against her;
Cause the horses to come up like the bristling locusts.
28 Prepare against her the nations,
With the kings of the Mēdes,
Its governors and all its rulers,
All the land of his dominion.
29 And the land will tremble and sorrow;
For every purpose of the LORD shall be performed against Babylon,
To make the land of Babylon a desolation without inhabitant.
30 The mighty men of Babylon have ceased fighting,
They have remained in their strongholds;
Their might has failed,
They became *like* women;
They have burned her dwelling places,
The bars of her *gate* are broken.
31 One runner will run to meet another,
And one messenger to meet another,
To show the king of Babylon that his city is taken on *all* sides;
32 The passages are blocked,
The reeds they have burned with fire,
And the men of war are terrified.

33 For thus says the LORD of hosts, the God of Israel:

51:20–23 You: Probably refers to the king of the Persians. He would be the Lord's weapon against every living creature in Babylon from the **horse** and **rider** to the **shepherd**, **farmer**, and **rulers**. No one would be exempt.

"The daughter of Babylon *is* like a threshing floor
When it is time to thresh her;
Yet a little while
And the time of her harvest will come."

34 "Ne·bū·chad·nez'zar the king of Babylon
Has devoured me, he has crushed me;
He has made me an empty vessel,
He has swallowed me up like a monster;
He has filled his stomach with my delicacies,
He has spit me out.
35 Let the violence *done* to me and my flesh *be* upon Babylon,"
The inhabitant of Zion will say;
"And my blood be upon the inhabitants of Chal·dē'a!"
Jerusalem will say.

36Therefore thus says the LORD:

"Behold, I will plead your case and take vengeance for you.
I will dry up her sea and make her springs dry.
37 Babylon shall become a heap,
A dwelling place for jackals,
An astonishment and a hissing,
Without an inhabitant.
38 They shall roar together like lions,
They shall growl like lions' whelps.
39 In their excitement I will prepare their feasts;
I will make them drunk,
That they may rejoice,
And sleep a perpetual sleep
And not awake," says the LORD.
40 "I will bring them down
Like lambs to the slaughter,
Like rams with male goats.

41 "Oh, how Shē'shach[a] is taken!
Oh, how the praise of the whole earth is seized!
How Babylon has become desolate among the nations!
42 The sea has come up over Babylon;
She is covered with the multitude of its waves.
43 Her cities are a desolation,
A dry land and a wilderness,
A land where no one dwells,
Through which no son of man passes.
44 I will punish Bel in Babylon,
And I will bring out of his mouth what he has swallowed;
And the nations shall not stream to him anymore.
Yes, the wall of Babylon shall fall.

45 "My people, go out of the midst of her!
And let everyone deliver himself from the fierce anger of the LORD.
46 And lest your heart faint,
And you fear for the rumor that *will be* heard in the land
(A rumor will come *one* year,
And after that, in *another* year
A rumor *will come*,
And violence in the land,
Ruler against ruler),
47 Therefore behold, the days are coming
That I will bring judgment on the carved images of Babylon;
Her whole land shall be ashamed,
And all her slain shall fall in her midst.

51:41 [a]A code word for Babylon (compare Jeremiah 25:26)

51:34, 35 devoured me: Judah and **Jerusalem** (v. 35) cry out about Nebuchadnezzar's attack against them.

51:42 The sea: A figure of speech for the conquering Medes.

51:45–51 go out of the midst: Prepare yourselves to return to **Jerusalem** (v. 50) after Babylon has fallen.

48 Then the heavens and the earth and
all that *is* in them
Shall sing joyously over Babylon;
For the plunderers shall come to her
from the north," says the LORD.

49 As Babylon *has caused* the slain of
Israel to fall,
So at Babylon the slain of all the earth
shall fall.
50 You who have escaped the sword,
Get away! Do not stand still!
Remember the LORD afar off,
And let Jerusalem come to your
mind.

51 We are ashamed because we have
heard reproach.
Shame has covered our faces,
For strangers have come into the
sanctuaries of the LORD's house.

52 "Therefore behold, the days are
coming," says the LORD,
"That I will bring judgment on her
carved images,
And throughout all her land the
wounded shall groan.
53 Though Babylon were to mount up to
heaven,
And though she were to fortify the
height of her strength,
Yet from Me plunderers would come
to her," says the LORD.

54 The sound of a cry *comes* from
Babylon,
And great destruction from the land
of the Chal·dē'ans,
55 Because the LORD is plundering
Babylon
And silencing her loud voice,
Though her waves roar like great
waters,
And the noise of their voice is
uttered,
56 Because the plunderer comes against
her, against Babylon,
And her mighty men are taken.
Every one of their bows is broken;
For the LORD *is* the God of
recompense,
He will surely repay.

57 "And I will make drunk
Her princes and wise men,
Her governors, her deputies, and her
mighty men.
And they shall sleep a perpetual sleep
And not awake," says the King,
Whose name *is* the LORD of hosts.

58 Thus says the LORD of hosts:

"The broad walls of Babylon shall be
utterly broken,
And her high gates shall be burned
with fire;
The people will labor in vain,
And the nations, because of the fire;
And they shall be weary."

Jeremiah's Command to Seraiah

59 The word which Jer·e·mī'ah the
prophet commanded Se·rāi'ah the son of
Ne·rī'ah, the son of Mah'sēi·ah, when he
went with Zed·e·kī'ah the king of Judah to
Babylon in the fourth year of his reign.
And Se·rāi'ah *was* the quartermaster. 60 So

51:50 Jerusalem: Although there was no magical connection between God and Jerusalem which would protect her from deserved punishment, still God's heart was, and is, upon that city.

51:59–64 Apparently Zedekiah was summoned to Babylon in 593 B.C. This may have been because those Jews already in Babylon may have participated in the revolt which occurred there in 595/594. At any rate Seraiah, who accompanied the king, was commissioned by Jeremiah to perform the symbolic acts noted here (vv. 61–64) while in Babylon to signify Babylon's eventual destruction. Evidently the incident is recounted here (out of chronological order) because the destruction of Babylon is the topic of ch. 51.

Jer·e·mī′ah wrote in a book all the evil that would come upon Babylon, all these words that are written against Babylon. [61]And Jer·e·mī′ah said to Se·rāi′ah, "When you arrive in Babylon and see it, and read all these words, [62]then you shall say, 'O LORD, You have spoken against this place to cut it off, so that none shall remain in it, neither man nor beast, but it shall be desolate forever.' [63]Now it shall be, when you have finished reading this book, *that* you shall tie a stone to it and throw it out into the Eū·phrā′tēs. [64]Then you shall say, 'Thus Babylon shall sink and not rise from the catastrophe that I will bring upon her. And they shall be weary.' "

Thus far *are* the words of Jer·e·mī′ah.

CHAPTER 52

The Fall of Jerusalem Reviewed

Zedekiah *was* twenty-one years old when he became king, and he reigned eleven years in Jerusalem. His mother's name *was* Ha·mū′tal the daughter of Jer·e·mī′ah of Lib′nah. [2]He also did evil in the sight of the LORD, according to all that Je·hoi′a·kim had done. [3]For because of the anger of the LORD *this* happened in Jerusalem and Judah, till He finally cast them out from His presence. Then Zed·e·kī′ah rebelled against the king of Babylon.

[4]Now it came to pass in the ninth year of his reign, in the tenth month, on the tenth *day* of the month, *that* Ne·bū·chad·nez′zar king of Babylon and all his army came against Jerusalem and encamped against it; and *they* built a siege wall against it all around. [5]So the city was besieged until the eleventh year of King Zed·e·kī′ah. [6]By the fourth month, on the ninth day of the month, the famine had become so severe in the city that there was no food for the people of the land. [7]Then the city wall was broken through, and all the men of war fled and went out of the city at night by way of the gate between the two walls, which *was* by the king's garden, even though the Chal·dē′ans *were* near the city all around. And they went by way of the plain.[a]

[8]But the army of the Chal·dē′ans pursued the king, and they overtook Zed·e·kī′ah in the plains of Jericho. All his army was scattered from him. [9]So they took the king and brought him up to the king of Babylon at Rib′lah in the land of Hā′math, and he pronounced judgment on him. [10]Then the king of Babylon killed the sons of Zed·e·kī′ah before his eyes. And he killed all the princes of Judah in Rib′lah. [11]He also put out the eyes of Zed·e·kī′ah; and the king of Babylon bound him in bronze fetters, took him to Babylon, and put him in prison till the day of his death.

The Temple and City Plundered and Burned

[12]Now in the fifth month, on the tenth *day* of the month (which *was* the nineteenth year of King Ne·bū·chad·nez′zar king of Babylon), Ne·bū·za·rad′an, the captain of the guard, *who* served the king of Babylon, came to Jerusalem. [13]He burned the house of the LORD and the king's house; all the houses of Jerusalem, that is, all the houses of the great, he burned with fire. [14]And all the army of the Chal·dē′ans who *were* with the captain of the guard broke down all the walls of Jerusalem all around. [15]Then Ne·bū·za·rad′an the captain of the guard carried away captive *some* of the poor people, the rest of the people who remained in the city, the defectors who had deserted to the king of Babylon, and the rest of the craftsmen. [16]But Ne·bū·za·rad′an the cap-

52:7 [a]Or *the Arabah,* that is, the Jordan Valley

51:64 The final words of this verse close the material left by Jeremiah.
52:1–34 An appendix which is almost identical to 2 Kin. 24:18—25:21, 27–30.
52:3 Zedekiah ignored the clear warning from Jeremiah (see 27:12–15) and rebelled.

tain of the guard left *some* of the poor of the
land as vinedressers and farmers.
17The bronze pillars that *were* in the
house of the LORD, and the carts and the
bronze Sea that *were* in the house of the
LORD, the Chal·dē'ans broke in pieces, and
carried all their bronze to Babylon. 18They
also took away the pots, the shovels, the
trimmers, the bowls, the spoons, and all
the bronze utensils with which the priests
ministered. 19The basins, the firepans, the
bowls, the pots, the lampstands, the
spoons, and the cups, whatever *was* solid
gold and whatever *was* solid silver, the
captain of the guard took away. 20The two
pillars, one Sea, the twelve bronze bulls
which *were* under *it, and* the carts, which
King Solomon had made for the house of
the LORD—the bronze of all these articles
was beyond measure. 21Now *concerning* the
pillars: the height of one pillar *was* eigh-
teen cubits, a measuring line of twelve cu-
bits could measure its circumference, and
its thickness *was* four fingers; *it was* hollow.
22A capital of bronze *was* on it; and the
height of one capital *was* five cubits, with a
network and pomegranates all around the
capital, all of bronze. The second pillar,
with pomegranates was the same. 23There
were ninety-six pomegranates on the
sides; all the pomegranates, all around on
the network, *were* one hundred.

The People Taken Captive to Babylonia

24The captain of the guard took Se·rāi'ah
the chief priest, Zeph·a·nī'ah the second
priest, and the three doorkeepers. 25He also
took out of the city an officer who had
charge of the men of war, seven men of the
king's close associates who were found in
the city, the principal scribe of the army
who mustered the people of the land, and
sixty men of the people of the land who
were found in the midst of the city. 26And
Ne·bū·za·rad'an the captain of the guard
took these and brought them to the king of
Babylon at Rib'lah. 27Then the king of
Babylon struck them and put them to
death at Rib'lah in the land of Hā'math.
Thus Judah was carried away captive from
its own land.
28These *are* the people whom Ne-
bū·chad·nez'zar carried away captive: in
the seventh year, three thousand and
twenty-three Jews; 29in the eighteenth year
of Ne·bū·chad·nez'zar he carried away
captive from Jerusalem eight hundred and
thirty-two persons; 30in the twenty-third
year of Ne·bū·chad·nez'zar, Ne·bū·za-
rad'an the captain of the guard carried
away captive of the Jews seven hundred
and forty-five persons. All the persons *were*
four thousand six hundred.

Jehoiachin Released from Prison

31Now it came to pass in the thirty-
seventh year of the captivity of Je·hoi'a-
chin king of Judah, in the twelfth month,
on the twenty-fifth *day* of the month, *that*
Ē'vil-Me·rō'dach[a] king of Babylon, in the
first *year* of his reign, lifted up the head of
Je·hoi'a·chin king of Judah and brought
him out of prison. 32And he spoke kindly to
him and gave him a more prominent seat
than those of the kings who *were* with him
in Babylon. 33So Je·hoi'a·chin changed
from his prison garments, and he ate bread
regularly before the king all the days of his
life. 34And as for his provisions, there was a
regular ration given him by the king of
Babylon, a portion for each day until the
day of his death, all the days of his life.

52:31 [a]Or *Awil-Marduk*

52:31–34 lifted up the head: A Hebrew phrase expressing the kindness and goodwill that Evil-Merodach showed toward Jehoiachin.

✦Lamentations✦

Lamentations contains five poems of mourning for the downfall of Jerusalem and was probably written about 587 B.C., shortly after the Babylonians invaded. The detailed descriptions of Jerusalem point to an eyewitness—Jeremiah—who prophesied during this time.

Jeremiah's five poems describe the destruction of Jerusalem, the anger of God, a prayer for mercy, the suffering of Jerusalem, and a prayer for restoration. These five lamentations contain three themes: mourning for the desolation of the city, confession of sin, and hope for the future (3:22–25). The hope that God would restore Jerusalem helped alleviate the pain of current punishment. Jeremiah found hope and comfort by remembering God's past faithfulness, just as we can view trials as an opportunity to recall past victories in the Lord.

From the early days of David's reign, Jerusalem had been the central location for sacrifice to God, and the dwelling of God's presence; it was later the primary site of the ministry of Jesus Christ. Lamentations highlights the role of this city in God's redemptive work in the world and offers hope for all people through its restoration. ✦

CHAPTER 1

Jerusalem in Affliction

How lonely sits the city
That was full of people!
How like a widow is she,
Who *was* great among the
nations!
The princess among the provinces
Has become a slave!

2 She weeps bitterly in the night,
Her tears *are* on her cheeks;
Among all her lovers
She has none to comfort *her*.
All her friends have dealt
treacherously with her;
They have become her enemies.

3 Judah has gone into captivity,
Under affliction and hard servitude;
She dwells among the nations,
She finds no rest;
All her persecutors overtake her in
dire straits.

4 The roads to Zion mourn
Because no one comes to the set
feasts.
All her gates are desolate;
Her priests sigh,
Her virgins are afflicted,
And she *is* in bitterness.

5 Her adversaries have become the
master,
Her enemies prosper;

1:1 princess: The previous Jerusalem. **widow . . . slave**: Jerusalem in ruins.
1:2 She: The city as a brokenhearted woman. **lovers**: Idols (see Jer. 2:23–28).

For the LORD has afflicted her
Because of the multitude of her
transgressions.
Her children have gone into captivity
before the enemy.

6 And from the daughter of Zion
All her splendor has departed.
Her princes have become like deer
That find no pasture,
That flee without strength
Before the pursuer.

7 In the days of her affliction and
roaming,
Jerusalem remembers all her pleasant
things
That she had in the days of old.
When her people fell into the hand of
the enemy,
With no one to help her,
The adversaries saw her
And mocked at her downfall.[a]

8 Jerusalem has sinned gravely,
Therefore she has become vile.[a]
All who honored her despise her
Because they have seen her
nakedness;
Yes, she sighs and turns away.

9 Her uncleanness *is* in her skirts;
She did not consider her destiny;
Therefore her collapse was awesome;
She had no comforter.
"O LORD, behold my affliction,
For *the* enemy is exalted!"

10 The adversary has spread his hand
Over all her pleasant things;
For she has seen the nations enter her
sanctuary,
Those whom You commanded
Not to enter Your assembly.

11 All her people sigh,
They seek bread;
They have given their valuables for
food to restore life.
"See, O LORD, and consider,
For I am scorned."

12 "*Is it* nothing to you, all you who pass
by?
Behold and see
If there is any sorrow like my
sorrow,
Which has been brought on me,
Which the LORD has inflicted
In the day of His fierce anger.

13 "From above He has sent fire into my
bones,
And it overpowered them;
He has spread a net for my feet
And turned me back;
He has made me desolate
And faint all the day.

14 "The yoke of my transgressions was
bound;[a]
They were woven together by His
hands,
And thrust upon my neck.
He made my strength fail;
The Lord delivered me into the hands
of *those whom* I am not able to
withstand.

1:7 [a]Vulgate reads *her Sabbaths.* 1:8 [a]Septuagint and Vulgate read *moved* or *removed.* 1:14 [a]Following Masoretic Text and Targum; Septuagint, Syriac, and Vulgate read *watched over.*

1:8 nakedness: Like a disgraced prostitute the people are forced to parade before their former allies.

1:10 The sanctuary (temple) had been violated by persons not prepared to come into God's presence.

1:12–22 A lament in the words of a personified Jerusalem, who speaks in all verses except v. 17.

1:14 yoke: Symbol for a heavy load of guilt.

15 "The Lord has trampled underfoot all
my mighty *men* in my midst;
He has called an assembly against me
To crush my young men;
The Lord trampled *as* in a winepress
The virgin daughter of Judah.

16 "For these *things* I weep;
My eye, my eye overflows with
water;
Because the comforter, who should
restore my life,
Is far from me.
My children are desolate
Because the enemy prevailed."

17 Zion spreads out her hands,
But no one comforts her;
The LORD has commanded concerning
Jacob
That those around him *become* his
adversaries;
Jerusalem has become an unclean
thing among them.

18 "The LORD is righteous,
For I rebelled against His
commandment.
Hear now, all peoples,
And behold my sorrow;
My virgins and my young men
Have gone into captivity.

19 "I called for my lovers,
But they deceived me;
My priests and my elders
Breathed their last in the city,
While they sought food
To restore their life.

20 "See, O LORD, that I *am* in distress;
My soul is troubled;
My heart is overturned within me,
For I have been very rebellious.
Outside the sword bereaves,
At home *it is* like death.

21 "They have heard that I sigh,
But no one comforts me.
All my enemies have heard of my
trouble;
They are glad that You have done *it*.
Bring on the day You have
announced,
That they may become like me.

22 "Let all their wickedness come before
You,
And do to them as You have done to
me
For all my transgressions;
For my sighs *are* many,
And my heart *is* faint."

CHAPTER 2

God's Anger with Jerusalem

How the Lord has covered the
daughter of Zion
With a cloud in His anger!
He cast down from heaven to the
earth
The beauty of Israel,
And did not remember His footstool
In the day of His anger.

2 The Lord has swallowed up and has
not pitied

1:15 winepress: A metaphor representing divine judgment. **virgin daughter**: Jerusalem and her people.

1:18–20 Both an affirmation of faith (v. 18) and a confession (vv. 18–20). Whenever we experience God's chastisement, we must recognize it as a consequence of our sin and acknowledge that His judgment is righteous. Once we confess and repent, fellowship will be restored.

1:21, 22 Bring on the day: The speaker arouses enough from grief to demand justice, the punishment of her enemies (see Jer. 50:33, 34).

2:1–9 These verses show a clear understanding of God's lordship in history. What has befallen Judah is neither accident nor a result of human power. It is God's work of judgment.

All the dwelling places of Jacob.
He has thrown down in His wrath
The strongholds of the daughter of
 Judah;
He has brought *them* down to the
 ground;
He has profaned the kingdom and its
 princes.

3 He has cut off in fierce anger
Every horn of Israel;
He has drawn back His right hand
From before the enemy.
He has blazed against Jacob like a
 flaming fire
Devouring all around.

4 Standing like an enemy, He has bent
 His bow;
With His right hand, like an
 adversary,
He has slain all *who were* pleasing to
 His eye;
On the tent of the daughter of Zion,
He has poured out His fury like fire.

5 The Lord was like an enemy.
He has swallowed up Israel,
He has swallowed up all her palaces;
He has destroyed her strongholds,
And has increased mourning and
 lamentation
In the daughter of Judah.

6 He has done violence to His
 tabernacle,
As if it were a garden;
He has destroyed His place of
 assembly;
The LORD has caused
The appointed feasts and Sabbaths to
 be forgotten in Zion.
In His burning indignation He has
 spurned the king and the priest.

7 The Lord has spurned His altar,
He has abandoned His sanctuary;
He has given up the walls of her
 palaces
Into the hand of the enemy.
They have made a noise in the house
 of the LORD
As on the day of a set feast.

8 The LORD has purposed to destroy
The wall of the daughter of Zion.
He has stretched out a line;
He has not withdrawn His hand from
 destroying;
Therefore He has caused the rampart
 and wall to lament;
They languished together.

9 Her gates have sunk into the ground;
He has destroyed and broken her
 bars.
Her king and her princes *are* among
 the nations;
The Law *is* no *more,*
And her prophets find no vision from
 the LORD.

10 The elders of the daughter of Zion
Sit on the ground *and* keep silence;
They throw dust on their heads
And gird themselves with sackcloth.
The virgins of Jerusalem
Bow their heads to the ground.

11 My eyes fail with tears,
My heart is troubled;
My bile is poured on the ground
Because of the destruction of the
 daughter of my people,
Because the children and the infants
Faint in the streets of the city.

12 They say to their mothers,
"Where *is* grain and wine?"

2:6–9 The Law is no more (v. 9): For devout Jews the most terrible result of the Fall of Jerusalem was the destruction of their temple and, as it seemed, their religion.

2:8 God had **stretched out** a measuring **line**, and Jerusalem had come up short (see Is. 34:11, 17).

As they swoon like the wounded
In the streets of the city,
As their life is poured out
In their mothers' bosom.

13 How shall I console you?
To what shall I liken you,
O daughter of Jerusalem?
What shall I compare with you, that I
may comfort you,
O virgin daughter of Zion?
For your ruin *is* spread wide as the
sea;
Who can heal you?

14 Your prophets have seen for you
False and deceptive visions;
They have not uncovered your
iniquity,
To bring back your captives,
But have envisioned for you false
prophecies and delusions.

15 All who pass by clap *their* hands at
you;
They hiss and shake their heads
At the daughter of Jerusalem:
"*Is* this the city that is called
'The perfection of beauty,
The joy of the whole earth'?"

16 All your enemies have opened their
mouth against you;
They hiss and gnash *their* teeth.
They say, "We have swallowed *her*
up!
Surely this *is* the day we have waited
for;
We have found *it*, we have seen *it*!"

17 The LORD has done what He
purposed;
He has fulfilled His word
Which He commanded in days of old.
He has thrown down and has not
pitied,
And He has caused an enemy to
rejoice over you;
He has exalted the horn of your
adversaries.

18 Their heart cried out to the Lord,
"O wall of the daughter of Zion,
Let tears run down like a river day
and night;
Give yourself no relief;
Give your eyes no rest.

19 "Arise, cry out in the night,
At the beginning of the watches;
Pour out your heart like water before
the face of the Lord.
Lift your hands toward Him
For the life of your young children,
Who faint from hunger at the head of
every street."

20 "See, O LORD, and consider!
To whom have You done this?
Should the women eat their offspring,
The children they have cuddled?[a]
Should the priest and prophet be
slain
In the sanctuary of the Lord?

21 "Young and old lie
On the ground in the streets;
My virgins and my young men
Have fallen by the sword;
You have slain *them* in the day of
Your anger,
You have slaughtered *and* not pitied.

22 "You have invited as to a feast day
The terrors that surround me.

2:20 [a]Vulgate reads *a span long.*

2:13–16 How shall I console you? God is distressed; He must punish, but He also weeps.

2:19 The Jews divided the **night** into three **watches** of four-hour intervals, beginning at sunset (6:00 P.M. to 10:00 P.M.), continuing with a middle watch (10:00 P.M. to 2:00 A.M.), and ending at sunrise (2:00 A.M. to 6:00 A.M.).

In the day of the LORD's anger
There was no refugee or survivor.
Those whom I have borne and
brought up
My enemies have destroyed."

CHAPTER 3

The Prophet's Anguish and Hope

I *am* the man *who* has seen affliction
by the rod of His wrath.
2 He has led me and made *me* walk
In darkness and not *in* light.
3 Surely He has turned His hand
against me
Time and time again throughout the
day.

4 He has aged my flesh and my skin,
And broken my bones.
5 He has besieged me
And surrounded *me* with bitterness
and woe.
6 He has set me in dark places
Like the dead of long ago.

7 He has hedged me in so that I cannot
get out;
He has made my chain heavy.
8 Even when I cry and shout,
He shuts out my prayer.
9 He has blocked my ways with hewn
stone;
He has made my paths crooked.

10 He *has been* to me a bear lying in wait,
Like a lion in ambush.
11 He has turned aside my ways and
torn me in pieces;
He has made me desolate.
12 He has bent His bow
And set me up as a target for the
arrow.

13 He has caused the arrows of His
quiver
To pierce my loins.[a]
14 I have become the ridicule of all my
people—
Their taunting song all the day.
15 He has filled me with bitterness,
He has made me drink wormwood.

16 He has also broken my teeth with
gravel,
And covered me with ashes.
17 You have moved my soul far from
peace;
I have forgotten prosperity.
18 And I said, "My strength and my
hope
Have perished from the LORD."

19 Remember my affliction and roaming,
The wormwood and the gall.
20 My soul still remembers
And sinks within me.
21 This I recall to my mind,
Therefore I have hope.

22 *Through* the LORD's mercies we are not
consumed,
Because His compassions fail not.

3:13 [a]Literally *kidneys*

3:2 The prophet Amos had warned northern Israel more than 150 years before that God's punishment would be a time of **darkness**, not of **light** (see Amos 5:18). Jerusalem had to experience the same for herself. (see also Is. 8:20–22).

3:8 shuts out my prayer: Because God's people have forgotten Him, He cannot respond to them as He would like; He is forced to turn His back (see Jer. 18:15, 17). Jeremiah knows that a holy God must act in this way (3:17, 18, 44) but also is assured that God will answer prayer when His people sincerely turn from sin (3:55–57).

3:15 wormwood: A symbol of **bitterness**.

3:19–42 One of the most remarkable statements of faith in all of Scripture, coming as it does after the awful cry of desolation in vv. 1–18.

3:22–24 Despite the immediate horror and God's seeming silence (v. 8), the writer remembers all the evidence of God's **compassions** and **faithfulness** in the past; he refuses

> ***I praise you, Lord, because through Your mercies I am not consumed, because Your compassions fail not. They are new every morning; great is Your faithfulness.***
>
> *adapted from* Lamentations 3:22, 23

23 *They are* new every morning;
Great *is* Your faithfulness.
24 "The LORD *is* my portion," says my soul,
"Therefore I hope in Him!"

25 The LORD *is* good to those who wait for Him,
To the soul *who* seeks Him.
26 *It is* good that *one* should hope and wait quietly
For the salvation of the LORD.
27 *It is* good for a man to bear
The yoke in his youth.

28 Let him sit alone and keep silent,
Because *God* has laid *it* on him;
29 Let him put his mouth in the dust—
There may yet be hope.
30 Let him give *his* cheek to the one who strikes him,
And be full of reproach.

31 For the Lord will not cast off forever.
32 Though He causes grief,
Yet He will show compassion
According to the multitude of His mercies.
33 For He does not afflict willingly,
Nor grieve the children of men.

34 To crush under one's feet
All the prisoners of the earth,
35 To turn aside the justice *due* a man
Before the face of the Most High,
36 Or subvert a man in his cause—
The Lord does not approve.

37 Who *is* he *who* speaks and it comes to pass,
When the Lord has not commanded *it?*
38 *Is it* not from the mouth of the Most High
That woe and well-being proceed?
39 Why should a living man complain,
A man for the punishment of his sins?

40 Let us search out and examine our ways,
And turn back to the LORD;

to give up hope now. Though every earthly possession is gone, God is the best **portion** (v. 24, inheritance) of all.

3:25–30 The Lord is found to be good by the one in distress who will **wait for Him** but also earnestly **seeks Him** (v. 25). The distressed person finds **good** in hoping and waiting for the Lord's **salvation** (v. 26). Sometimes this involves bearing the **yoke** of suffering patiently, learning to bear it **alone** while keeping **silent** (vv. 27, 28). It must include submitting totally (v. 29), as well as receiving punishment willingly and repenting (v. 30).

3:27 As we interact with young people, we should encourage them to learn to submit to God early in life. By recognizing His authority at a young age they can avoid the tragedy and heartache that results from rebellion.

3:29 The ancient custom of showing submission to a sovereign was to literally put one's **mouth in the dust**.

3:30 the one who strikes: God, when He disciplines us.

3:31 God's judgment is not simply a means of punishment in chastising us. He ultimately wants to restore fellowship. We can be confident that when we repent His judgment will turn to compassion.

3:40–42 Unconfessed sin results in God's chastisement, but self-examination and repentance lead to restoration and blessing.

41 Let us lift our hearts and hands
To God in heaven.
42 We have transgressed and rebelled;
You have not pardoned.

43 You have covered *Yourself* with anger
And pursued us;
You have slain *and* not pitied.
44 You have covered Yourself with a cloud,
That prayer should not pass through.
45 You have made us an offscouring and refuse
In the midst of the peoples.

46 All our enemies
Have opened their mouths against us.
47 Fear and a snare have come upon us,
Desolation and destruction.
48 My eyes overflow with rivers of water
For the destruction of the daughter of my people.

49 My eyes flow and do not cease,
Without interruption,
50 Till the LORD from heaven
Looks down and sees.
51 My eyes bring suffering to my soul
Because of all the daughters of my city.

52 My enemies without cause
Hunted me down like a bird.
53 They silenced[a] my life in the pit
And threw stones at me.
54 The waters flowed over my head;
I said, "I am cut off!"

55 I called on Your name, O LORD,
From the lowest pit.
56 You have heard my voice:
"Do not hide Your ear
From my sighing, from my cry for help."

57 You drew near on the day I called on You,
And said, "Do not fear!"

58 O Lord, You have pleaded the case for my soul;
You have redeemed my life.
59 O LORD, You have seen *how* I am wronged;
Judge my case.
60 You have seen all their vengeance,
All their schemes against me.

61 You have heard their reproach, O LORD,
All their schemes against me,
62 The lips of my enemies
And their whispering against me all the day.
63 Look at their sitting down and their rising up;
I *am* their taunting song.

64 Repay them, O LORD,
According to the work of their hands.
65 Give them a veiled[a] heart;
Your curse *be* upon them!
66 In Your anger,
Pursue and destroy them
From under the heavens of the LORD.

CHAPTER 4

The Degradation of Zion

How the gold has become dim!
How changed the fine gold!
The stones of the sanctuary are scattered
At the head of every street.

2 The precious sons of Zion,
Valuable as fine gold,
How they are regarded as clay pots,
The work of the hands of the potter!

3 Even the jackals present their breasts
To nurse their young;

3:53 [a]Septuagint reads *put to death.*
3:65 [a]A Jewish tradition reads *sorrow of.*

But the daughter of my people *is*
cruel,
Like ostriches in the wilderness.

4 The tongue of the infant clings
To the roof of its mouth for thirst;
The young children ask for bread,
But no one breaks *it* for them.

5 Those who ate delicacies
Are desolate in the streets;
Those who were brought up in scarlet
Embrace ash heaps.

6 The punishment of the iniquity of the
daughter of my people
Is greater than the punishment of the
sin of Sod'om,
Which was overthrown in a moment,
With no hand to help her!

7 Her Naz'ir·ītes[a] were brighter than
snow
And whiter than milk;
They were more ruddy in body than
rubies,
Like sapphire in their appearance.

8 *Now* their appearance is blacker than
soot;
They go unrecognized in the streets;
Their skin clings to their bones,
It has become as dry as wood.

9 *Those* slain by the sword are better off
Than *those* who die of hunger;
For these pine away,
Stricken *for lack* of the fruits of the
field.

10 The hands of the compassionate
women
Have cooked their own children;
They became food for them
In the destruction of the daughter of
my people.

11 The LORD has fulfilled His fury,
He has poured out His fierce anger.
He kindled a fire in Zion,
And it has devoured its foundations.

12 The kings of the earth,
And all inhabitants of the world,
Would not have believed
That the adversary and the enemy
Could enter the gates of Jerusalem—

13 Because of the sins of her prophets
And the iniquities of her priests,
Who shed in her midst
The blood of the just.

14 They wandered blind in the streets;
They have defiled themselves with
blood,
So that no one would touch their
garments.

15 They cried out to them,
"Go away, unclean!
Go away, go away,
Do not touch us!"
When they fled and wandered,
Those among the nations said,
"They shall no longer dwell *here*."

16 The face[a] of the LORD scattered them;
He no longer regards them.
The people do not respect the priests
Nor show favor to the elders.

4:7 [a]Or *nobles* 4:16 [a]Targum reads *anger.*

4:5 brought up in scarlet: A sign of luxury. Scarlet and purple were the costly colors of royal robes. (see Is. 3:18–26).

4:7 Nazirites: Not the same as the Nazirites who lived by stringent vows (Num. 6:1–8), but Jerusalem's "nobles," those who were separated to leadership positions. **ruddy**: The color of robust manhood (cf. David in 1 Sam. 16:12).

4:13–16 sins of her prophets: A heavy burden of responsibility and guilt rested on those false prophets. Even **the nations** (Gentile countries) rejected them.

17 Still our eyes failed us,
Watching vainly for our help;
In our watching we watched
For a nation *that* could not save *us*.

18 They tracked our steps
So that we could not walk in our
streets.
Our end was near;
Our days were over,
For our end had come.

19 Our pursuers were swifter
Than the eagles of the heavens.
They pursued us on the mountains
And lay in wait for us in the
wilderness.

20 The breath of our nostrils, the
anointed of the LORD,
Was caught in their pits,
Of whom we said, "Under his
shadow
We shall live among the nations."

21 Rejoice and be glad, O daughter of
Ē'dom,
You who dwell in the land of Uz!
The cup shall also pass over to you
And you shall become drunk and
make yourself naked.

22 *The punishment of* your iniquity is
accomplished,
O daughter of Zion;
He will no longer send you into
captivity.
He will punish your iniquity,
O daughter of Ē'dom;
He will uncover your sins!

CHAPTER 5

A Prayer for Restoration

Remember, O LORD, what has come
upon us;
Look, and behold our reproach!
2 Our inheritance has been turned over
to aliens,
And our houses to foreigners.
3 We have become orphans and waifs,
Our mothers *are* like widows.

4 We pay for the water we drink,
And our wood comes at a price.
5 *They* pursue at our heels;[a]
We labor *and* have no rest.
6 We have given our hand *to* the
Egyptians
And the Assyrians, to be satisfied
with bread.

7 Our fathers sinned *and are* no more,
But we bear their iniquities.
8 Servants rule over us;
There is none to deliver *us* from their
hand.
9 We get our bread *at the risk* of our lives,
Because of the sword in the
wilderness.

10 Our skin is hot as an oven,
Because of the fever of famine.
11 They ravished the women in Zion,
The maidens in the cities of Judah.
12 Princes were hung up by their hands,
And elders were not respected.

5:5 [a]Literally *necks*

4:17 a nation that could not save: Perhaps a reference to the false prophecies of help from Egypt (see Is. 31:1–3).

4:18–20 They: The Babylonian army.

4:20 anointed of the LORD: A reference to King Zedekiah who was captured, blinded, and led into captivity in 586 B.C. (see Jer. 39:4–7).

5:2–6 Our inheritance: The Promised Land. **to be satisfied with bread** (v. 6): They were forced to sell their land to bankers from surrounding countries in order to get money for food.

5:12 hung up by their hands: After death, in order to display the bodies of leaders who had suffered defeat (see 1 Sam. 31:8–13).

13 Young men ground at the millstones;
Boys staggered under *loads of* wood.
14 The elders have ceased *gathering at* the gate,
And the young men from their music.
15 The joy of our heart has ceased;
Our dance has turned into mourning.
16 The crown has fallen *from* our head.
Woe to us, for we have sinned!
17 Because of this our heart is faint;
Because of these *things* our eyes grow dim;
18 Because of Mount Zion which is desolate,
With foxes walking about on it.

19 You, O LORD, remain forever;
Your throne from generation to generation.
20 Why do You forget us forever,
And forsake us for so long a time?
21 Turn us back to You, O LORD, and we will be restored;
Renew our days as of old,
22 Unless You have utterly rejected us,
And are very angry with us!

5:21, 22 In a final burst of faith, this prayer lays hold of restoration and renewal in the Lord, but not without a nagging doubt. **Unless You have utterly rejected us**: To those not immediately in the distress, the answer was clear: The Lord must correct and punish them. But He would not make "a complete end" of them. "'I am with you,' says the LORD, 'to save you'" (Jer. 30:11).

✦Ezekiel✦

Ezekiel prophesied to the captives from Jerusalem while they were held in Babylon. His ministry lasted at least twenty-two years, and his book was probably completed around 565 B.C.

Taken captive to Babylon during the second of Nebuchadnezzar's three attacks on Jerusalem, Ezekiel tried to convince the Jewish exiles that they had no reason to hope for an immediate deliverance. However, not until Jerusalem was destroyed did the people abandon their false hopes. Like Jeremiah, Ezekiel used several metaphors for Judah: a useless vine (ch. 15), an adulterous wife (ch. 16), and a lioness (19:1–9).

While Isaiah and Jeremiah had warned against the coming judgment, Ezekiel reminded the generation born into captivity of the reason for Jerusalem's punishment. His actions indicate the importance of giving each new generation a legacy of faith in God. Ezekiel also prophesied the coming destruction of Babylon and proclaimed hope for the future restoration of Jerusalem. Chapters 33—48 focus on prophecies regarding the return of God's blessing and the gathering of His people. The vision of the valley of dry bones in chapter 37 illustrates the restoration of Israel. ✦

CHAPTER 1

Ezekiel's Vision of God

Now it came to pass in the thirtieth year,
in the fourth *month,* on the fifth *day* of the
month, as I *was* among the captives by the
River Chē'bar, *that* the heavens were
opened and I saw visions[a] of God. 2On the
fifth *day* of the month, which *was* in the
fifth year of King Je·hoi'a·chin's captivity,
3the word of the LORD came expressly to
E·zēk'i·el the priest, the son of Bū'zī, in the
land of the Chal·dē'ans[a] by the River
Chē'bar; and the hand of the LORD was
upon him there.
4Then I looked, and behold, a whirlwind
was coming out of the north, a great cloud
with raging fire engulfing itself; and
brightness *was* all around it and radiating
out of its midst like the color of amber, out
of the midst of the fire. 5Also from within it
came the likeness of four living creatures.
And this *was* their appearance: they had

1:1 [a]Following Masoretic Text, Septuagint, and Vulgate; Syriac and Targum read *a vision.*
1:3 [a]Or *Babylonians,* and so elsewhere in this book

1:1–3 thirtieth year: Probably the 30th year of Ezekiel's life. As a priest (v. 3), Ezekiel normally would have entered fully into his duties that year. As an exile in Babylon, he could not. God's call to be a prophet graciously replaced the lost priestly ministry. **the captives**: Judeans exiled to Babylon in 605 B.C. and/or in 597 B.C.

1:5 from within it: This cloud was not dark, but bright and apparently transparent. **four living creatures**: In 10:20, Ezekiel identifies them as cherubim, angelic servants of God.

the likeness of a man. 6Each one had four faces, and each one had four wings. 7Their legs *were* straight, and the soles of their feet *were* like the soles of calves' feet. They sparkled like the color of burnished bronze. 8The hands of a man *were* under their wings on their four sides; and each of the four had faces and wings. 9Their wings touched one another. *The creatures* did not turn when they went, but each one went straight forward.

10As for the likeness of their faces, *each* had the face of a man; each of the four had the face of a lion on the right side, each of the four had the face of an ox on the left side, and each of the four had the face of an eagle. 11Thus *were* their faces. Their wings stretched upward; two *wings* of each one touched one another, and two covered their bodies. 12And each one went straight forward; they went wherever the spirit wanted to go, and they did not turn when they went.

13As for the likeness of the living creatures, their appearance *was* like burning coals of fire, like the appearance of torches going back and forth among the living creatures. The fire was bright, and out of the fire went lightning. 14And the living creatures ran back and forth, in appearance like a flash of lightning.

15Now as I looked at the living creatures, behold, a wheel *was* on the earth beside each living creature with its four faces. 16The appearance of the wheels and their workings *was* like the color of beryl, and all four had the same likeness. The appearance of their workings *was*, as it were, a wheel in the middle of a wheel. 17When they moved, they went toward any one of four directions; they did not turn aside when they went. 18As for their rims, they were so high they were awesome; and their rims *were* full of eyes, all around the four of them. 19When the living creatures went, the wheels went beside them; and when the living creatures were lifted up from the earth, the wheels were lifted up. 20Wherever the spirit wanted to go, they went, *because* there the spirit went; and the wheels were lifted together with them, for the spirit of the living creatures[a] *was* in the wheels. 21When those went, *these* went; when those stood, *these* stood; and when those were lifted up from the earth, the wheels were lifted up together with them, for the spirit of the living creatures[a] *was* in the wheels.

22The likeness of the firmament above the heads of the living creatures[a] *was* like the color of an awesome crystal, stretched out over their heads. 23And under the firmament their wings *spread out* straight, one toward another. Each one had two which covered one side, and each one had two which covered the other side of the body. 24When they went, I heard the noise of their wings, like the noise of many waters, like the voice of the Almighty, a tumult like the noise of an army; and when they stood still, they let down their wings. 25A voice came from above the firmament that *was* over their heads; whenever they stood, they let down their wings.

26And above the firmament over their heads *was* the likeness of a throne, in appearance like a sapphire stone; on the like-

1:20 [a]Literally *living creature;* Septuagint and Vulgate read *spirit of life;* Targum reads *creatures.*
1:21 [a]Literally *living creature;* Septuagint and Vulgate read *spirit of life;* Targum reads *creatures.*
1:22 [a]Following Septuagint, Targum, and Vulgate; Masoretic Text reads *living creature.*

1:7 Their legs were straight: This and other details were intended to distinguish these creatures from the bull-men and other statues the Judeans would have seen in Babylonian temples. The living creatures walked upright, rather than on all fours.

1:16 a wheel in the middle of a wheel: Probably each wheel was, in reality, two wheels, each a solid disc bisecting the other at right angles. Thus no matter what the direction, each wheel could move forward.

1:26 a likeness with the appearance of: A sense of the awful holiness and transcendence

ness of the throne *was* a likeness with the
appearance of a man high above it. 27Also
from the appearance of His waist and up-
ward I saw, as it were, the color of amber
with the appearance of fire all around
within it; and from the appearance of His
waist and downward I saw, as it were, the
appearance of fire with brightness all
around. 28Like the appearance of a rainbow
in a cloud on a rainy day, so *was* the ap-
pearance of the brightness all around it.
This *was* the appearance of the likeness of
the glory of the LORD.

Ezekiel Sent to Rebellious Israel

So when I saw *it,* I fell on my face, and I
heard a voice of One speaking.

CHAPTER 2

And He said to me, "Son of man, stand
on your feet, and I will speak to you."
2Then the Spirit entered me when He
spoke to me, and set me on my feet; and I
heard Him who spoke to me. 3And He said
to me: "Son of man, I am sending you to
the children of Israel, to a rebellious nation
that has rebelled against Me; they and their
fathers have transgressed against Me to
this very day. 4For *they are* impudent and
stubborn children. I am sending you to
them, and you shall say to them, 'Thus
says the Lord GOD.' 5As for them, whether
they hear or whether they refuse—for they
are a rebellious house—yet they will know
that a prophet has been among them.
6"And you, son of man, do not be afraid

> It is more blessed to give than to receive, especially to those from whom you don't expect anything in return. The greatest gift of all is the promise of eternal life. If we are going to receive eternal life and God's blessings, we have a duty to give.
>
> Truett Cathy

of them nor be afraid of their words,
though briers and thorns *are* with you and
you dwell among scorpions; do not be
afraid of their words or dismayed by their
looks, though they *are* a rebellious house.
7You shall speak My words to them,
whether they hear or whether they refuse,
for they *are* rebellious. 8But you, son of
man, hear what I say to you. Do not be re-
bellious like that rebellious house; open
your mouth and eat what I give you."
9Now when I looked, there was a hand
stretched out to me; and behold, a scroll of
a book *was* in it. 10Then He spread it before
me; and *there was* writing on the inside and
on the outside, and written on it *were*
lamentations and mourning and woe.

CHAPTER 3

Moreover He said to me, "Son of man,
eat what you find; eat this scroll, and go,
speak to the house of Israel." 2So I opened
my mouth, and He caused me to eat that
scroll.
3And He said to me, "Son of man, feed

---

of God. Ezekiel can say only that he has seen a reflection of a reflection of God (see Rev. 1:13).

2:1 Son of man: God addresses Ezekiel almost 90 times in the book. Unlike the usage in Dan. 7:13 and the NT to refer to the Messiah, here and in Dan. 8:17 the term seems to emphasize that Ezekiel was only human. He was not responsible for the fulfillment of the message God gave him, only for its faithful proclamation. **stand on your feet**: God does not desire abject fear, but rather reverent obedience.

2:6–7 Just as Ezekiel's message was scorned by Israel, we can expect to encounter resistance to the message of the gospel. However, God did not call us to be popular; He called us to "preach the gospel to every creature."

2:10 inside . . . outside: That the scroll was written on both sides was unusual. This suggests that God had a full and complete message for Ezekiel to deliver to Israel.

your belly, and fill your stomach with this scroll that I give you." So I ate, and it was in my mouth like honey in sweetness.

4Then He said to me: "Son of man, go to the house of Israel and speak with My words to them. 5For you *are* not sent to a people of unfamiliar speech and of hard language, *but* to the house of Israel, 6not to many people of unfamiliar speech and of hard language, whose words you cannot understand. Surely, had I sent you to them, they would have listened to you. 7But the house of Israel will not listen to you, because they will not listen to Me; for all the house of Israel *are* impudent and hard-hearted. 8Behold, I have made your face strong against their faces, and your forehead strong against their foreheads. 9Like adamant stone, harder than flint, I have made your forehead; do not be afraid of them, nor be dismayed at their looks, though they *are* a rebellious house."

10Moreover He said to me: "Son of man, receive into your heart all My words that I speak to you, and hear with your ears. 11And go, get to the captives, to the children of your people, and speak to them and tell them, 'Thus says the Lord GOD,' whether they hear, or whether they refuse."

12Then the Spirit lifted me up, and I heard behind me a great thunderous voice: "Blessed *is* the glory of the LORD from His place!" 13*I* also *heard* the noise of the wings of the living creatures that touched one another, and the noise of the wheels beside them, and a great thunderous noise. 14So the Spirit lifted me up and took me away, and I went in bitterness, in the heat of my spirit; but the hand of the LORD was strong upon me. 15Then I came to the captives at Tel Ā'bib, who dwelt by the River Chē'bar; and I sat where they sat, and remained there astonished among them seven days.

Ezekiel Is a Watchman

16Now it came to pass at the end of seven days that the word of the LORD came to me, saying, 17"Son of man, I have made you a watchman for the house of Israel; therefore hear a word from My mouth, and give them warning from Me: 18When I say to the wicked, 'You shall surely die,' and you give him no warning, nor speak to warn the wicked from his wicked way, to save his life, that same wicked *man* shall die in his iniquity; but his blood I will require at your hand. 19Yet, if you warn the wicked, and he does not turn from his wickedness, nor from his wicked way, he shall die in his iniquity; but you have delivered your soul.

20"Again, when a righteous *man* turns from his righteousness and commits iniquity, and I lay a stumbling block before him, he shall die; because you did not give him warning, he shall die in his sin, and his righteousness which he has done shall not be remembered; but his blood I will require at your hand. 21Nevertheless if you warn the righteous *man* that the righteous should not sin, and he does not sin, he shall surely live because he took warning; also you will have delivered your soul."

22Then the hand of the LORD was upon me there, and He said to me, "Arise, go out into the plain, and there I shall talk with you."

23So I arose and went out into the plain, and behold, the glory of the LORD stood there, like the glory which I saw by the River Chē'bar; and I fell on my face. 24Then the Spirit entered me and set me on my feet, and spoke with me and said to me: "Go, shut yourself inside your house. 25And you, O son of man, surely they will put ropes on you and bind you with them, so that you cannot go out among them. 26I

3:14 in bitterness: Possibly an expression of Ezekiel's reluctance to be God's bearer of such a difficult message. Other prophets experienced a similar reluctance (see Jer. 1:6), but, like Ezekiel who overcame reluctance with a willingness to follow God's direction, they too obeyed.

will make your tongue cling to the roof of
your mouth, so that you shall be mute and
not be one to rebuke them, for they *are* a re-
bellious house. 27But when I speak with
you, I will open your mouth, and you shall
say to them, 'Thus says the Lord GOD.' He
who hears, let him hear; and he who re-
fuses, let him refuse; for they *are* a rebel-
lious house.

CHAPTER 4

The Siege of Jerusalem Portrayed

"You also, son of man, take a clay tablet
and lay it before you, and portray on it a
city, Jerusalem. 2Lay siege against it, build
a siege wall against it, and heap up a
mound against it; set camps against it also,
and place battering rams against it all
around. 3Moreover take for yourself an
iron plate, and set it *as* an iron wall be-
tween you and the city. Set your face
against it, and it shall be besieged, and you
shall lay siege against it. This *will be* a sign
to the house of Israel.

4"Lie also on your left side, and lay the
iniquity of the house of Israel upon it. *Ac-
cording* to the number of the days that you
lie on it, you shall bear their iniquity. 5For I
have laid on you the years of their iniquity,
according to the number of the days, three
hundred and ninety days; so you shall
bear the iniquity of the house of Israel.
6And when you have completed them, lie
again on your right side; then you shall
bear the iniquity of the house of Judah
forty days. I have laid on you a day for
each year.

7"Therefore you shall set your face to-
ward the siege of Jerusalem; your arm *shall
be* uncovered, and you shall prophesy
against it. 8And surely I will restrain you so
that you cannot turn from one side to an-
other till you have ended the days of your
siege.

9"Also take for yourself wheat, barley,
beans, lentils, millet, and spelt; put them
into one vessel, and make bread of them
for yourself. *During* the number of days
that you lie on your side, three hundred
and ninety days, you shall eat it. 10And
your food which you eat *shall be* by weight,
twenty shekels a day; from time to time
you shall eat it. 11You shall also drink water
by measure, one-sixth of a hin; from time
to time you shall drink. 12And you shall eat
it *as* barley cakes; and bake it using fuel of
human waste in their sight."

13Then the LORD said, "So shall the chil-
dren of Israel eat their defiled bread
among the Gentiles, where I will drive
them."

14So I said, "Ah, Lord GOD! Indeed I
have never defiled myself from my youth
till now; I have never eaten what died of it-
self or was torn by beasts, nor has abomi-
nable flesh ever come into my mouth."

15Then He said to me, "See, I am giving
you cow dung instead of human waste,
and you shall prepare your bread over it."

16Moreover He said to me, "Son of man,
surely I will cut off the supply of bread in
Jerusalem; they shall eat bread by weight
and with anxiety, and shall drink water by
measure and with dread, 17that they may
lack bread and water, and be dismayed

4:1—5:17 Ezekiel enacts before the exiles the coming siege of Jerusalem. The siege occurred in 587–586 B.C.; Ezekiel's prophecy was made about 593 (see 1:1–3).

4:3 iron plate: Normally set over the fire to bake flat bread. Ezekiel was to use it as an iron wall in his model of the siege, symbolizing God's firm intention to destroy Jerusalem.

4:10, 11 twenty shekels: About eight ounces (.23 kg) of bread. **from time to time**: Each day at the same time. **one-sixth of a hin**: Just over a pint (.5 l). These were starvation rations. Ezekiel would be demonstrating the coming famine in besieged Jerusalem.

4:14 defiled: The use of human waste for fuel would pollute whatever was cooked over it (see Deut. 23:12–14).

4:15 Dried **cow dung** is still widely used as fuel in many parts of Asia. Since the cow was a ritually clean animal, that would not have bothered Ezekiel.

with one another, and waste away because of their iniquity.

CHAPTER 5

A Sword Against Jerusalem

"And you, son of man, take a sharp sword, take it as a barber's razor, and pass *it* over your head and your beard; then take scales to weigh and divide the hair. 2You shall burn with fire one-third in the midst of the city, when the days of the siege are finished; then you shall take one-third and strike around *it* with the sword, and one-third you shall scatter in the wind: I will draw out a sword after them. 3You shall also take a small number of them and bind them in the edge of your *garment*. 4Then take some of them again and throw them into the midst of the fire, and burn them in the fire. From there a fire will go out into all the house of Israel.

5"Thus says the Lord GOD: 'This *is* Jerusalem; I have set her in the midst of the nations and the countries all around her. 6She has rebelled against My judgments by doing wickedness more than the nations, and against My statutes more than the countries that *are* all around her; for they have refused My judgments, and they have not walked in My statutes.' 7Therefore thus says the Lord GOD: 'Because you have multiplied *disobedience* more than the nations that *are* all around you, have not walked in My statutes nor kept My judgments, nor even done[a] according to the judgments of the nations that *are* all around you'— 8therefore thus says the Lord GOD: 'Indeed I, even I, *am* against you and will execute judgments in your midst in the sight of the nations. 9And I will do among you what I have never done, and the like of which I will never do again, because of all your abominations. 10Therefore fathers shall eat *their* sons in your midst, and sons shall eat their fathers; and I will execute judgments among you, and all of you who remain I will scatter to all the winds.

11'Therefore, *as* I live,' says the Lord GOD, 'surely, because you have defiled My sanctuary with all your detestable things and with all your abominations, therefore I will also diminish *you;* My eye will not spare, nor will I have any pity. 12One-third of you shall die of the pestilence, and be consumed with famine in your midst; and one-third shall fall by the sword all around you; and I will scatter another third to all the winds, and I will draw out a sword after them.

13'Thus shall My anger be spent, and I will cause My fury to rest upon them, and I will be avenged; and they shall know that I, the LORD, have spoken *it* in My zeal, when I have spent My fury upon them. 14Moreover I will make you a waste and a reproach among the nations that *are* all around you, in the sight of all who pass by.

15'So it[a] shall be a reproach, a taunt, a lesson, and an astonishment to the nations that *are* all around you, when I execute judgments among you in anger and in fury and in furious rebukes. I, the LORD, have spoken. 16When I send against them the terrible arrows of famine which shall be for destruction, which I will send to destroy you, I will increase the famine upon you and cut off your supply of bread. 17So I will send against you famine and wild beasts, and they will bereave you. Pestilence and blood shall pass through you, and I will

5:7 [a]Following Masoretic Text, Septuagint, Targum, and Vulgate; many Hebrew manuscripts and Syriac read *but have done* (compare 11:12). 5:15 [a]Septuagint, Syriac, Targum, and Vulgate read *you.*

5:1, 2 pass it over: So that his head and his beard would be shaved, as a sign of mourning or shame, or both.

5:10 This prophecy of cannibalism was fulfilled in the siege of Jerusalem; see the parallel prophecy in Jer. 19:9 and its gruesome fulfillment in Lam. 4:10.

5:12 a sword after them: Even some who survived the siege would be killed attempting to escape, or as punishment for the rebellion against Nebuchadnezzar.

bring the sword against you. I, the LORD,
have spoken.' "

CHAPTER 6

Judgment on Idolatrous Israel

Now the word of the LORD came to me,
saying: 2"Son of man, set your face toward
the mountains of Israel, and prophesy
against them, 3and say, 'O mountains of Is-
rael, hear the word of the Lord GOD! Thus
says the Lord GOD to the mountains, to the
hills, to the ravines, and to the valleys: "In-
deed I, *even* I, will bring a sword against
you, and I will destroy your high places.
4Then your altars shall be desolate, your
incense altars shall be broken, and I will
cast down your slain *men* before your
idols. 5And I will lay the corpses of the chil-
dren of Israel before their idols, and I will
scatter your bones all around your altars.
6In all your dwelling places the cities shall
be laid waste, and the high places shall be
desolate, so that your altars may be laid
waste and made desolate, your idols may
be broken and made to cease, your incense
altars may be cut down, and your works
may be abolished. 7The slain shall fall in
your midst, and you shall know that I *am*
the LORD.

8"Yet I will leave a remnant, so that you
may have *some* who escape the sword
among the nations, when you are scattered
through the countries. 9Then those of you
who escape will remember Me among the
nations where they are carried captive, be-
cause I was crushed by their adulterous
heart which has departed from Me, and by
their eyes which play the harlot after their
idols; they will loathe themselves for the
evils which they committed in all their
abominations. 10And they shall know that I
am the LORD; I have not said in vain that I
would bring this calamity upon them."

11'Thus says the Lord GOD: "Pound your
fists and stamp your feet, and say, 'Alas,
for all the evil abominations of the house of
Israel! For they shall fall by the sword, by
famine, and by pestilence. 12He who is far
off shall die by the pestilence, he who is
near shall fall by the sword, and he who re-
mains and is besieged shall die by the
famine. Thus will I spend My fury upon
them. 13Then you shall know that I *am* the
LORD, when their slain are among their
idols all around their altars, on every high
hill, on all the mountaintops, under every
green tree, and under every thick oak,
wherever they offered sweet incense to all
their idols. 14So I will stretch out My hand
against them and make the land desolate,
yes, more desolate than the wilderness to-
ward Dib'lah, in all their dwelling places.
Then they shall know that I *am* the
LORD.' " ' "

CHAPTER 7

Judgment on Israel Is Near

Moreover the word of the LORD came to
me, saying, 2"And you, son of man, thus
says the Lord GOD to the land of Israel:

'An end! The end has come upon the
four corners of the land.
3 Now the end *has come* upon you,
And I will send My anger against
you;
I will judge you according to your
ways,
And I will repay you for all your
abominations.
4 My eye will not spare you,
Nor will I have pity;

6:5 Corpses and bones strewn around the high places would defile them, making them unfit for worship. On Josiah's desecration of pagan high places see 1 Kin. 13:2; 2 Kin. 23:13–20 and notes.

6:8 This is Ezekiel's first explicit mention of the remnant who would be spared (but see 5:3).

7:4 My eye: The organ first to express pity would now be pitiless and unsparing.

But I will repay your ways,
And your abominations will be in your midst;
Then you shall know that I *am* the LORD!'

5 "Thus says the Lord GOD:

'A disaster, a singular disaster;
Behold, it has come!
6 An end has come,
The end has come;
It has dawned for you;
Behold, it has come!
7 Doom has come to you, you who dwell in the land;
The time has come,
A day of trouble *is* near,
And not of rejoicing in the mountains.
8 Now upon you I will soon pour out My fury,
And spend My anger upon you;
I will judge you according to your ways,
And I will repay you for all your abominations.

9 'My eye will not spare,
Nor will I have pity;
I will repay you according to your ways,
And your abominations will be in your midst.
Then you shall know that I *am* the LORD who strikes.

10 'Behold, the day!
Behold, it has come!
Doom has gone out;
The rod has blossomed,
Pride has budded.
11 Violence has risen up into a rod of wickedness;
None of them *shall remain,*
None of their multitude,
None of them;
Nor *shall there be* wailing for them.
12 The time has come,
The day draws near.

'Let not the buyer rejoice,
Nor the seller mourn,
For wrath *is* on their whole multitude.
13 For the seller shall not return to what has been sold,
Though he may still be alive;
For the vision concerns the whole multitude,
And it shall not turn back;
No one will strengthen himself
Who lives in iniquity.

14 'They have blown the trumpet and made everyone ready,
But no one goes to battle;
For My wrath *is* on all their multitude.
15 The sword *is* outside,
And the pestilence and famine within.
Whoever *is* in the field
Will die by the sword;
And whoever *is* in the city,
Famine and pestilence will devour him.

16 'Those who survive will escape and be on the mountains

> Crises reveal character. When we are put to the test the hidden resources of our character are revealed exactly.
> Oswald Chambers

7:9 the LORD who strikes: This description takes the same grammatical form as "The LORD will provide" (Gen. 22:14) and "The LORD our righteousness" (Jer. 33:16). How tragic that now He would be the Lord who strikes in judgment!

7:10 The rod has blossomed: A reminder of Aaron's rod, which blossomed as a sign of God's judgment on a rebellious people (see Num. 17:8, 10).

Like doves of the valleys,
All of them mourning,
Each for his iniquity.
17 Every hand will be feeble,
And every knee will be *as* weak *as* water.
18 They will also be girded with sackcloth;
Horror will cover them;
Shame *will be* on every face,
Baldness on all their heads.

19 'They will throw their silver into the streets,
And their gold will be like refuse;
Their silver and their gold will not be able to deliver them
In the day of the wrath of the LORD;
They will not satisfy their souls,
Nor fill their stomachs,
Because it became their stumbling block of iniquity.

20 'As for the beauty of his ornaments,
He set it in majesty;
But they made from it
The images of their abominations—
Their detestable things;
Therefore I have made it
Like refuse to them.
21 I will give it as plunder
Into the hands of strangers,
And to the wicked of the earth as spoil;
And they shall defile it.
22 I will turn My face from them,
And they will defile My secret place;
For robbers shall enter it and defile it.

23 'Make a chain,
For the land is filled with crimes of blood,
And the city is full of violence.
24 Therefore I will bring the worst of the Gentiles,
And they will possess their houses;
I will cause the pomp of the strong to cease,
And their holy places shall be defiled.
25 Destruction comes;
They will seek peace, but *there shall be* none.
26 Disaster will come upon disaster,
And rumor will be upon rumor.
Then they will seek a vision from a prophet;
But the law will perish from the priest,
And counsel from the elders.

27 'The king will mourn,
The prince will be clothed with desolation,
And the hands of the common people will tremble.
I will do to them according to their way,
And according to what they deserve I will judge them;
Then they shall know that I *am* the LORD!'"

CHAPTER 8

Abominations in the Temple

And it came to pass in the sixth year, in
the sixth *month,* on the fifth *day* of the
month, as I sat in my house with the elders
of Judah sitting before me, that the hand of
the Lord GOD fell upon me there. 2Then I
looked, and there was a likeness, like the
appearance of fire—from the appearance
of His waist and downward, fire; and from
His waist and upward, like the appearance
of brightness, like the color of amber. 3He
stretched out the form of a hand, and took

8:3 in visions of God: This phrase implies that Ezekiel was shown all the events of chs. 8—11. It was a vision in Babylon of events in Jerusalem. The **north gate** gave access to the king's palace, so the king was at least partly responsible for placing and maintaining the **image**, perhaps an Asherah pole like the one Manasseh had erected (2 Kin. 21:7). The **inner**

me by a lock of my hair; and the Spirit lifted me up between earth and heaven, and brought me in visions of God to Jerusalem, to the door of the north gate of the inner *court,* where the seat of the image of jealousy *was,* which provokes to jealousy. 4And behold, the glory of the God of Israel *was* there, like the vision that I saw in the plain.

5Then He said to me, "Son of man, lift your eyes now toward the north." So I lifted my eyes toward the north, and there, north of the altar gate, was this image of jealousy in the entrance.

6Furthermore He said to me, "Son of man, do you see what they are doing, the great abominations that the house of Israel commits here, to make Me go far away from My sanctuary? Now turn again, you will see greater abominations." 7So He brought me to the door of the court; and when I looked, there was a hole in the wall. 8Then He said to me, "Son of man, dig into the wall"; and when I dug into the wall, there was a door.

9And He said to me, "Go in, and see the wicked abominations which they are doing there." 10So I went in and saw, and there—every sort of creeping thing, abominable beasts, and all the idols of the house of Israel, portrayed all around on the walls. 11And there stood before them seventy men of the elders of the house of Israel, and in their midst stood Jā·az·a·nī'ah the son of Shā'phan. Each man had a censer in his hand, and a thick cloud of incense went up. 12Then He said to me, "Son of man, have you seen what the elders of the house of Israel do in the dark, every man in the room of his idols? For they say, 'The LORD does not see us, the LORD has forsaken the land.' "

13And He said to me, "Turn again, *and* you will see greater abominations that they are doing." 14So He brought me to the door of the north gate of the LORD's house; and to my dismay, women were sitting there weeping for Tam'mūz.

15Then He said to me, "Have you seen *this,* O son of man? Turn again, you will see greater abominations than these." 16So He brought me into the inner court of the LORD's house; and there, at the door of the temple of the LORD, between the porch and the altar, *were* about twenty-five men with their backs toward the temple of the LORD and their faces toward the east, and they were worshiping the sun toward the east.

17And He said to me, "Have you seen *this,* O son of man? Is it a trivial thing to the house of Judah to commit the abominations which they commit here? For they have filled the land with violence; then they have returned to provoke Me to anger. Indeed they put the branch to their nose. 18Therefore I also will act in fury. My eye will not spare nor will I have pity; and though they cry in My ears with a loud voice, I will not hear them."

---

court was off-limits to the ordinary Israelite. Here, at its entrance, where the floor plan of the temple was designed to begin emphasizing the holiness of Israel's God, the image of an unnamed foreign deity had been erected.

8:8–10 Dig into the wall suggests a secret chamber in the priests' quarters on either side of the Holy Place. **every sort . . . portrayed**: Relief carvings of many kinds of animals covered the walls. Judah's treaties with the nations required worship of those nations' animal gods.

8:15, 16 inner court: Where only the priests were allowed. **at the door**: At the very entrance to the Most Holy Place, God's dwelling place in the temple. **twenty-five men**: Not just priests, but elders of the priests (see 9:6). **worshiping . . . toward the east** meant facing away from the temple. This involved both a physical and a spiritual turning of their backs on God. The sun was the principal god of Egypt.

CHAPTER 9

The Wicked Are Slain

Then He called out in my hearing with a loud voice, saying, "Let those who have charge over the city draw near, each *with* a deadly weapon in his hand." 2And suddenly six men came from the direction of the upper gate, which faces north, each with his battle-ax in his hand. One man among them *was* clothed with linen and had a writer's inkhorn at his side. They went in and stood beside the bronze altar.

3Now the glory of the God of Israel had gone up from the cherub, where it had been, to the threshold of the temple.[a] And He called to the man clothed with linen, who *had* the writer's inkhorn at his side; 4and the LORD said to him, "Go through the midst of the city, through the midst of Jerusalem, and put a mark on the foreheads of the men who sigh and cry over all the abominations that are done within it."

5To the others He said in my hearing, "Go after him through the city and kill; do not let your eye spare, nor have any pity. 6Utterly slay old *and* young men, maidens and little children and women; but do not come near anyone on whom *is* the mark; and begin at My sanctuary." So they began with the elders who *were* before the temple. 7Then He said to them, "Defile the temple, and fill the courts with the slain. Go out!" And they went out and killed in the city.

8So it was, that while they were killing them, I was left *alone;* and I fell on my face and cried out, and said, "Ah, Lord GOD!

> The safest road to hell is the gradual one—the gentle slope, soft underfoot, without sudden turnings, without milestones, without guideposts.
>
> C. S. Lewis

Will You destroy all the remnant of Israel in pouring out Your fury on Jerusalem?"

9Then He said to me, "The iniquity of the house of Israel and Judah *is* exceedingly great, and the land is full of bloodshed, and the city full of perversity; for they say, 'The LORD has forsaken the land, and the LORD does not see!' 10And as for Me also, My eye will neither spare, nor will I have pity, *but* I will recompense their deeds on their own head."

11Just then, the man clothed with linen, who *had* the inkhorn at his side, reported back and said, "I have done as You commanded me."

CHAPTER 10

The Glory Departs from the Temple

And I looked, and there in the firmament that was above the head of the cherubim, there appeared something like a sapphire stone, having the appearance of the likeness of a throne. 2Then He spoke to the man clothed with linen, and said, "Go in among the wheels, under the cherub, fill your hands with coals of fire from among the cherubim, and scatter *them* over the city." And he went in as I watched.

3Now the cherubim were standing on the south side of the temple[a] when the man went in, and the cloud filled the inner

9:3 [a]Literally *house* 10:3 [a]Literally *house,* also in verses 4 and 18

9:2 six men: Angels. **The upper gate** was where the image of jealousy stood (8:3) and where the women were weeping for Tammuz (8:14). **One man**: A seventh angel, dressed and equipped as a scribe. All seven angels appeared in the form of men. **the bronze altar**: In the inner court of the temple.

9:4 We should be grieved when we see sin in the world. To be influenced by it or become indifferent to it indicates that our hearts are not sensitive to God's Word.

9:7 Corpses in the **temple** would recognizably **defile** it, whereas the people's abominable worship had defiled it without their recognition.

10:1–22 The glory of God departs from the temple.

court. 4 Then the glory of the LORD went up
from the cherub, *and paused* over the
threshold of the temple; and the house was
filled with the cloud, and the court was full
of the brightness of the LORD's glory. 5 And
the sound of the wings of the cherubim
was heard *even* in the outer court, like the
voice of Almighty God when He speaks.

6 Then it happened, when He com-
manded the man clothed in linen, saying,
"Take fire from among the wheels, from
among the cherubim," that he went in and
stood beside the wheels. 7 And the cherub
stretched out his hand from among the
cherubim to the fire that *was* among the
cherubim, and took *some of it* and put *it*
into the hands of the *man* clothed with
linen, who took *it* and went out. 8 The
cherubim appeared to have the form of a
man's hand under their wings.

9 And when I looked, there were four
wheels by the cherubim, one wheel by one
cherub and another wheel by each other
cherub; the wheels appeared *to have*
the color of a beryl stone. 10 *As for* their
appearance, all four looked alike—as it
were, a wheel in the middle of a wheel.
11 When they went, they went toward *any of*
their four directions; they did not turn
aside when they went, but followed in the
direction the head was facing. They did
not turn aside when they went. 12 And their
whole body, with their back, their hands,
their wings, and the wheels that the four
had, *were* full of eyes all around. 13 As for
the wheels, they were called in my hearing,
"Wheel."

14 Each one had four faces: the first face
was the face of a cherub, the second face the
face of a man, the third the face of a lion,
and the fourth the face of an eagle. 15 And
the cherubim were lifted up. This *was* the
living creature I saw by the River Chē′bar.
16 When the cherubim went, the wheels
went beside them; and when the cherubim
lifted their wings to mount up from the
earth, the same wheels also did not turn
from beside them. 17 When *the cherubim*[a]
stood still, *the wheels* stood still, and when
one[b] was lifted up, *the other*[c] lifted itself up,
for the spirit of the living creature *was* in
them.

18 Then the glory of the LORD departed
from the threshold of the temple and stood
over the cherubim. 19 And the cherubim
lifted their wings and mounted up from
the earth in my sight. When they went out,
the wheels *were* beside them; and they
stood at the door of the east gate of the
LORD's house, and the glory of the God of
Israel *was* above them.

20 This *is* the living creature I saw under
the God of Israel by the River Chē′bar, and
I knew they *were* cherubim. 21 Each one had
four faces and each one four wings, and
the likeness of the hands of a man *was* un-
der their wings. 22 And the likeness of their
faces *was* the same *as* the faces which I had
seen by the River Chē′bar, their appear-
ance and their persons. They each went
straight forward.

CHAPTER 11

Judgment on Wicked Counselors

Then the Spirit lifted me up and brought
me to the East Gate of the LORD's house,
which faces eastward; and there at the
door of the gate were twenty-five men,
among whom I saw Jā·az·a·nī′ah the son
of Az′zur, and Pel·a·tī′ah the son of
Be·nā′i·ah, princes of the people. 2 And He
said to me: "Son of man, these *are* the men
who devise iniquity and give wicked
counsel in this city, 3 who say, *'The time is*
not near to build houses; this *city is* the cal-

10:17 [a]Literally *they* [b]Literally *they* [c]Literally *they*

10:4 went up: A reference to God's leaving the Most Holy Place (see 9:3).

10:18, 19 The departure of God is described in stages, as though He were reluctant to leave. Though His holiness had been rejected so that He would not stay, He left with sorrow over the fate His people had brought upon themselves.

dron, and we *are* the meat.' 4Therefore
prophesy against them, prophesy, O son of
man!"
5Then the Spirit of the LORD fell upon
me, and said to me, "Speak! 'Thus says the
LORD: "Thus you have said, O house of Is-
rael; for I know the things that come into
your mind. 6You have multiplied your
slain in this city, and you have filled its
streets with the slain." 7Therefore thus says
the Lord GOD: "Your slain whom you have
laid in its midst, they *are* the meat, and this
city is the caldron; but I shall bring you out
of the midst of it. 8You have feared the
sword; and I will bring a sword upon
you," says the Lord GOD. 9"And I will
bring you out of its midst, and deliver you
into the hands of strangers, and execute
judgments on you. 10You shall fall by the
sword. I will judge you at the border of Is-
rael. Then you shall know that I *am* the
LORD. 11This *city* shall not be your caldron,
nor shall you be the meat in its midst. I will
judge you at the border of Israel. 12And you
shall know that I *am* the LORD; for you have
not walked in My statutes nor executed
My judgments, but have done according to
the customs of the Gentiles which *are* all
around you."'"
13Now it happened, while I was proph-
esying, that Pel·a·tī'ah the son of
Be·nā'i·ah died. Then I fell on my face and
cried with a loud voice, and said, "Ah,
Lord GOD! Will You make a complete end
of the remnant of Israel?"

God Will Restore Israel

14Again the word of the LORD came to
me, saying, 15"Son of man, your brethren,
your relatives, your countrymen, and all
the house of Israel in its entirety, *are* those
about whom the inhabitants of Jerusalem
have said, 'Get far away from the LORD;
this land has been given to us as a posses-
sion.' 16Therefore say, 'Thus says the Lord
GOD: "Although I have cast them far off
among the Gentiles, and although I have
scattered them among the countries, yet I
shall be a little sanctuary for them in the
countries where they have gone."'
17Therefore say, 'Thus says the Lord GOD:
"I will gather you from the peoples, assem-
ble you from the countries where you have
been scattered, and I will give you the land
of Israel."' 18And they will go there, and
they will take away all its detestable things
and all its abominations from there. 19Then
I will give them one heart, and I will put a
new spirit within them,[a] and take the stony
heart out of their flesh, and give them a

I pray that You will give Your people one heart and put a new spirit within us and take the stony hearts out of our flesh . . . that we shall be Your people and You will be our God.

adapted from Ezekiel 11:19, 20

11:19 [a]Literally *you*

11:7–12 bring you out: To be consumed in the fire of the Babylonian siege and its aftermath.

11:13 Pelatiah . . . died: A judgment on his sin of leading the people astray (11:1, 2) and, as a portent of the coming judgment, on all these men. **I fell on my face**: The prophecy did not cause Pelatiah's death, but Ezekiel saw his words as the catalyst in its timing, and was deeply disturbed.

11:16–20 God here announced that He would do just the opposite of what leaders in Jerusalem expected; He would protect the exiles as their **sanctuary**, and they would become the remnant.

11:19 one heart: Single devotion toward God, undivided in its loyalty and faithfulness to Him; this is the essence of holiness. **A new spirit** and a **heart of flesh** are the result, the evidence, of God's holiness imparted to those who love God only and serve Him faithfully.

heart of flesh, [20]that they may walk in My
statutes and keep My judgments and do
them; and they shall be My people, and I
will be their God. [21]But *as for those* whose
hearts follow the desire for their detestable
things and their abominations, I will rec-
ompense their deeds on their own heads,"
says the Lord GOD.

[22]So the cherubim lifted up their wings,
with the wheels beside them, and the glory
of the God of Israel *was* high above them.
[23]And the glory of the LORD went up from
the midst of the city and stood on the
mountain, which *is* on the east side of the
city.

[24]Then the Spirit took me up and
brought me in a vision by the Spirit of God
into Chal·dē'a,[a] to those in captivity. And
the vision that I had seen went up from me.
[25]So I spoke to those in captivity of all the
things the LORD had shown me.

CHAPTER 12

Judah's Captivity Portrayed

Now the word of the LORD came to me,
saying: [2]"Son of man, you dwell in the
midst of a rebellious house, which has eyes
to see but does not see, and ears to hear but
does not hear; for they *are* a rebellious
house.

[3]"Therefore, son of man, prepare your
belongings for captivity, and go into cap-
tivity by day in their sight. You shall go
from your place into captivity to another
place in their sight. It may be that they will
consider, though they *are* a rebellious
house. [4]By day you shall bring out your be-
longings in their sight, as though going
into captivity; and at evening you shall go
in their sight, like those who go into cap-
tivity. [5]Dig through the wall in their sight,
and carry your belongings out through it.
[6]In their sight you shall bear *them* on *your*
shoulders *and* carry *them* out at twilight;
you shall cover your face, so that you can-
not see the ground, for I have made you a
sign to the house of Israel."

[7]So I did as I was commanded. I brought
out my belongings by day, as though going
into captivity, and at evening I dug
through the wall with my hand. I brought
them out at twilight, *and* I bore *them* on *my*
shoulder in their sight.

[8]And in the morning the word of the
LORD came to me, saying, [9]"Son of man,
has not the house of Israel, the rebellious
house, said to you, 'What are you doing?'
[10]Say to them, 'Thus says the Lord GOD:
"This burden *concerns* the prince in Jerusa-
lem and all the house of Israel who are
among them." ' [11]Say, 'I *am* a sign to you.
As I have done, so shall it be done to them;
they shall be carried away into captivity.'
[12]And the prince who *is* among them shall
bear *his belongings* on *his* shoulder at twi-
light and go out. They shall dig through
the wall to carry *them* out through it. He
shall cover his face, so that he cannot see
the ground with *his* eyes. [13]I will also
spread My net over him, and he shall be
caught in My snare. I will bring him to
Babylon, *to* the land of the Chal·dē'ans; yet
he shall not see it, though he shall die
there. [14]I will scatter to every wind all who
are around him to help him, and all his
troops; and I will draw out the sword after
them.

[15]"Then they shall know that I *am* the
LORD, when I scatter them among the na-
tions and disperse them throughout the
countries. [16]But I will spare a few of their

11:24 [a]Or *Babylon*, and so elsewhere in this book

12:5 Dig through: As the exiles would go out through the breaches in Jerusalem's wall.
12:10 This burden: This prophecy. **prince**: Zedekiah. With the exception of 17:16, Ezekiel omits his name and calls him prince, not king.
12:12–14 Zedekiah did go through the **wall** of Jerusalem trying to flee. His **troops** were scattered, and he was captured near Jericho. He was led before Nebuchadnezzar, his eyes were put out, and then he was taken to **Babylon**. (see Jer. 39:4–7).

men from the sword, from famine, and from pestilence, that they may declare all their abominations among the Gentiles wherever they go. Then they shall know that I *am* the LORD."

Judgment Not Postponed

17Moreover the word of the LORD came to me, saying, 18"Son of man, eat your bread with quaking, and drink your water with trembling and anxiety. 19And say to the people of the land, 'Thus says the Lord GOD to the inhabitants of Jerusalem *and* to the land of Israel: "They shall eat their bread with anxiety, and drink their water with dread, so that her land may be emptied of all who are in it, because of the violence of all those who dwell in it. 20Then the cities that are inhabited shall be laid waste, and the land shall become desolate; and you shall know that I *am* the LORD." ' "

21And the word of the LORD came to me, saying, 22"Son of man, what *is* this proverb *that* you *people* have about the land of Israel, which says, 'The days are prolonged, and every vision fails'? 23Tell them therefore, 'Thus says the Lord GOD: "I will lay this proverb to rest, and they shall no more use it as a proverb in Israel." But say to them, "The days are at hand, and the fulfillment of every vision. 24For no more shall there be any false vision or flattering divination within the house of Israel. 25For I *am* the LORD. I speak, and the word which I speak will come to pass; it will no more be postponed; for in your days, O rebellious house, I will say the word and perform it," says the Lord GOD.' "

26Again the word of the LORD came to me, saying, 27"Son of man, look, the house of Israel is saying, 'The vision that he sees *is* for many days *from now,* and he prophesies of times far off.' 28Therefore say to them, 'Thus says the Lord GOD: "None of My words will be postponed any more, but the word which I speak will be done," says the Lord GOD.' "

CHAPTER 13

Woe to Foolish Prophets

And the word of the LORD came to me, saying, 2"Son of man, prophesy against the prophets of Israel who prophesy, and say to those who prophesy out of their own heart, 'Hear the word of the LORD!' "

3Thus says the Lord GOD: "Woe to the foolish prophets, who follow their own spirit and have seen nothing! 4O Israel, your prophets are like foxes in the deserts. 5You have not gone up into the gaps to build a wall for the house of Israel to stand in battle on the day of the LORD. 6They have envisioned futility and false divination, saying, 'Thus says the LORD!' But the LORD has not sent them; yet they hope that the word may be confirmed. 7Have you not seen a futile vision, and have you not spoken false divination? You say, 'The LORD says,' but I have not spoken."

8Therefore thus says the Lord GOD: "Because you have spoken nonsense and envisioned lies, therefore I *am* indeed against you," says the Lord GOD. 9"My hand will be against the prophets who envision futility and who divine lies; they shall not be in the assembly of My people, nor be written in the record of the house of Israel, nor

---

12:27 Just as the Israelites refused to believe that the prophecy of God's judgment was intended for them, so we often apply God's Word only to others. Somehow we can easily recognize sin in the lives of fellow believers while remaining blind to the evil in our own hearts.

13:2, 3 their own heart . . . own spirit: They prophesy without a message from God.

13:4 As **foxes** care nothing for the crumbling ruins about them, so these false prophets cared nothing for the true welfare of Israel.

13:5 to build a wall: Of spiritual protection. They contributed neither prayer, example, nor advice that would turn Judah back to God.

shall they enter into the land of Israel. Then you shall know that I *am* the Lord GOD.

10"Because, indeed, because they have seduced My people, saying, 'Peace!' when *there is* no peace—and one builds a wall, and they plaster it with untempered *mortar*— 11say to those who plaster *it* with untempered *mortar,* that it will fall. There will be flooding rain, and you, O great hailstones, shall fall; and a stormy wind shall tear *it* down. 12Surely, when the wall has fallen, will it not be said to you, 'Where *is* the mortar with which you plastered *it?'* "

13Therefore thus says the Lord GOD: "I will cause a stormy wind to break forth in My fury; and there shall be a flooding rain in My anger, and great hailstones in fury to consume *it.* 14So I will break down the wall you have plastered with untempered *mortar,* and bring it down to the ground, so that its foundation will be uncovered; it will fall, and you shall be consumed in the midst of it. Then you shall know that I *am* the LORD.

15"Thus will I accomplish My wrath on the wall and on those who have plastered it with untempered *mortar;* and I will say to you, 'The wall *is* no *more,* nor those who plastered it, 16*that is,* the prophets of Israel who prophesy concerning Jerusalem, and who see visions of peace for her when *there is* no peace,' " says the Lord GOD.

17"Likewise, son of man, set your face against the daughters of your people, who prophesy out of their own heart; prophesy against them, 18and say, 'Thus says the Lord GOD: "Woe to the *women* who sew *magic* charms on their sleeves[a] and make veils for the heads of people of every height to hunt souls! Will you hunt the souls of My people, and keep yourselves alive? 19And will you profane Me among My people for handfuls of barley and for pieces of bread, killing people who should not die, and keeping people alive who should not live, by your lying to My people who listen to lies?"

20'Therefore thus says the Lord GOD: "Behold, I *am* against your *magic* charms by which you hunt souls there like birds. I will tear them from your arms, and let the souls go, the souls you hunt like birds. 21I will also tear off your veils and deliver My people out of your hand, and they shall no longer be as prey in your hand. Then you shall know that I *am* the LORD.

22"Because with lies you have made the heart of the righteous sad, whom I have not made sad; and you have strengthened the hands of the wicked, so that he does not turn from his wicked way to save his life. 23Therefore you shall no longer envision futility nor practice divination; for I will deliver My people out of your hand, and you shall know that I *am* the LORD." ' "

CHAPTER 14

Idolatry Will Be Punished

Now some of the elders of Israel came to me and sat before me. 2And the word of the LORD came to me, saying, 3"Son of man, these men have set up their idols in their hearts, and put before them that which causes them to stumble into iniquity. Should I let Myself be inquired of at all by them?

4"Therefore speak to them, and say to them, 'Thus says the Lord GOD: "Everyone

13:18 [a]Literally *over all the joints of My hands;* Vulgate reads *under every elbow;* Septuagint and Targum read *on all elbows of the hands.*

13:10–16 The false prophets in Jerusalem were likened to builders who cheated on materials put into a city **wall**. Their fault was to prophesy **peace** and thus lull the people into believing they were not in need of any repentance (see v. 22). When the storm came, their shoddy work would be **uncovered** (v. 14).

13:18 sew . . . charms: To place on people, either to gain power over them or to make their wishes come true.

of the house of Israel who sets up his idols
in his heart, and puts before him what
causes him to stumble into iniquity, and
then comes to the prophet, I the LORD will
answer him who comes, according to the
multitude of his idols, 5that I may seize
the house of Israel by their heart, because
they are all estranged from Me by their
idols." '

6"Therefore say to the house of Israel,
'Thus says the Lord GOD: "Repent, turn
away from your idols, and turn your faces
away from all your abominations. 7For any-
one of the house of Israel, or of the strang-
ers who dwell in Israel, who separates him-
self from Me and sets up his idols in his
heart and puts before him what causes him
to stumble into iniquity, then comes to a
prophet to inquire of him concerning Me, I
the LORD will answer him by Myself. 8I will
set My face against that man and make him
a sign and a proverb, and I will cut him off
from the midst of My people. Then you
shall know that I *am* the LORD.

9"And if the prophet is induced to speak
anything, I the LORD have induced that
prophet, and I will stretch out My hand
against him and destroy him from among
My people Israel. 10And they shall bear
their iniquity; the punishment of the
prophet shall be the same as the punish-
ment of the one who inquired, 11that the
house of Israel may no longer stray from
Me, nor be profaned anymore with all their
transgressions, but that they may be My
people and I may be their God," says the
Lord GOD.' "

Judgment on Persistent Unfaithfulness

12The word of the LORD came again to
me, saying: 13"Son of man, when a land
sins against Me by persistent unfaithful-
ness, I will stretch out My hand against it; I
will cut off its supply of bread, send famine
on it, and cut off man and beast from it.
14Even *if* these three men, Noah, Daniel,
and Job, were in it, they would deliver *only*
themselves by their righteousness," says
the Lord GOD.

15"If I cause wild beasts to pass through
the land, and they empty it, and make it so
desolate that no man may pass through be-
cause of the beasts, 16*even though* these
three men *were* in it, *as* I live," says the Lord
GOD, "they would deliver neither sons nor
daughters; only they would be delivered,
and the land would be desolate.

17"Or *if* I bring a sword on that land, and
say, 'Sword, go through the land,' and I cut
off man and beast from it, 18even *though*
these three men *were* in it, *as* I live," says
the Lord GOD, "they would deliver neither
sons nor daughters, but only they them-
selves would be delivered.

19"Or *if* I send a pestilence into that land
and pour out My fury on it in blood, and
cut off from it man and beast, 20even *though*
Noah, Daniel, and Job *were* in it, *as* I live,"
says the Lord GOD, "they would deliver
neither son nor daughter; they would de-
liver *only* themselves by their righteous-
ness."

21For thus says the Lord GOD: "How
much more it shall be when I send My four
severe judgments on Jerusalem—the

14:7–9 If a prophet seeks a message from God encouraging an idol worshiper (a thing which was obviously wrong), God will give him a message, but it will be a message of destruction for both himself and the worshiper.

14:7 strangers: Resident aliens in the land, who were expected to worship Israel's God and follow His law.

14:14 Daniel: Probably Ezekiel's contemporary in exile. The Hebrew name is spelled differently here than in the Book of Daniel.

14:15–20 Just as the righteousness of their ancestors could not save the Israelites from God's judgment, we cannot rely on the faith of our parents and grandparents to go to heaven. Each of us is responsible for our personal decision to accept or reject the salvation offered by Jesus Christ.

sword and famine and wild beasts and pestilence—to cut off man and beast from it? 22Yet behold, there shall be left in it a remnant who will be brought out, *both* sons and daughters; surely they will come out to you, and you will see their ways and their doings. Then you will be comforted concerning the disaster that I have brought upon Jerusalem, all that I have brought upon it. 23And they will comfort you, when you see their ways and their doings; and you shall know that I have done nothing without cause that I have done in it," says the Lord GOD.

CHAPTER 15

The Outcast Vine

Then the word of the LORD came to me, saying: 2"Son of man, how is the wood of the vine *better* than any other wood, the vine branch which is among the trees of the forest? 3Is wood taken from it to make any object? Or can *men* make a peg from it to hang any vessel on? 4Instead, it is thrown into the fire for fuel; the fire devours both ends of it, and its middle is burned. Is it useful for *any* work? 5Indeed, when it was whole, no object could be made from it. How much less will it be useful for *any* work when the fire has devoured it, and it is burned?

6"Therefore thus says the Lord GOD: 'Like the wood of the vine among the trees of the forest, which I have given to the fire for fuel, so I will give up the inhabitants of Jerusalem; 7and I will set My face against them. They will go out from *one* fire, but *another* fire shall devour them. Then you shall know that I *am* the LORD, when I set My face against them. 8Thus I will make the land desolate, because they have persisted in unfaithfulness,' says the Lord GOD."

CHAPTER 16

God's Love for Jerusalem

Again the word of the LORD came to me, saying, 2"Son of man, cause Jerusalem to know her abominations, 3and say, 'Thus says the Lord GOD to Jerusalem: "Your birth and your nativity *are* from the land of Cā'naan; your father *was* an Am'o·rīte and your mother a Hit'tīte. 4*As for* your nativity, on the day you were born your navel cord was not cut, nor were you washed in water to cleanse *you;* you were not rubbed with salt nor wrapped in swaddling cloths. 5No eye pitied you, to do any of these things for you, to have compassion on you; but you were thrown out into the open field, when you yourself were loathed on the day you were born.

6"And when I passed by you and saw you struggling in your own blood, I said to you in your blood, 'Live!' Yes, I said to you in your blood, 'Live!' 7I made you thrive

---

14:22, 23 God Himself would spare a **remnant** of survivors from Jerusalem in spite of their wicked **ways** and **doings**. They would **come** to Babylon. The exiles there would see how wicked their countrymen had been, and how righteous God's judgment upon the city had been. Then the exiles would **be comforted**, perhaps because they had been spared the horrors of the siege, and because of the justice of God's actions.

16:2 cause . . . to know: Accuse; charge her in a legal sense. Jerusalem in this allegory represents all of Judah.

16:3–14 Judah is likened to an abandoned infant whom God rescued, cared for, and nurtured to adulthood.

16:3 Amorite . . . Hittite: God was calling Jerusalem an illegitimate child, with pagan religious tendencies.

16:4, 5 Not one of the things normally necessary for an infant's survival was done. **thrown out**: Abandonment of female infants was practiced in much of the ancient Near East. She was unwanted and unloved.

16:6 Live! It is God's deep desire for every child.

like a plant in the field; and you grew, matured, and became very beautiful. *Your* breasts were formed, your hair grew, but you *were* naked and bare.

[8]"When I passed by you again and looked upon you, indeed your time *was* the time of love; so I spread My wing over you and covered your nakedness. Yes, I swore an oath to you and entered into a covenant with you, and you became Mine," says the Lord GOD.

[9]"Then I washed you in water; yes, I thoroughly washed off your blood, and I anointed you with oil. [10]I clothed you in embroidered cloth and gave you sandals of badger skin; I clothed you with fine linen and covered you with silk. [11]I adorned you with ornaments, put bracelets on your wrists, and a chain on your neck. [12]And I put a jewel in your nose, earrings in your ears, and a beautiful crown on your head. [13]Thus you were adorned with gold and silver, and your clothing *was of* fine linen, silk, and embroidered cloth. You ate *pastry of* fine flour, honey, and oil. You were exceedingly beautiful, and succeeded to royalty. [14]Your fame went out among the nations because of your beauty, for it *was* perfect through My splendor which I had bestowed on you," says the Lord GOD.

Jerusalem's Harlotry

[15]"But you trusted in your own beauty, played the harlot because of your fame, and poured out your harlotry on everyone passing by who *would have* it. [16]You took some of your garments and adorned multicolored high places for yourself, and played the harlot on them. *Such* things should not happen, nor be. [17]You have also taken your beautiful jewelry from My gold and My silver, which I had given you, and made for yourself male images and played the harlot with them. [18]You took your embroidered garments and covered them, and you set My oil and My incense before them. [19]Also My food which I gave you—the pastry of fine flour, oil, and honey *which* I fed you—you set it before them as sweet incense; and *so* it was," says the Lord GOD.

[20]"Moreover you took your sons and your daughters, whom you bore to Me, and these you sacrificed to them to be devoured. *Were* your *acts* of harlotry a small matter, [21]that you have slain My children and offered them up to them by causing them to pass through *the fire?* [22]And in all your abominations and acts of harlotry you did not remember the days of your youth, when you were naked and bare, struggling in your blood.

[23]"Then it was so, after all your wickedness—'Woe, woe to you!' says the Lord GOD— [24]*that* you also built for yourself a shrine, and made a high place for yourself in every street. [25]You built your high places at the head of every road, and made your beauty to be abhorred. You offered yourself to everyone who passed by, and multiplied your acts of harlotry. [26]You also committed harlotry with the Egyptians, your very fleshly neighbors, and increased your acts of harlotry to provoke Me to anger.

[27]"Behold, therefore, I stretched out My hand against you, diminished your allotment, and gave you up to the will of those who hate you, the daughters of the Phi·lis'tines, who were ashamed of your lewd behavior. [28]You also played the harlot with the Assyrians, because you were insatiable; indeed you played the harlot with them and still were not satisfied. [29]Moreover you multiplied your acts of harlotry as far as the land of the trader, Chal·dē'a; and even then you were not satisfied.

16:8 My wing: "The corner of My garment," a standard and explicit statement of taking a woman as wife (see Ruth 3:9). **covenant**: The commitment God made with Israel at Sinai.

16:20, 21 pass through the fire: Burned their children as sacrifices to Molech (Lev. 18:21) or to Baal (Jer. 19:5).

> Believers may not often realize it, but even as believers we are either centered on God or centered on man. There is no alternative. Either God has become the center of our universe and we have become rightly adjusted to Him, or we have made ourselves the center and are attempting to make everything else orbit around us and for us.
>
> Paul Fromke

30"How degenerate is your heart!" says
the Lord GOD, "seeing you do all these
things, the deeds of a brazen harlot.

Jerusalem's Adultery

31"You erected your shrine at the head of
every road, and built your high place in
every street. Yet you were not like a harlot,
because you scorned payment. 32*You are* an
adulterous wife, *who* takes strangers in-
stead of her husband. 33Men make pay-
ment to all harlots, but you made your
payments to all your lovers, and hired
them to come to you from all around for
your harlotry. 34You are the opposite of
other women in your harlotry, because
no one solicited you to be a harlot. In
that you gave payment but no payment
was given you, therefore you are the oppo-
site."

Jerusalem's Lovers Will Abuse Her

35"Now then, O harlot, hear the word of
the LORD! 36Thus says the Lord GOD: "Be-
cause your filthiness was poured out and
your nakedness uncovered in your har-
lotry with your lovers, and with all your
abominable idols, and because of the blood
of your children which you gave to them,
37surely, therefore, I will gather all your
lovers with whom you took pleasure, all
those you loved, *and* all those you hated; I
will gather them from all around against
you and will uncover your nakedness to
them, that they may see all your naked-
ness. 38And I will judge you as women who
break wedlock or shed blood are judged; I
will bring blood upon you in fury and jeal-
ousy. 39I will also give you into their hand,
and they shall throw down your shrines
and break down your high places. They
shall also strip you of your clothes, take
your beautiful jewelry, and leave you
naked and bare.

40"They shall also bring up an assembly
against you, and they shall stone you with
stones and thrust you through with their
swords. 41They shall burn your houses
with fire, and execute judgments on you in
the sight of many women; and I will make
you cease playing the harlot, and you shall
no longer hire lovers. 42So I will lay to rest
My fury toward you, and My jealousy
shall depart from you. I will be quiet, and
be angry no more. 43Because you did not
remember the days of your youth, but agi-
tated Me[a] with all these *things*, surely I will
also recompense your deeds on *your own*
head," says the Lord GOD. "And you shall

16:43 [a]Following Septuagint, Syriac, Targum, and Vulgate; Masoretic Text reads *were agitated with Me.*

16:31–34 God emphasized again and again the excesses of Jerusalem's sin. Sinful people, like harlots, received money for their sins, but Jerusalem went so far as to pay her allies so she could consort with them. **head of every road** (also v. 25): Religious prostitutes plied their trade everywhere, making it possible for Tamar to resemble a harlot in an "open place" (see Gen. 38:14, 15).

16:36, 37 As Jerusalem had sought illicit pleasure in secret alliances, now she would experience shame in public exposure. Sin eventually ends that way (see Num. 32:23).

16:40, 41 A description of the destruction of Jerusalem.

16:42 Fury and **jealousy** are the righteous response of a wronged spouse. When Jerusalem had faced her just punishment, God's justice would be satisfied, and He would **be angry no more**.

not commit lewdness in addition to all
your abominations.

More Wicked than Samaria and Sodom

44“Indeed everyone who quotes
proverbs will use *this* proverb against you:
‘Like mother, like daughter!’ 45You *are* your
mother’s daughter, loathing husband and
children; and you *are* the sister of your sis-
ters, who loathed their husbands and chil-
dren; your mother *was* a Hit′tīte and your
father an Am′o·rīte.
46“Your elder sister *is* Samaria, who
dwells with her daughters to the north of
you; and your younger sister, who dwells
to the south of you, *is* Sod′om and her
daughters. 47You did not walk in their
ways nor act according to their abomina-
tions; but, as *if that were* too little, you be-
came more corrupt than they in all your
ways.
48“*As* I live,” says the Lord GOD, “neither
your sister Sod′om nor her daughters have
done as you and your daughters have
done. 49Look, this was the iniquity of your
sister Sod′om: She and her daughter had
pride, fullness of food, and abundance of
idleness; neither did she strengthen the
hand of the poor and needy. 50And they
were haughty and committed abomination
before Me; therefore I took them away as I
saw *fit*.[a]
51“Samaria did not commit half of your
sins; but you have multiplied your
abominations more than they, and have
justified your sisters by all the abomi-
nations which you have done. 52You
who judged your sisters, bear your own
shame also, because the sins which you
committed were more abominable than
theirs; they are more righteous than you.
Yes, be disgraced also, and bear your
own shame, because you justified your sis-
ters.
53“When I bring back their captives, the
captives of Sod′om and her daughters, and
the captives of Samaria and her daughters,
then *I will also bring back* the captives of
your captivity among them, 54that you may
bear your own shame and be disgraced by
all that you did when you comforted them.
55When your sisters, Sod′om and her
daughters, return to their former state,
and Samaria and her daughters return to
their former state, then you and your
daughters will return to your former
state. 56For your sister Sod′om was not
a byword in your mouth in the days of
your pride, 57before your wickedness was
uncovered. It was like the time of the
reproach of the daughters of Syria[a] and
all *those* around her, and of the daugh-
ters of the Phi·lis′tines, who despise you
everywhere. 58You have paid for your
lewdness and your abominations,” says
the LORD. 59For thus says the Lord GOD: “I
will deal with you as you have done, who
despised the oath by breaking the cove-
nant.

An Everlasting Covenant

60“Nevertheless I will remember My
covenant with you in the days of your
youth, and I will establish an everlasting
covenant with you. 61Then you will re-
member your ways and be ashamed, when
you receive your older and your younger
sisters; for I will give them to you for
daughters, but not because of My covenant
with you. 62And I will establish My
covenant with you. Then you shall know

16:50 [a]Vulgate reads *you saw;* Septuagint reads *he saw;* Targum reads *as was revealed to Me.*
16:57 [a]Following Masoretic Text, Septuagint, Targum, and Vulgate; many Hebrew manuscripts and Syriac read *Edom.*

16:46, 47 Samaria: The kingdom of Israel after Solomon’s death. In many ways, Israel led Judah into sin. **younger sister**: Sodom’s prominence and destruction came much earlier (Gen. 19:23–29).

16:56 Probably should be read as a question, Was not Sodom a **byword** (an item of gossip)?

that I *am* the LORD, 63that you may remem-
ber and be ashamed, and never open
your mouth anymore because of your
shame, when I provide you an atonement
for all you have done," says the Lord
GOD.' "

CHAPTER 17

The Eagles and the Vine

And the word of the LORD came to me,
saying, 2"Son of man, pose a riddle, and
speak a parable to the house of Israel, 3and
say, 'Thus says the Lord GOD:

"A great eagle with large wings and
long pinions,
Full of feathers of various colors,
Came to Lebanon
And took from the cedar the highest
branch.
4 He cropped off its topmost young
twig
And carried it to a land of trade;
He set it in a city of merchants.
5 Then he took some of the seed of the
land
And planted it in a fertile field;
He placed *it* by abundant waters
And set it like a willow tree.
6 And it grew and became a spreading
vine of low stature;
Its branches turned toward him,
But its roots were under it.
So it became a vine,
Brought forth branches,
And put forth shoots.

7 "But there was another[a] great eagle
with large wings and many
feathers;
And behold, this vine bent its roots
toward him,
And stretched its branches toward
him,
From the garden terrace where it had
been planted,
That he might water it.
8 It was planted in good soil by many
waters,
To bring forth branches, bear fruit,
And become a majestic vine." '

9"Say, 'Thus says the Lord GOD:

"Will it thrive?
Will he not pull up its roots,
Cut off its fruit,
And leave it to wither?
All of its spring leaves will wither,
And no great power or many people
Will be needed to pluck it up by its
roots.
10 Behold, *it is* planted,
Will it thrive?
Will it not utterly wither when the
east wind touches it?
It will wither in the garden terrace
where it grew." ' "

11Moreover the word of the LORD came
to me, saying, 12"Say now to the rebellious
house: 'Do you not know what these *things*

17:7 [a]Following Septuagint, Syriac, and Vulgate; Masoretic Text and Targum read *one*.

17:3 eagle: Nebuchadnezzar, king of the greatest empire to that time. **Lebanon**: Judah in her former glory. **highest branch**: King Jehoiachin, taken to Babylon in 597 B.C.

17:4 young twig: Jehoiachin was 18 years old when he went into captivity. **land of trade**: Babylon, a commercial as well as a military empire.

17:5, 6 seed of the land: Zedekiah and those left in Jerusalem. They became a low vine, rather than a tall cedar. Represented by the **branches**, Zedekiah **turned toward** Nebuchadnezzar, pretending to be a faithful vassal.

17:7 another great eagle: Egypt. **roots toward him**: Zedekiah at first made secret overtures toward Egypt. **branches toward him**: Finally, Zedekiah openly allied himself with Egypt, thus rebelling against Babylon.

17:8–10 Will it thrive? The alliance with Egypt would be futile. The **east wind** (Babylon's power) would soon destroy Judah and her ally.

mean?' Tell *them,* 'Indeed the king of Bab-
ylon went to Jerusalem and took its king
and princes, and led them with him to
Babylon. 13And he took the king's off-
spring, made a covenant with him, and put
him under oath. He also took away the
mighty of the land, 14that the kingdom
might be brought low and not lift itself up,
but that by keeping his covenant it might
stand. 15But he rebelled against him by
sending his ambassadors to Egypt, that
they might give him horses and many peo-
ple. Will he prosper? Will he who does
such *things* escape? Can he break a
covenant and still be delivered?

16'*As* I live,' says the Lord GOD, 'surely in
the place *where* the king *dwells* who made
him king, whose oath he despised and
whose covenant he broke—with him in the
midst of Babylon he shall die. 17Nor will
Pharaoh with *his* mighty army and great
company do anything in the war, when
they heap up a siege mound and build a
wall to cut off many persons. 18Since he de-
spised the oath by breaking the covenant,
and in fact gave his hand and still did all
these *things,* he shall not escape.' "

19Therefore thus says the Lord GOD: "*As*
I live, surely My oath which he despised,
and My covenant which he broke, I will
recompense on his own head. 20I will
spread My net over him, and he shall be
taken in My snare. I will bring him to
Babylon and try him there for the treason
which he committed against Me. 21All his
fugitives[a] with all his troops shall fall by
the sword, and those who remain shall be
scattered to every wind; and you shall
know that I, the LORD, have spoken."

Israel Exalted at Last

22Thus says the Lord GOD: "I will take
also *one* of the highest branches of the high
cedar and set *it* out. I will crop off from the
topmost of its young twigs a tender one,
and will plant *it* on a high and prominent
mountain. 23On the mountain height of Is-
rael I will plant it; and it will bring forth
boughs, and bear fruit, and be a majestic
cedar. Under it will dwell birds of every
sort; in the shadow of its branches they
will dwell. 24And all the trees of the field
shall know that I, the LORD, have brought
down the high tree and exalted the low
tree, dried up the green tree and made the
dry tree flourish; I, the LORD, have spoken
and have done *it.*"

CHAPTER 18

A False Proverb Refuted

The word of the LORD came to me again,
saying, 2"What do you mean when you use
this proverb concerning the land of Israel,
saying:

'The fathers have eaten sour grapes,
And the children's teeth are set on
edge'?

3"*As* I live," says the Lord GOD, "you
shall no longer use this proverb in Israel.

4 "Behold, all souls are Mine;
The soul of the father
As well as the soul of the son is Mine;
The soul who sins shall die.

17:21 [a]Following Masoretic Text and Vulgate; many Hebrew manuscripts and Syriac read *choice men;* Targum reads *mighty men;* Septuagint omits *All his fugitives.*

17:13 king's offspring: Zedekiah was King Josiah's son.

17:19 My oath . . . My covenant: Even though Zedekiah became a vassal of Nebuchadnezzar under duress, God recognized the oath he swore as binding. God's people are expected to keep all of their lawful agreements. (see Ps. 15:4).

17:22–24 I, the LORD, have spoken (v. 24): A promise to Judah that she would not be cut off completely; God Himself would replant her, and she again would be a great nation. David's line would rule again in splendor; this is ultimately a messianic promise.

18:2, 3 What do you mean? Some were apparently asking, "Why should we suffer for our ancestors' sins?" Ezekiel assures them they are suffering for their own misdeeds.

5 But if a man is just
And does what is lawful and right;
6 If he has not eaten on the mountains,
Nor lifted up his eyes to the idols of
the house of Israel,
Nor defiled his neighbor's wife,
Nor approached a woman during her
impurity;
7 If he has not oppressed anyone,
But has restored to the debtor his
pledge;
Has robbed no one by violence,
But has given his bread to the hungry
And covered the naked with
clothing;
8 If he has not exacted usury
Nor taken any increase,
But has withdrawn his hand from
iniquity
And executed true judgment between
man and man;
9 *If* he has walked in My statutes
And kept My judgments faithfully—
He *is* just;
He shall surely live!"
Says the Lord GOD.

10 "If he begets a son *who is* a robber
Or a shedder of blood,
Who does any of these *things*
11 And does none of those *duties,*
But has eaten on the mountains
Or defiled his neighbor's wife;
12 If he has oppressed the poor and
needy,
Robbed by violence,
Not restored the pledge,
Lifted his eyes to the idols,
Or committed abomination;
13 If he has exacted usury
Or taken increase—
Shall he then live?
He shall not live!
If he has done any of these abomina-
tions,
He shall surely die;
His blood shall be upon him.

14 "*If,* however, he begets a son
Who sees all the sins which his father
has done,
And considers but does not do
likewise;
15 *Who* has not eaten on the mountains,
Nor lifted his eyes to the idols of the
house of Israel,
Nor defiled his neighbor's wife;
16 Has not oppressed anyone,
Nor withheld a pledge,
Nor robbed by violence,
But has given his bread to the
hungry
And covered the naked with
clothing;
17 *Who* has withdrawn his hand from
the poor[a]
And not received usury or increase,
But has executed My judgments
And walked in My statutes—
He shall not die for the iniquity of his
father;
He shall surely live!

18 "*As for* his father,
Because he cruelly oppressed,
Robbed his brother by violence,
And did what *is* not good among his
people,
Behold, he shall die for his iniquity.

18:17 [a]Following Masoretic Text, Targum, and Vulgate; Septuagint reads *iniquity* (compare verse 8).

18:6 eaten on the mountains: Participated in the sacrifices and feasts of pagan gods.
18:7 pledge: see Deut. 24:12, 13.
18:10–13 A son who ignores his father's good example and does injustice condemns himself. He **shall not live.**
18:14–17 A child learning from the evil example of his father yet keeping God's statutes (v. 9) will **live**.

Turn and Live

19"Yet you say, 'Why should the son not
bear the guilt of the father?' Because the
son has done what is lawful and right, and
has kept all My statutes and observed
them, he shall surely live. 20The soul who
sins shall die. The son shall not bear the
guilt of the father, nor the father bear the
guilt of the son. The righteousness of
the righteous shall be upon himself, and
the wickedness of the wicked shall be
upon himself.

21"But if a wicked man turns from all his
sins which he has committed, keeps all My
statutes, and does what is lawful and right,
he shall surely live; he shall not die. 22None
of the transgressions which he has commit-
ted shall be remembered against him; be-
cause of the righteousness which he has
done, he shall live. 23Do I have any plea-
sure at all that the wicked should die?"
says the Lord GOD, "*and* not that he should
turn from his ways and live?

24"But when a righteous man turns
away from his righteousness and commits
iniquity, and does according to all the
abominations that the wicked *man* does,
shall he live? All the righteousness which
he has done shall not be remembered; be-
cause of the unfaithfulness of which he is
guilty and the sin which he has committed,
because of them he shall die.

25"Yet you say, 'The way of the Lord is
not fair.' Hear now, O house of Israel, is it
not My way which is fair, and your ways
which are not fair? 26When a righteous *man*
turns away from his righteousness, com-
mits iniquity, and dies in it, it is because of
the iniquity which he has done that he
dies. 27Again, when a wicked *man* turns
away from the wickedness which he com-
mitted, and does what is lawful and right,
he preserves himself alive. 28Because he
considers and turns away from all the
transgressions which he committed, he
shall surely live; he shall not die. 29Yet the
house of Israel says, 'The way of the Lord
is not fair.' O house of Israel, is it not My
ways which are fair, and your ways which
are not fair?

30"Therefore I will judge you, O house of
Israel, every one according to his ways,"
says the Lord GOD. "Repent, and turn from
all your transgressions, so that iniquity
will not be your ruin. 31Cast away from you
all the transgressions which you have com-
mitted, and get yourselves a new heart and
a new spirit. For why should you die, O
house of Israel? 32For I have no pleasure in
the death of one who dies," says the Lord
GOD. "Therefore turn and live!"

CHAPTER 19

Israel Degraded

"Moreover take up a lamentation for the
princes of Israel, 2and say:

'What *is* your mother? A lioness:
She lay down among the lions;
Among the young lions she
nourished her cubs.
3 She brought up one of her cubs,
And he became a young lion;

18:19, 20 shall be upon himself: Corporate responsibility does exist. But too much emphasis on it induces a fatalistic attitude and the evasion of individual responsibility. Ezekiel's message is a necessary corrective; the sins of the parents do not excuse the sins of the children.

18:25–29 The proverb of v. 2 is not true. The Lord does not hold a child accountable for the sins of the parents. Each individual is responsible for his or her own sins. The wicked cannot blame their wickedness or their judgment on anyone but themselves. Our sense of justice responds: Surely, **the way of the Lord is fair** (v. 29).

18:30–32 This passage demonstrates the balance between God's justice and His mercy. He desires that all people look to Him and live, and He has provided every opportunity for repentance. When we sincerely seek the Lord and repent of our sin, He has promised to save us.

He learned to catch prey,
And he devoured men.
4 The nations also heard of him;
He was trapped in their pit,
And they brought him with chains to
the land of Egypt.

5 'When she saw that she waited, *that*
her hope was lost,
She took another of her cubs *and*
made him a young lion.
6 He roved among the lions,
And became a young lion;
He learned to catch prey;
He devoured men.
7 He knew their desolate places,[a]
And laid waste their cities;
The land with its fullness was
desolated
By the noise of his roaring.
8 Then the nations set against him from
the provinces on every side,
And spread their net over him;
He was trapped in their pit.
9 They put him in a cage with chains,
And brought him to the king of
Babylon;
They brought him in nets,
That his voice should no longer be
heard on the mountains of Israel.

10 'Your mother *was* like a vine in your
bloodline,[a]
Planted by the waters,
Fruitful and full of branches
Because of many waters.
11 She had strong branches for scepters
of rulers.
She towered in stature above the
thick branches,
And was seen in her height amid the
dense foliage.
12 But she was plucked up in fury,
She was cast down to the ground,
And the east wind dried her fruit.
Her strong branches were broken and
withered;
The fire consumed them.
13 And now she *is* planted in the
wilderness,
In a dry and thirsty land.
14 Fire has come out from a rod of her
branches
And devoured her fruit,
So that she has no strong branch— a
scepter for ruling.' "

This *is* a lamentation, and has become a lamentation.

CHAPTER 20

The Rebellions of Israel

It came to pass in the seventh year, in the fifth *month*, on the tenth *day* of the month, *that* certain of the elders of Israel came to inquire of the LORD, and sat before me. [2]Then the word of the LORD came to me, saying, [3]"Son of man, speak to the elders of Israel, and say to them, 'Thus says the Lord GOD: "Have you come to inquire of Me? *As* I live," says the Lord GOD, "I will not be inquired of by you." ' [4]Will you judge them, son of man, will you judge

19:7 [a]Septuagint reads *He stood in insolence;* Targum reads *He destroyed its palaces;* Vulgate reads *He learned to make widows.* 19:10 [a]Literally *blood,* following Masoretic Text, Syriac, and Vulgate; Septuagint reads *like a flower on a pomegranate tree;* Targum reads *in your likeness.*

19:5–9 another: Jehoiachin. After a three-month reign, Jehoiachin was carried into Babylonian exile by Nebuchadnezzar in 597 B.C., at the same time that Ezekiel was taken.

19:13, 14 thirsty land: Judah was in tragic circumstances. **Fire has come out**: Ezekiel recognized that King Zedekiah's own faithlessness was bringing about the final undoing of the nation.

20:3, 4 In keeping with his own prohibition (14:3, 9), Ezekiel refused to prophesy in answer to their questions, but he did pronounce a judgment. **Judge** and **make known** are legal terms. Ezekiel was to bring an indictment against them.

Leaders on the Pilgrimage

No area of our lives carries more weight with grandchildren than our faith at work. As they begin as "babes in Christ" or start their lifelong spiritual pilgrimage, they are, even without knowing it, looking for spiritual maturity. They long to see consistency of life, habits of devotion, fruit of the Spirit, overcoming grace, and above all, the hope of eternal life. We cannot spare them most of the struggles and failures of life. We can, however, demonstrate that, after a long life filled with battles and victories, we can come out on the other side and do so with grace. ✦

them? Then make known to them the abominations of their fathers.
5"Say to them, 'Thus says the Lord GOD:
"On the day when I chose Israel and raised
My hand in an oath to the descendants of
the house of Jacob, and made Myself
known to them in the land of Egypt, I
raised My hand in an oath to them, saying,
'I *am* the LORD your God.' 6On that day I
raised My hand in an oath to them, to
bring them out of the land of Egypt into a
land that I had searched out for them,
'flowing with milk and honey,'[a] the glory
of all lands. 7Then I said to them, 'Each of
you, throw away the abominations which
are before his eyes, and do not defile yourselves with the idols of Egypt. I *am* the
LORD your God.' 8But they rebelled against
Me and would not obey Me. They did not
all cast away the abominations which were
before their eyes, nor did they forsake the
idols of Egypt. Then I said, 'I will pour out
My fury on them and fulfill My anger
against them in the midst of the land of
Egypt.' 9But I acted for My name's sake,
that it should not be profaned before the
Gentiles among whom they *were*, in whose
sight I had made Myself known to them, to
bring them out of the land of Egypt.
10"Therefore I made them go out of the
land of Egypt and brought them into the
wilderness. 11And I gave them My statutes
and showed them My judgments, 'which,
if a man does, he shall live by them.'[a]
12Moreover I also gave them My Sabbaths,
to be a sign between them and Me, that
they might know that I *am* the LORD who
sanctifies them. 13Yet the house of Israel rebelled against Me in the wilderness; they
did not walk in My statutes; they despised
My judgments, 'which, *if* a man does, he
shall live by them';[a] and they greatly defiled My Sabbaths. Then I said I would
pour out My fury on them in the wilderness, to consume them. 14But I acted for My
name's sake, that it should not be profaned
before the Gentiles, in whose sight I had
brought them out. 15So I also raised My
hand in an oath to them in the wilderness,
that I would not bring them into the land

20:6 [a]Exodus 3:8 20:11 [a]Leviticus 18:5
20:13 [a]Leviticus 18:5

20:5, 6 Searched out indicates the personal interest God had taken in Israel. He does the same for all His children.

20:8, 9 Ezekiel recalled Israel's habit of rebellion even in Egypt, which may be reflected in Ex. 5:21; 14:11, 12; Josh. 24:14. **for My name's sake**: God's name is God's glory. **profaned before the Gentiles**: See Num. 14:11–16. This recurring theme throughout ch. 20, namely that God will not destroy the Israelites totally lest the pagans should think He is either cruel or helpless to deliver, is the central theme of the restoration itself (see 36:3–15, 20–36; 37:28).

which I had given *them,* 'flowing with milk and honey,'[a] the glory of all lands, 16because they despised My judgments and did not walk in My statutes, but profaned My Sabbaths; for their heart went after their idols. 17Nevertheless My eye spared them from destruction. I did not make an end of them in the wilderness.

18"But I said to their children in the wilderness, 'Do not walk in the statutes of your fathers, nor observe their judgments, nor defile yourselves with their idols. 19I *am* the LORD your God: Walk in My statutes, keep My judgments, and do them; 20hallow My Sabbaths, and they will be a sign between Me and you, that you may know that I *am* the LORD your God.'

21"Notwithstanding, the children rebelled against Me; they did not walk in My statutes, and were not careful to observe My judgments, 'which, *if* a man does, he shall live by them';[a] but they profaned My Sabbaths. Then I said I would pour out My fury on them and fulfill My anger against them in the wilderness. 22Nevertheless I withdrew My hand and acted for My name's sake, that it should not be profaned in the sight of the Gentiles, in whose sight I had brought them out. 23Also I raised My hand in an oath to those in the wilderness, that I would scatter them among the Gentiles and disperse them throughout the countries, 24because they had not executed My judgments, but had despised My statutes, profaned My Sabbaths, and their eyes were fixed on their fathers' idols.

25"Therefore I also gave them up to statutes *that were* not good, and judgments by which they could not live; 26and I pronounced them unclean because of their ritual gifts, in that they caused all their firstborn to pass through *the fire,* that I might make them desolate and that they might know that I am the LORD." '

27"Therefore, son of man, speak to the house of Israel, and say to them, 'Thus says the Lord GOD: "In this too your fathers have blasphemed Me, by being unfaithful to Me. 28When I brought them into the land *concerning* which I had raised My hand in an oath to give them, and they saw all the high hills and all the thick trees, there they offered their sacrifices and provoked Me with their offerings. There they also sent up their sweet aroma and poured out their drink offerings. 29Then I said to them, 'What *is* this high place to which you go?' So its name is called Bā'mah[a] to this day." ' 30Therefore say to the house of Israel, 'Thus says the Lord GOD: "Are you defiling yourselves in the manner of your fathers, and committing harlotry according to their abominations? 31For when you offer your gifts and make your sons pass through the fire, you defile yourselves with all your idols, even to this day. So shall I be inquired of by you, O house of Israel? *As* I live," says the Lord GOD, "I will not be inquired of by you. 32What you have in your mind shall never be, when you say, 'We will be like the Gentiles, like the families in other countries, serving wood and stone.'

God Will Restore Israel

33"*As* I live," says the Lord GOD, "surely with a mighty hand, with an outstretched arm, and with fury poured out, I will rule over you. 34I will bring you out from the peoples and gather you out of the countries where you are scattered, with a mighty hand, with an outstretched arm,

20:15 [a]Exodus 3:8 20:21 [a]Leviticus 18:5
20:29 [a]Literally *High Place*

20:26 pass through the fire: Burned their children as sacrifices.

20:28 high hills . . . thick trees: The normal locations of pagan shrines which Israel adopted as her own.

20:32–34 shall never be: God would not give up Judah.

and with fury poured out. [35]And I will bring you into the wilderness of the peoples, and there I will plead My case with you face to face. [36]Just as I pleaded My case with your fathers in the wilderness of the land of Egypt, so I will plead My case with you," says the Lord GOD.

[37]"I will make you pass under the rod, and I will bring you into the bond of the covenant; [38]I will purge the rebels from among you, and those who transgress against Me; I will bring them out of the country where they dwell, but they shall not enter the land of Israel. Then you will know that I *am* the LORD.

[39]"As for you, O house of Israel," thus says the Lord GOD: "Go, serve every one of you his idols—and hereafter—if you will not obey Me; but profane My holy name no more with your gifts and your idols. [40]For on My holy mountain, on the mountain height of Israel," says the Lord GOD, "there all the house of Israel, all of them in the land, shall serve Me; there I will accept them, and there I will require your offerings and the firstfruits of your sacrifices, together with all your holy things. [41]I will accept you as a sweet aroma when I bring you out from the peoples and gather you out of the countries where you have been scattered; and I will be hallowed in you before the Gentiles. [42]Then you shall know that I *am* the LORD, when I bring you into the land of Israel, into the country *for* which I raised My hand in an oath to give to your fathers. [43]And there you shall remember your ways and all your doings with which you were defiled; and you shall loathe yourselves in your own sight because of all the evils that you have committed. [44]Then you shall know that I *am* the LORD, when I have dealt with you for My name's sake, not according to your wicked ways nor according to your corrupt doings, O house of Israel," says the Lord GOD.' "

Fire in the Forest

[45]Furthermore the word of the LORD came to me, saying, [46]"Son of man, set your face toward the south; preach against the south and prophesy against the forest land, the South,[a] [47]and say to the forest of the South, 'Hear the word of the LORD! Thus says the Lord GOD: "Behold, I will kindle a fire in you, and it shall devour every green tree and every dry tree in you; the blazing flame shall not be quenched, and all faces from the south to the north shall be scorched by it. [48]All flesh shall see that I, the LORD, have kindled it; it shall not be quenched." ' "

[49]Then I said, "Ah, Lord GOD! They say of me, 'Does he not speak parables?' "

CHAPTER 21

Babylon, the Sword of God

And the word of the LORD came to me, saying, [2]"Son of man, set your face toward Jerusalem, preach against the holy places, and prophesy against the land of Israel; [3]and say to the land of Israel, 'Thus says the LORD: "Behold, I *am* against you, and I will draw My sword out of its sheath and cut off both righteous and wicked from you. [4]Because I will cut off both righteous and wicked from you, therefore My sword shall go out of its sheath against all flesh from south *to* north, [5]that all flesh may know that I, the LORD, have drawn My sword out of its sheath; it shall not return

20:46 [a]Hebrew *Negev*

20:35, 36 the wilderness: Ezekiel compared the Babylonian exile with Israel's Sinai sojourn, where God first wooed and won her (see Jer. 2:2, 3). **plead My case**: What humility and compassion on the part of the Most High!

20:37–39 God would **pass** the exiles **under the rod**, as a shepherd does his sheep, in order to count them and to separate the righteous from **those who transgress** (v. 38).

anymore.” ’ 6 Sigh therefore, son of man,
with a breaking heart, and sigh with bitter-
ness before their eyes. 7 And it shall be
when they say to you, ‘Why are you sigh-
ing?’ that you shall answer, ‘Because of the
news; when it comes, every heart will melt,
all hands will be feeble, every spirit will
faint, and all knees will be weak *as* water.
Behold, it is coming and shall be brought
to pass,’ says the Lord GOD.”
8 Again the word of the LORD came to
me, saying, 9 “Son of man, prophesy and
say, ‘Thus says the LORD!’ Say:

‘A sword, a sword is sharpened
And also polished!
10 Sharpened to make a dreadful
slaughter,
Polished to flash like lightning!
Should we then make mirth?
It despises the scepter of My son,
As it does all wood.
11 And He has given it to be polished,
That it may be handled;
This sword is sharpened, and it is
polished
To be given into the hand of the
slayer.’

12 “Cry and wail, son of man;
For it will be against My people,
Against all the princes of Israel.
Terrors including the sword will be
against My people;
Therefore strike *your* thigh.

13 “Because *it is* a testing,
And what if *the sword* despises even
the scepter?
The scepter shall be no *more,*”
says the Lord GOD.

14 “You therefore, son of man, prophesy,
And strike *your* hands together.
The third time let the sword do
double *damage.*
It *is* the sword *that* slays,
The sword that slays the great *men,*
That enters their private chambers.
15 I have set the point of the sword
against all their gates,
That the heart may melt and many
may stumble.
Ah! *It is* made bright;
It is grasped for slaughter:

16 “Swords at the ready!
Thrust right!
Set your blade!
Thrust left—
Wherever your edge is ordered!

17 “I also will beat My fists together,
And I will cause My fury to rest;
I, the LORD, have spoken.”

18 The word of the LORD came to me
again, saying: 19 “And son of man, appoint
for yourself two ways for the sword of the
king of Babylon to go; both of them shall
go from the same land. Make a sign; put *it*
at the head of the road to the city. 20 Ap-
point a road for the sword to go to Rab′bah
of the Am′mon·ītes, and to Judah, into for-
tified Jerusalem. 21 For the king of Babylon
stands at the parting of the road, at the fork
of the two roads, to use divination: he
shakes the arrows, he consults the images,

21:6 a breaking heart: A true prophet of God never rejoices when he must announce to people the consequences of their sin.

21:12 strike your thigh: In a gesture of grief and despair.

21:13 The **scepter** of human kingly authority depends on the sword. But when God turned the sword of His judgment against the scepter of Judah's king, neither Judah nor her king could survive.

21:19, 20 the sword: Nebuchadnezzar was God's agent in the punishment of His people; he was God's sword.

21:21, 22 arrows . . . images . . . liver: Three different means of divination. All important decisions in the ancient Near East were made with the help of divination, attempting to

he looks at the liver. [22]In his right hand is
the divination for Jerusalem: to set up bat-
tering rams, to call for a slaughter, to lift
the voice with shouting, to set battering
rams against the gates, to heap up a *siege*
mound, and to build a wall. [23]And it will be
to them like a false divination in the eyes of
those who have sworn oaths with them;
but he will bring their iniquity to remem-
brance, that they may be taken.

[24]"Therefore thus says the Lord GOD:
'Because you have made your iniquity to
be remembered, in that your transgres-
sions are uncovered, so that in all your do-
ings your sins appear—because you have
come to remembrance, you shall be taken
in hand.

[25]'Now to you, O profane, wicked prince
of Israel, whose day has come, whose iniq-
uity *shall* end, [26]thus says the Lord GOD:

"Remove the turban, and take off the
crown;
Nothing *shall remain* the same.
Exalt the humble, and humble the
exalted.
27 Overthrown, overthrown,
I will make it overthrown!
It shall be no *longer,*
Until He comes whose right it is,
And I will give it *to Him.*" '

A Sword Against the Ammonites

[28]"And you, son of man, prophesy and
say, 'Thus says the Lord GOD concerning
the Am'mon·ītes and concerning their re-
proach,' and say:

'A sword, a sword *is* drawn,
Polished for slaughter,
For consuming, for flashing—
29 While they see false visions for you,
While they divine a lie to you,
To bring you on the necks of the
wicked, the slain
Whose day has come,
Whose iniquity *shall* end.

30 'Return *it* to its sheath.
I will judge you
In the place where you were created,
In the land of your nativity.
31 I will pour out My indignation on
you;
I will blow against you with the fire
of My wrath,
And deliver you into the hands of
brutal men *who are* skillful to
destroy.
32 You shall be fuel for the fire;
Your blood shall be in the midst of
the land.
You shall not be remembered,
For I the LORD have spoken.' "

CHAPTER 22

Sins of Jerusalem

Moreover the word of the LORD came to
me, saying, [2]"Now, son of man, will you
judge, will you judge the bloody city? Yes,
show her all her abominations! [3]Then say,
'Thus says the Lord GOD: "The city sheds
blood in her own midst, that her time may
come; and she makes idols within herself
to defile herself. [4]You have become guilty
by the blood which you have shed, and
have defiled yourself with the idols which
you have made. You have caused your
days to draw near, and have come to *the
end of* your years; therefore I have made
you a reproach to the nations, and a mock-
ery to all countries. [5]*Those* near and *those*

find the will of the gods in the matter. **right hand**: Coming from the north, the right-hand fork of the road would lead to Jerusalem.

21:25–27 take off the crown: The throne of Judah would be nonexistent **until** the time when **He comes**.

22:3 Ezekiel classed Judah's many sins in two categories: **sheds blood**—injustice toward people, and **makes idols**—unfaithfulness to God. All sin is a breach of one or both of these relationships.

far from you will mock you as infamous
and full of tumult.
[6]"Look, the princes of Israel: each one
has used his power to shed blood in you.
[7]In you they have made light of father and
mother; in your midst they have oppressed
the stranger; in you they have mistreated
the fatherless and the widow. [8]You have
despised My holy things and profaned My
Sabbaths. [9]In you are men who slander to
cause bloodshed; in you are those who eat
on the mountains; in your midst they com-
mit lewdness. [10]In you men uncover their
fathers' nakedness; in you they violate
women who are set apart during their im-
purity. [11]One commits abomination with
his neighbor's wife; another lewdly defiles
his daughter-in-law; and another in you
violates his sister, his father's daughter.
[12]In you they take bribes to shed blood; you
take usury and increase; you have made
profit from your neighbors by extortion,
and have forgotten Me," says the Lord
GOD.
[13]"Behold, therefore, I beat My fists at
the dishonest profit which you have made,
and at the bloodshed which has been in
your midst. [14]Can your heart endure, or
can your hands remain strong, in the days
when I shall deal with you? I, the LORD,
have spoken, and will do *it*. [15]I will scatter
you among the nations, disperse you
throughout the countries, and remove
your filthiness completely from you. [16]You
shall defile yourself in the sight of the na-
tions; then you shall know that I *am* the
LORD." ' "

Israel in the Furnace

[17]The word of the LORD came to me, say-
ing, [18]"Son of man, the house of Israel has
become dross to Me; they *are* all bronze,
tin, iron, and lead, in the midst of a fur-
nace; they have become dross from silver.
[19]Therefore thus says the Lord GOD: 'Be-
cause you have all become dross, therefore
behold, I will gather you into the midst of
Jerusalem. [20]*As men* gather silver, bronze,
iron, lead, and tin into the midst of a fur-
nace, to blow fire on it, to melt *it;* so I will
gather *you* in My anger and in My fury,
and I will leave *you there* and melt you.
[21]Yes, I will gather you and blow on you
with the fire of My wrath, and you shall be
melted in its midst. [22]As silver is melted in
the midst of a furnace, so shall you be
melted in its midst; then you shall know
that I, the LORD, have poured out My fury
on you.' "

Israel's Wicked Leaders

[23]And the word of the LORD came to me,
saying, [24]"Son of man, say to her: 'You *are* a
land that is not cleansed[a] or rained on in
the day of indignation.' [25]The conspiracy of
her prophets[a] in her midst is like a roaring
lion tearing the prey; they have devoured
people; they have taken treasure and pre-
cious things; they have made many wid-
ows in her midst. [26]Her priests have vio-
lated My law and profaned My holy
things; they have not distinguished be-
tween the holy and unholy, nor have they
made known *the difference* between the un-
clean and the clean; and they have hidden
their eyes from My Sabbaths, so that I am
profaned among them. [27]Her princes in her
midst *are* like wolves tearing the prey, to

22:24 [a]Following Masoretic Text, Syriac, and Vulgate; Septuagint reads *showered upon.* 22:25 [a]Following Masoretic Text and Vulgate; Septuagint reads *princes;* Targum reads *scribes.*

22:9 eat on the mountains: In feasting and sacrifice to pagan gods at the shrines of the high places.

22:21 blow on you: Image of the smith using bellows to make the fire hotter.

22:23–28 Judah's **prophets**, **priests** and **princes** had abused their power for personal **gain**. They had forfeited the trust of people and God.

22:26 Not to **distinguish** between what is **holy** and what is **unholy** is to make everything unholy, unclean, and profane.

NO PAIN, NO GAIN

Dr. Chris Thurman

Few of us like pain. Whether a trip to the dentist to have an aching tooth examined or a trip to the counselor to have an aching heart examined, we resist those things that might dig in and cause sharper pain. Most of us will do almost anything to avoid it.

But there is an inescapable "law" of personal growth: no pain, no gain. The simple truth is this: Any effort to change immediately increases our pain. Since we do not like pain, and since change requires a worsening of our pain for a period of time, *we do not like change.*

"Tremendous courage is required to walk through the pain of change."

Tremendous courage is required to go against our nature and walk through the pain of change—being willing to hurt worse now to reach new levels of happiness and health later on. ✦

shed blood, to destroy people, and to get
dishonest gain. 28Her prophets plastered
them with untempered *mortar,* seeing false
visions, and divining lies for them, saying,
'Thus says the Lord GOD,' when the LORD
had not spoken. 29The people of the land
have used oppressions, committed robbery, and mistreated the poor and needy;
and they wrongfully oppress the stranger.
30So I sought for a man among them who
would make a wall, and stand in the gap
before Me on behalf of the land, that I
should not destroy it; but I found no one.
31Therefore I have poured out My indignation on them; I have consumed them with
the fire of My wrath; and I have recompensed their deeds on their own heads,"
says the Lord GOD.

CHAPTER 23

Two Harlot Sisters

The word of the LORD came again to me, saying:

2 "Son of man, there were two women,
The daughters of one mother.
3 They committed harlotry in Egypt,
They committed harlotry in their youth;
Their breasts were there embraced,
Their virgin bosom was there pressed.
4 Their names: Ō·hŏ′lah[a] the elder and
Ō·hol′i·bah[b] her sister;

23:4 [a]Literally *Her Own Tabernacle* [b]Literally *My Tabernacle Is in Her*

22:28 Untempered mortar: Of deceit.

22:30, 31 stand in the gap: The figure is of a wall with a section broken down by a siege. If no soldier stands in the gap to repulse the enemy, the city surely will be taken. God represented Himself as against His people. Unable to find anyone who, by life or by intercession, could turn aside that judgment (see 14:13–20), He will pour out His **indignation** on the city.

23:2 one mother: Israel and Judah were aware of their common ancestry.

They were Mine,
And they bore sons and daughters.
As for their names,
Samaria *is* Ō·hō′lah, and Jerusalem *is*
Ō·hol′i·bah.

The Older Sister, Samaria

5 "Ō·hō′lah played the harlot even
though she was Mine;
And she lusted for her lovers, the
neighboring Assyrians,
6 *Who were* clothed in purple,
Captains and rulers,
All of them desirable young men,
Horsemen riding on horses.
7 Thus she committed her harlotry with
them,
All of them choice men of Assyria;
And with all for whom she lusted,
With all their idols, she defiled
herself.
8 She has never given up her harlotry
brought from Egypt,
For in her youth they had lain with
her,
Pressed her virgin bosom,
And poured out their immorality
upon her.

9 "Therefore I have delivered her
Into the hand of her lovers,
Into the hand of the Assyrians,
For whom she lusted.
10 They uncovered her nakedness,
Took away her sons and daughters,
And slew her with the sword;
She became a byword among women,
For they had executed judgment on
her.

The Younger Sister, Jerusalem

11 "Now although her sister Ō·hol′i·bah
saw *this,* she became more corrupt in her
lust than she, and in her harlotry more cor-
rupt than her sister's harlotry.

12 "She lusted for the neighboring
Assyrians,
Captains and rulers,
Clothed most gorgeously,
Horsemen riding on horses,
All of them desirable young men.
13 Then I saw that she was defiled;
Both *took* the same way.
14 But she increased her harlotry;
She looked at men portrayed on the
wall,
Images of Chal·dē′ans portrayed in
vermilion,
15 Girded with belts around their waists,
Flowing turbans on their heads,
All of them looking like captains,
In the manner of the Babylonians of
Chal·dē′a,
The land of their nativity.
16 As soon as her eyes saw them,
She lusted for them
And sent messengers to them in
Chal·dē′a.

17 "Then the Babylonians came to her,
into the bed of love,
And they defiled her with their
immorality;
So she was defiled by them, and
alienated herself from them.
18 She revealed her harlotry and
uncovered her nakedness.
Then I alienated Myself from her,
As I had alienated Myself from her
sister.

19 "Yet she multiplied her harlotry
In calling to remembrance the days of
her youth,
When she had played the harlot in
the land of Egypt.
20 For she lusted for her paramours,
Whose flesh *is like* the flesh of
donkeys,

23:5 she lusted: Israel took the initiative in her alliance with the Assyrians; she could not claim coercion (see 2 Kin. 16:7).

23:20 donkeys . . . horses: Unclean, coarse, and abhorrent.

And whose issue *is like* the issue of
horses.
21 Thus you called to remembrance the
lewdness of your youth,
When the Egyptians pressed your
bosom
Because of your youthful breasts.

Judgment on Jerusalem

22"Therefore, Ō·hol′i·bah, thus says the
Lord GOD:

'Behold, I will stir up your lovers
against you,
From whom you have alienated
yourself,
And I will bring them against you
from every side:
23 The Babylonians,
All the Chal·dē′ans,
Pē′kod, Shō′a, Kō′a,
All the Assyrians with them,
All of them desirable young men,
Governors and rulers,
Captains and men of renown,
All of them riding on horses.
24 And they shall come against you
With chariots, wagons, and
war-horses,
With a horde of people.
They shall array against you
Buckler, shield, and helmet all
around.

'I will delegate judgment to them,
And they shall judge you according
to their judgments.
25 I will set My jealousy against you,
And they shall deal furiously with
you;
They shall remove your nose and
your ears,
And your remnant shall fall by the
sword;
They shall take your sons and your
daughters,
And your remnant shall be devoured
by fire.
26 They shall also strip you of your
clothes
And take away your beautiful
jewelry.

27 'Thus I will make you cease your
lewdness and your harlotry
Brought from the land of Egypt,
So that you will not lift your eyes to
them,
Nor remember Egypt anymore.'

28"For thus says the Lord GOD: 'Surely I
will deliver you into the hand of those you
hate, into the hand *of those* from whom you
alienated yourself. 29They will deal hate-
fully with you, take away all you have
worked for, and leave you naked and bare.
The nakedness of your harlotry shall be
uncovered, both your lewdness and your
harlotry. 30I will do these *things* to you be-
cause you have gone as a harlot after the
Gentiles, because you have become defiled
by their idols. 31You have walked in the
way of your sister; therefore I will put her
cup in your hand.'
32"Thus says the Lord GOD:

'You shall drink of your sister's cup,
The deep and wide one;
You shall be laughed to scorn
And held in derision;
It contains much.
33 You will be filled with drunkenness
and sorrow,
The cup of horror and desolation,
The cup of your sister Samaria.
34 You shall drink and drain it,
You shall break its shards,
And tear at your own breasts;

23:25, 26 nose . . . ears: Judah's beauty would be disfigured so she could no longer attract **lovers** (foreign allies).

23:32–35 The outcome of Judah's sins is here revealed. Sin is always as horrible in its end as it is attractive in its beginning.

For I have spoken,'
Says the Lord GOD.

35"Therefore thus says the Lord GOD:

'Because you have forgotten Me and
cast Me behind your back,
Therefore you shall bear the *penalty*
Of your lewdness and your
harlotry.' "

Both Sisters Judged

36The LORD also said to me: "Son of man,
will you judge Ō·hō'lah and Ō·hol'i·bah?
Then declare to them their abominations.
37For they have committed adultery, and
blood *is* on their hands. They have com-
mitted adultery with their idols, and even
sacrificed their sons whom they bore to
Me, passing them through *the fire,* to de-
vour *them.* 38Moreover they have done this
to Me: They have defiled My sanctuary on
the same day and profaned My Sabbaths.
39For after they had slain their children for
their idols, on the same day they came into
My sanctuary to profane it; and indeed
thus they have done in the midst of My
house.

40"Furthermore you sent for men to
come from afar, to whom a messenger *was*
sent; and there they came. And you
washed yourself for them, painted your
eyes, and adorned yourself with orna-
ments. 41You sat on a stately couch, with a
table prepared before it, on which you had
set My incense and My oil. 42The sound of
a carefree multitude *was* with her, and
Sa·bē'ans *were* brought from the wilder-
ness with men of the common sort, who
put bracelets on their wrists and beautiful
crowns on their heads. 43Then I said con-
cerning *her who had grown* old in adulteries,
'Will they commit harlotry with her now,
and she *with them?'* 44Yet they went in to
her, as men go in to a woman who plays
the harlot; thus they went in to Ō·hō'lah
and Ō·hol'i·bah, the lewd women. 45But
righteous men will judge them after the
manner of adulteresses, and after the man-
ner of women who shed blood, because
they *are* adulteresses, and blood *is* on their
hands.

46"For thus says the Lord GOD: 'Bring up
an assembly against them, give them up to
trouble and plunder. 47The assembly shall
stone them with stones and execute them
with their swords; they shall slay their
sons and their daughters, and burn their
houses with fire. 48Thus I will cause lewd-
ness to cease from the land, that all women
may be taught not to practice your lewd-
ness. 49They shall repay you for your lewd-
ness, and you shall pay for your idolatrous
sins. Then you shall know that I *am* the
Lord GOD.' "

CHAPTER 24

Symbol of the Cooking Pot

Again, in the ninth year, in the tenth
month, on the tenth *day* of the month, the
word of the LORD came to me, saying,
2"Son of man, write down the name of the
day, this very day—the king of Babylon
started his siege against Jerusalem this
very day. 3And utter a parable to the rebel-
lious house, and say to them, 'Thus says
the Lord GOD:

"Put on a pot, set *it* on,
And also pour water into it.
4 Gather pieces *of meat* in it,

23:38, 39 Their religion had become so adulterated that they did not recognize that child sacrifice to an idol and worship of the Lord were totally incompatible.

23:40, 41 You sent . . . sat: As a harlot receiving her customers.

24:2 This very day marks the climax of the first section of Ezekiel's prophecies. The threatened judgment had begun. When the message came from Jerusalem verifying Ezekiel's date for the beginning of the siege, it reconfirmed him as God's true prophet to the exiles. This confirmation prepared the way for the second phase of his prophetic ministry to them.

Every good piece,
The thigh and the shoulder.
Fill *it* with choice cuts;
5 Take the choice of the flock.
Also pile *fuel* bones under it,
Make it boil well,
And let the cuts simmer in it."

6"Therefore thus says the Lord GOD:

"Woe to the bloody city,
To the pot whose scum *is* in it,
And whose scum is not gone from it!
Bring it out piece by piece,
On which no lot has fallen.
7 For her blood is in her midst;
She set it on top of a rock;
She did not pour it on the ground,
To cover it with dust.
8 That it may raise up fury and take
vengeance,
I have set her blood on top of a rock,
That it may not be covered."

9"Therefore thus says the Lord GOD:
"Woe to the bloody city!
I too will make the pyre great.
10 Heap on the wood,
Kindle the fire;
Cook the meat well,
Mix in the spices,
And let the cuts be burned up.

11 "Then set the pot empty on the coals,
That it may become hot and its
bronze may burn,
That its filthiness may be melted in it,
That its scum may be consumed.
12 She has grown weary with lies,
And her great scum has not gone
from her.
Let her scum *be* in the fire!
13 In your filthiness *is* lewdness.
Because I have cleansed you, and you
were not cleansed,
You will not be cleansed of your
filthiness anymore,
Till I have caused My fury to rest
upon you.
14 I, the LORD, have spoken *it;*
It shall come to pass, and I will do *it;*
I will not hold back,
Nor will I spare,
Nor will I relent;
According to your ways
And according to your deeds
They[a] will judge you,"
Says the Lord GOD.' "

The Prophet's Wife Dies

15Also the word of the LORD came to me,
saying, 16"Son of man, behold, I take away
from you the desire of your eyes with one
stroke; yet you shall neither mourn nor
weep, nor shall your tears run down.
17Sigh in silence, make no mourning for the
dead; bind your turban on your head, and
put your sandals on your feet; do not cover
your lips, and do not eat man's bread *of sorrow.*"
18So I spoke to the people in the morning,
and at evening my wife died; and the
next morning I did as I was commanded.
19And the people said to me, "Will you
not tell us what these *things signify* to us,
that you behave so?"
20Then I answered them, "The word of
the LORD came to me, saying, 21'Speak to
the house of Israel, "Thus says the Lord
GOD: 'Behold, I will profane My sanctuary,
your arrogant boast, the desire of your
eyes, the delight of your soul; and your
sons and daughters whom you left behind
shall fall by the sword. 22And you shall do

24:14 [a]Septuagint, Syriac, Targum, and Vulgate read *I.*

24:7, 8 did not . . . cover it with dust: In an attempt to keep the blood from calling for vengeance (see Gen. 4:10). Judah showed no shame for her sins, so God showed no mercy.

24:16, 17 desire of your eyes: Ezekiel's wife. **one stroke**: Suddenly, with little warning. The prophet was not to stop his normal activities, nor was he to perform any of the usual acts of mourning. Sometimes it is painful to obey God.

as I have done; you shall not cover *your*
lips nor eat man's bread *of sorrow.* 23Your
turbans shall be on your heads and your
sandals on your feet; you shall neither
mourn nor weep, but you shall pine away
in your iniquities and mourn with one an-
other. 24Thus E·zēk'i·el is a sign to you; ac-
cording to all that he has done you shall
do; and when this comes, you shall know
that I *am* the Lord GOD.' "

25'And you, son of man—*will it* not *be* in
the day when I take from them their
stronghold, their joy and their glory, the
desire of their eyes, and that on which they
set their minds, their sons and their daugh-
ters: 26on that day one who escapes will
come to you to let *you* hear *it* with *your*
ears; 27on that day your mouth will be
opened to him who has escaped; you shall
speak and no longer be mute. Thus you
will be a sign to them, and they shall know
that I *am* the LORD.' "

CHAPTER 25

Proclamation Against Ammon

The word of the LORD came to me, say-
ing, 2"Son of man, set your face against the
Am'mon·ītes, and prophesy against them.
3Say to the Am'mon·ītes, 'Hear the word of
the Lord GOD! Thus says the Lord GOD:
"Because you said, 'Aha!' against My sanc-
tuary when it was profaned, and against
the land of Israel when it was desolate, and
against the house of Judah when they went
into captivity, 4indeed, therefore, I will de-
liver you as a possession to the men of the
East, and they shall set their encampments
among you and make their dwellings
among you; they shall eat your fruit, and
they shall drink your milk. 5And I will
make Rab'bah a stable for camels and
Am'mon a resting place for flocks. Then
you shall know that I *am* the LORD."

6'For thus says the Lord GOD: "Because
you clapped *your* hands, stamped your
feet, and rejoiced in heart with all your dis-
dain for the land of Israel, 7indeed, there-
fore, I will stretch out My hand against

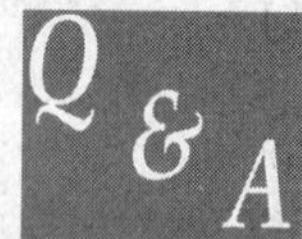

How can I better relate to those who are grieving? What can I do to comfort them?

Dr. Frank Minirth and Dr. Paul Meier

The Bible instructs us to weep with those who mourn just as we are to rejoice with those who are glad. Although we need to pray that the Holy Spirit will bring comfort when friends and loved ones suffer from grief, they need the freedom to express that grief naturally and openly. Putting on a false acceptance of the loss is not healthy, yet hearing clichés from their friends can make survivors feel that it is improper to hurt as badly as they do. Suppressing grief for the sake of appearing well adjusted can prolong the mourning period and even lead to clinical depression.

The best way to help grieving friends is with your presence. Just being there is comforting. It is not what you say that is needed; it is that you came, you stayed, you listened, you cared. They may remember little of what is said but much of what is done. ✦

you, and give you as plunder to the na-
tions; I will cut you off from the peoples,
and I will cause you to perish from the
countries; I will destroy you, and you shall
know that I *am* the LORD."

Proclamation Against Moab

[8]"Thus says the Lord GOD: "Because
Mō'ab and Sē'ir say, 'Look! The house of
Judah *is* like all the nations,' [9]therefore, be-
hold, I will clear the territory of Mō'ab of
cities, of the cities on its frontier, the glory
of the country, Beth Jesh'i·moth, Bā'al
Mē'on, and Kir·jath'a·im. [10]To the men of
the East I will give it as a possession, to-
gether with the Am'mon·ītes, that the
Am'mon·ītes may not be remembered
among the nations. [11]And I will execute
judgments upon Mō'ab, and they shall
know that I *am* the LORD."

Proclamation Against Edom

[12]"Thus says the Lord GOD: "Because of
what Ē'dom did against the house of Judah
by taking vengeance, and has greatly of-
fended by avenging itself on them,"
[13]therefore thus says the Lord GOD: "I will
also stretch out My hand against Ē'dom,
cut off man and beast from it, and make it
desolate from Tē'man; Dē'dan shall fall by
the sword. [14]I will lay My vengeance on
Ē'dom by the hand of My people Israel,
that they may do in Ē'dom according to
My anger and according to My fury; and
they shall know My vengeance," says the
Lord GOD.

Proclamation Against Philistia

[15]"Thus says the Lord GOD: "Because the
Phi·lis'tines dealt vengefully and took
vengeance with a spiteful heart, to destroy
because of the old hatred," [16]therefore thus
says the Lord GOD: "I will stretch out My
hand against the Phi·lis'tines, and I will
cut off the Cher'e·thītes and destroy the
remnant of the seacoast. [17]I will execute
great vengeance on them with furious re-
bukes; and they shall know that I *am* the
LORD, when I lay My vengeance upon
them." ' "

CHAPTER 26

Proclamation Against Tyre

And it came to pass in the eleventh year,
on the first *day* of the month, *that* the
word of the LORD came to me, saying,
[2]"Son of man, because Tȳre has said against
Jerusalem, 'Aha! She is broken who *was* the
gateway of the peoples; now she is turned
over to me; I shall be filled; she is laid
waste.'
[3]"Therefore thus says the Lord GOD: 'Be-
hold, I *am* against you, O Tȳre, and will
cause many nations to come up against
you, as the sea causes its waves to come
up. [4]And they shall destroy the walls of
Tȳre and break down her towers; I will
also scrape her dust from her, and make
her like the top of a rock. [5]It shall be *a place*
for spreading nets in the midst of the sea,
for I have spoken,' says the Lord GOD; 'it
shall become plunder for the nations. [6]Also

25:8 like all the nations: Moab's sin was her refusal to recognize God's presence with Israel and distinctive mission for her.

26:1, 2 gateway of the peoples: In her prime Judah was the commercial link between Tyre and Arabia. With Judah out of the way, Tyre imagined even greater opportunities for herself.

26:4 scrape her dust . . . top of a rock: Tyre would not merely be destroyed; even the rubble would be scraped away. This was literally fulfilled in 332 B.C. when Alexander the Great's armies used the rubble of the city to make a causeway over which they attacked the island citadel offshore.

26:5 midst of the sea: Tyre was originally a rocky islet. Fortified, it proved impregnable for centuries, but now would be plundered.

her daughter *villages* which *are* in the fields shall be slain by the sword. Then they shall know that I am the LORD.'

[7]"For thus says the Lord GOD: 'Behold, I will bring against Tyre from the north Ne·bū·chad·nez'zar[a] king of Babylon, king of kings, with horses, with chariots, and with horsemen, and an army with many people. [8]He will slay with the sword your daughter *villages* in the fields; he will heap up a siege mound against you, build a wall against you, and raise a defense against you. [9]He will direct his battering rams against your walls, and with his axes he will break down your towers. [10]Because of the abundance of his horses, their dust will cover you; your walls will shake at the noise of the horsemen, the wagons, and the chariots, when he enters your gates, as men enter a city that has been breached. [11]With the hooves of his horses he will trample all your streets; he will slay your people by the sword, and your strong pillars will fall to the ground. [12]They will plunder your riches and pillage your merchandise; they will break down your walls and destroy your pleasant houses; they will lay your stones, your timber, and your soil in the midst of the water. [13]I will put an end to the sound of your songs, and the sound of your harps shall be heard no more. [14]I will make you like the top of a rock; you shall be *a place for* spreading nets, and you shall never be rebuilt, for I the LORD have spoken,' says the Lord GOD.

[15]"Thus says the Lord GOD to Tyre: 'Will the coastlands not shake at the sound of your fall, when the wounded cry, when slaughter is made in the midst of you? [16]Then all the princes of the sea will come down from their thrones, lay aside their robes, and take off their embroidered garments; they will clothe themselves with trembling; they will sit on the ground, tremble *every* moment, and be astonished at you. [17]And they will take up a lamentation for you, and say to you:

"How you have perished,
O one inhabited by seafaring men,
O renowned city,
Who was strong at sea,
She and her inhabitants,
Who caused their terror *to be* on all
her inhabitants!
18 Now the coastlands tremble on the
day of your fall;
Yes, the coastlands by the sea are
troubled at your departure." '

[19]"For thus says the Lord GOD: 'When I make you a desolate city, like cities that are not inhabited, when I bring the deep upon you, and great waters cover you, [20]then I will bring you down with those who descend into the Pit, to the people of old, and I will make you dwell in the lowest part of the earth, in places desolate from antiquity, with those who go down to the Pit, so that you may never be inhabited; and I shall establish glory in the land of the living. [21]I will make you a terror, and you *shall be* no *more;* though you are sought for, you will never be found again,' says the Lord GOD."

CHAPTER 27

Lamentation for Tyre

The word of the LORD came again to me, saying, [2]"Now, son of man, take up a lamentation for Tyre, [3]and say to Tyre, 'You who are situated at the entrance of the sea,

26:7 [a]Hebrew *Nebuchadrezzar,* and so elsewhere in this book

26:7–14 A description of Nebuchadnezzar's 13-year siege of Tyre (586–573 B.C.). As Tyre rejoiced at the destruction of Jerusalem, little did she dream that her turn was next. The island fortress did not fall at this time (see v. 4) because Phoenician ships kept the defenders supplied and reinforced. But the mainland city was destroyed and Tyre's commercial strength crippled.

merchant of the peoples on many coastlands, thus says the Lord GOD:

"O Tȳre, you have said,
'I *am* perfect in beauty.'
4 Your borders *are* in the midst of the seas.
Your builders have perfected your beauty.
5 They made all *your* planks of fir trees from Sē'nir;
They took a cedar from Lebanon to make you a mast.
6 *Of* oaks from Bā'shan they made your oars;
The company of Ash'ur·ītes have inlaid your planks
With ivory from the coasts of Cyprus.[a]
7 Fine embroidered linen from Egypt was what you spread for your sail;
Blue and purple from the coasts of E·li'shah was what covered you.

8 "Inhabitants of Sī'don and Ar'vad were your oarsmen;
Your wise men, O Tȳre, were in you;
They became your pilots.
9 Elders of Gē'bal and its wise men
Were in you to caulk your seams;
All the ships of the sea
And their oarsmen were in you
To market your merchandise.

10 "Those from Persia, Lyd'i·a,[a] and Lib'ya[b]
Were in your army as men of war;
They hung shield and helmet in you;
They gave splendor to you.
11 Men of Ar'vad with your army *were* on your walls *all* around,
And the men of Gammad were in your towers;
They hung their shields on your walls *all* around;
They made your beauty perfect.

12 "Tar'shish *was* your merchant because
of your many luxury goods. They gave
you silver, iron, tin, and lead for your
goods. 13 Jā'van, Tū'bal, and Mē'shech *were*
your traders. They bartered human lives
and vessels of bronze for your merchandise.
14 Those from the house of Tō·gar'mah
traded for your wares with horses, steeds,
and mules. 15 The men of Dē'dan *were* your
traders; many isles *were* the market of your
hand. They brought you ivory tusks and
ebony as payment. 16 Syria *was* your merchant
because of the abundance of goods
you made. They gave you for your wares
emeralds, purple, embroidery, fine linen,
corals, and rubies. 17 Judah and the land of
Israel *were* your traders. They traded for
your merchandise wheat of Min'nith, millet,
honey, oil, and balm. 18 Damascus *was*
your merchant because of the abundance
of goods you made, because of your many
luxury items, with the wine of Hel'bon and
with white wool. 19 Dan and Jā'van paid for
your wares, traversing back and forth.
Wrought iron, cassia, and cane were
among your merchandise. 20 Dē'dan *was*
your merchant in saddlecloths for riding.
21 Arabia and all the princes of Kē'dar *were*
your regular merchants. They traded with
you in lambs, rams, and goats. 22 The merchants
of Shē'ba and Rā'a·mah *were* your
merchants. They traded for your wares the
choicest spices, all kinds of precious
stones, and gold. 23 Har'an, Can'neh, Eden,
the merchants of Shē'ba, Assyria, *and*
Chil'mad *were* your merchants. 24 These
were your merchants in choice items—in
purple clothes, in embroidered garments,
in chests of multicolored apparel, in sturdy
woven cords, which were in your marketplace.

25 "The ships of Tar'shish were carriers of your merchandise.
You were filled and very glorious in the midst of the seas.
26 Your oarsmen brought you into many waters,

27:6 [a]Hebrew *Kittim*, western lands, especially Cyprus
27:10 [a]Hebrew *Lud* [b]Hebrew *Put*

But the east wind broke you in the
midst of the seas.

27 "Your riches, wares, and merchandise,
Your mariners and pilots,
Your caulkers and merchandisers,
All your men of war who *are* in you,
And the entire company which *is* in
your midst,
Will fall into the midst of the seas on
the day of your ruin.
28 The common-land will shake at the
sound of the cry of your pilots.

29 "All who handle the oar,
The mariners,
All the pilots of the sea
Will come down from their ships *and*
stand on the shore.
30 They will make their voice heard
because of you;
They will cry bitterly and cast dust on
their heads;
They will roll about in ashes;
31 They will shave themselves
completely bald because of you,
Gird themselves with sackcloth,
And weep for you
With bitterness of heart *and* bitter
wailing.
32 In their wailing for you
They will take up a lamentation,
And lament for you:
'What *city is* like Tyre,
Destroyed in the midst of the sea?

33 'When your wares went out by sea,
You satisfied many people;
You enriched the kings of the earth
With your many luxury goods and
your merchandise.
34 But you are broken by the seas in the
depths of the waters;
Your merchandise and the entire
company will fall in your midst.
35 All the inhabitants of the isles will be
astonished at you;
Their kings will be greatly afraid,
And *their* countenance will be
troubled.
36 The merchants among the peoples
will hiss at you;
You will become a horror, and *be* no
more forever.' " ' "

CHAPTER 28

Proclamation Against the King of Tyre

The word of the LORD came to me again,
saying, 2"Son of man, say to the prince of
Tyre, 'Thus says the Lord GOD:

"Because your heart *is* lifted up,
And you say, 'I *am* a god,
I sit *in* the seat of gods,
In the midst of the seas,'
Yet you *are* a man, and not a god,
Though you set your heart as the
heart of a god
3 (Behold, you *are* wiser than Daniel!
There is no secret that can be hidden
from you!
4 With your wisdom and your
understanding
You have gained riches for yourself,
And gathered gold and silver into
your treasuries;
5 By your great wisdom in trade you
have increased your riches,
And your heart is lifted up because of
your riches),"

27:28–36 The greatness of Tyre meant that her destruction would cause astonishment and fear among all who had depended on her.

27:36 hiss: Not in derision, but in astonishment (see v. 35).

28:2 I am a god: Many people live their lives as though they were all-powerful, but few state that attitude so boldly. The prince was reflecting the attitude of his city. This pronouncement of God's judgment was upon both.

28:3–5 you are wiser: Sarcastic words; Tyre's prince was not really wise, even though he could accumulate wealth.

6"Therefore thus says the Lord GOD:

"Because you have set your heart as
the heart of a god,
7 Behold, therefore, I will bring
strangers against you,
The most terrible of the nations;
And they shall draw their swords
against the beauty of your wisdom,
And defile your splendor.
8 They shall throw you down into the
Pit,
And you shall die the death of the
slain
In the midst of the seas.

9 "Will you still say before him who
slays you,
'I *am* a god'?
But you *shall be* a man, and not a god,
In the hand of him who slays you.
10 You shall die the death of the uncir-
cumcised
By the hand of aliens;
For I have spoken," says the Lord
GOD.' "

Lamentation for the King of Tyre

11Moreover the word of the LORD came
to me, saying, 12"Son of man, take up a
lamentation for the king of Tyre, and say to
him, 'Thus says the Lord GOD:

"You *were* the seal of perfection,
Full of wisdom and perfect in beauty.
13 You were in Eden, the garden of God;
Every precious stone *was* your
covering:
The sardius, topaz, and diamond,
Beryl, onyx, and jasper,
Sapphire, turquoise, and emerald
with gold.
The workmanship of your timbrels
and pipes
Was prepared for you on the day you
were created.

14 "You *were* the anointed cherub who
covers;
I established you;
You were on the holy mountain of
God;
You walked back and forth in the
midst of fiery stones.
15 You *were* perfect in your ways from
the day you were created,
Till iniquity was found in you.

16 "By the abundance of your trading
You became filled with violence
within,
And you sinned;
Therefore I cast you as a profane
thing
Out of the mountain of God;
And I destroyed you, O covering
cherub,
From the midst of the fiery stones.

17 "Your heart was lifted up because of
your beauty;
You corrupted your wisdom for the
sake of your splendor;
I cast you to the ground,
I laid you before kings,
That they might gaze at you.

18 "You defiled your sanctuaries
By the multitude of your iniquities,
By the iniquity of your trading;
Therefore I brought fire from your
midst;

28:8 midst of the seas: Where Tyre's prince had established his wealth, power, and pride, he would be brought low.

28:12, 13 The blessings given to Tyre are likened to God's gifts to Adam in the Garden of **Eden**.

28:14–17 The **cherub** who **sinned** (v. 16), and whom God **cast** to the ground (v. 17), is Lucifer, expelled from heaven because of his pride and desire to be equal with God. See Is. 14:12–15.

28:17 The origin of the king's (and Lucifer's) sin was pride in his **beauty**. He allowed his **splendor** to corrupt his **wisdom**. Ultimately, all sin is rooted in this self-pride.

It devoured you,
And I turned you to ashes upon the earth
In the sight of all who saw you.
19 All who knew you among the peoples are astonished at you;
You have become a horror,
And *shall be* no more forever." ' "

Proclamation Against Sidon

[20]Then the word of the LORD came to me,
saying, [21]"Son of man, set your face toward
Sī'don, and prophesy against her, [22]and
say, 'Thus says the Lord GOD:

"Behold, I *am* against you, O Sī'don;
I will be glorified in your midst;
And they shall know that I *am* the LORD,
When I execute judgments in her and am hallowed in her.
23 For I will send pestilence upon her,
And blood in her streets;
The wounded shall be judged in her midst
By the sword against her on every side;
Then they shall know that I *am* the LORD.

[24]"And there shall no longer be a prick-
ing brier or a painful thorn for the house of
Israel from among all *who are* around them,
who despise them. Then they shall know
that I *am* the Lord GOD."

Israel's Future Blessing

[25]'Thus says the Lord GOD: "When I
have gathered the house of Israel from the
peoples among whom they are scattered,
and am hallowed in them in the sight of
the Gentiles, then they will dwell in their
own land which I gave to My servant Ja-
cob. [26]And they will dwell safely there,
build houses, and plant vineyards; yes,
they will dwell securely, when I execute
judgments on all those around them who
despise them. Then they shall know that I
am the LORD their God." ' "

CHAPTER 29

Proclamation Against Egypt

In the tenth year, in the tenth *month,* on
the twelfth *day* of the month, the word of
the LORD came to me, saying, [2]"Son of man,
set your face against Pharaoh king of
Egypt, and prophesy against him, and
against all Egypt. [3]Speak, and say, 'Thus
says the Lord GOD:

"Behold, I *am* against you,
O Pharaoh king of Egypt,
O great monster who lies in the midst of his rivers,
Who has said, 'My River[a] *is* my own;
I have made *it* for myself.'
4 But I will put hooks in your jaws,
And cause the fish of your rivers to stick to your scales;
I will bring you up out of the midst of your rivers,
And all the fish in your rivers will stick to your scales.
5 I will leave you in the wilderness,
You and all the fish of your rivers;
You shall fall on the open field;
You shall not be picked up or gathered.[a]

29:3 [a]That is, the Nile 29:5 [a]Following Masoretic Text, Septuagint, and Vulgate; some Hebrew manuscripts and Targum read *buried.*

29:3 My River: The Nile. **I have made it**: Pharaoh's and Egypt's sin was the same as Tyre's and her king's—overweening pride (see 28:2).

29:4, 5 I will put hooks: There is a greater God than Pharaoh. **Fish of your rivers** possibly refers to the peoples around Egypt who were dependent on, and supportive of, Egypt (see 30:5, 6).

I have given you as food
To the beasts of the field
And to the birds of the heavens.

6 "Then all the inhabitants of Egypt
Shall know that I *am* the LORD,
Because they have been a staff of reed
to the house of Israel.
7 When they took hold of you with the
hand,
You broke and tore all their
shoulders;[a]
When they leaned on you,
You broke and made all their backs
quiver."

8'Therefore thus says the Lord GOD:
"Surely I will bring a sword upon you and
cut off from you man and beast. 9And the
land of Egypt shall become desolate and
waste; then they will know that I *am* the
LORD, because he said, 'The River *is* mine,
and I have made *it*.' 10Indeed, therefore, I
am against you and against your rivers,
and I will make the land of Egypt utterly
waste and desolate, from Mig'dōl[a] *to*
Sy̅·ē'nē, as far as the border of Ethiopia.
11Neither foot of man shall pass through it
nor foot of beast pass through it, and it
shall be uninhabited forty years. 12I will
make the land of Egypt desolate in the
midst of the countries *that are* desolate; and
among the cities *that are* laid waste, her
cities shall be desolate forty years; and I
will scatter the Egyptians among the na-
tions and disperse them throughout the
countries."
13'Yet, thus says the Lord GOD: "At the
end of forty years I will gather the Egyp-
tians from the peoples among whom they
were scattered. 14I will bring back the cap-
tives of Egypt and cause them to return to
the land of Path'ros, to the land of their
origin, and there they shall be a lowly
kingdom. 15It shall be the lowliest of king-
doms; it shall never again exalt itself above
the nations, for I will diminish them so that
they will not rule over the nations any-
more. 16No longer shall it be the confidence
of the house of Israel, but will remind them
of *their* iniquity when they turned to follow
them. Then they shall know that I *am* the
Lord GOD." ' "

29:7 [a]Following Masoretic Text and Vulgate; Septuagint and Syriac read *hand*. 29:10 [a]Or *tower*

Babylonia Will Plunder Egypt

17And it came to pass in the twenty-sev-
enth year, in the first *month*, on the first *day*
of the month, *that* the word of the LORD
came to me, saying, 18"Son of man,
Ne·bū·chad·nez'zar king of Babylon
caused his army to labor strenuously
against Ty̅re; every head *was* made bald,
and every shoulder rubbed raw; yet
neither he nor his army received wages
from Ty̅re, for the labor which they ex-
pended on it. 19Therefore thus says the
Lord GOD: 'Surely I will give the land of
Egypt to Ne·bū·chad·nez'zar king of Bab-
ylon; he shall take away her wealth, carry
off her spoil, and remove her pillage; and
that will be the wages for his army. 20I have
given him the land of Egypt *for* his labor,

29:6 know that I am the LORD: God's purpose in displaying His power (see 6:7). As a **staff of reed** would break and injure the one leaning on it, so Egypt failed when Judah relied on her against Babylon (see Is. 36:6).

29:11–13 The **forty years** represent a period of exile and desolation like Jerusalem's.

29:15 they will not rule: Since her humiliation by Nebuchadnezzar, Egypt has never again been in the first rank of world powers. Until recent years, she has often been ruled by foreigners.

29:17 first day: Perhaps Apr. 26, 571 B.C., after Nebuchadnezzar's siege of Tyre had been broken off (see 26:7–14 and note). It is the latest of Ezekiel's dated prophecies.

29:18 bald: From the rubbing of constantly worn helmets through the 13 years of the siege. **raw**: From the friction of body armor and carrying material for the siege works. **from Tyre**: Presumably most of Tyre's treasure was carried to safety by the Phoenician fleet.

because they worked for Me,' says the Lord GOD.

21'In that day I will cause the horn of the house of Israel to spring forth, and I will open your mouth to speak in their midst. Then they shall know that I *am* the LORD.' "

CHAPTER 30

Egypt and Her Allies Will Fall

The word of the LORD came to me again, saying, 2"Son of man, prophesy and say, 'Thus says the Lord GOD:

"Wail, 'Woe to the day!'
3 For the day *is* near,
Even the day of the LORD *is* near;
It will be a day of clouds, the time of the Gentiles.
4 The sword shall come upon Egypt,
And great anguish shall be in Ethiopia,
When the slain fall in Egypt,
And they take away her wealth,
And her foundations are broken down.

5"Ethiopia, Lib'ya,[a] Lyd'i·a,[b] all the mingled people, Chub, and the men of the lands who are allied, shall fall with them by the sword."

6'Thus says the LORD:

"Those who uphold Egypt shall fall,
And the pride of her power shall come down.
From Mig'dōl *to* Sȳ·ē'nē
Those within her shall fall by the sword,"
Says the Lord GOD.
7 "They shall be desolate in the midst of the desolate countries,
And her cities shall be in the midst of the cities *that are* laid waste.
8 Then they will know that I *am* the LORD,
When I have set a fire in Egypt
And all her helpers are destroyed.
9 On that day messengers shall go forth from Me in ships
To make the careless Ethiopians afraid,
And great anguish shall come upon them,
As on the day of Egypt;
For indeed it is coming!"

10'Thus says the Lord GOD:

"I will also make a multitude of Egypt to cease
By the hand of Ne·bū·chad·nez'zar king of Babylon.
11 He and his people with him, the most terrible of the nations,
Shall be brought to destroy the land;
They shall draw their swords against Egypt,
And fill the land with the slain.
12 I will make the rivers dry,
And sell the land into the hand of the wicked;
I will make the land waste, and all that is in it,
By the hand of aliens.
I, the LORD, have spoken."

13'Thus says the Lord GOD:

"I will also destroy the idols,
And cause the images to cease from Noph;[a]
There shall no longer be princes from the land of Egypt;
I will put fear in the land of Egypt.
14 I will make Path'ros desolate,
Set fire to Zō'an,
And execute judgments in No.[a]
15 I will pour My fury on Sin,[a] the strength of Egypt;
I will cut off the multitude of No,
16 And set a fire in Egypt;
Sin shall have great pain,
No shall be split open,
And Noph *shall be in* distress daily.
17 The young men of Ā'ven[a] and Pī Bē'seth shall fall by the sword,
And these *cities* shall go into captivity.

30:5 [a]Hebrew *Put* [b]Hebrew *Lud* 30:13 [a]That is, ancient Memphis 30:14 [a]That is, ancient Thebes 30:15 [a]That is, ancient Pelusium 30:17 [a]That is, ancient On (Heliopolis)

18 At Te·haph'ne·hēs[a] the day shall also
be darkened,[b]
When I break the yokes of Egypt
there.
And her arrogant strength shall cease
in her;
As for her, a cloud shall cover her,
And her daughters shall go into
captivity.
19 Thus I will execute judgments on
Egypt,
Then they shall know that I *am* the
LORD." ' "

Proclamation Against Pharaoh

20And it came to pass in the eleventh
year, in the first *month,* on the seventh *day*
of the month, *that* the word of the LORD
came to me, saying, 21"Son of man, I have
broken the arm of Pharaoh king of Egypt;
and see, it has not been bandaged for heal-
ing, nor a splint put on to bind it, to make
it strong enough to hold a sword. 22There-
fore thus says the Lord GOD: 'Surely I *am*
against Pharaoh king of Egypt, and will
break his arms, both the strong one and the
one that was broken; and I will make the
sword fall out of his hand. 23I will scatter
the Egyptians among the nations, and dis-
perse them throughout the countries. 24I
will strengthen the arms of the king of
Babylon and put My sword in his hand;
but I will break Pharaoh's arms, and he
will groan before him with the groanings
of a mortally wounded *man.* 25Thus I will
strengthen the arms of the king of Babylon,
but the arms of Pharaoh shall fall down;
they shall know that I *am* the LORD, when I
put My sword into the hand of the king of
Babylon and he stretches it out against the
land of Egypt. 26I will scatter the Egyptians
among the nations and disperse them
throughout the countries. Then they shall
know that I *am* the LORD.' "

CHAPTER 31

Egypt Cut Down Like a Great Tree

Now it came to pass in the eleventh
year, in the third *month,* on the first *day* of
the month, *that* the word of the LORD came
to me, saying, 2"Son of man, say to
Pharaoh king of Egypt and to his multi-
tude:

'Whom are you like in your greatness?
3 Indeed Assyria *was* a cedar in
Lebanon,
With fine branches that shaded the
forest,
And of high stature;
And its top was among the thick
boughs.
4 The waters made it grow;
Underground waters gave it height,
With their rivers running around the
place where it was planted,
And sent out rivulets to all the trees
of the field.

5 'Therefore its height was exalted
above all the trees of the field;
Its boughs were multiplied,
And its branches became long
because of the abundance of water,
As it sent them out.
6 All the birds of the heavens made
their nests in its boughs;
Under its branches all the beasts of
the field brought forth their young;
And in its shadow all great nations
made their home.

30:18 [a]Spelled *Tahpanhes* in Jeremiah 43:7 and elsewhere [b]Following many Hebrew manuscripts, Bomberg, Septuagint, Syriac, Targum, and Vulgate; Masoretic Text reads *refrained.*

30:20–26 This prophecy of Babylon's increasing strength against a weakening Egypt was actually given earlier than the previous prophecy of 29:17–21. Verses 20–26 here possibly continue the prophecy of 29:1–16 which was given three months earlier. The present arrangement reflects a topical, rather than chronological, organization.

7 'Thus it was beautiful in greatness and
in the length of its branches,
Because its roots reached to abundant
waters.
8 The cedars in the garden of God
could not hide it;
The fir trees were not like its boughs,
And the chestnut[a] trees were not like
its branches;
No tree in the garden of God was like
it in beauty.
9 I made it beautiful with a multitude
of branches,
So that all the trees of Eden envied it,
That *were* in the garden of God.'

10"Therefore thus says the Lord GOD:
'Because you have increased in height, and
it set its top among the thick boughs, and
its heart was lifted up in its height, 11there-
fore I will deliver it into the hand of the
mighty one of the nations, and he shall
surely deal with it; I have driven it out for
its wickedness. 12And aliens, the most terri-
ble of the nations, have cut it down and left
it; its branches have fallen on the moun-
tains and in all the valleys; its boughs lie
broken by all the rivers of the land; and all
the peoples of the earth have gone from
under its shadow and left it.

13 'On its ruin will remain all the birds of
the heavens,
And all the beasts of the field will
come to its branches—

14'So that no trees by the waters may ever
again exalt themselves for their height, nor
set their tops among the thick boughs, that
no tree which drinks water may ever be
high enough to reach up to them.

'For they have all been delivered to
death,
To the depths of the earth,
Among the children of men who go
down to the Pit.'

15"Thus says the Lord GOD: 'In the day
when it went down to hell, I caused
mourning. I covered the deep because of it.
I restrained its rivers, and the great waters
were held back. I caused Lebanon to
mourn for it, and all the trees of the field
wilted because of it. 16I made the nations
shake at the sound of its fall, when I cast it
down to hell together with those who de-
scend into the Pit; and all the trees of Eden,
the choice and best of Lebanon, all that
drink water, were comforted in the depths
of the earth. 17They also went down to hell
with it, with those *slain* by the sword; and
those who were its *strong* arm dwelt in its
shadows among the nations.
18'To which of the trees in Eden will you
then be likened in glory and greatness? Yet
you shall be brought down with the trees
of Eden to the depths of the earth; you
shall lie in the midst of the uncircumcised,
with *those* slain by the sword. This *is*
Pharaoh and all his multitude,' says the
Lord GOD."

CHAPTER 32

Lamentation for Pharaoh and Egypt

And it came to pass in the twelfth year,
in the twelfth *month,* on the first *day* of the
month, *that* the word of the LORD came to

31:8 [a]Hebrew *armon*

31:9 After the detailed description of Assyria's majestic beauty, God asserted, **I made it beautiful**. All greatness of any kind comes from Him.

31:10 you: Addressed to Assyria. **it . . . its**: Again speaking of Assyria, but in the third person.

31:11, 12 mighty one: Babylon, which captured Nineveh, Assyria's capital, in 612 B.C. and put an end to Assyria herself with the capture of Haran in 610.

31:18 Egypt never could match Assyria's greatness, and Assyria had been brought down. What, then, was the basis for Pharaoh's pride? Like powerful Assyria, weak Egypt also would be **brought down**.

me, saying, [2]"Son of man, take up a lamentation for Pharaoh king of Egypt, and say to him:

'You are like a young lion among the nations,
And you *are* like a monster in the seas,
Bursting forth in your rivers,
Troubling the waters with your feet,
And fouling their rivers.'

[3]"Thus says the Lord GOD:

'I will therefore spread My net over you with a company of many people,
And they will draw you up in My net.
4 Then I will leave you on the land;
I will cast you out on the open fields,
And cause to settle on you all the birds of the heavens.
And with you I will fill the beasts of the whole earth.
5 I will lay your flesh on the mountains,
And fill the valleys with your carcass.
6 'I will also water the land with the flow of your blood,
Even to the mountains;
And the riverbeds will be full of you.
7 When *I* put out your light,
I will cover the heavens, and make its stars dark;
I will cover the sun with a cloud,
And the moon shall not give her light.
8 All the bright lights of the heavens I will make dark over you,
And bring darkness upon your land,'
Says the Lord GOD.

> Every day I see again that only You can teach me to pray, only You can set my heart at rest, only You can let me dwell in Your presence.
>
> No book, no idea, no concept or theory will ever bring me close to You unless You Yourself are the One who lets these instruments become the way to You.
>
> Henri J. M. Nouwen

[9]'I will also trouble the hearts of many
peoples, when I bring your destruction
among the nations, into the countries
which you have not known. [10]Yes, I will
make many peoples astonished at you, and
their kings shall be horribly afraid of you
when I brandish My sword before them;
and they shall tremble *every* moment,
every man for his own life, in the day of
your fall.'

[11]"For thus says the Lord GOD: 'The
sword of the king of Babylon shall come
upon you. [12]By the swords of the mighty
warriors, all of them the most terrible of
the nations, I will cause your multitude to
fall.

'They shall plunder the pomp of Egypt,
And all its multitude shall be destroyed.
13 Also I will destroy all its animals
From beside its great waters;
The foot of man shall muddy them no more,
Nor shall the hooves of animals muddy them.
14 Then I will make their waters clear,

32:2, 3 My net: The army of Babylon.

32:7, 8 The sun was the principal god of Egypt. God would put out that **light**; He was clearly sovereign over all supposed deities.

32:14 This is the quiet of desolation. Egypt's **rivers** would become smooth like **oil**; there would be no activity of living creatures.

And make their rivers run like oil,'
Says the Lord GOD.

15 'When I make the land of Egypt
desolate,
And the country is destitute of all
that once filled it,
When I strike all who dwell in it,
Then they shall know that I *am* the
LORD.

16 'This *is* the lamentation
With which they shall lament her;
The daughters of the nations shall
lament her;
They shall lament for her, for Egypt,
And for all her multitude,'
Says the Lord GOD."

Egypt and Others Consigned to the Pit

17 It came to pass also in the twelfth year,
on the fifteenth *day* of the month, *that* the
word of the LORD came to me, saying:

18 "Son of man, wail over the multitude
of Egypt,
And cast them down to the depths of
the earth,
Her and the daughters of the famous
nations,
With those who go down to the Pit:
19 'Whom do you surpass in beauty?
Go down, be placed with the
uncircumcised.'

20 "They shall fall in the midst of *those*
slain by the sword;
She is delivered to the sword,
Drawing her and all her multitudes.
21 The strong among the mighty
Shall speak to him out of the midst of
hell
With those who help him:
'They have gone down,
They lie with the uncircumcised, slain
by the sword.'

22 "Assyria *is* there, and all her company,
With their graves all around her,
All of them slain, fallen by the sword.
23 Her graves are set in the recesses of
the Pit,
And her company is all around her
grave,
All of them slain, fallen by the sword,
Who caused terror in the land of the
living.

24 "There *is* Ē'lam and all her multitude,
All around her grave,
All of them slain, fallen by the sword,
Who have gone down uncircumcised
to the lower parts of the earth,
Who caused their terror in the land of
the living;
Now they bear their shame with
those who go down to the Pit.
25 They have set her bed in the midst of
the slain,
With all her multitude,
With her graves all around it,
All of them uncircumcised, slain by
the sword;
Though their terror was caused
In the land of the living,
Yet they bear their shame
With those who go down to the Pit;
It was put in the midst of the slain.

26 "There *are* Mē'shech and Tū'bal and all
their multitudes,
With all their graves around it,
All of them uncircumcised, slain by
the sword,
Though they caused their terror in the
land of the living.

32:17–32 A catalog of the nations in Sheol (the OT place of the dead), whom Pharaoh would join. Through a roll call of five nations (vv. 22–30) and a cadenced repetitiveness in the announcement of their fates, Ezekiel heightened the sense of doom and horror approaching Pharaoh as he found his own place in Sheol. See also Is. 14 for a similar lament over the king of Babylon.

27 They do not lie with the mighty
Who are fallen of the uncircumcised,
Who have gone down to hell with
their weapons of war;
They have laid their swords under
their heads,
But their iniquities will be on their
bones,
Because of the terror of the mighty in
the land of the living.
28 Yes, you shall be broken in the midst
of the uncircumcised,
And lie with *those* slain by the sword.

29 "There *is* Ē′dom,
Her kings and all her princes,
Who despite their might
Are laid beside *those* slain by the
sword;
They shall lie with the uncircumcised,
And with those who go down to the
Pit.
30 There *are* the princes of the north,
All of them, and all the Sī·dō′ni·ans,
Who have gone down with the slain
In shame at the terror which they
caused by their might;
They lie uncircumcised with *those*
slain by the sword,
And bear their shame with those who
go down to the Pit.

31 "Pharaoh will see them
And be comforted over all his
multitude,
Pharaoh and all his army,
Slain by the sword,"
Says the Lord GOD.

32 "For I have caused My terror in the
land of the living;
And he shall be placed in the midst of
the uncircumcised
With *those* slain by the sword,
Pharaoh and all his multitude,"
Says the Lord GOD.

CHAPTER 33

The Watchman and His Message

Again the word of the LORD came to me,
saying, 2"Son of man, speak to the children
of your people, and say to them: 'When I
bring the sword upon a land, and the peo-
ple of the land take a man from their terri-
tory and make him their watchman, 3when
he sees the sword coming upon the land, if
he blows the trumpet and warns the peo-
ple, 4then whoever hears the sound of the
trumpet and does not take warning, if the
sword comes and takes him away, his
blood shall be on his *own* head. 5He heard
the sound of the trumpet, but did not take
warning; his blood shall be upon himself.
But he who takes warning will save his life.
6But if the watchman sees the sword com-
ing and does not blow the trumpet, and the
people are not warned, and the sword
comes and takes *any* person from among
them, he is taken away in his iniquity; but
his blood I will require at the watchman's
hand.'

7"So you, son of man: I have made you a

32:28 you: Pharaoh.

32:31, 32 Pharaoh will . . . be comforted: Only in the sense that "misery loves company."

33:1—48:35 This third major section of the book is a message of hope. Until Jerusalem had fallen, Ezekiel's message was predominantly negative, insisting the city would be destroyed. But after word of that event came (33:21), God's message immediately turned to hope: hope for new leadership (ch. 34), a new spirit (chs. 36; 37), a new victory (chs. 38; 39), and a new temple (chs. 40—48).

33:1–6 The watchman's responsibility is to see and warn of approaching danger. If he fails in that, he has failed in the purpose for which he was appointed.

33:7–9 I will require: Each watchman is accountable to God for the assignment He has given him. God holds us responsible to share the gospel with those around us: our family, friends, co-workers. Have we faithfully fulfilled our duty in this area?

watchman for the house of Israel; therefore you shall hear a word from My mouth and warn them for Me. 8When I say to the wicked, 'O wicked *man,* you shall surely die!' and you do not speak to warn the wicked from his way, that wicked *man* shall die in his iniquity; but his blood I will require at your hand. 9Nevertheless if you warn the wicked to turn from his way, and he does not turn from his way, he shall die in his iniquity; but you have delivered your soul.

10"Therefore you, O son of man, say to the house of Israel: 'Thus you say, "If our transgressions and our sins *lie* upon us, and we pine away in them, how can we then live?" ' 11Say to them: '*As* I live,' says the Lord GOD, 'I have no pleasure in the death of the wicked, but that the wicked turn from his way and live. Turn, turn from your evil ways! For why should you die, O house of Israel?'

The Fairness of God's Judgment

12"Therefore you, O son of man, say to the children of your people: 'The righteousness of the righteous man shall not deliver him in the day of his transgression; as for the wickedness of the wicked, he shall not fall because of it in the day that he turns from his wickedness; nor shall the righteous be able to live because of *his righteousness* in the day that he sins.' 13When I say to the righteous *that* he shall surely live, but he trusts in his own righteousness and commits iniquity, none of his righteous works shall be remembered; but because of the iniquity that he has committed, he shall die. 14Again, when I say to the wicked, 'You shall surely die,' if he turns from his sin and does what is lawful and right, 15*if* the wicked restores the pledge, gives back what he has stolen, and walks in the statutes of life without committing iniquity, he shall surely live; he shall not die. 16None of his sins which he has committed shall be remembered against him; he has done what is lawful and right; he shall surely live.

17"Yet the children of your people say, 'The way of the LORD is not fair.' But it is their way which is not fair! 18When the righteous turns from his righteousness and commits iniquity, he shall die because of it. 19But when the wicked turns from his wickedness and does what is lawful and right, he shall live because of it. 20Yet you say, 'The way of the LORD is not fair.' O house of Israel, I will judge every one of you according to his own ways."

The Fall of Jerusalem

21And it came to pass in the twelfth year of our captivity, in the tenth *month,* on the fifth *day* of the month, *that* one who had escaped from Jerusalem came to me and said, "The city has been captured!"

22Now the hand of the LORD had been upon me the evening before the man came who had escaped. And He had opened my mouth; so when he came to me in the morning, my mouth was opened, and I was no longer mute.

The Cause of Judah's Ruin

23Then the word of the LORD came to me, saying: 24"Son of man, they who inhabit those ruins in the land of Israel are saying, 'Abraham was only one, and he inherited the land. But we *are* many; the land has been given to us as a possession.'

25"Therefore say to them, 'Thus says the Lord GOD: "You eat *meat* with blood, you lift up your eyes toward your idols, and shed blood. Should you then possess the

---

33:23–29 they who inhabit those ruins: Even after the destruction of city and temple, the few who were left fancied themselves the righteous remnant, when in fact they, too, were wicked and marked for destruction. See Jer. 42:13–22.

33:25 eat meat with blood: In violation of the Mosaic law (see note on Lev. 7:22–27).

land? [26]You rely on your sword, you commit abominations, and you defile one another's wives. Should you then possess the land?" '

[27]"Say thus to them, 'Thus says the Lord GOD: "*As* I live, surely those who *are* in the ruins shall fall by the sword, and the one who *is* in the open field I will give to the beasts to be devoured, and those who *are* in the strongholds and caves shall die of the pestilence. [28]For I will make the land most desolate, her arrogant strength shall cease, and the mountains of Israel shall be so desolate that no one will pass through. [29]Then they shall know that I *am* the LORD, when I have made the land most desolate because of all their abominations which they have committed." '

Hearing and Not Doing

[30]"As for you, son of man, the children of your people are talking about you beside the walls and in the doors of the houses; and they speak to one another, everyone saying to his brother, 'Please come and hear what the word is that comes from the LORD.' [31]So they come to you as people do, they sit before you *as* My people, and they hear your words, but they do not do them; for with their mouth they show much love, *but* their hearts pursue their *own* gain. [32]Indeed you *are* to them as a very lovely song of one who has a pleasant voice and can play well on an instrument; for they hear your words, but they do not do them. [33]And when this comes to pass—surely it will come—then they will know that a prophet has been among them."

CHAPTER 34

Irresponsible Shepherds

And the word of the LORD came to me, saying, [2]"Son of man, prophesy against the shepherds of Israel, prophesy and say to them, 'Thus says the Lord GOD to the shepherds: "Woe to the shepherds of Israel who feed themselves! Should not the shepherds feed the flocks? [3]You eat the fat and clothe yourselves with the wool; you slaughter the fatlings, *but* you do not feed the flock. [4]The weak you have not strengthened, nor have you healed those who were sick, nor bound up the broken, nor brought back what was driven away, nor sought what was lost; but with force and cruelty you have ruled them. [5]So they were scattered because *there was* no shepherd; and they became food for all the beasts of the field when they were scattered. [6]My sheep wandered through all the mountains, and on every high hill; yes, My flock was scattered over the whole face of the earth, and no one was seeking or searching *for them.*"

[7]'Therefore, you shepherds, hear the word of the LORD: [8]"*As* I live," says the Lord GOD, "surely because My flock became a prey, and My flock became food for every beast of the field, because *there was* no shepherd, nor did My shepherds search for My flock, but the shepherds fed themselves and did not feed My flock"— [9]therefore, O shepherds, hear the word of the LORD! [10]Thus says the Lord GOD: "Behold, I *am* against the shepherds, and I will require My flock at their hand; I will cause them to cease feeding the sheep, and the shepherds shall feed themselves no more;

33:30–33 come and hear: Now that Ezekiel's predictions had come true, the people were entranced by his evident skill. Nevertheless, they did not apply what he was saying to their own lives. The prophets were first of all moral preachers and only secondarily tellers of the future. Today God expects us to apply His Word to our life, being "doers of the word, and not hearers only" (James 1:22).

34:2–4 shepherds: In Scripture and in other sources, kings are often portrayed as shepherds of the people. But many of Judah's kings had enriched themselves at the people's expense.

34:5, 6 beasts of the field: Wild beasts of prey. Here they represent the nations that had preyed on Judah.

for I will deliver My flock from their
mouths, that they may no longer be food
for them."

God, the True Shepherd

11'For thus says the Lord GOD: "Indeed I
Myself will search for My sheep and seek
them out. 12As a shepherd seeks out his
flock on the day he is among his scattered
sheep, so will I seek out My sheep and de-
liver them from all the places where they
were scattered on a cloudy and dark day.
13And I will bring them out from the peo-
ples and gather them from the countries,
and will bring them to their own land; I
will feed them on the mountains of Israel,
in the valleys and in all the inhabited
places of the country. 14I will feed them in
good pasture, and their fold shall be on the
high mountains of Israel. There they shall
lie down in a good fold and feed in rich
pasture on the mountains of Israel. 15I will
feed My flock, and I will make them lie
down," says the Lord GOD. 16"I will seek
what was lost and bring back what was
driven away, bind up the broken and
strengthen what was sick; but I will de-
stroy the fat and the strong, and feed them
in judgment."

17'And *as for* you, O My flock, thus says
the Lord GOD: "Behold, I shall judge be-
tween sheep and sheep, between rams and
goats. 18*Is it* too little for you to have eaten
up the good pasture, that you must tread
down with your feet the residue of your
pasture—and to have drunk of the clear
waters, that you must foul the residue with
your feet? 19And *as for* My flock, they eat
what you have trampled with your feet,
and they drink what you have fouled with
your feet."

20'Therefore thus says the Lord GOD to
them: "Behold, I Myself will judge be-
tween the fat and the lean sheep. 21Because
you have pushed with side and shoulder,
butted all the weak ones with your horns,
and scattered them abroad, 22therefore I
will save My flock, and they shall no
longer be a prey; and I will judge between
sheep and sheep. 23I will establish one
shepherd over them, and he shall feed
them—My servant David. He shall feed
them and be their shepherd. 24And I, the
LORD, will be their God, and My servant
David a prince among them; I, the LORD,
have spoken.

25"I will make a covenant of peace with
them, and cause wild beasts to cease from
the land; and they will dwell safely in the
wilderness and sleep in the woods. 26I will
make them and the places all around My
hill a blessing; and I will cause showers to
come down in their season; there shall be
showers of blessing. 27Then the trees of the
field shall yield their fruit, and the earth
shall yield her increase. They shall be safe
in their land; and they shall know that I *am*
the LORD, when I have broken the bands of
their yoke and delivered them from the
hand of those who enslaved them. 28And
they shall no longer be a prey for the na-
tions, nor shall beasts of the land devour
them; but they shall dwell safely, and no
one shall make *them* afraid. 29I will raise up
for them a garden of renown, and they
shall no longer be consumed with hunger

34:13 I will bring them out: From the Exile. This would be a truly miraculous event, because no dispersed people had ever before returned to their homeland.

34:14, 15 In that day the **high mountains** would be dedicated to the glory of God, and not to pagan deities. **rich pasture**: The best summer pasture in the Near East has always been in the mountains.

34:23, 24 The promise of **one shepherd . . . My servant David** looks ahead to Jesus, who called Himself "the good shepherd" (John 10:11).

34:25 covenant of peace: A new covenant, which will be effective. The **wilderness** and the **woods** are especially dangerous places for sheep. If they become safe, the whole land will be safe.

in the land, nor bear the shame of the Gen-
tiles anymore. 30Thus they shall know that
I, the LORD their God, *am* with them, and
they, the house of Israel, *are* My people,"
says the Lord GOD.' "

31"You are My flock, the flock of My pas-
ture; you *are* men, *and* I *am* your God," says
the Lord GOD.

CHAPTER 35

Judgment on Mount Seir

Moreover the word of the LORD came to
me, saying, 2"Son of man, set your face
against Mount Sē'ir and prophesy against
it, 3and say to it, 'Thus says the Lord GOD:

"Behold, O Mount Sē'ir, I *am* against
you;
I will stretch out My hand against
you,
And make you most desolate;
4 I shall lay your cities waste,
And you shall be desolate.
Then you shall know that I *am* the
LORD.

5"Because you have had an ancient ha-
tred, and have shed *the blood of* the children
of Israel by the power of the sword at the
time of their calamity, *when* their iniquity
came to an end, 6therefore, *as* I live," says
the Lord GOD, "I will prepare you for
blood, and blood shall pursue you; since
you have not hated blood, therefore blood
shall pursue you. 7Thus I will make Mount
Sē'ir most desolate, and cut off from it the
one who leaves and the one who returns.
8And I will fill its mountains with the slain;
on your hills and in your valleys and in all
your ravines those who are slain by the
sword shall fall. 9I will make you perpetu-
ally desolate, and your cities shall be unin-
habited; then you shall know that I *am* the
LORD.

10"Because you have said, 'These two
nations and these two countries shall be
mine, and we will possess them,' although
the LORD was there, 11therefore, *as* I live,"
says the Lord GOD, "I will do according to
your anger and according to the envy
which you showed in your hatred against
them; and I will make Myself known
among them when I judge you. 12Then you
shall know that I *am* the LORD. I have heard
all your blasphemies which you have spo-
ken against the mountains of Israel, say-
ing, 'They are desolate; they are given to us
to consume.' 13Thus with your mouth you
have boasted against Me and multiplied
your words against Me; I have heard
them."

14"Thus says the Lord GOD: "The whole
earth will rejoice when I make you deso-
late. 15As you rejoiced because the inheri-
tance of the house of Israel was desolate, so
I will do to you; you shall be desolate, O
Mount Sē'ir, as well as all of Ē'dom—all of
it! Then they shall know that I *am* the
LORD." '

CHAPTER 36

Blessing on Israel

"And you, son of man, prophesy to the
mountains of Israel, and say, 'O mountains
of Israel, hear the word of the LORD! 2Thus
says the Lord GOD: "Because the enemy
has said of you, 'Aha! The ancient heights
have become our possession,' " ' 3therefore
prophesy, and say, 'Thus says the Lord
GOD: "Because they made *you* desolate and
swallowed you up on every side, so that
you became the possession of the rest of

35:5 an ancient hatred: The Edomites were descended from Esau, whose grievance against his brother Jacob was carried on by his posterity, though Esau himself eventually forgave Jacob (Gen. 33:4).

36:1–7 The **mountains** are the characteristic feature of Israel's topography and were the site of her idolatry. Here personified, they were assured that their uncleanness would be purified and their fruitfulness restored.

the nations, and you are taken up by the lips of talkers and slandered by the people"— [4]therefore, O mountains of Israel, hear the word of the Lord GOD! Thus says the Lord GOD to the mountains, the hills, the rivers, the valleys, the desolate wastes, and the cities that have been forsaken, which became plunder and mockery to the rest of the nations all around— [5]therefore thus says the Lord GOD: "Surely I have spoken in My burning jealousy against the rest of the nations and against all Ē'dom, who gave My land to themselves as a possession, with wholehearted joy *and* spiteful minds, in order to plunder its open country." '

[6]"Therefore prophesy concerning the land of Israel, and say to the mountains, the hills, the rivers, and the valleys, 'Thus says the Lord GOD: "Behold, I have spoken in My jealousy and My fury, because you have borne the shame of the nations." [7]Therefore thus says the Lord GOD: "I have raised My hand in an oath that surely the nations that *are* around you shall bear their own shame. [8]But you, O mountains of Israel, you shall shoot forth your branches and yield your fruit to My people Israel, for they are about to come. [9]For indeed I *am* for you, and I will turn to you, and you shall be tilled and sown. [10]I will multiply men upon you, all the house of Israel, all of it; and the cities shall be inhabited and the ruins rebuilt. [11]I will multiply upon you man and beast; and they shall increase and bear young; I will make you inhabited as in former times, and do better *for you* than at your beginnings. Then you shall know that I *am* the LORD. [12]Yes, I will cause men to walk on you, My people Israel; they shall take possession of you, and you shall be their inheritance; no more shall you bereave them *of children*."

[13]'Thus says the Lord GOD: "Because they say to you, 'You devour men and bereave your nation *of children*,' [14]therefore you shall devour men no more, nor bereave your nation anymore," says the Lord GOD. [15]Nor will I let you hear the taunts of the nations anymore, nor bear the reproach of the peoples anymore, nor shall you cause your nation to stumble anymore," says the Lord GOD.' "

The Renewal of Israel

[16]Moreover the word of the LORD came to me, saying: [17]"Son of man, when the house of Israel dwelt in their own land, they defiled it by their own ways and deeds; to Me their way was like the uncleanness of a woman in her customary impurity. [18]Therefore I poured out My fury on them for the blood they had shed on the land, and for their idols *with which* they had defiled it. [19]So I scattered them among the nations, and they were dispersed throughout the countries; I judged them according to their ways and their deeds. [20]When they came to the nations, wherever they went, they profaned My holy name— when they said of them, 'These *are* the people of the LORD, *and* yet they have gone out of His land.' [21]But I had concern for My holy name, which the house of Israel had profaned among the nations wherever they went.

[22]"Therefore say to the house of Israel, 'Thus says the Lord GOD: "I do not do *this* for your sake, O house of Israel, but for My holy name's sake, which you have profaned among the nations wherever you went. [23]And I will sanctify My great name, which has been profaned among the nations, which you have profaned in their midst; and the nations shall know that I *am* the LORD," says the Lord GOD, "when I am

---

36:20–24 God's **concern** for His **holy name** would cause Him to bring the Exile to an end, and put His Spirit in His people (v. 27).

36:20 profaned My holy name: The Hebrew people by being in captivity made it appear that God was helpless to deliver them. We profane His name when we make God appear less than He is.

hallowed in you before their eyes. 24For I will take you from among the nations, gather you out of all countries, and bring you into your own land. 25Then I will sprinkle clean water on you, and you shall be clean; I will cleanse you from all your filthiness and from all your idols. 26I will give you a new heart and put a new spirit within you; I will take the heart of stone out of your flesh and give you a heart of flesh. 27I will put My Spirit within you and cause you to walk in My statutes, and you will keep My judgments and do *them.* 28Then you shall dwell in the land that I gave to your fathers; you shall be My people, and I will be your God. 29I will deliver you from all your uncleannesses. I will call for the grain and multiply it, and bring no famine upon you. 30And I will multiply the fruit of your trees and the increase of your fields, so that you need never again bear the reproach of famine among the nations. 31Then you will remember your evil ways and your deeds that *were* not good; and you will loathe yourselves in your own sight, for your iniquities and your abominations. 32Not for your sake do I do *this,*" says the Lord GOD, "let it be known to you. Be ashamed and confounded for your own ways, O house of Israel!"

33'Thus says the Lord GOD: "On the day that I cleanse you from all your iniquities, I will also enable *you* to dwell in the cities, and the ruins shall be rebuilt. 34The desolate land shall be tilled instead of lying desolate in the sight of all who pass by. 35So they will say, 'This land that was desolate has become like the garden of Eden; and the wasted, desolate, and ruined cities *are now* fortified *and* inhabited.' 36Then the nations which are left all around you shall know that I, the LORD, have rebuilt the ruined places *and* planted what was desolate. I, the LORD, have spoken *it,* and I will do *it.*"

37'Thus says the Lord GOD: "I will also let the house of Israel inquire of Me to do this for them: I will increase their men like a flock. 38Like a flock *offered as* holy *sacrifices,* like the flock at Jerusalem on its feast days, so shall the ruined cities be filled with flocks of men. Then they shall know that I *am* the LORD." ' "

CHAPTER 37

The Dry Bones Live

The hand of the LORD came upon me and brought me out in the Spirit of the LORD, and set me down in the midst of the valley; and it *was* full of bones. 2Then He caused me to pass by them all around, and behold, *there were* very many in the open valley; and indeed *they were* very dry. 3And He said to me, "Son of man, can these bones live?"

So I answered, "O Lord GOD, You know."

4Again He said to me, "Prophesy to

36:25–29 The cleansing of the Spirit, and the gift of the **new heart** and **new spirit**, enabling the believer to love God with an undivided love, were here promised as clearly as possible before these gifts were actually bestowed.

36:26 When God takes over a person's heart, He transforms that individual into a new creature. Christians should be identified by their tender hearts, filled with a love only God can give.

36:27 My Spirit within you: The new covenant has as its genius the change, not of the commandments, but of the human heart. It is by an infusion of God's Spirit that humans are enabled to obey.

36:32 Not for your sake: The Hebrew people had done nothing to deserve God's deliverance.

37:1–14 The vision of the valley of dry bones. The truths of 36:16–38 are restated in pictorial form.

Dry Bones

Claire Cloninger

When our lives are feeling as dry and disconnected as Ezekiel's bones, the Lord our God stands ready and waiting to gather the pieces and breathe into our dryness the breath of His incredible new life.

As we center our hearts on Him, He begins to give us eyes to see the beauty in others, the blessing hidden in the small disjointed moment, and the ability to stop and focus on each.

He longs to assemble the parts and pieces of who we are into lives of wholeness and continuity that only He can create.

"He longs to assemble the parts and pieces of who we are into lives of wholeness."

these bones, and say to them, 'O dry bones,
hear the word of the LORD! 5Thus says the
Lord GOD to these bones: "Surely I will
cause breath to enter into you, and you
shall live. 6I will put sinews on you and
bring flesh upon you, cover you with skin
and put breath in you; and you shall live.
Then you shall know that I *am* the
LORD." ' "

7So I prophesied as I was commanded;
and as I prophesied, there was a noise, and
suddenly a rattling; and the bones came to-
gether, bone to bone. 8Indeed, as I looked,
the sinews and the flesh came upon them,
and the skin covered them over; but *there
was* no breath in them.

9Also He said to me, "Prophesy to the
breath, prophesy, son of man, and say to
the breath, 'Thus says the Lord GOD:
"Come from the four winds, O breath, and
breathe on these slain, that they may
live." ' " 10So I prophesied as He com-
manded me, and breath came into them,
and they lived, and stood upon their feet,
an exceedingly great army.

11Then He said to me, "Son of man, these
bones are the whole house of Israel. They
indeed say, 'Our bones are dry, our hope is
lost, and we ourselves are cut off!' 12There-
fore prophesy and say to them, 'Thus says
the Lord GOD: "Behold, O My people, I will
open your graves and cause you to come
up from your graves, and bring you into
the land of Israel. 13Then you shall know
that I *am* the LORD, when I have opened
your graves, O My people, and brought
you up from your graves. 14I will put
My Spirit in you, and you shall live, and
I will place you in your own land. Then
you shall know that I, the LORD, have
spoken *it* and performed *it*," says the
LORD.' "

37:9 "Breath," "wind," and "spirit" all translate the same Hebrew word. Without breath or spirit, the bodies were still only corpses. **four winds**: From the four corners of the earth. The nation could be restored, given a new body as it were. But until the Spirit of God (v. 14) came upon them, there was no hope for them (see Is. 32:14–19; Joel 2:28, 29).

One Kingdom, One King

15Again the word of the LORD came to
me, saying, 16"As for you, son of man, take
a stick for yourself and write on it: 'For Ju-
dah and for the children of Israel, his com-
panions.' Then take another stick and
write on it, 'For Joseph, the stick of
Ē'phra·im, and *for* all the house of Israel,
his companions.' 17Then join them one to
another for yourself into one stick, and
they will become one in your hand.

18"And when the children of your peo-
ple speak to you, saying, 'Will you not
show us what you *mean* by these?'— 19say
to them, 'Thus says the Lord GOD: "Surely
I will take the stick of Joseph, which *is* in
the hand of Ē'phra·im, and the tribes of Is-
rael, his companions; and I will join them
with it, with the stick of Judah, and make
them one stick, and they will be one in My
hand." ' 20And the sticks on which you
write will be in your hand before their
eyes.

21"Then say to them, 'Thus says the Lord
GOD: "Surely I will take the children of Is-
rael from among the nations, wherever
they have gone, and will gather them from
every side and bring them into their own
land; 22and I will make them one nation in
the land, on the mountains of Israel; and
one king shall be king over them all; they
shall no longer be two nations, nor shall
they ever be divided into two kingdoms
again. 23They shall not defile themselves
anymore with their idols, nor with their
detestable things, nor with any of their
transgressions; but I will deliver them
from all their dwelling places in which
they have sinned, and will cleanse them.
Then they shall be My people, and I will be
their God.

24"David My servant *shall be* king over
them, and they shall all have one shep-
herd; they shall also walk in My judgments
and observe My statutes, and do them.
25Then they shall dwell in the land that I
have given to Jacob My servant, where
your fathers dwelt; and they shall dwell
there, they, their children, and their chil-
dren's children, forever; and My servant
David *shall be* their prince forever. 26More-
over I will make a covenant of peace with
them, and it shall be an everlasting
covenant with them; I will establish them
and multiply them, and I will set My sanc-
tuary in their midst forevermore. 27My
tabernacle also shall be with them; indeed
I will be their God, and they shall be My
people. 28The nations also will know that I,
the LORD, sanctify Israel, when My sanctu-
ary is in their midst forevermore." ' "

CHAPTER 38

Gog and Allies Attack Israel

Now the word of the LORD came to me,
saying, 2"Son of man, set your face against
Gog, of the land of Mā'gog, the prince of
Rosh,[a] Mē'shech, and Tū'bal, and proph-
esy against him, 3and say, 'Thus says the
Lord GOD: "Behold, I *am* against you, O
Gog, the prince of Rosh, Mē'shech, and
Tū'bal. 4I will turn you around, put hooks
into your jaws, and lead you out, with all
your army, horses, and horsemen, all

38:2 [a]Targum, Vulgate, and Aquila read *chief prince of* (also verse 3).

37:16, 17 The two sticks represent the two kingdoms of the Israelite people after the division following Solomon's death. **Joseph . . . Ephraim**: The northern kingdom, Israel. Many citizens of the northern kingdom had been carried into exile by the Assyrians nearly 150 years before. Yet some of their descendants would join in the return, when the two nations again would become one.

38:2 Gog, an aggressive foreign ruler, and **Magog**, first mentioned in Genesis 10:2 as a son of Japheth, settled to North Israel. Magog may be in Turkey because of its association with **Meshech** and **Tubal**. Gog and Magog have become bywords for barbarian invasions from the north (see Rev. 20:8). **Rosh** is probably a primitive form of Russia.

splendidly clothed, a great company *with* bucklers and shields, all of them handling swords. 5Persia, Ethiopia,[a] and Lib′ya[b] are with them, all of them *with* shield and helmet; 6Gō′mer and all its troops; the house of Tō·gar′mah *from* the far north and all its troops—many people *are* with you.

7"Prepare yourself and be ready, you and all your companies that are gathered about you; and be a guard for them. 8After many days you will be visited. In the latter years you will come into the land of those brought back from the sword *and* gathered from many people on the mountains of Israel, which had long been desolate; they were brought out of the nations, and now all of them dwell safely. 9You will ascend, coming like a storm, covering the land like a cloud, you and all your troops and many peoples with you."

10'Thus says the Lord GOD: "On that day it shall come to pass *that* thoughts will arise in your mind, and you will make an evil plan: 11You will say, 'I will go up against a land of unwalled villages; I will go to a peaceful people, who dwell safely, all of them dwelling without walls, and having neither bars nor gates'— 12to take plunder and to take booty, to stretch out your hand against the waste places *that are again* inhabited, and against a people gathered from the nations, who have acquired livestock and goods, who dwell in the midst of the land. 13Shē′ba, Dē′dan, the merchants of Tar′shish, and all their young lions will say to you, 'Have you come to take plunder? Have you gathered your army to take booty, to carry away silver and gold, to take away livestock and goods, to take great plunder?' " '

14"Therefore, son of man, prophesy and say to Gog, 'Thus says the Lord GOD: "On that day when My people Israel dwell safely, will you not know *it?* 15Then you will come from your place out of the far north, you and many peoples with you, all of them riding on horses, a great company and a mighty army. 16You will come up against My people Israel like a cloud, to cover the land. It will be in the latter days that I will bring you against My land, so that the nations may know Me, when I am hallowed in you, O Gog, before their eyes." 17Thus says the Lord GOD: "Are *you* he of whom I have spoken in former days by My servants the prophets of Israel, who prophesied for years in those days that I would bring you against them?

Judgment on Gog

18"And it will come to pass at the same time, when Gog comes against the land of Israel," says the Lord GOD, "*that* My fury will show in My face. 19For in My jealousy *and* in the fire of My wrath I have spoken: 'Surely in that day there shall be a great earthquake in the land of Israel, 20so that the fish of the sea, the birds of the heavens, the beasts of the field, all creeping things that creep on the earth, and all men who *are* on the face of the earth shall shake at My presence. The mountains shall be thrown down, the steep places shall fall, and every wall shall fall to the ground.' 21I will call for a sword against Gog throughout all My mountains," says the Lord GOD. "Every man's sword will be against his brother. 22And I will bring him to judgment with pestilence and bloodshed; I will rain down on him, on his troops, and on the many peoples who *are* with him, flooding rain, great hailstones, fire, and brimstone. 23Thus I will magnify Myself and sanctify Myself, and I will be known in the eyes of

38:5 [a]Hebrew *Cush* [b]Hebrew *Put*

38:5, 6 These nations of Ezekiel's own time were used as representatives of the opponents of God in the last days.

38:13 Merchants from the trading nations of **Sheba**, **Dedan**, and **Tarshish** would be interested in buying the **plunder** from the attacking armies or in trading for prisoners to be sold as slaves. **young lions**: Their leaders.

many nations. Then they shall know that I
am the LORD." '

CHAPTER 39

Gog's Armies Destroyed

"And you, son of man, prophesy
against Gog, and say, 'Thus says the Lord
GOD: "Behold, I *am* against you, O Gog, the
prince of Rosh,[a] Mē'shech, and Tū'bal;
2and I will turn you around and lead you
on, bringing you up from the far north,
and bring you against the mountains of Is-
rael. 3Then I will knock the bow out of your
left hand, and cause the arrows to fall out
of your right hand. 4You shall fall upon the
mountains of Israel, you and all your
troops and the peoples who *are* with you; I
will give you to birds of prey of every sort
and *to* the beasts of the field to be de-
voured. 5You shall fall on the open field;
for I have spoken," says the Lord GOD.
6"And I will send fire on Mā'gog and on
those who live in security in the coast-
lands. Then they shall know that I *am* the
LORD. 7So I will make My holy name
known in the midst of My people Israel,
and I will not *let them* profane My holy
name anymore. Then the nations shall
know that *I am* the LORD, the Holy One in
Israel. 8Surely it is coming, and it shall be
done," says the Lord GOD. "This *is* the day
of which I have spoken.

9"Then those who dwell in the cities of
Israel will go out and set on fire and burn
the weapons, both the shields and buck-
lers, the bows and arrows, the javelins and
spears; and they will make fires with them
for seven years. 10They will not take wood
from the field nor cut down *any* from the
forests, because they will make fires with
the weapons; and they will plunder those
who plundered them, and pillage those
who pillaged them," says the Lord GOD.

39:1 [a]Targum, Vulgate and Aquila read *chief prince of.*
39:11 [a]Literally *The Multitude of Gog* 39:14 [a]Literally *those who pass through*

The Burial of Gog

11"It will come to pass in that day *that* I
will give Gog a burial place there in Israel,
the valley of those who pass by east of the
sea; and it will obstruct travelers, because
there they will bury Gog and all his multi-
tude. Therefore they will call *it* the Valley
of Hā'mon Gog.[a] 12For seven months the
house of Israel will be burying them, in or-
der to cleanse the land. 13Indeed all the
people of the land will be burying, and
they will gain renown for it on the day that
I am glorified," says the Lord GOD. 14"They
will set apart men regularly employed,
with the help of a search party,[a] to pass
through the land and bury those bodies re-
maining on the ground, in order to cleanse
it. At the end of seven months they will
make a search. 15The search party will pass
through the land; and *when anyone* sees a
man's bone, he shall set up a marker by it,
till the buriers have buried it in the Valley
of Hā'mon Gog. 16*The* name of *the* city *will*
also *be* Ha·mō'nah. Thus they shall cleanse
the land." '

A Triumphant Festival

17"And as for you, son of man, thus says
the Lord GOD, 'Speak to every sort of bird
and to every beast of the field:

39:9, 10 God utterly destroys Israel's enemies, despite their having men and weapons so vast as to be humanly invincible.

39:11–16 A burial place is hardly the plunder Gog anticipated. He and his hordes will be buried **east of the sea** (Dead Sea), outside Israel's territory. The **seven months** of burial will **obstruct travelers** on the King's Highway, the major north-south road through that region.

39:17–20 Because Gog and his armies will neither acknowledge God nor sacrifice to Him, they will become a sacrificial feast which God will spread for all the carrion eaters of the land. This section is a detailed picture of the prediction made in v. 4. The feast for the birds and beasts precedes the burial.

"Assemble yourselves and come;
Gather together from all sides to My sacrificial meal
Which I am sacrificing for you,
A great sacrificial meal on the mountains of Israel,
That you may eat flesh and drink blood.
18 You shall eat the flesh of the mighty,
Drink the blood of the princes of the earth,
Of rams and lambs,
Of goats and bulls,
All of them fatlings of Bā'shan.
19 You shall eat fat till you are full,
And drink blood till you are drunk,
At My sacrificial meal
Which I am sacrificing for you.
20 You shall be filled at My table
With horses and riders,
With mighty men
And with all the men of war," says the Lord GOD.

Israel Restored to the Land

21"I will set My glory among the nations;
all the nations shall see My judgment
which I have executed, and My hand
which I have laid on them. 22So the house
of Israel shall know that I *am* the LORD their
God from that day forward. 23The Gentiles
shall know that the house of Israel went
into captivity for their iniquity; because
they were unfaithful to Me, therefore I hid
My face from them. I gave them into the
hand of their enemies, and they all fell by
the sword. 24According to their unclean-
ness and according to their transgressions I
have dealt with them, and hidden My face
from them." '

25"Therefore thus says the Lord GOD:
'Now I will bring back the captives of Ja-
cob, and have mercy on the whole house of
Israel; and I will be jealous for My holy
name— 26after they have borne their

Thank You, Lord, that You will bring back the captives of Jacob, and have mercy on Your people, the whole house of Israel.

adapted from Ezekiel 39:25

shame, and all their unfaithfulness in
which they were unfaithful to Me, when
they dwelt safely in their *own* land and no
one made *them* afraid. 27When I have
brought them back from the peoples and
gathered them out of their enemies' lands,
and I am hallowed in them in the sight
of many nations, 28then they shall know
that I *am* the LORD their God, who sent
them into captivity among the nations,
but also brought them back to their land,
and left none of them captive any longer.
29And I will not hide My face from them
anymore; for I shall have poured out My
Spirit on the house of Israel,' says the Lord
GOD."

CHAPTER 40

A New City, a New Temple

In the twenty-fifth year of our captivity,
at the beginning of the year, on the tenth
day of the month, in the fourteenth year af-
ter the city was captured, on the very same
day the hand of the LORD was upon me;
and He took me there. 2In the visions of
God He took me into the land of Israel and
set me on a very high mountain; on it to-
ward the south *was* something like the
structure of a city. 3He took me there, and
behold, *there was* a man whose appearance
was like the appearance of bronze. He had
a line of flax and a measuring rod in his
hand, and he stood in the gateway.

4And the man said to me, "Son of man,

39:18 Even the most powerful are destined for God's sacrificial feast.
40:1—48:35 Ezekiel's vision of the restored temple and land.
40:3 A man: An angelic guide.

look with your eyes and hear with your
ears, and fix your mind on everything I
show you; for you *were* brought here so
that I might show *them* to you. Declare to
the house of Israel everything you see."
5Now there was a wall all around the out-
side of the temple.[a] In the man's hand was
a measuring rod six cubits *long, each being a*
cubit and a handbreadth; and he measured
the width of the wall structure, one rod;
and the height, one rod.

The Eastern Gateway of the Temple

6Then he went to the gateway which
faced east; and he went up its stairs and
measured the threshold of the gateway,
which was one rod wide, and the other
threshold *was* one rod wide. 7Each gate
chamber *was* one rod long and one rod
wide; between the gate chambers *was a*
space of five cubits; and the threshold of the
gateway by the vestibule of the inside gate
was one rod. 8He also measured the
vestibule of the inside gate, one rod. 9Then
he measured the vestibule of the gateway,
eight cubits; and the gateposts, two cubits.
The vestibule of the gate *was* on the inside.
10In the eastern gateway *were* three gate
chambers on one side and three on the
other; the three *were* all the same size; also
the gateposts were of the same size on this
side and that side.

11He measured the width of the entrance
to the gateway, ten cubits; *and* the length of
the gate, thirteen cubits. 12*There was* a space
in front of the gate chambers, one cubit *on*
this side and one cubit on that side; the gate
chambers *were* six cubits on this side and
six cubits on that side. 13Then he measured
the gateway from the roof of *one* gate
chamber to the roof of the other; the width
was twenty-five cubits, as door faces door.
14He measured the gateposts, sixty cubits
high, and the court all around the gateway
extended to the gatepost. 15*From* the front of
the entrance gate to the front of the
vestibule of the inner gate *was* fifty cubits.
16*There were* beveled window *frames* in the
gate chambers and in their intervening
archways on the inside of the gateway all
around, and likewise in the vestibules.
There were windows all around on the
inside. And on each gatepost *were* palm
trees.

The Outer Court

17Then he brought me into the outer
court; and *there were* chambers and a pave-
ment made all around the court; thirty
chambers faced the pavement. 18The pave-
ment was by the side of the gateways, cor-
responding to the length of the gateways;
this was the lower pavement. 19Then he
measured the width from the front of the
lower gateway to the front of the inner
court exterior, one hundred cubits toward
the east and the north.

The Northern Gateway

20On the outer court was also a gateway
facing north, and he measured its length
and its width. 21Its gate chambers, three on
this side and three on that side, its
gateposts and its archways, had the same
measurements as the first gate; its length
was fifty cubits and its width twenty-five
cubits. 22Its windows and those of its arch-
ways, and also its palm trees, *had* the same
measurements as the gateway facing east;
it was ascended by seven steps, and its
archway *was* in front of it. 23A gate of the in-

40:5 [a]Literally *house,* and so elsewhere in this book

40:6–16 The eastern gate was the main entrance to the temple complex and also a gate in the city wall. As such, it was strong (three-chambered, v. 10), large (v. 14), and decorated (v. 16).

40:17–19 In all three of the temples that were constructed (Solomon's, Zerubbabel's, and Herod's) a **court** surrounded the main structure.

40:20–27 The northern and southern gates measured the same as the eastern gate, not for the security of the city, but for the majesty and symmetry of the temple.

ner court was opposite the northern gateway, just as the eastern *gateway;* and he measured from gateway to gateway, one hundred cubits.

The Southern Gateway

24After that he brought me toward the south, and there a gateway was facing south; and he measured its gateposts and archways according to these same measurements. 25*There were* windows in it and in its archways all around like those windows; its length *was* fifty cubits and its width twenty-five cubits. 26Seven steps led up to it, and its archway *was* in front of them; and it had palm trees on its gateposts, one on this side and one on that side. 27*There was* also a gateway on the inner court, facing south; and he measured from gateway to gateway toward the south, one hundred cubits.

Gateways of the Inner Court

28Then he brought me to the inner court through the southern gateway; he measured the southern gateway according to these same measurements. 29Also its gate chambers, its gateposts, and its archways *were* according to these same measurements; *there were* windows in it and in its archways all around; *it was* fifty cubits long and twenty-five cubits wide. 30*There were* archways all around, twenty-five cubits long and five cubits wide. 31Its archways faced the outer court, palm trees *were* on its gateposts, and going up to it *were* eight steps.

32And he brought me into the inner court facing east; he measured the gateway according to these same measurements. 33Also its gate chambers, its gateposts, and its archways *were* according to these same measurements; and *there were* windows in it and in its archways all around; *it was* fifty cubits long and twenty-five cubits wide. 34Its archways faced the outer court, and palm trees *were* on its gateposts on this side and on that side; and going up to it *were* eight steps.

35Then he brought me to the north gateway and measured *it* according to these same measurements— 36also its gate chambers, its gateposts, and its archways. It had windows all around; its length *was* fifty cubits and its width twenty-five cubits. 37Its gateposts faced the outer court, palm trees *were* on its gateposts on this side and on that side, and going up to it *were* eight steps.

Where Sacrifices Were Prepared

38*There was* a chamber and its entrance by the gateposts of the gateway, where they washed the burnt offering. 39In the vestibule of the gateway *were* two tables on this side and two tables on that side, on which to slay the burnt offering, the sin offering, and the trespass offering. 40At the outer side of the vestibule, as one goes up to the entrance of the northern gateway, *were* two tables; and on the other side of the vestibule of the gateway *were* two tables. 41Four tables *were* on this side and four tables on that side, by the side of the gateway, eight tables on which they slaughtered *the sacrifices.* 42*There were* also four tables of hewn stone for the burnt offering, one cubit and a half long, one cubit and a half wide, and one cubit high; on these they laid the instruments with which they slaughtered the burnt offering and the sacrifice. 43Inside *were* hooks, a handbreadth wide, fastened all around; and the flesh of the sacrifices *was* on the tables.

Chambers for Singers and Priests

44Outside the inner gate *were* the chambers for the singers in the inner court, one facing south at the side of the northern gateway, and the other facing north at the side of the southern gateway. 45Then he said to me, "This chamber which faces south *is* for the priests who have charge of the temple. 46The chamber which faces north *is* for the priests who have charge of the altar; these *are* the sons of Zā'dok, from the sons of Levi, who come near the LORD to minister to Him."

Dimensions of the Inner Court and Vestibule

47And he measured the court, one hun-
dred cubits long and one hundred cubits
wide, foursquare. The altar *was* in front of
the temple. 48Then he brought me to the
vestibule of the temple and measured the
doorposts of the vestibule, five cubits on
this side and five cubits on that side; and
the width of the gateway was three cubits
on this side and three cubits on that side.
49The length of the vestibule *was* twenty cu-
bits, and the width eleven cubits; and by
the steps which led up to it *there were* pil-
lars by the doorposts, one on this side and
another on that side.

CHAPTER 41

Dimensions of the Sanctuary

Then he brought me into the sanctuary[a]
and measured the doorposts, six cubits
wide on one side and six cubits wide on
the other side—the width of the taberna-
cle. 2The width of the entryway *was* ten cu-
bits, and the side walls of the entrance *were*
five cubits on this side and five cubits on
the other side; and he measured its length,
forty cubits, and its width, twenty cubits.
3Also he went inside and measured the
doorposts, two cubits; and the entrance,
six cubits *high;* and the width of the en-
trance, seven cubits. 4He measured the
length, twenty cubits; and the width,
twenty cubits, beyond the sanctuary; and
he said to me, "This *is* the Most Holy
Place."

The Side Chambers on the Wall

5Next, he measured the wall of the tem-
ple, six cubits. The width of each side
chamber all around the temple *was* four cu-
bits on every side. 6The side chambers *were*
in three stories, one above the other, thirty
chambers in each story; they rested on
ledges which *were* for the side chambers all
around, that they might be supported, but
not fastened to the wall of the temple. 7As
one went up from story to story, the side
chambers became wider all around, be-
cause their supporting ledges in the wall of
the temple ascended like steps; therefore
the width of the structure increased as one
went up *from* the lowest *story* to the highest
by way of the middle one. 8I also saw an el-
evation all around the temple; it was the
foundation of the side chambers, a full rod,
that is, six cubits *high.* 9The thickness of the
outer wall of the side chambers *was* five cu-
bits, and so also the remaining terrace by
the place of the side chambers of the tem-
ple. 10And between *it and* the *wall* chambers
was a width of twenty cubits all around
the temple on every side. 11The doors of the
side chambers opened on the terrace, one
door toward the north and another toward
the south; and the width of the terrace *was*
five cubits all around.

The Building at the Western End

12The building that faced the separating
courtyard at its western end *was* seventy
cubits wide; the wall of the building *was*
five cubits thick all around, and its length
ninety cubits.

Dimensions and Design of the Temple Area

13So he measured the temple, one hun-
dred cubits long; and the separating court-
yard with the building and its walls *was*
one hundred cubits long; 14also the width
of the eastern face of the temple, including
the separating courtyard, *was* one hundred

41:1 [a]Hebrew *heykal,* here the main room of the temple, sometimes called the *holy place* (compare Exodus 26:33)

41:1 As a priest, Ezekiel was permitted to enter the **sanctuary**.
41:3, 4 The angelic guide went **inside** the **Most Holy Place**, but Ezekiel did not. This was the inner, most sacred, room of the temple, which only the high priest entered, and he only once a year on the Day of Atonement (see Lev. 16:1–4, 34).

cubits. 15He measured the length of the
building behind it, facing the separating
courtyard, with its galleries on the one side
and on the other side, one hundred cubits,
as well as the inner temple and the porches
of the court, 16their doorposts and the
beveled window frames. And the galleries
all around their three stories opposite the
threshold were paneled with wood from
the ground to the windows—the windows
were covered— 17from the space above the
door, even to the inner room,[a] as well as
outside, and on every wall all around, in-
side and outside, by measure.
18And *it was* made with cherubim and
palm trees, a palm tree between cherub
and cherub. *Each* cherub had two faces, 19so
that the face of a man *was* toward a palm
tree on one side, and the face of a young
lion toward a palm tree on the other side;
thus *it was* made throughout the temple all
around. 20From the floor to the space above
the door, and on the wall of the sanctuary,
cherubim and palm trees *were* carved.
21The doorposts of the temple *were*
square, *as was* the front of the sanctuary;
their appearance was similar. 22The altar
was of wood, three cubits high, and its
length two cubits. Its corners, its length,
and its sides *were* of wood; and he said to
me, "This *is* the table that *is* before the
LORD."
23The temple and the sanctuary had two
doors. 24The doors had two panels *apiece,*
two folding panels: two *panels* for one
door and two panels for the other *door.*
25Cherubim and palm trees *were* carved on
the doors of the temple just as they *were*
carved on the walls. A wooden canopy *was*
on the front of the vestibule outside. 26*There
were* beveled window *frames* and palm
trees on one side and on the other, on the
sides of the vestibule—also on the side
chambers of the temple and on the
canopies.

CHAPTER 42

The Chambers for the Priests

Then he brought me out into the outer
court, by the way toward the north; and he
brought me into the chamber which *was*
opposite the separating courtyard, and
which *was* opposite the building toward
the north. 2Facing the length, *which was* one
hundred cubits (the width was fifty cu-
bits), was the north door. 3Opposite the in-
ner court of twenty *cubits,* and opposite the
pavement of the outer court, *was* gallery
against gallery in three *stories.* 4In front of
the chambers, toward the inside, *was* a
walk ten cubits wide, at a distance of one
cubit; and their doors faced north. 5Now
the upper chambers *were* shorter, because
the galleries took away *space* from them
more than from the lower and middle sto-
ries of the building. 6For they *were* in three
stories and did not have pillars like the pil-
lars of the courts; therefore *the upper level*
was shortened more than the lower and
middle levels from the ground up. 7And a
wall which *was* outside ran parallel to the
chambers, at the front of the chambers, to-
ward the outer court; its length *was* fifty
cubits. 8The length of the chambers toward
the outer court *was* fifty cubits, whereas
that facing the temple *was* one hundred cu-
bits. 9At the lower chambers *was* the en-
trance on the east side, as one goes into
them from the outer court.
10Also *there were* chambers in the thick-
ness of the wall of the court toward the
east, opposite the separating courtyard

41:17 [a]Literally *house,* here *the Most Holy Place*

41:18–20 Only **two faces** could be carved into the paneling of the walls, though the cherubim of Ezekiel's visions had four faces (see 1:6, 10).

41:22 the table: Corresponding to the table of showbread (see Ex. 25:23–30).

41:23, 24 The **temple** here means the holy place. The **sanctuary** means the Most Holy Place.

and opposite the building. [11]*There was* a
walk in front of them also, and their ap-
pearance *was* like the chambers which *were*
toward the north; they *were* as long and as
wide as the others, and all their exits and
entrances *were* according to plan. [12]And
corresponding to the doors of the cham-
bers that *were* facing south, as one enters
them, *there was* a door in front of the walk,
the way directly in front of the wall toward
the east.
[13]Then he said to me, "The north cham-
bers *and* the south chambers, which *are* op-
posite the separating courtyard, *are* the
holy chambers where the priests who ap-
proach the LORD shall eat the most holy of-
ferings. There they shall lay the most holy
offerings—the grain offering, the sin offer-
ing, and the trespass offering—for the
place *is* holy. [14]When the priests enter
them, they shall not go out of the holy
chamber into the outer court; but there they
shall leave their garments in which they
minister, for they *are* holy. They shall put
on other garments; then they may ap-
proach *that* which *is* for the people."

Outer Dimensions of the Temple

[15]Now when he had finished measuring
the inner temple, he brought me out
through the gateway that faces toward the
east, and measured it all around. [16]He mea-
sured the east side with the measuring
rod,[a] five hundred rods by the measuring
rod all around. [17]He measured the north
side, five hundred rods by the measuring
rod all around. [18]He measured the south
side, five hundred rods by the measuring
rod. [19]He came around to the west side *and*
measured five hundred rods by the mea-
suring rod. [20]He measured it on the four
sides; it had a wall all around, five hun-
dred *cubits* long and five hundred wide, to
separate the holy areas from the common.

CHAPTER 43

The Temple, the LORD's Dwelling Place

Afterward he brought me to the gate,
the gate that faces toward the east. [2]And
behold, the glory of the God of Israel came
from the way of the east. His voice *was* like
the sound of many waters; and the earth
shone with His glory. [3]*It was* like the ap-
pearance of the vision which I saw—like
the vision which I saw when I[a] came to de-
stroy the city. The visions *were* like the vi-
sion which I saw by the River Chē'bar; and
I fell on my face. [4]And the glory of the
LORD came into the temple by way of the
gate which faces toward the east.
[5]The Spirit lifted me up and brought me
into the inner court; and behold, the glory
of the LORD filled the temple.
[6]Then I heard *Him* speaking to me from
the temple, while a man stood beside me.
[7]And He said to me, "Son of man, *this is* the
place of My throne and the place of the
soles of My feet, where I will dwell in the
midst of the children of Israel forever. No
more shall the house of Israel defile My
holy name, they nor their kings, by their
harlotry or with the carcasses of their kings
on their high places. [8]When they set their
threshold by My threshold, and their door-
post by My doorpost, with a wall between

42:16 [a]Compare 40:5 43:3 [a]Some Hebrew manuscripts and Vulgate read *He*.

42:11 according to plan: A major reason for including all the measurements of these chapters is to show the perfection of all God's plans for His people (see 43:10–12).

43:1–5 God returns to dwell in the new temple. As He had left the old temple by the eastern gate, presaging its destruction (10:18, 19), so now He returned by way of the **gate** which faces **east**.

43:8, 9 their threshold: The structures for worship of pagan deities (and perhaps some of the kings' tombs) had been built within the very precincts of God's own temple, with only a **wall between**. This is a graphic picture of Judah's brazen unfaithfulness to God in her last days.

them and Me, they defiled My holy name by the abominations which they committed; therefore I have consumed them in My anger. [9]Now let them put their harlotry and the carcasses of their kings far away from Me, and I will dwell in their midst forever.

[10]"Son of man, describe the temple to the house of Israel, that they may be ashamed of their iniquities; and let them measure the pattern. [11]And if they are ashamed of all that they have done, make known to them the design of the temple and its arrangement, its exits and its entrances, its entire design and all its ordinances, all its forms and all its laws. Write *it* down in their sight, so that they may keep its whole design and all its ordinances, and perform them. [12]This *is* the law of the temple: The whole area surrounding the mountaintop *is* most holy. Behold, this *is* the law of the temple.

Dimensions of the Altar

[13]"These are the measurements of the altar in cubits (the *cubit is* one cubit and a handbreadth): the base one cubit high and one cubit wide, with a rim all around its edge of one span. This *is* the height of the altar: [14]from the base on the ground to the lower ledge, two cubits; the width of the ledge, one cubit; from the smaller ledge to the larger ledge, four cubits; and the width of the ledge, *one* cubit. [15]The altar hearth *is* four cubits high, with four horns extending upward from the hearth. [16]The altar hearth *is* twelve cubits long, twelve wide, square at its four corners; [17]the ledge, fourteen *cubits* long and fourteen wide on its four sides, with a rim of half a cubit around it; its base, one cubit all around; and its steps face toward the east."

Consecrating the Altar

[18]And He said to me, "Son of man, thus says the Lord GOD: 'These *are* the ordinances for the altar on the day when it is made, for sacrificing burnt offerings on it, and for sprinkling blood on it. [19]You shall give a young bull for a sin offering to the priests, the Lē′vītes, who are of the seed of Zā′dok, who approach Me to minister to Me,' says the Lord GOD. [20]You shall take some of its blood and put *it* on the four horns of the altar, on the four corners of the ledge, and on the rim around it; thus you shall cleanse it and make atonement for it. [21]Then you shall also take the bull of the sin offering, and burn it in the appointed place of the temple, outside the sanctuary. [22]On the second day you shall offer a kid of the goats without blemish for a sin offering; and they shall cleanse the altar, as they cleansed *it* with the bull. [23]When you have finished cleansing *it*, you shall offer a young bull without blemish, and a ram from the flock without blemish. [24]When you offer them before the LORD, the priests shall throw salt on them, and they will offer them up *as* a burnt offering to the LORD. [25]Every day for seven days you shall prepare a goat *for* a sin offering; they shall also prepare a young bull and a ram from the flock, both without blemish. [26]Seven days they shall make atonement for the altar and purify it, and so consecrate *it*. [27]When these days are over it shall be, on the eighth day and thereafter, that the priests shall offer your burnt offerings and your

---

43:10–12 that they may be ashamed: The symmetry, beauty, and purity of the new **temple** as Ezekiel described it to his fellow exiles would cause them to regret their profane treatment of Solomon's temple.

43:19 The **priests** are called **Levites** because they were from the tribe of Levi. Only priests descended from Zadok could attend the altar.

43:21 Burning the sin offering **outside the sanctuary** reflects the instructions of the Mosaic law which required the bull to be burned in a clean place "outside the camp" (see Lev. 4:12, 21).

CHRIST-CENTERED SERVICE

Anne Ortlund

Why do you do voluntary service? Because you enjoy it? Because it makes you a better person? Because it pleases your pastor or your spouse or someone else? Because you feel you need to pitch in and do your share?

God exposed certain "church workers" called Levites in Ezekiel 44 for serving for the reasons above!

They had their eyes on themselves and on others, but not on Him. And God said, "All right, from now on just please people, not Me. You weren't focused on Me before; from now on I won't allow you to be. You can keep on doing church 'busy work,' but I won't let you minister to Me."

It makes all the difference.

"You have access to the Lord Himself! Don't stop short in the vestibule."

An eye fixed on self is full of confusion: "How much commitment is commitment? If I teach a Sunday school class, can I ever go away weekends? If I join the choir, what happens when choir practice comes and I'm exhausted?"

This self-centered thinking says, "I can only be somewhat committed to you because I'm first committed to me."

But fix your eyes on Jesus, and you will be helped the most. You have access to the Lord Himself! Don't stop short in the vestibule.

Are you a "ministry-centered" person? You'll get depleted, irritated, abrasive, and exhausted.

Are you a "Christ-centered" person? Even as you serve Him, you'll stay nourished, happy, rested.

Fix your eyes on Jesus!

peace offerings on the altar; and I will accept you,' says the Lord GOD."

CHAPTER 44

The East Gate and the Prince

Then He brought me back to the outer
gate of the sanctuary which faces toward
the east, but it *was* shut. [2]And the LORD said
to me, "This gate shall be shut; it shall not
be opened, and no man shall enter by it,
because the LORD God of Israel has entered
by it; therefore it shall be shut. [3]*As for* the
prince, *because* he *is* the prince, he may sit
in it to eat bread before the LORD; he shall
enter by way of the vestibule of the gateway, and go out the same way."

Those Admitted to the Temple

[4]Also He brought me by way of the
north gate to the front of the temple; so I

44:2 the LORD . . . entered by it: That which has been used by God is no longer ordinary.
44:4 **I fell on my face**: Ezekiel's normal response in the presence of God. It ought to be everyone's response.

looked, and behold, the glory of the LORD
filled the house of the LORD; and I fell on
my face. 5And the LORD said to me, "Son of
man, mark well, see with your eyes and
hear with your ears, all that I say to you
concerning all the ordinances of the house
of the LORD and all its laws. Mark well who
may enter the house and all who go out
from the sanctuary.

6"Now say to the rebellious, to the
house of Israel, 'Thus says the Lord GOD:
"O house of Israel, let Us have no more of
all your abominations. 7When you brought
in foreigners, uncircumcised in heart and
uncircumcised in flesh, to be in My sanctu-
ary to defile it—My house—and when you
offered My food, the fat and the blood,
then they broke My covenant because of all
your abominations. 8And you have not
kept charge of My holy things, but you
have set *others* to keep charge of My sanc-
tuary for you." 9Thus says the Lord GOD:
"No foreigner, uncircumcised in heart or
uncircumcised in flesh, shall enter My
sanctuary, including any foreigner who *is*
among the children of Israel.

Laws Governing Priests

10"And the Lē'vītes who went far from
Me, when Israel went astray, who strayed
away from Me after their idols, they shall
bear their iniquity. 11Yet they shall be min-
isters in My sanctuary, *as* gatekeepers of
the house and ministers of the house; they
shall slay the burnt offering and the sacri-
fice for the people, and they shall stand be-
fore them to minister to them. 12Because
they ministered to them before their idols
and caused the house of Israel to fall into
iniquity, therefore I have raised My hand
in an oath against them," says the Lord
GOD, "that they shall bear their iniquity.
13And they shall not come near Me to min-
ister to Me as priest, nor come near any of
My holy things, nor into the Most Holy
Place; but they shall bear their shame and
their abominations which they have com-
mitted. 14Nevertheless I will make them
keep charge of the temple, for all its work,
and for all that has to be done in it.

15"But the priests, the Lē'vītes, the sons
of Zā'dok, who kept charge of My sanctu-
ary when the children of Israel went astray
from Me, they shall come near Me to min-
ister to Me; and they shall stand before Me
to offer to Me the fat and the blood," says
the Lord GOD. 16"They shall enter My sanc-
tuary, and they shall come near My table to
minister to Me, and they shall keep My
charge. 17And it shall be, whenever they
enter the gates of the inner court, that they
shall put on linen garments; no wool shall
come upon them while they minister
within the gates of the inner court or
within the house. 18They shall have linen
turbans on their heads and linen trousers
on their bodies; they shall not clothe them-
selves with *anything that causes* sweat.
19When they go out to the outer court, to
the *outer* court to the people, they shall
take off their garments in which they have
ministered, leave them in the holy cham-
bers, and put on other garments; and in
their holy garments they shall not sanctify
the people.

20"They shall neither shave their heads,
nor let their hair grow long, but they shall
keep their hair well trimmed. 21No priest
shall drink wine when he enters the inner
court. 22They shall not take as wife a
widow or a divorced woman, but take vir-
gins of the descendants of the house of Is-
rael, or widows of priests.

23"And they shall teach My people *the*

44:15, 16 The **sons of Zadok** were rewarded for faithfulness to God which goes back to Zadok's support of Solomon while the priest Abiathar followed Adonijah (see 1 Kin. 1:7, 8). Only they would be allowed as priests before God's **table**.

44:23 The priests were to **teach** the people about the holiness God required. In addition to precept and example, the symbolism of the temple design, its furnishings, and the sacrifice and other worship of the temple were all intended to have this teaching function.

difference between the holy and the unholy,
and cause them to discern between the un-
clean and the clean. 24In controversy they
shall stand as judges, *and* judge it accord-
ing to My judgments. They shall keep My
laws and My statutes in all My appointed
meetings, and they shall hallow My Sab-
baths.

25"They shall not defile *themselves* by
coming near a dead person. Only for father
or mother, for son or daughter, for brother
or unmarried sister may they defile them-
selves. 26After he is cleansed, they shall
count seven days for him. 27And on the day
that he goes to the sanctuary to minister in
the sanctuary, he must offer his sin offering
in the inner court," says the Lord GOD.

28"It shall be, in regard to their inheri-
tance, *that* I *am* their inheritance. You shall
give them no possession in Israel, for I *am*
their possession. 29They shall eat the grain
offering, the sin offering, and the trespass
offering; every dedicated thing in Israel
shall be theirs. 30The best of all firstfruits of
any kind, and every sacrifice of any kind
from all your sacrifices, shall be the
priest's; also you shall give to the priest the
first of your ground meal, to cause a bless-
ing to rest on your house. 31The priests
shall not eat anything, bird or beast, that
died naturally or was torn *by wild beasts*.

CHAPTER 45

The Holy District

"Moreover, when you divide the land
by lot into inheritance, you shall set apart a
district for the LORD, a holy section of the
land; its length *shall be* twenty-five thou-
sand *cubits*, and the width ten thousand. It
shall be holy throughout its territory all
around. 2Of this there shall be a square plot
for the sanctuary, five hundred by five
hundred *rods*, with fifty cubits around it
for an open space. 3So this is the district
you shall measure: twenty-five thousand
cubits long and ten thousand wide; in it
shall be the sanctuary, the Most Holy *Place*.
4It shall be a holy *section* of the land, be-
longing to the priests, the ministers of the
sanctuary, who come near to minister to
the LORD; it shall be a place for their houses
and a holy place for the sanctuary. 5*An area*
twenty-five thousand *cubits* long and ten
thousand wide shall belong to the Lē′vītes,
the ministers of the temple; they shall have
twenty chambers as a possession.[a]

Properties of the City and the Prince

6"You shall appoint as the property of
the city *an area* five thousand *cubits* wide
and twenty-five thousand long, adjacent to
the district of the holy *section*; it shall be-
long to the whole house of Israel.
7"The prince shall have *a section* on one
side and the other of the holy district and
the city's property; and bordering on the
holy district and the city's property, ex-
tending westward on the west side and
eastward on the east side, the length *shall
be* side by side with one of the *tribal* por-
tions, from the west border to the east bor-
der. 8The land shall be his possession in Is-
rael; and My princes shall no more oppress
My people, but they shall give *the rest of* the
land to the house of Israel, according to
their tribes."

Laws Governing the Prince

9"Thus says the Lord GOD: "Enough, O
princes of Israel! Remove violence and
plundering, execute justice and righteous-
ness, and stop dispossessing My people,"
says the Lord GOD. 10"You shall have hon-
est scales, an honest ephah, and an honest
bath. 11The ephah and the bath shall be of

45:5 [a]Following Masoretic Text, Targum, and Vulgate; Septuagint reads *a possession, cities of dwelling.*

44:24 The priests were to function as **judges**, because of their knowledge of the law. This probably reflects the origin of the scribes, the lawyers of NT times. At least once prior to Ezekiel's vision the priests acted as judges under appointment by King Jehoshaphat (see 2 Chr. 19:8–11).

the same measure, so that the bath con-
tains one-tenth of a homer, and the ephah
one-tenth of a homer; their measure shall
be according to the homer. 12The shekel
shall be twenty gerahs; twenty shekels,
twenty-five shekels, *and* fifteen shekels
shall be your mina.

13"This *is* the offering which you shall
offer: you shall give one-sixth of an ephah
from a homer of wheat, and one-sixth of an
ephah from a homer of barley. 14The ordi-
nance concerning oil, the bath of oil, *is* one-
tenth of a bath from a kor. A kor *is* a homer
or ten baths, for ten baths *are* a homer.
15And one lamb shall be given from a flock
of two hundred, from the rich pastures of
Israel. These shall be for grain offerings,
burnt offerings, and peace offerings, to
make atonement for them," says the Lord
GOD. 16"All the people of the land shall
give this offering for the prince in Israel.
17Then it shall be the prince's part *to give*
burnt offerings, grain offerings, and drink
offerings, at the feasts, the New Moons, the
Sabbaths, and at all the appointed seasons
of the house of Israel. He shall prepare the
sin offering, the grain offering, the burnt
offering, and the peace offerings to make
atonement for the house of Israel."

Keeping the Feasts

18'Thus says the Lord GOD: "In the first
month, on the first *day* of the month, you
shall take a young bull without blemish
and cleanse the sanctuary. 19The priest
shall take some of the blood of the sin of-
fering and put *it* on the doorposts of the
temple, on the four corners of the ledge of
the altar, and on the gateposts of the gate of
the inner court. 20And so you shall do on
the seventh *day* of the month for everyone
who has sinned unintentionally or in igno-
rance. Thus you shall make atonement for
the temple.

21"In the first *month,* on the fourteenth
day of the month, you shall observe the
Passover, a feast of seven days; unleavened
bread shall be eaten. 22And on that day the
prince shall prepare for himself and for all
the people of the land a bull *for* a sin offer-
ing. 23On the seven days of the feast he
shall prepare a burnt offering to the LORD,
seven bulls and seven rams without blem-
ish, daily for seven days, and a kid of the
goats daily *for* a sin offering. 24And he shall
prepare a grain offering of one ephah for
each bull and one ephah for each ram, to-
gether with a hin of oil for each ephah.

25"In the seventh *month,* on the fifteenth
day of the month, at the feast, he shall do
likewise for seven days, according to the
sin offering, the burnt offering, the grain
offering, and the oil."

CHAPTER 46

The Manner of Worship

'Thus says the Lord GOD: "The gateway
of the inner court that faces toward the east
shall be shut the six working days; but on
the Sabbath it shall be opened, and on the
day of the New Moon it shall be opened.
2The prince shall enter by way of the
vestibule of the gateway from the outside,
and stand by the gatepost. The priests shall
prepare his burnt offering and his peace of-
ferings. He shall worship at the threshold
of the gate. Then he shall go out, but the
gate shall not be shut until evening. 3Like-
wise the people of the land shall worship
at the entrance to this gateway before the
LORD on the Sabbaths and the New Moons.
4The burnt offering that the prince offers to
the LORD on the Sabbath day *shall be* six
lambs without blemish, and a ram without
blemish; 5and the grain offering *shall be one*
ephah for a ram, and the grain offering for
the lambs, as much as he wants to give, as
well as a hin of oil with every ephah. 6On
the day of the New Moon *it shall be* a young
bull without blemish, six lambs, and a ram;
they shall be without blemish. 7He shall
prepare a grain offering of an ephah for a
bull, an ephah for a ram, as much as he
wants to give for the lambs, and a hin of oil
with every ephah. 8When the prince enters,
he shall go in by way of the vestibule of the
gateway, and go out the same way.

9"But when the people of the land come
before the LORD on the appointed feast
days, whoever enters by way of the north
gate to worship shall go out by way of the
south gate; and whoever enters by way of
the south gate shall go out by way of the
north gate. He shall not return by way of
the gate through which he came, but shall
go out through the opposite gate. 10The
prince shall then be in their midst. When
they go in, he shall go in; and when they go
out, he shall go out. 11At the festivals and
the appointed feast days the grain offering
shall be an ephah for a bull, an ephah for a
ram, as much as he wants to give for the
lambs, and a hin of oil with every ephah.

12"Now when the prince makes a volun-
tary burnt offering or voluntary peace of-
fering to the LORD, the gate that faces to-
ward the east shall then be opened for him;
and he shall prepare his burnt offering and
his peace offerings as he did on the Sab-
bath day. Then he shall go out, and after he
goes out the gate shall be shut.

13"You shall daily make a burnt offering
to the LORD *of* a lamb of the first year with-
out blemish; you shall prepare it every
morning. 14And you shall prepare a grain
offering with it every morning, a sixth
of an ephah, and a third of a hin of oil
to moisten the fine flour. This grain offer-
ing is a perpetual ordinance, to be made
regularly to the LORD. 15Thus they shall
prepare the lamb, the grain offering, and
the oil, *as* a regular burnt offering every
morning."

The Prince and Inheritance Laws

16'Thus says the Lord GOD: "If the prince
gives a gift *of some* of his inheritance to any
of his sons, it shall belong to his sons; it is
their possession by inheritance. 17But if he
gives a gift of some of his inheritance to
one of his servants, it shall be his until the
year of liberty, after which it shall return to
the prince. But his inheritance shall belong
to his sons; it shall become theirs. 18More-
over the prince shall not take any of the
people's inheritance by evicting them from
their property; he shall provide an inheri-
tance for his sons from his own property,
so that none of My people may be scat-
tered from his property." ' "

How the Offerings Were Prepared

19Now he brought me through the en-
trance, which *was* at the side of the gate,
into the holy chambers of the priests which
face toward the north; and there a place
was situated at their extreme western end.
20And he said to me, "This *is* the place
where the priests shall boil the trespass of-
fering and the sin offering, *and* where they
shall bake the grain offering, so that they
do not bring *them* out into the outer court
to sanctify the people."

21Then he brought me out into the outer
court and caused me to pass by the four
corners of the court; and in fact, in every
corner of the court *there was another* court.
22In the four corners of the court *were* en-
closed courts, forty *cubits* long and thirty
wide; all four corners *were* the same size.
23*There was* a row *of building stones* all
around in them, all around the four of
them; and cooking hearths were made un-
der the rows of stones all around. 24And he
said to me, "These *are* the kitchens where
the ministers of the temple shall boil the
sacrifices of the people."

46:16–18 The **prince**, the civil ruler, is to be fair both to his sons and to his subjects; neither is to be turned out of his inheritance. Justice, not power, should be the goal of all who exercise authority.

46:21–24 The four kitchens in the **outer court** would be for the preparation of those parts of the **sacrifices** of the peace offering that the people were permitted to eat (see Deut. 12:18). Eating a sacrificial meal was an expression of fellowship, both with God and with one's fellow worshipers. Eating together can be, and should be, the same today.

CHAPTER 47

The Healing Waters and Trees

Then he brought me back to the door of
the temple; and there was water, flowing
from under the threshold of the temple to-
ward the east, for the front of the temple
faced east; the water was flowing from un-
der the right side of the temple, south of
the altar. 2He brought me out by way of the
north gate, and led me around on the out-
side to the outer gateway that faces east;
and there was water, running out on the
right side.

3And when the man went out to the east
with the line in his hand, he measured one
thousand cubits, and he brought me
through the waters; the water *came up to
my* ankles. 4Again he measured one thou-
sand and brought me through the waters;
the water *came up to my* knees. Again he
measured one thousand and brought me
through; the water *came up to my* waist.
5Again he measured one thousand, *and it
was* a river that I could not cross; for the
water was too deep, water in which one
must swim, a river that could not be
crossed. 6He said to me, "Son of man, have
you seen *this?"* Then he brought me and
returned me to the bank of the river.

7When I returned, there, along the bank
of the river, *were* very many trees on one
side and the other. 8Then he said to me:
"This water flows toward the eastern re-
gion, goes down into the valley, and enters
the sea. *When it* reaches the sea, *its* waters
are healed. 9And it shall be *that* every liv-
ing thing that moves, wherever the rivers
go, will live. There will be a very great
multitude of fish, because these waters go
there; for they will be healed, and every-
thing will live wherever the river goes. 10It
shall be *that* fishermen will stand by it from
En Ge'di to En Eg·lā'im; they will be *places*
for spreading their nets. Their fish will be
of the same kinds as the fish of the Great
Sea, exceedingly many. 11But its swamps
and marshes will not be healed; they will
be given over to salt. 12Along the bank of
the river, on this side and that, will grow
all *kinds of* trees used for food; their leaves
will not wither, and their fruit will not fail.
They will bear fruit every month, because
their water flows from the sanctuary. Their
fruit will be for food, and their leaves for
medicine."

Borders of the Land

13Thus says the Lord GOD: "These *are* the
borders by which you shall divide the land
as an inheritance among the twelve tribes
of Israel. Joseph *shall have two* portions.
14You shall inherit it equally with one an-
other; for I raised My hand in an oath to
give it to your fathers, and this land shall
fall to you as your inheritance.

15"This *shall be* the border of the land on
the north: from the Great Sea, *by* the road
to Heth'lon, as one goes to Zē'dad,
16Hā'math, Be·rō'thah, Sib'rā·im (which *is*
between the border of Damascus and the
border of Hā'math), to Hā'zar Hat'ti·con
(which *is* on the border of Hau'ran). 17Thus
the boundary shall be from the Sea to
Hā'zar Ē'nan, the border of Damascus; and
as for the north, northward, it is the border
of Hā'math. *This is* the north side.

18"On the east side you shall mark out
the border from between Hau'ran and Da-
mascus, and between Gil'ē·ad and the

47:1–12 The river flowing from the threshold of the temple, increasing in volume and bringing healing and prosperity to everything it touches, serves also to illustrate God's plan of salvation. The image of lifegiving water is present in Scripture from the Garden of Eden (Gen. 2:10) to the New Jerusalem (Rev. 22:1).

47:8 sea: The Dead Sea. **healed**: Changed from its salt content of over 25% to ordinary seawater, in which marine life can thrive (see v. 11).

47:13 The **two portions** for **Joseph** were for the two tribes named after his sons, Ephraim and Manasseh (see Gen. 48:1).

land of Israel, along the Jordan, and along the eastern side of the sea. *This is* the east side.

19“The south side, toward the South,[a] *shall be* from Tā′mar to the waters of Mer′i·bah by Kā′desh, along the brook to the Great Sea. *This is* the south side, toward the South.

20“The west side *shall be* the Great Sea, from the *southern* boundary until one comes to a point opposite Hā′math. This *is* the west side.

21“Thus you shall divide this land among yourselves according to the tribes of Israel. 22It shall be that you will divide it by lot as an inheritance for yourselves, and for the strangers who dwell among you and who bear children among you. They shall be to you as native-born among the children of Israel; they shall have an inheritance with you among the tribes of Israel. 23And it shall be *that* in whatever tribe the stranger dwells, there you shall give *him* his inheritance,” says the Lord GOD.

CHAPTER 48

Division of the Land

“Now these *are* the names of the tribes: From the northern border along the road to Heth′lon at the entrance of Hā′math, to Hā′zar Ē′nan, the border of Damascus northward, in the direction of Hā′math, *there shall be* one *section for* Dan from its east to its west side; 2by the border of Dan, from the east side to the west, one *section for* Ash′er; 3by the border of Ash′er, from the east side to the west, one *section for* Naph′ta·lī; 4by the border of Naph′ta·lī, from the east side to the west, one *section for* Ma·nas′seh; 5by the border of Ma·nas′seh, from the east side to the west, one *section for* Ē′phra·im; 6by the border of Ē′phra·im, from the east side to the west, one *section for* Reuben; 7by the border of Reuben, from the east side to the west, one *section for* Judah; 8by the border of Judah, from the east side to the west, shall be the district which you shall set apart, twenty-five thousand *cubits* in width, and *in* length the same as one of the *other* portions, from the east side to the west, with the sanctuary in the center.

9“The district that you shall set apart for the LORD *shall be* twenty-five thousand *cubits* in length and ten thousand in width. 10To these—to the priests—the holy district shall belong: on the north twenty-five thousand *cubits in length,* on the west ten thousand in width, on the east ten thousand in width, and on the south twenty-five thousand in length. The sanctuary of the LORD shall be in the center. 11*It shall be* for the priests of the sons of Zā′dok, who are sanctified, who have kept My charge, who did not go astray when the children of Israel went astray, as the Lē′vītes went astray. 12And *this* district of land that is set apart shall be to them a thing most holy by the border of the Lē′vītes.

13“Opposite the border of the priests, the Lē′vītes *shall have an area* twenty-five thousand *cubits* in length and ten thousand in width; its entire length *shall be* twenty-five thousand and its width ten thousand. 14And they shall not sell or exchange any of it; they may not alienate this best *part* of the land, for *it is* holy to the LORD.

15“The five thousand *cubits* in width that remain, along the edge of the twenty-five thousand, shall be for general use by the city, for dwellings and common-land; and the city shall be in the center. 16These *shall be* its measurements: the north side four thousand five hundred *cubits,* the south side four thousand five hundred, the east

47:19 [a]Hebrew *Negev*

47:22, 23 by lot: So no one could gain unfair advantage in the division of the land. **strangers**: A clear indication that Gentile converts will be part of the future commonwealth of Israel. All Gentile Christians are beneficiaries of this gracious provision.

48:11 sanctified: Set apart for the service of God.

side four thousand five hundred, and the
west side four thousand five hundred.
17The common-land of the city shall be: to
the north two hundred and fifty *cubits,* to
the south two hundred and fifty, to the east
two hundred and fifty, and to the west two
hundred and fifty. 18The rest of the length,
alongside the district of the holy *section,*
shall be ten thousand *cubits* to the east and
ten thousand to the west. It shall be adja-
cent to the district of the holy *section,* and
its produce shall be food for the workers of
the city. 19The workers of the city, from all
the tribes of Israel, shall cultivate it. 20The
entire district *shall be* twenty-five thousand
cubits by twenty-five thousand *cubits,*
foursquare. You shall set apart the holy
district with the property of the city.

21"The rest *shall belong* to the prince, on
one side and on the other of the holy dis-
trict and of the city's property, next to the
twenty-five thousand *cubits* of the *holy* dis-
trict as far as the eastern border, and west-
ward next to the twenty-five thousand as
far as the western border, adjacent to the
tribal portions; *it shall belong* to the prince.
It shall be the holy district, and the sanctu-
ary of the temple *shall be* in the center.
22Moreover, apart from the possession of
the Lē′vītes and the possession of the city
which are in the midst of what *belongs* to the
prince, *the area* between the border of Ju-
dah and the border of Benjamin shall be-
long to the prince.

23"As for the rest of the tribes, from the
east side to the west, Benjamin *shall have*
one *section;* 24by the border of Benjamin,
from the east side to the west, Sim′ē·on
shall have one *section;* 25by the border of
Sim′ē·on, from the east side to the west,
Is′sa·char *shall have* one *section;* 26by the
border of Is′sa·char, from the east side to
the west, Zeb′ū·lun *shall have* one *section;*
27by the border of Zeb′ū·lun, from the east
side to the west, Gad *shall have* one *section;*
28by the border of Gad, on the south side,
toward the South,[a] the border shall be from
Tā′mar *to* the waters of Mer′i·bah *by*
Kā′desh, along the brook to the Great Sea.
29This *is* the land which you shall divide by
lot as an inheritance among the tribes of Is-
rael, and these *are* their portions," says the
Lord GOD.

The Gates of the City and Its Name

30"These *are* the exits of the city. On the
north side, measuring four thousand five
hundred *cubits* 31(the gates of the city *shall*
be named after the tribes of Israel), the
three gates northward: one gate for Reu-
ben, one gate for Judah, and one gate for
Levi; 32on the east side, four thousand five
hundred *cubits,* three gates: one gate for Jo-
seph, one gate for Benjamin, and one gate
for Dan; 33on the south side, measuring
four thousand five hundred *cubits,* three
gates: one gate for Sim′ē·on, one gate for
Is′sa·char, and one gate for Zeb′ū·lun; 34on
the west side, four thousand five hundred
cubits with their three gates: one gate for
Gad, one gate for Ash′er, and one gate for
Naph′ta·lī. 35All the way around *shall be*
eighteen thousand *cubits;* and the name of
the city from *that* day *shall be:* THE LORD
IS THERE."[a]

48:28 [a]Hebrew *Negev* 48:35 [a]Hebrew *YHWH Shammah*

48:31–34 The 12 gates of the city were named for the 12 sons of Jacob with Levi and Joseph (vv. 31, 32) replacing Ephraim and Manasseh from the tribal allotments of the land.

48:35 The most sublime feature of **the city** is that **THE LORD IS THERE**. This is Ezekiel's passion throughout the book. God's people shall live so that God can dwell among them, sanctifying them with His presence.

✦Daniel✦

Daniel was a prophet and statesman taken as a captive to Babylon at age sixteen during the first siege in 605 B.C., and he was held until about 536 B.C. During this time, he wrote the book bearing his name, which is full of Daniel's prophecies concerning future events revealed in God-given visions. Daniel's ministry, from his youth through seventy years of Babylonian captivity, was characterized by faith, prayer, and consistency, providing an example for Christians of all ages.

Like Ezekiel, Daniel encouraged the captive Jews by revealing God's plan for renewing the covenant and establishing the messianic kingdom under Jesus Christ. Daniel's most important prophecy—the seventy weeks—pointed to the time of this coming kingdom. Seventy weeks alluded to seventy sevens, or 490 years until the ministry of Christ.

Yet these prophecies applied to more than the immediate. The symbolism of Daniel's language also points toward Christ's future return, and chapters 11—12 contain prophecies regarding the Antichrist and the Tribulation. ✦

CHAPTER 1

Daniel and His Friends Obey God

In the third year of the reign of
Je·hoi′a·kim king of Judah, Ne·bū-
chad·nez′zar king of Babylon came to Jeru-
salem and besieged it. 2And the Lord gave
Je·hoi′a·kim king of Judah into his hand,
with some of the articles of the house of
God, which he carried into the land of
Shī′nar to the house of his god; and he
brought the articles into the treasure house
of his god.
3Then the king instructed Ash′pe·naz,
the master of his eunuchs, to bring some of
the children of Israel and some of the
king's descendants and some of the nobles,
4young men in whom *there was* no blemish,
but good-looking, gifted in all wisdom,
possessing knowledge and quick to under-
stand, who *had* ability to serve in the king's
palace, and whom they might teach the
language and literature of the Chal·dē′ans.
5And the king appointed for them a daily
provision of the king's delicacies and of the
wine which he drank, and three years of
training for them, so that at the end of *that*
time they might serve before the king.
6Now from among those of the sons of Ju-
dah were Daniel, Han·a·nī′ah, Mish′a·el,

1:3 some of the children of Israel: The Babylonians took three different groups of captives: Daniel was in this one in 605 B.C.; Ezekiel (Ezek. 1:1, 2) in another in 597, and a third when Jerusalem was destroyed in 586. Jeremiah reports a fourth deportation five years after the fall of Jerusalem (see Jer. 52:30).

1:6 In these four typical Hebrew names the ending *el* represents the Hebrew word for "God"; the *ah* ending reflects *Yah*, the shortened form of the name *Yahweh*. The Babylonians would change these names to reflect Babylonian religion.

Beating the Bulge

Dr. Jenifer J. Mason

While Christians should not be obsessed with our physical appearance, we are responsible for the health of our bodies. National data show that older men and women weigh more than the recommended amount for optimal health. The best approach to weight loss (and *sustained* weight loss) continues to center on two fundamental principles: a balanced diet and physical activity. A low-fat, high-complex-carbohydrate diet—including more fruits, vegetables, and whole grains with less cheese, butter, oils, and fatty meats—is probably the most important measure in controlling obesity. Reduce caloric intake, but not to the point of losing more than one to two pounds per week. The slower the weight loss, the longer it stays off.

In general, the same exercise prescription for younger adults applies to seniors, too, but with greater caution and slower progression. Anyone over age fifty should seek medical advice before starting an exercise program. Exercising at least four to six days per week and slowly building up to thirty to forty-five minutes of continuous aerobic exercise per workout seems to work best for losing weight.

These two primary weapons in the "battle of the bulge"—a low-fat diet and daily exercise—will also help you feel better, look better, and improve your overall health status. And, as your physical health improves, you will discover you have more energy, which you can put to work for the Lord. ✦

and Az·a·rī'ah. 7To them the chief of the
eunuchs gave names: he gave Daniel *the*
name Bel·te·shaz'zar; to Han·a·nī'ah,
Shad'rach; to Mish'a·el, Mē'shach; and to
Az·a·rī'ah, A·bed'-Ne·gō'.
8But Daniel purposed in his heart that
he would not defile himself with the portion of the king's delicacies, nor with the
wine which he drank; therefore he requested of the chief of the eunuchs that he
might not defile himself. 9Now God had
brought Daniel into the favor and goodwill

1:8, 12 defile himself: Eating the king's rations would have violated the dietary restrictions of the Hebrew law (see Lev. 11). Meat would have defiled a Hebrew because the Babylonians did not properly drain the blood from carcasses (see Lev. 17:10–14) and ate pork. **requested**: Though he had determined to hold to principle, Daniel acted diplomatically.

1:8, 17 God will bless us when we obey His principles, even when surrounded by sin. Note that while Daniel is the only one specifically mentioned as determining not to defile himself, yet his three friends stood with him in his decision. When we stand firm in our beliefs, others—including our children and grandchildren—will draw strength from our example.

of the chief of the eunuchs. [10]And the chief
of the eunuchs said to Daniel, "I fear my
lord the king, who has appointed your
food and drink. For why should he see
your faces looking worse than the young
men who *are* your age? Then you would
endanger my head before the king."
[11]So Daniel said to the steward[a] whom
the chief of the eunuchs had set over Dan-
iel, Han·a·nī′ah, Mish′a·el, and Az·a·rī′ah,
[12]"Please test your servants for ten days,
and let them give us vegetables to eat and
water to drink. [13]Then let our appearance
be examined before you, and the appear-
ance of the young men who eat the portion
of the king's delicacies; and as you see fit,
so deal with your servants." [14]So he con-
sented with them in this matter, and tested
them ten days.
[15]And at the end of ten days their fea-
tures appeared better and fatter in flesh
than all the young men who ate the portion
of the king's delicacies. [16]Thus the steward
took away their portion of delicacies and
the wine that they were to drink, and gave
them vegetables.
[17]As for these four young men, God
gave them knowledge and skill in all liter-
ature and wisdom; and Daniel had under-
standing in all visions and dreams.
[18]Now at the end of the days, when the
king had said that they should be brought
in, the chief of the eunuchs brought them
in before Ne·bū·chad·nez′zar. [19]Then the
king interviewed[a] them, and among them
all none was found like Daniel, Han·a-
nī′ah, Mish′a·el, and Az·a·rī′ah; therefore
they served before the king. [20]And in all
matters of wisdom *and* understanding
about which the king examined them, he
found them ten times better than all the
magicians *and* astrologers who *were* in all
his realm. [21]Thus Daniel continued until
the first year of King Cyrus.

CHAPTER 2

Nebuchadnezzar's Dream

Now in the second year of
Ne·bū·chad·nez′zar's reign, Ne·bū-
chad·nez′zar had dreams; and his spirit
was *so* troubled that his sleep left him.
[2]Then the king gave the command to call
the magicians, the astrologers, the sorcer-
ers, and the Chal·dē′ans to tell the king his
dreams. So they came and stood before the
king. [3]And the king said to them, "I have
had a dream, and my spirit is anxious to
know the dream."
[4]Then the Chal·dē′ans spoke to the king
in Ar·a·mā′ic,[a] "O king, live forever! Tell
your servants the dream, and we will give
the interpretation."
[5]The king answered and said to the
Chal·dē′ans, "My decision is firm: if you
do not make known the dream to me, and
its interpretation, you shall be cut in
pieces, and your houses shall be made an
ash heap. [6]However, if you tell the dream
and its interpretation, you shall receive
from me gifts, rewards, and great honor.
Therefore tell me the dream and its inter-
pretation."
[7]They answered again and said, "Let the
king tell his servants the dream, and we
will give its interpretation."
[8]The king answered and said, "I know
for certain that you would gain time, be-
cause you see that my decision is firm: [9]if

1:11 [a]Hebrew *Melzar,* also in verse 16 1:19 [a]Literally *talked with them* 2:4 [a]The original language of Daniel 2:4b through 7:28 is Aramaic.

2:2 In Daniel, except for 1:4; 5:30; 9:1; and perhaps 3:8, the term **Chaldeans** denotes a class of priest/magicians. In those locations, it refers to a tribal confederation of lower Mesopotamia. The Babylonian kings were Chaldeans.

2:9 lying . . . words: The king did not say he had forgotten the dream. He was testing the Chaldeans' ability to interpret. Perhaps already in his reign he doubted their genuineness. **till the time has changed**: Hoping the king's mind would turn to other things, and he would forget his demands placed on them.

you do not make known the dream to me,
there is only one decree for you! For you
have agreed to speak lying and corrupt
words before me till the time has changed.
Therefore tell me the dream, and I shall
know that you can give me its interpreta-
tion."
10The Chal·dē'ans answered the king,
and said, "There is not a man on earth who
can tell the king's matter; therefore no
king, lord, or ruler has *ever* asked such
things of any magician, astrologer, or
Chal·dē'an. 11*It is* a difficult thing that the
king requests, and there is no other who
can tell it to the king except the gods,
whose dwelling is not with flesh."
12For this reason the king was angry and
very furious, and gave the command to de-
stroy all the wise *men* of Babylon. 13So the
decree went out, and they began killing the
wise *men;* and they sought Daniel and his
companions, to kill *them.*

God Reveals Nebuchadnezzar's Dream

14Then with counsel and wisdom Daniel
answered Ar'i·och, the captain of the
king's guard, who had gone out to kill the
wise *men* of Babylon; 15he answered and
said to Ar'i·och the king's captain, "Why is
the decree from the king so urgent?" Then
Ar'i·och made the decision known to Dan-
iel.
16So Daniel went in and asked the king
to give him time, that he might tell the king
the interpretation. 17Then Daniel went to
his house, and made the decision known to
Han·a·nī'ah, Mish'a·el, and Az·a·rī'ah, his
companions, 18that they might seek mer-
cies from the God of heaven concerning
this secret, so that Daniel and his compan-
ions might not perish with the rest of the
wise *men* of Babylon. 19Then the secret was
revealed to Daniel in a night vision. So
Daniel blessed the God of heaven.
20Daniel answered and said:

"Blessed be the name of God forever
and ever,
For wisdom and might are His.
21 And He changes the times and the
seasons;
He removes kings and raises up
kings;
He gives wisdom to the wise
And knowledge to those who have
understanding.
22 He reveals deep and secret things;
He knows what *is* in the darkness,
And light dwells with Him.

23 "I thank You and praise You,
O God of my fathers;
You have given me wisdom and
might,
And have now made known to me
what we asked of You,
For You have made known to us the
king's demand."

Daniel Explains the Dream

24Therefore Daniel went to Ar'i·och,
whom the king had appointed to destroy
the wise *men* of Babylon. He went and said
thus to him: "Do not destroy the wise *men*
of Babylon; take me before the king, and I
will tell the king the interpretation."
25Then Ar'i·och quickly brought Daniel
before the king, and said thus to him, "I
have found a man of the captives[a] of Ju-
dah, who will make known to the king the
interpretation."
26The king answered and said to Daniel,
whose name *was* Bel·te·shaz'zar, "Are you
able to make known to me the dream
which I have seen, and its interpretation?"
27Daniel answered in the presence of the
king, and said, "The secret which the king
has demanded, the wise *men,* the as-
trologers, the magicians, and the soothsay-

2:25 [a]Literally *of the sons of the captivity*

2:17, 18 When facing a crisis, we should immediately turn to the Lord for His help. In addition, we should seek the intercessory prayer of godly individuals on our behalf.

ers cannot declare to the king. [28]But there is
a God in heaven who reveals secrets, and
He has made known to King Ne·bū-
chad·nez'zar what will be in the latter
days. Your dream, and the visions of your
head upon your bed, were these: [29]As for
you, O king, thoughts came *to* your *mind
while* on your bed, *about* what would come
to pass after this; and He who reveals se-
crets has made known to you what will be.
[30]But as for me, this secret has not been re-
vealed to me because I have more wisdom
than anyone living, but for *our* sakes who
make known the interpretation to the king,
and that you may know the thoughts of
your heart.

[31]"You, O king, were watching; and be-
hold, a great image! This great image,
whose splendor *was* excellent, stood before
you; and its form *was* awesome. [32]This im-
age's head *was* of fine gold, its chest and
arms of silver, its belly and thighs[a] of
bronze, [33]its legs of iron, its feet partly of
iron and partly of clay.[a] [34]You watched
while a stone was cut out without hands,
which struck the image on its feet of iron
and clay, and broke them in pieces. [35]Then
the iron, the clay, the bronze, the silver, and
the gold were crushed together, and be-
came like chaff from the summer threshing
floors; the wind carried them away so that
no trace of them was found. And the stone
that struck the image became a great
mountain and filled the whole earth.

[36]"This *is* the dream. Now we will tell
the interpretation of it before the king.
[37]You, O king, *are* a king of kings. For the
God of heaven has given you a kingdom,
power, strength, and glory; [38]and wherever
the children of men dwell, or the beasts of
the field and the birds of the heaven, He
has given *them* into your hand, and has
made you ruler over them all—you *are* this
head of gold. [39]But after you shall arise an-
other kingdom inferior to yours; then an-
other, a third kingdom of bronze, which
shall rule over all the earth. [40]And the
fourth kingdom shall be as strong as iron,
inasmuch as iron breaks in pieces and shat-
ters everything; and like iron that crushes,
that kingdom will break in pieces and crush
all the others. [41]Whereas you saw the feet
and toes, partly of potter's clay and partly
of iron, the kingdom shall be divided; yet
the strength of the iron shall be in it, just as
you saw the iron mixed with ceramic clay.
[42]And *as* the toes of the feet *were* partly of
iron and partly of clay, *so* the kingdom
shall be partly strong and partly fragile.
[43]As you saw iron mixed with ceramic clay,
they will mingle with the seed of men; but
they will not adhere to one another, just as
iron does not mix with clay. [44]And in the
days of these kings the God of heaven will
set up a kingdom which shall never be de-
stroyed; and the kingdom shall not be left
to other people; it shall break in pieces and
consume all these kingdoms, and it shall
stand forever. [45]Inasmuch as you saw that
the stone was cut out of the mountain
without hands, and that it broke in pieces
the iron, the bronze, the clay, the silver, and
the gold—the great God has made known
to the king what will come to pass after
this. The dream is certain, and its interpre-
tation is sure."

Daniel and His Friends Promoted

[46]Then King Ne·bū·chad·nez'zar fell on
his face, prostrate before Daniel, and com-
manded that they should present an offer-
ing and incense to him. [47]The king an-
swered Daniel, and said, "Truly your God
is the God of gods, the Lord of kings, and a
revealer of secrets, since you could reveal
this secret." [48]Then the king promoted
Daniel and gave him many great gifts; and
he made him ruler over the whole

2:32 [a]Or *sides* 2:33 [a]Or *baked clay,* and so in verses 34, 35, and 42

2:37 king of kings: Not merely king over many kings—which Nebuchadnezzar was—but the kingliest of kings.

province of Babylon, and chief administra-
tor over all the wise *men* of Babylon. [49]Also
Daniel petitioned the king, and he set
Shad′rach, Mē′shach, and A·bed′-Ne·gō′
over the affairs of the province of Babylon;
but Daniel *sat* in the gate[a] of the king.

CHAPTER 3

The Image of Gold

Nebuchadnezzar the king made an im-
age of gold, whose height *was* sixty cubits
and its width six cubits. He set it up in the
plain of Dū′ra, in the province of Babylon.
[2]And King Ne·bū·chad·nez′zar sent *word*
to gather together the satraps, the adminis-
trators, the governors, the counselors, the
treasurers, the judges, the magistrates, and
all the officials of the provinces, to come to
the dedication of the image which King
Ne·bū·chad·nez′zar had set up. [3]So the
satraps, the administrators, the governors,
the counselors, the treasurers, the judges,
the magistrates, and all the officials of the
provinces gathered together for the dedi-
cation of the image that King Ne·bū-
chad·nez′zar had set up; and they stood
before the image that Ne·bū·chad·nez′zar
had set up. [4]Then a herald cried aloud: "To
you it is commanded, O peoples, nations,
and languages, [5]*that* at the time you hear
the sound of the horn, flute, harp, lyre, *and*
psaltery, in symphony with all kinds of
music, you shall fall down and worship
the gold image that King Ne·bū-
chad·nez′zar has set up; [6]and whoever
does not fall down and worship shall be
cast immediately into the midst of a burn-
ing fiery furnace."
[7]So at that time, when all the people
heard the sound of the horn, flute, harp,
and lyre, in symphony with all kinds of
music, all the people, nations, and lan-
guages fell down *and* worshiped the gold
image which King Ne·bū·chad·nez′zar
had set up.

Daniel's Friends Disobey the King

[8]Therefore at that time certain Chal-
dē′ans came forward and accused the
Jews. [9]They spoke and said to King Ne-
bū·chad·nez′zar, "O king, live forever!
[10]You, O king, have made a decree that
everyone who hears the sound of the horn,
flute, harp, lyre, *and* psaltery, in symphony
with all kinds of music, shall fall down and
worship the gold image; [11]and whoever
does not fall down and worship shall be
cast into the midst of a burning fiery fur-
nace. [12]There are certain Jews whom you
have set over the affairs of the province of
Babylon: Shad′rach, Mē′shach, and
A·bed′-Ne·gō′; these men, O king, have
not paid due regard to you. They do not
serve your gods or worship the gold image
which you have set up."
[13]Then Ne·bū·chad·nez′zar, in rage and
fury, gave the command to bring
Shad′rach, Mē′shach, and A·bed′-Ne·gō′.
So they brought these men before the king.
[14]Ne·bū·chad·nez′zar spoke, saying to
them, "*Is it* true, Shad′rach, Mē′shach, and
A·bed′-Ne·gō′, *that* you do not serve my
gods or worship the gold image which I
have set up? [15]Now if you are ready at the
time you hear the sound of the horn, flute,
harp, lyre, *and* psaltery, in symphony with
all kinds of music, and you fall down and

2:49 [a]That is, the king's court

3:5–7 The world is always trying to replace God in our worship.

3:8–12 the Jews: Daniel's three companions, named in v. 12. Why Daniel was not included is not told; **whom you have set**: Possibly the accusers were jealous of the foreigners who outranked them in authority.

3:12 While this example is often used to encourage young people, mature Christians can also learn from this passage. We do not become immune to the temptations society places before us when we reach a certain age; therefore we must remain in close fellowship with God so we will have the strength to withstand.

worship the image which I have made, *good!* But if you do not worship, you shall be cast immediately into the midst of a burning fiery furnace. And who *is* the god who will deliver you from my hands?"
16Shad'rach, Mē'shach, and A·bed'-Ne·gō' answered and said to the king, "O Ne·bū·chad·nez'zar, we have no need to answer you in this matter. 17If that *is the case,* our God whom we serve is able to deliver us from the burning fiery furnace, and He will deliver *us* from your hand, O
king. 18But if not, let it be known to you, O king, that we do not serve your gods, nor will we worship the gold image which you have set up."

Saved in Fiery Trial

19Then Ne·bū·chad·nez'zar was full of fury, and the expression on his face changed toward Shad'rach, Mē'shach, and A·bed'-Ne·gō'. He spoke and commanded that they heat the furnace seven times more than it was usually heated.
20And he commanded certain mighty men of valor who *were* in his army to bind Shad'rach, Mē'shach, and A·bed'-Ne·gō', *and* cast *them* into the burning fiery furnace.
21Then these men were bound in their coats, their trousers, their turbans, and their *other* garments, and were cast into the midst of the burning fiery furnace.
22Therefore, because

3:16–18 our God . . . is able (v. 17): A wonderful statement of faith. They do not believe God because He promises to deliver; they believe Him regardless of the short-term outcome. He can do what He wishes with them.

STANDING ON THE PROMISES

Billy Graham

The Bible is a book of promises, and unlike the books of men, it doesn't change or become outdated. The message I have been proclaiming for many years is basically the same—and God does not lie!

The Bible makes it clear that no problems in our lives are too great or too small for His concern. He cares about everything that affects His children.

"No problems in our lives are too great or too small for His concern."

If we have no knowledge of God's promises to us, we will not be able to appropriate them. The three Hebrews, Shadrach, Meshach, and Abed-Nego, had studied their Old Testament Scriptures. Of course, we do not know what promise they claimed when they defied Nebuchadnezzar's order, but it could have been from the Psalms. They might have remembered, "The LORD is my light and my salvation; whom shall I fear?" (Ps. 27:1). Their words to the king were, "Our God is able to deliver us—but if not, we still will not worship your image." They certainly knew some of the promises of God to give them the strength and faith they exhibited.

the king's command was urgent, and the
furnace exceedingly hot, the flame of the
fire killed those men who took up
Shad'rach, Mē'shach, and A·bed'-Ne·gō'.
23 And these three men, Shad'rach,
Mē'shach, and A·bed'-Ne·gō', fell down
bound into the midst of the burning fiery
furnace.

24 Then King Ne·bū·chad·nez'zar was
astonished; and he rose in haste *and* spoke,
saying to his counselors, "Did we not cast
three men bound into the midst of the
fire?"

They answered and said to the king,
"True, O king."

25 "Look!" he answered, "I see four men
loose, walking in the midst of the fire; and
they are not hurt, and the form of the
fourth is like the Son of God."[a]

Nebuchadnezzar Praises God

26 Then Ne·bū·chad·nez'zar went near
the mouth of the burning fiery furnace *and*
spoke, saying, "Shad'rach, Mē'shach, and
A·bed'-Ne·gō', servants of the Most High
God, come out, and come *here*." Then
Shad'rach, Mē'shach, and A·bed'-Ne·gō'
came from the midst of the fire. 27 And the
satraps, administrators, governors, and the
king's counselors gathered together, and
they saw these men on whose bodies the
fire had no power; the hair of their head
was not singed nor were their garments af-
fected, and the smell of fire was not on
them.

28 Ne·bū·chad·nez'zar spoke, saying,
"Blessed be the God of Shad'rach, Mē'-
shach, and A·bed'-Ne·gō', who sent His
Angel[a] and delivered His servants who
trusted in Him, and they have frustrated
the king's word, and yielded their bodies,
that they should not serve nor worship any
god except their own God! 29 Therefore I
make a decree that any people, nation, or
language which speaks anything amiss
against the God of Shad'rach, Mē'shach,
and A·bed'-Ne·gō' shall be cut in pieces,
and their houses shall be made an ash
heap; because there is no other God who
can deliver like this."

30 Then the king promoted Shad'rach,
Mē'shach, and A·bed'-Ne·gō' in the
province of Babylon.

CHAPTER 4

Nebuchadnezzar's Second Dream

Nebuchadnezzar the king,

To all peoples, nations, and languages
that dwell in all the earth:

Peace be multiplied to you.

2 I thought it good to declare the signs
and wonders that the Most High God
has worked for me.

3 How great *are* His signs,
And how mighty His wonders!
His kingdom *is* an everlasting
kingdom,

3:25 [a]Or *a son of the gods* 3:28 [a]Or *angel*

3:24, 25 I see four men: Nebuchadnezzar could look into the door of the furnace at its base, where it was fueled. **like the Son of God**: This may have been a preincarnate appearance of Jesus. If so, Nebuchadnezzar spoke more truly than he knew. He probably meant no more than "a divine being," recognizing this **fourth** person as more than human. Although the Lord will not always choose to keep us from trials, He will always walk with us through our trials.

3:29 This **decree**, while honoring God, was not yet a declaration of true faith on Nebuchadnezzar's part, as is clear from 4:28–33.

4:1–3 the Most High God: This declaration, while showing high honor to God, does not mean that Nebuchadnezzar had begun to worship Daniel's God exclusively. See v. 8 ("my god").

And His dominion *is* from generation
to generation.

4 I, Ne·bū·chad·nez'zar, was at rest in
my house, and flourishing in my
palace. [5]I saw a dream which made
me afraid, and the thoughts on my
bed and the visions of my head
troubled me. [6]Therefore I issued a
decree to bring in all the wise *men* of
Babylon before me, that they might
make known to me the interpretation
of the dream. [7]Then the magicians, the
astrologers, the Chal·dē'ans, and the
soothsayers came in, and I told them
the dream; but they did not make
known to me its interpretation. [8]But at
last Daniel came before me (his name
is Bel·te·shaz'zar, according to the
name of my god; in him *is* the Spirit of
the Holy God), and I told the dream
before him, *saying:* [9]"Bel·te·shaz'zar,
chief of the magicians, because I know
that the Spirit of the Holy God *is* in
you, and no secret troubles you,
explain to me the visions of my dream
that I have seen, and its interpretation.

10 "These *were* the visions of my head
while on my bed:

I was looking, and behold,
A tree in the midst of the earth,
And its height was great.
11 The tree grew and became strong;
Its height reached to the heavens,
And it could be seen to the ends of all
the earth.
12 Its leaves *were* lovely,
Its fruit abundant,
And in it *was* food for all.
The beasts of the field found shade
under it,
The birds of the heavens dwelt in its
branches,
And all flesh was fed from it.

13 "I saw in the visions of my head *while*
on my bed, and there was a watcher, a
holy one, coming down from heaven.
[14]He cried aloud and said thus:

'Chop down the tree and cut off its
branches,
Strip off its leaves and scatter its fruit.
Let the beasts get out from under it,
And the birds from its branches.
15 Nevertheless leave the stump and
roots in the earth,
Bound with a band of iron and
bronze,
In the tender grass of the field.
Let it be wet with the dew of heaven,
And *let* him graze with the beasts
On the grass of the earth.
16 Let his heart be changed from *that of* a
man,
Let him be given the heart of a beast,
And let seven times[a] pass over him.

17 'This decision *is* by the decree of the
watchers,
And the sentence by the word of the
holy ones,
In order that the living may know
That the Most High rules in the
kingdom of men,
Gives it to whomever He will,
And sets over it the lowest of men.'

4:16 [a]Possibly *seven years,* and so in verses 23, 25, and 32

4:8, 9 Spirit of the Holy God: As a pagan king uninstructed in the moral character of God's holiness, Nebuchadnezzar probably had reference merely to the evidence of divine power in Daniel's life. **God**: The Hebrew word *('elohim)* may be translated either "God" or "gods" depending on the context. Many interpreters believe it should be rendered "gods" here.

4:13 a holy one . . . from heaven: Almost certainly an angel.

4:16 Let his heart be changed: His thinking, feeling, and actions. **seven times**: Probably seven years. Seven is a biblical number for completeness.

18 "This dream I, King
Ne·bū·chad·nez'zar, have seen. Now
you, Bel·te·shaz'zar, declare its
interpretation, since all the wise *men*
of my kingdom are not able to make
known to me the interpretation; but
you *are* able, for the Spirit of the Holy
God *is* in you."

Daniel Explains the Second Dream

19 Then Daniel, whose name was
Bel·te·shaz'zar, was astonished for a
time, and his thoughts troubled him.
So the king spoke, and said,
"Bel·te·shaz'zar, do not let the dream
or its interpretation trouble you."
Bel·te·shaz'zar answered and said,
"My lord, *may* the dream concern
those who hate you, and its
interpretation concern your enemies!

20 "The tree that you saw, which grew
and became strong, whose height
reached to the heavens and which
could be seen by all the earth, 21whose
leaves *were* lovely and its fruit abun-
dant, in which *was* food for all, under
which the beasts of the field dwelt,
and in whose branches the birds of
the heaven had their home— 22it *is*
you, O king, who have grown and
become strong; for your greatness has
grown and reaches to the heavens,
and your dominion to the end of the
earth.

23 "And inasmuch as the king saw a
watcher, a holy one, coming down
from heaven and saying, 'Chop down
the tree and destroy it, but leave its
stump and roots in the earth, *bound*
with a band of iron and bronze in the
tender grass of the field; let it be wet
with the dew of heaven, and let him
graze with the beasts of the field, till
seven times pass over him'; 24this is
the interpretation, O king, and this is
the decree of the Most High, which
has come upon my lord the king:
25They shall drive you from men, your
dwelling shall be with the beasts of
the field, and they shall make you eat
grass like oxen. They shall wet you
with the dew of heaven, and seven
times shall pass over you, till you
know that the Most High rules in the
kingdom of men, and gives it to
whomever He chooses.

26 "And inasmuch as they gave the
command to leave the stump *and*
roots of the tree, your kingdom shall
be assured to you, after you come to
know that Heaven rules. 27Therefore,
O king, let my advice be acceptable to
you; break off your sins by *being*
righteous, and your iniquities by
showing mercy to *the* poor. Perhaps
there may be a lengthening of your
prosperity."

Nebuchadnezzar's Humiliation

28 All *this* came upon King
Ne·bū·chad·nez'zar. 29At the end of
the twelve months he was walking
about the royal palace of Babylon.
30The king spoke, saying, "Is not this
great Babylon, that I have built for a
royal dwelling by my mighty power
and for the honor of my majesty?"

31 While the word *was still* in the king's
mouth, a voice fell from heaven:
"King Ne·bū·chad·nez'zar, to you it is
spoken: the kingdom has departed
from you! 32And they shall drive you
from men, and your dwelling *shall be*
with the beasts of the field. They shall
make you eat grass like oxen; and

4:27 break off your sins: Righteousness and mercy are two of the marks of true conversion to God.

seven times shall pass over you, until
you know that the Most High rules in
the kingdom of men, and gives it to
whomever He chooses."

33 That very hour the word was fulfilled
concerning Ne·bū·chad·nez'zar; he
was driven from men and ate grass
like oxen; his body was wet with the
dew of heaven till his hair had grown
like eagles' *feathers* and his nails like
birds' *claws*.

Nebuchadnezzar Praises God

34 And at the end of the time[a] I,
Ne·bū·chad·nez'zar, lifted my eyes to
heaven, and my understanding
returned to me; and I blessed the
Most High and praised and honored
Him who lives forever:

For His dominion *is* an everlasting
dominion,
And His kingdom *is* from generation
to generation.
35 All the inhabitants of the earth *are*
reputed as nothing;
He does according to His will in the
army of heaven
And *among* the inhabitants of the
earth.
No one can restrain His hand
Or say to Him, "What have You
done?"

36 At the same time my reason returned
to me, and for the glory of my
kingdom, my honor and splendor
returned to me. My counselors and
nobles resorted to me, I was restored
to my kingdom, and excellent majesty
was added to me. 37Now I,
Ne·bū·chad·nez'zar, praise and extol
and honor the King of heaven, all of
whose works *are* truth, and His ways
justice. And those who walk in pride
He is able to put down.

CHAPTER 5

Belshazzar's Feast

Belshazzar the king made a great feast
for a thousand of his lords, and drank wine
in the presence of the thousand. 2While he
tasted the wine, Bel·shaz'zar gave the com-
mand to bring the gold and silver vessels
which his father Ne·bū·chad·nez'zar had
taken from the temple which *had been* in Je-
rusalem, that the king and his lords, his
wives, and his concubines might drink
from them. 3Then they brought the gold
vessels that had been taken from the tem-
ple of the house of God which *had been* in
Jerusalem; and the king and his lords, his
wives, and his concubines drank from
them. 4They drank wine, and praised the
gods of gold and silver, bronze and iron,
wood and stone.
5In the same hour the fingers of a man's
hand appeared and wrote opposite the
lampstand on the plaster of the wall of the
king's palace; and the king saw the part of
the hand that wrote. 6Then the king's coun-
tenance changed, and his thoughts trou-
bled him, so that the joints of his hips were

4:34 [a]Literally *days*

4:34–37 His dominion: There is only one King who rules the universe. Whoever rules under Him does so only as His agent. **I . . . honor the King of heaven**: God moves in mysterious ways but He makes Himself and His will known even to heathen kings who pay attention and respond to Him.

5:1 Belshazzar was regent for Nabonidus, his father, who ruled Babylon from 556 to 539 B.C. Nabonidus preferred to live at the Arabian oasis of Tema, leaving Belshazzar in charge in Babylon.

5:2 his father: Probably means no more than "predecessor" since no family connection is known (also in vv. 11, 13, 18, 22).

5:4 In drinking to pagan idols from the vessels set apart for God's use, Belshazzar blasphemed the Almighty.

loosened and his knees knocked against each other. 7The king cried aloud to bring in the astrologers, the Chal·dē'ans, and the soothsayers. The king spoke, saying to the wise *men* of Babylon, "Whoever reads this writing, and tells me its interpretation, shall be clothed with purple and *have* a chain of gold around his neck; and he shall be the third ruler in the kingdom." 8Now all the king's wise *men* came, but they could not read the writing, or make known to the king its interpretation. 9Then King Bel·shaz'zar was greatly troubled, his countenance was changed, and his lords were astonished.

10The queen, because of the words of the king and his lords, came to the banquet hall. The queen spoke, saying, "O king, live forever! Do not let your thoughts trouble you, nor let your countenance change. 11There is a man in your kingdom in whom *is* the Spirit of the Holy God. And in the days of your father, light and understanding and wisdom, like the wisdom of the gods, were found in him; and King Ne·bū·chad·nez'zar your father—your father the king—made him chief of the magicians, astrologers, Chal·dē'ans, *and* soothsayers. 12Inasmuch as an excellent spirit, knowledge, understanding, interpreting dreams, solving riddles, and explaining enigmas[a] were found in this Daniel, whom the king named Bel·te·shaz'zar, now let Daniel be called, and he will give the interpretation."

The Writing on the Wall Explained

13Then Daniel was brought in before the king. The king spoke, and said to Daniel, "*Are* you that Daniel who is one of the captives[a] from Judah, whom my father the king brought from Judah? 14I have heard of you, that the Spirit of God *is* in you, and *that* light and understanding and excellent wisdom are found in you. 15Now the wise *men*, the astrologers, have been brought in before me, that they should read this writing and make known to me its interpretation, but they could not give the interpretation of the thing. 16And I have heard of you, that you can give interpretations and explain enigmas. Now if you can read the writing and make known to me its interpretation, you shall be clothed with purple and *have* a chain of gold around your neck, and shall be the third ruler in the kingdom."

17Then Daniel answered, and said before the king, "Let your gifts be for yourself, and give your rewards to another; yet I will read the writing to the king, and make known to him the interpretation. 18O king, the Most High God gave Ne·bū-chad·nez'zar your father a kingdom and majesty, glory and honor. 19And because of the majesty that He gave him, all peoples, nations, and languages trembled and feared before him. Whomever he wished, he executed; whomever he wished, he kept alive; whomever he wished, he set up; and whomever he wished, he put down. 20But when his heart was lifted up, and his spirit was hardened in pride, he was deposed from his kingly throne, and they took his glory from him. 21Then he was driven from the sons of men, his heart was made like the beasts, and his dwelling *was* with the wild donkeys. They fed him with grass like oxen, and his body was wet with the dew of heaven, till he knew that the Most High God rules in the kingdom of men, and appoints over it whomever He chooses.

22"But you his son, Bel·shaz'zar, have not humbled your heart, although you knew all this. 23And you have lifted your-

5:12 [a]Literally *untying knots*, and so in verse 16
5:13 [a]Literally *of the sons of the captivity*

5:10 The queen: The wife of Nabonidus and mother of Belshazzar. This woman knew Daniel; the others present apparently did not. Belshazzar's own queen was also at the feast (v. 2).

5:23 No matter how successful or wealthy we may be, we must recognize God's role in

self up against the Lord of heaven. They
have brought the vessels of His house be-
fore you, and you and your lords, your
wives and your concubines, have drunk
wine from them. And you have praised the
gods of silver and gold, bronze and iron,
wood and stone, which do not see or hear
or know; and the God who *holds* your
breath in His hand and owns all your
ways, you have not glorified. 24Then the
fingers[a] of the hand were sent from Him,
and this writing was written.
25"And this is the inscription that was
written:

MENE,[a] MENE, TEKEL,[b] UPHARSIN.[c]

26This *is* the interpretation of *each* word.
MENE: God has numbered your kingdom,
and finished it; 27TEKEL: You have been
weighed in the balances, and found want-
ing; 28PERES: Your kingdom has been di-
vided, and given to the Mēdes and Per-
sians."[a] 29Then Bel·shaz'zar gave the
command, and they clothed Daniel with
purple and *put* a chain of gold around his
neck, and made a proclamation concerning
him that he should be the third ruler in the
kingdom.

Belshazzar's Fall

30That very night Bel·shaz'zar, king of
the Chal·dē'ans, was slain. 31And Da·rī'us
the Mēde received the kingdom, *being*
about sixty-two years old.

CHAPTER 6

The Plot Against Daniel

It pleased Da·rī'us to set over the king-
dom one hundred and twenty satraps, to
be over the whole kingdom; 2and over
these, three governors, of whom Daniel
was one, that the satraps might give ac-
count to them, so that the king would suf-
fer no loss. 3Then this Daniel distinguished
himself above the governors and satraps,
because an excellent spirit *was* in him; and
the king gave thought to setting him over
the whole realm. 4So the governors and
satraps sought to find *some* charge against
Daniel concerning the kingdom; but they
could find no charge or fault, because he
was faithful; nor was there any error or
fault found in him. 5Then these men said,
"We shall not find any charge against this
Daniel unless we find *it* against him con-
cerning the law of his God."
6So these governors and satraps
thronged before the king, and said thus to
him: "King Da·rī'us, live forever! 7All the
governors of the kingdom, the administra-
tors and satraps, the counselors and advi-
sors, have consulted together to establish a
royal statute and to make a firm decree,
that whoever petitions any god or man for
thirty days, except you, O king, shall be
cast into the den of lions. 8Now, O king, es-
tablish the decree and sign the writing, so
that it cannot be changed, according to the
law of the Mēdes and Persians, which does

5:24 [a]Literally *palm* 5:25 [a]Literally *a mina* (50 shekels) from the verb "to number" [b]Literally *a shekel* from the verb "to weigh" [c]Literally *and half-shekels* from the verb "to divide" 5:28 [a]Aramaic *Paras,* consonant with *Peres*

our lives; without Him we are absolutely nothing. The Lord who gives us our next breath deserves to be glorified for every blessing we receive.

5:25–28 Three words from everyday commerce are applied to the king's handling of the business of his kingdom. His accounts do not balance.

6:1, 2 satraps: Provincial governors. **governors**: Overseers of the satraps. **suffer no loss**: Through rebellion or financial corruption.

6:3, 4 Daniel performed his official duties blamelessly without **error or fault**. What an example for Christians today! Our conduct should be such that unbelievers cannot find fault in anything about our commitment to the Lord.

6:8, 9 does not alter: There is other evidence that royal decrees of the Medes and Persians were irrevocable (see Esth. 1:19; 8:8).

DANIEL: A MAN OF PURPOSE

As part of an elite force of exiled young Israelites, Daniel was hand-picked to serve the king because of his outstanding qualities. A handsome young man, he was "gifted in all wisdom, possessing knowledge and quick to understand" (Dan. 1:4). He took an active role in caring for his physical health. Rather than accept the rich Babylonian fare, which may have violated the dietary regulations of Leviticus 11, Daniel "purposed in his heart that he would not defile himself" (v. 8).

Although the chief of the eunuchs hesitated to consent to Daniel's request for a water-and-vegetable diet, the Lord worked in his heart and convinced him to conduct a test to determine which diet was more effective. God honored Daniel's faithfulness and self-control; the test successfully demonstrated the benefits of abstinence over self-indulgence in promoting health (v. 15).

The Bible also recounts the depth of Daniel's spiritual life. His integrity could not be challenged when his enemies sought to destroy him (6:4), and he regularly spent time alone with the Lord in prayer, even when such action was outlawed by the king (6:10). He is identified by Ezekiel as one of the three most righteous men in Old Testament history (Ezek. 14:14).

While we can be certain Daniel was not a perfect man, he is one of the few Bible heroes about whom we are told nothing negative. For more than sixty years, he lived a pure life in the midst of a corrupt land, just as he had purposed in his heart as a teenager.

Daniel provides a wonderful example of what God can do with those who commit themselves to living a life of spiritual, physical, and mental health despite difficult circumstances. ✦

not alter." 9Therefore King Da·rī'us signed the written decree.

Daniel in the Lions' Den

10Now when Daniel knew that the writing was signed, he went home. And in his upper room, with his windows open toward Jerusalem, he knelt down on his knees three times that day, and prayed and gave thanks before his God, as was his custom since early days.

11Then these men assembled and found Daniel praying and making supplication before his God. 12And they went before the

6:10 as was his custom: Daniel did not increase his prayer out of hypocrisy, nor did he try to conceal it out of fear. He did not allow anything to affect his relationship with God. So too ought our conduct to be based solely on God's will and not on the anticipated reactions of others.

king, and spoke concerning the king's de-
cree: "Have you not signed a decree that
every man who petitions any god or man
within thirty days, except you, O king,
shall be cast into the den of lions?"
The king answered and said, "The thing
is true, according to the law of the Mēdes
and Persians, which does not alter."
13 So they answered and said before the
king, "That Daniel, who is one of the cap-
tives[a] from Judah, does not show due re-
gard for you, O king, or for the decree that
you have signed, but makes his petition
three times a day."
14 And the king, when he heard *these*
words, was greatly displeased with him-
self, and set *his* heart on Daniel to deliver
him; and he labored till the going down of
the sun to deliver him. 15 Then these men
approached the king, and said to the king,
"Know, O king, that *it is* the law of the
Mēdes and Persians that no decree or
statute which the king establishes may be
changed."
16 So the king gave the command, and
they brought Daniel and cast *him* into the
den of lions. *But* the king spoke, saying to
Daniel, "Your God, whom you serve con-
tinually, He will deliver you." 17 Then a
stone was brought and laid on the mouth
of the den, and the king sealed it with his
own signet ring and with the signets of his
lords, that the purpose concerning Daniel
might not be changed.

Daniel Saved from the Lions

18 Now the king went to his palace and
spent the night fasting; and no musicians[a]
were brought before him. Also his sleep
went from him. 19 Then the king arose very
early in the morning and went in haste to
the den of lions. 20 And when he came to the
den, he cried out with a lamenting voice to
Daniel. The king spoke, saying to Daniel,
"Daniel, servant of the living God, has
your God, whom you serve continually,
been able to deliver you from the lions?"
21 Then Daniel said to the king, "O king,
live forever! 22 My God sent His angel and
shut the lions' mouths, so that they have
not hurt me, because I was found innocent
before Him; and also, O king, I have done
no wrong before you."
23 Now the king was exceedingly glad
for him, and commanded that they should
take Daniel up out of the den. So Daniel
was taken up out of the den, and no injury
whatever was found on him, because he
believed in his God.

Darius Honors God

24 And the king gave the command, and
they brought those men who had accused
Daniel, and they cast *them* into the den of
lions—them, their children, and their
wives; and the lions overpowered them,
and broke all their bones in pieces before
they ever came to the bottom of the den.
25 Then King Da·rī′us wrote:

To all peoples, nations, and languages
that dwell in all the earth:

Peace be multiplied to you.

26 I make a decree that in every
dominion of my kingdom *men must*
tremble and fear before the God of
Daniel.

For He *is* the living God,
And steadfast forever;
His kingdom *is the one* which shall
not be destroyed,
And His dominion *shall endure* to the
end.

6:13 [a]Literally *of the sons of the captivity* 6:18 [a]Exact meaning unknown

6:16 Your God . . . will deliver you: A remarkable statement of faith (see also 3:17, 18), especially from a heathen king. When our conduct is consistently holy, we will not fail to have an impact on those around us.

27 He delivers and rescues,
And He works signs and wonders
In heaven and on earth,
Who has delivered Daniel from the
power of the lions.

28 So this Daniel prospered in the reign of
Da·ri'us and in the reign of Cyrus the Per-
sian.

CHAPTER 7

Vision of the Four Beasts

In the first year of Bel·shaz'zar king of
Babylon, Daniel had a dream and visions
of his head *while* on his bed. Then he wrote
down the dream, telling the main facts.[a]

2 Daniel spoke, saying, "I saw in my vi-
sion by night, and behold, the four winds
of heaven were stirring up the Great Sea.
3 And four great beasts came up from the
sea, each different from the other. 4 The first
was like a lion, and had eagle's wings. I
watched till its wings were plucked off;
and it was lifted up from the earth and
made to stand on two feet like a man, and
a man's heart was given to it.

5 "And suddenly another beast, a sec-
ond, like a bear. It was raised up on one
side, and *had* three ribs in its mouth be-
tween its teeth. And they said thus to it:
'Arise, devour much flesh!'

6 "After this I looked, and there was an-
other, like a leopard, which had on its back
four wings of a bird. The beast also had
four heads, and dominion was given to it.

7 "After this I saw in the night visions,
and behold, a fourth beast, dreadful and
terrible, exceedingly strong. It had huge
iron teeth; it was devouring, breaking in
pieces, and trampling the residue with its
feet. It *was* different from all the beasts that
were before it, and it had ten horns. 8 I was
considering the horns, and there was an-
other horn, a little one, coming up among
them, before whom three of the first horns
were plucked out by the roots. And there,
in this horn, *were* eyes like the eyes of a
man, and a mouth speaking pompous
words.

Vision of the Ancient of Days

9 "I watched till thrones were put in
place,
And the Ancient of Days was seated;
His garment *was* white as snow,
And the hair of His head *was* like
pure wool.
His throne *was* a fiery flame,
Its wheels a burning fire;
10 A fiery stream issued
And came forth from before Him.
A thousand thousands ministered to
Him;
Ten thousand times ten thousand
stood before Him.
The court[a] was seated,
And the books were opened.

11 "I watched then because of the sound
of the pompous words which the horn was

7:1 [a]Literally *the head* (or *chief*) *of the words*
7:10 [a]Or *judgment*

7:2 In apocalyptic visions, the **sea** is often a symbol of all the earth's people.

7:4 **The first** beast was the Babylonian Empire. **lion**: King of the beasts. **eagle's wings**: King of the birds. **a man's heart**: Under Nebuchadnezzar, the Babylonian Empire became more humane (see 4:34–37).

7:5 **a bear**: The Medo-Persian Empire. **three ribs**: Parts of the empire, usually identified with Syria, Babylon, and Egypt, all of which were conquered by Cyrus and his son Cambyses.

7:6 **a leopard**: The Greek Empire established by Alexander. The **four wings** and **heads** may refer to the four parts into which Alexander's empire was divided after his death.

7:7 **a fourth beast**: The Roman Empire. **dreadful and terrible**: As unnerving as the three earlier beasts were, this one was obviously stronger and more destructive.

7:11, 12 While the fourth beast was totally **destroyed** (v. 11), the first three were spared, though left without power. The kingdom of the Antichrist (the "little horn" of v. 8) at the end of

speaking; I watched till the beast was slain, and its body destroyed and given to the burning flame. [12]As for the rest of the beasts, they had their dominion taken away, yet their lives were prolonged for a season and a time.

13 "I was watching in the night visions,
And behold, *One* like the Son of Man,
Coming with the clouds of heaven!
He came to the Ancient of Days,
And they brought Him near before
Him.
14 Then to Him was given dominion
and glory and a kingdom,
That all peoples, nations, and
languages should serve Him.
His dominion *is* an everlasting
dominion,
Which shall not pass away,
And His kingdom *the one*
Which shall not be destroyed.

Daniel's Visions Interpreted

[15]"I, Daniel, was grieved in my spirit
within *my* body, and the visions of my
head troubled me. [16]I came near to one of
those who stood by, and asked him the
truth of all this. So he told me and made
known to me the interpretation of these
things: [17]'Those great beasts, which are
four, *are* four kings[a] *which* arise out of the
earth. [18]But the saints of the Most High
shall receive the kingdom, and possess the
kingdom forever, even forever and ever.'

[19]"Then I wished to know the truth
about the fourth beast, which was different
from all the others, exceedingly dreadful,
with its teeth of iron and its nails of bronze,
which devoured, broke in pieces, and tram-
pled the residue with its feet; [20]and the ten
horns that *were* on its head, and the other
horn which came up, before which three
fell, namely, that horn which had eyes and
a mouth which spoke pompous words,
whose appearance *was* greater than his fellows.

[21]"I was watching; and the same horn
was making war against the saints, and
prevailing against them, [22]until the Ancient
of Days came, and a judgment was made
in favor of the saints of the Most High, and
the time came for the saints to possess the
kingdom.

[23]"Thus he said:

'The fourth beast shall be
A fourth kingdom on earth,
Which shall be different from all *other*
kingdoms,
And shall devour the whole earth,
Trample it and break it in pieces.
24 The ten horns *are* ten kings
Who shall arise from this kingdom.
And another shall rise after them;
He shall be different from the first
ones,
And shall subdue three kings.
25 He shall speak *pompous* words against
the Most High,
Shall persecute[a] the saints of the Most
High,
And shall intend to change times and
law.
Then *the saints* shall be given into his
hand
For a time and times and half a time.

26 'But the court shall be seated,
And they shall take away his
dominion,
To consume and destroy *it* forever.
27 Then the kingdom and dominion,

7:17 [a]Representing their kingdoms (compare verse 23)
7:25 [a]Literally *wear out*

the age will be completely destroyed. The other three empires were conquered, but their peoples and cultures continued for a **time**.

7:13, 14 Son of Man: Jesus frequently used this term to designate Himself, but only here in the OT are both humanity and deity intimated by this title. The prophecy must refer to the **kingdom** "of our Lord and of His Christ" (Rev. 11:15).

And the greatness of the kingdoms
under the whole heaven,
Shall be given to the people, the
saints of the Most High.
His kingdom *is* an everlasting
kingdom,
And all dominions shall serve and
obey Him.'

28 "This *is* the end of the account.[a] As for
me, Daniel, my thoughts greatly troubled
me, and my countenance changed; but I
kept the matter in my heart."

CHAPTER 8

Vision of a Ram and a Goat

In the third year of the reign of King
Bel·shaz'zar a vision appeared *to* me—to
me, Daniel—after the one that appeared to
me the first time. 2 I saw in the vision, and it
so happened while I was looking, that I
was in Shū'shan, the citadel, which *is* in the
province of Ē'lam; and I saw in the vision
that I was by the River Ū'laī. 3 Then I lifted
my eyes and saw, and there, standing be-
side the river, was a ram which had two
horns, and the two horns *were* high; but
one *was* higher than the other, and the
higher *one* came up last. 4 I saw the ram
pushing westward, northward, and south-
ward, so that no animal could withstand
him; nor *was there any* that could deliver
from his hand, but he did according to his
will and became great.

5 And as I was considering, suddenly a
male goat came from the west, across the
surface of the whole earth, without touch-
ing the ground; and the goat *had* a notable
horn between his eyes. 6 Then he came to
the ram that had two horns, which I had
seen standing beside the river, and ran at
him with furious power. 7 And I saw him
confronting the ram; he was moved with
rage against him, attacked the ram, and
broke his two horns. There was no power
in the ram to withstand him, but he cast
him down to the ground and trampled
him; and there was no one that could de-
liver the ram from his hand.

8 Therefore the male goat grew very
great; but when he became strong, the
large horn was broken, and in place of it
four notable ones came up toward the four
winds of heaven. 9 And out of one of them
came a little horn which grew exceedingly
great toward the south, toward the east,
and toward the Glorious *Land*. 10 And it
grew up to the host of heaven; and it cast
down *some* of the host and *some* of the stars
to the ground, and trampled them. 11 He
even exalted *himself* as high as the Prince of

7:28 [a]Literally *the word*

8:1–27 This vision deals with experiences of God's people under the rule of the Medes and Persians, represented by the ram, and under the Greeks, represented by the goat. These empires were the second and third of the four kingdoms that Daniel saw in his vision of ch. 7. **Belshazzar** was the last of the Babylonian kings, dying in 538 B.C., years after this vision which occurred about 551. Cyrus soon came to the throne, and in 537 B.C. decreed the return of the Jews to Jerusalem. The Persian Empire continued until 331 B.C. when Alexander's armies swept over the east. The Greeks ruled or influenced Palestine from 331 until 64 B.C. During this time the Jews suffered increasing persecution. The Romans, Daniel's fourth kingdom, conquered Palestine in 64 B.C. and continued the persecution until its culmination in the destruction of the temple in A.D. 70.

8:8 the large horn was broken: Alexander died at age 33. **four notable ones**: Four of Alexander's generals eventually established themselves in kingdoms carved from his empire.

8:9 a little horn: This is not the same person as the little horn of 7:8. The little horn of ch. 8 is Antiochus IV Epiphanes, who in 175 B.C. usurped the Seleucid kingdom. **Glorious Land**: Palestine (Ps. 106:24).

8:11 Antiochus dubbed himself "Epiphanes," (meaning "God Manifest"). He halted sacrifices and desecrated the temple.

the host; and by him the daily *sacrifices*
were taken away, and the place of His
sanctuary was cast down. [12]Because of
transgression, an army was given over *to
the horn* to oppose the daily *sacrifices;* and
he cast truth down to the ground. He did
all this and prospered.

[13]Then I heard a holy one speaking; and
another holy one said to that certain *one*
who was speaking, "How long *will* the vi-
sion *be, concerning* the daily *sacrifices* and
the transgression of desolation, the giving
of both the sanctuary and the host to be
trampled underfoot?"

[14]And he said to me, "For two thousand
three hundred days;[a] then the sanctuary
shall be cleansed."

Gabriel Interprets the Vision

[15]Then it happened, when I, Daniel, had
seen the vision and was seeking the mean-
ing, that suddenly there stood before me
one having the appearance of a man. [16]And
I heard a man's voice between *the banks of*
the Ū′laī, who called, and said, "Gabriel,
make this *man* understand the vision." [17]So
he came near where I stood, and when he
came I was afraid and fell on my face; but
he said to me, "Understand, son of man,
that the vision *refers* to the time of the end."

[18]Now, as he was speaking with me, I
was in a deep sleep with my face to the
ground; but he touched me, and stood me
upright. [19]And he said, "Look, I am making
known to you what shall happen in the lat-
ter time of the indignation; for at the ap-
pointed time the end *shall be.* [20]The ram
which you saw, having the two horns—
they are the kings of Media and Persia.
[21]And the male goat *is* the kingdom[a] of
Greece. The large horn that *is* between its
eyes *is* the first king. [22]As for the broken
horn and the four that stood up in its place,
four kingdoms shall arise out of that na-
tion, but not with its power.

23 "And in the latter time of their
kingdom,
When the transgressors have reached
their fullness,
A king shall arise,
Having fierce features,
Who understands sinister schemes.
24 His power shall be mighty, but not by
his own power;
He shall destroy fearfully,
And shall prosper and thrive;
He shall destroy the mighty, and *also*
the holy people.

25 "Through his cunning
He shall cause deceit to prosper
under his rule;[a]
And he shall exalt *himself* in his heart.
He shall destroy many in *their*
prosperity.
He shall even rise against the Prince
of princes;
But he shall be broken without *human*
means.[b]

26 "And the vision of the evenings and
mornings
Which was told is true;
Therefore seal up the vision,
For *it refers* to many days *in the
future.*"

[27]And I, Daniel, fainted and was sick for
days; afterward I arose and went about the
king's business. I was astonished by the vi-
sion, but no one understood it.

CHAPTER 9

Daniel's Prayer for the People

In the first year of Da·rī′us the son of
A·has·ū·ē′rus, of the lineage of the Mēdes,

8:14 [a]Literally *evening-mornings* 8:21 [a]Literally *king,* representing his kingdom (compare 7:17, 23)
8:25 [a]Literally *hand* [b]Literally *hand*

8:12 transgression: The apostasy of Jerusalem's ruling priests in the second century B.C. prompted Antiochus's blasphemous actions.

who was made king over the realm of the
Chal·dē'ans— 2in the first year of his reign
I, Daniel, understood by the books the
number of the years *specified* by the word
of the LORD through Jer·e·mī'ah the
prophet, that He would accomplish sev-
enty years in the desolations of Jerusalem.
3Then I set my face toward the Lord God
to make request by prayer and supplica-
tions, with fasting, sackcloth, and ashes.
4And I prayed to the LORD my God, and
made confession, and said, "O Lord, great
and awesome God, who keeps His
covenant and mercy with those who love
Him, and with those who keep His com-
mandments, 5we have sinned and commit-
ted iniquity, we have done wickedly and
rebelled, even by departing from Your pre-
cepts and Your judgments. 6Neither have
we heeded Your servants the prophets,
who spoke in Your name to our kings and
our princes, to our fathers and all the peo-
ple of the land. 7O Lord, righteousness *be-*
longs to You, but to us shame of face, as *it is*
this day—to the men of Judah, to the in-
habitants of Jerusalem and all Israel, those
near and those far off in all the countries to
which You have driven them, because of
the unfaithfulness which they have com-
mitted against You.
8"O Lord, to us *belongs* shame of face, to
our kings, our princes, and our fathers, be-
cause we have sinned against You. 9To the
Lord our God *belong* mercy and forgive-
ness, though we have rebelled against
Him. 10We have not obeyed the voice of the
LORD our God, to walk in His laws, which
He set before us by His servants the
prophets. 11Yes, all Israel has transgressed
Your law, and has departed so as not to
obey Your voice; therefore the curse and
the oath written in the Law of Moses the
servant of God have been poured out on
us, because we have sinned against Him.
12And He has confirmed His words, which
He spoke against us and against our
judges who judged us, by bringing upon
us a great disaster; for under the whole
heaven such has never been done as what
has been done to Jerusalem.
13"As *it is* written in the Law of Moses,
all this disaster has come upon us; yet we
have not made our prayer before the LORD
our God, that we might turn from our iniq-
uities and understand Your truth. 14There-
fore the LORD has kept the disaster in mind,
and brought it upon us; for the LORD our
God *is* righteous in all the works which He
does, though we have not obeyed His
voice. 15And now, O Lord our God, who
brought Your people out of the land of
Egypt with a mighty hand, and made
Yourself a name, as *it is* this day—we have
sinned, we have done wickedly!
16"O Lord, according to all Your right-
eousness, I pray, let Your anger and Your
fury be turned away from Your city Jerusa-
lem, Your holy mountain; because for our
sins, and for the iniquities of our fathers,
Jerusalem and Your people *are* a reproach
to all *those* around us. 17Now therefore, our
God, hear the prayer of Your servant, and
his supplications, and for the Lord's sake
cause Your face to shine on Your sanctuary,
which is desolate. 18O my God, incline
Your ear and hear; open Your eyes and see
our desolations, and the city which is
called by Your name; for we do not present
our supplications before You because of
our righteous deeds, but because of Your
great mercies. 19O Lord, hear! O Lord, for-
give! O Lord, listen and act! Do not delay
for Your own sake, my God, for Your city
and Your people are called by Your name."

The Seventy-Weeks Prophecy

20Now while I *was* speaking, praying,
and confessing my sin and the sin of my
people Israel, and presenting my supplica-
tion before the LORD my God for the holy
mountain of my God, 21yes, while I *was*
speaking in prayer, the man Gabriel,

9:21 Gabriel: The angel, appearing in human form. **the vision**: see 8:16–26.

whom I had seen in the vision at the beginning, being caused to fly swiftly, reached me about the time of the evening offering.
22And he informed *me,* and talked with me, and said, "O Daniel, I have now come forth to give you skill to understand. 23At the beginning of your supplications the command went out, and I have come to tell *you,* for you *are* greatly beloved; therefore consider the matter, and understand the vision:

24 "Seventy weeks[a] are determined
For your people and for your holy
city,
To finish the transgression,
To make an end of[a] sins,
To make reconciliation for iniquity,
To bring in everlasting righteousness,
To seal up vision and prophecy,
And to anoint the Most Holy.

25 "Know therefore and understand,
That from the going forth of the
command
To restore and build Jerusalem
Until Messiah the Prince,
There shall be seven weeks and
sixty-two weeks;
The street[a] shall be built again, and
the wall,[b]
Even in troublesome times.

26 "And after the sixty-two weeks
Messiah shall be cut off, but not for
Himself;
And the people of the prince who is
to come
Shall destroy the city and the
sanctuary.
The end of it *shall be* with a flood,
And till the end of the war
desolations are determined.
27 Then he shall confirm a covenant
with many for one week;
But in the middle of the week
He shall bring an end to sacrifice and
offering.
And on the wing of abominations
shall be one who makes desolate,
Even until the consummation, which
is determined,
Is poured out on the desolate."

CHAPTER 10

Vision of the Glorious Man

In the third year of Cyrus king of Persia
a message was revealed to Daniel, whose
name was called Bel·te·shaz'zar. The mes-
sage *was* true, but the appointed time *was*
long;[a] and he understood the message, and
had understanding of the vision. 2In those
days I, Daniel, was mourning three full
weeks. 3I ate no pleasant food, no meat or
wine came into my mouth, nor did I anoint
myself at all, till three whole weeks were
fulfilled.
4Now on the twenty-fourth day of the
first month, as I was by the side of the great
river, that *is,* the Tī'gris,[a] 5I lifted my eyes
and looked, and behold, a certain man
clothed in linen, whose waist *was* girded
with gold of Ū'phaz! 6His body *was* like
beryl, his face like the appearance of light-
ning, his eyes like torches of fire, his arms
and feet like burnished bronze in color,

9:24 [a]Literally *sevens,* and so throughout the chapter [b]Following Qere, Septuagint, Syriac, and Vulgate; Kethib and Theodotion read *To seal up.* 9:25 [a]Or *open square* [b]Or *moat* 10:1 [a]Or *and of great conflict* 10:4 [a]Hebrew *Hiddekel*

9:24–27 Seventy weeks: The "sevens" are God's own times. Although the vision contains no direct answer to Daniel's concern about Jeremiah's 70-year period (v. 2), God was giving Daniel an overview of events that must occur before his prayer was fully answered. The entire vision (vv. 24–27) refers to the Messiah and His purpose to make an end of sins.

9:26 Messiah . . . cut off: This can only refer to the death of Christ on the Cross. **not for Himself**: see Is. 53:4–6. **people of the prince**: The Romans under Titus, who destroyed Jerusalem in A.D. 70.

and the sound of his words like the voice
of a multitude.

7And I, Daniel, alone saw the vision, for
the men who were with me did not see the
vision; but a great terror fell upon them, so
that they fled to hide themselves. 8There-
fore I was left alone when I saw this great
vision, and no strength remained in me; for
my vigor was turned to frailty in me, and I
retained no strength. 9Yet I heard the sound
of his words; and while I heard the sound
of his words I was in a deep sleep on my
face, with my face to the ground.

Prophecies Concerning Persia and Greece

10Suddenly, a hand touched me, which
made me tremble on my knees and *on* the
palms of my hands. 11And he said to me,
"O Daniel, man greatly beloved, under-
stand the words that I speak to you, and
stand upright, for I have now been sent to
you." While he was speaking this word to
me, I stood trembling.

12Then he said to me, "Do not fear, Dan-
iel, for from the first day that you set your
heart to understand, and to humble your-
self before your God, your words were
heard; and I have come because of your
words. 13But the prince of the kingdom of
Persia withstood me twenty-one days; and
behold, Michael, one of the chief princes,
came to help me, for I had been left alone
there with the kings of Persia. 14Now I have
come to make you understand what will
happen to your people in the latter days,
for the vision *refers* to *many* days yet *to
come*."

15When he had spoken such words to
me, I turned my face toward the ground
and became speechless. 16And suddenly,
one having the likeness of the sons[a] of men
touched my lips; then I opened my mouth
and spoke, saying to him who stood before
me, "My lord, because of the vision my
sorrows have overwhelmed me, and I have
retained no strength. 17For how can this
servant of my lord talk with you, my lord?
As for me, no strength remains in me now,
nor is any breath left in me."

18Then again, *the one* having the likeness
of a man touched me and strengthened
me. 19And he said, "O man greatly
beloved, fear not! Peace *be* to you; be
strong, yes, be strong!"

So when he spoke to me I was strength-
ened, and said, "Let my lord speak, for you
have strengthened me."

20Then he said, "Do you know why I
have come to you? And now I must return
to fight with the prince of Persia; and when
I have gone forth, indeed the prince of
Greece will come. 21But I will tell you what
is noted in the Scripture of Truth. (No one
upholds me against these, except Michael
your prince.

CHAPTER 11

"Also in the first year of Da·rī'us the
Mēde, I, *even* I, stood up to confirm and
strengthen him.) 2And now I will tell you
the truth: Behold, three more kings will
arise in Persia, and the fourth shall be far
richer than *them* all; by his strength,
through his riches, he shall stir up all
against the realm of Greece. 3Then a
mighty king shall arise, who shall rule
with great dominion, and do according to
his will. 4And when he has arisen, his king-
dom shall be broken up and divided to-

10:16 [a]Theodotion and Vulgate read *the son;* Septuagint reads *a hand.*

10:13 Michael . . . came to help me: This verse, with v. 20 and 12:1, reveals that there are supernatural champions both for good and for evil taking part in earthly conflicts (see also James 4:7, 8; Rom. 8:26).

11:3 a mighty king: Alexander the Great in 333 B.C. defeated the Persian armies.

11:4 divided . . . four winds: Alexander's empire was divided into four kingdoms. **not . . . his posterity**: No relative of Alexander ruled after his death.

ward the four winds of heaven, but not
among his posterity nor according to his
dominion with which he ruled; for his
kingdom shall be uprooted, even for others besides these.

Warring Kings of North and South

5"Also the king of the South shall become strong, as well as *one* of his princes;
and he shall gain power over him and have
dominion. His dominion *shall be* a great
dominion. 6And at the end of *some* years
they shall join forces, for the daughter of
the king of the South shall go to the king of
the North to make an agreement; but she
shall not retain the power of her authority,[a]
and neither he nor his authority[b] shall
stand; but she shall be given up, with those
who brought her, and with him who begot
her, and with him who strengthened her in
those times. 7But from a branch of her roots
one shall arise in his place, who shall come
with an army, enter the fortress of the king
of the North, and deal with them and prevail. 8And he shall also carry their gods
captive to Egypt, with their princes[a] *and*
their precious articles of silver and gold;
and he shall continue *more* years than the
king of the North.

9"Also *the king of the North* shall come to
the kingdom of the king of the South, but
shall return to his own land. 10However his
sons shall stir up strife, and assemble a
multitude of great forces; and *one* shall certainly come and overwhelm and pass
through; then he shall return to his fortress
and stir up strife.

11"And the king of the South shall be
moved with rage, and go out and fight
with him, with the king of the North, who
shall muster a great multitude; but the
multitude shall be given into the hand of
his *enemy.* 12When he has taken away the
multitude, his heart will be lifted up; and
he will cast down tens of thousands, but he
will not prevail. 13For the king of the North
will return and muster a multitude greater
than the former, and shall certainly come
at the end of some years with a great army
and much equipment.

14"Now in those times many shall rise
up against the king of the South. Also, violent men[a] of your people shall exalt themselves in fulfillment of the vision, but they
shall fall. 15So the king of the North shall
come and build a siege mound, and take a
fortified city; and the forces[a] of the South
shall not withstand *him.* Even his choice
troops *shall have* no strength to resist. 16But
he who comes against him shall do according to his own will, and no one shall stand
against him. He shall stand in the Glorious
Land with destruction in his power.[a]

17"He shall also set his face to enter with
the strength of his whole kingdom, and
upright ones[a] with him; thus shall he do.
And he shall give him the daughter of
women to destroy it; but she shall not
stand *with him,* or be for him. 18After this he
shall turn his face to the coastlands, and
shall take many. But a ruler shall bring the
reproach against them to an end; and with
the reproach removed, he shall turn back
on him. 19Then he shall turn his face toward the fortress of his own land; but he
shall stumble and fall, and not be found.

20"There shall arise in his place one who
imposes taxes *on* the glorious kingdom;
but within a few days he shall be destroyed, but not in anger or in battle. 21And
in his place shall arise a vile person, to
whom they will not give the honor of

11:6 [a]Literally *arm* [b]Literally *arm* 11:8 [a]Or *molded images* 11:14 [a]Or *robbers,* literally *sons of breakage* 11:15 [a]Literally *arms* 11:16 [a]Literally *hand* 11:17 [a]Or *bring equitable terms*

11:14–19 A series of victories, but final defeat for the northern forces of Syria/Mesopotamia. Judah, in the **Glorious Land** (v. 16), will be caught in the middle between these warring kingdoms. These verses cover the years 323–175 B.C. Almost every event mentioned here is related in the secular history of the period.

royalty; but he shall come in peaceably, and seize the kingdom by intrigue. [22]With the force[a] of a flood they shall be swept away from before him and be broken, and also the prince of the covenant. [23]And after the league *is made* with him he shall act deceitfully, for he shall come up and become strong with a small *number of* people. [24]He shall enter peaceably, even into the richest places of the province; and he shall do *what* his fathers have not done, nor his forefathers: he shall disperse among them the plunder, spoil, and riches; and he shall devise his plans against the strongholds, but *only* for a time.

[25]"He shall stir up his power and his courage against the king of the South with a great army. And the king of the South shall be stirred up to battle with a very great and mighty army; but he shall not stand, for they shall devise plans against him. [26]Yes, those who eat of the portion of his delicacies shall destroy him; his army shall be swept away, and many shall fall down slain. [27]Both these kings' hearts *shall be* bent on evil, and they shall speak lies at the same table; but it shall not prosper, for the end *will* still *be* at the appointed time. [28]While returning to his land with great riches, his heart shall be *moved* against the holy covenant; so he shall do *damage* and return to his own land.

The Northern King's Blasphemies

[29]"At the appointed time he shall return and go toward the south; but it shall not be like the former or the latter. [30]For ships from Cyprus[a] shall come against him; therefore he shall be grieved, and return in rage against the holy covenant, and do *damage.*

"So he shall return and show regard for those who forsake the holy covenant. [31]And forces[a] shall be mustered by him, and they shall defile the sanctuary fortress; then they shall take away the daily *sacrifices,* and place *there* the abomination of desolation. [32]Those who do wickedly against the covenant he shall corrupt with flattery; but the people who know their God shall be strong, and carry out *great exploits.* [33]And those of the people who understand shall instruct many; yet *for many* days they shall fall by sword and flame, by captivity and plundering. [34]Now when they fall, they shall be aided with a little help; but many shall join with them by intrigue. [35]And *some* of those of understanding shall fall, to refine them, purify *them,* and make *them* white, *until* the time of the end; because *it is* still for the appointed time.

[36]"Then the king shall do according to his own will: he shall exalt and magnify himself above every god, shall speak blasphemies against the God of gods, and shall prosper till the wrath has been accomplished; for what has been determined shall be done. [37]He shall regard neither the God[a] of his fathers nor the desire of women, nor regard any god; for he shall exalt himself above *them* all. [38]But in their place he shall honor a god of fortresses; and a god which his fathers did not know he shall honor with gold and silver, with precious stones and pleasant things. [39]Thus he shall act against the strongest fortresses with a foreign god, which he shall acknowledge, *and* advance *its* glory; and

11:22 [a]Literally *arms* 11:30 [a]Hebrew *Kittim,* western lands, especially Cyprus 11:31 [a]Literally *arms* 11:37 [a]Or *gods*

11:30 Ships from Cyprus refers here to the Roman envoy who forced Antiochus to leave Egypt in 168 B.C. Thwarted in Egypt, Antiochus began in rage his desecrations and persecution of the faithful Jews.

11:31 The regular Jewish **sacrifices** were abolished. **the abomination**: A heathen altar was built on the Jewish altar of sacrifice (see Matt. 24:15).

11:36–45 A description of the future Antichrist, illustrated by Antiochus's self-deification. From this point on, the end of the age seems to be in view.

he shall cause them to rule over many, and divide the land for gain.

The Northern King's Conquests

[40]"At the time of the end the king of the South shall attack him; and the king of the North shall come against him like a whirlwind, with chariots, horsemen, and with many ships; and he shall enter the countries, overwhelm *them,* and pass through.
[41]He shall also enter the Glorious Land, and many *countries* shall be overthrown; but these shall escape from his hand: Ē'dom, Mō'ab, and the prominent people of Am'mon. [42]He shall stretch out his hand against the countries, and the land of Egypt shall not escape. [43]He shall have power over the treasures of gold and silver, and over all the precious things of Egypt; also the Lib'yans and Ethiopians *shall follow* at his heels. [44]But news from the east and the north shall trouble him; therefore he shall go out with great fury to destroy and annihilate many. [45]And he shall plant the tents of his palace between the seas and the glorious holy mountain; yet he shall come to his end, and no one will help him.

CHAPTER 12

Prophecy of the End Time

"At that time Michael shall stand up,
The great prince who stands *watch*
over the sons of your people;
And there shall be a time of
trouble,
Such as never was since there was a
nation,
Even to that time.
And at that time your people shall be
delivered,
Every one who is found written in the
book.
2 And many of those who sleep in the
dust of the earth shall awake,
Some to everlasting life,
Some to shame *and* everlasting
contempt.
3 Those who are wise shall shine
Like the brightness of the firmament,
And those who turn many to
righteousness
Like the stars forever and ever.

[4]"But you, Daniel, shut up the words, and seal the book until the time of the end; many shall run to and fro, and knowledge shall increase."

[5]Then I, Daniel, looked; and there stood two others, one on this riverbank and the other on that riverbank. [6]And *one* said to the man clothed in linen, who *was* above the waters of the river, "How long shall the fulfillment of these wonders *be?"*

[7]Then I heard the man clothed in linen, who *was* above the waters of the river, when he held up his right hand and his left hand to heaven, and swore by Him who lives forever, that *it shall be* for a time, times, and half *a time;* and when the power of the holy people has been completely shattered, all these *things* shall be finished.

[8]Although I heard, I did not understand. Then I said, "My lord, what *shall be* the end of these *things?"*

[9]And he said, "Go *your way,* Daniel, for the words *are* closed up and sealed till the time of the end. [10]Many shall be purified, made white, and refined, but the wicked shall do wickedly; and none of the wicked shall understand, but the wise shall understand.

12:1 Michael is called the archangel in Jude 9; here he is the champion of God's **people**, Israel. **the book**: The Book of Life (see Rev. 3:5).

12:2, 3 These verses contain the first explicit teaching of the general resurrection, with **everlasting life** awaiting the faithful, but eternal punishment for those who reject God (see Matt. 25:46).

12:4 seal the book: Not to conceal, but to authenticate and to preserve from loss.

[11]"And from the time *that* the daily *sacrifice* is taken away, and the abomination of desolation is set up, *there shall be* one thousand two hundred and ninety days.
[12]Blessed *is* he who waits, and comes to the one thousand three hundred and thirty-five days.

[13]"But you, go *your way* till the end; for you shall rest, and will arise to your inheritance at the end of the days."

✦Hosea✦

The first of the twelve minor prophets, Hosea lived during the reign of King Jeroboam II and prophesied in Israel from about 755 to 715 B.C. During this time, Israel was outwardly prosperous; however, the nation had become inwardly corrupt, worshiping false gods. Israel's gradual straying from the Lord shows the danger believers face of becoming more complacent and hardened to spiritual things through the passing of time. God's judgment for the sin of His people resulted in Assyria destroying the capital city in 722 B.C.

The first three chapters tell of Hosea's marriage to Gomer, who is unfaithful and deserts him. Gomer bore three children, named Jezreel ("God scatters"), Lo-Ruhamah ("not pitied"), and Lo-Ammi ("not my people"). The next chapters parallel Israel to Gomer: Israel deserted God just as Gomer deserted Hosea, and Gomer's degradation in chapter 2, as well as the symbolic names of Hosea's children, tells of God's coming judgment on the nation. Just as Hosea rescued Gomer from the slave market, God promises to one day restore His people.

Like Deuteronomy and John, the Book of Hosea contains proof of God's loyal love along with its prophecy of judgment. Hosea describes God's continued faithfulness and loyal love despite the backsliding of His people. ✦

CHAPTER 1

The word of the LORD that came to
Hō·sē′a the son of Be·ē′rī, in the days of
Uz·zī′ah, Jō′tham, Ā′haz, *and* Hez·e·kī′ah,
kings of Judah, and in the days of Jer-
o·bō′am the son of Jō′ash, king of Israel.

The Family of Hosea

2When the LORD began to speak by Hō-
sē′a, the LORD said to Hō·sē′a:

"Go, take yourself a wife of harlotry
And children of harlotry,
For the land has committed great
harlotry
By departing from the LORD."

3So he went and took Gō′mer the daughter
of Dib·lā′im, and she conceived and bore
him a son. 4Then the LORD said to him:

"Call his name Jez′rē·el,
For in a little *while*
I will avenge the bloodshed of
Jez′rē·el on the house of Jē′hū,
And bring an end to the kingdom of
the house of Israel.

1:3–5 Hosea's first son was given the symbolic name **Jezreel** signifying judgment on the **house of Jehu** for the massacre at Jezreel (2 Kin. 10:11). That judgment was fulfilled in Zechariah, the last of Jehu's dynasty as decreed in 2 Kin. 10:30 (see 2 Kin. 15:8–12). The massacre of Ahab's house was by God's appointment (2 Kin. 9:1–10), but judgment was administered either because Jehu went beyond the bounds of his commission or because of the vicious spirit in which it was done. See Is. 10:5–19 for a similar pattern with Assyria.

5 It shall come to pass in that day
That I will break the bow of Israel in
the Valley of Jez′rē•el."

6And she conceived again and bore a
daughter. Then *God* said to him:

"Call her name Lō-Rū•ha′mah,[a]
For I will no longer have mercy on
the house of Israel,
But I will utterly take them away.[b]
7 Yet I will have mercy on the house of
Judah,
Will save them by the LORD their God,
And will not save them by bow,
Nor by sword or battle,
By horses or horsemen."

8Now when she had weaned Lō-Rū-
ha′mah, she conceived and bore a son.
9Then *God* said:

"Call his name Lō-Am′mī,[a]
For you *are* not My people,
And I will not be your *God*.

The Restoration of Israel

10 "Yet the number of the children of
Israel
Shall be as the sand of the sea,
Which cannot be measured or
numbered.
And it shall come to pass
In the place where it was said to
them,
'You *are* not My people,'[a]
There it shall be said to them,
'*You are* sons of the living God.'
11 Then the children of Judah and the
children of Israel
Shall be gathered together,
And appoint for themselves one
head;
And they shall come up out of the
land,
For great *will be* the day of Jez′rē•el!

CHAPTER 2

Say to your brethren, 'My people,'[a]
And to your sisters, 'Mercy[b] *is shown*.'

God's Unfaithful People

2 "Bring charges against your mother,
bring charges;
For she *is* not My wife, nor *am* I her
Husband!
Let her put away her harlotries from
her sight,
And her adulteries from between her
breasts;
3 Lest I strip her naked
And expose her, as in the day she was
born,
And make her like a wilderness,
And set her like a dry land,
And slay her with thirst.

4 "I will not have mercy on her children,
For they *are* the children of harlotry.
5 For their mother has played the
harlot;
She who conceived them has behaved
shamefully.
For she said, 'I will go after my
lovers,
Who give *me* my bread and my water,
My wool and my linen,
My oil and my drink.'

1:6 [a]Literally *No-Mercy* [b]Or *That I may forgive them at all* 1:9 [a]Literally *Not-My-People* 1:10 [a]Hebrew *lo-ammi* (compare verse 9) 2:1 [a]Hebrew *Ammi* (compare 1:9, 10) [b]Hebrew *Ruhamah* (compare 1:6)

1:6, 7 Lo-Ruhamah means "Unpitied" and may imply that she was not Hosea's child. Prophetically the name signified the end of mercy for the northern kingdom.

1:8, 9 The third child was named **Lo-Ammi** meaning "Not My People," pointing to the culmination of Israel's persistent unfaithfulness. Many feel it also implied that Hosea was not the father.

6 "Therefore, behold,
I will hedge up your way with
thorns,
And wall her in,
So that she cannot find her paths.
7 She will chase her lovers,
But not overtake them;
Yes, she will seek them, but not find
them.
Then she will say,
'I will go and return to my first
husband,
For then *it was* better for me than
now.'
8 For she did not know
That I gave her grain, new wine, and
oil,
And multiplied her silver and gold—
Which they prepared for Bā'al.

9 "Therefore I will return and take away
My grain in its time
And My new wine in its season,
And will take back My wool and My
linen,
Given to cover her nakedness.
10 Now I will uncover her lewdness in
the sight of her lovers,
And no one shall deliver her from My
hand.
11 I will also cause all her mirth to cease,
Her feast days,
Her New Moons,
Her Sabbaths—
All her appointed feasts.

12 "And I will destroy her vines and her
fig trees,
Of which she has said,
'These *are* my wages that my lovers
have given me.'
So I will make them a forest,
And the beasts of the field shall eat
them.
13 I will punish her
For the days of the Bā'als to which
she burned incense.
She decked herself with her earrings
and jewelry,
And went after her lovers;
But Me she forgot," says the LORD.

God's Mercy on His People

14 "Therefore, behold, I will allure her,
Will bring her into the wilderness,
And speak comfort to her.
15 I will give her her vineyards from
there,
And the Valley of Ā'chor as a door of
hope;
She shall sing there,
As in the days of her youth,
As in the day when she came up from
the land of Egypt.

16 "And it shall be, in that day,"
Says the LORD,
"*That* you will call Me 'My Husband,'[a]
And no longer call Me 'My Master,'[b]
17 For I will take from her mouth the
names of the Bā'als,
And they shall be remembered by
their name no more.
18 In that day I will make a covenant for
them
With the beasts of the field,
With the birds of the air,

2:16 [a]Hebrew *Ishi* [b]Hebrew *Baali*

2:7 return to my first husband: Israel must realize that the Lord alone is the source of her sustenance. This would be the first step in her rehabilitation.

2:14–23 I will allure her: The second step (see note on v. 7) in Israel's return to God is depicted as a courtship.

2:16, 17 Israel was no longer to worship the Lord as if He were Baal. The Hebrew word *ba'al*, meaning "master," had become the name of the Canaanite god Baal. **take from her mouth**: God wanted them to remove the very word from their language. He would be Israel's **Husband** *('ish)*, not her **Master** *(ba'al)*.

And *with* the creeping things of the
ground.
Bow and sword of battle I will shatter
from the earth,
To make them lie down safely.

19 "I will betroth you to Me forever;
Yes, I will betroth you to Me
In righteousness and justice,
In lovingkindness and mercy;
20 I will betroth you to Me in
faithfulness,
And you shall know the LORD.

21 "It shall come to pass in that day
That I will answer," says the LORD;
"I will answer the heavens,
And they shall answer the earth.
22 The earth shall answer
With grain,
With new wine,
And with oil;
They shall answer Jez'rē·el.[a]
23 Then I will sow her for Myself in the
earth,
And I will have mercy on *her who had*
not obtained mercy;[a]
Then I will say to *those who were* not
My people,[b]
'You *are* My people!'
And they shall say, '*You are* my
God!' "

CHAPTER 3

Israel Will Return to God

Then the LORD said to me, "Go again,
love a woman *who is* loved by a lover[a] and
is committing adultery, just like the love of
the LORD for the children of Israel, who
look to other gods and love *the* raisin cakes
of the pagans."
2So I bought her for myself for fifteen
shekels of silver, and one and one-half
homers of barley. 3And I said to her, "You
shall stay with me many days; you shall
not play the harlot, nor shall you have a
man—so, too, *will* I *be* toward you."
4For the children of Israel shall abide
many days without king or prince, without
sacrifice or sacred pillar, without ephod or
teraphim. 5Afterward the children of Israel
shall return and seek the LORD their God
and David their king. They shall fear
the LORD and His goodness in the latter
days.

CHAPTER 4

God's Charge Against Israel

Hear the word of the LORD,
You children of Israel,
For the LORD *brings* a charge against
the inhabitants of the land:

"There is no truth or mercy
Or knowledge of God in the land.
2 *By* swearing and lying,
Killing and stealing and committing
adultery,
They break all restraint,
With bloodshed upon bloodshed.
3 Therefore the land will mourn;

2:22 [a]Literally *God Will Sow* 2:23 [a]Hebrew *lo-ruhamah* [b]Hebrew *lo-ammi* 3:1 [a]Literally *friend* or *husband*

2:21–23 in that day: A kind of formula which refers to a coming time of God's action, either in judgment or, as here, in deliverance. **earth shall answer**: The fertility of the soil would be renewed. **Jezreel**: Here the name means "God Will Sow" replacing the judgmental meaning of 1:4. **My people . . . my God**: The promise of the Exodus would be realized (v. 23; see Ex. 6:7).

3:1–5 Hosea's love for his errant wife and God's love for His rebellious people demonstrate the forgiving attitude we should have toward those who mistreat us. If God could forgive the sins of the entire world, what right have we to hold a grudge against anyone?

3:3, 4 nor shall you have a man: Just as Gomer would be deprived of her many lovers, Israel would be deprived in the Exile of all her political and religious trappings which she had loved. In exile she would be forced to trust in God alone, and in simplicity.

And everyone who dwells there will
waste away
With the beasts of the field
And the birds of the air;
Even the fish of the sea will be taken
away.

4 "Now let no man contend, or rebuke
another;
For your people *are* like those who
contend with the priest.
5 Therefore you shall stumble in the
day;
The prophet also shall stumble with
you in the night;
And I will destroy your mother.
6 My people are destroyed for lack of
knowledge.
Because you have rejected
knowledge,
I also will reject you from being priest
for Me;
Because you have forgotten the law of
your God,
I also will forget your children.

7 "The more they increased,
The more they sinned against Me;
I will change[a] their glory[b] into shame.
8 They eat up the sin of My people;
They set their heart on their iniquity.
9 And it shall be: like people, like
priest.
So I will punish them for their ways,
And reward them for their deeds.
10 For they shall eat, but not have
enough;
They shall commit harlotry, but not
increase;
Because they have ceased obeying the
LORD.

The Idolatry of Israel

11 "Harlotry, wine, and new wine enslave
the heart.
12 My people ask counsel from their
wooden *idols*,
And their staff informs them.
For the spirit of harlotry has caused
them to stray,
And they have played the harlot
against their God.
13 They offer sacrifices on the
mountaintops,
And burn incense on the hills,
Under oaks, poplars, and terebinths,
Because their shade *is* good.
Therefore your daughters commit
harlotry,
And your brides commit adultery.

14 "I will not punish your daughters
when they commit harlotry,
Nor your brides when they commit
adultery;
For *the men* themselves go apart with
harlots,
And offer sacrifices with a ritual
harlot.[a]
Therefore people *who* do not
understand will be trampled.

15 "Though you, Israel, play the harlot,
Let not Judah offend.
Do not come up to Gil'gal,
Nor go up to Beth Ā'ven,
Nor swear an oath, *saying,* 'As the
LORD lives'—

16 "For Israel is stubborn
Like a stubborn calf;
Now the LORD will let them forage
Like a lamb in open country.

4:7 [a]Following Masoretic Text, Septuagint, and Vulgate; scribal tradition, Syriac, and Targum read *They will change.* [b]Following Masoretic Text, Septuagint, Syriac, Targum, and Vulgate; scribal tradition reads *My glory.*
4:14 [a]Compare Deuteronomy 23:18

4:6 What we don't know can hurt us. In searching the Scriptures we will discover God's will and then we can serve Him faithfully. When we fail to read the Bible, we miss out on God's guidance and will inevitably fall into sin.

17 "Ē′phra·im *is* joined to idols,
Let him alone.
18 Their drink is rebellion,
They commit harlotry continually.
Her rulers dearly love dishonor.[a]
19 The wind has wrapped her up in its
wings,
And they shall be ashamed because
of their sacrifices.

CHAPTER 5

Impending Judgment on Israel and Judah

"Hear this, O priests!
Take heed, O house of Israel!
Give ear, O house of the king!
For yours *is* the judgment,
Because you have been a snare to
Miz′pah
And a net spread on Tā′bor.
2 The revolters are deeply involved in
slaughter,
Though I rebuke them all.
3 I know Ē′phra·im,
And Israel is not hidden from Me;
For now, O Ē′phra·im, you commit
harlotry;
Israel is defiled.

4 "They do not direct their deeds
Toward turning to their God,
For the spirit of harlotry is in their
midst,
And they do not know the LORD.
5 The pride of Israel testifies to his
face;
Therefore Israel and Ē′phra·im
stumble in their iniquity;
Judah also stumbles with them.

6 "With their flocks and herds
They shall go to seek the LORD,
But they will not find *Him;*
He has withdrawn Himself from
them.
7 They have dealt treacherously with
the LORD,
For they have begotten pagan
children.
Now a New Moon shall devour them
and their heritage.

8 "Blow the ram's horn in Gib′ē·ah,
The trumpet in Rā′mah!
Cry aloud *at* Beth Ā′ven,
'*Look* behind you, O Benjamin!'
9 Ē′phra·im shall be desolate in the day
of rebuke;
Among the tribes of Israel I make
known what is sure.

10 "The princes of Judah are like those
who remove a landmark;
I will pour out My wrath on them
like water.
11 Ē′phra·im is oppressed *and* broken in
judgment,
Because he willingly walked by
human precept.
12 Therefore I *will be* to Ē′phra·im like a
moth,
And to the house of Judah like
rottenness.

13 "When Ē′phra·im saw his sickness,
And Judah *saw* his wound,
Then Ē′phra·im went to Assyria
And sent to King Jā′reb;
Yet he cannot cure you,
Nor heal you of your wound.
14 For I *will be* like a lion to Ē′phra·im,
And like a young lion to the house of
Judah.
I, *even* I, will tear *them* and go away;

4:18 [a]Hebrew is difficult; a Jewish tradition reads *Her rulers shamefully love, 'Give!'*

5:10 Instead of supporting Judah's religious traditions, as they should, Judah's **princes** were tearing them down. To **remove a landmark** was an especially grievous sin because boundaries were originally set by the Lord (see Deut. 19:14).

I will take *them* away, and no one
shall rescue.
15 I will return again to My place
Till they acknowledge their offense.
Then they will seek My face;
In their affliction they will earnestly
seek Me."

CHAPTER 6

A Call to Repentance

Come, and let us return to the LORD;
For He has torn, but He will heal us;
He has stricken, but He will bind us
up.
2 After two days He will revive us;
On the third day He will raise us
up,
That we may live in His sight.
3 Let us know,
Let us pursue the knowledge of the
LORD.
His going forth is established as the
morning;
He will come to us like the rain,
Like the latter *and* former rain to the
earth.

Impenitence of Israel and Judah

4 "O Ē'phra·im, what shall I do to you?
O Judah, what shall I do to you?
For your faithfulness is like a
morning cloud,
And like the early dew it goes away.
5 Therefore I have hewn *them* by the
prophets,
I have slain them by the words of My
mouth;
And your judgments *are like* light *that*
goes forth.
6 For I desire mercy and not sacrifice,
And the knowledge of God more
than burnt offerings.

7 "But like men[a] they transgressed the
covenant;
There they dealt treacherously with
Me.
8 Gil'ē·ad *is* a city of evildoers
And defiled with blood.
9 As bands of robbers lie in wait for a
man,
So the company of priests murder on
the way to Shē'chem;
Surely they commit lewdness.
10 I have seen a horrible thing in the
house of Israel:
There *is* the harlotry of Ē'phra·im;
Israel is defiled.
11 Also, O Judah, a harvest is appointed
for you,
When I return the captives of My
people.

> A man has deprived himself of the best there is in the world who has deprived himself of this, a knowledge of the Bible. When you have read the Bible, you will know that it is the Word of God, because you will have found it the key to your own heart, your own happiness, and your own duty.
>
> Woodrow Wilson

6:7 [a]Or *like Adam*

6:1–3 At first glance, Israel's response seems to indicate genuine repentance. However, no specific confession of sin is included, and v. 1 seems to blame God for their trials rather than acknowledging that their troubles are a result of their sin. True repentance doesn't come until chapter 14.

6:4–11:11 A further recital of Israel's sins with an emphasis on their perverted love. Again, however, the warning ends on a note of hope. Israel's love may be fickle, but God's love is unchanging.

6:6 A verse, worthy of memorizing, that is considered by many as the key to the book. Religious behavior can never substitute for a heart wholly submitted to God. He places more value on our relationship with Him than on our adherence to rituals and rules.

CHAPTER 7

"When I would have healed Israel,
Then the iniquity of Ē′phra·im was uncovered,
And the wickedness of Samaria.
For they have committed fraud;
A thief comes in;
A band of robbers takes spoil outside.
2 They do not consider in their hearts
That I remember all their wickedness;
Now their own deeds have surrounded them;
They are before My face.
3 They make a king glad with their wickedness,
And princes with their lies.

4 "They *are* all adulterers.
Like an oven heated by a baker—
He ceases stirring *the fire* after kneading the dough,
Until it is leavened.
5 In the day of our king
Princes have made *him* sick, inflamed with wine;
He stretched out his hand with scoffers.
6 They prepare their heart like an oven,
While they lie in wait;
Their baker[a] sleeps all night;
In the morning it burns like a flaming fire.
7 They are all hot, like an oven,
And have devoured their judges;
All their kings have fallen.
None among them calls upon Me.

8 "Ē′phra·im has mixed himself among the peoples;
Ē′phra·im is a cake unturned.
9 Aliens have devoured his strength,
But he does not know *it;*
Yes, gray hairs are here and there on him,
Yet he does not know *it*.
10 And the pride of Israel testifies to his face,
But they do not return to the LORD their God,
Nor seek Him for all this.

Futile Reliance on the Nations

11 "Ē′phra·im also is like a silly dove, without sense—
They call to Egypt,
They go to Assyria.
12 Wherever they go, I will spread My net on them;
I will bring them down like birds of the air;
I will chastise them
According to what their congregation has heard.

13 "Woe to them, for they have fled from Me!
Destruction to them,
Because they have transgressed against Me!
Though I redeemed them,
Yet they have spoken lies against Me.
14 They did not cry out to Me with their heart
When they wailed upon their beds.

"They assemble together for[a] grain and new wine,

7:6 [a]Following Masoretic Text and Vulgate; Syriac and Targum read *Their anger;* Septuagint reads *Ephraim.*
7:14 [a]Following Masoretic Text and Targum; Vulgate reads *thought upon;* Septuagint reads *slashed themselves for* (compare 1 Kings 18:28).

7:1–16 By three metaphors Hosea describes Israel's attempt to survive by political maneuvers: Like a baker's **oven** (v. 4) their plots burned in their hearts. Like a **cake unturned** (v. 8) they were following a half-baked policy. Like a **silly dove** (v. 11) they flew first to one political alliance and then another. During Israel's last 25 years the nation went through six kings and five dynasties, each dynasty ending with violence.

They rebel against Me;[b]
15 Though I disciplined *and*
strengthened their arms,
Yet they devise evil against Me;
16 They return, *but* not to the Most
High;[a]
They are like a treacherous bow.
Their princes shall fall by the
sword
For the cursings of their tongue.
This *shall be* their derision in the land
of Egypt.

CHAPTER 8

The Apostasy of Israel

"*Set* the trumpet[a] to your mouth!
He shall come like an eagle against the
house of the LORD,
Because they have transgressed My
covenant
And rebelled against My law.
2 Israel will cry to Me,
'My God, we know You!'
3 Israel has rejected the good;
The enemy will pursue him.

4 "They set up kings, but not by Me;
They made princes, but I did not
acknowledge *them.*
From their silver and gold
They made idols for themselves—
That they might be cut off.
5 Your calf is rejected, O Samaria!
My anger is aroused against them—
How long until they attain to
innocence?
6 For from Israel *is* even this:
A workman made it, and it *is* not
God;
But the calf of Samaria shall be
broken to pieces.

7 "They sow the wind,
And reap the whirlwind.
The stalk has no bud;
It shall never produce meal.
If it should produce,
Aliens would swallow it up.
8 Israel is swallowed up;
Now they are among the Gentiles
Like a vessel in which *is* no
pleasure.
9 For they have gone up to Assyria,
Like a wild donkey alone by itself;
Ē'phra·im has hired lovers.
10 Yes, though they have hired among
the nations,
Now I will gather them;
And they shall sorrow a little,[a]
Because of the burden[b] of the king of
princes.

11 "Because Ē'phra·im has made many
altars for sin,
They have become for him altars for
sinning.
12 I have written for him the great
things of My law,
But they were considered a strange
thing.
13 *For* the sacrifices of My offerings they
sacrifice flesh and eat *it,*
But the LORD does not accept them.
Now He will remember their iniquity
and punish their sins.
They shall return to Egypt.

14 "For Israel has forgotten his Maker,
And has built temples;[a]
Judah also has multiplied fortified
cities;
But I will send fire upon his cities,
And it shall devour his palaces."

7:14 [b]Following Masoretic Text, Syriac, and Targum; Septuagint omits *They rebel against Me;* Vulgate reads *They departed from Me.* 7:16 [a]Or *upward* 8:1 [a]Hebrew *shophar,* ram's horn 8:10 [a]Or *begin to diminish* [b]Or *oracle* 8:14 [a]Or *palaces*

8:13 The **return to Egypt** is not intended in a literal sense. Israel would go out of their land into a new captivity, but that captivity would be in Assyria (11:5). Because they had not learned the truths of the Exodus, they must start over again.

CHAPTER 9

Judgment of Israel's Sin

Do not rejoice, O Israel, with joy like
other peoples,
For you have played the harlot
against your God.
You have made love *for* hire on every
threshing floor.
2 The threshing floor and the winepress
Shall not feed them,
And the new wine shall fail in her.

3 They shall not dwell in the LORD's
land,
But Ē'phra·im shall return to Egypt,
And shall eat unclean *things* in
Assyria.
4 They shall not offer wine *offerings* to
the LORD,
Nor shall their sacrifices be pleasing
to Him.
It shall be like bread of mourners to
them;
All who eat it shall be defiled.
For their bread *shall be* for their *own*
life;
It shall not come into the house of the
LORD.

5 What will you do in the appointed
day,
And in the day of the feast of the
LORD?
6 For indeed they are gone because of
destruction.
Egypt shall gather them up;
Memphis shall bury them.
Nettles shall possess their valuables
of silver;
Thorns *shall be* in their tents.

7 The days of punishment have come;
The days of recompense have come.
Israel knows!
The prophet *is* a fool,
The spiritual man *is* insane,
Because of the greatness of your
iniquity and great enmity.
8 The watchman of Ē'phra·im *is* with
my God;
But the prophet *is* a fowler's[a] snare in
all his ways—
Enmity in the house of his God.
9 They are deeply corrupted,
As in the days of Gib'ē·ah.
He will remember their iniquity;
He will punish their sins.

10 "I found Israel
Like grapes in the wilderness;
I saw your fathers
As the firstfruits on the fig tree in its
first season.
But they went to Bā'al Pē'or,
And separated themselves *to that*
shame;
They became an abomination like the
thing they loved.
11 *As for* Ē'phra·im, their glory shall fly
away like a bird—
No birth, no pregnancy, and no
conception!
12 Though they bring up their children,
Yet I will bereave them to the last
man.
Yes, woe to them when I depart from
them!
13 Just as I saw Ē'phra·im like Tȳre,
planted in a pleasant place,
So Ē'phra·im will bring out his
children to the murderer."

14 Give them, O LORD—
What will You give?
Give them a miscarrying womb
And dry breasts!

9:8 [a]That is, one who catches birds in a trap or snare

9:10 Baal Peor: Israel's tendency towards spiritual prostitution was as old as their wilderness days (Num. 25:1–5).

15 "All their wickedness *is* in Gil′gal,
For there I hated them.
Because of the evil of their deeds
I will drive them from My house;
I will love them no more.
All their princes *are* rebellious.
16 Ē′phra·im is stricken,
Their root is dried up;
They shall bear no fruit.
Yes, were they to bear children,
I would kill the darlings of their womb."

17 My God will cast them away,
Because they did not obey Him;
And they shall be wanderers among the nations.

CHAPTER 10

Israel's Sin and Captivity

Israel empties *his* vine;
He brings forth fruit for himself.
According to the multitude of his fruit
He has increased the altars;
According to the bounty of his land
They have embellished *his* sacred pillars.
2 Their heart is divided;
Now they are held guilty.
He will break down their altars;
He will ruin their sacred pillars.

3 For now they say,
"We have no king,
Because we did not fear the LORD.
And as for a king, what would he do for us?"
4 They have spoken words,
Swearing falsely in making a covenant.
Thus judgment springs up like hemlock in the furrows of the field.

5 The inhabitants of Samaria fear
Because of the calf[a] of Beth Ā′ven.
For its people mourn for it,
And its priests shriek for it—
Because its glory has departed from it.
6 *The idol* also shall be carried to Assyria
As a present for King Jā′reb.
Ē′phra·im shall receive shame,
And Israel shall be ashamed of his own counsel.
7 *As for* Samaria, her king is cut off
Like a twig on the water.
8 Also the high places of Ā′ven, the sin of Israel,
Shall be destroyed.
The thorn and thistle shall grow on their altars;
They shall say to the mountains, "Cover us!"
And to the hills, "Fall on us!"

9 "O Israel, you have sinned from the days of Gib′ē·ah;
There they stood.
The battle in Gib′ē·ah against the children of iniquity[a]
Did not overtake them.
10 When *it is* My desire, I will chasten them.
Peoples shall be gathered against them
When I bind them for their two transgressions.[a]

10:5 [a]Literally *calves* 10:9 [a]So read many Hebrew manuscripts, Septuagint, and Vulgate; Masoretic Text reads *unruliness.* 10:10 [a]Or *in their two habitations*

10:8 mountains, "Cover us!" Quoted by both Jesus (Luke 23:30) and John (Rev. 6:16) in describing the great fear of sinful men confronted by the judgment of a righteous God.

10:9, 10 Gibeah: The site of a shameful deed by the tribe of Benjamin against a Levite resulting in the near annihilation of the tribe (Judg. 19; 20). The analogy is drawn between this crime and Israel's treatment of Hosea. Israel shall likewise be destroyed.

11 Ē′phra·im *is* a trained heifer
That loves to thresh *grain;*
But I harnessed her fair neck,
I will make Ē′phra·im pull *a plow.*
Judah shall plow;
Jacob shall break his clods."

12 Sow for yourselves righteousness;
Reap in mercy;
Break up your fallow ground,
For *it is* time to seek the LORD,
Till He comes and rains righteousness
on you.

13 You have plowed wickedness;
You have reaped iniquity.
You have eaten the fruit of lies,
Because you trusted in your own
way,
In the multitude of your mighty men.
14 Therefore tumult shall arise among
your people,
And all your fortresses shall be
plundered
As Shal′man plundered Beth Ar′bel in
the day of battle—
A mother dashed in pieces upon *her*
children.
15 Thus it shall be done to you,
O Beth′el,
Because of your great wickedness.
At dawn the king of Israel
Shall be cut off utterly.

CHAPTER 11

God's Continuing Love for Israel

"When Israel *was* a child, I loved
him,
And out of Egypt I called My son.
2 *As* they called them,[a]
So they went from them;[b]
They sacrificed to the Bā′als,
And burned incense to carved
images.

3 "I taught Ē′phra·im to walk,
Taking them by their arms;[a]
But they did not know that I healed
them.
4 I drew them with gentle cords,[a]
With bands of love,
And I was to them as those who take
the yoke from their neck.[b]
I stooped *and* fed them.

5 "He shall not return to the land of
Egypt;
But the Assyrian shall be his king,
Because they refused to repent.
6 And the sword shall slash in his
cities,
Devour his districts,
And consume *them,*
Because of their own counsels.
7 My people are bent on backsliding
from Me.
Though they call to the Most High,[a]
None at all exalt *Him.*

8 "How can I give you up, Ē′phra·im?
How can I hand you over, Israel?
How can I make you like Ad′mah?
How can I set you like Ze·boi′im?
My heart churns within Me;
My sympathy is stirred.

11:2 [a]Following Masoretic Text and Vulgate; Septuagint reads *Just as I called them;* Targum interprets as *I sent prophets to a thousand of them.* [b]Following Masoretic Text, Targum, and Vulgate; Septuagint reads *from My face.* 11:3 [a]Some Hebrew manuscripts, Septuagint, Syriac, and Vulgate read *My arms.* 11:4 [a]Literally *cords of a man* [b]Literally *jaws* 11:7 [a]Or *upward*

10:12 Fallow ground can be viewed as the hardness of our hearts. When we sow righteousness by walking in obedience to the Lord, we cultivate holiness in our hearts and will reap blessings from God.

11:1–12 No chapter in the OT more graphically depicts the suffering love of God for His people. He is a gracious Father, tenderly teaching His little child to **walk** (vv. 3, 4); a lamenting Husband, agonizing over the waywardness of His faithless wife (v. 8); the loving Savior (vv. 9–11), not giving up on His people (see Ps. 139:7–10).

9 I will not execute the fierceness of My
anger;
I will not again destroy Ē′phra·im.
For I *am* God, and not man,
The Holy One in your midst;
And I will not come with terror.[a]

10 "They shall walk after the LORD.
He will roar like a lion.
When He roars,
Then *His* sons shall come trembling
from the west;
11 They shall come trembling like a bird
from Egypt,
Like a dove from the land of Assyria.
And I will let them dwell in their
houses,"
Says the LORD.

God's Charge Against Ephraim

12 "Ē′phra·im has encircled Me with
lies,
And the house of Israel with deceit;
But Judah still walks with God,
Even with the Holy One[a] *who is*
faithful.

CHAPTER 12

"Ephraim feeds on the wind,
And pursues the east wind;
He daily increases lies and desolation.
Also they make a covenant with the
Assyrians,
And oil is carried to Egypt.

2 "The LORD also *brings* a charge against
Judah,
And will punish Jacob according to
his ways;
According to his deeds He will
recompense him.
3 He took his brother by the heel in the
womb,
And in his strength he struggled with
God.[a]
4 Yes, he struggled with the Angel and
prevailed;
He wept, and sought favor from
Him.
He found Him *in* Beth′el,
And there He spoke to us—
5 That is, the LORD God of hosts.
The LORD *is* His memorable name.
6 So you, by *the help of* your God,
return;
Observe mercy and justice,
And wait on your God continually.

7 "A cunning Cā′naan·īte!
Deceitful scales *are* in his hand;
He loves to oppress.
8 And Ē′phra·im said,
'Surely I have become rich,
I have found wealth for myself;
In all my labors
They shall find in me no iniquity that
is sin.'

9 "But I *am* the LORD your God,
Ever since the land of Egypt;
I will again make you dwell in tents,
As in the days of the appointed feast.
10 I have also spoken by the prophets,
And have multiplied visions;
I have given symbols through the
witness of the prophets."

11 Though Gil′ē·ad *has* idols—
Surely they are vanity—
Though they sacrifice bulls in Gil′gal,
Indeed their altars *shall be* heaps in
the furrows of the field.

12 Jacob fled to the country of Syria;
Israel served for a spouse,
And for a wife he tended *sheep*.
13 By a prophet the LORD brought Israel
out of Egypt,
And by a prophet he was preserved.
14 Ē′phra·im provoked *Him* to anger
most bitterly;
Therefore his Lord will leave the guilt
of his bloodshed upon him,
And return his reproach upon him.

11:9 [a]Or *I will not enter a city*
11:12 [a]Or *holy ones*
12:3 [a]Compare Genesis 32:28

CHAPTER 13

Relentless Judgment on Israel

When Ē′phra·im spoke, trembling,
He exalted *himself* in Israel;
But when he offended through Bā′al
worship, he died.
2 Now they sin more and more,
And have made for themselves
molded images,
Idols of their silver, according to their
skill;
All of it *is* the work of craftsmen.
They say of them,
"Let the men who sacrifice[a] kiss the
calves!"
3 Therefore they shall be like the
morning cloud
And like the early dew that passes
away,
Like chaff blown off from a threshing
floor
And like smoke from a chimney.

4 "Yet I *am* the LORD your God
Ever since the land of Egypt,
And you shall know no God but Me;
For *there is* no savior besides Me.
5 I knew you in the wilderness,
In the land of great drought.
6 When they had pasture, they were
filled;
They were filled and their heart was
exalted;
Therefore they forgot Me.

7 "So I will be to them like a lion;
Like a leopard by the road I will
lurk;
8 I will meet them like a bear deprived
of her cubs;
I will tear open their rib cage,
And there I will devour them like a
lion.
The wild beast shall tear them.

9 "O Israel, you are destroyed,[a]
But your help[b] *is* from Me.
10 I will be your King;[a]
Where *is any other,*
That he may save you in all your
cities?
And your judges to whom you said,
'Give me a king and princes'?
11 I gave you a king in My anger,
And took *him* away in My wrath.

12 "The iniquity of Ē′phra·im *is* bound
up;
His sin *is* stored up.
13 The sorrows of a woman in childbirth
shall come upon him.
He *is* an unwise son,
For he should not stay long where
children are born.

14 "I will ransom them from the power of
the grave;[a]
I will redeem them from death.
O Death, I will be your plagues![b]
O Grave,[c] I will be your destruction![d]
Pity is hidden from My eyes."

15 Though he is fruitful among *his*
brethren,
An east wind shall come;
The wind of the LORD shall come up
from the wilderness.

13:2 [a]Or *those who offer human sacrifice*
13:9 [a]Literally *it* or *he destroyed you* [b]Literally *in your help* 13:10 [a]Septuagint, Syriac, Targum, and Vulgate read *Where is your king?* 13:14 [a]Or *Sheol* [b]Septuagint reads *where is your punishment?* [c]Or *Sheol* [d]Septuagint reads *where is your sting?*

13:1 The early dominance of the tribe of **Ephraim** resulted in other tribes **trembling** before it. But Ephraim **died** as a leader because he worshiped Baal. Faithlessness to the Lord results in the death sentence.

13:4 The essence of Hosea's theology: (1) The Lord is shown as the God of Israel because of the Exodus deliverance. (2) The Lord demands exclusive loyalty as the first commandment declares. (3) There is no effective help for Israel other than the Lord.

Then his spring shall become dry,
And his fountain shall be dried up.
He shall plunder the treasury of
every desirable prize.

16 Samaria is held guilty,[a]
For she has rebelled against her
God.
They shall fall by the sword,
Their infants shall be dashed in
pieces,
And their women with child ripped
open.

CHAPTER 14

Israel Restored at Last

O Israel, return to the LORD your
God,
For you have stumbled because of
your iniquity;
2 Take words with you,
And return to the LORD.
Say to Him,
"Take away all iniquity;
Receive *us* graciously,
For we will offer the sacrifices[a] of our
lips.
3 Assyria shall not save us,
We will not ride on horses,
Nor will we say anymore to the work
of our hands, *'You are* our gods.'
For in You the fatherless finds mercy."

4 "I will heal their backsliding,
I will love them freely,
For My anger has turned away from
him.
5 I will be like the dew to Israel;
He shall grow like the lily,
And lengthen his roots like Lebanon.
6 His branches shall spread;
His beauty shall be like an olive tree,
And his fragrance like Lebanon.
7 Those who dwell under his shadow
shall return;
They shall be revived *like* grain,
And grow like a vine.
Their scent[a] *shall be* like the wine of
Lebanon.

8 "Ē'phra·im *shall say,* 'What have I to
do anymore with idols?'
I have heard and observed him.
I *am* like a green cypress tree;
Your fruit is found in Me."

9 Who *is* wise?
Let him understand these things.
Who is prudent?
Let him know them.
For the ways of the LORD *are* right;
The righteous walk in them,
But transgressors stumble in them.

13:16 [a]Septuagint reads *shall be disfigured*
14:2 [a]Literally *bull calves;* Septuagint reads *fruit.*
14:7 [a]Literally *remembrance*

14:4–9 God's response to confession (vv. 1–3) is forgiveness, restoration, life, and healing.

14:9 Like the wise man in Eccl. 12:13, Hosea bids us to hear the conclusion of the whole matter: **the ways of the LORD are right**. True wisdom is serving Him wholeheartedly and walking consistently in the path down which He leads us.

✦Joel✦

Joel identifies himself only as the son of Pethuel, and the time of his writing cannot be dated with certainty. Since no king is mentioned, some scholars believe the Book of Joel was written in the ninth century B.C., when Jehoiada the high priest was regent during the boyhood years of Joash.

Joel believed that a recent plague of locusts, which devoured every green thing, was sent by God as a judgment for Judah's sin. He warned of even greater judgments to come during the terrible day of the Lord. He encouraged Judah to repent, promising that God would not punish the nation if it turned from its sin. Joel also predicted the future coming of the Holy Spirit (2:28–32), and Peter later used this passage to explain the event at Pentecost (Acts 2:16–21).

The Book of Joel shows that God's messages may come in the form of a natural disaster. The Lord will not allow evil to continue unpunished; however, those who repent—even late in life—will receive His mercy. God used the locust plague to stir the hearts of His people to repent and follow His will. ✦

CHAPTER 1

The word of the LORD that came to Jō'el the son of Pe·thū'el.

The Land Laid Waste

2 Hear this, you elders,
And give ear, all you inhabitants of the land!
Has *anything like* this happened in your days,
Or even in the days of your fathers?
3 Tell your children about it,
Let your children *tell* their children,
And their children another generation.

4 What the chewing locust[a] left, the swarming locust has eaten;
What the swarming locust left, the crawling locust has eaten;
And what the crawling locust left, the consuming locust has eaten.

5 Awake, you drunkards, and weep;
And wail, all you drinkers of wine,
Because of the new wine,
For it has been cut off from your mouth.
6 For a nation has come up against My land,

1:4 [a]Exact identity of these locusts is unknown.

1:2–20 In the light of a devastating locust plague, Joel calls for national mourning. Evidently there had been almost total destruction of vegetation with resultant drought and famine. The prophet interprets it as a judgment from God.

1:3 Christians are responsible to share their knowledge of the Lord with their children so that the legacy of faith may be passed from generation to generation.

Strong, and without number;
His teeth *are* the teeth of a lion,
And he has the fangs of a fierce lion.
7 He has laid waste My vine,
And ruined My fig tree;
He has stripped it bare and thrown *it* away;
Its branches are made white.

8 Lament like a virgin girded with sackcloth
For the husband of her youth.
9 The grain offering and the drink offering
Have been cut off from the house of the LORD;
The priests mourn, who minister to the LORD.
10 The field is wasted,
The land mourns;
For the grain is ruined,
The new wine is dried up,
The oil fails.

11 Be ashamed, you farmers,
Wail, you vinedressers,
For the wheat and the barley;
Because the harvest of the field has perished.
12 The vine has dried up,
And the fig tree has withered;
The pomegranate tree,
The palm tree also,
And the apple tree—
All the trees of the field are withered;
Surely joy has withered away from the sons of men.

Mourning for the Land

13 Gird yourselves and lament, you priests;
Wail, you who minister before the altar;
Come, lie all night in sackcloth,
You who minister to my God;
For the grain offering and the drink offering
Are withheld from the house of your God.
14 Consecrate a fast,
Call a sacred assembly;
Gather the elders
And all the inhabitants of the land
Into the house of the LORD your God,
And cry out to the LORD.

15 Alas for the day!
For the day of the LORD *is* at hand;
It shall come as destruction from the Almighty.
16 Is not the food cut off before our eyes,
Joy and gladness from the house of our God?
17 The seed shrivels under the clods,
Storehouses are in shambles;
Barns are broken down,
For the grain has withered.
18 How the animals groan!
The herds of cattle are restless,
Because they have no pasture;
Even the flocks of sheep suffer punishment.[a]

19 O LORD, to You I cry out;
For fire has devoured the open pastures,
And a flame has burned all the trees of the field.

1:18 [a]Septuagint and Vulgate read *are made desolate.*

1:8 a virgin: A young woman who lost her betrothed before the marriage.

1:11, 12 Be ashamed: The absence of a harvest was a disgrace for the farmer, as childlessness was for parents (Ps. 127:3–5).

1:14 Call a sacred assembly: It is one thing to wail over a catastrophe, but something more to turn to God in self-denial, repentance, and commitment when misfortune comes. This is the response God wants.

1:15–20 Joel's first announcement that the **day of the LORD** was impending. Like Amos, Joel warns God's own people of the approaching disaster. The locust plague was a symbol of that coming day of judgment at the hands of God. Israel was somehow never prepared to accept that the judgment was as much for her as for her enemies.

20 The beasts of the field also cry out to You,
For the water brooks are dried up,
And fire has devoured the open pastures.

CHAPTER 2

The Day of the LORD

Blow the trumpet in Zion,
And sound an alarm in My holy mountain!
Let all the inhabitants of the land tremble;
For the day of the LORD is coming,
For it is at hand:
2 A day of darkness and gloominess,
A day of clouds and thick darkness,
Like the morning *clouds* spread over the mountains.
A people *come,* great and strong,
The like of whom has never been;
Nor will there ever be any *such* after them,
Even for many successive generations.

3 A fire devours before them,
And behind them a flame burns;
The land *is* like the Garden of Eden before them,
And behind them a desolate wilderness;
Surely nothing shall escape them.
4 Their appearance is like the appearance of horses;
And like swift steeds, so they run.
5 With a noise like chariots
Over mountaintops they leap,
Like the noise of a flaming fire that devours the stubble,
Like a strong people set in battle array.
6 Before them the people writhe in pain;
All faces are drained of color.[a]
7 They run like mighty men,
They climb the wall like men of war;
Every one marches in formation,
And they do not break ranks.
8 They do not push one another;
Every one marches in his own column.[a]
Though they lunge between the weapons,
They are not cut down.[b]
9 They run to and fro in the city,
They run on the wall;
They climb into the houses,
They enter at the windows like a thief.

10 The earth quakes before them,
The heavens tremble;
The sun and moon grow dark,
And the stars diminish their brightness.
11 The LORD gives voice before His army,
For His camp is very great;
For strong *is the One* who executes His word.
For the day of the LORD *is* great and very terrible;
Who can endure it?

A Call to Repentance

12 "Now, therefore," says the LORD,
"Turn to Me with all your heart,
With fasting, with weeping, and with mourning."

2:6 [a]Septuagint, Targum, and Vulgate read *gather blackness.* 2:8 [a]Literally *his own highway* [b]That is, they are not halted by losses

2:12, 13 When the Lord reveals sin in our lives, we should immediately respond with confession and repentance. He has promised to forgive our sin when we turn to Him (1 John 1:9).

13 So rend your heart, and not your garments;
Return to the LORD your God,
For He *is* gracious and merciful,
Slow to anger, and of great kindness;
And He relents from doing harm.
14 Who knows *if* He will turn and relent,
And leave a blessing behind Him—
A grain offering and a drink offering
For the LORD your God?

15 Blow the trumpet in Zion,
Consecrate a fast,
Call a sacred assembly;
16 Gather the people,
Sanctify the congregation,
Assemble the elders,
Gather the children and nursing babes;
Let the bridegroom go out from his chamber,
And the bride from her dressing room.
17 Let the priests, who minister to the LORD,
Weep between the porch and the altar;
Let them say, "Spare Your people, O LORD,
And do not give Your heritage to reproach,
That the nations should rule over them.
Why should they say among the peoples,
'Where *is* their God?' "

The Land Refreshed

18 Then the LORD will be zealous for His land,
And pity His people.
19 The LORD will answer and say to His people,
"Behold, I will send you grain and new wine and oil,
And you will be satisfied by them;
I will no longer make you a reproach among the nations.

20 "But I will remove far from you the northern *army,*
And will drive him away into a barren and desolate land,
With his face toward the eastern sea
And his back toward the western sea;
His stench will come up,
And his foul odor will rise,
Because he has done monstrous things."

21 Fear not, O land;
Be glad and rejoice,
For the LORD has done marvelous things!
22 Do not be afraid, you beasts of the field;
For the open pastures are springing up,
And the tree bears its fruit;
The fig tree and the vine yield their strength.
23 Be glad then, you children of Zion,
And rejoice in the LORD your God;
For He has given you the former rain faithfully,[a]
And He will cause the rain to come down for you—
The former rain,
And the latter rain in the first *month.*
24 The threshing floors shall be full of wheat,

2:23 [a]Or *the teacher of righteousness*

2:14 Who knows? God's sovereignty is recognized, but Joel sees that God is also forgiving. However, He cannot be manipulated, and we must not presume upon His mercy.

2:18–27 It appears that Joel's appeals for repentance were heeded, resulting in national fasting and mourning. Now God's promised response provided a word of encouragement. That which had been destroyed by the locust plague would be restored, and the invading army would be repulsed. God had always been for His people, but now, because of their change of heart and life, He could express His love in redemption and restoration (v. 13).

And the vats shall overflow with new
wine and oil.

25 "So I will restore to you the years that
the swarming locust has eaten,
The crawling locust,
The consuming locust,
And the chewing locust,[a]
My great army which I sent among
you.

26 You shall eat in plenty and be
satisfied,
And praise the name of the LORD
your God,
Who has dealt wondrously with
you;
And My people shall never be put to
shame.

27 Then you shall know that I *am* in the
midst of Israel:
I *am* the LORD your God
And there is no other.
My people shall never be put to
shame.

God's Spirit Poured Out

28 "And it shall come to pass afterward
That I will pour out My Spirit on all
flesh;
Your sons and your daughters shall
prophesy,
Your old men shall dream dreams,
Your young men shall see visions.

29 And also on *My* menservants and on
My maidservants
I will pour out My Spirit in those
days.

30 "And I will show wonders in the
heavens and in the earth:
Blood and fire and pillars of smoke.

31 The sun shall be turned into
darkness,
And the moon into blood,
Before the coming of the great and
awesome day of the LORD.

32 And it shall come to pass
That whoever calls on the name of the
LORD
Shall be saved.
For in Mount Zion and in Jerusalem
there shall be deliverance,
As the LORD has said,
Among the remnant whom the LORD
calls.

CHAPTER 3

God Judges the Nations

"For behold, in those days and at that
time,
When I bring back the captives of
Judah and Jerusalem,

2 I will also gather all nations,
And bring them down to the Valley of
Je·hosh'a·phat;
And I will enter into judgment with
them there
On account of My people, My
heritage Israel,
Whom they have scattered among the
nations;
They have also divided up My
land.

3 They have cast lots for My people,

2:25 [a]Compare 1:4

2:28–32 The Hebrew Bible makes these verses a separate chapter because there seems to be a significant time break from v. 27. This is Joel's great promise of the universal outpouring of God's Spirit. Peter declared that the outpouring of the Holy Spirit on the Day of Pentecost was a fulfillment of this OT promise (Acts 2:16). In the same sermon he affirmed, "The promise is to you and to your children, and to all who are afar off, as many as the Lord our God will call" (Acts 2:39).

3:1–15 These verses depict the final judgment on the nations as one aspect of the day of the Lord. This is a common element in the prophetic books. That God used the nations to punish His people does not justify the brutality with which they carried out their charge. They are condemned especially for selling God's people into slavery (vv. 2, 3, 6). They are summoned to appear in the **Valley of Jehoshaphat**, God's place of judgment.

Have given a boy *as payment* for a
harlot,
And sold a girl for wine, that they
may drink.

4 "Indeed, what have you to do with
Me,
O Tȳre and Sī′don, and all the coasts
of Phi·lis′ti·a?
Will you retaliate against Me?
But if you retaliate against Me,
Swiftly and speedily I will return
your retaliation upon your own
head;
5 Because you have taken My silver
and My gold,
And have carried into your temples
My prized possessions.
6 Also the people of Judah and the
people of Jerusalem
You have sold to the Greeks,
That you may remove them far from
their borders.

7 "Behold, I will raise them
Out of the place to which you have
sold them,
And will return your retaliation upon
your own head.
8 I will sell your sons and your
daughters
Into the hand of the people of Judah,
And they will sell them to the
Sa·bē′ans,[a]
To a people far off;
For the LORD has spoken."

9 Proclaim this among the nations:
"Prepare for war!
Wake up the mighty men,
Let all the men of war draw near,
Let them come up.
10 Beat your plowshares into swords
And your pruning hooks into spears;
Let the weak say, 'I *am* strong.' "
11 Assemble and come, all you nations,
And gather together all around.
Cause Your mighty ones to go down
there, O LORD.

12 "Let the nations be wakened, and
come up to the Valley of
Je·hosh′a·phat;
For there I will sit to judge all the
surrounding nations.
13 Put in the sickle, for the harvest is
ripe.
Come, go down;
For the winepress is full,
The vats overflow—
For their wickedness *is* great."

14 Multitudes, multitudes in the valley
of decision!
For the day of the LORD *is* near in the
valley of decision.
15 The sun and moon will grow dark,
And the stars will diminish their
brightness.
16 The LORD also will roar from Zion,
And utter His voice from Jerusalem;
The heavens and earth will shake;
But the LORD will be a shelter for His
people,
And the strength of the children of
Israel.

17 "So you shall know that I *am* the LORD
your God,
Dwelling in Zion My holy mountain.
Then Jerusalem shall be holy,
And no aliens shall ever pass through
her again."

God Blesses His People

18 And it will come to pass in that day
That the mountains shall drip with
new wine,

3:8 [a]Literally *Shebaites* (compare Isaiah 60:6 and Ezekiel 27:22)

3:18 As God's judgment was symbolized by the desolation of the locust plague, so the restoration of His favor is by material plenty. **fountain shall flow**: A similar idea to that found in Ezek. 47:1–12.

The hills shall flow with milk,
And all the brooks of Judah shall be flooded with water;
A fountain shall flow from the house of the LORD
And water the Valley of Acacias.

19 "Egypt shall be a desolation,
And Ē'dom a desolate wilderness,
Because of violence *against* the people of Judah,
For they have shed innocent blood in their land.
20 But Judah shall abide forever,
And Jerusalem from generation to generation.
21 For I will acquit them of the guilt of bloodshed, whom I had not acquitted;
For the LORD dwells in Zion."

✦Amos✦

Amos was a shepherd in Tekoa, a village near Jerusalem in Judah. God called him to warn the northern kingdom of the coming judgment. He indicates that he prophesied during the reigns of King Uzziah in Judah and King Jeroboam II in Israel (about the time of Hosea), and he probably wrote his book sometime after 760 B.C.

Amos concentrated on the coming judgment of Israel because the nation had sinned repeatedly against a holy God and broken the covenant. Superstition and immorality abounded, while idolatry and hypocritical religious notions replaced true worship. After warning of the impending doom in eight prophecies, three sermons, and five visions, Amos related five promises for Israel's future (chapter 9), emphasizing the fulfillment of the Abrahamic, Davidic, and Palestinian covenants in the return of Christ.

Amos reveals the crisis long-time Christians can encounter when spiritual experience becomes a hollow habit rather than a dynamic relationship with Christ. He was known as the "prophet of righteousness" in the Old Testament because he taught that God demands righteousness. Following God is not simply observing holidays and offering sacrifices; it requires seeking God's will, following His commands, and treating others with love. ✦

CHAPTER 1

The words of Ā'mos, who was among the sheepbreeders[a] of Te•kō'a, which he saw concerning Israel in the days of Uz-zī'ah king of Judah, and in the days of Jer•o•bō'am the son of Jō'ash, king of Israel, two years before the earthquake.

2And he said:

"The LORD roars from Zion,
And utters His voice from Jerusalem;
The pastures of the shepherds mourn,
And the top of Car'mel withers."

Judgment on the Nations

3Thus says the LORD:

"For three transgressions of Damascus, and for four,
I will not turn away its *punishment*,
Because they have threshed Gil'ē•ad with implements of iron.
4 But I will send a fire into the house of Haz'a•el,
Which shall devour the palaces of Ben-Hā'dad.

1:1 [a]Compare 2 Kings 3:4

1:1 The prophecies of Amos were made during the reigns of **Uzziah**, king of Judah (792–740 B.C.) and **Jeroboam** of Israel (793–753 B.C.). They are also dated by an **earthquake** which occurred at that time (see Zech. 14:5). The period was an era of great prosperity and outward success in both kingdoms.

5 I will also break the *gate* bar of
Damascus,
And cut off the inhabitant from the
Valley of Ā′ven,
And the one who holds the scepter
from Beth Eden.
The people of Syria shall go captive
to Kir,"
Says the LORD.

6Thus says the LORD:

"For three transgressions of Gā′za, and
for four,
I will not turn away its *punishment*,
Because they took captive the whole
captivity
To deliver *them* up to Ē′dom.
7 But I will send a fire upon the wall of
Gā′za,
Which shall devour its palaces.
8 I will cut off the inhabitant from
Ash′dod,
And the one who holds the scepter
from Ash′ke·lon;
I will turn My hand against Ek′ron,
And the remnant of the Phi·lis′tines
shall perish,"
Says the Lord GOD.

9Thus says the LORD:

"For three transgressions of Tȳre, and
for four,
I will not turn away its *punishment*,
Because they delivered up the whole
captivity to Ē′dom,
And did not remember the covenant
of brotherhood.
10 But I will send a fire upon the wall of
Tȳre,
Which shall devour its palaces."

11Thus says the LORD:

"For three transgressions of Ē′dom,
and for four,
I will not turn away its *punishment*,
Because he pursued his brother with
the sword,
And cast off all pity;
His anger tore perpetually,
And he kept his wrath forever.
12 But I will send a fire upon Tē′man,
Which shall devour the palaces of
Boz′rah."

13Thus says the LORD:

"For three transgressions of the people
of Am′mon, and for four,
I will not turn away its *punishment*,
Because they ripped open the women
with child in Gil′ē·ad,
That they might enlarge their
territory.
14 But I will kindle a fire in the wall of
Rab′bah,
And it shall devour its palaces,
Amid shouting in the day of battle,
And a tempest in the day of the
whirlwind.
15 Their king shall go into captivity,
He and his princes together,"
Says the LORD.

CHAPTER 2

Thus says the LORD:

"For three transgressions of Mō′ab,
and for four,
I will not turn away its *punishment*,
Because he burned the bones of the
king of Ē′dom to lime.
2 But I will send a fire upon Mō′ab,
And it shall devour the palaces of
Ker′i·oth;
Mō′ab shall die with tumult,
With shouting *and* trumpet sound.
3 And I will cut off the judge from its
midst,

1:10 fire upon the wall: A figure of speech symbolizing complete destruction.

And slay all its princes with him,"
Says the LORD.

Judgment on Judah

4Thus says the LORD:

"For three transgressions of Judah, and for four,
I will not turn away its *punishment*,
Because they have despised the law of the LORD,
And have not kept His commandments.
Their lies lead them astray,
Lies which their fathers followed.
5 But I will send a fire upon Judah,
And it shall devour the palaces of Jerusalem."

Judgment on Israel

6Thus says the LORD:

"For three transgressions of Israel, and for four,
I will not turn away its *punishment*,
Because they sell the righteous for silver,
And the poor for a pair of sandals.
7 They pant after[a] the dust of the earth *which is* on the head of the poor,
And pervert the way of the humble.
A man and his father go in to the *same* girl,
To defile My holy name.
8 They lie down by every altar on clothes taken in pledge,
And drink the wine of the condemned *in* the house of their god.

9 "Yet *it was* I *who* destroyed the Am'o·rīte before them,
Whose height *was* like the height of the cedars,
And he *was as* strong as the oaks;
Yet I destroyed his fruit above
And his roots beneath.
10 Also *it was* I *who* brought you up from the land of Egypt,
And led you forty years through the wilderness,
To possess the land of the Am'o·rīte.
11 I raised up some of your sons as prophets,
And some of your young men as Naz'ir·ītes.
Is it not so, O you children of Israel?"
Says the LORD.
12 "But you gave the Naz'ir·ītes wine to drink,
And commanded the prophets saying,
'Do not prophesy!'

2:7 [a]Or *trample on*

2:4 An intimate knowledge of God's Word is essential to righteous living. Without such knowledge, we have nothing by which to judge the teaching we receive from others and we are vulnerable to the lies of false doctrine.

2:6–16 The climax of Amos's prophecies brings the measuring rod of God to bear on the life of Israel and finds God's chosen people seriously lacking. Amos's psychology begins with condemnation of Israel's enemies, thus holding the crowd's attention. But he climaxes with charges against Israel herself. Unlike the pagan nations who were condemned for what they had done to other peoples, Israel's sins were against fellow Israelites. They had taken men into slavery for nonpayment of debt and foreclosed on mortgages of trifling amounts (v. 6). And they had done all this in spite of God's efforts to teach them righteous ways (vv. 9–12).

2:8 If a creditor took a man's garment in pledge, it had to be returned before nightfall because it was probably all he had left (see Deut. 24:12, 13). But here, the lenders kept them. They got drunk even in the temple and lay down (perhaps a reference to sexual activity) on the garments.

13 "Behold, I am weighed down by you,
As a cart full of sheaves is weighed
down.
14 Therefore flight shall perish from the
swift,
The strong shall not strengthen his
power,
Nor shall the mighty deliver himself;
15 He shall not stand who handles the
bow,
The swift of foot shall not escape,
Nor shall he who rides a horse
deliver himself.
16 The most courageous men of might
Shall flee naked in that day,"
Says the LORD.

CHAPTER 3

Authority of the Prophet's Message

Hear this word that the LORD has spoken against you, O children of Israel, against the whole family which I brought up from the land of Egypt, saying:

2 "You only have I known of all the
families of the earth;
Therefore I will punish you for all
your iniquities."

3 Can two walk together, unless they
are agreed?
4 Will a lion roar in the forest, when he
has no prey?
Will a young lion cry out of his den, if
he has caught nothing?
5 Will a bird fall into a snare on the
earth, where there is no trap for it?
Will a snare spring up from the earth,
if it has caught nothing at all?
6 If a trumpet is blown in a city, will
not the people be afraid?
If there is calamity in a city, will not
the LORD have done *it?*

7 Surely the Lord GOD does nothing,
Unless He reveals His secret to His
servants the prophets.
8 A lion has roared!
Who will not fear?
The Lord GOD has spoken!
Who can but prophesy?

Punishment of Israel's Sins

9 "Proclaim in the palaces at Ash'dod,[a]
And in the palaces in the land of
Egypt, and say:
'Assemble on the mountains of
Samaria;
See great tumults in her midst,
And the oppressed within her.
10 For they do not know to do right,'
Says the LORD,
'Who store up violence and robbery in
their palaces.' "

11 Therefore thus says the Lord GOD:

"An adversary *shall be* all around the
land;
He shall sap your strength from you,
And your palaces shall be
plundered."

3:9 [a]Following Masoretic Text; Septuagint reads *Assyria.*

I pray that my spouse and I will always understand the significance of the question, "Can two walk together unless they are agreed?"

adapted from Amos 3:3

3:3–8 Eight rhetorical questions lead to the climax, **Who can but prophesy**? The questions show that "nothing happens without a cause." Amos has ample cause for prophesying: Israel has sinned; **GOD has spoken** (v. 8); His servant must prophesy.

12 Thus says the LORD:

"As a shepherd takes from the mouth
of a lion
Two legs or a piece of an ear,
So shall the children of Israel be taken
out
Who dwell in Samaria—
In the corner of a bed and on the
edge[a] of a couch!
13 Hear and testify against the house of
Jacob,"
Says the Lord GOD, the God of hosts,
14 "That in the day I punish Israel for
their transgressions,
I will also visit *destruction* on the
altars of Beth'el;
And the horns of the altar shall be cut
off
And fall to the ground.
15 I will destroy the winter house along
with the summer house;
The houses of ivory shall perish,
And the great houses shall have an
end,"
Says the LORD.

CHAPTER 4

Hear this word, you cows of Bā'shan,
who *are* on the mountain of
Samaria,
Who oppress the poor,
Who crush the needy,
Who say to your husbands,[a] "Bring
wine, let us drink!"
2 The Lord GOD has sworn by His
holiness:
"Behold, the days shall come upon you
When He will take you away with
fishhooks,
And your posterity with fishhooks.
3 You will go out *through* broken *walls*,
Each one straight ahead of her,
And you will be cast into Har'mon,"
Says the LORD.

4 "Come to Beth'el and transgress,
At Gil'gal multiply transgression;
Bring your sacrifices every morning,
Your tithes every three days.[a]
5 Offer a sacrifice of thanksgiving with
leaven,
Proclaim *and* announce the freewill
offerings;
For this you love,
You children of Israel!"
Says the Lord GOD.

Israel Did Not Accept Correction

6 "Also I gave you cleanness of teeth in
all your cities.
And lack of bread in all your places;
Yet you have not returned to Me,"
Says the LORD.

7 "I also withheld rain from you,
When *there were* still three months to
the harvest.
I made it rain on one city,
I withheld rain from another city.
One part was rained upon,
And where it did not rain the part
withered.
8 So two *or* three cities wandered to
another city to drink water,
But they were not satisfied;
Yet you have not returned to Me,"
Says the LORD.

9 "I blasted you with blight and mildew.
When your gardens increased,

3:12 [a]The Hebrew is uncertain. 4:1 [a]Literally *their lords* or *their masters* 4:4 [a]Or *years* (compare Deuteronomy 14:28)

4:1–3 cows of Bashan: A biting insult directed against the luxury-loving women who drove their husbands to dishonesty to provide for their extravagant tastes. Bashan was located southeast of Galilee and contained good pastureland so the animals were always "extra large."

4:4, 5 Satirical reference to Israel's false worship which had no effect on daily living.

Your vineyards,
Your fig trees,
And your olive trees,
The locust devoured *them;*
Yet you have not returned to Me,"
Says the LORD.

10 "I sent among you a plague after the manner of Egypt;
Your young men I killed with a sword,
Along with your captive horses;
I made the stench of your camps come up into your nostrils;
Yet you have not returned to Me,"
Says the LORD.

11 "I overthrew *some* of you,
As God overthrew Sod'om and Go·mor'rah,
And you were like a firebrand plucked from the burning;
Yet you have not returned to Me,"
Says the LORD.

12 "Therefore thus will I do to you, O Israel;
Because I will do this to you,
Prepare to meet your God, O Israel!"

13 For behold,
He who forms mountains,
And creates the wind,
Who declares to man what his[a] thought *is,*
And makes the morning darkness,
Who treads the high places of the earth—
The LORD God of hosts *is* His name.

CHAPTER 5

A Lament for Israel

Hear this word which I take up against you, a lamentation, O house of Israel:

2 The virgin of Israel has fallen;
She will rise no more.
She lies forsaken on her land;
There is no one to raise her up.

3For thus says the Lord GOD:

"The city that goes out by a thousand
Shall have a hundred left,
And that which goes out by a hundred
Shall have ten left to the house of Israel."

A Call to Repentance

4For thus says the LORD to the house of Israel:

"Seek Me and live;
5 But do not seek Beth'el,
Nor enter Gil'gal,
Nor pass over to Bē·er·shē'ba;
For Gil'gal shall surely go into captivity,
And Beth'el shall come to nothing.
6 Seek the LORD and live,
Lest He break out like fire *in* the house of Joseph,
And devour *it,*
With no one to quench *it* in Beth'el—
7 You who turn justice to wormwood,
And lay righteousness to rest in the earth!"

8 He made the Plēi'a·dēs and Ō·rī'on;
He turns the shadow of death into morning
And makes the day dark as night;
He calls for the waters of the sea
And pours them out on the face of the earth;
The LORD *is* His name.

4:13 [a]Or *His*

4:13 The God whom Israel must fight is not some idol, but the all-powerful Creator. This verse is the first of three hymn portions used by Amos (see 5:8, 9; 9:5, 6). They are identified as hymn portions because of their more exalted literary style.

9 He rains ruin upon the strong,
So that fury comes upon the fortress.

10 They hate the one who rebukes in the gate,
And they abhor the one who speaks uprightly.
11 Therefore, because you tread down the poor
And take grain taxes from him,
Though you have built houses of hewn stone,
Yet you shall not dwell in them;
You have planted pleasant vineyards,
But you shall not drink wine from them.
12 For I know your manifold transgressions
And your mighty sins:
Afflicting the just *and* taking bribes;
Diverting the poor *from justice* at the gate.
13 Therefore the prudent keep silent at that time,
For it *is* an evil time.

14 Seek good and not evil,
That you may live;
So the LORD God of hosts will be with you,
As you have spoken.
15 Hate evil, love good;
Establish justice in the gate.
It may be that the LORD God of hosts
Will be gracious to the remnant of Joseph.

The Day of the LORD

16Therefore the LORD God of hosts, the
Lord, says this:

"*There shall be* wailing in all streets,
And they shall say in all the highways,
'Alas! Alas!'
They shall call the farmer to mourning,
And skillful lamenters to wailing.
17 In all vineyards *there shall be* wailing,
For I will pass through you,"
Says the LORD.

18 Woe to you who desire the day of the LORD!
For what good *is* the day of the LORD to you?
It *will be* darkness, and not light.
19 It *will be* as though a man fled from a lion,
And a bear met him!
Or *as though* he went into the house,
Leaned his hand on the wall,
And a serpent bit him!
20 *Is* not the day of the LORD darkness, and not light?
Is it not very dark, with no brightness in it?

21 "I hate, I despise your feast days,
And I do not savor your sacred assemblies.
22 Though you offer Me burnt offerings and your grain offerings,

---

5:14, 15 This passage does not indicate salvation by works; true repentance alone can prevent God's judgment. Sincere repentance is reflected by a turning from evil.

5:18–20 the day of the LORD: The earliest discussion of an important theme among the prophets. The people evidently expected a time when God would deliver them from all their enemies. But Amos condemns their faulty expectations. God would establish Israel only as she followed His righteous laws. Amos puts the concept into its rightful ethical framework. This, in turn, shows that apostate Israel is not God's favorite, but is instead His enemy who would be destroyed on this Day of visitation. For all evildoers, the day of the Lord would be **darkness, and not light** (v. 20).

5:21–27 Amos's condemnation of Israel's unethical religion. God despises worship that is not accompanied by social justice and moral living. Verse 24 is the central thrust of Amos's message. **Justice** and **righteousness** in human relations are more important than ritual sacrifice, especially if that ritual is tainted with idolatry.

I will not accept *them,*
Nor will I regard your fattened peace
offerings.
23 Take away from Me the noise of your
songs,
For I will not hear the melody of your
stringed instruments.
24 But let justice run down like water,
And righteousness like a mighty
stream.

25 "Did you offer Me sacrifices and
offerings
In the wilderness forty years, O house
of Israel?
26 You also carried Sik'kuth[a] your
king[b]
And Chī'un,[c] your idols,
The star of your gods,
Which you made for yourselves.
27 Therefore I will send you into
captivity beyond Damascus,"
Says the LORD, whose name *is* the
God of hosts.

CHAPTER 6

Warnings to Zion and Samaria

Woe to you *who are* at ease in Zion,
And trust in Mount Samaria,
Notable persons in the chief nation,
To whom the house of Israel comes!
2 Go over to Cal'neh and see;
And from there go to Hā'math the
great;
Then go down to Gath of the
Phi·lis'tines.
Are you better than these kingdoms?
Or is their territory greater than your
territory?

3 *Woe to* you who put far off the day of
doom,
Who cause the seat of violence to
come near;
4 Who lie on beds of ivory,
Stretch out on your couches,
Eat lambs from the flock
And calves from the midst of the
stall;
5 Who sing idly to the sound of
stringed instruments,
And invent for yourselves musical
instruments like David;
6 Who drink wine from bowls,
And anoint yourselves with the best
ointments,
But are not grieved for the affliction
of Joseph.
7 Therefore they shall now go captive
as the first of the captives,
And those who recline at banquets
shall be removed.

8 The Lord GOD has sworn by Himself,
The LORD God of hosts says:
"I abhor the pride of Jacob,
And hate his palaces;
Therefore I will deliver up *the* city
And all that is in it."

9Then it shall come to pass, that if ten
men remain in one house, they shall die.
10And when a relative *of the dead,* with one
who will burn *the bodies,* picks up the bod-
ies[a] to take them out of the house, he will
say to one inside the house, "*Are there* any
more with you?"
Then someone will say, "None."
And he will say, "Hold your tongue! For
we dare not mention the name of the
LORD."

11 For behold, the LORD gives a
command:

5:26 [a]A pagan deity [b]Septuagint and Vulgate read *tabernacle of Moloch.* [c]A pagan deity 6:10 [a]Literally *bones*

6:8–14 The destruction of Samaria was complete. Verse 10 pictures a time when people would superstitiously be afraid of even casually invoking the Lord's name lest that should provoke further disasters from Him.

He will break the great house into
bits,
And the little house into pieces.
12 Do horses run on rocks?
Does *one* plow *there* with oxen?
Yet you have turned justice into gall,
And the fruit of righteousness into
wormwood,
13 You who rejoice over Lo Dē'bar,[a]
Who say, "Have we not taken
Kar·na'im[b] for ourselves
By our own strength?"

14 "But, behold, I will raise up a nation
against you,
O house of Israel,"
Says the LORD God of hosts;
"And they will afflict you from the
entrance of Hā'math
To the Valley of the Ar'a·bah."

CHAPTER 7

Vision of the Locusts

Thus the Lord GOD showed me: Behold,
He formed locust swarms at the beginning
of the late crop; indeed *it was* the late crop
after the king's mowings. 2And so it was,
when they had finished eating the grass of
the land, that I said:

"O Lord GOD, forgive, I pray!
Oh, that Jacob may stand,
For he *is* small!"
3 *So* the LORD relented concerning this.
"It shall not be," said the LORD.

Vision of the Fire

4Thus the Lord GOD showed me: Be-
hold, the Lord GOD called for conflict by
fire, and it consumed the great deep and
devoured the territory. 5Then I said:

"O Lord GOD, cease, I pray!
Oh, that Jacob may stand,
For he *is* small!"
6 *So* the LORD relented concerning this.
"This also shall not be," said the Lord
GOD.

Vision of the Plumb Line

7Thus He showed me: Behold, the Lord
stood on a wall *made* with a plumb line,
with a plumb line in His hand. 8And the
LORD said to me, "Ā'mos, what do you
see?"
And I said, "A plumb line."
Then the Lord said:

"Behold, I am setting a plumb line
In the midst of My people Israel;
I will not pass by them anymore.
9 The high places of Isaac shall be
desolate,
And the sanctuaries of Israel shall be
laid waste.
I will rise with the sword against the
house of Jer·o·bō'am."

Amaziah's Complaint

10Then Am·a·zī'ah the priest of Beth'el
sent to Jer·o·bō'am king of Israel, saying,
"Ā'mos has conspired against you in the
midst of the house of Israel. The land is not
able to bear all his words. 11For thus Ā'mos
has said:

'Jer·o·bō'am shall die by the sword,
And Israel shall surely be led away
captive
From their own land.'"

6:13 [a]Literally *Nothing* [b]Literally *Horns,* symbol of strength

7:1–3 A swarm of locusts suggests a vision of judgment upon Israel. The loss of the **late crop** in late spring and early summer would fall heaviest on the people because they depended on it for their living. Amos interceded, and God responded to his intercession.

7:7–9 plumb line: A builder's device to test whether a wall is straight up and down. God was holding the plumb line by Israel, and she was not straight. Like a dangerously leaning wall, she must be torn down.

[12]Then Am·a·zī′ah said to Ā′mos:

"Go, you seer!
Flee to the land of Judah.
There eat bread,
And there prophesy.
13 But never again prophesy at Beth′el,
For it *is* the king's sanctuary,
And it *is* the royal residence."

[14]Then Ā′mos answered, and said to Am·a·zī′ah:

"I *was* no prophet,
Nor *was* I a son of a prophet,
But I *was* a sheepbreeder[a]
And a tender of sycamore fruit.
15 Then the LORD took me as I followed
the flock,
And the LORD said to me,
'Go, prophesy to My people Israel.'
16 Now therefore, hear the word of the
LORD:
You say, 'Do not prophesy against Israel,
And do not spout against the house
of Isaac.'

[17]"Therefore thus says the LORD:

'Your wife shall be a harlot in the city;
Your sons and daughters shall fall by
the sword;
Your land shall be divided by *survey*
line;
You shall die in a defiled land;
And Israel shall surely be led away
captive
From his own land.' "

CHAPTER 8

Vision of the Summer Fruit

Thus the Lord GOD showed me: Behold,
a basket of summer fruit. [2]And He said,
"Ā′mos, what do you see?"
So I said, "A basket of summer fruit."
Then the LORD said to me:

"The end has come upon My people
Israel;
I will not pass by them anymore.
3 And the songs of the temple
Shall be wailing in that day,"
Says the Lord GOD—
"Many dead bodies everywhere,
They shall be thrown out in silence."

4 Hear this, you who swallow up[a] the
needy,
And make the poor of the land fail,

[5]Saying:

"When will the New Moon be past,
That we may sell grain?
And the Sabbath,
That we may trade wheat?
Making the ephah small and the
shekel large,
Falsifying the scales by deceit,
6 That we may buy the poor for silver,
And the needy for a pair of sandals—
Even sell the bad wheat?"

7 The LORD has sworn by the pride of
Jacob:

7:14 [a]Compare 2 Kings 3:4 8:4 [a]Or *trample on* (compare 2:7)

7:14, 15 Amos was probably denying that he was a professional **prophet**, appointed by the king. He testified, **the LORD took me**, indicating that he was God-called. **sycamore fruit**: Something like a mulberry. The fruit had to be bruised to ripen, generally a task of the very poor. This passage demonstrates that God uses people from all walks of life to bring His plan to completion.

8:1–3 Summer fruit came at the end of the season, so Israel was at the **end** of her season. This is a play on words in Hebrew where "summerfruit" and "end" are similar words. This vision completes the series of three in ch. 7—the locusts, the fire, and the plumb line. The message is the same: **The end has come upon My people**.

8:5, 6 New Moon . . . Sabbath: Their selfish concern was how soon worshiping God would be over so that they could get back to making money.

"Surely I will never forget any of their
works.
8 Shall the land not tremble for this,
And everyone mourn who dwells in
it?
All of it shall swell like the River,[a]
Heave and subside
Like the River of Egypt.

9 "And it shall come to pass in that day,"
says the Lord GOD,
"That I will make the sun go down at
noon,
And I will darken the earth in broad
daylight;
10 I will turn your feasts into mourning,
And all your songs into lamentation;
I will bring sackcloth on every waist,
And baldness on every head;
I will make it like mourning for an
only *son*,
And its end like a bitter day.

11 "Behold, the days are coming," says
the Lord GOD,
"That I will send a famine on the land,
Not a famine of bread,
Nor a thirst for water,
But of hearing the words of the LORD.
12 They shall wander from sea to sea,
And from north to east;
They shall run to and fro, seeking the
word of the LORD,
But shall not find *it*.

13 "In that day the fair virgins
And strong young men
Shall faint from thirst.
14 Those who swear by the sin[a] of
Samaria,
Who say,
'As your god lives, O Dan!'
And, 'As the way of Bē·er·shē'ba
lives!'
They shall fall and never rise again."

8:8 [a]That is, the Nile; some Hebrew manuscripts, Septuagint, Syriac, Targum, and Vulgate read *River;* Masoretic Text reads *the light.* 8:14 [a]Or *Ashima,* a Syrian goddess 9:2 [a]Or *Sheol* 9:5 [a]That is, the Nile

CHAPTER 9

The Destruction of Israel

I saw the Lord standing by the altar, and
He said:

"Strike the doorposts, that the
thresholds may shake,
And break them on the heads of them
all.
I will slay the last of them with the
sword.
He who flees from them shall not get
away,
And he who escapes from them shall
not be delivered.

2 "Though they dig into hell,[a]
From there My hand shall take them;
Though they climb up to heaven,
From there I will bring them down;
3 And though they hide themselves on
top of Car'mel,
From there I will search and take
them;
Though they hide from My sight at
the bottom of the sea,
From there I will command the
serpent, and it shall bite them;
4 Though they go into captivity before
their enemies,
From there I will command the
sword,
And it shall slay them.
I will set My eyes on them for harm
And not for good."

5 The Lord GOD of hosts,
He who touches the earth and it
melts,
And all who dwell there mourn;
All of it shall swell like the River,[a]
And subside like the River of Egypt.
6 He who builds His layers in the sky,
And has founded His strata in the
earth;
Who calls for the waters of the sea,
And pours them out on the face of
the earth—
The LORD *is* His name.

7 "*Are* you not like the people of
Ethiopia to Me,
O children of Israel?" says the LORD.
"Did I not bring up Israel from the
land of Egypt,
The Phi·lis'tines from Caph'tor,
And the Syrians from Kir?

8 "Behold, the eyes of the Lord GOD *are*
on the sinful kingdom,
And I will destroy it from the face of
the earth;
Yet I will not utterly destroy the
house of Jacob,"
Says the LORD.

9 "For surely I will command,
And will sift the house of Israel
among all nations,
As *grain* is sifted in a sieve;
Yet not the smallest grain shall fall to
the ground.
10 All the sinners of My people shall die
by the sword,
Who say, 'The calamity shall not
overtake nor confront us.'

Israel Will Be Restored

11 "On that day I will raise up
The tabernacle[a] of David, which has
fallen down,
And repair its damages;
I will raise up its ruins,
And rebuild it as in the days of old;
12 That they may possess the remnant of
Ē'dom,[a]
And all the Gentiles who are called
by My name,"
Says the LORD who does this thing.

13 "Behold, the days are coming," says
the LORD,
"When the plowman shall overtake the
reaper,
And the treader of grapes him who
sows seed;
The mountains shall drip with sweet
wine,
And all the hills shall flow *with it*.
14 I will bring back the captives of My
people Israel;
They shall build the waste cities and
inhabit *them;*
They shall plant vineyards and drink
wine from them;
They shall also make gardens and eat
fruit from them.
15 I will plant them in their land,
And no longer shall they be pulled
up
From the land I have given them,"
Says the LORD your God.

9:11 [a]Literally *booth*, figure of a deposed dynasty
9:12 [a]Septuagint reads *mankind.*

9:7 Amos recognized that Israel was not the only people whom the Lord loved. All people are subjects of God's mercy, and He acts on their behalf.

9:11 Here is a messianic prophecy. **The tabernacle of David** refers to the dynasty of David which would be reestablished in God's day of salvation.

9:14 God was going to punish Israel for her sins, but He promised to restore her. **I will bring back**: The transformation of the land assumes a prior transformation of the people. God says, "On the day that I cleanse you from all your iniquities, I will also enable you to dwell in the cities, and the ruins shall be rebuilt" (Ezek. 36:33). It is His gracious promise for our salvation and restoration.

✦Obadiah✦

Obadiah gave no clues to the time he wrote this book. He does mention a great humiliation of Israel, which could refer to the destruction of Jerusalem in 587 B.C., so he may have written the book shortly after this date.

The major theme of Obadiah is God's coming judgment against Edom for its cruelty toward Judah (vv. 10, 21). This cruelty stemmed from the long history of conflict between Jacob and Esau (Gen. 27; 36), and their descendants, the nations of Judah and Edom. Edom even helped loot Jerusalem after its destruction.

In Genesis, God promised He would bless the world through Abraham and protect his descendants against those who tried to harm them (12:1–3). The Book of Obadiah clearly demonstrates God's faithfulness to this promise, even though Judah was unworthy. Just as the strained relationship between Jacob and Esau affected their descendants for generations, Abraham's close fellowship with God brought blessings to his descendants for generations. ✦

The Coming Judgment on Edom

The vision of Ō·ba·dī'ah.

Thus says the Lord GOD concerning
Ē'dom
(We have heard a report from the
LORD,
And a messenger has been sent
among the nations, *saying,*
"Arise, and let us rise up against her
for battle"):

2 "Behold, I will make you small among
the nations;
You shall be greatly despised.
3 The pride of your heart has deceived
you,
You who dwell in the clefts of the
rock,
Whose habitation is high;
You who say in your heart, 'Who will
bring me down to the ground?'
4 Though you ascend *as* high as the
eagle,
And though you set your nest among
the stars,
From there I will bring you down,"
says the LORD.

5 "If thieves had come to you,
If robbers by night—
Oh, how you will be cut off!—
Would they not have stolen till they
had enough?

3, 4 No human success or accomplishment is out of the Lord's reach. Anything we achieve is due to His enabling and thus can just as easily be destroyed by Him.

5–9 had enough: Thieves generally do not take everything in sight but only the most valuable items they can carry off. So also **grape-gatherers** do not pick every grape. By contrast, Edom would have nothing left when the pillaging was over.

If grape-gatherers had come to you,
Would they not have left *some* gleanings?

6 "Oh, how Esau shall be searched out!
How his hidden treasures shall be sought after!
7 All the men in your confederacy
Shall force you to the border;
The men at peace with you
Shall deceive you *and* prevail against you.
Those who eat your bread shall lay a trap[a] for you.
No one is aware of it.

8 "Will I not in that day," says the LORD,
"Even destroy the wise *men* from Ē'dom,
And understanding from the mountains of Esau?
9 Then your mighty men, O Tē'man, shall be dismayed,
To the end that everyone from the mountains of Esau
May be cut off by slaughter.

Edom Mistreated His Brother

10 "For violence against your brother Jacob,
Shame shall cover you,
And you shall be cut off forever.
11 In the day that you stood on the other side—
In the day that strangers carried captive his forces,
When foreigners entered his gates
And cast lots for Jerusalem—
Even you *were* as one of them.

12 "But you should not have gazed on the day of your brother
In the day of his captivity;[a]
Nor should you have rejoiced over the children of Judah
In the day of their destruction;
Nor should you have spoken proudly
In the day of distress.
13 You should not have entered the gate of My people
In the day of their calamity.
Indeed, you should not have gazed on their affliction
In the day of their calamity,
Nor laid *hands* on their substance
In the day of their calamity.
14 You should not have stood at the crossroads
To cut off those among them who escaped;
Nor should you have delivered up those among them who remained
In the day of distress.

15 "For the day of the LORD upon all the nations *is* near;
As you have done, it shall be done to you;
Your reprisal shall return upon your own head.
16 For as you drank on My holy mountain,
So shall all the nations drink continually;
Yes, they shall drink, and swallow,

7 [a]Or *wound*, or *plot* 12 [a]Literally *on the day he became a foreigner*

10–14 Describe the reason for God's judgment. Edom had behaved like vultures at the attack on **Jerusalem** (v. 11; see 2 Chr. 21:16, 17), rejoicing over the resulting carrion. This was a greater evil because they were a **brother** to Judah. The word **day**, repeated 10 times in these verses, refers to the specific time when Edom perpetrated violence upon Judah.

15, 16 The judgment upon Edom is described as the **day of the LORD**. In contrast to the day of Edom's pleasure (vv. 11–14), the day of the Lord would be a time of retribution. **as though they had never been**: Edom later became extinct. See vv. 9, 18.

And they shall be as though they had
never been.

Israel's Final Triumph

17 "But on Mount Zion there shall be
deliverance,
And there shall be holiness;
The house of Jacob shall possess their
possessions.
18 The house of Jacob shall be a fire,
And the house of Joseph a flame;
But the house of Esau *shall be* stubble;
They shall kindle them and devour
them,
And no survivor shall *remain* of the
house of Esau,"
For the LORD has spoken.
19 The South[a] shall possess the
mountains of Esau,
And the Lowland shall possess
Phi·lis′ti·a.
They shall possess the fields of
Ē′phra·im
And the fields of Samaria.
Benjamin *shall possess* Gil′ē·ad.
20 And the captives of this host of the
children of Israel
Shall possess the land of the
Cā′naan·ītes
As far as Zar′e·phath.
The captives of Jerusalem who are in
Se·phar′ad
Shall possess the cities of the South.[a]
21 Then saviors[a] shall come to Mount
Zion
To judge the mountains of Esau,
And the kingdom shall be the LORD's.

19 [a]Hebrew *Negev* 20 [a]Hebrew *Negev* 21 [a]Or *deliverers*

> God whispers to us in our pleasures, speaks in our conscience, but shouts in our pains: it is His metaphor to rouse a deaf world.
>
> C. S. Lewis

✦Jonah✦

A native of Israel, Jonah prophesied during the reign of King Jeroboam II (793 to 753 B.C.). He probably wrote the book around 760 B.C. Unlike the other prophets, Jonah's writing focuses on his own life and experiences rather than on the judgment of God's people. Jonah was called to preach to Nineveh, the capital of the Assyrian empire—a great enemy of Israel.

Jonah was probably the most unwilling prophet; he had to be swallowed by a fish before he would obey God. His reluctance reflected his fear that the Assyrians would repent and be spared. And he was right! Jonah's message resulted in great revival and repentance in Nineveh. Jonah was unhappy with the positive results of his evangelism, and God used a plant, a worm, and the wind to teach him compassion.

Perhaps the most important theme, however, is God's love and concern for the Gentiles as well as the Jews. God calls all people of all nations to accept His gift of salvation. God's mercy is extended to all people, regardless of their ethnic or cultural background, and Christians of all ages should reflect His compassion. ✦

CHAPTER 1

Jonah's Disobedience

Now the word of the LORD came to Jo-
nah the son of A·mit'taī, saying, 2"Arise,
go to Nin'e·veh, that great city, and cry out
against it; for their wickedness has come
up before Me." 3But Jonah arose to flee to
Tar'shish from the presence of the LORD.
He went down to Jop'pa, and found a ship
going to Tar'shish; so he paid the fare, and
went down into it, to go with them to
Tar'shish from the presence of the LORD.

The Storm at Sea

4But the LORD sent out a great wind on
the sea, and there was a mighty tempest on
the sea, so that the ship was about to be
broken up.

5Then the mariners were afraid; and
every man cried out to his god, and threw
the cargo that *was* in the ship into the sea,
to lighten the load.[a] But Jonah had gone
down into the lowest parts of the ship, had
lain down, and was fast asleep.

6So the captain came to him, and said to

1:5 [a]Literally *from upon them*

1:1, 2 Unlike other prophets who received the **word of the LORD**, Jonah was not given a message for his own people. He was commissioned to go to a Gentile city with an implicit call for repentance. **Nineveh**, capital of Assyria, was a symbol of power and might, but was also hated by all peoples because of its heartless conquests. Jonah's mission was to go not just to Gentiles, but to especially hated ones.

1:4 We will never find peace apart from God's will; His plan will continue despite any rebellion on our part. We simply have to decide whether we will be used willingly or forcibly.

him, "What do you mean, sleeper? Arise,
call on your God; perhaps your God will
consider us, so that we may not perish."
7And they said to one another, "Come,
let us cast lots, that we may know for
whose cause this trouble *has come* upon
us." So they cast lots, and the lot fell on Jo-
nah. 8Then they said to him, "Please tell us!
For whose cause *is* this trouble upon us?
What is your occupation? And where do
you come from? What is your country?
And of what people are you?"
9So he said to them, "I *am* a Hebrew; and
I fear the LORD, the God of heaven, who
made the sea and the dry *land*."

Jonah Thrown into the Sea

10Then the men were exceedingly afraid,
and said to him, "Why have you done
this?" For the men knew that he fled from
the presence of the LORD, because he had
told them. 11Then they said to him, "What
shall we do to you that the sea may be calm
for us?"—for the sea was growing more
tempestuous.
12And he said to them, "Pick me up and
throw me into the sea; then the sea will be-
come calm for you. For I know that this
great tempest *is* because of me."
13Nevertheless the men rowed hard to
return to land, but they could not, for the
sea continued to grow more tempestuous
against them. 14Therefore they cried out to
the LORD and said, "We pray, O LORD,
please do not let us perish for this man's
life, and do not charge us with innocent
blood; for You, O LORD, have done as it
pleased You." 15So they picked up Jonah
and threw him into the sea, and the sea
ceased from its raging. 16Then the men
feared the LORD exceedingly, and offered a
sacrifice to the LORD and took vows.

Jonah's Prayer and Deliverance

17Now the LORD had prepared a great
fish to swallow Jonah. And Jonah was in
the belly of the fish three days and three
nights.

CHAPTER 2

Then Jonah prayed to the LORD his God
from the fish's belly. 2And he said:

"I cried out to the LORD because of my
affliction,
And He answered me.

"Out of the belly of Shē'ōl I cried,
And You heard my voice.
3 For You cast me into the deep,
Into the heart of the seas,
And the floods surrounded me;
All Your billows and Your waves
passed over me.
4 Then I said, 'I have been cast out of
Your sight;
Yet I will look again toward Your holy
temple.'
5 The waters surrounded me, *even* to
my soul;
The deep closed around me;
Weeds were wrapped around my
head.
6 I went down to the moorings of the
mountains;
The earth with its bars *closed* behind
me forever;
Yet You have brought up my life from
the pit,
O LORD, my God.

1:17—2:10 God's second effort to convert Jonah to the divine purpose (the first being the storm, wherein God used Jonah to make pagan sailors aware of Him). The prophet cannot escape God even in death. Jonah, like Israel, would serve God. This is not to say that Jonah's free will was abrogated, but just that his experiences taught him that he must choose God's way—any other is beset by sorrow and tragedy.

2:1–9 Jonah's prayer consists entirely of thanking God for saving him from drowning. There is no regret for escape from the whale, only a rededication in v. 9 that indicates his contrition.

7 "When my soul fainted within me,
I remembered the LORD;
And my prayer went *up* to You,
Into Your holy temple.

8 "Those who regard worthless idols
Forsake their own Mercy.
9 But I will sacrifice to You
With the voice of thanksgiving;
I will pay what I have vowed.
Salvation *is* of the LORD."

10 So the LORD spoke to the fish, and it
vomited Jonah onto dry *land*.

CHAPTER 3

Jonah Preaches at Nineveh

Now the word of the LORD came to Jo-
nah the second time, saying, 2 "Arise, go to
Nin'e·veh, that great city, and preach to it
the message that I tell you." 3 So Jonah
arose and went to Nin'e·veh, according
to the word of the LORD. Now Nin'e·veh
was an exceedingly great city, a three-
day journey[a] *in extent*. 4 And Jonah began
to enter the city on the first day's
walk. Then he cried out and said, "Yet
forty days, and Nin'e·veh shall be over-
thrown!"

The People of Nineveh Believe

5 So the people of Nin'e·veh believed
God, proclaimed a fast, and put on sack-
cloth, from the greatest to the least of them.
6 Then word came to the king of Nin'e·veh;
and he arose from his throne and laid aside
his robe, covered *himself* with sackcloth
and sat in ashes. 7 And he caused *it* to be
proclaimed and published throughout
Nin'e·veh by the decree of the king and his
nobles, saying,

Let neither man nor beast, herd nor
flock, taste anything; do not let them
eat, or drink water. 8 But let man and
beast be covered with sackcloth, and
cry mightily to God; yes, let every one
turn from his evil way and from the
violence that is in his hands. 9 Who can
tell *if* God will turn and relent, and
turn away from His fierce anger, so
that we may not perish?

10 Then God saw their works, that they
turned from their evil way; and God re-
lented from the disaster that He had said
He would bring upon them, and He did
not do it.

CHAPTER 4

Jonah's Anger and God's Kindness

But it displeased Jonah exceedingly, and
he became angry. 2 So he prayed to the
LORD, and said, "Ah, LORD, was not this
what I said when I was still in my country?
Therefore I fled previously to Tar'shish; for
I know that You *are* a gracious and merciful
God, slow to anger and abundant in
lovingkindness, One who relents from do-
ing harm. 3 Therefore now, O LORD, please
take my life from me, for *it is* better for me
to die than to live!"

4 Then the LORD said, *"Is it* right for you
to be angry?"

5 So Jonah went out of the city and sat on
the east side of the city. There he made
himself a shelter and sat under it in the
shade, till he might see what would be-
come of the city. 6 And the LORD God pre-
pared a plant[a] and made it come up over
Jonah, that it might be shade for his head

3:3 [a]Exact meaning unknown 4:6 [a]Hebrew *kikayon*, exact identity unknown

---

3:10 God relented: A remarkably clear insight into the nature of God. He responds to human action. This is not to say that God is vacillating or inconsistent. He is completely consistent in His intention to forgive repentant sinners, even Assyrians. Jonah knew about this divine consistency. That is why he had headed west to Tarshish (4:2).

4:3 An angry Jonah was ready to die rather than let God change his unforgiving spirit. Such a worldly mind resists the Spirit of God (see Rom. 8:7, 8).

Is It Right for You to Be Angry?

Anne Ortlund

If you are angry at someone right now, you know the feeling in the pit of your stomach, and you know the words that race through your mind—words to tell that person and words to tell others so they will be on your side.

Wait!

Wait. Cool down. Be quiet a minute. Think.

Look at Jesus. He "endured" (Heb. 12:2). He had every reason to be legitimately angry: Stupid, terrible people had unjustly done Him in—and yet He said, "Father, forgive them, for they do not know what they do" (Luke 23:34).

You see, the problem isn't really the person who is troubling you; it's within you. All your life, sinners around you will sin—it's what they do best!

But fix your eyes on Jesus. Remember Paul's words: "Love suffers long and is kind . . . is not provoked, thinks no evil . . . bears all things, believes all things, hopes all things, endures all things. Love never fails" (1 Cor. 13:4–8).

"If anger is your problem, you may suddenly realize that Jesus' eye is fixed on you."

If anger is your problem, you may suddenly realize that Jesus' eye is fixed on you, studying you, and He asks you simply, "Is it right for you to be angry?" ✦

to deliver him from his misery. So Jonah
was very grateful for the plant. 7But as
morning dawned the next day God pre-
pared a worm, and it *so* damaged the plant
that it withered. 8And it happened, when
the sun arose, that God prepared a vehe-
ment east wind; and the sun beat on Jo-
nah's head, so that he grew faint. Then he
wished death for himself, and said, *"It is*
better for me to die than to live."
9Then God said to Jonah, *"Is it* right for
you to be angry about the plant?"
And he said, *"It is* right for me to be an-
gry, even to death!"
10But the LORD said, "You have had pity
on the plant for which you have not la-
bored, nor made it grow, which came up in
a night and perished in a night. 11And
should I not pity Nin'e·veh, that great city,
in which are more than one hundred and
twenty thousand persons who cannot dis-
cern between their right hand and their
left—and much livestock?"

4:11 should I not pity Nineveh? God claims to be the Creator of all peoples, and this alone is sufficient to establish His love of His creation. Should our love have any narrower restrictions? Since God's great desire is that all should repent and live, we should rejoice at the salvation of others, knowing that Jesus died for even the most abominable of sinners.

✦Micah✦

Micah prophesied "in the days of Jotham, Ahaz, and Hezekiah, kings of Judah" (1:1), which stretched from 750 to 687 B.C. During this time, the Assyrians repeatedly attacked Israel until they conquered the nation in 722 B.C. Although he was a contemporary of Isaiah, Micah was of a humbler social class. His small village was located in a productive agricultural belt of Judah.

The Book of Micah is divided into thirds: the first section names the specific sins of Israel and Judah, the second predicts the punishment for those sins, and the third brings hope for deliverance. Micah looked beyond the doom to the time when the Messiah would reign and peace and justice would prevail.

In closing, Micah describes a courtroom scene with God calling the mountains and hills to serve as a jury as He tries Israel and Judah for their wrongs. Nevertheless, Micah contains promise as well as punishment. Chapter 7 describes God's mercy on His people and gives insights into His character. The prophet concludes by listing promises for God's forgiveness and blessing. Micah also points to the coming of Jesus Christ—the ultimate covenant with humanity. Regardless of age or situation, Christians can find encouragement in looking toward Christ's return. ✦

CHAPTER 1

The word of the LORD that came to
Mī′cah of Mō′re·sheth in the days of
Jō′tham, Ā′haz, *and* Hez·e·kī′ah, kings of
Judah, which he saw concerning Samaria
and Jerusalem.

The Coming Judgment on Israel

2 Hear, all you peoples!
Listen, O earth, and all that is in it!
Let the Lord GOD be a witness against
you,
The Lord from His holy temple.

3 For behold, the LORD is coming out of
His place;
He will come down
And tread on the high places of the
earth.
4 The mountains will melt under Him,
And the valleys will split
Like wax before the fire,
Like waters poured down a steep
place.
5 All this is for the transgression of
Jacob
And for the sins of the house of
Israel.

1:1 The kings named place Micah in the same period with the prophets Isaiah and Hosea (see Is. 1:1; Hos. 1:1).

1:2–5 God would no longer sit quietly over the sin of Jacob. It was not Assyria who would come, but a much more serious enemy: God Himself.

What *is* the transgression of Jacob?
Is it not Samaria?
And what *are* the high places of
Judah?
Are they not Jerusalem?

6 "Therefore I will make Samaria a heap
of ruins in the field,
Places for planting a vineyard;
I will pour down her stones into the
valley,
And I will uncover her foundations.
7 All her carved images shall be beaten
to pieces,
And all her pay as a harlot shall be
burned with the fire;
All her idols I will lay desolate,
For she gathered *it* from the pay of a
harlot,
And they shall return to the pay of a
harlot."

Mourning for Israel and Judah

8 Therefore I will wail and howl,
I will go stripped and naked;
I will make a wailing like the jackals
And a mourning like the ostriches,
9 For her wounds *are* incurable.
For it has come to Judah;
It has come to the gate of My
people—
To Jerusalem.
10 Tell *it* not in Gath,
Weep not at all;
In Beth Aph'rah[a]
Roll yourself in the dust.
11 Pass by in naked shame, you
inhabitant of Shā'phir;
The inhabitant of Zā'a·nan[a] does not
go out.
Beth Ē'zel mourns;
Its place to stand is taken away from
you.

12 For the inhabitant of Mā'roth pined[a]
for good,
But disaster came down from the
LORD
To the gate of Jerusalem.
13 O inhabitant of Lā'chish,
Harness the chariot to the swift steeds
(She *was* the beginning of sin to the
daughter of Zion),
For the transgressions of Israel were
found in you.

14 Therefore you shall give presents to
Mō're·sheth Gath;[a]
The houses of Ach'zib[b] *shall be* a lie to
the kings of Israel.
15 I will yet bring an heir to you,
O inhabitant of Ma·rē'shah;[a]
The glory of Israel shall come to
A·dul'lam.
16 Make yourself bald and cut off your
hair,
Because of your precious children;
Enlarge your baldness like an
eagle,
For they shall go from you into
captivity.

1:10 [a]Literally *House of Dust* 1:11 [a]Literally *Going Out* 1:12 [a]Literally *was sick* 1:14 [a]Literally *Possession of Gath* [b]Literally *Lie* 1:15 [a]Literally *Inheritance*

1:6 a heap of ruins: This prophecy was fulfilled in 722 B.C. The site of ancient Samaria sits desolate today as an eloquent testimony to the truth of the Word of God. History ultimately vindicates the divine pronouncement. **pour down her stones**: A graphic picture of the destruction of a Palestinian city. They stood on natural or artificial hills. Thus, it was easy for victorious attackers to roll the stones of the walls and buildings down the hill. Then, if the city was not immediately reinhabited, erosion would undermine foundations and topple whatever was left into the valley below.

1:8 In typical oriental language, God mourns over Samaria's impending death like a mourner at a funeral. The verse has great theological implications: God's judgment is always painful to Him; He loves His creation and takes no pleasure in its destruction (see Ezek. 18:23).

CHAPTER 2

Woe to Evildoers

Woe to those who devise iniquity,
And work out evil on their beds!
At morning light they practice it,
Because it is in the power of their hand.
2 They covet fields and take *them* by violence,
Also houses, and seize *them*.
So they oppress a man and his house,
A man and his inheritance.

3Therefore thus says the LORD:

"Behold, against this family I am devising disaster,
From which you cannot remove your necks;
Nor shall you walk haughtily,
For this *is* an evil time.
4 In that day *one* shall take up a proverb against you,
And lament with a bitter lamentation, saying:
'We are utterly destroyed!
He has changed the heritage of my people;
How He has removed *it* from me!
To a turncoat He has divided our fields.' "

5 Therefore you will have no one to determine boundaries[a] by lot
In the assembly of the LORD.

Lying Prophets

6 "Do not prattle," *you say to those* who prophesy.
So they shall not prophesy to you;[a]
They shall not return insult for insult.[b]
7 *You who are* named the house of Jacob:
"Is the Spirit of the LORD restricted?
Are these His doings?
Do not My words do good
To him who walks uprightly?

8 "Lately My people have risen up as an enemy—
You pull off the robe with the garment
From those who trust *you*, as they pass by,
Like men returned from war.
9 The women of My people you cast out
From their pleasant houses;
From their children
You have taken away My glory forever.

10 "Arise and depart,
For this *is* not *your* rest;
Because it is defiled, it shall destroy,
Yes, with utter destruction.
11 If a man should walk in a false spirit
And speak a lie, *saying*,
'I will prophesy to you of wine and drink,'
Even he would be the prattler of this people.

Israel Restored

12 "I will surely assemble all of you, O Jacob,
I will surely gather the remnant of Israel;
I will put them together like sheep of the fold,[a]
Like a flock in the midst of their pasture;
They shall make a loud noise because of *so many* people.
13 The one who breaks open will come up before them;
They will break out,
Pass through the gate,
And go out by it;
Their king will pass before them,
With the LORD at their head."

2:5 [a]Literally *one casting a surveyor's line*
2:6 [a]Literally *to these* [b]Vulgate reads *He shall not take shame.* 2:12 [a]Hebrew *Bozrah*

CHAPTER 3

Wicked Rulers and Prophets

And I said:
"Hear now, O heads of Jacob,
And you rulers of the house of Israel:
Is it not for you to know justice?
2 You who hate good and love evil;
Who strip the skin from My people,[a]
And the flesh from their bones;
3 Who also eat the flesh of My people,
Flay their skin from them,
Break their bones,
And chop *them* in pieces
Like *meat* for the pot,
Like flesh in the caldron."

4 Then they will cry to the LORD,
But He will not hear them;
He will even hide His face from them
at that time,
Because they have been evil in their
deeds.

5 Thus says the LORD concerning the
prophets
Who make my people stray;
Who chant "Peace"
While they chew with their teeth,
But who prepare war against him
Who puts nothing into their mouths:
6 "Therefore you shall have night
without vision,
And you shall have darkness without
divination;
The sun shall go down on the
prophets,
And the day shall be dark for them.
7 So the seers shall be ashamed,
And the diviners abashed;
Indeed they shall all cover their lips;
For *there is* no answer from God."

8 But truly I am full of power by the
Spirit of the LORD,
And of justice and might,
To declare to Jacob his transgression
And to Israel his sin.
9 Now hear this,
You heads of the house of Jacob
And rulers of the house of Israel,
Who abhor justice
And pervert all equity,
10 Who build up Zion with bloodshed
And Jerusalem with iniquity:
11 Her heads judge for a bribe,
Her priests teach for pay,
And her prophets divine for money.
Yet they lean on the LORD, and say,
"Is not the LORD among us?
No harm can come upon us."
12 Therefore because of you
Zion shall be plowed *like* a field,
Jerusalem shall become heaps of
ruins,
And the mountain of the temple[a]
Like the bare hills of the forest.

CHAPTER 4

The LORD's Reign in Zion

Now it shall come to pass in the latter
days

3:2 [a]Literally *them* 3:12 [a]Literally *house*

3:8 full of power: The false prophets promised a pleasant future, but Micah, under the **Spirit of the LORD**, denounced sin.

3:12 Jeremiah quoted these words 100 years later, referring to the approaching fall of Jerusalem in 586 B.C. (see Jer. 26:18).

4:1–13 One of the great prophetic visions of a future age of peace. The temple will be reestablished on Mt. Zion after its destruction (3:12), and all the people of the earth will flow into it to worship the one true God. Scholars debate whether this vision should be taken literally or spiritually. From the NT perspective it seems best to see both a spiritual fulfillment in the present age as a result of the work of Christ, but also a fuller consummation in the final day when the kingdom which was inaugurated at the first coming will be consummated in the Second Coming.

That the mountain of the LORD's
house
Shall be established on the top of the
mountains,
And shall be exalted above the hills;
And peoples shall flow to it.
2 Many nations shall come and say,
"Come, and let us go up to the
mountain of the LORD,
To the house of the God of Jacob;
He will teach us His ways,
And we shall walk in His paths."
For out of Zion the law shall go forth,
And the word of the LORD from
Jerusalem.
3 He shall judge between many
peoples,
And rebuke strong nations afar off;
They shall beat their swords into
plowshares,
And their spears into pruning hooks;
Nation shall not lift up sword against
nation,
Neither shall they learn war
anymore.[a]

4 But everyone shall sit under his vine
and under his fig tree,
And no one shall make *them* afraid;
For the mouth of the LORD of hosts
has spoken.
5 For all people walk each in the name
of his god,
But we will walk in the name of the
LORD our God
Forever and ever.

Zion's Future Triumph

6 "In that day," says the LORD,
"I will assemble the lame,
I will gather the outcast
And those whom I have afflicted;
7 I will make the lame a remnant,
And the outcast a strong nation;
So the LORD will reign over them in
Mount Zion
From now on, even forever.
8 And you, O tower of the flock,
The stronghold of the daughter of
Zion,
To you shall it come,
Even the former dominion shall
come,
The kingdom of the daughter of
Jerusalem."

9 Now why do you cry aloud?
Is there no king in your midst?
Has your counselor perished?
For pangs have seized you like a
woman in labor.
10 Be in pain, and labor to bring forth,
O daughter of Zion,
Like a woman in birth pangs.
For now you shall go forth from the
city,
You shall dwell in the field,
And to Babylon you shall go.
There you shall be delivered;
There the LORD will redeem you
From the hand of your enemies.

11 Now also many nations have
gathered against you,
Who say, "Let her be defiled,
And let our eye look upon Zion."
12 But they do not know the thoughts of
the LORD,
Nor do they understand His counsel;
For He will gather them like sheaves
to the threshing floor.

13 "Arise and thresh, O daughter of Zion;
For I will make your horn iron,
And I will make your hooves bronze;
You shall beat in pieces many
peoples;

4:3 [a]Compare Isaiah 2:2–4

4:6–15 Like his contemporaries Amos, Hosea, and Isaiah, Micah declared a captivity resulting from Israel's sin. But also like them, he saw a return which would bring back a **remnant** (v. 7) who would be the seed of a new beginning.

I will consecrate their gain to the
LORD,
And their substance to the Lord of the
whole earth."

CHAPTER 5

Now gather yourself in troops,
O daughter of troops;
He has laid siege against us;
They will strike the judge of Israel
with a rod on the cheek.

The Coming Messiah

2 "But you, Bethlehem Eph'ra·thah,
Though you are little among the
thousands of Judah,
Yet out of you shall come forth to Me
The One to be Ruler in Israel,
Whose goings forth *are* from of old,
From everlasting."

3 Therefore He shall give them up,
Until the time *that* she who is in labor
has given birth;
Then the remnant of His brethren
Shall return to the children of Israel.
4 And He shall stand and feed *His*
flock
In the strength of the LORD,
In the majesty of the name of the
LORD His God;
And they shall abide,
For now He shall be great
To the ends of the earth;
5 And this *One* shall be peace.

Judgment on Israel's Enemies

When the Assyrian comes into our
land,
And when he treads in our palaces,
Then we will raise against him
Seven shepherds and eight princely
men.
6 They shall waste with the sword the
land of Assyria,
And the land of Nim'rod at its
entrances;
Thus He shall deliver *us* from the
Assyrian,
When he comes into our land
And when he treads within our
borders.

7 Then the remnant of Jacob
Shall be in the midst of many
peoples,
Like dew from the LORD,
Like showers on the grass,
That tarry for no man
Nor wait for the sons of men.
8 And the remnant of Jacob
Shall be among the Gentiles,
In the midst of many peoples,
Like a lion among the beasts of the
forest,
Like a young lion among flocks of
sheep,
Who, if he passes through,
Both treads down and tears in pieces,
And none can deliver.
9 Your hand shall be lifted against your
adversaries,
And all your enemies shall be cut
off.

10 "And it shall be in that day," says the
LORD,
"That I will cut off your horses from
your midst
And destroy your chariots.
11 I will cut off the cities of your land
And throw down all your
strongholds.

5:7–9 in the midst of . . . peoples: The **remnant** is described as being both **dew** (v. 7), a symbol of God's grace to the nations, and a **lion** (v. 8), an agent of His judgment upon them.

5:10–15 Each item mentioned here as being slated for destruction represents an area in which Israel depended on something other than God. Today, rather than relying on money or power, we are called to depend solely on God in every area of our lives.

KEEP IT SIMPLE

Charles R. Swindoll

Micah's words (6:6–8) state exactly what many, to this day, wonder about—pleasing God. Teachers and preachers have made it so sacrificial . . . so complicated . . . so extremely difficult. To them, God is virtually impossible to please. Therefore, religion has become a series of long, drawn-out, deeply painful acts designed to appease this peevish Deity in the sky who takes delight in watching us squirm.

At the risk of overstepping proper bounds by putting God's preference in my own words: *God likes it simple.* He does *not* look for big-time, external displays.

"All God asks is simple faith."

Pause for a moment and look at how we have complicated what God said so simply. What is required? Slow down and read the list:

✦ To do justice
✦ To love kindness
✦ To walk humbly with your God

Period.

Faith is not a long series of religious performances. It is not doing a pile of pious things either to keep God from being angry or to impress others with how dedicated you are. The sooner we believe that and start living like that, the quicker we will understand the true meaning of the Christian life as God planned it—and the more contented we will be. All God asks is *simple faith.* ✦

12 I will cut off sorceries from your
hand,
And you shall have no soothsayers.
13 Your carved images I will also cut off,
And your sacred pillars from your
midst;
You shall no more worship the work
of your hands;
14 I will pluck your wooden images[a]
from your midst;
Thus I will destroy your cities.
15 And I will execute vengeance in
anger and fury
On the nations that have not heard."[a]

CHAPTER 6

God Pleads with Israel

Hear now what the LORD says:

"Arise, plead your case before the
mountains,
And let the hills hear your voice.
2 Hear, O you mountains, the LORD's
complaint,
And you strong foundations of the
earth;
For the LORD has a complaint against
His people,
And He will contend with Israel.
3 "O My people, what have I done to
you?
And how have I wearied you?
Testify against Me.
4 For I brought you up from the land of
Egypt,

5:14 [a]Hebrew *Asherim*, Canaanite deities 5:15 [a]Or *obeyed*

I redeemed you from the house of
bondage;
And I sent before you Moses, Aaron,
and Miriam.
5 O My people, remember now
What Bā′lak king of Mō′ab counseled,
And what Bā′laam the son of Bē′or
answered him,
From Acacia Grove[a] to Gil′gal,
That you may know the
righteousness of the LORD."

6 With what shall I come before the
LORD,
And bow myself before the High
God?
Shall I come before Him with burnt
offerings,
With calves a year old?
7 Will the LORD be pleased with
thousands of rams,
Ten thousand rivers of oil?
Shall I give my firstborn *for* my
transgression,
The fruit of my body *for* the sin of my
soul?

8 He has shown you, O man, what *is*
good;
And what does the LORD require of
you
But to do justly,
To love mercy,
And to walk humbly with your God?

Punishment of Israel's Injustice

9 The LORD's voice cries to the city—
Wisdom shall see Your name:

> The great test of a man's character is his tongue.
>
> Oswald Chambers

"Hear the rod!
Who has appointed it?
10 Are there yet the treasures of
wickedness
In the house of the wicked,
And the short measure *that is* an
abomination?
11 Shall I count pure *those* with the
wicked scales,
And with the bag of deceitful
weights?
12 For her rich men are full of violence,
Her inhabitants have spoken lies,
And their tongue is deceitful in their
mouth.

13 "Therefore I will also make *you* sick by
striking you,
By making *you* desolate because of
your sins.
14 You shall eat, but not be satisfied;
Hunger[a] *shall be* in your midst.
You may carry *some* away,[b] but shall
not save *them;*
And what you do rescue I will give
over to the sword.

15 "You shall sow, but not reap;
You shall tread the olives, but not
anoint yourselves with oil;
And *make* sweet wine, but not drink
wine.

6:5 [a]Hebrew *Shittim* (compare Numbers 25:1; Joshua 2:1; 3:1) 6:14 [a]Or *Emptiness* or *Humiliation* [b]Targum and Vulgate read *You shall take hold.*

6:6–8 These verses, probably the best known passage in Micah, are worth memorizing. The prophet proclaims an essential aspect of biblical religion. God does not desire sacrifice of material things—even of one's own **firstborn**, nor does He require us to follow a complicated system of rules and regulations (vv. 6, 7). He asks us to be just and merciful to our fellowman and to live in humble obedience to **God**. The message was also proclaimed by Jesus (see Matt. 22:36–40).

TESTIMONY IN ACTION

Charles R. Swindoll

You want to impact your family . . . your church . . . your community . . . your place of employment? You want to make a difference in the life of your mate, a family member, a friend (Christian or not), some person in the workplace?

Demonstrate the characteristics of Christ. No need to drop gospel tracts from a low-flying airplane or display a bright red twenty-foot-square "Jesus Saves" flag over your house. No need to stick a fish-shaped symbol on your car or quote verses every day to your neighbor or rant and rave against all the ills of society down at city hall. Just take the distilled essence of the Christian message as contained in the words of the Golden Rule and live it out. Morning to night. Day after day. Week after week. Month in, month out. As the prophet Micah put it: Act justly, love mercy, and walk humbly. You will be astounded at the impact that kind of simple-faith lifestyle will make.

It has been said that the only Bible most folks ever read is the daily life of the Christian. If that is true, I believe the world needs a revised version. Our problem is not that too many of us are being ignored, it's that we are all being observed!

If you think that words fitly spoken are powerful, they are nothing compared to the power of a life fitly lived. ✦

16 For the statutes of Om'rī are kept;
All the works of Ā'hab's house *are done;*
And you walk in their counsels,
That I may make you a desolation,
And your inhabitants a hissing.
Therefore you shall bear the reproach of My people."[a]

CHAPTER 7

Sorrow for Israel's Sins

Woe is me!
For I am like those who gather summer fruits,
Like those who glean vintage grapes;
There is no cluster to eat
Of the first-ripe fruit *which* my soul desires.
2 The faithful *man* has perished from the earth,
And *there is* no one upright among men.
They all lie in wait for blood;
Every man hunts his brother with a net.

3 That they may successfully do evil with both hands—
The prince asks *for gifts,*

6:16 [a]Following Masoretic Text, Targum, and Vulgate; Septuagint reads *of nations.*

7:1–7 No one upright (v. 2) describes a society bereft of righteousness and integrity. Each class and person had descended lower and lower into selfishness and rapacity until no one trusted anyone else (vv. 5, 6).

The judge *seeks* a bribe,
And the great *man* utters his evil
desire;
So they scheme together.
4 The best of them *is* like a brier;
The most upright *is sharper* than a
thorn hedge;
The day of your watchman and your
punishment comes;
Now shall be their perplexity.

5 Do not trust in a friend;
Do not put your confidence in a
companion;
Guard the doors of your mouth
From her who lies in your bosom.
6 For son dishonors father,
Daughter rises against her mother,
Daughter-in-law against her
mother-in-law;
A man's enemies *are* the men of his
own household.
7 Therefore I will look to the LORD;
I will wait for the God of my
salvation;
My God will hear me.

Israel's Confession and Comfort

8 Do not rejoice over me, my enemy;
When I fall, I will arise;
When I sit in darkness,
The LORD *will be* a light to me.
9 I will bear the indignation of the
LORD,
Because I have sinned against Him,
Until He pleads my case
And executes justice for me.
He will bring me forth to the light;
I will see His righteousness.
10 Then *she who is* my enemy will see,
And shame will cover her who said
to me,
"Where is the LORD your God?"
My eyes will see her;
Now she will be trampled down
Like mud in the streets.

11 *In* the day when your walls are to be
built,
In that day the decree shall go far and
wide.[a]
12 *In* that day they[a] shall come to you
From Assyria and the fortified cities,[b]
From the fortress[c] to the River,[d]
From sea to sea,
And mountain *to* mountain.
13 Yet the land shall be desolate
Because of those who dwell in it,
And for the fruit of their deeds.

God Will Forgive Israel

14 Shepherd Your people with Your staff,
The flock of Your heritage,
Who dwell solitarily *in* a woodland,
In the midst of Car′mel;
Let them feed *in* Bā′shan and
Gil′ē·ad,
As in days of old.

15 "As in the days when you came out of
the land of Egypt,
I will show them[a] wonders."

16 The nations shall see and be ashamed
of all their might;
They shall put *their* hand over *their*
mouth;
Their ears shall be deaf.
17 They shall lick the dust like a serpent;

7:11 [a]Or *the boundary shall be extended*
7:12 [a]Literally *he,* collective of the captives [b]Hebrew *arey mazor,* possibly *cities of Egypt* [c]Hebrew *mazor,* possibly *Egypt* [d]That is, the Euphrates
7:15 [a]Literally *him,* collective for the captives

7:8–20 When I fall, I will arise: A closing song of praise which recognizes that God's people must pay for their sin (vv. 8, 9) but confidently believes that restoration will occur. It is a confidence based on faith in God's love (vv. 18–20).

7:12 In that day: The day of return from captivity.

7:14 Shepherd Your people: The imagery of the divine Shepherd conveys God's personal care for His people and their individual needs.

They shall crawl from their holes like
snakes of the earth.
They shall be afraid of the LORD our
God,
And shall fear because of You.
18 Who *is* a God like You,
Pardoning iniquity
And passing over the transgression of
the remnant of His heritage?

He does not retain His anger forever,
Because He delights *in* mercy.
19 He will again have compassion on us,
And will subdue our iniquities.

You will cast all our[a] sins
Into the depths of the sea.
20 You will give truth to Jacob
And mercy to Abraham,
Which You have sworn to our fathers
From days of old.

7:19 [a]Literally *their*

7:20 give truth: God would be true to Jacob and faithful to the promises made to Abraham regarding their descendants as the people of God.

✦Nahum✦

God had allowed Assyria to conquer Israel in retribution for her sin, but later God's wrath turned on Assyria for its wicked ways. In 612 B.C., Babylon attacked Nineveh and, after three years of relentless fighting, defeated the mighty Assyrian empire. Nahum prophesied this event around 650 B.C.

Although revival had occurred under Jonah's preaching, by Nahum's time the Ninevites had returned to their sin; failure to pass the spiritual torch to following generations led to the Ninevites' downfall. Nahum predicted the destruction of Assyria's capital city, despite Nineveh's seeming invincibility. Nahum 1:2–8 describes God as powerful, holy, just, patient, and slow to wrath; however, He will not ignore sin forever.

Nahum teaches that God's judgment is fair and sure against the unrighteous. Even a pagan nation used as part of God's plan will be judged by God's standards of holiness. ✦

CHAPTER 1

The burden[a] against Nin'e·veh. The book of the vision of Nā'hum the El'kosh·īte.

God's Wrath on His Enemies

2 God *is* jealous, and the LORD
avenges;
The LORD avenges and *is* furious.
The LORD will take vengeance on His
adversaries,
And He reserves *wrath* for His
enemies;
3 The LORD *is* slow to anger and great
in power,
And will not at all acquit *the wicked.*
The LORD has His way
In the whirlwind and in the storm,
And the clouds *are* the dust of His
feet.
4 He rebukes the sea and makes it dry,
And dries up all the rivers.
Bā'shan and Car'mel wither,
And the flower of Lebanon wilts.
5 The mountains quake before Him,
The hills melt,
And the earth heaves[a] at His
presence,
Yes, the world and all who dwell in it.

6 Who can stand before His
indignation?
And who can endure the fierceness of
His anger?

1:1 [a]Or *oracle* 1:5 [a]Targum reads *burns.*

1:1 burden: A term indicating a prophetic message. **Nahum** means "The Comforter." His message of destruction to Israel's deadly enemies would be a comfort to God's people.

1:2 Jealousy, **vengeance**, and **wrath** are the appropriate responses of a holy and just God in the face of humanity's sin.

1:3 Although the Lord withholds His wrath for a time to provide an opportunity for repentance, He will not allow evil to continue unpunished.

I praise you, Lord, because You are good, a stronghold in the day of trouble; and You know those who trust in You.

Nahum 1:7

His fury is poured out like fire,
And the rocks are thrown down by
Him.

7 The LORD *is* good,
A stronghold in the day of trouble;
And He knows those who trust in
Him.
8 But with an overflowing flood
He will make an utter end of its place,
And darkness will pursue His
enemies.

9 What do you conspire against the
LORD?
He will make an utter end *of it*.
Affliction will not rise up a second
time.
10 For while tangled *like* thorns,
And while drunken *like* drunkards,
They shall be devoured like stubble
fully dried.
11 From you comes forth *one*
Who plots evil against the LORD,
A wicked counselor.

12 Thus says the LORD:

"Though *they are* safe, and likewise
many,
Yet in this manner they will be cut
down
When he passes through.
Though I have afflicted you,
I will afflict you no more;
13 For now I will break off his yoke from
you,
And burst your bonds apart."

14 The LORD has given a command
concerning you:
"Your name shall be perpetuated no
longer.
Out of the house of your gods
I will cut off the carved image and the
molded image.
I will dig your grave,
For you are vile."

15 Behold, on the mountains
The feet of him who brings good
tidings,
Who proclaims peace!
O Judah, keep your appointed feasts,
Perform your vows.
For the wicked one shall no more
pass through you;
He is utterly cut off.

CHAPTER 2

The Destruction of Nineveh

He who scatters[a] has come up before
your face.
Man the fort!
Watch the road!
Strengthen *your* flanks!
Fortify *your* power mightily.

2 For the LORD will restore the
excellence of Jacob

2:1 [a]Vulgate reads *he who destroys.*

1:7, 8 If people put their **trust** in God, they will experience Him as **good** and as a defense against **trouble**. If they follow wickedness, they will experience Him as destruction (see Ps. 1:1–6). **overflowing flood**: A remarkable anticipation of the method by which Nineveh was taken in 612 B.C. (see 2:6).

Like the excellence of Israel,
For the emptiers have emptied them out
And ruined their vine branches.

3 The shields of his mighty men *are* made red,
The valiant men *are* in scarlet.
The chariots *come* with flaming torches
In the day of his preparation,
And the spears are brandished.[a]
4 The chariots rage in the streets,
They jostle one another in the broad roads;
They seem like torches,
They run like lightning.

5 He remembers his nobles;
They stumble in their walk;
They make haste to her walls,
And the defense is prepared.
6 The gates of the rivers are opened,
And the palace is dissolved.
7 It is decreed:[a]
She shall be led away captive,
She shall be brought up;
And her maidservants shall lead *her* as with the voice of doves,
Beating their breasts.

8 Though Nin′e·veh of old *was* like a pool of water,
Now they flee away.
"Halt! Halt!" *they cry;*
But no one turns back.

9 Take spoil of silver!
Take spoil of gold!
There is no end of treasure,
Or wealth of every desirable prize.
10 She is empty, desolate, and waste!
The heart melts, and the knees shake;
Much pain *is* in every side,
And all their faces are drained of color.[a]

11 Where *is* the dwelling of the lions,
And the feeding place of the young lions,
Where the lion walked, the lioness *and* lion's cub,
And no one made *them* afraid?
12 The lion tore in pieces enough for his cubs,
Killed for his lionesses,
Filled his caves with prey,
And his dens with flesh.

13"Behold, I *am* against you," says the
LORD of hosts, "I will burn your[a] chariots in
smoke, and the sword shall devour your
young lions; I will cut off your prey from
the earth, and the voice of your messen-
gers shall be heard no more."

CHAPTER 3

The Woe of Nineveh

Woe to the bloody city!
It *is* all full of lies *and* robbery.
Its victim never departs.
2 The noise of a whip
And the noise of rattling wheels,
Of galloping horses,
Of clattering chariots!
3 Horsemen charge with bright sword and glittering spear.

2:3 [a]Literally *the cypresses are shaken;* Septuagint and Syriac read *the horses rush about;* Vulgate reads *the drivers are stupefied.* 2:7 [a]Hebrew *Huzzab* 2:10 [a]Compare Joel 2:6 2:13 [a]Literally *her*

2:7 Either Nineveh's queen or goddess Ishtar would be **led away captive**. This reflects Assyria's own practice of parading the religious representatives of her victims to demonstrate the superiority of her god to theirs. Paul uses this practice to illustrate the conquest of Christ over the powers of darkness (see Col. 2:15).

There is a multitude of slain,
A great number of bodies,
Countless corpses—
They stumble over the corpses—
4 Because of the multitude of harlotries
of the seductive harlot,
The mistress of sorceries,
Who sells nations through her
harlotries,
And families through her sorceries.

5 "Behold, I *am* against you," says the
LORD of hosts;
"I will lift your skirts over your face,
I will show the nations your
nakedness,
And the kingdoms your shame.
6 I will cast abominable filth upon you,
Make you vile,
And make you a spectacle.
7 It shall come to pass *that* all who look
upon you
Will flee from you, and say,
'Nin′e·veh is laid waste!
Who will bemoan her?'
Where shall I seek comforters for
you?"
8 Are you better than No Ā′mon[a]
That was situated by the River,[b]
That had the waters around her,
Whose rampart *was* the sea,
Whose wall *was* the sea?
9 Ethiopia and Egypt *were* her strength,
And *it was* boundless;
Put and Lū′bim were your[a] helpers.
10 Yet she *was* carried away,
She went into captivity;
Her young children also were dashed
to pieces
At the head of every street;
They cast lots for her honorable men,
And all her great men were bound in
chains.
11 You also will be drunk;
You will be hidden;
You also will seek refuge from the
enemy.

12 All your strongholds *are* fig trees with
ripened figs:
If they are shaken,
They fall into the mouth of the eater.
13 Surely, your people in your midst *are*
women!
The gates of your land are wide open
for your enemies;
Fire shall devour the bars of your
gates.

14 Draw your water for the siege!
Fortify your strongholds!
Go into the clay and tread the mortar!
Make strong the brick kiln!
15 There the fire will devour you,
The sword will cut you off;
It will eat you up like a locust.

Make yourself many—like the locust!
Make yourself many— like the
swarming locusts!
16 You have multiplied your merchants
more than the stars of heaven.
The locust plunders and flies away.
17 Your commanders *are* like *swarming*
locusts,
And your generals like great
grasshoppers,
Which camp in the hedges on a cold
day;
When the sun rises they flee away,
And the place where they *are* is not
known.

3:8 [a]That is, ancient Thebes; Targum and Vulgate read *populous Alexandria.* [b]Literally *rivers,* that is, the Nile and the surrounding canals 3:9 [a]Septuagint reads *her.*

3:12–17 Nineveh had tremendous provisions for defense—**strongholds** (v. 12), capable **people**, **gates** (v. 13), **water** supplies, and **brick** walls (v. 14). All would be too weak to protect her against the attackers because God had decreed her fall.

18 Your shepherds slumber, O king of
Assyria;
Your nobles rest *in the dust.*
Your people are scattered on the
mountains,
And no one gathers them.

19 Your injury *has* no healing,
Your wound is severe.
All who hear news of you
Will clap *their* hands over you,
For upon whom has not your
wickedness passed continually?

3:18 Ninevah fell in 612 B.C. and its destruction was so thorough that the site of the city was not identified until the nineteenth century.

✦Habakkuk✦

Habakkuk tells nothing about himself except his name, but since he warns of the coming destruction of Judah, the book must have been written about 600 B.C., before Jerusalem was defeated by Babylon. During this period, Babylon had gained control of much of the world by defeating Assyria in 612 B.C.

Habakkuk contemplates these questions frequently asked by Christians: Why does God sometimes allow sin to go unpunished? Why do certain men violate God's law without fear? In the last chapter, God showed Habakkuk that He was in control of all circumstances and would judge in His perfect time. The last three verses show Habakkuk's change from questions to answers, from complaint to confidence.

Habakkuk's question-and-answer writing style shows that God is patient enough to allow His followers to think, to wonder, and to question Him. Rather than discouraging young Christians from asking questions, mentors can point to Habakkuk, who directed his questions right to God and received an answer. The book also teaches that God judges according to His fairness, righteousness, and mercy. We never need to wonder whether God will have the last word. ✦

CHAPTER 1

The burden[a] which the prophet Habak'kuk saw.

The Prophet's Question

2 O LORD, how long shall I cry,
And You will not hear?
Even cry out to You, "Violence!"
And You will not save.
3 Why do You show me iniquity,
And cause *me* to see trouble?
For plundering and violence *are* before me;
There is strife, and contention arises.
4 Therefore the law is powerless,
And justice never goes forth.
For the wicked surround the righteous;
Therefore perverse judgment proceeds.

The LORD's Reply

5 "Look among the nations and watch—
Be utterly astounded!
For *I will* work a work in your days

1:1 [a]Or *oracle*

✦ ✦

1:3 Like many today, Habakkuk wondered why the Lord allowed the righteous to suffer while the wicked prospered. We can take heart from God's answer that He will respond in His perfect time (2:3).

1:5–11 God answers Habakkuk's insistent question with the words **I will work**. But God's way of dealing with the wicked causes more problems for Judah: He is raising up the fierce and violent **Chaldeans** (v. 6) as an instrument to visit judgment on the Judeans. Nabopolassar led the Chaldeans in an alliance with the Medes to destroy Nineveh in 612 B.C. The Chaldean-Babylonian Empire would remain a force until defeated by the Persians in 539 B.C.

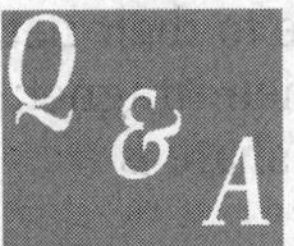

Why is there so much evil and suffering in the world today?

J. Vernon McGee

The prophet Habakkuk had the same question. Habakkuk walked about in his nation and saw iniquity, evil, injustice, and violence taking place and asked, "Why do You show me iniquity, and cause me to see trouble? For plundering and violence are before me; there is strife, and contention arises" (Hab. 1:3).

Is this not a fundamental question of the human race?

Now the questions of Habakkuk were precisely this: Why was God permitting evil to manifest itself and run rampant in the nation of Israel? Why does God permit evil? Why would a holy, gracious, good God permit these things to take place?

Those questions are not new. They are as old as the human family. Beginning in the Garden of Eden, the enemy has always used that same method—the "why does God permit evil" question—to destroy confidence in the goodness of God.

God says to us many times, "My child, I am asking you to walk with Me and believe Me." He did not say He would give us the answers, but "the just shall live by his faith" (Hab. 2:4). This is such an important statement that the three major epistles in the New Testament not only quote it but make it very basic in their teaching.

Today the world asks, "Why does God not do something about sin?" My friend, God *has* done something about it! Over nineteen hundred years ago He gave His Son to die. He intruded into the affairs of the world. Through Jesus Christ—His death and burial and resurrection—the human family can be forgiven of their sins. My beloved, without doubt this is one of the most wonderful examples of the fact that the hand of God is in the glove of human events!

Why does God permit evil? He permits it because He is longsuffering. He is not willing that any should perish, and He has provided a Cross—a crucified Savior—so that no one needs to perish. ✦

Which you would not believe, though
it were told *you*.

6 For indeed I am raising up the
Chal·dē′ans,
A bitter and hasty nation
Which marches through the breadth
of the earth,
To possess dwelling places *that are* not
theirs.

7 They are terrible and dreadful;
Their judgment and their dignity
proceed from themselves.

8 Their horses also are swifter than
leopards,
And more fierce than evening wolves.
Their chargers charge ahead;
Their cavalry comes from afar;
They fly as the eagle *that* hastens to
eat.

9 "They all come for violence;
Their faces are set *like* the east wind.
They gather captives like sand.
10 They scoff at kings,
And princes are scorned by them.
They deride every stronghold,
For they heap up earthen *mounds* and
seize it.
11 Then *his* mind[a] changes, and he
transgresses;
He commits offense,
Ascribing this power to his god."

The Prophet's Second Question

12 Are You not from everlasting,
O LORD my God, my Holy One?
We shall not die.
O LORD, You have appointed them for
judgment;
O Rock, You have marked them for
correction.
13 *You are* of purer eyes than to behold
evil,
And cannot look on wickedness.
Why do You look on those who deal
treacherously,
And hold Your tongue when the
wicked devours
A *person* more righteous than he?
14 *Why* do You make men like fish of the
sea,
Like creeping things *that have* no ruler
over them?

15 They take up all of them with a hook,
They catch them in their net,
And gather them in their dragnet.
Therefore they rejoice and are glad.
16 Therefore they sacrifice to their net,
And burn incense to their dragnet;
Because by them their share *is*
sumptuous
And their food plentiful.
17 Shall they therefore empty their net,
And continue to slay nations without
pity?

CHAPTER 2

I will stand my watch
And set myself on the rampart,
And watch to see what He will say to
me,
And what I will answer when I am
corrected.

The Just Live by Faith

2Then the LORD answered me and said:

"Write the vision
And make *it* plain on tablets,
That he may run who reads it.
3 For the vision *is* yet for an appointed
time;
But at the end it will speak, and it
will not lie.
Though it tarries, wait for it;
Because it will surely come,
It will not tarry.

4 "Behold the proud,
His soul is not upright in him;
But the just shall live by his faith.

1:11 [a]Literally *spirit* or *wind*

1:9 east wind: A particularly devastating wind off the desert.

1:12–17 In light of the cruel power of the Chaldeans, Habakkuk pondered a further problem: How could a **holy** God use such a wicked people to punish those more righteous than they? He queries, "How could God whose **eyes** are too pure to **behold evil** (v. 13) permit the cruel deeds of the Chaldeans?" **more righteous than he**: The Judean people might be wicked, but not as wicked as the Babylonians. As God had suggested, His response to the prophet's first request for justice was shocking (v. 5).

2:1 The prophet retreats to his watchtower to hear what God will say about his questions. He expects to be rebuked, but is not. God welcomes sincere questions (Judges 6:39). True prayer is a two-way conversation; we must be alert to hear God's response.

2:4 The **proud** man's **soul is not upright**. He deludes himself to think he can oppress others, and in so doing take care of himself. But the **just** live by the principle of **faithfulness**

Woe to the Wicked

5 "Indeed, because he transgresses by
wine,
He is a proud man,
And he does not stay at home.
Because he enlarges his desire as
hell,[a]
And he *is* like death, and cannot be
satisfied,
He gathers to himself all nations
And heaps up for himself all peoples.

6 "Will not all these take up a proverb
against him,
And a taunting riddle against him,
and say,
'Woe to him who increases
What is not his—how long?
And to him who loads himself with
many pledges'?[a]
7 Will not your creditors[a] rise up
suddenly?
Will they not awaken who oppress
you?
And you will become their booty.
8 Because you have plundered many
nations,
All the remnant of the people shall
plunder you,
Because of men's blood
And the violence of the land *and* the
city,
And of all who dwell in it.

9 "Woe to him who covets evil gain for
his house,
That he may set his nest on high,
That he may be delivered from the
power of disaster!
10 You give shameful counsel to your
house,
Cutting off many peoples,
And sin *against* your soul.
11 For the stone will cry out from the
wall,
And the beam from the timbers will
answer it.

12 "Woe to him who builds a town with
bloodshed,
Who establishes a city by iniquity!
13 Behold, *is it* not of the LORD of
hosts
That the peoples labor to feed the
fire,[a]
And nations weary themselves in
vain?
14 For the earth will be filled
With the knowledge of the glory of
the LORD,
As the waters cover the sea.

15 "Woe to him who gives drink to his
neighbor,
Pressing[a] *him to* your bottle,
Even to make *him* drunk,
That you may look on his
nakedness!
16 You are filled with shame instead of
glory.
You also—drink!
And be exposed as uncircumcised![a]
The cup of the LORD's right hand *will
be* turned against you,
And utter shame will be on your
glory.
17 For the violence *done to* Lebanon will
cover you,
And the plunder of beasts *which*
made them afraid,
Because of men's blood

2:5 [a]Or *Sheol* 2:6 [a]Syriac and Vulgate read *thick clay.* 2:7 [a]Literally *those who bite you*
2:13 [a]Literally *for what satisfies fire,* that is, for what is of no lasting value 2:15 [a]Literally *Attaching* or *Joining*
2:16 [a]Dead Sea Scrolls and Septuagint read *And reel!;* Syriac and Vulgate read *And fall fast asleep!*

(the literal meaning of the word translated **faith**). Being faithful to God and to others, trusting God to supply personal needs, and doing what is right regardless of the short-term results are all part of living by faith. It is trusting God and His word enough to live by His precepts. This verse became the text for Paul's doctrine of justification (see Rom. 1:17; 3:1—4:25).

And the violence of the land *and* the city,
And of all who dwell in it.

18 "What profit is the image, that its maker should carve it,
The molded image, a teacher of lies,
That the maker of its mold should trust in it,
To make mute idols?
19 Woe to him who says to wood, 'Awake!'
To silent stone, 'Arise! It shall teach!'
Behold, it is overlaid with gold and silver,
Yet in it there is no breath at all.

20 "But the LORD is in His holy temple.
Let all the earth keep silence before Him."

CHAPTER 3

The Prophet's Prayer

A prayer of Ha·bak'kuk the prophet, on Shig·i·ōn'oth.[a]

2 O LORD, I have heard Your speech *and* was afraid;
O LORD, revive Your work in the midst of the years!
In the midst of the years make *it* known;
In wrath remember mercy.

3 God came from Tē'man,
The Holy One from Mount Par'an. Sē'lah

His glory covered the heavens,
And the earth was full of His praise.
4 *His* brightness was like the light;
He had rays *flashing* from His hand,
And there His power *was* hidden.
5 Before Him went pestilence,
And fever followed at His feet.
6 He stood and measured the earth;
He looked and startled the nations.
And the everlasting mountains were scattered,
The perpetual hills bowed.
His ways *are* everlasting.
7 I saw the tents of Cūsh'an in affliction;
The curtains of the land of Mid'i·an trembled.

8 O LORD, were *You* displeased with the rivers,
Was Your anger against the rivers,
Was Your wrath against the sea,
That You rode on Your horses,
Your chariots of salvation?
9 Your bow was made quite ready;
Oaths were sworn over *Your* arrows.[a] Sē'lah
You divided the earth with rivers.
10 The mountains saw You *and* trembled;
The overflowing of the water passed by.
The deep uttered its voice,
And lifted its hands on high.
11 The sun and moon stood still in their habitation;
At the light of Your arrows they went,
At the shining of Your glittering spear.

12 You marched through the land in indignation;

3:1 [a]Exact meaning unknown 3:9 [a]Literally *rods* or *tribes* (compare verse 14)

3:2 revive Your work: A prayer for God to once again manifest His redemptive power on behalf of His people as He did at the Exodus.

3:8–15 A fairly thorough merging of images from the Exodus (vv. 8, 10, 15), the conquest of Canaan (vv. 12–14), and the judges period (v. 11). All are put in a poetic setting designed to show God's complete and overwhelming sovereignty in all times.

You trampled the nations in anger.
13 You went forth for the salvation of
Your people,
For salvation with Your Anointed.
You struck the head from the house of
the wicked,
By laying bare from foundation to
neck. Sē'lah

14 You thrust through with his own
arrows
The head of his villages.
They came out like a whirlwind to
scatter me;
Their rejoicing was like feasting on
the poor in secret.
15 You walked through the sea with
Your horses,
Through the heap of great waters.

16 When I heard, my body trembled;
My lips quivered at *the* voice;
Rottenness entered my bones;
And I trembled in myself,
That I might rest in the day of
trouble.
When he comes up to the people,
He will invade them with his troops.

I praise You, the Lord God, because You are my strength.

adapted from Habakkuk 3:19

A Hymn of Faith

17 Though the fig tree may not blossom,
Nor fruit be on the vines;
Though the labor of the olive may
fail,
And the fields yield no food;
Though the flock may be cut off from
the fold,
And there be no herd in the stalls—
18 Yet I will rejoice in the LORD,
I will joy in the God of my salvation.

19 The LORD God[a] is my strength;
He will make my feet like deer's *feet*,
And He will make me walk on my
high hills.

To the Chief Musician. With my stringed instruments.

3:19 [a]Hebrew *YHWH Adonai*

3:16 Like Job (Job 42:1–6) and Isaiah (Is. 6:1–5), Habakkuk was overcome at the revelation of God's overwhelming power.

3:17–19 How we react to negative circumstances is a true measure of our faith. Like the prophet Habakkuk, we must base our actions on God and His righteousness, rather than on the world around us.

✦Zephaniah✦

Zephaniah, a descendant of King Hezekiah, wrote his book sometime between 641 and 609 B.C., during his ministry in Judah under King Josiah. Israel had already fallen to Assyria because of its sin and idolatry, and Zephaniah sensed that a similar fate would befall Judah, since the people had begun worshiping false gods under kings Manasseh and Amon. Unfortunately, the spiritual reforms that took place under King Josiah did not change the hearts of the people, and they returned to their sin soon after his death.

Zephaniah prophesied both the judgment during the day of the Lord and the restoration that would follow. Israel would again be established as a nation and inherit the blessings which God had promised in His covenant. Zephaniah gives a reminder that, in teaching new generations about the nature of God, equal coverage should be given to both His holiness and His love.

Since God is holy and righteous, He had to judge His people for their rebellion; however, He kept His promise and later restored His blessing to them. God's character contains both wrath and mercy, and each nation must account for its actions. ✦

CHAPTER 1

The word of the LORD which came to
Zeph·a·nī'ah the son of Cū'shī, the son of
Ged·a·lī'ah, the son of Am·a·rī'ah, the son
of Hez·e·kī'ah, in the days of Jō·sī'ah the
son of Ā'mon, king of Judah.

The Great Day of the LORD

2 "I will utterly consume everything
From the face of the land,"
Says the LORD;
3 "I will consume man and beast;
I will consume the birds of the heavens,
The fish of the sea,
And the stumbling blocks[a] along with the wicked.
I will cut off man from the face of the land,"
Says the LORD.

4 "I will stretch out My hand against Judah,
And against all the inhabitants of Jerusalem.
I will cut off every trace of Bā'al from this place,
The names of the idolatrous priests[a] with the *pagan* priests—
5 Those who worship the host of heaven on the housetops;
Those who worship and swear *oaths* by the LORD,

1:3 [a]Figurative of idols 1:4 [a]Hebrew *chemarim*

1:1 The genealogy related here demonstrates Zephaniah's kinship with the godly king Hezekiah.

1:5, 6 host of heaven: The heavenly bodies which many were worshiping. **Milcom**: Mo-

But who *also* swear by Mil'com;[a]
6 Those who have turned back from
following the LORD,
And have not sought the LORD, nor
inquired of Him."

7 Be silent in the presence of the Lord
GOD;
For the day of the LORD *is* at hand,
For the LORD has prepared a sacrifice;
He has invited[a] His guests.

8 "And it shall be,
In the day of the LORD's sacrifice,
That I will punish the princes and the
king's children,
And all such as are clothed with
foreign apparel.
9 In the same day I will punish
All those who leap over the
threshold,[a]
Who fill their masters' houses with
violence and deceit.

10 "And there shall be on that day," says
the LORD,
"The sound of a mournful cry from the
Fish Gate,
A wailing from the Second Quarter,
And a loud crashing from the hills.
11 Wail, you inhabitants of Mak'tesh![a]
For all the merchant people are cut
down;
All those who handle money are cut
off.

12 "And it shall come to pass at that time
That I will search Jerusalem with
lamps,
And punish the men
Who are settled in complacency,[a]
Who say in their heart,
'The LORD will not do good,
Nor will He do evil.'
13 Therefore their goods shall become
booty,
And their houses a desolation;
They shall build houses, but not
inhabit *them;*
They shall plant vineyards, but not
drink their wine."

14 The great day of the LORD *is* near;
It is near and hastens quickly.
The noise of the day of the LORD is
bitter;
There the mighty men shall cry out.
15 That day *is* a day of wrath,
A day of trouble and distress,
A day of devastation and desolation,
A day of darkness and gloominess,
A day of clouds and thick darkness,
16 A day of trumpet and alarm
Against the fortified cities
And against the high towers.

17 "I will bring distress upon men,
And they shall walk like blind men,
Because they have sinned against the
LORD;

1:5 [a]Or *Malcam,* an Ammonite god, also called *Molech* (compare Leviticus 18:21)
1:7 [a]Literally *set apart, consecrated*
1:9 [a]Compare 1 Samuel 5:5
1:11 [a]Literally *Mortar,* a market district of Jerusalem
1:12 [a]Literally *on their lees,* that is, settled like the dregs of wine

lech, an Ammonite god associated with child sacrifice (Jer. 32:35). Many in Judah attempted to combine idol worship with loyalty to God, but the Lord admits no shared obedience.

1:8, 9 Condemnation of the royal family. **King's children** refers to the dynasty. **foreign apparel**: A violation of God's commands to keep themselves separate from the pagan nations. **Leap over the threshold** perhaps refers to the plunder of private citizens by the king's people. It may also refer to some superstitious act associated with idolatry (see 1 Sam. 5:2).

1:12 settled in complacency: Lit. "settled on their lees," a metaphor from wine making implying laziness and indifference.

1:14 While "the day of the Lord" referred to in this verse was partially fulfilled by the Babylonian invasion in 586 B.C., the messianic fulfillment will take place when Christ comes again. Unlike the Jews of Zephaniah's time, we must not become complacent or cynical, but maintain an attitude of anticipation regarding the Second Coming.

Their blood shall be poured out like
dust,
And their flesh like refuse."

18 Neither their silver nor their gold
Shall be able to deliver them
In the day of the LORD's wrath;
But the whole land shall be devoured
By the fire of His jealousy,
For He will make speedy riddance
Of all those who dwell in the land.

CHAPTER 2

A Call to Repentance

Gather yourselves together, yes,
gather together,
O undesirable[a] nation,
2 Before the decree is issued,
Or the day passes like chaff,
Before the LORD's fierce anger comes
upon you,
Before the day of the LORD's anger
comes upon you!
3 Seek the LORD, all you meek of the
earth,
Who have upheld His justice.
Seek righteousness, seek humility.
It may be that you will be hidden
In the day of the LORD's anger.

Judgment on Nations

4 For Gā'za shall be forsaken,
And Ash'ke·lon desolate;
They shall drive out Ash'dod at
noonday,
And Ek'ron shall be uprooted.
5 Woe to the inhabitants of the
seacoast,
The nation of the Cher'e·thītes!
The word of the LORD *is* against you,
O Cā'naan, land of the Phi·lis'tines:
"I will destroy you;
So there shall be no inhabitant."

6 The seacoast shall be pastures,
With shelters[a] for shepherds and folds
for flocks.
7 The coast shall be for the remnant of
the house of Judah;
They shall feed *their* flocks there;
In the houses of Ash'ke·lon they shall
lie down at evening.
For the LORD their God will intervene
for them,
And return their captives.

8 "I have heard the reproach of Mō'ab,
And the insults of the people of
Am'mon,
With which they have reproached My
people,
And made arrogant threats against
their borders.
9 Therefore, as I live,"
Says the LORD of hosts, the God of
Israel,
"Surely Mō'ab shall be like Sod'om,
And the people of Am'mon like
Go·mor'rah—
Overrun with weeds and saltpits,
And a perpetual desolation.
The residue of My people shall
plunder them,
And the remnant of My people shall
possess them."

10 This they shall have for their pride,
Because they have reproached and
made arrogant threats
Against the people of the LORD of
hosts.
11 The LORD *will be* awesome to them,
For He will reduce to nothing all the
gods of the earth;
People shall worship Him,
Each one from his place,
Indeed all the shores of the nations.

2:1 [a]Or *shameless* 2:6 [a]Literally *excavations*, either underground huts or cisterns

2:7 house of Judah: Assumes a captivity from which a **remnant** would return to possess the coastlands of Palestine (see also v. 9).

12 "You Ethiopians also,
You shall be slain by My sword."

13 And He will stretch out His hand
against the north,
Destroy Assyria,
And make Nin'e·veh a desolation,
As dry as the wilderness.
14 The herds shall lie down in her
midst,
Every beast of the nation.
Both the pelican and the bittern
Shall lodge on the capitals *of* her
pillars;
Their voice shall sing in the windows;
Desolation *shall be* at the threshold;
For He will lay bare the cedar work.
15 This is the rejoicing city
That dwelt securely,
That said in her heart,
"I *am it,* and *there is* none besides me."
How has she become a desolation,
A place for beasts to lie down!
Everyone who passes by her
Shall hiss and shake his fist.

CHAPTER 3

The Wickedness of Jerusalem

Woe to her who is rebellious and
polluted,
To the oppressing city!
2 She has not obeyed *His* voice,
She has not received correction;
She has not trusted in the LORD,
She has not drawn near to her God.

3 Her princes in her midst *are* roaring
lions;
Her judges *are* evening wolves
That leave not a bone till morning.
4 Her prophets are insolent,
treacherous people;
Her priests have polluted the
sanctuary,
They have done violence to the
law.
5 The LORD *is* righteous in her
midst,
He will do no unrighteousness.
Every morning He brings His justice
to light;
He never fails,
But the unjust knows no shame.

6 "I have cut off nations,
Their fortresses are devastated;
I have made their streets desolate,
With none passing by.
Their cities are destroyed;
There is no one, no inhabitant.
7 I said, 'Surely you will fear Me,
You will receive instruction'—
So that her dwelling would not be cut
off,
Despite everything for which I
punished her.
But they rose early and corrupted all
their deeds.

A Faithful Remnant

8 "Therefore wait for Me," says the
LORD,
"Until the day I rise up for
plunder;[a]
My determination *is* to gather the
nations
To My assembly of kingdoms,
To pour on them My indignation,
All My fierce anger;
All the earth shall be devoured
With the fire of My jealousy.

3:8 [a]Septuagint and Syriac read *for witness;* Targum reads *for the day of My revelation for judgment;* Vulgate reads *for the day of My resurrection that is to come.*

2:12 A one-verse prophecy against Ethiopia which was considered the ruler of Egypt at that time.

3:8 wait for Me: An expression of complete dependence. The person who waits has surrendered the situation and its solution into God's hand.

9 "For then I will restore to the peoples a
pure language,
That they all may call on the name of
the LORD,
To serve Him with one accord.
10 From beyond the rivers of Ethiopia
My worshipers,
The daughter of My dispersed ones,
Shall bring My offering.
11 In that day you shall not be shamed
for any of your deeds
In which you transgress against Me;
For then I will take away from your
midst
Those who rejoice in your pride,
And you shall no longer be haughty
In My holy mountain.
12 I will leave in your midst
A meek and humble people,
And they shall trust in the name of
the LORD.
13 The remnant of Israel shall do no
unrighteousness
And speak no lies,
Nor shall a deceitful tongue be found
in their mouth;
For they shall feed *their* flocks and lie
down,
And no one shall make *them* afraid."

Joy in God's Faithfulness

14 Sing, O daughter of Zion!
Shout, O Israel!
Be glad and rejoice with all *your*
heart,
O daughter of Jerusalem!
15 The LORD has taken away your
judgments,
He has cast out your enemy.
The King of Israel, the LORD, *is* in
your midst;
You shall see[a] disaster no more.
16 In that day it shall be said to
Jerusalem:
"Do not fear;
Zion, let not your hands be weak.
17 The LORD your God in your midst,
The Mighty One, will save;
He will rejoice over you with
gladness,
He will quiet *you* with His love,
He will rejoice over you with
singing."
18 "I will gather those who sorrow over
the appointed assembly,
Who are among you,
To whom its reproach *is* a burden.
19 Behold, at that time
I will deal with all who afflict you;
I will save the lame,
And gather those who were driven
out;
I will appoint them for praise and
fame
In every land where they were put to
shame.
20 At that time I will bring you back,
Even at the time I gather you;
For I will give you fame and praise
Among all the peoples of the earth,
When I return your captives before
your eyes,"
Says the LORD.

3:15 [a]Some Hebrew manuscripts, Septuagint, and Bomberg read *see;* Masoretic Text and Vulgate read *fear.*

3:9, 10 pure language: Lit. "a pure lip." It may symbolize the inner state of one's being (see Is. 6:5). God promises a purified heart resulting in purified behavior. The NT indicates this would be effected by the sanctifying Spirit of God (see 1 Pet. 1:2, 22). The result of purified lives would be purified worship. They would serve God with **one accord**.

3:14–20 The redeemed shall be returned and their enemy **cast out** (v. 15). Thus there will be no **fear** (v. 16). Zephaniah shares a common vision with other Hebrew prophets: Sin will bring punishment, but will be followed by deliverance in the form of a restoration to the homeland.

✦Haggai✦

Haggai probably spent years of captivity in Babylon with the rest of the people of Judah. His name means "festive," and he gave encouraging messages to the remnant that returned to Jerusalem beginning in 530 B.C. He began his book "in the second year of King Darius" (1:1), 520 B.C.

When the first group of Jewish captives left Babylon and returned to Jerusalem to rebuild the temple, they became discouraged by various hardships. The people turned their attention to personal affairs and ceased work on the temple. Just as the temple builders sinned in allowing their personal affairs to interfere with God's business, believers today must avoid neglecting spiritual matters for the busyness of everyday activities.

Haggai called the builders to a renewed faith and reordered priorities, and he told the people that they must complete the temple before God would bless them again. Having a place of worship and sacrifice was crucial to their relationship with God. Haggai also gave prophecies concerning the Tribulation and Christ's Second Coming (2:6–9). ✦

CHAPTER 1

The Command to Build God's House

In the second year of King Da·rī'us, in
the sixth month, on the first day of the
month, the word of the LORD came by
Hag'gaī the prophet to Ze·rub'ba·bel the
son of She·al'ti·el, governor of Judah, and
to Joshua the son of Je·hoz'a·dak, the high
priest, saying, 2"Thus speaks the LORD of
hosts, saying: 'This people says, "The time
has not come, the time that the LORD's
house should be built." ' "
3Then the word of the LORD came by
Hag'gaī the prophet, saying, 4"*Is it* time for
you yourselves to dwell in your paneled
houses, and this temple[a] *to lie* in ruins?"
5Now therefore, thus says the LORD of
hosts: "Consider your ways!

6"You have sown much, and bring in
little;
You eat, but do not have enough;
You drink, but you are not filled with
drink;
You clothe yourselves, but no one is
warm;
And he who earns wages,
Earns wages *to put* into a bag with
holes."

7Thus says the LORD of hosts: "Consider
your ways! 8Go up to the mountains and

1:4 [a]Literally *house*, and so in verse 8

✦ ✦

1:3, 4 They had spent their time and energy building their own homes but had neglected their responsibilities to God. The work of God should always be a priority of the Christian. As good stewards, we must commit both our time and our money to Him.

1:7–11 The prophet calls his people to action based on the faith that if they would move, God would provide. When they had not moved, He had not provided.

bring wood and build the temple, that I may take pleasure in it and be glorified," says the LORD. 9"*You* looked for much, but indeed *it came to* little; and when you brought it home, I blew it away. Why?" says the LORD of hosts. "Because of My house that *is in* ruins, while every one of you runs to his own house. 10Therefore the heavens above you withhold the dew, and the earth withholds its fruit. 11For I called for a drought on the land and the mountains, on the grain and the new wine and the oil, on whatever the ground brings forth, on men and livestock, and on all the labor of *your* hands."

The People's Obedience

12Then Ze·rub'ba·bel the son of She·al'ti·el, and Joshua the son of Je·hoz'a·dak, the high priest, with all the remnant of the people, obeyed the voice of the LORD their God, and the words of Hag'gai the prophet, as the LORD their God had sent him; and the people feared the presence of the LORD. 13Then Hag'gai, the LORD's messenger, spoke the LORD's message to the people, saying, "I *am* with you, says the LORD." 14So the LORD stirred up the spirit of Ze·rub'ba·bel the son of She·al'ti·el, governor of Judah, and the spirit of Joshua the son of Je·hoz'a·dak, the high priest, and the spirit of all the remnant of the people; and they came and worked on the house of the LORD of hosts, their God, 15on the twenty-fourth day of the sixth month, in the second year of King Da·ri'us.

CHAPTER 2

The Coming Glory of God's House

In the seventh *month,* on the twenty-first of the month, the word of the LORD came by Hag'gai the prophet, saying: 2"Speak now to Ze·rub'ba·bel the son of She·al'ti·el, governor of Judah, and to Joshua the son of Je·hoz'a·dak, the high priest, and to the remnant of the people, saying: 3'Who is left among you who saw this temple[a] in its former glory? And how do you see it now? In comparison with it, *is this* not in your eyes as nothing? 4Yet now be strong, Ze·rub'ba·bel,' says the LORD; 'and be strong, Joshua, son of Je·hoz'a·dak, the high priest; and be strong, all you people of the land,' says the LORD, 'and work; for I *am* with you,' says the LORD of hosts. 5'*According to* the word that I covenanted with you when you came out of Egypt, so My Spirit remains among you; do not fear!'

6"For thus says the LORD of hosts: 'Once more (it *is* a little while) I will shake heaven and earth, the sea and dry land; 7and I will shake all nations, and they shall come to the Desire of All Nations,[a] and I will fill this temple with glory,' says the LORD of hosts. 8'The silver *is* Mine, and the gold *is* Mine,' says the LORD of hosts. 9'The glory of this latter temple shall be greater than the former,' says the LORD of hosts. 'And in this place I will give peace,' says the LORD of hosts."

The People Are Defiled

10On the twenty-fourth *day* of the ninth *month,* in the second year of Da·ri'us, the word of the LORD came by Hag'gai the prophet, saying, 11"Thus says the LORD of hosts: 'Now, ask the priests *concerning the* law, saying, 12"If one carries holy meat in the fold of his garment, and with the edge he touches bread or stew, wine or oil, or any food, will it become holy?" ' "

2:3 [a]Literally *house,* and so in verses 7 and 9
2:7 [a]Or *the desire of all nations*

2:7 Desire of All Nations: The Messiah, who would come to the temple.

2:11–14 The discussion emphasizes that it is easier to become unholy than to become holy. The implication is that the Babylonian captivity had rendered them unclean and it would take a long time to be purified. That is why the anticipated glorious future was so long in coming.

Then the priests answered and said,
"No."
13 And Hag'gaī said, "If *one who is* un-
clean *because* of a dead body touches any of
these, will it be unclean?"
So the priests answered and said, "It
shall be unclean."
14 Then Hag'gaī answered and said,
" 'So is this people, and so is this nation be-
fore Me,' says the LORD, 'and so is every
work of their hands; and what they offer
there is unclean.

Promised Blessing

15 'And now, carefully consider from this
day forward: from before stone was laid
upon stone in the temple of the LORD—
16 since those *days,* when *one* came to a heap
of twenty ephahs, there were *but* ten; when
one came to the wine vat to draw out fifty
baths from the press, there were *but*
twenty. 17 I struck you with blight and
mildew and hail in all the labors of your
hands; yet you did not *turn* to Me,' says the
LORD. 18 'Consider now from this day for-
ward, from the twenty-fourth day of the
ninth month, from the day that the founda-
tion of the LORD's temple was laid—con-
sider it: 19 Is the seed still in the barn? As yet
the vine, the fig tree, the pomegranate, and
the olive tree have not yielded *fruit. But*
from this day I will bless *you.*' "

Zerubbabel Chosen as a Signet

20 And again the word of the LORD came
to Hag'gaī on the twenty-fourth day of the
month, saying, 21 "Speak to Ze·rub'ba·bel,
governor of Judah, saying:

'I will shake heaven and earth.
22 I will overthrow the throne of
kingdoms;
I will destroy the strength of the
Gentile kingdoms.
I will overthrow the chariots
And those who ride in them;
The horses and their riders shall come
down,
Every one by the sword of his
brother.

23 'In that day,' says the LORD of hosts, 'I
will take you, Ze·rub'ba·bel My servant,
the son of She·al'ti·el,' says the LORD, 'and
will make you like a signet *ring;* for I have
chosen you,' says the LORD of hosts."

2:20–23 Zerubbabel, governor: Can it be that tiny Judah, only a part of vast Persia, would indeed worship the one true God? Would her local governor really be on a par with kings and emperors? Haggai asserted that God would make it so.

2:23 Here the promises made to Zerubbabel of the Davidic line seem to foreshadow David's greater Son, Jesus Christ. This is a promise that God still honors the Davidic Covenant, just as He always keeps His word.

✦Zechariah✦

Zechariah was born in Babylon while the Jews were held captive, and he accompanied the Jewish exiles on the first return to Palestine around 530 B.C. Both a priest and a prophet, Zechariah was a younger contemporary of Haggai the prophet.

Like Haggai, Zechariah encouraged the returning Jews to complete the temple. He reminded the people that blessings for future generations depended upon the obedience of the present generation. In the first eight chapters, he addressed the future importance of the temple; it would be used by the Messiah during His ministry. The last six chapters contain various prophecies regarding the coming Messiah, including His entry into Jerusalem (9:9), His betrayal for thirty pieces of silver (11:12, 13), and His Second Coming to the Mount of Olives (14:3–8). Zechariah's visual and symbolic language is similar to that in Daniel and Revelation. ✦

CHAPTER 1

A Call to Repentance

In the eighth month of the second year
of Da·rī′us, the word of the LORD came to
Zech·a·rī′ah the son of Ber·e·chī′ah, the
son of Id′dō the prophet, saying, 2"The
LORD has been very angry with your
fathers. 3Therefore say to them, 'Thus says
the LORD of hosts: "Return to Me," says
the LORD of hosts, "and I will return to
you," says the LORD of hosts. 4"Do not
be like your fathers, to whom the former
prophets preached, saying, 'Thus says
the LORD of hosts: "Turn now from your
evil ways and your evil deeds." ' But
they did not hear nor heed Me," says the
LORD.

5 "Your fathers, where *are* they?
And the prophets, do they live
forever?
6 Yet surely My words and My statutes,
Which I commanded My servants the
prophets,
Did they not overtake your fathers?

"So they returned and said:

'Just as the LORD of hosts determined
to do to us,
According to our ways and according
to our deeds,
So He has dealt with us.' " ' "

Vision of the Horses

7On the twenty-fourth day of the
eleventh month, which is the month

1:1–6 Zechariah is concerned that his people had not learned the lessons of the Exile.

1:1 October–November, 520 B.C. The foundation of the second temple had been sitting abandoned some 15 or 16 years by this time.

1:6 they returned: The fathers. God always keeps His word in regard to both blessing and punishment.

1:7–17 The man among the myrtle trees (v. 8) is a message to encourage the people

She·bat′, in the second year of Da·rī′us, the
word of the LORD came to Zech·a·rī′ah the
son of Ber·e·chī′ah, the son of Id′dō the
prophet: 8 I saw by night, and behold, a
man riding on a red horse, and it stood
among the myrtle trees in the hollow; and
behind him *were* horses: red, sorrel, and
white. 9 Then I said, "My lord, what *are*
these?" So the angel who talked with me
said to me, "I will show you what they
are."
10 And the man who stood among the
myrtle trees answered and said, "These *are*
the ones whom the LORD has sent to walk to
and fro throughout the earth."
11 So they answered the Angel of the
LORD, who stood among the myrtle trees,
and said, "We have walked to and fro
throughout the earth, and behold, all the
earth is resting quietly."

The LORD Will Comfort Zion

12 Then the Angel of the LORD answered
and said, "O LORD of hosts, how long will
You not have mercy on Jerusalem and on
the cities of Judah, against which You were
angry these seventy years?"
13 And the LORD answered the angel who
talked to me, *with* good *and* comforting
words. 14 So the angel who spoke with me
said to me, "Proclaim, saying, 'Thus says
the LORD of hosts:

"I am zealous for Jerusalem
And for Zion with great zeal.
15 I am exceedingly angry with the
nations at ease;
For I was a little angry,
And they helped—*but* with evil
intent."

16 'Therefore thus says the LORD:

"I am returning to Jerusalem with
mercy;
My house shall be built in it," says
the LORD of hosts,
"And a *surveyor's* line shall be
stretched out over Jerusalem." '

17 "Again proclaim, saying, 'Thus says
the LORD of hosts:

"My cities shall again spread out
through prosperity;
The LORD will again comfort Zion,
And will again choose Jerusalem." ' "

Vision of the Horns

18 Then I raised my eyes and looked, and
there *were* four horns. 19 And I said to the
angel who talked with me, "What *are*
these?"
So he answered me, "These *are* the
horns that have scattered Judah, Israel, and
Jerusalem."
20 Then the LORD showed me four crafts-
men. 21 And I said, "What are these coming
to do?"
So he said, "These *are* the horns that
scattered Judah, so that no one could lift
up his head; but the craftsmen[a] are coming
to terrify them, to cast out the horns of the
nations that lifted up *their* horn against the
land of Judah to scatter it."

1:21 [a]Literally *these*

with the comforting word that God cares for them in spite of their depressed condition. Three angelic groups are mentioned: (1) the messengers on **red**, **sorrel**, and **white** horses, (2) the Angel of the LORD who sat on the red horse, and (3) the angel who spoke to Zechariah. But it is possible the latter two are identical. If not, then the Angel of the LORD in v. 11 may be the same as the man among the myrtle trees (vv. 8, 10).

1:18–21 This vision addresses the first obstacle that must be removed if the temple is to be rebuilt: obstruction by outside forces (see Ezra 4:1–5). **four horns**: Foreign powers which had defeated God's people. In the OT "horn" represents force or power. **four craftsmen**: Supernatural powers that would overthrow the enemy forces. In His own way God would eliminate the opposition to the rebuilding.

CHAPTER 2

Vision of the Measuring Line

Then I raised my eyes and looked, and
behold, a man with a measuring line in his
hand. 2So I said, "Where are you going?"

And he said to me, "To measure Jerusa-
lem, to see what *is* its width and what *is* its
length."

3And there *was* the angel who talked
with me, going out; and another angel was
coming out to meet him, 4who said to him,
"Run, speak to this young man, saying: 'Je-
rusalem shall be inhabited *as* towns with-
out walls, because of the multitude of men
and livestock in it. 5For I,' says the LORD,
'will be a wall of fire all around her, and I
will be the glory in her midst.' "

Future Joy of Zion and Many Nations

6"Up, up! Flee from the land of the
north," says the LORD; "for I have spread
you abroad like the four winds of heaven,"
says the LORD. 7"Up, Zion! Escape, you
who dwell with the daughter of Babylon."

8For thus says the LORD of hosts: "He
sent Me after glory, to the nations which
plunder you; for he who touches you
touches the apple of His eye. 9For surely I
will shake My hand against them, and they
shall become spoil for their servants. Then
you will know that the LORD of hosts has
sent Me.

10"Sing and rejoice, O daughter of Zion!
For behold, I am coming and I will dwell in
your midst," says the LORD. 11"Many na-
tions shall be joined to the LORD in that day,
and they shall become My people. And I
will dwell in your midst. Then you will
know that the LORD of hosts has sent Me to
you. 12And the LORD will take possession of
Judah as His inheritance in the Holy Land,
and will again choose Jerusalem. 13Be
silent, all flesh, before the LORD, for He is
aroused from His holy habitation!"

CHAPTER 3

Vision of the High Priest

Then he showed me Joshua the high
priest standing before the Angel of the
LORD, and Satan standing at his right hand
to oppose him. 2And the LORD said to Sa-
tan, "The LORD rebuke you, Satan! The
LORD who has chosen Jerusalem rebuke
you! *Is* this not a brand plucked from the
fire?"

3Now Joshua was clothed with filthy
garments, and was standing before the An-
gel.

4Then He answered and spoke to those
who stood before Him, saying, "Take away
the filthy garments from him." And to him
He said, "See, I have removed your iniq-
uity from you, and I will clothe you with
rich robes."

5And I said, "Let them put a clean tur-
ban on his head."

So they put a clean turban on his head,
and they put the clothes on him. And the
Angel of the LORD stood by.

The Coming Branch

6Then the Angel of the LORD admon-
ished Joshua, saying, 7"Thus says the LORD
of hosts:

'If you will walk in My ways,
And if you will keep My command,
Then you shall also judge My house,

2:4, 5 A city **without walls** for protection was unheard of in the ancient world. It is literally true in Jerusalem today—no walls.

3:1–10 The accusation by **Satan** against the high priest **Joshua** may symbolize the uncleanness of the people in the person of their priestly representative. It could also represent uncertainty about the sanctity of the priesthood, another obstacle that needed to be removed in preparation for the establishment of the restored nation. The earlier prophets had accused the priests of having failed, so there needed to be a reaffirmation that God still honored the priesthood in the person of the present high priest, Joshua.

And likewise have charge of My
courts;
I will give you places to walk
Among these who stand here.

8 'Hear, O Joshua, the high priest,
You and your companions who sit
before you,
For they are a wondrous sign;
For behold, I am bringing forth My
Servant the BRANCH.
9 For behold, the stone
That I have laid before Joshua:
Upon the stone *are* seven eyes.
Behold, I will engrave its inscription,'
Says the LORD of hosts,
'And I will remove the iniquity of that
land in one day.
10 In that day,' says the LORD of hosts,
'Everyone will invite his neighbor
Under his vine and under his fig
tree.' "

CHAPTER 4

Vision of the Lampstand and Olive Trees

Now the angel who talked with me
came back and wakened me, as a man who
is wakened out of his sleep. 2And he said to
me, "What do you see?"
So I said, "I am looking, and there *is* a
lampstand of solid gold with a bowl on top
of it, and on the *stand* seven lamps with
seven pipes to the seven lamps. 3Two olive
trees *are* by it, one at the right of the bowl
and the other at its left." 4So I answered
and spoke to the angel who talked with
me, saying, "What *are* these, my lord?"
5Then the angel who talked with me an-
swered and said to me, "Do you not know
what these are?"
And I said, "No, my lord."
6So he answered and said to me:

"This *is* the word of the LORD to
Ze·rub'ba·bel:
'Not by might nor by power, but by
My Spirit,'
Says the LORD of hosts.
7 'Who *are* you, O great mountain?
Before Ze·rub'ba·bel *you shall become* a
plain!
And he shall bring forth the capstone
With shouts of "Grace, grace to it!" ' "

8Moreover the word of the LORD came to
me, saying:

9 "The hands of Ze·rub'ba·bel
Have laid the foundation of this
temple;[a]
His hands shall also finish *it*.
Then you will know
That the LORD of hosts has sent Me to
you.
10 For who has despised the day of
small things?

4:9 [a]Literally *house*

3:8 My Servant the BRANCH: The term used by Jeremiah (Jer. 23:5) to refer to the Messiah. Joshua, the religious leader of the community, may be the symbol of the Coming One.

4:3 olive trees: An unceasing supply of the Spirit is symbolized by the oil for the lamps (see vv. 11–14).

4:6 Not by might: God declares that the coming kingdom would not be the result of human ability, but by His Spirit. Just as the rebuilding of the temple could only be accomplished by the power of the Holy Spirit, so anything we attempt for God must be done through reliance on Him alone. Human strength is ineffective without God's blessing.

4:9 this temple: The first time the rebuilding of the temple is explicitly mentioned. Zerubbabel had **laid the foundation** in 537 or 536 B.C. Because it had lain idle until this time (520 B.C.), some were undoubtedly saying he would never **finish it**.

4:10 small things: Reflects the lack of grandeur that characterized Zerubbabel's temple (see Hag. 2:3). **these seven**: The eyes of the Lord (see also 3:9).

For these seven rejoice to see
The plumb line in the hand of
Ze·rub'ba·bel.
They are the eyes of the LORD,
Which scan to and fro throughout the
whole earth."

11Then I answered and said to him,
"What *are* these two olive trees—at the
right of the lampstand and at its left?"
12And I further answered and said to him,
"What *are these* two olive branches that *drip*
into the receptacles[a] of the two gold pipes
from which the golden *oil* drains?"
13Then he answered me and said, "Do
you not know what these *are?*"
And I said, "No, my lord."
14So he said, "These *are* the two anointed
ones, who stand beside the Lord of the
whole earth."

CHAPTER 5

Vision of the Flying Scroll

Then I turned and raised my eyes, and
saw there a flying scroll.
2And he said to me, "What do you see?"
So I answered, "I see a flying scroll. Its
length *is* twenty cubits and its width ten
cubits."
3Then he said to me, "This *is* the curse
that goes out over the face of the whole
earth: 'Every thief shall be expelled,' ac-
cording *to* this side of *the scroll;* and, 'Every
perjurer shall be expelled,' according *to*
that side of it."

4 "I will send out *the curse,*" says the
LORD of hosts;
"It shall enter the house of the thief
And the house of the one who swears
falsely by My name.
It shall remain in the midst of his
house
And consume it, with its timber and
stones."

Vision of the Woman in a Basket

5Then the angel who talked with me
came out and said to me, "Lift your eyes
now, and see what this *is* that goes forth."
6So I asked, "What *is* it?" And he said,
"It *is* a basket[a] that is going forth."
He also said, "This *is* their resemblance
throughout the earth: 7Here *is* a lead disc
lifted up, and this *is* a woman sitting inside
the basket"; 8then he said, "This *is* Wicked-
ness!" And he thrust her down into the
basket, and threw the lead cover[a] over its
mouth. 9Then I raised my eyes and looked,
and there *were* two women, coming with
the wind in their wings; for they had wings
like the wings of a stork, and they lifted up
the basket between earth and heaven.
10So I said to the angel who talked with
me, "Where are they carrying the basket?"
11And he said to me, "To build a house
for it in the land of Shī'nar;[a] when it is
ready, *the basket* will be set there on its
base."

CHAPTER 6

Vision of the Four Chariots

Then I turned and raised my eyes and
looked, and behold, four chariots *were*
coming from between two mountains, and
the mountains *were* mountains of bronze.
2With the first chariot *were* red horses, with
the second chariot black horses, 3with the
third chariot white horses, and with the

4:12 [a]Literally *into the hands of* 5:6 [a]Hebrew *ephah,* a measuring container, and so elsewhere
5:8 [a]Literally *stone* 5:11 [a]That is, Babylon

4:14 two anointed ones: Immediately the reference is to Joshua and Zerubbabel, but prophetically it signifies the union of kingly and priestly functions in Jesus Christ.

5:5–11 The **woman** in **the basket** (v. 7) symbolizes **Wickedness**, the principle of sin, which must be removed from God's people. Only God Himself can do this.

5:11 Shinar: Babylon, the epitome of evil (see Rev. 17; 18).

fourth chariot dappled horses—strong
steeds. 4Then I answered and said to the an-
gel who talked with me, "What *are* these,
my lord?"

5And the angel answered and said to
me, "These *are* four spirits of heaven, who
go out from *their* station before the Lord of
all the earth. 6The one with the black horses
is going to the north country, the white are
going after them, and the dappled are go-
ing toward the south country." 7Then the
strong *steeds* went out, eager to go, that
they might walk to and fro throughout the
earth. And He said, "Go, walk to and fro
throughout the earth." So they walked to
and fro throughout the earth. 8And He
called to me, and spoke to me, saying,
"See, those who go toward the north coun-
try have given rest to My Spirit in the north
country."

The Command to Crown Joshua

9Then the word of the LORD came to me,
saying: 10"Receive *the gift* from the cap-
tives—from Hel'daī, Tō·bī'jah, and Je-
daī'ah, who have come from Babylon—
and go the same day and enter the house of
Jō·sī'ah the son of Zeph·a·nī'ah. 11Take the
silver and gold, make an elaborate crown,
and set *it* on the head of Joshua the son of
Je·hoz'a·dak, the high priest. 12Then speak
to him, saying, 'Thus says the LORD of
hosts, saying:

"Behold, the Man whose name *is* the
BRANCH!
From His place He shall branch out,
And He shall build the temple of the
LORD;
13 Yes, He shall build the temple of the
LORD.
He shall bear the glory,
And shall sit and rule on His throne;
So He shall be a priest on His throne,
And the counsel of peace shall be
between them both." '

14"Now the elaborate crown shall be for
a memorial in the temple of the LORD for
Hē'lem,[a] Tō·bī'jah, Je·daī'ah, and Hen the
son of Zeph·a·nī'ah. 15Even those from afar
shall come and build the temple of the
LORD. Then you shall know that the LORD
of hosts has sent Me to you. And *this* shall
come to pass if you diligently obey the
voice of the LORD your God."

CHAPTER 7

Obedience Better than Fasting

Now in the fourth year of King Da·rī'us
it came to pass *that* the word of the LORD
came to Zech·a·rī'ah, on the fourth day of
the ninth month, Chis'lev, 2when *the people*[a]
sent She·rē'zer,[b] with Reg'em-Mel'ech and
his men, *to* the house of God,[c] to pray be-
fore the LORD, 3*and* to ask the priests who
were in the house of the LORD of hosts, and
the prophets, saying, "Should I weep in the
fifth month and fast as I have done for so
many years?"

4Then the word of the LORD of hosts

6:14 [a]Following Masoretic Text, Targum, and Vulgate; Syriac reads *for Heldai* (compare verse 10); Septuagint reads *for the patient ones.* 7:2 [a]Literally *they* (compare verse 5) [b]Or *Sar-Ezer* [c]Hebrew *Bethel*

6:8 given rest to My Spirit: Implies "they have pacified My anger," indicating that Babylon had been fully subdued by the Persians.

7:1–3 The occasion for this message was the arrival of a deputation, probably of Samaritans from Bethel, in December, 518 B.C. Since work on the new temple was going forward again, they wondered whether to continue the fasts commemorating the burning of the city and temple in the fifth month (v.3) of 587 B.C. (see 2 Kin. 25:8–10).

7:4 Zechariah's answer, like the messages of the earlier prophets, shows that God cares more for righteousness than religious forms. Zechariah reminds them that their fasting was intended to be symbolic of changed hearts demonstrated in changed lives. In and of itself their fasting, like their eating and drinking, did not affect God, but only themselves (v.6). Religious acts are meaningless unless accompanied by the attitudes and actions of a righteous heart and holy life.

came to me, saying, 5"Say to all the people of the land, and to the priests: 'When you fasted and mourned in the fifth and seventh *months* during those seventy years, did you really fast for Me—for Me? 6When you eat and when you drink, do you not eat and drink *for yourselves?* 7*Should you* not *have obeyed* the words which the LORD proclaimed through the former prophets when Jerusalem and the cities around it were inhabited and prosperous, and the South[a] and the Lowland were inhabited?' "

Disobedience Resulted in Captivity

8Then the word of the LORD came to Zech·a·rī'ah, saying, 9"Thus says the LORD of hosts:

'Execute true justice,
Show mercy and compassion
Everyone to his brother.
10 Do not oppress the widow or the
fatherless,
The alien or the poor.
Let none of you plan evil in his heart
Against his brother.'

11But they refused to heed, shrugged their shoulders, and stopped their ears so that they could not hear. 12Yes, they made their hearts like flint, refusing to hear the law and the words which the LORD of hosts had sent by His Spirit through the former prophets. Thus great wrath came from the LORD of hosts. 13Therefore it happened, *that* just as He proclaimed and they would not hear, so they called out and I would not listen," says the LORD of hosts. 14"But I scattered them with a whirlwind among all the nations which they had not known. Thus the land became desolate after them, so that no one passed through or returned; for they made the pleasant land desolate."

CHAPTER 8

Jerusalem, Holy City of the Future

Again the word of the LORD of hosts came, saying, 2"Thus says the LORD of hosts:

'I am zealous for Zion with great zeal;
With great fervor I am zealous for
her.'

3"Thus says the LORD:

'I will return to Zion,
And dwell in the midst of Jerusalem.
Jerusalem shall be called the City of
Truth,
The Mountain of the LORD of hosts,
The Holy Mountain.'

4"Thus says the LORD of hosts:

'Old men and old women shall again
sit
In the streets of Jerusalem,
Each one with his staff in his hand
Because of great age.
5 The streets of the city
Shall be full of boys and girls
Playing in its streets.'

6"Thus says the LORD of hosts:

'If it is marvelous in the eyes of the
remnant of this people in these
days,
Will it also be marvelous in My eyes?'
Says the LORD of hosts.

7"Thus says the LORD of hosts:

'Behold, I will save My people from
the land of the east

7:7 [a]Hebrew *Negev*

7:13 I would not listen: When the Spirit is moving in convicting power is the time to respond. Some other time, when judgment is already underway, may be too late.

And from the land of the west;
8 I will bring them *back*,
And they shall dwell in the midst of Jerusalem.
They shall be My people
And I will be their God,
In truth and righteousness.'

9"Thus says the LORD of hosts:

'Let your hands be strong,
You who have been hearing in these days
These words by the mouth of the prophets,
Who *spoke* in the day the foundation was laid
For the house of the LORD of hosts,
That the temple might be built.
10 For before these days
There were no wages for man nor any hire for beast;
There was no peace from the enemy for whoever went out or came in;
For I set all men, everyone, against his neighbor.

11But now I *will* not *treat* the remnant of this
people as in the former days,' says the
LORD of hosts.

12 'For the seed *shall be* prosperous,
The vine shall give its fruit,
The ground shall give her increase,
And the heavens shall give their dew—
I will cause the remnant of this people
To possess all these.
13 And it shall come to pass
That just as you were a curse among the nations,
O house of Judah and house of Israel,
So I will save you, and you shall be a blessing.
Do not fear,
Let your hands be strong.'

14"For thus says the LORD of hosts:

'Just as I determined to punish you
When your fathers provoked Me to wrath,'
Says the LORD of hosts,
'And I would not relent,
15 So again in these days
I am determined to do good
To Jerusalem and to the house of Judah.
Do not fear.
16 These *are* the things you shall do:
Speak each man the truth to his neighbor;
Give judgment in your gates for truth, justice, and peace;
17 Let none of you think evil in your[a] heart against your neighbor;
And do not love a false oath.
For all these *are things* that I hate,'
Says the LORD."

18Then the word of the LORD of hosts
came to me, saying, 19"Thus says the LORD
of hosts:

'The fast of the fourth *month*,
The fast of the fifth,
The fast of the seventh,
And the fast of the tenth,
Shall be joy and gladness and cheerful feasts

8:17 [a]Literally *his*

8:8 They shall be My people: This is God's desire for all persons, in all the earth, in every circumstance (see John 3:16; 4:23).

8:9–13 Words of encouragement to the temple builders. **Before these days** (v. 10) refers to the period from 536 to 520 B.C. when the work had languished. **But now** (v. 11): Since the work had begun again, conditions had already started to improve and would continue to do so.

For the house of Judah.
Therefore love truth and peace.'

20"Thus says the LORD of hosts:

'Peoples shall yet come,
Inhabitants of many cities;
21 The inhabitants of one *city* shall go to another, saying,
"Let us continue to go and pray before the LORD,
And seek the LORD of hosts.
I myself will go also."
22 Yes, many peoples and strong nations
Shall come to seek the LORD of hosts in Jerusalem,
And to pray before the LORD.'

23"Thus says the LORD of hosts: 'In those
days ten men from every language of the
nations shall grasp the sleeve of a Jewish
man, saying, "Let us go with you, for we
have heard *that* God *is* with you." ' "

CHAPTER 9

Israel Defended Against Enemies

The burden[a] of the word of the LORD
Against the land of Had'rach,
And Damascus its resting place
(For the eyes of men
And all the tribes of Israel
Are on the LORD);
2 Also *against* Hā'math, *which* borders on it,
And *against* Tȳre and Sī'don, though they are very wise.

3 For Tȳre built herself a tower,
Heaped up silver like the dust,
And gold like the mire of the streets.
4 Behold, the LORD will cast her out;
He will destroy her power in the sea,
And she will be devoured by fire.

5 Ash'ke•lon shall see *it* and fear;
Gā'za also shall be very sorrowful;
And Ek'ron, for He dried up her expectation.
The king shall perish from Gā'za,
And Ash'ke•lon shall not be inhabited.

6 "A mixed race shall settle in Ash'dod,
And I will cut off the pride of the Phi•lis'tines.
7 I will take away the blood from his mouth,
And the abominations from between his teeth.
But he who remains, even he *shall be* for our God,
And shall be like a leader in Judah,
And Ek'ron like a Jeb'ū•sīte.
8 I will camp around My house
Because of the army,
Because of him who passes by and him who returns.
No more shall an oppressor pass through them,
For now I have seen with My eyes.

The Coming King

9 "Rejoice greatly, O daughter of Zion!
Shout, O daughter of Jerusalem!
Behold, your King is coming to you;
He *is* just and having salvation,
Lowly and riding on a donkey,
A colt, the foal of a donkey.

9:1 [a]Or *oracle*

8:20–23 Israel's ultimate reason for existence was an experience with God that would draw all **nations** (v. 22) to Him. The same vision applies to Christ's church. When she is what God has called her to be, the result will be effective missionary service.

9:9 The messianic King appears as a bringer of peace. In his Gospel Matthew applied this prophecy to Jesus (see Matt. 21:4, 5). **having salvation**: Lit. "being saved," as in the sense of being vindicated. This is precisely what the Resurrection did. It vindicated the lowly Jesus as God's Messiah.

10 I will cut off the chariot from
Ē′phra·im
And the horse from Jerusalem;
The battle bow shall be cut off.
He shall speak peace to the nations;
His dominion *shall be* 'from sea to sea,
And from the River to the ends of the
earth.'[a]

God Will Save His People

11 "As for you also,
Because of the blood of your
covenant,
I will set your prisoners free from the
waterless pit.
12 Return to the stronghold,
You prisoners of hope.
Even today I declare
That I will restore double to you.
13 For I have bent Judah, My *bow,*
Fitted the bow with Ē′phra·im,
And raised up your sons, O Zion,
Against your sons, O Greece,
And made you like the sword of a
mighty man."

14 Then the LORD will be seen over
them,
And His arrow will go forth like
lightning.
The Lord GOD will blow the trumpet,
And go with whirlwinds from the
south.
15 The LORD of hosts will defend them;
They shall devour and subdue with
slingstones.
They shall drink *and* roar as if with
wine;
They shall be filled *with blood* like
basins,
Like the corners of the altar.

16 The LORD their God will save them in
that day,
As the flock of His people.
For they *shall be like* the jewels of a
crown,
Lifted like a banner over His land—
17 For how great is its[a] goodness
And how great its[b] beauty!
Grain shall make the young men
thrive,
And new wine the young women.

CHAPTER 10

Restoration of Judah and Israel

Ask the LORD for rain
In the time of the latter rain.[a]
The LORD will make flashing
clouds;
He will give them showers of rain,
Grass in the field for everyone.

2 For the idols[a] speak delusion;
The diviners envision lies,
And tell false dreams;
They comfort in vain.
Therefore *the people* wend their way
like sheep;
They are in trouble because *there is* no
shepherd.

3 "My anger is kindled against the
shepherds,
And I will punish the goatherds.
For the LORD of hosts will visit His
flock,
The house of Judah,
And will make them as His royal
horse in the battle.
4 From him comes the cornerstone,
From him the tent peg,
From him the battle bow,
From him every ruler[a] together.

9:10 [a]Psalm 72:8 9:17 [a]Or *His* [b]Or *His*
10:1 [a]That is, spring rain 10:2 [a]Hebrew *teraphim*
10:4 [a]Or *despot*

10:1, 2 A transition passage. It is God, not **idols**, who gives the **rain**. People had fallen for the **delusion** of idols because, **like sheep**, they had not been guided rightly. Who was at fault? The shepherds, the leaders of God's people. **Shepherd** becomes a major figure of speech in this section.

5 They shall be like mighty men,
Who tread down *their enemies*
In the mire of the streets in the battle.
They shall fight because the LORD is with them,
And the riders on horses shall be put to shame.

6 "I will strengthen the house of Judah,
And I will save the house of Joseph.
I will bring them back,
Because I have mercy on them.
They shall be as though I had not cast them aside;
For I *am* the LORD their God,
And I will hear them.
7 *Those of* Ē′phra·im shall be like a mighty man,
And their heart shall rejoice as if with wine.
Yes, their children shall see *it* and be glad;
Their heart shall rejoice in the LORD.
8 I will whistle for them and gather them,
For I will redeem them;
And they shall increase as they once increased.

9 "I will sow them among the peoples,
And they shall remember Me in far countries;
They shall live, together with their children,
And they shall return.
10 I will also bring them back from the land of Egypt,
And gather them from Assyria.
I will bring them into the land of Gil′ē·ad and Lebanon,
Until no *more room* is found for them.
11 He shall pass through the sea with affliction,
And strike the waves of the sea:
All the depths of the River[a] shall dry up.
Then the pride of Assyria shall be brought down,
And the scepter of Egypt shall depart.

12 "So I will strengthen them in the LORD,
And they shall walk up and down in His name,"
Says the LORD.

CHAPTER 11

Desolation of Israel

Open your doors, O Lebanon,
That fire may devour your cedars.
2 Wail, O cypress, for the cedar has fallen,
Because the mighty *trees* are ruined.
Wail, O oaks of Bā′shan,
For the thick forest has come down.
3 *There is* the sound of wailing shepherds!
For their glory is in ruins.
There is the sound of roaring lions!
For the pride[a] of the Jordan is in ruins.

Prophecy of the Shepherds

4Thus says the LORD my God, "Feed the
flock for slaughter, 5whose owners slaugh-
ter them and feel no guilt; those who sell
them say, 'Blessed be the LORD, for I am
rich'; and their shepherds do not pity
them. 6For I will no longer pity the inhabi-
tants of the land," says the LORD. "But in-
deed I will give everyone into his neigh-
bor's hand and into the hand of his king.
They shall attack the land, and I will not
deliver *them* from their hand."
7So I fed the flock for slaughter, in par-

10:11 [a]That is, the Nile 11:3 [a]Or *floodplain, thicket*

11:4–14 The prophet is told to become a good shepherd of the flock and thus enact a prophecy of Christ. He was to **feed the flock** even though they were destined for **slaughter**. This he did (v. 7).

ticular the poor of the flock.[a] I took for my-
self two staffs: the one I called Beauty,[b] and
the other I called Bonds;[c] and I fed the
flock. 8I dismissed the three shepherds in
one month. My soul loathed them, and
their soul also abhorred me. 9Then I said, "I
will not feed you. Let what is dying die,
and what is perishing perish. Let those that
are left eat each other's flesh." 10And I took
my staff, Beauty, and cut it in two, that I
might break the covenant which I had
made with all the peoples. 11So it was bro-
ken on that day. Thus the poor[a] of the flock,
who were watching me, knew that it *was*
the word of the LORD. 12Then I said to them,
"If it is agreeable to you, give *me* my
wages; and if not, refrain." So they
weighed out for my wages thirty *pieces* of
silver.

13And the LORD said to me, "Throw it to
the potter"—that princely price they set on
me. So I took the thirty *pieces* of silver and
threw them into the house of the LORD for
the potter. 14Then I cut in two my other
staff, Bonds, that I might break the brother-
hood between Judah and Israel.

15And the LORD said to me, "Next, take
for yourself the implements of a foolish
shepherd. 16For indeed I will raise up a
shepherd in the land *who* will not care for
those who are cut off, nor seek the young,
nor heal those that are broken, nor feed
those that still stand. But he will eat the
flesh of the fat and tear their hooves in
pieces.

17 "Woe to the worthless shepherd,
Who leaves the flock!
A sword *shall be* against his arm
And against his right eye;
His arm shall completely wither,
And his right eye shall be totally
blinded."

CHAPTER 12

The Coming Deliverance of Judah

The burden[a] of the word of the LORD
against Israel. Thus says the LORD, who
stretches out the heavens, lays the founda-
tion of the earth, and forms the spirit of
man within him: 2"Behold, I will make Je-
rusalem a cup of drunkenness to all the
surrounding peoples, when they lay siege
against Judah and Jerusalem. 3And it shall
happen in that day that I will make Jerusa-
lem a very heavy stone for all peoples; all
who would heave it away will surely be
cut in pieces, though all nations of the
earth are gathered against it. 4In that day,"
says the LORD, "I will strike every horse
with confusion, and its rider with mad-
ness; I will open My eyes on the house of
Judah, and will strike every horse of the
peoples with blindness. 5And the gover-
nors of Judah shall say in their heart, 'The
inhabitants of Jerusalem *are* my strength in
the LORD of hosts, their God.' 6In that day I
will make the governors of Judah like a

11:7 [a]Following Masoretic Text, Targum, and Vulgate; Septuagint reads *for the Canaanites.* [b]Or *Grace,* and so in verse 10 [c]Or *Unity,* and so in verse 14
11:11 [a]Following Masoretic Text, Targum, and Vulgate; Septuagint reads *the Canaanites.* 12:1 [a]Or *oracle*

11:8 three shepherds: Kings who used the sheep for their own ends, not looking out for the good of the flock. Their identity is uncertain.

11:12–14 give me my wages: Having resigned his post, the Shepherd asked for his pay. He was given **thirty pieces of silver**, the price of a slave. It is ironically called by the prophet a **princely price**. The **potter** (v. 13) was among the lowest of society. The striking similarity between these details and those relating to the rejection of Jesus makes it plain that the prophetic reference is to the Good Shepherd. See Matt. 27:3–10 for the application of these details to Judas's betrayal of Christ.

12:1—14:21 Whereas ch. 11 deals with Christ's first coming, chs. 12—14 deal with His second.

12:2 The **cup of drunkenness** represents the wrath of God which the nations that would attack Jerusalem must face (see Is. 51:17–23).

firepan in the woodpile, and like a fiery
torch in the sheaves; they shall devour all
the surrounding peoples on the right hand
and on the left, but Jerusalem shall be in-
habited again in her own place—Jerusa-
lem.
7"The LORD will save the tents of Judah
first, so that the glory of the house of David
and the glory of the inhabitants of Jerusa-
lem shall not become greater than that of
Judah. 8In that day the LORD will defend
the inhabitants of Jerusalem; the one who
is feeble among them in that day shall be
like David, and the house of David *shall be*
like God, like the Angel of the LORD before
them. 9It shall be in that day *that* I will seek
to destroy all the nations that come against
Jerusalem.

Mourning for the Pierced One

10"And I will pour on the house of Da-
vid and on the inhabitants of Jerusalem the
Spirit of grace and supplication; then they
will look on Me whom they pierced. Yes,
they will mourn for Him as one mourns for
his only *son,* and grieve for Him as one
grieves for a firstborn. 11In that day there
shall be a great mourning in Jerusalem,
like the mourning at Hā′dad Rim′mon in
the plain of Me·gid′dō.[a] 12And the land
shall mourn, every family by itself: the
family of the house of David by itself, and
their wives by themselves; the family of
the house of Nathan by itself, and their
wives by themselves; 13the family of the
house of Levi by itself, and their wives by
themselves; the family of Shim′ē·ī by itself,
and their wives by themselves; 14all the
families that remain, every family by itself,
and their wives by themselves.

CHAPTER 13

Idolatry Cut Off

"In that day a fountain shall be opened
for the house of David and for the inhabi-
tants of Jerusalem, for sin and for unclean-
ness.
2"It shall be in that day," says the LORD
of hosts, "*that* I will cut off the names of the
idols from the land, and they shall no
longer be remembered. I will also cause the
prophets and the unclean spirit to depart
from the land. 3It shall come to pass *that* if
anyone still prophesies, then his father and
mother who begot him will say to him,
'You shall not live, because you have spo-
ken lies in the name of the LORD.' And his
father and mother who begot him shall
thrust him through when he prophesies.
4"And it shall be in that day *that* every
prophet will be ashamed of his vision
when he prophesies; they will not wear a
robe of coarse hair to deceive. 5But he will
say, 'I *am* no prophet, I *am* a farmer; for a
man taught me to keep cattle from my
youth.' 6And *one* will say to him, 'What are
these wounds between your arms?'[a] Then
he will answer, '*Those* with which I was
wounded in the house of my friends.'

The Shepherd Savior

7 "Awake, O sword, against My
Shepherd,
Against the Man who is My
Companion,"
Says the LORD of hosts.
"Strike the Shepherd,
And the sheep will be scattered;

12:11 [a]Hebrew *Megiddon* 13:6 [a]Or *hands*

13:2–6 Religion shall be purified of its two curses: idolatry and false prophecy.

13:3–5 Prophecy had been discredited because it had been perverted so consistently.

13:6 wounds: In OT times pagan prophets would sometimes lacerate themselves as they worked themselves into a frenzy seeking inspiration (see Deut. 14:1; 1 Kin. 18:28). In Israel's new day anything even hinting of devotion to something other than God will be looked at with suspicion.

13:7–9 This poetic section uses the shepherd metaphor to speak of purifying leaders and people in the last days. Jesus applied the last part of v. 7 to Himself and His disciples (Mark 14:27). **one-third** (vv. 8, 9): As in the Exile, a remnant would survive this event.

Then I will turn My hand against the
little ones.
8 And it shall come to pass in all the
land,"
Says the LORD,
"*That* two-thirds in it shall be cut off
and die,
But *one*-third shall be left in it:
9 I will bring the *one*-third through the
fire,
Will refine them as silver is refined,
And test them as gold is tested.
They will call on My name,
And I will answer them.
I will say, 'This *is* My people';
And each one will say, 'The LORD *is*
my God.' "

CHAPTER 14

The Day of the LORD

Behold, the day of the LORD is
coming,
And your spoil will be divided in
your midst.
2 For I will gather all the nations to
battle against Jerusalem;
The city shall be taken,
The houses rifled,
And the women ravished.
Half of the city shall go into captivity,
But the remnant of the people shall
not be cut off from the city.

3 Then the LORD will go forth
And fight against those nations,
As He fights in the day of battle.
4 And in that day His feet will stand on
the Mount of Olives,
Which faces Jerusalem on the east.
And the Mount of Olives shall be
split in two,
From east to west,
Making a very large valley;
Half of the mountain shall move
toward the north
And half of it toward the south.
5 Then you shall flee *through* My
mountain valley,
For the mountain valley shall reach to
Ā'zal.
Yes, you shall flee
As you fled from the earthquake
In the days of Uz·zī'ah king of
Judah.

Thus the LORD my God will come,
And all the saints with You.[a]

6 It shall come to pass in that day
That there will be no light;
The lights will diminish.
7 It shall be one day
Which is known to the LORD—
Neither day nor night.
But at evening time it shall happen
That it will be light.

8 And in that day it shall be
That living waters shall flow from
Jerusalem,
Half of them toward the eastern sea
And half of them toward the western
sea;
In both summer and winter it shall
occur.
9 And the LORD shall be King over all
the earth.
In that day it shall be—
"The LORD *is* one,"[a]
And His name one.

10 All the land shall be turned into a plain
from Gē'ba to Rim'mon south of Jerusa-
lem. *Jerusalem*[a] shall be raised up and in-
habited in her place from Benjamin's Gate
to the place of the First Gate and the Cor-
ner Gate, and *from* the Tower of Ha·nan'el
to the king's winepresses.

11 *The people* shall dwell in it;
And no longer shall there be utter
destruction,
But Jerusalem shall be safely
inhabited.

14:5 [a]Or *you;* Septuagint, Targum, and Vulgate read *Him.* 14:9 [a]Compare Deuteronomy 6:4
14:10 [a]Literally *She*

[12]And this shall be the plague with which the LORD will strike all the people who fought against Jerusalem:

Their flesh shall dissolve while they
 stand on their feet,
Their eyes shall dissolve in their
 sockets,
And their tongues shall dissolve in
 their mouths.

13 It shall come to pass in that day
That a great panic from the LORD will
 be among them.
Everyone will seize the hand of his
 neighbor,
And raise his hand against his
 neighbor's hand;
14 Judah also will fight at Jerusalem.
And the wealth of all the surrounding
 nations
Shall be gathered together:
Gold, silver, and apparel in great
 abundance.

15 Such also shall be the plague
On the horse *and* the mule,
On the camel and the donkey,
And on all the cattle that will be in
 those camps.
So *shall* this plague *be*.

The Nations Worship the King

[16]And it shall come to pass *that* everyone
who is left of all the nations which came
against Jerusalem shall go up from year to
year to worship the King, the LORD of
hosts, and to keep the Feast of Tabernacles.
[17]And it shall be *that* whichever of the fam-
ilies of the earth do not come up to Jerusa-
lem to worship the King, the LORD of hosts,
on them there will be no rain. [18]If the fam-
ily of Egypt will not come up and enter
in, they *shall have* no *rain;* they shall re-
ceive the plague with which the LORD
strikes the nations who do not come up to
keep the Feast of Tabernacles. [19]This shall
be the punishment of Egypt and the pun-
ishment of all the nations that do not come
up to keep the Feast of Tabernacles.

[20]In that day "HOLINESS TO THE
LORD" shall be *engraved* on the bells of the
horses. The pots in the LORD's house shall
be like the bowls before the altar. [21]Yes,
every pot in Jerusalem and Judah shall be
holiness to the LORD of hosts.[a] Everyone
who sacrifices shall come and take them
and cook in them. In that day there shall no
longer be a Cā'naan·īte in the house of the
LORD of hosts.

14:21 [a]Or *on every pot . . . . shall be (engraved)* "HOLINESS TO THE LORD OF HOSTS"

14:20, 21 When the kingdom of God fully comes, His **holiness** will permeate every part of life (see Matt. 6:10). **Canaanite**: Symbolic of all that is ceremonially defiled or unclean.

✦Malachi✦

Malachi wrote his book about 450 B.C., nearly one hundred years after the Jews returned from their captivity in Babylon. After rebuilding the temple, the people began to question God's providence, lose their enthusiasm, and become cynical. They wondered whether serving God was worth the trouble and developed an insensitivity to God's moral law.

To break through their discouragement, Malachi delivered an oracle with a divine dialogue to reveal God's continual love. The people had to understand that their problems were caused by their disobedience of the covenant, not by God's apathy. The Lord assured His people that the wicked would be judged and the righteous would be blessed. Malachi ended with a dramatic prophecy of the coming of the Messiah and John the Baptist (3:1). Just as Malachi reminded the people of their high calling to encourage them in their spiritual walk, Christians must strive to retain enthusiasm in serving God and inspire others to do the same. ✦

CHAPTER 1

The burden[a] of the word of the LORD to Israel by Mal'a·chī.

Israel Beloved of God

2 "I have loved you," says the LORD.
"Yet you say, 'In what way have You loved us?'
Was not Esau Jacob's brother?"
Says the LORD.
"Yet Jacob I have loved;
3 But Esau I have hated,
And laid waste his mountains and his heritage
For the jackals of the wilderness."

4 Even though Ē'dom has said,
"We have been impoverished,
But we will return and build the desolate places,"

Thus says the LORD of hosts:

"They may build, but I will throw down;
They shall be called the Territory of Wickedness,
And the people against whom the LORD will have indignation forever.
5 Your eyes shall see,
And you shall say,
'The LORD is magnified beyond the border of Israel.'

1:1 [a]Or *oracle*

1:2–5 The prophet shows that God's choice of Israel instead of the Edomites, Esau's descendants, is evidence of His love for Israel. Being older than **Jacob**, his twin brother, **Esau** was the rightful heir of the family tradition. But God, in His wisdom and love, reversed the natural order and chose the younger.

1:2, 3 loved . . . hated: This is not to be taken in terms of human emotion as arising from the conduct of either Jacob or Esau. The purpose of God was expressed before either child had been born, or could have done either good or evil (Rom. 9:11).

Polluted Offerings

6 "A son honors *his* father,
And a servant *his* master.
If then I am the Father,
Where *is* My honor?
And if I *am* a Master,
Where *is* My reverence?
Says the LORD of hosts
To you priests who despise My
name.
Yet you say, 'In what way have we
despised Your name?'

7 "You offer defiled food on My altar,
But say,
'In what way have we defiled You?'
By saying,
'The table of the LORD is
contemptible.'
8 And when you offer the blind as a
sacrifice,
Is it not evil?
And when you offer the lame and
sick,
Is it not evil?
Offer it then to your governor!
Would he be pleased with you?
Would he accept you favorably?"
Says the LORD of hosts.

9 "But now entreat God's favor,
That He may be gracious to us.
While this is being *done* by your
hands,
Will He accept you favorably?"
Says the LORD of hosts.
10 "Who *is there* even among you who
would shut the doors,
So that you would not kindle fire *on*
My altar in vain?
I have no pleasure in you,"
Says the LORD of hosts,
"Nor will I accept an offering from
your hands.
11 For from the rising of the sun, even to
its going down,
My name *shall be* great among the
Gentiles;
In every place incense *shall be* offered
to My name,
And a pure offering;
For My name shall be great among
the nations,"
Says the LORD of hosts.

12 "But you profane it,
In that you say,
'The table of the LORD[a] is defiled;
And its fruit, its food, *is*
contemptible.'
13 You also say,
'Oh, what a weariness!'
And you sneer at it,"
Says the LORD of hosts.
"And you bring the stolen, the lame,
and the sick;
Thus you bring an offering!
Should I accept this from your
hand?"
Says the LORD.
14 "But cursed *be* the deceiver
Who has in his flock a male,
And takes a vow,
But sacrifices to the Lord what is
blemished—
For I *am* a great King,"
Says the LORD of hosts,
"And My name *is to be* feared among
the nations.

CHAPTER 2

Corrupt Priests

"And now, O priests, this
commandment is for you.
2 If you will not hear,
And if you will not take *it* to
heart,
To give glory to My name,"
Says the LORD of hosts,
"I will send a curse upon you,
And I will curse your blessings.
Yes, I have cursed them already,
Because you do not take *it* to heart.

1:12 [a]Following Bomberg; Masoretic Text reads *Lord.*

3 "Behold, I will rebuke your
descendants
And spread refuse on your faces,
The refuse of your solemn feasts;
And *one* will take you away with it.
4 Then you shall know that I have sent
this commandment to you,
That My covenant with Levi may
continue,"
Says the LORD of hosts.
5 "My covenant was with him, *one* of life
and peace,
And I gave them to him *that he might*
fear *Me;*
So he feared Me
And was reverent before My name.
6 The law of truth[a] was in his mouth,
And injustice was not found on his
lips.
He walked with Me in peace and
equity,
And turned many away from
iniquity.

7 "For the lips of a priest should keep
knowledge,
And *people* should seek the law from
his mouth;
For he is the messenger of the LORD of
hosts.
8 But you have departed from the way;
You have caused many to stumble at
the law.
You have corrupted the covenant of
Levi,"
Says the LORD of hosts.
9 "Therefore I also have made you
contemptible and base
Before all the people,
Because you have not kept My ways
But have shown partiality in the law."

Treachery of Infidelity

10 Have we not all one Father?
Has not one God created us?
Why do we deal treacherously with
one another
By profaning the covenant of the
fathers?
11 Judah has dealt treacherously,
And an abomination has been
committed in Israel and in
Jerusalem,
For Judah has profaned
The LORD's holy *institution* which He
loves:
He has married the daughter of a
foreign god.
12 May the LORD cut off from the tents of
Jacob
The man who does this, being awake
and aware,[a]
Yet who brings an offering to the
LORD of hosts!

13 And this is the second thing you do:
You cover the altar of the LORD with
tears,
With weeping and crying;
So He does not regard the offering
anymore,

2:6 [a]Or *true instruction* 2:12 [a]Talmud and Vulgate read *teacher and student.*

2:5 them: **Life** and **peace** which were part of the covenant with Levi (see v. 4). That covenant had been instituted through Phinehas, the grandson of Aaron (see Num. 25:10–13).

2:7 messenger: A key word in the book. Malachi was God's messenger; that was the meaning of his name. Also, God would ultimately send His greater Messenger, Christ, to deal with His people (3:1). Thus, it was the more tragic that the priests who served as messengers of the Lord had failed in their calling.

2:8, 9 covenant of Levi: God had offered the tribe of Levi a perpetual ministry if they would surrender their claims to territory and a life like everyone else lived. But the priests had failed to keep their part of the agreement.

2:13–16 Jewish men were divorcing the wives with whom they had made a **covenant** in **youth** and marrying younger women, perhaps young pagan women referred to in vv. 10–12. Malachi's words are plain; God **hates divorce** (v. 16).

Nor receive *it* with goodwill from
your hands.
14 Yet you say, "For what reason?"
Because the LORD has been witness
Between you and the wife of your
youth,
With whom you have dealt
treacherously;
Yet she is your companion
And your wife by covenant.
15 But did He not make *them* one,
Having a remnant of the Spirit?
And why one?
He seeks godly offspring.
Therefore take heed to your spirit,
And let none deal treacherously with
the wife of his youth.

16 "For the LORD God of Israel says
That He hates divorce,
For it covers one's garment with
violence,"
Says the LORD of hosts.
"Therefore take heed to your spirit,
That you do not deal treacherously."

17 You have wearied the LORD with your
words;
Yet you say,
"In what way have we wearied *Him?*"
In that you say,
"Everyone who does evil
Is good in the sight of the LORD,
And He delights in them,"
Or, "Where *is* the God of justice?"

CHAPTER 3

The Coming Messenger

"Behold, I send My messenger,
And he will prepare the way before
Me.
And the Lord, whom you seek,
Will suddenly come to His temple,
Even the Messenger of the covenant,
In whom you delight.
Behold, He is coming,"
Says the LORD of hosts.

2 "But who can endure the day of His
coming?
And who can stand when He
appears?
For He *is* like a refiner's fire
And like launderers' soap.
3 He will sit as a refiner and a purifier
of silver;
He will purify the sons of Levi,
And purge them as gold and silver,
That they may offer to the LORD
An offering in righteousness.

4 "Then the offering of Judah and
Jerusalem
Will be pleasant to the LORD,
As in the days of old,
As in former years.
5 And I will come near you for
judgment;
I will be a swift witness
Against sorcerers,
Against adulterers,
Against perjurers,
Against those who exploit wage
earners and widows and orphans,
And against those who turn away an
alien—
Because they do not fear Me,"
Says the LORD of hosts.

6 "For I *am* the LORD, I do not change;
Therefore you are not consumed,
O sons of Jacob.

2:17 Although His timing is often different from our expectation, we can be sure that God always judges evil conduct appropriately. We have no right to question His sense of justice.

3:2 who can stand? The people expected the Coming One to defeat their enemies and enthrone His followers as rulers of the world. Malachi says He will come like fire and purify His own. **refiner's fire**: A metaphor from smelting ore to extract pure metal. **launderers' soap**: The launderer used strong lye soap to bleach the impurities from cloth and make it white (see Mark 9:3).

7 Yet from the days of your fathers
You have gone away from My
ordinances
And have not kept *them.*
Return to Me, and I will return to
you,"
Says the LORD of hosts.
"But you said,
'In what way shall we return?'

Do Not Rob God

8 "Will a man rob God?
Yet you have robbed Me!
But you say,
'In what way have we robbed You?'
In tithes and offerings.
9 You are cursed with a curse,
For you have robbed Me,
Even this whole nation.
10 Bring all the tithes into the
storehouse,
That there may be food in My house,
And try Me now in this,"
Says the LORD of hosts,
"If I will not open for you the
windows of heaven
And pour out for you *such* blessing
That *there will* not *be room* enough *to
receive it.*

11 "And I will rebuke the devourer for
your sakes,
So that he will not destroy the fruit of
your ground,
Nor shall the vine fail to bear fruit for
you in the field,"
Says the LORD of hosts;
12 And all nations will call you
blessed,
For you will be a delightful land,"
Says the LORD of hosts.

The People Complain Harshly

13 "Your words have been harsh against
Me,"
Says the LORD,
"Yet you say,
'What have we spoken against You?'
14 You have said,
'It is useless to serve God;
What profit *is it* that we have kept
His ordinance,
And that we have walked as
mourners
Before the LORD of hosts?
15 So now we call the proud blessed,
For those who do wickedness are
raised up;
They even tempt God and go free.' "

A Book of Remembrance

16 Then those who feared the LORD
spoke to one another,
And the LORD listened and heard
them;
So a book of remembrance was
written before Him
For those who fear the LORD
And who meditate on His name.

17 "They shall be Mine," says the LORD of
hosts,
"On the day that I make them My
jewels.[a]
And I will spare them

3:17 [a]Literally *special treasure*

3:10 When we practice tithing—realizing that all we have belongs to God—He will bless us immeasurably. We should give joyously to the Lord in thanks for the privilege of serving Him.

3:13–15 What profit is it? Here the people's wrong motive for serving God becomes very clear. If we serve God only for prosperity, we shall think of the wealthy **proud** as blessed, and the wealthy wicked as honorable and righteous.

3:16–18 The prophet's answer to the sad attitude that it is useless to serve the Lord. He declares that God will finally honor those who are faithful to Him. We cannot judge the value of right action by the immediate results. But everything is recorded in God's **book of remembrance**, and His eventual rewards are certain.

As a man spares his own son who
  serves him."
18 Then you shall again discern
Between the righteous and the
  wicked,
Between one who serves God
And one who does not serve
  Him.

CHAPTER 4

The Great Day of God

"For behold, the day is coming,
Burning like an oven,
And all the proud, yes, all who do
  wickedly will be stubble.
And the day which is coming shall
  burn them up,"
Says the LORD of hosts,
"That will leave them neither root nor
  branch.
2 But to you who fear My name
The Sun of Righteousness shall arise
With healing in His wings;
And you shall go out
And grow fat like stall-fed calves.
3 You shall trample the wicked,
For they shall be ashes under the
  soles of your feet
On the day that I do *this*,"
Says the LORD of hosts.

4 "Remember the Law of Moses, My
  servant,
Which I commanded him in Hō′reb
  for all Israel,
With the statutes and judgments.
5 Behold, I will send you E·lī′jah the
  prophet
Before the coming of the great and
  dreadful day of the LORD.
6 And he will turn
The hearts of the fathers to the
  children,
And the hearts of the children to their
  fathers,
Lest I come and strike the earth with
  a curse."

4:1, 2 A promise that on a **day** yet to be, the wicked and the righteous will both receive just rewards. The same Sun whose heat will **burn** up the wicked will bring **healing** to those who **fear** His **name**. **Sun of Righteousness**: A beautiful figure fulfilled by Jesus Christ.

THE
NEW TESTAMENT

✦Matthew✦

Matthew, a Jew, wrote his Gospel to a Jewish audience to convince them that their promised King had come. Matthew emphasizes that Jesus is the long-awaited Messiah foretold by Old Testament prophets. The fact that this Gospel refers more to Old Testament writings and the Law of Moses than the others is probably the reason it was placed first in the canon; it is a natural bridge between the Testaments with extensive teaching on the Messiah, Israel, the Law, the kingdom of God, and prophecy.

Jesus did not seek His disciples from among the elite of society, indicating that even the most humble people can be used to fulfill His purpose. Matthew, also called Levi, was a tax collector for the Roman government and despised by the Jews. When Jesus called him to discipleship, his quick response probably indicated that he had already been stirred by Jesus' public preaching. Luke tells us that Matthew made a great feast for Jesus, inviting other tax gatherers and some persons regarded as sinners. Shortly afterward Matthew forsook all to follow Christ.

The key theme of this Gospel shows Jesus as the culmination of promises delivered by the prophets: Christ the King. Even in His death, seeming defeat is turned to victory by the Resurrection, and the message again echoes forth: the King of the Jews lives. ✦

CHAPTER 1

The Genealogy of Jesus Christ

The book of the genealogy of Jesus
Christ, the Son of David, the Son of Abra-
ham:
2Abraham begot Isaac, Isaac begot Ja-
cob, and Jacob begot Judah and his broth-
ers. 3Judah begot Per'ez and Zē'rah by
Tā'mar, Per'ez begot Hez'ron, and Hez'ron
begot Ram. 4Ram begot Am·min'a·dab,
Am·min'a·dab begot Nah'shon, and
Nah'shon begot Sal'mon. 5Sal'mon begot
Bō'az by Rā'hab, Bō'az begot Ō'bed by
Ruth, Ō'bed begot Jesse, 6and Jesse begot
David the king.
David the king begot Solomon by her
who had been the wife[a] of Ū·rī'ah. 7Solomon
begot Rē·ho·bō'am, Rē·ho·bō'am begot
A·bī'jah, and A·bī'jah begot Ā'sa.[a] 8Ā'sa be-
got Je·hosh'a·phat, Je·hosh'a·phat begot
Jō'ram, and Jō'ram begot Uz·zī'ah. 9Uz-
zī'ah begot Jō'tham, Jō'tham begot Ā'haz,
and Ā'haz begot Hez·e·kī'ah. 10Hez·e-
kī'ah begot Ma·nas'seh, Ma·nas'seh begot
Ā'mon,[a] and Ā'mon begot Jō·sī'ah. 11Jō-
sī'ah begot Jec·o·nī'ah and his brothers
about the time they were carried away to
Babylon.
12And after they were brought to Bab-
ylon, Jec·o·nī'ah begot She·al'ti·el, and
She·al'ti·el begot Ze·rub'ba·bel. 13Ze·rub'-
ba·bel begot A·bī'ud, A·bī'ud begot
E·lī'a·kim, and E·lī'a·kim begot Ā'zor.
14Ā'zor begot Zā'dok, Zā'dok begot

1:6 [a]Words in italic type have been added for clarity. They are not found in the original Greek. 1:7 [a]NU-Text reads *Asaph.* 1:10 [a]NU-Text reads *Amos.*

Ā'chim, and Ā'chim begot E·lī'ud. 15E·lī'ud begot El·ē·ā'zar, El·ē·ā'zar begot Mat'than, and Mat'than begot Jacob. 16And Jacob begot Joseph the husband of Mary, of whom was born Jesus who is called Christ.

17So all the generations from Abraham to David *are* fourteen generations, from David until the captivity in Babylon *are* fourteen generations, and from the captivity in Babylon until the Christ *are* fourteen generations.

Christ Born of Mary

18Now the birth of Jesus Christ was as follows: After His mother Mary was betrothed to Joseph, before they came together, she was found with child of the Holy Spirit. 19Then Joseph her husband, being a just *man,* and not wanting to make her a public example, was minded to put her away secretly. 20But while he thought about these things, behold, an angel of the Lord appeared to him in a dream, saying, "Joseph, son of David, do not be afraid to take to you Mary your wife, for that which is conceived in her is of the Holy Spirit. 21And she will bring forth a Son, and you shall call His name JESUS, for He will save His people from their sins."

22So all this was done that it might be fulfilled which was spoken by the Lord through the prophet, saying: 23*"Behold, the virgin shall be with child, and bear a Son, and they shall call His name Imman'ū·el,"*[a] which is translated, "God with us."

24Then Joseph, being aroused from sleep, did as the angel of the Lord commanded him and took to him his wife, 25and did not know her till she had brought forth her firstborn Son.[a] And he called His name JESUS.

CHAPTER 2

Wise Men from the East

Now after Jesus was born in Bethlehem of Judea in the days of Her'od the king, behold, wise men from the East came to Jerusalem, 2saying, "Where is He who has been born King of the Jews? For we have seen His star in the East and have come to worship Him."

3When Her'od the king heard *this,* he was troubled, and all Jerusalem with him. 4And when he had gathered all the chief priests and scribes of the people together, he inquired of them where the Christ was to be born.

5So they said to him, "In Bethlehem of Judea, for thus it is written by the prophet:

6 *'But you, Bethlehem, in the land of Judah,*
Are not the least among the rulers of Judah;
For out of you shall come a Ruler
Who will shepherd My people Israel.'"[a]

1:23 [a]Isaiah 7:14. Words in oblique type in the New Testament are quoted from the Old Testament.
1:25 [a]NU-Text reads *a Son.* 2:6 [a]Micah 5:2

1:16 The pattern of the genealogy is broken. It is not said that **Joseph** begot **Jesus**. In Greek the words "of whom" can refer only to Mary. The genealogy establishes Jesus as a legal descendant of David through His adoptive father. **Christ**: The Anointed One, the long-expected "King of the Jews" (2:2). Christ is a title, not a name.

1:18–20 betrothed: Engagement in Palestine was a legally binding contract, usually arranged by parents. Custom suggests that **Mary** was a young teenager and **Joseph** around 30. Sexual relations were forbidden until after marriage. **before they came together**: Apparently Mary and Joseph engaged in normal sexual relations after the birth of Jesus (see v. 25). Because of the binding character of Jewish engagements, Joseph is called Mary's **husband**, and she his "wife" (v. 24). **a just man**: Joseph's character is shown by his decision to take private legal action to break the engagement instead of publicly humiliating Mary. After he had decided upon a gentle course of action, the Lord revealed to him the special circumstances of Mary's pregnancy.

7Then Her′od, when he had secretly
called the wise men, determined from
them what time the star appeared. 8And he
sent them to Bethlehem and said, "Go and
search carefully for the young Child, and
when you have found *Him,* bring back
word to me, that I may come and worship
Him also."

9When they heard the king, they de-
parted; and behold, the star which they
had seen in the East went before them, till
it came and stood over where the young
Child was. 10When they saw the star, they
rejoiced with exceedingly great joy. 11And
when they had come into the house, they
saw the young Child with Mary His
mother, and fell down and worshiped
Him. And when they had opened their
treasures, they presented gifts to Him:
gold, frankincense, and myrrh.

12Then, being divinely warned in a
dream that they should not return to
Her′od, they departed for their own coun-
try another way.

The Flight into Egypt

13Now when they had departed, behold,
an angel of the Lord appeared to Joseph in
a dream, saying, "Arise, take the young
Child and His mother, flee to Egypt, and
stay there until I bring you word; for
Her′od will seek the young Child to de-
stroy Him."

14When he arose, he took the young
Child and His mother by night and de-
parted for Egypt, 15and was there until the
death of Her′od, that it might be fulfilled
which was spoken by the Lord through the
prophet, saying, *"Out of Egypt I called My
Son."*[a]

Massacre of the Innocents

16Then Her′od, when he saw that he was
deceived by the wise men, was exceed-
ingly angry; and he sent forth and put to
death all the male children who were in
Bethlehem and in all its districts, from two
years old and under, according to the time
which he had determined from the wise
men. 17Then was fulfilled what was spoken
by Jer·e·mī′ah the prophet, saying:

18 *"A voice was heard in Rā′mah,*
Lamentation, weeping, and great
mourning,
Rachel weeping for her children,
Refusing to be comforted,
Because they are no more."[a]

The Home in Nazareth

19Now when Her′od was dead, behold,
an angel of the Lord appeared in a dream
to Joseph in Egypt, 20saying, "Arise, take
the young Child and His mother, and go to
the land of Israel, for those who sought the
young Child's life are dead." 21Then he
arose, took the young Child and His
mother, and came into the land of Israel.

22But when he heard that Ar·che·lā′us
was reigning over Judea instead of his
father Her′od, he was afraid to go there.
And being warned by God in a dream, he
turned aside into the region of Galilee.
23And he came and dwelt in a city called
Nazareth, that it might be fulfilled which
was spoken by the prophets, "He shall be
called a Naz′a·rēne."

CHAPTER 3

John the Baptist Prepares the Way

In those days John the Baptist came
preaching in the wilderness of Judea, 2and

2:15 [a]Hosea 11:1 2:18 [a]Jeremiah 31:15

2:15 that it might be fulfilled: God saved the Israelites by bringing them out of Egypt. Matthew sees this first exodus as a picture of God's providing our salvation by bringing the child Jesus back from Egypt. Herod died in 4 B.C. and v. 16 suggests that Jesus may have been about two years old at that time. An error in the calendar accounts for Jesus being born between 7 and 4 B.C.

2:23 spoken by the prophets: No single OT prophecy provides this quote; however, several call the Messiah the "Branch" (Hebrew *nezer,* see Is. 4:2; Zech. 3:8).

JESUS: THE PERFECT BALANCE

As the only perfect man ever to walk on earth, Jesus epitomized healthy living, achieving physical, spiritual, and mental balance as no one else could hope to do. While His entire life provides the ideal model for Christians to follow, the temptation in the wilderness most clearly demonstrates His flawlessly balanced perspective.

Having fasted for forty days and nights, Jesus' human body must have been crying out for food, so Satan's first attack came on the physical level. He said, "If You are the Son of God, command that these stones become bread" (Matt. 4:3). Despite His hunger, Jesus recognized Satan's ploy for what it was, and He kept His priorities in focus: "It is written, 'Man shall not live by bread alone, but by every word that proceeds from the mouth of God'" (v. 4).

Next, Satan tested Jesus' mental stability, misquoting Scripture in an attempt to trip Him up with pride: "If You are the Son of God, throw Yourself down. For it is written: 'He shall give His angels charge over you,' and, 'In their hands they shall bear you up, / Lest you dash your foot against a stone'" (v. 6).

What a challenge! Many of us might have responded to this dare with an "I'll show you!" Not Jesus. He replied, "It is written again, 'You shall not tempt the LORD your God'" (v. 7).

Failing at his first two attempts, Satan pulled out one last trick. He tried to convince Jesus to trade His spiritual well-being for the power and glory of this world. Showing Him all the kingdoms and splendor of the earth, he said, "All these things I will give You if You will fall down and worship me" (v. 9).

Now this may seem a foolish attempt on Satan's part, since Jesus, of course, knew that only God had the power to fulfill such an extravagant vow. Yet how often do we fall prey to similar temptations, despite our knowledge that God alone has the power to meet our needs and desires?

Jesus, however, stood firm. "Away with you, Satan!" he said. "For it is written, 'You shall worship the LORD your God, and Him only you shall serve'" (v. 10).

Since Satan had the audacity to tempt the Son of God, we can be assured that no matter how long we serve the Lord, we will never be immune from the wiles of the devil. As with Jesus, Satan usually chooses our most vulnerable point to begin his attack, so careful attention to all aspects of our health is vital for Christians. Our best defense is to study Scripture, establish our priorities, and follow Christ's example as closely as we can. ✦

saying, "Repent, for the kingdom of heaven is at hand!" [3]For this is he who was spoken of by the prophet Ī·sāi'ah, saying:

"The voice of one crying in the
wilderness:
'Prepare the way of the L*ORD;*
Make His paths straight.'"[a]

[4]Now John himself was clothed in camel's hair, with a leather belt around his waist; and his food was locusts and wild honey. [5]Then Jerusalem, all Judea, and all the region around the Jordan went out to him [6]and were baptized by him in the Jordan, confessing their sins.

[7]But when he saw many of the Phar'i·sees and Sad'dū·cees coming to his baptism, he said to them, "Brood of vipers! Who warned you to flee from the wrath to come? [8]Therefore bear fruits worthy of repentance, [9]and do not think to say to yourselves, 'We have Abraham as *our* father.' For I say to you that God is able to raise up children to Abraham from these stones. [10]And even now the ax is laid to the root of the trees. Therefore every tree which does not bear good fruit is cut down and thrown into the fire. [11]I indeed baptize you with water unto repentance, but He who is coming after me is mightier than I, whose sandals I am not worthy to carry. He will baptize you with the Holy Spirit and fire.[a] [12]His winnowing fan *is* in His hand, and He will thoroughly clean out His threshing floor, and gather His wheat into the barn; but He will burn up the chaff with unquenchable fire."

John Baptizes Jesus

[13]Then Jesus came from Galilee to John at the Jordan to be baptized by him. [14]And John *tried to* prevent Him, saying, "I need to be baptized by You, and are You coming to me?"

[15]But Jesus answered and said to him, "Permit *it to be so* now, for thus it is fitting for us to fulfill all righteousness." Then he allowed Him.

[16]When He had been baptized, Jesus came up immediately from the water; and behold, the heavens were opened to Him, and He[a] saw the Spirit of God descending like a dove and alighting upon Him. [17]And suddenly a voice *came* from heaven, saying, "This is My beloved Son, in whom I am well pleased."

CHAPTER 4

Satan Tempts Jesus

Then Jesus was led up by the Spirit into the wilderness to be tempted by the devil. [2]And when He had fasted forty days and forty nights, afterward He was hungry. [3]Now when the tempter came to Him, he said, "If You are the Son of God, command that these stones become bread."

[4]But He answered and said, "It is written, *'Man shall not live by bread alone, but by every word that proceeds from the mouth of God.'"*[a]

[5]Then the devil took Him up into the holy city, set Him on the pinnacle of the

3:3 [a]Isaiah 40:3 3:11 [a]M-Text omits *and fire.* 3:16 [a]Or *he* 4:4 [a]Deuteronomy 8:3

4:1–11 God used these three temptations (vv. 2–4, 5–7, 8–10) by the **devil** to test Jesus' loyalty. During forty years in the wilderness Israel put comfort before obedience. She complained about the food and hardships, failed to trust God, and fell into idolatry. **The Son of God** (v. 3) is the ideal Israel who by overcoming these temptations shows His obedience in all these areas. As Christ's disciples, we also will face temptations, but we can find strength in following the sinless example, using God's Word to overcome Satan's lies.

4:5–7 The devil **took** Jesus to the highest point of the temple, the southeast corner, overlooking the Kidron Valley. **throw Yourself down**: The person who really trusts God does not challenge God to prove Himself by such an artificial test. The Scripture can be twisted, leading God's people astray. We must therefore study and apply the Bible thoughtfully and prayerfully. Jesus answered by quoting a verse that had been used to correct Israel's

> ***I pray that my children put into practice the fact that they shall not live by bread alone, but by every word that proceeds from the mouth of God.***
>
> *adapted from* Matthew 4:4

temple, 6and said to Him, "If You are
the Son of God, throw Yourself down. For
it is written:

'He shall give His angels charge over
you,'

and,

'In their hands they shall bear you up,
Lest you dash your foot against a
stone.'"[a]

7Jesus said to him, "It is written again,
'You shall not tempt the LORD *your*
God.'"[a]
8Again, the devil took Him up on an ex-
ceedingly high mountain, and showed
Him all the kingdoms of the world and
their glory. 9And he said to Him, "All these
things I will give You if You will fall down
and worship me."
10Then Jesus said to him, "Away with
you,[a] Satan! For it is written, *'You shall*
worship the LORD *your God, and Him only*
you shall serve.'"[b]
11Then the devil left Him, and behold,
angels came and ministered to Him.

Jesus Begins His Galilean Ministry

12Now when Jesus heard that John had
been put in prison, He departed to Galilee.
13And leaving Nazareth, He came and
dwelt in Ca·per'na·um, which is by the
sea, in the regions of Zeb'ū·lun and
Naph'ta·lī, 14that it might be fulfilled
which was spoken by Ī·sāi'ah the prophet,
saying:

15 *"The land of Zeb'ū·lun and the land of*
Naph'ta·lī,
By the way of the sea, beyond the
Jordan,
Galilee of the Gentiles:
16 *The people who sat in darkness have*
seen a great light,
And upon those who sat in the region
and shadow of death
Light has dawned."[a]

17From that time Jesus began to preach
and to say, "Repent, for the kingdom of
heaven is at hand."

Four Fishermen Called as Disciples

18And Jesus, walking by the Sea of Gali-
lee, saw two brothers, Simon called Peter,
and Andrew his brother, casting a net into
the sea; for they were fishermen. 19Then He
said to them, "Follow Me, and I will make
you fishers of men." They immediately left
their nets and followed Him.
21Going on from there, He saw two other
brothers, James *the son* of Zeb'e·dee, and
John his brother, in the boat with Zeb'e·dee
their father, mending their nets. He called
them, 22and immediately they left the boat
and their father, and followed Him.

Jesus Heals a Great Multitude

23And Jesus went about all Galilee,
teaching in their synagogues, preaching
the gospel of the kingdom, and healing all
kinds of sickness and all kinds of disease
among the people. 24Then His fame went
throughout all Syria; and they brought to
Him all sick people who were afflicted

4:6 [a]Psalm 91:11, 12 4:7 [a]Deuteronomy 6:16
4:10 [a]M-Text reads *Get behind Me.* [b]Deuteronomy 6:13
4:16 [a]Isaiah 9:1, 2

demand for God to prove His presence by a miracle (Ex. 17:1–7). We are to trust the Father's providential care, not put Him to the test to prove it.

with various diseases and torments, and
those who were demon-possessed, epilep-
tics, and paralytics; and He healed them.
25 Great multitudes followed Him—from
Galilee, and *from* De·cap'o·lis, Jerusalem,
Judea, and beyond the Jordan.

CHAPTER 5

The Beatitudes

And seeing the multitudes, He went up
on a mountain, and when He was seated
His disciples came to Him. 2 Then He
opened His mouth and taught them, saying:

3 "Blessed *are* the poor in spirit,
For theirs is the kingdom of
heaven.
4 Blessed *are* those who mourn,
For they shall be comforted.
5 Blessed *are* the meek,
For they shall inherit the earth.
6 Blessed *are* those who hunger and
thirst for righteousness,
For they shall be filled.
7 Blessed *are* the merciful,
For they shall obtain mercy.
8 Blessed *are* the pure in heart,
For they shall see God.
9 Blessed *are* the peacemakers,
For they shall be called sons of
God.
10 Blessed *are* those who are persecuted
for righteousness' sake,
For theirs is the kingdom of
heaven.

11 "Blessed are you when they revile and
persecute you, and say all kinds of evil
against you falsely for My sake. 12 Rejoice
and be exceedingly glad, for great *is* your
reward in heaven, for so they persecuted
the prophets who were before you.

Believers Are Salt and Light

13 "You are the salt of the earth; but if the
salt loses its flavor, how shall it be sea-
soned? It is then good for nothing but to be
thrown out and trampled underfoot by men.
14 "You are the light of the world. A city
that is set on a hill cannot be hidden. 15 Nor
do they light a lamp and put it under a bas-
ket, but on a lampstand, and it gives light
to all *who are* in the house. 16 Let your light
so shine before men, that they may see
your good works and glorify your Father
in heaven.

Christ Fulfills the Law

17 "Do not think that I came to destroy
the Law or the Prophets. I did not come to
destroy but to fulfill. 18 For assuredly, I say
to you, till heaven and earth pass away,
one jot or one tittle will by no means pass
from the law till all is fulfilled. 19 Whoever
therefore breaks one of the least of these
commandments, and teaches men so, shall
be called least in the kingdom of heaven;
but whoever does and teaches *them*, he
shall be called great in the kingdom of
heaven. 20 For I say to you, that unless your
righteousness exceeds *the righteousness* of
the scribes and Phar'i·sees, you will by no
means enter the kingdom of heaven.

Murder Begins in the Heart

21 "You have heard that it was said to
those of old, *'You shall not murder,*[a] and

5:21 [a]Exodus 20:13; Deuteronomy 5:17

5:13 Salt was a sign of God's covenant with Israel (see Lev. 2:13). It is a preservative, a flavor enhancer, and a purifying agent. Jews called the law the **salt of the earth**. Jesus claimed that His disciples exerted this influence. Rather than withdrawing from this world, we are to walk through the world with uncompromising holiness, allowing God to reach others by our example.

5:21–26 Jesus brought out the deeper meaning of the OT command against murder. Not only is the act forbidden, but the **angry** spirit which leads to it is wrong. Jesus is not saying that the angry person might as well commit murder, but that he is guilty of sin. While human courts punish obvious crimes, God judges the hidden sins.

SACRED SEASONING

Charles R. Swindoll

Before refrigeration, salt served a vital purpose. Fishermen, for example, knew its value. As soon as they got their catch, they packed the fish in layers of salt to preserve the meat until they could get it to market. Our forefathers who crossed the rugged plains and mountains in prairie schooners often layered their meat in salt or carried meat that had been soaked in brine to preserve it for as long as possible. Salt has a preserving effect. In other words, it arrests corruption.

"Salty Christians make the surrounding world thirsty for the very water of life."

Salt also adds flavor to food. Just a little shake of salt can dramatically change the taste of a dish. One of salt's most valuable contributions is the "bite" it adds to food. However, it can also lose that bite.

Look at a Christian who has absorbed the world system and you will see salt that has lost its flavor—a tasteless, useless seasoning. The worse our world becomes, the greater is its need of salt because that is another important property: salt causes thirst. Salty Christians make the surrounding world thirsty for the very water of life. And, by the way, I am not just talking about huge piles of salt (like big churches and evangelistic crusades) that make folks thirsty for the things of God. I am talking about consistent, everyday, lifestyle things.

Think about it: Do people feel more alive when they are around you? Do you create a thirst as you "shake the salt?" Does anyone ever wonder why you are so unselfish, so thoughtful, so caring? Do the neighborhood children want to be in your home because of the way you treat your children? And how about teenagers? Is there some kind of "salty magnet" that draws them toward you? ✦

whoever murders will be in danger of the
judgment.' 22But I say to you that whoever
is angry with his brother without a cause[a]
shall be in danger of the judgment. And
whoever says to his brother, 'Ra'ca!' shall
be in danger of the council. But whoever
says, 'You fool!' shall be in danger of hell
fire. 23Therefore if you bring your gift to the
altar, and there remember that your
brother has something against you, 24leave
your gift there before the altar, and go your
way. First be reconciled to your brother,
and then come and offer your gift. 25Agree
with your adversary quickly, while you are
on the way with him, lest your adversary
deliver you to the judge, the judge hand
you over to the officer, and you be thrown
into prison. 26Assuredly, I say to you, you
will by no means get out of there till you
have paid the last penny.

5:22 [a]NU-Text omits *without a cause.*

Adultery in the Heart

27"You have heard that it was said to those of old,[a] *'You shall not commit adultery.'*[b] 28But I say to you that whoever looks at a woman to lust for her has already committed adultery with her in his heart. 29If your right eye causes you to sin, pluck it out and cast *it* from you; for it is more profitable for you that one of your members perish, than for your whole body to be cast into hell. 30And if your right hand causes you to sin, cut it off and cast *it* from you; for it is more profitable for you that one of your members perish, than for your whole body to be cast into hell.

Marriage Is Sacred and Binding

31"Furthermore it has been said, 'Whoever divorces his wife, let him give her a certificate of divorce.' 32But I say to you that whoever divorces his wife for any reason except sexual immorality[a] causes her to commit adultery; and whoever marries a woman who is divorced commits adultery.

Jesus Forbids Oaths

33"Again you have heard that it was said to those of old, 'You shall not swear falsely, but shall perform your oaths to the Lord.' 34But I say to you, do not swear at all: neither by heaven, for it is God's throne; 35nor by the earth, for it is His footstool; nor by Jerusalem, for it is the city of the great King. 36Nor shall you swear by your head, because you cannot make one hair white or black. 37But let your 'Yes' be 'Yes,' and your 'No,' 'No.' For whatever is more than these is from the evil one.

Go the Second Mile

38"You have heard that it was said, *'An eye for an eye and a tooth for a tooth.'*[a] 39But I tell you not to resist an evil person. But whoever slaps you on your right cheek, turn the other to him also. 40If anyone wants to sue you and take away your tunic, let him have *your* cloak also. 41And whoever compels you to go one mile, go with him two. 42Give to him who asks you, and from him who wants to borrow from you do not turn away.

Love Your Enemies

43"You have heard that it was said, *'You shall love your neighbor*[a] and hate your enemy.' 44But I say to you, love your enemies, bless those who curse you, do good to those who hate you, and pray for those who spitefully use you and persecute you,[a] 45that you may be sons of your Father in heaven; for He makes His sun rise on the evil and on the good, and sends rain on the

5:27 [a]NU-Text and M-Text omit *to those of old.* [b]Exodus 20:14; Deuteronomy 5:18 5:32 [a]Or *fornication* 5:38 [a]Exodus 21:24; Leviticus 24:20; Deuteronomy 19:21 5:43 [a]Compare Leviticus 19:18 5:44 [a]NU-Text omits three clauses from this verse, leaving, *"But I say to you, love your enemies and pray for those who persecute you."*

5:38–42 An eye for an eye: The OT law was intended to limit revenge so that retaliation would fit the crime rather than far exceeding it (see Deut. 19:21). Jesus urged His followers to go even further: to forego revenge rather than insist on legal rights, and to forgive rather than to seek retaliation or even strict justice. Jesus has set the example that we should adopt for our Christian lifestyle. As we make a conscious effort to release any bitterness we hold toward others, we are taking an important step that will have a positive impact on our physical health as well.

5:40, 41 tunic: Undergarment. **cloak**: Outer garment. **compels**: Roman soldiers could legally force Jews to serve as porters for a set distance. Jesus urged His followers not to let their oppressors destroy their Christian love, which should even go beyond what the Roman law demanded (see Rom. 12:21).

5:42 Give to him who asks: To aid the poor the OT forbade charging interest on loans made to fellow Jews (Deut. 15:7–11). Many refused to make such interest-free loans. Jesus asks His followers not to put material gain above human need.

just and on the unjust. 46For if you love
those who love you, what reward have
you? Do not even the tax collectors do the
same? 47And if you greet your brethren[a]
only, what do you do more *than others?* Do
not even the tax collectors[b] do so? 48There-
fore you shall be perfect, just as your
Father in heaven is perfect.

CHAPTER 6

Do Good to Please God

"Take heed that you do not do your
charitable deeds before men, to be seen by
them. Otherwise you have no reward from
your Father in heaven. 2Therefore, when
you do a charitable deed, do not sound
a trumpet before you as the hypocrites do
in the synagogues and in the streets, that
they may have glory from men. Assuredly,
I say to you, they have their reward. 3But
when you do a charitable deed, do not let
your left hand know what your right hand
is doing, 4that your charitable deed may be
in secret; and your Father who sees in se-
cret will Himself reward you openly.[a]

The Model Prayer

5"And when you pray, you shall not be
like the hypocrites. For they love to pray
standing in the synagogues and on the cor-
ners of the streets, that they may be seen by
men. Assuredly, I say to you, they have
their reward. 6But you, when you pray, go
into your room, and when you have shut
your door, pray to your Father who *is*
in the secret *place;* and your Father who
sees in secret will reward you openly.[a]
7And when you pray, do not use vain repe-
titions as the heathen *do.* For they think
that they will be heard for their many
words.
8"Therefore do not be like them. For
your Father knows the things you have
need of before you ask Him. 9In this man-
ner, therefore, pray:

Our Father in heaven,
Hallowed be Your name.
10 Your kingdom come.
Your will be done
On earth as *it is* in heaven.
11 Give us this day our daily bread.
12 And forgive us our debts,
As we forgive our debtors.
13 And do not lead us into temptation,
But deliver us from the evil one.
For Yours is the kingdom and the
power and the glory forever.
Amen.[a]

> God always gives a greater blessing to humble beginnings than to those that start with the chiming of bells.
>
> St. Vincent de Paul

14"For if you forgive men their tres-
passes, your heavenly Father will also for-
give you. 15But if you do not forgive men
their trespasses, neither will your Father
forgive your trespasses.

Fasting to Be Seen Only by God

16"Moreover, when you fast, do not be
like the hypocrites, with a sad counte-
nance. For they disfigure their faces that
they may appear to men to be fasting. As-
suredly, I say to you, they have their re-
ward. 17But you, when you fast, anoint
your head and wash your face, 18so that
you do not appear to men to be fasting, but
to your Father who *is* in the secret *place;*
and your Father who sees in secret will re-
ward you openly.[a]

Lay Up Treasures in Heaven

19"Do not lay up for yourselves trea-
sures on earth, where moth and rust de-
stroy and where thieves break in and steal;
20but lay up for yourselves treasures in

5:47 [a]M-Text reads *friends.* [b]NU-Text reads *Gentiles.* 6:4 [a]NU-Text omits *openly.* 6:6 [a]NU-Text omits *openly.* 6:13 [a]NU-Text omits *For Yours* through *Amen.* 6:18 [a]NU-Text and M-Text omit *openly.*

heaven, where neither moth nor rust destroys and where thieves do not break in and steal. [21]For where your treasure is, there your heart will be also.

The Lamp of the Body

[22]"The lamp of the body is the eye. If therefore your eye is good, your whole body will be full of light. [23]But if your eye is bad, your whole body will be full of darkness. If therefore the light that is in you is darkness, how great *is* that darkness!

You Cannot Serve God and Riches

[24]"No one can serve two masters; for either he will hate the one and love the other, or else he will be loyal to the one and despise the other. You cannot serve God and mammon.

Do Not Worry

[25]"Therefore I say to you, do not worry about your life, what you will eat or what you will drink; nor about your body, what you will put on. Is not life more than food and the body more than clothing? [26]Look at the birds of the air, for they neither sow nor reap nor gather into barns; yet your heavenly Father feeds them. Are you not of more value than they? [27]Which of you by worrying can add one cubit to his stature?

[28]"So why do you worry about clothing? Consider the lilies of the field, how they grow: they neither toil nor spin; [29]and yet I say to you that even Solomon in all his glory was not arrayed like one of these. [30]Now if God so clothes the grass of the field, which today is, and tomorrow is thrown into the oven, *will He* not much more *clothe* you, O you of little faith?

[31]"Therefore do not worry, saying, 'What shall we eat?' or 'What shall we drink?' or 'What shall we wear?' [32]For after all these things the Gentiles seek. For your

> The future is something which everyone reaches at the rate of sixty minutes an hour, whatever he does, whoever he is.
>
> C. S. Lewis

heavenly Father knows that you need all these things. [33]But seek first the kingdom of God and His righteousness, and all these things shall be added to you. [34]Therefore do not worry about tomorrow, for tomorrow will worry about its own things. Sufficient for the day *is* its own trouble.

CHAPTER 7

Do Not Judge

"Judge not, that you be not judged. [2]For with what judgment you judge, you will be judged; and with the measure you use, it will be measured back to you. [3]And why do you look at the speck in your brother's eye, but do not consider the plank in your own eye? [4]Or how can you say to your brother, 'Let me remove the speck from your eye'; and look, a plank *is* in your own eye? [5]Hypocrite! First remove the plank from your own eye, and then you will see clearly to remove the speck from your brother's eye.

[6]"Do not give what is holy to the dogs; nor cast your pearls before swine, lest they trample them under their feet, and turn and tear you in pieces.

Keep Asking, Seeking, Knocking

[7]"Ask, and it will be given to you; seek, and you will find; knock, and it will be opened to you. [8]For everyone who asks receives, and he who seeks finds, and to him who knocks it will be opened. [9]Or what

6:22, 23 The **lamp** and the **eye** stand for our intentions and choices. The person with a **good** eye focuses on God alone and is totally loyal to His kingdom. His life is full of God's **light**. The person with a **bad** eye makes other things the goal of his life. Because he has purposefully turned from God, his **darkness** is **great**.

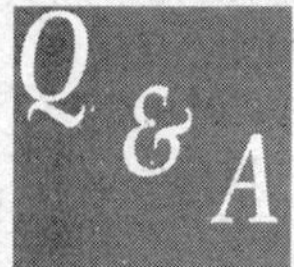

What are some biblical ways to reduce my anxiety and fears?

Dr. Frank Minirth and Dr. Paul Meier

First, you must understand that worry and the anger and frustration that often accompany it are normal human emotions. Scripture tells us in several passages not to succumb to worry (Matt. 6:25–34; Phil. 4:6, 7) and offers the belief in Christ as the alternative.

Where can you begin? Here are some ideas.

✦ *Organize your worries.* When generalized anxiety crops up during the day, do not allow yourself to surrender to its debilitating effect. Instead, identify its source, write down the worry, and save it for a "worry time," maybe from nine to ten at night. During that time concentrate on the specific worry (or worries) you have listed, and pray about it, asking God what He would have you do about the situation.

✦ *Ask others for advice.* Do not be too proud to go to friends for advice and counsel. The Bible says that friends can sharpen friends as iron sharpens iron (Prov. 27:17), and that many advisors make victory sure (Prov. 11:14; 15:22; and 24:6). The advice of committed Christian companions may give you some valuable insight, since it comes from a viewpoint that is more objective than yours.

✦ *Consider the worst that can happen.* Ask yourself, "What would happen if my worst worry came true?" Then ask, "What would God teach me from that?" The majority of things we worry about never happen, and those that do usually are not as devastating as we expected them to be.

✦ *Make definite plans to deal with specific worries.* Then consider sharing your plans and ideas with others, especially fellow Christians who have been supportive in the past. They can give you valuable feedback about the option you have chosen. Revise your plan as necessary. Having a well-considered solution to a problem can dispel much anxiety.

Remember, the stronger our faith in God, the less we will worry. ✦

man is there among you who, if his son
asks for bread, will give him a stone? 10Or if
he asks for a fish, will he give him a ser-
pent? 11If you then, being evil, know how
to give good gifts to your children, how
much more will your Father who is in
heaven give good things to those who ask
Him! 12Therefore, whatever you want men
to do to you, do also to them, for this is the
Law and the Prophets.

The Narrow Way

13"Enter by the narrow gate; for wide *is*
the gate and broad *is* the way that leads to

destruction, and there are many who go in by it. [14]Because[a] narrow *is* the gate and difficult *is* the way which leads to life, and there are few who find it.

You Will Know Them by Their Fruits

[15]"Beware of false prophets, who come to you in sheep's clothing, but inwardly they are ravenous wolves. [16]You will know them by their fruits. Do men gather grapes from thornbushes or figs from thistles? [17]Even so, every good tree bears good fruit, but a bad tree bears bad fruit. [18]A good tree cannot bear bad fruit, nor *can* a bad tree bear good fruit. [19]Every tree that does not bear good fruit is cut down and thrown into the fire. [20]Therefore by their fruits you will know them.

I Never Knew You

[21]"Not everyone who says to Me, 'Lord, Lord,' shall enter the kingdom of heaven, but he who does the will of My Father in heaven. [22]Many will say to Me in that day, 'Lord, Lord, have we not prophesied in Your name, cast out demons in Your name, and done many wonders in Your name?' [23]And then I will declare to them, 'I never knew you; depart from Me, you who practice lawlessness!'

Build on the Rock

[24]"Therefore whoever hears these sayings of Mine, and does them, I will liken him to a wise man who built his house on the rock: [25]and the rain descended, the floods came, and the winds blew and beat on that house; and it did not fall, for it was founded on the rock.

[26]"But everyone who hears these sayings of Mine, and does not do them, will be like a foolish man who built his house on the sand: [27]and the rain descended, the floods came, and the winds blew and beat on that house; and it fell. And great was its fall."

[28]And so it was, when Jesus had ended these sayings, that the people were astonished at His teaching, [29]for He taught them as one having authority, and not as the scribes.

CHAPTER 8

Jesus Cleanses a Leper

When He had come down from the mountain, great multitudes followed Him. [2]And behold, a leper came and worshiped Him, saying, "Lord, if You are willing, You can make me clean."

[3]Then Jesus put out *His* hand and touched him, saying, "I am willing; be cleansed." Immediately his leprosy was cleansed.

[4]And Jesus said to him, "See that you tell no one; but go your way, show yourself to the priest, and offer the gift that Moses commanded, as a testimony to them."

Jesus Heals a Centurion's Servant

[5]Now when Jesus had entered Ca-per'na·um, a centurion came to Him, pleading with Him, [6]saying, "Lord, my servant is lying at home paralyzed, dreadfully tormented."

[7]And Jesus said to him, "I will come and heal him."

[8]The centurion answered and said, "Lord, I am not worthy that You should come under my roof. But only speak a word, and my servant will be healed. [9]For I also am a man under authority, having soldiers under me. And I say to this *one,* 'Go,' and he goes; and to another, 'Come,' and he comes; and to my servant, 'Do this,' and he does *it.*"

7:14 [a]NU-Text and M-Text read *How . . . !*

7:28, 29 one having authority: Jesus did not quote other authorities as did the rabbis. He did not even say "Thus says the LORD" as did the prophets. Rather He spoke with direct authority, "I say to you" (see 5:18, 28, 44). He called people to be loyal to Himself and declared that He would be their judge (vv. 21–23).

10When Jesus heard *it,* He marveled, and
said to those who followed, "Assuredly, I
say to you, I have not found such great
faith, not even in Israel! 11And I say to you
that many will come from east and west,
and sit down with Abraham, Isaac, and Ja-
cob in the kingdom of heaven. 12But the
sons of the kingdom will be cast out into
outer darkness. There will be weeping and
gnashing of teeth." 13Then Jesus said to the
centurion, "Go your way; and as you have
believed, *so* let it be done for you." And his
servant was healed that same hour.

Peter's Mother-in-Law Healed

14Now when Jesus had come into Peter's
house, He saw his wife's mother lying sick
with a fever. 15So He touched her hand, and
the fever left her. And she arose and served
them.[a]

Many Healed After Sabbath Sunset

16When evening had come, they brought
to Him many who were demon-possessed.
And He cast out the spirits with a word,
and healed all who were sick, 17that it
might be fulfilled which was spoken by
Ī·sāi'ah the prophet, saying:

"He Himself took our infirmities
And bore our sicknesses."[a]

The Cost of Discipleship

18And when Jesus saw great multitudes
about Him, He gave a command to depart
to the other side. 19Then a certain scribe
came and said to Him, "Teacher, I will fol-
low You wherever You go."

20And Jesus said to him, "Foxes have
holes and birds of the air *have* nests, but the
Son of Man has nowhere to lay *His* head."

21Then another of His disciples said to
Him, "Lord, let me first go and bury my
father."

22But Jesus said to him, "Follow Me, and
let the dead bury their own dead."

Wind and Wave Obey Jesus

23Now when He got into a boat, His dis-
ciples followed Him. 24And suddenly a

> How sweet the name of Jesus sounds
> In a believer's ear!
> It soothes his sorrows, heals his
> wounds,
> And drives away his fear.
>
> Edward Perronet

great tempest arose on the sea, so that the
boat was covered with the waves. But He
was asleep. 25Then His disciples came to
Him and awoke Him, saying, "Lord, save
us! We are perishing!"

26But He said to them, "Why are you
fearful, O you of little faith?" Then He
arose and rebuked the winds and the sea,
and there was a great calm. 27So the men
marveled, saying, "Who can this be, that
even the winds and the sea obey Him?"

Two Demon-Possessed Men Healed

28When He had come to the other side,
to the country of the Ger'ge·sēnes,[a] there
met Him two demon-possessed *men,* com-
ing out of the tombs, exceedingly fierce, so
that no one could pass that way. 29And
suddenly they cried out, saying, "What
have we to do with You, Jesus, You Son of
God? Have You come here to torment us
before the time?"

30Now a good way off from them there
was a herd of many swine feeding. 31So the
demons begged Him, saying, "If You cast
us out, permit us to go away[a] into the herd
of swine."

32And He said to them, "Go." So when
they had come out, they went into the herd
of swine. And suddenly the whole herd of
swine ran violently down the steep place
into the sea, and perished in the water.

33Then those who kept *them* fled; and
they went away into the city and told
everything, including what *had happened* to
the demon-possessed *men.* 34And behold,
the whole city came out to meet Jesus. And

8:15 [a]NU-Text and M-Text read *Him.*
8:17 [a]Isaiah 53:4 8:28 [a]NU-Text reads *Gadarenes.*
8:31 [a]NU-Text reads *send us.*

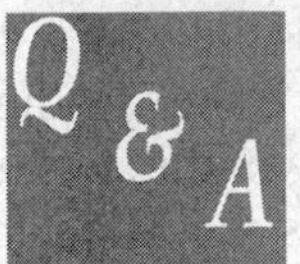

What can one do for a spouse with a terminal illness?

Elmer L. Gray

How hard it is to undergo a spouse's decline with terminal illness! No wonder people who pray for someone who is dying often ask the Lord to strengthen and comfort the surviving spouse as well.

Memories of the good times together may help you bear the sadness and despair. Your faith can also help. Above all, trust God. When people greatly need the Lord, they can ask for His help, and He will be close to them. Be open and honest with Him. You can say things to Him that you could not say to anyone else. Remember how frank Job was with God.

Patience will help you bear your burden and it will also contribute to your spiritual growth. Impatience will not help you and can even destroy your health.

Reading the Bible also helps. Read Psalm 23 again and again. The Lord is indeed your shepherd, and He will take as good care of you as a good shepherd does of his sheep (v. 1). He will walk with you all of the way through the valley of the shadow of death, and His presence with you will give you the strength to overcome fear (v. 4).

Taking care of a dying loved one is one of the hardest things in the world. As you go through this ordeal, remember that this difficult experience can have an amazing blessing if you trust yourself completely to God.

Jesus gave an invitation you can take personally: "Come to Me, all you who labor and are heavy laden, and I will give you rest" (Matt. 11:28).

Ask God for strength, wisdom, and love. ✦

when they saw Him, they begged *Him* to depart from their region.

CHAPTER 9

Jesus Forgives and Heals a Paralytic

So He got into a boat, crossed over, and
came to His own city. [2]Then behold, they
brought to Him a paralytic lying on a bed.
When Jesus saw their faith, He said to the
paralytic, "Son, be of good cheer; your sins
are forgiven you."
[3]And at once some of the scribes said
within themselves, "This Man blasphemes!"
[4]But Jesus, knowing their thoughts,
said, "Why do you think evil in your
hearts? [5]For which is easier, to say, '*Your*
sins are forgiven you,' or to say, 'Arise and
walk'? [6]But that you may know that the
Son of Man has power on earth to forgive
sins"—then He said to the paralytic,
"Arise, take up your bed, and go to your
house." [7]And he arose and departed to his
house.
[8]Now when the multitudes saw *it*, they

9:1–8 Matthew omits many details reported in Mark 2:1–12. He focuses on Jesus' authority **to forgive sins** (v. 6). Underlying the incident is the unstated Jewish assumption, which Jesus rejected (John 9:1–3), that all sickness was a result of sin.

marveled[a] and glorified God, who had
given such power to men.

Matthew the Tax Collector

9As Jesus passed on from there, He saw
a man named Matthew sitting at the tax of-
fice. And He said to him, "Follow Me." So
he arose and followed Him.
10Now it happened, as Jesus sat at the
table in the house, *that* behold, many tax
collectors and sinners came and sat down
with Him and His disciples. 11And when
the Phar'i·sees saw *it,* they said to His dis-
ciples, "Why does your Teacher eat with
tax collectors and sinners?"
12When Jesus heard *that,* He said to
them, "Those who are well have no need of
a physician, but those who are sick. 13But
go and learn what *this* means: *'I desire
mercy and not sacrifice.'*[a] For I did not
come to call the righteous, but sinners, to
repentance."[b]

Jesus Is Questioned About Fasting

14Then the disciples of John came to
Him, saying, "Why do we and the Phar'-
i·sees fast often,[a] but Your disciples do not
fast?"
15And Jesus said to them, "Can the
friends of the bridegroom mourn as long
as the bridegroom is with them? But the
days will come when the bridegroom will
be taken away from them, and then they
will fast. 16No one puts a piece of unshrunk
cloth on an old garment; for the patch pulls
away from the garment, and the tear is
made worse. 17Nor do they put new wine
into old wineskins, or else the wineskins
break, the wine is spilled, and the wine-
skins are ruined. But they put new wine
into new wineskins, and both are pre-
served."

A Girl Restored to Life and a Woman Healed

18While He spoke these things to them,
behold, a ruler came and worshiped Him,
saying, "My daughter has just died, but
come and lay Your hand on her and she
will live." 19So Jesus arose and followed
him, and so *did* His disciples.
20And suddenly, a woman who had a
flow of blood for twelve years came from
behind and touched the hem of His gar-
ment. 21For she said to herself, "If only I
may touch His garment, I shall be made
well." 22But Jesus turned around, and
when He saw her He said, "Be of good
cheer, daughter; your faith has made you
well." And the woman was made well
from that hour.
23When Jesus came into the ruler's
house, and saw the flute players and the
noisy crowd wailing, 24He said to them,
"Make room, for the girl is not dead, but
sleeping." And they ridiculed Him. 25But
when the crowd was put outside, He went
in and took her by the hand, and the girl
arose. 26And the report of this went out into
all that land.

Two Blind Men Healed

27When Jesus departed from there, two
blind men followed Him, crying out and
saying, "Son of David, have mercy on us!"
28And when He had come into the
house, the blind men came to Him. And
Jesus said to them, "Do you believe that I
am able to do this?"
They said to Him, "Yes, Lord."
29Then He touched their eyes, saying,
"According to your faith let it be to you."
30And their eyes were opened. And Jesus

9:8 [a]NU-Text reads *were afraid.* 9:13 [a]Hosea 6:6 [b]NU-Text omits *to repentance.* 9:14 [a]NU-Text brackets *often* as disputed.

9:12, 13 Those who are well . . . sick: A popular proverb of the day, which Jesus applied to the healing of the souls of sinners. **I desire mercy**: The words from Hos. 6:6 condemned the Pharisees as people who were more concerned about religious forms than about compassion. Jesus cannot help those who think they are **righteous** and need no help.

sternly warned them, saying, "See *that* no
one knows *it*." 31But when they had de-
parted, they spread the news about Him in
all that country.

A Mute Man Speaks

32As they went out, behold, they
brought to Him a man, mute and demon-
possessed. 33And when the demon was
cast out, the mute spoke. And the multi-
tudes marveled, saying, "It was never seen
like this in Israel!"

34But the Phar'i·sees said, "He casts out
demons by the ruler of the demons."

The Compassion of Jesus

35Then Jesus went about all the cities and
villages, teaching in their synagogues,
preaching the gospel of the kingdom, and
healing every sickness and every disease
among the people.[a] 36But when He saw the
multitudes, He was moved with compas-
sion for them, because they were weary[a]
and scattered, like sheep having no shep-
herd. 37Then He said to His disciples, "The
harvest truly *is* plentiful, but the laborers
are few. 38Therefore pray the Lord of the har-
vest to send out laborers into His harvest."

CHAPTER 10

The Twelve Apostles

And when He had called His twelve
disciples to *Him,* He gave them power *over*
unclean spirits, to cast them out, and to
heal all kinds of sickness and all kinds of
disease. 2Now the names of the twelve
apostles are these: first, Simon, who is
called Peter, and Andrew his brother;
James the *son* of Zeb'e·dee, and John his
brother; 3Philip and Bartholomew; Thomas
and Matthew the tax collector; James the
son of Al·phaē'us, and Leb·baē'us, whose
surname was[a] Thad·daē'us; 4Simon the
Can'a·nīte,[a] and Judas Is·car'i·ot, who also
betrayed Him.

Sending Out the Twelve

5These twelve Jesus sent out and com-
manded them, saying: "Do not go into the
way of the Gentiles, and do not enter a city
of the Samaritans. 6But go rather to the lost
sheep of the house of Israel. 7And as you
go, preach, saying, 'The kingdom of
heaven is at hand.' 8Heal the sick, cleanse
the lepers, raise the dead,[a] cast out demons.
Freely you have received, freely give. 9Pro-
vide neither gold nor silver nor copper in
your money belts, 10nor bag for *your* jour-
ney, nor two tunics, nor sandals, nor staffs;
for a worker is worthy of his food.

11"Now whatever city or town you en-
ter, inquire who in it is worthy, and stay
there till you go out. 12And when you go
into a household, greet it. 13If the house-
hold is worthy, let your peace come upon
it. But if it is not worthy, let your peace re-
turn to you. 14And whoever will not re-
ceive you nor hear your words, when you
depart from that house or city, shake off
the dust from your feet. 15Assuredly, I say
to you, it will be more tolerable for the land
of Sod'om and Go·mor'rah in the day of
judgment than for that city!

9:35 [a]NU-Text omits *among the people.*
9:36 [a]NU-Text and M-Text read *harassed.*
10:3 [a]NU-Text omits *Lebbaeus, whose surname was.*
10:4 [a]NU-Text reads *Cananaean.* 10:8 [a]NU-Text reads *raise the dead, cleanse the lepers;* M-Text omits *raise the dead.*

10:2–6 the twelve apostles: *Disciple* means "learner"; *apostle* means "one who is sent out." An apostle is someone sent to represent another. The disciples became apostles when they shared in Jesus' mission. The Twelve—and later Paul—were apostles in a special sense, being chosen by Jesus to be witnesses to His resurrection and the foundation of His church (see 16:16–18; Acts 1:21, 22). During His earthly ministry Jesus sent His apostles only to the **house of Israel**. But after His resurrection (see 28:19) He would commission them to go to all the world. The Israelites who accepted Him were to proclaim Him to all humankind. **the Samaritans**: See note on Luke 10:29–35.

> No suffering that one of Christ's own endures for Him is ever in vain. Living for Christ, walking in His way, will not be an easy path. The way of the cross is a hard one, but He never said it would be easy.
>
> Billy Graham

Persecutions Are Coming

16“Behold, I send you out as sheep in the
midst of wolves. Therefore be wise as ser-
pents and harmless as doves. 17But beware
of men, for they will deliver you up to
councils and scourge you in their syna-
gogues. 18You will be brought before gov-
ernors and kings for My sake, as a testi-
mony to them and to the Gentiles. 19But
when they deliver you up, do not worry
about how or what you should speak. For
it will be given to you in that hour what
you should speak; 20for it is not you who
speak, but the Spirit of your Father who
speaks in you.
21“Now brother will deliver up brother
to death, and a father *his* child; and chil-
dren will rise up against parents and cause
them to be put to death. 22And you will be
hated by all for My name's sake. But he
who endures to the end will be saved.
23When they persecute you in this city, flee
to another. For assuredly, I say to you, you
will not have gone through the cities of Is-
rael before the Son of Man comes.
24“A disciple is not above *his* teacher, nor
a servant above his master. 25It is enough
for a disciple that he be like his teacher,
and a servant like his master. If they have
called the master of the house Bē•el'-
ze•bub,[a] how much more *will they call* those
of his household! 26Therefore do not fear
them. For there is nothing covered that will
not be revealed, and hidden that will not
be known.

Jesus Teaches the Fear of God

27“Whatever I tell you in the dark, speak
in the light; and what you hear in the ear,
preach on the housetops. 28And do not fear
those who kill the body but cannot kill the
soul. But rather fear Him who is able to de-
stroy both soul and body in hell. 29Are not
two sparrows sold for a copper coin? And
not one of them falls to the ground apart
from your Father's will. 30But the very
hairs of your head are all numbered. 31Do
not fear therefore; you are of more value
than many sparrows.

Confess Christ Before Men

32“Therefore whoever confesses Me be-
fore men, him I will also confess before My
Father who is in heaven. 33But whoever de-
nies Me before men, him I will also deny
before My Father who is in heaven.

Christ Brings Division

34“Do not think that I came to bring
peace on earth. I did not come to bring
peace but a sword. 35For I have come to *'set*
a man against his father, a daughter
against her mother, and a daughter-in-law
against her mother-in-law'; 36and *'a man's*
enemies will be those of his own house-
hold.'[a] 37He who loves father or mother
more than Me is not worthy of Me. And he
who loves son or daughter more than Me
is not worthy of Me. 38And he who does

10:25 [a]NU-Text and M-Text read *Beelzebul.*
10:36 [a]Micah 7:6

10:38, 39 take his cross: Those who carried a cross were condemned to die. The disciple must die to self-will; God's will must become his will. He may have to give up his own plans and ambitions, perhaps even his life. Those who follow the crucified One should expect suffering. He whose goal is merely to preserve his physical **life** will **lose** all that makes life worthwhile. He who gives up his own interests for Jesus will **find** a fulfilled life here and blessing throughout eternity. As important as it is to plan for our financial future, we must keep our priorities in order and focus our efforts on matters of eternal importance.

not take his cross and follow after Me is not worthy of Me. [39]He who finds his life will lose it, and he who loses his life for My sake will find it.

A Cup of Cold Water

[40]"He who receives you receives Me, and he who receives Me receives Him who sent Me. [41]He who receives a prophet in the name of a prophet shall receive a prophet's reward. And he who receives a righteous man in the name of a righteous man shall receive a righteous man's reward. [42]And whoever gives one of these little ones only a cup of cold *water* in the name of a disciple, assuredly, I say to you, he shall by no means lose his reward."

CHAPTER 11

John the Baptist Sends Messengers to Jesus

Now it came to pass, when Jesus finished commanding His twelve disciples, that He departed from there to teach and to preach in their cities.

[2]And when John had heard in prison about the works of Christ, he sent two of[a] his disciples [3]and said to Him, "Are You the Coming One, or do we look for another?"

[4]Jesus answered and said to them, "Go and tell John the things which you hear and see: [5]*The* blind see and *the* lame walk; *the* lepers are cleansed and *the* deaf hear; *the* dead are raised up and *the* poor have the gospel preached to them. [6]And blessed is he who is not offended because of Me."

[7]As they departed, Jesus began to say to the multitudes concerning John: "What did you go out into the wilderness to see? A reed shaken by the wind? [8]But what did you go out to see? A man clothed in soft garments? Indeed, those who wear soft *clothing* are in kings' houses. [9]But what did you go out to see? A prophet? Yes, I say to you, and more than a prophet. [10]For this is *he* of whom it is written:

'Behold, I send My messenger before
Your face,
Who will prepare Your way before
You.'[a]

[11]"Assuredly, I say to you, among those born of women there has not risen one greater than John the Baptist; but he who is least in the kingdom of heaven is greater than he. [12]And from the days of John the Baptist until now the kingdom of heaven suffers violence, and the violent take it by force. [13]For all the prophets and the law prophesied until John. [14]And if you are willing to receive *it,* he is E·lī'jah who is to come. [15]He who has ears to hear, let him hear!

[16]"But to what shall I liken this generation? It is like children sitting in the marketplaces and calling to their companions, [17]and saying:

'We played the flute for you,
And you did not dance;
We mourned to you,
And you did not lament.'

[18]For John came neither eating nor drinking, and they say, 'He has a demon.' [19]The

11:2 [a]NU-Text reads *by* for *two of.* 11:10 [a]Malachi 3:1

11:4, 5 hear . . . see: The words and deeds of Jesus. In his Gospel Matthew has already shown Jesus performing all of the miracles reported in v. 5. The OT prophets had prophesied that the Messiah, the Coming One (v. 3), would do these **things** (see Is. 35:5; 61:1). Jesus encouraged **John** the Baptist's faith by reminding him that even though He had not yet come as Judge (see 3:11, 12), He had more than fulfilled the prophets' expectations.

ONE DAY AT A TIME
Charles R. Swindoll

One day at a time. You have heard it before: do not contaminate today by corrupting it with tomorrow's troubles. Refuse—yes, refuse—to allow tomorrow's lagoon of worries to drain into today's lake. Today is challenge enough! And since you will need fresh energy and new insight to handle what tomorrow throws at you, wait until it dawns before taking it on. Some of the things you do today may seem totally insignificant so far as tomorrow is concerned, but stay at it. Keep life simple. Do what you have to do today, and to your surprise, it may make an enormous difference in the world you wake up to tomorrow.

And while I'm tossing out all this advice, never underestimate the importance of even the most menial tasks you carry out each day. Don't think that some slight contribution you make on a given day is not worth the effort . . . or will not make any difference tomorrow. ✦

Son of Man came eating and drinking, and
they say, 'Look, a glutton and a wine-
bibber, a friend of tax collectors and
sinners!' But wisdom is justified by her
children."[a]

Woe to the Impenitent Cities

20 Then He began to rebuke the cities in
which most of His mighty works had been
done, because they did not repent: 21 "Woe
to you, Chō·rā'zin! Woe to you, Beth-
sā'i·da! For if the mighty works which
were done in you had been done in Tȳre
and Sī'don, they would have repented
long ago in sackcloth and ashes. 22 But I
say to you, it will be more tolerable
for Tȳre and Sī'don in the day of judg-
ment than for you. 23 And you, Ca·per'-
na·um, who are exalted to heaven, will
be[a] brought down to Hā'dēs; for if the
mighty works which were done in you had
been done in Sod'om, it would have re-
mained until this day. 24 But I say to you
that it shall be more tolerable for the land
of Sod'om in the day of judgment than for
you."

Jesus Gives True Rest

25 At that time Jesus answered and said,
"I thank You, Father, Lord of heaven and
earth, that You have hidden these things
from *the* wise and prudent and have re-
vealed them to babes. 26 Even so, Father, for
so it seemed good in Your sight. 27 All
things have been delivered to Me by My
Father, and no one knows the Son except
the Father. Nor does anyone know the
Father except the Son, and *the one* to whom
the Son wills to reveal *Him*. 28 Come to Me,
all *you* who labor and are heavy laden, and
I will give you rest. 29 Take My yoke upon
you and learn from Me, for I am gentle and
lowly in heart, and you will find rest for
your souls. 30 For My yoke *is* easy and My
burden is light."

11:19 [a]NU-Text reads *works.* 11:23 [a]NU-Text reads *will you be exalted to heaven? No, you will be.*

CHAPTER 12

Jesus Is Lord of the Sabbath

At that time Jesus went through the
grainfields on the Sabbath. And His disci-
ples were hungry, and began to pluck
heads of grain and to eat. 2And when the
Phar'i·sees saw *it,* they said to Him, "Look,
Your disciples are doing what is not lawful
to do on the Sabbath!"

3But He said to them, "Have you not
read what David did when he was hungry,
he and those who were with him: 4how he
entered the house of God and ate the
showbread which was not lawful for him
to eat, nor for those who were with him,
but only for the priests? 5Or have you not
read in the law that on the Sabbath the
priests in the temple profane the Sabbath,
and are blameless? 6Yet I say to you that in
this place there is *One* greater than the tem-
ple. 7But if you had known what *this*
means, *'I desire mercy and not sacrifice,'*[a]
you would not have condemned the guilt-
less. 8For the Son of Man is Lord even[a] of
the Sabbath."

Healing on the Sabbath

9Now when He had departed from
there, He went into their synagogue. 10And
behold, there was a man who had a with-
ered hand. And they asked Him, saying,
"Is it lawful to heal on the Sabbath?"—that
they might accuse Him.
11Then He said to them, "What man is
there among you who has one sheep, and
if it falls into a pit on the Sabbath, will not
lay hold of it and lift *it* out? 12Of how much
more value then is a man than a sheep?
Therefore it is lawful to do good on the
Sabbath." 13Then He said to the man,
"Stretch out your hand." And he stretched
it out, and it was restored as whole as the
other. 14Then the Phar'i·sees went out and
plotted against Him, how they might de-
stroy Him.

Behold, My Servant

15But when Jesus knew *it,* He withdrew
from there. And great multitudes[a] fol-
lowed Him, and He healed them all. 16Yet
He warned them not to make Him known,
17that it might be fulfilled which was spo-
ken by Ī·sāi'ah the prophet, saying:

18 *"Behold! My Servant whom I have chosen,*
My Beloved in whom My soul is well pleased!
I will put My Spirit upon Him,
And He will declare justice to the Gentiles.
19 *He will not quarrel nor cry out,*
Nor will anyone hear His voice in the streets.
20 *A bruised reed He will not break,*
And smoking flax He will not quench,
Till He sends forth justice to victory;
21 *And in His name Gentiles will trust."*[a]

12:7 [a]Hosea 6:6 12:8 [a]NU-Text and M-Text omit *even.* 12:15 [a]NU-Text brackets *multitudes* as disputed. 12:21 [a]Isaiah 42:1–4

12:1–8 Sabbath: The Jewish holy day of rest (see Ex. 20:8–11). **pluck . . . eat**: The **Pharisees** claimed that picking a few heads of grain to eat was the same as harvesting and therefore not **lawful** on the **Sabbath** (but see Deut. 23:25). In reply, Jesus appealed to Scripture. **David** (v. 3) broke the ceremonial law because he was **hungry**, thus because of human need (see 1 Sam. 21:6). The **priests** (v. 5) broke the Sabbath law in the **temple** itself and were not blamed. As God come in the flesh, Jesus is the **One** who is **greater** (v. 6) than David, the priests, or even the temple. As **Lord** of the **Sabbath** (v. 8), He explains its true meaning. God wants **mercy** (v. 7)—concern for people, put before **sacrifice**—legalistic ritual observance (see notes on 9:12, 13; Mark 2:23, 24).

12:15–21 The reason Jesus would not allow people to **make** His miracles **known** (v. 16) is explained by a quotation from Is. 42:1–4. He did not come to be a military Messiah. He came in humility and gentleness as the prophesied **Servant** (v. 18), who would be concerned for the weak and would accomplish our salvation by suffering.

A House Divided Cannot Stand

22Then one was brought to Him who
was demon-possessed, blind and mute;
and He healed him, so that the blind and[a]
mute man both spoke and saw. 23And all
the multitudes were amazed and said,
"Could this be the Son of David?"
24Now when the Phar′i·sees heard *it*
they said, "This *fellow* does not cast out
demons except by Bē·el′ze·bub,[a] the ruler
of the demons."
25But Jesus knew their thoughts, and
said to them: "Every kingdom divided
against itself is brought to desolation, and
every city or house divided against itself
will not stand. 26If Satan casts out Satan, he
is divided against himself. How then will
his kingdom stand? 27And if I cast out
demons by Bē·el′ze·bub, by whom do
your sons cast *them* out? Therefore they
shall be your judges. 28But if I cast out
demons by the Spirit of God, surely the
kingdom of God has come upon you. 29Or
how can one enter a strong man's house
and plunder his goods, unless he first
binds the strong man? And then he will
plunder his house. 30He who is not with
Me is against Me, and he who does not
gather with Me scatters abroad.

The Unpardonable Sin

31"Therefore I say to you, every sin and
blasphemy will be forgiven men, but the
blasphemy *against* the Spirit will not be
forgiven men. 32Anyone who speaks a
word against the Son of Man, it will be for-
given him; but whoever speaks against the
Holy Spirit, it will not be forgiven him, ei-
ther in this age or in the *age* to come.

A Tree Known by Its Fruit

33"Either make the tree good and its fruit
good, or else make the tree bad and its fruit
bad; for a tree is known by *its* fruit. 34Brood
of vipers! How can you, being evil, speak
good things? For out of the abundance of
the heart the mouth speaks. 35A good man
out of the good treasure of his heart[a] brings
forth good things, and an evil man out of
the evil treasure brings forth evil things.
36But I say to you that for every idle word
men may speak, they will give account of it
in the day of judgment. 37For by your
words you will be justified, and by your
words you will be condemned."

The Scribes and Pharisees Ask for a Sign

38Then some of the scribes and Phar′-
i·sees answered, saying, "Teacher, we want
to see a sign from You."
39But He answered and said to them,
"An evil and adulterous generation seeks
after a sign, and no sign will be given to it
except the sign of the prophet Jonah. 40For
as Jonah was three days and three nights
in the belly of the great fish, so will the
Son of Man be three days and three nights
in the heart of the earth. 41The men of
Nin′e·veh will rise up in the judgment
with this generation and condemn it, be-
cause they repented at the preaching of
Jonah; and indeed a greater than Jonah *is*
here. 42The queen of the South will rise up
in the judgment with this generation and
condemn it, for she came from the ends of
the earth to hear the wisdom of Solomon;
and indeed a greater than Solomon *is*
here.

An Unclean Spirit Returns

43"When an unclean spirit goes out of a
man, he goes through dry places, seeking

12:22 [a]NU-Text omits *blind and.* 12:24 [a]NU-Text and M-Text read *Beelzebul.* 12:35 [a]NU-Text and M-Text omit *of his heart.*

12:22–37 He healed him: When Jesus cast out this demon, He divided His audience. The crowd wondered if He was the Messiah, the **Son of David**. But the **Pharisees** charged Him with using satanic power (v. 24; see 9:32–34). Jesus declared this accusation to be absurd (vv. 25–30); Satan would not use his power to release demon-possessed persons.

rest, and finds none. [44]Then he says, 'I will
return to my house from which I came.'
And when he comes, he finds *it* empty,
swept, and put in order. [45]Then he goes and
takes with him seven other spirits more
wicked than himself, and they enter and
dwell there; and the last *state* of that man is
worse than the first. So shall it also be with
this wicked generation."

Jesus' Mother and Brothers Send for Him

[46]While He was still talking to the mul-
titudes, behold, His mother and broth-
ers stood outside, seeking to speak
with Him. [47]Then one said to Him,
"Look, Your mother and Your brothers are
standing outside, seeking to speak with
You."

[48]But He answered and said to the one
who told Him, "Who is My mother and
who are My brothers?" [49]And He stretched
out His hand toward His disciples and
said, "Here are My mother and My
brothers! [50]For whoever does the will of
My Father in heaven is My brother and
sister and mother."

CHAPTER 13

The Parable of the Sower

On the same day Jesus went out of
the house and sat by the sea. [2]And great
multitudes were gathered together to
Him, so that He got into a boat and sat;
and the whole multitude stood on the
shore.

[3]Then He spoke many things to them in
parables, saying: "Behold, a sower went
out to sow. [4]And as he sowed, some *seed*
fell by the wayside; and the birds came and
devoured them. [5]Some fell on stony places,
where they did not have much earth; and
they immediately sprang up because they
had no depth of earth. [6]But when the sun
was up they were scorched, and because
they had no root they withered away. [7]And
some fell among thorns, and the thorns
sprang up and choked them. [8]But others
fell on good ground and yielded a crop:
some a hundredfold, some sixty, some
thirty. [9]He who has ears to hear, let him
hear!"

The Purpose of Parables

[10]And the disciples came and said to
Him, "Why do You speak to them in para-
bles?"

[11]He answered and said to them, "Be-
cause it has been given to you to know the
mysteries of the kingdom of heaven, but
to them it has not been given. [12]For who-
ever has, to him more will be given, and he
will have abundance; but whoever does
not have, even what he has will be taken
away from him. [13]Therefore I speak to
them in parables, because seeing they do
not see, and hearing they do not hear, nor
do they understand. [14]And in them the
prophecy of Ī·sāi′ah is fulfilled, which
says:

'Hearing you will hear and shall not
understand,
And seeing you will see and not
perceive;
15 *For the hearts of this people have*
grown dull.
Their ears are hard of hearing,
And their eyes they have closed,
Lest they should see with their eyes
and hear with their ears,
Lest they should understand with
their hearts and turn,
So that I should[a] *heal them.'*[b]

[16]But blessed *are* your eyes for they see, and
your ears for they hear; [17]for assuredly, I
say to you that many prophets and right-
eous *men* desired to see what you see, and
did not see *it*, and to hear what you hear,
and did not hear *it*.

13:15 [a]NU-Text and M-Text read *would.* [b]Isaiah 6:9, 10

The Parable of the Sower Explained

18"Therefore hear the parable of the sower: 19When anyone hears the word of the kingdom, and does not understand *it,* then the wicked *one* comes and snatches away what was sown in his heart. This is he who received seed by the wayside. 20But he who received the seed on stony places, this is he who hears the word and immediately receives it with joy; 21yet he has no root in himself, but endures only for a while. For when tribulation or persecution arises because of the word, immediately he stumbles. 22Now he who received seed among the thorns is he who hears the word, and the cares of this world and the deceitfulness of riches choke the word, and he becomes unfruitful. 23But he who received seed on the good ground is he who hears the word and understands *it,* who indeed bears fruit and produces: some a hundredfold, some sixty, some thirty."

The Parable of the Wheat and the Tares

24Another parable He put forth to them, saying: "The kingdom of heaven is like a man who sowed good seed in his field; 25but while men slept, his enemy came and sowed tares among the wheat and went his way. 26But when the grain had sprouted and produced a crop, then the tares also appeared. 27So the servants of the owner came and said to him, 'Sir, did you not sow good seed in your field? How then does it have tares?' 28He said to them, 'An enemy has done this.' The servants said to him, 'Do you want us then to go and gather them up?' 29But he said, 'No, lest while you gather up the tares you also uproot the wheat with them. 30Let both grow together until the harvest, and at the time of harvest I will say to the reapers, "First gather together the tares and bind them in bundles to burn them, but gather the wheat into my barn." ' "

The Parable of the Mustard Seed

31Another parable He put forth to them, saying: "The kingdom of heaven is like a mustard seed, which a man took and sowed in his field, 32which indeed is the least of all the seeds; but when it is grown it is greater than the herbs and becomes a tree, so that the birds of the air come and nest in its branches."

The Parable of the Leaven

33Another parable He spoke to them: "The kingdom of heaven is like leaven, which a woman took and hid in three measures[a] of meal till it was all leavened."

Prophecy and the Parables

34All these things Jesus spoke to the multitude in parables; and without a parable He did not speak to them, 35that it might be fulfilled which was spoken by the prophet, saying:

"I will open My mouth in parables;
I will utter things kept secret from the foundation of the world."[a]

13:33 [a]Greek *sata,* approximately two pecks in all
13:35 [a]Psalm 78:2

13:30 Let both grow together: Now is the time when those who reject Christ become more hardened and those who believe become more Christlike. Thus at the judgment the fate of each group will be clearly just. As the years go by, we may feel increasingly discouraged by the wickedness surrounding us, but the Lord has promised eternal rewards to those who hold fast to the faith.

13:31–33 when it is grown: These two short parables picture the small beginnings of the Christian movement in Palestine which would eventually be followed by blessed results in the Gentile mission. God's work often appears insignificant at first, but has far-reaching results.

The Parable of the Tares Explained

36Then Jesus sent the multitude away
and went into the house. And His disciples
came to Him, saying, "Explain to us the
parable of the tares of the field."
37He answered and said to them: "He
who sows the good seed is the Son of Man.
38The field is the world, the good seeds are
the sons of the kingdom, but the tares are
the sons of the wicked *one*. 39The enemy
who sowed them is the devil, the harvest is
the end of the age, and the reapers are the
angels. 40Therefore as the tares are gath-
ered and burned in the fire, so it will be at
the end of this age. 41The Son of Man will
send out His angels, and they will gather
out of His kingdom all things that offend,
and those who practice lawlessness, 42and
will cast them into the furnace of fire.
There will be wailing and gnashing of
teeth. 43Then the righteous will shine forth
as the sun in the kingdom of their Father.
He who has ears to hear, let him hear!

The Parable of the Hidden Treasure

44"Again, the kingdom of heaven is like
treasure hidden in a field, which a man
found and hid; and for joy over it he goes
and sells all that he has and buys that field.

The Parable of the Pearl of Great Price

45"Again, the kingdom of heaven is like
a merchant seeking beautiful pearls, 46who,
when he had found one pearl of great
price, went and sold all that he had and
bought it.

The Parable of the Dragnet

47"Again, the kingdom of heaven is like
a dragnet that was cast into the sea and
gathered some of every kind, 48which,
when it was full, they drew to shore; and
they sat down and gathered the good into
vessels, but threw the bad away. 49So it will
be at the end of the age. The angels will
come forth, separate the wicked from
among the just, 50and cast them into the
furnace of fire. There will be wailing and
gnashing of teeth."
51Jesus said to them,[a] "Have you under-
stood all these things?"
They said to Him, "Yes, Lord."[b]
52Then He said to them, "Therefore
every scribe instructed concerning[a] the
kingdom of heaven is like a householder
who brings out of his treasure *things* new
and old."

Jesus Rejected at Nazareth

53Now it came to pass, when Jesus had
finished these parables, that He departed
from there. 54When He had come to His
own country, He taught them in their syn-
agogue, so that they were astonished and
said, "Where did this *Man* get this wisdom
and *these* mighty works? 55Is this not the
carpenter's son? Is not His mother called
Mary? And His brothers James, Jō'sēs,[a] Si-
mon, and Judas? 56And His sisters, are they
not all with us? Where then did this *Man*
get all these things?" 57So they were of-
fended at Him.
But Jesus said to them, "A prophet is not
without honor except in his own country
and in his own house." 58Now He did not
do many mighty works there because of
their unbelief.

CHAPTER 14

John the Baptist Beheaded

At that time Her'od the tetrarch heard
the report about Jesus 2and said to his
servants, "This is John the Baptist; he is
risen from the dead, and therefore these
powers are at work in him." 3For Her'od
had laid hold of John and bound him,
and put *him* in prison for the sake of
He·rō'di·as, his brother Philip's wife.
4Because John had said to him, "It is not
lawful for you to have her." 5And although
he wanted to put him to death, he feared

13:51 [a]NU-Text omits *Jesus said to them.* [b]NU-Text omits *Lord.* 13:52 [a]Or *for* 13:55 [a]NU-Text reads *Joseph.*

the multitude, because they counted him
as a prophet.
6But when Her′od′s birthday was cele-
brated, the daughter of He·rō′di·as danced
before them and pleased Her′od. 7There-
fore he promised with an oath to give her
whatever she might ask.
8So she, having been prompted by her
mother, said, "Give me John the Baptist's
head here on a platter."
9And the king was sorry; nevertheless,
because of the oaths and because of those
who sat with him, he commanded *it* to be
given to *her.* 10So he sent and had John be-
headed in prison. 11And his head was
brought on a platter and given to the
girl, and she brought *it* to her mother.
12Then his disciples came and took away
the body and buried it, and went and told
Jesus.

Feeding the Five Thousand

13When Jesus heard *it,* He departed from
there by boat to a deserted place by Him-
self. But when the multitudes heard it, they
followed Him on foot from the cities.
14And when Jesus went out He saw a great
multitude; and He was moved with com-
passion for them, and healed their sick.
15When it was evening, His disciples came
to Him, saying, "This is a deserted place,
and the hour is already late. Send the mul-
titudes away, that they may go into the vil-
lages and buy themselves food."
16But Jesus said to them, "They do not
need to go away. You give them something
to eat."
17And they said to Him, "We have here
only five loaves and two fish."
18He said, "Bring them here to Me."
19Then He commanded the multitudes to
sit down on the grass. And He took the five
loaves and the two fish, and looking up to
heaven, He blessed and broke and gave the
loaves to the disciples; and the disciples
gave to the multitudes. 20So they all ate and
were filled, and they took up twelve bas-
kets full of the fragments that remained.
21Now those who had eaten were about
five thousand men, besides women and
children.

Jesus Walks on the Sea

22Immediately Jesus made His disciples
get into the boat and go before Him to the
other side, while He sent the multitudes
away. 23And when He had sent the multi-
tudes away, He went up on the mountain
by Himself to pray. Now when evening
came, He was alone there. 24But the boat
was now in the middle of the sea,[a] tossed
by the waves, for the wind was contrary.
25Now in the fourth watch of the night
Jesus went to them, walking on the sea.
26And when the disciples saw Him walk-
ing on the sea, they were troubled, saying,
"It is a ghost!" And they cried out for fear.
27But immediately Jesus spoke to them,
saying, "Be of good cheer! It is I; do not be
afraid."
28And Peter answered Him and said,
"Lord, if it is You, command me to come to
You on the water."
29So He said, "Come." And when Peter
had come down out of the boat, he walked
on the water to go to Jesus. 30But when he
saw that the wind *was* boisterous,[a] he was
afraid; and beginning to sink he cried out,
saying, "Lord, save me!"
31And immediately Jesus stretched out
His hand and caught him, and said to him,
"O you of little faith, why did you doubt?"
32And when they got into the boat, the
wind ceased.
33Then those who were in the boat came
and[a] worshiped Him, saying, "Truly You
are the Son of God."

Many Touch Him and Are Made Well

34When they had crossed over, they
came to the land of[a] Gen·nes′a·ret. 35And
when the men of that place recognized
Him, they sent out into all that surround-

14:24 [a]NU-Text reads *many furlongs away from the land.* 14:30 [a]NU-Text brackets *that* and *boisterous* as disputed. 14:33 [a]NU-Text omits *came and.* 14:34 [a]NU-Text reads *came to land at.*

ing region, brought to Him all who were
sick, 36and begged Him that they might
only touch the hem of His garment. And as
many as touched *it* were made perfectly
well.

CHAPTER 15

Defilement Comes from Within

Then the scribes and Phar′i·sees who
were from Jerusalem came to Jesus, saying,
2"Why do Your disciples transgress the tra-
dition of the elders? For they do not wash
their hands when they eat bread."
3He answered and said to them, "Why
do you also transgress the commandment
of God because of your tradition? 4For God
commanded, saying, *'Honor your father
and your mother';*[a] and, *'He who curses
father or mother, let him be put to death.'*[b]
5But you say, 'Whoever says to his father or
mother, "Whatever profit you might have
received from me *is* a gift *to God*"— 6then
he need not honor his father or mother.'[a]
Thus you have made the commandment[b]
of God of no effect by your tradition. 7Hyp-
ocrites! Well did Ī·sāi′ah prophesy about
you, saying:

8 *'These people draw near to Me with*
their mouth,
And[a] *honor Me with their lips,*
But their heart is far from Me.
9 *And in vain they worship Me,*
Teaching as doctrines the
commandments of men.'"[a]

10When He had called the multitude to
Himself, He said to them, "Hear and under-
stand: 11Not what goes into the mouth de-
files a man; but what comes out of the
mouth, this defiles a man."
12Then His disciples came and said to
Him, "Do You know that the Phar′i·sees
were offended when they heard this say-
ing?"
13But He answered and said, "Every
plant which My heavenly Father has not
planted will be uprooted. 14Let them alone.
They are blind leaders of the blind. And if
the blind leads the blind, both will fall into
a ditch."
15Then Peter answered and said to Him,
"Explain this parable to us."
16So Jesus said, "Are you also still with-
out understanding? 17Do you not yet
understand that whatever enters the
mouth goes into the stomach and is elimi-
nated? 18But those things which proceed
out of the mouth come from the heart, and
they defile a man. 19For out of the heart
proceed evil thoughts, murders, adulter-

15:4 [a]Exodus 20:12; Deuteronomy 5:16 [b]Exodus 21:17
15:6 [a]NU-Text omits *or mother.* [b]NU-Text reads *word.*
15:8 [a]NU-Text omits *draw near to Me with their mouth, And.* 15:9 [a]Isaiah 29:13

15:2 tradition of the elders: The interpretive guide to Scripture passed down by the rabbis. It was supposed to ensure that one kept God's law. The accusation against the disciples had nothing to do with hygiene. The rules dealt with ceremonial hand washings, required in Jewish worship (see Lev. 22:4–6). Matthew did not explain these customs which were familiar to his Jewish readers. Mark's Gentile audience required explanation (see Mark 7:2–4).

15:3–6 Jesus showed that their **tradition** actually allowed them to disobey God's law. **God commanded** that a person take care of the needs of his aged parents (v. 4). Their tradition said that a person was released from this obligation if he declared his wealth a **gift to God** (v. 5). However, the tradition allowed one merely to utter the declaration and then to continue holding the money for his own use, instead of actually using it for religious purposes. In addition to condemning hypocrisy, this passage indicates that we are expected to provide for our parents' needs—both financial and physical—whenever necessary.

15:12–14 Israel was often referred to as the **plant** sustained by God (see Luke 13:6–9). Jesus claimed that the Pharisees would be **uprooted** because they were not truly God's people. These religious leaders were **blind** to spiritual truth because they refused to accept Jesus.

ies, fornications, thefts, false witness, blas-
phemies. 20These are *the things* which defile
a man, but to eat with unwashed hands
does not defile a man."

A Gentile Shows Her Faith

21Then Jesus went out from there and
departed to the region of Tȳre and Sī'don.
22And behold, a woman of Cā'naan came
from that region and cried out to Him, say-
ing, "Have mercy on me, O Lord, Son of
David! My daughter is severely demon-
possessed."

23But He answered her not a word.

And His disciples came and urged Him,
saying, "Send her away, for she cries out
after us."

24But He answered and said, "I was not
sent except to the lost sheep of the house of
Israel."

25Then she came and worshiped Him,
saying, "Lord, help me!"

26But He answered and said, "It is not
good to take the children's bread and
throw *it* to the little dogs."

27And she said, "Yes, Lord, yet even the
little dogs eat the crumbs which fall from
their masters' table."

28Then Jesus answered and said to her,
"O woman, great *is* your faith! Let it be to
you as you desire." And her daughter was
healed from that very hour.

Jesus Heals Great Multitudes

29Jesus departed from there, skirted the
Sea of Galilee, and went up on the moun-
tain and sat down there. 30Then great mul-
titudes came to Him, having with them *the*
lame, blind, mute, maimed, and many oth-
ers; and they laid them down at Jesus' feet,
and He healed them. 31So the multitude
marveled when they saw *the* mute speak-
ing, *the* maimed made whole, *the* lame
walking, and *the* blind seeing; and they
glorified the God of Israel.

Feeding the Four Thousand

32Now Jesus called His disciples to *Him-
self* and said, "I have compassion on the
multitude, because they have now con-
tinued with Me three days and have
nothing to eat. And I do not want to send
them away hungry, lest they faint on the
way."

33Then His disciples said to Him,
"Where could we get enough bread in the
wilderness to fill such a great multitude?"

34Jesus said to them, "How many loaves
do you have?"

And they said, "Seven, and a few little
fish."

35So He commanded the multitude to sit
down on the ground. 36And He took the
seven loaves and the fish and gave thanks,
broke *them* and gave *them* to His disciples;
and the disciples *gave* to the multitude. 37So
they all ate and were filled, and they took
up seven large baskets full of the frag-
ments that were left. 38Now those who ate
were four thousand men, besides women
and children. 39And He sent away the mul-
titude, got into the boat, and came to the
region of Mag'da·la.[a]

CHAPTER 16

The Pharisees and Sadducees Seek a Sign

Then the Phar'i·sees and Sad'dū·cees
came, and testing Him asked that He
would show them a sign from heaven. 2He
answered and said to them, "When it is
evening you say, '*It will be* fair weather, for

15:39 [a]NU-Text reads *Magadan*.

15:26 Jesus pictures **children** sitting at the dining table with their pet dogs on the floor below them. The children will be fed first, then the dogs, who must wait their turn. The gospel must first be preached to the Jews, then to the Gentiles. Jesus makes this statement to test the woman's faith and humility. **little dogs**: Puppies. Perhaps Jesus softened the abusive term "dogs" that Jews often used for Gentiles (see Phil. 3:2).

the sky is red'; 3and in the morning, *'It will
be* foul weather today, for the sky is red and
threatening.' Hypocrites![a] You know how
to discern the face of the sky, but you can-
not *discern* the signs of the times. 4A wicked
and adulterous generation seeks after a
sign, and no sign shall be given to it except
the sign of the prophet[a] Jonah." And He
left them and departed.

The Leaven of the Pharisees and Sadducees

5Now when His disciples had come to
the other side, they had forgotten to take
bread. 6Then Jesus said to them, "Take
heed and beware of the leaven of the
Phar'i·sees and the Sad'dū·cees."
7And they reasoned among themselves,
saying, *"It is* because we have taken no
bread."
8But Jesus, being aware of *it,* said to
them, "O you of little faith, why do you
reason among yourselves because you
have brought no bread?[a] 9Do you not yet
understand, or remember the five loaves of
the five thousand and how many baskets
you took up? 10Nor the seven loaves of the
four thousand and how many large bas-
kets you took up? 11How is it you do not
understand that I did not speak to you con-
cerning bread?—*but* to beware of the
leaven of the Phar'i·sees and Sad'dū·cees."
12Then they understood that He did not tell
them to beware of the leaven of bread, but
of the doctrine of the Phar'i·sees and
Sad'dū·cees.

Peter Confesses Jesus as the Christ

13When Jesus came into the region of
Caes·a·rē'a Phi·lip'pī, He asked His disci-
ples, saying, "Who do men say that I, the
Son of Man, am?"
14So they said, "Some *say* John the Bap-
tist, some E·lī'jah, and others Jer·e·mī'ah
or one of the prophets."
15He said to them, "But who do you say
that I am?"
16Simon Peter answered and said, "You
are the Christ, the Son of the living God."
17Jesus answered and said to him,
"Blessed are you, Simon Bar-Jō'nah, for
flesh and blood has not revealed *this* to
you, but My Father who is in heaven.
18And I also say to you that you are Peter,
and on this rock I will build My church,
and the gates of Hā'dēs shall not prevail
against it. 19And I will give you the keys of
the kingdom of heaven, and whatever you
bind on earth will be bound in heaven, and
whatever you loose on earth will be
loosed[a] in heaven."
20Then He commanded His disciples
that they should tell no one that He was
Jesus the Christ.

Jesus Predicts His Death and Resurrection

21From that time Jesus began to show to
His disciples that He must go to Jerusalem,
and suffer many things from the elders
and chief priests and scribes, and be killed,
and be raised the third day.

16:3 [a]NU-Text omits *Hypocrites.* 16:4 [a]NU-Text omits *the prophet.* 16:8 [a]NU-Text reads *you have no bread.* 16:19 [a]Or *will have been bound . . . will have been loosed*

16:16–18 By calling Jesus **the Christ**, Peter acknowledged that He was Israel's promised Savior; by calling Him **Son of . . . God**, He acknowledged His divine power (see 14:33). **Bar-Jonah**: Son of Jonah or John. No mere human made of **flesh and blood**, but the **Father** Himself gave Peter this insight. **Peter** is the English translation of the Greek *Petros*, meaning "stone" or "rock"; the Aramaic equivalent is Cephas (see John 1:42). The **church** is built on **this rock** (petra, a large mass of stone). This could refer to Peter and the apostles, who witnessed Christ's resurrection and first preached the gospel (see Eph. 3:20). The different Greek words and the preceding verse suggest, however, that the bedrock is Peter's statement of faith in v. 16: that Jesus is God and Messiah. Ultimately it is He Himself who builds His church so that even the **gates of Hades** and all of the powers of evil will not be able to stop it.

22Then Peter took Him aside and began
to rebuke Him, saying, "Far be it from You,
Lord; this shall not happen to You!"
23But He turned and said to Peter, "Get
behind Me, Satan! You are an offense to
Me, for you are not mindful of the things of
God, but the things of men."

Take Up the Cross and Follow Him

24Then Jesus said to His disciples, "If
anyone desires to come after Me, let him
deny himself, and take up his cross, and
follow Me. 25For whoever desires to save
his life will lose it, but whoever loses his
life for My sake will find it. 26For what
profit is it to a man if he gains the whole
world, and loses his own soul? Or what
will a man give in exchange for his soul?
27For the Son of Man will come in the glory
of His Father with His angels, and then
He will reward each according to his
works.

Jesus Transfigured on the Mount

28Assuredly, I say to you, there are some
standing here who shall not taste death till
they see the Son of Man coming in His
kingdom."

CHAPTER 17

Now after six days Jesus took Peter,
James, and John his brother, led them up
on a high mountain by themselves; 2and
He was transfigured before them. His face
shone like the sun, and His clothes became
as white as the light. 3And behold, Moses
and E·lī′jah appeared to them, talking with
Him. 4Then Peter answered and said to
Jesus, "Lord, it is good for us to be here; if
You wish, let us[a] make here three taberna-
cles: one for You, one for Moses, and one
for E·lī′jah."
5While he was still speaking, behold, a
bright cloud overshadowed them; and
suddenly a voice came out of the cloud,
saying, "This is My beloved Son, in whom
I am well pleased. Hear Him!" 6And when
the disciples heard *it*, they fell on their
faces and were greatly afraid. 7But Jesus
came and touched them and said, "Arise,
and do not be afraid." 8When they had

Jesus Loves the Little Ones

Jerry and Jack Schreur

Grandpa Jim is on the board of his church. People need to see him. But he aggravates some of the people at church. Why? Because when they are looking all over for him after the service, he is not available. They invariably find him in his grandson's Sunday school classroom (with Mom and Dad's permission). He will be sprawled on the floor, eye-to-eye with little Christopher, listening to an account of a trip to the supermarket with his mom. This is his grandson's time, and he doesn't let anyone rob him of it. He feels that he is applying these words of Christ: "Let the little children come to Me, and do not forbid them; for of such is the kingdom of heaven" (Matt. 19:14). Jim feels that if Jesus esteemed the little ones, so should he.

Creative grandparents build time into their schedules to listen to their grandchildren. One grandmother likes to take hers "out to lunch," often to a place of the child's choosing. The child who is given the opportunity to choose is being sent an important message about her worth, her value as a person. Besides, these lunch dates open up wonderful opportunities for conversation, and the most amazing things may surface. ✦

17:4 aNU-Text reads *I will.*

lifted up their eyes, they saw no one but
Jesus only.
9Now as they came down from the
mountain, Jesus commanded them, say-
ing, "Tell the vision to no one until the Son
of Man is risen from the dead."
10And His disciples asked Him, saying,
"Why then do the scribes say that E·lī'jah
must come first?"
11Jesus answered and said to them, "In-
deed, E·lī'jah is coming first[a] and will re-
store all things. 12But I say to you that
E·lī'jah has come already, and they did not
know him but did to him whatever they
wished. Likewise the Son of Man is also
about to suffer at their hands." 13Then the
disciples understood that He spoke to
them of John the Baptist.

A Boy Is Healed

14And when they had come to the multi-
tude, a man came to Him, kneeling down
to Him and saying, 15"Lord, have mercy on
my son, for he is an epileptic[a] and suffers
severely; for he often falls into the fire and
often into the water. 16So I brought him to
Your disciples, but they could not cure
him."
17Then Jesus answered and said, "O
faithless and perverse generation, how
long shall I be with you? How long shall I
bear with you? Bring him here to Me."
18And Jesus rebuked the demon, and it
came out of him; and the child was cured
from that very hour.
19Then the disciples came to Jesus pri-
vately and said, "Why could we not cast it
out?"
20So Jesus said to them, "Because of your
unbelief;[a] for assuredly, I say to you, if you
have faith as a mustard seed, you will say
to this mountain, 'Move from here to
there,' and it will move; and nothing will
be impossible for you. 21However, this
kind does not go out except by prayer and
fasting."[a]

Jesus Again Predicts His Death and Resurrection

22Now while they were staying[a] in Gali-
lee, Jesus said to them, "The Son of Man is
about to be betrayed into the hands of
men, 23and they will kill Him, and the third
day He will be raised up." And they were
exceedingly sorrowful.

Peter and His Master Pay Their Taxes

24When they had come to Ca·per'-
na·um,[a] those who received the *temple* tax
came to Peter and said, "Does your
Teacher not pay the *temple* tax?"
25He said, "Yes."
And when he had come into the house,
Jesus anticipated him, saying, "What do
you think, Simon? From whom do the
kings of the earth take customs or taxes,
from their sons or from strangers?"
26Peter said to Him, "From strangers."
Jesus said to him, "Then the sons are
free. 27Nevertheless, lest we offend them,
go to the sea, cast in a hook, and take the
fish that comes up first. And when you
have opened its mouth, you will find a
piece of money;[a] take that and give it to
them for Me and you."

CHAPTER 18

Who Is the Greatest?

At that time the disciples came to Jesus,
saying, "Who then is greatest in the king-
dom of heaven?"
2Then Jesus called a little child to Him,
set him in the midst of them, 3and said,
"Assuredly, I say to you, unless you are
converted and become as little children,
you will by no means enter the kingdom of
heaven. 4Therefore whoever humbles him-
self as this little child is the greatest in the
kingdom of heaven. 5Whoever receives
one little child like this in My name re-
ceives Me.

17:11 [a]NU-Text omits *first.* 17:15 [a]Literally *moon-struck* 17:20 [a]NU-Text reads *little faith.* 17:21 [a]NU-Text omits this verse. 17:22 [a]NU-Text reads *gathering together.* 17:24 [a]NU-Text reads *Capharnaum* (here and elsewhere). 17:27 [a]Greek *stater,* the exact amount to pay the temple tax (didrachma) for two

Beacons of Faith

Jay Kesler

In today's world, grandchildren—and their parents—need the support of grandparents who have walked with God through adversity and struggle. They need to see what faith in God can do when times are difficult, what supernatural strength and endurance the Spirit gives in time of need.

Grandparents can be that for their grandchildren—a beacon of faith. As they offer time and security and acceptance and love to their grandchildren, they demonstrate by living example the availability and faithfulness of God. ✦

Jesus Warns of Offenses

6"Whoever causes one of these little
ones who believe in Me to sin, it would be
better for him if a millstone were hung
around his neck, and he were drowned in
the depth of the sea. 7Woe to the world be-
cause of offenses! For offenses must come,
but woe to that man by whom the offense
comes!

8"If your hand or foot causes you to sin,
cut it off and cast *it* from you. It is better for
you to enter into life lame or maimed,
rather than having two hands or two feet,
to be cast into the everlasting fire. 9And if
your eye causes you to sin, pluck it out and
cast *it* from you. It is better for you to enter
into life with one eye, rather than having
two eyes, to be cast into hell fire.

The Parable of the Lost Sheep

10"Take heed that you do not despise
one of these little ones, for I say to you that
in heaven their angels always see the face
of My Father who is in heaven. 11For the
Son of Man has come to save that which
was lost.[a]

12"What do you think? If a man has a
hundred sheep, and one of them goes
astray, does he not leave the ninety-nine
and go to the mountains to seek the one
that is straying? 13And if he should find it,
assuredly, I say to you, he rejoices more
over that *sheep* than over the ninety-nine
that did not go astray. 14Even so it is not the
will of your Father who is in heaven that
one of these little ones should perish.

Dealing with a Sinning Brother

15"Moreover if your brother sins against
you, go and tell him his fault between you
and him alone. If he hears you, you have
gained your brother. 16But if he will not
hear, take with you one or two more, that
'by the mouth of two or three witnesses
every word may be established.'[a] 17And if
he refuses to hear them, tell *it* to the
church. But if he refuses even to hear the
church, let him be to you like a heathen
and a tax collector.

18"Assuredly, I say to you, whatever you
bind on earth will be bound in heaven, and
whatever you loose on earth will be loosed
in heaven.

19"Again I say[a] to you that if two of you
agree on earth concerning anything that
they ask, it will be done for them by My
Father in heaven. 20For where two or three

18:11 [a]NU-Text omits this verse. 18:16 [a]Deuteronomy 19:15 18:19 [a]NU-Text and M-Text read *Again, assuredly, I say.*

18:17 Only after all efforts have failed to win a sinning Christian brother back should he be excluded from the church.

18:20 Jewish regulations required the presence of at least 10 males to establish a synagogue, but **two or three** believers establishes the Christian fellowship, because Christ is in their midst.

are gathered together in My name, I am there in the midst of them."

The Parable of the Unforgiving Servant

21Then Peter came to Him and said, "Lord, how often shall my brother sin against me, and I forgive him? Up to seven times?"

22Jesus said to him, "I do not say to you, up to seven times, but up to seventy times seven. 23Therefore the kingdom of heaven is like a certain king who wanted to settle accounts with his servants. 24And when he had begun to settle accounts, one was brought to him who owed him ten thousand talents. 25But as he was not able to pay, his master commanded that he be sold, with his wife and children and all that he had, and that payment be made. 26The servant therefore fell down before him, saying, 'Master, have patience with me, and I will pay you all.' 27Then the master of that servant was moved with compassion, released him, and forgave him the debt.

28"But that servant went out and found one of his fellow servants who owed him a hundred denarii; and he laid hands on him and took *him* by the throat, saying, 'Pay me what you owe!' 29So his fellow servant fell down at his feet[a] and begged him, saying, 'Have patience with me, and I will pay you all.'[b] 30And he would not, but went and threw him into prison till he should pay the debt. 31So when his fellow servants saw what had been done, they were very grieved, and came and told their master all that had been done. 32Then his master, after he had called him, said to him, 'You wicked servant! I forgave you all that debt because you begged me. 33Should you not also have had compassion on your fellow servant, just as I had pity on you?' 34And his master was angry, and delivered him to the torturers until he should pay all that was due to him.

35"So My heavenly Father also will do to you if each of you, from his heart, does not forgive his brother his trespasses."[a]

CHAPTER 19

Marriage and Divorce

Now it came to pass, when Jesus had finished these sayings, *that* He departed from Galilee and came to the region of Judea beyond the Jordan. 2And great multitudes followed Him, and He healed them there.

3The Phar'i·sees also came to Him, testing Him, and saying to Him, "Is it lawful for a man to divorce his wife for *just* any reason?"

4And He answered and said to them, "Have you not read that He who made[a] *them* at the beginning *'made them male and female,'*[b] 5and said, *'For this reason a man shall leave his father and mother and be joined to his wife, and the two shall become one flesh'*?[a] 6So then, they are no longer two but one flesh. Therefore what God has joined together, let not man separate."

7They said to Him, "Why then did Moses command to give a certificate of divorce, and to put her away?"

8He said to them, "Moses, because of the hardness of your hearts, permitted you to divorce your wives, but from the beginning it was not so. 9And I say to you, whoever divorces his wife, except for sexual immorality,[a] and marries another, commits adultery; and whoever marries her who is divorced commits adultery."

10His disciples said to Him, "If such is the case of the man with *his* wife, it is better not to marry."

Jesus Teaches on Celibacy

11But He said to them, "All cannot accept this saying, but only *those* to whom it has been given: 12For there are eunuchs

18:29 [a]NU-Text omits *at his feet.* [b]NU-Text and M-Text omit *all.* 18:35 [a]NU-Text omits *his trespasses.* 19:4 [a]NU-Text reads *created.* [b]Genesis 1:27; 5:2 19:5 [a]Genesis 2:24 19:9 [a]Or *fornication*

who were born thus from *their* mother's womb, and there are eunuchs who were made eunuchs by men, and there are eunuchs who have made themselves eunuchs for the kingdom of heaven's sake. He who is able to accept *it,* let him accept *it.*"

Jesus Blesses Little Children

13Then little children were brought to Him that He might put *His* hands on them and pray, but the disciples rebuked them. 14But Jesus said, "Let the little children come to Me, and do not forbid them; for of such is the kingdom of heaven." 15And He laid *His* hands on them and departed from there.

Jesus Counsels the Rich Young Ruler

16Now behold, one came and said to Him, "Good[a] Teacher, what good thing shall I do that I may have eternal life?"

17So He said to him, "Why do you call Me good?[a] No one *is* good but One, *that is,* God.[b] But if you want to enter into life, keep the commandments."

18He said to Him, "Which ones?"

Jesus said, "*'You shall not murder,' 'You shall not commit adultery,' 'You shall not steal,' 'You shall not bear false witness,'* 19*'Honor your father and your mother,'*[a] and, *'You shall love your neighbor as yourself.'*"[b]

20The young man said to Him, "All these things I have kept from my youth.[a] What do I still lack?"

21Jesus said to him, "If you want to be perfect, go, sell what you have and give to the poor, and you will have treasure in heaven; and come, follow Me."

22But when the young man heard that saying, he went away sorrowful, for he had great possessions.

With God All Things Are Possible

23Then Jesus said to His disciples, "Assuredly, I say to you that it is hard for a rich man to enter the kingdom of heaven. 24And again I say to you, it is easier for a camel to go through the eye of a needle than for a rich man to enter the kingdom of God."

25When His disciples heard *it,* they were greatly astonished, saying, "Who then can be saved?"

26But Jesus looked at *them* and said to them, "With men this is impossible, but with God all things are possible."

27Then Peter answered and said to Him, "See, we have left all and followed You. Therefore what shall we have?"

28So Jesus said to them, "Assuredly I say to you, that in the regeneration, when the Son of Man sits on the throne of His glory, you who have followed Me will also sit on twelve thrones, judging the twelve tribes of Israel. 29And everyone who has left houses or brothers or sisters or father or mother or wife[a] or children or

I pray that my children will remember that with You, God, all things are possible.

adapted from Matthew 19:26

19:16 [a]NU-Text omits *Good.* 19:17 [a]NU-Text reads *Why do you ask Me about what is good?* [b]NU-Text reads *There is One who is good.* 19:19 [a]Exodus 20:12–16; Deuteronomy 5:16–20 [b]Leviticus 19:18 19:20 [a]NU-Text omits *from my youth.* 19:29 [a]NU-Text omits *or wife.*

19:17 No one is good but . . . God: Jesus was not admitting sinfulness. He was rejecting this man's idea that he could earn salvation by doing good. Salvation is based on God's goodness, not ours. If a person could **keep the commandments**, he would be considered good—but except for Christ, no human being has.

19:21 to be perfect: He must give to God that complete loyalty demanded by the Ten Commandments (see Deut. 6:5). In his case this meant giving away his wealth. For every seeker it means giving up whatever is loved more than God. To be perfect in this sense means to be ready to give up what we love most if Christ asks for it.

lands, for My name's sake, shall receive a hundredfold, and inherit eternal life. 30But many *who are* first will be last, and the last first.

CHAPTER 20

The Parable of the Workers in the Vineyard

"For the kingdom of heaven is like a landowner who went out early in the morning to hire laborers for his vineyard. 2Now when he had agreed with the laborers for a denarius a day, he sent them into his vineyard. 3And he went out about the third hour and saw others standing idle in the marketplace, 4and said to them, 'You also go into the vineyard, and whatever is right I will give you.' So they went. 5Again he went out about the sixth and the ninth hour, and did likewise. 6And about the eleventh hour he went out and found others standing idle,[a] and said to them, 'Why have you been standing here idle all day?' 7They said to him, 'Because no one hired us.' He said to them, 'You also go into the vineyard, and whatever is right you will receive.'[a]

8"So when evening had come, the owner of the vineyard said to his steward, 'Call the laborers and give them *their* wages, beginning with the last to the first.' 9And when those came who *were hired* about the eleventh hour, they each received a denarius. 10But when the first came, they supposed that they would receive more; and they likewise received each a denarius. 11And when they had received *it,* they complained against the landowner, 12saying, 'These last *men* have worked *only* one hour, and you made them equal to us who have borne the burden and the heat of the day.' 13But he answered one of them and said, 'Friend, I am doing you no wrong. Did you not agree with me for a denarius? 14Take *what is* yours and go your way. I wish to give to this last man *the same* as to you. 15Is it not lawful for me to do what I wish with my own things? Or is your eye evil because I am good?' 16So the last will be first, and the first last. For many are called, but few chosen."[a]

Jesus a Third Time Predicts His Death and Resurrection

17Now Jesus, going up to Jerusalem, took the twelve disciples aside on the road and said to them, 18"Behold, we are going up to Jerusalem, and the Son of Man will be betrayed to the chief priests and to the scribes; and they will condemn Him to death, 19and deliver Him to the Gentiles to mock and to scourge and to crucify. And the third day He will rise again."

Greatness Is Serving

20Then the mother of Zeb'e·dee's sons came to Him with her sons, kneeling down and asking something from Him.

21And He said to her, "What do you wish?"

She said to Him, "Grant that these two sons of mine may sit, one on Your right hand and the other on the left, in Your kingdom."

22But Jesus answered and said, "You do not know what you ask. Are you able to drink the cup that I am about to drink, and be baptized with the baptism that I am baptized with?"[a]

They said to Him, "We are able."

23So He said to them, "You will indeed drink My cup, and be baptized with the baptism that I am baptized with;[a] but to sit on My right hand and on My left is not Mine to give, but *it is for those* for whom it is prepared by My Father."

24And when the ten heard *it,* they were greatly displeased with the two brothers. 25But Jesus called them to *Himself* and said,

20:6 [a]NU-Text omits *idle.* 20:7 [a]NU-Text omits the last clause of this verse. 20:16 [a]NU-Text omits the last sentence of this verse. 20:22 [a]NU-Text omits *and be baptized with the baptism that I am baptized with.* 20:23 [a]NU-Text omits *and be baptized with the baptism that I am baptized with.*

"You know that the rulers of the Gentiles
lord it over them, and those who are great
exercise authority over them. 26Yet it shall
not be so among you; but whoever desires
to become great among you, let him be
your servant. 27And whoever desires to be
first among you, let him be your slave—
28just as the Son of Man did not come to be
served, but to serve, and to give His life a
ransom for many."

Two Blind Men Receive Their Sight

29Now as they went out of Jericho, a
great multitude followed Him. 30And be-
hold, two blind men sitting by the road,
when they heard that Jesus was passing
by, cried out, saying, "Have mercy on us,
O Lord, Son of David!"

31Then the multitude warned them that
they should be quiet; but they cried out all
the more, saying, "Have mercy on us,
O Lord, Son of David!"

32So Jesus stood still and called them,
and said, "What do you want Me to do for
you?"

33They said to Him, "Lord, that our eyes
may be opened." 34So Jesus had compas-
sion and touched their eyes. And immedi-
ately their eyes received sight, and they
followed Him.

CHAPTER 21

The Triumphal Entry

Now when they drew near Jerusalem,
and came to Beth'pha·gē,[a] at the Mount of
Olives, then Jesus sent two disciples, 2say-
ing to them, "Go into the village opposite
you, and immediately you will find a don-
key tied, and a colt with her. Loose *them*
and bring *them* to Me. 3And if anyone says
anything to you, you shall say, 'The Lord
has need of them,' and immediately he will
send them."

4All[a] this was done that it might be ful-
filled which was spoken by the prophet,
saying:

5 *"Tell the daughter of Zion,*
'Behold, your King is coming to you,
Lowly, and sitting on a donkey,
A colt, the foal of a donkey.' "[a]

6So the disciples went and did as Jesus
commanded them. 7They brought the
donkey and the colt, laid their clothes on
them, and set *Him*[a] on them. 8And a very
great multitude spread their clothes on
the road; others cut down branches from
the trees and spread *them* on the road.
9Then the multitudes who went before
and those who followed cried out, say-
ing:

"Hō·san'na to the Son of David!
'Blessed is He who comes in the name
of the Lord!'[a]
Hō·san'na in the highest!"

10And when He had come into Jerusa-
lem, all the city was moved, saying, "Who
is this?"

11So the multitudes said, "This is Jesus,
the prophet from Nazareth of Galilee."

Jesus Cleanses the Temple

12Then Jesus went into the temple of
God[a] and drove out all those who bought
and sold in the temple, and overturned the
tables of the money changers and the seats
of those who sold doves. 13And He said to
them, "It is written, *'My house shall be*

21:1 [a]M-Text reads *Bethsphage.* 21:4 [a]NU-Text omits *All.* 21:5 [a]Zechariah 9:9 21:7 [a]NU-Text reads *and He sat.* 21:9 [a]Psalm 118:26 21:12 [a]NU-Text omits *of God.*

21:1–11 Verse 4 indicates that Jesus intentionally fulfilled the prophecy of Zechariah (v. 5) by entering Jerusalem as the King coming on a humble **colt** (v. 7) to give Himself for His people.

STEEL AND VELVET

Ron Lee Davis

A man of steel, Jesus confronted the religious evil of His day. He called the corrupt religious leaders vipers, hypocrites, white-washed tombs full of dead bones. Like steel, He cleared the money changers out of the temple. Like steel, He confronted Peter, told him he could be a rock, that he should be consistent, that he should stop wavering.

Yet it was a man of velvet who wept over the death of His friend Lazarus. It was the velvet in the man that gave Him compassion for a woman caught in adultery. It was the velvet in Him that led Him to reach out to the little children who crowded around Him. It was the velvet in Him that compelled Him, just hours before the Cross, to kneel before His disciples and wash their feet.

Our task as mentors is to imitate the Master Mentor, Jesus Himself. Our lives must be marked both with Christ's toughness and His tenderness, both His steel and His velvet. This means that those of us who are tender Christians will have to become a bit more tough, and those of us who are tough will have to learn a little more tenderness.

The tender Christian who avoids building toughness into his or her life soon becomes little more than a weak sentimentalist. The tough Christian who has no use for tenderness inevitably hardens into a harshly critical Pharisee. To be Christlike, we must have these complementary qualities in dynamic balance in our lives. ✦

called a house of prayer,'[a] but you have
made it a *'den of thieves.'"*[b]
[14]Then *the* blind and *the* lame came to
Him in the temple, and He healed them.
[15]But when the chief priests and scribes
saw the wonderful things that He did, and
the children crying out in the temple and
saying, "Hō·san'na to the Son of David!"
they were indignant [16]and said to Him,
"Do You hear what these are saying?"

And Jesus said to them, "Yes. Have you never read,

'Out of the mouth of babes and
nursing infants
You have perfected praise'?"[a]

[17]Then He left them and went out of the
city to Beth'a·ny, and He lodged there.

The Fig Tree Withered

[18]Now in the morning, as He returned to
the city, He was hungry. [19]And seeing a fig
tree by the road, He came to it and found
nothing on it but leaves, and said to it, "Let
no fruit grow on you ever again." Immediately the fig tree withered away.

21:13 [a]Isaiah 56:7 [b]Jeremiah 7:11 21:16 [a]Psalm 8:2

21:18–22 Cursing the **fig tree** was an enacted parable describing Jesus' rejection at Jerusalem. The tree represented the hypocritical Jewish leaders. Its **leaves** symbolized outward religious observances. **found nothing**: Lack of fruit stood for their rejection of Jesus. Such failure called for judgment. Jesus used the amazement of the disciples as an opportunity to teach the importance of **faith** in **prayer** to release the power of God (see 17:19, 20).

The Lesson of the Withered Fig Tree

[20]And when the disciples saw *it*, they
marveled, saying, "How did the fig tree
wither away so soon?"
[21]So Jesus answered and said to them,
"Assuredly, I say to you, if you have faith
and do not doubt, you will not only do
what was done to the fig tree, but also if
you say to this mountain, 'Be removed and
be cast into the sea,' it will be done. [22]And
whatever things you ask in prayer, believ-
ing, you will receive."

Jesus' Authority Questioned

[23]Now when He came into the temple,
the chief priests and the elders of the peo-
ple confronted Him as He was teaching,
and said, "By what authority are You do-
ing these things? And who gave You this
authority?"
[24]But Jesus answered and said to them,
"I also will ask you one thing, which if you
tell Me, I likewise will tell you by what au-
thority I do these things: [25]The baptism of
John—where was it from? From heaven or
from men?"

And they reasoned among themselves,
saying, "If we say, 'From heaven,' He will
say to us, 'Why then did you not believe
him?' [26]But if we say, 'From men,' we fear
the multitude, for all count John as a
prophet." [27]So they answered Jesus and
said, "We do not know."

And He said to them, "Neither will I
tell you by what authority I do these
things.

The Parable of the Two Sons

[28]"But what do you think? A man had
two sons, and he came to the first and said,
'Son, go, work today in my vineyard.' [29]He
answered and said, 'I will not,' but after-
ward he regretted it and went. [30]Then he
came to the second and said likewise. And
he answered and said, 'I *go,* sir,' but he did
not go. [31]Which of the two did the will of
his father?"

They said to Him, "The first."

Jesus said to them, "Assuredly, I say to
you that tax collectors and harlots enter the
kingdom of God before you. [32]For John
came to you in the way of righteousness,
and you did not believe him; but tax col-
lectors and harlots believed him; and when
you saw *it,* you did not afterward relent
and believe him.

The Parable of the Wicked Vinedressers

[33]"Hear another parable: There was a
certain landowner who planted a vineyard
and set a hedge around it, dug a winepress
in it and built a tower. And he leased it to
vinedressers and went into a far country.
[34]Now when vintage-time drew near, he
sent his servants to the vinedressers, that
they might receive its fruit. [35]And the vine-
dressers took his servants, beat one, killed
one, and stoned another. [36]Again he sent
other servants, more than the first, and
they did likewise to them. [37]Then last of all
he sent his son to them, saying, 'They will
respect my son.' [38]But when the vine-
dressers saw the son, they said among
themselves, 'This is the heir. Come, let us
kill him and seize his inheritance.' [39]So
they took him and cast *him* out of the vine-
yard and killed *him.*
[40]"Therefore, when the owner of the

21:23–27 By what authority? The **chief priests** were in charge of the temples. They received their authority by birth into aristocratic priestly families and by appointment. Neither John nor Jesus had such credentials. **these things**: Especially the cleansing of the temple. Jesus' question (v. 25) offered the Jewish leaders a chance to recognize the work of both John and Jesus as from God (see v. 32). John had said that Jesus was greater than he (see 3:11–15). If **John** had God's authority, then Jesus must have had it to a much greater degree. At this time Jesus was making no effort to conceal His claim to be God's Son (see v. 37).

vineyard comes, what will he do to those
vinedressers?"
41They said to Him, "He will destroy
those wicked men miserably, and lease
his vineyard to other vinedressers who
will render to him the fruits in their sea-
sons."
42Jesus said to them, "Have you never
read in the Scriptures:

'The stone which the builders rejected
Has become the chief cornerstone.
This was the LORD*'s doing,*
And it is marvelous in our eyes'?[a]

43"Therefore I say to you, the kingdom
of God will be taken from you and given to
a nation bearing the fruits of it. 44And who-
ever falls on this stone will be broken; but
on whomever it falls, it will grind him to
powder."
45Now when the chief priests and
Phar'i·sees heard His parables, they per-
ceived that He was speaking of them. 46But
when they sought to lay hands on Him,
they feared the multitudes, because they
took Him for a prophet.

CHAPTER 22

The Parable of the Wedding Feast

And Jesus answered and spoke to them
again by parables and said: 2"The kingdom
of heaven is like a certain king who
arranged a marriage for his son, 3and sent
out his servants to call those who were in-
vited to the wedding; and they were not
willing to come. 4Again, he sent out other
servants, saying, 'Tell those who are in-
vited, "See, I have prepared my dinner; my
oxen and fatted cattle *are* killed, and all
things *are* ready. Come to the wedding." '
5But they made light of it and went their
ways, one to his own farm, another to his
business. 6And the rest seized his servants,
treated *them* spitefully, and killed *them*.
7But when the king heard *about it*, he was
furious. And he sent out his armies, de-
stroyed those murderers, and burned up
their city. 8Then he said to his servants,
'The wedding is ready, but those who were
invited were not worthy. 9Therefore go into
the highways, and as many as you find, in-
vite to the wedding.' 10So those servants
went out into the highways and gathered
together all whom they found, both bad
and good. And the wedding *hall* was filled
with guests.
11"But when the king came in to see the
guests, he saw a man there who did not
have on a wedding garment. 12So he said to
him, 'Friend, how did you come in here
without a wedding garment?' And he was
speechless. 13Then the king said to the ser-
vants, 'Bind him hand and foot, take him
away, and[a] cast *him* into outer darkness;
there will be weeping and gnashing of
teeth.'
14"For many are called, but few *are* cho-
sen."

The Pharisees: Is It Lawful to Pay Taxes to Caesar?

15Then the Phar'i·sees went and plotted
how they might entangle Him in *His* talk.
16And they sent to Him their disciples with
the He·rō'di·ans, saying, "Teacher, we
know that You are true, and teach the way
of God in truth; nor do You care about any-
one, for You do not regard the person of
men. 17Tell us, therefore, what do You
think? Is it lawful to pay taxes to Caesar, or
not?"
18But Jesus perceived their wickedness,
and said, "Why do you test Me, *you* hyp-
ocrites? 19Show Me the tax money."
So they brought Him a denarius.
20And He said to them, "Whose image
and inscription *is* this?"
21They said to Him, "Caesar's."
And He said to them, "Render therefore
to Caesar the things that are Caesar's, and
to God the things that are God's." 22When
they had heard *these words*, they marveled,
and left Him and went their way.

21:42 [a]Psalm 118:22, 23 22:13 [a]NU-Text omits *take him away, and*.

The Sadducees: What About the Resurrection?

23The same day the Sad′dū·cees, who
say there is no resurrection, came to Him
and asked Him, 24saying: "Teacher, Moses
said that if a man dies, having no children,
his brother shall marry his wife and raise
up offspring for his brother. 25Now there
were with us seven brothers. The first died
after he had married, and having no off-
spring, left his wife to his brother. 26Like-
wise the second also, and the third, even to
the seventh. 27Last of all the woman died
also. 28Therefore, in the resurrection,
whose wife of the seven will she be? For
they all had her."
29Jesus answered and said to them, "You
are mistaken, not knowing the Scriptures
nor the power of God. 30For in the resurrec-
tion they neither marry nor are given in
marriage, but are like angels of God[a] in
heaven. 31But concerning the resurrection
of the dead, have you not read what was
spoken to you by God, saying, 32*'I am the
God of Abraham, the God of Isaac, and the
God of Jacob'*?[a] God is not the God of
the dead, but of the living." 33And when
the multitudes heard *this,* they were aston-
ished at His teaching.

The Scribes: Which Is the First Commandment of All?

34But when the Phar′i·sees heard that He
had silenced the Sad′dū·cees, they gath-
ered together. 35Then one of them, a lawyer,
asked *Him a question,* testing Him, and say-
ing, 36"Teacher, which *is* the great com-
mandment in the law?"
37Jesus said to him, " *'You shall love the
LORD your God with all your heart, with all
your soul, and with all your mind.'*[a] 38This
is *the* first and great commandment. 39And
the second *is* like it: *'You shall love your
neighbor as yourself.'*[a] 40On these two com-
mandments hang all the Law and the
Prophets."

Jesus: How Can David Call His Descendant Lord?

41While the Phar′i·sees were gathered
together, Jesus asked them, 42saying,
"What do you think about the Christ?
Whose Son is He?"
They said to Him, "*The* Son of David."
43He said to them, "How then does Da-
vid in the Spirit call Him *'Lord,'* saying:

44 *'The LORD said to my Lord,*
"Sit at My right hand,
Till I make Your enemies Your
footstool" '?[a]

45If David then calls Him *'Lord,'* how is He
his Son?" 46And no one was able to answer
Him a word, nor from that day on did any-
one dare question Him anymore.

CHAPTER 23

Woe to the Scribes and Pharisees

Then Jesus spoke to the multitudes and
to His disciples, 2saying: "The scribes and
the Phar′i·sees sit in Moses' seat. 3There-
fore whatever they tell you to observe,[a]
that observe and do, but do not do accord-
ing to their works; for they say, and do not
do. 4For they bind heavy burdens, hard to
bear, and lay *them* on men's shoulders; but
they *themselves* will not move them with
one of their fingers. 5But all their works
they do to be seen by men. They make their
phylacteries broad and enlarge the borders
of their garments. 6They love the best
places at feasts, the best seats in the syna-

22:30 [a]NU-Text omits *of God.* 22:32 [a]Exodus 3:6, 15
22:37 [a]Deuteronomy 6:5 22:39 [a]Leviticus 19:18
22:44 [a]Psalm 110:1 23:3 [a]NU-Text omits *to observe.*

23:2, 3 sit in Moses' seat: As teachers of the Mosaic Law. **whatever they tell you**: "That is, all those things which they read out of the law and prophets, and all things which they teach consistently with them" (Adam Clarke). Jesus was not advising His followers to observe the false teachings of the Pharisees (see 16:12).

gogues, 7greetings in the marketplaces,
and to be called by men, 'Rabbi, Rabbi.'
8But you, do not be called 'Rabbi'; for One
is your Teacher, the Christ,[a] and you are all
brethren. 9Do not call anyone on earth your
father; for One is your Father, He who is in
heaven. 10And do not be called teachers;
for One is your Teacher, the Christ. 11But he
who is greatest among you shall be your
servant. 12And whoever exalts himself will
be humbled, and he who humbles himself
will be exalted.

13"But woe to you, scribes and Phar'-
i·sees, hypocrites! For you shut up the
kingdom of heaven against men; for you
neither go in *yourselves,* nor do you allow
those who are entering to go in. 14Woe to
you, scribes and Phar'i·sees, hypocrites!
For you devour widows' houses, and for a
pretense make long prayers. Therefore you
will receive greater condemnation.[a]

15"Woe to you, scribes and Phar'i·sees,
hypocrites! For you travel land and sea to
win one proselyte, and when he is won,
you make him twice as much a son of hell
as yourselves.

16"Woe to you, blind guides, who say,
'Whoever swears by the temple, it is noth-
ing; but whoever swears by the gold of the
temple, he is obliged *to perform it.*' 17Fools
and blind! For which is greater, the gold or
the temple that sanctifies[a] the gold? 18And,
'Whoever swears by the altar, it is nothing;
but whoever swears by the gift that is on it,
he is obliged *to perform it.*' 19Fools and
blind! For which is greater, the gift or the
altar that sanctifies the gift? 20Therefore he
who swears by the altar, swears by it and
by all things on it. 21He who swears by the
temple, swears by it and by Him who
dwells[a] in it. 22And he who swears by
heaven, swears by the throne of God and
by Him who sits on it.

23"Woe to you, scribes and Phar'i·sees,
hypocrites! For you pay tithe of mint and
anise and cummin, and have neglected the
weightier *matters* of the law: justice and
mercy and faith. These you ought to have
done, without leaving the others undone.
24Blind guides, who strain out a gnat and
swallow a camel!

25"Woe to you, scribes and Phar'i·sees,
hypocrites! For you cleanse the outside of
the cup and dish, but inside they are full of
extortion and self-indulgence.[a] 26Blind
Phar'i·see, first cleanse the inside of the
cup and dish, that the outside of them may
be clean also.

27"Woe to you, scribes and Phar'i·sees,
hypocrites! For you are like whitewashed
tombs which indeed appear beautiful out-
wardly, but inside are full of dead *men's*
bones and all uncleanness. 28Even so you
also outwardly appear righteous to men,
but inside you are full of hypocrisy and
lawlessness.

29"Woe to you, scribes and Phar'i·sees,
hypocrites! Because you build the tombs of
the prophets and adorn the monuments of
the righteous, 30and say, 'If we had lived
in the days of our fathers, we would not
have been partakers with them in the
blood of the prophets.'

31"Therefore you are witnesses against
yourselves that you are sons of those who
murdered the prophets. 32Fill up, then, the
measure of your fathers' *guilt.* 33Serpents,
brood of vipers! How can you escape the

23:8 [a]NU-Text omits *the Christ.* 23:14 [a]NU-Text omits this verse. 23:17 [a]NU-Text reads *sanctified.* 23:21 [a]M-Text reads *dwelt.* 23:25 [a]M-Text reads *unrighteousness.*

23:13, 14 kingdom of heaven: The salvation of God. The Pharisees not only exempted themselves from God's rule, they excluded others by trying to keep them from following Jesus. **Woe** means that God's judgment is upon these religious leaders because they are hypocrites—they claim to do good while they do evil. Each time this phrase is used (vv. 14–16, 23, 25, 27, 29) a different type of sinful hypocrisy is described. As mature Christians we must avoid becoming mired in legalism. When discipling young believers we should encourage them to seek the truth rather than simply following our example.

condemnation of hell? [34]Therefore, indeed, I send you prophets, wise men, and scribes: *some* of them you will kill and crucify, and *some* of them you will scourge in your synagogues and persecute from city to city, [35]that on you may come all the righteous blood shed on the earth, from the blood of righteous Abel to the blood of Zech·a·rī′ah, son of Ber·e·chī′ah, whom you murdered between the temple and the altar. [36]Assuredly, I say to you, all these things will come upon this generation.

Jesus Laments over Jerusalem

[37]"O Jerusalem, Jerusalem, the one who kills the prophets and stones those who are sent to her! How often I wanted to gather your children together, as a hen gathers her chicks under *her* wings, but you were not willing! [38]See! Your house is left to you desolate; [39]for I say to you, you shall see Me no more till you say, *'Blessed is He who comes in the name of the Lord!'* "[a]

CHAPTER 24

Jesus Predicts the Destruction of the Temple

Then Jesus went out and departed from the temple, and His disciples came up to show Him the buildings of the temple. [2]And Jesus said to them, "Do you not see all these things? Assuredly, I say to you, not *one* stone shall be left here upon another, that shall not be thrown down."

The Signs of the Times and the End of the Age

[3]Now as He sat on the Mount of Olives, the disciples came to Him privately, saying, "Tell us, when will these things be? And what *will be* the sign of Your coming, and of the end of the age?"

[4]And Jesus answered and said to them: "Take heed that no one deceives you. [5]For many will come in My name, saying, 'I am the Christ,' and will deceive many. [6]And you will hear of wars and rumors of wars. See that you are not troubled; for all[a] *these things* must come to pass, but the end is not yet. [7]For nation will rise against nation, and kingdom against kingdom. And there will be famines, pestilences,[a] and earthquakes in various places. [8]All these *are* the beginning of sorrows.

[9]"Then they will deliver you up to tribulation and kill you, and you will be hated by all nations for My name's sake. [10]And then many will be offended, will betray one another, and will hate one another. [11]Then many false prophets will rise up and deceive many. [12]And because lawlessness will abound, the love of many will grow cold. [13]But he who endures to the end shall be saved. [14]And this gospel of the kingdom will be preached in all the world as a witness to all the nations, and then the end will come.

The Great Tribulation

[15]"Therefore when you see the *'abomination of desolation,'*[a] spoken of by Daniel the prophet, standing in the holy place" (whoever reads, let him understand), [16]"then let those who are in Judea flee to the mountains. [17]Let him who is on the housetop not go down to take anything out of his house. [18]And let him who is in the field not go back to get his clothes.

23:39 [a]Psalm 118:26 24:6 [a]NU-Text omits *all.* 24:7 [a]NU-Text omits *pestilences.* 24:15 [a]Daniel 11:31; 12:11

24:15 Daniel prophesied that the **abomination of desolation** would be set up in the temple (see Dan. 11:31; 12:11). For Daniel, this could possibly refer to the heathen altar of Antiochus IV Epiphanes in 168 B.C. However, for Jesus' time it had a further fulfillment in the Roman armies which attacked Jerusalem in A.D. 70 (see Luke 21:20). Beyond this, many interpreters expect a yet future fulfillment when the Antichrist will exalt himself above God (see 2 Thess. 2:3, 4). **whoever reads**: The writer assumed that readers would know what his veiled reference meant.

19But woe to those who are pregnant and to
those who are nursing babies in those
days! 20And pray that your flight may not
be in winter or on the Sabbath. 21For then
there will be great tribulation, such as has
not been since the beginning of the world
until this time, no, nor ever shall be. 22And
unless those days were shortened, no flesh
would be saved; but for the elect's sake
those days will be shortened.

23"Then if anyone says to you, 'Look,
here *is* the Christ!' or 'There!' do not be-
lieve *it*. 24For false christs and false
prophets will rise and show great signs
and wonders to deceive, if possible, even
the elect. 25See, I have told you beforehand.

26"Therefore if they say to you, 'Look,
He is in the desert!' do not go out; *or* 'Look,
He is in the inner rooms!' do not believe *it*.
27For as the lightning comes from the east
and flashes to the west, so also will the
coming of the Son of Man be. 28For wher-
ever the carcass is, there the eagles will be
gathered together.

The Coming of the Son of Man

29"Immediately after the tribulation of
those days the sun will be darkened, and
the moon will not give its light; the stars
will fall from heaven, and the powers of
the heavens will be shaken. 30Then the sign
of the Son of Man will appear in heaven,
and then all the tribes of the earth will
mourn, and they will see the Son of Man
coming on the clouds of heaven with
power and great glory. 31And He will send
His angels with a great sound of a trumpet,
and they will gather together His elect
from the four winds, from one end of
heaven to the other.

The Parable of the Fig Tree

32"Now learn this parable from the fig
tree: When its branch has already become
tender and puts forth leaves, you know
that summer *is* near. 33So you also, when
you see all these things, know that it[a] is
near—at the doors! 34Assuredly, I say to
you, this generation will by no means pass
away till all these things take place.
35Heaven and earth will pass away, but My
words will by no means pass away.

No One Knows the Day or Hour

36"But of that day and hour no one
knows, not even the angels of heaven,[a] but
My Father only. 37But as the days of Noah
were, so also will the coming of the Son of
Man be. 38For as in the days before the
flood, they were eating and drinking, mar-
rying and giving in marriage, until the day
that Noah entered the ark, 39and did not
know until the flood came and took them
all away, so also will the coming of the Son
of Man be. 40Then two *men* will be in the
field: one will be taken and the other left.
41Two *women will be* grinding at the mill:
one will be taken and the other left.
42Watch therefore, for you do not know
what hour[a] your Lord is coming. 43But
know this, that if the master of the house
had known what hour the thief would
come, he would have watched and not
allowed his house to be broken into.
44Therefore you also be ready, for the Son
of Man is coming at an hour you do not ex-
pect.

The Faithful Servant and the Evil Servant

45"Who then is a faithful and wise ser-
vant, whom his master made ruler over his
household, to give them food in due sea-
son? 46Blessed *is* that servant whom his
master, when he comes, will find so doing.
47Assuredly, I say to you that he will make
him ruler over all his goods. 48But if that
evil servant says in his heart, 'My master is
delaying his coming,' [a] 49and begins to beat
his fellow servants, and to eat and drink
with the drunkards, 50the master of that
servant will come on a day when he is
not looking for *him* and at an hour that
he is not aware of, 51and will cut him in
two and appoint *him* his portion with the

24:33 [a]Or *He* 24:36 [a]NU-Text adds *nor the Son.*
24:42 [a]NU-Text reads *day.* 24:48 [a]NU-Text omits *his coming.*

Prosperity: More than Possessions

Ron Blue

Prosperity is simply advancing in wealth or any good—making progress in anything desirable. This definition of prosperity (from a spiritual standpoint) means that wealth, materialism, houses, or boats may be a part of, but not the essence of, the definition. Prosperity occurs when someone progresses in pursuing and accomplishing a desired end.

"We must see our possessions and assets from a balanced perspective."

We must see our possessions and assets from a balanced perspective. While we must live as though our true wealth lies in heaven, we must also wisely handle the wealth God has entrusted to us on earth. ✦

hypocrites. There shall be weeping and
gnashing of teeth.

CHAPTER 25

The Parable of the Wise and Foolish Virgins

"Then the kingdom of heaven shall be
likened to ten virgins who took their lamps
and went out to meet the bridegroom.
2Now five of them were wise, and five *were*
foolish. 3Those who *were* foolish took their
lamps and took no oil with them, 4but the
wise took oil in their vessels with their
lamps. 5But while the bridegroom was delayed, they all slumbered and slept.
6"And at midnight a cry was *heard:* 'Behold, the bridegroom is coming;[a] go out to
meet him!' 7Then all those virgins arose
and trimmed their lamps. 8And the foolish
said to the wise, 'Give us *some* of your oil,
for our lamps are going out.' 9But the wise
answered, saying, '*No,* lest there should
not be enough for us and you; but go
rather to those who sell, and buy for yourselves.' 10And while they went to buy, the
bridegroom came, and those who were
ready went in with him to the wedding;
and the door was shut.
11"Afterward the other virgins came
also, saying, 'Lord, Lord, open to us!' 12But
he answered and said, 'Assuredly, I say to
you, I do not know you.'
13"Watch therefore, for you know neither the day nor the hour[a] in which the Son
of Man is coming.

25:6 [a]NU-Text omits *is coming.* 25:13 [a]NU-Text omits the rest of this verse.

25:3, 5, 8, 9 lamps: They burned only long enough for a wedding procession that began on time. **oil**: Spiritual preparedness. **they all slumbered**: Sleeping sometimes symbolizes unreadiness (Rom. 13:11; 1 Thess. 5:6). The point of the parable, however, is not to be awake, but to be prepared. Although everyone slept, only the wise had the necessary oil when they needed it. **lest there should not be enough**: This was not selfishness. Rather, it illustrates the truth that spiritual preparedness cannot be shared.

The Parable of the Talents

14"For *the kingdom of heaven is* like a man
traveling to a far country, *who* called his
own servants and delivered his goods to
them. 15And to one he gave five talents, to
another two, and to another one, to each
according to his own ability; and immedi-
ately he went on a journey. 16Then he who
had received the five talents went and
traded with them, and made another five
talents. 17And likewise he who *had received*
two gained two more also. 18But he who
had received one went and dug in the
ground, and hid his lord's money. 19After a
long time the lord of those servants came
and settled accounts with them.

20"So he who had received five talents
came and brought five other talents, say-
ing, 'Lord, you delivered to me five talents;
look, I have gained five more talents be-
sides them.' 21His lord said to him, 'Well
done, good and faithful servant; you were
faithful over a few things, I will make you
ruler over many things. Enter into the joy
of your lord.' 22He also who had received
two talents came and said, 'Lord, you de-
livered to me two talents; look, I have
gained two more talents besides them.'
23His lord said to him, 'Well *done,* good and
faithful servant; you have been faithful
over a few things, I will make you ruler
over many things. Enter into the joy of
your lord.'

24"Then he who had received the one
talent came and said, 'Lord, I knew you to
be a hard man, reaping where you have
not sown, and gathering where you have
not scattered seed. 25And I was afraid, and
went and hid your talent in the ground.
Look, *there* you have *what is* yours.'

26"But his lord answered and said to
him, 'You wicked and lazy servant, you
knew that I reap where I have not sown,
and gather where I have not scattered
seed. 27So you ought to have deposited my
money with the bankers, and at my com-
ing I would have received back my own
with interest. 28So take the talent from him,
and give *it* to him who has ten talents.

29'For to everyone who has, more will be
given, and he will have abundance; but
from him who does not have, even what he
has will be taken away. 30And cast the un-
profitable servant into the outer darkness.
There will be weeping and gnashing of
teeth.'

The Son of Man Will Judge the Nations

31"When the Son of Man comes in His
glory, and all the holy[a] angels with Him,
then He will sit on the throne of His glory.
32All the nations will be gathered before
Him, and He will separate them one from
another, as a shepherd divides *his* sheep
from the goats. 33And He will set the sheep
on His right hand, but the goats on the left.
34Then the King will say to those on His
right hand, 'Come, you blessed of My
Father, inherit the kingdom prepared for
you from the foundation of the world: 35for
I was hungry and you gave Me food; I was
thirsty and you gave Me drink; I was a
stranger and you took Me in; 36I *was* naked
and you clothed Me; I was sick and you
visited Me; I was in prison and you came
to Me.'

37"Then the righteous will answer Him,
saying, 'Lord, when did we see You hun-
gry and feed *You,* or thirsty and give *You*
drink? 38When did we see You a stranger
and take *You* in, or naked and clothe *You?*
39Or when did we see You sick, or in

25:31 [a]NU-Text omits *holy.*

25:21, 23 ruler over many things: The reward for responsible stewardship is greater responsibilities (see v. 29) and the **joy** of fellowship with Christ. **Well done**: He who had five talents received the same commendation as he who had two. With God, the basis of reward is not how much we have, but how faithfully we serve. Thus we must determine not to become careless in our spiritual walk, despite the pressures we may face as retirement approaches.

> All that is not eternal is eternally out of date.
>
> C. S. Lewis

prison, and come to You?' 40And the King
will answer and say to them, 'Assuredly, I
say to you, inasmuch as you did *it* to one of
the least of these My brethren, you did *it* to
Me.'
41"Then He will also say to those on the
left hand, 'Depart from Me, you cursed,
into the everlasting fire prepared for the
devil and his angels: 42for I was hungry
and you gave Me no food; I was thirsty
and you gave Me no drink; 43I was a stran-
ger and you did not take Me in, naked and
you did not clothe Me, sick and in prison
and you did not visit Me.'
44"Then they also will answer Him,[a] say-
ing, 'Lord, when did we see You hungry or
thirsty or a stranger or naked or sick or in
prison, and did not minister to You?'
45Then He will answer them, saying, 'As-
suredly, I say to you, inasmuch as you did
not do *it* to one of the least of these, you
did not do *it* to Me.' 46And these will go
away into everlasting punishment, but the
righteous into eternal life."

CHAPTER 26

The Plot to Kill Jesus

Now it came to pass, when Jesus had
finished all these sayings, *that* He said to
His disciples, 2"You know that after two
days is the Passover, and the Son of Man
will be delivered up to be crucified."
3Then the chief priests, the scribes,[a] and
the elders of the people assembled at the
palace of the high priest, who was called
Cā'i·a·phas, 4and plotted to take Jesus by
trickery and kill *Him.* 5But they said, "Not
during the feast, lest there be an uproar
among the people."

The Anointing at Bethany

6And when Jesus was in Beth'a·ny at the
house of Simon the leper, 7a woman came
to Him having an alabaster flask of very
costly fragrant oil, and she poured *it* on
His head as He sat *at the table.* 8But when
His disciples saw *it,* they were indignant,
saying, "Why this waste? 9For this fragrant
oil might have been sold for much and
given to *the* poor."
10But when Jesus was aware of *it,* He
said to them, "Why do you trouble the
woman? For she has done a good work for
Me. 11For you have the poor with you al-
ways, but Me you do not have always.
12For in pouring this fragrant oil on My
body, she did *it* for My burial. 13Assuredly,
I say to you, wherever this gospel is
preached in the whole world, what this
woman has done will also be told as a
memorial to her."

Judas Agrees to Betray Jesus

14Then one of the twelve, called Judas
Is·car'i·ot, went to the chief priests 15and
said, "What are you willing to give me if I
deliver Him to you?" And they counted
out to him thirty pieces of silver. 16So from
that time he sought opportunity to betray
Him.

Jesus Celebrates Passover with His Disciples

17Now on the first *day of the Feast* of
the Unleavened Bread the disciples came
to Jesus, saying to Him, "Where do You
want us to prepare for You to eat the
Passover?"
18And He said, "Go into the city to a cer-
tain man, and say to him, 'The Teacher
says, "My time is at hand; I will keep the
Passover at your house with My disci-
ples." ' "
19So the disciples did as Jesus had di-
rected them; and they prepared the
Passover.
20When evening had come, He sat down
with the twelve. 21Now as they were eat-

25:44 [a]NU-Text and M-Text omit *Him.* 26:3 [a]NU-Text omits *the scribes.*

> Forgiveness, which is so easy for us to accept, cost God the agony of Calvary.
> Oswald Chambers

ing, He said, "Assuredly, I say to you, one
of you will betray Me."
22And they were exceedingly sorrowful,
and each of them began to say to Him,
"Lord, is it I?"
23He answered and said, "He who
dipped *his* hand with Me in the dish will
betray Me. 24The Son of Man indeed goes
just as it is written of Him, but woe to that
man by whom the Son of Man is betrayed!
It would have been good for that man if he
had not been born."
25Then Judas, who was betraying Him,
answered and said, "Rabbi, is it I?"
He said to him, "You have said it."

Jesus Institutes the Lord's Supper

26And as they were eating, Jesus took
bread, blessed[a] and broke *it,* and gave *it* to
the disciples and said, "Take, eat; this is
My body."
27Then He took the cup, and gave
thanks, and gave *it* to them, saying, "Drink
from it, all of you. 28For this is My blood of
the new[a] covenant, which is shed for many
for the remission of sins. 29But I say to you,
I will not drink of this fruit of the vine from
now on until that day when I drink it new
with you in My Father's kingdom."
30And when they had sung a hymn, they
went out to the Mount of Olives.

Jesus Predicts Peter's Denial

31Then Jesus said to them, "All of you
will be made to stumble because of Me this
night, for it is written:

'I will strike the Shepherd,
And the sheep of the flock will be
scattered.'[a]

32But after I have been raised, I will go be-
fore you to Galilee."
33Peter answered and said to Him,
"Even if all are made to stumble because of
You, I will never be made to stumble."
34Jesus said to him, "Assuredly, I say to
you that this night, before the rooster
crows, you will deny Me three times."
35Peter said to Him, "Even if I have to
die with You, I will not deny You!"
And so said all the disciples.

The Prayer in the Garden

36Then Jesus came with them to a place
called Geth·sem′a·nē, and said to the disci-
ples, "Sit here while I go and pray over
there." 37And He took with Him Peter and
the two sons of Zeb′e·dee, and He began to
be sorrowful and deeply distressed. 38Then
He said to them, "My soul is exceedingly
sorrowful, even to death. Stay here and
watch with Me."
39He went a little farther and fell on His
face, and prayed, saying, "O My Father, if
it is possible, let this cup pass from Me;
nevertheless, not as I will, but as You *will.*"
40Then He came to the disciples and
found them sleeping, and said to Peter,
"What! Could you not watch with Me one
hour? 41Watch and pray, lest you enter into
temptation. The spirit indeed *is* willing,
but the flesh *is* weak."

26:26 [a]M-Text reads *gave thanks for.* 26:28 [a]NU-Text omits *new.* 26:31 [a]Zechariah 13:7

26:24 as it is written of Him: Of Jesus, whose death was predicted. Perhaps the reference is to Is. 53. **good . . . if he had not been born**: Judas freely chose to betray Jesus (vv. 14–16), but in doing so he helped to fulfill the Scriptures. God's sovereignty does not destroy human freedom or responsibility for willful actions (see 18:7).

26:26–30 The bread and wine of the Passover commemorated deliverance from Egypt. Jesus' **body** (v. 26) and **blood** (v. 28) are now identified as the true Passover sacrifice of the **new covenant** (v. 28) that brings deliverance from **sins**.

42 Again, a second time, He went away
and prayed, saying, "O My Father, if this
cup cannot pass away from Me unless[a] I
drink it, Your will be done." 43 And He
came and found them asleep again, for
their eyes were heavy.
44 So He left them, went away again, and
prayed the third time, saying the same
words. 45 Then He came to His disciples
and said to them, "Are *you* still sleeping
and resting? Behold, the hour is at hand,
and the Son of Man is being betrayed into
the hands of sinners. 46 Rise, let us be going.
See, My betrayer is at hand."

Betrayal and Arrest in Gethsemane

47 And while He was still speaking, be-
hold, Judas, one of the twelve, with a great
multitude with swords and clubs, came
from the chief priests and elders of the peo-
ple.
48 Now His betrayer had given them a
sign, saying, "Whomever I kiss, He is the
One; seize Him." 49 Immediately he went
up to Jesus and said, "Greetings, Rabbi!"
and kissed Him.
50 But Jesus said to him, "Friend, why
have you come?"
Then they came and laid hands on Jesus
and took Him. 51 And suddenly, one of
those *who were* with Jesus stretched out
his hand and drew his sword, struck the
servant of the high priest, and cut off his
ear.
52 But Jesus said to him, "Put your sword
in its place, for all who take the sword will
perish[a] by the sword. 53 Or do you think
that I cannot now pray to My Father, and
He will provide Me with more than twelve
legions of angels? 54 How then could the
Scriptures be fulfilled, that it must happen
thus?"
55 In that hour Jesus said to the multi-
tudes, "Have you come out, as against a
robber, with swords and clubs to take Me?
I sat daily with you, teaching in the temple,
and you did not seize Me. 56 But all this was
done that the Scriptures of the prophets
might be fulfilled."
Then all the disciples forsook Him and
fled.

Jesus Faces the Sanhedrin

57 And those who had laid hold of Jesus
led *Him* away to Cā'i·a·phas the high
priest, where the scribes and the elders
were assembled. 58 But Peter followed Him
at a distance to the high priest's courtyard.
And he went in and sat with the servants
to see the end.
59 Now the chief priests, the elders,[a] and
all the council sought false testimony
against Jesus to put Him to death, 60 but
found none. Even though many false wit-
nesses came forward, they found none.[a]
But at last two false witnesses[b] came for-
ward 61 and said, "This *fellow* said, 'I am
able to destroy the temple of God and to
build it in three days.' "
62 And the high priest arose and said to
Him, "Do You answer nothing? What *is it*
these men testify against You?" 63 But Jesus
kept silent. And the high priest answered
and said to Him, "I put You under oath by
the living God: Tell us if You are the Christ,
the Son of God!"
64 Jesus said to him, "*It is as* you said.
Nevertheless, I say to you, hereafter you
will see the Son of Man sitting at the right
hand of the Power, and coming on the
clouds of heaven."

26:42 [a]NU-Text reads *if this may not pass away unless.* 26:52 [a]M-Text reads *die.* 26:59 [a]NU-Text omits *the elders.* 26:60 [a]NU-Text puts a comma after *but found none,* does not capitalize *Even,* and omits *they found none.* [b]NU-Text omits *false witnesses.*

26:61, 62 destroy the temple: Taken literally, this charge against Jesus was false. The statement which they misquoted was a prophecy of His death and resurrection. See John 2:19–21. **Do You answer nothing**? Caiaphas tried to get Jesus to publicly claim to be the Son of God (v. 63). In the minds of the court this would be a blasphemy punishable by death (see vv. 65, 66).

[65]Then the high priest tore his clothes,
saying, "He has spoken blasphemy! What
further need do we have of witnesses?
Look, now you have heard His blasphemy!
[66]What do you think?"

They answered and said, "He is deserv-
ing of death."

[67]Then they spat in His face and beat
Him; and others struck *Him* with the palms
of their hands, [68]saying, "Prophesy to
us, Christ! Who is the one who struck
You?"

Peter Denies Jesus, and Weeps Bitterly

[69]Now Peter sat outside in the court-
yard. And a servant girl came to him,
saying, "You also were with Jesus of Gali-
lee."

[70]But he denied it before *them* all, saying,
"I do not know what you are saying."

[71]And when he had gone out to the gate-
way, another *girl* saw him and said to those
who were there, "This *fellow* also was with
Jesus of Nazareth."

[72]But again he denied with an oath, "I do
not know the Man!"

[73]And a little later those who stood by
came up and said to Peter, "Surely you also
are *one* of them, for your speech betrays
you."

[74]Then he began to curse and swear, *say-
ing,* "I do not know the Man!"

Immediately a rooster crowed. [75]And
Peter remembered the word of Jesus who
had said to him, "Before the rooster crows,
you will deny Me three times." So he went
out and wept bitterly.

27:2 [a]NU-Text omits *Pontius.* 27:10 [a]Jeremiah 32:6–9

CHAPTER 27

Jesus Handed Over to Pontius Pilate

When morning came, all the chief
priests and elders of the people plotted
against Jesus to put Him to death. [2]And
when they had bound Him, they led Him
away and delivered Him to Pon'ti·us[a] Pi-
late the governor.

Judas Hangs Himself

[3]Then Judas, His betrayer, seeing that
He had been condemned, was remorseful
and brought back the thirty pieces of silver
to the chief priests and elders, [4]saying, "I
have sinned by betraying innocent blood."

And they said, "What *is that* to us? You
see *to it!*"

[5]Then he threw down the pieces of sil-
ver in the temple and departed, and went
and hanged himself.

[6]But the chief priests took the silver
pieces and said, "It is not lawful to put
them into the treasury, because they are the
price of blood." [7]And they consulted to-
gether and bought with them the potter's
field, to bury strangers in. [8]Therefore that
field has been called the Field of Blood to
this day.

[9]Then was fulfilled what was spoken by
Jer·e·mī'ah the prophet, saying, *"And they
took the thirty pieces of silver, the value of
Him who was priced,* whom they of the
children of Israel priced, [10]*and gave them
for the potter's field, as the* LORD *directed
me."*[a]

Jesus Faces Pilate

[11]Now Jesus stood before the governor.
And the governor asked Him, saying, "Are
You the King of the Jews?"

27:3–8 What is that to us? (v. 4): The religious leaders had no concern for killing an innocent person. They were careful only to avoid breaking the ritual requirement of not putting the **price of blood** (v. 6) in the temple treasury. According to Acts 1:18 Judas bought the field. Because it was blood money that came from Judas, the Jewish leaders may have bought the field in his name. The rope with which he hung himself (v. 5) or the tree branch to which it was tied probably broke so that his body fell and burst open as recorded in Acts 1:18.

Jesus said to him, "*It is as* you say."
12And while He was being accused by the
chief priests and elders, He answered
nothing.
13Then Pilate said to Him, "Do You not
hear how many things they testify against
You?" 14But He answered him not one
word, so that the governor marveled
greatly.

Taking the Place of Barabbas

15Now at the feast the governor was
accustomed to releasing to the multitude
one prisoner whom they wished. 16And at
that time they had a notorious prisoner
called Ba·rab'bas.[a] 17Therefore, when they
had gathered together, Pilate said to them,
"Whom do you want me to release to you?
Ba·rab'bas, or Jesus who is called Christ?"
18For he knew that they had handed Him
over because of envy.
19While he was sitting on the judgment
seat, his wife sent to him, saying, "Have
nothing to do with that just Man, for I have
suffered many things today in a dream be-
cause of Him."
20But the chief priests and elders per-
suaded the multitudes that they should
ask for Ba·rab'bas and destroy Jesus. 21The
governor answered and said to them,
"Which of the two do you want me to re-
lease to you?"

They said, "Ba·rab'bas!"
22Pilate said to them, "What then shall I
do with Jesus who is called Christ?"

They all said to him, "Let Him be cruci-
fied!"
23Then the governor said, "Why, what
evil has He done?"

But they cried out all the more, saying,
"Let Him be crucified!"
24When Pilate saw that he could not pre-
vail at all, but rather *that* a tumult was ris-
ing, he took water and washed *his* hands
before the multitude, saying, "I am inno-
cent of the blood of this just Person.[a] You
see *to it*."
25And all the people answered and said,
"His blood *be* on us and on our chil-
dren."
26Then he released Ba·rab'bas to them;
and when he had scourged Jesus, he deliv-
ered *Him* to be crucified.

The Soldiers Mock Jesus

27Then the soldiers of the governor took
Jesus into the Praetorium and gathered the
whole garrison around Him. 28And they
stripped Him and put a scarlet robe on
Him. 29When they had twisted a crown of
thorns, they put *it* on His head, and a reed
in His right hand. And they bowed the
knee before Him and mocked Him, saying,
"Hail, King of the Jews!" 30Then they spat
on Him, and took the reed and struck Him
on the head. 31And when they had mocked
Him, they took the robe off Him, put His
own clothes on Him, and led Him away to
be crucified.

The King on a Cross

32Now as they came out, they found a
man of Cȳ·rē'nē, Simon by name. Him
they compelled to bear His cross. 33And
when they had come to a place called
Gol'go·tha, that is to say, Place of a Skull,
34they gave Him sour[a] wine mingled with
gall to drink. But when He had tasted *it*,
He would not drink.
35Then they crucified Him, and divided
His garments, casting lots,[a] that it might be
fulfilled which was spoken by the prophet:

27:16 [a]NU-Text reads *Jesus Barabbas.*
27:24 [a]NU-Text omits *just.* 27:34 [a]NU-Text omits *sour.* 27:35 [a]NU-Text and M-Text omit the rest of this verse.

27:34 Gall can refer to various substances that have a bitter taste. It may have been offered to Jesus as a mild narcotic to deaden pain. Mark 15:23 identifies this substance as myrrh. Jesus' refusal reflects His determination to avoid nothing that the Father had in store for Him.

"They divided My garments among them,
And for My clothing they cast lots."[b]

36 Sitting down, they kept watch over Him there. 37 And they put up over His head the accusation written against Him:

THIS IS JESUS
THE KING OF THE JEWS.

38 Then two robbers were crucified with Him, one on the right and another on the left.

39 And those who passed by blasphemed Him, wagging their heads 40 and saying, "You who destroy the temple and build *it* in three days, save Yourself! If You are the Son of God, come down from the cross."

41 Likewise the chief priests also, mocking with the scribes and elders,[a] said, 42 "He saved others; Himself He cannot save. If He is the King of Israel,[a] let Him now come down from the cross, and we will believe Him.[b] 43 He trusted in God; let Him deliver Him now if He will have Him; for He said, 'I am the Son of God.' "

44 Even the robbers who were crucified with Him reviled Him with the same thing.

Jesus Dies on the Cross

45 Now from the sixth hour until the ninth hour there was darkness over all the land. 46 And about the ninth hour Jesus cried out with a loud voice, saying, "Ē'lī, Ē'lī, lama sabachthani?" that is, *"My God, My God, why have You forsaken Me?"*[a]

47 Some of those who stood there, when they heard *that,* said, "This Man is calling for E·lī'jah!" 48 Immediately one of them ran and took a sponge, filled *it* with sour wine and put *it* on a reed, and offered it to Him to drink.

49 The rest said, "Let Him alone; let us see if E·lī'jah will come to save Him."

50 And Jesus cried out again with a loud voice, and yielded up His spirit.

51 Then, behold, the veil of the temple was torn in two from top to bottom; and the earth quaked, and the rocks were split, 52 and the graves were opened; and many bodies of the saints who had fallen asleep were raised; 53 and coming out of the graves after His resurrection, they went into the holy city and appeared to many.

54 So when the centurion and those with him, who were guarding Jesus, saw the earthquake and the things that had happened, they feared greatly, saying, "Truly this was the Son of God!"

55 And many women who followed Jesus from Galilee, ministering to Him, were there looking on from afar, 56 among whom were Mary Mag'da·lēne, Mary the mother of James and Jō'sēs,[a] and the mother of Zeb'e·dee's sons.

Jesus Buried in Joseph's Tomb

57 Now when evening had come, there came a rich man from Ar·i·ma·thē'a, named Joseph, who himself had also become a disciple of Jesus. 58 This man went to Pilate and asked for the body of Jesus. Then Pilate commanded the body to be given to him. 59 When Joseph had taken the body, he wrapped it in a clean linen cloth,

27:35 [b]Psalm 22:18 27:41 [a]M-Text reads *with the scribes, the Pharisees, and the elders.* 27:42 [a]NU-Text reads *He is the King of Israel!* [b]NU-Text and M-Text read *we will believe in Him.* 27:46 [a]Psalm 22:1 27:56 [a]NU-Text reads *Joseph.*

27:45 During the Crucifixion there was a supernatural **darkness** over Israel from noon until 3:00 P.M. This was not due to a solar eclipse because at Passover the moon was always full. For other supernatural occurrences see vv. 51–53.

27:51 The tearing of the **veil** of the temple at the time of Jesus' death conveyed in visible form God's plan of salvation under the new covenant. Direct access to God is available through the death of Jesus. See Heb. 10:19–22.

60 and laid it in his new tomb which he had
hewn out of the rock; and he rolled a large
stone against the door of the tomb, and de-
parted. 61 And Mary Mag'da·lēne was
there, and the other Mary, sitting opposite
the tomb.

Pilate Sets a Guard

62 On the next day, which followed the
Day of Preparation, the chief priests and
Phar'i·sees gathered together to Pilate,
63 saying, "Sir, we remember, while He was
still alive, how that deceiver said, 'After
three days I will rise.' 64 Therefore com-
mand that the tomb be made secure until
the third day, lest His disciples come by
night[a] and steal Him *away,* and say to the
people, 'He has risen from the dead.' So
the last deception will be worse than the
first."

65 Pilate said to them, "You have a guard;
go your way, make *it* as secure as you
know how." 66 So they went and made the
tomb secure, sealing the stone and setting
the guard.

CHAPTER 28

He Is Risen

Now after the Sabbath, as the first *day* of
the week began to dawn, Mary Mag'da-
lēne and the other Mary came to see the
tomb. 2 And behold, there was a great
earthquake; for an angel of the Lord de-
scended from heaven, and came and rolled
back the stone from the door,[a] and sat on it.
3 His countenance was like lightning, and
his clothing as white as snow. 4 And the
guards shook for fear of him, and became
like dead *men.*

5 But the angel answered and said to the
women, "Do not be afraid, for I know that
you seek Jesus who was crucified. 6 He is
not here; for He is risen, as He said. Come,
see the place where the Lord lay. 7 And go
quickly and tell His disciples that He is
risen from the dead, and indeed He is go-
ing before you into Galilee; there you will
see Him. Behold, I have told you."

8 So they went out quickly from the tomb
with fear and great joy, and ran to bring
His disciples word.

The Women Worship the Risen Lord

9 And as they went to tell His disciples,[a]
behold, Jesus met them, saying, "Rejoice!"
So they came and held Him by the feet and
worshiped Him. 10 Then Jesus said to them,
"Do not be afraid. Go *and* tell My brethren
to go to Galilee, and there they will see
Me."

The Soldiers Are Bribed

11 Now while they were going, behold,
some of the guard came into the city and
reported to the chief priests all the things
that had happened. 12 When they had as-
sembled with the elders and consulted to-
gether, they gave a large sum of money to
the soldiers, 13 saying, "Tell them, 'His dis-

27:64 [a]NU-Text omits *by night.* 28:2 [a]NU-Text omits *from the door.* 28:9 [a]NU-Text omits the first clause of this verse.

27:60 new tomb: Family burial crypts were common in Palestine. Newly deceased bodies were placed in the same tomb with their ancestors' bones. Had Jesus' body been placed in a used grave, it would have been impossible to validate the claim that His tomb was empty (see 28:1–8).

27:65, 66 as secure as you know how: Once the stone was in place, soft wax was poured over the crevice between the stone and the wall of the opening. The official Roman government seal was then pressed into the wax. The penalty for breaking the seal was death. See 28:11–15.

28:11–15 An attempt to conceal the truth of the Resurrection. **while we slept** (v. 13): This was a failure of duty punishable by death. In return for testifying to a falsehood, the guards received from the chief priests not only money (v. 12), but also protection from the penalty.

NEVER ALONE

Anne Ortlund

Jesus on the Cross became truly lonely so that you and I would never need to be.

Listen carefully: *Your loneliness is unnecessary.*

Do you know that?

In fact, if loneliness is long-term and chronic with you, it is disobedient. It is not taking seriously His promise, "I am with you always, even to the end of the age" (Matt. 28:20).

You see, when on the Cross, Jesus found out what real loneliness felt like. He made sure it need never happen to you.

This is your secret to overcoming loneliness: Fix your eyes on Him. People suggest lots of prescriptions: get busy, get involved in your church and community, do things for others, find a friend, join a small group—no, no! Not first!

First in your loneliness, draw from Jesus. See how He drew and drew from His Father, His ever-flowing Source of all love and comfort and hope and pleasure and fullness: "Now in the morning, having risen a long while before daylight, He went out and . . . prayed (Mark 1:35).

He even deliberately sought aloneness for the best togetherness of all: "Great multitudes came together to hear. . . . So He Himself often withdrew into the wilderness and prayed" (Luke 5:15, 16).

"Sit at His feet and spread out your loneliness before Him."

So do the same. Sit at His feet, and spread out your loneliness before Him. Apologize! Admit you have been fixing your eyes on yourself.

He is complete in the Father, and He says you are complete in Him (Col. 2:9, 10). He—and only He—is full of fullness for you. When, humanly speaking, you feel all alone, your heart can still be happy and satisfied: You are complete in Him. ✦

ciples came at night and stole Him *away*
while we slept.' [14]And if this comes to the
governor's ears, we will appease him and
make you secure." [15]So they took the
money and did as they were instructed;
and this saying is commonly reported
among the Jews until this day.

The Great Commission

[16]Then the eleven disciples went away
into Galilee, to the mountain which Jesus
had appointed for them. [17]When they saw
Him, they worshiped Him; but some
doubted.
[18]And Jesus came and spoke to them,

28:18, 19 Since His resurrection Jesus reigns sovereign over **heaven** and **earth** (see Acts 2:36; 1 Cor. 15:20–28; Phil. 2:9–11). **therefore**: The central task of the church, its Great Commission, is to **make disciples of all the nations**. Jesus is not merely continuing John's baptism of repentance. In Christian baptism the believer promises loyalty to all three

saying, "All authority has been given to Me in heaven and on earth. 19Go therefore[a] and make disciples of all the nations, baptizing them in the name of the Father and of the Son and of the Holy Spirit, 20teaching them to observe all things that I have commanded you; and lo, I am with you always, *even* to the end of the age." Amen.[a]

28:19 [a]M-Text omits *therefore*.
28:20 [a]NU-Text omits *Amen*.

members of the Trinity (see 2 Cor. 13:14). The Christian's salvation is through the grace, mercy, and love of the **Father**; the sacrificial death of the **Son**; and the cleansing and empowerment of the **Holy Spirit**.

28:20 We can find comfort in Jesus' promise to be with us always, even when we experience suffering and trials for our faith.

✦Mark✦

Mark, the shortest and simplest of the four Gospels, was written to Gentiles not familiar with Old Testament theology. The writer, known as John Mark, unfolds the dual focus of Christ's life: service and sacrifice. Jesus is portrayed as a servant on the move, instantly responsive to the will of the Father and the needs of every person.

In his portrayal of Christ as a servant, Mark demonstrates that, rather than relying on past accomplishments, a mature Christian should continue to minister throughout life. A traveling companion and friend of both Paul and Peter, Mark understandably desired to show his readers what the gospel message is: Jesus' life, death, and Resurrection.

The emotions of Jesus are emphasized in this Gospel more than in any other. The Lord is presented as an active, compassionate, and obedient servant who constantly ministers to the physical and spiritual needs of others. Miracles are predominate in this book, and they are used to demonstrate not only the power of Christ but also His sensitivity to suffering. By preaching, teaching, and healing, He ministered to others—even to the point of death. Almost 40 percent of this Gospel is devoted to a detailed account of the last eight days of Jesus' life, climaxing in His Resurrection. ✦

CHAPTER 1

John the Baptist Prepares the Way

The beginning of the gospel of Jesus
Christ, the Son of God. [2]As it is written in
the Prophets:[a]

"Behold, I send My messenger before
Your face,
Who will prepare Your way before
You."[b]

3 *"The voice of one crying in the*
wilderness:
'Prepare the way of the LORD;
Make His paths straight.' "[a]

[4]John came baptizing in the wilderness
and preaching a baptism of repentance for
the remission of sins. [5]Then all the land of
Judea, and those from Jerusalem, went out
to him and were all baptized by him in the
Jordan River, confessing their sins.

[6]Now John was clothed with camel's
hair and with a leather belt around his
waist, and he ate locusts and wild honey.
[7]And he preached, saying, "There comes
One after me who is mightier than I, whose
sandal strap I am not worthy to stoop
down and loose. [8]I indeed baptized you

1:2 [a]NU-Text reads *Isaiah the prophet.* [b]Malachi 3:1
1:3 [a]Isaiah 40:3

1:1 the gospel: Mark's message of Good News concerns Jesus Christ as the fulfillment of the promise of salvation.

JOHN THE BAPTIST: THE MESSIAH'S MESSENGER

As the last of the Old Testament-style prophets, John the Baptist heralded the Messiah and the beginning of the church age. His dedication to God in every area of his life provides a challenging example for Christians today.

John's appearance and actions were considered strange, even for his day. He was "clothed in camel's hair and with a leather belt around his waist" (Mark 1:6). This style of dress, similar to that worn by Elijah (2 Kin. 1:8), may have been typical for Old Testament prophets (Zech. 13:4), but it had not been seen for some time.

His diet consisted of locusts and wild honey (Mark 1:6). Locusts, considered a "clean" food according to Old Testament law (Lev. 11:22), were primarily eaten by the poorest of people. As the son of a priest, John had access to much better food, yet he sacrificed this privilege for a life in the wilderness (Luke 1:80).

This meager diet did not impress his critics: "John came neither eating nor drinking, and they say, 'He has a demon.' The Son of Man came eating and drinking, and they say, 'Look, a glutton and a winebibber' " (Matt. 11:18, 19). But neither John nor Jesus was deterred by these comments, showing us that each Christian must follow God in the way revealed to him or her through Scripture, regardless of the opinions expressed by others.

Although his ascetic lifestyle might not be practical today, it reflected John's whole-hearted dedication to the Lord and his calling. He performed no miracles (John 10:41), but his ministry drew many followers, including some of the self-righteous Pharisees and Sadducees. His holy lifestyle convicted even a miscreant like Herod (Mark 6:20), and he courageously refused to soften his message for anyone (Matt. 3:7; 14:4; Mark 6:18).

John the Baptist had been chosen for an awesome task—to prepare the people for the ministry of the Messiah—and he fulfilled his calling to the utmost of his ability. Jesus honored John for his faithfulness: "Among those born of women there has not risen one greater than John the Baptist" (Matt. 11:11).

Yet despite his prominent role, John continually expressed humility: "One mightier than I is coming, whose sandal strap I am not worthy to loose" (Luke 3:16). "He must increase, but I must decrease" (John 3:30). John was not intimidated by Jesus' effect on his own ministry, but he rejoiced as a friend of the Bridegroom (v. 29).

John's zeal for the Lord provides a challenge to all Christians. Each of us should serve faithfully, courageously, and humbly in every area of our lives so that Jesus could say of us as He said of John: "He was the burning and shining lamp" (John 5:35). ✦

with water, but He will baptize you with
the Holy Spirit."

John Baptizes Jesus

9It came to pass in those days *that* Jesus
came from Nazareth of Galilee, and was
baptized by John in the Jordan. 10And im-
mediately, coming up from[a] the water, He
saw the heavens parting and the Spirit de-
scending upon Him like a dove. 11Then a
voice came from heaven, "You are My
beloved Son, in whom I am well pleased."

Satan Tempts Jesus

12Immediately the Spirit drove Him into
the wilderness. 13And He was there in the
wilderness forty days, tempted by Satan,
and was with the wild beasts; and the an-
gels ministered to Him.

Jesus Begins His Galilean Ministry

14Now after John was put in prison,
Jesus came to Galilee, preaching the gospel
of the kingdom[a] of God, 15and saying, "The
time is fulfilled, and the kingdom of God
is at hand. Repent, and believe in the
gospel."

Four Fishermen Called as Disciples

16And as He walked by the Sea of Gali-
lee, He saw Simon and Andrew his brother
casting a net into the sea; for they were
fishermen. 17Then Jesus said to them, "Fol-
low Me, and I will make you become fish-
ers of men." 18They immediately left their
nets and followed Him.

19When He had gone a little farther from
there, He saw James the *son* of Zeb'e·dee,
and John his brother, who also *were* in the
boat mending their nets. 20And immedi-
ately He called them, and they left their
father Zeb'e·dee in the boat with the hired
servants, and went after Him.

Jesus Casts Out an Unclean Spirit

21Then they went into Ca·per'na·um,
and immediately on the Sabbath He en-
tered the synagogue and taught. 22And
they were astonished at His teaching, for
He taught them as one having authority,
and not as the scribes.

23Now there was a man in their syna-
gogue with an unclean spirit. And he cried
out, 24saying, "Let *us* alone! What have we
to do with You, Jesus of Nazareth? Did You
come to destroy us? I know who You are—
the Holy One of God!"

25But Jesus rebuked him, saying, "Be
quiet, and come out of him!" 26And when
the unclean spirit had convulsed him and
cried out with a loud voice, he came out of
him. 27Then they were all amazed, so that
they questioned among themselves, say-
ing, "What is this? What new doctrine *is*
this? For with authority[a] He commands
even the unclean spirits, and they obey
Him." 28And immediately His fame spread
throughout all the region around Galilee.

1:10 [a]NU-Text reads *out of.* 1:14 [a]NU-Text omits *of the kingdom.* 1:27 [a]NU-Text reads *What is this? A new doctrine with authority.*

1:9 Since Jesus was sinless, His baptism did not indicate repentance; rather it signaled His approval of John's ministry and served to identify Him with the sinful people He came to save.

1:17 Follow Me: Jesus spoke with authority as King. Those who would enter the kingdom are called upon to give Him absolute obedience. Following Jesus is one of Mark's main themes. Through Jesus' interaction with His disciples we learn how to follow Him. **fishers of men:** His disciples would lead others to Him. As Jesus' disciples, we too are called to lead others to Him by our words and actions.

1:18–20 left their nets . . . their father: Let neither occupation nor family keep you from following Christ. **immediately**: One of Mark's favorite words (see vv. 12, 18, 20, 28). Although we may have difficulty maintaining a proper perspective in the midst of pressing obligations, it is vital that our relationship with God be our top priority.

1:27 Jesus had spoken with God's **authority** (v. 22); now with that same power He cast out unclean **spirits**.

Peter's Mother-in-Law Healed

29 Now as soon as they had come out of
the synagogue, they entered the house of
Simon and Andrew, with James and John.
30 But Simon's wife's mother lay sick with a
fever, and they told Him about her at once.
31 So He came and took her by the hand and
lifted her up, and immediately the fever
left her. And she served them.

Many Healed After Sabbath Sunset

32 At evening, when the sun had set, they
brought to Him all who were sick and
those who were demon-possessed. 33 And
the whole city was gathered together at the
door. 34 Then He healed many who were
sick with various diseases, and cast out
many demons; and He did not allow the
demons to speak, because they knew Him.

Preaching in Galilee

35 Now in the morning, having risen a
long while before daylight, He went out
and departed to a solitary place; and there
He prayed. 36 And Simon and those *who
were* with Him searched for Him. 37 When
they found Him, they said to Him, "Every-
one is looking for You."
38 But He said to them, "Let us go into
the next towns, that I may preach there
also, because for this purpose I have come
forth."
39 And He was preaching in their syna-
gogues throughout all Galilee, and casting
out demons.

Jesus Cleanses a Leper

40 Now a leper came to Him, imploring
Him, kneeling down to Him and saying to
Him, "If You are willing, You can make me
clean."
41 Then Jesus, moved with compassion,
stretched out *His* hand and touched him,
and said to him, "I am willing; be
cleansed." 42 As soon as He had spoken, im-
mediately the leprosy left him, and he was
cleansed. 43 And He strictly warned him
and sent him away at once, 44 and said to
him, "See that you say nothing to anyone;
but go your way, show yourself to the
priest, and offer for your cleansing those
things which Moses commanded, as a tes-
timony to them."
45 However, he went out and began to
proclaim *it* freely, and to spread the matter,
so that Jesus could no longer openly enter
the city, but was outside in deserted places;
and they came to Him from every direc-
tion.

CHAPTER 2

Jesus Forgives and Heals a Paralytic

And again He entered Ca·per'na·um af-
ter *some* days, and it was heard that He was
in the house. 2 Immediately[a] many gath-
ered together, so that there was no longer
room to receive *them,* not even near the
door. And He preached the word to them.
3 Then they came to Him, bringing a para-
lytic who was carried by four *men.* 4 And
when they could not come near Him be-
cause of the crowd, they uncovered the
roof where He was. So when they had bro-
ken through, they let down the bed on
which the paralytic was lying.
5 When Jesus saw their faith, He said to
the paralytic, "Son, your sins are forgiven
you."
6 And some of the scribes were sitting
there and reasoning in their hearts, 7 "Why
does this *Man* speak blasphemies like this?
Who can forgive sins but God alone?"
8 But immediately, when Jesus perceived
in His spirit that they reasoned thus within
themselves, He said to them, "Why do you
reason about these things in your hearts?
9 Which is easier, to say to the paralytic,
'*Your* sins are forgiven you,' or to say,

2:2 [a]NU-Text omits *Immediately.*

2:7 Jesus agreed with these Jewish officials that only God **can forgive sins**. For them to accept Jesus' claim would have been to recognize Him as God's Son.

'Arise, take up your bed and walk'? [10]But that you may know that the Son of Man has power on earth to forgive sins"—He said to the paralytic, [11]"I say to you, arise, take up your bed, and go to your house." [12]Immediately he arose, took up the bed, and went out in the presence of them all, so that all were amazed and glorified God, saying, "We never saw *anything* like this!"

Matthew the Tax Collector

[13]Then He went out again by the sea; and all the multitude came to Him, and He taught them. [14]As He passed by, He saw Levi the *son* of Al·phae'us sitting at the tax office. And He said to him, "Follow Me." So he arose and followed Him.

[15]Now it happened, as He was dining in *Levi's* house, that many tax collectors and sinners also sat together with Jesus and His disciples; for there were many, and they followed Him. [16]And when the scribes and[a] Phar'i·sees saw Him eating with the tax collectors and sinners, they said to His disciples, "How *is it* that He eats and drinks with tax collectors and sinners?"

[17]When Jesus heard *it,* He said to them, "Those who are well have no need of a physician, but those who are sick. I did not come to call *the* righteous, but sinners, to repentance."[a]

Jesus Is Questioned About Fasting

[18]The disciples of John and of the Phar'i·sees were fasting. Then they came and said to Him, "Why do the disciples of John and of the Phar'i·sees fast, but Your disciples do not fast?"

[19]And Jesus said to them, "Can the friends of the bridegroom fast while the bridegroom is with them? As long as they have the bridegroom with them they cannot fast. [20]But the days will come when the bridegroom will be taken away from them, and then they will fast in those days. [21]No one sews a piece of unshrunk cloth on an old garment; or else the new piece pulls away from the old, and the tear is made worse. [22]And no one puts new wine into old wineskins; or else the new wine bursts the wineskins, the wine is spilled, and the wineskins are ruined. But new wine must be put into new wineskins."

Jesus Is Lord of the Sabbath

[23]Now it happened that He went through the grainfields on the Sabbath; and as they went His disciples began to pluck the heads of grain. [24]And the Phar'i·sees said to Him, "Look, why do they do what is not lawful on the Sabbath?"

[25]But He said to them, "Have you never read what David did when he was in need and hungry, he and those with him: [26]how he went into the house of God *in the days* of A·bi'a·thar the high priest, and ate the showbread, which is not lawful to eat except for the priests, and also gave some to those who were with him?"

[27]And He said to them, "The Sabbath was made for man, and not man for the Sabbath. [28]Therefore the Son of Man is also Lord of the Sabbath."

CHAPTER 3

Healing on the Sabbath

And He entered the synagogue again, and a man was there who had a withered

2:16 [a]NU-Text reads *of the.* 2:17 [a]NU-Text omits *to repentance.*

2:15 Because **tax collectors** worked for the Romans or their representation, such as Herod Antipas, the Jews hated them and considered them great sinners. By eating with these people, Jesus showed that God's forgiveness is extended even to the worst. As His followers we have no right to withhold the testimony of the gospel from those we deem unworthy; His love and mercy are extended to all.

2:23, 24 pluck the . . . grain: It was legal for a hungry person to eat a handful of grain while passing through another's field (see Deut. 23:25). The Pharisees complained that thus picking a handful violated the law against harvesting on the Sabbath (see Ex. 34:21).

hand. 2So they watched Him closely, whether He would heal him on the Sabbath, so that they might accuse Him. 3And He said to the man who had the withered hand, "Step forward." 4Then He said to them, "Is it lawful on the Sabbath to do good or to do evil, to save life or to kill?" But they kept silent. 5And when He had looked around at them with anger, being grieved by the hardness of their hearts, He said to the man, "Stretch out your hand." And he stretched *it* out, and his hand was restored as whole as the other.[a] 6Then the Phar′i•sees went out and immediately plotted with the He•rō′di•ans against Him, how they might destroy Him.

A Great Multitude Follows Jesus

7But Jesus withdrew with His disciples to the sea. And a great multitude from Galilee followed Him, and from Judea 8and Jerusalem and Id•ū•mē′a and beyond the Jordan; and those from Tȳre and Sī′don, a great multitude, when they heard how many things He was doing, came to Him. 9So He told His disciples that a small boat should be kept ready for Him because of the multitude, lest they should crush Him. 10For He healed many, so that as many as had afflictions pressed about Him to touch Him. 11And the unclean spirits, whenever they saw Him, fell down before Him and cried out, saying, "You are the Son of God." 12But He sternly warned them that they should not make Him known.

The Twelve Apostles

13And He went up on the mountain and called to *Him* those He Himself wanted. And they came to Him. 14Then He appointed twelve,[a] that they might be with Him and that He might send them out to preach, 15and to have power to heal sicknesses and[a] to cast out demons: 16Simon,[a] to whom He gave the name Peter; 17James the *son* of Zeb′e•dee and John the brother of James, to whom He gave the name Bō•a•ner′gēs, that is, "Sons of Thunder"; 18Andrew, Philip, Bartholomew, Matthew, Thomas, James the *son* of Al•phae̅′us, Thad•dae̅′us, Simon the Can′a•nīte; 19and Judas Is•car′i•ot, who also betrayed Him. And they went into a house.

A House Divided Cannot Stand

20Then the multitude came together again, so that they could not so much as eat bread. 21But when His own people heard *about this,* they went out to lay hold of Him, for they said, "He is out of His mind."

22And the scribes who came down from Jerusalem said, "He has Bē•el′ze•bub," and, "By the ruler of the demons He casts out demons."

23So He called them to *Himself* and said to them in parables: "How can Satan cast out Satan? 24If a kingdom is divided against itself, that kingdom cannot stand. 25And if a house is divided against itself, that house cannot stand. 26And if Satan has risen up against himself, and is divided, he cannot stand, but has an end. 27No one can enter a strong man's house and plunder his goods, unless he first binds the strong man. And then he will plunder his house.

The Unpardonable Sin

28"Assuredly, I say to you, all sins will be forgiven the sons of men, and whatever blasphemies they may utter; 29but he who

3:5 [a]NU-Text omits *as whole as the other.*
3:14 [a]NU-Text adds *whom He also named apostles.*
3:15 [a]NU-Text omits *to heal sicknesses and.*
3:16 [a]NU-Text reads *and He appointed the twelve: Simon* . . . .

3:27 The **strong man** is Satan. Jesus was the One who entered his house, bound him, and was releasing people from his power.

3:28–30 blasphemes against the Holy Spirit: They had taken a deliberate attitude of hardened resistance to the Spirit who was working through Christ (see Is. 61:1–3). Such opposition, in this face-to-face confrontation, would not be forgiven.

blasphemes against the Holy Spirit never
has forgiveness, but is subject to eternal
condemnation"— 30because they said, "He
has an unclean spirit."

Jesus' Mother and Brothers Send for Him

31Then His brothers and His mother
came, and standing outside they sent to
Him, calling Him. 32And a multitude was
sitting around Him; and they said to Him,
"Look, Your mother and Your brothers[a] are
outside seeking You."

33But He answered them, saying, "Who
is My mother, or My brothers?" 34And He
looked around in a circle at those who sat
about Him, and said, "Here are My mother
and My brothers! 35For whoever does the
will of God is My brother and My sister
and mother."

CHAPTER 4

The Parable of the Sower

And again He began to teach by the sea.
And a great multitude was gathered to
Him, so that He got into a boat and sat *in it*
on the sea; and the whole multitude was
on the land facing the sea. 2Then He taught
them many things by parables, and said to
them in His teaching:

3"Listen! Behold, a sower went out to
sow. 4And it happened, as he sowed, *that*
some *seed* fell by the wayside; and the birds
of the air[a] came and devoured it. 5Some fell
on stony ground, where it did not have
much earth; and immediately it sprang up
because it had no depth of earth. 6But
when the sun was up it was scorched, and
because it had no root it withered away.
7And some *seed* fell among thorns; and the
thorns grew up and choked it, and it
yielded no crop. 8But other *seed* fell on
good ground and yielded a crop that
sprang up, increased and produced: some
thirtyfold, some sixty, and some a hundred."

9And He said to them,[a] "He who has
ears to hear, let him hear!"

The Purpose of Parables

10But when He was alone, those around
Him with the twelve asked Him about the
parable. 11And He said to them, "To you it
has been given to know the mystery of the
kingdom of God; but to those who are outside,
all things come in parables, 12so that

'Seeing they may see and not perceive,
And hearing they may hear and not
understand;
Lest they should turn,
And their sins be forgiven them.'"[a]

The Parable of the Sower Explained

13And He said to them, "Do you not understand
this parable? How then will you
understand all the parables? 14The sower
sows the word. 15And these are the ones by
the wayside where the word is sown.
When they hear, Satan comes immediately
and takes away the word that was sown in
their hearts. 16These likewise are the ones
sown on stony ground who, when they
hear the word, immediately receive it with
gladness; 17and they have no root in themselves,
and so endure only for a time. Afterward,
when tribulation or persecution
arises for the word's sake, immediately
they stumble. 18Now these are the ones
sown among thorns; *they are* the ones who
hear the word, 19and the cares of this
world, the deceitfulness of riches, and the
desires for other things entering in choke

3:32 [a]NU-Text and M-Text add *and Your sisters.*
4:4 [a]NU-Text and M-Text omit *of the air.*
4:9 [a]NU-Text and M-Text omit *to them.*
4:12 [a]Isaiah 6:9, 10

3:31–35 Jesus teaches that to be united with Him is a closer bond than even the ties of human families. Whoever does **the will of God** (v. 35) is not merely Jesus' disciple; he belongs to the family of God. On those occasions when we feel slighted by our human families, we can take comfort in our position as children of the King.

the word, and it becomes unfruitful. 20But
these are the ones sown on good ground,
those who hear the word, accept *it*, and
bear fruit: some thirtyfold, some sixty, and
some a hundred."

Light Under a Basket

21Also He said to them, "Is a lamp
brought to be put under a basket or under
a bed? Is it not to be set on a lampstand?
22For there is nothing hidden which will
not be revealed, nor has anything been
kept secret but that it should come to light.
23If anyone has ears to hear, let him hear."
24Then He said to them, "Take heed
what you hear. With the same measure you
use, it will be measured to you; and to you
who hear, more will be given. 25For who-
ever has, to him more will be given; but
whoever does not have, even what he has
will be taken away from him."

The Parable of the Growing Seed

26And He said, "The kingdom of God is
as if a man should scatter seed on the
ground, 27and should sleep by night and
rise by day, and the seed should sprout and
grow, he himself does not know how. 28For
the earth yields crops by itself: first the
blade, then the head, after that the full
grain in the head. 29But when the grain
ripens, immediately he puts in the sickle,
because the harvest has come."

The Parable of the Mustard Seed

30Then He said, "To what shall we liken
the kingdom of God? Or with what para-
ble shall we picture it? 31*It is* like a mustard
seed which, when it is sown on the
ground, is smaller than all the seeds on
earth; 32but when it is sown, it grows up
and becomes greater than all herbs, and
shoots out large branches, so that the birds
of the air may nest under its shade."

Jesus' Use of Parables

33And with many such parables He
spoke the word to them as they were able
to hear *it*. 34But without a parable He did
not speak to them. And when they were
alone, He explained all things to His disci-
ples.

Wind and Wave Obey Jesus

35On the same day, when evening had
come, He said to them, "Let us cross over
to the other side." 36Now when they had
left the multitude, they took Him along in
the boat as He was. And other little boats
were also with Him. 37And a great wind-
storm arose, and the waves beat into the
boat, so that it was already filling. 38But He
was in the stern, asleep on a pillow. And
they awoke Him and said to Him,
"Teacher, do You not care that we are per-
ishing?"
39Then He arose and rebuked the wind,
and said to the sea, "Peace, be still!" And
the wind ceased and there was a great
calm. 40But He said to them, "Why are you
so fearful? How *is it* that you have no
faith?"[a] 41And they feared exceedingly, and

4:40 [a]NU-Text reads *Have you still no faith?*

4:21–23 Just as a **lamp** put on a **lampstand** makes things visible, so the gospel message brings God's truth **to light**. Those who have **ears** are persons who willingly receive this truth. Only they can truly understand and obey it.

4:30–32 The **kingdom of God** appeared very small and weak in the person of Jesus and His little band, but it was destined to be a blessing worldwide. Sometimes the church appears weak, but we should not be discouraged; God will accomplish His worldwide purpose through it. As members of the Body of Christ, we too are vital to His plan, no matter how small our roles may seem to us.

4:35 The disciples were obeying Jesus' command, **Let us cross over**, when the storm came. Obedience does not save us from the storms of life, but when we obey, Jesus is with us to see us through them. Sometimes He delivers us from difficulties. Sometimes He gives us grace to pass through them. In dealing with the challenges we face during the second half of life, we must remember to rely on His strength and presence.

said to one another, "Who can this be, that even the wind and the sea obey Him!"

CHAPTER 5

A Demon-Possessed Man Healed

Then they came to the other side of the sea, to the country of the Gad′a·rēnes.[a] [2]And when He had come out of the boat, immediately there met Him out of the tombs a man with an unclean spirit, [3]who had *his* dwelling among the tombs; and no one could bind him,[a] not even with chains, [4]because he had often been bound with shackles and chains. And the chains had been pulled apart by him, and the shackles broken in pieces; neither could anyone tame him. [5]And always, night and day, he was in the mountains and in the tombs, crying out and cutting himself with stones.

[6]When he saw Jesus from afar, he ran and worshiped Him. [7]And he cried out with a loud voice and said, "What have I to do with You, Jesus, Son of the Most High God? I implore You by God that You do not torment me."

[8]For He said to him, "Come out of the man, unclean spirit!" [9]Then He asked him, "What *is* your name?"

And he answered, saying, "My name *is* Legion; for we are many." [10]Also he begged Him earnestly that He would not send them out of the country.

[11]Now a large herd of swine was feeding there near the mountains. [12]So all the demons begged Him, saying, "Send us to the swine, that we may enter them." [13]And at once Jesus[a] gave them permission. Then the unclean spirits went out and entered the swine (there were about two thousand); and the herd ran violently down the steep place into the sea, and drowned in the sea.

5:1 [a]NU-Text reads *Gerasenes.* 5:3 [a]NU-Text adds *anymore.* 5:13 [a]NU-Text reads *And He gave.*

[14]So those who fed the swine fled, and they told *it* in the city and in the country. And they went out to see what it was that had happened. [15]Then they came to Jesus, and saw the one *who had been* demon-possessed and had the legion, sitting and clothed and in his right mind. And they were afraid. [16]And those who saw it told them how it happened to him *who had been* demon-possessed, and about the swine. [17]Then they began to plead with Him to depart from their region.

[18]And when He got into the boat, he who had been demon-possessed begged Him that he might be with Him. [19]However, Jesus did not permit him, but said to him, "Go home to your friends, and tell them what great things the Lord has done for you, and how He has had compassion on you." [20]And he departed and began to proclaim in De·cap′o·lis all that Jesus had done for him; and all marveled.

A Girl Restored to Life and a Woman Healed

[21]Now when Jesus had crossed over again by boat to the other side, a great multitude gathered to Him; and He was by the sea. [22]And behold, one of the rulers of the synagogue came, Jā·ī′rus by name. And when he saw Him, he fell at His feet [23]and begged Him earnestly, saying, "My little daughter lies at the point of death. Come and lay Your hands on her, that she may be healed, and she will live." [24]So *Jesus* went with him, and a great multitude followed Him and thronged Him.

[25]Now a certain woman had a flow of blood for twelve years, [26]and had suffered many things from many physicians. She had spent all that she had and was no better, but rather grew worse. [27]When she heard about Jesus, she came behind *Him* in the crowd and touched His garment. [28]For

5:19, 20 For this man the call to follow Jesus and witness for Him was a command to **go home** and tell his experience of the power and love of God. Sometimes home is the most needed place to witness for Christ.

> You rarely hear a man who has been through the real agony of suffering who says he disbelieves in God; it is the one who watches others going through suffering who says he disbelieves in God.
>
> Oswald Chambers

she said, "If only I may touch His clothes, I shall be made well."

[29]Immediately the fountain of her blood was dried up, and she felt in *her* body that she was healed of the affliction. [30]And Jesus, immediately knowing in Himself that power had gone out of Him, turned around in the crowd and said, "Who touched My clothes?"

[31]But His disciples said to Him, "You see the multitude thronging You, and You say, 'Who touched Me?' "

[32]And He looked around to see her who had done this thing. [33]But the woman, fearing and trembling, knowing what had happened to her, came and fell down before Him and told Him the whole truth. [34]And He said to her, "Daughter, your faith has made you well. Go in peace, and be healed of your affliction."

[35]While He was still speaking, *some* came from the ruler of the synagogue's *house* who said, "Your daughter is dead. Why trouble the Teacher any further?"

[36]As soon as Jesus heard the word that was spoken, He said to the ruler of the synagogue, "Do not be afraid; only believe." [37]And He permitted no one to follow Him except Peter, James, and John the brother of James. [38]Then He came to the house of the ruler of the synagogue, and saw a tumult and those who wept and wailed loudly. [39]When He came in, He said to them, "Why make this commotion and weep? The child is not dead, but sleeping."

[40]And they ridiculed Him. But when He had put them all outside, He took the father and the mother of the child, and those *who were* with Him, and entered where the child was lying. [41]Then He took the child by the hand, and said to her, "Tal'i·tha, cumi," which is translated, "Little girl, I say to you, arise." [42]Immediately the girl arose and walked, for she was twelve years *of age.* And they were overcome with great amazement. [43]But He commanded them strictly that no one should know it, and said that *something* should be given her to eat.

CHAPTER 6

Jesus Rejected at Nazareth

Then He went out from there and came to His own country, and His disciples followed Him. [2]And when the Sabbath had come, He began to teach in the synagogue. And many hearing *Him* were astonished, saying, "Where *did* this Man *get* these things? And what wisdom *is* this which is given to Him, that such mighty works are performed by His hands! [3]Is this not the carpenter, the Son of Mary, and brother of James, Jō'sēs, Judas, and Simon? And are not His sisters here with us?" So they were offended at Him.

[4]But Jesus said to them, "A prophet is not without honor except in his own country, among his own relatives, and in his own house." [5]Now He could do no mighty work there, except that He laid His hands on a few sick people and healed *them.* [6]And He marveled because of their unbelief. Then He went about the villages in a circuit, teaching.

6:2, 3 Even Jesus' **wisdom** and **mighty works** meant little to those who would not believe. They were **offended at Him** because they knew Him. Does the marvel of the message about Jesus become dull because we hear it often? If so, we need to draw aside and meditate long enough to recover the wonder. As mature Christians we must guard against a tendency toward indifference to the life-changing power of the gospel.

Sending Out the Twelve

[7]And He called the twelve to *Himself,* and began to send them out two *by* two, and gave them power over unclean spirits. [8]He commanded them to take nothing for the journey except a staff—no bag, no bread, no copper in *their* money belts—[9]but to wear sandals, and not to put on two tunics.

[10]Also He said to them, "In whatever place you enter a house, stay there till you depart from that place. [11]And whoever[a] will not receive you nor hear you, when you depart from there, shake off the dust under your feet as a testimony against them.[b] Assuredly, I say to you, it will be more tolerable for Sod′om and Go·mor′rah in the day of judgment than for that city!"

[12]So they went out and preached that *people* should repent. [13]And they cast out many demons, and anointed with oil many who were sick, and healed *them.*

John the Baptist Beheaded

[14]Now King Her′od heard *of Him,* for His name had become well known. And he said, "John the Baptist is risen from the dead, and therefore these powers are at work in him."

[15]Others said, "It is E·lī′jah."

And others said, "It is the Prophet, or[a] like one of the prophets."

[16]But when Her′od heard, he said, "This is John, whom I beheaded; he has been raised from the dead!" [17]For Her′od himself had sent and laid hold of John, and bound him in prison for the sake of He·rō′di·as, his brother Philip's wife; for he had married her. [18]Because John had said to Her′od, "It is not lawful for you to have your brother's wife."

6:11 [a]NU-Text reads *whatever place.* [b]NU-Text omits the rest of this verse. 6:15 [a]NU-Text and M-Text omit *or.*

[19]Therefore He·rō′di·as held it against him and wanted to kill him, but she could not; [20]for Her′od feared John, knowing that he *was* a just and holy man, and he protected him. And when he heard him, he did many things, and heard him gladly.

[21]Then an opportune day came when Her′od on his birthday gave a feast for his nobles, the high officers, and the chief *men* of Galilee. [22]And when He·rō′di·as′ daughter herself came in and danced, and pleased Her′od and those who sat with him, the king said to the girl, "Ask me whatever you want, and I will give *it* to you." [23]He also swore to her, "Whatever you ask me, I will give you, up to half my kingdom."

[24]So she went out and said to her mother, "What shall I ask?"

And she said, "The head of John the Baptist!"

[25]Immediately she came in with haste to the king and asked, saying, "I want you to give me at once the head of John the Baptist on a platter."

[26]And the king was exceedingly sorry; *yet,* because of the oaths and because of those who sat with him, he did not want to refuse her. [27]Immediately the king sent an executioner and commanded his head to be brought. And he went and beheaded him in prison, [28]brought his head on a platter, and gave it to the girl; and the girl gave it to her mother. [29]When his disciples heard *of it,* they came and took away his corpse and laid it in a tomb.

Feeding the Five Thousand

[30]Then the apostles gathered to Jesus and told Him all things, both what they had done and what they had taught. [31]And He said to them, "Come aside by yourselves to a deserted place and rest a while." For there were many coming and going,

6:8–10 take nothing: Their mission was urgent. They were to depend on God and the hospitality of the people (see Matt. 10:11–13). **stay there**: Trying to find a nicer place would cast suspicion on their motives.

A Resting Place

Dr. Frank Minirth, Dr. Paul Meier, and Don Hawkins

When the twelve disciples of Jesus returned home after their first preaching and healing mission, Jesus listened to their reports, then made a suggestion: "Come aside by yourselves to a deserted place and rest a while" (Mark 6:31). The kind of rest He prescribed for them was physical and mental, and it contained the same three components that are so valuable today in reducing anxiety and stress: a change of scene, a change of activity, and adequate time to rejuvenate.

Note that Christ didn't merely suggest that they get a good night's sleep, and neither did He dismiss them with the old platitude, "You'll feel better in the morning." He clearly instructed them to leave their obligations behind, even though their work was far from complete, and retreat to a place that was remote and quiet. He knew they could never rest where they were, no matter how determined they might be.

The same is true for us today. No matter how busy we feel we ought to be, nothing is more essential to a balanced life than setting aside a time and place for regular devotions. When we separate ourselves from the pressing demands that surround us and spend some time alone with the Lord, we return to our work refreshed and revitalized. As we daily fellowship with God and leave our worries in His hands, we can say along with David, "He restores my soul" (Ps. 23:3). ✦

and they did not even have time to eat. 32So
they departed to a deserted place in the
boat by themselves.
33But the multitudes[a] saw them departing, and many knew Him and ran there on foot from all the cities. They arrived before
them and came together to Him. 34And
Jesus, when He came out, saw a great multitude and was moved with compassion for them, because they were like sheep not having a shepherd. So He began to teach
them many things. 35When the day was
now far spent, His disciples came to Him and said, "This is a deserted place, and already the hour *is* late. 36Send them away,
that they may go into the surrounding country and villages and buy themselves bread;[a] for they have nothing to eat."
37But He answered and said to them,
"You give them something to eat."

And they said to Him, "Shall we go and buy two hundred denarii worth of bread and give them *something* to eat?"

6:33 [a]NU-Text and M-Text read *they.*
6:36 [a]NU-Text reads *something to eat* and omits the rest of this verse.

6:37, 38 You give them something to eat: The disciples would serve the needs of the people, but not in their own strength. Jesus took what they had and made it more than enough.

[38]But He said to them, "How many loaves do you have? Go and see."

And when they found out they said, "Five, and two fish."

[39]Then He commanded them to make them all sit down in groups on the green grass. [40]So they sat down in ranks, in hundreds and in fifties. [41]And when He had taken the five loaves and the two fish, He looked up to heaven, blessed and broke the loaves, and gave *them* to His disciples to set before them; and the two fish He divided among *them* all. [42]So they all ate and were filled. [43]And they took up twelve baskets full of fragments and of the fish. [44]Now those who had eaten the loaves were about[a] five thousand men.

Jesus Walks on the Sea

[45]Immediately He made His disciples get into the boat and go before Him to the other side, to Beth·sā′i·da, while He sent the multitude away. [46]And when He had sent them away, He departed to the mountain to pray. [47]Now when evening came, the boat was in the middle of the sea; and He *was* alone on the land. [48]Then He saw them straining at rowing, for the wind was against them. Now about the fourth watch of the night He came to them, walking on the sea, and would have passed them by. [49]And when they saw Him walking on the sea, they supposed it was a ghost, and cried out; [50]for they all saw Him and were troubled. But immediately He talked with them and said to them, "Be of good cheer! It is I; do not be afraid." [51]Then He went up into the boat to them, and the wind ceased. And they were greatly amazed in themselves beyond measure, and marveled. [52]For they had not understood about the loaves, because their heart was hardened.

Many Touch Him and Are Made Well

[53]When they had crossed over, they came to the land of Gen·nes′a·ret and anchored there. [54]And when they came out of the boat, immediately the people recognized Him, [55]ran through that whole surrounding region, and began to carry about on beds those who were sick to wherever they heard He was. [56]Wherever He entered, into villages, cities, or the country, they laid the sick in the marketplaces, and begged Him that they might just touch the hem of His garment. And as many as touched Him were made well.

CHAPTER 7

Defilement Comes from Within

Then the Phar′i·sees and some of the scribes came together to Him, having come from Jerusalem. [2]Now when[a] they saw some of His disciples eat bread with defiled, that is, with unwashed hands, they found fault. [3]For the Phar′i·sees and all the Jews do not eat unless they wash *their* hands in a special way, holding the tradition of the elders. [4]*When they come* from the marketplace, they do not eat unless they wash. And there are many other things which they have received and hold, *like* the washing of cups, pitchers, copper vessels, and couches.

[5]Then the Phar′i·sees and scribes asked Him, "Why do Your disciples not walk according to the tradition of the elders, but eat bread with unwashed hands?"

[6]He answered and said to them, "Well did Ī·sāi′ah prophesy of you hypocrites, as it is written:

6:44 [a]NU-Text and M-Text omit *about*.
7:2 [a]NU-Text omits *when* and *they found fault*.

6:48 passed them by: Jesus was not planning to leave His disciples in their trouble. Just as God had once revealed His saving presence to Moses (Ex. 33:19) and to Elijah (1 Kin. 19:11), so Jesus was revealing His true deity to His disciples.

6:50 It is I could be translated "I am." In these words God revealed Himself to Moses (Ex. 3:14). **do not be afraid**: This revelation of Jesus' deity brought fear to their hearts. In a similar revelation God reassured Abram (Gen. 15:1).

'This people honors Me with their lips,
But their heart is far from Me.
7 *And in vain they worship Me,*
Teaching as doctrines the
commandments of men.'[a]

8 For laying aside the commandment of
God, you hold the tradition of men[a]—the
washing of pitchers and cups, and many
other such things you do."
9 He said to them, "*All too* well you reject
the commandment of God, that you may
keep your tradition. 10 For Moses said,
'Honor your father and your mother';[a]
and, *'He who curses father or mother, let*
him be put to death.'[b] 11 But you say, 'If a
man says to his father or mother, "What-
ever profit you might have received from
me *is* Cor'ban"—' (that is, a gift *to God*),
12 then you no longer let him do anything
for his father or his mother, 13 making the
word of God of no effect through your tra-
dition which you have handed down. And
many such things you do."
14 When He had called all the multitude
to *Himself*, He said to them, "Hear Me,
everyone, and understand: 15 There is noth-
ing that enters a man from outside which
can defile him; but the things which come
out of him, those are the things that defile a
man. 16 If anyone has ears to hear, let him
hear!"[a]
17 When He had entered a house away
from the crowd, His disciples asked Him
concerning the parable. 18 So He said to
them, "Are you thus without understand-
ing also? Do you not perceive that what-
ever enters a man from outside cannot de-
file him, 19 because it does not enter his
heart but his stomach, and is eliminated,
thus purifying all foods?"[a] 20 And He said,
"What comes out of a man, that defiles a
man. 21 For from within, out of the heart of
men, proceed evil thoughts, adulteries,
fornications, murders, 22 thefts, covetous-
ness, wickedness, deceit, lewdness, an evil
eye, blasphemy, pride, foolishness. 23 All
these evil things come from within and de-
file a man."

A Gentile Shows Her Faith

24 From there He arose and went to the
region of Tȳre and Sī'don.[a] And He en-
tered a house and wanted no one to know
it, but He could not be hidden. 25 For a
woman whose young daughter had an un-
clean spirit heard about Him, and she
came and fell at His feet. 26 The woman was
a Greek, a Sȳ'rō-Phoe•ni'cian by birth, and
she kept asking Him to cast the demon out
of her daughter. 27 But Jesus said to her,
"Let the children be filled first, for it is not
good to take the children's bread and
throw *it* to the little dogs."
28 And she answered and said to Him,
"Yes, Lord, yet even the little dogs under
the table eat from the children's crumbs."
29 Then He said to her, "For this saying
go your way; the demon has gone out of
your daughter."
30 And when she had come to her house,
she found the demon gone out, and her
daughter lying on the bed.

Jesus Heals a Deaf-Mute

31 Again, departing from the region of
Tȳre and Sī'don, He came through the

7:7 [a]Isaiah 29:13 7:8 [a]NU-Text omits the rest of this verse. 7:10 [a]Exodus 20:12; Deuteronomy 5:16 [b]Exodus 21:17 7:16 [a]NU-Text omits this verse. 7:19 [a]NU-Text ends quotation with *eliminated*, setting off the final clause as Mark's comment that Jesus has declared all foods clean. 7:24 [a]NU-Text omits *and Sidon*.

7:9–13 An example of Jewish human tradition evading God's law. God clearly said, **Honor your father and your mother** (v. 10). But the scribes annulled this by their rules which said if a man vowed the resources he would have used to help his parents as **Corban** (dedicated to God), he could not give them to his parents. These things were dedicated verbally, but not actually given, to the temple. Having said "Corban," he could withdraw them for personal use. Thus with one hypocritical word he acted selfishly, lied to God, and deprived his parents of needed support. We never serve God by mistreating another.

midst of the region of De·cap′o·lis to the
Sea of Galilee. [32]Then they brought to Him
one who was deaf and had an impediment
in his speech, and they begged Him to put
His hand on him. [33]And He took him aside
from the multitude, and put His fingers in
his ears, and He spat and touched his
tongue. [34]Then, looking up to heaven, He
sighed, and said to him, "Eph′pha·tha,"
that is, "Be opened."

[35]Immediately his ears were opened,
and the impediment of his tongue was
loosed, and he spoke plainly. [36]Then He
commanded them that they should tell no
one; but the more He commanded them,
the more widely they proclaimed *it*. [37]And
they were astonished beyond measure,
saying, "He has done all things well. He
makes both the deaf to hear and the mute
to speak."

CHAPTER 8

Feeding the Four Thousand

In those days, the multitude being very
great and having nothing to eat, Jesus
called His disciples *to Him* and said to
them, [2]"I have compassion on the multi-
tude, because they have now continued
with Me three days and have nothing to
eat. [3]And if I send them away hungry to
their own houses, they will faint on the
way; for some of them have come from
afar."

[4]Then His disciples answered Him,
"How can one satisfy these people with
bread here in the wilderness?"

[5]He asked them, "How many loaves do
you have?"

And they said, "Seven."

[6]So He commanded the multitude to sit
down on the ground. And He took the
seven loaves and gave thanks, broke *them*
and gave *them* to His disciples to set before
them; and they set *them* before the multi-
tude. [7]They also had a few small fish; and
having blessed them, He said to set them
also before *them*. [8]So they ate and were
filled, and they took up seven large baskets
of leftover fragments. [9]Now those who had
eaten were about four thousand. And He
sent them away, [10]immediately got into the
boat with His disciples, and came to the re-
gion of Dal·ma·nū′tha.

The Pharisees Seek a Sign

[11]Then the Phar′i·sees came out and be-
gan to dispute with Him, seeking from
Him a sign from heaven, testing Him. [12]But
He sighed deeply in His spirit, and said,
"Why does this generation seek a sign? As-
suredly, I say to you, no sign shall be given
to this generation."

Beware of the Leaven of the Pharisees and Herod

[13]And He left them, and getting into the
boat again, departed to the other side.
[14]Now the disciples[a] had forgotten to take
bread, and they did not have more than
one loaf with them in the boat. [15]Then He
charged them, saying, "Take heed, beware
of the leaven of the Phar′i·sees and the
leaven of Her′od."

[16]And they reasoned among themselves,
saying, "*It is* because we have no bread."

[17]But Jesus, being aware of *it*, said to
them, "Why do you reason because you
have no bread? Do you not yet perceive
nor understand? Is your heart still[a] hard-
ened? [18]Having eyes, do you not see? And
having ears, do you not hear? And do you
not remember? [19]When I broke the five
loaves for the five thousand, how many
baskets full of fragments did you take up?"

They said to Him, "Twelve."

[20]"Also, when I broke the seven for the
four thousand, how many large baskets
full of fragments did you take up?"

And they said, "Seven."

[21]So He said to them, "How *is it* you do
not understand?"

A Blind Man Healed at Bethsaida

[22]Then He came to Beth·sā′i·da; and
they brought a blind man to Him, and

8:14 [a]NU-Text and M-Text read *they*. 8:17 [a]NU-Text omits *still*.

begged Him to touch him. 23So He took the
blind man by the hand and led him out of
the town. And when He had spit on his
eyes and put His hands on him, He asked
him if he saw anything.
24And he looked up and said, "I see men
like trees, walking."
25Then He put *His* hands on his eyes
again and made him look up. And he was
restored and saw everyone clearly. 26Then
He sent him away to his house, saying,
"Neither go into the town, nor tell anyone
in the town."[a]

Peter Confesses Jesus as the Christ

27Now Jesus and His disciples went out
to the towns of Caes·a·rē′a Phi·lip′pī;
and on the road He asked His disciples,
saying to them, "Who do men say that
I am?"
28So they answered, "John the Baptist;
but some *say,* E·lī′jah; and others, one of
the prophets."
29He said to them, "But who do you say
that I am?"
Peter answered and said to Him, "You
are the Christ."
30Then He strictly warned them that
they should tell no one about Him.

Jesus Predicts His Death and Resurrection

31And He began to teach them that the
Son of Man must suffer many things, and
be rejected by the elders and chief priests

> Those who have suffered most are often able to comfort others best.
> Billy Graham

and scribes, and be killed, and after three
days rise again. 32He spoke this word
openly. Then Peter took Him aside and began to rebuke Him. 33But when He had
turned around and looked at His disciples,
He rebuked Peter, saying, "Get behind
Me, Satan! For you are not mindful of
the things of God, but the things of
men."

Take Up the Cross and Follow Him

34When He had called the people to
Himself, with His disciples also, He said to
them, "Whoever desires to come after Me,
let him deny himself, and take up his cross,
and follow Me. 35For whoever desires to
save his life will lose it, but whoever loses
his life for My sake and the gospel's will
save it. 36For what will it profit a man if he
gains the whole world, and loses his own
soul? 37Or what will a man give in exchange for his soul? 38For whoever is
ashamed of Me and My words in this adulterous and sinful generation, of him the
Son of Man also will be ashamed when He
comes in the glory of His Father with the
holy angels."

8:26 [a]NU-Text reads *"Do not even go into the town."*

8:27—9:1 Peter's confession of Jesus as the **Christ** (8:27–30) is the turning point of Mark's Gospel. Jesus immediately explained that to be the Christ meant He must suffer (8:31–33), and His disciples must follow Him in suffering (8:34—9:1). Even today, true discipleship requires total dedication to Christ and selfless service to others.

8:33 Peter was so wrong that Jesus **rebuked** him as He had the unclean spirits in 1:25. **things of God**: The disciples were thinking like the average man—not from the divine perspective.

8:34 Deny himself does not mean to hate himself or to go without something, but to give full control of his life to Christ. **take up his cross**: The person who carried a cross was on the way to execution. Thus it is a graphic picture of one who is dead to his own will. He is ready to accept whatever costs are involved in a life of complete Christian commitment. Have you placed your life—including your goals and dreams—in the hands of Christ?

8:36–38 Our eternal destiny is reflected in our relationship to Christ in this life.

CHAPTER 9

Jesus Transfigured on the Mount

And He said to them, "Assuredly, I say
to you that there are some standing here
who will not taste death till they see the
kingdom of God present with power."
[2]Now after six days Jesus took Peter,
James, and John, and led them up on a
high mountain apart by themselves; and
He was transfigured before them. [3]His
clothes became shining, exceedingly
white, like snow, such as no launderer
on earth can whiten them. [4]And E·lī′jah
appeared to them with Moses, and they
were talking with Jesus. [5]Then Peter an-
swered and said to Jesus, "Rabbi, it is good
for us to be here; and let us make three
tabernacles: one for You, one for Moses,
and one for E·lī′jah"— [6]because he did not
know what to say, for they were greatly
afraid.
[7]And a cloud came and overshadowed
them; and a voice came out of the cloud,
saying, "This is My beloved Son. Hear
Him!" [8]Suddenly, when they had looked
around, they saw no one anymore, but
only Jesus with themselves.
[9]Now as they came down from the
mountain, He commanded them that they
should tell no one the things they had seen,
till the Son of Man had risen from the dead.
[10]So they kept this word to themselves,
questioning what the rising from the dead
meant.
[11]And they asked Him, saying, "Why do
the scribes say that E·lī′jah must come
first?"
[12]Then He answered and told them,
"Indeed, E·lī′jah is coming first and re-
stores all things. And how is it written
concerning the Son of Man, that He must
suffer many things and be treated with
contempt? [13]But I say to you that E·lī′jah
has also come, and they did to him what-
ever they wished, as it is written of him."

A Boy Is Healed

[14]And when He came to the disciples,
He saw a great multitude around them,
and scribes disputing with them. [15]Imme-
diately, when they saw Him, all the peo-
ple were greatly amazed, and running to
Him, greeted Him. [16]And He asked the
scribes, "What are you discussing with
them?"
[17]Then one of the crowd answered and
said, "Teacher, I brought You my son, who
has a mute spirit. [18]And wherever it seizes
him, it throws him down; he foams at the
mouth, gnashes his teeth, and becomes
rigid. So I spoke to Your disciples, that
they should cast it out, but they could
not."
[19]He answered him and said, "O faith-
less generation, how long shall I be with
you? How long shall I bear with you?
Bring him to Me." [20]Then they brought him
to Him. And when he saw Him, immedi-
ately the spirit convulsed him, and he fell
on the ground and wallowed, foaming at
the mouth.
[21]So He asked his father, "How long has
this been happening to him?"
And he said, "From childhood. [22]And
often he has thrown him both into the fire
and into the water to destroy him. But if
You can do anything, have compassion on
us and help us."
[23]Jesus said to him, "If you can believe,[a]

9:23 [a]NU-Text reads *" 'If You can!' All things. . . ."*

9:5, 6 Peter did not understand what was happening. **Three tabernacles** suggests that he wanted to stay on the mountain. But this experience was to prepare him to carry his cross in the day-to-day world. His answer tended to put Jesus, **Moses**, and **Elijah** on the same level. **greatly afraid**: Awed at the revelation of Jesus' divine glory.

9:7 The **cloud** represented God's presence. The voice declared that Jesus was God's **Son** in a way that no one else was—not even Moses and Elijah. **Hear Him**! Obey Him above all others (Deut. 18:15).

all things *are* possible to him who believes."

24Immediately the father of the child
cried out and said with tears, "Lord, I believe; help my unbelief!"

25When Jesus saw that the people came
running together, He rebuked the unclean
spirit, saying to it, "Deaf and dumb spirit, I
command you, come out of him and enter
him no more!" 26Then *the spirit* cried out,
convulsed him greatly, and came out of
him. And he became as one dead, so that
many said, "He is dead." 27But Jesus took
him by the hand and lifted him up, and he
arose.

28And when He had come into the
house, His disciples asked Him privately,
"Why could we not cast it out?"

29So He said to them, "This kind can
come out by nothing but prayer and fasting."[a]

Jesus Again Predicts His Death and Resurrection

30Then they departed from there and
passed through Galilee, and He did not
want anyone to know *it*. 31For He taught
His disciples and said to them, "The Son of
Man is being betrayed into the hands of
men, and they will kill Him. And after He
is killed, He will rise the third day." 32But
they did not understand this saying, and
were afraid to ask Him.

Who Is the Greatest?

33Then He came to Ca·per'na·um. And
when He was in the house He asked them,
"What was it you disputed among yourselves on the road?" 34But they kept silent,
for on the road they had disputed among
themselves who *would be the* greatest.
35And He sat down, called the twelve, and
said to them, "If anyone desires to be first,
he shall be last of all and servant of all."
36Then He took a little child and set him in
the midst of them. And when He had taken
him in His arms, He said to them, 37"Whoever receives one of these little children in
My name receives Me; and whoever receives Me, receives not Me but Him who
sent Me."

Jesus Forbids Sectarianism

38Now John answered Him, saying,
"Teacher, we saw someone who does not
follow us casting out demons in Your
name, and we forbade him because he
does not follow us."

39But Jesus said, "Do not forbid him, for
no one who works a miracle in My name
can soon afterward speak evil of Me. 40For
he who is not against us is on our[a] side.
41For whoever gives you a cup of water to
drink in My name, because you belong to
Christ, assuredly, I say to you, he will by
no means lose his reward.

Jesus Warns of Offenses

42"But whoever causes one of these little
ones who believe in Me to stumble, it
would be better for him if a millstone were
hung around his neck, and he were thrown
into the sea. 43If your hand causes you to
sin, cut it off. It is better for you to enter
into life maimed, rather than having two
hands, to go to hell, into the fire that shall
never be quenched— 44where

9:29 [a]NU-Text omits *and fasting*. 9:40 [a]M-Text reads *against you is on your side.*

9:36, 37 Children were given little status in the ancient world. The child here represents all needy people, but especially needy believers. Christ's disciples take a lowly place by ministering to the needs of the lowly. **receives Me**: This service is accepted as if done to Jesus who made Himself lowest of all. Despite what the world would have us believe, true greatness is found in rendering selfless service to others rather than in striving for personal advancement.

9:41 a cup of water: The most trivial service given to encourage a Christian receives God's blessing. It is not the size of the task, but loving faithfulness that counts with God.

'Their worm does not die
And the fire is not quenched.'[a]

45And if your foot causes you to sin, cut it
off. It is better for you to enter life lame,
rather than having two feet, to be cast into
hell, into the fire that shall never be
quenched— 46where

'Their worm does not die
And the fire is not quenched.'[a]

47And if your eye causes you to sin, pluck it
out. It is better for you to enter the king-
dom of God with one eye, rather than hav-
ing two eyes, to be cast into hell fire—
48where

'Their worm does not die
And the fire is not quenched.'[a]

Tasteless Salt Is Worthless

49"For everyone will be seasoned with
fire,[a] and every sacrifice will be seasoned
with salt. 50Salt *is* good, but if the salt loses
its flavor, how will you season it? Have salt
in yourselves, and have peace with one an-
other."

CHAPTER 10

Marriage and Divorce

Then He arose from there and came to the region of Judea by the other side of the Jordan. And multitudes gathered to Him again, and as He was accustomed, He taught them again.

2The Phar'i·sees came and asked Him,
"Is it lawful for a man to divorce *his* wife?"
testing Him.
3And He answered and said to them,
"What did Moses command you?"
4They said, "Moses permitted *a man* to
write a certificate of divorce, and to dis-
miss *her*."
5And Jesus answered and said to them,
"Because of the hardness of your heart he
wrote you this precept. 6But from the be-
ginning of the creation, God *'made them
male and female.'*[a] 7*'For this reason a man
shall leave his father and mother and be
joined to his wife, 8and the two shall be-
come one flesh';*[a] so then they are no longer
two, but one flesh. 9Therefore what God
has joined together, let not man separate."
10In the house His disciples also asked
Him again about the same *matter*. 11So He
said to them, "Whoever divorces his wife
and marries another commits adultery
against her. 12And if a woman divorces her
husband and marries another, she commits
adultery."

Jesus Blesses Little Children

13Then they brought little children to
Him, that He might touch them; but the
disciples rebuked those who brought *them*.
14But when Jesus saw *it*, He was greatly
displeased and said to them, "Let the little
children come to Me, and do not forbid
them; for of such is the kingdom of God.
15Assuredly, I say to you, whoever does not
receive the kingdom of God as a little child
will by no means enter it." 16And He took
them up in His arms, laid *His* hands on
them, and blessed them.

Jesus Counsels the Rich Young Ruler

17Now as He was going out on the road,
one came running, knelt before Him, and
asked Him, "Good Teacher, what shall I do
that I may inherit eternal life?"
18So Jesus said to him, "Why do you call
Me good? No one *is* good but One, *that is*,
God. 19You know the commandments: *'Do*

9:44 [a]NU-Text omits this verse. 9:46 [a]NU-Text omits the last clause of verse 45 and all of verse 46. 9:48 [a]Isaiah 66:24 9:49 [a]NU-Text omits the rest of this verse. 10:6 [a]Genesis 1:27; 5:2 10:8 [a]Genesis 2:24

10:15 receive . . . as a little child: Just as a child trustingly receives the necessities of life from his parents, so we are to receive the kingdom of God. We can no more earn the kingdom than a child can earn his livelihood.

Friends, Young and Old

Sherwood Eliot Wirt

Dr. Samuel Johnson said, "If a man does not make new acquaintances as he advances through life, he will soon find himself left alone." He could have said the same of a woman.

Old friends are choice, but so are new friends, and we find them in many places and of various ages. We should never let pass an opportunity to meet them. It's a major blunder for us to make friends exclusively among people our own age. If we do that, we let the world segregate us! Young people whose dress makes them seem to our generation as if they came from outer space are actually eager to make friends with us. Many of them covet a warmhearted relationship with an older person.

Similarly, middle-aged people now in their forties and fifties would like to become friends with older people because they see what they will be shortly. They are curious to know how life will treat them, how they will feel, what works, and what doesn't.

One of the most heartwarming experiences of life is becoming grandparents. To make friends with little children, especially if they are one's own progeny, is a free ticket to happiness. Yet many Americans are finding distance a real obstacle to grandparenting. Families move away, taking the children, and visits are few and far between. In such cases many are becoming "adoptive grandparents" to children in the neighborhood or in the church family. Children are quick to respond to such a relationship. And the resulting outpouring of affection is a blessing to young and old alike. If no children are around you, and your own family is not nearby, find yourself some little friends. You won't be sorry. ✦

not commit adultery,' 'Do not murder,' 'Do not steal,' 'Do not bear false witness,' ' Do not defraud,' 'Honor your father and your mother.' "[a]

20And he answered and said to Him,
"Teacher, all these things I have kept from
my youth."

21Then Jesus, looking at him, loved him,
and said to him, "One thing you lack: Go
your way, sell whatever you have and give
to the poor, and you will have treasure in
heaven; and come, take up the cross, and
follow Me."

22But he was sad at this word, and went
away sorrowful, for he had great posses-
sions.

With God All Things Are Possible

23Then Jesus looked around and said to
His disciples, "How hard it is for those

10:19 [a]Exodus 20:12–16; Deuteronomy 5:16–20

10:21 One thing: The young man needed to dethrone the idol of riches and to love God instead. He had seemingly kept several commandments, but had violated the first: "You shall have no other gods before Me" (Ex. 20:3). To **take up the cross** is to give that loyalty to God which we normally give to ourselves (Deut. 6:5). We need to stop and examine ourselves to determine whether we are giving top priority to anything other than God, including family or work.

who have riches to enter the kingdom of
God!" 24And the disciples were astonished
at His words. But Jesus answered again
and said to them, "Children, how hard it
is for those who trust in riches[a] to enter
the kingdom of God! 25It is easier for a
camel to go through the eye of a needle
than for a rich man to enter the kingdom
of God."
26And they were greatly astonished, say-
ing among themselves, "Who then can be
saved?"
27But Jesus looked at them and said,
"With men *it is* impossible, but not with
God; for with God all things are possible."
28Then Peter began to say to Him, "See,
we have left all and followed You."
29So Jesus answered and said, "As-
suredly, I say to you, there is no one who
has left house or brothers or sisters or
father or mother or wife[a] or children or
lands, for My sake and the gospel's, 30who
shall not receive a hundredfold now in this
time—houses and brothers and sisters and
mothers and children and lands, with per-
secutions—and in the age to come, eternal
life. 31But many *who are* first will be last,
and the last first."

Jesus a Third Time Predicts His Death and Resurrection

32Now they were on the road, going up
to Jerusalem, and Jesus was going before
them; and they were amazed. And as they
followed they were afraid. Then He took
the twelve aside again and began to tell
them the things that would happen to
Him: 33"Behold, we are going up to Jerusa-
lem, and the Son of Man will be betrayed
to the chief priests and to the scribes; and
they will condemn Him to death and de-
liver Him to the Gentiles; 34and they will
mock Him, and scourge Him, and spit on
Him, and kill Him. And the third day He
will rise again."

10:24 [a]NU-Text omits *for those who trust in riches.*
10:29 [a]NU-Text omits *or wife.*

Greatness Is Serving

35Then James and John, the sons of
Zeb'-e•dee, came to Him, saying, "Teacher,
we want You to do for us whatever we
ask."
36And He said to them, "What do you
want Me to do for you?"
37They said to Him, "Grant us that we
may sit, one on Your right hand and the
other on Your left, in Your glory."
38But Jesus said to them, "You do not
know what you ask. Are you able to drink
the cup that I drink, and be baptized with
the baptism that I am baptized with?"
39They said to Him, "We are able."
So Jesus said to them, "You will indeed
drink the cup that I drink, and with the
baptism I am baptized with you will be
baptized; 40but to sit on My right hand and
on My left is not Mine to give, but *it is for*
those for whom it is prepared."
41And when the ten heard *it,* they began
to be greatly displeased with James and
John. 42But Jesus called them to *Himself* and
said to them, "You know that those who
are considered rulers over the Gentiles
lord it over them, and their great ones ex-
ercise authority over them. 43Yet it shall not
be so among you; but whoever desires to
become great among you shall be your ser-
vant. 44And whoever of you desires to be
first shall be slave of all. 45For even the Son
of Man did not come to be served, but to
serve, and to give His life a ransom for
many."

Jesus Heals Blind Bartimaeus

46Now they came to Jericho. As He went
out of Jericho with His disciples and a
great multitude, blind Bar•ti•maē'us, the
son of Ti•maē'us, sat by the road begging.
47And when he heard that it was Jesus of
Nazareth, he began to cry out and say,
"Jesus, Son of David, have mercy on me!"
48Then many warned him to be quiet;
but he cried out all the more, "Son of Da-
vid, have mercy on me!"
49So Jesus stood still and commanded
him to be called.

Then they called the blind man, saying
to him, "Be of good cheer. Rise, He is call-
ing you."
50And throwing aside his garment, he
rose and came to Jesus.
51So Jesus answered and said to him,
"What do you want Me to do for you?"
The blind man said to Him, "Rab·bō′nī,
that I may receive my sight."
52Then Jesus said to him, "Go your way;
your faith has made you well." And imme-
diately he received his sight and followed
Jesus on the road.

CHAPTER 11

The Triumphal Entry

Now when they drew near Jerusalem, to
Beth′pha·gē[a] and Beth′a·ny, at the Mount
of Olives, He sent two of His disciples;
2and He said to them, "Go into the village
opposite you; and as soon as you have en-
tered it you will find a colt tied, on which
no one has sat. Loose it and bring *it*. 3And
if anyone says to you, 'Why are you doing
this?' say, 'The Lord has need of it,' and im-
mediately he will send it here."
4So they went their way, and found the[a]
colt tied by the door outside on the street,
and they loosed it. 5But some of those who
stood there said to them, "What are you
doing, loosing the colt?"
6And they spoke to them just as Jesus
had commanded. So they let them go.
7Then they brought the colt to Jesus and
threw their clothes on it, and He sat on it.
8And many spread their clothes on the
road, and others cut down leafy branches
from the trees and spread *them* on the road.
9Then those who went before and those
who followed cried out, saying:

"Hō·san′na!
'Blessed is He who comes in the name
of the Lord!'[a]
10 Blessed *is* the kingdom of our father
David
That comes in the name of the Lord![a]
Hō·san′na in the highest!"

11And Jesus went into Jerusalem and into
the temple. So when He had looked
around at all things, as the hour was al-
ready late, He went out to Beth′a·ny with
the twelve.

The Fig Tree Withered

12Now the next day, when they had
come out from Beth′a·ny, He was hungry.
13And seeing from afar a fig tree having
leaves, He went to see if perhaps He would
find something on it. When He came to it,
He found nothing but leaves, for it was not
the season for figs. 14In response Jesus said
to it, "Let no one eat fruit from you ever
again."
And His disciples heard *it*.

Jesus Cleanses the Temple

15So they came to Jerusalem. Then Jesus
went into the temple and began to drive
out those who bought and sold in the tem-
ple, and overturned the tables of the
money changers and the seats of those
who sold doves. 16And He would not allow
anyone to carry wares through the temple.
17Then He taught, saying to them, "Is it not
written, *'My house shall be called a house
of prayer for all nations'*?[a] But you have
made it a *'den of thieves.'*"[b]

11:1 [a]M-Text reads *Bethsphage.* 11:4 [a]NU-Text and M-Text read *a.* 11:9 [a]Psalm 118:26 11:10 [a]NU-Text omits *in the name of the Lord.* 11:17 [a]Isaiah 56:7 [b]Jeremiah 7:11

11:9, 10 This song from Ps. 118:26 was often sung by pilgrims on their way to the Passover. Here the song clearly reflected the people's expectation of the promised Messiah. **our father David**: The disciples believed that, in Jesus, God would fulfill His promises to David. See 10:47; 12:35–37.

11:12–14 An enacted parable describing Jesus' rejection at Jerusalem. The **fig tree** represented the Jewish nation. Its **leaves** were Judaism's outward religious observances. **found nothing**: Lack of fruit stood for the rejection of Jesus, which would be followed by judgment.

Righteous Anger

Gloria Gaither

Many people who have not read the Bible think that Jesus was a passive person who simply preached positive messages of peace. But Jesus was often angry when confronted by sin and injustice. He drove the money changers out of the temple (Mark 11:15, 16), criticized His disciples for their doubts (Matt. 8:26; John 20:27), and condemned the Pharisees over their hypocrisy (Matt. 23; Mark 3:5).

Jesus calls His followers to speak out against injustice and other moral issues boldly and not in a meek and quiet voice. He expects us to know the difference between right and wrong (Heb. 5:14; 1 John 4:6) and to call attention to the problems of the world (Rom. 12:9, 21; Heb. 3:12, 13). He does not want us to sit quietly by when sin is winning out.

"Jesus calls His followers to speak out against injustice."

We are not to be angry out of bitterness or rage (Eph. 4:31), but when we see a wrong we must speak against it. If it is not righted, we must speak out again, even if we have to do so forcefully. In order to be salt and light to the world (Matt. 5:13, 14), we may, at times, need to raise our voices in righteous anger. ✦

18And the scribes and chief priests heard
it and sought how they might destroy Him;
for they feared Him, because all the people
were astonished at His teaching. 19When
evening had come, He went out of the city.

The Lesson of the Withered Fig Tree

20Now in the morning, as they passed
by, they saw the fig tree dried up from the
roots. 21And Peter, remembering, said to
Him, "Rabbi, look! The fig tree which You
cursed has withered away."

22So Jesus answered and said to them,
"Have faith in God. 23For assuredly, I say to
you, whoever says to this mountain, 'Be removed
and be cast into the sea,' and does
not doubt in his heart, but believes that
those things he says will be done, he will
have whatever he says. 24Therefore I say to
you, whatever things you ask when you
pray, believe that you receive *them*, and
you will have *them*.

Forgiveness and Prayer

25"And whenever you stand praying, if
you have anything against anyone, forgive
him, that your Father in heaven may also
forgive you your trespasses. 26But if you do
not forgive, neither will your Father in
heaven forgive your trespasses."[a]

Jesus' Authority Questioned

27Then they came again to Jerusalem.
And as He was walking in the temple, the
chief priests, the scribes, and the elders
came to Him. 28And they said to Him, "By
what authority are You doing these things?

11:26 [a]NU-Text omits this verse.

And who gave You this authority to do
these things?"
29But Jesus answered and said to them,
"I also will ask you one question; then an-
swer Me, and I will tell you by what au-
thority I do these things: 30The baptism of
John—was it from heaven or from men?
Answer Me."
31And they reasoned among themselves,
saying, "If we say, 'From heaven,' He will
say, 'Why then did you not believe him?'
32But if we say, 'From men' "—they feared
the people, for all counted John to have
been a prophet indeed. 33So they answered
and said to Jesus, "We do not know."
And Jesus answered and said to them,
"Neither will I tell you by what authority I
do these things."

CHAPTER 12

The Parable of the Wicked Vinedressers

Then He began to speak to them in
parables: "A man planted a vineyard and
set a hedge around *it,* dug *a place for* the
wine vat and built a tower. And he leased it
to vinedressers and went into a far country.
2Now at vintage-time he sent a servant to
the vinedressers, that he might receive
some of the fruit of the vineyard from the
vinedressers. 3And they took *him* and beat
him and sent *him* away empty-handed.
4Again he sent them another servant, and
at him they threw stones,[a] wounded *him* in
the head, and sent *him* away shamefully
treated. 5And again he sent another, and
him they killed; and many others, beating
some and killing some. 6Therefore still
having one son, his beloved, he also sent
him to them last, saying, 'They will respect
my son.' 7But those vinedressers said
among themselves, 'This is the heir. Come,
let us kill him, and the inheritance will be
ours.' 8So they took him and killed *him* and
cast *him* out of the vineyard.
9"Therefore what will the owner of the
vineyard do? He will come and destroy the
vinedressers, and give the vineyard to oth-
ers. 10Have you not even read this Scrip-
ture:

'The stone which the builders rejected
Has become the chief cornerstone.
11 *This was the LORD's doing,*
And it is marvelous in our eyes'?"[a]

12And they sought to lay hands on Him,
but feared the multitude, for they knew He
had spoken the parable against them. So
they left Him and went away.

The Pharisees: Is It Lawful to Pay Taxes to Caesar?

13Then they sent to Him some of the
Phar'i·sees and the He·rō'di·ans, to catch
Him in *His* words. 14When they had come,
they said to Him, "Teacher, we know that
You are true, and care about no one; for
You do not regard the person of men, but
teach the way of God in truth. Is it lawful
to pay taxes to Caesar, or not? 15Shall we
pay, or shall we not pay?"
But He, knowing their hypocrisy, said to
them, "Why do you test Me? Bring Me a
denarius that I may see *it.*" 16So they
brought *it.*
And He said to them, "Whose image
and inscription *is* this?" They said to Him,
"Caesar's."
17And Jesus answered and said to them,
"Render to Caesar the things that are

12:4 [a]NU-Text omits *and at him they threw stones.*
12:11 [a]Psalm 118:22, 23

12:1–8 Jesus probably applied Isaiah's parable (Is. 5:1–7) to His own situation. **A man**: God. **vineyard**: God's blessings to the nation of Israel. **vinedressers**: The rulers of the Jews (see v. 12). **servant . . . another servant** (vv. 2–5): The OT prophets. **They will respect my son**: A human landlord would never have sent his son into such danger, but God's love risks all to save us from our rebellion.

Caesar's, and to God the things that are God's."

And they marveled at Him.

The Sadducees: What About the Resurrection?

[18]Then *some* Sad'dū·cees, who say there
is no resurrection, came to Him; and they
asked Him, saying: [19]"Teacher, Moses
wrote to us that if a man's brother dies, and
leaves *his* wife behind, and leaves no chil-
dren, his brother should take his wife and
raise up offspring for his brother. [20]Now
there were seven brothers. The first took a
wife; and dying, he left no offspring. [21]And
the second took her, and he died; nor did
he leave any offspring. And the third like-
wise. [22]So the seven had her and left no off-
spring. Last of all the woman died also.
[23]Therefore, in the resurrection, when they
rise, whose wife will she be? For all seven
had her as wife."

[24]Jesus answered and said to them, "Are
you not therefore mistaken, because you
do not know the Scriptures nor the power
of God? [25]For when they rise from the
dead, they neither marry nor are given in
marriage, but are like angels in heaven.
[26]But concerning the dead, that they rise,
have you not read in the book of Moses, in
the *burning* bush *passage,* how God spoke
to him, saying, *'I am the God of Abraham,
the God of Isaac, and the God of Jacob'*?[a]
[27]He is not the God of the dead, but the
God of the living. You are therefore greatly
mistaken."

12:26 [a]Exodus 3:6, 15 12:28 [a]NU-Text reads *seeing.* 12:30 [a]Deuteronomy 6:4, 5 [b]NU-Text omits this sentence. 12:31 [a]Leviticus 19:18
12:33 [a]NU-Text omits *with all the soul.*

I pray that I will always love You, the Lord my God, with all my heart, with all my soul, with all my mind, and with all my strength and that I will love my neighbor as myself.

adapted from Mark 12:30, 31

The Scribes: Which Is the First Commandment of All?

[28]Then one of the scribes came, and
having heard them reasoning together,
perceiving[a] that He had answered them
well, asked Him, "Which is the first com-
mandment of all?"

[29]Jesus answered him, "The first of all
the commandments *is: 'Hear, O Israel, the
LORD our God, the LORD is one.* [30]*And you
shall love the LORD your God with all your
heart, with all your soul, with all your
mind, and with all your strength.'*[a] This *is*
the first commandment.[b] [31]And the second,
like *it, is* this: *'You shall love your neighbor
as yourself.'*[a] There is no other command-
ment greater than these."

[32]So the scribe said to Him, "Well *said,*
Teacher. You have spoken the truth, for
there is one God, and there is no other but
He. [33]And to love Him with all the heart,
with all the understanding, with all the
soul,[a] and with all the strength, and to love
one's neighbor as oneself, is more than all
the whole burnt offerings and sacrifices."

[34]Now when Jesus saw that he answered
wisely, He said to him, "You are not far
from the kingdom of God."

12:29–31 love the Lord . . . with all: Jesus asks total devotion from His disciples. Love for our **neighbor** is the practical outworking of our love for God. **as yourself**: Care for his welfare as you care for your own. We need to avoid becoming wrapped up in ourselves and our families and reach out to the needy and lonely people who surround us.

12:34 Because of this scribe's humility and understanding of God's true purpose he was **not far** from accepting Jesus as the Christ.

But after that no one dared question Him.

Jesus: How Can David Call His Descendant Lord?

[35]Then Jesus answered and said, while
He taught in the temple, "How *is it* that the
scribes say that the Christ is the Son of David? [36]For David himself said by the Holy
Spirit:

'The LORD said to my Lord,
"Sit at My right hand,
Till I make Your enemies Your footstool."'[a]

[37]Therefore David himself calls Him *'Lord'*;
how is He *then* his Son?"

And the common people heard Him gladly.

Beware of the Scribes

[38]Then He said to them in His teaching,
"Beware of the scribes, who desire to go
around in long robes, *love* greetings in the
marketplaces, [39]the best seats in the syna-
gogues, and the best places at feasts, [40]who
devour widows' houses, and for a pretense
make long prayers. These will receive
greater condemnation."

The Widow's Two Mites

[41]Now Jesus sat opposite the treasury
and saw how the people put money into
the treasury. And many *who were* rich put
in much. [42]Then one poor widow came and
threw in two mites,[a] which make a quad-
rans. [43]So He called His disciples to *Himself*
and said to them, "Assuredly, I say to you
that this poor widow has put in more than
all those who have given to the treasury;
[44]for they all put in out of their abundance,
but she out of her poverty put in all that
she had, her whole livelihood."

CHAPTER 13

Jesus Predicts the Destruction of the Temple

Then as He went out of the temple, one
of His disciples said to Him, "Teacher, see
what manner of stones and what buildings
are here!"
[2]And Jesus answered and said to him,
"Do you see these great buildings? Not *one*
stone shall be left upon another, that shall
not be thrown down."

The Signs of the Times and the End of the Age

[3]Now as He sat on the Mount of Olives
opposite the temple, Peter, James, John,
and Andrew asked Him privately, [4]"Tell
us, when will these things be? And what
will be the sign when all these things will be
fulfilled?"
[5]And Jesus, answering them, began to
say: "Take heed that no one deceives you.
[6]For many will come in My name, saying,
'I am *He*,' and will deceive many. [7]But
when you hear of wars and rumors of
wars, do not be troubled; for *such things*
must happen, but the end *is* not yet. [8]For
nation will rise against nation, and king-
dom against kingdom. And there will be
earthquakes in various places, and there
will be famines and troubles.[a] These *are* the
beginnings of sorrows.

12:36 [a]Psalm 110:1 12:42 [a]Greek *lepta*, very small copper coins worth a fraction of a penny 13:8 [a]NU-Text omits *and troubles.*

12:35–37 Jesus challenged their false understanding of who **Christ** would be. He would not be a mere **Son of David**, a military deliverer. David called Him Lord. As Christ, the Anointed One from God, He brings more than military deliverance.

12:38–44 Jesus gives two illustrations, one negative and one positive, of what it means to truly love God. The **scribes** loved themselves and took advantage of others. The **widow** (v. 42) had little, but put in **all that she had**. Her love was not calculating. God may not want us to give all of our money, but He wants us to have that spirit. With such an attitude we become true followers of Jesus, who gave His all for us.

9"But watch out for yourselves, for they
will deliver you up to councils, and you
will be beaten in the synagogues. You will
be brought[a] before rulers and kings for My
sake, for a testimony to them. 10And the
gospel must first be preached to all the na-
tions. 11But when they arrest *you* and de-
liver you up, do not worry beforehand, or
premeditate[a] what you will speak. But
whatever is given you in that hour, speak
that; for it is not you who speak, but the
Holy Spirit. 12Now brother will betray
brother to death, and a father *his* child; and
children will rise up against parents and
cause them to be put to death. 13And you
will be hated by all for My name's sake.
But he who endures to the end shall be
saved.

The Great Tribulation

14"So when you see the *'abomination of
desolation,'*[a] spoken of by Daniel the
prophet,[b] standing where it ought not" (let
the reader understand), "then let those
who are in Judea flee to the mountains.
15Let him who is on the housetop not go
down into the house, nor enter to take any-
thing out of his house. 16And let him who is
in the field not go back to get his clothes.
17But woe to those who are pregnant and to
those who are nursing babies in those
days! 18And pray that your flight may not
be in winter. 19For *in* those days there will
be tribulation, such as has not been since
the beginning of the creation which God
created until this time, nor ever shall be.
20And unless the Lord had shortened those
days, no flesh would be saved; but for the
elect's sake, whom He chose, He shortened
the days.

21"Then if anyone says to you, 'Look,
here *is* the Christ!' or, 'Look, *He is* there!' do
not believe it. 22For false christs and false
prophets will rise and show signs and
wonders to deceive, if possible, even the
elect. 23But take heed; see, I have told you
all things beforehand.

The Coming of the Son of Man

24"But in those days, after that tribula-
tion, the sun will be darkened, and the
moon will not give its light; 25the stars of
heaven will fall, and the powers in the
heavens will be shaken. 26Then they will
see the Son of Man coming in the clouds
with great power and glory. 27And then He
will send His angels, and gather together
His elect from the four winds, from the far-
thest part of earth to the farthest part of
heaven.

The Parable of the Fig Tree

28"Now learn this parable from the fig
tree: When its branch has already become
tender, and puts forth leaves, you know
that summer is near. 29So you also, when
you see these things happening, know that
it[a] is near—at the doors! 30Assuredly, I say
to you, this generation will by no means
pass away till all these things take place.
31Heaven and earth will pass away, but My
words will by no means pass away.

No One Knows the Day or Hour

32"But of that day and hour no one
knows, not even the angels in heaven, nor
the Son, but only the Father. 33Take heed,
watch and pray; for you do not know
when the time is. 34*It is* like a man going to
a far country, who left his house and gave
authority to his servants, and to each his
work, and commanded the doorkeeper to
watch. 35Watch therefore, for you do not

13:9 [a]NU-Text and M-Text read *will stand.*
13:11 [a]NU-Text omits *or premeditate.* 13:14 [a]Daniel 11:31; 12:11 [b]NU-Text omits *spoken of by Daniel the prophet.* 13:29 [a]Or *He*

13:14–20 abomination of desolation: Events fitting this description occurred when Jerusalem was destroyed in A.D. 70; they will also occur at the time of Christ's return.

13:31 by no means pass away: Only God's words are eternal. This statement makes Jesus' words equal to the Father's words.

know when the master of the house is
coming—in the evening, at midnight, at
the crowing of the rooster, or in the morn-
ing— 36lest, coming suddenly, he find you
sleeping. 37And what I say to you, I say to
all: Watch!"

CHAPTER 14

The Plot to Kill Jesus

After two days it was the Passover and
the Feast of Unleavened Bread. And the
chief priests and the scribes sought how
they might take Him by trickery and put
Him to death. 2But they said, "Not during
the feast, lest there be an uproar of the peo-
ple."

The Anointing at Bethany

3And being in Beth'a·ny at the house of
Simon the leper, as He sat at the table, a
woman came having an alabaster flask of
very costly oil of spikenard. Then she
broke the flask and poured *it* on His head.
4But there were some who were indignant
among themselves, and said, "Why was
this fragrant oil wasted? 5For it might have
been sold for more than three hundred de-
narii and given to the poor." And they crit-
icized her sharply.

6But Jesus said, "Let her alone. Why do
you trouble her? She has done a good work
for Me. 7For you have the poor with you al-
ways, and whenever you wish you may do
them good; but Me you do not have al-
ways. 8She has done what she could. She
has come beforehand to anoint My body
for burial. 9Assuredly, I say to you, wher-
ever this gospel is preached in the whole
world, what this woman has done will also
be told as a memorial to her."

Judas Agrees to Betray Jesus

10Then Judas Is·car'i·ot, one of the
twelve, went to the chief priests to betray
Him to them. 11And when they heard *it*,
they were glad, and promised to give him
money. So he sought how he might conve-
niently betray Him.

Jesus Celebrates the Passover with His Disciples

12Now on the first day of Unleavened
Bread, when they killed the Passover *lamb*,
His disciples said to Him, "Where do You
want us to go and prepare, that You may
eat the Passover?"

13And He sent out two of His disciples
and said to them, "Go into the city, and a
man will meet you carrying a pitcher of
water; follow him. 14Wherever he goes in,
say to the master of the house, 'The
Teacher says, "Where is the guest room in
which I may eat the Passover with My dis-
ciples?"' 15Then he will show you a large
upper room, furnished *and* prepared; there
make ready for us."

16So His disciples went out, and came
into the city, and found it just as He had
said to them; and they prepared the
Passover.

17In the evening He came with the
twelve. 18Now as they sat and ate, Jesus
said, "Assuredly, I say to you, one of you
who eats with Me will betray Me."

19And they began to be sorrowful, and
to say to Him one by one, "*Is* it I?" And an-
other *said*, "*Is* it I?"[a]

20He answered and said to them, "*It is*
one of the twelve, who dips with Me in the
dish. 21The Son of Man indeed goes just as
it is written of Him, but woe to that man by

14:19 [a]NU-Text omits this sentence.

14:11 They were glad because Judas's help would enable them to arrest Jesus without a riot by the people (see vv. 1, 2).

14:21 as it is written: It was God's purpose that Jesus be betrayed, but Judas did not have to do it. God's sovereignty and our responsibility for choosing flow side by side. Neither destroys the other.

whom the Son of Man is betrayed! It
would have been good for that man if he
had never been born."

Jesus Institutes the Lord's Supper

22 And as they were eating, Jesus took
bread, blessed and broke *it*, and gave *it* to
them and said, "Take, eat;[a] this is My
body."
23 Then He took the cup, and when He
had given thanks He gave *it* to them, and
they all drank from it. 24 And He said to
them, "This is My blood of the new[a]
covenant, which is shed for many. 25 As-
suredly, I say to you, I will no longer drink
of the fruit of the vine until that day when
I drink it new in the kingdom of God."
26 And when they had sung a hymn, they
went out to the Mount of Olives.

Jesus Predicts Peter's Denial

27 Then Jesus said to them, "All of you
will be made to stumble because of Me this
night,[a] for it is written:

'I will strike the Shepherd,
And the sheep will be scattered.'[b]

28 "But after I have been raised, I will go
before you to Galilee."
29 Peter said to Him, "Even if all are
made to stumble, yet I *will* not *be*."
30 Jesus said to him, "Assuredly, I say to
you that today, *even* this night, before the
rooster crows twice, you will deny Me
three times."
31 But he spoke more vehemently, "If
I have to die with You, I will not deny
You!"
And they all said likewise.

The Prayer in the Garden

32 Then they came to a place which was
named Geth·sem'a·nē; and He said to His
disciples, "Sit here while I pray." 33 And He
took Peter, James, and John with Him, and
He began to be troubled and deeply dis-
tressed. 34 Then He said to them, "My soul
is exceedingly sorrowful, *even* to death.
Stay here and watch."
35 He went a little farther, and fell on the
ground, and prayed that if it were possible,
the hour might pass from Him. 36 And He
said, "Abba, Father, all things *are* possible
for You. Take this cup away from Me;
nevertheless, not what I will, but what You
will."
37 Then He came and found them sleep-
ing, and said to Peter, "Simon, are you
sleeping? Could you not watch one hour?
38 Watch and pray, lest you enter into temp-
tation. The spirit indeed *is* willing, but the
flesh *is* weak."
39 Again He went away and prayed, and
spoke the same words. 40 And when He re-
turned, He found them asleep again, for
their eyes were heavy; and they did not
know what to answer Him.
41 Then He came the third time and said
to them, "Are you still sleeping and rest-
ing? It is enough! The hour has come; be-
hold, the Son of Man is being betrayed into
the hands of sinners. 42 Rise, let us be going.
See, My betrayer is at hand."

Betrayal and Arrest in Gethsemane

43 And immediately, while He was still
speaking, Judas, one of the twelve, with a
great multitude with swords and clubs,
came from the chief priests and the scribes
and the elders. 44 Now His betrayer had
given them a signal, saying, "Whomever I
kiss, He is the One; seize Him and lead
Him away safely."

14:22 [a]NU-Text omits *eat*. 14:24 [a]NU-Text omits *new*. 14:27 [a]NU-Text omits *because of Me this night*. [b]Zechariah 13:7

14:22–25 The Passover meal commemorated God's deliverance of Israel from Egypt. When Jesus associated the Passover bread with His **body** (v. 22) and the **cup** (v. 23) with His **blood** (v. 24), He identified Himself as the true Passover sacrifice that would bring forgiveness of sins. Those who participate in this sacrifice share in the **new covenant** (v. 24); they are part of the true people of God.

Silence Is Golden

Claire Cloninger

Quiet time may be hard to come by in our busy lives, but finding it is worth our best efforts. Being silent in God's presence results in a clarity of vision and purpose that truly sets us apart from the strident clamor of this world.

Even Jesus, the Son of God, needed regular times of silence in God's presence. He came to do only what His Father revealed to Him in secret (John 5:19, 20, 30). Hearing that still, small voice was vital to His life and ministry. Luke's Gospel tells us that "He Himself often withdrew into the wilderness and prayed" (Luke 5:16).

"Being silent in God's presence results in a clarity of vision and purpose."

If Jesus needed quiet times of communion with the Father, how much more do we? Only by pulling away into our hidden hearts to listen for the voice of our God can we experience Him deeply. A special room has been prepared within the heart of each believer which can only be unlocked by the key of silence. When we are willing to sit still, expectantly waiting, He will meet us there.

[45]As soon as he had come, immediately
he went up to Him and said to Him,
"Rabbi, Rabbi!" and kissed Him.
[46]Then they laid their hands on Him and
took Him. [47]And one of those who stood by
drew his sword and struck the servant of
the high priest, and cut off his ear.
[48]Then Jesus answered and said to them,
"Have you come out, as against a robber,
with swords and clubs to take Me? [49]I was
daily with you in the temple teaching, and
you did not seize Me. But the Scriptures
must be fulfilled."
[50]Then they all forsook Him and fled.

A Young Man Flees Naked

[51]Now a certain young man followed
Him, having a linen cloth thrown around
his naked *body*. And the young men laid
hold of him, [52]and he left the linen cloth
and fled from them naked.

Jesus Faces the Sanhedrin

[53]And they led Jesus away to the high
priest; and with him were assembled all
the chief priests, the elders, and the scribes.
[54]But Peter followed Him at a distance,
right into the courtyard of the high priest.
And he sat with the servants and warmed
himself at the fire.
[55]Now the chief priests and all the coun-
cil sought testimony against Jesus to put
Him to death, but found none. [56]For many
bore false witness against Him, but their
testimonies did not agree.
[57]Then some rose up and bore false
witness against Him, saying, [58]"We heard
Him say, 'I will destroy this temple made
with hands, and within three days I will
build another made without hands.' "
[59]But not even then did their testimony
agree.
[60]And the high priest stood up in the

midst and asked Jesus, saying, "Do You
answer nothing? What *is it* these men tes-
tify against You?" [61]But He kept silent and
answered nothing.

Again the high priest asked Him, saying
to Him, "Are You the Christ, the Son of the
Blessed?"

[62]Jesus said, "I am. And you will see the
Son of Man sitting at the right hand of the
Power, and coming with the clouds of
heaven."

[63]Then the high priest tore his clothes
and said, "What further need do we have
of witnesses? [64]You have heard the blas-
phemy! What do you think?"

And they all condemned Him to be de-
serving of death.

[65]Then some began to spit on Him, and
to blindfold Him, and to beat Him, and to
say to Him, "Prophesy!" And the officers
struck Him with the palms of their hands.[a]

Peter Denies Jesus, and Weeps

[66]Now as Peter was below in the court-
yard, one of the servant girls of the high
priest came. [67]And when she saw Peter
warming himself, she looked at him and
said, "You also were with Jesus of Naza-
reth."

[68]But he denied it, saying, "I neither
know nor understand what you are say-
ing." And he went out on the porch, and a
rooster crowed.

[69]And the servant girl saw him again,
and began to say to those who stood by,
"This is one of them." [70]But he denied it
again.

And a little later those who stood by
said to Peter again, "Surely you are *one* of
them; for you are a Galilean, and your
speech shows *it*."[a]

[71]Then he began to curse and swear, "I
do not know this Man of whom you
speak!"

[72]A second time *the* rooster crowed.
Then Peter called to mind the word that
Jesus had said to him, "Before the rooster
crows twice, you will deny Me three
times." And when he thought about it, he
wept.

CHAPTER 15

Jesus Faces Pilate

Immediately, in the morning, the chief
priests held a consultation with the elders
and scribes and the whole council; and
they bound Jesus, led *Him* away, and deliv-
ered *Him* to Pilate. [2]Then Pilate asked Him,
"Are You the King of the Jews?"

He answered and said to him, "*It is as*
you say."

[3]And the chief priests accused Him of
many things, but He answered nothing.
[4]Then Pilate asked Him again, saying, "Do
You answer nothing? See how many things
they testify against You!"[a] [5]But Jesus still
answered nothing, so that Pilate marveled.

Taking the Place of Barabbas

[6]Now at the feast he was accustomed to
releasing one prisoner to them, whomever
they requested. [7]And there was one named
Ba·rab′bas, *who was* chained with his fel-
low rebels; they had committed murder in
the rebellion. [8]Then the multitude, crying
aloud,[a] began to ask *him to do* just as he had
always done for them. [9]But Pilate an-

14:65 [a]NU-Text reads *received Him with slaps.*
14:70 [a]NU-Text omits *and your speech shows it.*
15:4 [a]NU-Text reads *of which they accuse You.*
15:8 [a]NU-Text reads *going up.*

14:61, 62 Are You the Christ? See 1:1. Up to this point Jesus had not even let His disciples openly confess Him as Christ (see 8:30; 9:9). Now there was no more need of caution. **I am**: A clear claim to deity (see note on 6:50). **right hand of the Power**: An exalted position next to God Himself from which the King will come again in judgment.

15:5 answered nothing: Throughout His trial and crucifixion Jesus was the only one who did not act from fear, jealousy, or self-interest. We should strive to follow His example when we encounter persecution for His sake.

swered them, saying, "Do you want me to
release to you the King of the Jews?" [10]For
he knew that the chief priests had handed
Him over because of envy.

[11]But the chief priests stirred up the
crowd, so that he should rather release
Ba·rab′bas to them. [12]Pilate answered and
said to them again, "What then do you
want me to do *with Him* whom you call the
King of the Jews?"

[13]So they cried out again, "Crucify
Him!"

[14]Then Pilate said to them, "Why, what
evil has He done?"

But they cried out all the more, "Crucify
Him!"

[15]So Pilate, wanting to gratify the crowd,
released Ba·rab′bas to them; and he delivered
Jesus, after he had scourged *Him,* to
be crucified.

The Soldiers Mock Jesus

[16]Then the soldiers led Him away into
the hall called Praetorium, and they called
together the whole garrison. [17]And they
clothed Him with purple; and they
twisted a crown of thorns, put it on His
head, [18]and began to salute Him, "Hail,
King of the Jews!" [19]Then they struck Him
on the head with a reed and spat on Him;
and bowing the knee, they worshiped
Him. [20]And when they had mocked Him,
they took the purple off Him, put His own
clothes on Him, and led Him out to crucify
Him.

The King on a Cross

[21]Then they compelled a certain man, Simon
a Cȳ·rē′ni·an, the father of Alexander
and Rū′fus, as he was coming out of the
country and passing by, to bear His cross.
[22]And they brought Him to the place
Gol′go·tha, which is translated, Place of a
Skull. [23]Then they gave Him wine mingled
with myrrh to drink, but He did not take *it.*
[24]And when they crucified Him, they divided
His garments, casting lots for them
to determine what every man should take.

[25]Now it was the third hour, and they
crucified Him. [26]And the inscription of His
accusation was written above:

THE KING OF THE JEWS.

[27]With Him they also crucified two robbers,
one on His right and the other on His
left. [28]So the Scripture was fulfilled[a] which
says, *"And He was numbered with the
transgressors."*[b]

[29]And those who passed by blasphemed
Him, wagging their heads and saying,
"Aha! *You* who destroy the temple and
build *it* in three days, [30]save Yourself, and
come down from the cross!"

[31]Likewise the chief priests also, mocking
among themselves with the scribes,
said, "He saved others; Himself He cannot
save. [32]Let the Christ, the King of Israel, descend
now from the cross, that we may see
and believe."[a]

Even those who were crucified with
Him reviled Him.

Jesus Dies on the Cross

[33]Now when the sixth hour had come,
there was darkness over the whole land
until the ninth hour. [34]And at the ninth
hour Jesus cried out with a loud voice, saying,
"Ē′lō·ī, Ē′lō·ī, lama sabachthani?"
which is translated, *"My God, My God,
why have You forsaken Me?"*[a]

[35]Some of those who stood by, when
they heard *that,* said, "Look, He is calling
for E·lī′jah!" [36]Then someone ran and filled
a sponge full of sour wine, put *it* on a reed,
and offered *it* to Him to drink, saying, "Let
Him alone; let us see if E·lī′jah will come to
take Him down."

15:28 [a]Isaiah 53:12 [b]NU-Text omits this verse.
15:32 [a]M-Text reads *believe Him.* 15:34 [a]Psalm 22:1

15:25 the third hour: 9:00 A.M. (see note on John 19:14–16).
15:33 sixth hour: 12:00 noon. **ninth hour**: 3:00 P.M. See note on v. 25.

[37]And Jesus cried out with a loud voice,
and breathed His last.
[38]Then the veil of the temple was torn in
two from top to bottom. [39]So when the cen-
turion, who stood opposite Him, saw that
He cried out like this and breathed His
last,[a] he said, "Truly this Man was the Son
of God!"
[40]There were also women looking on
from afar, among whom were Mary
Mag'da·lēne, Mary the mother of James
the Less and of Jō'sēs, and Sa·lō'mē, [41]who
also followed Him and ministered to Him
when He was in Galilee, and many other
women who came up with Him to Jerusa-
lem.

Jesus Buried in Joseph's Tomb

[42]Now when evening had come, because
it was the Preparation Day, that is, the day
before the Sabbath, [43]Joseph of Ar·i·ma-
thē'a, a prominent council member, who
was himself waiting for the kingdom of
God, coming and taking courage, went in
to Pilate and asked for the body of Jesus.
[44]Pilate marveled that He was already
dead; and summoning the centurion, he
asked him if He had been dead for some
time. [45]So when he found out from the cen-
turion, he granted the body to Joseph.
[46]Then he bought fine linen, took Him
down, and wrapped Him in the linen. And
he laid Him in a tomb which had been
hewn out of the rock, and rolled a stone
against the door of the tomb. [47]And Mary
Mag'da·lēne and Mary *the mother* of Jō'sēs
observed where He was laid.

CHAPTER 16

He Is Risen

Now when the Sabbath was past, Mary
Mag'da·lēne, Mary *the mother* of James,
and Sa·lō'mē bought spices, that they
might come and anoint Him. [2]Very early
in the morning, on the first *day* of the
week, they came to the tomb when the sun
had risen. [3]And they said among them-
selves, "Who will roll away the stone from
the door of the tomb for us?" [4]But when
they looked up, they saw that the stone
had been rolled away—for it was very
large. [5]And entering the tomb, they saw a
young man clothed in a long white robe
sitting on the right side; and they were
alarmed.
[6]But he said to them, "Do not be
alarmed. You seek Jesus of Nazareth, who
was crucified. He is risen! He is not here.
See the place where they laid Him. [7]But go,
tell His disciples—and Peter—that He is
going before you into Galilee; there you
will see Him, as He said to you."
[8]So they went out quickly[a] and fled from
the tomb, for they trembled and were
amazed. And they said nothing to anyone,
for they were afraid.

Mary Magdalene Sees the Risen Lord

[9]Now when *He* rose early on the first *day*
of the week, He appeared first to Mary
Mag'da·lēne, out of whom He had cast

15:39 [a]NU-Text reads *that He thus breathed His last.*
16:8 [a]NU-Text and M-Text omit *quickly.*

15:38 The veil . . . was torn symbolizing that Jesus' sacrifice of Himself on the Cross made the temple sacrifices unnecessary. See Heb. 10:19, 20.

16:3 roll away the stone: It was extremely difficult to remove the heavy stone disc once it had been rolled into position in front of the entrance. They had come to apply spices to a corpse, to counteract the odors of decay (see v. 1); they expected to find a normal, closed tomb.

16:7 The **disciples** who had forsaken Jesus (14:50) would be restored—even **Peter** who had denied his Lord. **Galilee**: Where Jesus had first called them. **as He said**: See 14:28. Jesus is always ready to restore those who forsake Him if they turn to Him in faith to make a new start. Although Satan may try to use the failures of our past to discourage us in our spiritual walk, we can find victory in claiming God's promise of forgiveness and turning back to Him in repentance.

seven demons. 10She went and told those
who had been with Him, as they mourned
and wept. 11And when they heard that He
was alive and had been seen by her, they
did not believe.

Jesus Appears to Two Disciples

12After that, He appeared in another
form to two of them as they walked and
went into the country. 13And they went and
told *it* to the rest, *but* they did not believe
them either.

The Great Commission

14Later He appeared to the eleven as
they sat at the table; and He rebuked their
unbelief and hardness of heart, because
they did not believe those who had seen
Him after He had risen. 15And He said to
them, "Go into all the world and preach
the gospel to every creature. 16He who be-
lieves and is baptized will be saved; but he
who does not believe will be condemned.
17And these signs will follow those who be-
lieve: In My name they will cast out
demons; they will speak with new
tongues; 18they[a] will take up serpents; and
if they drink anything deadly, it will by no
means hurt them; they will lay hands on
the sick, and they will recover."

Christ Ascends to God's Right Hand

19So then, after the Lord had spoken to
them, He was received up into heaven, and
sat down at the right hand of God. 20And
they went out and preached everywhere,
the Lord working with *them* and confirm-
ing the word through the accompanying
signs. Amen.[a]

16:18 [a]NU-Text reads *and in their hands they will.*
16:20 [a]Verses 9–20 are bracketed in NU-Text as not original. They are lacking in Codex Sinaiticus and Codex Vaticanus, although nearly all other manuscripts of Mark contain them.

✦Luke✦

Luke, a physician, writes with the compassion and warmth of a family doctor as he carefully documents the perfect humanity of Jesus Christ. His style of written Greek is of a higher quality than the other writers of the Gospels, and the beauty, grace, and tenderness of his book have made it one of the most beloved in the Bible. He portrays Christ in His fullest humanity by writing more of Christ's feelings than any other Gospel.

Luke wanted to create an accurate, chronological, and comprehensive account of the unique life of Jesus to strengthen the faith of Gentile believers and stimulate saving faith among nonbelievers. He records details not found elsewhere, including the response of the prophetess Anna at seeing the baby Jesus. Anna, a long-time widow, refused to succumb to grief or bitterness, choosing instead to spend her life in service to God. Her dedication was rewarded when she saw the young Messiah.

Luke was a close associate and traveling companion of Paul and, like Paul, emphasized faith, repentance, mercy, and forgiveness. In Luke's Gospel, as in Paul's Epistles, key themes include the universality of salvation, the boundlessness of divine grace, and the promise of joy to the followers of Christ.

Tradition says that Luke was from Syrian Antioch, remained unmarried, and died at age eighty-four. *Kata Loukon,* "According to Luke," is the Greek title added to this Gospel at a very early date. The name "Luke" appears only three times in the New Testament (Col. 4:14; 2 Tim. 4:11; Philem. 24). ✦

CHAPTER 1

Dedication to Theophilus

Inasmuch as many have taken in hand
to set in order a narrative of those things
which have been fulfilled[a] among us, 2just
as those who from the beginning were
eyewitnesses and ministers of the word
delivered them to us, 3it seemed good to
me also, having had perfect understanding
of all things from the very first, to write to
you an orderly account, most excellent
Thē·oph'i·lus, 4that you may know the certainty of those things in which you were
instructed.

John's Birth Announced to Zacharias

5There was in the days of Her'od, the
king of Judea, a certain priest named
Zach·a·rī'as, of the division of A·bī'jah.
His wife *was* of the daughters of Aaron,
and her name *was* Elizabeth. 6And they
were both righteous before God, walking
in all the commandments and ordinances

1:1 [a]Or *are most surely believed*

✦ ✦

1:5 Herod the Great was king not only of Judea, but of all Palestine from 37 to 4 B.C. **Division of Abijah** identifies **Zacharias** as a member of one of 24 groups of priests that took turns ministering at the Jerusalem temple.

of the Lord blameless. [7]But they had no
child, because Elizabeth was barren, and
they were both well advanced in years.

[8]So it was, that while he was serving as
priest before God in the order of his divi-
sion, [9]according to the custom of the priest-
hood, his lot fell to burn incense when he
went into the temple of the Lord. [10]And the
whole multitude of the people was pray-
ing outside at the hour of incense. [11]Then
an angel of the Lord appeared to him,
standing on the right side of the altar of in-
cense. [12]And when Zach·a·rī′as saw *him,*
he was troubled, and fear fell upon him.

[13]But the angel said to him, "Do not be
afraid, Zach·a·rī′as, for your prayer is
heard; and your wife Elizabeth will bear
you a son, and you shall call his name
John. [14]And you will have joy and glad-
ness, and many will rejoice at his birth.
[15]For he will be great in the sight of the
Lord, and shall drink neither wine nor
strong drink. He will also be filled with the
Holy Spirit, even from his mother's womb.
[16]And he will turn many of the children of
Israel to the Lord their God. [17]He will also
go before Him in the spirit and power of
E·lī′jah, *'to turn the hearts of the fathers to
the children,'*[a] and the disobedient to the
wisdom of the just, to make ready a people
prepared for the Lord."

[18]And Zach·a·rī′as said to the angel,
"How shall I know this? For I am an old
man, and my wife is well advanced in
years."

[19]And the angel answered and said to
him, "I am Gabriel, who stands in the pres-
ence of God, and was sent to speak to you
and bring you these glad tidings. [20]But be-
hold, you will be mute and not able to
speak until the day these things take place,
because you did not believe my words
which will be fulfilled in their own time."

[21]And the people waited for Zach-
a·rī′as, and marveled that he lingered so
long in the temple. [22]But when he came
out, he could not speak to them; and they
perceived that he had seen a vision in the
temple, for he beckoned to them and re-
mained speechless.

[23]So it was, as soon as the days of his ser-
vice were completed, that he departed to
his own house. [24]Now after those days his
wife Elizabeth conceived; and she hid her-
self five months, saying, [25]"Thus the Lord
has dealt with me, in the days when He
looked on *me,* to take away my reproach
among people."

Christ's Birth Announced to Mary

[26]Now in the sixth month the angel Ga-
briel was sent by God to a city of Galilee
named Nazareth, [27]to a virgin betrothed to
a man whose name was Joseph, of the
house of David. The virgin's name *was*
Mary. [28]And having come in, the angel said
to her, "Rejoice, highly favored *one,* the
Lord *is* with you; blessed *are* you among
women!"[a]

[29]But when she saw *him,*[a] she was trou-
bled at his saying, and considered what
manner of greeting this was. [30]Then the an-
gel said to her, "Do not be afraid, Mary, for
you have found favor with God. [31]And be-
hold, you will conceive in your womb and
bring forth a Son, and shall call His name
JESUS. [32]He will be great, and will be called
the Son of the Highest; and the Lord God
will give Him the throne of His father Da-
vid. [33]And He will reign over the house of
Jacob forever, and of His kingdom there
will be no end."

[34]Then Mary said to the angel, "How
can this be, since I do not know a man?"

[35]And the angel answered and said to

1:17 [a]Malachi 4:5, 6 1:28 [a]NU-Text omits *blessed are you among women.* 1:29 [a]NU-Text omits *when she saw him.*

1:18 How shall I know? When God makes a promise, we are wise to trust Him (see v. 45). This promise even had scriptural precedent (see Gen.18:10, 14; 21:1–7); Zacharias had no excuse for not believing it.

1:31 JESUS means "The LORD Will Save" or "The LORD Is Salvation."

her, "*The* Holy Spirit will come upon you, and the power of the Highest will overshadow you; therefore, also, that Holy One who is to be born will be called the Son of God. 36 Now indeed, Elizabeth your relative has also conceived a son in her old age; and this is now the sixth month for her who was called barren. 37 For with God nothing will be impossible."

38 Then Mary said, "Behold the maidservant of the Lord! Let it be to me according to your word." And the angel departed from her.

Mary Visits Elizabeth

39 Now Mary arose in those days and went into the hill country with haste, to a city of Judah, 40 and entered the house of Zach·a·rī′as and greeted Elizabeth. 41 And it happened, when Elizabeth heard the greeting of Mary, that the babe leaped in her womb; and Elizabeth was filled with the Holy Spirit. 42 Then she spoke out with a loud voice and said, "Blessed *are* you among women, and blessed *is* the fruit of your womb! 43 But why *is* this *granted* to me, that the mother of my Lord should come to me? 44 For indeed, as soon as the voice of your greeting sounded in my ears, the babe leaped in my womb for joy. 45 Blessed *is* she who believed, for there will be a fulfillment of those things which were told her from the Lord."

The Song of Mary

46 And Mary said:

"My soul magnifies the Lord,
47 And my spirit has rejoiced in God my Savior.
48 For He has regarded the lowly state of His maidservant;
For behold, henceforth all generations will call me blessed.
49 For He who is mighty has done great things for me,
And holy *is* His name.
50 And His mercy *is* on those who fear Him
From generation to generation.
51 He has shown strength with His arm;
He has scattered *the* proud in the imagination of their hearts.
52 He has put down the mighty from *their* thrones,
And exalted *the* lowly.
53 He has filled *the* hungry with good things,
And *the* rich He has sent away empty.
54 He has helped His servant Israel,
In remembrance of *His* mercy,
55 As He spoke to our fathers,
To Abraham and to his seed forever."

56 And Mary remained with her about three months, and returned to her house.

Birth of John the Baptist

57 Now Elizabeth's full time came for her to be delivered, and she brought forth a son. 58 When her neighbors and relatives heard how the Lord had shown great mercy to her, they rejoiced with her.

1:38 According to your word is Mary's commitment to God's will. She faced overwhelming social pressures because she would be pregnant with Jesus before marrying Joseph. Her humble willingness is a model of trust for all of us. Her faith (v. 45) contrasts with the unbelief of Zacharias (vv. 18–20).

1:41–44 The **Holy Spirit**, who filled Elizabeth even as Mary spoke, gave Elizabeth supernatural insight into the meaning of what she heard. She immediately pronounced Mary the **mother** of her **Lord** (v. 43). A vigorous movement of Elizabeth's unborn child provided a kind of physical confirmation (v. 44).

1:46–55 Mary spontaneously burst into a song of praise to God. Its traditional name is "Magnificat" from **magnifies**; the name is also the song's first word in the Latin Bible. For Hannah's similar song see 1 Sam. 2:1–10.

Circumcision of John the Baptist

[59]So it was, on the eighth day, that they
came to circumcise the child; and they
would have called him by the name of his
father, Zach·a·rī′as. [60]His mother an-
swered and said, "No; he shall be called
John."

[61]But they said to her, "There is no one
among your relatives who is called by this
name." [62]So they made signs to his father—
what he would have him called.

[63]And he asked for a writing tablet, and
wrote, saying, "His name is John." So they
all marveled. [64]Immediately his mouth
was opened and his tongue *loosed*, and
he spoke, praising God. [65]Then fear came
on all who dwelt around them; and all
these sayings were discussed throughout
all the hill country of Judea. [66]And all
those who heard *them* kept *them* in their
hearts, saying, "What kind of child will
this be?" And the hand of the Lord was
with him.

Zacharias' Prophecy

[67]Now his father Zach·a·rī′as was filled
with the Holy Spirit, and prophesied, say-
ing:

68 "Blessed *is* the Lord God of Israel,
For He has visited and redeemed His people,
69 And has raised up a horn of salvation for us
In the house of His servant David,
70 As He spoke by the mouth of His holy prophets,
Who *have been* since the world began,
71 That we should be saved from our enemies
And from the hand of all who hate us,
72 To perform the mercy *promised* to our fathers
And to remember His holy covenant,
73 The oath which He swore to our father Abraham:
74 To grant us that we,
Being delivered from the hand of our enemies,
Might serve Him without fear,
75 In holiness and righteousness before Him all the days of our life.

76 "And you, child, will be called the prophet of the Highest;
For you will go before the face of the Lord to prepare His ways,
77 To give knowledge of salvation to His people
By the remission of their sins,
78 Through the tender mercy of our God,
With which the Dayspring from on high has visited[a] us;
79 To give light to those who sit in darkness and the shadow of death,
To guide our feet into the way of peace."

[80]So the child grew and became strong
in spirit, and was in the deserts till the day
of his manifestation to Israel.

CHAPTER 2

Christ Born of Mary

And it came to pass in those days *that* a
decree went out from Caesar Au·gus′tus
that all the world should be registered.

1:78 [a]NU-Text reads *shall visit.*

1:68–79 Zacharias' song, called the *Benedictus*, proclaims the fulfillment of the promise of salvation and relates John's role as the forerunner of the Messiah.

2:1 registered: To pay taxes. **Caesar Augustus**: Roman emperor from 31 B.C. to A.D. 14. His decree was used by God to bring Joseph and Mary to Bethlehem where the prophet had foretold that Jesus would be born (Mic. 5:2).

MARY: A WOMAN OF BALANCE

The Bible does not reveal a great deal about Mary, the mother of Jesus. We know, of course, that she must have been a very special woman to have been chosen for the privilege of bringing the Savior into the world. From this and certain passages of Scripture we can see ways that Mary exemplified balanced living.

The angel Gabriel revealed the state of her spiritual life when he said she was blessed among women and had found favor with God (Luke 1:28, 30). Mary's mature faith is confirmed by her immediate submission to the angel's announcement of her role in God's plan: "Behold the maidservant of the Lord! Let it be to me according to your word" (v. 38). And her *Magnificat,* or song of praise, demonstrates her faith, piety, and knowledge of Scripture.

Mary's reaction to the shepherds' visit and Jesus' comments in the temple reflect a woman of thought (2:19, 51). Her resourceful use of the manger in the midst of giving birth to the Savior illustrates her creativity (v. 7). And her confidence in Jesus' ability to remedy the shortage of wine at the wedding in Cana shows that she had full knowledge of who He was (John 2:3–5). The Lord obviously selected a woman of intelligence to rear the Messiah.

While nothing is said regarding Mary's physical health, we can assume the Lord would choose a healthy vessel for His only begotten Son. Mary must have been especially careful of her health during her pregnancy, knowing the miracle she carried in her body.

Today, the Holy Spirit lives inside all Christians. Although His presence is not physical, the Holy Spirit considers our bodies His temple (1 Cor. 3:16, 17; 6:19). Our efforts to maintain our spiritual, mental, and physical health should reflect our appreciation of this awesome privilege. ✦

[2]This census first took place while Quī-rin'i·us was governing Syria. [3]So all went to be registered, everyone to his own city.

[4]Joseph also went up from Galilee, out of the city of Nazareth, into Judea, to the city of David, which is called Bethlehem, because he was of the house and lineage of David, [5]to be registered with Mary, his betrothed wife,[a] who was with child. [6]So it was, that while they were there, the days were completed for her to be delivered. [7]And she brought forth her firstborn Son,

2:5 [a]NU-Text omits *wife.*

2:7 swaddling cloths: long, narrow strips of cloth used to wrap infants.

and wrapped Him in swaddling cloths,
and laid Him in a manger, because there
was no room for them in the inn.

Glory in the Highest

8Now there were in the same country
shepherds living out in the fields, keeping
watch over their flock by night. 9And be-
hold,[a] an angel of the Lord stood before
them, and the glory of the Lord shone
around them, and they were greatly afraid.
10Then the angel said to them, "Do not be
afraid, for behold, I bring you good tidings
of great joy which will be to all people.
11For there is born to you this day in the
city of David a Savior, who is Christ the
Lord. 12And this *will be* the sign to you: You
will find a Babe wrapped in swaddling
cloths, lying in a manger."
13And suddenly there was with the an-
gel a multitude of the heavenly host prais-
ing God and saying:

14 "Glory to God in the highest,
And on earth peace, goodwill toward
men!"[a]

15So it was, when the angels had gone
away from them into heaven, that the
shepherds said to one another, "Let us now
go to Bethlehem and see this thing that has
come to pass, which the Lord has made
known to us." 16And they came with haste
and found Mary and Joseph, and the Babe
lying in a manger. 17Now when they had
seen *Him,* they made widely[a] known the
saying which was told them concerning
this Child. 18And all those who heard *it*
marveled at those things which were told
them by the shepherds. 19But Mary kept all
these things and pondered *them* in her
heart. 20Then the shepherds returned, glo-
rifying and praising God for all the things
that they had heard and seen, as it was told
them.

Circumcision of Jesus

21And when eight days were completed
for the circumcision of the Child,[a] His
name was called JESUS, the name given by
the angel before He was conceived in the
womb.

Jesus Presented in the Temple

22Now when the days of her purification
according to the law of Moses were com-
pleted, they brought Him to Jerusalem to
present *Him* to the Lord 23(as it is written in
the law of the Lord, *"Every male who
opens the womb shall be called holy to the
LORD"*),[a] 24and to offer a sacrifice accord-
ing to what is said in the law of the Lord,
*"A pair of turtledoves or two young pi-
geons."*[a]

Simeon Sees God's Salvation

25And behold, there was a man in Jeru-
salem whose name was Sim'ē·on, and this
man was just and devout, waiting for the
Consolation of Israel, and the Holy Spirit
was upon him. 26And it had been revealed
to him by the Holy Spirit that he would not
see death before he had seen the Lord's
Christ. 27So he came by the Spirit into the
temple. And when the parents brought in
the Child Jesus, to do for Him according to
the custom of the law, 28he took Him up in
his arms and blessed God and said:

2:9 [a]NU-Text omits *behold.* 2:14 [a]NU-Text reads *toward men of goodwill.* 2:17 [a]NU-Text omits *widely.* 2:21 [a]NU-Text reads *for His circumcision.* 2:23 [a]Exodus 13:2, 12, 15 2:24 [a]Leviticus 12:8

2:21–24 eight days: Since the Jews considered the day of birth as the first day, this would be seven days by our way of counting. The mother of a newborn son was deemed ceremonially unclean for seven days (Lev. 12:1, 2), after which the parents had to take the child to the temple for **circumcision**. She was then considered unclean for an additional 33 days, after which she would go to the temple to offer a sacrifice for her purification. Mary and Joseph offered **turtledoves** or **young pigeons** for the purification **sacrifice** because they were too poor to offer a lamb.

29 "Lord, now You are letting Your
servant depart in peace,
According to Your word;
30 For my eyes have seen Your
salvation
31 Which You have prepared before the
face of all peoples,
32 A light to *bring* revelation to the
Gentiles,
And the glory of Your people Israel."

33And Joseph and His mother[a] mar-
veled at those things which were spoken
of Him. 34Then Sim'ē·on blessed them,
and said to Mary His mother, "Behold,
this *Child* is destined for the fall and rising
of many in Israel, and for a sign which
will be spoken against 35(yes, a sword will
pierce through your own soul also), that
the thoughts of many hearts may be re-
vealed."

Anna Bears Witness to the Redeemer

36Now there was one, Anna, a prophet-
ess, the daughter of Phan'ū·el, of the tribe
of Ash'er. She was of a great age, and had
lived with a husband seven years from her
virginity; 37and this woman *was* a widow
of about eighty-four years,[a] who did not
depart from the temple, but served *God*
with fastings and prayers night and day.
38And coming in that instant she gave
thanks to the Lord,[a] and spoke of Him to
all those who looked for redemption in Je-
rusalem.

The Family Returns to Nazareth

39So when they had performed all
things according to the law of the Lord,
they returned to Galilee, to their *own* city,
Nazareth. 40And the Child grew and be-
came strong in spirit,[a] filled with wis-
dom; and the grace of God was upon
Him.

2:33 [a]NU-Text reads *And His father and mother.*
2:37 [a]NU-Text reads *a widow until she was eighty-four.*
2:38 [a]NU-Text reads *to God.* 2:40 [a]NU-Text omits *in spirit.*

God Is Listening

Sherwood Eliot Wirt

The prophetess Anna was not praying for herself; she was thinking about Jerusalem. Such prayer is called intercession. If you would like your prayer life to come alive and make your growing old a delightful experience, get rolling on a personal program of praying for other people.

It takes some practice at first. Someone comes to you with a problem. Let's suppose it is a granddaughter who is worried about a stiff competitive examination. What if she fails? What if she disappoints her parents? What if . . . ? Your response is to take charge and say, "Let's pray about this." You put your hand on the grandchild's head or shoulder and talk to God, asking for His help in removing fear and giving a clear mind. Request that He remove the worry about her parents' reaction because it is irrelevant. If the youngster does not know Christ, you have an opportunity to talk to the Lord about it right then. Don't miss it!

The minute we stop asking something for ourselves and begin praying for someone else, we begin to sense the joy of prayer. We forget to think about whether we are "getting through," whether we are praying "spiritually," whether we are "really sincere," or whether God is "real." All such introverted thoughts become academic; we are now intercessors, on the battlefield for the Lord and on behalf of our brother or sister. Is God listening? You had better believe it! ✦

The Boy Jesus Amazes the Scholars

41His parents went to Jerusalem every year at the Feast of the Passover. 42And when He was twelve years old, they went up to Jerusalem according to the custom of the feast. 43When they had finished the days, as they returned, the Boy Jesus lingered behind in Jerusalem. And Joseph and His mother[a] did not know *it;* 44but supposing Him to have been in the company, they went a day's journey, and sought Him among *their* relatives and acquaintances. 45So when they did not find Him, they returned to Jerusalem, seeking Him. 46Now so it was *that* after three days they found Him in the temple, sitting in the midst of the teachers, both listening to them and asking them questions. 47And all who heard Him were astonished at His understanding and answers. 48So when they saw Him, they were amazed; and His mother said to Him, "Son, why have You done this to us? Look, Your father and I have sought You anxiously."

49And He said to them, "Why did you seek Me? Did you not know that I must be about My Father's business?" 50But they did not understand the statement which He spoke to them.

Jesus Advances in Wisdom and Favor

51Then He went down with them and came to Nazareth, and was subject to them, but His mother kept all these things in her heart. 52And Jesus increased in wisdom and stature, and in favor with God and men.

CHAPTER 3

John the Baptist Prepares the Way

Now in the fifteenth year of the reign of Tī·bē′ri·us Caesar, Pon′ti·us Pilate being governor of Judea, Her′od being tetrarch of Galilee, his brother Philip tetrarch of Ī·tu·rē′a and the region of Trach·o·nī′tis, and Lȳ·sā′ni·as tetrarch of Ab·i·lē′nē, 2while An′nas and Cā′i·a·phas were high priests,[a] the word of God came to John the son of Zach·a·rī′as in the wilderness. 3And he went into all the region around the Jordan, preaching a baptism of repentance for the remission of sins, 4as it is written in the book of the words of Ī·sāi′ah the prophet, saying:

"The voice of one crying in the
wilderness:
'Prepare the way of the LORD;
Make His paths straight.
5 *Every valley shall be filled*
And every mountain and hill brought
low;
The crooked places shall be made
straight
And the rough ways smooth;
6 *And all flesh shall see the salvation of*
God.' "[a]

2:43 [a]NU-Text reads *And His parents.* 3:2 [a]NU-Text and M-Text read *in the high priesthood of Annas and Caiaphas.* 3:6 [a]Isaiah 40:3–5

2:41–49 When a Jewish boy was **twelve years old** he formally joined the religious community as a man responsible to keep the law, including celebrating **Passover** at Jerusalem (see Ex. 23:14–17). Jesus was obedient to His parents (see v. 51), but He had now reached the age of religious responsibility. He used this incident at the temple to make a statement about the priority of His relationship with His heavenly Father. Our lives should reflect His example, as we strive to keep our priorities in proper order.

3:1 The gospel is for all the world; therefore, Luke puts the beginning of the ministry of John the Baptist, and Jesus, in historical context. **Tiberius** was the Roman emperor from A.D. 14 to 37. The **fifteenth year** would be about A.D. 28. **Pilate** was the Roman governor of **Judea** including Samaria (A.D. 26–36). **Tetrarch** means "ruler of a fourth." Two sons of Herod the Great were tetrarchs: **Herod** Antipas ruled **Galilee** and Perea, the center of much of Jesus' ministry, from 4 B.C. to A.D. 39. **Philip**, whose capital was Caesarea Philippi, ruled areas northeast of Galilee from 4 B.C. to A.D. 34. **Lysanias**, who ruled **Abilene** northwest of Damascus, was not related to Herod.

John Preaches to the People

[7]Then he said to the multitudes that came out to be baptized by him, "Brood of vipers! Who warned you to flee from the wrath to come? [8]Therefore bear fruits worthy of repentance, and do not begin to say to yourselves, 'We have Abraham as *our* father.' For I say to you that God is able to raise up children to Abraham from these stones. [9]And even now the ax is laid to the root of the trees. Therefore every tree which does not bear good fruit is cut down and thrown into the fire."

[10]So the people asked him, saying, "What shall we do then?"

[11]He answered and said to them, "He who has two tunics, let him give to him who has none; and he who has food, let him do likewise."

[12]Then tax collectors also came to be baptized, and said to him, "Teacher, what shall we do?"

[13]And he said to them, "Collect no more than what is appointed for you."

[14]Likewise the soldiers asked him, saying, "And what shall we do?"

So he said to them, "Do not intimidate anyone or accuse falsely, and be content with your wages."

[15]Now as the people were in expectation, and all reasoned in their hearts about John, whether he was the Christ *or* not, [16]John answered, saying to all, "I indeed baptize you with water; but One mightier than I is coming, whose sandal strap I am not worthy to loose. He will baptize you with the Holy Spirit and fire. [17]His winnowing fan *is* in His hand, and He will thoroughly clean out His threshing floor, and gather the wheat into His barn; but the chaff He will burn with unquenchable fire."

[18]And with many other exhortations he preached to the people. [19]But Her'od the tetrarch, being rebuked by him concerning He·rō'di·as, his brother Philip's wife,[a] and for all the evils which Her'od had done, [20]also added this, above all, that he shut John up in prison.

John Baptizes Jesus

[21]When all the people were baptized, it came to pass that Jesus also was baptized; and while He prayed, the heaven was opened. [22]And the Holy Spirit descended in bodily form like a dove upon Him, and a voice came from heaven which said, "You are My beloved Son; in You I am well pleased."

The Genealogy of Jesus Christ

[23]Now Jesus Himself began *His ministry at* about thirty years of age, being (as was supposed) *the* son of Joseph, *the son* of Hē'lī, [24]*the son* of Mat'that,[a] *the son* of Levi, *the son* of Mel'chī, *the son* of Jan'na, *the son* of Joseph, [25]*the son* of Mat·ta·thī'ah, *the son* of Ā'mos, *the son* of Nā'hum, *the son* of Es'lī, *the son* of Nag'ga·ī, [26]*the son* of Mā'ath, *the son* of Mat·ta·thī'ah, *the son* of Sem'e·ī, *the son* of Joseph, *the son* of Judah, [27]*the son* of Jō·an'nas, *the son* of Rhē'sa, *the son* of Ze·rub'ba·bel, *the son* of She·al'ti·el, *the son* of Nē'rī, [28]*the son* of Mel'chī, *the son*

3:19 [a]NU-Text reads *his brother's wife.*
3:24 [a]This and several other names in the genealogy are spelled somewhat differently in the NU-Text. Since the New King James Version uses the Old Testament spelling for persons mentioned in the New Testament, these variations, which come from the Greek, have not been footnoted.

3:19, 20 Herodias was both the niece of Herod and the wife of his brother, Philip. When Herod divorced his first wife and married Herodias, John the Baptist publicly challenged him, causing John's arrest.

3:23 Jesus began His ministry at about **thirty** years of age. Since He ministered for only about three years, He clearly demonstrated that length of life is no measure of its quality. A person of any age who is wholly dedicated to God can have a vital impact on the lives of others. **as was supposed**: Joseph was not the actual father of Jesus, though he was His legal father and raised Him as his son.

of Ad′dī, *the son* of Cō′sam, *the son* of
El·mō′dam, *the son* of Er, 29*the son* of Jō′sē,
the son of El·i·ē′zer, *the son* of Jō′rim, *the son*
of Mat′that, *the son* of Levi, 30*the son* of
Sim′ē·on, *the son* of Judah, *the son* of Jo-
seph, *the son* of Jō′nan, *the son* of E·lī′a·kim,
31*the son* of Mē′le·a, *the son* of Mē′nan, *the*
son of Mat′ta·thah, *the son* of Nathan, *the*
son of David, 32*the son* of Jesse, *the son* of
Ō′bed, *the son* of Bō′az, *the son* of Sal′mon,
the son of Nah′shon, 33*the son* of Am·min′-
a·dab, *the son* of Ram, *the son* of Hez′ron,
the son of Per′ez, *the son* of Judah, 34*the son*
of Jacob, *the son* of Isaac, *the son* of Abra-
ham, *the son* of Tē′rah, *the son* of Nā′hor,
35*the son* of Sē′rug, *the son* of Rē′ū, *the son* of
Pē′leg, *the son* of Ē′ber, *the son* of Shē′lah,
36*the son* of Cā·ī′nan, *the son* of Ar·phā′xad,
the son of Shem, *the son* of Noah, *the son* of
Lā′mech, 37*the son* of Me·thū′se·lah, *the son*
of Ē′noch, *the son* of Jar′ed, *the son* of
Ma·hal′a·lel, *the son* of Cā·ī′nan, 38*the son* of
Ē′nosh, *the son* of Seth, *the son* of Adam, *the*
son of God.

CHAPTER 4

Satan Tempts Jesus

Then Jesus, being filled with the Holy
Spirit, returned from the Jordan and was
led by the Spirit into[a] the wilderness, 2be-
ing tempted for forty days by the devil.
And in those days He ate nothing, and af-
terward, when they had ended, He was
hungry.

3And the devil said to Him, "If You are
the Son of God, command this stone to be-
come bread."

4But Jesus answered him, saying,[a] "It is
written, *'Man shall not live by bread alone,*
but by every word of God.'"[b]

5Then the devil, taking Him up on a
high mountain, showed Him[a] all the king-
doms of the world in a moment of time.
6And the devil said to Him, "All this au-
thority I will give You, and their glory; for
this has been delivered to me, and I give it
to whomever I wish. 7Therefore, if You will
worship before me, all will be Yours."

8And Jesus answered and said to him,
"Get behind Me, Satan![a] For[b] it is written,
'You shall worship the LORD your God, and
Him only you shall serve.'"[c]

9Then he brought Him to Jerusalem, set
Him on the pinnacle of the temple, and
said to Him, "If You are the Son of God,
throw Yourself down from here. 10For it is
written:

> *'He shall give His angels charge over*
> *you,*
> *To keep you,'*

11and,

> *'In their hands they shall bear you up,*
> *Lest you dash your foot against a*
> *stone.'*"[a]

12And Jesus answered and said to him,
"It has been said, *'You shall not tempt the*
LORD your God.'"[a]

13Now when the devil had ended every
temptation, he departed from Him until an
opportune time.

Jesus Begins His Galilean Ministry

14Then Jesus returned in the power of
the Spirit to Galilee, and news of Him went

4:1 [a]NU-Text reads *in.* 4:4 [a]Deuteronomy 8:3 [b]NU-Text omits *but by every word of God.* 4:5 [a]NU-Text reads *And taking Him up, he showed Him.* 4:8 [a]NU-Text omits *Get behind Me, Satan.* [b]NU-Text and M-Text omit *For.* [c]Deuteronomy 6:13 4:11 [a]Psalm 91:11, 12 4:12 [a]Deuteronomy 6:16

3:38 son of Adam: Matthew traced Jesus' genealogy back to Abraham, the father of the Jews (Matt. 1:1, 2). He wanted to prove that Jesus was their promised Messiah. Luke emphasizes that salvation is for the whole world. Therefore he traces Jesus' ancestry back to Adam, the father of the human race.

4:10 Satan's misuse of Scripture should prompt us to beware of those who twist God's Word to support false doctrine.

out through all the surrounding region.
15And He taught in their synagogues, be-
ing glorified by all.

Jesus Rejected at Nazareth

16So He came to Nazareth, where He
had been brought up. And as His custom
was, He went into the synagogue on the
Sabbath day, and stood up to read. 17And
He was handed the book of the prophet
Ī·sāi'ah. And when He had opened the
book, He found the place where it was
written:

18 *"The Spirit of the LORD is upon*
Me,
Because He has anointed Me
To preach the gospel to the poor;
He has sent Me to heal the
brokenhearted,[a]
To proclaim liberty to the captives
And recovery of sight to the blind,
To set at liberty those who are
oppressed;
19 *To proclaim the acceptable year of the*
LORD."[a]

20Then He closed the book, and gave *it*
back to the attendant and sat down. And
the eyes of all who were in the synagogue
were fixed on Him. 21And He began to say
to them, "Today this Scripture is fulfilled
in your hearing." 22So all bore witness
to Him, and marveled at the gracious
words which proceeded out of His
mouth. And they said, "Is this not Joseph's
son?"
23He said to them, "You will surely say
this proverb to Me, 'Physician, heal your-
self! Whatever we have heard done in
Ca·per'na·um,[a] do also here in Your coun-
try.' " 24Then He said, "Assuredly, I say to
you, no prophet is accepted in his own
country. 25But I tell you truly, many wid-
ows were in Israel in the days of E·lī'jah,
when the heaven was shut up three years
and six months, and there was a great
famine throughout all the land; 26but to
none of them was E·lī'jah sent except to
Zar'e·phath,[a] *in the region* of Sī'don, to a
woman *who was* a widow. 27And many lep-
ers were in Israel in the time of E·lī'sha the
prophet, and none of them was cleansed
except Nā'a·man the Syrian."
28So all those in the synagogue, when
they heard these things, were filled with
wrath, 29and rose up and thrust Him out of
the city; and they led Him to the brow of
the hill on which their city was built, that
they might throw Him down over the cliff.
30Then passing through the midst of them,
He went His way.

Jesus Casts Out an Unclean Spirit

31Then He went down to Ca·per'na·um,
a city of Galilee, and was teaching them on
the Sabbaths. 32And they were astonished
at His teaching, for His word was with au-
thority. 33Now in the synagogue there was
a man who had a spirit of an unclean de-
mon. And he cried out with a loud voice,
34saying, "Let *us* alone! What have we to do
with You, Jesus of Nazareth? Did You
come to destroy us? I know who You are—
the Holy One of God!"
35But Jesus rebuked him, saying, "Be
quiet, and come out of him!" And when
the demon had thrown him in *their* midst,

4:18 [a]NU-Text omits *to heal the brokenhearted.*
4:19 [a]Isaiah 61:1, 2 4:23 [a]Here and elsewhere the NU-Text spelling is *Capharnaum.* 4:26 [a]Greek *Sarepta*

4:18, 19 acceptable year: An allusion to the OT Jubilee year which proclaimed liberation for indentured servants and for the land (Lev. 25:8–55). However, Jesus would proclaim a greater liberation—a time of reconciliation with God and freedom from the results of human sin. He uses the quotation from Isaiah to announce His ministry and describe six aspects of it.

4:20, 21 Following the custom of the Jewish synagogue, Jesus stood to read the Scripture (v. 16), then **sat down** to teach or preach. **Scripture . . . fulfilled**: This prophecy came true when Jesus read it. The Spirit of the Lord was on Him. He was the One sent to bring the full benefits of salvation promised to God's people.

it came out of him and did not hurt him.
36Then they were all amazed and spoke
among themselves, saying, "What a word
this *is!* For with authority and power He
commands the unclean spirits, and they
come out." 37And the report about Him
went out into every place in the surround-
ing region.

Peter's Mother-in-Law Healed

38Now He arose from the synagogue
and entered Simon's house. But Simon's
wife's mother was sick with a high fever,
and they made request of Him concerning
her. 39So He stood over her and rebuked
the fever, and it left her. And immediately
she arose and served them.

Many Healed After Sabbath Sunset

40When the sun was setting, all those
who had any that were sick with various
diseases brought them to Him; and He laid
His hands on every one of them and
healed them. 41And demons also came out
of many, crying out and saying, "You are
the Christ,[a] the Son of God!"

And He, rebuking *them,* did not allow
them to speak, for they knew that He was
the Christ.

Jesus Preaches in Galilee

42Now when it was day, He departed
and went into a deserted place. And the
crowd sought Him and came to Him, and
tried to keep Him from leaving them; 43but
He said to them, "I must preach the king-
dom of God to the other cities also, because
for this purpose I have been sent." 44And
He was preaching in the synagogues of
Galilee.[a]

CHAPTER 5

Four Fishermen Called as Disciples

So it was, as the multitude pressed
about Him to hear the word of God, that
He stood by the Lake of Gen·nes'a·ret,
2and saw two boats standing by the lake;
but the fishermen had gone from them and
were washing *their* nets. 3Then He got into
one of the boats, which was Simon's, and
asked him to put out a little from the land.
And He sat down and taught the multi-
tudes from the boat.

4When He had stopped speaking,
He said to Simon, "Launch out into
the deep and let down your nets for a
catch."

5But Simon answered and said to Him,
"Master, we have toiled all night and
caught nothing; nevertheless at Your word
I will let down the net." 6And when they
had done this, they caught a great number
of fish, and their net was breaking. 7So they
signaled to *their* partners in the other boat
to come and help them. And they came
and filled both the boats, so that they
began to sink. 8When Simon Peter saw *it,*
he fell down at Jesus' knees, saying, "De-
part from me, for I am a sinful man,
O Lord!"

9For he and all who were with him were
astonished at the catch of fish which they
had taken; 10and so also *were* James
and John, the sons of Zeb'e·dee, who
were partners with Simon. And Jesus
said to Simon, "Do not be afraid.
From now on you will catch men." 11So
when they had brought their boats
to land, they forsook all and followed
Him.

Jesus Cleanses a Leper

12And it happened when He was in a
certain city, that behold, a man who was
full of leprosy saw Jesus; and he fell on
his face and implored Him, saying, "Lord,
if You are willing, You can make me
clean."

4:41 [a]NU-Text omits *the Christ.* 4:44 [a]NU-Text reads *Judea.*

5:1 the Lake of Gennesaret: the Sea of Galilee.

LUKE: A BALANCED PERSPECTIVE

The viewpoint of Jesus' life provided in the Gospel of Luke clearly reflects the background of its author. As a physician during the New Testament era, Luke could be considered a scientist of his day. He belonged to the intellectual community, much like his fellow laborer, Paul, and most scholars believe Luke wrote the best Greek of any New Testament author.

It is no accident that Luke was chosen as one of the four gospel writers. In contrast to Matthew, Mark, and John, his narrative provides the most complete historical background. His frequent references to the institutions, customs, geography, and history of the period indicate a man devoted to scientific accuracy. Luke's precision as an historian authenticates the beliefs of the Christian church as little else can. In fact, he explicitly set forth this objective in writing to Theophilus: "That you may know the certainty of those things in which you were instructed" (Luke 1:4).

But Luke did not limit himself to the scientific. He alone, of the four gospel writers, recorded the songs of Christmas: The *Ave Maria,* the words of the angel Gabriel to Mary (1:28–33); Mary's *Magnificat* (1:46–55); Zechariah's *Benedictus* (1:68–79); the *Gloria in Excelsis* of the angels (2:13–14); and Simeon's prayer of praise, the *Nunc Dimittis* (2:29–32). Luke's version of the Christmas story, in addition to providing the most detail, shows an appreciation for the beauty and joy of the occasion.

Not only was Luke a man of intellect and emotion, but he was a man of action. He accompanied Paul on his second missionary journey and stayed close to that great apostle throughout much of his persecution and suffering (2 Tim. 4:11; Philem. 24). So close was their relationship that Paul refers to his companion as "Luke the beloved physician" (Col. 4:14).

Luke shows us the essence of a balanced Christian life: As a doctor, he demonstrated concern with sickness and healing in his account of the ministry of Christ. As a scientist, he held himself to the strictest standards of accuracy and pursued the highest level of knowledge. And as a believer, Luke ministered to fellow Christians, rejoiced in the message of the gospel, and shared the Good News with others. ✦

13Then He put out *His* hand and touched
him, saying, "I am willing; be cleansed."
Immediately the leprosy left him. 14And
He charged him to tell no one, "But go and
show yourself to the priest, and make an
offering for your cleansing, as a testimony
to them, just as Moses commanded."
15However, the report went around concerning Him all the more; and great multitudes came together to hear, and to be

healed by Him of their infirmities. 16So He Himself *often* withdrew into the wilderness and prayed.

Jesus Forgives and Heals a Paralytic

17Now it happened on a certain day, as He was teaching, that there were Phar′i·sees and teachers of the law sitting by, who had come out of every town of Galilee, Judea, and Jerusalem. And the power of the Lord was *present* to heal them.[a] 18Then behold, men brought on a bed a man who was paralyzed, whom they sought to bring in and lay before Him. 19And when they could not find how they might bring him in, because of the crowd, they went up on the housetop and let him down with *his* bed through the tiling into the midst before Jesus.

20When He saw their faith, He said to him, "Man, your sins are forgiven you."

21And the scribes and the Phar′i·sees began to reason, saying, "Who is this who speaks blasphemies? Who can forgive sins but God alone?"

22But when Jesus perceived their thoughts, He answered and said to them, "Why are you reasoning in your hearts? 23Which is easier, to say, 'Your sins are forgiven you,' or to say, 'Rise up and walk'? 24But that you may know that the Son of Man has power on earth to forgive sins"—He said to the man who was paralyzed, "I say to you, arise, take up your bed, and go to your house."

25Immediately he rose up before them, took up what he had been lying on, and departed to his own house, glorifying God. 26And they were all amazed, and they glorified God and were filled with fear, saying, "We have seen strange things today!"

Matthew the Tax Collector

27After these things He went out and saw a tax collector named Levi, sitting at the tax office. And He said to him, "Follow Me." 28So he left all, rose up, and followed Him.

29Then Levi gave Him a great feast in his own house. And there were a great number of tax collectors and others who sat down with them. 30And their scribes and the Phar′i·sees[a] complained against His disciples, saying, "Why do You eat and drink with tax collectors and sinners?"

31Jesus answered and said to them, "Those who are well have no need of a physician, but those who are sick. 32I have not come to call *the* righteous, but sinners, to repentance."

Jesus Is Questioned About Fasting

33Then they said to Him, "Why do[a] the disciples of John fast often and make prayers, and likewise those of the Phar′i·sees, but Yours eat and drink?"

34And He said to them, "Can you make the friends of the bridegroom fast while

5:17 [a]NU-Text reads *present with Him to heal.*
5:30 [a]NU-Text reads *But the Pharisees and their scribes.*
5:33 [a]NU-Text omits *Why do,* making the verse a statement.

5:24 With the exception of Acts 7:56, Jesus is called **the Son of Man** by no one but Himself. Here He uses the title to emphasize His present authority. In other places it refers to His preexistence, coming authority as Judge, and/or identification with humanity. For the OT background of this title see Dan. 7:13, 14.

5:27, 28 tax collector: The Romans sold the right to collect their taxes to private contractors, who then charged enough to make a profit. Tax collectors' methods were so oppressive that they were despised by the people and classified with gross sinners such as prostitutes. Thus Jesus broke social convention and showed His ability and desire to forgive even the worst of sinners by inviting **Levi** to become one of the 12 disciples. Levi is called Matthew in the lists of the Twelve. Matthew identifies himself as a tax collector in Matt. 9:9; 10:3, thus indicating that he is Levi.

the bridegroom is with them? 35But the days will come when the bridegroom will be taken away from them; then they will fast in those days."

36Then He spoke a parable to them: "No one puts a piece from a new garment on an old one;[a] otherwise the new makes a tear, and also the piece that was *taken* out of the new does not match the old. 37And no one puts new wine into old wineskins; or else the new wine will burst the wineskins and be spilled, and the wineskins will be ruined. 38But new wine must be put into new wineskins, and both are preserved.[a] 39And no one, having drunk old *wine,* immediately[a] desires new; for he says, 'The old is better.' "[b]

CHAPTER 6

Jesus Is Lord of the Sabbath

Now it happened on the second Sabbath after the first[a] that He went through the grainfields. And His disciples plucked the heads of grain and ate *them,* rubbing *them* in *their* hands. 2And some of the Phar′i·sees said to them, "Why are you doing what is not lawful to do on the Sabbath?"

3But Jesus answering them said, "Have you not even read this, what David did when he was hungry, he and those who were with him: 4how he went into the house of God, took and ate the showbread, and also gave some to those with him, which is not lawful for any but the priests to eat?" 5And He said to them, "The Son of Man is also Lord of the Sabbath."

Healing on the Sabbath

6Now it happened on another Sabbath, also, that He entered the synagogue and taught. And a man was there whose right hand was withered. 7So the scribes and Phar′i·sees watched Him closely, whether He would heal on the Sabbath, that they might find an accusation against Him. 8But He knew their thoughts, and said to the man who had the withered hand, "Arise and stand here." And he arose and stood. 9Then Jesus said to them, "I will ask you one thing: Is it lawful on the Sabbath to do good or to do evil, to save life or to destroy?"[a] 10And when He had looked around at them all, He said to the man,[a] "Stretch out your hand." And he did so, and his hand was restored as whole as the other.[b] 11But they were filled with rage, and discussed with one another what they might do to Jesus.

The Twelve Apostles

12Now it came to pass in those days that He went out to the mountain to pray, and continued all night in prayer to God. 13And when it was day, He called His disciples to *Himself;* and from them He chose twelve whom He also named apostles: 14Simon, whom He also named Peter, and Andrew his brother; James and John; Philip and Bartholomew; 15Matthew and Thomas; James the *son* of Al·phae̅′us, and Simon called the Zealot; 16Judas *the son* of James,

5:36 [a]NU-Text reads *No one tears a piece from a new garment and puts it on an old one.* 5:38 [a]NU-Text omits *and both are preserved.* 5:39 [a]NU-Text omits *immediately.* [b]NU-Text reads *good.* 6:1 [a]NU-Text reads *on a Sabbath.* 6:9 [a]M-Text reads *to kill.* 6:10 [a]NU-Text and M-Text read *to him.* [b]NU-Text omits *as whole as the other.*

6:1, 2 second Sabbath: Sabbaths were numbered following Passover. The first Sabbath was during Passover week; the second during the following week. According to the interpretation of the Pharisees, Jesus' disciples were harvesting and threshing when they plucked **heads of grain** and rubbed off the husks.

6:3, 4 Jesus rejected an interpretation of the Sabbath law that lacked compassion and forgot the needs of people. He responded: "The Sabbath was made for man, and not man for the Sabbath" (see Mark 2:27). He justified His disciples' action with the OT example in which David ate bread reserved for priests.

6:12 Even the Son of God found it necessary to spend time in prayer, setting an example for us as we face the pressures of daily life.

and Judas Is·car′i·ot who also became a
traitor.

Jesus Heals a Great Multitude

17 And He came down with them and
stood on a level place with a crowd of His
disciples and a great multitude of people
from all Judea and Jerusalem, and from the
seacoast of Tȳre and Sī′don, who came to
hear Him and be healed of their diseases,
18 as well as those who were tormented
with unclean spirits. And they were
healed. 19 And the whole multitude sought
to touch Him, for power went out from
Him and healed *them* all.

The Beatitudes

20 Then He lifted up His eyes toward His
disciples, and said:

"Blessed *are you* poor,
For yours is the kingdom of God.
21 Blessed *are you* who hunger now,
For you shall be filled.
Blessed *are you* who weep now,
For you shall laugh.
22 Blessed are you when men hate you,
And when they exclude you,
And revile *you*, and cast out your
name as evil,
For the Son of Man's sake.
23 Rejoice in that day and leap for joy!
For indeed your reward *is* great in
heaven,
For in like manner their fathers did
to the prophets.

Jesus Pronounces Woes

24 "But woe to you who are rich,
For you have received your
consolation.
25 Woe to you who are full,
For you shall hunger.
Woe to you who laugh now,
For you shall mourn and weep.
26 Woe to you[a] when all[b] men speak
well of you,
For so did their fathers to the false
prophets.

Love Your Enemies

27 "But I say to you who hear: Love your
enemies, do good to those who hate you,
28 bless those who curse you, and pray for
those who spitefully use you. 29 To him who
strikes you on the *one* cheek, offer the other
also. And from him who takes away your
cloak, do not withhold *your* tunic either.
30 Give to everyone who asks of you. And
from him who takes away your goods do
not ask *them* back. 31 And just as you want
men to do to you, you also do to them like-
wise.

32 "But if you love those who love you,
what credit is that to you? For even sinners
love those who love them. 33 And if you do
good to those who do good to you, what
credit is that to you? For even sinners do
the same. 34 And if you lend *to those* from
whom you hope to receive back, what
credit is that to you? For even sinners lend
to sinners to receive as much back. 35 But
love your enemies, do good, and lend,
hoping for nothing in return; and your re-
ward will be great, and you will be sons of
the Most High. For He is kind to the un-
thankful and evil. 36 Therefore be merciful,
just as your Father also is merciful.

Do Not Judge

37 "Judge not, and you shall not be
judged. Condemn not, and you shall not
be condemned. Forgive, and you will be

6:26 [a]NU-Text and M-Text omit *to you.* [b]M-Text omits *all.*

6:27–31 Positively, Christian **love** means doing **good** even to those who **hate** us (vv. 27, 28). Negatively, it means not holding a grudge or seeking revenge against those who have wronged us (vv. 29, 30). Jesus' teachings are meant to be taken seriously; love is the guiding spirit of a Christian's life. But this does not mean we never oppose evil. Genuine love resists evil and challenges wrongs directed against other persons. Verse 31 is a dependable and practical rule by which to determine our behavior.

The Math-defying Principle of Tithing

Jay Kesler

Grandparents have the opportunity and responsibility to remind young people that God will never leave them nor forsake them, that He has been faithful to us in the past and, therefore, He will be faithful in the present. We can share stories of answered prayer, of times when God came to our rescue, when He did things for us that we didn't understand.

Janie and I have told our children the story of our own experience with tithing, how God has never disappointed us. We have not only attempted to tithe, but to go above the tithe in our giving to Christ and His church and to the needy and poor. We have tried to explain to them that mathematically it does not work. In math, nine-tenths should not go as far as ten-tenths; but in life's experience, if you lay aside the first portion and give it to the Lord and His work, God will bless you, "pressed down, shaken together, and running over" (Luke 6:38).

We have been gratified to see our children practicing the same principles and passing them on to our grandchildren. These testimonies to God's faithfulness, of seeing us through, have value. Our children and grandchildren live in a demanding and competitive culture, where expenses rise to meet income and every dollar has a couple of places to be used. It is easy to rationalize that charitable needs are covered by our taxes, that somebody else can take care of them, that a lot of people richer than we are should carry the responsibility. But our example of tithing has made an impact on our lives, and we want to pass it on to our children and our children's children. ✦

forgiven. 38Give, and it will be given to
you: good measure, pressed down, shaken
together, and running over will be put into
your bosom. For with the same measure
that you use, it will be measured back to
you."

39And He spoke a parable to them: "Can
the blind lead the blind? Will they not both
fall into the ditch? 40A disciple is not above
his teacher, but everyone who is perfectly
trained will be like his teacher. 41And why
do you look at the speck in your brother's
eye, but do not perceive the plank in your
own eye? 42Or how can you say to your
brother, 'Brother, let me remove the speck
that *is* in your eye,' when you yourself do
not see the plank that *is* in your own eye?
Hypocrite! First remove the plank from
your own eye, and then you will see
clearly to remove the speck that is in your
brother's eye.

A Tree Is Known by Its Fruit

43"For a good tree does not bear bad
fruit, nor does a bad tree bear good fruit.
44For every tree is known by its own fruit.
For *men* do not gather figs from thorns, nor
do they gather grapes from a bramble
bush. 45A good man out of the good trea-
sure of his heart brings forth good; and an
evil man out of the evil treasure of

6:41 Jesus' illustration calls us to honest self-examination, a vital prerequisite for mentoring younger Christians.

his heart[a] brings forth evil. For out of the abundance of the heart his mouth speaks.

Build on the Rock

46"But why do you call Me 'Lord, Lord,' and not do the things which I say? 47Whoever comes to Me, and hears My sayings and does them, I will show you whom he is like: 48He is like a man building a house, who dug deep and laid the foundation on the rock. And when the flood arose, the stream beat vehemently against that house, and could not shake it, for it was founded on the rock.[a] 49But he who heard and did nothing is like a man who built a house on the earth without a foundation, against which the stream beat vehemently; and immediately it fell.[a] And the ruin of that house was great."

CHAPTER 7

Jesus Heals a Centurion's Servant

Now when He concluded all His sayings in the hearing of the people, He entered Ca·per'na·um. 2And a certain centurion's servant, who was dear to him, was sick and ready to die. 3So when he heard about Jesus, he sent elders of the Jews to Him, pleading with Him to come and heal his servant. 4And when they came to Jesus, they begged Him earnestly, saying that the one for whom He should do this was deserving, 5"for he loves our nation, and has built us a synagogue."

6Then Jesus went with them. And when He was already not far from the house, the centurion sent friends to Him, saying to Him, "Lord, do not trouble Yourself, for I am not worthy that You should enter under my roof. 7Therefore I did not even think myself worthy to come to You. But say the word, and my servant will be healed. 8For I also am a man placed under authority, having soldiers under me. And I say to one, 'Go,' and he goes; and to another, 'Come,' and he comes; and to my servant, 'Do this,' and he does *it*."

9When Jesus heard these things, He marveled at him, and turned around and said to the crowd that followed Him, "I say to you, I have not found such great faith, not even in Israel!" 10And those who were sent, returning to the house, found the servant well who had been sick.[a]

Jesus Raises the Son of the Widow of Nain

11Now it happened, the day after, *that* He went into a city called Nā'in; and many of His disciples went with Him, and a large crowd. 12And when He came near the gate of the city, behold, a dead man was being carried out, the only son of his mother; and she was a widow. And a large crowd from the city was with her. 13When the Lord saw her, He had compassion on her and said to

6:45 [a]NU-Text omits *treasure of his heart.*
6:48 [a]NU-Text reads *for it was well built.*
6:49 [a]NU-Text reads *collapsed.* 7:10 [a]NU-Text omits *who had been sick.*

7:2–6 A **centurion** was commander of 100 men in the Roman army, a responsible and well-paid position. Historical study indicates that there were probably no Roman soldiers in Galilee at this time. If this is true, then this centurion was possibly part of Herod Antipas's army. He was a Gentile who believed in the God of Judaism without becoming a Jew.

7:9 such great faith: We must have a faith that believes in the power of Jesus although He is not physically present with us. This Gentile outsider showed more faith than God's own people of **Israel**.

7:11–17 This story illustrates Jesus' great **compassion** (v. 13) and prepares the way for His report to John the Baptist's disciples ("the dead are raised"; see v. 22). **Nain**: A village in Galilee, a little south of Nazareth. A **widow** whose **only son** had died was among the most destitute. She had no one to help her, and her family line was cut off. **great prophet**: Raising the dead was a miracle performed by the great OT prophets (Elijah, 1 Kin. 17:17–24; Elisha, 2 Kin. 4:18–37). **God has visited**: The miracle was recognized as God's working in Jesus' ministry.

her, "Do not weep." 14Then He came and touched the open coffin, and those who carried *him* stood still. And He said, "Young man, I say to you, arise." 15So he who was dead sat up and began to speak. And He presented him to his mother.

16Then fear came upon all, and they glorified God, saying, "A great prophet has risen up among us"; and, "God has visited His people." 17And this report about Him went throughout all Judea and all the surrounding region.

John the Baptist Sends Messengers to Jesus

18Then the disciples of John reported to him concerning all these things. 19And John, calling two of his disciples to *him,* sent *them* to Jesus,[a] saying, "Are You the Coming One, or do we look for another?"

20When the men had come to Him, they said, "John the Baptist has sent us to You, saying, 'Are You the Coming One, or do we look for another?' " 21And that very hour He cured many of infirmities, afflictions, and evil spirits; and to many blind He gave sight.

22Jesus answered and said to them, "Go and tell John the things you have seen and heard: that *the* blind see, *the* lame walk, *the* lepers are cleansed, *the* deaf hear, *the* dead are raised, *the* poor have the gospel preached to them. 23And blessed is *he* who is not offended because of Me."

24When the messengers of John had departed, He began to speak to the multitudes concerning John: "What did you go out into the wilderness to see? A reed shaken by the wind? 25But what did you go out to see? A man clothed in soft garments? Indeed those who are gorgeously appareled and live in luxury are in kings' courts. 26But what did you go out to see? A prophet? Yes, I say to you, and more than a prophet. 27This is *he* of whom it is written:

'Behold, I send My messenger before
Your face,
Who will prepare Your way before
You.'[a]

28For I say to you, among those born of women there is not a greater prophet than John the Baptist;[a] but he who is least in the kingdom of God is greater than he."

29And when all the people heard *Him,* even the tax collectors justified God, having been baptized with the baptism of John. 30But the Phar'i·sees and lawyers rejected the will of God for themselves, not having been baptized by him.

31And the Lord said,[a] "To what then shall I liken the men of this generation, and what are they like? 32They are like children sitting in the marketplace and calling to one another, saying:

'We played the flute for you,
And you did not dance;
We mourned to you,
And you did not weep.'

33For John the Baptist came neither eating bread nor drinking wine, and you say, 'He has a demon.' 34The Son of Man has come eating and drinking, and you say, 'Look, a glutton and a winebibber, a friend of tax collectors and sinners!' 35But wisdom is justified by all her children."

A Sinful Woman Forgiven

36Then one of the Phar'i·sees asked Him to eat with him. And He went to the

7:19 [a]NU-Text reads *the Lord.* 7:27 [a]Malachi 3:1
7:28 [a]NU-Text reads *there is none greater than John.*
7:31 [a]NU-Text and M-Text omit *And the Lord said.*

7:31–34 Children who say they will not play funeral because it is too sad and will not play wedding because it is too happy simply do not want to play. Those who rejected John the Baptist for his abstinence and Jesus because He was joyful did not want to accept what God was doing. We must be careful not to deny God's hand in events around us simply because He works in unexpected ways.

Phar′i·see's house, and sat down to eat. [37]And behold, a woman in the city who was a sinner, when she knew that *Jesus* sat at the table in the Phar′i·see's house, brought an alabaster flask of fragrant oil, [38]and stood at His feet behind *Him* weeping; and she began to wash His feet with her tears, and wiped *them* with the hair of her head; and she kissed His feet and anointed *them* with the fragrant oil. [39]Now when the Phar′i·see who had invited Him saw *this,* he spoke to himself, saying, "This Man, if He were a prophet, would know who and what manner of woman *this is* who is touching Him, for she is a sinner."

[40]And Jesus answered and said to him, "Simon, I have something to say to you."

So he said, "Teacher, say it."

[41]"There was a certain creditor who had two debtors. One owed five hundred denarii, and the other fifty. [42]And when they had nothing with which to repay, he freely forgave them both. Tell Me, therefore, which of them will love him more?"

[43]Simon answered and said, "I suppose the *one* whom he forgave more."

And He said to him, "You have rightly judged." [44]Then He turned to the woman and said to Simon, "Do you see this woman? I entered your house; you gave Me no water for My feet, but she has washed My feet with her tears and wiped *them* with the hair of her head. [45]You gave Me no kiss, but this woman has not ceased to kiss My feet since the time I came in. [46]You did not anoint My head with oil, but this woman has anointed My feet with fragrant oil. [47]Therefore I say to you, her sins, *which are* many, are forgiven, for she loved much. But to whom little is forgiven, *the same* loves little."

[48]Then He said to her, "Your sins are forgiven."

[49]And those who sat at the table with Him began to say to themselves, "Who is this who even forgives sins?"

[50]Then He said to the woman, "Your faith has saved you. Go in peace."

CHAPTER 8

Many Women Minister to Jesus

Now it came to pass, afterward, that He went through every city and village, preaching and bringing the glad tidings of the kingdom of God. And the twelve *were* with Him, [2]and certain women who had been healed of evil spirits and infirmities—Mary called Mag′da·lēne, out of whom had come seven demons, [3]and Jō·an′na the wife of Chū′za, Her′od's steward, and Susanna, and many others who provided for Him[a] from their substance.

The Parable of the Sower

[4]And when a great multitude had gathered, and they had come to Him from every city, He spoke by a parable: [5]"A sower went out to sow his seed. And as he sowed, some fell by the wayside; and it was trampled down, and the birds of the air devoured it. [6]Some fell on rock; and as soon as it sprang up, it withered away because it lacked moisture. [7]And some fell among thorns, and the thorns sprang up with it and choked it. [8]But others fell on

8:3 [a]NU-Text and M-Text read *them.*

7:44–46 no water: The Pharisee had not provided the common courtesy of washing the guest's dusty feet. **no kiss**: Simon had neglected to give the customary kiss of peace when his guest arrived. **anoint My head**: This practice was reserved for an honored guest on a festive day (see Ps. 23:5).

7:47 she loved much: The woman's love was evidence of having been forgiven rather than the cause of her forgiveness. The Pharisee, on the other hand, had felt little need for forgiveness; consequently, his love was small. As we grow spiritually, we become more aware of the depth of our sin and the greatness of God's mercy; thus our love for the Lord should increase throughout our lives.

> Gloria and I have two mature collies now, but when they were puppies I remember walking into the kitchen and accidentally stepping on one of their tails. He yipped, then immediately licked my foot, as if to say, "You didn't mean it, did you?"
>
> I told Gloria, "What a wonderful example of grace! Wouldn't it be wonderful if everyone in the world reacted like that when they got hurt? To say, in effect, 'I know you love me and mean to do me good.'"
>
> Bill Gaither

good ground, sprang up, and yielded a
crop a hundredfold." When He had said
these things He cried, "He who has ears to
hear, let him hear!"

The Purpose of Parables

9Then His disciples asked Him, saying,
"What does this parable mean?"
10And He said, "To you it has been given
to know the mysteries of the kingdom of
God, but to the rest *it is given* in parables,
that

'Seeing they may not see,
And hearing they may not
understand.'[a]

The Parable of the Sower Explained

11"Now the parable is this: The seed is
the word of God. 12Those by the wayside
are the ones who hear; then the devil
comes and takes away the word out of
their hearts, lest they should believe and
be saved. 13But the ones on the rock *are*
those who, when they hear, receive the
word with joy; and these have no root,
who believe for a while and in time of
temptation fall away. 14Now the ones *that*
fell among thorns are those who, when
they have heard, go out and are choked
with cares, riches, and pleasures of life,
and bring no fruit to maturity. 15But the
ones *that* fell on the good ground are those
who, having heard the word with a noble
and good heart, keep *it* and bear fruit with
patience.

The Parable of the Revealed Light

16"No one, when he has lit a lamp, cov-
ers it with a vessel or puts *it* under a bed,
but sets *it* on a lampstand, that those who
enter may see the light. 17For nothing is se-
cret that will not be revealed, nor *anything*
hidden that will not be known and come to
light. 18Therefore take heed how you hear.
For whoever has, to him *more* will be
given; and whoever does not have, even
what he seems to have will be taken from
him."

Jesus' Mother and Brothers Come to Him

19Then His mother and brothers came to
Him, and could not approach Him because
of the crowd. 20And it was told Him *by*
some, who said, "Your mother and Your
brothers are standing outside, desiring to
see You."
21But He answered and said to them,
"My mother and My brothers are these
who hear the word of God and do it."

Wind and Wave Obey Jesus

22Now it happened, on a certain day,
that He got into a boat with His disciples.
And He said to them, "Let us cross over to
the other side of the lake." And they
launched out. 23But as they sailed He fell
asleep. And a windstorm came down on

8:10 [a]Isaiah 6:9

8:19–21 These verses do not indicate lack of appreciation for Jesus' earthly family. But membership in God's family is based on spiritual relationships. We **hear** and **do** the will of God when we become part of His family. Obedience must be the highest concern of the Christian. Human relationships take second place to our relationship with God.

the lake, and they were filling *with water,*
and were in jeopardy. 24And they came to
Him and awoke Him, saying, "Master,
Master, we are perishing!"

Then He arose and rebuked the wind
and the raging of the water. And they
ceased, and there was a calm. 25But He said
to them, "Where is your faith?"

And they were afraid, and marveled,
saying to one another, "Who can this be?
For He commands even the winds and water, and they obey Him!"

A Demon-Possessed Man Healed

26Then they sailed to the country of the
Gad′a·rēnes,[a] which is opposite Galilee.
27And when He stepped out on the land,
there met Him a certain man from the city
who had demons for a long time. And he
wore no clothes,[a] nor did he live in a house
but in the tombs. 28When he saw Jesus, he
cried out, fell down before Him, and with a
loud voice said, "What have I to do with
You, Jesus, Son of the Most High God? I
beg You, do not torment me!" 29For He had
commanded the unclean spirit to come out
of the man. For it had often seized him,
and he was kept under guard, bound with
chains and shackles; and he broke the
bonds and was driven by the demon into
the wilderness.

30Jesus asked him, saying, "What is your
name?"

And he said, "Legion," because many
demons had entered him. 31And they
begged Him that He would not command
them to go out into the abyss.

32Now a herd of many swine was feeding there on the mountain. So they begged
Him that He would permit them to enter
them. And He permitted them. 33Then the
demons went out of the man and entered
the swine, and the herd ran violently
down the steep place into the lake and
drowned.

34When those who fed *them* saw what
had happened, they fled and told *it* in the
city and in the country. 35Then they went
out to see what had happened, and came
to Jesus, and found the man from whom
the demons had departed, sitting at the
feet of Jesus, clothed and in his right mind.
And they were afraid. 36They also who had
seen *it* told them by what means he who
had been demon-possessed was healed.
37Then the whole multitude of the surrounding region of the Gad′a·rēnes[a] asked
Him to depart from them, for they were
seized with great fear. And He got into the
boat and returned.

38Now the man from whom the demons
had departed begged Him that he might be
with Him. But Jesus sent him away, saying,
39"Return to your own house, and tell what
great things God has done for you." And
he went his way and proclaimed throughout the whole city what great things Jesus
had done for him.

A Girl Restored to Life and a Woman Healed

40So it was, when Jesus returned, that
the multitude welcomed Him, for they
were all waiting for Him. 41And behold,
there came a man named Jā·ī′rus, and he
was a ruler of the synagogue. And he fell
down at Jesus' feet and begged Him to
come to his house, 42for he had an only
daughter about twelve years of age, and
she was dying.

But as He went, the multitudes
thronged Him. 43Now a woman, having a
flow of blood for twelve years, who had

8:26 [a]NU-Text reads *Gerasenes.* 8:27 [a]NU-Text reads *who had demons and for a long time wore no clothes.* 8:37 [a]NU-Text reads *Gerasenes.*

8:25 Where is your faith? Deep faith in God brings a steadiness in life's greatest crises. Excessive fear of death is often an indication of lack of spiritual maturity. Christians need not be afraid to die. As we grow older, it is natural to make preparations for death, but we should not dwell on the subject nor should we fear its arrival. **Who can this be**? They would soon confess Him as the Christ (9:20).

> Faith is necessary for physical as well as spiritual well-being.
> Smiley Blanton, M.D.

spent all her livelihood on physicians and
could not be healed by any, 44came from
behind and touched the border of His gar-
ment. And immediately her flow of blood
stopped.
45And Jesus said, "Who touched Me?"
When all denied it, Peter and those with
him[a] said, "Master, the multitudes throng
and press You, and You say, 'Who touched
Me?' "[b]
46But Jesus said, "Somebody touched
Me, for I perceived power going out from
Me." 47Now when the woman saw that she
was not hidden, she came trembling; and
falling down before Him, she declared to
Him in the presence of all the people the
reason she had touched Him and how she
was healed immediately.
48And He said to her, "Daughter, be of
good cheer;[a] your faith has made you well.
Go in peace."
49While He was still speaking, someone
came from the ruler of the synagogue's
house, saying to him, "Your daughter is
dead. Do not trouble the Teacher."[a]
50But when Jesus heard *it,* He answered
him, saying, "Do not be afraid; only
believe, and she will be made well."
51When He came into the house, He per-
mitted no one to go in[a] except Peter, James,
and John,[b] and the father and mother of the
girl. 52Now all wept and mourned for her;
but He said, "Do not weep; she is not dead,
but sleeping." 53And they ridiculed Him,
knowing that she was dead.
54But He put them all outside,[a] took her
by the hand and called, saying, "Little girl,
arise." 55Then her spirit returned, and she
arose immediately. And He commanded
that she be given *something* to eat. 56And
her parents were astonished, but He
charged them to tell no one what had hap-
pened.

CHAPTER 9

Sending Out the Twelve

Then He called His twelve disciples to-
gether and gave them power and authority
over all demons, and to cure diseases. 2He
sent them to preach the kingdom of God
and to heal the sick. 3And He said to them,
"Take nothing for the journey, neither
staffs nor bag nor bread nor money; and do
not have two tunics apiece.
4"Whatever house you enter, stay there,
and from there depart. 5And whoever will
not receive you, when you go out of that
city, shake off the very dust from your feet
as a testimony against them."
6So they departed and went through the
towns, preaching the gospel and healing
everywhere.

Herod Seeks to See Jesus

7Now Her'od the tetrarch heard of all
that was done by Him; and he was per-
plexed, because it was said by some that
John had risen from the dead, 8and by
some that E·lī'jah had appeared, and by
others that one of the old prophets had
risen again. 9Her'od said, "John I have
beheaded, but who is this of whom I
hear such things?" So he sought to see
Him.

8:45 [a]NU-Text omits *and those with him.* [b]NU-Text omits *and You say, 'Who touched Me?'* 8:48 [a]NU-Text omits *be of good cheer.* 8:49 [a]NU-Text adds *anymore.* 8:51 [a]NU-Text adds *with Him.* [b]NU-Text and M-Text read *Peter, John, and James.* 8:54 [a]NU-Text omits *put them all outside.*

9:1–6 Jesus sent the Twelve to **preach** and **heal** (v. 2) just as He had been doing. He gave them the **power and authority** (v. 1) necessary to carry out His commands, and received a report from them (see v. 10). Their ministry was an extension of His. Jesus always gives us help to do what He tells us to do, and He always holds us accountable for our obedience.

Feeding the Five Thousand

[10]And the apostles, when they had returned, told Him all that they had done. Then He took them and went aside privately into a deserted place belonging to the city called Beth·sā′i·da. [11]But when the multitudes knew *it,* they followed Him; and He received them and spoke to them about the kingdom of God, and healed those who had need of healing. [12]When the day began to wear away, the twelve came and said to Him, "Send the multitude away, that they may go into the surrounding towns and country, and lodge and get provisions; for we are in a deserted place here."

[13]But He said to them, "You give them something to eat."

And they said, "We have no more than five loaves and two fish, unless we go and buy food for all these people." [14]For there were about five thousand men.

Then He said to His disciples, "Make them sit down in groups of fifty." [15]And they did so, and made them all sit down.

[16]Then He took the five loaves and the two fish, and looking up to heaven, He blessed and broke *them,* and gave *them* to the disciples to set before the multitude. [17]So they all ate and were filled, and twelve baskets of the leftover fragments were taken up by them.

Peter Confesses Jesus as the Christ

[18]And it happened, as He was alone praying, *that* His disciples joined Him, and He asked them, saying, "Who do the crowds say that I am?"

[19]So they answered and said, "John the Baptist, but some *say* E·lī′jah; and others *say* that one of the old prophets has risen again."

[20]He said to them, "But who do you say that I am?"

Peter answered and said, "The Christ of God."

Jesus Predicts His Death and Resurrection

[21]And He strictly warned and commanded them to tell this to no one, [22]saying, "The Son of Man must suffer many things, and be rejected by the elders and chief priests and scribes, and be killed, and be raised the third day."

Take Up the Cross and Follow Him

[23]Then He said to *them* all, "If anyone desires to come after Me, let him deny himself, and take up his cross daily,[a] and follow Me. [24]For whoever desires to save his life will lose it, but whoever loses his life for My sake will save it. [25]For what profit is it to a man if he gains the whole world, and is himself destroyed or lost? [26]For whoever is ashamed of Me and My words, of him the Son of Man will be ashamed when He comes in His *own* glory, and *in His* Father's, and of the holy angels. [27]But I tell you truly, there are some standing here who shall not taste death till they see the kingdom of God."

Jesus Transfigured on the Mount

[28]Now it came to pass, about eight days after these sayings, that He took Peter,

9:23 [a]M-Text omits *daily.*

9:23 deny himself: Jesus does not speak of denying ourselves something. We are to deny ourselves, our ambitions, our self-interests. Self must no longer rule our lives. **take up his cross**: Jesus pictures His disciples as condemned to death and carrying their crosses along with Him to the place of crucifixion. We must live dead to self-centeredness. **to them all**: Not only the Twelve, but to all who would follow Him. While it is normal for us at this stage of life to have dreams and goals for the future, we must be willing to sacrifice all to follow God's will for our lives.

9:28–36 In the experience of the Transfiguration Jesus confirmed Peter's confession, given about a week earlier. There on the **mountain** Jesus mentioned His coming departure and gave three disciples a vision of His resurrection glory.

John, and James and went up on the moun-
tain to pray. [29]As He prayed, the appear-
ance of His face was altered, and His robe
became white *and* glistening. [30]And behold,
two men talked with Him, who were Mo-
ses and E·lī'jah, [31]who appeared in glory
and spoke of His decease which He was
about to accomplish at Jerusalem. [32]But Pe-
ter and those with him were heavy with
sleep; and when they were fully awake,
they saw His glory and the two men who
stood with Him. [33]Then it happened, as
they were parting from Him, *that* Peter
said to Jesus, "Master, it is good for us to be
here; and let us make three tabernacles:
one for You, one for Moses, and one for
E·lī'jah"—not knowing what he said.

[34]While he was saying this, a cloud came
and overshadowed them; and they were
fearful as they entered the cloud. [35]And a
voice came out of the cloud, saying, "This
is My beloved Son.[a] Hear Him!" [36]When
the voice had ceased, Jesus was found
alone. But they kept quiet, and told no one
in those days any of the things they had
seen.

A Boy Is Healed

[37]Now it happened on the next day,
when they had come down from the
mountain, that a great multitude met Him.
[38]Suddenly a man from the multitude cried
out, saying, "Teacher, I implore You, look
on my son, for he is my only child. [39]And
behold, a spirit seizes him, and he sud-
denly cries out; it convulses him so that he
foams *at the mouth;* and it departs from him
with great difficulty, bruising him. [40]So I
implored Your disciples to cast it out, but
they could not."

[41]Then Jesus answered and said,
"O faithless and perverse generation, how
long shall I be with you and bear with you?
Bring your son here." [42]And as he was still
coming, the demon threw him down and
convulsed *him*. Then Jesus rebuked the un-
clean spirit, healed the child, and gave him
back to his father.

Jesus Again Predicts His Death

[43]And they were all amazed at the
majesty of God.

But while everyone marveled at all the
things which Jesus did, He said to His dis-
ciples, [44]"Let these words sink down into
your ears, for the Son of Man is about to be
betrayed into the hands of men." [45]But they
did not understand this saying, and it was
hidden from them so that they did not per-
ceive it; and they were afraid to ask Him
about this saying.

Who Is the Greatest?

[46]Then a dispute arose among them as to
which of them would be greatest. [47]And
Jesus, perceiving the thought of their heart,
took a little child and set him by Him,
[48]and said to them, "Whoever receives this
little child in My name receives Me; and
whoever receives Me receives Him who
sent Me. For he who is least among you all
will be great."

Jesus Forbids Sectarianism

[49]Now John answered and said, "Mas-
ter, we saw someone casting out demons in
Your name, and we forbade him because
he does not follow with us."

[50]But Jesus said to him, "Do not forbid
him, for he who is not against us[a] is on our[b]
side."

A Samaritan Village Rejects the Savior

[51]Now it came to pass, when the time
had come for Him to be received up, that

9:35 [a]NU-Text reads *This is My Son, the Chosen One.*
9:50 [a]NU-Text reads *you.* [b]NU-Text reads *your.*

9:51 be received up: A reference to Jesus' ascension, although His death and resurrection were included in this climax of His earthly ministry. **set His face**: He determined to move steadfastly toward His death.

A Humble Heart

Claire Cloninger

When we examine the life and teachings of Jesus, we will note how frequently He encourages us to adopt the heart position of the small and humble. We are told that the least person shall be the greatest (Luke 9:48), that to be faithful with a small number of things will result in our being put in charge of a large number of things (Matt. 25:21), and even that to minister to the "least" of men constitutes ministry to the Lord Himself (Matt. 25:40). Indeed, the hallmark of the Lord's very life was His desire to identify with the humble, the needy, the destitute. And the heart of His message to us who would follow after Him is that we must be willing to do the same.

"He encourages us to adopt the heart position of the small and humble."

So often we rush out in our fervent desire to do "great things" for the kingdom, forgetting the necessary first step of ministry—which is a humble heart-attitude before the Lord. I believe that many well-intended plans have gone awry in the church today because of our misplaced emphasis on the size and greatness of our endeavors. We become carried away with the number of converts filling the pews and the amounts listed on pledge cards, forgetting that the first focus of our Lord is not upon the grand scale of our efforts, but upon the humbleness and obedience of every heart that comes to Him. ✦

He steadfastly set His face to go to Jerusa-
lem, [52]and sent messengers before His face.
And as they went, they entered a village of
the Samaritans, to prepare for Him. [53]But
they did not receive Him, because His face
was *set* for the journey to Jerusalem. [54]And
when His disciples James and John saw
this, they said, "Lord, do You want us to
command fire to come down from heaven
and consume them, just as E·lī′jah did?"[a]
[55]But He turned and rebuked them,[a] and
said, "You do not know what manner of
spirit you are of. [56]For the Son of Man did
not come to destroy men's lives but to save
them."[a] And they went to another village.

The Cost of Discipleship

[57]Now it happened as they journeyed on
the road, *that* someone said to Him, "Lord,
I will follow You wherever You go."
[58]And Jesus said to him, "Foxes have
holes and birds of the air *have* nests, but
the Son of Man has nowhere to lay *His*
head."
[59]Then He said to another, "Follow Me."
But he said, "Lord, let me first go and
bury my father."

9:54 [a]NU-Text omits *just as Elijah did.*
9:55 [a]NU-Text omits the rest of this verse.
9:56 [a]NU-Text omits the first sentence of this verse.

60Jesus said to him, "Let the dead bury
their own dead, but you go and preach the
kingdom of God."
61And another also said, "Lord, I will
follow You, but let me first go *and* bid them
farewell who are at my house."
62But Jesus said to him, "No one, having
put his hand to the plow, and looking back,
is fit for the kingdom of God."

CHAPTER 10

The Seventy Sent Out

After these things the Lord appointed
seventy others also,[a] and sent them two by
two before His face into every city and
place where He Himself was about to go.
2Then He said to them, "The harvest truly
is great, but the laborers *are* few; therefore
pray the Lord of the harvest to send out la-
borers into His harvest. 3Go your way; be-
hold, I send you out as lambs among
wolves. 4Carry neither money bag, knap-
sack, nor sandals; and greet no one along
the road. 5But whatever house you enter,
first say, 'Peace to this house.' 6And if a son
of peace is there, your peace will rest on it;
if not, it will return to you. 7And remain in
the same house, eating and drinking such
things as they give, for the laborer is wor-
thy of his wages. Do not go from house to
house. 8Whatever city you enter, and they
receive you, eat such things as are set be-
fore you. 9And heal the sick there, and say
to them, 'The kingdom of God has come
near to you.' 10But whatever city you enter,
and they do not receive you, go out into its
streets and say, 11'The very dust of your city
which clings to us[a] we wipe off against
you. Nevertheless know this, that the king-
dom of God has come near you.' 12But[a] I
say to you that it will be more tolerable in
that Day for Sod′om than for that city.

> Christianity is not a spectator sport, it's something in which we become totally involved.
>
> Billy Graham

Woe to the Impenitent Cities

13"Woe to you, Chō·rā′zin! Woe to you,
Beth·sā′i·da! For if the mighty works
which were done in you had been done in
Tȳre and Sī′don, they would have re-
pented long ago, sitting in sackcloth and
ashes. 14But it will be more tolerable for
Tȳre and Sī′don at the judgment than for
you. 15And you, Ca·per′na·um, who are ex-
alted to heaven, will be brought down to
Hā′dēs.[a] 16He who hears you hears Me, he
who rejects you rejects Me, and he who re-
jects Me rejects Him who sent Me."

The Seventy Return with Joy

17Then the seventy[a] returned with joy,
saying, "Lord, even the demons are subject
to us in Your name."
18And He said to them, "I saw Satan fall
like lightning from heaven. 19Behold, I give
you the authority to trample on serpents
and scorpions, and over all the power of
the enemy, and nothing shall by any means
hurt you. 20Nevertheless do not rejoice in
this, that the spirits are subject to you, but

10:1 [a]NU-Text reads *seventy-two others.*
10:11 [a]NU-Text reads *our feet.* 10:12 [a]NU-Text and M-Text omit *But.* 10:15 [a]NU-Text reads *will you be exalted to heaven? You will be thrust down to Hades!*
10:17 [a]NU-Text reads *seventy-two.*

9:60 Jesus is saying to let the spiritually dead bury the physically dead. He is not promoting disrespect for the dead; He is warning against postponing obedience to God for the sake of worldly affairs.

10:13–16 Chorazin . . . Bethsaida . . . Capernaum: Towns in Galilee in which Jesus had done **mighty works**. **Tyre and Sidon**: Gentile cities of Phoenicia located on the Mediterranean seacoast. Jesus did not excuse the wickedness of those Gentiles; however, the Jews who heard the gospel and rejected the Savior were more guilty than they.

rather[a] rejoice because your names are
written in heaven."

Jesus Rejoices in the Spirit

21 In that hour Jesus rejoiced in the Spirit
and said, "I thank You, Father, Lord of
heaven and earth, that You have hidden
these things from *the* wise and prudent
and revealed them to babes. Even so,
Father, for so it seemed good in Your sight.
22 All[a] things have been delivered to Me by
My Father, and no one knows who the Son
is except the Father, and who the Father is
except the Son, and *the one* to whom the
Son wills to reveal *Him.*"

23 Then He turned to *His* disciples and
said privately, "Blessed *are* the eyes which
see the things you see; 24 for I tell you that
many prophets and kings have desired to
see what you see, and have not seen *it,* and
to hear what you hear, and have not heard
it."

The Parable of the Good Samaritan

25 And behold, a certain lawyer stood up
and tested Him, saying, "Teacher, what
shall I do to inherit eternal life?"

26 He said to him, "What is written in the
law? What is your reading *of it?*"

27 So he answered and said, "*'You shall
love the LORD your God with all your
heart, with all your soul, with all your
strength, and with all your mind,'*[a] and
'your neighbor as yourself.'"[b]

28 And He said to him, "You have an-
swered rightly; do this and you will live."

29 But he, wanting to justify himself, said
to Jesus, "And who is my neighbor?"

30 Then Jesus answered and said: "A cer-
tain *man* went down from Jerusalem to Jer-
icho, and fell among thieves, who stripped
him of his clothing, wounded *him,* and de-
parted, leaving *him* half dead. 31 Now by
chance a certain priest came down that
road. And when he saw him, he passed by
on the other side. 32 Likewise a Lē'vīte,
when he arrived at the place, came and
looked, and passed by on the other side.
33 But a certain Samaritan, as he journeyed,
came where he was. And when he saw
him, he had compassion. 34 So he went to
him and bandaged his wounds, pouring on
oil and wine; and he set him on his own an-
imal, brought him to an inn, and took care
of him. 35 On the next day, when he de-
parted,[a] he took out two denarii, gave *them*
to the innkeeper, and said to him, 'Take
care of him; and whatever more you
spend, when I come again, I will repay
you.' 36 So which of these three do you
think was neighbor to him who fell among
the thieves?"

37 And he said, "He who showed mercy
on him."

Then Jesus said to him, "Go and do like-
wise."

Mary and Martha Worship and Serve

38 Now it happened as they went that He
entered a certain village; and a certain
woman named Martha welcomed Him
into her house. 39 And she had a sister

10:20 [a]NU-Text and M-Text omit *rather.*
10:22 [a]M-Text reads *And turning to the disciples He said, "All . . . .* 10:27 [a]Deuteronomy 6:5 [b]Leviticus 19:18 10:35 [a]NU-Text omits *when he departed.*

10:25–28 A **lawyer** asked Jesus two questions (vv. 25, 29). In the first he raised humanity's most important issue, **What shall I do to inherit eternal life**? In answer Jesus asked him what he knew about God's requirements, and he responded correctly (see Matt. 22:37–40). Like so many who have heard the gospel, the man knew what God required—but he did not want to do it (see 6:46).

10:29–35 The parable is Jesus' answer to the question, **Who is my neighbor**? The **priest** and the **Levite** were highly respected Jewish religious leaders, perhaps on their way to the temple at Jerusalem. The Samaritans were half-breeds, descended from Israelites who intermarried with the Gentile settlers brought into Palestine by the Assyrians after the fall of Samaria in 722 B.C. Although the Jews hated these neighbors, this Samaritan had compassion on the wounded Jew.

Get Involved

Billy Graham

When the Good Samaritan found a man robbed, beaten, and left for dead, he did not continue on his trip and "report the accident." He did not call 911 and leave the scene or pay someone else to go back and care for the man. The Samaritan himself got involved.

He tenderly lifted the wounded body onto his own donkey and continued on the journey to Jericho. When he reached the city, he found a place to stay and probably cared for the patient. The next day, he made arrangements with the innkeeper to pay all the financial debts that the patient would incur.

His actions demonstrate what bearing one another's burdens is all about. It is so easy to give to a charity or a ministry and feel good about it. It is not so easy to provide the personal charity. It is easier to give to someone overseas than it is to take a casserole next door. May God give us the sensitivity to recognize the needs of those around us and lend a helping hand. ✦

"May God give us the sensitivity to recognize the needs of those around us."

called Mary, who also sat at Jesus'[a] feet and
heard His word. [40]But Martha was dis-
tracted with much serving, and she ap-
proached Him and said, "Lord, do You not
care that my sister has left me to serve
alone? Therefore tell her to help me."
[41]And Jesus[a] answered and said to her,
"Martha, Martha, you are worried and
troubled about many things. [42]But one
thing is needed, and Mary has chosen that
good part, which will not be taken away
from her."

CHAPTER 11

The Model Prayer

Now it came to pass, as He was praying
in a certain place, when He ceased, *that* one
of His disciples said to Him, "Lord, teach
us to pray, as John also taught his disci-
ples."
[2]So He said to them, "When you pray,
say:

Our Father in heaven,[a]
Hallowed be Your name.
Your kingdom come.[b]
Your will be done
On earth as *it is* in heaven.
3 Give us day by day our daily bread.
4 And forgive us our sins,
For we also forgive everyone who is
indebted to us.
And do not lead us into temptation,
But deliver us from the evil one." [a]

A Friend Comes at Midnight

[5]And He said to them, "Which of you
shall have a friend, and go to him at mid-
night and say to him, 'Friend, lend me

10:39 [a]NU-Text reads *the Lord's*. 10:41 [a]NU-Text reads *the Lord*. 11:2 [a]NU-Text omits *Our* and *in heaven*. [b]NU-Text omits the rest of this verse.
11:4 [a]NU-Text omits *But deliver us from the evil one.*

three loaves; 6for a friend of mine has come
to me on his journey, and I have nothing to
set before him'; 7and he will answer from
within and say, 'Do not trouble me; the
door is now shut, and my children are with
me in bed; I cannot rise and give to you'? 8I
say to you, though he will not rise and give
to him because he is his friend, yet because
of his persistence he will rise and give him
as many as he needs.

Keep Asking, Seeking, Knocking

9"So I say to you, ask, and it will be
given to you; seek, and you will find;
knock, and it will be opened to you. 10For
everyone who asks receives, and he who
seeks finds, and to him who knocks it will
be opened. 11If a son asks for bread[a] from
any father among you, will he give him a
stone? Or if *he asks* for a fish, will he give
him a serpent instead of a fish? 12Or if he
asks for an egg, will he offer him a scor-
pion? 13If you then, being evil, know how
to give good gifts to your children, how
much more will *your* heavenly Father give
the Holy Spirit to those who ask Him!"

A House Divided Cannot Stand

14And He was casting out a demon, and
it was mute. So it was, when the demon
had gone out, that the mute spoke; and the
multitudes marveled. 15But some of them
said, "He casts out demons by Bē·el′-
ze·bub,[a] the ruler of the demons."

16Others, testing *Him,* sought from Him
a sign from heaven. 17But He, knowing
their thoughts, said to them: "Every king-
dom divided against itself is brought to
desolation, and a house *divided* against a
house falls. 18If Satan also is divided
against himself, how will his kingdom
stand? Because you say I cast out demons
by Bē·el′ze·bub. 19And if I cast out demons
by Bē·el′ze·bub, by whom do your sons
cast *them* out? Therefore they will be your
judges. 20But if I cast out demons with the
finger of God, surely the kingdom of God
has come upon you. 21When a strong man,
fully armed, guards his own palace, his
goods are in peace. 22But when a stronger
than he comes upon him and overcomes
him, he takes from him all his armor in
which he trusted, and divides his spoils.
23He who is not with Me is against Me,
and he who does not gather with Me
scatters.

An Unclean Spirit Returns

24"When an unclean spirit goes out of a
man, he goes through dry places, seeking
rest; and finding none, he says, 'I will re-
turn to my house from which I came.'
25And when he comes, he finds *it* swept
and put in order. 26Then he goes and takes
with *him* seven other spirits more wicked
than himself, and they enter and dwell
there; and the last *state* of that man is worse
than the first."

Keeping the Word

27And it happened, as He spoke these
things, that a certain woman from the
crowd raised her voice and said to Him,
"Blessed *is* the womb that bore You, and
the breasts which nursed You!"

28But He said, "More than that, blessed
are those who hear the word of God and
keep it!"

Seeking a Sign

29And while the crowds were thickly
gathered together, He began to say, "This is
an evil generation. It seeks a sign, and no
sign will be given to it except the sign of Jo-
nah the prophet.[a] 30For as Jonah became a
sign to the Nin′e·vītes, so also the Son of
Man will be to this generation. 31The queen

11:11 [a]NU-Text omits the words from *bread* through *for* in the next sentence. 11:15 [a]NU-Text and M-Text read *Beelzebul.* 11:29 [a]NU-Text omits *the prophet.*

11:23 Neutrality is impossible where Christ is concerned; we are either committed to Him or opposed to Him.

of the South will rise up in the judgment
with the men of this generation and con-
demn them, for she came from the ends of
the earth to hear the wisdom of Solomon;
and indeed a greater than Solomon *is* here.
32The men of Nin'e·veh will rise up in the
judgment with this generation and con-
demn it, for they repented at the preaching
of Jonah; and indeed a greater than Jonah
is here.

The Lamp of the Body

33"No one, when he has lit a lamp, puts
it in a secret place or under a basket, but on
a lampstand, that those who come in may
see the light. 34The lamp of the body is the
eye. Therefore, when your eye is good,
your whole body also is full of light. But
when *your eye* is bad, your body also *is* full
of darkness. 35Therefore take heed that the
light which is in you is not darkness. 36If
then your whole body *is* full of light, hav-
ing no part dark, *the* whole *body* will be full
of light, as when the bright shining of a
lamp gives you light."

Woe to the Pharisees and Lawyers

37And as He spoke, a certain Phar'i·see
asked Him to dine with him. So He went in
and sat down to eat. 38When the Phar'i·see
saw *it,* he marveled that He had not first
washed before dinner.

39Then the Lord said to him, "Now you
Phar'i·sees make the outside of the cup
and dish clean, but your inward part is full
of greed and wickedness. 40Foolish ones!
Did not He who made the outside make
the inside also? 41But rather give alms of
such things as you have; then indeed all
things are clean to you.

42"But woe to you Phar'i·sees! For you
tithe mint and rue and all manner of herbs,
and pass by justice and the love of God.
These you ought to have done, without
leaving the others undone. 43Woe to you
Phar'i·sees! For you love the best seats in
the synagogues and greetings in the mar-
ketplaces. 44Woe to you, scribes and
Phar'i·sees, hypocrites![a] For you are like
graves which are not seen, and the men
who walk over *them* are not aware *of them.*"

45Then one of the lawyers answered and
said to Him, "Teacher, by saying these
things You reproach us also."

46And He said, "Woe to you also,
lawyers! For you load men with burdens
hard to bear, and you yourselves do not
touch the burdens with one of your fin-
gers. 47Woe to you! For you build the tombs
of the prophets, and your fathers killed
them. 48In fact, you bear witness that you
approve the deeds of your fathers; for they
indeed killed them, and you build their
tombs. 49Therefore the wisdom of God also
said, 'I will send them prophets and apos-
tles, and *some* of them they will kill and
persecute,' 50that the blood of all the
prophets which was shed from the founda-
tion of the world may be required of this
generation, 51from the blood of Abel to the
blood of Zech·a·rī'ah who perished be-
tween the altar and the temple. Yes, I say
to you, it shall be required of this genera-
tion.

11:44 [a]NU-Text omits *scribes and Pharisees, hypocrites.*

11:44 For a Jew to touch a grave was ceremonially defiling (see Num. 19:16). Because the Pharisees were supposed to be righteous teachers, their wrong example led the unsuspecting into sin.

11:47–51 you build the tombs: The Jews of Jesus' day were busy building memorial tombs for famous religious figures from the past (v. 47). Jesus accused them of approving and finishing the work of their fathers, who had killed the prophets (v. 48). **The wisdom of God** (v. 49) is God's predictions in Scripture. By killing Jesus, they would be guilty of the blood of all the **prophets** who looked forward to Jesus' coming (vv. 50, 51).

11:51 The Jewish Bible put 2 Chronicles at the end of the OT. Thus the murder of **Abel** was recorded in the first book (Gen. 4:8) and the murder of **Zechariah** in the last (2 Chr. 24:20–22). Jesus was referring to all the OT martyrs from the beginning of the Jewish Scriptures to the end.

[52]"Woe to you lawyers! For you have taken away the key of knowledge. You did not enter in yourselves, and those who were entering in you hindered."

[53]And as He said these things to them,[a] the scribes and the Phar'i·sees began to assail *Him* vehemently, and to cross-examine Him about many things, [54]lying in wait for Him, and seeking to catch Him in something He might say, that they might accuse Him.[a]

CHAPTER 12

Beware of Hypocrisy

In the meantime, when an innumerable multitude of people had gathered together, so that they trampled one another, He began to say to His disciples first *of all*, "Beware of the leaven of the Phar'i·sees, which is hypocrisy. [2]For there is nothing covered that will not be revealed, nor hidden that will not be known. [3]Therefore whatever you have spoken in the dark will be heard in the light, and what you have spoken in the ear in inner rooms will be proclaimed on the housetops.

Jesus Teaches the Fear of God

[4]"And I say to you, My friends, do not be afraid of those who kill the body, and after that have no more that they can do. [5]But I will show you whom you should fear: Fear Him who, after He has killed, has

11:53 [a]NU-Text reads *And when He left there.*
11:54 [a]NU-Text omits *and seeking* and *that they might accuse Him.*

12:1 leaven: yeast. The hypocrisy of the Pharisees was spreading like yeast in dough.

EMISSARIES FOR THE LORD

Lloyd Ogilvie

Every day you and I encounter people in trouble—friends with heartaches beneath their polished surfaces, fellow workers who long for someone to care. The Lord has deployed us in our families, workplaces, churches, and communities so we can be used decisively when He wants to communicate His love, forgiveness, and sometimes confrontational truth.

The Lord has a strategy for each situation and relationship. Prolonged time in prayer prepares us for them. Often the Lord shows us beforehand what we are to say and do. Other times, He reveals His will at that moment. We do not need to excuse ourselves from a conversation or meeting for private prayer, for when we open the channel of our minds to the Lord daily, we can expect the fulfillment of Jesus' promise, "Do not worry about how or what you should answer, or what you should say. For the Holy Spirit will teach you in that very hour what you ought to say" (Luke 12:11, 12). ✦

"The Lord has a strategy for each situation and relationship."

power to cast into hell; yes, I say to you,
fear Him!
6"Are not five sparrows sold for two
copper coins?[a] And not one of them is forgotten before God.
7But the very hairs of
your head are all numbered. Do not fear
therefore; you are of more value than many
sparrows.

Confess Christ Before Men

8"Also I say to you, whoever confesses
Me before men, him the Son of Man also
will confess before the angels of God.
9But
he who denies Me before men will be denied before the angels of God.
10"And anyone who speaks a word
against the Son of Man, it will be forgiven
him; but to him who blasphemes against
the Holy Spirit, it will not be forgiven.
11"Now when they bring you to the synagogues and magistrates and authorities,
do not worry about how or what you
should answer, or what you should say.
12For the Holy Spirit will teach you in that
very hour what you ought to say."

The Parable of the Rich Fool

13Then one from the crowd said to Him,
"Teacher, tell my brother to divide the inheritance with me."
14But He said to him, "Man, who made
Me a judge or an arbitrator over you?"
15And He said to them, "Take heed and beware of covetousness,[a] for one's life does
not consist in the abundance of the things
he possesses."
16Then He spoke a parable to them, saying: "The ground of a certain rich man
yielded plentifully.
17And he thought
within himself, saying, 'What shall I do,
since I have no room to store my crops?'
18So he said, 'I will do this: I will pull down
my barns and build greater, and there I will
store all my crops and my goods.
19And I
will say to my soul, "Soul, you have many
goods laid up for many years; take your
ease; eat, drink, *and* be merry." '
20But God
said to him, 'Fool! This night your soul will
be required of you; then whose will those
things be which you have provided?'
21"So *is* he who lays up treasure for himself, and is not rich toward God."

> We may let go all things which we cannot carry into the eternal life.
> Anna R. Brown Lindsay

Do Not Worry

22Then He said to His disciples, "Therefore I say to you, do not worry about your
life, what you will eat; nor about the body,
what you will put on.
23Life is more than
food, and the body *is more* than clothing.
24Consider the ravens, for they neither sow
nor reap, which have neither storehouse
nor barn; and God feeds them. Of how
much more value are you than the birds?
25And which of you by worrying can add
one cubit to his stature?
26If you then are
not able to do *the* least, why are you anxious for the rest?
27Consider the lilies, how
they grow: they neither toil nor spin; and
yet I say to you, even Solomon in all his
glory was not arrayed like one of these.
28If

12:6 [a]Greek *assarion*, a coin of very small value
12:15 [a]NU-Text reads *all covetousness.*

12:13 divide the inheritance: Jewish civil law allotted a double portion of a family's inheritance to the oldest brother, along with the responsibility for the welfare of the mother and unmarried sisters. Younger heirs received a single portion.

12:16–20 Jesus' parable warns against the dangers of materialism. We should look on our possessions as blessings from God to be shared unselfishly.

12:22–34 Disciples of Jesus are to **seek** His **kingdom** (v. 31) more than material blessings (see Matt. 6:33). True security lies in always doing God's will, not in amassing possessions. God will take care of His own (v. 24). While we should do what we can to prepare financially for the future, we must recognize God's sovereignty and rely on Him to supply our needs.

then God so clothes the grass, which today
is in the field and tomorrow is thrown into
the oven, how much more *will He clothe*
you, O *you* of little faith?
29"And do not seek what you should eat
or what you should drink, nor have an
anxious mind. 30For all these things the na-
tions of the world seek after, and your
Father knows that you need these things.
31But seek the kingdom of God, and all
these things[a] shall be added to you.
32"Do not fear, little flock, for it is your
Father's good pleasure to give you the
kingdom. 33Sell what you have and give
alms; provide yourselves money bags
which do not grow old, a treasure in the
heavens that does not fail, where no thief
approaches nor moth destroys. 34For where
your treasure is, there your heart will be
also.

The Faithful Servant and the Evil Servant

35"Let your waist be girded and *your*
lamps burning; 36and you yourselves be
like men who wait for their master, when
he will return from the wedding, that
when he comes and knocks they may open
to him immediately. 37Blessed *are* those ser-
vants whom the master, when he comes,
will find watching. Assuredly, I say to you
that he will gird himself and have them sit
down *to eat,* and will come and serve them.
38And if he should come in the second
watch, or come in the third watch, and find
them so, blessed are those servants. 39But
know this, that if the master of the house
had known what hour the thief would
come, he would have watched and[a] not
allowed his house to be broken into.
40Therefore you also be ready, for the Son
of Man is coming at an hour you do not ex-
pect."
41Then Peter said to Him, "Lord, do You
speak this parable *only* to us, or to all *peo-*
ple?"
42And the Lord said, "Who then is that
faithful and wise steward, whom *his* mas-
ter will make ruler over his household, to
give *them their* portion of food in due sea-
son? 43Blessed *is* that servant whom his
master will find so doing when he comes.
44Truly, I say to you that he will make him
ruler over all that he has. 45But if that ser-
vant says in his heart, 'My master is delay-
ing his coming,' and begins to beat the
male and female servants, and to eat and
drink and be drunk, 46the master of that
servant will come on a day when he is not
looking for *him,* and at an hour when he is
not aware, and will cut him in two and ap-
point *him* his portion with the unbelievers.
47And that servant who knew his master's
will, and did not prepare *himself* or do ac-
cording to his will, shall be beaten with
many *stripes.* 48But he who did not know,
yet committed things deserving of stripes,
shall be beaten with few. For everyone to
whom much is given, from him much will
be required; and to whom much has been
committed, of him they will ask the more.

Christ Brings Division

49"I came to send fire on the earth, and
how I wish it were already kindled! 50But I
have a baptism to be baptized with, and
how distressed I am till it is accomplished!
51Do *you* suppose that I came to give peace
on earth? I tell you, not at all, but rather
division. 52For from now on five in one

12:31 [a]NU-Text reads *His kingdom, and these things.*
12:39 [a]NU-Text reads *he would not have allowed.*

12:33 Sell what you have and give alms: Jesus did not intend this command to be taken literally by all Christians. Some must give up material wealth because, like the rich young ruler (see 18:18–30), it keeps them from following Christ. Others are able to keep and administer their wealth for God's glory and the world's benefit. Jesus teaches that material goods are to be used to further God's kingdom, not for personal indulgence or power. He also warns how easy it is to depend on wealth instead of trusting in God (see 18:24, 25). True peace comes in reliance on God, not on current circumstances.

house will be divided: three against two, and two against three. [53]Father will be divided against son and son against father, mother against daughter and daughter against mother, mother-in-law against her daughter-in-law and daughter-in-law against her mother-in-law."

Discern the Time

[54]Then He also said to the multitudes, "Whenever *you see* a cloud rising out of the west, immediately you say, 'A shower is coming'; and so it is. [55]And when you see the south wind blow, you say, 'There will be hot weather'; and there is. [56]Hypocrites! You can discern the face of the sky and of the earth, but how *is it* you do not discern this time?

Make Peace with Your Adversary

[57]"Yes, and why, even of yourselves, do you not judge what is right? [58]When you go with your adversary to the magistrate, make every effort along the way to settle with him, lest he drag you to the judge, the judge deliver you to the officer, and the officer throw you into prison. [59]I tell you, you shall not depart from there till you have paid the very last mite."

CHAPTER 13

Repent or Perish

There were present at that season some who told Him about the Galileans whose blood Pilate had mingled with their sacrifices. [2]And Jesus answered and said to them, "Do you suppose that these Galileans were worse sinners than all *other* Galileans, because they suffered such things? [3]I tell you, no; but unless you repent you will all likewise perish. [4]Or those eighteen on whom the tower in Sī·lō'am fell and killed them, do you think that they were worse sinners than all *other* men who dwelt in Jerusalem? [5]I tell you, no; but unless you repent you will all likewise perish."

The Parable of the Barren Fig Tree

[6]He also spoke this parable: "A certain *man* had a fig tree planted in his vineyard, and he came seeking fruit on it and found none. [7]Then he said to the keeper of his vineyard, 'Look, for three years I have come seeking fruit on this fig tree and find none. Cut it down; why does it use up the ground?' [8]But he answered and said to him, 'Sir, let it alone this year also, until I dig around it and fertilize *it*. [9]And if it bears fruit, *well*. But if not, after that[a] you can cut it down.' "

A Spirit of Infirmity

[10]Now He was teaching in one of the synagogues on the Sabbath. [11]And behold, there was a woman who had a spirit of infirmity eighteen years, and was bent over and could in no way raise *herself* up. [12]But when Jesus saw her, He called *her* to *Him* and said to her, "Woman, you are loosed from your infirmity." [13]And He laid *His* hands on her, and immediately she was made straight, and glorified God.

[14]But the ruler of the synagogue answered with indignation, because Jesus had healed on the Sabbath; and he said to the crowd, "There are six days on which men ought to work; therefore come and be healed on them, and not on the Sabbath day."

[15]The Lord then answered him and said, "Hypocrite![a] Does not each one of you on the Sabbath loose his ox or donkey from the stall, and lead *it* away to water it? [16]So

13:9 [a]NU-Text reads *And if it bears fruit after that, well. But if not, you can cut it down.* 13:15 [a]NU-Text and M-Text read *Hypocrites.*

13:1, 4, 5 blood . . . mingled with their sacrifices: Pilate had killed some Galileans when they were making their Passover sacrifices. **those eighteen . . . killed**: Another group, probably well known to Jesus' listeners, who met with tragic death. Jesus challenged the concept that misfortune is always the result of sinful living and thus fell only upon the sinful.

ought not this woman, being a daughter of Abraham, whom Satan has bound—think of it—for eighteen years, be loosed from this bond on the Sabbath?" [17]And when He said these things, all His adversaries were put to shame; and all the multitude rejoiced for all the glorious things that were done by Him.

The Parable of the Mustard Seed

[18]Then He said, "What is the kingdom of God like? And to what shall I compare it? [19]It is like a mustard seed, which a man took and put in his garden; and it grew and became a large[a] tree, and the birds of the air nested in its branches."

The Parable of the Leaven

[20]And again He said, "To what shall I liken the kingdom of God? [21]It is like leaven, which a woman took and hid in three measures[a] of meal till it was all leavened."

The Narrow Way

[22]And He went through the cities and villages, teaching, and journeying toward Jerusalem. [23]Then one said to Him, "Lord, are there few who are saved?"

And He said to them, [24]"Strive to enter through the narrow gate, for many, I say to you, will seek to enter and will not be able. [25]When once the Master of the house has risen up and shut the door, and you begin to stand outside and knock at the door, saying, 'Lord, Lord, open for us,' and He will answer and say to you, 'I do not know you, where you are from,' [26]then you will begin to say, 'We ate and drank in Your presence, and You taught in our streets.' [27]But He will say, 'I tell you I do not know you, where you are from. Depart from Me, all you workers of iniquity.' [28]There will be weeping and gnashing of teeth, when you see Abraham and Isaac and Jacob and all the prophets in the kingdom of God, and yourselves thrust out. [29]They will come from the east and the west, from the north and the south, and sit down in the kingdom of God. [30]And indeed there are last who will be first, and there are first who will be last."

[31]On that very day[a] some Phar'i·sees came, saying to Him, "Get out and depart from here, for Her'od wants to kill You."

[32]And He said to them, "Go, tell that fox, 'Behold, I cast out demons and perform cures today and tomorrow, and the third *day* I shall be perfected.' [33]Nevertheless I must journey today, tomorrow, and the *day* following; for it cannot be that a prophet should perish outside of Jerusalem.

Jesus Laments over Jerusalem

[34]"O Jerusalem, Jerusalem, the one who kills the prophets and stones those who are sent to her! How often I wanted to gather your children together, as a hen *gathers* her brood under *her* wings, but you were not willing! [35]See! Your house is left to you desolate; and assuredly,[a] I say to you, you shall not see Me until *the time* comes when you say, *'Blessed is He who comes in the name of the LORD!'"*[b]

13:19 [a]NU-Text omits *large.* 13:21 [a]Greek *sata,* approximately two pecks in all 13:31 [a]NU-Text reads *In that very hour.* 13:35 [a]NU-Text and M-Text omit *assuredly.* [b]Psalm 118:26

13:23–30 Strive to enter: Entering God's kingdom is not so much a matter of being religious (v. 26) as it is a personal decision to place one's trust in Christ. Any other strategy to gain God's acceptance is **iniquity** (v. 27).

13:31–33 depart: From Herod's territory of Galilee. **Fox** designates Herod's cunning. **today and tomorrow**: No matter what Herod did, Jesus' earthly ministry would continue for a short period of time as God had planned. **be perfected**: Soon Jesus' work would be completed by His death and resurrection. **I must journey**: In order to fulfill God's will, Jesus had to go to Jerusalem and be crucified. **outside of Jerusalem**: Because the city was notorious for killing prophets, it was appropriate that Jesus die there.

CHAPTER 14

A Man with Dropsy Healed on the Sabbath

Now it happened, as He went into the
house of one of the rulers of the Phar'i·sees
to eat bread on the Sabbath, that they
watched Him closely. [2]And behold, there
was a certain man before Him who had
dropsy. [3]And Jesus, answering, spoke to
the lawyers and Phar'i·sees, saying, "Is it
lawful to heal on the Sabbath?"[a]
[4]But they kept silent. And He took *him*
and healed him, and let him go. [5]Then He
answered them, saying, "Which of you,
having a donkey[a] or an ox that has fallen
into a pit, will not immediately pull him
out on the Sabbath day?" [6]And they could
not answer Him regarding these things.

Take the Lowly Place

[7]So He told a parable to those who were
invited, when He noted how they chose
the best places, saying to them: [8]"When
you are invited by anyone to a wedding
feast, do not sit down in the best place, lest
one more honorable than you be invited by
him; [9]and he who invited you and him
come and say to you, 'Give place to this
man,' and then you begin with shame to
take the lowest place. [10]But when you are
invited, go and sit down in the lowest
place, so that when he who invited you
comes he may say to you, 'Friend, go up
higher.' Then you will have glory in the
presence of those who sit at the table with
you. [11]For whoever exalts himself will be
humbled, and he who humbles himself
will be exalted."
[12]Then He also said to him who invited
Him, "When you give a dinner or a supper,
do not ask your friends, your brothers,
your relatives, nor rich neighbors, lest they
also invite you back, and you be repaid.
[13]But when you give a feast, invite *the* poor,
the maimed, *the* lame, *the* blind. [14]And you
will be blessed, because they cannot repay
you; for you shall be repaid at the resurrection of the just."

The Parable of the Great Supper

[15]Now when one of those who sat at the
table with Him heard these things, he said
to Him, "Blessed *is* he who shall eat bread[a]
in the kingdom of God!"
[16]Then He said to him, "A certain man
gave a great supper and invited many,
[17]and sent his servant at supper time to say
to those who were invited, 'Come, for all
things are now ready.' [18]But they all with
one *accord* began to make excuses. The first
said to him, 'I have bought a piece of
ground, and I must go and see it. I ask you
to have me excused.' [19]And another said, 'I
have bought five yoke of oxen, and I am
going to test them. I ask you to have me excused.' [20]Still another said, 'I have married
a wife, and therefore I cannot come.' [21]So
that servant came and reported these
things to his master. Then the master of the
house, being angry, said to his servant, 'Go
out quickly into the streets and lanes of the
city, and bring in here *the* poor and *the*
maimed and *the* lame and *the* blind.' [22]And

14:3 [a]NU-Text adds *or not.* 14:5 [a]NU-Text and M-Text read *son.* 14:15 [a]M-Text reads *dinner.*

14:2 dropsy: swelling caused by excessive water retention.

14:12–14 Here is further teaching on kingdom conduct. Jesus did not mean to forbid entertaining **friends** and **relatives**. He Himself took part in such social fellowship. He means that the unfortunate should be entertained and no repayment expected in this life. God accepts the poor (vv. 15–24) and so should we.

14:15 eat bread in the kingdom: The man referred to the Jewish expectation of a future feast in the Messiah's kingdom (Is. 25:6; Rev. 19:9). **Blessed is he**: Jesus responded, "Do not expect selfish enjoyment in the kingdom; respond to it." The central teaching of the parable is that we should accept the invitation when it comes. The duty of the servant is to extend the invitation to others.

the servant said, 'Master, it is done as you
commanded, and still there is room.'
23Then the master said to the servant, 'Go
out into the highways and hedges, and
compel *them* to come in, that my house
may be filled. 24For I say to you that none
of those men who were invited shall taste
my supper.' "

Leaving All to Follow Christ

25Now great multitudes went with Him.
And He turned and said to them, 26"If any-
one comes to Me and does not hate his
father and mother, wife and children,
brothers and sisters, yes, and his own life
also, he cannot be My disciple. 27And who-
ever does not bear his cross and come after
Me cannot be My disciple. 28For which of
you, intending to build a tower, does not
sit down first and count the cost, whether
he has *enough* to finish *it*— 29lest, after he
has laid the foundation, and is not able to
finish, all who see *it* begin to mock him,
30saying, 'This man began to build and was
not able to finish.' 31Or what king, going to
make war against another king, does not
sit down first and consider whether he is
able with ten thousand to meet him who
comes against him with twenty thousand?
32Or else, while the other is still a great way
off, he sends a delegation and asks condi-
tions of peace. 33So likewise, whoever of
you does not forsake all that he has cannot
be My disciple.

Tasteless Salt Is Worthless

34"Salt *is* good; but if the salt has lost its
flavor, how shall it be seasoned? 35It is nei-
ther fit for the land nor for the dunghill, *but*
men throw it out. He who has ears to hear,
let him hear!"

CHAPTER 15

The Parable of the Lost Sheep

Then all the tax collectors and the sin-
ners drew near to Him to hear Him. 2And
the Phar'i·sees and scribes complained,
saying, "This Man receives sinners and
eats with them." 3So He spoke this parable
to them, saying:

4"What man of you, having a hundred
sheep, if he loses one of them, does not
leave the ninety-nine in the wilderness,
and go after the one which is lost until he
finds it? 5And when he has found *it,* he lays
it on his shoulders, rejoicing. 6And when
he comes home, he calls together *his*
friends and neighbors, saying to them, 'Re-
joice with me, for I have found my sheep
which was lost!' 7I say to you that likewise
there will be more joy in heaven over one
sinner who repents than over ninety-nine
just persons who need no repentance.

The Parable of the Lost Coin

8"Or what woman, having ten silver
coins,[a] if she loses one coin, does not light a
lamp, sweep the house, and search care-
fully until she finds *it?* 9And when she has
found *it,* she calls *her* friends and neigh-
bors together, saying, 'Rejoice with me, for
I have found the piece which I lost!' 10Like-
wise, I say to you, there is joy in the pres-
ence of the angels of God over one sinner
who repents."

The Parable of the Lost Son

11Then He said: "A certain man had two
sons. 12And the younger of them said to *his*
father, 'Father, give me the portion of
goods that falls *to me.*' So he divided to

15:8 [a]Greek *drachma,* a valuable coin often worn in a ten-piece garland by married women

14:26 Rather than commanding His disciples to hate their families, Jesus is saying that our love for Him should be so great that, in comparison, our love for family is as hate.

15:1–32 Three stories with one point. Jesus wants us to remember God's concern for the lost. He loves sinners and actively seeks them; His **joy** is great when they turn to Him. There is hope even for the proud Pharisees if they will repent. Verses 1, 2 set the context for the whole chapter.

them *his* livelihood. 13And not many days
after, the younger son gathered all to-
gether, journeyed to a far country, and
there wasted his possessions with prodigal
living. 14But when he had spent all, there
arose a severe famine in that land, and he
began to be in want. 15Then he went and
joined himself to a citizen of that country,
and he sent him into his fields to feed
swine. 16And he would gladly have filled
his stomach with the pods that the swine
ate, and no one gave him *anything.*

17"But when he came to himself, he said,
'How many of my father's hired servants
have bread enough and to spare, and I per-
ish with hunger! 18I will arise and go to my
father, and will say to him, "Father, I have
sinned against heaven and before you,
19and I am no longer worthy to be called
your son. Make me like one of your hired
servants." '

20"And he arose and came to his father.
But when he was still a great way off, his
father saw him and had compassion, and
ran and fell on his neck and kissed him.
21And the son said to him, 'Father, I have
sinned against heaven and in your sight,
and am no longer worthy to be called your
son.'

22"But the father said to his servants,
'Bring[a] out the best robe and put *it* on him,
and put a ring on his hand and sandals on
his feet. 23And bring the fatted calf here and
kill *it,* and let us eat and be merry; 24for this
my son was dead and is alive again; he was
lost and is found.' And they began to be
merry.

25"Now his older son was in the field.
And as he came and drew near to the
house, he heard music and dancing. 26So he
called one of the servants and asked what
these things meant. 27And he said to him,
'Your brother has come, and because he
has received him safe and sound, your
father has killed the fatted calf.'

28"But he was angry and would not go
in. Therefore his father came out and
pleaded with him. 29So he answered and
said to *his* father, 'Lo, these many years I
have been serving you; I never trans-
gressed your commandment at any time;
and yet you never gave me a young goat,
that I might make merry with my friends.
30But as soon as this son of yours came,
who has devoured your livelihood with
harlots, you killed the fatted calf for him.'

31"And he said to him, 'Son, you are al-
ways with me, and all that I have is yours.
32It was right that we should make merry
and be glad, for your brother was dead
and is alive again, and was lost and is
found.' "

CHAPTER 16

The Parable of the Unjust Steward

He also said to His disciples: "There
was a certain rich man who had a steward,
and an accusation was brought to him that
this man was wasting his goods. 2So he
called him and said to him, 'What is this I
hear about you? Give an account of your
stewardship, for you can no longer be
steward.'

3"Then the steward said within himself,
'What shall I do? For my master is taking
the stewardship away from me. I cannot
dig; I am ashamed to beg. 4I have resolved
what to do, that when I am put out of the
stewardship, they may receive me into
their houses.'

5"So he called every one of his master's
debtors to *him,* and said to the first, 'How

15:22 [a]NU-Text reads *Quickly bring.*

15:25–32 The elder son represents the Pharisee who fails to enjoy his inheritance. Jesus does not tell us how this elder son responded after his father's appeal. It was up to the Pharisees to finish the story by making a decision for or against God's love in Christ.

16:1–30 Previously Luke has emphasized that the gospel is for the poor. Here Jesus warns about the dangers of wealth. A Christian must invest it to bring a profit in eternity (vv. 1–13). Religion must not become a hypocritical cover for a greedy heart (vv. 14–30).

FAITHFUL STEWARDSHIP

Evelyn Christenson

Are you secretly longing to get out of your status quo and into something you think would be more glamorous, more important for the Lord? Paul explained the secret of God's being able to do greater things through us: "It is required in stewards that one be found faithful" (1 Cor. 4:2).

Stewards are those to whom something has been entrusted for which they are responsible and accountable. Each of us has been entrusted with the differing gifts of God—a household, children, a civic position, work in the church, money, and the mysteries of God—making us all stewards. And according to God's Word, stewards are required to be faithful—trustworthy.

So how can being a steward determine whether or not God can trust us with bigger things? Our track record. Jesus said, "He who is faithful in what is least is faithful also in much" (Luke 16:10). So he who is faithful over a few things can be entrusted with greater things. We demonstrate our faithfulness and trustworthiness by what we have done with what God has given us in the past. ✦

"Each of us has been entrusted with the differing gifts of God."

much do you owe my master?' 6And he
said, 'A hundred measures[a] of oil.' So he
said to him, 'Take your bill, and sit down
quickly and write fifty.' 7Then he said to
another, 'And how much do you owe?' So
he said, 'A hundred measures[a] of wheat.'
And he said to him, 'Take your bill, and
write eighty.' 8So the master commended
the unjust steward because he had dealt
shrewdly. For the sons of this world are
more shrewd in their generation than the
sons of light.
9"And I say to you, make friends for
yourselves by unrighteous mammon, that
when you fail,[a] they may receive you into
an everlasting home. 10He who *is* faithful in
what is least is faithful also in much; and he
who is unjust in *what is* least is unjust also
in much. 11Therefore if you have not been
faithful in the unrighteous mammon, who
will commit to your trust the true *riches?*
12And if you have not been faithful in what
is another man's, who will give you what
is your own?
13"No servant can serve two masters; for
either he will hate the one and love the
other, or else he will be loyal to the one and
despise the other. You cannot serve God
and mammon."

16:6 [a]Greek *batos*, eight or nine gallons each (Old Testament *bath*) 16:7 [a]Greek *koros*, ten or twelve bushels each (Old Testament *kor*) 16:9 [a]NU-Text reads *it fails.*

16:8–13 The **master** commended the **steward** not because of his dishonesty, but because he was shrewd enough to grasp an opportunity. Jesus suggests that believers would do well to be as alert in establishing an eternal reward as the unjust steward was in working for security in this world.

The Law, the Prophets, and the Kingdom

[14]Now the Phar'i·sees, who were lovers of money, also heard all these things, and they derided Him. [15]And He said to them, "You are those who justify yourselves before men, but God knows your hearts. For what is highly esteemed among men is an abomination in the sight of God.

[16]"The law and the prophets *were* until John. Since that time the kingdom of God has been preached, and everyone is pressing into it. [17]And it is easier for heaven and earth to pass away than for one tittle of the law to fail.

[18]"Whoever divorces his wife and marries another commits adultery; and whoever marries her who is divorced from *her* husband commits adultery.

The Rich Man and Lazarus

[19]"There was a certain rich man who was clothed in purple and fine linen and fared sumptuously every day. [20]But there was a certain beggar named Laz'a·rus, full of sores, who was laid at his gate, [21]desiring to be fed with the crumbs which fell[a] from the rich man's table. Moreover the dogs came and licked his sores. [22]So it was that the beggar died, and was carried by the angels to Abraham's bosom. The rich man also died and was buried. [23]And being in torments in Hā'dēs, he lifted up his eyes and saw Abraham afar off, and Laz'a·rus in his bosom.

[24]"Then he cried and said, 'Father Abraham, have mercy on me, and send Laz'a·rus that he may dip the tip of his finger in water and cool my tongue; for I am tormented in this flame.' [25]But Abraham said, 'Son, remember that in your lifetime you received your good things, and likewise Laz'a·rus evil things; but now he is comforted and you are tormented. [26]And besides all this, between us and you there is a great gulf fixed, so that those who want to pass from here to you cannot, nor can those from there pass to us.'

[27]"Then he said, 'I beg you therefore, father, that you would send him to my father's house, [28]for I have five brothers, that he may testify to them, lest they also come to this place of torment.' [29]Abraham said to him, 'They have Moses and the prophets; let them hear them.' [30]And he said, 'No, father Abraham; but if one goes to them from the dead, they will repent.' [31]But he said to him, 'If they do not hear Moses and the prophets, neither will they be persuaded though one rise from the dead.' "

CHAPTER 17

Jesus Warns of Offenses

Then He said to the disciples, "It is impossible that no offenses should come, but woe *to him* through whom they do come! [2]It would be better for him if a millstone were hung around his neck, and he were thrown into the sea, than that he should offend one of these little ones. [3]Take heed to yourselves. If your brother sins against you,[a] rebuke him; and if he repents, forgive him. [4]And if he sins against you seven times in a day, and seven times in a day returns to you,[a] saying, 'I repent,' you shall forgive him."

Faith and Duty

[5]And the apostles said to the Lord, "Increase our faith."

[6]So the Lord said, "If you have faith as a

16:21 [a]NU-Text reads *with what fell.* 17:3 [a]NU-Text omits *against you.* 17:4 [a]M-Text omits *to you.*

16:22, 23 Abraham's bosom: A place of honor in the abode of the righteous dead, and a place of comfort (v. 25). **Hades**: The place of the dead, but in this case clearly a place of **torments** characterized by fire (v. 24). A chasm between the two places prevented passage from one to the other (v. 26).

17:1 offenses: actions or attitudes that lead others to sin.

> ***I pray that You, Lord, will increase my grandchildren's faith.***
>
> *adapted from* Luke 17:5

mustard seed, you can say to this mulberry
tree, 'Be pulled up by the roots and be
planted in the sea,' and it would obey you.
7And which of you, having a servant plow-
ing or tending sheep, will say to him when
he has come in from the field, 'Come at
once and sit down to eat'? 8But will he not
rather say to him, 'Prepare something for
my supper, and gird yourself and serve me
till I have eaten and drunk, and afterward
you will eat and drink'? 9Does he thank
that servant because he did the things that
were commanded him? I think not.[a] 10So
likewise you, when you have done all
those things which you are commanded,
say, 'We are unprofitable servants. We have
done what was our duty to do.' "

Ten Lepers Cleansed

11Now it happened as He went to Jerusa-
lem that He passed through the midst of
Samaria and Galilee. 12Then as He entered
a certain village, there met Him ten men
who were lepers, who stood afar off. 13And
they lifted up *their* voices and said, "Jesus,
Master, have mercy on us!"

14So when He saw *them,* He said to them,
"Go, show yourselves to the priests." And
so it was that as they went, they were
cleansed.

15And one of them, when he saw that he
was healed, returned, and with a loud
voice glorified God, 16and fell down on *his*
face at His feet, giving Him thanks. And he
was a Samaritan.

17So Jesus answered and said, "Were
there not ten cleansed? But where *are* the
nine? 18Were there not any found who re-
turned to give glory to God except this
foreigner?" 19And He said to him, "Arise,
go your way. Your faith has made you
well."

The Coming of the Kingdom

20Now when He was asked by the
Phar'i·sees when the kingdom of God
would come, He answered them and said,
"The kingdom of God does not come with
observation; 21nor will they say, 'See here!'
or 'See there!'[a] For indeed, the kingdom of
God is within you."

22Then He said to the disciples, "The
days will come when you will desire to see
one of the days of the Son of Man, and you
will not see *it.* 23And they will say to you,
'Look here!' or 'Look there!'[a] Do not go af-
ter *them* or follow *them.* 24For as the light-
ning that flashes out of one *part* under
heaven shines to the other *part* under
heaven, so also the Son of Man will be in
His day. 25But first He must suffer many

17:9 [a]NU-Text ends verse with *commanded;* M-Text omits *him.* 17:21 [a]NU-Text reverses *here* and *there.* 17:23 [a]NU-Text reverses *here* and *there.*

17:9, 10 Thanks were considered unnecessary for a slave. Because he belonged to his master, the slave could never do more than his duty. Jesus tells us this is the right attitude for us to take toward God. We can never do all, or even a significant part, to repay God for what He has done for us. Rather than relying on our past accomplishments, we should continue in the work of the Lord with a cheerful heart.

17:20–37 Jesus taught about the present and future **kingdom of God**. It had come in the person of Jesus, though the Pharisees did not recognize that fact. However, Jesus must die (v. 25) and His disciples go through an indefinite period of waiting (vv. 22, 23) before He returns. There is no point in asking when He will return because His coming will be as evident as a flash of **lightning** (v. 24). Worldly concerns will cause many to be unprepared for Jesus' coming (vv. 26–30), but His disciples must not let such concerns entangle them (vv. 31–33). We must at all times be ready for Christ's return because there will be no chance to prepare when He comes (vv. 34–36).

things and be rejected by this generation.
[26]And as it was in the days of Noah, so it
will be also in the days of the Son of Man:
[27]They ate, they drank, they married
wives, they were given in marriage, until
the day that Noah entered the ark, and
the flood came and destroyed them all.
[28]Likewise as it was also in the days of
Lot: They ate, they drank, they bought,
they sold, they planted, they built; [29]but
on the day that Lot went out of Sod'om it
rained fire and brimstone from heaven
and destroyed *them* all. [30]Even so will it be
in the day when the Son of Man is revealed.

[31]"In that day, he who is on the housetop, and his goods *are* in the house, let him
not come down to take them away. And
likewise the one who is in the field, let him
not turn back. [32]Remember Lot's wife.
[33]Whoever seeks to save his life will lose it,
and whoever loses his life will preserve it.
[34]I tell you, in that night there will be two
men in one bed: the one will be taken and
the other will be left. [35]Two *women* will be
grinding together: the one will be taken
and the other left. [36]Two *men* will be in the
field: the one will be taken and the other
left."[a]

[37]And they answered and said to Him,
"Where, Lord?"

So He said to them, "Wherever the body is, there the eagles will be gathered together."

CHAPTER 18

The Parable of the Persistent Widow

Then He spoke a parable to them, that
men always ought to pray and not lose

> ***I pray that my children will always pray and not lose heart.***
>
> *adapted from* Luke 18:1

heart, [2]saying: "There was in a certain city
a judge who did not fear God nor regard
man. [3]Now there was a widow in that city;
and she came to him, saying, 'Get justice
for me from my adversary.' [4]And he would
not for a while; but afterward he said
within himself, 'Though I do not fear God
nor regard man, [5]yet because this widow
troubles me I will avenge her, lest by her
continual coming she weary me.' "

[6]Then the Lord said, "Hear what the unjust judge said. [7]And shall God not avenge
His own elect who cry out day and night to
Him, though He bears long with them? [8]I
tell you that He will avenge them speedily.
Nevertheless, when the Son of Man comes,
will He really find faith on the earth?"

The Parable of the Pharisee and the Tax Collector

[9]Also He spoke this parable to some
who trusted in themselves that they were
righteous, and despised others: [10]"Two
men went up to the temple to pray, one a
Phar'i·see and the other a tax collector.
[11]The Phar'i·see stood and prayed thus
with himself, 'God, I thank You that I am
not like other men—extortioners, unjust,
adulterers, or even as this tax collector. [12]I
fast twice a week; I give tithes of all that I
possess.' [13]And the tax collector, standing
afar off, would not so much as raise *his*
eyes to heaven, but beat his breast, saying,

17:36 [a]NU-Text and M-Text omit verse 36.

17:32 Lot's wife was absorbed by material possessions; her fate is a warning against being concerned with worldly matters.

18:2 This parable contrasts the unrighteous judge with our just God, who is ready and willing to execute justice.

18:9–14 Genuine prayer is more a matter of attitude than of words or persistence. When we converse with God, we should recognize His grace and our unworthiness apart from Christ.

'God, be merciful to me a sinner!' [14]I tell you, this man went down to his house justified *rather* than the other; for everyone who exalts himself will be humbled, and he who humbles himself will be exalted."

Jesus Blesses Little Children

[15]Then they also brought infants to Him that He might touch them; but when the disciples saw *it,* they rebuked them. [16]But Jesus called them to *Him* and said, "Let the little children come to Me, and do not forbid them; for of such is the kingdom of God. [17]Assuredly, I say to you, whoever does not receive the kingdom of God as a little child will by no means enter it."

Jesus Counsels the Rich Young Ruler

[18]Now a certain ruler asked Him, saying, "Good Teacher, what shall I do to inherit eternal life?"

[19]So Jesus said to him, "Why do you call Me good? No one *is* good but One, *that is,* God. [20]You know the commandments: *'Do not commit adultery,' 'Do not murder,' 'Do not steal,' 'Do not bear false witness,' 'Honor your father and your mother.'*"[a]

[21]And he said, "All these things I have kept from my youth."

[22]So when Jesus heard these things, He said to him, "You still lack one thing. Sell all that you have and distribute to the poor, and you will have treasure in heaven; and come, follow Me."

[23]But when he heard this, he became very sorrowful, for he was very rich.

With God All Things Are Possible

[24]And when Jesus saw that he became very sorrowful, He said, "How hard it is for those who have riches to enter the kingdom of God! [25]For it is easier for a camel to go through the eye of a needle than for a rich man to enter the kingdom of God."

[26]And those who heard it said, "Who then can be saved?"

[27]But He said, "The things which are impossible with men are possible with God."

[28]Then Peter said, "See, we have left all[a] and followed You."

[29]So He said to them, "Assuredly, I say to you, there is no one who has left house or parents or brothers or wife or children, for the sake of the kingdom of God, [30]who shall not receive many times more in this present time, and in the age to come eternal life."

Jesus a Third Time Predicts His Death and Resurrection

[31]Then He took the twelve aside and said to them, "Behold, we are going up to Jerusalem, and all things that are written by the prophets concerning the Son of Man will be accomplished. [32]For He will be delivered to the Gentiles and will be mocked and insulted and spit upon. [33]They will scourge *Him* and kill Him. And the third day He will rise again."

[34]But they understood none of these things; this saying was hidden from them, and they did not know the things which were spoken.

A Blind Man Receives His Sight

[35]Then it happened, as He was coming near Jericho, that a certain blind man sat by

18:20 [a]Exodus 20:12–16; Deuteronomy 5:16–20
18:28 [a]NU-Text reads *our own.*

18:22, 23 The significant part of the invitation is not **sell all**, but **follow Me**. Whatever keeps us from following Christ is the **one thing** separating us from eternal life.

18:30 many times more: You can never outgive God. Jesus' promise points primarily to spiritual rather than material blessings, but it includes God's care for our needs in this **present time** (see 12:29–31). And in the **age to come** we have God's promise of **eternal life**. That is the best of both worlds!

the road begging. 36And hearing a multi-
tude passing by, he asked what it meant.
37So they told him that Jesus of Nazareth
was passing by. 38And he cried out, say-
ing, "Jesus, Son of David, have mercy on
me!"
39Then those who went before warned
him that he should be quiet; but he cried
out all the more, "Son of David, have
mercy on me!"
40So Jesus stood still and commanded
him to be brought to Him. And when
he had come near, He asked him, 41say-
ing, "What do you want Me to do for
you?"

He said, "Lord, that I may receive my sight."

42Then Jesus said to him, "Receive your
sight; your faith has made you well."
43And immediately he received his sight,
and followed Him, glorifying God. And all the people, when they saw *it*, gave praise to God.

CHAPTER 19

Jesus Comes to Zacchaeus' House

Then *Jesus* entered and passed through
Jericho. 2Now behold, *there was* a man
named Zac·chae'us who was a chief tax
collector, and he was rich. 3And he sought
to see who Jesus was, but could not be-
cause of the crowd, for he was of short
stature. 4So he ran ahead and climbed up
into a sycamore tree to see Him, for He was
going to pass that *way*. 5And when Jesus
came to the place, He looked up and saw
him,[a] and said to him, "Zac·chae'us, make
haste and come down, for today I must
stay at your house." 6So he made haste and
came down, and received Him joyfully.
7But when they saw *it*, they all complained,

19:5 [a]NU-Text omits *and saw him.*

Making Restitution

Evelyn Christenson

Zacchaeus and other tax collectors did not receive a salary for their work, but they collected as much money as they could so they would have a handsome income after paying the Roman government its appointed sum. But when Zacchaeus had "received [Jesus] joyfully," he made this startling declaration of his restitution intentions, "Look, Lord, I give half of my goods to the poor; and if I have taken anything from anyone by false accusation, I restore fourfold" (Luke 19:8).

"Should we today do less than Zacchaeus?"

Should we today do less than Zacchaeus? Should we not only have the blush of a first love that comes with new life in Jesus, but also an ever-growing awareness of how we damage, hurt, and wound our victims even in everyday life?

Since Zacchaeus's words, "I give" and "I restore," are both in the present tense in the Greek, we know that he intended a future ongoing process of making restitution. Should we not also strive to keep alive that sensitivity to those hurts we bring to people—even those we love?✦

saying, "He has gone to be a guest with a man who is a sinner."

8Then Zac·chaē'us stood and said to the Lord, "Look, Lord, I give half of my goods to the poor; and if I have taken anything from anyone by false accusation, I restore fourfold."

9And Jesus said to him, "Today salvation has come to this house, because he also is a son of Abraham; 10for the Son of Man has come to seek and to save that which was lost."

The Parable of the Minas

11Now as they heard these things, He spoke another parable, because He was near Jerusalem and because they thought the kingdom of God would appear immediately. 12Therefore He said: "A certain nobleman went into a far country to receive for himself a kingdom and to return. 13So he called ten of his servants, delivered to them ten minas,[a] and said to them, 'Do business till I come.' 14But his citizens hated him, and sent a delegation after him, saying, 'We will not have this *man* to reign over us.'

15"And so it was that when he returned, having received the kingdom, he then commanded these servants, to whom he had given the money, to be called to him, that he might know how much every man had gained by trading. 16Then came the first, saying, 'Master, your mina has earned ten minas.' 17And he said to him, 'Well *done,* good servant; because you were faithful in a very little, have authority over ten cities.' 18And the second came, saying, 'Master, your mina has earned five minas.' 19Likewise he said to him, 'You also be over five cities.'

20"Then another came, saying, 'Master, here is your mina, which I have kept put away in a handkerchief. 21For I feared you, because you are an austere man. You collect what you did not deposit, and reap what you did not sow.' 22And he said to him, 'Out of your own mouth I will judge you, *you* wicked servant. You knew that I was an austere man, collecting what I did not deposit and reaping what I did not sow. 23Why then did you not put my money in the bank, that at my coming I might have collected it with interest?'

24"And he said to those who stood by, 'Take the mina from him, and give *it* to him who has ten minas.' 25(But they said to him, 'Master, he has ten minas.') 26'For I say to you, that to everyone who has will be given; and from him who does not have, even what he has will be taken away from him. 27But bring here those enemies of mine, who did not want me to reign over them, and slay *them* before me.' "

The Triumphal Entry

28When He had said this, He went on ahead, going up to Jerusalem. 29And it came to pass, when He drew near to Beth'pha·gē[a] and Beth'a·ny, at the mountain called Ol'i·vet, *that* He sent two of His disciples, 30saying, "Go into the village opposite *you,* where as you enter you will find a colt tied, on which no one has ever

19:13 [a]The *mina* (Greek *mna,* Hebrew *minah*) was worth about three months' salary. 19:29 [a]M-Text reads *Bethsphage.*

19:8 half of my goods: Half of his annual income. A **fourfold** restoration went beyond the usual requirements of the law (see Num. 5:6, 7; Lev. 6:1–6). **Zacchaeus** seems to have been complying with Roman law, which sometimes required a fourfold repayment. In gratitude to God, he announced what he intended to do from then on.

19:13 mina: a Greek monetary unit.

19:20–26 The unfaithful servant represents the man who has let resentment destroy love and loyalty. The **wicked** servant tried to shift the blame for his negligence to the **austere** character of his master. But even if the master had been austere, it would not have excused disobedience. The servant could have put his money in the **bank** and gained **interest** with no fear of loss. How often do we blame our disobedience on others or on God? As mature Christians we must take responsiblity for our actions.

sat. Loose it and bring *it here.* [31]And if anyone asks you, 'Why are you loosing *it?*' thus you shall say to him, 'Because the Lord has need of it.' "

[32]So those who were sent went their way and found *it* just as He had said to them. [33]But as they were loosing the colt, the owners of it said to them, "Why are you loosing the colt?"

[34]And they said, "The Lord has need of him." [35]Then they brought him to Jesus. And they threw their own clothes on the colt, and they set Jesus on him. [36]And as He went, *many* spread their clothes on the road.

[37]Then, as He was now drawing near the descent of the Mount of Olives, the whole multitude of the disciples began to rejoice and praise God with a loud voice for all the mighty works they had seen, [38]saying:

" *'Blessed is the King who comes in the*
name of the L*ORD*!'[a]
Peace in heaven and glory in the
highest!"

[39]And some of the Phar'i·sees called to Him from the crowd, "Teacher, rebuke Your disciples."

[40]But He answered and said to them, "I tell you that if these should keep silent, the stones would immediately cry out."

Jesus Weeps over Jerusalem

[41]Now as He drew near, He saw the city and wept over it, [42]saying, "If you had known, even you, especially in this your day, the things *that make* for your peace! But now they are hidden from your eyes. [43]For days will come upon you when your enemies will build an embankment around you, surround you and close you in on every side, [44]and level you, and your children within you, to the ground; and they will not leave in you one stone upon another, because you did not know the time of your visitation."

Jesus Cleanses the Temple

[45]Then He went into the temple and began to drive out those who bought and sold in it,[a] [46]saying to them, "It is written, *'My house is*[a] *a house of prayer,'*[b] but you have made it a *'den of thieves.'* "[c]

[47]And He was teaching daily in the temple. But the chief priests, the scribes, and the leaders of the people sought to destroy Him, [48]and were unable to do anything; for all the people were very attentive to hear Him.

CHAPTER 20

Jesus' Authority Questioned

Now it happened on one of those days, as He taught the people in the temple and preached the gospel, *that* the chief priests and the scribes, together with the elders, confronted *Him* [2]and spoke to Him, saying, "Tell us, by what authority are You doing these things? Or who is he who gave You this authority?"

[3]But He answered and said to them, "I also will ask you one thing, and answer Me: [4]The baptism of John—was it from heaven or from men?"

[5]And they reasoned among themselves, saying, "If we say, 'From heaven,' He will

19:38 [a]Psalm 118:26 19:45 [a]NU-Text reads *those who were selling.* 19:46 [a]NU-Text reads *shall be.* [b]Isaiah 56:7 [c]Jeremiah 7:11

19:41–44 Jesus **wept** over the city (1) because in spite of the acclamation at the Triumphal Entry He knew that He was being rejected by the majority of the people (v. 42; see v. 39) and (2) because He knew that destruction lay ahead for them (vv. 43, 44). This destruction occurred in the Roman occupation of A.D. 70. **the time of your visitation**: When their long-awaited Messiah had come to them.

19:46 Jesus quoted from Is. 56:7 and Jer. 7:11. **house of prayer**: The temple's true purpose. **den of thieves**: The vendors made outrageous profits, and the money changers (see Mark 11:15) cheated the pilgrims when changing their foreign money to "the shekel of the sanctuary," required by law to pay the temple tax (Ex. 30:13–16).

say, 'Why then[a] did you not believe him?'
[6]But if we say, 'From men,' all the people will stone us, for they are persuaded that John was a prophet." [7]So they answered that they did not know where *it was* from.

[8]And Jesus said to them, "Neither will I tell you by what authority I do these things."

The Parable of the Wicked Vinedressers

[9]Then He began to tell the people this parable: "A certain man planted a vineyard, leased it to vinedressers, and went into a far country for a long time. [10]Now at vintage-time he sent a servant to the vinedressers, that they might give him some of the fruit of the vineyard. But the vinedressers beat him and sent *him* away empty-handed. [11]Again he sent another servant; and they beat him also, treated *him* shamefully, and sent *him* away empty-handed. [12]And again he sent a third; and they wounded him also and cast *him* out.

[13]"Then the owner of the vineyard said, 'What shall I do? I will send my beloved son. Probably they will respect *him* when they see him.' [14]But when the vinedressers saw him, they reasoned among themselves, saying, 'This is the heir. Come, let us kill him, that the inheritance may be ours.' [15]So they cast him out of the vineyard and killed *him*. Therefore what will the owner of the vineyard do to them? [16]He will come and destroy those vinedressers and give the vineyard to others."

And when they heard *it* they said, "Certainly not!"

[17]Then He looked at them and said, "What then is this that is written:

'The stone which the builders rejected
Has become the chief cornerstone'?[a]

[18]Whoever falls on that stone will be broken; but on whomever it falls, it will grind him to powder."

[19]And the chief priests and the scribes that very hour sought to lay hands on Him, but they feared the people[a]—for they knew He had spoken this parable against them.

The Pharisees: Is It Lawful to Pay Taxes to Caesar?

[20]So they watched *Him*, and sent spies who pretended to be righteous, that they might seize on His words, in order to deliver Him to the power and the authority of the governor.

[21]Then they asked Him, saying, "Teacher, we know that You say and teach rightly, and You do not show personal favoritism, but teach the way of God in truth: [22]Is it lawful for us to pay taxes to Caesar or not?"

[23]But He perceived their craftiness, and said to them, "Why do you test Me?[a] [24]Show Me a denarius. Whose image and inscription does it have?"

They answered and said, "Caesar's."

[25]And He said to them, "Render therefore to Caesar the things that are Caesar's, and to God the things that are God's."

[26]But they could not catch Him in His words in the presence of the people. And they marveled at His answer and kept silent.

The Sadducees: What About the Resurrection?

[27]Then some of the Sad'dū·cees, who deny that there is a resurrection, came to *Him* and asked Him, [28]saying: "Teacher, Moses wrote to us *that* if a man's brother dies, having a wife, and he dies without

20:5 [a]NU-Text and M-Text omit *then*. 20:17 [a]Psalm 118:22 20:19 [a]M-Text reads *but they were afraid.* 20:23 [a]NU-Text omits *Why do you test Me?*

20:16, 17 Certainly not! Jesus' listeners refused to be identified with the wicked vinedressers. They would not believe that God would judge them for rejecting Jesus. In response Jesus quoted the Scripture predicting both that He would be **rejected** by those to whom He had been sent, and that He would triumph.

children, his brother should take his wife
and raise up offspring for his brother.
29Now there were seven brothers. And the
first took a wife, and died without chil-
dren. 30And the second[a] took her as wife,
and he died childless. 31Then the third took
her, and in like manner the seven also; and
they left no children,[a] and died. 32Last of all
the woman died also. 33Therefore, in the
resurrection, whose wife does she become?
For all seven had her as wife."

34Jesus answered and said to them, "The
sons of this age marry and are given in
marriage. 35But those who are counted
worthy to attain that age, and the resurrec-
tion from the dead, neither marry nor are
given in marriage; 36nor can they die any-
more, for they are equal to the angels and
are sons of God, being sons of the resurrec-
tion. 37But even Moses showed in the *burn-
ing* bush *passage* that the dead are raised,
when he called the Lord *'the God of Abra-
ham, the God of Isaac, and the God of Ja-
cob.'*[a] 38For He is not the God of the dead
but of the living, for all live to Him."

39Then some of the scribes answered
and said, "Teacher, You have spoken well."
40But after that they dared not question
Him anymore.

Jesus: How Can David Call His Descendant Lord?

41And He said to them, "How can they
say that the Christ is the Son of David?
42Now David himself said in the Book of
Psalms:

'The LORD said to my Lord,
"Sit at My right hand,
43 *Till I make Your enemies Your*
footstool."'[a]

44Therefore David calls Him *'Lord'*; how is
He then his Son?"

Beware of the Scribes

45Then, in the hearing of all the people,
He said to His disciples, 46"Beware of the
scribes, who desire to go around in long
robes, love greetings in the marketplaces,
the best seats in the synagogues, and the
best places at feasts, 47who devour wid-
ows' houses, and for a pretense make long
prayers. These will receive greater
condemnation."

CHAPTER 21

The Widow's Two Mites

And He looked up and saw the rich
putting their gifts into the treasury, 2and
He saw also a certain poor widow putting
in two mites. 3So He said, "Truly I say to
you that this poor widow has put in more
than all; 4for all these out of their abun-
dance have put in offerings for God,[a] but
she out of her poverty put in all the liveli-
hood that she had."

Jesus Predicts the Destruction of the Temple

5Then, as some spoke of the temple, how
it was adorned with beautiful stones and
donations, He said, 6"These things which
you see—the days will come in which not
one stone shall be left upon another that
shall not be thrown down."

The Signs of the Times and the End of the Age

7So they asked Him, saying, "Teacher,
but when will these things be? And what
sign *will there be* when these things are
about to take place?"

20:30 [a]NU-Text ends verse 30 here. 20:31 [a]NU-Text and M-Text read *the seven also left no children.*
20:37 [a]Exodus 3:6, 15 20:43 [a]Psalm 110:1
21:4 [a]NU-Text omits *for God.*

20:41–44 In Matthew's account (22:42) we are told that Jesus asked the Pharisees whose Son Christ would be. They replied, "The Son of David." While not denying that He was descended from David, Jesus argues that He is much more than a **Son of David**, an earthly king. David himself had called the Messiah his **Lord**. How then could the Pharisees call Him anything less?

> Example is not the main thing in influencing others. It is the only thing.
> Albert Schweitzer

8And He said: "Take heed that you not
be deceived. For many will come in My
name, saying, 'I am *He*,' and, 'The time has
drawn near.' Therefore[a] do not go after
them. 9But when you hear of wars and
commotions, do not be terrified; for these
things must come to pass first, but the end
will not come immediately."

10Then He said to them, "Nation will
rise against nation, and kingdom against
kingdom. 11And there will be great earth-
quakes in various places, and famines and
pestilences; and there will be fearful sights
and great signs from heaven. 12But before
all these things, they will lay their hands
on you and persecute *you*, delivering *you*
up to the synagogues and prisons. You will
be brought before kings and rulers for My
name's sake. 13But it will turn out for you
as an occasion for testimony. 14Therefore
settle *it* in your hearts not to meditate be-
forehand on what you will answer; 15for I
will give you a mouth and wisdom which
all your adversaries will not be able to con-
tradict or resist. 16You will be betrayed
even by parents and brothers, relatives and
friends; and they will put *some* of you to
death. 17And you will be hated by all for
My name's sake. 18But not a hair of your
head shall be lost. 19By your patience pos-
sess your souls.

The Destruction of Jerusalem

20"But when you see Jerusalem sur-
rounded by armies, then know that its des-
olation is near. 21Then let those who are in
Judea flee to the mountains, let those who
are in the midst of her depart, and let not
those who are in the country enter her.
22For these are the days of vengeance, that
all things which are written may be ful-
filled. 23But woe to those who are pregnant
and to those who are nursing babies in
those days! For there will be great distress
in the land and wrath upon this people.
24And they will fall by the edge of the
sword, and be led away captive into all na-
tions. And Jerusalem will be trampled by
Gentiles until the times of the Gentiles are
fulfilled.

The Coming of the Son of Man

25"And there will be signs in the sun, in
the moon, and in the stars; and on the earth
distress of nations, with perplexity, the sea
and the waves roaring; 26men's hearts fail-
ing them from fear and the expectation of
those things which are coming on the
earth, for the powers of the heavens will be
shaken. 27Then they will see the Son of Man
coming in a cloud with power and great
glory. 28Now when these things begin to
happen, look up and lift up your heads, be-
cause your redemption draws near."

The Parable of the Fig Tree

29Then He spoke to them a parable:
"Look at the fig tree, and all the trees.

21:8 [a]NU-Text omits *Therefore*.

21:20–24 Jesus prophesies the destruction of **Jerusalem** with its temple. This destruction occurred in A.D. 70, when the Romans crushed the Jewish revolt.

21:24 edge of the sword: The event was as gruesome as Jesus indicated. The Jewish historian Josephus tells us that 1,000,000 Jews perished in that war, and that 97,000 were led captive to Egypt. **times of the Gentiles**: The period when Israel is subservient to or dependent on Gentile powers.

21:29–33 This parable is given as an encouragement to believers so that they will know God's future **kingdom** is near (v. 31). **these things**: The signs of Christ's return described in vv. 8–19 and the destruction of Jerusalem in vv. 20–24. The signs do not allow us to fix the time of His return. They do, however, assure us that He is coming and that His coming could always be near.

30When they are already budding, you see
and know for yourselves that summer is
now near. 31So you also, when you see
these things happening, know that the
kingdom of God is near. 32Assuredly, I say
to you, this generation will by no means
pass away till all things take place.
33Heaven and earth will pass away, but My
words will by no means pass away.

The Importance of Watching

34"But take heed to yourselves, lest your
hearts be weighed down with carousing,
drunkenness, and cares of this life, and
that Day come on you unexpectedly. 35For
it will come as a snare on all those who
dwell on the face of the whole earth.
36Watch therefore, and pray always that
you may be counted worthy[a] to escape all
these things that will come to pass, and to
stand before the Son of Man."

37And in the daytime He was teaching
in the temple, but at night He went out
and stayed on the mountain called
Ol'i·vet. 38Then early in the morning all the
people came to Him in the temple to hear
Him.

CHAPTER 22

The Plot to Kill Jesus

Now the Feast of Unleavened Bread
drew near, which is called Passover. 2And
the chief priests and the scribes sought
how they might kill Him, for they feared
the people.

3Then Satan entered Judas, surnamed
Is·car'i·ot, who was numbered among the
twelve. 4So he went his way and conferred
with the chief priests and captains, how he
might betray Him to them. 5And they were
glad, and agreed to give him money. 6So he
promised and sought opportunity to be-
tray Him to them in the absence of the
multitude.

Jesus and His Disciples Prepare the Passover

7Then came the Day of Unleavened
Bread, when the Passover must be killed.
8And He sent Peter and John, saying, "Go
and prepare the Passover for us, that we
may eat."

9So they said to Him, "Where do You
want us to prepare?"

10And He said to them, "Behold, when
you have entered the city, a man will meet
you carrying a pitcher of water; follow him
into the house which he enters. 11Then you
shall say to the master of the house, 'The
Teacher says to you, "Where is the guest
room where I may eat the Passover with
My disciples?" ' 12Then he will show you a
large, furnished upper room; there make
ready."

13So they went and found it just as He
had said to them, and they prepared the
Passover.

Jesus Institutes the Lord's Supper

14When the hour had come, He sat
down, and the twelve[a] apostles with Him.
15Then He said to them, "With *fervent* de-
sire I have desired to eat this Passover with
you before I suffer; 16for I say to you, I will
no longer eat of it until it is fulfilled in the
kingdom of God."

17Then He took the cup, and gave
thanks, and said, "Take this and divide *it*
among yourselves; 18for I say to you,[a] I will
not drink of the fruit of the vine until the
kingdom of God comes."

19And He took bread, gave thanks and

21:36 [a]NU-Text reads *may have strength.*
22:14 [a]NU-Text omits *twelve.* 22:18 [a]NU-Text adds *from now on.*

22:1 The **Feast of Unleavened Bread** was a week-long celebration of the Exodus that immediately followed **Passover** (see Ex. 12:1–20). The evening Passover meal merged with the beginning of the Feast of Unleavened Bread. By NT times the two feasts were closely identified.

22:19, 20 My body . . . My blood: Jesus transformed the **bread** and **cup** of the Passover meal into a sacrament for Christian believers. The bread and wine symbolize our Lord's body and

broke *it*, and gave *it* to them, saying, "This
is My body which is given for you; do this
in remembrance of Me."
[20]Likewise He also *took* the cup after
supper, saying, "This cup *is* the new
covenant in My blood, which is shed for
you. [21]But behold, the hand of My betrayer
is with Me on the table. [22]And truly the
Son of Man goes as it has been determined,
but woe to that man by whom He is betrayed!"
[23]Then they began to question among
themselves, which of them it was who
would do this thing.

The Disciples Argue About Greatness

[24]Now there was also a dispute among
them, as to which of them should be considered the greatest. [25]And He said to
them, "The kings of the Gentiles exercise
lordship over them, and those who exercise authority over them are called 'benefactors.' [26]But not so *among* you; on the
contrary, he who is greatest among you,
let him be as the younger, and he who
governs as he who serves. [27]For who *is*
greater, he who sits at the table, or he who
serves? *Is* it not he who sits at the table?
Yet I am among you as the One who
serves.
[28]"But you are those who have continued with Me in My trials. [29]And I bestow
upon you a kingdom, just as My Father bestowed *one* upon Me, [30]that you may eat
and drink at My table in My kingdom, and
sit on thrones judging the twelve tribes of
Israel."

Jesus Predicts Peter's Denial

[31]And the Lord said,[a] "Simon, Simon!
Indeed, Satan has asked for you, that he
may sift *you* as wheat. [32]But I have prayed
for you, that your faith should not fail; and
when you have returned to *Me*, strengthen
your brethren."
[33]But he said to Him, "Lord, I am ready
to go with You, both to prison and to
death."
[34]Then He said, "I tell you, Peter, the
rooster shall not crow this day before you
will deny three times that you know Me."

Supplies for the Road

[35]And He said to them, "When I sent
you without money bag, knapsack, and
sandals, did you lack anything?"
So they said, "Nothing."
[36]Then He said to them, "But now, he
who has a money bag, let him take *it*, and
likewise a knapsack; and he who has no
sword, let him sell his garment and buy
one. [37]For I say to you that this which is
written must still be accomplished in Me:
'And He was numbered with the transgressors.'[a] For the things concerning Me
have an end."
[38]So they said, "Lord, look, here *are* two
swords."
And He said to them, "It is enough."

The Prayer in the Garden

[39]Coming out, He went to the Mount of
Olives, as He was accustomed, and His
disciples also followed Him. [40]When He
came to the place, He said to them, "Pray
that you may not enter into temptation."
[41]And He was withdrawn from them
about a stone's throw, and He knelt down
and prayed, [42]saying, "Father, if it is Your

22:31 [a]NU-Text omits *And the Lord said.*
22:37 [a]Isaiah 53:12

blood. The sacrament celebrates God's **new covenant** with His people. By keeping the Lord's Supper, we show our dependence upon Christ and our spiritual participation in His death.

22:22 it has been determined: The death of Jesus was in God's plan, but Judas freely chose to betray Him and was therefore responsible for his actions.

22:31, 32 Satan has asked for you: Satan wanted to sidetrack Peter as he had Judas. In that temptation Jesus **prayed** for Peter as He prays for all who follow Him (John 17:9–11).

22:36–38 Jesus is not condoning force but urging His disciple to be prepared for persecution; however the disciples take him literally. He dismisses the subject, saying, "It is enough."

will, take this cup away from Me; never-
theless not My will, but Yours, be done."
[43]Then an angel appeared to Him from
heaven, strengthening Him. [44]And being in
agony, He prayed more earnestly. Then His
sweat became like great drops of blood
falling down to the ground.[a]
[45]When He rose up from prayer, and
had come to His disciples, He found them
sleeping from sorrow. [46]Then He said to
them, "Why do you sleep? Rise and pray,
lest you enter into temptation."

Betrayal and Arrest in Gethsemane

[47]And while He was still speaking, be-
hold, a multitude; and he who was called
Judas, one of the twelve, went before them
and drew near to Jesus to kiss Him. [48]But
Jesus said to him, "Judas, are you betray-
ing the Son of Man with a kiss?"
[49]When those around Him saw what
was going to happen, they said to Him,

22:44 [a]NU-Text brackets verses 43 and 44 as not in the original text.

Follow Closely in His Steps

Jill Briscoe

The Bible does not say Peter failed to follow Jesus after His arrest; it says he failed to follow closely. When we follow Jesus closely, we can hear His voice and sense His presence. When we deliberately put distance between us, we hear only the clamor of the opposition and lose sight of God Himself! It is then that we panic as Peter did, and we end up failing both Jesus and ourselves.

If we are to keep near the Lord, we must keep praying. Earlier that night, Jesus had taken His men to the beautiful Garden of Gethsemane. Jesus particularly asked Peter, James, and John to watch and pray with Him as He battled out His last agony of submission to the Father's will. The Lord knew the Cross was just around the corner.

But the garden was so peaceful, it was hard to believe the need to watch and pray. The smell of flowers and the soft, sweet night breezes lulled the tired disciples to sleep.

Very few of us pray *before* trouble comes. Most of us wait until the soldiers arrive on the scene, the arrests are made, the trial is in progress, and the cross is in sight before we get around to praying. But the problem is that no one prays well on the way to the cross! The praying must be done beforehand, when Gethsemane is peaceful and the trauma is yet to come. If we fail to be fortified by prayer, we will not do well when Judas arrives—or when we find ourselves at a charcoal fire, surrounded by a hostile crowd.

"When we follow Jesus closely, we can hear His voice and sense His presence."

Before—not after—is the critical time to pray. Therefore, says Jesus, "Why do you sleep? Rise and pray, lest you enter into temptation" (Luke 22:46).✦

"Lord, shall we strike with the sword?"
50 And one of them struck the servant of the
high priest and cut off his right ear.
51 But Jesus answered and said, "Permit
even this." And He touched his ear and
healed him.
52 Then Jesus said to the chief priests,
captains of the temple, and the elders who
had come to Him, "Have you come out, as
against a robber, with swords and clubs?
53 When I was with you daily in the temple,
you did not try to seize Me. But this is your
hour, and the power of darkness."

Peter Denies Jesus, and Weeps Bitterly

54 Having arrested Him, they led *Him*
and brought Him into the high priest's
house. But Peter followed at a distance.
55 Now when they had kindled a fire in the
midst of the courtyard and sat down to-
gether, Peter sat among them. 56 And a cer-
tain servant girl, seeing him as he sat by
the fire, looked intently at him and said,
"This man was also with Him."
57 But he denied Him,[a] saying, "Woman,
I do not know Him."
58 And after a little while another saw
him and said, "You also are of them."
But Peter said, "Man, I am not!"
59 Then after about an hour had passed,
another confidently affirmed, saying,
"Surely this *fellow* also was with Him, for
he is a Galilean."
60 But Peter said, "Man, I do not know
what you are saying!"
Immediately, while he was still speak-
ing, the rooster[a] crowed. 61 And the Lord
turned and looked at Peter. Then Peter re-
membered the word of the Lord, how He
had said to him, "Before the rooster crows,[a]
you will deny Me three times." 62 So Peter
went out and wept bitterly.

Jesus Mocked and Beaten

63 Now the men who held Jesus mocked
Him and beat Him. 64 And having blind-
folded Him, they struck Him on the face
and asked Him,[a] saying, "Prophesy! Who
is the one who struck You?" 65 And many
other things they blasphemously spoke
against Him.

Jesus Faces the Sanhedrin

66 As soon as it was day, the elders of the
people, both chief priests and scribes, came
together and led Him into their council,
saying, 67 "If You are the Christ, tell us."
But He said to them, "If I tell you, you
will by no means believe. 68 And if I also ask
you, you will by no means answer Me or let
Me go.[a] 69 Hereafter the Son of Man will sit
on the right hand of the power of God."
70 Then they all said, "Are You then the
Son of God?"
So He said to them, "You *rightly* say that
I am."
71 And they said, "What further testi-
mony do we need? For we have heard it
ourselves from His own mouth."

CHAPTER 23

Jesus Handed Over to Pontius Pilate

Then the whole multitude of them arose
and led Him to Pilate. 2 And they began to
accuse Him, saying, "We found this *fellow*
perverting the[a] nation, and forbidding to

22:57 [a]NU-Text reads *denied it.* 22:60 [a]NU-Text and M-Text read *a rooster.* 22:61 [a]NU-Text adds *today.* 22:64 [a]NU-Text reads *And having blindfolded Him, they asked Him.* 22:68 [a]NU-Text omits *also* and *Me or let Me go.* 23:2 [a]NU-Text reads *our.*

22:51–53 Permit . . . this: Do not resist any more. **chief priests**: The temple authorities themselves were present. **your hour**: The time when evil reveals itself and exercises its powers. Dark times come even in God's most significant work, but He will always triumph.

23:1, 2 Pilate, as the Roman governor, alone had the power to execute criminals. **accuse Him**: The Jewish leaders made three false charges. They twisted the facts to make Jesus appear to be a threat to Pilate and the Roman government.

pay taxes to Caesar, saying that He Himself is Christ, a King."

[3]Then Pilate asked Him, saying, "Are You the King of the Jews?"

He answered him and said, "*It is as* you say."

[4]So Pilate said to the chief priests and the crowd, "I find no fault in this Man."

[5]But they were the more fierce, saying, "He stirs up the people, teaching throughout all Judea, beginning from Galilee to this place."

Jesus Faces Herod

[6]When Pilate heard of Galilee,[a] he asked if the Man were a Galilean. [7]And as soon as he knew that He belonged to Her'od's jurisdiction, he sent Him to Her'od, who was also in Jerusalem at that time. [8]Now when Her'od saw Jesus, he was exceedingly glad; for he had desired for a long *time* to see Him, because he had heard many things about Him, and he hoped to see some miracle done by Him. [9]Then he questioned Him with many words, but He answered him nothing. [10]And the chief priests and scribes stood and vehemently accused Him. [11]Then Her'od, with his men of war, treated Him with contempt and mocked *Him,* arrayed Him in a gorgeous robe, and sent Him back to Pilate. [12]That very day Pilate and Her'od became friends with each other, for previously they had been at enmity with each other.

Taking the Place of Barabbas

[13]Then Pilate, when he had called together the chief priests, the rulers, and the people, [14]said to them, "You have brought this Man to me, as one who misleads the people. And indeed, having examined *Him* in your presence, I have found no fault in this Man concerning those things of which you accuse Him; [15]no, neither did Her'od, for I sent you back to him;[a] and indeed nothing deserving of death has been done by Him. [16]I will therefore chastise Him and release *Him*" [17](for it was necessary for him to release one to them at the feast).[a]

[18]And they all cried out at once, saying, "Away with this *Man,* and release to us Ba·rab'bas"— [19]who had been thrown into prison for a certain rebellion made in the city, and for murder.

[20]Pilate, therefore, wishing to release Jesus, again called out to them. [21]But they shouted, saying, "Crucify *Him,* crucify Him!"

[22]Then he said to them the third time, "Why, what evil has He done? I have found no reason for death in Him. I will therefore chastise Him and let *Him* go."

[23]But they were insistent, demanding with loud voices that He be crucified. And the voices of these men and of the chief priests prevailed.[a] [24]So Pilate gave sentence that it should be as they requested. [25]And he released to them[a] the one they requested, who for rebellion and murder had been thrown into prison; but he delivered Jesus to their will.

The King on a Cross

[26]Now as they led Him away, they laid hold of a certain man, Simon a Cȳ·rē'ni·an, who was coming from the country, and on him they laid the cross that he might bear *it* after Jesus.

[27]And a great multitude of the people followed Him, and women who also mourned and lamented Him. [28]But Jesus, turning to them, said, "Daughters of Jerusalem, do not weep for Me, but weep for yourselves and for your children. [29]For in-

23:6 [a]NU-Text omits *of Galilee.* 23:15 [a]NU-Text reads *for he sent Him back to us.* 23:17 [a]NU-Text omits verse 17. 23:23 [a]NU-Text omits *and of the chief priests.* 23:25 [a]NU-Text and M-Text omit *to them.*

23:7, 12 Herod Antipas ruled Galilee and Perea, the center of much of Jesus' ministry. **at enmity**: Perhaps over Pilate's killing some Galileans (13:1, 2). Pilate's deference to Herod apparently healed the breach.

deed the days are coming in which they will say, 'Blessed *are* the barren, wombs that never bore, and breasts which never nursed!' 30Then they will begin *'to say to the mountains, "Fall on us!" and to the hills, "Cover us!"'*[a] 31For if they do these things in the green wood, what will be done in the dry?"

32There were also two others, criminals, led with Him to be put to death. 33And when they had come to the place called Calvary, there they crucified Him, and the criminals, one on the right hand and the other on the left. 34Then Jesus said, "Father, forgive them, for they do not know what they do."[a]

And they divided His garments and cast lots. 35And the people stood looking on. But even the rulers with them sneered, saying, "He saved others; let Him save Himself if He is the Christ, the chosen of God."

36The soldiers also mocked Him, coming and offering Him sour wine, 37and saying, "If You are the King of the Jews, save Yourself."

38And an inscription also was written over Him in letters of Greek, Latin, and Hebrew:[a]

THIS IS THE KING OF THE JEWS.

39Then one of the criminals who were hanged blasphemed Him, saying, "If You are the Christ,[a] save Yourself and us."

40But the other, answering, rebuked him, saying, "Do you not even fear God, seeing you are under the same condemnation? 41And we indeed justly, for we receive the due reward of our deeds; but this Man has done nothing wrong." 42Then he said to Jesus, "Lord,[a] remember me when You come into Your kingdom."

43And Jesus said to him, "Assuredly, I say to you, today you will be with Me in Paradise."

Jesus Dies on the Cross

44Now it was[a] about the sixth hour, and there was darkness over all the earth until the ninth hour. 45Then the sun was darkened,[a] and the veil of the temple was torn in two. 46And when Jesus had cried out with a loud voice, He said, "Father, *'into Your hands I commit My spirit.'*"[a] Having said this, He breathed His last.

47So when the centurion saw what had happened, he glorified God, saying, "Certainly this was a righteous Man!"

48And the whole crowd who came together to that sight, seeing what had been done, beat their breasts and returned. 49But all His acquaintances, and the women who followed Him from Galilee, stood at a distance, watching these things.

Jesus Buried in Joseph's Tomb

50Now behold, *there was* a man named Joseph, a council member, a good and just man. 51He had not consented to their decision and deed. *He was* from Ar·i·ma·thē'a, a city of the Jews, who himself was also waiting[a] for the kingdom of God. 52This man went to Pilate and asked for the body of Jesus. 53Then he took it down, wrapped it in linen, and laid it in a tomb *that was* hewn out of the rock, where no one had ever lain before. 54That day was the Preparation, and the Sabbath drew near.

23:30 [a]Hosea 10:8 23:34 [a]NU-Text brackets the first sentence as a later addition. 23:38 [a]NU-Text omits *written* and *in letters of Greek, Latin, and Hebrew.* 23:39 [a]NU-Text reads *Are You not the Christ?* 23:42 [a]NU-Text reads *And he said, "Jesus, remember me.* 23:44 [a]NU-Text adds *already.* 23:45 [a]NU-Text reads *obscured.* 23:46 [a]Psalm 31:5 23:51 [a]NU-Text reads *who was waiting.*

23:43 Paradise: Originally a Persian word meaning "park" or "garden." The Greek OT and some Jewish writers referred to the Garden of Eden as "Paradise." By NT times it came to mean the abode of the righteous after death, thus heaven (see 2 Cor. 12:4; Rev. 2:7).

23:44 The Jewish times **sixth hour** and **ninth hour** indicate that the **darkness** lasted from 12:00 noon to 3:00 P.M.

23:54 the Preparation: the day before the Sabbath.

55And the women who had come with
Him from Galilee followed after, and they
observed the tomb and how His body was
laid. 56Then they returned and prepared
spices and fragrant oils. And they rested
on the Sabbath according to the command-
ment.

CHAPTER 24

He Is Risen

Now on the first *day* of the week, very
early in the morning, they, and certain
other women with them,[a] came to the tomb
bringing the spices which they had pre-
pared. 2But they found the stone rolled
away from the tomb. 3Then they went in
and did not find the body of the Lord
Jesus. 4And it happened, as they were
greatly[a] perplexed about this, that behold,
two men stood by them in shining gar-
ments. 5Then, as they were afraid and
bowed *their* faces to the earth, they said to
them, "Why do you seek the living among
the dead? 6He is not here, but is risen! Re-
member how He spoke to you when He
was still in Galilee, 7saying, 'The Son of
Man must be delivered into the hands of
sinful men, and be crucified, and the third
day rise again.' "

8And they remembered His words.
9Then they returned from the tomb and
told all these things to the eleven and to all
the rest. 10It was Mary Mag'da·lēne,
Jō·an'na, Mary *the mother* of James, and the
other *women* with them, who told these
things to the apostles. 11And their words
seemed to them like idle tales, and they did
not believe them. 12But Peter arose and ran
to the tomb; and stooping down, he saw
the linen cloths lying[a] by themselves; and
he departed, marveling to himself at what
had happened.

The Road to Emmaus

13Now behold, two of them were travel-
ing that same day to a village called
Em·mā'us, which was seven miles[a] from
Jerusalem. 14And they talked together of all
these things which had happened. 15So it
was, while they conversed and reasoned,
that Jesus Himself drew near and went
with them. 16But their eyes were restrained,
so that they did not know Him.

17And He said to them, "What kind of
conversation *is* this that you have with one
another as you walk and are sad?"[a]

18Then the one whose name was
Clē'o·pas answered and said to Him, "Are
You the only stranger in Jerusalem, and
have You not known the things which hap-
pened there in these days?"

19And He said to them, "What things?"

So they said to Him, "The things con-
cerning Jesus of Nazareth, who was a
Prophet mighty in deed and word before
God and all the people, 20and how the
chief priests and our rulers delivered Him
to be condemned to death, and crucified
Him. 21But we were hoping that it was
He who was going to redeem Israel. In-
deed, besides all this, today is the third day
since these things happened. 22Yes, and
certain women of our company, who ar-
rived at the tomb early, astonished us.
23When they did not find His body, they
came saying that they had also seen a vi-
sion of angels who said He was alive.
24And certain of those *who were* with us
went to the tomb and found *it* just as the
women had said; but Him they did not
see."

25Then He said to them, "O foolish ones,
and slow of heart to believe in all that the

24:1 [a]NU-Text omits *and certain other women with them.* 24:4 [a]NU-Text omits *greatly.* 24:12 [a]NU-Text omits *lying.* 24:13 [a]Literally *sixty stadia* 24:17 [a]NU-Text reads *as you walk? And they stood still, looking sad.*

24:13–35 These two disciples thought Jesus would set up a political kingdom; therefore, His death was a tragedy (v. 21). Jesus, however, showed them that it was according to God's plan (v. 26) and had been taught throughout the OT (v. 27). His death was the way for Him to accomplish salvation for humankind.

FISHERS OF MEN

Jill Briscoe

My father was a fisherman. I never ever heard him return from a day's fishing and announce, "I influenced a lot of fish today!" He either said, "I caught one" or "I lost one!" But how many of us stop short of actually catching our "fish?" Perhaps the work involved is just too hard for us. Maybe we are scared of actually talking to someone about receiving Jesus—in case they laugh at us or reject us.

"Jesus is living inside us, and it is His job to win souls," I was told almost as soon as I had come to Christ. I remember saying to the girl who led me to Him, "Oh, I could never share my faith with anyone else." "Yes, you can," she replied cheerfully.

"Our job is to be so enamored with our Savior that we 'launch out' into the deep things of the Christian faith."

You don't become an expert fisherman overnight—but there have been many big fish caught by little boys with a pole and a bent pin. The important thing is enthusiasm! Our job is to be so thoroughly enamored with our Savior that we "launch out" into the deep things of the Christian faith, let our nets down in the place He tells us to, then rely on Him as we do the hard work of hauling in the consequences of such a Christ-directed operation. ✦

prophets have spoken! 26Ought not the
Christ to have suffered these things and to
enter into His glory?" 27And beginning at
Moses and all the Prophets, He expounded
to them in all the Scriptures the things concerning Himself.

The Disciples' Eyes Opened

28Then they drew near to the village
where they were going, and He indicated
that He would have gone farther. 29But
they constrained Him, saying, "Abide with
us, for it is toward evening, and the day is
far spent." And He went in to stay with
them.

30Now it came to pass, as He sat at the
table with them, that He took bread,
blessed and broke *it*, and gave it to them.
31Then their eyes were opened and they
knew Him; and He vanished from their
sight.

32And they said to one another, "Did not
our heart burn within us while He talked
with us on the road, and while He opened
the Scriptures to us?" 33So they rose up that
very hour and returned to Jerusalem, and

24:31 vanished from their sight: The LORD's body was real and not just apparent. Yet it was not hampered by the common limitations of the human body. See vv. 36–43; John 21:1–14; Acts 1:9.

found the eleven and those *who were* with
them gathered together, [34]saying, "The
Lord is risen indeed, and has appeared to
Simon!" [35]And they told about the things
that had happened on the road, and how He
was known to them in the breaking of
bread.

Jesus Appears to His Disciples

[36]Now as they said these things, Jesus
Himself stood in the midst of them, and
said to them, "Peace to you." [37]But they
were terrified and frightened, and sup-
posed they had seen a spirit. [38]And He said
to them, "Why are you troubled? And why
do doubts arise in your hearts? [39]Behold
My hands and My feet, that it is I Myself.
Handle Me and see, for a spirit does not
have flesh and bones as you see I have."
[40]When He had said this, He showed
them His hands and His feet.[a] [41]But while
they still did not believe for joy, and mar-
veled, He said to them, "Have you any
food here?" [42]So they gave Him a piece of a
broiled fish and some honeycomb.[a] [43]And
He took *it* and ate in their presence.

The Scriptures Opened

[44]Then He said to them, "These *are* the
words which I spoke to you while I was
still with you, that all things must be ful-
filled which were written in the Law of
Moses and *the* Prophets and *the* Psalms
concerning Me." [45]And He opened their
understanding, that they might compre-
hend the Scriptures.
[46]Then He said to them, "Thus it is writ-
ten, and thus it was necessary for the
Christ to suffer and to rise[a] from the dead
the third day, [47]and that repentance and re-
mission of sins should be preached in His
name to all nations, beginning at Jerusa-
lem. [48]And you are witnesses of these
things. [49]Behold, I send the Promise of My
Father upon you; but tarry in the city of Je-
rusalem[a] until you are endued with power
from on high."

The Ascension

[50]And He led them out as far as
Beth'a·ny, and He lifted up His hands and
blessed them. [51]Now it came to pass, while
He blessed them, that He was parted from
them and carried up into heaven. [52]And
they worshiped Him, and returned to Jeru-
salem with great joy, [53]and were continu-
ally in the temple praising and[a] blessing
God. Amen.[b]

24:40 [a]Some printed New Testaments omit this verse. It is found in nearly all Greek manuscripts. 24:42 [a]NU-Text omits *and some honeycomb.* 24:46 [a]NU-Text reads *written, that the Christ should suffer and rise.* 24:49 [a]NU-Text omits *of Jerusalem.* 24:53 [a]NU-Text omits *praising and.* [b]NU-Text omits *Amen.*

24:34 appeared to Simon: Scripture nowhere tells what took place at that meeting. But Jesus sent a special word to a repentant disciple (Mark 16:7), and Paul records that appearance (1 Cor. 15:5).

24:36–43 The risen Christ is identified with the earthly Jesus, emphasizing the reality of His resurrected body. **a spirit**: A ghost. **ate in their presence**: Not because He needed nourishment, but as proof that His body was real.

24:44 Law . . . Prophets . . . Psalms: The three major divisions of the Hebrew Scriptures. The Law corresponds to the first five books of the OT. The prophets were grouped into the Former Prophets (Joshua, Judges, Samuel, Kings) and the Latter Prophets (Isaiah, Jeremiah, Ezekiel, the 12 Minor Prophets). The Psalms may stand for the section of Hebrew Scriptures called the Writings, containing the remaining books of the Christian OT.

✦John✦

John, the disciple whom Jesus loved and who was His closest earthly friend, presents the most powerful case in the Bible for the deity of the incarnate Son of God. John's purpose for writing the book is crystal clear: to set forth Christ in His deity, to spark believing faith in his readers and that, in believing, they would have life in His name.

John was evidently among the Galileans who followed John the Baptist until they were called to follow Jesus at the outset of His public ministry. Selected to be among the twelve apostles, John became part of the inner circle of disciples and was closely associated with Peter and James. As an eye witness to the life of Jesus, he wrote of Christ's unending love for man and the intimate, personal relationship Jesus offers to those who believe. The conversation between Jesus and Nicodemus (ch. 3) reflects the divine insight Jesus had into the hearts of the people and His desire that all find salvation in Him. That account of their discussion should prompt us to pause and determine whether we are relying on our own morality or on Jesus Christ for salvation.

John's Gospel is topical, not primarily chronological, and it revolves around seven miracles and seven "I Am" statements of Christ. Following an extended first-hand description of the Upper Room meal and Discourse, John records events leading up to the Resurrection, the final climactic proof that Jesus is the Son of God. ✦

CHAPTER 1

The Eternal Word

In the beginning was the Word, and the
Word was with God, and the Word was
God. 2He was in the beginning with God.
3All things were made through Him, and
without Him nothing was made that was
made. 4In Him was life, and the life was the
light of men. 5And the light shines in the
darkness, and the darkness did not com-
prehend[a] it.

John's Witness: The True Light

6There was a man sent from God, whose
name *was* John. 7This man came for a wit-
ness, to bear witness of the Light, that all
through him might believe. 8He was not

1:5 [a]Or *overcome*

1:1, 2 In the beginning: See Gen. 1:1. John affirms three vital truths about **the Word** (Christ): He existed in the **beginning**; He was **with God** (lit. "face-to-face with God"); and in His divine nature He **was** indeed **God**.

1:4, 5 "Life" and "light" are favorite terms used frequently by John throughout this book. Here he shows that Christ came to give us life and open our eyes to the light of salvation, which conquers the **darkness** of this world.

that Light, but *was sent* to bear witness of that Light. [9]That was the true Light which gives light to every man coming into the world.[a]

[10]He was in the world, and the world was made through Him, and the world did not know Him. [11]He came to His own,[a] and His own[b] did not receive Him. [12]But as many as received Him, to them He gave the right to become children of God, to those who believe in His name: [13]who were born, not of blood, nor of the will of the flesh, nor of the will of man, but of God.

The Word Becomes Flesh

[14]And the Word became flesh and dwelt among us, and we beheld His glory, the glory as of the only begotten of the Father, full of grace and truth.

[15]John bore witness of Him and cried out, saying, "This was He of whom I said, 'He who comes after me is preferred before me, for He was before me.' "

[16]And[a] of His fullness we have all received, and grace for grace. [17]For the law was given through Moses, *but* grace and truth came through Jesus Christ. [18]No one has seen God at any time. The only begotten Son,[a] who is in the bosom of the Father, He has declared *Him*.

A Voice in the Wilderness

[19]Now this is the testimony of John, when the Jews sent priests and Le′vītes from Jerusalem to ask him, "Who are you?"

[20]He confessed, and did not deny, but confessed, "I am not the Christ."

[21]And they asked him, "What then? Are you E·lī′jah?"

He said, "I am not."

"Are you the Prophet?"

And he answered, "No."

[22]Then they said to him, "Who are you, that we may give an answer to those who sent us? What do you say about yourself?"

[23]He said: "I *am*

'The voice of one crying in the wilderness:
"Make straight the way of the LORD,*" '*[a]

as the prophet Ī·sāi′ah said."

[24]Now those who were sent were from the Phar′i·sees. [25]And they asked him, saying, "Why then do you baptize if you are not the Christ, nor E·lī′jah, nor the Prophet?"

[26]John answered them, saying, "I baptize with water, but there stands One among you whom you do not know. [27]It is He who, coming after me, is preferred before me, whose sandal strap I am not worthy to loose."

[28]These things were done in Beth·ab′a·ra[a] beyond the Jordan, where John was baptizing.

The Lamb of God

[29]The next day John saw Jesus coming toward him, and said, "Behold! The Lamb of God who takes away the sin of the world! [30]This is He of whom I said, 'After me comes a Man who is preferred before

1:9 [a]Or *That was the true Light which, coming into the world, gives light to every man.* 1:11 [a]That is, His own things or domain [b]That is, His own people 1:16 [a]NU-Text reads *For.* 1:18 [a]NU-Text reads *only begotten God.* 1:23 [a]Isaiah 40:3 1:28 [a]NU-Text and M-Text read *Bethany.*

1:14 the Word became flesh: A central truth of the Christian faith. The divine Christ became a man and **dwelt** temporarily **among us**. The God who dwelt in the OT tabernacle now came as a human being. The apostles and other witnesses **beheld His** divine **glory** in His miracles (2:11), crucifixion (19:34, 35), and resurrection (20:24–29). They knew that God was indeed among them.

1:18 John demonstrates the intimate, loving relationship between the Father and the Son.

1:19 The phrase **the Jews** occurs frequently in John and usually signifies the Jewish authorities—Pharisees and scribes, who opposed Jesus' ministry.

REAPING THE HARVEST

Sherwood Eliot Wirt

How many times have you heard it? "I'm no good any more. I feel so useless. Why, when I was younger I could do anything, go anywhere. But now . . ." Does it sound familiar? Perhaps you have even muttered something like that yourself.

God has given us older people the opportunity of a lifetime. In a world in which being old is a social problem, God Almighty Himself pays us honor. He gives us high responsibility, puts us to work, and rewards us for it.

It is a great boon to us to find that in God's work program of harvesting, the age of the harvester only increases his or her value. The harvest is what Christianity is all about. Whether we are eight years old or eighty, bringing souls into the kingdom, winning men and women to faith in Jesus Christ and preparing them for heaven, is what we have been commissioned to do. ✦

me, for He was before me.' 31I did not
know Him; but that He should be revealed
to Israel, therefore I came baptizing with
water."

32And John bore witness, saying, "I saw
the Spirit descending from heaven like a
dove, and He remained upon Him. 33I
did not know Him, but He who sent
me to baptize with water said to me,
'Upon whom you see the Spirit descending,
and remaining on Him, this is He who
baptizes with the Holy Spirit.' 34And I have
seen and testified that this is the Son of
God."

The First Disciples

35Again, the next day, John stood with
two of his disciples. 36And looking at Jesus
as He walked, he said, "Behold the Lamb
of God!"

37The two disciples heard him speak,
and they followed Jesus. 38Then Jesus
turned, and seeing them following, said to
them, "What do you seek?"

They said to Him, "Rabbi" (which is to
say, when translated, Teacher), "where are
You staying?"

39He said to them, "Come and see."
They came and saw where He was staying,
and remained with Him that day (now it
was about the tenth hour).

40One of the two who heard John *speak,*
and followed Him, was Andrew, Simon
Peter's brother. 41He first found his own
brother Simon, and said to him, "We have
found the Messiah" (which is translated,
the Christ). 42And he brought him to Jesus.

Now when Jesus looked at him, He said,
"You are Simon the son of Jonah.[a] You shall
be called Cē'phas" (which is translated, A
Stone).

Philip and Nathanael

43The following day Jesus wanted to go
to Galilee, and He found Philip and said to
him, "Follow Me." 44Now Philip was from
Beth·sā'i·da, the city of Andrew and Peter.
45Philip found Na·than'a·el and said to
him, "We have found Him of whom Moses
in the law, and also the prophets, wrote—
Jesus of Nazareth, the son of Joseph."

46And Na·than'a·el said to him, "Can
anything good come out of Nazareth?"

1:42 [a]NU-Text reads *John.*

Philip said to him, "Come and see."
[47]Jesus saw Na·than'a·el coming toward
Him, and said of him, "Behold, an Israelite
indeed, in whom is no deceit!"
[48]Na·than'a·el said to Him, "How do
You know me?"
Jesus answered and said to him, "Before
Philip called you, when you were under
the fig tree, I saw you."
[49]Na·than'a·el answered and said to
Him, "Rabbi, You are the Son of God! You
are the King of Israel!"
[50]Jesus answered and said to him, "Be-
cause I said to you, 'I saw you under the fig
tree,' do you believe? You will see greater
things than these." [51]And He said to him,
"Most assuredly, I say to you, hereafter[a]
you shall see heaven open, and the angels
of God ascending and descending upon
the Son of Man."

CHAPTER 2

Water Turned to Wine

On the third day there was a wedding in
Cā'na of Galilee, and the mother of Jesus
was there. [2]Now both Jesus and His disci-
ples were invited to the wedding. [3]And
when they ran out of wine, the mother of
Jesus said to Him, "They have no wine."
[4]Jesus said to her, "Woman, what does
your concern have to do with Me? My
hour has not yet come."
[5]His mother said to the servants, "What-
ever He says to you, do *it*."
[6]Now there were set there six waterpots
of stone, according to the manner of purifi-
cation of the Jews, containing twenty or
thirty gallons apiece. [7]Jesus said to them,
"Fill the waterpots with water." And they
filled them up to the brim. [8]And He said to
them, "Draw *some* out now, and take *it* to
the master of the feast." And they took *it*.
[9]When the master of the feast had tasted
the water that was made wine, and did not
know where it came from (but the servants
who had drawn the water knew), the mas-
ter of the feast called the bridegroom.
[10]And he said to him, "Every man at the be-
ginning sets out the good wine, and when
the *guests* have well drunk, then the infe-
rior. You have kept the good wine until
now!"
[11]This beginning of signs Jesus did in
Cā'na of Galilee, and manifested His glory;
and His disciples believed in Him.
[12]After this He went down to Ca·per'-
na·um, He, His mother, His brothers, and
His disciples; and they did not stay there
many days.

Jesus Cleanses the Temple

[13]Now the Passover of the Jews was at
hand, and Jesus went up to Jerusalem.
[14]And He found in the temple those who
sold oxen and sheep and doves, and the
money changers doing business. [15]When
He had made a whip of cords, He drove
them all out of the temple, with the sheep
and the oxen, and poured out the chang-
ers' money and overturned the tables.
[16]And He said to those who sold doves,
"Take these things away! Do not make My
Father's house a house of merchandise!"
[17]Then His disciples remembered that it

1:51 [a]NU-Text omits *hereafter*.

2:1—12:50 John records seven **signs** (2:11) and seven discourses through which Jesus revealed Himself to the world.

2:3–5 The shortage of **wine** on such an occasion was a great social embarrassment. Bringing the problem to Jesus and reacting to His response as she did showed Mary's profound confidence in Him. **Woman** (v. 4) was not a disrespectful form of address; He spoke to her in exactly the same way from the Cross (19:26). **My hour has not yet come** refers to the time of His passion (see 17:1). His acts must be in accordance with the divine timetable.

2:14–16 The business of **money changers** and the sale of animals and doves was permitted in the court of the temple for the convenience of pilgrims to the Passover. It made it easier for them to offer the appropriate sacrifices and gifts at the temple. But the practice had become characterized by irreverence and greed.

was written, *"Zeal for Your house has
eaten[a] Me up."*[b]
18So the Jews answered and said to Him,
"What sign do You show to us, since You
do these things?"
19Jesus answered and said to them, "De-
stroy this temple, and in three days I will
raise it up."
20Then the Jews said, "It has taken forty-
six years to build this temple, and will You
raise it up in three days?"
21But He was speaking of the temple of
His body. 22Therefore, when He had risen
from the dead, His disciples remembered
that He had said this to them;[a] and they be-
lieved the Scripture and the word which
Jesus had said.

The Discerner of Hearts

23Now when He was in Jerusalem at the
Passover, during the feast, many believed
in His name when they saw the signs
which He did. 24But Jesus did not commit
Himself to them, because He knew all *men,*
25and had no need that anyone should tes-
tify of man, for He knew what was in man.

CHAPTER 3

The New Birth

There was a man of the Phar'i·sees
named Nic·o·dē'mus, a ruler of the Jews.
2This man came to Jesus by night and said
to Him, "Rabbi, we know that You are a
teacher come from God; for no one can do
these signs that You do unless God is with
him."
3Jesus answered and said to him, "Most
assuredly, I say to you, unless one is born
again, he cannot see the kingdom of God."
4Nic·o·dē'mus said to Him, "How can a
man be born when he is old? Can he enter
a second time into his mother's womb and
be born?"
5Jesus answered, "Most assuredly, I say
to you, unless one is born of water and the
Spirit, he cannot enter the kingdom of
God. 6That which is born of the flesh is
flesh, and that which is born of the Spirit is
spirit. 7Do not marvel that I said to you,
'You must be born again.' 8The wind blows
where it wishes, and you hear the sound of
it, but cannot tell where it comes from and
where it goes. So is everyone who is born
of the Spirit."
9Nic·o·dē'mus answered and said to
Him, "How can these things be?"
10Jesus answered and said to him, "Are
you the teacher of Israel, and do not know
these things? 11Most assuredly, I say to you,
We speak what We know and testify what
We have seen, and you do not receive Our
witness. 12If I have told you earthly things
and you do not believe, how will you be-
lieve if I tell you heavenly things? 13No one
has ascended to heaven but He who came
down from heaven, *that is,* the Son of Man
who is in heaven.[a] 14And as Moses lifted up
the serpent in the wilderness, even so must
the Son of Man be lifted up, 15that whoever
believes in Him should not perish but[a]
have eternal life. 16For God so loved the

2:17 [a]NU-Text and M-Text read *will eat.* [b]Psalm 69:9
2:22 [a]NU-Text and M-Text omit *to them.* 3:13 [a]NU-Text omits *who is in heaven.* 3:15 [a]NU-Text omits *not perish but.*

2:23–25 We must be careful to distinguish between genuine faith and superficial belief prompted by enthusiasm of the moment.

3:5 born of water: Physical birth or, perhaps, cleansing through the word of God (see 15:3; Eph. 5:26; Titus 3:5). **Born of . . . the Spirit** refers to the new life given by the Holy Spirit. Spiritual birth is necessary to enter God's **kingdom**.

3:14, 15 Jesus illustrated the simplicity of God's plan of salvation by faith in Christ. As Israelites were saved from death simply by looking at the bronze image of a **serpent** (Num. 21:4–9), so anyone may be saved by looking in faith to Christ. **Lifted up** foreshadows Jesus' death on the Cross. **whoever**: Salvation is available to all who accept God's plan. **eternal life**: Life in fellowship with God, which the believer receives now when he accepts Christ.

world that He gave His only begotten Son, that whoever believes in Him should not perish but have everlasting life. 17For God did not send His Son into the world to condemn the world, but that the world through Him might be saved.

18"He who believes in Him is not condemned; but he who does not believe is condemned already, because he has not believed in the name of the only begotten Son of God. 19And this is the condemnation, that the light has come into the world, and men loved darkness rather than light, because their deeds were evil. 20For everyone practicing evil hates the light and does not come to the light, lest his deeds should be exposed. 21But he who does the truth comes to the light, that his deeds may be clearly seen, that they have been done in God."

John the Baptist Exalts Christ

22After these things Jesus and His disciples came into the land of Judea, and there He remained with them and baptized. 23Now John also was baptizing in Aē′non near Sā′lim, because there was much water there. And they came and were baptized. 24For John had not yet been thrown into prison.

25Then there arose a dispute between *some* of John's disciples and the Jews about purification. 26And they came to John and said to him, "Rabbi, He who was with you beyond the Jordan, to whom you have testified—behold, He is baptizing, and all are coming to Him!"

27John answered and said, "A man can receive nothing unless it has been given to him from heaven. 28You yourselves bear me witness, that I said, 'I am not the Christ,' but, 'I have been sent before Him.' 29He who has the bride is the bridegroom; but the friend of the bridegroom, who stands and hears him, rejoices greatly because of the bridegroom's voice. Therefore this joy of mine is fulfilled. 30He must increase, but I *must* decrease. 31He who comes from above is above all; he who is of the earth is earthly and speaks of the earth. He who comes from heaven is above all. 32And what He has seen and heard, that He testifies; and no one receives His testimony. 33He who has received His testimony has certified that God is true. 34For He whom God has sent speaks the words of God, for God does not give the Spirit by measure. 35The Father loves the Son, and has given all things into His hand. 36He who believes in the Son has everlasting life; and he who does not believe the Son shall not see life, but the wrath of God abides on him."

CHAPTER 4

A Samaritan Woman Meets Her Messiah

Therefore, when the Lord knew that the Phar′i·sees had heard that Jesus made and baptized more disciples than John 2(though Jesus Himself did not baptize, but His disciples), 3He left Judea and departed again to Galilee. 4But He needed to go through Samaria.

5So He came to a city of Samaria which

3:29, 30 In NT times the best man brought the bride to **the bridegroom**. John had brought the people of Israel to Jesus.

3:36 Those who reject Christ also reject His gift of life. In consequence, such individuals will experience the **wrath of God**, not in a fleeting moment, but as a permanent state of existence.

4:4 Because of the history of antagonism between the two peoples, Jews usually traveled the longer route to avoid contact with Samaritans. However, Jesus' love extended even to these undesirables and compelled Him to go through Samaria.

4:5, 6 plot of ground: Gen. 33:18, 19 and Josh. 24:32 tell how this ground was acquired by **Jacob** and designated for the family of **Joseph**. **being wearied from His journey**: A simple but telling reference to Jesus' humanity. He too knows the feeling of exhaustion we experience after a hard day's work.

is called Sȳ'char, near the plot of ground
that Jacob gave to his son Joseph. 6Now Ja-
cob's well was there. Jesus therefore, being
wearied from *His* journey, sat thus by the
well. It was about the sixth hour.
7A woman of Samaria came to draw wa-
ter. Jesus said to her, "Give Me a drink."
8For His disciples had gone away into the
city to buy food.
9Then the woman of Samaria said to
Him, "How is it that You, being a Jew, ask
a drink from me, a Samaritan woman?"
For Jews have no dealings with Samari-
tans.
10Jesus answered and said to her, "If you
knew the gift of God, and who it is who
says to you, 'Give Me a drink,' you would
have asked Him, and He would have
given you living water."
11The woman said to Him, "Sir, You
have nothing to draw with, and the well is
deep. Where then do You get that living
water? 12Are You greater than our father Ja-
cob, who gave us the well, and drank from
it himself, as well as his sons and his live-
stock?"
13Jesus answered and said to her, "Who-
ever drinks of this water will thirst again,
14but whoever drinks of the water that I
shall give him will never thirst. But the wa-
ter that I shall give him will become in him
a fountain of water springing up into ever-
lasting life."
15The woman said to Him, "Sir, give me
this water, that I may not thirst, nor come
here to draw."
16Jesus said to her, "Go, call your hus-
band, and come here."
17The woman answered and said, "I
have no husband."
Jesus said to her, "You have well said, 'I
have no husband,' 18for you have had five
husbands, and the one whom you now
have is not your husband; in that you
spoke truly."
19The woman said to Him, "Sir, I per-
ceive that You are a prophet. 20Our fathers
worshiped on this mountain, and you *Jews*
say that in Jerusalem is the place where
one ought to worship."
21Jesus said to her, "Woman, believe
Me, the hour is coming when you will
neither on this mountain, nor in Jerusa-
lem, worship the Father. 22You worship
what you do not know; we know what
we worship, for salvation is of the Jews.
23But the hour is coming, and now is,
when the true worshipers will wor-
ship the Father in spirit and truth; for
the Father is seeking such to worship
Him. 24God *is* Spirit, and those who wor-
ship Him must worship in spirit and
truth."
25The woman said to Him, "I know that
Messiah is coming" (who is called Christ).
"When He comes, He will tell us all
things."
26Jesus said to her, "I who speak to you
am *He.*"

The Whitened Harvest

27And at this *point* His disciples came,
and they marveled that He talked with
a woman; yet no one said, "What do
You seek?" or, "Why are You talking with
her?"
28The woman then left her waterpot,
went her way into the city, and said to the
men, 29"Come, see a Man who told me all
things that I ever did. Could this be the
Christ?" 30Then they went out of the city
and came to Him.

4:22 you do not know: Because of the mixture of pagan ideas with the true faith, the Samaritans were confused in their **worship** (see 2 Kin. 17:29–41). **salvation is of the Jews**: God chose to reveal Himself to the Jews, and through them to bring true worship and the Savior to the whole world.

4:23 Jesus' death ushered in a new age of worship, removing the barrier imposed by sin. True worship is now a matter of having a proper, sincere, and active relationship with God.

4:27 Talking to a woman in public was considered improper conduct for a Jewish man.

31In the meantime His disciples urged Him, saying, "Rabbi, eat."

32But He said to them, "I have food to eat of which you do not know."

33Therefore the disciples said to one another, "Has anyone brought Him *anything* to eat?"

34Jesus said to them, "My food is to do the will of Him who sent Me, and to finish His work. 35Do you not say, 'There are still four months and *then* comes the harvest'? Behold, I say to you, lift up your eyes and look at the fields, for they are already white for harvest! 36And he who reaps receives wages, and gathers fruit for eternal life, that both he who sows and he who reaps may rejoice together. 37For in this the saying is true: 'One sows and another reaps.' 38I sent you to reap that for which you have not labored; others have labored, and you have entered into their labors."

The Savior of the World

39And many of the Samaritans of that city believed in Him because of the word of the woman who testified, "He told me all that I *ever* did." 40So when the Samaritans had come to Him, they urged Him to stay with them; and He stayed there two days. 41And many more believed because of His own word.

42Then they said to the woman, "Now we believe, not because of what you said, for we ourselves have heard *Him* and we know that this is indeed the Christ,[a] the Savior of the world."

Welcome at Galilee

43Now after the two days He departed from there and went to Galilee. 44For Jesus Himself testified that a prophet has no honor in his own country. 45So when He came to Galilee, the Galileans received Him, having seen all the things He did in Jerusalem at the feast; for they also had gone to the feast.

A Nobleman's Son Healed

46So Jesus came again to Cā'na of Galilee where He had made the water wine. And there was a certain nobleman whose son was sick at Ca·per'na·um. 47When he heard that Jesus had come out of Judea into Galilee, he went to Him and implored Him to come down and heal his son, for he was at the point of death. 48Then Jesus said to him, "Unless you *people* see signs and wonders, you will by no means believe."

49The nobleman said to Him, "Sir, come down before my child dies!"

50Jesus said to him, "Go your way; your son lives." So the man believed the word that Jesus spoke to him, and he went his way. 51And as he was now going down, his servants met him and told *him*, saying, "Your son lives!"

52Then he inquired of them the hour when he got better. And they said to him, "Yesterday at the seventh hour the fever left him." 53So the father knew that *it was* at the same hour in which Jesus said to him,

4:42 [a]NU-Text omits *the Christ.*

4:37, 38 One sows . . . another reaps: A vital lesson in discipleship. There are various tasks and laborers in the work of the LORD, but all receive honor alike (see 1 Cor. 3:6, 7). We should never feel that our particular role in ministry is trivial.

4:43–54 This healing of the nobleman's son is the **second** (v. 54) of seven miraculous signs that John recounts. It shows that Jesus requires trust of those who would receive a blessing from Him (v. 50). The first sign was the turning of water into wine (2:1–11).

4:46, 47 nobleman: Probably an official of Herod Antipas, ruler of Galilee and Perea (see Luke 3:1).

4:53 Jesus did not perform miracles simply to show His power but to bring observers to faith in Him.

"Your son lives." And he himself believed, and his whole household.

54This again *is* the second sign Jesus did when He had come out of Judea into Galilee.

CHAPTER 5

A Man Healed at the Pool of Bethesda

After this there was a feast of the Jews, and Jesus went up to Jerusalem. 2Now there is in Jerusalem by the Sheep *Gate* a pool, which is called in Hebrew, Bethes'da,[a] having five porches. 3In these lay a great multitude of sick people, blind, lame, paralyzed, waiting for the moving of the water. 4For an angel went down at a certain time into the pool and stirred up the water; then whoever stepped in first, after the stirring of the water, was made well of whatever disease he had.[a] 5Now a certain man was there who had an infirmity thirty-eight years. 6When Jesus saw him lying there, and knew that he already had been *in that condition* a long time, He said to him, "Do you want to be made well?"

7The sick man answered Him, "Sir, I have no man to put me into the pool when the water is stirred up; but while I am coming, another steps down before me."

8Jesus said to him, "Rise, take up your bed and walk." 9And immediately the man was made well, took up his bed, and walked.

And that day was the Sabbath. 10The Jews therefore said to him who was cured, "It is the Sabbath; it is not lawful for you to carry your bed."

11He answered them, "He who made me well said to me, 'Take up your bed and walk.' "

12Then they asked him, "Who is the Man who said to you, 'Take up your bed and walk'?" 13But the one who was healed did not know who it was, for Jesus had withdrawn, a multitude being in *that* place. 14Afterward Jesus found him in the temple, and said to him, "See, you have been made well. Sin no more, lest a worse thing come upon you."

15The man departed and told the Jews that it was Jesus who had made him well.

Honor the Father and the Son

16For this reason the Jews persecuted Jesus, and sought to kill Him,[a] because He had done these things on the Sabbath. 17But Jesus answered them, "My Father has been working until now, and I have been working."

18Therefore the Jews sought all the more to kill Him, because He not only broke the Sabbath, but also said that God was His Father, making Himself equal with God. 19Then Jesus answered and said to them, "Most assuredly, I say to you, the Son can do nothing of Himself, but what He sees the Father do; for whatever He does, the Son also does in like manner. 20For the Father loves the Son, and shows Him all things that He Himself does; and He will show Him greater works than these, that you may marvel. 21For as the Father raises

5:2 [a]NU-Text reads *Bethzatha.* 5:4 [a]NU-Text omits *waiting for the moving of the water* at the end of verse 3, and all of verse 4. 5:16 [a]NU-Text omits *and sought to kill Him.*

5:5–7 Thirty-eight years of confinement and affliction had left the man weak and hopeless. Jesus' question (v. 6) seems intended to challenge the man's will and his openness toward another source of help.

5:16–18 These verses explain why **the Jews** were so angry with Jesus. God had instituted the **Sabbath**, so by claiming authority over it, Jesus had claimed equality with God. **My Father has been working until now** (v. 17): God rested on the Sabbath (see Gen. 2:3), but He did not cease from doing good. He has been giving His blessing ever since. **I have been working**: Jesus too did good on the Sabbath. The Lord's day is a time for us also to be engaged in the work of God.

Do You Want to Be Made Well?

Gloria Gaither

I have always been intrigued by Jesus' statement to the crippled man near the pool of Bethesda, "Do you want to be made well?" On the surface, that sounds like a stupid question. "Of course he wants to be well!" I would probably have said had I been there. "He's been lying here, helpless for thirty-eight years, totally dependent on the others to feed him, clothe him, carry him from place to place. Why, he can't even help himself to the edge of the therapeutic waters when they are troubled. Then you ask if he wants to be well. Anyone in his right mind wants to be well!"

But Jesus knew human nature. He knew the way we cling to the familiar, even when it is painful, to avoid the risk of the unknown. He knew how frightening it can be to face responsibility. He was, no doubt, asking the man, "Are you ready to begin living as a whole person? Are you willing to take the responsibility of making and following through on your own decisions instead of letting others decide for you? Are you ready to live without excuses, to have no one or nothing but yourself to blame for the direction of your life? *Do you want to be made well?*" It was a good question.

"Forsaking the past demands that we move toward and deal with the future."

It is also a question we each must answer, for forgiveness and redemption are only the beginning. Forsaking the past demands that we move toward and deal with the future. The decision to become a "new creation" is the first in a whole lifetime of new choices that have to be made (2 Cor. 5:17). "Forgetting those things which are behind" (Phil. 3:13) is only the beginning. The greatest amount of energy is required for the rest of the task, that of "reaching forward to those things which are ahead" and pressing on "toward the goal" (v. 14). ✦

the dead and gives life to *them,* even so the
Son gives life to whom He will. [22]For the
Father judges no one, but has committed
all judgment to the Son, [23]that all should
honor the Son just as they honor the Father.
He who does not honor the Son does not
honor the Father who sent Him.

Life and Judgment Are Through the Son

[24]"Most assuredly, I say to you, he who
hears My word and believes in Him who
sent Me has everlasting life, and shall not
come into judgment, but has passed from

5:24 Everlasting life begins now. He who **believes** in Christ already has that **life**; he will not be subject to condemnation under the **judgment** of God.

death into life. 25Most assuredly, I say to
you, the hour is coming, and now is, when
the dead will hear the voice of the Son of
God; and those who hear will live. 26For as
the Father has life in Himself, so He has
granted the Son to have life in Himself,
27and has given Him authority to execute
judgment also, because He is the Son of
Man. 28Do not marvel at this; for the hour is
coming in which all who are in the graves
will hear His voice 29and come forth—
those who have done good, to the resurrec-
tion of life, and those who have done evil,
to the resurrection of condemnation. 30I can
of Myself do nothing. As I hear, I judge;
and My judgment is righteous, because I
do not seek My own will but the will of the
Father who sent Me.

The Fourfold Witness

31"If I bear witness of Myself, My wit-
ness is not true. 32There is another who
bears witness of Me, and I know that the
witness which He witnesses of Me is true.
33You have sent to John, and he has borne
witness to the truth. 34Yet I do not receive
testimony from man, but I say these things
that you may be saved. 35He was the burn-
ing and shining lamp, and you were will-
ing for a time to rejoice in his light. 36But I
have a greater witness than John's; for the
works which the Father has given Me to
finish—the very works that I do—bear wit-
ness of Me, that the Father has sent Me.
37And the Father Himself, who sent Me,
has testified of Me. You have neither heard
His voice at any time, nor seen His form.
38But you do not have His word abiding in
you, because whom He sent, Him you do
not believe. 39You search the Scriptures, for
in them you think you have eternal life;
and these are they which testify of Me.
40But you are not willing to come to Me
that you may have life.

41"I do not receive honor from men.
42But I know you, that you do not have
the love of God in you. 43I have come
in My Father's name, and you do not re-
ceive Me; if another comes in his own
name, him you will receive. 44How can
you believe, who receive honor from one
another, and do not seek the honor that
comes from the only God? 45Do not think
that I shall accuse you to the Father;
there is *one* who accuses you—Moses, in
whom you trust. 46For if you believed Mo-
ses, you would believe Me; for he wrote
about Me. 47But if you do not believe his
writings, how will you believe My
words?"

CHAPTER 6

Feeding the Five Thousand

After these things Jesus went over the
Sea of Galilee, which is *the Sea* of Tī·bē′-
ri·as. 2Then a great multitude followed
Him, because they saw His signs which He
performed on those who were diseased.
3And Jesus went up on the mountain, and
there He sat with His disciples.

4Now the Passover, a feast of the Jews,
was near. 5Then Jesus lifted up *His* eyes,
and seeing a great multitude coming to-
ward Him, He said to Philip, "Where shall
we buy bread, that these may eat?" 6But
this He said to test him, for He Himself
knew what He would do.

7Philip answered Him, "Two hundred
denarii worth of bread is not sufficient for
them, that every one of them may have a
little."

5:31–47 The term **witness** (testimony, v. 34) is a prominent concept in John. Though Jesus' testimony about Himself was true, under Jewish law one's self-testimony was not admissible in legal proceedings. **another**: The Father is Jesus' primary and ultimate witness (see v. 37). Jesus also points His hearers to three other witnesses: **John** the Baptist, Jesus' own **works**, and the **Scriptures**, especially the writings of **Moses**.

6:7 denarii: One denarius was equal to a laborer's daily wage.

8One of His disciples, Andrew, Simon
Peter's brother, said to Him, 9"There is a
lad here who has five barley loaves and
two small fish, but what are they among so
many?"
10Then Jesus said, "Make the people sit
down." Now there was much grass in the
place. So the men sat down, in number
about five thousand. 11And Jesus took the
loaves, and when He had given thanks He
distributed *them* to the disciples, and the
disciples[a] to those sitting down; and like-
wise of the fish, as much as they wanted.
12So when they were filled, He said to His
disciples, "Gather up the fragments that
remain, so that nothing is lost." 13Therefore
they gathered *them* up, and filled twelve
baskets with the fragments of the five bar-
ley loaves which were left over by those
who had eaten. 14Then those men, when
they had seen the sign that Jesus did, said,
"This is truly the Prophet who is to come
into the world."

Jesus Walks on the Sea

15Therefore when Jesus perceived that
they were about to come and take Him by
force to make Him king, He departed
again to the mountain by Himself alone.
16Now when evening came, His disci-
ples went down to the sea, 17got into the
boat, and went over the sea toward
Ca·per'na·um. And it was already dark,
and Jesus had not come to them. 18Then the
sea arose because a great wind was blow-
ing. 19So when they had rowed about three
or four miles,[a] they saw Jesus walking on
the sea and drawing near the boat; and
they were afraid. 20But He said to them, "It
is I; do not be afraid." 21Then they willingly
received Him into the boat, and immedi-
ately the boat was at the land where they
were going.

The Bread from Heaven

22On the following day, when the people
who were standing on the other side of the
sea saw that there was no other boat there,
except that one which His disciples had
entered,[a] and that Jesus had not entered
the boat with His disciples, but His disci-
ples had gone away alone— 23however,
other boats came from Tī·bē'ri·as, near the
place where they ate bread after the Lord
had given thanks— 24when the people
therefore saw that Jesus was not there, nor
His disciples, they also got into boats and
came to Ca·per'na·um, seeking Jesus.
25And when they found Him on the other
side of the sea, they said to Him, "Rabbi,
when did You come here?"
26Jesus answered them and said, "Most
assuredly, I say to you, you seek Me, not
because you saw the signs, but because
you ate of the loaves and were filled. 27Do
not labor for the food which perishes, but
for the food which endures to everlasting
life, which the Son of Man will give you,
because God the Father has set His seal on
Him."
28Then they said to Him, "What shall
we do, that we may work the works of
God?"

6:11 [a]NU-Text omits *to the disciples, and the disciples.*
6:19 [a]Literally *twenty-five or thirty stadia*
6:22 [a]NU-Text omits *that* and *which His disciples had entered.*

6:9 barley loaves: bread eaten by the very poor. **small fish**: essentially large dried minnows.

6:15 king: A political savior. They wanted Jesus on their terms to use for their ends. But we can have Him only on His terms.

6:16–21 This miracle shows that Jesus is Lord even of nature. He is much more powerful than any political king (see v. 15), able to help His followers in every situation. We have no need to fear the storms of life, for our God is all-powerful.

6:28, 29 There is one essential **work of God**—to **believe** in the One **sent** by Him. Every other deed that pleases God is founded on this one. All our good deeds mean nothing unless they are prompted by our faith in and acceptance of Jesus Christ.

29 Jesus answered and said to them,
"This is the work of God, that you believe
in Him whom He sent."
30 Therefore they said to Him, "What
sign will You perform then, that we may
see it and believe You? What work will You
do? 31 Our fathers ate the manna in the
desert; as it is written, *'He gave them bread
from heaven to eat.'*"[a]
32 Then Jesus said to them, "Most as-
suredly, I say to you, Moses did not give
you the bread from heaven, but My Father
gives you the true bread from heaven. 33 For
the bread of God is He who comes down
from heaven and gives life to the world."
34 Then they said to Him, "Lord, give us
this bread always."
35 And Jesus said to them, "I am the
bread of life. He who comes to Me shall
never hunger, and he who believes in Me
shall never thirst. 36 But I said to you that
you have seen Me and yet do not believe.
37 All that the Father gives Me will come to
Me, and the one who comes to Me I will by
no means cast out. 38 For I have come down
from heaven, not to do My own will, but
the will of Him who sent Me. 39 This is the
will of the Father who sent Me, that of all
He has given Me I should lose nothing, but
should raise it up at the last day. 40 And this
is the will of Him who sent Me, that every-
one who sees the Son and believes in Him
may have everlasting life; and I will raise
him up at the last day."

Rejected by His Own

41 The Jews then complained about Him,
because He said, "I am the bread which
came down from heaven." 42 And they said,
"Is not this Jesus, the son of Joseph, whose
father and mother we know? How is it
then that He says, 'I have come down from
heaven'?"
43 Jesus therefore answered and said to
them, "Do not murmur among yourselves.
44 No one can come to Me unless the Father
who sent Me draws him; and I will raise
him up at the last day. 45 It is written in the
prophets, *'And they shall all be taught by
God.'*[a] Therefore everyone who has heard
and learned[b] from the Father comes to Me.
46 Not that anyone has seen the Father, ex-
cept He who is from God; He has seen the
Father. 47 Most assuredly, I say to you, he
who believes in Me[a] has everlasting life.
48 I am the bread of life. 49 Your fathers ate
the manna in the wilderness, and are dead.
50 This is the bread which comes down from
heaven, that one may eat of it and not die.
51 I am the living bread which came down
from heaven. If anyone eats of this bread,
he will live forever; and the bread that I
shall give is My flesh, which I shall give for
the life of the world."
52 The Jews therefore quarreled among
themselves, saying, "How can this Man
give us *His* flesh to eat?"
53 Then Jesus said to them, "Most as-
suredly, I say to you, unless you eat the
flesh of the Son of Man and drink His
blood, you have no life in you. 54 Whoever
eats My flesh and drinks My blood has
eternal life, and I will raise him up at the
last day. 55 For My flesh is food indeed,[a] and
My blood is drink indeed. 56 He who eats
My flesh and drinks My blood abides
in Me, and I in him. 57 As the living Father
sent Me, and I live because of the Father,
so he who feeds on Me will live because
of Me. 58 This is the bread which came
down from heaven—not as your fathers

6:31 [a]Exodus 16:4; Nehemiah 9:15; Psalm 78:24
6:45 [a]Isaiah 54:13 [b]M-Text reads *hears and has learned.* 6:47 [a]NU-Text omits *in Me.*
6:55 [a]NU-Text reads *true food* and *true drink.*

6:35, 36 I am: This is the first of Jesus' seven "I am" discourses through which He expressed His power and the work He had come to do. He Himself is the **bread of life**; to partake of that bread one must **believe** in Him. **never hunger . . . never thirst**: Jesus fully satisfies the deepest need of the human heart, but that satisfaction is forfeited by those who **do not believe**.

ate the manna, and are dead. He who eats this bread will live forever."

59These things He said in the synagogue as He taught in Ca·per'na·um.

Many Disciples Turn Away

60Therefore many of His disciples, when they heard *this,* said, "This is a hard saying; who can understand it?"

61When Jesus knew in Himself that His disciples complained about this, He said to them, "Does this offend you? 62*What* then if you should see the Son of Man ascend where He was before? 63It is the Spirit who gives life; the flesh profits nothing. The words that I speak to you are spirit, and *they* are life. 64But there are some of you who do not believe." For Jesus knew from the beginning who they were who did not believe, and who would betray Him. 65And He said, "Therefore I have said to you that no one can come to Me unless it has been granted to him by My Father."

66From that *time* many of His disciples went back and walked with Him no more. 67Then Jesus said to the twelve, "Do you also want to go away?"

68But Simon Peter answered Him, "Lord, to whom shall we go? You have the words of eternal life. 69Also we have come to believe and know that You are the Christ, the Son of the living God."[a]

70Jesus answered them, "Did I not choose you, the twelve, and one of you is a devil?" 71He spoke of Judas Is·car'i·ot, *the son* of Simon, for it was he who would betray Him, being one of the twelve.

CHAPTER 7

Jesus' Brothers Disbelieve

After these things Jesus walked in Galilee; for He did not want to walk in Judea, because the Jews[a] sought to kill Him. 2Now the Jews' Feast of Tabernacles was at hand. 3His brothers therefore said to Him, "Depart from here and go into Judea, that Your disciples also may see the works that You are doing. 4For no one does anything in secret while he himself seeks to be known openly. If You do these things, show Yourself to the world." 5For even His brothers did not believe in Him.

6Then Jesus said to them, "My time has not yet come, but your time is always ready. 7The world cannot hate you, but it hates Me because I testify of it that its works are evil. 8You go up to this feast. I am not yet[a] going up to this feast, for My time has not yet fully come." 9When He had said these things to them, He remained in Galilee.

The Heavenly Scholar

10But when His brothers had gone up, then He also went up to the feast, not openly, but as it were in secret. 11Then the Jews sought Him at the feast, and said, "Where is He?" 12And there was much complaining among the people concerning Him. Some said, "He is good"; others said, "No, on the contrary, He deceives the people." 13However, no one spoke openly of Him for fear of the Jews.

6:69 [a]NU-Text reads *You are the Holy One of God.*
7:1 [a]That is, the ruling authorities 7:8 [a]NU-Text omits *yet.*

6:64, 65 An early indication of the unbelief of Judas who would **betray** Jesus (see vv. 70, 71).

7:2–5 The **Feast of Tabernacles** (see Lev. 23:33–44) was observed on the 15th day of the month of Tishri, corresponding to the beginning of October. The remarks of Jesus' **brothers** appear to be sarcastic: "If You are who You claim to be, and Your works are so great and worthy, display them openly in Judea, and You will be duly noted." However, after the resurrection, Jesus' brothers were counted among the believers (Acts 1:14).

7:6–9 Jesus' **time** was not governed by the world's schedule, but by the Father. The **hate** of **the world** was a natural response to Jesus' pointing out its **evil**. If our lives reflect Jesus clearly, the unsaved people we encounter will be convicted by their own sinfulness and may even hate us for the guilt they feel.

14 Now about the middle of the feast Je-
sus went up into the temple and taught.
15 And the Jews marveled, saying, "How
does this Man know letters, having never
studied?"

16 Jesus[a] answered them and said, "My
doctrine is not Mine, but His who sent Me.
17 If anyone wills to do His will, he shall
know concerning the doctrine, whether it
is from God or *whether* I speak on My own
authority. 18 He who speaks from himself
seeks his own glory; but He who seeks the
glory of the One who sent Him is true, and
no unrighteousness is in Him. 19 Did not
Moses give you the law, yet none of you
keeps the law? Why do you seek to kill
Me?"

20 The people answered and said, "You
have a demon. Who is seeking to kill You?"

21 Jesus answered and said to them, "I
did one work, and you all marvel. 22 Moses
therefore gave you circumcision (not that it
is from Moses, but from the fathers), and
you circumcise a man on the Sabbath. 23 If a
man receives circumcision on the Sabbath,
so that the law of Moses should not be
broken, are you angry with Me because
I made a man completely well on the
Sabbath? 24 Do not judge according to ap-
pearance, but judge with righteous judg-
ment."

Could This Be the Christ?

25 Now some of them from Jerusalem
said, "Is this not He whom they seek to
kill? 26 But look! He speaks boldly, and they
say nothing to Him. Do the rulers know in-
deed that this is truly[a] the Christ? 27 How-
ever, we know where this Man is from; but
when the Christ comes, no one knows
where He is from."

28 Then Jesus cried out, as He taught in
the temple, saying, "You both know Me,
and you know where I am from; and I have
not come of Myself, but He who sent Me is
true, whom you do not know. 29 But[a] I know
Him, for I am from Him, and He sent Me."

30 Therefore they sought to take Him; but
no one laid a hand on Him, because His
hour had not yet come. 31 And many of the
people believed in Him, and said, "When
the Christ comes, will He do more signs
than these which this *Man* has done?"

Jesus and the Religious Leaders

32 The Phar'i·sees heard the crowd mur-
muring these things concerning Him, and
the Phar'i·sees and the chief priests sent of-
ficers to take Him. 33 Then Jesus said to
them,[a] "I shall be with you a little while
longer, and *then* I go to Him who sent Me.
34 You will seek Me and not find *Me,* and
where I am you cannot come."

35 Then the Jews said among themselves,
"Where does He intend to go that we shall
not find Him? Does He intend to go to the
Dispersion among the Greeks and teach
the Greeks? 36 What is this thing that He
said, 'You will seek Me and not find Me,
and where I am you cannot come'?"

The Promise of the Holy Spirit

37 On the last day, that great *day* of the
feast, Jesus stood and cried out, saying, "If
anyone thirsts, let him come to Me and

7:16 [a]NU-Text and M-Text read *So Jesus.* 7:26 [a]NU-Text omits *truly.* 7:29 [a]NU-Text and M-Text omit *But.* 7:33 [a]NU-Text and M-Text omit *to them.*

7:15 The Jews are amazed at Jesus' knowledge of Scriptures despite His lack of rabbinical training. Jesus' words ring with authority because the source of His doctrinal understanding is God Himself.

7:21 one work: healing the crippled man at the pool of Bethesda.

7:30 they: The rulers **sought** to arrest Him. **His hour**: The time for His suffering and death. The Father was in control.

7:32 officers: Temple guards directed by the priests.

7:35 the Dispersion: Jews scattered throughout the Greek world.

7:37, 38 great day of the feast: Probably the seventh day. Water was poured out at the altar

drink. 38He who believes in Me, as the
Scripture has said, out of his heart will
flow rivers of living water." 39But this He
spoke concerning the Spirit, whom those
believing[a] in Him would receive; for the
Holy[b] Spirit was not yet *given*, because
Jesus was not yet glorified.

Who Is He?

40Therefore many[a] from the crowd,
when they heard this saying, said, "Truly
this is the Prophet." 41Others said, "This is
the Christ."

But some said, "Will the Christ come
out of Galilee? 42Has not the Scripture said
that the Christ comes from the seed of Da-
vid and from the town of Bethlehem,
where David was?" 43So there was a divi-
sion among the people because of Him.
44Now some of them wanted to take Him,
but no one laid hands on Him.

Rejected by the Authorities

45Then the officers came to the chief
priests and Phar'i·sees, who said to them,
"Why have you not brought Him?"

46The officers answered, "No man ever
spoke like this Man!"

47Then the Phar'i·sees answered them,
"Are you also deceived? 48Have any of the
rulers or the Phar'i·sees believed in Him?
49But this crowd that does not know the
law is accursed."

50Nic·o·dē'mus (he who came to Jesus
by night,[a] being one of them) said to them,
51"Does our law judge a man before it hears
him and knows what he is doing?"

52They answered and said to him, "Are
you also from Galilee? Search and look, for
no prophet has arisen[a] out of Galilee."

An Adulteress Faces the Light of the World

53And everyone went to his *own* house.[a]

CHAPTER 8

But Jesus went to the Mount of Olives.
2Now early[a] in the morning He came
again into the temple, and all the people
came to Him; and He sat down and taught
them. 3Then the scribes and Phar'i·sees
brought to Him a woman caught in adul-
tery. And when they had set her in the
midst, 4they said to Him, "Teacher, this
woman was caught[a] in adultery, in the
very act. 5Now Moses, in the law, com-
manded[a] us that such should be stoned.[b]
But what do You say?"[c] 6This they said,
testing Him, that they might have *some-
thing* of which to accuse Him. But Jesus
stooped down and wrote on the ground
with *His* finger, as though He did not hear.[a]

7So when they continued asking Him,
He raised Himself up[a] and said to them,
"He who is without sin among you, let him
throw a stone at her first." 8And again He

7:39 [a]NU-Text reads *who believed.* [b]NU-Text omits *Holy.* 7:40 [a]NU-Text reads *some.* 7:50 [a]NU-Text reads *before.* 7:52 [a]NU-Text reads *is to rise.* 7:53 [a]The words *And everyone* through *sin no more* (8:11) are bracketed by NU-Text as not original. They are present in over 900 manuscripts. 8:2 [a]M-Text reads *very early.* 8:4 [a]M-Text reads *we found this woman.* 8:5 [a]M-Text reads *in our law Moses commanded.* [b]NU-Text and M-Text read *to stone such.* [c]M-Text adds *about her.* 8:6 [a]NU-Text and M-Text omit *as though He did not hear.* 8:7 [a]M-Text reads *He looked up.*

---

as part of that day's ritual. This furnished a fitting framework for Jesus' call to **come . . . and drink**, and for His promise of **rivers of living water**.

7:41–44 Those who objected that Jesus was from **Galilee**, and so could not be **the Christ**, were obviously unaware of His birth in **Bethlehem** (v. 42).

7:45–49 The **officers** were so impressed with our Lord's teachings that they risked the ire of the **chief priests** and **Pharisees** rather than arrest Jesus. **this crowd** (v. 49): Disdain for those who supported Jesus.

8:3–11 The Pharisees did not bring the adulteress to Jesus out of a passion for righteousness but because of their desire to trap Him. If He said, "Let the woman go," they could accuse Him of breaking the law of Moses; if He upheld the law and said, "Stone her," He would be violating Roman law, which prohibited executions without government approval.

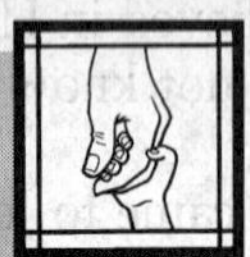

LIVING ON . . . AND ON . . .

Ron Lee Davis

We live on after our death in two ways: First, we live on in eternity with Jesus. Second, we live on in the lives of those whom we have mentored.

Whenever I spend time with someone who has been profoundly influenced by the life of my father or my brother, I feel refreshment and joy. It's as if I am actually in the presence of that departed loved one and, in a very real sense, I *am*.

A part of my brother lives on in the scores of lives he affected as a teacher, coach, and mentor in Colorado and across the country. A part of my father lives on in the scores of lives he touched and imprinted during his twenty-five years as a pastor in Iowa.

Every time I go back to my hometown of Clarinda, Iowa, people tell me how much they loved my dad and how they fondly recall the things he did to help people in the church and the community. But more than that, I can see that something of the Christlikeness of my father has become embedded in the lives of these people, making them more like Christ.

Just think of it: You and I can be immortal, not only in eternity but here on earth. Even after your death, you can reach out and touch unborn generations through the life of someone you have mentored. You can continue to impact countless lives, long after you have gone to be with the Lord, because you have lived the lifestyle of a mentor. ✦

stooped down and wrote on the ground.
9Then those who heard *it,* being convicted
by *their* conscience,[a] went out one by one,
beginning with the oldest *even* to the last.
And Jesus was left alone, and the woman
standing in the midst. 10When Jesus had
raised Himself up and saw no one but the
woman, He said to her,[a] "Woman, where
are those accusers of yours?[b] Has no one
condemned you?"
11She said, "No one, Lord."
And Jesus said to her, "Neither do I condemn you; go and[a] sin no more."

12Then Jesus spoke to them again, saying, "I am the light of the world. He who follows Me shall not walk in darkness, but have the light of life."

Jesus Defends His Self-Witness

13The Phar'i·sees therefore said to Him,
"You bear witness of Yourself; Your witness is not true."

8:9 [a]NU-Text and M-Text omit *being convicted by their conscience.* 8:10 [a]NU-Text omits *and saw no one but the woman;* M-Text reads *He saw her and said.* [b]NU-Text and M-Text omit *of yours.* 8:11 [a]NU-Text and M-Text add *from now on.*

8:9 the oldest even to the last: This order was followed because of the elders' natural seniority and perhaps because of their greater sense of guilt. Where matters of righteousness are concerned, we who are older should lead the way.

8:12 I am the light of the world: The second great "I am" of Jesus (see 6:35, 36 and note), spoken with divine authority. Jesus is the source of spiritual enlightenment. He picks up this theme again when He heals the blind man (see 9:5).

I pray that my grandchildren shall know the truth, and the truth shall make them free.

adapted from John 8:32

14Jesus answered and said to them,
"Even if I bear witness of Myself, My
witness is true, for I know where I came
from and where I am going; but you
do not know where I come from and where
I am going. 15You judge according to the
flesh; I judge no one. 16And yet if I
do judge, My judgment is true; for I am
not alone, but I *am* with the Father who
sent Me. 17It is also written in your law that
the testimony of two men is true. 18I
am One who bears witness of Myself, and
the Father who sent Me bears witness of
Me."
19Then they said to Him, "Where is Your
Father?"
Jesus answered, "You know neither Me
nor My Father. If you had known Me, you
would have known My Father also."
20These words Jesus spoke in the trea-
sury, as He taught in the temple; and no
one laid hands on Him, for His hour had
not yet come.

Jesus Predicts His Departure

21Then Jesus said to them again, "I am
going away, and you will seek Me, and will
die in your sin. Where I go you cannot
come."
22So the Jews said, "Will He kill Himself,
because He says, 'Where I go you cannot
come'?"
23And He said to them, "You are from
beneath; I am from above. You are of this
world; I am not of this world. 24Therefore I
said to you that you will die in your sins;
for if you do not believe that I am *He,* you
will die in your sins."
25Then they said to Him, "Who are
You?"
And Jesus said to them, "Just what I
have been saying to you from the begin-
ning. 26I have many things to say and to
judge concerning you, but He who sent Me
is true; and I speak to the world those
things which I heard from Him."
27They did not understand that He
spoke to them of the Father.
28Then Jesus said to them, "When you
lift up the Son of Man, then you will know
that I am *He,* and *that* I do nothing of My-
self; but as My Father taught Me, I speak
these things. 29And He who sent Me is with
Me. The Father has not left Me alone, for I
always do those things that please Him."
30As He spoke these words, many believed
in Him.

The Truth Shall Make You Free

31Then Jesus said to those Jews who be-
lieved Him, "If you abide in My word, you
are My disciples indeed. 32And you shall
know the truth, and the truth shall make
you free."
33They answered Him, "We are Abra-
ham's descendants, and have never been
in bondage to anyone. How *can* You say,
'You will be made free'?"
34Jesus answered them, "Most as-
suredly, I say to you, whoever commits sin

8:23–26 Jesus' divine identity is established because His origin is **from above** and His nature is **not of this world** (v. 23). He is claiming to be God as well as the promised Messiah. In vv. 28, 58 He declares, **I am**, a statement reminiscent of God's words to Moses (Ex. 3:14).

8:31, 32 Though many **believed Him**, Jesus says it is necessary to go beyond initial acceptance of His **word**. We must **abide** in His teaching. Those who thus continue to live by the **truth** are made **free** from the bondage of sin.

is a slave of sin. 35And a slave does not
abide in the house forever, *but* a son abides
forever. 36Therefore if the Son makes you
free, you shall be free indeed.

Abraham's Seed and Satan's

37"I know that you are Abraham's de-
scendants, but you seek to kill Me, because
My word has no place in you. 38I speak
what I have seen with My Father, and you
do what you have seen with[a] your father."
39They answered and said to Him,
"Abraham is our father."
Jesus said to them, "If you were Abra-
ham's children, you would do the works of
Abraham. 40But now you seek to kill Me, a
Man who has told you the truth which I
heard from God. Abraham did not do this.
41You do the deeds of your father."
Then they said to Him, "We were not
born of fornication; we have one Father—
God."
42Jesus said to them, "If God were your
Father, you would love Me, for I proceeded
forth and came from God; nor have I come
of Myself, but He sent Me. 43Why do you
not understand My speech? Because you
are not able to listen to My word. 44You are
of *your* father the devil, and the desires of
your father you want to do. He was a mur-
derer from the beginning, and does not
stand in the truth, because there is no truth
in him. When he speaks a lie, he speaks
from his own *resources,* for he is a liar and
the father of it. 45But because I tell the truth,
you do not believe Me. 46Which of you con-
victs Me of sin? And if I tell the truth, why
do you not believe Me? 47He who is of God
hears God's words; therefore you do not
hear, because you are not of God."

Before Abraham Was, I AM

48Then the Jews answered and said to
Him, "Do we not say rightly that You are a
Samaritan and have a demon?"
49Jesus answered, "I do not have a de-
mon; but I honor My Father, and you dis-
honor Me. 50And I do not seek My *own*
glory; there is One who seeks and judges.
51Most assuredly, I say to you, if anyone
keeps My word he shall never see death."
52Then the Jews said to Him, "Now we
know that You have a demon! Abraham is
dead, and the prophets; and You say, 'If
anyone keeps My word he shall never taste
death.' 53Are You greater than our father
Abraham, who is dead? And the prophets
are dead. Who do You make Yourself out to
be?"
54Jesus answered, "If I honor Myself, My
honor is nothing. It is My Father who hon-
ors Me, of whom you say that He is your[a]
God. 55Yet you have not known Him, but I
know Him. And if I say, 'I do not know
Him,' I shall be a liar like you; but I do
know Him and keep His word. 56Your
father Abraham rejoiced to see My day,
and he saw *it* and was glad."
57Then the Jews said to Him, "You are
not yet fifty years old, and have You seen
Abraham?"

8:38 [a]NU-Text reads *heard from.*
8:54 [a]NU-Text and M-Text read *our.*

8:41 born of fornication: Used figuratively. They realized that Jesus had been talking about a spiritual relationship in vv. 37–40. They claim they are not opposing God. He is truly their **Father**.

8:48–51 They could not have insulted Jesus more than to call Him a **Samaritan** and charge that His ministry was empowered by a demon. Jesus ignored the Samaritan slur but again called attention to His **Father** (v. 49). Here **death** (v. 51) refers to eternal death.

8:54–59 The issue between Jesus and the Pharisees was basic; He was right and they were wrong. In this there can be no compromise. God, His **Father**, was on Jesus' side. The Pharisees really had no fellowship with Him (v. 55). **Abraham** saw Jesus' **day** when the pre-incarnate Christ acted on his behalf (see Gen. 18:10; 21:1, 2; 22:11–13). **I AM** (v. 58) expresses Jesus' eternal existence and deity. This statement would be rank blasphemy to the Jews. See note on vv. 23–26.

58Jesus said to them, "Most assuredly, I
say to you, before Abraham was, I AM."
59Then they took up stones to throw at
Him; but Jesus hid Himself and went out
of the temple,[a] going through the midst of
them, and so passed by.

CHAPTER 9

A Man Born Blind Receives Sight

Now as *Jesus* passed by, He saw a man
who was blind from birth. 2And His disci-
ples asked Him, saying, "Rabbi, who
sinned, this man or his parents, that he was
born blind?"
3Jesus answered, "Neither this man nor
his parents sinned, but that the works of
God should be revealed in him. 4I[a] must
work the works of Him who sent Me while
it is day; *the* night is coming when no one
can work. 5As long as I am in the world, I
am the light of the world."
6When He had said these things, He
spat on the ground and made clay with the
saliva; and He anointed the eyes of the
blind man with the clay. 7And He said to
him, "Go, wash in the pool of Sī·lō'am"
(which is translated, Sent). So he went and
washed, and came back seeing.
8Therefore the neighbors and those who
previously had seen that he was blind[a]
said, "Is not this he who sat and begged?"
9Some said, "This is he." Others *said*,
"He is like him."[a]
He said, "I am *he*."
10Therefore they said to him, "How were
your eyes opened?"
11He answered and said, "A Man called
Jesus made clay and anointed my eyes and
said to me, 'Go to the pool of[a] Sī·lō'am and
wash.' So I went and washed, and I re-
ceived sight."
12Then they said to him, "Where is He?"
He said, "I do not know."

The Pharisees Excommunicate the Healed Man

13They brought him who formerly was
blind to the Phar'i·sees. 14Now it was a
Sabbath when Jesus made the clay and
opened his eyes. 15Then the Phar'i·sees also
asked him again how he had received his
sight. He said to them, "He put clay on my
eyes, and I washed, and I see."
16Therefore some of the Phar'i·sees said,
"This Man is not from God, because He
does not keep the Sabbath."
Others said, "How can a man who is a
sinner do such signs?" And there was a
division among them.
17They said to the blind man again,
"What do you say about Him because He
opened your eyes?"
He said, "He is a prophet."
18But the Jews did not believe concern-
ing him, that he had been blind and re-
ceived his sight, until they called the par-
ents of him who had received his sight.
19And they asked them, saying, "Is this
your son, who you say was born blind?
How then does he now see?"
20His parents answered them and said,
"We know that this is our son, and that he
was born blind; 21but by what means he
now sees we do not know, or who opened
his eyes we do not know. He is of age; ask
him. He will speak for himself." 22His par-
ents said these *things* because they feared
the Jews, for the Jews had agreed already
that if anyone confessed *that* He *was* Christ,
he would be put out of the synagogue.
23Therefore his parents said, "He is of age;
ask him."
24So they again called the man who was
blind, and said to him, "Give God the
glory! We know that this Man is a sinner."

8:59 [a]NU-Text omits the rest of this verse. 9:4 [a]NU-Text reads *We*. 9:8 [a]NU-Text reads *a beggar*. 9:9 [a]NU-Text reads *"No, but he is like him."* 9:11 [a]NU-Text omits *the pool of*.

9:7 The sixth of seven miraculous signs detailed by John.

25 He answered and said, "Whether He is
a sinner *or not* I do not know. One thing I
know: that though I was blind, now I see."
26 Then they said to him again, "What
did He do to you? How did He open your
eyes?"
27 He answered them, "I told you al-
ready, and you did not listen. Why do you
want to hear *it* again? Do you also want to
become His disciples?"
28 Then they reviled him and said, "You
are His disciple, but we are Moses' disci-
ples. 29 We know that God spoke to Moses;
as for this *fellow,* we do not know where He
is from."
30 The man answered and said to them,
"Why, this is a marvelous thing, that you
do not know where He is from; yet He has
opened my eyes! 31 Now we know that God
does not hear sinners; but if anyone is a
worshiper of God and does His will, He
hears him. 32 Since the world began it has
been unheard of that anyone opened the
eyes of one who was born blind. 33 If this
Man were not from God, He could do
nothing."
34 They answered and said to him, "You
were completely born in sins, and are you
teaching us?" And they cast him out.

True Vision and True Blindness

35 Jesus heard that they had cast him out;
and when He had found him, He said to
him, "Do you believe in the Son of God?"[a]
36 He answered and said, "Who is He,
Lord, that I may believe in Him?"
37 And Jesus said to him, "You have both
seen Him and it is He who is talking with
you."
38 Then he said, "Lord, I believe!" And he
worshiped Him.
39 And Jesus said, "For judgment I have
come into this world, that those who do
not see may see, and that those who see
may be made blind."
40 Then *some* of the Phar'i·sees who were
with Him heard these words, and said to
Him, "Are we blind also?"
41 Jesus said to them, "If you were blind,
you would have no sin; but now you say,
'We see.' Therefore your sin remains.

CHAPTER 10

Jesus the True Shepherd

"Most assuredly, I say to you, he who
does not enter the sheepfold by the door,
but climbs up some other way, the same is
a thief and a robber. 2 But he who enters by
the door is the shepherd of the sheep. 3 To
him the doorkeeper opens, and the sheep
hear his voice; and he calls his own sheep
by name and leads them out. 4 And when
he brings out his own sheep, he goes be-
fore them; and the sheep follow him, for
they know his voice. 5 Yet they will by no
means follow a stranger, but will flee from
him, for they do not know the voice of
strangers." 6 Jesus used this illustration, but
they did not understand the things which
He spoke to them.

Jesus the Good Shepherd

7 Then Jesus said to them again, "Most
assuredly, I say to you, I am the door of the
sheep. 8 All who *ever* came before Me[a] are

9:35 [a]NU-Text reads *Son of Man.* 10:8 [a]M-Text omits *before Me.*

10:1–30 Jesus explains the parable of the sheepfold (vv. 1–6) by two more "I am" statements: **I am the door** (v. 7) and **I am the good shepherd**. The background of this parable is Ezek. 34. There the rulers of God's people were unfaithful, so God promised to send a true Shepherd to be their Savior.

10:7–10 A shepherd would often sleep at the entrance to the sheepfold, literally making his body the door of the fold. In the analogy, Jesus is first the door—the only way to be saved (v. 9). Those who came before Him (v. 8) would include false messiahs who arose following the Exile, and perhaps also the Jewish authorities of Jesus' day. Go in and out and find pasture (v. 9) indicates the peace and safety of the sheep in their shepherd's care.

thieves and robbers, but the sheep did not hear them. 9I am the door. If anyone enters by Me, he will be saved, and will go in and out and find pasture. 10The thief does not come except to steal, and to kill, and to destroy. I have come that they may have life, and that they may have *it* more abundantly.

11"I am the good shepherd. The good shepherd gives His life for the sheep. 12But a hireling, *he who is* not the shepherd, one who does not own the sheep, sees the wolf coming and leaves the sheep and flees; and the wolf catches the sheep and scatters them. 13The hireling flees because he is a hireling and does not care about the sheep. 14I am the good shepherd; and I know My *sheep,* and am known by My own. 15As the Father knows Me, even so I know the Father; and I lay down My life for the sheep. 16And other sheep I have which are not of this fold; them also I must bring, and they will hear My voice; and there will be one flock *and* one shepherd.

17"Therefore My Father loves Me, because I lay down My life that I may take it again. 18No one takes it from Me, but I lay it down of Myself. I have power to lay it down, and I have power to take it again. This command I have received from My Father."

19Therefore there was a division again among the Jews because of these sayings. 20And many of them said, "He has a demon and is mad. Why do you listen to Him?"

21Others said, "These are not the words of one who has a demon. Can a demon open the eyes of the blind?"

The Shepherd Knows His Sheep

22Now it was the Feast of Dedication in Jerusalem, and it was winter. 23And Jesus walked in the temple, in Solomon's porch. 24Then the Jews surrounded Him and said to Him, "How long do You keep us in doubt? If You are the Christ, tell us plainly."

25Jesus answered them, "I told you, and you do not believe. The works that I do in My Father's name, they bear witness of Me. 26But you do not believe, because you are not of My sheep, as I said to you.[a] 27My sheep hear My voice, and I know them, and they follow Me. 28And I give them eternal life, and they shall never perish; neither shall anyone snatch them out of My hand. 29My Father, who has given *them* to Me, is greater than all; and no one is able to snatch *them* out of My Father's hand. 30I and *My* Father are one."

Renewed Efforts to Stone Jesus

31Then the Jews took up stones again to stone Him. 32Jesus answered them, "Many good works I have shown you from My Father. For which of those works do you stone Me?"

33The Jews answered Him, saying, "For a good work we do not stone You, but for blasphemy, and because You, being a Man, make Yourself God."

34Jesus answered them, "Is it not written in your law, *'I said, "You are gods"'*?[a] 35If

10:26 [a]NU-Text omits *as I said to you.* 10:34 [a]Psalm 82:6

10:11–13 Though a Palestinian shepherd cared for his sheep, it would be unusual for him to die defending them. But Jesus is the **good shepherd** because His purpose is to willingly give **His life for the sheep**. In contrast, the **hireling** represents religious leaders who use their people for their own selfish purposes.

10:16 other sheep: Non-Jewish believers and, by extension, future believers of all nations. **One flock . . . one shepherd** expresses the kind of unity for which Jesus prayed in 17:21.

10:17, 18 I lay down my life: No man could kill Jesus because He is God; thus He willingly gave up His life to fulfill His Father's plan.

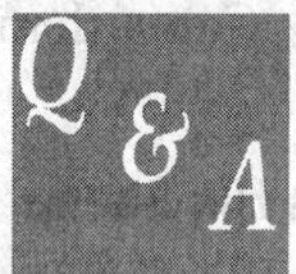

How long does it usually take to work through the grieving process?

The normal grief process includes five distinct stages, although one or more stages may overlap. First is denial or disbelief. This period may last as little as a few moments to as much as several days (or even years in rare cases).

Next is usually anger. "This is so unfair!" says the grieving one. This stage often includes anger toward God for "allowing" this to happen. The distorted logic of grief may even make the mourner wonder, "How could this have happened to a Christian?"

Then the grieving person typically will move to guilt and say many sentences starting with, "If only I had . . ." Some of this guilt may have validity and need to be resolved, but most is false guilt prompted by the turmoil of emotional pain and a sense of loss.

Once the extent of the loss settles in, true grief will appear, usually manifested by deep sadness and tears. This normal reaction is necessary and important. Although one does not have to be overcome with emotion to release the stress of grief, holding back feelings prolongs and worsens the pain.

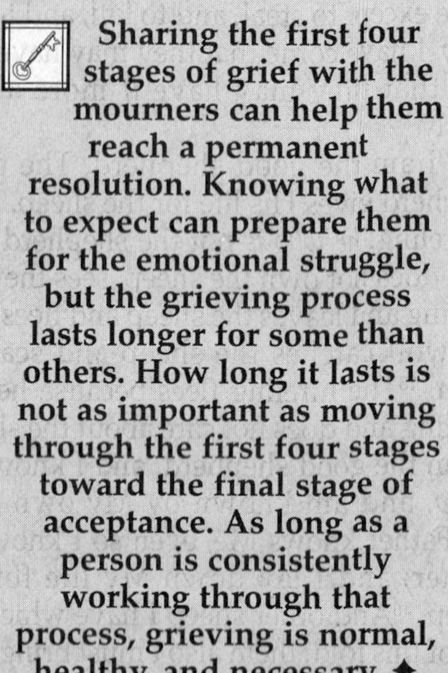

Sharing the first four stages of grief with the mourners can help them reach a permanent resolution. Knowing what to expect can prepare them for the emotional struggle, but the grieving process lasts longer for some than others. How long it lasts is not as important as moving through the first four stages toward the final stage of acceptance. As long as a person is consistently working through that process, grieving is normal, healthy, and necessary. ✦

He called them gods, to whom the word of
God came (and the Scripture cannot be
broken), [36]do you say of Him whom the
Father sanctified and sent into the world,
'You are blaspheming,' because I said, 'I
am the Son of God'? [37]If I do not do the
works of My Father, do not believe Me;
[38]but if I do, though you do not believe Me,
believe the works, that you may know and
believe[a] that the Father *is* in Me, and I in
Him." [39]Therefore they sought again to
seize Him, but He escaped out of their
hand.

The Believers Beyond Jordan

[40]And He went away again beyond the
Jordan to the place where John was baptizing at first, and there He stayed. [41]Then
many came to Him and said, "John performed no sign, but all the things that John
spoke about this Man were true." [42]And
many believed in Him there.

10:38 [a]NU-Text reads *understand.*

Martha and Mary: A Matter of Priorities

So often when we think of Martha, the sister of Mary and Lazarus, we picture a harried woman, impatient and perhaps a bit overbearing. We condemn her poor judgment in being more concerned with serving than with learning.

But God gave Martha the gift of serving, and He certainly expected her to exercise it. By opening her home to Jesus in loving hospitality, Martha provided her sister Mary the opportunity to sit and learn at Jesus' feet (Luke 10:38).

The few glimpses of Martha in Scripture show a woman of energy and action (Luke 10:40; John 11:20; 12:2). She enjoyed serving others, and they apparently appreciated her ministrations. Mary, however, expressed her love for others by her calm, listening presence.

When Jesus came to them following Lazarus's death, Martha characteristically went out to meet Him (John 11:20). Mary, on the other hand, sat at home, waiting for the appropriate time to talk with Jesus. Yet she expressed her faith in exactly the same words as Martha: "Lord, if You had been here, my brother would not have died" (see vv. 21, 32).

The contrast between Mary and Martha reminds us that, although our faith may be equally strong, not everyone can serve the Lord in the same capacity. Each must seek an area of ministry that fits his or her personality. Jesus loved the activity-oriented Martha just as much as He loved the quieter, more reflective Mary (John 11:5).

Martha's problem was not her serving—which was simply an expression of her personality—but her tendency to put service above spiritual nourishment. Her concern with appearances distracted her from the more important need to spend time with Jesus (Luke 10:41, 42). She placed others' physical needs above her own spiritual health.

How often Christians become so caught up in serving the Lord—teaching Sunday school, leading Bible studies, preparing fellowship suppers, attending to church matters—that we neglect our own personal time with the Lord. The activities in themselves are not wrong, but they must take second place to our spiritual nourishment. If we're not caring for our own spiritual health, how can we effectively help others in their walk with the Lord?

When we're too busy serving the Lord to spend time with Him, we're busier than He wants us to be. ✦

CHAPTER 11

The Death of Lazarus

Now a certain *man* was sick, Laz'a·rus
of Beth'a·ny, the town of Mary and her sis-
ter Martha. 2It was *that* Mary who anointed
the Lord with fragrant oil and wiped His
feet with her hair, whose brother Laz'a·rus
was sick. 3Therefore the sisters sent to Him,
saying, "Lord, behold, he whom You love
is sick."

4When Jesus heard *that,* He said, "This
sickness is not unto death, but for the glory
of God, that the Son of God may be glori-
fied through it."

5Now Jesus loved Martha and her sister
and Laz'a·rus. 6So, when He heard that he
was sick, He stayed two more days in the
place where He was. 7Then after this He
said to *the* disciples, "Let us go to Judea
again."

8*The* disciples said to Him, "Rabbi, lately
the Jews sought to stone You, and are You
going there again?"

9Jesus answered, "Are there not twelve
hours in the day? If anyone walks in the
day, he does not stumble, because he sees
the light of this world. 10But if one walks in
the night, he stumbles, because the light is
not in him." 11These things He said, and
after that He said to them, "Our friend
Laz'a·rus sleeps, but I go that I may wake
him up."

12Then His disciples said, "Lord, if he
sleeps he will get well." 13However, Jesus
spoke of his death, but they thought that
He was speaking about taking rest in
sleep.

14Then Jesus said to them plainly,
"Laz'a·rus is dead. 15And I am glad for
your sakes that I was not there, that you
may believe. Nevertheless let us go to
him."

16Then Thomas, who is called the Twin,
said to his fellow disciples, "Let us also go,
that we may die with Him."

I Am the Resurrection and the Life

17So when Jesus came, He found that he
had already been in the tomb four days.
18Now Beth'a·ny was near Jerusalem,
about two miles[a] away. 19And many of the
Jews had joined the women around Mar-
tha and Mary, to comfort them concerning
their brother.

20Now Martha, as soon as she heard that
Jesus was coming, went and met Him, but
Mary was sitting in the house. 21Now Mar-
tha said to Jesus, "Lord, if You had been
here, my brother would not have died.
22But even now I know that whatever You
ask of God, God will give You."

23Jesus said to her, "Your brother will
rise again."

24Martha said to Him, "I know that he
will rise again in the resurrection at the last
day."

25Jesus said to her, "I am the resurrection
and the life. He who believes in Me,
though he may die, he shall live. 26And
whoever lives and believes in Me shall
never die. Do you believe this?"

27She said to Him, "Yes, Lord, I believe
that You are the Christ, the Son of God,
who is to come into the world."

11:18 [a]Literally *fifteen stadia*

11:1–57 The raising of Lazarus is the last of seven miracle signs in John's Gospel. It shows what Jesus meant when He declared, **I am the resurrection and the life** (v. 25). Those who rejected this sign had no alternative but to kill the One who performed the miracle (v. 53).

11:5, 6 stayed . . . where He was: On the surface, a strange way to show love. But Jesus always knows what He is going to do—now as then. When trials and tragedies occur and it seems as if even God has forgotten us, we can rely on the knowledge that He is in control. While He may not always do what we desire, we know that He will always do what is best.

11:17–19 Jesus may have waited **four days** because of a common belief that the spirit hovered near the body for three days after death. Hence, a resurrection after four days would be conclusive.

11:24–26 The fifth "I am" declaration, which shows Jesus as **the resurrection and the life**.

MEN HAVE FEELINGS, TOO

Charles R. Swindoll

Many of the men I spend time with are extremely caring. Often as men we were not taught how to present that side, and, for fear of appearing feminine, we hold our care back, especially around women. Men tend to act hard, lest they seem too affectionate or give the wrong impression. Unless they are in a very safe environment, they will not be as vulnerable as a woman.

The best letters I have received come from very caring women who write deeply and wonderfully of their feelings. And I know men who have similar feelings, but they just don't know how to express them. A man is often like a deep river. Current, depth, and movement are there, but on the surface it looks glassy and unruffled.

I find men are very sensitive to spiritual things. When you reach a man regarding his home or his family or something that he cares about, I find more men willing to weep over their sorrow now than before. In a safe context, a man will release more feelings.

"Men are very sensitive to spiritual things."

In my own case, although I may appear to be strong and stable, I really am not, and I have learned to give myself permission to let that be. I learned to be more open by going through difficulties with our family and through learning more about my wife and myself.

Cynthia timed her confrontations very wisely so they would touch me. She reached me when I was reachable. She knew my moods, and she knew I was tender underneath. She knew I cared. She knew it was a blind spot.

When a woman confronts a man with anger, he is going to put up his dukes; he has been taught to do that. When a woman is vulnerable, he is more open. Tears say more than screams. ✦

Jesus and Death, the Last Enemy

28And when she had said these things,
she went her way and secretly called Mary
her sister, saying, "The Teacher has come
and is calling for you." 29As soon as she
heard *that,* she arose quickly and came to
Him. 30Now Jesus had not yet come into
the town, but was[a] in the place where
Martha met Him. 31Then the Jews who
were with her in the house, and comforting her, when they saw that Mary rose up
quickly and went out, followed her, saying, "She is going to the tomb to weep
there."[a]

32Then, when Mary came where Jesus
was, and saw Him, she fell down at His
feet, saying to Him, "Lord, if You had been
here, my brother would not have
died."

33Therefore, when Jesus saw her weeping, and the Jews who came with her

11:30 [a]NU-Text adds *still.* 11:31 [a]NU-Text reads *supposing that she was going to the tomb to weep there.*

weeping, He groaned in the spirit and was
troubled. 34And He said, "Where have you
laid him?"

They said to Him, "Lord, come and
see."

35Jesus wept. 36Then the Jews said, "See
how He loved him!"

37And some of them said, "Could not
this Man, who opened the eyes of the
blind, also have kept this man from dy-
ing?"

Lazarus Raised from the Dead

38Then Jesus, again groaning in Himself,
came to the tomb. It was a cave, and a
stone lay against it. 39Jesus said, "Take
away the stone."

Martha, the sister of him who was dead,
said to Him, "Lord, by this time there is a
stench, for he has been *dead* four days."

40Jesus said to her, "Did I not say to you
that if you would believe you would see
the glory of God?" 41Then they took away
the stone *from the place* where the dead man
was lying.[a] And Jesus lifted up *His* eyes
and said, "Father, I thank You that You
have heard Me. 42And I know that You al-
ways hear Me, but because of the people
who are standing by I said *this*, that they
may believe that You sent Me." 43Now
when He had said these things, He cried
with a loud voice, "Laz'a·rus, come forth!"
44And he who had died came out bound
hand and foot with graveclothes, and his
face was wrapped with a cloth. Jesus said
to them, "Loose him, and let him go."

The Plot to Kill Jesus

45Then many of the Jews who had come
to Mary, and had seen the things Jesus did,
believed in Him. 46But some of them went
away to the Phar'i·sees and told them the
things Jesus did. 47Then the chief priests
and the Phar'i·sees gathered a council and
said, "What shall we do? For this Man
works many signs. 48If we let Him alone
like this, everyone will believe in Him, and
the Romans will come and take away both
our place and nation."

49And one of them, Cā'i·a·phas, being
high priest that year, said to them, "You
know nothing at all, 50nor do you consider
that it is expedient for us[a] that one man
should die for the people, and not that the
whole nation should perish." 51Now this
he did not say on his own *authority;* but be-
ing high priest that year he prophesied
that Jesus would die for the nation, 52and
not for that nation only, but also that He
would gather together in one the children
of God who were scattered abroad.

53Then, from that day on, they plotted to
put Him to death. 54Therefore Jesus no
longer walked openly among the Jews, but
went from there into the country near the
wilderness, to a city called Ē'phra·im, and
there remained with His disciples.

55And the Passover of the Jews was near,
and many went from the country up to
Jerusalem before the Passover, to purify

11:41 [a]NU-Text omits *from the place where the dead man was lying.* 11:50 [a]NU-Text reads *you.*

11:35, 36 The people mistakenly believe Jesus is weeping out of sorrow for His friend's death; however, His tears express His sadness at the blindness and unbelief of the people. As His followers, we too should be moved with compassion for the unsaved, unseeing world.

11:43, 44 Graveclothes (lit. "windings") reflects the way in which bodies were prepared for burial. The **cloth** on his face was a separate small napkin. Jesus' body was prepared in a similar way (see 19:40; 20:7).

11:49–52 That year may indicate that the Romans controlled the office of high priest and rotated it annually. **one man should die for the people** (v. 50): Caiaphas meant that Jesus must die so that the Romans would not take away the privileges of the Jewish nation (see v. 48). But God intended these words to mean that Jesus would die for the salvation of the Jews and of people everywhere who would believe in Him.

11:55 The Jews would **purify themselves** in preparation for **the Passover** by washing their bodies and their clothing so that they could enter the temple for worship.

themselves. [56]Then they sought Jesus, and spoke among themselves as they stood in the temple, "What do you think—that He will not come to the feast?" [57]Now both the chief priests and the Phar′i·sees had given a command, that if anyone knew where He was, he should report *it,* that they might seize Him.

CHAPTER 12

The Anointing at Bethany

Then, six days before the Passover, Jesus came to Beth′a·ny, where Laz′a·rus was who had been dead,[a] whom He had raised from the dead. [2]There they made Him a supper; and Martha served, but Laz′a·rus was one of those who sat at the table with Him. [3]Then Mary took a pound of very costly oil of spikenard, anointed the feet of Jesus, and wiped His feet with her hair. And the house was filled with the fragrance of the oil.

[4]But one of His disciples, Judas Is·car′i·ot, Simon's *son,* who would betray Him, said, [5]"Why was this fragrant oil not sold for three hundred denarii[a] and given to the poor?" [6]This he said, not that he cared for the poor, but because he was a thief, and had the money box; and he used to take what was put in it.

[7]But Jesus said, "Let her alone; she has kept[a] this for the day of My burial. [8]For the poor you have with you always, but Me you do not have always."

The Plot to Kill Lazarus

[9]Now a great many of the Jews knew that He was there; and they came, not for Jesus' sake only, but that they might also see Laz′a·rus, whom He had raised from the dead. [10]But the chief priests plotted to put Laz′a·rus to death also, [11]because on account of him many of the Jews went away and believed in Jesus.

The Triumphal Entry

[12]The next day a great multitude that had come to the feast, when they heard that Jesus was coming to Jerusalem, [13]took branches of palm trees and went out to meet Him, and cried out:

"Hō·san′na!
'Blessed is He who comes in the name of the LORD!'[a]
The King of Israel!"

[14]Then Jesus, when He had found a young donkey, sat on it; as it is written:

15 *"Fear not, daughter of Zion;*
Behold, your King is coming,
Sitting on a donkey's colt."[a]

[16]His disciples did not understand these things at first; but when Jesus was glorified, then they remembered that these things were written about Him and *that* they had done these things to Him.

[17]Therefore the people, who were with Him when He called Laz′a·rus out of his tomb and raised him from the dead, bore witness. [18]For this reason the people also met Him, because they heard that He had done this sign. [19]The Phar′i·sees therefore said among themselves, "You see that you

12:1 [a]NU-Text omits *who had been dead.*
12:5 [a]About one year's wages for a worker
12:7 [a]NU-Text reads *that she may keep.*
12:13 [a]Psalm 118:26 12:15 [a]Zechariah 9:9

12:3 spikenard: a costly, perfumed ointment reserved for special occasions. Mary's action is a symbol of her consecration and dedication.

12:7, 8 Jesus was not dismissing the importance of helping the poor; He was simply showing that our ministry *to* the Lord should be a higher priority than our ministry *for* the Lord.

12:12–15 The **multitude** excitedly hailed Jesus as a conquering King. **Palm** branches were used to welcome royalty. The addition of **King of Israel** (v. 13) to the quotation from Ps. 118:25, 26 shows the crowd intended to make Jesus King. **Hosanna** means "Save us now." By riding on a **young donkey** (v. 14) and fulfilling Zech. 9:9 quoted in v. 15, Jesus proclaimed Himself a King who was humble and peaceful. He came to free the people from the bondage of sin, not from the oppression of Rome.

are accomplishing nothing. Look, the world has gone after Him!"

The Fruitful Grain of Wheat

[20]Now there were certain Greeks among
those who came up to worship at the feast.
[21]Then they came to Philip, who was from
Beth·sā'i·da of Galilee, and asked him, saying, "Sir, we wish to see Jesus."

[22]Philip came and told Andrew, and in turn Andrew and Philip told Jesus.

[23]But Jesus answered them, saying, "The hour has come that the Son of Man should
be glorified. [24]Most assuredly, I say to you, unless a grain of wheat falls into the ground and dies, it remains alone; but if it
dies, it produces much grain. [25]He who
loves his life will lose it, and he who hates his life in this world will keep it for eternal
life. [26]If anyone serves Me, let him follow Me; and where I am, there My servant will be also. If anyone serves Me, him *My* Father will honor.

Jesus Predicts His Death on the Cross

[27]"Now My soul is troubled, and what shall I say? 'Father, save Me from this hour'? But for this purpose I came to this
hour. [28]Father, glorify Your name."

Then a voice came from heaven, *saying,* "I have both glorified *it* and will glorify *it* again."

[29]Therefore the people who stood by and heard *it* said that it had thundered. Others said, "An angel has spoken to Him."

[30]Jesus answered and said, "This voice did not come because of Me, but for your
sake. [31]Now is the judgment of this world; now the ruler of this world will be cast out.
[32]And I, if I am lifted up from the earth, will
draw all *peoples* to Myself." [33]This He said, signifying by what death He would die.
[34]The people answered Him, "We have heard from the law that the Christ remains forever; and how *can* You say, 'The Son of Man must be lifted up'? Who is this Son of Man?"

[35]Then Jesus said to them, "A little while longer the light is with you. Walk while you have the light, lest darkness overtake you; he who walks in darkness does not
know where he is going. [36]While you have the light, believe in the light, that you may become sons of light." These things Jesus spoke, and departed, and was hidden from them.

Who Has Believed Our Report?

[37]But although He had done so many signs before them, they did not believe in
Him, [38]that the word of Ī·sāi'ah the prophet might be fulfilled, which he spoke:

> *"Lord, who has believed our report?*
> *And to whom has the arm of the*
> *LORD been revealed?"*[a]

[39]Therefore they could not believe, because Ī·sāi'ah said again:

> 40 *"He has blinded their eyes and*
> *hardened their hearts,*
> *Lest they should see with their eyes,*
> *Lest they should understand with*
> *their hearts and turn,*
> *So that I should heal them."*[a]

[41]These things Ī·sāi'ah said when[a] he saw His glory and spoke of Him.

12:38 [a]Isaiah 53:1 12:40 [a]Isaiah 6:10
12:41 [a]NU-Text reads *because.*

12:24–26 A powerful illustration of Christian discipleship. The **grain of wheat** must die before it can reproduce itself. So the individual who would follow Jesus must die to all purposes in life that are contrary to the will of God. **hates his life in this world**: Values life as less important than serving Christ. To everyone who serves Christ, v. 26 offers a challenge: **let him follow Me**. But with that challenge Christ gives two promises: He will be **where I am**, and **him My Father will honor**. Thrilling challenge! Glorious promises!
12:32 lifted up: John uses this phrase to refer to the Cross. **all peoples**: Jews and Gentiles alike.

THE ORDER OF THE TOWEL

Jill Briscoe

The Savior's attitude of humility startled the disciples. After all, He was their Master and Lord. But toward the end of His ministry, as they went up to Jerusalem for the Passover feast, they knew He must not only be followed and obeyed but emulated as well. To live as Jesus lived, however, was not the easiest thing in the world to do. To enter "the order of the towel," for instance, was an unexpected challenge for the disciples—especially, I suspect, for Peter!

But then, humility is a tough assignment for all of us! Which of us wakes up in the morning racking our brains for new ways to be humble and serve others? Usually our waking moments are filled with thoughts about ourselves and who is going to serve us.

"Humility is a tough assignment for all of us!"

How often do we look at others and ask, "Who do they think they are? They obviously think they are as important as I am!" Oh, yes, the human heart has much to learn from Jesus! ✦

Walk in the Light

42Nevertheless even among the rulers
many believed in Him, but because of the
Phar'i·sees they did not confess *Him,* lest
they should be put out of the synagogue;
43for they loved the praise of men more
than the praise of God.

44Then Jesus cried out and said, "He
who believes in Me, believes not in Me but
in Him who sent Me. 45And he who sees
Me sees Him who sent Me. 46I have come *as*
a light into the world, that whoever believes in Me should not abide in darkness.
47And if anyone hears My words and does
not believe,[a] I do not judge him; for I did
not come to judge the world but to save the
world. 48He who rejects Me, and does not
receive My words, has that which judges
him—the word that I have spoken will
judge him in the last day. 49For I have not
spoken on My own *authority;* but the
Father who sent Me gave Me a command,
what I should say and what I should
speak. 50And I know that His command is
everlasting life. Therefore, whatever I
speak, just as the Father has told Me, so I
speak."

12:47 [a]NU-Text reads *keep them.*

CHAPTER 13

Jesus Washes the Disciples' Feet

Now before the Feast of the Passover,
when Jesus knew that His hour had come
that He should depart from this world to

13:1—17:26 The seven signs and seven discourses completed (see note on 2:1—12:50), John's Gospel turns its primary focus from Jesus' public ministry to the time He spent teaching His disciples before His Crucifixion.

13:1 His own: The Twelve, but also all **in the world** who would believe in Him. **To the end**

the Father, having loved His own who were
in the world, He loved them to the end.
2And supper being ended,[a] the devil
having already put it into the heart of
Judas Is·car'i·ot, Simon's *son,* to betray
Him, 3Jesus, knowing that the Father had
given all things into His hands, and that
He had come from God and was going to
God, 4rose from supper and laid aside His
garments, took a towel and girded Him-
self. 5After that, He poured water into a
basin and began to wash the disciples' feet,
and to wipe *them* with the towel with
which He was girded. 6Then He came to Si-
mon Peter. And *Peter* said to Him, "Lord,
are You washing my feet?"
7Jesus answered and said to him, "What
I am doing you do not understand now,
but you will know after this."
8Peter said to Him, "You shall never
wash my feet!"
Jesus answered him, "If I do not wash
you, you have no part with Me."
9Simon Peter said to Him, "Lord, not my
feet only, but also *my* hands and *my* head!"
10Jesus said to him, "He who is bathed
needs only to wash *his* feet, but is com-
pletely clean; and you are clean, but not all
of you." 11For He knew who would betray
Him; therefore He said, "You are not all
clean."
12So when He had washed their feet,
taken His garments, and sat down again,
He said to them, "Do you know what I
have done to you? 13You call Me Teacher
and Lord, and you say well, for *so* I am. 14If
I then, *your* Lord and Teacher, have
washed your feet, you also ought to wash
one another's feet. 15For I have given you
an example, that you should do as I have
done to you. 16Most assuredly, I say to you,
a servant is not greater than his master; nor
is he who is sent greater than he who sent
him. 17If you know these things, blessed
are you if you do them.

Jesus Identifies His Betrayer

18"I do not speak concerning all of you.
I know whom I have chosen; but that the
Scripture may be fulfilled, *'He who eats
bread with Me[a] has lifted up his heel
against Me.'[b]* 19Now I tell you before it
comes, that when it does come to pass, you
may believe that I am *He.* 20Most assuredly,
I say to you, he who receives whomever I
send receives Me; and he who receives Me
receives Him who sent Me."
21When Jesus had said these things, He
was troubled in spirit, and testified and
said, "Most assuredly, I say to you, one of
you will betray Me." 22Then the disciples
looked at one another, perplexed about
whom He spoke.
23Now there was leaning on Jesus' bo-
som one of His disciples, whom Jesus
loved. 24Simon Peter therefore motioned to
him to ask who it was of whom He spoke.
25Then, leaning back[a] on Jesus' breast, he
said to Him, "Lord, who is it?"

13:2 [a]NU-Text reads *And during supper.*
13:18 [a]NU-Text reads *My bread.* [b]Psalm 41:9
13:25 [a]NU-Text and M-Text add *thus.*

---

refers to intensity; Jesus **loved them** in the highest degree. His act of service (vv. 3–10) and His coming death demonstrated the extent of that love.

13:5 The custom called for a low-ranking servant to wash the guests' feet, but as no servant was present and none of the disciples wished to lower himself to that role, Jesus took the opportunity to give a lesson in humility and servanthood.

13:10 Christians have already been "bathed" through salvation and need to simply take time daily for cleansing from defilement accumulated during the day.

13:18, 19 eats bread with Me: Has enjoyed My close fellowship. **lifted up his heel**: Has turned against Me. Jesus made this prediction so that His betrayal would strengthen, not weaken, the faith of His disciples.

13:23–26 Leaning on Jesus' bosom indicates a place of special favor and intimacy at the table fellowship. The apostle John is probably the disciple **whom Jesus loved**. The phrase is used often, but only in this Gospel.

26Jesus answered, "It is he to whom
I shall give a piece of bread when I have
dipped *it*." And having dipped the bread,
He gave *it* to Judas Is·car'i·ot, *the son* of Si-
mon. 27Now after the piece of bread, Satan
entered him. Then Jesus said to him,
"What you do, do quickly." 28But no one at
the table knew for what reason He said this
to him. 29For some thought, because Judas
had the money box, that Jesus had said to
him, "Buy *those things* we need for the
feast," or that he should give something to
the poor.
30Having received the piece of bread, he
then went out immediately. And it was
night.

The New Commandment

31So, when he had gone out, Jesus said,
"Now the Son of Man is glorified, and God
is glorified in Him. 32If God is glorified in
Him, God will also glorify Him in Himself,
and glorify Him immediately. 33Little chil-
dren, I shall be with you a little while
longer. You will seek Me; and as I said to
the Jews, 'Where I am going, you cannot
come,' so now I say to you. 34A new com-
mandment I give to you, that you love one
another; as I have loved you, that you also
love one another. 35By this all will know
that you are My disciples, if you have love
for one another."

Jesus Predicts Peter's Denial

36Simon Peter said to Him, "Lord, where
are You going?"
Jesus answered him, "Where I am going
you cannot follow Me now, but you shall
follow Me afterward."
37Peter said to Him, "Lord, why can I
not follow You now? I will lay down my
life for Your sake."
38Jesus answered him, "Will you lay
down your life for My sake? Most as-
suredly, I say to you, the rooster shall not
crow till you have denied Me three times.

CHAPTER 14

The Way, the Truth, and the Life

"Let not your heart be troubled; you be-
lieve in God, believe also in Me. 2In My
Father's house are many mansions;[a] if *it
were* not *so,* I would have told you. I go to
prepare a place for you.[b] 3And if I go and
prepare a place for you, I will come again
and receive you to Myself; that where I am,
there you may be also. 4And where I go you
know, and the way you know."
5Thomas said to Him, "Lord, we do not
know where You are going, and how can
we know the way?"
6Jesus said to him, "I am the way, the
truth, and the life. No one comes to the
Father except through Me.

The Father Revealed

7"If you had known Me, you would
have known My Father also; and from now
on you know Him and have seen Him."
8Philip said to Him, "Lord, show us the
Father, and it is sufficient for us."
9Jesus said to him, "Have I been with
you so long, and yet you have not known
Me, Philip? He who has seen Me has seen
the Father; so how can you say, 'Show us
the Father'? 10Do you not believe that I am
in the Father, and the Father in Me? The
words that I speak to you I do not speak on
My own *authority;* but the Father who
dwells in Me does the works. 11Believe Me

14:2 [a]Literally *dwellings* [b]NU-Text adds a word which would cause the text to read either *if it were not so, would I have told you that I go to prepare a place for you?* or *if it were not so I would have told you; for I go to prepare a place for you.*

14:7–11 Jesus is the Father's revelation of Himself to the world. Therefore, Jesus could say, **You know** [God] **and have seen Him**. In response to **Philip**, Jesus spoke even more plainly: **He who has seen Me has seen the Father** (v. 9). This unique relationship is expressed in three ways: the Father and Jesus are **in** one another; the **words** of Jesus come with the **authority** of the Father; His **works** are done by the indwelling Father.

ONLY ONE WAY

J. Vernon McGee

When Jesus said, "I am the way," He didn't mean that He would *show* the way. He said, "I *am* the way." He said, "I am the truth"—not I *tell* the truth (although He did tell the truth)—but I *am* the touchstone of truth, I am the bureau of standards of truth. Also He said, "I am the life," not the *source* of life.

"It is the characteristic of truth to be dogmatic."

That statement is dogmatic. Several years ago I was speaking at a Bible club at UCLA, using John 14:6. A young fellow came up to me afterward and said, "Dr. McGee, I have one criticism of that verse. It is too dogmatic." I said to him, "I agree with you. It is dogmatic. In fact, it is the most dogmatic statement I can think of. But it is the characteristic of truth to be dogmatic."

Then I gave him the illustration of a teacher I had when I was first starting school. She taught me that two plus two equals four. She was not broad-minded about it. She had no tolerance for anything else. To be honest with you, I was very broad-minded in those days. As far as I was concerned, two plus two could equal three or five. But she insisted that under every circumstance, two plus two equals four! You just cannot get any more dogmatic than that. But I have thanked God for her since then because I now do business with a bank that is equally narrow-minded. Also, when I figure out my income tax, I have found that the government has the same narrow-minded idea about two plus two.

May I say to you, my beloved, truth is always dogmatic. And if it is not dogmatic, it is not truth. ✦

that I *am* in the Father and the Father in
Me, or else believe Me for the sake of the
works themselves.

The Answered Prayer

12"Most assuredly, I say to you, he who
believes in Me, the works that I do he will
do also; and greater *works* than these he
will do, because I go to My Father. 13And
whatever you ask in My name, that I will
do, that the Father may be glorified in the
Son. 14If you ask[a] anything in My name, I
will do *it*.

Jesus Promises Another Helper

15"If you love Me, keep[a] My command-
ments. 16And I will pray the Father, and He

14:14 [a]NU-Text adds *Me.* 14:15 [a]NU-Text reads *you will keep.*

14:15 The acid test: genuine love for Jesus results in genuine obedience (see 1 John 5:3). We cannot fulfill our obligations to the Lord through mere lip-service; we must put our faith into action.

14:16–18 The Holy Spirit as the Christians' **Helper** would remain with them **forever**, in con-

will give you another Helper, that He may
abide with you forever— 17the Spirit of
truth, whom the world cannot receive, be-
cause it neither sees Him nor knows Him;
but you know Him, for He dwells with
you and will be in you. 18I will not leave
you orphans; I will come to you.

Indwelling of the Father and the Son

19"A little while longer and the world
will see Me no more, but you will see
Me. Because I live, you will live also. 20At
that day you will know that I *am* in My
Father, and you in Me, and I in you. 21He
who has My commandments and keeps
them, it is he who loves Me. And he who
loves Me will be loved by My Father, and
I will love him and manifest Myself to
him."

22Judas (not Is·car′i·ot) said to Him,
"Lord, how is it that You will manifest
Yourself to us, and not to the world?"

23Jesus answered and said to him, "If
anyone loves Me, he will keep My word;
and My Father will love him, and We will
come to him and make Our home with
him. 24He who does not love Me does not
keep My words; and the word which you
hear is not Mine but the Father's who sent
Me.

The Gift of His Peace

25"These things I have spoken to you
while being present with you. 26But the
Helper, the Holy Spirit, whom the Father
will send in My name, He will teach you
all things, and bring to your remembrance
all things that I said to you. 27Peace I leave
with you, My peace I give to you; not as
the world gives do I give to you. Let not
your heart be troubled, neither let it be
afraid. 28You have heard Me say to you,
'I am going away and coming *back* to you.'
If you loved Me, you would rejoice be-
cause I said,[a] 'I am going to the Father,' for
My Father is greater than I.

29"And now I have told you before it
comes, that when it does come to pass, you
may believe. 30I will no longer talk much
with you, for the ruler of this world is com-
ing, and he has nothing in Me. 31But that
the world may know that I love the Father,
and as the Father gave Me commandment,
so I do. Arise, let us go from here.

CHAPTER 15

The True Vine

"I am the true vine, and My Father is the
vinedresser. 2Every branch in Me that does
not bear fruit He takes away;[a] and every
branch that bears fruit He prunes, that it
may bear more fruit. 3You are already clean

14:28 [a]NU-Text omits *I said.* 15:2 [a]Or *lifts up*

trast to Jesus, who was soon to depart (v. 16). **He dwells with you and will be in you** (v. 17): Jesus seems to indicate a limited presence of the Spirit with the disciples prior to Pentecost, and then afterward in a fuller measure as Spirit-filled, Spirit-empowered witnesses.

14:21 The one who **loves** Jesus will obey His **commandments**. He will experience more of the love of the Father and of Jesus. To him Jesus will **manifest** (reveal) Himself in a special way. See also v. 23.

14:22–24 Judas (not Iscariot): The son of James (see Luke 6:16; Acts 1:13). **make Our home** (v. 23): Jesus speaks of the inner spiritual union produced by **love** and the keeping of His **word**. Obedience is a sign of genuine **love**; disobedience proves a lack of love.

15:1–4 In the OT disobedient Israel was God's "degenerate" vine (Jer. 2:21). In the seventh of the "I am" pronouncements, Jesus is the **true vine**, the source of all spiritual life for God's people. As the **vinedresser**, the **Father** removes what is unfruitful and **prunes** (v. 2; disciplines) fruitbearing lives to make us even more Christlike in character and witness. The lives of the disciples were **already** (v. 3) being shaped by obedience to the **word** that Jesus had taught them. **Abide in Me** (v. 4): Total, continued dependence on Christ is the only way to grow in Christian character and witness. As mature Christians, we must guard against a tendency toward reliance on our own wisdom and strength.

PEACE AND PRIORITIES

Bill Gaither

At each stage of life, you have to reevaluate all the busy-ness in your life against what you *need* to be doing to be the person God wants you to be. Give up the frantic rushing around. Give up the merely "interesting" for the truly valuable. What a simple way to uncomplicate your life!

One wonderful thing about growing older is that whatever new thing comes up, in some way or another I have seen it before. With that feeling of *deja vu* comes that ability to think it through, to keep calm. In this day, when we are all dealing with high levels of stress, we need to act on our belief that the living Christ is at our side with His hand on our shoulder saying, "Son, Daughter, don't panic. Take My peace. Take My peace. Take My peace." ✦

"We need to act on our belief that the living Christ is at our side."

because of the word which I have spoken
to you. [4]Abide in Me, and I in you. As the
branch cannot bear fruit of itself, unless it
abides in the vine, neither can you, unless
you abide in Me.

[5]"I am the vine, you *are* the branches. He
who abides in Me, and I in him, bears
much fruit; for without Me you can do
nothing. [6]If anyone does not abide in Me,
he is cast out as a branch and is withered;
and they gather them and throw *them* into
the fire, and they are burned. [7]If you abide
in Me, and My words abide in you, you
will[a] ask what you desire, and it shall be
done for you. [8]By this My Father is glori-
fied, that you bear much fruit; so you will
be My disciples.

Love and Joy Perfected

[9]"As the Father loved Me, I also have
loved you; abide in My love. [10]If you keep
My commandments, you will abide in My
love, just as I have kept My Father's com-
mandments and abide in His love.

[11]"These things I have spoken to you,
that My joy may remain in you, and *that*
your joy may be full. [12]This is My com-
mandment, that you love one another as
I have loved you. [13]Greater love has no one
than this, than to lay down one's life for his
friends. [14]You are My friends if you do
whatever I command you. [15]No longer do
I call you servants, for a servant does not
know what his master is doing; but I have
called you friends, for all things that
I heard from My Father I have made
known to you. [16]You did not choose Me,
but I chose you and appointed you that
you should go and bear fruit, and *that* your
fruit should remain, that whatever you ask

15:7 [a]NU-Text omits *you will.*

15:7 Abiding in Christ is essential to an effective prayer life.

the Father in My name He may give you.
[17]These things I command you, that you
love one another.

The World's Hatred

[18]"If the world hates you, you know that
it hated Me before *it hated* you. [19]If you
were of the world, the world would love
its own. Yet because you are not of the
world, but I chose you out of the world,
therefore the world hates you. [20]Remember
the word that I said to you, 'A servant is
not greater than his master.' If they persecuted Me, they will also persecute you. If
they kept My word, they will keep yours
also. [21]But all these things they will do to
you for My name's sake, because they do
not know Him who sent Me. [22]If I had not
come and spoken to them, they would
have no sin, but now they have no excuse
for their sin. [23]He who hates Me hates My
Father also. [24]If I had not done among them
the works which no one else did, they
would have no sin; but now they have
seen and also hated both Me and My
Father. [25]But *this happened* that the word
might be fulfilled which is written
in their law, *'They hated Me without a
cause.'*[a]

The Coming Rejection

[26]"But when the Helper comes, whom I
shall send to you from the Father, the Spirit
of truth who proceeds from the Father, He
will testify of Me. [27]And you also will bear
witness, because you have been with Me
from the beginning.

15:25 [a]Psalm 69:4 16:3 [a]NU-Text and M-Text omit *to you.* 16:4 [a]NU-Text reads *their.*

> ***I pray, Jesus, that my spouse and I will follow Your commandment that we love one another as You have loved us.***
>
> *adapted from* John 15:12

CHAPTER 16

"These things I have spoken to you, that
you should not be made to stumble. [2]They
will put you out of the synagogues; yes,
the time is coming that whoever kills you
will think that he offers God service. [3]And
these things they will do to you[a] because
they have not known the Father nor Me.
[4]But these things I have told you, that
when the[a] time comes, you may remember
that I told you of them.

"And these things I did not say to you at
the beginning, because I was with you.

The Work of the Holy Spirit

[5]"But now I go away to Him who sent
Me, and none of you asks Me, 'Where are
You going?' [6]But because I have said these
things to you, sorrow has filled your heart.
[7]Nevertheless I tell you the truth. It is to
your advantage that I go away; for if I do
not go away, the Helper will not come to
you; but if I depart, I will send Him to you.
[8]And when He has come, He will convict
the world of sin, and of righteousness, and
of judgment: [9]of sin, because they do not
believe in Me; [10]of righteousness, because I
go to My Father and you see Me no more;

16:1–4 made to stumble: Rejection by the world should confirm, not weaken, our faith. Both predictions of v. 2 were fulfilled in the lives of the apostles. If we find ourselves in favor with those who have rejected Christ, we need to pause and determine whether our everyday actions reflect our Christian faith, or have we become caught up in the things of the world?

16:8–11 Through the preaching of believers the Holy Spirit will **convict the world of sin**. Refusal to believe in Jesus is the most basic sin (v. 9), because the Cross and the empty tomb have shown that Jesus was in the right. In Christ the **ruler of this world**, Satan, and those who follow him have been defeated and condemned.

11 of judgment, because the ruler of this
world is judged.
12 "I still have many things to say to you,
but you cannot bear *them* now. 13 However,
when He, the Spirit of truth, has come, He
will guide you into all truth; for He will not
speak on His own *authority,* but whatever
He hears He will speak; and He will tell
you things to come. 14 He will glorify Me,
for He will take of what is Mine and de-
clare *it* to you. 15 All things that the Father
has are Mine. Therefore I said that He will
take of Mine and declare *it* to you.[a]

Sorrow Will Turn to Joy

16 "A little while, and you will not see
Me; and again a little while, and you will
see Me, because I go to the Father."
17 Then *some* of His disciples said among
themselves, "What is this that He says to
us, 'A little while, and you will not see Me;
and again a little while, and you will see
Me'; and, 'because I go to the Father'?"
18 They said therefore, "What is this that He
says, 'A little while'? We do not know what
He is saying."
19 Now Jesus knew that they desired to
ask Him, and He said to them, "Are you
inquiring among yourselves about what I
said, 'A little while, and you will not see
Me; and again a little while, and you will
see Me'? 20 Most assuredly, I say to you that
you will weep and lament, but the world
will rejoice; and you will be sorrowful, but
your sorrow will be turned into joy. 21 A
woman, when she is in labor, has sorrow
because her hour has come; but as soon as
she has given birth to the child, she no
longer remembers the anguish, for joy that
a human being has been born into the
world. 22 Therefore you now have sorrow;
but I will see you again and your heart will
rejoice, and your joy no one will take from
you.
23 "And in that day you will ask Me
nothing. Most assuredly, I say to you,
whatever you ask the Father in My name
He will give you. 24 Until now you have
asked nothing in My name. Ask, and you
will receive, that your joy may be full.

Jesus Christ Has Overcome the World

25 "These things I have spoken to you in
figurative language; but the time is coming
when I will no longer speak to you in figu-
rative language, but I will tell you plainly
about the Father. 26 In that day you will ask
in My name, and I do not say to you that I
shall pray the Father for you; 27 for the
Father Himself loves you, because you
have loved Me, and have believed that I
came forth from God. 28 I came forth from
the Father and have come into the world.
Again, I leave the world and go to the
Father."
29 His disciples said to Him, "See, now
You are speaking plainly, and using no fig-
ure of speech! 30 Now we are sure that You
know all things, and have no need that
anyone should question You. By this we
believe that You came forth from God."
31 Jesus answered them, "Do you now
believe? 32 Indeed the hour is coming, yes,
has now come, that you will be scattered,
each to his own, and will leave Me alone.
And yet I am not alone, because the Father
is with Me. 33 These things I have spoken to
you, that in Me you may have peace. In the

16:15 [a]NU-Text and M-Text read *He takes of Mine and will declare it to you.*

16:12–15 when He . . . has come (v. 13): The **Spirit** had not yet come to the disciples as He would come on the Day of Pentecost (Acts 1:4, 5). Jesus promised that the Holy Spirit would **guide** His disciples. **all truth . . . things to come**: The Spirit fulfilled these functions in large measure by inspiring the NT. **He will glorify Me** (v. 14): The Holy Spirit glorifies Christ by reminding us of what He taught and by giving us deeper appreciation for Him and His work. The Spirit will make us Christlike.

16:26 In Jesus' **name**—i.e., as though representing Him—His followers could make their petitions personally to the **Father**.

> We are here for a short time. We will have eternity to be free of boundaries, evil, and afflictions. Our time on earth is just our opportunity to invest in eternity.
>
> Joni Eareckson Tada

world you will[a] have tribulation; but be of
good cheer, I have overcome the world."

CHAPTER 17

Jesus Prays for Himself

Jesus spoke these words, lifted up His
eyes to heaven, and said: "Father, the hour
has come. Glorify Your Son, that Your Son
also may glorify You, 2 as You have given
Him authority over all flesh, that He
should[a] give eternal life to as many as You
have given Him. 3 And this is eternal life,
that they may know You, the only true
God, and Jesus Christ whom You have
sent. 4 I have glorified You on the earth. I
have finished the work which You have
given Me to do. 5 And now, O Father, glo-
rify Me together with Yourself, with the
glory which I had with You before the
world was.

Jesus Prays for His Disciples

6 "I have manifested Your name to the
men whom You have given Me out of the
world. They were Yours, You gave them to
Me, and they have kept Your word. 7 Now
they have known that all things which You
have given Me are from You. 8 For I have
given to them the words which You have
given Me; and they have received *them,*
and have known surely that I came forth
from You; and they have believed that You
sent Me.

9 "I pray for them. I do not pray for the
world but for those whom You have given
Me, for they are Yours. 10 And all Mine are
Yours, and Yours are Mine, and I am glori-
fied in them. 11 Now I am no longer in the
world, but these are in the world, and I
come to You. Holy Father, keep through
Your name those whom You have given
Me,[a] that they may be one as We *are.*
12 While I was with them in the world,[a] I
kept them in Your name. Those whom You
gave Me I have kept;[b] and none of them is
lost except the son of perdition, that the
Scripture might be fulfilled. 13 But now I
come to You, and these things I speak in
the world, that they may have My joy ful-
filled in themselves. 14 I have given them
Your word; and the world has hated them
because they are not of the world, just as I
am not of the world. 15 I do not pray that
You should take them out of the world, but
that You should keep them from the evil
one. 16 They are not of the world, just as I
am not of the world. 17 Sanctify them by
Your truth. Your word is truth. 18 As You
sent Me into the world, I also have sent
them into the world. 19 And for their sakes I
sanctify Myself, that they also may be
sanctified by the truth.

Jesus Prays for All Believers

20 "I do not pray for these alone, but also
for those who will[a] believe in Me through
their word; 21 that they all may be one, as

16:33 [a]NU-Text and M-Text omit *will.* 17:2 [a]M-Text reads *shall.* 17:11 [a]NU-Text and M-Text read *keep them through Your name which You have given Me.* 17:12 [a]NU-Text omits *in the world.* [b]NU-Text reads *in Your name which You gave Me. And I guarded them;* (or *it;*). 17:20 [a]NU-Text and M-Text omit *will.*

17:2, 3 all flesh: He gives **eternal life** to all who receive Him. This eternal life consists in fellowship with God through saving faith in **Jesus Christ**.

17:6 Your name: Jesus had revealed the nature of the Father to His disciples. The disciples, like all believers (see v. 2), were the Father's gift to Jesus.

17:17 Sanctify them: The joy and protection of vv. 13–16 were to come through the Father's answer to this prayer of the Son. Jesus asked the Father to set apart and purify the disciples for holy service. The instrument for such setting apart is the **truth** of **God's Word**.

You, Father, *are* in Me, and I in You; that
they also may be one in Us, that the world
may believe that You sent Me. 22And the
glory which You gave Me I have given
them, that they may be one just as We are
one: 23I in them, and You in Me; that they
may be made perfect in one, and that the
world may know that You have sent Me,
and have loved them as You have loved
Me.

24"Father, I desire that they also whom
You gave Me may be with Me where I am,
that they may behold My glory which You
have given Me; for You loved Me before
the foundation of the world. 25O righteous
Father! The world has not known You, but
I have known You; and these have known
that You sent Me. 26And I have declared to
them Your name, and will declare *it*, that
the love with which You loved Me may be
in them, and I in them."

CHAPTER 18

Betrayal and Arrest in Gethsemane

When Jesus had spoken these words,
He went out with His disciples over the
Brook Kid′ron, where there was a garden,
which He and His disciples entered. 2And
Judas, who betrayed Him, also knew the
place; for Jesus often met there with His
disciples. 3Then Judas, having received a
detachment *of troops*, and officers from the
chief priests and Phar′i·sees, came there
with lanterns, torches, and weapons. 4Jesus
therefore, knowing all things that would
come upon Him, went forward and said to
them, "Whom are you seeking?"

5They answered Him, "Jesus of Naza-
reth."

Jesus said to them, "I am *He*." And Ju-
das, who betrayed Him, also stood with
them. 6Now when He said to them, "I am
He," they drew back and fell to the ground.

7Then He asked them again, "Whom are
you seeking?"

And they said, "Jesus of Nazareth."

8Jesus answered, "I have told you that I
am *He*. Therefore, if you seek Me, let these
go their way," 9that the saying might be
fulfilled which He spoke, "Of those whom
You gave Me I have lost none."

10Then Simon Peter, having a sword,
drew it and struck the high priest's ser-
vant, and cut off his right ear. The servant's
name was Mal′chus.

11So Jesus said to Peter, "Put your sword
into the sheath. Shall I not drink the cup
which My Father has given Me?"

Before the High Priest

12Then the detachment *of troops* and the
captain and the officers of the Jews ar-
rested Jesus and bound Him. 13And they
led Him away to An′nas first, for he was
the father-in-law of Cā′i·a·phas who was
high priest that year. 14Now it was
Cā′i·a·phas who advised the Jews that it
was expedient that one man should die for
the people.

Peter Denies Jesus

15And Simon Peter followed Jesus, and
so *did* another[a] disciple. Now that disciple
was known to the high priest, and went
with Jesus into the courtyard of the high
priest. 16But Peter stood at the door out-
side. Then the other disciple, who was
known to the high priest, went out and
spoke to her who kept the door, and
brought Peter in. 17Then the servant girl
who kept the door said to Peter, "You are
not also *one* of this Man's disciples, are
you?"

He said, "I am not."

18Now the servants and officers who

18:15 [a]M-Text reads *the other.*

18:5, 6 Jesus' statement, "I am He" is both personal identification and a revelation of His deity. The troops are involuntarily thrown to the ground at this manifestation of divine power.

18:16–18 You are not . . . are you? (v. 17): The question assumed a negative response; thus, it was convenient for Peter to declare firmly, "I am not."

had made a fire of coals stood there, for it was cold, and they warmed themselves. And Peter stood with them and warmed himself.

Jesus Questioned by the High Priest

[19]The high priest then asked Jesus about His disciples and His doctrine.

[20]Jesus answered him, "I spoke openly to the world. I always taught in synagogues and in the temple, where the Jews always meet,[a] and in secret I have said nothing. [21]Why do you ask Me? Ask those who have heard Me what I said to them. Indeed they know what I said."

[22]And when He had said these things, one of the officers who stood by struck Jesus with the palm of his hand, saying, "Do You answer the high priest like that?"

[23]Jesus answered him, "If I have spoken evil, bear witness of the evil; but if well, why do you strike Me?"

[24]Then An′nas sent Him bound to Cā′i·a·phas the high priest.

Peter Denies Twice More

[25]Now Simon Peter stood and warmed himself. Therefore they said to him, "You are not also *one* of His disciples, are you?"

He denied *it* and said, "I am not!"

[26]One of the servants of the high priest, a relative *of him* whose ear Peter cut off, said, "Did I not see you in the garden with Him?" [27]Peter then denied again; and immediately a rooster crowed.

In Pilate's Court

[28]Then they led Jesus from Cā′i·a·phas to the Prae·tō′ri·um, and it was early morning. But they themselves did not go into the Praetorium, lest they should be defiled, but that they might eat the Passover. [29]Pilate then went out to them and said, "What accusation do you bring against this Man?"

[30]They answered and said to him, "If He were not an evildoer, we would not have delivered Him up to you."

[31]Then Pilate said to them, "You take Him and judge Him according to your law."

Therefore the Jews said to him, "It is not lawful for us to put anyone to death," [32]that the saying of Jesus might be fulfilled which He spoke, signifying by what death He would die.

[33]Then Pilate entered the Praetorium again, called Jesus, and said to Him, "Are You the King of the Jews?"

[34]Jesus answered him, "Are you speaking for yourself about this, or did others tell you this concerning Me?"

[35]Pilate answered, "Am I a Jew? Your own nation and the chief priests have delivered You to me. What have You done?"

[36]Jesus answered, "My kingdom is not of this world. If My kingdom were of this world, My servants would fight, so that I should not be delivered to the Jews; but now My kingdom is not from here."

[37]Pilate therefore said to Him, "Are You a king then?"

Jesus answered, "You say *rightly* that I am a king. For this cause I was born, and for this cause I have come into the world, that I should bear witness to the truth. Everyone who is of the truth hears My voice."

[38]Pilate said to Him, "What is truth?"

18:20 [a]NU-Text reads *where all the Jews meet.*

18:28 the Praetorium: the temporary residence of the Roman governor during the Jewish festival.

18:29, 30 What accusation? Motivated by spite and envy, the Jews offered no charge against Jesus that would be accepted under Roman law. They thus wanted Pilate to pass sentence on Him with no questions asked.

18:31, 32 not lawful: The Jews could not inflict the death penalty without the Roman governor's authority. Death under Roman law would ensure that Jesus would be crucified, thus fulfilling what **He spoke** about His **death** (see 3:14; 12:32, 33). If the Jews had carried out the death penalty themselves, Jesus would have been stoned.

And when he had said this, he went out again to the Jews, and said to them, "I find no fault in Him at all.

Taking the Place of Barabbas

39"But you have a custom that I should release someone to you at the Passover. Do you therefore want me to release to you the King of the Jews?"

40Then they all cried again, saying, "Not this Man, but Ba·rab'bas!" Now Ba·rab'bas was a robber.

CHAPTER 19

The Soldiers Mock Jesus

So then Pilate took Jesus and scourged *Him.* 2And the soldiers twisted a crown of thorns and put *it* on His head, and they put on Him a purple robe. 3Then they said,[a] "Hail, King of the Jews!" And they struck Him with their hands.

4Pilate then went out again, and said to them, "Behold, I am bringing Him out to you, that you may know that I find no fault in Him."

Pilate's Decision

5Then Jesus came out, wearing the crown of thorns and the purple robe. And *Pilate* said to them, "Behold the Man!"

6Therefore, when the chief priests and officers saw Him, they cried out, saying, "Crucify *Him,* crucify *Him!*"

Pilate said to them, "You take Him and crucify *Him,* for I find no fault in Him."

7The Jews answered him, "We have a law, and according to our[a] law He ought to die, because He made Himself the Son of God."

8Therefore, when Pilate heard that saying, he was the more afraid, 9and went again into the Prae·tō'ri·um, and said to Jesus, "Where are You from?" But Jesus gave him no answer.

10Then Pilate said to Him, "Are You not speaking to me? Do You not know that I have power to crucify You, and power to release You?"

11Jesus answered, "You could have no power at all against Me unless it had been given you from above. Therefore the one who delivered Me to you has the greater sin."

12From then on Pilate sought to release Him, but the Jews cried out, saying, "If you let this Man go, you are not Caesar's friend. Whoever makes himself a king speaks against Caesar."

13When Pilate therefore heard that saying, he brought Jesus out and sat down in the judgment seat in a place that is called *The* Pavement, but in Hebrew, Gab'ba·tha. 14Now it was the Preparation Day of the Passover, and about the sixth hour. And he said to the Jews, "Behold your King!"

15But they cried out, "Away with *Him,* away with *Him!* Crucify Him!"

Pilate said to them, "Shall I crucify your King?"

The chief priests answered, "We have no king but Caesar!"

16Then he delivered Him to them to be crucified. Then they took Jesus and led *Him* away.[a]

The King on a Cross

17And He, bearing His cross, went out to a place called *the Place* of a Skull, which is

19:3 [a]NU-Text reads *And they came up to Him and said.* 19:7 [a]NU-Text reads *the law.* 19:16 [a]NU-Text omits *and led Him away.*

19:8–11 Mistreating a divine person, Pilate feared, would bring retribution on him. Jesus' response (v. 11) shows plainly the primary responsibility of the Jewish high priest and his associates for Jesus' death.

19:14–16 The trial began at the **sixth hour**, which is Roman time for 6:00 A.M. The Crucifixion occurred three hours later at "the third hour" (Mark 15:25), Jewish time for 9:00 A.M. See Luke 23:44 and note.

19:17, 18 The place where Jesus was **crucified** has never been firmly identified. Many be-

called in Hebrew, Gol′go·tha, 18where they
crucified Him, and two others with Him,
one on either side, and Jesus in the center.
19Now Pilate wrote a title and put *it* on the
cross. And the writing was:

JESUS OF NAZARETH,
THE KING OF THE JEWS.

20Then many of the Jews read this title, for
the place where Jesus was crucified was
near the city; and it was written in Hebrew,
Greek, *and* Latin.

21Therefore the chief priests of the Jews
said to Pilate, "Do not write, 'The King of
the Jews,' but, 'He said, "I am the King of
the Jews." ' "

22Pilate answered, "What I have written,
I have written."

23Then the soldiers, when they had cru-
cified Jesus, took His garments and made
four parts, to each soldier a part, and also
the tunic. Now the tunic was without
seam, woven from the top in one piece.
24They said therefore among themselves,
"Let us not tear it, but cast lots for it, whose
it shall be," that the Scripture might be ful-
filled which says:

"They divided My garments among
them,
And for My clothing they cast lots."[a]

Therefore the soldiers did these things.

Behold Your Mother

25Now there stood by the cross of Jesus
His mother, and His mother's sister, Mary
the *wife* of Clō′pas, and Mary Mag′da·lēne.
26When Jesus therefore saw His mother,
and the disciple whom He loved standing
by, He said to His mother, "Woman, be-
hold your son!" 27Then He said to the disci-
ple, "Behold your mother!" And from that
hour that disciple took her to his own
home.

It Is Finished

28After this, Jesus, knowing[a] that all
things were now accomplished, that the
Scripture might be fulfilled, said, "I thirst!"
29Now a vessel full of sour wine was sitting
there; and they filled a sponge with sour
wine, put *it* on hyssop, and put *it* to His
mouth. 30So when Jesus had received the
sour wine, He said, "It is finished!" And
bowing His head, He gave up His spirit.

Jesus' Side Is Pierced

31Therefore, because it was the Prepara-
tion *Day,* that the bodies should not remain
on the cross on the Sabbath (for that Sab-
bath was a high day), the Jews asked Pilate
that their legs might be broken, and *that*
they might be taken away. 32Then the sol-
diers came and broke the legs of the first
and of the other who was crucified with
Him. 33But when they came to Jesus and
saw that He was already dead, they did
not break His legs. 34But one of the soldiers
pierced His side with a spear, and immedi-
ately blood and water came out. 35And he
who has seen has testified, and his testi-
mony is true; and he knows that he is
telling the truth, so that you may believe.
36For these things were done that the Scrip-
ture should be fulfilled, *"Not one of His*
bones shall be broken."[a] 37And again

19:24 [a]Psalm 22:18 19:28 [a]M-Text reads *seeing.*
19:36 [a]Exodus 12:46; Numbers 9:12; Psalm 34:20

lieve it to be a skull-shaped knoll just outside Jerusalem, giving credence to the name **Place of a Skull**.

19:30 It is finished: The task for which Jesus came to earth was complete.

19:31, 32 The Jewish Sabbath law would have been violated by leaving the bodies on the crosses overnight, and the Sabbath began at sundown on Friday. **Preparation Day**: Friday, the day before the **Sabbath**. This Sabbath was **a high day** because it was the first day of unleavened bread during Passover week. The soldiers **broke the legs** of victims still living to hasten death.

19:33, 34 The thrust with a **spear** was to make sure that **Jesus** was indeed **dead**.

another Scripture says, *"They shall look on Him whom they pierced."*[a]

Jesus Buried in Joseph's Tomb

38After this, Joseph of Ar·i·ma·thē′a, being a disciple of Jesus, but secretly, for fear of the Jews, asked Pilate that he might take away the body of Jesus; and Pilate gave *him* permission. So he came and took the body of Jesus. 39And Nic·o·dē′mus, who at first came to Jesus by night, also came, bringing a mixture of myrrh and aloes, about a hundred pounds. 40Then they took the body of Jesus, and bound it in strips of linen with the spices, as the custom of the Jews is to bury. 41Now in the place where He was crucified there was a garden, and in the garden a new tomb in which no one had yet been laid. 42So there they laid Jesus, because of the Jews' Preparation *Day,* for the tomb was nearby.

CHAPTER 20

The Empty Tomb

Now the first *day* of the week Mary Mag′da·lēne went to the tomb early, while it was still dark, and saw *that* the stone had been taken away from the tomb. 2Then she ran and came to Simon Peter, and to the other disciple, whom Jesus loved, and said to them, "They have taken away the Lord out of the tomb, and we do not know where they have laid Him."

3Peter therefore went out, and the other disciple, and were going to the tomb. 4So they both ran together, and the other disciple outran Peter and came to the tomb first. 5And he, stooping down and looking in, saw the linen cloths lying *there;* yet he did not go in. 6Then Simon Peter came, following him, and went into the tomb; and he saw the linen cloths lying *there,* 7and the handkerchief that had been around His head, not lying with the linen cloths, but folded together in a place by itself. 8Then the other disciple, who came to the tomb first, went in also; and he saw and believed. 9For as yet they did not know the Scripture, that He must rise again from the dead. 10Then the disciples went away again to their own homes.

Mary Magdalene Sees the Risen Lord

11But Mary stood outside by the tomb weeping, and as she wept she stooped down *and looked* into the tomb. 12And she saw two angels in white sitting, one at the head and the other at the feet, where the body of Jesus had lain. 13Then they said to her, "Woman, why are you weeping?"

She said to them, "Because they have taken away my Lord, and I do not know where they have laid Him."

14Now when she had said this, she turned around and saw Jesus standing *there,* and did not know that it was Jesus. 15Jesus said to her, "Woman, why are you weeping? Whom are you seeking?"

She, supposing Him to be the gardener, said to Him, "Sir, if You have carried Him away, tell me where You have laid Him, and I will take Him away."

16Jesus said to her, "Mary!"

She turned and said to Him,[a] "Rab·bō′nī!" (which is to say, Teacher).

17Jesus said to her, "Do not cling to Me,

19:37 [a]Zechariah 12:10   20:16 [a]NU-Text adds *in Hebrew.*

19:38, 39 Joseph of Arimathea: A wealthy member of the Jewish Sanhedrin and now a **disciple of Jesus** (Matt. 27:57; Mark 15:43). **Nicodemus** apparently accepted Jesus' teaching and was born of the Spirit (see 3:1–21).

19:40–42 The burial place was probably a private **garden**. Because the time before the Sabbath was short, Jesus had to be buried nearby.

20:8–10 Having seen the undisturbed graveclothes, the **other disciple**, John, **believed** that Jesus had risen. **the Scripture**: Ps. 16:9–11 is cited by Peter in connection with the Resurrection (see Acts 2:24–31).

for I have not yet ascended to My Father;
but go to My brethren and say to them, 'I
am ascending to My Father and your
Father, and *to* My God and your God.' "
18 Mary Mag′da•lēne came and told the
disciples that she had seen the Lord,[a] and
that He had spoken these things to her.

The Apostles Commissioned

19 Then, the same day at evening, being
the first *day* of the week, when the doors
were shut where the disciples were assem-
bled,[a] for fear of the Jews, Jesus came and
stood in the midst, and said to them,
"Peace *be* with you." 20 When He had said
this, He showed them *His* hands and His
side. Then the disciples were glad when
they saw the Lord.
21 So Jesus said to them again, "Peace to
you! As the Father has sent Me, I also send
you." 22 And when He had said this, He
breathed on *them,* and said to them, "Re-
ceive the Holy Spirit. 23 If you forgive the
sins of any, they are forgiven them; if you
retain the *sins* of any, they are retained."

Seeing and Believing

24 Now Thomas, called the Twin, one of
the twelve, was not with them when Jesus
came. 25 The other disciples therefore said
to him, "We have seen the Lord."
So he said to them, "Unless I see in His
hands the print of the nails, and put my
finger into the print of the nails, and put
my hand into His side, I will not believe."
26 And after eight days His disciples
were again inside, and Thomas with them.
Jesus came, the doors being shut, and
stood in the midst, and said, "Peace to
you!" 27 Then He said to Thomas, "Reach
your finger here, and look at My hands;
and reach your hand *here,* and put *it* into
My side. Do not be unbelieving, but believ-
ing."
28 And Thomas answered and said to
Him, "My Lord and my God!"
29 Jesus said to him, "Thomas,[a] because
you have seen Me, you have believed.
Blessed *are* those who have not seen and
yet have believed."

That You May Believe

30 And truly Jesus did many other signs
in the presence of His disciples, which
are not written in this book; 31 but these
are written that you may believe that
Jesus is the Christ, the Son of God, and
that believing you may have life in His
name.

CHAPTER 21

Breakfast by the Sea

After these things Jesus showed Him-
self again to the disciples at the Sea of
Tī•bē′ri•as, and in this way He showed
Himself: 2 Simon Peter, Thomas called the
Twin, Na•than′a•el of Cā′na in Galilee, the
sons of Zeb′e•dee, and two others of His
disciples were together. 3 Simon Peter said
to them, "I am going fishing."
They said to him, "We are going with
you also." They went out and immedi-
ately[a] got into the boat, and that night they
caught nothing. 4 But when the morning
had now come, Jesus stood on the shore;
yet the disciples did not know that it was
Jesus. 5 Then Jesus said to them, "Children,
have you any food?"
They answered Him, "No."
6 And He said to them, "Cast the net on
the right side of the boat, and you will find
some." So they cast, and now they were not
able to draw it in because of the multitude
of fish.
7 Therefore that disciple whom Jesus

20:18 [a]NU-Text reads *disciples, "I have seen the Lord,"*. . . 20:19 [a]NU-Text omits *assembled.*
20:29 [a]NU-Text and M-Text omit *Thomas.*
21:3 [a]NU-Text omits *immediately.*

20:22 breathed on them: The Greek *pneuma* may mean either "breath" or "spirit." Thus Jesus graphically portrayed His gift of the **Holy Spirit**. This was a foretaste of what would happen at Pentecost. See Jesus' promise and command (Acts 1:4, 5, 8) and its fulfillment (Acts 2:1–4).

loved said to Peter, "It is the Lord!" Now
when Simon Peter heard that it was the
Lord, he put on *his* outer garment (for he
had removed it), and plunged into the sea.
8But the other disciples came in the little
boat (for they were not far from land, but
about two hundred cubits), dragging the
net with fish. 9Then, as soon as they had
come to land, they saw a fire of coals there,
and fish laid on it, and bread. 10Jesus said
to them, "Bring some of the fish which you
have just caught."

11Simon Peter went up and dragged the
net to land, full of large fish, one hundred
and fifty-three; and although there were
so many, the net was not broken. 12Jesus
said to them, "Come *and* eat breakfast."
Yet none of the disciples dared ask
Him, "Who are You?"—knowing that it
was the Lord. 13Jesus then came and took
the bread and gave it to them, and likewise
the fish.

14This *is* now the third time Jesus
showed Himself to His disciples after He
was raised from the dead.

Jesus Restores Peter

15So when they had eaten breakfast, Jesus said to Simon Peter, "Simon, *son* of Jonah,[a] do you love Me more than these?"

He said to Him, "Yes, Lord; You know that I love You."

He said to him, "Feed My lambs."

16He said to him again a second time, "Simon, *son* of Jonah,[a] do you love Me?"

He said to Him, "Yes, Lord; You know that I love You."

He said to him, "Tend My sheep."

17He said to him the third time, "Simon, *son* of Jonah,[a] do you love Me?" Peter was grieved because He said to him the third time, "Do you love Me?"

And he said to Him, "Lord, You know all things; You know that I love You."

Jesus said to him, "Feed My sheep.
18Most assuredly, I say to you, when you
were younger, you girded yourself and
walked where you wished; but when you
are old, you will stretch out your hands,
and another will gird you and carry *you*
where you do not wish." 19This He spoke,
signifying by what death he would glorify
God. And when He had spoken this, He
said to him, "Follow Me."

The Beloved Disciple and His Book

20Then Peter, turning around, saw the
disciple whom Jesus loved following, who
also had leaned on His breast at the supper, and said, "Lord, who is the one who
betrays You?" 21Peter, seeing him, said to
Jesus, "But Lord, what *about* this man?"

22Jesus said to him, "If I will that he remain till I come, what *is that* to you? You follow Me."

23Then this saying went out among the brethren that this disciple would not die. Yet Jesus did not say to him that he would not die, but, "If I will that he remain till I come, what *is that* to you?"

24This is the disciple who testifies of these things, and wrote these things; and we know that his testimony is true.

25And there are also many other things that Jesus did, which if they were written one by one, I suppose that even the world itself could not contain the books that would be written. Amen.

21:15 [a]NU-Text reads *John.* 21:16 [a]NU-Text reads *John.* 21:17 [a]NU-Text reads *John.*

21:18, 19 stretch out your hands: Jesus' prediction was fulfilled when Peter was crucified in Rome. **Follow Me** is a present imperative giving the sense: Follow Me—now, and always.

21:21, 22 Peter's question may have been prompted by curiosity or by jealousy: If I am to die, what about John? Jesus' response is wise counsel for Christians of all time: Do not be jealously concerned about God's role for others—**you follow Me**.

ETERNITY BEGINS TODAY

Leslie E. Moser, Ph.D.

Let me tell you something that may change the way you think about heaven. I believe that this eternal life of which we speak and toward which we yearn has already begun. Today is the day of salvation, and now is the time to serve the Lord. Now we see through the dark glass—we do not see the Lord as clearly as we will in heaven—but at least we do see (1 Cor. 13:1).

"Our Savior came that our joy might be full even before we get to heaven."

Think about it. Isn't it true that today, this day, is the first remaining day of your eternity? Eternity for you will not begin at death; it began the moment Christ entered your life. Christ came that we might have life. He does not teach us how to live in heaven. He teaches us how to live on earth. His constant message is *hope* for the kingdom to come but *help* for the kingdom at hand. We certainly should be exuberant about the reality of our heavenly abode, joyful about our heavenly fellowship with Christ, and confident in the promise that all things will be new. In heaven, we will see through the glass clearly; we will know Christ face-to-face.

You and I must keep looking forward to heaven—that glorious place where we will be able to sit at the feet of Jesus, that place which is down the road just past the milestone of death. But as Christians, we look forward to the joys of heaven at the same time that we embrace the joys of this life. Although life can be filled with frustrations, pain, and misery, it is also a time for joy—joy not just because we shall soon be home with Christ, but joy that comes through living daily with and for Him. Our Savior came that our joy might be full even before we get to heaven (John 15:11), and we are to appropriate that promise daily! ✦

✦Acts✦

Acts is an extension of Luke and is the historical link between the Gospels, as biographies of Jesus Christ, and the Epistles, as commentaries on Jesus' life and teachings. While the four Gospels provide an account of the life of Christ, Acts is the only book that carries on the story from His Ascension to the spread of the new faith throughout the world.

The title, Acts of the Apostles, is a bit misleading, for it mainly records the acts of Peter among the Jews and Paul among the other people of the then-known world. Written by Luke, the book tells the story of men and women who took Christ's Great Commission seriously and began to spread the news of the risen Savior to the corners of the world. In their zeal for God, these individuals demonstrated what He can do with a life fully committed to His service. Because of Luke's strong emphasis on the ministry of the Holy Spirit, this book could be regarded as the Acts of the Spirit of Christ working in and through the apostles. In fact, the coming of the Spirit is mentioned in Acts more than in any other New Testament book. ✦

CHAPTER 1

Prologue

The former account I made, O Thē-
oph'i·lus, of all that Jesus began both to do
and teach, 2until the day in which He was
taken up, after He through the Holy Spirit
had given commandments to the apostles
whom He had chosen, 3to whom He also
presented Himself alive after His suffering
by many infallible proofs, being seen by
them during forty days and speaking of
the things pertaining to the kingdom of
God.

The Holy Spirit Promised

4And being assembled together with
them, He commanded them not to depart
from Jerusalem, but to wait for the Promise
of the Father, "which," *He said,* "you have
heard from Me; 5for John truly baptized
with water, but you shall be baptized with
the Holy Spirit not many days from now."
6Therefore, when they had come together,
they asked Him, saying, "Lord, will You at
this time restore the kingdom to Israel?"
7And He said to them, "It is not for you to
know times or seasons which the Father
has put in His own authority. 8But you

1:1 The former account: the gospel of Luke.

1:4 the Promise of the Father: The coming of the Holy Spirit, announced by Joel (Joel 2:28, 29; see Ezek. 36:25–27) and Jesus (Luke 24:49; John 14:16).

1:8 witnesses to Me: In Acts, as in the Gospels, the message is about Jesus. The Christian agenda is aggressive evangelism worldwide. In this one verse lies the theme of the entire book and the mandate for believers today. Every Christian, regardless of specific talents or spiritual gifts, is called to be a witness to the world of the saving power of Jesus Christ.

shall receive power when the Holy Spirit has come upon you; and you shall be witnesses to Me[a] in Jerusalem, and in all Judea and Samaria, and to the end of the earth."

Jesus Ascends to Heaven

9 Now when He had spoken these things, while they watched, He was taken up, and a cloud received Him out of their sight. 10 And while they looked steadfastly toward heaven as He went up, behold, two men stood by them in white apparel, 11 who also said, "Men of Galilee, why do you stand gazing up into heaven? This *same* Jesus, who was taken up from you into heaven, will so come in like manner as you saw Him go into heaven."

The Upper Room Prayer Meeting

12 Then they returned to Jerusalem from the mount called Ol′i·vet, which is near Jerusalem, a Sabbath day's journey. 13 And when they had entered, they went up into the upper room where they were staying: Peter, James, John, and Andrew; Philip and Thomas; Bartholomew and Matthew; James *the son* of Al·phæ′us and Simon the Zealot; and Judas *the son* of James. 14 These all continued with one accord in prayer and supplication,[a] with the women and Mary the mother of Jesus, and with His brothers.

Matthias Chosen

15 And in those days Peter stood up in the midst of the disciples[a] (altogether the number of names was about a hundred and twenty), and said, 16 "Men *and* brethren, this Scripture had to be fulfilled, which the Holy Spirit spoke before by the mouth of David concerning Judas, who became a guide to those who arrested Jesus; 17 for he was numbered with us and obtained a part in this ministry."

18 (Now this man purchased a field with the wages of iniquity; and falling headlong, he burst open in the middle and all his entrails gushed out. 19 And it became known to all those dwelling in Jerusalem; so that field is called in their own language, Akel Da′ma, that is, Field of Blood.)

20 "For it is written in the Book of Psalms:

> *'Let his dwelling place be desolate,*
> *And let no one live in it';*[a]

and,

> *'Let*[b] *another take his office.'*[c]

21 "Therefore, of these men who have accompanied us all the time that the Lord Jesus went in and out among us, 22 beginning from the baptism of John to that day when He was taken up from us, one of these must become a witness with us of His resurrection."

23 And they proposed two: Joseph called Bar′sa·bas, who was surnamed Jus′tus,

1:8 [a]NU-Text reads *My witnesses.* 1:14 [a]NU-Text omits *and supplication.* 1:15 [a]NU-Text reads *brethren.* 1:20 [a]Psalm 69:25 [b]Psalm 109:8 [c]Greek *episkopen*, position of overseer

1:9–11 Luke is the only Gospel writer who records the Ascension of Christ (Luke 24:49–53).

1:15 Peter stood up: Peter's formal leadership begins.

1:18 This is not a contradiction of the description in Matt. 27:5–10 but rather an expansion. The priests purchased the field in Judas' name with the money He returned to them (Matt. 27:3–7). After Judas hanged himself, his body either fell down or was cut down and "burst open."

1:20 Let another take his office: They felt it essential to maintain the number of 12 apostles, perhaps to represent the 12 tribes of Israel (see Matt. 19:28); hence, it was necessary to fill the vacancy left by Judas.

1:21, 22 become a witness with us: In order to witness to the Resurrection, Judas's replacement had to have been with Jesus during His public ministry and to have seen the risen Christ. Paul supported his call to be an apostle by the fact that he also had seen the resurrected Christ (1 Cor. 15:8).

and Mat·thī′as. 24And they prayed and
said, "You, O Lord, who know the hearts of
all, show which of these two You have cho-
sen 25to take part in this ministry and apos-
tleship from which Judas by transgression
fell, that he might go to his own place."
26And they cast their lots, and the lot fell on
Mat·thī′as. And he was numbered with the
eleven apostles.

CHAPTER 2

Coming of the Holy Spirit

When the Day of Pentecost had fully
come, they were all with one accord[a] in one
place. 2And suddenly there came a sound
from heaven, as of a rushing mighty wind,
and it filled the whole house where they
were sitting. 3Then there appeared to them
divided tongues, as of fire, and *one* sat
upon each of them. 4And they were all
filled with the Holy Spirit and began to
speak with other tongues, as the Spirit
gave them utterance.

The Crowd's Response

5And there were dwelling in Jerusalem
Jews, devout men, from every nation un-
der heaven. 6And when this sound oc-
curred, the multitude came together, and
were confused, because everyone heard
them speak in his own language. 7Then
they were all amazed and marveled, say-
ing to one another, "Look, are not all these
who speak Galileans? 8And how *is it that*
we hear, each in our own language in
which we were born? 9Par′thi·ans and
Mēdes and Ē′lam·ītes, those dwelling in
Mes·o·po·tā′mi·a, Judea and Cap·pa-
dō′ci·a, Pon′tus and Asia, 10Phryg′i·a and
Pam·phyl′i·a, Egypt and the parts of
Lib′ya adjoining Cȳ·rē′nē, visitors from
Rome, both Jews and proselytes, 11Crē′tans
and Arabs—we hear them speaking in our
own tongues the wonderful works of
God." 12So they were all amazed and per-
plexed, saying to one another, "Whatever
could this mean?"

13Others mocking said, "They are full of
new wine."

Peter's Sermon

14But Peter, standing up with the eleven,
raised his voice and said to them, "Men of
Judea and all who dwell in Jerusalem, let
this be known to you, and heed my words.
15For these are not drunk, as you suppose,
since it is *only* the third hour of the day.
16But this is what was spoken by the
prophet Jō′el:

17 *'And it shall come to pass in the last days, says God,*
That I will pour out of My Spirit on all flesh;
Your sons and your daughters shall prophesy,
Your young men shall see visions,
Your old men shall dream dreams.
18 *And on My menservants and on My maidservants*
I will pour out My Spirit in those days;
And they shall prophesy.
19 *I will show wonders in heaven above*
And signs in the earth beneath:
Blood and fire and vapor of smoke.
20 *The sun shall be turned into darkness,*

2:1 [a]NU-Text reads *together.*

1:26 they cast their lots: An OT method of determining the will of God (Josh. 18:6). There is no record of casting lots after Pentecost.

2:1 Pentecost: a yearly Jewish festival held to celebrate the first buds of harvest. Also known as the "Feast of Weeks" or the "Day of First fruits."

2:4 other tongues: spoken human languages not known to the speakers.

2:5 Every nation in the Roman world was represented in this gathering of pilgrims who had traveled to Jerusalem to celebrate the festival of Pentecost.

2:14, 15 The miracle obviously was not drunkenness because it was too early in the day (9:00 A.M.).

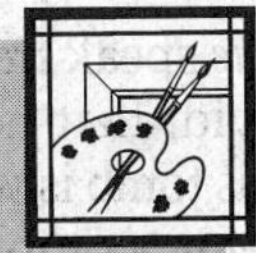

Peter: From a Reed to a Rock

Just as parents often find it difficult to view their adult children as "all grown up," more mature Christians sometimes fail to acknowledge the changes in younger believers. We may continue to act on our first impression of an immature individual long after the Lord has transformed him or her into a faithful and balanced servant of God.

But the Lord does not make that mistake, as we see in the life of Simon Peter. Despite his early imprudence and pride, this headstrong disciple eventually matured into a stable and loving apostle whom God used in a marvelous way.

When he was first called to follow Jesus, Peter's habit of speaking and acting impulsively often placed him in awkward situations, as in his attempt to walk on the water (Matt. 14:28–30). In addition to being presumptuous (16:22; 17:4), he was self-seeking (19:27) and conceited (26:33). His commitment wavered like a reed blowing in the wind.

Yet Simon Peter belonged to Jesus' inner circle, along with James and John. What could the Lord have possibly seen in such an immature man?

Jesus recognized Peter's potential—his tender heart (John 13:6) and his spiritual sensitivity (Matt. 16:16). He knew that once Peter fully surrendered to the Lord's will, his impetuous nature could be harnessed for God's purposes and his self-centeredness could be transformed into love for others.

Peter himself caught a true glimpse of his failures following his denial of Christ (Mark 14:67–72). The harsh reality of his own shortcomings prompted this brash, proud man to weep over what he had done. Although he still had much to learn, this moment marked the beginning of Peter's transformation.

The events at Pentecost further impacted his character. In Acts, we see Peter as a powerful preacher. The leader of the early church movement, he spread the gospel to the Jews (Acts 2), to the Samaritans (8:14–17), and to the Gentiles (ch. 10). He performed many miracles in the name of Jesus Christ and courageously suffered much persecution for his testimony.

By the time he wrote his two epistles, Peter had become the rock Jesus described years earlier (John 1:42). The power of the Holy Spirit, along with years of suffering, had transformed the apostle into a man of wisdom, love, and spiritual strength. He could speak with the authority of experience and righteous living.

No matter how far from our ideal a young Christian may be, we should never forget the power of God to change that person into an effective servant of Jesus Christ. Just as Peter's precarious disposition was stabilized by the Holy Spirit, each of us can be similarly changed into spiritually and emotionally balanced people when we allow God to work in our lives. ✦

And the moon into blood,
Before the coming of the great and
awesome day of the LORD.
21 *And it shall come to pass*
That whoever calls on the name of the
LORD
Shall be saved.'[a]

[22]"Men of Israel, hear these words: Jesus
of Nazareth, a Man attested by God to you
by miracles, wonders, and signs which
God did through Him in your midst, as
you yourselves also know— [23]Him, being
delivered by the determined purpose and
foreknowledge of God, you have taken[a] by
lawless hands, have crucified, and put to
death; [24]whom God raised up, having
loosed the pains of death, because it was
not possible that He should be held by it.
[25]For David says concerning Him:

'I foresaw the LORD *always before my*
face,
For He is at my right hand, that I may
not be shaken.
26 *Therefore my heart rejoiced, and my*
tongue was glad;
Moreover my flesh also will rest in
hope.
27 *For You will not leave my soul in*
Hā'dēs,
Nor will You allow Your Holy One to
see corruption.
28 *You have made known to me the*
ways of life;
You will make me full of joy in Your
presence.'[a]

[29]"Men *and* brethren, let *me* speak freely
to you of the patriarch David, that he is
both dead and buried, and his tomb is with
us to this day. [30]Therefore, being a prophet,
and knowing that God had sworn with an
oath to him that of the fruit of his body, ac-
cording to the flesh, He would raise up the
Christ to sit on his throne,[a] [31]he, foreseeing
this, spoke concerning the resurrection of
the Christ, that His soul was not left in
Hā'dēs, nor did His flesh see corruption.
[32]This Jesus God has raised up, of which
we are all witnesses. [33]Therefore being ex-
alted to the right hand of God, and having
received from the Father the promise of the
Holy Spirit, He poured out this which you
now see and hear.
[34]"For David did not ascend into the
heavens, but he says himself:

'The LORD *said to my Lord,*
"Sit at My right hand,
35 *Till I make Your enemies Your*
footstool."'[a]

[36]"Therefore let all the house of Israel
know assuredly that God has made this Je-
sus, whom you crucified, both Lord and
Christ."
[37]Now when they heard *this*, they were
cut to the heart, and said to Peter and the
rest of the apostles, "Men *and* brethren,
what shall we do?"

2:21 [a]Joel 2:28–32 2:23 [a]NU-Text omits *have taken.* 2:28 [a]Psalm 16:8–11 2:30 [a]NU-Text omits *according to the flesh, He would raise up the Christ* and completes the verse with *He would seat one on his throne.* 2:35 [a]Psalm 110:1

2:19–21 These verses refer primarily to the end of this age at Christ's Second Coming (see Matt. 24:29).

2:22, 23 Peter solemnly charged the Jewish leaders with crucifying the **Man attested by God**, their Messiah. They were responsible, but our Lord's death was no accident. He was **delivered by the determined purpose and foreknowledge of God**. The theology of the Bible blends belief in the total sovereignty of God with recognition of the full responsibility of human agents. This still holds true today: although our omniscient God knows our actions and thoughts before they take place, each of us is responsible for the choices we make.

2:32 The evidence for the Resurrection is twofold: the empty tomb (v. 29) and the appearances of the risen Christ. Peter and his companions (1:13, 14) were **all witnesses** of these resurrection appearances.

[38]Then Peter said to them, "Repent, and let every one of you be baptized in the name of Jesus Christ for the remission of sins; and you shall receive the gift of the Holy Spirit. [39]For the promise is to you and to your children, and to all who are afar off, as many as the Lord our God will call."

A Vital Church Grows

[40]And with many other words he testified and exhorted them, saying, "Be saved from this perverse generation." [41]Then those who gladly[a] received his word were baptized; and that day about three thousand souls were added *to them.* [42]And they continued steadfastly in the apostles' doctrine and fellowship, in the breaking of bread, and in prayers. [43]Then fear came upon every soul, and many wonders and signs were done through the apostles. [44]Now all who believed were together, and had all things in common, [45]and sold their possessions and goods, and divided them among all, as anyone had need.

[46]So continuing daily with one accord in the temple, and breaking bread from house to house, they ate their food with gladness and simplicity of heart, [47]praising God and having favor with all the people. And the Lord added to the church[a] daily those who were being saved.

CHAPTER 3

A Lame Man Healed

Now Peter and John went up together to the temple at the hour of prayer, the ninth *hour.* [2]And a certain man lame from his mother's womb was carried, whom they laid daily at the gate of the temple which is called Beautiful, to ask alms from those who entered the temple; [3]who, seeing Peter and John about to go into the temple, asked for alms. [4]And fixing his eyes on him, with John, Peter said, "Look at us." [5]So he gave them his attention, expecting to receive something from them. [6]Then Peter said, "Silver and gold I do not have, but what I do have I give you: In the name of Jesus Christ of Nazareth, rise up and walk." [7]And he took him by the right hand and lifted *him* up, and immediately his feet and ankle bones received strength. [8]So he, leaping up, stood and walked and entered the temple with them—walking, leaping, and praising God. [9]And all the people saw him walking and praising God. [10]Then they knew that it was he who sat begging alms at the Beautiful Gate of the temple; and they were filled with wonder and amazement at what had happened to him.

Preaching in Solomon's Portico

[11]Now as the lame man who was healed held on to Peter and John, all the people ran together to them in the porch which is called Solomon's, greatly amazed. [12]So when Peter saw *it,* he responded to the people: "Men of Israel, why do you marvel at this? Or why look so intently at us, as though by our own power or godliness we had made this man walk? [13]The God of Abraham, Isaac, and Jacob, the God of our fathers, glorified His Servant Jesus, whom you delivered up and denied in the presence of Pilate, when he was determined to

2:41 [a]NU-Text omits *gladly.* 2:47 [a]NU-Text omits *to the church.*

2:43 fear: awe.

2:44, 45 all things in common: Christian love prompted a sharing of goods for the benefit of the less fortunate, and thus a whole new dimension of stewardship. As stewards of our God-given blessings, we must be ready and willing to give generously when the Lord prompts.

3:13 glorified His Servant: Jesus fulfills the role of the Suffering Servant of the Lord described in Is. 52; 53 (see v. 26; 4:27, 30). Peter identifies the Messiah as the Holy One, the Just (v. 14), Prince of life (v. 15), Christ (vv. 18, 20), Prophet (v. 23), and Servant (v. 26).

SPIRITUALLY CRIPPLED

Jill Briscoe

One thing is certain: the man at the temple gate was used to the disinterest of the worshipers and was not expecting too much from Peter and John. He certainly got the shock of his life! Peter, fastening his eyes on him, said, "Look at us" (Acts 3:4). So the man gave them his attention. Two seconds later, he was on his feet for the very first time in his life!

When Christians witness about the Lord Jesus, in effect they are saying, "Look at us! We have something to give you." Maybe crippled people do not expect very much, but we can always surprise them. The greatest thing we can ever give a spiritually disabled man is not a crutch or even a handout, but a word from God that will stand him up on his own two feet and set him off on the right road.

"The greatest thing we can ever give a spiritually disabled man is a word from God that will stand him up."

"Then Peter said, 'Silver and gold I do not have, but what I do have I give you: In the name of Jesus Christ of Nazareth, rise up and walk.' And he took him by the right hand and lifted him up, and immediately his feet and ankle bones received strength. So he, leaping up, stood and walked and entered the temple with them—walking, leaping, and praising God" (Acts 3:6–8).

We, like Peter and John, must tell a hurting world to look to us so we can point them to Him. We can witness to the fact that we were once crippled, too, until Jesus walked by and took us by the hand and told us to get up and walk. It is in His name and power, not our own, that we can do this and so can they. ✦

let *Him* go. [14]But you denied the Holy One
and the Just, and asked for a murderer to
be granted to you, [15]and killed the Prince of
life, whom God raised from the dead, of
which we are witnesses. [16]And His name,
through faith in His name, has made this
man strong, whom you see and know. Yes,
the faith which *comes* through Him has
given him this perfect soundness in the
presence of you all.
[17]"Yet now, brethren, I know that you
did *it* in ignorance, as *did* also your rulers.
[18]But those things which God foretold by
the mouth of all His prophets, that the
Christ would suffer, He has thus fulfilled.
[19]Repent therefore and be converted, that
your sins may be blotted out, so that times
of refreshing may come from the presence
of the Lord, [20]and that He may send Jesus
Christ, who was preached to you before,[a]

3:20 [a]NU-Text and M-Text read *Christ Jesus, who was ordained for you before.*

3:16 Peter disclaimed the glory for the miracle, explaining that Jesus healed the man.

21whom heaven must receive until the
times of restoration of all things, which
God has spoken by the mouth of all His
holy prophets since the world began. 22For
Moses truly said to the fathers, *'The LORD
your God will raise up for you a Prophet
like me from your brethren. Him you shall
hear in all things, whatever He says to you.*
23*And it shall be that every soul who will
not hear that Prophet shall be utterly de-
stroyed from among the people.'*[a] 24Yes,
and all the prophets, from Samuel and
those who follow, as many as have spoken,
have also foretold[a] these days. 25You are
sons of the prophets, and of the covenant
which God made with our fathers, saying
to Abraham, *'And in your seed all the fam-
ilies of the earth shall be blessed.'*[a] 26To you
first, God, having raised up His Servant Je-
sus, sent Him to bless you, in turning away
every one *of you* from your iniquities."

CHAPTER 4

Peter and John Arrested

Now as they spoke to the people, the
priests, the captain of the temple, and the
Sad'dū·cees came upon them, 2being
greatly disturbed that they taught the peo-
ple and preached in Jesus the resurrection
from the dead. 3And they laid hands on
them, and put *them* in custody until the
next day, for it was already evening. 4How-
ever, many of those who heard the word
believed; and the number of the men came
to be about five thousand.

Addressing the Sanhedrin

5And it came to pass, on the next day,
that their rulers, elders, and scribes, 6as
well as An'nas the high priest, Cā'i·a·phas,
John, and Alexander, and as many as were
of the family of the high priest, were gath-
ered together at Jerusalem. 7And when
they had set them in the midst, they asked,
"By what power or by what name have
you done this?"

8Then Peter, filled with the Holy Spirit,
said to them, "Rulers of the people and el-
ders of Israel: 9If we this day are judged for
a good deed *done* to a helpless man, by
what means he has been made well, 10let it
be known to you all, and to all the people
of Israel, that by the name of Jesus Christ of
Nazareth, whom you crucified, whom God
raised from the dead, by Him this man
stands here before you whole. 11This is the
*'stone which was rejected by you builders,
which has become the chief cornerstone.'*[a]
12Nor is there salvation in any other, for
there is no other name under heaven given
among men by which we must be saved."

The Name of Jesus Forbidden

13Now when they saw the boldness of
Peter and John, and perceived that they
were uneducated and untrained men, they
marveled. And they realized that they had
been with Jesus. 14And seeing the man who
had been healed standing with them, they
could say nothing against it. 15But when

3:23 [a]Deuteronomy 18:15, 18, 19 3:24 [a]NU-Text and M-Text read *proclaimed.* 3:25 [a]Genesis 22:18; 26:4; 28:14 4:11 [a]Psalm 118:22

3:25 In repeating the Abrahamic covenant, Peter reminded the Jewish leaders that God never intended to make Abraham's descendants the sole recipients of His blessing.

4:1, 2 The **Sadducees** were **disturbed** because the disciples **preached in Jesus the resurrection**. Unlike the Pharisees, the Sadducees did not believe in a resurrection (23:8; see John 11:24).

4:12 no other name: Jesus is the only way to God and salvation (John 14:6).

4:13 The boldness of Peter and John, despite their lack of technical religious training, was another miracle. It was the result of the Holy Spirit who came to them in fulfillment of Jesus' promise (John 15:26, 27). Our own personal relationship with God and His Spirit should be so evident as to cause those who hear us to conclude that we have **been with Jesus**.

they had commanded them to go aside out
of the council, they conferred among them-
selves, [16]saying, "What shall we do to these
men? For, indeed, that a notable miracle
has been done through them *is* evident to
all who dwell in Jerusalem, and we cannot
deny *it*. [17]But so that it spreads no further
among the people, let us severely threaten
them, that from now on they speak to no
man in this name."

[18]So they called them and commanded
them not to speak at all nor teach in the
name of Jesus. [19]But Peter and John an-
swered and said to them, "Whether it is
right in the sight of God to listen to you
more than to God, you judge. [20]For we can-
not but speak the things which we have
seen and heard." [21]So when they had fur-
ther threatened them, they let them go,
finding no way of punishing them, be-
cause of the people, since they all glorified
God for what had been done. [22]For the man
was over forty years old on whom this mir-
acle of healing had been performed.

Prayer for Boldness

[23]And being let go, they went to their
own *companions* and reported all that the
chief priests and elders had said to them.
[24]So when they heard that, they raised their
voice to God with one accord and said:
"Lord, You *are* God, who made heaven and
earth and the sea, and all that is in them,
[25]who by the mouth of Your servant David[a]
have said:

'Why did the nations rage,
And the people plot vain things?
26 *The kings of the earth took their stand,*
And the rulers were gathered
together
Against the LORD *and against His*
Christ.'[a]

[27]"For truly against Your holy Servant
Jesus, whom You anointed, both Her'od
and Pon'ti·us Pilate, with the Gentiles and
the people of Israel, were gathered to-
gether [28]to do whatever Your hand and
Your purpose determined before to be
done. [29]Now, Lord, look on their threats,
and grant to Your servants that with all
boldness they may speak Your word, [30]by
stretching out Your hand to heal, and that
signs and wonders may be done through
the name of Your holy Servant Jesus."

[31]And when they had prayed, the place
where they were assembled together was
shaken; and they were all filled with the
Holy Spirit, and they spoke the word of
God with boldness.

Sharing in All Things

[32]Now the multitude of those who be-
lieved were of one heart and one soul; nei-
ther did anyone say that any of the things
he possessed was his own, but they had all
things in common. [33]And with great power
the apostles gave witness to the resurrec-
tion of the Lord Jesus. And great grace was
upon them all. [34]Nor was there anyone
among them who lacked; for all who were
possessors of lands or houses sold them,
and brought the proceeds of the things that
were sold, [35]and laid *them* at the apostles'
feet; and they distributed to each as any-
one had need.

[36]And Jō'sēs,[a] who was also named
Bar'na·bas by the apostles (which is trans-
lated Son of Encouragement), a Lē'vīte of
the country of Cyprus, [37]having land, sold
it, and brought the money and laid *it* at the
apostles' feet.

4:25 [a]NU-Text reads *who through the Holy Spirit, by the mouth of our father, Your servant David.*
4:26 [a]Psalm 2:1, 2 4:36 [a]NU-Text reads *Joseph.*

4:16 The Sanhedrin did not deny the God-given power of the apostles, but they feared losing their control over the people.

4:29 grant to Your servants . . . boldness: It was not a cry for deliverance from danger but for courage to face the challenge. Their boldness after Pentecost contrasts sharply with their hiding "for fear of the Jews" before Pentecost (John 20:19).

CHAPTER 5

Lying to the Holy Spirit

But a certain man named An·a·nī′as,
with Sap·phī′ra his wife, sold a possession.
[2]And he kept back *part* of the proceeds, his
wife also being aware *of it*, and brought a
certain part and laid *it* at the apostles' feet.
[3]But Peter said, "An·a·nī′as, why has Satan
filled your heart to lie to the Holy Spirit
and keep back *part* of the price of the land
for yourself? [4]While it remained, was it not
your own? And after it was sold, was it not
in your own control? Why have you con-
ceived this thing in your heart? You have
not lied to men but to God."

[5]Then An·a·nī′as, hearing these words,
fell down and breathed his last. So great
fear came upon all those who heard these
things. [6]And the young men arose and
wrapped him up, carried *him* out, and
buried *him*.

[7]Now it was about three hours later
when his wife came in, not knowing what
had happened. [8]And Peter answered her,
"Tell me whether you sold the land for so
much?"

She said, "Yes, for so much."

[9]Then Peter said to her, "How is it that
you have agreed together to test the Spirit
of the Lord? Look, the feet of those who
have buried your husband *are* at the
door, and they will carry you out."
[10]Then immediately she fell down at
his feet and breathed her last. And the
young men came in and found her dead,
and carrying *her* out, buried *her* by her hus-
band. [11]So great fear came upon all the
church and upon all who heard these
things.

Continuing Power in the Church

[12]And through the hands of the apostles
many signs and wonders were done
among the people. And they were all with
one accord in Solomon's Porch. [13]Yet none
of the rest dared join them, but the people
esteemed them highly. [14]And believers
were increasingly added to the Lord, mul-
titudes of both men and women, [15]so that
they brought the sick out into the streets
and laid *them* on beds and couches, that at
least the shadow of Peter passing by might
fall on some of them. [16]Also a multitude
gathered from the surrounding cities to Je-
rusalem, bringing sick people and those
who were tormented by unclean spirits,
and they were all healed.

Imprisoned Apostles Freed

[17]Then the high priest rose up, and all
those who *were* with him (which is the sect
of the Sad′dū·cees), and they were filled
with indignation, [18]and laid their hands on
the apostles and put them in the common
prison. [19]But at night an angel of the Lord
opened the prison doors and brought them
out, and said, [20]"Go, stand in the temple
and speak to the people all the words of
this life."

[21]And when they heard *that*, they en-
tered the temple early in the morning and
taught. But the high priest and those with
him came and called the council together,
with all the elders of the children of Israel,
and sent to the prison to have them
brought.

Apostles on Trial Again

[22]But when the officers came and did not
find them in the prison, they returned and

5:1, 2 The sin of **Ananias** and **Sapphira** was not in keeping back money but in lying about it. Peter seems to have had a Spirit-given discernment of this deception.

5:12 Signs and wonders are mentioned repeatedly in Acts. These miracles seem to accompany crises in the history of God's people: at the Exodus (Ex. 7—12); during a threat to the nation at the time of Elisha (2 Kin. 6; 7); at the beginning of Jesus' ministry (John 4—6); and here at the birth of the church. **Solomon's Porch**: The colonnade to the east of Herod's temple.

5:20 in the temple: An appropriate place. It represented God's presence in Israel.

reported, [23]saying, "Indeed we found the
prison shut securely, and the guards stand-
ing outside[a] before the doors; but when we
opened them, we found no one inside!"
[24]Now when the high priest,[a] the captain of
the temple, and the chief priests heard
these things, they wondered what the out-
come would be. [25]So one came and told
them, saying,[a] "Look, the men whom you
put in prison are standing in the temple
and teaching the people!"

[26]Then the captain went with the officers
and brought them without violence,
for they feared the people, lest they
should be stoned. [27]And when they had
brought them, they set *them* before the
council. And the high priest asked them,
[28]saying, "Did we not strictly command
you not to teach in this name? And look,
you have filled Jerusalem with your doc-
trine, and intend to bring this Man's blood
on us!"

[29]But Peter and the *other* apostles an-
swered and said: "We ought to obey
God rather than men. [30]The God of our fa-
thers raised up Jesus whom you murdered
by hanging on a tree. [31]Him God has ex-
alted to His right hand *to be* Prince and
Savior, to give repentance to Israel and for-
giveness of sins. [32]And we are His wit-
nesses to these things, and *so* also *is* the
Holy Spirit whom God has given to those
who obey Him."

Gamaliel's Advice

[33]When they heard *this,* they were furi-
ous and plotted to kill them. [34]Then one in
the council stood up, a Phar'i·see named
Ga·mā'li·el, a teacher of the law held in re-
spect by all the people, and commanded
them to put the apostles outside for a little
while. [35]And he said to them: "Men of Is-
rael, take heed to yourselves what you in-
tend to do regarding these men. [36]For some
time ago Theū'das rose up, claiming to be
somebody. A number of men, about four
hundred, joined him. He was slain, and all
who obeyed him were scattered and came
to nothing. [37]After this man, Judas of Gali-
lee rose up in the days of the census, and
drew away many people after him. He also
perished, and all who obeyed him were
dispersed. [38]And now I say to you, keep
away from these men and let them alone;
for if this plan or this work is of men, it will
come to nothing; [39]but if it is of God, you
cannot overthrow it—lest you even be
found to fight against God."

[40]And they agreed with him, and when
they had called for the apostles and beaten
them, they commanded that they should
not speak in the name of Jesus, and let
them go. [41]So they departed from the pres-
ence of the council, rejoicing that they were
counted worthy to suffer shame for His[a]
name. [42]And daily in the temple, and in
every house, they did not cease teaching
and preaching Jesus *as* the Christ.

CHAPTER 6

Seven Chosen to Serve

Now in those days, when *the number of*
the disciples was multiplying, there arose a
complaint against the Hebrews by the
Hel'len·ists,[a] because their widows were

5:41 [a]NU-Text reads *the name;* M-Text reads *the name of Jesus.* 6:1 [a]That is, Greek-speaking Jews

5:28 bring this Man's blood on us: A response to the apostles' accusation that the Jewish leaders had personally crucified Jesus (see v. 30; 4:10). They were not rid of Jesus yet and felt increasingly on the defensive. They refused to accept Jesus as Messiah because they did not want to lose their authority.

5:41 We are never promised uninterrupted happiness as followers of Christ, but we can experience a boundless joy in serving Him.

6:1 Hebrews: Aramaic-speaking Jews native to Palestine. **Hellenists**: Greek-speaking Jews, usually born outside of Palestine. After Pentecost the believers had "all things in common" in a unity of love. But tensions developed because of alleged discrimination on the

neglected in the daily distribution. 2Then
the twelve summoned the multitude of the
disciples and said, "It is not desirable that
we should leave the word of God and
serve tables. 3Therefore, brethren, seek
out from among you seven men of *good*
reputation, full of the Holy Spirit and wis-
dom, whom we may appoint over this
business; 4but we will give ourselves con-
tinually to prayer and to the ministry of the
word."

5And the saying pleased the whole mul-
titude. And they chose Stephen, a man full
of faith and the Holy Spirit, and Philip,
Proch′o·rus, Nī·cā′nor, Tī′mon, Par′me-
nas, and Nic′o·las, a proselyte from An′-
ti·och, 6whom they set before the apostles;
and when they had prayed, they laid
hands on them.

7Then the word of God spread, and the
number of the disciples multiplied greatly
in Jerusalem, and a great many of the
priests were obedient to the faith.

Stephen Accused of Blasphemy

8And Stephen, full of faith[a] and power,
did great wonders and signs among the
people. 9Then there arose some from what
is called the Synagogue of the Freedmen
(Cȳ·rē′ni·ans, Alexandrians, and those
from Ci·li′ci·a and Asia), disputing with
Stephen. 10And they were not able to resist
the wisdom and the Spirit by which he
spoke. 11Then they secretly induced men to
say, "We have heard him speak blasphe-
mous words against Moses and God."
12And they stirred up the people, the el-
ders, and the scribes; and they came upon
him, seized him, and brought *him* to the
council. 13They also set up false witnesses
who said, "This man does not cease to
speak blasphemous[a] words against this
holy place and the law; 14for we have heard
him say that this Jesus of Nazareth will de-
stroy this place and change the customs
which Moses delivered to us." 15And all
who sat in the council, looking steadfastly
at him, saw his face as the face of an angel.

CHAPTER 7

Stephen's Address: The Call of Abraham

Then the high priest said, "Are these
things so?"

2And he said, "Brethren and fathers, lis-
ten: The God of glory appeared to our fa-
ther Abraham when he was in Mes·o-
po·tā′mi·a, before he dwelt in Har′an, 3and
said to him, *'Get out of your country and
from your relatives, and come to a land
that I will show you.'*[a] 4Then he came out of
the land of the Chal·dē′ans and dwelt in
Har′an. And from there, when his father
was dead, He moved him to this land in
which you now dwell. 5And *God* gave him
no inheritance in it, not even *enough* to set
his foot on. But even when *Abraham* had no
child, He promised to give it to him for a
possession, and to his descendants after
him. 6But God spoke in this way: that his
descendants would dwell in a foreign
land, and that they would bring them into
bondage and oppress *them* four hundred
years. 7*'And the nation to whom they will*

6:8 [a]NU-Text reads *grace.* 6:13 [a]NU-Text omits *blasphemous.* 7:3 [a]Genesis 12:1

basis of language and culture. In the intertestamental period Jews who spoke Greek, rather than Aramaic or Hebrew, were considered liberal or worldly.

6:2 Although the church should not neglect its less fortunate members, the spreading of the gospel must be the primary focus of church leaders. By assigning men to handle this specific area, the apostles preserved the reputation and fulfilled the duty of the church, while ensuring that their time and energy could be fully devoted to preaching the Word of God.

6:9 The **Synagogue of the Freedmen** included Greek-speaking Jews whose ancestors were slaves of the Romans, later set free. The synagogue was a local assembly of Jews meeting for prayer and scripture exposition. Synagogues were the focal point of Jewish life in the cities of the Roman world.

be in bondage I will judge,'[a] said God, *'and after that they shall come out and serve Me in this place.'*[b] [8]Then He gave him the covenant of circumcision; and so *Abraham* begot Isaac and circumcised him on the eighth day; and Isaac *begot* Jacob, and Jacob *begot* the twelve patriarchs.

The Patriarchs in Egypt

[9]"And the patriarchs, becoming envious, sold Joseph into Egypt. But God was with him [10]and delivered him out of all his troubles, and gave him favor and wisdom in the presence of Pharaoh, king of Egypt; and he made him governor over Egypt and all his house. [11]Now a famine and great trouble came over all the land of Egypt and Cā'naan, and our fathers found no sustenance. [12]But when Jacob heard that there was grain in Egypt, he sent out our fathers first. [13]And the second *time* Joseph was made known to his brothers, and Joseph's family became known to the Pharaoh. [14]Then Joseph sent and called his father Jacob and all his relatives to *him,* seventy-five[a] people. [15]So Jacob went down to Egypt; and he died, he and our fathers. [16]And they were carried back to Shē'chem and laid in the tomb that Abraham bought for a sum of money from the sons of Hā'mor, *the father* of Shē'chem.

God Delivers Israel by Moses

[17]"But when the time of the promise drew near which God had sworn to Abraham, the people grew and multiplied in Egypt [18]till another king arose who did not know Joseph. [19]This man dealt treacherously with our people, and oppressed our forefathers, making them expose

7:7 [a]Genesis 15:14 [b]Exodus 3:12 7:14 [a]Or *seventy* (compare Exodus 1:5)

7:16 While **Abraham bought** burial ground in Hebron (Mamre) from the Hittite Ephron (Gen. 23:16–20), it was Jacob who purchased land in **Shechem** from the **sons of Hamor** (Gen. 33:18, 19). Stephen combines these two events as he recounts that Jacob and the fathers (see v. 15) were **carried back** to Canaan and buried in Abraham's **tomb** (see Gen. 49:29–33; 50:12, 13). **they**: An ancient tradition by Josephus records that Joseph's brothers were also buried in Hebron. Josh. 24:32 notes that Joseph was buried in Shechem.

SHARE AND SHARE ALIKE

Janette Oke

My grandson Nate was celebrating his fifth birthday. Some of the gifts I gave him were books because Nate loves to read. He tore away the birthday wrap but left the books in their cellophane packages while he reached for another gift. Jessica, two years younger, decided to take over. She was busily tearing off the wrap when an adult reminded her that the gift belonged to Nate.

But Nate spoke up quickly. "That's okay. I'll share with Jessica. She can have two and I'll have two."

"Whatever I have, I will willingly share."

Oh, what a nice world it would be if everyone had the same philosophy: Whatever I have, I will willingly share. ✦

their babies, so that they might not live. 20At this time Moses was born, and was well pleasing to God; and he was brought up in his father's house for three months. 21But when he was set out, Pharaoh's daughter took him away and brought him up as her own son. 22And Moses was learned in all the wisdom of the Egyptians, and was mighty in words and deeds.

23"Now when he was forty years old, it came into his heart to visit his brethren, the children of Israel. 24And seeing one of *them* suffer wrong, he defended and avenged him who was oppressed, and struck down the Egyptian. 25For he supposed that his brethren would have understood that God would deliver them by his hand, but they did not understand. 26And the next day he appeared to two of them as they were fighting, and *tried to* reconcile them, saying, 'Men, you are brethren; why do you wrong one another?' 27But he who did his neighbor wrong pushed him away, saying, *'Who made you a ruler and a judge over us? 28Do you want to kill me as you did the Egyptian yesterday?'*[a] 29Then, at this saying, Moses fled and became a dweller in the land of Mid'i·an, where he had two sons.

30"And when forty years had passed, an Angel of the Lord[a] appeared to him in a flame of fire in a bush, in the wilderness of Mount Sinai. 31When Moses saw *it,* he marveled at the sight; and as he drew near to observe, the voice of the Lord came to him, 32*saying, 'I am the God of your fathers—the God of Abraham, the God of Isaac, and the God of Jacob.'*[a] And Moses trembled and dared not look. 33*'Then the LORD said to him, "Take your sandals off your feet, for the place where you stand is holy ground. 34I have surely seen the oppression of My people who are in Egypt; I have heard their groaning and have come down to deliver them. And now come, I will send you to Egypt."'*[a]

35"This Moses whom they rejected, saying, *'Who made you a ruler and a judge?'*[a] is the one God sent *to be* a ruler and a deliverer by the hand of the Angel who appeared to him in the bush. 36He brought them out, after he had shown wonders and signs in the land of Egypt, and in the Red Sea, and in the wilderness forty years.

Israel Rebels Against God

37"This is that Moses who said to the children of Israel,[a] *'The LORD your God will raise up for you a Prophet like me from your brethren. Him you shall hear.'*[b]

38"This is he who was in the congregation in the wilderness with the Angel who spoke to him on Mount Sinai, and *with* our fathers, the one who received the living oracles to give to us, 39whom our fathers would not obey, but rejected. And in their hearts they turned back to Egypt, 40saying to Aaron, *'Make us gods to go before us; as for this Moses who brought us out of the land of Egypt, we do not know what has become of him.'*[a] 41And they made a calf in those days, offered sacrifices to the idol, and rejoiced in the works of their own hands. 42Then God turned and gave them up to worship the host of

7:28 [a]Exodus 2:14 7:30 [a]NU-Text omits *of the Lord.*
7:32 [a]Exodus 3:6, 15 7:34 [a]Exodus 3:5, 7, 8, 10
7:35 [a]Exodus 2:14 7:37 [a]Deuteronomy 18:15
[b]NU-Text and M-Text omit *Him you shall hear.*
7:40 [a]Exodus 32:1, 23

7:27, 28 When Moses intervened to help a Hebrew slave, his offer was rejected and his authority challenged. This was an ominous parallel to the rejection of Jesus. See Mark 11:28; 12:7.

7:35, 36 The **deliverer**, whom his people had rejected, was God's choice to bring salvation; the parallel to Christ was becoming obvious.

7:37, 38 Prophet like me: Stephen was drawing the net around his accusers. Deut. 18:15 was generally accepted as a prediction of the Messiah; it was fulfilled in Jesus (see 3:22, 23). When they rejected Him, they rejected Moses.

heaven, as it is written in the book of the
Prophets:

'Did you offer Me slaughtered animals
and sacrifices during forty years in
the wilderness,
O house of Israel?
43 *You also took up the tabernacle of*
Mō'loch,
And the star of your god Rem'phan,
Images which you made to worship;
And I will carry you away beyond
Babylon.'[a]

God's True Tabernacle

44"Our fathers had the tabernacle of wit-
ness in the wilderness, as He appointed,
instructing Moses to make it according to
the pattern that he had seen, 45which our
fathers, having received it in turn, also
brought with Joshua into the land pos-
sessed by the Gentiles, whom God drove
out before the face of our fathers until the
days of David, 46who found favor before
God and asked to find a dwelling for the
God of Jacob. 47But Solomon built Him a
house.
48"However, the Most High does not
dwell in temples made with hands, as the
prophet says:

49 *'Heaven is My throne,*
And earth is My footstool.
What house will you build for Me?
says the L*ORD*,
Or what is the place of My rest?
50 *Has My hand not made all these*
things?'[a]

Israel Resists the Holy Spirit

51"*You* stiff-necked and uncircumcised
in heart and ears! You always resist the
Holy Spirit; as your fathers *did*, so *do* you.
52Which of the prophets did your fathers
not persecute? And they killed those who
foretold the coming of the Just One, of
whom you now have become the betrayers
and murderers, 53who have received the
law by the direction of angels and have not
kept *it*."

Stephen the Martyr

54When they heard these things they
were cut to the heart, and they gnashed at
him with *their* teeth. 55But he, being full of
the Holy Spirit, gazed into heaven and saw
the glory of God, and Jesus standing at the
right hand of God, 56and said, "Look! I see
the heavens opened and the Son of Man
standing at the right hand of God!"
57Then they cried out with a loud voice,
stopped their ears, and ran at him with one
accord; 58and they cast *him* out of the city
and stoned *him*. And the witnesses laid
down their clothes at the feet of a young
man named Saul. 59And they stoned
Stephen as he was calling on *God* and say-
ing, "Lord Jesus, receive my spirit." 60Then
he knelt down and cried out with a loud
voice, "Lord, do not charge them with this
sin." And when he had said this, he fell
asleep.

CHAPTER 8

Saul Persecutes the Church

Now Saul was consenting to his death.
At that time a great persecution arose
against the church which was at Jerusalem;
and they were all scattered throughout the
regions of Judea and Samaria, except the

7:43 [a]Amos 5:25–27 7:50 [a]Isaiah 66:1, 2

7:58 they . . . stoned Stephen in violation of the law. The Romans did not permit the Jews to inflict capital punishment; Pilate had to authorize the death of Jesus. This is the first mention of Saul of Tarsus.

8:1 Saul was not only **consenting**, but also sharing responsibility for Stephen's **death** because he was custodian for the stone throwers (7:58). Saul was his Hebrew name; Paul his name as a Roman citizen. He remained "Saul" until in Paphos on the first missionary

apostles. 2And devout men carried
Stephen *to his burial,* and made great
lamentation over him.
3As for Saul, he made havoc of the
church, entering every house, and
dragging off men and women, committing
them to prison.

Christ Is Preached in Samaria

4Therefore those who were scattered
went everywhere preaching the word.
5Then Philip went down to the[a] city of Sa-
maria and preached Christ to them. 6And
the multitudes with one accord heeded the
things spoken by Philip, hearing and see-
ing the miracles which he did. 7For unclean
spirits, crying with a loud voice, came out
of many who were possessed; and many
who were paralyzed and lame were
healed. 8And there was great joy in that
city.

The Sorcerer's Profession of Faith

9But there was a certain man called Si-
mon, who previously practiced sorcery in
the city and astonished the people of Sa-
maria, claiming that he was someone
great, 10to whom they all gave heed, from
the least to the greatest, saying, "This man
is the great power of God." 11And they
heeded him because he had astonished
them with his sorceries for a long time.
12But when they believed Philip as he
preached the things concerning the king-
dom of God and the name of Jesus Christ,
both men and women were baptized.
13Then Simon himself also believed; and
when he was baptized he continued with
Philip, and was amazed, seeing the mira-
cles and signs which were done.

The Sorcerer's Sin

14Now when the apostles who were at
Jerusalem heard that Samaria had received
the word of God, they sent Peter and John
to them, 15who, when they had come
down, prayed for them that they might re-
ceive the Holy Spirit. 16For as yet He had
fallen upon none of them. They had only
been baptized in the name of the Lord Je-
sus. 17Then they laid hands on them, and
they received the Holy Spirit.
18And when Simon saw that through the
laying on of the apostles' hands the Holy
Spirit was given, he offered them money,
19saying, "Give me this power also, that
anyone on whom I lay hands may receive
the Holy Spirit."
20But Peter said to him, "Your money
perish with you, because you thought that
the gift of God could be purchased with
money! 21You have neither part nor portion
in this matter, for your heart is not right in
the sight of God. 22Repent therefore of this
your wickedness, and pray God if perhaps
the thought of your heart may be forgiven
you. 23For I see that you are poisoned by
bitterness and bound by iniquity."
24Then Simon answered and said, "Pray
to the Lord for me, that none of the things
which you have spoken may come upon
me."
25So when they had testified and
preached the word of the Lord, they re-
turned to Jerusalem, preaching the gospel
in many villages of the Samaritans.

Christ Is Preached to an Ethiopian

26Now an angel of the Lord spoke to
Philip, saying, "Arise and go toward the
south along the road which goes down
from Jerusalem to Gā'za." This is desert.

8:5 [a]Or *a*

journey when he emerged as leader of the mission (13:9–13). The believers **scattered** from Jerusalem either because of fear or because they followed their Master's instruction to move to a more receptive locale (see Matt. 10:23).

8:22–24 Pray . . . for me: The account does not tell us enough to determine whether Simon did truly repent and receive pardon, or was only seeking to avoid the consequences of his wrong motive.

27So he arose and went. And behold, a man
of Ethiopia, a eunuch of great authority
under Can·dā′cē the queen of the Ethio-
pians, who had charge of all her treasury,
and had come to Jerusalem to worship,
28was returning. And sitting in his chariot,
he was reading Ī·sāi′ah the prophet. 29Then
the Spirit said to Philip, "Go near and over-
take this chariot."

30So Philip ran to him, and heard him
reading the prophet Ī·sāi′ah, and said, "Do
you understand what you are reading?"

31And he said, "How can I, unless some-
one guides me?" And he asked Philip to
come up and sit with him. 32The place in
the Scripture which he read was this:

"He was led as a sheep to the
slaughter;
And as a lamb before its shearer is
silent,
So He opened not His mouth.
33 *In His humiliation His justice was*
taken away,
And who will declare His generation?
For His life is taken from the earth."[a]

34So the eunuch answered Philip and
said, "I ask you, of whom does the prophet
say this, of himself or of some other man?"
35Then Philip opened his mouth, and be-
ginning at this Scripture, preached Jesus to
him. 36Now as they went down the road,
they came to some water. And the eunuch
said, "See, *here is* water. What hinders me
from being baptized?"

37Then Philip said, "If you believe with
all your heart, you may."

And he answered and said, "I believe
that Jesus Christ is the Son of God."[a]

38So he commanded the chariot to stand
still. And both Philip and the eunuch went
down into the water, and he baptized him.
39Now when they came up out of the water,
the Spirit of the Lord caught Philip away,
so that the eunuch saw him no more; and
he went on his way rejoicing. 40But Philip
was found at A·zō′tus. And passing
through, he preached in all the cities till he
came to Caes·a·rē′a.

CHAPTER 9

The Damascus Road: Saul Converted

Then Saul, still breathing threats and
murder against the disciples of the Lord,
went to the high priest 2and asked letters
from him to the synagogues of Damascus,
so that if he found any who were of the
Way, whether men or women, he might
bring them bound to Jerusalem.

3As he journeyed he came near Damas-
cus, and suddenly a light shone around
him from heaven. 4Then he fell to the
ground, and heard a voice saying to him,
"Saul, Saul, why are you persecuting
Me?"

5And he said, "Who are You, Lord?"

Then the Lord said, "I am Jesus, whom
you are persecuting.[a] It *is* hard for you to
kick against the goads."

8:33 [a]Isaiah 53:7, 8 8:37 [a]NU-Text and M-Text omit this verse. It is found in Western texts, including the Latin tradition. 9:5 [a]NU-Text and M-Text omit the last sentence of verse 5 and begin verse 6 with *But arise and go.*

8:27 man of Ethiopia: a high-ranking court official of a Gentile queen who worshipped the Jewish God.

8:39, 40 the Spirit . . . caught Philip away: He disappeared from sight. **was found at**: He appeared in Azotus. He seems to have settled in Caesarea (see 21:8).

9:1, 2 Because of extradition permits authorized by Rome, these **letters** from the **high priest** gave Saul jurisdiction over Jews in **Damascus**. The expression **the Way** was an early designation of Jesus' followers (22:4). These early Christians believed that faith in Christ was the fulfillment of the OT, the true **way** of worshiping God.

9:5 goads: a staff with a sharp piece of metal, used to drive oxen and donkeys. Paul may have been feeling the pricks of his conscience regarding his persecution of the early church.

6So he, trembling and astonished, said,
"Lord, what do You want me to do?"
Then the Lord *said* to him, "Arise and go
into the city, and you will be told what you
must do."
7And the men who journeyed with him
stood speechless, hearing a voice but see-
ing no one. 8Then Saul arose from the
ground, and when his eyes were opened
he saw no one. But they led him by the
hand and brought *him* into Damascus.
9And he was three days without sight, and
neither ate nor drank.

Ananias Baptizes Saul

10Now there was a certain disciple at Da-
mascus named An·a·nī'as; and to him the
Lord said in a vision, "An·a·nī'as."
And he said, "Here I am, Lord."
11So the Lord *said* to him, "Arise and
go to the street called Straight, and inquire
at the house of Judas for *one* called Saul
of Tar'sus, for behold, he is praying.
12And in a vision he has seen a man named
An·a·nī'as coming in and putting *his*
hand on him, so that he might receive his
sight."
13Then An·a·nī'as answered, "Lord, I
have heard from many about this man,
how much harm he has done to Your saints
in Jerusalem. 14And here he has authority
from the chief priests to bind all who call
on Your name."
15But the Lord said to him, "Go, for he
is a chosen vessel of Mine to bear My
name before Gentiles, kings, and the chil-
dren of Israel. 16For I will show him how
many things he must suffer for My name's
sake."
17And An·a·nī'as went his way and en-
tered the house; and laying his hands on
him he said, "Brother Saul, the Lord Jesus,[a]
who appeared to you on the road as you
came, has sent me that you may receive
your sight and be filled with the Holy
Spirit." 18Immediately there fell from his
eyes *something* like scales, and he received
his sight at once; and he arose and was
baptized.
19So when he had received food, he was
strengthened. Then Saul spent some days
with the disciples at Damascus.

Saul Preaches Christ

20Immediately he preached the Christ[a]
in the synagogues, that He is the Son of
God.
21Then all who heard were amazed, and
said, "Is this not he who destroyed those
who called on this name in Jerusalem, and
has come here for that purpose, so that he
might bring them bound to the chief
priests?"
22But Saul increased all the more in
strength, and confounded the Jews who
dwelt in Damascus, proving that this *Jesus*
is the Christ.

Saul Escapes Death

23Now after many days were past, the
Jews plotted to kill him. 24But their plot be-
came known to Saul. And they watched
the gates day and night, to kill him. 25Then
the disciples took him by night and let *him*
down through the wall in a large basket.

Saul at Jerusalem

26And when Saul had come to Jerusa-
lem, he tried to join the disciples; but they

9:17 [a]M-Text omits *Jesus.* 9:20 [a]NU-Text reads *Jesus.*

9:7 At first glance, Luke seems to contradict himself in 22:9; however a closer look at the Greek shows that Luke is saying that Saul's companions heard the voice but could not comprehend the message.

9:11 street called Straight: So called because most streets in old Damascus were not straight. It bears this name today, now a covered and crowded bazaar.

9:24, 25 To avoid capture and death Saul was secretly lowered over the city wall by friends. Houses were often built on, or into, the city walls (see 2 Cor. 11:33). Such a house is visible today in Damascus.

TABITHA: SHINE WHERE YOU ARE!

The New Testament does not provide many female role models, and the few mentioned are not characterized in great detail. However, we know that Jesus initiated a new respect for women through His compassionate treatment of Martha, Mary, and others. Throughout His ministry and the early days of the Christian church, the role of women began slowly to expand; but for the most part, women had to find ways to express their love for God through activities outside of the church or synagogue.

Tabitha, also known as Dorcas, worked for the Lord in Joppa. This compassionate woman expressed her love for God by loving others. The Bible says she "was full of good works and charitable deeds which she did" (Acts 9:36).

As one of the early Christians, she did not have the opportunities available to women today. But she found something she could do: she sewed clothing for the widows and other less fortunate people. She discovered her gift for service and performed it with all her heart.

The impact of her seemingly small role was revealed at the scene of her death. When Peter arrived, he found the room filled with people Dorcas had helped: "And all the widows stood by him weeping, showing the tunics and garments which Dorcas had made while she was with them" (v. 39).

After praying, Peter called her name and raised her from the dead. Although nothing further is mentioned of her in Scripture, we can be certain Dorcas continued to shine her light of love through her handiwork as soon as she was able. After all, she had more reason than ever to love the Lord.

Christian service is not limited to those with leadership or speaking skills. The Lord can use anyone who surrenders body, mind, and soul to Him. We should never feel our area of ministry is unimportant, but we must answer the Lord's call whenever and however it comes.

What can you do today to show your love for the Lord? ✦

were all afraid of him, and did not believe
that he was a disciple. 27But Bar'na·bas
took him and brought *him* to the apostles.
And he declared to them how he had seen
the Lord on the road, and that He had spo-
ken to him, and how he had preached
boldly at Damascus in the name of Jesus.
28So he was with them at Jerusalem,
coming in and going out. 29And he
spoke boldly in the name of the Lord Jesus
and disputed against the Hel'len·ists, but
they attempted to kill him. 30When the

brethren found out, they brought him down to Caes·a·rē′a and sent him out to Tar′sus.

The Church Prospers

[31]Then the churches[a] throughout all Judea, Galilee, and Samaria had peace and were edified. And walking in the fear of the Lord and in the comfort of the Holy Spirit, they were multiplied.

Aeneas Healed

[32]Now it came to pass, as Peter went
through all *parts of the country,* that he also came down to the saints who dwelt in
Lyd′da. [33]There he found a certain man named Aē·nē′as, who had been bedridden
eight years and was paralyzed. [34]And Peter said to him, "Aē·nē′as, Jesus the Christ heals you. Arise and make your bed."
Then he arose immediately. [35]So all who dwelt at Lyd′da and Sharon saw him and turned to the Lord.

Dorcas Restored to Life

[36]At Jop′pa there was a certain disciple named Tab′i·tha, which is translated Dor′cas. This woman was full of good works and charitable deeds which she did.
[37]But it happened in those days that she became sick and died. When they had washed her, they laid *her* in an upper
room. [38]And since Lyd′da was near Jop′pa, and the disciples had heard that Peter was there, they sent two men to him, imploring
him not to delay in coming to them. [39]Then
Peter arose and went with them. When he had come, they brought *him* to the upper room. And all the widows stood by him weeping, showing the tunics and garments which Dor′cas had made while she was
with them. [40]But Peter put them all out, and knelt down and prayed. And turning to the body he said, "Tab′i·tha, arise." And she opened her eyes, and when she saw
Peter she sat up. [41]Then he gave her *his* hand and lifted her up; and when he had called the saints and widows, he presented
her alive. [42]And it became known throughout all Jop′pa, and many believed on the
Lord. [43]So it was that he stayed many days in Jop′pa with Simon, a tanner.

CHAPTER 10

Cornelius Sends a Delegation

There was a certain man in Caes·a·rē′a called Cornelius, a centurion of what was
called the Italian Regiment, [2]a devout *man* and one who feared God with all his household, who gave alms generously to the people, and prayed to God always.
[3]About the ninth hour of the day he saw clearly in a vision an angel of God coming in and saying to him, "Cornelius!"

[4]And when he observed him, he was afraid, and said, "What is it, lord?"

So he said to him, "Your prayers and your alms have come up for a memorial
before God. [5]Now send men to Jop′pa, and send for Simon whose surname is Peter.
[6]He is lodging with Simon, a tanner, whose house is by the sea.[a] He will tell you what
you must do." [7]And when the angel who spoke to him had departed, Cornelius

9:31 [a]NU-Text reads *church . . . was edified.*
10:6 [a]NU-Text and M-Text omit the last sentence of this verse.

9:39 Widows were the most helpless people in ancient society. Both Jews and Christians considered it their religious duty to care for them (see 1 Tim. 5:3–16).

9:43 a tanner: Jewish law considered the handling of dead animals defiling. Such outcasts would be more receptive of the gospel; they had no status in Jewish religious life that would be threatened.

10:1 centurion: Non-commissioned Roman military officer in charge of one hundred men.

10:2 Although Cornelius was essentially a "good" man, he could not obtain eternal life without accepting the gift of salvation.

10:3 The **ninth hour** (3:00 P.M.) was the hour of prayer in Jerusalem (3:1).

called two of his household servants and a
devout soldier from among those who
waited on him continually. 8So when he
had explained all *these* things to them, he
sent them to Jop′pa.

Peter's Vision

9The next day, as they went on their
journey and drew near the city, Peter went
up on the housetop to pray, about the sixth
hour. 10Then he became very hungry and
wanted to eat; but while they made ready,
he fell into a trance 11and saw heaven
opened and an object like a great sheet
bound at the four corners, descending to
him and let down to the earth. 12In it were
all kinds of four-footed animals of the
earth, wild beasts, creeping things, and
birds of the air. 13And a voice came to him,
"Rise, Peter; kill and eat."
14But Peter said, "Not so, Lord! For I
have never eaten anything common or un-
clean."
15And a voice *spoke* to him again the sec-
ond time, "What God has cleansed you
must not call common." 16This was done
three times. And the object was taken up
into heaven again.

Summoned to Caesarea

17Now while Peter wondered within
himself what this vision which he had seen
meant, behold, the men who had been sent
from Cornelius had made inquiry for Si-
mon's house, and stood before the gate.
18And they called and asked whether Si-
mon, whose surname was Peter, was lodg-
ing there.
19While Peter thought about the vision,
the Spirit said to him, "Behold, three men
are seeking you. 20Arise therefore, go down
and go with them, doubting nothing; for I
have sent them."
21Then Peter went down to the men who
had been sent to him from Cornelius,[a] and
said, "Yes, I am he whom you seek. For
what reason have you come?"
22And they said, "Cornelius *the* centu-
rion, a just man, one who fears God and
has a good reputation among all the nation
of the Jews, was divinely instructed by a
holy angel to summon you to his house,
and to hear words from you." 23Then he in-
vited them in and lodged *them*.
On the next day Peter went away with
them, and some brethren from Jop′pa ac-
companied him.

Peter Meets Cornelius

24And the following day they entered
Caes·a·rē′a. Now Cornelius was waiting
for them, and had called together his rela-
tives and close friends. 25As Peter was com-
ing in, Cornelius met him and fell down at
his feet and worshiped *him*. 26But Peter
lifted him up, saying, "Stand up; I myself
am also a man." 27And as he talked with
him, he went in and found many who had
come together. 28Then he said to them,
"You know how unlawful it is for a Jewish
man to keep company with or go to one of
another nation. But God has shown me
that I should not call any man common or
unclean. 29Therefore I came without objec-
tion as soon as I was sent for. I ask, then,
for what reason have you sent for me?"
30So Cornelius said, "Four days ago I
was fasting until this hour; and at the ninth
hour[a] I prayed in my house, and behold, a
man stood before me in bright clothing,

10:21 [a]NU-Text and M-Text omit *who had been sent to him from Cornelius.* 10:30 [a]NU-Text reads *Four days ago to this hour, at the ninth hour.*

10:9, 10 The **sixth hour** (noon) was the usual lunchtime among Romans.

10:12 In his "trance" (v. 10) Peter saw **all kinds** of **animals**, most of them forbidden for food. The three things a Jew must observe in order to remain a true Jew were (1) sanctity of the Sabbath, (2) circumcision, and (3) the dietary laws.

10:25, 26 Cornelius . . . worshiped him: The Greek term indicates veneration of God or of an important person. But Peter was quick to disclaim deity (see 14:15).

[31]and said, 'Cornelius, your prayer has been heard, and your alms are remembered in the sight of God. [32]Send therefore to Jop'pa and call Simon here, whose surname is Peter. He is lodging in the house of Simon, a tanner, by the sea.[a] When he comes, he will speak to you.' [33]So I sent to you immediately, and you have done well to come. Now therefore, we are all present before God, to hear all the things commanded you by God."

Preaching to Cornelius' Household

[34]Then Peter opened *his* mouth and said: "In truth I perceive that God shows no partiality. [35]But in every nation whoever fears Him and works righteousness is accepted by Him. [36]The word which *God* sent to the children of Israel, preaching peace through Jesus Christ—He is Lord of all— [37]that word you know, which was proclaimed throughout all Judea, and began from Galilee after the baptism which John preached: [38]how God anointed Jesus of Nazareth with the Holy Spirit and with power, who went about doing good and healing all who were oppressed by the devil, for God was with Him. [39]And we are witnesses of all things which He did both in the land of the Jews and in Jerusalem, whom they[a] killed by hanging on a tree. [40]Him God raised up on the third day, and showed Him openly, [41]not to all the people, but to witnesses chosen before by God, *even* to us who ate and drank with Him after He arose from the dead. [42]And He commanded us to preach to the people, and to testify that it is He who was ordained by God *to be* Judge of the living and the dead. [43]To Him all the prophets witness that, through His name, whoever believes in Him will receive remission of sins."

The Holy Spirit Falls on the Gentiles

[44]While Peter was still speaking these words, the Holy Spirit fell upon all those who heard the word. [45]And those of the circumcision who believed were astonished, as many as came with Peter, because the gift of the Holy Spirit had been poured out on the Gentiles also. [46]For they heard them speak with tongues and magnify God.

Then Peter answered, [47]"Can anyone forbid water, that these should not be baptized who have received the Holy Spirit just as we *have?*" [48]And he commanded them to be baptized in the name of the Lord. Then they asked him to stay a few days.

CHAPTER 11

Peter Defends God's Grace

Now the apostles and brethren who were in Judea heard that the Gentiles had also received the word of God. [2]And when Peter came up to Jerusalem, those of the circumcision contended with him, [3]saying, "You went in to uncircumcised men and ate with them!"

[4]But Peter explained *it* to them in order from the beginning, saying: [5]"I was in the city of Jop'pa praying; and in a trance I saw a vision, an object descending like a great sheet, let down from heaven by four corners; and it came to me. [6]When I observed it intently and considered, I saw four-footed animals of the earth, wild beasts,

10:32 [a]NU-Text omits the last sentence of this verse.
10:39 [a]NU-Text and M-Text add *also.*

10:34 God shows no partiality: the gift of salvation is available to all, despite any of the world's social barriers.

10:46 The Gentiles spoke with **tongues** and magnified God. This was objective evidence of God's decision to include the Gentiles (11:17; 15:9). He gave them the same experience He had given the Jewish Christians on the Day of Pentecost.

11:3 You . . . ate with . . . uncircumcised men: Peter had violated one of the three tests of Jewish fidelity to the law (see note on 10:12). In their eyes this failure invalidated his Judaism.

creeping things, and birds of the air. 7And I heard a voice saying to me, 'Rise, Peter; kill and eat.' 8But I said, 'Not so, Lord! For nothing common or unclean has at any time entered my mouth.' 9But the voice answered me again from heaven, 'What God has cleansed you must not call common.' 10Now this was done three times, and all were drawn up again into heaven. 11At that very moment, three men stood before the house where I was, having been sent to me from Caes·a·rē′a. 12Then the Spirit told me to go with them, doubting nothing. Moreover these six brethren accompanied me, and we entered the man's house. 13And he told us how he had seen an angel standing in his house, who said to him, 'Send men to Jop′pa, and call for Simon whose surname is Peter, 14who will tell you words by which you and all your household will be saved.' 15And as I began to speak, the Holy Spirit fell upon them, as upon us at the beginning. 16Then I remembered the word of the Lord, how He said, 'John indeed baptized with water, but you shall be baptized with the Holy Spirit.' 17If therefore God gave them the same gift as *He gave* us when we believed on the Lord Jesus Christ, who was I that I could withstand God?"

18When they heard these things they became silent; and they glorified God, saying, "Then God has also granted to the Gentiles repentance to life."

Barnabas and Saul at Antioch

19Now those who were scattered after the persecution that arose over Stephen traveled as far as Phoe·ni′ci·a, Cyprus, and An′ti·och, preaching the word to no one but the Jews only. 20But some of them were men from Cyprus and Cȳ·rē′nē, who, when they had come to An′ti·och, spoke to the Hel′len·ists, preaching the Lord Jesus. 21And the hand of the Lord was with them, and a great number believed and turned to the Lord.

22Then news of these things came to the ears of the church in Jerusalem, and they sent out Bar′na·bas to go as far as An′ti·och. 23When he came and had seen the grace of God, he was glad, and encouraged them all that with purpose of heart they should continue with the Lord. 24For he was a good man, full of the Holy Spirit and of faith. And a great many people were added to the Lord.

25Then Bar′na·bas departed for Tar′sus to seek Saul. 26And when he had found him, he brought him to An′ti·och. So it was that for a whole year they assembled with the church and taught a great many people. And the disciples were first called Christians in An′ti·och.

Relief to Judea

27And in these days prophets came from Jerusalem to An′ti·och. 28Then one of them, named Ag′a·bus, stood up and showed by the Spirit that there was going to be a great famine throughout all the world, which also happened in the days of Clau′di·us Caesar. 29Then the disciples, each according to his ability, determined to send relief to the brethren dwelling in Judea. 30This they also did, and sent it to the elders by the hands of Bar′na·bas and Saul.

11:14, 15 will be saved . . . the Holy Spirit fell upon them: Apparently Cornelius was not yet a Christian, but he was devout and ready to receive the gospel. He was converted and filled with the Holy Spirit when Peter visited him. **at the beginning**: On the Day of Pentecost (see 2:1–4).

11:19–30 The church at Antioch was the first to include Gentile Christians. More innovative than the Jerusalem church, Antioch became the center of missionary outreach to Gentiles.

11:26 called Christians: Followers of Christ (literally, "little Christs"). Outsiders had called them Nazarenes and a sect (24:5, 14); they called themselves followers of the Way (9:2).

CHAPTER 12

Herod's Violence to the Church

Now about that time Her′od the king
stretched out *his* hand to harass some from
the church. [2]Then he killed James the
brother of John with the sword. [3]And be-
cause he saw that it pleased the Jews, he
proceeded further to seize Peter also. Now
it was *during* the Days of Unleavened
Bread. [4]So when he had arrested him, he
put *him* in prison, and delivered *him* to
four squads of soldiers to keep him, in-
tending to bring him before the people af-
ter Passover.

Peter Freed from Prison

[5]Peter was therefore kept in prison, but
constant[a] prayer was offered to God for
him by the church. [6]And when Her′od was
about to bring him out, that night Peter
was sleeping, bound with two chains be-
tween two soldiers; and the guards before
the door were keeping the prison. [7]Now
behold, an angel of the Lord stood by *him,*
and a light shone in the prison; and he
struck Peter on the side and raised him up,
saying, "Arise quickly!" And his chains fell
off *his* hands. [8]Then the angel said to him,
"Gird yourself and tie on your sandals";
and so he did. And he said to him, "Put on
your garment and follow me." [9]So he went
out and followed him, and did not know
that what was done by the angel was real,
but thought he was seeing a vision. [10]When
they were past the first and the second
guard posts, they came to the iron gate that
leads to the city, which opened to them of
its own accord; and they went out and
went down one street, and immediately
the angel departed from him.

[11]And when Peter had come to himself,
he said, "Now I know for certain that the
Lord has sent His angel, and has delivered
me from the hand of Her′od and *from* all
the expectation of the Jewish people."

[12]So, when he had considered *this,* he
came to the house of Mary, the mother of
John whose surname was Mark, where
many were gathered together praying.
[13]And as Peter knocked at the door of the
gate, a girl named Rhō′da came to answer.
[14]When she recognized Peter's voice, be-
cause of *her* gladness she did not open the
gate, but ran in and announced that Peter
stood before the gate. [15]But they said to her,
"You are beside yourself!" Yet she kept in-
sisting that it was so. So they said, "It is his
angel."

[16]Now Peter continued knocking; and
when they opened *the door* and saw him,
they were astonished. [17]But motioning to
them with his hand to keep silent, he de-
clared to them how the Lord had brought
him out of the prison. And he said, "Go,
tell these things to James and to the
brethren." And he departed and went to
another place.

[18]Then, as soon as it was day, there was
no small stir among the soldiers about
what had become of Peter. [19]But when
Her′od had searched for him and not
found him, he examined the guards and
commanded that *they* should be put to
death.

And he went down from Judea to Caes-
a•rē′a, and stayed *there.*

Herod's Violent Death

[20]Now Her′od had been very angry with
the people of Tȳre and Sī′don; but they
came to him with one accord, and having
made Blas′tus the king's personal aide

12:5 [a]NU-Text reads *constantly* (or *earnestly*).

12:2 James was the first of the twelve apostles to be martyred.
12:3 Days of Unleavened Bread: part of the Passover festival.
12:5–17 Prayer should be a major part of every church ministry, and we should pray in faith, expecting God to answer.
12:17 James: The brother of Jesus (15:13; 21:18; Mark 6:3). **the brethren**: Other leaders of the church.

their friend, they asked for peace, because
their country was supplied with food by
the king's *country*.
21So on a set day Her′od, arrayed in
royal apparel, sat on his throne and gave
an oration to them. 22And the people kept
shouting, "The voice of a god and not of a
man!" 23Then immediately an angel of the
Lord struck him, because he did not give
glory to God. And he was eaten by worms
and died.
24But the word of God grew and multi-
plied.

Barnabas and Saul Appointed

25And Bar′na·bas and Saul returned
from[a] Jerusalem when they had fulfilled
their ministry, and they also took with
them John whose surname was Mark.

CHAPTER 13

Now in the church that was at An′ti·och
there were certain prophets and teachers:
Bar′na·bas, Sim′ē·on who was called
Nī′ger, Lū′cius of Cȳ·rē′nē, Man′a·en who
had been brought up with Her′od the
tetrarch, and Saul. 2As they ministered to
the Lord and fasted, the Holy Spirit said,
"Now separate to Me Bar′na·bas and
Saul for the work to which I have called
them." 3Then, having fasted and prayed,
and laid hands on them, they sent *them*
away.

Preaching in Cyprus

4So, being sent out by the Holy Spirit,
they went down to Se·leū′ci·a, and from
there they sailed to Cyprus. 5And when
they arrived in Sal′a·mis, they preached
the word of God in the synagogues of the
Jews. They also had John as *their* assistant.
6Now when they had gone through the
island[a] to Pā′phos, they found a certain
sorcerer, a false prophet, a Jew whose
name *was* Bar-Jē′sus, 7who was with the
proconsul, Ser′gi·us Paul′us, an intelligent
man. This man called for Bar′na·bas and
Saul and sought to hear the word of God.
8But El′y·mas the sorcerer (for so his name
is translated) withstood them, seeking to
turn the proconsul away from the faith.
9Then Saul, who also *is called* Paul, filled
with the Holy Spirit, looked intently at him
10and said, "O full of all deceit and all
fraud, *you* son of the devil, *you* enemy of all
righteousness, will you not cease pervert-
ing the straight ways of the Lord? 11And
now, indeed, the hand of the Lord *is* upon
you, and you shall be blind, not seeing the
sun for a time."

And immediately a dark mist fell on
him, and he went around seeking someone
to lead him by the hand. 12Then the pro-
consul believed, when he saw what had

12:25 [a]NU-Text and M-Text read *to*. 13:6 [a]NU-Text reads *the whole island*.

12:23 The Jewish historian Josephus corroborates Luke's account of Herod's unusual death.

13:1—28:31 The gospel had already spread beyond the Jews to Samaria (8:5–25), to Ethiopia (8:26–40), to God-fearing Gentiles as in the household of Cornelius (10:1—11:18), and to the Greeks at Antioch (11:19–30). The remainder of Acts describes how the gospel was carried into the Gentile world under the leadership of the Holy Spirit. This new initiative was begun by the church at Antioch sending out Barnabas and Saul (13:2). The change of thrust towards pagan non-Jews rather than skeptical Jews is made clear by Paul's announcement in Antioch of Pisidia: **we turn to the Gentiles** (13:46).

13:4–12 This is the beginning of Paul's first missionary journey. It was natural for them to evangelize first in **Cyprus** since it was Barnabas's home (see 4:36).

13:5 Since **the synagogues** were the centers of Jewish community life in the cities that Paul visited, they were the most appropriate places to begin preaching Christ. **John**: John Mark, Barnabas's cousin (12:25; Col. 4:10).

13:6 Bar-Jesus: son of Jesus. Jesus, or Joshua, was a common name, so this reference does not imply a relationship to Jesus Christ.

been done, being astonished at the teach-
ing of the Lord.

At Antioch in Pisidia

13 Now when Paul and his party set sail
from Pā′phos, they came to Per′ga in
Pam·phyl′i·a; and John, departing from
them, returned to Jerusalem. 14 But when
they departed from Per′ga, they came to
An′ti·och in Pi·sid′i·a, and went into the
synagogue on the Sabbath day and sat
down. 15 And after the reading of the Law
and the Prophets, the rulers of the
synagogue sent to them, saying, "Men *and*
brethren, if you have any word of exhorta-
tion for the people, say on."

16 Then Paul stood up, and motioning
with *his* hand said, "Men of Israel, and you
who fear God, listen: 17 The God of this peo-
ple Israel[a] chose our fathers, and exalted
the people when they dwelt as strangers in
the land of Egypt, and with an uplifted
arm He brought them out of it. 18 Now for a
time of about forty years He put up with
their ways in the wilderness. 19 And when
He had destroyed seven nations in the
land of Cā′naan, He distributed their land
to them by allotment.

20 "After that He gave *them* judges for
about four hundred and fifty years, until
Samuel the prophet. 21 And afterward they
asked for a king; so God gave them Saul
the son of Kish, a man of the tribe of Benja-
min, for forty years. 22 And when He had
removed him, He raised up for them Da-
vid as king, to whom also He gave testi-
mony and said, *'I have found David*[a] the
son of Jesse, *a man after My own heart,* who
will do all My will.'[b] 23 From this man's
seed, according to *the* promise, God raised
up for Israel a Savior—Jesus—[a] 24 after John
had first preached, before His coming, the
baptism of repentance to all the people of
Israel. 25 And as John was finishing his
course, he said, 'Who do you think I am? I
am not *He*. But behold, there comes One af-
ter me, the sandals of whose feet I am not
worthy to loose.'

26 "Men *and* brethren, sons of the family
of Abraham, and those among you who
fear God, to you the word of this salvation
has been sent. 27 For those who dwell in Je-
rusalem, and their rulers, because they did
not know Him, nor even the voices of the
Prophets which are read every Sabbath,
have fulfilled *them* in condemning *Him*.
28 And though they found no cause for
death *in Him*, they asked Pilate that He
should be put to death. 29 Now when they
had fulfilled all that was written concern-
ing Him, they took *Him* down from the tree
and laid *Him* in a tomb. 30 But God raised
Him from the dead. 31 He was seen for
many days by those who came up with
Him from Galilee to Jerusalem, who are
His witnesses to the people. 32 And we de-
clare to you glad tidings—that promise
which was made to the fathers. 33 God has
fulfilled this for us their children, in that
He has raised up Jesus. As it is also written
in the second Psalm:

> *'You are My Son,*
> *Today I have begotten You.'*[a]

34 And that He raised Him from the dead,
no more to return to corruption, He has
spoken thus:

> *'I will give you the sure mercies of*
> *David.'*[a]

35 Therefore He also says in another *Psalm:*

> *'You will not allow Your Holy One to*
> *see corruption.'*[a]

13:17 [a]M-Text omits *Israel.* 13:22 [a]Psalm 89:20 [b]1 Samuel 13:14 13:23 [a]M-Text reads *for Israel salvation.* 13:33 [a]Psalm 2:7 13:34 [a]Isaiah 55:3 13:35 [a]Psalm 16:10

13:15 It was customary for the **rulers of the synagogue** to invite guests to speak to the congregation.

13:16 Paul stood up: The rabbis usually remained seated to teach; Paul stood perhaps to be heard better.

RELEVANT CHRISTIANITY

George Barna

Millions of adults are still baffled about the true purpose and value of the Christian faith. Consequently, they consistently and stubbornly resist efforts to become involved in the life of a local church.

Can you conceptualize or implement, through your own personal relationships with unchurched or nonbelieving people and through the course of your ongoing church involvement, ways that make the life of the church more attractive and transforming for those who venture in from the outside? Building the church family is more than simply a career challenge for pastors and their staff. Every Christian has the privilege and responsibility of making Christianity sufficiently real and practical so that every adult will find true, deep value in what the church has to offer.

One means of making the church relevant in the lives of those who have rejected it is to establish significant relationships with those people. Consciously prepare for a time when you might have an opportunity to expose them to the benefits that Christianity—through an outward-looking, Christ-centered, people-sensitive church—has to offer. Engaging with the unchurched on their turf is sometimes scary, sometimes uncomfortable. However, if your church is sensitive to the needs and backgrounds of your unchurched friends, what better gift could you ever provide them than the chance to know Christ personally and share in the eternal grace available by God through His Son? ✦

36"For David, after he had served his
own generation by the will of God, fell
asleep, was buried with his fathers, and
saw corruption; 37but He whom God raised
up saw no corruption. 38Therefore let it be
known to you, brethren, that through this
Man is preached to you the forgiveness of
sins; 39and by Him everyone who believes
is justified from all things from which you
could not be justified by the law of Moses.
40Beware therefore, lest what has been spoken in the prophets come upon you:

41 *'Behold, you despisers,*
Marvel and perish!
For I work a work in your days,
A work which you will by no means
believe,
Though one were to declare it to
you.' "[a]

Blessing and Conflict at Antioch

42So when the Jews went out of the synagogue,[a] the Gentiles begged that these
words might be preached to them the next
Sabbath. 43Now when the congregation
had broken up, many of the Jews and devout proselytes followed Paul and
Bar'na·bas, who, speaking to them, per-

13:41 [a]Habakkuk 1:5 13:42 [a]Or *And when they went out of the synagogue of the Jews;* NU-Text reads *And when they went out of the synagogue, they begged.*

13:39 justified: set free.

suaded them to continue in the grace of
God.
[44]On the next Sabbath almost the whole
city came together to hear the word of
God. [45]But when the Jews saw the multi-
tudes, they were filled with envy; and con-
tradicting and blaspheming, they opposed
the things spoken by Paul. [46]Then Paul and
Bar′na·bas grew bold and said, "It was
necessary that the word of God should be
spoken to you first; but since you reject it,
and judge yourselves unworthy of ever-
lasting life, behold, we turn to the Gentiles.
[47]For so the Lord has commanded us:

'I have set you as a light to the
Gentiles,
That you should be for salvation to
the ends of the earth.'"[a]

[48]Now when the Gentiles heard this,
they were glad and glorified the word of
the Lord. And as many as had been ap-
pointed to eternal life believed.
[49]And the word of the Lord was being
spread throughout all the region. [50]But the
Jews stirred up the devout and prominent
women and the chief men of the city, raised
up persecution against Paul and Bar′-
na·bas, and expelled them from their re-
gion. [51]But they shook off the dust from
their feet against them, and came to
Ī·cō′ni·um. [52]And the disciples were filled
with joy and with the Holy Spirit.

CHAPTER 14

At Iconium

Now it happened in Ī·cō′ni·um that they
went together to the synagogue of the
Jews, and so spoke that a great multitude
both of the Jews and of the Greeks be-
lieved. [2]But the unbelieving Jews stirred
up the Gentiles and poisoned their minds
against the brethren. [3]Therefore they
stayed there a long time, speaking boldly
in the Lord, who was bearing witness to
the word of His grace, granting signs and
wonders to be done by their hands.
[4]But the multitude of the city was di-
vided: part sided with the Jews, and part
with the apostles. [5]And when a violent at-
tempt was made by both the Gentiles and
Jews, with their rulers, to abuse and stone
them, [6]they became aware of it and fled to
Lys′tra and Der′bē, cities of Lyc·ā·ō′ni·a,
and to the surrounding region. [7]And they
were preaching the gospel there.

Idolatry at Lystra

[8]And in Lys′tra a certain man without
strength in his feet was sitting, a cripple
from his mother's womb, who had never
walked. [9]*This* man heard Paul speaking.
Paul, observing him intently and seeing
that he had faith to be healed, [10]said with a
loud voice, "Stand up straight on your
feet!" And he leaped and walked. [11]Now
when the people saw what Paul had done,
they raised their voices, saying in the
Lyc·ā·ō′ni·an *language,* "The gods have
come down to us in the likeness of men!"
[12]And Bar′na·bas they called Zeūs, and
Paul, Her′mēs, because he was the chief
speaker. [13]Then the priest of Zeūs, whose
temple was in front of their city, brought
oxen and garlands to the gates, intending
to sacrifice with the multitudes.
[14]But when the apostles Bar′na·bas and
Paul heard this, they tore their clothes and
ran in among the multitude, crying out

13:47 [a]Isaiah 49:6

13:46 since you reject . . . we turn to the Gentiles: One of the most important verses in the NT. Henceforth Paul was the apostle to the Gentiles (see Gal. 2:9; Eph. 3:8).

14:6–20 In Lystra Paul and Barnabas first addressed a purely pagan Gentile audience. When God healed a **cripple** (v. 8), as had been done in Jerusalem (see 3:6–8), the people tried to worship Barnabas and Paul.

14:10 Stand up: This was asking the impossible. But when the man willed to obey, God furnished the power.

15and saying, "Men, why are you doing these things? We also are men with the same nature as you, and preach to you that you should turn from these useless things to the living God, who made the heaven, the earth, the sea, and all things that are in them, 16who in bygone generations allowed all nations to walk in their own ways. 17Nevertheless He did not leave Himself without witness, in that He did good, gave us rain from heaven and fruitful seasons, filling our hearts with food and gladness." 18And with these sayings they could scarcely restrain the multitudes from sacrificing to them.

Stoning, Escape to Derbe

19Then Jews from An′ti·och and Ī·cō′-ni-um came there; and having persuaded the multitudes, they stoned Paul *and* dragged *him* out of the city, supposing him to be dead. 20However, when the disciples gathered around him, he rose up and went into the city. And the next day he departed with Bar′na·bas to Der′bē.

Strengthening the Converts

21And when they had preached the gospel to that city and made many disciples, they returned to Lys′tra, Ī·cō′ni·um, and An′ti·och, 22strengthening the souls of the disciples, exhorting *them* to continue in the faith, and *saying,* "We must through many tribulations enter the kingdom of God." 23So when they had appointed elders in every church, and prayed with fasting, they commended them to the Lord in whom they had believed. 24And after they had passed through Pi·sid′i·a, they came to Pam·phyl′i·a. 25Now when they had preached the word in Per′ga, they went down to At·ta·lī′a. 26From there they sailed to An′ti·och, where they had been commended to the grace of God for the work which they had completed.

27Now when they had come and gathered the church together, they reported all that God had done with them, and that He had opened the door of faith to the Gentiles. 28So they stayed there a long time with the disciples.

CHAPTER 15

Conflict over Circumcision

And certain *men* came down from Judea and taught the brethren, "Unless you are circumcised according to the custom of Moses, you cannot be saved." 2Therefore, when Paul and Bar′na·bas had no small dissension and dispute with them, they determined that Paul and Bar′na·bas and certain others of them should go up to Jerusalem, to the apostles and elders, about this question.

3So, being sent on their way by the church, they passed through Phoe·ni′ci·a and Samaria, describing the conversion of the Gentiles; and they caused great joy to all the brethren. 4And when they had come to Jerusalem, they were received by the church and the apostles and the elders; and they reported all things that God had done with them. 5But some of the sect of the

14:15–17 God, who made . . . all things: Creation is cited as evidence of the power and goodness of the living God (see Ps. 19:1; Rom. 1:19, 20).

14:19 After preparing to worship Paul, **they stoned** him. That he could have survived this assault was a miracle.

14:22 The apostles are not saying that one can earn salvation or a place in heaven by enduring suffering but that persecution and suffering automatically accompany salvation.

14:23 appointed elders in every church: The missionaries were more than itinerant evangelists; they conserved the converts with leaders who would continue to train them.

15:1–5 Unless . . . circumcised . . . you cannot be saved: Evidence was accumulating that the uncircumcised **Gentiles** (v. 3) were being **saved**. The problem was how to reconcile these events with the **custom** of circumcision commanded in the law. Hence they appealed to the leaders in **Jerusalem** (v. 4).

Phar'i·sees who believed rose up, saying,
"It is necessary to circumcise them, and to
command *them* to keep the law of Moses."

The Jerusalem Council

6Now the apostles and elders came to-
gether to consider this matter. 7And when
there had been much dispute, Peter rose
up and said to them: "Men and brethren,
you know that a good while ago God chose
among us, that by my mouth the Gentiles
should hear the word of the gospel and be-
lieve. 8So God, who knows the heart, ac-
knowledged them by giving them the
Holy Spirit, just as *He did* to us, 9and made
no distinction between us and them, puri-
fying their hearts by faith. 10Now therefore,
why do you test God by putting a yoke on
the neck of the disciples which neither our
fathers nor we were able to bear? 11But we
believe that through the grace of the Lord
Jesus Christ[a] we shall be saved in the same
manner as they."

12Then all the multitude kept silent and
listened to Bar'na·bas and Paul declaring
how many miracles and wonders God had
worked through them among the Gentiles.
13And after they had become silent, James
answered, saying, "Men *and* brethren, lis-
ten to me: 14Simon has declared how God
at the first visited the Gentiles to take out
of them a people for His name. 15And with
this the words of the prophets agree, just as
it is written:

16 *'After this I will return*
And will rebuild the tabernacle of
David, which has fallen down;
I will rebuild its ruins,
And I will set it up;
17 *So that the rest of mankind may seek*
the LORD,
Even all the Gentiles who are called
by My name,
Says the LORD who does all these
things.'[a]

18"Known to God from eternity are all
His works.[a] 19Therefore I judge that we
should not trouble those from among the
Gentiles who are turning to God, 20but that
we write to them to abstain from things
polluted by idols, *from* sexual immorality,[a]
from things strangled, and *from* blood. 21For
Moses has had throughout many genera-
tions those who preach him in every city,
being read in the synagogues every Sab-
bath."

The Jerusalem Decree

22Then it pleased the apostles and el-
ders, with the whole church, to send cho-
sen men of their own company to An'-
ti·och with Paul and Bar'na·bas, *namely,*
Judas who was also named Bar'sa·bas,[a]
and Silas, leading men among the
brethren.

23They wrote this, *letter* by them:

The apostles, the elders, and the
brethren,

To the brethren who are of the Gen-
tiles in An'ti·och, Syria, and Ci·li'ci·a:

Greetings.

24 Since we have heard that some who
went out from us have troubled you
with words, unsettling your souls,

15:11 [a]NU-Text and M-Text omit *Christ.*
15:17 [a]Amos 9:11, 12 15:18 [a]NU-Text (combining with verse 17) reads *Says the Lord, who makes these things known from eternity (of old).* 15:20 [a]Or *fornication* 15:22 [a]NU-Text and M-Text read *Barsabbas.*

15:22–29 Salvation was by faith in Jesus, not by keeping the law (see v. 11). This principle was settled. The Gentiles were not required to keep the law or to be circumcised. They were directed to **abstain from things offered to idols**, **from blood**, and **from things strangled** (v. 29). These practices were offensive to the Jews and made it particularly hard for them to have table fellowship with Gentiles. We too should be sensitive to the feelings of others. All Christians must abstain from **sexual immorality**, emphasized because it was a prominent sin in the Gentile world.

saying, "*You must* be circumcised and
keep the law"[a]—to whom we gave no
such commandment—25it seemed
good to us, being assembled with one
accord, to send chosen men to you
with our beloved Bar'na·bas and Paul,
26men who have risked their lives for
the name of our Lord Jesus Christ.
27We have therefore sent Judas and
Silas, who will also report the same
things by word of mouth. 28For it
seemed good to the Holy Spirit, and
to us, to lay upon you no greater bur-
den than these necessary things: 29that
you abstain from things offered to
idols, from blood, from things stran-
gled, and from sexual immorality.[a] If
you keep yourselves from these, you
will do well.

Farewell.

Continuing Ministry in Syria

30So when they were sent off, they
came to An'ti·och; and when they had
gathered the multitude together, they
delivered the letter. 31When they had
read it, they rejoiced over its encourage-
ment. 32Now Judas and Silas, them-
selves being prophets also, exhorted
and strengthened the brethren with
many words. 33And after they had stayed
there for a time, they were sent back
with greetings from the brethren to the
apostles.[a]

34However, it seemed good to Silas to re-
main there.[a] 35Paul and Bar'na·bas also re-
mained in An'ti·och, teaching and preach-
ing the word of the Lord, with many others
also.

Division over John Mark

36Then after some days Paul said to
Bar'na·bas, "Let us now go back and visit
our brethren in every city where we have
preached the word of the Lord, *and see* how
they are doing." 37Now Bar'na·bas was de-
termined to take with them John called
Mark. 38But Paul insisted that they should
not take with them the one who had de-
parted from them in Pam·phyl'i·a, and
had not gone with them to the work.
39Then the contention became so sharp that
they parted from one another. And so
Bar'na·bas took Mark and sailed to
Cyprus; 40but Paul chose Silas and de-
parted, being commended by the brethren
to the grace of God. 41And he went through
Syria and Ci·li'ci·a, strengthening the
churches.

CHAPTER 16

Timothy Joins Paul and Silas

Then he came to Der'bē and Lys'tra.
And behold, a certain disciple was there,
named Timothy, *the* son of a certain Jewish
woman who believed, but his father *was*
Greek. 2He was well spoken of by the
brethren who were at Lys'tra and
Ī·cō'ni·um. 3Paul wanted to have him go
on with him. And he took *him* and circum-
cised him because of the Jews who were in
that region, for they all knew that his fa-
ther was Greek. 4And as they went through
the cities, they delivered to them the de-
crees to keep, which were determined by

15:24 [a]NU-Text omits *saying, "You must be circumcised and keep the law,"* 15:29 [a]Or *fornication*
15:33 [a]NU-Text reads *to those who had sent them.*
15:34 [a]NU-Text and M-Text omit this verse.

15:36–41 Barnabas was determined: He was people-oriented (v. 37). **Paul insisted**: He was idea-oriented (v. 38). God uses both. In this case Barnabas was right (see 2 Tim. 4:11), but God used the disagreement to make two missions instead of only one.

16:3 because of the Jews: His mother was Jewish (v. 1), so circumcision was appropriate. Then, as now, the mother determined Jewishness. His Greek father may have delayed the rite. Without circumcision Timothy's ministry among Jews would have been hampered. Social and cultural differences should never be allowed to interfere with the spread of the gospel.

the apostles and elders at Jerusalem. 5So
the churches were strengthened in the
faith, and increased in number daily.

The Macedonian Call

6Now when they had gone through
Phryg′i·a and the region of Galatia, they
were forbidden by the Holy Spirit to
preach the word in Asia. 7After they had
come to Mys′i·a, they tried to go into
Bi·thyn′i·a, but the Spirit[a] did not permit
them. 8So passing by Mys′i·a, they came
down to Trō′as. 9And a vision appeared to
Paul in the night. A man of Mac·e·dō′ni·a
stood and pleaded with him, saying,
"Come over to Mac·e·dō′ni·a and help us."
10Now after he had seen the vision, imme-
diately we sought to go to Mac·e·dō′ni·a,
concluding that the Lord had called us to
preach the gospel to them.

Lydia Baptized at Philippi

11Therefore, sailing from Trō′as, we ran a
straight course to Sam′o·thrāce, and the
next *day* came to Nē·ap′o·lis, 12and from
there to Phi·lip′pī, which is the foremost
city of that part of Mac·e·dō′ni·a, a colony.
And we were staying in that city for some
days. 13And on the Sabbath day we went
out of the city to the riverside, where
prayer was customarily made; and we sat
down and spoke to the women who met
there. 14Now a certain woman named
Lyd′i·a heard *us.* She was a seller of purple
from the city of Thy̅·a·tī′ra, who wor-
shiped God. The Lord opened her heart to
heed the things spoken by Paul. 15And
when she and her household were bap-
tized, she begged *us,* saying, "If you have
judged me to be faithful to the Lord, come
to my house and stay." So she persuaded us.

Paul and Silas Imprisoned

16Now it happened, as we went to
prayer, that a certain slave girl possessed
with a spirit of divination met us, who
brought her masters much profit by
fortune-telling. 17This girl followed Paul
and us, and cried out, saying, "These men
are the servants of the Most High God,
who proclaim to us the way of salvation."
18And this she did for many days.

But Paul, greatly annoyed, turned and
said to the spirit, "I command you in the
name of Jesus Christ to come out of her."
And he came out that very hour. 19But
when her masters saw that their hope of
profit was gone, they seized Paul and Silas
and dragged *them* into the marketplace to
the authorities.

20And they brought them to the magis-
trates, and said, "These men, being Jews,
exceedingly trouble our city; 21and they
teach customs which are not lawful for us,
being Romans, to receive or observe."
22Then the multitude rose up together
against them; and the magistrates tore off
their clothes and commanded *them* to be
beaten with rods. 23And when they had
laid many stripes on them, they threw *them*
into prison, commanding the jailer to keep
them securely. 24Having received such a
charge, he put them into the inner prison
and fastened their feet in the stocks.

16:7 [a]NU-Text adds *of Jesus.*

16:9 Macedonia: Northern Greece

16:12–40 Philippi was a Roman **colony**. This explains why Paul was accused of teaching customs not **lawful for . . . Romans** (v. 21) and why the **magistrates** were so concerned because they had beaten Paul and Silas, who were Roman citizens (vv. 37–39). The demonstration of God's power in this pagan city led to the conversion of the **keeper of the prison** (v. 27).

16:13 spoke to the women . . . there: Luke gives special attention to women in his Gospel and Acts. Apparently few Jews lived in this Roman colony, because if there were as many as 10 heads of families in a community, the Jews were required to form a synagogue. Jewish women were not obliged to attend public worship, but these devout ladies **customarily** prayed outside the city.

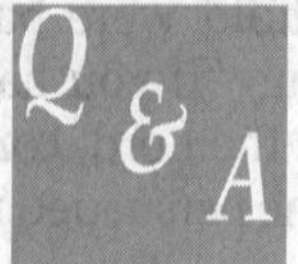

What can we do as we realize death is coming?

Elmer L. Gray

Medical science has done much to heal our diseases and to prolong life. However, as the years pass, we become more aware of death's approach. Some older adults lose their dread of death and even begin to anticipate it.

The thing about dying is to be ready for it and for what comes after it. I am like the fellow who said, "I am ready to go anytime, but I am not in a hurry." People need to be serious about life and death. A father, concerned about his son who had no sense of responsibility, said, "Son, if I died tomorrow, where would you be?" The son answered, "Why, I would be here. The question, Dad, is, Where would you be?" We can joke about it but we should not postpone answering the question of death and the hereafter.

What must you do in the face of death? Paul said, "Believe on the Lord Jesus Christ, and you will be saved" (Acts 16:31).

If we are assured of our own salvation, we need to do all we can to help those who will live on after us. Do your best to provide for them physically and spiritually. Help them to know of your faith in Christ and of your love for God. Be sure also that they are aware of your love for them, your appreciation for them and their good qualities, and your confidence that they will make the most of their lives. ✦

The Philippian Jailer Saved

25But at midnight Paul and Silas were
praying and singing hymns to God, and
the prisoners were listening to them. 26Sud-
denly there was a great earthquake, so that
the foundations of the prison were shaken;
and immediately all the doors were
opened and everyone's chains were
loosed. 27And the keeper of the prison,
awaking from sleep and seeing the prison
doors open, supposing the prisoners had
fled, drew his sword and was about to kill
himself. 28But Paul called with a loud
voice, saying, "Do yourself no harm, for
we are all here."

29Then he called for a light, ran in, and
fell down trembling before Paul and Silas.
30And he brought them out and said, "Sirs,
what must I do to be saved?"

31So they said, "Believe on the Lord
Jesus Christ, and you will be saved, you
and your household." 32Then they spoke
the word of the Lord to him and to all
who were in his house. 33And he took them
the same hour of the night and washed
their stripes. And immediately he and
all his family were baptized. 34Now when
he had brought them into his house, he
set food before them; and he rejoiced, hav-
ing believed in God with all his house-
hold.

✦

16:25 What an example we have in Paul and Silas, who rejoiced in the face of injustice and suffering!

Paul Refuses to Depart Secretly

35 And when it was day, the magistrates
sent the officers, saying, "Let those men
go."
36 So the keeper of the prison reported
these words to Paul, saying, "The magis-
trates have sent to let you go. Now there-
fore depart, and go in peace."
37 But Paul said to them, "They have
beaten us openly, uncondemned Romans,
and have thrown *us* into prison. And now
do they put us out secretly? No indeed! Let
them come themselves and get us out."
38 And the officers told these words to
the magistrates, and they were afraid
when they heard that they were Romans.
39 Then they came and pleaded with them
and brought *them* out, and asked *them* to
depart from the city. 40 So they went out of
the prison and entered *the house of* Lyd′i·a;
and when they had seen the brethren, they
encouraged them and departed.

CHAPTER 17

Preaching Christ at Thessalonica

Now when they had passed through
Am·phip′o·lis and Ap·ol·lō′ni·a, they
came to Thes·sa·lo·nī′ca, where there was
a synagogue of the Jews. 2 Then Paul, as his
custom was, went in to them, and for three
Sabbaths reasoned with them from the
Scriptures, 3 explaining and demonstrating
that the Christ had to suffer and rise again
from the dead, and *saying*, "This Jesus
whom I preach to you is the Christ." 4 And
some of them were persuaded; and a great
multitude of the devout Greeks, and not a
few of the leading women, joined Paul and
Silas.

Assault on Jason's House

5 But the Jews who were not persuaded,
becoming envious,[a] took some of the evil
men from the marketplace, and gathering
a mob, set all the city in an uproar and at-
tacked the house of Jason, and sought to
bring them out to the people. 6 But when
they did not find them, they dragged Jason
and some brethren to the rulers of the city,
crying out, "These who have turned the
world upside down have come here too.
7 Jason has harbored them, and these are all
acting contrary to the decrees of Caesar,
saying there is another king—Jesus." 8 And
they troubled the crowd and the rulers of
the city when they heard these things. 9 So
when they had taken security from Jason
and the rest, they let them go.

Ministering at Berea

10 Then the brethren immediately sent
Paul and Silas away by night to Be·rē′a.
When they arrived, they went into the syn-
agogue of the Jews. 11 These were more fair-
minded than those in Thes·sa·lo·nī′ca, in
that they received the word with all readi-
ness, and searched the Scriptures daily *to
find out* whether these things were
so. 12 Therefore many of them believed,
and also not a few of the Greeks, promi-
nent women as well as men. 13 But
when the Jews from Thes·sa·lo·nī′ca
learned that the word of God was
preached by Paul at Be·rē′a, they came
there also and stirred up the crowds.
14 Then immediately the brethren sent Paul
away, to go to the sea; but both Silas and
Timothy remained there. 15 So those who
conducted Paul brought him to Athens;
and receiving a command for Silas and
Timothy to come to him with all speed,
they departed.

17:5 [a]NU-Text omits *who were not persuaded;* M-Text omits *becoming envious.*

17:1–4 Besides some Jews, a **multitude** of **devout Greeks**, and several **leading women**, many pagans were also converted (1 Thess. 1:9). These early converts in Macedonia were the recipients of one of the earliest Christian documents: several months later Paul wrote 1 Thessalonians to them from Corinth.

17:11 Mature Christians follow the example set by the Bereans, checking everything against the authority of Scripture.

The Philosophers at Athens

16Now while Paul waited for them at
Athens, his spirit was provoked within
him when he saw that the city was given
over to idols. 17Therefore he reasoned in
the synagogue with the Jews and with the
Gentile worshipers, and in the marketplace
daily with those who happened to be
there. 18Then[a] certain Ep·i·cū·rē'an and
Stoic philosophers encountered him. And
some said, "What does this babbler want
to say?"

Others said, "He seems to be a pro-
claimer of foreign gods," because he
preached to them Jesus and the resurrec-
tion.

19And they took him and brought him to
the Ar·e·op'a·gus, saying, "May we know
what this new doctrine *is* of which you
speak? 20For you are bringing some strange
things to our ears. Therefore we want to
know what these things mean." 21For all
the A·thē'ni·ans and the foreigners who
were there spent their time in nothing
else but either to tell or to hear some new
thing.

Addressing the Areopagus

22Then Paul stood in the midst of the
Ar·e·op'a·gus and said, "Men of Athens, I
perceive that in all things you are very reli-
gious; 23for as I was passing through and
considering the objects of your worship, I
even found an altar with this inscription:

TO THE UNKNOWN GOD.

Therefore, the One whom you worship
without knowing, Him I proclaim to you:
24God, who made the world and every-
thing in it, since He is Lord of heaven and
earth, does not dwell in temples made
with hands. 25Nor is He worshiped with
men's hands, as though He needed any-
thing, since He gives to all life, breath, and
all things. 26And He has made from one
blood[a] every nation of men to dwell on all
the face of the earth, and has determined
their preappointed times and the bound-
aries of their dwellings, 27so that they
should seek the Lord, in the hope that they
might grope for Him and find Him,
though He is not far from each one of us;
28for in Him we live and move and have
our being, as also some of your own poets
have said, 'For we are also His offspring.'
29Therefore, since we are the offspring of
God, we ought not to think that the Divine
Nature is like gold or silver or stone, some-
thing shaped by art and man's devising.
30Truly, these times of ignorance God over-
looked, but now commands all men every-
where to repent, 31because He has ap-
pointed a day on which He will judge the
world in righteousness by the Man whom
He has ordained. He has given assurance
of this to all by raising Him from the
dead."

32And when they heard of the resurrec-
tion of the dead, some mocked, while oth-
ers said, "We will hear you again on this
matter." 33So Paul departed from among
them. 34However, some men joined him
and believed, among them Dī·o·nys'i·us
the Ar·e·op'a·gīte, a woman named
Dam'a·ris, and others with them.

17:18 [a]NU-Text and M-Text add *also*. 17:26 [a]NU-Text omits *blood*.

17:19–21 The Areopagus, or Mars' Hill, overlooked the marketplace. It served as a court and a place for discussion and debate. There Paul was invited to explain his **new doctrine**.

17:22–31 Addressing pagans who did not know the Scriptures, Paul did not appeal explicitly to Jewish writings. The content of his message was thoroughly biblical, however. It included the role of God as Creator, the futility of idols, the coming judgment, and—as the climax—the resurrection of Christ.

17:31 will judge the world in righteousness: The gods worshiped by the Greeks were often more immoral than their worshipers. The **Man** Jesus will be both the judge and the measure of the righteousness required by God.

CHAPTER 18

Ministering at Corinth

After these things Paul departed from Athens and went to Corinth. 2And he found a certain Jew named A·qui′la, born in Pon′tus, who had recently come from Italy with his wife Pri·scil′la (because Clau′di·us had commanded all the Jews to depart from Rome); and he came to them. 3So, because he was of the same trade, he stayed with them and worked; for by occupation they were tentmakers. 4And he reasoned in the synagogue every Sabbath, and persuaded both Jews and Greeks.

5When Silas and Timothy had come from Mac·e·dō′ni·a, Paul was compelled by the Spirit, and testified to the Jews *that* Jesus *is* the Christ. 6But when they opposed him and blasphemed, he shook *his* garments and said to them, "Your blood *be* upon your *own* heads; I *am* clean. From now on I will go to the Gentiles." 7And he departed from there and entered the house of a certain *man* named Jus′tus,[a] *one* who worshiped God, whose house was next door to the synagogue. 8Then Cris′pus, the ruler of the synagogue, believed on the Lord with all his household. And many of the Corinthians, hearing, believed and were baptized.

9Now the Lord spoke to Paul in the night by a vision, "Do not be afraid, but speak, and do not keep silent; 10for I am with you, and no one will attack you to hurt you; for I have many people in this city." 11And he continued *there* a year and six months, teaching the word of God among them.

12When Gal′li·ō was proconsul of A·chā′i·a, the Jews with one accord rose up against Paul and brought him to the judgment seat, 13saying, "This *fellow* persuades men to worship God contrary to the law."

14And when Paul was about to open *his* mouth, Gal′li·ō said to the Jews, "If it were a matter of wrongdoing or wicked crimes, O Jews, there would be reason why I should bear with you. 15But if it is a question of words and names and your own law, look *to it* yourselves; for I do not want to be a judge of such *matters*." 16And he drove them from the judgment seat. 17Then all the Greeks[a] took Sos′the·nēs, the ruler of the synagogue, and beat *him* before the judgment seat. But Gal′li·ō took no notice of these things.

Paul Returns to Antioch

18So Paul still remained a good while. Then he took leave of the brethren and sailed for Syria, and Pri·scil′la and A·qui′la *were* with him. He had *his* hair cut off at Cen′chrē·a, for he had taken a vow. 19And he came to Eph′e·sus, and left them there; but he himself entered the synagogue and reasoned with the Jews. 20When they asked *him* to stay a longer time with them, he did not consent, 21but took leave of them, saying, "I must by all means keep this coming feast in Jerusalem;[a] but I will return again to you, God willing." And he sailed from Eph′e·sus.

22And when he had landed at Caes·a·rē′a, and gone up and greeted the church, he went down to An′ti·och. 23After he had spent some time *there*, he departed and went over the region of Galatia and

18:7 [a]NU-Text reads *Titius Justus.* 18:17 [a]NU-Text reads *they all.* 18:21 [a]NU-Text omits *I must* through *Jerusalem.*

18:3 With his brilliant gift for oration, Paul was not too proud to perform manual labor.

18:12–17 Paul was brought before Gallio in A.D. 51 in **Achaia** (southern Greece). At that time the Roman officials would not become involved with religious quarrels. This worked to the advantage of the gospel. The reverse was true later on.

18:18 Jews sometimes shaved their **hair** at the conclusion of a **vow** and offered the hair as part of their sacrifice in the temple (see Num. 6:5, 6; Acts 21:23–26). Paul may have taken this vow in thanksgiving for protection and for the success of his mission.

Phryg′i•a in order, strengthening all the
disciples.

Ministry of Apollos

[24]Now a certain Jew named A•pol′los,
born at Alexandria, an eloquent man *and*
mighty in the Scriptures, came to Eph′-
e•sus. [25]This man had been instructed in
the way of the Lord; and being fervent in
spirit, he spoke and taught accurately the
things of the Lord, though he knew only
the baptism of John. [26]So he began to speak
boldly in the synagogue. When A•qui′la
and Pri•scil′la heard him, they took him
aside and explained to him the way of God
more accurately. [27]And when he desired to
cross to A•cha′i•a, the brethren wrote, ex-
horting the disciples to receive him; and
when he arrived, he greatly helped those
who had believed through grace; [28]for he
vigorously refuted the Jews publicly,
showing from the Scriptures that Jesus is
the Christ.

CHAPTER 19

Paul at Ephesus

And it happened, while A•pol′los was
at Corinth, that Paul, having passed
through the upper regions, came to Eph′-
e•sus. And finding some disciples [2]he said
to them, "Did you receive the Holy Spirit
when you believed?"

So they said to him, "We have not so
much as heard whether there is a Holy
Spirit."

[3]And he said to them, "Into what then
were you baptized?"

So they said, "Into John's baptism."

[4]Then Paul said, "John indeed baptized
with a baptism of repentance, saying to the
people that they should believe on Him
who would come after him, that is, on
Christ Jesus."

[5]When they heard *this*, they were bap-
tized in the name of the Lord Jesus. [6]And
when Paul had laid hands on them, the
Holy Spirit came upon them, and they
spoke with tongues and prophesied. [7]Now
the men were about twelve in all.

[8]And he went into the synagogue and
spoke boldly for three months, reasoning
and persuading concerning the things of
the kingdom of God. [9]But when some were
hardened and did not believe, but spoke
evil of the Way before the multitude, he de-
parted from them and withdrew the disci-
ples, reasoning daily in the school of
Ty̆•ran′nus. [10]And this continued for two
years, so that all who dwelt in Asia heard
the word of the Lord Jesus, both Jews and
Greeks.

Miracles Glorify Christ

[11]Now God worked unusual miracles by
the hands of Paul, [12]so that even handker-
chiefs or aprons were brought from his
body to the sick, and the diseases left them
and the evil spirits went out of them.

18:24 Paul's third missionary journey begins.

18:24–26 Apollos was probably more eloquent than Paul (see 2 Cor. 10:10) and became his rival in Corinth, though probably unintended (see 1 Cor. 1:12). How much better it was for **Aquila** and **Priscilla** to explain privately to this sincere brother **the way of God more accurately** than to denounce him publicly.

19:2 when you believed: Probably after hearing of John's baptism of repentance from Apollos before he had talked with Aquila and Priscilla (see 18:25). These people were looking for the coming Messiah (see Matt. 3:11), unaware that He not only had already come but also had sent the **Holy Spirit** (see John 7:39).

19:6 The Holy Spirit came upon them with accompanying signs, as in Jerusalem and Caesarea. The coming of the Holy Spirit on Jewish believers at Pentecost (2:1–4), on Samaritans (8:14–17), on Gentiles at Cornelius's house (10:44, 45; 11:15–17), and now on John's followers in Ephesus completed the incorporation of four distinct groups into the church of Christ.

13Then some of the itinerant Jewish exor-
cists took it upon themselves to call the
name of the Lord Jesus over those who had
evil spirits, saying, "We[a] exorcise you by
the Jesus whom Paul preaches." 14Also
there were seven sons of Scē′va, a Jewish
chief priest, who did so.
15And the evil spirit answered and said,
"Jesus I know, and Paul I know; but who
are you?"
16Then the man in whom the evil spirit
was leaped on them, overpowered[a] them,
and prevailed against them,[b] so that they
fled out of that house naked and wounded.
17This became known both to all Jews and
Greeks dwelling in Eph′e·sus; and fear fell
on them all, and the name of the Lord Jesus
was magnified. 18And many who had be-
lieved came confessing and telling their
deeds. 19Also, many of those who had
practiced magic brought their books to-
gether and burned *them* in the sight of all.
And they counted up the value of them,
and *it* totaled fifty thousand *pieces* of silver.
20So the word of the Lord grew mightily
and prevailed.

The Riot at Ephesus

21When these things were accomplished,
Paul purposed in the Spirit, when he had
passed through Mac·e·dō′ni·a and
A·chā′i·a, to go to Jerusalem, saying, "Af-
ter I have been there, I must also see
Rome." 22So he sent into Mac·e·dō′ni·a two
of those who ministered to him, Timothy
and Ē·ras′tus, but he himself stayed in Asia
for a time.
23And about that time there arose a great
commotion about the Way. 24For a certain
man named De·mē′tri·us, a silversmith,
who made silver shrines of Diana,[a]
brought no small profit to the craftsmen.
25He called them together with the workers
of similar occupation, and said: "Men, you
know that we have our prosperity by this
trade. 26Moreover you see and hear that
not only at Eph′e·sus, but throughout al-
most all Asia, this Paul has persuaded and
turned away many people, saying that
they are not gods which are made with
hands. 27So not only is this trade of ours in
danger of falling into disrepute, but also
the temple of the great goddess Diana may
be despised and her magnificence de-
stroyed,[a] whom all Asia and the world
worship."
28Now when they heard *this,* they were
full of wrath and cried out, saying, "Great
is Diana of the E·phē′si·ans!" 29So the
whole city was filled with confusion, and
rushed into the theater with one accord,
having seized Gā′i·us and Ar·is·tar′chus,
Mac·e·dō′ni·ans, Paul's travel compan-
ions. 30And when Paul wanted to go in to
the people, the disciples would not allow
him. 31Then some of the officials of Asia,
who were his friends, sent to him pleading
that he would not venture into the theater.
32Some therefore cried one thing and some
another, for the assembly was confused,
and most of them did not know why they
had come together. 33And they drew Alex-
ander out of the multitude, the Jews
putting him forward. And Alexander mo-
tioned with his hand, and wanted to make
his defense to the people. 34But when they
found out that he was a Jew, all with one
voice cried out for about two hours, "Great
is Diana of the E·phē′si·ans!"
35And when the city clerk had quieted
the crowd, he said: "Men of Eph′e·sus,
what man is there who does not know that

19:13 [a]NU-Text reads *I.* 19:16 [a]M-Text reads *and they overpowered.* [b]NU-Text reads *both of them.* 19:24 [a]Greek *Artemis* 19:27 [a]NU-Text reads *she be deposed from her magnificence.*

19:19 Fifty thousand pieces of silver: probably refers to 50,000 Greek drachmae, each of which was approximately equal to one day's wages.

19:31 The **officials of Asia** were prominent citizens and were also friends of Paul.

19:35–37 The city clerk, responsible for law and order, rebuked the unauthorized assembly. He argued that the prestige of **Diana** was such that she needed no defense, and

the city of the E·phē′si·ans is temple guardian of the great goddess Diana, and of the *image* which fell down from Zeūs? 36Therefore, since these things cannot be denied, you ought to be quiet and do nothing rashly. 37For you have brought these men here who are neither robbers of temples nor blasphemers of your[a] goddess. 38Therefore, if De·mē′tri·us and his fellow craftsmen have a case against anyone, the courts are open and there are proconsuls. Let them bring charges against one another. 39But if you have any other inquiry to make, it shall be determined in the lawful assembly. 40For we are in danger of being called in question for today's uproar, there being no reason which we may give to account for this disorderly gathering." 41And when he had said these things, he dismissed the assembly.

CHAPTER 20

Journeys in Greece

After the uproar had ceased, Paul called the disciples to *himself*, embraced *them*, and departed to go to Mac·e·dō′ni·a. 2Now when he had gone over that region and encouraged them with many words, he came to Greece 3and stayed three months. And when the Jews plotted against him as he was about to sail to Syria, he decided to return through Mac·e·dō′ni·a. 4And Sop′a·ter of Be·rē′a accompanied him to Asia—also Ar·is·tar′chus and Secundus of the Thes·sa·lō′ni·ans, and Gā′i·us of Der′bē, and Timothy, and Tych′i·cus and Troph′i·mus of Asia. 5These men, going ahead, waited for us at Trō′as. 6But we sailed away from Phi·lip′pī after the Days of Unleavened Bread, and in five days joined them at Trō′as, where we stayed seven days.

Ministering at Troas

7Now on the first *day* of the week, when the disciples came together to break bread, Paul, ready to depart the next day, spoke to them and continued his message until midnight. 8There were many lamps in the upper room where they[a] were gathered together. 9And in a window sat a certain young man named Eū′ty·chus, who was sinking into a deep sleep. He was overcome by sleep; and as Paul continued speaking, he fell down from the third story and was taken up dead. 10But Paul went down, fell on him, and embracing *him* said, "Do not trouble yourselves, for his life is in him." 11Now when he had come up, had broken bread and eaten, and talked a long while, even till daybreak, he departed. 12And they brought the young man in alive, and they were not a little comforted.

From Troas to Miletus

13Then we went ahead to the ship and sailed to As′sos, there intending to take Paul on board; for so he had given orders, intending himself to go on foot. 14And when he met us at As′sos, we took him on board and came to Mit·y·lē′nē. 15We sailed from there, and the next *day* came opposite

> Make sure that you let God's grace work in your souls by accepting whatever He gives you, and giving Him whatever He takes from you. True holiness consists of doing God's work with a smile.
>
> Mother Teresa of Calcutta

19:37 [a]NU-Text reads *our*. 20:8 [a]NU-Text and M-Text read *we*.

that **these men** had not attacked their **goddess**. A legend of their heathen religion told of an **image which fell down from Zeus**. Changed lives threatened paganism.

20:7 It was on the **first day of the week** that the **disciples came together**. This suggests a transition from Saturday to Sunday as the day of worship.

20:11 This verse illustrates the joy we should experience in true Christian fellowship.

Chī′os. The following *day* we arrived at
Sā′mos and stayed at Trō·gyl′li·um. The
next *day* we came to Mī·lē′tus. 16For Paul
had decided to sail past Eph′e·sus, so that
he would not have to spend time in Asia;
for he was hurrying to be at Jerusalem, if
possible, on the Day of Pentecost.

The Ephesian Elders Exhorted

17From Mī·lē′tus he sent to Eph′e·sus
and called for the elders of the church.
18And when they had come to him, he said
to them: "You know, from the first day that
I came to Asia, in what manner I always
lived among you, 19serving the Lord with
all humility, with many tears and trials
which happened to me by the plotting of
the Jews; 20how I kept back nothing that
was helpful, but proclaimed it to you, and
taught you publicly and from house to
house, 21testifying to Jews, and also to
Greeks, repentance toward God and faith
toward our Lord Jesus Christ. 22And see,
now I go bound in the spirit to Jerusalem,
not knowing the things that will happen to
me there, 23except that the Holy Spirit testi-
fies in every city, saying that chains and
tribulations await me. 24But none of these
things move me; nor do I count my life
dear to myself,[a] so that I may finish my
race with joy, and the ministry which I re-
ceived from the Lord Jesus, to testify to the
gospel of the grace of God.

25"And indeed, now I know that you all,
among whom I have gone preaching the
kingdom of God, will see my face no more.
26Therefore I testify to you this day that I
am innocent of the blood of all *men*. 27For I
have not shunned to declare to you the
whole counsel of God. 28Therefore take
heed to yourselves and to all the flock,
among which the Holy Spirit has made

20:24 [a]NU-Text reads *But I do not count my life of any value or dear to myself.* 20:28 [a]M-Text reads *of the Lord and God.* 20:34 [a]NU-Text and M-Text omit *Yes.*

> ***I pray that my children will remember it is more blessed to give than to receive.***
>
> *adapted from* Acts 20:35

you overseers, to shepherd the church of
God[a] which He purchased with His own
blood. 29For I know this, that after my de-
parture savage wolves will come in among
you, not sparing the flock. 30Also from
among yourselves men will rise up, speak-
ing perverse things, to draw away the dis-
ciples after themselves. 31Therefore watch,
and remember that for three years I did not
cease to warn everyone night and day with
tears.

32"So now, brethren, I commend you to
God and to the word of His grace, which is
able to build you up and give you an in-
heritance among all those who are sancti-
fied. 33I have coveted no one's silver or
gold or apparel. 34Yes,[a] you yourselves
know that these hands have provided for
my necessities, and for those who were
with me. 35I have shown you in every way,
by laboring like this, that you must sup-
port the weak. And remember the words of
the Lord Jesus, that He said, 'It is more
blessed to give than to receive.' "

36And when he had said these things, he
knelt down and prayed with them all.
37Then they all wept freely, and fell on
Paul's neck and kissed him, 38sorrowing
most of all for the words which he spoke,
that they would see his face no more. And
they accompanied him to the ship.

CHAPTER 21

Warnings on the Journey to Jerusalem

Now it came to pass, that when we had
departed from them and set sail, running a

20:28 take heed to yourselves: leaders must keep themselves pure if their ministry is to be effective.

20:31 three years: The approximate length of Paul's ministry in Ephesus.

straight course we came to Cōs, the follow-
ing *day* to Rhōdes, and from there to
Pat′a·ra. 2And finding a ship sailing over
to Phoe·ni′ci·a, we went aboard and set
sail. 3When we had sighted Cyprus, we
passed it on the left, sailed to Syria, and
landed at Tȳre; for there the ship was to
unload her cargo. 4And finding disciples,[a]
we stayed there seven days. They told Paul
through the Spirit not to go up to Jerusa-
lem. 5When we had come to the end of
those days, we departed and went on our
way; and they all accompanied us, with
wives and children, till *we were* out of the
city. And we knelt down on the shore and
prayed. 6When we had taken our leave of
one another, we boarded the ship, and they
returned home.

7And when we had finished *our* voyage
from Tȳre, we came to Ptol·e·mā′is,
greeted the brethren, and stayed with them
one day. 8On the next *day* we who were
Paul's companions[a] departed and came to
Caes·a·rē′a, and entered the house of
Philip the evangelist, who was *one* of the
seven, and stayed with him. 9Now this
man had four virgin daughters who
prophesied. 10And as we stayed many
days, a certain prophet named Ag′a·bus
came down from Judea. 11When he had
come to us, he took Paul's belt, bound his
own hands and feet, and said, "Thus says
the Holy Spirit, 'So shall the Jews at Jerusa-
lem bind the man who owns this belt, and
deliver *him* into the hands of the Gen-
tiles.' "

12Now when we heard these things,
both we and those from that place pleaded
with him not to go up to Jerusalem. 13Then
Paul answered, "What do you mean by
weeping and breaking my heart? For I am
ready not only to be bound, but also to die
at Jerusalem for the name of the Lord Je-
sus."

14So when he would not be persuaded,
we ceased, saying, "The will of the Lord be
done."

Paul Urged to Make Peace

15And after those days we packed and
went up to Jerusalem. 16Also some of the
disciples from Caes·a·rē′a went with us
and brought with them a certain Mnā′son
of Cyprus, an early disciple, with whom
we were to lodge.

17And when we had come to Jerusalem,
the brethren received us gladly. 18On the
following *day* Paul went in with us to
James, and all the elders were present.
19When he had greeted them, he told in de-
tail those things which God had done
among the Gentiles through his ministry.
20And when they heard *it*, they glorified
the Lord. And they said to him, "You see,
brother, how many myriads of Jews there
are who have believed, and they are all
zealous for the law; 21but they have been
informed about you that you teach all the
Jews who are among the Gentiles to for-
sake Moses, saying that they ought not to
circumcise *their* children nor to walk ac-
cording to the customs. 22What then? The

21:4 [a]NU-Text reads *the disciples.* 21:8 [a]NU-Text omits *who were Paul's companions.*

21:8, 9 Philip the evangelist apparently settled in Caesarea, his last reported stop (8:40).

21:10–12 The stay of **many days** seems strange in view of Paul's eagerness to arrive in Jerusalem (see 20:16). The **prophet . . . Agabus** followed OT precedent, reinforcing his verbal prediction by dramatic action (see Jer. 27:1–9; 28:10, 11). The gift of prophecy included the ability to predict events.

21:20–22 The leaders of the church rejoiced over the conversion of Gentiles, but they were worried about Jewish hostility. Many Christian **Jews** in Jerusalem had heard that Paul taught the **Jews** living outside Palestine not to keep the Jewish law. What Paul actually taught, in agreement with the other apostles, was that **Gentile** believers did not have to keep the law to be saved (v. 25). Probably many Jews began to see that if the law was not necessary for Gentiles, it was not necessary for Jews either.

assembly must certainly meet, for they will[a] hear that you have come. 23Therefore do what we tell you: We have four men who have taken a vow. 24Take them and be purified with them, and pay their expenses so that they may shave *their* heads, and that all may know that those things of which they were informed concerning you are nothing, but *that* you yourself also walk orderly and keep the law. 25But concerning the Gentiles who believe, we have written *and* decided that they should observe no such thing,[a] except that they should keep themselves from *things* offered to idols, from blood, from things strangled, and from sexual immorality."

Arrested in the Temple

26Then Paul took the men, and the next day, having been purified with them, entered the temple to announce the expiration of the days of purification, at which time an offering should be made for each one of them.

27Now when the seven days were almost ended, the Jews from Asia, seeing him in the temple, stirred up the whole crowd and laid hands on him, 28crying out, "Men of Israel, help! This is the man who teaches all *men* everywhere against the people, the law, and this place; and furthermore he also brought Greeks into the temple and has defiled this holy place." 29(For they had previously[a] seen Troph′i·mus the E·phē′si·an with him in the city, whom they supposed that Paul had brought into the temple.)

30And all the city was disturbed; and the people ran together, seized Paul, and dragged him out of the temple; and immediately the doors were shut. 31Now as they were seeking to kill him, news came to the commander of the garrison that all Jerusalem was in an uproar. 32He immediately took soldiers and centurions, and ran down to them. And when they saw the commander and the soldiers, they stopped beating Paul. 33Then the commander came near and took him, and commanded *him* to be bound with two chains; and he asked who he was and what he had done. 34And some among the multitude cried one thing and some another.

So when he could not ascertain the truth because of the tumult, he commanded him to be taken into the barracks. 35When he reached the stairs, he had to be carried by the soldiers because of the violence of the mob. 36For the multitude of the people followed after, crying out, "Away with him!"

Addressing the Jerusalem Mob

37Then as Paul was about to be led into the barracks, he said to the commander, "May I speak to you?"

He replied, "Can you speak Greek? 38Are you not the Egyptian who some time ago stirred up a rebellion and led the four thousand assassins out into the wilderness?"

39But Paul said, "I am a Jew from Tar′sus, in Ci·li′ci·a, a citizen of no mean city; and I implore you, permit me to speak to the people."

40So when he had given him permission,

21:22 [a]NU-Text reads *What then is to be done? They will certainly.* 21:25 [a]NU-Text omits *that they should observe no such thing, except.* 21:29 [a]M-Text omits *previously.*

21:23, 24 To avoid a dispute Paul was urged to join with **four men** who had **taken a vow**. This observance would demonstrate that as a Jew he was keeping the law, despite his witnessing to Gentiles. **be purified . . . shave their heads**: Requirements of the Nazirite vow (see Num. 6:2–8 and note). **pay their expenses**: of the offerings connected with the vow (see v. 26; Num. 6:10–12).

21:30 All the city was disturbed because Paul was accused of profaning the temple. Gentiles were allowed in the outer court, called appropriately the Court of the Gentiles. But they were forbidden to come into the Court of Women or the Court of Israel. Signs warned that Gentiles entering these courts would be put to death.

FOLLOWING GOD'S PLAN

Evelyn Christenson

One of the most difficult aspects of obedience is being willing *not* to do something. Obedience is not only going and doing, it also is *not* going and *not* doing. This is especially hard when we feel that the job or activity is so right and so necessary.

Paul must have been surprised and even confused when the Spirit did not permit him to speak the Word to those in Asia when he was so convinced that they needed to hear about Jesus (Acts 16:6). But God's plan was right, and Paul's obedience opened Europe to the gospel.

"Obedience is not only going and doing, it also is *not* going and *not* doing."

When a position or job would bring prestige, honor, and favorable exposure to the world, it is especially hard to release it back to God. But when we are willing to decrease so that He and His kingdom may increase—this is real obedience.

Surprisingly for me, it frequently is only after I have prayed a prayer of release that God flings the door open wide to what He originally called me to do. To God, my complete obedience seems to include being willing not to do it; then He says, "Now go!" ✦

Paul stood on the stairs and motioned with
his hand to the people. And when there
was a great silence, he spoke to *them* in the
Hebrew language, saying,

CHAPTER 22

"Brethren and fathers, hear my defense
before you now." 2And when they heard
that he spoke to them in the Hebrew lan-
guage, they kept all the more silent.

Then he said: 3"I am indeed a Jew, born
in Tar'sus of Ci·li'ci·a, but brought up in
this city at the feet of Ga·mā'li·el, taught
according to the strictness of our fathers'
law, and was zealous toward God as you
all are today. 4I persecuted this Way to the
death, binding and delivering into prisons
both men and women, 5as also the high
priest bears me witness, and all the council
of the elders, from whom I also received
letters to the brethren, and went to Damas-
cus to bring in chains even those who were
there to Jerusalem to be punished.

6"Now it happened, as I journeyed and
came near Damascus at about noon, sud-
denly a great light from heaven shone
around me. 7And I fell to the ground and
heard a voice saying to me, 'Saul, Saul,
why are you persecuting Me?' 8So I an-

22:1–5 Brethren and fathers: Paul identified with his accusers by inheritance as a **Jew** (v. 3), training **at the feet of Gamaliel**, zeal for the **law**, and persecution of the church (v. 4). Because of this background, his conversion (vv. 6–16) was the more miraculous and incredible.

swered, 'Who are You, Lord?' And He said
to me, 'I am Jesus of Nazareth, whom you
are persecuting.'
9 "And those who were with me indeed
saw the light and were afraid,[a] but they did
not hear the voice of Him who spoke to
me. 10 So I said, 'What shall I do, Lord?'
And the Lord said to me, 'Arise and go into
Damascus, and there you will be told all
things which are appointed for you to do.'
11 And since I could not see for the glory of
that light, being led by the hand of those
who were with me, I came into Damascus.
12 "Then a certain An·a·nī'as, a devout
man according to the law, having a good
testimony with all the Jews who dwelt
there, 13 came to me; and he stood and said
to me, 'Brother Saul, receive your sight.'
And at that same hour I looked up at him.
14 Then he said, 'The God of our fathers has
chosen you that you should know His will,
and see the Just One, and hear the voice of
His mouth. 15 For you will be His witness to
all men of what you have seen and heard.
16 And now why are you waiting? Arise
and be baptized, and wash away your sins,
calling on the name of the Lord.'
17 "Now it happened, when I returned to
Jerusalem and was praying in the temple,
that I was in a trance 18 and saw Him saying
to me, 'Make haste and get out of Jerusa-
lem quickly, for they will not receive your
testimony concerning Me.' 19 So I said,
'Lord, they know that in every synagogue I
imprisoned and beat those who believe on
You. 20 And when the blood of Your martyr
Stephen was shed, I also was standing by
consenting to his death,[a] and guarding the
clothes of those who were killing him.'
21 Then He said to me, 'Depart, for I will
send you far from here to the Gentiles.' "

Paul's Roman Citizenship

22 And they listened to him until this
word, and *then* they raised their voices and
said, "Away with such a *fellow* from the
earth, for he is not fit to live!" 23 Then, as
they cried out and tore off *their* clothes and
threw dust into the air, 24 the commander
ordered him to be brought into the bar-
racks, and said that he should be examined
under scourging, so that he might know
why they shouted so against him. 25 And as
they bound him with thongs, Paul said to
the centurion who stood by, "Is it lawful
for you to scourge a man who is a Roman,
and uncondemned?"
26 When the centurion heard *that,* he
went and told the commander, saying,
"Take care what you do, for this man is a
Roman."
27 Then the commander came and said to
him, "Tell me, are you a Roman?"
He said, "Yes."
28 The commander answered, "With a
large sum I obtained this citizenship."
And Paul said, "But I was born *a citi-
zen."*
29 Then immediately those who were
about to examine him withdrew from him;
and the commander was also afraid after
he found out that he was a Roman, and be-
cause he had bound him.

The Sanhedrin Divided

30 The next day, because he wanted to
know for certain why he was accused by
the Jews, he released him from *his* bonds,
and commanded the chief priests and all
their council to appear, and brought Paul
down and set him before them.

CHAPTER 23

Then Paul, looking earnestly at the
council, said, "Men *and* brethren, I have

22:9 [a]NU-Text omits *and were afraid.* 22:20 [a]NU-Text omits *to his death.*

22:25, 28 Is it lawful? Citizens of Rome had special privileges including freedom from punishment until they had been tried and convicted. **I was born a citizen**: Paul's rank was higher than the centurion's. Paul's father had probably acquired citizenship by meritorious service in Tarsus.

lived in all good conscience before God
until this day." 2And the high priest
An·a·nī'as commanded those who stood
by him to strike him on the mouth. 3Then
Paul said to him, "God will strike you,
you whitewashed wall! For you sit to judge
me according to the law, and do you
command me to be struck contrary to the
law?"

4And those who stood by said, "Do you
revile God's high priest?"

5Then Paul said, "I did not know,
brethren, that he was the high priest; for it
is written, *'You shall not speak evil of a
ruler of your people.'*"[a]

6But when Paul perceived that one part
were Sad'dū·cees and the other Phar'-
i·sees, he cried out in the council, "Men
and brethren, I am a Phar'i·see, the son of
a Phar'i·see; concerning the hope and
resurrection of the dead I am being
judged!"

7And when he had said this, a dissen-
sion arose between the Phar'i·sees and the
Sad'dū·cees; and the assembly was di-
vided. 8For Sad'dū·cees say that there is no
resurrection—and no angel or spirit; but
the Phar'i·sees confess both. 9Then there
arose a loud outcry. And the scribes of the
Phar'i·sees' party arose and protested, say-
ing, "We find no evil in this man; but if a
spirit or an angel has spoken to him, let us
not fight against God."[a]

10Now when there arose a great dissen-
sion, the commander, fearing lest Paul
might be pulled to pieces by them, com-
manded the soldiers to go down and take
him by force from among them, and bring
him into the barracks.

The Plot Against Paul

11But the following night the Lord stood
by him and said, "Be of good cheer, Paul;
for as you have testified for Me in Jerusa
lem, so you must also bear witness at
Rome."

12And when it was day, some of the Jews
banded together and bound themselves
under an oath, saying that they would nei-
ther eat nor drink till they had killed Paul.
13Now there were more than forty who had
formed this conspiracy. 14They came to the
chief priests and elders, and said, "We
have bound ourselves under a great oath
that we will eat nothing until we have
killed Paul. 15Now you, therefore, together
with the council, suggest to the comman-
der that he be brought down to you tomor-
row,[a] as though you were going to make
further inquiries concerning him; but we
are ready to kill him before he comes near."

16So when Paul's sister's son heard of
their ambush, he went and entered the bar-
racks and told Paul. 17Then Paul called one
of the centurions to *him* and said, "Take
this young man to the commander, for he
has something to tell him." 18So he took
him and brought *him* to the commander
and said, "Paul the prisoner called me to
him and asked *me* to bring this young man
to you. He has something to say to you."

19Then the commander took him by the
hand, went aside, and asked privately,
"What is it that you have to tell me?"

20And he said, "The Jews have agreed to
ask that you bring Paul down to the coun-

23:5 [a]Exodus 22:28 23:9 [a]NU-Text omits last clause and reads *what if a spirit or an angel has spoken to him?* 23:15 [a]NU-Text omits *tomorrow.*

23:2 Ananias, the high priest, is not the same as the Ananias of 5:1 and 9:10.
23:3 contrary to the law: Ananias's command (v. 2) violated Jewish law which required judgment to be executed with fairness and justice.
23:6–10 I am a Pharisee: Paul adroitly divided his opposition by announcing his belief in the **resurrection of the dead** (23:6), a doctrine that the **Sadducees** (23:8) rejected.
23:9 let us not fight against God: Perhaps they remembered the warning of their famous teacher Gamaliel (23:9).
23:16–22 Paul's sister's son probably saved Paul's life. The **commander** (v. 22) took the threat seriously and acted promptly.

cil tomorrow, as though they were going to
inquire more fully about him. 21But do not
yield to them, for more than forty of them
lie in wait for him, men who have bound
themselves by an oath that they will nei-
ther eat nor drink till they have killed him;
and now they are ready, waiting for the
promise from you."
22So the commander let the young man
depart, and commanded *him,* "Tell no one
that you have revealed these things to me."

Sent to Felix

23And he called for two centurions, say-
ing, "Prepare two hundred soldiers, sev-
enty horsemen, and two hundred spear-
men to go to Caes·a·rē'a at the third hour
of the night; 24and provide mounts to set
Paul on, and bring *him* safely to Felix the
governor." 25He wrote a letter in the fol-
lowing manner:

26 Clau'di·us Lys'i·as,

To the most excellent governor Felix:

Greetings.

27 This man was seized by the Jews and
was about to be killed by them. Com-
ing with the troops I rescued him,
having learned that he was a Roman.
28And when I wanted to know the rea-
son they accused him, I brought him
before their council. 29I found out that
he was accused concerning questions
of their law, but had nothing charged
against him deserving of death or
chains. 30And when it was told me
that the Jews lay in wait for the man,[a]
I sent him immediately to you, and
also commanded his accusers to state
before you the charges against him.

Farewell.

31Then the soldiers, as they were com-
manded, took Paul and brought *him* by
night to An·tip'a·tris. 32The next day they
left the horsemen to go on with him, and
returned to the barracks. 33When they
came to Caes·a·rē'a and had delivered the
letter to the governor, they also presented
Paul to him. 34And when the governor had
read *it,* he asked what province he was
from. And when he understood that *he was*
from Ci·li'ci·a, 35he said, "I will hear you
when your accusers also have come." And
he commanded him to be kept in Her'od's
Praetorium.

CHAPTER 24

Accused of Sedition

Now after five days An·a·nī'as the high
priest came down with the elders and a
certain orator *named* Ter·tul'lus. These
gave evidence to the governor against
Paul.
2And when he was called upon,
Ter·tul'lus began his accusation, saying:
"Seeing that through you we enjoy great
peace, and prosperity is being brought to
this nation by your foresight, 3we accept *it*
always and in all places, most noble Felix,
with all thankfulness. 4Nevertheless, not to
be tedious to you any further, I beg you to
hear, by your courtesy, a few words from
us. 5For we have found this man a plague,

23:30 [a]NU-Text reads *there would be a plot against the man.*

23:23–29 Paul, escorted by 470 Roman soldiers, left Jerusalem at 9:00 P.M. (vv. 23, 24). The Roman commander, **Claudius Lysias** (v. 26), was taking no chances because Paul was a **Roman** citizen (v. 27).

23:24 Felix served as governor of Judea from A.D. 52–59.

23:35 Herod's Praetorium: The governor's residence and place of judgment (see Mark 15:16). Paul was secure at last and en route to Rome; all was in the providence of God.

24:5 dissension . . . throughout the world: An accusation designed to interest Rome

a creator of dissension among all the Jews throughout the world, and a ringleader of the sect of the Naz'a·rēnes. 6He even tried to profane the temple, and we seized him,[a] and wanted to judge him according to our law. 7But the commander Lys'i·as came by and with great violence took *him* out of our hands, 8commanding his accusers to come to you. By examining him yourself you may ascertain all these things of which we accuse him." 9And the Jews also assented,[a] maintaining that these things were so.

The Defense Before Felix

10Then Paul, after the governor had nodded to him to speak, answered: "Inasmuch as I know that you have been for many years a judge of this nation, I do the more cheerfully answer for myself, 11because you may ascertain that it is no more than twelve days since I went up to Jerusalem to worship. 12And they neither found me in the temple disputing with anyone nor inciting the crowd, either in the synagogues or in the city. 13Nor can they prove the things of which they now accuse me. 14But this I confess to you, that according to the Way which they call a sect, so I worship the God of my fathers, believing all things which are written in the Law and in the Prophets. 15I have hope in God, which they themselves also accept, that there will be a resurrection of *the* dead,[a] both of *the* just and *the* unjust. 16This *being* so, I myself always strive to have a conscience without offense toward God and men.

17"Now after many years I came to bring alms and offerings to my nation, 18in the midst of which some Jews from Asia found me purified in the temple, neither with a mob nor with tumult. 19They ought to have been here before you to object if they had anything against me. 20Or else let those who are *here* themselves say if they found any wrongdoing[a] in me while I stood before the council, 21unless *it is* for this one statement which I cried out, standing among them, 'Concerning the resurrection of the dead I am being judged by you this day.' "

Felix Procrastinates

22But when Felix heard these things, having more accurate knowledge of *the* Way, he adjourned the proceedings and said, "When Lys'i·as the commander comes down, I will make a decision on your case." 23So he commanded the centurion to keep Paul and to let *him* have liberty, and told him not to forbid any of his friends to provide for or visit him.

24And after some days, when Felix came with his wife Drū·sil'la, who was Jewish, he sent for Paul and heard him concerning the faith in Christ. 25Now as he reasoned about righteousness, self-control, and the judgment to come, Felix was afraid and answered, "Go away for now; when I have a convenient time I will call for you." 26Meanwhile he also hoped that money would be given him by Paul, that he might release him.[a] Therefore he sent for him more often and conversed with him.

24:6 [a]NU-Text ends the sentence here and omits the rest of verse 6, all of verse 7, and the first clause of verse 8. 24:9 [a]NU-Text and M-Text read *joined the attack.* 24:15 [a]NU-Text omits *of the dead.* 24:20 [a]NU-Text and M-Text read *say what wrongdoing they found.* 24:26 [a]NU-Text omits *that he might release him.*

in trying the case. **Nazarenes**: This name, used of Christians only here in the NT (see Matt. 2:23), may have been a term of contempt (see John 1:46).

24:14 Paul explained that he had not abandoned Jewish Scriptures; he simply viewed them from a new perspective.

24:17 offerings to my nation: Paul had brought a gift from the Gentile churches to the Christians at Jerusalem as an expression of thanks for the gospel (see 1 Cor. 16:1–4; 2 Cor. 8; 9; Rom. 15:25–33).

27But after two years Por′ci·us Fes′tus succeeded Felix; and Felix, wanting to do the Jews a favor, left Paul bound.

CHAPTER 25

Paul Appeals to Caesar

Now when Fes′tus had come to the province, after three days he went up from Caes·a·rē′a to Jerusalem. 2Then the high priest[a] and the chief men of the Jews informed him against Paul; and they petitioned him, 3asking a favor against him, that he would summon him to Jerusalem—while *they* lay in ambush along the road to kill him. 4But Fes′tus answered that Paul should be kept at Caes·a·rē′a, and that he himself was going *there* shortly. 5"Therefore," he said, "let those who have authority among you go down with *me* and accuse this man, to see if there is any fault in him."

6And when he had remained among them more than ten days, he went down to Caes·a·rē′a. And the next day, sitting on the judgment seat, he commanded Paul to be brought. 7When he had come, the Jews who had come down from Jerusalem stood about and laid many serious complaints against Paul, which they could not prove, 8while he answered for himself, "Neither against the law of the Jews, nor against the temple, nor against Caesar have I offended in anything at all."

9But Fes′tus, wanting to do the Jews a favor, answered Paul and said, "Are you willing to go up to Jerusalem and there be judged before me concerning these things?"

10So Paul said, "I stand at Caesar's judgment seat, where I ought to be judged. To the Jews I have done no wrong, as you very well know. 11For if I am an offender, or have committed anything deserving of death, I do not object to dying; but if there is nothing in these things of which these men accuse me, no one can deliver me to them. I appeal to Caesar."

12Then Fes′tus, when he had conferred with the council, answered, "You have appealed to Caesar? To Caesar you shall go!"

Paul Before Agrippa

13And after some days King A·grip′pa and Ber·nī′cē came to Caes·a·rē′a to greet Fes′tus. 14When they had been there many days, Fes′tus laid Paul's case before the king, saying: "There is a certain man left a prisoner by Felix, 15about whom the chief priests and the elders of the Jews informed *me,* when I was in Jerusalem, asking for a judgment against him. 16To them I answered, 'It is not the custom of the Romans to deliver any man to destruction[a] before the accused meets the accusers face to face, and has opportunity to answer for himself concerning the charge against him.' 17Therefore when they had come together, without any delay, the next day I sat on the judgment seat and commanded the man to be brought in. 18When the accusers stood up, they brought no accusation against him of such things as I supposed, 19but had some questions against him about their own religion and about a certain Jesus, who had died, whom Paul affirmed to be

25:2 [a]NU-Text reads *chief priests.* 25:16 [a]NU-Text omits *to destruction,* although it is implied.

24:27 During these two years Paul was in prison, he produced several books of the NT in the forms of letters to various churches. These were called "Prison Epistles".

25:9–12 Festus, like Felix, wanting to please the **Jews**, asked Paul to stand trial in **Jerusalem**. Paul refused, saying: **I stand at Caesar's judgment seat**. Thus he used his prerogative as a Roman citizen to appeal, over the jurisdiction of the governor, to the emperor.

25:13 Festus decided to present the problem to King Agrippa II (A.D. 53 to about 100). He and **Bernice** were children of Herod Agrippa I who died at Caesarea (12:23). Although Agrippa was king of only a small area in northern Palestine, he had the right of appointing the Jewish high priest and was considered an expert on Jewish affairs (see 26:3).

alive. [20]And because I was uncertain of such questions, I asked whether he was willing to go to Jerusalem and there be judged concerning these matters. [21]But when Paul appealed to be reserved for the decision of Au·gus′tus, I commanded him to be kept till I could send him to Caesar."

[22]Then A·grip′pa said to Fes′tus, "I also would like to hear the man myself."

"Tomorrow," he said, "you shall hear him."

[23]So the next day, when A·grip′pa and Ber·nī′cē had come with great pomp, and had entered the auditorium with the commanders and the prominent men of the city, at Fes′tus′ command Paul was brought in. [24]And Fes′tus said: "King A·grip′pa and all the men who are here present with us, you see this man about whom the whole assembly of the Jews petitioned me, both at Jerusalem and here, crying out that he was not fit to live any longer. [25]But when I found that he had committed nothing deserving of death, and that he himself had appealed to Au·gus′tus, I decided to send him. [26]I have nothing certain to write to my lord concerning him. Therefore I have brought him out before you, and especially before you, King A·grip′pa, so that after the examination has taken place I may have something to write. [27]For it seems to me unreasonable to send a prisoner and not to specify the charges against him."

CHAPTER 26

Paul's Early Life

Then A·grip′pa said to Paul, "You are permitted to speak for yourself."

So Paul stretched out his hand and answered for himself: [2]"I think myself happy, King A·grip′pa, because today I shall answer for myself before you concerning all the things of which I am accused by the Jews, [3]especially because you are expert in all customs and questions which have to do with the Jews. Therefore I beg you to hear me patiently.

[4]"My manner of life from my youth, which was spent from the beginning among my own nation at Jerusalem, all the Jews know. [5]They knew me from the first, if they were willing to testify, that according to the strictest sect of our religion I lived a Phar′i·see. [6]And now I stand and am judged for the hope of the promise made by God to our fathers. [7]To this *promise* our twelve tribes, earnestly serving *God* night and day, hope to attain. For this hope's sake, King A·grip′pa, I am accused by the Jews. [8]Why should it be thought incredible by you that God raises the dead?

[9]"Indeed, I myself thought I must do many things contrary to the name of Jesus of Nazareth. [10]This I also did in Jerusalem, and many of the saints I shut up in prison, having received authority from the chief priests; and when they were put to death, I cast my vote against *them.* [11]And I punished them often in every synagogue and compelled *them* to blaspheme; and being exceedingly enraged against them, I persecuted *them* even to foreign cities.

Paul Recounts His Conversion

[12]"While thus occupied, as I journeyed to Damascus with authority and commission from the chief priests, [13]at midday, O king, along the road I saw a light from heaven, brighter than the sun, shining around me and those who journeyed with

---

25:26 my lord: The Roman emperor, Nero (A.D. 54–68).

26:1 Stretched out his hand: In salutation to the king.

26:4, 5 I lived a Pharisee: In Jerusalem while studying under Gamaliel. Paul had good credentials (see 22:3).

26:6–8 the promise made by God to our fathers: Paul claimed this promise (v. 6) was fulfilled in Jesus and His resurrection (v. 8). The Jewish authorities claimed it was not. This disagreement was the real issue.

me. [14]And when we all had fallen to the
ground, I heard a voice speaking to me and
saying in the Hebrew language, 'Saul,
Saul, why are you persecuting Me? *It is*
hard for you to kick against the goads.' [15]So
I said, 'Who are You, Lord?' And He said, 'I
am Jesus, whom you are persecuting. [16]But
rise and stand on your feet; for I have appeared to you for this purpose, to make
you a minister and a witness both of the
things which you have seen and of the
things which I will yet reveal to you. [17]I
will deliver you from the *Jewish* people, as
well as *from* the Gentiles, to whom I now[a]
send you, [18]to open their eyes, *in order* to
turn *them* from darkness to light, and *from*
the power of Satan to God, that they may
receive forgiveness of sins and an inheritance among those who are sanctified by
faith in Me.'

Paul's Post-Conversion Life

[19]"Therefore, King A·grip'pa, I was not
disobedient to the heavenly vision, [20]but
declared first to those in Damascus and in
Jerusalem, and throughout all the region of
Judea, and *then* to the Gentiles, that they
should repent, turn to God, and do works
befitting repentance. [21]For these reasons
the Jews seized me in the temple and tried
to kill *me*. [22]Therefore, having obtained
help from God, to this day I stand, witnessing both to small and great, saying no
other things than those which the prophets
and Moses said would come— [23]that the
Christ would suffer, that He would be the
first to rise from the dead, and would proclaim light to the *Jewish* people and to the
Gentiles."

26:17 [a]NU-Text and M-Text omit *now*.

> The assured Christian is more motion than notion, more work than word, more life than lip, more hand than tongue.
> Thomas Brooks

Agrippa Parries Paul's Challenge

[24]Now as he thus made his defense,
Fes'tus said with a loud voice, "Paul, you
are beside yourself! Much learning is
driving you mad!"

[25]But he said, "I am not mad, most noble
Fes'tus, but speak the words of truth and
reason. [26]For the king, before whom I also
speak freely, knows these things; for I am
convinced that none of these things escapes his attention, since this thing was not
done in a corner. [27]King A·grip'pa, do you
believe the prophets? I know that you do
believe."

[28]Then A·grip'pa said to Paul, "You almost persuade me to become a Christian."

[29]And Paul said, "I would to God that
not only you, but also all who hear me today, might become both almost and altogether such as I am, except for these
chains."

[30]When he had said these things, the
king stood up, as well as the governor and
Ber·nī'cē and those who sat with them;

26:14 against the goads: Like an ox that kicks against its master's sharp goading stick, Paul was struggling against his conscience and the call of God upon his life.

26:17 Gentiles, to whom I now send you: Paul's primary calling was Gentile evangelism (see Eph. 3:6, 7). The fact that Paul was born in the Gentile city of Tarsus uniquely qualified him for this ministry.

26:24–29 the king . . . knows these things: The Roman Festus did not really comprehend the gospel message preached by Paul. Agrippa, however, understood but tried to avoid Paul's compelling witness with his lighthearted response: **You almost persuade me to become a Christian** (v. 28).

26:30–32 All the participants in this trial, even **Agrippa**, agreed that Paul was innocent. Christianity was not a crime before this Roman court. Paul should rightfully have been **set free** (v. 32).

I Forgive You

Colleen Townsend Evans

At the very core, forgiveness is a choice. You and I must choose to forgive. If you carry a load of guilt over something you have done or a grudge of unforgiveness because of something someone else has done to you or to those you love, that excess baggage is hindering you in running the race that God has marked out for you. I urge you to let it go.

When we find we cannot forgive someone, we have to say, "God, I can't, but You can, and I allow You to so invade and fill my life that You will literally forgive that person through me. Not I, but Christ living in me. Not I, but Christ loving through me. Not I, but Christ forgiving through me."

"There is absolutely nothing you have done that God will not forgive."

That is the secret: allowing Jesus Christ in us to do that which we cannot do.

Remember, there is absolutely nothing you have done that God will not forgive if you confess and if, in His power, you choose to go a new direction. ✦

[31]and when they had gone aside, they
talked among themselves, saying, "This
man is doing nothing deserving of death
or chains."
[32]Then A·grip'pa said to Fes'tus, "This
man might have been set free if he had not
appealed to Caesar."

CHAPTER 27

The Voyage to Rome Begins

And when it was decided that we
should sail to Italy, they delivered Paul and
some other prisoners to *one* named Julius,
a centurion of the Au·gus'tan Regiment.
[2]So, entering a ship of Ad·ra·myt'ti·um, we
put to sea, meaning to sail along the coasts
of Asia. Ar·is·tar'chus, a Mac·e·dō'ni·an of
Thes·sa·lo·nī'ca, was with us. [3]And the
next *day* we landed at Sī'don. And Julius
treated Paul kindly and gave *him* liberty
to go to his friends and receive care.
[4]When we had put to sea from there, we
sailed under *the shelter of* Cyprus, because the winds were contrary. [5]And
when we had sailed over the sea which
is off Ci·li'ci·a and Pam·phyl'i·a, we
came to Mȳ'ra, *a city* of Ly'ci·a. [6]There
the centurion found an Alexandrian
ship sailing to Italy, and he put us on
board.
[7]When we had sailed slowly many days,
and arrived with difficulty off Cnī'dus, the
wind not permitting us to proceed, we

✦ ✦

27:1 Augustan Regiment: one of five Roman regiments stationed near the seaport city of Caesarea.

27:2 The phrase "**we put to sea**" indicates that Luke accompanied Paul on his journey to Rome.

Give Me a Vision!

Sherwood Eliot Wirt

A well-worn saying expresses the idea that we are immortal until our work is done. I would supplement the statement by saying that we are immortal until the vision fades.

Put me in a rocking chair without a vision, and I would languish. Put me in a room full of people sitting in rocking chairs with nothing to do, and I would not last long. If I had to stay there, I would certainly organize something—perhaps a game or even a prayer meeting. But give me a vision of something new and challenging God would have me do—something that would fire my spirit, get the élan flowing, and give me an opportunity to use my life to help others—and I will feel as young as I do now and as I did at forty. The difference is, today I am a lot smarter! ✦

sailed under *the shelter of* Crēte off Sal-
mō′nē. 8Passing it with difficulty, we came
to a place called Fair Havens, near the city
of La·sē′a.

Paul's Warning Ignored

9Now when much time had been spent,
and sailing was now dangerous because
the Fast was already over, Paul advised
them, 10saying, "Men, I perceive that this
voyage will end with disaster and much
loss, not only of the cargo and ship, but
also our lives." 11Nevertheless the centu-
rion was more persuaded by the helms-
man and the owner of the ship than by
the things spoken by Paul. 12And because
the harbor was not suitable to winter in,
the majority advised to set sail from there
also, if by any means they could reach
Phoenix, a harbor of Crēte opening toward
the southwest and northwest, *and* winter
there.

In the Tempest

13When the south wind blew softly, sup-
posing that they had obtained *their* desire,
putting out to sea, they sailed close by
Crēte. 14But not long after, a tempestuous
head wind arose, called Eū·roc′ly·don.[a]
15So when the ship was caught, and could
not head into the wind, we let *her* drive.
16And running under *the shelter of* an island
called Clau′da,[a] we secured the skiff with
difficulty. 17When they had taken it on
board, they used cables to undergird the
ship; and fearing lest they should run
aground on the Syr′tis[a] *Sands,* they struck
sail and so were driven. 18And because
we were exceedingly tempest-tossed, the
next *day* they lightened the ship. 19On the
third *day* we threw the ship's tackle over-
board with our own hands. 20Now when
neither sun nor stars appeared for many
days, and no small tempest beat on *us,* all
hope that we would be saved was finally
given up.
21But after long abstinence from food,

27:14 [a]NU-Text reads *Euraquilon.* 27:16 [a]NU-Text reads *Cauda.* 27:17 [a]M-Text reads *Syrtes.*

27:19 the ship's tackle: Everything that added weight to the hull.

then Paul stood in the midst of them and
said, "Men, you should have listened to
me, and not have sailed from Crēte and in-
curred this disaster and loss. 22And now I
urge you to take heart, for there will be no
loss of life among you, but only of the ship.
23For there stood by me this night an angel
of the God to whom I belong and whom I
serve, 24saying, 'Do not be afraid, Paul; you
must be brought before Caesar; and indeed
God has granted you all those who sail
with you.' 25Therefore take heart, men, for I
believe God that it will be just as it was
told me. 26However, we must run aground
on a certain island."

27Now when the fourteenth night had
come, as we were driven up and down in
the Ā·dri·at'ic *Sea,* about midnight the
sailors sensed that they were drawing near
some land. 28And they took soundings and
found *it* to be twenty fathoms; and when
they had gone a little farther, they took
soundings again and found *it* to be fifteen
fathoms. 29Then, fearing lest we should run
aground on the rocks, they dropped four
anchors from the stern, and prayed for day
to come. 30And as the sailors were seeking
to escape from the ship, when they had let
down the skiff into the sea, under pretense
of putting out anchors from the prow,
31Paul said to the centurion and the sol-
diers, "Unless these men stay in the ship,
you cannot be saved." 32Then the soldiers
cut away the ropes of the skiff and let it fall
off.

33And as day was about to dawn, Paul
implored *them* all to take food, saying, "To-
day is the fourteenth day you have waited
and continued without food, and eaten
nothing. 34Therefore I urge you to take
nourishment, for this is for your survival,
since not a hair will fall from the head of
any of you." 35And when he had said these
things, he took bread and gave thanks to
God in the presence of them all; and when
he had broken *it* he began to eat. 36Then
they were all encouraged, and also took
food themselves. 37And in all we were two
hundred and seventy-six persons on the
ship. 38So when they had eaten enough,
they lightened the ship and threw out the
wheat into the sea.

Shipwrecked on Malta

39When it was day, they did not recog-
nize the land; but they observed a bay with
a beach, onto which they planned to run
the ship if possible. 40And they let go the
anchors and left *them* in the sea, mean-
while loosing the rudder ropes; and they
hoisted the mainsail to the wind and made
for shore. 41But striking a place where two
seas met, they ran the ship aground; and
the prow stuck fast and remained immov-
able, but the stern was being broken up by
the violence of the waves.

42And the soldiers' plan was to kill the
prisoners, lest any of them should swim
away and escape. 43But the centurion,
wanting to save Paul, kept them from *their*
purpose, and commanded that those who
could swim should jump *overboard* first
and get to land, 44and the rest, some on
boards and some on *parts* of the ship. And
so it was that they all escaped safely to
land.

CHAPTER 28

Paul's Ministry on Malta

Now when they had escaped, they then
found out that the island was called Malta.
2And the natives showed us unusual kind-
ness; for they kindled a fire and made us

27:41 place where two seas met: A shoal on the north side of Malta bears the name "Bay of St. Paul." Since Paul's visit in A.D. 60, without interruption, the inhabitants of the island have been Christian.

27:44 some on boards: Perhaps some on planks and some on other debris from the broken ship.

28:1 Malta: a small island just south of Italy and Sicily.

all welcome, because of the rain that was
falling and because of the cold. 3But when
Paul had gathered a bundle of sticks and
laid *them* on the fire, a viper came out be-
cause of the heat, and fastened on his
hand. 4So when the natives saw the crea-
ture hanging from his hand, they said to
one another, "No doubt this man is a mur-
derer, whom, though he has escaped the
sea, yet justice does not allow to live." 5But
he shook off the creature into the fire and
suffered no harm. 6However, they were ex-
pecting that he would swell up or sud-
denly fall down dead. But after they had
looked for a long time and saw no harm
come to him, they changed their minds
and said that he was a god.
7In that region there was an estate of the
leading citizen of the island, whose name
was Pub′li·us, who received us and enter-
tained us courteously for three days.
8And it happened that the father of
Pub′li·us lay sick of a fever and dysentery.
Paul went in to him and prayed, and he
laid his hands on him and healed him.
9So when this was done, the rest of those
on the island who had diseases also came
and were healed. 10They also honored us
in many ways; and when we departed,
they provided such things as were neces-
sary.

Arrival at Rome

11After three months we sailed in an
Alexandrian ship whose figurehead
was the Twin Brothers, which had win-
tered at the island. 12And landing at
Syracuse, we stayed three days. 13From
there we circled round and reached
Rhē′gi·um. And after one day the south
wind blew; and the next day we came
to Pū·tē′o·lī, 14where we found brethren,
and were invited to stay with them seven
days. And so we went toward Rome.
15And from there, when the brethren heard
about us, they came to meet us as far as
Ap′pi·ī Forum and Three Inns. When Paul
saw them, he thanked God and took
courage.
16Now when we came to Rome, the cen-
turion delivered the prisoners to the cap-
tain of the guard; but Paul was permitted
to dwell by himself with the soldier who
guarded him.

Paul's Ministry at Rome

17And it came to pass after three days
that Paul called the leaders of the Jews to-
gether. So when they had come together,
he said to them: "Men *and* brethren,
though I have done nothing against our
people or the customs of our fathers, yet I
was delivered as a prisoner from Jerusalem
into the hands of the Romans, 18who, when
they had examined me, wanted to let *me*
go, because there was no cause for putting
me to death. 19But when the Jews[a] spoke
against *it,* I was compelled to appeal to
Caesar, not that I had anything of which to
accuse my nation. 20For this reason there-
fore I have called for you, to see *you* and
speak with *you,* because for the hope of Is-
rael I am bound with this chain."

28:19 [a]That is, the ruling authorities

28:2 natives: The people spoke their own dialect instead of using Greek, the language of cultured people.

28:4 justice does not allow to live: Justice may refer to the goddess of that name. In any case the Maltese believed the universe was under moral law.

28:7 Publius was the highest ranking Roman official on the island.

28:12–14 Syracuse, founded by Greeks in 734 B.C., was the chief city of Sicily. The ancient temple of Athena at Syracuse is now a Christian church. **Puteoli**: A suburb of Naples and its ancient harbor. Here the apostle was welcomed by Christian **brethren**.

28:16 permitted to dwell by himself: A kind of house arrest.

28:17 called the leaders of the Jews: It was the Jews who had made charges against Paul. He therefore sought to explain his situation to the Jews in Rome before his trial date (see v. 20).

[21]Then they said to him, "We neither re-
ceived letters from Judea concerning you,
nor have any of the brethren who came re-
ported or spoken any evil of you. [22]But we
desire to hear from you what you think; for
concerning this sect, we know that it is
spoken against everywhere."
[23]So when they had appointed him a
day, many came to him at *his* lodging, to
whom he explained and solemnly testified
of the kingdom of God, persuading them
concerning Jesus from both the Law of Mo-
ses and the Prophets, from morning till
evening. [24]And some were persuaded by
the things which were spoken, and some
disbelieved. [25]So when they did not agree
among themselves, they departed after
Paul had said one word: "The Holy Spirit
spoke rightly through Ī·sāi'ah the prophet
to our[a] fathers, [26]saying,

'Go to this people and say:
" Hearing you will hear, and shall not
understand;
And seeing you will see, and not
perceive;
[27] *For the hearts of this people have*
grown dull.
Their ears are hard of hearing,
And their eyes they have closed,
Lest they should see with their eyes
and hear with their ears,
Lest they should understand with
their hearts and turn,
So that I should heal them." '[a]

[28]"Therefore let it be known to you that
the salvation of God has been sent to the
Gentiles, and they will hear it!" [29]And
when he had said these words, the Jews
departed and had a great dispute among
themselves.[a]
[30]Then Paul dwelt two whole years in
his own rented house, and received all
who came to him, [31]preaching the kingdom
of God and teaching the things which con-
cern the Lord Jesus Christ with all confi-
dence, no one forbidding him.

28:25 [a]NU-Text reads *your.* 28:27 [a]Isaiah 6:9, 10
28:29 [a]NU-Text omits this verse.

28:26, 27 you will see, and not perceive: This quotation (Is. 6:9, 10) is cited five times in the NT to explain rejections of gospel truth.

✦Romans✦

Romans, which is Paul's greatest work and most systematic statement of Christian belief, sums up the essentials of the faith. While the Gospels present the words and works of Jesus Christ, Romans explores the significance of His sacrificial death and the doctrine of justification for all who place their faith in Him. His death and Resurrection are the basis for the believer's redemption, justification, reconciliation, salvation, and glorification. Romans is more than a book of theology; it is also a book of practical exhortation.

Paul had never visited Rome which, at the time of his writing, was the greatest city in the world with more than one million inhabitants. The church was well-known and had been established for several years by the time of his letter. Written during his stay in Corinth when he was planning his trip to Rome, Paul wanted to introduce himself, tell of his missionary work, and let the believers know of his future plans. He hoped that his letter would provide the Jewish and Gentile members of the Roman church with a clear statement of faith, stressing their union in Christ. Furthermore, he wanted his readers to know that the Good News of Jesus Christ is more than a set of facts to be believed; it is also a life to be lived. No matter what our age, profession, or social standing, we are called to lead a life of righteousness befitting the person, "justified freely by [God's] grace through the redemption that is in Christ Jesus" (3:24).✦

CHAPTER 1

Greeting

Paul, a bondservant of Jesus Christ,
called *to be* an apostle, separated to the
gospel of God 2which He promised before
through His prophets in the Holy Scrip-
tures, 3concerning His Son Jesus Christ our
Lord, who was born of the seed of David
according to the flesh, 4*and* declared *to be*
the Son of God with power according to
the Spirit of holiness, by the resurrection
from the dead. 5Through Him we have re-
ceived grace and apostleship for obedience
to the faith among all nations for His
name, 6among whom you also are the
called of Jesus Christ;

7To all who are in Rome, beloved of God, called *to be* saints:

Grace to you and peace from God our Father and the Lord Jesus Christ.

Desire to Visit Rome

8First, I thank my God through Jesus
Christ for you all, that your faith is spoken

1:1 bondservant: a paid servant or slave with many responsibilities. Such an employee, while usually treated well, was prohibited from changing employers.
1:3 according to the flesh: So far as Jesus' human nature is concerned.
1:7 saints: Holy ones, people set apart for God. This includes all believers.

of throughout the whole world. [9]For God is
my witness, whom I serve with my spirit
in the gospel of His Son, that without ceas-
ing I make mention of you always in my
prayers, [10]making request if, by some
means, now at last I may find a way in the
will of God to come to you. [11]For I long to
see you, that I may impart to you some
spiritual gift, so that you may be estab-
lished— [12]that is, that I may be encouraged
together with you by the mutual faith both
of you and me.

[13]Now I do not want you to be unaware,
brethren, that I often planned to come to
you (but was hindered until now), that I
might have some fruit among you also,
just as among the other Gentiles. [14]I am a
debtor both to Greeks and to barbarians,
both to wise and to unwise. [15]So, as much
as is in me, *I am* ready to preach the gospel
to you who are in Rome also.

The Just Live by Faith

[16]For I am not ashamed of the gospel of
Christ,[a] for it is the power of God to salva-
tion for everyone who believes, for the Jew
first and also for the Greek. [17]For in it the
righteousness of God is revealed from faith
to faith; as it is written, *"The just shall live
by faith."*[a]

God's Wrath on Unrighteousness

[18]For the wrath of God is revealed from
heaven against all ungodliness and un-
righteousness of men, who suppress the
truth in unrighteousness, [19]because what
may be known of God is manifest in them,
for God has shown *it* to them. [20]For since
the creation of the world His invisible
attributes are clearly seen, being under-
stood by the things that are made, *even* His
eternal power and Godhead, so that they
are without excuse, [21]because, although
they knew God, they did not glorify *Him* as
God, nor were thankful, but became futile
in their thoughts, and their foolish hearts
were darkened. [22]Professing to be wise,
they became fools, [23]and changed the glory
of the incorruptible God into an image
made like corruptible man—and birds and
four-footed animals and creeping things.

[24]Therefore God also gave them up to
uncleanness, in the lusts of their hearts, to
dishonor their bodies among themselves,
[25]who exchanged the truth of God for the
lie, and worshiped and served the creature
rather than the Creator, who is blessed for-
ever. Amen.

> I am not interested in the past. I am interested in the future, for that is where I expect to spend the rest of my life.
>
> Charles F. Kettering

1:16 [a]NU-Text omits *of Christ.* 1:17 [a]Habakkuk 2:4

1:9 Mature Christians should strive to fellowship with God throughout the day. Although it is important to set aside a specific time each day for prayer, we should not hesitate to bring our requests and give our praise to God any time our hearts are so moved.

1:14 debtor: Paul considered himself especially obligated to the Gentiles because God had called him to be an apostle to them (Acts 9:15; Gal. 2:7). **Greeks and . . . barbarians**: The total Gentile population. Our hearts should also be burdened by our Lord's call to declare the gospel to all, regardless of cultural or social differences.

1:17, 18 the righteousness of God: A key concept in Romans. God is righteous because He always acts in accord with His holy character and His promises. Because He is righteous, He condemns sin and judges sinners (1:18—3:20). Because of that same righteousness, He has provided through Christ forgiveness for all who believe (justification; 3:21—5:21) and power for living a holy life in right relationship to Himself (sanctification; 6:1—8:39). God's righteousness shows itself in His faithful keeping of His promise to the Jews (9:1—11:36), and in His careful instructions for the Christian's daily walk of holiness (12:1—15:13). **wrath of God**: Not an uncontrolled emotional outburst. Rather, the consistent reaction of God's character against sin.

[26]For this reason God gave them up to vile passions. For even their women exchanged the natural use for what is against nature. [27]Likewise also the men, leaving the natural use of the woman, burned in their lust for one another, men with men committing what is shameful, and receiving in themselves the penalty of their error which was due.

[28]And even as they did not like to retain God in *their* knowledge, God gave them over to a debased mind, to do those things which are not fitting; [29]being filled with all unrighteousness, sexual immorality,[a] wickedness, covetousness, maliciousness; full of envy, murder, strife, deceit, evil-mindedness; *they are* whisperers, [30]backbiters, haters of God, violent, proud, boasters, inventors of evil things, disobedient to parents, [31]undiscerning, untrustworthy, unloving, unforgiving,[a] unmerciful; [32]who, knowing the righteous judgment of God, that those who practice such things are deserving of death, not only do the same but also approve of those who practice them.

CHAPTER 2

God's Righteous Judgment

Therefore you are inexcusable, O man, whoever you are who judge, for in whatever you judge another you condemn yourself; for you who judge practice the same things. [2]But we know that the judgment of God is according to truth against those who practice such things. [3]And do you think this, O man, you who judge those practicing such things, and doing the same, that you will escape the judgment of God? [4]Or do you despise the riches of His goodness, forbearance, and longsuffering, not knowing that the goodness of God leads you to repentance? [5]But in accordance with your hardness and your impenitent heart you are treasuring up for yourself wrath in the day of wrath and revelation of the righteous judgment of God, [6]who *"will render to each one according to his deeds"*:[a] [7]eternal life to those who by patient continuance in doing good seek for glory, honor, and immortality; [8]but to those who are self-seeking and do not obey the truth, but obey unrighteousness—indignation and wrath, [9]tribulation and anguish, on every soul of man who does evil, of the Jew first and also of the Greek; [10]but glory, honor, and peace to everyone who works what is good, to the Jew first and also to the Greek. [11]For there is no partiality with God.

[12]For as many as have sinned without law will also perish without law, and as many as have sinned in the law will be judged by the law [13](for not the hearers of the law *are* just in the sight of God, but the doers of the law will be justified; [14]for when Gentiles, who do not have the law, by nature do the things in the law, these, although not having the law, are a law to themselves, [15]who show the work of the law written in their hearts, their conscience also bearing witness, and between themselves *their* thoughts accusing or else

1:29 [a]NU-Text omits *sexual immorality.* 1:31 [a]NU-Text omits *unforgiving.* 2:6 [a]Psalm 62:12; Proverbs 24:12

2:1–16 How does God judge? He judges justly (v. 2), according to one's **deeds** (vv. 6–10) and in the light of what one knows (vv. 11–16).

2:7 eternal life: The life of the age to come—a comprehensive expression for God's blessings on His people. This is no contradiction to the teaching that eternal life is through faith. True faith includes doing good (see Eph. 2:10).

2:9 No sinner will be excused from judgment on the basis of religion or ethnic background.

2:12 law: Law of Moses. God does not judge Gentiles according to Jewish law, because Gentiles do not know that law. People are responsible only for the light they have or could have.

PRACTICE WHAT YOU PREACH

Ron Lee Davis

There is no such thing in this world as cheap integrity. Integrity is absolute, and integrity has a price.

To have integrity is to be the same person alone, when no one is watching, as you are in the glare of the spotlight. As Howard Hendricks put it, "You show me a leader who is great in public and I will show you a leader who is even greater in private." That means that your secret inner self is seamlessly joined to your outer self. And that's very hard, isn't it? But to live any other way is to live a lie.

In those moments of solitude when no one else can see, our goal as mentors is to strive to exceed our public reputation as servants of Jesus Christ. As biblical mentors, we are called to live out our lives with total congruence between the way we live and what we say we believe. That is the only way to have an authentic and lasting effect on the lives of others. ✦

excusing *them*) [16]in the day when God will
judge the secrets of men by Jesus Christ,
according to my gospel.

The Jews Guilty as the Gentiles

[17]Indeed[a] you are called a Jew, and rest
on the law, and make your boast in God,
[18]and know *His* will, and approve the
things that are excellent, being instructed
out of the law, [19]and are confident that you
yourself are a guide to the blind, a light to
those who are in darkness, [20]an instructor
of the foolish, a teacher of babes, having
the form of knowledge and truth in the
law. [21]You, therefore, who teach another,
do you not teach yourself? You who preach
that a man should not steal, do you steal?
[22]You who say, "Do not commit adultery,"
do you commit adultery? You who abhor
idols, do you rob temples? [23]You who make
your boast in the law, do you dishonor
God through breaking the law? [24]For *"the
name of God is blasphemed among the
Gentiles because of you,"*[a] as it is written.

Circumcision of No Avail

[25]For circumcision is indeed profitable if
you keep the law; but if you are a breaker
of the law, your circumcision has become
uncircumcision. [26]Therefore, if an uncir-
cumcised man keeps the righteous require-
ments of the law, will not his uncircumci-
sion be counted as circumcision? [27]And
will not the physically uncircumcised, if he
fulfills the law, judge you who, *even* with
your written *code* and circumcision, *are* a
transgressor of the law? [28]For he is not a
Jew who *is one* outwardly, nor *is* circumci-
sion that which *is* outward in the flesh;
[29]but *he is* a Jew who *is one* inwardly; and

2:17 [a]NU-Text reads *But if.* 2:24 [a]Isaiah 52:5; Ezekiel 36:22

2:24 As Christians, we need to examine our lives for any sin that will hinder the unsaved from seeking the truth.

2:26–28 counted as circumcision: The Gentile who does not have God's written law but lives according to its intent receives more praise from God than a Jew who has God's law but does not obey it.

circumcision *is that* of the heart, in the Spirit, not in the letter; whose praise *is* not from men but from God.

CHAPTER 3

God's Judgment Defended

What advantage then has the Jew, or
what *is* the profit of circumcision? [2]Much
in every way! Chiefly because to them
were committed the oracles of God. [3]For
what if some did not believe? Will their unbelief make the faithfulness of God without effect? [4]Certainly not! Indeed, let God
be true but every man a liar. As it is written:

"That You may be justified in Your words,
And may overcome when You are judged."[a]

[5]But if our unrighteousness demonstrates the righteousness of God, what
shall we say? *Is* God unjust who inflicts
wrath? (I speak as a man.) [6]Certainly not!
For then how will God judge the world?
[7]For if the truth of God has increased
through my lie to His glory, why am I also
still judged as a sinner? [8]And *why* not *say,*
"Let us do evil that good may come"?—as
we are slanderously reported and as some
affirm that we say. Their condemnation is just.

All Have Sinned

[9]What then? Are we better *than they?*
Not at all. For we have previously charged
both Jews and Greeks that they are all under sin.

[10]As it is written:

"There is none righteous, no, not one;
11 *There is none who understands;*
There is none who seeks after God.
12 *They have all turned aside;*
They have together become unprofitable;
There is none who does good, no, not one."[a]
13 *"Their throat is an open tomb;*
With their tongues they have practiced deceit";[a]
"The poison of asps is under their lips";[b]
14 *"Whose mouth is full of cursing and bitterness."*[a]
15 *"Their feet are swift to shed blood;*
16 *Destruction and misery are in their ways;*
17 *And the way of peace they have not known."*[a]
18 *"There is no fear of God before their eyes."*[a]

[19]Now we know that whatever the law
says, it says to those who are under the
law, that every mouth may be stopped,
and all the world may become guilty
before God. [20]Therefore by the deeds of
the law no flesh will be justified in His
sight, for by the law *is* the knowledge of sin.

God's Righteousness Through Faith

[21]But now the righteousness of God
apart from the law is revealed, being witnessed by the Law and the Prophets,
[22]even the righteousness of God, through
faith in Jesus Christ, to all and on all[a] who
believe. For there is no difference; [23]for all
have sinned and fall short of the glory of
God, [24]being justified freely by His grace
through the redemption that is in Christ

3:4 [a]Psalm 51:4 3:12 [a]Psalms 14:1–3; 53:1–3; Ecclesiastes 7:20 3:13 [a]Psalm 5:9 [b]Psalm 140:3 3:14 [a]Psalm 10:7 3:17 [a]Isaiah 59:7, 8 3:18 [a]Psalm 36:1 3:22 [a]NU-Text omits *and on all.*

3:24 justified: declared innocent in God's sight. The shed blood of Jesus Christ provides the believer a righteous standing before God.

Jesus, 25 whom God set forth *as* a propitia-
tion by His blood, through faith, to demon-
strate His righteousness, because in His
forbearance God had passed over the
sins that were previously committed, 26 to
demonstrate at the present time His
righ-teousness, that He might be just and
the justifier of the one who has faith in Je-
sus.

Boasting Excluded

27 Where *is* boasting then? It is excluded.
By what law? Of works? No, but by the
law of faith. 28 Therefore we conclude that
a man is justified by faith apart from
the deeds of the law. 29 Or *is He* the God of
the Jews only? *Is He* not also the God
of the Gentiles? Yes, of the Gentiles also,
30 since *there is* one God who will justify the
circumcised by faith and the uncircum-
cised through faith. 31 Do we then make
void the law through faith? Certainly not!
On the contrary, we establish the law.

CHAPTER 4

Abraham Justified by Faith

What then shall we say that Abraham
our father has found according to the
flesh?[a] 2 For if Abraham was justified by
works, he has *something* to boast about, but
not before God. 3 For what does the Scrip-
ture say? *"Abraham believed God, and it
was accounted to him for righteousness."*[a]
4 Now to him who works, the wages are not
counted as grace but as debt.

David Celebrates the Same Truth

5 But to him who does not work but be-
lieves on Him who justifies the ungodly,
his faith is accounted for righteousness,
6 just as David also describes the blessed-
ness of the man to whom God imputes
righteousness apart from works:

7 *"Blessed are those whose lawless deeds
are forgiven,
And whose sins are covered;*
8 *Blessed is the man to whom the* LORD
shall not impute sin."[a]

Abraham Justified Before Circumcision

9 *Does* this blessedness then *come* upon
the circumcised *only,* or upon the uncir-
cumcised also? For we say that faith was
accounted to Abraham for righteousness.
10 How then was it accounted? While he
was circumcised, or uncircumcised? Not
while circumcised, but while uncircum-
cised. 11 And he received the sign of circum-
cision, a seal of the righteousness of the
faith which *he had while still* uncircumcised,
that he might be the father of all those who
believe, though they are uncircumcised,
that righteousness might be imputed to
them also, 12 and the father of circumcision
to those who not only *are* of the circumci-
sion, but who also walk in the steps of the

4:1 [a]Or *Abraham our (fore)father according to the flesh has found?* 4:3 [a]Genesis 15:6
4:8 [a]Psalm 32:1, 2

3:25, 26 The wrath of God judges and punishes sin. Jesus is a **propitiation** (satisfaction) in that His sacrificial death paid the penalty for our sin, satisfying the righteous wrath of God. It is God Himself in Christ who provided this sacrifice. **His blood**: The sacrificial death of Jesus. **through faith**: The way to receive the benefits of Christ's sacrifice. **His righteousness**: God is righteous; He cannot condone sin. The sacrifice of Christ demonstrates that He always takes sin seriously. In the past God left **sins** unpunished, because He knew that He Himself would take their punishment in Christ. Today He **justifies** the sinner who has **faith in Jesus** because He Himself has taken the sinner's punishment. God can thus forgive and yet be **just**. He has not compromised His hatred of sin, yet He has kept His promise to bless humankind.

4:9–12 Abraham was justified (accepted by God) before the covenant sign of circumcision was given. This was done in order that He might be the model of salvation by **faith** for all people, whether Jews or Gentiles.

faith which our father Abraham *had while*
still uncircumcised.

The Promise Granted Through Faith

[13]For the promise that he would be the
heir of the world *was* not to Abraham or to
his seed through the law, but through the
righteousness of faith. [14]For if those who
are of the law *are* heirs, faith is made void
and the promise made of no effect, [15]be-
cause the law brings about wrath; for
where there is no law *there is* no transgres-
sion.

[16]Therefore *it is* of faith that *it might be*
according to grace, so that the promise
might be sure to all the seed, not only to
those who are of the law, but also to those
who are of the faith of Abraham, who is the
father of us all [17](as it is written, *"I have*
made you a father of many nations"[a]) in
the presence of Him whom he believed—
God, who gives life to the dead and calls
those things which do not exist as though
they did; [18]who, contrary to hope, in hope
believed, so that he became the father of
many nations, according to what was spo-
ken, *"So shall your descendants be."*[a]
[19]And not being weak in faith, he did not
consider his own body, already dead (since
he was about a hundred years old), and the

4:17 [a]Genesis 17:5 4:18 [a]Genesis 15:5

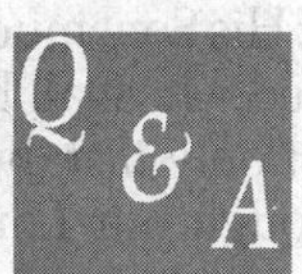

What does a person have to do to have contentment in his or her heart?

J. Vernon McGee

If you want peace of mind, the Scripture is very clear: "Therefore, having been justified by faith, we have peace with God through our Lord Jesus Christ" (Rom. 5:1). That present benefit is yours if you can see that, by faith in the substitutionary death of Christ, you are saved; God has extended grace to you—not because of merit but because you have a need.

You cannot save yourself; He has agreed to do it for you. If you can believe Christ and rest in Him, then you can have peace of mind.

However, if you mean by "security" that you expect to go through this life wrapped in plastic or packed in cotton, you are entirely wrong. For instance, when you are on a plane and you fly into a storm and the plane begins to wobble up and down, you would be a very strange individual if you did not lose a little of your peace and become a bit concerned about the situation. If you do not get a feeling of insecurity, you are entirely without feeling.

In every situation, you can have that deeper peace of mind that comes through Jesus Christ. ✦

4:16 Salvation is based on faith, an attitude of dependence on God, so that all people can receive it as a gift from God that cannot be earned.

4:18 contrary to hope: unlike ordinary human expectation. **In hope**: in faith in God to keep His promises.

deadness of Sarah's womb. [20]He did not
waver at the promise of God through un-
belief, but was strengthened in faith,
giving glory to God, [21]and being fully con-
vinced that what He had promised He
was also able to perform. [22]And therefore
*"it was accounted to him for righteous-
ness."*[a]

[23]Now it was not written for his sake
alone that it was imputed to him, [24]but also
for us. It shall be imputed to us who be-
lieve in Him who raised up Jesus our Lord
from the dead, [25]who was delivered up be-
cause of our offenses, and was raised be-
cause of our justification.

CHAPTER 5

Faith Triumphs in Trouble

Therefore, having been justified by
faith, we have[a] peace with God through
our Lord Jesus Christ, [2]through whom also
we have access by faith into this grace in
which we stand, and rejoice in hope of the
glory of God. [3]And not only *that,* but we
also glory in tribulations, knowing that
tribulation produces perseverance; [4]and
perseverance, character; and character,
hope. [5]Now hope does not disappoint, be-
cause the love of God has been poured out
in our hearts by the Holy Spirit who was
given to us.

Christ in Our Place

[6]For when we were still without
strength, in due time Christ died for the
ungodly. [7]For scarcely for a righteous man
will one die; yet perhaps for a good man
someone would even dare to die. [8]But God
demonstrates His own love toward us, in
that while we were still sinners, Christ
died for us. [9]Much more then, having now
been justified by His blood, we shall be
saved from wrath through Him. [10]For if
when we were enemies we were reconciled
to God through the death of His Son, much
more, having been reconciled, we shall be
saved by His life. [11]And not only *that,* but
we also rejoice in God through our Lord
Jesus Christ, through whom we have now
received the reconciliation.

> ***I pray that I will glory in tribulations, knowing that tribulation produces perseverance; and perseverance, character; and character, hope.***
>
> *adapted from* Romans 5:3, 4

Death in Adam, Life in Christ

[12]Therefore, just as through one man sin
entered the world, and death through sin,
and thus death spread to all men, because
all sinned— [13](For until the law sin was in

4:22 [a]Genesis 15:6 5:1 [a]Another ancient reading is, *let us have peace.*

4:20, 21 He did not waver: Abraham could not understand how God could give them a child (Gen. 17:17, 18), but he took God's promise at face value. He obeyed the command to be circumcised in acceptance of God's covenant (see Gen. 17:23). To give glory to God is to acknowledge Him as God and to do what He commands. When we face a seemingly insurmountable obstacle to fulfilling God's will, we can follow Abraham's example and allow the test to strengthen our faith.

5:3, 4 The trials we experience today will teach us perseverance and thus build our character. Then, having survived and grown, our faith in God's ability to fulfill His promises grows stronger.

5:12 The **death** that follows sin is (1) physical death (Gen. 3:19); (2) spiritual death, the separation of the self from God by an act of disobedience (Rom. 7:9); and, as a final outcome, (3) eternal death (Matt. 10:28).

the world, but sin is not imputed when
there is no law. 14Nevertheless death
reigned from Adam to Moses, even over
those who had not sinned according to the
likeness of the transgression of Adam, who
is a type of Him who was to come. 15But the
free gift *is* not like the offense. For if by the
one man's offense many died, much more
the grace of God and the gift by the grace
of the one Man, Jesus Christ, abounded to
many. 16And the gift *is* not like *that which
came* through the one who sinned. For the
judgment *which came* from one *offense re-
sulted* in condemnation, but the free gift
which came from many offenses *resulted*
in justification. 17For if by the one man's of-
fense death reigned through the one,
much more those who receive abundance
of grace and of the gift of righteousness
will reign in life through the One, Jesus
Christ.)

18Therefore, as through one man's of-
fense *judgment* came to all men, result-
ing in condemnation, even so through one
Man's righteous act *the free gift came* to
all men, resulting in justification of
life. 19For as by one man's disobedience
many were made sinners, so also by one
Man's obedience many will be made righ-
teous.

20Moreover the law entered that the of-
fense might abound. But where sin
abounded, grace abounded much more,
21so that as sin reigned in death, even so
grace might reign through righteousness
to eternal life through Jesus Christ our
Lord.

> For every one look at your problems, your weaknesses, your failures—take ten looks at Jesus.
>
> Robert Murray McCheyne

CHAPTER 6

Dead to Sin, Alive to God

What shall we say then? Shall we con-
tinue in sin that grace may abound? 2Cer-
tainly not! How shall we who died to sin
live any longer in it? 3Or do you not know
that as many of us as were baptized into
Christ Jesus were baptized into His death?
4Therefore we were buried with Him
through baptism into death, that just as
Christ was raised from the dead by the
glory of the Father, even so we also should
walk in newness of life.

5For if we have been united together in
the likeness of His death, certainly we also
shall be *in the likeness* of *His* resurrection,
6knowing this, that our old man was cruci-
fied with *Him*, that the body of sin might
be done away with, that we should no
longer be slaves of sin. 7For he who has
died has been freed from sin. 8Now if we
died with Christ, we believe that we shall
also live with Him, 9knowing that Christ,
having been raised from the dead, dies no
more. Death no longer has dominion over
Him. 10For *the death* that He died, He
died to sin once for all; but *the life* that He
lives, He lives to God. 11Likewise you
also, reckon yourselves to be dead indeed to

5:14–19 type: a living prediction or model. Paul draws a comparison between Adam and Christ and the effect their respective actions have had on the human race.

6:1, 2 To prevent people from twisting his teaching on grace, Paul explains that a true Christian has died to sin and will not continue in it as a way of life.

6:6, 7 Our **old man** and **the body of sin** both refer, in some sense, to our fallen nature and the person we used to be when we were under the control of sin. When this "person" is **done away with**, we are no longer controlled by sin. When we have **died** with Christ, we are **freed from sin**.

6:11 reckon: Accept as true what God has done in Christ and let His resurrection life be a reality in yours. **dead indeed to sin**: While we are not immune form sin's influence, it is no longer the controlling power in our lives.

sin, but alive to God in Christ Jesus our Lord.

12Therefore do not let sin reign in your mortal body, that you should obey it in its lusts. 13And do not present your members *as* instruments of unrighteousness to sin, but present yourselves to God as being alive from the dead, and your members *as* instruments of righteousness to God. 14For sin shall not have dominion over you, for you are not under law but under grace.

From Slaves of Sin to Slaves of God

15What then? Shall we sin because we are not under law but under grace? Certainly not! 16Do you not know that to whom you present yourselves slaves to obey, you are that one's slaves whom you obey, whether of sin *leading* to death, or of obedience *leading* to righteousness? 17But God be thanked that *though* you were slaves of sin, yet you obeyed from the heart that form of doctrine to which you were delivered. 18And having been set free from sin, you became slaves of righteousness. 19I speak in human *terms* because of the weakness of your flesh. For just as you presented your members *as* slaves of uncleanness, and of lawlessness *leading* to *more* lawlessness, so now present your members *as* slaves *of* righteousness for holiness.

20For when you were slaves of sin, you were free in regard to righteousness. 21What fruit did you have then in the things of which you are now ashamed? For the end of those things *is* death. 22But now having been set free from sin, and having become slaves of God, you have your fruit to holiness, and the end, everlasting life. 23For the wages of sin *is* death, but the gift of God *is* eternal life in Christ Jesus our Lord.

CHAPTER 7

Freed from the Law

Or do you not know, brethren (for I speak to those who know the law), that the law has dominion over a man as long as he lives? 2For the woman who has a husband is bound by the law to *her* husband as long as he lives. But if the husband dies, she is released from the law of *her* husband. 3So then if, while *her* husband lives, she marries another man, she will be called an adulteress; but if her husband dies, she is free from that law, so that she is no adulteress, though she has married another man. 4Therefore, my brethren, you also have become dead to the law through the body of Christ, that you may be married to another—to Him who was raised from the dead, that we should bear fruit to God. 5For when we were in the flesh, the sinful passions which were aroused by the law were at work in our members to bear fruit to death. 6But now we have been delivered from the law, having died to what we were held by, so that we should serve in the newness of the Spirit and not *in* the oldness of the letter.

Sin's Advantage in the Law

7What shall we say then? *Is* the law sin? Certainly not! On the contrary, I would not

---

6:13 members: various parts of our bodies, representing all aspects of our lives.

6:17 that form of doctrine: Christian teaching that shapes our lives according to the perfect will of God (12:2).

6:23 wages of sin: The wages paid by sin. **Death** can be earned. **Eternal life** is God's gift.

7:7–12 Sin and **the law** both held me in bondage. Is the law, then, something evil like sin? Not at all. The specific commandments of the law made the knowledge of sin clearer. Sin takes advantage of that clearer knowledge to stir us to rebel and thus leads us into greater sin. The good purpose of the law was to show us how to please God in order that we could have **life**. Sin twisted God's purpose for the law so that it actually brought spiritual **death** (v. 10).

have known sin except through the law. For I would not have known covetousness unless the law had said, *"You shall not covet."*[a] [8]But sin, taking opportunity by the commandment, produced in me all *manner of* evil desire. For apart from the law sin *was* dead. [9]I was alive once without the law, but when the commandment came, sin revived and I died. [10]And the commandment, which *was* to *bring* life, I found to *bring* death. [11]For sin, taking occasion by the commandment, deceived me, and by it killed *me*. [12]Therefore the law *is* holy, and the commandment holy and just and good.

Law Cannot Save from Sin

[13]Has then what is good become death to me? Certainly not! But sin, that it might appear sin, was producing death in me through what is good, so that sin through the commandment might become exceedingly sinful. [14]For we know that the law is spiritual, but I am carnal, sold under sin. [15]For what I am doing, I do not understand. For what I will to do, that I do not practice; but what I hate, that I do. [16]If, then, I do what I will not to do, I agree with the law that *it is* good. [17]But now, *it is* no longer I who do it, but sin that dwells in me. [18]For I know that in me (that is, in my flesh) nothing good dwells; for to will is present with me, but *how* to perform what is good I do not find. [19]For the good that I will *to do,* I do not do; but the evil I will not *to do,* that I practice. [20]Now if I do what I will not *to do,* it is no longer I who do it, but sin that dwells in me.

[21]I find then a law, that evil is present with me, the one who wills to do good. [22]For I delight in the law of God according to the inward man. [23]But I see another law in my members, warring against the law of my mind, and bringing me into captivity to the law of sin which is in my members. [24]O wretched man that I am! Who will deliver me from this body of death? [25]I thank God—through Jesus Christ our Lord!

So then, with the mind I myself serve the law of God, but with the flesh the law of sin.

CHAPTER 8

Free from Indwelling Sin

There is therefore now no condemnation to those who are in Christ Jesus,[a] who do not walk according to the flesh, but according to the Spirit. [2]For the law of the Spirit of life in Christ Jesus has made me free from the law of sin and death. [3]For what the law could not do in that it was weak through the flesh, God *did* by sending His own Son in the likeness of sinful flesh, on account of sin: He condemned sin in the flesh, [4]that the righteous requirement of the law might be fulfilled in us who do not walk according to the flesh but according to the Spirit. [5]For those who live according to the flesh set their minds on the things of the flesh, but those *who live* according to the Spirit, the things of the Spirit. [6]For to be carnally minded *is* death, but to be spiritually minded *is* life and peace. [7]Because the carnal mind *is* enmity against God; for it is not subject to the law of God, nor indeed can be. [8]So then, those who are in the flesh cannot please God.

[9]But you are not in the flesh but in the Spirit, if indeed the Spirit of God dwells in you. Now if anyone does not have the Spirit of Christ, he is not His. [10]And if Christ *is* in you, the body *is* dead because

7:7 [a]Exodus 20:17; Deuteronomy 5:21

8:1 [a]NU-Text omits the rest of this verse.

8:3 The OT law was powerless to produce righteousness because it relied on sinful human nature to meet its demands. **in the likeness of sinful flesh**: Although Jesus came in human form, He was sinless.

8:9 The Holy Spirit's presence or lack thereof, determines whether or not a person has been saved.

8:10, 11 Even if **Christ** lives in us through the Holy **Spirit**, our physical bodies still must

of sin, but the Spirit *is* life because of righteousness. [11]But if the Spirit of Him who raised Jesus from the dead dwells in you, He who raised Christ from the dead will also give life to your mortal bodies through His Spirit who dwells in you.

Sonship Through the Spirit

[12]Therefore, brethren, we are debtors—not to the flesh, to live according to the flesh. [13]For if you live according to the flesh you will die; but if by the Spirit you put to death the deeds of the body, you will live. [14]For as many as are led by the Spirit of God, these are sons of God. [15]For you did not receive the spirit of bondage again to fear, but you received the Spirit of adoption by whom we cry out, "Abba, Father." [16]The Spirit Himself bears witness with our spirit that we are children of God, [17]and if children, then heirs—heirs of God and joint heirs with Christ, if indeed we suffer with *Him,* that we may also be glorified together.

From Suffering to Glory

[18]For I consider that the sufferings of this present time are not worthy *to be compared* with the glory which shall be revealed in us. [19]For the earnest expectation of the creation eagerly waits for the revealing of the sons of God. [20]For the creation was subjected to futility, not willingly, but because of Him who subjected *it* in hope; [21]because the creation itself also will be de-

✦ ✦

die **because of sin**. But the indwelling Spirit assures us of eternal **life** because we have been justified by Christ. God will also raise our **mortal bodies** to a glorious new life at the resurrection.

THE FATHER KNOWS BEST

Billy Graham

I do not believe we should cancel our newspapers and cut off our televisions so that we do not know what is happening in the world. But when we see the terrible injustice, the cruelty, the numbing madness that exists, we cannot help but ask, "Has the world gone crazy?"

It is reassuring to know that God is still all-powerful, that nothing touches my life without His permission. Things happen to me that I cannot understand, but I never doubt God's love. In the hour of trial I may not be able to see His design, but I am confident it must be in line with His purpose.

"Things happen to me that I cannot understand, but I never doubt God's love."

People in the midst of suffering often quote (or are quoted) Romans 8:28. Christians look at the circumstances and say, "How can this possibly work together for my good?" We cannot answer that. Only God can make it work for good, and He cannot do it unless we cooperate with Him. In all of our praying we must ask that His will be done. ✦

livered from the bondage of corruption into the glorious liberty of the children of God. 22 For we know that the whole creation groans and labors with birth pangs together until now. 23 Not only *that,* but we also who have the firstfruits of the Spirit, even we ourselves groan within ourselves, eagerly waiting for the adoption, the redemption of our body. 24 For we were saved in this hope, but hope that is seen is not hope; for why does one still hope for what he sees? 25 But if we hope for what we do not see, we eagerly wait for *it* with perseverance.

26 Likewise the Spirit also helps in our weaknesses. For we do not know what we should pray for as we ought, but the Spirit Himself makes intercession for us[a] with groanings which cannot be uttered. 27 Now He who searches the hearts knows what the mind of the Spirit *is,* because He makes intercession for the saints according to *the will of* God.

28 And we know that all things work together for good to those who love God, to those who are the called according to *His* purpose. 29 For whom He foreknew, He also predestined *to be* conformed to the image of His Son, that He might be the firstborn among many brethren. 30 Moreover whom He predestined, these He also called; whom He called, these He also justified; and whom He justified, these He also glorified.

God's Everlasting Love

31 What then shall we say to these things? If God *is* for us, who *can be* against us? 32 He who did not spare His own Son, but delivered Him up for us all, how shall He not with Him also freely give us all things? 33 Who shall bring a charge against God's elect? *It is* God who justifies. 34 Who *is* he who condemns? *It is* Christ who died, and furthermore is also risen, who is even at the right hand of God, who also makes intercession for us. 35 Who shall separate us from the love of Christ? *Shall* tribulation, or distress, or persecution, or famine, or nakedness, or peril, or sword? 36 As it is written:

"For Your sake we are killed all day long;
We are accounted as sheep for the slaughter."[a]

37 Yet in all these things we are more than conquerors through Him who loved us. 38 For I am persuaded that neither death nor life, nor angels nor principalities nor powers, nor things present nor things to come, 39 nor height nor depth, nor any other created thing, shall be able to separate us from the love of God which is in Christ Jesus our Lord.

I pray that my husband realizes that in all these things he is more than a conqueror through You who loved him.

adapted from Romans 8:37

8:26 [a]NU-Text omits *for us.* 8:36 [a]Psalm 44:22

8:28 God causes **all things** to work for the spiritual **good** and ultimate salvation of those who respond to Him in love. They have been **called according to His purpose**. We are confident that nothing can hurt God's people so deeply that God cannot turn it around for their good. When tragedy or sorrow strikes our families, we must rely on God's promise and trust Him to use it ultimately for good.

8:35–39 No matter what obstacles we face as we grow older, no problem could cause greater discouragement than those mentioned by Paul in this passage. And if none of these tragedies can separate us from Christ's love, then surely we can be "more than conquerors" in every trial we face.

CHAPTER 9

Israel's Rejection of Christ

I tell the truth in Christ, I am not lying,
my conscience also bearing me witness in
the Holy Spirit, [2]that I have great sorrow
and continual grief in my heart. [3]For I
could wish that I myself were accursed
from Christ for my brethren, my
countrymen[a] according to the flesh, [4]who
are Israelites, to whom *pertain* the adop-
tion, the glory, the covenants, the giving of
the law, the service *of God,* and the
promises; [5]of whom *are* the fathers and
from whom, according to the flesh, Christ
came, who is over all, *the* eternally blessed
God. Amen.

Israel's Rejection and God's Purpose

[6]But it is not that the word of God has
taken no effect. For they *are* not all Israel
who *are* of Israel, [7]nor *are they* all children
because they are the seed of Abraham; but,
"In Isaac your seed shall be called."[a] [8]That
is, those who *are* the children of the flesh,
these *are* not the children of God; but the
children of the promise are counted as the
seed. [9]For this *is* the word of promise: *"At this
time I will come and Sarah shall have a son."*[a]

[10]And not only *this,* but when Rebecca
also had conceived by one man, *even* by
our father Isaac [11](for *the children* not yet be-
ing born, nor having done any good or
evil, that the purpose of God according to
election might stand, not of works but of
Him who calls), [12]it was said to her, *"The
older shall serve the younger."*[a] [13]As it is
written, *"Jacob I have loved, but Esau I
have hated."*[a]

Israel's Rejection and God's Justice

[14]What shall we say then? *Is there* un-
righteousness with God? Certainly not!
[15]For He says to Moses, *"I will have mercy
on whomever I will have mercy, and I will
have compassion on whomever I will have
compassion."*[a] [16]So then *it is* not of him
who wills, nor of him who runs, but of God
who shows mercy. [17]For the Scripture says
to the Pharaoh, *"For this very purpose I
have raised you up, that I may show My
power in you, and that My name may be
declared in all the earth."*[a] [18]Therefore He
has mercy on whom He wills, and whom
He wills He hardens.

[19]You will say to me then, "Why does He
still find fault? For who has resisted His
will?" [20]But indeed, O man, who are you to
reply against God? Will the thing formed
say to him who formed *it,* "Why have you

9:3 [a]Or *relatives* 9:7 [a]Genesis 21:12
9:9 [a]Genesis 18:10, 14 9:12 [a]Genesis 25:23
9:13 [a]Malachi 1:2, 3 9:15 [a]Exodus 33:19
9:17 [a]Exodus 9:16

9:1—11:36 A great number of the Israelites, God's chosen people, were not saved (9:1–5). Does this mean that God's promise has failed (9:6)? The remainder of chs. 9—11 answers this pressing question. It is the true Israel, made up of Jews who believe, like Abraham, that inherits the promise (9:6–29). The majority of the Israelites were rejected because they sought righteousness by works rather than by faith (9:30—10:21). But Israel's rejection is not final because in the end Israel as a whole will believe and be saved (11:1–36). Therefore God is faithful to His promise. He is reliable.

9:3 Paul's fervor to see those around him saved should inspire each of us to work harder at winning souls to the Lord.

9:15, 16 God declares His freedom to show mercy on His own terms. He is not, however, arbitrary and capricious in having mercy on certain individuals and withholding it from others. Furthermore, His disposition is to show mercy. Our human thinking should never set limits to His **compassion** (see Matt. 20:8–15).

9:19, 20 Some would claim that if God is totally sovereign, humans are not responsible for their actions: "How can God fault us if He makes all decisions and we have no choice?" We can always approach God with honest questions when we are spiritually perplexed (Ps. 73:21–24). But our questioning must not challenge the divine sovereignty of the God who created us (Is. 45:9).

made me like this?" 21Does not the potter
have power over the clay, from the same
lump to make one vessel for honor and an-
other for dishonor?
22*What* if God, wanting to show *His*
wrath and to make His power known, en-
dured with much longsuffering the vessels
of wrath prepared for destruction, 23and
that He might make known the riches of
His glory on the vessels of mercy, which
He had prepared beforehand for glory,
24*even* us whom He called, not of the Jews
only, but also of the Gentiles?
25As He says also in Hō·sē'a:

"I will call them My people, who were
not My people,
And her beloved, who was not
beloved."[a]
26 *"And it shall come to pass in the place*
where it was said to them,
'You are *not My people,'*
There they shall be called sons of the
living God."[a]

27Ī·sāi'ah also cries out concerning Is-
rael:[a]

"Though the number of the children of
Israel be as the sand of the sea,
The remnant will be saved.
28 *For He will finish the work and cut it*
short in righteousness,
Because the LORD *will make a short*
work upon the earth."[a]

9:25 [a]Hosea 2:23 9:26 [a]Hosea 1:10
9:27 [a]Isaiah 10:22, 23 9:28 [a]NU-Text reads *For the* LORD *will finish the work and cut it short upon the earth.*
9:29 [a]Literally, in Hebrew, *Hosts* [b]Isaiah 1:9
9:31 [a]NU-Text omits *of righteousness.* 9:32 [a]NU-Text reads *by works.* 9:33 [a]Isaiah 8:14; 28:16
10:1 [a]NU-Text reads *them.* 10:5 [a]Leviticus 18:5

29And as Ī·sāi'ah said before:

"Unless the LORD *of Sab'a·ōth*[a] *had left*
us a seed,
We would have become like Sod'om,
And we would have been made like
Go·mor'rah."[b]

Present Condition of Israel

30What shall we say then? That Gentiles,
who did not pursue righteousness, have
attained to righteousness, even the righ-
teousness of faith; 31but Israel, pursuing
the law of righteousness, has not attained
to the law of righteousness.[a] 32Why? Be-
cause *they did* not *seek it* by faith, but as it
were, by the works of the law.[a] For they
stumbled at that stumbling stone. 33As it is
written:

"Behold, I lay in Zion a stumbling
stone and rock of offense,
And whoever believes on Him will
not be put to shame."[a]

CHAPTER 10

Israel Needs the Gospel

Brethren, my heart's desire and prayer
to God for Israel[a] is that they may be saved.
2For I bear them witness that they have a
zeal for God, but not according to knowl-
edge. 3For they being ignorant of God's
righteousness, and seeking to establish
their own righteousness, have not submit-
ted to the righteousness of God. 4For Christ
is the end of the law for righteousness to
everyone who believes.
5For Moses writes about the righteous-
ness which is of the law, *"The man who*
does those things shall live by them."[a] 6But

9:29 Unless God had been merciful, Israel would have been utterly destroyed.

9:32 that stumbling stone: Jesus Christ. Those who sought to attain salvation by works refused to humble themselves and accept the Messiah's offer of salvation by faith.

10:4 Christ fulfilled the requirements of the law and He put an end to the law as a way to achieve righteousness in one's own strength. This is not to be interpreted as a license to ignore God's moral standards, but as a confirmation that everyone who believes can find righteousness in Christ.

the righteousness of faith speaks in this
way, *"Do not say in your heart, 'Who will
ascend into heaven?' "*[a] (that is, to bring
Christ down *from above*) 7or, *" 'Who will
descend into the abyss?' "*[a] (that is, to bring
Christ up from the dead). 8But what does it
say? *"The word is near you, in your mouth
and in your heart"*[a] (that is, the word of
faith which we preach): 9that if you confess
with your mouth the Lord Jesus and be-
lieve in your heart that God has raised
Him from the dead, you will be saved.
10For with the heart one believes unto
righteousness, and with the mouth confes-
sion is made unto salvation. 11For the Scrip-
ture says, *"Whoever believes on Him will
not be put to shame."*[a] 12For there is no dis-
tinction between Jew and Greek, for the
same Lord over all is rich to all who call
upon Him. 13For *"whoever calls on the
name of the LORD shall be saved."*[a]

Israel Rejects the Gospel

14How then shall they call on Him in
whom they have not believed? And how
shall they believe in Him of whom they
have not heard? And how shall they hear
without a preacher? 15And how shall they
preach unless they are sent? As it is writ-
ten:

*"How beautiful are the feet of those
who preach the gospel of peace,*[a]
*Who bring glad tidings of good
things!"*[b]

16But they have not all obeyed the gospel.
For Ī·sāi'ah says, *"LORD, who has believed
our report?"*[a] 17So then faith *comes* by hear-
ing, and hearing by the word of God.
18But I say, have they not heard? Yes in-
deed:

*"Their sound has gone out to all the
earth,
And their words to the ends of the
world."*[a]

19But I say, did Israel not know? First
Moses says:

*"I will provoke you to jealousy by
those who are not a nation,
I will move you to anger by a foolish
nation."*[a]

20But Ī·sāi'ah is very bold and says:

*"I was found by those who did not
seek Me;
I was made manifest to those who
did not ask for Me."*[a]

21But to Israel he says:

*"All day long I have stretched out My
hands
To a disobedient and contrary
people."*[a]

CHAPTER 11

Israel's Rejection Not Total

I say then, has God cast away His peo-
ple? Certainly not! For I also am an Israel-
ite, of the seed of Abraham, *of* the tribe of
Benjamin. 2God has not cast away His peo-
ple whom He foreknew. Or do you not
know what the Scripture says of E·lī'jah,
how he pleads with God against Israel,
saying, 3*"LORD, they have killed Your*

10:6 [a]Deuteronomy 30:12 10:7 [a]Deuteronomy 30:13
10:8 [a]Deuteronomy 30:14 10:11 [a]Isaiah 28:16
10:13 [a]Joel 2:32 10:15 [a]NU-Text omits *preach the gospel of peace, Who.* [b]Isaiah 52:7; Nahum 1:15
10:16 [a]Isaiah 53:1 10:18 [a]Psalm 19:4
10:19 [a]Deuteronomy 32:21 10:20 [a]Isaiah 65:1
10:21 [a]Isaiah 65:2

10:8, 9 The **word** is the message of salvation by **faith** in Christ. It is as **near** as believing in your heart and confessing with your **mouth**, and available to all who hear. **Lord Jesus**: The word *Lord* was used in the Greek translation of the OT for the name of God. Paul applied the title to Jesus showing that to confess Jesus as Lord is to accept Him as the Lord God.

prophets and torn down Your altars, and I alone am left, and they seek my life"?[a] 4But what does the divine response say to him? *"I have reserved for Myself seven thousand men who have not bowed the knee to Bā'al."*[a] 5Even so then, at this present time there is a remnant according to the election of grace. 6And if by grace, then *it is* no longer of works; otherwise grace is no longer grace.[a] But if *it is* of works, it is no longer grace; otherwise work is no longer work.

7What then? Israel has not obtained what it seeks; but the elect have obtained it, and the rest were blinded. 8Just as it is written:

"God has given them a spirit of stupor,
Eyes that they should not see
And ears that they should not hear,
To this very day."[a]

9And David says:

"Let their table become a snare and a
trap,
A stumbling block and a recompense
to them.
10 *Let their eyes be darkened, so that*
they do not see,
And bow down their back always."[a]

Israel's Rejection Not Final

11I say then, have they stumbled that they should fall? Certainly not! But through their fall, to provoke them to jealousy, salvation *has come* to the Gentiles. 12Now if their fall *is* riches for the world, and their failure riches for the Gentiles, how much more their fullness!

13For I speak to you Gentiles; inasmuch as I am an apostle to the Gentiles, I magnify my ministry, 14if by any means I may provoke to jealousy *those who are* my flesh and save some of them. 15For if their being cast away *is* the reconciling of the world, what *will* their acceptance *be* but life from the dead?

16For if the firstfruit *is* holy, the lump *is* also *holy;* and if the root *is* holy, so *are* the branches. 17And if some of the branches were broken off, and you, being a wild olive tree, were grafted in among them, and with them became a partaker of the root and fatness of the olive tree, 18do not boast against the branches. But if you do boast, *remember that* you do not support the root, but the root supports you.

19You will say then, "Branches were broken off that I might be grafted in." 20Well *said.* Because of unbelief they were broken off, and you stand by faith. Do not be haughty, but fear. 21For if God did not spare the natural branches, He may not spare you either. 22Therefore consider the goodness and severity of God: on those who fell, severity; but toward you, goodness,[a] if you continue in *His* goodness. Otherwise you also will be cut off. 23And they also, if they do not continue in unbelief, will be grafted in, for God is able to graft them in again. 24For if you were cut out of the olive tree which is wild by nature, and were grafted contrary to nature into a cultivated olive tree, how much more will these, who

11:3 [a]1 Kings 19:10, 14 11:4 [a]1 Kings 19:18
11:6 [a]NU-Text omits the rest of this verse.
11:8 [a]Deuteronomy 29:4; Isaiah 29:10
11:10 [a]Psalm 69:22, 23 11:22 [a]NU-Text adds *of God.*

11:11 that they should fall: Into final ruin. The Israelites' temporary rejection of the gospel could be used by God for good. Their rejection, **their fall**, provided the occasion for salvation to come to the Gentiles. The Gentiles' acceptance, in turn, would provoke the Jews to jealousy and ultimately bring about their repentance.

11:16–18 firstfruit: The first part of the dough was made into a cake to be offered to God (see Num. 15:17–21). Here firstfruit refers to the godly patriarchs of Israel. The entire lump of dough represents Israel. Paul calls the lump **holy** to show that God still plans to save Israel.

are natural *branches,* be grafted into their
own olive tree?
25For I do not desire, brethren, that you
should be ignorant of this mystery, lest you
should be wise in your own opinion, that
blindness in part has happened to Israel
until the fullness of the Gentiles has come
in. 26And so all Israel will be saved,[a] as it is
written:

"The Deliverer will come out of Zion,
And He will turn away ungodliness
from Jacob;
27 *For this is My covenant with them,*
When I take away their sins."[a]

28Concerning the gospel *they are* enemies
for your sake, but concerning the election
they are beloved for the sake of the fathers.
29For the gifts and the calling of God *are* ir-
revocable. 30For as you were once disobedi-
ent to God, yet have now obtained mercy
through their disobedience, 31even so these
also have now been disobedient, that
through the mercy shown you they also
may obtain mercy. 32For God has commit-
ted them all to disobedience, that He might
have mercy on all.
33Oh, the depth of the riches both of the
wisdom and knowledge of God! How un-
searchable *are* His judgments and His
ways past finding out!

34 *"For who has known the mind of the*
LORD?
Or who has become His counselor?"[a]
35 *"Or who has first given to Him*
And it shall be repaid to him?"[a]

36For of Him and through Him and to
Him *are* all things, to whom *be* glory for-
ever. Amen.

CHAPTER 12

Living Sacrifices to God

I beseech you therefore, brethren, by the
mercies of God, that you present your bod-
ies a living sacrifice, holy, acceptable to
God, *which is* your reasonable service.
2And do not be conformed to this world,
but be transformed by the renewing of
your mind, that you may prove what *is*
that good and acceptable and perfect will
of God.

Serve God with Spiritual Gifts

3For I say, through the grace given to
me, to everyone who is among you, not to
think *of himself* more highly than he ought
to think, but to think soberly, as God has
dealt to each one a measure of faith. 4For as
we have many members in one body, but
all the members do not have the same
function, 5so we, *being* many, are one body
in Christ, and individually members of
one another. 6Having then gifts differing
according to the grace that is given to us,
let us use them: if prophecy, *let us prophesy* in
proportion to our faith; 7or ministry, *let us*
use it in *our* ministering; he who teaches, in
teaching; 8he who exhorts, in exhortation;
he who gives, with liberality; he who
leads, with diligence; he who shows mercy,
with cheerfulness.

11:26 [a]Or *delivered* 11:27 [a]Isaiah 59:20, 21
11:34 [a]Isaiah 40:13; Jeremiah 23:18 11:35 [a]Job
41:11

11:25 A **mystery** is something unknown until it is revealed by God. This mystery is that the temporary blindness of Israel will lead to the salvation of the Gentiles and finally to the salvation of Israel. Thus Gentiles should not be proud of what God has done for them. **the fullness of the Gentiles**: The complete number of Gentiles who will come to Christ. **come in**: Been saved.

12:1 Like the OT Jews, we are to offer sacrifices to God. However, rather than animal sacrifices, we are to give ourselves, all that we are, in unconditional devotion to God.

12:3–6 God has given each of us gifts to be used to minister to the church. We are to fulfill our individual responsibilities, knowing that no one person is more important than another.

THINK POSITIVELY

Dr. Frank Minirth

Your mental diet is important because your mind controls your behavior. Avoid negative input as much as possible by staying away from the people, places, and things that bring out the worst in you. "And do not be conformed to this world, but be transformed by the renewing of your mind, that you may prove what is that good and acceptable and perfect will of God" (Rom. 12:2).

People who have nibbled or feasted on negativism over the years cannot expect to transform their thought patterns and behaviors overnight. But they *can* commit to working on them. Criticism, put-downs, and pessimism can be replaced with praise, encouragement, and comfort. This requires time and effort, but it is a worthwhile investment.

We should focus on positive things by studying meaningful passages in the Bible, reading good books, and spending more time with the people who care about us and give us positive support. The apostle Paul tells us that we can change our lives by seizing control of our thoughts and concentrating on "whatever things are true, whatever things are noble, whatever things are just, whatever things are pure, whatever things are lovely, whatever things are of good report, if there is any virtue and if there is anything praiseworthy—meditate on these things" (Phil. 4:8). ✦

Behave Like a Christian

[9]*Let* love *be* without hypocrisy. Abhor
what is evil. Cling to what is good. [10]*Be*
kindly affectionate to one another with
brotherly love, in honor giving preference
to one another; [11]not lagging in diligence,
fervent in spirit, serving the Lord; [12]rejoic-
ing in hope, patient in tribulation, continu-
ing steadfastly in prayer; [13]distributing to
the needs of the saints, given to hospitality.
[14]Bless those who persecute you; bless
and do not curse. [15]Rejoice with those who
rejoice, and weep with those who weep.
[16]Be of the same mind toward one another.
Do not set your mind on high things, but
associate with the humble. Do not be wise
in your own opinion.
[17]Repay no one evil for evil. Have regard
for good things in the sight of all men. [18]If
it is possible, as much as depends on you,
live peaceably with all men. [19]Beloved, do
not avenge yourselves, but *rather* give
place to wrath; for it is written, *"Vengeance
is Mine, I will repay,"*[a] says the Lord.
[20]Therefore

"If your enemy is hungry, feed him;
If he is thirsty, give him a drink;
For in so doing you will heap coals of
fire on his head."[a]

[21]Do not be overcome by evil, but over-
come evil with good.

12:19 [a]Deuteronomy 32:35 12:20 [a]Proverbs 25:21, 22

THE MYTH OF THE PERFECT HOST
Jill Briscoe

It's a huge release to know you don't need to be the perfect host before you invite anyone into your home. I have observed that many church people have been reluctant about using their homes for the Lord because they don't think the furniture is nice enough—it doesn't match—or they feel awkward because they can't do gourmet cooking.

Well, join the club; I have felt that way, too. But when I discovered that people wanted to spend time with me, not my furniture, and to eat the Bread of Life, not my questionable baking, I was home safe. This does not mean that I cover my furniture with dropcloths and poison my guests; on the contrary, I have worked very hard at making the most of what we have, and I have even learned to make a mean apple pie. But I also try to remember that it is Jesus they want and Jesus they need and Jesus they come to see!

When someone's marriage is falling apart, it matters not that my sofa needs recovering. When a child has been discovered taking "crack," a distraught parent will not be interested to see how I set the table. And when an empty, hungry person wants a spiritual answer, he or she will not be looking at the pile of wash on the floor I have not had time to do. ✦

CHAPTER 13

Submit to Government

Let every soul be subject to the govern-
ing authorities. For there is no authority
except from God, and the authorities that
exist are appointed by God. 2Therefore
whoever resists the authority resists the or-
dinance of God, and those who resist will
bring judgment on themselves. 3For rulers
are not a terror to good works, but to evil.
Do you want to be unafraid of the author-
ity? Do what is good, and you will have
praise from the same. 4For he is God's min-
ister to you for good. But if you do evil, be
afraid; for he does not bear the sword in
vain; for he is God's minister, an avenger
to *execute* wrath on him who practices evil.
5Therefore *you* must be subject, not only
because of wrath but also for conscience'
sake. 6For because of this you also pay
taxes, for they are God's ministers attend-
ing continually to this very thing. 7Render
therefore to all their due: taxes to whom
taxes *are due,* customs to whom customs,
fear to whom fear, honor to whom honor.

Love Your Neighbor

8Owe no one anything except to love
one another, for he who loves another has
fulfilled the law. 9For the commandments,
"You shall not commit adultery," "You

13:1–7 God has established civil government (vv. 1, 2) for the purpose of rewarding good and punishing evil (vv. 3, 4). Therefore the Christian should submit to civil authorities not only because they can punish him but also because God requires it (vv. 5–7). If the civil authority should try to compel the Christian to do evil, he may be forced to disobey civil authority out of loyalty to God. **wrath** (v. 4): Punishment administered by civil authorities.

shall not murder," "You shall not steal,"
"You shall not bear false witness,"[a] *"You*
shall not covet,"[b] and if *there is* any other
commandment, are *all* summed up in this
saying, namely, *"You shall love your*
neighbor as yourself."[c] 10Love does no
harm to a neighbor; therefore love *is* the
fulfillment of the law.

Put on Christ

11And *do* this, knowing the time, that
now *it is* high time to awake out of sleep;
for now our salvation *is* nearer than when
we *first* believed. 12The night is far spent,
the day is at hand. Therefore let us cast off
the works of darkness, and let us put on
the armor of light. 13Let us walk properly,
as in the day, not in revelry and drunken-
ness, not in lewdness and lust, not in strife
and envy. 14But put on the Lord Jesus
Christ, and make no provision for the
flesh, to *fulfill its* lusts.

CHAPTER 14

The Law of Liberty

Receive one who is weak in the faith, *but*
not to disputes over doubtful things. 2For
one believes he may eat all things, but he
who is weak eats *only* vegetables. 3Let not
him who eats despise him who does not
eat, and let not him who does not eat judge
him who eats; for God has received him.
4Who are you to judge another's servant?
To his own master he stands or falls. In-
deed, he will be made to stand, for God is
able to make him stand.

5One person esteems *one* day above an-
other; another esteems every day *alike*. Let
each be fully convinced in his own mind.
6He who observes the day, observes *it* to
the Lord;[a] and he who does not observe the
day, to the Lord he does not observe *it*. He
who eats, eats to the Lord, for he gives God
thanks; and he who does not eat, to the
Lord he does not eat, and gives God
thanks. 7For none of us lives to himself,
and no one dies to himself. 8For if we live,
we live to the Lord; and if we die, we die to
the Lord. Therefore, whether we live or
die, we are the Lord's. 9For to this end
Christ died and rose[a] and lived again, that
He might be Lord of both the dead and the
living. 10But why do you judge your
brother? Or why do you show contempt
for your brother? For we shall all stand be-
fore the judgment seat of Christ.[a] 11For it is
written:

> *"As I live, says the LORD,*
> *Every knee shall bow to Me,*
> *And every tongue shall confess to*
> *God."*[a]

12So then each of us shall give account of
himself to God. 13Therefore let us not judge
one another anymore, but rather resolve
this, not to put a stumbling block or a
cause to fall in *our* brother's way.

The Law of Love

14I know and am convinced by the Lord
Jesus that *there is* nothing unclean of itself;

13:9 [a]NU-Text omits *"You shall not bear false witness."* [b]Exodus 20:13–15, 17; Deuteronomy 5:17–19, 21 [c]Leviticus 19:18 14:6 [a]NU-Text omits the rest of this sentence. 14:9 [a]NU-Text omits *and rose.* 14:10 [a]NU-Text reads *of God.* 14:11 [a]Isaiah 45:23

> Duty does not have to be dull. Love can make it beautiful and fill it with life.
> Thomas Merton

14:1—15:7 Paul provides some practical guidelines regarding things that are neither forbidden nor commanded in Scripture. This passage is of special import as we struggle daily to balance our Christian freedom with our Christian responsibility.

14:4, 5 another's servant: Christ's follower.

14:10 In matters not specifically addressed in Scripture, we are each individually responsible to God and He is the only One with a right to judge.

Young at Heart

Dr. Dale Matthews

Study after study reveals that what we do or do not eat affects our life spans. The number-one killers in America today are heart disease and heart attacks. One-third of all deaths in the United States are from heart disease. But many heart problems are related more to saturated fat intake, cholesterol level, high blood pressure, and smoking (things we can control) than genetics (which we cannot control).

If we are eating "to the Lord" (Rom. 14:6), we should be careful about what we put into our bodies. From that perspective, these common-sense suggestions for good eating should be taken to "heart!"

✦ Eat a variety of foods: not too much fat, protein, or sugar. In general, keep your fat intake less than 20 to 30 percent of the total. After age thirty, the average individual loses muscle fiber at a rate of about 3 to 5 percent every ten years; decrease the amount you eat, especially of fat, by that amount. Your total blood cholesterol shouldn't be greater than two hundred.

✦ Maintain a healthy weight.

✦ Choose a diet with plenty of vegetables, fruit, and grain products. Think fiber.

✦ Use simple sugars in moderation. Eat cakes, pies, and candies very rarely. Since your metabolism decreases by 2 percent every decade, as you age, decrease the amount of sugar you consume. Sugars are empty calories.

✦ Use salt and sodium in moderation. Be particularly careful if you have a tendency toward high blood pressure. ✦

but to him who considers anything to be
unclean, to him *it is* unclean. [15]Yet if your
brother is grieved because of *your* food,
you are no longer walking in love. Do not
destroy with your food the one for whom
Christ died. [16]Therefore do not let your
good be spoken of as evil; [17]for the king-
dom of God is not eating and drinking, but
righteousness and peace and joy in the
Holy Spirit. [18]For he who serves Christ in
these things[a] *is* acceptable to God and ap-
proved by men.
[19]Therefore let us pursue the things
which make for peace and the things by
which one may edify another. [20]Do not de-
stroy the work of God for the sake of food.
All things indeed *are* pure, but *it is* evil for
the man who eats with offense. [21]*It is* good
neither to eat meat nor drink wine nor *do
anything* by which your brother stumbles
or is offended or is made weak.[a] [22]Do you

14:18 [a]NU-Text reads *this*. 14:21 [a]NU-Text omits *or is offended or is made weak.*

14:19, 20 edify: To help another grow stronger in the Christian faith. **work of God**: Here means the brother weak in faith, whom God is building up. **eats with offense**: Offends a fellow Christian by the liberty he allows himself.

have faith?[a] Have *it* to yourself before God.
Happy *is* he who does not condemn him-
self in what he approves. 23But he who
doubts is condemned if he eats, because *he*
does not *eat* from faith; for whatever *is* not
from faith is sin.[a]

CHAPTER 15

Bearing Others' Burdens

We then who are strong ought to bear
with the scruples of the weak, and not to
please ourselves. 2Let each of us please *his*
neighbor for *his* good, leading to edifica-
tion. 3For even Christ did not please Him-
self; but as it is written, *"The reproaches of*
those who reproached You fell on Me."[a]
4For whatever things were written before
were written for our learning, that we
through the patience and comfort of the
Scriptures might have hope. 5Now may the
God of patience and comfort grant you to
be like-minded toward one another, ac-
cording to Christ Jesus, 6that you may with
one mind *and* one mouth glorify the God
and Father of our Lord Jesus Christ.

Glorify God Together

7Therefore receive one another, just as
Christ also received us,[a] to the glory of
God. 8Now I say that Jesus Christ has be-
come a servant to the circumcision for the
truth of God, to confirm the promises
made to the fathers, 9and that the Gentiles
might glorify God for *His* mercy, as it is
written:

"For this reason I will confess to You
among the Gentiles,
And sing to Your name."[a]

10And again he says:

"Rejoice, O Gentiles, with His
people!"[a]

11And again:

"Praise the LORD, all you Gentiles!
Laud Him, all you peoples!"[a]

12And again, I·sai'ah says:

"There shall be a root of Jesse;
And He who shall rise to reign over
the Gentiles,
In Him the Gentiles shall hope."[a]

13Now may the God of hope fill you
with all joy and peace in believing, that
you may abound in hope by the power of
the Holy Spirit.

From Jerusalem to Illyricum

14Now I myself am confident concerning
you, my brethren, that you also are full of
goodness, filled with all knowledge, able
also to admonish one another.[a] 15Neverthe-
less, brethren, I have written more boldly
to you on *some* points, as reminding you,
because of the grace given to me by God,
16that I might be a minister of Jesus Christ
to the Gentiles, ministering the gospel of
God, that the offering of the Gentiles might
be acceptable, sanctified by the Holy Spirit.
17Therefore I have reason to glory in Christ
Jesus in the things *which pertain* to God.
18For I will not dare to speak of any of those
things which Christ has not accomplished

14:22 [a]NU-Text reads *The faith which you have—have.*
14:23 [a]M-Text puts Romans 16:25–27 here.
15:3 [a]Psalm 69:9 15:7 [a]NU-Text and M-Text read *you.* 15:9 [a]2 Samuel 22:50; Psalm 18:49
15:10 [a]Deuteronomy 32:43 15:11 [a]Psalm 117:1
15:12 [a]Isaiah 11:10 15:14 [a]M-Text reads *others.*

15:1–6 Christ is to be the example we follow in our relationships. When we practice His principles of love and acceptance, the church will find unity.

15:8, 9 servant to the circumcision: Jesus came as a Jew (1) in order to fulfill God's promises to them, and (2) so that the Gentiles might also receive God's mercy.

15:14 When the body of Christ is unified, its members can provide good counsel to one another, based on their understanding and application of Scripture.

THE ULTIMATE RELATIONSHIP

Sherwood Eliot Wirt

Bumper stickers keep informing us that "Happiness is being a grandparent." Grandchildren are certainly a blessing; in our house their affection always gives us a lift. Real inner joy, however, does not stem from dependence on relationships with other individuals, including grandchildren. It comes from a vision of what life is for and the translation of that vision into reality. It does not derive from Social Security or Medicare, great as these helps are to retirement. True joy derives from acknowledging that the Creator of the universe is our heavenly Father, that Jesus Christ is His Son, and that we belong to Him forever. ✦

through me, in word and deed, to make
the Gentiles obedient— 19in mighty signs
and wonders, by the power of the Spirit of
God, so that from Jerusalem and round
about to Il·lyr′i·cum I have fully preached
the gospel of Christ. 20And so I have made
it my aim to preach the gospel, not where
Christ was named, lest I should build on
another man's foundation, 21but as it is
written:

"To whom He was not announced,
they shall see;
And those who have not heard shall
understand."[a]

Plan to Visit Rome

22For this reason I also have been much
hindered from coming to you. 23But now
no longer having a place in these parts,
and having a great desire these many years
to come to you, 24whenever I journey to
Spain, I shall come to you.[a] For I hope to
see you on my journey, and to be helped on
my way there by you, if first I may enjoy
your *company* for a while. 25But now I am
going to Jerusalem to minister to the saints.
26For it pleased those from Mac·e·dō′ni·a
and A·chā′i·a to make a certain contribution for the poor among the saints who are
in Jerusalem. 27It pleased them indeed, and
they are their debtors. For if the Gentiles
have been partakers of their spiritual
things, their duty is also to minister to
them in material things. 28Therefore, when
I have performed this and have sealed to
them this fruit, I shall go by way of you to
Spain. 29But I know that when I come to
you, I shall come in the fullness of the
blessing of the gospel[a] of Christ.
30Now I beg you, brethren, through the
Lord Jesus Christ, and through the love of
the Spirit, that you strive together with me
in prayers to God for me, 31that I may be

15:21 [a]Isaiah 52:15 15:24 [a]NU-Text omits *I shall come to you* (and joins *Spain* with the next sentence). 15:29 [a]NU-Text omits *of the gospel.*

15:24 Paul had his eyes on **Spain**, the frontier of the Roman Empire in the West. He hoped the Romans would support him in his mission farther west.

15:28 when I . . . have sealed: Delivered this collection to the Jewish Christians and helped them understand its significance.

delivered from those in Judea who do not
believe, and that my service for Jerusalem
may be acceptable to the saints, 32that I
may come to you with joy by the will of
God, and may be refreshed together with
you. 33Now the God of peace *be* with you
all. Amen.

CHAPTER 16

Sister Phoebe Commended

I commend to you Phoē′bē our sister,
who is a servant of the church in Cen′-
chrē·a, 2that you may receive her in the
Lord in a manner worthy of the saints, and
assist her in whatever business she has
need of you; for indeed she has been a
helper of many and of myself also.

Greeting Roman Saints

3Greet Pri·scil′la and A·qui′la, my fel-
low workers in Christ Jesus, 4who risked
their own necks for my life, to whom not
only I give thanks, but also all the churches
of the Gentiles. 5Likewise *greet* the church
that is in their house.

Greet my beloved E·paē′ne·tus, who is
the firstfruits of A·chā′i·a[a] to Christ. 6Greet
Mary, who labored much for us. 7Greet
An·dron′i·cus and Jū′ni·a, my countrymen
and my fellow prisoners, who are of note
among the apostles, who also were in
Christ before me.

8Greet Am′pli·as, my beloved in the
Lord. 9Greet Ur·bā′nus, our fellow worker
in Christ, and Stā′chys, my beloved.
10Greet A·pel′lēs, approved in Christ. Greet
those who are of the *household* of Ar-
is·tob′ū·lus. 11Greet He·rō′di·on, my coun-
tryman.[a] Greet those who are of the *house-
hold* of Nar·cis′sus who are in the Lord.

12Greet Trȳ·phē′na and Trȳ·phō′sa, who
have labored in the Lord. Greet the
beloved Per′sis, who labored much in the
Lord. 13Greet Rū′fus, chosen in the Lord,
and his mother and mine. 14Greet A·syn′-
cri·tus, Phlē′gon, Her′mas, Pat′ro·bas,
Her′mēs, and the brethren who are with
them. 15Greet Phi·lol′o·gus and Julia,
Ne′rē·us and his sister, and Ō·lym′pas,
and all the saints who are with them.

16Greet one another with a holy kiss.
The[a] churches of Christ greet you.

Avoid Divisive Persons

17Now I urge you, brethren, note those
who cause divisions and offenses, contrary
to the doctrine which you learned, and
avoid them. 18For those who are such do
not serve our Lord Jesus[a] Christ, but their
own belly, and by smooth words and flat-
tering speech deceive the hearts of the sim-
ple. 19For your obedience has become
known to all. Therefore I am glad on your
behalf; but I want you to be wise in what is
good, and simple concerning evil. 20And
the God of peace will crush Satan under
your feet shortly.

The grace of our Lord Jesus Christ *be*
with you. Amen.

Greetings from Paul's Friends

21Timothy, my fellow worker, and
Lū′cius, Jason, and Sō·sip′a·ter, my coun-
trymen, greet you.

16:5 [a]NU-Text reads *Asia.* 16:11 [a]Or *relative*
16:16 [a]NU-Text reads *All the churches.*
16:18 [a]NU-Text and M-Text omit *Jesus.*

16:3–5 Priscilla and **Aquila** were tentmakers who had earlier been coworkers with Paul in Corinth (see Acts 18:1–3). **the church . . . in their house**: In NT times churches met in private houses for worship.

16:19 Once we have discovered something evil, we should avoid it rather than trying to learn all the explicit details. Such innocence will enable us to keep our minds and hearts pure, rather than dwelling on sin.

16:21–23 Timothy: Paul's fellow missionary (Acts 16:1–5; Acts 20:4). **Tertius** was Paul's secretary. **Gaius**: One of the few Christians baptized by Paul personally in Corinth (see 1 Cor. 1:14). He had a large house and acted as **host** for the church services there. Because of his hospitality, he is usually identified with Titius Justus in Acts 18:7.

[22]I, Ter'ti·us, who wrote *this* epistle,
greet you in the Lord.
[23]Gā'i·us, my host and *the host* of the
whole church, greets you. Ē·ras'tus, the
treasurer of the city, greets you, and
Quar'tus, a brother. [24]The grace of our Lord
Jesus Christ *be* with you all. Amen.[a]

Benediction

[25]Now to Him who is able to establish
you according to my gospel and the
preaching of Jesus Christ, according to the
revelation of the mystery kept secret since
the world began [26]but now made manifest,
and by the prophetic Scriptures made
known to all nations, according to the com-
mandment of the everlasting God, for obe-
dience to the faith— [27]to God, alone wise,
be glory through Jesus Christ forever.
Amen.[a]

God be in my head, and in my understanding;
God be in mine eyes, and in my looking;
God be in my mouth, and in my speaking;
God be in my heart, and in my thinking;
God be at mine end, and at my departing.

Sarum Primer, 1558

16:24 [a]NU-Text omits this verse. 16:27 [a]M-Text puts Romans 16:25–27 after Romans 14:23.

1 Corinthians

Corinth, one of the most important cities in Greece during Paul's day, was a major commercial center which thrived in vice and corruption. During his second missionary journey, Paul stayed in the city for about a year and a half, and in spite of the obstacles the gospel faced, he was able to establish a church there.

When Paul was on his third missionary journey in Ephesus, he received word from the household of Chloe that the churches in Corinth were being infected by the surrounding evil culture. He was asked to help answer some of the questions raised about the teachings and practices of some of the congregations. Shortly after receiving this news, three men from Corinth visited Paul in Ephesus and discussed the need for his judgment on these matters.

As a response to these questions, Paul wrote this epistle, which proclaims the relevance of Christ Jesus to every area of the believer's life. In urging Christians to make use of the spiritual gifts they have been given, Paul showed that everyone should recognize his or her importance in the church. Paul's concern for the Corinthians as their spiritual father was tempered with love, and he wanted to avoid visiting them "with a rod." The basic theme is applying Christian principles to carnality in the individual and the church. The Cross of Christ transforms lives and should make believers and the church different from the surrounding world. ✦

CHAPTER 1

Greeting

Paul, called *to be* an apostle of Jesus
Christ through the will of God, and Sos'-
the·nēs *our* brother,

2To the church of God which is at
Corinth, to those who are sanctified
in Christ Jesus, called *to be* saints, with
all who in every place call on the name
of Jesus Christ our Lord, both theirs and
ours:

3Grace to you and peace from God our
Father and the Lord Jesus Christ.

Spiritual Gifts at Corinth

4I thank my God always concerning you
for the grace of God which was given to
you by Christ Jesus, 5that you were en-
riched in everything by Him in all utter-
ance and all knowledge, 6even as the testi-
mony of Christ was confirmed in you, 7so
that you come short in no gift, eagerly
waiting for the revelation of our Lord Jesus
Christ, 8who will also confirm you to the

1:1 apostle of Jesus Christ: Because some were challenging Paul's apostleship, he claimed the apostle's authority to correct their errors (see 9:1, 2; 15:9, 10).

1:6 The power of Christ was confirmed by the changed lives of the Corinthians.

PAUL: STRENGTH IN WEAKNESS

Christians often think of Paul as the "ultimate Christian." His remarkable testimony of conversion and the ensuing change in his lifestyle are rivaled only by his unquenchable zeal and love for the lost as revealed in Acts and his epistles. Yet, while we may long for a testimony as inspiring as Paul's, few of us would embrace the agony and suffering he endured for his faithfulness.

This man, who had the status of a free-born Roman citizen (Acts 22:27, 28) and who had studied under Gamaliel, the most prominent Hebrew teacher in Jerusalem (22:3), worked as a humble tentmaker in order to support himself and those who were with him (18:3; 20:34). His passion for souls led him to endure beatings, shipwrecks, sleeplessness, hunger and thirst, and a battery of perils—all because of his deep concern for the churches and the lost (2 Cor. 11:24–28).

The Lord obviously ordained Paul to preach the Word and He blessed the apostle's efforts; but God also selected Paul for the less glamorous task of suffering: "He is a chosen vessel of Mine to bear My name before Gentiles, kings, and the children of Israel. For I will show him how many things he must suffer for My name's sake" (Acts 9:15, 16).

Not only did he suffer from outside persecution, but Paul was also reviled by fellow believers, especially for his unimpressive physique and poor oratorical skills. His critics disparaged him, saying, "His bodily presence is weak, and his speech contemptible" (2 Cor. 10:10).

Paul's physical presence obviously did not match his spiritual and mental strength. In addition, he struggled with a "thorn in the flesh" (12:7), which many scholars believe to be a physical infirmity, such as eye trouble (see Gal. 4:13–15).

How did Paul live a successful Christian life despite such an imbalance between spiritual, mental, and physical health? The Lord supplied his need.

The apostle prayed three times to have the thorn removed, but the Lord declined his request: "My grace is sufficient for you, for My strength is made perfect in weakness" (2 Cor. 12:9). Paul accepted this answer, glad to suffer since it meant receiving the power of Christ on his life.

Paul's suffering and health problems demonstrate God's all-sufficient grace. As with all of His servants, God supplied exactly what Paul needed to complete the task set before him. While our lives will not be free of trouble, if we are walking in obedience to God, we can expect Him to answer our needs and keep our physical, spiritual, and mental health in balance. ✦

end, *that you may be* blameless in the day of our Lord Jesus Christ. [9]God *is* faithful, by whom you were called into the fellowship of His Son, Jesus Christ our Lord.

Sectarianism Is Sin

[10]Now I plead with you, brethren, by the name of our Lord Jesus Christ, that you all speak the same thing, and *that* there be no divisions among you, but *that* you be perfectly joined together in the same mind and in the same judgment. [11]For it has been declared to me concerning you, my brethren, by those of Chlō'ē's *household,* that there are contentions among you. [12]Now I say this, that each of you says, "I am of Paul," or "I am of A·pol'los," or "I am of Cē'phas," or "I am of Christ." [13]Is Christ divided? Was Paul crucified for you? Or were you baptized in the name of Paul?

[14]I thank God that I baptized none of you except Cris'pus and Gā'i·us, [15]lest anyone should say that I had baptized in my own name. [16]Yes, I also baptized the household of Steph'a·nas. Besides, I do not know whether I baptized any other. [17]For Christ did not send me to baptize, but to preach the gospel, not with wisdom of words, lest the cross of Christ should be made of no effect.

Christ the Power and Wisdom of God

[18]For the message of the cross is foolishness to those who are perishing, but to us who are being saved it is the power of God. [19]For it is written:

"I will destroy the wisdom of the wise,
And bring to nothing the
understanding of the prudent."[a]

[20]Where *is* the wise? Where *is* the scribe? Where *is* the disputer of this age? Has not God made foolish the wisdom of this world? [21]For since, in the wisdom of God, the world through wisdom did not know God, it pleased God through the foolishness of the message preached to save those who believe. [22]For Jews request a sign, and Greeks seek after wisdom; [23]but we preach Christ crucified, to the Jews a stumbling block and to the Greeks[a] foolishness, [24]but to those who are called, both Jews and Greeks, Christ the power of God and the wisdom of God. [25]Because the foolishness of God is wiser than men, and the weakness of God is stronger than men.

Glory Only in the Lord

[26]For you see your calling, brethren, that not many wise according to the flesh, not many mighty, not many noble, *are called.* [27]But God has chosen the foolish things of the world to put to shame the wise, and God has chosen the weak things of the world to put to shame the things which are mighty; [28]and the base things of the world and the things which are despised God has chosen, and the things which are not, to bring to nothing the things that are, [29]that no flesh should glory in His presence. [30]But of Him you are in Christ Jesus, who became for us wisdom from God—and righteousness and sanctification and redemption— [31]that, as it is written, *"He who glories, let him glory in the* LORD.*"*[a]

1:19 [a]Isaiah 29:14 1:23 [a]NU-Text reads *Gentiles.*
1:31 [a]Jeremiah 9:24

1:10 speak the same thing: Paul does not ask that they agree with one another in all points, but he pleads for a common basic understanding of the Christian faith. He asks that different judgments not create broken fellowship. The Corinthians were still brethren, yet they needed to be restored to their former condition of full fellowship in Christ.

1:22, 23 The Jews wanted a **sign**, a Christ who through God's power would overthrow their enemies and establish their nation. **stumbling block**: How could God's blessing be on a Christ who was crucified? The **Greeks** (Gentiles) sought God through speculative wisdom. The thought of finding Him through a man on a cross was sheer **foolishness** to them.

CHAPTER 2

Christ Crucified

And I, brethren, when I came to you,
did not come with excellence of speech or
of wisdom declaring to you the testimony[a]
of God. 2For I determined not to know any-
thing among you except Jesus Christ and
Him crucified. 3I was with you in weak-
ness, in fear, and in much trembling. 4And
my speech and my preaching *were* not with
persuasive words of human[a] wisdom, but
in demonstration of the Spirit and of
power, 5that your faith should not be in the
wisdom of men but in the power of God.

Spiritual Wisdom

6However, we speak wisdom among
those who are mature, yet not the wisdom
of this age, nor of the rulers of this age,
who are coming to nothing. 7But we speak
the wisdom of God in a mystery, the hid-
den *wisdom* which God ordained before the
ages for our glory, 8which none of the
rulers of this age knew; for had they
known, they would not have crucified the
Lord of glory.
9But as it is written:

"Eye has not seen, nor ear heard,
Nor have entered into the heart of
man
The things which God has prepared
for those who love Him."[a]

10But God has revealed *them* to us through
His Spirit. For the Spirit searches all things,
yes, the deep things of God. 11For what
man knows the things of a man except the
spirit of the man which is in him? Even so
no one knows the things of God except the
Spirit of God. 12Now we have received, not
the spirit of the world, but the Spirit who is
from God, that we might know the things
that have been freely given to us by God.
13These things we also speak, not in
words which man's wisdom teaches but
which the Holy[a] Spirit teaches, comparing
spiritual things with spiritual. 14But the
natural man does not receive the things of
the Spirit of God, for they are foolishness
to him; nor can he know *them,* because they
are spiritually discerned. 15But he who is
spiritual judges all things, yet he himself is
rightly judged by no one. 16For *"who has
known the mind of the* LORD *that he may
instruct Him?"*[a] But we have the mind of
Christ.

CHAPTER 3

Sectarianism Is Carnal

And I, brethren, could not speak to you
as to spiritual *people* but as to carnal, as to

2:1 [a]NU-Text reads *mystery.* 2:4 [a]NU-Text omits *human.* 2:9 [a]Isaiah 64:4 2:13 [a]NU-Text omits *Holy.* 2:16 [a]Isaiah 40:13

I pray that I will have the mind of Christ.

adapted from 1 Corinthians 2:16

Never live on memories. Do not remember in your testimony what you once were; let the Word of God be always living and active in you, and give the best you have every time and all the time.

Oswald Chambers

2:10 searches all things: The Holy Spirit is omniscient.

2:13 Paul is saying that his very words are inspired by the Holy Spirit.

2:14 the natural man: Here, the person who trusts in his or her own earthly wisdom and takes no account of God's help. **spiritually discerned**: Examined with the assistance of the Holy Spirit.

3:1–4 Although the Corinthians were Christians, they were not fully **spiritual** (v. 1); they

babes in Christ. [2]I fed you with milk and not with solid food; for until now you were not able *to receive it,* and even now you are still not able; [3]for you are still carnal. For where *there are* envy, strife, and divisions among you, are you not carnal and behaving like *mere* men? [4]For when one says, "I am of Paul," and another, "I *am* of A·pol′los," are you not carnal?

Watering, Working, Warning

[5]Who then is Paul, and who *is* A·pol′los, but ministers through whom you believed, as the Lord gave to each one? [6]I planted, A·pol′los watered, but God gave the increase. [7]So then neither he who plants is anything, nor he who waters, but God who gives the increase. [8]Now he who plants and he who waters are one, and each one will receive his own reward according to his own labor.

[9]For we are God's fellow workers; you are God's field, *you are* God's building. [10]According to the grace of God which was given to me, as a wise master builder I have laid the foundation, and another builds on it. But let each one take heed how he builds on it. [11]For no other foundation can anyone lay than that which is laid, which is Jesus Christ. [12]Now if anyone builds on this foundation *with* gold, silver, precious stones, wood, hay, straw, [13]each one's work will become clear; for the Day will declare it, because it will be revealed by fire; and the fire will test each one's work, of what sort it is. [14]If anyone's work which he has built on *it* endures, he will receive a reward. [15]If anyone's work is burned, he will suffer loss; but he himself will be saved, yet so as through fire.

[16]Do you not know that you are the temple of God and *that* the Spirit of God dwells in you? [17]If anyone defiles the temple of God, God will destroy him. For the temple of God is holy, which *temple* you are.

Avoid Worldly Wisdom

[18]Let no one deceive himself. If anyone among you seems to be wise in this age, let him become a fool that he may become wise. [19]For the wisdom of this world is foolishness with God. For it is written, *"He catches the wise in their own craftiness"*;[a] [20]and again, *"The LORD knows the thoughts of the wise, that they are futile."*[a] [21]Therefore let no one boast in men. For all things are yours: [22]whether Paul or A·pol′los or Cē′phas, or the world or life or death, or things present or things to come—all are yours. [23]And you *are* Christ's, and Christ *is* God's.

CHAPTER 4

Stewards of the Mysteries of God

Let a man so consider us, as servants of Christ and stewards of the mysteries of God. [2]Moreover it is required in stewards that one be found faithful. [3]But with me it is a very small thing that I should be judged by you or by a human court.[a] In fact, I do not even judge myself. [4]For I know of nothing against myself, yet I am not justified by this; but He who judges me is the Lord. [5]Therefore judge nothing

3:19 [a]Job 5:13 3:20 [a]Psalm 94:11 4:3 [a]Literally *day*

did not live in full obedience to the Spirit. Neither were they **mere** natural **men** (v. 3; see 2:14), people who did not know Christ. Rather they were **carnal** Christians (vv. 1, 3) who still lived in **envy** and **divisions** like the unsaved (vv. 3, 4).

3:6, 7 planted: Paul took the gospel to new areas. **watered**: Apollos encouraged new converts with teachings from Scripture (see Acts 18:24–28). **God . . . gives the increase**: It is His gracious activity that should be exalted; without Him, His ministers are nothing. We should be careful to keep our pride in check, not allowing ourselves to think our ministry is more important than another person's. Anything accomplished through our actions happens only because God chose to use us to fulfill His purpose.

> The most eloquent prayer is the prayer through hands that heal and bless. The highest form of worship is the worship of unselfish Christian service. The greatest form of praise is the sound of consecrated feet seeking out the lost and helpless.
>
> Billy Graham

before the time, until the Lord comes, who will both bring to light the hidden things of darkness and reveal the counsels of the hearts. Then each one's praise will come from God.

Fools for Christ's Sake

6Now these things, brethren, I have figuratively transferred to myself and A·pol'los for your sakes, that you may learn in us not to think beyond what is written, that none of you may be puffed up on behalf of one against the other. 7For who makes you differ *from another?* And what do you have that you did not receive? Now if you did indeed receive *it,* why do you boast as if you had not received *it?*

8You are already full! You are already rich! You have reigned as kings without us—and indeed I could wish you did reign, that we also might reign with you! 9For I think that God has displayed us, the apostles, last, as men condemned to death; for we have been made a spectacle to the world, both to angels and to men. 10We *are* fools for Christ's sake, but you *are* wise in Christ! We *are* weak, but you *are* strong! You *are* distinguished, but we *are* dishonored! 11To the present hour we both hunger and thirst, and we are poorly clothed, and beaten, and homeless. 12And we labor, working with our own hands. Being reviled, we bless; being persecuted, we endure; 13being defamed, we entreat. We have been made as the filth of the world, the offscouring of all things until now.

Paul's Paternal Care

14I do not write these things to shame you, but as my beloved children I warn *you.* 15For though you might have ten thousand instructors in Christ, yet *you do* not *have* many fathers; for in Christ Jesus I have begotten you through the gospel. 16Therefore I urge you, imitate me. 17For this reason I have sent Timothy to you, who is my beloved and faithful son in the Lord, who will remind you of my ways in Christ, as I teach everywhere in every church.

18Now some are puffed up, as though I were not coming to you. 19But I will come to you shortly, if the Lord wills, and I will know, not the word of those who are puffed up, but the power. 20For the kingdom of God *is* not in word but in power. 21What do you want? Shall I come to you with a rod, or in love and a spirit of gentleness?

CHAPTER 5

Immorality Defiles the Church

It is actually reported *that there is* sexual immorality among you, and such sexual immorality as is not even named[a] among

5:1 [a]NU-Text omits *named.*

4:8 The Corinthians thought that Christians were to be **full**, **rich**, and to **reign** in the present. But Paul knew that we must go through trials now if we are to reign when Christ returns. **I could wish**: That you were indeed involved in the **reign** of Christ and that we might be united in His true kingdom.

4:12 **Labor** was esteemed in the Hebrew tradition, but despised by the Greeks. Paul, himself a tentmaker (Acts 18:3), is speaking here of hard, manual work.

4:13 **offscouring**: The ill treatment the apostles suffered for the sake of Christ. The **world** considered them to be refuse and outcasts.

5:1, 2 **his father's wife**: Probably a second wife, younger than his father. **not . . .**

the Gentiles—that a man has his father's wife! 2And you are puffed up, and have not rather mourned, that he who has done this deed might be taken away from among you. 3For I indeed, as absent in body but present in spirit, have already judged (as though I were present) him who has so done this deed. 4In the name of our Lord Jesus Christ, when you are gathered together, along with my spirit, with the power of our Lord Jesus Christ, 5deliver such a one to Satan for the destruction of the flesh, that his spirit may be saved in the day of the Lord Jesus.[a]

6Your glorying *is* not good. Do you not know that a little leaven leavens the whole lump? 7Therefore purge out the old leaven, that you may be a new lump, since you truly are unleavened. For indeed Christ, our Passover, was sacrificed for us.[a] 8Therefore let us keep the feast, not with old leaven, nor with the leaven of malice and wickedness, but with the unleavened *bread* of sincerity and truth.

Immorality Must Be Judged

9I wrote to you in my epistle not to keep company with sexually immoral people. 10Yet *I* certainly *did* not *mean* with the sexually immoral people of this world, or with the covetous, or extortioners, or idolaters, since then you would need to go out of the world. 11But now I have written to you not to keep company with anyone named a brother, who is sexually immoral, or covetous, or an idolater, or a reviler, or a drunkard, or an extortioner—not even to eat with such a person.

12For what *have* I *to do* with judging those also who are outside? Do you not judge those who are inside? 13But those who are outside God judges. Therefore *"put away from yourselves the evil person."*[a]

CHAPTER 6

Do Not Sue the Brethren

Dare any of you, having a matter against another, go to law before the unrighteous, and not before the saints? 2Do you not know that the saints will judge the world? And if the world will be judged by you, are you unworthy to judge the smallest matters? 3Do you not know that we shall judge angels? How much more, things that pertain to this life? 4If then you have judgments concerning things pertaining to this life, do you appoint those who are least esteemed by the church to judge? 5I say this to your shame. Is it so, that there is not a wise man among you, not even one, who will be able to judge between his brethren? 6But brother goes to law against brother, and that before unbelievers!

7Now therefore, it is already an utter failure for you that you go to law against one another. Why do you not rather accept wrong? Why do you not rather *let yourselves* be cheated? 8No, you yourselves do wrong and cheat, and *you do* these things *to your* brethren! 9Do you not know that the unrighteous will not inherit the kingdom

5:5 [a]NU-Text omits *Jesus.* 5:7 [a]NU-Text omits *for us.* 5:13 [a]Deuteronomy 17:7; 19:19; 22:21, 24; 24:7

---

mourned: For the sin of this church member and for the embarrassment brought on the church.

5:7, 8 In Scripture **leaven** is often used figuratively of evil or the past life. The Jews removed all leaven before killing the **Passover** sacrifice and celebrating the feast that followed (see Ex. 12:15), which commemorated their deliverance from Egypt. Because Christ is our true **Passover** sacrifice, we must get rid of all **malice** and **wickedness**, which characterized our former life. The rest of life is to be lived in Christlike **sincerity** and **truth**.

5:13 Paul urges the church to administer strict discipline to those who claim to be believers yet persist in immorality. He makes a clear distinction between employing corrective discipline within the fellowship and attempting to impose Christian morals on the world, which could never be successful and is not part of the church's mission.

Time to Repair Your Temple?

Leslie E. Moser, Ph.D.

Most of us abuse our bodies in one way or another even though our bodies are the dwelling place of the Holy Spirit (1 Cor. 6:19). That fact makes our abuse of our bodies sinful. And consider the contrast. When a valued guest visits, most of us put our houses in order. We vacuum the carpets, dust the furniture, and pick up the mess.

But we do not always do that for the Holy Spirit. The Spirit often dwells in bodies which are unkept, unhealthy, and unfit. Ideally, keeping your body healthy means making it the best temple possible—and we all benefit from that. So what shall we present to the Holy Spirit as a dwelling place? Only the very best our bodies can be!

We have no choice. Whatever our age, we must dedicate ourselves to preserving our health, stamina, and vitality. Appearance is not the issue; physical health is. While we must avoid vanity, less than total dedication to physical fitness is an affront to the God who created us. He will accept nothing less than our best effort to keep physically fit. We glorify God when we are conscientious stewards of our bodies, our minds, and our spirits. ✦

of God? Do not be deceived. Neither forni-
cators, nor idolaters, nor adulterers, nor
homosexuals,[a] nor sodomites, [10]nor
thieves, nor covetous, nor drunkards, nor
revilers, nor extortioners will inherit the
kingdom of God. [11]And such were some of
you. But you were washed, but you were
sanctified, but you were justified in the
name of the Lord Jesus and by the Spirit of
our God.

Glorify God in Body and Spirit

[12]All things are lawful for me, but all
things are not helpful. All things are lawful
for me, but I will not be brought under the
power of any. [13]Foods for the stomach and
the stomach for foods, but God will de-
stroy both it and them. Now the body *is*
not for sexual immorality but for the Lord,
and the Lord for the body. [14]And God both
raised up the Lord and will also raise us up
by His power.

[15]Do you not know that your bodies are
members of Christ? Shall I then take the
members of Christ and make *them* mem-
bers of a harlot? Certainly not! [16]Or do you
not know that he who is joined to a harlot
is one body *with her*? For *"the two,"* He

6:9 [a]That is, catamites

6:11 Although acceptance of salvation cleanses us from all sin, God calls all believers to change their lifestyles and live in accordance with their new life in Christ.

6:12 All things are lawful: Perhaps a common saying among the Corinthians used to excuse sinful actions. Though we may be free to do many things, we should do only those which strengthen the spiritual lives of ourselves and others. See Rom. 14:1—15:7 for practical guidelines on balancing Christian freedom with Christian responsibility.

Bought at a Price

Charles R. Swindoll

Since the believer's body is considered the "temple of the Holy Spirit," it stands to reason that He should be glorified through it (1 Cor. 6:19, 20). He owns it! This completely rearranges our reason for existence. When you operate your life from this perspective, everything is changed. That explains why it is so important to view every day—sunup to sundown—from the spiritual perspective. When we do, nothing is accidental, coincidental, meaningless, or superficial. Things that happen to us are under our Lord's supervision because we are His, and we are to glorify Him, regardless. Since we belong to Him and His Spirit lives in us, we are in good hands. We occupy, in fact, the best possible situation on earth.

"It is important to view every day from the spiritual perspective."

This means that words like "accidents" or "coincidences" should be removed from our vocabulary. Seriously! When events transpire that we cannot understand or explain, we are reminded that we are not our own. Rather than being upset, frustrated, or confused, we need to allow His Spirit to fill us with the divine fuel we need to serve Him and honor Him in those events—to glorify Him. ✦

says, *"shall become one flesh."*[a] 17But he
who is joined to the Lord is one spirit *with*
Him.
18Flee sexual immorality. Every sin that
a man does is outside the body, but he who
commits sexual immorality sins against his
own body. 19Or do you not know that your
body is the temple of the Holy Spirit *who is*
in you, whom you have from God, and
you are not your own? 20For you were
bought at a price; therefore glorify God in
your body[a] and in your spirit, which are
God's.

6:16 [a]Genesis 2:24 6:20 [a]NU-Text ends the verse at *body.*

CHAPTER 7

Principles of Marriage

Now concerning the things of which
you wrote to me:
It is good for a man not to touch a
woman. 2Nevertheless, because of sexual
immorality, let each man have his own
wife, and let each woman have her own
husband. 3Let the husband render to his
wife the affection due her, and likewise
also the wife to her husband. 4The wife
does not have authority over her own
body, but the husband *does*. And likewise
the husband does not have authority over

6:19 Because the Holy Spirit dwells inside believers, we should consider our bodies sanctuaries of God and, as such, keep them from sexual immorality.

his own body, but the wife *does*. [5]Do not de-
prive one another except with consent for a
time, that you may give yourselves to fast-
ing and prayer; and come together again
so that Satan does not tempt you because
of your lack of self-control. [6]But I say this
as a concession, not as a commandment.
[7]For I wish that all men were even as I my-
self. But each one has his own gift from
God, one in this manner and another in
that.

[8]But I say to the unmarried and to the
widows: It is good for them if they remain
even as I am; [9]but if they cannot exercise
self-control, let them marry. For it is better
to marry than to burn *with passion*.

Keep Your Marriage Vows

[10]Now to the married I command, *yet*
not I but the Lord: A wife is not to depart
from *her* husband. [11]But even if she does
depart, let her remain unmarried or be rec-
onciled to *her* husband. And a husband is
not to divorce *his* wife.

[12]But to the rest I, not the Lord, say: If
any brother has a wife who does not be-
lieve, and she is willing to live with him,
let him not divorce her. [13]And a woman
who has a husband who does not believe,
if he is willing to live with her, let her not
divorce him. [14]For the unbelieving hus-
band is sanctified by the wife, and the
unbelieving wife is sanctified by the hus-
band; otherwise your children would be
unclean, but now they are holy. [15]But if the
unbeliever departs, let him depart; a
brother or a sister is not under bondage in
such *cases*. But God has called us to peace.

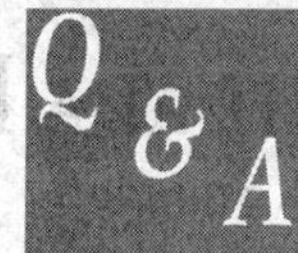

Is it all right to marry again after a divorce?

J. Vernon McGee

I believe the following scripture pertains to situations of this nature: "But if the unbeliever departs, let him depart; a brother or a sister is not under bondage in such cases. But God has called us to peace" (1 Cor. 7:15).

If the unbeliever walks out of the marriage, then the believer is free. Is one free to marry again? I believe that under certain circumstances, Paul would have given permission for that. I do not think one can put down a categorical rule either way for today. I think that each case stands or falls on its own merits. I am afraid this can easily be abused, even by Christians. I am afraid that sometimes a husband or a wife tries to get rid of the other and forces the spouse to leave in order to have a "scriptural ground" for divorce. In cases like this I always urge people to talk to their pastor who knows them personally and is familiar with the background of the previous marital relationship.

7:5 Neither partner has the right to refuse physical relations with the other unless such abstinence is by mutual agreement, for a limited time, based on spiritual, rather than selfish, reasons.

7:10, 12 but the Lord: Paul quotes a command given by Jesus when He was on earth (Mark 10:2–12). **not the Lord**: For this situation Paul did not have a command given by Jesus while He was on earth (see v. 25); therefore, he gives his own judgment which he believed was directed by the Holy Spirit (see v. 40).

7:14 sanctified . . . children . . . are holy: Unbelievers benefit from the blessings that God gives to their believing mates. These blessings include a witness to the unsaved marriage partner and to the children of God's reality.

16 For how do you know, O wife, whether
you will save *your* husband? Or how do
you know, O husband, whether you will
save *your* wife?

Live as You Are Called

17 But as God has distributed to each one,
as the Lord has called each one, so let him
walk. And so I ordain in all the churches.
18 Was anyone called while circumcised?
Let him not become uncircumcised. Was
anyone called while uncircumcised? Let
him not be circumcised. 19 Circumcision is
nothing and uncircumcision is nothing,
but keeping the commandments of God *is*
what matters. 20 Let each one remain in the
same calling in which he was called. 21 Were
you called *while* a slave? Do not be con-
cerned about it; but if you can be made
free, rather use *it*. 22 For he who is called in
the Lord *while* a slave is the Lord's freed-
man. Likewise he who is called *while* free is
Christ's slave. 23 You were bought at a price;
do not become slaves of men. 24 Brethren,
let each one remain with God in that *state*
in which he was called.

To the Unmarried and Widows

25 Now concerning virgins: I have no
commandment from the Lord; yet I give
judgment as one whom the Lord in His
mercy *has made* trustworthy. 26 I suppose
therefore that this is good because of the
present distress—that *it is* good for a man
to remain as he is: 27 Are you bound to a
wife? Do not seek to be loosed. Are you
loosed from a wife? Do not seek a wife.
28 But even if you do marry, you have not
sinned; and if a virgin marries, she has not
sinned. Nevertheless such will have trou-
ble in the flesh, but I would spare you.

29 But this I say, brethren, the time *is*
short, so that from now on even those who
have wives should be as though they had
none, 30 those who weep as though they did
not weep, those who rejoice as though they
did not rejoice, those who buy as though
they did not possess, 31 and those who use
this world as not misusing *it*. For the form
of this world is passing away.

32 But I want you to be without care. He
who is unmarried cares for the things of
the Lord—how he may please the Lord.
33 But he who is married cares about the
things of the world—how he may please
his wife. 34 There is[a] a difference between a
wife and a virgin. The unmarried woman
cares about the things of the Lord, that she
may be holy both in body and in spirit. But
she who is married cares about the things
of the world—how she may please *her* hus-
band. 35 And this I say for your own profit,
not that I may put a leash on you, but for
what is proper, and that you may serve the
Lord without distraction.

36 But if any man thinks he is behaving
improperly toward his virgin, if she is past
the flower of youth, and thus it must be, let
him do what he wishes. He does not sin; let
them marry. 37 Nevertheless he who stands
steadfast in his heart, having no necessity,
but has power over his own will, and has
so determined in his heart that he will keep
his virgin,[a] does well. 38 So then he who
gives *her*[a] in marriage does well, but he
who does not give *her* in marriage does
better.

39 A wife is bound by law as long as her
husband lives; but if her husband dies, she
is at liberty to be married to whom she
wishes, only in the Lord. 40 But she is hap-
pier if she remains as she is, according to
my judgment—and I think I also have the
Spirit of God.

CHAPTER 8

Be Sensitive to Conscience

Now concerning things offered to idols:
We know that we all have knowledge.
Knowledge puffs up, but love edifies.
2 And if anyone thinks that he knows any-
thing, he knows nothing yet as he ought to
know. 3 But if anyone loves God, this one is
known by Him.

4 Therefore concerning the eating of

7:34 [a]M-Text adds *also.* 7:37 [a]Or *virgin daughter*
7:38 [a]NU-Text reads *his own virgin.*

things offered to idols, we know that an idol *is* nothing in the world, and that *there is* no other God but one. [5]For even if there are so-called gods, whether in heaven or on earth (as there are many gods and many lords), [6]yet for us *there is* one God, the Father, of whom *are* all things, and we for Him; and one Lord Jesus Christ, through whom *are* all things, and through whom we *live.*

[7]However, *there is* not in everyone that knowledge; for some, with consciousness of the idol, until now eat *it* as a thing offered to an idol; and their conscience, being weak, is defiled. [8]But food does not commend us to God; for neither if we eat are we the better, nor if we do not eat are we the worse.

[9]But beware lest somehow this liberty of yours become a stumbling block to those who are weak. [10]For if anyone sees you who have knowledge eating in an idol's temple, will not the conscience of him who is weak be emboldened to eat those things offered to idols? [11]And because of your knowledge shall the weak brother perish, for whom Christ died? [12]But when you thus sin against the brethren, and wound their weak conscience, you sin against Christ. [13]Therefore, if food makes my brother stumble, I will never again eat meat, lest I make my brother stumble.

CHAPTER 9

A Pattern of Self-Denial

Am I not an apostle? Am I not free? Have I not seen Jesus Christ our Lord? Are you not my work in the Lord? [2]If I am not an apostle to others, yet doubtless I am to you. For you are the seal of my apostleship in the Lord.

[3]My defense to those who examine me is this: [4]Do we have no right to eat and drink? [5]Do we have no right to take along a believing wife, as *do* also the other apostles, the brothers of the Lord, and Cē'phas? [6]Or *is it* only Bar'na·bas and I *who* have no right to refrain from working? [7]Who ever goes to war at his own expense? Who plants a vineyard and does not eat of its fruit? Or who tends a flock and does not drink of the milk of the flock?

[8]Do I say these things as a *mere* man? Or does not the law say the same also? [9]For it is written in the law of Moses, *"You shall not muzzle an ox while it treads out the grain."*[a] Is it oxen God is concerned about? [10]Or does He say *it* altogether for our sakes? For our sakes, no doubt, *this* is written, that he who plows should plow in hope, and he who threshes in hope should be partaker of his hope. [11]If we have sown spiritual things for you, *is it* a great thing if we reap your material things? [12]If others are partakers of *this* right over you, *are* we not even more?

Nevertheless we have not used this right, but endure all things lest we hinder the gospel of Christ. [13]Do you not know that those who minister the holy things eat *of the things* of the temple, and those who serve at the altar partake of *the offerings of* the altar? [14]Even so the Lord has commanded that those who preach the gospel should live from the gospel.

[15]But I have used none of these things, nor have I written these things that it

9:9 [a]Deuteronomy 25:4

8:9 As Christians we have **liberty** in Christ; however, we must exercise our freedom in love, refraining from using it, if necessary, so that we do not become stumbling blocks for others.

9:5 brothers of the Lord: The children of Mary and Joseph. **Cephas** (see 1:12): Peter, whose wife's mother is mentioned in Mark 1:30.

9:13 Both Jewish and pagan priests received their living from offerings. God's plan is similar for Christian ministers.

should be done so to me; for it *would be* bet-
ter for me to die than that anyone should
make my boasting void. 16For if I preach
the gospel, I have nothing to boast of, for
necessity is laid upon me; yes, woe is me if
I do not preach the gospel! 17For if I do this
willingly, I have a reward; but if against
my will, I have been entrusted with a stew-
ardship. 18What is my reward then? That
when I preach the gospel, I may present
the gospel of Christ[a] without charge, that
I may not abuse my authority in the
gospel.

Serving All Men

19For though I am free from all *men,*
I have made myself a servant to all, that
I might win the more; 20and to the Jews I
became as a Jew, that I might win Jews; to
those *who are* under the law, as under the
law,[a] that I might win those *who are* under
the law; 21to those *who are* without law, as
without law (not being without law to-
ward God,[a] but under law toward Christ[b]),
that I might win those *who are* without law;
22to the weak I became as[a] weak, that I
might win the weak. I have become all
things to all *men,* that I might by all means
save some. 23Now this I do for the gospel's
sake, that I may be partaker of it with *you.*

Striving for a Crown

24Do you not know that those who run
in a race all run, but one receives the prize?
Run in such a way that you may obtain *it.*
25And everyone who competes *for the prize*
is temperate in all things. Now they *do it* to
obtain a perishable crown, but we *for* an
imperishable *crown.* 26Therefore I run thus:
not with uncertainty. Thus I fight: not as
one who beats the air. 27But I discipline my
body and bring *it* into subjection, lest,
when I have preached to others, I myself
should become disqualified.

CHAPTER 10

Old Testament Examples

Moreover, brethren, I do not want you
to be unaware that all our fathers were un-
der the cloud, all passed through the sea,
2all were baptized into Moses in the cloud
and in the sea, 3all ate the same spiritual
food, 4and all drank the same spiritual
drink. For they drank of that spiritual Rock
that followed them, and that Rock was
Christ. 5But with most of them God was
not well pleased, for *their bodies* were scat-
tered in the wilderness.

6Now these things became our exam-
ples, to the intent that we should not lust
after evil things as they also lusted. 7And
do not become idolaters as *were* some of
them. As it is written, *"The people sat
down to eat and drink, and rose up to
play."*[a] 8Nor let us commit sexual immoral-
ity, as some of them did, and in one day
twenty-three thousand fell; 9nor let us
tempt Christ, as some of them also
tempted, and were destroyed by serpents;
10nor complain, as some of them also com-
plained, and were destroyed by the

9:18 [a]NU-Text omits *of Christ.* 9:20 [a]NU-Text adds *though not being myself under the law.*
9:21 [a]NU-Text reads *God's law.* [b]NU-Text reads *Christ's law.* 9:22 [a]NU-Text omits *as.*
10:7 [a]Exodus 32:6

9:20, 21 To persuade the **Jews** of the gospel truth Paul joined them in observing the requirements and customs of the OT law. He thus placed himself **under the law** in such matters as circumcision (Acts 16:3), the Nazirite vow (Acts 18:18), and purification (Acts 21:24, 26). **those . . . without law**: Gentiles who did not observe the Jewish OT law. To evangelize the Gentiles Paul was willing to be **as without law**—to adopt their customs and culture. However, this process did not include disregard for God's law; Paul always remained under Christ's teachings.

9:27 disqualified: Paul is not talking about loss of salvation, but about losing his influence as a minister of the gospel.

10:7–10 The Israelites' basic sin was that they became **idolaters. sat down . . . rose up to play**: A description of their participation in idolatrous feasts.

Part of the Family

Lucibel Van Atta

The past puts into context who we are—and where we fit. It shows us where we have come from, and it shines a light on where we are going. Memories have security, but recalling and sorting out the past is difficult for youngsters. That's why God entrusts to grandparents the special privilege of preserving and nurturing a family's understanding of who they are.

I have chosen to write a monthly birthday letter during the first year of my nine grandchildren's lives. I include glimpses of his or her parent's early years, words about the meaning of Baby's name, a specific prayer, plus humorous anecdotes and insights. Although Grandbaby cannot read these letters for a few years, he or she can help parents and siblings see God's goodness in everyday events. ✦

destroyer. 11Now all[a] these things hap-
pened to them as examples, and they were
written for our admonition, upon whom
the ends of the ages have come.
12Therefore let him who thinks he stands
take heed lest he fall. 13No temptation has
overtaken you except such as is common
to man; but God *is* faithful, who will not al-
low you to be tempted beyond what you
are able, but with the temptation will also
make the way of escape, that you may be
able to bear *it*.

Flee from Idolatry

14Therefore, my beloved, flee from idol-
atry. 15I speak as to wise men; judge for
yourselves what I say. 16The cup of blessing
which we bless, is it not the communion of
the blood of Christ? The bread which we
break, is it not the communion of the body
of Christ? 17For we, *though* many, are one
bread *and* one body; for we all partake of
that one bread.
18Observe Israel after the flesh: Are not
those who eat of the sacrifices partakers of
the altar? 19What am I saying then? That an
idol is anything, or what is offered to idols
is anything? 20Rather, that the things which
the Gentiles sacrifice they sacrifice to
demons and not to God, and I do not want
you to have fellowship with demons. 21You
cannot drink the cup of the Lord and the
cup of demons; you cannot partake of the
Lord's table and of the table of demons.
22Or do we provoke the Lord to jealousy?
Are we stronger than He?

All to the Glory of God

23All things are lawful for me,[a] but not
all things are helpful; all things are lawful
for me,[b] but not all things edify. 24Let no
one seek his own, but each one the other's
well-being.
25Eat whatever is sold in the meat mar-
ket, asking no questions for conscience'
sake; 26for *"the earth is the* LORD*'s, and all
its fullness."*[a]

10:11 [a]NU-Text omits *all.* 10:23 [a]NU-Text omits *for me.* [b]NU-Text omits *for me.* 10:26 [a]Psalm 24:1

10:12, 13 Paul warns against confidence in one's own moral strength. Satan is most likely to attack where we least suspect it. We must anticipate temptation and rely on God's strength to guide us safely through.

10:23, 24 All things are lawful: A common statement among the Corinthians (see note on 6:12). Paul does not directly attack their position, but quotes a still higher principle: They should guide their conduct not merely by what is lawful, but by what will **edify** or build up another.

27If any of those who do not believe invites you *to dinner,* and you desire to go, eat whatever is set before you, asking no question for conscience' sake. 28But if anyone says to you, "This was offered to idols," do not eat it for the sake of the one who told you, and for conscience' sake;[a] for *"the earth is the LORD's, and all its fullness."*[b] 29"Conscience," I say, not your own, but that of the other. For why is my liberty judged by another *man's* conscience? 30But if I partake with thanks, why am I evil spoken of for *the food* over which I give thanks?

31Therefore, whether you eat or drink, or whatever you do, do all to the glory of God. 32Give no offense, either to the Jews or to the Greeks or to the church of God, 33just as I also please all *men* in all *things,* not seeking my own profit, but the *profit* of many, that they may be saved.

CHAPTER 11

Imitate me, just as I also *imitate* Christ.

Head Coverings

2Now I praise you, brethren, that you remember me in all things and keep the traditions just as I delivered *them* to you. 3But I want you to know that the head of every man is Christ, the head of woman *is* man, and the head of Christ *is* God. 4Every man praying or prophesying, having *his* head covered, dishonors his head. 5But every woman who prays or prophesies with *her* head uncovered dishonors her head, for that is one and the same as if her head were shaved. 6For if a woman is not covered, let her also be shorn. But if it is shameful for a woman to be shorn or shaved, let her be covered. 7For a man indeed ought not to cover *his* head, since he is the image and glory of God; but woman is the glory of man. 8For man is not from woman, but woman from man. 9Nor was man created for the woman, but woman for the man. 10For this reason the woman ought to have *a symbol of* authority on *her* head, because of the angels. 11Nevertheless, neither *is* man independent of woman, nor woman independent of man, in the Lord. 12For as woman *came* from man, even so man also *comes* through woman; but all things are from God.

13Judge among yourselves. Is it proper for a woman to pray to God with her head uncovered? 14Does not even nature itself teach you that if a man has long hair, it is a dishonor to him? 15But if a woman has long hair, it is a glory to her; for *her* hair is given to her[a] for a covering. 16But if anyone seems to be contentious, we have no such custom, nor *do* the churches of God.

Conduct at the Lord's Supper

17Now in giving these instructions I do not praise *you,* since you come together not for the better but for the worse. 18For first of all, when you come together as a church, I hear that there are divisions among you, and in part I believe it. 19For there must also be factions among you, that those who are approved may be recognized among you. 20Therefore when you come together in one place, it is not to eat the Lord's Supper. 21For in eating, each one takes his own supper ahead of *others;* and one is hungry

10:28 [a]NU-Text omits the rest of this verse. [b]Psalm 24:1 11:15 [a]M-Text omits *to her.*

10:27, 28 The Christian may eat whatever is put before him in a pagan household unless it appears to others that he is involved in idolatry. Then he should abstain so that he does not give them a wrong impression. Even so, Christians today are free to do things not forbidden by God's word, unless such actions would jeopardize their testimony. If a certain act would cause people to identify us with the world, then we should abstain.

11:6 In ancient Greece it was a shame for a woman to have her hair **shaved** or cut short because it made her look like a man. Paul argues that for a woman not to cover her head in public worship would have the same effect.

and another is drunk. 22What! Do you not have houses to eat and drink in? Or do you despise the church of God and shame those who have nothing? What shall I say to you? Shall I praise you in this? I do not praise *you.*

Institution of the Lord's Supper

23For I received from the Lord that which I also delivered to you: that the Lord Jesus on the *same* night in which He was betrayed took bread; 24and when He had given thanks, He broke *it* and said, "Take, eat;[a] this is My body which is broken[b] for you; do this in remembrance of Me." 25In the same manner *He* also *took* the cup after supper, saying, "This cup is the new covenant in My blood. This do, as often as you drink *it,* in remembrance of Me."

26For as often as you eat this bread and drink this cup, you proclaim the Lord's death till He comes.

Examine Yourself

27Therefore whoever eats this bread or drinks *this* cup of the Lord in an unworthy manner will be guilty of the body and blood[a] of the Lord. 28But let a man examine himself, and so let him eat of the bread and drink of the cup. 29For he who eats and drinks in an unworthy manner[a] eats and drinks judgment to himself, not discerning the Lord's[b] body. 30For this reason many *are* weak and sick among you, and many sleep. 31For if we would judge ourselves, we would not be judged. 32But when we are judged, we are chastened by the Lord, that we may not be condemned with the world.

33Therefore, my brethren, when you come together to eat, wait for one another. 34But if anyone is hungry, let him eat at home, lest you come together for judgment. And the rest I will set in order when I come.

CHAPTER 12

Spiritual Gifts: Unity in Diversity

Now concerning spiritual *gifts* brethren, I do not want you to be ignorant: 2You know that[a] you were Gentiles, carried away to these dumb idols, however you were led. 3Therefore I make known to you that no one speaking by the Spirit of God calls Jesus accursed, and no one can say that Jesus is Lord except by the Holy Spirit.

4There are diversities of gifts, but the same Spirit. 5There are differences of ministries, but the same Lord. 6And there are diversities of activities, but it is the same God who works all in all. 7But the manifestation of the Spirit is given to each one for the profit *of all:* 8for to one is given the word of wisdom through the Spirit, to another the word of knowledge through the same Spirit, 9to another faith by the same Spirit, to another gifts of healings by the same[a] Spirit, 10to another the working of miracles, to another prophecy, to another discerning of spirits, to another *different* kinds of tongues, to another the interpretation of tongues. 11But one and the same

11:24 [a]NU-Text omits *Take, eat.* [b]NU-Text omits *broken.* 11:27 [a]NU-Text and M-Text read *the blood.* 11:29 [a]NU-Text omits *in an unworthy manner.* [b]NU-Text omits *Lord's.* 12:2 [a]NU-Text and M-Text add *when.* 12:9 [a]NU-Text reads *one.*

11:24, 25 1 Corinthians was written before the Gospels; therefore, these are the earliest recorded words of Jesus. The Lord **broke** the bread as a symbol of His **body** broken on the Cross. Likewise, drinking of the **cup** represented participation in the **new covenant** foretold in Jer. 31:31–34 and now available through Christ's shed blood. See note on Heb. 8:8–10. **in remembrance**: By taking communion in faith, we experience the salvation for which it stands.

11:29 judgment: Not eternal damnation, but the corrective discipline of God. **not discerning**: Not understanding that all Christians are part of Christ's **body** through their faith in His death.

Spirit works all these things, distributing to each one individually as He wills.

Unity and Diversity in One Body

[12]For as the body is one and has many members, but all the members of that one body, being many, are one body, so also *is* Christ. [13]For by one Spirit we were all baptized into one body—whether Jews or Greeks, whether slaves or free—and have all been made to drink into[a] one Spirit. [14]For in fact the body is not one member but many.

[15]If the foot should say, "Because I am not a hand, I am not of the body," is it therefore not of the body? [16]And if the ear should say, "Because I am not an eye, I am not of the body," is it therefore not of the body? [17]If the whole body *were* an eye, where *would be* the hearing? If the whole *were* hearing, where *would be* the smelling? [18]But now God has set the members, each one of them, in the body just as He pleased. [19]And if they *were* all one member, where *would* the body *be?*

[20]But now indeed *there are* many members, yet one body. [21]And the eye cannot say to the hand, "I have no need of you"; nor again the head to the feet, "I have no need of you." [22]No, much rather, those members of the body which seem to be weaker are necessary. [23]And those *members* of the body which we think to be less honorable, on these we bestow greater honor; and our unpresentable *parts* have greater modesty, [24]but our presentable *parts* have no need. But God composed the body, hav-

12:13 [a]NU-Text omits *into.*

12:14–26 Evidently some Corinthians felt superior and were claiming the more spectacular gifts, such as speaking in tongues. Others felt inferior because their gifts were not so obvious. Paul uses the imagery of one **body** with many **members** to illustrate that all believers are dependent on one another.

12:24, 25 Since God has chosen the parts of the body that appear insignificant to accom-

Room to Grow

Ruth Ann Ridley

By the time we reach our mature years in marriage, most of us give each other *physical* space. We have learned through the years how much time our spouses need alone. And in these situations, we withdraw so our spouses can experience rest from the pressures of relating. We understand that their need for solitude is not rejecting us—that is just how God made them.

Psychological space means giving each other the same kind of latitude in the mental, emotional, and spiritual realms. We give others psychological space when we allow them to share their feelings and thoughts, refusing to fence them in with our personal preferences and solutions. Giving our spouses psychological space means being quiet when the other one shares. We let our partner's words flow and rise and turn and ebb. We attend to what she or he is saying, but we resist the temptation to expound our own views. Such acceptance is a priceless gift called love, the kind that gives another room to grow.✦

ing given greater honor to that *part* which
lacks it, [25]that there should be no schism in
the body, but *that* the members should
have the same care for one another. [26]And
if one member suffers, all the members suf-
fer with *it;* or if one member is honored, all
the members rejoice with *it.*

[27]Now you are the body of Christ, and
members individually. [28]And God has ap-
pointed these in the church: first apostles,
second prophets, third teachers, after that
miracles, then gifts of healings, helps, ad-
ministrations, varieties of tongues. [29]*Are* all
apostles? *Are* all prophets? *Are* all teach-
ers? *Are* all workers of miracles? [30]Do all
have gifts of healings? Do all speak with
tongues? Do all interpret? [31]But earnestly
desire the best[a] gifts. And yet I show you a
more excellent way.

CHAPTER 13

The Greatest Gift

Though I speak with the tongues of men
and of angels, but have not love, I have be-
come sounding brass or a clanging cymbal.
[2]And though I have *the gift of* prophecy,
and understand all mysteries and all
knowledge, and though I have all faith, so
that I could remove mountains, but have

12:31 [a]NU-Text reads *greater.*

plish some important purpose, we should show equal concern **for one another** in the Christian family, regardless of individual gifts.

13:1 the tongues of men and of angels: Paul exaggerates, "Even if I have some spiritual gift that enables me to speak the language of both earth and heaven, if I do not match my words with actions of love, I am just making noise." The **sounding brass** and **clanging cymbal** were familiar to the Corinthians who witnessed the use of gongs and cymbals in pagan worship.

Helping Your Hurting Children

Barbara Johnson

Sometimes parents endure ongoing pain, not because their kids have rebelled or rejected them, but because life has dealt their children a severe blow. For example, one of the most painful things parents can endure is to give a child in marriage and see that marriage disintegrate for any number of reasons.

When a grown child's marriage ends in divorce, parents can be supportive but not patronizing. The same principle about every child making his or her choices applies. Perhaps your son or daughter chose an individual you really didn't approve of. It will do no good now to criticize and say, "I told you so."

The best thing to do is back off and let your children live their own lives. You may be tempted to step in, take over, and start parenting again, but avoid that at all costs. Instead, try to give them lots of emotional support because their self-esteem is probably at an all-time low.

Remember that you walk a very fine line. You are needed—sometimes desperately—but you must wait to be invited. When your kids ask for your help or advice, you can give it. Always remember, however, Coleridge's words: "Advice is like snow, the softer it falls, . . . the deeper it sinks into the mind." ✦

not love, I am nothing. 3And though I be-
stow all my goods to feed *the poor,* and
though I give my body to be burned,[a] but
have not love, it profits me nothing.
4Love suffers long *and* is kind; love does
not envy; love does not parade itself, is not
puffed up; 5does not behave rudely, does
not seek its own, is not provoked, thinks
no evil; 6does not rejoice in iniquity, but re-
joices in the truth; 7bears all things, be-
lieves all things, hopes all things, endures
all things.
8Love never fails. But whether *there are*
prophecies, they will fail; whether *there*
are tongues, they will cease; whether *there is*
knowledge, it will vanish away. 9For we
know in part and we prophesy in part. 10But
when that which is perfect has come, then
that which is in part will be done away.
11When I was a child, I spoke as a child,
I understood as a child, I thought as a
child; but when I became a man, I put
away childish things. 12For now we see in a
mirror, dimly, but then face to face. Now I
know in part, but then I shall know just as
I also am known.
13And now abide faith, hope, love, these
three; but the greatest of these *is* love.

CHAPTER 14

Prophecy and Tongues

Pursue love, and desire spiritual *gifts,*
but especially that you may prophesy. 2For
he who speaks in a tongue does not speak
to men but to God, for no one understands
him; however, in the spirit he speaks mys-
teries. 3But he who prophesies speaks edifi-
cation and exhortation and comfort to men.
4He who speaks in a tongue edifies himself,
but he who prophesies edifies the church. 5I
wish you all spoke with tongues, but even
more that you prophesied; for[a] he who
prophesies *is* greater than he who speaks
with tongues, unless indeed he interprets,
that the church may receive edification.

Tongues Must Be Interpreted

6But now, brethren, if I come to you
speaking with tongues, what shall I profit
you unless I speak to you either by revela-
tion, by knowledge, by prophesying, or by
teaching? 7Even things without life,
whether flute or harp, when they make a
sound, unless they make a distinction in
the sounds, how will it be known what is
piped or played? 8For if the trumpet makes
an uncertain sound, who will prepare for
battle? 9So likewise you, unless you utter
by the tongue words easy to understand,
how will it be known what is spoken? For
you will be speaking into the air. 10There
are, it may be, so many kinds of languages
in the world, and none of them *is* without
significance. 11Therefore, if I do not know
the meaning of the language, I shall be a
foreigner to him who speaks, and he who
speaks *will be* a foreigner to me. 12Even so
you, since you are zealous for spiritual
gifts, let it be for the edification of the
church *that* you seek to excel.
13Therefore let him who speaks in a
tongue pray that he may interpret. 14For if I
pray in a tongue, my spirit prays, but my
understanding is unfruitful. 15What is *the*

13:3 [a]NU-Text reads *so I may boast.* 14:5 [a]NU-Text reads *and.*

13:9–11 when that which is perfect has come: In eternity there will be no more need for the gifts of prophecies, tongues, or knowledge (v. 8) to build up the body of Christ. **childish things**: These lesser virtues will be **put away**.

13:13 Spiritual gifts are of value only in this life and only as they are used to build up **faith**, **hope**, and **love**. These greater realities have eternal significance. Eventually faith will become sight (see 2 Cor. 5:7); hope will be fulfilled; however, love, the greatest of all, will remain unchanged.

14:15 with the spirit: The emotions. **with the understanding**: The mind grasping an understandable message and communicating it to the congregation (see v. 19). Christianity has never been an anti-intellectual religion. Jesus commanded us to love God with all our minds (see Matt. 22:37).

conclusion then? I will pray with the spirit, and I will also pray with the understanding. I will sing with the spirit, and I will also sing with the understanding. [16]Otherwise, if you bless with the spirit, how will he who occupies the place of the uninformed say "Amen" at your giving of thanks, since he does not understand what you say? [17]For you indeed give thanks well, but the other is not edified.

[18]I thank my God I speak with tongues more than you all; [19]yet in the church I would rather speak five words with my understanding, that I may teach others also, than ten thousand words in a tongue.

Tongues a Sign to Unbelievers

[20]Brethren, do not be children in understanding; however, in malice be babes, but in understanding be mature.

[21]In the law it is written:

"With men of other tongues and other lips
I will speak to this people;
And yet, for all that, they will not hear Me,"[a]

says the Lord.

[22]Therefore tongues are for a sign, not to those who believe but to unbelievers; but prophesying is not for unbelievers but for those who believe. [23]Therefore if the whole church comes together in one place, and all speak with tongues, and there come in *those who are* uninformed or unbelievers, will they not say that you are out of your mind? [24]But if all prophesy, and an unbeliever or an uninformed person comes in, he is convinced by all, he is convicted by all. [25]And thus[a] the secrets of his heart are revealed; and so, falling down on *his* face, he will worship God and report that God is truly among you.

Order in Church Meetings

[26]How is it then, brethren? Whenever you come together, each of you has a psalm, has a teaching, has a tongue, has a revelation, has an interpretation. Let all things be done for edification. [27]If anyone speaks in a tongue, *let there be* two or at the most three, *each* in turn, and let one interpret. [28]But if there is no interpreter, let him keep silent in church, and let him speak to himself and to God. [29]Let two or three prophets speak, and let the others judge. [30]But if *anything* is revealed to another who sits by, let the first keep silent. [31]For you can all prophesy one by one, that all may learn and all may be encouraged. [32]And the spirits of the prophets are subject to the prophets. [33]For God is not *the author* of confusion but of peace, as in all the churches of the saints.

[34]Let your[a] women keep silent in the churches, for they are not permitted to speak; but *they are* to be submissive, as the law also says. [35]And if they want to learn something, let them ask their own husbands at home; for it is shameful for women to speak in church.

I pray that when my grandchildren feel confused they will remember and understand that You, God, are not the author of confusion but of peace.

adapted from 1 Corinthians 14:33

14:21 [a]Isaiah 28:11, 12 14:25 [a]NU-Text omits *And thus.* 14:34 [a]NU-Text omits *your.*

14:32, 33 subject to the prophets: The gift of prophecy does not overpower the prophet so that he cannot control himself and wait his turn. God's design for Christian worship requires that procedures avoid confusion and contribute to peace.

36Or did the word of God come *originally*
from you? Or *was it* you only that it
reached? 37If anyone thinks himself to be a
prophet or spiritual, let him acknowledge
that the things which I write to you are the
commandments of the Lord. 38But if any-
one is ignorant, let him be ignorant. [a]

39Therefore, brethren, desire earnestly to
prophesy, and do not forbid to speak with
tongues. 40Let all things be done decently
and in order.

CHAPTER 15

The Risen Christ, Faith's Reality

Moreover, brethren, I declare to you the
gospel which I preached to you, which also
you received and in which you stand, 2by
which also you are saved, if you hold fast
that word which I preached to you—
unless you believed in vain.

3For I delivered to you first of all that
which I also received: that Christ died for
our sins according to the Scriptures, 4and
that He was buried, and that He rose again
the third day according to the Scriptures,
5and that He was seen by Cē'phas, then by
the twelve. 6After that He was seen by over
five hundred brethren at once, of whom
the greater part remain to the present, but
some have fallen asleep. 7After that He was
seen by James, then by all the apostles.
8Then last of all He was seen by me also, as
by one born out of due time.

9For I am the least of the apostles, who
am not worthy to be called an apostle, be-
cause I persecuted the church of God. 10But
by the grace of God I am what I am, and
His grace toward me was not in vain; but I
labored more abundantly than they all, yet
not I, but the grace of God *which was* with
me. 11Therefore, whether *it was* I or they, so
we preach and so you believed.

The Risen Christ, Our Hope

12Now if Christ is preached that He has
been raised from the dead, how do some
among you say that there is no resurrection
of the dead? 13But if there is no resurrection
of the dead, then Christ is not risen. 14And
if Christ is not risen, then our preaching *is*
empty and your faith *is* also empty. 15Yes,
and we are found false witnesses of God,
because we have testified of God that He
raised up Christ, whom He did not raise
up—if in fact the dead do not rise. 16For if
the dead do not rise, then Christ is not
risen. 17And if Christ is not risen, your faith
is futile; you are still in your sins! 18Then
also those who have fallen asleep in Christ
have perished. 19If in this life only we have
hope in Christ, we are of all men the most
pitiable.

The Last Enemy Destroyed

20But now Christ is risen from the dead,
and has become the firstfruits of those who
have fallen asleep. 21For since by man *came*
death, by Man also *came* the resurrection of
the dead. 22For as in Adam all die, even so
in Christ all shall be made alive. 23But each
one in his own order: Christ the firstfruits,
afterward those *who are* Christ's at His
coming. 24Then *comes* the end, when He de-
livers the kingdom to God the Father,

14:38 [a]NU-Text reads *if anyone does not recognize this, he is not recognized.*

15:5–8 A list of witnesses to the reality of Christ's resurrection. **the twelve**: Jesus' first group of disciples, reduced to 11 by the death of Judas, was restored to 12 by the addition of Matthias (see Acts 1:15–26). **the greater part remain**: Most of the 500 to whom Jesus appeared were still alive when Paul wrote this letter about A.D. 55. **James**: Perhaps the half brother of Jesus (see Matt. 13:55; Acts 1:14). **out of due time**: The risen Jesus did not appear to Paul until after the Ascension.

15:12–19 The resurrection of Christ is an essential tenet of the Christian faith. If a literal, physical resurrection had not taken place, the entire gospel would be false.

15:20 As surely as the sheaf of the **firstfruits** was followed by the whole harvest (see Lev. 23:10, 11), Christ's resurrection guarantees the resurrection of all who follow Him.

Facing the Future

Joni Eareckson Tada

Less than a year after my father's passing, I signed a durable power of attorney for health care and designated my husband, Ken, as my health-care proxy. I shared very specifically my wishes with him because as a quadriplegic I have outlived statistics. I have some views as to how "extraordinary" I would want measures taken on my behalf. We have had to talk very specifically about what "till death do us part" really means.

It is very complicated. How do you approach death and not make it a worse evil than it is? How do you honor God's name and Scripture and still do what is best for this person you love? We want to know what is right and wrong, black and white. But the Bible does not deal with death this way.

My situation is unique, but so is every situation. Most of us will have to face this with a loved one, so we should discuss this with each other. ✦

when He puts an end to all rule and all au-
thority and power. 25For He must reign till
He has put all enemies under His feet.
26The last enemy *that* will be destroyed *is*
death. 27For *"He has put all things under
His feet."*[a] But when He says "all things
are put under *Him,"* *it is* evident that
He who put all things under Him is
excepted. 28Now when all things are made
subject to Him, then the Son Himself
will also be subject to Him who put all
things under Him, that God may be all in
all.

Effects of Denying the Resurrection

29Otherwise, what will they do who are
baptized for the dead, if the dead do not
rise at all? Why then are they baptized for
the dead? 30And why do we stand in jeop-
ardy every hour? 31I affirm, by the boasting
in you which I have in Christ Jesus our
Lord, I die daily. 32If, in the manner of men,
I have fought with beasts at Eph'e·sus,
what advantage *is it* to me? If *the* dead do
not rise, *"Let us eat and drink, for tomor-
row we die!"*[a]
33Do not be deceived: "Evil company
corrupts good habits." 34Awake to righ-
teousness, and do not sin; for some do not
have the knowledge of God. I speak *this* to
your shame.

A Glorious Body

35But someone will say, "How are the
dead raised up? And with what body do
they come?" 36Foolish one, what you sow is
not made alive unless it dies. 37And what
you sow, you do not sow that body that

15:27 [a]Psalm 8:6 15:32 [a]Isaiah 22:13

15:33, 34 This quotation from the Greek poet Menander had probably become a popular saying. Paul is warning the Corinthians to avoid the **evil company** of those who denied the resurrection. **do not sin**: Paul would not ask his readers to live up to a standard that he knew was impossible. The standard for God's people is a life without sin (see 1 John 2:1).

shall be, but mere grain—perhaps wheat
or some other *grain.* 38But God gives it a
body as He pleases, and to each seed its
own body.
39All flesh *is* not the same flesh, but *there*
is one *kind of* flesh[a] of men, another flesh of
animals, another of fish, *and* another of
birds.
40*There are* also celestial bodies and ter-
restrial bodies; but the glory of the celestial
is one, and the *glory* of the terrestrial *is* an-
other. 41*There is* one glory of the sun, an-
other glory of the moon, and another glory
of the stars; for *one* star differs from *another*
star in glory.
42So also *is* the resurrection of the dead.
The body is sown in corruption, it is raised
in incorruption. 43It is sown in dishonor, it
is raised in glory. It is sown in weakness, it
is raised in power. 44It is sown a natural
body, it is raised a spiritual body. There is a
natural body, and there is a spiritual body.
45And so it is written, *"The first man Adam*
became a living being."[a] The last Adam *be-*
came a life-giving spirit.
46However, the spiritual is not first, but
the natural, and afterward the spiritual.
47The first man *was* of the earth, *made* of
dust; the second Man *is* the Lord[a] from
heaven. 48As *was* the *man* of dust, so also *are*
those *who are* made of dust; and as *is* the
heavenly *Man,* so also *are* those *who are*
heavenly. 49And as we have borne the im-
age of the *man* of dust, we shall also bear[a]
the image of the heavenly *Man.*

Our Final Victory

50Now this I say, brethren, that flesh and
blood cannot inherit the kingdom of God;
nor does corruption inherit incorruption.
51Behold, I tell you a mystery: We shall not
all sleep, but we shall all be changed— 52in
a moment, in the twinkling of an eye, at the
last trumpet. For the trumpet will sound,
and the dead will be raised incorruptible,
and we shall be changed. 53For this cor-
ruptible must put on incorruption, and this
mortal *must* put on immortality. 54So when
this corruptible has put on incorruption,
and this mortal has put on immortality,
then shall be brought to pass the saying
that is written: *"Death is swallowed up in*
victory."[a]

55 *"O Death, where is your sting?*[a]
O Hā'dēs, where is your victory?"[b]

56The sting of death *is* sin, and the strength
of sin *is* the law. 57But thanks *be* to God,
who gives us the victory through our Lord
Jesus Christ.
58Therefore, my beloved brethren, be
steadfast, immovable, always abounding
in the work of the Lord, knowing that your
labor is not in vain in the Lord.

CHAPTER 16

Collection for the Saints

Now concerning the collection for the
saints, as I have given orders to the
churches of Galatia, so you must do also:
2On the first *day* of the week let each one of
you lay something aside, storing up as he
may prosper, that there be no collections
when I come. 3And when I come, whom-
ever you approve by *your* letters I will send

15:39 [a]NU-Text and M-Text omit *of flesh.*
15:45 [a]Genesis 2:7 15:47 [a]NU-Text omits *the Lord.*
15:49 [a]M-Text reads *let us also bear.* 15:54 [a]Isaiah 25:8 15:55 [a]Hosea 13:14 [b]NU-Text reads *O Death, where is your victory? O Death, where is your sting?*

15:51 a mystery: God's plan not previously understood. Some Christians will be alive when Christ comes; they will be given resurrection bodies without dying. Both the living and those already dead will **be changed** to immortality.

16:2 Note that Paul assumes that the Corinthian church was meeting on Sundays. Christians set aside the first day of the week for worship to mark the day of Christ's victory over the grave. This change creates a clear distinction between Judaism and Christianity (see also Acts 20:7).

to bear your gift to Jerusalem. 4But if it is
fitting that I go also, they will go with me.

Personal Plans

5Now I will come to you when I pass
through Mac·e·dō'ni·a (for I am passing
through Mac·e·dō'ni·a). 6And it may be
that I will remain, or even spend the winter
with you, that you may send me on my
journey, wherever I go. 7For I do not wish
to see you now on the way; but I hope to
stay a while with you, if the Lord permits.
8But I will tarry in Eph'e·sus until Pente-
cost. 9For a great and effective door has
opened to me, and *there are* many adver-
saries.
10And if Timothy comes, see that he may
be with you without fear; for he does the
work of the Lord, as I also *do.* 11Therefore
let no one despise him. But send him on his
journey in peace, that he may come to me;
for I am waiting for him with the brethren.
12Now concerning *our* brother A·pol'los,
I strongly urged him to come to you with
the brethren, but he was quite unwilling to
come at this time; however, he will come
when he has a convenient time.

Final Exhortations

13Watch, stand fast in the faith, be brave,
be strong. 14Let all *that* you *do* be done with
love.

> ***I pray that my child will watch, stand fast in the faith, and be brave and strong.***
>
> *adapted from* 1 Corinthians 16:13

> To go against one's conscience is neither safe nor right. Here I stand. I cannot do otherwise.
>
> Martin Luther

15I urge you, brethren—you know the
household of Steph'a·nas, that it is the
firstfruits of A·chā'i·a, and *that* they have
devoted themselves to the ministry of the
saints— 16that you also submit to such, and
to everyone who works and labors with *us.*
17I am glad about the coming of Steph'-
a·nas, For·tu·nā'tus, and A·chā'i·cus, for
what was lacking on your part they sup-
plied. 18For they refreshed my spirit and
yours. Therefore acknowledge such men.

Greetings and a Solemn Farewell

19The churches of Asia greet you.
A·qui'la and Pri·scil'la greet you heartily
in the Lord, with the church that is in their
house. 20All the brethren greet you.
Greet one another with a holy kiss.
21The salutation with my own hand—
Paul's.
22If anyone does not love the Lord Jesus
Christ, let him be accursed.[a] O Lord,
come![b]
23The grace of our Lord Jesus Christ *be*
with you. 24My love *be* with you all in
Christ Jesus. Amen.

16:22 [a]Greek *anathema* [b]Aramaic *Maranatha*

✦2 Corinthians✦

While Paul was ministering in Ephesus, Timothy brought word from Corinth that Paul's first letter had not resolved the problems addressed or united the factions. Furthermore, Paul learned that opposition to his apostolic authority was being preached in some of the congregations. In response, Paul went to Corinth to confront personally this false teaching. Returning to Ephesus after a brief and painful visit, Paul wrote a sorrowful letter to urge the church to discipline the leader of the opposition. Titus carried this letter to Corinth, and Paul journeyed to Macedonia to await Titus's word of the results.

Paul was elated by Titus's report that the majority of Corinthians had repented; however, a minority opposition still persisted in denying that Paul was a genuine apostle. With this word of mixed response, Paul wrote 2 Corinthians with a dual purpose—rejoicing over the good news of reconciliation with the majority of believers and defending his apostolic credentials and authority with his detractors. He told the church that throughout their trials, Christian brotherhood must be at the heart of their faith and relationships. Dissension within the church always hinders the work of God, and like the Corinthian Christians, we need to strive for unity.

Christ is presented as the believer's comfort (1:5), triumph (2:14), Lord (4:5), light (4:6), judge (5:10), reconciliation (5:19), substitute (5:21), gift (9:15), owner (10:7), and power (12:9). ✦

CHAPTER 1

Greeting

Paul, an apostle of Jesus Christ by the will of God, and Timothy *our* brother,

To the church of God which is at Corinth, with all the saints who are in all A·chā'i·a:

2Grace to you and peace from God our Father and the Lord Jesus Christ.

Comfort in Suffering

3Blessed *be* the God and Father of our
Lord Jesus Christ, the Father of mercies
and God of all comfort, 4who comforts us
in all our tribulation, that we may be able
to comfort those who are in any trouble,
with the comfort with which we ourselves
are comforted by God. 5For as the suffer-
ings of Christ abound in us, so our consola-
tion also abounds through Christ. 6Now if
we are afflicted, *it is* for your consolation
and salvation, which is effective for endur-

1:1 an apostle: sent one. A major purpose of this letter is to affirm Paul's authority as an apostle. He wants his readers to realize that he represents the Lord Jesus and is following the will of God.

1:4 Paul explains one reason Christians suffer. While it may be difficult to comprehend during a trial, we can often look back and see how our suffering has enabled us to help others.

HE STILL HOLDS THE WORLD IN HIS HANDS

Claire Cloninger

Many Christians are reluctant to acknowledge any connection between God and suffering. Some see Satan as the only cause for the hard times we all go through. Others blame every difficulty in this life on the fact that we are members of a fallen creation whose rebellion has inflicted suffering on the world.

I believe that these views are interrelated and that both are true. Satan does cause suffering. Scripture describes him as a thief, a liar, and a destroyer, and we are encouraged to learn to do battle with him, wearing the whole armor of God (see Eph. 6:10–18).

It is also true that tremendous suffering has resulted from humankind's choice to follow Satan into rebellion against God's way. The world is reaping the *natural consequences* of man's fallen condition—in the wars that rage among nations, in the breakdown of the family, in the appalling spread of sexually transmitted diseases.

"Whatever happens in His universe has happened with God's knowledge and permission."

But I believe it is important for us Christians to know that regardless of where suffering originates, God is now, has always been, and always will be in control of His universe. Satan has not "pulled any fast ones" on the King of kings and Lord of lords. Sinful mankind has not managed to foil heaven's best intentions while some powerless deity was catching a catnap! God is sovereign! He is God! Whatever happens in His universe has happened with God's knowledge and permission. And this includes suffering. ✦

ing the same sufferings which we also suffer. Or if we are comforted, *it is* for your consolation and salvation.
7And our hope for you *is* steadfast, because we know that as you are partakers of the sufferings, so also *you will partake* of the consolation.

Delivered from Suffering

8For we do not want you to be ignorant, brethren, of our trouble which came to us in Asia: that we were burdened beyond measure, above strength, so that we despaired even of life.
9Yes, we had the sentence of death in ourselves, that we should not trust in ourselves but in God who raises the dead,
10who delivered us from so great a death, and does[a] deliver us; in whom we trust that He will still deliver *us,*
11you also helping together in prayer for

1:10 [a]NU-Text reads *shall.*

1:8–10 We do not know why Paul **despaired**. The threat was so great that no helper was sufficient except the **God who raises the dead**.

Coping with Divorce
Jay Kesler

When they have been victimized by divorce, grandchildren are confused and hurt and often filled with anger, resentment, and guilt that they really don't understand. The role of the grandparent at this time is providing a fair, objective listening ear and a place of security, faith, and love. A compassionate grandparent who is willing to let the child talk performs a necessary function. Wise grandparents are careful not to take sides, even on the side of their own child against the other parent. ✦

us, that thanks may be given by many persons on our[a] behalf for the gift *granted* to us through many.

Paul's Sincerity

12For our boasting is this: the testimony of our conscience that we conducted ourselves in the world in simplicity and godly sincerity, not with fleshly wisdom but by the grace of God, and more abundantly toward you. 13For we are not writing any other things to you than what you read or understand. Now I trust you will understand, even to the end 14(as also you have understood us in part), that we are your boast as you also *are* ours, in the day of the Lord Jesus.

Sparing the Church

15And in this confidence I intended to come to you before, that you might have a

second benefit— 16to pass by way of you to Mac·e·dō′ni·a, to come again from Mac·e·dō′ni·a to you, and be helped by you on my way to Judea. 17Therefore, when I was planning this, did I do it lightly? Or the things I plan, do I plan according to the flesh, that with me there should be Yes, Yes, and No, No? 18But *as* God *is* faithful, our word to you was not Yes and No. 19For the Son of God, Jesus Christ, who was preached among you by us—by me, Sil-vā′nus, and Timothy—was not Yes and No, but in Him was Yes. 20For all the promises of God in Him *are* Yes, and in Him Amen, to the glory of God through us. 21Now He who establishes us with you in Christ and has anointed us *is* God, 22who also has sealed us and given us the Spirit in our hearts as a guarantee.

23Moreover I call God as witness against my soul, that to spare you I came no more to Corinth. 24Not that we have dominion over your faith, but are fellow workers for your joy; for by faith you stand.

CHAPTER 2

But I determined this within myself, that I would not come again to you in sorrow. 2For if I make you sorrowful, then who is he who makes me glad but the one who is made sorrowful by me?

Forgive the Offender

3And I wrote this very thing to you, lest, when I came, I should have sorrow over those from whom I ought to have joy, having confidence in you all that my joy is *the joy* of you all. 4For out of much affliction and anguish of heart I wrote to you, with many tears, not that you should be grieved, but that you might know the love which I have so abundantly for you.

5But if anyone has caused grief, he has not grieved me, but all of you to some extent—not to be too severe. 6This

1:11 [a]M-Text reads *your behalf.*

1:22 sealed us: marked us as belonging to Him.

punishment which *was inflicted* by the ma-
jority *is* sufficient for such a man, 7so that,
on the contrary, you *ought* rather to forgive
and comfort *him,* lest perhaps such a one
be swallowed up with too much sorrow.
8Therefore I urge you to reaffirm *your* love
to him. 9For to this end I also wrote, that I
might put you to the test, whether you are
obedient in all things. 10Now whom you
forgive anything, I also *forgive.* For if in-
deed I have forgiven anything, I have for-
given that one[a] for your sakes in the pres-
ence of Christ, 11lest Satan should take
advantage of us; for we are not ignorant of
his devices.

Triumph in Christ

12Furthermore, when I came to Trō′as to
preach Christ's gospel, and a door was
opened to me by the Lord, 13I had no rest in
my spirit, because I did not find Titus my
brother; but taking my leave of them, I de-
parted for Mac·e·dō′ni·a.
14Now thanks *be* to God who always
leads us in triumph in Christ, and through
us diffuses the fragrance of His knowledge
in every place. 15For we are to God the fra-
grance of Christ among those who are be-
ing saved and among those who are per-
ishing. 16To the one *we are* the aroma of
death *leading* to death, and to the other the
aroma of life *leading* to life. And who *is* suf-
ficient for these things? 17For we are not, as
so many,[a] peddling the word of God; but as
of sincerity, but as from God, we speak in
the sight of God in Christ.

CHAPTER 3

Christ's Epistle

Do we begin again to commend our-
selves? Or do we need, as some *others,*
epistles of commendation to you or *letters*
of commendation from you? 2You are our
epistle written in our hearts, known and
read by all men; 3clearly *you are* an epistle
of Christ, ministered by us, written not
with ink but by the Spirit of the living God,
not on tablets of stone but on tablets of
flesh, *that is,* of the heart.

The Spirit, Not the Letter

4And we have such trust through Christ
toward God. 5Not that we are sufficient of
ourselves to think of anything as *being*
from ourselves, but our sufficiency *is* from
God, 6who also made us sufficient as min-
isters of the new covenant, not of the letter
but of the Spirit;[a] for the letter kills, but the
Spirit gives life.

Glory of the New Covenant

7But if the ministry of death, written *and*
engraved on stones, was glorious, so that
the children of Israel could not look
steadily at the face of Moses because of the
glory of his countenance, which *glory* was
passing away, 8how will the ministry of the
Spirit not be more glorious? 9For if the min-
istry of condemnation *had* glory, the min-

2:10 [a]NU-Text reads *For indeed, what I have forgiven, if I have forgiven anything, I did it.* 2:17 [a]M-Text reads *the rest.* 3:6 [a]Or *spirit*

2:10, 11 I also forgive: How important it is for Christians to forgive. If we do not forgive a penitent backslider, **Satan** will **take advantage** of that person by suggesting he is beyond forgiveness. He will also take advantage of our unforgiving spirit to separate us from Christ.

2:14 triumph in Christ: Paul pictures the spread of the gospel as a parade of victory. The message of Christ is likened to the **fragrance** of incense diffused everywhere as a result of preaching. For the unsaved the gospel is an aroma of death, but for believers it is the aroma of life.

2:16 sufficient: worthy or capable.

3:5, 6 our sufficiency: It was not Paul who changed the lives of the Corinthians. He had been made **sufficient** for this life-changing ministry only by the power of God. **The new covenant**: foretold by Jeremiah (see Jer. 31:31–34) involves the work of the Holy Spirit. The **letter** of the Law of Moses **kills** because it only shows our failures. The Holy **Spirit gives life** by making us like Christ (see v. 18; John 16:13–15).

istry of righteousness exceeds much more in glory. [10]For even what was made glorious had no glory in this respect, because of the glory that excels. [11]For if what is passing away *was* glorious, what remains *is* much more glorious.

[12]Therefore, since we have such hope, we use great boldness of speech— [13]unlike Moses, *who* put a veil over his face so that the children of Israel could not look steadily at the end of what was passing away. [14]But their minds were blinded. For until this day the same veil remains unlifted in the reading of the Old Testament, because the *veil* is taken away in Christ. [15]But even to this day, when Moses is read, a veil lies on their heart. [16]Nevertheless when one turns to the Lord, the veil is taken away. [17]Now the Lord is the Spirit; and where the Spirit of the Lord *is,* there *is* liberty. [18]But we all, with unveiled face, beholding as in a mirror the glory of the Lord, are being transformed into the same image from glory to glory, just as by the Spirit of the Lord.

CHAPTER 4

The Light of Christ's Gospel

Therefore, since we have this ministry, as we have received mercy, we do not lose heart. [2]But we have renounced the hidden things of shame, not walking in craftiness nor handling the word of God deceitfully, but by manifestation of the truth commending ourselves to every man's conscience in the sight of God. [3]But even if our gospel is veiled, it is veiled to those who are perishing, [4]whose minds the god of this age has blinded, who do not believe, lest the light of the gospel of the glory of Christ, who is the image of God, should shine on them. [5]For we do not preach ourselves, but Christ Jesus the Lord, and ourselves your bondservants for Jesus' sake. [6]For it is the God who commanded light to shine out of darkness, who has shone in our hearts to *give* the light of the knowledge of the glory of God in the face of Jesus Christ.

Cast Down but Unconquered

[7]But we have this treasure in earthen vessels, that the excellence of the power may be of God and not of us. [8]*We are* hard-pressed on every side, yet not crushed; *we are* perplexed, but not in despair; [9]persecuted, but not forsaken; struck down, but not destroyed— [10]always carrying about in the body the dying of the Lord Jesus, that the life of Jesus also may be manifested in our body. [11]For we who live are always delivered to death for Jesus' sake, that the life of Jesus also may be manifested in our mortal flesh. [12]So then death is working in us, but life in you.

[13]And since we have the same spirit of faith, according to what is written, *"I believed and therefore I spoke,"*[a] we also believe and therefore speak, [14]knowing that He who raised up the Lord Jesus will also raise us up with Jesus, and will present *us* with you. [15]For all things *are* for your sakes, that grace, having spread through the many, may cause thanksgiving to abound to the glory of God.

4:13 [a]Psalm 116:10

3:18 When we turn in repentance and faith to look at Christ through the mirror of God's word, we are gloriously **transformed** more and more fully into His **image** by the Holy **Spirit**. Although we are saved once and for all, we are continually in the process of growing more like Christ. This transformation will not be complete in this world.

4:4 the god of this age: Satan.

4:7–9 This treasure is God's transcendent power. Paul emphasizes the weakness of our humanity by comparing Christians to common clay pots. The commonness of the vessel reveals the **excellence** of the **power**. Because God's power is at work in us, we may suffer, but we need never be **crushed** or **destroyed**. Common trials can bring uncommon grace.

Models of the Faith

Dr. Randy Reese

The secret to growing older gracefully is to allow others to minister to you—physically, emotionally, and spiritually. Every individual longs to be loved and accepted. As they approach retirement, most individuals have given much of their time, effort, and energy to lovingly supporting their children, church, and community. They still have much to give others, but it is now time for them to receive support from others.

Daily, we make choices that can help or hinder our ability to grow older gracefully and continue to bear fruit. What's more, we can invest our remaining years in personal spiritual growth, sharing our relationship with Christ with the generations that follow—those children and grandchildren who look to us as models of the faith.

As you grow older, heed the admonition of the apostle Paul: "Therefore we do not lose heart. Even though our outward man is perishing, yet the inward man is being renewed day by day. For our light affliction, which is but for a moment, is working for us a far more exceeding and eternal weight of glory, while we do not look at the things which are seen, but at the things which are not seen. For the things which are seen are temporary, but the things which are not seen are eternal" (2 Cor. 4:16–18). ✦

Seeing the Invisible

16Therefore we do not lose heart. Even
though our outward man is perishing, yet
the inward *man* is being renewed day by
day. 17For our light affliction, which is but
for a moment, is working for us a far more
exceeding *and* eternal weight of glory,
18while we do not look at the things which
are seen, but at the things which are not
seen. For the things which are seen *are* temporary, but the things which are not seen
are eternal.

CHAPTER 5

Assurance of the Resurrection

For we know that if our earthly house,
this tent, is destroyed, we have a building
from God, a house not made with hands,
eternal in the heavens. 2For in this we
groan, earnestly desiring to be clothed
with our habitation which is from heaven,
3if indeed, having been clothed, we shall
not be found naked. 4For we who are in *this*
tent groan, being burdened, not because
we want to be unclothed, but further
clothed, that mortality may be swallowed
up by life. 5Now He who has prepared us
for this very thing *is* God, who also has
given us the Spirit as a guarantee.
6So *we are* always confident, knowing
that while we are at home in the body we
are absent from the Lord. 7For we walk by
faith, not by sight. 8We are confident, yes,

4:16 outward man . . . inward man: As a human being Paul was subject to progressive physical decay and, finally, death. But as a new person in Christ his spiritual life became stronger daily.

4:18 We must view the temporary events of this world in light of eternity. Such an outlook precludes materialism and helps us through present trials.

Trivial Pursuits

Jay Kesler

Grandparents have a wonderful opportunity to watch their grandchildren grow, to remember how important the small things are and provide affirmation, encouragement, and support when doubt and rejection inevitably creep in. In our youth we all struggled with acceptance in our peer groups. Nothing has changed. All of us need friends and will do almost anything to have one.

Children are usually proud of their grandparents and want to show us off. A willingness to show interest in them is important in making grandchildren want to be around us. Sometimes kids will show up with strange clothes, haircuts, and earrings. We don't need to panic; these are simply the fads of their generation.

A wise grandparent is able to separate the trivial from the serious. ✦

well pleased rather to be absent from the body and to be present with the Lord.

The Judgment Seat of Christ

9Therefore we make it our aim, whether
present or absent, to be well pleasing to
Him. 10For we must all appear before the
judgment seat of Christ, that each one may
receive the things *done* in the body, according to what he has done, whether good or
bad. 11Knowing, therefore, the terror of the
Lord, we persuade men; but we are well

I pray that my children will walk by faith, not by sight.

adapted from 2 Corinthians 5:7

known to God, and I also trust are well known in your consciences.

Be Reconciled to God

12For we do not commend ourselves
again to you, but give you opportunity to boast on our behalf, that you may have *an answer* for those who boast in appearance
and not in heart. 13For if we are beside ourselves, *it is* for God; or if we are of sound
mind, *it is* for you. 14For the love of Christ
compels us, because we judge thus: that if
One died for all, then all died; 15and He
died for all, that those who live should live no longer for themselves, but for Him who died for them and rose again.

16Therefore, from now on, we regard no
one according to the flesh. Even though we have known Christ according to the flesh,
yet now we know *Him thus* no longer.
17Therefore, if anyone *is* in Christ, *he is* a new creation; old things have passed away; behold, all things have become new.
18Now all things *are* of God, who has reconciled us to Himself through Jesus Christ, and has given us the ministry of reconcilia-
tion, 19that is, that God was in Christ reconciling the world to Himself, not imputing their trespasses to them, and has committed to us the word of reconciliation.

20Now then, we are ambassadors for
Christ, as though God were pleading through us: we implore *you* on Christ's be-
half, be reconciled to God. 21For He made
Him who knew no sin *to be* sin for us, that we might become the righteousness of God in Him.

✦

5:9, 10 Paul's aim, to be **well pleasing** to Christ, has judgment-day seriousness. The Christian's reward will be according to **things done in the body**. Faith must lead to a changed life. Who we shall be depends on the life we now live (see 1 Cor. 3:12–15).

Ambassador for Christ

George Barna

As an "ambassador for Christ" (2 Cor. 5:20), how consciously and conscientiously do you model His values, His purposes, and His heart to a skeptical but observing world? Most committed Christians fail to consistently view themselves as His representatives. Perhaps recognizing that we are called to be His reflection in this world—and that the world watches us more closely than we may realize—will better enable us to shape our thinking and behavior to conform to His calling on our lives.

If we take on a more Christlike demeanor in all aspects of our existence, perhaps the tendency to embrace situational ethics would be replaced by a biblical standard for decision making. The evidence must be clear that our society has fallen prey to serious ethical and moral decline at least partially because of the absence of a sense of the proper foundation for ethical choices.

Are you prepared to integrate Scripture into the decisions you make every day, backing your choices with a logical, defensible, biblical understanding of the choice that Christ would have made in that same situation? Making decisions on the basis of what is easy (the path of least resistance), what is socially acceptable or in vogue (the path of cultural relativism), or as a result of a snap judgment (the path of emotional inertia), rarely results in sound choices. ✦

CHAPTER 6

Marks of the Ministry

We then, *as* workers together *with Him* also plead with *you* not to receive the grace of God in vain. [2]For He says:

"In an acceptable time I have heard you,
And in the day of salvation I have helped you."[a]

Behold, now *is* the accepted time; behold, now *is* the day of salvation.

[3]We give no offense in anything, that our ministry may not be blamed. [4]But in all *things* we commend ourselves as ministers of God: in much patience, in tribulations, in needs, in distresses, [5]in stripes, in imprisonments, in tumults, in labors, in sleeplessness, in fastings; [6]by purity, by

6:2 [a]Isaiah 49:8

6:4–10 Paul describes his apostolic labors, all of which recommend him as a faithful minister of God seeking to serve others, not himself. Verses 4, 5 depict the sufferings he had endured. **Labors**, **sleeplessness**, and **fastings** represent self-imposed disciplines that would allow him to devote more time to his ministry. Verses 6, 7 describe his moral character: **purity**, **kindness** and **love** result from the riches received through Christ. Each pair of words in vv. 8–10 contrasts the way the world looks at Paul's ministry with the way God looks at it. In the eyes of the world he receives **dishonor**; but from God, **honor**. The world thinks he is **nothing**, but in God he has all that matters.

knowledge, by longsuffering, by kindness, by the Holy Spirit, by sincere love, 7by the word of truth, by the power of God, by the armor of righteousness on the right hand and on the left, 8by honor and dishonor, by evil report and good report; as deceivers, and *yet* true; 9as unknown, and *yet* well known; as dying, and behold we live; as chastened, and *yet* not killed; 10as sorrowful, yet always rejoicing; as poor, yet making many rich; as having nothing, and *yet* possessing all things.

Be Holy

11O Corinthians! We have spoken openly to you, our heart is wide open. 12You are not restricted by us, but you are restricted by your *own* affections. 13Now in return for the same (I speak as to children), you also be open.

14Do not be unequally yoked together with unbelievers. For what fellowship has righteousness with lawlessness? And what communion has light with darkness? 15And what accord has Christ with Bē′li·al? Or what part has a believer with an unbeliever? 16And what agreement has the temple of God with idols? For you[a] are the temple of the living God. As God has said:

"I will dwell in them
And walk among them.
I will be their God,
And they shall be My people."[b]

17Therefore

"Come out from among them
And be separate, says the Lord.
Do not touch what is unclean,
And I will receive you."[a]

18 *"I will be a Father to you,*
And you shall be My sons and daughters,
Says the LORD Almighty."[a]

6:16 [a]NU-Text reads *we.* [b]Leviticus 26:12; Jeremiah 32:38; Ezekiel 37:27 6:17 [a]Isaiah 52:11; Ezekiel 20:34, 41 6:18 [a]2 Samuel 7:14

CHAPTER 7

Therefore, having these promises, beloved, let us cleanse ourselves from all filthiness of the flesh and spirit, perfecting holiness in the fear of God.

The Corinthians' Repentance

2Open *your hearts* to us. We have wronged no one, we have corrupted no one, we have cheated no one. 3I do not say *this* to condemn; for I have said before that you are in our hearts, to die together and to live together. 4Great *is* my boldness of speech toward you, great *is* my boasting on your behalf. I am filled with comfort. I am exceedingly joyful in all our tribulation.

5For indeed, when we came to Mac·e·dō′ni·a, our bodies had no rest, but we were troubled on every side. Outside *were* conflicts, inside *were* fears. 6Nevertheless God, who comforts the downcast, comforted us by the coming of Titus, 7and not only by his coming, but also by the consolation with which he was comforted in you, when he told us of your earnest desire, your mourning, your zeal for me, so that I rejoiced even more.

8For even if I made you sorry with my letter, I do not regret it; though I did regret it. For I perceive that the same epistle made you sorry, though only for a while. 9Now I rejoice, not that you were made sorry, but that your sorrow led to repentance. For you were made sorry in a godly manner, that you might suffer loss from us in nothing. 10For godly sorrow produces repentance *leading* to salvation, not to be regretted; but the sorrow of the world produces death. 11For observe this very thing, that you sorrowed in a godly manner: What diligence it produced in you, *what* clearing of *yourselves, what* indignation, *what* fear, *what* vehement desire, *what* zeal, *what* vindication! In all *things* you proved yourselves to be clear in this matter. 12Therefore, although I wrote to you, *I did* not *do it* for

the sake of him who had done the wrong,
nor for the sake of him who suffered
wrong, but that our care for you in the
sight of God might appear to you.

The Joy of Titus

13Therefore we have been comforted in
your comfort. And we rejoiced exceed-
ingly more for the joy of Titus, because his
spirit has been refreshed by you all. 14For if
in anything I have boasted to him about
you, I am not ashamed. But as we spoke all
things to you in truth, even so our boasting
to Titus was found true. 15And his affec-
tions are greater for you as he remembers
the obedience of you all, how with fear and
trembling you received him. 16Therefore I
rejoice that I have confidence in you in
everything.

CHAPTER 8

Excel in Giving

Moreover, brethren, we make known to
you the grace of God bestowed on the
churches of Mac·e·dō′ni·a: 2that in a great
trial of affliction the abundance of their joy
and their deep poverty abounded in the
riches of their liberality. 3For I bear witness
that according to *their* ability, yes, and be-
yond *their* ability, *they were* freely willing,
4imploring us with much urgency that we
would receive[a] the gift and the fellowship
of the ministering to the saints. 5And not
only as we had hoped, but they first gave
themselves to the Lord, and *then* to us by
the will of God. 6So we urged Titus, that as
he had begun, so he would also complete
this grace in you as well. 7But as you
abound in everything—in faith, in speech,
in knowledge, in all diligence, and in your
love for us—*see* that you abound in this
grace also.

Christ Our Pattern

8I speak not by commandment, but I am
testing the sincerity of your love by the
diligence of others. 9For you know the
grace of our Lord Jesus Christ, that though
He was rich, yet for your sakes He became
poor, that you through His poverty might
become rich.

10And in this I give advice: It is to your
advantage not only to be doing what you
began and were desiring to do a year ago;
11but now you also must complete the do-
ing *of it;* that as *there was* a readiness to de-
sire *it,* so *there* also *may be* a completion out
of what *you* have. 12For if there is first a
willing mind, *it is* accepted according to
what one has, *and* not according to what he
does not have.

13For *I do* not *mean* that others should be
eased and you burdened; 14but by an
equality, *that* now at this time your abun-
dance *may supply* their lack, that their
abundance also may supply your lack—
that there may be equality. 15As it is writ-
ten, *"He who gathered much had nothing
left over, and he who gathered little had no
lack."*[a]

8:4 [a]NU-Text and M-Text omit *that we would receive,* thus changing text to *urgency for the favor and fellowship . . .* 8:15 [a]Exodus 16:18

7:14 I am not ashamed: "You did not let me down."

8:12–15 Three principles of Christian giving: (1) Give from a **willing mind**. (2) Give in proportion to what you have. The larger your income, the greater proportion you can give. (3) Give from love to supply another's lack (v. 14). These principles should guide us in handling our current finances as well as in planning our financial future.

8:14, 15 equality: The Christians in Corinth, a great commercial center, were better off financially than those in Macedonia and Jerusalem. The future possibility of the Jewish Christians in the Jerusalem church supplying the needs of the Gentile Christians in Corinth was unlikely, except as abundance includes the gifts of grace and the gospel (see Rom. 15:27). God wants us to meet each other's needs, just as His manna supplied Israel's exact dietary needs in the wilderness (see Ex. 16:18).

Collection for the Judean Saints

16But thanks *be* to God who puts[a] the same earnest care for you into the heart of Titus. 17For he not only accepted the exhortation, but being more diligent, he went to you of his own accord. 18And we have sent with him the brother whose praise *is* in the gospel throughout all the churches, 19and not only *that,* but who was also chosen by the churches to travel with us with this gift, which is administered by us to the glory of the Lord Himself and *to show* your ready mind, 20avoiding this: that anyone should blame us in this lavish gift which is administered by us— 21providing honorable things, not only in the sight of the Lord, but also in the sight of men.

22And we have sent with them our brother whom we have often proved diligent in many things, but now much more diligent, because of the great confidence which *we have* in you. 23If *anyone inquires* about Titus, *he is* my partner and fellow worker concerning you. Or if our brethren *are inquired about, they are* messengers of the churches, the glory of Christ. 24Therefore show to them, and[a] before the churches, the proof of your love and of our boasting on your behalf.

CHAPTER 9

Administering the Gift

Now concerning the ministering to the saints, it is superfluous for me to write to you; 2for I know your willingness, about which I boast of you to the Mac·e·dō′ni·ans, that A·chā′i·a was ready a year ago; and your zeal has stirred up the majority. 3Yet I have sent the brethren, lest our boasting of you should be in vain in this respect, that, as I said, you may be ready; 4lest if *some* Mac·e·dō′ni·ans come with me and find you unprepared, we (not to mention you!) should be ashamed of this confident boasting.[a] 5Therefore I thought it necessary to exhort the brethren to go to you ahead of time, and prepare your generous gift beforehand, which *you had* previously promised, that it may be ready as *a matter of* generosity and not as a grudging obligation.

The Cheerful Giver

6But this *I say:* He who sows sparingly will also reap sparingly, and he who sows bountifully will also reap bountifully. 7*So let* each one *give* as he purposes in his heart, not grudgingly or of necessity; for God loves a cheerful giver. 8And God *is* able to make all grace abound toward you, that you, always having all sufficiency in all *things,* may have an abundance for every good work. 9As it is written:

"He has dispersed abroad,
He has given to the poor;
His righteousness endures forever."[a]

10Now may[a] He who supplies seed to the sower, and bread for food, supply and multiply the seed you have *sown* and increase the fruits of your righteousness,

8:16 [a]NU-Text reads *has put.* 8:24 [a]NU-Text and M-Text omit *and.* 9:4 [a]NU-Text reads *this confidence.* 9:9 [a]Psalm 112:9 9:10 [a]NU-Text reads *Now He who supplies. . . will supply. . . .*

8:16–24 Paul made careful plans for handling the money given for the work of the church. He wanted his actions to be honest in the sight of **the Lord**. But he was also concerned that other people be able to check his honesty (vv. 20, 21), because mistrust discredits the gospel. Thus three people would handle this money: **Titus** was known and trusted by both Paul and the Corinthians (vv. 16, 17). Another **brother** (vv. 18, 19) was well known for his ministry throughout the **churches**, and had been **chosen** by them. The third **brother** (v. 22) was from Paul's party. Trust in the administration of the church's money encourages more generous giving (see 1 Cor. 16:3, 4).

9:7 of necessity: against one's will

9:10 may He . . . multiply the seed: When we give ourselves and our money to God's

11while *you are* enriched in everything for
all liberality, which causes thanksgiving
through us to God. 12For the administra-
tion of this service not only supplies the
needs of the saints, but also is abounding
through many thanksgivings to God,
13while, through the proof of this ministry,
they glorify God for the obedience of your
confession to the gospel of Christ, and for
your liberal sharing with them and all *men,*
14and by their prayer for you, who long for
you because of the exceeding grace of God
in you. 15Thanks *be* to God for His inde-
scribable gift!

CHAPTER 10

The Spiritual War

Now I, Paul, myself am pleading with
you by the meekness and gentleness of
Christ—who in presence *am* lowly among
you, but being absent am bold toward you.
2But I beg *you* that when I am present I may
not be bold with that confidence by which
I intend to be bold against some, who think
of us as if we walked according to the
flesh. 3For though we walk in the flesh, we
do not war according to the flesh. 4For the
weapons of our warfare *are* not carnal but
mighty in God for pulling down strong-
holds, 5casting down arguments and every
high thing that exalts itself against the
knowledge of God, bringing every thought
into captivity to the obedience of Christ,
6and being ready to punish all disobedi-
ence when your obedience is fulfilled.

Reality of Paul's Authority

7Do you look at things according to the
outward appearance? If anyone is con-
vinced in himself that he is Christ's, let him
again consider this in himself, that just as
he *is* Christ's, even so we *are* Christ's.[a] 8For
even if I should boast somewhat more
about our authority, which the Lord gave
us[a] for edification and not for your de-
struction, I shall not be ashamed— 9lest I
seem to terrify you by letters. 10"For *his*
letters," they say, "*are* weighty and power-
ful, but *his* bodily presence *is* weak, and
his speech contemptible." 11Let such a
person consider this, that what we are
in word by letters when we are absent,
such *we will* also *be* in deed when we are
present.

Limits of Paul's Authority

12For we dare not class ourselves or
compare ourselves with those who com-
mend themselves. But they, measuring
themselves by themselves, and comparing
themselves among themselves, are not
wise. 13We, however, will not boast beyond
measure, but within the limits of the
sphere which God appointed us—a sphere
which especially includes you. 14For we are
not overextending ourselves (as though
our authority did not extend to you), for it
was to you that we came with the gospel of
Christ; 15not boasting of things beyond
measure, *that is,* in other men's labors, but
having hope, *that* as your faith is increased,
we shall be greatly enlarged by you in our
sphere, 16to preach the gospel in the *regions*
beyond you, *and* not to boast in another
man's sphere of accomplishment.

17But *"he who glories, let him glory in*

10:7 [a]NU-Text reads *even as we are.* 10:8 [a]NU-Text omits *us.*

---

work, He multiplies the results beyond the expectations of natural cause and effect (see Matt. 14:14–21).

10:10 Paul's opponents criticized his appearance and his speaking ability.

10:13–16 Paul would **boast** only within the **sphere** of ministry that **God** had given him. **to you that we came** (v. 14): The Corinthian Christians were within the sphere of Paul's work because he had brought the **gospel of Christ** to them, founding the church in Corinth. By their help he planned to extend his ministry to others in **regions beyond** where no one had yet preached (vv. 15, 16). He would not be like the false teachers who tried to take over **another man's sphere** (v. 16).

Striving for Excellence

Gary Rosberg, Ed. D.

Sometimes we experience life just as our cars do. We have sudden starts and stops, the sun scorches our "finish," and yet we can be washed to look almost new. At a distance even an old car can look great, but up close, the scratches and dings are a little more evident. I believe the "flaws" reflect the character of the car rather than its problems.

At times I look at other people and think they look better than I do, until I remember that we all look good at a distance. A closer look shows that we all have needs. God created me with certain talents, and I need to utilize those as best I can. I do not have to compete with others to be acceptable to them or myself; I just need to do my best.

The apostle Paul explained the dangers of comparison, noting that it can lead to boasting and criticism (2 Cor. 10:7–18). Measuring our worth against that of others may also lead to a poor self-image. We should judge ourselves only against God's rule of holiness.

"We should judge ourselves only against God's rule of holiness."

I once heard a man describe the difference between perfectionism and excellence: the person trying to be perfect is comparing himself with others, but the person pursuing excellence is just trying to be the best he can be. Go for excellence! You do not have any control over how you measure up to others. ✦

the LORD."[a] 18For not he who commends
himself is approved, but whom the Lord
commends.

CHAPTER 11

Concern for Their Faithfulness

Oh, that you would bear with me in a
little folly—and indeed you do bear with
me. 2For I am jealous for you with godly
jealousy. For I have betrothed you to one
husband, that I may present *you as* a chaste
virgin to Christ. 3But I fear, lest somehow,
as the serpent deceived Eve by his crafti-
ness, so your minds may be corrupted
from the simplicity[a] that is in Christ. 4For if
he who comes preaches another Jesus
whom we have not preached, or *if* you re-
ceive a different spirit which you have not
received, or a different gospel which you
have not accepted—you may well put up
with it!

10:17 [a]Jeremiah 9:24 11:3 [a]NU-Text adds *and purity.*

10:18 This verse expresses the main thrust of ch. 10. The Christlike pattern of Paul's life (see 4:10; 11:23–29) and the fruit of his labor among the Corinthians and others showed that he was **approved** by God.

11:1 Paul must cite some of his own virtues in order to counter the criticisms against him. To him this boasting of self was **folly**, even though in this case a necessary self-defense.

Paul and False Apostles

5For I consider that I am not at all infe-
rior to the most eminent apostles. 6Even
though *I am* untrained in speech, yet *I am* not
in knowledge. But we have been thoroughly
manifested[a] among you in all things.

7Did I commit sin in humbling myself
that you might be exalted, because I
preached the gospel of God to you free of
charge? 8I robbed other churches, taking
wages *from them* to minister to you. 9And
when I was present with you, and in need,
I was a burden to no one, for what I lacked
the brethren who came from Mac·e·dō'ni·a
supplied. And in everything I kept myself
from being burdensome to you, and so I
will keep *myself*. 10As the truth of Christ is
in me, no one shall stop me from this
boasting in the regions of A·chā'i·a.
11Why? Because I do not love you? God
knows!

12But what I do, I will also continue to
do, that I may cut off the opportunity from
those who desire an opportunity to be re-
garded just as we are in the things of which
they boast. 13For such *are* false apostles, de-
ceitful workers, transforming themselves
into apostles of Christ. 14And no wonder!
For Satan himself transforms himself into
an angel of light. 15Therefore *it is* no great
thing if his ministers also transform them-
selves into ministers of righteousness,
whose end will be according to their works.

Reluctant Boasting

16I say again, let no one think me a fool.
If otherwise, at least receive me as a fool,
that I also may boast a little. 17What I
speak, I speak not according to the Lord,
but as it were, foolishly, in this confidence
of boasting. 18Seeing that many boast ac-
cording to the flesh, I also will boast. 19For
you put up with fools gladly, since you
yourselves are wise! 20For you put up with it
if one brings you into bondage, if one de-
vours *you*, if one takes *from you*, if one ex-
alts himself, if one strikes you on the face.
21To *our* shame I say that we were too weak
for that! But in whatever anyone is bold—I
speak foolishly—I am bold also.

Suffering for Christ

22Are they Hebrews? So *am* I. Are they
Israelites? So *am* I. Are they the seed of
Abraham? So *am* I. 23Are they ministers of
Christ?—I speak as a fool—I *am* more: in
labors more abundant, in stripes above
measure, in prisons more frequently, in
deaths often. 24From the Jews five times I
received forty *stripes* minus one. 25Three
times I was beaten with rods; once I was
stoned; three times I was shipwrecked; a
night and a day I have been in the deep;
26*in* journeys often, *in* perils of waters, *in*
perils of robbers, *in* perils of *my own* coun-
trymen, *in* perils of the Gentiles, *in* perils in
the city, *in* perils in the wilderness, *in* perils
in the sea, *in* perils among false brethren;
27in weariness and toil, in sleeplessness
often, in hunger and thirst, in fastings
often, in cold and nakedness— 28besides
the other things, what comes upon me

11:6 [a]NU-Text omits *been.*

11:7–12 To distinguish himself from so-called apostles who ministered from selfish motives, Paul supported himself financially through the craft of tentmaking, rather than asking the Corinthian church for money. Such manual labor was held in contempt by the Greeks, so Paul is defending his actions to his critics.

11:16–18 To **boast** about one's own achievements is foolish and not **according to the Lord**. Paul did so only because the false teachers were boasting in this way. Arguing on their own premises was an attempt to counteract their influence over the Corinthians. But even such boasting by Paul is boasting over what the Lord has done. Four times he declares he will boast only of his weaknesses in which Christ's power has been shown in his life (11:30; 12:5, 9, 10).

11:24, 25 five times . . . three times: This list of imprisonments, beatings, and shipwrecks indicates how little the Book of Acts tells us about Paul's sufferings.

daily: my deep concern for all the churches. 29Who is weak, and I am not weak? Who is made to stumble, and I do not burn *with indignation?*

30If I must boast, I will boast in the things which concern my infirmity. 31The God and Father of our Lord Jesus Christ, who is blessed forever, knows that I am not lying. 32In Damascus the governor, under Ar'e·tas the king, was guarding the city of the Dam'a·scēnes with a garrison, desiring to arrest me; 33but I was let down in a basket through a window in the wall, and escaped from his hands.

CHAPTER 12

The Vision of Paradise

It is doubtless[a] not profitable for me to boast. I will come to visions and revelations of the Lord: 2I know a man in Christ who fourteen years ago—whether in the body I do not know, or whether out of the body I do not know, God knows—such a one was caught up to the third heaven. 3And I know such a man—whether in the body or out of the body I do not know, God knows— 4how he was caught up into Paradise and heard inexpressible words, which it is not lawful for a man to utter. 5Of such a one I will boast; yet of myself I will not boast, except in my infirmities. 6For though I might desire to boast, I will not be a fool; for I will speak the truth. But I refrain, lest anyone should think of me above what he sees me *to be* or hears from me.

> ***I pray that I will take pleasure in infirmities, in reproaches, in needs, in persecutions, in distresses, for Christ's sake. For when I am weak, then I am strong.***
> *adapted from* 2 Corinthians 12:10

The Thorn in the Flesh

7And lest I should be exalted above measure by the abundance of the revelations, a thorn in the flesh was given to me, a messenger of Satan to buffet me, lest I be exalted above measure. 8Concerning this thing I pleaded with the Lord three times that it might depart from me. 9And He said to me, "My grace is sufficient for you, for My strength is made perfect in weakness." Therefore most gladly I will rather boast in my infirmities, that the power of Christ may rest upon me. 10Therefore I take pleasure in infirmities, in reproaches, in needs, in persecutions, in distresses, for Christ's sake. For when I am weak, then I am strong.

Signs of an Apostle

11I have become a fool in boasting;[a] you have compelled me. For I ought to have been commended by you; for in nothing was I behind the most eminent apostles, though I am nothing. 12Truly the signs of an apostle were accomplished among you with all perseverance, in signs and wonders and mighty deeds. 13For what is it in which you were inferior to other churches,

12:1 [a]NU-Text reads *necessary, though not profitable, to boast.* 12:11 [a]NU-Text omits *in boasting.*

11:32, 33 In Damascus: Paul mentioned this incident perhaps because it was the first of his many sufferings for Christ. **Aretas** was the title of the kings of the Arabian kingdom of Nabatea which bordered Damascus. The **governor** here may have been his representative responsible to look after the Nabatean citizens in Damascus. The Jews (see Acts 9:23–25) and the Nabateans cooperated in their attempt to seize Paul.

12:1 the third heaven: the presence of God.

12:1–10 Bible commentators almost unanimously agree that Paul is referring to himself in this description of a vision of Paradise.

except that I myself was not burdensome to you? Forgive me this wrong!

Love for the Church

14Now *for* the third time I am ready to come to you. And I will not be burdensome to you; for I do not seek yours, but you. For the children ought not to lay up for the parents, but the parents for the children.
15And I will very gladly spend and be spent for your souls; though the more abundantly I love you, the less I am loved.
16But be that *as it may,* I did not burden you. Nevertheless, being crafty, I caught you by cunning! 17Did I take advantage of you by any of those whom I sent to you? 18I urged Titus, and sent our brother with *him.* Did Titus take advantage of you? Did we not walk in the same spirit? Did *we* not *walk* in the same steps?
19Again, do you think[a] that we excuse ourselves to you? We speak before God in Christ. But *we do* all things, beloved, for your edification. 20For I fear lest, when I come, I shall not find you such as I wish, and *that* I shall be found by you such as you do not wish; lest *there be* contentions, jealousies, outbursts of wrath, selfish ambitions, backbitings, whisperings, conceits, tumults; 21lest, when I come again, my God will humble me among you, and I shall mourn for many who have sinned before and have not repented of the uncleanness, fornication, and lewdness which they have practiced.

CHAPTER 13

Coming with Authority

This *will be* the third *time* I am coming to you. *"By the mouth of two or three witnesses every word shall be established."*[a] 2I have told you before, and foretell as if I were present the second time, and now being absent I write[a] to those who have sinned before, and to all the rest, that if I come again I will not spare— 3since you seek a proof of Christ speaking in me, who is not weak toward you, but mighty in you.
4For though He was crucified in weakness, yet He lives by the power of God. For we also are weak in Him, but we shall live with Him by the power of God toward you.
5Examine yourselves *as to* whether you are in the faith. Test yourselves. Do you not know yourselves, that Jesus Christ is in you?—unless indeed you are disqualified.
6But I trust that you will know that we are not disqualified.

> No matter how long you've been married or how difficult you find communication, you must make the effort to share thoughts and feelings often.
>
> Bob Dyer

Paul Prefers Gentleness

7Now I[a] pray to God that you do no evil, not that we should appear approved, but that you should do what is honorable, though we may seem disqualified. 8For we can do nothing against the truth, but for the truth. 9For we are glad when we are weak and you are strong. And this also we pray, that you may be made complete.

12:19 [a]NU-Text reads *You have been thinking for a long time. . . .* 13:1 [a]Deuteronomy 19:15 13:2 [a]NU-Text omits *I write.* 13:7 [a]NU-Text reads *we.*

13:1 In the OT it took **two or three witnesses** to establish the truth of an accusation. Paul felt that the **third time** he came and warned the Corinthians about their misconduct would be crucial.

13:5, 6 Examine yourselves implies that they could be **disqualified** (exposed as never having actually believed). The test of our relationship to Christ is the ethical quality of our behavior. But Paul trusts that they are indeed in the **faith**. On examination they will see that **Jesus Christ** is in them. Thus they will know that Paul, who led them to Christ, is not a disqualified apostle.

[10]Therefore I write these things being absent, lest being present I should use sharpness, according to the authority which the Lord has given me for edification and not for destruction.

Greetings and Benediction

[11]Finally, brethren, farewell. Become complete. Be of good comfort, be of one mind, live in peace; and the God of love and peace will be with you.

[12]Greet one another with a holy kiss.

[13]All the saints greet you.

[14]The grace of the Lord Jesus Christ, and the love of God, and the communion of the Holy Spirit *be* with you all. Amen.

13:12 It was common in NT times for people to greet each other with a **kiss** on the forehead or shoulder. By following this custom in the church, Christians demonstrated that they were members of the same spiritual family.

✦Galatians✦

Paul's missionary work during his first journey to Galatia met great success as large numbers of Gentiles accepted the Good News and committed their lives to the risen Christ. Having launched their Christian experience by faith, this early church of new believers was soon under the influence of the false teaching that required converts, if they wanted to be real Christians, to live under the requirements of the Mosaic Law. Paul's letter to the Galatian Christians is a vigorous attack against the gospel of works and a defense of the gospel of faith.

The central theme of the letter is justification by faith alone. Using Abraham as an example, Paul declared the believer to be free from bondage to the law (legalism) and sin (license). The law declares humans guilty and imprisons them; faith sets us free to enjoy liberty in Christ. He urged the Galatians to balance this liberty with a sense of responsibility. His note of encouragement (Gal. 6:9) should be heeded by Christians who find themselves weary after years of service. Freedom in Christ means freedom to produce the fruits of righteousness through a Spirit-led lifestyle. Galatians, then, is the Christian's great charter of liberty. ✦

CHAPTER 1

Greeting

Paul, an apostle (not from men nor
through man, but through Jesus Christ and
God the Father who raised Him from the
dead), [2]and all the brethren who are with
me,

To the churches of Galatia:

[3]Grace to you and peace from God
the Father and our Lord Jesus Christ,
[4]who gave Himself for our sins, that He
might deliver us from this present evil age,
according to the will of our God and
Father, [5]to whom *be* glory forever and ever.
Amen.

Only One Gospel

[6]I marvel that you are turning away so
soon from Him who called you in the grace
of Christ, to a different gospel, [7]which is
not another; but there are some who trouble you and want to pervert the gospel of
Christ. [8]But even if we, or an angel from
heaven, preach any other gospel to you
than what we have preached to you, let
him be accursed. [9]As we have said before,
so now I say again, if anyone preaches any

1:6 turning away: Not only changing doctrinal position, but also abandoning loyalty to **Him who called**, God Himself.

1:8, 9 Paul's statements reflect how strongly he feels about any attempt to rewrite the gospel of Christ. We too must be intolerant of any doctrine that is not centered on the grace of God through the death and resurrection of Christ.

other gospel to you than what you have re-
ceived, let him be accursed.
10For do I now persuade men, or God?
Or do I seek to please men? For if I still
pleased men, I would not be a bondservant
of Christ.

Call to Apostleship

11But I make known to you, brethren,
that the gospel which was preached by me
is not according to man. 12For I neither re-
ceived it from man, nor was I taught *it,* but
it came through the revelation of Jesus
Christ.
13For you have heard of my former con-
duct in Judaism, how I persecuted the
church of God beyond measure and *tried to*
destroy it. 14And I advanced in Judaism be-
yond many of my contemporaries in my
own nation, being more exceedingly zeal-
ous for the traditions of my fathers.
15But when it pleased God, who sepa-
rated me from my mother's womb and
called *me* through His grace, 16to reveal His
Son in me, that I might preach Him among
the Gentiles, I did not immediately confer
with flesh and blood, 17nor did I go up to
Jerusalem to those *who were* apostles before
me; but I went to Arabia, and returned
again to Damascus.

Contacts at Jerusalem

18Then after three years I went up to Je-
rusalem to see Peter,[a] and remained with
him fifteen days. 19But I saw none of the
other apostles except James, the Lord's
brother. 20(Now *concerning* the things
which I write to you, indeed, before God, I
do not lie.)
21Afterward I went into the regions of
Syria and Ci·li'ci·a. 22And I was unknown
by face to the churches of Judea which *were*
in Christ. 23But they were hearing only,
"He who formerly persecuted us now
preaches the faith which he once *tried to*
destroy." 24And they glorified God in me.

CHAPTER 2

Defending the Gospel

Then after fourteen years I went up
again to Jerusalem with Bar'na·bas, and
also took Titus with *me.* 2And I went up by
revelation, and communicated to them
that gospel which I preach among the Gen-
tiles, but privately to those who were of
reputation, lest by any means I might run,
or had run, in vain. 3Yet not even Titus who
was with me, being a Greek, was com-
pelled to be circumcised. 4And *this occurred*
because of false brethren secretly brought
in (who came in by stealth to spy out our
liberty which we have in Christ Jesus, that
they might bring us into bondage), 5to
whom we did not yield submission even

1:18 [a]NU-Text reads *Cephas.*

> Truth has no special time of its own. Its hour is now-always.
>
> Albert Schweitzer

1:13–16 Only divine intervention could prompt such a miraculous transformation as took place in Paul's life, but the same thing can happen to any life surrendered to God.

2:1, 2 Fourteen years after his conversion (1:15) Paul went to Jerusalem a second time. This visit is probably referred to in Acts 11:27–30. **communicated to them**: Paul did not ask the apostles what he should preach; he told them what he was preaching, thus indicating that he had received the message from the Lord Himself. **run, in vain**: Paul wanted the church leaders to agree that circumcision was not necessary for Christians so that the false teachers would not be able to force circumcision on his Gentile converts and ruin his ministry.

2:5 not . . . even for an hour: Paul was unwilling to allow Titus to be circumcised because he understood that such a demand would be a crucial test case. Freedom from Jewish laws was essential to **the truth of the gospel**.

for an hour, that the truth of the gospel
might continue with you.
6But from those who seemed to be
something—whatever they were, it makes
no difference to me; God shows personal
favoritism to no man—for those who
seemed *to be something* added nothing to
me. 7But on the contrary, when they saw
that the gospel for the uncircumcised had
been committed to me, as *the gospel* for the
circumcised *was* to Peter 8(for He who
worked effectively in Peter for the apostle-
ship to the circumcised also worked effec-
tively in me toward the Gentiles), 9and
when James, Cē′phas, and John, who
seemed to be pillars, perceived the grace
that had been given to me, they gave me
and Bar′na·bas the right hand of fellow-
ship, that we *should go* to the Gentiles and
they to the circumcised. 10*They desired* only
that we should remember the poor, the
very thing which I also was eager to do.

No Return to the Law

11Now when Peter[a] had come to
An′ti·och, I withstood him to his face, be-
cause he was to be blamed; 12for before cer-
tain men came from James, he would eat
with the Gentiles; but when they came, he
withdrew and separated himself, fearing
those who were of the circumcision. 13And
the rest of the Jews also played the hyp-
ocrite with him, so that even Bar′na·bas
was carried away with their hypocrisy.
14But when I saw that they were not
straightforward about the truth of the
gospel, I said to Peter before *them* all, "If
you, being a Jew, live in the manner of
Gentiles and not as the Jews, why do you[a]
compel Gentiles to live as Jews?[b] 15We *who*
are Jews by nature, and not sinners of the
Gentiles, 16knowing that a man is not justi-
fied by the works of the law but by faith in
Jesus Christ, even we have believed in
Christ Jesus, that we might be justified by
faith in Christ and not by the works of the
law; for by the works of the law no flesh
shall be justified.
17"But if, while we seek to be justified by
Christ, we ourselves also are found sin-
ners, *is* Christ therefore a minister of sin?
Certainly not! 18For if I build again those
things which I destroyed, I make myself a
transgressor. 19For I through the law died
to the law that I might live to God. 20I have
been crucified with Christ; it is no longer I
who live, but Christ lives in me; and the *life*
which I now live in the flesh I live by faith
in the Son of God, who loved me and

> It is one thing to go through a crisis grandly, and another thing to go through every day glorifying God when nobody is paying any attention to you.
>
> Oswald Chambers

2:11 [a]NU-Text reads *Cephas.* 2:14 [a]NU-Text reads *how can you.* [b]Some interpreters stop the quotation here.

2:9 The repeated expression **seemed to be** (vv. 6, 9) underscores Paul's own claim to divine revelation for the truth he preached.

2:11 This confrontation between Peter and Paul demonstrates the importance of communication in resolving conflicts within the church. Instead of criticizing Peter behind his back, Paul approached him openly and expressed his concern. What a difference it would make if we followed his example in our churches today!

2:12, 13 The issue here was not whether Gentile Christians must keep the Jewish law, but whether Jewish Christians must continue to keep the law. **Certain men**, Jews from Jerusalem, argued that salvation for Jewish Christians meant keeping the law as well as having faith in Christ. Thus they should not violate the Jewish prohibition against eating with Gentiles—even Gentile Christians. Peter's withdrawal from table fellowship with Gentiles because of his fear of reprisal from these Jews made him a **hypocrite**. He knew that Jewish law was no longer binding upon Jewish Christians for salvation, yet denied this by his conduct. Even **Barnabas**, who had helped Paul found Gentile churches, was led astray.

gave Himself for me. 21I do not set aside the
grace of God; for if righteousness *comes*
through the law, then Christ died in vain."

CHAPTER 3

Justification by Faith

O foolish Galatians! Who has bewitched
you that you should not obey the truth,[a]
before whose eyes Jesus Christ was clearly
portrayed among you[b] as crucified? 2This
only I want to learn from you: Did you re-
ceive the Spirit by the works of the law, or
by the hearing of faith? 3Are you so fool-
ish? Having begun in the Spirit, are you
now being made perfect by the flesh?
4Have you suffered so many things in
vain—if indeed *it was* in vain?

5Therefore He who supplies the Spirit to
you and works miracles among you, *does
He do it* by the works of the law, or by the
hearing of faith?— 6just as Abraham *"be-
lieved God, and it was accounted to him
for righteousness."*[a] 7Therefore know that
only those who are of faith are sons of
Abraham. 8And the Scripture, foreseeing
that God would justify the Gentiles by
faith, preached the gospel to Abraham be-
forehand, *saying, "In you all the nations
shall be blessed."*[a] 9So then those who *are* of
faith are blessed with believing Abraham.

The Law Brings a Curse

10For as many as are of the works of the
law are under the curse; for it is written,
*"Cursed is everyone who does not con-
tinue in all things which are written in
the book of the law, to do them."*[a] 11But
that no one is justified by the law in the
sight of God *is* evident, for *"the just shall*

> Every act leaves the world with a
> deeper or a fainter impression of God.
> Alfred North Whitehead

live by faith."[a] 12Yet the law is not of faith,
but *"the man who does them shall live by
them."*[a]

13Christ has redeemed us from the curse
of the law, having become a curse for us
(for it is written, *"Cursed is everyone who
hangs on a tree"*[a]), 14that the blessing of
Abraham might come upon the Gentiles in
Christ Jesus, that we might receive the
promise of the Spirit through faith.

The Changeless Promise

15Brethren, I speak in the manner of
men: Though *it is* only a man's covenant,
yet *if it is* confirmed, no one annuls or
adds to it. 16Now to Abraham and his Seed
were the promises made. He does not say,
"And to seeds," as of many, but as of one,
"And to your Seed,"[a] who is Christ.
17And this I say, *that* the law, which was
four hundred and thirty years later, cannot
annul the covenant that was confirmed be-
fore by God in Christ,[a] that it should make
the promise of no effect. 18For if the inheri-
tance *is* of the law, *it is* no longer of
promise; but God gave *it* to Abraham by
promise.

Purpose of the Law

19What purpose then *does* the law *serve?*
It was added because of transgressions, till
the Seed should come to whom the
promise was made; *and it was* appointed
through angels by the hand of a mediator.
20Now a mediator does not *mediate* for one
only, but God is one.

21*Is* the law then against the promises of
God? Certainly not! For if there had been a
law given which could have given life,

3:1 [a]NU-Text omits *that you should not obey the truth.* [b]NU-Text omits *among you.* 3:6 [a]Genesis 15:6
3:8 [a]Genesis 12:3; 18:18; 22:18; 26:4; 28:14
3:10 [a]Deuteronomy 27:26 3:11 [a]Habakkuk 2:4
3:12 [a]Leviticus 18:5 3:13 [a]Deuteronomy 21:23
3:16 [a]Genesis 12:7; 13:15; 24:7 3:17 [a]NU-Text omits *in Christ.*

2:21 If salvation could be earned simply through obedience to the law, there would have been no reason for Christ to give His life.

We Are One

Evelyn Christenson

Contrary to popular thought, Jesus did not ask His children to be reconciled so that they could become one but because they were one! So whenever we pray, asking God with which Christians we should pray, He answers, "but you are one!" "There is neither Jew nor Greek, there is neither slave nor free, there is neither male nor female; for you are all one in Christ Jesus" (Gal. 3:28).

God's requirement for reconciliation is broader than just the body of Christ. It includes individual reconciliation to mates, parents, in-laws, children, brothers, sisters, pastors, neighbors, employees, employers, competitors, and our enemies (Luke 6:27, 28)—all of whom may or may not be Christians. So as long as we are not reconciled to even one of them, we are not obeying Jesus' plan for us. "Forgiving one another, if anyone has a complaint against another; even as Christ forgave you, so you also must do" (Col. 3:13).

"God's requirement for reconciliation is broader than just the body of Christ."

Thus, being unwilling to be reconciled to other people is a sin which must be confessed, repented of, forgiven, and turned from if we are to be reconciled back to God. ✦

truly righteousness would have been by
the law. 22But the Scripture has confined all
under sin, that the promise by faith in Je-
sus Christ might be given to those who be-
lieve. 23But before faith came, we were kept
under guard by the law, kept for the faith
which would afterward be revealed.
24Therefore the law was our tutor *to bring*
us to Christ, that we might be justified by
faith. 25But after faith has come, we are no
longer under a tutor.

Sons and Heirs

26For you are all sons of God through
faith in Christ Jesus. 27For as many of you
as were baptized into Christ have put on
Christ. 28There is neither Jew nor Greek,
there is neither slave nor free, there is nei-
ther male nor female; for you are all one in
Christ Jesus. 29And if you *are* Christ's, then
you are Abraham's seed, and heirs accord-
ing to the promise.

CHAPTER 4

Now I say *that* the heir, as long as he is a
child, does not differ at all from a slave,
though he is master of all, 2but is under
guardians and stewards until the time ap-
pointed by the father. 3Even so we, when
we were children, were in bondage under
the elements of the world. 4But when the
fullness of the time had come, God sent
forth His Son, born[a] of a woman, born un-
der the law, 5to redeem those who were un-
der the law, that we might receive the
adoption as sons.

4:4 [a]Or *made*

6And because you are sons, God has sent forth the Spirit of His Son into your hearts, crying out, "Abba, Father!" 7Therefore you are no longer a slave but a son, and if a son, then an heir of[a] God through Christ.

Fears for the Church

8But then, indeed, when you did not know God, you served those which by nature are not gods. 9But now after you have known God, or rather are known by God, how *is it that* you turn again to the weak and beggarly elements, to which you desire again to be in bondage? 10You observe days and months and seasons and years. 11I am afraid for you, lest I have labored for you in vain.

12Brethren, I urge you to become like me, for I *became* like you. You have not injured me at all. 13You know that because of physical infirmity I preached the gospel to you at the first. 14And my trial which was in my flesh you did not despise or reject, but you received me as an angel of God, *even* as Christ Jesus. 15What[a] then was the blessing you *enjoyed?* For I bear you witness that, if possible, you would have plucked out your own eyes and given them to me. 16Have I therefore become your enemy because I tell you the truth?

17They zealously court you, *but* for no good; yes, they want to exclude you, that you may be zealous for them. 18But it is good to be zealous in a good thing always, and not only when I am present with you. 19My little children, for whom I labor in birth again until Christ is formed in you, 20I would like to be present with you now and to change my tone; for I have doubts about you.

Two Covenants

21Tell me, you who desire to be under the law, do you not hear the law? 22For it is written that Abraham had two sons: the one by a bondwoman, the other by a freewoman. 23But he *who was* of the bondwoman was born according to the flesh, and he of the freewoman through promise, 24which things are symbolic. For these are the[a] two covenants: the one from Mount Sinai which gives birth to bondage, which is Hā'gar— 25for this Hā'gar is Mount Sinai in Arabia, and corresponds to Jerusalem which now is, and is in bondage with her children— 26but the Jerusalem above is free, which is the mother of us all. 27For it is written:

"Rejoice, O barren,
You who do not bear!

4:7 [a]NU-Text reads *through God* and omits *through Christ.* 4:15 [a]NU-Text reads *Where.* 4:24 [a]NU-Text and M-Text omit *the.*

4:6 Abba: intimate Aramaic word for "Father," equivalent to "Daddy."

4:13, 14 We do not know the nature of Paul's **physical infirmity**; perhaps the Galatians knew without further description. It was apparently something that would normally cause people to despise or reject him—perhaps an eye problem (see v. 15). The fact that he continued his ministry despite this affliction tells volumes about his character and probably helped to convince his listeners of his sincerity. How we cope with our difficulties can greatly affect our witness for Christ.

4:24–28 symbolic: God's dealings with Abraham present a pattern for us. Seeking the birth of a son by **Hagar** was Abraham's attempt to fulfill God's promise by his own efforts. Thus Hagar and her son are appropriate symbols of the **Mount Sinai** covenant, the Judaism of **Jerusalem** (v. 25), representing people who try to earn salvation through good deeds.

God, however, in fulfillment of His **promise** to bring salvation, caused **Isaac** (v. 28) to be born to Abraham and Sarah because they trusted Him. Thus Isaac is a fitting type of those who are **children** (v. 28) of God through faith in Jesus. This plan of salvation by faith is called the **Jerusalem above** (v. 26). In contrast, those who follow the way of works are under **bondage** (v. 25) to a law they cannot keep. Those who trust Christ are **free** (v. 25) for joyful obedience.

A Conversation with Daddy

Gloria Gaither

Prayer is intimate and loving communion between a human person and a holy God. It is the privilege given us by God, then extended to its fullest by the death and sacrifice of Jesus. When Jesus died for us, He tore away all that kept us at arm's length from God, separated from Him by our sin. Because of Jesus we can go directly to God without fear and call Him "Abba, Father." That really means "Daddy" to me, for "Abba" was the affectionate personal word children used for addressing their fathers. There's no distance there, no religiosity, just a comfortable, natural relationship. God invites us, because of Jesus, just to be at home in His presence, to call Him "Daddy" and openly tell Him what we need (Gal. 4:6, 7).

"When Jesus died for us, He tore away all that kept us at arm's length from God."

I love the verse that says, "Be anxious for nothing, but in everything by prayer and supplication, with thanksgiving, let your requests be made known to God" (Phil. 4:6). Now, that part about thanksgiving is important, too, especially for us. It helps us avoid the "taker" mentality.

God wants to "freely give us all things" (Rom. 8:32), but we need gratitude in our lives so that greed will not destroy our openness to God or our love for Him. Greed does not destroy God's love for us; it destroys *our* ability to love.✦

Break forth and shout,
You who are not in labor!
For the desolate has many more
children
Than she who has a husband."[a]

[28]Now we, brethren, as Isaac *was*, are
children of promise. [29]But, as he who was
born according to the flesh then persecuted
him *who was born* according to the Spirit,
even so *it is* now. [30]Nevertheless what does
the Scripture say? *"Cast out the bond-*
woman and her son, for the son of the
bondwoman shall not be heir with the son
of the freewoman."[a] [31]So then, brethren, we
are not children of the bondwoman but of
the free.

CHAPTER 5

Christian Liberty

Stand fast therefore in the liberty by
which Christ has made us free,[a] and do not
be entangled again with a yoke of
bondage. [2]Indeed I, Paul, say to you that if

4:27 [a]Isaiah 54:1 4:30 [a]Genesis 21:10
5:1 [a]NU-Text reads *For freedom Christ has made us free; stand fast therefore.*

5:2–4 Why is Christ of no **profit** to the person who chooses to be **circumcised** (v. 2)? Because circumcision is a commitment to seek salvation by keeping the **law** in its entirety

KEEP WALKING

J. Vernon McGee

We walk without thinking. We can go down the street thinking about something else while we are walking. But, you know, we had a great problem getting started. You may have forgotten, but notice that little fellow trying to take his first wobbly step and toppling over. If stopped for one second, walking is not walking; it is standing. You have to keep going. You put one foot in front, then you have to bring up the other foot, and then you have to do it all over again. It is a moment-by-moment, continual, habitual thing.

It is interesting how the Word of God has brought together metaphors. The Christian life is a conflict, and in the conflict we are told to *stand*—"Stand therefore," Paul said to the Ephesians (6:14). Also, the Christian life is a race, and we are told to *run* the race (1 Cor. 9:24). But the greater part of the Christian life is just plain living, and that means *walking*—which is the most difficult. Many of us can move out into the arena of life and when applause comes from the gallery, we can draw our sword and stand our ground. Or when those on the sidelines are urging us to run, we can exert great effort. But when we get up in the morning to a sink full of dirty dishes or go down to the office to a desk loaded with accumulated work, we fail. It is then that we are to *walk* by the power of the Holy Spirit (Gal. 5:16). ✦

"The Christian life is just plain living, and that means *walking*—which is the most difficult."

you become circumcised, Christ will profit
you nothing. 3And I testify again to every
man who becomes circumcised that he is a
debtor to keep the whole law. 4You have
become estranged from Christ, you who
attempt to be justified by law; you have
fallen from grace. 5For we through the
Spirit eagerly wait for the hope of righ-
teousness by faith. 6For in Christ Jesus nei-
ther circumcision nor uncircumcision
avails anything, but faith working through
love.

Love Fulfills the Law

7You ran well. Who hindered you from
obeying the truth? 8This persuasion does
not *come* from Him who calls you. 9A little
leaven leavens the whole lump. 10I have
confidence in you, in the Lord, that you
will have no other mind; but he who trou-
bles you shall bear his judgment, whoever
he is.

11And I, brethren, if I still preach circum-
cision, why do I still suffer persecution?
Then the offense of the cross has ceased. 12I

(v. 3). It is exactly opposite of salvation by trusting Christ. Thus the person who relies on keeping the law is separated from Christ and from salvation by **grace** (v. 4).

could wish that those who trouble you would even cut themselves off!

13For you, brethren, have been called to liberty; only do not *use* liberty as an opportunity for the flesh, but through love serve one another. 14For all the law is fulfilled in one word, *even* in this: *"You shall love your neighbor as yourself."*[a] 15But if you bite and devour one another, beware lest you be consumed by one another!

Walking in the Spirit

16I say then: Walk in the Spirit, and you shall not fulfill the lust of the flesh. 17For the flesh lusts against the Spirit, and the Spirit against the flesh; and these are contrary to one another, so that you do not do the things that you wish. 18But if you are led by the Spirit, you are not under the law.

19Now the works of the flesh are evident, which are: adultery,[a] fornication, uncleanness, lewdness, 20idolatry, sorcery, hatred, contentions, jealousies, outbursts of wrath, selfish ambitions, dissensions, heresies, 21envy, murders,[a] drunkenness, revelries, and the like; of which I tell you beforehand, just as I also told *you* in time past, that those who practice such things will not inherit the kingdom of God.

22But the fruit of the Spirit is love, joy, peace, longsuffering, kindness, goodness, faithfulness, 23gentleness, self-control. Against such there is no law. 24And those *who are* Christ's have crucified the flesh with its passions and desires. 25If we live in the Spirit, let us also walk in the Spirit. 26Let us not become conceited, provoking one another, envying one another.

CHAPTER 6

Bear and Share the Burdens

Brethren, if a man is overtaken in any trespass, you who *are* spiritual restore such a one in a spirit of gentleness, considering yourself lest you also be tempted. 2Bear one another's burdens, and so fulfill the law of Christ. 3For if anyone thinks himself to be something, when he is nothing, he deceives himself. 4But let each one examine his own work, and then he will have rejoicing in himself alone, and not in another. 5For each one shall bear his own load.

Be Generous and Do Good

6Let him who is taught the word share in all good things with him who teaches.

7Do not be deceived, God is not mocked; for whatever a man sows, that he will also reap. 8For he who sows to his flesh will of the flesh reap corruption, but he who sows to the Spirit will of the Spirit reap everlasting life. 9And let us not grow weary while doing good, for in due season we shall

5:14 [a]Leviticus 19:18 5:19 [a]NU-Text omits *adultery.*
5:21 [a]NU-Text omits *murders.*

I pray that my wife does not grow weary while doing good, for in due season she shall reap if she does not lose heart.

adapted from Galatians 6:9

5:13–15 The gospel frees us from bondage to legalism and replaces it with the law of love.

5:22, 23 Fruit signifies that all nine are normal results of the life of the **Spirit**. These qualities stand in sharp contrast to the disruptive "works of the flesh" (v. 19).

6:2, 5 These verses do not contradict each other. Verse 2 refers to helping one another with spiritual burdens and guiding each other out from under the burden of sin. Verse 5 stresses each individual's responsibility to do the work to which the Lord has called him or her.

The Mighty Pen

Jay Kesler

Several years ago it dawned on me that most teenagers have never received a first-class personal letter from an adult. They receive letters from friends and get advertisements from people selling things, but they seldom receive a thoughtful letter. I began writing letters to kids and encouraging parents and grandparents to do the same. I have been amazed at how powerful the tradition of a letter on a birthday, Christmas, or the anniversary of a special occasion can be. As one student put it, "My grandfather never misses my birthday. He is sort of a poet and always writes a birthday poem for me and the other grandchildren, mostly about nature and life. I read them over and over. Some day we'll have a collection of those in our family. I think that's pretty special."

Not all of us are poets, but then again, this granddad is probably no Robert Frost, either. He is simply a grandfather who understands how powerful even small predictabilities—traditions, if you please—can be. ✦

reap if we do not lose heart. [10]Therefore, as
we have opportunity, let us do good to all,
especially to those who are of the house-
hold of faith.

Glory Only in the Cross

[11]See with what large letters I have writ-
ten to you with my own hand! [12]As many
as desire to make a good showing in the
flesh, these *would* compel you to be circum-
cised, only that they may not suffer perse-
cution for the cross of Christ. [13]For not even
those who are circumcised keep the law,
but they desire to have you circumcised
that they may boast in your flesh. [14]But
God forbid that I should boast except in
the cross of our Lord Jesus Christ, by
whom[a] the world has been crucified to
me, and I to the world. [15]For in Christ Jesus
neither circumcision nor uncircumcision
avails anything, but a new creation.

Blessing and a Plea

[16]And as many as walk according to this
rule, peace and mercy *be* upon them, and
upon the Israel of God.

[17]From now on let no one trouble me, for
I bear in my body the marks of the Lord Je-
sus.

[18]Brethren, the grace of our Lord Jesus
Christ *be* with your spirit. Amen.

6:14 [a]Or *by which* (the cross)

6:12, 13 Paul exposes the selfish motives of the false teachers. They wanted the Galatian Christians to be **circumcised** so that as teachers they would not **suffer persecution** from other Jews for failing to support the law. These teachers also wanted to boast in the converts they had made. But those who were advocating circumcision were not keeping other parts of the **law** themselves and thus were the ultimate hypocrites.

6:17 Paul's scars reflected the suffering he had endured for his faith at the hand of his persecutors.

✦Ephesians✦

Ephesians is the first of Paul's "Prison Epistles" written during his first Roman imprisonment. It may have been a circular letter intended to be sent to a number of churches, even though it addresses the problems of the church in Ephesus. The book focuses on the nature of salvation and the believer's life in Christ.

Paul admonishes believers to accept their responsibility to walk in accordance with their heavenly calling in Christ Jesus (4:1). Ephesians details the resources God has provided to every Christian, young and old, for ministering within the church and for battling Satan. It was also written to encourage the body to maturity in Christ and to make believers more aware of their position in Christ. This spiritual wealth we have in Christ is the basis for our practice in every level of life.✦

CHAPTER 1

Greeting

Paul, an apostle of Jesus Christ by the will of God,

To the saints who are in Eph′e•sus, and faithful in Christ Jesus:

2Grace to you and peace from God our Father and the Lord Jesus Christ.

Redemption in Christ

3Blessed *be* the God and Father of our Lord Jesus Christ, who has blessed us with every spiritual blessing in the heavenly *places* in Christ, 4just as He chose us in Him before the foundation of the world, that we should be holy and without blame before Him in love, 5having predestined us to adoption as sons by Jesus Christ to Himself, according to the good pleasure of His will, 6to the praise of the glory of His grace, by which He made us accepted in the Beloved.

7In Him we have redemption through
His blood, the forgiveness of sins, according to the riches of His grace 8which He
made to abound toward us in all wisdom
and prudence, 9having made known to us
the mystery of His will, according to His good pleasure which He purposed in Himself, 10that in the dispensation of the fullness of the times He might gather together in one all things in Christ, both[a] which are in heaven and which are on earth—in Him.
11In Him also we have obtained an inheritance, being predestined according to the purpose of Him who works all things according to the counsel of His will, 12that we
who first trusted in Christ should be to the praise of His glory.

1:10 [a]NU-Text and M-Text omit *both*.

1:11 counsel of His will: God's eternal and immutable plan.

A Confident Hope

Lloyd Ogilvie

Hope is more than wishing, yearning, or optimism. As it is used in the Bible, the word "hope" means confident expectations rooted in the Lord's promises. Hope never exists by itself. It springs forth in response to His gracious assurance, "For I know the thoughts that I think toward you, says the LORD, thoughts of peace and not of evil, to give you a future and a hope" (Jer. 29:11).

"Hope is not something Christ *gives*; it is what He *is*."

In Ephesians Paul uses the word "hope" in relation to the plans of God for us as they are focused in Christ (5:18). These plans are that we know Christ, be filled with His Spirit, and consistently become more like Him. We are given a clear picture of the person we are meant to be. In spite of our vacillating human nature, Christ pushes us forward. He loves us as we are but never leaves us stagnant. He empowers us with hope, based on His promise that He will never leave us nor forsake us.

More than this, we are given confident hope that He will use all that we go through to enable us to grow in maturity as saints. Nothing is wasted. With this hope we can endure the pressures and pain of adversity.

Hope is not something Christ *gives;* it is what He *is.* We receive lasting hope when He lives in us. This quality of hope makes us resilient, confident, and bold. Because Christ never gives up on us, we can endure without giving up. ✦

13In Him you also *trusted,* after you
heard the word of truth, the gospel of your
salvation; in whom also, having believed,
you were sealed with the Holy Spirit of
promise, 14who[a] is the guarantee of our in-
heritance until the redemption of the pur-
chased possession, to the praise of His
glory.

Prayer for Spiritual Wisdom

15Therefore I also, after I heard of your
faith in the Lord Jesus and your love for all
the saints, 16do not cease to give thanks for
you, making mention of you in my
prayers: 17that the God of our Lord Jesus
Christ, the Father of glory, may give to you
the spirit of wisdom and revelation in the
knowledge of Him, 18the eyes of your un-
derstanding[a] being enlightened; that you
may know what is the hope of His calling,

1:14 [a]NU-Text reads *which.* 1:18 [a]NU-Text and M-Text read *hearts.*

1:14 guarantee: down payment. The Holy Spirit is God's deposit for purchasing us and owning us forever.

1:15 Intercessory prayer should have a part in the spiritual life of every Christian. How often do we take time to give thanks for our fellow believers?

Clearly Different

George Barna

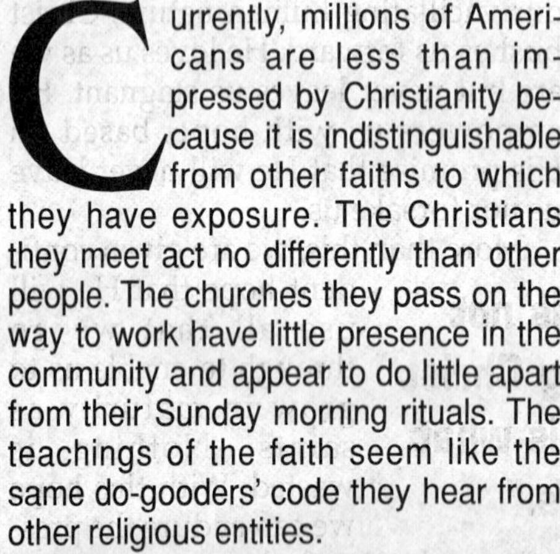

Currently, millions of Americans are less than impressed by Christianity because it is indistinguishable from other faiths to which they have exposure. The Christians they meet act no differently than other people. The churches they pass on the way to work have little presence in the community and appear to do little apart from their Sunday morning rituals. The teachings of the faith seem like the same do-gooders' code they hear from other religious entities.

Somehow, many Americans have heard about and accepted the notion that a fellow named Jesus Christ once lived and did some rather unusual things, but the connection between those events and their own lives is missing. Even their view of God has frequently remained untouched by the teachings of the Bible. Until we get our own house (of faith) in order, the chances of our leaving a lasting, life-changing impression on others is negligible.

Ultimately, we must impress upon America that there is a crucial difference between Christianity and the pop religion of the day. God has clearly stated that, regardless of how hard we try and how many good deeds we do, entry into heaven is not available for purchase through the sweat of our brow (Eph. 2:8, 9). In a driven culture, this is hard to sell. Our job, as God's ambassadors to a confused and sinful world, is to continually use the resources He has provided—including our intelligence—to proclaim His way and to pray for His blessing upon those efforts. ✦

what are the riches of the glory of His in-
heritance in the saints, [19]and what *is* the ex-
ceeding greatness of His power toward us
who believe, according to the working of
His mighty power [20]which He worked in
Christ when He raised Him from the dead
and seated *Him* at His right hand in the
heavenly *places,* [21]far above all principality
and power and might and dominion, and
every name that is named, not only in this
age but also in that which is to come.
[22]And He put all *things* under His feet,
and gave Him *to be* head over all *things* to
the church, [23]which is His body, the full-
ness of Him who fills all in all.

CHAPTER 2

By Grace Through Faith

And you *He made alive,* who were dead
in trespasses and sins, [2]in which you once
walked according to the course of this
world, according to the prince of the
power of the air, the spirit who now works

1:19–21 The **power** which works in **us who believe** is the same power which God **worked in Christ**. This power is seen in Christ's resurrection and exaltation **in the heavenly places**, above all other powers—present and future. How can we fail to have spiritual victory if we allow this power to fill our lives? If our problem is no bigger than raising Christ from the dead, God can take care of it.

in the sons of disobedience, [3]among whom
also we all once conducted ourselves in the
lusts of our flesh, fulfilling the desires
of the flesh and of the mind, and were by
nature children of wrath, just as the
others.

[4]But God, who is rich in mercy, because
of His great love with which He loved us,
[5]even when we were dead in trespasses,
made us alive together with Christ (by
grace you have been saved), [6]and raised *us*
up together, and made *us* sit together in the
heavenly *places* in Christ Jesus, [7]that in the
ages to come He might show the exceeding
riches of His grace in *His* kindness toward
us in Christ Jesus. [8]For by grace you have
been saved through faith, and that not of
yourselves; *it is* the gift of God, [9]not of
works, lest anyone should boast. [10]For we
are His workmanship, created in Christ Jesus for good works, which God prepared
beforehand that we should walk in them.

Brought Near by His Blood

[11]Therefore remember that you, once
Gentiles in the flesh—who are called
Uncircumcision by what is called the Circumcision made in the flesh by hands—
[12]that at that time you were without Christ,
being aliens from the commonwealth of Israel and strangers from the covenants of
promise, having no hope and without God
in the world. [13]But now in Christ Jesus you
who once were far off have been brought
near by the blood of Christ.

Christ Our Peace

[14]For He Himself is our peace, who has
made both one, and has broken down the
middle wall of separation, [15]having abolished in His flesh the enmity, *that is,* the
law of commandments *contained* in ordinances, so as to create in Himself one new
man *from* the two, *thus* making peace, [16]and
that He might reconcile them both to God
in one body through the cross, thereby
putting to death the enmity. [17]And He
came and preached peace to you who were
afar off and to those who were near. [18]For
through Him we both have access by one
Spirit to the Father.

Christ Our Cornerstone

[19]Now, therefore, you are no longer
strangers and foreigners, but fellow citizens with the saints and members of the
household of God, [20]having been built on
the foundation of the apostles and
prophets, Jesus Christ Himself being the
chief corner*stone,* [21]in whom the whole
building, being fitted together, grows into
a holy temple in the Lord, [22]in whom you
also are being built together for a dwelling
place of God in the Spirit.

CHAPTER 3

The Mystery Revealed

For this reason I, Paul, the prisoner of
Christ Jesus for you Gentiles— [2]if indeed
you have heard of the dispensation of the

2:3 children of wrath: Whether we are Jew or Gentile, living according to our fallen **nature** deserves the wrath of God. His wrath is His refusal to compromise with evil and His commitment to punish wrongdoing.

2:10 we are His workmanship: God made us what we are now. He gave us both our salvation and the faith by which we received it. We have been **created** anew, given a new beginning and a new nature, so that we can do the **good works** that, from the beginning, He planned for us to do. "It is not against works that we contend, but against trust in works" (Luther).

2:11 Uncircumcision: used here to explain that the Gentiles did not have a covenant relationship with God as did the Jews.

2:14 Jesus' death united all believers into one group; Jews and Gentiles could worship together.

3:1–13 The revealed **mystery** of the Gentiles' inclusion in God's people (vv. 1–6) is the basis for Paul's ministry to them (vv. 7–13).

PRISONERS OF CHRIST

Lloyd Ogilvie

In the apostle Paul's conversion experience on the Damascus road, Jesus Christ had conscripted and captivated him. Paul became a prisoner of the Lord (Eph. 3:1). From that time on, his only passion was Christ—to know Christ, to be filled with Christ, to communicate Christ, and to see everything in the perspective of Christ. He became the most free human being who ever lived because he knew he belonged to Christ—mind, soul, and body.

"We are prisoners of Christ's unchanging, unqualified grace."

The only way to be released from the tension and pressure of life's tough times is to know that we are prisoners, not of fate or people or circumstances, but of Christ's unchanging, unqualified grace. We can take anything if we understand that, according to His plan, He is using what we are going through for His glory. ✦

grace of God which was given to me for
you, [3]how that by revelation He made
known to me the mystery (as I have briefly
written already, [4]by which, when you read,
you may understand my knowledge in the
mystery of Christ), [5]which in other ages
was not made known to the sons of men,
as it has now been revealed by the Spirit to
His holy apostles and prophets: [6]that the
Gentiles should be fellow heirs, of the
same body, and partakers of His promise
in Christ through the gospel, [7]of which I
became a minister according to the gift of
the grace of God given to me by the effective working of His power.

Purpose of the Mystery

[8]To me, who am less than the least of all
the saints, this grace was given, that I
should preach among the Gentiles the unsearchable riches of Christ, [9]and to make
all see what *is* the fellowship[a] of the mystery, which from the beginning of the ages
has been hidden in God who created all
things through Jesus Christ;[b] [10]to the intent
that now the manifold wisdom of God
might be made known by the church to the
principalities and powers in the heavenly
places, [11]according to the eternal purpose
which He accomplished in Christ Jesus our
Lord, [12]in whom we have boldness and access with confidence through faith in Him.
[13]Therefore I ask that you do not lose heart
at my tribulations for you, which is your
glory.

Appreciation of the Mystery

[14]For this reason I bow my knees to the
Father of our Lord Jesus Christ,[a] [15]from
whom the whole family in heaven and
earth is named, [16]that He would grant you,
according to the riches of His glory, to be
strengthened with might through His

3:9 [a]NU-Text and M-Text read *stewardship* (dispensation). [b]NU-Text omits *through Jesus Christ.*
3:14 [a]NU-Text omits *of our Lord Jesus Christ.*

Spirit in the inner man, 17that Christ may
dwell in your hearts through faith; that
you, being rooted and grounded in love,
18may be able to comprehend with all the
saints what *is* the width and length and
depth and height— 19to know the love of
Christ which passes knowledge; that you
may be filled with all the fullness of
God.

20Now to Him who is able to do exceed-
ingly abundantly above all that we ask or
think, according to the power that works
in us, 21to Him *be* glory in the church by
Christ Jesus to all generations, forever and
ever. Amen.

CHAPTER 4

Walk in Unity

I, therefore, the prisoner of the Lord, be-
seech you to walk worthy of the calling
with which you were called, 2with all low-
liness and gentleness, with longsuffering,
bearing with one another in love, 3endeav-
oring to keep the unity of the Spirit in the
bond of peace. 4*There is* one body and one
Spirit, just as you were called in one hope
of your calling; 5one Lord, one faith, one
baptism; 6one God and Father of all, who *is*
above all, and through all, and in you[a] all.

Spiritual Gifts

7But to each one of us grace was given
according to the measure of Christ's gift.
8Therefore He says:

"When He ascended on high,
He led captivity captive,
And gave gifts to men."[a]

9(Now this, *"He ascended"*—what does it
mean but that He also first[a] descended into
the lower parts of the earth? 10He who de-
scended is also the One who ascended far
above all the heavens, that He might fill all
things.)

11And He Himself gave some *to be* apos-
tles, some prophets, some evangelists, and
some pastors and teachers, 12for the equip-
ping of the saints for the work of ministry,
for the edifying of the body of Christ, 13till
we all come to the unity of the faith and of
the knowledge of the Son of God, to a per-
fect man, to the measure of the stature of
the fullness of Christ; 14that we should no
longer be children, tossed to and fro and
carried about with every wind of doctrine,
by the trickery of men, in the cunning
craftiness of deceitful plotting, 15but,
speaking the truth in love, may grow up in
all things into Him who is the head—
Christ— 16from whom the whole body,
joined and knit together by what every
joint supplies, according to the effective
working by which every part does its
share, causes growth of the body for the
edifying of itself in love.

The New Man

17This I say, therefore, and testify in the
Lord, that you should no longer walk as
the rest of[a] the Gentiles walk, in the futility
of their mind, 18having their understand-
ing darkened, being alienated from the life
of God, because of the ignorance that is in
them, because of the blindness of their
heart; 19who, being past feeling, have given
themselves over to lewdness, to work all
uncleanness with greediness.

20But you have not so learned Christ, 21if
indeed you have heard Him and have been
taught by Him, as the truth is in Jesus:

4:6 [a]NU-Text omits *you;* M-Text reads *us.*
4:8 [a]Psalm 68:18 4:9 [a]NU-Text omits *first.*
4:17 [a]NU-Text omits *the rest of.*

3:18 comprehend: experience.

4:1 prisoner of the Lord: The letter was written from a Roman prison. How we live is a testimony to our faith. At work, at home, everywhere we go, our lives should present consistent evidence of the power of God.

4:17 Daily we must examine our hearts and minds and ask the Lord to purify them from worldly thinking.

ABOVE AND BEYOND

Evelyn Christenson

No matter how much I expect from God, He always gives more. No matter how much faith I have, I never seem to have enough to equal the fabulous amount of whatever God is ready, willing, and anxious to do—when there is enough prayer. God's intention is to exceed by His answer even the far-reaching petitions of His pray-ers and the aspirations that prompted them.

Paul gives us a tremendous look into God's mind (Eph. 3:20). And I have found that life bathed in, saturated by, and directed through prayer has been exhilarating and exciting. I feel as if I am continuously standing on tiptoe, straining to peer into God's mind, wondering how and what He is going to do this time. Yes, I have learned about His "exceedingly abundantly above all that (any of us could) ask or think."

How much power is God releasing because of *your* prayers? Then again, how much power is God waiting for you to unlock with your key of prayer? ✦

"Life bathed in, saturated by, and directed through prayer has been exhilarating and exciting."

[22]that you put off, concerning your former
conduct, the old man which grows corrupt
according to the deceitful lusts, [23]and be re-
newed in the spirit of your mind, [24]and that
you put on the new man which was cre-
ated according to God, in true righteous-
ness and holiness.

Do Not Grieve the Spirit

[25]Therefore, putting away lying, *"Let each one of you speak truth with his neighbor,"*[a] for we are members of one another.
[26]*"Be angry, and do not sin"*:[a] do not let the
sun go down on your wrath, [27]nor give
place to the devil. [28]Let him who stole steal
no longer, but rather let him labor, working
with *his* hands what is good, that he may
have something to give him who has need.
[29]Let no corrupt word proceed out of your
mouth, but what is good for necessary edification, that it may impart grace to the
hearers. [30]And do not grieve the Holy
Spirit of God, by whom you were sealed
for the day of redemption. [31]Let all bitter-
ness, wrath, anger, clamor, and evil speak-
ing be put away from you, with all malice.

4:25 [a]Zechariah 8:16 4:26 [a]Psalm 4:4

4:22, 23 By the grace of God we have **put off** the **old man**, the person we used to be when we were controlled by sin. The human spirit is to be transformed by the power of the Holy Spirit.

4:30 do not grieve: Do not push the Spirit away, ignore Him, or cause Him to grieve by rejecting His counsel.

Never Too Old to Change

Charles R. Swindoll

You and I are growing older. That's automatic. But that does not necessarily mean we are growing up. How important it is that we do so! And it will not happen unless we get control of our attitudes, which turn us in the right direction. Let me urge you not to feed your mind with thoughts like: *I'm too far gone to change*; or, *Having been through all the things I've been through, I cannot alter my attitude*. Wrong!

"God's specialty is bringing renewal to our strength."

It is childish to play in the traffic of fear or let the hobgoblins of habit impede our progress. No one can win a race by continually looking back at where he or she has been. That will only demoralize, immobilize, and ultimately paralyze. God is for us. God's goal is that we move toward maturity, all our past failures and faults and hang-ups notwithstanding (Eph. 4:14). Attitudes can soar even if our circumstances lag and our past record sags.

God's specialty is bringing renewal to our strength, not reminders of our weakness. Take it by faith—He is well aware of your weaknesses; He just sovereignly chooses not to stop there. They become the platform upon which He does His best work. Cheer up! There is great hope. You will not be the first He helped from puberty to maturity. ✦

32And be kind to one another, tender-
hearted, forgiving one another, even as
God in Christ forgave you.

CHAPTER 5

Walk in Love

Therefore be imitators of God as dear
children. 2And walk in love, as Christ also
has loved us and given Himself for us, an
offering and a sacrifice to God for a sweet-
smelling aroma.

5:5 [a]NU-Text reads *For know this.*

3But fornication and all uncleanness or
covetousness, let it not even be named
among you, as is fitting for saints; 4neither
filthiness, nor foolish talking, nor coarse
jesting, which are not fitting, but rather
giving of thanks. 5For this you know,[a] that
no fornicator, unclean person, nor cov-
etous man, who is an idolater, has any in-
heritance in the kingdom of Christ and
God. 6Let no one deceive you with empty
words, for because of these things the
wrath of God comes upon the sons of
disobedience. 7Therefore do not be par-
takers with them.

4:32 This verse should be our guide in our relationships with spouses, children, friends, coworkers, every believer we come in contact with.

5:1, 2 As Christians we should pattern our lives after Jesus and His example of perfect love.

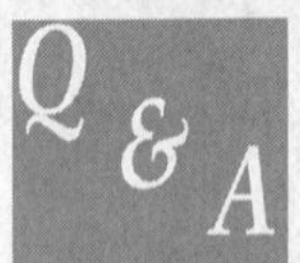

How can the Bible help me overcome my destructive emotions?

Dr. Frank Minirth and Dr. Paul Meier

Usually those who struggle with emotional problems will struggle spiritually, too. "Sanctification" (becoming more like Christ) includes recognizing emotional conflicts as signals from God that we need to monitor our behavior. For example, anger can be a warning to slow down, examine the situation, and take the necessary steps to dissipate hostility constructively.

Holding in anger and bitterness solves nothing. The bitterness churns away, tearing up an individual's emotions and often doing physical damage. Prolonged bitterness can lead to chronic, clinical depression. Yet if the bitter person had applied the basic principles of forgiveness as taught in Ephesians, the anger would have been put away long before it became bitterness (4:26–32). It is a pay-now-or-pay-later proposition because forgiveness is frequently the key to overcoming depression. Unless forgiveness is applied, the emotional despair will remain.

In other instances, meditating on verses of encouragement (such as Ps. 27:14; Is. 41:10; 1 Pet. 5:10) can make us take a positive look at our problems and help us find solutions. Also, Scripture reminds us that this life is only the beginning, not the end. If life on earth was all we had to look forward to, who would not be anxious or depressed? In God's eternal kingdom, the believer will be able to say, "Can you believe how uptight we were over the silliest things?!"

Remember, daily adherence to biblical guidelines improves our sense of worth and generally bolsters our mental and spiritual health. ✦

I pray that no one deceives my grandchildren with empty words.

Adapted from Ephesians 5:6

Walk in Light

8For you were once darkness, but now
you are light in the Lord. Walk as children
of light 9(for the fruit of the Spirit[a] *is* in all
goodness, righteousness, and truth),
10finding out what is acceptable to the
Lord. 11And have no fellowship with the
unfruitful works of darkness, but rather
expose *them*. 12For it is shameful even to
speak of those things which are done by
them in secret. 13But all things that are ex-
posed are made manifest by the light, for
whatever makes manifest is light. 14There-
fore He says:

"Awake, you who sleep,
Arise from the dead,
And Christ will give you light."

5:9 [a]NU-Text reads *light.*

Walk in Wisdom

15See then that you walk circumspectly,
not as fools but as wise, 16redeeming the
time, because the days are evil.
17Therefore do not be unwise, but un-
derstand what the will of the Lord *is.* 18And
do not be drunk with wine, in which is dis-
sipation; but be filled with the Spirit,
19speaking to one another in psalms and
hymns and spiritual songs, singing and
making melody in your heart to the Lord,
20giving thanks always for all things to
God the Father in the name of our Lord Je-
sus Christ, 21submitting to one another in
the fear of God.[a]

Marriage—Christ and the Church

22Wives, submit to your own husbands,
as to the Lord. 23For the husband is head of
the wife, as also Christ is head of the
church; and He is the Savior of the body.
24Therefore, just as the church is subject to
Christ, so *let* the wives *be* to their own hus-
bands in everything.
25Husbands, love your wives, just as
Christ also loved the church and gave
Himself for her, 26that He might sanctify
and cleanse her with the washing of water
by the word, 27that He might present her to
Himself a glorious church, not having spot
or wrinkle or any such thing, but that she
should be holy and without blemish. 28So
husbands ought to love their own wives as
their own bodies; he who loves his wife
loves himself. 29For no one ever hated his
own flesh, but nourishes and cherishes it,
just as the Lord *does* the church. 30For we
are members of His body,[a] of His flesh and
of His bones. 31*"For this reason a man shall
leave his father and mother and be joined
to his wife, and the two shall become one
flesh."*[a] 32This is a great mystery, but I
speak concerning Christ and the church.
33Nevertheless let each one of you in par-
ticular so love his own wife as himself, and
let the wife *see* that she respects *her* hus-
band.

CHAPTER 6

Children and Parents

Children, obey your parents in the Lord,
for this is right. 2*"Honor your father and
mother,"* which is the first commandment
with promise: 3*"that it may be well with
you and you may live long on the earth."*[a]
4And you, fathers, do not provoke your
children to wrath, but bring them up in the
training and admonition of the Lord.

Bondservants and Masters

5Bondservants, be obedient to those
who are your masters according to the
flesh, with fear and trembling, in sincerity
of heart, as to Christ; 6not with eyeservice,
as men-pleasers, but as bondservants of
Christ, doing the will of God from the
heart, 7with goodwill doing service, as to
the Lord, and not to men, 8knowing that
whatever good anyone does, he will re-
ceive the same from the Lord, whether *he is*
a slave or free.

5:21 [a]NU-Text reads *Christ.* 5:30 [a]NU-Text omits the rest of this verse. 5:31 [a]Genesis 2:24
6:3 [a]Deuteronomy 5:16

5:15 circumspectly: cautiously.

5:18 Be filled with the Spirit is a command to be obeyed, not an option for the Christian. "Be filled" is a present tense meaning "go on being filled with the Spirit." It is also plural; all believers are to "be filled."

The image is of a container so full that there is no room for anything else. The Spirit-filled Christian is so given over to the Spirit's leadership that other conflicting influences have no place.

6:1–4 Children, obey your parents in the Lord, that is, in all things lawful and Christian. In 5:22 wives are told to be submissive, but here children are ordered to "obey", a far stronger word. **do not provoke**: Parents, do not be unreasonably severe with children or ridicule them. **bring them up**: Instruct and correct them consistently in ways that will teach them to serve **the Lord**.

MORE THAN FIFTY-FIFTY

Kevin Leman

We each walk into marriage with our own rule books. Most couples never exchange rule books, but each person knows that his or hers is right. We say that two people are married, but really it is more like six people are married. You have married each other's families and all of their expectations.

When expectations are not fulfilled, disillusionment comes into a marriage. After disillusionment comes anger, and with anger comes license. At that point a person feels that if he or she is not getting what is needed at home, he or she can go elsewhere.

"To really make a marriage work, you have to put your spouse's feelings first."

Too many people today have a fifty-fifty marriage. They have their own towels, their own checking accounts, and they go their own ways. I call them married singles. To really make a marriage work, you have to put your spouse's feelings first. It's difficult. It takes things like asking your husband or wife what you could do to be a better spouse. But I can tell you that the rewards are worth it. ✦

9And you, masters, do the same things
to them, giving up threatening, knowing
that your own Master also[a] is in heaven,
and there is no partiality with Him.

The Whole Armor of God

10Finally, my brethren, be strong in the
Lord and in the power of His might. 11Put
on the whole armor of God, that you may
be able to stand against the wiles of the
devil. 12For we do not wrestle against flesh
and blood, but against principalities,
against powers, against the rulers of the
darkness of this age,[a] against spiritual *hosts*
of wickedness in the heavenly *places*.
13Therefore take up the whole armor of
God, that you may be able to withstand in
the evil day, and having done all, to stand.
14Stand therefore, having girded your
waist with truth, having put on the breast-
plate of righteousness, 15and having shod
your feet with the preparation of the
gospel of peace; 16above all, taking the
shield of faith with which you will be able

6:9 [a]NU-Text reads *He who is both their Master and yours.* 6:12 [a]NU-Text reads *rulers of this darkness.*

6:11, 12 whole armor of God: God provides complete armor to protect us from all kinds of evil and temptation. **The wiles of the devil** are the result of superhuman craftiness, capable of drawing careless Christians into sin. **wrestle**: The Christian life is a struggle; it requires decision and effort. Our real enemy is not human **flesh and blood**, but the devil and his hosts. These **rulers of the darkness of this age** have so blinded the world to spiritual values that unregenerate people cannot understand God or His will. The forces of evil are superhuman, but they are not all-powerful. God has adequate power for us. See Acts 1:8.

Finding Balance in Marriage

Dr. Robert Hemfelt

Couples, no matter how long they have been together, need to see clearly how their old family ties affect their marital relationships. What kind of communication techniques were learned in childhood? Consider traditions, hobbies, habits, work ethics, prejudices, and household chores.

It's hard to find a new balance point in all areas. Marriage partners are constantly teeter-tottering up and down, trying to find a comfortable balance between the old and new ways of doing things. They are seeking a union that is tailor-made for them, a compromise—that final, fragile destination of new balance in each area.

We all have a built-in tendency to be creatures of extreme—of imbalance. Couples often swing from intense infatuation to periods of disenchantment and conflict, then back again. It can take years to maintain a balance of habits, expectations, and emotional closeness without the extreme or constant ups and downs that threaten a marriage. But if we are following the guidelines for marriage outlined in the second half of Ephesians 5, our commitment will outlast and be strengthened by these challenges.

Be patient and flexible and the teeter-tottering will slow down and become a pleasant ride you both can enjoy. ✦

to quench all the fiery darts of the wicked
one. 17And take the helmet of salvation,
and the sword of the Spirit, which is the
word of God; 18praying always with all
prayer and supplication in the Spirit, being
watchful to this end with all perseverance
and supplication for all the saints— 19and
for me, that utterance may be given to me,
that I may open my mouth boldly to make
known the mystery of the gospel, 20for
which I am an ambassador in chains; that
in it I may speak boldly, as I ought to
speak.

A Gracious Greeting

21But that you also may know my affairs
and how I am doing, Tych'i·cus, a beloved
brother and faithful minister in the Lord,
will make all things known to you; 22whom
I have sent to you for this very purpose,
that you may know our affairs, and *that* he
may comfort your hearts.

23Peace to the brethren, and love with
faith, from God the Father and the Lord Jesus Christ. 24Grace *be* with all those who
love our Lord Jesus Christ in sincerity.
Amen.

6:18 Praying always: Because we cannot win without God's help. **Being watchful**: Because God does not give us victory without our full commitment and best effort. **supplication**: Earnest prayer for other Christians.

LEAD BY EXAMPLE

Ron Lee Davis

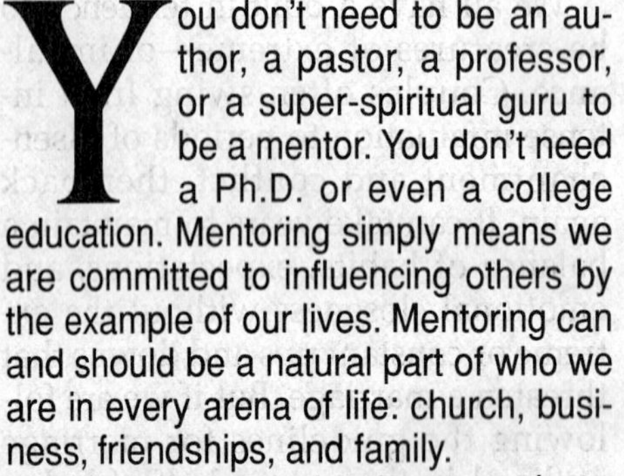

You don't need to be an author, a pastor, a professor, or a super-spiritual guru to be a mentor. You don't need a Ph.D. or even a college education. Mentoring simply means we are committed to influencing others by the example of our lives. Mentoring can and should be a natural part of who we are in every arena of life: church, business, friendships, and family.

Although mentoring has an educational dimension (Paul instructs us to pass on the teachings and doctrine of our faith as well as our character), the purpose of mentoring is not only to impart knowledge to others. Rather, authentic Christian mentoring deals primarily with issues of maturity and integrity, and only secondarily with information and skills. It has much more to do with modeling character than with verbal teaching. It has more to do with what is *caught* than what is *taught*. ✦

✦Philippians✦

While in prison in Rome, Paul received a money offering from the church in Philippi, the first church he founded in Macedonia during the early part of his second missionary journey. He wrote this letter to thank the believers for their generous support and sent the letter to the church by the hand of Epaphroditus, who had delivered the offering.

Paul also included some instruction on Christian unity; he taught that true unity and joy are only possible in Christ. Although Paul's life was at stake, he wrote the letter almost entirely as an expression of joy. "Rejoice" is the key word in the epistle, reflecting Paul's confidence that He who had begun a good work would complete it until the day of Jesus Christ (1:6). Sixteen times throughout the epistle Paul mentioned "joy" and "rejoicing," demonstrating that, for Christians of any age, triumph over circumstances is simply a matter of trusting Christ.

Every chapter resounds with the theme of the centrality of Jesus in the Christian's life. To live was to be in Christ and to die was to gain (1:21). For us today, we are reminded that with Christ as our model of humility and service, we can enjoy a oneness of purpose, attitude, goal, and labor—a truth that Paul demonstrated in his own life and that the Philippians—and believers throughout time—needed to hear. ✦

CHAPTER 1

Greeting

Paul and Timothy, bondservants of Jesus Christ,

To all the saints in Christ Jesus who are in Phi·lip′pī, with the bishops[a] and deacons:

[2]Grace to you and peace from God our Father and the Lord Jesus Christ.

1:1 [a]Literally *overseers*

Thankfulness and Prayer

[3]I thank my God upon every remembrance of you, [4]always in every prayer of mine making request for you all with joy, [5]for your fellowship in the gospel from the first day until now, [6]being confident of this very thing, that He who has begun a good work in you will complete *it* until the day of Jesus Christ; [7]just as it is right for me to think this of you all, because I have you in my heart, inasmuch as both in my chains and in the defense and confirmation of the gospel, you all are partakers with me of grace. [8]For God is my witness, how greatly

✦ ✦

1:1 bishops: overseers, spiritual leaders, pastors. Both bishops and deacons were recognized officers of the early church.

I long for you all with the affection of Jesus Christ.

9And this I pray, that your love may
abound still more and more in knowledge
and all discernment, 10that you may ap-
prove the things that are excellent, that you
may be sincere and without offense till the
day of Christ, 11being filled with the fruits
of righteousness which *are* by Jesus Christ,
to the glory and praise of God.

I pray that my child will be confident of this very thing, that You who have begun a good work in him will complete it until the day of Jesus Christ.

adapted from Philippians 1:6

Christ Is Preached

12But I want you to know, brethren, that
the things *which happened* to me have actu-
ally turned out for the furtherance of the
gospel, 13so that it has become evident to
the whole palace guard, and to all the rest,
that my chains are in Christ; 14and most of
the brethren in the Lord, having become
confident by my chains, are much more
bold to speak the word without fear.
15Some indeed preach Christ even from
envy and strife, and some also from good-
will: 16The former[a] preach Christ from self-
ish ambition, not sincerely, supposing to
add affliction to my chains; 17but the latter
out of love, knowing that I am appointed
for the defense of the gospel. 18What then?
Only *that* in every way, whether in pre-
tense or in truth, Christ is preached; and in
this I rejoice, yes, and will rejoice.

To Live Is Christ

19For I know that this will turn out for
my deliverance through your prayer and
the supply of the Spirit of Jesus Christ, 20ac-
cording to my earnest expectation and
hope that in nothing I shall be ashamed,
but with all boldness, as always, so now
also Christ will be magnified in my body,
whether by life or by death. 21For to me, to
live *is* Christ, and to die *is* gain. 22But if *I*
live on in the flesh, this *will mean* fruit from
my labor; yet what I shall choose I cannot
tell. 23For[a] I am hard-pressed between the
two, having a desire to depart and be with
Christ, *which is* far better. 24Nevertheless to
remain in the flesh *is* more needful for you.
25And being confident of this, I know that I
shall remain and continue with you all for
your progress and joy of faith, 26that your
rejoicing for me may be more abundant
in Jesus Christ by my coming to you
again.

Striving and Suffering for Christ

27Only let your conduct be worthy of the
gospel of Christ, so that whether I come
and see you or am absent, I may hear of
your affairs, that you stand fast in one
spirit, with one mind striving together for

1:16 [a]NU-Text reverses the contents of verses 16 and 17. 1:23 [a]NU-Text and M-Text read *But*.

1:9, 10 knowledge . . . discernment: Information about God's truth, and sound judgment in applying it. **approve the . . . excellent**: Love guided by knowledge and discernment enables the Christian to make right choices in the situations of life. **the day of Christ**: Of His return.

1:12–14 turned out: Even difficult situations can be used for advancing the work of the **gospel**. Through Paul's imprisonment many others, including the **palace guard** (v. 13), heard about Christ. Because of Paul's courageous example, other Christians were made **bold to speak the word** without fear (v. 14). How we cope with adversity is not only a test of our faith but also an opportunity to impact the lives of those around us.

1:27 As God's children, our conduct is to be holy. As members of the body of Christ, we must work together to advance the gospel of Christ, striving for unity and cooperation.

Should death be delayed by artificial life support?

Elmer L. Gray

"When my life forces are failing and it is only a matter of time, do not keep me here with artificial means." That is what I have told my family.

A "living will" is a legal document through which you can authorize the authorities not to prolong your life when you are dying. This relieves your survivors and the authorities of the responsibility for the decision.

Find out about the laws in your state. Check with your doctor, a hospital, or a senior adult group. If you choose to make a living will, do it in agreement with your spouse and other members of the family. Your signature will need to be appropriately witnessed.

We need not fear death nor resist it. Paul said, "For me, to live is Christ, and to die is gain" (Phil. 1:21). Jesus said, "Be faithful unto death, and I will give you the crown of life" (Rev. 2:10).

Ask God to guide you in making necessary decisions for the sake of others. ✦

the faith of the gospel, 28and not in any way
terrified by your adversaries, which is to
them a proof of perdition, but to you of sal-
vation,[a] and that from God. 29For to you it
has been granted on behalf of Christ, not
only to believe in Him, but also to suffer
for His sake, 30having the same conflict
which you saw in me and now hear *is* in
me.

CHAPTER 2

Unity Through Humility

Therefore if *there is* any consolation in
Christ, if any comfort of love, if any fellow-
ship of the Spirit, if any affection and
mercy, 2fulfill my joy by being like-
minded, having the same love, *being* of one
accord, of one mind. 3*Let* nothing *be done*
through selfish ambition or conceit, but in
lowliness of mind let each esteem others
better than himself. 4Let each of you look
out not only for his own interests, but also
for the interests of others.

The Humbled and Exalted Christ

5Let this mind be in you which was also
in Christ Jesus, 6who, being in the form of
God, did not consider it robbery to be
equal with God, 7but made Himself of no
reputation, taking the form of a bondser-
vant, *and* coming in the likeness of men.
8And being found in appearance as a man,

1:28 [a]NU-Text reads *of your salvation.*

2:1 if: since. In the Greek, these three "if" clauses are not used to express doubt, but to emphasize these realities.

2:3 Let nothing be done implies a complete mastery of selfishness and **conceit** through the power of God's love within us.

2:5–8 Let: An exhortation that calls for continued action. The believer's attitude of complete submission to God is to be continually like that of Christ as depicted in vv. 6–8 (see Luke 22:42). **being in the form of God**: A clear testimony to Jesus' deity. **not . . . robbery**: Jesus' equality with God was a natural right and heritage. **made Himself of no reputation**

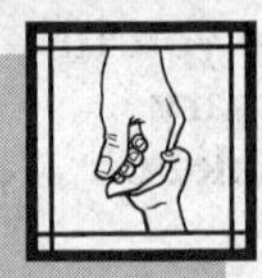

Keep Your Antenna Up

Lucibel Van Atta

I have learned that some young people will never ask for help—even from their friends. Unless you and I are looking for their silent pleas, we may be unaware that they would welcome a mentoring relationship. Be willing to seek out these younger people with the guidance of the Holy Spirit. At times I have said: "How about our getting together for an hour or so each week—for some Bible study and talking together?" Practice alerting yourself to the younger person's plea for nurture, whether expressed directly or indirectly. Sensitivity to other people's feelings—having your "antenna" up—makes the difference. ✦

He humbled Himself and became obedient
to *the point of* death, even the death of the
cross. [9]Therefore God also has highly ex-
alted Him and given Him the name which
is above every name, [10]that at the name of
Jesus every knee should bow, of those in
heaven, and of those on earth, and of those
under the earth, [11]and *that* every tongue
should confess that Jesus Christ *is* Lord, to
the glory of God the Father.

Light Bearers

[12]Therefore, my beloved, as you have al-
ways obeyed, not as in my presence only,
but now much more in my absence, work
out your own salvation with fear and trem-
bling; [13]for it is God who works in you both
to will and to do for *His* good pleasure.
[14]Do all things without complaining and
disputing, [15]that you may become blame-
less and harmless, children of God without
fault in the midst of a crooked and per-
verse generation, among whom you shine
as lights in the world, [16]holding fast the
word of life, so that I may rejoice in the day
of Christ that I have not run in vain or la-
bored in vain.
[17]Yes, and if I am being poured out *as a*
drink offering on the sacrifice and service of
your faith, I am glad and rejoice with you
all. [18]For the same reason you also be glad
and rejoice with me.

Timothy Commended

[19]But I trust in the Lord Jesus to send
Timothy to you shortly, that I also may be
encouraged when I know your state. [20]For I
have no one like-minded, who will sin-
cerely care for your state. [21]For all seek
their own, not the things which are of
Christ Jesus. [22]But you know his proven
character, that as a son with *his* father he
served with me in the gospel. [23]Therefore I
hope to send him at once, as soon as I see
how it goes with me. [24]But I trust in the
Lord that I myself shall also come shortly.

(literally, "emptied Himself"): He was willing to lay aside the glory of His deity. **death of the cross**: A form of punishment reserved for slaves and common criminals.

2:20, 21 As Christians, we are to be concerned with the things of Jesus, which in turn means being more concerned with the welfare of others than of ourselves. How many of us have a truly unselfish devotion to Christ?

MODEL OF AN UNSELFISH ATTITUDE

Charles R. Swindoll

The hidden secret of a happy life is becoming so interested in helping others that we become self-forgetful in the process.

Being unselfish in attitude strikes at the very core of our being. It means we are willing to forego our own comfort, our own preferences, our own schedules, our own desires for another's benefit. And that brings us to Christ. Perhaps you never realized that it was His attitude of unselfishness that launched Him from the splendor of heaven to a humble manger in Bethlehem . . . and later to the Cross at Calvary. How did He accept all that? Willingly.

"Being unselfish in attitude strikes at the very core of our being."

Everything that was involved in Jesus' becoming human began with an attitude of submission . . . a willingness to cooperate with God's plan for salvation. Rather than lobbying for His right to remain in heaven and continuing to enjoy all the benefits of that exalted role as the second member of the Godhead and Lord of the created world, He willingly said yes. He agreed to cooperate with a plan that would require His releasing ecstasy and accepting agony. In a state of absolute perfection and undiminished deity, He willingly came to earth. Leaving the angelic hosts who flooded His presence with adoring praise, He unselfishly accepted a role that would require His being misunderstood, abused, cursed, and crucified (Phil. 2:5–8). He unhesitatingly surrendered the fellowship and protection of the Father's glory for the lonely path of obedience and torturous death. ✦

Epaphroditus Praised

25Yet I considered it necessary to send to
you E·paph·ro·dī′tus, my brother, fellow
worker, and fellow soldier, but your mes-
senger and the one who ministered to my
need; 26since he was longing for you all,
and was distressed because you had heard
that he was sick. 27For indeed he was sick
almost unto death; but God had mercy on
him, and not only on him but on me also,
lest I should have sorrow upon sorrow.
28Therefore I sent him the more eagerly,
that when you see him again you may re-
joice, and I may be less sorrowful. 29Re-
ceive him therefore in the Lord with all
gladness, and hold such men in esteem;
30because for the work of Christ he came
close to death, not regarding his life, to
supply what was lacking in your service
toward me.

CHAPTER 3

All for Christ

Finally, my brethren, rejoice in the Lord. For me to write the same things to you *is* not tedious, but for you *it is* safe.

[2]Beware of dogs, beware of evil work-
ers, beware of the mutilation! [3]For we are
the circumcision, who worship God in the
Spirit,[a] rejoice in Christ Jesus, and have no
confidence in the flesh, [4]though I also
might have confidence in the flesh. If any-
one else thinks he may have confidence in
the flesh, I more so: [5]circumcised the eighth
day, of the stock of Israel, *of* the tribe of
Benjamin, a Hebrew of the Hebrews; con-
cerning the law, a Phar'i·see; [6]concerning
zeal, persecuting the church; concerning
the righteousness which is in the law,
blameless.

[7]But what things were gain to me, these
I have counted loss for Christ. [8]Yet indeed I
also count all things loss for the excellence
of the knowledge of Christ Jesus my Lord,

3:3 [a]NU-Text and M-Text read *who worship in the Spirit of God.*

3:2 Paul is warning the Philippians about the Judaizers, those who insisted that circumcision and keeping the Law of Moses were necessary for salvation.

3:4–7 Paul could boast as much as anyone in his Jewish religious achievements. He was **circumcised** a Jew at the correct age, came from pure Jewish stock within the esteemed **tribe of Benjamin**, and was thoroughly steeped in the **Hebrew** language and tradition. Paul was a Pharisee, the sect that interpreted the Mosaic law most strictly. He had been so enthusiastic for Judaism that he persecuted the church of Christ. Indeed, no one could find fault with the way he kept the Jewish **law**. **counted loss**: Paul deliberately turned from his heritage and earlier religious training because none of these things could bring him to God. Only **Christ** could do that.

LEANING FORWARD

Charles R. Swindoll

What is your particular quest? For what are you leaning forward? Something is wonderfully exciting about reaching into the future with excited anticipation, and those who pursue new adventures through life stay younger, think better, and laugh louder! I just spoke with a middle-aged man who told me he hopes to teach himself Mandarin, one of the Chinese dialects, so that when he takes an early retirement in a few years, he can go to China and teach English as a second language. He was smiling from ear to ear as he shared his plans, and I encouraged him to keep reaching forward for what lies before.

Cynthia and I recently had lunch with a wonderful couple in their thirties who are seriously considering a mid-career change. He will go to seminary and she will go to work to put him through. They have been thinking about it for years. Both are so excited, so motivated. They said we were the first ones to sound enthusiastic; all the others they had mentioned this to were quick to point out all the things that could possibly go wrong, all the sacrifices they would have to endure. Why focus on that? I told them to keep reaching forward . . . to pursue their dream. And do I need to mention it? Both were laughing again as they walked away. ✦

A Model Grandmother

Ingrid Trobisch

I am told that I cried often as a young child. My parents rarely picked me up to comfort me since the rules of child-rearing advised against it. I have often wondered if that "weeping child," which my husband said he sometimes detected in me, would have been healed earlier if my mother had ignored the "experts." By the time her last child arrived, she had forgotten those rules and had learned to listen to her own inner mother-voice. At any rate, it must have been a difficult time, and my grandmother, living next door, realized it. She took me in from time to time, and I had "only child" status in her home.

My playthings were stored in a box tucked underneath the legs of her electric stove. The stove was a table model, under which I found the quietness and shelter I needed. After a period of "hiding out" under her watchful eye, I was ready to return to the company of my brothers and my new baby sister. Perhaps that is what grandmothers do best—take each child separately and give them the individual attention that a busy mother cannot always provide.

The bond that began in these first years of my life was completed when I lived with her for two years as a young teenager. I loved her with a love founded on deep respect. Now, four decades later, I realize that her life has formed the pattern for my own. She has become for me, consciously or unconsciously, the model on which I base my life. ✦

for whom I have suffered the loss of all
things, and count them as rubbish, that I
may gain Christ 9and be found in Him, not
having my own righteousness, which *is*
from the law, but that which *is* through
faith in Christ, the righteousness which is
from God by faith; 10that I may know Him
and the power of His resurrection, and the
fellowship of His sufferings, being conformed to His death, 11if, by any means, I
may attain to the resurrection from the
dead.

Pressing Toward the Goal

12Not that I have already attained, or am
already perfected; but I press on, that I
may lay hold of that for which Christ Jesus
has also laid hold of me. 13Brethren, I do
not count myself to have apprehended; but
one thing *I do,* forgetting those things
which are behind and reaching forward to
those things which are ahead, 14I press toward the goal for the prize of the upward
call of God in Christ Jesus.

15Therefore let us, as many as are mature, have this mind; and if in anything
you think otherwise, God will reveal even
this to you. 16Nevertheless, to *the degree*
that we have already attained, let us walk
by the same rule,[a] let us be of the same
mind.

3:16 [a]NU-Text omits *rule* and the rest of the verse.

✦

3:13, 14 We must not allow ourselves to be hindered by the guilt of the past. Once we are saved, we must focus on the goal before us: to become more like Christ.

REJOICE ALWAYS!

Charles R. Swindoll

I have discovered that a joyful countenance has nothing to do with one's age, one's occupation (or lack of it), or one's geography or education or marital status or good looks or circumstances. Joy is a choice. It is a matter of attitude that stems from one's confidence in God—that He is at work, that He is in full control, that He is in the midst of whatever has happened, is happening, and will happen. Either we fix our minds on that and determine to laugh again, or we wail and whine our way through life, complaining that we never got a fair shake. We are the ones who consciously determine which way we shall go.

"We are the ones who consciously determine which way we shall go."

Rejoicing is clearly a scriptural command (Phil. 4:4). To ignore it is disobedience. In place of worry, start spending time enjoying the release of humor. Find the bright side, the sunny side of life. Deliberately look for things that are funny during your day. Loosen up and laugh more often. Consciously stay aware of the importance of a cheerful countenance. Live lightheartedly! Stop reading only the grim sections of the newspaper. Watch less television and start reading more books that bring a smile instead of a frown. Feed your mind more uplifting "thought food."

Locate a few acquaintances who will help you laugh more at life. Ideally, find Christian friends who see life through Christ's eyes, which is, in itself, more encouraging. Have fun together. Share funny stories with each other. Affirm one another. ✦

Our Citizenship in Heaven

17Brethren, join in following my exam-
ple, and note those who so walk, as you
have us for a pattern. 18For many walk, of
whom I have told you often, and now tell
you even weeping, *that they are* the ene-
mies of the cross of Christ: 19whose end *is*
destruction, whose god *is their* belly, and
whose glory *is* in their shame—who set
their mind on earthly things. 20For our citi-
zenship is in heaven, from which we also
eagerly wait for the Savior, the Lord Jesus
Christ, 21who will transform our lowly
body that it may be conformed to His glo-
rious body, according to the working by
which He is able even to subdue all things
to Himself.

CHAPTER 4

Therefore, my beloved and longed-for brethren, my joy and crown, so stand fast in the Lord, beloved.

Be United, Joyful, and in Prayer

2I implore Eū·ō′di·a and I implore Syn′-
ty·chē to be of the same mind in the Lord.

TRUE GRATITUDE

Evelyn Christenson

People tend to insert their thanksgiving at different places in the prayer process. Some never bother to thank God no matter how great and wonderful the answers He sends. Most people, but not all, are thankful when God answers the way they requested and has given them what they wanted. Then, some Christians have matured enough spiritually to thank Him in spite of how He has answered, trusting His divine wisdom.

But the Bible has an even greater requirement as to where the thanksgiving belongs in the whole prayer process. Philippians 4:6, surprisingly, reads, "Be anxious for nothing, but in everything by prayer and supplication, with thanksgiving, let your requests be made known to God."

"It takes deep maturity indeed to be able to thank God *before* He answers."

It is rare indeed to find those who actually put their thanksgiving right in with the request. Few are able to be thankful *while* they are asking, because they are concentrating on the way they want God to answer. And the deeper the personal need or hurt, the more difficult it becomes to be thankful while begging God to intervene. Our minds usually are totally consumed by the problem, not with thanksgiving, during our wrestling and striving in prayer. It takes deep maturity indeed to be able to thank God *before* He answers, to be able to include the thanks with the request! ✦

3And[a] I urge you also, true companion,
help these women who labored with me in
the gospel, with Clem′ent also, and the rest
of my fellow workers, whose names *are* in
the Book of Life.
4Rejoice in the Lord always. Again I will
say, rejoice!

4:3 [a]NU-Text and M-Text read *Yes.*

5Let your gentleness be known to all
men. The Lord *is* at hand.
6Be anxious for nothing, but in every-
thing by prayer and supplication, with
thanksgiving, let your requests be made
known to God; 7and the peace of God,
which surpasses all understanding, will
guard your hearts and minds through
Christ Jesus.

4:4 Paul found reason to rejoice in the Lord even in the midst of adversity, and he urges us to do the same. Even when financial struggles or family troubles seem insurmountable, we can rejoice in our union with Christ.

4:6, 7 Be anxious for nothing: Do not worry. Paul reflects Jesus' own counsel (Matt. 6:25–34). To worry is to doubt God's ability to help. Instead, we are counseled to tell God our needs. The Greek suggests that the peace of Christ guards our hearts like a squad of soldiers guarding a town.

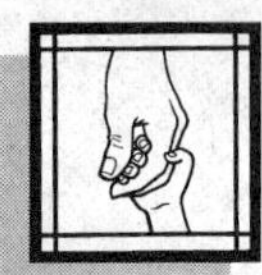

THE BADGE OF CONTENTMENT

Sherwood Eliot Wirt

The apostle Paul had a wonderful way with people that bespoke his inner ease of mind. He wrote to the church at Philippi, "I have learned in whatever state I am, to be content: I know how to be abased, and I know how to abound . . . to be full and to be hungry" (Phil. 4:11, 12).

Content while he clung for hours to a piece of wood in the Mediterranean sea? Content while he yearned for the salvation of his kinsmen? Content with much or little, in freedom or in chains? Yes, Paul was content.

No wonder this amazing Jew from Tarsus appealed to Greeks and Romans and Asians and Jews and Arabs alike. More often than is realized, people become Christians after they have encountered a contented Christian; they want to be like him or her. That explains why the Galilean fishermen left their nets when they heard Jesus say, "Follow me."

We who are older can have a far more effective ministry than we had in our younger days if we are wearing the badge of contentment. It tells the world that we have learned to trust a Friend who is working behind the scenes to take care of things. We can relax; everything is not on us. Contentment, without question, is one of God's supreme gifts. ✦

Meditate on These Things

[8]Finally, brethren, whatever things are
true, whatever things *are* noble, whatever
things *are* just, whatever things *are* pure,
whatever things *are* lovely, whatever
things *are* of good report, if *there is* any
virtue and if *there is* anything praise-
worthy—meditate on these things. [9]The
things which you learned and received
and heard and saw in me, these do, and the
God of peace will be with you.

Philippian Generosity

[10]But I rejoiced in the Lord greatly that
now at last your care for me has flourished
again; though you surely did care, but you
lacked opportunity. [11]Not that I speak in re-
gard to need, for I have learned in what-
ever state I am, to be content: [12]I know how
to be abased, and I know how to abound.
Everywhere and in all things I have
learned both to be full and to be hungry,
both to abound and to suffer need. [13]I can
do all things through Christ[a] who strength-
ens me.

[14]Nevertheless you have done well that
you shared in my distress. [15]Now you
Phi·lip′pi·ans know also that in the begin-
ning of the gospel, when I departed from
Mac·e·dō′ni·a, no church shared with me
concerning giving and receiving but you
only. [16]For even in Thes·sa·lo·nī′ca you
sent *aid* once and again for my necessities.

4:13 [a]NU-Text reads *Him who.*

✦ ✦

4:8 As we make choices throughout the day, deciding what to watch on television, which book to read, or what to discuss with our friends, we need to remember Paul's admonition to focus on things that will keep our minds pure.

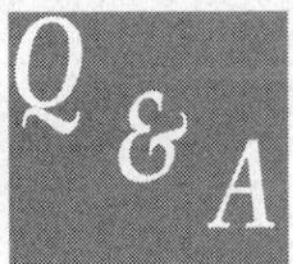

Is it wrong to pray about every little thing?

J. Vernon McGee

"Be anxious for nothing, but in everything by prayer and supplication, with thanksgiving, let your requests be made known to God" (Phil. 4:6).

We are to worry about nothing because we are to pray about everything. This means that we are to talk to the Lord about everything in our lives. Nothing should be left out. Some years ago, I am told, a dowager in Philadelphia came to Dr. G. Campbell Morgan with this question: "Dr. Morgan, do you think we should pray about the *little* things in our lives?" Dr. Morgan, in his characteristically British manner, said, "Madam, can you mention anything in your life that is *big* to God?"

"With thanksgiving, let your requests be made known to God." Paul never lets prayer become a leap in the dark; it rests on a foundation. "So then faith comes by hearing, and hearing by the word of God" (Rom. 10:17). Prayer rests on faith, and faith rests on the Word of God. ✦

17Not that I seek the gift, but I seek the fruit
that abounds to your account. 18Indeed I
have all and abound. I am full, having re-
ceived from E·paph·ro·dī′tus the things
sent from you, a sweet-smelling aroma, an
acceptable sacrifice, well pleasing to God.
19And my God shall supply all your need
according to His riches in glory by Christ
Jesus. 20Now to our God and Father *be*
glory forever and ever. Amen.

Greeting and Blessing

21Greet every saint in Christ Jesus. The
brethren who are with me greet you. 22All
the saints greet you, but especially those
who are of Caesar's household.

23The grace of our Lord Jesus Christ be
with you all.[a] Amen.

I praise You, God, because You supply all my needs according to Your riches in glory by Christ Jesus.

adapted from Philippians 4:19

4:23 [a]NU-Text reads *your spirit.*

4:17–19 He who gives to support God's work receives **fruit** (credit) to his **account** before God (v. 17). A gift given and accepted in love is a **sacrifice** that is pleasing to God (v. 18). Through Christ God will supply every need of His generous people (v. 19). We cannot outgive God.

Living on a Fixed Income

Charles Ross

Retirement can be a time of uncertainty. The average couple retires with their home paid for but very little in the bank. A financial plan can ease the stress.

Your retirement years are a period of major adjustment, both personally and financially. From this point on, you will probably be living on a fixed income. Even though you may have planned during your working years, you will find that inflation requires the use of more income than expected to meet your expenses.

To protect yourself, think about these ideas:

✦ Consider a part-time job if supplementing your income becomes a necessity.

✦ Avoid unnecessary spending by budgeting to live on your income.

✦ Review your insurance again, especially your health coverage. Make sure it is adequate.

✦ Try to eliminate all debt. A retirement budget should be free from all interest expense and other unnecessary monthly payments.

Remember that, while no financial plan is absolutely fail-safe, as Christians we can trust the Lord to faithfully meet our needs. If we place our trust in Him, we have no need to worry. ✦

✦Colossians✦

The last of the four "Prison Epistles" written during Paul's Roman imprisonment, Colossians was written as a response to news Paul had received from Epaphras that a dangerous heresy was beginning to spread in the church. This mystery cult combined Greek, Jewish, and Oriental thought and included the worship of angels as intermediaries between man and God.

Paul declared that nothing exists apart from Christ. Christ is preeminent—the first and foremost in everything—and the Christian's life should reflect that priority. Because believers are rooted in Him, hidden in Him, and complete in Him, it is utterly inconsistent for them to live life without Him.

Although Paul never visited the church at Colosse, he was clearly concerned that any false teaching be confronted immediately with the truth to avoid confusion. In perhaps the most Christ-centered book in the Bible, Jesus is declared all-sufficient, and the believer is complete in Him alone, lacking nothing because "in Him dwells all the fullness of the Godhead bodily" (2:9). Christians need to recognize that a relationship with God is not based on ceremonial rituals or legalistic self-denial but on submission to Jesus Christ. ✦

CHAPTER 1

Greeting

Paul, an apostle of Jesus Christ by the will of God, and Timothy our brother,

2To the saints and faithful brethren in Christ *who are* in Co·los′sē:

Grace to you and peace from God our Father and the Lord Jesus Christ.[a]

Their Faith in Christ

3We give thanks to the God and Father
of our Lord Jesus Christ, praying always
for you, 4since we heard of your faith in
Christ Jesus and of your love for all the
saints; 5because of the hope which is laid
up for you in heaven, of which you heard
before in the word of the truth of the
gospel, 6which has come to you, as *it has*
also in all the world, and is bringing forth
fruit,[a] as *it is* also among you since the day
you heard and knew the grace of God in
truth; 7as you also learned from Ep′a-
phras, our dear fellow servant, who is a
faithful minister of Christ on your behalf,

1:2 [a]NU-Text omits *and the Lord Jesus Christ.*
1:6 [a]NU-Text and M-Text add *and growing.*

1:4 The apostle had not visited Colosse, but had heard of the Christians there through Epaphras (vv. 7, 8). Our relationship with God through faith leads to a relationship with other Christians through love.

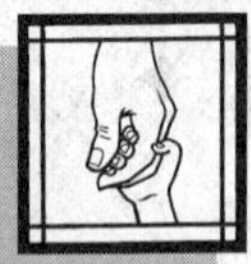

MENTORING IS A TWO-WAY STREET

Lucibel Van Atta

One of the most powerful parts of nurturing comes in praying. The mentor may do most of the praying, especially at first, but God works strongly during these times of prayer.

Remember Jesus' willingness to be vulnerable? God uses role models who are transparent. We need to tell others of the sore places within our hearts as well as the joys. When I have told what God is doing in my life and what I want Him to do, it becomes easier for others to do the same. Asking for support—and admitting our hurts and hurdles—will affirm our desire to become a better spouse or roommate or parent. I have asked for prayer about starting a neighborhood Bible study, terminating an uncomfortable community responsibility, needed attitude changes, my husband's impending job changes, financial struggles, and hassles with my ailing refrigerator.

Each time we are together I ask, "How can I most effectively pray for you this week?" I write down those requests so that I will be praying on a daily basis. This list serves as a tool for follow-up and accountability as well.

This two-way vulnerability helps our partners grasp how much we need their prayers, and it helps both of us as we pray specifically for each other during the week. ✦

8who also declared to us your love in the
Spirit.

Preeminence of Christ

9For this reason we also, since the day
we heard it, do not cease to pray for you,
and to ask that you may be filled with the
knowledge of His will in all wisdom and
spiritual understanding; 10that you may
walk worthy of the Lord, fully pleasing
Him, being fruitful in every good work and
increasing in the knowledge of God;
11strengthened with all might, according to
His glorious power, for all patience and
longsuffering with joy; 12giving thanks to
the Father who has qualified us to be partakers of the inheritance of the saints in the
light. 13He has delivered us from the power
of darkness and conveyed *us* into the kingdom of the Son of His love, 14in whom we
have redemption through His blood,[a] the
forgiveness of sins.

15He is the image of the invisible God,
the firstborn over all creation. 16For by Him

1:14 [a]NU-Text and M-Text omit *through His blood.*

1:10 For a Christian to "walk worthy" means to live a life characterized by continual fruitfulness and growth in godly knowledge. We should examine our conduct and determine if anything is causing us to stray from the course.

1:15, 17 Firstborn does not mean that Christ was "born" to the Father. Rather, as the firstborn Jewish son had a certain preeminence, so Christ has authority and preeminence over all creation. **before all things**: Both in time and in supremacy. Because of Christ's supreme authority and oversight, all things consist (hold together).

all things were created that are in heaven
and that are on earth, visible and invisible,
whether thrones or dominions or principalities or powers. All things were created
through Him and for Him. [17]And He is before all things, and in Him all things consist. [18]And He is the head of the body, the
church, who is the beginning, the firstborn
from the dead, that in all things He may
have the preeminence.

Reconciled in Christ

[19]For it pleased *the Father that* in Him all
the fullness should dwell, [20]and by Him to
reconcile all things to Himself, by Him,
whether things on earth or things in
heaven, having made peace through the
blood of His cross.

[21]And you, who once were alienated
and enemies in your mind by wicked
works, yet now He has reconciled [22]in
the body of His flesh through death, to
present you holy, and blameless, and
above reproach in His sight— [23]if indeed
you continue in the faith, grounded and
steadfast, and are not moved away from
the hope of the gospel which you heard,
which was preached to every creature under heaven, of which I, Paul, became a
minister.

Sacrificial Service for Christ

[24]I now rejoice in my sufferings for you,
and fill up in my flesh what is lacking in
the afflictions of Christ, for the sake of His
body, which is the church, [25]of which I became a minister according to the stewardship from God which was given to me for
you, to fulfill the word of God, [26]the mystery which has been hidden from ages and
from generations, but now has been revealed to His saints. [27]To them God willed
to make known what are the riches of the
glory of this mystery among the Gentiles:
which[a] is Christ in you, the hope of glory.
[28]Him we preach, warning every man and
teaching every man in all wisdom, that we
may present every man perfect in Christ
Jesus. [29]To this *end* I also labor, striving according to His working which works in me
mightily.

CHAPTER 2

Not Philosophy but Christ

For I want you to know what a great
conflict I have for you and those in
Lā·o·di·cē'a, and *for* as many as have not
seen my face in the flesh, [2]that their hearts
may be encouraged, being knit together in
love, and *attaining* to all riches of the full
assurance of understanding, to the knowledge of the mystery of God, both of the
Father and[a] of Christ, [3]in whom are hidden
all the treasures of wisdom and knowledge.

[4]Now this I say lest anyone should deceive you with persuasive words. [5]For
though I am absent in the flesh, yet I am
with you in spirit, rejoicing to see your
good order and the steadfastness of your
faith in Christ.

[6]As you therefore have received Christ
Jesus the Lord, so walk in Him, [7]rooted and
built up in Him and established in the
faith, as you have been taught, abounding
in it[a] with thanksgiving.

[8]Beware lest anyone cheat you through
philosophy and empty deceit, according to
the tradition of men, according to the basic

1:27 [a]M-Text reads *who.* 2:2 [a]NU-Text omits *both of the Father and.* 2:7 [a]NU-Text omits *in it.*

1:22, 23 The purpose of God's reconciling us to Himself is to make us **holy** and **blameless**—not blameless as all others may see us, but blameless **in His sight**. By His grace we can be what He expects us to be. **preached to every creature**: Not all have heard, but this gospel is designed to be preached to all people.

1:28 Notice that Paul is not preaching a code of ethics or a list of rules and regulations. Our faith is based solely on the person of Christ.

principles of the world, and not according to Christ. 9For in Him dwells all the fullness of the Godhead bodily; 10and you are complete in Him, who is the head of all principality and power.

Not Legalism but Christ

11In Him you were also circumcised with the circumcision made without hands, by putting off the body of the sins[a] of the flesh, by the circumcision of Christ, 12buried with Him in baptism, in which you also were raised with *Him* through faith in the working of God, who raised Him from the dead. 13And you, being dead in your trespasses and the uncircumcision of your flesh, He has made alive together with Him, having forgiven you all trespasses, 14having wiped out the handwriting of requirements that was against us, which was contrary to us. And He has taken it out of the way, having nailed it to the cross. 15Having disarmed principalities and powers, He made a public spectacle of them, triumphing over them in it.

16So let no one judge you in food or in drink, or regarding a festival or a new moon or sabbaths, 17which are a shadow of things to come, but the substance is of Christ. 18Let no one cheat you of your reward, taking delight in *false* humility and worship of angels, intruding into those things which he has not[a] seen, vainly puffed up by his fleshly mind, 19and not holding fast to the Head, from whom all the body, nourished and knit together by joints and ligaments, grows with the increase *that is* from God.

20Therefore,[a] if you died with Christ from the basic principles of the world, why, as *though* living in the world, do you subject yourselves to regulations— 21"Do not touch, do not taste, do not handle," 22which all concern things which perish with the using—according to the commandments and doctrines of men? 23These things indeed have an appearance of wisdom in self-imposed religion, *false* humility, and neglect of the body, *but are* of no value against the indulgence of the flesh.

> The closer we are to God, the closer we are to those who are close to Him. We can understand others only by loving Him who understands them from within the depths of their own being. Otherwise we know them only by the surmises that are formed within the mirror of our own soul.
>
> Thomas Merton

CHAPTER 3

Not Carnality but Christ

If then you were raised with Christ, seek those things which are above, where Christ is, sitting at the right hand of God. 2Set your mind on things above, not on things on the earth. 3For you died, and your life is hidden with Christ in God. 4When Christ *who is* our life appears, then you also will appear with Him in glory.

5Therefore put to death your members which are on the earth: fornication, uncleanness, passion, evil desire, and cov-

2:11 [a]NU-Text omits *of the sins.* 2:18 [a]NU-Text omits *not.* 2:20 [a]NU-Text and M-Text omit *Therefore.*

2:16 Paul urges the Colossians not to be enslaved by legalism. As we disciple younger Christians, we must be careful to focus on the principles in the Bible rather than attempting to force our personal preferences on them.

3:1 if: since.

3:2 Although we are wise to plan for our financial future, we must not allow ourselves to get caught up in acquiring money or material possessions. We should instead be consumed by heavenly concerns.

Live in the Present

Dr. Verle Bell

It has been said that the depressed person lives in the past. The obsessive person lives for tomorrow. The healthy person lives in today. Where do you live?

Those who choose to dwell in the past tend to focus on "shoulds" and "coulds." What should they have done? What could they have done differently? Some people look at their pasts, assume the future is going to be the same way, and give up. True, some have had difficult past experiences, but God is in the present and can make a difference.

We can deal with the past in the sense that we can forgive people and forgive ourselves, but we cannot live the past over. This is not to say we are to ignore the past. Some people figure they must never think about the past; if they do, it must mean they have not forgiven those who hurt them. This negative rigidity usually indicates that they really have not worked through the pain to choose forgiveness. When this is the case, the patterns from the past generally repeat in the present and future. When people "gloss over" the past, they get mired in bitterness.

"The healthy person lives in today. Where do you live?"

The goal is not to push the past from our memories but to get to the place where we are not embittered by it, where we do not dwell on it or let it control us.

etousness, which is idolatry. [6]Because of
these things the wrath of God is coming
upon the sons of disobedience, [7]in which
you yourselves once walked when you
lived in them.

[8]But now you yourselves are to put off
all these: anger, wrath, malice, blasphemy,
filthy language out of your mouth. [9]Do not
lie to one another, since you have put off
the old man with his deeds, [10]and have put
on the new *man* who is renewed in knowl-
edge according to the image of Him who
created him, [11]where there is neither Greek
nor Jew, circumcised nor uncircumcised,
barbarian, Scyth'i·an, slave *nor* free, but
Christ *is* all and in all.

Character of the New Man

[12]Therefore, as *the* elect of God, holy and
beloved, put on tender mercies, kindness,
humility, meekness, longsuffering; [13]bear-
ing with one another, and forgiving one
another, if anyone has a complaint against
another; even as Christ forgave you, so you
also *must do.* [14]But above all these things
put on love, which is the bond of perfec-
tion. [15]And let the peace of God rule in
your hearts, to which also you were called
in one body; and be thankful. [16]Let the
word of Christ dwell in you richly in all
wisdom, teaching and admonishing one
another in psalms and hymns and spiritual
songs, singing with grace in your hearts to

> ***I pray that whatever I do, I do it heartily, as to You, Lord, and not to men.***
>
> *adapted from* Colossians 3:23

the Lord. [17]And *whatever* you do in word or
deed, *do* all in the name of the Lord Jesus,
giving thanks to God the Father through
Him.

The Christian Home

[18]Wives, submit to your own husbands,
as is fitting in the Lord.

[19]Husbands, love your wives and do not
be bitter toward them.

[20]Children, obey your parents in all
things, for this is well pleasing to the Lord.

[21]Fathers, do not provoke your children,
lest they become discouraged.

[22]Bondservants, obey in all things your
masters according to the flesh, not with
eyeservice, as men-pleasers, but in sincer-
ity of heart, fearing God. [23]And whatever
you do, do it heartily, as to the Lord and
not to men, [24]knowing that from the Lord
you will receive the reward of the inheri-
tance; for[a] you serve the Lord Christ. [25]But
he who does wrong will be repaid for what
he has done, and there is no partiality.

CHAPTER 4

Masters, give your bondservants what
is just and fair, knowing that you also have
a Master in heaven.

Christian Graces

[2]Continue earnestly in prayer, being
vigilant in it with thanksgiving; [3]mean-
while praying also for us, that God would
open to us a door for the word, to speak the
mystery of Christ, for which I am also in
chains, [4]that I may make it manifest, as I
ought to speak.

[5]Walk in wisdom toward those *who are*
outside, redeeming the time. [6]*Let* your
speech always *be* with grace, seasoned
with salt, that you may know how you
ought to answer each one.

Final Greetings

[7]Tych'i·cus, a beloved brother, faithful
minister, and fellow servant in the Lord,
will tell you all the news about me. [8]I am
sending him to you for this very purpose,
that he[a] may know your circumstances and
comfort your hearts, [9]with O̅·nes'i·mus, a
faithful and beloved brother, who is *one* of
you. They will make known to you all
things which *are happening* here.

[10]Ar·is·tar'chus my fellow prisoner
greets you, with Mark the cousin of
Bar'na·bas (about whom you received in-
structions: if he comes to you, welcome
him), [11]and Jesus who is called Jus'tus.
These *are my* only fellow workers for the
kingdom of God who are of the circumci-
sion; they have proved to be a comfort to
me.

[12]Ep'a·phras, who is *one* of you, a

3:24 [a]NU-Text omits *for.* 4:8 [a]NU-Text reads *you may know our circumstances and he may.*

3:20 Children, **obey** because this is your part in the Christian home. This obedience does not extend to commands by non-Christian parents to do sinful things. Such compliance could not be **well pleasing to the Lord**.

3:21 The command for children to obey (v. 20) is balanced by the command for parents not to **provoke**. **Fathers**, be careful and kind in your discipline so that you do not cause your child to **become discouraged**. Correct your children lovingly, praying for guidance, maturity, and skill.

4:5 We are to conduct ourselves wisely and prudently, avoiding actions that might hinder the unsaved from seeking Christ.

4:6 Speak with **grace** and let your words be as appealing as meat **seasoned with salt**. Such beauty of character attracts sinners to Christ.

4:11 of the circumcision: Jews.

AMAZING GRACE

Bill Gaither

I thank God for grace because without grace I wouldn't have a friend. Who would put up with my idiosyncrasies? I'm not the easiest person in the world to get along with. I'm impatient. I have a short fuse. Thank God some people have extended grace to me. I have to be willing to do the same for them and for everyone with whom I come in contact.

The body of Christ, the family of God, is a place where you can fail and still not be a failure. No matter how many times you think you've failed, there is still grace at the foot of the Cross, where you can start again and be whole. Now, we can give ourselves to the idea that it has always been like this, that we are from a long list of failures so nothing will ever change, or we can be willing to fill the shoes of the good and godly examples of those who have gone before us.

"The body of Christ is a place where you can fail and still not be a failure."

bondservant of Christ, greets you, always laboring fervently for you in prayers, that you may stand perfect and complete[a] in all the will of God. 13For I bear him witness that he has a great zeal[a] for you, and those who are in Lā·o·di·cē'a, and those in Hī·er·ap'o·lis. 14Luke the beloved physician and Dē'mas greet you. 15Greet the brethren who are in Lā·o·di·cē'a, and Nym'phas and the church that *is* in his[a] house.

4:12 [a]NU-Text reads *fully assured.* 4:13 [a]NU-Text reads *concern.* 4:15 [a]NU-Text reads *Nympha . . . her house.*

Closing Exhortations and Blessing

16Now when this epistle is read among you, see that it is read also in the church of the Lā·o·di·cē'ans, and that you likewise read the epistle from Lā·o·di·cē'a. 17And say to Ar·chip'pus, "Take heed to the ministry which you have received in the Lord, that you may fulfill it."

18This salutation by my own hand—Paul. Remember my chains. Grace *be* with you. Amen.

✦1 Thessalonians✦

While ministering in Thessalonica during his second missionary journey, Paul was forced to leave town. He traveled first to Berea, about fifty miles to the west, then through Athens and eventually to Corinth. Paul was concerned about the condition of the Thessalonians' faith, and he sent Timothy to see how they were doing in his absence. When he received the good word that this young church's faith was holding fast during its tribulations, Paul wrote to commend them on their hope, love, and perseverance.

However, the Thessalonians had many questions regarding the Second Coming and the last days. Every chapter of the epistle contains some positive reference to the promised return of Christ and its significance to the believers. Christ is seen as the believer's hope of salvation now and at His coming. When He returns, He will deliver (1:10), reward (2:19), perfect (3:13), resurrect (4:13–18), and sanctify (5:23) all who trust Him.

Throughout this letter, Paul encouraged the church to excel in their newfound faith; to increase their love for one another; and to rejoice, pray, and give thanks always. ✦

CHAPTER 1

Greeting

Paul, Sil·vā′nus, and Timothy,

To the church of the Thes·sa·lō′ni·ans in
God the Father and the Lord Jesus Christ:

Grace to you and peace from God our
Father and the Lord Jesus Christ.[a]

Their Good Example

2We give thanks to God always for you
all, making mention of you in our prayers,
3remembering without ceasing your work
of faith, labor of love, and patience of hope
in our Lord Jesus Christ in the sight of our
God and Father, 4knowing, beloved
brethren, your election by God. 5For our
gospel did not come to you in word only,
but also in power, and in the Holy Spirit
and in much assurance, as you know what
kind of men we were among you for your
sake.
6And you became followers of us and of
the Lord, having received the word in
much affliction, with joy of the Holy Spirit,
7so that you became examples to all in
Mac·e·dō′ni·a and A·chā′i·a who believe.
8For from you the word of the Lord has
sounded forth, not only in Mac·e·dō′ni·a
and A·chā′i·a, but also in every place. Your
faith toward God has gone out, so that we
do not need to say anything. 9For they
themselves declare concerning us what
manner of entry we had to you, and how
you turned to God from idols to serve the
living and true God, 10and to wait for His

1:1 [a]NU-Text omits *from God our Father and the Lord Jesus Christ.*

1:1 Silvanus: Silas, as mentioned in Acts.

Son from heaven, whom He raised from
the dead, *even* Jesus who delivers us from
the wrath to come.

CHAPTER 2

Paul's Conduct

For you yourselves know, brethren, that
our coming to you was not in vain. 2But
even[a] after we had suffered before and
were spitefully treated at Phi·lip'pī, as you
know, we were bold in our God to speak to
you the gospel of God in much conflict.
3For our exhortation *did* not *come* from er-
ror or uncleanness, nor *was it* in deceit.

4But as we have been approved by God
to be entrusted with the gospel, even so we
speak, not as pleasing men, but God who
tests our hearts. 5For neither at any time
did we use flattering words, as you know,
nor a cloak for covetousness—God *is* wit-
ness. 6Nor did we seek glory from men, ei-
ther from you or from others, when we
might have made demands as apostles of
Christ. 7But we were gentle among you,
just as a nursing *mother* cherishes her own
children. 8So, affectionately longing for
you, we were well pleased to impart to you
not only the gospel of God, but also our
own lives, because you had become dear to
us. 9For you remember, brethren, our labor
and toil; for laboring night and day, that
we might not be a burden to any of you, we
preached to you the gospel of God.

10You *are* witnesses, and God *also,* how
devoutly and justly and blamelessly we
behaved ourselves among you who be-
lieve; 11as you know how we exhorted, and
comforted, and charged[a] every one of you,
as a father *does* his own children, 12that you
would walk worthy of God who calls you
into His own kingdom and glory.

Their Conversion

13For this reason we also thank God
without ceasing, because when you re-
ceived the word of God which you heard
from us, you welcomed *it* not *as* the word
of men, but as it is in truth, the word of
God, which also effectively works in you
who believe. 14For you, brethren, became
imitators of the churches of God which are
in Judea in Christ Jesus. For you also suf-
fered the same things from your own
countrymen, just as they *did* from the
Judeans, 15who killed both the Lord Jesus
and their own prophets, and have perse-
cuted us; and they do not please God and
are contrary to all men, 16forbidding us to
speak to the Gentiles that they may be
saved, so as always to fill up *the measure of*
their sins; but wrath has come upon them
to the uttermost.

Longing to See Them

17But we, brethren, having been taken
away from you for a short time in pres-
ence, not in heart, endeavored more ea-
gerly to see your face with great desire.
18Therefore we wanted to come to you—
even I, Paul, time and again—but Satan
hindered us. 19For what *is* our hope, or joy,
or crown of rejoicing? *Is it* not even you in
the presence of our Lord Jesus Christ at His
coming? 20For you are our glory and joy.

CHAPTER 3

Concern for Their Faith

Therefore, when we could no longer en-
dure it, we thought it good to be left in
Athens alone, 2and sent Timothy, our

2:2 [a]NU-Text and M-Text omit *even.* 2:11 [a]NU-Text and M-Text read *implored.*

1:8, 9 The missionary zeal of the Thessalonian Christians in the face of severe persecution is a marvelous testimony of faith in God.

2:12 Paul's charge to "walk worthy of God" refers to proper Christian conduct, which, now as then, is at variance with the ways of the world.

3:1–10 From Thessalonica the missionaries had gone to Berea (Acts 17:10–15). Silas and Timothy stayed there, while Paul went on to Athens. Anxious because of the severe

IT'S OK TO CRY

Charles R. Swindoll

I have found that my feelings often represent some of the most sensitive areas in my life touched by the Spirit of God. Not infrequently do my emotions play a vital role in how and where the Spirit is guiding me. How else but through feelings are we prompted to "rejoice with those who rejoice, and weep with those who weep?" (Rom. 12:15).

We are strange creatures: proud of our brains, stubborn in our wills, but ashamed of our emotions. By warming up to our emotions, we allow ourselves the freedom to be real, to be whole.

"By warming up to our emotions, we allow ourselves the freedom to be whole."

Becoming a Christian is not synonymous with becoming superhuman. Expressing one's emotions is not a mark of immaturity or carnality. The loss of a loved one is just as much a loss for the believer as it is for the nonbeliever. At such times tears are not only acceptable, they are appropriate and expected. It is part of being real, being human. Nothing is gained by denial or proven by remaining stoic.

The apostle Paul did not write that Christians are not to grieve, but that we do not grieve as if we "have no hope" (1 Thess. 4:13). Our theology should have room for feelings of loss and tears, as well as feelings of lighthearted joy and great laughter. The Spirit of God prompts both. I have been concerned for years that too many so-called mature evangelical Christians have little room in their lives for either. ✦

brother and minister of God, and our fellow laborer in the gospel of Christ, to establish you and encourage you concerning your faith, [3]that no one should be shaken by these afflictions; for you yourselves know that we are appointed to this. [4]For, in fact, we told you before when we were with you that we would suffer tribulation, just as it happened, and you know. [5]For this reason, when I could no longer endure it, I sent to know your faith, lest by some means the tempter had tempted you, and our labor might be in vain.

Encouraged by Timothy

[6]But now that Timothy has come to us from you, and brought us good news of your faith and love, and that you always have good remembrance of us, greatly desiring to see us, as we also *to see* you—

persecution at Thessalonica, he asked Timothy to return to that city and encourage the believers (v. 2). Timothy later joined him in Corinth with a very positive and encouraging report (Acts 18:1, 5).

7therefore, brethren, in all our affliction
and distress we were comforted concern-
ing you by your faith. 8For now we live, if
you stand fast in the Lord.
9For what thanks can we render to God
for you, for all the joy with which we re-
joice for your sake before our God, 10night
and day praying exceedingly that we may
see your face and perfect what is lacking in
your faith?

Prayer for the Church

11Now may our God and Father Him-
self, and our Lord Jesus Christ, direct our
way to you. 12And may the Lord make you
increase and abound in love to one another
and to all, just as we *do* to you, 13so that He
may establish your hearts blameless in ho-
liness before our God and Father at the
coming of our Lord Jesus Christ with all
His saints.

CHAPTER 4

Plea for Purity

Finally then, brethren, we urge and ex-
hort in the Lord Jesus that you should
abound more and more, just as you re-
ceived from us how you ought to walk and
to please God; 2for you know what com-
mandments we gave you through the Lord
Jesus.
3For this is the will of God, your sanctifi-
cation: that you should abstain from sexual
immorality; 4that each of you should know
how to possess his own vessel in sanctifi-
cation and honor, 5not in passion of lust,
like the Gentiles who do not know God;
6that no one should take advantage of and
defraud his brother in this matter, because
the Lord *is* the avenger of all such, as we
also forewarned you and testified. 7For
God did not call us to uncleanness, but in
holiness. 8Therefore he who rejects *this*
does not reject man, but God, who has also
given[a] us His Holy Spirit.

A Brotherly and Orderly Life

9But concerning brotherly love you have
no need that I should write to you, for you
yourselves are taught by God to love one
another; 10and indeed you do so toward all
the brethren who are in all Mac·e·dō′ni·a.
But we urge you, brethren, that you in-
crease more and more; 11that you also as-
pire to lead a quiet life, to mind your own
business, and to work with your own
hands, as we commanded you, 12that you
may walk properly toward those who are
outside, and *that* you may lack nothing.

The Comfort of Christ's Coming

13But I do not want you to be ignorant,
brethren, concerning those who have
fallen asleep, lest you sorrow as others
who have no hope. 14For if we believe
that Jesus died and rose again, even so God
will bring with Him those who sleep in Je-
sus.[a]
15For this we say to you by the word of
the Lord, that we who are alive *and* remain
until the coming of the Lord will by no

4:8 [a]NU-Text reads *who also gives.* 4:14 [a]Or *those who through Jesus sleep*

3:11 Paul trusts in the Lord to clear the way to return to Thessalonica, if it is His will. In the same way we must rely on God to open appropriate doors as we pursue His will for our lives.

4:3–8 Immorality was common to pagan religion. But the Thessalonians now served "the living and true God" (1:9). **Sexual immorality** is sin against both God and people. It takes **advantage** of (1) the unmarried person by causing loss of virginity that should be saved for marriage, and of (2) the married person along with his or her spouse by violating their marriage vows. The **Lord** punishes this sin because it rejects **God** and is incompatible with **His Holy Spirit**.

4:10–12 To maintain an impeccable testimony, believers should work to support their own families, live a quiet life, and avoid conflict with others.

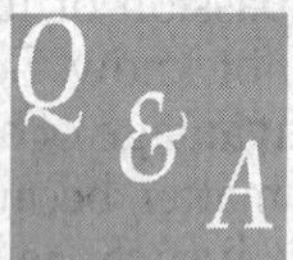

How can I cope with the imminent death of my spouse?

Elmer L. Gray

Coping with the illness and death of a beloved individual is one of life's most difficult experiences, and advance preparation for certain things can help. Some people buy cemetery plots and make arrangements with a mortuary. You may plan together the program for the funeral or memorial service. Such advance preparation can ease some of the stress at the time of the death.

No two people grieve exactly alike, but if you realize that your feelings during the grief period are natural, your grieving can help you rather than disturb you. People differ in how much they depend on others, but most find comfort when friends join with them in grieving over the loss of a loved one. Later, returning as much as possible to your normal activities will help you regain your emotional balance. Plan for the days and years ahead.

Draw close to the Lord and be comforted by your assurance of heaven and the reunion we look forward to there. The Bible promises: "Then we who are alive and remain shall be caught up together with them in the clouds to meet the Lord in the air. And thus we shall always be with the Lord. Therefore comfort one another with these words" (1 Thess. 4:17, 18).

Ask the Lord to walk close to you and to comfort you. ✦

means precede those who are asleep. 16For
the Lord Himself will descend from
heaven with a shout, with the voice of an
archangel, and with the trumpet of God.
And the dead in Christ will rise first.
17Then we who are alive *and* remain shall
be caught up together with them in the
clouds to meet the Lord in the air. And thus
we shall always be with the Lord. 18Therefore comfort one another with these words.

CHAPTER 5

The Day of the Lord

But concerning the times and the seasons, brethren, you have no need that I
should write to you. 2For you yourselves
know perfectly that the day of the Lord so
comes as a thief in the night. 3For when
they say, "Peace and safety!" then sudden
destruction comes upon them, as labor
pains upon a pregnant woman. And they
shall not escape. 4But you, brethren, are not
in darkness, so that this Day should overtake you as a thief. 5You are all sons of light

4:16, 17 It is **the Lord** Jesus **Himself** who will return. **Shout** is a military term used for ordering troops to assemble. This shout calls the dead to life. **The voice of an archangel** and the **trumpet** emphasize the divine authority and the victory of this command. Christians already dead will **rise** before those still alive. **shall be caught up**: The word *rapture* comes from the Latin translation of this phrase. Throughout Scripture **clouds** are representative of the divine glory (see Acts 1:9).

I pray that my child will put on the breastplate of faith and love, and as his helmet the hope of salvation.

adapted from 1 Thessalonians 5:8

and sons of the day. We are not of the night
nor of darkness. [6]Therefore let us not sleep,
as others *do,* but let us watch and be sober.
[7]For those who sleep, sleep at night, and
those who get drunk are drunk at night.
[8]But let us who are of the day be sober,
putting on the breastplate of faith and love,
and *as* a helmet the hope of salvation. [9]For
God did not appoint us to wrath, but to ob-
tain salvation through our Lord Jesus
Christ, [10]who died for us, that whether we
wake or sleep, we should live together
with Him.
[11]Therefore comfort each other and edify
one another, just as you also are doing.

Various Exhortations

[12]And we urge you, brethren, to recog-
nize those who labor among you, and are
over you in the Lord and admonish you,
[13]and to esteem them very highly in love
for their work's sake. Be at peace among
yourselves.
[14]Now we exhort you, brethren, warn
those who are unruly, comfort the faint-
hearted, uphold the weak, be patient with
all. [15]See that no one renders evil for evil to
anyone, but always pursue what is good
both for yourselves and for all.
[16]Rejoice always, [17]pray without ceasing,
[18]in everything give thanks; for this is the
will of God in Christ Jesus for you.
[19]Do not quench the Spirit. [20]Do not de-

5:11 One of the primary reasons we fellowship together in the church is to fulfill our obligation to encourage and build up one another. Perhaps our failure to do so helps explain why so many view church-goers as hypocrites.

5:19 quench: A metaphor taken from the picture of the **Spirit** as fire. We quench the Spirit when we ignore or disobey Him. It is the Holy Spirit who draws us to God and makes forgiveness, cleansing, and power for service a reality in our lives. "Stop treating lightly the things of the Spirit" is Paul's strong admonition.

The Attitude Factor

Dr. Kenneth Cooper

Attitude is a major factor in success or failure. If I had said twenty years ago, "I can't do the impossible," I would not be here today. I accomplished what I did through the Lord answering my prayers.

We may not be able to do everything but we can try. We can achieve. And working toward the goal is half of it. Attitude is extremely important in all aspects of life, whether physical, emotional, work-related, or family-related. Attitude is extremely important.

They all work together: physical fitness, a positive attitude, and spiritual fitness. ✦

spise prophecies. [21]Test all things; hold fast
what is good. [22]Abstain from every form of
evil.

Blessing and Admonition

[23]Now may the God of peace Himself
sanctify you completely; and may your
whole spirit, soul, and body be preserved
blameless at the coming of our Lord Jesus
Christ. [24]He who calls you *is* faithful, who
also will do *it*.

[25]Brethren, pray for us.

[26]Greet all the brethren with a holy kiss.

[27]I charge you by the Lord that this epis-
tle be read to all the holy[a] brethren.

[28]The grace of our Lord Jesus Christ *be*
with you. Amen.

5:27 [a]NU-Text omits *holy.*

THE SECRET TO HEALTHY AGING

Philip Walker

As we age, we become more concerned with the quality of our lives. We look for the latest research on staying healthy through diet, fitness, and just plain good habits. Fads seem to come and go, and new studies pop up consistently, showing us amazing facts we never thought possible.

But surprisingly, one of the best ways to age gracefully involves aerobic exercise—a well-known form of conditioning that has been around for about twenty-five years. Aerobic exercise is not just a fitness fad. It has been shown to substantially increase the quality of health during the retirement years, and it is still advocated by authorities around the world as the basis of a good health and fitness program.

The term *aerobic* means "living with air" or "utilizing oxygen." Aerobic exercises include activities that require oxygen for prolonged periods and place demands on the body to improve its capacity to handle oxygen. These activities bring beneficial changes in the lungs, heart, and vascular system. Common aerobic exercises include jogging, walking, cycling, aerobic dance, and swimming.

As we seek to be good stewards of our bodies, aerobic exercise can help us keep our "temples" healthy. In addition, good physical fitness enables us to think more clearly, so we can consider exercise an investment in our Bible study as well. ✦

✦2 Thessalonians✦

Not long after the Thessalonians received the first letter from Paul, they fell prey to the false teaching that the day of the Lord had already begun. Some of the believers had abandoned their work and had begun to live off others, apparently assuming that the end was at hand.

The return of Christ is mentioned more times (318) in the New Testament than any other doctrine, and it is a major concept in this epistle. Paul encouraged the Thessalonians to follow his example by supporting themselves, and he instructs the rest of the church to discipline them if they fail to do so. Just as Paul cautioned the church at Thessalonica, Christians today should continue steadfastly in the work of the Lord, even while looking forward to Christ's return. ✦

CHAPTER 1

Greeting

Paul, Sil·vā′nus, and Timothy,

To the church of the Thes·sa·lō′ni·ans in God our Father and the Lord Jesus Christ:

2Grace to you and peace from God our Father and the Lord Jesus Christ.

God's Final Judgment and Glory

3We are bound to thank God always for
you, brethren, as it is fitting, because your
faith grows exceedingly, and the love of
every one of you all abounds toward each
other, 4so that we ourselves boast of you
among the churches of God for your pa-
tience and faith in all your persecutions
and tribulations that you endure, 5*which is*
manifest evidence of the righteous judg-
ment of God, that you may be counted
worthy of the kingdom of God, for which
you also suffer; 6since *it is* a righteous thing
with God to repay with tribulation those
who trouble you, 7and to *give* you who are
troubled rest with us when the Lord Jesus
is revealed from heaven with His mighty
angels, 8in flaming fire taking vengeance
on those who do not know God, and on
those who do not obey the gospel of our
Lord Jesus Christ. 9These shall be punished
with everlasting destruction from the pres-
ence of the Lord and from the glory of His
power, 10when He comes, in that Day, to be
glorified in His saints and to be admired
among all those who believe,[a] because our
testimony among you was believed.

11Therefore we also pray always for you
that our God would count you worthy of
this calling, and fulfill all the good pleasure
of *His* goodness and the work of faith with
power, 12that the name of our Lord Jesus
Christ may be glorified in you, and you in
Him, according to the grace of our God
and the Lord Jesus Christ.

1:10 [a]NU-Text and M-Text read *have believed.*

1:8 Fire is often associated with God's coming in judgment. **vengeance**: God will act in justice, giving to the unrighteous what is the appropriate return for their conduct. **those who do not know God**: A term used often for the heathen world (1 Thess. 4:5). Here it refers to all who have refused to know God because they have refused to obey the gospel of our Lord Jesus Christ. There is no saving knowledge of God for those who reject Christ.

CHAPTER 2

The Great Apostasy

Now, brethren, concerning the coming
of our Lord Jesus Christ and our gathering
together to Him, we ask you, 2not to be
soon shaken in mind or troubled, either by
spirit or by word or by letter, as if from us,
as though the day of Christ[a] had come. 3Let
no one deceive you by any means; for *that
Day will not come* unless the falling away
comes first, and the man of sin[a] is revealed,
the son of perdition, 4who opposes and ex-
alts himself above all that is called God or
that is worshiped, so that he sits as God[a] in
the temple of God, showing himself that he
is God.

5Do you not remember that when I was
still with you I told you these things? 6And
now you know what is restraining, that he
may be revealed in his own time. 7For the
mystery of lawlessness is already at work;
only He[a] who now restrains *will do so* until
He[b] is taken out of the way. 8And then the
lawless one will be revealed, whom the
Lord will consume with the breath of His
mouth and destroy with the brightness of
His coming. 9The coming of the *lawless one*
is according to the working of Satan, with
all power, signs, and lying wonders, 10and
with all unrighteous deception among
those who perish, because they did not
receive the love of the truth, that they
might be saved. 11And for this reason
God will send them strong delusion, that
they should believe the lie, 12that they all
may be condemned who did not believe
the truth but had pleasure in unrighteous-
ness.

Stand Fast

13But we are bound to give thanks to
God always for you, brethren beloved by
the Lord, because God from the beginning
chose you for salvation through sanctifica-
tion by the Spirit and belief in the truth, 14to
which He called you by our gospel, for the
obtaining of the glory of our Lord Jesus
Christ. 15Therefore, brethren, stand fast
and hold the traditions which you were
taught, whether by word or our epistle.

16Now may our Lord Jesus Christ Him-
self, and our God and Father, who has
loved us and given *us* everlasting consola-
tion and good hope by grace, 17comfort
your hearts and establish you in every
good word and work.

CHAPTER 3

Pray for Us

Finally, brethren, pray for us, that the
word of the Lord may run *swiftly* and be
glorified, just as *it is* with you, 2and that we
may be delivered from unreasonable and
wicked men; for not all have faith.

3But the Lord is faithful, who will estab-
lish you and guard *you* from the evil one.
4And we have confidence in the Lord con-
cerning you, both that you do and will do
the things we command you.

5Now may the Lord direct your hearts
into the love of God and into the patience
of Christ.

2:2 [a]NU-Text reads *the Lord.* 2:3 [a]NU-Text reads *lawlessness.* 2:4 [a]NU-Text omits *as God.* 2:7 [a]Or *he* [b]Or *he*

I pray, Lord, that Your faithfulness will establish my grandchild and guard her from the evil one.

adapted from 2 Thessalonians 3:3

2:11, 12 God will send them strong delusion: God is not the author of deception, but He allows those who reject the truth to be misled by falsehood. Following such falsehood, they are eternally condemned.

3:1 We should pray consistently for the leaders in our church.

Warning Against Idleness

[6]But we command you, brethren, in the
name of our Lord Jesus Christ, that you
withdraw from every brother who walks
disorderly and not according to the tradi-
tion which he[a] received from us. [7]For you
yourselves know how you ought to follow
us, for we were not disorderly among you;
[8]nor did we eat anyone's bread free of
charge, but worked with labor and toil
night and day, that we might not be a bur-
den to any of you, [9]not because we do not
have authority, but to make ourselves an
example of how you should follow us.

[10]For even when we were with you, we
commanded you this: If anyone will not
work, neither shall he eat. [11]For we hear
that there are some who walk among you
in a disorderly manner, not working at all,
but are busybodies. [12]Now those who are
such we command and exhort through our
Lord Jesus Christ that they work in quiet-
ness and eat their own bread.

[13]But *as for* you, brethren, do not grow
weary *in* doing good. [14]And if anyone does
not obey our word in this epistle, note that
person and do not keep company with
him, that he may be ashamed. [15]Yet do not
count *him* as an enemy, but admonish *him*
as a brother.

Benediction

[16]Now may the Lord of peace Himself
give you peace always in every way. The
Lord *be* with you all.

[17]The salutation of Paul with my own
hand, which is a sign in every epistle; so I
write.

[18]The grace of our Lord Jesus Christ *be*
with you all. Amen.

A Higher Rate of Interest

Jay Kesler

The older generation is often highly critical of the younger one. Some people believe that an innate generation gap separates us from one another; yet I find that young people, who often seem so far away and so strange, frequently have a great thirst for a little interest shown by somebody.

Perhaps their fascination with MTV and video games may simply demonstrate that nature abhors a vacuum. Perhaps these people we criticize for being crassly commercial and preying on our youth are simply moving into areas left open to them by the preoccupation, fears, and selfishness of an adult generation who will not take the time to show interest in young people.

As grandparents, we need to look up from the hymnal, look around the church, and find young people to befriend. We can share a smile, ask a question, show interest in these children; and perhaps we can provide more than simply our tithes and offerings to the church of Jesus Christ in this modern and very needy age. ✦

3:6 [a]NU-Text and M-Text read *they.*

3:7, 8 follow us: A daring thing to say. Yet every effective Christian teacher has the responsibility to back his teaching with his lifestyle (see 1 Thess. 1:6).

3:14, 15 do not keep company with him: Do not have close fellowship with the disobedient lest you become involved with his disobedience. Do not associate with him in any way that will cause him, or others, to think that you approve of his conduct. Your good conduct should make him **ashamed**. But rather than avoid him, do your best to **admonish** and reclaim him, remembering that he is your **brother** in the Lord. The object of discipline in the church is to restore fellowship with the one who has strayed.

✦1 Timothy✦

1 and 2 Timothy and Titus are commonly called the "Pastoral Epistles" because they provide instruction and guidance for the care and protection of the churches. Each of the letters focuses on church life as well as leadership qualifications and responsibilities. The need for sound doctrine and a godly life are recurring themes throughout these three letters written by Paul.

1 Timothy was written from Macedonia while Timothy was serving as Paul's representative in Ephesus. Timothy's responsibilities included appointing elders, combating false doctrine, and supervising the churches. He probably worked directly with pastors of both the small and large congregations that met in homes throughout Ephesus and the surrounding provinces of Asia. Since no formal training institutions existed for pastors, Paul wrote to the young pastor Timothy to provide a foundation for his teaching and leadership responsibilities.

In addition to erasing false doctrines, Paul admonished Timothy to avoid greedy motives and pursue righteousness, godliness, faith, love, perseverance, and the gentleness that befits a man of God. This epistle served as a leadership manual for Timothy; Paul encouraged his young assistant to become an example to others, to exercise his spiritual gifts, to "fight the good fight of faith" (6:12), and to keep his personal and public life above reproach. Paul's relationship with Timothy illustrates the mentoring process mature Christians should follow in befriending members of younger generations and grounding them in the basics of the faith. ✦

CHAPTER 1

Greeting

Paul, an apostle of Jesus Christ, by the
commandment of God our Savior and the
Lord Jesus Christ, our hope,

[2]To Timothy, a true son in the faith:

Grace, mercy, *and* peace from God our
Father and Jesus Christ our Lord.

No Other Doctrine

[3]As I urged you when I went into Mac-
e·dō'ni·a—remain in Eph'e·sus that you
may charge some that they teach no other
doctrine, [4]nor give heed to fables and end-
less genealogies, which cause disputes
rather than godly edification which is in
faith. [5]Now the purpose of the command-
ment is love from a pure heart, *from* a good
conscience, and *from* sincere faith, [6]from
which some, having strayed, have turned
aside to idle talk, [7]desiring to be teachers of
the law, understanding neither what they
say nor the things which they affirm.

[8]But we know that the law *is* good if one
uses it lawfully, [9]knowing this: that the law
is not made for a righteous person, but for

1:2 Paul was instrumental in Timothy's conversion and thus considered Timothy his spiritual son.

1:5 the commandment: Clear Christian teaching. Speculations do not preoccupy Paul. We should beware of anyone whose teaching raises doubts rather than strengthens faith.

> ***I pray that my grandchild will have a pure heart, a good conscience, and sincere faith.***
>
> *adapted from* 1 Timothy 1:5

the lawless and insubordinate, for *the* ungodly and for sinners, for *the* unholy and profane, for murderers of fathers and murderers of mothers, for manslayers, [10]for fornicators, for sodomites, for kidnappers, for liars, for perjurers, and if there is any other thing that is contrary to sound doctrine, [11]according to the glorious gospel of the blessed God which was committed to my trust.

Glory to God for His Grace

[12]And I thank Christ Jesus our Lord who has enabled me, because He counted me faithful, putting *me* into the ministry, [13]although I was formerly a blasphemer, a persecutor, and an insolent man; but I obtained mercy because I did *it* ignorantly in unbelief. [14]And the grace of our Lord was exceedingly abundant, with faith and love which are in Christ Jesus. [15]This *is* a faithful saying and worthy of all acceptance, that Christ Jesus came into the world to save sinners, of whom I am chief. [16]However, for this reason I obtained mercy, that in me first Jesus Christ might show all longsuffering, as a pattern to those who are going to believe on Him for everlasting life. [17]Now to the King eternal, immortal, invisible, to God who alone is wise,[a] *be* honor and glory forever and ever. Amen.

Fight the Good Fight

[18]This charge I commit to you, son Timothy, according to the prophecies previously made concerning you, that by them you may wage the good warfare, [19]having faith and a good conscience, which some having rejected, concerning the faith have suffered shipwreck, [20]of whom are Hȳ-me·naē′us and Alexander, whom I delivered to Satan that they may learn not to blaspheme.

CHAPTER 2

Pray for All Men

Therefore I exhort first of all that supplications, prayers, intercessions, *and* giving of thanks be made for all men, [2]for kings and all who are in authority, that we may lead a quiet and peaceable life in all godliness and reverence. [3]For this *is* good and acceptable in the sight of God our Savior, [4]who desires all men to be saved and to come to the knowledge of the truth. [5]For *there is* one God and one Mediator between God and men, *the* Man Christ Jesus, [6]who gave Himself a ransom for all, to be testified in due time, [7]for which I was appointed a preacher and an apostle—I am speaking the truth in Christ[a] *and* not lying—a teacher of the Gentiles in faith and truth.

Men and Women in the Church

[8]I desire therefore that the men pray everywhere, lifting up holy hands, without wrath and doubting; [9]in like manner also,

1:17 [a]NU-Text reads *to the only God.* 2:7 [a]NU-Text omits *in Christ.*

1:13 Paul's conduct had been wrong, but it was not as if he had clearly understood the truth and purposefully rebelled against Christ. We are judged in the light of our knowledge (Luke 12:47, 48).

1:20 delivered to Satan: may refer to discipline through excommunication or punishment through physical judgment, as in the case of Ananias and Sapphira (Acts 5:1–11).

2:2 Christians have a responsibility to pray for those in authority.

2:9 Paul is not forbidding women to dress tastefully; he is emphasizing the importance of modesty, propriety, and humility. A godly woman is more concerned with her inner beauty than with outward adornment.

Fitness Is Fundamental

Dr. Sharon Sneed and Dr. David Sneed

Happiness and vitality during the later years of life will partially depend on your own level of fitness. Other things in life are surely important and can affect your outlook, but if you constantly feel fatigued, frustrated, depressed, or sick (much of which can improve with a realistic and well-planned fitness program), then you are settling for less of the good things in life and may not be able to do your best for the Lord.

While a truly balanced perspective must take into account all aspects of your health—spiritual, mental, and physical—one of the most important components is consistent exercise. To be as effective as possible in our work for the Lord, we need to allot some time for physical fitness. Certainly a good diet and other preventive-medicine health measures impact your level of fitness; but without some exercise, you just cannot be fit. ✦

that the women adorn themselves in mod-
est apparel, with propriety and modera-
tion, not with braided hair or gold or
pearls or costly clothing, 10but, which is
proper for women professing godliness,
with good works. 11Let a woman learn in
silence with all submission. 12And I do not
permit a woman to teach or to have au-
thority over a man, but to be in silence.
13For Adam was formed first, then Eve.
14And Adam was not deceived, but the
woman being deceived, fell into trans-
gression. 15Nevertheless she will be
saved in childbearing if they continue in
faith, love, and holiness, with self-control.

CHAPTER 3

Qualifications of Overseers

This *is* a faithful saying: If a man desires
the position of a bishop,[a] he desires a good
work. 2A bishop then must be blameless,
the husband of one wife, temperate, sober-
minded, of good behavior, hospitable, able
to teach; 3not given to wine, not violent,
not greedy for money,[a] but gentle, not
quarrelsome, not covetous; 4one who rules
his own house well, having *his* children in
submission with all reverence 5(for if a man
does not know how to rule his own house,
how will he take care of the church of
God?); 6not a novice, lest being puffed up
with pride he fall into the *same* condemna-

3:1 [a]Literally *overseer* 3:3 [a]NU-Text omits *not greedy for money.*

2:11–15 Paul himself did not disapprove of women praying and prophesying in public provided they were properly attired (see 1 Cor. 11:4, 5). Also Paul freely acknowledged his debt to a considerable group of women who helped in the NT church (Rom. 16:1–15). Public teaching, which involves making authoritative statements of doctrine, is another matter. It is improper for a woman to exercise such authority over males who have reached the age of religious responsibility in the church.

3:1 bishop: overseer or pastor.

3:2 This passage is a prohibition of polygamy; it is not intended to exclude from service a widower who has remarried or a man who has never been married. Paul is simply saying that a bishop's conduct must be above reproach.

tion as the devil. 7Moreover he must have a
good testimony among those who are out-
side, lest he fall into reproach and the snare
of the devil.

Qualifications of Deacons

8Likewise deacons *must be* reverent, not
double-tongued, not given to much wine,
not greedy for money, 9holding the mys-
tery of the faith with a pure conscience.
10But let these also first be tested; then let
them serve as deacons, being *found* blame-
less. 11Likewise, *their* wives *must be* rever-
ent, not slanderers, temperate, faithful in all
things. 12Let deacons be the husbands
of one wife, ruling *their* children and
their own houses well. 13For those who
have served well as deacons obtain for
themselves a good standing and great bold-
ness in the faith which is in Christ Jesus.

The Great Mystery

14These things I write to you, though I
hope to come to you shortly; 15but if I am
delayed, *I write* so that you may know how
you ought to conduct yourself in the house
of God, which is the church of the living
God, the pillar and ground of the truth.
16And without controversy great is the
mystery of godliness:

God[a] was manifested in the flesh,
Justified in the Spirit,
Seen by angels,
Preached among the Gentiles,
Believed on in the world,
Received up in glory.

CHAPTER 4

The Great Apostasy

Now the Spirit expressly says that in lat-
ter times some will depart from the faith,
giving heed to deceiving spirits and doc-
trines of demons, 2speaking lies in
hypocrisy, having their own conscience
seared with a hot iron, 3forbidding to
marry, *and commanding* to abstain from
foods which God created to be received
with thanksgiving by those who believe
and know the truth. 4For every creature of
God *is* good, and nothing is to be refused if
it is received with thanksgiving; 5for it is
sanctified by the word of God and prayer.

A Good Servant of Jesus Christ

6If you instruct the brethren in these
things, you will be a good minister of Jesus
Christ, nourished in the words of faith and
of the good doctrine which you have care-
fully followed. 7But reject profane and old
wives' fables, and exercise yourself toward
godliness. 8For bodily exercise profits a lit-
tle, but godliness is profitable for all
things, having promise of the life that now
is and of that which is to come. 9This *is* a
faithful saying and worthy of all accep-
tance. 10For to this *end* we both labor and
suffer reproach,[a] because we trust in the
living God, who is *the* Savior of all men,
especially of those who believe. 11These
things command and teach.

Take Heed to Your Ministry

12Let no one despise your youth, but be
an example to the believers in word, in
conduct, in love, in spirit,[a] in faith, in pu-
rity. 13Till I come, give attention to reading,
to exhortation, to doctrine. 14Do not neglect
the gift that is in you, which was given to
you by prophecy with the laying on of the
hands of the eldership. 15Meditate on these
things; give yourself entirely to them, that
your progress may be evident to all.
16Take heed to yourself and to the doctrine.
Continue in them, for in doing this you

3:16 [a]NU-Text reads *Who.* 4:10 [a]NU-Text reads *we labor and strive.* 4:12 [a]NU-Text omits *in spirit.*

3:8 Although the office of deacon is not clearly defined in the NT, the word deacon means "servant" or "attendant" and suggests that such a role involved easing the pastor's burden by handling the tasks that would distract him from prayer and ministry (see Acts 6:1–4).

4:14 Every Christian has been entrusted with at least one spiritual gift, and we are to put these to work in the church.

will save both yourself and those who hear you.

CHAPTER 5

Treatment of Church Members

Do not rebuke an older man, but exhort *him* as a father, younger men as brothers, 2older women as mothers, younger women as sisters, with all purity.

Honor True Widows

3Honor widows who are really widows. 4But if any widow has children or grandchildren, let them first learn to show piety at home and to repay their parents; for this is good and[a] acceptable before God. 5Now she who is really a widow, and left alone, trusts in God and continues in supplications and prayers night and day. 6But she who lives in pleasure is dead while she lives. 7And these things command, that they may be blameless. 8But if anyone does not provide for his own, and especially for those of his household, he has denied the faith and is worse than an unbeliever.

9Do not let a widow under sixty years old be taken into the number, *and not unless* she has been the wife of one man, 10well reported for good works: if she has brought up children, if she has lodged strangers, if she has washed the saints' feet, if she has relieved the afflicted, if she has diligently followed every good work.

11But refuse *the* younger widows; for when they have begun to grow wanton against Christ, they desire to marry, 12having condemnation because they have cast off their first faith. 13And besides they learn *to be* idle, wandering about from house to house, and not only idle but also gossips and busybodies, saying things which they ought not. 14Therefore I desire that *the* younger *widows* marry, bear children, manage the house, give no opportunity to the adversary to speak reproachfully. 15For some have already turned aside after Satan. 16If any believing man or[a] woman has widows, let them relieve them, and do not let the church be burdened, that it may relieve those who are really widows.

Honor the Elders

17Let the elders who rule well be counted worthy of double honor, especially those who labor in the word and doctrine. 18For the Scripture says, *"You shall not muzzle an ox while it treads out the grain,"*[a] and, "The laborer *is* worthy of his wages."[b] 19Do not receive an accusation against an elder except from two or three witnesses. 20Those who are sinning rebuke in the presence of all, that the rest also may fear.

21I charge *you* before God and the Lord Jesus Christ and the elect angels that you observe these things without prejudice, doing nothing with partiality. 22Do not lay hands on anyone hastily, nor share in other people's sins; keep yourself pure.

23No longer drink only water, but use a little wine for your stomach's sake and your frequent infirmities.

24Some men's sins are clearly evident, preceding *them* to judgment, but those of some *men* follow later. 25Likewise, the good works *of some* are clearly evident, and those that are otherwise cannot be hidden.

5:4 [a]NU-Text and M-Text omit *good and.*
5:16 [a]NU-Text omits *man or.* 5:18 [a]Deuteronomy 25:4 [b]Luke 10:7

5:1 We are to treat all our brothers and sisters in Christ with respect, no matter what their age or station.

5:3, 4 really widows: Those who have no relatives to support them and who fulfill the qualifications of v. 5. Children, as adults, are expected, as a matter of piety (religious duty), to care for their parents. The obligation is also extended to grandchildren (see v. 8).

5:19 Discipline must be based on corroborated evidence, not gossip.

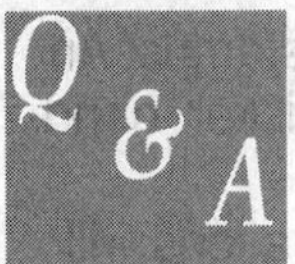

How can I handle being dependent on others?

Elmer L. Gray

A preacher friend told me the most loving person in his large circle of kinfolk is a cousin who is almost completely helpless. Relatives take turns waiting on him. The cousin is so appreciative and loving that even the children enjoy being with him and waiting on him. Although absolutely dependent on others, he greatly blesses them. The preacher said this helpless cousin, with his appreciation of love, leaves everyone feeling happy and worthwhile.

Even though dependent persons are aware of their condition and recognize their limitations, they should realize that they have something worth more than gold. Let them care greatly for others and show their appreciation and love.

Doing things for others is good. However, letting others do something nice for you is usually the same as doing something for them. It is hard to let someone help, but you can do more than you realize. Ask them what they do, what they like, where they go, and so forth. Listen to them and respond. Thank them for sharing with you. The experience will bless them and also give you something to think and pray about.

In His Sermon on the Mount, Jesus said, "Let your light so shine before men, that they may see your good works and glorify your Father in heaven" (Matt. 5:16).

Ask God to help you let others do things for you and then to enable you to show them loving appreciation. ✦

CHAPTER 6

Honor Masters

Let as many bondservants as are under
the yoke count their own masters worthy
of all honor, so that the name of God and
His doctrine may not be blasphemed. [2]And
those who have believing masters, let them
not despise *them* because they are brethren,
but rather serve *them* because those who
are benefited are believers and beloved.
Teach and exhort these things.

Error and Greed

[3]If anyone teaches otherwise and does
not consent to wholesome words, *even* the
words of our Lord Jesus Christ, and to the
doctrine which accords with godliness, [4]he
is proud, knowing nothing, but is obsessed
with disputes and arguments over words,
from which come envy, strife, reviling, evil
suspicions, [5]useless wranglings[a] of men of
corrupt minds and destitute of the truth,
who suppose that godliness is a *means of*
gain. From such withdraw yourself.[b]
[6]Now godliness with contentment is

6:5 [a]NU-Text and M-Text read *constant friction.* [b]NU-Text omits this sentence.

6:6–8 True **godliness** brings **contentment** with the material blessings that God has provided (vv. 7, 8). This is **great** spiritual **gain** because it keeps us from the temptations caused by covetousness (vv. 9, 10). After all, material things are only for this life (v. 7). To be content we must keep our values in right order (see Matt. 6:33).

I dare you to be healthy, live a long time, and never think old age.

William H. Danforth

Long-Distance Love

Irene M. Endicott

When a grandchild moves away, how can a grandparent maintain a relationship with the child? It is possible. And it can be fun. All it takes is a little planning and a lot of love. Even if separated by a half-century and a whole continent, you and your grandchild can be best friends.

Try a Sunday morning phone call before church. Hearing that familiar voice will hold you for the rest of the week. Make more than small talk. Build on past discussions. Talk about school projects, upcoming recitals, and sporting events. Know what is going on in your grandchild's life. What is his or her favorite TV program? Watch it; then call and discuss it. Then go and pray for your grandchild.

Write your grandchild regularly, maybe every two weeks or so, and encourage a written response. Print for the young ones. Enclose colorful paper, envelopes, and stamps. An occasional dollar bill, sticker, or riddle adds to the fun.

That way, both generations will look forward to visits from the mailman. Children adore getting mail addressed to them, even if they can't read it themselves. It demonstrates your love. By including magazine clippings about other youngsters their age, animals, funny tales, or sports, you might help the child's reading skills without it seeming like homework. ✦

great gain. 7For we brought nothing into
this world, *and it is* certain[a] we can carry
nothing out. 8And having food and cloth-
ing, with these we shall be content. 9But
those who desire to be rich fall into temp-
tation and a snare, and *into* many foolish
and harmful lusts which drown men in de-
struction and perdition. 10For the love of
money is a root of all *kinds of* evil, for which
some have strayed from the faith in their
greediness, and pierced themselves
through with many sorrows.

The Good Confession

11But you, O man of God, flee these
things and pursue righteousness, godli-
ness, faith, love, patience, gentleness.
12Fight the good fight of faith, lay hold on
eternal life, to which you were also called
and have confessed the good confession in
the presence of many witnesses. 13I urge
you in the sight of God who gives life to all
things, and *before* Christ Jesus who wit-
nessed the good confession before Pon'-
ti·us Pilate, 14that you keep *this* command-
ment without spot, blameless until our
Lord Jesus Christ's appearing, 15which He
will manifest in His own time, *He who is*
the blessed and only Potentate, the King of
kings and Lord of lords, 16who alone has
immortality, dwelling in unapproachable
light, whom no man has seen or can see, to
whom *be* honor and everlasting power.
Amen.

6:7 [a]NU-Text omits *and it is certain.*

Instructions to the Rich

[17]Command those who are rich in this present age not to be haughty, nor to trust in uncertain riches but in the living God, who gives us richly all things to enjoy. [18]*Let them* do good, that they be rich in good works, ready to give, willing to share, [19]storing up for themselves a good foundation for the time to come, that they may lay hold on eternal life.

Guard the Faith

[20]O Timothy! Guard what was committed to your trust, avoiding the profane *and* idle babblings and contradictions of what is falsely called knowledge— [21]by professing it some have strayed concerning the faith.

Grace *be* with you. Amen.

6:17–19 Having money is not a sin, but trusting in that wealth rather than relying on God is. The secret to true contentment is to use the material blessings we receive from God for the benefit of others.

6:21 Christianity is based on **the faith**—the content of the gospel as revealed by God in Christ and recorded in the Bible. Those who teach contrary views have **strayed** (Greek "missed the mark"). Paul begins (1:3–7) and concludes (6:20, 21) this letter on the same note: whatever is contrary to sound doctrine leads to spiritual ruin.

Pursuit of Happiness

Charles R. Swindoll

When Christ becomes our central focus—our reason for existence—contentment replaces our anxiety as well as our fears and insecurities. This cannot help but impact three of the most prevalent joy stealers in all of life.

"Once fear is removed, it is remarkable how quickly peace fills the vacuum."

1. He broadens the dimensions of our circumstances. This gives us new confidence. Chains that once bound and irritated us no longer seem so irksome. Our limitations become a challenge rather than a chore.

2. He delivers us from preoccupation with others. This causes our contentment level to rise. Other people's opinions, motives, and criticisms no longer seem all that important. What a wonderful deliverance!

3. He calms our fears regarding ourselves and our futures. This provides a burst of fresh hope on a daily basis. Once fear is removed, it is remarkable how quickly peace fills the vacuum. And when we get those three ducks in a row, it isn't long before we begin to laugh again. What a way to live! Let me urge you not to let anything keep you from it.

Since it is your inalienable right to pursue happiness, I suggest that you get with it right away. ✦

✦2 Timothy✦

Many historians believe that Nero burned Rome in A.D. 64 so he could rebuild a city of even greater grandeur. The people of the city suspected this, and Nero decided to blame the Christians to avoid a revolution against his reign. He ordered their punishment and, in many cases, their death. Paul was rearrested as one of the Christian church's leaders and imprisoned in Rome. Paul writes his last letter to Timothy during his trial, knowing that his execution is imminent.

Under these circumstances, Paul wrote 2 Timothy to encourage his young helper, who was facing churches plagued with false doctrine and persecution. He assured Timothy of his love and prayers and reminded him of his spiritual heritage and responsibilities. Paul commissioned Timothy to faithfully carry on the work that the condemned apostle had to relinquish.

Perhaps one reason Paul had such confidence in Timothy was the knowledge that the younger man had a supportive Christian mother and godly grandmother (1:5). Grandparents have a wonderful example to follow in the person of Lois, whose genuine faith influenced her grandson Timothy and, through him, changed the lives of countless others. ✦

CHAPTER 1

Greeting

Paul, an apostle of Jesus Christ[a] by the
will of God, according to the promise of
life which is in Christ Jesus,

[2]To Timothy, a beloved son:

Grace, mercy, *and* peace from God the
Father and Christ Jesus our Lord.

Timothy's Faith and Heritage

[3]I thank God, whom I serve with a pure
conscience, as *my* forefathers *did*, as with-
out ceasing I remember you in my prayers
night and day, [4]greatly desiring to see you,
being mindful of your tears, that I may be
filled with joy, [5]when I call to remembrance
the genuine faith that is in you, which
dwelt first in your grandmother Lō'is and
your mother Eū'nice, and I am persuaded
is in you also. [6]Therefore I remind you to
stir up the gift of God which is in you
through the laying on of my hands. [7]For
God has not given us a spirit of fear, but of
power and of love and of a sound mind.

1:1 [a]NU-Text and M-Text read *Christ Jesus.*

1:4 Paul had left Timothy at Ephesus sometime between his first imprisonment at Rome (see Acts 28:16–31) and his later arrest and return to Rome. **your tears**: Acts 20:37, 38 is an example of an earlier sorrowful parting between Paul and his friends.

1:7 spirit of fear: Was timidity Timothy's particular weakness? The apostle reminds him that God has given **power** to overcome difficulties, love for the unlovely, and good judgment with self-control necessary to carry out his ministry. Whatever spiritual gifts God has given us are accompanied by the power to put them to use.

The Power of Genuine Faith

Jerry and Jack Schreur

Children develop their first perceptions of God during the wonder years. They try to picture Him in their minds. They become aware that their parents and grandparents read the Bible, pray, go to church, and try to follow Jesus. Creative grandparents know the importance of modeling a real and personal relationship with Christ.

Living in obedience to God and His Word, with Christ a part of everyday conversation, makes a powerful statement about the reality of your faith to your grandchildren. They know what Grandma and Grandpa believe because they watch you so closely. You cannot fake it very long in front of them. Do you see what this does? It gives you the responsibility of forging a real, live faith of your own, lived out with all its complexities and ambiguities, for their questioning, impressionable minds to see.

The Bible testifies to the power of this kind of faith in a grandparent. When the apostle Paul charged Timothy with the task of carrying out the work of the gospel, he wrote, "I call to remembrance the genuine faith that is in you, which dwelt first in your grandmother Lois and your mother Eunice, and I am persuaded is in you also" (2 Tim. 1:5).

Love Jesus with your grandchildren. There is no greater way to care for them! ✦

Not Ashamed of the Gospel

[8]Therefore do not be ashamed of the tes-
timony of our Lord, nor of me His prisoner,
but share with me in the sufferings for the
gospel according to the power of God,
[9]who has saved us and called *us* with a
holy calling, not according to our works,
but according to His own purpose and
grace which was given to us in Christ Jesus
before time began, [10]but has now been re-
vealed by the appearing of our Savior
Jesus Christ, *who* has abolished death
and brought life and immortality to light
through the gospel, [11]to which I was ap-
pointed a preacher, an apostle, and a
teacher of the Gentiles.[a] [12]For this reason I
also suffer these things; nevertheless I am
not ashamed, for I know whom I have be-
lieved and am persuaded that He is able to
keep what I have committed to Him until
that Day.

Be Loyal to the Faith

[13]Hold fast the pattern of sound words
which you have heard from me, in faith
and love which are in Christ Jesus. [14]That
good thing which was committed to you,
keep by the Holy Spirit who dwells in us.

[15]This you know, that all those in Asia
have turned away from me, among whom
are Phy′gel·lus and Her·mog′e·nes. [16]The
Lord grant mercy to the household of
On·e·siph′o·rus, for he often refreshed me,
and was not ashamed of my chain; [17]but
when he arrived in Rome, he sought me
out very zealously and found *me.* [18]The
Lord grant to him that he may find mercy
from the Lord in that Day—and you know
very well how many ways he ministered *to
me*[a] at Eph′e·sus.

CHAPTER 2

Be Strong in Grace

You therefore, my son, be strong in the
grace that is in Christ Jesus. [2]And the
things that you have heard from me
among many witnesses, commit these to
faithful men who will be able to teach

1:11 [a]NU-Text omits *of the Gentiles.*
1:18 [a]*To me* is from the Vulgate and a few Greek manuscripts.

TOTAL WELL-BEING

Dr. Kenneth Cooper

Having a good, powerful, solid body goes along with a powerful, sound mind (2 Tim. 1:7). That's why there are fewer mental problems in people who are physically fit. Psychiatrists are now using exercise as a means of treating depression and various types of psychological and psychiatric problems.

This total concept of well-being is not complete without putting the spiritual in the proper place. I emphasize the physical, but if the spiritual is not in the proper order, the physical does not make any difference.

Bodily fitness is important, but spiritual fitness is really what is needed because it prepares you not only for life now but also for the life hereafter. ✦

others also. [3]You therefore must endure[a]
hardship as a good soldier of Jesus Christ.
[4]No one engaged in warfare entangles
himself with the affairs of *this* life, that he
may please him who enlisted him as a sol-
dier. [5]And also if anyone competes in ath-
letics, he is not crowned unless he com-
petes according to the rules. [6]The
hardworking farmer must be first to par-
take of the crops. [7]Consider what I say, and
may[a] the Lord give you understanding in
all things.

[8]Remember that Jesus Christ, of the seed
of David, was raised from the dead accord-
ing to my gospel, [9]for which I suffer trou-
ble as an evildoer, *even* to the point of
chains; but the word of God is not chained.
[10]Therefore I endure all things for the sake
of the elect, that they also may obtain the
salvation which is in Christ Jesus with eter-
nal glory.

[11]*This is* a faithful saying:

For if we died with *Him*,
We shall also live with *Him*.
12 If we endure,
We shall also reign with *Him*.
If we deny *Him*,
He also will deny us.
13 If we are faithless,
He remains faithful;
He cannot deny Himself.

Approved and Disapproved Workers

[14]Remind *them* of these things, charging
them before the Lord not to strive about
words to no profit, to the ruin of the hear-
ers. [15]Be diligent to present yourself ap-
proved to God, a worker who does not
need to be ashamed, rightly dividing the
word of truth. [16]But shun profane *and* idle
babblings, for they will increase to more
ungodliness. [17]And their message will
spread like cancer. Hy̆·me·naē′us and
Phi·lē′tus are of this sort, [18]who have
strayed concerning the truth, saying that
the resurrection is already past; and they
overthrow the faith of some. [19]Neverthe-
less the solid foundation of God stands,
having this seal: "The Lord knows those
who are His," and, "Let everyone who
names the name of Christ[a] depart from in-
iquity."

[20]But in a great house there are not only
vessels of gold and silver, but also of wood

2:3 [a]NU-Text reads *You must share.* 2:7 [a]NU-Text reads *the Lord will give you.*

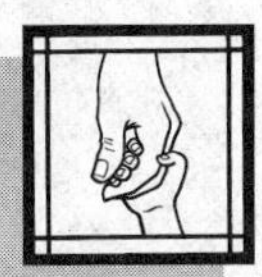

COMMIT YOURSELF

Dr. Richard Meier

In his second letter to Timothy, the apostle Paul encouraged the young pastor to pass along to other faithful believers the things he has seen and heard from Paul (2:2). This is the ultimate goal of a mentoring relationship—passing on truth, training people who will train others, and thereby positively affecting the world for Jesus Christ.

A word of caution: Anyone who aspires to be a mentor should also be involved in a mentoring relationship as a protégé. It's an ongoing, lifetime commitment to growth. If you give and give without receiving in return, eventually you will dry up. And you cannot give what you do not possess.

Don't wait until you feel you have it all together before getting started. That day will never come this side of heaven! But consider the commitment carefully. It will take time and energy. Be careful to balance the demands of the relationship with healthy, appropriate boundaries. Commit yourself to seeing the potential in a person, not the problems and mistakes. ✦

and clay, some for honor and some for dishonor. [21]Therefore if anyone cleanses himself from the latter, he will be a vessel for honor, sanctified and useful for the Master, prepared for every good work. [22]Flee also youthful lusts; but pursue righteousness, faith, love, peace with those who call on the Lord out of a pure heart. [23]But avoid foolish and ignorant disputes, knowing that they generate strife. [24]And a servant of the Lord must not quarrel but be gentle to all, able to teach, patient, [25]in humility correcting those who are in opposition, if God perhaps will grant them repentance, so that they may know the truth, [26]and *that* they may come to their senses *and escape* the snare of the devil, having been taken captive by him to *do* his will.

CHAPTER 3

Perilous Times and Perilous Men

But know this, that in the last days perilous times will come: [2]For men will be lovers of themselves, lovers of money, boasters, proud, blasphemers, disobedient to parents, unthankful, unholy, [3]unloving, unforgiving, slanderers, without self-control, brutal, despisers of good, [4]traitors, headstrong, haughty, lovers of pleasure rather than lovers of God, [5]having a form of godliness but denying its power. And from such people turn away! [6]For of this sort are those who creep into households and make captives of gullible women loaded down with sins, led away by various lusts, [7]always learning and never able to come to the knowledge of the truth. [8]Now as Jan'nēs and Jam'brēs resisted Moses, so do these also resist the truth: men of corrupt minds, disapproved concerning the faith; [9]but they will progress no further, for their folly will be manifest to all, as theirs also was.

The Man of God and the Word of God

[10]But you have carefully followed my doctrine, manner of life, purpose, faith, longsuffering, love, perseverance, [11]persecutions, afflictions, which happened to me at An'ti·och, at Ī·cō'ni·um, at Lys'tra—

2:19 [a]NU-Text and M-Text read *the Lord.*

SEARCHING THE SCRIPTURES

Gloria Gaither

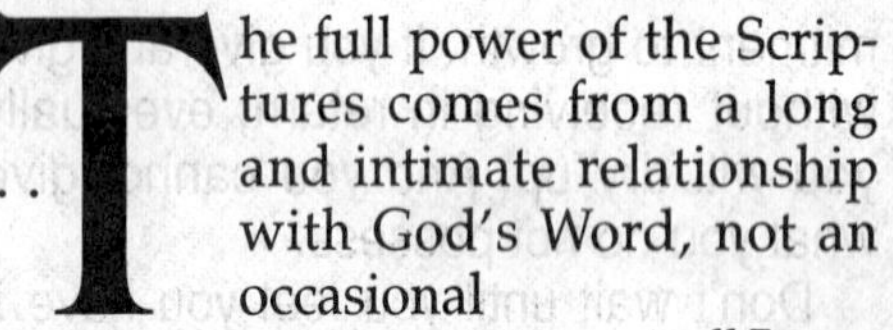

The full power of the Scriptures comes from a long and intimate relationship with God's Word, not an occasional brief encounter. The Bible is not a spiritual "rabbit's foot." We can't treat it like a sort of "panic potion" and expect it to have power in our lives. If we wait until we are face to face with a crisis before we dust off the "black book," we aren't too likely to find any relevant answers.

"A continuing companionship with God's Word will truly equip us to think clearly."

"Searching the Scriptures" doesn't mean letting the Bible fall open at random and stabbing an index finger at its pages with our eyes shut, hoping to find a magic remedy that will fix everything. On the contrary, only a continuing companionship with God's Word will truly equip us to think clearly when we are faced with choices to make. The Bible helps us know God better. If our motive for reading God's Word is to know God more intimately, then the Book that at one time may have seemed to be dull and difficult will take on the excitement of a living adventure. ✦

what persecutions I endured. And out of
them all the Lord delivered me. 12Yes, and
all who desire to live godly in Christ Jesus
will suffer persecution. 13But evil men and
impostors will grow worse and worse, de-
ceiving and being deceived. 14But you
must continue in the things which you
have learned and been assured of, know-
ing from whom you have learned *them*,
15and that from childhood you have known
the Holy Scriptures, which are able to
make you wise for salvation through faith
which is in Christ Jesus.

16All Scripture *is* given by inspiration of
God, and *is* profitable for doctrine, for re-
proof, for correction, for instruction in
righteousness, 17that the man of God may
be complete, thoroughly equipped for
every good work.

CHAPTER 4

Preach the Word

I charge *you* therefore before God and
the Lord Jesus Christ, who will judge the
living and the dead at[a] His appearing and
His kingdom: 2Preach the word! Be ready
in season *and* out of season. Convince, re-
buke, exhort, with all longsuffering and
teaching. 3For the time will come when
they will not endure sound doctrine, but
according to their own desires, *because* they
have itching ears, they will heap up for
themselves teachers; 4and they will turn
their ears away from the truth, and be
turned aside to fables. 5But you be watch-
ful in all things, endure afflictions, do the
work of an evangelist, fulfill your ministry.

4:1 [a]NU-Text omits *therefore* and reads *and by* for *at.*

I pray that my grandchild will fight the good fight, that he will finish the race, and that he will keep the faith.

adapted from 2 Timothy 4:7

Paul's Valedictory

[6]For I am already being poured out as a drink offering, and the time of my departure is at hand. [7]I have fought the good fight, I have finished the race, I have kept the faith. [8]Finally, there is laid up for me the crown of righteousness, which the Lord, the righteous Judge, will give to me on that Day, and not to me only but also to all who have loved His appearing.

The Abandoned Apostle

[9]Be diligent to come to me quickly; [10]for Dē′mas has forsaken me, having loved this present world, and has departed for Thes·sa·lo·nī′ca—Crescens for Galatia, Titus for Dal·mā′tia. [11]Only Luke is with me. Get Mark and bring him with you, for he is useful to me for ministry. [12]And Tych′i·cus I have sent to Eph′e·sus. [13]Bring the cloak that I left with Car′pus at Trō′as when you come—and the books, especially the parchments.

[14]Alexander the coppersmith did me much harm. May the Lord repay him according to his works. [15]You also must beware of him, for he has greatly resisted our words.

[16]At my first defense no one stood with me, but all forsook me. May it not be charged against them.

The Lord Is Faithful

[17]But the Lord stood with me and strengthened me, so that the message might be preached fully through me, and *that* all the Gentiles might hear. Also I was delivered out of the mouth of the lion. [18]And the Lord will deliver me from every evil work and preserve *me* for His heavenly kingdom. To Him *be* glory forever and ever. Amen!

Come Before Winter

[19]Greet Pris′ca and A·qui′la, and the household of On·e·siph′o·rus. [20]Ē·ras′tus stayed in Corinth, but Troph′i·mus I have left in Mī·lē′tus sick.

[21]Do your utmost to come before winter.

Eū·bū′lus greets you, as well as Pū′dens, Lī′nus, Clau′di·a, and all the brethren.

Farewell

[22]The Lord Jesus Christ[a] be with your spirit. Grace be with you. Amen.

4:22 [a]NU-Text omits *Jesus Christ.*

4:11 Luke, the author of Acts and the Gospel of Luke, was a companion of Paul on many of his earlier missionary travels. When John **Mark** deserted Paul and Barnabas on the first missionary journey (Acts 13:13), Paul refused to take him on his second journey (Acts 15:36–40). Later, however, he accepted Mark as a coworker in the gospel (Col. 4:10; Philem. 24).

4:13 books . . . parchments: Perhaps (1) Paul's legal papers, (2) the OT Scriptures, (3) written accounts of Jesus' words and works, or (4) other NT materials, including copies of Paul's epistles.

4:16 first defense: Evidently a preliminary hearing when Paul was called to answer the charges against him.

✦Titus✦

Titus was one of Paul's closest and most trusted companions. Paul gave Titus a huge challenge—go to Crete and set it in order. Crete was already an ancient city in Titus's time, famous as the legendary birthplace of the mythical Greek god Zeus, and full of liars and immorality. Because of the decadence of the Cretans, Titus had to stress the need for righteousness in Christian living.

Paul advised Titus to appoint elders, men and women of proven spiritual character, to oversee the work of the church. Men and women, young and old, each have their own vital functions to fulfill in the church to be living examples of the doctrine they profess. Throughout this letter, Paul stressed working out salvation in the daily lives of both the elders and the congregation. He set forth rules of conduct for mature Christians, emphasizing their role in teaching appropriate behavior to younger generations. ✦

CHAPTER 1

Greeting

Paul, a bondservant of God and an
apostle of Jesus Christ, according to the
faith of God's elect and the acknowledg-
ment of the truth which accords with god-
liness, 2in hope of eternal life which God,
who cannot lie, promised before time be-
gan, 3but has in due time manifested His
word through preaching, which was com-
mitted to me according to the command-
ment of God our Savior;

4To Titus, a true son in *our* common
faith:

Grace, mercy, *and* peace from God the
Father and the Lord Jesus Christ[a] our
Savior.

Qualified Elders

5For this reason I left you in Crēte, that
you should set in order the things that are
lacking, and appoint elders in every city as
I commanded you— 6if a man is blameless,
the husband of one wife, having faithful
children not accused of dissipation or
insubordination. 7For a bishop[a] must be
blameless, as a steward of God, not self-
willed, not quick-tempered, not given to
wine, not violent, not greedy for money,
8but hospitable, a lover of what is good,
sober-minded, just, holy, self-controlled,
9holding fast the faithful word as he has
been taught, that he may be able, by sound
doctrine, both to exhort and convict those
who contradict.

The Elders' Task

10For there are many insubordinate,
both idle talkers and deceivers, especially
those of the circumcision, 11whose mouths
must be stopped, who subvert whole

1:4 [a]NU-Text reads *and Christ Jesus.*
1:7 [a]Literally *overseer*

1:11, 12 mouths . . . stopped: The Greek can be translated "mouths muzzled." They

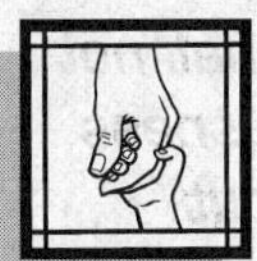

A Good Act to Follow

Sherwood Eliot Wirt

The older Christian man is expected to be a role model for younger men to follow. He is to set an example of integrity and sound character. He is to be held worthy of respect and to be full of faith, love, fortitude, and self-control. He should give evidence of good habits and enjoy a solid reputation outside the church as well as within the Christian community.

And here is the point: He is to teach these principles to young Christian men. He is to instruct them in ethics, morals, marriage and family matters, and service to the community. Instead of just being an example, he is to reproduce that example in others who are younger.

Older Christian women also have a holy task to teach younger women what it means to be true servants of the Lord in this generation. They are to instruct young women in worship, in morals, in character building, in family matters, and in assistance to those in need.

Instead of being "out to pasture," the Christian elder is given a sacred and hallowed trust. For centuries God's key people have discipled the succeeding generation and so transmitted the unsearchable riches of Christ. ✦

households, teaching things which they
ought not, for the sake of dishonest gain.
12One of them, a prophet of their own, said,
"Crē'tans *are* always liars, evil beasts, lazy
gluttons." 13This testimony is true. There-
fore rebuke them sharply, that they may be
sound in the faith, 14not giving heed to Jew-
ish fables and commandments of men who
turn from the truth. 15To the pure all things
are pure, but to those who are defiled
and unbelieving nothing is pure; but even
their mind and conscience are defiled.
16They profess to know God, but in
works they deny Him, being abominable,
disobedient, and disqualified for every
good work.

CHAPTER 2

Qualities of a Sound Church

But as for you, speak the things which
are proper for sound doctrine: 2that the
older men be sober, reverent, temperate,
sound in faith, in love, in patience; 3the
older women likewise, that they be rev-
erent in behavior, not slanderers, not
given to much wine, teachers of good
things— 4that they admonish the young

had to be stopped because **whole households** were being turned aside from the faith. **for . . . dishonest gain**: Their motivation was perverted (see v. 7). **One of them**: Epimenides, a sixth century B.C. Cretan philosopher. He was regarded as an inspired **prophet**, and highly honored. **liars**: So notorious that the verb "to Cretize" was a slang expression meaning to lie or cheat.

2:2–5 As mature Christians, we have a responsiblity to teach the principles of Christian living to those younger than we are. When we set a proper example for them to follow, we are reinforcing the Word of God.

women to love their husbands, to love their children, 5to be discreet, chaste, homemakers, good, obedient to their own husbands, that the word of God may not be blasphemed.

6Likewise, exhort the young men to be sober-minded, 7in all things showing yourself *to be* a pattern of good works; in doctrine *showing* integrity, reverence, incorruptibility,[a] 8sound speech that cannot be condemned, that one who is an opponent may be ashamed, having nothing evil to say of you.[a]

9*Exhort* bondservants to be obedient to their own masters, to be well pleasing in all *things,* not answering back, 10not pilfering, but showing all good fidelity, that they may adorn the doctrine of God our Savior in all things.

Trained by Saving Grace

11For the grace of God that brings salvation has appeared to all men, 12teaching us that, denying ungodliness and worldly lusts, we should live soberly, righteously, and godly in the present age, 13looking for the blessed hope and glorious appearing of our great God and Savior Jesus Christ, 14who gave Himself for us, that He might redeem us from every lawless deed and purify for Himself *His* own special people, zealous for good works.

15Speak these things, exhort, and rebuke with all authority. Let no one despise you.

CHAPTER 3

Graces of the Heirs of Grace

Remind them to be subject to rulers and authorities, to obey, to be ready for every good work, 2to speak evil of no one, to be peaceable, gentle, showing all humility to all men. 3For we ourselves were also once foolish, disobedient, deceived, serving various lusts and pleasures, living in malice and envy, hateful and hating one another. 4But when the kindness and the love of God our Savior toward man appeared, 5not by works of righteousness which we have done, but according to His mercy He saved us, through the washing of regeneration and renewing of the Holy Spirit, 6whom He poured out on us abundantly through Jesus Christ our Savior, 7that having been justified by His grace we should become heirs according to the hope of eternal life.

8This is a faithful saying, and these things I want you to affirm constantly, that those who have believed in God should be careful to maintain good works. These things are good and profitable to men.

Avoid Dissension

9But avoid foolish disputes, genealogies, contentions, and strivings about the law; for they are unprofitable and useless. 10Reject a divisive man after the first and second admonition, 11knowing that such a person is warped and sinning, being self-condemned.

> ***I praise you, Lord, that not by works of righteousness which I have done, but according to Your mercy You saved me.***
>
> *adapted from* Titus 3:5

2:7 [a]NU-Text omits *incorruptibility.* 2:8 [a]NU-Text and M-Text read *us.*

2:13 glorious appearing: The Second Coming of our Lord **Jesus Christ**.

3:1 Although we are citizens of heaven, we must fulfill our responsibilities in civil matters, so we won't bring reproach upon the church.

3:10 a devisive man: one who chooses to believe what he wants and acts upon it rather than accepting the biblical position.

Final Messages

[12]When I send Ar′te·mas to you, or Tych′i·cus, be diligent to come to me at Ni·cop′o·lis, for I have decided to spend the winter there. [13]Send Zē′-nas the lawyer and A·pol′los on their journey with haste, that they may lack nothing. [14]And let our *people* also learn to maintain good works, to *meet* urgent needs, that they may not be unfruitful.

Farewell

[15]All who *are* with me greet you. Greet those who love us in the faith.

Grace *be* with you all. Amen.

✦Philemon✦

Paul wrote this personal letter to his close friend Philemon, a wealthy businessman in Colosse with whom Paul had stayed during his visits and missionary journeys through the area. Evidently a slave named Onesimus stole some money from Philemon and escaped to Rome as a fugitive. Alone and on the run, Onesimus found Paul, whom he would have known from Paul's visits to the home of Philemon. Paul led Onesimus to Christ, and soon he became a valuable asset to Paul and his ministry in Rome.

Paul asked Philemon to receive Onesimus, not as the thief and deserter he was, but as the brother in Christ he had become while in Rome. Paul encouraged Philemon to receive Onesimus as he would receive Paul himself. Paul even laid aside his rights and became Onesimus's substitute by assuming his debt.

Every Christian can follow Paul's example. Just as Paul stepped in as a peacemaker between Onesimus and Philemon, all Christians should look for ways to resolve potential conflicts within the church. ✦

Greeting

Paul, a prisoner of Christ Jesus, and Timothy *our* brother,

To Phī·lē′mon our beloved *friend* and fellow laborer, 2to the beloved[a] Ap′phi·a, Ar·chip′pus our fellow soldier, and to the church in your house:

3Grace to you and peace from God our Father and the Lord Jesus Christ.

Philemon's Love and Faith

4I thank my God, making mention of you always in my prayers, 5hearing of your love and faith which you have toward the Lord Jesus and toward all the saints, 6that the sharing of your faith may become effective by the acknowledgment of every good thing which is in you[a] in Christ Jesus. 7For we have[a] great joy[b] and consolation in your love, because the hearts of the saints have been refreshed by you, brother.

The Plea for Onesimus

8Therefore, though I might be very bold in Christ to command you what is fitting, 9*yet* for love's sake I rather appeal *to you*—being such a one as Paul, the aged, and now also a prisoner of Jesus Christ— 10I appeal to you for my son Ō·nes′i·mus, whom I have begotten *while* in my chains, 11who

2 [a]NU-Text reads *to our sister Apphia.* 6 [a]NU-Text and M-Text read *us.* 7 [a]NU-Text reads *had.* [b]M-Text reads *thanksgiving.*

---

4 Paul's prayer life is an example for all believers. We should strive to continually remember our Christian brothers and sisters in prayer.

9 Paul knew the most effective decision would result from free choice, not from compulsion. Thus he appealed to Philemon's **love** (see v. 5).

> ***I pray that the sharing of my faith may become effective by the acknowledgment of every good thing which is in Christ Jesus.***
>
> *adapted from* Philemon 1:6

once was unprofitable to you, but now is profitable to you and to me.

[12]I am sending him back.[a] You therefore receive him, that is, my own heart, [13]whom I wished to keep with me, that on your behalf he might minister to me in my chains for the gospel. [14]But without your consent I wanted to do nothing, that your good deed might not be by compulsion, as it were, but voluntary.

[15]For perhaps he departed for a while for this *purpose,* that you might receive him forever, [16]no longer as a slave but more than a slave—a beloved brother, especially to me but how much more to you, both in the flesh and in the Lord.

Philemon's Obedience Encouraged

[17]If then you count me as a partner, receive him as *you would* me. [18]But if he has wronged you or owes anything, put that on my account. [19]I, Paul, am writing with my own hand. I will repay—not to mention to you that you owe me even your own self besides. [20]Yes, brother, let me have joy from you in the Lord; refresh my heart in the Lord.

[21]Having confidence in your obedience, I write to you, knowing that you will do even more than I say. [22]But, meanwhile, also prepare a guest room for me, for I trust that through your prayers I shall be granted to you.

Farewell

[23]Ep'a·phras, my fellow prisoner in Christ Jesus, greets you, [24]*as do* Mark, Ar·is·tar'chus, Dē'mas, Luke, my fellow laborers.

[25]The grace of our Lord Jesus Christ *be* with your spirit. Amen.

12 [a]NU-Text reads *back to you in person, that is, my own heart.*

14, 15 Two reasons Paul would not keep Onesimus: he did not have Philemon's **consent** (v. 14), and perhaps God wanted Onesimus to be permanently with Philemon as his spiritual brother (v. 15). **not . . . by compulsion**: In Christ, our own right actions are always freely chosen.

18, 19 if he . . . owes: Paul assumed that Onesimus owed Philemon something—perhaps stolen when the slave escaped. The apostle was willing to take responsibility for that debt. However, if Philemon kept a close ledger, he should be reminded that he was indebted to Paul for his own spiritual life.

22 prepare a . . . room: Directed to Philemon. The pronouns **your** and **you** are now plural. The whole house church would be praying for Paul and he hoped to see them all. Since Paul often used a stenographer, he has written this letter in his own handwriting, perhaps to emphasize his deep personal concern.

✦Hebrews✦

Many of the Jewish believers, having converted to Christianity, were tempted to reverse their course to escape the persecution of their countrymen. During Jesus' ministry, He had predicted the destruction of the temple which, to these first-century Jewish Christians, was still the center of their worship. The writer of Hebrews addressed each of these issues and exhorted readers to "go on to perfection" (6:1). Hebrews appeals to the superiority of Christ over the Judaic system, which was committed to following the temple rights and sacrifices. The imminent destruction of the temple would begin the new order, and the writer wanted to prepare the Jewish believers for this time.

This profound work supports the superiority of Christ by arguing that Christ is "better" in every respect. Christ is better than the angels because they worship Him. He is better than Moses, for He created him. He is better than the Aaronic priesthood, for His sacrifice was once and for all. He is better than the Law, for He mediates a better covenant. In short, more can be gained in Christ than lost in Judaism. Pressing on in Christ produces tested faith, self-discipline, and a visible love seen in good works. The author urged the new believers to encourage one another to remain steadfast in the faith. Today, many Christians are discouraged by the challenge of consistent church attendance; however, fellowship with other believers is a vital component of a dynamic spiritual life.

Although the author, origin, and audience of the book are unknown, Hebrews stands alone in the New Testament declaring Jesus to be the "High Priest." It is an excellent defense of the Christian faith against those who would look elsewhere for redemption, salvation, and eternal life. ✦

CHAPTER 1

God's Supreme Revelation

God, who at various times and in various ways spoke in time past to the fathers
by the prophets, 2has in these last days
spoken to us by *His* Son, whom He has appointed heir of all things, through
whom also He made the worlds; 3who being the brightness of *His* glory and the express image of His person, and upholding all things by the word of His power, when He had by Himself[a] purged our[b] sins, sat down at the right hand of the
Majesty on high, 4having become so
much better than the angels, as He has by

1:3 [a]NU-Text omits *by Himself.* [b]NU-Text omits *our.*

1:4 The writer is emphasizing Christ's superiority to **angels** to counteract the mistaken belief held by some first-century Christians that Christ Himself was an angel.

inheritance obtained a more excellent name than they.

The Son Exalted Above Angels

5For to which of the angels did He ever say:

"You are My Son,
Today I have begotten You"?[a]

And again:

"I will be to Him a Father,
And He shall be to Me a Son"?[b]

6But when He again brings the firstborn into the world, He says:

"Let all the angels of God worship
Him."[a]

7And of the angels He says:

"Who makes His angels spirits
And His ministers a flame of fire."[a]

8But to the Son *He says:*

"Your throne, O God, is forever and
ever;
A scepter of righteousness is the
scepter of Your kingdom.
9 *You have loved righteousness and*
hated lawlessness;
Therefore God, Your God, has
anointed You
With the oil of gladness more than
Your companions."[a]

1:5 [a]Psalm 2:7 [b]2 Samuel 7:14 1:6 [a]Deuteronomy 32:43 (Septuagint, Dead Sea Scrolls); Psalm 97:7 1:7 [a]Psalm 104:4 1:9 [a]Psalm 45:6, 7 1:12 [a]Psalm 102:25–27 1:13 [a]Psalm 110:1

10And:

"You, LORD, in the beginning laid the
foundation of the earth,
And the heavens are the work of Your
hands.
11 *They will perish, but You remain;*
And they will all grow old like a
garment;
12 *Like a cloak You will fold them up,*
And they will be changed.
But You are the same,
And Your years will not fail."[a]

13But to which of the angels has He ever said:

"Sit at My right hand,
Till I make Your enemies Your
footstool"?[a]

14Are they not all ministering spirits sent forth to minister for those who will inherit salvation?

CHAPTER 2

Do Not Neglect Salvation

Therefore we must give the more
earnest heed to the things we have heard,
lest we drift away. 2For if the word spoken
through angels proved steadfast, and
every transgression and disobedience re-
ceived a just reward, 3how shall we escape

> The measure of the worth of our public activity to God is the private, profound communion we have with Him.
> Oswald Chambers

1:10–12 The Son is called **LORD**. He is the eternal, unchanging Creator, not part of the ever-changing and transitory creation (see 13:8).

2:1 Therefore: Because of Christ's greatness.

2:2 The NT (Acts 7:38; Gal. 3:19), and later, Judaism indicate that **angels** were present and active at the giving of the law on Sinai. God's **steadfast** word always comes to pass. Without exception, all who disobeyed God's previous lesser revelation were appropriately punished.

if we neglect so great a salvation, which at
the first began to be spoken by the Lord,
and was confirmed to us by those who
heard *Him*, 4God also bearing witness both
with signs and wonders, with various mir-
acles, and gifts of the Holy Spirit, accord-
ing to His own will?

The Son Made Lower than Angels

5For He has not put the world to come,
of which we speak, in subjection to angels.
6But one testified in a certain place, saying:

> *"What is man that You are mindful of*
> *him,*
> *Or the son of man that You take care*
> *of him?*
> 7 *You have made him a little lower*
> *than the angels;*
> *You have crowned him with glory*
> *and honor,*[a]
> *And set him over the works of Your*
> *hands.*
> 8 *You have put all things in subjection*
> *under his feet."*[a]

For in that He put all in subjection under
him, He left nothing *that is* not put under
him. But now we do not yet see all things
put under him. 9But we see Jesus, who was
made a little lower than the angels, for the
suffering of death crowned with glory and
honor, that He, by the grace of God, might
taste death for everyone.

Bringing Many Sons to Glory

10For it was fitting for Him, for whom
are all things and by whom *are* all things, in
bringing many sons to glory, to make the
captain of their salvation perfect through
sufferings. 11For both He who sanctifies
and those who are being sanctified *are* all
of one, for which reason He is not ashamed
to call them brethren, 12saying:

> *"I will declare Your name to My*
> *brethren;*
> *In the midst of the assembly I will*
> *sing praise to You."*[a]

13And again:

> *"I will put My trust in Him."*[a]

And again:

> *"Here am I and the children whom*
> *God has given Me."*[b]

14Inasmuch then as the children have
partaken of flesh and blood, He Himself
likewise shared in the same, that through
death He might destroy him who had the
power of death, that is, the devil, 15and re-
lease those who through fear of death were
all their lifetime subject to bondage. 16For
indeed He does not give aid to angels, but
He does give aid to the seed of Abraham.
17Therefore, in all things He had to be
made like *His* brethren, that He might be a
merciful and faithful High Priest in things
pertaining to God, to make propitiation for
the sins of the people. 18For in that He Him-
self has suffered, being tempted, He is able
to aid those who are tempted.

CHAPTER 3

The Son Was Faithful

Therefore, holy brethren, partakers of
the heavenly calling, consider the Apostle

2:7 [a]NU-Text and M-Text omit the rest of verse 7.
2:8 [a]Psalm 8:4–6 2:12 [a]Psalm 22:22
2:13 [a]2 Samuel 22:3; Isaiah 8:17 [b]Isaiah 8:18

2:10 for Him: For God the Father. **the captain of . . . salvation**: Jesus Christ, the Son. **perfect through sufferings**: If He had not suffered, He could not save (5:9).

3:1–6 The author now begins to show how Christ's work of salvation fulfills and supersedes the order of salvation established through **Moses** (v. 2) and carried out through the Aaronic priesthood. Such a comparison/contrast had to begin by comparing **Christ** (v. 6) with Moses, the great mediator of the old order.

and High Priest of our confession, Christ Jesus, [2]who was faithful to Him who appointed Him, as Moses also *was faithful* in all His house. [3]For this One has been counted worthy of more glory than Moses, inasmuch as He who built the house has more honor than the house. [4]For every house is built by someone, but He who built all things *is* God. [5]And Moses indeed *was* faithful in all His house as a servant, for a testimony of those things which would be spoken *afterward*, [6]but Christ as a Son over His own house, whose house we are if we hold fast the confidence and the rejoicing of the hope firm to the end.[a]

Be Faithful

[7]Therefore, as the Holy Spirit says:

"Today, if you will hear His voice,
8 *Do not harden your hearts as in the rebellion,*
In the day of trial in the wilderness,
9 *Where your fathers tested Me, tried Me,*
And saw My works forty years.
10 *Therefore I was angry with that generation,*
And said, 'They always go astray in their heart,
And they have not known My ways.'
11 *So I swore in My wrath,*
'They shall not enter My rest.'"[a]

[12]Beware, brethren, lest there be in any of you an evil heart of unbelief in departing from the living God; [13]but exhort one another daily, while it is called *"Today,"* lest any of you be hardened through the deceitfulness of sin. [14]For we have become partakers of Christ if we hold the beginning of our confidence steadfast to the end, [15]while it is said:

"Today, if you will hear His voice,
Do not harden your hearts as in the rebellion."[a]

> Age irons out the highs and lows; it offers less joy but more contentment.
> David Myers

Failure of the Wilderness Wanderers

[16]For who, having heard, rebelled? Indeed, *was it* not all who came out of Egypt, *led* by Moses? [17]Now with whom was He angry forty years? *Was it* not with those who sinned, whose corpses fell in the wilderness? [18]And to whom did He swear that they would not enter His rest, but to those who did not obey? [19]So we see that they could not enter in because of unbelief.

CHAPTER 4

The Promise of Rest

Therefore, since a promise remains of entering His rest, let us fear lest any of you seem to have come short of it. [2]For indeed the gospel was preached to us as well as to them; but the word which they heard did not profit them,[a] not being mixed with

3:6 [a]NU-Text omits *firm to the end.* 3:11 [a]Psalm 95:7–11 3:15 [a]Psalm 95:7, 8 4:2 [a]NU-Text and M-Text read *profit them,* since they were not united by faith with those who heeded it.

3:7–11 By attributing this OT quotation to the Holy Spirit, the writer testifies to the inspiration of Scripture.

3:12, 13 Fellowship with other believers who hold us accountable is a vital part of a faithful Christian walk.

3:14 To be faithful is to hold firmly to **our confidence** in the salvation provided by **Christ** until He comes for us. There is no fellowship with Christ without faithfulness to Him.

3:16–19 Even God's own people who had experienced His grace were rejected by Him when they refused to obey (see 6:4–6; 10:26–29).

4:2 Simply hearing the gospel is ineffective; we must believe its message to obtain salvation.

THE LIVING WORD

Evelyn Christenson

The Bible differs from all other books ever written in that it is alive. "For the word of God is living and powerful, and sharper than any two-edged sword . . . and is a discerner of the thoughts and intents of the heart" (Heb. 4:12). This is only possible because God Himself, its Author, is active in its convicting, enlightening, and instructing process. Thus, the Bible can be applied practically only through spiritual involvement with God Himself. And this interaction is prayer.

This is not true of any other book. When we obey the traffic rule book and stop our car when the light turns red, we have no personal involvement with the person who at some time decided we "stop on red" and "go on green." With textbooks, it is also not necessary to become personally involved with the author to put into practice the laws, information, rules, or suggestions being taught. Learning and using a mathematical formula is not dependent upon a personal relationship with its originator. Not so with the Bible. The reader must exhibit a spiritual response to the Author to ensure adequate and meaningful application of its precepts.

"The Bible can be applied through spiritual involvement with God Himself."

To be confronted by God's prerecorded answers in the Bible is to be confronted by God Himself. ✦

faith in those who heard *it.* 3For we who
have believed do enter that rest, as He has
said:

"So I swore in My wrath,
'They shall not enter My rest,'"[a]

although the works were finished from the
foundation of the world. 4For He has spo-
ken in a certain place of the seventh *day* in
this way: *"And God rested on the seventh*
day from all His works";[a] 5and again in
this *place: "They shall not enter My*
rest."[a]

6Since therefore it remains that some
must enter it, and those to whom it was
first preached did not enter because of
disobedience, 7again He designates a cer-
tain day, saying in David, *"Today,"* after
such a long time, as it has been said:

"Today, if you will hear His voice,
Do not harden your hearts."[a]

8For if Joshua had given them rest, then
He would not afterward have spoken of
another day. 9There remains therefore a
rest for the people of God. 10For he who has
entered His rest has himself also ceased
from his works as God *did* from His.

The Word Discovers Our Condition

11Let us therefore be diligent to enter
that rest, lest anyone fall according to the

4:3 [a]Psalm 95:11 4:4 [a]Genesis 2:2 4:5 [a]Psalm 95:11 4:7 [a]Psalm 95:7, 8

same example of disobedience. 12For the
word of God *is* living and powerful, and
sharper than any two-edged sword, pierc-
ing even to the division of soul and spirit,
and of joints and marrow, and is a dis-
cerner of the thoughts and intents of the
heart. 13And there is no creature hidden
from His sight, but all things *are* naked and
open to the eyes of Him to whom we *must
give* account.

Our Compassionate High Priest

14Seeing then that we have a great High
Priest who has passed through the heav-
ens, Jesus the Son of God, let us hold fast
our confession. 15For we do not have a High
Priest who cannot sympathize with our
weaknesses, but was in all *points* tempted
as *we are,* yet without sin. 16Let us therefore
come boldly to the throne of grace, that we
may obtain mercy and find grace to help in
time of need.

CHAPTER 5

Qualifications for High Priesthood

For every high priest taken from among
men is appointed for men in things *pertain-
ing* to God, that he may offer both gifts and
sacrifices for sins. 2He can have compas-
sion on those who are ignorant and going
astray, since he himself is also subject to
weakness. 3Because of this he is required as
for the people, so also for himself, to offer
sacrifices for sins. 4And no man takes this
honor to himself, but he who is called by
God, just as Aaron *was.*

A Priest Forever

5So also Christ did not glorify Himself to
become High Priest, *but it* was He who
said to Him:

"You are My Son,
Today I have begotten You."[a]

6As *He* also *says* in another *place:*

"You are a priest forever
According to the order of
Mel·chiz′e·dek.";[a]

7who, in the days of His flesh, when He
had offered up prayers and supplications,
with vehement cries and tears to Him who
was able to save Him from death, and was
heard because of His godly fear, 8though
He was a Son, *yet* He learned obedience by
the things which He suffered. 9And having
been perfected, He became the author of
eternal salvation to all who obey Him,
10called by God as High Priest *"according
to the order of Mel·chiz′e·dek,"* 11of whom
we have much to say, and hard to explain,
since you have become dull of hearing.

Spiritual Immaturity

12For though by this time you ought to
be teachers, you need *someone* to teach you
again the first principles of the oracles of
God; and you have come to need milk and
not solid food. 13For everyone who par-
takes *only* of milk *is* unskilled in the word
of righteousness, for he is a babe. 14But
solid food belongs to those who are of full
age, *that is,* those who by reason of use

5:5 [a]Psalm 2:7 5:6 [a]Psalm 110:4

4:12 the word of God is living: It is effective and accomplishes God's purpose. It penetrates to the depths of the human personality, standing in judgment on our deepest **thoughts** and **intents**.

4:13 God's word exposes us completely to Him. Therefore He requires an answering word of **account** from us.

5:3 The sinfulness of the OT priest was shown by his need to **offer** sacrifice for **himself**. Thus his sacrifice for others could not take away sins. We understand when OT people believed in God's promise and performed those sacrifices they were accepted because of Christ. The sacrifices themselves became a way of expressing their faith.

5:12, 13 We should be continually growing in spiritual knowledge. If we cannot get beyond the basics, how can we disciple others?

> ***I pray that my children will imitate those who through faith and patience inherit the promises.***
>
> *adapted from* Hebrews 6:12

have their senses exercised to discern both good and evil.

CHAPTER 6

The Peril of Not Progressing

Therefore, leaving the discussion of the elementary *principles* of Christ, let us go on to perfection, not laying again the foundation of repentance from dead works and of faith toward God, [2]of the doctrine of baptisms, of laying on of hands, of resurrection of the dead, and of eternal judgment. [3]And this we will[a] do if God permits.

[4]For *it is* impossible for those who were once enlightened, and have tasted the heavenly gift, and have become partakers of the Holy Spirit, [5]and have tasted the good word of God and the powers of the age to come, [6]if they fall away,[a] to renew them again to repentance, since they crucify again for themselves the Son of God, and put *Him* to an open shame.

[7]For the earth which drinks in the rain that often comes upon it, and bears herbs useful for those by whom it is cultivated, receives blessing from God; [8]but if it bears thorns and briers, *it is* rejected and near to being cursed, whose end *is* to be burned.

A Better Estimate

[9]But, beloved, we are confident of better things concerning you, yes, things that accompany salvation, though we speak in this manner. [10]For God *is* not unjust to forget your work and labor of[a] love which you have shown toward His name, *in that* you have ministered to the saints, and do minister. [11]And we desire that each one of you show the same diligence to the full assurance of hope until the end, [12]that you do not become sluggish, but imitate those who through faith and patience inherit the promises.

God's Infallible Purpose in Christ

[13]For when God made a promise to Abraham, because He could swear by no one greater, He swore by Himself, [14]saying, *"Surely blessing I will bless you, and multiplying I will multiply you."*[a] [15]And so, after he had patiently endured, he obtained the promise. [16]For men indeed swear by the greater, and an oath for confirmation *is* for them an end of all dispute. [17]Thus God, determining to show more abundantly to the heirs of promise the immutability of His counsel, confirmed *it* by an oath, [18]that by two immutable things, in which it *is* impossible for God to lie, we might[a] have strong consolation, who have fled for refuge to lay hold of the hope set before *us*.

[19]This *hope* we have as an anchor of the soul, both sure and steadfast, and which enters the *Presence* behind the veil, [20]where the forerunner has entered for us, *even*

6:3 [a]M-Text reads *let us do.* 6:6 [a]Or *and have fallen away* 6:10 [a]NU-Text omits *labor of.* 6:14 [a]Genesis 22:17 6:18 [a]M-Text omits *might.*

6:4–8 These verses have caused considerable debate among interpreters because they seem at first reading to say that a truly converted person can be lost—something Christ clearly denied (see, for example, John 10:27–30). It seems easiest to view the person described here as never having actually believed, even though—like Judas Iscariot—he has participated in the community of believers and shared, to a degree, in the benefits pertaining thereto. However we appear to others, only we and God know whether we are truly trusting Christ for our salvation.

Jesus, having become High Priest forever according to the order of Mel·chiz′e·dek.

CHAPTER 7

The King of Righteousness

For this Mel·chiz′e·dek, king of Sā′lem, priest of the Most High God, who met Abraham returning from the slaughter of the kings and blessed him, [2]to whom also Abraham gave a tenth part of all, first being translated "king of righteousness," and then also king of Sā′lem, meaning "king of peace," [3]without father, without mother, without genealogy, having neither beginning of days nor end of life, but made like the Son of God, remains a priest continually.

[4]Now consider how great this man *was,* to whom even the patriarch Abraham gave a tenth of the spoils. [5]And indeed those who are of the sons of Levi, who receive the priesthood, have a commandment to receive tithes from the people according to the law, that is, from their brethren, though they have come from the loins of Abraham; [6]but he whose genealogy is not derived from them received tithes from Abraham and blessed him who had the promises. [7]Now beyond all contradiction the lesser is blessed by the better. [8]Here mortal men receive tithes, but there he *receives them,* of whom it is witnessed that he lives. [9]Even Levi, who receives tithes, paid tithes through Abraham, so to speak, [10]for he was still in the loins of his father when Mel·chiz′e·dek met him.

Need for a New Priesthood

[11]Therefore, if perfection were through the Le·vit′i·cal priesthood (for under it the people received the law), what further need *was there* that another priest should rise according to the order of Mel·chiz′e·dek, and not be called according to the order of Aaron? [12]For the priesthood being changed, of necessity there is also a change of the law. [13]For He of whom these things are spoken belongs to another tribe, from which no man has officiated at the altar.

[14]For *it is* evident that our Lord arose from Judah, of which tribe Moses spoke nothing concerning priesthood.[a] [15]And it is yet far more evident if, in the likeness of Mel·chiz′e·dek, there arises another priest [16]who has come, not according to the law of a fleshly commandment, but according to the power of an endless life. [17]For He testifies:[a]

"You are a priest forever
According to the order of
Mel·chiz′e·dek."[b]

[18]For on the one hand there is an annulling of the former commandment because of its weakness and unprofitableness, [19]for the law made nothing perfect;

7:14 [a]NU-Text reads *priests.* 7:17 [a]NU-Text reads *it is testified.* [b]Psalm 110:4

7:3 remains a priest continually: If a Levitical priest failed to prove his ancestry, he was disqualified. Melchizedek's ancestry was unknown, and he is not portrayed as having been succeeded in the priesthood by any of his descendants, yet he was a priest. Thus his depiction in Scripture is an excellent illustration of the eternal priesthood of the Son.

7:4–10 The writer of Hebrews notes three indications that Melchizedek was greater than **Abraham** and **the sons of Levi**: First, the Levites received tithes only from their fellow Israelites. But Melchizedek was given tithes by Abraham, the patriarch (v. 4), the father of all the Israelites. Second, Melchizedek was great enough to bless Abraham, who had received God's special **promises** (see 6:14–20). Third, Melchizedek's portrayal lacks the usual OT information about the ancestry, birth, death, and descendants of the great men of God. The author of Hebrews considers the absence of such information about Melchizedek to be a witness **that he lives** as a prototype of Christ (see v. 3).

7:13, 14 Jesus was of the tribe of Judah, rather than of Levi, indicating establishment of a new priestly order.

on the other hand, *there is the* bringing in of
a better hope, through which we draw
near to God.

Greatness of the New Priest

20And inasmuch as *He was* not *made*
priest without an oath 21(for they have be-
come priests without an oath, but He with
an oath by Him who said to Him:

"The LORD *has sworn*
And will not relent,
'You are a priest forever[a]
According to the order of
Mel·chiz'e·dek' "),[b]

22by so much more Jesus has become a
surety of a better covenant.

23Also there were many priests, because
they were prevented by death from contin-
uing. 24But He, because He continues for-
ever, has an unchangeable priesthood.
25Therefore He is also able to save to the ut-
termost those who come to God through
Him, since He always lives to make inter-
cession for them.

26For such a High Priest was fitting for
us, *who is* holy, harmless, undefiled, sepa-
rate from sinners, and has become higher
than the heavens; 27who does not need
daily, as those high priests, to offer up sac-
rifices, first for His own sins and then for
the people's, for this He did once for all
when He offered up Himself. 28For the law
appoints as high priests men who have
weakness, but the word of the oath, which
came after the law, *appoints* the Son who
has been perfected forever.

CHAPTER 8

The New Priestly Service

Now *this is* the main point of the things
we are saying: We have such a High Priest,
who is seated at the right hand of the
throne of the Majesty in the heavens, 2a
Minister of the sanctuary and of the true
tabernacle which the Lord erected, and not
man.

3For every high priest is appointed to of-
fer both gifts and sacrifices. Therefore *it is*
necessary that this One also have some-
thing to offer. 4For if He were on earth, He
would not be a priest, since there are
priests who offer the gifts according to the
law; 5who serve the copy and shadow of
the heavenly things, as Moses was divinely
instructed when he was about to make the
tabernacle. For He said, *"See that you make*
all things according to the pattern shown
you on the mountain."[a] 6But now He has
obtained a more excellent ministry, inas-
much as He is also Mediator of a better
covenant, which was established on better
promises.

A New Covenant

7For if that first *covenant* had been fault-
less, then no place would have been
sought for a second. 8Because finding fault
with them, He says: *"Behold, the days are*
coming, says the LORD*, when I will make a*
new covenant with the house of Israel and
with the house of Judah— 9*not according*
to the covenant that I made with their

7:21 [a]NU-Text ends the quotation here. [b]Psalm 110:4
8:5 [a]Exodus 25:40

8:6 Christ's priestly **ministry** is **more excellent** than the ministry of the Aaronic priests because He is a **Mediator** who can really bring people to God. The **covenant** is **better** (see 1:4) because it really works (see 7:19). This covenant is based on **promises** that offer us something **better** than ritual cleansing (see vv. 10–12).

8:8–10 The **new covenant** with its better promises is found in Jer. 31:31–34, quoted by the author here in full. How is this covenant new? God's people **did not continue** in His first covenant; therefore, under the new covenant God will put His **laws** in the **mind** and **hearts** of His people. They will both want to obey and be given power to obey. Thus they will have intimate fellowship with God. This change of heart promised in the OT is now made possible by the sanctifying work of Christ the Mediator (see 13:12).

fathers in the day when I took them by the
hand to lead them out of the land of Egypt;
because they did not continue in My
covenant, and I disregarded them, says the
LORD. 10*For this is the covenant that I will*
make with the house of Israel after those
days, says the LORD: I will put My laws in
their mind and write them on their hearts;
and I will be their God, and they shall be
My people. 11*None of them shall teach his*
neighbor, and none his brother, saying,
'Know the LORD,' for all shall know Me,
from the least of them to the greatest of
them. 12*For I will be merciful to their un-*
righteousness, and their sins and their law-
less deeds[a] *I will remember no more."*[b]
13In that He says, *"A new covenant,"* He
has made the first obsolete. Now what is
becoming obsolete and growing old is
ready to vanish away.

CHAPTER 9

The Earthly Sanctuary

Then indeed, even the first *covenant* had
ordinances of divine service and the
earthly sanctuary. 2For a tabernacle was
prepared: the first *part,* in which *was* the
lampstand, the table, and the showbread,
which is called the sanctuary; 3and behind
the second veil, the part of the tabernacle
which is called the Holiest of All, 4which
had the golden censer and the ark of the
covenant overlaid on all sides with gold, in
which *were* the golden pot that had the
manna, Aaron's rod that budded, and the
tablets of the covenant; 5and above it were
the cherubim of glory overshadowing the
mercy seat. Of these things we cannot now
speak in detail.

Limitations of the Earthly Service

6Now when these things had been thus
prepared, the priests always went into the
first part of the tabernacle, performing *the*
services. 7But into the second part the high
priest *went* alone once a year, not without
blood, which he offered for himself and *for*
the people's sins *committed* in ignorance;
8the Holy Spirit indicating this, that the
way into the Holiest of All was not yet
made manifest while the first tabernacle
was still standing. 9It *was* symbolic for the
present time in which both gifts and sacri-
fices are offered which cannot make him
who performed the service perfect in re-
gard to the conscience— 10*concerned* only
with foods and drinks, various washings,
and fleshly ordinances imposed until the
time of reformation.

The Heavenly Sanctuary

11But Christ came *as* High Priest of the
good things to come,[a] with the greater and
more perfect tabernacle not made with
hands, that is, not of this creation. 12Not
with the blood of goats and calves, but
with His own blood He entered the Most
Holy Place once for all, having obtained
eternal redemption. 13For if the blood of
bulls and goats and the ashes of a heifer,
sprinkling the unclean, sanctifies for the
purifying of the flesh, 14how much more
shall the blood of Christ, who through the
eternal Spirit offered Himself without spot
to God, cleanse your conscience from dead
works to serve the living God? 15And for
this reason He is the Mediator of the new
covenant, by means of death, for the re-
demption of the transgressions under the
first covenant, that those who are called
may receive the promise of the eternal in-
heritance.

The Mediator's Death Necessary

16For where there *is* a testament, there
must also of necessity be the death of the
testator. 17For a testament *is* in force after
men are dead, since it has no power at all
while the testator lives. 18Therefore not
even the first *covenant* was dedicated with-
out blood. 19For when Moses had spoken
every precept to all the people according to
the law, he took the blood of calves
and goats, with water, scarlet wool, and

8:12 [a]NU-Text omits *and their lawless deeds.* [b]Jeremiah 31:31–34 9:11 [a]NU-Text reads *that have come.*

GRACEFULLY GROWING OLD

Dr. Randy Reese

Growing old is the natural progression of life. Medical science and the Word of God agree that physical death is inevitable (Rom. 6:23; Heb. 9:27). We know that death originally came into the world as a consequence of Adam's sin. But why do we physically age, as if our bodies were gradually wearing out?

Many scientists speculate that it has to do with problems in our immune system. Other researchers point to mutational theory in which chromosomal deviations increase with age. Still others embrace the "free radical theory" in which toxic substances (the breakdown or byproducts of normal metabolism) accumulate within the body, eventually destroying molecules and tissues. Another plausible theory has to do with environmental factors, including radiation exposure from the sun.

Various lifestyle and environmental factors can accelerate the aging process and shorten the life span, but many of these lifestyle factors are within our control. As good stewards of our time here on earth, each of us should make the most of the life span God gives us. By keeping our bodies in the best possible health, we will find more energy to use for the Lord's work. Choose to grow old more gracefully and feel more youthful instead of "letting nature take its course." ✦

hyssop, and sprinkled both the book itself
and all the people, [20]saying, *"This is the
blood of the covenant which God has com-
manded you."*[a] [21]Then likewise he sprin-
kled with blood both the tabernacle and all
the vessels of the ministry. [22]And according
to the law almost all things are purified
with blood, and without shedding of blood
there is no remission.

Greatness of Christ's Sacrifice

[23]Therefore *it was* necessary that the
copies of the things in the heavens should
be purified with these, but the heavenly
things themselves with better sacrifices
than these. [24]For Christ has not entered the
holy places made with hands, *which are*
copies of the true, but into heaven itself,
now to appear in the presence of God for
us; [25]not that He should offer Himself of-
ten, as the high priest enters the Most Holy
Place every year with blood of another—
[26]He then would have had to suffer often
since the foundation of the world; but now,
once at the end of the ages, He has ap-
peared to put away sin by the sacrifice of
Himself. [27]And as it is appointed for men
to die once, but after this the judgment, [28]so

9:20 [a]Exodus 24:8

9:25, 26 Christ's sacrifice gains access because He offered **Himself**, not the **blood of another**. His sacrifice **at the end of the ages** (the OT era) was the climax and turning point of history. There He **put away sin**, completely overcoming its power and guilt. Thus He never needed to repeat the offering.

Christ was offered once to bear the sins of
many. To those who eagerly wait for Him
He will appear a second time, apart from
sin, for salvation.

CHAPTER 10

Animal Sacrifices Insufficient

For the law, having a shadow of the
good things to come, *and* not the very im-
age of the things, can never with these
same sacrifices, which they offer continu-
ally year by year, make those who
approach perfect. 2For then would they
not have ceased to be offered? For the
worshipers, once purified, would have
had no more consciousness of sins. 3But in
those *sacrifices there is* a reminder of sins
every year. 4For *it is* not possible that the
blood of bulls and goats could take away
sins.

Christ's Death Fulfills God's Will

5Therefore, when He came into the
world, He said:

"Sacrifice and offering You did not
desire,
But a body You have prepared for
Me.
6 *In burnt offerings and sacrifices for*
sin
You had no pleasure.
7 *Then I said, 'Behold, I have come—*
In the volume of the book it is written
of Me—
To do Your will, O God.' "[a]

8Previously saying, *"Sacrifice and offering,*
burnt offerings, and offerings for sin You
did not desire, nor had pleasure in them"
(which are offered according to the law),
9then He said, *"Behold, I have come to do*
Your will, O God."[a] He takes away the first
that He may establish the second. 10By that
will we have been sanctified through the
offering of the body of Jesus Christ once *for*
all.

Christ's Death Perfects the Sanctified

11And every priest stands ministering
daily and offering repeatedly the same sac-
rifices, which can never take away sins.
12But this Man, after He had offered one
sacrifice for sins forever, sat down at the
right hand of God, 13from that time waiting
till His enemies are made His footstool.
14For by one offering He has perfected for-
ever those who are being sanctified.

15But the Holy Spirit also witnesses to
us; for after He had said before,

16*"This is the covenant that I will make*
with them after those days, says the LORD:
I will put My laws into their hearts, and in
their minds I will write them,"[a] 17*then He*
adds, "Their sins and their lawless deeds I
will remember no more."[a] 18Now where
there is remission of these, *there is* no
longer an offering for sin.

Hold Fast Your Confession

19Therefore, brethren, having boldness
to enter the Holiest by the blood of Jesus,
20by a new and living way which He conse-
crated for us, through the veil, that is, His
flesh, 21and *having* a High Priest over the
house of God, 22let us draw near with a
true heart in full assurance of faith, having
our hearts sprinkled from an evil con-
science and our bodies washed with pure
water. 23Let us hold fast the confession of
our hope without wavering, for He who
promised *is* faithful. 24And let us consider
one another in order to stir up love and

10:7 [a]Psalm 40:6–8 10:9 [a]NU-Text and M-Text omit *O God.* 10:16 [a]Jeremiah 31:33 10:17 [a]Jeremiah 31:34

10:11–13 Normally a **priest stands** so that he can offer sacrifice. But Christ **sat down**, an indication that His sacrifice is complete. He has dealt with sin and taken the place of ultimate authority **at the right hand of God** (see 1:3; 8:1). **waiting**: He need do nothing more to do away with sin. **till His enemies are made His footstool**: At His Second Coming.

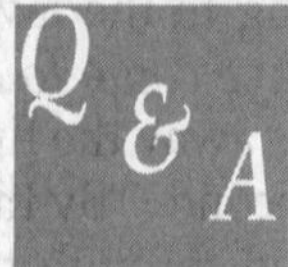

Is it worth the trouble for me to go to church on Sunday?

Elmer L. Gray

Preparing for church and getting there can sometimes be a big problem, but it is worth your trouble.

Christians need to meet together. The Bible says, "And let us consider one another in order to stir up love and good works, not forsaking the assembling of ourselves together, as is the manner of some, but exhorting one another" (Heb. 10:24, 25).

Meeting with other Christians is good for you in several ways:

✦ Jesus said we could experience His presence by meeting together: "Where two or three are gathered together in My name, I am there in the midst of them" (Matt. 18:20).

✦ We need to meet together for the same reason the early Christians did. They met to study Christian teachings, to share with each other, to break bread together, and to pray (Acts 2:42). They were blessed by divine awe coming upon them and by seeing wonderful things happen. The Bible describes that experience as follows: "Fear came upon every soul, and many wonders and signs were done through the apostles" (v. 43).

You have gifts to share with others and they with you. You could miss something great by not meeting with your fellow Christians.

✦ You can be a blessing to others by meeting with them for prayer. "Confess your trespasses to one another, and pray for one another, that you may be healed. The effective, fervent prayer of a righteous man avails much" (James 5:16).

Ask God to bless His people as they meet together. ✦

good works, [25]not forsaking the assem-
bling of ourselves together, as *is* the man-
ner of some, but exhorting *one another,* and
so much the more as you see the Day ap-
proaching.

The Just Live by Faith

[26]For if we sin willfully after we have re-
ceived the knowledge of the truth, there no
longer remains a sacrifice for sins, [27]but a
certain fearful expectation of judgment,
and fiery indignation which will devour
the adversaries. [28]Anyone who has rejected
Moses' law dies without mercy on the tes-
timony of two or three witnesses. [29]Of how
much worse punishment, do you suppose,
will he be thought worthy who has tram-
pled the Son of God underfoot, counted
the blood of the covenant by which he was
sanctified a common thing, and insulted
the Spirit of grace? [30]For we know Him
who said, *"Vengeance is Mine, I will re-*

10:25 This verse reinforces the importance of consistent fellowship with a local community of believers. While personal prayer and devotions are important, they clearly are not sufficient to give us the encouragement we need.

pay,"[a] says the Lord.[b] And again, *"The*
LORD will judge His people."[c] 31It is a fear-
ful thing to fall into the hands of the living
God.
32But recall the former days in which, af-
ter you were illuminated, you endured a
great struggle with sufferings: 33partly
while you were made a spectacle both by
reproaches and tribulations, and partly
while you became companions of those
who were so treated; 34for you had com-
passion on me[a] in my chains, and joyfully
accepted the plundering of your goods,
knowing that you have a better and an
enduring possession for yourselves in
heaven.[b] 35Therefore do not cast away your
confidence, which has great reward. 36For
you have need of endurance, so that after
you have done the will of God, you may
receive the promise:

37 *"For yet a little while,*
And He[a] *who is coming will come*
and will not tarry.
38 *Now the*[a] *just shall live by faith;*
But if anyone draws back,
My soul has no pleasure in him."[b]

39But we are not of those who draw back to
perdition, but of those who believe to the
saving of the soul.

CHAPTER 11

By Faith We Understand

Now faith is the substance of things
hoped for, the evidence of things not seen.
2For by it the elders obtained a *good* testi-
mony.

10:30 [a]Deuteronomy 32:35 [b]NU-Text omits *says the Lord.* [c]Deuteronomy 32:36 10:34 [a]NU-Text reads *the prisoners* instead of *me in my chains.* 10:34 [b]NU-Text omits *in heaven.* 10:37 [a]Or *that which* 10:38 [a]NU-Text reads *My just one.* [b]Habakkuk 2:3, 4 11:5 [a]Genesis 5:24

I pray that my friend will always remember that faith is the substance of things hoped for, the evidence of things not seen.

adapted from Hebrews 11:1

3By faith we understand that the worlds
were framed by the word of God, so that
the things which are seen were not made of
things which are visible.

Faith at the Dawn of History

4By faith Abel offered to God a more ex-
cellent sacrifice than Cain, through which
he obtained witness that he was righteous,
God testifying of his gifts; and through it
he being dead still speaks.
5By faith Ē'noch was taken away so that
he did not see death, *"and was not found,*
because God had taken him";[a] for before
he was taken he had this testimony, that he
pleased God. 6But without faith *it is* impos-
sible to please *Him,* for he who comes to
God must believe that He is, and *that* He is a
rewarder of those who diligently seek Him.
7By faith Noah, being divinely warned
of things not yet seen, moved with godly
fear, prepared an ark for the saving of his
household, by which he condemned the
world and became heir of the righteous-
ness which is according to faith.

Faithful Abraham

8By faith Abraham obeyed when he was
called to go out to the place which he
would receive as an inheritance. And he
went out, not knowing where he was go-
ing. 9By faith he dwelt in the land of

11:1 The **faith** by which the righteous live (10:38) is certain that **things hoped for**, God's promised blessings, will be fulfilled. It is also confident of **things not seen**, God's power and faithfulness in life today.

11:6 We cannot please God simply through good works; faith in Him and in His promises is absolutely necessary if we are to please Him.

promise as *in* a foreign country, dwelling in tents with Isaac and Jacob, the heirs with him of the same promise; 10for he waited for the city which has foundations, whose builder and maker *is* God.

11By faith Sarah herself also received strength to conceive seed, and she bore a child[a] when she was past the age, because she judged Him faithful who had promised. 12Therefore from one man, and him as good as dead, were born *as many* as the stars of the sky in multitude—innumerable as the sand which is by the seashore.

The Heavenly Hope

13These all died in faith, not having received the promises, but having seen them afar off were assured of them,[a] embraced *them* and confessed that they were strangers and pilgrims on the earth. 14For those who say such things declare plainly that they seek a homeland. 15And truly if they had called to mind that *country* from which they had come out, they would have had opportunity to return. 16But now they desire a better, that is, a heavenly *country.* Therefore God is not ashamed to be called their God, for He has prepared a city for them.

The Faith of the Patriarchs

17By faith Abraham, when he was tested, offered up Isaac, and he who had received the promises offered up his only begotten *son,* 18of whom it was said, *"In Isaac your seed shall be called,"*[a] 19concluding that God *was* able to raise *him* up, even from the dead, from which he also received him in a figurative sense.

20By faith Isaac blessed Jacob and Esau concerning things to come.

21By faith Jacob, when he was dying, blessed each of the sons of Joseph, and worshiped, *leaning* on the top of his staff.

22By faith Joseph, when he was dying, made mention of the departure of the children of Israel, and gave instructions concerning his bones.

The Faith of Moses

23By faith Moses, when he was born, was hidden three months by his parents, because they saw *he was* a beautiful child; and they were not afraid of the king's command.

24By faith Moses, when he became of age, refused to be called the son of Pharaoh's daughter, 25choosing rather to suffer affliction with the people of God than to enjoy the passing pleasures of sin, 26esteeming the reproach of Christ greater riches than the treasures in[a] Egypt; for he looked to the reward.

27By faith he forsook Egypt, not fearing the wrath of the king; for he endured as seeing Him who is invisible. 28By faith he kept the Passover and the sprinkling of blood, lest he who destroyed the firstborn should touch them.

29By faith they passed through the Red Sea as by dry *land, whereas* the Egyptians, attempting *to do* so, were drowned.

By Faith They Overcame

30By faith the walls of Jericho fell down after they were encircled for seven days.

11:11 [a]NU-Text omits *she bore a child.*
11:13 [a]NU-Text and M-Text omit *were assured of them.*
11:18 [a]Genesis 21:12 11:26 [a]NU-Text and M-Text read *of.*

11:12 Abraham was only **one man**, and as far as reproduction was concerned, he was as **good as dead**. But because he trusted the promise, God made him the father of a nation as numerous as the **stars** or the **sand**.

11:24–26 When **Moses** identified himself with **the people of God** (v. 25), he identified with Christ's people—the faithful of all time. Thus the affliction (v. 25) he suffered can be correctly called **the reproach of Christ** (v. 26). This reproach is great **riches** because of the heavenly **reward** it brings (see Matt. 5:10, 11). In Moses we see the courage that comes from faith.

[31]By faith the harlot Rā'hab did not perish
with those who did not believe, when she
had received the spies with peace.
[32]And what more shall I say? For the
time would fail me to tell of Gideon and
Bar'ak and Samson and Jeph'thah, also *of*
David and Samuel and the prophets: [33]who
through faith subdued kingdoms, worked
righteousness, obtained promises, stopped
the mouths of lions, [34]quenched the vio-
lence of fire, escaped the edge of the
sword, out of weakness were made strong,
became valiant in battle, turned to flight
the armies of the aliens. [35]Women received
their dead raised to life again.

"Looking unto Jesus" (Heb. 12:2). Only three little words, but in those three little words is the whole secret of life.
Theodore Monod

Others were tortured, not accepting de-
liverance, that they might obtain a better
resurrection. [36]Still others had trial of
mockings and scourgings, yes, and of
chains and imprisonment. [37]They were
stoned, they were sawn in two, were
tempted,[a] were slain with the sword. They
wandered about in sheepskins and
goatskins, being destitute, afflicted, tor-

11:37 [a]NU-Text omits *were tempted.*

11:35 Some would not accept **deliverance** because to do so would have meant denying their faith. They preferred **a better resurrection** (see 10:34), choosing reward in the life to come rather than a longer life here and now.

STRETCH YOURSELF!

Philip Walker

Flexibility—the ability to move joints through a full range of motion—generally decreases with age and inactivity. Flexibility is specific to each joint. Muscles, tendons, and ligaments attached to bones determine the amount of movement possible at each joint. Unfortunately, joints are hit hard by aging. Many women over age seventy are 20 to 30 percent less flexible than they were at twenty-five.

Tight muscles and joints may lead to muscle soreness, less stability, poor posture, limited range of joint movement, and possible injury. More than 75 percent of lower back pain is due to inadequate abdominal muscle tone and inadequate lower back flexibility. Maintaining flexibility is important for general health and total well-being. We can be more effective for God when our bodies are as healthy as they can be for our individual circumstances.

A regular program of stretching can keep people limber well into their fifties and sixties. Many well-supervised classes throughout the country provide excellent stretching programs. And it's never too late to start a stretching routine; a study at the University of Wisconsin found that women over age seventy could improve the range of motion of their necks, hips, and backs more than 25 percent after only twelve weeks of a simple stretching routine. ✦

> Hate and fear can poison the body as surely as any toxic chemicals.
> Joseph Krimsky, M.D.

mented— [38]of whom the world was not worthy. They wandered in deserts and mountains, *in* dens and caves of the earth.

[39]And all these, having obtained a good testimony through faith, did not receive the promise, [40]God having provided something better for us, that they should not be made perfect apart from us.

CHAPTER 12

The Race of Faith

Therefore we also, since we are surrounded by so great a cloud of witnesses, let us lay aside every weight, and the sin which so easily ensnares *us,* and let us run with endurance the race that is set before us, [2]looking unto Jesus, the author and finisher of *our* faith, who for the joy that was set before Him endured the cross, despising the shame, and has sat down at the right hand of the throne of God.

The Discipline of God

[3]For consider Him who endured such hostility from sinners against Himself, lest you become weary and discouraged in your souls. [4]You have not yet resisted to bloodshed, striving against sin. [5]And you have forgotten the exhortation which speaks to you as to sons:

"My son, do not despise the
chastening of the LORD,
Nor be discouraged when you are
rebuked by Him;
6 *For whom the* L*ORD loves He*
chastens,
And scourges every son whom He
receives."[a]

[7]If[a] you endure chastening, God deals with you as with sons; for what son is there whom a father does not chasten? [8]But if you are without chastening, of which all have become partakers, then you are illegitimate and not sons. [9]Furthermore, we have had human fathers who corrected *us,* and we paid *them* respect. Shall we not much more readily be in subjection to the Father of spirits and live? [10]For they indeed for a few days chastened *us* as seemed *best* to them, but He for *our* profit, that *we* may be partakers of His holiness. [11]Now no chastening seems to be joyful for the present, but painful; nevertheless, afterward it yields the peaceable fruit of righteousness to those who have been trained by it.

Renew Your Spiritual Vitality

[12]Therefore strengthen the hands which hang down, and the feeble knees, [13]and make straight paths for your feet, so that what is lame may not be *dislocated,* but rather be healed.

[14]Pursue peace with all *people,* and holiness, without which no one will see the Lord: [15]looking carefully lest anyone fall short of the grace of God; lest any root of bitterness springing up cause trouble, and

12:6 [a]Proverbs 3:11, 12 12:7 [a]NU-Text and M-Text read *It is for discipline that you endure; God . . . .*

12:1 cloud of witnesses: The OT saints witnessed God's work in their lives, and have testified through Scripture. **so easily ensnares**: It is the nature of sin to entangle us.

12:2 As we run the race, we must keep our eyes on the goal: becoming more like Christ. We cannot allow ourselves to be distracted by past shortcomings or present worldly concerns, nor should we compare ourselves to other believers.

12:14 Christians are to strive to maintain the peace unless it will compromise holiness. Before we commit ourselves to a dispute, we should determine whether it's an issue of personal preference or a matter of holiness.

by this many become defiled; [16]lest there *be*
any fornicator or profane person like Esau,
who for one morsel of food sold his
birthright. [17]For you know that afterward,
when he wanted to inherit the blessing, he
was rejected, for he found no place for repentance, though he sought it diligently
with tears.

The Glorious Company

[18]For you have not come to the mountain that[a] may be touched and that burned
with fire, and to blackness and darkness[b]
and tempest, [19]and the sound of a trumpet
and the voice of words, so that those who
heard *it* begged that the word should not
be spoken to them anymore. [20](For they
could not endure what was commanded:
*"And if so much as a beast touches the
mountain, it shall be stoned*[a] *or shot with
an arrow."*[b] [21]And so terrifying was the
sight *that* Moses said, *"I am exceedingly
afraid* and trembling."[a])
[22]But you have come to Mount Zion and
to the city of the living God, the heavenly
Jerusalem, to an innumerable company of
angels, [23]to the general assembly and
church of the firstborn *who are* registered in
heaven, to God the Judge of all, to the spirits of just men made perfect, [24]to Jesus the
Mediator of the new covenant, and to the
blood of sprinkling that speaks better
things than *that of* Abel.

Hear the Heavenly Voice

[25]See that you do not refuse Him who
speaks. For if they did not escape who refused Him who spoke on earth, much
more *shall we not escape* if we turn away
from Him who *speaks* from heaven,
[26]whose voice then shook the earth; but
now He has promised, saying, *"Yet once
more I shake*[a] *not only the earth, but also
heaven."*[b] [27]Now this, *"Yet once more,"* indicates the removal of those things that are
being shaken, as of things that are made,
that the things which cannot be shaken
may remain.
[28]Therefore, since we are receiving a
kingdom which cannot be shaken, let us
have grace, by which we may[a] serve God
acceptably with reverence and godly fear.
[29]For our God *is* a consuming fire.

12:18 [a]NU-Text reads *to that which.* [b]NU-Text reads *gloom.* 12:20 [a]NU-Text and M-Text omit the rest of this verse. [b]Exodus 19:12, 13 12:21 [a]Deuteronomy 9:19 12:26 [a]NU-Text reads *will shake.* [b]Haggai 2:6 12:28 [a]M-Text omits *may.*

> But all God's angels come to us disguised:
>
> Sorrow and sickness, poverty and death,
> One after other lift their frowning masks,
> And we behold the Seraph's face beneath,
> All radiant with the glory and the calm
> Of having looked upon the front of God.
>
> James Russell Lowell

CHAPTER 13

Concluding Moral Directions

Let brotherly love continue. [2]Do not forget to entertain strangers, for by so *doing*
some have unwittingly entertained angels.
[3]Remember the prisoners as if chained
with them—those who are mistreated—
since you yourselves are in the body also.
[4]Marriage *is* honorable among all, and

13:2 entertain strangers: God always blesses those who show hospitality. **some**: For Abraham (Gen. 18:1–8), Lot (Gen. 19:1–3), and Manoah (Judg. 13:15–18), the strangers were actually **angels**. Sometimes enduring a bit of inconvenience brings innumerable blessings. We should always be willing to open our homes to Christians in need.

13:4 Sexual relationships are completely **honorable** within and only within **marriage**. **Fornicators** are those who participate in sexual sin other than adultery. **Adulterers** are unfaithful married people.

MARTYRED SAINTS: KEEPSAKE WORDS

John Gilmore

Pressed flowers crumble, cheap paper disintegrates, and iron rusts. Part of the preservation problem is environmental conditions. Another part is the nature of the material preserved. The Bible's words endure because the Bible is God's Word.

In the coronation ceremony of England's kings and queens, the Archbishop of Canterbury steps forward and places into the hands of the new monarch a copy of the Bible. He says, "We present to you this Book, the most valuable thing that this world affords. Here is wisdom; this is the Royal law; these are the lively oracles of God."

"Remember those who rule over you, who have spoken the word of God to you, whose faith follow, considering the outcome of their conduct" (Heb. 13:7). Henry Martyn had a brilliant academic career, but he spent the last part of his life as a missionary in India. Thomas Babington Macaulay, who was raised in a staunchly evangelical Anglican family, wrote about Martyn's life:

> Here Martyn lies. In manhood's early bloom
> The Christian Hero finds a Pagan tomb.
> Religion, sorrowing o'er her favorite son,
> Points to the glorious trophies that he won,
> Eternal trophies! not with carnage red,
> Not stained with tears by hapless Captives shed,
> But trophies of the Cross! for that dear name,
> Through every form of danger, death, and shame
> Onward he journeyed to a happier shore,
> Where danger, death, and shame assault no more.

"Bearers of God's Good News provide spiritual refreshment."

Bearers of God's Good News provide spiritual refreshment. Their departure grieves those thirsting after righteousness. Many giants in faith and spiritual knowledge have left their moving words and witness for future generations.

The memory of God's messengers in every age are found in Christian biographies and church history. We should read about the saints, scholars, and preachers who have laid down their lives to make Christ known.

Begin by reading Scripture to restore faith. Then learn how believers in former ages suffered and triumphed. A healthy nostalgia allows the biblical past to shape us and heeds the reminders of Christian faith in other creatures who summon us to newness. ✦

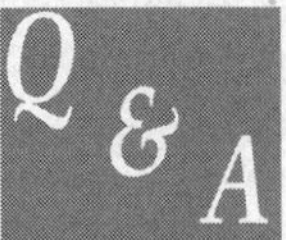

At what point does an individual reach maturity?

Elmer L. Gray

When we were children and youth, adults scolded us saying, "When are you going to grow up? Why don't you act your age?" No one has said that to me for years. Does that mean that at last I am mature? Not necessarily. It may mean folks have given up on me.

Let us test our maturity with these questions:

✦ Am I mature enough to love all persons and to keep on loving them the way Christ loves me?

✦ Am I mature enough to trust the Lord so much that I will do anything He wants me to do?

✦ Am I mature enough to keep my hope bright regardless of what happens to me?

✦ Am I mature enough to cooperate with my fellow Christians in reaching and teaching people the way Christ commanded?

✦ Am I mature enough to give at least as much as God commanded people in the Old Testament to give?

✦ Am I mature enough to forgive people and not to hold bad feelings toward them?

✦ Am I mature enough to work hard at becoming more like Christ?

These Scriptures will help us: "Till we all come to the unity of the faith and of the knowledge of the Son of God, to a perfect man, to the measure of the stature of the fullness of Christ" (Eph. 4:13). "May the God of peace . . . make you complete in every good work to do His will, working in you what is well pleasing in His sight" (Heb. 13:20, 21). ✦

the bed undefiled; but fornicators and
adulterers God will judge.
5*Let your* conduct *be* without covetous-
ness; *be* content with such things as you
have. For He Himself has said, *"I will never leave you nor forsake you."*[a] 6So we
may boldly say:

"The LORD is my helper;
I will not fear.
What can man do to me?"[a]

Concluding Religious Directions

7Remember those who rule over you,
who have spoken the word of God to you,
whose faith follow, considering the out-
come of *their* conduct. 8Jesus Christ *is* the
same yesterday, today, and forever. 9Do not
be carried about[a] with various and strange
doctrines. For *it is* good that the heart be
established by grace, not with foods which
have not profited those who have been oc-
cupied with them.

13:5 [a]Deuteronomy 31:6, 8; Joshua 1:5 13:6 [a]Psalm 118:6 13:9 [a]NU-Text and M-Text read *away.*

YESTERDAY, TODAY, AND FOREVER

Lucibel Van Atta

Mentoring requires no special talent or God-given quality. All God asks is for us to take seriously the task of nurturing and building up other believers.

By the example of our lives and by our encouragement, we can show a younger person what it means to be godly. Because we have experienced God's grace and moment-by-moment support through the years of our own discouragements and crises, we have the privilege of passing on some of the lessons we have learned. Today's younger people face difficult, granite-hard situations. They need the special kind of encouragement and assurance promised in Scripture: "Jesus Christ is the same yesterday, today, and forever" (Heb. 13:8). ✦

10We have an altar from which those
who serve the tabernacle have no right to
eat. 11For the bodies of those animals,
whose blood is brought into the sanctuary
by the high priest for sin, are burned outside the camp. 12Therefore Jesus also, that
He might sanctify the people with His own
blood, suffered outside the gate. 13Therefore let us go forth to Him, outside the
camp, bearing His reproach. 14For here we
have no continuing city, but we seek the
one to come. 15Therefore by Him let us continually offer the sacrifice of praise to God,
that is, the fruit of *our* lips, giving thanks to
His name. 16But do not forget to do good
and to share, for with such sacrifices God is
well pleased.

17Obey those who rule over you, and be
submissive, for they watch out for your
souls, as those who must give account.
Let them do so with joy and not with
grief, for that would be unprofitable for
you.

Prayer Requested

18Pray for us; for we are confident that
we have a good conscience, in all things
desiring to live honorably. 19But I especially urge *you* to do this, that I may be restored to you the sooner.

Benediction, Final Exhortation, Farewell

20Now may the God of peace who
brought up our Lord Jesus from the dead,
that great Shepherd of the sheep, through
the blood of the everlasting covenant,
21make you complete in every good work
to do His will, working in you[a] what is

13:21 [a]NU-Text and M-Text read *us.*

13:11, 12 Just as the bodies of the animals sacrificed on the Day of Atonement were burned outside the camp (Lev. 16:27), so Jesus also died outside the gate in order to sanctify the people by purifying them from sin.

13:13, 14 outside the camp: Excluded from social and religious acceptance. We must forgo the approval of the world and accept the **reproach** of Jesus if we wish to find that **continuing city** established by God (see 11:10). We cannot let our human desire for popularity jeopardize our witness for Christ.

well pleasing in His sight, through Jesus
Christ, to whom *be* glory forever and ever.
Amen.
22And I appeal to you, brethren, bear
with the word of exhortation, for I have
written to you in few words. 23Know
that *our* brother Timothy has been set free,
with whom I shall see you if he comes
shortly.
24Greet all those who rule over you, and
all the saints. Those from Italy greet you.
25Grace *be* with you all. Amen.

✦James✦

The purpose of this book is practical instead of doctrinal or apologetic. James, the author, challenges Jewish believers living outside Palestine, probably in Egypt and Syria, to examine the quality of their daily attitudes and actions. A genuine faith will produce real changes in a person's character, and the absence of change is a symptom of a dead faith.

Throughout his epistle, James integrates faith and practical experience by stressing that true faith must manifest itself in works. Faith must work—it must produce, it must inspire action, and it must wait patiently for the coming of the Lord.

James also addressed the issue of faith-testing trials, explaining their purpose in building spiritual maturity. Rather than diminishing through the years, trials may become more frequent, and Christians should recognize them as tests of faith along the path to perfection. ✦

CHAPTER 1

Greeting to the Twelve Tribes

James, a bondservant of God and of the
Lord Jesus Christ,

To the twelve tribes which are scattered
abroad:

Greetings.

Profiting from Trials

2My brethren, count it all joy when you
fall into various trials, 3knowing that the
testing of your faith produces patience.
4But let patience have *its* perfect work, that
you may be perfect and complete, lacking
nothing. 5If any of you lacks wisdom, let
him ask of God, who gives to all liberally
and without reproach, and it will be given
to him. 6But let him ask in faith, with no
doubting, for he who doubts is like a wave
of the sea driven and tossed by the wind.
7For let not that man suppose that he will
receive anything from the Lord; 8*he is* a
double-minded man, unstable in all his
ways.

The Perspective of Rich and Poor

9Let the lowly brother glory in his exal-
tation, 10but the rich in his humiliation, be-
cause as a flower of the field he will pass
away. 11For no sooner has the sun risen

I pray that if my child lacks wisdom, he will ask of You, God, who gives to all liberally and without reproach, and it will be given to him.

adapted from James 1:5

1:2, 3 As Christians we can rejoice in the midst of **trials** because we know such hardship serves a purpose: to strengthen our faith and make us more like Christ.

with a burning heat than it withers the
grass; its flower falls, and its beautiful ap-
pearance perishes. So the rich man also
will fade away in his pursuits.

Loving God Under Trials

12Blessed *is* the man who endures temp-
tation; for when he has been approved, he
will receive the crown of life which the
Lord has promised to those who love Him.
13Let no one say when he is tempted, "I am
tempted by God"; for God cannot be
tempted by evil, nor does He Himself
tempt anyone. 14But each one is tempted
when he is drawn away by his own desires
and enticed. 15Then, when desire has con-
ceived, it gives birth to sin; and sin, when it
is full-grown, brings forth death.
16Do not be deceived, my beloved
brethren. 17Every good gift and every per-
fect gift is from above, and comes down
from the Father of lights, with whom there
is no variation or shadow of turning.
18Of His own will He brought us forth by

1:12 the crown of life: not a reward in the hereafter but a more abundant life now.
1:18 Of His own will: God is the One who initiated our salvation, the greatest of the good gifts (v. 17) He has given us. **brought us forth**: He has made us new persons in Christ by the **word of truth** found in the gospel. James calls his readers **firstfruits**, implying that many others would also believe in Christ.

The Gift That Always Fits

Charles Ross

Whenever the holiday season approaches, your thoughts probably turn to gift ideas for your children, grandchildren, nieces, nephews, brothers, and/or sisters. Along with the latest toys, dolls, and games, another "good gift" option you might consider is a financial investment.

Financial gifts, just like toys or clothing, come in all shapes and sizes. With a little bit of shopping around, you can find one that matches your budget and also meets the needs of the recipient—whether the gift be college tuition in fifteen years or money for summer camp in three years.

The key is giving money to children early and using appropriate investment vehicles. During their growing-up years, the dividends and interest from their investments will compound at their low tax rate or will be completely tax-free. However, to qualify for the tax advantage, the money must ultimately be used for acceptable purposes such as school tuition, ballet lessons, or summer camp, and not for the child's everyday living expenses. Check your state's laws to find out exactly how this money may be used.

No matter what material gift you choose, remember that the greatest present you can give is to share the love of God. Let your loved ones know that, ultimately, "every good gift . . . is from above" (James 1:17). ✦

the word of truth, that we might be a kind of firstfruits of His creatures.

Qualities Needed in Trials

19So then,[a] my beloved brethren, let every man be swift to hear, slow to speak, slow to wrath; 20for the wrath of man does not produce the righteousness of God.

Doers—Not Hearers Only

21Therefore lay aside all filthiness and overflow of wickedness, and receive with meekness the implanted word, which is able to save your souls.

22But be doers of the word, and not hearers only, deceiving yourselves. 23For if anyone is a hearer of the word and not a doer, he is like a man observing his natural face in a mirror; 24for he observes himself, goes away, and immediately forgets what kind of man he was. 25But he who looks into the perfect law of liberty and continues *in it,* and is not a forgetful hearer but a doer of the work, this one will be blessed in what he does.

26If anyone among you[a] thinks he is religious, and does not bridle his tongue but deceives his own heart, this one's religion *is* useless. 27Pure and undefiled religion before God and the Father is this: to visit orphans and widows in their trouble, *and* to keep oneself unspotted from the world.

CHAPTER 2

Beware of Personal Favoritism

My brethren, do not hold the faith of our Lord Jesus Christ, *the Lord* of glory, with partiality. 2For if there should come into your assembly a man with gold rings, in fine apparel, and there should also come in a poor man in filthy clothes, 3and you pay attention to the one wearing the fine clothes and say to him, "You sit here in a good place," and say to the poor man, "You stand there," or, "Sit here at my footstool," 4have you not shown partiality among yourselves, and become judges with evil thoughts?

5Listen, my beloved brethren: Has God not chosen the poor of this world *to be* rich in faith and heirs of the kingdom which He promised to those who love Him? 6But you have dishonored the poor man. Do not the rich oppress you and drag you into the courts? 7Do they not blaspheme that noble name by which you are called?

8If you really fulfill *the* royal law according to the Scripture, *"You shall love your neighbor as yourself,"*[a] you do well; 9but if you show partiality, you commit sin, and are convicted by the law as transgressors. 10For whoever shall keep the whole law, and yet stumble in one *point,* he is guilty of all. 11For He who said, *"Do not commit adultery,"*[a] also said, *"Do not murder."*[b] Now if you do not commit adultery, but you do murder, you have become a transgressor of the law. 12So speak and so do as those who will be judged by the law of liberty. 13For judgment is without mercy to the one who has shown no mercy. Mercy triumphs over judgment.

1:19 [a]NU-Text reads *Know this* or *This you know.*
1:26 [a]NU-Text omits *among you.* 2:8 [a]Leviticus 19:18 2:11 [a]Exodus 20:14; Deuteronomy 5:18 [b]Exodus 20:13; Deuteronomy 5:17

1:19, 20 Self-centered anger leads to bitterness and ruins our Christian testimony.

2:2–4 The gift of salvation was made available to every person, regardless of economic, social, or political status. When we show partiality to the wealthy or socially important, or when we hesitate to shake the hand of the newly-converted down-and-outer, we are not reflecting the love of Jesus accurately; we are sinning.

Faith Without Works Is Dead

[14]What *does it* profit, my brethren, if
someone says he has faith but does not
have works? Can faith save him? [15]If a
brother or sister is naked and destitute of
daily food, [16]and one of you says to them,
"Depart in peace, be warmed and filled,"
but you do not give them the things which
are needed for the body, what *does it* profit?
[17]Thus also faith by itself, if it does not have
works, is dead.

[18]But someone will say, "You have faith,
and I have works." Show me your faith
without your[a] works, and I will show you
my faith by my[b] works. [19]You believe that
there is one God. You do well. Even the
demons believe—and tremble! [20]But do
you want to know, O foolish man, that
faith without works is dead?[a] [21]Was not
Abraham our father justified by works
when he offered Isaac his son on the altar?
[22]Do you see that faith was working to-
gether with his works, and by works faith
was made perfect? [23]And the Scripture was
fulfilled which says, *"Abraham believed
God, and it was accounted to him for righ-
teousness."*[a] And he was called the friend
of God. [24]You see then that a man is justi-
fied by works, and not by faith only.

[25]Likewise, was not Rā'hab the harlot
also justified by works when she received
the messengers and sent *them* out another
way?

[26]For as the body without the spirit is
dead, so faith without works is dead also.

2:18 [a]NU-Text omits *your.* [b]NU-Text omits *my.*
2:20 [a]NU-Text reads *useless.* 2:23 [a]Genesis 15:6
3:3 [a]NU-Text reads *Now if.*

Help Your Neighbor

Colleen Townsend Evans

Many of us have a vision for faraway people in faraway lands. We are good at writing checks—and we should be. But we should not limit ourselves to writing checks. It is too easy, and we think that gets us off the hook.

Meanwhile, we remain blind to the needs of people in our own communities, maybe because they are somehow different from us. I think we need to ask God for a vision for our neighbors, to enable us to let go of our reticence and our fear and follow Jesus across town, across the freeway, across the street. ✦

CHAPTER 3

The Untamable Tongue

My brethren, let not many of you be-
come teachers, knowing that we shall re-
ceive a stricter judgment. [2]For we all stum-
ble in many things. If anyone does not
stumble in word, he *is* a perfect man, able
also to bridle the whole body. [3]Indeed,[a] we
put bits in horses' mouths that they may
obey us, and we turn their whole body.
[4]Look also at ships: although they are so

2:14–19 Faith is more than an intellectual belief in God. If that belief does not produce righteousness and mercy, it is not a saving faith (see Matt. 7:21–23). James gives three arguments in support of this truth: (1) Faith without **works** is no better than words without deeds (vv. 15–17). (2) Faith can be neither seen nor verified unless it shows itself in works (v. 18). (3) Even the **demons** have an intellectual belief in God, but it does not lead to their salvation (v. 19).

3:1 God has given each of us different spiritual gifts and we should use those for His glory, not seeking to be something we are not called to be.

3:2–8 Each time we succumb to the temptation of gossip, slander, or criticism, we not only harm our Christian testimony but we also drive a wedge between ourselves and the recipient, hindering the ministry of the church.

large and are driven by fierce winds, they are turned by a very small rudder wherever the pilot desires. 5Even so the tongue is a little member and boasts great things.

See how great a forest a little fire kindles! 6And the tongue *is* a fire, a world of iniquity. The tongue is so set among our members that it defiles the whole body, and sets on fire the course of nature; and it is set on fire by hell. 7For every kind of beast and bird, of reptile and creature of the sea, is tamed and has been tamed by mankind. 8But no man can tame the tongue. *It is* an unruly evil, full of deadly poison. 9With it we bless our God and Father, and with it we curse men, who have been made in the similitude of God. 10Out of the same mouth proceed blessing and cursing. My brethren, these things ought not to be so. 11Does a spring send forth fresh *water* and bitter from the same opening? 12Can a fig tree, my brethren, bear olives, or a grapevine bear figs? Thus no spring yields both salt water and fresh.[a]

Heavenly Versus Demonic Wisdom

13Who *is* wise and understanding among you? Let him show by good conduct *that* his works *are done* in the meekness of wisdom. 14But if you have bitter envy and self-seeking in your hearts, do not boast and lie against the truth. 15This wisdom does not descend from above, but *is* earthly, sensual, demonic. 16For where envy and self-seeking *exist*, confusion and every evil thing *are* there. 17But the wisdom that is from above is first pure, then peaceable, gentle, willing to yield, full of mercy and good fruits, without partiality and without hypocrisy. 18Now the fruit of righteousness is sown in peace by those who make peace.

> ***I pray that my child will submit to You, God. I pray that she will resist the devil, and he will flee from her.***
>
> *adapted from* James 4:7

CHAPTER 4

Pride Promotes Strife

Where do wars and fights *come* from among you? Do *they* not *come* from your *desires for* pleasure that war in your members? 2You lust and do not have. You murder and covet and cannot obtain. You fight and war. Yet[a] you do not have because you do not ask. 3You ask and do not receive, because you ask amiss, that you may spend *it* on your pleasures. 4Adulterers and[a] adulteresses! Do you not know that friendship with the world is enmity with God? Whoever therefore wants to be a friend of the world makes himself an enemy of God. 5Or do you think that the Scripture says in vain, "The Spirit who dwells in us yearns jealously"?

6But He gives more grace. Therefore He says:

"God resists the proud,
But gives grace to the humble."[a]

3:12 [a]NU-Text reads *Neither can a salty spring produce fresh water.* 4:2 [a]NU-Text and M-Text omit *Yet.* 4:4 [a]NU-Text omits *Adulterers and.* 4:6 [a]Proverbs 3:34

3:13–18 Practical wisdom that comes from God is reflected by our actions. A self-centered attitude indicates a reliance on worldly wisdom.

4:1 Conflicts between believers demonstrate a divided commitment to the things of God and the things of the world. We can promote peace within our churches by confessing sin and allowing the Holy Spirit to cultivate the fruit of self-control.

4:5 Although the OT source of this quotation is uncertain, it reflects God's desire for our complete loyalty, as described in Ex. 20:5; 34:14. **Dwells** is the NT word to indicate the presence of God's Spirit.

Humility Cures Worldliness

[7]Therefore submit to God. Resist the
devil and he will flee from you. [8]Draw near
to God and He will draw near to you.
Cleanse *your* hands, *you* sinners; and
purify *your* hearts, *you* double-minded.
[9]Lament and mourn and weep! Let your
laughter be turned to mourning and
your joy to gloom. [10]Humble yourselves
in the sight of the Lord, and He will lift
you up.

Do Not Judge a Brother

[11]Do not speak evil of one another,
brethren. He who speaks evil of a brother
and judges his brother, speaks evil of the
law and judges the law. But if you judge
the law, you are not a doer of the law but a
judge. [12]There is one Lawgiver,[a] who is able
to save and to destroy. Who[b] are you to
judge another?[c]

Do Not Boast About Tomorrow

[13]Come now, you who say, "Today or to-
morrow we will[a] go to such and such a city,
spend a year there, buy and sell, and make
a profit"; [14]whereas you do not know what
will happen tomorrow. For what *is* your life?
It is even a vapor that appears for a little
time and then vanishes away. [15]Instead you
ought to say, "If the Lord wills, we shall live
and do this or that." [16]But now you boast
in your arrogance. All such boasting is
evil.

[17]Therefore, to him who knows to do
good and does not do *it*, to him it is sin.

4:12 [a]NU-Text adds *and Judge.* [b]NU-Text and M-Text read *But who.* [c]NU-Text reads *a neighbor.*
4:13 [a]M-Text reads *let us.* 5:4 [a]Literally, in Hebrew, *Hosts* 5:5 [a]NU-Text omits *as.* 5:9 [a]NU-Text and M-Text read *judged.*

CHAPTER 5

Rich Oppressors Will Be Judged

Come now, *you* rich, weep and howl for
your miseries that are coming upon *you!*
[2]Your riches are corrupted, and your gar-
ments are moth-eaten. [3]Your gold and sil-
ver are corroded, and their corrosion will
be a witness against you and will eat your
flesh like fire. You have heaped up treasure
in the last days. [4]Indeed the wages of the
laborers who mowed your fields, which
you kept back by fraud, cry out; and the
cries of the reapers have reached the ears
of the Lord of Sab'a·ōth.[a] [5]You have lived
on the earth in pleasure and luxury; you
have fattened your hearts as[a] in a day of
slaughter. [6]You have condemned, you
have murdered the just; he does not resist
you.

Be Patient and Persevering

[7]Therefore be patient, brethren, until the
coming of the Lord. See *how* the farmer
waits for the precious fruit of the earth,
waiting patiently for it until it receives the
early and latter rain. [8]You also be patient.
Establish your hearts, for the coming of the
Lord is at hand.

[9]Do not grumble against one another,
brethren, lest you be condemned.[a] Behold,
the Judge is standing at the door! [10]My
brethren, take the prophets, who spoke in
the name of the Lord, as an example of suf-
fering and patience. [11]Indeed we count
them blessed who endure. You have heard
of the perseverance of Job and seen the end
intended by the Lord—that the Lord is very
compassionate and merciful.

[12]But above all, my brethren, do not
swear, either by heaven or by earth or with

4:13–16 Careful planning is a characteristic of a responsible steward; however, our behavior should consistently reflect our dependence on the Lord and acknowledge His control over the course of our lives.

5:12 do not swear: Neither these words nor Jesus' teaching in Matt. 5:34–37 forbid official oath taking. Rather, they forbid the use of an oath in casual conversation to convince others of our integrity. Such usage is disrespectful of God's name. **Yes . . . No**: Our word should be so above reproach that others will accept without an oath what we affirm or deny.

any other oath. But let your "Yes" be "Yes," and *your* "No," "No," lest you fall into judgment.[a]

Meeting Specific Needs

13 Is anyone among you suffering? Let him pray. Is anyone cheerful? Let him sing psalms. 14 Is anyone among you sick? Let him call for the elders of the church, and let them pray over him, anointing him with oil in the name of the Lord. 15 And the prayer of faith will save the sick, and the Lord will raise him up. And if he has committed sins, he will be forgiven. 16 Confess *your* trespasses[a] to one another, and pray for one another, that you may be healed. The effective, fervent prayer of a righteous man avails much. 17 E·lī′jah was a man with a nature like ours, and he prayed earnestly that it would not rain; and it did not rain on the land for three years and six months. 18 And he prayed again, and the heaven gave rain, and the earth produced its fruit.

Bring Back the Erring One

19 Brethren, if anyone among you wanders from the truth, and someone turns him back, 20 let him know that he who turns a sinner from the error of his way will save a soul[a] from death and cover a multitude of sins.

5:12 [a]M-Text reads *hypocrisy.* 5:16 [a]NU-Text reads *Therefore confess your sins.* 5:20 [a]NU-Text reads *his soul.*

✦1 Peter✦

Nero's persecution of the early Christian church in Rome also encouraged other local authorities to punish this new group of believers. In light of the trials, tribulations, and even death which Christians were facing throughout the Roman Empire and Asia Minor, Peter used this letter to give counsel and comfort, stressing their living hope in the Lord.

Peter was one of the first converts to Jesus. He traveled with Christ during His three years of ministry and became the leader of the inner circle, comprised of James, John, and himself. Knowing firsthand of Jesus' suffering and death, Peter presented Christ as the believer's example in difficult times. He knew that persecution could cause either growth or bitterness, and he encouraged believers to conduct themselves courageously for Christ. Both their character and their conduct must be above reproach.

Peter pointed out that suffering for Christ is the Christian's privilege. Furthermore, Peter reminded these early believers that the One they followed also suffered and died, so they should not be surprised at their own ordeals. This epistle still serves as a guidebook for any Christian suffering persecution or ridicule because of his or her faith; it demonstrates that such trials are cause for rejoicing. ✦

CHAPTER 1

Greeting to the Elect Pilgrims

Peter, an apostle of Jesus Christ,
To the pilgrims of the Dispersion in
Pon'tus, Galatia, Cap·pa·dō'ci·a, Asia,
and Bi·thyn'i·a, 2elect according to the
fore-knowledge of God the Father, in
sanctification of the Spirit, for obedience
and sprinkling of the blood of Jesus
Christ:

Grace to you and peace be multiplied.

A Heavenly Inheritance

3Blessed *be* the God and Father of our
Lord Jesus Christ, who according to His
abundant mercy has begotten us again to a
living hope through the resurrection of
Jesus Christ from the dead, 4to an inheri-
tance incorruptible and undefiled and that
does not fade away, reserved in heaven for
you, 5who are kept by the power of God
through faith for salvation ready to be re-
vealed in the last time.

6In this you greatly rejoice, though now
for a little while, if need be, you have
been grieved by various trials, 7that the

1:1 pilgrims of the Dispersion: God's people live in this world, but their citizenship is in heaven.

1:3 begotten us again: has given us new life.

1:7 genuineness: True faith is that which is still in place after the artificial layers have

Keep Your Eyes on the Master

Anne Ortlund

"Sin and pain and sorrow"—all your troubles—are so limited and weak, they're not worthy of your full concentration.

Your troubles can't shut off the power of God's Spirit to work on your behalf.

They can't change His long-range plans for you.

They can't thwart the ability of His Word to comfort and direct you.

"Fix your eyes on Jesus, and ask Him for godly optimism, steadiness, endurance."

They can't lessen the availability of your Christian brothers and sisters to encourage you.

They can't reduce your eternal life!

Then don't let them overcome you.

Fix your eyes on Jesus, and ask Him for godly optimism, steadiness, endurance.

Take courage from Psalm 25:

"My eyes are ever toward the Lord,
For He shall pluck my feet out of the net" (v. 15). ✦

genuineness of your faith, *being* much
more precious than gold that perishes,
though it is tested by fire, may be found to
praise, honor, and glory at the revelation of
Jesus Christ, 8whom having not seen[a] you
love. Though now you do not see *Him,* yet
believing, you rejoice with joy inexpress-
ible and full of glory, 9receiving the end of
your faith—the salvation of *your* souls.

10Of this salvation the prophets have in-
quired and searched carefully, who proph-
esied of the grace *that would come* to you,
11searching what, or what manner of time,
the Spirit of Christ who was in them was
indicating when He testified beforehand
the sufferings of Christ and the glories that
would follow. 12To them it was revealed
that, not to themselves, but to us[a] they
were ministering the things which now
have been reported to you through those
who have preached the gospel to you by
the Holy Spirit sent from heaven—things
which angels desire to look into.

Living Before God Our Father

13Therefore gird up the loins of your
mind, be sober, and rest *your* hope fully

1:8 [a]M-Text reads *known.* 1:12 [a]NU-Text and M-Text read *you.*

been stripped away by trials and testings. The Christian who proves faithful through trials will receive God's praise at the return of Christ and share in God's own honor and glory. As we experience these trials, we can find comfort in clinging to this promise and in knowing that Christ has already experienced ultimate suffering on our behalf and will help us make it through.

1:13 gird up . . . your mind: In the ancient world people had to gather up the long robes they wore in order to be free to do anything energetic. The modern equivalent would

> The miracle of the Christian life is that God can give a man joy in the midst of external misery, a joy which gives him power to work until the misery is removed.
>
> Oswald Chambers

upon the grace that is to be brought to you
at the revelation of Jesus Christ; 14as obedi-
ent children, not conforming yourselves to
the former lusts, *as* in your ignorance; 15but
as He who called you *is* holy, you also be
holy in all *your* conduct, 16because it is
written, *"Be holy, for I am holy."*[a]
17And if you call on the Father, who
without partiality judges according to each
one's work, conduct yourselves through-
out the time of your stay *here* in fear;
18knowing that you were not redeemed
with corruptible things, *like* silver or
gold, from your aimless conduct *received*
by tradition from your fathers, 19but
with the precious blood of Christ, as of a
lamb without blemish and without spot.
20He indeed was foreordained before
the foundation of the world, but was
manifest in these last times for you 21who
through Him believe in God, who
raised Him from the dead and gave Him
glory, so that your faith and hope are in
God.

The Enduring Word

22Since you have purified your souls in
obeying the truth through the Spirit[a] in sin-
cere love of the brethren, love one another
fervently with a pure heart, 23having been
born again, not of corruptible seed but in-
corruptible, through the word of God
which lives and abides forever,[a] 24because

"All flesh is as grass,
And all the glory of man[a] *as the*
flower of the grass.
The grass withers,
And its flower falls away,
25 *But the word of the LORD endures*
forever."[a]

Now this is the word which by the gospel
was preached to you.

CHAPTER 2

Therefore, laying aside all malice, all de-
ceit, hypocrisy, envy, and all evil speaking,
2as newborn babes, desire the pure milk of
the word, that you may grow thereby,[a] 3if
indeed you have tasted that the Lord *is*
gracious.

The Chosen Stone and His Chosen People

4Coming to Him *as to* a living stone, re-
jected indeed by men, but chosen by God
and precious, 5you also, as living stones,
are being built up a spiritual house, a holy
priesthood, to offer up spiritual sacrifices
acceptable to God through Jesus Christ.
6Therefore it is also contained in the Scrip-
ture,

1:16 [a]Leviticus 11:44, 45; 19:2; 20:7 1:22 [a]NU-Text omits *through the Spirit.* 1:23 [a]NU-Text omits *forever.* 1:24 [a]NU-Text reads *all its glory.* 1:25 [a]Isaiah 40:6–8 2:2 [a]NU-Text adds *up to salvation.*

be "Roll up the shirt-sleeves of your mind." We must be ready for mental and spiritual activity. The distractions of this world must not be allowed to rule in our lives, and we must keep ourselves in the best possible health—spiritually, mentally, and physically. **sober**: Self-disciplined. **rest your hope fully**: That entire commitment to Christ which prepares us for His coming. **grace**: Here equivalent to God's gift of salvation. **revelation**: The return of Jesus Christ.

1:17 fear: reverence.

1:22 When we are obedient to God's truth through Holy living, we will discover a sincere love for our brothers and sisters in Christ.

"Behold, I lay in Zion
A chief cornerstone, elect, precious,
And he who believes on Him will by
no means be put to shame."[a]

7Therefore, to you who believe, *He is*
precious; but to those who are disobe-
dient,[a]

"The stone which the builders rejected
Has become the chief cornerstone,"[b]

8and

"A stone of stumbling
And a rock of offense."[a]

They stumble, being disobedient to the
word, to which they also were appointed.
9But you *are* a chosen generation, a royal
priesthood, a holy nation, His own special
people, that you may proclaim the praises
of Him who called you out of darkness
into His marvelous light; 10who once *were*
not a people but *are* now the people of
God, who had not obtained mercy but now
have obtained mercy.

Living Before the World

11Beloved, I beg *you* as sojourners and
pilgrims, abstain from fleshly lusts which
war against the soul, 12having your con-
duct honorable among the Gentiles, that
when they speak against you as evildoers,
they may, by *your* good works which they
observe, glorify God in the day of visita-
tion.

Submission to Government

13Therefore submit yourselves to every
ordinance of man for the Lord's sake,
whether to the king as supreme, 14or to
governors, as to those who are sent by him
for the punishment of evildoers and *for the*
praise of those who do good. 15For this is
the will of God, that by doing good you
may put to silence the ignorance of foolish
men— 16as free, yet not using liberty as a
cloak for vice, but as bondservants of God.
17Honor all *people.* Love the brotherhood.
Fear God. Honor the king.

Submission to Masters

18Servants, *be* submissive to *your* mas-
ters with all fear, not only to the good and
gentle, but also to the harsh. 19For this *is*
commendable, if because of conscience to-
ward God one endures grief, suffering
wrongfully. 20For what credit *is it* if, when
you are beaten for your faults, you take it
patiently? But when you do good and suf-
fer, if you take it patiently, this *is* com-
mendable before God. 21For to this you
were called, because Christ also suffered
for us,[a] leaving us[b] an example, that you
should follow His steps:

22 *"Who committed no sin,*
Nor was deceit found in His mouth";[a]

23who, when He was reviled, did not revile
in return; when He suffered, He did not
threaten, but committed *Himself* to Him
who judges righteously; 24who Himself
bore our sins in His own body on the tree,
that we, having died to sins, might live for
righteousness—by whose stripes you were

2:6 [a]Isaiah 28:16 2:7 [a]NU-Text reads *to those who disbelieve.* [b]Psalm 118:22 2:8 [a]Isaiah 8:14 2:21 [a]NU-Text reads *you.* [b]NU-Text and M-Text read *you.* 2:22 [a]Isaiah 53:9

2:11, 12 fleshly lusts: The whole of fallen human nature in alienation from God—pride, selfishness, the drive for power, and overindulgence in physical desires. Since we don't really belong to this world, we should not become caught up in worldly matters. Instead, our lives should so clearly reflect God's holiness that the unsaved will be caused to glorify Him.

2:21–23 to this: The call to follow Christ often involves a call to suffer for righteousness. The way He bore the suffering of crucifixion is our example in difficult situations. He **committed Himself** to God who always **judges righteously** and thus vindicates the innocent. We too can rely on God to work His ultimate justice in every situation.

healed. [25]For you were like sheep going astray, but have now returned to the Shepherd and Overseer[a] of your souls.

CHAPTER 3

Submission to Husbands

Wives, likewise, *be* submissive to your own husbands, that even if some do not obey the word, they, without a word, may be won by the conduct of their wives, [2]when they observe your chaste conduct *accompanied* by fear. [3]Do not let your adornment be *merely* outward—arranging the hair, wearing gold, or putting on *fine* apparel— [4]rather *let it be* the hidden person of the heart, with the incorruptible *beauty* of a gentle and quiet spirit, which is very precious in the sight of God. [5]For in this manner, in former times, the holy women who trusted in God also adorned themselves, being submissive to their own husbands, [6]as Sarah obeyed Abraham, calling him lord, whose daughters you are if you do good and are not afraid with any terror.

How can an older couple get the most out of their marriage?
Elmer L. Gray

A couple's relationship to God flavors everything else. This includes going to church together and sharing your awareness of God's will; prayer at the table; and discussing church activities, God's will in decisions, concern for others, and the Sunday school lesson.

The relationship between the two of you is more important than ever because you are together so much. Being together more, you can discuss future plans and finances more. My wife and I approach ideas tentatively so we can change our minds. We talk a lot, but we are comfortable not saying anything for hours. We have learned to make up more quickly.

Find things to enjoy together every day. That is the way to live—celebrate life together. If husbands and wives will act like Christians, they will get along and be better able to work out problems. Couples need to read Peter's advice to them (1 Pet. 3:1–7), then his advice to all Christians in the next two verses. He said that Christians should be harmonious, sympathetic, loving like a family, humble-minded, with no aim to get even or to hurt each other (vv. 8, 9).

Ask God to help you to treat each other like Christians. ✦

A Word to Husbands

[7]Husbands, likewise, dwell with *them* with understanding, giving honor to the wife, as to the weaker vessel, and as *being* heirs together of the grace of life, that your prayers may not be hindered.

Called to Blessing

[8]Finally, all *of you be* of one mind, having compassion for one another; love as brothers, *be* tenderhearted, *be* courteous;[a] [9]not returning evil for evil or reviling for reviling, but on the contrary blessing, knowing that you were called to this, that you may inherit a blessing. [10]For

2:25 [a]Greek *Episkopos* 3:8 [a]NU-Text reads *humble.*

"He who would love life
And see good days,
Let him refrain his tongue from evil,
And his lips from speaking deceit.
11 *Let him turn away from evil and do good;*
Let him seek peace and pursue it.
12 *For the eyes of the* LORD *are on the righteous,*
And His ears are *open to their prayers;*
But the face of the LORD *is against those who do evil."*[a]

Suffering for Right and Wrong

13And who *is* he who will harm you if
you become followers of what is good?
14But even if you should suffer for righ-
teousness' sake, *you are* blessed. *"And do
not be afraid of their threats, nor be trou-
bled."*[a] 15But sanctify the Lord God[a] in your
hearts, and always *be* ready to *give* a de-
fense to everyone who asks you a reason
for the hope that is in you, with meekness
and fear; 16having a good conscience, that
when they defame you as evildoers, those
who revile your good conduct in Christ
may be ashamed. 17For *it is* better, if it is the
will of God, to suffer for doing good than
for doing evil.

Christ's Suffering and Ours

18For Christ also suffered once for sins,
the just for the unjust, that He might bring
us[a] to God, being put to death in the flesh
but made alive by the Spirit, 19by whom
also He went and preached to the spirits in
prison, 20who formerly were disobedient,
when once the Divine longsuffering
waited[a] in the days of Noah, while *the* ark
was being prepared, in which a few, that is,
eight souls, were saved through water.
21There is also an antitype which now
saves us—baptism (not the removal of the
filth of the flesh, but the answer of a good
conscience toward God), through the res-
urrection of Jesus Christ, 22who has gone
into heaven and is at the right hand of
God, angels and authorities and powers
having been made subject to Him.

CHAPTER 4

Therefore, since Christ suffered for us[a]
in the flesh, arm yourselves also with the
same mind, for he who has suffered in the
flesh has ceased from sin, 2that he no
longer should live the rest of *his* time in the
flesh for the lusts of men, but for the will of
God. 3For we *have spent* enough of our past
lifetime[a] in doing the will of the Gentiles—
when we walked in lewdness, lusts,
drunkenness, revelries, drinking parties,
and abominable idolatries. 4In regard to
these, they think it strange that you do not
run with *them* in the same flood of dissipa-
tion, speaking evil of *you*. 5They will give
an account to Him who is ready to judge
the living and the dead. 6For this reason
the gospel was preached also to those who

3:12 [a]Psalm 34:12–16 3:14 [a]Isaiah 8:12
3:15 [a]NU-Text reads *Christ as Lord.* 3:18 [a]NU-Text and M-Text read *you.* 3:20 [a]NU-Text and M-Text read *when the longsuffering of God waited patiently.*
4:1 [a]NU-Text omits *for us.* 4:3 [a]NU-Text reads *time.*

3:15 sanctify the Lord God in your hearts: Be sure you are filled with His Spirit and have no attitude contrary to love. We should give our testimony with **meekness** (humility) toward others and with **fear** (reverence) toward God for what He has done. As we witness to others we must avoid any hint of self-righteousness, knowing that we are saved by God's mercy and not by achievements of our own.

3:21 antitype: Noah's experience is a picture of ours. He was delivered by the Flood from a world corrupted by sinful humanity. After the Flood he entered a new world. Baptism is a symbol of our deliverance from the old life of sin. We can now begin a new way of life. It is by the **resurrection** power of Christ that we have been delivered.

4:4, 5 think it strange: Unbelievers cannot understand Christians when their habits of **dissipation** have been changed. They may speak **evil** of Christians now, but they will have to give an account to God.

Not What We Deserve

Colleen Townsend Evans

Scripture abounds with examples of grace in the midst of imperfection and unfairness. When I read the story of the prodigal son, I always identify with the older brother who was faithful and did it all right. The younger brother squandered everything and came back and received gifts. The father put a ring on his finger and a robe on his shoulders. He called for a party, and there was the sound of music and dancing and celebration. This son got it all! And I can almost hear the older brother saying, "But, Father, it just isn't fair!"

Again and again, God chooses unfair situations to reveal His love and His power and His grace.

It was certainly so in the life of Jesus. Jesus was the only perfect human being, the only totally faithful man, yet He ended up being treated with the most outrageous injustice that a culture and a society could inflict on anyone. But through that unjust, outrageous event, our lives have been saved, our lives have been filled, and our lives have been changed forever (1 Pet. 3:18).

"Always we will have the choice of how to respond."

And so it will be in our lives. We will have unfair events. We will have times when we are treated unjustly and have no control over those events. But always we will have the choice of how to respond. And if we choose to accept God's power and grace to go through those events as His people, God will be able to use us in ways that will be powerful and real. ✦

are dead, that they might be judged according to men in the flesh, but live according to God in the spirit.

Serving for God's Glory

7But the end of all things is at hand; therefore be serious and watchful in your prayers. 8And above all things have fervent love for one another, for *"love will cover a multitude of sins."*[a] 9*Be* hospitable to one another without grumbling. 10As each one has received a gift, minister it to one another, as good stewards of the manifold grace of God. 11If anyone speaks, *let him speak* as the oracles of God. If anyone ministers, *let him do it* as with the ability which God supplies, that in all things God may be glorified through Jesus Christ, to whom belong the glory and the dominion forever and ever. Amen.

4:8 [a]Proverbs 10:12

4:8 Our ultimate responsibility as Christians is to love one another. Such love will guide our actions and compensate for any shortcomings in our relationships.

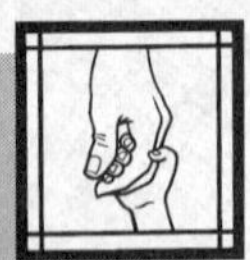

Still Leading the Way

Leslie E. Moser, Ph.D.

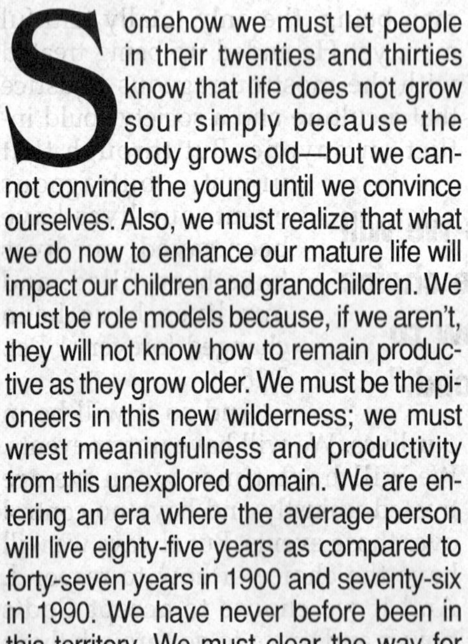

Somehow we must let people in their twenties and thirties know that life does not grow sour simply because the body grows old—but we cannot convince the young until we convince ourselves. Also, we must realize that what we do now to enhance our mature life will impact our children and grandchildren. We must be role models because, if we aren't, they will not know how to remain productive as they grow older. We must be the pioneers in this new wilderness; we must wrest meaningfulness and productivity from this unexplored domain. We are entering an era where the average person will live eighty-five years as compared to forty-seven years in 1900 and seventy-six in 1990. We have never before been in this territory. We must clear the way for those who will follow.

And why must we? Simply because no one else can accomplish for God and for our country what we can accomplish. We were the power base of the sixties and seventies, and we must continue to be. It is good for us to continue, and we can continue. We must make the world understand that active, meaningful, productive life does not necessarily end or even wane at age forty, fifty, sixty, seventy, or even eighty. Most of all, we must communicate the good news that God has given us extra years on this planet. We are now spending a few more years of our everlasting life here on earth. Thanks be to God that our extra years on earth take nothing away from our time in heaven! ✦

Suffering for God's Glory

12Beloved, do not think it strange con-
cerning the fiery trial which is to try you,
as though some strange thing happened to
you; 13but rejoice to the extent that you par-
take of Christ's sufferings, that when His
glory is revealed, you may also be glad
with exceeding joy. 14If you are reproached
for the name of Christ, blessed *are you,* for
the Spirit of glory and of God rests upon
you.[a] On their part He is blasphemed, but
on your part He is glorified. 15But let none
of you suffer as a murderer, a thief, an evil-
doer, or as a busybody in other people's
matters. 16Yet if *anyone suffers* as a Chris-
tian, let him not be ashamed, but let him
glorify God in this matter.[a]
17For the time *has come* for judgment to
begin at the house of God; and if *it begins*
with us first, what will *be* the end of
those who do not obey the gospel of God?
18Now

4:14 [a]NU-Text omits the rest of this verse.
4:16 [a]NU-Text reads *name.*

4:12, 13 Suffering should not come as a surprise to the Christian. We are told repeatedly throughout Scripture to expect trials. Rather than having a "Why me?" attitude, we should rejoice in the opportunity to partake in Christ's sufferings and view the experience as a reminder that we shall one day also partake in His glory.

"If the righteous one is scarcely saved,
Where will the ungodly and the sin-
ner appear?"[a]

19Therefore let those who suffer according
to the will of God commit their souls *to*
Him in doing good, as to a faithful Creator.

CHAPTER 5

Shepherd the Flock

The elders who are among you I exhort,
I who am a fellow elder and a witness of
the sufferings of Christ, and also a partaker
of the glory that will be revealed: 2Shep-
herd the flock of God which is among you,
serving as overseers, not by compulsion
but willingly,[a] not for dishonest gain but
eagerly; 3nor as being lords over those en-
trusted to you, but being examples to the
flock; 4and when the Chief Shepherd ap-
pears, you will receive the crown of glory
that does not fade away.

Submit to God, Resist the Devil

5Likewise you younger people, submit
yourselves to *your* elders. Yes, all of *you* be
submissive to one another, and be clothed
with humility, for

"God resists the proud,
But gives grace to the humble."[a]

4:18 [a]Proverbs 11:31 5:2 [a]NU-Text adds *according to God.* 5:5 [a]Proverbs 3:34 5:8 [a]NU-Text and M-Text omit *because.* 5:10 [a]NU-Text reads *But the God of all grace . . .* will perfect, establish, strengthen, and settle you. [b]NU-Text and M-Text read *you.*

I pray that my grandchild will cast all his cares upon You, God, for You care for him.

adapted from 1 Peter 5:7

6Therefore humble yourselves under the
mighty hand of God, that He may exalt
you in due time, 7casting all your care
upon Him, for He cares for you.
8Be sober, be vigilant; because[a] your ad-
versary the devil walks about like a roar-
ing lion, seeking whom he may devour.
9Resist him, steadfast in the faith, knowing
that the same sufferings are experienced
by your brotherhood in the world. 10But
may[a] the God of all grace, who called us[b] to
His eternal glory by Christ Jesus, after you
have suffered a while, perfect, establish,
strengthen, and settle *you.* 11To Him *be* the
glory and the dominion forever and ever.
Amen.

Farewell and Peace

12By Sil·vā'nus, our faithful brother as I
consider him, I have written to you briefly,
exhorting and testifying that this is the true
grace of God in which you stand.
13She who is in Babylon, elect together
with *you,* greets you; and *so does* Mark my
son. 14Greet one another with a kiss of love.
Peace to you all who are in Christ Jesus.
Amen.

CAST OFF YOUR CARES

Dr. Sharon Sneed and Dr. David Sneed

A healthy balanced person is one who has a controlled level of incoming stressors, adequate coping skills, and a high level of social support. Anticipating life-cycle changes can ease a certain amount of inherent stress. Recognizing the difference between stressors which are controllable and those which are uncontrollable will allow you to focus your coping skills where they can really make a difference.

As with most things in life, and certainly matters pertaining to our health, preventing a problem is much easier and more desirable than trying to correct a disease which has already occurred. Preventing stress is no exception. Once you become overwhelmed with incoming stress, it is easy to "fall to pieces" very quickly if you do not have appropriate coping methods.

By casting your cares upon the Lord (1 Pet. 5:7), and by incorporating sound stress management techniques into your everyday life now, you will be better able to withstand the effects of acute stress when it does occur. Physical, mental, and spiritual health all contribute to wellness. Maintaining a balance in these areas of life is one of the most important health rules to follow. ✦

✦2 Peter✦

Peter's second letter to the churches of Asia Minor begins and ends with a call to grow in the grace and knowledge of God and Jesus the Lord. First, Peter dealt with problems from outside the church (persecution); second, he dealt with problems from inside the church (false doctrine). False teachers were perverting the doctrine of justification and promoting rebellious and immoral living.

Since Christian maturity is the best defense against spiritual counterfeits, Peter urged believers to watch their personal lives closely. They should live godly, blameless, and steadfast lives. Even though false teachers scoff at the thought of future judgment and practice all forms of immorality, and even though God may be longsuffering in sending judgment, ultimately it will come.

Peter's warning to be on the lookout for false prophets is also vital for today's believers, who bear great responsibility for keeping the faith pure for succeeding generations. ✦

CHAPTER 1

Greeting the Faithful

Simon Peter, a bondservant and apostle
of Jesus Christ,

To those who have obtained like precious faith with us by the righteousness of our God and Savior Jesus Christ:

2Grace and peace be multiplied to you
in the knowledge of God and of Jesus our
Lord, 3as His divine power has given to us
all things that *pertain* to life and godliness,
through the knowledge of Him who called
us by glory and virtue, 4by which have
been given to us exceedingly great and
precious promises, that through these you
may be partakers of the divine nature, having escaped the corruption *that is* in the world through lust.

Fruitful Growth in the Faith

5But also for this very reason, giving all
diligence, add to your faith virtue, to
virtue knowledge, 6to knowledge self-
control, to self-control perseverance, to
perseverance godliness, 7to godliness
brotherly kindness, and to brotherly kind-
ness love. 8For if these things are yours

1:2 True **knowledge** is not found in philosophy; it can only be obtained through learning more about God.

1:5–7 for this very reason: Because God's promised power is a present reality, we must with **diligence** grow as Christians by cultivating the characteristics listed in vv. 5–7. **knowledge**: Discernment of true from false teaching, of right from wrong. **Self-control** in the face of temptation and perseverance amid difficulties helps us live a life that pleases God. We must show **brotherly kindness** through practical concern for fellow Christians, and demonstrate **love** by being interested in the well-being of all people. Building these characteristics is an ongoing process in our lives; we should never consider ourselves to be fully mature.

I praise You, Lord, because You have given to me exceedingly great and precious promises, that through these I might be a partaker of the divine nature.

adapted from 2 Peter 1:4

and abound, *you will be* neither barren nor unfruitful in the knowledge of our Lord Jesus Christ. 9For he who lacks these things is shortsighted, even to blindness, and has forgotten that he was cleansed from his old sins.

10Therefore, brethren, be even more diligent to make your call and election sure, for if you do these things you will never stumble; 11for so an entrance will be supplied to you abundantly into the everlasting kingdom of our Lord and Savior Jesus Christ.

Peter's Approaching Death

12For this reason I will not be negligent to remind you always of these things, though you know and are established in the present truth. 13Yes, I think it is right, as long as I am in this tent, to stir you up by reminding *you,* 14knowing that shortly I *must* put off my tent, just as our Lord Jesus Christ showed me. 15Moreover I will be careful to ensure that you always have a reminder of these things after my decease.

The Trustworthy Prophetic Word

16For we did not follow cunningly devised fables when we made known to you the power and coming of our Lord Jesus Christ, but were eyewitnesses of His majesty. 17For He received from God the Father honor and glory when such a voice came to Him from the Excellent Glory: "This is My beloved Son, in whom I am well pleased." 18And we heard this voice which came from heaven when we were with Him on the holy mountain.

19And so we have the prophetic word confirmed,[a] which you do well to heed as a light that shines in a dark place, until the day dawns and the morning star rises in your hearts; 20knowing this first, that no prophecy of Scripture is of any private interpretation,[a] 21for prophecy never came by the will of man, but holy men of God[a] spoke *as they were* moved by the Holy Spirit.

CHAPTER 2

Destructive Doctrines

But there were also false prophets among the people, even as there will be false teachers among you, who will secretly bring in destructive heresies, even denying the Lord who bought them, *and* bring on themselves swift destruction. 2And many will follow their destructive ways, because of whom the way of truth will be blasphemed. 3By covetousness they will exploit you with deceptive words; for a long time their judgment has not been idle, and their destruction does[a] not slumber.

Doom of False Teachers

4For if God did not spare the angels who sinned, but cast *them* down to hell and delivered *them* into chains of darkness, to be

1:19 [a]Or *We also have the more sure prophetic word.* 1:20 [a]Or *origin* 1:21 [a]NU-Text reads *but men spoke from God.* 2:3 [a]M-Text reads *will not.*

1:20, 21 private interpretation: Thus, not of private origin. Scripture has been revealed by God to **holy men** who recorded it. The OT came from God just as truly as the voice from heaven at the Transfiguration (see vv. 17, 18). We are not permitted to interpret the Scriptures to suit our personal preferences, and we should beware of teachers who use verses out of context to support their own views.

reserved for judgment; 5and did not spare the ancient world, but saved Noah, *one of* eight *people,* a preacher of righteousness, bringing in the flood on the world of the ungodly; 6and turning the cities of Sod′om and Go·mor′rah into ashes, condemned *them* to destruction, making *them* an example to those who afterward would live ungodly; 7and delivered righteous Lot, *who was* oppressed by the filthy conduct of the wicked 8(for that righteous man, dwelling among them, tormented *his* righteous soul from day to day by seeing and hearing *their* lawless deeds)— 9*then* the Lord knows how to deliver the godly out of temptations and to reserve the unjust under punishment for the day of judgment, 10and especially those who walk according to the flesh in the lust of uncleanness and despise authority. *They are* presumptuous, self-willed. They are not afraid to speak evil of dignitaries, 11whereas angels, who are greater in power and might, do not bring a reviling accusation against them before the Lord.

Depravity of False Teachers

12But these, like natural brute beasts made to be caught and destroyed, speak evil of the things they do not understand, and will utterly perish in their own corruption, 13*and* will receive the wages of unrighteousness, *as* those who count it pleasure to carouse in the daytime. *They are* spots and blemishes, carousing in their own deceptions while they feast with you, 14having eyes full of adultery and that cannot cease from sin, enticing unstable souls. *They have* a heart trained in covetous practices, *and are* accursed children. 15They have forsaken the right way and gone astray, following the way of Bā′laam the *son* of Bē′or, who loved the wages of unrighteousness; 16but he was rebuked for his iniquity: a dumb donkey speaking with a man's voice restrained the madness of the prophet.

17These are wells without water, clouds[a] carried by a tempest, for whom is reserved the blackness of darkness forever.[b]

Deceptions of False Teachers

18For when they speak great swelling *words* of emptiness, they allure through the lusts of the flesh, through lewdness, the ones who have actually escaped[a] from those who live in error. 19While they promise them liberty, they themselves are slaves of corruption; for by whom a person is overcome, by him also he is brought into bondage. 20For if, after they have escaped the pollutions of the world through the knowledge of the Lord and Savior Jesus Christ, they are again entangled in them and overcome, the latter end is worse for them than the beginning. 21For it would have been better for them not to have known the way of righteousness, than having known *it,* to turn from the holy commandment delivered to them. 22But it has happened to them according to the true proverb: *"A dog returns to his own vomit,"*[a] and, "a sow, having washed, to her wallowing in the mire."

CHAPTER 3

God's Promise Is Not Slack

Beloved, I now write to you this second epistle (in *both of* which I stir up your pure minds by way of reminder), 2that you may be mindful of the words which were

2:17 [a]NU-Text reads *and mists.* [b]NU-Text omits *forever.*
2:18 [a]NU-Text reads *are barely escaping.*
2:22 [a]Proverbs 26:11

2:17 The message of the false teachers was as unsatisfying as **wells without water** and **clouds** of a **tempest**, blown past before they can release needed rain. If we are not being fed spiritually or we feel something is lacking from our church's teaching, it's time to evaluate and perhaps find a different place of worship.

> Our faith is not dependent upon human knowledge and scientific advance, but upon the unmistakable message of the Word of God.
>
> Billy Graham

spoken before by the holy prophets, and of
the commandment of us,[a] the apostles of
the Lord and Savior, [3]knowing this first:
that scoffers will come in the last days,
walking according to their own lusts, [4]and
saying, "Where is the promise of His coming? For since the fathers fell asleep, all
things continue as *they were* from the beginning of creation." [5]For this they willfully forget: that by the word of God the
heavens were of old, and the earth standing out of water and in the water, [6]by
which the world *that* then existed perished, being flooded with water. [7]But the
heavens and the earth *which* are now preserved by the same word, are reserved for
fire until the day of judgment and perdition of ungodly men.

[8]But, beloved, do not forget this one
thing, that with the Lord one day *is* as a
thousand years, and a thousand years as
one day. [9]The Lord is not slack concerning
His promise, as some count slackness, but
is longsuffering toward us,[a] not willing
that any should perish but that all should
come to repentance.

The Day of the Lord

[10]But the day of the Lord will come as a
thief in the night, in which the heavens will
pass away with a great noise, and the elements will melt with fervent heat; both the
earth and the works that are in it will be
burned up.[a] [11]Therefore, since all these
things will be dissolved, what manner *of
persons* ought you to be in holy conduct
and godliness, [12]looking for and hastening
the coming of the day of God, because of
which the heavens will be dissolved, being
on fire, and the elements will melt with fervent heat? [13]Nevertheless we, according to

3:2 [a]NU-Text and M-Text read *commandment of the apostles of your Lord and Savior* or *commandment of your apostles of the Lord and Savior.* 3:9 [a]NU-Text reads *you.* 3:10 [a]NU-Text reads *laid bare* (literally *found*).

Umbrellas Can't Stop the Rain

J. Vernon McGee

Did you know that you cannot keep God from loving you? You can reject His love, but you cannot keep Him from loving you. You cannot keep it from raining, but you can raise an umbrella to keep the rain from falling on you. At this moment God's love is falling around you—certainly showers of mercy are falling on this earth—and you can raise the umbrella of indifference, you can raise the umbrella of skepticism, you can raise the umbrella of your own self-will, but you cannot keep God from loving you. ✦

3:8, 9 When we become disheartened by the increasing amount of evil in the world and wonder why God allows it to continue, we should remember these verses. Our merciful God may temporarily withhold His wrath to provide opportunity for repentance, but He will take action against those who persist in evil in His own time.

3:10 Peter's description reminds us of Isaiah's vision (Is. 13:10–13) and of the words of Jesus (Matt. 24:29, 35).

3:13 new heavens . . . new earth: God's new creation will be completely free from the effects of sin (see Is. 65:17–25; Rev. 21:1, 2.

His promise, look for new heavens and a
new earth in which righteousness dwells.

Be Steadfast

[14]Therefore, beloved, looking forward to
these things, be diligent to be found by
Him in peace, without spot and blameless;
[15]and consider *that* the longsuffering of our
Lord *is* salvation—as also our beloved
brother Paul, according to the wisdom
given to him, has written to you, [16]as also
in all his epistles, speaking in them of these
things, in which are some things hard to
understand, which untaught and unstable
people twist to their own destruction, as
they do also the rest of the Scriptures.

[17]You therefore, beloved, since you
know *this* beforehand, beware lest you also
fall from your own steadfastness, being led
away with the error of the wicked; [18]but
grow in the grace and knowledge of our
Lord and Savior Jesus Christ.

To Him *be* the glory both now and forever. Amen.

✦1 John✦

This is the first of three letters written by the author of the fourth Gospel. John was one of the fishermen Jesus called to be His disciples. After the Resurrection, John left Jerusalem and ministered in and around Ephesus; he also ministered to the seven churches in the Roman province of Asia (Rev. 2; 3).

John wrote this fatherly epistle out of loving concern for his "children" whose steadfastness in the truth was being threatened by the temptations of the world and the deceptions of false teaching. The major theme is fellowship with God and assurance of His indwelling through an abiding relationship with Jesus Christ.

Gnosticism, a popular teaching of the day, taught that matter is inherently evil, and a divine being, therefore, could not take on human flesh. This resulted in a distinction between the man Jesus and the spiritual Christ, whom the Gnostics believed came upon Jesus at His baptism and departed prior to His crucifixion. In one of the clearest arguments in the New Testament, John stressed the reality of the Incarnation and the emptiness of profession without practice.

This epistle prompts Christians to put love into action, not simply into words; all believers should seek opportunities to show love to hurting people. ✦

CHAPTER 1

What Was Heard, Seen, and Touched

That which was from the beginning,
which we have heard, which we have seen
with our eyes, which we have looked
upon, and our hands have handled, con-
cerning the Word of life— 2the life was
manifested, and we have seen, and bear
witness, and declare to you that eternal life
which was with the Father and was mani-
fested to us— 3that which we have seen
and heard we declare to you, that you also
may have fellowship with us; and truly
our fellowship *is* with the Father and with
His Son Jesus Christ. 4And these things
we write to you that your[a] joy may be
full.

Fellowship with Him and One Another

5This is the message which we have
heard from Him and declare to you, that
God is light and in Him is no darkness at
all. 6If we say that we have fellowship with
Him, and walk in darkness, we lie and do
not practice the truth. 7But if we walk in
the light as He is in the light, we have
fellowship with one another, and the
blood of Jesus Christ His Son cleanses us
from all sin.
8If we say that we have no sin, we de-

1:4 [a]NU-Text and M-Text read *our.*

1:6, 7 John indicates that true believers, those who have been cleansed from all sin, will reflect God in their lifestyles.

> ***I praise You because when I confess my sins, You, God, are faithful and just to forgive my sins and to cleanse me from all unrighteousness.***
>
> *adapted from* 1 John 1:9

ceive ourselves, and the truth is not in us.
9If we confess our sins, He is faithful and
just to forgive us *our* sins and to cleanse us
from all unrighteousness. 10If we say that
we have not sinned, we make Him a liar,
and His word is not in us.

CHAPTER 2

My little children, these things I write to
you, so that you may not sin. And if any-
one sins, we have an Advocate with the
Father, Jesus Christ the righteous. 2And He
Himself is the propitiation for our sins, and
not for ours only but also for the whole
world.

The Test of Knowing Him

3Now by this we know that we know
Him, if we keep His commandments. 4He
who says, "I know Him," and does not
keep His commandments, is a liar, and the
truth is not in him. 5But whoever keeps His
word, truly the love of God is perfected in
him. By this we know that we are in Him.
6He who says he abides in Him ought him-
self also to walk just as He walked.

7Brethren,[a] I write no new command-
ment to you, but an old commandment
which you have had from the beginning.
The old commandment is the word which
you heard from the beginning.[b] 8Again, a
new commandment I write to you, which
thing is true in Him and in you, because
the darkness is passing away, and the true
light is already shining.

9He who says he is in the light, and
hates his brother, is in darkness until now.
10He who loves his brother abides in the
light, and there is no cause for stumbling in
him. 11But he who hates his brother is in
darkness and walks in darkness, and does
not know where he is going, because the
darkness has blinded his eyes.

Their Spiritual State

12I write to you, little children,
Because your sins are forgiven you
for His name's sake.
13I write to you, fathers,
Because you have known Him *who
is* from the beginning.
I write to you, young men,
Because you have overcome the
wicked one.
I write to you, little children,
Because you have known the
Father.

2:7 [a]NU-Text reads *Beloved.* [b]NU-Text omits *from the beginning.*

2:1 that you may not sin: God's plan for every believer. The cure for backsliding is to hurry to our **Advocate**, Jesus Christ. Because He is **righteous**, He will plead our case and obtain our forgiveness.

2:3–6 After we are saved, we will sin at times and vv. 1, 2 tell us how to deal with such situations; however, a true relationship with God will be outwardly evident by consistent obedience to His commandments.

2:7–11 The command to love is an **old commandment** because from **the beginning** God has expected His people to love (see Lev. 19:18). Yet it is a **new commandment** because Jesus' coming has fully shown us God's love, and He enables us to live in love.

2:12–14 The commandment to love fits all ages and all stages of the Christian life. **Children** in Christ can love because their **sins** are forgiven. **Fathers** have longer memories of past grace. **Young men** rejoice in power to overcome evil. As we grow older, we have more and more opportunities and reasons to express God's love.

> Sanctity does not consist merely in *doing* the will of God. It consists in *willing* the will of God.
>
> Thomas Merton

14I have written to you, fathers,
Because you have known Him *who is* from the beginning.
I have written to you, young men,
Because you are strong, and the word of God abides in you,
And you have overcome the wicked one.

Do Not Love the World

15Do not love the world or the things in the world. If anyone loves the world, the love of the Father is not in him. 16For all that *is* in the world—the lust of the flesh, the lust of the eyes, and the pride of life—is not of the Father but is of the world. 17And the world is passing away, and the lust of it; but he who does the will of God abides forever.

Deceptions of the Last Hour

18Little children, it is the last hour; and as you have heard that the[a] Antichrist is coming, even now many antichrists have come, by which we know that it is the last hour. 19They went out from us, but they were not of us; for if they had been of us, they would have continued with us; but *they went out* that they might be made manifest, that none of them were of us.

20But you have an anointing from the Holy One, and you know all things.[a] 21I have not written to you because you do not know the truth, but because you know it, and that no lie is of the truth.

22Who is a liar but he who denies that Jesus is the Christ? He is antichrist who denies the Father and the Son. 23Whoever denies the Son does not have the Father either; he who acknowledges the Son has the Father also.

Let Truth Abide in You

24Therefore let that abide in you which you heard from the beginning. If what you heard from the beginning abides in you, you also will abide in the Son and in the Father. 25And this is the promise that He has promised us—eternal life.

26These things I have written to you concerning those who *try to* deceive you. 27But the anointing which you have received from Him abides in you, and you do not need that anyone teach you; but as the same anointing teaches you concerning all things, and is true, and is not a lie, and just as it has taught you, you will[a] abide in Him.

The Children of God

28And now, little children, abide in Him, that when[a] He appears, we may have confidence and not be ashamed before Him at His coming. 29If you know that He is righteous, you know that everyone who practices righteousness is born of Him.

CHAPTER 3

Behold what manner of love the Father has bestowed on us, that we should be called children of God![a] Therefore the world does not know us,[b] because it did

2:18 [a]NU-Text omits *the.* 2:20 [a]NU-Text reads *you all know.* 2:27 [a]NU-Text reads *you abide.* 2:28 [a]NU-Text reads *if.* 3:1 [a]NU-Text adds *And we are.* [b]M-Text reads *you.*

2:15, 16 lust of the flesh: The desires of our sin-tainted human nature. **lust of the eyes**: Greed for more and more things. **pride of life**: Empty boasting in our status and achievements. Contrary to popular belief, these temptations grow stronger, not weaker, as we grow older.

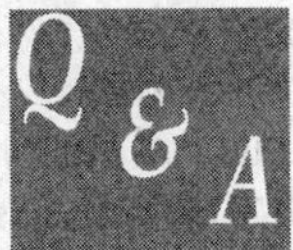

What Scriptures prove a living body in the Spirit can live without sin?

J. Vernon McGee

1 John 2:1 says, "My little children, these things I write to you, so that you may not sin." God has made every arrangement so that we can live without sin, but He adds this: "And if anyone sins, we have an Advocate with the Father, Jesus Christ the righteous."

Although God has made ample and adequate provision for us not to sin, our entrance into His provision is imperfect because of our imperfection. Notice that this verse does not say that we *cannot* sin, but John is writing to us that we *may not* sin. God wants us to walk in a manner that is well pleasing to Him; that is, He wants us to walk in obedience to His Word.

Let me say that I have never met anyone who lived without sinning. I have met some who thought they had reached that grandiose plane, but they had not impressed the people around them that they were sinless. God is not impressed, either; back up one verse to 1 John 1:10: "If we say that we have not sinned, we make Him a liar, and His word is not in us." That is pretty plain. ✦

not know Him. [2]Beloved, now we are chil-
dren of God; and it has not yet been re-
vealed what we shall be, but we know that
when He is revealed, we shall be like Him,
for we shall see Him as He is. [3]And every-
one who has this hope in Him purifies
himself, just as He is pure.

Sin and the Child of God

[4]Whoever commits sin also commits
lawlessness, and sin is lawlessness. [5]And
you know that He was manifested to take
away our sins, and in Him there is no sin.
[6]Whoever abides in Him does not sin.
Whoever sins has neither seen Him nor
known Him.

[7]Little children, let no one deceive you.
He who practices righteousness is righ-
teous, just as He is righteous. [8]He who sins
is of the devil, for the devil has sinned from
the beginning. For this purpose the Son of
God was manifested, that He might de-
stroy the works of the devil. [9]Whoever has
been born of God does not sin, for His seed

3:6 A person cannot abide in Christ (see John 15:1–10) and continue in sin at the same time. "Sins" in this context indicates a continual, habitual action. The person living in sin is not living in Christ and, in that sense, has not **seen Him** (v. 6). Unless he repents, he has no biblical assurance of salvation.

3:9 he cannot sin: It is inconceivable for the person **born of God** to live a life of sin. If he does, he is denying what God did when He saved him. Sin is incompatible with Christ's new nature given to the Christian.

remains in him; and he cannot sin, because
he has been born of God.

The Imperative of Love

[10]In this the children of God and the chil-
dren of the devil are manifest: Whoever
does not practice righteousness is not of
God, nor *is* he who does not love his
brother. [11]For this is the message that you
heard from the beginning, that we should
love one another, [12]not as Cain *who* was of
the wicked one and murdered his brother.
And why did he murder him? Because his
works were evil and his brother's righ-
teous.

[13]Do not marvel, my brethren, if the
world hates you. [14]We know that we have
passed from death to life, because we love
the brethren. He who does not love *his*
brother[a] abides in death. [15]Whoever hates
his brother is a murderer, and you know
that no murderer has eternal life abiding in
him.

The Outworking of Love

[16]By this we know love, because He laid
down His life for us. And we also ought to
lay down *our* lives for the brethren. [17]But
whoever has this world's goods, and sees
his brother in need, and shuts up his heart
from him, how does the love of God abide
in him?

[18]My little children, let us not love in
word or in tongue, but in deed and in
truth. [19]And by this we know[a] that we are
of the truth, and shall assure our hearts be-
fore Him. [20]For if our heart condemns us,
God is greater than our heart, and knows
all things. [21]Beloved, if our heart does not
condemn us, we have confidence toward
God. [22]And whatever we ask we receive

> Don't be so hardheaded about your prayer requests that you miss God's clues about *His* will in a situation. The deepest prayer of our hearts must always be, "Thy will be done."
>
> Claire Cloninger

from Him, because we keep His com-
mandments and do those things that are
pleasing in His sight. [23]And this is His
commandment: that we should believe on
the name of His Son Jesus Christ and love
one another, as He gave us[a] command-
ment.

The Spirit of Truth and the Spirit of Error

[24]Now he who keeps His command-
ments abides in Him, and He in him. And
by this we know that He abides in us, by
the Spirit whom He has given us.

CHAPTER 4

Beloved, do not believe every spirit, but
test the spirits, whether they are of God;
because many false prophets have gone
out into the world. [2]By this you know the
Spirit of God: Every spirit that confesses
that Jesus Christ has come in the flesh is of
God, [3]and every spirit that does not con-
fess that[a] Jesus Christ has come in the
flesh is not of God. And this is the *spirit*
of the Antichrist, which you have heard

3:14 [a]NU-Text omits *his brother.* 3:19 [a]NU-Text reads *we shall know.* 3:23 [a]M-Text omits *us.* 4:3 [a]NU-Text omits *that* and *Christ has come in the flesh.*

4:1–3 do not believe every spirit: Do not be gullible. **Test** the moral and spiritual implications of any new idea. Does it agree with Scripture? Will it make me more like Christ? **By this you know**: Sometimes one can recognize the work of Satan at a glance. Any idea is false if it denies the deity, humanity, or saving work of **Jesus Christ**. Anything less than full acceptance of, and obedience to, the divine-human Christ is following **the Antichrist**.

was coming, and is now already in the
world.
[4]You are of God, little children, and have
overcome them, because He who is in you
is greater than he who is in the world.
[5]They are of the world. Therefore they
speak *as* of the world, and the world hears
them. [6]We are of God. He who knows God
hears us; he who is not of God does not
hear us. By this we know the spirit of truth
and the spirit of error.

Knowing God Through Love

[7]Beloved, let us love one another, for
love is of God; and everyone who loves is
born of God and knows God. [8]He who
does not love does not know God, for God
is love. [9]In this the love of God was mani-
fested toward us, that God has sent His
only begotten Son into the world, that
we might live through Him. [10]In this is
love, not that we loved God, but that He
loved us and sent His Son *to be* the propiti-
ation for our sins. [11]Beloved, if God so
loved us, we also ought to love one an-
other.

Seeing God Through Love

[12]No one has seen God at any time. If we
love one another, God abides in us, and
His love has been perfected in us. [13]By this
we know that we abide in Him, and He in
us, because He has given us of His Spirit.
[14]And we have seen and testify that the
Father has sent the Son *as* Savior of the
world. [15]Whoever confesses that Jesus is
the Son of God, God abides in him, and he
in God. [16]And we have known and be-
lieved the love that God has for us. God is
love, and he who abides in love abides in
God, and God in him.

Show Your Love

Jerry and Jack Schreur

Grandparents cannot express their love too much, too often, or in too many ways to their grandchildren. We are not spoiling them when we give them constant reassurances of our love. On the contrary, we will find it easier to say no to them because they already know that we love them.

Creative grandparents make an unflagging commitment to finding new ways to say "I love you." We accept this biblical principle as our mandate: "My little children, let us not love in word or in tongue, but in deed and in truth." ✦

The Consummation of Love

[17]Love has been perfected among us
in this: that we may have boldness in the
day of judgment; because as He is, so
are we in this world. [18]There is no fear
in love; but perfect love casts out fear,
because fear involves torment. But he
who fears has not been made perfect in
love. [19]We love Him[a] because He first
loved us.

Obedience by Faith

[20]If someone says, "I love God," and
hates his brother, he is a liar; for he who
does not love his brother whom he has
seen, how can[a] he love God whom he has
not seen? [21]And this commandment we
have from Him: that he who loves God
must love his brother also.

4:19 [a]NU-Text omits *Him*. 4:20 [a]NU-Text reads *he cannot*.

4:20, 21 A sincere love for God will reveal itself in love for others. The Holy Spirit enables us to love the unlovable.

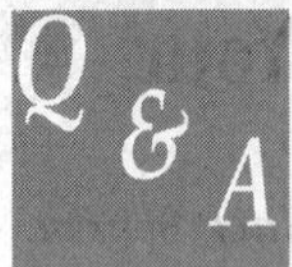

Can you tell whether Jesus is always in your life?

J. Vernon McGee

I think your primary problem is that you are trusting your feelings. One day you feel good, and another day you may feel bad. Frankly, I feel very good today, but I felt wretched yesterday. I was just down, that is all. We cannot trust our feelings, either when we are up or down. Our salvation rests upon what the Word of God says: "And this is the testimony: that God has given us eternal life, and this life is in His Son. He who has the Son has life; he who does not have the Son of God does not have life" (1 John 5:11, 12).

"He who has the Son has life." It is as simple as that. Do you have Christ? Are you trusting Him? If you are, then you are saved. It may have rained on your parade, but your salvation rests upon what the Word of God has to say—not upon your feelings. ✦

CHAPTER 5

Whoever believes that Jesus is the
Christ is born of God, and everyone who
loves Him who begot also loves him who
is begotten of Him. 2By this we know
that we love the children of God, when
we love God and keep His command-
ments. 3For this is the love of God, that we
keep His commandments. And His com-
mandments are not burdensome. 4For
whatever is born of God overcomes the
world. And this is the victory that has
overcome the world—our[a] faith. 5Who is
he who overcomes the world, but he
who believes that Jesus is the Son of
God?

The Certainty of God's Witness

6This is He who came by water and
blood—Jesus Christ; not only by water, but
by water and blood. And it is the Spirit
who bears witness, because the Spirit is
truth. 7For there are three that bear witness
in heaven: the Father, the Word, and the
Holy Spirit; and these three are one. 8And
there are three that bear witness on earth:[a]
the Spirit, the water, and the blood; and
these three agree as one.

9If we receive the witness of men, the
witness of God is greater; for this is the
witness of God which[a] He has testified of
His Son. 10He who believes in the Son of
God has the witness in himself; he who
does not believe God has made Him a liar,

5:4 [a]M-Text reads *your.* 5:8 [a]NU-Text and M-Text omit the words from *in heaven* (verse 7) through *on earth* (verse 8). Only four or five very late manuscripts contain these words in Greek. 5:9 [a]NU-Text reads *God, that.*

5:6 by water: Jesus' baptism showed He was God's Son and yet truly one of us. **blood**: His death. He died for us. The Holy **Spirit** bears witness to Jesus' divine sonship, true humanity, and atoning death.

5:7, 8 Most scholars agree that the words beginning with **in heaven** (v. 7) and continuing through **on earth** (v. 8) were not in the original manuscript.

because he has not believed the testimony
that God has given of His Son. [11]And this is
the testimony: that God has given us eter-
nal life, and this life is in His Son. [12]He who
has the Son has life; he who does not have
the Son of God does not have life. [13]These
things I have written to you who believe in
the name of the Son of God, that you may
know that you have eternal life,[a] and that
you may *continue to* believe in the name of
the Son of God.

Confidence and Compassion in Prayer

[14]Now this is the confidence that we
have in Him, that if we ask anything ac-
cording to His will, He hears us. [15]And if
we know that He hears us, whatever we
ask, we know that we have the petitions
that we have asked of Him.
[16]If anyone sees his brother sinning a sin
which does not *lead* to death, he will ask,
and He will give him life for those who
commit sin not *leading* to death. There is
sin *leading* to death. I do not say that he
should pray about that. [17]All unrighteous-
ness is sin, and there is sin not *leading* to
death.

Knowing the True—Rejecting the False

[18]We know that whoever is born of God
does not sin; but he who has been born of
God keeps himself,[a] and the wicked one
does not touch him.
[19]We know that we are of God, and the
whole world lies *under the sway of* the
wicked one.
[20]And we know that the Son of God has
come and has given us an understanding,
that we may know Him who is true; and
we are in Him who is true, in His Son Jesus
Christ. This is the true God and eternal life.
[21]Little children, keep yourselves from
idols. Amen.

5:13 [a]NU-Text omits the rest of this verse. 5:18 [a]NU-Text reads *him.*

5:14, 15 The fundamental requirement for answered prayer is that we ask according to His will. Of course, if we are abiding in Christ and living in holy accordance with His commands, we will not be inclined to request something that is out of God's will.

5:21 Here **idols** probably refers to teaching that is contrary to Scripture, particularly teaching that denies the full deity and humanity of Jesus. God can be known only through His Son (see v. 20).

THE JOY OF CHRISTIAN FELLOWSHIP

Leslie E. Moser, Ph.D.

The fellowship of Christians continues to be a thing of beauty as well as a necessity. Even critics of the organized church and of Christianity in general profess amazement at Christian fellowship. These critics do not understand how Christianity is not merely surviving, and they marvel over the way the church grows and thrives. They shake their heads in disbelief: "How can this be? Why doesn't Christianity crumble?" Indeed, today's enemies of the faith, though different from those of the early church, are more tenacious. The tools Satan uses to try to destroy the church of Christ are sharp and subtle, but still Christianity and its followers survive.

"No other fellowship can be found like that which grows out of love for Christ."

In fact, the church has become a haven for young and old, for people of every walk of life. People are flocking with great zeal to their churches, seeking a fellowship that cannot be found in country clubs, discos, gambling casinos, or social ventures developed by modern entrepreneurs. No other fellowship can be found like that which grows out of love for Christ and one another! In part, the renewal of churches everywhere can be credited to godly folk who seek companionship, fellowship, and social contact that do not conform to the world's patterns of sex, violence, drugs, and a general flaunting of the laws of God. Society cannot provide the wholesome social outlets found in Christian fellowship. ✦

✦2 John✦

This brief epistle is addressed to an unidentified woman who may have been the head of a household and who had Christian children. Some scholars, however, interpret John's reverential "elect lady" as a reference to the church—thus, his letter is addressed to all believers in the Lord Jesus Christ.

John cautioned his readers about receiving heretics into their homes and churches. His advice still holds true. Modern-day Christians should heed John's admonition and be alert to detect subtle digressions from the true gospel. Even though Christians are to exercise love and have fellowship with other believers, this love must discriminate. Genuine love does not include accepting false doctrine or having fellowship with false teachers. ✦

Greeting the Elect Lady

The Elder,

To the elect lady and her children,
whom I love in truth, and not only I, but
also all those who have known the truth,
2 because of the truth which abides in us
and will be with us forever:

3 Grace, mercy, *and* peace will be with
you[a] from God the Father and from the
Lord Jesus Christ, the Son of the Father, in
truth and love.

Walk in Christ's Commandments

4 I rejoiced greatly that I have found *some*
of your children walking in truth, as we re-
ceived commandment from the Father.
5 And now I plead with you, lady, not as
though I wrote a new commandment to
you, but that which we have had from the
beginning: that we love one another. 6 This
is love, that we walk according to His com-
mandments. This is the commandment,
that as you have heard from the beginning,
you should walk in it.

Beware of Antichrist Deceivers

7 For many deceivers have gone out into
the world who do not confess Jesus Christ
as coming in the flesh. This is a deceiver
and an antichrist. 8 Look to yourselves, that
we[a] do not lose those things we worked
for, but *that* we[b] may receive a full reward.
9 Whoever transgresses[a] and does not
abide in the doctrine of Christ does not
have God. He who abides in the doctrine
of Christ has both the Father and the Son.
10 If anyone comes to you and does not
bring this doctrine, do not receive him into

3 [a]NU-Text and M-Text read *us.* 8 [a]NU-Text reads *you.* [b]NU-Text reads *you.* 9 [a]NU-Text reads *goes ahead.*

---

4 "Walking in the truth" means living in obedience to the message of Christ.

7 Besides knowing and doing the truth, we must also be able to recognize destructive heresy. The central doctrine of the Christian faith is that **Jesus Christ** is the eternal Son of God who became human and died for our sins. Anyone who denies this doctrine is both a **deceiver** and **an antichrist**—the very opposite of what a Christian should be.

your house nor greet him; [11]for he who greets him shares in his evil deeds.

John's Farewell Greeting

[12]Having many things to write to you, I did not wish *to do so* with paper and ink; but I hope to come to you and speak face to face, that our joy may be full.

[13]The children of your elect sister greet you. Amen.

13 If "the elect lady" (v.1) refers to a church, then "your elect sister" would be another church.

✦3 John✦

3 John is the shortest book in the New Testament, but it is personal and vivid. As a leader of the church in and around Ephesus, John would have been responsible for the teaching ministry carried out by a number of itinerant preachers under his direction. This letter was written to Gaius, who was commended for his hospitality to John's messengers when they visited his area. The hospitality shown by Gaius toward missionaries of the early church provides a relevant example for believers seeking an opportunity to serve. The letter also addressed Diotrephes, who was chastised for his arrogance and obstruction of the truth.

The basic theme is similar to John's first two letters: Believers should continue in fellowship with God and their Christian brethren, and they should not allow false doctrines and teachers to enter their hearts or homes. ✦

Greeting to Gaius

The Elder,

To the beloved Gă'i·us, whom I love in truth:

[2]Beloved, I pray that you may prosper in
all things and be in health, just as your soul
prospers. [3]For I rejoiced greatly when
brethren came and testified of the truth
that is in you, just as you walk in the truth.
[4]I have no greater joy than to hear that my
children walk in truth.[a]

4 [a]NU-Text reads *the truth.* 5 [a]NU-Text adds *especially.*

> ***I pray that my friend may prosper in all things and be in health, just as his soul prospers.***
>
> *adapted from* 3 John 1:2

Gaius Commended for Generosity

[5]Beloved, you do faithfully whatever
you do for the brethren and[a] for strangers,
[6]who have borne witness of your love before the church. *If* you send them forward
on their journey in a manner worthy of
God, you will do well, [7]because they went

2 John provides a model for intercessory prayer on behalf of other believers.

5, 6 Gaius acted faithfully by supporting both the brethren in his local church and visiting strangers. These were Christians traveling from other towns, particularly those engaged in evangelistic outreach.

7, 8 These missionaries had gone out for the sake of Jesus' name, not for gain. They took nothing from the unconverted Gentiles to whom they preached lest they be accused of preaching for money as the pagan philosophers did.

Vital Vaccines

Dr. Sharon Sneed and Dr. David Sneed

Immunization programs have been highly successful in preventing many illnesses, especially children's diseases. However, many adults mistakenly think they no longer require immunization and go unprotected against several potentially serious illnesses. The Centers for Disease Control estimate that each year there are more than twenty-five thousand unnecessary deaths due to vaccine-preventable diseases. Recognizing our bodies as the temple of Christ (1 Cor. 3:16), we should take every practical step in keeping them healthy, including immunization.

Adults should be aware of their need to be immunized against seven diseases. These are tetanus, diphtheria, influenza, pneumococcal infection, hepatitis B, measles, and rubella.

Measles and rubella vaccines are primarily for young adult women in their childbearing years. Hepatitis B vaccine is important for certain health-care workers who are exposed to blood products. There is a definite need for all adults to receive immunizations against some or all of the remaining four diseases. ✦

forth for His name's sake, taking nothing
from the Gentiles. 8We therefore ought to
receive[a] such, that we may become fellow
workers for the truth.

Diotrephes and Demetrius

9I wrote to the church, but Dī·ot′-
re·phēs, who loves to have the preemi-
nence among them, does not receive us.
10Therefore, if I come, I will call to mind his
deeds which he does, prating against us
with malicious words. And not content
with that, he himself does not receive the
brethren, and forbids those who wish to,
putting *them* out of the church.
11Beloved, do not imitate what is evil,
but what is good. He who does good is of
God, but[a] he who does evil has not seen
God.
12De·mē′tri·us has a *good* testimony
from all, and from the truth itself. And we
also bear witness, and you know that our
testimony is true.

Farewell Greeting

13I had many things to write, but I do not
wish to write to you with pen and ink;
14but I hope to see you shortly, and we shall
speak face to face.

Peace to you. Our friends greet you. Greet the friends by name.

8 [a]NU-Text reads *support.*
11 [a]NU-Text and M-Text omit *but.*

✦Jude✦

Jude, the brother of James and half brother of Christ, minced no words in attacking the deceptive nature of false teachers and their destructive influence on the church. Anyone who rejects Christ's deity and lordship must be denied fellowship with the body of Christ.

When apostasy arises, we should fight for the faith; when required, each believer should be able to speak the truth with knowledge and authority. Mature Christians who are grounded in the Word must be prepared to rescue weaker brothers and sisters enticed by false doctrines.

Jude reminded false teachers of God's past dealings with unbelieving Israel and with Sodom and Gomorrah. In the face of such danger, Christians should not be caught off guard. Jesus is Lord now and forever. Therefore, He is to be followed both in doctrine and in deed. ✦

Greeting to the Called

Jude, a bondservant of Jesus Christ, and
brother of James,

To those who are called, sanctified[a] by
God the Father, and preserved in Jesus
Christ:

2Mercy, peace, and love be multiplied to
you.

Contend for the Faith

3Beloved, while I was very diligent to
write to you concerning our common sal-
vation, I found it necessary to write to you
exhorting you to contend earnestly for the
faith which was once for all delivered to
the saints. 4For certain men have crept in
unnoticed, who long ago were marked out
for this condemnation, ungodly men, who
turn the grace of our God into lewdness
and deny the only Lord God[a] and our Lord
Jesus Christ.

Old and New Apostates

5But I want to remind you, though you
once knew this, that the Lord, having
saved the people out of the land of Egypt,
afterward destroyed those who did not be-
lieve. 6And the angels who did not keep
their proper domain, but left their own
abode, He has reserved in everlasting
chains under darkness for the judgment of
the great day; 7as Sod'om and Go·mor'rah,
and the cities around them in a similar
manner to these, having given themselves
over to sexual immorality and gone after
strange flesh, are set forth as an example,
suffering the vengeance of eternal fire.
8Likewise also these dreamers defile the

1 [a]NU-Text reads *beloved.* 4 [a]NU-Text omits *God.*

1 Jude's spiritual relationship as a **bondservant of Jesus Christ** was more important to him than his physical relationship as a half brother of Jesus (Jude is called Judas in Mark 6:3). Jude's readers had been called by God to be His people, as are all believers. **sanctified**: Made holy, set apart for God's service. **preserved**: Enabled to live victoriously.

flesh, reject authority, and speak evil of
dignitaries. 9 Yet Michael the archangel, in
contending with the devil, when he dis-
puted about the body of Moses, dared not
bring against him a reviling accusation,
but said, "The Lord rebuke you!" 10 But
these speak evil of whatever they do not
know; and whatever they know naturally,
like brute beasts, in these things they cor-
rupt themselves. 11 Woe to them! For they
have gone in the way of Cain, have run
greedily in the error of Bā'laam for profit,
and perished in the rebellion of Kō'rah.

Apostates Depraved and Doomed

12 These are spots in your love feasts,
while they feast with you without fear,
serving *only* themselves. *They are* clouds
without water, carried about[a] by the
winds; late autumn trees without fruit,
twice dead, pulled up by the roots; 13 raging
waves of the sea, foaming up their own
shame; wandering stars for whom is re-
served the blackness of darkness forever.
14 Now Ē'noch, the seventh from Adam,
prophesied about these men also, saying,
"Behold, the Lord comes with ten thou-
sands of His saints, 15 to execute judgment
on all, to convict all who are ungodly
among them of all their ungodly deeds
which they have committed in an ungodly
way, and of all the harsh things which un-
godly sinners have spoken against Him."

Apostates Predicted

16 These are grumblers, complainers,
walking according to their own lusts; and
they mouth great swelling *words*, flattering
people to gain advantage. 17 But you,
beloved, remember the words which were
spoken before by the apostles of our Lord

> Prayer is meant to be a part of our lives, like breathing and thinking and talking.
> Gloria Gaither

Jesus Christ: 18 how they told you that there
would be mockers in the last time who
would walk according to their own un-
godly lusts. 19 These are sensual persons,
who cause divisions, not having the Spirit.

Maintain Your Life with God

20 But you, beloved, building yourselves
up on your most holy faith, praying in the
Holy Spirit, 21 keep yourselves in the love of
God, looking for the mercy of our Lord
Jesus Christ unto eternal life.
22 And on some have compassion, mak-
ing a distinction;[a] 23 but others save with
fear, pulling *them* out of the fire,[a] hating
even the garment defiled by the flesh.

Glory to God

24 Now to Him who is able to keep you[a]
from stumbling,
And to present *you* faultless
Before the presence of His glory with
exceeding joy,
25 To God our Savior,[a]
Who alone is wise,[b]
Be glory and majesty,
Dominion and power,[c]
Both now and forever.
Amen.

12 [a]NU-Text and M-Text read *along.* 22 [a]NU-Text reads *who are doubting* (or *making distinctions*). 23 [a]NU-Text adds *and on some have mercy with fear* and omits *with fear* in first clause. 24 [a]M-Text reads *them.* 25 [a]NU-Text reads *To the only God our Savior.* [b]NU-Text omits *Who . . . is wise* and adds *Through Jesus Christ our Lord.* [c]NU-Text adds *Before all time.*

12 love feasts: fellowship meals of early Christians. **clouds without water**: The false teachers promise spiritual refreshment but cannot give it.

14, 15 Many early Christians held **Enoch** in high regard. He had "walked with God" (Gen. 5:24). He represented the **seventh** generation **from Adam** (Gen. 5:3–23; 1 Chr. 1:1–3), the number seven symbolizing perfection.

23 We cannot allow fellow believers to falter in the faith, but in brotherly love we must confront them and snatch them back from the brink of disaster.

✦Revelation✦

Just as Genesis is the book of beginnings, Revelation is the book of consummation. Written by the apostle John to the churches in Asia Minor, Revelation is the only book in the New Testament that focuses primarily on prophetic events. The title "Revelation" is derived from the combination of two Greek words, *kalupto* meaning "veil," and *apo* meaning "from"—hence "to remove the veil" or "to reveal." John received the contents by a series of visions intended to reveal the character and program of God.

The church was facing hostility, and Christians suffered overt persecution during the latter half of the first century. John's effective ministry led the Roman authorities to exile him to the small, desolate island of Patmos in the Aegean Sea. In these circumstances, John wrote to the seven churches and described the contents of several visions he had received during his exile.

John was commissioned to record three things: "the things which [he had] seen"—the vision of the resurrected and glorified Christ (Rev. 1); "the things which are"—a message to the churches (Rev. 2; 3); and "the things which will take place after this"—a prophetic look at God's program (Rev. 4—21).

Because of its complex imagery and symbolism, Revelation is the most difficult book to interpret. However, advocates of all interpretative approaches to Revelation agree it was written to assure recipients of the ultimate victory of Christ over the forces of evil. They needed encouragement to persevere by standing firm in Christ in view of God's plan for the righteous and the wicked. The book was also intended to challenge complacent Christians to stop compromising with the world.

Every Christian who despairs at the evil of this world can take heart in knowing that one day Satan will be conquered, and Jesus Christ will reign with His church. ✦

CHAPTER 1

Introduction and Benediction

The Revelation of Jesus Christ, which
God gave Him to show His servants—
things which must shortly take place. And
He sent and signified *it* by His angel to His
servant John, 2who bore witness to the
word of God, and to the testimony of Jesus
Christ, to all things that he saw. 3Blessed *is*
he who reads and those who hear the
words of this prophecy, and keep those

1:1 The purpose of this book is to show believers what they should expect to happen in the future, specifically regarding the actions of **Jesus Christ**.

1:3 the time is near: a call to obedience and preparation, not a reference to a specific time. All events in Revelation are seen from the perspective of the Lord and cannot be assigned to a human frame of reference.

things which are written in it; for the time *is* near.

Greeting the Seven Churches

4John, to the seven churches which are in Asia:

Grace to you and peace from Him who is and who was and who is to come, and from the seven Spirits who are before His throne, 5and from Jesus Christ, the faithful witness, the firstborn from the dead, and the ruler over the kings of the earth.

To Him who loved us and washed[a] us from our sins in His own blood, 6and has

1:5 aNU-Text reads *loves us and freed;* M-Text reads *loves us and washed.*

1:4 John addressed the real problems of **seven churches** in the Roman province of Asia Minor (see v. 11), yet these problems afflict churches in every age.

Look to the Lord

John Gilmore

John got a state-sponsored trip to Patmos courtesy of the Roman emperor Domitian, but the small island was no pleasure resort. Patmos was containment without comfort.

On Patmos, John saw the persecution of Christians as the high tide of evil, but he was not drowned by its undertow. He looked to the Lord, and Christ appeared to him, giving him a graphic analysis of history's ups and downs. What John wrote was not an escapist dream, a vision of despair, or a bitter anticipation of the future. It was a tapestry of victory, a symphony of praise to the triumphs of the Lamb that was slain but is alive forevermore.

John did not write to unload his frustrations or release bottled-up outrage against persecution. The Apocalypse does not spill personal spite and seething anger. His visions were not even a manifesto against Rome, as such, but an overview of the hidden war being waged from earlier to later times. Revelation was a verbal canvas where cosmic figures clashed.

"What John wrote was a tapestry of victory, a symphony of praise."

John saw God in control of history. Evil was defeated; the devil was destroyed. John's message was not that brighter days were ahead, but that dark days were already bright, for Christ was in charge. Christ gave John comfort, confidence, and cheerfulness. The church would win, for Christ had defeated death.

We sometimes may feel exiled or abandoned. We can feel rundown and may lack energy for "seizing the day." Whenever we feel depressed by circumstances or world events, we can look forward with John to Christ's Second Coming and His glorious reign over the earth. ✦

made us kings[a] and priests to His God and
Father, to Him *be* glory and dominion for-
ever and ever. Amen.
[7]Behold, He is coming with clouds, and
every eye will see Him, even they who
pierced Him. And all the tribes of the earth
will mourn because of Him. Even so, Amen.
[8]"I am the Alpha and the Omega, *the* Be-
ginning and *the* End,"[a] says the Lord,[b]
"who is and who was and who is to come,
the Almighty."

Vision of the Son of Man

[9]I, John, both[a] your brother and com-
panion in the tribulation and kingdom
and patience of Jesus Christ, was on the
island that is called Pat'mos for the word
of God and for the testimony of
Jesus Christ. [10]I was in the Spirit on the
Lord's Day, and I heard behind me a
loud voice, as of a trumpet, [11]saying, "I
am the Alpha and the Omega, the First and
the Last,"[a] and, "What you see, write in a
book and send *it* to the seven churches
which are in Asia:[b] to Eph'e·sus, to
Smyrna, to Per'ga·mos, to Thȳ·a·tī'ra, to
Sar'dis, to Philadelphia, and to Lā·o-
di·cē'a."

1:6 [a]NU-Text and M-Text read *a kingdom.*
1:8 [a]NU-Text and M-Text omit *the Beginning and the End.* [b]NU-Text and M-Text add *God.* 1:9 [a]NU-Text and M-Text omit *both.* 1:11 [a]NU-Text and M-Text omit *I am* through third *and.* [b]NU-Text and M-Text omit *which are in Asia.* 1:17 [a]NU-Text and M-Text omit *to me.* 1:19 [a]NU-Text and M-Text read *Therefore, write.* 1:20 [a]NU-Text and M-Text omit *which you saw.*

[12]Then I turned to see the voice that
spoke with me. And having turned I saw
seven golden lampstands, [13]and in the
midst of the seven lampstands *One* like the
Son of Man, clothed with a garment down
to the feet and girded about the chest with
a golden band. [14]His head and hair *were*
white like wool, as white as snow, and His
eyes like a flame of fire; [15]His feet *were*
like fine brass, as if refined in a furnace,
and His voice as the sound of many
waters; [16]He had in His right hand seven
stars, out of His mouth went a sharp two-
edged sword, and His countenance *was*
like the sun shining in its strength. [17]And
when I saw Him, I fell at His feet as dead.
But He laid His right hand on me, saying
to me,[a] "Do not be afraid; I am the First and
the Last. [18]I *am* He who lives, and was
dead, and behold, I am alive forevermore.
Amen. And I have the keys of Hā'dēs and
of Death. [19]Write[a] the things which you
have seen, and the things which are, and
the things which will take place after this.
[20]The mystery of the seven stars which you
saw in My right hand, and the seven
golden lampstands: The seven stars are
the angels of the seven churches, and the
seven lampstands which you saw[a] are the
seven churches.

CHAPTER 2

The Loveless Church

"To the angel of the church of Eph'e·sus
write,

1:12 These **lampstands** represent the churches, bearing the light of God's truth (see note on v. 20).

1:13–16 The first of many descriptions of Christ in the Revelation (see 2:1, 8, 18; 3:1, 7, 14). **the Son of Man**: Jesus came to earth as a man, yet He is the eternal, sovereign Lord of the universe (Dan. 7:13, 14). His **garment** speaks of kingly dignity; the **golden band** and **white . . . hair** reflect authority; the flaming **eyes** reveal that nothing is hidden from Him. His **feet** like **brass** depict strength, and His **voice** is as impressive as the thunder of the sea. His **right hand** holds the destiny of the church, and His word is a **sword** that brings judgment on the disobedient. John sees His **countenance** shine with divine glory.

1:18 Jesus is Lord of both the realm of the soul (Hades) and the realm of the physical body (Death).

1:20 The **stars** and **angels** are figures for the church protected in Christ's **right hand.** Some think that the **angels** are the pastors of the churches (see 2:1, 8, 12, 18).

WHITE HAIR

John Gilmore

When Christ appeared with white hair to John on Patmos (Rev. 1:14), He was not wearing a white wig; the ageless Christ appeared aged. He who pre-existed the universe came to John as the Bible's Ancient of Days.

Christ was eternity appearing in time. White hair came close to communicating the message of His dignity due to duration. It was symbolic of wisdom, of long life, and of seasoned experience. White hair was a traditional emblem of an elder. Besides the blessing of adornment, it held the message of age. Age alone and the years that back it cannot spare us from missteps and misfortune. God, however, carries and delivers us through old age (Is. 46:4).

Solomon compared old age to the white almond tree blossom (Eccl. 12:5). White hair does not indicate that we are finished, but like the almond tree, white blossoms indicate that fruit is near. And fruit does not come singly on an almond tree! In latter years, look for a harvest of goods—white symbolizes production, not conclusion!

"Christ was eternity appearing in time."

White hair was seen on the Ancient of Days (Dan. 7:9) in addition to the risen Christ by John on Patmos (Rev. 1:14). White hair marks the longevity, strength, wisdom, and durability of those worthy to wear that color atop their heads. ✦

'These things says He who holds the
seven stars in His right hand, who walks in
the midst of the seven golden lampstands:
2"I know your works, your labor, your pa-
tience, and that you cannot bear those who
are evil. And you have tested those who
say they are apostles and are not, and have
found them liars; 3and you have perse-
vered and have patience, and have labored
for My name's sake and have not become
weary. 4Nevertheless I have *this* against
you, that you have left your first love. 5Re-
member therefore from where you have
fallen; repent and do the first works, or
else I will come to you quickly and remove
your lampstand from its place—unless you
repent. 6But this you have, that you hate the
deeds of the Nic·ō·lā'i·tans, which I also
hate.

7"He who has an ear, let him hear what
the Spirit says to the churches. To him who
overcomes I will give to eat from the tree of

2:4 left your first love: See Mark 12:29–31. Although the Ephesians hated evil, they no longer gave God first place in their lives. Nor did they reflect His love to others as they should.

2:6 the Nicolaitans: Some of the "evil" people in v. 2.

life, which is in the midst of the Paradise of God." '

The Persecuted Church

[8]"And to the angel of the church in Smyrna write,

'These things says the First and the Last, who was dead, and came to life: [9]"I know your works, tribulation, and poverty (but you are rich); and *I know* the blasphemy of those who say they are Jews and are not, but *are* a synagogue of Satan. [10]Do not fear any of those things which you are about to suffer. Indeed, the devil is about to throw *some* of you into prison, that you may be tested, and you will have tribulation ten days. Be faithful until death, and I will give you the crown of life.

[11]"He who has an ear, let him hear what the Spirit says to the churches. He who overcomes shall not be hurt by the second death." '

The Compromising Church

[12]"And to the angel of the church in Per'ga·mos write,

'These things says He who has the sharp two-edged sword: [13]"I know your works, and where you dwell, where Satan's throne *is*. And you hold fast to My name, and did not deny My faith even in the days in which An'ti·pas *was* My faithful martyr, who was killed among you, where Satan dwells. [14]But I have a few things against you, because you have there those who hold the doctrine of Bā'laam, who taught Bā'lak to put a stumbling block before the children of Israel, to eat things sacrificed to idols, and to commit sexual immorality. [15]Thus you also have those who hold the doctrine of the Nic·ō·lā'i·tans, which thing I hate.[a] [16]Repent, or else I will come to you quickly and will fight against them with the sword of My mouth.

[17]"He who has an ear, let him hear what the Spirit says to the churches. To him who overcomes I will give some of the hidden manna to eat. And I will give him a white stone, and on the stone a new name written which no one knows except him who receives *it*." '

The Corrupt Church

[18]"And to the angel of the church in Thy̅·a·tī'ra write,

'These things says the Son of God, who has eyes like a flame of fire, and His feet like fine brass: [19]"I know your works, love, service, faith,[a] and your patience; and *as* for your works, the last *are* more than the first. [20]Nevertheless I have a few things against you, because you allow[a] that woman[b] Jez'e·bel, who calls herself a prophetess, to teach and seduce[c] My servants to commit sexual immorality and eat things sacrificed to idols. [21]And I gave her time to repent of her sexual immorality, and she did not repent.[a] [22]Indeed I will cast her into a sickbed, and those who commit adultery with her into great tribulation, unless they repent of their[a] deeds. [23]I will kill her children with death, and all the

2:15 [a]NU-Text and M-Text read *likewise* for *which thing I hate.* 2:19 [a]NU-Text and M-Text read *faith, service.* 2:20 [a]NU-Text and M-Text read *I have against you that you tolerate.* [b]M-Text reads *your wife Jezebel.* [c]NU-Text and M-Text read *and teaches and seduces.*
2:21 [a]NU-Text and M-Text read *time to repent, and she does not want to repent of her sexual immorality.*
2:22 [a]NU-Text and M-Text read *her.*

2:9 Although the church at Smyrna was economically poor, John identified them as spiritually rich because of their faith.

2:11 the second death: eternal separation from God.

2:17 Three gifts symbolic of heavenly reward: (1) **hidden manna**: The manna Moses gave Israel in the wilderness brought physical blessing. Christ gives the manna of eternal life. (2) **white stone**: A widely used symbol for victory or special privilege, here probably signifying admission to eternal reward. (3) **new name**: The new and glorified existence of the age to come. **no one knows**: Each Christian has a unique relationship to Christ and a unique part to play in God's eternal kingdom.

churches shall know that I am He who
searches the minds and hearts. And I will
give to each one of you according to your
works.
24"Now to you I say, and[a] to the rest in
Thȳ·a·tī′ra, as many as do not have
this doctrine, who have not known the
depths of Satan, as they say, I will[b] put
on you no other burden. 25But hold fast
what you have till I come. 26And he who
overcomes, and keeps My works until the
end, to him I will give power over the na-
tions—

27 *'He shall rule them with a rod of iron;*
They shall be dashed to pieces like
the potter's vessels'[a]—

as I also have received from My Father;
28and I will give him the morning star.
29"He who has an ear, let him hear what
the Spirit says to the churches." '

CHAPTER 3

The Dead Church

"And to the angel of the church in
Sar′dis write,
'These things says He who has the
seven Spirits of God and the seven stars: "I
know your works, that you have a name
that you are alive, but you are dead. 2Be
watchful, and strengthen the things which
remain, that are ready to die, for I have not
found your works perfect before God.[a]
3Remember therefore how you have re-
ceived and heard; hold fast and repent.
Therefore if you will not watch, I will come
upon you as a thief, and you will not know
what hour I will come upon you. 4You[a]
have a few names even in Sar′dis who
have not defiled their garments; and they
shall walk with Me in white, for they are
worthy. 5He who overcomes shall be
clothed in white garments, and I will not
blot out his name from the Book of Life;
but I will confess his name before My
Father and before His angels.
6"He who has an ear, let him hear what
the Spirit says to the churches." '

The Faithful Church

7"And to the angel of the church in
Philadelphia write,
'These things says He who is holy,
He who is true, *"He who has the key of Da-*
vid, He who opens and no one shuts,
and shuts and no one opens":[a] 8"I know
your works. See, I have set before you an
open door, and no one can shut it;[a] for
you have a little strength, have kept
My word, and have not denied My name.
9Indeed I will make *those* of the synagogue
of Satan, who say they are Jews and are
not, but lie—indeed I will make them
come and worship before your feet, and to
know that I have loved you. 10Because
you have kept My command to persevere,
I also will keep you from the hour of trial
which shall come upon the whole world,
to test those who dwell on the earth.
11Behold,[a] I am coming quickly! Hold
fast what you have, that no one may
take your crown. 12He who overcomes, I
will make him a pillar in the temple of My
God, and he shall go out no more. I will
write on him the name of My God and the
name of the city of My God, the New Jeru-
salem, which comes down out of heaven
from My God. And *I will write on him* My
new name.
13"He who has an ear, let him hear what
the Spirit says to the churches." '

2:24 [a]NU-Text and M-Text omit *and.* [b]NU-Text and M-Text omit *will.* 2:27 [a]Psalm 2:9 3:2 [a]NU-Text and M-Text read *My God.* 3:4 [a]NU-Text and M-Text read *Nevertheless you have a few names in Sardis.* 3:7 [a]Isaiah 22:22 3:8 [a]NU-Text and M-Text read *which no one can shut.* 3:11 [a]NU-Text and M-Text omit *Behold.*

3:5 This verse emphatically promises that once a person has become a true believer, nothing can erase that individual's name from the **Book of Life**, God's record of the redeemed.

The Lukewarm Church

14"And to the angel of the church of the
Lā·o·di·cē′ans[a] write,
'These things says the Amen, the Faith-
ful and True Witness, the Beginning of the
creation of God: 15"I know your works, that
you are neither cold nor hot. I could wish
you were cold or hot. 16So then, because
you are lukewarm, and neither cold nor
hot,[a] I will vomit you out of My mouth.
17Because you say, 'I am rich, have become
wealthy, and have need of nothing'—and
do not know that you are wretched, miser-
able, poor, blind, and naked— 18I counsel
you to buy from Me gold refined in the fire,
that you may be rich; and white garments,
that you may be clothed, *that* the shame of
your nakedness may not be revealed; and
anoint your eyes with eye salve, that you
may see. 19As many as I love, I rebuke and
chasten. Therefore be zealous and repent.
20Behold, I stand at the door and knock. If
anyone hears My voice and opens the
door, I will come in to him and dine with
him, and he with Me. 21To him who over-
comes I will grant to sit with Me on My
throne, as I also overcame and sat down
with My Father on His throne.
22"He who has an ear, let him hear what
the Spirit says to the churches." ' "

CHAPTER 4

The Throne Room of Heaven

After these things I looked, and behold,
a door *standing* open in heaven. And the
first voice which I heard *was* like a trumpet
speaking with me, saying, "Come up here,
and I will show you things which must
take place after this."
2Immediately I was in the Spirit; and be-
hold, a throne set in heaven, and *One* sat
on the throne. 3And He who sat there was[a]
like a jasper and a sardius stone in appear-
ance; and *there was* a rainbow around the
throne, in appearance like an emerald.
4Around the throne *were* twenty-four
thrones, and on the thrones I saw twenty-
four elders sitting, clothed in white robes;
and they had crowns[a] of gold on their
heads. 5And from the throne proceeded
lightnings, thunderings, and voices.[a]
Seven lamps of fire *were* burning before
the throne, which are the[b] seven Spirits of
God.
6Before the throne *there* was[a] a sea of
glass, like crystal. And in the midst of the
throne, and around the throne, *were* four
living creatures full of eyes in front and in
back. 7The first living creature *was* like a
lion, the second living creature like a calf,
the third living creature had a face like a
man, and the fourth living creature *was*

3:14 [a]NU-Text and M-Text read *in Laodicea.*
3:16 [a]NU-Text and M-Text read *hot nor cold.*
4:3 [a]M-Text omits *And He who sat there was* (which makes the description in verse 3 modify the throne rather than God). 4:4 [a]NU-Text and M-Text read *robes, with crowns.* 4:5 [a]NU-Text and M-Text read *voices, and thunderings.* [b]M-Text omits *the.*
4:6 [a]NU-Text and M-Text add *something like.*

3:14 the Amen: Christ, the God of truth and the ultimate Authority.

3:15, 16 It is often easier to reach the **cold** unbeliever than to stir the **lukewarm** Christian who has a form of religion but no real commitment or power. **vomit you out**: Christ will judge the lukewarm if they do not repent. The mineral springs of Laodicea produced hot water for therapy, cold water for refreshment, and lukewarm water that would make a person sick.

4:1 the first voice: The Lord Jesus Christ summoned John so that He might see, from a heavenly perspective, the events that must transpire.

4:4 Many interpreters believe that the **twenty-four elders** represent the church or its representatives—God's redeemed people enjoying their ultimate fellowship with God in heaven. The numbers may symbolize the 12 tribes of Israel in the OT and the 12 apostles of Jesus in the NT. Others believe that they are exalted angels who continually praise God. Because they offer incense and present the prayers of the saints, they have been compared to the 24 priestly divisions under David (see 1 Chr. 24:1–19 and note). Both interpretations emphasize the majesty and dominion of God (see v. 10).

like a flying eagle. 8*The* four living creatures, each having six wings, were full of eyes around and within. And they do not rest day or night, saying:

"Holy, holy, holy,[a]
Lord God Almighty,
Who was and is and is to come!"

9Whenever the living creatures give glory and honor and thanks to Him who sits on the throne, who lives forever and ever, 10the twenty-four elders fall down before Him who sits on the throne and worship Him who lives forever and ever, and cast their crowns before the throne, saying:

11 "You are worthy, O Lord,[a]
To receive glory and honor and
power;
For You created all things,
And by Your will they exist[b] and were
created."

CHAPTER 5

The Lamb Takes the Scroll

And I saw in the right *hand* of Him who sat on the throne a scroll written inside and on the back, sealed with seven seals. 2Then I saw a strong angel proclaiming with a loud voice, "Who is worthy to open the scroll and to loose its seals?" 3And no one in heaven or on the earth or under the earth was able to open the scroll, or to look at it.

4So I wept much, because no one was found worthy to open and read[a] the scroll, or to look at it. 5But one of the elders said to me, "Do not weep. Behold, the Lion of the tribe of Judah, the Root of David, has prevailed to open the scroll and to loose[a] its seven seals."

6And I looked, and behold,[a] in the midst of the throne and of the four living creatures, and in the midst of the elders, stood a Lamb as though it had been slain, having seven horns and seven eyes, which are the seven Spirits of God sent out into all the earth. 7Then He came and took the scroll out of the right hand of Him who sat on the throne.

Worthy Is the Lamb

8Now when He had taken the scroll, the four living creatures and the twenty-four elders fell down before the Lamb, each having a harp, and golden bowls full of incense, which are the prayers of the saints. 9And they sang a new song, saying:

"You are worthy to take the scroll,
And to open its seals;
For You were slain,
And have redeemed us to God by
Your blood
Out of every tribe and tongue and
people and nation,
10 And have made us[a] kings[b] and priests
to our God;
And we[c] shall reign on the earth."

11Then I looked, and I heard the voice of many angels around the throne, the living creatures, and the elders; and the number of them was ten thousand times ten thou-

4:8 [a]M-Text has *holy* nine times. 4:11 [a]NU-Text and M-Text read *our Lord and God.* [b]NU-Text and M-Text read *existed.* 5:4 [a]NU-Text and M-Text omit *and read.* 5:5 [a]NU-Text and M-Text omit *to loose.* 5:6 [a]NU-Text and M-Text read *I saw in the midst . . . a Lamb standing.* 5:10 [a]NU-Text and M-Text read *them.* [b]NU-Text reads *a kingdom.* [c]NU-Text and M-Text read *they.*

5:5 Christ is the greatest member, or **Lion**, of the **tribe of Judah**. He is also the **Root of David** spoken of in prophecy (Is. 11:1, 10).

5:6 The **seven horns** show that Christ has all power and the **seven eyes** that He has all knowledge.

5:8 The **bowls** of **incense** represent the **prayers of the saints**, sinners who have been redeemed.

sand, and thousands of thousands, 12say-
ing with a loud voice:

"Worthy is the Lamb who was slain
To receive power and riches and
wisdom,
And strength and honor and glory
and blessing!"

13And every creature which is in heaven
and on the earth and under the earth and
such as are in the sea, and all that are in
them, I heard saying:

"Blessing and honor and glory and
power
Be to Him who sits on the throne,
And to the Lamb, forever and ever!"[a]

14Then the four living creatures said,
"Amen!" And the twenty-four[a] elders fell
down and worshiped Him who lives for-
ever and ever.[b]

CHAPTER 6

First Seal: The Conqueror

Now I saw when the Lamb opened one
of the seals;[a] and I heard one of the four liv-
ing creatures saying with a voice like thun-
der, "Come and see." 2And I looked, and
behold, a white horse. He who sat on it had
a bow; and a crown was given to him, and
he went out conquering and to conquer.

Second Seal: Conflict on Earth

3When He opened the second seal, I
heard the second living creature saying,
"Come and see."[a] 4Another horse, fiery
red, went out. And it was granted to the
one who sat on it to take peace from the
earth, and that *people* should kill one an-
other; and there was given to him a great
sword.

Third Seal: Scarcity on Earth

5When He opened the third seal, I heard
the third living creature say, "Come and
see." So I looked, and behold, a black
horse, and he who sat on it had a pair of
scales in his hand. 6And I heard a voice in
the midst of the four living creatures say-
ing, "A quart[b] of wheat for a denarius,[a] and
three quarts of barley for a denarius; and
do not harm the oil and the wine."

Fourth Seal: Widespread Death on Earth

7When He opened the fourth seal, I
heard the voice of the fourth living crea-
ture saying, "Come and see." 8So I looked,
and behold, a pale horse. And the name of
him who sat on it was Death, and Hā′dēs
followed with him. And power was given
to them over a fourth of the earth, to kill
with sword, with hunger, with death, and
by the beasts of the earth.

Fifth Seal: The Cry of the Martyrs

9When He opened the fifth seal, I saw
under the altar the souls of those who had
been slain for the word of God and for the
testimony which they held. 10And they
cried with a loud voice, saying, "How

5:13 [a]M-Text adds *Amen.* 5:14 [a]NU-Text and M-Text omit *twenty-four.* [b]NU-Text and M-Text omit *Him who lives forever and ever.* 6:1 [a]NU-Text and M-Text read *seven seals.* 6:3 [a]NU-Text and M-Text omit *and see.* 6:6 [a]Greek *choinix;* that is, approximately one quart [b]This was approximately one day's wage for a worker.

6:1–8 The first four **seals** reveal God's judgment on the world. The **white horse** (v. 2) represents the rise of Antichrist (see note on 13:1–3). The **red horse** (v. 4) symbolizes an increase in wars; the **black horse** (v. 5), the ensuing famine. The **pale horse** (v. 8) represents the death caused by these three scourges.

6:6 Wheat and **barley** will be scarce and thus expensive, but there will still be **oil** and **wine**. The famine will be severe, but not total. The judgment described in vv. 5, 6 is preliminary, not final.

6:9, 10 under the altar: Safe in God's presence. **until You judge**: The saints do not cry for revenge. They ask for judgment on the wicked so that God's righteousness will be displayed and His kingdom established.

long, O Lord, holy and true, until You judge and avenge our blood on those who dwell on the earth?" 11Then a white robe was given to each of them; and it was said to them that they should rest a little while longer, until both *the number of* their fellow servants and their brethren, who would be killed as they *were,* was completed.

Sixth Seal: Cosmic Disturbances

12I looked when He opened the sixth seal, and behold,[a] there was a great earthquake; and the sun became black as sackcloth of hair, and the moon[b] became like blood. 13And the stars of heaven fell to the earth, as a fig tree drops its late figs when it is shaken by a mighty wind. 14Then the sky receded as a scroll when it is rolled up, and every mountain and island was moved out of its place. 15And the kings of the earth, the great men, the rich men, the commanders,[a] the mighty men, every slave and every free man, hid themselves in the caves and in the rocks of the mountains, 16and said to the mountains and rocks, "Fall on us and hide us from the face of Him who sits on the throne and from the wrath of the Lamb! 17For the great day of His wrath has come, and who is able to stand?"

CHAPTER 7

The Sealed of Israel

After these things I saw four angels standing at the four corners of the earth, holding the four winds of the earth, that the wind should not blow on the earth, on the sea, or on any tree. 2Then I saw another angel ascending from the east, having the seal of the living God. And he cried with a loud voice to the four angels to whom it was granted to harm the earth and the sea, 3saying, "Do not harm the earth, the sea, or the trees till we have sealed the servants of our God on their foreheads." 4And I heard the number of those who were sealed. One hundred *and* forty-four thousand of all the tribes of the children of Israel *were* sealed:

5 of the tribe of Judah twelve thousand
were sealed;[a]
of the tribe of Reuben twelve
thousand *were* sealed;
of the tribe of Gad twelve thousand
were sealed;
6 of the tribe of Ash'er twelve thousand
were sealed;
of the tribe of Naph'ta·lī twelve
thousand *were* sealed;
of the tribe of Ma·nas'seh twelve
thousand *were* sealed;
7 of the tribe of Sim'ē·on twelve
thousand *were* sealed;
of the tribe of Levi twelve thousand
were sealed;
of the tribe of Is'sa·char twelve
thousand *were* sealed;
8 of the tribe of Zeb'ū·lun twelve
thousand *were* sealed;
of the tribe of Joseph twelve thousand
were sealed;
of the tribe of Benjamin twelve
thousand *were* sealed.

A Multitude from the Great Tribulation

9After these things I looked, and behold, a great multitude which no one could number, of all nations, tribes, peoples, and tongues, standing before the throne and before the Lamb, clothed with white robes, with palm branches in their hands, 10and

6:12 [a]NU-Text and M-Text omit *behold.* [b]NU-Text and M-Text read *the whole moon.* 6:15 [a]NU-Text and M-Text read *the commanders, the rich men.*
7:5 [a]In NU-Text and M-Text *were sealed* is stated only in verses 5a and 8c; the words are understood in the remainder of the passage.

7:3, 4 Seals signify possession and ownership. Believers are **sealed** by the Holy Spirit to proclaim that they belong to God, as opposed to those who bear the mark of the beast (13:17).

7:9 White robes symbolize holiness; **palm branches** represent victory.

crying out with a loud voice, saying, "Salvation *belongs* to our God who sits on the throne, and to the Lamb!" 11All the angels stood around the throne and the elders and the four living creatures, and fell on their faces before the throne and worshiped God, 12saying:

"Amen! Blessing and glory and
wisdom,
Thanksgiving and honor and power
and might,
Be to our God forever and ever.
Amen."

13Then one of the elders answered, saying to me, "Who are these arrayed in white robes, and where did they come from?"

14And I said to him, "Sir,[a] you know."

So he said to me, "These are the ones who come out of the great tribulation, and washed their robes and made them white in the blood of the Lamb. 15Therefore they are before the throne of God, and serve Him day and night in His temple. And He who sits on the throne will dwell among them. 16They shall neither hunger anymore nor thirst anymore; the sun shall not strike them, nor any heat; 17for the Lamb who is in the midst of the throne will shepherd them and lead them to living fountains of waters.[a] And God will wipe away every tear from their eyes."

CHAPTER 8

Seventh Seal: Prelude to the Seven Trumpets

When He opened the seventh seal, there was silence in heaven for about half an hour. 2And I saw the seven angels who stand before God, and to them were given seven trumpets. 3Then another angel, having a golden censer, came and stood at the altar. He was given much incense, that he should offer *it* with the prayers of all the saints upon the golden altar which was before the throne. 4And the smoke of the incense, with the prayers of the saints, ascended before God from the angel's hand. 5Then the angel took the censer, filled it with fire from the altar, and threw *it* to the earth. And there were noises, thunderings, lightnings, and an earthquake.

6So the seven angels who had the seven trumpets prepared themselves to sound.

First Trumpet: Vegetation Struck

7The first angel sounded: And hail and fire followed, mingled with blood, and they were thrown to the earth.[a] And a third of the trees were burned up, and all green grass was burned up.

Second Trumpet: The Seas Struck

8Then the second angel sounded: And *something* like a great mountain burning with fire was thrown into the sea, and a third of the sea became blood. 9And a third of the living creatures in the sea died, and a third of the ships were destroyed.

Third Trumpet: The Waters Struck

10Then the third angel sounded: And a great star fell from heaven, burning like a torch, and it fell on a third of the rivers and on the springs of water. 11The name of the star is Wormwood. A third of the waters became wormwood, and many men died from the water, because it was made bitter.

Fourth Trumpet: The Heavens Struck

12Then the fourth angel sounded: And a third of the sun was struck, a third of the

7:14 [a]NU-Text and M-Text read *My lord.* 7:17 [a]NU-Text and M-Text read *to fountains of the waters of life.* 8:7 [a]NU-Text and M-Text add *and a third of the earth was burned up.*

8:1 the phrase "about half an hour" does not indicate a specific amount of time but it does signify a brief period.

8:6–13 The disasters following each of the first four **trumpets** recall the plagues that God sent on the Egyptians. A **third** (vv. 8–12): God restrained these judgments so that people would have opportunity to repent (see also 6:8).

moon, and a third of the stars, so that a
third of them were darkened. A third of the
day did not shine, and likewise the night.
13And I looked, and I heard an angel[a]
flying through the midst of heaven, saying
with a loud voice, "Woe, woe, woe to the
inhabitants of the earth, because of the re-
maining blasts of the trumpet of the three
angels who are about to sound!"

CHAPTER 9

Fifth Trumpet: The Locusts from the Bottomless Pit

Then the fifth angel sounded: And I saw
a star fallen from heaven to the earth. To
him was given the key to the bottomless
pit. 2And he opened the bottomless pit,
and smoke arose out of the pit like the
smoke of a great furnace. So the sun and
the air were darkened because of the
smoke of the pit. 3Then out of the smoke lo-
custs came upon the earth. And to them
was given power, as the scorpions of the
earth have power. 4They were commanded
not to harm the grass of the earth, or any
green thing, or any tree, but only those
men who do not have the seal of God on
their foreheads. 5And they were not given
authority to kill them, but to torment them
for five months. Their torment *was* like the
torment of a scorpion when it strikes a
man. 6In those days men will seek death
and will not find it; they will desire to die,
and death will flee from them.
7The shape of the locusts was like horses
prepared for battle. On their heads were
crowns of something like gold, and their
faces *were* like the faces of men. 8They had
hair like women's hair, and their teeth
were like lions' *teeth*. 9And they had breast-
plates like breastplates of iron, and the
sound of their wings *was* like the sound of
chariots with many horses running into
battle. 10They had tails like scorpions, and
there were stings in their tails. Their power
was to hurt men five months. 11And they
had as king over them the angel of the bot-
tomless pit, whose name in Hebrew *is*
A·bad'don, but in Greek he has the name
A·pol'lyon.
12One woe is past. Behold, still two more
woes are coming after these things.

Sixth Trumpet: The Angels from the Euphrates

13Then the sixth angel sounded: And I
heard a voice from the four horns of the
golden altar which is before God, 14saying
to the sixth angel who had the trumpet,
"Release the four angels who are bound at
the great river Eū·phrā'tēs." 15So the four
angels, who had been prepared for the
hour and day and month and year, were
released to kill a third of mankind. 16Now
the number of the army of the horsemen
was two hundred million; I heard the num-
ber of them. 17And thus I saw the horses in

8:13 [a]NU-Text and M-Text read *eagle*.

9:1–12 This horde of **locusts** (v. 3) is reminiscent of the plague of locusts on Egypt (Ex. 10:12–15) and of Joel's prediction of a plague of locusts before the day of God's judgment (Joel 1:1–20). But the locusts of Revelation are demonic forces, released from their place of confinement in the **bottomless pit** (see 20:1, 2).

9:1 star: Perhaps an angel or perhaps Satan himself. **key to the . . . pit**: God determines how far evil is allowed to go (see vv. 4, 5).

9:3–6 Real **locusts** destroy plant life, but these demonic beings torture the ungodly who do not have God's **seal** (see 7:3). The sting of a **scorpion** is painful, but seldom fatal. Thus these demons **torment**, but do not kill. The Lord allows this onslaught not to destroy sinners but to prompt them to repent. In Palestine the **five** dry **months** of the year were the season for locusts, but a normal attack lasted only a few days. These demonic hordes will ravage rebellious humanity for a much longer time than the usual locust plague. **seek death**: This was Jeremiah's phrase to predict the suffering of Jerusalem under siege (Jer. 8:3).

9:11, 12 Again, these locusts are not physical insects; they are demonic forces being led like an army by a fallen **angel**.

the vision: those who sat on them had
breastplates of fiery red, hyacinth blue,
and sulfur yellow; and the heads of the
horses *were* like the heads of lions; and out
of their mouths came fire, smoke, and
brimstone. 18By these three *plagues* a third
of mankind was killed—by the fire and the
smoke and the brimstone which came out
of their mouths. 19For their power[a] is in
their mouth and in their tails; for their tails
are like serpents, having heads; and with
them they do harm.

20But the rest of mankind, who were not
killed by these plagues, did not repent of
the works of their hands, that they should
not worship demons, and idols of gold, sil-
ver, brass, stone, and wood, which can nei-
ther see nor hear nor walk. 21And they did
not repent of their murders or their sorcer-
ies[a] or their sexual immorality or their
thefts.

CHAPTER 10

The Mighty Angel with the Little Book

I saw still another mighty angel coming
down from heaven, clothed with a cloud.
And a rainbow *was* on his head, his face
was like the sun, and his feet like pillars of
fire. 2He had a little book open in his hand.
And he set his right foot on the sea and *his*
left *foot* on the land, 3and cried with a loud
voice, as *when* a lion roars. When he cried
out, seven thunders uttered their voices.
4Now when the seven thunders uttered
their voices,[a] I was about to write; but I
heard a voice from heaven saying to me,[b]
"Seal up the things which the seven thun-
ders uttered, and do not write them."

5The angel whom I saw standing on the
sea and on the land raised up his hand[a] to
heaven 6and swore by Him who lives for-
ever and ever, who created heaven and
the things that are in it, the earth and the
things that are in it, and the sea and
the things that are in it, that there should
be delay no longer, 7but in the days of the
sounding of the seventh angel, when he is
about to sound, the mystery of God would
be finished, as He declared to His servants
the prophets.

John Eats the Little Book

8Then the voice which I heard from
heaven spoke to me again and said, "Go,
take the little book which is open in the
hand of the angel who stands on the sea
and on the earth."

9So I went to the angel and said to him,
"Give me the little book."

And he said to me, "Take and eat it; and
it will make your stomach bitter, but it will
be as sweet as honey in your mouth."

10Then I took the little book out of the
angel's hand and ate it, and it was as sweet
as honey in my mouth. But when I had
eaten it, my stomach became bitter. 11And
he[a] said to me, "You must prophesy again
about many peoples, nations, tongues, and
kings."

CHAPTER 11

The Two Witnesses

Then I was given a reed like a measur-
ing rod. And the angel stood,[a] saying,

9:19 [a]NU-Text and M-Text read *the power of the horses.* 9:21 [a]NU-Text and M-Text read *drugs.* 10:4 [a]NU-Text and M-Text read *sounded.* [b]NU-Text and M-Text omit *to me.* 10:5 [a]NU-Text and M-Text read *right hand.* 10:11 [a]NU-Text and M-Text read *they.* 11:1 [a]NU-Text and M-Text omit *And the angel stood.*

9:20, 21 did not repent: Punishment does not always bring repentance or reformation, although it should. **works of their hands**: Every action described here either is forbidden in the Ten Commandments (Ex. 20:2–17) or is a capital offense according to the laws found in the Book of the Covenant (Ex. 20:22—23:33).

10:9, 10 A renewal of John's prophetic call. He eats the **little book**, representing God's word, so that he can proclaim it (see Ezek. 3:1–3). **sweet . . . bitter**: John finds God's word a joy to receive but painful to deliver. It is a message of judgment on unbelievers and therefore a message that may bring persecution to the prophet.

"Rise and measure the temple of God, the altar, and those who worship there. [2]But leave out the court which is outside the temple, and do not measure it, for it has been given to the Gentiles. And they will tread the holy city underfoot *for* forty-two months. [3]And I will give *power* to my two witnesses, and they will prophesy one thousand two hundred and sixty days, clothed in sackcloth."

[4]These are the two olive trees and the two lampstands standing before the God[a] of the earth. [5]And if anyone wants to harm them, fire proceeds from their mouth and devours their enemies. And if anyone wants to harm them, he must be killed in this manner. [6]These have power to shut heaven, so that no rain falls in the days of their prophecy; and they have power over waters to turn them to blood, and to strike the earth with all plagues, as often as they desire.

The Witnesses Killed

[7]When they finish their testimony, the beast that ascends out of the bottomless pit will make war against them, overcome them, and kill them. [8]And their dead bodies *will lie* in the street of the great city which spiritually is called Sod′om and Egypt, where also our[a] Lord was crucified. [9]Then *those* from the peoples, tribes, tongues, and nations will see their dead bodies three-and-a-half days, and not allow[a] their dead bodies to be put into graves. [10]And those who dwell on the earth will rejoice over them, make merry, and send gifts to one another, because these two prophets tormented those who dwell on the earth.

The Witnesses Resurrected

[11]Now after the three-and-a-half days the breath of life from God entered them, and they stood on their feet, and great fear fell on those who saw them. [12]And they[a] heard a loud voice from heaven saying to them, "Come up here." And they ascended to heaven in a cloud, and their enemies saw them. [13]In the same hour there was a great earthquake, and a tenth of the city fell. In the earthquake seven thousand people were killed, and the rest were afraid and gave glory to the God of heaven.

[14]The second woe is past. Behold, the third woe is coming quickly.

Seventh Trumpet: The Kingdom Proclaimed

[15]Then the seventh angel sounded: And there were loud voices in heaven, saying, "The kingdoms[a] of this world have become *the kingdoms* of our Lord and of His Christ, and He shall reign forever and ever!" [16]And the twenty-four elders who sat before God on their thrones fell on their faces and worshiped God, [17]saying:

"We give You thanks, O Lord God
Almighty,
The One who is and who was and
who is to come,[a]

11:4 [a]NU-Text and M-Text read *Lord.* 11:8 [a]NU-Text and M-Text read *their.* 11:9 [a]NU-Text and M-Text read *nations see . . . and will not allow.* 11:12 [a]M-Text reads *I.* 11:15 [a]NU-Text and M-Text read *kingdom . . . has become.* 11:17 [a]NU-Text and M-Text omit *and who is to come.*

11:2 Forty-two months is a three-and-a-half-year period equivalent to the 1,260 days of 12:6 and the "time and times and half a time" of 12:14 (see Dan. 12:7). It follows a similar period identified in v. 3. The two periods total seven years, corresponding to the two halves of the final "week" of Dan. 9:27.

11:4 Jewish law required two witnesses to verify a fact (see Deut. 19:15); thus, the number **two** shows that their witness is true. In Zech. 4:11–14 the **olive trees** represent the king and priest.

11:8 Sodom and Egypt: Figurative language for Jerusalem where Jesus **was crucified.** Sodom represents wickedness and Egypt represents oppression.

11:9 To leave a dead body unburied is considered a tremendous insult.

Because You have taken Your great
power and reigned.
18 The nations were angry, and Your
wrath has come,
And the time of the dead, that they
should be judged,
And that You should reward Your
servants the prophets and the saints,
And those who fear Your name, small
and great,
And should destroy those who
destroy the earth."

19 Then the temple of God was opened in
heaven, and the ark of His covenant[a] was
seen in His temple. And there were light-
nings, noises, thunderings, an earthquake,
and great hail.

CHAPTER 12

The Woman, the Child, and the Dragon

Now a great sign appeared in heaven: a
woman clothed with the sun, with the
moon under her feet, and on her head a
garland of twelve stars. 2 Then being with
child, she cried out in labor and in pain to
give birth.
3 And another sign appeared in heaven:
behold, a great, fiery red dragon having
seven heads and ten horns, and seven di-
adems on his heads. 4 His tail drew a third
of the stars of heaven and threw them to
the earth. And the dragon stood before the
woman who was ready to give birth, to de-
vour her Child as soon as it was born. 5 She
bore a male Child who was to rule all na-
tions with a rod of iron. And her Child was
caught up to God and His throne. 6 Then
the woman fled into the wilderness, where
she has a place prepared by God, that they
should feed her there one thousand two
hundred and sixty days.

Satan Thrown Out of Heaven

7 And war broke out in heaven: Michael
and his angels fought with the dragon; and
the dragon and his angels fought, 8 but they
did not prevail, nor was a place found for
them[a] in heaven any longer. 9 So the great
dragon was cast out, that serpent of old,
called the Devil and Satan, who deceives
the whole world; he was cast to the earth,
and his angels were cast out with him.
10 Then I heard a loud voice saying in
heaven, "Now salvation, and strength, and
the kingdom of our God, and the power of
His Christ have come, for the accuser of
our brethren, who accused them before our
God day and night, has been cast down.
11 And they overcame him by the blood of
the Lamb and by the word of their testi-
mony, and they did not love their lives to
the death. 12 Therefore rejoice, O heavens,
and you who dwell in them! Woe to the in-
habitants of the earth and the sea! For the
devil has come down to you, having great
wrath, because he knows that he has a
short time."

The Woman Persecuted

13 Now when the dragon saw that he had
been cast to the earth, he persecuted the
woman who gave birth to the male *Child.*
14 But the woman was given two wings of a
great eagle, that she might fly into the
wilderness to her place, where she is nour-
ished for a time and times and half a time,
from the presence of the serpent. 15 So the
serpent spewed water out of his mouth
like a flood after the woman, that he might
cause her to be carried away by the flood.
16 But the earth helped the woman, and the
earth opened its mouth and swallowed up
the flood which the dragon had spewed

11:19 [a]M-Text reads *the covenant of the Lord.*
12:8 [a]M-Text reads *him.*

12:1–6 The **woman** represents the faithful in Israel. The **Child** is Jesus.
12:3 red dragon: Satan
12:11 The key to overcoming Satan is to accept the gift of salvation through the blood of Christ and be a faithful witness to the grace of God, even unto **death**.

out of his mouth. 17And the dragon was enraged with the woman, and he went to make war with the rest of her offspring, who keep the commandments of God and have the testimony of Jesus Christ.[a]

CHAPTER 13

The Beast from the Sea

Then I[a] stood on the sand of the sea. And I saw a beast rising up out of the sea, having seven heads and ten horns,[b] and on his horns ten crowns, and on his heads a blasphemous name. 2Now the beast which I saw was like a leopard, his feet were like *the feet of* a bear, and his mouth like the mouth of a lion. The dragon gave him his power, his throne, and great authority. 3And *I saw* one of his heads as if it had been mortally wounded, and his deadly wound was healed. And all the world marveled and followed the beast. 4So they worshiped the dragon who gave authority to the beast; and they worshiped the beast, saying, "Who *is* like the beast? Who is able to make war with him?"

5And he was given a mouth speaking great things and blasphemies, and he was given authority to continue[a] for forty-two months. 6Then he opened his mouth in blasphemy against God, to blaspheme His name, His tabernacle, and those who dwell in heaven. 7It was granted to him to make war with the saints and to overcome them. And authority was given him over every tribe,[a] tongue, and nation. 8All who dwell on the earth will worship him, whose names have not been written in the Book of Life of the Lamb slain from the foundation of the world.

9If anyone has an ear, let him hear. 10He who leads into captivity shall go into captivity; he who kills with the sword must be killed with the sword. Here is the patience and the faith of the saints.

The Beast from the Earth

11Then I saw another beast coming up out of the earth, and he had two horns like a lamb and spoke like a dragon. 12And he exercises all the authority of the first beast in his presence, and causes the earth and those who dwell in it to worship the first beast, whose deadly wound was healed. 13He performs great signs, so that he even makes fire come down from heaven on the earth in the sight of men. 14And he deceives those[a] who dwell on the earth by those signs which he was granted to do in the sight of the beast, telling those who dwell on the earth to make an image to the beast who was wounded by the sword and lived. 15He was granted *power* to give breath to the image of the beast, that the image of the beast should both speak and cause as many as would not worship the image of the beast to be killed. 16He causes all, both small and great, rich and poor, free and slave, to receive a mark on their right hand or on their foreheads, 17and that no one may buy or sell except one who has

12:17 [a]NU-Text and M-Text omit *Christ.*
13:1 [a]NU-Text reads *he.* [b]NU-Text and M-Text read *ten horns and seven heads.* 13:5 [a]M-Text reads *make war.* 13:7 [a]NU-Text and M-Text add *and people.*
13:14 [a]M-Text reads *my own people.*

13:1–3 The **beast** from the **sea** is best understood as the Antichrist, Satan's counterpart to the true Christ. The **heads**, **horns**, and **crowns** show his claim to full authority and power (see 12:3; 17:3). In Dan. 7:2–8 the **leopard**, **bear**, and **lion** represented successive world empires; here they symbolize the Antichrist's political **power**, which, like all human empires, has roots in its predecessors. Just as Christ shares God's throne, so the Antichrist shares Satan's **throne**. **mortally wounded . . . healed**: Perhaps literal, to imitate Christ's resurrection; perhaps figurative of the seeming death and later revival of Rome (see 17:9; Dan. 7:7).

13:11 Whereas the first beast (v. 1) represents evil in the form of political and social power, this second **beast** is concerned with religious power, a false prophet who attempts to imitate the ministry of Christ.

the mark or[a] the name of the beast, or the
number of his name.
18Here is wisdom. Let him who has un-
derstanding calculate the number of the
beast, for it is the number of a man: His
number *is* 666.

CHAPTER 14

The Lamb and the 144,000

Then I looked, and behold, a[a] Lamb
standing on Mount Zion, and with Him
one hundred *and* forty-four thousand, hav-
ing[b] His Father's name written on their
foreheads. 2And I heard a voice from
heaven, like the voice of many waters, and
like the voice of loud thunder. And I heard
the sound of harpists playing their harps.
3They sang as it were a new song before the
throne, before the four living creatures,
and the elders; and no one could learn that
song except the hundred *and* forty-four
thousand who were redeemed from the
earth. 4These are the ones who were not de-
filed with women, for they are virgins.
These are the ones who follow the Lamb
wherever He goes. These were redeemed[a]
from *among* men, *being* firstfruits to God
and to the Lamb. 5And in their mouth was
found no deceit,[a] for they are without fault
before the throne of God.[b]

The Proclamations of Three Angels

6Then I saw another angel flying in the
midst of heaven, having the everlasting
gospel to preach to those who dwell on the
earth—to every nation, tribe, tongue, and
people— 7saying with a loud voice, "Fear
God and give glory to Him, for the hour of
His judgment has come; and worship Him
who made heaven and earth, the sea and
springs of water."
8And another angel followed, saying,
"Babylon[a] is fallen, is fallen, that great
city, because she has made all nations
drink of the wine of the wrath of her forni-
cation."
9Then a third angel followed them, say-
ing with a loud voice, "If anyone worships
the beast and his image, and receives *his*
mark on his forehead or on his hand, 10he
himself shall also drink of the wine of the
wrath of God, which is poured out full
strength into the cup of His indignation.
He shall be tormented with fire and brim-
stone in the presence of the holy angels
and in the presence of the Lamb. 11And the
smoke of their torment ascends forever
and ever; and they have no rest day or
night, who worship the beast and his im-
age, and whoever receives the mark of his
name."
12Here is the patience of the saints; here
are those[a] who keep the commandments of
God and the faith of Jesus.
13Then I heard a voice from heaven say-
ing to me,[a] "Write: 'Blessed *are* the dead
who die in the Lord from now on.' "
"Yes," says the Spirit, "that they may
rest from their labors, and their works fol-
low them."

Reaping the Earth's Harvest

14Then I looked, and behold, a white
cloud, and on the cloud sat *One* like the
Son of Man, having on His head a golden
crown, and in His hand a sharp sickle.

13:17 [a]NU-Text and M-Text omit *or.* 14:1 [a]NU-Text and M-Text read *the.* [b]NU-Text and M-Text add *His name and.* 14:4 [a]M-Text adds *by Jesus.* 14:5 [a]NU-Text and M-Text read *falsehood.* [b]NU-Text and M-Text omit *before the throne of God.* 14:8 [a]NU-Text reads *Babylon the great is fallen,* is fallen, which has made; M-Text reads *Babylon the great is fallen. She has made.* 14:12 [a]NU-Text and M-Text omit *here are those.* 14:13 [a]NU-Text and M-Text omit *to me.*

14:4 The term "virgins" should be understood here in a spiritual sense, meaning they have kept themselves pure from idolatry.

14:14–20 Two visions of the end times: the first, under the figure of a grain harvest (vv. 14–16), probably depicts the gathering of the righteous; it is the **Son of Man** coming for His own. The second, described as a grape harvest (vv. 17–20), refers to the terrible judgment of the wicked.

15And another angel came out of the tem-
ple, crying with a loud voice to Him who
sat on the cloud, "Thrust in Your sickle and
reap, for the time has come for You[a] to
reap, for the harvest of the earth is ripe."
16So He who sat on the cloud thrust in His
sickle on the earth, and the earth was
reaped.

Reaping the Grapes of Wrath

17Then another angel came out of the
temple which is in heaven, he also having
a sharp sickle.
18And another angel came out from the
altar, who had power over fire, and he
cried with a loud cry to him who had the
sharp sickle, saying, "Thrust in your sharp
sickle and gather the clusters of the vine of
the earth, for her grapes are fully ripe."
19So the angel thrust his sickle into the
earth and gathered the vine of the earth,
and threw *it* into the great winepress of the
wrath of God. 20And the winepress was
trampled outside the city, and blood came
out of the winepress, up to the horses' bri-
dles, for one thousand six hundred fur-
longs.

CHAPTER 15

Prelude to the Bowl Judgments

Then I saw another sign in heaven, great
and marvelous: seven angels having the
seven last plagues, for in them the wrath of
God is complete.
2And I saw *something* like a sea of glass
mingled with fire, and those who have the
victory over the beast, over his image and
over his mark[a] *and* over the number of his
name, standing on the sea of glass, having
harps of God. 3They sing the song of Mo-
ses, the servant of God, and the song of the
Lamb, saying:

"Great and marvelous *are* Your works,
Lord God Almighty!
Just and true *are* Your ways,
O King of the saints![a]
4 Who shall not fear You, O Lord, and
glorify Your name?
For *You* alone *are* holy.
For all nations shall come and
worship before You,
For Your judgments have been
manifested."

5After these things I looked, and be-
hold,[a] the temple of the tabernacle of the
testimony in heaven was opened. 6And out
of the temple came the seven angels hav-
ing the seven plagues, clothed in pure
bright linen, and having their chests
girded with golden bands. 7Then one of the
four living creatures gave to the seven an-
gels seven golden bowls full of the wrath
of God who lives forever and ever. 8The
temple was filled with smoke from the
glory of God and from His power, and no
one was able to enter the temple till the
seven plagues of the seven angels were
completed.

CHAPTER 16

Then I heard a loud voice from the tem-
ple saying to the seven angels, "Go and
pour out the bowls[a] of the wrath of God on
the earth."

14:15 [a]NU-Text and M-Text omit *for You.* 15:2 [a]NU-Text and M-Text omit *over his mark.* 15:3 [a]NU-Text and M-Text read *nations.* 15:5 [a]NU-Text and M-Text omit *behold.* 16:1 [a]NU-Text and M-Text read *seven bowls.*

15:3 song of Moses . . . of the Lamb: Just as Israel praised God for victory over Pharaoh at the Red Sea (see Ex. 15:1–18), so the saints praise God for their much greater victory over the Antichrist (see v. 2).

15:5, 6 The **tabernacle** was built by Moses as a dwelling place for God. It contained the ark of the Testimony (or covenant) which held the tablets on which were inscribed the Ten Commandments. The symbolism suggests that God Himself is judging those who have violated His law. **clothed in . . . linen**: Like the priests who served God.

First Bowl: Loathsome Sores

2So the first went and poured out his
bowl upon the earth, and a foul and loathsome sore came upon the men who had the mark of the beast and those who worshiped his image.

Second Bowl: The Sea Turns to Blood

3Then the second angel poured out his
bowl on the sea, and it became blood as of a dead *man;* and every living creature in the sea died.

Third Bowl: The Waters Turn to Blood

4Then the third angel poured out his
bowl on the rivers and springs of water,
and they became blood. 5And I heard the
angel of the waters saying:

"You are righteous, O Lord,[a]
The One who is and who was and
who is to be,[b]
Because You have judged these
things.
6 For they have shed the blood of saints
and prophets,
And You have given them blood to
drink.
For[a] it is their just due."

7And I heard another from[a] the altar
saying, "Even so, Lord God Almighty, true and righteous *are* Your judgments."

Fourth Bowl: Men Are Scorched

8Then the fourth angel poured out his
bowl on the sun, and power was given to
him to scorch men with fire. 9And men
were scorched with great heat, and they blasphemed the name of God who has power over these plagues; and they did not repent and give Him glory.

Fifth Bowl: Darkness and Pain

10Then the fifth angel poured out his
bowl on the throne of the beast, and his kingdom became full of darkness; and they gnawed their tongues because of the
pain. 11They blasphemed the God of
heaven because of their pains and their sores, and did not repent of their deeds.

Sixth Bowl: Euphrates Dried Up

12Then the sixth angel poured out his
bowl on the great river Eū·phrā'tēs, and its water was dried up, so that the way of the kings from the east might be prepared.
13And I saw three unclean spirits like frogs
coming out of the mouth of the dragon, out of the mouth of the beast, and out of the
mouth of the false prophet. 14For they are
spirits of demons, performing signs, *which* go out to the kings of the earth and[a] of the whole world, to gather them to the battle of that great day of God Almighty.
15"Behold, I am coming as a thief.
Blessed *is* he who watches, and keeps his garments, lest he walk naked and they see his shame."
16And they gathered them together to
the place called in Hebrew, Ar·ma·ged'-don.[a]

Seventh Bowl: The Earth Utterly Shaken

17Then the seventh angel poured out his
bowl into the air, and a loud voice came out of the temple of heaven, from the
throne, saying, "It is done!" 18And there
were noises and thunderings and lightnings; and there was a great earthquake,

16:5 [a]NU-Text and M-Text omit *O Lord.* [b]NU-Text and M-Text read *who was, the Holy One.* 16:6 [a]NU-Text and M-Text omit *For.* 16:7 [a]NU-Text and M-Text omit *another from.* 16:14 [a]NU-Text and M-Text omit *of the earth and.* 16:16 [a]M-Text reads *Megiddo.*

16:2 Those who follow the **beast** are stricken with a physical disease, similar to the sixth plague on Egypt (Ex. 9:9–11).

16:3, 4 every living creature: This final series of plagues describes the full force of God's judgment during the Tribulation. In 8:9 only one-third of the sea creatures died. And unlike the Egyptian plague, every source of fresh water on earth is affected.

such a mighty and great earthquake as had not occurred since men were on the earth. 19 Now the great city was divided into three parts, and the cities of the nations fell. And great Babylon was remembered before God, to give her the cup of the wine of the fierceness of His wrath. 20 Then every island fled away, and the mountains were not found. 21 And great hail from heaven fell upon men, *each hailstone* about the weight of a talent. Men blasphemed God because of the plague of the hail, since that plague was exceedingly great.

CHAPTER 17

The Scarlet Woman and the Scarlet Beast

Then one of the seven angels who had the seven bowls came and talked with me, saying to me,[a] "Come, I will show you the judgment of the great harlot who sits on many waters, 2 with whom the kings of the earth committed fornication, and the inhabitants of the earth were made drunk with the wine of her fornication."

3 So he carried me away in the Spirit into the wilderness. And I saw a woman sitting on a scarlet beast *which was* full of names of blasphemy, having seven heads and ten horns. 4 The woman was arrayed in purple and scarlet, and adorned with gold and precious stones and pearls, having in her hand a golden cup full of abominations and the filthiness of her fornication.[a] 5 And on her forehead a name *was* written:

MYSTERY,
BABYLON THE GREAT,
THE MOTHER OF HARLOTS AND
OF THE ABOMINATIONS OF THE
EARTH.

6 I saw the woman, drunk with the blood of the saints and with the blood of the martyrs of Jesus. And when I saw her, I marveled with great amazement.

The Meaning of the Woman and the Beast

7 But the angel said to me, "Why did you marvel? I will tell you the mystery of the woman and of the beast that carries her, which has the seven heads and the ten horns. 8 The beast that you saw was, and is not, and will ascend out of the bottomless pit and go to perdition. And those who dwell on the earth will marvel, whose names are not written in the Book of Life from the foundation of the world, when they see the beast that was, and is not, and yet is.[a]

9 "Here *is* the mind which has wisdom: The seven heads are seven mountains on which the woman sits. 10 There are also seven kings. Five have fallen, one is, *and* the other has not yet come. And when he comes, he must continue a short time. 11 The beast that was, and is not, is himself also the eighth, and is of the seven, and is going to perdition.

12 "The ten horns which you saw are ten

17:1 [a]NU-Text and M-Text omit *to me.*
17:4 [a]M-Text reads *the filthiness of the fornication of the earth.* 17:8 [a]NU-Text and M-Text read *and shall be present.*

17:1–6 The great harlot, identified with **Babylon** (v. 5), is a powerful and wealthy system of false religion. Since the days of Nimrod (see Gen. 10:8–10 and note on 1 Chr. 1:10) and the tower of Babel in Shinar (see Gen. 11:2–9), Babylon has been synonymous with idolatry as well as militarism. False religion, furthermore, has often allied itself with government throughout history (v. 2). Chapter 17 thus uses the figure of Babylon to depict the religious aspect of mankind's final attempt at self-government, and ch. 18 portrays its political aspect. **sits on many waters**: See v. 15. **sitting on a scarlet beast**: This **woman**, the great harlot, is empowered by the beast, the Antichrist. **names of blasphemy**: The beast claims to be God. **seven heads and ten horns**: See 12:3; 13:1. The **saints** and **martyrs** (witnesses) of Jesus are the victims of the system's power, as they were under Rome during the first centuries of the church.

kings who have received no kingdom as
yet, but they receive authority for one hour
as kings with the beast. [13]These are of one
mind, and they will give their power and
authority to the beast. [14]These will make
war with the Lamb, and the Lamb will
overcome them, for He is Lord of lords and
King of kings; and those *who are* with Him
are called, chosen, and faithful."
[15]Then he said to me, "The waters which
you saw, where the harlot sits, are peoples,
multitudes, nations, and tongues. [16]And
the ten horns which you saw on[a] the beast,
these will hate the harlot, make her deso-
late and naked, eat her flesh and burn her
with fire. [17]For God has put it into their
hearts to fulfill His purpose, to be of one
mind, and to give their kingdom to the
beast, until the words of God are fulfilled.
[18]And the woman whom you saw is that
great city which reigns over the kings of
the earth."

CHAPTER 18

The Fall of Babylon the Great

After these things I saw another angel
coming down from heaven, having great
authority, and the earth was illuminated
with his glory. [2]And he cried mightily[a]
with a loud voice, saying, "Babylon the
great is fallen, is fallen, and has become a
dwelling place of demons, a prison for
every foul spirit, and a cage for every un-
clean and hated bird! [3]For all the nations
have drunk of the wine of the wrath of her
fornication, the kings of the earth have
committed fornication with her, and the
merchants of the earth have become rich
through the abundance of her luxury."
[4]And I heard another voice from heaven

> Let nothing disturb you, let nothing frighten you: everything passes away except God; God alone is sufficient.
> St. Theresa

saying, "Come out of her, my people, lest
you share in her sins, and lest you receive
of her plagues. [5]For her sins have reached[a]
to heaven, and God has remembered her
iniquities. [6]Render to her just as she ren-
dered to you,[a] and repay her double ac-
cording to her works; in the cup which she
has mixed, mix double for her. [7]In the mea-
sure that she glorified herself and lived
luxuriously, in the same measure give her
torment and sorrow; for she says in her
heart, 'I sit *as* queen, and am no widow,
and will not see sorrow.' [8]Therefore her
plagues will come in one day—death and
mourning and famine. And she will be ut-
terly burned with fire, for strong *is* the
Lord God who judges[a] her.

The World Mourns Babylon's Fall

[9]"The kings of the earth who committed
fornication and lived luxuriously with her
will weep and lament for her, when they
see the smoke of her burning, [10]standing at
a distance for fear of her torment, saying,
'Alas, alas, that great city Babylon, that
mighty city! For in one hour your judg-
ment has come.'
[11]"And the merchants of the earth will
weep and mourn over her, for no one buys
their merchandise anymore: [12]merchandise
of gold and silver, precious stones and
pearls, fine linen and purple, silk and scar-
let, every kind of citron wood, every kind
of object of ivory, every kind of object of
most precious wood, bronze, iron, and
marble; [13]and cinnamon and incense, fra-
grant oil and frankincense, wine and oil,

17:16 [a]NU-Text and M-Text read *saw, and the beast.*
18:2 [a]NU-Text and M-Text omit *mightily.*
18:5 [a]NU-Text and M-Text read *have been heaped up.*
18:6 [a]NU-Text and M-Text omit *to you.*
18:8 [a]NU-Text and M-Text read *has judged.*

18:2 place of demons: The destruction will be complete, leaving a desert where only evil lurks. In the OT a similar prophecy was made against the literal Babylon in Chaldea (see Is. 13:19–22).

fine flour and wheat, cattle and sheep,
horses and chariots, and bodies and souls
of men. 14The fruit that your soul longed
for has gone from you, and all the things
which are rich and splendid have gone
from you,[a] and you shall find them no
more at all. 15The merchants of these
things, who became rich by her, will
stand at a distance for fear of her torment,
weeping and wailing, 16and saying,
'Alas, alas, that great city that was clothed
in fine linen, purple, and scarlet, and
adorned with gold and precious stones
and pearls! 17For in one hour such great
riches came to nothing.' Every shipmaster,
all who travel by ship, sailors, and as many
as trade on the sea, stood at a distance
18and cried out when they saw the smoke
of her burning, saying, 'What *is* like this
great city?'

19"They threw dust on their heads and
cried out, weeping and wailing, and say-
ing, 'Alas, alas, that great city, in which all
who had ships on the sea became rich by
her wealth! For in one hour she is made
desolate.'

20"Rejoice over her, O heaven, and *you*
holy apostles[a] and prophets, for God has
avenged you on her!"

Finality of Babylon's Fall

21Then a mighty angel took up a stone
like a great millstone and threw *it* into the
sea, saying, "Thus with violence the great
city Babylon shall be thrown down, and
shall not be found anymore. 22The sound of
harpists, musicians, flutists, and trum-
peters shall not be heard in you anymore.
No craftsman of any craft shall be found in
you anymore, and the sound of a millstone
shall not be heard in you anymore. 23The
light of a lamp shall not shine in you any-
more, and the voice of bridegroom and
bride shall not be heard in you anymore.
For your merchants were the great men of
the earth, for by your sorcery all the na-
tions were deceived. 24And in her was
found the blood of prophets and saints,
and of all who were slain on the earth."

CHAPTER 19

Heaven Exults over Babylon

After these things I heard[a] a loud voice
of a great multitude in heaven, saying, "Al-
leluia! Salvation and glory and honor and
power *belong* to the Lord[b] our God! 2For
true and righteous *are* His judgments, be-
cause He has judged the great harlot who
corrupted the earth with her fornication;
and He has avenged on her the blood of
His servants *shed* by her." 3Again they said,
"Alleluia! Her smoke rises up forever and
ever!" 4And the twenty-four elders and the
four living creatures fell down and wor-
shiped God who sat on the throne, saying,
"Amen! Alleluia!" 5Then a voice came from
the throne, saying, "Praise our God, all you
His servants and those who fear Him,
both[a] small and great!"

6And I heard, as it were, the voice of a
great multitude, as the sound of many wa-
ters and as the sound of mighty thunder-
ings, saying, "Alleluia! For the[a] Lord God
Omnipotent reigns! 7Let us be glad and re-
joice and give Him glory, for the marriage
of the Lamb has come, and His wife has

18:14 [a]NU-Text and M-Text read *been lost to you.* 18:20 [a]NU-Text and M-Text read *saints and apostles.* 19:1 [a]NU-Text and M-Text add *something like.* [b]NU-Text and M-Text omit *the Lord.* 19:5 [a]NU-Text and M-Text omit *both.* 19:6 [a]NU-Text and M-Text read *our.*

18:22–24 a lamp shall not shine . . . anymore (v. 23): When sin has run its course at the end of time, the loss is everything that we value most: music, art, the familiar sounds of home (v. 22), **light**, love, and marriage (v. 23). "Sin, when it is full-grown, brings forth death" (James 1:15).

19:1–6 The word "Alleluia" ("praise the Lord") occurs four times in this passage but appears nowhere else in the NT.

19:7 His wife: the church.

made herself ready.” 8And to her it was
granted to be arrayed in fine linen, clean
and bright, for the fine linen is the righ-
teous acts of the saints.
9Then he said to me, “Write: ‘Blessed *are*
those who are called to the marriage sup-
per of the Lamb!’ ” And he said to me,
“These are the true sayings of God.” 10And
I fell at his feet to worship him. But he said
to me, “See *that you do* not *do that!* I am
your fellow servant, and of your brethren
who have the testimony of Jesus. Worship
God! For the testimony of Jesus is the spirit
of prophecy.”

Christ on a White Horse

11Now I saw heaven opened, and be-
hold, a white horse. And He who sat on
him *was* called Faithful and True, and in
righteousness He judges and makes war.
12His eyes *were* like a flame of fire, and on
His head *were* many crowns. He had[a] a
name written that no one knew except
Himself. 13He *was* clothed with a robe
dipped in blood, and His name is called
The Word of God. 14And the armies in
heaven, clothed in fine linen, white and
clean,[a] followed Him on white horses.
15Now out of His mouth goes a sharp[a]
sword, that with it He should strike the na-
tions. And He Himself will rule them with
a rod of iron. He Himself treads the wine-
press of the fierceness and wrath of
Almighty God. 16And He has on *His* robe
and on His thigh a name written:

KING OF KINGS
AND LORD OF LORDS.

The Beast and His Armies Defeated

17Then I saw an angel standing in the
sun; and he cried with a loud voice, saying
to all the birds that fly in the midst of
heaven, “Come and gather together for the
supper of the great God,[a] 18that you may
eat the flesh of kings, the flesh of captains,
the flesh of mighty men, the flesh of horses
and of those who sit on them, and the flesh
of all *people,* free[a] and slave, both small and
great.”
19And I saw the beast, the kings of the
earth, and their armies, gathered together
to make war against Him who sat on the
horse and against His army. 20Then the
beast was captured, and with him the false
prophet who worked signs in his presence,
by which he deceived those who received
the mark of the beast and those who wor-
shiped his image. These two were cast
alive into the lake of fire burning with
brimstone. 21And the rest were killed with
the sword which proceeded from the
mouth of Him who sat on the horse.
And all the birds were filled with their
flesh.

CHAPTER 20

Satan Bound 1000 Years

Then I saw an angel coming down from
heaven, having the key to the bottomless
pit and a great chain in his hand. 2He
laid hold of the dragon, that serpent of
old, who is *the* Devil and Satan, and bound
him for a thousand years; 3and he cast
him into the bottomless pit, and shut him
up, and set a seal on him, so that he should
deceive the nations no more till the thou-
sand years were finished. But after these
things he must be released for a little
while.

19:12 [a]M-Text adds *names written, and.*
19:14 [a]NU-Text and M-Text read *pure white linen.*
19:15 [a]M-Text adds *two-edged.* 19:17 [a]NU-Text and M-Text read *the great supper of God.* 19:18 [a]NU-Text and M-Text read *both free.*

19:11 The **white horse** symbolizes victory.
19:13 robe dipped in blood: See Is. 63:1, 2.
19:15 The **sharp sword** of Christ’s mouth is His Word. All He needs to do to defeat His enemies is to pronounce their judgment.
20:1–3 The defeat of the earthly allies of the devil (19:20, 21) leaves him without forces to do his work.

The Saints Reign with Christ 1000 Years

4And I saw thrones, and they sat on them, and judgment was committed to them. Then *I saw* the souls of those who had been beheaded for their witness to Jesus and for the word of God, who had not worshiped the beast or his image, and had not received *his* mark on their foreheads or on their hands. And they lived and reigned with Christ for a[a] thousand years. 5But the rest of the dead did not live again until the thousand years were finished. This *is* the first resurrection. 6Blessed and holy *is* he who has part in the first resurrection. Over such the second death has no power, but they shall be priests of God and of Christ, and shall reign with Him a thousand years.

Satanic Rebellion Crushed

7Now when the thousand years have expired, Satan will be released from his prison 8and will go out to deceive the nations which are in the four corners of the earth, Gog and Mā′gog, to gather them together to battle, whose number *is* as the sand of the sea. 9They went up on the breadth of the earth and surrounded the camp of the saints and the beloved city. And fire came down from God out of heaven and devoured them. 10The devil, who deceived them, was cast into the lake of fire and brimstone where[a] the beast and the false prophet *are*. And they will be tormented day and night forever and ever.

The Great White Throne Judgment

11Then I saw a great white throne and Him who sat on it, from whose face the earth and the heaven fled away. And there was found no place for them. 12And I saw the dead, small and great, standing before God,[a] and books were opened. And another book was opened, which is *the Book* of Life. And the dead were judged according to their works, by the things which were written in the books. 13The sea gave up the dead who were in it, and Death and Hā′dēs delivered up the dead who were in them. And they were judged, each one according to his works. 14Then Death and Hā′dēs were cast into the lake of fire. This is the second death.[a] 15And anyone not found written in the Book of Life was cast into the lake of fire.

CHAPTER 21

All Things Made New

Now I saw a new heaven and a new earth, for the first heaven and the first earth had passed away. Also there was no more sea. 2Then I, John,[a] saw the holy

> ***I praise You for Your promise that You, God, will wipe away every tear from our eyes; there shall be no more death, nor sorrow, nor crying; and there shall be no more pain.***
>
> *adapted from* Revelation 21:4

20:4 [a]M-Text reads *the.* 20:10 [a]NU-Text and M-Text add *also.* 20:12 [a]NU-Text and M-Text read *the throne.* 20:14 [a]NU-Text and M-Text add *the lake of fire.* 21:2 [a]NU-Text and M-Text omit *John.*

20:7, 8 A **thousand years** will not change Satan's nature. He will seek to deceive **the nations**.

20:11–15 The final judgment, also called the Great White Judgment, demonstrates God's perfect justice. At this time, the spiritually dead will be sentenced to eternal doom.

21:1, 2 Because the first creation has **passed away**, the pattern for a new creation and a **New Jerusalem** for God's people comes down from **heaven**, shining and pure like a **bride**. The combination **heaven . . . earth** refers to the whole created universe, which will be **new** in quality, not just recently made. It is a new world without Satan and sin (see v. 5).

THE BEAUTY OF HEAVEN

Billy Graham

Imagine some of the most beautiful places in the world: Switzerland when the sun breaks over the snow-capped peaks and spills onto the slopes filled with wildflowers. A crystal clear lake, nestled among pine trees. A beach with white sand and the gentle lapping of warm Caribbean waters. A night in the desert west with a million stars against a velvet backdrop. An autumn day on a quiet road in New England. An easy chair, a good book, a cup of hot chocolate, and a glowing fire when the snow is falling at home.

Heaven will be more than that because it is the Father's house, and He is a God of beauty. The same hand that prepared this world has a more beautiful place prepared for us.

We have polluted so much of our earth, but in heaven there will be no environmental concerns. The water will be pure, the air clean, and there will be no need for landfills or recycled paper and cans.

"The same hand that prepared this world has a more beautiful place prepared for us."

In Revelation, when John caught a glimpse of heaven, the only thing he could think to compare it to was a bride on her wedding day (21:2). I have three daughters and two daughters-in-law, and every one was a beautiful bride, but their beauty was just a dim reflection of heaven.

If we are amazed and thrilled when we view some of the beauty the Lord gave us on earth, I am sure we are in for some wonderful surprises in heaven. ✦

city, New Jerusalem, coming down out of
heaven from God, prepared as a bride
adorned for her husband. 3And I heard a
loud voice from heaven saying, "Behold,
the tabernacle of God *is* with men, and He
will dwell with them, and they shall be His
people. God Himself will be with them *and*
be their God. 4And God will wipe away
every tear from their eyes; there shall be no
more death, nor sorrow, nor crying. There
shall be no more pain, for the former
things have passed away."
5Then He who sat on the throne said,
"Behold, I make all things new." And He
said to me,[a] "Write, for these words are
true and faithful."
6And He said to me, "It is done![a] I am
the Alpha and the Omega, the Beginning

21:5 [a]NU-Text and M-Text omit *to me*.
21:6 [a]M-Text omits *It is done*.

21:4, 5 When God dwells with humanity, He Himself will tenderly remove every **sorrow** and **pain** just as He promised (see 7:17). These evils are so much a part of this world that to remove them God must **make all things new**. He will do this because His promises are **true** and **faithful**.

and the End. I will give of the fountain of the water of life freely to him who thirsts. 7He who overcomes shall inherit all things,[a] and I will be his God and he shall be My son. 8But the cowardly, unbelieving,[a] abominable, murderers, sexually immoral, sorcerers, idolaters, and all liars shall have their part in the lake which burns with fire and brimstone, which is the second death."

The New Jerusalem

9Then one of the seven angels who had the seven bowls filled with the seven last plagues came to me[a] and talked with me, saying, "Come, I will show you the bride, the Lamb's wife."[b] 10And he carried me away in the Spirit to a great and high mountain, and showed me the great city, the holy[a] Jerusalem, descending out of heaven from God, 11having the glory of God. Her light *was* like a most precious stone, like a jasper stone, clear as crystal. 12Also she had a great and high wall with twelve gates, and twelve angels at the gates, and names written on them, which are *the names* of the twelve tribes of the children of Israel: 13three gates on the east, three gates on the north, three gates on the south, and three gates on the west.

14Now the wall of the city had twelve foundations, and on them were the names[a] of the twelve apostles of the Lamb. 15And he who talked with me had a gold reed to measure the city, its gates, and its wall. 16The city is laid out as a square; its length is as great as its breadth. And he measured the city with the reed: twelve thousand furlongs. Its length, breadth, and height are equal. 17Then he measured its wall: one hundred *and* forty-four cubits, *according* to the measure of a man, that is, of an angel. 18The construction of its wall was *of* jasper; and the city *was* pure gold, like clear glass. 19The foundations of the wall of the city *were* adorned with all kinds of precious stones: the first foundation *was* jasper, the second sapphire, the third chalcedony, the fourth emerald, 20the fifth sardonyx, the sixth sardius, the seventh chrysolite, the eighth beryl, the ninth topaz, the tenth chrysoprase, the eleventh jacinth, and the twelfth amethyst. 21The twelve gates *were* twelve pearls: each individual gate was of one pearl. And the street of the city *was* pure gold, like transparent glass.

The Glory of the New Jerusalem

22But I saw no temple in it, for the Lord God Almighty and the Lamb are its temple. 23The city had no need of the sun or of the moon to shine in it,[a] for the glory[b] of God illuminated it. The Lamb *is* its light. 24And the nations of those who are saved[a] shall walk in its light, and the kings of the earth bring their glory and honor into it.[b] 25Its gates shall not be shut at all by day (there shall be no night there). 26And they shall bring the glory and the honor of the nations into it.[a] 27But there shall by no means enter it anything that defiles, or causes[a] an abomination or a lie, but only those who are written in the Lamb's Book of Life.

CHAPTER 22

The River of Life

And he showed me a pure[a] river of water of life, clear as crystal, proceeding from

21:7 [a]M-Text reads *overcomes, I shall give him these things.* 21:8 [a]M-Text adds *and sinners.*
21:9 [a]NU-Text and M-Text omit *to me.* [b]M-Text reads *I will show you the woman, the Lamb's bride.*
21:10 [a]NU-Text and M-Text omit *the great* and read *the holy city, Jerusalem.* 21:14 [a]NU-Text and M-Text read *twelve names.* 21:23 [a]NU-Text and M-Text omit *in it.* [b]M-Text reads *the very glory.* 21:24 [a]NU-Text and M-Text omit *of those who are saved.* [b]M-Text reads *the glory and honor of the nations to Him.*
21:26 [a]M-Text adds *that they may enter in.*
21:27 [a]NU-Text and M-Text read *anything profane, nor one who causes.* 22:1 [a]NU-Text and M-Text omit *pure.*

21:7 He who overcomes: the believer.

the throne of God and of the Lamb. 2In the middle of its street, and on either side of the river, *was* the tree of life, which bore twelve fruits, each *tree* yielding its fruit every month. The leaves of the tree *were* for the healing of the nations. 3And there shall be no more curse, but the throne of God and of the Lamb shall be in it, and His servants shall serve Him. 4They shall see His face, and His name *shall be* on their foreheads. 5There shall be no night there: They need no lamp nor light of the sun, for the Lord God gives them light. And they shall reign forever and ever.

The Time Is Near

6Then he said to me, "These words *are* faithful and true." And the Lord God of the holy[a] prophets sent His angel to show His servants the things which must shortly take place.

7"Behold, I am coming quickly! Blessed *is* he who keeps the words of the prophecy of this book."

8Now I, John, saw and heard[a] these things. And when I heard and saw, I fell down to worship before the feet of the angel who showed me these things.

9Then he said to me, "See *that you do* not *do that*. For[a] I am your fellow servant, and of your brethren the prophets, and of those who keep the words of this book. Worship God." 10And he said to me, "Do not seal the words of the prophecy of this book, for the time is at hand. 11He who is unjust, let him be unjust still; he who is filthy, let him be filthy still; he who is righteous, let him be righteous[a] still; he who is holy, let him be holy still."

Jesus Testifies to the Churches

12"And behold, I am coming quickly, and My reward *is* with Me, to give to every one according to his work. 13I am the Alpha and the Omega, *the* Beginning and *the* End, the First and the Last."[a]

14Blessed *are* those who do His commandments,[a] that they may have the right to the tree of life, and may enter through the gates into the city. 15But[a] outside *are* dogs and sorcerers and sexually immoral and murderers and idolaters, and whoever loves and practices a lie.

16"I, Jesus, have sent My angel to testify to you these things in the churches. I am the Root and the Offspring of David, the Bright and Morning Star."

17And the Spirit and the bride say, "Come!" And let him who hears say, "Come!" And let him who thirsts come. Whoever desires, let him take the water of life freely.

A Warning

18For[a] I testify to everyone who hears the words of the prophecy of this book: If

22:6 [a]NU-Text and M-Text read *spirits of the prophets.*
22:8 [a]NU-Text and M-Text read *am the one who heard and saw.* 22:9 [a]NU-Text and M-Text omit *For.*
22:11 [a]NU-Text and M-Text read *do right.*
22:13 [a]NU-Text and M-Text read *the First and the Last, the Beginning and the End.* 22:14 [a]NU-Text reads *wash their robes.* 22:15 [a]NU-Text and M-Text omit *But.* 22:18 [a]NU-Text and M-Text omit *For.*

22:2 The **tree of life** provides abundantly everything necessary for fullness of life.

22:3 The **curse** which resulted from the sin of Adam and Eve is gone (see Gen. 3:14–19).

22:12 according to his work: Keeping the word of God and the testimony of Jesus is the key to overcoming, but God deals justly with the fruit of our lives (see 20:12).

22:13 Alpha . . . Omega: The first and last letters in the Greek alphabet. God is the sovereign Lord of all that happens from the **Beginning** to the **End**. This title is appropriate for Christ when He comes to judge.

22:16 I, Jesus: Our Lord's own validation of John's prophecy. As **the Root**, Jesus established God's plan to send the Savior through David's descendants, and created David's ancestral line beginning with Adam. As the **Offspring**, He brought that plan to fulfillment. From the beginning to the end He is our Savior. As the **Morning Star**, He is our full reward. When He comes, darkness flees.

HE'S COMING BACK

J. Vernon McGee

In World War II when General Douglas MacArthur withdrew from the Philippines—after Pearl Harbor and before the surrender of Corregidor—he issued his now famous statement: "I shall return." For several years millions of people in the Orient hung onto these three words as the only ray of light in the darkness of tyranny and oppression. They were words of hope; they were words of promised deliverance for people around the world.

MacArthur did return. He returned with a vengeance. Not stopping at Manila, he went on to Tokyo to receive the surrender of the proud nation of Japan on the deck of the battleship *Missouri.* Although he was, after all, a frail human being, he kept his promise. He did return.

Before the Lord Jesus Christ left this earth to return to heaven, He said, "I will come again" (John 14:3). These words have been the hope and comfort of millions of believers for the past twenty centuries. He, as the glorified Christ, repeated these words to the apostle John on the lonely island of Patmos. Here He sharpened His promise and delivered it in a dramatic way, "And behold, I am coming quickly, and My reward is with Me" (Rev. 22:12). He did not mean that He was coming *soon*—that is not what He said. He said that His coming, with all that it entailed, would occupy a very brief time—"I am coming *quickly.*" The Book of Revelation closes the Bible with His affirmation, "He who testifies to these things says, 'Surely I am coming quickly.' Amen" (v. 20). This is the last promise that has come to us from heaven. "I am coming quickly." And these words have been the comfort of His own for twenty centuries. ✦

"I will come again." These words have been the hope and comfort of millions.

anyone adds to these things, God will add[b]
to him the plagues that are written in this
book; [19]and if anyone takes away from the
words of the book of this prophecy, God
shall take away[a] his part from the Book[a] of
Life, from the holy city, and *from* the things
which are written in this book.

I Am Coming Quickly

[20]He who testifies to these things says,
"Surely I am coming quickly."
Amen. Even so, come, Lord Jesus!
[21]The grace of our Lord Jesus Christ *be*
with you all.[a] Amen.

22:18 [b]M-Text reads *may God add.*
22:19 [a]M-Text reads *may God take away.* [b]NU-Text and M-Text read *tree of life.* 22:21 [a]NU-Text reads *with all;* M-Text reads *with all the saints.*

✦ *Concordance* ✦

✦ *Bible Reading Plan* ✦

✦ *Acknowledgments* ✦

✦ *Personal Journal Pages* ✦

CONCORDANCE

A

ABBA
And He said, "*A*. . . . . .Mark 14:36
whom we cry out, "*A*. . . . . .Rom 8:15
crying out, "*A*. . . . . .Gal 4:6

ABIDE
LORD, who may *a*. . . . . .Ps 15:1
the Most High shall *a*. . . . . . . .Ps 91:1
Helper, that He may *a*. . . .John 14:16
"If you *a* in Me . . . . .John 15:7
does the love of God *a*. . .1 John 3:17

ABIDES
He who *a* in Me. . . . . .John 15:5

ABOMINATION
the *a* of desolation. . . . . .Dan 12:11
the *'a of desolation'* . . . . . .Matt 24:15

ABUNDANTLY
may have it more *a* . . . . . .John 10:10

ACCEPTABLE
a time I have heard . . . . .Is 49:8
Proclaim the a year . . . . . . .Luke 4:19

ACCESS
whom also we have *a*. . . . . . .Rom 5:2

ACCORD
daily with one *a*. . . . . .Acts 2:46

ACCURSED
he who is hanged is *a* . . . .Deut 21:23
not know the law is *a* . . . . .John 7:49
that I myself were *a*. . . . . . . .Rom 9:3
of God calls Jesus *a* . . . . . .1 Cor 12:3

ACCUSATION
over His head the *a*. . . . . .Matt 27:37
they might find an *a*. . . . . . . .Luke 6:7
Do not receive an *a*. . . . . .1 Tim 5:19

ACCUSER
the *a* of our brethren . . . . . .Rev 12:10

ACKNOWLEDGE
in all your ways *a* . . . . .Prov 3:6

ACQUAINTED
are *a* with all my ways. . . . .Ps 139:3
a Man of sorrows and *a* . . . . . .Is 53:3

ADOPTION
received the Spirit of *a*. . . . .Rom 8:15
we might receive the *a*. . . . . . Gal 4:5

ADULTERERS
nor idolaters, nor *a* . . . . .1 Cor 6:9
a God will judge . . . . .Heb 13:4

ADULTERY
You shall not commit *a*. . . . .Ex 20:14
already committed *a*. . . . . . .Matt 5:28
a woman caught in *a* . . . . . . .John 8:3

ADVANTAGE
Satan should take *a* . . . . . .2 Cor 2:11
no one should take *a*. . . . .1 Thess 4:6

ADVERSARY
your *a* the devil walks. . . . . . 1 Pet 5:8

ADVOCATE
sins, we have an *A* . . . . . . 1 John 2:1

AFFECTION
to his wife the *a* . . . . .1 Cor 7:3

AFFLICTION
is my comfort in my *a* . . . . .Ps 119:50
For our light *a*. . . . . .2 Cor 4:17

AFRAID
garden, and I was *a* . . . . .Gen 3:10
I will not be *a* of ten . . . . .Ps 3:6

AGE
and in the *a* to come . . . . .Mark 10:30
the powers of the *a*. . . . . .Heb 6:5

AGES
ordained before the *a* . . . . . .1 Cor 2:7
a was not made known. . . . . .Eph 3:5
at the end of the *a* . . . . .Heb 9:26

AGREE
that if two of you *a*. . . . . . .Matt 18:19
and these three *a*. . . . . .1 John 5:8

AIR
of the power of the *a*. . . . . . . .Eph 2:2

ALIVE
I kill and I make *a* . . . . . . .Deut 32:39
go down *a* into hell . . . . .Ps 55:15
presented Himself *a* . . . . .Acts 1:3
all shall be made *a* . . . . . . 1 Cor 15:22
trespasses, made us *a* . . . . . . .Eph 2:5
flesh, He has made *a*. . . . . . . .Col 2:13
that we who are *a* . . . . . . 1 Thess 4:15
the flesh but made *a* . . . . . . 1 Pet 3:18
and behold, I am *a* . . . . .Rev 1:18
These two were cast *a*. . . . .Rev 19:20

ALPHA
"I am the *A* and the . . . . Rev 1:8
"I am the *A* and the . . . . Rev 22:13

ALTAR
Then Noah built an *a*. . . . . . . Gen 8:20
your gift to the *a* . . . . Matt 5:23
Isaac his son on the *a* . . . . James 2:21

ALWAYS
lo, I am with you *a* . . . . Matt 28:20
thus we shall *a* . . . . 1 Thess 4:17

AM
to Moses, "I *A* WHO I *A* . . . . . Ex 3:14
Abraham was, I *A*. . . . . John 8:58

ANGEL
Now the *A* of the LORD . . . . . Gen 16:7
"Behold, I send an *A* . . . . Ex 23:20
And behold, an *a* . . . . Luke 2:9
For an *a* went down at. . . . . . . John 5:4
A who appeared to him . . . . Acts 7:35

ANGELS
give His a charge. . . . . Matt 4:6
but are like *a* . . . . Matt 22:30
twelve legions of *a* . . . . . . Matt 26:53

ANGER
For His *a* is but for a . . . . Ps 30:5
harsh word stirs up *a*. . . . . . Prov 15:1
fierceness of His *a* . . . . Nah 1:6

ANOINT
you shall *a* for Me the. . . . 1 Sam 16:3
a my head with oil . . . . Ps 23:5

ANOINTING
them pray over him, *a*. . . . James 5:14
But you have an *a*. . . . . . . 1 John 2:20

ANT
Go to the *a*. . . . . Prov 6:6

ANTICHRIST
have heard that the *A*. . . . 1 John 2:18
is a deceiver and an *a* . . . . . . 2 John 7

ANXIOUS
Be *a* for nothing . . . . Phil 4:6

APOSTLE
called to be an *a*. . . . . Rom 1:1
the signs of an *a* were . . . 2 Cor 12:12
a preacher and an *a* . . . . 1 Tim 2:7
consider the *A* . . . . Heb 3:1

APOSTLES
of the twelve *a* . . . . Matt 10:2
am the least of the *a*. . . . . . 1 Cor 15:9
gave some to be *a*. . . . . Eph 4:11

APPEARING
Lord Jesus Christ's *a* . . . . . 1 Tim 6:14
who have loved His *a*. . . . . . . 2 Tim 4:8

APPOINTED
You have *a* his limits . . . . Job 14:5
And as it is *a* for men . . . . . . Heb 9:27

APPROVE
do the same but also *a*. . . . . Rom 1:32
a the things that are. . . . . Phil 1:10

ARCHANGEL
with the voice of an *a*. . . 1 Thess 4:16
Yet Michael the *a* . . . . Jude 9

ARISE
A, shine . . . . Is 60:1

ARK
"Make yourself an *a* . . . . Gen 6:14
Let us bring the *a*. . . . . 1 Sam 4:3

ARM
with an outstretched *a*. . . . . Ex 6:6
You have a mighty *a* . . . . Ps 89:13
therefore His own *a*. . . . . Is 59:16

ARMIES
"I defy the *a*. . . . . 1 Sam 17:10
any number to His *a*. . . . . Job 25:3
And the *a* in heaven. . . . . . . Rev 19:14

ARMOR
let us put on the *a*. . . . . Rom 13:12
Put on the whole *a*. . . . . Eph 6:11

AROMA
smelled a soothing *a* . . . . Gen 8:21
a sweet-smelling *a* . . . . Phil 4:18

ARROW
a that flies by day . . . . Ps 91:5
Their tongue is an *a*. . . . . Jer 9:8

ASCEND
Who may *a* into the . . . . Ps 24:3
If I *a* into heaven . . . . Ps 139:8
'I will *a* into heaven . . . . Is 14:13
see the Son of Man *a* . . . . . . John 6:62

ASCRIBE
a greatness to our God . . . . Deut 32:3
A strength to God . . . . Ps 68:34

ASHAMED
Let me not be *a* . . . . Ps 25:2
am not *a* of the gospel . . . . . Rom 1:16

ASK
when your children *a* . . . . Josh 4:6
a, and it will be . . . . Luke 11:9
a anything in My name. . . John 14:14
in that day you will *a*. . . . . John 16:23

ASLEEP
down, and was fast *a* . . . . Jon 1:5
but some have fallen *a* . . . . 1 Cor 15:6
those who are *a* . . . . 1 Thess 4:15

ASSEMBLING
not forsaking the *a*. . . . . Heb 10:25

ASSURANCE
to the full *a* of hope . . . . Heb 6:11

ASTONISHED
Just as many were *a* . . . . Is 52:14
that the people were *a* . . . . . Matt 7:28

ASTRAY
and one of them goes *a* . . . Matt 18:12

ATONEMENT
a year he shall make *a* . . . . . Ex 30:10
for it is the Day of *A* . . . . . . Lev 23:28

AUTHOR
For God is not the *a* . . . . . 1 Cor 14:33
unto Jesus, the *a*. . . . . Heb 12:2

AUTHORITY
"All *a* has been given. . . . . . Matt 28:18

AVAILS
of a righteous man *a* . . . . . James 5:16

AVENGE
for He will *a* the . . . . Deut 32:43
Beloved, do not *a*. . . . . Rom 12:19
a our blood on those . . . . Rev 6:10

AWAKE
be satisfied when I *a*. . . . . Ps 17:15

AWAY
Do not cast me *a* . . . . Ps 51:11
and earth will pass *a* . . . . . Matt 24:35

AWESOME
Your great and *a* name . . . . . . Ps 99:3
with me as a mighty, *a*. . . . . Jer 20:11
"O Lord, great and *a*. . . . . Dan 9:4

B

BABE
You will find a *B*. . . . . Luke 2:12

BACKSLIDINGS
and I will heal your *b* . . . . Jer 3:22
b have increased. . . . . Jer 5:6

BALM
Is there no *b* in Gilead . . . . . . Jer 8:22

BAPTISM
"The *b* of John . . . . Matt 21:25
"But I have a *b* . . . . Luke 12:50
with Him through *b* . . . . Rom 6:4
Lord, one faith, one *b* . . . . Eph 4:5
buried with Him in *b*. . . . . Col 2:12
now saves us—*b* . . . . 1 Pet 3:21

BAPTISMS
of the doctrine of *b*. . . . . Heb 6:2

BAPTIZE
"I indeed *b* you with. . . . . . . Matt 3:11

BAPTIZED
b will be saved . . . . Mark 16:16
every one of you be *b*. . . . . . Acts 2:38
were *b* into Christ . . . . Rom 6:3
Spirit we were all *b*. . . . . . 1 Cor 12:13
of you as were *b* . . . . Gal 3:27

BAPTIZING
b them in the name of . . . . Matt 28:19

BARREN
"Sing, O *b* . . . . Is 54:1

BASKETS
they took up twelve *b*. . . . . Matt 14:20

BATTLE
b is the LORD's. . . . . 1 Sam 17:47
the *b* to the strong . . . . Eccl 9:11

BEAR
they shall *b* you up . . . . Ps 91:12
B one another's . . . . Gal 6:2

BEAST
the mark of the *b* . . . . Rev 19:20

BEAT
spat in His face and *b* . . . . Matt 26:67

BEAUTIFUL
has made everything *b* . . . . . Eccl 3:11
my love, you are as *b* . . . . . . Song 6:4
How *b* upon the. . . . . Is 52:7

BED
If I make my *b* in hell. . . . . . . Ps 139:8
Arise, take up your *b* . . . . Matt 9:6

BEGINNING
In the *b* God created . . . . Gen 1:1
In the *b* was the Word. . . . . . John 1:1
and the Omega, the *B* . . . . Rev 21:6

BEGOTTEN
glory as of the only *b*. . . . . . John 1:14

BEHOLD
B the Lamb of God. . . . . John 1:36
B what manner of love. . . . 1 John 3:1

BELIEVE
B in the LORD your God. . 2 Chr 20:20
because they did not *b* . . . Mark 16:14
even to those who *b*. . . . . John 1:12
the Lord Jesus and *b* . . . . Rom 10:9

comes to God must *b*....... Heb 11:6
Even the demons *b* ...... James 2:19

BELIEVED
Abraham b God............ Rom 4:3
I know whom I have *b*.... 2 Tim 1:12

BELIEVES
that whoever *b* in Him..... John 3:16
with the heart one *b*...... Rom 10:10

BELIEVING
you ask in prayer, *b*...... Matt 21:22

BELLY
And Jonah was in the *b*..... Jon 1:17

BELOVED
My *b* is mine .... Song 2:16
a song of my *B*............... Is 5:1
for you are greatly *b*....... Dan 9:23

BESTOWED
love the Father has *b* ..... 1 John 3:1

BETRAY
you, one of you will *b* .... Matt 26:21

BETRAYED
Man is about to be *b*...... Matt 17:22

BETROTHED
to a virgin *b* to a man ..... Luke 1:27

BETTER
b than sacrifice .... 1 Sam 15:22
For it is *b* to marry .... 1 Cor 7:9
Christ, which is far *b*....... Phil 1:23
b things concerning .... Heb 6:9
b things than that.......... Heb 12:24

BEWARE
"*B* of false prophets .... Matt 7:15

BEWITCHED
b you that you should........ Gal 3:1

BIRTH
Now the *b* of Jesus .... Matt 1:18
conceived, it gives *b* ..... James 1:15

BIRTHRIGHT
of food sold his *b* .... Heb 12:16

BISHOP
the position of a *b*......... 1 Tim 3:1
b must be blameless......... Titus 1:7

BITTERNESS
root of *b* springing up..... Heb 12:15

BLAMELESS
you holy, and *b*............ Col 1:22
without spot and *b*........ 2 Pet 3:14

BLASPHEME
may learn not to *b*........ 1 Tim 1:20
God, to *b* His name......... Rev 13:6

BLASPHEMED
the name of God is b ...... Rom 2:24

BLEMISH
LORD, a ram without *b*....... Lev 6:6
as of a lamb without *b* .... 1 Pet 1:19

BLESS
b those who *b* you .... Gen 12:3
"The LORD *b* you and...... Num 6:24
b those who curse.......... Luke 6:28
B those who persecute.... Rom 12:14

BLESSED
B is the man to whom .... Ps 32:2
B is the nation whose...... Ps 33:12
rise up and call her *b*..... Prov 31:28
b is He who comes .... Matt 21:9
It is more *b* to give ...... Acts 20:35

BLESSING
I will command My *b*...... Lev 25:21
shall be showers of *b*..... Ezek 34:26
that the *b* of Abraham ...... Gal 3:14

BLIND
To open *b* eyes .... Is 42:7
The *b* see and the lame .... Matt 11:5

BLOOD
b that makes atonement ... Lev 17:11
For this is My *b* .... Matt 26:28
new covenant in My *b*.... Luke 22:20
with His own *b*........... Acts 20:28
justified by His *b* .... Rom 5:9
peace through the *b* .... Col 1:20
with the precious *b*........ 1 Pet 1:19
b of Jesus Christ His...... 1 John 1:7
our sins in His own *b*........ Rev 1:5
overcame him by the *b* ... Rev 12:11

BOAST
lest anyone should *b* .... Eph 2:9

BODIES
b a living sacrifice......... Rom 12:1
also celestial *b* .... 1 Cor 15:40
wives as their own *b*....... Eph 5:28

BODILY
b exercise profits.......... 1 Tim 4:8

BODY
this is My *b*.............. Matt 26:26
many members in one *b* .. Rom 12:4
b which is broken .... 1 Cor 11:24
are the *b* of Christ....... 1 Cor 12:27

BOLD
the righteous are *b* . . . . Prov 28:1
are much more *b*. . . . . Phil 1:14

BOLDNESS
in whom we have *b* . . . . Eph 3:12
but with all *b* . . . . Phil 1:20

BONES
I can count all My *b* . . . . Ps 22:17
say to them, 'O dry *b*. . . . . . Ezek 37:4

BOOK
in the Lamb's *B* . . . . Rev 21:27

BOOKS
God, and *b* were opened . . . Rev 20:12

BORE
b the sin of many . . . . Is 53:12
b our sicknesses. . . . . Matt 8:17

BORN
"Man who is *b* . . . . Job 14:1
A time to be *b* . . . . Eccl 3:2
unto us a Child is *b* . . . . Is 9:6
unless one is *b* again . . . . John 3:3

BOTTOMLESS
the key to the *b* . . . . Rev 20:1

BRANCH
B shall grow out of. . . . . Is 11:1
grow up to David a *B* . . . . . Jer 33:15
forth My Servant the *B* . . . . . Zech 3:8

BRANCHES
vine, you are the *b* . . . . John 15:5

BREAD
Cast your *b* upon the. . . . . . . Eccl 11:1
not live by b alone. . . . . Matt 4:4
"I am the *b* of life . . . . John 6:48
He was betrayed took *b*. . 1 Cor 11:23

BREASTPLATE
righteousness as a *b*. . . . . Is 59:17
having put on the *b* . . . . Eph 6:14

BREASTS
doe, let her *b* satisfy . . . . Prov 5:19

BREATH
nostrils the *b* of life . . . . Gen 2:7
everything that has *b* . . . . Ps 150:6

BRETHREN
least of these My *b* . . . . . . Matt 25:40
firstborn among many *b* . . . Rom 8:29
over five hundred *b*. . . . . . 1 Cor 15:6

BRIDE
the Spirit and the *b* . . . . Rev 22:17

BRIDEGROOM
b fast while the . . . . Mark 2:19

BRIGHTNESS
and kings to the *b*. . . . . Is 60:3
who being the *b*. . . . . Heb 1:3

BRIMSTONE
the lake of fire and *b* . . . . . Rev 20:10

BROKEN
is My body which is *b* . . . 1 Cor 11:24

BROKENHEARTED
He heals the *b* and . . . . Ps 147:3

BROTHER
Where is Abel your *b* . . . . Gen 4:9
and a *b* is born for . . . . Prov 17:17
how often shall my *b* . . . . . Matt 18:21

BROTHER'S
Am I my *b* keeper. . . . . Gen 4:9

BROTHERS
b did not believe . . . . John 7:5

BRUISE
He shall *b* your head . . . . . . Gen 3:15
the LORD to *b* Him . . . . Is 53:10

BRUISED
He was *b* for our. . . . . Is 53:5

BUILDER
me, as a wise master *b*. . . . 1 Cor 3:10
foundations, whose *b* . . . . . Heb 11:10

BUILDING
field, you are God's *b* . . . . . . 1 Cor 3:9

BURDEN
Cast your *b* on the. . . . . Ps 55:22
easy and My *b* is light . . . . Matt 11:30

BURDENS
Bear one another's *b*. . . . . Gal 6:2

BURIAL
she did it for My *b* . . . . Matt 26:12

BURIED
b with Him in baptism . . . . . . Col 2:12

BUSYBODIES
but also gossips and *b* . . . . 1 Tim 5:13

C

CALF
and made a molded *c*. . . . . Ex 32:4
And bring the fatted *c*. . . . Luke 15:23

CALL
c upon Him while He........Is 55:6
'C to Me ....Jer 33:3
They will *c* on My name...Zech 13:9
c His name JESUS..........Matt 1:21
How then shall they *c* ....Rom 10:14

CALLED
to those who are the *c* .....Rom 8:28
But God has *c* us to.......1 Cor 7:15

CALLING
the gifts and the *c* ....Rom 11:29
to walk worthy of the *c*......Eph 4:1

CAMEL
it is easier for a *c*.........Matt 19:24
and swallow a *c*...........Matt 23:24

CAPTIVITY
every thought into *c* ....2 Cor 10:5

CARE
casting all your *c* ....1 Pet 5:7

CARNAL
c mind is enmity ....Rom 8:7
for you are still *c* ....1 Cor 3:3

CARNALLY
c minded is death ....Rom 8:6

CAST
Why are you *c* down ....Ps 42:5
c all our sins into ....Mic 7:19
In My name they will *c* ..Mark 16:17
c away your confidence ... Heb 10:35

CATCH
down your nets for a *c* .....Luke 5:4

CHARIOT
and overtake this *c* ....Acts 8:29

CHASTEN
C your son while there ...Prov 19:18
a father does not *c* ....Heb 12:7

CHASTENING
do not despise the *c* ....Job 5:17

CHASTENS
the LORD loves He c.........Heb 12:6

CHASTISEMENT
the *c* for our peace ....Is 53:5

CHEERFUL
God loves a *c* giver ....2 Cor 9:7

CHERUBIM
dwell between the *c* ....Ps 80:1

CHILD
c is known by his ....Prov 20:11
Train up a *c* in the ....Prov 22:6
For unto us a C ....Is 9:6
c shall lead them.............Is 11:6
He took a little *c*..........Mark 9:36

CHILDBEARING
she will be saved in *c*.....1 Tim 2:15

CHILDREN
c are a heritage ....Ps 127:3
and become as little *c* .....Matt 18:3
the right to become *c*......John 1:12

CHOSE
just as He *c* us in Him.......Eph 1:4
from the beginning *c*....2 Thess 2:13

CHOSEN
But you are a *c* ....1 Pet 2:9

CHRIST
"You are the C...........Matt 16:16
It is C who died ....Rom 8:34
to be justified by *C* ....Gal 2:17
been crucified with *C* ....Gal 2:20
to me, to live is C ....Phil 1:21
confess that Jesus *C*........Phil 2:11
Jesus C is the same ....Heb 13:8
that Jesus is the C.........1 John 5:1

CHRISTIAN
anyone suffers as a *C* .....1 Pet 4:16

CHRISTIANS
were first called C........Acts 11:26

CHURCH
rock I will build My *c*.....Matt 16:18
body, which is the *c* ....Col 1:24

CHURCHES
strengthening the *c*.......Acts 15:41

CIRCUMCISE
c the foreskin of your ....Deut 10:16
is necessary to *c* them .....Acts 15:5

CIRCUMCISION
c is that of the heart.......Rom 2:29
C is nothing and..........1 Cor 7:19

CITY
How lonely sits the *c*........Lam 1:1
c that is set on a ....Matt 5:14

CLAY
Shall the *c* say to him ....Is 45:9

CLEAN
He who has *c* hands and.....Ps 24:4

CLEANSE
C me from secret...........Ps 19:12

And *c* me from my sin . . . . . . Ps 51:2
How can a young man *c* . . . . Ps 119:9
c the lepers, raise . . . . Matt 10:8

CLOTHED
all her household is *c* . . . . . Prov 31:21
I was naked and you *c* . . . . Matt 25:36
that you may be *c* . . . . Rev 3:18

CLOTHING
to you in sheep's *c* . . . . Matt 7:15

CLOUD
c received Him out of . . . . Acts 1:9
great a *c* of witnesses . . . . . . Heb 12:1

CLOUDS
of Man coming on the *c* . . Matt 24:30

COLD
of many will grow *c* . . . . . . Matt 24:12
that you are neither *c* . . . . . . Rev 3:15

COME
who have no money, *c*. . . . . Is 55:1
C to Me, all you who . . . . . Matt 11:28
the bride say, "*C* . . . . Rev 22:17

COMFORT
and Your staff, they *c* . . . . Ps 23:4
yes, *c* My people . . . . Is 40:1
For the LORD will *c*. . . . . Is 51:3
she has none to *c* her . . . . Lam 1:2
in Christ, if any *c* . . . . Phil 2:1

COMING
but He who is *c* . . . . Matt 3:11
see the Son of Man *c* . . . . Mark 13:26
the promise of His *c*. . . . . 2 Pet 3:4

COMMAND
c fire to come down . . . . Luke 9:54
if you do whatever I *c* . . . . John 15:14

COMMANDMENT
"A new *c* I give to. . . . . . . John 13:34
And this is His *c* . . . . 1 John 3:23

COMMANDMENTS
covenant, the Ten *C* . . . . Ex 34:28

COMMITTED
"Who c no sin . . . . 1 Pet 2:22
c Himself to Him who . . . . . 1 Pet 2:23

COMMON
had all things in *c* . . . . Acts 2:44
not call any man *c*. . . . . Acts 10:28

COMMUNION
bless, is it not the *c* . . . . . . 1 Cor 10:16
c of the Holy Spirit . . . . . . 2 Cor 13:14

COMPANY
not to keep *c* with . . . . 1 Cor 5:9
c corrupts good habits . . . 1 Cor 15:33
and do not keep *c* . . . . . . 2 Thess 3:14

COMPASSION
He, being full of *c* . . . . Ps 78:38
show mercy and *c*. . . . . Zech 7:9
He was moved with *c*. . . . . . Matt 9:36

COMPASSIONS
because His *c* fail not . . . . . . Lam 3:22

COMPLETE
that you may be made *c* . . 2 Cor 13:9
work in you will *c*. . . . . Phil 1:6
and you are *c* in Him . . . . Col 2:10

CONCEIVE
the virgin shall *c* . . . . Is 7:14
And behold, you will *c* . . . . Luke 1:31

CONDEMN
world to *c* the world. . . . . . . John 3:17

CONDEMNATION
therefore now no *c* . . . . Rom 8:1

CONFESS
that if you *c* with . . . . Rom 10:9
every tongue shall c . . . . . . Rom 14:11
If we *c* our sins. . . . . 1 John 1:9

CONFESSES
prosper, but whoever *c* . . . Prov 28:13
c that Jesus is the . . . . 1 John 4:15

CONFESSION
with the mouth *c* . . . . Rom 10:10
High Priest of our *c* . . . . Heb 3:1
let us hold fast our *c* . . . . Heb 4:14

CONFIDENCE
Jesus, and have no *c* . . . . Phil 3:3
if we hold fast the *c* . . . . Heb 3:6

CONFORMED
And do not be *c* . . . . Rom 12:2
sufferings, being *c* . . . . Phil 3:10

CONQUERORS
we are more than *c*. . . . . Rom 8:37

CONSCIENCE
having a good *c*. . . . . 1 Pet 3:16

CONSIDER
C the lilies of the . . . . Matt 6:28

CONSOLATION
if there is any *c* . . . . Phil 2:1
we might have strong *c*. . . . . Heb 6:18

CONSUMED
mercies we are not *c*. . . . . Lam 3:22

CONSUMING
our God is a *c* fire . . . . Heb 12:29

CONTEND
c earnestly for the. . . . . Jude 3

CONTENT
state I am, to be *c* . . . . Phil 4:11

CONTRITE
saves such as have a *c*. . . . . . Ps 34:18
poor and of a *c* spirit . . . . Is 66:2

CORD
this line of scarlet *c*. . . . . . . Josh 2:18
And a threefold *c* . . . . Eccl 4:12

CORNERSTONE
stone, a precious *c* . . . . Is 28:16
Has become the chief c . . . Matt 21:42
in Zion a chief c . . . . 1 Pet 2:6

CORRECT
C your son. . . . . Prov 29:17

CORRUPT
have together become *c*. . . . . . Ps 14:3
men of *c* minds . . . . 2 Tim 3:8

CORRUPTIBLE
For this *c* must put on . . . 1 Cor 15:53

CORRUPTION
Your Holy One to see *c* . . . . . Ps 16:10
The body is sown in *c* . . . 1 Cor 15:42

COUNSEL
and strength, He has *c*. . . . . Job 12:13
is this who darkens *c*. . . . . . Job 38:2
We took sweet *c*. . . . . Ps 55:14
Where there is no *c* . . . . . . Prov 11:14

COUNSELOR
be called Wonderful, *C* . . . . Is 9:6

COUNTENANCE
The LORD lift up His *c* . . . . . Num 6:26
up the light of Your *c* . . . . Ps 4:6

COUNTRY
and went into a far *c* . . . . . Matt 21:33
that is, a heavenly *c*. . . . . . . Heb 11:16

COURAGE
strong and of good *c* . . . . . . Deut 31:6

COURTS
And into His *c* . . . . Ps 100:4

COVENANT
I will establish My *c*. . . . . Gen 6:18
day the LORD made a *c* . . . . Gen 15:18
as a perpetual *c* . . . . Ex 31:16
the Messenger of the *c*. . . . . . . Mal 3:1
This cup is the new *c*. . . . . Luke 22:20
Mediator of a better *c* . . . . Heb 8:6
Mediator of the new *c*. . . . . Heb 12:24

COVER
not to *c* his head . . . . 1 Cor 11:7
c a multitude of sins . . . . . James 5:20

COVERING
given to her for a *c* . . . . . . 1 Cor 11:15

COVET
"You shall not *c* . . . . Ex 20:17

COVETOUSNESS
heed and beware of *c* . . . . Luke 12:15
conduct be without *c* . . . . Heb 13:5

CREATED
So God *c* man in His . . . . Gen 1:27
Has not one God *c* . . . . Mal 2:10
c in Christ Jesus . . . . Eph 2:10
Him all things were *c* . . . . Col 1:16

CREATION
c was subjected . . . . Rom 8:20
Christ, he is a new *c* . . . . . . 2 Cor 5:17

CREATOR
Remember now your *C*. . . . . Eccl 12:1
rather than the *C*. . . . . Rom 1:25

CREATURE
the gospel to every *c*. . . . . Mark 16:15
For every *c* of God is . . . . . . 1 Tim 4:4

CROOKED
c places straight . . . . Is 45:2
c places shall be made . . . . Luke 3:5
in the midst of a *c*. . . . . Phil 2:15

CROSS
does not take his *c* . . . . . . Matt 10:38
come down from the *c*. . . . Matt 27:40
lest the *c* of Christ. . . . . 1 Cor 1:17
boast except in the *c*. . . . . Gal 6:14
Him endured the *c* . . . . Heb 12:2

CROWN
c has fallen from our . . . . . . Lam 5:16
they had twisted a *c* . . . . . Matt 27:29
laid up for me the *c*. . . . . 2 Tim 4:8
he will receive the *c*. . . . . . James 1:12

CROWNED
have c him with glory . . . . Heb 2:7

CROWNS
and they had *c* of gold. . . . . . . Rev 4:4

CRUCIFIED
"Let Him be *c*. . . . . Matt 27:22
Calvary, there they *c* . . . . . Luke 23:33
lawless hands, have *c*. . . . . Acts 2:23

that our old man was *c* . . . . . Rom 6:6
Jesus Christ and Him *c* . . . . 1 Cor 2:2
I have been *c* with . . . . Gal 2:20

CRUCIFY
out again, "C Him . . . . Mark 15:13

CRY
and their *c* came up to . . . . . . Ex 2:23
heart and my flesh *c* . . . . Ps 84:2
I *c* out with my whole . . . . Ps 119:145
Does not wisdom *c* . . . . Prov 8:1
"What shall I *c* . . . . Is 40:6
His own elect who *c* . . . . Luke 18:7

CRYING
"The voice of one *c* . . . . Matt 3:3
nor sorrow, nor *c* . . . . Rev 21:4

CRYSTAL
a sea of glass, like *c* . . . . Rev 4:6

CUP
My *c* runs over . . . . Ps 23:5
Then He took the *c* . . . . Matt 26:27
c is the new covenant . . . . 1 Cor 11:25

CURSE
c the ground for man's . . . . . Gen 8:21
c a ruler of your . . . . Ex 22:28
shall not *c* the deaf . . . . Lev 19:14
C God and die . . . . Job 2:9
Do not *c* the king . . . . Eccl 10:20
are cursed with a *c* . . . . Mal 3:9
law are under the *c* . . . . Gal 3:10

CURSES
I will curse him who *c* . . . . . . Gen 12:3
c his father or his . . . . Prov 20:20

CYMBAL
or a clanging *c* . . . . 1 Cor 13:1

D

DAILY
Give us this day our *d* . . . . . Matt 6:11
I sat *d* with you . . . . Matt 26:55
take up his cross *d* . . . . Luke 9:23
the Scriptures *d* . . . . Acts 17:11
our Lord, I die *d* . . . . 1 Cor 15:31

DANCE
mourn, and a time to *d* . . . . . . Eccl 3:4
And you did not *d* . . . . Matt 11:17

DANCED
Then David *d* before . . . . . 2 Sam 6:14
daughter of Herodias *d* . . . . Matt 14:6

DANCING
saw the calf and the *d* . . . . . Ex 32:19
me my mourning into *d* . . . . . Ps 30:11

DARKNESS
d He called Night . . . . Gen 1:5
d have seen a great . . . . Is 9:2
cast out into outer *d* . . . . Matt 8:12
For you were once *d* . . . . Eph 5:8
us from the power of *d* . . . . Col 1:13
called you out of *d* . . . . 1 Pet 2:9
and in Him is no *d* . . . . 1 John 1:5

DARTS
quench all the fiery *d* . . . . Eph 6:16

DAUGHTER
Rejoice greatly, O *d* . . . . Zech 9:9
"Fear not, d of Zion . . . . . . John 12:15
the son of Pharaoh's *d* . . . . Heb 11:24

DAUGHTERS
d shall prophesy . . . . Acts 2:17

DAY
God called the light *D* . . . . Gen 1:5
Remember the Sabbath *d* . . . . Ex 20:8
d the LORD has made . . . . . . Ps 118:24
For the *d* of the LORD . . . . Joel 2:11
again the third *d* . . . . 1 Cor 15:4

DEACONS
d be the husbands . . . . 1 Tim 3:12

DEAD
d are raised up and . . . . Matt 11:5
for this my son was *d* . . . . Luke 15:24
resurrection of the *d* . . . . . 1 Cor 15:12
made alive, who were *d* . . . . . Eph 2:1
And the *d* in Christ . . . . . 1 Thess 4:16

DEADLY
they drink anything *d* . . . . Mark 16:18
d wound was healed . . . . Rev 13:3

DEAF
d shall hear the words . . . . Is 29:18
are cleansed and the *d* . . . . . Matt 11:5

DEATH
Let me die the *d* . . . . Num 23:10
d parts you and me . . . . Ruth 1:17
For in *d* there is no . . . . Ps 6:5
D and life are in the . . . . . . Prov 18:21
the wages of sin is *d* . . . . Rom 6:23
proclaim the Lord's *d* . . . 1 Cor 11:26
is sin leading to *d* . . . . 1 John 5:16
which is the second *d* . . . . . . Rev 21:8

DEBTORS
As we forgive our *d* . . . . . . Matt 6:12

DECEITFUL
"The heart is *d* . . . . Jer 17:9

DECEIVE
Let no one *d* himself . . . . . . 1 Cor 3:18
Let no one *d* you with . . . . Eph 5:6

DECISION
in the valley of *d*. . . . . Joel 3:14

DECLARE
The heavens *d* the. . . . . Ps 19:1
d His generation . . . . Is 53:8
"I will d Your name. . . . . Heb 2:12

DEEDS
shares in his evil *d* . . . . 2 John 11

DEEP
LORD God caused a *d*. . . . . . . Gen 2:21
D calls unto *d* . . . . Ps 42:7
Launch out into the *d* . . . . . Luke 5:4

DEFEND
D the poor and. . . . . Ps 82:3

DEFILES
mouth, this *d* a man . . . . . . Matt 15:11
d the temple of God . . . . . . 1 Cor 3:17

DELIGHT
D yourself also in the. . . . . Ps 37:4

DELIVER
d you from the immoral. . . . Prov 2:16
we serve is able to *d* . . . . Dan 3:17
d the godly out of . . . . 2 Pet 2:9

DELUSION
send them strong *d*. . . . . 2 Thess 2:11

DEMON
Jesus rebuked the *d* . . . . . . Matt 17:18

DEMONS
They sacrificed to *d* . . . . . . Deut 32:17
authority over all *d*. . . . . Luke 9:1
even the *d* are subject . . . . Luke 10:17
Even the *d* believe . . . . James 2:19

DEN
it a *'d of thieves*. . . . . Matt 21:13

DENIED
Peter then *d* again. . . . . John 18:27

DENY
let him *d* himself . . . . Matt 16:24
He cannot *d* Himself. . . . . . 2 Tim 2:13

DEPTH
nor height nor *d*. . . . . Rom 8:39
Oh, the *d* of the . . . . Rom 11:33

DESCENDANTS
"We are Abraham's *d* . . . . . John 8:33

DESIRE
d shall be for your . . . . Gen 3:16
Behold, You *d* truth in . . . . Ps 51:6

DESIRES
shall give you the *d*. . . . . Ps 37:4

DESOLATION
the *'abomination of d*. . . . . Matt 24:15

DESPISE
if you *d* My statutes . . . . Lev 26:15
d Me shall be lightly . . . . . 1 Sam 2:30
d the riches of His. . . . . Rom 2:4

DESPISING
the cross, *d* the shame. . . . . Heb 12:2

DESTROY
shall not hurt nor *d* . . . . Is 11:9
I did not come to *d* . . . . Matt 5:17
'I will *d* this temple . . . . . . Mark 14:58

DESTRUCTION
d that lays waste . . . . Ps 91:6
your life from *d* . . . . Ps 103:4
Pride goes before *d*. . . . . . . Prov 16:18

DEVIL
of your father the *d* . . . . John 8:44
give place to the *d* . . . . Eph 4:27
the wiles of the *d* . . . . Eph 6:11
the snare of the *d* . . . . 2 Tim 2:26
Resist the *d* and he. . . . . James 4:7

DEVOUT
d men carried . . . . Acts 8:2

DIE
I shall not *d*. . . . . Ps 118:17
that one man should *d*. . . . John 11:50
For as in Adam all *d*. . . . . 1 Cor 15:22
and to *d* is gain . . . . Phil 1:21
for men to *d* once . . . . Heb 9:27

DIED
in due time Christ *d* . . . . Rom 5:6
Christ *d* for us . . . . Rom 5:8

DILIGENT
d shall be made rich . . . . Prov 13:4
Let us therefore be *d*. . . . . . . Heb 4:11

DIM
His eyes were not *d* . . . . Deut 34:7

DISCERNED
they are spiritually *d*. . . . . . 1 Cor 2:14

DISCIPLE
d is not above his . . . . Matt 10:24
he cannot be My *d* . . . . Luke 14:26

DISCIPLES
My word, you are My *d*. . . John 8:31
so you will be My *d* . . . . John 15:8

DISCRETION
woman who lacks *d* . . . . Prov 11:22

DISOBEDIENT
out My hands to a d......Rom 10:21

DISPUTES
foolish and ignorant *d*....2 Tim 2:23
But avoid foolish *d*........Titus 3:9

DISQUALIFIED
myself should become *d*..1 Cor 9:27

DIVIDED
"Every kingdom *d*........Matt 12:25
and a house *d* against....Luke 11:17

DIVIDING
rightly *d* the word of .....2 Tim 2:15

DIVINATION
shall you practice *d* ....Lev 19:26
a spirit of *d* met us ....Acts 16:16

DIVINE
d power has given ....2 Pet 1:3

DIVISIONS
note those who cause *d*...Rom 16:17

DIVISIVE
Reject a *d* man after.......Titus 3:10

DIVORCE
her a certificate of *d*.......Deut 24:1
a certificate of *d*..........Mark 10:4

DO
men to *d* to you, *d*.........Matt 7:12
without Me you can *d*.....John 15:5
good that I will to *d*.......Rom 7:19
or whatever you *d*, *d*.....1 Cor 10:31
d all things through........Phil 4:13

DOCTRINE
with every wind of *d*.......Eph 4:14
is contrary to sound *d*....1 Tim 1:10
is profitable for *d*.........2 Tim 3:16

DOERS
But be *d* of the word.....James 1:22

DOG
d returns to his own.......2 Pet 2:22

DOGS
what is holy to the *d*........Matt 7:6
d eat the crumbs which...Matt 15:27

DOMINION
let them have *d*............Gen 1:26
made him to have *d*.........Ps 8:6

DONKEY
colt, the foal of a d.......Matt 21:5

DOOR
sin lies at the *d*.............Gen 4:7
to you, I am the *d*........John 10:7
I stand at the *d*.............Rev 3:20

DOORKEEPER
I would rather be a *d*.......Ps 84:10

DOUBLE
worthy of *d* honor.........1 Tim 5:17

DOUBLE-MINDED
he is a *d* man..............James 1:8

DOUBTS
doubting, for he who *d*....James 1:6

DOVE
d found no resting ....Gen 8:9
I had wings like a *d*..........Ps 55:6
descending like a *d*.........Matt 3:16

DRAGON
a great, fiery red *d*.........Rev 12:3
they worshiped the *d*.......Rev 13:4

DRAW
You have nothing to *d*.....John 4:11
D near to God and He.....James 4:8

DREAM
prophet who has a *d*.......Jer 23:28
to Joseph in a *d*............Matt 2:13
your old men shall d.......Acts 2:17

DRINK
gave me vinegar to *d*.......Ps 69:21
to her, "Give Me a *d*........John 4:7
d wine nor do anything...Rom 14:21
do, as often as you *d*....1 Cor 11:25

DROVE
So He *d* out the man ....Gen 3:24
a whip of cords, He *d*.....John 2:15

DRUNK
For these are not *d*........Acts 2:15

DRUNKARD
to and fro like a *d*..........Is 24:20
or a reviler, or a *d*........1 Cor 5:11

DRUNKENNESS
Jerusalem a cup of *d*......Zech 12:2
envy, murders, *d*............Gal 5:21

DULL
heart of this people *d*..........Is 6:10
people have grown d.....Matt 13:15

DUMB
Deaf and *d* spirit..........Mark 9:25

DUST
formed man of the *d* .... Gen 2:7
descendants as the *d* ...... Gen 13:16

DWELL
Who may *d* in Your holy .... Ps 15:1
that Christ may *d* .... Eph 3:17
the word of Christ *d* .... Col 3:16

DWELLS
He who *d* in the secret .... Ps 91:1
d all the fullness .... Col 2:9

E

EAGLE
As an *e* stirs up its .... Deut 32:11
fly away like an *e* .... Prov 23:5
had the face of an *e* .... Ezek 1:10

EAR
Bow down Your *e* .... Ps 31:2
what you hear in the *e* .... Matt 10:27
not seen, nor e heard .... 1 Cor 2:9
"He who has an *e* .... Rev 2:7

EARS
they have itching *e* .... 2 Tim 4:3

EARTH
coming to judge the *e* .... 1 Chr 16:33
e is the LORD's .... Ps 24:1
e is My footstool .... Is 66:1
e as it is in heaven .... Matt 6:10
new heaven and a new *e* ... Rev 21:1

EARTHQUAKES
And there will be *e* .... Mark 13:8

EAST
As far as the *e* .... Ps 103:12
many will come from *e* .... Matt 8:11

EAT
you may freely *e* .... Gen 2:16
e this scroll, and go .... Ezek 3:1

EDIFICATION
his good, leading to *e* ...... Rom 15:2
prophesies speaks *e* .... 1 Cor 14:3

EDIFIES
puffs up, but love *e* .... 1 Cor 8:1
he who prophesies *e* .... 1 Cor 14:4

ELDER
against an *e* except .... 1 Tim 5:19

ELDERS
e who rule well be .... 1 Tim 5:17
Let him call for the *e* .... James 5:14

ELECTION
call and *e* sure .... 2 Pet 1:10

ELEMENTS
weak and beggarly *e* .... Gal 4:9
e will melt with .... 2 Pet 3:10

END
Declaring the *e* .... Is 46:10
He loved them to the *e* .... John 13:1

ENDURANCE
For you have need of *e* .... Heb 10:36
run with *e* the race that .... Heb 12:1

ENEMIES
to you, love your *e* .... Matt 5:44

ENEMY
If your *e* is hungry .... Prov 25:21
last *e* that will be .... 1 Cor 15:26

ENJOY
richly all things to *e* ...... 1 Tim 6:17
than to *e* the passing ...... Heb 11:25

ENMITY
And I will put *e* .... Gen 3:15

ENTER
E into His gates .... Ps 100:4

ENTERED
Then Satan *e* Judas .... Luke 22:3
e the Most Holy Place ...... Heb 9:12

ENTREAT
E me not to leave you ..... Ruth 1:16

EQUAL
making Himself *e* .... John 5:18
it robbery to be *e* .... Phil 2:6

ESCAPE
and how shall we *e* .... Is 20:6
also make the way of *e* . 1 Cor 10:13
how shall we *e* if we .... Heb 2:3

ESTABLISH
E your hearts .... James 5:8

ESTEEM
and we did not *e* .... Is 53:3
and hold such men in *e* .... Phil 2:29
e them very highly ..... 1 Thess 5:13

ETERNAL
I do that I may have *e* .... Matt 19:16
not perish but have *e* ..... John 3:15
"And this is *e* life .... John 17:3
e weight of glory .... 2 Cor 4:17
lay hold on *e* life .... 1 Tim 6:12

EUNUCH
of Ethiopia, a *e* .... Acts 8:27

EVANGELIST
house of Philip the *e*. . . . . . . Acts 21:8
do the work of an *e*. . . . . 2 Tim 4:5

EVANGELISTS
some prophets, some *e* . . . . . Eph 4:11

EVERLASTING
awake, some to *e* life. . . . . . . Dan 12:2
believes in Me has *e*. . . . . . . John 6:47

EVIDENCE
e of things not seen . . . . Heb 11:1

EVIL
I will fear no *e* . . . . Ps 23:4
Whoever rewards *e*. . . . . . . Prov 17:13
deliver us from the *e* . . . . . . Matt 6:13
Repay no one *e* for . . . . Rom 12:17
not be overcome by *e*. . . . . Rom 12:21

EVILDOER
suffer trouble as an *e* . . . . . . 2 Tim 2:9

EXALTED
valley shall be *e* . . . . Is 40:4
"Him God has *e* . . . . Acts 5:31
also has highly *e*. . . . . Phil 2:9

EXALTS
Righteousness *e*. . . . . Prov 14:34

EXAMINE
But let a man *e*. . . . . 1 Cor 11:28
But let each one *e* . . . . Gal 6:4

EXCHANGED
e the truth of God for. . . . . . Rom 1:25

EXCUSE
they are without *e*. . . . . Rom 1:20

EXERCISE
e profits a little. . . . . 1 Tim 4:8

EXHORT
e him as a father . . . . 1 Tim 5:1
e one another. . . . . Heb 3:13

EXHORTATION
you have any word of *e*. . . Acts 13:15

EXPECTATION
a certain fearful *e*. . . . . Heb 10:27

EXPOSED
his deeds should be *e*. . . . . . John 3:20

EYE
e for *e*, tooth for tooth. . . . . Ex 21:24
guide you with My *e*. . . . . Ps 32:8
the apple of His *e* . . . . Zech 2:8
plank in your own *e*. . . . . Matt 7:3
the *e* of a needle . . . . Luke 18:25
the twinkling of an *e*. . . . . 1 Cor 15:52
every *e* will see Him. . . . . Rev 1:7

EYES
The *e* of the LORD are. . . . . . . Ps 34:15
I will lift up my *e*. . . . . Ps 121:1
Who have *e* and see not . . . . . . Jer 5:21
plucked out your own *e*. . . . . Gal 4:15

F

FABLES
cunningly devised *f* . . . . 2 Pet 1:16

FACE
the LORD make His *f*. . . . . . . Num 6:25
sins have hidden His *f*. . . . . Is 59:2

FAIL
faith should not *f* . . . . Luke 22:32

FAILS
Love never *f* . . . . 1 Cor 13:8

FAITH
shall live by his *f* . . . . Hab 2:4
f as a mustard seed. . . . . . . Matt 17:20
f comes by hearing . . . . Rom 10:17
For we walk by *f* . . . . 2 Cor 5:7
f working through love . . . . . . Gal 5:6
been saved through *f*. . . . . Eph 2:8
taking the shield of *f* . . . . Eph 6:16
for not all have *f*. . . . . 2 Thess 3:2
f is the substance . . . . Heb 11:1
without *f* it is impossible . . . Heb 11:6
f will save the sick . . . . James 5:15

FAITHFUL
He who promised is *f* . . . . Heb 10:23
He is *f* and just to . . . . 1 John 1:9

FAITHFULNESS
great is Your *f*. . . . . Lam 3:23

FALL
a righteous man may *f*. . . . Prov 24:16

FALSE
You shall not bear *f* . . . . Ex 20:16
I hate every *f* way . . . . Ps 119:104

FAMILIES
in you all the *f*. . . . . Gen 12:3
in your seed all the f. . . . . . . Acts 3:25

FAMINE
Now there was a *f* . . . . Gen 12:10

FAR
their heart is f from Me . . . . Matt 15:8
you who once were *f* . . . . Eph 2:13

FAST
Moreover, when you *f* . . . . . Matt 6:16

FASTING
except by prayer and *f*....Matt 17:21

FATHER
man shall leave his *f*.......Gen 2:24
and you shall be a *f*.........Gen 17:4
I was a *f* to the poor.......Job 29:16
Our *F* in heaven...............Matt 6:9
that he might be the *f*......Rom 4:11

FAVOR
A good man obtains *f*......Prov 12:2
and seek the LORD's *f*........Jer 26:19
and stature, and in *f*.......Luke 2:52

FEAR
The *f* of the LORD is..........Ps 19:9
The *f* of man brings a.....Prov 29:25
f Him who is able ....Matt 10:28
given us a spirit of *f*.........2 Tim 1:7
love casts out *f*...........1 John 4:18

FEAST
hate, I despise your *f*.....Amos 5:21
every year at the *F*........Luke 2:41

FEED
to him, "*F* My lambs ....John 21:15
enemy is hungry, f ....Rom 12:20

FEET
beautiful are the f..........Rom 10:15
all things under His f.....1 Cor 15:27
and having shod your *f*.....Eph 6:15

FELLOWSHIP
the right hand of *f*...........Gal 2:9
And have no *f* with the.....Eph 5:11

FERVENT
and being *f* in spirit.......Acts 18:25
f prayer of a.............James 5:16
all things have *f* love ....1 Pet 4:8

FEW
but the laborers are *f*......Matt 9:37
called, but *f* chosen.......Matt 20:16

FIERY
of a burning *f* furnace.......Dan 3:6
concerning the *f* trial......1 Pet 4:12

FIG
f leaves together ....Gen 3:7
f tree may not blossom.....Hab 3:17
"Look at the *f* ....Luke 21:29

FIGHT
"The LORD will *f* for ....Ex 14:14
Our God will *f* for us.......Neh 4:20
F the good *f*.............1 Tim 6:12
have fought the good *f*......2 Tim 4:7

FILL
f the earth and subdue ......Gen 1:28
F the waterpots ....John 2:7
that He might *f* ....Eph 4:10

FILLED
the whole earth be *f*.........Ps 72:19
that you may be *f*...........Eph 3:19

FILTHINESS
ourselves from all *f*........2 Cor 7:1
lay aside all *f*..............James 1:21

FIND
sure your sin will *f*.......Num 32:23
seek, and you will *f*..........Matt 7:7
f grace to help in............Heb 4:16

FINISHED
He said, "It is *f*...........John 19:30
I have *f* the race.........2 Tim 4:7

FIRE
rained brimstone and *f*....Gen 19:24
like a refiner's *f*..............Mal 3:2
f is not quenched ....Mark 9:44
"I came to send *f* ....Luke 12:49
into the lake of *f*.........Rev 20:14

FIREBRAND
f plucked from the........Amos 4:11

FIRMAMENT
Thus God made the *f*.........Gen 1:7
f shows His handiwork ......Ps 19:1

FIRST
love Him because He *f*...1 John 4:19
you have left your *f* ....Rev 2:4

FIRSTBORN
LORD struck all the *f*.........Ex 12:29
I will make him My *f* ....Ps 89:27
brought forth her *f* ....Matt 1:25
that He might be the *f* .....Rom 8:29

FIRSTFRUITS
also who have the *f*.........Rom 8:23
and has become the *f* ....1 Cor 15:20
might be a kind of *f*......James 1:18

FISH
had prepared a great *f*......Jon 1:17
belly of the great *f*........Matt 12:40

FISHERS
and I will make you *f*......Matt 4:19

FLAME
and His ministers a f........Heb 1:7
and His eyes like a *f*.........Rev 1:14

FLEE
F sexual immorality ......1 Cor 6:18
devil and he will *f*...........James 4:7

FLESH
bone of my bones and *f* . . . . Gen 2:23
"All *f* is grass, and . . . . Is 40:6
out My Spirit on all *f* . . . . Joel 2:28
two shall become one f . . . . Mark 10:8
And the Word became *f* . . . John 1:14
have crucified the *f* . . . . Gal 5:24

FLOOD
the waters of the *f* . . . . Gen 7:10

FLOWER
grass withers, the *f* . . . . Is 40:7

FLOWING
'a land *f* with milk . . . . Deut 6:3

FOLLOW
He said to him, "*F* Me . . . . . Matt 9:9
up his cross, and *f* . . . . Mark 8:34

FOOL
f has said in his . . . . Ps 14:1
f is right in his own. . . . . . . Prov 12:15
whoever says, 'You *f* . . . . . . Matt 5:22

FOOLISHNESS
F is bound up in the . . . . . . Prov 22:15
of the cross is *f* . . . . 1 Cor 1:18

FOOLS
f despise wisdom . . . . Prov 1:7
We are *f* for Christ's . . . . . . 1 Cor 4:10

FOOT
will not allow your *f* . . . . Ps 121:3

FOOTSTOOL
Your enemies Your f . . . . . Matt 22:44

FOREKNOWLEDGE
according to the *f* . . . . 1 Pet 1:2

FOREVER
His mercy endures *f* . . . . Ps 136:1
will not cast off *f* . . . . Lam 3:31
And they shall reign *f* . . . . . . Rev 22:5

FORGAVE
even as Christ *f* . . . . Col 3:13

FORGIVE
f their sin and heal . . . . 2 Chr 7:14
And *f* us our debts. . . . . Matt 6:12
f the sins of any. . . . . John 20:23
f us our sins and to . . . . 1 John 1:9

FORGIVEN
transgression is *f* . . . . Ps 32:1
to whom little is *f* . . . . Luke 7:47

FORGIVENESS
God belong mercy and *f* . . . . Dan 9:9

FORGIVING
tenderhearted, *f* . . . . Eph 4:32
and *f* one another . . . . Col 3:13

FORM
earth was without *f* . . . . Gen 1:2
who, being in the *f* . . . . Phil 2:6
having a *f* of godliness . . . . . 2 Tim 3:5

FORMED
And the LORD God *f* . . . . Gen 2:7
f my inward parts . . . . Ps 139:13

FORNICATOR
you know, that no *f* . . . . Eph 5:5
lest there be any *f* . . . . Heb 12:16

FORSAKE
never leave you nor f . . . . . . Heb 13:5

FORSAKEN
My God, why have You *f* . . . . . Ps 22:1
seen the righteous *f* . . . . Ps 37:25
My God, why have You f . . . Matt 27:46

FORTRESS
LORD is my rock, my *f* . . . . 2 Sam 22:2

FOUND
LORD while He may be *f* . . . . . . Is 55:6
be diligent to be *f* . . . . 2 Pet 3:14

FOUNDATION
and justice are the *f* . . . . Ps 89:14
loved Me before the *f* . . . . . John 17:24
Lamb slain from the *f* . . . . . . Rev 13:8

FOXES
f that spoil the vines. . . . . . . Song 2:15
F have holes and birds . . . . . Luke 9:58

FREE
if the Son makes you *f* . . . . . John 8:36
Jesus has made me *f* . . . . Rom 8:2
Christ has made us *f* . . . . Gal 5:1

FRIEND
f loves at all times. . . . . Prov 17:17
f who sticks closer. . . . . Prov 18:24
a *f* of tax collectors . . . . Matt 11:19

FRUIT
that you bear much *f* . . . . . . John 15:8
But the *f* of the Spirit . . . . Gal 5:22
yields the peaceable *f* . . . . . Heb 12:11

FULFILL
f the law of Christ . . . . Gal 6:2

FULFILLED
all things must be *f* . . . . . . Luke 24:44
loves another has *f* . . . . Rom 13:8
For all the law is *f* . . . . Gal 5:14

FULL
that your joy may be *f*... John 15:11
chose Stephen, a man *f* ..... Acts 6:5

FULLNESS
Him dwells all the *f*.......... Col 2:9

FURNACE
tested you in the *f*........... Is 48:10
of a burning fiery *f*.......... Dan 3:6

G

GAIN
and to die is *g* .... Phil 1:21
contentment is great *g*..... 1 Tim 6:6

GARDEN
LORD God planted a *g* .... Gen 2:8
g a new tomb in which ... John 19:41

GATE
by the narrow *g*........... Matt 7:13
suffered outside the *g* .... Heb 13:12

GENERATION
and adulterous *g* .... Matt 12:39

GENTILES
as a light to the *G*........... Is 42:6
all these things the *G*...... Matt 6:32
bear My name before *G*.... Acts 9:15

GIFT
but the *g* of God is .... Rom 6:23
it is the *g* of God............ Eph 2:8
Do not neglect the *g*...... 1 Tim 4:14
you to stir up the *g* .... 2 Tim 1:6

GIFTS
and desire spiritual *g* ..... 1 Cor 14:1
captive, and gave g.......... Eph 4:8

GIVE
G us this day our.......... Matt 6:11
but what I do have I *g* ...... Acts 3:6

GLAD
I was *g* when they said ..... Ps 122:1

GLADNESS
receive it with *g* .... Mark 4:16

GLORIFY
"Father, *g* Your name .... John 12:28

GLORY
"*G* to God in the .... Luke 2:14
and we beheld His *g*....... John 1:14

GO
'Let My people *g* .... Ex 5:1
Where can I *g* from.......... Ps 139:7
I *g* to prepare a place...... John 14:2

GOAL
I press toward the *g*......... Phil 3:14

GOD
the *G* of Abraham............ Ex 3:6
G is a consuming fire...... Deut 4:24
my people, and your *G* .... Ruth 1:16
G is our refuge .... Ps 46:1
Counselor, Mighty *G* .... Is 9:6
and I will be their *G* .... Jer 31:33
in G my Savior .... Luke 1:47
"For *G* so loved the .... John 3:16
Christ is the Son of *G*..... Acts 8:37
Indeed, let *G* be true........ Rom 3:4
G shall supply all .... Phil 4:19
for *G* is love............... 1 John 4:8

GODHEAD
the fullness of the *G* .... Col 2:9

GODLINESS
having a form of *g* .... 2 Tim 3:5
pertain to life and *g* .... 2 Pet 1:3

GOLD
is like apples of *g* .... Prov 25:11
more precious than *g*....... 1 Pet 1:7
of the city was pure *g* .... Rev 21:21

GOOD
who went about doing *g* .. Acts 10:38
g man someone would..... Rom 5:7
overcome evil with *g* .... Rom 12:21

GOODNESS
Surely *g* and mercy.......... Ps 23:6

GOODS
and plunder his *g* .... Matt 12:29
Soul, you have many *g*.... Luke 12:19
has this world's *g*........ 1 John 3:17

GOSPEL
and believe in the *g*....... Mark 1:15
not ashamed of the *g* ...... Rom 1:16

GOVERNMENT
and the *g* will be upon.......... Is 9:6

GRACE
But Noah found *g*........... Gen 6:8
G to you and peace.......... Rom 1:7
My *g* is sufficient .... 2 Cor 12:9
g you have been saved ...... Eph 2:8
But He gives more *g* ...... James 4:6

GRAIN
unless a *g* of wheat....... John 12:24

GRAPES
brought forth wild *g*........... Is 5:2
have eaten sour *g* .... Ezek 18:2

GRASS
The *g* withers . . . . Is 40:7
"All flesh is as g . . . . 1 Pet 1:24

GREAT
and make your name *g* . . . . . Gen 12:2
g is Your faithfulness . . . . . . Lam 3:23
one pearl of *g* price . . . . Matt 13:46
Then I saw a *g* white . . . . Rev 20:11

GREATER
g things than these . . . . John 1:50
G love has no one . . . . John 15:13

GREATEST
little child is the *g* . . . . Matt 18:4
be considered the *g* . . . . . . Luke 22:24

GREEK
is neither Jew nor *G* . . . . Gal 3:28

GRIEVE
g the Holy Spirit . . . . Eph 4:30

GROUND
"Cursed is the *g* . . . . Gen 3:17
you stand is holy *g* . . . . Ex 3:5
others fell on good *g* . . . . Matt 13:8

GUARANTEE
us the Spirit as a *g* . . . . 2 Cor 5:5

GUARD
will be your rear *g* . . . . Is 52:12
G what was committed . . . 1 Tim 6:20

H

HABITATION
from His holy *h* . . . . Zech 2:13

HADES
gates of *H* shall not . . . . Matt 16:18
being in torments in *H* . . . Luke 16:23
not leave my soul in H . . . . Acts 2:27
H were cast into the . . . . Rev 20:14

HAIR
if a woman has long *h* . . . 1 Cor 11:15
not with braided *h* . . . . 1 Tim 2:9

HALLOWED
heaven, *h* be Your name . . . . Matt 6:9

HAND
My times are in Your *h* . . . . Ps 31:15
at the right *h* of God . . . . . . Acts 7:55

HANDIWORK
firmament shows His *h* . . . . . . Ps 19:1

HANDS
"Behold My *h* and My . . . Luke 24:39
h the print of the . . . . John 20:25

lifting up holy *h* . . . . 1 Tim 2:8
the laying on of the *h* . . . . 1 Tim 4:14

HAPPY
H are the people who . . . . . . Ps 144:15
trusts in the LORD, *h* . . . . . . Prov 16:20

HARD
"Is anything too *h* . . . . Gen 18:14
I knew you to be a *h* . . . . . . Matt 25:24
This is a *h* saying . . . . John 6:60

HARDENED
But Pharaoh *h* his . . . . Ex 8:32
their heart was *h* . . . . Mark 6:52
lest any of you be *h* . . . . Heb 3:13

HARDSHIP
h as a good soldier . . . . 2 Tim 2:3

HARLOT
of a *h* named Rahab . . . . Josh 2:1
h is a deep pit . . . . Prov 23:27
h is one body with her . . . . 1 Cor 6:16

HARVEST
seedtime and *h* . . . . Gen 8:22
"The *h* is past . . . . Jer 8:20
pray the Lord of the *h* . . . . . Matt 9:38
already white for *h* . . . . John 4:35

HATE
love the LORD, *h* evil . . . . Ps 97:10
love, and a time to *h* . . . . Eccl 3:8

HAUGHTY
h spirit before a fall . . . . . . Prov 16:18

HEAD
He shall bruise your *h* . . . . . . Gen 3:15
The whole *h* is sick . . . . Is 1:5
For the husband is *h* . . . . Eph 5:23

HEAL
O LORD, *h* me . . . . Ps 6:2
h your backslidings . . . . Jer 3:22
"*H* the sick . . . . Matt 10:8

HEALED
His stripes we are *h* . . . . Is 53:5
and He *h* them . . . . Matt 4:24
he had faith to be *h* . . . . Acts 14:9
that you may be *h* . . . . James 5:16

HEALS
h all your diseases . . . . Ps 103:3
Jesus the Christ *h* . . . . Acts 9:34

HEAR
"*H*, O Israel . . . . Deut 6:4
And how shall they *h* . . . . . Rom 10:14

HEARD
Have you not *h* . . . . Is 40:21
not seen, nor ear h . . . . 1 Cor 2:9

HEARERS
of the word, and not *h* . . . James 1:22

HEARING
or by the *h* of faith . . . . Gal 3:2

HEART
LORD looks at the *h* . . . . . . 1 Sam 16:7
My *h* and my flesh cry . . . . . . Ps 84:2
as he thinks in his *h* . . . . . . Prov 23:7
h is deceitful above . . . . Jer 17:9
and take the stony *h* . . . . . Ezek 11:19
are the pure in *h* . . . . Matt 5:8
h will flow rivers . . . . John 7:38
"Let not your *h* . . . . John 14:1

HEARTS
And he will turn the *h* . . . . Mal 4:6
h failing them from . . . . . . Luke 21:26
will guard your *h* . . . . Phil 4:7
of God rule in your *h* . . . . Col 3:15

HEAVEN
on earth as it is in *h* . . . . Matt 6:10
"*H* and earth will . . . . Matt 24:35
laid up for you in *h* . . . . Col 1:5

HEAVENLY
your *h* Father will . . . . Matt 6:14
h host praising God . . . . Luke 2:13

HEAVENS
h declare the glory . . . . Ps 19:1
For as the *h* are high . . . . . . Ps 103:11
h are the work of Your . . . . . Heb 1:10

HEEL
you shall bruise His *h* . . . . . . Gen 3:15

HEIGHT
nor *h* nor depth . . . . Rom 8:39
length and depth and *h* . . . . . Eph 3:18

HEIRS
of God and joint *h* . . . . Rom 8:17
should be fellow *h* . . . . Eph 3:6

HELL
go down alive into *h* . . . . Ps 55:15
his soul from *h* . . . . Prov 23:14
"*H* from beneath is . . . . Is 14:9
to be cast into *h* . . . . Matt 18:9
power to cast into *h* . . . . Luke 12:5
it is set on fire by *h* . . . . James 3:6

HELMET
And take the *h* of . . . . Eph 6:17

HELP
A very present *h* . . . . Ps 46:1

HELPER
I will make him a *h* . . . . Gen 2:18
"But when the *H* . . . . John 15:26

HELPS
the Spirit also *h* . . . . Rom 8:26

HERESIES
in destructive *h* . . . . 2 Pet 2:1

HIDDEN
Your word I have *h* . . . . Ps 119:11
h that will not . . . . Matt 10:26

HIGH
know that the Most *H* . . . . . . Dan 4:17
h thing that exalts . . . . 2 Cor 10:5
and faithful *H* Priest . . . . Heb 2:17

HOLY
where you stand is *h* . . . . Ex 3:5
priests and a *h* nation . . . . Ex 19:6
the LORD your God am *h* . . . . Lev 19:2
God, in His *h* mountain . . . . . . Ps 48:1
"*H, h, h* is the LORD . . . . Is 6:3
baptize you with the *H* . . . . . Mark 1:8
all filled with the *H* . . . . Acts 2:4
receive the *H* Spirit . . . . Acts 19:2
it is written, "*Be h* . . . . 1 Pet 1:16

HOME
to him and make Our *h* . . . John 14:23
to show piety at *h* . . . . 1 Tim 5:4

HONOR
H your father and your . . . . Matt 15:4
worthy of double *h* . . . . 1 Tim 5:17

HONORABLE
Marriage is *h* among . . . . Heb 13:4

HOPE
For You are my *h* . . . . Ps 71:5
O the *H* of Israel . . . . Jer 14:8
good that one should *h* . . . . . Lam 3:26
h does not disappoint . . . . Rom 5:5
And now abide faith, *h* . . 1 Cor 13:13
were called in one *h* . . . . Eph 4:4
h which is laid . . . . Col 1:5
Christ in you, the *h* . . . . Col 1:27
Jesus Christ, our *h* . . . . 1 Tim 1:1
to lay hold of the *h* . . . . Heb 6:18
us again to a living *h* . . . . 1 Pet 1:3

HORN
h will be exalted . . . . Ps 112:9

HORSE
The *h* and its rider He . . . . Ex 15:1
h is a vain hope . . . . Ps 33:17

HOSPITABLE
Be *h* to one another . . . . 1 Pet 4:9

HOSTS
LORD of *h* is His name . . . . Is 47:4
against spiritual *h* . . . . Eph 6:12

HOUR
day and *h* no one knows. . Matt 24:36

HOUSE
But as for me and my *h*. . . Josh 24:15
'Set your *h* in order . . . . Is 38:1
h divided against . . . . Matt 12:25
h are many mansions. . . . . . John 14:2

HOUSEHOLD
saved, you and your *h* . . . . Acts 16:31

HUMBLE
man Moses was very *h* . . . . Num 12:3
h shall hear of it and . . . . Ps 34:2
associate with the *h* . . . . . . Rom 12:16
h yourselves under the . . . . . 1 Pet 5:6

HUNGER
are those who *h* . . . . Matt 5:6

HUNGRY
gives food to the *h*. . . . . Ps 146:7
your soul to the *h* . . . . Is 58:10
'for I was *h* and you . . . . . . Matt 25:35

HUSBAND
She also gave to her *h*. . . . . . . Gen 3:6
h safely trusts her . . . . Prov 31:11
For the unbelieving *h* . . . . . 1 Cor 7:14
For the *h* is head of . . . . Eph 5:23
the *h* of one wife . . . . 1 Tim 3:2

HUSBANDS
H, love your wives . . . . Eph 5:25

HYPOCRISY
Pharisees, which is *h*. . . . . . Luke 12:1
Let love be without *h* . . . . Rom 12:9

HYSSOP
Purge me with *h*. . . . . Ps 51:7

I

IDLE
i word men may speak . . . Matt 12:36
they learn to be *i*. . . . . 1 Tim 5:13

IDOLS
stolen the household *i*. . . . . Gen 31:19
This was offered to *i*. . . . . 1 Cor 10:28
keep yourselves from *i*. . . 1 John 5:21

IMITATE
I urge you, *i* me . . . . 1 Cor 4:16
i those who through. . . . . Heb 6:12

IMMORALITY
except sexual *i* . . . . Matt 5:32
abstain from sexual *i*. . . . . 1 Thess 4:3

IMMORTALITY
mortal must put on *i*. . . . . 1 Cor 15:53

IMPOSSIBLE
and nothing will be *i* . . . . . Matt 17:20
God nothing will be *i*. . . . . . Luke 1:37
without faith it is *i* . . . . Heb 11:6

INCORRUPTIBLE
dead will be raised *i* . . . . . 1 Cor 15:52
corruptible seed but *i*. . . . . . 1 Pet 1:23

INFIRMITIES
He Himself took our i. . . . . . Matt 8:17
boast, except in my *i*. . . . . . 2 Cor 12:5

INHERITANCE
we have obtained an *i*. . . . . . Eph 1:11
i incorruptible . . . . 1 Pet 1:4

INIQUITIES
forgives all your *i* . . . . Ps 103:3
was bruised for our *i* . . . . Is 53:5
i have separated you . . . . Is 59:2

INIQUITY
If I regard *i* in my . . . . Ps 66:18
has laid on Him the *i*. . . . . Is 53:6

INTEGRITY
In the *i* of my heart . . . . Gen 20:5
he holds fast to his *i* . . . . Job 2:3
I have walked in my *i*. . . . . Ps 26:1
The *i* of the upright. . . . . Prov 11:3

INTERCESSION
of many, and made *i* . . . . Is 53:12
Spirit Himself makes *i*. . . . Rom 8:26
always lives to make *i*. . . . . Heb 7:25

INTERPRET
pray that he may *i*. . . . . . . 1 Cor 14:13

ISRAEL
be called Jacob, but *I* . . . . . Gen 32:28
"Hear, O *I* . . . . Deut 6:4
shepherd My people *I* . . . . . 2 Sam 7:7
and upon the *I* of God . . . . . . Gal 6:16

J

JEALOUS
your God, am a *j* God. . . . . Ex 20:5
LORD, whose name is *J* . . . . . Ex 34:14

JESUS
shall call His name *J*. . . . . . . Matt 1:21
J wept. . . . . John 11:35
J was crucified. . . . . John 19:20
This *J* God has raised . . . . . . Acts 2:32
your mouth the Lord *J*. . . . . Rom 10:9
looking unto *J* . . . . Heb 12:2

JOT
one *j* or one tittle . . . . Matt 5:18

JOY
is fullness of *j* . . . . Ps 16:11
j comes in the morning . . . . . . Ps 30:5
To God my exceeding *j* . . . . . . Ps 43:4
in my womb for *j* . . . . Luke 1:44
My *j* may remain in you . . John 15:11
the Spirit is love, *j* . . . . Gal 5:22
count it all *j* . . . . James 1:2

JOYFUL
Make a *j* shout to the . . . . Ps 100:1

JUDGE
"*J* not, that you be. . . . . Matt 7:1
j who did not fear God . . . Luke 18:2

JUDGES
he who is spiritual *j*. . . . . . . 1 Cor 2:15

JUDGMENT
be in danger of the *j* . . . . . . Matt 5:21
after this the *j* . . . . Heb 9:27
receive a stricter *j*. . . . . James 3:1

JUDGMENTS
righteous are His *j* . . . . Rev 19:2

JUST
j shall live by faith . . . . Rom 1:17
j men made perfect . . . . Heb 12:23

JUSTICE
for all His ways are *j* . . . . . . Deut 32:4
j as the noonday. . . . . Ps 37:6

JUSTIFICATION
because of our *j* . . . . Rom 4:25
offenses resulted in *j*. . . . . . Rom 5:16

JUSTIFIED
law no flesh will be *j* . . . . . Rom 3:20
having been *j* by . . . . Rom 5:1

JUSTIFIES
It is God who *j* . . . . Rom 8:33

K

KEEP
day, to *k* it holy . . . . Ex 20:8

KEEPER
Am I my brother's *k*. . . . . Gen 4:9
The LORD is your *k* . . . . Ps 121:5

KEYS
I will give you the *k* . . . . . . Matt 16:19
And I have the *k* . . . . Rev 1:18

KILL
k the Passover . . . . Ex 12:21
I *k* and I make alive . . . . . Deut 32:39
k and eat . . . . Acts 10:13

KINDNESS
anger, abundant in *k*. . . . . . . Neh 9:17
k shall not depart . . . . Is 54:10
longsuffering, *k* . . . . Gal 5:22

KING
said, "Give us a *k*. . . . . 1 Sam 8:6
K of kings and Lord of . . . . Rev 19:16

KINGDOM
"Repent, for the *k* . . . . Matt 3:2
are not far from the *k*. . . . Mark 12:34
back, is fit for the *k* . . . . Luke 9:62
for the *k* of God is. . . . . Rom 14:17
will not inherit the *k*. . . . . Gal 5:21

KINGDOMS
have become the *k* . . . . Rev 11:15

KISS
Let him *k* me with the. . . . . Song 1:2
"You gave Me no *k* . . . . Luke 7:45
another with a holy *k*. . . . Rom 16:16

KNEE
of Jesus every *k*. . . . . Phil 2:10

KNEW
Adam *k* Eve his wife . . . . Gen 4:1
in the womb I *k*. . . . . Jer 1:5
to them, 'I never *k*. . . . . Matt 7:23
k what was in man . . . . John 2:25

KNOCK
k, and it will be . . . . Matt 7:7
at the door and *k*. . . . . Rev 3:20

KNOW
k that my Redeemer. . . . . . . Job 19:25
k that I am God . . . . Ps 46:10
We speak what We *k*. . . . . . John 3:11
k what we worship . . . . John 4:22

KNOWLEDGE
and the tree of the *k* . . . . Gen 2:9
k is too wonderful . . . . Ps 139:6
Wise people store up *k* . . . Prov 10:14
k shall increase. . . . . Dan 12:4
you have rejected *k* . . . . Hos 4:6
K puffs up. . . . . 1 Cor 8:1

KNOWS
searches the hearts *k* . . . . . . Rom 8:27
k the things of God . . . . 1 Cor 2:11
k those who are His . . . . . . 2 Tim 2:19

L

LABOR
Six days you shall *l* . . . . Ex 20:9
to Me, all you who *l*. . . . . . . Matt 11:28
but rather let him *l*. . . . . Eph 4:28

LABORERS
but the *l* are few. . . . . Matt 9:37

LACK
"One thing you *l* . . . . Mark 10:21

LINE
upon precept, *l* upon *l* . . . . Is 28:10
I am setting a plumb *l* . . . . . Amos 7:8

LIVE
but the just shall *l*. . . . . Hab 2:4
'Man shall not l . . . . Matt 4:4
to me, to *l* is Christ. . . . . Phil 1:21

LOAVES
have here only five *l*. . . . . . Matt 14:17

LONGSUFFERING
is love, joy, peace, *l*. . . . . Gal 5:22

LOOK
"*L* to Me, and be saved. . . . . . Is 45:22

LOOKING
l unto Jesus. . . . . Heb 12:2

LOOSE
and whatever you *l*. . . . . . . Matt 16:19

LORD
L is a man of war . . . . Ex 15:3
L our God, the *L* . . . . Deut 6:4
L is near to all who. . . . . Ps 145:18
L is a God of justice. . . . . Is 30:18
L Our Righteousness. . . . . Jer 23:6
L God is my strength. . . . . . . Hab 3:19
shall worship the L. . . . . Matt 4:10
why do you call Me *'L*. . . . . Luke 6:46
'Who are You, *L*. . . . . Acts 26:15
that Jesus Christ is *L*. . . . . . . Phil 2:11
L God Omnipotent . . . . Rev 19:6

LOTS
garments, casting *l* . . . . . . Mark 15:24

LOVE
l your neighbor as. . . . . Lev 19:18
l the LORD your God . . . . Deut 6:5
l covers all sins . . . . Prov 10:12
a time to *l* . . . . Eccl 3:8
banner over me was *l* . . . . . . Song 2:4
to you, *l* your enemies . . . . . Matt 5:44
"If you *l* Me . . . . John 14:15
l one another as I . . . . John 15:12
Let *l* be without . . . . Rom 12:9
up, but *l* edifies. . . . . 1 Cor 8:1
L never fails . . . . 1 Cor 13:8
greatest of these is *l* . . . . . 1 Cor 13:13
For the *l* of Christ . . . . 2 Cor 5:14
fruit of the Spirit is *l*. . . . . . . Gal 5:22
Husbands, *l* your wives. . . . . Eph 5:25
l their husbands. . . . . Titus 2:4
for "*l will cover a* . . . . 1 Pet 4:8
we *l* the brethren . . . . 1 John 3:14
know God, for God is *l*. . . . 1 John 4:8
have left your first *l* . . . . Rev 2:4

LOVINGKINDNESS
l is better than life. . . . . Ps 63:3

LUKEWARM
because you are *l* . . . . Rev 3:16

LYING
I hate and abhor *l* . . . . Ps 119:163
righteous man hates *l*. . . . . . Prov 13:5
signs, and *l* wonders . . . . . 2 Thess 2:9

M

MAGNIFIED
For You have *m* Your. . . . . . . Ps 138:2

MAJESTY
splendor of Your *m*. . . . . Ps 145:5
eyewitnesses of His *m*. . . . . 2 Pet 1:16
wise, be glory and *m* . . . . Jude 25

MAKE
Let Us *m* man in Our. . . . . . . Gen 1:26
m Our home with him. . . . John 14:23

MALICE
laying aside all *m* . . . . 1 Pet 2:1

MAN
"Let Us make *m* . . . . Gen 1:26
"You are the *m* . . . . 2 Sam 12:7
"Behold the *M* . . . . John 19:5
since by *m* came death . . 1 Cor 15:21
in Himself one new *m*. . . . . . Eph 2:15

MANGER
and laid Him in a *m*. . . . . Luke 2:7

MANIFESTED
"I have *m* Your name . . . . . John 17:6
God was *m* in the flesh . . . 1 Tim 3:16
the love of God was *m*. . . . 1 John 4:9

MANNA
of Israel ate *m* . . . . Ex 16:35
Our fathers ate the *m*. . . . . . John 6:31
of the hidden *m*. . . . . Rev 2:17

MANNER
in an unworthy *m* . . . . . . 1 Cor 11:27
as is the *m* of some . . . . Heb 10:25

MANSIONS
house are many *m* . . . . John 14:2

MARK
And the LORD set a *m* . . . . . . Gen 4:15
M the blameless man . . . . Ps 37:37
whoever receives the *m* . . . Rev 14:11

MARRED
so His visage was *m*. . . . . Is 52:14

MARRIAGE
nor are given in *m*. . . . . . . Matt 22:30
her in *m* does well. . . . . 1 Cor 7:38
M is honorable among . . . . . Heb 13:4
the *m* of the Lamb has . . . . . Rev 19:7

MARRY
it is better not to *m*....... Matt 19:10
they neither *m* nor are.... Matt 22:30
let them *m* .... 1 Cor 7:9
forbidding to *m* .... 1 Tim 4:3
the younger widows *m* ... 1 Tim 5:14

MARVELED
Jesus heard it, He *m*....... Matt 8:10
And the multitudes *m*...... Matt 9:33

MARVELOUS
m are Your works......... Ps 139:14
of darkness into His *m* ..... 1 Pet 2:9

MASTER
not greater than his *m*.... John 15:20
m builder I have laid ..... 1 Cor 3:10

MASTERS
can serve two *m* .... Luke 16:13

MEASURE
to each one a *m* .... Rom 12:3

MEDIATOR
is one God and one *M* ..... 1 Tim 2:5
as He is also *M* .... Heb 8:6
to Jesus the *M* of the..... Heb 12:24

MEEK
Blessed are the *m* .... Matt 5:5

MEMBERS
that your bodies are *m*.... 1 Cor 6:15

MENSERVANTS
And on My m and on My .. Acts 2:18

MERCIFUL
Blessed are the *m* .... Matt 5:7
saying, 'God be *m*....... Luke 18:13

MERCY
but showing *m* to .... Ex 20:6
and abundant in *m*....... Num 14:18
m endures forever....... 1 Chr 16:34
do justly, to love *m*.......... Mic 6:8
that we may obtain *m*...... Heb 4:16

MERRY
m heart makes a .... Prov 15:13
eat, drink, and be *m* .... Eccl 8:15

MESSIAH
until *M* the Prince .... Dan 9:25
"We have found the *M* .... John 1:41

MIDST
I am there in the *m*....... Matt 18:20

MIGHT
'Not by *m* nor by.......... Zech 4:6

MIGHTY
How the *m* have fallen ... 2 Sam 1:19
The LORD *m* in battle .... Ps 24:8
their Redeemer is *m*...... Prov 23:11
Woe to men *m* at............. Is 5:22

MIND
perfect peace, whose *m*....... Is 26:3
Be of the same *m*.......... Rom 12:16

MINISTERS
angels spirits, His *m* .... Ps 104:4
commend ourselves as *m*... 2 Cor 6:4

MIRACLES
God worked unusual *m* ... Acts 19:11
the working of *m*........ 1 Cor 12:10

MITES
widow putting in two *m* ... Luke 21:2

MOCKED
knee before Him and *m*... Matt 27:29
deceived, God is not *m*........ Gal 6:7

MONEY
tables of the *m* changers.. Matt 21:12
and hid his lord's *m* ...... Matt 25:18
not greedy for *m* .... 1 Tim 3:3

MORNING
Lucifer, son of the *m* .... Is 14:12
the Bright and *M* Star ..... Rev 22:16

MOTHER
because she was the *m*..... Gen 3:20
leave his father and m..... Matt 19:5
"Behold your *m*!" .... John 19:27

MOUNTAIN
you will say to this *m*..... Matt 17:20
with Him on the holy *m* ... 2 Pet 1:18

MOUNTAINS
in Judea flee to the *m*..... Matt 24:16

MOURN
a time to *m*................ Eccl 3:4
are those who *m* .... Matt 5:4
of the earth will *m* .... Rev 1:7

MOURNING
I will turn their *m*.......... Jer 31:13

MULTIPLY
"Be fruitful and *m* .... Gen 1:22
m your descendants....... Gen 16:10

MULTITUDE
compassion on the *m*..... Matt 15:32

MURDER
'You shall not m .... Matt 5:21
threats and *m* against......... Acts 9:1

MUZZLE
"You shall not m..........1 Tim 5:18

MYSTERIES
the spirit he speaks *m* ....1 Cor 14:2

MYSTERY
Behold, I tell you a *m*....1 Cor 15:51
made known to us the *m* .....Eph 1:9

N

NAKED
And they were both *n* ......Gen 2:25
N I came from my..........Job 1:21
'I was *n* and you ....Matt 25:36

NAME
Abram called on the *n*.......Gen 13:4
The *n* of the LORD is a ....Prov 18:10
A good *n* is to be..........Prov 22:1
They will call on My *n*....Zech 13:9
to you who fear My *n*.........Mal 4:2
hallowed be Your *n*..........Matt 6:9
who believe in His *n*.......John 1:12
through faith in His *n*......Acts 3:16
there is no other *n*.........Acts 4:12
which is above every *n*......Phil 2:9
deed, do all in the *n* ....Col 3:17
reproached for the *n* ......1 Pet 4:14
you hold fast to My *n*........Rev 2:13

NARROW
"Enter by the *n* gate.......Matt 7:13
n is the gate and ....Matt 7:14

NATION
make you a great *n* ....Gen 12:2
I will make them one *n*...Ezek 37:22
n will rise against ....Matt 24:7
tribe, tongue, and *n* ....Rev 13:7

NEED
the things you have *n*.......Matt 6:8
'The Lord has *n* ....Matt 21:3
each as anyone had *n*......Acts 4:35
supply all your *n*...........Phil 4:19

NEIGHBOR
every man teach his *n*......Jer 31:34
You shall love your n......Matt 5:43
And who is my *n* ....Luke 10:29
You shall love your n......Rom 13:9

NET
catch them in their *n*........Hab 1:15
I will let down the *n*.........Luke 5:5
to them, "Cast the *n*.......John 21:6

NEW
and there is nothing *n*.......Eccl 1:9
n every morning.............Lam 3:23
of the *n* covenant...........Matt 26:28
n commandment I give ...John 13:34
he is a *n* creation..........2 Cor 5:17

NINETY-NINE
he not leave the *n* ....Matt 18:12

NUMBER
teach us to *n* our days ......Ps 90:12
His *n* is 666.................Rev 13:18

O

OATH
I may establish the *o*.........Jer 11:5
he denied with an *o* ......Matt 26:72

OBEY
o is better than ....1 Sam 15:22
o God rather than men......Acts 5:29
and do not *o* the truth ......Rom 2:8
o your parents in all ....Col 3:20
O those who rule ....Heb 13:17

OFFERING
you shall bring your *o* ....Lev 1:2
You make His soul an *o* ....Is 53:10

OIL
like the precious *o*..........Ps 133:2
o might have been sold ....Matt 26:9

OLD
your o men shall dream....Acts 2:17
o man was crucified ....Rom 6:6

OLIVE
a freshly plucked *o*.........Gen 8:11
of the *o* may fail ....Hab 3:17
o tree which is wild ......Rom 11:24

OPPORTUNITY
But sin, taking *o*............Rom 7:8
as we have *o*..................Gal 6:10

OPPRESSED
He was *o* and He was ....Is 53:7
healing all who were *o*....Acts 10:38

ORDER
swept, and put in *o*.......Matt 12:44
done decently and in *o*...1 Cor 14:40
according to the o............Heb 5:6

ORPHANS
I will not leave you *o*.....John 14:18
to visit *o* and widows ....James 1:27

OUTSIDE
Pharisees make the *o*.....Luke 11:39
to Him, *o* the camp ....Heb 13:13
But *o* are dogs and ....Rev 22:15

OVERCOME
good cheer, I have *o*......John 16:33

because you have *o*......1 John 2:13
and the Lamb will *o*........Rev 17:14

OVERCOMES
of God *o* the world ....1 John 5:4
o I will give to eat...........Rev 2:7
o shall inherit all...........Rev 21:7

OVERSEERS
you, serving as *o*...........1 Pet 5:2

OVERTAKEN
if a man is *o* in any...........Gal 6:1

P

PAIN
p you shall bring...........Gen 3:16
Why is my *p* perpetual......Jer 15:18
shall be no more *p* ....Rev 21:4

PALACES
Out of the ivory *p* ....Ps 45:8

PARADISE
will be with Me in *P*......Luke 23:43
was caught up into *P*.....2 Cor 12:4
in the midst of the *P*.........Rev 2:7

PARDON
p your transgressions ......Ex 23:21
O LORD, *p* my iniquity ......Ps 25:11
He will abundantly *p*...........Is 55:7

PARENTS
will rise up against *p* .....Matt 10:21
has left house or *p* ....Luke 18:29
disobedient to *p*...........Rom 1:30

PART
has chosen that good *p*...Luke 10:42
you, you have no *p*.........John 13:8

PARTIALITY
that God shows no *p*.......Acts 10:34
For there is no *p* ....Rom 2:11

PASSOVER
It is the LORD's *P*............Ex 12:11
I will keep the *P*..........Matt 26:18
indeed Christ, our *P* ....1 Cor 5:7
By faith he kept the *P*.....Heb 11:28

PASTURES
to lie down in green *p* ....Ps 23:2

PATHS
He leads me in the *p*.........Ps 23:3
and all her *p* are ....Prov 3:17
p they have not ....Is 42:16
make His p straight ....Matt 3:3

PATIENCE
'Master, have *p* ....Matt 18:26
Now may the God of *p*.....Rom 15:5
labor of love, and *p* ......1 Thess 1:3
faith, love, *p* ....1 Tim 6:11
p have its perfect ....James 1:4

PEACE
you, and give you *p* ....Num 6:26
both lie down in *p*............Ps 4:8
Pray for the *p* of ....Ps 122:6
keep him in perfect *p*.........Is 26:3
and on earth *p*.............Luke 2:14
in Me you may have *p*.....John 16:33
by faith, we have *p* ....Rom 5:1
He Himself is our *p* ....Eph 2:14
and the *p* of God............Phil 4:7
meaning "king of *p*,".........Heb 7:2

PEACEMAKERS
Blessed are the *p* ....Matt 5:9

PEARLS
nor cast your *p*.............Matt 7:6
gates were twelve *p* ....Rev 21:21

PEOPLE
p shall be my *p* ....Ruth 1:16
We are His *p* and the.......Ps 100:3
and they shall be My *p*......Jer 24:7
for you are not My *p* ....Hos 1:9

PERDITION
except the son of *p*.......John 17:12
to them a proof of *p*.........Phil 1:28
revealed, the son of *p*....2 Thess 2:3
who draw back to *p*.......Heb 10:39
day of judgment and *p* .....2 Pet 3:7

PERFECT
Noah was a just man, *p* ....Gen 6:9
for God, His way is *p*.......Ps 18:30
Father in heaven is *p* ......Matt 5:48
and *p* will of God..........Rom 12:2
present every man *p*........Col 1:28
of just men made *p* ....Heb 12:23

PERISH
All flesh would *p*...........Job 34:15
little ones should *p* ....Matt 18:14
will all likewise *p* ....Luke 13:3
in Him should not *p* ....John 3:16
that any should *p* ....2 Pet 3:9

PERSECUTE
p me wrongfully ....Ps 119:86
when they revile and *p* ....Matt 5:11
Bless those who *p*.........Rom 12:14

PERSEVERANCE
tribulation produces *p* ....Rom 5:3
to this end with all *p* ....Eph 6:18

PERSON
express image of His *p* ......Heb 1:3
let it be the hidden *p* ....1 Pet 3:4

PERSUADE
"You almost *p* me . . . . Acts 26:28
the Lord, we *p* men. . . . . . . 2 Cor 5:11
For do I now *p* men . . . . Gal 1:10

PERSUADED
p that He is able . . . . 2 Tim 1:12

PERVERSE
p lips far from you . . . . Prov 4:24
from this *p* generation . . . . . Acts 2:40

PHYSICIAN
Gilead, is there no *p* . . . . Jer 8:22
have no need of a *p* . . . . . . Matt 9:12
Luke the beloved *p* . . . . Col 4:14

PIERCED
p My hands and My feet . . . . Ps 22:16
Me whom they have *p*. . . . Zech 12:10
of the soldiers *p*. . . . . John 19:34
and they also who *p*. . . . . Rev 1:7

PILLAR
and she became a *p*. . . . . . . Gen 19:26
and by night in a *p*. . . . . Ex 13:21

PIT
cast him into some *p*. . . . . . Gen 37:20
who go down to the *p*. . . . . Ps 28:1
a harlot is a deep *p*. . . . . . . Prov 23:27
up my life from the *p*. . . . . Jon 2:6
if it falls into a *p* . . . . Matt 12:11
into the bottomless *p*. . . . . . . Rev 20:3

PITY
"Have *p* on me. . . . . Job 19:21
for someone to take *p*. . . . . . . Ps 69:20
And should I not *p* . . . . Jon 4:11

PLACE
Come, see the *p* . . . . Matt 28:6
I go to prepare a *p* . . . . John 14:2
might go to his own *p*. . . . . . Acts 1:25

PLAGUES
I will send all My *p*. . . . . Ex 9:14
p that are written . . . . Rev 22:18

PLANT
a time to *p* . . . . Eccl 3:2
Him as a tender *p*. . . . . Is 53:2
p which My heavenly. . . . . Matt 15:13

PLANTED
I *p*, Apollos watered . . . . 1 Cor 3:6

PLAY
p skillfully with a. . . . . Ps 33:3
nursing child shall *p* . . . . Is 11:8

PLEASANT
how good and how *p* . . . . Ps 133:1
P words are like a. . . . . Prov 16:24

PLEASE
in the flesh cannot *p*. . . . . Rom 8:8
is impossible to *p* Him. . . . . . Heb 11:6

PLEASURE
not a God who takes *p*. . . . . Ps 5:4
for He has no *p*. . . . . Eccl 5:4
shall perform all My *p*. . . . . . . Is 44:28
your Father's good *p* . . . . . Luke 12:32

PLEASURES
Your right hand are *p* . . . . . . Ps 16:11
to enjoy the passing *p*. . . . . Heb 11:25

PLOW
put his hand to the *p* . . . . . . Luke 9:62

PLUMB
a *p* line, with a *p* . . . . Amos 7:7

POISON
"The p of asps is . . . . Rom 3:13
evil, full of deadly *p*. . . . . . . James 3:8

POOR
p will never cease. . . . . Deut 15:11
soul grieved for the *p*. . . . . . Job 30:25
p man cried out . . . . Ps 34:6
a slack hand becomes *p*. . . . Prov 10:4
the alien or the *p*. . . . . Zech 7:10
p have the gospel. . . . . Matt 11:5
your sakes He became *p* . . . 2 Cor 8:9
should remember the *p* . . . . . Gal 2:10
wretched, miserable, *p* . . . . . Rev 3:17

PORTION
I will divide Him a *p* . . . . Is 53:12
"The LORD is my *p*. . . . . Lam 3:24
and appoint him his *p* . . . . Matt 24:51
Father, give me the *p*. . . . Luke 15:12

POSSIBLE
God all things are *p* . . . . . . Matt 19:26
p that the blood. . . . . Heb 10:4

POUR
p My Spirit on your . . . . Is 44:3
that I will *p* out My . . . . Joel 2:28

POURED
I am *p* out like water . . . . Ps 22:14
I am already being *p* . . . . . . 2 Tim 4:6

POVERTY
but it leads to *p* . . . . Prov 11:24
p might become rich . . . . 2 Cor 8:9

POWER
that I may show My *p* . . . . Ex 9:16
Not by might nor by *p*. . . . . . Zech 4:6
you are endued with *p* . . . Luke 24:49
you shall receive *p*. . . . . Acts 1:8
for it is the *p*. . . . . Rom 1:16

greatness of His *p*.......... Eph 1:19
by the word of His *p*........ Heb 1:3

PRAISE
that has breath *p*.......... Ps 150:6
Let another man *p*.......... Prov 27:2
for You are my *p*.......... Jer 17:14
You have perfected p..... Matt 21:16
should be to the *p*.......... Eph 1:12
the sacrifice of *p*.......... Heb 13:15
saying, "*P* our God.......... Rev 19:5

PRAISES
enthroned in the *p*.......... Ps 22:3
it is good to sing *p*.......... Ps 147:1

PRAY
LORD in ceasing to *p*.... 1 Sam 12:23
"But you, when you *p*...... Matt 6:6
to the mountain to *p*...... Mark 6:46
"Lord, teach us to *p*....... Luke 11:1
men always ought to *p*.... Luke 18:1
I do not *p* for the.......... John 17:9
know what we should *p*.... Rom 8:26
p without ceasing....... 1 Thess 5:17
Let him *p*.............. James 5:13

PRAYER
continually to *p*.......... Acts 6:4
steadfastly in *p*.......... Rom 12:12
to fasting and *p*.......... 1 Cor 7:5
but in everything by *p*...... Phil 4:6
And the *p* of faith........ James 5:15

PREACH
that great city, and *p*....... Jon 3:2
time Jesus began to *p*..... Matt 4:17
p the gospel to the....... Luke 4:18
And how shall they *p*.... Rom 10:15
p Christ crucified........ 1 Cor 1:23
For we do not *p*.......... 2 Cor 4:5
p Christ even from......... Phil 1:15
P the word.............. 2 Tim 4:2

PREDESTINED
He foreknew, He also *p*.... Rom 8:29
having *p* us to.......... Eph 1:5
inheritance, being *p*........ Eph 1:11

PRESENCE
themselves from the *p*....... Gen 3:8
p is fullness of joy.......... Ps 16:11
Be silent in the *p*.......... Zeph 1:7

PRESENT
p your bodies a living .... Rom 12:1
absent in body but *p*...... 1 Cor 5:3
p you faultless............ Jude 24

PREVAIL
our tongue we will *p*........ Ps 12:4
of Hades shall not *p*..... Matt 16:18

PRIDE
P goes before.......... Prov 16:18

PRIEST
so He shall be a *p*........ Zech 6:13
and faithful High *P*......... Heb 2:17
we have a great High *P*..... Heb 4:14
p forever according......... Heb 5:6

PRIESTHOOD
has an unchangeable *p*..... Heb 7:24
house, a holy *p*.......... 1 Pet 2:5
generation, a royal *p*...... 1 Pet 2:9

PRIESTS
to Me a kingdom of *p*........ Ex 19:6
made us kings and *p*....... Rev 1:6
but they shall be *p*....... Rev 20:6

PRINCE
"Who made you a *p*......... Ex 2:14
everlasting Father, *P*......... Is 9:6
according to the *p*.......... Eph 2:2

PRISON
and put him into the *p*.... Gen 39:20
to the spirits in *p*.......... 1 Pet 3:19

PRIZE
the goal for the *p*.......... Phil 3:14

PROCLAIM
began to *p* it freely......... Mark 1:45
knowing, Him I *p*......... Acts 17:23
drink this cup, you *p*..... 1 Cor 11:26

PRODIGAL
with *p* living............ Luke 15:13

PROMISE
but to wait for the *P*....... Acts 1:4
is made void and the *p*.... Rom 4:14
it is no longer of *p*.......... Gal 3:18
Therefore, since a *p*.......... Heb 4:1

PROMISES
For all the *p* of God....... 2 Cor 1:20
patience inherit the *p*....... Heb 6:12

PROPHECY
miracles, to another *p*... 1 Cor 12:10
for *p* never came by the ... 2 Pet 1:21

PROPHESIED
Lord, have we not *p*....... Matt 7:22
virgin daughters who *p*.... Acts 21:9

PROPHESY
prophets, "Do not *p*......... Is 30:10
the prophets *p* falsely....... Jer 5:31
saying, "*P* to us.......... Matt 26:68
your daughters shall p.... Acts 2:17
if prophecy, let us *p*....... Rom 12:6
know in part and we *p*.... 1 Cor 13:9
desire earnestly to *p*..... 1 Cor 14:39

PROPHET
raise up for you a *P*....... Deut 18:15

RECONCILE
and that He might *r* . . . . Eph 2:16
r all things to. . . . . Col 1:20

RECONCILED
were enemies we were *r* . . . Rom 5:10

RED
though they are *r* . . . . Is 1:18
for the sky is *r* . . . . Matt 16:2

REDEEM
r their life from. . . . . Ps 72:14
And He shall *r* Israel . . . . Ps 130:8
us, that He might *r*. . . . . Titus 2:14

REDEEMED
Christ has *r* us from . . . . Gal 3:13

REDEEMER
For I know that my *R*. . . . . . Job 19:25
for their *R* is mighty . . . . . . Prov 23:11
Their *R* is strong. . . . . Jer 50:34

REDEMPTION
heads, because your *r* . . . . Luke 21:28
sanctification and *r* . . . . 1 Cor 1:30
In Him we have *r* . . . . Eph 1:7

REFUGE
six cities of *r*. . . . . Num 35:6
eternal God is your *r* . . . . . Deut 33:27
God is our *r* and. . . . . Ps 46:1
who have fled for *r*. . . . . Heb 6:18

REGENERATION
the washing of *r* . . . . Titus 3:5

REIGN
righteousness will *r*. . . . . Rom 5:17
do not let sin *r* . . . . Rom 6:12

REJECTED
He is despised and *r*. . . . . Is 53:3

REJOICE
R in the LORD . . . . Ps 33:1
R, O young man . . . . Eccl 11:9
and your heart will *r*. . . . . John 16:22
R with those who . . . . Rom 12:15
R in the Lord always . . . . Phil 4:4

RELIGION
in self-imposed *r* . . . . Col 2:23
and undefiled *r* . . . . James 1:27

REMEMBER
R the Sabbath day . . . . Ex 20:8
R now your Creator. . . . . Eccl 12:1
R those who rule. . . . . Heb 13:7

REMEMBRANCE
Put Me in *r* . . . . Is 43:26
do this in *r* of Me . . . . Luke 22:19
do this in *r* of Me. . . . . 1 Cor 11:24

REMISSION
repentance for the *r*. . . . . Mark 1:4
Jesus Christ for the *r* . . . . . . Acts 2:38
where there is *r*. . . . . Heb 10:18

RENDER
R therefore to Caesar. . . . . . Matt 22:21

RENEWED
that your youth is *r*. . . . . Ps 103:5
inward man is being *r* . . . . 2 Cor 4:16
and be *r* in the spirit . . . . . . Eph 4:23
the new man who is *r*. . . . . . . Col 3:10

REPENT
I abhor myself, and *r* . . . . Job 42:6
R, for the kingdom . . . . Matt 3:2
said to them, "*R* . . . . Acts 2:38
be zealous and *r* . . . . Rev 3:19

REPENTANCE
will grant them *r* . . . . 2 Tim 2:25
renew them again to *r*. . . . . . . Heb 6:6
all should come to *r* . . . . 2 Pet 3:9

REPUTATION
seven men of good *r*. . . . . Acts 6:3
made Himself of no *r* . . . . Phil 2:7

RESIST
r the Holy Spirit . . . . Acts 7:51
R the devil and he . . . . James 4:7

RESISTS
"God r the proud. . . . . James 4:6

REST
and I will give you *r*. . . . . . Matt 11:28
remains therefore a *r*. . . . . Heb 4:9

RESTORE
R to me the joy. . . . . Ps 51:12
For I will *r* health to . . . . Jer 30:17
and will *r* all things. . . . . . . Matt 17:11
who are spiritual *r*. . . . . Gal 6:1

RESTORES
He *r* my soul . . . . Ps 23:3

RESURRECTION
who say there is no *r* . . . . . Matt 22:23
to her, "I am the *r*. . . . . John 11:25
and the power of His *r* . . . . . Phil 3:10

REVELATION
spirit of wisdom and *r*. . . . . . Eph 1:17

REWARDER
and that He is a *r* . . . . Heb 11:6

RICH
Abram was very *r*. . . . . Gen 13:2
you say, 'I am *r* . . . . Rev 3:17

RICHES
do you despise the *r* . . . . Rom 2:4
the unsearchable *r* . . . . Eph 3:8
trust in uncertain *r* . . . . 1 Tim 6:17

RIGHTEOUS
also destroy the *r* . . . . Gen 18:23
r are bold as a lion . . . . Prov 28:1

RIGHTEOUSNESS
r delivers from death . . . . . Prov 10:2
R exalts a nation . . . . Prov 14:34
r will be peace . . . . Is 32:17
r as a breastplate . . . . Is 59:17
The LORD Our *R* . . . . Jer 23:6
accounted to him for r . . . . . Rom 4:22
we might become the *r*. . . . 2 Cor 5:21
the breastplate of *r*. . . . . Eph 6:14

RISE
third day He will *r*. . . . . Matt 20:19

RISEN
disciples that He is *r*. . . . . . Matt 28:7
"The Lord is *r* . . . . Luke 24:34

RIVER
peace to her like a *r*. . . . . Is 66:12
he showed me a pure *r* . . . . . Rev 22:1

RIVERS
his heart will flow *r* . . . . John 7:38

ROB
"Will a man *r* God . . . . Mal 3:8

ROCK
you shall strike the *r* . . . . Ex 17:6
R who begot you. . . . . Deut 32:18
"The LORD is my *r* . . . . 2 Sam 22:2
For You are my *r*. . . . . Ps 31:3
been mindful of the *R* . . . . Is 17:10
his house on the *r* . . . . Matt 7:24
"Some fell on *r* . . . . Luke 8:6

ROD
And Moses took the *r*. . . . . Ex 4:20
Your *r* and Your staff. . . . . Ps 23:4
The *r* and rebuke give . . . . Prov 29:15
shall come forth a *R*. . . . . Is 11:1
rule them with a r. . . . . Rev 2:27

ROOTED
that you, being *r* . . . . Eph 3:17
r and built up in Him . . . . Col 2:7

ROSE
I am the *r* of Sharon. . . . . Song 2:1
and blossom as the *r* . . . . Is 35:1
buried, and that He *r* . . . . . 1 Cor 15:4

RUBIES
of wisdom is above *r* . . . . Job 28:18
worth is far above *r* . . . . . . Prov 31:10

RULE
and he shall *r*. . . . . Gen 3:16
let the peace of God *r*. . . . . . . Col 3:15
Let the elders who *r* . . . . . . 1 Tim 5:17
Remember those who *r*. . . . Heb 13:7

RUN
r and not be weary . . . . Is 40:31
that I have not *r* . . . . Phil 2:16

S

SABBATH
"Remember the *S* . . . . Ex 20:8
S was made for man . . . . . . Mark 2:27

SACRIFICE
desire mercy and not s. . . . Matt 9:13
God a more excellent *s* . . . . . Heb 11:4
offer the *s* of praise . . . . Heb 13:15

SACRIFICES
The *s* of God are a. . . . . Ps 51:17
burnt offerings and *s*. . . . . Mark 12:33
s God is well pleased. . . . . . Heb 13:16

SAINTS
is the death of His *s* . . . . Ps 116:15
war against the *s* . . . . Dan 7:21
the least of all the *s* . . . . Eph 3:8
shed the blood of *s*. . . . . Rev 16:6

SALT
"You are the *s* . . . . Matt 5:13
s loses its flavor . . . . Mark 9:50

SALVATION
the good news of His *s*. . . 1 Chr 16:23
And He has become my *s* . . Ps 118:14
joy in the God of my *s* . . . . . Hab 3:18
"Nor is there *s* . . . . Acts 4:12
the power of God to *s*. . . . . Rom 1:16
work out your own *s* . . . . Phil 2:12
neglect so great a *s*. . . . . Heb 2:3

SAMARITAN
But a certain *S*. . . . . Luke 10:33
a drink from me, a *S* . . . . . . John 4:9

SANCTIFICATION
righteousness and *s*. . . . . . . 1 Cor 1:30
will of God, your *s*. . . . . . 1 Thess 4:3

SANCTIFIED
husband is *s* by the . . . . . . 1 Cor 7:14
those who are being *s* . . . . . Heb 2:11
who are called, *s*. . . . . Jude 1

SANCTUARY
let them make Me a *s*. . . . . Ex 25:8
and the earthly *s* . . . . Heb 9:1

SATAN
S stood up against . . . . 1 Chr 21:1

before the LORD, and *S*....... Job 1:6
"Away with you, *S* .... Matt 4:10
"How can *S* cast out ...... Mark 3:23
S has asked for you...... Luke 22:31

SATISFIES
s your mouth with good..... Ps 103:5
s the longing soul .... Ps 107:9

SATISFY
s us early with Your......... Ps 90:14
long life I will *s* .... Ps 91:16

SAVE
mighty to *s* .... Is 63:1
JESUS, for He will *s* .... Matt 1:21
the world to *s* sinners..... 1 Tim 1:15

SAVED
through Him might be *s* ... John 3:17
what must I do to be *s* .... Acts 16:30
is that they may be *s* .... Rom 10:1
grace you have been *s*.......... Eph 2:8

SAVIOR
of Israel, your *S*................ Is 43:3
the city of David a *S* ...... Luke 2:11
the Christ, the *S*.............. John 4:42
to be Prince and *S*.............. Acts 5:31
and He is the *S* .... Eph 5:23
God, who is the *S* .... 1 Tim 4:10
of our *S* Jesus Christ ..... 2 Tim 1:10
God and *S* Jesus Christ..... Titus 2:13

SCEPTER
s shall not depart .... Gen 49:10
S shall rise out of .... Num 24:17

SCORPIONS
on serpents and *s* .... Luke 10:19

SCRIPTURE
"Today this *S*............ Luke 4:21
S has confined all .... Gal 3:22
All *S* is given by .... 2 Tim 3:16
that no prophecy of *S* ..... 2 Pet 1:20

SEA
drowned in the Red *S* .... Ex 15:4
the waters cover the *s*...... Hab 2:14

SEAT
shall make a mercy *s*...... Ex 25:17
before the judgment *s*.... 2 Cor 5:10
the mercy *s*................... Heb 9:5

SEED
He shall see His *s* .... Is 53:10
s is the word of God....... Luke 8:11
had left us a s............. Rom 9:29
you are Abraham's *s*........ Gal 3:29
of corruptible *s* .... 1 Pet 1:23

SEEK
will find Him if you *s*...... Deut 4:29
early will I *s* You .... Ps 63:1
"*S* Me and live .... Amos 5:4
of Man has come to *s* .... Luke 19:10

SEEN
s Me has *s* the .... John 14:9
things which are not *s* .... 2 Cor 4:18
heard, which we have *s* ... 1 John 1:1

SELF-CONTROL
they cannot exercise *s* ..... 1 Cor 7:9
gentleness, *s* .... Gal 5:23
slanderers, without *s* ...... 2 Tim 3:3

SELL
s whatever you have....... Mark 10:21
no one may buy or *s* ...... Rev 13:17

SEND
"Whom shall I *s* .... Is 6:8
s them a Savior.............. Is 19:20
"Behold, I *s* you out .... Matt 10:16
whom the Father will *s*... John 14:26

SEPARATE
let not man *s*................ Matt 19:6
Who shall *s* us from .... Rom 8:35

SERPENT
s was more cunning......... Gen 3:1
"Make a fiery *s* .... Num 21:8
will he give him a *s*....... Matt 7:10
Moses lifted up the *s* ...... John 3:14
was cast out, that *s*......... Rev 12:9

SERVANT
good and faithful *s* .... Matt 25:21

SERVE
LORD your God and *s* ...... Deut 6:13
You cannot *s* God and..... Matt 6:24
but through love *s* .... Gal 5:13

SEVENTY
S weeks are .... Dan 9:24
up to *s* times seven....... Matt 18:22
Then the *s* returned ...... Luke 10:17

SHADOW
in the *s* of His hand .... Is 49:2
which are a *s* of .... Col 2:17
the law, having a *s*......... Heb 10:1
is no variation or *s*...... James 1:17

SHAKE
s the earth.................... Is 2:19
I will *s* all nations............ Hag 2:7
s not only the earth ...... Heb 12:26

SHAME
hate Zion be put to *s*....... Ps 129:5
is a son who causes *s*..... Prov 10:5
hide My face from *s*.......... Is 50:6
their glory into *s* .... Hos 4:7

worthy to suffer *s*. . . . . Acts 5:41
will not be put to s . . . . Rom 9:33

SHARE
is taught the word *s* . . . . Gal 6:6
to do good and to *s* . . . . . . Heb 13:16

SHED
which is *s* for many . . . . . . Matt 26:28

SHEDDING
blood, and without *s* . . . . Heb 9:22

SHEEP
slaughter, and as a *s* . . . . Is 53:7
s will be scattered. . . . . Zech 13:7
having a hundred *s*. . . . . Luke 15:4
and I know My *s*. . . . . John 10:14
"He was led as a s. . . . . Acts 8:32
like *s* going astray . . . . 1 Pet 2:25

SHEOL
down to the gates of *S*. . . . . . . Job 17:16
not leave my soul in *S* . . . . . . Ps 16:10
the belly of *S* I cried. . . . . Jon 2:2

SHEPHERD
s My people Israel . . . . 2 Sam 5:2
The LORD is my *s*. . . . . Ps 23:1
His flock like a *s*. . . . . Is 40:11
'I will strike the S . . . . Matt 26:31
"I am the good *s* . . . . John 10:11
S the flock of God. . . . . 1 Pet 5:2
of the throne will *s*. . . . . Rev 7:17

SHIELD
He is a *s* to all who . . . . . 2 Sam 22:31
God is a sun and *s*. . . . . Ps 84:11
all, taking the *s* . . . . Eph 6:16

SHINE
cause His face to *s*. . . . . Ps 67:1
who are wise shall *s* . . . . Dan 12:3
the righteous will *s*. . . . . . . Matt 13:43
among whom you *s* . . . . Phil 2:15

SHIPWRECK
faith have suffered *s*. . . . . . 1 Tim 1:19

SHOUT
S joyfully to the LORD. . . . . . . Ps 98:4
from heaven with a *s* . . . 1 Thess 4:16

SHOWBREAD
s which had been taken . . 1 Sam 21:6
s which was not lawful . . . . Matt 12:4

SICK
I was *s* and you . . . . Matt 25:36
many are weak and *s* . . . . 1 Cor 11:30
faith will save the *s* . . . . . . James 5:15

SICKLE
Put in the *s*. . . . . Joel 3:13
"Thrust in Your *s* . . . . Rev 14:15

SIGHT
by faith, not by *s* . . . . 2 Cor 5:7

SIGN
will give you a *s* . . . . Is 7:14
we want to see a *s*. . . . . Matt 12:38
For Jews request a *s*. . . . . . 1 Cor 1:22
Now a great *s* appeared . . . . Rev 12:1

SILVER
have refined us as *s* . . . . Ps 66:10
chosen rather than *s*. . . . . . Prov 16:16
s has become dross . . . . Is 1:22
may buy the poor for *s* . . . . Amos 8:6
him thirty pieces of *s* . . . . . Matt 26:15

SIMPLE
making wise the *s* . . . . Ps 19:7
LORD preserves the *s*. . . . . Ps 116:6

SIN
and be sure your *s* . . . . Num 32:23
in *s* my mother . . . . Ps 51:5
"He who is without *s* . . . . John 8:7
died to *s* once for all. . . . . . . Rom 6:10
Him who knew no *s* . . . . 2 Cor 5:21
appeared to put away *s*. . . . . Heb 9:26
"Who committed no s . . . . . 1 Pet 2:22
say that we have no *s*. . . . . 1 John 1:8

SING
"S to the LORD . . . . Ex 15:21
I will *s* of mercy and. . . . . Ps 101:1
S us one of the songs . . . . Ps 137:3
Let him *s* psalms . . . . James 5:13

SINNED
You only, have I *s* . . . . Ps 51:4
for all have *s* and. . . . . Rom 3:23
say that we have not *s* . . . 1 John 1:10

SINNER
s who repents than. . . . . Luke 15:7

SINNERS
the righteous, but *s* . . . . Matt 9:13
tax collectors and *s*. . . . . . . Matt 11:19
the world to save *s* . . . . 1 Tim 1:15

SINS
s have hidden His face . . . . Is 59:2
the soul who *s* shall . . . . Ezek 18:4
If we confess our *s* . . . . 1 John 1:9

SIT
but to *s* on My right . . . . . . Matt 20:23
"S at My right hand. . . . . Heb 1:13
I will grant to *s* . . . . Rev 3:21

SLAIN
s his thousands . . . . 1 Sam 18:7
Those *s* by the sword . . . . Lam 4:9
the prophets, I have *s* . . . . Hos 6:5
is the Lamb who was *s* . . . . . Rev 5:12

SPARE
I will not pity nor *s* .... Jer 13:14
He who did not *s* .... Rom 8:32
s the natural branches .... Rom 11:21

SPARES
s his rod hates his .... Prov 13:24

SPARROWS
more value than many *s* .. Matt 10:31

SPEAK
oh, that God would *s* .... Job 11:5
and a time to *s* .... Eccl 3:7
s anymore in His name...... Jer 20:9
or what you should *s* ..... Matt 10:19
I would rather *s* .... 1 Cor 14:19

SPIRIT
S shall not strive .... Gen 6:3
I have put My *S*.............. Is 42:1
new heart and a new *s* ... Ezek 18:31
S descending upon Him ... Mark 1:10
gifts, but the same *S* ...... 1 Cor 12:4
but the *S* gives life .... 2 Cor 3:6
he who sows to the *S* .... Gal 6:8
and may your whole *s* .. 1 Thess 5:23
division of soul and *s* .... Heb 4:12
S who dwells in us .... James 4:5
has given us of His *S* .... 1 John 4:13

SPOT
and there is no *s* .... Song 4:7
church, not having *s* .... Eph 5:27
commandment without *s* .. 1 Tim 6:14
Himself without *s* .... Heb 9:14

SPREAD
their message will *s* ...... 2 Tim 2:17

SPRINKLE
He *s* many nations .... Is 52:15

STAFF
Your rod and Your *s* .... Ps 23:4

STAND
ungodly shall not *s* .... Ps 1:5
that kingdom cannot *s* .... Mark 3:24
Watch, *s* fast in the ...... 1 Cor 16:13
having done all, to *s* .... Eph 6:13
"Behold, I *s* at the .... Rev 3:20

STANDARD
LORD will lift up a *s* .... Is 59:19

STANDS
him who thinks he *s* ..... 1 Cor 10:12

STAR
S shall come out of .... Num 24:17
For we have seen His *s* ..... Matt 2:2
Bright and Morning *S* ..... Rev 22:16

STEADFAST
O God, my heart is *s* .... Ps 57:7
beloved brethren, be *s* ... 1 Cor 15:58
faith, grounded and *s* .... Col 1:23
Resist him, *s* in the .... 1 Pet 5:9

STEAL
"You shall not *s* .... Ex 20:15
thieves break in and *s* ..... Matt 6:19
not come except to *s* ...... John 10:10
Let him who stole *s* .... Eph 4:28

STEPS
The *s* of a good man .... Ps 37:23
A man's *s* are of the ...... Prov 20:24

STEWARD
faithful and wise *s* .... Luke 12:42
commended the unjust *s* ... Luke 16:8

STIFF-NECKED
"Now do not be *s* .... 2 Chr 30:8
"You *s* and .... Acts 7:51

STILL
sea, "Peace, be *s* .... Mark 4:39

STIR
S up Yourself .... Ps 35:23
I remind you to *s* .... 2 Tim 1:6

STONE
s shall be a witness .... Josh 24:27
I lay in Zion a *s* .... Is 28:16
take the heart of *s* .... Ezek 36:26
will give him a *s* .... Matt 7:9
s which the builders ..... Luke 20:17
Him as to a living *s* .... 1 Pet 2:4
like a jasper *s* .... Rev 21:11

STONED
s Stephen as he was .... Acts 7:59
once I was *s* .... 2 Cor 11:25

STONES
Abraham from these *s* ...... Matt 3:9
command that these *s* ...... Matt 4:3
also, as living *s* .... 1 Pet 2:5

STRAIGHT
make *s* in the desert a .... Is 40:3
LORD; make His paths s ..... Luke 3:4

STREET
s called Straight .... Acts 9:11
And the *s* of the city ...... Rev 21:21

STRENGTH
the God of my *s* .... 2 Sam 22:3
Him are wisdom and *s* .... Job 12:13
You have ordained *s* .... Ps 8:2
They go from *s* to .... Ps 84:7
S and honor are her ..... Prov 31:25
might He increases *s* ...... Is 40:29

WIFE
w finds a good thing. . . . . . Prov 18:22
with the *w* of his . . . . Mal 2:15
Whoever divorces his *w*. . Mark 10:11
'I have married a *w* . . . . . . Luke 14:20
so love his own *w*. . . . . Eph 5:33
the husband of one *w* . . . . . . Titus 1:6
giving honor to the *w* . . . . . . 1 Pet 3:7
bride, the Lamb's *w* . . . . Rev 21:9

WILDERNESS
wasteland, a howling *w* . . Deut 32:10
of one crying in the w . . . . . . Matt 3:3

WILL
w be done on earth as . . . . . Matt 6:10
nevertheless not My *w* . . Luke 22:42
I do not seek My own *w* . . . John 5:30
w is present with me . . . . . . Rom 7:18
works in you both to *w*. . . . . Phil 2:13
the knowledge of His *w* . . . . . Col 1:9
come to do Your w. . . . . Heb 10:9
but he who does the *w*. . . 1 John 2:17

WINE
W is a mocker . . . . Prov 20:1
love is better than *w* . . . . Song 1:2
when they ran out of *w*. . . . . John 2:3
do not be drunk with *w* . . . . Eph 5:18
not given to much *w* . . . . Titus 2:3

WINESKINS
new wine into old *w*. . . . . Matt 9:17

WINGS
the shadow of Your *w* . . . . Ps 36:7
each one had six *w*. . . . . Is 6:2
with healing in His *w*. . . . . Mal 4:2

WIPE
the Lord GOD will *w*. . . . . Is 25:8
w away every tear . . . . Rev 21:4

WISDOM
is the beginning of *w* . . . . . . Prov 9:10
w is justified by her . . . . . . Matt 11:19
If any of you lacks *w*. . . . . . James 1:5
and glory and *w* . . . . Rev 7:12

WISE
Do not be *w* in your . . . . Prov 3:7
Therefore be *w* as . . . . Matt 10:16
not as fools but as *w* . . . . Eph 5:15
are able to make you *w*. . . 2 Tim 3:15

WITCHCRAFT
is as the sin of *w*. . . . . 1 Sam 15:23

WITNESS
all the world as a *w* . . . . . . Matt 24:14

WITNESSES
of two or three *w*. . . . . Deut 17:6
so great a cloud of *w*. . . . . . . Heb 12:1

WOLF
The *w* and the lamb . . . . Is 65:25
the sheep, sees the *w*. . . . . John 10:12

WOMB
nations are in your *w* . . . . . Gen 25:23
in the *w* I knew you. . . . . Jer 1:5
is the fruit of your *w* . . . . . . Luke 1:42

WOMEN
w will be grinding. . . . . Matt 24:41
are you among *w* . . . . Luke 1:28
times, the holy *w*. . . . . 1 Pet 3:5
not defiled with *w*. . . . . Rev 14:4

WONDERFUL
Your testimonies are *w* . . . Ps 119:129
name will be called *W*. . . . . Is 9:6

WORD
Your *w* I have hidden . . . . . Ps 119:11
w is a lamp to my feet . . . . Ps 119:105
w be that goes forth. . . . . Is 55:11
for every idle *w* . . . . Matt 12:36
beginning was the *W*. . . . . . . John 1:1
W became flesh and. . . . . . . John 1:14
For the *w* of God is . . . . Heb 4:12
name is called The *W* . . . . . Rev 19:13

WORK
day God ended His *w* . . . . Gen 2:2
know that all things *w*. . . . . Rom 8:28
If anyone will not *w* . . . . 2 Thess 3:10

WORKER
w is worthy of his . . . . Matt 10:10
Timothy, my fellow *w* . . . . Rom 16:21
w who does not need . . . . . 2 Tim 2:15

WORKS
not of *w*, lest anyone . . . . Eph 2:9
He might destroy the *w* . . . 1 John 3:8

WORLD
For God so loved the *w* . . . . John 3:16
I have overcome the *w* . . . John 16:33
without God in the *w*. . . . . . . Eph 2:12
Do not love the *w* . . . . 1 John 2:15

WORM
But I am a *w* . . . . Ps 22:6
w does not die and the . . . . Mark 9:44

WORMWOOD
end she is bitter as *w* . . . . . . Prov 5:4
of the star is *W* . . . . Rev 8:11

WORSHIP
Oh come, let us *w* . . . . Ps 95:6
w what you do not know . . John 4:22

WORTHY
"I am not *w* of the . . . . Gen 32:10
sandals I am not *w* . . . . Matt 3:11
and I am no longer *w* . . . . Luke 15:19

Read Your Bible Through In a Year

A systematic division of the books of the Bible, primarily for reading.

JANUARY

Date	MORNING	EVENING
	MATT.	GEN.
1	1	1, 2, 3
2	2	4, 5, 6
3	3	7, 8, 9
4	4	10, 11, 12
5	5: 1–26	13, 14, 15
6	5:27–48	16, 17
7	6: 1–18	18, 19
8	6:19–34	20, 21, 22
9	7	23, 24
10	8: 1–17	25, 26
11	8:18–34	27, 28
12	9: 1–17	29, 30
13	9:18–38	31, 32
14	10: 1–20	33, 34, 35
15	10:21–42	36, 37, 38
16	11	39, 40
17	12: 1–23	41, 42
18	12:24–50	43, 44, 45
19	13: 1–30	46, 47, 48
20	13:31–58	49, 50
		EX.
21	14: 1–21	1, 2, 3
22	14:22–36	4, 5, 6
23	15: 1–20	6, 8
24	15:21–39	9, 10, 11
25	16	12, 13
26	17	14, 15
27	18: 1–20	16, 17, 18
28	18:21–35	19, 20
29	19	21, 22
30	20: 1–16	23, 24
31	20:17–34	25, 26

FEBRUARY

Date	MORNING	EVENING
	MATT.	EX.
1	21: 1–22	27, 28
2	21:23–46	29, 30
3	22: 1–22	31, 32, 33
4	22:23–46	34, 35
5	23: 1–22	36, 37, 38
6	23:23–39	39, 40
		LEV.
7	24: 1–28	1, 2, 3
8	24:29–51	4, 5
9	25: 1–30	6, 7
10	25:31–46	8, 9, 10
11	26: 1–25	11, 12
12	26:26–50	13
13	26:51–75	14
14	27: 1–26	15, 16
15	27:27–50	17, 18
16	27:51–66	19, 20
17	28	21, 22
	MARK	
18	1: 1–22	23, 24
19	1:23–45	25
20	2	26, 27
		NUM.
21	3: 1–19	1, 2
22	3:20–35	3, 4
23	4: 1–20	5, 6
24	4:21–41	7, 8
25	5: 1–20	9, 10, 11
26	5:21–43	12, 13, 14
27	6: 1–29	15, 16
28	6:30–56	17, 18, 19
29	7: 1–13	20, 21, 22

MARCH

Date	MORNING	EVENING
	MARK	NUM.
1	7:14–37	23, 24, 25
2	8: 1–21	26, 27
3	8:22–38	28, 29, 30
4	9: 1–29	31, 32, 33
5	9:30–50	34, 35, 36
		DEUT.
6	10: 1–31	1, 2
7	10:32–52	3, 4
8	11: 1–18	5, 6, 7
9	11:19–33	8, 9, 10
10	12: 1–27	11, 12, 13
11	12:28–44	14, 15, 16
12	13: 1–20	17, 18, 19
13	13:21–37	20, 21, 22
14	14: 1–26	23, 24, 25
15	14:27–53	26, 27
16	14:54–72	28, 29
17	15: 1–25	30, 31
18	15:26–47	32, 33, 34
		JOSH.
19	16	1, 2, 3
	LUKE	
20	1: 1–20	4, 5, 6
21	1:21–38	7, 8, 9
22	1:39–56	10, 11, 12
23	1:57–80	13, 14, 15
24	2: 1–24	16, 17, 18
25	2:25–52	19, 20, 21
26	3	22, 23, 24
		JUDG.
27	4: 1–30	1, 2, 3
28	4:31–44	4, 5, 6
29	5: 1–16	7, 8
30	5:17–39	9, 10
31	6: 1–26	11, 12

APRIL

Date	MORNING	EVENING
	LUKE	JUDG.
1	6:27–49	13, 14, 15
2	7: 1–30	16, 17, 18
3	7:31–50	19, 20, 21
4	8: 1–25	RUTH
		1 SAM.
5	8:26–56	1, 2, 3
6	9: 1–17	4, 5, 6
7	9:18–36	7, 8, 9
8	9:37–62	10, 11, 12
9	10: 1–24	13, 14
10	10:25–42	15, 16
11	11: 1–28	17, 18
12	11:29–54	19, 20, 21
13	12: 1–31	22, 23, 24
14	12:32–59	25, 26
15	13: 1–22	27, 28, 29
16	13:23–35	30, 31
		2 SAM.
17	14: 1–24	1, 2
18	14:25–35	3, 4, 5
19	15: 1–10	6, 7, 8
20	15:11–32	9, 10, 11
21	16	12, 13
22	17: 1–19	14, 15
23	17:20–37	16, 17, 18
24	18: 1–23	19, 20
25	18:24–43	21, 22
26	19: 1–27	23, 24
		1 KIN.
27	19:28–48	1, 2
28	20: 1–26	3, 4, 5
29	20:27–47	6, 7
30	21: 1–19	8, 9

MAY

Date	MORNING	EVENING
	LUKE	1 KIN.
1	21:20–38	10, 11
2	22: 1–20	12, 13
3	22:21–46	14, 15
4	22:47–71	16, 17, 18
5	23: 1–25	19, 20
6	23:26–56	21, 22
		2 KIN.
7	24: 1–35	1, 2, 3
8	24:36–53	4, 5, 6
	JOHN	
9	1: 1–28	7, 8, 9
10	1:29–51	10, 11, 12
11	2	13, 14
12	3: 1–18	15, 16
13	3:19–38	17, 18
14	4: 1–30	19, 20, 21
15	4:31–54	22, 23
16	5: 1–24	24, 25
		1 CHR.
17	5:25–47	1, 2, 3
18	6: 1–21	4, 5, 6
19	6:22–44	7, 8, 9
20	6:45–71	10, 11, 12
21	7: 1–27	13, 14, 15
22	7:28–53	16, 17, 18
23	8: 1–27	19, 20, 21
24	8:28–59	22, 23, 24
25	9: 1–23	25, 26, 27
26	9:24–41	28, 29
		2 CHR.
27	10: 1–23	1, 2, 3
28	10:24–42	4, 5, 6
29	11: 1–29	7, 8, 9
30	11:30–57	10, 11, 12
31	12: 1–26	13, 14

JUNE

Date	MORNING	EVENING
	JOHN	2 CHR.
1	12:27–50	15, 16
2	13: 1–20	17, 18
3	13:21–38	19, 20
4	14	21, 22
5	15	23, 24
6	16	25, 26, 27
7	17	28, 29
8	18: 1–18	30, 31
9	18:19–40	32, 33
10	19: 1–22	34, 35, 36
		EZRA
11	19:23–42	1, 2
12	20	3, 4, 5
13	21	6, 7, 8
	ACTS	
14	1	9, 10
		NEH.
15	2: 1–21	1, 2, 3
16	2:22–47	4, 5, 6
17	3	7, 8, 9
18	4: 1–22	10, 11
19	4:23–37	12, 13
		ESTH.
20	5: 1–21	1, 2
21	5:22–42	3, 4, 5
22	6	6, 7, 8
23	7: 1–21	9, 10
		JOB
24	7:22–43	1, 2
25	7:44–60	3, 4
26	8: 1–25	5, 6, 7
27	8:26–40	8, 9, 10
28	9: 1–21	11, 12, 13
29	9:22–43	14, 15, 16
30	10: 1–23	17, 18, 19

JULY

Date	MORNING	EVENING
	ACTS	**JOB**
1	10:24–48	20, 21
2	11	22, 23, 24
3	12	25, 26, 27
4	13: 1–25	28, 29
5	13:26–52	30, 31
6	14	32, 33
7	15: 1–21	34, 35
8	15:22–41	36, 37
9	16: 1–21	38, 39, 40
10	16:22–40	41, 42
		PS.
11	17: 1–15	1, 2, 3
12	17:16–34	4, 5, 6
13	18	7, 8, 9
14	19: 1–20	10, 11, 12
15	19:21–41	13, 14, 15
16	20: 1–16	16, 17
17	20:17–38	18, 19
18	21: 1–17	20, 21, 22
19	21:18–40	23, 24, 25
20	22	26, 27, 28
21	23: 1–15	29, 30
22	23:16–35	31, 32
23	24	33, 34
24	25	35, 36
25	26	37, 38, 39
26	27: 1–26	40, 41, 42
27	27:27–44	43, 44, 45
28	28	46, 47, 48
	ROM.	
29	1	49, 50
30	2	51, 52, 53
31	3	54, 55, 56

AUGUST

Date	MORNING	EVENING
	ROM.	**PS.**
1	4	57, 58, 59
2	5	60, 61, 62
3	6	63, 64, 65
4	7	66, 67
5	8: 1–21	68, 69
6	8:22–39	70, 71
7	9: 1–15	72, 73
8	9:16–33	74, 75, 76
9	10	77, 78
10	11: 1–18	79, 80
11	11:19–36	81, 82, 83
12	12	84, 85, 86
13	13	87, 88
14	14	89, 90
15	15: 1–13	91, 92, 93
16	15:14–33	94, 95, 96
17	16	97, 98, 99
	1 COR.	
18	1	100, 101, 102
19	2	103, 104
20	3	105, 106
21	4	107, 108, 109
22	5	110, 111, 112
23	6	113, 114, 115
24	7: 1–19	116, 117, 118
25	7:20–40	119: 1–88
26	8	119: 89–176
27	9	120, 121, 122
28	10: 1–18	123, 124, 125
29	10:19–33	126, 127, 128
30	11: 1–16	129, 130, 131
31	11:17–34	132, 133, 134

SEPTEMBER

Date	MORNING	EVENING
	1 COR.	**PS.**
1	12	135, 136
2	13	137, 138, 139
3	14: 1–20	140, 141, 142
4	14:21–40	143, 144, 145
5	15: 1–28	146, 147
6	15:29–58	148, 149, 150
		PROV.
7	16	1, 2
	2 COR.	
8	1	3, 4, 5
9	2	6, 7
10	3	8, 9
11	4	10, 11, 12
12	5	13, 14, 15
13	6	16, 17, 18
14	7	19, 20, 21
15	8	22, 23, 24
16	9	25, 26
17	10	27, 28, 29
18	11: 1–15	30, 31
		ECCL.
19	11:16–33	1, 2, 3
20	12	4, 5, 6
21	13	7, 8, 9
	GAL.	
22	1	10, 11, 12
		SONG
23	2	1, 2, 3
24	3	4, 5
25	4	6, 7, 8
		IS.
26	5	1, 2
27	6	3, 4
	EPH.	
28	1	5, 6
29	2	7, 8
30	3	9, 10

OCTOBER

Date	MORNING	EVENING
	EPH.	IS.
1	4	11, 12, 13
2	5: 1–16	14, 15, 16
3	5:17–33	17, 18, 19
4	6	20, 21, 22
	PHIL.	
5	1	23, 24, 25
6	2	26, 27
7	3	28, 29
8	4	30, 31
	COL.	
9	1	32, 33
10	2	34, 35, 36
11	3	37, 38
12	4	39, 40
	1 THESS.	
13	1	41, 42
14	2	43, 44
15	3	45, 46
16	4	47, 48, 49
17	5	50, 51, 52
	2 THESS.	
18	1	53, 54, 55
19	2	56, 57, 58
20	3	59, 60, 61
	1 TIM.	
21	1	62, 63, 64
22	2	65, 66
		JER.
23	3	1, 2
24	4	3, 4, 5
25	5	6, 7, 8
26	6	9, 10, 11
	2 TIM.	
27	1	12, 13, 14
28	2	15, 16, 17
29	3	18, 19
30	4	20, 21
	TITUS	
31	1	22, 23

NOVEMBER

Date	MORNING	EVENING
	TITUS	JER.
1	2	24, 25, 26
2	3	27, 28, 29
3	PHILEM.	30, 31
	HEB.	
4	1	32, 33
5	2	34, 35, 36
6	3	37, 38, 39
7	4	40, 41, 42
8	5	43, 44, 45
9	6	46, 47
10	7	48, 49
11	8	50
12	9	51, 52
		LAM.
13	10: 1–18	1, 2
14	10:19–39	3, 4, 5
		EZEK.
15	11: 1–19	1, 2
16	11:20–40	3, 4
17	12	5, 6, 7
18	13	8, 9, 10
	JAMES	
19	1	11, 12, 13
20	2	14, 15
21	3	16, 17
22	4	18, 19
23	5	20, 21
	1 PET.	
24	1	22, 23
25	2	24, 25, 26
26	3	27, 28, 29
27	4	30, 31, 32
28	5	33, 34
	2 PET.	
29	1	35, 36
30	2	37, 38, 39

DECEMBER

Date	MORNING	EVENING
	2 PET.	EZEK.
1	3	40, 41
	1 JOHN	
2	1	42, 43, 44
3	2	45, 46
4	3	47, 48
		DAN.
5	4	1, 2
6	5	3, 4
7	2 JOHN	5, 6, 7
8	3 JOHN	8, 9, 10
9	JUDE	11, 12
	REV.	HOS.
10	1	1, 2, 3, 4
11	2	5, 6, 7, 8
12	3	9, 10, 11
13	4	12, 13, 14
14	5	JOEL
		AMOS
15	6	1, 2, 3
16	7	4, 5, 6
17	8	7, 8, 9
18	9	OBAD.
19	10	JON.
		MIC.
20	11	1, 2, 3
21	12	4, 5
22	13	6, 7
23	14	NAH.
24	15	HAB.
25	16	ZEPH.
26	17	HAG.
		ZECH.
27	18	1, 2, 3, 4
28	19	5, 6, 7, 8
29	20	9, 10, 11, 12
30	21	13, 14
31	22	MAL.

Acknowledgments

Barna, George, from *Absolute Confusion*. Copyright © 1993 by George Barna. Regal Books, Ventura, CA 93003. Used by permission.

Bell, Dr. Verle. "Where Do You Live?" *Today's Better Life* (Spring 1992). Reprinted by permission of Thomas Nelson Publishers.

Blue, Ron. "Living a Better Tomorrow," *A Better Tomorrow* (Fall 1993). Reprinted by permission of Thomas Nelson Publishers.

Blue, Ron. "Prosperity vs. Posterity," *A Better Tomorrow* (Premiere 1992). Reprinted by permission of Thomas Nelson Publishers.

Bourke, Dale Hanson. "Dr. Ken Cooper: An Ounce of Prevention," *Possibilities* (September/October 1989). Reprinted by permission of Crystal Cathedral Ministries.

Briscoe, Jill, from *By Hook or By Crook*, copyright © 1987, Word, Inc., Dallas, Texas. Used with permission.

Christenson, Evelyn, reprinted from *What Happens When God Answers* by Evelyn Christenson, published by Victor Books, copyright 1986 and 1994, SP Publications, Inc., Wheaton, IL 60187.

Cloninger, Claire, from *The Kaleidoscope*, copyright © 1988, Word, Inc., Dallas, Texas. Used with permission.

Cloud, Dr. Henry. "Strengthening Our Fences," *Today's Better Life* (Fall 1993). Reprinted by permission of Thomas Nelson Publishers.

Davis, Ron Lee, from the book *Mentoring*. Reprinted by permission of Thomas Nelson Publishers. Copyright © 1991 by Ron Lee Davis.

Endicott, Irene, excerpts from *Grandparenting Redefined*, Aglow Publications, 1992. Reprinted by permission.

Enlow, David R. "Talk to God," *A Better Tomorrow* (Fall 1993). Reprinted by permission of Thomas Nelson Publishers.

Gaither, Bill, from the book *I Almost Missed the Sunset*. Reprinted by permission of Thomas Nelson Publishers. Copyright © 1992 by William J. Gaither.

Gaither, Gloria, from *Decision Vision* by Gloria Gaither, copyright © 1991. Warner Press, Inc.

Gaither, Gloria with Dale Hanson Bourke. "Deeply Rooted," *Today's Better Life* (Spring 1993). Reprinted by permission of Thomas Nelson Publishers.

Gilmore, John. "Too Old to Be Tempted?" *A Better Tomorrow* (Fall 1993). Reprinted by permission of Thomas Nelson Publishers.

Graham, Billy, from *Hope for the Troubled Heart*, copyright © 1991, Word, Inc., Dallas, Texas. Used with permission.

Gray, Elmer L., *The Bible Answers Senior Adult Questions* (Nashville: Broadman Press, 1991). All rights reserved. Used by permission.

Hemfelt, Robert. "Ghosts of the Past," *Today's Better Life* (Fall/Winter 1991). Reprinted by permission of Thomas Nelson Publishers.

Johnson, Barbara, from *Pack Up Your Gloomees*, copyright © 1993, Word, Inc., Dallas, Texas. Used with permission.

Kesler, Jay, from *Grandparenting*, © 1993 by Jay Kesler. Published by Servant Publications, Box 8617, Ann Arbor, Michigan 48107. Used with permission.

Koons, Carolyn with John Archer. "Becoming Unstuck," *A Better Tomorrow* (Winter 1993). Reprinted by permission of Thomas Nelson Publishers.

Leman, Kevin with Dale Hanson Bourke. "Fighting for Relationships," *Today's Better Life* (Summer 1993). Reprinted by permission of Thomas Nelson Publishers.

ACKNOWLEDGMENTS

"Living Water," *Today's Better Life* (Fall 1992). Reprinted by permission of Thomas Nelson Publishers.

Mason, Dr. Jenifer J. "Beating the Bulge," *A Better Tomorrow* (Winter 1993). Reprinted by permission of Thomas Nelson Publishers.

Matthews, Dr. Dale. "Staying Young," *Today's Better Life* (Summer 1992). Reprinted by permission of Thomas Nelson Publishers.

McGee, J. Vernon, from the book *Feasting on the Word*. Reprinted by permission of Thomas Nelson Publishers. Copyright © 1992 by J. Vernon McGee.

McGee, J. Vernon, from the book *Questions and Answers*. Reprinted by permission of Thomas Nelson Publishers. Copyright © 1990 by J. Vernon McGee.

McManus, Una. "Write Your Life," *A Better Tomorrow* (Fall 1993). Reprinted by permission of Thomas Nelson Publishers.

Mehl, Ron. "Facing Death," *A Better Tomorrow* (Spring 1994). Reprinted by permission of Thomas Nelson Publishers.

Meier, Dr. Richard. "Looking for a Few Good Mentors," *Today's Better Life* (Fall 1992). Reprinted by permission of Thomas Nelson Publishers.

Minirth, Dr. Frank. "When Opportunity Whispers," *Today's Better Life* (Fall 1993). Reprinted by permission of Thomas Nelson Publishers.

Minirth, Dr. Frank B. and Meier, Dr. Paul D., from *Ask the Doctors*. Copyright © 1991 by Baker Book House Company.

Minirth, Dr. Frank; Meier, Dr. Paul; and Hawkins, Don, from the book *Worry-Free Living*. Reprinted by permission of Thomas Nelson Publishers. Copyright © 1989 by Dr. Frank Minirth, Dr. Paul Meier, Don Hawkins.

Moser, Leslie E., from *September Song*, © 1991 by Star Song Publishing Group, 2325 Crestmoor, Nashville, TN 37215. All rights reserved.

Moser, Leslie E. "Stretch Your Mind," *A Better Tomorrow* (Spring 1993). Reprinted by permission.

Ogilvie, Lloyd, from *Enjoying God*, copyright © 1989, Word, Inc., Dallas, Texas. Used with permission.

Oke, Janette. "A Child Shall Lead Us," *A Better Tomorrow* (Spring 1994). Reprinted by permission of Thomas Nelson Publishers.

Ortlund, Anne, from *Fix Your Eyes on Jesus*, copyright © 1991, Word, Inc., Dallas, Texas. Used with permission.

Parachin, Victor. "The Lord Is My Shepherd," *A Better Tomorrow* (Spring 1994). Reprinted by permission of Thomas Nelson Publishers.

Reese, Dr. Randy. "Growing Old Gracefully," *Today's Better Life* (Spring 1992). Reprinted by permission of Thomas Nelson Publishers.

Ridley, RuthAnn. "I Need Space," *A Better Tomorrow* (Spring 1994). Reprinted by permission of Thomas Nelson Publishers.

Rosberg, Dr. Gary. "Living, Loving, Learning," *A Better Tomorrow* (Premiere 1992). Reprinted by permission of Thomas Nelson Publishers.

Rosberg, Dr. Gary. "Living, Loving, Learning," *A Better Tomorrow* (Fall 1993). Reprinted by permission of Thomas Nelson Publishers.

Rosberg, Dr. Gary. "Living, Loving, Learning," *A Better Tomorrow* (Spring 1994). Reprinted by permission of Thomas Nelson Publishers.

Ross, Charles, from the book *Your Commonsense Guide to Financial Planning*. Reprinted by permission of Thomas Nelson Publishers. Copyright © 1993 by Charles Ross.

Schreur, Jerry and Jack, from the book *Creative Grandparenting*. Reprinted by permission of Thomas Nelson Publishers. Copyright © 1992 by Jerry Schreur and Jack Schreur.

Shaw, Luci. "Journal of Life," *A Better Tomorrow* (Spring 1993). Reprinted by permission of Thomas Nelson Publishers.

Smith, Pam. "Fighting Stress," *A Better Tomorrow* (Fall 1993). Reprinted by permission of Thomas Nelson Publishers.

Smith, Pam. "Small Steps Make a Big Difference," *A Better Tomorrow* (Spring 1993). Reprinted by permission of Thomas Nelson Publishers.

Sneed, Dr. Sharon and Sneed, Dr. David, from *Prime Time*, copyright © 1989, Word, Inc., Dallas, Texas. Used with permission.

Swindoll, Charles, from *Flying Closer to the Flame*, copyright © 1993, Word, Inc., Dallas, Texas. Used with permission.

Swindoll, Charles, from *Laugh Again*, copyright © 1992, Word, Inc., Dallas, Texas. Used with permission.

Swindoll, Charles, from *Simple Faith*, copyright © 1991, Word, Inc., Dallas, Texas. Used with permission.

Swindoll, Charles with Dale Hanson Bourke. "The Joy of Being a Man," *Today's Better Life* (Fall 1992). Reprinted by permission of Thomas Nelson Publishers.

Tada, Joni Eareckson with Dale Hanson Bourke. "Joni Eareckson Tada: Celebrating the Confines of Life," *Today's Better Life* (Fall 1993). Reprinted by permission of Thomas Nelson Publishers.

Thurman, Dr. Chris. "The Truth About Change," *Today's Better Life* (Summer 1992). Reprinted by permission of Thomas Nelson Publishers.

Trobisch, Ingrid, from *Heroes*, © 1983 and 1985 by Servant Publications. Previously published under the title of *Bright Legacy*. Published by Servant Publications, Box 8617, Ann Arbor, Michigan 48107. Used with permission.

Van Atta, Lucibel, excerpted from the book *Women Encouraging Women* by Lucibel Van Atta; Multnomah Books; copyright © 1987 by Lucibel Van Atta.

Van Atta, Lucibel, from *Family Traditions That Last a Lifetime*. Copyright © 1993 by Karen M. Ball and Karen L. Tornberg. Used by permission of Tyndale House Publishers, Inc. All rights reserved.

Walker, Philip. "Loosen Up!" *A Better Tomorrow* (Fall 1993). Reprinted by permission of Thomas Nelson Publishers.

Walker, Philip. "The Secret to Healthy Aging," *A Better Tomorrow* (Spring 1994). Reprinted by permission of Thomas Nelson Publishers.

Wirt, Sherwood Eliot, from the book *I Don't Know What Old Is, But Old Is Older Than Me.* Reprinted by permission of Thomas Nelson Publishers. Copyright © 1992 by Sherwood Eliot Wirt.

✦ *Personal Journal* ✦

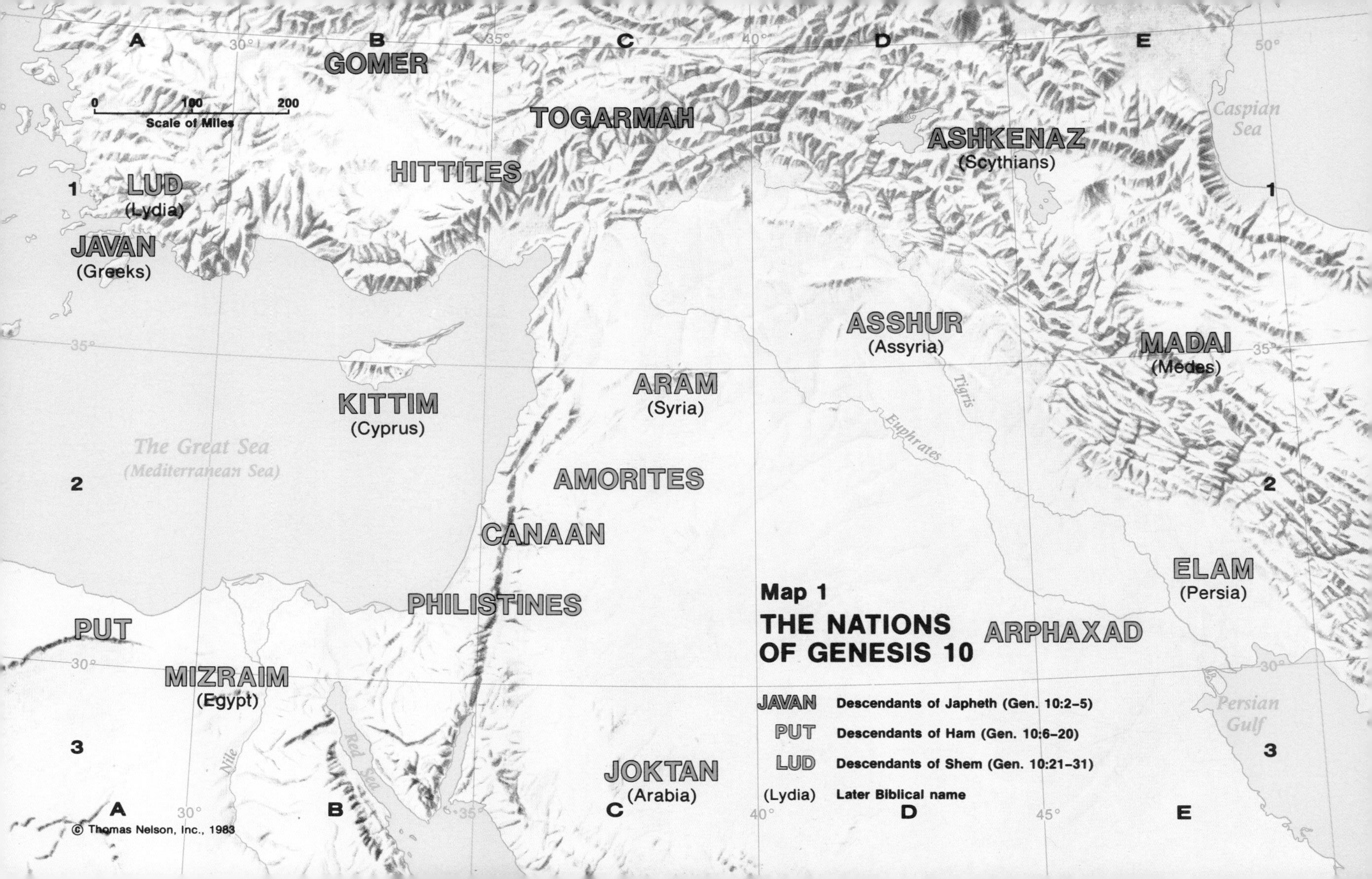
Map 1
THE NATIONS OF GENESIS 10
JAVAN Descendants of Japheth (Gen. 10:2–5)
PUT Descendants of Ham (Gen. 10:6–20)
LUD Descendants of Shem (Gen. 10:21–31)
(Lydia) Later Biblical name
GOMER
TOGARMAH
ASHKENAZ
(Scythians)
HITTITES
LUD
(Lydia)
JAVAN
(Greeks)
Caspian Sea
ASSHUR
(Assyria)
MADAI
(Medes)
ARAM
(Syria)
KITTIM
(Cyprus)
The Great Sea
(Mediterranean Sea)
Tigris
Euphrates
AMORITES
CANAAN
ELAM
(Persia)
PHILISTINES
ARPHAXAD
PUT
MIZRAIM
(Egypt)
Persian Gulf
Red Sea
Nile
JOKTAN
(Arabia)
Scale of Miles
0 100 200
A B C D E
1 2 3
30° 35° 40° 45° 50°

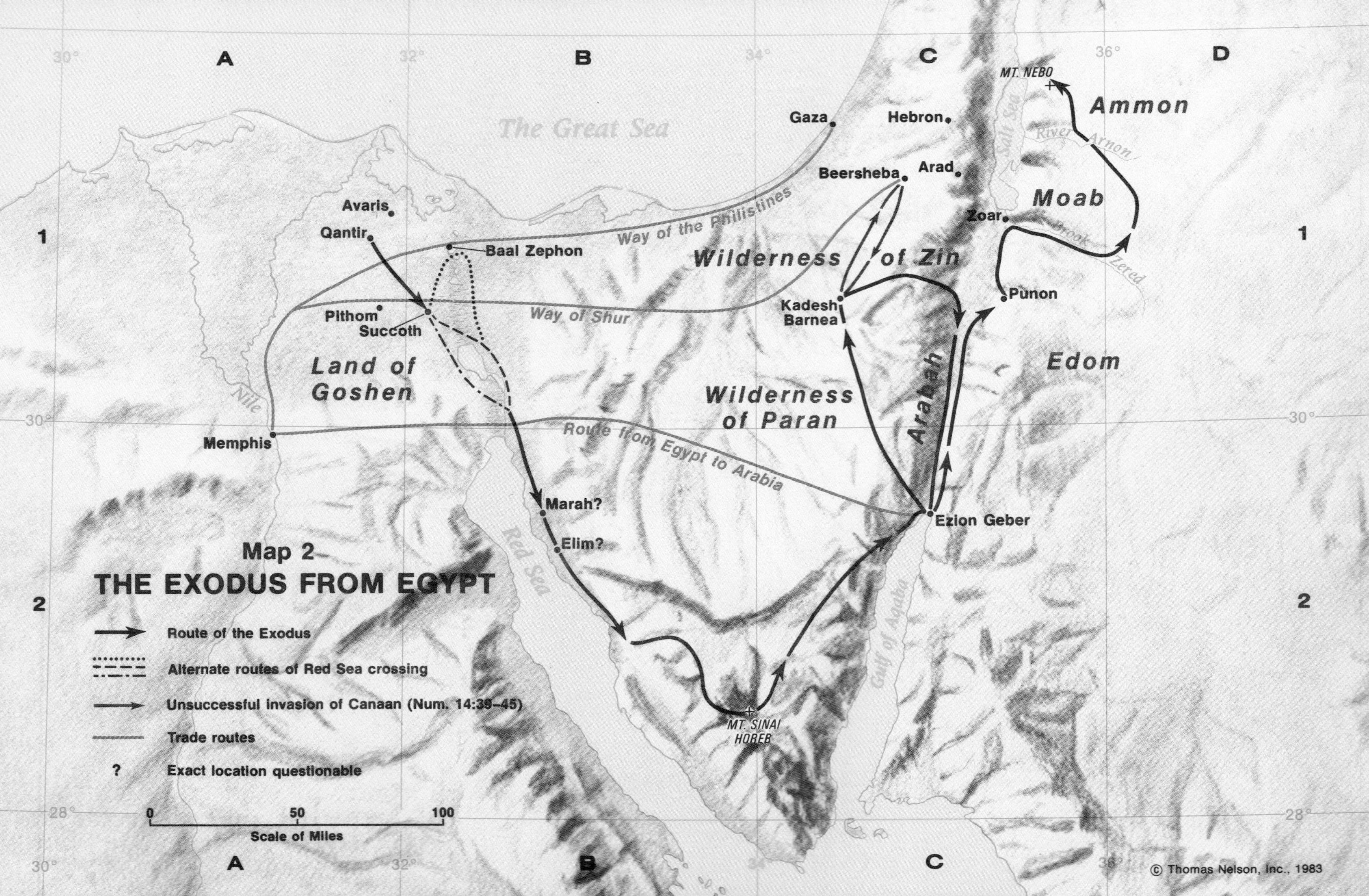

Map 2
THE EXODUS FROM EGYPT
Route of the Exodus
Alternate routes of Red Sea crossing
Unsuccessful invasion of Canaan (Num. 14:39–45)
Trade routes
? Exact location questionable
0 50 100
Scale of Miles
The Great Sea
Gaza
Hebron
Arad
Beersheba
Avaris
Qantir
Baal Zephon
Way of the Philistines
Wilderness of Zin
Kadesh Barnea
Pithom
Succoth
Way of Shur
Land of Goshen
Nile
Memphis
Wilderness of Paran
Route from Egypt to Arabia
Marah?
Elim?
Red Sea
MT. SINAI HOREB
Gulf of Aqaba
Ezion Geber
Arabah
Salt Sea
MT. NEBO
Ammon
River Arnon
Moab
Zoar
Brook Zered
Punon
Edom
A B C D
1 2
30° 32° 34° 36° 28°

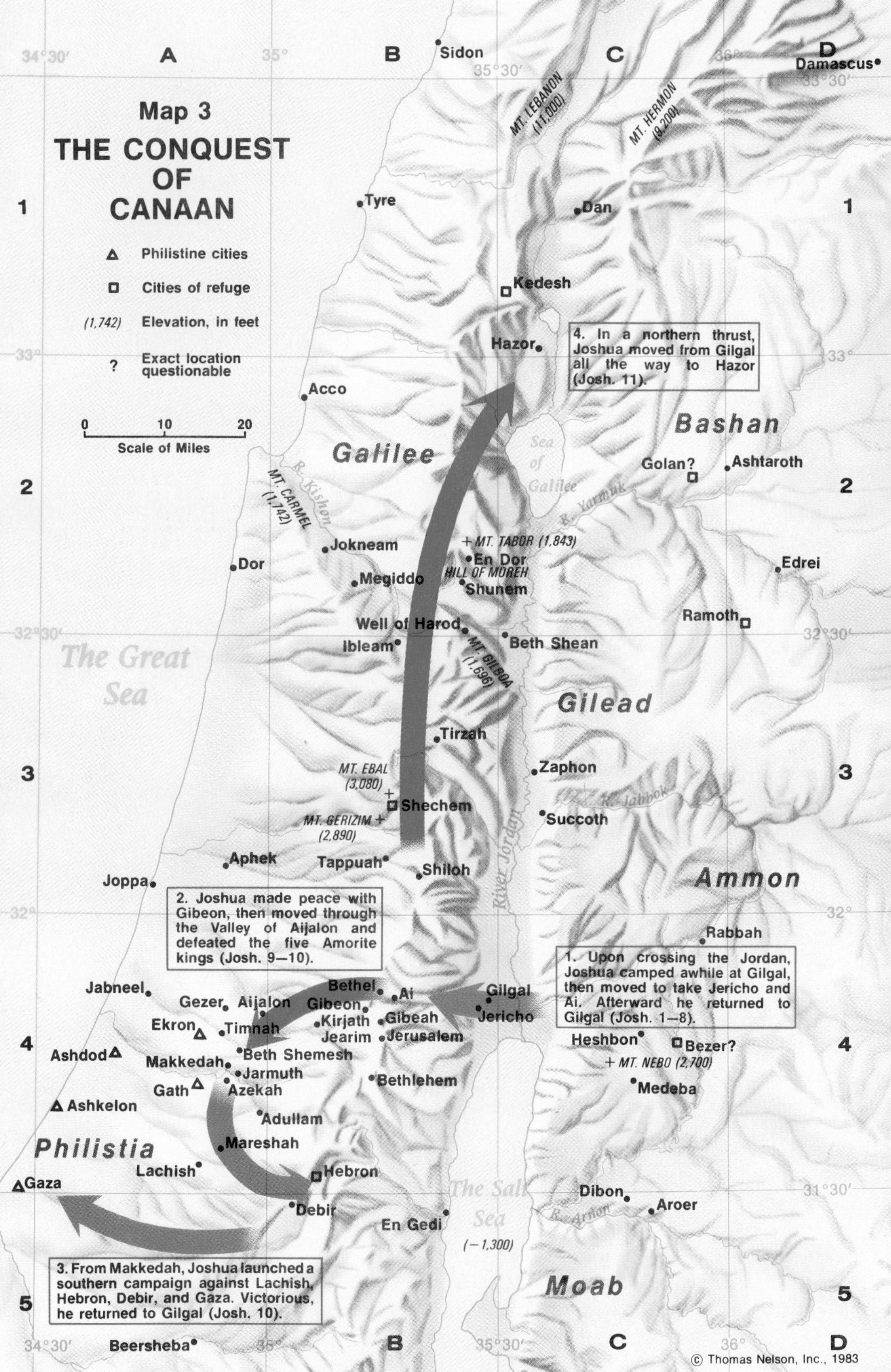
Map 3
THE CONQUEST OF CANAAN
Philistine cities
Cities of refuge
(1,742) Elevation, in feet
? Exact location questionable
0 10 20
Scale of Miles
4. In a northern thrust, Joshua moved from Gilgal all the way to Hazor (Josh. 11).
2. Joshua made peace with Gibeon, then moved through the Valley of Aijalon and defeated the five Amorite kings (Josh. 9—10).
1. Upon crossing the Jordan, Joshua camped awhile at Gilgal, then moved to take Jericho and Ai. Afterward he returned to Gilgal (Josh. 1—8).
3. From Makkedah, Joshua launched a southern campaign against Lachish, Hebron, Debir, and Gaza. Victorious, he returned to Gilgal (Josh. 10).
Sidon
Damascus
MT. LEBANON (11,000)
MT. HERMON (9,200)
Tyre
Dan
Kedesh
Hazor
Acco
Bashan
Galilee
Sea of Galilee
MT. CARMEL (1,742)
R. Kishon
Golan?
Ashtaroth
R. Yarmuk
Jokneam
MT. TABOR (1,843)
En Dor
Dor
Megiddo
HILL OF MOREH
Shunem
Edrei
Well of Harod
Ramoth
Ibleam
Beth Shean
MT. GILBOA (1,696)
The Great Sea
Gilead
Tirzah
MT. EBAL (3,080)
Zaphon
Shechem
R. Jabbok
MT. GERIZIM (2,890)
Succoth
Aphek
Tappuah
Shiloh
River Jordan
Joppa
Ammon
Rabbah
Jabneel
Bethel
Ai
Gilgal
Gezer
Aijalon
Gibeon
Jericho
Ekron
Timnah
Kirjath Jearim
Gibeah
Jerusalem
Heshbon
Bezer?
Ashdod
Beth Shemesh
Makkedah
Jarmuth
MT. NEBO (2,700)
Gath
Azekah
Bethlehem
Medeba
Ashkelon
Adullam
Mareshah
Philistia
Lachish
Hebron
Gaza
The Salt Sea (−1,300)
Dibon
Aroer
Debir
En Gedi
R. Arnon
Moab
Beersheba
A B C D
1 2 3 4 5
34°30′ 35° 35°30′ 36° 33°30′ 33° 32°30′ 32° 31°30′

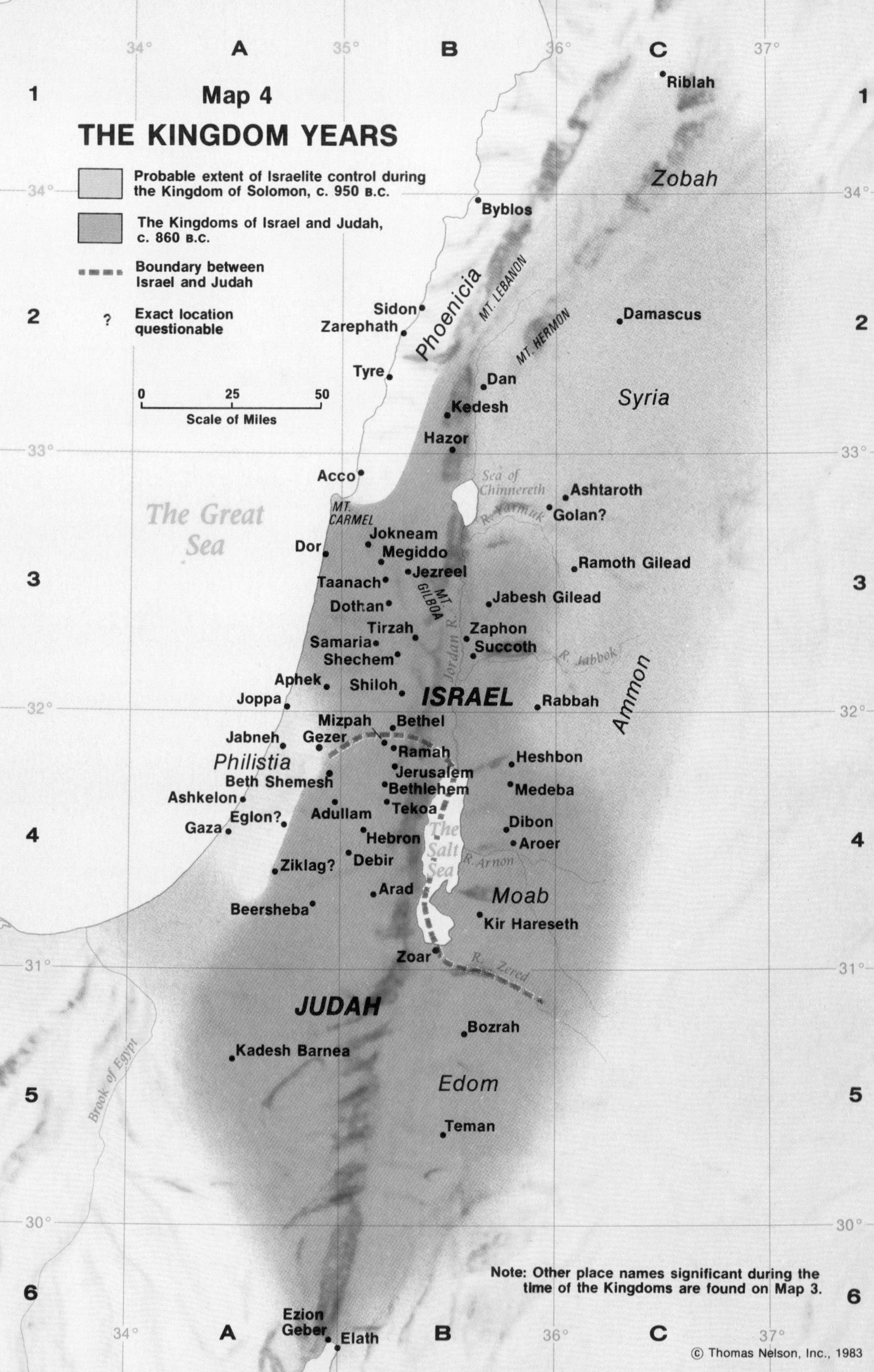

Map 4
THE KINGDOM YEARS
Probable extent of Israelite control during the Kingdom of Solomon, c. 950 B.C.
The Kingdoms of Israel and Judah, c. 860 B.C.
Boundary between Israel and Judah
? Exact location questionable
0 25 50
Scale of Miles
A B C
1 2 3 4 5 6
34° 35° 36° 37°
34° 33° 32° 31° 30°
Riblah
Zobah
Byblos
Phoenicia
MT. LEBANON
MT. HERMON
Sidon
Zarephath
Damascus
Tyre
Dan
Kedesh
Syria
Hazor
Acco
Sea of Chinnereth
Ashtaroth
R. Yarmuk
Golan?
The Great Sea
MT. CARMEL
Jokneam
Dor
Megiddo
Ramoth Gilead
Jezreel
Taanach
MT. GILBOA
Jabesh Gilead
Dothan
Tirzah
Zaphon
Samaria
Succoth
Jordan R.
R. Jabbok
Shechem
Ammon
Aphek
Shiloh
ISRAEL
Rabbah
Joppa
Mizpah
Bethel
Jabneh
Gezer
Ramah
Heshbon
Philistia
Jerusalem
Beth Shemesh
Bethlehem
Medeba
Ashkelon
Tekoa
Adullam
Eglon?
The Salt Sea
Dibon
Gaza
Hebron
Aroer
R. Arnon
Ziklag?
Debir
Arad
Moab
Beersheba
Kir Hareseth
Zoar
R. Zered
JUDAH
Bozrah
Kadesh Barnea
Brook of Egypt
Edom
Teman
Note: Other place names significant during the time of the Kingdoms are found on Map 3.
Ezion Geber
Elath

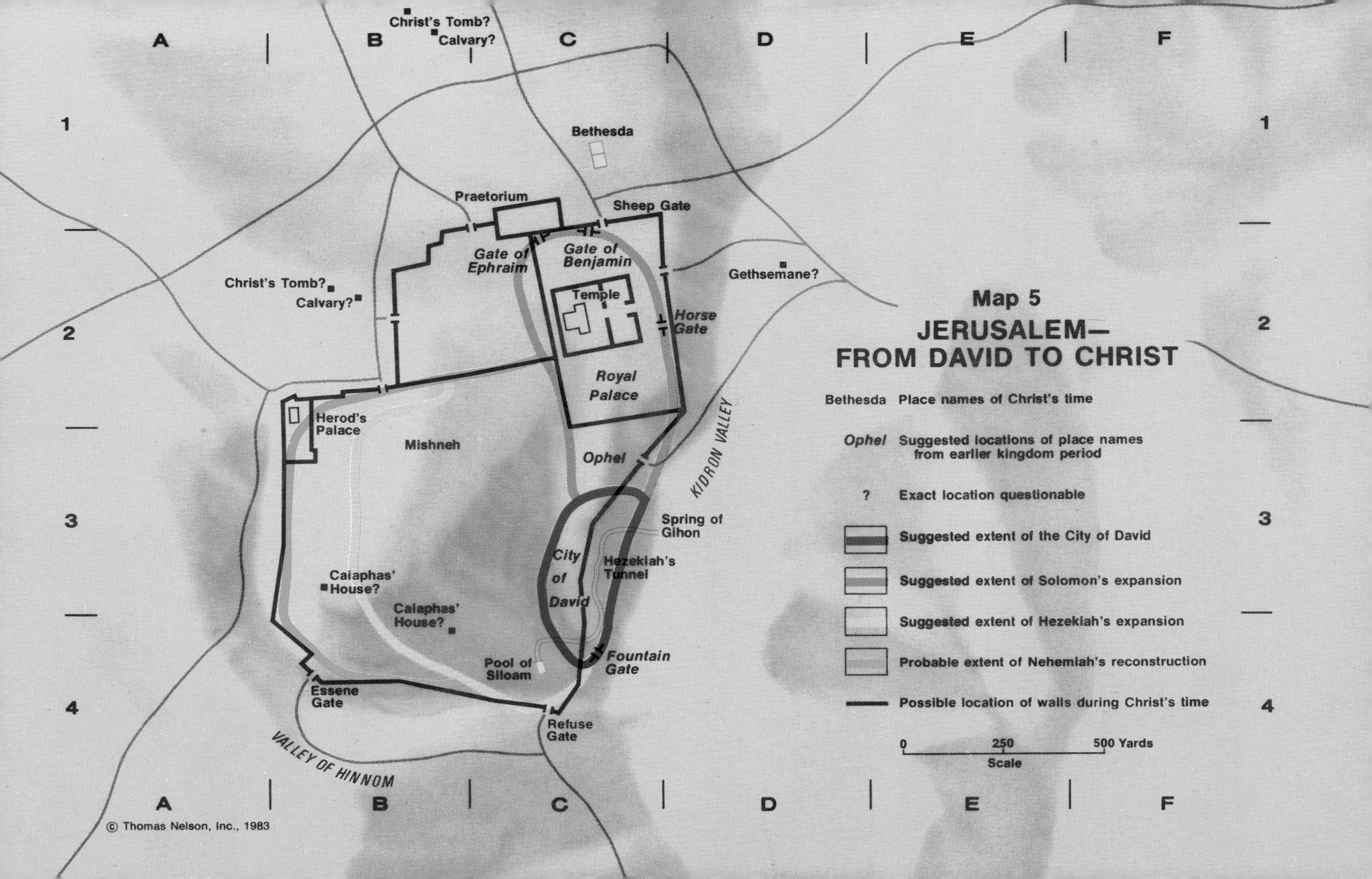
Map 5
JERUSALEM—
FROM DAVID TO CHRIST
Bethesda Place names of Christ's time
Ophel Suggested locations of place names from earlier kingdom period
? Exact location questionable
Suggested extent of the City of David
Suggested extent of Solomon's expansion
Suggested extent of Hezekiah's expansion
Probable extent of Nehemiah's reconstruction
Possible location of walls during Christ's time
0
250
500 Yards
Scale
Christ's Tomb?
Calvary?
Bethesda
Praetorium
Sheep Gate
Gate of Ephraim
Gate of Benjamin
Gethsemane?
Christ's Tomb?
Calvary?
Temple
Horse Gate
Royal Palace
Herod's Palace
Mishneh
Ophel
KIDRON VALLEY
Spring of Gihon
City of David
Hezekiah's Tunnel
Caiaphas' House?
Caiaphas' House?
Pool of Siloam
Fountain Gate
Essene Gate
Refuse Gate
VALLEY OF HINNOM
A
B
C
D
E
F
1
2
3
4

Map 6
PALESTINE
IN
CHRIST'S TIME
(1,742) Elevation, in feet
? Exact location questionable
0 10 20
Scale of Miles
34°30′
A
35°
B
35°30′
C
36°
D
33°30′
33°
32°30′
32°
31°30′
1
2
3
4
5
Sidon
Damascus
Zarephath
MT. LEBANON (11,000)
MT. HERMON (9,200)
Phoenicia
Iturea
Tyre
Panias
(Caesarea Philippi)
Trachonitis
Galilee
Ptolemais
Chorazin
Bethsaida?
Capernaum
Sea of Chinnereth
Magdala
Gergesa
Cana
Tiberias
R. Kishon
MT. CARMEL (1,742)
R. Yarmuk
Nazareth
MT. TABOR (1,843)
Gadara?
Nain
Esdraelon
R. Jezreel
Scythopolis
MT. GILBOA (1,696)
The Great Sea
Caesarea
Decapolis
Samaria
Samaria
Gerasa
Sychar
R. Jabbok
MT. GERIZIM (2,890)
River Jordan
Antipatris
Joppa
Perea
Arimathea
Gadara?
Ephraim
Lydda
Philadelphia
Emmaus
Jericho
Kirjath Jearim
Bethabara
Jerusalem
Bethany
Azotus
Beth Haccerem
Qumran
Bethlehem
Medeba
Ashkelon
Herodium
Judea
Machaerus
Hebron
Gaza
The Salt Sea
(−1,300)
R. Arnon
Masada
Idumea
Beersheba
© Thomas Nelson, Inc., 1983

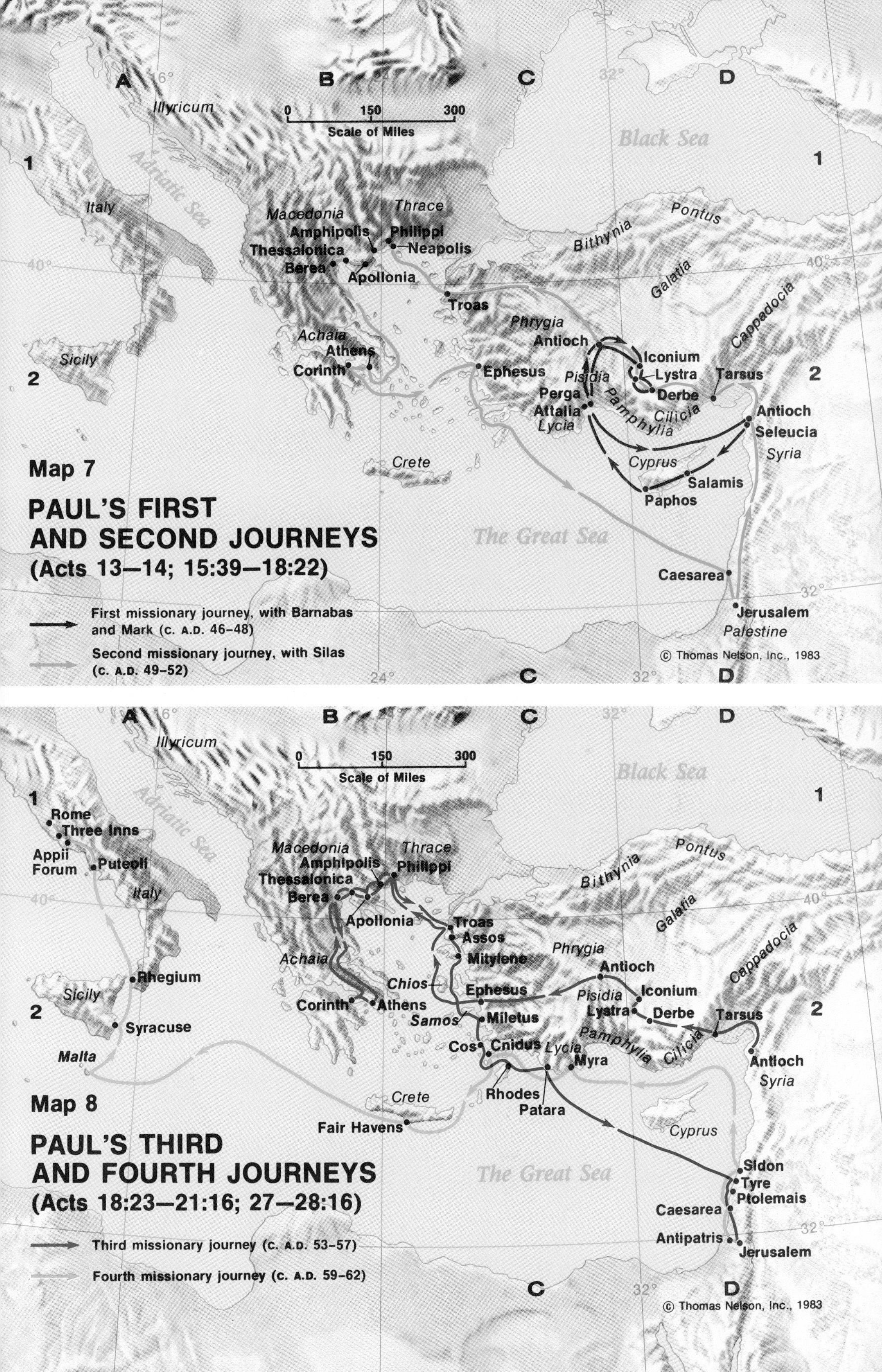
A
B
C
D
Illyricum
0
150
300
Scale of Miles
Black Sea
1
Adriatic Sea
Italy
Macedonia
Thrace
Pontus
Amphipolis
Philippi
Thessalonica
Neapolis
Bithynia
Berea
Apollonia
Galatia
Troas
Cappadocia
Phrygia
Achaia
Athens
Antioch
Iconium
Sicily
Corinth
Ephesus
Pisidia
Lystra
Tarsus
2
Perga
Derbe
Attalia
Pamphylia
Cilicia
Lycia
Antioch
Seleucia
Syria
Crete
Cyprus
Salamis
Paphos
The Great Sea
Caesarea
Jerusalem
Palestine
Map 7
PAUL'S FIRST AND SECOND JOURNEYS
(Acts 13—14; 15:39—18:22)
First missionary journey, with Barnabas and Mark (c. A.D. 46–48)
Second missionary journey, with Silas (c. A.D. 49–52)
© Thomas Nelson, Inc., 1983
Rome
Three Inns
Appii Forum
Puteoli
Italy
Macedonia
Thrace
Amphipolis
Philippi
Thessalonica
Berea
Apollonia
Troas
Assos
Mitylene
Achaia
Chios
Rhegium
Sicily
Corinth
Athens
Ephesus
Pisidia
Iconium
Lystra
Derbe
Tarsus
Samos
Miletus
Syracuse
Malta
Cos
Cnidus
Lycia
Myra
Pamphylia
Cilicia
Antioch
Syria
Rhodes
Patara
Crete
Fair Havens
Cyprus
Sidon
Tyre
Ptolemais
Caesarea
Antipatris
Jerusalem
Map 8
PAUL'S THIRD AND FOURTH JOURNEYS
(Acts 18:23—21:16; 27—28:16)
Third missionary journey (c. A.D. 53–57)
Fourth missionary journey (c. A.D. 59–62)
© Thomas Nelson, Inc., 1983

Map 9
THE HOLY LAND
IN MODERN TIMES
Area occupied by Israel since June, 1967
0
25
50
Scale of Miles
A
B
C
D
E
1
2
3
4
5
6
34°
35°
36°
37°
33°
32°
31°
30°
LEBANON
SYRIA
JORDAN
ISRAEL
EGYPT
Tripoli
Beirut
Sidon
Tyre
Dan
Qiryat Shemona
Damascus
BEKAA VALLEY
LEBANON MTS.
ANTI-LEBANON MTS.
U.N. Buffer Zone
1973 Line
Quneitra
1967 Cease-Fire Line
Golan Heights
Nahariyya
Akko
Safad
Sea of Galilee
Haifa
Tiberias
Nazareth
Afula
Mediterranean Sea
Dera
Ramtha
Beth Shean
Hadera
Netanya
Tulkarm
Nablus
Jordan River
Jarash
Herzliyya
Tel Aviv
Yafo
Petah Tiqwa
West Bank
Rishon le Zion
Lod
Ramla
Ramalah
Amman
Ashdod
Jericho
Jerusalem
Bethlehem
Ashqelon
Madaba
Gaza
Qiryat Gat
Hebron
Dead Sea
En Gedi
Dhiban
Beersheba
Al-Arish
Karak
Negev
Arabah
Sinai
Elat
Aqaba